THE ESSENTIAL WORKS OF THOMAS MORE

D0023524

THE ESSENTIAL WORKS OF
THOMAS MORE

Edited by Gerard B. Wegemer and Stephen W. Smith

Yale UNIVERSITY PRESS

New Haven and London

Published with support from the Fund established in memory of Oliver Baty Cunningham, a distinguished graduate of the Class of 1917, Yale College, Captain, 15th United States Field Artillery, born in Chicago September 17, 1894, and killed while on active duty near Thiaucourt, France, September 17, 1918, the twenty-fourth anniversary of his birth.

Copyright © 2020 by Gerard B. Wegemer and Stephen W. Smith. All rights reserved.
This book may not be reproduced, in whole or in part, including the illustrations, in any form (beyond the copying permitted by Sections 107 and 108 of the U.S. Copyright Law and except by reviewers for the public press), without written permission from the publishers.

Yale University Press books may be purchased in quantity for educational, business, or promotional use. For information, please e-mail sales. press@yale.edu (U.S. office) or sales@yaleup.co.uk (U.K. office).

Designed by Gregg Chase.
Set by Julie Allred in Garamond Premier Pro customized by Charles Ellertson.
Printed in the United States of America.

Library of Congress Control Number: 2019933373
ISBN 978-0-300-22337-8 (hardcover : alk. paper)

A catalogue record for this book is available from the British Library.

This paper meets the requirements of ANSI/NISO Z39.48-1992 (Permanence of Paper).

10 9 8 7 6 5 4 3 2 1

Frontispiece: *Thomas More* (2013), bronze, 8', by Pablo Eduardo, Boston College Law School. He has *The City of God* and *Utopia* in one hand and a palm branch in the other as he faces rising winds.

To the more than thirty editors and translators and the many dedicated members of Yale University Press who worked thirty-nine years (1958–1997) to produce *The Yale Edition of the Complete Works of St. Thomas More*, guided by Executive Editors Richard S. Sylvester and Clarence H. Miller and Editorial Board Chair Louis L. Martz — collaborative international scholarship at its best; and to Germain Marc'hadour, *CW* advisor and editor as well as founding editor of *Moreana*, who traveled the world for almost fifty years fostering that international collaboration.

CONTENTS

ILLUSTRATIONS

cover: *Sir Thomas More,* detail, Hans Holbein the Younger, 1527, © The Frick Collection, New York

front endpapers: *Thomas More's London,* © 2018 by Michael Hall

frontispiece: *Thomas More,* 2013, sculpture by Pablo Eduardo, Boston College Law School; photo by J. F. Keefe, © CTMS

ILLUSTRATIONS IN THE TEXT

*All of the Beinecke images are from the General Collection of the Beinecke Rare Book and Manuscript Library at Yale University.

PLATES

A distinguished lawyer and judge and the first major author of early modern England, Sir Thomas More (1478–1535) wrote in poetry and prose, in Latin and English, throughout a lifetime of no little fame and still lingering controversy. Called both "a man for all seasons" and "Master Mock" during his career, and likened to Cicero and Socrates after his death, Thomas More was executed for high treason on July 6, 1535, following a historic trial. In the 1540s, Tudor historian Edward Hall wondered over More. "I cannot tell," he wrote frankly, "whether I should call him a foolish wise man, or a wise foolish man," especially when he considered the spectacle of More's death. While conversation and dialogue will no doubt continue over his writings, life, and legacy, one necessary means for advancing these labors remains a better knowledge of More's varied and voluminous writings in poetry, history, literature, law, theology, and contemporary controversies.

The Essential Works of Thomas More gathers together—for the first time in a one-volume standardized edition—More's writings in poetry and prose from his Latin and English works. The only other one-volume editions of More date from earlier centuries, and focus on either his English or Latin compositions. William Rastell's 1557 folio edition, *The Workes of Sir Thomas More Knight,* was published in London during the reign of Queen Mary and gathered together principally More's English writings, while the *Opera omnia,* published in Louvain in 1565 and 1566, collected and presented his Latin writings to the wider European audience. A later one-volume Latin edition would follow in the seventeenth century, and Rastell's edition of the English works would be reprinted in the twentieth century, but only in its original "blackletter" Gothic script, an impediment for many contemporary readers.

The Essential Works offers those texts considered necessary for a general view and understanding of More, presented in modernized English and with updated glosses, based on recent scholarly advances and made after the model of today's single-volume editions of William Shakespeare and other major authors. In publishing *The Essential Works,* we hope to facilitate the study of More's place in the early modern period by providing the reader with those texts and other helps that prove essential for a clearer understanding of More's complex life and works.

A reliable single volume of More's essential writings has become possible because of the Yale University Press's critical edition of *The Complete Works of Saint Thomas More.* Yale's model project of international scholarship and collaboration, *The Complete Works* involved the work of twenty-five scholars from 1963 to 1997 and totaled twenty-one books in its fifteen-volume set. *The Essential Works* is profoundly indebted to the labors of these editors and scholars and includes many fruits of the Yale critical edition, presenting them to contemporary readers with the help needed for a closer encounter with More's early sixteenth-century writings. This type of project was envisioned by the founders and editors of Yale's *Complete Works,* who began what they called "modernized" editions of More's works. That useful but incomplete series included More's *Selected Letters* (1961), *Utopia* (1964), *The History of King Richard III and Selections from the English and Latin Poems* (1976), *A Dialogue of Comfort against Tribulation* (1977), and *The Tower Works* (1980). *The Essential Works of Thomas More* aims to build upon and continue that work by presenting Thomas More anew to the great variety of readers and scholars interested in his life and writings, and in this remarkable historical period.

More's writings are presented chronologically, with brief introductions, content outlines, relevant images, and glosses, all of which seek to assist the reader and facilitate careful study; in preparing the edition, we have had particularly in mind those for whom More's works are less familiar, but who nevertheless wish to make a solid beginning of studying his writings. This edition endeavors to present a comprehensive More to the contemporary reader, as fully as limitations of space and wit allow.

To provide this fuller view, a detailed chronology situates More's life and writings in their historical, social, and intellectual contexts. A reconstructed version of More's fateful trial is also included, based on the most recent scholarship, as well as texts of the relevant legal acts and oaths. *The Essential*

Works is rounded off by an illuminating selection of the earliest biographical accounts of More, mostly from those contemporaries who witnessed him in action, in one form or another: his humanist friend, Erasmus; his son-in-law, William Roper; his rival in theological controversy, William Tyndale; the court historian, Edward Hall; the anonymous author of the *Paris Newsletter* account of his trial and death; and fellow humanist and later polemicist Reginald Pole. This final section also includes the full text of *Sir Thomas More,* the first dramatic depiction of More's life, written by a group of London dramatists, including William Shakespeare.

On Editing Thomas More's English. More's English texts have been edited and standardized in spelling and punctuation, per modern usage, but with exceptions made on occasion for his poetry. While original spelling and punctuation remain indispensable and illuminating, we follow the lead of other editors of one-volume editions of major authors (e.g., Shakespeare and Milton) and present to readers a modern More. (See the "Note on This Edition" at the end of this preface, for some detail.) We do, however, reference Yale's critical editions on most pages to facilitate further study and cross referencing.

Glosses are provided throughout *The Essential Works* for both the Latin and English works. Our authority for English glosses is the second edition of the *Oxford English Dictionary.* English glosses are rendered as concisely as possible; the nuances, valences, and subtleties of More's English are suggested within reason. We gloss obsolete and archaic words, as well as syntactical and morphological archaisms. We also gloss historical references, as well as intertextual references, when they are explicit, clear, or important. Of the making of glosses there is no ending; we can only hope to have achieved a thorough yet tempered approach, one especially helpful for less experienced readers of sixteenth-century literature and English.

One page from a letter to King Henry VIII, in More's own hand (see page xvi), gives the reader some sense of the challenges involved in editing More's English. In *The Essential Works,* punctuation is edited to clarify syntax while respecting More's style as much as possible. Some Moreanisms have been retained, such as comma-less serial adjectives in phrases like "a seely rude roaring ass" or "Christ's dear bitter passion."

One prominent editorial change, especially in the English dialogues, is the replacement of More's virgule—the mark "/"—with modern punctuation. The following selection gives the reader some sense of the difference between the original punctuation with virgules and the standardized, modern punctuation used in this edition:

> while the thing shall not apere so terrible vnto them / reason shall bettre entre, & thorow grace workying with their diligens / engendre & set sure, not a sodayne sleyght affeccion of sufferaunce for godes sake / but by a long contynuaunce, a strong depe rotid habit. (*CW* 12: 205)

> while the thing shall not appear so terrible unto them—reason shall better enter, and, through grace working with their diligence, engender and set sure not a sudden slight affection of sufferance for God's sake, but, by a long continuance, a strong deep-rooted habit.

Proper names are standardized in spelling and always capitalized. For recognizable historical personages, literary characters, places, battles, and so on, the spelling used is the standard (first-listed) spelling given in *The Oxford Dictionary of National Biography* and *Contemporaries of Erasmus: A Biographical Register of the Renaissance and Reformation.*

Nouns which refer to God, such as "Maker, Creator, Redeemer, etc.," titles of Jesus and Mary, royal and noble honorifics, and the word "Church" (when it does not refer to a building) are capitalized. For example, in *Richard III,* King Edward IV is called "his Highness"; Bishop Morton, "your Grace"; and Christ, "our Lord." The titles of secular and ecclesiastical offices as well as references to current holders of those offices are also capitalized, so that Morton was made "Archbishop of Canterbury and Chancellor of England, whereunto the Pope joined the honor of Cardinal," and in Letter 200 (for example) the following phrases appear: "my Lord Chancellor," "the King's Highness," "my Lord of Canterbury," and "the King's Grace."

Quotations in Latin are italicized, often followed by More's own translation given in parentheses and enclosed in quotation marks, as in this example from his *Dialogue of Comfort*:

> For as Saint James saith, *Omne datum optimum, et omne donum perfectum, de sursum est, descendens*

a Patre luminum ("Every good gift, and every perfect gift, is given from above, descending from the Father of lights").

By editing and glossing More's English in these ways, the hope is to facilitate the reader's encounter with More's mind, art, and wit. The precise cross-referencing to *The Complete Works* throughout this edition is done so that interested readers may easily refer to the Yale critical edition texts with original spelling and punctuation, along with their notes and commentaries, to which we are also indebted.

On Translations from More's Latin. For More's Latin writings, the Yale *Complete Works* translations have generally been used, but with several exceptions. An English translation of More's Latin translations of Lucian's dialogues was sorely needed because the translations provided in the Yale critical edition are from the Loeb Classical Library edition of Lucian, and are not translations of More's striking Latin. For *Utopia,* we offer Clarence Miller's astute translation from the Yale *Nota Bene* series. For the remaining Latin writings (the *Epigrams,* the humanist letters, the selections from *Response to Luther,* and the *Sadness of Christ*), we use the translations from the Yale critical editions. Translations for many of the other letters are from Yale's *St. Thomas More: Selected Letters,* supplemented by additional translations, as noted in the contents page for each section. Erasmus's letters and comments on More are drawn from the Toronto edition of his complete works, except for the letter to John Faber, which we present in a new translation.

On Complete Texts versus Selections. As much as possible, complete texts have been chosen, but for reasons of space, selections are sometimes offered: for two of the controversial works — the long *Response to Luther* and the massive *Confutation of Tyndale's* Answer — only representative selections are given; for More's exchange with the legal scholar Christopher St. German, the complete *Apology of Sir Thomas More, Knight* is provided, but not the complete text of More's follow-up response to St. German, *The Debellation of Salem and Bizance.* Standardized versions of *Confutation* and *Debellation* are, however, available as online resources at www.essentialmore.org, along with the full text of *Responsio ad Lutherum.*

On More's Correspondence. More's wide-ranging correspondence is presented in three separate sections: (1) his general correspondence, dating from 1501 to 1534, the year of his arrest and imprisonment; (2) his "humanist letters," often treatise-like in length and more public in character; and (3) his prison letters, dating from 1534 to the week of his death in July 1535. Considered together, the correspondence provides the reader with a valuable window into More's mind, his keen sense of rhetoric and truth, and all the little particularities of his times, friends, family, and associates. As much of More's "essential" correspondence as possible has been included since the two-part volume that the Yale *Complete Works* planned for his correspondence has not yet been done — a much needed labor for the future to contemplate and undertake, one hopes.

A wealth of materials and tools for further study of Thomas More and his time is also available online at www.essentialmore.org. This website includes texts from More in English and Latin, a library of supporting historical documents and images, study guides, and links to the complete International Thomas More Bibliography, maintained by Romuald Lakowski. Specially useful are complete concordances for both the English and Latin works, as well as three cumulative concordances — one for the English works, one for the Latin works, and one for the complete works. Readers should also consult the archives of *Moreana: Thomas More and Renaissance Studies,* digitized and available from Edinburgh University Press at http://www.euppublishing.com/loi/more.

Two recent collections of helpful scholarly materials are *The Cambridge Companion to Thomas More,* edited by George M. Logan (Cambridge University Press, 2011) and *A Companion to Thomas More,* edited by A. D. Cousins and Damian Grace (Fairleigh Dickinson University Press, 2009).

To help improve this book in future editions, you are encouraged to contact us with corrections and suggestions, through www.essentialmore.org. To conclude with a merry variation on what Ben Jonson wrote for the first folio of Shakespeare in 1623: it's no longer time to look on prefaces about Thomas More, gentle readers, but on "his book."

Center for Thomas More Studies
February 7, 2019

This is a facsimile of the first page of Thomas More's 5 March <1534> letter to King Henry VIII. See pages 1470–72 for the other facsimiles, transcribed on pages 381–82.

Hit may lyke yor highnes to call to yor graciouse rememberaunce / that at
such tyme as of that great weighty rome & office of your chauncellor
(with which so far aboue my meritis or qualitees able & mete therfore
yor highnes had of yor incomparable goodnes honored & exalted me)
ye were so good & graciouse vn to me as at my pore humble suit
to discharge & disburden me, geving me licence with yor graciouse
favor / to bestow the residew of my life in myn age now to come / abowt
the provision for my soule in the service of god, & to be yor gracys
bedisman & pray for you, it pleased yor highnes ferther to say vnto
me, that for the service which I byfore had done you, (Which it than
lyked yor goodnes far aboue my deserving to commend) that in eny suit
that I should after haue un to yor highness / which either should concerne
myn honor (that word it lyked your highnes to vse vn to me) or that
should perteyne vn to my profit / I should fynd yor highnes good
& graciouse lord vn to me . So is it now graciouse soverayn,
that worldly honor ys the thing wherof I haue resigned both the
possession & the desire / in the resignation of yor moost honorable
office . And wordlely profit I trust experience proveth & dayly more
& more shall prove, that I never was very gredy theron . ¶But now
ys my most humble suit vn to yor excellent highnes / partely to
beseche the same some what to tendre my pore honestie . But principally
that of yor accustumed goodnes no sinistre information move yor
noble grace / to have eny more distruste of my trouth ~~toward~~
& devotion toward you, than I have or shall duryng my life geve
the cause . For in this mater of the wykked woman of canterbery
I have vn to yor trusty counsaylour @ Thomas Cromwell by my

NOTE ON THIS EDITION

Spelling is standardized to accord with the headwords of the Oxford English Dictionary. In the following instances, however, spelling has been modernized to assist the general reader: "eath" to "easy," "egall" to "equal," "en/sample" to "example," "fro" to "from," "leese" to "lose," "minish" to "diminish," "mo" to "more," "natheless" to "nevertheless," "quod" to "quoth," "seld" to "seldom," "sith(en)" to "since," "shew" to "show," "throughly" to "thoroughly," "the tone…the tother" to "the one…the other"; and (where appropriate) "knowledge" to "acknowledge." In addition, all reflexive pronouns are given modern forms, so "self" becomes "itself"; "themself" and plural "yourself" are changed to "themselves" and "yourselves." Final "s" is added wherever modern usage requires it, such as: "allthing" to "all things"; "alway" to "always"; "mean" (in the sense of "way") to "means"; "many time" to "many times"; and (where appropriate) "sometime" to "sometimes"; "beside" to "besides"; "other" to "others," and to show possession ("fox" to "fox's").

Archaic verb number and tense forms are standardized in spelling: "doutest" becomes "doubtest." Irregular past tense forms are standardized to the modern form, so that "bare" becomes "bore," "brake" becomes "broke," "celebrate" becomes "celebrated," "drave" becomes "drove," "fet" becomes "fetched," "forbare" becomes "forbore," "forboden" becomes "forbidden," "gat" becomes "got," "holpen" becomes "helped," "infect" becomes "infected," "spake" becomes "spoke," "sware" becomes "swore." Past participles ending in –en are also standardized, and –en is added to verbs as needed, such as "been" instead of "be" or "strengthen" instead of "strength."

Archaic plurals are standardized: for example, "eyen" becomes "eyes" and "shoon," "shoes." The abbreviations "wt," "&," "yt," and "ye" are expanded to "with," "and," "that," and "the," respectively. The abbreviations "S" and "St" are expanded to "Saint." Before an aspirated "h," "an" becomes "a."

One distinctive Latinate feature of More's English style is the "continuative relative clause," similar to a then-common type of Latin syntax in which a relative pronoun (such as *which, who, whom, whose*) is the grammatically independent subject of its own sentence or clause and refers to an antecedent in the previous sentence. This type of construction is meant to indicate a close relationship between the two sentences, but the two sentences are separate. In this edition, these continuative relative clauses are sometimes treated as independent clauses, but often they follow semicolons or commas and are treated as part of the previous sentence.

ACKNOWLEDGMENTS

Special thanks to managing editor Katherine Stearns; to Latin editor Gerald Malsbary; to the Center for Thomas More Studies' directors Steve Bennett, Myles Harrington, Tom Jodziewicz, Tom Spence, Shane Tucker; to senior advisors Clarence Miller, Elizabeth McCutcheon, Marie-Claire Phélippeau, Seymour House; to the many individuals who helped at various stages of development including Joshua Avery, Hubert Baudet, John Boyle, Emma Curtis, Travis Curtright, Jenny Fast, Andrea Frank, Mary Gottschalk, Joseph Koterski, Tamara Kuykendall, Jacquelyn Lee, Leonard Leo, Matthew Mehan, Frank Mitjans, Carle Mock, Matthew Post, Bradley Ritter, Michael Simmons, Katherine Sorensen, Mary Taneyhill, Alex Taylor, and Eliot Wondercheck; to book designers Gregg Chase and Julie Allred; to artist Mike Hall for his beautiful recreations of More's London and Chelsea manor; and to the editorial team at Yale University Press, especially Sarah Miller, Ash Lago, Margaret Otzel, and Joyce Ippolito for their patient and expert help to bring this challenging work to completion.

We are grateful to the institutions who granted permission to use their materials: all those given in our List of Illustrations; *Moreana* for translations of Letters 106a, 106b, 106c, 106d, 108a, 135, 138, 139, 142, 155, 155a, 155b; University of Toronto for translations of the following letters from *The Collected Works of Erasmus:* Letters 191, 513, 601, 623, 683, 684, 688, 706, 999, 1087, 1090, 1093, 1096, 1106, 1233; Boydell Press for translations of trial documents; and of course, special gratitude to Yale University Press for permission to quote from *The Complete Works of St. Thomas More.*

ABBREVIATIONS

ASD   *Opera omnia Desiderii Erasmi Roterodami,* Amsterdam, 1969–

CC   *The Cambridge Companion to Thomas More,* ed. George M. Logan, Cambridge University Press, 2011

Corr   *Correspondence of Sir Thomas More,* ed. Elizabeth F. Rogers, Princeton University Press, 1947

CWE   *The Collected Works of Erasmus,* 86 vols., Toronto University Press, 1974–

CW   *The Complete Works of St. Thomas More,* 15 vols., Yale University Press, 1963–97

EE   *Erasmi Epistolae,* ed. P.S. Allen et al, 12 vols., Oxford University Press, 1906–55

Harpsfield   Nicholas Harpsfield's *The life and death of Sir Thomas Moore, knight,* EETS, 1932

Lehmberg   Stanford E. Lehmberg's *The Reformation Parliament 1529–35,* Cambridge University Press, 1970

LP   *Letters and Papers, Foreign and Domestic, of the Reign of Henry VIII,* 1862–1932

OCEL   *Oxford Companion to English Literature,* ed. Margaret Drabble, Oxford University Press, 1985

ODCC   *Oxford Dictionary of the Christian Church,* eds. F. L. Cross and E. A. Livingstone, Oxford University Press, 2005

OED   *Oxford English Dictionary,* second edition (1989) and online (2017)

OLD   *Oxford Latin Dictionary,* 2005

Opera omnia   *Opera omnia Latina Thomae Mori,* Louvain, Bogard, 1565

PG   *Patrologia cursus completus: series graeca,* ed. J. P. Migne, 161 vols., Paris, 1857–66

PL   *Patrologia cursus completus: series latina,* ed. J. P. Migne, 221 vols., Paris, 1844–1903

Ps   Psalm: the Vulgate numbering is given first, e.g., Ps 117(118):14

Roper   William Roper's *The Lyfe of Sir Thomas Moore, knight,* EETS, 1935

Stapleton   Thomas Stapleton's *The Life and Illustrious Martyrdom of Sir Thomas More,* Burns & Oates, 1928

SL   *St. Thomas More: Selected Letters,* ed. Elizabeth F. Rogers, Yale University Press, 1961

Til   M. P. Tilley's *A Dictionary of the Proverbs in England in the Sixteenth and Seventeenth Centuries,* University of Michigan Press, 1950

WA   Martin Luther's *Werks,* ed. J. K. F. Knaake et al, 93 vols., Weimar, 1883–1978

Whit   B. J. Whiting's *Proverbs, Sentences, and Proverbial Phrases,* Harvard University Press, 1968

Workes   *The Workes of Sir Thomas More Knight…wrytten by him in the Englysh tonge,* London, 1557

CHRONOLOGY OF
THOMAS MORE'S LIFE AND WRITINGS

1478 Born February 7 in London to law student John More and his wife, Agnes Granger.

1483 Richard III becomes king in July; Edward V and his younger brother disappear.

1484 Begins his studies at St. Anthony's School on Threadneedle Street, London.

1485 Richard III dies at Bosworth Field August 22, ending the Wars of the Roses (1455–85); Henry VII assumes the throne.

1486 John Morton becomes Archbishop of Canterbury.

1487 John Morton becomes Lord Chancellor of England.

1489 Serves as page for Archbishop and Lord Chancellor Morton at Lambeth Palace.

1491 Grocyn returns from studies in Italy and teaches at Oxford.

1492 Studies at Canterbury College, Oxford, at Morton's urging.

1494 Begins pre-law studies at New Inn, London, and writes "Pageant Verses." Falls in love with Elizabeth; writes later about the experience in Epigram 263, composed in 1519.

1496 Begins law studies at Lincoln's Inn. John Colet returns to London from studies in Italy and proceeds to Oxford to teach.

1497 Writes epitaphs for Abingdon the Singer: Epigrams 159–61.

1498 Writes epigrams satirizing astrology: Epigrams 60–65, 67, 101, 118, 169, and 182. About this time, also writes Epigrams 273–74 for Holt's Latin grammar, *Lac Puerorum,* dedicated to Morton.

1499 Meets Erasmus for the first time and introduces Erasmus to Prince Henry. Linacre settles in London after completing a doctorate in medicine at Padua.

1500 Morton dies. Grocyn moves to London as rector of St. Lawrence Jewry (stays until 1506). Erasmus finishes the textual editing of Cicero's *De officiis* (published in Paris 1501).

1501 Moves in or near the Carthusians' Charterhouse (stays until 1504). Attends Grocyn's lectures on Dionysius the Areopagite; begins Greek studies with Grocyn; writes comedy about Solomon; lectures on *City of God* at St. Lawrence Jewry at Grocyn's invitation; finishes formal study of law; becomes an utter barrister. Prince Arthur marries Catherine of Aragon.

1502 Prince Arthur dies in April; Prince Henry is now heir to Henry VII's throne. More becomes Reader at Furnivall's Inn (serves through 1506).

1503 More's father becomes a sergeant-at-law; More writes "A Merry Jest" about a sergeant. Queen Elizabeth dies; More writes his "Rueful Lamentation" after her death.

1504 Serves in Parliament as a burgess representing London and leads opposition to Henry VII's tax plan. Writes "Letter to Colet" about the need for good counsel; writes the "Book of Fortune" poem. Continues studying Greek with Linacre and Lily; begins his study and translations from Giofrancesco's *Life of Pico.*

1505 Marries Joanna Colt, *ca.* January; rents Bucklersbury in London. Erasmus visits a second time; he stays with More and they translate Lucian. More's daughter Margaret is born.

1506 Daughter Elizabeth is born. More visits the Rastells at Coventry; encounters an angry friar promising easy salvation. More's Lucian translations are published; he dedicates these to Henry VII's secretary, Thomas Ruthall.

1507 Daughter Cecily is born. More is appointed pensioner (financial secretary) of Lincoln's Inn.

1508 Acts as Latin spokesman and orator for Mercer's Company in dealing with Antwerp representatives; visits Paris and Louvain.

1509 Son John is born. More is admitted to Mercers' Company "frank and free"; joins his father on a Middlesex Commission; acts as Mercers' negotiator with chief magistrate of Antwerp. Henry VII dies. Henry VIII crowned at age seventeen after marrying Catherine; More writes "Coronation Ode" and Epigrams 20–23. Erasmus makes his third and longest visit (stays until August 1514). Erasmus writes *Praise of Folly* at More's urging and edits Seneca as well. Linacre appointed royal physician.

1510 Chosen undersheriff of London (serves until 1518). Represents London in the 1510 Parliament; elected as Marshall of Lincoln's Inn. Competes with Lily in translating Greek epigrams. Publishes *The Life of John Pico*. On February 6, Colet gives his speech to the Convocation, focusing on reform and criticism of the war between England and France.

1511 Wife Joanna dies. Marries Alice Middleton within a month. Named Autumn Reader for Lincoln's Inn. On January 1, Prince Henry is born but dies February 22. England allies with Spain and Rome to war against France. Henry VIII has Parliament order all men to practice the longbow. On November 18, Ammonius writes that More sees Lord Chancellor and Archbishop William Warham daily. Richard Hunne's infant son, Stephen, is buried; Hunne refuses to pay the mortuary fee.

1512 On February 4, Warham opens Parliament with a speech on peace and justice. In April, England declares war on France, with Wolsey as war minister. In May, Cuthbert Tunstall (Chancellor to Archbishop Warham) hears

Hunne's case. On June 7, an English expedition lands on the Spanish coast. On August 10, the English *Regent* and French *Cordelière* blow up and sink. On August 28, the English army abandons the field. In November, Brixius's *Chordigera* is published and addressed to Queen Anne; More responds with epigrams satirizing Brixius: Epigrams 188–95, and 209, written through 1513. During the winter, Henry prepares to lead his army into France, over objections of his counselors. More becomes one of Lincoln Inn's four governors. Lily becomes the first master of Colet's school, St. Paul's, and John Clement is one of the first pupils. More writes Epigram 275 for Linacre's Latin grammar.

1513 Begins drafting *The History of King Richard III* and *Historia Richardi Tertii,* published in 1557 and 1565, respectively. Hunne files suit under Praemunire against the English Church. In February, Pope Julius dies; Leo X is elected Pope. On March 27, Colet preaches about war in King's presence. The satiric invective *Julius Excluded from Heaven* is published anonymously, likely written by Erasmus. In June, Henry lands in France with the English army. In July, Erasmus dedicates to Henry VIII his translation of Plutarch's *How to Tell a Flatterer from a Friend.* In August, Queen Catherine and the Earl of Surrey quell the Scottish uprising, and More writes Epigrams 183, 184, and 271. In September, Henry conquers Tournai, and More writes Epigrams 243 and 244. On September 17, Prince Henry is born to Henry and Catherine, but dies the same day. In October, Henry returns in triumph and plans to continue war. In October–November, More writes Epigram 277 satirizing two friars for their lack of friendship. Machiavelli's *The Prince* circulates in manuscript.

1514 Elected to the Doctors' Commons; joins his father as a commissioner of sewers. Asked to serve on embassy to Flanders to ease tensions between merchants of London and foreign traders in the Steelyard. On July 10, the peace treaty between England and France is signed. In December, Hunne is found hanged in the Bishop of London's prison.

1515 Serves as orator for London to receive the Venetian ambassador in January. On January 8, Prince Arthur is born to Henry and Catherine, but dies the same day. On February 16, More is included in the peace commission of Hampshire. Appointed Lenten Reader for Lincoln's Inn. In May, goes on embassy to Bruges and Antwerp to negotiate commercial treaties. In July, meets Giles and begins *Utopia*. Writes Epigram 259, "To Himself . . . Having Escaped from a Storm," and Epigrams 250, 252, and 279 to Busleyden. Erasmus visits again; More helps alleviate Erasmus's financial difficulties. On October 21, More writes from Bruges the "Letter to Dorp," defending Erasmus. Erasmus publishes *Against War* as part of his *Adages*.

1516 Erasmus publishes his edition of the Greek New Testament. More writes Epigram 255 on Erasmus's edition; writes Epigrams 256–57 presenting Erasmus's edition to Cardinal Wolsey. In February, More writes to Erasmus that he plans to decline an annual pension of £100 offered by the King, because of a conflict of interest. In March, the sixteen-year-old Charles (nephew of Catherine of Aragon) becomes king of Spain. In May, John More enters the King's service as a judge. In July and August, Erasmus is in England; his *Education of a Christian Prince* is written for young Charles V. On August 24, the Turks occupy Jerusalem. In the fall, More becomes a member of the court of Star Chamber. Around November, More's *Utopia* is published. In December, Norfolk remarks that the "whole of this kingdom wishes for a general peace."

1517 John More becomes a judge of the Court of Common Pleas. In the spring, the English-financed expedition against France fails. In March, Leo X's bull is published, imposing a five-year truce and calling for united action against the Turks. Bishop Fox founds Corpus Christi College to advance humanism at Oxford; Fox opposes further war. In April, Erasmus makes his last trip to England. In May, Wolsey and the Royal Council ask More to help investigate the Evil May Day riots. In July, Erasmus publishes his *Complaint of Peace*. On September 8, Erasmus rededicates his translation of Plutarch's *How to Tell a Flatterer from a Friend* to King Henry. On September 29, More goes on his second embassy to Calais to help settle disputes between English and French merchants. On October 7, More writes Epigram 276 on friendship to thank Peter Giles and Erasmus for their pictures sent. More's second edition of *Utopia* published, in Paris. In November, Luther publishes his "Disputation on the Power and Efficacy of Indulgences," also known as the "95 Theses." In December, More successfully defends in Star Chamber the Pope's interest in a shipping dispute over those of the Crown.

1518 In January, Wolsey presents his plan for Universal Peace. In January–March, More decides to enter the King's service; Henry tells More to adhere to God and his conscience, "the most virtuous lesson that ever a prince taught his servant," as More later wrote. Wolsey employs More as official secretary between Westminster and the royal Court and for much judicial work. On February 18, Princess Mary is born. On March 6, a five-year truce of peace is proclaimed in Rome. In March, More publishes the *Epigrams* with the third edition of *Utopia*, printed by John Froben. On March 29, writes the "Letter to Oxford." In April, Erasmus writes to More that "you are lost to literature, and to us." Erasmus tells Tunstall he regrets More's advancement. In the spring, More publicly refutes the clergyman who preached against Greek studies in the King's presence. On May 17, Wolsey is made papal legate *a latere*. In the summer, More joins the Privy Council. On June 21, receives first payment of his annuity. In July, gives the welcoming oration to Campeggio; on July 23, resigns as undersheriff. On October 2, Wolsey's "Treaty of Universal Peace" is signed. In November, More's *Epigrams* and *Utopia* are published again. In December, Wolsey summons the bishops for March 1519 to consider Church reform.

1519 In January, Maximilian dies and Henry, Francis, and Charles all vie to be Holy Roman Emperor. On March 14, Wolsey's legatine meeting of bishops is held, and Fisher gives his speech for reform. On June 28, Charles V is elected Holy Roman Emperor. More defends Erasmus in the "Letter to Lee" and the "Letter to a Monk." Erasmus publishes a second edition of his Greek New Testament. Colet and Grocyn die. Wolsey sets up permanent court at White Hall, later known as the Court of Requests.

1520   Brixius writes *Antimorus* and More publishes "Letter to Brixius." John More becomes judge of the King's Bench. On May 26–29, Charles and Henry meet in Dover and Canterbury. On June 11, the Field of the Cloth of Gold at Calais solemnizes peace with the French, with More present. Over the next three months, More negotiates in Bruges, and Erasmus introduces him to Cranevelt. On June 20, the papal condemnation of Luther is made; Luther is given sixty days to admit his errors. In August, Luther publishes *Address to the Christian Nobility of the German Nation.* In October, Luther publishes *On the Babylonian Captivity of the Church.* In November, Luther publishes *Liberty of a Christian Man.* Charles V is crowned emperor. On December 10, Luther publicly burns the papal bull and decretals. Responding to Luther's *Babylonian Captivity,* Henry VIII publishes *In Defense of the Seven Sacraments,* More having cautioned him not to exaggerate the Pope's secular authority.

1521   Daughter Margaret marries William Roper. On January 3, Luther is excommunicated. On April 17–18, Luther speaks before Charles V at the imperial Diet at Worms and refuses to recant. On April 19, Charles V condemns Luther and bans him from the empire. In the spring, More accompanies Wolsey to Calais and Bruges for negotiations with French and Imperial envoys; wins a legal battle of wits against the Imperial lawyer by stumping him with an issue about rural English law: "Whether cattle taken in withernam are irrepleviable." Meets for the last time Erasmus, who introduces to More the Valencian humanist Juan Vives (later is advisor to Catherine and teacher to Princess Mary). In May, knighted and made under-treasurer of the Exchequer. On May 12, Wolsey burns heretical books before a large crowd. On

May 17, the Duke of Buckingham is executed. In August, the Turks under Suleiman take Belgrade. Wolsey concludes the Anglo-Imperial Treaty at Bruges and delays large-scale war. In September, More joins Wolsey in Calais; in mid-October, More is sent to the King in England but contracts a tertian fever, making him both hot and cold at the same time. In October, the Pope declares Henry the Defender of the Faith. On December 2, Leo X dies and Wolsey puts his name forward at the papal election.

1522   On January 9, Adrian VI is elected Pope; on January 21, Suleiman captures Rhodes after five-month siege; on May 19, England declares war on France. During the summer, Emperor Charles V visits England, and More gives the welcoming oration. More is given wardship of Giles Heron. Surrey leads 11,000 as an expeditionary force into France. Luther publishes *Against Henry, King of the English.* More expresses reservations about the war. In December, the Turks under Suleiman capture Rhodes. More's *Last Things,* Erasmus's *Colloquies,* and Vives's edition of Augustine's *City of God* are published. Tunstall dedicates his treatise on arithmetic, *De arte supputandi,* to More. More serves as Henry's secretary.

1523   Gives oration defending free speech as Speaker of the House of Commons. At Henry VIII's request, writes *Response to Luther* against Luther's vituperative *Against Henry.* Wolsey appoints Vives to lecture at Oxford. England signs a treaty to invade France; Suffolk leads 10,000 troops in an attempted march on Paris. Erasmus announces his decision to combat Luther in print.

1524   Moves to Chelsea; publishes a second edition of *Response to Luther*; appointed High Steward to Oxford; given wardship of Anne Cresacre. The Turks invade Hungary. Erasmus publishes *On Free Choice of the Will,* responding to Luther. In October, Linacre dies. In November, the army in France retreats, but Henry still orders a winter campaign. More remarks to Roper: "If my head could win [the King] a castle in France, . . . it would not fail to go." Bishop

Tunstall warns booksellers not to import heretical books.

1525 Elizabeth marries William Dauncey and Cecily marries Giles Heron in a double wedding ceremony. More is made High Steward of Cambridge. On February 14, the French king is captured by Charles V at Pavia; in March, Henry plans to lead an army against France; in April, Warham reports the commoners' aversion to paying for the French war. Wolsey removes Vives from Oxford for opposing war. In June, More attends ceremonies making Henry VIII's illegitimate son, Henry, the Duke of Richmond. During the summer, the peasants revolt in Germany; Luther writes "Against the Murderous, Thieving Hordes of Peasants"; 60,000–100,000 peasants are killed. In August, More helps negotiate a peace agreement with France. In September, appointed the Chancellor of Duchy of Lancaster. In December, Luther publishes *On the Servitude of the Will* (reprinted six times in two months) as a response to Erasmus, but writes a submissive letter to King Henry as well. More begins but does not publish *Letter to Bugenhagen*, in response to the Lutheran controversies.

1526 In January, Wolsey orders raids upon Steelyard for Luther's writings, and More leads one of these. On February 11, Robert Barnes abjures heresy before Fisher and Wolsey. In March, Henry receives Luther's letter. More helps in making the King's reply, and so does not publish his *Letter to Bugenhagen* (later published in 1568). In March, Francis I is released by Charles V. In the spring, Henry's infatuation with Anne Boleyn begins. In April, More continues to help negotiate a peace treaty with France and is among those who sign the agreement. In June, Erasmus publishes his response to Luther, *Hyperaspistes I* (*Shield-Bearer I*, running through seven editions in six months) and an edition of Irenaeus's *Against Heresies*. On August 28, the Turks achieve victory at Mohacz, Hungary, with Buda occupied. In the autumn, Tunstall has copies of Tyndale's New Testament burned; Barnes helps distribute it. More's daughters dispute philosophy before King Henry. On December 18, More

asks Erasmus to complete *Hyperaspites II*. In December, Vives complains that the English do nothing to help resist the Turks; Holbein arrives to More's home from Antwerp.

1527 Holbein paints the portrait of More's family at Chelsea, along with More's own portrait. In April, More is with Wolsey in France for final negotiations and the formal signing of the Anglo-French Treaty. On May 17, Henry appears before the secret court of Wolsey and Warham, and Catherine objects. Wolsey explains to Henry the difficulties involved with the divorce. Henry informs Catherine of his scruple about their marriage. Imperial troops under Bourbon sack Rome without Charles V's knowledge. In September, Erasmus publishes *Hyperaspistes II*. Henry consults More on the marriage and invites Erasmus to England as a consultant. With one of the worst harvests of the century because of the continual rain, wheat prices are doubled. On November 21, the heresy trial of Bilney takes place, and More abjures.

1528 More feeds one hundred people a day at Chelsea after the bad harvest of 1527. In January, war is declared against Charles V. In March, Bishop Tunstall commissions More to defend the Church in England through writing. In the spring, Margaret almost dies from illness. In the autumn, Cardinal Campeggio arrives in London to hear the case of Henry and Catherine's annulment. In November, Henry gives official arguments for his divorce: not the lack of a male heir, but concern for Mary's legitimacy. Catherine gives her public statement that the consummation with Arthur never occurred. Endangered by his sympathy for Catherine, Vives leaves England. Christopher St. German's first dialogue of *Doctor and Student* appears, along with William Tyndale's *Obedience of a Christian Man* (the first divine right theory in English), which Anne Boleyn gives to Henry. Simon Fish dedicates his anticlerical *Supplication of Beggars* to King Henry. More is chosen as alternate Master of Revels, Lincoln's Inn. Castiglione's *The Book of the Courtier* is published in Venice. More tells Roper his three great wishes: that Christian princes would cease to make war and learn to work peace; that the afflicted Church would settle into uniformity of belief again; and that the matter of the King's marriage "to the glory of God and quietness of all parties" would be brought "to a good conclusion."

1529 More's son John marries Anne Cresacre. More publishes *Dialogue of Sir Thomas More, Knight* "under royal favor." Serves as delegate at the Peace of Cambrai. In July, Wolsey fails to get Henry's marriage annulled at London legatine court. In August, Cranmer suggests use of himself, the universities, and *Collectanea* to resolve marriage issue, not Rome. In September, More counters Fish in *The Supplication of Souls*. More's family suffers a fire at Chelsea. Chapuys becomes the new Imperial ambassador. In October, Henry consults More a second time on marriage. Wolsey is dismissed and charged with Praemunire. More appointed Lord Chancellor; writes Erasmus that "this post involves the interests of Christendom." In November, Parliament is convened. More as Lord Chancellor calls for reformation of laws and condemns Wolsey's failures. The Commons' "Supplication" (with corrections in Thomas Cromwell's hand) lists clerical grievances. Henry VIII makes a partial defense of Luther to ambassador Eustace Chapuys and says he will reform the Church by Parliament.

1530 The opening of Parliament is delayed several times. Cromwell enters royal service. Agents are sent to enlist Tyndale's and Frith's help in the King's "Great Matter"; other royal agents are sent to universities and private scholars to gain support for Henry's marriage annulment and to gather materials for Cranmer's *Collectanea*. St. German adds a second dialogue to *Doctor and Student,* arguing that common law has precedence over canon law. On February 23, Thomas Hitton is burned for heresy at Maidstone. In March, Charles V is crowned emperor by the Pope. In September, Archbishop Cranmer presents *Collectanea satis copiosa* to Henry VIII, arguing for the English king's divine right and imperial status. Henry studies and annotates *Collectanea* carefully, then uses royal prerogative forbidding

the exercise of foreign authority in England. On September 20, Chapuys reports that More is nearly dismissed for opposing Henry's designs. In October, Henry argues that his imperial power allows him to prevent appeals to foreign powers; chief lawyers and clerics say no. Cromwell joins the King's Council. In November, More's father, John, dies. Tyndale's *Practice of Prelates* denounces Henry's divorce. On November 4, Wolsey is arrested. He is tried for treason, but dies on November 29. In December, the King's Council decides on Praemunire charges against all the clergy for illegal use of ecclesiastical courts.

1531 King Henry charges the clergy with Praemunire and requires that they recognize him as "Supreme Head of the Church of England." They do so "as far as Christ's law allows" and submit to paying a £100,000 penalty. On March 30, More is required to report to Parliament the universities' approval of the royal divorce (citing *Collectanea*). In the spring, More refuses to accept a letter from Charles V (Letter 183a). More publishes the second edition of *Dialogue of Sir Thomas More, Knight.* In the summer, Tyndale publishes his *Answer to Sir More Thomas More's* Dialogue. Henry is enraged, yet Cromwell still seeks Tyndale's support. St. German publishes his *New Additions* — arguing for Parliament's authority over the Church — and drafts reform legislation. On August 16, Thomas Bilney is burned at Norwich for heresy. In December, Richard Bayfield and John Tewkesbury are burned at Smithfield in London for heresy. Cromwell becomes a principal counselor of King Henry. Thomas Elyot's *The Book of the Governor* is published, dedicated to Henry VIII.

1532 Thomas Benet is burned at Exeter. Fisher and Tunstall are not called for January's Parliament session. Pole leaves England, having refused the See of York. In February, Warham, Archbishop of Canterbury, formally dissociates himself from the anticlerical laws promulgated since 1529. In March, More publishes *The Confutation of Tyndale's* Answer, Books 1–3. On March 15, there is an open clash over divorce tactics between Henry VIII and Archbishop

Warham. On March 18, the Commons submit *Supplication against the Ordinaries* to Henry VIII, who shows little interest. On March 19, the Conditional Restraint of Annates Act passes the House of Lords after Henry VIII visits the House three times; all bishops, two abbots and the Earl of Arundel oppose the act. On March 26, the Conditional Restraint of Annates Act passes the House of Commons after Henry VIII "causes the House to divide" for voting, for the first time in English history. On March 31, Henry is enraged by Friar Peto's Easter sermon against his intended divorce. After this sermon, which likens Henry to King Ahab and Anne to Jezebel, Friar Peto (the Queen's chaplain) is arrested. On April 12, Henry presents the Commons' *Supplication* to Warham to answer; Henry receives the bishops' reply on April 27. On April 30, an enraged Henry VIII finds the bishops' *Answer* "very slender"; James Bainham (husband of Simon Fish's widow) is burned in London. On May 10, the King sends his demands to the Convocation who are described by the King as "half our subjects . . . scarce our subjects." On May 14, Henry VIII dismisses Parliament after it refuses, under More's leadership, to pass the Submission of the Clergy Act. On May 15, a few members of the Upper House of Convocation approve the Submission of the Clergy after disbanding the Lower House. On May 16, More resigns as Lord Chancellor, saying he is "not up to the work." During the summer, More writes his epitaph, and has it engraved on his tombstone. More gives his advice to Cromwell on working with lions. In July, Frith returns to England to support the Protestant effort. In August, Warham dies leaving a speech defending the liberties of the English Church and repeatedly invoking St. Thomas Becket. In October, Frith is arrested and Cromwell visits him. In December, More's "Letter against Frith" is published. Anne Boleyn becomes pregnant. Machiavelli's *The Prince* is published posthumously in Italy.

1533   On January 25, Henry and Anne are secretly married. On January 26, Audley becomes Lord Chancellor. In February, St. German's anonymous *Treatise on the Division Between the Spiritualty and Temporalty* is published by the royal printer (runs to five editions by 1537). In the February–April Parliament, the Act in Restraint of Appeals declares England to be an empire and begins the transfer of power to Henry as Head of the Church. On March 30, Cranmer is consecrated Archbishop of Canterbury. In April, More publishes his *Apology* responding to "the Pacifier," a reference to St. German. In the spring, More also publishes *The Confutation of Tyndale's* Answer, Books 4–8. In April, More refuses the bishops' invitation to attend Anne's coronation, lest he be "deflowered, then devoured." In May, Cranmer grants Henry's divorce. On June 1, Anne is crowned queen, and Henry drafts revisions to the coronation oath. More sends his "Epitaph, a public declaration of the actual facts," to Erasmus and urges Erasmus not to delay in publishing it (Letter 191). In July, Pope Clement VII condemns the divorce; Elizabeth Barton, the Nun of Kent, is arrested; John Frith is burned at Smithfield in London. On September 7, Anne gives birth to Elizabeth. In September, St. German anonymously publishes his *Salem and Bizance;* in November, More responds by publishing his *Debellation of Salem and Bizance.* In December, More publishes his *Answer to a Poisoned Book,* responding to the anonymous *Supper of the Lord.* The Royal Council publishes a book of nine Articles defending Henry's marriage and denouncing the Pope; Tunstall writes to Henry to object; Henry replies.

1534   Fisher, Tunstall, Lee, Darcy, and others are told not to attend the January Parliament session. In February, Henry VIII includes More's name in the bill of attainder against the Nun of Kent. In February–March, More writes to Cromwell and Henry denying any guilt (Letters 197–99). The House of Lords requests to hear More's case; instead, Henry has More appear before the royal commission of Cromwell, Cranmer, Audley, and Norfolk. More is removed from attainder, but his salary as royal councillor is stopped. Parliament formalizes, through the Act of Submission of the Clergy, the 1532 Convocation statute: all appeals of Church law must now go to the King's Court of Chancery. The Act Restraining Annates confirms the 1532 Conditional Act: abbots and bishops will now be appointed by Henry VIII. The Act Ratifying the Oath to the Succession authorizes penalty of high treason for writing or acting against succession, and misprision of treason for refusing an oath concerning it. On April 13, More is interrogated at Lambeth Palace (Letter 200). On April 17, More is imprisoned (illegally) for refusing to take the oath of succession. On April 20, the Nun of Kent and five priest-supporters are executed at Tyburn. In mid-May, Margaret begins visiting More in prison. In August, Chancellor Audley sends a warning to More through Alice Alington (Letters 205–6). In November–December, the Act Recognizing the King as Supreme Head of the Church in England passes. The Second Act of Succession, giving the text of the required oath, passes. The Treason Act makes it high treason to maliciously deprive the King and Queen of the dignity, title, or name of their royal estates, by word, deed, or thought. An Act of Attainder is made against Bishop Fisher and others, convicting them of misprision of treason for refusing the oath of Succession. An Act of Attainder of Thomas More follows: misprision of treason for refusing the oath of Succession. This act, retrospectively, makes More's earlier imprisonment legal. More begins *A Treatise upon the Passion* before his imprisonment, continuing More's commission by Tunstall to defend the Church's teachings. Writes *A Dialogue of Comfort against Tribulation* and *A Treatise to Receive the Blessed Body* after imprisonment.

1535   Cromwell is made Viceregent in spiritual affairs, to visit ecclesiastical foundations and make a detailed list of property. On April 28, the treason trial of three Carthusian and one Bridgettine priors occurs. On April 30, More is interrogated in the Tower by Cromwell and others (Letter 214). On May 4, the Charterhouse and Bridgettine priors are placed on pallets to be taken to Tyburn and hanged in their habits; the process begins below More's cell window and while Margaret is visiting. The priors are dragged to Tyburn and hung, drawn, and quartered. *Ca.* May–June, More writes *De tristitia Christi* (published in 1565, with an English translation in 1557). On June 3, More is interrogated again, this time by members of the Royal Council. Tunstall gives full support to the King's Supremacy. On June 12, Richard Rich removes More's books and writing materials from his cell, and their disputed conversation about Parliament's proper powers occurs. On June 14, More's formal interrogation is recorded by a notary before Council members and witnesses. On June 17 and 22, Bishop John Fisher is tried and executed. *Ca.* June 18: Cromwell makes a "Remembrances" note to himself to find out the King's "pleasure touching Master More" after informing the King about "the opinion of the judges thereon." On June 25, Henry VIII gives the order to publicize the guilt of Fisher and More. On June 28, the Grand Jury of Middlesex County indicts Thomas More. On July 1, More is tried at Westminster Hall and found guilty of malicious treason. On July 1–5, More writes his final prayer. On July 6, More is executed, not as decreed at trial (by hanging, drawing, quartering), but by beheading, a mercy from the King. On October 6, William Tyndale is executed in Brussels.

1536   On January 8, Queen Catherine of Aragon dies. From February 4 to April 14, the Seventh Parliamentary Session is held. On March 11, Henry delivers a speech to the House of Commons on the *Dissolution of the Lesser Monasteries Act*. On May 17, Henry's marriage to Anne Boleyn is annulled by Thomas Cranmer. On May 19, Anne is executed for witchcraft, incest, and adultery. On May 20, Henry is betrothed to Jane Seymour. On May 30, Henry and Jane marry. In June, a New Parliament is called. In July, Princess Mary and her sister Elizabeth are bastardized by the Second Act of Succession. On July 31, the Act Extinguishing the Authority of the Bishop of Rome passes. On October 8, rebellions begin in Lincolnshire and Yorkshire (the "Pilgrimage of Grace") and continue on until June 1537.

English Poetry

While Thomas More wrote vastly more prose than poetry during his life, the early poetry remains a revealing testimony to the author's wit and skill, and an intriguing foreshadowing of his later concerns as a writer and thinker. Erasmus wrote in *Ciceronianus* that More was "a poet even in his prose," and More scholar Richard Sylvester concluded "that there is a great deal of 'poetry' in More's dialectic and an almost equal amount of 'dialectic' in his poetry."

The "Pageant Verses," written to accompany tapestries in his father's house, are most likely More's earliest poems, written sometime before 1503. Composed in rhyme royal meter, the poems strikingly mingle both English and Petrarchan iconographic traditions (*CW* 1: xx). The sequence culminates in a Latin poem, "The Poet," which places the earlier meditations on Childhood, Manhood, Venus and Cupid, Age, Death, Fame, Time, and Eternity in a comprehensive perspective that cautions against trusting and hoping in lesser goods that "will fade away." The only source for these "Pageant Verses" is Rastell's 1557 English edition.

More's "Rueful Lamentation" was inspired by the untimely death of Elizabeth of York, King Henry VII's wife, on February 11, 1502/3, her thirty-seventh birthday. The poem was probably composed shortly after her death, and may have been written to be hung beside Elizabeth's tomb, given the young More's connections to her family (*CW* 1: xxiii). Anthony Edwards notes that More's provocative "integration" of first person lamentation, *de casibus* tragedy (see Lydgate's *Fall of Princes*), and verse epitaph may be unique to the author (xxiv). As in "Pageant Verses," the poetry addresses itself—through the dead queen's voice—to those who put "trust and confidence / In worldly riches and frail prosperity." By juxtaposing earthly realities and desires with Elizabeth's repeated lament, "Lo, here I lie," the poem explores favorite themes of the later More, such as the transience of life and the danger of human blindness, and the poem counsels the reader to "love and magnify" true and lasting goods, what Elizabeth calls "heavenly things," and to avoid "worldly vanity" and "earthly folly." Her "Rueful

Lamentation" survives in two manuscripts, marked by many differences. Our edition follows the text of *CW* 1.

"A Merry Jest," More's rollicking comic poem on one form of human folly, was probably composed either for the occasion of his father's election to sargeant of law in 1503, or later in 1509, for the occasion of young More's appointment as an honorary mercer (*CW* 1: xxvi–xxvii). In this youthful jest, the reader encounters for the first time a favorite form of the author, the "merry tale." More's later writings are replete with merry tales as well, but in prose. "A Merry Jest" is written in "tail rhyme"—two rhymed lines followed by a longer "tail" line—a poetic form used in Chaucer's "Tale of Sir Topaz" and other medieval poems (*OCEL* 959). Through its satirical portrait of a man who pretends to be a friar, the poem directs readers away from "feigning" and toward diligent work in areas where one has proper competence, or "skill."

Regarding More's "Fortune Verses," William Rastell writes that these rhyme royal poems were "written by Master Thomas More in his youth," and were intended to serve as a preface to a "Book of Fortune." The poems were written sometime earlier than 1505, though how much earlier is difficult to say, and identifying the "Book of Fortune" has proved elusive as well (*CW* 1: xxviii–xxix). In the "Fortune Verses," young More focuses on issues of credence and trust, in regard to fortune, described as "inconstant, slipper, frail, and full of treason." The poetry reveals both blindness and the governance of pride in human life. "Fortune Verses" attempt to alter the "eye" of those that trust in fortune by praising the surprising freedom to be found in poverty, challenging the reader to choose "bondage, or free liberty." The dialectical structure of this poem shows More's lifelong interest in the dialogue form and its role in fostering active reflection and free choice. As More writes later in the 1529 *Dialogue*, pursuits such as poetry and dialectical inquiry help foster "a good mother wit," without which human learning is "half lame."

The last two poems in this section, the rhyme royal "Lewis the Lost Lover" and "Davey the Dicer," are described by Rastell as "two short ballads which Sir Thomas More made for his pastime" during his imprisonment in the Tower of London. More's son-in-law William Roper attests that "Lewis the Lost Lover" was composed after a visit from Thomas Cromwell, who "pretended much friendship" toward More, and "for his comfort told [More] that the King's Highness was his good and gracious Lord, and minded not with any matter wherein he should have any cause of scruple, from henceforth to trouble his conscience." The poem records More's response and reveals the imprisoned author's vigilance about fortune's flatteries and beguilements—returning to a topic treated in his earliest poetry. In these prison verses, More stresses the need to be prepared for whatever "storm" will arise in human life, a need consistently pondered across his writing career.

More's last known poem, "Davey the Dicer," may have been composed along with "Lewis the Lost Lover" or close in time (*CW* 1: xxxii). More's habitual humor—his way of "speaking the truth through jests," an art learned from Chaucer, Lucian, and others—sparkles again in this poem. Fortune's sharp downward turn, though it has ruined poor Davey in obvious ways, has nevertheless also provided "some leisure" for writing poetry again, a happy development.

In addition to the English poems given here, More also included four rhyme royal poems in the concluding part of his *Life of John Pico*. Moreover, he composed 281 poems in Latin, published as his *Epigrams* in 1518 and 1520, with additions and corrections. These poems are found in those sections of *Essential Works*.

CONTENTS

English Poetry

Pageant Verses

Master Thomas More in his youth devised in his father's house in London a goodly hanging of fine painted cloth, with nine pageants,[1] and verses over every of those pageants, which verses expressed and declared what the images in those pageants represented; and also in those pageants were painted the things that the verses over them did, in effect, declare; which verses here follow.

In the first pageant was painted a boy playing at the top and scourge.[2] And over this pageant was written as followeth:

CHILDHOOD

I am called Childhood; in play is all my mind,
To cast a quoit,[3] a cock-stele,[4] and a ball.
A top can I set, and drive it in his kind.[5]
But would to God these hateful bookés all
Were in a fire brent[6] to powder small.
Then might I lead my life always in play:
Which life God send me to mine ending day.

In the second pageant was painted a goodly fresh young man riding upon a goodly horse, having a hawk on his fist and a brace[7] of greyhounds following him. And under the horse feet was painted the same boy that in the first pageant was playing at the top and scourge. And over this second pageant the writing was thus:

MANHOOD

Manhood I am; therefore I me delight
To hunt and hawk, to nourish up and feed[8]
The greyhound to the course,[9] the hawk to the flight.[10]
And to bestride a good and lusty[11] steed.
These things become a very man indeed,

Yet thinketh this boy his peevish[12] game swetter,[13]
But what, no force,[14] his reason is no better.

In the third pageant was painted the goodly young man in the second pageant lying on the ground. And upon him stood Lady Venus, goddess of love, and by her upon this man stood the little god Cupid. And over this third pageant, this was the writing that followeth:

VENUS AND CUPID

Whoso ne[15] knoweth the strength, pow'r, and might
Of Venus and me, her little son Cupide,
Thou, Manhood, shalt a mirror been[16] aright,
By us subduéd for all thy great pride.
My fiery dart pierceth thy tender side.
Now thou which erst[17] despised'st children small,
Shall wax[18] a child again and be my thrall.[19]

In the fourth pageant was painted an old sage father sitting in a chair. And lying under his feet was painted the image of Venus and Cupid, that[20] were in the third pageant. And over this fourth pageant the scripture[21] was thus:

AGE

Old Age am I, with lockés thin and hore,[22]
Of our short life, the last and best part.
Wise and discreet: the public weal[23] therefore,
I help to rule to my labor and smart.[24]
Therefore, Cupid, withdraw thy fiery dart,
Chargeable[25] matters shall of love oppress[26]
Thy childish game[27] and idle busyness.

In the fifth pageant was painted an image of Death, and under his feet lay the old man in the fourth pageant. And above this fifth pageant, this was the saying:

1 pictorial illustrations   2 *top and scourge:* child's top, spun with a detached whip-like string   3 iron ring for throwing   4 stick thrown in sport at a tethered rooster   5 *A top . . . kind:* i.e., I can spin a top and keep it going in its way   6 burned   7 pair   8 *nourish . . . feed:* raise and train   9 *the course:* chase hares or game with greyhounds   10 *the flight:* hawk's pursuit of game in sport   11 *good and lusty:* strong and spirited   12 foolish   13 sweeter   14 matter   15 does not   16 *a mirror been:* an example be   17 *which erst:* who before   18 become   19 slave   20 who   21 inscription   22 hoar, gray, aged, venerable   23 well-being   24 pain   25 weighty, requiring responsibility   26 *of love oppress:* deprive love of   27 pleasure, amusement

DEATH

Though I be foul, ugly, lean, and misshape,[28]
Yet there is none in all this worlde wide,
70 That may my power withstand or escape.
Therefore, sage father, greatly magnified,[29]
Descend from your chair,[30] set apart your pride,
Witsafe[31] to lend (though it be to your pain)
To me, a fool,[32] some of your wise brain.

75 *In the sixth pageant was painted Lady Fame. And*
under her feet was the picture of Death that was in
the fifth pageant. And over this sixth pageant the
writing was as followeth:

FAME

80 Fame I am called; marvel you nothing,
Though with tongues am compasséd all round
For in voice of people is my chief living.
O cruel death, thy power I confound.[33]
When thou a noble man hast brought to ground,
85 Maugré thy teeth,[34] to live cause him shall I,
Of people in perpetual memory.

In the seventh pageant was painted the image of
Time, and under his feet was lying the picture of
Fame that was in the sixth pageant. And this was
90 *the scripture over this seventh pageant:*

TIME

I, whom thou seest with horologe[35] in hand,
Am named Time, the lord of every hour;
I shall in space[36] destroy both sea and land.
95 O simple Fame, how darest thou man honour
Promising of his name an endless flour?[37]
Who may in the world have a name eternall,
When I shall, in process,[38] destroy the world and
all?

In the eighth pageant was pictured the image of Lady
100 *Eternity, sitting in a chair under a sumptuous cloth*
of estate,[39] crowned with an imperial crown. And
under her feet lay the picture of Time, that was in the
seventh pageant. And above this eighth pageant, was
it written as followeth:

ETERNITY   105

Me needeth not to boast; I am Eternity.
The very name signifieth well
That mine empire infinite shall be.
Thou mortal Time, every man can tell,
Art nothing else but the mobility   110
Of sun and moon changing in every degree.
When they shall leave their course, thou shalt be
brought,
For all thy pride and boasting, into nought.[40]

In the ninth pageant was painted a Poet sitting in a
chair. And over this pageant were there written these 115
verses in Latin following:

THE POET

Has fictas quemcunque iuvat spectare figuras,
Sed mira veros quas putat arte homines,
Ille potest veris, animum sic pascere rebus,   120
Ut pictis oculos pascit imaginibus.
Namque videbit uti fragilis bona lubrica mundi,
Tam cito non veniunt, quam cito pretereunt,
Gaudia laus et honor, celeri pede omnia cedunt,
Qui manet excepto semper amore dei?   125
Ergo homines, levibus iamiam diffidite rebus,
Nulla recessuro spes adhibenda bono.
Qui dabit eternam nobis pro munere vitam,
In permansuro ponite vota deo.

[Translation:[41]
Whoever delights to behold these fashioned figures,
But thinks them, by a wondrous art, to be true to life,
Is able to nourish his soul on true things,
As he nourishes his eyes on the painted images.
For indeed he will see how the slippery goods of the
fragile world
No more quickly come than they quickly pass away.
Joys, praise, and honor, all things move past at a swift
pace;
What remains always, except for the love of God?
Therefore, O mortals, distrust fickle things right now,
No hope should be attached to a good that will fade
away.
It is God who will give us the gift of eternal life;
Place your prayers with him who ever will remain.]

---

28 ill-shaped, deformed, monstrous
29 praised; enlarged to the sight
30 throne **31** deign to **32** The original
spelling, "fole," could be read as two
syllables, which renders a regular iambic
line. **33** defeat **34** *Maugré thy teeth:*
despite your resistance **35** hourglass
36 time **37** flowering **38** due course
39 *cloth of estate:* tapestry used by monarchs **40** nothing **41** For an alternate
translation of this poem, see Epigram 272.

A Rueful Lamentation[1]

Ye that put your trust and confidence
In worldly riches and frail prosperity,
That so live here as ye should never hence,[2]
5   Remember death and look here upon me.
In sample[3] I think there may no better be.
Yourself wot[4] well that in this realm was I
Your queen but late.[5] Lo, here I lie.

Was I not born of old worthy lin'age?[6]
10   Was not my mother queen and my father king?
Was I not a king's fere[7] in marriáge?[8]
Had I not plenty of every pleasant thing?
Merciful God, this is a strange reckoning:
Riches, honor, wealth, and ancestry
15   Hath me forsake. Lo, here I lie.

If worship[9] might have kept me, I had not[10] gone.
If wealth might me have served, I needed not to
    fear.
If money might have hold,[11] I lackéd none.
But O good God, what availeth all this gear?[12]
20   When death cometh, thy mighty messenger,
Obey we must; there is no remedye,
He hath me summoned. Lo, here I lie.

Yet was I lately promised otherwise:[13]
This year to live in wealth and delice.[14]
25   Lo, whereto cometh thy blandishing[15] promise,
O false astrology divinatrice,[16]
Of Godés secretés making thee so wise!
How true is for this year the prophecy?
The year yet lasteth, and lo, now here I lie.

30   O brittle wealth, aye[17] full of bitterness,
Thy sing'lar pleasure ay doubled is with pain.

Accompt[18] my sorrow first and my distress,
Sundry wise,[19] and reckon there again
The joy that I have had, I dare not fain.[20]
For all my honor, enduréd yet have I   35
More woe than wealth, and lo, here I lie.

Where are our castlés now and our towers?
Goodly Richmond,[21] soon art thou gone from me.
At Westminster that goodly work of yours,[22]
Mine own dear Lord, now shall I never see.   40
Almighty God witsave[23] to grant that ye
And your children well may edify.[24]
My place builded is,[25] for lo, here I lie.

Adieu, my true spouse, my worthy lord;
The faithful love, that did us two combine   45
In marriáge and peaceable concord,
Unto your handés here I clean resign,
To be bestowed on your children and mine.
Erst[26] were ye father; now must ye supply
The mother's part also. Lo, here I lie.   50

Farewell, my daughter Lady Margarete.
God wot full sore[27] it grievéd hath my mind,
That ye should go where we should seldom meet.[28]
Now am I gone, and have left you behind.
O mortal folk, what, we ever blind![29]   55
That we least fear, full oft it is full nigh.[30]
From you depart I first. Lo, here I lie.

Farewell, Madam, my lordés worthy mother,
Comfort your son, and be ye of good cheer.
Take all in worth,[31] for it will be none other.[32]   60
Farewell, my daughter Katherine,[33] late the fere[34]
To Prince Arthur, my own child so dear.
It booteth[35] not for me to weep and cry;
Pray for my soul, for now, lo here I lie.

1 The full title as given in the 1557 *Workes* is "A Rueful Lamentation written by Master Thomas More in his youth, of the death of Queen Elizabeth, mother to King Henry the Eighth, wife to King Henry the Seventh, and eldest daughter to King Edward the Fourth, which Queen Elizabeth died in childbed in February in the year of our Lord 1503 and in the 18th year of the reign of King Henry the Seventh." 2 (depart) from here   3 *In sample:* As an example or warning   4 know   5 *but late:* not long ago   6 Elizabeth was the daughter of Elizabeth Woodville and Edward IV, and hence a descendent of the royal Plantagenet line. 7 consort, spouse   8 Elizabeth married Henry VII on January 18, 1486.   9 honor 10 *had not:* would not have   11 helped 12 stuff   13 differently, i.e., by the court astrologer, William Parron, who published two optimistic predictions in the months preceding Elizabeth's death   14 delight 15 flattering   16 a female seer or diviner   17 always   18 account, consider 19 *Sundry wise:* In various ways   20 (be) glad   21 new name for Henry VII's palace, given when rebuilt after a fire soon before Elizabeth's death   22 Henry VII's new chapel, under construction at the time of Elizabeth's death   23 deign   24 *well may edify:* may build well   25 *my place builded is:* i.e., her tomb is complete, in contrast to the castle and chapel   26 before 27 *full sore:* very bitterly   28 Just before Elizabeth's death, negotiations had been completed for Margaret's marriage to James IV of Scotland.   29 *what…blind:* This text follows the L edition for a clearer metrical reading.   30 *full oft…nigh:* very often is very near   31 *Take…worth:* Be content   32 *none other:* no other way 33 Not included in Yale, but appears in L and 1557. This emendation clarifies meaning and increases the line to a full ten syllables. 34 *late the fere:* recently the wife. Catherine of Aragon had married Elizabeth's eldest son, Prince Arthur, on November 14, 1501. He died on April 2, 1502.   35 helps

65 Adieu, Lord Harry, my lovely son adieu.
    Our Lord increase your honor and your estate;[36]
    Adieu, my daughter Mary, bright of hue.[37]
    God make you virtuous, wise, and fortunáte.
    Adieu, sweet heart, my Lady daughter Kate;[38]
70 Thou shalt, good babe, such is thy destiny,
    Thy mother never know: for lo here I lie.

    O Lady Cécil', Anne, and Katheríne,
    Farewell, my well-beloved sisters three.
    O Lady Bridget, dear sister mine,
75 Lo, here the end of worldly vanity;[39]
    Lo, well are you that earthly folly flee
    And heavenly things love and magnify.[40]
    Farewell, and pray for me, for lo here I lie.

    Adieu, my lords, adieu my ladies all,[41]
80 Adieu, my faithful servants every chone;[42]
    Adieu, my commons[43] whom I never shall
    See in this world. Wherefore to thee alone,
    Immortal God, very[44] three in one,
    I me commend. Thy infinite mercy
85 Show to thy servant now, for lo here I lie.

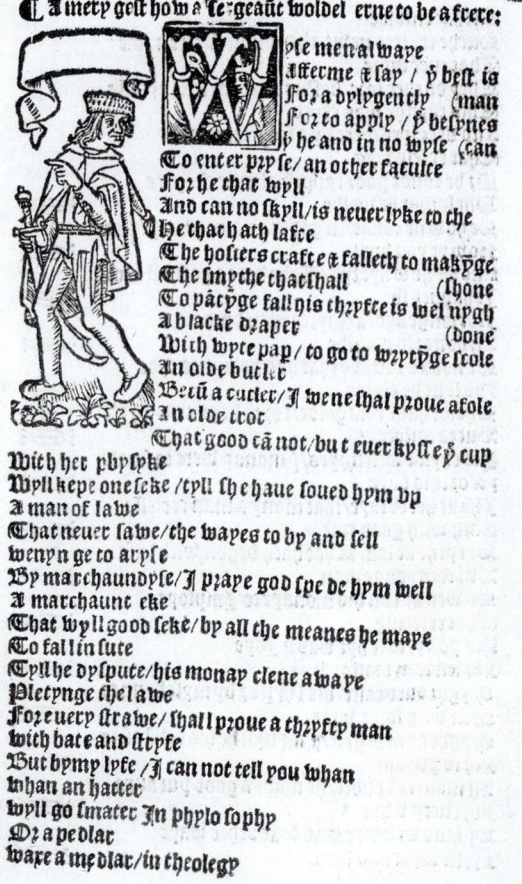

Title page, *Mery Gest, ca.* 1516. Courtesy Huntington Library, RB 31484.

36 position   37 complexion   38 Elizabeth's last child, Katherine, was born on February 2, 1503, just over a week before her mother's death.   39 *here . . .* *vanity:* proverbial, from "This world is but a vanity" (cf. Eccl 1:2)   40 praise   41 *Adieu . . . all:* Text is emended to follow L and 1557, rendering the line metrically more regular.   42 *every chone:* everyone (dialect)   43 common people   44 truly

A Merry Jest: How a Sergeant Would Learn to Play the Frère[1]

Wise men always
Affirm and say
    That best is for a man
Diligently
For to apply
    The business that he can[2]
And in no wise[3]
To enterprise[4]
    Another faculty;[5]
For he that will,
And can[6] no skill,
    Is never like to thee.[7]
He that hath laft[8]
The hosier's[9] craft,
    And falleth to making shone,[10]
The smith that shall
To painting fall,
    His thrift[11] is well-nigh[12] done.
A black draper,[13]
With white paper
    To go to writing school,
An old butler,
Become a cutler,
    I ween[14] shall prove a fool.
An old trot,[15]
That good can not
    But ever kiss the cup,[16]
With her physic[17]
Will keep one sick
    Till she have soused[18] him up.
A man of law
That never saw
    The ways to buy and sell,
Weening to arise
By merchandise,
    I pray God speed him well.
A merchant eke,[19]
That will go seke,[20]
    By all the means he may,

To fall in suit[21]
Till he dispute
    His money clean away,
Pleading the law
For every straw,
    Shall prove a thrifty man
With bate[22] and strife;
But by my life,
    I cannot tell you whan.[23]
When an hatter
Will go smatter[24]
    In philosophy,
Or a peddler
Wax[25] a meddler
    In theology;
All that ensue[26]
Such craftés new,
    They drive so far a-cast[27]
That evermore
They do, therefore,
    Beshrew[28] themself at last.
This thing was tried
And verified
    Here by a sergeant late[29]
That rifely[30] was,
Or[31] he could pass,[32]
    Rapped about the pate,[33]
While that he would[34]
See how he could
    In God's name play the frère;
Now if you wyll[35]
Know how it fyll,[36]
    Take heed and ye shall hear.
It happéd so,
Not long ago,
    A thrifty[37] man there[38] died.
An hundred pound
Of nobles[39] round,
    That had he laid aside,
His son he would[40]
Should have this gold,
    For to begin with all:

---

1 French for brother, monk   2 knows
3 way   4 undertake   5 skill, occupation   6 knows   7 *like to thee:* likely
to prosper   8 left   9 one who makes
or sells stockings and socks   10 shoes
11 prosperity   12 almost completely
13 cloth maker or dealer   14 think,
surmise   15 hag   16 i.e., the drinking
cup   17 medicine   18 intoxicated
19 also   20 seek   21 lawsuit   22 conflict
23 when   24 dabble   25 become
26 follows   27 astray   28 cause
misfortune on   29 recently   30 commonly; amply   31 before   32 leave;
accomplish his deception (i.e., pass for a
friar)   33 *Rapped … pate:* Beaten on the
crown of his head   34 *While … would:*
When he wanted to   35 will, want
to   36 happened, befell   37 prosperous
38 "there" is added in the 1557 edition, and
added here to fill out the trimester line.
39 gold coins   40 wished

But to suffice
85 His child, well thrice
   That money were too small.
Yet or[41] this day
I have heard say,
   That many a man certesse[42]
90 Hath, with good cast,[43]
Be rich at last
   That hath begun with less.
But this young man
So well began
95   His money to employ,
That certainly,
His policy,[44]
   To see it was a joy.
For lest some blast[45]
100 Might over cast
   His ship, or by mischance
Men with some wile
Might him beguile
   And minish[46] his substance;
105 For to put out
All manner doubt,
   He made a good purvey[47]
For every whyt,[48]
(By his own wyt)
110   And took another way.
First, fair and wele,[49]
A great dele,[50]
   He dight[51] it in a pot;
But then him thought,
115 That way was nought,[52]
   And there he left it not.
So was he fain,[53]
From thence again,
   To put it in a cup;
120 And, by and by,[54]
Covetously,
   He suppéd it fair up.[55]
In his own breast,
He thought it best,
125   His money to enclose.
Then wist[56] he well,
Whatever fell,

He could it never lose.
He borrowed than,[57]
Of another man, 130
   Money and merchandise.
Never paid it;
Up he laid it,
   In like manner wise.[58]
Yet on the gear,[59] 135
That he would wear,
   He rought[60] not what he spent,
So it were nice,
As for the price
   Could him not miscontent. 140
With lusty sport,
And with resort[61]
   Of jolly company,
In mirth and play,
Full many a day 145
   He livéd merrily.
And men had sworn,
Some man is born
   To have a goodly flour,[62]
And so was he, 150
For such degree[63]
   He gat,[64] and such honour,
That without doubt,
When he went out,
   A sergeant well and fair 155
Was ready straight,[65]
On him to wait
   As soon as on the may'r.[66]
But he, doubtless
Of his meekness, 160
   Hated such pomp and pride,
And would not go
Comp'nied[67] so,
   But drew himself aside,
To Saint Katherine,[68] 165
Straight as a line,[69]
   He gat him at a tide.[70]
For devotion,
Or promotion,[71]
   There would he needs abide. 170
There spent he fast

---

41 before   42 assuredly   43 fortune   44 shrewdness   45 storm   46 diminish   47 plan, arrangement   48 creature   49 well   50 deal   51 hid; also, misused   52 not good   53 obliged   54 *by and by:* immediately   55 *supped…up:* drank it up completely   56 knew   57 then   58 *in…wise:* in the same way; i.e., he drank it   59 apparel   60 cared   61 help   62 flowering   63 degree   64 got   65 immediately   66 mayor   67 accompanied   68 *Saint Katherine:* Hospital by the Tower; a sanctuary for debtors   69 *Straight as a line:* immediately (proverbial)   70 *at a…tide:* for a time   71 informing against someone; here, gather information against those to whom he owes money

Till all was past,
    And to him came there many
To ask their debt,
175 But none could get
    The valor[72] of a penny.
With visage stout,[73]
He bare it out[74]
    Unto the hard hedge,[75]
180 A month or twain,[76]
Till he was fain[77]
    To lay his gown to pledge.
Then was he there,
In greater fere,[78]
185 Then, or[79] that he came thither,
And would as fain[80]
Depart again,
    But that he wist[81] not whither.
Then, after this,
190 To a friend of his
    He went and there abode,
Where, as he lay
So sick alway,
    He might not come abrode.[82]
195 It happéd than,
A merchant man
    That he ought[83] money to,
Of an officer
Then 'gan[84] inquire,
200   What him was best to do.
And he answered,
    "Be not afeared,
    Take an action[85] therefore;
I you behest,[86]
205 I shall him 'rest,[87]
    And then care for no more."[88]
"I fear," quod he,
"It will not be,
    For he will not come out."
210 The sergeant sayd,
    "Be not afraid,
    It shall be brought about.
In many a game,
Like to the same,[89]
215   Have I been well in ure,[90]

And for your sake,
Let me be bake,[91]
    But if[92] I do this cure."
Thus part they both,
And forth him go'th   220
    Apace, this officere,
And for a day,
All his array
    He changéd with a frère.
So was he dight[93]   225
That no man might
    Him for a frère deny,
He dopped and douked,[94]
He spake and loked
    So religiously.   230
Yet in a glass,[95]
Or he would pass,[96]
    He touted[97] and he peered:
His heart for pride
Leapt in his side,   235
    To see how well he frèred.[98]
Then forth apace,
Unto the place,
    He goeth, in God's name,
To do this deed.   240
But now take heed,
    For here beginneth the game.
He drew him nigh[99]
And softly
    At the door he knocked;   245
A demoiselle,[100]
That heard him well,
    Came and it unlocked.
The frère sayd,
"God speed,[101] fair maid;   250
    Here lodgeth such a man,
It is told me…"
"Well, sir," quod[102] she
    "And if he do, what than?"
Quod he, "Mistress,   255
No harm, doubtless;
    It 'longeth for our order
To hurt no man,
But, as we can,

---

72 value   73 brave; also proud or arrogant
74 *bare it out:* endured   75 *Unto…
hedge:* to the very edge (proverbial)
76 two   77 obliged   78 fear   79 before
80 willingly (as he had come)   81 know
82 abroad   83 owed   84 began

85 legal action   86 promise   87 arrest
88 *care…more:* no longer be troubled (by
him)   89 *the same:* this situation   90 *in
ure:* accustomed to   91 baked (an exclamation)   92 *But if:* Unless   93 dressed
94 *dopped and douked:* bowed and cringed

95 mirror   96 *Or…pass:* Before he would
depart   97 gazed   98 to act the part of a
friar (More's playful invention)   99 near
100 young, unmarried woman   101 make
you prosper   102 said

260 Every wight[103] to forder.[104]
With him, truly,
Fain[105] speak would I."
     "Sir," quod she, "By my fay,[106]
He is so sike,[107]
265 Ye be not like[108]
     To speak with him today."
Quod he, "Fair may,[109]
Yet I you pray,
     This much, at my desire,
270 Vouchsafe[110] to do,
As to go him to
     And say an Austen frère[111]
Would with him speak
And matters break[112]
275   For his avail[113] certain."
Quod she, "I will;
Stand ye here still
     Till I come down again."
Up is she go
280 And told him so
     As she was bode[114] to say.
He, mistrusting
No manner thing,
     Said, "Maiden, go thy way
285 And fetch him hither,
That we together
     May talk. Adown she go'th,
And up she brought
No harm, she thought;
290   But it made some folk wroth.
But this officere,
This feigned frère,
     When he was come aloft,
He dopped[115] than,
295 And greet this man
     Religiously and oft.
And he, again
Right glad and fain,[116]
     Took him there by the hand.
300 The frère then sayd,
"Ye be dismayed
     With trouble, I understand."
"Indeed," quod he,
"It hath with me

Been better than it is." 305
"Sir," quod the frère,
"Be of good chere;
     Yet shall it after this.
For Christ's sake,
Look that you take 310
     No thought in your breast;
God may turn all —
And so he shall,
     I trust — unto the best.[117]
But I would now 315
Come in with you
     In counsel, if you please —
Or else nat[118] —
Of matters that
     Shall set your heart at ease." 320
Down went the maid.
The merchant said,
     "Now say on, gentle frère.
Of all this tiding
That ye me bring, 325
     I long full sore to hear."
When there was none
But they alone,
     The frère, with evil grace,
Said, "I 'rest[119] thee. 330
Come on with me,"
     And out he took his mace.
"Thou shalt obey.
Come on thy way,
     I have thee in my clouch.[120] 335
Thou goest not hence
For all the pence
     The mayor hasth in his pouch."
This merchant there,
For wrath and fere,[121] 340
     Waxed well-nigh wood,[122]
Said, "Whoreson thief,
With a mischief,[123]
     Who hath taught thee good?"
And with his fist,
Upon the list[124] 345
     He gave him such a blow
That backward down,
Almost in swown,[125]

---

103 person   **104** help   **105** gladly
106 faith   **107** sick   **108** unlikely
109 maiden   **110** deign, agree   **111** *Austen frère*: Augustinian friar (St. Katherine's, where the man had sought refuge

previously, was an Augustinian hospital)
112 disclose   **113** benefit   **114** bidden
115 bowed his head   **116** well-pleased
117 See Rom 8:28.   **118** not   **119** arrest
120 clutch   **121** fear   **122** crazy, mad

123 *with a mischief*: expletive; misfortune on you   **124** ear   **125** *in swown*: fallen down; in a swoon

350 The frère is overthrow.
Yet was this man
Well fearder,¹²⁶ than,
   Lest he the frère had slain,
Till with good raps
355 And heavy claps,
   He dawed¹²⁷ him up again.
The frère took heart,
And up he start,
   And well he laid about,¹²⁸
360 And so there go'th
Between them both
   Many a lusty clout.¹²⁹
They rent¹³⁰ and tear
Each other hair,
365   And clave ¹³¹ together fast,
Till with lugging,
Hauling, and tugging,
   They fell down both at last.
Then on the ground,
370 Together, 'round,
   With many sadde¹³² stroke,
They roll and rumble,
They turn and tumble,
   Like pigges in a poke.¹³³
375 So long above,
They heave and shove
   Together, that at the last
The maid, the wife,
To break the strife,
380   Hied¹³⁴ them upward fast.
And when they spy
The captains lie,
   Waltering on¹³⁵ the place,
The frère's hood
385 They pulled a-good
   Adown about his face.
While he was blind,
The wench behind
   Lent him, on the floor,
390 Many a joll¹³⁶
About the noll¹³⁷
   With a great battledore.¹³⁸
The wife came yet,

And with her fete¹³⁹
   She holp¹⁴⁰ to keep him down, 395
And with her rock¹⁴¹
Many a knock
   She gave him on the crown.
They laid his mace
About his face,
   That he was wood¹⁴² for pain; 400
The frère frappe¹⁴³
Gat many a swappe,¹⁴⁴
   Till he was full nigh¹⁴⁵ slain.
Up they him lift, 405
And, with evil thrift,
   Headling¹⁴⁶ all the stair,
Down they him threw,
And said, "Adieu.
   Commend us to the may'r!" 410
The frère arose,
But I suppose
   Amazéd was his head.
He shook his ears,¹⁴⁷
And from great fears, 415
   He thought him well afled.¹⁴⁸
Quod he, "Now lost
Is all this cost,
   We be never the nere.¹⁴⁹
Ill mote he thee¹⁵⁰ 420
That causéd me
   To make myself a frère."
Now, masters all,
And now I shall
   End there, as I began: 425
In any wise,¹⁵¹
I would advise
   And counsel every man
His own craft use,
All new refuse, 430
   And utterly let them gone.
Play not the frère;
Now make good chere,
   And welcome every chone.¹⁵²

FINIS 435

126 *well fearder:* much more afraid **127** revived, woke **128** *laid about:* dealt violent blows on all sides **129** heavy blow **130** pulled at **131** held **132** heavy **133** sack **134** hurried; exerted **135** *Waltering on:* Rolling around **136** blow **137** head **138** a large wooden paddle-like implement used in washing **139** feet **140** helped **141** distaff, spindle **142** mad **143** beaten **144** blows **145** nearly **146** head-first **147** *shook his ears:* roused himself **148** escaped **149** nearer **150** *mote he thee:* may he prosper **151** case **152** *every chone:* everyone (dialect)

THE FORTUNE VERSES

THE PROLOGUE

As often as I consider these old noble clerks,[1]
Poets, Orators, and Philosophers, sects[2] three,
5 How wonderful they were, in all their works
How eloquent, how inventive in every degree,
Half amazed I am, and as a dead tree
Stand still, over-rude[3] for to bring forth
Any fruit or sentence that is ought worth.[4]

10 Nevertheless, though rude[5] I be in all contriving
Of matters, yet somewhat[6] to make, I need not to care;
I see many a one occupied in the same thing.
Lo, unlearned men nowadays will not spare
To write, to babble, their mindés to declare,
15 Trowing[7] themself gay fantasies to draw,
When all their cunning is not worth a straw.

Some in French chronicles gladly doth presume.
Some in English blindly wade and wander.
Another in Latin bloweth forth a dark fume,[8]
20 As wise as a great-headed Ass of Alexander.[9]
Some in philosophy, like a gaggling[10] gander,
Beginneth lustily[11] the brows to set up,[12]
And at the last concludeth in the good ale cup.

Finis Prologus,[13]
25 quod[14] T. M.

Fortune perverse
Qui le monde verses
Tout à ton désire
Jamais tu ne cesses
30 Pleine de finesse
Et y prends plaisir.
Par toi viennent maux
Et guerres mortelles
Tous inconvénients,
35 Par monts et par vaux

Et aux hôpitaux
Meurent tant de gens.[15]

Fortune, O mighty and variable,[16]
What rule thou claimest, with thy cruel power!
Good folk thou stroyest,[17] and lovest reprovable.[18]   40
Thou mayst not warrant[19] thy gifts for one hour.
Fortune unworthy men setteth in honor.
Through Fortune, th'innocent in woe and sorrow
    shritcheth.[20]
The just man she spoileth,[21] and the unjust
    enricheth.

Young men she killeth, and letteth old men live,   45
Unrighteously dividing time and season.
That[22] good men leeseth,[23] to wicked doth she
    give.
She hath no difference,[24] but judgeth all good
    reason:[25]
Inconstant, slipper,[26] frail, and full of treason,
Neither forever cherishing whom she taketh,   50
Nor forever oppressing whom she forsaketh.

Finish, quod T. M.

THE WORDS OF FORTUNE TO THE PEOPLE

Mine high estate,[27] power, and auctority,
If ye ne[28] know, ensearch and ye shall spy   55
That riches, worship, and dignity,
Joy, rest, and peace, and all-thing finally
That any pleasure or profit may come by
To mannés[29] comfort, aid, and sustenance,
Is all at my device[30] and ordinance.[31]   60

Without my favor, there is nothing won.
Many a matter have I brought at last
To good conclusion, that fondly[32] was begun.
And many a purpose, bounden sure and fast
With wise provision, I have overcast.   65
Without good hap,[33] there may no wit[34] suffice:
Better is to be fortunate than wise.

---

1 scholars   **2** kinds of people   **3** too unlearned   **4** *ought worth:* having any value   **5** unlearned   **6** something worthwhile   **7** believing   **8** smoke   **9** *Ass of Alexander:* reference unclear; possibly expressing contempt for Alexander the Great's excess and drunkenness   **10** cackling   **11** with vigor   **12** *the brows to set up:* to be full of contempt   **13** *Finis Prologus:* End Prologue   **14** said   **15** *Fortune…*

gens: Perverse Fortune, / Who turn the world / All at your desire, / You never cease, / Full of cunning; / And you take pleasure in it. / Through you come evils / And mortal wars, / All disadvantages; / On the mountains and in the valleys / And in the hospitals / So many people die.   **16** *Fortune…forsaketh:* These two stanzas are a translation of a Latin epigram, attributed to Caelius Firmianus Symphosius

(4th–5th century AD). More's version strengthens the indictment of Fortune and omits any mention of poverty.   **17** destroys   **18** those deserving reproof   **19** guarantee   **20** screech   **21** robs   **22** what   **23** loses   **24** *hath no difference:* does not discern   **25** rational conduct   **26** slippery, unreliable   **27** state, position   **28** (do) not   **29** man's   **30** planning   **31** decree   **32** foolishly   **33** luck   **34** intelligence

And, therefore, hath some men been, or[35] this,
My deadly foes, and written many a book
70 To my dispraise. And other cause there n'is,[36]
But for me list[37] not friendly on them look.
Thus, like the fox they fare, that once forsook
The pleasant grapes, and 'gan[38] for to defy[39] them,
Because he leapt and leapt and could not come by
    them.

75 But let them write; the labor is in vain.
For well ye wot,[40] mirth, honor, and richesse[41]
Better is than shame, penury, and pain.
The needy wretch that lingereth in distress
Without mine help is ever comfortless,
80 A weary burden, odious and loath
To all the world, and to himself, both.

But he that by my favor may ascend
To mighty power and excellent degree,
A commonweal to govern and defend,
85 O in how blessed condition standeth he:
Himself in honor and felicity,
And over[42] that, may further and increase
An whole region in joy, rest, and peace.

Now in this point there is no more to say;
90 Each man hath of himself the governance.
Let every wight[43] then take his own way.
And he that out of poverty and mischance
List[44] for to live, and will himself enhance[45]
In wealth and riches, come forth and wait on me;
95 And he that will be a beggar, let him be.

TO THEM THAT TRUSTETH IN FORTUNE

Thou that are proud of honor, shape,[46] or kin,
That heapest up this wretched worldés treasure,[47]
Thy fingers shined with gold, thy tawny skin
100 With fresh apparel garnished out of measure,[48]
And weenest[49] to have Fortune alway at thy
    pleasure,
Cast up thine eye, and look how slipper[50] Chance
Eludeth her men with change and variance.

Sometime she looketh as lovely, fair, and bright
As goodly Venus, mother of Cupide,   105
She becketh[51] and smileth upon every wight.
But this feignéd cheer may not abide;
There cometh a cloud, and farewell all our pride.
Like any serpent, she beginneth to swell,
And looketh as fierce as any fury of hell.   110

Yet for all that, we brittle men are fain,[52]
So wretched is our nature and so blind,
As soon as Fortune list to laugh again,
With fair countenance and deceitful mind,
To crouch and kneel and gape after the wind.   115
Not one or twain,[53] but thousands on a rout,[54]
Like swarming bees, come flattering her about.

Then, as a bait, she bringeth forth her ware:
Silver, gold, rich pearl, and precious stone,
On which the mazéd[55] people gaze and stare,   120
And gape[56] therefor, as doggés for the bone.
Fortune at them laugheth; and in her trone,[57]
Amid her treasure and wavering richesse,
Proudly she hoveth[58] as Lady and Empress.

Fast by her side doth weary Labor stand,   125
Pale Fear also, and Sorrow all bewept,
Disdain and Hatred on that other hand,
Eke[59] restless Watch, from sleep with travail[60] kept,
His eyes drowsy and looking as he slept;
Before her standeth Danger and Envy,   130
Flattery, Deceit, Mischief, and Tyranny.

About her cometh all the world to beg:
He asketh land; and he to pass would bring
This toy and that, and all not worth an egg;
He would in love prosper above all-thing;   135
He kneeleth down and would be made a king;
He forceth not, so[61] he may money have,
Though all the world accompt[62] him for a knave.

Lo, thus diveris[63] heads, diveris wittes.
Fortune alone, as diveris as they all,   140
Unstable, here and there among them flittes:
And, at adventure,[64] down her giftés fall,
Catch whoso may; she throweth great and small

---

35 before **36** is not **37** please
38 began **39** despise **40** know
41 wealth **42** besides **43** person
44 Desires **45** *will…enhance:* wishes
to increase **46** beauty **47** *That…*

treasure: Mt 6:19–20 **48** excessively
49 hope **50** fickle **51** beckons, or
curtsies to show respect **52** glad **53** two
54 *on a rout:* in a crowd **55** amazed
56 desire, long for **57** throne; a weighing

scale **58** hovers, remains above **59** Also
60 toil **61** *forceth not, so:* doesn't care,
provided that **62** account; reckon
63 different, various **64** random

Not to all men, as cometh sun or dew,
145   But, for the most part, all among a few.

And yet, her brotel[65] giftés may not last.
He that[66] she gave them looketh proud and high;
She whirleth about and plucketh away as fast,
And giveth them to another by and by.
150   And thus, from man to man continually,
She useth[67] to give and take, and slyly toss
One man to winning of another's loss.

And when she robbeth one, down go'th his pride;
He weepeth and waileth and curseth her full sore.[68]
155   But he that receiveth it, on that other side,
Is glad, and blesseth her a thousand times therefore.
But in a while, when she loveth him no more,
She glideth from him, and her giftés too,
And he her cuseth,[69] as other foolés do.

160   Alas, the foolish people cannot cease
Ne void[70] her train,[71] till they the harm feel.
About her alway, busily they prese.[72]
But Lord, what he thinketh himself wele,[73]
That may set once his hand upon her wheel.
165   He holdeth fast, but upward as he stieth,[74]
She whippeth her wheel about, and there he lieth.

Thus fell Julius[75] from his mighty power.
Thus fell Darius,[76] the worthy king of Perse.[77]
Thus fell Alexander,[78] the sovereign conqueror.
170   Thus many mo[79] than I may well rehearse.
Thus, double[80] Fortune, when she list[81] reverse
Her slipper[82] favor from them that in her trust,
She flieth her way,[83] and layeth them in the dust.

She suddenly enhanceth them aloft,
175   And suddenly mischieveth[84] all the flock.
The head that late lay easily and soft,
Instead of pillows, li'th after on the block.[85]
And yet, alas, the cruel proud mock:[86]

The dainty mouth, that ladies kissed have,
She bringeth in the case[87] to kiss a knave.   180

Thus when she changeth her uncertain course,
Up starteth a knave, and down there falleth a
    knight;
The beggar rich, and the rich man poor is;
Hatred is turned to love, love to despite.[88]
This is her sport; thus proveth she her might.   185
Great boast she maketh if one, by her power,
Wealthy and wretched both in an howre.

Poverty, that of her gifts will nothing take,
With merry cheer she looketh on the prese,[89]
And seeth how Fortune's household go'th to   190
    wrack.[90]
Fast by her standeth the wise Socrates,
Aristippus,[91] Pythagoras,[92] and many a lese[93]
Of old philosophers; and eke[94] against the sun
Beeketh him[95] poor Diogenes[96] in his tun.[97]

With her is Bias,[98] whose country lacked defense,   195
And whilom[99] of their foes stood in doubt,
That each man hastily gan[100] to carry thence,[101]
And askéd him why he nought[102] carried out.
"I bear," quod[103] he, "all mine with me about."
Wisdom he meant, no[104] Fortune's brittle fees;[105]   200
For nought[106] he counted his that he might leese.[107]

Heraclitus,[108] eke, list[109] fellowship to keep
With glad Poverty; Democritus[110] also;
Of which the first can never cease but weep
To see how thick[111] the blind people go   205
With great labor to purchase care and woe.
That other laugheth to see the foolish apes,
How earnestly they walk about their japes.[112]

Of this poor sect, it is the usage
Only to take that nature may sustain,   210
Banishing clean[113] all other surplusage,[114]

---

65 frail, perishable **66** to whom **67** is accustomed **68** bitterly **69** accuses **70** *Ne void:* Nor leave **71** entourage; also trap **72** press **73** well-off **74** rises up **75** Julius Caesar, 100–44 BC **76** Darius the Great, 550–486 BC, was King of Persia at that empire's height. **77** Persia **78** Alexander the Great, 356–323 BC **79** more **80** deceitful **81** desires to **82** fickle **83** *her way:* following 1556 and 1557 texts **84** harms **85** i.e., the executioner's block **86** mockery

87 *in the case:* perhaps **88** disdain **89** throng **90** ruin **91** Aristippus of Cyrene, 435–356 BC, pupil of Socrates, founder of the Cyrenaic school of philosophy **92** Pythagoras of Samos, 570–495 BC, philosopher and mathematician **93** group of three (hunting term) **94** also **95** *beekith him:* warms himself **96** Diogenes the Cynic, 412–323 BC, was a founder of the Cynic school of philosophy, famous for mocking Alexander the Great, sleeping in a large jar

in the marketplace (the "tun" of this line). **97** barrel or cask **98** Bias of Priene, 6th century BC, pre-Socratic philosopher **99** while **100** began **101** away from there **102** nothing **103** said **104** not **105** goods **106** nothing **107** lose **108** Heraclitus of Ephesus, 535–475 BC **109** desires **110** Democritus, 460–370 BC, famous for his atomic hypothesis of matter **111** numerous **112** tricks; playthings **113** completely **114** excess; surplus

They be content, and of nothing complain.
No niggard eke is of his goods so fain,[115]
But they more pleasure have a thousandfold,
215 The secret draughts[116] of nature to behold.

Set Fortune's servants by themself and ye wull,[117]
That one is free, that other ever thrall,[118]
That one content, that other never full,
That one in sur'ty,[119] that other like[120] to fall.
220 Who list to advise them both, perceive he shall
As great difference between them as we see
Betwixt wretchedness and felicity.

Now have I showed you both: choose which ye list,
Stately Fortune, or humble Poverty;
225 That is to say, now lieth it in your fist[121]
To take you to bondage, or free liberty.
But in this point, and ye do after me,
Draw thee to Fortune and labor her to please
If that ye think yourself too well at ease.

230 And first, upon thee, lovely shall she smile,
And friendly on thee cast her wandering eyes,
Embrace thee in her arms, and, for a while,
Put thee into a foolés paradise.
And forthwith, all whatso you list devise,[122]
235 She will thee grant it liberally, perhaps.
But for all that, beware of afterclaps.[123]

Reckon you never of her favor sure:
Ye may in the clouds as easily trace[124] an hare,
Or in dry land cause fishes to endure,
240 And make the brenning[125] fire his heat to spare,
And all this world encompass to forfare,[126]
As her to make by craft of engine[127] stable,
That of her nature is ever variable.

Serve her day and night as reverently
245 Upon thy knees as any[128] servant may,
And in conclusion, that[129] thou shalt win thereby
Shall not be worth thy service, I dare say.
And look yet; what she giveth thee today,
With labor won, she shall haply[130] tomorrow
250 Pluck it out of thine hand again[131] with sorrow.

Wherefore, if thou in sur'ty list[132] to stand,
Take Poverty's part and let proud Fortune go;
Receive nothing that cometh from her hand.
Love manner[133] and virtue, for they be only tho[134]
Which double[135] Fortune may never take thee fro.[136]   255
Then mayst thou boldly defy her, turning[137]
    Chance:
She can thee neither hinder nor advance.

But and thou wilt needes[138] meddle with her
    treasure,
Trust not therein, and spend it liberally.
Bear[139] thee not proud, nor take not out of   260
    measure.
Build not thine house high up in the sky.
None falleth far, but he that climbeth high;
Remember, nature sent thee hither bare;
The gifts of Fortune, count them borrowed ware.

TO THEM THAT SEEKETH FORTUNE   265

Whoso delighteth to prove and assay,[140]
Of wavering Fortune, the full uncertain lot,
If that the answer please thee not alway,
Blame not me: for I command you not
Fortune to trust; and eke[141] full well ye wot,[142]   270
I have of her no bridle in my fist.
She runneth loose, and turneth where she list.

The rolling dice, in whom your luck doth stand,
With whose unhappy chance ye be so wroth,
Ye know yourself came never in mine hand.   275
Lo, in this pond be fish and frogs both.
Cast in your net; but be you lief[143] or loath,[144]
Hold you content as Fortune list[145] assign;
It is your own fishing, and not mine.

And though, in one chance, Fortune you offend,   280
Grutch[146] not thereat, but bear a merry face;
In many another she shall it amend.
There is no man so far out of her grace
But he sometime hath comfort and solace;
Ne none[147] again so far-forth[148] in her favor   285
That fully satisfied is with her behavior.

---

[115] glad   [116] plans, designs   [117] *and ye wull:* if you will   [118] enslaved   [119] surety, security   [120] likely   [121] grasp   [122] *list devise:* desire to contrive   [123] unexpected consequences   [124] pursue   [125] burning   [126] destroy

[127] ingenuity   [128] following 1556 and 1557 texts   [129] what   [130] perhaps   [131] 1556 and 1557 add "again" to produce the decasyllabic line.   [132] *sur'ty list:* security wish   [133] moderation   [134] those (things)   [135] deceitful   [136] *thee fro:*

from you   [137] revolving   [138] *and thou wilt needes:* if you must   [139] behave   [140] test   [141] also   [142] know   [143] glad   [144] reluctant   [145] desires to   [146] Murmur, complain   [147] *Ne none:* Not one (is)   [148] *so far-forth:* to such an extent

Fortune is stately, solemn, proud, and high,
And riches giveth to have service therefore.
The needy beggar catcheth an halfpenny;
290 Some man a thousand pound, some less, some
    more.
But for all that, she keepeth ever in store
From every man some parcel of his will,
That he may pray therefor, and serve her still.

Some man hath good,[149] but children hath he
    none.
295 Some man hath both, but he can get none health.
Some hath all three, but up to honor's trone[150]
Can he not creep, by no manner[151] stealth.
To some she sendeth children, riches, wealth,
Honor, worship, and reverence all his life;
300 But yet she plucketh[152] him with a shrewd[153] wife.

Then, forasmuch as it is Fortune's guise[154]
To grant no man all-thing that he will ask,[155]
But as herself list[156] order and devise,
Doth every man his part divide and tax.
305 I counsel you: either truss up your packs,
And take nothing at all; or be content
With such reward as Fortune hath you sent.

All things in this book that ye shall read,
Do as ye list; there shall no man you bind
310 Them to believe as surely as your creed.[157]
But, notwithstanding, certes[158] in my mind
I durst well swear: as true shall ye them find
In every point, each answer, by and by,
As are the judgments of astronomy.

LEWIS THE LOST LOVER

Eye flattering Fortune, look thou never so fair,
Nor never so pleasantly begin to smile,
As though thou wouldst[159] my ruin all repair,
During my life thou shalt me not beguile.   5
Trust shall I God, to enter in awhile
His haven of heaven ever sure and uniform:[160]
Ever after thy calm, look I for a storm.

DAVY THE DICER

Long was I, Lady Luck, your serving man,
And now have I lost again all that I gat,[161]
Wherefore, when I think on you now and than,
And in my mind remember this and that,   5
You may not blame me, though I beshrew your
    cat,[162]
But in faith I bless you again a thousand times,
For lending me now some leisure to make rhymes.

149 goods (wealth)   **150** throne
151 kind of way   **152** afflicts; humbles
153 bad tempered, irksome   **154** practice,
custom   **155** desires   **156** More uses
the spelling variant *axe* here.   **157** *you*
bind … believe: force you to believe
them   **158** certainly   **159** intend, desire
to   **160** unchanging   **161** got, gained
162 *beshrew your cat:* curse any deceptive
plans you may have made for me (probably
from "to turn the cat," a phrase from
dicing, meaning to reverse a situation
so that it appears as the opposite of its
previous state)

Lucian Dialogues and Declamations
Thomas More's Translations and Response

These translations of Lucian of Samosata (*ca.* 125–80 AD) are among Thomas More's earliest Latin writings. More had begun his study of Greek by 1501, and these translations are, as he puts it, the "first fruits of my Greek studies," published in 1506 in collaboration with Erasmus. The first of More's Latin writings to be published, these translations proved More's most popular work during his lifetime. Reprinted nine times between 1506 and 1534, the translations exceed even *Utopia* on this count, and attest to the general interest in Lucian during More's lifetime, and to the skills and reputations of the translators (*CW* 3.1: xxv).

For this volume, More contributed three dialogue translations, along with his prefatory letter to Thomas Ruthall, and an original declamation in response to Lucian's *Tyrannicide*, which he also translated. Erasmus offered his own dialogue translations, and he too supplied a declamation in response to Lucian's *Tyrannicide*, part of what he called a "contest of wits" with More, "that most congenial of all my friends, in whose company I enjoy combining jest and earnest" (*CWE* 2: 113).

So why translate Lucian? More's letter to Ruthall praises Lucian as an author who "everywhere reprimands and censures, with very honest and at the same time very entertaining wit, our human frailties." Lucian does so with such art that "although no one pricks more deeply, nobody resents his stinging words." Lucian, in More's judgment, fulfills Horace's famous maxim of mingling delight and learning as well as any author does, a position echoed by Erasmus too, who claims that Lucian's "superb wit" invites us to see human beings "with our own eyes" so successfully that "whether you look for pleasure or edification, there is not a comedy or satire that challenges comparison with his dialogues" (*CWE* 2: 116). While More and Erasmus admired Lucian for his wit and vision, Lucian was also associated with skepticism, scoffing, and irreverence at the time, and More himself was even termed a Lucian during later controversies (*CW* 3.1: xxii–xxiv).

More chooses his three dialogues — *The Cynic, Menippus,* and *Lover of Lies* — because they exhibit Lucian's art "exceptionally well" and "particularly struck my fancy," likely on account of their irony, a figure that More uses repeatedly across his writings. A classical figure, irony has a range of meanings for Lucian and More. As Craig Thompson explains, irony may mean: "first, ironical speech, (a) the rhetorical tactic of saying one thing while meaning another and usually contrary thing, e.g. praising when one is blaming and vice versa, (b) understatement or *litotes*; (c) intentional over-simplification; second, an habitual manner or cast of mind, specifically an assumed self-depreciation such as that practiced by Socrates; third, the irony of situation or fortune, when decisions and actions planned or carried out for supposedly sound, logical, dependable reasons produce instead wholly unforeseen and often catastrophic results" (*CW* 3.1: l–li). More explicitly discusses irony as a manner of speech that "every man uses," for example, when he chooses to call a naughty boy "a good son" (*CW* 10: 24), and in his last work, written in the Tower, More argues that understanding irony as a figure of speech is necessary to grasp the "real sense" of speech, literary or ordinary (*CW* 14: 295–97). Later in 1560, Thomas Wilson compares More with Socrates for their use of irony or "pleasant dissembling," in his *Art of Rhetoric*. Like Socrates and Plato, More uses irony as a strategy to awaken and engage the intellect, in the service of discovery and deeper insight.

In addition to his irony, Lucian's fusion of comedy and dialogue no doubt struck More as well. As Lucian explains in *Bis accusatus*, comedy and dialogue do not "easily tolerate partnership," because dialogue loves to ponder "nature and virtue," while comedy delights in jests, quips, and "liberties." Despite this tension, Lucian claims that he has "dared to combine them as they are into a harmony," a combination More explores in writings such as *Utopia* and *A Dialogue of Sir Thomas More, Knight,* with their serious play of wit, pleasure, and reason.

The last work More includes is also his most

original: the declamation in response to Lucian's *Tyrannicide.* In rhetorical declamation exercises like this, a common part of education at the time, the writer "professedly commits himself to an imagined, fictive argument and thereby claims immunity from being taken literally" (*CW* 3.1: xxxv–xxxvi). More's reply to Lucian is made in the voice of a citizen-orator. Offering his services to his country and speaking with a concern for law and liberty, the speaker critiques the tyrannicide's fanciful arguments. More's declamation not only demonstrates his rhetorical skill but also serves as an example of his lifelong interest in tyranny. As Erasmus wrote in his letter to von Hutton, More had a "special hatred for tyranny" and a corresponding love of equality and friendship. The treatment of tyranny here curiously anticipates his later considerations in *Richard the Third, Utopia,* the *Epigrams,* and elsewhere. More's declamation was praised by Erasmus as an example of the author's eloquence and discerning mind.

The three Lucian dialogues and Lucian's "Tyrannicide" are translated from More's Latin into English by Gerald Malsbary. Modern scholarship has cast doubts on the Lucianic authorship of *The Cynic,* but that is of little consequence for the study of More. The other translations of More's Letter to Ruthall and More's response to Lucian's "Tyrannicide" are by Craig R. Thompson, from volume 3.1 of *The Complete Works of St. Thomas More* (New Haven: Yale University Press, 1974). The Greek references are from the Loeb Classical Library's *Lucian,* ed. M. D. McLeod (Cambridge, MA: Harvard University Press, 1967). The section numbers are taken from this Greek edition and are included to assist the reader; they did not appear in More's Latin editions.

CONTENTS

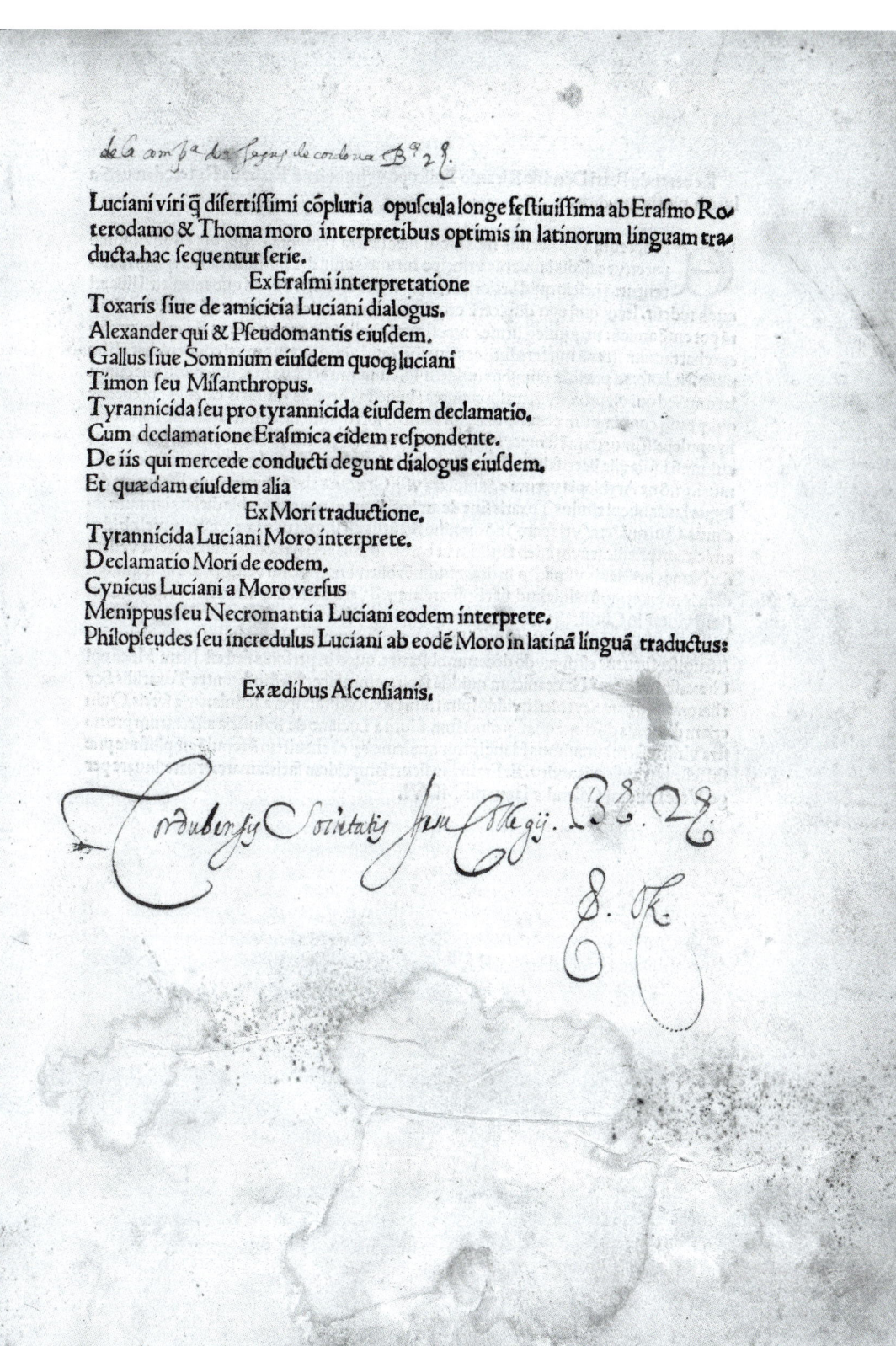

de la ampa de ſegus de cordoua Bª 2 ӡ.

Luciani viri q̃ diſertiſſimi copluria opuſcula longe feſtiuiſſima ab Eraſmo Ro
terodamo & Thoma moro interpretibus optimis in latinorum linguam tra
ducta,hac ſequentur ſerie.

 Ex Eraſmi interpretatione

Toxaris ſiue de amicicia Luciani dialogus.

Alexander qui & Pſeudomantis eiuſdem.

Gallus ſiue Somnium eiuſdem quoq̃ luciani

Timon ſeu Miſanthropus.

Tyrannicida ſeu pro tyrannicida eiuſdem declamatio.

Cum declamatione Eraſmica eidem reſpondente.

De iis qui mercede conducti degunt dialogus eiuſdem.

Et quædam eiuſdem alia

Ex Mori traductione

Tyrannicida Luciani Moro interprete.

Declamatio Mori de eodem.

Cynicus Luciani a Moro verſus

Menippus ſeu Necromantia Luciani eodem interprete.

Philopſeudes ſeu incredulus Luciani ab eodē Moro in latinā linguā traductus:

Ex ædibus Aſcenſianis.

Corduberſis Soꞓietatis Jeꞓu Collegij. Bᴼ 2ᴾ.
E. Ʀ.

Title page of Erasmus's and More's Lucian translations, first edition, 1506, Paris, Josse Badius Ascensius.

5. To Thomas Ruthall.

<London 1506>

To the most illustrious and learned Thomas Ruthall, English Royal Secretary, Thomas More sends
5 greeting.

If, most learned sir, there was ever anyone who
fulfilled the Horatian maxim and combined delight
with instruction,[1] I think Lucian certainly ranked
among the foremost in this respect. Refraining
10 from the arrogant pronouncements of the philosophers as well as from the wanton wiles of the poets,
he everywhere reprimands and censures, with very
honest and at the same time very entertaining wit,
our human frailties. And this he does so cleverly
15 and effectively that although no one pricks more
deeply, nobody resents his stinging words.[2] He is
always first-rate at this, but in my opinion he has
done it exceptionally well in these three dialogues,
which for this very reason I have chosen, from
20 such an abundance of exceedingly pleasant ones,
to translate, though perhaps other persons might
much prefer other dialogues. For just as, among
girls, all men do not love the same one, but each has
his own preference as fancy dictates and adores not
25 the one he can prove is best but the one who seems
best to him — so of the most agreeable dialogues of
Lucian, one man likes a certain one best, another
prefers another; and these have particularly struck
my fancy, yet not without reason, I trust, nor mine
30 alone.

For to begin with the shortest, which is called
Cynicus, and which might appear unacceptable on
account of its very brevity, did not Horace[3] remind
us that the greater strength is often to be found in a
35 slight body, and did not we ourselves see that even
the smallest jewels are prized? My choice of it is
endorsed by the estimable approval of Saint John
Chrysostom, a man of the most acute judgment,
of all learned men perhaps the most Christian and
40 (at least in my opinion) of all Christians the most
learned. So much did this dialogue delight him that
he introduced a large part of it into a homily he
composed on the Gospel of Saint John.[4] And not
without reason: for what should have pleased that

grave and truly Christian man more than this dialogue in which, while the severe life of Cynics, satis- 45
fied with little, is defended and the soft, enervating
luxury of voluptuaries denounced, by the same token Christian simplicity, temperance, and frugality,
and finally that strait and narrow path which leads 50
to life eternal, are praised?

Next *Necromantia,* for this is what the second dialogue is called — not very auspicious in its title but
felicitous in content — how wittily it rebukes the
jugglery of magicians or the silly fictions of poets 55
or the fruitless contentions of philosophers among
themselves on any question whatever!

There remains *Philopseudes,* which, with a measure of Socratic irony, is entirely concerned (as its
title indicates) with ridiculing and reproving the 60
inordinate passion for lying. Whether this dialogue is more amusing or more instructive is hard
to say. I'm not much troubled by the fact that the
author seems to have been disposed to doubt his
own immortality, and to have been in the same er- 65
ror as Democritus, Lucretius, Pliny, and many others likewise were. For what difference does it make
to me what a pagan thinks about those articles contained in the principal mysteries of the Christian
faith? Surely the dialogue will teach us this lesson: 70
that we should put no trust in magic and that we
should eschew superstition, which obtrudes everywhere under the guise of religion. It teaches us also
that we should live a life less distracted by anxiety;
less fearful, that is, of any gloomy and superstitious 75
untruths. Very many of these are related with such
a show of confidence and authority that some cunning rogue or other even induced the most blessed
father Augustine, a man of complete sobriety and
a zealous enemy of lies,[5] to tell as a truth, as some- 80
thing that occurred in his own lifetime, that yarn
about two *Spurinnae* — one coming back to life
and the other departing from it — which Lucian
made fun of in this dialogue, with only the names
changed, so many years before Augustine was born. 85

You should not be surprised, therefore, if the common herd are taken in by the fictions of those who
think they've done a great work, and put Christ in
their debt forever, if they've feigned a story about a

---

1 *The Art of Poetry* 333–34, 343   **2** or literally: "…that although no one pricks more
deeply, yet no one would receive his barbs
without equanimity" (*nemo tamen sit, qui
non aequo animo illius aculeos admittat*).

See note 27 of *The Cynic.*   **3** uncertain;
perhaps *Epistle* 1.17.40 or 1.20.19–24
4 The last part of Chrysostom's Homily 80
on John 17:1–5 treats the slavery that comes
from excessive attachment to material

goods as opposed to the "true wisdom"
and freedom of a Christ who paradoxically
"emptied himself, taking the nature of a
slave."   **5** See *De mendacio* 10.17.

saint or a horrendous tale of hell to drive some old woman to tears or make her tremble with fear. And so there is scarcely a martyr's or a virgin's life which they have passed over without inserting some falsehoods of this kind—with pious intent, to be sure, for otherwise there was danger lest truth could not stand by its own strength but had to be bolstered with lies! They have not shrunk from defiling with their tales that religion which Truth itself established and which it intended to consist of truth unadorned; and they have not considered that fables of this kind, so far from helping at all, do more deadly harm than anything else. Surely, as the aforementioned father Augustine testifies, when the added falsehood is detected, the authority of truth is immediately diminished and weakened. Wherefore I have often suspected that a large portion of such fables has been concocted by certain crafty, wicked wretches and heretics whose object was partly to amuse themselves by the thoughtless credulity of the simple-minded (rather than the wise), partly to undermine trust in the true stories of Christians by traffic in mere fictions; since they often invent things so nearly resembling those in Sacred Scripture that they easily reveal that by playing upon those stories they have been ridiculing them. Therefore we ought to place unquestioning trust in the stories commended to us by divinely inspired Scripture, but testing the others carefully and deliberately by the teaching of Christ (as though applying the rule of Critolaus[6]), we should either accept or reject them if we wish to free ourselves both from foolish confidence and superstitious dread.

But where am I headed? This epistle already rivals a book in length, yet I haven't said a word so far in praise of you; another man would have dwelt perhaps on that theme exclusively. I had abundant resources for doing so, without being open to the slightest suspicion of flattery. There is—quite apart from the rest of your virtues—your distinction in learning and your unsurpassed wisdom in practical affairs, attested by numerous diplomatic missions carried out in various lands with such difficult negotiations and with such success. Or there is your extraordinary trustworthiness and dignity. Unless he had regarded this as tried and tested, a sagacious prince would never have appointed you to be Secretary. But your singular modesty, which makes you unwilling to hear yourself praised for the praiseworthy things you so willingly do, balks at publication of your other virtues. Accordingly I spare your sense of propriety, begging only that you kindly accept these first fruits of my Greek studies and treat them as a token, in some sort, of my affection and my duty toward you. I have ventured to submit them to you with the greater confidence because, although your judgment is so keen that nobody would more quickly detect any error there may be, yet your nature is so kind that none would more readily condone it. Farewell.

6 See Cicero, *Tusculan Disputations* 5.51.

The Cynic

Characters: Cynic, Lucian

1. LUCIAN:[1] So what are you, then? You have a beard and long hair, but you don't have any shirt; you look naked; you're not wearing shoes—and no wonder, having chosen a roaming, inhuman, bestial way of life, treating your body always unsuitably, and in a manner opposite to the way most people do, wandering about here and there, sleeping besides on bare hard ground so that your worn-out cloak[2] acquires even more dirt,[3] not to mention that it is neither finely woven nor soft nor attractive.

CYNIC: Nor certainly do I need one like that, since one like this is very easy to acquire and gives the least possible trouble to its master,[4] and that kind of cloak, I say, is sufficient for me.

2. But tell me, by the gods, don't you think there is vice in luxury?[5]

LUCIAN: Of course I do.

CYNIC: And, by contrast, that frugality[6] is a virtue?

LUCIAN: Yes.

CYNIC: Then, when you see me living more frugally than most people and them living more luxuriously, why do you correct me, and not them?

LUCIAN: Because, by Jove, you do not seem to me to be living more frugally than they do, but simply in greater poverty: in fact, you are living a poor and needy life. You are no different than beggars who beg for their food every day.

3. CYNIC: Then would you like to examine, now that the conversation has gone this far, what neediness is and then abundance?[7]

LUCIAN: If you want to, yes.

CYNIC: So then, wouldn't you say that "enough" for any person is what satisfies that person's necessity? Or is it something else?

LUCIAN: Okay, let that be granted.

CYNIC: But neediness is whatever falls short of what someone has, and does not reach the point that is necessary?

LUCIAN: Of course.

CYNIC: Nothing then is lacking in my possessions, since there is nothing that does not satisfy my necessity.

4. LUCIAN: How can you say that?

CYNIC: You will understand if you consider the purpose why each of the things we need was made,[8] such as a house. Is it not for the purpose of shelter?

LUCIAN: Yes, very much so.

CYNIC: So then, what is the purpose of clothing? Isn't it also a kind of shelter?

LUCIAN: Of course.[9]

CYNIC: And by the gods, what do we need shelter for? Isn't it for the betterment of what is sheltered?

LUCIAN: So it seems.

CYNIC: Do my feet, then, seem to be in worse shape?

LUCIAN: I don't know.

CYNIC: But here's how you will find out. What is the duty[10] of feet?

LUCIAN: To walk.

CYNIC: Do my feet seem to you to walk less well than the feet of other[11] people?

1 More changes the interlocutor's name from "Lycinus" to "Lucian." **2** More translates the Greek word *tribōn* in two words (*tritum...pallium*, "worn-out cloak") to bring out the etymology of the Greek word for a "philosopher's cloak" (from the verb *tribō*, "to wear down"). **3** *sordium:* can mean "dirt or filth of any kind," "the dark or soiled clothing of mourners," "squalor" associated with poverty, or "meanness of character or conduct" **4** More uses the Latin *domino* ("master") for the Greek *ktēsaménōi* (literally "possessor"). **5** *luxuria:* unruly or willful behavior; disregard for moral restraints, licentiousness; indulgence in extravagance, or good living **6** More consistently translates the Greek *euteles* ("economical, thrifty") with the Latin *frugalis.* **7** More translates the Greek *endees, hikanon* ("lacking," "sufficient") with the Latin *inopia, copia* ("neediness," "abundance"). **8** Greek *gégonen* ("happened, came about"); Latin *paratum est* **9** *sane:* This term is commonly used ironically. **10** More chooses *officium* ("duty, function, fitting behavior") for the Greek *ergon* ("work, deed, task"). **11** More has *aliorum* ("other people") for the Greek *pollōn* ("the many people").

LUCIAN: In this case, perhaps not.

CYNIC: But regardless of whether they were in better or in worse shape, would they not be able to perform their own duty?

5   LUCIAN: Perhaps.

CYNIC: So with regard to my feet, do I appear to be any worse off than other people?

LUCIAN: You don't seem to.

CYNIC: What then? Is my body in worse shape
10   than the rest of the people? Because if it is, it would be weaker, since strength is bodily health. Is my body any weaker?

LUCIAN: It does not appear to be.

CYNIC: Well then, neither my feet nor the rest
15   of my body needs shelter. If they did need it, they would be in a bad condition. For poverty is always bad and makes worse off anything near it. But in fact my body does not seem to be less well nourished, since it is nourished by whatever it happens
20   to get.

LUCIAN: That at least is clear.

CYNIC: Nor would it be healthy and strong, if it were badly nourished. And this is because bad foods weaken bodies.

25   LUCIAN: Yes, that is the case.

5. CYNIC: So tell me, since this is the way things are, why do you find fault with me? Why do you disapprove of my way of life and say it is miserable?

LUCIAN: Because, by Jove, nature (which you cher-
30   ish) and the gods have established the earth for us all in common,[12] and have produced, of course,[13] many good things from it so that we have everything in abundant supply, and not only for necessity, but for pleasure[14] as well. You nonetheless take no part in
35   any of these, or at least not in most of them, and you take no more advantage of them than the animals. You drink the water the animals drink; you eat whatever you find like the dogs, and your bed is no better than what dogs have; straw is as good for
40   you as it is for them; the cloak you wear is no better than a beggar's. But if you are correct in thinking

that this is good enough, then the god was wrong to make sheep have plush fleeces, and grapes sweet for wine, and all the other wonderful variety, such as ol-
45   ives and honey and the rest, so that we have all sorts of food and sweet drink and money and soft bedding, lovely houses as well, and finally all the other marvelous provisions.[15] And in fact the benefits of the arts are gifts of the gods. To live deprived of all
50   these things is truly miserable if someone has been deprived of them by someone else, as are people in prison. But much more miserable it is if someone deprives himself of all these goods. For that is really plain madness.

55   6. CYNIC: Well, perhaps you are right. But tell me: say there is a wealthy man who very eagerly and generously invites people to a banquet and hosts many guests at once, some weak, some in good health, and then serves them all kinds of things, but he himself
60   grabs and eats everything, not only what is near him, but also what is put farther away for the sick guests, even though he is himself in good health and only in possession of one stomach, needing to be nourished only by a little, but taking up more time in doing it
65   than many others. What does such a man seem like to you? Does he seem a good man[16] to you?

LUCIAN: No, not to me.

CYNIC: Self-controlled?

LUCIAN: No, not that, either.

70   7. CYNIC: What if somebody sitting at the same banquet takes no thought for the great variety of delicacies and chooses only one item from the things that are set near him since he considers that enough for his needs, and he eats it decently,[17] and
75   only eats that, without even looking at the other things? Wouldn't you think this man more self-controlled and a better man than the other?

LUCIAN: Of course I would.

CYNIC: Well, do you understand yet, or do I have
80   to tell you?

LUCIAN: What?

CYNIC: That god is just like a host who sets out a beautiful banquet, who serves many and various

---

12 More translates the Greek *en mésōi* ("in our midst, in the middle of us all") by *in communi*.   13 More adds *nimirum* ("and no wonder," "of course").   14 Greek *pros hēdonén*; Latin *ad volputatem*   15 Greek *kataskeuásmata*; Latin *praeparata*   16 More uses *probus* ("good, upright, honest") for Greek *phronimos* ("prudent")   17 Greek *kosmíōs*; Latin *decenter*

things, all kinds of things, to be suitable for each person: some things for the healthy, other things for the sick, some things for the strong, others for the weak — not that every one of us gets everything, but that each of us makes use of what most fits his own nature, selecting from just those things whatever happens to be most needed.

8. But you people resemble the one who snatches everything without being satisfied and without self-control, as if you wanted to use everything, no matter where they are taken from, and not being content with things that are at hand; you think neither your own land nor sea is enough, but you import your pleasures from the very ends of the earth and prefer foreign goods to native things, luxurious things to frugal ones, things that are difficult to obtain to things that are easy to obtain. To sum it all up, you prefer troubles and evils to living without troubles. But those many precious provisions for happiness by which you exalt yourselves only come to you through great misery and wretchedness. Think, if you like, of gold itself — so much desired — or think of silver, of expensive homes, and fancy clothing, and everything of that kind: how much trouble it costs, how many labors and risks are involved in getting them, how much blood and how much murder. Not only in sailing the seas do many perish for the sake of these things, suffering greatly in finding and getting them, but also many sword battles are caused, and plots are laid because of these things, by friends against friends, children against parents, wives against husbands. This, I think, is why Eriphyle[18] betrayed her husband: for the sake of gold.

9. And all this happens even though those different clothes cannot bring a bit more warmth; those golden buildings give no better shelter; those silver goblets add nothing to the drink. Nor do those golden or ivory beds bring any sweeter sleep; in fact, you frequently see those blessed people not being able to sleep in that ivory bed or in that luxurious bedding. Furthermore, all those many anxieties about food do not nourish anyone the more, but rather spoil bodies and even generate illness in them.

10. What would be the point in saying how many

mortal miseries are created and suffered for the sake of their lust?[19] Yet it would be easy to remedy this desire if not for wanting to indulge in wanton pleasures. But not even this insanity and corruption seem to be enough for mortals since they actually pervert the use of things, using them for what they were not in the least made for, just like someone wanting to use a bed in place of a wagon, and as a carriage.

LUCIAN: And who would do that?

CYNIC: You do, I say, when you use people like beasts of burden. For you command them to bear your litters on their shoulders as if they were carriages. And all the while you lie up high in luxury, and from that position you drive human beings like mules, commanding them to go here and there, and those of you who do this the most, consider yourselves the most well off.

11. Then there are the people who not only use fish flesh for food, but even make certain colors out of it; I am talking about the people who dye things purple: don't they use these things made[20] by god contrary to their nature?

LUCIAN: No, by Jove! After all, the meat of the purple-fish can be used for dye as well as for eating.

CYNIC: But it was not born[21] for this. Somebody can torture a soup dish contrary to its nature and can use it in place of a jug, but it was not made[22] for that. But how could anybody describe fully the complete unhappiness of these people, so great as it is? But you hold it against me that I refuse to participate in this. And yet I am living just like that decent one,[23] using only those things put before me and using them most frugally, not panting for variety or for all sorts of things.

12. And then, since I make use of a few things and do not use many, I seem to you to be living a bestial life. But by that reasoning, surely the gods themselves run the risk of becoming worse than the beasts, because they have need of absolutely nothing. But in order for you to understand more precisely the difference between these two — to need a few things or to need many things — consider this: children need more than adults, women need more

18 *Eriphyle:* the wife of the seer Amphiaraeus in the Theban saga, who was bribed to send her husband to war 19 Greek *aphrodisíōn*; Latin *libidinis* 20 Greek *kataskeuásmasin*; Latin *praeparata* 21 Greek *ou...gegonen* ("did not... come to be"); Latin *nata est* ("was not born for this") 22 Greek *ou...gegonen* ("did not...come to be"); Latin *paratum est* 23 Greek *kósmios*; Latin *modestus*; the reference is to the ideal banqueter in section 7.

than men, the sick need more than the healthy, and in general and as a whole, inferior things need more than superior things, just as the gods need nothing at all, and those who come closest to the gods need the least.

13. Or do you think that Hercules — the most outstanding human being of all, seeing that he was a divine man, and rightly considered a god — was unhappy going around naked, clothed only in a skin, and not needing any of our things? But surely he was not miserable, but drove off the misery of others; nor again was he poor, who had the mastery of land and sea. And wherever he turned his force, he conquered everyone in all directions; nor did he encounter anyone in his time who equaled or overcame him until he left the mortal realm altogether. Do you think he needed fancy coverings or shoes? Or that such a man walked around the world in search of them? That must not be said. Rather, he was temperate and brave, and desired to live modestly²⁴ and not to indulge in pleasures. What do you think about Theseus, his follower? Was he not king of all the Athenians, and even, as they say, the son of Neptune and the bravest man of his time?

14. But he too wanted to go without shoes and walk about naked; he liked having a beard and long hair, and he was not alone, but all the men of old did, because they were better than you, and none of them would have put up with these things, no more than a lion would submit to having his hair shaved off. They felt that softness and smoothness of skin are fit for women, but they wanted to appear as men, just as they were, and they believed that the beard was a man's ornamentation, the same as a mane for horses and as a beard for lions: to them god gave splendor and decoration, just as he gave men beards. Therefore I envy those men of old, I say, and I want to imitate them, but I do not envy the men of this age for their marvelous happiness that consists in their dining and clothing habits, shaving and smoothing all the parts of their bodies, and not allowing even the most private parts to be as nature established them²⁵ to be.

15. But I would like to have feet no different from a horse's, such as they say Chiron²⁶ had. Then

I would not need any coverings, the way lions are, nor would I need food any better than what dogs eat. And let any ground be good enough for my bed, since I would think of this world as my home. Let me choose the food that is easiest to come by. May I never want gold or silver — neither I myself nor any of my friends, because all evils arise among men from the desire for these things: rebellions, wars, plots, and slaughters. All such things originate in the desire of possessing more. Let them depart far away from us; let me never desire more than enough, and let me be able to bear with equanimity²⁷ less than what I have.

16. Well, that's our way. It is very different from what the vulgar crowd thinks. No wonder, therefore, we differ in clothing as much as in way of life.²⁸ But I wonder about you, when you grant a musician his own clothing and style, or a flute player or tragic actor his own costume, but you think there should not be a distinctive costume and style for a good man, thinking he should wear the same clothing as the crowd, although the crowd is evil. If there should be a distinctive clothing for the good, what would be more fitting than mine, which those extravagantly luxuriant²⁹ people would be most ashamed of? And which they shun more than anything?

17. Therefore my own way is this: to be rough, shaggy, wear a plain cloak, let my hair grow, and go without shoes. But your³⁰ way is like that of luxurious people,³¹ and nobody could distinguish you from them by the color of your clothes, or by the softness or quantity of your shirts, by your cloaks, your footwear, your hair style, or your cologne. In fact you smell very much like them, you, O so very fortunate ones! And yet what is to be done when someone has the same smell as the luxurious? In fact, you are no better than they are when it comes to undertaking hard work. You are overcome by pleasures no less than they are, you eat the same things, you sleep the same way, you walk around — actually you don't like walking: you would rather be carried like baggage, either by other human beings or by beasts of burden. But my feet take me wherever I have to go. I am able to put up with cold and heat and whatever the gods grant me; I endure

24 More's *moderate vivere* translates the Greek *kratein* in an ethical sense ("to be powerful"). **25** Greek *hēi péphyken* ("as naturally [became]"); Latin *ita ut instituit natura* **26** *Chiron:* the centaur,

half man and half beast **27** More adds *aequo animo*. **28** More translates the Greek *prohairesis* ("life choice") with the Latin word *institutum* ("design; mode of life"). **29** More uses *luxuriosis* for the

Greek *akolastois* ("uncontrolled, insolent"). **30** plural second person **31** More's word here and a little below is *cinaedi*, following Lucian's Greek.

with the least trouble possible, just because I am a "sad" man.[32] But you, because of your "happiness," are not content with any fortune that comes your way;[33] you are sorry about everything, unable to bear the things that are at hand; you long for things that are absent, wish for summer in the winter and winter in the summer, for heat during cold and for cold during heat, just like sick people, always peevish and complaining; and what their illness causes in them, your habits[34] cause in you.

18. And so, since this is the way things are, you now think it right to tell us to live like you and to damage our way of life, when the things that you do are often badly thought out, and you yourselves are not at all careful in your own business, doing nothing with judgment and reason, but by your habitual desire. Therefore you differ in no way from those who are carried by a torrent. Such persons are carried wherever the flow of water goes, and you are carried wherever your emotions go. You are just like the fellow who mounted a raving horse. The horse took him away, and he couldn't get off the horse. When a passerby asked him where he was going, the man said, "Wherever he wants to go," pointing to the horse. If somebody should ask you people where you are going, you will all in general say, "Wherever we feel like" — but individually, sometimes it is for pleasure, sometimes for ambition, sometimes for profit. And sometimes it is anger, sometimes fear, sometimes something else of this kind that seems to be carrying you off. And you don't appear to have mounted one horse only, but ride off on many horses, now this one, now that one, and all of them mad horses. And they will take you off cliffs and into the abyss. You have no idea where you will end up until you land there.

19. But this cloak of mine and my hair and my appearance, you laugh at — the things that give me the power to live a quiet life, to do whatever I want, to live with whom I want.[35] In fact, none of the ignorant and uninformed wishes to come near me, thanks to my clothes. The faint-hearted turn aside when they are still far away. But the most knowledgeable and the most self-controlled and the lovers of virtue come toward me most of all, and I am delighted by their constant company. I do not frequent the doorsteps of those who are called human beings;[36] I despise their golden crowns and think their purple is arrogance, and the people themselves I scoff at.

20. So when you understand that this outfit of mine suits[37] not only good men but the gods themselves, if you still want to laugh at it, just consider the statues of the gods and decide if they appear more like me or like you, and take a look at the temples not just of the Greeks but of the foreigners as well to see if the gods themselves are bearded and have long hair like me, or if they are smooth shaven and painted like yourselves. You will even see many with no cloaks at all, just as you see me now. From this time forward, how will you dare to find fault with this way of being when it is seen to suit[38] even the gods?

THE END
THOMAS MORE, TRANSLATOR

---

32 Greek *áthlios*; Latin *miser*. The Cynic is speaking with sarcasm here.   **33** More uses *fortuna*, for the Greek *gignomena* ("what comes to be").   **34** Greek *nósos…trópos*; Latin *morbus…mores*   **35** *ut vitam… atque agam quicquid volo…volo*. Compare with Raphael's *vivo ut volo* in *Utopia* at *CW* 4: 56/1; *sic vivere ut velis* at 1.70 of Cicero's *De officiis*, and *vivit ut vult* at 14.25 of Augustine's *City of God*.   **36** More substitutes *homines* for *eudaimonōn* ("happy ones"): Lucian's "so-called blessed ones" becomes More's "so called human beings" (*qui vocantur homines*).   **37** Greek *prepontos* ("is proper, is fitting"); Latin *decet* **38** Greek *prepon*; Latin *decere* ("to suit, be fitting, be proper")

Menippus *or* A Consultation with the Dead[1]

Characters: Menippus, Philonides[2]

1. Menippus [Dressed like Hercules]:
>   Hail, O hall and vestibule of my house!
5 >   How glad am I to see you, now restored to light![3]

Philonides: Well, isn't that Menippus, the cynic? By Hercules — it is no other! Unless perhaps I am hallucinating Menippuses everywhere![4] But what is the meaning of this strange attire? A club,[5] a
10 lyre, a lion-skin cape? I must approach him, anyway.
   Greetings, Menippus. From where have you come to us? It's been a long time since we've seen you in the city.

2. Menippus:
15 >   Here, returned from the hidden chambers of
>   the dead,
>   And from the black gates of the shadows sad,
>   Where the departed shades dwell below, far
>   from the gods above.[6]

20 **Philonides:** Hercules! Did Menippus die on us without our knowing, and then come back to life again?

Menippus:
>   No; hell received me, while still alive —[7]

25 **Philonides:** And what was the cause of this strange and incredible journey?

Menippus:
>   Youth spurred me on, and audacity,
>   By no means weaker than my youth.[8]

30 **Philonides:** Give up the tragedy, my good man, and climbing down from your iambic lines, just tell me simply: what is all this get-up? What was the reason for your journey to the land below? It certainly could not have been a very pleasant or enjoy-
35 able trip for you.

Menippus: Dear friend,
>   'Twas serious business drove me to the shades
>   below
>   To consult the ghost of Prophet Tiresias —[9]

Philonides: But you're mad. Otherwise, why 40 would you sing in such rhapsodic verses to your friends?

Menippus: Do not wonder, my friend, for I have just been keeping company with Euripides and Homer, and I am somehow so filled up with their verses 45 that the lines come spontaneously to my mouth. But tell me, how are human affairs here on earth[10] and what's going on in the city?

Philonides: Nothing new. Just like they ever did: people steal, lie, lend money, collect interest. 50

Menippus: O sad, unfortunate people. They just don't realize what decrees have lately been made about our lives by the people in the underworld. What voting pebbles have been tossed against the wealthy — by Cerberus, they will never escape them. 55

Philonides: What's that you say? Something new has been decreed about our lives by the dead?

Menippus: By Jupiter, yes, many things! But I am not at liberty to say: I cannot reveal the secrets, lest someone accuse me to Rhadamanthus[11] of impiety. 60

Philonides: No, Menippus! By Jupiter, don't begrudge such information to your friend. You will be telling someone who knows how to keep a secret; and besides, I was once initiated into the mysteries.

Menippus: You drive a hard bargain, and it's not 65 very safe.... Oh well, I'll take the chance for your sake. So it has been decided then that all those rich and really well-off people who hoard their money like Danae[12] in a prison —

---

1 Lucian's Greek title is *Menippos e Nekyomantia,* which More translates *Menippus sive Necromantia,* both alluding to Odysseus's visit to Hades in Book 11 of Homer's *Odyssey* (commonly referred to as the Necromancy). **2** *Philonides,* in Greek, means "son of a friend." **3** Menippus quotes Hercules' exclamation on returning home from the underworld in Euripides' play on the madness of Hercules (*Herakles Furens* 523–24). More's Latin is, like Lucian's quoted lines, in iambic trimeter. **4** More has added "By Hercules" to Lucian's Greek text. **5** Here and later, More has replaced Lucian's "felt cap" (*pilos*) with a club (*clava*). **6** See Euripides, *Hekabe* 1–2. **7** trimeter verse, source unknown **8** trimeter verse, source unknown **9** Homer's *Odyssey* 11.164–65, but with this adjustment: where Odysseus addresses his dead mother in the underworld as "O mother mine," Lucian has "O friend"; More has changed the meter to epic hexameter. **10** *res humanae...in terris* for *ta huper ges* ("the things on earth") **11** son of Zeus and Europa and one of the judges of the dead. See Homer's *Iliad* 14.322 and *Odyssey* 4.564, 7.323; Plato's *Gorgias* 524a; Virgil's *Aeneid* 6.566. **12** In this mythical story, Danae (Perseus's mother) is held captive by her father to prevent her from conceiving a child, but she is impregnated by Zeus in the form of a shower of golden rain.

PHILONIDES: My good man, don't tell me what has been decreed before you run through everything that I really want to hear from you most: What was the reason for your journey down there? Who was your guide? And then tell me in order what you saw and what you heard. It is very likely, since you are very curious about seeing beautiful sights, that you did not miss a single thing worth seeing or hearing about.

3. MENIPPUS: Well, I will do as you say in regards to that too. After all, what can you do when a friend urges? So first I will tell you the reasons that compelled me to this descent. Now when I was still a boy and heard Homer and Hesiod singing of wars and quarrels — not only of the demi-gods but even of the gods themselves — and also adulteries, assaults, rapes, tortures, banishing fathers, and marriages between brothers and sisters, by Hercules,[13] I thought all this was great and I was really fascinated by it. But after I reached the age of manhood, then there I am, hearing[14] the laws commanding the opposite of the poets: saying *not* to commit adultery, plot revolts or rape and pillage. So there I stood, completely uncertain how I should conduct myself. For I never thought the gods would be adulterers or raise rebellions against each other unless they had decided that those were really good actions to perform; nor, on the other hand, would the law-makers have commanded the opposite things, if they hadn't thought that would be helpful.

4. So, since I was in doubt, I decided to go to the philosophers, put myself in their hands, and ask them to have their will with me by showing me a simple and certain way to live. So with such thoughts in mind, off I go to them, and foolishly too, since, as they say, I was only throwing myself from the smoke into the fire. For, observing them very carefully, I found the utmost ignorance and everything even more uncertain — so much so, in fact, that compared with them, right away even the life of ordinary people[15] seemed golden to me. One of them told me to pursue pleasure alone, and to direct the entire course of my life to that goal. That, he said, is where happiness itself is located. Another

advised that I just work hard, subject my body to thirst and lack of sleep and squalor, feel wretched at all times, and be constantly the subject of insults; and he praised Hesiod's widely known poetry about virtue and, of course, the strenuous and sweaty ascent up the steep mountain. Still another commanded me to despise money, and to think possession of it a matter of indifference. Another instead declared wealth as good. And what about the cosmos? All I heard about it, one day after another, was incorporeal ideas, substances, atoms, the void, and a certain mass of words fighting against each other; and the most absurd of all the absurd things I heard was when each one of them asserted contrary things, and brought forward such unassailable and persuasive arguments that I was not able to utter a single thing against someone who said cold and hot were the same thing, even though I clearly knew it could never happen that the same thing could be both cold and hot. And something happened to me that happens to people who are dozing off, that I would sometimes nod my head in assent and at other times shake my head in disagreement.

5. Besides, much more absurd than this was when, watching carefully their way of life, I discovered that their lives greatly conflicted with their words and teachings. Those who held that money must be spurned were, I noticed, most eagerly gaping at the collection of riches, going to court over the collection of debts, and instructing people how to make a profit. They would put up with anything for the sake of cash. And those who decried fame in their speeches were directing their whole way of life for the sake of winning fame. On the other hand, while everybody fairly openly attacked pleasure, secretly they were all gladly flocking after[16] pleasure alone.

6. And so, disappointed in this hope, I was even more miserable and irritated. Nevertheless, I was able to console myself a little bit with the fact that I was unwise along with many wise and very famous persons, and was still really wandering about in ignorance. Finally, one day as I was sleepless and thinking about this, it came into my head to go to Babylon and meet up with a Magi, one of Zoroaster's[17] disciples and successors. I had heard, you see, that

---

13 More adds the interjection *hercle*.
14 More uses the vivid present *audio* here and elsewhere, even though Lucian uses past tenses throughout. **15** Greek *idiotōn*; Latin *idiotarum* — also used at the end of the dialogue **16** More translates

Lucian's *prosartáomai* ("attach oneself to") with the Latin *confluere*, evoking an image of a crowd of people "streaming" into a place. **17** Zoroaster (*ca.* 628–*ca.* 551 BC), or Zarathustra, is credited with founding Zoroastrianism, a religion with dualistic

and monotheistic elements that became the dominant religion of Ancient Persia. The Hellenistic world associated him with astrology, alchemy, and magic.

they could open the doors of the underworld with their chants and secret rituals, and could take anybody they wanted down there and safely bring them back again. So I thought I would be doing a most excellent thing if I could engage someone to take me down to consult the Boeotian seer Tiresias[18] and learn from him (since he was, after all, a wise man and a prophet) what the best life is, and what life the wisest person would especially choose.[19] And so, leaping up on the spot, I headed for Babylon the fastest way I could. When I got there, I spent[20] some time with a Chaldaean man, certainly a very wise and skilled one, very venerable with white hair and a long beard. His name was Mithrobarzanes.[21] Begging and pleading with him, I barely managed, at any price he wanted, **7.** to get him to take me on that trip below. So at long last, beginning with a new moon, for twenty-nine days he cleansed me, taking me at dawn eastwards to the Euphrates, and mumbling a long speech of some kind, which I did not hear very well. He was shouting (the way incompetent announcers do at the games) something rather loud and incoherent, except that he seemed to be calling on certain *daemons*.[22] After that incantation, he spat in my face three times, and led me back the way we came, never turning his eyes toward anyone we met coming the other way. Our food was only nuts; our drink was milk mixed with honey and the water of Choaspus; our bed was in the grass, under the sky. Now after we had been prepared by this regimen, in the silence of midnight[23] he brought me to the Tigris River, cleansed me and wiped me off, brandished a torch around me and sea-weed and many other things in the same way, mumbling a magical chant at the same time; and after casting a complete spell upon me, circling around me, so that I would be safe from any specters, he led me back home just as I was, walking backwards, and for the rest of the night we made ready for the journey. **8.** He donned a certain magical cloak himself, very similar to a Median cloak,[24] and he outfitted me as you see me now,

with a club,[25] a lion skin, and a lyre as well. Then he instructed me that if anyone asked me my name, I should not say "Menippus," but "Hercules," "Ulysses," or "Orpheus."

PHILONIDES: Why did he do that, Menippus? I don't understand the reason for the name or the costume.

MENIPPUS: It's obvious, really—nothing secret about it. Regarding the men who had descended alive to the underworld before our time, he reasoned that if I looked similar to them, it would be easier for me to elude the guards of Aeacus,[26] and pass through without anybody stopping me, since I would be a more familiar figure if I were sent out in that really dramatic outfit.

9. Now day was already dawning when we reached the river and attended to our departure below. The raft, the sacrifices, the honey-drinks were ready, and whatever else was necessary for the mystic rite. Therefore, after we had loaded whatever was ready to hand, we "sadly stepped in ourselves, our eyes filling with tears,"[27] and after we were borne along by the river for a while, we were carried into a wood, and a kind of lake into which the Euphrates was channeled. After we crossed that, we came to a lonely region, forested and dark, and climbing down (Mithrobarzanes was leading the way), we dug a pit and slaughtered sheep and sprinkled their blood into it. Meanwhile the Magus, holding a burning torch, and no longer with just a low murmur, but speaking as loudly as he could, called upon all the *daemons* at once—the Punishments, the Avengers, Hecate of the night, lofty Proserpina—and at the same time he mixed in as well some unknown barbarian names with many syllables.

10. Immediately everything began to shake; cracks in the ground were caused by his incantations; you could hear Cerberus barking; it was a sad and miserable business, "and Orcus the King of shadows felt fear

---

18 *consult…Tiresias:* as Odysseus is commanded to do in Homer's *Odyssey* **19** More adds two superlatives to Lucian's Greek, which is without superlatives: "What life a wise person would choose." **20** More is using historical presents, which are more usual in Latin than in Greek or English narratives.   **21** A Roman general by this name was defeated in 69 BC, but no Chaldean by this name has been identified.

In *Utopia,* the old name of the ruler was Barzanes (*CW* 4: 132/8); their name for the supreme being is Mithras (*CW* 4: 216/20, 232/13).   **22** The Greek *daímones*— and again below in section 9—were translated literally by More as *daemones* in the Latin. **23** More adds a Virgilian touch by adding "silent" to "midnight": cf. *"nocte silenti"*; see *Aeneid* 4.527, 7.87, 7.102.   **24** *Median cloak:* a luxurious cloak with sleeves,

sometimes ornamented with gold **25** Again More has substituted "club" (Latin *clava*) for Greek *pilos* ("felt hat"). **26** one of the three mythological judges of departed shades, along with Radamanthus and Minos   **27** Here Lucian quotes Homer's *Odyssey* 11.5, and More translated it as prose. More, or a later editor, may have adapted a line from Virgil's *Aeneid* 4.30: *sic effata sinum lacrimis implevit obortis.*

in his deep abodes,"[28] and right away, many things of the underworld could be seen: the lake, Periphlegethon, the kingdoms of Pluto. Then, climbing down, we encountered Rhadamanthus, who was nearly frightened to death. Cerberus at first was barking and moving himself about, but when I quickly took up my lyre and strummed it, he instantly fell into a deep sleep. Afterwards, when we reached the lake, we were almost not able to cross it. For the ferry was already loaded, and was certainly filled with lamentation. Everybody riding in it was wounded: this one in his leg, that one in the head, everybody with some part of his body out of order, so much so that they looked to me like they had all come from some war. But good old Charon, when he saw my lion skin, thought I was Hercules and let us aboard and gladly brought us over, and after we got out of the boat even showed us the path to follow. **11.** Since we were already in the darkness then, Mithrobarzanes led the way, and I stuck right behind him until we came to some huge meadow planted with asphodel, where we were followed by the screaming shades of the dead surrounding us on all sides. Then going on a little further we came to the actual court of Minos. He happened to be sitting on some very high stool, with Punishments, Tortures, Genii, and Furies standing by in attendance. From the other side a very great number, bound by a long rope, were standing in order. They were said to be adulterers, pimps, fornicators, murderers, flatterers, informants, and such a crowd of people who had perpetrated something in life. Separate from them were coming along wealthy ones and creditors, pale, with big bellies, suffering from gout, and each one was strapped to a beam of iron weighing two talents each. While we are standing there, watching everything that is happening and hearing everything that is being said, some amazing, strange attorneys were accusing them.

PHILONIDES: And who were they, by Jupiter? Don't hesitate to tell me that too.

MENIPPUS: Are you familiar with the shadows that bodies make when they are in the sunlight?

PHILONIDES: Yes, what of it?

MENIPPUS: Well, these are the ones who, as soon as we die, accuse, bear witness, and prove whatever wrong we have done in life. Some of them are apparently very trustworthy witnesses, since they have kept our company constantly, never leaving our bodies. **12.** So Minos, consequently, carefully examining each one, was assigning them to the group of evil-doers, where they would undergo the penalties worthy of their crimes. He was especially incensed against those whose wealth and honors had puffed them up while they lived, and who expected to be almost worshiped; he detested their haughtiness, of course, and their pride that would so quickly disappear, since they had forgotten that because they were mortals, they were only acquiring mortal and perishable goods. But now they had shed all those splendid things—wealth, I mean, and noble birth, and privileges; they stood there naked, with downcast faces, thinking over this human felicity as if it was a dream, and to such an extent that I was more than delighted to see it. And if I happened to recognize anybody, I walked up and quietly spoke in his ear to tell him what he had been in life, how greatly he had been puffed up then, when so many people, waiting at his door in the morning for him to come out, were pushed away and shut out by his servants and then, how he would emerge like the rising sun, dressed in gold or purple or rainbow colors, thinking he would make them happy and blessed if he stretched forth his side or hand to be kissed. They did not take it well when they heard this.

13. But once Minos did make a favorable judgment. For Dionysius the Sicilian tyrant,[29] who was accused of many atrocious crimes by Dion, and convicted by the grave witness brought by the Stoics[30]—Aristippus the Cyrenean philosopher intervened (the shades in the underworld revere him, you know, and his authority is very great there) and got him released from his punishment, just when he was about to be strapped onto the Chimaera,[31] by asserting that he had helped out many learned men by financially supporting them.

14. Next, leaving the court of judgment, we came to the place of punishment. There, my friend, could numerous and miserable things be both seen and heard. All at one time could be heard the sound of

---

28 In Lucian, this line is from Homer (*Iliad* 20.61); More, or a later editor, has adapted it, perhaps with reference to Virgil's *Georgics* 4.471 and 4.507. **29** a famous Greek despot in Sicily, *ca.* 432–367 BC **30** As Thompson notes, More's text read *stoas* ("porch" or the "Stoic school"), whereas the correct reading is *skias* ("shadow"). In Lucian's version, Menippus is saying that Dionysius's shadow accused him with Dion's help. **31** *Chimaera:* a fabled monster part lion, part dragon, part goat

burning flames and the screams of people burning in the fire; then the wheels and tortures, the chains; Cerberus tearing with his teeth; the Chimaera ripping apart; and everybody being equally put to torture, captives, kings, prefects, paupers, beggars, wealthy people — and they were all sorry for their crimes. And we recognized certain of them as we watched, who had recently departed from life. But these individuals were hiding in shame, and took themselves out of our sight, or if some of them were looking at us, they did so very abjectly and in a servile manner — and how proud and difficult do you think these people once were in life? But half of the evils were taken away for the poor, and after they had taken a break for a while, they were taken back to their punishment. But I also saw those famous figures told of in myths: Ixion, Sisyphus, and Tantalus the Phrygian,[32] that man so grievously punished; and how big — good gods! — was that earth-born Tityos?[33] He took up a whole field, spread out.

15. Finally passing by these, we came to the Acherusian plain, where we found the demi-gods, heroines, and at the same time another multitude of the dead, divided up into nations and tribes, some old, some shrunken and (as Homer says) strengthless, others young and hale — and these were especially Egyptians, thanks to their very efficient burial practices. But it was scarcely easy to distinguish any one of them, since they all looked very much alike with their exposed skeletons, unless we stared at them for a very long time, and then we could make them out. After all, they were sitting there together, all dark and dreary, and preserving no trace of their original beauty.[34] When then many of those bony figures stood there together, completely alike each other, giving you a rather terrifying stare through their empty eye hollows, showing their teeth all exposed, I really hesitated, thinking by what mark I could distinguish Thersites[35] from lovely Nireus,[36] the beggar Irus[37] from the King of the Phaeacians,[38] Pyrrhias the cook[39] from Agamemnon.[40] There was just nothing left to them of any former distinguishing mark; their bones were all alike, unrecognizable, with no labels written on them, or anything recognizable to anyone.

16. So as I was watching all this, human life seemed to me very much like some long pageant for which Fortune supplied and arranged everything by fitting various costumes to each of those in the pageant. And so, one she liked and equipped with royal trappings (placing a tiara on him, providing him with servants, putting a crown on his head); another she gave the accoutrement of a servant; one she made beautiful, another deformed and ridiculous, since the display, I think, had to include all kinds. In fact, the costumes of certain ones she changed frequently, even in the midst of the pageant, not permitting them to go all the time in the same order and with the same costume as they had when they first came out. Croesus[41] she forced, with changed dress, to put on the clothes of a servant and prisoner of war, but Meandrius,[42] who was at first walking along with the servants, she adorned, on the other hand,[43] with the imperial style of Polycrates.[44] And she permitted him to use the costume for some time; but afterwards, when the time for the pageant was past, each one returned his trappings, and leaving aside both his clothes and his body, became what he was before, no different from his neighbor. But some, because of their inexperience,[45] when Fortune demanded back her trappings, took it hard and were indignant, as if they had been deprived of their own

---

32 Ixion is bound to a wheel in the Underworld that turns forever; Sisyphus is condemned to roll a large stone to the top of a hill, only to have it roll down again when it reaches the top; Tantalus is set in a pool of water that eternally recedes when he tries to drink from it.   **33** Tityos is stretched out in Tartarus, where two vultures feed on his liver, which grows back each night.   **34** More has *nullum pristinae formae vestigium* for Lucian's *ouden tōn par' hēmin kalōn* ("nothing of the things that are beautiful with us").   **35** an ill-favored Greek soldier in Homer's *Iliad*   **36** one of the Greek leaders in the Trojan War, known for his beauty   **37** a beggar with whom Odysseus fights in Book 18 of Homer's *Odyssey*   **38** King Alcinous offers Odysseus the hospitality of his palace and a ship to Ithaka in the *Odyssey*.   **39** a slave in Menander's *Dyskolos*   **40** the commander of the Greek army in the Trojan War   **41** Croesus, the last king of Lydia, who was renowned for his riches, was defeated and captured by Cyrus in 546 BC at Sardis. In a fictitious account by Herodotus (*Histories* 1.29–33), the Athenian Solon warned Croesus that good fortune rather than wealth was the source of happiness.   **42** According to Herodotus (*Histories* 3.123, 142–43), Meandrius was the tyrant Polycrates' scribe, who ruled Samos after Polycrates' assassination. At first, he sought to reestablish democratic rule, but soon he also became a tyrant.   **43** More adds *vicissim* ("in turn, by contrast") for clarity.   **44** Polycrates was a tyrant of the island of Samos (ca. 535–522 BC). According to Herodotus (*Histories* 3.40–43), even when Polycrates was counseled to throw his most treasured possession — an emerald ring — into the sea in order to avoid the jealousy of the gods over his good fortune, shortly afterwards, a fisherman presented him with a fish that was discovered to have the ring in its belly. However, he was later assassinated during a visit to the Persian governor of Sardis.   **45** *inscitiam:* also "inattention, unskilledness, absence of knowledge" for the Greek *agnomosunes* ("want of sense")

proper goods, and had not merely changed out of the clothing that belonged to others and that they had used a little while. I think that you have frequently seen those tragic actors on the stage who, as the plot of the play demands, are Kreons[46] now, and now Priams,[47] and now Agamemnons. And the same actor, if chance should allow it, who had a little while before portrayed so gravely the figure of Cecrops or Erechtheus,[48] then shortly thereafter, at the playwright's command, comes forth as a servant. But when the end of the play has come, and he has taken off those golden clothes and stopped playing that role, climbing out of the raised boots of the dramatic actors, he walks about humble and poor, no longer Agamemnon the son of Atreus or Creon the son of Menoeceus, but Polus[49] the son of Charicles or Satyrus[50] the son of Theogiton of Marathon. This is the way of mortal affairs,[51] the way it seemed to me as I watched it then.

17. PHILONIDES: Tell me, Menippus: those people who have magnificent and high tombs on the earth, with columns, statues, and inscriptions—are they not in any way more honored among the people below than the other shades?

MENIPPUS: You are joking, of course: if you had seen Mausolus (I mean that Carian man famous for his pyramid),[52] I know very well that you would never have stopped laughing, he was so shamefully flung into some out-of-the-way cave, hidden among the crowd of the dead. The only good he gained from that monument, it seems to me, was that he suffered all the more, being pressed under such a great weight. For, my friend, when Aeacus measures out a place for someone, he gives at the most scarcely more than a foot, and each one has to be content with that and squeeze himself into the place. But you would have laughed a lot more, I think, if you had seen these kings of ours and satraps among the beggars, selling pickled goods or learning how to write under duress of poverty, or how they were being afflicted with reproaches by anybody coming along, or being struck in the jaws just like the most worthless of slaves. Looking at

Philip of Macedon, I was really not able to control myself: he was pointed out to me in some corner, repairing old shoes for pay. You could even see many others begging at the street corners—like Xerxes, Darius, and Polycrates.

18. PHILONIDES: You are telling me amazing things about those kings; it's almost incredible. But what is Socrates doing? And Diogenes?[53] Were there any other men of wisdom?

MENIPPUS: Socrates is there too, refuting everybody. Palamedes, Ulysses, and Nestor are keeping company with him and whoever else is a great talker among the dead. His legs were still puffy and swollen from when he had drunk the poison. But excellent Diogenes stays close to Sardanapalus the Assyrian and Midas the Phrygian and many others of that crowd of lavish spenders; when Diogenes heard them moaning as they thought over the greatness of their former good fortune, he laughed and enjoyed himself enormously, falling onto his back and singing out loudly, and with his harsh and unpleasant voice he drowned out their complaints so much that they took it very hard and were not able to put up with Diogenes, and were thinking about changing their location.

19. PHILONIDES: Okay, enough about these. What was it you said was decreed when you said something was decreed against the wealthy?

MENIPPUS: You are right to remind me: I don't know how, but although I first intended to talk about that, I wandered far off the subject I had planned. Well, while I was spending time there, the magistrates[54] called together an assembly to deliberate about what would be for their common good. Seeing so many of them gathering together, I mingled with them myself, and became one of the members of the assembly. Many other things were discussed, and finally the business about the wealthy, against whom very many things were alleged— violence, pride, arrogance, injustices—and finally a certain leading man of the people[55] stood up and read this decree.

---

46 the king of Thebes, who takes the throne after Oedipus chooses exile in Sophocles' Theban plays   47 the king of Troy during the Trojan War   48 Cecrops and Erechtheus were legendary kings of Athens.   49 Polus of Aegina (4th century BC) was a celebrated Greek tragic actor.   50 an actor who, according to Plutarch, helped Demosthenes improve his rhetoric (*Demosthenes* 7.1–2)   51 Here More's *mortalium res* closely mirrors Lucian's *tà tōn anthrōpōn prágmata*.   52 Mausolus of Caria had himself buried in a huge sepulcher; hence our "mausoleum" for a lavish tomb.   53 a Greek philosopher and a founder of the Cynic school of philosophy (d. *ca.* 320 BC)   54 *magistratus* for *prutaneis* (chiefs, in Athens, members of the *boule*, a council of 500)   55 *ex populo primas* for the Greek *demagogon*

20. Since the wealthy perpetrate many things in life by their thefts and use of force and their despising of the poor in every way, it has been decided by the assembly and the people[56] that when they have departed from life, their bodies are to pay their penalties along with the other criminals' bodies; but their souls will re-emerge into life, and become donkeys, until they have spent two hundred and fifty thousand years in that state, always as donkeys being reborn from donkeys, carrying loads, and driven around by poor men. After that, they will be allowed to be released from life. This is the sentence of Calvarius,[57] son of Aridellus,[58] of Manica, the tribe of Styx.[59]

When this law was read out, the leaders[60] approved, the people voted for it, Proserpina raged, Cerberus howled—that's how the folks in the world below confirm statutes and make them official.

21. And that's what happened in the assembly. Then I immediately went to see Tiresias, who was my reason for going there, and after I had explained my business in order, I made my plea to him, that he tell me what he thought was the best kind of life. Smiling at me (he's a little old man blind and pale, with a frail voice) he said, "My son, I know that the cause of your perplexity comes from those men of wisdom, who hardly ever think the same as one another about the same things; but it's not lawful for me to speak to you: it's prohibited by Rhadamanthus."

"By no means," I said, "little father, but please tell me; do not despise me, who wander about in life more blind than you."

And so leading me aside, very far away from the others, he leaned to speak in my ear: "The life of private and ordinary citizens[61] is the best life and the most prudent one. So leaving off this most empty consideration of lofty matters, give up seeking for origins and ends;[62] spit out of your mouth those blabbering syllogisms, and, realizing that all that kind of thing is but foolishness, seek throughout your whole life[63] only this: having put things into good order, without being curious or being anxious about anything,[64] spend your life as cheerfully as you can,[65] and smiling."

"So he spoke and hastened back to the meadow of asphodels."[66]

22. Then—it was already evening now—I said, "Well, Mithrobarzanes, why are we waiting around? Shouldn't we go back to life now?" To which he replied: "Trust me, O Menippus, since I am going to show you a short and easy path." And straightaway he led me off to a certain region more shadowy than the first, and pointing out with his hand a dim[67] and faint light pouring through a crack, he said, "That is the temple of Trophonius, and this is the way people descend to the underworld from Boeotia; if you climb out this way, you will immediately be in Greece." So, delighted by these words, and saying farewell to the Magus, I crawled with much difficulty through the narrow passage of a cave, and arrived, I do not know how, in Lebedaia.[68]

THE END
THOMAS MORE, TRANSLATOR

---

56 More uses *Curiae et populo visum est* for Lucian's *Dedóchthōi tēi boulēi kai tōi dēmōi*. **57** or "Mr. Skull"; *Calvarius* is a translation of Lucian's *Kraníōn* (cf. cranium) **58** *Aridellus* or "Little dried up one," an equivalent for Lucian's *Skeletíōn* **59** *Manica*, as Thompson suggests (*CW* 3.1: 145), is from Latin *manes* ("departed shade"), translating the Greek *Nekyieus* ("Dead One"); *Stygiana* is More's suitable replacement for *Alibantídos*, an obscure Greek word for "corpse." The wordplay of this sentence is translated by Harmon in the Loeb Lucian as "On motion of Scully Fitzbones of Corpsebury, Cadavershire." **60** For Lucian's *archaí*, More uses *principes*; the same word used for the ruler of each city in *Utopia*. **61** More's *idiotarum privatorumque vita* and Lucian's *idiōtou* both probably recall Plato's *Republic* 620c where, in the "Myth of Er," the shade of Odysseus chooses "the life of a private, quiet-living citizen" (*bíon andrós idiōtou aprágmonos*). **62** *principia…fines:* or "principles and final causes" **63** *in tota vita* for *ex hapantos* ("above all") **64** Here More gives *minime curiosus, nulla re sollicitus* for Lucian's *perì mēdèn espoudakós* ("taking nothing seriously"). **65** More adds *quam plurimum potes hilaris* ("being cheerful as you can") to *ridens* ("smiling"), where Lucian has only *gelōn tà pollà* ("laughing at many things"). **66** Homer's *Odyssey* 11.539; More translates it as prose. **67** *subobscurum,* for the Greek *amauron* **68** Lebedaia in Boeotia is the location of the temple of Trophonius, who helped build Apollo's temple at Delphi.

The Lover of Lies *or* The Skeptic

Characters: Tychiades, Philocles

1. TYCHIADES: Can you tell me, Philocles, just what is it that leads so many to the love of lying, so that they are just as happy to say nothing worth-while themselves, as they are to pay the utmost attention to other people who say such things?

PHILOCLES: There are many things, Tychiades, that compel some mortals to lie, because they see a profit in doing so.

TYCHIADES: That has nothing to do with it (as they say) and I was not asking about the people who lie when they have to, since of course such people deserve forgiveness, or even praise whenever they deceive their enemies, or make use of lying as a kind of drug[1] to survive in emergencies. Ulysses did many things of that kind, in order to win his own life and the return of his companions.[2] I am asking, rather, my excellent man, about those who, with no need whatsoever, greatly prefer falsehood itself to truth, and take delight in the thing itself, engaging in lying without any regard for what is fitting for the occasion — I want to know, therefore, for the sake of what benefit[3] these people do this?

2. PHILOCLES: So have you somewhere already detected some of these, in whom this desire to lie is engrained?

TYCHIADES: Really, there are very many like this.

PHILOCLES: What other reason is there for them to lie, except madness? Because they are prefering something very bad in place of something very good.

TYCHIADES: That's nothing. I could show you many people who are sensible in other respects and wonderfully wise, but somehow or other they are taken in by this evil, and are enthusiastic about lying to such an extent that I really am annoyed that such men who are excellent in all other respects nevertheless take pleasure in fooling both themselves and the people they meet. You know better than I do how those men of old — Herodotus and Ktesias the Cnidian[4] and before them going back finally to Homer himself, renowned men — made use of the lies they wrote down, not only so as to deceive the ones who heard them in person, but even to the extent that the deception has been handed down to us, preserved in the loveliest verses and meters. Consequently I often feel ashamed on account of those verses whenever they tell of the cutting of heaven or the chains of Prometheus or the rebellion of the Giants and all that sad story about the people in the underworld. And the way Jupiter was turned into a bull or a swan for the sake of love affairs, and how someone was changed from a woman into a little bird or a bear. Then there are the Pegasuses, the Chimaeras, the Gorgons, and the Cyclopes, and all that sort of thing — really monstrous and absurd stories, the kind that can affect the minds of children who still fear goblins and ghosts. Even so, the poetry is perhaps somewhat tolerable.

3. But what about cities and whole nations who lie publicly and in unison — isn't that ridiculous? Such as when the Cretans are not ashamed to show people the grave of Jupiter; or the Athenians who say that Erichthonius came out of the earth, and that the first people in Attica grew out of the ground like vegetables. But they are more modest than the Thebans who tell how certain men germinated from the planted teeth of a dragon; now if someone, carefully examining them, does not believe these things are true because they are so ridiculous and thinks that it would require the mind of a Coroebus[5] or a Margites[6] for someone to believe that Triptolemos[7] was borne through the air on dragon's wings, or that Pan came from Arcadia to help at Marathon, or that Orithyia[8] was snatched by the North Wind — anybody with that view is considered impious and insane to them, since he does not believe obvious truths; that's how far lying has gone.

---

1 More uses the same Greek word as Lucian here (*pharmacum*), rather than Latin *medicamentum*. **2** In Lucian's Greek the words closely recall Homer's *Odyssey* 1.5, but More translates in prose. **3** Lucian's *agathon* is rendered by More as *commodum*, a frequent word in *Utopia*. **4** a Greek physician and historian (5th century BC) **5** a character of Greek legend who convinced Aeneas and other Trojans to fight the Greeks in disguise (*Aeneid* 2.385–95) **6** the eponymous hero of the lost mock-epic *Margites*, who is extremely dull-witted **7** a priest of Demeter and the inventor of agriculture in Greek mythology **8** the mythological daughter of King Erectheus, who is abducted by Boreas (Ovid, *Metamorphoses* 6.683)

4. PHILOCLES: But you could forgive the poets and the cities perhaps, Tychiades: after all, they had to mix in with their poetry the pleasure that comes from fables and make it as alluring as possible for their audience. And the Athenians and the Thebans and some others win more magnificence for their native land by these kinds of fictions; but if somebody removed the myths from Greece, nothing would keep their story-tellers from dying of hunger, when nobody will go as a tourist there who wants to hear the truth, even for free. But when someone does it for no reason at all, but simply enjoys lying—such people seem completely ridiculous, for good reason.

5. TYCHIADES: You speak rightly, for I just now came from visiting that famous Eucrates, and after hearing many incredible and mythical things, I left right in the middle of the conversation, being unable to stand such stories that went so far beyond belief—but it was as if the Furies drove me away, while so many monstrous and absurd things were being told.

PHILOCLES: But, Tychiades, Eucrates is a serious man; certainly nobody would believe that a man with such a long beard, sixty years of age, and well versed in philosophy to boot, would permit anybody to hear some person lying in his presence, let alone dare to do such a thing himself.

TYCHIADES: But you don't know, my friend, what he was saying, how consistently he asserted it, and then how solemnly he swore about so many things, even when his sons were brought into his presence, and so much so that when I saw him I wondered much to myself how it had eluded my notice what an imposter he was and how much time he had been "leading an ape around in a lion's cloak," so absurd were the things he spoke of.

PHILOCLES: By the gods of the hearth, Tychiades, what were they? I want to know what kind of imposture he was hiding under his long beard.

6. TYCHIADES: Well, Philocles, I used to visit him from time to time—whenever, that is, I had plenty of leisure at my disposal.

And today, because I had to see Leontichus (he's a friend of mine, as you know), I was informed by his servant, that he had gone to see Eucrates, to examine his illness, so I went there for both reasons, to meet Leontichus and see Eucrates, although I hadn't known he was sick. But I didn't find Leontichus there, for he had left just before I arrived, as they told me; I did, however, find many others gathered there, among whom were Cleodemus the Peripatetic, Dinomachus the Stoic, and Ion—do you know the man? He's the one who hopes to get great admiration for his Platonism, as if he were the only one who rightly detected Plato's meaning, and who alone is capable of explaining his oracular sayings to others; you see the kind of men I am naming: endowed of course with all wisdom and every virtue, each one the head of a school, all very respectable, by Hercules, and almost terrifying to behold. In addition, Antigonus the medical doctor was present, who, I think, was called there to give medical assistance, and Eucrates seemed to be already on the mend since his illness was one of the familiar ones, for the humor had descended into his feet. So when he caught sight of me, Eucrates, in a relaxed and quiet sort of voice told me to sit down on the bed next to him, although when I was entering the room I had heard him speaking loudly with exertion in his voice; nevertheless, being very careful not to touch his feet, after I had excused myself with the usual niceties—saying that I did not know he was sick, but as soon as I found out, came at a run—I proceeded to sit next to him. **7.** They were talking about the illness: they had already said some things about it, and were still discussing it then, each one proposing some remedy.

Then Cleodemus said, "If someone picks up, with his left hand, the tooth of a weasel, killed in the way I just said, and ties it into a lion's skin (a lion that has recently been skinned), and then puts it around your shin, the pain will immediately cease."

"Not in a lion's skin," said Dinomachus, "according to what I heard, but rather in the skin of a female deer, young and not yet mated, and this is more likely for the following reason: a doe is very fast, and very strong in the feet, whereas although a lion is very strong, since a lion's fat and right forepaw and the hairs that stick straight out from his beard have a lot of strength as well if someone knows how to use them along with the appropriate spells—nevertheless these things promise little help for the feet."

"I too," said Cleodemus, "once thought a deer's skin should be used, because a deer is swift, but recently a certain Libyan man, very skilled in these matters, taught me the opposite, by pointing out that lions were faster than deer: "After all," he said, "they can hunt them down and capture them."

8. The others who were present praised the Libyan for speaking correctly. Then I said, "Do you think that such maladies are cured by certain spells? Or by things hung on the outside, when the trouble is inside the body?" They laughed at what I said, and openly condemned my great foolishness, my ignorance of very obvious things, which no one with any sense would dispute how they are. But the doctor Antigonus, to be sure, seemed to be pleased by my questioning. I think he was already being ignored for a long time, since he wanted to bring Eucrates some help from the medical art, advising him to abstain from wine, eat vegetables, and in general, limit the strain on his mind.

Cleodemus meanwhile, said with a grin, "What do you say, Tychiades? Does it seem unbelievable to you that remedies against disease can be made from things like that?"

"It seems certain to me," said I, "unless my nose is running too much for me to believe that what is applied externally, and has no communication at all with what is causing the disease on the inside, can work through a few little words, as you say, to work some magic and, when tied to the body, introduce healing powers—*that* can surely never happen, not even if you put sixteen weasel's teeth into the skin of the Nemean lion. I once saw a lion limping from pains, still in his own whole skin."

9. "You are just not very well informed," said Dinomachus, "and you've never taken the trouble to learn how things like this do battle against diseases,[9] when they are applied; and it seems to me that you would not accept even the most well known: the repellents, I mean, of those fevers that recur at regular intervals, and the de-toxifying of snakes, the healings of swellings, and the rest—whatever old wives do; and if they all really happen, why will you not think that these too happen through similar means?"

"Dinomachus," I said, "you are heaping up an infinite number of things, and driving in one nail on top of another, as the saying goes. Nor is it certain that what you are talking about happens by that kind of a power. Consequently, unless you first persuade me by a logical argument that it can naturally

happen that a fever or a tumor is frightened by a divine name, everything you have reported is nothing but old wives' tales."

10. "When you talk like that," Dinomachus replied, "you seem to me not even to believe that the gods exist, if you think it cannot happen that remedies are brought to diseases through sacred spells."

"My good man," I said, "do not speak so. Even if the gods fully exist, that does not keep the things you are talking about from being nonsense. In fact, I worship the gods and I see their acts of healing, the assistance they give to those who are in pain, namely, restoring them by medicines and the art of doctoring. And hence Asclepius and his successors have been healing by bringing healing medicines to their patients, but not by tying lions or weasels to them."

11. "Let him alone," said Ion. "But I will tell you something marvelous. I was still a teenager, about fourteen years old, when a fellow came up to my father to inform him that Midas, his vine-dresser servant, although a strong and hard-working man in other respects, about the time of the crowded forum,[10] had been bitten by a snake and was lying down with a putrefying leg. He had been tying palm-branches together and weaving them into fences when the little creature crawled up and bit him on his big toe, then immediately slithered away and hid himself again. The man was howling, and wracked to death with pains. While we were hearing about all this, we saw Midas himself being carried on a litter by his fellow servants: he was all swollen and discolored and his skin looked like it was decaying—he was breathing with great difficulty. My father was very upset about this, and one of his friends, who was standing near, said, 'Take courage. Right away, I am going to bring in a certain Babylonian, one of the people they call the Chaldaeans, and he will cure the man.' And so, lest I take up the whole day telling the story, the Babylonian came and restored Midas to health. He drove the poison out of his body with a certain spell, and by tying to his foot a pebble that he had taken from a column that marked the grave of a deceased virgin.

12. "So far this was nothing very spectacular. Then Midas went back to the fields, and carried his litter away: so much was accomplished by a spell and

9 For the Greek *homileî toîs nosémasi*, More gives *adversus morbos...conferunt*. Lucian uses a military metaphor, which More accurately reproduces, since Greek *homileō* with dative means "join battle with."   **10** around noontime, when the agora or forum is full of people

by that stone from a grave-column. But the Babylonian clearly did other divine things. For going out into the fields the next morning, after declaiming from an old volume seven sacred names, and walking in a circle three times with burning sulfur and a torch, he stirred up and summoned all the snakes that were in the area. And many serpents came, as if drawn by the spell: the aspids, vipers, horned snakes, jumping snakes, poisonous frogs and puff-toads, all except one old python that (I think) was too old to crawl very well, and did not obey the summons. But the Magus said, "Not all are present." Then he chose one of the snakes—the youngest one there—and sent him as a messenger to the old snake, and after a little while that one came too. After they were all collected there, the Babylonian hissed[11] at them, and suddenly they were all burned up by his breath, as we watched in amazement."

13. Then I said, "Tell me, Ion: did that messenger snake—I mean the young one—did he lead the old snake back by the hand or did the old one use a cane?" "You joke," said Cleodemus, "but I myself, who used to be even less believing of such things than you, and thought there was no way I could ever be made to believe them, when I first saw the flying man, that foreign traveler (they say he came from the Hyperboreans),[12] *then* I believed, then I was won over, even though I fought hard against it for a long time, since what could I do when I saw him flying in the air, in broad daylight, and also walking on water, and walking slowly, step by step, right through the midst of a fire?" "So," I said, "you really saw that? A Hyperborean man flying, and walking on water?" "Yes, I really did," he said, "and with canvas shoes on, which is the kind of shoes those people mostly use. And what would be the point of me telling all the minor things he did— how he conjured up love affairs, or drove out demons, or brought decayed dead persons back to life, or made Hecate herself appear to bystanders, and dragged the moon from the sky?

14. "But I might as well tell you what I saw he did for Glaucias, the son of Alexicles. When this Glaucias had inherited the wealth left behind by his recently dead father, he fell in love with Chrysis, the daughter of Demaenetus; he was a pupil of mine in arts education, and if his love interest had not

drawn him away, he would have learned the whole Peripatetic doctrine, since he was eighteen and had already finished with analytics, and had reached the end of my lectures on the physics. But he was overcome by love, and told me all about it. Well then, as was only right, since I was his teacher, I brought the Hyperborean Magus to him. He was hired right away at the price of four *minae* cash up front, since he had to get some sacrifices ready, and then would need to be paid another sixteen *minae* if Glaucias did succeed in winning Chrysis. So, waiting for the waxing moon (that's when sacred rituals like that are usually done), after digging a trench in the open-air part of his house, under the night sky at midnight, he first summoned the spirit of Alexicles, the father of Glaucias, who had died seven months before. The old man was enraged about the love affair, quite against it. But he finally gave his permission. Then the Magus brought up Hecate, who brought Cerberus along with her, then brought down the moon from the sky and made it have many forms, looking different at different times: first it showed a womanly shape, then it was turned into a beautiful calf, and finally it looked like a little dog. Then the Hyperborean, after making a kind of figurine of Cupid from clay, said: "Now go away, and bring back Chrysis." The clay figurine instantly rushed off, and soon after, the girl was knocking on the door. Coming inside, she embraced Glaucias, being madly in love with him, and they spent their time together until we heard the cocks crowing. Then the moon flew up to the sky, Hecate went back underground, the other spectres disappeared, and we sent Chrysis on her way when it was just about dawn.

15. "If you had seen this, Tychiades, you would surely no longer doubt that there are many benefits in those spells." "You are right," I said. "I would believe, if I had seen them, but I think you should forgive me if I am not able to see as clearly and sharply the kinds of things you see; that Chrysis you mention, by the way, I know, is a very loose woman—a prostitute—so I surely do not see why you would need the clay figurine messenger, the Hyperborean Magus, and the moon, to boot. You could have brought her all the way to the Hyperboreans for twenty drachmas. The woman is marvelously responsive to the charm, and her case is the opposite

---

11 For the Greek *enephusēsen*; More's *insibulavit* humorously recalls the "hissing" sound of snakes.　　**12** a race of giants in Greek mythology

of the ghosts: if they hear any sound of bronze or iron, they run away (that's what you say), but if she hears anything like the sound of money, she comes running to the sound of the jingling. And I also wonder at the Magus: since he can get the richest women to fall in love with him, and get whole talents from them, why would he be so desperate for such a tiny profit of four *minae*, just so Glaucias could get Chrysis's affections?" "You joke because you believe nothing," said Ion.

16. "Let me ask you what you might say about those who liberate possessed persons from their terrors, so very clearly casting out those ghosts by means of spells? I don't have to tell you about this, since everybody knows it: that Syrian fellow from Palestine, who is an artist in these matters, how many poor souls he has helped, who fall down at the moon, twist their eyes and foam at the mouth, but he raises them up and sends them away healed, freeing them from those fearful evils for a substantial profit. And when he stands over them as they lie there, asking them whence they had come into the body, the sick man is quiet, but the *daemon* replies in either Greek or barbarian, depending on where he was from, both how and whence he entered into the man. And then the Magus, adjuring him and threatening him if he does not cooperate, drives out the *daemon*. I have even seen one coming out, all black and smoky in color."

"It was not something great, O Ion," I said, "for you to see such things—you, to whom the very Ideas appear, which the father of your family Plato reveals: that is, a thing barely to be seen and vanishing as far as concerns us blind mortals."

17. "So, did only Ion," Eucrates said, "see that kind of sight? Did not many others come upon *daemones*: some at night, others even in daytime? To be sure, I have seen such things not once but a thousand times, and at first I was troubled about them, but soon, because of habituation, it seemed I was not seeing anything strange or marvelous, especially since that Arabian gave me a ring made of iron made from a cross,[13] and taught me a spell filled with many names—just in case you won't believe me either, Tychiades."

"But how can it be," I said, "that I would dis-

believe Eucrates, the son of Dino? A man especially wise, and freely telling, with authority, in his own home and in private, what was seen by him?"

18. "Haven't you heard," said Eucrates, "that bit about the statue that appears to everyone in the house every night—the boys, the teenagers, the older men? You might have heard that, I say, not only from me, but from any of my people." "About what statue?" I said. "Didn't you see," he said, "as you came in, that statue in the atrium, a quite beautiful one, a work by Demetrius, who customarily makes statues of the human form?" "You don't mean the one throwing a discus? It's bent over, as if going to throw, leaning back toward the side where he's holding the discus, with the other leg bent somewhat, and seeming about to straighten up at the throw of the discus?" "No, not that one," he said. "You are talking about that discus-thrower; that's one of the works of Myron.[14] Nor do I mean the one next to it: I mean the one with fillets on his head, a real beauty, that one—it's the work of Polycleitus.[15] But forget the ones to the right hand side as you come in, among whom are the images of the tyrannicides Critias and Nesiotes;[16] but didn't you see, beside the water fountain, a statue with a protruding belly, bald, half-undressed, and some hairs of the beard plucked out, with clearly visible veins, but very similar to a human being? It appears to be Pelichus, the Corinthian general."

19. "By Jupiter," I said, "I saw a certain statue to the right side of Saturn with head-bands and dry-leaf crowns, and some gold leaves on his chest." "I had that gold put on it," Eucrates said, "when he healed me when I was being ruined by three-day fever. "Was that noble Pelichus also a medical doctor?" I said. "He is," said Eucrates, "and don't laugh—or the man will attack you not long afterwards. I certainly know how strong that statue is, at which you are laughing. But don't you think that it would be in the power of a statue to send fevers into any people it wants if that same statue has the power to expel them?" "Let that statue, that has so much strength, be favorable and kindly to me!" I said. "What else have the people in the house seen him doing?" "As soon as it is night," he said, "that statue, climbing down from the pedestal on which

13 More gives the singular *cruce* ("cross, crucifix") for the Greek *ek tôn staurôn*, "[made] from stakes." **14** Greek sculptor (fl. *ca.* 480–440 BC) known for his bronze depictions of athletes in action **15** (fl. *ca.* 450–415 BC) Greek sculptor known for his sculptures of athletes **16** Critias and Nesiotes were sculptors in Athens, 5th century BC, of a work called *The Tyrant-Slayers*.

it was standing, walks in a circle around the entire house. Everyone has met up with him, sometimes singing. He has not hurt anyone; you only have to move out of his way. And the statue goes past without a hostile expression while it bathes itself and plays all night, as you can hear from the splash of the water." "Look," I said, "that statue may not be of Pelichus but of Talus[17] the Cretan that was supposed to belong to Minos. He was made of bronze, and was the guard of Crete. But if he[18] had been made out of bronze, and not out of wood, nothing would keep him from appearing to be, not the work of Demetrius, but one of the devices created by Daedalus! After all, that statue also climbed off his pedestal, as you said this one does."

20. "Look here, Tychiades," said he, "and be careful you don't regret making this joke afterwards. I know what happened to the fellow who stole the obols[19] that we offer the statue every new moon." "Really horrible things must have happened," said Ion, "since that was a sacrilege. How did he punish him, Eucrates? I want to hear, even if Tychiades will be very disbelieving." "There were many obols lying at his feet, as well as other coins, and even some silver ones stuck on his legs with wax, and silver foil too: they were each person's thanksgiving offerings or rewards for healing from anyone who was freed by him, when oppressed by fever. But we had a servant, a Libyan scoundrel, a horse groomer. He approached at night and took all the money, watching when the statue was away from its pedestal. But because the moment he came back, Pelichus knew he had been a victim of sacrilegious robbery, consider how he got revenge and exposed the theft of the Libyan: all night long, the man wandered around the atrium, miserable, not able to go outside, as if he had been trapped in a Labyrinth, until at sunrise he was apprehended holding the money he had taken, and then, once captured, he received not a few blows, nor did he survive very long after that and, as an evil man, died evilly, being beaten up every night so that welts appeared on his body the next day. So go ahead, Tychiades, and laugh at Pelichus now that you have heard this, and think of me as if I were just some hold-over from the age of

Minos, gone mad." "But Eucrates," I said, "as long as bronze is bronze, Demetrius the Alopecian will be a sculptor who specializes in making humans, not gods. I will never revere the statue of Pelichus, of whom I would not have been afraid even if he were still alive and making threats at me."

21. At this point Antigonus the medical doctor said, "Eucrates, I have a statue of Hippocrates, a bronze one, about one cubit[20] high. As soon as the lamp is extinguished, he goes around the whole house, making noise and overturning jars, mixing up the drugs, and overturning the sacrifice, especially if we delay any of the sacrifices we offer him on a yearly basis." "So, then," said I, "even Hippocrates the doctor demands sacrifices to be made to him, and he gets angry if he is not entertained at the proper time by the correct sacrificial offerings. Of course, someone should have had the good idea to pour him a libation or sprinkle some sacrificial meal or put a crown on his head."

22. "Listen, then," said Eucrates, "I can prove with certainty by means of witnesses something that I saw five years ago. It was about harvest time. About the middle of the day, I sent the workers into the vineyards, and walked alone into the woods, thinking and pondering about something. After I reached the wild pasture, I heard the sound of dogs barking. I guessed it was my son Mnason coming along with his friends to play and hunt, as usual. But it was something altogether different: a little later, there was an earthquake and a sound like thunder, and I saw a woman coming up to me, terrible to behold. She was almost half a stadium tall, with a torch in her left hand, and a sword in her right about twenty cubits long. Down below, her feet were serpents, and up above, she had, you see, a face that reminded me of the Gorgon and was terrifying in appearance. She had snakes for hair that was tied back, and snakes around her neck and still others spread over her shoulders. Look, my friends, how terrified I am just telling you about it," and saying this, Eucrates showed everybody there how the hairs on his arms were sticking straight up with fear.

23. Now Ion and Dinomachus and Cleodemus were listening, agape with wonder, all old men

---

17 See Apollonius Rhodius, *Argonautika* 4.1638–88. **18** i.e., the statue of Pelichus. More appears to have corrected his Greek text by adding a negative (*non*). The thought is then clear: if the statue of Pelichus had been bronze and *not* wood, it would be just like something made by Daedalus (i.e., like Talos, who was made of bronze) rather than by Demetrius (who, presumably, worked in wood). More makes an intelligible joke to avoid some obscurity in Lucian's Greek text. **19** a silver coin in Ancient Greece, one-sixth of a drachma **20** about eighteen inches

giving reverence to such an unbelievable Colossus in their midst: a woman half a stadium high, a kind of giant monster. Now, I was pondering in the interim, what sort of men these were who, in the name of wisdom, consorted with youth and were popularly held up for admiration, when they differ from children only by having beards and white hair. But they are even more easily led to believe lies than children. "Tell me, Eucrates," said Dinomachus. "Those dogs of the woman—what size were they?"

24. "Taller," said he, "than the elephants of India, black and shagged and with filthy dirty tufts of hair. Now when I saw her, I stood still, and turned the seal of the ring (that the Arab had given me) to the inside of my finger. And so, Hecate, striking the ground with those snaky feet of hers, created a huge chasm, so large that it went all the way down to Tartarus. Shortly after, she leaped into it and disappeared. But I had the presence of mind to bend down and look, holding on to a tree that stood nearby, taking care not to fall headlong into the shadows and steep chasm before me; then I saw everything down below: Pyriphlegethon, the lake, Cerberus, the shades of the dead, so that I could even recognize some of them. I clearly saw my father, clothed in the very same things we buried him in."

"O Eucrates," said Ion, "what were the souls doing?" "What else," said he, "but hanging around with their friends and relations, divided into families and tribes, and settled upon the asphodel?" "Let the Epicureans try," said Ion, "to contradict holy Plato and his arguments about the soul. But did you see Socrates and Plato himself among the shades?" "I saw Socrates," he said, "although none too clearly, apart from guessing that he was bald and had a protruding stomach. I didn't see Plato—among friends one must tell the truth, of course. As soon as I saw everything, the chasm closed up, and some of my servants came looking for me, among them Pyrrhias here, and they got there before the chasm had closed all the way up—right, Pyrrhias? Don't I speak the truth?" "By Jupiter," said Pyrrhias, "I even heard howling through the gap, and fire seemed to me to be blazing, as from a torch." And then I really laughed, when the eye-witness added the howling and the fire to top it all off.

25. Then Cleodemus said, "This is hardly new, and what you saw has not been unseen by others. For I myself not too long ago, when I was sick, saw something like that. Antigonus here was looking out for me and tending to me, and it was the seventh day of my illness. What kind of fever was it? It was certainly stronger than burning. Everybody had left me alone, and they were waiting outside with the doors closed. Indeed, those were your orders, Antigonus—so that I could get some sleep. Well, then a young man was standing by me, as I lay there still awake. Very handsome he was, and clothed in a bright white garb. And when he had gotten me up, he led me through some kind of opening to the lower regions, as I immediately understood when I saw Tantalus and Tityus and Sisyphus. Why should I rehearse the rest to you? After I reached the judges' stand (Aeacus was there, and Charon, the Fates and the Furies), some kind of king (he seemed to me, of course, to be Pluto) took his seat to review the names of each person who was about to die who had happened to evade their appointed last day of life. So the young man brought me up and showed me to Pluto. Pluto got blazing mad and said to the one who led me there, "His thread is not finished yet. Let him go. But bring me the carpenter Demylus; he's already living 'beyond the spool.'" Then I was very happy to leave, and coming back I was free of my fever and told everybody that Demylus was going to die. He lived in our neighborhood, and even he was a little sick, as it was reported. And a little afterwards we heard the wailing of his mourners."

26. "What is so marvelous about that?" said Antigonus. "For I knew someone who was resurrected twenty days after he was buried. I took care of the man both before he died and after he came back to life."[21] "And how," I said, "in those twenty days did the body not spoil or become decayed through starvation, unless you had some Epimenides[22] for your patient?"

27. When we were saying this, the sons of Eucrates came in, just returning home from the palestra.[23] One had just outgrown the ephebes,[24] the other was about fifteen years old. After the exchange of greetings, they took a seat next to their father on the bed, and a chair was brought for me to sit in. Then Eucrates, as if reminded of something by the sight of his sons, said, "By the joy I take in

21 Greek *anastánta...anéstē*; Latin *resurrexisse...resurrexit*. Lucian appears to have used the Christian terminology rather than the Platonic *anabiôsthai*. **22** A Cretan seer (fl. *ca*. 6th century BC) who, according to legend, miraculously slept for fifty-seven years **23** a gymnasium for wrestling and other sports **24** military training for citizens between eighteen and twenty

these boys," and he put his arms around them, "I will tell you the truth, Tychiades. Everyone knows my wife of happy memory, the mother of these two, how I loved her; and I declared it in the things I did for her not only while she lived but even after she died. Because, you see, I included in her grave all her personal affects and the clothing she was delighted by when alive. On the seventh day after her death, I was lying here on this same bed, the way I am now, trying to lessen the grief that I felt for her. I was silently reading Plato's volume on the soul. And then Demanete herself came into the room, and sat next to me, just the way Eucratides is here," he said, pointing to his younger son. And the son was trembling very much like a boy, and for a while was pale at hearing the story. "But when I saw her," said Eucrates, "I embraced her and wept and sobbed. But she would not allow me to talk, but accused me, saying that although I was pleasing to her with everything else, nevertheless I had not cremated one of her golden sandals, which she said was still to be found, because it had fallen under the chest, and because we could not find it, we only had burned the one sandal. While we were talking about this, a certain most rascally dog, one of my pets, that was lying on the bed,[25] barked, and she vanished at the barking. But the sandal was found under the chest, and we burned it afterwards.

28. "So, Tychiades, will you refuse to believe these things too, even though they are so evident and happen every day?" "By Jupiter," I said, "if any people don't believe these things and still so impudently resist them, they deserve to have their behinds spanked, like children, with a golden sandal."

29. Meanwhile Arignotus the Pythagorean had entered the room, most venerable in appearance, and you know that he is famous by reason of his learning; he has been given the name "holy." Well, when I saw him, I breathed easily again, thinking, as the saying goes, that he had come to my rescue, a veritable axe to cut falsehoods: "That wise man will close their mouths, who are telling such monstrous tales," and immediately, according to that old adage, I thought that a god had suddenly been sent down to me by fortune. So after he took a seat (Cleodemus meanwhile getting up and giving him room to

sit), he asked, first of all, about the illness, and said that he had heard that Eucrates was getting better. "But what are you all philosophizing about?" he said. "For while I was coming in, I overheard you a little, and you seemed to be involved in a lovely conversation."

"What else," said Eucrates, "but trying to persuade this block of marble (pointing at me) that *daemones* and ghosts exist and that the souls of dead persons walk the earth and can show themselves to whomsoever they please!" Well, I blushed at that, and looked down, feeling some shame before Arignotus. But he said, "Look, Eucrates, is Tychiades saying that? The only souls that wander about are the souls of those who have died violently, say by being strangled or beheaded or crucified or departing from life in some such way as that; those, however, who have died a natural kind of death no longer wander at all. If *that* is what he is saying, he has not said anything really that absurd."

"By Jupiter!" said Dinomachus, "he doesn't think they even exist, or can be seen as present at all."

30. "What's that you say?" said Arignotus, looking at me rather sternly. "You don't think any of this happens? Especially when everybody, so to speak, sees it?" "Please forgive me," I said, "if I do not believe, since I am the only one who doesn't see them. I am sure that if I had seen them, I would have surely believed in them just the way you do." "But if you go to Corinth, "he said," ask where the house of Eubatides is, and when it is pointed out to you (it's near the Cranion), go on in, and tell the doorman Tibius that you want to see the place where Arignotus the Pythagorean brought forth the *daemon* and drove it away, and made the house habitable again."

31. "What was that all about, Arignotus?" asked Eucrates. "The house was uninhabitable for a long time because of some frightening things so that if anybody lived there, he became terrified and was chased away by a horrifying and terrible ghost. It was already falling down, the roof had caved in, and there was nobody who even dared to go in it at all. Now, when I heard about it, taking some books with me (I own quite a few Egyptian books about these very matters), I went into the house about the first

---

25 More makes a small change here, perhaps to humanize the scene: Lucian's Greek says, "a little dog, a Maltese (Greek *Melitaîon*), which was under (*hypò*) the bed, barked"; More omits mentioning the kind of dog (as *CW* 3.1 editor Thompson points out, p. 147), but instead makes it "a pet he loves" (*in deliciis*) and has it lying *on* the bed (in *lecto*) instead of *under* it.

watch of the night, even though the homeowner was pleading with me and almost forcing me not to go in, when he learned where I was headed—he thought I was going surely to destruction. Holding a lamp, I went in alone. Entering a very large room, I set down the lamp and began to read silently. The *daemon* shows up, thinking he was dealing with just another common person, and intending to frighten me the same way he had the others—he was shaggy and filthy and darker than the shadows. As he stood there, he tried to get at me from every which way, changing into a dog, a bull, and a lion. But holding in my hands the most terrifying spell I had, and making my voice sound Egyptian, chanting the spell, I drove him into a corner of the dark house. When I saw where he hid himself in the ground, I left off. In the morning, when everyone had given up hope, and thought they would find me dead the way they had found the rest, out I came to everyone's surprise! Going up to Eubatides, I cheerfully announced to him that his house was now clean and free of ghosts and that he could live there again. So bringing him and many others (they were following in curiosity over this unexpected event) to the place where I had seen the *daemon* burying himself, I told them to get picks and shovels and dig it up. When they had done so, about six feet under they found a decayed cadaver, with only an intact skeleton to show the human shape. Digging it out, we gave it a proper burial, and after that the house stopped being haunted.

32. When Arignotus—a man of haunting[26] wisdom, and respected by all—told this story, nobody was there who failed to think me quite mad for not believing such things, especially when Arignotus was telling them. But I had no regard for his long hair, nor for their high opinion of him. "What is this, Arignotus? You, in whom all my hopes were placed, have been full of smoke and images like this? Well then, I have experienced in your case the old proverb, 'Look for a treasure, but only find charcoal.'" "But listen, you," said Arignotus. "If you don't believe me or Dinomachus or Cleodemus here, or Eucrates himself, tell me whom do you find worthier of belief concerning these matters? Who is telling you differently?" "By Jupiter," said I, "a most admirable man, Democritus from Abdera, whose firm conviction that nothing of this kind can exist was made clear, when he enclosed himself outside the gates of the city in a sepulcher, and spent days and nights there, composing and writing, and some youths who wanted to scare him and play tricks on him dressed themselves in black and put on masks to look like corpses, stood around him and jumped and danced a lot; he had no fear of their deceptions and didn't even look at them, but just spoke to them while he kept on writing: 'Stop being fools.' That's how firmly he believed that souls are nothing after they depart from bodies." "So you say," said Eucrates, "that there was a madman like Democritus? And that he thought like that?

33. "I will tell you something else, something that happened to me, and not something I heard from somebody else; perhaps even you, Tychiades, will be forced to give in, when you have heard it, and be compelled by the truth of the story. When I was spending time in Egypt, still a young man—having been sent there by my father for the purpose of education—I wanted to hear that miraculous sound. Leaving by boat for Coptus, I wanted to go from there to Memnon, to hear that sound that he gives at the rising sun. And I heard him, but not in the common way, whereby other people hear some silly noise, but Memnon himself divulged oracles to me, opening his mouth to speak in seven verses, and if it weren't pointless for me to do so, I would now recite them for you. **34.** While we were sailing, we met a certain man from Memphis who was travelling with us, one of those sacred scribes, of wonderful wisdom, thoroughly versed in the whole doctrine of the Egyptians. He was said to have spent twenty-three years in subterranean chambers, and to have learned magic from Isis. Arignotus my teacher said, 'You speak of Pancrates, a holy man with a shaved head, clothed in linen, learned and speaking very good Greek, tall, with a snub nose, protruding lips and slender legs.' The other said, 'That's him, Pancrates, but at first I didn't know who he was. After we came to harbor, and I saw him in addition to many other wonders, riding on crocodiles and consorting with animals, while they fawned on him and wagged their tails, I realized that he was a holy man, and by keeping company with him, I gradually insinuated myself into his confidence and friendship

---

26 Latin *vir prodigiosa sapientia:* a humorous touch introduced by More; the Latin word *prodigiosa* ("spooky") picks up More's own translation of the sentence before *turbari prodigiis* "to be disturbed by prodigies." Lucian's Greek says simply that the man's wisdom was "godlike" (*daimonios*).

so much so that he told me all his secrets. At last he persuaded me to leave all my servants behind in Memphis and follow him by myself; he said we would not be lacking our own assistants. And this was how we lived from that time forwards.

35. When we came to an inn, the man would take something—a pestle, or a little broom, or a door-bolt—and wrapping it up in his cloak, would chant a certain spell upon it, and make it walk, and appear to others like a human being. So the thing would go away and fetch water, make dinner, set the table, and in all respects served us and ministered to us comfortably. After the service was accomplished, reciting another spell, he made the broom turn back into a broom or the pestle turn back into a pestle. And though I tried very hard, there was no way I could fish the secret out of him. He begrudged me that, even though he was very generous in everything else. One day, while hiding in a shadowy place where he didn't notice me, I overheard the spell at closer range. It had three syllables. He gave a pestle some orders to do something, then left for the forum.

36. The next day, when he was busy at the forum, I took the pestle, wrapped it up and, pronouncing the syllables exactly as I heard them pronounced, commanded it to fetch water. When it brought me the amphora full of water, I said, 'Stop. Don't bring me any more water, and become a pestle again.' But it did not want to obey me anymore and kept bringing water without stopping until he filled up our whole house with water. And when I was not able to stop the thing, fearing that Pancrates would be angry when he returned (and he did in fact return), I picked up an axe and cut the pestle into two pieces. But then each part picked up a jug and fetched water, and it now began to be two servants instead of one. That's when Pancrates arrived and, grasping the situation, changed the pieces back into the wood they were to begin with. Then he disappeared from my sight, going off someplace secretly." "But are you still able," said Dinomachus, "to make a pestle into a human?" "By Jupiter," said the other, "I know half of it, but I was never able to turn it back into its original form, once it became a water-carrier. We would have to get out of a house full of water."

37. Then I said, "Old men, will you not stop telling these monstrous stories? At least for the sake of the young people, leave to another time the telling of these incredible and terrifying stories lest they be filled, without your noticing it, with terrors and scary tales. You should spare them from getting used to hearing such things which will stick with them and disturb them all their lives and make them jumpy at every little sound, let alone fill them with every kind of superstition."

38. "You are right," said Eucrates, "to warn me about superstition. But what do you think about these kind of things, Tychiades: I mean oracles and prophecies, and whatever people proclaim who are inspired by some divinity, things heard from caverns? Or when a virgin prophetess speaking in elegant verses predicts the future? Don't you even believe that? Well, I won't tell you that I have a sacred ring that has a signet with the image of Pythian Apollo, nor will I tell you what this Apollo says to me lest you think I am telling incredible things for my own glory. But what I heard in the presence of Amphilochus in Mallus, when the hero spoke to me for a long time, getting advice from the god about my affairs, as well as what I saw myself—*that* is what I would like to tell you about. Then what I saw in Pergamum, and next what I heard in Patara, in order. So then, when I came back home from Egypt, and I heard that that very clear prophecy in Mallus, at the same time as being very truthful, would also give out oracles in such a way that they would exactly answer whatever somebody wrote on a tablet and handed to the prophet. I thought I would be acting rightly, if I experienced the oracle, while I was sailing near the place anyway, and consult the god about the future."

39. Eucrates was still speaking, when I saw how long the thing was going to take, since he had started no brief tragic tale about the oracle. Deciding it would not do any good for me alone to contradict everybody there, I left him sailing from Egypt to Mallum. You see, I also gathered that my presence was obnoxious to them since I was disagreeing with them and refuting their lies. "Okay, I am leaving," I said. "I want to find Leonticus, whom I still need to talk to about something. Since you all believe that human things are not enough for you, you call the gods themselves to aid you with their myths." As soon as I said that, I left. And they, delighted to have their liberty, as you can truly imagine, toasted each other generously and drowned themselves in lies. O Philocles! After hearing all that at Eucrates's house, I come here with a stomach bursting, like people who have been drinking sweet wine—I need to vomit! I would gladly buy for a high price some drug that would bring forgetfulness of what I heard, to keep the memory of it from damaging me: I think I see monsters, daimons, Hecates!

40. PHILOCLES: Actually, Tychiades, this story of yours has brought something similar to me: they say that not only people who have been bitten by rabid dogs go crazy and become hydrophobic,[27] but even if a man who has been bitten like that bites another, that bite will be no less powerful than the dog bite, and the next man will be just as hydrophobic. So, since you have been bitten by many lies at Eucrates',

you appear now to have communicated that same bite to me, so much have you filled my mind with *daemones*!

TYCHIADES: Let's be of good cheer, my friend, since we have a great remedy against things of this kind: truth and right reason in all things, and if we use that, we will never be disturbed by these vain and stupid lies.

THE END
THOMAS MORE, TRANSLATOR

27 The fear of water was considered a symptom of rabies.

The Tyrannicide *or* Declamation on Behalf of the Tyrant-slayer

THE ARGUMENT
OF THE DECLAMATION

5 A man went up into the citadel in order to kill[1] the tyrant; although he did not find him, after he slew the tyrant's son, he left his sword in the body. The tyrant himself came up, and, seeing his son already dead, drove himself through with the very same 10 sword; the man who had gone up and slain the tyrant's son requests reward as a tyrant-slayer.

THE DECLAMATION

1. Since, judges, I have killed two tyrants in a single day—one already advanced in age, the other in the 15 prime of youth and thus fit for taking up the succession of crimes—I am here today, all the same, to ask for a single reward for the double action, and I do this, even though I am the only one of those who have assassinated tyrants to dispatch and destroy 20 two wicked persons with one blow: I killed the son by means of my sword, but the father by means of the excessive love he had for his son. Therefore the tyrant paid a sufficient penalty for what he had done, in so far as he saw his own son killed while he was 25 still alive himself, and at the last (and this was especially beyond all expectation) was forced to become his own tyrannicide. And therefore the son was slain by me, and even when dead, acted as my assistant toward another death: for he who, when alive, to-30 gether with his father committed injustices, when dead, killed his father as only he could have done it.

2. I am the one who removed the tyranny; mine is the sword that accomplished everything; I only switched the order of their deaths: removing the 35 stronger one, the one who could have taken revenge, and leaving the old man only to the sword.

3. Now because of these things I was actually expecting something extra from you, and would hope to receive rewards equaling the number of the slain, 40 seeing that I have snatched you not only from present evils, but also from the fear of future crimes,

and have given you certain freedom, with no living heir of wickedness. But in the meanwhile, I run the risk of going away from you without receiving any reward at all, to be alone deprived of the payment 45 which the very laws, rescued by me, have decreed. Therefore, this adversary of mine here is apparently not doing this out of love of country,[2] as he claims, but rather, has been stirred up by the killing of the tyrants to avenge himself on the one who was the 50 cause of their death.

4. But, judges, listen to me a little, while I present the evils of the tyranny (even though you yourselves are quite aware of them); in this way you will better grasp the extent of my service, and you will 55 also rejoice more, when you think over the ills from which you have been delivered. For, the way it often happens to many others, it has not in the same way happened to us also: to have suffered a simple tyranny and a single servitude; nor have we put up with 60 the passion of a single master, but alone of all those whom a similar unhappiness has ever oppressed, have had two tyrants in place of one, and been wretchedly distraught into double the injuries. But the old man was much more moderate: milder in his 65 anger, less keen to enforce punishments, slower to act on his desires, since his old age restrained the excessiveness of his drive, and reined in his passions for pleasures. In fact, he was said to have been pushed unwillingly into starting injustices, since he was not 70 extremely tyrannical himself, except when he gave in to the other, for, as he showed, he was overly fond of his son. That son was everything to him: the father obeyed him, did whatever injustice he commanded, and punished whomever the son wished; in a word, 75 he lived under his tyranny, and had become the willing[3] accomplice of his son's desires.

5. The young man yielded in honor to the father because of his age, and abstained from the title alone of tyranny; in actual fact, however, he was 80 himself the tyranny's head. The stability and the safety of the rulership[4] depended upon him, since

---

1 Lucian used the same Greek verb for "kill" (*apokténein*) three times; More varies it: *occidere, perimere, interemere.* **2** Greek *kēdómenos...tôn koinôn* ("caring for the things that are in common"); Latin *nullo Reipublicae studio* **3** More has added *ultroneus* ("willing")—perhaps to bring out further the contradiction in the father's behavior. **4** Greek *dynasteías*; Latin *principatus*

he alone enjoyed the results of the injustices. He was the one who directed the henchmen, who ruled the bodyguards, who struck down the tyrannized, who terrified the rebellious. He was the one who kidnapped the young men and violated weddings, the one to whom maidens were brought. If there were any killings, any forced exiles, any confiscations, any tortures or insults—all that was the work of the young one, for the old one followed his lead, was his companion in crime, and had only approval for his son's misdeeds. The whole business became intolerable to us, since, when the mind's desires get a license from political power, they bring no end of injustices.

6. But the most burning thing[5] of all to us was that we knew it was going to be a long-lasting—even a permanent—enslavement, and that the republic[6] and people were going to be handed down in succession, moving as an inheritance from one criminal overlord to the next. Of course, others have no little hope about this situation, and can rationalize and say to themselves: "It will be over soon," and "he will die, then we will be free." But nothing of the kind could be hoped for with those, but we saw the heir prepared for succession to the rule, and none of the braver men dared do anything, even the ones who longed for the same outcome as I. Freedom was completely despaired of, and the tyranny appeared invincible, since so many had to be attacked.

7. But these things frightened me not at all, nor did thinking of the difficulty of the business make me shirk from it, or dread the danger. I alone, I alone advanced against so strong and extensive a tyranny—well, not really alone, with my trusty sword, my comrade in tyrannicide—having my own death before my eyes, but counterbalancing my own slaughter with the freedom of all.[7] After I made my first attack on the guards, and had pushed aside—not easily—the bodyguards, killing whomever I encountered, and overcoming whatever stood in the way, I flew at the very head of the problem, the one bulwark of the tyranny, the very source of our woes. And standing there amid the guards of the citadel, when I caught sight of him manfully defending

himself and resisting, with many wounds, nevertheless, I killed him.

8. The tyranny was removed, the exploit was accomplished, and from that point forward we were all free. The old man alone remained, unarmed, stripped of his guards, and now with that one henchman of his gone, he was deserted, and no longer worthy of any noble foe's hand. At that moment, judges, these were my thoughts: "My entire project has turned out well: everything is done; all has been vigorously accomplished. In what way, now, is the one who survives to be punished? He is, of course, unworthy of my hand, and especially, now that my noble, youthful exploit has been done, I would only subtract from the glory of it by adding[8] such a lackluster killing. It would be worthwhile to look for an executioner—but after the catastrophe, then, let him get no benefit from it. Let him see, let him be punished, let him have the sword at his disposal: I entrust the rest of the business to the sword!" Once I decided this, I removed myself from there. But he acted just as I had divined he would, and killing a tyrant, added the final act to my fable.[9]

9. Therefore I am present today, bringing back popular government[10] to you, proclaiming safety to all, joyfully proclaiming freedom. So therefore, make use now of what I have accomplished. As you see, the citadel is freed of criminals; nobody is giving orders, but it is permitted to bestow honors, to make judgments, to plead cases on the basis of laws; and these are results that derive from me, that have proceeded from my daring deed and from that one killing, after which the father could no longer live. Therefore for these reasons I judge it worthy, that the reward be given me, not because I am eager for profit, or because I make a lot out of a little, or because I have set my heart on getting paid for helping the fatherland, but because I want my services to be approved by your reward, that my daring attempt not be belittled or become inglorious, abandoned as if maimed by you, and judged unworthy of reward.

10. But this fellow disputes it, and says I act unjustly because I want to be honored and win a reward, for he says I am not a tyrant-slayer, and that

---

5 Greek *elúpei* ("pained"); Latin *urebat* ("burned"). More has specified a particular kind of pain. **6** Here More uses *respublica* for the Greek *pólis.* **7** More adds *propria* and brings out the juxtaposition of private sacrifice and public service: *propria, communi.* **8** More adds a playful paradox,

"I would subtract [*minuerem*] . . . by adding [*addita*]," where Lucian's Greek is "he, being despatched . . . would put shame on that killing [of mine]." **9** Greek *drámati*, Latin *fabulae.* More uses the traditional Latin word for a tragedy. The Greek word *drama* has not yet become a standard word

in Latin Europe. **10** Greek *dēmokratían*; Latin *popularem gubernationem.* Like *drama, democratia* has apparently not yet become a familiar word in Latin Christendom.

nothing has been done by me in accordance with the law, but that something is still lacking to my action for it to be rewarded. And so I ask him: What more do you want from me? Did I not will the act? Did I not go up into the citadel? Did I not I kill? Did I not liberate? Does anybody give orders? Does anyone give commands? Is any overlord making threats? Has any criminal escaped? You will not say so. But everything is full of peace; all the laws have been restored; our freedom is manifest; the popular government is stable; marriages are not violated; boys are out of danger; maids are safe; and the state[11] is celebrating festival days because of the general happiness. What is, then, the reason for all this? Who took away those things, and brought about these things? In fact, if someone is more deserving of this honor than myself, I let him have the gift; I abstain from the reward. But if I alone have done everything—daring, risking, attacking, killing, punishing, avenging the one upon the other—why do you slander my services? Why do you make me unappreciated by the people?

11. "But you did not kill the tyrant," you say; "the law decrees a reward for a tyrant-slayer." So tell me: is there a difference between killing him and providing the cause of his death? I certainly don't think there is any difference, and I think the law-maker had only this in mind: freedom, and a state for the people,[12] the removal of ill-doers; that is what he honored, that is what he counted worthy of thanks, and you cannot deny that this is what has been done by me. For if I killed the one person without whom he could not go on living, then, of course, I killed him. The killing was mine; the hand was his. So do not quibble over-curiously about the mode of death, nor investigate how he died, but rather, whether or not he is still alive, and whether or not it was through me that he is no longer still alive. Indeed, you seem to me about to discuss this too, and become a persecutor of benefactors, asking whether somebody killed him with a sword or a rock or a stick or in some other way.

But what if I had blockaded the tyrant and by starvation driven him to death? Even then would you demand a killing carried out by my own hand? Or would you still say that something was lacking toward the fulfillment of the law? And this, even though the evil-doer had died by a harsher punishment? Investigate one thing only; interrogate about this; be inquisitive to find out this: who of those wicked men is still living? What fear of injury still hangs over us? What traces of those calamities? If everything has been cleaned up and pacified, it is the role of a sycophant to besmirch the way things are done and to wish to deprive actual deeds of their deserved reward.

12. Now I also recall that this was stated in the law (unless perhaps, owing to our long enslavement, I have forgotten what is said in them), that there are two causes of death, either someone killed,[13] or, without killing the person himself or doing it by his own hand, nevertheless forced it and provided the occasion of the killing. The law judges that this latter man too should be punished, and quite justly, for the supplying of the cause of death it has judged to be no less than the actual fact, and any remaining question about the mode of killing is superfluous. Therefore, someone who murdered a man in that way, you would think justly to be punished as a homicide, and would in no way absolve him; but when someone has benefited the state in the same way, will you consider him undeserving of the reward of a benefactor?

13. Nor can you say this: that I simply did it, but a particular good result followed by chance, without my intending it. What further cause would I have had to fear, once the stronger one had been slain? Why would I have left my sword in the wound, unless I had foreseen completely what was going to happen? Unless perhaps you will say that he who was killed was not the tyrant, nor had acquired that name, nor that you would have gladly offered many rewards for it, if he had been slain. But you will never say this.

Therefore, now that the tyrant is dead, you will not give a reward to the one who supplied the cause for it? Oh, what quibbling! You are concerned about how he was killed, when you enjoy your freedom, or you demand something more from the one who restored the republic.[14] And yet the law, as you say, investigates the core of things, but bids all the intermediate issues farewell, and quibbles

---

11 Greek *hè pólis*; Latin *civitas*   12 Greek *dēmokratían*; Latin *popularem statum*   13 More adds this short clause to make the two categories of murder more explicit.

He has not changed the meaning.   **14** The use of *rempublicam* in the earlier editions listed by Thompson (1506, 1516, 1519) is preferable to *democratiam*, which,

apparently, first appeared in a marginal gloss and was then brought into the text. More does not use Latin *democratia* for the Greek word elsewhere in the work.

no further. Why indeed—would not one who had driven a tyrant into exile, not have received the honor of a tyrannicide? Well, of course, and justly so, since that man too has brought liberty in the place of servitude. But what was done by me was not exile, nor any fear that a rebellion would be repeated, but a complete removal, the destruction of the whole family, the evil entirely cut out at its root.

14. And now, by the gods, examine everything in my case from the beginning to end, and determine whether anything has been left out in fulfilling the law, if I lack anything that a tyrant-slayer ought to have. Above all, then, it is becoming that a generous spirit should be present, passionate for the republic,[15] prepared to undergo dangers for the common welfare, and to purchase with his own death the safety of the many: so was anything lacking to me, in doing it? Was I broken in spirit? Or, foreseeing what I had to go through, did I shrink before the danger? That you would not say. Dwell, then, on this point alone: imagine that only on the basis that I wanted to do it, and had a plan to do it, and even though no good came from it, that still, just because of my serious intention in itself, I was seeking a reward as a benefactor, but nevertheless I did not do it, but some other person came after me and killed the tyrant, wouldn't it be discordant (tell me!) or absurd to award me, especially if I were to say, "O men of the jury! I wanted to do it, I longed to do it, I went right up, I made signs of my intention, and I alone am worthy of honor." What would you say in reply to that?

15. But that is not what I am saying. I climbed up; I put myself in danger; I accomplished countless feats before I killed the young man. And do not think that it is all so easy a matter to overcome the guards, defeat the henchmen, and, although alone, turn aside so many: this is really the biggest thing in the slaying of a tyrant, the very core of the matter. For the tyrant himself, in fact, is not a big deal, nor a great problem to take care of, nor difficult to fight down, but rather those are that protect and preserve the tyranny. He who overcomes those, overcomes everything; the rest is rather little. Indeed, I could not have been allowed to get through all the way to the tyrants unless I had first been victor over the guards and the henchmen who encircled them, if I had not first defeated them all. I add nothing more, but again insist on these things: I overcame the guards and the henchmen, I say, and I made the tyrant guardless, armless, stripped. Do I not seem worthy of reward because of this? Do you still require of me his actual killing?

16. But if you also want a killing, that is not absent. Nor am I without blood on my hands, but I have perpetrated the great and noble killing of the young man in his flower, when he was feared by all, through whom even the tyrant was safe from plots, in whom alone he trusted, and was all he needed, taking the place of many henchmen for him. So then, am I not worthy of a reward? Shall I be deprived of the honor of such great deeds? What if I had killed one of the henchmen, or some servant of the tyrant? Or some rather distinguished retainer? Would not this seem big to you, also: if I went up to the middle of the citadel and in the midst of the weapons had accomplished the killing of one of the tyrant's friends? But as it is, just consider the one who has been slain: he was the son of the tyrant, but really a worse tyrant, a more pitiless master, a more cruel torturer, a more violent extortionist. Then, and most of all, the heir and successor of all that; finally, someone who was capable of extending our calamities for a long time.

17. Do you wish I had only done that, with the tyrant still alive, having made his escape? This is what I am asking to be rewarded for. What do you say? You won't give it? Didn't you also consider the son wicked? Wasn't he an overlord? A bad one? An intolerable one?

But now, understand the heart of the matter. What this adversary of mine is demanding from me, I accomplished, and it was done the best way it could have been: I killed one tyrant by the killing[16] of another, and not just any old way,[17] nor with a single blow, which is the most he could have wished for, considering all the crimes he committed. But I did it by giving him a lot of pain first: showing him, laid out wretchedly before his eyes, what was most dear to him, his son—an evil man, but in the prime of life, and just like his father—lying there, covered in blood and gore. Here are wounds for fathers, here

---

15 Greek *philópolin* ("city-loving"); More periphrases: *reipublicae studiosum*
16 More adds a wordplay with the Latin *nex* (*paranomasia* or *polyptoton*) that is not

in Lucian: *tyrannum alterius nece necavi.*
17 More adds a touch of emphasis, translating Greek *haplôs* ("simply") with *vulgariter* ("in the cheap, common way"),

strengthening the idea that the killing was "fit" for a bad tyrant.

the swords of legitimate tyrant-slayers! This was a death to befit cruel tyrants; this was a punishment fit for such huge crimes. To die instantly, at the same instant to be unaware, not to see such a sight — that holds nothing worthy for a tyrant's punishment.

18. For I was not unaware — listen to me — I was not, I say, unaware, nor in fact was anyone else, of how much love he had for his son, and that he did not think it worthwhile to outlive him for even a short time. And perhaps all fathers are this way toward their sons. But he certainly had this trait more than others, and for good reason, since he saw the son as the lone caretaker and guardian of the tyranny, saw him alone undergoing dangers before his father, and providing strength to the rule.[18] Consequently, I knew he would soon die — although not for love, at least out of desperation — since he thought his life would be useless to him once the security his son provided was gone. Thus I surrounded him with all these things at once: nature, grief, separation, terror, and apprehension for what the future would bring. I made use of all these as my allies, and forced him to make plans for death. He died on us[19] bereaved, afflicted, grieving, weeping, and engaged in a mourning that was brief, but enough for a father, and, most grievously of all, at his own hand: the most miserable kind of death, much more bitter than if caused by someone else.

19. Where is my sword? Can anybody else recognize it? Does it belong to anyone else? Who brought it up to the citadel? Who used it before the tyrant did? Who sent it to the tyrant? O sword, who shared in my deeds, and succeeded to the legacy of my actions, after so many risks, after so many deaths, we are despised, and appear unworthy of honor and reward! For, if because of this reason alone I were seeking honor from you, if I were to say, "O men, when the tyrant was longing for death and was caught without a weapon, that's when my sword came to serve, and contributed its work to acquiring liberty for all," would you have thought it unworthy of honor and reward? Wouldn't you have exchanged[20] your overlord for such a public possession? Wouldn't you have listed it among your benefactors? Wouldn't you have set my sword among the sacred objects? And not have revered it along with the gods?

20. Now, think over with me, what kinds of things it is likely that the tyrant himself said and did before he died, once I had killed his son, and pierced him with many wounds in the visible parts of the body, in order, namely, that the father be burned[21] with suffering, and be struck dumb at first sight as soon as he saw it. He screamed out for his father, and shouted at him, not to come to help or aid in battle, he being old and infirm, but to behold his family's misfortunes. I departed from the place, the author of the entire tragedy, and left to the stage-actor the dead body, the scene, the sword and what remained to be performed. But when he came on the scene, and saw his son, the only one he had, breathing his last, covered with deadly slashes, bearing those many lethal wounds, he shouted: "O son! We are destroyed, we are slain, we are tyrants who have been assassinated. Where is the killer? Why did he spare me? For what evil is he saving me, who am already dead, by you being dead? Perhaps he despises me as an old man, and having decided to kill me slowly, stretches out my death, in order to prolong his act of killing me."

21. And at the same time as he said this, he looked for a sword. He was unarmed, being a man who had placed all his hopes in his son. But even this was not lacking to him, since it had been made ready by me long before, and had been left behind to work a future exploit. And so, tearing it out of the body, and removing the sword from the wound, "You have already cut me down, killed me, so now make an end, O sword," he said; "come to console a grieving father, and help the unlucky hand of an old man; slaughter a tyrant, kill me, and release me from grief. How I wish I had met with you first, that I had begun the series of slaughters, and had fallen, but just as a tyrant, still hoping for an avenger; as it is, I die bereaved, and not even able to provide an executioner." And as he said these words, he gave

---

18 Greek *têi arché*; Latin *imperio*. Yet another word for "state" (cf. *civitas, respublica, principatus, popularis status, popularis gubernatio*). The Greek word *arché* ("beginning, principle") emphasizes where the chain of command "begins"; the Latin word *imperium,* the "command"

as such.   **19** Greek *humîn* ("on you"); More has changed it to "us" (*nobis*), which makes a little more sense, considering the pathos of the immediate context. **20** Greek *ēmeípsasthe*; Latin *retaliassetis*. In her edition of the *Utopia*, Delcourt lists *retaliare* as one of the rare words More

uses; it is used twice in the *Utopia*: once with reference to pain and pleasure (*CW* 4: 167/10) and once in close association with tyranny and tyrannicide (*CW* 4: 200.10). **21** Greek *lypésein*; Latin *ureretur*

himself the wound with trembling hand, weakly, but still desiring it, without the strength needed to administer such a deed.

22. How many punishments are there here? How many wounds? How many deaths? How many assassinations of tyrants? How many rewards? And yet you have all seen the young one lying there, no small deed, and no easy one: the old man poured out upon him, the blood of both clinging to them, that funereal libation-rite that engendered us our freedom,[22] and the work of my sword. The sword itself was in display between them, showing that it was not unworthy of its owner, and giving witness that it faithfully obeyed me. Had this been done by me, it would have been more obscurely done, but now it has been made more brilliant by its very novelty. The one who removed the whole tyranny is I, but the work was distributed among many, as in the acting of a play.[23] I played the leading part;[24] the son played the second, the tyrant the third, and the sword played the servant to all.

THE END
THOMAS MORE, TRANSLATOR

---

22 More introduces a Roman religious term *Libitinam,* the goddess of death and funerals, as a kind of play on the similar Latin word *libationem*; Greek *spondén* ("libation"). He also modifies *Libitinam* with the adjective *parentem:* the goddess of death; the father-tyrant's suicide is thus the "parent" or "engenderer" of liberty, something missing from Lucian's Greek. 23 Greek *drámati*; Latin *fabula* 24 More uses the plural of *pars* for an actor's (single) role, an idiom in Terence and Cicero.

Thomas More's Declamation in Response
to Lucian's "Tyrannicide"

I had not imagined, gentlemen of the jury, that one who undertook to plead a case in the public interest, as I now do, would need to explain why he resolved to do this. For there would be no danger of his seeming to be impelled by malice rather than by a sense of duty, since he offers as indisputable proof of his thorough integrity his willingness to exert himself, on his own initiative, for the general welfare. Though I suppose all pleaders of cases such as this can defend themselves justly from every suspicion of calumny, yet I can do this most justly of all. I have not only taken this task upon myself for the sake of the public weal but have incurred the personal enmity of this man who boasts that he killed the tyrants. But since I see that nothing is attempted, however rightly, which the malevolence of the wicked does not carp at and distort; and since even now I hear the murmurings of some who, convinced by his speech, are prejudiced against my performance of duty — I have resolved, gentlemen of the jury, to explain to you the reasons for this lawsuit of mine, lest any spiteful critic try to ascribe my zeal to grief, hatred, or envy.

First of all, why should I be thought to mourn the death of the tyrant, as my opponent has lately charged? He offered no proof, to be sure, content merely with having made the assertion; and he asks to be believed without evidence, without a witness. Nay, more than that: "Unless you were mourning," he says, "unless you desired to avenge the tyrant's death, you would not oppose me." Hence do you demonstrate that I sorrow at the tyrant's death merely by the fact that I have justly opposed you in your unjust claim to the reward for his violent end? Do you want to see how empty that retort is? If you could prove you killed the tyrant, I could not bring suit against you if I would, nor would if I could. Why indeed am I going to oppose you now, except that you did *not* kill him? If you had slain him, I would not complain; on the contrary I would praise and admire you, and I would be the first to vote for a reward. Now, in fact, it is for this very reason that I speak against you, for this very reason I deny the honor to you, for this very reason I appear against you, for this very reason I object: that *you did not*

kill the tyrant. I do not seem on that account to be plunged into sorrow for his death, do I? My opponent ought rather to have shown, gentlemen, that I was connected with the tyrant by blood or marriage ties, or obligated to him for favors, or leagued with him in crimes! But he has been unable even to pretend anything of the sort. If therefore I was neither related to him nor connected with him, if he never employed my services to the injury of anyone, if no benefit accrued to me from him, if he oppressed me along with others by bitter slavery, if his destruction restored me as well as you to freedom, what reason is there that I should lament his death, the good omen of my safety and liberty?

Yet surely there is just as little reason for hatred on my part. What has he done to provoke my hatred? First, he killed the tyrant's son. Afterward, when the tyrant had slain himself by his own hand, this man here demanded reward as a tyrannicide. Consider, for one thing, that he did kill the youth, though with too little forethought and without benefit to the public had not the gods been gracious to us. Yet he did it, so far as I can conjecture, from no unworthy motive. The other point is that he seeks the reward. Although he has not deserved it, men's dispositions are such nowadays that I am not surprised by his seeking it, and I excuse him if he can carry it off.

Neither of these actions excites my animosity toward him. Excepting these, he never did anything that pertains to me in any way. Am I therefore so unfair that I should gratuitously prosecute, out of hatred, a man hardly known to me by looks or reputation, who had never offended me by word or deed?

There remains to be explained the suspicion of jealousy, which is such a thing that from no fault would I more earnestly wish to be free. For although all vices are of their own nature pernicious, none is more destructive than envy, which excites with exceptionally grievous torments the breast wherein it has once lodged. Surely to deem another's good fortune one's own misfortune, to rage at the success of others, to be vexed by praise of others, to be tormented by another's happiness — is not this the greatest misery, is it not the most extreme madness? And so, if I am free from any other fault, gentlemen of the jury, I am certainly the furthest of all from this. Whose fortune have I ever attacked? Whose achievements have I disparaged? Whose praises have I ever belittled? Whose reputation have I besmirched? Assuredly if my own modest fortune—not so mean that I must envy the resources and rewards of other men—does not free me from suspicion of this fault; if I am not vindicated by the record of my life, which has not been so lacking in achievements that I should waste away with envy at another's praise, by Hercules this suit itself straightway absolves me. It is such as deserves the indulgence of everyone rather than the jealousy of anyone. I ask you, jurors, what mark of hatred, what example of envy do I exhibit?

I utter no challenge, I am not angry, I make no accusation; I am only defending the city, which is summoned to the bar by him. But since there are others sitting here, all of them keeping silence, and among them many distinguished men and persons eminent in authority and much more skilled in speaking than I am, why do I of all others rise and oppose him when he seeks rewards? I doubt not that they feel the same as I do, and that there are many among them who would willingly have undertaken this duty had I not done so; yet I am not to be blamed because I was the first to offer my services to my country. I am not bound by the reasons for others' silence, whatever they are. Beyond question the public welfare and, secondly, reverence for the immortal gods, urged me to speak.

When I considered the meager resources of our treasury, the present scarcity of funds, and the fact that many occasions of necessary expense confront us, I could not bear it that the state be drained of money by this extra, unnecessary expenditure. You are not unaware how large the reward for tyrannicide is—and rightly so; for what sum is large enough if it means recovery of fields, homes, fortunes, children, wives, the liberty and safety of all people and finally the very altars and temples of the gods? The more burdensome this sum is to the city, the more care we must take lest it be awarded rashly. The vast expenditures with which we are threatened, judges—quite apart from what is demanded by this man, to whom we owe nothing—are enough to empty our treasury.

Besides, since this slaying of the tyrant came about only by the mercy of the gods, who, so often implored, at last took pity on our calamities and pleased to liberate us from the yoke of that cruelest of tyrants and restore us to freedom, it would in my opinion be intolerable if the city withheld homage and gratitude owed to the gods and gave them instead to a man who does not deserve them. I shall demonstrate by the plainest proofs that this whole affair is due to fortune and divine clemency, with no thanks at all to this man. While I do this, gentlemen of the jury, I request your close attention.

There are three reasons, any one of which he thinks sufficient ground for seeking this honor: because he slew the tyrant's son, or because he attempted to kill the tyrant, or because the father, moved by the murder of his son, committed suicide with the sword this man left behind.

Does the murder of that youth seem tyrannicide? "Why not? Surely he too was a tyrant." Who would believe, jurors, that one city satisfied two tyrants? That two tyrants lived in concord within the same walls? That they could be contained within the circuit of a single city, when the whole world would scarcely have been room enough for either one? Whoever asks us to believe that seems to me to have a very inadequate notion of the nature of tyranny. Even legitimate authorities, not only governing by laws but also obeying laws, and so very much milder than a tyranny, are nevertheless so dominated by the desire for power that they spare not the lives of intimate friends rather than allow them to share their rule. Is it credible that a tyrant, cruel and violent by nature, suffers any associate to share his power, which he prizes so passionately that he has trampled on the laws of men, scorned those of gods, had no respect for life? Nearly all beasts living by prey (the characteristic of tyrants), on whom hunger alone has stamped certain marks of a tyrannical nature, rage against their own offspring rather than accept them as companions of the hunt. And do we imagine that a human tyrant, puffed up by pride, driven by the lust of power, impelled by greed, provoked by thirst for fame, can share his tyranny with anyone?

Now my adversary not only supposes two tyrants but even wants to make the youth appear more than tyrant; for (it is said) he committed dreadful crimes against the citizens—murder, robbery, rape—in brief, all known forms of crime. The title he eschewed; but in reality he was the head of the tyranny and more powerful than the parent, whom he governed as he pleased.

But the truth is far otherwise, gentlemen of the

jury. Certainly tyranny is always a violent and fear-some thing. If the son had had power, he would not have endured his father; nor would the father for his part have allowed the son to gain so much power that he could take control. No one is more suspect to tyrants than the heir, who, the more he gives vent to his savage nature and tyrannical practices, the more he terrifies his parent. There-fore he restrained his son's passions and checked rather than loosened his reins over the boy, lest the youth, growing too powerful, eager for rule and ar-rogant in his strength, no longer master of him-self, at length would not spare even his parent; nay, the gods might prefer Jove to Saturn. If from time to time he committed outrages, what was that but proof that he was his father's accomplice? Of such persons, how few are there who would not rob, vio-late marriages, plunder homes, despoil temples, kill those who stand in the way, and murder the leading citizens? But since there is one man under whose power and protection they commit such outrageous crimes — else they would be punished for their deeds, either by him or by the laws, as thieves, mur-derers, bandits, adulterers — he alone, the sole mas-ter under whose title they all take shelter, is tyrant. And that youth, when he committed some extraor-dinarily outrageous deed, would always say his fa-ther had so commanded; nor do I doubt that he did command it. Though the son's temperament was such that he gave promise of some day — if he lived long enough — matching his father in shameful deeds and enormities, nevertheless in his youth, by comparison with his parent's cruelty and savagery (already thoroughly familiar to him from child-hood), he was still a raw recruit, scarcely a beginner, and did scarcely anything of importance unless or-dered and instructed by his father.

But whether he did not do those deeds unless commanded or whether he dared to do them him-self without orders, yet, since he acted *as if* under orders; since he neither usurped the name of tyrant, nor bore himself as tyrant, but made plain that he was acting in obedience to his father and referred the reasons for his exploits to him; since he ac-knowledged another (in whose power he trusted) was stronger than he and the sole source of his im-punity — call him robber or sacrilege if you like, or any other name you please, but assuredly he is not one against whom tyrannicide could be committed. If you contend that he alone had absolute power

and was actually tyrant, and that, as you boasted a short time ago, the state became free immediately after his death, let us imagine, I beg you, the par-ent as still alive though not put to flight; I do not know why you feigned that, when you had neither put him to flight nor done anything to make him flee. For though his son had been so treacherously slain, his other forces were left intact; I fail to see what reason there would have been for the father to despair or to flee, any more than if he had not had a son or the son had died of plague. Let us therefore, as I said, imagine the father living and bereft of his only son, but nevertheless surrounded by his palace guard, bewailing the murder of his son, yet threat-ening the murderer and intending all kinds of pun-ishments. Let us imagine him with mournful but grim countenance rushing into the forum and, dis-playing the sword you left behind, promising vast rewards if anyone makes known the owner of that sword. With the forum here already occupied by him and his retinue, and inquiry already directed toward you, rush forward, brave tyrannicide, and, dashing into the midst of the crowd, announce that you have killed the tyrant, proclaim liberty for all, and demand a tyrannicide's reward! Why do you run away? Why look for a hiding-place? Why are you, the tyrannicide, afraid? Is not the common-wealth free? Has not the tyrant been killed? — Then the one you slew was *not* the tyrant but rather some accomplice of the tyrant; nor was the city by his death restored to liberty, which, as you said a short time ago, was the sole end the proposer of this law had in view.

"But," he says, "I killed the heir." Why mention heirs to me? Why remind me of laws in a tyranny? They are laws in name only. Succession is a matter of legal right. If a pirate's son filled the place of the dead father, who would speak of the "heir"? A ty-rant always dies intestate, since the laws, which alone can make a will valid, are held captive by him. In like manner, he who succeeds to the place of a de-ceased tyrant is not an heir but a new tyrant, for he does not succeed but usurps. "We would have been in subjection to him even now." Why assume that? I say, on the contrary, that the people are free the instant the tyrant dies. Otherwise the law decreed a reward for the tyrannicide in vain, if at the death of one tyrant we fell into the hands of another.

But the case is far different, gentlemen; for when the tyrant died, by whatever chance, then — while

his friends are busy with lamentation, his accomplices stunned by his death — the people already
free, would thereupon have proclaimed their liberty. The son could no more have resisted their
5 strength than can anyone now, either the strongest
of the tyrant's cronies or whoever in his family was
closest to him after the son; to whom, if the title of
inheritance and succession is to be considered, the
tyranny belongs as much as it would have belonged
10 to the son. For this reason, whoever slays an agent,
a friend, a relative, a son of the tyrant, boasts of tyrannicide in vain. It is the tyrant alone whose death
the state[1] buys with so great a reward.

   "But I determined to do something," he says; "I
15 made an attempt, I ventured; and you cannot deny
that with the tyrant's son dead, the expectation of
future tyranny eliminated, I have left behind distinguished proof of my resolution; and this alone, I
think, merits the honor."
20   Observe here, I beg you, how fairly, how frankly,
I argue everything with you; how I expound your
whole case with the minimum of mistrust. If another person were arguing this case, not one of your
enemies either but one of the keener advocates,
25 who scrutinize every point, and ply with doubt, and
press upon you as roughly as possible, by Hercules
he would so handle this point as to make it an argument that you never attempted the deed or planned
to do it! If you voiced astonishment that anyone
30 could be so surpassingly impudent as to dare to say
such things when the tyrant's son was slain in that
very attempt, he will reply directly to the effect that
it could not fail to be the case that you climbed to
the stronghold not to free your country (which you
35 did not accomplish), not to kill the tyrant (whom
you did not touch), but rather to slay the very youth
whom you did murder: you did that in revenge or
retaliation for some private injury done to you. If
he should plead, urge, press this, and demand some
40 certain proofs of your "resolution" and intention,
you see, I am sure, into what difficult positions you
would be drawn.

   But I shall not deal with you in this manner,
since in matters extremely obscure, like this, I am
45 accustomed always to incline to the more lenient
interpretation. So I grant that you appear to have

committed the deed with patriotic motive. You
wished, and forthwith attempted, to destroy the
tyranny. Does this seem to you to merit this reward?
That, first of all, you wished to do it: who does not   50
see how poor a reason that is? For by this logic we
should all seek reward for tyrannicide. Who was so
lacking in patriotism that he did not long to destroy
that cruelest of tyrants? By making an attempt what
have you shown except that you wished to be a ty-   55
rannicide? Moreover, that you exposed yourself to
dangers, and whether that deserved any reward, we
shall consider afterward. I hope it is clear to you,
gentlemen of the jury, merely from a recital of the
law, that it did not. Since the law provides no re-   60
ward *except to a tyrannicide,* and since he who has
not killed a tyrant cannot be a tyrannicide, however
much he has attempted, however many risks he has
run, he will seek a tyrannicide's reward in vain unless the tyrant was killed. To one who in trying to   65
kill him forced him into exile, a reward should be
given; but I would not grant as big a one, or the
same kind of one, as to a tyrannicide.

   If, struggling with some sickness, I announce that
whoever heals me will receive three talents when I   70
recover, some one led by hope of gain might come
to undertake my cure. Later, when he had given
me medicines, found that his efforts failed, confessed that his skill was baffled by the disease, and
left me sorely afflicted but nonetheless somewhat   75
improved, I do not owe him a fee for restoring my
health, because he did not restore it; on the other
hand, because he helped me, it is unfair for me to
dismiss him empty handed. But if, after trying a
thousand drugs, he leaves me no whit better, he de-   80
serves no reward who gave me no help; indeed deserves only the thanks due to one who tried to cure
me for his own sake and not for mine. If, grossly ignorant of medical science, he nevertheless ventured
to attack the disease, and after a time abandoned the   85
case, with me miserably poisoned — not only having failed to help me but making me worse, even
though he offered his services gratis — is he worthy of affection because, by his own exertion over
so long period of time, without hope of reward, he   90
maltreated me so obligingly? Does he not, rather,
deserve the strongest condemnation for rashly med-

---

1 *respublica*: Here and throughout, More
changes Lucian's setting from a democracy
to a republic. At 53/77 and 58/10, 26, 41, 91

and 59/28–29, this term has been translated
as "commonwealth" or "state" or "republic."

dling, to my danger, in this matter in which he was unskilled?

The present case, gentlemen, seems to me not far different from this. The law is very ready to hire a tyrannicide from somewhere, and it promises him a specific reward when the tyrant has been slain. But when it says tyrannicide, gentlemen, it seeks a resourceful man, one not only strong-handed but (much more) strong-hearted; able in stratagem rather than in force; one who knows how to lay plots, hide his traps, make the most of opportunities. If one who has undertaken a business of this sort attacks the tyrant himself by means of some clever stratagem, overpowers him when attacked, and slays him when overpowered, and does not desist from his work, once begun, until it is finished— this man may boldly demand the reward for tyrannicide. If he were unable to do this but instead did something approximate and related to it, for instance drove the tyrant into exile or forced him to surrender, his life being spared, or compelled him to relinquish his tyranny on a certain condition—this man I deem worthy of some reward, yet not the reward for tyrannicide.

If a person physically powerful but slow-witted, and utterly unfamiliar with the skill a tyrannicide must possess, who supposed the job could be done by force alone and not with careful planning; who, finally, would be much more like Ajax than Ulysses but like Ajax running mad when the arms have been awarded and slashing at cattle instead of men; if, I say, such a person took upon himself the execution of so great a business and then, failing to devise a stratagem or choose the proper time for awaiting his chance, rushed forward in his attack but instead of beginning with the tyrant himself sprang at his guards, the tyrant meanwhile having opportunity to look out for himself; and after that, the tyrant having escaped, the affair rashly attempted, stupidly managed, abandoned through cowardice, and wholly unfinished, he thinks only of his own flight, even throwing his sword away; and later, when the tyrant has died or has been killed, he should appear in public and claim the reward as if he were the tyrannicide, and make a speech of this kind: "I resolved, jurors, I made an attempt, I tried, I essayed it"—would you give him the reward for tyrannicide, gentlemen of the jury, because he *tried* to kill the tyrant? Or would you, rather, bear him ill will and esteem him deserving of punishment because,

by his recklessness, he had not only exposed himself alone, uselessly, to dangers, but at the same time had thrown the entire city into extreme peril, since by foolishly inciting him he made the tyrant more menacing to the citizens and more wary of plots?

You see, therefore, gentlemen, how that which he relied on to be sufficient in itself is so far from helping him that it damages his case considerably. Accordingly, if the man he killed was *not* the tyrant, and it was *not* enough to have killed the tyrant's son, but to have made the attempt recklessly was more than vain, it remains for us to examine the last point, the death of the tyrant himself, which this man contends we owe to him.

This is the crux of the whole matter. If he persuades you of his view on this, there is nothing to prevent his winning; and if on the contrary I win this point and, as they say, cut away his sheet anchor, must he not at once, of necessity, be tossed about and perish in the shipwreck? For this reason, gentlemen of the jury, I hereby request you again and again to be as attentive as possible while I demonstrate that the death of the tyrant, on which this entire controversy hangs, has no connection at all with my opponent.

You recall that this whole ground was covered by him in the manner of one who wanted to persuade you to believe that even at the time he slew the son he knew in advance the parent would do what afterward he did. "I knew it was enough to kill the son," he says. "I knew the father would take his own life instantly after the death of his son." Nay, rather you knew quite well that when you thus argued this case it was incumbent on you to appear to have foreknown those facts! Else you would seek the reward for tyrannicide in vain if you had not yourself killed the tyrant, or at least done that as a result of which you knew his destruction was close at hand. This is why, gentlemen of the jury, he wanted the result of his act to seem so certain: that he might tell you, his listeners, it was for that very reason he withheld his hand from the tyrant and left him to himself— and to this man's sword as well. Otherwise he could easily have killed him—so he says—and would have done so except that, sure of his death, he purposely refrained in order that the tyrant shortly after would die the more wretched death.

So then, what am I to do with this story? Where can I possibly turn? Where find arguments to show that this man is not able to foretell future events?

Rather let us question him and demand some of the reasons for which he would have us believe a thing so far beyond credibility; whence he got such marvelous skill in prophecy; whether he learned it from 5 a teacher or grasped it rather by divine inspiration.

Tell us, then, Tiresias, how will you demonstrate that you have achieved this knowledge of future events? Dig up buried treasure somewhere, disclose our thoughts, bring forth something mysterious 10 and secret, which we may all wonder at; for to declare what present events lie hidden and to predict what future ones will be is, I suppose, the function of this art. Or, if you can only foretell future happenings, inform us now of some events that will oc-15 cur some years hence; or, if it please you, events of future ages. When all these will have come to pass in accordance with your promise, then return and declare that you had foreknown the future. Meantime you will have difficulty, I suspect, in persuading us 20 that you knew before it happened what occurred without your knowledge. If, then, when you killed the son you did not know that the father would slay himself, as afterward he did, why do you now demand the reward for his murder—which, unless 25 you are willing to be a brazen liar, you must confess was committed without your being aware of it or even thinking of it?

But perhaps this is the very reason he considers himself the one responsible for the tyrant's death, 30 since the murder he *did* commit was in some manner (though beyond expectation) the cause of it. On this subject I dare say you, gentlemen of the jury, are of a very different opinion. If someone had killed the tyrant by chance, or in a fit of madness, you 35 would not have given the reward for tyrannicide to him. Why? Surely because in either case the killer had killed without knowing it and without intending it. *This* man's plea, it seems to me, is somewhat weaker. For if either of those others claimed the re-40 ward, though the one who had killed unwittingly would therefore demand it in vain, nevertheless that claimant had, after all, killed him. But in the present circumstances the tyrant was slain without this man's knowing about it at all and by no act of his.

45 "But," he says, "I did nothing by accident or without knowing it. I murdered the son deliberately, and thus designedly and knowingly provided the father with a reason to die—who, had I not killed his son, would still be living as tyrant." Permit me to exam-50 ine this more closely.

If you attacked the tyrant in order to kill him and then, overcome by him and throwing your sword away, you fled; and if when he was pursuing you on horseback his horse stumbled and he very opportunely fell headlong on your sword, so that he was 55 pierced through by it; could you not say all these same things here, namely that you had intended it and that intending it you attacked him, hence by intending and planning it you caused his death— since unless you had attacked him he would not 60 have been killed? But do you not see that in the same manner you could, rather, boast of your flight and seek reward for your cowardice? For unless you had fled, he would not have fallen; unless you had disgracefully thrown your sword away, he would 65 not have been transfixed. Finally, by this reasoning cowards also may be tyrannicides! Just as in that case, what followed after would not be deemed your doing, though you would have attacked to kill (but ran away with the deed unperformed), and though 70 it would not have followed unless you had done something earlier:—so, even though you did climb to the citadel to kill the tyrant, and while searching for the father slew the son, yet since what you had undertaken to perform you either dared not do be-75 cause of fear, would not do because of negligence, or could not do because of chance, but straightway returned with the deed unachieved, and then afterward something occurred unknown to you and unexpected by you, you cannot say it was effected by 80 you. Even if any of it could be called yours, it ceased to be so then and there when you abandoned your enterprise.

Now it may be that he will not concede that this is a fair representation of what he did but will con-85 tradict me again, in this fashion: "This man you imagine did not attack the tyrant with the thought that afterward the victorious tyrant, in pursuit of his defeated and fugitive foe, would fall to his death. Hence what he did not intend he cannot 90 justly call his. But as for me, I *did* slay the son with the intention that the father, overwhelmed by grief, would kill himself; and in my mind's eye I foresaw this would happen." Do you see, gentlemen of the jury, that once more he confronts us with that div-95 ination of his? We ought, therefore, to demand of him how he perceived it would happen. Did he have foreknowledge of it? Or did he surmise it? If he replies that he foreknew it, I am confident no one will believe him. If he says he surmised it, he confesses 100

meanwhile that he did not know it but only supposed it; confesses, that is, that he was doubtful,
uncertain—what else, finally, but that he did not
know it at all? Yet let us consider by what signs,
what clear evidence, he thus inferred the eventuality of a thing so conjectural that what nobody else
could have hoped, this man imagined to himself as
sure and inevitable. "I had known how desperately
he loved his son," he says. So that made you certain
and confident, did it, that you could determine his
death would follow, not so much through chance
but of necessity? I am aware, gentlemen, of the extraordinary affection for their children that nature
has planted in the hearts of parents. But I would
not have believed it to be either so great, or so thoroughly tested, that one would dare promise himself what this man says he did: that a father would
be the voluntary companion of his son in death.
How many of those whose sons—their only, dearly
loved sons—die every day from disease or perish by
reason of treachery or fall in battle or die by accident are so overwhelmed by grief that they commit
suicide?

"But," he says, "besides love, desperation was
equally a reason for his desiring death." So then, I ask
you, when you slew the son, did you kill all his surviving followers too? You will not affirm, I dare say,
that you made so big a slaughter! So he still had the
others; he had plenty of wealth, plenty of resources.
And therefore, when a single person was slain and
so many were safe, including—most important of
all—this man, the tyrant, why was it so great a grief
to him that he should flee in haste, not from the city
but from the earth? Are we to believe that there is
anyone in the world today who would have done
what that tyrant did? Why ask about others?

Let us question you instead, for probably you had
made this supposition about yourself and viewed
the tyrant by the light of your own character. If
your son perished, and your fortune and your life
seemed threatened, you would not choose to join
your son rather than avenge his death, would you?
Or would you kill yourself to avoid being killed by
others? Of course not. (I will answer for you.) Then
how could you have imagined that the tyrant would
do what others have not done, what nobody would
have done, and what you yourself would not do?

"But clearly I was thinking of it," he retorts, "else
why would I have left my sword there?" You do well,
surely, to remind us of your cowardice! For when he

says this, gentlemen of the jury, does he not seem
to you to be saying, "Of course I knew what would
happen, else why had I fled from that place?" For
what difference is there between "Else why would
I have left my sword there?" and "Else why did I
basely throw my sword aside and run away?" Now
of what use was it to leave the sword for the tyrant?
To make certain he would not lack means of dying?
So the man who feared everybody's sword lacked
a sword himself, did he? Was he ever without a
sword—he who got by the sword, held by the sword,
and guarded by the sword whatever he possessed? A
wondrous prodigy, jurors: a tyrant without a sword!
No: he did not lack a sword; nor did this man here
leave a sword behind for him. He threw it away; and
he did *not* foresee what was going to happen in the
future, even by the slightest guess. But after he had
rashly broken into the citadel—I know not how—
and there suddenly attacked and overpowered the
young man, who (with the carelessness of youth)
was alone, off guard, not in the least suspicious; and,
advancing farther, might perhaps have been able to
deal with the tyrant in the same manner—at that
instant fright took hold of him, fearful as he was
lest, already betrayed to the tyrant's retinue by the
cry and groans of the dying youth, he would be captured. Already before his eyes were the chains, dungeon, tortures, and a thousand deaths, a thousand
punishments. Terrified by this empty fancy, fearful
now of every noise, every sound, and at last afraid of
his own shadow, suddenly as timid as before he was
rash, he rushed from the citadel; he did not even
dare to carry his sword with him, for fear his flight
would be slowed or, arrested with a sword in his
possession, he would be accused of having plotted
against the tyrant—at whose death he now returns
arrogantly and demands the reward for tyrannicide,
as if he had killed him!

Bear in mind, then, that I am not asking whether
you killed the tyrant himself. I ask only this: *could*
you have killed him? If not, then you did not await
opportunity, you did not choose a suitable place,
you did not seize the proper moment; but recklessly, rashly, without plan, without thought, you
undertook what you were unable to carry through
to completion. Do not boast, therefore, of having
killed him whom you confess you were not able to
kill. But if you *were* able, it was due to great want of
skill, or cowardice, that you did not do so.

"Not at all," he says. "I could have done it but

refrained deliberately. I had already done enough; I had killed the son. The father I left to his grief and to my sword, with which—I foresaw—he would kill himself."

Shameless man, if you are lying! Insane, if you are not! If you invented things so incredible we marvel at your impudence; if you reasoned so absurdly we marvel at your stupidity. Were you so mad that when able at a single stroke to ensure your own life and the safety of the republic, you preferred to leave everything exposed to mere chance and to promise yourself as a future occurrence what no sane man would dare to hope? What if the tyrant had been disposed to do what you yourself would doubtless have done, and what it is far more likely he would have done than what he actually did—summon his guard, call his ruffians together, arm his scoundrels; and, when the body of his son was brought before him, his cruel nature and his rage at so horrid a sight would have caused him to vent his wrath and fury first of all on you, by whom his son was slain, and then on the entire city for which he was slain? Had these things happened (as, thanks to your folly, they came close to happening), you would not be alive today, you miserable wretch, to seek this reward, nor would we have any commonwealth of which it could be sought.

But the immortal gods, jurors, remembered our prayers and entreaties; the gods took pity on the miseries of our enslavement; the gods came to our aid in our worst, most extreme perils. Though they had always intended to rescue this city, they chose the most opportune occasion especially to bestow their blessing on us. For though the tyrant was always oppressive when the son was alive, yet he was less burdensome to citizens for that very reason; he did not want to bequeath to his son a city internally miserable and exhausted. But with the murder of him on whose account he had forborne previously, who can doubt that he would have totally destroyed everything? After the state had fallen into the gravest danger, first because of this man's rashness, then by his cowardice, the gods, thinking the time had come to fashion for us an everlasting memorial of their favor, suddenly diverted all the calamities pressing so closely on us to the head of the tyrant himself, and so swiftly that we knew we were freed from danger before we realized we had been in danger—before dread of so great a crisis could even move us. Who would have thought,

gentlemen of the jury, that after the body of his son had been found the tyrant would have turned his sword on himself rather than on this city, unless the gods, through concern for us, had driven him to his own destruction by loosing the Furies upon him?

Even now I seem to see the glittering eyes of the brigand, the knitted brows, the contracted forehead, the pale cheeks, the gnashing teeth, the swelling lips; in short, as the poets describe Pentheus, showing his madness with his whole face, his whole countenance. When he first came in and found his son slain, what might we suppose he did, what exclaimed? What else, accursed and frenzied as he was, but to have vomited from his filthy mouth insane abuse against the gods? "O wrath of the gods, O hatred of the divine powers! I see the manifestations of your ill-will, you denizens of heaven. I see the signs of your dark malice. Nothing exists more wicked, more vainglorious and malevolent than you. You wish to rule alone, to govern alone; yet, not sufficiently contented with your own happiness, you are always consumed by envy of others' happiness. Why did you not come down to earth to oppose me? Why did you send instead a cowardly plotter against my son? Whoever he was, he did not even dare to match his strength with the tyrant's. This at any rate I rejoice in, that no one will be able to call himself a tyrannicide, no one seek the reward for tyrannicide, because no one will kill the tyrant today—except the tyrant. I shall die today as tyrant, despite the displeasure of the gods." When he had babbled frantic words of this sort, at length, frenzied and distraught, he fell upon the sword.

The tyrant, then, lies dead, transfixed by this man's sword—no, no, not by *his*, since he had previously thrown it away (by his own hand, in truth), but through the act of the gods alone. Yet now this man, who played no part at all there, claims the leading role. And so I ask you who called me cheat to consider which of us is closer to this fault, I who today clash with you on behalf of the state and the gods—yet without demanding a victor's reward—or you, a deserter and fugitive, who strive for a triumph when others—and those the gods—are the real victors? Cease, cease to arrogate to yourself the victory produced by another power than yours. Cease to becloud so signal a favor of the gods upon this city. Cease to obstruct our praises of the gods, and refrain from this presumptuous claim.

But if he continues to be troublesome, gentlemen

of the jury, weigh the fact in even scales. What else did he do but warn the tyrant to be on his guard? The gods brought it about that the tyrant could not guard himself, and that there should be no further need of plots. What else did he do than arm the tyrant with his own sword against us all? The gods diverted that sword from us to the throat of the tyrant. Finally, what else did he do than plunge the whole city into the greatest danger by his folly? The gods, amending his madness, suddenly turned that danger into the most fortunate safety. I entreat you, then, jurors, by the immortal gods, the gods who are the sources of this most precious freedom, this unlooked-for happiness, not to allow what came to us through the design and power of all the gods to be ascribed to the madness of one man; nor to allow this city ever to be so ungrateful to the gods their liberators; nor to suffer it to confess that its safety is owed to the temerity of a human being rather than to the benevolence of the gods, who we may now hope will always be propitious toward this city if we, mindful of what they have bestowed, acknowledge them (as is right) the authors of their blessings. But if — may it never come about! — we prove ungrateful, ascribing their deeds to others, and giving to men the gratitude owed to gods, we must fear in turn, by Hercules, lest the gods curtail their favor toward us and leave off the protection of our commonwealth as unworthy of their guardianship.

To conclude, at last, what I have to say: since this man erred in a dutiful act, and blundered with good intentions, but the gods turned his misdeed to our benefit; and since it was the gods who caused the tyrant's death, though the tyrant actually killed himself; and moreover, since they who brought it about do not seek a reward, and the man who committed the murder cannot seek one — in your decision, gentlemen of the jury, give pardon to this man and thanks to the gods; and absolve the city of the obligation of this reward, for which the gods wanted it to be free.

I have finished.

A ¶ The life of John Picus Erle of Myrandula, a great Lorde of Italy, an excellent connyng man in all sciences, & vertuous of liuing: with diuers epistles & other workes of ý sayd John Picus, full of greate science, vertue, and wisedome: whose life and workes bene worthy and digne to be read, and often to be had in memory.

B ¶ Translated out of latin into Englische by maister Thomas More.

(∵)

¶ Unto his right entierly beloued sister in Christ, Joyeuce Leigh, Thomas More greting in our lorde.

IT is, and of longe time hath bene (my well beloued sister) a custome in the beginnyng of the new yere, frendes to sende betwene, presentes or gyftes, as the witnesses of their loue and frendship, & also signifying, that thei desire eche to other that yere a good continuance and prosperous ende of that lucky beginnyng. But commonly all those presentes, that are vsed custommably all in this maner betwene frendes to be sent: be such thinges as perteine only vnto the body, either to be fed, or to be clad, or some other wise delited: by whiche it semeth, that their frendship is but fleshly, and stretcheth in maner to the body only. But for asmuch as the loue & amitie of christen folke should be rather ghostly frendship then bodily: sith that all faithfull people are rather spirituall then carnall. (For, as thapostle saith: we be not now in flesh, but in spirit, if Christ abide in vs.) I therfore myne hertely beloued sister, in good lucke of this new yere, haue sent you suche a present, as maie beare witnesse of my tender loue and zele to the happy continuaunce & graciouse encrease of vertue in your soule. And whereas the giftes of other folke declare that thei wissh their frendes to be worldly fortunate: myne testifieth, that I desire to haue you godly prosperous. These workes more profitable the

(margin left:) The intet or meanynge of new yeres gyftes.
(margin left:) Presentes bodily.
(margin left:) Christen loue.
(margin left:) Rom.8.
C
D

(margin top right:) I

large, were made in latine by one John Picus Erle of Mirandula, a lordship in Italye: of whose connyng and vertue we nede here nothing to speake: forasmuch as hereafter we peruse the course of his whole life, rather after our litle power slenderly, then after his merites sufficiently. The workes are suche, ý trewly good sister, I suppose of the quantitie ther cometh none in your hande more profitable, neither to thatchieuyng of temperace in prosperitie, nor to the purchasing of paciece in aduersitie, nor to the dispising of worldly vanitie, nor to the desiring of heauely felicitie: which workes I wolde require you gladly to receiue: ne were it, that thei be such, that for the godly mater (how so euer thei be translated) maie delite & please any person, that hath any meane desire and loue to God: and that your selfe is such one, as for your vertue and feruent zele to god, can not but ioyously receiue any thing, that meanely soundeth either to the reproch of vice, commendacion of vertue, or honoure and laude of God, who preserue you.

(margin right:) E — John Picus.
(margin right:) The profit of his workes.
(margin right:) F

¶ The life of John Picus Erle of Mirandula. G

IOhn Picus of the fathers side, desceded of the worthy linage of themperoure Constantyne, by a neuewe of the sayde Emperour called Picus, by whom al the auncessers of this John Picus, vndoutedly beare that name. But we shall lette his auncessers passe, to whom (though they were right excellent) he gaue agayn as much honour, as he received: & we shall speake of him self, rehearsing in part his learning, & his vertue. For these be the thinges, whiche we may accompt for our owne: of which euery man is more properly to be comeded, the of the noblenes of his auncessers: whose honour maketh vs not honorable. For either they were themself verteouse or not: if not, the had thei none honour theself: had thei neuer so great possessios: for honour is the reward of vertue. And howe maie they clayme the rewarde ý properly longeth to vertue: if they lacke the vertue, that the rewarde longeth to: Then if theself had

(margin right:) The linage of J. Picus.
(margin right:) H
(margin right:) Noblenesse of auncesters.
(margin right:) Honour.

a.j.   had

This facsimile of page 1 of the 1557 *Workes of Sir Thomas More* shows the variety of font sizes and the care taken in this large folio of 1,490 pages. The letters in the margin are to help in locating and referencing specific passages. The book features a detailed "Table of many matters contained in this book."

The Life of John Pico
Earl of Mirandola

Thomas More's first book published in English, *The Life of John Pico, Earl of Mirandola*, is an unusual work in five parts, only the first of which is biographical. Dead at thirty-one in 1494, the famous intellectual Pico grew in stature posthumously through the publication of his *Opera omnia* in 1496. His nephew Gianfrancesco edited the collection and contributed a Latin Vita of his uncle to serve as an "extremely laudatory preface" to the volume (*CW* 1: xli). More probably based his translations on the 1504 Strassburg edition of the *Opera omnia* (xlii). While Gianfrancesco's large folio of Pico's life and works was 531 folio pages, More's is only thirty-four. More was probably introduced to Pico's life and writings by either John Colet, Thomas Linacre, or Cuthbert Tunstall, all of whom had studied in Italy and had returned during the time that More was struggling, as had Pico, to discern his own path in life.

Prefaced by a dedication to young nun Joyce Leigh on friendship, virtue, and true nobility, More's *Life* opens with his translation — characterized by revealing additions and deletions — of Gianfrancesco's biography. After this much abbreviated biographical portrait, More includes English translations of three Pico letters and a translation of Pico's "Commentary on Psalm 15." After these works, More offers his own English poetry, loosely based on what are originally short prose texts from Pico: "Twelve Rules of Spiritual Battle," "Twelve Weapons of Spiritual Battle," and a list of "Twelve Properties of a Lover." The volume concludes with More's translation of Pico's *Deprecatoria ad Deum*, "A Prayer of Picus Mirandola unto God." As Anthony Edwards observes, More's *Life* is really "both biography and anthology" (*CW* 1: xxxvii), a carefully edited and curious whole, a work mingling prose and verse that continues to make readers wonder about the author's intentions in sharing this *Life*, or in undertaking the work of translation.

While early biographers Thomas Stapleton and Cresacre More have claimed that the young More found in Pico a model or pattern for the layman, More's *Life* is considerably more ambiguous in its presentation and probing of Pico's character. One can imagine other models of living, for example, than a precocious intellectual who dies prematurely and ends in the "dark fire" of purgatory, at least according to the testimony of Pico's most controversial advisor, Savonarola, whom More leaves unnamed but Gianfrancesco highly praised. The combination of admiration and ambivalence, irony and adulation, makes More's *Life* a challenging portrait to judge. Throughout More's later writings, he will continue his consideration of prominent intellectual figures and their varying works. More's Pico is the first in a series of portraits that will grow to include: Raphael Hythloday in *Utopia*; the lawyers and theological doctors in *The History of King Richard the Third*; Martin Luther, William Tyndale, and John Frith; the Messenger from *A Dialogue of Sir Thomas More, Knight*; his own daughter, Margaret Roper (Letter 206); and the interlocutors of *A Dialogue of Comfort against Tribulation*.

The Life of John Pico was published around 1510 by John Rastell, but earlier dates of composition have been proposed. More's *Life* is presented as a "New Year's gift," an act of "ghostly friendship," from the young More to a nun, Joyce Leigh, sister to Edward Lee, later Archbishop of York and the addressee of one of More's humanist letters. In the prefatory letter to this *Life*, More identifies his intention as the hope that the reader will become "godly prosperous," especially through a study of "cunning and virtue" in the life of Pico, Earl of Mirandola.

This edition of *Pico* indicates, through the use of half brackets (⌐¬), More's additions to the text, especially prominent in the biographical section. More's changes to Gianfrancesco's *Vita* tend to intensify the "focus on the figure of Pico himself," and serve to make the text "a meditative or exemplary life appropriate for study" (*CW* 1: xlv). *The Life of John Pico* was the first English work of More's to be reprinted; the prominent publisher de Worde produced his edition of the text in 1525, featuring a specially designed woodcut of Christ crucified (lvi). After the 1557 edition of More's English works, there are references to *The Life of John Pico* in Robert Parsons's *Treatise of Three Conversions of England* (1603), but the work would not be reprinted again until the early eighteenth century (lviii).

CONTENTS

TIMELINE

24 February 1463	Pico is born; his father dies shortly after.
1477	His mother sends him to Bologna to study canon law and become a priest.
August 1478	His mother dies; Pico goes to Florence to study.
May 1479	Goes to Ferrara to study philosophy and Greek; meets Savonarola
August 1480–82	University of Padua; introduced to Cabala; writes love poetry he later burns
Fall 1482	Studies philosophy, Greek, rhetoric in Pavia; asks Ficino to send *Th. Platonica*
1483–85	Studies in Florence and at Sorbonne
1486	Leaves for Rome with *900 Theses*; abducts Margherita de Medici; wounded, arrested, released
	Letter to Corneo (although More's *Life of Pico* gives 1492 as the date)
February 1487	Pope Innocent VIII cancels conference Pico helped organize.
March 1487	Seven of his theses are condemned; six are declared dubious.
May 1487	Publishes *Apologia* defending Cabala and magic—taken as insubordination by Pope
July 1487	Retracts officially his *900 Theses*; leaves Rome to escape arrest
January 1488	Arrested and briefly imprisoned at Lyons by order of Innocent VIII
June 1488	Permitted to return to Florence if he does not discuss his *900 Theses*
1489	Innocent VIII's advice is reported to Lorenzo de'Medici: have Pico write poetry.
	Pico writes *Heptaplus* (on Mosaic account of creation in Genesis)
1491	Sells patrimony; writes *De ente et uno* on reconciliation of Aristotelianism and Platonism
	Tells Gianfrancesco he sees his vocation to Friars Preachers as "God's special command"
15 May 1492	First letter to Francis
2 July 1492	Second letter to Francis
18 June 1493	Pope Alexander VI absolves Pico of heresy
14 November 1494	Contracts fever; King's two physicians do not succeed in restoring health
17 November 1494	Dies; appears shortly afterwards to Savonarola (as reported by Savonarola)
1496	Nephew Gianfrancesco publishes Pico's life and collected works in a 531-page folio.
1497	Savonarola excommunicated
1498	Savonarola executed for heresy and for conspiring to depose Pope Alexander VI
1498–1500	Thomas More's likely introduction to Pico's writings by Colet or Linacre
ca. 1504	Thomas More decides on marriage, not priesthood.
ca. 1510	More publishes in thirty-four folio pages Pico's life and selected works.

The Life of John Pico

Earl of Mirandola, a great lord of Italy, an excellent
cunning man in all sciences, ⌐and virtuous of living;
with diverse epistles and other works of the said John Pico,
full of great science, virtue, and wisdom: whose life
and works been worthy and digne[1] to be read,
and often to be had in memory.⌐
⌐Translated out of Latin into English
by Master Thomas More.⌐

Unto his right entirely beloved sister
in Christ, Joyce Leigh: Thomas More,
greeting in our Lord.⌐

It is, and of long time hath been, my well-beloved
sister, a custom in the beginning of the new year,
friends to send between[2] presents or gifts, as the
witnesses of their love and friendship, and also
signifying that they desire each to other that year
a good continuance and prosperous end of that
lucky[3] beginning. But commonly all those presents,
that are used customably all in this manner between
friends to be sent,[4] be such things as pertain only
unto the body, either to be fed or to be clad or some
other wise[5] delighted, by which it seemeth that their
friendship is but fleshly,[6] and stretcheth[7] in manner
to the body only. But forasmuch as the love and
amity of Christian folk should be rather ghostly[8]
friendship than bodily, since that all faithful[9] people are rather spiritual than carnal (for as the Apostle[10] saith, "We be not now in flesh but in spirit, if
Christ abide in us"),[11] I therefore, mine heartily beloved sister, in good luck of this new year have sent
you such a present as may bear witness of my tender
love and zeal to the happy continuance and gracious
increase of virtue in your soul; and whereas the gifts
of other folk declare that they wish their friends to
be worldly-fortunate, mine testifieth that I desire to
have you godly prosperous. These works, more profitable than large, were made in Latin by one John
Pico, Earl of Mirandola (a lordship in Italy), of
whose cunning[12] and virtue we need here nothing to
speak forasmuch as hereafter we peruse the course
of his whole life, rather after[13] our little power slenderly, than after his merits sufficiently. The works
are such that truly, good sister, I suppose of the
quantity[14] there cometh none in your hand more
profitable, neither to the achieving of temperance
in prosperity, nor to the purchasing of patience in
adversity, nor to the despising of worldly vanity, nor
to the desiring of heavenly felicity. Which[15] works
I would require[16] you gladly to receive, ne[17] were it
that they be such that, for the goodly matter (howsoever they be translated), may delight and please
any person that hath any mean[18] desire and love to
God, and that yourself is such one as for your virtue and fervent zeal to God cannot but joyously receive anything that meanly soundeth[19] either to the
reproach of vice, commendation of virtue, or honor
and laud of God, who preserve you.

---

1 deserving **2** *send between*: exchange
3 auspicious; fortunate; prosperous
4 *used…sent*: sent customarily between
friends **5** way **6** worldly **7** extends

8 spiritual **9** having the Christian faith
10 Saint Paul **11** Rom 8:9 **12** knowledge; cleverness; learning **13** in accord
with **14** *of the quantity*: for the size

15 These **16** ask **17** nor **18** moderate;
average **19** *meanly soundeth*: moderately
tends

Life of Pico

THE LIFE OF JOHN PICO
Earl of Mirandola

John Pico of the father's side descended of the worthy lineage of the Emperor Constantine, by a
5 nephew of the said emperor called Pico, by whom all the ancestors of this John Pico undoubtedly bear that name. But we shall let his ancestors pass,[20] to whom ⌐(though they were right excellent)⌐ he gave again[21] as much honor as he received, ⌐and
10 we shall speak of himself, rehearsing[22] in part his learning and his virtue. For these be the things which we may account for our own of which every man is more properly to be commended than of the nobleness of his ancestors, whose honor ma-
15 keth us not honorable. For either they were themselves virtuous or not. If not, then had they none honor themselves, had they never so great possessions. For honor is the reward of virtue. And how may they claim the reward that properly longeth[23]
20 to virtue, if they lack the virtue that the reward longeth to? Then, if themselves had none honor, how might they leave to their heirs that thing which they had not themselves? On the other side, if they be virtuous and so, consequently, honorable, yet may
25 they not leave their honor to us as inheritance, no more than the virtue that themselves were honorable for. For never the more noble be we for their nobleness if ourselves lack those things for which they were noble. But rather the more worshipful[24]
30 that our ancestors were, the more vile and shameful be we, if we decline from the steps of their worshipful living, the clear beauty of whose virtue maketh the dark spot of our vice the more evidently to appear and to be the more marked. But Pico,
35 of whom we speak, was himself so honorable, for the great plenteous abundance of all such virtues the possession whereof very[25] honor followeth (as a shadow followeth a body), that he was to all them that aspire to honor a very spectacle in whose con-
40 ditions, as in a clear polished mirror, they might behold in what points very honor standeth:[26] whose marvelous cunning and excellent virtue, though my rude[27] learning be far unable sufficiently to express, yet forasmuch as if no man should do it but
45 he that might sufficiently do it, no man should do

it—and better it were to be insufficiently done than utterly undone—I shall, therefore, as I can, briefly rehearse you his whole life, at the leastwise to give some other man hereafter (that can do it better) oc-
50 casion to take it in hand when it shall haply[28] grieve him to see the life of such an excellent cunning man so far uncunningly written.⌐

⌐*Of His Parents and Time of His Birth.*⌐
In the year of our Lord God 1463, Pius the Second being then the general vicar of Christ in his
55 Church, and Frederick, the third of that name, ruling the Empire,[29] this nobleman was born, the last child of his mother, Julia, a woman comen of a noble stock, his father, hight[30] John Francis, ⌐a lord of great honor and authority.⌐
60

⌐*Of the Wonder That Appeared before His Birth.*⌐
A marvelous sight was there seen before his birth: there appeared a fiery garland standing over the chamber of his mother while she travailed,[31] and suddenly vanished away; which appearance was per-
65 adventure a token[32] that he which should that hour in the company of mortal men be born, in the perfection[33] of understanding should be like the perfect figure of that round circle, or garland, and that his excellent name should round about the circle
70 of this whole world be magnified,[34] whose mind should always, as the fire, aspire upward to heavenly things, and whose fiery eloquence should, with an ardent heart, in time to come worship and praise Almighty God with all his strength; and as that
75 flame suddenly vanished, so should this fire soon from the eyes of mortal people be hid. We have oftentimes read that such unknown and strange tokens hath gone before or followeth the nativities of excellent, wise, and virtuous men, departing,[35] as it
80 were (and by God's commandment), severing[36] the cradles of such special children from the company of others of the common sort, and showing that they be born to the achieving of some great thing. But to pass over[37] others, the great Saint Ambrose:
85 a swarm of bees flew about his mouth in his cradle, and some entered into his mouth, and after that, issuing out again and flying upon high, hiding themselves among the clouds, escaped both the sight of

---

20 go unmentioned 21 in turn; back 22 telling 23 belongs 24 honorable 25 true 26 consists 27 rudimentary; 28 perhaps 29 i.e., the Holy Roman Empire 30 named 31 was in labor 32 *peradventure a token:* perhaps a portent 33 maturity; fullness 34 praised 35 separating 36 setting apart 37 *to pass over:* not mentioning

his father and of all them that were present. Which prognostication, one Paulinus,[38] making much of, expounded it to signify[39] to us the ⌐sweet¬ honeycombs of his ⌐pleasant¬ writing, which should show out the celestial gifts of God and should lift up the minds of men from earth into heaven.

⌐Of His Person¬

He was of feature and shape seemly and beauteous: of stature, goodly and high; of flesh, tender and soft; his visage lovely and fair; his color white, intermingled with comely ruds;[40] his eyes grey, and quick of look; his teeth white and even; his hair yellow, and not too picked.[41]

⌐Of His Setting Forth to School, and Study in Humanity¬

Under the rule and governance of his mother, he was set to masters[42] and to learning, where with so ardent mind he labored the studies of humanity that within short while he was (and not without a cause) accounted among the chief orators and poets of that time: in learning marvelously swift, and of so ready a wit that the verses which he heard once read, he would again[43]—both forward and backward, to the great wonder of the hearers—rehearse; and, over that, would hold it in sure remembrance; which in other folk is wont commonly to happen contrary. For they that are swift in taking be oftentimes slow in remembering; and they that with more labor and difficulty receive it, more fast[44] and surely hold it.

⌐Of His Study in Canon[45]¬

In the fourteenth year of his age, by the commandment of his mother (which[46] longed very sore[47] to have him priest), he departed to Bologna to study in the laws of the Church. Which, when he had two years tasted, perceiving that the faculty leaned to[48] nothing but only mere traditions and ordinances, his mind fell from it. Yet lost he not his time therein; for in that two years, yet being a child, he compiled a breviary or a sum upon all the decretals,[49] in which, as briefly as possible was, he comprised the effect of all that whole great volume and made a book, no slender thing to right cunning and perfect doctors.

⌐Of His Study in Philosophy and Divinity¬

After this, as a desirous ensearcher of the secrets of nature, he left these common-trodden paths and gave himself wholly to speculation and philosophy, as well human as divine. For the purchasing[50] whereof (after the manner of Plato and Apollonius[51]), he scrupulously sought out all the famous doctors of his time, visiting studiously all the universities and schools not only through Italy, but also through France. And so[52] indefatigable labor gave he to those studies that, yet a child and beardless, he was both reputed, and was indeed, both a perfect philosopher and a perfect divine.[53]

⌐Of His Mind and Vainglorious Dispicions[54] at Rome¬

Now had he been seven years conversant[55] in these studies when, ⌐full of pride, and desirous of glory and man's praise¬ (for yet was he not kindled in the love of God), he went to Rome, and there (coveting to make a show of his cunning and little considering how great envy he should raise against himself), nine hundred questions[56] he purposed[57] of diverse and sundry matters, as well in logic and philosophy as divinity, with great study picked and sought out as well of the Latin authors as the Greeks, and partly fetched out of the secret mysteries of the Hebrews, Chaldeans, and Arabians, and many things drawn out of the old obscure philosophy of Pythagoras, Trismegistus, and Orpheus, and many other things strange and to all folk (except right few special excellent men) before that day not unknown only, but also unheard of. All which questions in open[58] places (that they might be to all people the better known) he fastened and set up, offering also himself to bear the costs of all such as would come thither out of far countries to dispute. But through the envy of his malicious enemies (which envy, like the fire, ever draweth to the highest), he could never bring about to have a day to his dispicions appointed.[59] For this cause he tarried at Rome a whole year; in all which time, his enviers

---

38 See Paulinus, *The Life of St. Ambrose of Milan* 2.   **39** *expounded it to signify:* explained it as signifying   **40** ruddiness; red   **41** ornate, fastidious   **42** tutors   **43** in turn; in reply   **44** steadfastly

45 Canon Law   **46** who   **47** greatly   **48** *faculty leaned to:* professors relied on   **49** canon-law decrees   **50** obtaining   **51** Apollonius of Tyana (*ca.* AD 15–100) traveled to India, Babylon, and Egypt in search of teachers.   **52** such   **53** theologian   **54** Disputations   **55** engaged in   **56** theses   **57** proposed   **58** public   **59** *to…appointed:* scheduled for his disputations

never durst openly, with open dispicions, attempt[60] him, but rather, with craft and sleight[61] and, as it were, with privy trenches,[62] enforced to undermine him — for none other cause but for malice and for they were (as many men thought) corrupt with a pestilent envy. This envy, as men deemed, was specially raised against him for this cause: that where there were many which had many years, some for glory, some for covetise, given themselves to learning, they thought that it should haply deface their fame and diminish the opinion of their cunning if so young a man, plenteous of substance[63] and great doctrine, durst in the chief city of the world, make a proof of his wit and his learning, as well in things natural as in divinity and in many such things as men many years never attained to. Now when they perceived that they could not against his cunning anything openly prevail, they brought forth the serpentines[64] of false crime[65] and cried out that there were thirteen of his nine hundred questions suspect of heresy. Then joined they to them some good simple folk that should, of zeal to the faith and pretense of religion, impugn those questions as new things, and with which their ears had not been in ure.[66] In which impugnation, though some of them haply[67] lacked not good mind, yet lacked they erudition and learning, which questions notwithstanding, before that, not a few famous doctors of divinity had approved as good and clean, and subscribed their names under them. But he, not bearing the loss of his fame, made a defense for those thirteen questions — a work of great erudition, and elegant, and stuffed with the cognition of many things worthy to be learned (which work he compiled in twenty nights) — in which it evidently appeareth not only that those conclusions were good and standing with the faith, but also that they which had barked at them were of folly and rudeness[68] to be reproved. Which defense, and all other things that he should write, he committed, like a good Christian man, to the most holy judgment of our mother, holy Church. Which defense received, and the thirteen questions duly by deliberation examined, our holy father the

Pope approved Pico,[69] and tenderly favored him, as by a bull of our holy father Pope Alexander the VI it plainly appeareth; but the book in which the whole nine hundred questions with their conclusions were contained — forasmuch as there were in them many things strange and not fully declared[70] and were more meet for secret[71] communication of learned men than for open[72] hearing of common people, which for lack of cunning might take hurt thereby — Pico desired[73] himself that it should not be read. And so was the reading thereof forbidden. ⌐Lo, this end had Pico of his high mind and proud purpose: that where he thought to have gotten perpetual praise, there had he much work to keep himself upright, that he ran not in perpetual infamy and slander.⌐

⌐*Of the Change of His Life*⌐

But, as himself told his nephew, he judged that this came thus to pass by the especial provision and singular goodness of almighty God: that by this false crime[74] untruly put upon him by his evil-willers, he should correct his very[75] errors, and that this should be to him (wandering in darkness) as a shining light in which he might behold and consider how far he had gone out of the way of truth. For before this, he had been both desirous of glory and kindled in vain love, and held in voluptuous use of women. The comeliness[76] of his body with the lovely favor of his visage, and therewith all his marvelous fame, his excellent learning, great riches, and noble kindred, set many women afire on him. From the desire of whom he not abhorring (the way of life set aside) was somewhat fallen into wantonness.[77] But after that he was once with this variance wakened, he drew back his mind flowing in riot, and turned it to Christ. Womanish blandishments[78] he changed into the desire of heavenly joys, and despising the blast of vainglory, which he before desired, now with all his mind he began to seek the glory and profit of Christ's Church, and so began he to order his conditions that from thenceforth he might have been approved and though[79] his enemy were his judge.

---

60 attack   61 underhanded trickery
62 *privy trenches:* hidden earthworks
or tunnels   63 wealth   64 malicious
actions   65 accusation   66 familiarity
67 perhaps   68 ignorance   69 Not so

by Pope Innocent VIII, who ordered the
suppression of Pico's book in 1487. Only in
June 1493 did Pope Alexander VI absolve
Pico of heresy charges.   70 explained
71 *meet . . . secret:* suitable for private

72 public   73 asked   74 accusation
75 true   76 attractiveness   77 lustfulness
78 allurements   79 *and though:* even if

⌐Of the Fame of His Virtue, and the Resort unto Him Therefore⌐

Hereupon shortly,[80] the fame of his ⌐noble cunning and excellent virtue⌐ both far and nigh[81] began gloriously to spring, for which many worthy[82] philosophers (and that were taken in number of[83] the most cunning) resorted busily unto him as to a market of good doctrine: some for to move[84] questions and dispute, some (that were of more godly mind) to hear and to take the wholesome lessons and instruction of good living, which lessons were so much the more set by[85] in how much they came from a more noble man and a more wise man and him also which had himself some time followed the crooked hills of delicious pleasure. To the fastening of good discipline in the minds of the hearers, those things seem to be of great effect which be both of their own nature good and also be spoken of such a master as is converted to the way of justice from the crooked and ragged path of voluptuous living.

⌐The Burning of Wanton Books⌐

Five books, that in his youth of wanton verses of[86] love with other like fantasies, he had made in his vulgar tongue,[87] altogether (⌐in detestation of his vice past, and lest these trifles might be some evil occasion afterward⌐) he burned.

⌐Of His Study and Diligence in Holy Scripture⌐

From thenceforth he gave himself day and night most fervently to the studies of Scripture, ⌐in which he wrote many noble books, which well testify[88] both his angelic wit, his ardent labor, and his profound erudition, of which books some we have and some (as an inestimable treasure) we have lost. Great libraries—it is incredible to consider with how marvelous celerity[89] he read them over and wrote out what he liked. Of the old fathers of the Church, so great knowledge he had as it were hard for him to have that hath lived long and all his life hath done nothing else but read them. Of these newer divines,[90] so good judgment he had that it might appear there were nothing in any of them that were unknown to him, but all things as ripe as[91] though he had all their works ever before his eyes. But of all these new doctors he specially commendeth Saint Thomas[92] as him that enforceth[93] himself in a sure pillar of truth.⌐ He was very quick, wise, and subtle in dispicions,[94] and had great felicity[95] therein, while he had that high stomach.[96] But now a great while he had bidden such conflicts farewell, and every day more and more hated them, and so greatly abhorred them that when Ercole d'Este, Duke of Ferrara, first by messengers and after by himself, desired[97] him to dispute at Ferrara (because the general chapter of Friars Preachers[98] was held there), long it was ere[99] he could be brought thereto. But at the instant[100] request of the Duke, which very singularly loved him, he came thither, where he so behaved himself that was wonder to behold how all the audience rejoiced to hear him, for it were not possible for a man to utter neither more cunning, nor more cunningly. But it was a common saying with him that such altercations were for a logician and not meetly[101] for a philosopher. He said also that such disputations greatly profited as were exercised with a peaceable mind, to the ensearching of the truth in secret[102] company, without great audience; but he said that those dispicions did great hurt that were held openly[103] to the ostentation of learning and to win the favor of the common people and the commendation of fools. He thought that utterly[104] it could uneath[105] be but that with the desire of worship[106] (which these gazing disputers[107] gape after[108]) there is with an inseparable bond annexed[109] the appetite of his confusion and rebuke whom they argue with. Which appetite is a deadly wound to the soul and a mortal[110] poison to charity. There was nothing passed[111] him of those captions, subtleties, and cavillations[112] of sophistry; nor again there was nothing that he more hated and abhorred, considering that they served of nought[113] but to the shaming of such other folk as were in very[114] science much better learned and in those trifles ignorant, and that unto the ensearching of the

---

80 *Hereupon shortly:* Soon after this
81 near 82 distinguished 83 *taken in number of:* considered to be among
84 *for to move:* in order to raise 85 *set by:* valued 86 *wanton verses of:* lustful poems about 87 *vulgar tongue:* native language
88 attest to 89 *how marvelous celerity:* what astonishing speed 90 theologians

91 *as ripe:* as ready; as maturely considered 92 Aquinas 93 strengthens
94 disputations; debates 95 success; delight 96 *high stomach:* proud heart
97 asked 98 i.e., the Dominicans
99 before 100 insistent 101 suitable
102 private 103 in public 104 truly; entirely 105 scarcely 106 honor;

distinction 107 *gazing disputers:* debaters looking around at the audience 108 *gape after:* long for 109 attached 110 deadly
111 that got by 112 *captions . . . cavillations:* fallacies, verbal tricks, frivolous quibbles 113 *of nought:* for nothing
114 true

truth (to which he gave continual labor) they profited little or nought.

⌐*Of His Learning Universally*⌐

But because we will hold the reader no longer in hand,[115] we will speak of his learning but a word or twain[116] generally. Some man hath shined in eloquence, but ignorance of natural things hath dishonested[117] him. Some man hath flowered in the knowledge of diverse strange[118] languages, but he hath wanted[119] all the cognition of philosophy. Some man hath read the inventions[120] of the old philosophers, but he hath not been exercised in the new schools. Some man hath sought cunning, as well philosophy as divinity,[121] for praise and vainglory, and not for any profit or increase of Christ's Church. But Pico all these things with equal study hath so received that they might seem by heaps, as a plenteous stream, to have flowed into him. For he was not of the condition of some folk (which to be excellent in one thing set all others aside) but he in all sciences profited so excellently that which of them soever ye had considered in him, ye would have thought that he had taken that one for his only study. And all these things were in him so much the more marvelous in that he came thereto by himself with the strength of his own wit, ⌐for the love of God and profit of His Church,⌐ without masters, so that we may say of him that Epicurus the philosopher said of himself, that he was his own master.[122]

⌐*Five Causes That in So Short Time Brought Him to So Marvelous Cunning*⌐

To the bringing forth of so wonderful effects in so small time, I consider five causes to have come together: first, an incredible wit; secondly, a marvelous fast memory; thirdly, great substance,[123] by the which, to the buying of his books as well Latin as Greek and other tongues, he was especially helped. (Seven thousand ducats[124] he had laid out in the gathering together of volumes of all manner of literature.) The fourth cause was his busy and indefatigable study. The fifth was the despising of all earthly things.

⌐*Of His Conditions and His Virtue*⌐

But now let us pass over those powers of his soul which appertain to understanding and knowledge, and let us speak of them that belong to the achieving of noble acts. Let us, as we can, declare his excellent conditions, that his mind inflamed to Godward may appear, and his riches given out to poor folk may be understood, to the intent that they ⌐which shall hear his virtue⌐ may have occasion thereby to give especial laud and thanks therefor to almighty God, of whose infinite goodness all grace and virtue cometh.

⌐*Of the Sale of His Lordships,*[125] *and Alms*⌐

Three years before his death (to the end that, all the charge[126] and business of rule or lordship set aside, he might lead his life in rest and peace, well considering to what end this earthly honor and worldly dignity cometh), all his patrimony and dominions—that is to say, the third part[127] of the earldom of Mirandola and of Concordia, unto John Francis, his nephew, he sold and that so good cheap[128] that it seemed rather a gift than a sale. All that ever he received of this bargain, partly he gave out to poor folk, partly he bestowed in the buying of a little land to the finding of him[129] and his household. And over that,[130] much silver vessel and plate, with other precious and costly utensils of household, he divided among poor people. He was content with mean[131] fare at his table, howbeit somewhat yet retaining of the old plenty in dainty viand[132] and silver vessels. Every day at certain hours he gave himself to prayer. To poor men always, if any came, he ⌐plenteously⌐ gave out his money; and not content only to give that he had himself ready, he wrote over that to one Jerome Benivieni, a Florentine, a well-lettered man (whom for his great love toward him and the integrity of his conditions he singularly favored), that he should with his own money ever help poor folk, and give maidens money to their marriage, and always send him word what he had laid out that he might pay it him again. This office[133] he committed to him that he might the more easily by him, as by a faithful messenger,

---

115 suspense   **116** two   **117** discredited
118 foreign   **119** lacked   **120** discoveries
121 theology   **122** See Diogenes Laërtius's
Lives and Opinions of Eminent Philosophers

10.13.   **123** wealth   **124** gold coins
125 domains; lands one has a right to
rule   **126** burden; responsibility   **127** *the
third part*: one-third   **128** *so good cheap*:

at such a low price   **129** *finding of him*:
supporting of himself   **130** *over that*:
moreover   **131** moderate   **132** *dainty
viand*: fancy foods   **133** responsibility

relieve the necessity and misery of poor needy people such as himself haply[134] could not come by the knowledge of.

⌐Of the Voluntary Affliction and Paining of His Own Body⌐

Over all this, many times (which is not to be kept secret) he gave alms of his own body. We know many men which, as Saint Jerome saith, put forth their hand to poor folk, but with the pleasure of the flesh they be overcomen.[135] But he, many days—and namely[136] those days which represent unto us[137] the Passion and death that Christ suffered for our sake—beat and scourged his own flesh in the remembrance of that great benefit, and for cleansing of his old offenses.

⌐Of His Placability, or Benign Nature⌐

He was of cheer always merry, and of so benign nature that he was never troubled with anger. And he said once to his nephew that whatsoever should happen (fell there never so great misadventure) he could never, as him thought, be moved to wrath but if[138] his chests perished in which his books lay, that he had with great travail and watch[139] compiled. But forasmuch as he considered that he labored only for the love of God and profit of his Church, and that he had dedicated unto him all his works, his studies, and his doings; and since he saw that, ⌐since God is almighty,⌐ they could not miscarry but if it were either by his commandment or by his sufferance,[140] he verily trusted, ⌐since God is all good,⌐ that he would not suffer him to have that occasion of heaviness.[141] O ⌐very⌐ happy mind, which none adversity might oppress, which no prosperity might enhance: not the cunning of all philosophy was able to make him proud; not the knowledge of the Hebrew, Chaldean, and Arabian languages, besides Greek and Latin, could make him vainglorious; not his great substance,[142] not his noble blood could blow up his heart; not the beauty of his body, not the great occasion of sin were able to pull him back into the voluptuous

broad way ⌐that leadeth to hell.[143]⌐ What thing was there of so marvelous strength that might overturn the mind of him which now (as Seneca saith) was "gotten above fortune"[144] as he which as well her favor as her malice hath set at nought,[145] that he might be coupled with a spiritual knot unto Christ and his heavenly citizens?

⌐How He Eschewed Dignities⌐

When he saw many men with great labor and money desire[146] and busily purchase the offices and dignities of the Church (which are nowadays, alas the while,[147] commonly bought and sold), himself refused to receive them when two kings offered them. When another man offered him great worldly promotion if he would go to the king's court, he gave him such an answer that he should well know that he neither desired worship[148] nor worldly riches, but rather set them at nought, that he might the more quietly give himself to study and the service of God. This was he persuaded: that to a philosopher and him that seeketh for wisdom, it was no praise to gather riches but to refuse them.

⌐Of the Despising of Worldly Glory⌐

All praise of people and all earthly glory he reputed utterly for nothing, but in the renaying[149] of this shadow of glory, he labored for very[150] glory, which evermore followeth virtue as an inseparable servant. He said that fame oftentimes did hurt to men while they live, and never good when they be dead. So much only set he by[151] his learning: in how much he knew that it was profitable to the Church and to the extermination of errors. And over that, he was come to that prick[152] of perfect humility that he little forced[153] whether his works went out under his own name or not, so that[154] they might as much profit[155] as if they were given out under his name. And now set he little by[156] any other books save only the Bible, in the only study of which he had appointed himself[157] to spend the residue of his life, saving[158] that the common profit pricked[159] him when he considered so many and so great works as

---

134 perhaps   135 See St. Jerome, *Letter to Eustochium* (Letter 108) 17.   136 especially 137 *represent unto us:* call to our minds 138 *but if:* unless   139 keeping awake and vigilant   140 allowing it   141 dejectedness of mind; sadness   142 wealth

143 See Mt 7:13–14.   144 Seneca, *On the Shortness of Life* 5   145 *set at nought:* value as nothing   146 ask for   147 *alas the while:* sad to say   148 honor; prestige 149 refusing; renouncing   150 true 151 *set he by:* did he value   152 height

153 cared   154 *so that:* as long as 155 *might as much profit:* could do as much good   156 *set he little by:* he placed little value on   157 *appointed himself:* decided 158 except   159 spurred; goaded

he had conceived and long travailed upon, how they were of every man, by and by,[160] desired and looked after.

⌐How Much He Set More by Devotion Than Cunning⌐

The little affection of an old man or an old woman to Godward (were it never so small) he set more by than by all his own knowledge as well of natural things as godly. And oftentimes in communication[161] he would admonish his familiar friends how greatly these mortal things bow and draw[162] to an end: how slipper[163] and how falling[164] it is that we live in now; how firm, how stable that shall be that we shall hereafter live in, whether we be thrown down into hell or lifted up into heaven. Wherefore he exhorted them to turn up their minds to love God, which was a thing far excelling all the cunning that is possible for us in this life to obtain. The same thing also in his book which he entitled *De Ente et Uno*[165] lightsomely[166] he treateth, where he interrupteth the course of his dispicion[167] and turning his words to Angelo Poliziano (to whom he dedicateth that book), he writeth in this wise: "But now behold, O my well-beloved Angel, what madness holdeth us. Love God (while we be in this body) we rather[168] may, than either know him or by speech utter[169] him. In loving him, also we more profit ourselves; we labor less and serve him more. And yet had we liefer[170] always by knowledge never find that thing that we seek than by love to possess that thing which also, without love, were in vain found."

⌐Of His Liberality and Contempt of Riches⌐

Liberality only in him passed measure,[171] for so far was he from the giving of any diligence to earthly things that he seemed somewhat besprent[172] with the freckle[173] of ⌐negligence.⌐ His friends oftentimes admonished him that he should not all utterly despise riches, showing him that it was his dishonesty and rebuke when it was reported (were it true or false) ⌐that his negligence and setting nought by[174] money⌐ gave his servants occasion of deceit and robbery. Nevertheless, that mind of his (which evermore on high cleaved fast in[175] contemplation and in the ensearching[176] of nature's counsel[177]) could never let down itself to the consideration and overseeing of these base, abject, and vile earthly trifles. His high steward came on a time to him and desired[178] him to receive his account of such money as he had in many years received of him, and brought forth his books of reckoning.[179] Pico answered him in this wise: "My friend," saith he, "I know well ye have might oftentimes, and yet may, deceive me and ye list;[180] wherefore the examination of these expenses shall not need.[181] ⌐There is no more to do.⌐ If I be aught[182] in your debt, I shall pay you by and by.[183] If ye be in mine, pay me — either now if ye have it, or hereafter if ye be now not able."

⌐Of His Loving Mind and Virtuous Behavior to His Friends⌐

His ⌐lovers and⌐ friends with great benignity ⌐and courtesy⌐ he entreated. Whom he used in all secret communing[184] virtuously to exhort to Godward. Whose godly words ⌐so effectually wrought[185] in the hearers⌐ that, where a ⌐cunning⌐ man ⌐(but not so good as cunning) came to him on a day⌐ for the great fame of his learning to commune[186] with him, as they fell in talking of virtue, he was with two words[187] of Pico so thoroughly pierced that forthwithal[188] he forsook his accustomed vice and reformed his conditions. The words that he said unto him were these: "If we had evermore before our eyes the ⌐painful⌐ death of Christ which he suffered for the love of us, and then if we would again[189] think upon our death, we should well beware of sin." Marvelous benignity and courtesy he showed unto them, not whom strength of body or goods of fortune magnified, but to them whom learning and conditions bound him to favor, for similitude of manners is a cause of love and friendship. A likeness of conditions is, as Apollonius saith, an affinity.[190]

---

160 *by and by:* on and on, continuously
161 conversation **162** *bow and draw:* decline and come **163** unreliable; uncertain **164** transitory **165** "On Being and Unity" **166** clearly, lucidly **167** discussion **168** sooner **169** reveal **170** rather **171** *passed measure:* went beyond moderation **172** spotted **173** blemish **174** *setting nought by:* caring nothing about **175** *cleaved fast in:* clung steadfastly to **176** probing **177** secret design **178** asked **179** accounting **180** *and ye list:* if you wish **181** be necessary **182** at all **183** *by and by:* directly, immediately **184** *all secret communing:* every personal conversation **185** worked **186** talk **187** utterances **188** immediately **189** further; in turn **190** Philostratus, *The Life of Apollonius of Tyana* 6.40

⌐What He Hated, and What He Loved⌐

There was nothing more odious nor more intolerable to him than (as Horace saith) the proud palaces of stately lords.[191] Wedding and worldly business he fled almost alike; notwithstanding, when he was asked once in sport whether[192] of those two burdens seemed lighter, and which he would choose if he should of necessity be driven to that one and at his election, which he sticked thereat[193] a while but at the last he shook his head and a little smiling he answered that he had liefer[194] take him to marriage, as that thing in which was less servitude and not so much jeopardy. Liberty above all things he loved to which both his own natural affection and the study of philosophy inclined him, and for that was he always wandering and flitting and would never take himself to any certain dwelling.

⌐Of His Fervent Love to God⌐

Of outward[195] observances he gave no very great force.[196] We speak not of those observances which the Church commandeth to be observed, for in those he was diligent; but we speak of those ceremonies which folk bring up, setting the very[197] service of God aside, which is, ⌐as Christ saith,⌐ to be worshipped "in spirit and in truth."[198] But in the inward affects of the mind he cleaved to God with very fervent love ⌐and devotion.⌐ Sometimes that marvelous alacrity languished and almost fell, and eft[199] again with great strength rose up into God. In the love of whom he so fervently burned that on a time as he walked with John Francis (his nephew) in an orchard at Ferrara in the talking of the love of Christ, he broke out into these words: "Nephew," said he, "this will I show thee; I warn thee, keep it secret: the substance[200] that I have left after certain books of mine finished,[201] I intend to give out to poor folk; and fencing[202] myself with the crucifix, barefoot walking about the world in every town and castle I purpose[203] to preach of Christ." Afterward I understand, ⌐by the especial commandment of God,⌐ he changed that purpose and appointed[204] to profess himself[205] in the Order of Friars Preachers.[206]

⌐Of His Death⌐

In the year of our Redemption 1494, when himself had fulfilled the thirty-second year of his age and abode at Florence, he was suddenly taken with a fervent access[207] which so far-forth crept into the interior parts of his body that it despised[208] all medicines and overcame all remedy, and compelled him within three days to satisfy nature and ⌐repay her the life which he received of her.⌐

⌐Of His Behavior in the Extremes of His Life⌐

After that he had received the holy Body of our Savior, when they offered unto him the crucifix (that in the image of Christ's ineffable Passion suffered for our sake, he might, ere[209] he gave up the ghost, receive his full draught of love and compassion in the beholding of that pitiful figure as a strong defense against all adversity and a sure portcullis[210] against wicked spirits) the priest demanded[211] him whether he firmly believed that crucifix to be the image of him that was very[212] God and very man: which in his Godhead was before all time begotten of his Father, to whom he is also equal in all things and which of the Holy Ghost, God also, of him and of the Father coeternally going forth (which three Persons be one God) was in the chaste womb of our Lady, a perpetual virgin, conceived in time; which suffered hunger, thirst, heat, ⌐cold,⌐ labor, travail, and watch;[213] and which at the last, for washing of our spotty[214] sin contracted and drawn unto us in the sin of Adam, for the sovereign love that he had to mankind, in the altar of the cross willingly and gladly shed out his most precious blood. When the priest inquired of him these things and such others as they be wont to inquire of folk in such case, Pico answered him that he not only believed it, but also certainly knew it.

When that one Albert, his sister's son, a young man both of wit, cunning, and conditions excellent, began to comfort him against death, and by natural reason to show him why it was not to be feared but strongly to be taken—as that only thing which maketh an end of all the labor, pain, trouble, and sorrow of this short, miserable, ⌐deadly⌐

---

191 Horace, *Epodes* 2.7–8   192 which
193 *sticked thereat:* hesitated about for
194 rather   195 external   196 importance   197 true   198 Jn 4:24
199 afterward   200 wealth   201 are
finished   202 protecting   203 intend
204 decided   205 *profess himself:* take
religious vows   206 Dominican Order
207 *fervent access:* burning or intense
fever   208 defied; was impervious to
209 before   210 an iron gate used to
defend castles   211 asked   212 true
213 sleeplessness   214 staining

life — he answered that this was not the chief thing that should make him content to die (because the death determineth[215] the manifold incommodities[216] and painful wretchedness of this life) but rather, this cause should make him not content only but also glad to die: for that[217] death maketh an end of sin, inasmuch as he trusted the shortness of his life should leave him no space to sin and offend. He asked also all his servants' forgiveness if he had ever before that day offended any of them for whom he had provided by his testament[218] eight years before: for some of them meat[219] and drink; for some, money; each of them after their deserving. He showed also, to the above-named Albert and many other credible persons, that the Queen of heaven came to him that night with a marvelous fragrant odor, refreshing all his members that were bruised and frushed[220] with that fever, and promised him that he should not utterly die. He lay always with a pleasant and a merry countenance,[221] and in the very twitches and pangs of death he spoke as though he beheld the heavens open. And all that came to him and saluted[222] him, offering their service, with very loving words he received, thanked, and kissed. The executor of his movable goods he made one Anthony, his brother. The heir of his lands he made the poor people of the hospital of Florence. ⌐And in this wise, into the hands of our Savior he gave up his spirit.⌐

⌐*How His Death Was Taken*⌐

What sorrow and heaviness[223] his departing out of this world was, both to rich and poor, high and low, well testifieth the princes of Italy, well witnesseth the cities and people, well recordeth the great benignity and singular courtesy of Charles, King of France, which as he came to Florence (intending from thence to Rome, and so forth, in his voyage[224] against the realm of Naples), hearing of the sickness of Pico, in all convenient[225] haste he sent him two of his own physicians as ambassadors both to visit him and to do him all the help they might, and over that, sent unto him letters, subscribed[226] with his own hand, full of such humanity and courteous offers as the benevolent mind of such a noble prince and the worthy virtues of Pico required.

⌐*Of the State of His Soul*⌐

⌐After his death (and not long after),⌐ one Jeronimus,[227] a Friar Preacher[228] of Ferrara, a man as well in cunning[229] as holiness of living most famous, in a sermon which he rehearsed in the chief church of all Florence, said unto the people in this wise: "O thou city of Florence, I have a secret thing to show thee which is as true as the Gospel of Saint John. I would have kept it secret, but I am compelled to show it. For he that hath authority to command me hath bid me publish[230] it. I suppose verily that there be none of you but ye knew John Pico, Earl of Mirandola, a man in whom God had heaped many great gifts and singular graces. The Church had of him an inestimable loss. For I suppose if he might have had the space of his life prorogued,[231] he should have excelled (by such works as he should have left behind him) all them that died this eight hundred years before him. He was wont to be conversant with me and to break[232] to me the secrets of his heart, in which I perceived that he was by privy[233] inspiration called of God unto religion.[234] Wherefore he purposed[235] oftentimes to obey this inspiration and follow his calling.

Howbeit, not being kind[236] enough for so great benefices[237] of God, or called back by the tenderness of his flesh (as he was a man of delicate complexion) he shrank from the labor or thinking haply[238] that the religion[239] had no need of him, deferred it for a time. Howbeit, this I speak only by conjecture. But for this delay I threatened him two years together[240] that he would be punished if he forslothed[241] that purpose which our Lord had put in his mind. And certainly I prayed to God myself (I will not lie therefor[242]) that he might be somewhat beaten, to compel him to take that way which God had from above showed him. But I desired not this scourge upon him that he was beaten with; I looked not for that. But our Lord had so decreed that he should forsake[243] this present life and lose a part of that noble crown that he should have had in heaven. Notwithstanding,

---

215 put an end to   216 harms and discomforts   217 *for that:* because   218 will   219 food   220 crushed; disabled   221 look on his face   222 greeted   223 grief   224 military expedition   225 due   226 signed

227 Savonarola, as stated in More's source document   228 *Friar Preacher:* Dominican   229 knowledge; cleverness; learning   230 publicize   231 extended   232 reveal   233 private   234 life in a religious order   235 intended   236 grateful   237 benefits;

gifts   238 perhaps   239 religious order   240 uninterruptedly   241 through sloth neglected   242 about that; on that account   243 give up

the most benign Judge hath dealt mercifully with him and for his plenteous alms given out with a free and liberal hand unto poor people, and for the devout prayers which he most instantly[244] offered unto God, this favor he hath: though his soul be not yet in the bosom of our Lord in the heavenly joy, yet is it not on the other side deputed[245] unto perpetual pain, but he is adjudged[246] for a while to the fire of purgatory, there to suffer pain for a season. Which I am the gladder to show you in this behalf,[247] to the intent that they which knew him — and such, in especially,[248] as for his manifold benefices are singularly beholden unto him — should now with their prayers, alms, and other suffrages[249] help him." These things this holy man Jerome, this servant of God, openly[250] affirmed and also said that he knew well if he lied in that place,[251] he were worthy[252] eternal damnation. And over that, he said that he had known all those things within a certain time, but the words which Pico had said in his sickness of the appearing of our Lady caused him to doubt and to fear lest Pico had been deceived by some illusion of the devil, inasmuch as the promise of our Lady seemed to have been frustrated by his death. But afterward he understood that Pico was deceived in the equivocation of the word, while she spoke of the second death and everlasting, and he undertook her of[253] the first death and temporal. And after this the same Jerome showed to his acquaintance that Pico had after his death appeared unto him all compassed in fire, and showed unto him that he was suchwise in purgatory punished for ⌐his negligence and⌐ his unkindness.[254] ⌐Now, since it is so — that he is adjudged[255] to that fire from which he shall undoubtedly depart unto glory and no man is sure how long it shall be first, and may be the shorter time for our intercessions — let every Christian body show their charity upon him to help to speed him thither where, after the long habitation with the inhabitants of this dark world (to whom his goodly conversation gave great light), and after the dark fire of purgatory (in which venial offenses be cleansed), he may shortly (if he be not already) enter the inaccessible and infinite light of heaven, where he may in the presence of the sovereign Godhead so pray for us that we may the rather by his intercession be partners of that unspeakable joy which we have prayed to bring him speedily to. Amen.⌐

⌐Here endeth the life of John Pico, Earl of Mirandola.⌐

⌐*Finis*⌐

---

244 persistently   245 consigned   offered for the dead   250 publicly   took her as referring to   254 ingratitude;
246 sentenced   247 *in this behalf:* for   251 *in that place:* i.e., in the church pulpit   unnatural conduct   255 sentenced
this reason   248 particular   249 prayers   252 deserving of   253 *undertook her of:*

⌐Here Followeth Three Epistles
of the Said Pico⌐
of which three, two be written unto
John Francis, his nephew; the third unto
one Andrew Corneo, a nobleman of Italy.⌐

⌐*The argument and matter of the first epistle of Pico
unto his nephew John Francis*⌐

It appeareth by this epistle that John Francis, the
nephew of Pico, had broken²⁵⁶ his mind unto Pico
and had made him of counsel in some secret godly
purpose which he intended to take upon him;²⁵⁷
but what this purpose should be, upon²⁵⁸ this letter
can we not fully perceive. Now after that he thus intended, there fell unto him many impediments and
diverse occasions which withstood his intent and in
manner letted²⁵⁹ him and pulled him back. Wherefore Pico comforteth him in this epistle and exhorteth him to perseverance, by such means as are in the
epistle evident and plain enough. Notwithstanding,
in the beginning of this letter, where he saith that
the flesh shall, but if²⁶⁰ we take good heed, "make
us drunk in the cups of Circe" and misshape us into
the likeness and figure of brute beasts: those words,
if ye perceive them not, be in this wise understood.
There was sometime in [Aeaea]²⁶¹ a woman called
Circe, which by enchantment (as Virgil maketh
mention) used with a drink to turn as many men as
received it into diverse likenesses and figures of sundry beasts—some into lions, some into bears, some
into swine, some into wolves—which afterward
walked ever tame about her house and waited upon
her in such use or service as she list²⁶² to put unto
them.²⁶³ In like wise²⁶⁴ the flesh, if it make us drunk
in the wine of voluptuous pleasure or make the
soul leave the noble use of his²⁶⁵ reason and incline
unto sensuality and affections²⁶⁶ of the body, then
the flesh changeth us from the figure of reasonable
men into the likeness of unreasonable beasts, and
that diversely, after the convenience²⁶⁷ and similitude between our sensual affections and the brutish
properties of sundry beasts: as the proud-hearted
man into a lion, the irous²⁶⁸ into a bear, the lecherous into a goat, the drunken glutton into a swine,
the ravenous extortioner into a wolf, the false²⁶⁹

deceiver into a fox, the mocking jester into an ape.
From which beastly shape may we never be restored
to our own likeness again unto²⁷⁰ the time we have
cast up again the drink of the bodily affections by
which we were into these figures enchanted. When
there cometh sometime a monstrous beast to the
town, we run and are glad to pay some money to
have the sight thereof. But I fear if men would look
upon themselves advisedly, they should see a more
monstrous beast nearer home; for they should perceive themselves, by the wretched inclination to diverse beastly passions, changed in their soul, not
into the shape of one, but of many beasts: that is to
say, of all them whose brutish appetites they follow.
Let us then beware, as Pico counseleth us, that we
be not drunken in the cups of Circe—that is to say,
in the sensual affections of the flesh—lest we deform the image of God in our souls, after whose image we be made,²⁷¹ and make ourselves worse than
idolaters. For if he be odious to God which²⁷² turneth the image of a beast into God,²⁷³ how much is
he more odious which turneth the image of God
into a beast?⌐

John Pico, Earl of Mirandola, to John Francis,
his nephew by his brother: health in him that is
very²⁷⁴ health.

That thou hast had many evil occasions after thy
departing which trouble thee and stand against the
virtuous purpose that thou hast taken, there is no
cause, my son, why thou shouldst either marvel
thereof, be sorry therefor, or dread it. But rather,
how great a wonder were this: if only to thee among
mortal men the way lay open to heaven without
sweat, as though that now at erst²⁷⁵ the deceitful
world and the cursed devil failed, and as though
thou were not yet²⁷⁶ in the flesh, which "coveteth
against the spirit,"²⁷⁷ and which false flesh (but if²⁷⁸
we watch and look well to ourselves) shall make us
drunk in the cups of Circe and so deform us into
monstrous shapes of brutish and unreasonable
beasts. ⌐Remember also that of these evil occa-
sions⌐ the holy apostle Saint James saith thou hast
cause to be glad, writing in this wise: *Gaudete, fratres, cum in tentationes varias incideritis* ("Be glad,"

256 revealed   **257** *take upon him:*
undertake   **258** from   **259** prevented;
hindered   **260** *but if:* unless   **261** For this
missing place name, see *Aeneid* 3.386 and
Odyssey 10.135.   **262** chose   **263** See

Aeneid, 7.15–20; *Odyssey,* 10.208–43.
264 manner   **265** i.e., the soul's
266 inclinations; passions; appetites
267 *after the convenience:* according to
the correspondence   **268** irascible;

hot-tempered   **269** unfaithful
270 until   **271** Gn 1:26–27   **272** who
273 Ex 20:3–6   **274** true   **275** *at
erst:* for the first time   **276** still
277 Gal 5:17   **278** *but if:* unless

saith he, "my brethren, when ye fall in diverse temptations"),[279] and not causeless. For what hope is there of glory if there be none hope of victory? Or what place is there for victory where there is no battle? He is called to the crown and triumph which is provoked to the conflict, and namely[280] to that conflict in which no man may be overcome against his will, and in which we need none other strength to vanquish but that we list[281] ourselves to vanquish. Very happy is a Christian man, since that the victory is both put in his own free will, and the reward of the victory shall be far greater than we can either hope or wish. Tell me, I pray[282] thee, my most dear son, if there be aught[283] in this life—of all those things the delight whereof so vexeth and tosseth these earthly minds—is there, I say, any of those trifles in the getting of which a man must not suffer many labors, many displeasures, and many miseries ere[284] he get it? The merchant thinketh himself well served if, after ten years sailing, after a thousand incommodities,[285] after a thousand jeopardies of his life, he may at last have a little the more gathered together. Of the court and service of this world there is nothing that I need to write unto thee the wretchedness whereof the experience itself hath taught thee, and daily teacheth. In obtaining the favor of the princes, in purchasing the friendship of the company,[286] in ambitious labor for offices and honors, what a heap of heaviness[287] there is. How great anguish, how much business and trouble, I may rather learn of thee than teach thee, which, holding myself content with my books and rest, of a child have learned to live within my degree and (as much as I may), dwelling with myself, nothing out of myself labor for or long for. Now then, these earthly things—slipper,[288] uncertain, vile, and common also to us and brute beasts—sweating and panting we shall uneath[289] obtain. And look we, then, to heavenly things and godly—which "neither eye hath seen nor ear hath heard, nor heart hath thought"[290]—to be drawn slumbery[291] and sleeping maugre our teeth,[292] as though neither God might reign nor those heavenly citizens live without us? Certainly if this worldly felicity were gotten to us with idleness and ease, then might some man that shrinketh from labor rather choose to serve the world than God. But now, if we be forlabored[293] in the way of sin as much as in the way of God and much more—whereof the damned wretches cry out, *Lassati sumus in via iniquitatis*! ("We be wearied in the way of wickedness!")[294]—then must it needs be a point of extreme madness if we had not liefer[295] labor there where we go from labor to reward than where we go from labor to pain. I pass over how great peace and felicity it is to the mind when a man hath nothing that grudgeth[296] his conscience, nor is not appalled with the secret twitch of any privy[297] crime. This pleasure undoubtedly far excelleth all the pleasures that in this life may be obtained or desired. What thing is there to be desired among the delights of this world, which in the seeking weary us, in the having blindeth us, in the losing paineth us? Doubtest thou, my son, whether the minds of wicked men be vexed or not with continual thought and torment? It is the word of God which neither may deceive nor be deceived: *Cor impii quasi mare fervens, quod quiescere non potest* ("The wicked man's heart is like a stormy sea, that may not rest").[298] There is to him nothing sure, nothing peaceable, but all things fearful, all things sorrowful, all things deadly. Shall we, then, envy these men? Shall we follow them? And forgetting our own country (heaven) and our own heavenly Father, where we were freeborn, shall we willfully make ourselves their bondsmen? And with them wretchedly living, more wretchedly die and at the last most wretchedly in everlasting fire be punished? O the dark minds of men! O the blind hearts! Who seeth not more clear than light that all these things be (as they say) truer than truth itself? And yet do we not that that we know is to be done. In vain we would pluck our foot out of the clay, but we stick still. There shall come to thee, my son, doubt it not (in these places namely where thou art conversant[299]) innumerable impediments every hour, which might fear thee from the purpose of good and virtuous living (and but if[300] thou be wary) shall throw thee down headlong. But among all things, the very[301] deadly pestilence is this: to be conversant day and night among them whose life is

---

279 Jas 1:2   **280** especially   **281** want
282 ask, beg   **283** anything   **284** before
285 inconveniences   **286** group of other
courtiers   **287** grief   **288** slippery;
unreliable; having no stability or certainty
289 not easily; with difficulty   **290** 1 Cor
2:9   **291** lethargic   **292** *maugre our teeth:*
despite our resistance   **293** exhausted
294 Ws 5:7   **295** *had not liefer:* would
not rather   **296** disturbs   **297** private
298 Is 57:20   **299** familiar   **300** *but if:*
unless   **301** truly

not only on every side an allective[302] to sin, but over that all set in the expugnation[303] of virtue, under their captain the devil, under the banner of death, under the stipend[304] of hell, fighting against heaven, against our Lord God, and against his Christ. But cry thou, therefore, with the prophet, *Dirumpamus vincula eorum, et proiiciamus a nobis iugum ipsorum* ("Let us break the bands of them, and let us cast off the yoke of them").[305] These be they whom, ⌐as the glorious apostle Saint Paul saith,¬ our Lord hath "delivered into the passions of rebuke" and "to a reprovable sense[306] to do those things that are not convenient,[307] full of all iniquity, full of envy, manslaughter, contention, guile, and malice; backbiters, odious to God, contumelious,[308] proud, stately finders[309] of evil things, foolish, dissolute; without affection, without covenant, without mercy; which when they daily see the justice of God, yet understand they not that such as[310] these things commit are worthy death—not only they that do such things, but also they which consent to the doing."[311] Wherefore, my child, go thou never about to please them whom virtue displeaseth; but evermore let these words of the Apostle[312] be before thine eyes: *Oportet magis Deo placere quam hominibus* ("We must rather please God than men").[313] And ⌐remember¬ these ⌐words of Saint Paul also¬: *Si hominibus placerem, servus Christi non essem* ("If I should please men, I were not Christ's servant").[314] Let enter into thine heart a holy pride, and have disdain to take them for masters of thy living which have more need to take thee for a master of theirs. It were far more seeming[315] that they should with thee by good living begin to be men than thou shouldst with them, by the leaving of thy good purpose,[316] shamefully begin to be a beast. There holdeth me sometimes, by almighty God, as it were even a swoon and an insensibility for wonder when I begin in myself: I wot[317] never whether I shall say to remember or to sorrow, to marvel or to bewail the appetites of men, or, if I shall more plainly speak, the very madness. For it is verily a great madness not to believe the Gospel, whose truth the blood of martyrs crieth, the voice of apostles soundeth,

miracles proveth, reason confirmeth, the world testifieth, the elements speaketh, devils confesseth.[318] But a far greater madness is it, if thou doubt not but[319] that the Gospel is true, to live then as though thou doubtest not but that it were[320] false. For if these words of the Gospel be true—that it is "very hard for a rich man to enter the kingdom of heaven"[321]—why do we daily then gape after[322] the heaping up of riches? And if this be true—that we should seek for the glory and praise not that cometh of men, but that cometh of God—why do we then ever hang upon the judgment and opinion of men, and no man recketh[323] whether God like him or not? And if we surely[324] believe that once the time shall come in which our Lord shall say, "Go, ye cursed people, into everlasting fire,"[325] and again, "Come, ye my blessed children, possess ye the kingdom that hath been prepared for you from the forming of the world,"[326] why is there nothing then that we less fear than hell, or that we less hope for than the kingdom of God? What shall we say else but that there be many Christian men in name, but few in deed? But thou, my son, enforce[327] thyself to enter by the strait[328] gate ⌐that leadeth to heaven[329]¬ and take no heed what thing many men do, but what thing the very law of nature, what thing very reason, what thing our Lord himself showeth thee to be done. For neither thy glory shall be less if thou be happy with few, nor thy pain more easy if thou be wretched with many. Thou shalt have two specially effectual remedies against the world and the devil, with which two, as with two wings, thou shalt out of this vale of misery be lifted up into heaven: that is to say, almsdeed[330] and prayer. What may we do without the help of God? Or how shall he help us if he be not called upon?

But over that, certainly he shall not hear thee when thou callest on him if thou hear not first the poor man when he calleth upon thee. And verily it is according[331] that God should despise thee, being a man, when thou, being a man, despisest a man. For it is written, "In what measure that ye mete,[332] it shall be meted you again."[333] And in another place of the Gospel it is said, "Blessed be merciful men, for

---

302 allurement   **303** vanquishing; overcoming   **304** *under the stipend:* in the pay   **305** Ps 2:3   **306** *reprovable sense:* reprehensible idea   **307** appropriate   **308** insolent   **309** *stately finders:* arrogant devisers   **310** *such as:* those

who   **311** Rom 1:26, 28–32   **312** St. Peter   **313** Acts 5:29   **314** Gal 1:10   **315** fitting   **316** resolution   **317** know   **318** acknowledge   **319** *doubt not but:* do no doubt   **320** *doubtest . . . were:* had no doubt that it was   **321** Lk 18:24   **322** *gape after:* long

for   **323** cares   **324** definitely; firmly   **325** Mt 25:41   **326** Mt 25:24   **327** exert; strengthen   **328** narrow   **329** See Mt 7:13–14.   **330** almsgiving   **331** fitting   **332** measure   **333** Mt 7:2

they shall get mercy."³³⁴ When I stir thee to prayer, I stir thee not to the prayer which standeth in many words, but to that prayer which in the secret chamber of the mind, in the privy closet of the soul, with
⁵ very affect³³⁵ speaketh to God, and in the most lightsome³³⁶ darkness of contemplation not only presenteth the mind to the Father but also uniteth it with him by unspeakable ways which only they know that have assayed.³³⁷ Nor I care not how long ⌜or
¹⁰ how short⌝ thy prayer be, but how effectual, how ardent, and rather interrupted and broken between with sighs than drawn on length with a continual row³³⁸ and number of words. If thou love thine health; if thou desire to be sure³³⁹ from the grins³⁴⁰
¹⁵ of the devil, from the storms of this world, from the await³⁴¹ of thine enemies; if thou long to be acceptable to God; if thou covet to be happy at the last, let no day pass thee but thou once, at the leastwise, present thyself to God by prayer, and, falling
²⁰ down before him flat to the ground with a humble affect of devout mind—not from the extremity of thy lips, but out of the inwardness of thine heart—cry these words of the prophet: *Delicta iuventutis meae, et ignorantias meas, ne memineris; sed*
²⁵ *secundum misericordiam tuam memento mei, propter bonitatem tuam, Domine* ("The offenses of my youth, and mine ignorances, remember not, good Lord; but after³⁴² thy mercy, Lord, for thy goodness, remember me").³⁴³ What thou shalt in thy prayer
³⁰ ask of God—both the Holy Spirit which³⁴⁴ prayeth for us and, eke³⁴⁵ thine own necessity shall every hour put in thy mind, and also what thou shalt pray for—thou shalt find matter enough in the reading of Holy Scripture; which that thou wouldst now
³⁵ (setting poets' fables and trifles aside) take ever in thine hand, I heartily pray thee. Thou mayst do nothing more pleasant to God, nothing more profitable to thyself, than if thine hand cease not day nor night to turn and read the volumes of Holy
⁴⁰ Scripture. There lieth privily in them a certain heavenly strength, quick³⁴⁶ and effectual, which with a marvelous power transformeth and changeth the reader's mind into the love of God if they be clean and lowly entreated.³⁴⁷ But I have passed now the
⁴⁵ bounds of a letter, the matter drawing me forth and the great love that I have had to thee, both ever

before and specially since that hour in which I have had first knowledge of thy most holy purpose.

Now to make an end with this one thing, I warn
⁵⁰ thee (of which, when we were last together, I often talked with thee) that thou never forget these two things: that both the Son of God died for thee and that thou shalt also thyself die shortly live thou never so³⁴⁸ long. With these twain,³⁴⁹ as with two
⁵⁵ spurs—that one of fear, that other of love—spur forth thine horse through the short way of this momentary life to the reward of eternal felicity since we neither ought nor may prefix³⁵⁰ ourselves any other end than the endless fruition³⁵¹ of the in-
⁶⁰ finite goodness both to soul and body in everlasting peace. Farewell and fear God.³⁵²

⌜*The Matter or Argument of the Epistle of Pico to Andrew Corneo*⌝

⌜This Andrew, a worshipful³⁵³ man and an es-
⁶⁵ pecial friend of Pico, had by his letters given him counsel to leave the study of philosophy, as a thing in which he thought Pico to have spent time enough, and which, but if³⁵⁴ it were applied to the use of some actual business, he judged a thing vain
⁷⁰ and unprofitable. Wherefore he counseled Pico to surcease of study and put himself with some of the great princes of Italy. With whom (as this Andrew said) he should be much more fruitfully occupied than always in the study and learning of philoso-
⁷⁵ phy. To whom Pico answered as in this present epistle appeareth. Where he saith these words—"By this it should follow that it were either servile or at the leastwise not princely to make the study of philosophy other than mercenary"—thus he mea-
⁸⁰ neth: "Mercenary" we call all those things which we do for hire or reward. Then he maketh philosophy mercenary, and useth it not as cunning but as merchandise, which studieth it not for pleasure of itself, or for the instruction of his mind in moral vir-
⁸⁵ tue, but to apply it to such things where he may get some lucre or worldly advantage.⌝

John Pico, Earl of Mirandola, to Andrew Corneo: greeting.

Ye exhort me by your letters to the civil³⁵⁵ and
⁹⁰ active life, saying that in vain—and, in manner, to

334 Mt 5:7   335 *very affect*: real feeling   336 luminous   337 experienced (them)   338 string   339 safe   340 snares   341 ambush   342 according to   343 Ps   24(25):7   344 who   345 also   346 living   347 treated, handled   348 *never so*: no matter how   349 two   350 intend   for   351 enjoyment   352 More omits   this place and date: Ferrara, May 15, 1492.   353 distinguished   354 *but if*: unless   355 civic; public; political

my rebuke and shame—have I so long studied in philosophy, but if I would at the last exercise that learning in the entreating[356] of some profitable acts and outward business. Certainly, my well-beloved Andrew, I had cast away both cost and labor of my study if I were so minded that I could find in my heart in this matter to assent unto you and follow your counsel. This is a very deadly and monstrous persuasion which hath entered the minds of men: believing that the studies of philosophy are of estates[357] and princes, either utterly not to be touched, or, at the leastwise, with extreme lips[358] to be sipped and—rather to the pomp and ostentation of their wit than to the culture ⌐and profit⌐ of their minds—to be little and easily tasted. The words of Neoptolemus[359] they hold utterly for a sure decree, that philosophy is to be studied either never or not long;[360] but the sayings of wise men they repute for japes[361] and very fables: that sure and steadfast felicity standeth only in the goodness of the mind, and that these outward things of the body or of fortune little or nought[362] pertain unto us. But here ye will say to me thus: ⌐"I am content ye study, but I would have you outwardly occupied also.⌐ And I desire[363] you not so to embrace Martha that ye should utterly forsake Mary.[364] ⌐Love them and use them both: as well study as worldly occupation."⌐ ⌐Truly, my well-beloved friend,⌐ in this point I gainsay[365] you not: they that so do, I find no fault in, nor I blame them not; but certainly it is not all one to say "We do well if we do so" and to say "We do evil but if we do so." This is far out of the way: to think that from contemplation to the active living—⌐that is to say, from the better to the worse⌐—is none error to decline and to think that it were shame to abide still in the better and not decline. Shall a man then be rebuked because that he desireth and ensueth[366] virtue only for itself? Because he studieth the mysteries of God? Because he ensearcheth the counsel[367] of nature? Because he useth continually this pleasant ease and rest, seeking none outward thing, despising all other things, since those things are able sufficiently to satisfy the desire of their followers? By this reckoning it is a thing either servile or at the leastwise

not princely to make the study of wisdom other than mercenary. Who may well hear this? Who may suffer[368] it? Certainly he never studied for wisdom which so studied therefor that in time to come either he might not or would not study therefor. This man rather exercised the study of merchandise[369] than of wisdom. Ye write unto me that it is time for me now to put myself ⌐in household with⌐ some of the great princes of Italy. But I see well that as yet ye have not known the opinion that philosophers have of themselves which, as Horace saith, repute[370] themselves "kings of kings."[371] ⌐They love liberty;⌐ they cannot bear the proud manners of estates; they cannot serve. They dwell with themselves and be content with the tranquility of their own mind. They suffice themselves and more; they seek nothing out of themselves. The things that are had in honor among the common people, among them be not holden honorable. All that ever the voluptuous desire of men thirsteth for, or ambition sigheth for, they set at nought and despise. Which, while it belongeth to all men, yet undoubtedly it pertaineth most properly to them whom fortune hath so liberally favored that they may live not only well and plenteously but also nobly. These great fortunes lift up a man high and setteth him out to the show; but oftentimes, as a fierce and a skittish horse, they cast off their master. Certainly, always they grieve and vex him, and rather tear him than bear him. The golden mediocrity,[372] ⌐the mean estate,⌐[373] is to be desired, which shall bear us, as it were, in hands more easily; which shall obey us, and not master us. I, therefore, abiding firmly in this opinion, set more by[374] my little house, my study, the pleasure of my books, the ⌐rest and⌐ peace of my mind, than by all your kings' palaces, all your common business, ⌐all your glory,⌐ all the advantage that ye hawk after, and all the favor of the court. Nor I look not for this fruit of my study—that I may thereby hereafter be tossed in the flood and rumbling of your worldly business—but that I may once bring forth the children that I travail on:[375] that I may give out some books of mine own, to the common[376] profit, which may somewhat savor, if not of cunning, yet

---

356 undertaking 357 *of estates:* by nobility 358 *with extreme lips:* i.e., delicately, superficially; in small amounts 359 a son of Achilles. The words quoted are from a fragment of a play by Ennius (*ca.* 239–169 BC). 360 See Cicero, *Tusculan Disputations* 2.1; *On the Republic* 1.18. 361 trifles; tricks 362 nothing 363 ask 364 See Lk 10:38–42. 365 oppose; contradict 366 pursues 367 secret designs 368 tolerate 369 commerce 370 regard 371 Horace, *Epistles* 1.1.106–7 372 *golden mediocrity:* golden mean; happy medium 373 *mean estate:* middle position 374 *set more by:* value more highly 375 *travail on:* am in labor with 376 public

at the leastwise of wit and diligence. And because[377] ye shall not think that my travail and diligence in study is anything remitted[378] or slacked, I give you knowledge that after great fervent labor, with much watch and infatigable[379] travail, I have learned both the Hebrew language and the Chaldean, and now have I set hand to overcome the great difficulty of the Arabic tongue. These, my dear friend, be things which to appertain to[380] a noble prince, I have ever thought and yet think.

⌐Fare ye well.⌐ Written at Paris, the 15ᵗʰ day of October, the year of grace 1492.[381]

⌐*The Argument of the Epistle Following*

After that John Francis, the nephew of Pico, had (as it appeareth in the first epistle of Pico to him) begun a change in his living,[382] it seemeth, by this letter, that the company of the court where he was conversant,[383] diversely (as it is their unmannerly manner) descanted thereof,[384] to his rebuke as them[385] thought, but as truth was unto their own. Some of them judged it folly; some called it hypocrisy; some scorned him; some slandered him. Of all which demeanor (as we may of this epistle conjecture) he wrote unto this earl Pico, his uncle; which in this letter comforteth and encourageth him, as it is in the course thereof evident.⌐

John Pico, Earl of Mirandola, to Francis, his nephew: greeting ⌐in our Lord.⌐

Happy art thou, my son, when that our Lord not only giveth thee grace well to live, but also that while thou livest well, he giveth thee grace to bear evil words of evil people for thy living well. Certainly, as great a praise as it is to be commended of them that are commendable, as great a commendation it is to be reproved of them that are reprovable. Notwithstanding, ⌐my son,⌐ I call thee not therefor[386] happy because this false reproof is worshipful[387] and glorious unto thee, but for because that our Lord Jesus Christ (which is not only true, but also Truth itself[388]) affirmeth that our reward shall be plenteous in heaven when men speak evil to us and speak all evil against us, lying, for his name.[389] This is an apostle's dignity: to be reputed digne[390] ⌐afore God⌐ to be defamed of[391] wicked folk for his name. For we read in the Gospel of Luke that the apostles went joyful and glad from the council house of the Jews because God had accepted them as worthy to suffer wrong and reproof for his sake.[392] Let us therefore joy and be glad if we be worthy so great worship before God that his worship[393] be showed in our rebuke. And if we suffer of the world anything that is grievous or bitter, let this sweet voice of our Lord be our consolation: *Si mundus vos odio habet, scitote quia priorem me vobis odio habuit* ("If the world," saith our Lord, "hate you, know ye that it hated me before you").[394] If the world, then, hated him by whom the world was made, we most vile and simple men—and worthy[395] (if we consider our wretched living well) all shame and reproof—if folk backbite us and say evil of us, shall we so grievously take it that, lest they should say evil, we should begin to do evil? Let us rather gladly receive these evil words, and if we be not so happy to suffer for virtue and truth as the old saints suffered—beatings, binding, prison, swords, ⌐and death⌐—let us think, at the leastwise we be well served if we have the grace to suffer chiding, detraction, and hatred of wicked men, lest that, if all occasion of deserving be taken away, there be left us none hope of reward. If men for thy good living praise thee—thy virtue, certainly, in that it is virtue, maketh thee like unto Christ—but in that it is praised it maketh thee unlike him, which for the reward of his virtue received the ⌐opprobrious⌐ death of the cross, for which, as the Apostle[396] saith, "God hath exalted him and given him a name that is above all names."[397] More desireful is then to be condemned of the world and exalted of God, than to be exalted of the world and condemned of God. The world condemneth to life; God exalteth to glory. The world exalteth to a fall; God condemneth to the fire of hell. Finally, if the world fawn upon thee, uneath it may be[398] but that thy virtue (which, all lifted upward, should have God alone to please) shall somewhat unto the blandishing[399] of the world and favor of the people incline. And so, though[400] it lose nothing of the

---

377 so that   **378** diminished   **379** untiring   **380** *appertain to:* befit; suit   **381** The actual date of the letter is 1486, the year before Pico's alleged conversion. More omits Pico's excuses for the affair with Margherita de' Medici.   **382** way of living   **383** familiar   **384** *descanted thereof:* made comments about it   **385** they   **386** for that reason   **387** honorable   **388** See Jn 14:6.   **389** See Mt 5:11–12.   **390** worthy   **391** *defamed of:* slandered by   **392** Acts 5:27–41   **393** honor   **394** Jn 15:18   **395** deserving of   **396** Saint Paul   **397** Phil 2:9   **398** *uneath . . . be:* scarcely can it be   **399** flattery   **400** even if

integrity ⌐of our perfection,¬ yet it loseth of the reward; which reward, while it beginneth to be paid in the world, where all things is little, it shall be less in heaven, where all-thing is great. O happy rebukes which make us sure that neither the flower of our virtue shall wither with the pestilent blast of vainglory, nor our eternal reward be diminished for the vain promotion of a little popular fame. Let us, my son, love these rebukes; and only of the ignominy and reproof of our Lord's cross let us, like faithful servants, with a holy ambition be proud. "We," saith Saint Paul, "preach Christ crucified, which is unto the Jews despite,⁴⁰¹ unto the Gentiles folly, unto us the virtue and wisdom of God."⁴⁰² "The wisdom of this world is foolishness afore God,"⁴⁰³ and the folly of Christ is that by which he hath overcome the wisdom of the world, by which it hath pleased God to make his believing people safe.⁴⁰⁴

If that thou doubt not but that they be mad which backbite thy virtue—which the Christian living, that is very⁴⁰⁵ wisdom, reputeth for madness—consider, then, how much were thy madness if thou shouldst for the judgment of madmen swerve from the good institution⁴⁰⁶ of thy life namely since all error is with amendment to be taken away and not, with imitation and following, to be increased. Let them therefore neigh, let them bawl, let them bark; go thou boldly forth thy journey as thou hast begun, and of their wickedness and misery consider how much thyself art beholden to God, which hath illumined thee sitting in the shadow of death and, translating⁴⁰⁷ thee out of the company of them which, like drunken men without a guide wander hither and thither in obscure darkness, hath associated thee to the children of light. Let that same sweet voice of our Lord always sound in thine ears: *Sine mortuos sepelire mortuos suos; tu Me sequere* ("Let dead men alone with dead men; follow thou me").⁴⁰⁸ Dead be they that live not to God and in the space of this temporal death laboriously purchase themselves eternal death. Of whom, if thou ask whereto they draw,⁴⁰⁹ whereto they refer their studies, their works, and their business, and finally what end they have appointed⁴¹⁰ themselves in the adeption⁴¹¹ whereof

they should be happy, either they shall have utterly nothing to answer or they shall bring forth words repugnant in themselves and contrary each to other, like the raving of Bedlam⁴¹² people. Nor they wot never⁴¹³ themselves what they do, but like them that swim in swift floods, they be borne forth with the violence of evil custom as⁴¹⁴ it were with the boistous⁴¹⁵ course of the stream. And their wickedness blinding them on this side, and the devil pricking⁴¹⁶ them forthward on that side, they run forth headlong into all mischief as blind guides of blind men, till that death set on them unware,⁴¹⁷ and till that it be said unto them ⌐that Christ saith in the Gospel:¬ "My friend, this night ⌐the devils¬ shall take thy soul from thee. These goods, then, that thou hast gathered, whose shall they be?"⁴¹⁸ Then shall they envy them whom they despised. Then shall they commend them that they mocked. Then shall they covet to ensue⁴¹⁹ them in living when they may not, whom when they might have ensued they pursued.⁴²⁰ Stop therefore thine ears, my most dear son, and whatsoever men say of thee, whatsoever men think on thee, account it for nothing, but regard only "the judgment of God," which shall "yield every man after his own works"⁴²¹ "when he shall show himself from heaven with the angels of his virtue,⁴²² in flame of fire doing vengeance upon them that have not known God nor obeyed his Gospel," which, as the Apostle⁴²³ saith, "shall suffer in death eternal pain from the face of our Lord and from the glory of his virtue, when he shall come to be glorified of his saints and to be made marvelous in all them that have believed."⁴²⁴ It is written, *Nolite timere qui corpus possunt occidere, sed qui animam potest mittere in gehennam* ("Fear not them," saith our Lord, "that may slay the body; but fear him that may cast the soul into hell").⁴²⁵ How much less, then, be they to be feared that may neither hurt soul nor body? Which, if they now backbite thee living virtuously, they shall do the same never the less if, virtue forsaken, thou were overwhelmed with vice—not for that⁴²⁶ vice displeaseth them, but for that the vice of backbiting always pleaseth them. Flee if thou love thine health; flee as far as thou mayest

---

401 an insult   **402** 1 Cor 1:23–24   **403** 1 Cor 3:19   **404** saved   **405** true   **406** ordering   **407** moving   **408** Mt 8:22   **409** *whereto they draw:* what they're aiming for   **410** set

411 acquiring; attaining   **412** an insane asylum   **413** *Nor…never:* Nor they ever know   **414** as if   **415** stormy; rough   **416** spurring; goading   **417** unaware, unexpectedly   **418** Lk 12:20   **419** follow

420 persecuted   **421** *yield…after:* render to every man according to; Rom 2:5–6; Rv 22:12; Mt 16:27   **422** power, might   **423** Saint Paul   **424** 2 Thes 1:7–10   **425** Mt 10:28   **426** *for that:* because

their company; and, returning to thyself, oftentimes secretly pray unto the most benign Father ⌐of
heaven,⌐ crying with the prophet, *Ad te, Domine,*
levavi animam meam; Deus meus, in te confido. Non
erubescam, etiam si irrideant me inimici mei. Etenim
universi qui sperant in te non confundentur. Con-
fundantur iniqua agentes supervacue. Vias tuas, Do-
mine, demonstra mihi, et semitas tuas edoce me; di-
rige me in veritate tua et doce me. Quia tu es Deus
salvator meus, et in te sperabo tota die—that is to say,
"To thee, Lord, I lift up my soul; in thee I trust. I
shall not be shamed, and though[427] mine enemies
mock me. Certainly all they that trust in thee shall
not be ashamed. Let them be ashamed that work
wickedness in vain. Thy ways, good Lord, show me,
and thy paths teach me; direct me in thy truth and
teach me for thou art God my Savior; in thee shall
I trust all the day."[428] Remember also, my son, that
the death lieth at hand. Remember that all the time
of our life is but a moment and yet less than a moment. Remember how cursed our old enemy is,
which offereth us the kingdoms of this world that
he might bereave us[429] the kingdom of heaven; how
false the fleshly pleasures which therefor embrace

us that they might strangle us; how deceitful these
⌐worldly⌐ honors, which therefor lift us up, that
they might throw us down; how deadly these riches,
which, the more they feed us, the more they poison us; how short, how uncertain, how shadow-
like, false, imaginary it is that all these things together may bring us, and though they flow to us as
we would wish them. Remember again[430] how great
things be promised and prepared for them which,
despising these present things, desire and long for
that country whose king is the Godhead, whose law
is charity, whose measure is eternity. Occupy thy
mind with these meditations and such others that
may waken thee when thou sleepest, kindle thee
when thou waxest[431] cold, confirm thee when thou
waverest, and exhibit[432] thee wings of the love of
God while thou laborest to heavenward, that when
thou comest home to us (which with great desire
we look for), we may see not only him that we covet
but also such a manner one as we covet.

Farewell and love God, whom of old thou hast
begun to fear.

At Ferrara, the 2nd day of July, ⌐the year of our
Redemption⌐ 1492.

---

427 *and though:* even if   **428** Ps 24(25):1–5   **429** *bereave us:* deprive us of   **430** in addition; further   **431** are becoming   **432** provide

⌐The Interpretation of John Pico
upon This Psalm,
"*Conserva me Domine*"⌐

[1]*Conserva me, Domine,* [2]*quoniam speravi in te.*
5 [3]*Dixi Domino, 'Deus meus es tu,* [4]*quoniam bono-*
rum meorum non eges.' [5]*Sanctis qui sunt in terra,*
mirificavit voluntates suas. [6]*Multiplicatae sunt in-*
firmitates, postea acceleraverunt. [7]*Non congregabo*
conventicula eorum de sanguinibus; nec memor ero
10 *nominum eorum per labia mea.* [8]*Dominus pars he-*
reditatis meae et calicis mei: [9]*tu es qui restitues he-*
reditatem meam mihi. [10]*Funes ceciderunt mihi in*
praeclaris: [11]*etenim hereditas mea praeclara est mihi.*
[12]*Benedicam Dominum, qui tribuit mihi intellec-*
15 *tum: insuper* [13]*et usque ad noctem increpuerunt me*
renes mei. [14]*Providebam Dominum in conspectu*
meo semper, quoniam [15]*a dextris est mihi, ne com-*
movear. Propter hoc [16]*laetatum est cor meum, et ex-*
ultavit lingua mea; insuper [17]*et caro mea requiescet*
20 *in spe.* [18]*Quoniam non derelinques animam meam*
in inferno, [19]*nec dabis sanctum tuum videre corrup-*
tionem. [20]*Notas mihi fecisti vias vitae;* [21]*adimplebis*
me laetitia cum vultu tuo. [22]*Delectationes in dextera*
tua usque in finem.⌐433

25 [1]*Conserva me Domine:* "Keep me, good Lord."
If any perfect434 man look upon his own estate,435
there is one peril therein: that is to wit,436 lest he
wax437 proud of his virtue. And therefore David,
speaking in the person of a righteous man of his
30 estate, beginneth with these words: "*Conserva me,*
Domine" — that is to say, "Keep me good Lord" —
which word "keep me," if it be well considered, taketh away all occasion of pride. For he that is able
of himself anything to get, is able of himself that
35 same thing to keep. He that asketh, then, of God
to be kept in the state of virtue signifieth in that
asking that from the beginning he got not that virtue by himself. He, then, which remembereth that
he attained his virtue, not by his own power but by
40 the power of God, may not be proud thereof but
rather humbled before God, after438 those words of
the Apostle *Quid habes quod non accepisti*? ("What
hast thou that thou hast not received?") and "if
thou hast received it, why art thou proud thereof, as

though thou hadst not received it?"439 Two words,   45
then, be there which we should ever have in our
mouth: that one, *Miserere mei, Deus* ("Have mercy
on me, Lord"),440 when we remember our vice; that
other, *Conserva me, Deus* ("Keep me good Lord"),
when we remember our virtue.   50

[2]*Quoniam speravi in te:* "For I have trusted in thee."
This one thing is it that maketh us obtain of God
our petition: that is to wit, when we have a full hope
and trust that we shall speed.441 And if we observe
these two things in our requests — that is to wit, that 55
we require442 nothing but that which is good for us,
and that we require it ardently with a sure443 hope
that God shall hear us — our prayers shall never be
void. Wherefore, when we miss the effect of our petition, either it is for that we ask such thing as is   60
noyous444 unto us — for, as Christ saith, we "wot445
never what we ask";446 and Jesus said, "Whatsoever
ye shall ask in my name, it shall be given you"447
(This name "Jesus" signifieth a Savior, and therefore there is nothing asked in the name of Jesus but 65
⌐that is wholesome and helping⌐ to the salvation of
the asker) — or else God heareth not our prayer because that though the thing that we require be good
yet we ask it not well, for we ask it with little hope.
And he that asketh doubtingly asketh coldly; and   70
therefore Saint James biddeth us ask in faith, nothing doubting.448

[3]*Dixi Domino, 'Deus meus es tu':* "I have said to our
Lord, 'My God art thou.'" After that he hath warded
and fenced449 himself against pride, he describeth in   75
these words his estate. All the estate of a righteous
man standeth450 in these words: *Dixi Domino, 'Deus*
meus es tu' ("I have said to our Lord, 'My God art
thou.'"). Which words, though they seem common
to all folk, yet are there very few that may say them   80
truly. That thing a man taketh for his god that he
taketh for his chief good. And that thing taketh
he for his chief good which only had, though451 all
other things lack, he thinketh himself happy, and
which only lacking, though he have all other things,   85
he thinketh himself unhappy. The niggard,452 then,
saith to his money, *Deus meus es tu* ("My God art
thou"). For though honor fail, and health and

433 Ps 15(16) 434 righteous 435 state
of soul, general condition 436 say
437 become 438 in keeping with
439 1 Cor 4:7 440 Ps 50(51):1

441 succeed 442 ask for 443 secure;
steadfast 444 harmful 445 know
446 See Mt 20:22. 447 See Jn 14:13,
15:16, 16:23–26. 448 See Jas 1:5–8.

449 *warded and fenced:* guarded and
protected 450 consists 451 even if
452 miser

strength and friends, so[453] he have money he thinketh himself well. And if he have all those things
that we have spoken of, if money fail, he thinketh
himself unhappy. The glutton saith unto his fleshly
lust, the ambitious man saith to his vainglory, "My
God art thou." See, then, how few may truly say
these words: "I have said to our Lord, 'My God art
thou.'" For only he may truly say it which is content
with God alone, so that if there were offered him all
the kingdoms of the world, and all the good that is
in earth, and all the good that is in heaven, he would
not once offend God to have them all. In these
words, then — "I have said to our Lord, 'My God art
thou'" — standeth all the state of a right wise man.

[4]*Quoniam bonorum meorum non eges:* "For thou
hast no need of my goods." In these words he
showeth the cause why he saith only to our Lord
"*Deus meus es tu*" ("My God art thou"). The cause is
for that[454] only our Lord hath no need of our goods.
There is no creature but that it needeth other creatures, and though[455] they be of less perfection than
itself, as philosophers and divines[456] proven. For if
these ⌐more imperfect creatures⌐ were not, the others ⌐that are more perfect⌐ could not be. For if any
part of the whole university[457] of creatures were destroyed and fallen to nought, all the whole were
subverted. For certainly, ⌐one part of⌐ that university perishing, all parts perish; and all creatures be
parts of that university; of which university God
is no part, but he is the beginning, nothing thereupon depending. For nothing truly won he by the
creation of this world, nor nothing should he lose
if the world were annihilated and turned to nought
again. Then, only God is he which hath no need of
our goods. Well ought we certainly to be ashamed to
take such thing for God as hath need of us, and such
is every creature. Moreover, we should not accept
for God — that is to say, for the chief goodness —
but only[458] that thing which is the most sovereign
goodness of all things, and that is not the goodness
of any creature. Only therefore to Our Lord ought
we to say, "My God art thou."

[5]*Sanctis qui sunt in terra eius, mirificavit voluntates
suas:* "To his saints that are in the land of him, he

hath made marvelous his wills." After God should
we specially love them which are nearest joined unto
God, as be the holy angels and blessed saints that are
in their country of heaven. Therefore, after that he
had said to our Lord, "My God art thou," he addeth
thereunto that our Lord "hath made marvelous his
wills": that is to say, he hath made marvelous his
loves and his desires toward his saints that are "in
the land of him" — that is to wit,[459] in the country of
heaven, which is called "the land of God"[460] and the
"land of living people."[461] And verily if we inwardly
consider how great is the felicity of that country
and how much is the misery of this world, how
great is the goodness and charity of those ⌐blessed⌐
citizens, we shall continually desire to be hence, that
we were there. These things and such others when
we remember, we should ⌐evermore⌐ take heed that
our meditations be not unfruitful, but that of every
meditation we should always purchase[462] one virtue
or other, as, for example, by this meditation of the
goodness of that heavenly country we should win
this virtue: that we should not only strongly[463] suffer death and patiently when our time cometh or
if it were put unto us for the faith of Christ, but
also we should willingly and gladly long therefor,[464]
desiring to be departed out of this vale of wretchedness, that we may reign in the heavenly country
with God and his holy saints.

[6]*Multiplicate sunt infirmitates eorum, postea acceleraverunt:* "Their infirmities be multiplied, and after
they hasted."[465] These words the prophet speaketh
of wicked men. By "infirmities" he understandeth
idols, and so it is in the Hebrew text. For as good
folk have but one God whom they worship, so evil
folk have many gods and idols for they have many
voluptuous pleasures, many vain desires, many diverse passions which they serve. And wherefore seek
they many sundry pleasures? Certainly for because
they can find none that can set their heart at rest.
And for that[466] ⌐(as the prophet saith),⌐ "wicked
men walk about in a circuit" ⌐or "compass"[467]
whereof there is none end.⌐ Now, after these words
⌐"Their idols be multiplied"⌐ it followeth, "after
they hasted" — that is to say, ⌐after their idols,⌐ after
their ⌐passions and beastly desires,⌐ they run forth

---

453 so long as   **454** *for that:* because
455 *and though:* even if   **456** theologians
457 universe; universality   **458** *but only:*
anything but   **459** say   **460** i.e., in

this psalm, and also Zech 9:16   **461** Ps
26(27):13, 115(116):9   **462** endeavor to
bring about; strive to achieve   **463** stal-
wartly   **464** for it   **465** hastened

466 *for that:* because   **467** circular course;
Ps 1(2):8

headlong unadvisedly without any consideration. And in this be we taught that we should as speedily run to virtue as they run to vice, and that we should with no less diligence serve our Lord God than they serve their lord, the devil. The just man, considering the estate of evil folk, determineth firmly with himself (as we should also) that utterly he will in no wise follow them, and therefore he saith:

[7]*Non congregabo conventiculam* [*sic*] *eorum de sanguinibus, nec memor nominum:* "I shall not gather the congregation of them from the blood, nor I shall not remember their names." He saith "from the blood" both because idolaters were wont to gather the blood of their sacrifice together and thereabout to do their ceremonies, and also for that⁴⁶⁸ all the life of evil men forsakes reason, ⌐which standeth all in the soul,⌐ and follows sensuality, that standeth all in the blood. ⌐The prophet saith not only that he will not "gather their congregation" together "from the blood" (that is to say, that he would do no sacrifice to those idols) but also that he would not "remember their names" — that is to say, that he would not talk nor speak of the voluptuous delights which are evil people's gods,⌐ which we might yet lawfully do, showing us by that, that a perfect man should abstain not only from unlawful pleasures but also from lawful, to the end that he may altogether whole have his mind into heavenward and the more purely intend unto the contemplation of heavenly things. And forasmuch as some man would peradventure⁴⁶⁹ think that it were folly for a man utterly to deprive himself from all pleasures, therefore the prophet addeth:

[8]*Dominus pars hereditatis meae:* "Our Lord is the part⁴⁷⁰ of mine inheritance," as though he would say, "Marvel ye not though I forsake all things to the intent that I may have the possession of God, in whom all other things also be possessed." This should be the voice of every good Christian man: *Dominus pars hereditatis meae* ("God is the part of mine inheritance"). For ⌐certainly⌐ we Christian people, to whom God is promised for an inheritance, ought to be ashamed to desire anything besides him. But for that some man might haply⁴⁷¹ repute it for a great presumption that a man should

promise himself God for his inheritance, therefore the prophet putteth thereto:⁴⁷²

[9]*Tu es qui restitues hereditatem meam mihi:* "Thou, good Lord, art he that shall restore mine inheritance unto me," as though he would say, "O good Lord, my God, I know well that I am nothing in respect of thee. I wot⁴⁷³ well I am unable to ascend by mine own strength so high, to have thee in possession; but thou art he that shalt draw me to thee, by thy grace; thou art he that shalt give thyself in possession unto me." Let a righteous man then consider how great a felicity it is to have God fall unto him as his inheritance. It followeth ⌐in the psalm:⌐

[10]*Funes ceciderunt mihi in praeclaris:* "The cords have fallen to me nobly." The parts and lots⁴⁷⁴ ⌐of inheritances⌐ were of old time meted out and divided by ⌐cords or ropes.⌐ ⌐These words, then — "The ropes" (or "cords") "have fallen to me nobly" — be as much to say as, "The part" (or "lot") "of mine inheritance is noble."⌐ But forasmuch as there be many men which, though they be called to this great felicity (as, indeed, all Christian people are), yet they set little thereby and oftentimes change it for a small simple delight, therefore the prophet saith suingly:⁴⁷⁵

[11]*Hereditas mea praeclara est mihi:* "Mine inheritance is noble to me," as though he would say that "as it is noble in itself, so it is noble to me" — ⌐that is to say, "I repute⁴⁷⁶ it noble.⌐ And all other things in respect of it I repute, as Saint Paul saith, 'for dung.'"⁴⁷⁷ But forasmuch⁴⁷⁸ as to have this light of understanding whereby a man may know this gift that is given him of God to be the gift of God, therefore ⌐the prophet suingly⌐ saith:

[12]*Benedicam Dominum, qui tribuit intellectum* — that is to say, "I shall bless our Lord, which hath given me understanding." But insomuch as a man oftentimes intendeth after⁴⁷⁹ reason to serve God, and that notwithstanding, yet sensuality and the flesh repugneth,⁴⁸⁰ then is a man perfect when that, not his soul only, but also his flesh draw forth to Godward, after those words ⌐of the prophet in another psalm:⌐ *Cor meum et caro mea exultaverunt*

---

468 *for that:* because   **469** maybe   *thereto:* adds to that   **473** know   **476** consider   **477** Phil 3:8   **478** so
470 portion   **471** perhaps   **472** *putteth*   **474** allotments   **475** accordingly   **479** in accord with   **480** resists

in Deum vivum — that is to say, "My mind and my flesh, both, have joyed into living God."[481] And for[482] this, the prophet saith here suingly:[483]

[13]*Et usque ad noctem increpuerunt me renes mei:* "My reins" ⌐(or "kidneys[484]")⌐ "hath chidden[485] me unto the night" — that is to say, "My reins (in which is wont to be the greatest inclination to concupiscence) not only now inclineth me not to sin but also chideth me (that is to say, withdraw me from sin) 'unto the night' — that is to say, they so far-forth withdraw me from sin that willingly[486] they afflict and pain my body." Affliction is ⌐in Scripture⌐ oftentimes signified by the night ⌐because it is the most discomfortable[487] season.⌐ Then ⌐suingly,[488] the prophet⌐ showeth what is the root of this privation ⌐or taking away of fleshly concupiscence in a man,⌐ saying:

[14]*Providebam Deum semper in conspectu meo:* "I provided[489] God always before my sight." For if a man had God always before his eyes as a ruler of all his works, and in all his works he should neither seek his own lucre,[490] his glory, nor his own pleasure, but only to the pleasure of God, he should shortly be perfect. And forasmuch as he that so doth prospereth in all thing, therefore it followeth:

[15]*Ipse a dextris est mihi ne commovear:* "He is on my right hand, that I be not moved" — or troubled. Then the prophet declareth how great is the felicity of a just man, which shall be everlastingly blessed both in body and in soul, and therefore he saith,

[16]*Laetatum est cor meum:* "My soul is glad," knowing that after death heaven is made ready for him,

[17]*Et caro mea requiescet in spe:* "And my flesh shall rest in hope" — that is to say, that though it joy not by and by,[491] as in receiving his glorious estate immediately after the death, yet it resteth in the sepulchre with this hope: that it shall arise in the Day of Judgment immortal and shining with his soul. And also the prophet more expressly declareth in the verse following. For where he said thus — "My soul is glad" — he addeth the cause, saying:

[18]*Quoniam non derelinques animam in inferno:* "For thou shalt not leave my soul in hell." Also, where the prophet said that his "flesh" should "rest in hope" he showeth the cause, saying:

[19]*Nec dabis sanctum tuum videre corruptionem:* "Nor thou shalt not suffer[492] thy saint to see corruption" — ⌐that is to say, "Thou shalt not suffer the flesh of a good man to be corrupted."⌐ "For that that was corruptible shall arise incorruptible."[493] And forasmuch as Christ was the first which entered paradise, and opened the life unto us, and was the first that rose again and the cause of our resurrection, therefore these words that we have spoken of the resurrection be principally understood of Christ, as Saint Peter the apostle hath declared;[494] and secondarily they may be understood of us, in that we be the members of Christ — which only[495] never saw corruption, for his ⌐holy⌐ body was in his sepulcher nothing putrefied. Forasmuch, then, as the way of good living bringeth us to perpetual life of soul and body, therefore the prophet saith:

[20]*Notas mihi fecisti vias vitae:* "Thou hast made the ways of life known unto me." And because that all the felicity of that standeth[496] in the clear beholding and fruition[497] of God, therefore it followeth:

[21]*Adimplebis me laetitiis* [*sic*] *cum vultu tuo:* "Thou shalt fill me full of gladness with thy cheer." And for that[498] our felicity shall be everlasting, therefore he saith:

[22]*Delectationes in dextra tua usque in finem:* "Delectation[499] and joy shall be on thy right hand forever." He saith "on thy right hand" because that our felicity is fulfilled in the vision and fruition of the humanity of Christ (which sitteth in heaven on the right hand of his Father's majesty), after[500] the words of Saint John: *Haec est tota merces, ut videamus Deum et quem misisti, Iesum Christum* ("This is all our reward: that we may behold God, and Jesus Christ, whom thou hast sent"). To which reward he bring us, that sitteth there and prayeth for us. Amen.

---

481 See Ps 83(84):3.   482 because of   483 next   484 *reins…kidneys:* the seat of the feelings or of sexual desire   485 rebuked   486 deliberately   487 distressing   488 right after that   489 took steps to keep   490 financial gain   491 *by and by:* right away   492 allow   493 1 Cor 15:42   494 Acts 2:25–32   495 alone   496 consists   497 enjoying   498 *for that:* because   499 delight   500 according to

Twelve Rules of John Pico, Earl of Mirandola Partly Exciting, Partly Directing, a Man in Spiritual Battle

5 Whoso to virtue esteemeth hard the way,[501]
Because we must have war continual
Against the world, the flesh, the devil, ⌐that ay[502]
Enforce[503] themselves to make us bond[504] and
   thrall,⌐
Let him remember that choose what way he shall[505]
10 Even after[506] the world, yet must he need sustain[507]
Sorrow, adversity, labor, grief, and pain.

THE SECOND RULE

Think in this wretched world's busy woe
The battle more sharp and longer is iwis[508]
15 With more labor and lessé fruit also,
In which the end of labor, labor is.
⌐And when the world hath left us after this
Void of all virtue, the reward when we die
Is nought[509] but fire⌐ and pain perpetually.

20   ### THE THIRD RULE

Consider ⌐well⌐ that folly it is ⌐and vain[510]⌐
To look for heaven ⌐with pleasure and delight⌐
Since Christ, our ⌐Lord and sovereign⌐ captain
Ascended never but by manly fight
25 And bitter passion.[511] Then were it no right
That any servant, ⌐ye will yourself record,[512]⌐
Should stand in better condition than his lord.[513]

THE FOURTH RULE

Think how that we not only should not grudge[514]
30 But eke[515] be ⌐glad and joyful⌐ of this fight,
And long therefor although[516] we could not judge
How that thereby redound[517] unto us might
Any ⌐profit, but only ⌐for delight⌐
To be conformed and like in some behavior
35 To Jesus Christ, our blessed Lord and Savior.

As often as thou dost warré[518] and strive,
By the resistance of any sinful motion,[519]
Against any of thy sensual wits five,
Cast[520] in thy mind as oft[521] ⌐with good devotion⌐
How thou resemblest Christ, as with sour potion[522] 40
If thou pain thy taste: remember therewithal[523]
How Christ for thee tasted eisell[524] and gall.[525]

If thou withdraw[526] thine handés and forbear[527]
The ravin of anything, remember then
How his ⌐innocent⌐ handés nailéd were.[528] 45
If thou be tempt with pride, think how that "when
He was in form of God, yet of a bondsman[529]
He took the shape and humbled himself" for thee
To the ⌐most odious and vile⌐ death of a tree.[530]

Consider when thou art moved to be wroth 50
He who that was God, and of all men the best,
Seeing himself scornéd and scourgéd both,[531]
And as a thief between two thievés threst[532]
With all rebuke and shame, yet from his breast
Came never sign of wrath or of disdain, 55
But patiently enduréd all the pain.

Thus every snare and engine[533] of the devil
If thou this wise[534] peruse them by and by,[535]
There can be none so curséd or so evil
But ⌐to some virtue thou mayst it apply 60
For oft thou shalt, resisting valiantly
The fiendé's[536] might and subtle fiery dart,⌐
Our Savior Christ resemble in some part.

THE FIFTH RULE

Remember well that we in no wise[537] must, 65
Neither in the foresaid espiritual[538] armor
Nor any other remedy, put our trust,
But only in the strength of our Savior
For he it is by whose mighty power
The world was vanquished and his[539] prince cast out 70
Which reigned before in all the earth about.[540]

In him let us trust to overcome all evil;
In him let us put our hope and confidence
To subdue the flesh and master the devil;

---

501 *Whoso . . . way:* Whoever thinks the way to virtue is hard **502** ever; always **503** Exert **504** enslaved **505** *choose what way he shall:* whatever way he chooses **506** according to **507** endure **508** certainly **509** nothing **510** futile; conceited **511** suffering **512** recall;

remember **513** Mt 10:24; Jn 15:20 **514** complain about; be discontented **515** also **516** even if **517** return **518** war **519** impulse, instigation, incitement **520** Consider **521** *as oft:* just as often **522** medicine **523** with that **524** vinegar **525** Mt 27:34 **526** keep

back **527** refrain from **528** Jn 20:25; Lk 24:39–40 **529** slave **530** Phil 2:6–8 **531** Mt 27:26–31 **532** thrust, Lk 23:32–33 **533** plot; cunning trick **534** way **535** *by and by:* presently; straightway **536** fiend's **537** way **538** spiritual **539** its **540** See Jn 12:31; 1 Jn 5:19; 2 Cor 4:4; Rv 12:9.

75 To him be all honor and lowly reverence.
Oft should we require[541] with all our diligence,
With prayer, ⌐with tears, and lamentable plaints,[542]⌐
The aid of his grace and his holy saints.

THE SIXTH RULE

80 One sinné vanquished, ⌐look thou not tarry[543]⌐
But lie in await[544] for another every hour
For "as a wood[545] lion, the fiend our adversary
Runneth about seeking whom he may devour."[546]
Wherefore continually upon thy tower,[547]
85 Lest he thee unpurveyed[548] and unready catch,
Thou must with the prophet "stand and keep
    watch."[549]

THE SEVENTH RULE

Enforce[550] thyself not only for to stand
Unvanquishéd against the devil's might
90 But over[551] that take valiantly on hand
To vanquish him and put him unto flight,
And that is when of the same deed, thought, or
    sight
By which he would have thee with sin contract,
Thou takest occasion of[552] some good ⌐virtuous⌐
    act.

95 Sometimes he secretly casteth in thy mind
Some laudable deed to steer thee to pride
As vainglory maketh many a man blind;
But let humility be thy sure guide,
Thy good work to God let it be applied.[553]
100 Think it not thine but a gift of his
Of whose grace undoubtedly all goodness is.

THE EIGHTH RULE

In time of battle so put thyself in preace[554]
As though thou shouldest after that victory
105 Enjoy forever a perpetual peace
For God ⌐of His goodness and liberal mercy⌐
May grant the gift, and eke[555] thy proud enemy,
Confounded and ⌐rebuked[556]⌐ by thy battail,[557]
Shall thee no more haply[558] for very shame assail.

But when thou mayest once the triumph obtain, 110
Prepare thyself and trim thee in thy gear[559]
As[560] thou shouldest incontinent[561] fight again:
⌐For if thou be ready, the devil will thee fear.⌐
Wherefore, in any wise,[562] so evin though thee bear[563]
That thou remember and have ever in memory: 115
In victory, battle; in battle, victory.

THE NINTH RULE

If thou think thyself well fenced and sure[564]
Against every subtle suggestion of vice,
⌐Consid'r: frail glass may no distress[565] endure 120
And great adventurers oft curse the dice.
Jeopard[566] not too far therefore and[567] ye be wise,⌐
But evermore eschew[568] the occasions of sin
For "he that loveth peril shall perish therein."[569]

THE TENTH RULE   125

In all temptation, withstand the beginning.
The cursed infants of wretched Babylon
⌐To suffer them wax[570] is a jeopardous[571] thing.⌐
Beat out their brainés therefore at[572] the stone.[573]
⌐Perilous is the canker that catcheth[574] the bone.⌐ 130
Too late cometh the medicine if thou let the sore
By long continuance increase more and more.

THE ELEVENTH RULE

Though in the time of the battle and war
The conflict seemé[575] bitter, sharp, and sore,[576] 135
Yet consider it is more pleasure far
Over the devil to be a conqueror
Than is in the use of thy beastly pleasure.
⌐Of virtue more joy the conscience hath within
Than outward the body of all his filthy sin.⌐ 140

In this point many men err ⌐for[577] negligence⌐
For they compare not the joy of the victory
To the sensual pleasure of their concupiscence,
But like rude beastés unadvisedly,
Lacking discretion, they compare and apply[578] 145
Of their foul sin the voluptuous delight
To the laborous travail[579] of the conflict and fight.

541 ask   **542** wailings, moanings
543 (to) delay   **544** watchfulness
545 raging   **546** 1 Pt 5:8   **547** lookout   **548** unprepared   **549** Hb 2:1
550 Strengthen; Exert   **551** beyond
552 *takest occasion of:* take as an opportunity for   **553** ascribed   **554** the thick of
the fight   **555** also   **556** *confounded and
refuted:* utterly defeated and forced back

557 battle   **558** perhaps   **559** *trim…
gear:* dress yourself in your armor   **560** As
if   **561** immediately   **562** *Wherefore…
wise:* For which reason, in any habitual
manner of action   **563** *so evin though
thee bear:* in such a way steadily yet
conduct yourself   **564** *fenced and sure:*
protected and secure   **565** pressure, strain
566 Risk   **567** if   **568** avoid, shun

569 Ecclus(Sir) 3:26   **570** *suffer them
wax:* allow them to grow   **571** dangerous
572 against   **573** See Ps 136(137):8–9.
574 *canker that catcheth:* corruption that
attacks   **575** seem   **576** grievous, severe
577 out of   **578** liken; weigh against;
make use   **579** oppressive toil

And yet, alas, he that ofté hath known
What grief it is by long experience
150 Of his cruel enemy to be overthrown,
Should once at the leastwise do his diligence
To prove and assay[580] with manly defense
What pleasure there is, what honor, peace, and rest,
In glorious victory, triumph, and conquest.

155   THE TWELFTH RULE

Though thou be tempted, despair thee nothing.
Remember the glorious apostle Saint Paul:
When he had seen God in his perfect being,
Lest such revelation should his heart extol,
160 His flesh was suffered[581] rebel against the soul.
This did almighty God of his goodness provide
To preserve his servant from the danger of pride.

And here take heed that he whom God did love,
And for his most especial vessel chose,[582]
165 "Ravished[583] into the third heaven" above,
Yet stood in peril lest pride might him depose.[584]
Well ought we then our heartés fence[585] and close
Against[586] vainglory, ⌐the mother of reprief,[587]¬
The ⌐very crop[588] and¬ root of all mischief.

170 Against this ⌐pomp and wretched worldé's gloss,[589]¬
Consider how Christ the Lord sovereign power
Humbled himself for us unto the cross—
And ⌐peradventure[590]¬ death ⌐within one hour¬
⌐Shall us bereave wealth,[591] riches, and honor,¬
175 And bring us down full low, ⌐both small and great,¬
To[592] ⌐vile carrion and wretched¬ wormés' meat.

⌐THE TWELVE WEAPONS OF
SPIRITUAL BATTLE
which every man should have at
hand when the pleasure of a sinful
temptation cometh to his mind¬   5

The pleasure little and short.
The followers grief and heaviness.[593]
The loss of a better thing.
This life a dream and a shadow.
The death at our hand and unware.   10
The fear of impenitent departing.
Eternal joy, eternal pain.
The nature and dignity of man.
The peace of a good mind.
The ⌐great¬ benefits of God.   15
The ⌐painful¬ cross of Christ.
The witness of martyrs and example of saints.

⌐THE TWELVE WEAPONS
have we more at length
declared,[594] as it followeth.

THE PLEASURE LITTLE AND SHORT

Consider well the pleasure that thou hast: 5
Stand it in touching or in wanton[595] sight,
In vain smell or in thy lickerous tast,[596]
Or finally in whatsoever delight
Occupied is thy wretched appetite,
Thou shalt it find, when thou hast all cast,[597]   10
Little, simple, short, and suddenly past.

THE FOLLOWERS GRIEF AND HEAVINESS

Any good work if thou with labor do,
The labor go'th, the goodness doth remain.
If thou do evil with pleasure joined thereto,   15
The pleasure which thine evil work doth contain
Glideth his way; thou mayst him[598] not restrain.
The evil then in thy breast cleaveth behind
With grudge[599] of heart and heaviness of mind.

---

580 test   **581** allowed to   **582** Acts 9:15
583 Transported   **584** 2 Cor 12:1–10
585 safeguard   **586** In contrast to
587 fault, censure, opprobrious behavior

588 topmost branch   **589** superficial
luster   **590** (that) perhaps   **591** *us bereave
wealth:* strip us of well-being   **592** To the
status of   **593** sadness   **594** set forth

595 unrestrained; lewd   **596** *lickerous
tast:* pleasant or dainty taste   **597** cal-
culated, reckoned   **598** the pleasure
599 discontent

THE LOSS OF A BETTER THING

20   When thou laborest thy pleasure for to buy,
Upon the price look thou thee well advise;[600]
Thou sellest thy soul therefor even by and by[601]
To thy most utter[602] dispiteous enemies.
25   O mad merchant, O foolish merchandise,[603]
To buy a trifle — O childish reckoning[604] —
And pay therefor[605] so dear[606] a precious thing.

⌐THIS⌐ LIFE A DREAM AND A SHADOW

This wretched life (the trust and confidence
30   Of whose continuance maketh us bold to sin)
Thou perceivest well by experience:
Since that hour in which it did begin,
It holdeth on the course and will not lin[607]
But fast it runneth on and passen shall[608]
35   As doth a dream or shadow on the wall.[609]

DEATH AT OUR HAND AND UNWARE[610]

Consider well that ever night and day
While that we busily provide and care
For our disport,[611] revel, mirth, and play,
40   For pleasant melody and dainty fare,[612]
Death stealeth on full slyly and unware:
He lieth at hand and shall us enterprise[613]
We n'wot[614] how soon nor in what manner wise.[615]

FEAR OF IMPENITENT DEPARTING

45   If thou shouldest God offend, think how therefor[616]
Thou were forthwith in very jeopardous case
For haply[617] thou shouldest not live an hour more
Thy sin to cleanse;[618] and though thou haddest space[619]
Yet peradventure[620] shouldest thou lack the grace.
50   Well ought we then be fear'd to done[621] offense
Impenitent lest we departen hence.

ETERNAL REWARD, ETERNAL PAIN

Thou seest this world is but a thoroughfare.
See thou behave thee wisely with thine host.

Hence must thou needs depart naked and bare   55
And after thy desert[622] look to what coast[623]
Thou art conveyed at such time as thy ghost[624]
From this wretched carcass shall dissever:
Be it joy or pain, endure it shall forever.

THE NATURE AND DIGNITY OF MAN   60

Remember how God hath made thee reasonable
Like unto his image and figure.[625]
And for thee suffered pains intolerable
That he for angel never would endure.
Regard, O man, thine excellent nature,   65
Thou that with angel art made to been equall,[626]
For very shame be not the devil's thrall.[627]

THE PEACE OF A GOOD MIND

Why lovest thou so this brittle[628] worldé's joy?
Take all the mirth, take all the fantasies,   70
Take every game, take every wanton[629] toy,
Take every sport[630] that men can thee devise,
And among them all on warrantise[631]
Thou shalt no pleasure comparable find
To th'inward gladness of a virtuous mind.   75

THE ⌐GREAT⌐ BENEFICES OF GOD

Besides that God thee bought and forméd both,[632]
Many a benefit hast thou received of his:
Though thou have moved him often to be wroth
Yet he thee kept hath[633] and brought us up to this,   80
And daily calleth upon[634] thee to his bliss.
How mayst thou then to him unloving be
That ever hath been so loving unto thee?

THE ⌐PAINFUL⌐ CROSS OF CHRIST

When thou in flame of the temptation fry'st   85
Think on the very lamentable pain,
Think on the piteous cross of woeful Christ.
Think on his blood beat out at every vein,
Think on his precious heart carved in twain,[635]
Think how for thy redemption all was wrought:[636]   90
Let him not lose that he so dear[637] hath bought.

---

600 consider 601 *even by and by:* quite directly; right then and there 602 complete 603 transaction 604 calculation 605 for it 606 expensive, valuable 607 cease to do so 608 *passen shall:* will pass 609 See Ps 143(144): 4; Eccl 6:12, 8:13; Ws 2:5; Plato's *Republic* 514a–518d. 610 unexpected; unnoticed 611 entertainment 612 *dainty fare:* choice foods

613 attack 614 do not know 615 *manner wise:* kind of way 616 on account of that 617 perhaps 618 *Thy sin to cleanse:* (in which to get) your sin absolved 619 i.e., time 620 perhaps 621 do 622 *after thy desert:* according to what you have merited 623 place 624 soul 625 See Gn 1:26–28. 626 *been equall:* be equal 627 slave 628 fragile; perishable;

unreliable 629 carefree; lustful 630 entertainment 631 *on warrantise:* it can be guaranteed 632 *bought and formed both:* both redeemed and created 633 *thee kept hath:* has kept (taken care) of you 634 *calleth upon:* invites 635 two 636 done 637 *so dear:* at such a high cost

THE WITNESS OF MARTYRS
AND EXAMPLE OF SAINTS

Sin to withstand[638] say not thou lackest might:[639]

95 Such allegations[640] folly it is to use;

The witness of saints' and martyrs' constant fight

Shall thee of slothful cowardice accuse;

God will thee help if thou do not refuse.

If others have stood ere[641] this, thou mayst
    eftsone;[642]

100 Nothing impossible is that hath been done.

THE TWELVE PROPERTIES OR
CONDITIONS[643] OF A LOVER

To love one alone and contemn[644] all others for
    that one.

To think him unhappy that is not with his love.

5 To adorn himself for the pleasure of his love.

To suffer all-thing, though[645] it were death, to be
    with his love.

To desire also to suffer harm for his love and to
    think that hurt sweet.

To be with his love ever[646] as he may, if not in deed,
    yet in thought.

To love all-thing that pertaineth unto his love.

10 To covet the praise of his love and not to suffer any
    dispraise.[647]

To believe of his love all things excellent and to
    desire that all folk should think the same.

To weep often with his love: in presence for joy, in
    absence for sorrow.

To languish ever and ever to burn in the desire of
    his love.

To serve his love, nothing thinking of any reward
    or profit.

THE TWELVE PROPERTIES

15 we have at length more openly[648]
expressed in ballade[649] as it followeth.

The first point is to love but one alone

And for that one all others to forsake,[650]

For whoso loveth many, loveth none:

20 The flood that is in many channels take,[651]

In each of them shall feeble streamés[652] make;

The love that is divided among many

Uneath[653] sufficeth that every part have any.

25 So that thou hast thy love set unto God

In thy remembrance this imprint and grave:[654]

As he in sovereign dignity is odd[655]

So will he in love no parting fellows[656] have.

Love him therefore with all that he thee gave,

30 For body, soul, wit, cunning, mind, and thought

Part will he none, but either all or nought.[657]

THE SECOND PROPERTY

Of his love, lo, the sight and company

To the lover so glad and pleasant is

35 That whoso[658] hath the grace to come thereby

He judgeth him in perfect joy and bliss,

And whoso of that company doth miss,[659]

Live he in never so prosperous estate,[660]

He thinketh him wretched and infortunate.

40 So should the lover of God esteem that he

Which[661] all the pleasure hath, mirth and
    disport,[662]

That in this world is possible to be —

Yet till the time that he may once resort[663]

Unto that blessed joyful heavenly port

45 Where he of God may have the glorious sight —

Is void of perfect joy and sure delight.

THE THIRD PROPERTY

The third point of a perfect lover is

To make him fresh, to see that all-thing been

50 Appointed[664] well and nothing set amiss

But all well-fashioned, proper, goodly, clean,

That in his person there be nothing seen

---

638 resist 639 power, ability
640 excuses 641 before 642 again
643 Characteristics 644 disregard
645 even if 646 always 647 *suffer any
dispraise:* tolerate any denigrating (of his

lover) 648 clearly 649 stanzaic verse
(rhyme royal) 650 renounce, give up
651 carried 652 streams 653 Scarcely
654 engrave 655 matchless; unique;
alone 656 *parting fellows:* partners;

sharers 657 nothing 658 whoever
659 *of … miss:* is lacking that company
660 condition or state 661 Who
662 entertainment 663 *may once resort:*
can finally go 664 Put in order, arranged

In speech, apparel, gesture, look, or pace[665]
That may offend or minish[666] any grace.

55 So thou that wilt[667] with God get into favor,
Garnish[668] thyself up in as goodly wise[669] —
As comely[670] be as honest in behavior
As it is possible for thee to devise:
I mean not hereby that thou shouldest arise
60 And in the glass[671] upon thy body prowl[672]
But with fair virtue to adorn thy soul.

THE FOURTH PROPERTY

If love be strong, hot, mighty, and fervent,
There may no trouble, grief, or sorrow fall[673]
65 But that the lover would be well content
All to endure and think it eke[674] too small,
Though[675] it were death, so he might therewithal[676]
The joyful presence of that person get
On whom he hath his heart and love i-set.[677]

70 Thus should of God the lover[678] be content
Any distress or sorrow to endure
Rather than to be from God absent,
And glad to die so[679] that he may be sure
By his departing hence for to procure
75 After this valley dark, the heavenly light,
And of his love, the glorious blessed sight.

THE FIFTH PROPERTY

Not only a lover content is in his heart
But coveteth eke[680] and longeth to sustain
80 Some labor, incommodity, or smart,[681]
Loss, adversity, trouble, grief, or pain,
And of his sorrow joyful is and fain[682]
And happy thinketh himself that he may take
Some misadventure for his lover's sake.

85 Thus shouldest thou that lovest God also
In thine heart wisshe, covet, and be glad
For him to suffer trouble, pain, and woe,
For whom, if thou be never so woe-bestead,[683]
Yet thou ne shalt[684] sustain (be not a-dread[685])

Half the dolor, grief, and adversity   90
That he already suffered hath for thee.

THE SIXTH PROPERTY

The perfect lover longeth for to be
In presence of his love both night and day,
And if it haply[686] so befall that he   95
May not as he would, he will yet as he may
Ever be with his love: that is to say,
Where his heavy body n'ill[687] be brought
He will be conversant[688] in mind and thought.

Lo, in like manner the lover of God should   100
At the least in such wise as he may,
If he may not in such wise as he would,
Be present with God and conversant alway,
For certes[689] whoso list,[690] he may purvey[691] —
Though all the world would him there from   105
    bereaven[692] —
To bear his body in earth, his mind in heaven.

THE SEVENTH PROPERTY

There is no page or servant, most or least,
That doth upon his love attend and wait —
There is no little worm, no simple beast,   110
Ne[693] none so small a trifle or conceit[694]
(Lace, girdle, point,[695] or proper glove strait[696]) —
But that if to his love it have been near,
The lover hath[697] it precious, lief,[698] and dear.

So every relic, image, or picture   115
That doth pertain to God's magnificence,
The lover of God should with all busy cure[699]
Have[700] it in love, honor, and reverence,
And specially give them preeminence
Which,[701] daily done, his blessed Body wurch[702] 120
The quick[703] relics, the ministers of his Church.

THE EIGHTH PROPERTY

A very[704] lover above all earthly thing
Coveteth and longeth evermore to hear
Th' honor, laud, commendation, and praising,   125

---

665 gait; manner of movement
666 diminish 667 want to 668 Spruce;
clothe in an elegant fashion 669 a way
670 attractive 671 mirror 672 carefully
inspect 673 come; happen 674 moreover, also 675 Even if 676 along with
it 677 set 678 *of God the lover:* the
lover of God 679 provided 680 in

addition 681 *incommodity, or smart:*
inconvenience, or pain 682 glad
683 *never so woe-bestead:* no matter how
beset by affliction 684 *ne shalt:* shall
not 685 afraid 686 by chance; perhaps
687 will not 688 speaking and interact-
ing with, dwelling habitually 689 certainly 690 *whoso list:* whoever wants to

691 arrange; make plans 692 deprive him
693 Nor 694 ornament 695 needle-
point; embroidery 696 tight-fitting
697 holds 698 beloved 699 concern
700 Holds 701 Who 702 works; i.e.,
makes (at the Consecration) 703 living
704 true

And everything that may the fame clear[705]
Of his love; he may in no manner
Endure to hear that therefrom mighten vary[706]
Or anything sound into[707] the contrary.

130 The lover of God should covet in like wise[708]
To hear his honor, worship, laud, and praise,
Whose sovereign goodness none heart may
    comprise,[709]
Whom hell, earth, and all the heaven obeys,
Whose perfect lover ought by no manner ways[710]
135 To suffer[711] the cursed words of blasphemy
Or anything spoken of God unreverently.

THE NINTH PROPERTY

A very lover believeth in his mind
On whomsoever he hath his heart i-bent[712]
140 That in that person men may nothing find
But honorable, worthy, and excellent,
And eke[713] surmounting far in his intent
All others that he hath known by sight or name,
And would that every man should think the same.

145 Of God likewise so wonderful and high
All-thing esteem and judge his lover ought —
So reverence, worship, honor, and magnify[714] —
That all the creatures in this world i-wrought[715]
In comparison should he set at nought[716]
150 And glad be if he might the means devise
That all the world would thinken in like wise.[717]

THE TENTH PROPERTY

The lover is of color dead and pale;
There will no sleep into his eyen stalk;[718]
155 He savoreth neither meat, wine, nor ale;
He mindeth not what men about him talk;
But eat he, drink he, sit, lie down, or walk,
He burneth ever as it were with a fire
In the fervent heat of his desire.

160 Here should the lover of God ensample[719] take
To have him continually in remembrance,

With him in prayer and meditation wake[720]
While others play, revel, sing, and dance:
None earthly joy, disport,[721] or vain pleasance[722]
Should him delight, or anything remove   165
His ardent mind from God, his heavenly love.

THE ELEVENTH PROPERTY

Diversely passioned is the lover's heart:
Now pleasant hope, now dread and grievous fere;[723]
Now perfect bliss, now bitter sorrow smart.[724]   170
And whether his love be with him or elésewhere,
Oft from his eyen there falleth many a tere:[725]
For very joy, when they together be;
When they be sundered, for adversity.

Like affectionés[726] feeleth eke[727] the breast   175
Of Godé's lover in prayer and meditation:
When that his love liketh in him rest[728]
With inward gladness of pleasant contemplation,
Out break the tears for joy and delectation;[729]
And when his love list eft[730] to part him fro,   180
Out break the tears again for pain and woe.

THE TWELFTH PROPERTY

A very[731] lover will his love obey:
His joy it is and all his appetite
To pain himself in all that ever he may   185
That person in whom he set hath[732] his delight
Diligently to serve both day and night
For very love, without any regard
To any profit, guerdon,[733] or reward.

So thou likewise that hast thine heart i-set[734]   190
Upward to God, so well thyself endeavor,
So studiously, that nothing may thee let[735]
Nor from his service any wise dissever:[736]
Freely, look eke[737] thou serve — that thereto[738] never
Trust of reward or profit do thee bind   195
But only faithful heart and loving mind.⌐

Wageless to serve, three thingés may us move:[739]
First, if the service self[740] be desirable;

---

705 i.e., make clear or known   706 be
at odds with   707 *sound into:* spoken
to   708 manner   709 comprehend
710 *by no manner ways:* in no kind of way
711 tolerate   712 bent   713 moreover;
also   714 praise   715 wrought, made
716 *set at nought:* regard as nothing

717 *in like wise:* the same way   718 *eyen
stalk:* eyes enter stealthily   719 example
720 keep vigil   721 entertainment
722 pleasure   723 fear   724 keen
725 tear   726 emotions   727 also
728 *liketh . . . rest:* desires to remain
729 delight   730 *list eft:* chooses

afterward   731 true   732 *set hath:*
has placed   733 recompense   734 set
735 hinder   736 *any wise dissever:* in any
way cut you off   737 also   738 i.e., to
his service   739 *Wageless . . . move:* Three
things may motivate us to serve without
pay   740 itself

Second, if they whom that we serve and love
200 Be very good and very amiable;
Thirdly, ⌐of reason⌐[741] be we serviceable[742]
Without the gaping after any[743] more⌐
To such as[744] have done much for us before.

Serve God for love then, not for hope of meed.[745]
205 What service may so desirable be
As where all turneth to thine own speed?[746]
Who is so good, so lovely eke,[747] as he
Who hath already done so much for thee?
As he that first thee made, and on the rood[748]
210 Eft[749] thee redeeméd with his precious blood?

A PRAYER OF
PICO MIRANDOLA UNTO GOD

O holy God of dreadful[750] majesty,
Verily one in three and three in one,
5 Whom angels serve, whose work all creatures be,
Which[751] heaven and earth directest all alone:
We thee beseech, good Lord, with woeful moan,
Spare us wretches and wash away our guilt
That we be not by thy just anger spilt.[752]

10 In strait balance[753] of rigorous judgment
If thou shouldest our sin ponder and weigh,
Who able were to bear thy punishment?[754]
The whole engine[755] of all this world, ⌐I say,⌐
The engine that enduren shall for ay,[756]
15 ⌐With such examination⌐ might not stand
⌐Space of a moment[757] in⌐ thine angry hand.

Who is not born in sin original?
Who doth not actual[758] sin in sundry wise?[759]
But thou, good Lord, art he that sparest all
20 With piteous mercy tempering justice;
For as thou dost rewardés us devise
Above our merit,[760] so dost thou dispense
Thy punishment far under our offense.

More is thy mercy far than all our sin:
To give[761] them also that unworthy be   25
More godly is, ⌐and more mercy therein.⌐
Howbeit, worthy enough are they, pardie,[762]
Be they never so[763] unworthy, whom that he
List[764] to accept, which wheresoever he taketh
Whom he unworthy findeth, worthy maketh.[765]   30

Wherefore, ⌐good Lord, that ay[766] merciful art,
Unto thy grace and sovereign dignity
We seely[767] wretches cry with humble heart:
Our sin forget and our malignity;⌐
With piteous eyes of thy benignity   35
Friendly look on us once;[768] thine own we be,
Servants or sinners, whether it liketh thee.

Sinners, if thou our crime behold certain,
Our crime, the work of our uncourteous mind,
But if thy giftés thou behold again[769]—   40
Thy giftés noble, wonderful, and kind—
Thou shalt us then the same personés find
Which[770] are to thee, and have be long space,[771]
Servants by nature, children by thy grace.

But this thy goodness wringeth[772] us, alas;   45
For we whom grace had made thy children dear
Are made thy guilty folk by our trespass.
Sin hath us guilty made this many a year,
But let thy grace, thy grace that hath no peer,
Of our offense surmounten all the preace[773]   50
That in our sin thine honor may increase.

For though thy wisdom, though thy sovereign
    power,
May otherwise appear sufficiently—
As thingés which thy creatures every hour
All with one voice declare and testify   55
Thy goodness—yet thy singular mercy,
Thy piteous heart, thy gracious indulgence
Nothing so clearly showeth as our offense.

---

741 *of reason:* as is reasonable   **742** ready and willing to do service   **743** *gaping… any:* striving after anything   **744** *such as:* those who   **745** reward; pay   **746** success   **747** *lovely eke:* lovable also   **748** cross   **749** Afterwards   **750** awe-inspiring   **751** Who   **752** destroyed   **753** *In strait balance:* On a strict scale   **754** See Ps 129(130):3, 142(143):2.   **755** *whole engine:* universal frame   **756** forever   **757** *Space… moment:* Even for a moment   **758** personally committed, as opposed to inherited (original)   **759** *sundry wise:* many different ways   **760** *rewardés… merit:* provide us rewards beyond what we deserve   **761** give to   **762** from "by God" (French); certainly   **763** *never so:* no matter how   **764** Chooses   **765** *which… he maketh:* who, (referring to God) no matter where or how unworthy he finds them, God makes them worthy   **766** always   **767** poor; pitiful   **768** under any circumstance; as an emphatic: simply   **769** in turn   **770** Who   **771** *be… space:* been for a long time   **772** pains   **773** distress; difficulty

What but our sin hath showed that mighty love,
60   Which able was thy dreadful majesty
To draw down into earth from heaven above
And crucify God, that we, poor wretches we,
Should from our filthy sin i-cleansèd[774] be
With blood and water of thine own side[775]
65   That streamèd from thy blessèd woundés wide.[776]

Thy love and pity thus, O heavenly King,
Our evil maketh matter of[777] thy goodness.
O love, O pity, our wealth ay providing,[778]
O goodness, serving thy servants ⌐in distress,⌐
70   O love, O pity, well nigh now thankless,
O goodness ⌐mighty, gracious, and wise⌐ —
And yet almost now vanquished with our vice —

Grant, I thee pray, such heat into mine heart
That to this love of thine may be egall;[779]

Grant me from Satana's service to astart[780]   75
With whom me rueth[781] so long to have be thrall;
Grant me, ⌐good Lord and Creator of all,⌐
The flame to quench of all sinful desire
And in thy love set all mine heart afire,

That when the journey of this deadly[782] life   80
My seely ghost[783] hath finished, and thence
Departen must ⌐without his fleshly wife,[784]⌐
Alone, into his Lordé's ⌐high⌐ presence,
He may thee find, ⌐O well of indulgence,⌐
⌐In thy lordship⌐ not as a lord, but rather   85
As ⌐a very tender loving⌐ father.
                    ⌐Amen.⌐

Imprinted at London by John Rastell
dwelling at the Fleet Bridge at the Abbot
of Winchcombe, his[785] place.   90

---

774 cleansed   **775** Jn 19:34   **776** i.e.,
far and wide   **777** for   **778** *ay
providing:* always arranging for

779 equal   **780** escape   **781** *me rueth:*
I regret   **782** mortal   **783** *seely ghost:*

poor soul   **784** *fleshly wife:* i.e., the body
785 *Winchcombe, his:* Winchcombe's

The History of King Richard III

Unpublished during More's life, *The History of Richard the Third* exists in two distinct versions, English and Latin. According to William Rastell, who published the English text in the 1557 *Workes*, More wrote the *History* "about 1513," while serving as undersheriff of London. Although More may have started the *History* in 1513, he worked on it until at least 1514, and likely through 1518, if not beyond (*CW* 2: lxv). After More's death in 1535, the English *History* circulated in manuscript before it was incorporated, with corruptions, into the English chronicle histories of John Harding and Edward Hall. A more accurate English version was not published until Rastell's 1557 edition, while the Latin version first saw print in the 1565 *Opera omnia*. Both versions are apparently unfinished.

As early biographer Thomas Stapleton relates, More "studied with avidity all the historical works he could find," both contemporary and classical. Following Cicero, Renaissance humanists understood history as a part of rhetoric, especially demonstrative rhetoric. For More, the classical historians provide the best models for imitation, particularly Sallust and Tacitus, and help explain why More was less concerned with modern "accuracy" in certain details. After Sallust and Tacitus, St. Augustine emerges as another major influence on More's understanding of history. More lectured publicly on *The City of God* in London in 1501, "not from a theological point of view, but from the standpoint of history and philosophy," as Stapleton relates.

In humanist fashion, More's *imitatio* is more creative than simple repetition or echoing. As Petrarch wrote of imitation, "we must write just as bees make honey, not keeping the flowers but turning them into a sweetness of our own, blending many different flavors into one." Articulating what More "turns" his sources into through the *History* remains the reader's challenge, an invitation to consider what's uniquely Morean about this artful "blending."

More's *History* is mediated through its narrator, whose ironic voice suggests that discovering the truth will prove a challenge. The narrator introduces characters, makes asides, and relates what he has heard from various sources. He also conveys a sense of limits: "But of all this point there is no certainty," he admits regarding one question, "and whosoever divines upon conjectures may as well shoot too far as too short." Throughout the *History*, the narrator frequently withholds his judgment, and instead offers the reader two or more possibilities, leaving interpretation open. Confronted with multiple possibilities, readers must consider matters carefully and exercise their own judgment. As More contends in his 1518 "Letter to Oxford University," such serious study of history and literature helps foster "prudence in human affairs," and even "prepares the soul for virtue."

Throughout the *History*, More is further concerned with the questions of fate, freedom, and law. Considering how Richard obtained the office of Protector, for example, the narrator asks whether Richard rose through "destiny" or "folly," and leaves the question unanswered. Another emphasis in the *History* is the role law plays in Richard's unfolding tyranny. The "sanctuary scene," for example, raises questions about the purposes of law, the relationship between various kinds of law (divine law, natural law, and positive law), and the relationship between law and royal power. An experienced lawyer and judge, the author brings to bear the historical knowledge and practice of law, well aware of its abuses. However one approaches this work, More's *History* remains a provocative study of tyranny, a representation of a country and characters in the throes of violence — and in need of a renaissance.

Note on the text: Our text of the English *History* follows Richard Sylvester's edition in *CW* 2, based on Rastell's text from the 1557 *Workes* — with references to its many proverbs given by Andrea Frank. See her "Proverbs and Irony: Their Literary Role in Thomas More's *Richard III*" (*Moreana* nos. 195–96 [June 2014]: 211–36). For the Latin text and translation, see *CW* 15. The Latin text is also available on-line at www.essentialmore.org. More's *History* would go on to serve as a major source for Shakespeare's tragedy.

The History of King Richard III

DATES

28 June 1461: Edward IV is crowned king.

1 May 1464: Edward secretly marries Elizabeth Grey.

9 April 1483: Edward IV dies at Westminster.

24 April: Edward V and his escort depart Wales for London.

30 April or 1 May: Anthony Woodville, Richard Grey, and Thomas Vaughan are arrested by Richard; Elizabeth Woodville, Edward IV's queen, enters sanctuary with her younger son.

10 May: Richard is named Lord Protector.

19 May: Edward V enters the Tower of London.

13 June: Hastings is executed and Bishop Morton is arrested.

16 June: Edward V's younger brother Richard is removed from sanctuary and enters the Tower.

22 June: Dr. Shaw preaches a sermon which describes Edward IV's children as illegitimate.

24 June: The Duke of Buckingham gives a speech at the Guildhall supporting Richard's claim.

25 June: Anthony Woodville, Richard Grey, and Thomas Vaughan are executed.

25 or 26 June: Buckingham publicly offers Richard the crown at Baynard's Castle.

26 June: Richard accepts the crown at Westminster Hall.

6 July: Richard III is formally crowned.

22 August 1485: Richard is killed at Bosworth Field.

CONTENTS

KINGS AND NOBLES

King Edward IV, oldest son of Richard Duke of York

Edward, Prince of Wales, later King Edward V; oldest son of Edward IV

Richard, Duke of York, second son of Edward IV

George, Duke of Clarence, second son of Richard Duke of York

Richard, Duke of Gloucester, youngest son of Richard Duke of York, later King Richard III

Henry, Earl of Richmond, later King Henry VII

Henry, Duke of Buckingham, Richard's principal collaborator

Richard Neville, Earl of Warwick, "King Maker"

Lord William Hastings, King Edward's Chamberlain

Lord Thomas Stanley, Steward of Edward IV's household

QUEENS AND NOBLES

Queen Elizabeth, wife of Edward IV; formerly Lady Grey

Lord Rivers, Sir Anthony Woodville, her brother; arrested and beheaded

Lord Richard Grey, her second son by Squire John Grey; arrested and beheaded

Marquis of Dorset, Thomas Grey, her oldest son by Squire John Grey

Lord Thomas Vaughan, relative of the Queen; counselor to Edward IV; arrested and beheaded

Duchess of York, mother of Edward IV, Clarence, and Richard III

Elizabeth Lucy, mistress of Edward IV; known only as "a girl of noble blood"

Elizabeth of York, wife of Henry VII, daughter of Edward IV

CLERGY

Cardinal Bourchier, Archbishop of Canterbury

Archbishop of York, Thomas Rotherham

Bishop of Ely, John Morton, Thomas More's early patron; see *Utopia*, Book 1

Bishop of London, John Russell

Doctor Shaa, brother of Mayor Shaa, doctor of divinity

Friar Penker, Provincial of Augustinian Friars

CITIZENS

Edmund Shaa, Mayor of London

Sir William Catesby, lawyer; manager of Hastings's estates

Jane Shore, wife of William Shore; mistress of Edward IV, then of Lord Hastings

Sir John Markham, Chief Justice under Edward IV; resigned rather than illicitly cooperate against Cook

Sir Thomas Cook, a prosperous Londoner brought to trial for political reasons

Thomas Fitzwilliam, Recorder of London

Sir Richard Radcliff, strong supporter of Richard; brother-in-law to Catesby

Sir Robert Brackenbury, Constable of the Tower

Sir James Tyrell, coordinates murder of princes

John Dighton, Tower guard of the princes, enlisted by Tyrell to perform princes' murder

Miles Forest, Tyrell's horsekeeper, enlisted to perform princes' murder

the king (fo2 so was he from that time called) and the people departed, talking diuerslie of the matter, euerie man as his fantasie gaue him. But much they talked and marueiled of the maner of this dealing, that the matter was on both parts made so strange, as though neither had euer communed with other thereof before, when that themselues wist there was no man so dull that heard them, but he perceiued well inough that all the matter was made betwéene them. Howbeit some excused that againe, and said all must be done in god o2der though: and men must sometime fo2 the maners sake, not be aknowen what they know (though it be hard to ontreach the circumspect, wise, & vigilant minded man; as the poet saith:

I made match to cousen the people.

Iuuenal.sat.3.

—————*non facile est tibi*
Decipere Vlyssem.]
Fo2 at the consecration of a bishop, euerie man wooteth well by the paieng fo2 his buls, that he purpo-

seth to be one, & though he paie fo2 nothing else. And yet must he be twise asked whether he will be bishop o2 no, and he must twise saie naie, and the third time take it, as compelled therevnto by his owne will. And in a stage plaie, all the people know right well, that one plaieng the Soldan, is percase a sowter: yet if one should can so litle good, to shew out of season what aquaintance he hath with him, and call him by his owne name while he standeth in his maiestie, one of his to2mento2s might hap to breake his head (and wo2thie, fo2 marring of the plaie. And so they said, that these matters be kings games, as it were stage plaies, and fo2 the mo2e part plaied vpon scaffolds, in which po2e men be but the lookers on. And they that wise be will meddle no further. Fo2 they that sometime step vp, and plaie with them, when they can not plaie their parts, they diso2der the plaie, and do themselues no good.

Thus farre Edward the fift, who was neuer king crowned, but shamefullie
by his vncle slaine, as in the processe following appeereth.

Richard the third, third sonne
to Richard duke of Yorke, and vncle
to Edward the fift.

Anno Reg.1
1483

(*) This that is here be-
twéene this marke & this
marke (*) was not written by maister
More in this histo2ie writt-
en by him in English, but is translated
out of this hi-
sto2ie which he wrote in
Latine,

THe next daie the p2otec-
to2 with a great traine went to Westminster hall, & there when he had placed himselfe in the court of the kings bench, declared to the audi-
ence, that he would take vpon him the crowne in that place there, where the king himselfe sitteth and ministreth the law, bicause he considered that it was the chiefest dutie of a king to minister the lawes. Then with as pleasant an o2ation as he could, he went about to win vnto him the nobles, the merchants, the artificers, and in conclusion all kind of men, but especial-
lie the lawiers of this realme. And finallie, to the in-
tent that no man should hate him fo2 feare, and that his deceitfull clemencie might get him the good will of the people, when he had declared the discommodi-
ties of disco2d, & the commodities of concord & vnitie, he made an open p2oclamation, that he did put out of his mind all enmities, and that he there did openlie pardon all offenses committed against him.

And to the intent that he might shew a p2oofe ther-
of, he commanded that one Fog, whom he had long deadlie hated, should be b2ought then before him, who being b2ought out of the sanctuarie (fo2 thither had he fled fo2 feare of him) in the sight of the people, he tooke him by the hand. Which thing the common people re-
ioised at, and p2aised, but wise men tooke it fo2 a vani-
tie. In his returne homeward, whom so euer he met, he saluted. Fo2 a mind that knoweth it selfe guiltie,

is in a manner deiected to a seruile flatterie (which refuseth no dutifulnesse, tend the same to neuer so vile a degrée of indignitie; which one noteth, saieng:

—————*rides? maiore cachinno*
Concutitur; flet, si lachrymas aspexit amici;
Frigescis? frigets? si dixerit, æstuo, sudat.]
When he had begun his reigne in the moneth of June, after this mockish election, then was he crowned king in the verie same moneth. And that so-
lemnitie was furnished, fo2 the most part, with the selfe same p2ouision that was appointed fo2 the co2o-
nation of his nephue. (*) But here to shew the man-
ner of his co2onation, as the same is inserted in this pamphlet by maister Thomas More, by maister Edward Hall and Richard Grafton (although not found in the same pamphlet) thus line we find it by them repo2ted. (*) First, to be sure of all enmies (as he thought) he sent fo2 fiue thousand men of the no2th against his co2onation, which came vp euill apparelled, and wo2se harnessed, in rustie harnesse, neither defensible, no2 scou2ed to the sale, which mustered in Finsburie field to the great disdaine of the lookers on. By which beginning it apéered to the wo2ld that he had his state in suspicion, otherwise he would not haue p2ocured such a power to be attendant at his commandement, and that at such time as (all weapons laid aside) peace and tranquillitie should haue béene sought after fo2 the comfo2ts of the peoples minds, & the safetie of his owne person; but being verie mistrustfull & fraught with carefull thoughts, he was in a maze betwéene hope and feare, according to this verie true saieng:

Solicita

From this marke (*) to this (*) is not found in the Thomas More, but in maister Hall and Grafton.

Holinshed's *Chronicles*, 1587 (the edition Shakespeare would have used), p. 732, credits Thomas More in its marginal notes, indicating what portion is translated from his Latin *Richardi Tertii* and what portion is taken from Hall's and Grafton's edition of More's English *History of King Richard III*.

The History of King Richard III

(unfinished), written by Master Thomas More, then one of the undersheriffs of London, about the year of our Lord 1513. Which work hath been before this time printed, in Harding's Chronicle and in Hall's Chronicle, but very much corrupt in many places, sometimes having less and sometimes having more, and altered in words and whole sentences, much varying from the copy of his own hand, by which this is printed.

King Edward of that name the Fourth, after that[1] he had lived fifty and three years, seven months, and six days, and thereof[2] reigned two and twenty years, one month, and eight days, died at Westminster the ninth day of April, the year of our redemption a thousand four hundred fourscore and three, leaving much fair issue, that is to wit,[3] Edward the Prince,[4] a thirteen year of age; Richard Duke of York, two years younger; Elizabeth, whose fortune and grace was after to be queen, wife unto King Henry the Seventh and mother unto the Eighth; Cecily, not so fortunate as fair; Bridget, which,[5] representing[6] the virtue of her whose name she bore, professed and observed a religious life in Dartford, a house of close[7] nuns; Anne, that[8] was after honorably married unto Thomas, then Lord Howard, and after Earl of Surrey; and Katherine, which[9] long-time tossed in either fortune—sometimes in wealth, oft in adversity[10]—at the last (if this be the last, for yet she liveth) is by the benignity of her nephew King Henry the Eighth in very prosperous estate, and worthy her birth and virtue.

This noble prince deceased at his palace of Westminster, and with great funeral honor and heaviness[11] of his people from thence conveyed, was interred at Windsor: a king of such governance and behavior in time of peace (for in war each party must needs be other's enemy) that there was never any prince of this land attaining the crown by battle so heartily beloved with the substance[12] of the people, nor he himself so specially[13] in any part of his life as at the time of his death. Which[14] favor and affection yet after his decease, by the cruelty, mischief, and trouble of the tempestuous world that followed, highly toward him more increased. At such time as he died, the displeasure of those that bore him grudge for King Henry's sake the Sixth, whom he deposed, was well assuaged, and in effect quenched, in that that many of them were dead in more than twenty years of his reign, a great part of a long life—and many of them in the mean season[15] grown into his favor, of which he was never strange.[16] He was a goodly personage and very princely to behold; of heart courageous, politic[17] in counsel; in adversity nothing abashed, in prosperity rather joyful than proud; in peace just and merciful, in war sharp and fierce; in the field bold and hardy, and nevertheless no farther than wisdom would, adventurous.[18] Whose[19] wars whoso[20] well consider, he shall no less commend his wisdom where he voided,[21] than his manhood where he vanquished. He was of visage lovely, of body mighty, strong, and clean-made,[22] howbeit[23] in

1 *after that:* after   2 of all that time
(Edward in fact died at age forty.)   3 say
4 *the Prince:* the Crown Prince, first in line
for the throne   5 who   6 demonstrating,
showing   7 cloistered   8 who   9 who
10 *either... adversity:* Whit F523; Til F606

11 heavy-heartedness, sadness   12 *with the
substance:* by the majority   13 especially
(beloved)   14 This (a continuative relative
pronoun; see Preface, p. xviii)   15 *mean
season:* meantime   16 stinting, miserly
17 prudent; shrewd; crafty   18 *no...*

adventurous: no more than it would be wise
for him to be bold or seeking adventures
19 i.e., Edward's (a continuative relative)
20 whoever   21 withdrew; retreated
22 properly; proportioned   23 although

his latter days with over-liberal diet somewhat corpulent and burly, and nevertheless not uncomely; he was of[24] youth greatly given to fleshly wantonness, from which health of body in great prosperity and fortune, without a special grace, hardly refraineth. This fault not greatly grieved the people, for neither could any one man's pleasure stretch and extend to the displeasure of very many, and was without violence, and, over[25] that, in his latter days, lessed[26] and well left. In which time of his latter days, this realm was in quiet and prosperous estate: no fear of outward enemies, no war in hand, nor none toward,[27] but such as no man looked for; the people toward[28] the prince, not in a constrained fear, but in a willing and loving obedience; among themselves, the commons[29] in good peace. The lords whom he knew at variance,[30] himself in his deathbed appeased. He had left all gathering of money (which is the only thing that withdraweth the hearts of Englishmen from the prince), nor anything intended he to take in hand, by which he should be driven thereto, for his tribute out of France he had before obtained, and the year foregoing his death, he had obtained Berwick.[31]

And albeit that[32] all the time of his reign, he was with his people so benign, courteous, and so familiar that no part of his virtues was more esteemed, yet that condition in the end of his days (in which many princes by a long-continued sovereignty decline into a proud port[33] from debonair[34] behavior of their beginning) marvelously in him grew and increased: so far-forth that in the summer, the last that ever he saw, his Highness being at Windsor[35] in hunting, sent for the mayor and aldermen of London to him for none other errand but to have them hunt and be merry with him, where he made them not so stately, but so friendly and so familiar cheer, and sent venison from thence so freely into the city, that no one thing in many days before got him either more hearts or more hearty favor among the common people, which oftentimes more esteem and take for greater kindness a little courtesy than a great benefit.

So deceased (as I have said) this noble king in that time in which his life was most desired. Whose[36] love of his people and their entire affection toward him had been to his noble children (having in themselves also as many gifts of nature, as many princely virtues, as much goodly towardness,[37] as their age could receive) a marvelous fortress and sure armor, if division and dissension of their friends had not unarmed them and left them destitute, and the execrable desire of sovereignty provoked him to their destruction which, if either kind or kindness had holden place,[38] must needs have been their chief defense.[39] For Richard the Duke of Gloucester, by nature their uncle, by office their protector, to their father beholden, to themselves by oath and allegiance bounden, all the bands broken that binden man and man together, without any respect of God or the world, unnaturally contrived to bereave them[40] not only their dignity, but also their lives. But forasmuch as[41] this duke's demeanor ministreth[42] in effect all the whole matter whereof this book shall entreat,[43] it is therefore convenient[44] somewhat to show you, ere[45] we farther go, what manner of man this was, that could find in his heart so much mischief to conceive.

Richard Duke of York, a noble man and a mighty, began not by war, but by law, to challenge the crown, putting his claim into the Parliament, where his cause was either for right or favor[46] so far-forth advanced that, King Henry his blood[47] (albeit he[48] had a goodly prince) utterly rejected, the crown was by authority of Parliament entailed[49] unto the Duke of York and his issue male in remainder[50] immediately after the death of King Henry. But the Duke, not enduring so long to tarry, but intending, under pretext of dissension and debate arising in the realm, to prevent[51] his time and to take upon him the rule in King Harry his[52] life, was with many nobles of the realm at Wakefield[53] slain, leaving three sons: Edward, George, and Richard.

All three as they were great states of[54] birth, so were they great and stately of stomach,[55] greedy and

24 since his 25 besides 26 lessened
27 impending 28 in service to 29 commoners 30 dispute, state of discord
31 Berwick Castle, on the Scottish border
32 *albeit that:* although 33 deportment, bearing 34 gracious 35 Windsor, about twenty miles from London, was an important royal residence. 36 Edward's
37 aptitude, disposition 38 *which…*

place: who, if either nature or kinship had prevailed 39 *the execrable…defense:* Whit D167 40 them of 41 *forasmuch as:* because 42 provides 43 treat
44 appropriate 45 before 46 *either… favor:* Til R126 47 *King Henry his blood:* (with) King Henry's bloodline, descendants 48 King Henry VI 49 bestowed in such a way that the designated person

may not bequeath the possessions to others
50 a legal property right that comes into existence only upon the death of the heir
51 act before 52 *Harry his:* Harry's (i.e., King Henry's) 53 a battle in Yorkshire, on Deccember 30, 1460 54 *states of:* noblemen by 55 *stately of stomach:* proud in disposition

ambitious of authority, and impatient of partners. Edward, revenging his father's death, deprived[56] King Henry and attained the crown. George Duke of Clarence was a goodly noble prince and at all points fortunate, if either his own ambition had not set him against his brother, or the envy of his enemies, his brother against him. For were it by the Queen and the lords of her blood, which highly maligned the King's kindred (as women commonly, not of malice but of nature, hate them whom their husbands love),[57] or were it a proud appetite of the Duke himself intending to be king, at the leastwise heinous treason was there laid to his charge, and finally, were he faulty, were he faultless, attainted[58] was he by Parliament, and judged to the death, and thereupon hastily drowned in a butt of malmsey,[59] whose death King Edward (albeit he commanded it), when he wist[60] it was done, piteously bewailed and sorrowfully repented.

Richard, the third son, of whom we now entreat,[61] was in wit and courage equal with either of them, in body and prowess[62] far under them both: little of stature, ill-featured of limbs, crookbacked,[63] his left shoulder much higher than his right, hard-favored[64] of visage, and such as is in states[65] called warly,[66] in other men otherwise. He was malicious, wrathful, envious, and, from afore his birth, ever froward.[67] It is for truth reported that the duchess his mother had so much ado in her travail[68] that she could not be delivered of him uncut, and that he came into the world with the feet forward,[69] as men be borne outward,[70] and (as the fame runneth) also not untoothed—whether men of hatred report above the truth,[71] or else that nature changed her course in his beginning, which[72] in the course of his life many things unnaturally committed.

None evil[73] captain was he in the war, as to which his disposition was more meetly[74] than for peace. Sundry victories had he, and sometimes overthrows, but never in default[75] as for his own person,[76] either of hardiness or politic order. Free was he called of dispense,[77] and somewhat above his power liberal;[78]

with large gifts he got him unsteadfast friendship, for which he was fain to pill and spoil[79] in other places, and get him steadfast hatred.

He was close[80] and secret, a deep dissimuler,[81] lowly of countenance,[82] arrogant of heart, outwardly companable[83] where he inwardly hated,[84] not letting[85] to kiss whom he thought to kill:[86] dispiteous and cruel, not for evil will always, but often for ambition, and either for the surety or increase of his estate. Friend and foe was muchwhat[87] indifferent: where his advantage grew, he spared no man's death whose life withstood his purpose. He slew with his own hands King Henry the Sixth, being prisoner in the Tower, as men constantly say, and that without commandment or knowledge of the King, which[88] would undoubtedly, if he had intended that thing, have appointed that butcherly office to some other than his own born brother.

Some wise men also ween[89] that his drift,[90] covertly conveyed, lacked not in helping forth his brother of Clarence to his death, which he resisted openly, howbeit[91] somewhat (as men deemed) more faintly than he that were heartily minded to his wealth.[92] And they that thus deem, think that he long-time in King Edward's life forethought to be king in case that the King his brother (whose life he looked that evil diet should shorten) should happen to decease (as indeed he did) while his children were young. And they deem that for this intent he was glad of his brother's death, the Duke of Clarence, whose life must needs have hindered him so intending, whether the same Duke of Clarence had kept him true to his nephew the young king or enterprised to be king himself. But of all this point is there no certainty, and whoso divineth upon conjectures may as well shoot too far as too short.

Howbeit,[93] this have I by credible information learned, that the self[94] night in which King Edward died, one Mistlebrook, long ere[95] morning, came in great haste to the house of one Potter dwelling in Redcross Street without[96] Cripplegate; and when he was with hasty rapping quickly letten in, he showed

---

56 deposed　**57** *women … husbands love:* Whit W540; Euripides' *Andromache* 181–82　**58** convicted　**59** *butt of malmsey:* barrel of a strong, sweet wine　**60** knew　**61** treat　**62** virtue; excellence　**63** hunchbacked　**64** ugly **65** noblemen　**66** warlike　**67** perverse **68** *ado … travail:* trouble in her labor **69** *he … forward:* Til T234　**70** out of

the world　**71** *men … truth:* Whit M310 **72** who　**73** *none evil:* not an unskillful **74** suitable　**75** *in default:* lacking **76** *as … person:* personally　**77** spending **78** *above … liberal:* generous beyond his means　**79** *fain … spoil:* inclined to pillage and steal　**80** private　**81** dissembler. *He … dissimuler:* Til D386　**82** *lowly of countenance:* humble in appearance

83 companionable　**84** *arrogant … hated:* Whit C174, S138　**85** refraining　**86** *to kiss … to kill:* Whit J68; Til J92　**87** pretty much　**88** who　**89** believe　**90** scheme, plot, design　**91** although　**92** well-being **93** However　**94** same　**95** before **96** outside

unto Potter that King Edward was departed. "By my troth,[97] man," quoth Potter, "then will my master, the Duke of Gloucester, be king." What cause he had so to think, hard it is to say — whether he, being toward[98] him, anything knew that he such thing purposed, or otherwise had any inkling thereof[99] — for he was not likely to speak it of nought.[100]

But now to return to the course of this history: were it that the Duke of Gloucester had of old foreminded[101] this conclusion, or was now at erst[102] thereunto moved and put in hope by the occasion of the tender age of the young princes, his nephews (as opportunity and likelihood of speed[103] putteth a man in courage of that he never intended),[104] certain is it that he contrived their destruction, with the usurpation of the regal dignity upon himself. And, forasmuch as he well wist[105] and helped to maintain a long-continued grudge and heartburning[106] between the Queen's kindred and the King's blood, either party envying other's authority, he now thought that their division should be (as it was indeed) a furtherly[107] beginning to the pursuit of his intent, and a sure ground for the foundation of all his building,[108] if he might first, under the pretext of revenging of old displeasure, abuse the anger and ignorance of the one party to the destruction of the other, and then win to his purpose as many as he could; and those that could not be won might be lost ere they looked therefor.[109] For of one thing was he certain: that if his intent were perceived, he should soon have made peace between the both parties, with his own blood.

King Edward in his life, albeit that[110] this dissension between his friends somewhat irked him, yet in his good health he somewhat the less regarded it, because he thought, whatsoever business should fall between them, himself should always be able to rule both the parties. But in his last sickness, when he perceived his natural strength so sore[111] enfeebled that he despaired all recovery, then he, considering the youth of his children — albeit he nothing less mistrusted than that that happened, yet well

foreseeing that many harms might grow by their debate[112] while the youth of his children should lack discretion of themselves and good counsel of their friends, of which either party should counsel for their own commodity[113] and rather by pleasant advice to win themselves favor than by profitable advertisement[114] to do the children good — he called some of them before him that were at variance,[115] and in especial[116] the Lord Marquis Dorset,[117] the Queen's son by her first husband, and Richard the Lord Hastings, a noble man, then Lord Chamberlain, again[118] whom the Queen specially grudged for the great favor the King bore him, and also for that[119] she thought him secretly familiar with the King in wanton company. Her kindred also bore him sore,[120] as well for that the King had made him captain of Calais[121] (which office the Lord Rivers,[122] brother to the Queen, claimed of the King's former promise) as for diverse other great gifts which he received, that they looked for.

When these lords, with diverse others of both the parties, were come in presence,[123] the King, lifting up himself and underset with pillows, as it is reported, on this wise[124] said unto them: "My lords, my dear kinsmen and allies,[125] in what plight I lie, you see and I feel. By which, the less while[126] I look to live with you, the more deeply am I moved to care in what case I leave you; for such as I leave you, such be my children like[127] to find you. Which,[128] if they should (that God forbid) find you at variance, might hap to fall themselves at war ere their discretion would serve to set you at peace. Ye see their youth, of which I reckon the only surety[129] to rest in your concord. For it sufficeth not that all you love them, if each of you hate other. If they were men, your faithfulness haply[130] would suffice. But childhood must be maintained[131] by men's authority, and slipper[132] youth underpropped with elder counsel,[133] which neither they can have but[134] ye give it, nor ye give it if ye gree[135] not. For where each laboreth to break that[136] the other maketh, and for hatred of each of other's person impugneth each other's

97 *By my troth:* Upon my truth or faithfulness **98** in attendance upon **99** *had... thereof:* Whit I46; Til I79 **100** *of nought:* for nothing **101** planned, intended **102** first **103** success **104** *opportunity... intended:* Whit E27; Til O71 **105** knew **106** burning jealousy **107** favorable, adapted to further **108** *a sure... building:* Til F619 **109** *ere they looked therefor:* before they expected it **110** *albeit that:* although **111** greatly **112** strife, dispute **113** advantage **114** instruction, warning **115** dispute **116** *in especial:* in particular **117** Thomas Grey **118** against **119** *for that:* because **120** grievously **121** Calais, in France, was under English control at the time **122** Anthony Woodville **123** the royal presence **124** *on this wise:* in this manner **125** in-laws. See Sallust, *Jugurtha* 9–10. **126** *less while:* shorter time **127** likely **128** Who (the children) **129** security, safety **130** perhaps **131** supported; ruled **132** likely to slip; unreliable **133** *slipper... counsel:* Whit Y36 **134** unless **135** reconcile **136** what counsel, there must it needs be long ere[137] any good conclusion go forward. And also, while either party laboreth to be chief, flattery shall have more place than plain and faithful advice, of which must needs ensue the evil bringing-up of the Prince, whose mind in tender youth infect,[138] shall readily fall to mischief and riot and draw down with this noble realm to ruin, but if[139] grace turn him to wisdom; which, if God send, then they that by evil means before pleased him best, shall after fall farthest out of favor, so that ever at length evil drifts[140] drive to nought,[141] and good plain ways prosper.[142]

"Great variance[143] hath there long been between you, not always for great causes. Sometimes a thing right well intended, our misconstruction turneth unto worse; or a small displeasure done us, either our own affection or evil tongues aggrieveth.[144] But this wot[145] I well: ye never had so great cause of hatred as ye have of love. That we be all men, that we be Christian men, this shall I leave for preachers to tell you (and yet I wot nere[146] whether any preacher's words ought more to move you than his that is, by and by, going to the place that they all preach of). But this shall I desire you to remember, that the one party of you is of my blood, the other of mine allies,[147] and each of you with other, either of kindred or affinity;[148] which spiritual kindred[149] of affinity, if the sacraments of Christ's Church bear that weight with us that would God they did, should no less move us to charity than the respect of fleshly consanguinity.[150] Our Lord forbid that you love together the worse, for the self[151] cause that you ought to love the better. And yet that happeneth. And nowhere find we so deadly debate as among them which by nature and law most ought to agree together. Such a pestilent serpent is ambition and desire of vainglory and sovereignty, which among states[152] where he once entereth creepeth forth so far till with division and variance he turneth all to mischief—first longing to be next the best, afterward equal with the best, and at last chief and above the best. Of which immoderate appetite of worship,[153] and thereby of debate and dissension, what loss, what sorrow, what trouble hath within these

few years grown in this realm, I pray God as well forget as we well remember. Which things if I could as well have foreseen, as I have with my more pain than pleasure proved,[154] by God's blessed Lady"— that was ever his oath—"I would never have won the courtesy of men's knees with the loss of so many heads. But since things past cannot be gaincalled,[155] much ought we the more beware, by what occasion we have taken so great hurt afore, that we eftsoons[156] fall not in that occasion again.

"Now be those griefs past, and all is (God be thanked) quiet, and likely right well to prosper in wealthful peace under your cousins,[157] my children, if God send them life and you love. Of which two things, the less loss were they by whom though God did his pleasure,[158] yet should the realm always find kings, and peradventure[159] as good kings. But if you among yourselves in a child's reign fall at debate, many a good man shall perish and haply[160] he too, and ye too, ere this land find peace again. Wherefore in these last words that ever I look to speak with you, I exhort you and require[161] you all, for the love that you have ever borne to me, for the love that I have ever borne to you, for the love that our Lord beareth to us all, from this time forward, all griefs forgotten, each of you love other.[162] Which I verily[163] trust you will, if ye anything earthly regard— either God or your king, affinity or kindred, this realm, your own country, or your own surety."[164]

And therewithal the King, no longer enduring to sit up, laid him down on his right side, his face toward them; and none was there present that could refrain from weeping. But the lords, recomforting[165] him with as good words as they could, and answering for the time as they thought to stand with his pleasure, there in his presence (as by their words appeared) each forgave other, and joined their hands together, when (as it after appeared by their deeds) their hearts were far asunder.

As soon as the King was departed, the noble Prince his son drew toward London, which at the time of his decease, kept his household at Ludlow in Wales. Which country, being far off from the law and recourse to justice, was begun to be far out of

---

137 before   138 infected   139 *but if:* unless   140 schemes, devices 141 nothing; *evil…nought:* Whit D392 142 *good…prosper:* Til W163; Whit W118 143 disagreement   144 *Sometimes… aggrieveth:* Til T31   145 know   146 *wot*

nere: know not   147 in-laws   148 related by marriage   149 kinship   150 blood-relationship   151 very same   152 noblemen   153 distinction; prestige, renown 154 learned by experience   155 called back again; *things…gaincalled:* Whit D287,

P45; Til T203   156 soon after   157 kins-folk; relatives   158 *his pleasure:* i.e., taking them young   159 perhaps   160 perhaps 161 ask   162 See Jn 13:34–35.   163 truly 164 safety   165 reassuring good will and waxen[166] wild, robbers and reavers[167] walking at liberty uncorrected. And for this encheason[168] the Prince was in the life of his father sent thither, to the end that the authority of his presence should refrain evil-disposed persons from the boldness of their former outrages. To the governance and ordering[169] of this young Prince, at his sending thither, was there appointed Sir Anthony Woodville (Lord Rivers and brother unto the Queen), a right honorable man, as valiant of hand[170] as politic[171] in counsel. Adjoined were there unto him others of the same party, and in effect everyone, as he was nearest of kin unto the Queen, so was planted next about the Prince.

That drift[172] by the Queen not unwisely devised, whereby her blood might of[173] youth be rooted in the Prince's favor, the Duke of Gloucester turned unto their destruction, and upon that ground set the foundation of all his unhappy building. For whomsoever he perceived either at variance[174] with them or bearing himself their favor, he broke[175] unto them, some by mouth, some by writing and secret messengers, that it neither was reason[176] nor in any wise[177] to be suffered that the young King, their master and kinsman, should be in the hands and custody of his mother's kindred, sequestered in manner[178] from their company and attendance, of which every one owed him as faithful service as they, and many of them far more honorable part of kin than his mother's side, "whose blood," quoth he, "saving the King's pleasure, was full unmeetly[179] to be matched with his—which[180] now to be, as who[181] say, removed from the King and the less noble to be left about him, is," quoth he, "neither honorable to his Majesty nor unto us, and also to his Grace no surety,[182] to have the mightiest of his friends from him, and unto us no little jeopardy to suffer[183] our well-proved evil-willers to grow in over-great authority with the Prince in youth, namely which is light of belief[184] and soon persuaded.[185]

"Ye remember, I trow,[186] King Edward himself, albeit[187] he was a man of age and of discretion, yet was he in many things ruled by the bend,[188] more than stood either with his honor or our profit, or with the commodity[189] of any man else, except only the immoderate advancement of themselves. Which,[190] whether they sorer[191] thirsted after their own weal[192] or our woe, it were hard, I ween,[193] to guess. And if some folks' friendship had not holden better place with the King than any respect of kindred, they might peradventure[194] easily have betrapped and brought to confusion[195] some of us ere[196] this. Why not, as easily as they have done some other[197] already, as near of his royal blood as we? But our Lord hath wrought his will, and, thanks be to his grace that peril is past. Howbeit,[198] as great[199] is growing, if we suffer this young king in our enemies' hand, which, without his witting,[200] might abuse the name of his commandment to any of our undoing, which thing God and good provision[201] forbid. Of which good provision none of us hath anything the less need for the late-made atonement,[202] in which the King's pleasure had more place than the parties' wills. Nor none of us, I believe, is so unwise oversoon to trust a new friend made of an old foe,[203] or to think that a hoverly[204] kindness, suddenly contract[205] in one hour, continued yet scant[206] a fortnight, should be deeper settled in their stomachs than a long-accustomed malice many years rooted."

With these words and writings and such other, the Duke of Gloucester soon set afire them that were of themselves easy to kindle,[207] and in especial twain:[208] Edward Duke of Buckingham, and Richard Lord Hastings and Chamberlain—both men of honor and of great power, the one by long succession from his ancestry, the other by his office and the King's favor. These two, not bearing each to other so much love as hatred both unto the Queen's party, in this point accorded together with the Duke of Gloucester, that they would utterly amove[209] from the King's company all his mother's friends, under the name of their enemies.

Upon this concluded, the Duke of Gloucester, understanding that the lords which at that time

166 grown, become 167 raiders
168 reason 169 training, raising
170 *of hand:* in combat 171 prudent;
shrewd; crafty 172 scheme 173 from
his 174 disagreement 175 revealed
176 reasonable 177 way 178 effect
179 *full unmeetly:* completely inappropriate 180 the blood-relations
of Edward's 181 they 182 safety

183 allow 184 *light of belief:* credulous,
gullible 185 *youth . . . persuaded:* Til
Y44 186 trust 187 although 188 *the
bend:* the (Queen's) faction 189 benefit
190 Who (i.e., those who sought their
own advancement) 191 more intensely
192 well-being, advantage 193 think
194 perhaps 195 ruin, destruction
196 before 197 *some other:* George, the

Duke of Clarence 198 However 199 as
great a peril 200 knowing 201 foresight, planning 202 *late-made atonement:*
recent reconciliation 203 *unwise . . .
foe:* Whit F662; Til 373 204 superficial
205 contracted 206 hardly 207 *soon . . .
kindle:* Til N308 208 two 209 remove

were about the King intended to bring him up to his coronation, accompanied with such power[210] of their friends that it should be hard for him to bring his purpose to pass without the gathering and great assembly of people and in manner of open war, whereof the end he wist[211] was doubtous,[212] and in which, the King being on their side, his party should have the face and name of a rebellion, he secretly therefore by diverse means caused the Queen to be persuaded and brought in the mind that it neither were need, and also should be jeopardous, the King to come up strong.[213] For whereas now every lord loved other, and none other thing studied upon but about the coronation and honor of the King, if the lords of her kindred should assemble in the King's name much people, they should give the lords atwixt[214] whom and them had been sometimes debate, to fear and suspect, lest they should gather this people, not for the King's safeguard, whom no man impugned,[215] but for their destruction, having more regard to their old variance[216] than their new atonement. For which cause they should assemble, on the other party, much people again for their defense, whose power, she wist well, far stretched. And thus should all the realm fall on a roar.[217] And of all the hurt that thereof should ensue, which was likely not to be little,[218] and the most harm there like[219] to fall where she least would, all the world would put her and her kindred in the wight,[220] and say that they had unwisely, and untruly also, broken the amity and peace that the King her husband so prudently made between his kin and hers in his deathbed, and which the other party faithfully observed.

The Queen, being in this wise[221] persuaded, such word sent unto her son[222] and unto her brother,[223] being about the King; and over[224] that, the Duke of Gloucester himself and other lords, the chief of his bend,[225] wrote unto the King so reverently, and to the Queen's friends there so lovingly, that they, nothing earthly[226] mistrusting, brought the King up in great haste, not in good speed,[227] with a sober[228] company.

Now was the King in his way to London gone from Northampton, when these Dukes of Gloucester and Buckingham came thither. Where[229] remained behind the Lord Rivers, the King's uncle, intending on the morrow to follow the King and be with him at Stony Stratford (eleven miles thence), early before he departed. So was there made that night much friendly cheer between these dukes and the Lord Rivers a great while.

But incontinent[230] after that they were openly with great courtesy[231] departed and the Lord Rivers lodged, the dukes secretly with a few of their most privy friends set them down in council, wherein they spent a great part of the night. And at their rising in the dawning of the day, they sent about privily to their servants in their inns and lodgings about, giving them commandment to make themselves shortly ready, for their lords were to horsebackward.[232] Upon which messages, many of their folk were attendant, when many of the Lord Rivers's servants were unready. Now had these dukes taken also into their custody the keys of the inn, that none should pass forth without their license. And over[233] this, in the highway toward Stony Stratford where the King lay, they had bestowed[234] certain of their folk that should send back again and compel to return any man that were gotten out of Northampton toward Stony Stratford, till they should give other license, forasmuch as the dukes themselves intended, for the show of their diligence, to be the first that should that day attend upon the King's Highness out of that town: thus bore they folk in hand.[235]

But when the Lord Rivers understood the gates closed and the ways on every side beset, neither his servants nor himself suffered[236] to go out, perceiving well so great a thing without his knowledge not begun for nought, comparing this manner present with this last night's cheer, in so few hours so great a change marvelously misliked. Howbeit,[237] since he could not get away—and keep himself close[238] he would not, lest he should seem to hide himself for some secret fear of his own fault, whereof he saw no such cause in himself—he determined, upon the surety of[239] his own conscience, to go boldly to them and inquire what this matter might mean. Whom,[240] as soon as they saw, they began to quarrel

---

210 a military presence   **211** knew
212 doubtful; *war … doubtous:* Whit B65;
Til C223   **213** with a strong military escort
214 between   **215** attacked   **216** disputes
217 *on a roar:* into turmoil   **218** *of
all … little:* Til E191, M1012   **219** likely
220 blame   **221** way   **222** Richard Grey

223 Anthony Woodville, the second Earl
Rivers   **224** besides   **225** band, faction
226 in all the world   **227** *in great … speed:*
Til H197; Whit H167   **228** moderate in
number   **229** There (in Northampton)
230 immediately   **231** *with … courtesy:*
Til C732   **232** mount their horses

233 besides   **234** stationed   **235** *bore …
hand:* they tricked people   **236** allowed
237 However   **238** enclosed, confined;
keep … close: keep himself confined
239 *surety of:* security given him by
240 Lord Rivers

with him and say that he intended to set distance between the King and them, and to bring them to confusion,[241] but it should not lie in his power. And when he began (as he was a very well-spoken man) in goodly wise to excuse himself, they tarried not the end of his answer, but shortly took him and put him in ward,[242] and, that done, forthwith[243] went to horseback and took the way to Stony Stratford, where they found the King with his company ready to leap on horseback, and depart forward, to leave that lodging for them, because it was too strait[244] for both companies.

And as soon as they came in his presence, they light a-down, with all their company about them. To whom the Duke of Buckingham said, "Go afore, gentlemen and yeomen; keep your rooms."[245] And thus in a goodly array they came to the King, and on their knees in very humble wise saluted his Grace, which received them in very joyous and amiable manner, nothing earthly knowing nor mistrusting as yet. But even by and by,[246] in his presence they picked a quarrel to the Lord Richard Grey, the King's other brother by his mother, saying that he, with the Lord Marquis[247] his brother and the Lord Rivers his uncle, had compassed[248] to rule the King and the realm, and to set variance[249] among the states,[250] and to subdue and destroy the noble blood of the realm. Toward the accomplishing whereof, they said that the Lord Marquis had entered into the Tower of London, and thence taken out the King's treasure, and sent men to the sea. All which things these dukes wist[251] well were done for good purposes and necessary by the whole Council at London, saving that somewhat they must say.[252] Unto which words the King answered, "What my brother Marquis hath done, I cannot say. But in good faith, I dare well answer for mine uncle Rivers and my brother here, that they be innocent of any such matters."

"Yea, my liege," quoth the Duke of Buckingham, "they have kept their dealing in these matters far from the knowledge of your good Grace." And forthwith they arrested the Lord Richard and Sir Thomas Vaughan, Knight, in the King's presence, and brought the King and all back unto Northampton, where they took again further counsel. And there they sent away from the King whom it pleased them, and set new servants about him, such as liked better them than him. At which dealing he wept and was nothing content, but it booted[253] not. And at dinner the Duke of Gloucester sent a dish from his own table to the Lord Rivers, praying him to be of good cheer, all should be well enough. And he thanked the Duke, and prayed the messenger to bear it to his nephew the Lord Richard with the same message for his comfort, who he thought had more need of comfort, as one to whom such adversity was strange. But himself had been all his days in ure therewith,[254] and therefore could bear it the better. But for all this comfortable[255] courtesy of the Duke of Gloucester, he sent the Lord Rivers and the Lord Richard with Sir Thomas Vaughan into the north country into diverse places to prison, and afterward all to Pomfret,[256] where they were in conclusion beheaded.

In this wise[257] the Duke of Gloucester took upon himself the order and governance of the young King, whom with much honor and humble reverence he conveyed upward toward the city. But anon[258] the tidings of this matter came hastily to the Queen, a little before the midnight following, and that in the sorest wise,[259] that the King her son was taken, her brother, her son,[260] and her other friends arrested, and sent no man wist whither, to be done with God wot[261] what. With which tidings the Queen in great flight and heaviness,[262] bewailing her child's ruin, her friends' mischance, and her own infortune,[263] damning the time that ever she dissuaded the gathering of power[264] about the King, got herself in all the haste possible, with her younger son and her daughters, out of the Palace of Westminster, in which she then lay, into the sanctuary, lodging herself and her company there in the abbot's place.

Now came there one in likewise[265] not long after midnight, from the Lord Chamberlain unto the Archbishop of York,[266] then Chancellor of England, to his place not far from Westminster. And for that[267] he showed his[268] servants that he had tidings of so great importance that his master gave him

241 ruin **242** custody **243** immediately **244** small **245** places, stations **246** *by and by:* right away; before long **247** Dorset (Thomas Grey) **248** plotted **249** strife **250** noblemen **251** knew **252** *saving . . . say:* but they had to say

something **253** mattered, helped **254** *in ure therewith:* used to it **255** encouraging **256** also known as Pontefract **257** way **258** at once **259** *sorest wise:* most grievous way **260** Richard Grey **261** knew **262** *flight and heaviness:* agitation and

heavy-heartedness **263** misfortune **264** armed men **265** the same manner **266** Thomas Rotherham **267** *for that:* because **268** the Archbishop's

in charge not to forbear[269] his rest, they letted[270] not to wake him, nor he to admit this messenger into his bedside. Of whom he heard that these dukes were gone back with the King's Grace from Stony Stratford unto Northampton. "Notwithstanding, sir," quoth he, "my lord sendeth your Lordship word that there is no fear. For he assureth you that all shall be well."

"I assure him," quoth the Archbishop, "be it as well as it will, it will never be so well as we have seen it."[271] And thereupon, by and by,[272] after the messenger departed, he caused in all the haste all his servants to be called up; and so with his own household about him, and every man weaponed, he took the Great Seal with him and came, yet before day, unto the Queen. About whom he found much heaviness, rumble,[273] haste, and busyness, carriage and conveyance of her stuff into sanctuary (chests, coffers, packs, fardels, trusses,[274] all on men's backs), no man unoccupied, some lading,[275] some going, some discharging,[276] some coming for more, some breaking down the walls to bring in the next way,[277] and some yet drew to them that helped to carry a wrong way. The Queen herself sat alone, alow on the rushes, all desolate and dismayed, whom the Archbishop comforted in the best manner he could, showing her that he trusted the matter was nothing so sore[278] as she took it for,[279] and that he was put in good hope and out of fear by the message sent him from the Lord Chamberlain.

"Ah, woe worth him"[280] quoth she, "for he is one of them that laboreth to destroy me and my blood."

"Madam," quoth he, "be ye of good cheer. For I assure you, if they crown any other king than your son whom they now have with them, we shall on the morrow crown his brother whom you have here with you. And here is the Great Seal, which in like wise as that noble prince your husband delivered it unto me, so here I deliver it unto you to the use and behoof[281] of your son." And therewith he betook her the Great Seal, and departed home again, yet in the dawning of the day. By which time he might in his chamber window see all the Thames full of boats of the Duke of Gloucester's servants, watching that

no man should go to sanctuary, nor none could pass unsearched. Then was there great commotion and murmur as well in other places about, as specially in the city, the people diversely divining upon this dealing.[282] And some lords, knights, and gentlemen, either for favor of the Queen or for fear of themselves, assembled in sundry companies, and went flock-meal in harness,[283] and many also for that[284] they reckoned this demeanor attempted not so specially against the other lords as against the King himself in the disturbance of his coronation.

But then, by and by, the lords assembled together at London. Toward which meeting, the Archbishop of York, fearing that it would be ascribed (as it was indeed) to his overmuch lightness that he so suddenly had yielded up the Great Seal to the Queen, to whom the custody thereof nothing pertained without especial commandment of the King, secretly sent for the Seal again, and brought it with him after the customable manner. And at this meeting the Lord Hastings, whose troth[285] toward the King no man doubted nor needed to doubt, persuaded the lords to believe that the Duke of Gloucester was sure and fastly faithful to his prince and that the Lord Rivers and Lord Richard, with the other knights, were, for matters attempted by them against the Dukes of Gloucester and Buckingham, put under arrest for their surety, not for the King's jeopardy, and that they were also in safeguard, and there no longer should remain than till the matter were, not by the dukes only but also by all the other lords of the King's Council, indifferently[286] examined and by other discretions ordered, and either judged or appeased. But one thing he advised them beware: that they judged not the matter too far-forth ere[287] they knew the truth,[288] nor turning their private grudges into the common hurt, irritating and provoking men unto anger, and disturbing the King's coronation, toward which the dukes were coming up, that they might peradventure[289] bring the matter so far out of joint[290] that it should never be brought in frame[291] again. Which strife if it should hap as it were likely to come to a field,[292] though both parties were in all other things equal,

---

269 spare 270 hesitated 271 *it will… it:* Whit B277; Til B332 272 *by and by:* directly, soon 273 commotion 274 *fardels, trusses:* parcels, bundles 275 loading 276 unloading 277 *in… way:* in by the nearest possible way 278 grievous

279 *the matter… for:* Til T31 280 *woe worth him:* may evil befall him 281 benefit 282 *the people… dealing:* Whit F370 283 *flock-meal in harness:* by companies in armor 284 *for that:* because 285 loyalty, faithfulness 286 impartially 287 before

288 *judged… truth:* Whit J77 289 perhaps 290 *out of joint:* Whit J54; Til J75 291 *in frame:* in shape, right order; Whit F607 292 battlefield

yet should the authority be on that side where the King is himself.

With these persuasions of the Lord Hastings — whereof part himself believed, of part he wist[293] the contrary — these commotions were somewhat appeased. But specially by that that[294] the Dukes of Gloucester and Buckingham were so near, and came so shortly on with the King, in none other manner, with none other voice or semblance, than to his coronation — causing the fame to be blown about[295] that these lords and knights which were taken had contrived the destruction of the Dukes of Gloucester and Buckingham and of other the noble blood of the realm, to the end that themselves would alone demean[296] and govern the King at their pleasure. And for the colorable[297] proof thereof, such of the dukes' servants as rode with the carts of their stuff that were taken (among which stuff no marvel though some were harness,[298] which at the breaking-up of that household must needs either be brought away or cast away), they showed unto the people all the way as they went: "Lo, here be the barrels of harness that these traitors had privily conveyed in their carriage to destroy the noble lords withal." This device, albeit that[299] it made the matter to wise men more unlikely, well perceiving that the intenders of such a purpose would rather have had their harness on their backs than to have bound them up in barrels, yet much part of the common people were therewith very well satisfied, and said it were alms[300] to hang them.[301]

When the King approached near to the city, Edmund Shaa, goldsmith, then mayor, with William White and John Mathew, sheriffs, and all the other aldermen in scarlet, with five hundred horse of the citizens in violet, received him reverently at Hornsea, and riding from thence, accompanied him into the city, which he entered the fourth day of May, the first and last year of his reign. But the Duke of Gloucester bore him in open sight so reverently to the Prince, with all semblance of lowliness, that from the great obloquy[302] in which he was so late before, he was suddenly fallen in so great trust that at the Council next assembled, he was made the only man chosen and thought most meet[303] to be

Protector of the King and his realm, so that (were it destiny or were it folly) the lamb was betaken to the wolf to keep.[304] At which Council also the Archbishop of York, Chancellor of England, which had delivered up the Great Seal to the Queen, was thereof greatly reproved, and the Seal taken from him and delivered to Doctor Russell, Bishop of Lincoln, a wise man and a good and of much experience, and one of the best-learned men undoubtedly that England had in his time. Diverse lords and knights were appointed unto diverse rooms.[305] The Lord Chamberlain and some others kept still their offices that they had before.

Now, all were it so that the Protector so sore[306] thirsted for the finishing of that he had begun that thought every day a year till it were achieved, yet durst[307] he no further attempt as long as he had but half his prey in his hand, well witting[308] that if he deposed the one brother, all the realm would fall to the other if he either remained in sanctuary or should haply[309] be shortly conveyed to his farther liberty.[310] Wherefore incontinent[311] at the next meeting of the lords at the Council, he proposed unto them that it was a heinous deed of the Queen, and proceeding of great malice toward the King's Councillors, that she should keep in sanctuary the King's brother from him, whose special pleasure and comfort were to have his brother with him — and that by her done to none other intent, but to bring all the lords in obloquy and murmur of the people, as though they were not to be trusted with the King's brother, that[312] by the assent of the nobles of the land were appointed as the King's nearest friends, to the tuition[313] of his own royal person.

"The prosperity whereof standeth," quoth he, "not all in keeping from enemies or ill viand,[314] but partly also in recreation and moderate pleasure, which he cannot in his tender youth take in the company of ancient persons,[315] but in the familiar conversation of those that be neither far under nor far above his age, and nevertheless of estate convenient[316] to accompany his noble Majesty. Wherefore, with whom rather than with his own brother? And if any man think this consideration light (which I think no man thinketh that loveth the King), let him consider

293 knew   **294** *by that that:* by reason that   **295** *fame... blown about:* Whit 643; Til 833   **296** handle, control   **297** ostensible   **298** armor   **299** *albeit that:* although   **300** a good deed; act of charity   **301** *it... them:* Til A2; Whit A113   **302** disrepute, infamy   **303** fit, appropriate   **304** *the lamb... to keep:* Til W602; Whit S215   **305** offices, positions   **306** greatly   **307** dared   **308** knowing   **309** perhaps   **310** *to... liberty:* i.e., out of the country   **311** right away   **312** who   **313** protection, guardianship   **314** *ill viand:* bad food   **315** *which... persons:* Whit Y33; Til Y43   **316** appropriate, fitting

that sometimes without small things greater cannot stand.[317] And verily it redoundeth[318] greatly to the dishonor both of the King's Highness and of all us that are about his Grace, to have it run in every man's mouth, not in this realm only, but also in other lands (as evil words walk far)[319] that the King's brother should be fain[320] to keep sanctuary. For every man will ween[321] that no man will so do for nought.[322] And such evil opinion once fastened in men's hearts, hard it is to wrest out,[323] and may grow to more grief than any man here can divine.

"Wherefore methinketh it were not worst to send unto the Queen, for the redress of this matter, some honorable trusty man, such as both tendereth[324] the King's weal[325] and the honor of his Council, and is also in favor and credence with her. For all which considerations, none seemeth me more meetly[326] than our Reverend Father here present, my Lord Cardinal,[327] who may in this matter do most good of any man, if it please him to take the pain. Which I doubt not of his goodness he will not refuse, for the King's sake and ours, and wealth[328] of the young Duke himself, the King's most honorable brother and, after my Sovereign Lord himself, my most dear nephew — considering that thereby shall be ceased the slanderous rumor and obloquy[329] now going, and the hurts avoided that thereof might ensue, and much rest and quiet grow to all the realm. And if she be percase[330] so obstinate, and so precisely set upon her own will, that neither his wise and faithful advertisement[331] can move her, nor any man's reason content her, then shall we, by mine advice, by the King's authority fetch him out of that prison and bring him to his noble presence, in whose continual company he shall be so well cherished and so honorably entreated[332] that all the world shall, to our honor and her reproach, perceive that it was only malice, frowardness,[333] or folly that caused her to keep him there. This is my mind in this matter for this time, except[334] any of your lordships anything perceive to the contrary. For never shall I, by God's grace, so wed myself to mine own will[335] but that I shall be ready to change it upon your better advices."

When the Protector had said, all the Council affirmed that the motion was good and reasonable, and to the King and the Duke his brother honorable, and a thing that should cease great murmur in the realm, if the mother might be by good means induced to deliver him. Which thing the Archbishop of [Canterbury],[336] whom they all agreed also to be thereto most convenient,[337] took upon him to move her, and therein to do his uttermost devoir.[338] Howbeit,[339] if she could be in no wise entreated with her good will to deliver him, then thought he and such others as were of the spiritualty[340] present that it were not in any wise to be attempted to take him out against her will. For it would be a thing that should turn to the great grudge of all men, and high displeasure of God, if the privilege of that holy place should now be broken, which had so many years been kept, which both kings and popes so good had granted, so many had confirmed, and which holy ground was more than five hundred years ago by Saint Peter, his own person in spirit, accompanied with great multitude of angels, by night so specially hallowed and dedicate to God (for the proof whereof they have yet in the abbey Saint Peter's cope[341] to show) that from that time hitherward[342] was there never so undevout a king that durst that sacred place violate, or so holy a bishop that durst[343] it presume to consecrate. "And therefore," quoth the Archbishop,[344] "God forbid that any man should, for anything earthly, enterprise to break the immunity and liberty of that sacred sanctuary, that hath been the safeguard of so many a good man's life. And I trust," quoth he, "with God's grace, we shall not need it. But for any manner need, I would not we should do it. I trust that she shall be with reason contented, and all things in good manner[345] obtained. And if it happen that I bring it not so to pass, yet shall I toward it so farforth do my best, that ye shall all well perceive, that no lack of my devoir, but the mother's dread and womanish fear, shall be the let."[346]

"Womanish fear? Nay, womanish frowardness,"[347] quoth the Duke of Buckingham. "For I dare take it upon my soul, she well knoweth she needeth no such thing to fear, either for her son or for herself.

---

317 *without...stand:* Whit T203
318 contributes   319 *evil words walk far:*
Whit W580   320 obliged   321 think
322 no reason, nothing   323 *evil...
out:* Til O68   324 holds dear, cares
for   325 well-being   326 suitable
327 Thomas Bourchier, Archbishop

of Canterbury   328 well-being;
prosperity   329 disgrace, slander,
reproach   330 by chance   331 advice
332 treated   333 perversity, contrariness
334 unless   335 *wed...will:* Til W392
336 The 1557 text has York, but the other
early texts correct this to Canterbury.

337 appropriate   338 effort; duty
339 However   340 clergy   341 a long
cloak worn by priests and monks   342 till
now   343 dared   344 The 1557 text mistakenly adds "of York."   345 *all things...
manner:* Whit M363, M464; Til 806
346 obstacle   347 perversity; contrariness

For as for her, here is no man that will be at war with women.[348] Would God some of the men of her kin were women too, and then should all be soon in rest. Howbeit, there is none of her kin the less loved for that[349] they be her kin, but for their own evil deserving. And nevertheless if we loved neither her nor her kin, yet were there no cause to think that we should hate the King's noble brother, to whose Grace we ourselves be of kin. Whose honor, if she as much desired as our dishonor, and as much regard took to his wealth[350] as to her own will, she would be as loath to suffer[351] him from the King as any of us be. For if she have any wit (as would God she had as good will as she hath shrewd[352] wit), she reckoneth herself no wiser than she thinketh some that be here, of whose faithful mind she nothing doubteth, but verily[353] believeth and knoweth that they would be as sorry of his harm as herself, and yet would have him from her if she bide[354] there. And we all, I think, content that both be with her if she come thence and bide in such place where they may with their honor be.

"Now then if she refuse in the deliverance of him to follow the counsel of them whose wisdom she knoweth, whose troth[355] she well trusteth, it is easy to perceive that frowardness letteth[356] her, and not fear. But go to,[357] suppose that she fear (as who may let her to fear her own shadow?);[358] the more she feareth to deliver him, the more ought we fear to leave him in her hands. For if she cast such fond doubts[359] that she fear his hurt, then will she fear that he shall be fetched thence. For she will soon think that if men were set (which God forbid) upon so great a mischief, the sanctuary would little let[360] them. Which good men might, as methinketh, without sin somewhat less regard than they do.

"Now then, if she doubt lest he might be fetched from her, is it not likely enough that she shall send him somewhere out of the realm? Verily, I look for none other. And I doubt not but she now as sore mindeth[361] it, as we the let[362] thereof. And if she might happen to bring that to pass (as it were no great mastery,[363] we letting her alone), all the world

would say that we were a wise sort of councillors about a king, that let his brother be cast away under our noses. And therefore I ensure[364] you faithfully, for my mind, I will rather, maugre[365] her mind, fetch him away than leave him there, till her frowardness or fond[366] fear convey him away.

And yet will I break no sanctuary therefor. For verily, since the privileges of that place and others like have been of long continued, I am not he that would be about to break them. And in good faith if they were now to begin, I would not be he that should be about to make them. Yet will I not say nay, but that it is a deed of pity that such men as the sea or their evil debtors have brought in poverty should have some place of liberty, to keep their bodies out of the danger of their cruel creditors. And also if the crown happen (as it hath done) to come in question, while either party taketh other as traitors, I will well there be some places of refuge for both.

But as for thieves, of which these places be full, and which never fall from the craft after they once fall thereto,[367] it is pity the sanctuary should serve them. And much more manquellers,[368] whom God bade[369] to take from the altar and kill them if their murder were willful. And where it is otherwise, there need we not the sanctuaries that God appointed in the Old Law.[370] For if either necessity, his own defense, or misfortune draw him to that deed, a pardon serveth which either the law granteth of course, or the King of pity may.

"Then look me[371] now how few sanctuary men there be whom any favorable necessity compelled to go thither. And then see on the other side what a sort[372] there be commonly therein, of them whom willful unthriftiness[373] hath brought to nought.[374] What a rabble of thieves, murderers, and malicious heinous traitors, and that in two places specially: the one at the elbow of the city, the other in the very bowels.[375] I dare well avow it: weigh the good that they do with the hurt that cometh of them, and ye shall find it much better to lack both, than have both. And this I say, although they were not abused as they now be, and so long have been, that I fear

---

348 *here...women:* Til W685   **349** *for that:* because   **350** well-being   **351** allow   **352** clever; shrewish; malicious   **353** truly   **354** *would...there:* want him to be away from her if she stays there (in the sanctuary)   **355** faithfulness, trustworthiness; truthfulness   **356** *frowardness letteth:* perversity prevents   **357** *go to:*

come now (interjection)   **358** *to fear... shadow:* Whit S177; Til S261   **359** *if... doubts:* if she devises such foolish doubt; Til D571   **360** prevent   **361** *sore mindeth:* seriously intends   **362** *the let:* (intend) the prevention   **363** achievement   **364** assure   **365** despite   **366** *frowardness or fond:* perversity or foolish   **367** *thieves...thereto:*

Til K133   **368** murderers   **369** See Ex 21:14.   **370** See Ex 21:13; Nm 35:22.   **371** *look me:* consider for me   **372** group   **373** dissoluteness   **374** *them...to nought:* Til W81   **375** *elbow...bowels:* Westminster Abbey is outside, while St. Martin le Grand is inside London.

me ever they will be while men be afeard to set their hands to the amendment—as though God and Saint Peter were the patrons of ungracious living.

"Now unthrifts riot and run in debt upon the boldness[376] of these places; yea, and rich men run thither with poor men's goods; there they build, there they spend and bid their creditors go whistle them.[377] Men's wives run thither with their husbands' plate[378] and say they dare not abide with their husbands, for[379] beating. Thieves bring thither their stolen goods, and there live thereon. There devise they new robberies; nightly they steal out, they rob and reave[380] and kill, and come in again as though those places gave them not only a safeguard for the harm they have done, but a license also to do more. Howbeit,[381] much of this mischief, if wise men would set their hands to,[382] it might be amended with great thanks of God and no breach of the privilege. The residue, since so long ago I wot nere[383] what pope and what prince more piteous[384] than politic[385] hath granted it and other men since of a certain religious fear have not broken it, let us take a pain therewith and let it a[386] God's name stand in force as far-forth as reason will. Which is not fully so far-forth as may serve to let[387] us of the fetching forth of this nobleman, to his honor and wealth, out of that place in which he neither is nor can be a sanctuary man.

"A sanctuary serveth always to defend the body of that man that standeth in danger abroad, not of great hurt only, but also of lawful hurt. For against unlawful harms, never pope nor king intended to privilege any one place. For that privilege hath every place. Knoweth any man any place wherein it is lawful one man to do another wrong? That[388] no man unlawfully take hurt, that liberty[389] the king, the law, and very nature[390] forbiddeth in every place, and maketh to that regard[391] for every man every place a sanctuary. But where a man is by lawful means in peril, there needeth he the tuition[392] of some special privilege, which is the only ground and cause of all sanctuaries. From which necessity this noble prince is far, whose love to his king, nature and kindred proveth, whose innocence to all the world his tender youth proveth. And so sanctuary, as for him, neither none he needeth, nor also none can have. Men come not to sanctuary as they come to baptism, to require[393] it by their godfathers. He must ask it himself that must have it. And reason,[394] since no man hath cause to have it but whose conscience of his own fault maketh him have need to require it, what will[395] then hath yonder babe? Which, and[396] if he had discretion to require it, if need were, I dare say would now be right angry with them that keep him there. And I would think, without any scruple of conscience, without any breach of privilege, to be somewhat more homely[397] with them that be there sanctuary men indeed. For if one go to sanctuary with another man's goods, why should not the King, leaving his body at liberty, satisfy the party of[398] his goods even within the sanctuary? For neither king nor pope can give any place such a privilege that it shall discharge a man of his debts, being able to pay."

And with that, diverse of the clergy that were present—whether they said it for his pleasure, or as they thought—agreed plainly that, by the law of God and of the Church, the goods of a sanctuary man should be delivered in payment of his debts, and stolen goods to the owner, and only liberty reserved him to get his living with the labor of his hands.

"Verily,"[399] quoth the Duke, "I think you say very truth. And what if a man's wife will take sanctuary because she list[400] to run from her husband? I would ween[401] if she can allege none other cause, he may lawfully, without any displeasure to Saint Peter, take her out of Saint Peter's church by the arm. And if nobody may be taken out of sanctuary that saith he will bide there, then if a child will take sanctuary because he feareth to go to school, his master must let him alone. And as simple as that example is, yet is there less reason in our case than in that. For therein though it be a childish fear, yet is there at the leastwise some fear. And herein is there none at all. And verily I have often heard of sanctuary men. But I never heard erst[402] of sanctuary children. And therefore as for the conclusion of my mind, whoso

---

376 *upon the boldness:* relying on the security   **377** *go whistle them:* a contemptuous dismissal; *bid...them:* Til W313   **378** items of precious metal   **379** due to   **380** pillage; make raids   **381** However   **382** *if...hands to:* Whit H81; Til H97   **383** *wot nere:* know not   **384** pious   **385** prudent, cunning, shrewd   **386** in   **387** hinder   **388** In order that   **389** *that liberty:* i.e., the liberty to do others wrong   **390** *very nature:* nature itself   **391** *to that regard:* in that respect   **392** protection   **393** ask   **394** that stands to reason   **395** desire or cause (for it)   **396** even   **397** unceremonious; direct   **398** with   **399** Truly   **400** wants   **401** think   **402** before

may have deserved to need it, if they think it for their surety,[403] let them keep it. But he can be no sanctuary man that neither hath wisdom to desire it, nor malice to deserve it, whose life or liberty can by no lawful process stand in jeopardy. And he that taketh one out of sanctuary to do him good, I say plainly that he breaketh no sanctuary."

When the Duke had done, the temporal men whole, and good part of the spiritual also, thinking none hurt earthly meant toward the young babe, condescended[404] in effect, that if he were not delivered, he should be fetched. Howbeit,[405] they thought it all best, in the avoiding of all manner of rumor, that the Lord Cardinal should first assay[406] to get him with her good will. And thereupon all the Council came unto the Star Chamber at Westminster. And the Lord Cardinal, leaving the Protector with the Council in the Star Chamber, departed into the sanctuary to the Queen, with diverse other lords with him—were it for the respect of his honor, or that she should by presence of so many perceive that this errand was not one man's mind, or were it for that[407] the Protector intended not in this matter to trust any one man alone, or else that if she finally were determined to keep him, some of that company had haply[408] secret instruction incontinent, maugre[409] her mind, to take him and to leave her no respite[410] to convey him, which she was likely to mind[411] after this matter broken[412] to her, if her time would in any wise serve her.

When the Queen and these lords were come together in presence,[413] the Lord Cardinal showed unto her that it was thought unto[414] the Protector and unto the whole Council that her keeping of the King's brother in that place was the thing which highly sounded,[415] not only to the great rumor of the people and their obloquy,[416] but also to the important[417] grief and displeasure of the King's royal majesty. To whose Grace it were as singular comfort to have his natural brother in company, as it was their both dishonor and all theirs and hers also, to suffer him in sanctuary. As though the one brother stood in danger and peril of the other. And he showed her that the Council therefore had sent him

unto her, to require[418] her the delivery of him, that he might be brought unto the King's presence at his liberty, out of that place which they reckoned as a prison. And there should he be demeaned[419] according to his estate. And she in this doing should both do great good to the realm, pleasure to the Council, and profit to herself, succor to her friends that were in distress, and over[420] that (which he wist[421] well she specially tendered[422]), not only great comfort and honor to the King, but also to the young Duke himself, whose both great wealth[423] it were to be together, as well for many greater causes, as also for their both disport[424] and recreation; which thing the lords esteemed not slight, though it seem light, well pondering that their youth without recreation and play cannot endure, nor any estranger[425] for the convenience of[426] their both ages and estates so meetly[427] in that point for any of them as either of them for other.

"My lord," quoth the Queen, "I say not nay but that it were very convenient[428] that this gentleman, whom ye require,[429] were in the company of the King, his brother. And in good faith methinketh it were as great commodity[430] to them both, as for yet a while, to be in the custody of their mother, the tender age considered of the elder of them both, but special the younger, which besides his infancy, that also needeth good looking to, hath a while been so sore[431] diseased, vexed with sickness, and is so newly rather a little amended than well-recovered, that I dare put no person earthly in trust with his keeping but myself only, considering that there is, as physicians say and as we also find, double the peril in the recidivation[432] that was in the first sickness,[433] with which disease, nature—being forelabored, forewearied and weakened—waxeth[434] the less able to bear out a new surfeit.[435] And albeit[436] there might be founden others that would haply do their best unto him, yet is there none that either knoweth better how to order him than I that so long have kept him, or is more tenderly like to cherish him than his own mother that bore him."

"No man denieth, good madam," quoth the Cardinal, "but that your Grace were of all folk most

403 safety **404** agreed **405** However
406 endeavor **407** *for that:* because
408 perhaps **409** *incontinent, maugre:*
immediately, despite **410** opportunity
411 intend **412** was told, revealed
413 in formal presence of royalty

414 by **415** gave rise **416** reproach
417 unbearable **418** ask **419** treated
420 besides **421** knew **422** cared about
423 happiness; well-being **424** fun
425 *any estranger:* anyone outside the
family **426** *convenience of:* suitability to

427 appropriately **428** fitting **429** ask
for **430** a benefit **431** grievously
432 relapse **433** *double . . . sickness:*
Til R62 **434** becomes **435** illness
436 although

necessary about your children, and so would all the Council not only be content but also glad that ye were, if it might stand with your pleasure to be in such place as might stand with their honor. But if you appoint yourself to tarry[437] here, then think they yet more convenient[438] that the Duke of York were with the King, honorably at his liberty to the comfort of them both, than here as a sanctuary man to their both dishonor and obloquy;[439] since there is not always so great necessity to have the child be with the mother, but that occasion may sometimes be such that it should be more expedient to keep him elsewhere. Which in this well appeareth that at such time as your dearest son, then prince and now king, should for his honor and good order of the country, keep household in Wales, far out of your company, your Grace was well content therewith yourself."

"Not very well content," quoth the Queen. "And yet the case is not like, for the one was then in health, and the other is now sick. In which case I marvel greatly that my Lord Protector is so desirous to have him in his keeping, where if the child in his sickness miscarried by nature,[440] yet might he run into slander and suspicion of fraud. And where[441] they call it a thing so sore[442] against my child's honor and theirs also that he bideth[443] in this place, it is all their honors there to suffer him bide, where no man doubteth, he shall be best kept. And that is here, while I am here, which[444] as yet intend not to come forth and jeopard[445] myself after[446] others of my friends, which would God were rather here in surety[447] with me than I were there in jeopardy with them."

"Why, madam," quoth another lord, "know you anything why they should be in jeopardy?"

"Nay, verily,[448] sir," quoth she, "nor why they should be in prison neither, as they now be. But it is, I trow,[449] no great marvel though I fear, lest those that have not letted[450] to put them in duress[451] without color,[452] will let as little to procure their destruction without cause."

The Cardinal made a countenance to the other lord that he should harp no more upon that string.[453] And then said he to the Queen that he nothing doubted but that those lords of her honorable kin, which as yet remained under arrest,

should, upon the matter examined, do well enough. And as toward her noble person, neither was nor could be, any manner[454] jeopardy.

"Whereby should I trust that?" quoth the Queen. "In that I am guiltless? As though they were guilty. In that I am with their enemies better beloved than they? When they hate them for my sake? In that I am so near of kin to the King? And how far be they off?—if that would help, as God send grace it hurt not. And therefore as for me, I purpose not as yet to depart hence. And as for this gentleman, my son, I mind that he shall be where I am till I see further. For I assure you, for that[455] I see some men so greedy without any substantial cause to have him, this maketh me much the more fearder[456] to deliver him."

"Truly, madam," quoth he, "and the fearder that you be to deliver him, the fearder be other men to suffer[457] you to keep him, lest your causeless fear might cause you farther to convey him. And many be there that think that he can have no privilege in this place which neither can have will to ask it nor malice to deserve it. And therefore they reckon no privilege broken, though they fetch him out. Which, if ye finally refuse to deliver him, I verily think they will. So much dread hath my lord his uncle, for the tender love he beareth him, lest your Grace should hap to send him away."

"Ah, sir," quoth the Queen, "hath the Protector so tender zeal to him that he feareth nothing but lest he should escape him? Thinketh he that I would send him hence which neither is in the plight[458] to send out, and in what place could I reckon him sure, if he be not sure in this the sanctuary whereof was there never tyrant yet so devilish that durst[459] presume to break? And I trust God is as strong now to withstand his adversaries, as ever he was.

But my son 'can deserve no sanctuary, and therefore he cannot have it'? Forsooth,[460] he hath founden a goodly gloss[461] by which that place that may defend a thief may not save an innocent. But 'he is in no jeopardy, nor hath no need thereof.' Would God he had not. Troweth the Protector[462] (I pray God he may prove a protector), troweth he that I perceive not whereunto his painted process draweth?[463] 'It is not honorable that the Duke bide here.' 'It were

---

437 appoint . . . tarry: decide to remain
438 appropriate **439** disgrace **440** miscarried by nature: died of natural causes
441 whereas **442** terribly **443** stays
444 who (i.e., she herself) **445** endanger
446 like **447** safety **448** truly

449 believe **450** hesitated **451** forcible restraint; imprisonment **452** justifiable evidence **453** harp . . . that string: Whit S838; Til S934 **454** kind of **455** for that: because **456** afraid **457** allow
458 condition **459** dared **460** In truth

461 pretext **462** Troweth the Protector: Does the Protector believe **463** painted process draweth: pretended proceeding leads to

comfortable for them both that he were with his brother, because the King lacketh a playfellow'— be ye sure.[464] I pray God send them both better playfellows than him, that maketh so high a matter upon such a trifling pretext, as though there could none be founden to play with the King but if[465] his brother (that hath no lust to play, for sickness) come out of sanctuary, out of his safeguard, to play with him. As though princes, as young as they be, could not play but with their peers, or children could not play but with their kindred, with whom for the more part they agree much worse than with strangers.[466] But the child 'cannot require[467] the privilege.' Who told him so? He shall hear him ask it, an he will.[468] Howbeit, this is a gay[469] matter: suppose he could not ask it; suppose he would not ask it; suppose he would ask to go out. If I say he shall not, if I ask the privilege but for myself, I say: he that against my will taketh out him, breaketh the sanctuary. Serveth this liberty for my person only, or for my goods too? Ye may not hence take my horse from me, and may you take my child from me? He is also my ward, for, as my learned counsel showeth me, since he hath nothing by descent holden by knight's service,[470] the law maketh his mother his guardian. Then may no man, I suppose, take my ward from me out of sanctuary without the breach of the sanctuary. And if my privilege could not serve him, nor he ask it for himself, yet since the law committeth to me the custody of him, I may require it for him—except[471] the law give a child a guardian only for his goods and his lands, discharging him of the cure[472] and safekeeping of his body, for which only both lands and goods serve.

‡[473]And if examples be sufficient to obtain privilege for my child, I need not far to seek. For in this place in which we now be (and which is now in question whether my child may take benefit of it), mine other son, now king, was born and kept in his cradle, and preserved to a more prosperous fortune, which I pray God long to continue. And as all you know, this is not the first time that I have taken sanctuary, for when my lord my husband was banished and thrust out of his kingdom, I fled hither being great

with child, and here I bore the Prince. And when my lord my husband returned safe again and had the victory, then went I hence to welcome him home, and from hence I brought my babe the Prince unto his father, when he first took him in his arms. And I pray God that my son's palace may be as great safeguard to him now reigning, as this place was sometimes to the King's enemy. In which place I intend to keep his brother, since* man's law serveth[474] the guardian to keep the infant. The law of nature willeth the mother keep her child. God's law privilegeth the sanctuary, and the sanctuary my son, since I fear to put him in the Protector's hands that hath his brother already, and were, if both failed, inheritor to the crown. The cause of my fear hath no man to do[475] to examine. And yet fear I no further than the law feareth, which, as learned men tell me, forbiddeth every man the custody of them by whose death he may inherit less land than a kingdom. I can[476] no more, but whosoever he be that breaketh this holy sanctuary, I pray God shortly send him need of sanctuary, when he may not come to it. For taken out of sanctuary would I not my mortal enemy were."

The Lord Cardinal, perceiving that the Queen waxed ever the longer the farther off,[477] and also that she began to kindle and chafe, and speak sore[478] biting words against the Protector, and such as he neither believed and was also loath to hear, he said unto her for a final conclusion, that he would no longer dispute the matter. But if she were content to deliver the Duke to him and to the other lords there present, he durst[479] lay his own body and soul both in pledge, not only for his surety[480] but also for his estate.[481] And if she would give them a resolute answer to the contrary, he would forthwith[482] depart therewithal, and shift[483] whoso would with this business afterward; for he never intended more to move her in that matter in which she thought that he and all others also, save herself, lacked either wit or troth:[484] wit, if they were so dull that they could nothing perceive what the Protector intended; troth, if they should procure her son to be delivered into his hands, in whom they should perceive toward the child any evil intended.

464 *be ye sure:* oh sure! **465** *but if:* unless **466** *children…strangers:* Til K38, K97; Whit K63 **467** ask for **468** *an he will:* if he wants **469** specious **470** *knight's service:* land ownership given to those who served the king in war **471** unless **472** care **473** ‡: The editor of the 1557 *Workes* added this note: "This that is here between this mark ‡ and this mark* was not written by Mr. More in this history written by him in English, but is translated out of this history which he wrote in Latin." **474** appoints (as legal heir) **475** *hath…to do:* is no one's business **476** can say **477** *waxed… off:* grew evermore, the longer she talked, farther from giving up her son **478** harsh **479** dared **480** safety **481** condition **482** immediately **483** deal **484** *wit or troth:* intelligence or trustworthiness/ truthfulness

The Queen with these words stood a good while in a great study.[485] And forasmuch her seemed the Cardinal[486] more ready to depart than some of the remnant, and the Protector himself ready at hand, so that she verily[487] thought she could not keep him there, but that he should incontinent[488] be taken thence; and to convey him elsewhere, neither had she time to serve her, nor place determined, nor persons appointed, all things unready (this message came on her so suddenly), nothing less looking for than to have him fetched out of sanctuary, which she thought to be now beset in such places about that he could not be conveyed out untaken, and partly as she thought it might fortune[489] her fear to be false, so well she wist[490] it was either needless or bootless,[491] wherefore, if she should needs go from him, she deemed it best to deliver him. And over[492] that, of the Cardinal's faith she nothing doubted, nor of some other lords neither, whom she there saw, which as she feared lest they might be deceived, so was she well assured they would not be corrupted. Then thought she it should yet make them the more warily to look to him, and the more circumspectly to see to his surety, if she with her own hands betook him to them of trust.

And at the last she took the young duke by the hand, and said unto the lords: "My lord," quoth she, "and all my lords, I neither am so unwise to mistrust your wits, nor so suspicious to mistrust your troths. Of which thing I purpose to make you such a proof as, if either of both lacked in you, might turn both me to great sorrow, the realm to much harm, and you to great reproach. For lo, here is," quoth she, "this gentleman, whom I doubt not but I could here keep safe if I would, whatsoever any man say. And I doubt not also but there be some abroad so deadly enemies unto my blood that if they wist where any of it lay in their own body, they would let it out. We have also had experience that the desire of a kingdom knoweth no kindred.[493] The brother hath been the brother's bane.[494] And may the nephews be sure of their uncle? Each of these children is other's defense while they be asunder,[495] and each of their lives lieth in the other's body. Keep one safe and both be

sure, and nothing for them both more perilous than to be both in one place. For what wise merchant adventureth[496] all his goods in one ship?[497] All this notwithstanding, here I deliver him, and his brother in him, to keep into your hands, of whom I shall ask them both afore God and the world. Faithful ye be, that wot[498] I well, and I know well you be wise. Power and strength to keep him, if ye list,[499] neither lack ye of yourself, nor can lack help in this cause. And if ye cannot elsewhere, then may you leave him here. But only one thing I beseech you, for the trust that his father put in you ever, and for the trust that I put in you now, that as far as ye think that I fear too much, be you well ware[500] that you fear not as far too little."[501]

And therewithal[502] she said unto the child, "Farewell, my own sweet son; God send you good keeping. Let me kiss you once yet ere[503] you go, for God knoweth when we shall kiss together again." And therewith she kissed him, and blessed him, turned her back and wept and went her way, leaving the child weeping as fast.

When the Lord Cardinal and these other lords with him had received this young duke, they brought him into the Star Chamber, where the Protector took him in his arms and kissed him with these words: "Now welcome, my lord, even with all my very heart." And he said, in that, of likelihood as he thought.

Thereupon forthwith[504] they brought him to the King his brother, into the bishop's palace at Paul's, and from thence through the city honorably into the Tower, out of which after that day they never came abroad.

‡[505]When the Protector had both the children in his hands, he opened himself more boldly, both to certain other men, and also chiefly to the Duke of Buckingham, although I know that many thought that this duke was privy to all the Protector's counsel, even from the beginning. And some of the Protector's friends said that the Duke was the first mover of the Protector to this matter, sending a privy messenger unto him straight, after King Edward's death. But others again, which knew better

485 *in a great study:* Whit S854; Til S945
486 *her seemed the Cardinal:* the Cardinal seemed to her   **487** truly   **488** immediately   **489** chance   **490** knew
491 useless   **492** besides   **493** *the desire of…no kindred:* Whit D167   **494** *The*

brother…bane: Til H211   **495** separated
496 risks   **497** *what wise…one ship:* Til A209   **498** know   **499** want; choose to   **500** wary   **501** *as far…too little:* Whit W685; Til W912   **502** with that
503 before   **504** at once   **505** ‡: The

editor of the 1557 *Workes* added this note: "This that is here between this mark ‡ and this mark* was not written by Mr. More in this history written by him in English, but is translated out of this history which he wrote in Latin."

the subtle wit of the Protector, deny that he ever opened his enterprise to the Duke until he had brought to pass the things before rehearsed.[506] But when he had imprisoned the Queen's kinsfolks, and gotten both her sons into his own hands, then he opened the rest of his purpose with less fear to them whom he thought meet[507] for the matter, and specially to the Duke, who being won to his purpose, he thought his strength more than half increased.

The matter was broken[508] unto the Duke by subtle folks, and such as were their craft-masters in the handling of such wicked devices,[509] who declared unto him that the young King was offended with him for his kinsfolk's sakes, and that if he were ever able, he would revenge them, who would prick[510] him forward thereunto, if they escaped (for they would remember their imprisonment). Or else if they were put to death, without doubt the young King would be careful for[511] their deaths, whose imprisonment was grievous unto him. And that with repenting, the Duke should nothing avail for there was no way left to redeem his offense by benefits, but he should sooner destroy himself than save the King, who with his brother and his kinsfolks he saw in such places imprisoned, as the Protector might with a beck[512] destroy them all; and that it were no doubt but he would do it indeed, if there were any new enterprise attempted. And that it was likely that as the Protector had provided privy guard for himself, so had he spials[513] for the Duke, and trains[514] to catch him if he should be against him, and that peradventure[515] from them, whom he least suspected. For the state of things and the dispositions of men were then such that a man could not well tell whom he might trust, or whom he might fear. These things and suchlike, being beaten into the Duke's mind, brought him to that point that, where he had repented the way that he had entered, yet would he go forth in the same; and since he had once begun, he would stoutly go through. And therefore to this wicked enterprise, which he believed could not be voided,[516] he bent himself and went through, and determined that since the common mischief could not be amended, he would turn it as much as he might to his own commodity.[517]

Then it was agreed that the Protector should have the Duke's aid to make him king, and that the Protector's only lawful son should marry the Duke's daughter, and that the Protector should grant him the quiet[518] possession of the earldom of Hereford, which he claimed as his inheritance, and could never obtain it in King Edward's time. Besides these requests of the Duke, the Protector of his own mind promised him a great quantity of the King's treasure and of his household stuff. And when they were thus at a point[519] between themselves, they went about to prepare for the coronation of the young King, as they would have it seem. And that they might turn both the eyes and minds of men from perceiving of their drifts[520] otherwhere,[521] the lords, being sent for from all parts of the realm, came thick to that solemnity. But the Protector and the Duke, after that, that they had set the Lord Cardinal,[522] the Archbishop of York[523] [with] the Lord Chancellor,[524] the Bishop of Ely,[525] the Lord Stanley,[526] and the Lord Hastings (then Lord Chamberlain), with many other noblemen, to commune and devise[527] about the coronation in one place, as fast were they in another place contriving the contrary, and to make the Protector king. To which council, albeit[528] there were adhibit[529] very few, and they very secret, yet began there, here and there about, some manner of muttering among the people, as though all should not long be well, though they neither wist[530] what they feared nor wherefore:[531] were it that before such great things, men's hearts of a secret instinct of nature misgiveth them[532] (as the sea without wind swelleth of himself sometimes before a tempest), or were it that some one man haply somewhat perceiving,[533] filled many men with suspicion, though he showed few men what he knew. Howbeit,[534] somewhat the dealing itself made men to muse on the matter, though the council were close.[535] For little and[536] little all folk withdrew from the Tower and drew to Crosby's Place in Bishopsgate's Street where the Protector kept his household. The Protector had the resort;[537]

506 related   **507** suitable   **508** told, revealed   **509** schemes   **510** spur, drive   **511** *careful for:* grief-stricken over   **512** nod   **513** spies   **514** traps   **515** perhaps   **516** avoided   **517** advantage   **518** uncontestable legally   **519** *at a point:* agreed   **520** schemes   **521** elsewhere;

turn…otherwhere: Whit S309; Til S438   **522** Thomas Bourchier   **523** Thomas Rotherham   **524** *[with]…Chancellor:* John Russell, Bishop of London (corrected from the Latin)   **525** John Morton   **526** Thomas Stanley   **527** *commune and devise:* confer and plan   **528** although

529 admitted   **530** knew   **531** why   **532** *misgiveth them:* give them a foreboding; *men's…them:* Til M475   **533** *haply somewhat perceiving:* perhaps perceiving something   **534** However   **535** secret   **536** by   **537** assemblage of people

the King, in manner desolate.[538] While some for their business made suit to them that had the doing, some were by their friends secretly warned that it might haply[539] turn them to no good to be too much attendant about the King without the Protector's appointment—which[540] removed also diverse of the Prince's old servants from him and set new about him.

Thus many things coming together, partly by chance, partly of purpose, caused at length not common people only that wave with the wind,[541] but wise men also and some lords eke,[542] to mark the matter and muse thereon, so far-forth that the Lord Stanley (that was after Earl of Derby) wisely mistrusted it, and said unto the Lord Hastings that he much misliked these two several[543] councils. "For while we," quoth he, "talk of one matter in the one place, little wot[544] we whereof they talk in the other place."

"My lord," quoth the Lord Hastings, "on my life, never doubt[545] you. For while one man is there, which is never thence, never can there be thing once minded that should sound amiss toward me but it should be in mine ears ere[546] it were well out of their mouths."

This meant he by[547] Catesby, which was of his near secret counsel and whom he very familiarly used, and in his most weighty matters put no man in so special trust, reckoning himself to no man so lief,[548] since he well wist[549] there was no man to him so much beholden as was this Catesby, which was a man well learned in the laws of this land and, by the special favor of the Lord Chamberlain,[550] in good authority, and much rule bore in all the county of Leicester where the Lord Chamberlain's power chiefly lay. But surely great pity was it that he had not had either more troth[551] or less wit. For his dissimulation only, kept all that mischief up. In whom if the Lord Hastings had not put so special trust, the Lord Stanley and he had departed with diverse other lords, and broken all the dance,[552] for many ill signs that he saw, which he now construed all to the best. So surely thought he that there could be none

harm toward him in that council intended where Catesby was.

And of truth, the Protector and the Duke of Buckingham made very good semblance unto the Lord Hastings, and kept him much in company. And undoubtedly the Protector loved him well, and loath was to have lost him, saving for fear lest his life[553] should have quailed[554] their purpose. For which cause he moved Catesby to prove[555] with some words cast out afar off, whether he could think it possible to win the Lord Hastings into their party. But Catesby, whether he assayed him[556] or assayed him not, reported unto them that he found him so fast,[557] and heard him speak so terrible words, that he durst no further break.[558] And of troth[559] the Lord Chamberlain of very trust showed unto Catesby the mistrust that others began to have in the matter. And therefore he, fearing lest their motions might with the Lord Hastings diminish his credence, whereunto only all the matter leaned, procured[560] the Protector hastily to rid[561] him. And much the rather,[562] for that[563] he trusted by his death to obtain much of the rule that the Lord Hastings bore in his country, the only desire whereof[564] was the allective[565] that induced him to be partner and one special contriver of all this horrible treason.

Whereupon soon after, that is to wit,[566] on the Friday the thirteenth day of June, many lords assembled in the Tower and there sat in council, devising the honorable solemnity of the King's coronation, of which the time appointed then so near approached that the pageants and subtleties[567] were in making day and night at Westminster, and much victual[568] killed therefor that afterward was cast away. These lords so sitting together communing of[569] this matter, the Protector came in among them, first about nine of the clock, saluting them courteously, and excusing himself that he had been from them so long, saying merrily that he had been asleep that day. And after a little talking with them, he said unto the Bishop of Ely, "My lord, you have very good strawberries at your garden in Holborn; I require[570] you, let us have a mess of them."

---

538 *the King . . . desolate:* the King was, as it were, isolated **539** perhaps **540** who **541** *that wave with the wind:* Til W 439; Whit W 339 **542** also **543** separate **544** knew **545** fear **546** before **547** concerning **548** dear **549** knew **550** Lord Hastings **551** trustworthiness

552 *broken . . . dance:* ended the whole conspiracy; Whit D 11 **553** staying alive **554** destroyed **555** test **556** *assayed him:* put him to the test **557** steadfast **558** *durst . . . break:* dared not reveal more **559** truthfulness; faithfulness **560** persuaded **561** do away with **562** more

readily **563** *for that:* because **564** for which **565** allurement, enticement **566** say **567** *pageants and subtleties:* stage platforms and props or decorations **568** food **569** *communing of:* conferring about **570** ask of

"Gladly, my lord," quoth he. "Would God I had some better thing as ready to your pleasure as that." And therewith in all the haste he sent his servant for a mess of strawberries.

5   The Protector set the lords fast in communing, and thereupon, praying them to spare him for a little while, departed thence.

And soon, after one hour, between ten and eleven, he returned into the chamber among them,
10 all changed with a wonderful sour, angry countenance, knitting the brows, frowning and fretting and gnawing on his lips, and so sat him down in his place, all the lords much dismayed and sore[571] marveling of this manner of sudden change, and what
15 thing should him ail. Then when he had sitten still a while, thus he began: "What were they worthy to have, that compass and imagine[572] the destruction of me, being so near of blood unto the King and Protector of his royal person and his realm?"
20 At this question, all the lords sat sore astonied,[573] musing much by whom this question should be meant, of which every man wist[574] himself clear. Then the Lord Chamberlain, as he that for the love between them thought he might be boldest with
25 him, answered and said that they were worthy to be punished as heinous traitors, whatsoever they were. And all the others affirmed the same.

"That is," quoth he, "yonder sorceress my brother's wife — and others with her," meaning the Queen.
30 At these words many of the other lords were greatly abashed that favored her. But the Lord Hastings was in his mind better content that it was moved by[575] her than by any other whom he loved better, albeit[576] his heart somewhat grudged that he
35 was not afore made of counsel in this matter, as he was of the taking of her kindred and of their putting to death, which were by his assent before devised to be beheaded at Pomfret this selfsame day, in which he was not ware[577] that it was by others de-
40 vised that himself should the same day be beheaded at London.

Then said the Protector, "Ye shall all see in what wise[578] that sorceress and that other witch of her counsel, Shore's wife, with their affinity,[579] have by
45 their sorcery and witchcraft wasted my body." And therewith he plucked up his doublet sleeve to his elbow upon his left arm, where he showed a wearish,[580] withered arm and small — as it was never other.[581]

And thereupon every man's mind sore misgave   50
them, well perceiving that this matter was but a quarrel. For well they wist that the Queen was too wise to go about any such folly. And also if she would, yet would she of all folk least make Shore's wife of counsel, whom of all women she most hated,   55
as that concubine whom the King, her husband, had most loved. And also no man was there present but well knew that his arm was ever such, since his birth.

Nevertheless, the Lord Chamberlain (which from   60
the death of King Edward kept Shore's wife, on whom he somewhat doted in the King's life, saving, as it is said, he that while[582] forbore her of reverence toward his King, or else of a certain kind of fidelity to his friend) answered and said, "Certainly, my   65
lord, if they have so heinously done, they be worthy heinous punishment."

"What?" quoth the Protector. "Thou servest me, I ween,[583] with 'if's and with 'and's![584] I tell thee, they have so done, and that I will make good on thy   70
body, traitor!"

And therewith, as in a great anger, he clapped his fist upon the board,[585] a great rap. At which token given, one cried "Treason!" without the chamber. Therewith a door clapped, and in came there   75
rushing men in harness,[586] as many as the chamber might hold. And anon[587] the Protector said to the Lord Hastings, "I arrest thee, traitor."

"What? Me, my lord?" quoth he.

"Yea, thee, traitor!" quoth the Protector.   80

And another let fly at the Lord Stanley, which[588] shrank at the stroke and fell under the table, or else his head had been cleft to the teeth; for as shortly[589] as he shrank, yet ran the blood about his ears.

Then were they all quickly bestowed in diverse   85
chambers, except the Lord Chamberlain, whom the Protector bade speed and shrive him apace,[590] "for by Saint Paul," quoth he, "I will not to dinner till I see thy head off." It booted[591] him not to ask why, but heavily[592] he took a priest at adventure,[593]   90
and made a short shrift,[594] for a longer would not be suffered,[595] the Protector made so much haste

571 greatly   **572** *compass and imagine:* plot and plan   **573** astonished   **574** knew   **575** *moved by:* said about   **576** although   **577** aware   **578** way   **579** allies

580 shriveled   **581** otherwise   **582** *that while:* during that time   **583** think   **584** *with 'if's . . . 'and's:* Til I.16   **585** table   **586** armor   **587** at once   **588** who

589 quickly   **590** *shrive . . . apace:* give him a quick confession   **591** helped   **592** sadly   **593** *at adventure:* at random   **594** confession of his sins   **595** allowed to dinner—which he might not go to till this were done, for saving of his oath. So was he brought forth into the green beside the chapel within the Tower, and his head laid down upon a long log of timber, and there stricken off, and afterward his body with the head interred at Windsor beside the body of King Edward, whose both souls our Lord pardon.

A marvelous case is it to hear either the warnings of that he should have voided[596] or the tokens of that he could not void. For the self night next[597] before his death, the Lord Stanley sent a trusty secret messenger unto him at midnight in all the haste, requiring[598] him to rise and ride away with him, for he was disposed utterly no longer to bide;[599] he had so fearful a dream, in which him thought that a boar with his tusks so razed them both by the heads that the blood ran about both their shoulders.[600] And forasmuch as the Protector gave the boar for his cognizance,[601] this dream made so fearful an impression in his heart that he was thoroughly determined no longer to tarry, but had his horse ready, if the Lord Hastings would go with him to ride so far yet the same night, that they should be out of danger ere[602] day.

"Ay, good lord," quoth the Lord Hastings to this messenger, "leaneth my lord thy master so much to such trifles, and hath such faith in dreams, which either his own fear fantasieth[603] or do rise in the night's rest by reason of his day thoughts? Tell him it is plain witchcraft to believe in such dreams—which if they were tokens of things to come, why thinketh he not that we might be as likely to make them true by our going if we were caught and brought back (as friends fail fleers)?[604] For then had the boar a cause likely to raze us with his tusks, as folk that fled for some falsehood, wherefore either is there no peril—nor none there is indeed—or if any be, it is rather in going than biding.[605] And if we should needs cost[606] fall in peril one way or other, yet had I liefer[607] that men should see it were by other men's falsehood than think it were either our own fault or faint heart. And therefore go to thy master, man, and commend me to him, and pray

him be merry and have no fear: for I ensure[608] him I am as sure of the man that he wotteth[609] of as I am of my own hand."[610]

"God send grace, sir," quoth the messenger, and went his way.

Certain is it also that in the riding toward the Tower, the same morning in which he was beheaded, his horse twice or thrice stumbled with him almost to the falling;[611] which thing, albeit each man wot well daily happeneth to them to whom no such mischance is toward,[612] yet hath it been of an old rite[613] and custom observed as a token oftentimes notably foregoing some great misfortune.

Now this that followeth was no warning, but an enemious scorn. The same morning ere he were up, came a knight unto him, as[614] it were of courtesy to accompany him to the Council, but of troth[615] sent by the Protector to haste him thitherward, with whom he was of secret confederacy in that purpose, a mean[616] man at that time, and now of great authority. This knight, when it happed the Lord Chamberlain by the way to stay his horse and commune[617] a while with a priest whom he met in the Tower street, broke[618] his tale and said merrily to him, "What, my lord, I pray you come on. Whereto[619] talk you so long with that priest? You have no need of a priest yet." And therewith he laughed upon him, as though he would say, "Ye shall have soon." But so little wist[620] the other what he meant, and so little mistrusted, that he was never merrier nor never so full of good hope in his life—which self[621] thing is often seen a sign of change. But I shall rather let anything pass[622] me than the vain surety[623] of man's mind so near his death.[624]

Upon the very Tower wharf, so near the place where his head was off so soon after, there met he with one Hastings, a pursuivant of his own name.[625] And of their meeting in that place, he was put in remembrance of another time, in which it had happened them before, to meet in like manner together in the same place. At which other time the Lord Chamberlain had been accused unto King Edward by the Lord Rivers, the Queen's brother, in such wise that he was for the while (but it lasted not long) far

---

596 avoided   **597** *self night next:* very last night   **598** asking   **599** stay   **600** *a boar…shoulders:* Til R7   **601** coat of arms   **602** before   **603** *dreams… fantasieth:* Whit S952, D387; Til D587   **604** *friends fail fleers:* those who flee

lack friends; Whit F637   **605** staying   **606** *needs cost:* of necessity   **607** rather   **608** assure   **609** knows   **610** *I am… own hand:* Whit H76   **611** *stumbled… falling:* Til T9   **612** impending   **613** practice   **614** as if   **615** *of troth:*

in truth   **616** low-ranking   **617** talk   **618** revealed   **619** Why   **620** knew   **621** very   **622** go uncommented upon by   **623** security   **624** *vain… death:* Til T223   **625** *pursuivant… name:* royal messenger by same name (i.e., Hastings)

fallen into the King's indignation, and stood in great fear of[626] himself. And forasmuch as he now met this pursuivant in the same place, that jeopardy so well past, it gave him great pleasure to talk with him thereof with whom he had before talked thereof, in the same place while he was therein.

And therefore he said, "Ah, Hastings, art thou remembered when I met thee here once with a heavy heart?"

"Yea, my Lord," quoth he, "that remember I well; and thanked be God they got no good, nor ye none harm thereby."

"Thou wouldst say so," quoth he, "if thou knewest as much as I know, which few know else as yet and more shall shortly." That meant he by[627] the lords of the Queen's kindred that were taken before and should that day be beheaded at Pomfret—which he well wist, but nothing ware[628] that the axe hung over his own head.[629]

"In faith, man," quoth he, "I was never so sorry,[630] nor never stood in so great dread in my life as I did when thou and I met here. And lo, how the world is turned:[631] now stand mine enemies in the danger (as thou mayest hap to hear more hereafter), and I never in my life so merry, nor never in so great surety."[632]

O good God, the blindness of our mortal nature! When he most feared, he was in good surety; when he reckoned himself surest, he lost his life,[633] and that within two hours after.

Thus ended this honorable man, a good knight and a gentle, of great authority with his prince, of living somewhat dissolute, plain and open to his enemy and secret to his friend, easy to beguile, as he that of good heart and courage[634] forestudied no perils; a loving man and passing well beloved; very faithful, and trusty enough, trusting too much.[635]

Now flew the fame of this lord's death swiftly through the city, and so forth farther about like a wind[636] in every man's ear. But the Protector immediately after dinner, intending to set some color[637] upon the matter, sent in all the haste for many substantial men out of the city into the Tower. And at their coming, himself, with the Duke of

Buckingham, stood harnessed in old ill-faring briganders,[638] such as no man should ween[639] that they would vouchsafe[640] to have put upon their backs, except that some sudden necessity had constrained them. And then the Protector showed them that the Lord Chamberlain and others of his conspiracy had contrived to have suddenly destroyed him and the Duke there, the same day, in the Council. And what they intended further was as yet not well known. Of which their treason he never had knowledge before ten of the clock the same forenoon. Which sudden fear drove them to put on for their defense such harness[641] as came next to hand. And so had God helped them, that the mischief turned upon them that would have done it. And this he required[642] them to report.

Every man answered him fair,[643] as though no man mistrusted the matter which of troth no man believed.[644] Yet for the further appeasing of the people's mind, he sent immediately after dinner, in all the haste, one herald of arms with a proclamation to be made through the city in the King's name, containing that the Lord Hastings, with diverse others of his traitorous purpose, had before conspired the same day to have slain the Lord Protector and the Duke of Buckingham sitting in the Council, and after to have taken upon them to rule the King and the realm at their pleasure, and thereby to pill and spoil[645] whom they list,[646] uncontrolled. And much matter was there in the proclamation devised to the slander of the Lord Chamberlain, as that he was an evil counselor to the King's father, enticing him to many things highly redounding to the diminishing of his honor and to the universal hurt of his realm, by his evil company, sinister procuring, and ungracious example, as well in many other things as in the vicious living and inordinate abusion[647] of his body, both with many others and also specially with Shore's wife, which was one also of his most secret counsel of this heinous treason, with whom he lay nightly, and namely the night last past next before his death, so that it was the less marvel if ungracious living brought him to an unhappy ending,[648] which he was now put unto, by the most dread

---

626 for   **627** *That…by:* By that he meant   **628** aware, wary   **629** *nothing…head:* Whit S979   **630** sad; distressed   **631** *lo…turned:* Whit W672; Til W901   **632** safety, security   **633** *when…life:* Til T223   **634** spirit,

disposition   **635** *trusty…too much:* Whit T492; Til T549   **636** *Now…wind:* Whit W294   **637** reasonable excuse; justification   **638** body armor   **639** think   **640** be willing   **641** armor   **642** asked   **643** agreeably   **644** *Every…believed:*

Whit W581, D122, F50   **645** *pill and spoil:* pillage and steal from   **646** wished   **647** misuse   **648** *ungracious…ending:* Whit E186, L0; Til L392, L247

commandment of the King's Highness and of his honorable and faithful Council, both for his demerits, being so openly taken in his falsely conceived treason, and also lest the delaying of his execution might have encouraged other mischievous persons, partners of his conspiracy, to gather and assemble themselves together in making some great commotion for his deliverance, whose hope now being by his well-deserved death politicly[649] repressed, all the realm should by God's grace rest in good quiet and peace.

Now was this proclamation made within two hours after that he was beheaded, and it was so curiously indited,[650] and so fair written in parchment in so well a set hand, and therewith of itself so long a process, that every child might well perceive that it was prepared before. For all the time between his death and the proclaiming could scant[651] have sufficed unto the bare writing alone, all had it been but in paper and scribbled forth in haste at adventure.[652] So that upon the proclaiming thereof, one that was schoolmaster of Paul's, of chance standing by, and comparing the shortness of the time with the length of the matter, said unto them that stood about him, "Here is a gay goodly cast, foul cast[653] away for haste."[654] And a merchant answered him that it was written by prophecy.

Now then, by and by,[655] as it were for anger not for covetise, the Protector sent into the house of Shore's wife (for her husband dwelled not with her) and spoiled[656] her of all that ever she had, above the value of two or three thousand marks,[657] and sent her body to prison. And when he had a while laid unto[658] her, for the manner sake,[659] that she went about to bewitch him and that she was of counsel[660] with the Lord Chamberlain to destroy him, in conclusion, when that no color[661] could fasten upon these matters, then he laid heinously to her charge the thing that herself could not deny, that all the world wist[662] was true, and that nevertheless every man laughed at to hear it then so suddenly so highly[663] taken: that she was naught[664] of her body.

And for this cause (as a goodly continent prince, clean and faultless of himself, sent out of heaven into this vicious world for the amendment of men's manners) he caused the Bishop of London to put her to open[665] penance, going before the cross in procession upon a Sunday with a taper[666] in her hand. In which she went in countenance and pace demure so womanly, and albeit[667] she were out of all array[668] save her kirtle[669] only, yet went she so fair and lovely, namely[670] while the wondering of the people cast a comely rud[671] in her cheeks (of which she before had most miss), that her great shame won her much praise among those that were more amorous of[672] her body than curious of her soul.[673] And many good folk also, that hated her living and glad were to see sin corrected, yet pitied they more her penance than rejoiced therein, when they considered that the Protector procured it more of a corrupt intent than any virtuous affection.

This woman was born in London, worshipfully friended,[674] honestly brought up, and very well married (saving somewhat too soon), her husband an honest citizen, young and goodly and of good substance.[675] But forasmuch as they were coupled ere[676] she were well ripe, she not very fervently loved for whom she never longed. Which was haply[677] the thing that the more easily made her incline unto the King's appetite when he required[678] her. Howbeit,[679] the respect of his royalty, the hope of gay apparel, ease, pleasure, and other wanton wealth was able soon to pierce a soft tender heart. But when the King had abused her, anon[680] her husband (as he was an honest man and one that could his good,[681] not presuming to touch a King's concubine) left her up to him altogether. When the King died, the Lord Chamberlain took her. Which in the King's days, albeit[682] he was sore[683] enamored upon her, yet he forbore her, either for reverence or for a certain friendly faithfulness.

Proper she was and fair, nothing in her body that you would have changed, but if[684] you would have wished her somewhat higher. Thus say they that

---

649 prudently; shrewdly; craftily **650** *curiously indited:* elaborately composed **651** hardly **652** random **653** *cast . . . cast:* trick . . . thrown (a play on words) **654** *a gay . . . haste:* Whit H162; Til H189 **655** *by and by:* immediately **656** despoiled **657** *two . . . marks:* i.e., about £1,500–2,000 (a considerable sum in those days) **658** *laid unto:* brought

charges against **659** *manner sake:* sake of appearances; Til M806; Whit M464, M363 **660** *of counsel:* in a plot **661** pretext, appearance **662** knew **663** seriously **664** immoral, wicked **665** public **666** candle **667** although **668** attire **669** simple gown or petticoat **670** especially **671** *comely rud:* beautiful redness **672** about **673** *much . . .*

soul: Til F13 **674** *worshipfully friended:* befriended by honorable persons **675** wealth **676** before **677** perhaps **678** asked **679** However **680** immediately **681** *could his good:* knew what was good for him; Til G321 **682** although **683** greatly **684** *but if:* unless

knew her in her youth, albeit some that now see her (for yet she liveth) deem her never to have been well-visaged.[685] Whose judgment seemeth me somewhat like as though men should guess the beauty of one long before departed by her scalp[686] taken out of the charnel house:[687] for now is she old, lean, withered, and dried up, nothing left but riveled[688] skin and hard bone.[689] And yet being even such, whoso well advise her visage,[690] might guess and devise[691] which parts how filled would make it a fair face.

Yet delighted not men so much in her beauty as in her pleasant behavior. For a proper wit[692] had she, and could both read well and write, merry in company, ready and quick of answer, neither mute nor full of babble,[693] sometimes taunting without displeasure and not without disport.[694] The King would say that he had three concubines, which in three diverse properties diversely excelled: one the merriest, another the wiliest, the third the holiest harlot in his realm, as one whom no man could get out of the church lightly[695] to any place, but[696] it were to his bed. The other two were somewhat greater personages, and nevertheless of their humility content to be nameless, and to forbear[697] the praise of those properties. But the merriest was this Shore's wife, in whom the King therefore took special pleasure. For many he had, but her he loved, whose favor, to say the truth (for sin it were to belie the devil),[698] she never abused to any man's hurt, but to many a man's comfort and relief. Where the King took displeasure, she would mitigate and appease his mind; where men were out of favor, she would bring them in his grace. For many that had highly offended, she obtained pardon. Of great forfeitures she got men remission. And finally in many weighty suits,[699] she stood many men in great stead, either for none, or very small rewards, and those rather gay than rich — either for that[700] she was content with the deed itself well done, or for that she delighted to be sued unto and to show what she was able to do with the King, or for that wanton women and wealthy be not always covetous.

I doubt not some shall think this woman too slight a thing to be written of and set among the remembrances of great matters, which they shall specially think that haply[701] shall esteem her only by that they now see her. But meseemeth the chance[702] so much the more worthy to be remembered, in how much she is now in the more beggarly condition: unfriended and worn-out of acquaintance,[703] after good substance,[704] after as great favor with the Prince, after as great suit and seeking-to[705] with all those that those days had business to speed,[706] as many other men were in their times, which[707] be now famous only by the infamy of their ill deeds. Her doings were not much less, albeit they be much less remembered because they were not so evil. For men use,[708] if they have an evil turn, to write it in marble; and whoso doth us a good turn, we write it in dust[709] — which is not worst proved by her, for at this day she beggeth of many at this day living, that at this day had begged if she had not been.[710]

Now was it so devised by the Protector and his Council that the self[711] day in which the Lord Chamberlain was beheaded in the Tower of London, and about the selfsame hour, was there (not without his assent) beheaded at Pomfret the fore-remembered lords and knights that were taken from the King at Northampton and Stony Stratford. Which thing was done in the presence and by the order of Sir Richard Radcliff, knight, whose service the Protector specially used in the counsel[712] and in the execution of such lawless enterprises, as a man that had been long secret with him, having experience of the world and a shrewd[713] wit, short[714] and rude in speech, rough and boisterous of behavior, bold in mischief, as far from pity as from all fear of God. This knight — bringing them out of the prison to the scaffold, and showing to the people about that they were traitors, not suffering[715] them to speak and declare their innocence lest their words might have inclined men to pity them, and to hate the Protector and his party — caused them hastily, without judgment, process,[716] or manner of order to be beheaded, and without other earthly guilt but only

---

685 pretty faced   **686** skull   **687** *the charnel house:* a building in which skulls and bones are piled up   **688** wrinkled   **689** *riveled . . . bone:* Whit S362   **690** *advise her visage:* considers her face   **691** imagine   **692** *proper wit:* fine mind   **693** *full of babble:* Til F465   **694** entertainment   **695** easily   **696** unless

697 avoid   **698** *sin . . . devil:* Whit S337; Til S470   **699** appeals (to the King)   **700** *for that:* because   **701** perhaps   **702** event, circumstances   **703** *worn . . . acquaintance:* having no companions left   **704** wealth   **705** *suit and seeking-to:* petition and searching to obtain things from   **706** expedite   **707** who   **708** are

accustomed   **709** *men . . . dust:* Whit T531   **710** *she begged . . . not been:* Til B223   **711** very same. They actually occurred, however, on June 25, not June 13.   **712** planning   **713** cunning; wicked   **714** curt   **715** allowing   **716** legal process

that they were good men, too true to the King and too nigh[717] to the Queen.

Now when the Lord Chamberlain and these other lords and knights were thus beheaded and rid out of the way, then thought the Protector that while men mused what the matter meant, while the lords of the realm were about him, out of their own strengths, while no man wist[718] what to think nor whom to trust, ere ever they should have space to dispute and digest the matter and make parties, it were best hastily to pursue his purpose and put himself in possession of the crown, ere men could have time to devise any ways to resist. But now was all the study[719] by what means this matter, being of itself so heinous, might be first broken[720] to the people, in such wise[721] that it might be well taken. To this counsel[722] they took diverse,[723] such as they thought meetly[724] to be trusted, likely to be induced to that party, and able to stand them in stead,[725] either by power or policy.

Among whom they made of counsel Edmund Shaa, knight, then Mayor of London, which upon trust of his own advancement whereof he was of a proud heart highly desirous, should frame[726] the city to their appetite. Of spiritual men they took such as had wit and were in authority among the people for opinion of their learning, and had no scrupulous conscience. Among these had they John Shaa, clerk,[727] brother to the Mayor, and Friar Penker,[728] Provincial of the Augustinian Friars, both doctors of divinity, both great preachers, both of more learning than virtue, of more fame than learning. For they were before greatly esteemed among the people, but after that never.

Of these two the one had a sermon in praise of the Protector before the coronation, the other after; both so full of tedious flattery that no man's ears could abide them. Penker in his sermon so lost his voice that he was fain[729] to leave off and come down in the mids.[730] Doctor Shaa by his sermon lost his honesty, and soon after his life, for very shame of the world, into which he durst[731] never after come abroad. But the friar forced[732] for no shame, and

so it harmed him the less. Howbeit, some doubt[733] and many thinken that Penker was not of counsel of the matter before the coronation, but, after the common manner, fell to flattery after—namely since his sermon was not incontinent upon[734] it, but at St. Mary Hospital at the Easter after. But certain is it that Doctor Shaa was of counsel in the beginning, so far-forth[735] that they determined that he should first break the matter in a sermon at Paul's Cross,[736] in which he should by the authority of his preaching incline the people to the Protector's ghostly[737] purpose.

But now was all the labor and study[738] in the devise of some convenient[739] pretext for which the people should be content to depose the Prince and accept the Protector for king. In which, diverse things they devised. But the chief thing and the weighty of all that invention rested in this:[740] that they should allege bastardy, either in King Edward himself or in his children, or both, so that he should seem disabled to inherit the crown by the Duke of York, and the Prince by him.

To lay bastardy in King Edward sounded openly to the rebuke[741] of the Protector's own mother, which was mother to them both; for in that point could be none other color[742] but to pretend that his own mother was an adulteress—which, notwithstanding, to further this purpose he letted[743] not. But nevertheless he would the point should be less and more favorably handled, not even fully plain and directly, but that the matter should be touched aslope,[744] craftily, as though men spared in that point to speak all the truth for fear of his displeasure. But the other point concerning the bastardy that they devised to surmise[745] in King Edward's children—that, would he[746] should be openly declared and enforced[747] to the uttermost.

The color and pretext whereof cannot be well perceived but if[748] we first repeat you some things long before done about King Edward's marriage. After that King Edward the Fourth had deposed King Henry the Sixth and was in peaceable possession of the realm, determining himself to marry (as it was requisite both for himself and for the realm),

717 near   **718** knew   **719** *all the study:* Whit S854   **720** revealed
721 a way   **722** *To this counsel:* Into this plot   **723** several (individuals)
724 fit   **725** *stand them in stead:* be of benefit to them   **726** shape, dispose
727 cleric   **728** Thomas Penker (d. 1487)

729 obliged   **730** middle   **731** dared
732 cared   **733** suspect   **734** *incontinent upon:* immediately following (the coronation)   **735** *so far-forth:* to such an extent
736 *Paul's Cross:* an open-air pulpit on the grounds of St. Paul's Cathedral   **737** shadowy; spiritual   **738** *all the labor and*

study: Whit S854   **739** suitable   **740** *the chief... in this:* Til W5   **741** *sounded... rebuke:* suggested clearly the disgrace
742 pretext; justification   **743** hesitated, refrained   **744** indirectly   **745** allege, accuse   **746** *would he:* he wanted that it
747 emphasized   **748** *but if:* unless

he sent over in embassiate[749] the Earl of Warwick,[750] with other noblemen in his company, unto Spain, to entreat[751] and conclude a marriage between King Edward and the King's daughter of Spain. In which thing the Earl of Warwick found the parties so toward[752] and willing that he speedily, according to his instructions, without any difficulty brought the matter to very good conclusion.

Now happed it that in the mean season[753] there came, to make a suit[754] by petition to the King, Dame Elizabeth Grey (which was after his queen, at that time a widow), born of noble blood, specially by her mother, which was Duchess of Bedford ere[755] she married the Lord Woodville, her father. Howbeit,[756] this Dame Elizabeth, herself being in service with Queen Margaret, wife unto King Henry the Sixth, was married unto one John Grey, a squire, whom King Henry made knight upon the field[757] that he had on Shrove Tuesday[758] at Saint Albans against King Edward. And little while enjoyed he that knighthood, for he was at the same field slain. After which done, and the Earl of Warwick being in his embassiate[759] about the aforeremembered[760] marriage, this poor lady made humble suit unto the King that she might be restored unto such small lands as her late husband had given her in jointure.[761] Whom, when the King beheld and heard her speak — as she was both fair, of a good favor, moderate of stature, well-made, and very wise — he not only pitied her, but also waxed[762] enamored on her. And taking her afterward secretly aside, began to enter in talking more familiarly. Whose appetite when she perceived, she virtuously denied him. But that did she so wisely, and with so good manner, and words so well set, that she rather kindled his desire than quenched it. And finally, after many a meeting, much wooing, and many great promises, she well espied the King's affection toward her so greatly increased that she durst[763] somewhat the more boldly say her mind, as to him whose heart she perceived more firmly set than to fall off for a word. And in conclusion she showed him plain that, as she wist[764] herself too

simple to be his wife, so thought she herself too good to be his concubine.

The King, much marveling of her constancy, as he that had not been wont elsewhere to be so stiffly said nay, so much esteemed her continence and chastity that he set her virtue in the stead of possession and riches.[765] And thus taking counsel of his desire, determined in all possible haste to marry her.

And after he was thus appointed,[766] and had between them twain ensured[767] her, then asked he counsel of his other friends, and that in such manner as they might easily perceive it booted[768] not greatly to say nay. Notwithstanding, the Duchess of York, his mother, was so sore[769] moved therewith that she dissuaded the marriage as much as she possibly might, alleging that it was his honor, profit, and surety[770] also, to marry in a noble progeny out of his realm, whereupon depended great strength to his estate by the affinity[771] and great possibility of increase of his possessions — and that he could not well otherwise do, standing[772] that the Earl of Warwick had so far moved already. Which[773] were not likely to take it well if all his voyage[774] were in such wise frustrate and his appointments deluded.[775]

And she said also that it was not princely to marry his own subject, no great occasion leading thereunto, no possessions or other commodities depending thereupon, but only as[776] it were a rich man that would marry his maid,[777] only for a little wanton dotage upon her person. In which marriage many more commend the maiden's fortune than the master's wisdom. And yet therein she said was more honesty than honor in this marriage, forasmuch as there is between no merchant and his own maid so great difference as between the King and this widow. In whose person, albeit[778] there was nothing to be misliked, yet was there, she said, "nothing so excellent but that it might be founden in diverse others that were more meetly,"[779] quoth she, "for your estate, and maidens also; whereas the only widowhood[780] of Elizabeth Grey, though she were in all other things convenient[781] for you, should yet suffice, as meseemeth, to refrain you from her

749 *in embassiate:* as an ambassador
750 Richard Neville, a cousin of
Edward IV   **751** negotiate   **752** obliging
753 *mean season:* meantime   **754** an
appeal   **755** before   **756** However
757 battlefield   **758** *Shrove Tuesday:* the
day before Ash Wednesday   **759** *in his
embassiate:* on his ambassadorial mission

760 *aforeremembered:* aforementioned
761 *in jointure:* as property to be hers
in the event of his death   **762** grew
763 dared   **764** knew   **765** *set … riches:*
Til N22; Whit N112, H447   **766** decided
767 *twain ensured:* two become engaged
to   **768** helped   **769** greatly   **770** safety
771 marriage alliance   **772** considering

773 Who   **774** undertaking; journey
775 mocked   **776** as if   **777** *it was …
maid:* Whit M175, M4   **778** although
779 appropriate   **780** *the only widowhood:* the widowhood alone   **781** suitable,
appropriate

marriage, since it is an unsitting[782] thing, and a very blemish and high disparagement to the sacred majesty of a prince, that ought as nigh to approach priesthood in cleanness as he doth in dignity, to be
5 defouled with bigamy[783] in his first marriage."

The King, when his mother had said, made her answer, part in earnest, part in play merrily, as he that wist himself out of her rule. And albeit he would gladly that she should take it well, yet was at
10 a point[784] in his own mind, took she it well or otherwise. Howbeit, somewhat to satisfy her, he said that albeit marriage, being a spiritual thing, ought rather to be made for the respect of God where his grace inclineth the parties to love together as he trusted it
15 was in his than for the regard of any temporal advantage, yet nevertheless him seemed[785] that this marriage, even worldly considered, was not unprofitable. For he reckoned the amity of no earthly nation so necessary for him as the friendship of his own,
20 which he thought likely to bear him so much the more hearty favor in that he disdained not to marry with one of his own land. And yet if outward[786] alliance were thought so requisite, he would find the means to enter thereinto much better by other of his
25 kin, where all the parties could be contented, than to marry himself whom he should haply[787] never love, and for the possibility of more possessions, lose the fruit and pleasure of this that he had already. For small pleasure taketh a man of all that ever he hath
30 beside, if he be wived against his appetite.

"And I doubt not," quoth he, "but there be, as ye say, others that be in every point comparable with her. And therefore I let[788] not them that like them to wed them. No more is it reason that it mislike[789] any
35 man that I marry where it liketh me. And I am sure that my cousin of Warwick neither loveth me so little to grudge at that I love, nor is so unreasonable to look that I should, in choice of a wife, rather be ruled by his eye than by mine own, as though I were a ward
40 that were bound to marry by the appointment of a guardian. I would not be a king with that condition, to forbear[790] mine own liberty in choice of my own marriage. As for possibility of more inheritance by new affinity in estrange[791] lands, is oft the occasion of
45 more trouble than profit. And we have already title

by that means to so much as sufficeth to get and keep well in one man's days.[792] That she is a widow and hath already children, by God's blessed Lady, I am a bachelor and have some too, and so each of us hath
50 a proof that neither of us is like to be barren. And therefore, madam, I pray you be content; I trust in God she shall bring forth a young prince that shall please you. And as for the bigamy, let the bishop hardily[793] lay it in my way when I come to take orders.[794]
55 For I understand it is forbidden a priest, but I never wist[795] it yet that it was forbidden a prince."

The Duchess, with these words nothing appeased, and seeing the King so set thereon that she could not pull him back, so highly she disdained[796]
60 it that, under pretext of her duty to Godward,[797] she devised to disturb this marriage, and rather to help that he should marry one Dame Elizabeth Lucy, whom the King had also not long before gotten with child. Wherefore the King's mother objected
65 openly against his marriage, as[798] it were in discharge of her conscience, that the King was sure[799] to Dame Elizabeth Lucy and her husband before God. By reason of which words, such obstacle was made in the matter that either the bishops durst[800]
70 not, or the King would not, proceed to the solemnization of this wedding till these same[801] were clearly purged and the truth well and openly testified. Whereupon Dame Elizabeth Lucy was sent for.

And albeit that[802] she was by the King's mother
75 and many others put in good comfort to affirm that she was ensured[803] unto the King, yet when she was solemnly sworn to say the truth, she confessed that they were never ensured. Howbeit,[804] she said his Grace spoke so loving words unto her that she verily[805] hoped he would have married her, and that if it
80 had not been for such kind words, she would never have showed such kindness to him, to let him so kindly get her with child.

This examination solemnly taken, when it was clearly perceived that there was none impediment,
85 the King with great feast and honorable solemnity married Dame Elizabeth Grey, and her crowned Queen that was his enemy's wife and many times had prayed full heartily for his loss. In which God loved her better than to grant her her boon.[806]
90

782 unbecoming 783 marriage to a widowed person 784 decision 785 *him seemed:* it seemed to him 786 foreign 787 perhaps 788 prevent 789 displease 790 do without; give up 791 *affinity…*

lands: alliance by marriage in foreign lands 792 *so…days:* Til E163 793 by all means 794 *take orders:* receive holy orders, be ordained a priest 795 knew 796 was offended by 797 *to Godward:* toward

God 798 as if 799 engaged, legally betrothed 800 dared 801 i.e., charges 802 *albeit that:* although 803 engaged 804 However 805 truly 806 wish, prayer

But when the Earl of Warwick understood of this marriage, he took it so highly[807] that his embassiate was deluded[808] that, for very anger and disdain, he at his return assembled a great puissance[809] against the King, and came so fast upon him ere[810] he could be able to resist, that he was fain to void[811] the realm and flee into Holland for succor, where he remained for the space of two years, leaving his new wife in Westminster in sanctuary, where she was delivered of Edward the Prince, of whom we before have spoken. In which meantime the Earl of Warwick took out of prison and set up again King Henry the Sixth, which was before by King Edward deposed and that muchwhat[812] by the power of the Earl of Warwick, which was a wise man and a courageous warrior, and of such strength, what for[813] his lands, his alliance,[814] and favor with all the people, that he made kings and put down kings almost at his pleasure, and not impossible to have attained it himself, if he had not reckoned it a greater thing to make a king than to be a king.

But nothing lasteth always;[815] for in conclusion King Edward returned, and, with much less number than he[816] had, at Barnet on the Easter Day field, slew the Earl of Warwick with many other great estates[817] of that party, and so stably attained the crown again that he peaceably enjoyed it until his dying day, and in such plight left it that it could not be lost but by the discord of his very friends, or falsehood of his feigned friends.

I have rehearsed[818] this business about this marriage somewhat the more at length because it might thereby the better appear upon how slipper[819] a ground the Protector builded his color,[820] by which he pretended King Edward's children to be bastards. But that invention simple as it was, it liked them to whom it sufficed to have somewhat to say, while they were sure to be compelled to no larger proof than themselves list[821] to make.

Now then, as I began to show you, it was by the Protector and his Council concluded that this Doctor Shaa should in a sermon at Paul's Cross signify to the people that neither King Edward himself nor the Duke of Clarence were lawfully begotten, nor were not the very children of the Duke of York, but begotten unlawfully by other persons by the adultery of the Duchess, their mother; and that also Dame Elizabeth Lucy was verily the wife of King Edward, and so the Prince and all his children bastards that were gotten upon the Queen.

According to this device,[822] Doctor Shaa, the Sunday after[823] at Paul's Cross in a great audience (as always assembled great number to his preaching), he took for his theme *Spuria vitulamina non agent radices altas*, that is to say, "Bastard slips[824] shall never take deep root."[825] Thereupon when he had showed the great grace that God giveth and secretly infoundeth[826] in right generation after the laws of matrimony, then declared he that commonly those children lacked that grace, and for the punishment of their parents, were for the more part unhappy, which were gotten in bast[827] and specially in adultery. Of which, though some by the ignorance of the world and the truth hid from knowledge inherited for the season other men's lands, yet God always so provideth that it continueth not in their blood long, but the truth coming to light,[828] the rightful inheritors be restored and the bastard slip pulled up ere it can be rooted deep.

And when he had laid for the proof and confirmation of this sentence certain examples taken out of the Old Testament and other ancient histories, then began he to descend into the praise of the Lord Richard, late Duke of York, calling him father to the Lord Protector, and declared the title of his heirs unto the crown, to whom it was, after the death of King Henry the Sixth, entailed by authority of Parliament. Then showed he that his very right heir of his body, lawfully begotten, was only the Lord Protector. For he declared then that King Edward was never lawfully married unto the Queen, but was, before God, husband unto Dame Elizabeth Lucy, and so his children bastards. And besides that, neither King Edward himself nor the Duke of Clarence, among those that were secret in the household, were reckoned very surely for the children of the noble Duke, as those that by their favors[829] more resembled other known men than him, from whose virtuous conditions he said also that King Edward was far off. "But the Lord Protector,"

---

807 indignantly   **808** frustrated, mocked   **809** military force   **810** before **811** *fained to void:* forced to leave   **812** to a great extent   **813** *what for:* what with, because of   **814** connections

815 *nothing lasteth always:* Whit N158 **816** the Earl   **817** nobles   **818** related **819** slippery, false   **820** justification **821** wished   **822** plan, scheme   **823** after Hastings's execution   **824** shoots;

offspring   **825** See Wis 4:3.   **826** infuses **827** *in bast:* in bastardy, out of wedlock **828** *God…light:* Til T324   **829** looks, faces

he said, "that very noble prince, the special pattern of knightly prowess, as well in all princely behavior as in the lineaments[830] and favor of his visage, represented the very face of the noble Duke his father. This is," quoth he, "the father's own figure; this is his own countenance, the very print[831] of his visage, the sure undoubted image, the plain express likeness of that noble duke."

Now was it before devised that in the speaking of these words the Protector should have comen in among the people to the sermonward,[832] to the end that those words, meeting with his presence, might have been taken among the hearers as though the Holy Ghost had put them in the preacher's mouth, and should have moved the people even there to cry: "King Richard! King Richard!" — that it might have been after said that he was specially chosen by God and, in manner,[833] by miracle. But this device quailed,[834] either by the Protector's negligence or the preacher's overmuch diligence. For while the Protector found, by the way, tarrying[835] (lest he should prevent[836] those words), and the Doctor (fearing that he should come ere his sermon could come to those words) hasted his matter thereto, he was come to them and past them and entered into other matters ere the Protector came. Whom, when he beheld coming, he suddenly left the matter with which he was in hand and, without any deduction[837] thereunto, out of all order and out of all frame, began to repeat those words again: "This is the very noble prince, the special pattern of knightly prowess, which as well in all princely behavior as in the lineaments and favor of his visage representeth the very face of the noble Duke of York his father. This is the father's own figure, this his own countenance, the very print of his visage, the sure undoubted image, the plain express likeness of the noble Duke, whose remembrance can never die while he liveth."

While these words were in speaking, the Protector, accompanied with the Duke of Buckingham, went through the people into the place where the doctors commonly stand, in the upper story, where he stood to hearken the sermon. But the people were so far from crying "King Richard!" that they stood as they had been turned into stones,[838] for wonder of this shameful sermon. After which once ended, the preacher got him home and never after durst look out, for shame, but kept him out of sight like an owl.[839] And when he once asked one that had been his old friend what the people talked of him, all were it that[840] his own conscience well showed him that they talked no good, yet when the other answered him that there was in every man's mouth spoken of him much shame, it so struck him to the heart that, within few days after, he withered and consumed away.

Then on the Tuesday following this sermon, there came unto the Guildhall in London the Duke of Buckingham, accompanied with diverse lords and knights, more than haply[841] knew the message that they brought. And there, in the east end of the hall where the Mayor keepeth the Hustings,[842] the Mayor and all the aldermen being assembled about him, all the commons[843] of the city gathered before them, after silence commanded upon great pain in the Protector's name, the Duke stood up, and (as he was neither unlearned and of nature marvelously well-spoken) he said unto the people with a clear and a loud voice, in this manner of wise:[844]

"Friends, for the zeal and hearty favor that we bear you, we be comen to break[845] unto you of a matter right great and weighty, and no less weighty than pleasing to God and profitable to all the realm — nor to no part of the realm more profitable than to you, the citizens of this noble city. For why? That thing that we wot[846] well ye have long-time lacked and sore[847] longed for, that ye would have given great good for, that ye would have gone far to fetch,[848] that thing we be come hither to bring you, without your labor, pain, cost, adventure, or jeopardy.

"What thing is that? Certes,[849] the surety[850] of your own bodies, the quiet of your wives and your daughters, the safeguard of your goods — of all which things in times past ye stood evermore in doubt.[851] For who was there of you all that would reckon himself lord of his own good, among so many grins[852] and traps as was set therefor, among so much pilling and polling,[853] among so many taxes

---

830 distinctive features   831 imprint
832 *to the sermonward:* to listen to the sermon   833 *in manner:* as it were
834 failed   835 *found...tarrying:* created, on the way, means of delay   836 arrive before   837 introduction   838 *they...*

stones: Whit S786   839 *kept...owl:* Whit O73   840 *all...that:* even though
841 perhaps   842 highest London court for civil matters   843 commoners
844 *this manner of wise:* words to this effect   845 reveal   846 know

847 greatly   848 *That thing...fetch:* Whit F58   849 Certainly   850 security, safety
851 *ye...in doubt:* Til S817   852 snares
853 *pilling and polling:* robbing and extorting

and tallages,[854] of which there was never end and oftentime no need; or if any were, it rather grew of riot[855] and unreasonable waste than any necessary or honorable charge.[856] So that there was daily pilled from good men and honest, great substance of goods to be lashed out[857] among unthrifts so far-forth[858] that fifteens[859] sufficed not—nor any usual names of known taxes—but under an easy[860] name of 'benevolence and good will,'[861] the commissioners so much of every man took as no man would with his good will have given. As though the name of 'benevolence' had signified that every man should pay, not what himself of his good will list[862] to grant, but what the King of his good will list to take. Which[863] never asked little, but everything was hawsed[864] above the measure:[865] amercements[866] turned into fines,[867] fines into ransoms, small trespass to misprision,[868] misprision into treason.

"Whereof, I think, no man looketh that we should remember[869] you of examples by name, as though Burdet were forgotten, that was for a word spoken in haste cruelly beheaded[870] by the misconstruing of the laws of this realm for the Prince's pleasure; with no less honor to Markham, then Chief Justice, that left his office rather than he would assent to that judgment, than to the dishonesty of those that, either for fear or flattery, gave that judgment. What[871] Cook, your own worshipful[872] neighbor, alderman and mayor of this noble city? Who is of you either so negligent that he knoweth not, or so forgetful that he remembreth not, or so hard-hearted that he pitieth not, that worshipful man's loss? What[873] speak we of loss? His utter spoil[874] and undeserved destruction, only for that[875] it happed those to favor him whom the Prince favored not. We need not, I suppose, to rehearse of[876] these any more by name, since there be, I doubt not, many here present that either in themselves or their nigh[877] friends have known as well their goods as their persons greatly endangered, either by feigned quarrels or small matters aggrieved[878] with heinous names.

"And also there was no crime so great of which

there could lack a pretext. For since the King, preventing[879] the time of his inheritance, attained the crown by battle, it sufficed in a rich man for a pretext of treason to have been of kindred or alliance,[880] near familiarity or leger[881] acquaintance with any of those that were at any time the King's enemies, which was at one time and other, more than half the realm. Thus were neither your goods in surety,[882] and yet they brought your bodies in jeopardy—besides the common adventure[883] of open war, which, albeit that[884] it is ever the well[885] and occasion of much mischief, yet is it never so mischievous as where any people fall at distance[886] among themselves, nor in none earthly nation so deadly and so pestilent as when it happeneth among us, and among us never so long-continued dissension, nor so many battles in the season, nor so cruel and so deadly foughten, as was in the King's days that dead is, God forgive it his soul. In whose time and by whose occasion—what about[887] the getting of the garland,[888] keeping it, losing and winning again—it hath cost more English blood than hath twice the winning of France. In which inward war among ourselves hath been so great effusion of the ancient noble blood of this realm that scarcely the half remaineth, to the great enfeebling of this noble land, besides many a good town ransacked and spoiled[889] by them that have been going to the field[890] or coming from thence. And peace long after not much surer than war.[891] So that no time was there in which rich men for their money and great men for their lands, or some other for some fear or some displeasure were not out of peril. For whom trusted he that mistrusted his own brother? Whom spared he that killed his own brother?[892] Or who could perfectly love him, if his own brother could not?

"What manner of folk he most favored, we shall, for his honor, spare to speak of.[893] Howbeit, this wot you well all: that whoso was best bore always least rule, and more suit was in his days unto Shore's wife, a vile and an abominable strumpet, than to all the lords in England—except unto those that made her

---

854 levies **855** extravagance **856** *honorable charge:* legitimate expense **857** *lashed out:* squandered **858** *so far-forth:* to such an extent **859** taxes on personal property, equivalent to one-fifteenth of it **860** convenient **861** *benevolence… good will:* Edward was the first to levy what he termed "benevolences" and "good will" offerings: taxes imposed, without approval by Parliament. **862** chose **863** Who

(the King) **864** raised **865** *limit; everything… measure:* Whit M463 **866** small fees or penalties set by the judge **867** fees or penalties set by statute **868** offense similar to but less serious than treason or felony **869** remind **870** *that… beheaded:* Whit W591 **871** What of **872** honorable **873** Why **874** robbery **875** *for that:* because **876** *rehearse of:* mention **877** close **878** exaggerated

879 anticipating, preceding **880** connection by marriage **881** slight **882** safety **883** *common adventure:* shared risk **884** *albeit that:* although **885** wellspring, source **886** discord, dissension **887** with **888** crown **889** plundered **890** battlefield **891** *peace… war:* Til C223 **892** Edward's brother George **893** *we… speak of:* Whit R100; Til R93

their proctor[894]—which simple woman was well-named and honest till the King, for his wanton lust and sinful affection, bereft her from her husband, a right honest substantial[895] young man among you. And in that point, which in good faith I am sorry to speak of, saving that it is in vain to keep in counsel that thing that all men know: the King's greedy appetite was insatiable, and everywhere over all the realm intolerable. For no woman was there anywhere—young or old, rich or poor, whom he set his eye upon, in whom he anything liked, either person or favor, speech, pace, or countenance—but without any fear of God or respect of his honor, murmur or grudge of the world, he would importunately[896] pursue his appetite and have her, to the great destruction of many a good woman, and great dolor to their husbands and their other friends, which being honest people of themselves so much regard the cleanness of their house, the chastity of their wives and their children that them were liefer[897] to lose all that they have beside than to have such a villainy done them.

"And all were it that[898] with this and other importable[899] dealing the realm was in every part annoyed,[900] yet specially ye here, the citizens of this noble city, as well for that[901] among you is most plenty of all such things as minister[902] matter to such injuries, as for that you were nearest at hand, since that near hereabout was commonly his most abiding. And yet be ye the people whom he had as singular cause well and kindly to entreat as any part of his realm, not only for that the Prince by this noble city (as his special chamber and the special well-renowned city of his realm) much honorable fame receiveth among all other nations, but also for that ye, not without your great cost and sundry perils and jeopardies in all his wars, bore ever your special favor to his party, which your kind minds [have] borne to the house of York, since he hath nothing worthily acquitted,[903] there is of that house that now, by God's grace, better shall; which thing to show you is the whole sum and effect of this our present errand.

"It shall not, I wot well, need that I rehearse you again that ye have already heard of him that can better tell it, and of whom, I am sure, ye will better believe it. And reason is, that it so be. I am not

so proud to look therefor, that ye should reckon my words of as great authority as the preacher's of the word of God, namely a man so cunning and so wise that no man better wotteth what he should say, and thereto[904] so good and virtuous that he would not say the thing which he wist[905] he should not say in the pulpit, namely, into which none honest man cometh to lie. Which honorable preacher, ye well remember, substantially declared unto you, at Paul's Cross on Sunday last past, the right and title that the most excellent prince, Richard Duke of Gloucester, now Protector of this realm, hath unto the crown and kingdom of the same.

"For as that worshipful[906] man groundly[907] made open unto you, the children of King Edward the Fourth were never lawfully begotten, forasmuch as the King (living his very[908] wife, Dame Elizabeth Lucy) was never lawfully married unto the Queen, their mother—whose blood, saving that he set his voluptuous pleasure before his honor, was full unmeetly[909] to be matched with his, and the mingling of whose bloods together hath been the effusion of great part of the noble blood of this realm. Whereby it may well seem that marriage not well made, of which there is so much mischief grown.[910] For lack of which lawful accoupling and also of other things which the said worshipful doctor rather signified than fully explained, and which things shall not be spoken for me, as the thing wherein[911] every man forbeareth[912] to say that he knoweth in avoiding displeasure of my noble Lord Protector, bearing, as nature requireth a filial reverence to the Duchess, his mother—for these causes, I say, before remembered, that is to wit,[913] for lack of other issue lawfully coming of the late noble prince Richard Duke of York, to whose royal blood the crown of England and of France is by the high authority of Parliament entailed—the right and title of the same is by the just course of inheritance, according to the common law of this land, devolute[914] and comen unto the most excellent prince the Lord Protector as to the very lawfully begotten son of the fore-remembered[915] noble Duke of York.

"Which thing well considered, and the great knightly prowess pondered, with manifold virtues which in his noble person singularly abound, the

894 advocate   **895** well-to-do
896 persistently, imploringly   **897** *them were liefer:* they would prefer   **898** *all were it that:* although   **899** intolerable

900 injured, offended   **901** *for that:* because   **902** furnish   **903** requited, repaid   **904** also   **905** knew   **906** honorable   **907** soundly   **908** true

909 unfit   **910** *marriage…grown:* Til M679   **911** of which   **912** refrains   **913** say   **914** transmitted to, inherited by   **915** previously mentioned nobles and commons also of this realm, and specially of the north parts, not willing any bastard blood to have the rule of the land, nor the abusions[916] before in the same used[917] any longer to continue, have condescended[918] and fully determined to make humble petition unto the most puissant[919] prince the Lord Protector that it may like his Grace, at our humble request, to take upon him the guiding and governance of this realm to the wealth and increase of the same, according to his very right and just title. Which thing, I wot[920] it well, he will be loath to take upon him, as he whose wisdom well perceiveth the labor and study both of mind and of body that shall come therewith to whomsoever so well occupy that room,[921] as I dare say he will if he take it. Which room, I warn you well, is no child's office.[922] And that, the great wise man[923] well perceived when he said, *Vae regno cuius rex puer est,* 'Woe is that realm that hath a child to[924] their king.'

"Wherefore, so much the more cause have we to thank God that this noble personage, which is so righteously entitled thereunto, is of so sad[925] age, and thereto of so great wisdom joined with so great experience; which[926]—albeit[927] he will be loath, as I have said, to take it upon him—yet shall he, to our petition in that behalf, the more graciously incline if ye, the worshipful citizens of this the chief city of this realm, join with us, the nobles, in our said request. Which for your own weal[928] we doubt not but ye will, and nevertheless I heartily pray[929] you so to do; whereby you shall do great profit to all this realm beside, in choosing them so good a king, and unto yourselves special commodity,[930] to whom his Majesty shall ever after bear so much the more tender favor, in how much he shall perceive you the more prone and benevolently minded toward his election. Wherein, dear friends, what mind you have, we require[931] you plainly to show us."

When the Duke had said—and looked that the people, whom he hoped the Mayor had framed[932] before, should, after this proposition made, have cried "King Richard! King Richard!"—all was hushed and mute, and not one word answered thereunto. Wherewith the Duke was marvelously abashed, and taking the Mayor nearer to him, with others that were about him privy to that matter, said unto them softly, "What meaneth this, that this people be so still?"

"Sir," quoth the Mayor, "percase[933] they perceive you not well."

"That shall we mend," quoth he, "if that will help." And by and by,[934] somewhat louder, he rehearsed[935] them the same matter again in other order and other words, so well and ornately, and nevertheless so evidently and plain, with voice, gesture, and countenance so comely and so convenient,[936] that every man much marveled that heard him, and thought that they never had in their lives heard so evil a tale so well told. But were it for wonder or fear, or that each look that other should speak first, not one word was there answered of all the people that stood before, but all was as still as the midnight,[937] not so much as rounding[938] among them, by which they might seem to commune[939] what was best to do.

When the Mayor saw this, he, with other partners of that counsel, drew about the Duke and said that the people had not been accustomed there to be spoken unto but by the Recorder, which is the mouth of the city, and haply[940] to him they will answer.

With that, the Recorder, called Fitzwilliam, a sad[941] man and an honest, which was so new come into that office that he never had spoken to the people before—and loath was with that matter to begin, notwithstanding, thereunto commanded by the Mayor, made rehearsal to the commons[942] of that[943] the Duke had twice rehearsed them himself. But the Recorder so tempered his tale that he showed everything as the Duke's words and no part his own. But all this nothing no change[944] made in the people, which always, after[945] one, stood as they had been men amazed.

Whereupon the Duke rounded[946] unto the Mayor and said, "This is a marvelous obstinate silence," and therewith he turned unto the people again, with these words: "Dear friends, we come to move you to that thing which peradventure[947] we not so greatly needed, but that the lords of this realm and

916 abuses **917** allowed **918** agreed **919** mighty **920** know **921** office **922** *Which... office:* Whit 436; Til W600 **923** *the great wise man:* Solomon. See Eccl 10:16. **924** for **925** mature **926** who **927** although **928** well-being; advantage

929 ask **930** benefit **931** ask **932** shaped, prepared **933** perhaps **934** *by and by:* immediately **935** told **936** appropriate **937** *all... midnight:* Whit M532 **938** whispering **939** discuss, confer **940** perhaps **941** sober;

grave **942** commoners **943** what **944** *nothing no change:* no change whatsoever **945** as **946** whispered **947** perhaps

the commons of other parts might have sufficed, saving that we such love bear you, and so much set by you, that we would not gladly do without you that thing in which to be partners is your weal and honor, which, as it seemeth, either you see not or weigh not. Wherefore we require[948] you give us answer one or other: whether you be minded as all the nobles of the realm be, to have this noble prince, now Protector, to be your king or not."

At these words the people began to whisper among themselves secretly, that the voice was neither loud nor distinct, but, as it were, the sound of a swarm of bees,[949] till at the last, in the nether[950] end of the hall, a bushment[951] of the Duke's servants and Nashfield's, and others longing[952] to the Protector, with some prentices and lads that thrust[953] into the hall among the press,[954] began suddenly at men's backs to cry out as loud as their throats would give, "King Richard! King Richard!"—and threw up their caps in token of joy. And they that stood before[955] cast back their heads, marveling thereof, but nothing they said. And when the Duke and the Mayor saw this manner, they wisely turned it to their purpose, and said it was a goodly cry and a joyful to hear, every man with one voice, no man saying nay.

"Wherefore, friends," quoth the Duke, "since that we perceive it is all your whole minds to have this noble man for your king, whereof we shall make his Grace so effectual[956] report that we doubt not but it shall redound unto your great weal and commodity,[957] we require ye that ye tomorrow go with us and we with you unto his noble Grace, to make our humble request unto him in manner before remembered."[958]

And therewith the lords came down, and the company dissolved and departed, the more part all sad, some with glad semblance that were not very merry, and some of those that came thither with the Duke, not able to dissemble their sorrow, were fain[959] at his back to turn their face to the wall while the dolor of their heart burst out at their eyes.

Then on the morrow after, the Mayor, with all the aldermen and chief commoners of the city, in their best manner appareled, assembling themselves together, resorted unto Baynard's Castle, where the Protector lay. To which place repaired also, according to their appointment, the Duke of Buckingham, with diverse noblemen with him, beside many knights and other gentlemen. And thereupon the Duke sent word unto the Lord Protector of the being-there of a great and honorable company, to move a great matter unto his Grace.

Whereupon the Protector made difficulty to come out unto them, but if[960] he first knew some part of their errand, as though he doubted and partly distrusted the coming of such number unto him so suddenly, without any warning or knowledge whether they came for good or harm. Then the Duke, when he had showed this unto the Mayor and others, that they might thereby see how little the Protector looked for this matter, they sent unto him by the messenger such loving message again, and therewith so humbly besought him to vouchsafe[961] that they might resort to[962] his presence to purpose their intent, of which they would unto none other person any part disclose, that at the last he came forth of[963] his chamber, and yet not down unto them, but stood above in a gallery over them, where they might see him and speak to him, as though he would not yet come too near them till he wist[964] what they meant.

And thereupon the Duke of Buckingham first made humble petition unto him, on the behalf of them all, that his Grace would pardon them and license them to purpose[965] unto his Grace the intent of their coming without his displeasure, without which pardon obtained, they durst[966] not be bold to move him of that matter. In which, albeit[967] they meant as much honor to his Grace as wealth to all the realm beside, yet were they not sure how his Grace would take it, whom they would in no wise[968] offend.

Then the Protector, as he was very gentle of himself and also longed sore to wit[969] what they meant, gave him leave to purpose what him liked, verily trusting, for the good mind that he bore them all, none of them anything would intend unto himward wherewith he ought to be grieved. When the Duke had this leave and pardon to speak, then waxed[970] he bold to show him their intent and purpose, with all the causes moving them thereunto, as ye before

948 ask that   **949** *the sound…bees:* Whit S937   **950** lower   **951** secretly planted group; ambush   **952** belonging   **953** forcibly made their way   **954** crowd

955 in front   **956** enthusiastic; effective   **957** advantage   **958** previously mentioned   **959** obliged   **960** *but if:* unless   **961** grant   **962** *resort to:*

come into   **963** from   **964** knew   **965** propose   **966** dared   **967** although   **968** way   **969** *sore to wit:* greatly to know   **970** became have heard, and finally to beseech his Grace that it would like him, of his accustomed goodness and zeal unto the realm, now with his eye of pity, to behold the long-continued distress and decay of the same and to set his gracious hands to the redress and amendment thereof, by taking upon him the crown and governance of this realm, according to his right and title lawfully descended unto him, and to the laud of God, profit of the land, and unto his Grace so much the more honor and less pain, in that that never prince reigned upon any people that were so glad to live under his obeisance[971] as the people of this realm under his.

When the Protector had heard the proposition, he looked very strangely thereat, and answered that, all were it that[972] he partly knew the things by them alleged to be true, yet such entire love he bore unto King Edward and his children, and so much more regarded his honor in other realms about than the crown of any one, of which he was never desirous, that he could not find in his heart in this point to incline to their desire. For in all other nations where the truth were not well known, it should peradventure[973] be thought that it were his own ambitious mind and device to depose the Prince and take himself the crown. With which infamy he would not have his honor stained for any crown. In which, he had ever perceived much more labor and pain than pleasure to him that so would use it as he that would not were not worthy to have it. Notwithstanding, he not only pardoned them the motion that they made him, but also thanked them for the love and hearty favor they bore him, praying them for his sake to give and bear the same to the Prince, under whom he was and would be content to live; and with his labor and counsel, as far as should like the King to use him, he would do his uttermost devoir[974] to set the realm in good state. Which was already in this little while of his protectorship (the praise given to God) well begun, in that the malice of such as were before occasion of the contrary and of new[975] intended to be, were now (partly by good policy, partly more by God's special providence than man's provision[976]) repressed.

Upon this answer given, the Duke, by the Protector's license, a little rounded[977] as well with other noblemen about him as with the Mayor and Recorder of London. And after that, upon like pardon desired and obtained, he showed aloud unto the Protector that, for a final conclusion, that the realm was appointed[978] King Edward's line should not any longer reign upon them, both for that[979] they had so far gone that it was now no surety to retreat, as for that they thought it for the weal universal[980] to take that way, although they had not yet begun it. Wherefore, if it would like his Grace to take the crown upon him, they would humbly beseech him thereunto. If he would give them a resolute answer to the contrary, which they would be loath to hear,[981] then must they needs seek and should not fail to find some other nobleman that would.

These words much moved the Protector, which else,[982] as every man may wit, would never of likelihood have inclined thereunto. But when he saw there was none other way, but that either he must take it or else he and his[983] both go from it,[984] he said unto the lords and commons: "Since we perceive well that all the realm is so set, whereof we be very sorry that they will not suffer[985] in any wise King Edward's line to govern them, whom no man earthly[986] can govern again[987] their wills, and we well also perceive that no man is there to whom the crown can by so just title appertain[988] as to ourselves, as very right heir, lawfully begotten of the body of our most dear father Richard, late Duke of York, to which title is now joined your election, the nobles and commons of this realm, which we of all titles possible take for most effectual:[989] we be content, and agree favorably to incline to your petition and request and, according to the same, here we take upon us the royal estate, preeminence, and kingdom of the two noble realms England and France — the one from this day forward by us and our heirs to rule, govern, and defend; the other, by God's grace and your good help, to get again and subdue, and establish forever in due obedience unto this realm of England, the advancement whereof we never ask of God longer to live than we intend to procure."

With this there was a great shout crying "King Richard! King Richard!"

And then the lords went up to the King (for so was he from that time called), and the people

---

971 rule; obedience, submission
972 *all…that:* although **973** perhaps
974 effort **975** *of new:* recently
976 foresight, planning; *more…provision:*

Whit M162; Til M298 **977** whispered **978** determined **979** *for that:* because **980** *weal universal:* good of all **981** *which…hear:* Whit L418 **982** *which*

else: who otherwise **983** his nephew **984** *he must…from it:* Whit T14; Til T28 **985** allow **986** in the world **987** against **988** belong **989** valid

departed, talking diversely of the matter, every man as his fantasy gave him.

But much they talked and marveled of the manner of this dealing, that the matter was on both parts made so strange, as though neither had ever communed with other thereof before, when that themselves well wist there was no man so dull that heard them but he perceived well enough that all the matter was made between them. Howbeit,[990] some excused that again, and said all must be done in good order though. And men must sometimes for the manner sake[991] not be acknown[992] what they know.[993] For at the consecration of a bishop, every man wotteth[994] well, by the paying for his bulls,[995] that he purposeth to be one, and[996] though he pay for nothing else. And yet must he be twice asked whether he will be bishop or no, and he must twice say nay, and at the third time take it as compelled thereunto by his own will.

And in a stage play all the people know right well that he that playeth the soudan[997] is percase[998] a souter.[999] Yet if one should can so little good[1] to show out of season what acquaintance he hath with him, and call him by his own name while he standeth in his majesty, one of his tormentors might hap to break his head — and worthy,[2] for marring of the play. And so they said that these matters be kings' games, as it were, stage plays, and for the more part played upon scaffolds,[3] in which poor men be but the lookers-on. And they that wise be, will meddle no farther. For they that sometimes step up and play with them, when they cannot play their parts, they disorder the play and do themselves no good.

‡[4]The next day the Protector, with a great train,[5] went to Westminster Hall, and there, when he had placed himself in the Court of the King's Bench, declared to the audience that he would take upon him the crown in that place there, where the king himself sitteth and ministreth the law, because he considered that it was the chiefest duty of a king to minister the laws. Then, with as pleasant an oration as he could, he went about to win unto him the nobles, the merchants, the artificers, and, in

conclusion, all kind of men — but specially the lawyers of this realm. And finally, to the intent that no man should hate him for fear, and that his deceitful clemency might get him the good will of the people, when he had declared the discommodity[6] of discord and the commodities[7] of concord and unity, he made an open[8] proclamation that he did put out of his mind all enmities, and that he there did openly pardon all offenses committed against him. And to the intent that he might show a proof thereof, he commanded that one Fogge, whom he had long deadly hated, should be brought then before him. Who, being brought out of the sanctuary by[9] (for thither had he fled, for fear of him), in the sight of the people he took him by the hand. Which thing the common people rejoiced at and praised, but wise men took it for a vanity. In his return homeward, whomsoever he met, he saluted. For a mind that knoweth itself guilty is in a manner dejected[10] to a servile flattery.

When he had begun his reign the twenty-sixth day of June after this mockish election, then was he crowned the sixth day of July. And that solemnity was furnished for the most part with the selfsame provision that was appointed for the coronation of his nephew.*

Now fell there mischiefs thick.[11] And as the thing evil-gotten is never well-kept,[12] through all the time of his reign never ceased there cruel death and slaughter, till his own destruction ended it. But as he finished his time with the best death and the most righteous, that is to wit,[13] his own, so began he with the most piteous and wicked, I mean the lamentable murder of his innocent nephews, the young King and his tender brother, whose death and final infortune[14] hath nevertheless so far comen in question that some remain yet in doubt whether they were in his days destroyed or no. Not for that only that[15] Perkin Warbeck, by many folks' malice and more folks' folly so long space abusing[16] the world, was as well with princes as the poorer people reputed and taken for the younger of those two, but for that also that[17] all things were in late days so

---

990 However　**991** *for the manner sake:* for the sake of custom; Whit M363, M464; Til 806　**992** *be acknown:* acknowledge　**993** *men . . . know:* Whit W691; Til K173　**994** knows　**995** the papal documents authorizing that he be made a bishop　**996** even　**997** sultan　**998** perhaps　**999** shoemaker　**1** *can . . . good:* have so

little sense as　**2** deservedly　**3** stages for plays; platforms for executions　**4** ‡: The editor of the 1557 *Workes* added this note: "This that is here between this mark ‡ and this mark* was not written by Mr. More in this history written by him in English, but is translated out of this history which he wrote in Latin."　**5** retinue, entourage

6 unprofitability　**7** advantages　**8** public　**9** nearby　**10** abased　**11** *Now . . . thick:* Whit H139　**12** *as . . . well-kept:* Whit G333, G342; Til G305　**13** say　**14** misfortune　**15** *Not . . . that:* Not only because　**16** *so . . . abusing:* for so long a time misleading　**17** *for that also that:* also because

covertly demeaned,[18] one thing pretended and another meant,[19] that there was nothing so plain and openly proved, but that yet for[20] the common custom of close[21] and covert dealing, men had it ever inwardly suspect, as many well-counterfeited jewels make the true mistrusted.[22] Howbeit,[23] concerning that opinion, with the occasions moving either party, we shall have place more at large to entreat[24] if we hereafter happen to write the time of the late noble prince of famous memory King Henry the Seventh, or percase[25] that history of Perkin in any compendious process[26] by itself.

But in the meantime, for this present matter, I shall rehearse you the dolorous end of those babes, not after every way that I have heard, but after that way that I have so heard by such men and by such means as methinketh it were hard but it should be true. King Richard, after his coronation — taking his way to Gloucester to visit, in his new honor, the town of which he bore the name of his old[27] — devised, as he rode, to fulfill that thing which he before had intended. And forasmuch as his mind gave him that, his nephews living, men would not reckon that he could have right to the realm, he thought therefore without delay to rid them, as though the killing of his kinsmen could amend his cause and make him a kindly king.

Whereupon he sent one John Green, whom he specially trusted, unto Sir Robert Brackenbury, Constable of the Tower, with a letter and credence[28] also that the same Sir Robert should in any wise[29] put the two children to death. This John Green did his errand[30] unto Brackenbury, kneeling before our Lady in the Tower, who plainly answered that he would never put them to death — to die therefor — with which answer John Green, returning, recounted the same to King Richard at Warwick, yet in[31] his way.

Wherewith he took such displeasure and thought that the same night he said unto a secret[32] page of his, "Ah, whom shall a man trust?[33] Those that I have brought up myself, those that I had weened[34] would most surely serve me — even those fail me and at my commandment will do nothing for me."

"Sir," quoth his page, "there lieth one on your pallet without, that,[35] I dare well say, to do your Grace pleasure, the thing were right hard that he would refuse," meaning this by Sir James Tyrell, which was a man of right goodly personage, and for nature's gifts, worthy to have served a much better prince, if he had well served God and by grace obtained as much troth[36] and good will as he had strength and wit. The man had a high[37] heart and sore[38] longed upward, not rising yet so fast as he had hoped, being hindered and kept under by the means of Sir Richard Radcliff and Sir William Catesby, which,[39] longing for no more partners of the Prince's favor, and namely not for him whose pride they wist[40] would bear no peer, kept him by secret drifts[41] out of all secret trust. Which thing this page well had marked and known. Wherefore, this occasion offered, of very special friendship he took his time to put him forward, and by such wise do him good that all the enemies he had except the devil could never have done him so much hurt.[42]

For upon this page's words, King Richard arose (for this communication had he sitting at the draught,[43] a convenient carpet[44] for such a council) and came out into the pallet chamber,[45] on which he found in bed Sir James and Sir Thomas Tyrell, of person like and brethren of blood, but nothing of kin in conditions.

Then said the King merrily to them, "What, sirs? Be ye in bed so soon?" — and calling up Sir James, broke[46] to him secretly his mind in this mischievous matter, in which he found him nothing strange.[47] Wherefore on the morrow he sent him to Brackenbury with a letter by which he was commanded to deliver Sir James all the keys of the Tower for one night, to the end he might there accomplish the King's pleasure in such thing as he had given him commandment. After which letter delivered and the keys received, Sir James appointed the night next ensuing to destroy them, devising before and preparing the means.

The Prince, as soon as the Protector left that name and took himself as king, had it showed unto him that he should not reign, but his uncle should

---

18 conducted; managed **19** *one . . . meant:* Whit T189 **20** because of **21** secret **22** *as . . . mistrusted:* Whit J44 **23** However **24** treat **25** perhaps **26** *compendious process:* succinct narrative **27** *of his old:* in

his previous one (Duke of Gloucester) **28** a document furnishing credentials **29** manner **30** *did his errand:* delivered his message **31** on **32** personal, private **33** *whom . . . trust:* Whit W423; Til M198 **34** thought **35** who **36** faithfulness;

truthfulness **37** haughty **38** greatly **39** who **40** knew **41** schemes **42** *of . . . hurt:* Whit F673, G219; Til F739 **43** toilet **44** *convenient carpet:* appropriate setting **45** *pallet chamber:* waiting room **46** revealed **47** unwilling

have the crown. At which word the Prince, sore abashed,[48] began to sigh and said, "Alas, I would my uncle would let me have my life yet, though I lose my kingdom." Then he that told him the tale used him with good words, and put him in the best comfort he could.[49] But forthwith[50] was the Prince and his brother both shut up, and all others removed from them, only one called "Black Will" or "William Slaughter" except, set to serve them and see them sure.[51] After which time the Prince never tied his points,[52] nor aught rought of[53] himself, but with that young babe his brother lingered in thought and heaviness[54] till this traitorous death delivered them of that wretchedness.

For Sir James Tyrell devised that they should be murdered in their beds. To the execution whereof, he appointed Miles Forest, one of the four that kept them, a fellow fleshed[55] in murder beforetime. To him he joined one John Dighton, his own horsekeeper: a big, broad, square, strong knave. Then, all the others being removed from them, this Miles Forest and John Dighton about midnight (the seely[56] children lying in their beds) came into the chamber and suddenly lapped them up among the clothes[57] — so bewrapped them and entangled them, keeping down by force the featherbed[58] and pillows hard unto their mouths, that within a while, smored[59] and stifled, their breath failing, they gave up to God their innocent souls into the joys of heaven, leaving to the tormentors their bodies dead in the bed. Which,[60] after that the wretches perceived[61] — first by the struggling with the pains of death, and after, long lying still — to be thoroughly dead, they laid their bodies naked out upon the bed, and fetched Sir James to see them. Which,[62] upon the sight of them, caused those murderers to bury them at the stair-foot, meetly[63] deep in the ground, under a great heap of stones.

Then rode Sir James in great haste to King Richard, and showed him all the manner of the murder, who gave him great thanks and (as some say) there made him knight. But he allowed not, as I have heard, the burying in so vile a corner, saying that he would have them buried in a better place because

they were a king's sons. Lo, the honorable courage[64] of a king! Whereupon they say that a priest of Sir Robert Brackenbury took up the bodies again and secretly interred them in such place as, by the occasion of his death which only[65] knew it, could never since come to light. Very truth is it and well known that at such time as Sir James Tyrell was in the Tower for treason committed against the most famous prince King Henry the Seventh, both Dighton and he were examined, and confessed the murder in manner above-written, but whither the bodies were removed, they could nothing tell.

And thus, as I have learned of them that much knew and little cause had to lie, were these two noble princes — these innocent tender children, born of most royal blood, brought up in great wealth, likely long to live to reign and rule in the realm — by traitorous tyranny taken, deprived of their estate, shortly[66] shut up in prison, and privily slain and murdered, their bodies cast God wot[67] where by the cruel ambition of their unnatural uncle and his dispiteous tormentors. Which things on every part well pondered, God never gave this world a more notable example neither in what unsurety standeth this worldly weal,[68] or what mischief worketh the proud enterprise of a high heart,[69] or finally, what wretched end ensueth such dispiteous cruelty.[70]

For first to begin with the ministers: Miles Forest at Saint Martin's[71] piecemeal rotted away. Dighton, indeed, yet walketh on alive in good possibility to be hanged ere[72] he die. But Sir James Tyrell died at Tower Hill, beheaded for treason. King Richard himself, as ye shall hereafter hear, slain in the field, hacked and hewed of[73] his enemies' hands, harried[74] on horseback dead, his hair in despite[75] torn and tugged like a cur dog. And the mischief that he took, within less than three years of the mischief that he did, in three months be not comparable.[76] And yet all the meantime spent in much pain and trouble outward; much fear, anguish, and sorrow within. For I have heard by credible report of such as were secret with his chamberers that after this abominable deed done, he never had quiet in his mind;[77] he never thought himself sure.[78] Where

---

48 distraught **49** *used…could:* Til U26
50 immediately **51** safe, secure **52** laces for attaching hose to doublet **53** *aught rought of:* took any care for **54** sadness
55 experienced **56** poor, helpless
57 bedclothes **58** mattress **59** smothered **60** Who (i.e., the executioners)

61 *wretches perceived:* i.e., the children were perceived **62** Who (Sir James)
63 suitably **64** spirit, disposition
65 *which only:* who alone **66** abruptly, speedily **67** knows **68** prosperity; *in…weal:* Whit W671 **69** *what… heart:* Whit P384 **70** *what…cruelty:*

Til L247; Whit L250, L412 **71** *Saint Martin's:* a sanctuary **72** before **73** by **74** dragged around **75** contempt **76** *the mischief…comparable:* Til L247; Whit L250, L412 **77** *after…mind:* Til F139
78 safe, secure

he went abroad, his eyes whirled about, his body privily fenced,[79] his hand ever on his dagger, his countenance and manner like one always ready to strike again;[80] he took ill rest a-nights, lay long waking and musing, sore[81] wearied with care and watch, rather slumbered than slept, troubled with fearful dreams, suddenly sometimes start up, leap out of his bed and run about the chamber — so was his restless heart continually tossed and tumbled with the tedious[82] impression and stormy remembrance of his abominable deed.

Now, had he outward[83] no long time in rest. For hereupon soon after began the conspiracy, or rather good confederation, between the Duke of Buckingham and many other gentlemen against him. The occasion whereupon the King and the Duke fell out is of diverse folk diverse wise pretended.[84] This duke, as I have for certain been informed, as soon as the Duke of Gloucester,[85] upon the death of King Edward, came to York, and there had solemn funeral service for King Edward, sent thither, in the most secret wise he could, one Percival, his[86] trusty servant, who came to John Ward, a chamberer of like secret trust with the Duke of Gloucester, desiring that in the most close[87] and covert manner he[88] might be admitted to the presence and speech of his master.[89] And the Duke of Gloucester, advertised[90] of his desire, caused him in the dead of the night, after all other folk avoided,[91] to be brought unto him in his secret[92] chamber, where Percival, after his master's recommendation, showed him that he had secretly sent him to show him that in this new world he would take such part as he would, and wait upon him with a thousand good fellows if need were. The messenger, sent back with thanks and some secret instruction of the Protector's mind, yet met him again with further message from the duke his master,[93] within few days after at Nottingham, whither the Protector from York, with many gentlemen of the north country, to the number of six hundred horses,[94] was comen on his way to Londonward. And after secret meeting and communication had, eftsoon,[95] departed.

Whereupon at Northampton the Duke met with the Protector himself, with 300 horses, and from thence still continued with him as partner of all his devices, till that after his coronation they departed, as it seemed, very great friends at Gloucester. From whence, as soon as the Duke came home, he so lightly turned from him and so highly conspired against him that a man would marvel whereof that change grew. And surely the occasion of their variance[96] is of diverse men diversely reported.[97] Some have I heard say that the Duke, a little before the coronation, among other things required[98] of the Protector the Duke of Hereford's lands, to which he pretended himself just inheritor. And forasmuch as the title which he claimed by inheritance was somewhat interlaced with the title to the crown by the line of King Henry, before deprived,[99] the Protector conceived such indignation that he rejected the Duke's request with many spiteful and minatory[100] words, which so wounded his heart with hatred and mistrust that he never after could endure to look aright[101] on King Richard, but ever feared[102] his own life so far-forth that, when the Protector rode through London toward his coronation, he feigned himself sick, because he would not ride with him. And the other, taking it in evil part,[103] sent him word to rise and come ride or he would make him be carried. Whereupon he rode on with evil will and, that notwithstanding, on the morrow rose from the feast feigning himself sick; and King Richard said it was done in hatred and despite[104] of him. And they say that ever after, continually, each of them lived in such hatred and distrust of other that the Duke verily looked[105] to have been murdered at Gloucester. From which, nevertheless, he in fair manner departed.

But surely some right secret at the days[106] deny this; and many right wise men think it unlikely (the deep dissimulating nature of those both men considered, and what need in that green world the Protector had of the Duke, and in what peril the Duke stood if he fell once in suspicion of the tyrant) that either the Protector would give the Duke occasion of displeasure, or the Duke, the Protector occasion of mistrust. And utterly men think that if King

---

79 *privily fenced:* secretly shielded
80 back   **81** very   **82** troublesome
83 publicly   **84** alleged; *diverse…pretended:* Whit F370   **85** *Duke of Gloucester:* Richard's title before he became Protector
86 Buckingham's   **87** secret   **88** Percival

89 Richard (Ward's master)   **90** notified
91 had left   **92** private   **93** Buckingham
94 horsemen; cavalry   **95** soon after, again
96 falling out   **97** *diverse…reported:* Whit F370   **98** requested   **99** deposed
100 menacing, threatening   **101** directly;

correctly   **102** feared for   **103** *taking…part:* taking it badly; taking offense at it
104 contempt   **105** *verily looked:* truly expected   **106** *right…days:* especially privy to secrets at that time

Richard had any such opinion conceived, he would never have suffered[107] him to escape his hands. Very truth it is, the Duke was a high-minded[108] man, and evil[109] could bear the glory of another — so that I have heard, of some that said they saw it, that the Duke, at such time as the crown was first set upon the Protector's head, his eye could not abide the sight thereof, but wried[110] his head another way. But men say that he was of troth not well at ease, and that both to King Richard well known and not ill taken, nor any demand[111] of the Duke's uncourteously rejected, but he, both with great gifts and high behests,[112] in most loving and trusty manner departed at Gloucester.

But soon after his coming home to Brecknock, having there in his custody, by the commandment of King Richard, Doctor Morton, Bishop of Ely (who, as ye before heard, was taken[113] in the Council at the Tower), waxed with him familiar.[114] Whose wisdom abused[115] his pride to his own deliverance and the Duke's destruction.[116] The Bishop was a man of great natural wit, very well-learned, and honorable in behavior, lacking no wise ways to win favor. He had been fast[117] upon the party of King Henry while that party was in wealth,[118] and nevertheless left it not nor forsook it in woe,[119] but fled the realm with the Queen and the Prince while King Edward had the King[120] in prison — never came home but to the field. After which lost, and that party utterly subdued, the other,[121] for his fast faith[122] and wisdom, not only was content to receive him, but also wooed him to come and had him from thenceforth both in secret trust and very special favor, which he nothing deceived. For he — being, as ye have heard, after King Edward's death first taken[123] by the tyrant for his troth[124] to the King[125] — found the means to set this duke in his top:[126] joined gentlemen together in aid of King Henry,[127] devising first the marriage between him and King Edward's daughter,[128] by which his faith declared and good service to both his masters at once, with infinite benefit to the realm by the conjunction of those two bloods in one, whose several titles had long inquieted the land. He fled the realm, went to Rome, never minding more to meddle with the world till the noble prince King Henry the Seventh got him home again, made him Archbishop of Canterbury and Chancellor of England, whereunto the Pope joined the honor of Cardinal. Thus living many days in as much honor as one man might well wish, ended them so godly that his death, with God's mercy, well-changed his life.

This man, therefore, as I was about to tell you, by the long and often alternate proof,[129] as well of prosperity as adverse fortune, had gotten by great experience, the very mother and mistress of wisdom,[130] a deep insight in politic worldly drifts.[131] Whereby, perceiving now this duke glad to commune[132] with him, fed him with fair words and many pleasant praises.[133] And perceiving by the process of their communications the Duke's pride now and then bolk out[134] a little braid[135] of envy toward the glory of the King, and thereby feeling him easy to fall out if the matter were well-handled, he craftily sought the ways to prick him forward, taking always the occasion of his coming, and so keeping himself close within his bonds that he rather seemed him to follow him than to lead him.

For when the Duke first began to praise and boast[136] the King and show how much profit the realm should take by his reign, my lord Morton answered: "Surely, my Lord, folly were it for me to lie, for if I would swear the contrary, your Lordship would not, I ween,[137] believe but that if the world would have gone as I would have wished, King Henry's son[138] had had the crown, and not King Edward. But after that God had ordered him to lose it, and King Edward to reign, I was never so mad that I would with a dead man strive against the quick.[139] So was I to King Edward faithful chaplain, and glad would have been that his child had succeeded him. Howbeit,[140] if the secret judgment of God have otherwise provided, I purpose not to spurn against a prick,[141] nor labor to set up that[142] God pulleth down. And as for the late Protector and now King — "

And even there he left,[143] saying that he had

---

107 allowed   108 haughty   109 ill
110 turned   111 request   112 promises
113 taken prisoner   114 *waxed…familiar:*
became friendly with him   115 deceived
116 *Whose…destruction:* Whit L381,
W418   117 steadfastly   118 prosperity
119 *had…woe:* Whit W132, W432; Til
W188   120 Henry VI   121 *the other:* i.e.,

Edward IV   122 *his fast faith:* the Bishop's
steadfast loyalty   123 taken captive
124 loyalty   125 Edward IV   126 *set…
top:* attack this duke (Richard III); Whit
T422   127 Henry VII   128 Elizabeth
of York (eldest daughter of Edward IV)
129 experience, test, trial   130 *experience…wisdom:* Til E221   131 schemes

132 talk   133 *fed…praises:* Whit W584
134 bolk out: let escape   135 outburst
136 extol   137 think   138 Prince
Edward, son of Henry VI   139 living;
I was…quick: Til Q12   140 However
141 *spurn…prick:* kick against the goad.
See Acts 26:14; Whit P377.   142 *set up
that:* advance forward what   143 left off

already meddled too much with the world, and would from that day meddle with his book[144] and his beads,[145] and no further. Then longed the Duke sore[146] to hear what he would have said, because he ended with the King and there so suddenly stopped, and exhorted him so familiarly between the twain,[147] to be bold to say whatsoever he thought; whereof he faithfully promised there should never come hurt and peradventure[148] more good than he would ween,[149] and that himself intended to use his faithful secret advice and counsel, which he said was the only cause for which he procured of the King to have him in his custody, where he might reckon himself at home, and else had he been put in the hands of them with whom he should not have founden the like favor.

The Bishop right humbly thanked him and said, "In good faith, my Lord, I love not much to talk much of princes, as thing not all out of peril, though the word be without fault—forasmuch as it shall not be taken as the party meant it, but as it pleaseth the Prince to construe it.[150] And ever I think on Aesop's tale,[151] that when the lion had proclaimed that on pain of death there should none horned beast abide in that wood, one that had in his forehead a bunch[152] of flesh fled away[153] a great pace. The fox, that saw him run so fast, asked him whither he made all that haste. And he answered, 'In faith, I neither wot nor reck,[154] so I were once

hence, because of this proclamation made of[155] horned beasts.'

'What, fool?' quoth the fox. 'Thou mayest abide well enough; the lion meant not by thee, for it is none horn that is in thine head.'

'No, marry,' quoth he, 'that wot I well enough. But what and[156] he call it a horn, where am I then?'"

The Duke laughed merrily at the tale, and said, "My Lord, I warrant you, neither the lion nor the boar[157] shall pick any matter at[158] anything here spoken, for it shall never come near their ear."

"In good faith, Sir," said the Bishop, "if it did, the thing that I was about to say, taken as well as afore God I meant it, could deserve but thanks. And yet taken as I ween it would, might happen to turn me to little good and you to less."

Then longed the Duke yet much more to wit[159] what it was. Whereupon the Bishop said, "In good faith, my Lord, as for the late Protector, since he is now king in possession, I purpose not to dispute his title. But for the weal[160] of this realm whereof his Grace hath now the governance, and whereof I am myself one poor member, I was about to wish that, to those good abilities whereof he hath already right many little needing my praise, it might yet have pleased God, for the better store,[161] to have given him some of such other excellent virtues meet[162] for the rule of a realm, as our Lord hath planted in the person of your Grace."

---

144 prayer book, breviary   **145** rosary
146 greatly   **147** two   **148** perhaps
149 suppose   **150** *it shall…construe it:*
Til T31   **151** *Aesop's tale:* not known from any fable collection; perhaps Morton's

invention   **152** growth; lump   **153** away
at   **154** *wot nor reck:* know nor care
155 about   **156** if   **157** *the lion nor boar:*
i.e., Richard, whose royal arms included the lion and the boar   **158** *pick…at:* find

fault with   **159** know   **160** well-being
161 provision, supply for future use
162 suitable, fitting

Ben Jonson marked over half of the 3,000 lines in More's *Historia Regis Richardi Tertii* in his 1566 Louvain edition of More's *Opera omnia*. Shown here are 51v and 52r; for facsimiles of each page, see www.thomasmorestudies.org, courtesy of the Dean and Chapter of Canterbury Cathedral and its Library.

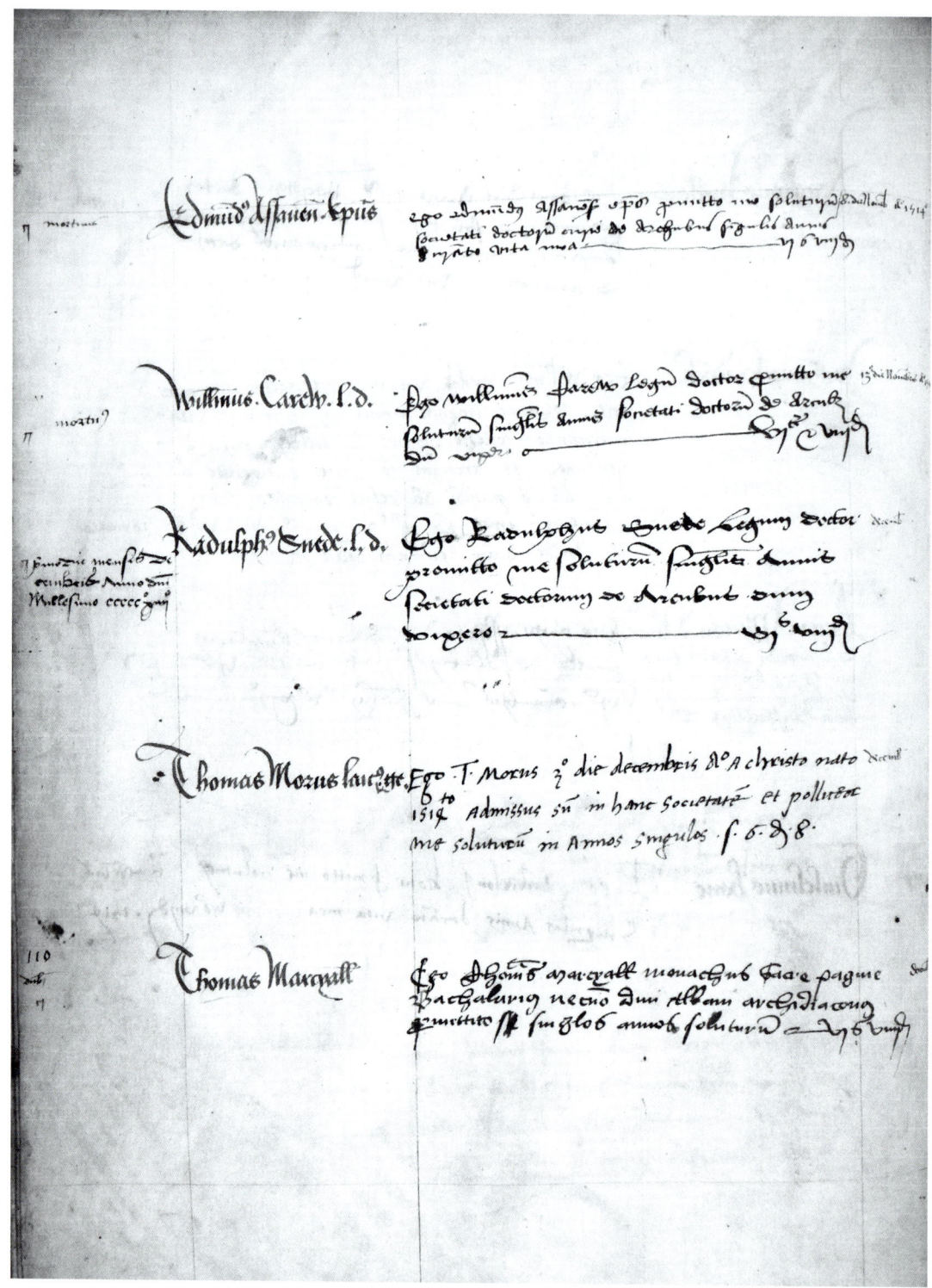

In this official register of the Doctors' Commons, after *Thomas Morus laicus*, More writes in his own hand: *Ego T. Morus 3°*
die decembris a[nno] a christo nato 1514° admissus sum in hanc societatem et polliceor me soluturum in annos singulos s.6.d.8.
["I, Thomas More, on December 3 of the year 1514 since Christ's birth, have been admitted into this society and I promise
that I will pay, each year, 6 shillings, 8 pence."] Other members in this register include More's teachers and friends John
Colet, Polydore Vergil, William Grocyn, and Andreas Ammonius. The Doctors' Commons was a society of canon and
civil lawyers.

140

Utopia

More's most famous and thought-provoking book, *Utopia* has its sources in the author's long study of the classical and Christian traditions of reflection on vital questions such as: What is the best way for human beings to live, both personally and politically? What does humanity need to flourish in justice, peace, friendship, and concord? What kind of citizens and leaders does a commonwealth (*respublica*) need to achieve such ends?

Informed by More's habitual irony and merry wit, the work records a conversation between Thomas More, whose last name means "fool," and a wandering traveler named Raphael Hythloday, whose last name suggests "peddler of nonsense," though his first name means "God heals." In the course of an afternoon, the two characters discuss the demands of public service, and then Raphael recounts the customs, laws, and culture of the island commonwealth of "Utopia," a word that means "no place," or perhaps "good place" if one hears "eu-topia" in the name.

Written in Latin with puns in Greek, *Utopia* features a witty play of names that prompts bemusement and spurs reflection in the "sharp-sighted" reader: What could such a work of art possibly mean? Is this just silly banter, or some kind of learned game? In *Utopia*, More challenges the reader to exercise discerning judgment over the subjects discussed—in particular the best way to order a commonwealth, a concern linking the work to Plato, Cicero, and Augustine, and the roles that "soundly and wisely trained citizens" play in such a commonwealth. Where might this playful conversation about "no place," the experience of the "truly golden book," be leading the interlocutors—and the curious reader? How does the work of this "eloquent author" and "citizen," as the title page describes Thomas More, delight and educate?

Utopia is divided into two parts, but also features a provocative array of supporting materials such as commendatory letters from humanist friends, a map of Utopia, a sample of its alphabet, and even a poem on Utopia by their much-lauded laureate, Anemolius ("Wind-bag"). Far from unimportant, these paratexts or "Parerga" help create the rich intellectual experience and the perplexing whole that is *Utopia*. Taken together, they reveal More's understanding of authorship, reading, conversation, and friendship—all in the context of an emerging European humanism and its distinctive concerns. As Dominic Baker-Smith points out, the "most important thing" in recent readings of *Utopia* has been "the rediscovery of the work as a dialogue," where the "interplay" between characters and voices is vital and leads to the heart of the book's concerns (*CC* 162).

Book 1, known as the "The Dialogue of Counsel," takes place in Antwerp. With the help of his friend Peter Giles, Thomas More (away from home on diplomatic business) encounters Raphael Hythloday, an old and bearded philosophical traveler. Their discussion quickly centers on the question: Does a gifted intellectual, like Hythloday, have a duty to enter the service of a prince and counsel him for the best? They disagree pointedly, and their conversation ranges across a number of controversial subjects, including labor and greed, crime and punishment, leadership and corruption, private property and pride—and the question of justice. At the end of Book 1, Raphael tells More that he fundamentally misunderstands things because of the faulty "image" of a commonwealth that he has in his mind. If only More could visit Utopia, Raphael contends, he would see things differently.

Book 2 is Hythloday's eloquent monologue on behalf of Utopia, its cities and their organization, its households and their way of life, its philosophies and religions, its approach to peace and war, and the virtues of its citizens. After explaining the remarkable founding of Utopia, Raphael offers an account of Utopian life in some detail. Again, the strange names invite and stir our consideration. The great Utopian capital, for example, is called Amaurot ("City of Darkness"), and one kind of Utopian leader is called a phylarch ("fond of power"). Striking too are the names for the river Anyder ("Waterless") and the *princeps* or city leader Ademos ("Without a People"). Like the puzzling names, the events and practices described in Book 2, along with some apparent contradictions and tensions in Raphael's tale, work to elicit wonder and inspire fresh reasoning. Book 2 ends with More leading Raphael to dinner, after which More hopes for further conversation about Utopia, a detail that invites the reader to think of the book as a propaedeutic to more—but what exactly? The conversation about *Utopia* has continued for over five hundred years, with More's work reprinted and translated into many languages around the globe. One of the most playful yet controversial works of modernity, *Utopia* is a book that continues to launch a thousand reflections on philosophy, public service, and the best way to live, or the worst.

Written while More served as undersheriff of London, *Utopia* was first published in 1516, in 1517, and then again in two revised editions in 1518 under the direction of Erasmus. In that same year, Thomas More would choose to enter the service of King Henry VIII and so commence the political drama of his maturity. An important discussion of these early editions of *Utopia* can be found in Elizabeth McCutcheon's "More's *Utopia* and its Parerga (1516–1518)," reprinted in *Moreana* nos. 201–2 (December 2015), pp. 133–48. John Guy's chapter "Social Reformer?" ably explores the "enigma" of More's *Utopia* and unfolds the long argument over the work's possible meanings (*Thomas More* [Oxford University Press, 2000], 84–105). In her essay "'The Best State of a Commonwealth': Thomas More and Quentin Skinner," Cathy Curtis probes the rich array of sources informing *Utopia* (Greek, Roman, and Christian) and More's potent form of authorship: "More appropriated, fused, and transformed earlier traditions so as to comment on the utility of those traditions in contemporary society and to generate debate and new insight" (*Rethinking the Foundations of Modern Political Thought* [Cambridge University Press, 2006], 111).

The March 1518 edition of *Utopia* is the basis for the text here. That edition is noteworthy, among other things, for the inclusion of More's complete Latin *Epigrams*, as well as a selection of epigrams by Erasmus. It is intriguing to read More's *Utopia*—sometimes judged ironic and ambivalent beyond all attempts at resolution—in light of his *Epigrams*, which share many of the major themes of *Utopia*, addressed in playful and trenchant verse.

The translation of Books 1 and 2 and More's two letters to Giles are by Clarence H. Miller (Yale University Press, 2001), and most of the footnotes are from Miller's commentary. The other translated texts are from *CW* 4, ed. Edward Surtz and J. H. Hexter (Yale University Press, 1965).

TIMELINE

244 BC: Utopia founded (Raphael's account)

ca. 1497: Raphael meets and speaks with Morton.

ca. 1504–9: Raphael then spends "more than five years" in Utopia.

ca. 1504: *Four Voyages of Amerigo Vespucci*, a best seller (and a forgery), is published in Vienna.

1514: First printing of Hesychius's Greek dictionary, which Raphael says he brought to Utopia

1515: More's trip to Antwerp where he meets Giles and Raphael and then writes most of *Utopia*

1516: First edition of *Utopia* published in Louvain

1517: Second edition of *Utopia* published in Paris

1518: March and November; third and fourth editions published in Basle by J. Froben

1519–22: Magellan is first to circumnavigate the globe, unless Raphael's claim is correct.

CONTENTS[1]

1 The order and illustrations are those of the March 1518 edition of *Utopia*, except for the additions noted in Parerga II. For a careful study of the different Parergas in the first four editions of *Utopia*, see Elizabeth McCutcheon's "More's *Utopia* and Its Parerga (1516–1518)," *Moreana* nos. 201–2 (2015): 133–48.
2 "something accessory to the main work." This is not a term used by More; recently these supporting materials have been called "Paratexts."

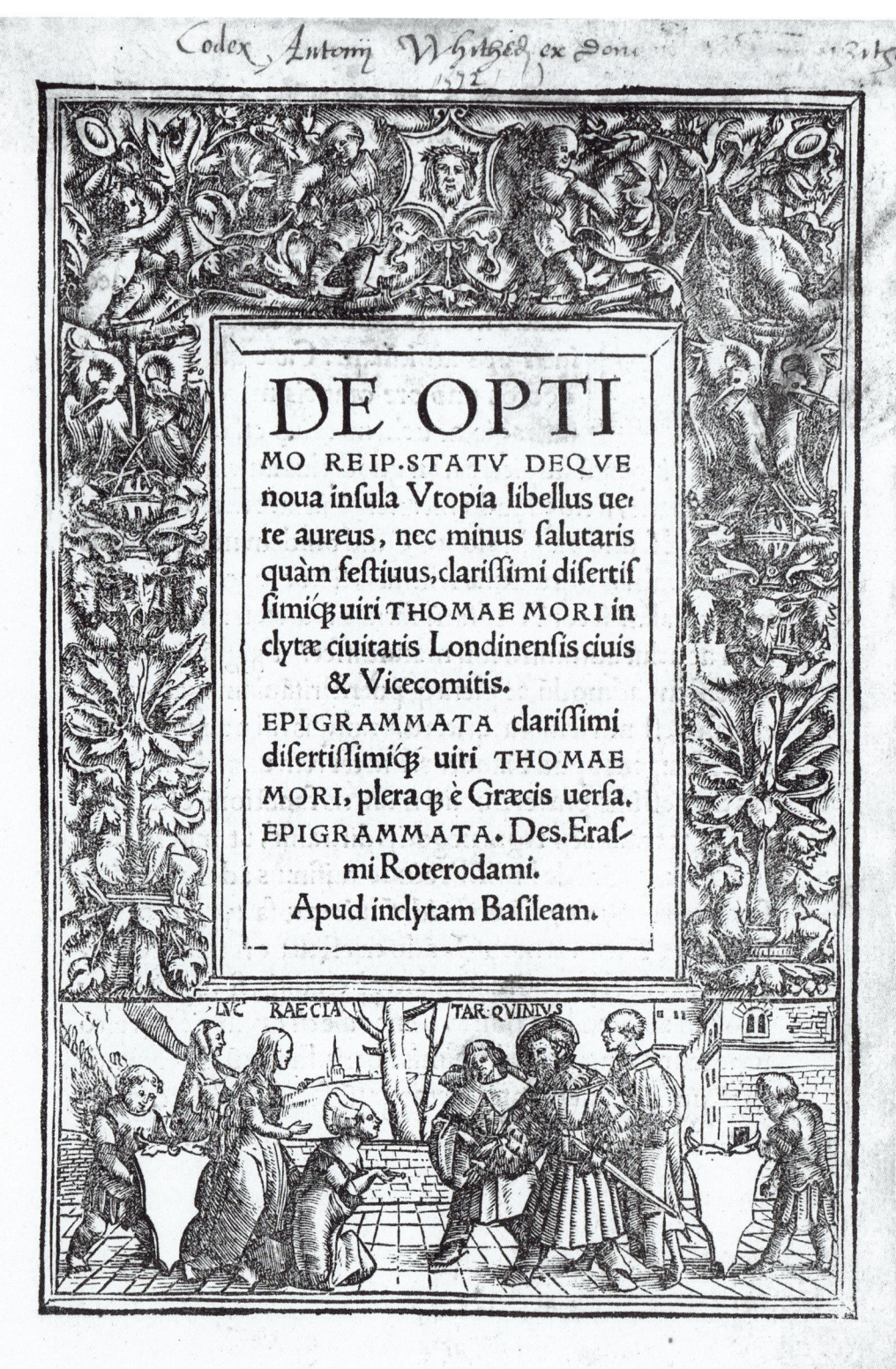

This elaborate title page of Froben's March 1518 *Utopia* depicts the thorn-crowned head of Christ at the top and the suicide of Lucretia (Livy 1.58) at the bottom. Both depictions are removed from Froben's November 1518 *Utopia*, replaced by a cherub with trumpet and a small snakes-and-dove etching. For the full title of *On the Best State of a Commonwealth and on the New Island of Utopia . . .*, see the formal title page ahead.

144

On the Best State of a Commonwealth
and on the New Island of Utopia
a truly golden handbook, no less beneficial than
entertaining, by the most distinguished and
eloquent author THOMAS MORE, citizen
and undersheriff of the famous city of London

ERASMUS OF ROTTERDAM
TO JOHN FROBEN, DEAREST FATHER
OF HIS GODSON, GREETINGS.

Hitherto I have ever been exceedingly pleased with all my friend More's writings, but, on account of our very close friendship, I somewhat distrusted my own judgment. Now, however, I see that all learned men unanimously subscribe to my opinion and admire the man's superhuman genius even more warmly than I—not that they have more affection but that they have greater critical discernment. I therefore openly approve of my verdict rather late, but I shall not hesitate in future to express my sentiment publicly.

What would this wonderful, rich nature not have accomplished if his talent had been trained in Italy, if it were now totally devoted to the service of the muses, if it had ripened to its proper harvest and, as it were, its own autumnal plenty? When a mere youth, he amused himself with epigrams, most of them written when he was but a lad. He has never left his native England except twice when serving his king on an embassy in Flanders. Not only is he married, not only has he family cares to attend to, not only does he hold a public office and handle an overwhelming number of legal cases, but he is distracted by so many and weighty affairs of the realm that you wonder he finds time even to think of books.

For these reasons we have sent you his *Progymnasmata* or *Early Exercises* and his *Utopia* so that, if you think well, they may go out to the world and to posterity with the recommendation of having been printed by you. Such is the reputation of your press that, if it is known that a book has come from the house of Froben, that is enough to have it please the learned world.

Farewell to you and your excellent father-in-law, sweetest wife, and most delightful children. Erasmus, the godson whom I share in common with you, has been born in an atmosphere of learning: so mind that he is trained in all good learning.

Louvain, 25 August 1517

WILLIAM BUDÉ
TO THOMAS LUPSET,
ENGLISHMAN, GREETINGS.

I owe you really immense thanks, Lupset, most learned of young men, for having handed me Thomas More's *Utopia* and thereby drawn my attention to what is very pleasant reading as well as reading likely to be profitable. It was not long ago that you strove to obtain from me by entreaties what of my own free will I had strongly desired, namely, the reading of the six books of *The Preservation of Health* by Galen. Thomas Linacre, the physician outstanding in both Greek and Latin, had recently rendered them the service, or rather paid them the compliment, of translating them from the extant originals into elegant Latin. He has performed the task so well that, if all of Galen's works (which I judge to be worth the whole of medicine) are at length translated into Latin, the society of physicians seems unlikely to feel the lack of knowledge of Greek.

I consider your courteous loan of Linacre's manuscript to me for a lengthy period a favor of the highest type. My hasty and cursory reading has caused me to conclude that the perusal profited me a great deal and also to promise myself still greater profit after the publication of the book on which you are now busily engaged at the presses of this city of Paris. On this account I believed myself to be under sufficient obligation to you. But, behold, you have given me, as an appendix or a supplement to your previous favor, the *Utopia* of Thomas More, a man of keen discernment, of pleasant disposition, and of great experience in the appraisal of human affairs.

I had the book by me in the country as I ran up and down very busily and gave directions to the workmen, for, as you have partly come to know by yourself and partly heard from others, I had been expending much energy on the business of my country estate now for the second year. As I learned and weighed the customs and laws of the Utopians, the reading of the book impressed me so much that I almost neglected and even forsook the management of household affairs. I perceived the trumpery in all the theory and practice of domestic economy and in absolutely all anxiety for increasing one's revenue.

By the latter, as by some inner and innate horsefly, the whole human race is stung, as everyone sees and understands. The result I almost went as far as to say, is that one must necessarily confess the object of legal and civil arts and sciences to be this: with spiteful and watchful cunning a man should behave toward his neighbor, with whom he is joined by rights of citizenship and sometimes of family, so as always to be taking something or other away, drawing it away, shaving it away, swearing it away, squeezing it out, beating it out, scooping it out, twisting it out, shaking it out, hammering it out, taking it quietly, stealing it away, plucking it away, pouncing upon it, and—partly with the connivance and partly with the sanction of the laws—purloining it and embezzling it.

This condition prevails all the more in those countries where the so-called civil law and canonical law have greater authority in both forums. Their procedures and decrees, as everyone sees, have been pervaded more and more by the view that men who are skilled in bailing out—or rather in taking in, who prey like hawks on unadvised citizens, who are artists in formulas—that is, in duperies, who are adepts in contractual law, who are fixers of suits, and who are lawyers of a contraverted, perverted, inverted law, are to be upheld as the high priests of justice and equity. They are to be the only persons worthy to give definitive replies on what is good and fair and, what is far more, worthy to determine with authority and power what each man should be allowed to have, what not to have and how much and how long to have it—and all this according to the declaration of the common feelings of mankind dreaming up the nonsense!

The truth is that most of us, blind with the thick rheum of ignorance, presume that, as a rule, each person's case usually is right insofar as it satisfies the demands of the law or insofar as it is supported by the law. But suppose we were to estimate laws by the standard of truth and by the command of the Gospel to be simple. Anyone with a spark of intelligence and sense would admit, if pressed, that there is a vast difference between true equity and law as expressed in canonical censures (at present and for a long time past) and between true equity and the law as expressed in civil statutes and royal decrees, just as there is a vast difference between the principles of Christ, who established the moral law, and the conduct of his disciples and the opposing doctrines and tenets of those who regard the golden heaps of Croesus and Midas as the ultimate goal and the essence of happiness. Hence, if you should now wish to explain justice according to the definition acceptable to ancient writers, namely, as the virtue which gives his due to every man, either you would find it nowhere in evidence or we should have to confess that it is treated, if I may allow myself such a comparison, like a scullery maid, whether you observe the morality of contemporary rulers or the feelings of fellow citizens and countrymen toward one another.

This situation obtains unless you admit their contention that the real and world-old justice which is called the natural law has been the source of that law of theirs. According to the latter, the stronger a man is the more he should possess, and the more he does possess the more eminent among his fellow citizens he ought to be. The result is that we see it accepted by the law of nations that persons who cannot help their fellow citizens by any art or practice worth mentioning, provided only they control the knotty bonds of pacts and contracts which they use to entangle men's patrimonies and which the ignorant multitude and the humanistic scholars, living far from public business for the sake of relaxation or for the investigation of truth, account a combination of Gordian knots and charlatan methods hardly admirable—well, we see it accepted by the law of nations that such persons should each have an income equal to that of a thousand of his fellow citizens and often of individual states, or even more than that, and that these same persons should be hailed by the honorable titles of wealthy men, honest men, magnificent fortune-builders.

This happens, of course, in those generations, those institutions, those customs, in those nations which have pronounced it lawful that every man should have reputation and power in proportion to the resources by which he has built up his own family fortunes—he and his heirs. This process snowballs as great-great-great-grandchildren and their great-great-grandchildren vie in increasing by splendid additions the patrimonies received from their forefathers—which amounts to saying that it snowballs as they oust, far and wide, their neighbors, their kindred by marriage, their relations by blood, and even their brothers and sisters!

Yet Christ, the founder and supervisor of possessions, left among his followers a Pythagorean communion and charity ratified by significant example when Ananias was condemned to death for breaking the law of communion. Certainly, by this arrangement, Christ seems to me to have abolished, among his own at least, the whole arrangement set up by the civil and canonical law of fairly recent date in contentious volumes. This law we see today holding the highest position in jurisprudence and controlling our destinies.

Now, the island of Utopia, which I hear is called also Udepotia, is said, by a singularly wonderful stroke of fortune (if we are to believe the story), to have adopted the customs and the true wisdom of Christianity for public and private life and to have kept this wisdom uncorrupted even to this day. It has done so by holding in close combat (as they say) to three divine principles: (1) the equality of all things, good and bad, among fellow-citizens or, if you prefer, their civic sharing of them, absolute on all counts; (2) the resolute and tenacious love of peace and quiet; and (3) the contempt of gold and silver. These are the three overthrowers, I may say, of all frauds, impostures, swindles, rogueries, and wicked deceptions.

Would that the inhabitants of heaven for their own name's sake would cause these three principles of Utopian legislation to be fixed in the minds of all mortals by the beam-spikes of a strong and settled conviction! You would immediately see pride, avarice, mad strife, and almost all the other wound-inflicting darts of the Stygian adversary fall to the ground and lie inert. You would see that interminable array of legal tomes, engrossing the attention of so many excellent and solid intellects even until death, viewed as hollow and empty and therefore consigned to bookworms or used as wrapping paper in shops.

Immortal beings above! What sort of holiness did the Utopians possess to merit the heavenly grace of not having avarice and cupidity break or creep into that island alone for so many centuries, of not having them drive out and expel justice and decency by their audacity and shamelessness?

Would that the great and good God had behaved as benignly with those regions which hold fast and cling to the surname of Christian derived from his most holy name! Beyond the shadow of a doubt, avarice, the vice which perverts and ruins so many minds otherwise extraordinary and lofty, would depart hence once for all, and the golden age of Saturn would return. In Utopia the assertion could be made that Aratus and the ancient poets were dangerously close to being mistaken when they stationed Justice in the zodiac after her flight from the earth. If we are to believe Hythloday, she must have remained behind on the island of Utopia and not yet have made her way to the sky.

I personally, however, have made investigation and discerned for certain that Utopia lies outside the limits of the known world. Undoubtedly it is one of the Fortunate Isles, perhaps close to the Elysian Fields, for More himself testifies that Hythloday has not yet stated its position by giving its definite bearings. It is itself divided into many cities, but they all unite and harmonize in one state, named Hagnopolis. The latter is content with its own institutions and possessions, blessed in its innocence, and leading a kind of heavenly life which is below the level of heaven but above the rabble of this known world. Amid countless mortal pursuits, as empty and disappointing as they are painful and vehement, the rabble is hurled headlong wildly and feverishly.

We owe the knowledge of this island to Thomas More, who has made public for our age this model of the happy life and this rule of living. The discoverer, as More himself reveals, is Hythloday, to whom he ascribes the whole account. On the one hand, Hythloday is the one who has built their city for the Utopians and established customs and laws for them; that is to say, he has borrowed from them and brought home to us the pattern of the good life. On the other hand, beyond question it is More who has adorned the island and its holy institutions by his style and eloquence, who has embellished the very city of the Hagnopolitans according to precept and rule, and who has added all those touches that bring grace and beauty and impressiveness to the magnificent work—although in the help which he has given he has claimed for himself only the role of an arranger of the materials.

Manifestly it was a point of conscience with him not to arrogate to himself the major part in the work. Otherwise Hythloday could rightly complain that, if he ever would have decided to commit his own experiences to paper, More had left him a prematurely plucked and deflowered glory. *More was afraid, I suppose, that Hythloday himself, now residing of his own choice on the island of Udepotia but appearing at some time in Europe, would be displeased and vexed at More's unfairness in leaving him but the deflowered glory of this discovery of his. Such a persuasion is the part of men who are good and wise.*[1]

It was the testimony of Peter Giles of Antwerp which caused me to have full faith in More, who of himself carries weight and relies on great authority. I have never known More in person—I am now passing over the recommendation given his learning and character—but I love him on account of his sworn friendship with the illustrious Erasmus, who has deserved exceedingly well of sacred and profane letters of all kinds. With Erasmus himself, I have long ago formed an association of friendship sealed by an exchange of letters.

Farewell, my dearest Lupset. Give my greetings—whether in person or by a go-between letter, and that at the first opportunity—to Linacre, that pillar of the British name in all that concerns good learning. He is now, I hope, no more yours than ours. He is one of the few whose approbation I should be very glad to gain if possible. During his personal sojourn here, he himself gained the highest approbation of me and of Jehan Ruelle, my friend, who is privy to my studies. Especially shall I esteem and try to emulate Linacre's singular learning and careful diligence.

I should like also to have you greet More once and again at my request, either by written message, as I said before, or by word of mouth. Both in my mind and in my talk I have long ago entered his name in Minerva's album of greater immortals. Now I pay him the highest possible love and veneration for his island in the new world, Utopia. The reason is that our age and succeeding ages will hold his account as a nursery of correct and useful institutions from which every man may introduce and adapt transplanted customs to his own city. Farewell.

Paris, 31 July [1517]

---

1 Budé wrote this italicized section in Greek.

This map by Ambrosius Holbein appeared in the March and November 1518 *Utopia*.

VTOPIENSIVM ALPHABETVM. 13

a b c d e f g h i k l m n o p q r s t u x y

○⊖⊕⊙⊖⊝⊙⊙⊙⊙⊙⊗△⅃⎍⎚⎚⊡⊞⊟⊡⊡

TETRASTICHON VERNACVLA VTO-
PIENSIVM LINGVA.

Vtopos   ha   Boccas   peula   chama.

polta   chamaan

Bargol   he   maglomi   baccan

foma   gymnofophaon

Agrama   gymnofophon   labarem

bacha   bodamilomin

Voluala   barchin   heman   la

lauoluola   dramme   pagloni.

HORVM VERSVVM AD VERBVM HAEC
EST SENTENTIA.

Vtopus me dux ex non infula fecit infulam.
Vna ego terrarum omnium abfᵹ philofophia
Ciuitatem philofophicam expreffi mortalibus.
Libenter impartio mea, non grauatim accipio meliora.

b 3

LITERAL TRANSLATION OF THE ABOVE LINES

Utopus, my ruler, converted me, formerly not an island, into an island.
Alone of all lands, without the aid of abstract philosophy,
I have represented for mortals the philosophical city.
Ungrudgingly do I share my benefits with others; undemurringly
   do I adopt whatever is better from others.

SIX LINES ON THE ISLAND
OF UTOPIA BY
ANEMOLIUS, POET LAUREATE,
NEPHEW OF HYTHLODAY
BY HIS SISTER

The ancients called me Utopia or Nowhere
because of my isolation. At present, however,
I am a rival of Plato's republic, perhaps even a
victor over it. The reason is that what he has
delineated in words I alone have exhibited
in men and resources and laws of surpassing
excellence. Deservedly ought I to be called by
the name of Eutopia or Happy Land.

TO THE MOST ILLUSTRIOUS
JEROME BUSLEYDEN,
PROVOST OF AIRE AND COUNCILOR
TO THE CATHOLIC KING CHARLES,
PETER GILES OF ANTWERP
SENDS GREETINGS.

Most excellent Busleyden, the other day, Thomas
More, the greatest ornament of this age of ours,
as you too can testify because of your intimate acquaintance with him, sent me his *Island of Utopia*.
It is known as yet to few mortals, but it is eminently
worthy of everyone's knowledge as being superior
to Plato's republic. This statement is true especially
because a man of great eloquence has represented,
painted, and set it before our eyes in such a way
that, as often as I read it, I think I see far more than
when, being as much a part of the conversation as
More himself, I heard Raphael Hythloday's own
words sounding in my ears.

And yet this Hythloday, a man endowed with no
ordinary power of expression, so described his subject as to make it readily apparent that he was not
repeating what he had learned from the accounts
of others but telling what he had taken in directly
with his own eyes and what he had long experienced
personally. To my mind he was a man superior even
to Ulysses himself in his knowledge of countries,
men, and affairs. I think he has had no equal anywhere in the last eight hundred years; in comparison with him Vespucci himself may be thought to
have seen nothing. Apart from the fact that we tell
more effectively what we have seen than what we

have heard, the man had a special skill of his own in
unfolding his narrative.

Nevertheless, when I contemplate the same picture as painted by More's brush, I am as affected as
if I were sometimes actually living in Utopia itself.
By heaven, I am even disposed to believe that in all
the five years which Raphael spent on the island, he
did not see as much as one may perceive in More's
description. In the latter, such a quantity of marvelous things presents itself everywhere that I am at a
loss which I should admire first or most: the faithfulness of a most happy memory which could repeat almost word for word many matters which he
had merely heard; or the sagacity with which he has
noted the sources from which all evils actually arise
in the commonwealth or from which all blessings
possibly could arise, all quite unknown to ordinary
folk; or the force and fluency of his discourse by
which in pure Latin style and forceful expression he
has united numerous topics. This is especially amazing since he is a man distracted by a mass of public
business and domestic affairs. But all these remarks
will not much surprise you, most learned Busleyden, for by intimate contact you really know him
for a man of superhuman and almost divine genius.

For the rest, there is nothing I can add to what he
has written. There was only a poem of four lines in
the Utopian vernacular which, after More's departure, Hythloday happened to show me. This verse,
preceded by the Utopian alphabet, I have caused to
be added to the book. I have appended also some
brief annotations in the margins.

As to More's difficulty about the geographical position of the island, Raphael did not fail to mention
even that, but in very few words and as it were in
passing, as if reserving the topic for another place.
But, somehow or other, an unlucky accident caused
us both to fail to catch what he said. While Raphael
was speaking on the topic, one of More's servants
had come up to him to whisper something or other
in his ear. I was therefore listening all the more intently when one of our company who had, I suppose, caught cold on shipboard, coughed so loudly
that I lost some phrases of what Raphael said. I shall
not rest, however, till I have full information on this
point so that I shall be able to tell you exactly not
only the location of the island but even the longi-
tude and latitude—provided that our friend Hythloday be alive and safe.

There are various reports circulating about the

man. Some say that he died during his travel. Others declare that, after his return to his native land, partly because he could not endure his countrymen's ways and partly because he was moved by his longing for Utopia, he made his way back again to that country.

As to the difficulty that the name of this island is to be found nowhere in the cosmographers, that was well explained by Hythloday himself. It was possible, he said, either that the name used by the ancients had afterward been changed or that this island had escaped even their notice, just as nowadays we find very many lands cropping up which were unknown to the ancient geographers.

But what is the use of finding arguments to make the account more credible when we have the distinguished More himself to vouch for it?

In conclusion, his hesitation about publication makes me praise and acknowledge his modesty. From every point of view, however, I considered it unfitting to suppress the work for long and most fitting to place it in men's hands, especially since it is recommended to the world by your patronage. This latter is true not only because you are unusually well acquainted with More's talents but because no man is better qualified than you to assist with good counsels the government of the commonwealth in which you have labored for many years, winning the highest praise for wisdom and integrity. Farewell, Maecenas of learned pursuits and ornament of our age.

Antwerp, 1 November 1516

Preface[1]

THOMAS MORE
TO PETER GILES, GREETINGS.

I am almost ashamed, my dear Peter Giles,[2] to have delayed for almost a year in sending you this little book about the Utopian[3] commonwealth, which I'm sure you expected within six weeks.[4] You knew, after all, that I was spared the labor of finding my matter, and did not have to give any thought to its arrangement; all I had to do was repeat what you and I heard Raphael[5] say. For that reason there was no need to strive for eloquence,[6] since his language could hardly be polished, first because it was informal and extemporaneous, and also because he is a person, as you know, not as well versed in Latin as in Greek; the closer my language came to his casual simplicity,[7] the more accurate it would be, and in this matter accuracy is all that I ought to, and in fact do, aim for.

I grant you, Peter, that with all this already taken care of, I was relieved of so much effort that there was almost nothing left for me to do. If this had not been so, thinking up the subject matter and arranging it might have required not a little time and study, even from someone of not inconsiderable intelligence and not totally without learning. But if I had been required to write not only accurately but also elegantly, no amount of time or study would have enabled me to do it. As it is, all these concerns, which would have cost me so much labor, are removed and all that remained to do was to write what I heard — not a difficult task.

But nevertheless, even to perform this trifling task, other chores left me almost no time at all. I am constantly pleading one case, hearing another, acting as arbitrator, handing down decisions as a judge, visiting one person or another on business or because it is my duty to do so; I am out practically

---

1 This letter is described as a "preface" in the running heads of the two Basel editions of 1518; both editions also begin this section with a title page having an elaborate border (see next page). The first edition (Louvain, 1516) has this heading: *Prefatio in opus de optimo reipublicae statu.* 2 Peter Giles (*ca.* 1486–1533) was a humanist friend of More and Erasmus. He was a corrector at the press of Dirk Martens in his native city of Antwerp and was a clerk of that city from 1512 on. 3 The name "Utopia" derives from Greek *ou* ("not") and *topos*

("place"), meaning "no place" (More also called it by the equivalent Latin name "nusquama"). "Utopia" includes a pun because the initial "u" may also be derived from Greek *eu* ("good"). Hence Utopia is a good place which is no place. 4 More visited Giles in Antwerp in September 1515; together with a letter dated September 3, 1516, he sent the manuscript of *Utopia* to Erasmus for publication. 5 The angel Raphael is a saving guide and healer in the biblical book of Tobias. Raphael's surname, Hythloday, is derived from Greek

words meaning "peddler of nonsense." 6 More refers to the principal divisions of rhetoric according to the classical tradition: invention (finding matter), disposition (arranging it), and eloquence (stylistic elaboration). 7 This description applies to most of Hythloday's description of Utopia itself, but hardly to the elaborate and often passionate eloquence of Hythloday's language in much of Book 1 and in his peroration at the end of Book 2. Almost nothing in this letter (or in *Utopia* itself, for that matter) can be taken at face value.

THOMAS
MORVS PETRO
AEGIDIO
S. D.

Vdet me prope
modum charisͦ
sime Petre Aegi
di libellum húc,
de Vtopiana re
publica, post an
num fermè ad te mittere, quem te
nõ dubito intra sesquimésem exͭ
pectasse. quippe quum scires miͭ
hi demptum in hoc opere inueni
c endi

This title page to *Utopia*'s "Preface," More's Letter to Giles, appeared in the 1518 editions.

all day dealing with others, and the rest of my time is devoted to my family, and so I leave nothing for myself, that is for writing.[8]

When I get home, I have to talk with my wife, chat with my children, confer with the servants. All this I count as part of my obligations, since it needs to be done (and it does if you do not wish to be a stranger in your own home); and you must do everything you can to make yourself as agreeable as possible to the persons you live with, whether they were provided by nature, chance, or your own choice, as long as you do not spoil them by your familiarity or turn servants into masters through over-indulgence. As I am doing such things, as I said, a day, a month, a year slips by.

When do I write then? And as yet I have said nothing about sleep and nothing at all about eating, and for many that takes up no less time than sleep itself, which consumes almost half our lives. The only time I get for myself is what I steal from sleep and eating. Because that is so little, I progressed slowly, but because it was at least something, I did make progress, and I sent *Utopia* to you, my dear Peter, so that you can read it and let me know if I have missed anything. For, though on that score I do not lack all confidence in myself (and I only wish that my intelligence and learning were a match for my not inconsiderable memory), still I am not confident enough to think that nothing has escaped me.

As you know, John Clement,[9] my young assistant, was there with us, for I do not allow him to miss out on any conversation which could be profitable to him because from this sprout which is beginning to grow green with proficiency in Latin and Greek I expect someday a marvelous harvest. He has made me feel very doubtful about one point: as far as I remember Hythloday told us that the bridge which spans the river Anyder at Amaurot[10] is five hundred yards long, but my boy John says that is two hundred yards too many and that the river is no more than three hundred wide. Please try to remember that point. For if you agree with him, I will go along with you

both and believe I am mistaken. But if you do not recall, I will stand by what I think I remember myself, for just as I have taken great pains to prevent any inaccuracy in the book, so too, when I am in doubt, I would rather say something inaccurate than tell a lie, because I would rather be honest than clever.[11]

Note the theological distinction between lying and speaking a falsehood

In fact, it would be easy to remedy this defect if you would find out from Raphael himself about it, in person or by letter. And you need to do the same concerning another difficulty which has arisen— who is more to blame for it, I or you or Raphael himself, I do not know. For it did not occur to us to ask, or him to mention, in what part of that new world Utopia is located. Indeed, to remedy this oversight I would be willing to give a sizeable sum, partly because I am ashamed not to know in which ocean the island lies about which I have recounted so much, partly because there are one or two people here, but especially one person, a devout man and a theologian by profession, who is amazingly eager to go to Utopia, not out of idle curiosity or any hankering after novelties but in order to nourish and spread our religion, which has made such a good beginning there. To do this properly he has decided to see to it beforehand that he is sent by the pope and made the bishop of the Utopians. He has no scruples whatever about begging for this bishopric, since he considers such ambition to be holy if it is not based on honor or gain but rather springs from piety.

A holy ambition

Therefore, my dear Peter, I beg you to contact Hythloday, either in person if that is convenient or by letter if you are separated, and see to it that this work of mine contains nothing false and lacks nothing true. And perhaps it would be best to show him the book. For there is no one else capable of correcting any errors and even he cannot do so unless he reads through what I have written. Then too, this will let you see whether he is pleased or annoyed at me for writing this work. For if he himself has decided to commit his labors to writing, he

---

8 More describes himself (accurately) as devoted to the active life which Hythloday rejects.   **9** John Clement (*ca.* 1500–1572), one of the first students at Colet's humanist school, St. Paul's, became a page and pupil in More's household about 1514; later he became a distinguished physician.

10 "Anyder" is coined from the Greek for "waterless"; "Amaurot" from the Greek for "made dark or dim."   **11** Though it is apparently not found among the theologians, the distinction between *mentiri* (tell a lie) and *mendacium dicere* (speak a falsehood, with no intention of

deceiving) derives from Aulus Gellius (11.11.1–4) and was well known. Peter Giles, and perhaps Erasmus, probably added the sidenotes that appeared in the margins of the original edition.

may not want me to do so. And I certainly would not want to deprive his narrative of the bloom and charm of novelty by making the commonwealth of Utopia public.

But in fact, to tell you the truth, I myself have not yet made up my mind whether or not to publish it at all. For the tastes of mortals are so various, the temperaments of some are so bitter, their minds so ungrateful, their judgments so preposterous that a person would do far better to follow his own bent and lead a merry life than to wear himself out trying to publish something useful or entertaining for an audience so finicky and ungrateful. Most people know nothing about learning; many despise it. Dummies reject as too hard whatever is not dumb. The literati look down their noses at anything not swarming with obsolete words. Some like only ancient authors; many like only their own writing. One person is so dour that he cannot abide jokes; another is so witless that he cannot stand anything witty. Some have so little nose for satire that they dread it the way someone bitten by a rabid dog fears water. Others are so changeable that their approval depends on whether they are sitting down or standing up.

Human judgments are ungrateful

Persons with no "nose" he calls "flat-nosed"

They sit around in taverns and over their cups they pontificate about the talents of writers, condemning each author just as they please, pulling him down through his writings as if they had grabbed him by the hair, while they themselves are safe and out of harm's way,[12] as the saying goes, because these good men have their whole heads smooth-shaven so that there is not a single hair to grab on to.[13]

A proverb

Furthermore, some are so ungrateful that, even though a work has given them great pleasure, they still do not like the author any better because of it. They are not unlike ill-mannered guests who, after they have been lavishly entertained at a splendid banquet, finally go home stuffed without saying a word of thanks to the host who invited them. Go on, now, and at your own expense provide a banquet for persons of such delicate palates and various tastes, who will remember and repay you with such gratitude!

A remarkable comparison

Nevertheless, my dear Peter, raise with Hythloday the points I mentioned. Afterwards I will be free to consider the matter once more. But in fact, if he himself gives his consent — since it is late to be wise[14] now that I have finished all the work — in all other considerations about publishing I will follow the advice of my friends, and especially yours. Farewell, my dearest Peter Giles, with regards to your excellent wife, and be as fond of me as ever, since I am fonder of you than ever.

---

12 See Erasmus, *Adages* 293 (*CWE* 31: 311).   **13** The metaphor seems to be drawn from wrestling.   **14** Erasmus, *Adages* 28 (*CWE* 31: 76–77)

Io. Clemens.   Hythlodæus.,   Tho. Morus.   Pet. Aegid.

A DISCOURSE SPOKEN BY
THE REMARKABLE
RAPHAEL HYTHLODAY
ON THE BEST FORM OF A COMMONWEALTH
AS REPORTED BY THE ILLUSTRIOUS
THOMAS MORE, A CITIZEN AND
THE UNDERSHERIFF OF THE FAMOUS
BRITISH CITY OF LONDON

Book 1

Recently the invincible king of England,[1] Henry the eighth of that name, who is lavishly endowed with all skills necessary for an outstanding ruler,[2] had some matters of no small moment[3] which had to be worked out with Charles, the most serene prince of Castile.[4] To discuss and resolve these differences he sent me to Flanders as his ambassador; I was the companion and colleague of the incomparable Cuthbert Tunstall, whom he recently appointed to be Master of the Rolls, to the enormous satisfaction of everyone.[5] I will say nothing in his praise, not because I am afraid that my friendship might seem to make me an unreliable witness, but because his virtue and learning are beyond my power to proclaim them and because they are everywhere so renowned and well known that there is no need for me to do so, unless I intend to display the sun by the light of a lantern, as they say.[6]

Cuthbert Tunstall

An adage

As had been agreed, we were met at Bruges by those to whom the prince had entrusted the negotiations, all of them outstanding men. Their leader

1 In August 1513 Henry's army had been victorious at the Battle of the Spurs and briefly occupied Thérouanne and Tournai; but his French campaigns, then and later, were as futile and destructive as those of the French kings in Italy. **2** The word here is *princeps,* a term used five times but in different ways in these opening two paragraphs. This is the word used for the head-leader of each Utopian city. It has a long and complex history, as indicated in David Baker's "First Among Equals: The Utopian *Princeps*" in *Moreana* nos. 115–16 (Dec. 1993): 33–45. **3** The difficulties were mainly connected with the wool trade between England and Flanders. They were serious enough for Wolsey to be worried early in 1515 that Charles would seize the English fleet for back taxes. **4** By 1515 Charles V, later Holy Roman Emperor (1519), was Duke of Burgundy and Prince of Castile. **5** Tunstall (1474–1559), Bishop of London (1522) and later Durham (1530), was a close friend whom More admired throughout his lifetime. On May 12, 1516 Tunstall became Master of the Rolls and Vice-Chancellor; as such he was chief of the twelve assistants to the Lord Chancellor. **6** See Erasmus, *Adages* 1406–7 (*CWE* 33: 245).

and chief was the Mayor of Bruges,[7] a splendid man, but their spokesman and mastermind was George de Themsecke, the Provost of Cassel, who is not only a trained orator but also a naturally eloquent speaker; he is very skilled in the law as well, and also an extraordinarily deft negotiator because he is both intelligent and very experienced.[8] After one or two meetings we could not reach agreement on some points, and so they bade us farewell for some days and set out for Brussels to ask for the pronouncement of their prince.[9]

Meanwhile, as my business required, I made my way to Antwerp. While I was staying there, I was often visited by Peter Giles,[10] among others, though no other visitor was more delightful to me. A native of Antwerp, he holds a post of great responsibility and prestige (and he is worthy of the most prestigious), since for this young man it would be hard to say which is greater, his learning or his virtue.[11] For he is most virtuous and very widely read, and also good-natured toward everyone, but toward his friends he is so responsive, warmhearted, loyal, and unfeignedly affectionate that it would be hard to find even one or two anywhere that you would think comparable to him in every aspect of friendship. He has a modesty rarely to be found; no one is further from false poses; no one combines more prudence with simplicity.[12] Then, too, his elegant speech and his innocent wit are so attractive that his delightful companionship and his charming conversation alleviated my longing for my country, household, wife, and children, though I was tormented by my desire to see them again, for at that time I had been away from home for more than four months.[13]

One day, after I had heard mass at the church of Saint Mary, which is remarkable for its beautiful architecture and its large congregation, when the service was over and I was getting ready to return to my lodgings, I happened to see Giles conversing with a

Peter Giles

stranger who was getting up in years. His face was sunburned, his beard untrimmed, his cloak hanging carelessly from his shoulder; from his face and bearing I thought he looked like a sea captain. But then, when Peter saw me, he came up and greeted me. When I tried to answer, he took me a little aside and said, "Do you see this man?" (At the same time he indicated the person I had seen him talking to.) "He is the one," he said, "I was just getting ready to bring straight to you."

"He would have been all the more welcome to me on your account."

"Actually on his own," he said, "if you knew him. For there is no mortal alive today who can give more information about unknown peoples and lands, and I know that you are very eager to hear about them."

"My guess was not far off, then," I said, "for when I first set eyes on him, I immediately thought he was a sea captain."

"But in fact," he said, "you were far off the mark. Certainly he has sailed, not like Palinurus, but rather like Ulysses, or even better like Plato.[14] This man, who is named Raphael—his family name is Hythloday—has no mean knowledge of the Latin language but is especially proficient in Greek; he has devoted himself to Greek more than to Latin because he has totally committed himself to philosophy and he knew that in that field there is nothing of any importance in Latin except some works of Seneca and Cicero.[15] Out of a desire to see the world he left to his brothers his heritage in his homeland (he is from Portugal),[16] joined Amerigo Vespucci, and was his constant companion in the first three of the four voyages which everyone is now reading about; but on the last voyage he did not come back with him. He sought and practically wrested from Amerigo permission to be one of the twenty-four who were left behind in a fort at the farthest point of the last voyage.[17] And so he was left behind in

7 Jean (or perhaps Jacques) de Halewyn, Seigneur de Maldeghem   8 De Themsecke (d. *ca.* 1536), a doctor of the law and a member of Charles V's council at Mechlin, was employed on many diplomatic missions. (Cassel is now in northern France.) 9 on or before July 25, 1515   10 In Flemish his name is "Gillis" or "Gilles," but the usual English translation of his Latin name ("Aegidius") is "Giles."   11 Giles (1486–1533) was learned in the law and edited classical and humanist works. Since

1512 he had been chief clerk of the court of justice at Antwerp.   12 Cf. Mt 10:16 ("wise as serpents, innocent as doves"). The same combination was part of the printer's mark of Johann Froben, who printed the two 1518 editions of *Utopia*.   13 More left England May 12, 1515.   14 Palinurus, Aeneas's steersman, dozed at the helm, fell overboard, and drowned (*Aeneid* 5.833–61), unlike Odysseus and Plato, who learned much from their travels (*Odyssey* 1.1–4; Diogenes Laertius 3.6–7, 18–22).

15 More expressed the same opinion in his *Letter to Oxford* (*CW* 15: 143).   16 In 1515 the Portuguese excelled in exploration, especially in the Far East.   17 The voyages (1503–4) of the Florentine explorer Amerigo Vespucci (1451–1512), who was in the employ of the King of Portugal, were described in two Latin narratives (of disputed authenticity) published about 1507; one of the versions mentions the twenty-four mariners left behind in a fort at the farthest point of the voyage (Cape

accordance with his outlook, since he was more concerned about his travels than his tomb. Indeed he often used to say, 'Who-

Aphorism

ever does not have an urn has the sky to cover him,'[18] and 'from everywhere it is the same distance to heaven.'[19] This attitude of his would have cost him dearly if God had not been merciful to him. However, after the departure of Vespucci, he traveled through many lands with five companions from the fort, and finally, by an extraordinary stroke of luck, he was transported to Ceylon and from there he reached Calicut,[20] where he opportunely found some Portuguese ships and at last, beyond all expectation, he got home again."

When Peter had told me this I thanked him for his kindness in taking so much trouble to introduce me to someone whose conversation he hoped I would enjoy, and then I turned to Raphael. After we had greeted each other and spoken the usual amenities that are exchanged when strangers meet for the first time, we went off to my house, where we conversed sitting in the garden on a bench covered with grassy turf.[21]

And so he told us how, after the departure of Vespucci, he and his companions who had remained in the fort gradually began to win the good graces of the people of that land by encountering and speaking well of them, and then they started to interact with them not only with no danger but even on friendly terms, and finally they gained the affection and favor of some ruler, whose name and country escape me. He told how, through the generosity of the ruler, he and five of his companions were liberally supplied with provisions and ships on the sea and wagons on the land—together with a trustworthy guide who took them to other rulers to whom he heartily recommended them. After many days' journey, he said, he discovered towns and cities and commonwealths that were very populous and not badly governed.

On both sides of the equator, it is true, extending almost as far as the space covered by the orbit of the sun there lie vast empty wastelands, scorched with perpetual heat.[22] The whole region is barren

and ugly, rugged and uncultivated, inhabited by wild beasts and serpents and by people who are no less wild than the beasts and no less dangerous. But when you have traveled further, everything gradually becomes milder. The heavens are less fierce, the ground is green and pleasant, the creatures are more gentle, and finally one sees peoples, cities, towns, which not only trade continually among themselves and with near neighbors but also carry on commerce with distant nations by land and sea. From that point on they were able to visit many countries in all directions since there was no ship traveling anywhere in which he and his comrades were not eagerly welcomed.

He told us that in the first regions they traveled they saw flat-bottomed vessels, spreading sails made of wickerwork or of stitched papyrus, and in other places of leather. But afterwards they found ships with curved keels, canvas sails, and in fact all the features of our own vessels. The sailors were not unskilled in seamanship and celestial navigation, but he told us that they were extremely grateful to him for introducing them to the magnetic compass, with which they had been totally unfamiliar. For that reason they usually were afraid to commit themselves to the open sea and they did not venture to do so except during the summer. But now they have such confidence in the compass that they scorn the winter weather and are careless rather than secure; thus there is a danger that the device which they thought would do them so much good will do them great harm because of their imprudence.

To present what he told us about the things he saw in each and every place would take a long time and would be beyond the scope of this work. And perhaps I will speak of it elsewhere, especially those points of which it would be useful not to be ignorant, above all whatever correct and prudent provisions he observed among civilized nations. We asked him very eagerly about such matters, and he was quite willing to explain them, but we paid no attention to monsters, for nothing is less novel than they are. Indeed, there is almost no place where you will not find Scyllas and rapacious Celaenos and

Frio in southeast Brazil). **18** Lucan, *Pharsalia* 7.818–19; cf. Augustine, *City of God* 1.12 **19** Cf. Erasmus, *Apophthegmata* 7, Anaxagorus Clazomenus 4, and Cicero, *Tusculan Disputations* 1.43.104. **20** The Portuguese had visited Calicut (a city on the west coast of India, not Calcutta) by 1487 and established a station there in 1511. **21** This is not an ordinary bench covered with sod. The small woodcut of the scene in the two editions of 1518 shows that it was a long wooden box filled with earth and covered on top with growing grass. **22** The torrid zone between the Tropic of Cancer and the Tropic of Capricorn, the northern and southern limits between which the sun's orbit was thought to move.

man-eating Laestrigonians and such prodigious monsters,[23] but it is not everywhere that you will find soundly and wisely trained citizens. But just as he noted many ill-considered practices among those newly discovered nations, so too he recounted not a few features that could serve as patterns to correct the errors of our own cities, nations, peoples, and kingdoms. These, as I said, will have to be presented elsewhere. At present I intend to relate only what he told us about the customs and institutions of the Utopians,[24] but first I will present the conversation which led him on, as it were, to mention that commonwealth. For after Raphael had very judiciously analyzed some of our errors and some of theirs (and certainly there are plenty in both places) and had presented some wiser provisions both here and there—and he had such a mastery of the customs and institutions of every nation he visited that you would imagine he had spent his whole life there—Peter was amazed by him and said, "My dear Raphael, why do you not enter into the service of some king, for I am convinced that there is none who would not be extremely glad to have you, because this learning of yours and your knowledge of peoples and places would not only serve to delight him but would also make you fit to inform him of precedents and aid him with advice. In this manner you could at one and the same time promote your own interests enormously and be of great assistance to your relatives and friends."

"As for my relatives and friends, I am not much concerned about them because I have done my duty by them well enough: others do not give up their possessions until they are old and sick, and even then they do so reluctantly, when they can no longer retain them; but I divided my possessions up among my relatives and friends when I was not only healthy and vigorous but also young. I think they ought to be satisfied with my generosity, and beyond that they should not demand and expect me to hand myself over into servitude to kings for their sake."

"A fine thing to say," said Peter. "I want you to go into the service of kings, not be in servitude to them."

"There is," he said, "only one syllable's difference between them."

"But I am of the opinion," said Peter, "that, whatever name you give it, it is still the course by which you can not only profit others, both privately and publicly, but also make your own position a happier one."

"Would I make it happier by following a course which is abhorrent to me? But as it is, I live as I please,[25] and I certainly suspect that is very seldom the case with the grandees of court. Surely there are plenty of people who strive to gain the favor of powerful men, so that you need not consider it any great loss if I and one or two like me are not among them."

Then I said, "It is clear, my dear Raphael, that you are not greedy for wealth or power; I respect and revere a person with your attitude no less than I do any of the high and mighty. But it seems obvious to me that you would be acting in a fashion worthy of yourself and of your noble and truly philosophical nature if you could bring yourself to apply your intelligence and industry to public affairs, even at the cost of some private inconvenience. You will never be able to do this to such good effect as you could if you became a counsellor to some great prince[26] and urged upon him what is right and honorable, as I am sure you would. For the stream of good and evil, as if from a never-failing spring, flows from the prince down upon the whole people. And your learning is so complete, even if you had no great experience, and your experience is so full, even if you had no learning at all, that you would be an outstanding counsellor to any king whatever."

"You are wrong on two counts, my dear More," he said. "First about me, and then about the way things are. For I do not have the ability you attribute to me, and even if I had it in full measure, I would sacrifice my contemplative leisure to active endeavor without contributing anything to the common good. First of all, the princes themselves, almost all

23 Scylla was a six-headed sea monster (*Odyssey* 12.73–100, 234–59; *Aeneid* 3.424–32); Celaeno was one of the harpies, disgusting birds with women's faces (*Aeneid* 3.209–58); the Laestrigonians were giant cannibals (*Odyssey* 10.17–133). 24 It seems likely that at this point More inserted the bulk of Book 1, the dialogue about counseling kings, which was written after Book 2, when More had returned to London. In this addition More does not limit himself to describing Utopian institutions but gives Raphael's narration about the Polylerites, Achorians, and Macarians. 25 Hythloday paraphrases a definition of liberty given by Cicero in a context similar to this one (*De officiis* 1.69–70). See *Pico*, *CW* 1: 69/21–22 and 87/4–5, and Augustine's *City of God* 14.25 for different uses of this proclamation of liberty. 26 As indicated in the opening paragraph, the term More uses here and frequently elsewhere is *princeps*.

of them, are more devoted to military pursuits (in which I neither have nor desire any skill) than they are to the beneficent pursuits of peacetime; and they are far more interested in how to acquire new kingdoms by hook or crook than in how to govern well those they have already acquired. Moreover, among the counsellors to kings, there is none who is not so truly wise as not to need—or at least thinks he is so wise as not to tolerate—the advice of any other counsellor, except that they support and fawn on any and all absurdities propounded by the prince's favorites, whose favor they strive to win by flattery. Certainly nature seems to have arranged it so that everyone is delighted with his own insights. So the crow dotes on its chick, and the monkey on its whelp.[27]

"But in a conclave made up of those who envy the insights of others or exalt their own, if anyone should propose something which he has read was done in other eras or which he has seen done in other places, his listeners there immediately act as if their whole reputation for wisdom were at risk, as if they would thereafter be considered totally stupid if they cannot propose something to undermine the proposals of others. If all else fails, then this is their last resort: these things pleased our ancestors, they say, and would that we were as wise as they! And with this remark they take their seat thinking they have said the last word on the subject, as if it were a very dangerous matter if anyone were detected to be wiser than his ancestors on any point. In fact if those ancestors have instituted some truly excellent policy, we are quite content to dismiss it. But if they might have taken a wiser course on some point, we immediately and eagerly seize the pretext of tradition to maintain it. And I have encountered such arrogant, absurd, and captious judgments often enough in other places, but once even in England."

"What," I said, "you were in our country?"

"I was," he said, "and I spent some months there, not long after the revolt of the Englishmen from the west against the king was put down with such a miserable slaughter of the rebels.[28] While there I was much obliged to the most Reverend Father John Morton, Cardinal Archbishop of Canterbury, and

at that time also Lord Chancellor of England.[29] He was a man, my dear Peter (for More already knows what I am about to say) no more venerable for his authority than for his prudence and character. He was of medium height, not stooped over though he was of an advanced age. His looks inspired reverence, not fear. In company he was not standoffish, but grave and serious. Sometimes he enjoyed handling suitors roughly, but harmlessly, so as to gauge the intelligence and presence of mind each would display. He was delighted with such qualities, provided they were devoid of all impudence, since they were related to his own character, and he embraced them as valuable in getting things done. His speech was polished and pointed; he was very skilled in the law; his intelligence was incomparable; his memory was so excellent as to be prodigious. These extraordinary natural gifts he had improved by study and practice. The king seemed to rely very much on his advice and while I was there he seemed to be the mainstay of the commonwealth. This was not surprising: thrust immediately from school into the court at a very young age, active in important affairs throughout his life, continually whirled about by violent changes of fortune, he had learned practical wisdom in the midst of many and serious perils, and wisdom so won is not easily forgotten.

"One day when I happened to be dining at his table, a layman who was skilled in the laws of your country was there. Following up some remark or other, he launched on an elaborate encomium of the *Laws hardly just* rigorous justice which was at that time applied to thieves in England. They were executed everywhere, he said, sometimes as many as twenty at a time hanging on one gallows,[30] and he remarked that he was all the more amazed that the country was cursed to have so many of them prowling about everywhere, since so few escaped punishment. Then I said (and I dared to speak my mind freely in the presence of the Cardinal): 'You should not be at all surprised. For this punishment of thieves is both beyond the limits of justice and not in the public interest. As a punishment for theft it is too harsh, and even so it is not a sufficient deterrent: simple theft is

---

27 Cf. Erasmus, *Adages* 115, 121, 3064 (*CWE* 31: 158–60, 167–68)   **28** A Cornish rebellion was crushed at the Battle of Blackheath on June 22, 1497.   **29** More had admired Morton (1420–1500) since the time he was a page in his household (*ca.* 1490–92). He is portrayed as skilled and shrewd in More's *Richard III* (*CW* 2: 90–92).   **30** In his *Description of England* (1587), ed. Georges Edelen (Ithaca, NY: Cornell University Press, 1968), 193, William Harrison reported that in the reign of Henry VIII alone 72,000 thieves and vagabonds were hanged.

not so serious a crime as to deserve capital punishment, and no penalty is great enough to keep people from stealing if they have no other way to make a living. Thus, in this matter, not only you but most of the world seem to imitate bad teachers who are more eager to beat their pupils than to instruct them. For heavy and horrible punishments are imposed on thieves when it would be much better to make some provision for their livelihood, so that no one should labor under the cruel necessity first of stealing and then of dying for it.'

A feasible method for reducing the number of thieves

"'We have made sufficient provision for that,' he said. 'There are trades; there is farming. From them they can make a living, as long as they do not willingly prefer to be criminals.'

"'You will not get out of it that way,' I said. 'First of all, we will overlook the many soldiers who come home crippled from foreign or domestic wars, as they recently did from the battle against the Cornishmen and not long before that from the French wars.[31] They have sacrificed their limbs for the commonwealth or the king; their disability does not allow them to practice their former trades and they are too old to learn a new one. These,' I said, 'let us overlook, since wars happen only now and then. Let us consider what is never not happening. Now there is a multitude of noblemen who not only live like drones on the labor of others[32] — namely the tenants of their estates whom they bleed white by raising their rents (for this is the only kind of frugality they recognize, and otherwise they are so prodigal as to reduce themselves to beggary) — but they also travel with a huge crowd of retainers, none of whom has ever learned how to make a living. As soon as their master dies or they get sick, they are immediately thrown out. For lords would rather support idle men than invalids, and often the heir of a dying master cannot support a household as large as his father's, at least at first. Meanwhile the outcasts vigorously starve unless they vigorously steal. For what are they to do? After tramping around a bit

they will have ruined their clothes and their health. Disfigured as they are by disease and clad in rags, no nobleman will deign to take them in and no farmer dares to do so. For the farmers are not unaware that a person who has been brought up in idle ease and pleasure and who has been used to swaggering about like a bully, girt with sword and buckler, looking down his nose at the whole neighborhood and despising everyone but himself, is hardly likely to be a reliable and faithful servant for a poor farmer, working with hoe and mattock for miserable wages and scanty keep.'

"To this the lawyer replied, 'But this is precisely the sort of person we should cherish the most. For since they are more high-spirited and lofty-minded than artisans and farmers, they provide the strength and power of an army if we ever have to fight a war.'

"'Indeed,' I said, 'you might as well say that we should cherish thieves for the sake of warfare, for you will never lack for thieves as long as you have the retainers. In fact robbers are no slouches as soldiers and soldiers are not the most lethargic of thieves — so finely matched are the two callings.[33] But this problem, though it is widespread among you, is not peculiar to you; it is shared by almost all nations.

But France is infected with another pestilence besides, one that is even more virulent: the whole country is occupied and filled with mercenaries, even during peacetime (if it can be called that).[34] Their justification is the same as yours for maintaining idle retainers here: those foolosophers[35] think that the public welfare consists in having strong and stout armed forces in a state of readiness, especially veterans, for they have no confidence in untried troops, just as if they should seek out a war precisely to avoid having inexperienced soldiers, and people should be gratuitously slaughtered (as Sallust nicely puts it) lest hand and spirit should grow sluggish through inactivity.[36] Just how deadly it is to maintain such beasts France has learned to her cost,[37] and the same

The disaster produced by standing military garrisons

31 Since Hythloday was in England in late 1497 and early 1498, he may be referring to English skirmishes in France in the early 1490s. But as he speaks in 1515, he may also be thinking of the much heavier casualties in Henry VIII's futile French campaigns of 1512–13. **32** Plato uses the figure of the drones to describe an oligarchy ruled by rich men who exploit the poor and contribute nothing to society (*Republic* 8.552b–c). **33** The parallel between soldiers and robbers is a frequent theme among humanists; see, for example, Erasmus, *Complaint of Peace* (*CWE* 27: 317). **34** In the time of Francis I, the French relied mostly on Swiss and German mercenaries. **35** The Latin *morosophi* (transliterated from Greek) means literally "foolish wisemen" (the reverse of the modern "sophomore"). See Lucian, *Alexander* 40. Erasmus uses it in *The Praise of Folly* 13; in *De copia, Opera omnia* 1.12c; and in *Adagia* (prol., *CWE* 31: 23). **36** *Bellum Catilinae* 16.3 **37** Foreign mercenaries often wreaked

is made clear by the examples of the Romans, the Carthaginians, and the Syrians,[38] and of many other nations as well:[39] standing armies of mercenaries, on one occasion after another, destroyed not only their government but also their fields and even their cities. How little this was necessary is made clear by the fact that not even French soldiers, thoroughly trained in warfare to their very fingertips, can very often boast that they came off better than your draftees — not to put it more strongly lest I seem to be flattering present company.[40] But your troops, whether urban artisans or rough and untrained farmers, are not thought to be very much afraid of the idle retainers of noblemen, except for some whose physique does not lend itself to strength and boldness or whose brave spirit has been broken by the poverty of their families. There is little enough danger that those retainers whose vigorous and strong bodies (for noblemen do not deign to ruin any but choice physiques) are now either grown flabby with idleness or soft with almost ladylike activities, no danger, I say, that such retainers would be unmanned if they were taught a good craft to earn a living and were exercised in manly labors. However that may be, I certainly do not see that it can ever contribute to the common good to prepare for war (which you never have unless you wish to) by maintaining such a huge crowd of people who undermine the peace, to which we ought to pay so much more attention than to war. But this is not the only problem which makes it necessary to steal. There is another, more peculiar (so far as I know) to you Englishmen.'

"'What is that?' said the Cardinal.

"'Your sheep,' I said, 'which are ordinarily so meek and require so little to maintain them, now begin (so they say) to be so voracious and fierce that they devour even the people themselves; they destroy and despoil fields, houses, towns.[41] I mean that wherever in the realm finer and therefore more expensive wool is produced, noblemen, gentlemen, and even some abbots (holy men are they), not content with the annual rents and produce which their ancestors were accustomed to derive from their estates, not thinking it sufficient to live idly and comfortably, contributing nothing to the common good, unless they also undermine it, these drones leave nothing for cultivation; they enclose everything as pasture; they destroy homes, level towns, leaving only the church as a stable for the sheep; and as if too little ground among you were lost as game preserves or hunting forests, these good men turn all habitations and cultivated lands into a wilderness. And so that one glutton, a dire and insatiable plague to his native country, may join the fields together and enclose thousands of acres within one hedge, the farmers are thrown out: some are stripped of their possessions, circumvented by fraud or overcome by force; or worn out by injustices, they are forced to sell. One way or another, the poor wretches depart, men, women, husbands, wives, orphans, widows, parents with little children and a household which is numerous rather than rich, since agriculture requires many hands, they depart, I say, from hearth and home, all that was known and familiar to them, and they cannot find any place to go to. All their household furnishings, which could not be sold for much even if they could wait for a buyer, are sold for a song now that they must be removed. They soon spend that pittance in their wanderings, and then finally what else is left but to steal and to hang — justly, to be sure — or else to bum around and beg? For that matter, even as vagrants they are thrown into jail because they are wandering around idly, though no one will hire them, even when they offer their services most eagerly. For since no seed is sown, there is no farm labor, and that is all they are accustomed to. One herdsman or shepherd is sufficient to graze livestock on ground that would require many hands to cultivate and grow crops.

"'And for this reason the price of grain has risen sharply in many places. Even the price of wool has gone up so high that poorer people who ordinarily make cloth out of it in this country cannot buy it,

havoc in France during the Hundred Years' War (1337–1453). **38** The Greek historian Herodian (mentioned in Book 2 as one of the authors Hythloday brought to Utopia) describes how several emperors were murdered by the barbarian mercenaries of the Praetorian guard. After the first Punic War, foreign mercenaries revolted against their Carthaginian employers. From the thirteenth to the sixteenth centuries, the

Mamelukes (originally mercenaries from Turkey and Circassia) ruled despotically a large empire consisting of Egypt, Syria, and other parts of the Middle East. **39** Especially Italy, which was often devastated by foreign mercenaries; Machiavelli, who firmly opposed the use of mercenaries, gives many examples of the harm they caused. **40** The English defeated the French decisively at Crècy (1346), Poitiers

(1356), and Agincourt (1415). **41** Between the thirteenth and eighteenth centuries, much arable land was enclosed by hedges or ditches and used to pasture sheep. Hythloday's arguments against enclosure were widespread, and though it had its supporters (mostly because of the profitability of the wool trade), it undoubtedly caused much suffering to farm laborers and destroyed many villages.

and for that reason many of them are out of a job and reduced to idleness. For after pastureland was expanded, huge herds of sheep were carried off by a murrain, as if God were punishing the owners' greed by visiting on the sheep a pestilence which might more justly have been hurled at the heads of their owners. But even if the number of sheep should increase enormously, the price still does not go down, because, though the sellers cannot be said to have a monopoly since more than one is selling, still it is certainly an oligopoly. For the sheep have almost all come into the hands of a few, and these men are so rich that they are under no necessity to sell until they want to, and they do not want to until they get the price they want.

"'For the same reason other kinds of livestock are similarly high-priced, and all the more so because, once the farmhouses have been torn down and agriculture neglected, there is no one to see to the breeding of animals. For even those rich landholders do not rear other animals as they do sheep. Rather they buy them lean and cheap in some distant market and then sell them dear after fattening them up in their pastures. And for that reason, I think, the full disadvantage of this system has not yet been felt. I mean that up to now they have raised the prices only in the places where the animals are sold. But when the time comes that they are taken from the breeders faster than they can be bred, then finally the numbers will also gradually decrease where they are bought, so that here also there must needs be a severe shortage. Thus the very feature that seemed to make your island extremely fortunate has been turned into an instrument of its destruction by the wicked greed of a few men. For these high food prices are the reason why everyone dismisses as many as he can from his household— to go where, I ask you, except to go begging or else, as a noble spirit can more easily be persuaded to do, to turn to robbery.

"'What shall we say when this miserable poverty and want is coupled with wanton luxury?[42] For the retainers of noblemen, artisans, and one might say even some peasants and, in sum, all classes of society indulge in extravagant sartorial display and excessive, luxurious cuisine. And then the cookshops, the brothels, the bawdy houses, and those other sorts of bawdy houses, the wine bars and alehouses, and then so many crooked games of chance, dice, cards, backgammon, tennis, bowling, quoits, don't all these quickly empty pockets and send their votaries off to rob someone? Get rid of these pernicious plagues, make laws requiring that villages and towns be rebuilt by those who have torn them down or be handed over to those who are willing to restore and rebuild them. Keep the rich from cornering the market and from having a licensed monopoly, as it were.[43] Let fewer people be supported in idleness, let agriculture be restored, let cloth working be reinstated as an honest trade which will give useful employment to this idle mob, whether those whom poverty has already turned into thieves or those who are now vagabonds or idle servants—in either case they will turn out to be thieves.

"'Certainly unless you remedy these evils, it is pointless for you to boast of the justice administered in the punishment of thieves, a justice which is specious rather than either just or expedient. In fact when you bring people up with the worst sort of education and allow their morals to be corrupted little by little from their earliest years, and then punish them at last as grown men when they commit the crimes which from childhood they have given every prospect of committing, what else are you doing, I ask you, but making them into thieves and then punishing them for it?'

"As I was saying this, the lawyer was already getting ready to speak and had decided to employ that common method of disputants who are more diligent in repeating than in replying—so high is their opinion of memory. 'A very fine speech indeed,' he said, 'especially for a stranger who has only had more opportunity to hear about these matters than to get any precise knowledge of them, as I shall make clear in a few words. For first I shall recount in an orderly way what you have said; then I shall show on what points your ignorance of our affairs has misled you; finally, I shall rebut and refute all your arguments. Therefore, to begin with the first task I promised to undertake, you seem to have made four—'

"'Be quiet,' said the Cardinal, 'for it seems hardly likely that you will reply in a few words after such a

---

42 Long before and after 1515 many sumptuary laws were passed against extravagant display, especially in clothing, but they were honored more in the breach than the observance. **43** During the reigns of Henry VII and Henry VIII, laws were passed forbidding gaming and alehouses, limiting enclosure, restoring land from pasture to tillage, and restricting monopolies, but with little effect.

beginning. Hence, for the present we will relieve you of the trouble of replying, but we reserve that whole task for you when you two meet again, which I wish to be tomorrow, if nothing prevents you or Raphael here from meeting then. But meanwhile, my dear Raphael, I would very much like to hear why you think theft should not be punished with execution, or what other punishment you would enact that would contribute more to the common good. For even you do not think we should put up with it. But if people rush into thievery now when it is punishable by death, and then if they could once be sure of their lives, what force, what fear could possibly restrain criminals? They would interpret the mitigation of the punishment almost as an incentive or reward for wrongdoing.'

This shows the Cardinal's usual way of interrupting anyone who talks too much

"'Most gracious Father,' I said, 'it seems to me to be entirely and absolutely unjust to take a person's life because he has taken some money. For a human life cannot be equated with the goods of fortune, not even the whole sum of them. But if they say that this punishment is redress not for money but for the transgression of justice or the violation of laws, would it not be right to call this extreme justice extreme injury?[44] For we ought not to approve of legal decrees so Manlian[45] that the slightest infraction causes the sword to be unsheathed nor should we accept the Stoic maxim that all sins are equal,[46] making no distinction between killing a person or stealing a coin from him, for between these two crimes (if fairness means anything at all) there is no similarity or relationship. God forbade us to kill anyone,[47] and are we so ready to kill someone because he has taken a bit of money? But if someone should interpret that command to mean that the power to kill anyone is taken away except when human law declares a person should be killed, what is to prevent human beings from using the same principle to decide to what degree rape,

Manlian edicts from Livy

adultery, or perjury are permissible? In fact, God has deprived us of the right to kill not only others but also ourselves, but if the mutual consent of human beings to specific laws allowing them to kill one another has enough force to release their agents from the bonds of God's commandment and enable them, with no precedent from God, to execute anyone condemned to death by human law, will that not mean that God's commandment has only as much force as is granted to it by human law? And indeed on this principle human beings may decide to what degree God's commands are to be observed in all fields. Finally, the law of Moses, though it was harsh and severe because it was made for slaves, and stubborn ones at that, still punished theft with a fine, not death.[48] Let us not think that in his new law of mercy, by which he commands us as a father does his children, God has granted us greater license to be cruel to one another.[49]

"'These are the reasons why I think this punishment is wrong. And I think there is no one who does not understand how absurd and even dangerous it is to society to punish theft and murder in the same way. For when a thief sees that he is in no less danger if he is convicted of theft than if he had also been condemned for murder, that consideration alone will drive him to kill someone whom otherwise he would only have robbed. For apart from the fact that there is no more danger if he is caught, murder makes him more safe and gives him a greater hope of concealing his crime, since the witness to it has been eliminated. Thus by using excessively harsh measures to terrify thieves we encourage them to kill the innocent.

"'As for the usual question of what punishment would be more advantageous, in my judgment it would be quite a bit easier to find a better one than to find one that is worse. For why should we doubt the utility of that way of punishing criminals which we know was once preferred for so long by the Romans, who were quite expert in the art of governing? Those convicted of serious crimes were condemned

---

44 a proverbial saying (Erasmus, *Adages* 924, *CWE* 32: 244), derived primarily from Cicero, *De officiis* 1.10.33 **45** Proverbial for "harshly unjust" (Erasmus, *Adages* 987, *CWE* 32: 274–75). The Roman consul Manlius executed his son for winning a victory without having permission to do so (Livy 8.7.1–22). **46** Stoics such as Zeno, Seneca, and Epictetus believed that

virtue consisted in ignoring exterior forces and remaining faithful to the interior dictates of reason about what is right; such faithfulness has no degrees but is either kept or not. Cicero presents and refutes the paradox in *De finibus* 4.10.21–23; Horace ridicules it in *Satires* 1.3.113–24. **47** Ex 20:13; Dt 5:17 (All scriptural references are to the Vulgate text and numbering.)

48 Ex 22:1–4 **49** The Mosaic law does, of course, prescribe death as a punishment for various crimes. And even under the more merciful Christian dispensation, Hythloday does not always condemn capital punishment; as the remedy of last resort, it is employed by the Polylerites and the Utopians.

to quarry stone or dig out ore, constantly shackled and guarded. But as for me, on this point I reserve my highest approval for the system practiced by a people generally called the Polylerites[50] whom I encountered in the course of my travels in Persia. Their population is not small and their institutions are not lacking in prudence; except that they pay an annual tribute to the king of Persia, they are otherwise free and allowed to make their own laws. But because they are a long way from the ocean and almost entirely surrounded by mountains, and because they are content with the produce of their land, which is by no means infertile, they neither visit others nor are visited very often themselves. In accord with the ancient policy of their country, they do not seek to extend their territory, and what they already have is easily protected by the mountains and the tribute paid to their overlord. They have absolutely no armed forces, their lifestyle is hardly splendid but it is comfortable, and they are happy rather than renowned or illustrious. Indeed, even their name, I think, is not very well known except to their immediate neighbors.

The commonwealth of the Polylerites in Persia

"'And so, among them whoever is convicted of theft restores what was taken to its owner, not (as elsewhere) to the prince, for they consider he has no more right to stolen goods than the thief himself.[51] If the goods have been lost, their equivalent is paid from the possessions of the thief, and whatever is left is handed over intact to his wife and children. He himself is condemned to hard labor.

We should note this, since we do otherwise

"'Moreover, unless the theft was committed with violence, they are not shackled or imprisoned but left free and unconstrained as they work on public projects. Shirkers and slackers are not restrained with shackles but egged on with the lash. If they work energetically, they are subjected to no humiliation; they are locked up in their cells only at nighttime after roll call. Except for constant labor their lives are not uncomfortable. Since they are doing public works they are fed at public expense, and not badly, but in different ways in different places. In some places what is spent on them is collected as alms; and this method, though it is unpredictable, has nevertheless been found to be the most productive because the people there are compassionate. In other places public revenues are set aside for that purpose. There are places where they levy a tax on private individuals to support the prisoners. Actually, in other places they do not do public works, but when a private person needs workmen he goes to the city square and hires some of them for that day at a fixed wage, which is a little less than what a freeman would cost. Moreover, if a slave is lazy it is permissible to whip him. Thus no one ever lacks work. And over and above his keep, each of them brings something into the public treasury every day.

"'They are all dressed in one color and they are the only ones who wear it. Their hair is not shaved off but it is clipped a bit short above the ears. A little piece of one ear is cut off. Their friends are allowed to give any of them food, drink, and clothing of the right color. But it is death to give them money, both for the donor and the recipient, nor is it any less dangerous for a freeman to take money from them for any reason whatsoever or for a slave (for that is what they call the convicts) to lay a hand on a weapon. Each district has its own distinguishing badge, which it is a capital crime to throw away, just as it is to be seen outside the district boundaries or to say anything to a slave from another district. To plan an escape is no safer than to attempt it. In fact, to be an accessory to such a plan is death for a slave and enslavement for a freeman. On the other hand, rewards are allotted to informers: for a freeman money, for a slave freedom, and for either one pardon and amnesty for their complicity, to keep it from seeming safer to carry out a criminal plan than to repent of it.

But nowadays the servants of noblemen find such a haircut attractive

"'This law and the system I have described constitute their policy in this matter. It is perfectly obvious how humane and advantageous it is since vengeance is managed in such a way as to eliminate the vice and preserve the person, and to handle him in such a way that he has to be good and will spend the rest of his life making up for the harm he has done. Furthermore, there is so little fear that they

50 a name formed from Greek *polus* ("much") and *leros* ("nonsense")
51 Erasmus expresses the same opinion in *The Education of a Christian Prince* (*CWE* 27: 270).

will revert to their former ways that travelers who intend to make a journey consider no guides to be safer than these slaves, whom they exchange from district to district. For there is no opportunity whatever to commit robbery: they are unarmed; money is of no use except as evidence of a crime; punishment is in store for them if they are caught; and there is absolutely no hope of escaping anywhere. For how could a person whose clothes are totally different from anyone else's cover up his escape and disguise himself unless he ran away naked? And even then his ear would give him away. But couldn't they at least conspire to overthrow the republic?—that surely is the real danger. As if any district could hope to do so without sounding out and enlisting the slave gangs of many other districts! They are so far from being able to conspire that they cannot even meet or converse or greet one another. And then how can we believe anyone would dare to trust his companions with such a plot, since it is dangerous for them to remain silent and most advantageous to reveal it? On the other hand, if they are patient and obedient, if they give good reason to believe that they will lead reformed lives in the future, none need despair of regaining his freedom; indeed not a year goes by in which some slaves who have recommended themselves by their patience are not reinstated.'

"When I had said this, and had added that I saw no reason why this system could not be set up also in England, and with much more benefit than the justice which the lawyer had praised so highly, then he (namely the lawyer) said: 'This system could never be established in England without enormous danger to the commonwealth.' As he said this he shook his head, puckered his mouth, and fell silent. And everyone there jumped on his bandwagon.[52]

"Then the Cardinal said, 'It is not easy to predict whether the outcome would be favorable or not without at least trying it out. But when the death sentence has been pronounced, if the prince were to grant a reprieve without any right of asylum[53] in order to see how the system would work, and then if in fact it turned out to be useful, it would be right to establish it. If not, then thieves who had been condemned earlier could be executed at that time; on the part of the government this would be neither

less nor more unjust than immediate execution, and during the trial period it would pose no danger. In fact, it seems clear to me that it would not be a bad idea to treat vagabonds also in the same way, for in spite of the many laws made against them, we have still made no progress.'

"When the Cardinal had said this, there was no one there who did not vie with the others in praising what they had scorned when I proposed it, but especially the part about the vagabonds because the Cardinal himself had added it on.

"I do not know whether or not it would be better to say nothing about what happened then, for it was quite silly. But I will tell it anyway, for it was not malicious and it has some bearing on our subject. A certain hanger-on was standing around. It seems he wanted to play the fool, but he did it so well that he seemed to be one, raising a laugh with such witless jokes that the laughter was directed more often at him than at the jokes. But every now and then he came up with something not entirely absurd, so as to confirm the proverb 'Throw the dice often enough and you will sooner or later get a lucky combination.'[54] One of the guests said that in my discourse I had made good provision for thieves and the Cardinal had also taken care of the vagabonds, and now all that remained was to make public provision for those whom disease or old age had rendered destitute and who were incapable of returning to the jobs by which they had earned their living. 'Leave that to me,' said the hanger-on. 'I will see to it that this is also properly taken care of. In fact, I am desperately anxious to ship off this sort of person somewhere out of my sight; they annoy me so much with their wailing and whining and pleas for money, though they can never sing so pretty a tune as to extract a penny from me. Actually, one of two things happens: either I don't want to give them anything or I don't have anything to give. And so they have now begun to get wise. To keep from wasting their effort, they keep silent when they see me passing by. Good lord, they no more hope for anything from me than if I were a priest.[55] I would decree by law that all such

An entertaining exchange between a friar and a fool

A proverb frequently bandied about among beggars

---

52 Erasmus, *Adages* 1612 (*CWE* 34: 8–10)
53 If a criminal could reach a place of asylum or sanctuary (usually a church)

he could not be arrested, though during the reign of Henry VII the privilege was discussed and somewhat curtailed. It is

debated in More's *Richard III* (*CW* 2: 27–33). **54** Cf. Erasmus, *Adages* 113 (*CWE* 31: 154–55) **55** There seems to

beggars be divided up and parceled out among the Benedictine monasteries where they would become lay brothers (as they are called);[56] and the women I would order to become nuns.'

5   "The Cardinal smiled and took it as a joke, but the others took it seriously. A certain friar, however, a theologian, was so delighted by a joke aimed at priests and monks that he himself also began to make merry, though he was otherwise so serious as 10 to be almost sour. 'But even this,' he said, 'will not free you from beggars unless you also look out for us friars.'

  "But that is already taken care of,' said the hanger-on. 'For the Cardinal looked out for you 15 marvelously well when he proposed that vagabonds should be confined and put to work, for you are the greatest vagabonds of all.'

  "After they all had looked at the Cardinal and saw that he did not reject this joke either, they were not 20 at all loath to enjoy it, all except the friar. Needled in this fashion,[57] he was indignant and furious (nor am I surprised that he was), so much so that he couldn't 25 even refrain from hurling insults. He called the fellow a scoundrel, a backbiter, a sneak, and a son of perdition,[58] all the while citing terrible threats from Holy Scripture. Now the buffoon began to do some serious buffoonery, for he was clearly on his own 30 ground.

He alludes to the Horatian phrase "doused with Italian vinegar"

  "'Do not grow angry, my good friar,' he said, 'for it is written, "In your patience you shall possess your souls."'[59]

  "The friar replied (and I will give his very own 35 words), 'I am not angry, you jailbird, or at least I do not sin. For the psalmist says, "Be angry and do not sin."'[60]

How well the people in the story speak in character!

  "Then the friar was gently advised by the Cardinal 40 to control his emotions, but he said, 'No, my lord, my language springs from nothing but good zeal, as it should, for holy men have had good zeal, whence

it is said, "Zeal for your house has consumed me,"[61] and we sing in church, "Those who mock Elisha as he goes up to the house of God feel the zeal of the bald man," just as perhaps this mocking and ribald rascal will feel it.'[62]

Apparently the friar, in his ignorance, misuses zelus *as if it were neuter like* scelus

45

  "'Perhaps you are acting out of a laudable feeling,' said the Cardinal, 'but it seems to me that you 50 would act, if not in a holier, then certainly in a wiser way, if you would not put yourself on the level of a fool and set out to cap his absurdities with your own.' 55

  "'No, my lord,' he said, 'I would not act more wisely. For Solomon, the wisest of men, says, "Reply to a fool in accord with his folly,"[63] as I am now doing, and I am showing him the pit into which he will fall[64] if he does not watch out. For if the mul- 60 titude which mocked Elisha, who was just one bald man, felt the zeal of the bald man, how much more will be heaped on a single person who mocks a multitude of friars, for many of them are bald. And also we have a papal bull which excommunicates anyone 65 who makes fun of us.'

  "When the Cardinal saw there would be no end to it, he sent the hanger-on away with a motion of his head and opportunely turned the conversation to another subject. A little later he arose from the 70 table and, dismissing us, devoted himself to hearing the petitions of suitors.

  "See, my dear More, how I have burdened you with a long discourse, and I would be quite ashamed of myself for doing so if you had not eagerly im- 75 portuned me and seemed to listen as if you wanted no detail of this conversation omitted. Though I should have been more brief, still I did at least feel obliged to tell it to show how judiciously they scorned the plan when I proposed it and how the 80 very same persons immediately reversed themselves and approved it when the Cardinal did not disapprove of it. Their flattery of him went so far that they seriously favored and almost accepted the ideas

be no recorded or recognized proverb here (though it might still have been a frequent saying among beggars); there may be some allusion to the priest who passed by the wounded Samaritan (Luke 10:31).   **56** Unordained members of religious orders were called "lay brothers." **57** See *Satires* 1.7.32 and Erasmus, *Adages* 1252 (*CWE* 33: 164). The phrase is here

translated as "needled."   **58** Jn 17:12; 2 Thes 2:3   **59** Lk 21:19   **60** Ps 4:5 **61** Ps 68(69):10   **62** In 2(4) Kgs 2:23–25, some children mocked Elisha because of his baldness; when he cursed them two bears came out of the woods and tore forty-two of them to pieces. The friar quotes a hymn attributed to Adam of St. Victor, sung within the octave of Easter. In the ordinary

pronunciation of Erasmus's time *zelus* ("zeal") could sound like *scelus* ("crime"). The confusion produces the following result: those who mocked Elisha . . . feel the crime of the bald man.   **63** Prv 26:5. But the preceding verse says: "Do not answer the fool according to his folly lest you become like him."   **64** perhaps alluding to Ps 7:16

of his hanger-on because his master took them as a joke and hence did not scorn them. From this you can judge how high an estimation courtiers would have of me and my advice."

"Indeed, my dear Raphael," I said, "you have given me much pleasure, you told the whole story so judiciously and so deftly. Moreover, while you spoke I seemed not only to have returned to my homeland but also to have grown young again because of fond memories of the Cardinal, in whose household I was educated as a boy. When you honored his memory so highly, you cannot imagine how much dearer you became to me on that account, though you were already most dear. But I am by no means ready to change my mind yet. No, I am convinced if you could bring yourself not to shrink from the courts of princes, you could contribute a great deal to the common good through your advice. No duty of a good man (and you are one, of course) is more important than that. Then too, since your friend Plato thinks that commonwealths will be happy only when philosophers become kings or kings become philosophers,[65] how far will we be from happiness if philosophers will not even deign to impart their advice to kings."

"They are not so disagreeable as that; they would do so gladly. Indeed they have already done so by publishing many books, if those in power were prepared to accept their good advice. But undoubtedly Plato clearly foresaw that unless kings became philosophers, they would never give their approval to the advice of philosophers, because since childhood they have been thoroughly imbued and infected with misguided notions. He also found this out for himself when he was with Dionysius.[66] But don't you think that, if I proposed sound measures to some king and tried to eradicate from his mind the seeds of corruption, I would be banished or held up as a laughingstock!

"Come now,[67] imagine that I serve the French king[68] and sit in his council chamber, as the king himself presides in a secret session, surrounded by a most judicious circle of advisers who are very eagerly seeking out wiles and stratagems to keep Milan and win back Naples (which is always slipping from his fingers),[69] and then to overthrow Venice and make all of Italy subject to him,[70] and then to bring Flanders, Brabant, and finally all of Burgundy into his control,[71] and other peoples as well, whose realms he has long had it in mind to invade. At this meeting, while one urges that a treaty be struck with Venice, to last only as long as it suits the French, and that the French share their plans with them and even give them some share of the spoils, which they can reclaim when matters have been satisfactorily settled; while another advises them to hire German mercenaries, another to soothe the Swiss with payments of money;[72] someone else, on the other hand, thinks that his divine majesty the emperor ought to be propitiated with a votive offering, as it were, of gold;[73] while another thinks it best to strike a bargain with the king of Aragon, granting him the kingdom of Navarre (which belongs to someone else) as the price of peace;[74] and on the same occasion another suggests that the prince of Castile should be snared by the prospect of a marriage alliance[75] and that some nobles of his court

Indirectly he is discouraging the French from acquiring Italy

Swiss mercenaries

65 *Republic* 5.473c–d; *Epistles* 7.326a–b
66 During his three sojourns at Syracuse, Plato failed in his attempt to reform the tyrant Dionysius or his son (also Dionysius); see his *Epistles* 7 and Plutarch, *Dion* 4.1–5.3, 10.1–20.2. **67** Here Hythloday launches into a 464-word sentence, suspended, unrealistically intricate, interminable (as Lupton called it), which ends with "react to this speech." Though translators (with the exception of Robinson) have generally broken up this sentence to make it easier, such manipulation is unjustified: the sentence is no easier in Latin than in English. Its difficulty springs from Hythloday's difficult outlook. See Gerald Malsbary's "Hythlodeus' 464-Word 'Marathon Sentence': How Does It Work?," *Moreana* nos. 195–96 (June 2014): 153–75. **68** In

1515, the time of More's imagined interview with Hythloday, the king of France was Francis I, who continued the policy of his predecessors Charles VII and Louis XII. All three invented claims to Milan and Naples, but their military adventures in Italy foundered in confusion and intrigue. **69** The French won Milan in 1499, lost it in 1512, and regained it in 1515. They won Naples in 1495, lost it in 1496, regained it in 1501, and lost it in 1503. **70** At the battle of Agnadello (1509), France defeated Venice and deprived it of its territory on the mainland. By 1515, when the Venetians helped Francis I in his campaign against Milan, the French king restored Verona to his Venetian ally. Hythloday wonders if the French king is ready to turn on his recent ally once more. **71** After the death of Charles the Rash, Duke of Burgundy

(1477), Louis XI of France tried to seize all the vast Burgundian holdings, though many parts clearly did not belong to France. **72** The German mercenary footsoldiers were surpassed only by the Swiss; both were despised and excoriated by Erasmus and many humanists. **73** Emperor Maximilian of Hapsburg, grandfather of Charles V, was usually impecunious and totally unreliable. A votive offering was normally an expensive gift left in a church or shrine in thanksgiving for a favor from God or a saint. **74** With the help of troops sent by a duped Henry VIII, Ferdinand II, King of Aragon and regent of Castile, occupied southern Navarre in 1512 and annexed it to Castile in 1515. **75** Charles V, prince of Castile and the future emperor (1519), was often affianced for dynastic reasons, especially to French brides.

should be brought over to the French side by giving them reliable pensions; when the greatest difficulty of all is encountered, namely what to do in the meantime about England; but they agree that a peace treaty should be negotiated with them,[76] for a weak bond should always be tightened by the strictest terms; let them be called friends but be suspected as enemies; and that therefore the Scots should be stationed in readiness, poised on all occasions to attack immediately if the English make any moves;[77] moreover, that some exiled noblemen be supported secretly (for treaties forbid that it be done openly) who can claim that the kingdom is rightfully his so that the French king will have a rein to check an English king he does not trust[78] — at this council, I say, amidst such a mass of suggestions, surrounded by such distinguished men, all vying to give advice about going to war, if such a nobody as I were to stand up and give an order to tack in a different direction,[79] expressing the opinion that Italy should be ignored and that the king should stay at home, that France is a kingdom so large that it is not easy for one man to rule it (much less should the king imagine he should consider adding others to it);[80] and then if I should put before them the measures adopted by the Achorians,[81] whose country faces the island of Utopia on the southeast side; if I should tell them that they had once fought a war to gain for their king a realm which he claimed to inherit because of some ancient marriage tie, and that, when they finally won it, they saw that they would endure no less suffering in keeping it than they did in gaining it, but rather that the seeds of war were always sprouting up, either rebellion within or incursions from without against the subjected people, so that they were always having to fight either for them or against them; that they never had an opportunity to disband their army, and that at the same time they were being stripped of their resources, their money was being carried out of the country, their blood was being spilled to provide someone else a smidgeon of glory, that they were no

A notable example

safer during peacetime; that at home the war had corrupted morals, imbued the citizens with a lust for robbery, that slaughter in warfare made them completely reckless, that they scorned the laws because the king was so distracted by trying to take care of two kingdoms that he couldn't concentrate on either one. When they saw that otherwise there would be no end to these great troubles, they finally took counsel together and very courteously gave their king the choice of retaining whichever of the kingdoms he wished; but they said he could not have power over both because they were too numerous to be governed by half a king (indeed no one is willing to share even a muledriver with someone else). And so the good prince left his new kingdom to one of his friends (who was soon afterwards banished) and was forced to be content with his old one. Furthermore, if I showed that all these abortive wars, which had thrown so many countries into turmoil for his sake would exhaust his treasury, destroy his people, and in the end still come to nothing through some mishap or other; and that therefore he should care for the kingdom of his ancestors, improve it as much as he could, make it as flourishing as possible;[82] he should love his own and be loved by them; he should live with them, govern them kindly and leave other kingdoms alone, since the kingdom which has fallen to his lot is enough, and more than enough, for him — how do you imagine, my dear More, my listeners would react to this speech?"

"Certainly not very favorably," I said.

"Let us proceed, then," he said.[83] "If counsellors were in a discussion with some king or other and were thinking up schemes to fill up his treasury, while one person suggests increasing the value of the currency when the king pays out money and decreasing it exorbitantly when he collects it so that he can discharge a large debt with a little money and collect a great deal when he is owed only a little;[84] while another urges him to pretend he is going to war and to use that pretext to raise money and then, when it suits him, to make peace with religious ceremonies, pulling the wool over the people's eyes and

---

76 Francis I did make a treaty with England in April 1515. **77** The Scots were traditionally allies of France against England. **78** The French had supported several pretenders to the English throne during the reigns of Henry VII and Henry VIII: Lambert Simnel, Perkin Warbeck, and Edmund de la Pole and his brother Richard. **79** Erasmus, *Adages* 860 (*CWE* 32: 215) **80** Cf. More's epigram no. 243, "On Lust for Power," in *CW* 3.2. **81** From Greek *a-* ("without") and *choros* ("place, country") **82** More here echoes Erasmus's *Adages* 1401 (*CWE* 33: 237–43): "Sparta is your portion; make it flourish." **83** Hythloday presents his second imaginary council in an even longer marathon sentence (926 words); it is just as extravagant in Latin as in this English translation. **84** Fraudulent manipulation of the currency was practiced by Edward IV, Henry VII, and (later) Henry VIII.

making them think that he is a conscientious, merciful prince[85] who wishes to spare them bloodshed;[86] while another reminds him of certain antiquated, moth-eaten laws, long since fallen into disuse, laws which everyone ignores since no one even remembers that they were passed, and advises that he should therefore enforce them with fines, noting that no source of revenue could be more productive, none more honorable, since it has the appearance of a concern for justice;[87] while another advises him to prohibit many practices with heavy fines, especially those that are contrary to the public interest, noting that later he can make a monetary arrangement with those whose interests are hurt by the laws and that thus he can win the gratitude of the people and make a double profit, first from fining those whom greed has led into his trap and then by selling dispensations to others (the higher the price the better the prince, since he is reluctant to grant a private person the right to obstruct the common good, and therefore does it only for a high price); while someone else persuades him to put pressure on judges to rule in his favor in all cases and advises him to summon them to his palace where they are to discuss his affairs in his own presence, saying that thus no case will seem so flimsy that his judges (whether out of love of contradiction, or a desire to seem original, or a wish to curry favor) cannot, in his presence, find some loophole for a false verdict, noting that when the judges give differing opinions and argue about a case that is as clear as day, the truth can be called into question and the king will have a convenient handle to interpret the law in his own favor, pointing out that the others will acquiesce out of shame or fear and thus the judgment can be fearlessly rendered in court, nor can there be any lack of pretexts for someone ruling in the prince's favor, since he has on his side either equity or the letter of the law or a twisted interpretation of the language, or something that outweighs all laws in the minds of conscientious judges,

the indisputable royal prerogative;[88] while everyone agrees completely with that saying of Crassus that no amount of gold is sufficient for a king, since he has to maintain an army,[89] and

The saying of Crassus, a rich man

moreover that a king can do no wrong, no matter how much he wants to, since all the possessions of all his subjects, and even their own persons, belong to him, and since nothing belongs to anyone unless the king graciously refrains from taking it away from him, and that he should leave as little as possible to his subjects since his safety consists in keeping the people from enjoying too much wealth or freedom, which render them less willing to put up with harsh and unjust commands, whereas on the other hand poverty and privation break their spirits and make them patient, depriving the oppressed of the lofty aspirations needed for rebellion;[90] at this point, if I should stand up and contend that all this advice is both dishonorable and harmful to the king, for not only his honor but also his safety depends more on the people's wealth than on his own; if I were to show that the people choose a king for their own sake, not his, since his labor and effort enable them to live in comfort and safety; and that therefore a prince should be more concerned with the welfare of his people than with his own, just as it is the duty of a shepherd, insofar as he is a real one, to feed his sheep and not himself;[91] that experience itself shows how wrong they are in thinking that the poverty of the people is the safeguard of peace, for where can you find more quarrels than among beggars? who is more intent on changing things than someone who is most dissatisfied with his present state in life? or, finally, who is more driven to create a general disturbance in the hope of gaining something than someone who has nothing to lose? But if a king is so scorned and hated by his subjects that he cannot make them do their duty unless he harasses them with maltreatment, plundering, and confiscation and reduces them to

---

85 The Latin phrase used here, *pius princeps,* would immediately remind a renaissance humanist of Virgil's epic hero, *pius* Aeneas. More uses this phrase in *History of King Richard III* at *CW* 15: 424/8–9 and in Epigram 111.   **86** In 1492 Henry VII not only levied taxes for a pretended war against France but accepted a bribe from Charles VIII of France for not fighting it.   **87** Henry VII's ministers Empson and Dudley were notorious for

such chicanery.   **88** The royal prerogative, the special, inherited claims of the king apart from common law, was a subject of considerable dispute even in More's time, though it became more heated in the following century.   **89** Hythloday adapts Cicero's statement in *De officiis* 1.25: "Recently Marcus Crassus said that no amount of money is enough for one who wishes to be head of state unless it produces enough income to maintain an army."

90 Among the techniques mentioned by Aristotle by which tyrants maintain their power are keeping subjects poor and humble-spirited and pretending to rule for the advantage of the citizens (*Politics* 5.9.4, 8, 11, 1313b, 1314a–b).   **91** The biblical and Homeric figure of kings as shepherds was widespread; in his speech at the opening of Parliament in 1529 More compared kings to shepherds. See also his Latin epigrams against tyranny (*CW* 3.2: 65, 168–69).

poverty, it would certainly be better for him to ab-
dicate his throne than to retain it by methods which
may keep the name of authority but have certainly
lost all of its majesty, for it does not befit the dignity
of a king to rule over beggars but rather over
wealthy and happy subjects; that was certainly what
was meant by that upright and lofty spirit Fabricius,
when he replied that he would rather rule over the
rich than be rich himself.⁹² Indeed, for one person
to wallow in pleasure and luxury while he is surrounded on all sides by grieving and groaning, that
is to be the guardian not of a kingdom but of a
prison; finally, just as a physician is totally incompetent if he cannot cure a disease except by means of
another disease, so too someone who does not know
how to improve the lives of citizens except by depriving them of the comforts of life is admitting
that he does not know how to rule over a free people; instead he should cure either his sloth or his
pride, for these are usually the vices that make his
people despise and hate him; he should live harmlessly on his own income, adapt his expenses to his
income; he should curb crime and, by educating his
people properly, prevent it rather than allow it to
increase and then punish it; he should not be hasty
to revive laws which are customarily ignored, especially those which are long disused because they
were never desirable; he should never take something as a fine which a private person would not be
allowed to accept because to do so would be criminal and deceitful. At this point, what if I told them

The marvelous law of the Macarians

that the Macarians,⁹³ who
are also not very far from
the Utopians, have a law re-
quiring their king to swear formally and solemnly
on the very first day of his reign that he will never
have in his treasury at one time more than a thousand pounds in gold or the equivalent amount of
silver?⁹⁴ They say that a king who was more concerned about the welfare of his land than about his
own wealth made this law to prevent the heaping

up of so much treasure as to impoverish his people;
for he saw that this amount would be enough either
for the king to fight against rebels or for the kingdom to repel a hostile invasion but would be too little to encourage him to invade other countries —
and that was the primary reason for making the law.
A secondary reason was that he thought it would
make enough money available for the ordinary
business transactions of the citizens; and since any
money which accrues over that limit has to be paid
back, he reckoned that a king would not seek out
methods of extortion. A king such as this would be
feared by malefactors and loved by his law-abiding
subjects. If I should obtrude such notions and others like them on persons who are violently opposed
to them, don't you suppose
they would turn deaf ears as   *A proverb*
I told my tale?"⁹⁵

"Deaf as a post, undoubtedly," I said. "And, by
heaven I am not surprised, and, to tell you the truth,
I don't think you should obtrude such speeches or
give advice which you are certain they will never accept. For how can it do any good or how can such
an odd discourse influence the thinking of those
whose minds are prejudiced and dead set against
such notions? In private conversation with good
friends this academic philosophy is not unpleasant.
But there is no room for it in the council chambers
of kings, where great matters are handled with great
authority."⁹⁶

"That is what I said," he replied. "Among princes
there is no room for philosophy."

"Yes indeed, there is," I said, "but not for this academic philosophy⁹⁷ which
considers anything appro-   *An academic philosophy*
priate anywhere. But there is another sort of philosophy better suited to public affairs. It knows its role
and adapts to it, keeping to its part in the play at
hand with harmony and decorum. This is the sort
you should use. Otherwise, during a performance of
a comedy by Plautus, when the slaves are joking

92 The saying derives from Manlius Curius Dentatus (Plutarch, *Moralia* 194f), but it was also attributed to Gaius Fabricius Luscinus by classical and medieval authors. 93 From the Greek *makarios* ("happy"). This Greek word introduces each of the beatitudes (Mt 5:3–11). 94 More may be thinking of Henry VII, who had an enormous sum in his treasury when he died. 95 See Erasmus, *Adages* 1387 (*CWE*

31: 376). 96 The following argument centers on the moral and rhetorical notion of decorum (Cicero, *De officiis* 1.27.93–39.141, *Orator* 21.69–22.74, and *De oratore* 3.55.109–12). It is also based on the conflict between rhetorical persuasion, which deals with probable truths, and philosophical logic, which produces demonstrable truths. 97 In the text and side note, this philosophy is designated

scholastica. The only academic philosophy in More's time was that of the universities, which we nowadays call scholasticism, so that in this case "academic" and "scholastic" are practically synonymous. The humanists generally attacked the hair-splitting excesses of scholastic philosophy and favored a more rhetorical approach to literature and life. See, for example, More's *Letter to Dorp* (*CW* 15: 29–39, 49–70).

around together, if you should come out onto the stage dressed like a philosopher and recite the passage from *Octavia* where Seneca argues with Nero,[98]

A marvelous comparison

wouldn't it have been better for you to have a non-speaking part[99] than to jumble together tragedy and

A mute role

comedy by reciting something inappropriate? By hauling in something quite diverse, you would spoil and distort the play then being presented, even if what you add were better in itself. Whatever play is being presented, play your part as best you can and do not disturb the whole performance just because a more elegant play by someone else comes to mind.

"That's how it is in the commonwealth; that's how it is in the councils of princes. If you cannot thoroughly eradicate corrupt opinions or cure long-standing evils to your own satisfaction, that is still no reason to abandon the commonwealth, deserting the ship in a storm because you cannot control the winds. You should not din into people's ears odd and peculiar language which you know will have no effect on those who believe otherwise, but rather by indirection you should strive and struggle as hard as you can to handle everything deftly, and if you cannot turn something to good at least make it as little bad as you can. For everything will not be done well until all men are good, and I do not expect to see that for quite a few years yet."

"In that way," he said, "I would be doing no more than trying to remedy the madness of others by succumbing to their madness myself. For if I want to tell the truth, then I have to say such things. I do not know whether it is proper for a philosopher to say what is false,[100] but it certainly isn't for me. Though that discourse of mine might perhaps have been irksome and repugnant to them, I do not see why it should seem odd to the point of absurdity. If I were to describe everything Plato imagines in his *Republic*

The institutions of the Utopians

or what the Utopians do in theirs, these things might be better (as they surely are), but they might still seem strange, because here we have private property and there all things are held in common.

"As for my speech (except that those who have decided to run headlong down a different path cannot be pleased by someone who calls them back and points out the dangers), but otherwise what was there in it that it is not fitting and even obligatory to say anywhere? Indeed if we are to avoid as odd or absurd everything that has been made to seem alien by the corrupt morals of mankind, we Christians will have to ignore almost all Christ's teachings, and he forbade us to ignore them, so much so that the teachings which he himself whispered in the ears of his disciples, he commanded them to preach openly from the rooftops.[101] And most of his teachings are far more alien to our common customs than that speech of mine was, except that preachers (following your advice, I imagine), whenever mankind refuses to make their behavior conform to the rule of Christ, adapt Christ's teaching to the behavior as if it were a ruler made of lead,[102] so as to make the two match in some way or other. I don't see what good that does except to allow people to be wicked with a better conscience.

"And that, indeed, is all the good I would do in the councils of princes. For my opinion would either be different, and that would amount to having no opinion at all, or it would be the same, and I would be the abettor, as Terence's Mitio says, of their madness.[103] For I do not see what you mean by that indirect approach of yours which you think enables you to manage things deftly even if you cannot make everything good, and at least make them as little bad as you can. For there is no room there to dissemble or to look the other way: you must approve of advice that is clearly quite bad and subscribe to measures that are utterly pestilential. Anyone who gave faint praise to wicked advice would be taken for a spy or perhaps a traitor. There will be no occasions on which you can do any good, since you have fallen among colleagues who will corrupt the best of men before they themselves will be reformed; either you will be depraved by their evil way of life or, if you remain honest and innocent, you will be made a screen for the wickedness and folly of others. That is how far you are from being able to improve anything by that indirect approach.

---

98 *Octavia* is a tragedy once attributed to Seneca in which Seneca discusses the abuse of power with Nero. Cf. Erasmus, "to be subservient to your role" (*Adages* 91, *CWE* 31: 131–32).　**99** John Clement plays such a part in *Utopia*.　**100** Plato allows rulers (even presumably philosopher-kings) to lie to their subjects for a useful purpose (*Republic* 3.21.414b–415d, 5.8.459c–d). Quintilian says that "everyone must allow, what even the sternest of the Stoics admit, that the good man will sometimes tell a lie" (*Institutes* 12.1.38).　**101** Mt 10:27; Lk 12:3　**102** The so-called Lesbian ruler was made of lead so as to accommodate itself to measuring curved surfaces; see Erasmus, *Adages* 493 (*CWE* 31: 465).　**103** *Adelphoe* 1.2.145–47

"That is why Plato, in a very elegant simile, explains why wise men are right to refrain from taking on governmental tasks: when they see people rushing out on the streets only to be soaked by never-ending rain and they cannot persuade them to get under a roof and out of the rain, they get under shelter themselves, knowing that they will accomplish nothing by going out except to get drenched together with the rest and considering it sufficient, when they cannot cure the folly of others, at least to remain in safety themselves.[104]

"But actually, my dear More (to tell you truly what I really think), it seems to me that wherever there is private property, where everything is measured in terms of money, it is hardly ever possible for the common good to be served with justice and prosperity, unless you think justice is served when all the best things go to the worst people or that happiness is possible when everything is shared among very few, who themselves are not entirely happy, while the rest are plunged into misery.

"Therefore, when I turn over in my mind the most prudent and holy institutions of the Utopians, who have very few laws and yet manage so well that virtue is rewarded and yet, since everything is equalized, everyone has plenty of everything, and then when I contrast their customs with those of other nations, always issuing ordinances but none of them all ever achieving order, where whatever a person can get he calls his own private property, where a mass of laws, enacted day after day, are never enough to ensure that anyone can protect what each calls his own private property or even adequately distinguish it from what belongs to someone else (as can easily be seen from the infinite lawsuits which are always being filed and are never finished), when I consider these things, I say, I have a higher opinion of Plato and I am not surprised that he would not deign to make any laws for people who would not accept laws requiring that all goods be shared equally by all. In his great wisdom he easily foresaw that the one and only path to the welfare of the public is the equal allocation of goods; and I doubt whether such equality can be maintained where every individual has his own property.[105] For

where everyone tries to get clear title to whatever he can scrape together, then however abundant things are, a few men divide up everything among themselves, leaving everyone else in poverty. And it usually happens that each sort deserves the lot of the other, since the one is rapacious, wicked, and worthless, and the other is made up of simple, modest men who by their daily labor contribute more to the common good than to themselves.

"Thus I am firmly persuaded that there is no way property can be equitably and justly distributed or the affairs of mortal men managed so as to make them happy unless private property is utterly abolished. But if it remains, there will also always remain a distressing and unavoidable burden of poverty and anxiety on the backs of the largest and best part of the human race. I grant their misery may be somewhat alleviated but I contend that it cannot be fully eliminated. I mean, if you decreed that no one could own more than a certain amount of land and that there be a legal limit to the money anyone can possess, if some laws were enacted that could keep the prince from being too powerful or the people too headstrong, that would keep offices from being solicited or put up for sale, or keep them from entailing many expenses (for otherwise they provide opportunities to rake in money by fraud and spoliation or it becomes necessary to put rich men in offices which ought to be held by wise men), such laws, I say, could mitigate and alleviate these ills, just as applying continual poultices can relieve the symptoms of sick bodies that are beyond healing. But as long as everyone has his own property, there is no hope whatever of curing them and putting society back into good condition. In fact, while you are trying to cure one part you aggravate the malady in other parts; curing one disease causes another to break out in its place, since you cannot give something to one person without taking it away from someone else."

"Quite the contrary," I said, "it seems to me that no one can live comfortably where everything is held in common. For how can there be any abundance of goods when everyone stops working because he is no longer motivated by making a profit, and grows lazy because he relies on the labors of

104 *Republic* 6.496d–e **105** According to Diogenes Laertius (3.23), "the Arcadians and Thebans, when they were founding Megalopolis, invited Plato to be their legislator; but ... when he discovered that they were opposed to equality of possessions, he refused to go." In the *Republic*, Plato prescribes community of property (and of wives and children) only for the guardians (5.464b–e), but in the *Laws* he says that in the best state it would be observed by the whole populace (5.739b–d).

others. And then, when people are driven by want and there is no law which enables them to keep their acquisitions for their own use, wouldn't everyone necessarily suffer from continual bloodshed and turmoil? Especially when the magistrates no longer have any respect or authority, for I cannot conceive how they could have any among people who are all placed on one level."[106]

"I am not surprised that you think so," he said, "since you have no conception of the matter, or only a false one. But if you had been with me in Utopia and had seen their customs and institutions in person as I did (for I lived there more than five years, and I would never have wanted to leave except to reveal that new world to others) you would quite agree that you had never seen a people well governed anywhere but there."

"But you would surely have a hard time persuading me," said Peter Giles, "that a better governed people can be found in that new world than in the one we know, since our intellects are no worse than theirs and our governments are older, I imagine, than theirs, so that long experience has brought to light many features which make our lives more comfortable, to say nothing of some things we have discovered by chance which no amount of ingenuity would have sufficed to invent."

"As for the antiquity of governments," said Raphael, "you could give a more accurate judgment if you had read through the histories of that world: if they are trustworthy, there were cities there before there were people here. As for what ingenuity has invented or chance revealed up till now, that could have happened in either place. But certainly I think that even though we may surpass them in intelligence, they still leave us far behind in diligence and zeal to learn.

"According to their chronicles before we landed there they had never heard anything about us Ultra-equatorials (for that is what they call us) except that some twelve hundred years ago a ship was driven to Utopia by a storm and shipwrecked there.

Some Romans and Egyptians were cast upon the shore and never left there again. Notice how their diligence turned this single occasion to their advantage. There was no useful skill in the whole Roman empire which they did not learn from the explanations of the strangers or did not manage to discover from the hints and clues they were given. Such was the enormous gain they made on this one occasion when some men from here were driven to their shores. But if a similar accident ever brought one of them from there to here, the incident has been completely forgotten, just as posterity perhaps will also forget that I was once there. One meeting alone was enough for them to appropriate all of our useful inventions, but I think it will be a long time before we will accept any institution of theirs which is better than ours. And I think that is the only reason why they manage their affairs more prudently and live more happily than we do, though we are not inferior to them in intelligence or resources."

"Therefore, my dear Raphael," I said, "I beg and implore you, describe the island to us. And do not try to be brief but explain in order their fields, rivers, cities, population, customs, institutions, laws, and, in short, whatever you think we would want to know. And you should think we want to know whatever we don't know yet."

"There is nothing I would rather do," he said, "for I have all this at my fingertips. But it will take some free time."

"Then let us go inside to eat lunch," I said. "Afterwards we will take as much time as we want."

"Agreed," he said. And so we went in to eat lunch. After lunch we came back to the same place and sat down on the same bench, and having instructed the servants that we were not to be interrupted, Peter Giles and I urged Raphael to keep his promise. When he saw that we were attentive and eager to hear, he sat there quiet and thoughtful for a little while, and then began as follows.

THE END OF THE FIRST BOOK

---

106 More summarizes Aristotle's arguments in the *Politics* (2.1.2.1260b–4.13.1267b) against Plato's advocacy of communism. Aristotle's arguments had been adopted by the medieval scholastics such as Thomas Aquinas in his commentary on Aristotle's *Politics* (2.1–7).

THE DISCOURSE OF
RAPHAEL HYTHLODAY
ON THE BEST FORM OF A COMMONWEALTH
AS REPORTED BY THOMAS MORE, CITIZEN
AND UNDERSHERIFF OF LONDON

Book 2

The island of the Utopians is two hundred miles across in the middle, where it is widest, and throughout most of the island it is not much narrower, but toward both ends it narrows a bit. These ends, curling around into a circle *Site and shape of the new island of Utopia* with a circumference of five hundred miles, make the whole island look like a new moon. The sea flows in between the horns through a strait about eleven miles wide and then spreads out into a huge empty space protected from the wind on all sides, like an enormous, smooth, unruffled lake; thus almost the whole inner coast serves as a harbor and allows ships to go from shore to shore in all directions, much to the advantage of the people. The jaws of the strait are dangerous, on one side because of shallows, on the other *A place safe by nature is defended by one garrison* because of rocks. In just about the middle of the channel, one rock stands out, visible and hence harmless; they have built and garrisoned a tower on it. The other rocks are hidden and treacherous. The channels are known only to the Utopians themselves, and hence it hardly ever happens that a foreigner enters the bay without a Utopian pilot. Indeed *The stratagem of shifting the signals* they themselves find it hard to enter it safely, except that they set their course by means of some signals on the shore. By moving these to different locations, they can easily lure an enemy fleet to shipwreck, no matter how large it is.

On the outside coast there are not a few ports. But everywhere the landing places are so well defended, either naturally or artificially, that a few troops can keep a huge army from coming ashore. According to report, however (and the appearance of the place bears it out), their land was once not surrounded by the ocean. But Utopus, who conquered the island and named it after himself (for before that time it had been called Abraxa)[1] and *The island Utopia named for General Utopus* who brought its crude and rustic mob to a level of culture and humanity beyond almost all other mortals, after he won the victory at his first assault, had a channel cut fifteen miles wide at the point where the land adjoined the continent, and thus caused the sea to flow all around the land.[2] And since he set not only the inhabitants to *A greater task than cutting through the Isthmus* this task but also employed his own soldiers (to keep the inhabitants from thinking the work was imposed on them as a humiliation), the labor was shared by a great multitude of workers and was finished in an incredibly short time, *Common effort lightens a burden* so that the neighboring peoples (who at first ridiculed the project as silly) were overwhelmed with wonder and fear.

The island has fifty-four cities,[3] all of them large and *The cities of Utopia* splendid and having exactly the same language, customs, institutions, and laws. They have the same layout and they look the same, insofar as the terrain allows. *Likeness breeds concord* Those which are closest to each other are separated by twenty-four miles. None is so isolated that it is more than a day's journey on foot from another city. *A moderate distance between cities* Every year each city sends three old and experienced citizens to Amaurot to discuss problems common to the whole island. For that city, which is located at the navel of the land, so to speak, and hence is most convenient as a meeting place for the delegates from everywhere, is the capital and chief city.

The land is so well distributed that no city has *Land distribution* less than twelve miles of ground on all sides, though

---

1 The numerical equivalents of the Greek letters in "Abraxas" (the usual form, rather than "Abraxa") add up to 365. The name was given to the highest of the 365 heavens invented by the heretic Basilides. 2 Several attempts to dig a canal across the Isthmus of Corinth failed so that the attempt became proverbial for failure (Erasmus, *Adages* 3326, *CWE* 36: 76–77). 3 According to Erasmus, in Utopia More "represented the English commonwealth in particular" (*CWE* 7: 23/281). In 1587, according to William Harrison's *Description of England* (1587), ed. Georges Edelen (Ithaca, NY: Cornell University Press, 1968, pp. 86–87), England had fifty-three counties, which, together with London, make it match the city-states of Utopia. The city-states are mostly independent but loosely federated, each having its own governor; they are united only by codes and customs, as well as a triennial meeting of a senate.

it may have much more in some directions, namely where the cities are furthest apart from one another.

But today such a desire is the plague of all commonwealths

None of them is driven by any desire to extend its boundaries. Indeed, whatever land they have, they consider themselves its tenant-farmers, not its landlords. In the countryside, throughout the fields, they have conveniently located houses, each provided with farming tools. They are inhabited by the citizens, who take turns going out to live there. No country household has fewer than forty men and women, besides the two slaves bound to the land; it is presided over by a master and mistress who are sober and mature. Every thirty households are ruled by one phylarch.[4] Every year twenty from each household return to the city, having fulfilled their two-year stint in the country. They are replaced by twenty substitutes from the city, who are to be trained by those who have already been there a year and hence are more skilled in farmwork; the substitutes themselves will train another group the following year, for if everyone were new and equally ignorant of farming, the crops would suffer from lack of skill. Although this system of exchanging farmers is customary, to keep anyone from being forced to live this hard life for a long time, nevertheless many who have a natural bent for agricultural pursuits apply for and are allowed additional years.

The care of agriculture is first

Farm duties

They farm the land, raise cattle, cut wood, and convey it to the cities by the most convenient route, whether by sea or by land. They raise a huge number of chickens, and they have a marvelous method of doing it. The hens do not sit on the eggs. For the Utopians themselves tend a great number of eggs, keeping them alive and hatching them in constant warmth.[5] As soon as the chicks emerge from the shell, they recognize and follow human beings around as if they were their mothers.

A wondrous method of hatching eggs

Use of horses

They raise very few horses and none but high-spirited ones, which serve no other purpose than the training of young people in horsemanship. For ploughing and hauling they use oxen; they grant that they are inferior to horses in short sprints, but they consider them superior over the long haul and less subject to diseases; moreover, they require less effort and expense to maintain, and when they have served out their term, they can be used for food.

Use of oxen

Grain they use only for bread.[6] For they drink either wine made from grapes or cider made from apples or pears or else plain water, which they often boil with honey or licorice, of which they have plenty. Although they know (and they know it very well) how much produce is needed by a city and its surrounding population, they plant far more grain and raise far more cattle than they need for their own use, giving the surplus to their neighbors. All the supplies that are necessary but not available in the country they get from the city, giving nothing in exchange; the city magistrates provide them the goods with no bargaining. For every month many of them gather there on the feast day. On the day of harvesting, the phylarchs of the farmers inform the city magistrates how many citizens should be sent out; since they arrive at precisely the right time, such a large crowd of workers gets the harvest almost completely done in one day if they have good weather.

Food and drink

The method of sowing

The advantage of communal labor

THEIR CITIES, ESPECIALLY AMAUROT

If you know one of their cities, you know them all, so similar are they in all respects (so far as the terrain allows). And so I will describe one of them (it doesn't much matter which one). But why choose any one except Amaurot? For it is the most notable and takes precedence over the others because the senate meets there; and no other is better known to me, since I lived there for five whole years.

The description of Amaurotum, capital city of Utopia

Amaurot, then, is situated on the gentle slope of a mountain; its shape is almost square. Beginning almost at the crest of the hill, it stretches two miles down to the river Anyder;[7] its width is slightly

---

4 from a Greek compound meaning "ruler of a tribe" **5** Pliny mentions artificial incubation (*Natural History* 10.76.154–55),

but it seems not to have been practiced in More's time. **6** That is, they do not use it to make beer or ale, as the English do.

7 From a Greek adjective meaning "without water." Amaurot resembles London in its tidal river (the Thames) and smaller stream

greater along the river than it is at the hilltop. The source of the Anyder is

A description of the river Anydrus

eighty miles above Amaurot, a small spring which is amplified by tributaries, two of them sizeable, until, when it reaches the city itself, it is five hundred yards wide. Then for sixty miles it flows on, getting wider and finally flowing into the ocean. In the space between the city and the coast, and also for some miles above the city, the tide flows and ebbs for six whole hours in a swift current. Seawater flows in to a point thirty miles upstream, filling the whole channel of the Any-

The same thing happens to the Thames in England

der and driving the river water upstream. It also makes the water salty somewhat higher up; from there the river gradually grows fresh and it is pure when it flows by the city. And at ebb tide it flows pure and fresh nearly all the way to the mouth of the river.

The city is connected to the opposite bank of the river by a bridge made not of pilings and planks but

In this feature London is also like Amaurot

of beautifully arched stonework; it is placed at a point furthest from the sea so that ships can sail unobstructed along that whole side of the city.[8] They also have another stream, not large but very gentle and pleasant, which gushes from a spring on the same mountain where the city is located; it flows down through the middle of the city into the Anyder. The Amaurotians have fortified the

Use of drinkable water

head and spring of this stream, which is located a little outside the city, surrounding it with walls that link it to the city, so that if an enemy ever attacks them, the water cannot be diverted or contaminated. From this stream the water is channeled in tile conduits to the various districts in the lower parts of the city. Where the terrain makes this impossible, rainwater collected in large cisterns serves the same purpose.

Fortifications of the city walls

The city is surrounded by a high, thick wall with many towers and bastions. On three sides the wall is surrounded by a moat that is dry but wide and deep and blocked by thorn hedges; on the fourth side the river itself serves as a moat. The streets are laid out to facilitate traffic and to offer protection from the wind. The buildings are by

The kinds of streets

no means ugly; the houses extend in a continuous row along the whole block, facing the row on the other

The buildings

side of the street; the housefronts along each block are separated by a street twenty feet wide. Behind the houses, a large garden, as long on each side as the block itself, is hemmed in on all sides by the backs of the rowhouses.

Gardens attached to the houses

There is no house which does not have a door opening on the street and a backdoor into the garden. The double doors, which open easily with a push of the hand and close again automatically, allow anyone to come in—so there is nothing private anywhere.[9] For every ten years

This is reminiscent of Plato

they exchange the houses themselves by drawing lots. The Utopians place great stock by these gardens; in them they grow vines, fruit trees, herbs, and flowers, all so bright and well tended that I have never seen anything more flourishing and elegant. In gardening they are motivated not only by their own pleasure but also by competition among the various blocks to see which has the best garden. And certainly you will not easily find any feature of the

Vergil also praised the usefulness of gardens

whole city that is of greater use to the citizens or gives them more pleasure.[10] For that reason the founder of the city seems to have devoted more attention to these gardens than he did to anything else.

For they say that in the very beginning Utopus himself laid out the whole plan of the city. But he left it to succeeding ages to complete the adornment and landscaping that could not be completed during one lifetime. Thus in their annals, which have been diligently and scrupulously kept up since the island was captured 1,760 years ago,[11] it is

(Fleet Ditch, except that London's stream was foul and unpleasant). **8** But Amaurot has the advantage of having its bridge above the city, not below it. **9** See *Republic* 3.22.416a. **10** See *Georgics* 4.116–48. **11** That is, 244 BC, when Aegis IV became

king of Sparta; he was killed because of the egalitarian reforms he wished to introduce. See Richard Schoeck, "More, Plutarch, and King Aegis: Spartan History and the Meaning of History," *Philological Quarterly* 35 (1956): 366–75; reprinted in

Essential Articles for the Study of Thomas More, ed. Richard Sylvester and Germain Marc'hadour (Hamden, CT.: Archon Books, 1977), pp. 275–80.

recorded that at first their dwellings were humble, mere huts and shacks, built of wood gathered at random, the walls plastered with mud. The roofs came to a point and were thatched with straw. But now all houses have a handsome appearance and are built three stories high. The outer sections of the walls are made of fieldstone, quarried rock, or brick, and the space between is filled up with gravel and cement. The roofs are flat and are coated with a sort of plaster which is not expensive but is formulated so as to be fireproof and more weather-resistant than lead.[12] They commonly use glass (which is very plentiful there) to keep out the wind; sometimes they also use thin linen, soaked in clear oil or treated with resin — a method which has two advantages: it lets in more light and keeps out more drafts.[13]

Glass or linen windows

THEIR MAGISTRATES

Every year each group of thirty families elects its magistrate, who in their ancient language was called a syphogrant but is known as a phylarch in the modern tongue. Ten syphogrants with their households are presided over by an official once called a tranibor, now known as a protophylarch.[14] Finally, all the syphogrants, who number two hundred,[15] having sworn to choose the person they consider the most capable, elect the ruler[16] by secret ballot, choosing him from the four candidates named by the people. For each of the four quarters of the city names one person and proposes him to the senate. The ruler remains in office for life, unless his tenure is interrupted because he is suspected of trying to become a tyrant. They elect the tranibors every year, but they do

In the Utopian language "tranibor" means "chief director"

A remarkable way of electing officials

Tyranny is hateful to the well-ordered commonwealth

not lightly change them. All the other magistrates hold office for one year.[17]

Every third day, and sometimes oftener if circumstances require it, the tranibors gather to advise the ruler. They make decisions about public affairs; if there are any disputes among private persons (and there are very few) they settle them in a timely fashion. They always invite two syphogrants into the senate, different ones on every occasion; and they have provided that no measures concerning public affairs be adopted unless they have been discussed in the senate three days before a decision is reached. To enter into schemes concerning affairs of state outside the senate or public assemblies is a capital crime. These measures were taken, they say, to make it hard for the ruler and the tranibors to conspire to change the form of government and set up a tyranny over the people. And for the same reason matters of great moment are presented at the assemblies of the syphogrants, who report the matter to the households, take counsel among themselves, and report their recommendations to the senate. Sometimes a matter will be referred to the council of the whole island.[18]

Disputes should be settled quickly, but nowadays they are deliberately and lengthily prolonged

Nothing should be decided hastily

Then, too, the senate has a rule that no point is discussed on the same day it is brought up, but rather it is put off till the next meeting; they do this so that someone who blurts out the first thing that occurs to him will not proceed to think up arguments to defend his position instead of looking for what is of use to the commonwealth, being willing to damage the public welfare

Would that the same thing were done in our councils

This is the meaning of the proverb "take counsel at night"

12 In More's time, lead was commonly used to roof important buildings. William Harrison, in his *Description of England* (1587), ed. Georges Edelen (Ithaca, NY: Cornell University Press, 1968), speaks of "fine alabaster burned, which they call plaster of Paris, whereof in some places we have great plenty and that very profitable against the rage of fire," but he is describing the plastering of interior walls, not roofs, which he says are covered with shingles, straw, sedge, reeds, or slate (p. 196). **13** Glass windows were uncommon in homes during More's time; oiled linen,

sheets of horn, or lattices of wicker or wood were used instead. Hythloday means that oiled linen is brighter and more impervious than linen alone, not that it is superior to glass. **14** "Syphogrant" seems to be derived from the Greek compound meaning "wise old man" (or perhaps "old man of the sty" = steward). "Tranibor" seems to come from a Greek compound meaning "plain eater." But other meanings have also been suggested. In fact, Hythloday continues to use the older terms "syphogrant" and "tranibor," not "phylarch" (ruler of a tribe) or "protophylarch"

(chief phylarch). **15** Thus there are six thousand families in Utopia, excluding the countryside. **16** The term used here and throughout Book 2 is *princeps*. For its significance, see the note to the opening paragraph of Book 1. **17** Utopia is presented as a federation of democratic republics: the households elect the syphogrants, who elect the tranibors and governor (whom they can also remove from office). The syphogrants also select the class of scholars, from which all high officials are chosen. **18** But for the whole island of Utopia there is no single executive branch

rather than his own reputation, ashamed, as it were, in a perverse and wrong-headed way, to admit that his first view was short-sighted.[19] From the start such a person should have taken care to speak with deliberation rather than haste.

OCCUPATIONS

Farming is the one occupation in which all of them are skilled, men and women alike. They are all trained in it from childhood on, partly by instruction in the classroom, partly by being taken out to play at it,[20] as it were, in the fields near the city, not merely looking on but doing the work themselves for bodily exercise.

Farming is an occupation common to everyone, though here it is fobbed off on a few despised workers

Besides farming (which, as I said, is common to all of them) everyone is taught some trade of his own. The ordinary ones are working with wool or linen or laboring as a stone mason, blacksmith, or carpenter. No other trade there employs any number worth mentioning. As for their clothing—which is uniform throughout the island for all age groups and varies only to indicate sex or marital status, and which is not unappealing to the eye, allows freedom of movement, and is adapted to either heat or cold—as for their clothing, I say, each household makes its own.

Trades should be learned to satisfy needs, not luxury

Uniform clothing

Everybody learns one or the other of these trades, including women as well as men. But women, as the weaker sex, engage in lighter crafts, mostly working with wool or linen. The other trades, which require more strength, are relegated to the men. Generally children take up their father's trade, for most are naturally inclined to it. But if anyone is drawn to another occupation, he is transferred by adoption into another household where he can work at the trade he wants to pursue. The move is supervised not only by his father but also by the

No citizen without a trade

Let everyone learn the trade for which he has a natural aptitude

magistrates, to make sure the master of his adoptive household is respectable and responsible. Actually, if someone has mastered one trade and wants to learn another besides, he gets permission to do so by the same procedure. When he has mastered both, he practices whichever he wants to, unless the city has a greater need for the other.[21]

The chief and practically the only function of the syphogrants is to take care and see to it that no one lounges around in idleness but rather that everyone practices his trade diligently, but not working from early morning till late at night, exhausted by constant labor like a beast of burden.[22] For such grievous labor is fit only for slaves, and yet almost everywhere it is the way workmen live, except in Utopia. Dividing the day and night into twenty-four equal hours, they devote only six to work, three before noon, when they go to lunch. After lunch they take two hours of rest in the afternoon, then three more given over to work, after which they have dinner. Counting the first hour after noon as ending at one o'clock, it is eight o'clock when they go to bed. Sleep takes up eight hours.

The idle are to be expelled from the commonwealth

The work of laborers should be kept within bounds

The intervals between work, meals, and sleep they are allowed to spend however they like, provided that the time they have free from work is not wasted in debauchery and idleness but spent well in some other pursuit, according to their preference. Many devote these intervals to intellectual activities. For every day they have regular lectures in the hours before dawn; attendance is required only from those who have been specially chosen to devote themselves to learning. But a great number of men, and also women, from all orders of society flock to hear these lectures, some one sort, some another, as each is naturally inclined. But if someone wishes to spend this same time practicing his trade (as do many whose temperaments are not suited to any abstract discipline), they are quite free to do so;

Scholarly pursuits

to carry out or enforce the deliberations or decisions of this council. **19** See Erasmus, *Adages* 1143 (*CWE* 33: 96). **20** Plato (*Republic* 7.797a–b) and Aristotle (*Politics* 7.15.5.1336a). Plato specifically advises that "to make a good farmer [a man] must play [in childhood] at tilling land" (*Republic* 1.643a–c). **21** Unlike the Utopians, Plato insists that each craftsman must have only one trade (*Republic* 2.11.370a–c, 2.13.474b–c; *Laws* 8.846d–e). **22** Statutes during the reign of Henry VII required laborers to work from daybreak to nightfall in spring and summer and from before 5 A.M. to between 7 and 8 P.M. in fall and winter.

indeed they are also praised for doing so, since their labor contributes to the common good.

After dinner they devote one hour to recreation, during the summer in the gardens, during the winter in the common rooms where they have their meals. There they either play music or entertain themselves with conversation. They do not so much as know about dice and other such pointless and pernicious games, but they do play two games not unlike chess. In one of them numbers fight against each other, one taking over the other; in the other game virtues are lined up in a battlefront against the vices. This game shows very cleverly both how the vices fight among themselves but join forces against the virtues, and also which vices are opposed to which virtues, what forces they bring to bear openly, what instruments they use to attack indirectly, what defenses the virtues use to fend off the forces of the vices, how they evade their assaults, and finally by what methods one side or the other wins the victory.

Play at supper

But nowadays playing at dice is the sport of princes

Even their games are useful

But at this point, it is necessary to examine the matter in more detail to avoid making a mistake. If only six hours are devoted to work, you might think that there would necessarily be some shortage of supplies. But that is so far from being true that six hours is not only enough to produce abundantly all the necessities and comforts of life but is even more than enough. This you, too, will understand if you consider what a large part of the population in other countries live their lives in idleness. First, almost all the women do,[23] and they make up almost half the population. Or in places where the women work, the men take their place and lie around snoring. Add to that the huge idle crowd of priests and religious, as they are called.[24] Throw in all the rich, especially the landlords of estates who are commonly called gentlemen and nobles. Include with them their retainers, that rank cesspool of worthless swashbucklers. Add, finally, the strong and sturdy beggars who feign some disease as a pretext for their idleness. You will certainly

Kinds of idle men

The bodyguard of the nobles

find that it takes far fewer than you thought to produce everything that mortals use.

A very prudent statement

Now consider how few of these workers are occupied in necessary trades, since, where money is the measure of everything, many completely futile and superfluous crafts must be practiced just to support over-indulgence and wanton luxury. Now if that same crowd who are presently working were divided up among the few trades needed to produce the few commodities that nature requires, the resulting abundance of goods would drive prices down so low that craftsmen could not make a living. But if all those who work away at pointless tasks and, together with them, that whole crowd of lazy, languid idlers (any single one of whom consumes twice as much as any of the workers who produce the goods), if they all were put to work — and useful work at that — you can easily see how little time would be enough and more than enough time to produce all the goods required for human needs and conveniences — and pleasures, too, as long as they are true and natural ones.

And this very point is confirmed by the experience of the Utopians. For there, in the whole city and the surrounding territory, out of all the men and women who are old enough and strong enough to work, barely five hundred are exempted from work.[25] Among them the syphogrants, who are legally relieved from work, nevertheless do not exempt themselves; they work so as to motivate others to work by giving a good example. The same immunity is enjoyed by those to whom the people give total leisure to pursue various branches of learning, but only after the priests have recommended them and the syphogrants have chosen them by a secret ballot. If any of them disappoints the hopes they had in him, he is put back to work; and on the other hand, it happens, not infrequently, that an artisan, devoting his free time to intellectual pursuits, works so diligently and makes such progress that he is exempted from working at his trade and promoted to the scholarly class. From this order of scholars are chosen ambassadors, priests, tranibors, and finally

Not even the magistrates stop working

Only scholars are designated for the magistrates

---

23 More surely knew how inaccurate Hythloday is here, since women in his time had duties at least as heavy as they have now.
24 that is, members of the religious orders
25 This number would be made up of the governor, the two hundred syphogrants,

the twenty tranibors, the thirteen priests, the scholars, and the ambassadors.

the ruler himself, who was called Barzanes in their ancient language, but is named Ademus in the modern tongue.[26] The remaining group, which is neither idle nor devoted to useless trades, is so large that it is easy to imagine how many goods they produce in so few hours.

Apart from what I have just said, they have it easier because in most of the necessary trades they do not need to expend as much labor as in other nations. First of all, building or repairing structures everywhere else requires the continuous effort of so many workers for the simple reason that what a father has built his worthless heir allows to fall gradually into disrepair. Thus what could have been maintained with a minimum of effort has to be totally rebuilt, at great expense, by the next heir. Moreover, it often happens that a house that cost someone enormous sums to build seems contemptible to someone of more fastidious taste; after a short time it falls into ruin through neglect and the owner builds another house somewhere else, at no less expense. But among the Utopians, from the time when everything was settled and the commonwealth was established, it very rarely happens that a new site is chosen on which to build houses; and they not only repair damage quickly when it happens but they take preventive measures against it. The result is that their buildings last a very long time and require very little work, and sometimes construction workers have so little to do that they are set to shaping timbers or squaring and fitting stones at home, so that if they ever need to build anything, it can be constructed more quickly.

How house building costs could be avoided

Now as for their clothing, notice how little labor it requires. First of all, at work they wear informal garments made of leather or skins which last for seven years. When they go out in public they put on cloaks which cover these rough clothes; throughout the island they are all of the same color, that of the natural wool. Thus they not only get along with much less woolen cloth than anywhere else, but it also costs much less. But linen is easier to work and hence they use more of it; they are concerned only about the whiteness of linen

How to avoid cost in clothing

and the neatness of wool, for they place no value on fineness of weave. The result is that in other places four or five woolen cloaks and the same number of silk shirts are not enough for one person, and if he is a bit fastidious, not even ten will do, but there everybody is content with one, which generally lasts for two years. Naturally there is no reason why he should want any more, for if he got them he would have no more protection against the cold, and his clothing would not look the least bit more fashionable.

Therefore, since everyone is employed in a useful trade and the trades themselves require less labor, the result is a great abundance of everything, so that sometimes they bring out an enormous number of people to repair the public roads, if any have deteriorated. It happens very often, when there is no occasion even for that kind of work, that they publicly decree a shorter workday. For the magistrates do not compel anyone to engage in superfluous labor against his will, since the structure of the commonwealth is primarily designed to relieve all the citizens from as much bodily labor as possible, so that they can devote their time to the freedom and cultivation of the mind. For that, they think, constitutes a happy life.

SOCIAL RELATIONS

Now is the time, I think, to explain how they treat each other, how they interact with one another, and what system they have for distributing goods.

And so, while the city is made up of households, the households themselves consist mostly of blood relatives. Girls, when they grow up and marry, move into the dwellings of their husbands. But sons and, after them, grandsons remain in the household and are subject to the oldest parent, unless his mind is failing because of old age; in that case he is replaced by the next oldest. But to keep the city from being either over- or underpopulated, they see to it that no household (and each city, apart from its territory, has six thousand of them) has fewer than ten or more than sixteen adults. For it is not possible to set a limit for children.[27] This limit is easily maintained by transferring persons from households with too

Number of citizens

---

26 "Barzanes" derives from the Hebrew for "son of" and the Greek Doric form for "of Zeus." A Chaldean named "Mithrobarzanes" appears in Lucian's *Menippus,* which More translated. "Ademus" derives from the Greek for "without a people." **27** An average of twelve adults in each household would produce a population of seventy-two thousand in each city. Adding children and slaves would probably bring it to more than one hundred thousand (of whom only five hundred are exempt from work).

many people to those with too few. But if it should happen that the whole city grows too large, they use the excess to supply underpopulated cities. But if it should happen that throughout the island the whole mass of the population should swell inordinately, they sign up citizens from each city and send them as colonists to live under their own laws on the nearest part of the continent, wherever the natives have a lot of land left over and uncultivated; they adopt any natives who choose to live with them. Assenting willingly to the same style of life and the same customs, the natives are easily assimilated, and that to the advantage of both groups. For by means of their institutions the Utopians make the land easily support both peoples, whereas before it provided a meager and skimpy living for only one. The natives who refuse to live under their laws are driven out of the territory the Utopians have marked off for their use; if they resist, the Utopians make war against them. For they think it is quite just to wage war against someone who has land which he himself does not use, leaving it fallow and unproductive, but denying its possession and use to someone else who has a right, by the law of nature, to be maintained by it.[28] If any of their cities is ever accidentally so reduced in population that they cannot replenish it from other parts of the island and still keep the full quota in those cities (which they say has only happened twice in their whole history because of a virulent plague), then they resupply it with citizens immigrating from a colony. For they would rather allow the colonies to disappear than let any of the cities on the island shrink in size.

But, to return to the citizens' way of life, the oldest man, as I said, presides over a household. Wives

Thus they avoid having a crowd of idle servants

serve their husbands and children their parents, and generally the younger serve the older. Each city is divided into four equal districts. In the middle of each district is a marketplace for all sorts of commodities. The products of each household are taken to designated houses there and each kind of goods is separately stored in a warehouse. From them each head of household goes to get whatever he and his household need, and he takes away whatever he wants, paying no money and giving absolutely nothing in exchange for it. For

why should he be denied anything, since there is plenty of everything and no one need fear that anyone would want to ask for more than he needs? For why should anyone be suspected of asking for too much if he is certain he will never lack for anything? Certainly fear of want makes all kinds of animals greedy and rapacious, but only mankind is made so by pride, which makes

The cause of rapaciousness

them consider their own glory enhanced if they excel others in displaying superfluous possessions; in the Utopian scheme of things there is no place at all for such a vice.

Adjoining the marketplaces I mentioned are food markets, to which vegetables, fruit, and bread are brought, and also fish and edible birds and beasts are conveyed from designated places outside the city where there is a stream to wash away refuse and offal. From here they bring

Gore and filth carry the plague into cities

the cattle which have been slaughtered and cleaned by the hands of bondsmen. For they do not allow their own citizens to become accustomed to butchering animals; they think that to do so gradually eliminates compassion, the finest feeling of human na-

From slaughtering cattle we learned even to kill humans

ture. They do not allow anything filthy or foul to be brought into the city, for air tainted by such rottenness might engender disease.

Furthermore, each block has spacious halls located at equal intervals, each known by its own name. The syphogrants look after them, and to each of them are assigned thirty families (namely fifteen on either side) who eat their meals there.[29] Stewards from each hall gather in the market at a designated hour and get food according to the number of mouths they have to feed.

But their first priority is the sick, who are cared for

Care for the sick

in public hospitals. They have four of them on the outskirts of the city, a little outside the walls; they are as capacious as four little towns so that no matter how many people are sick they do not need to be crowded uncomfortably together, and so that those who have contagious diseases that can be transferred from one person to another can be kept

---

28 Hythloday's and the Utopians' rather facile justification of colonialism offers many difficulties. For example, if no one is using or occupying the land, why does anyone have to be driven from it by force? Is farming the only satisfactory use of land?

29 That is, each of the four sides of a block has thirty houses, with a hall in the middle of each side.

at a distance from the main body of the patients. These hospitals are so equipped and provided with everything that promotes health, the care provided in them is so gentle and solicitous, the doctors who are in constant attendance are so skilled that, although no one is sent there against his will, there is still almost no one in the whole city who would not rather be lodged there than at home when he is in failing health.

After the stewards of the hospitals have received the food prescribed by the physicians, the best of what is left is divided equitably among the halls, according to the number fed by each one, except that they pay special attention to the ruler, the high priest, and the tranibors, and also to ambassadors and all foreigners (if there are any, for they are few and far between); but when there are any, designated residences are furnished and prepared for them. At the times fixed for lunch and dinner, the whole syphograncy, alerted by the blast of a bronze trumpet, convenes in these halls, except for those who are bedridden in the hospitals or at home. Nevertheless, no one is forbidden to take home food from the marketplace once the halls have been supplied with their quotas, for they know that no one would lightly choose to do so; though no one is prohibited from eating at home, still no one does it willingly, for it is not considered proper and it would be foolish to go to the trouble of preparing an inferior meal at home when a splendid and sumptuous one is ready and waiting in a hall nearby.

Common and mixed dining

They always take freedom into account lest anyone act under compulsion

In this hall slaves perform all the chores which are somewhat heavy or dirty. But the women are solely[30] responsible for preparing and cooking the food and making arrangements for the whole meal, each household taking its turn. They sit at three tables or more, according to the number of diners. The men sit with their backs to the wall, the women on the outside, so that if they should suddenly feel ill, as happens, sometimes, when they are pregnant, they can get up and go out to the nurses without disturbing the seating arrangement.

Women serve at feasts

The nurses are seated separately with the nursing infants in a little room assigned to them; it never lacks a fire and clean water and also cradles so that when they want they can either lay them down or take off their swaddling clothes and let them refresh themselves by playing freely. Every mother nurses her own child unless death or disease prevents it. When that happens, the wives of the syphogrants immediately find a nurse, and that is not hard to do. For those who can are more than willing because everyone praises their compassion and the infant who is brought up this way takes the nurse as its natural mother.

Praise and a sense of duty are the best way to encourage citizens to act properly

Children who are under five sit in the nurses' den. Other minors, among whom they include members of both sexes who are not yet old enough to marry, either serve the diners, or, if they are too young and not strong enough for that, stand by— and that in absolute silence. Both groups eat what is handed to them by those seated at table, nor is any other time set aside for them to eat.

The education of the young

The syphogrant and his wife sit at the head table, which is the place of honor and overlooks the whole assembly, since it is placed crosswise in the highest part of the chamber. Next to them sit two of the oldest persons, for they sit in groups of four at all the tables. But if a church is located in that syphograncy, the priest and his wife sit with the syphogrant so as to preside. On both sides of them sit younger people, and then older people again, and so on throughout the whole hall. And so people sit with their coevals, and yet they are mixed in with a different age group. They say that this arrangement was adopted so that the dignity of the elders and the respect due them would keep the young people from indulging in improper language or behavior, since nothing can be done or said at table which would escape the notice of the persons sitting nearby on all sides.

Priests above the prince, though nowadays even bishops are the lackies of princes

Younger mixed with the elder

The dishes of food are not served to the highest places and then downward to the others, but rather the choicest pieces are served first to the old people

Respect for the elders

---

30 that is, without the help of servants

(whose places are marked) and then equitable shares are served to the rest. But some of the delicacies which are not in sufficient supply to be distributed to the whole hall are given by the old people, as they see fit, to those sitting near them. Thus respect for the elders is maintained and yet everyone has the same advantage from it.

Nowadays even monks rarely observe this custom

Lunch and dinner always begin with some reading that concerns morals, but it is brief lest it be tedious. Taking off from this, the elders begin the discussion, but not in a gloomy and sour fashion. And they do not take up the whole meal

Talk at meals

with long disquisitions. No, they would much rather listen to the young people, and they even deliberately challenge them so as to learn about the temperament and intelligence of each of them as revealed in the free give and take of tabletalk.

Nowadays physicians condemn this practice

Lunches are quite brief, dinners more ample because the one is followed by work and the other by rest and sleep during the night, which they think contribute more to good digestion. They never dine

Music at meals

without music and after dinner they never lack for tasty desserts. They light incense and sprinkle perfumes and spare no effort to cheer up the diners. For they tend to incline to

Harmless pleasure should not be spurned

the position that no kind of pleasure ought to be forbidden as long as no harm comes of it.

This is the way they live in the city. But in the country, since they live far apart, they all eat in their own homes. No household has any shortage of food, since, after all, everything eaten by the city-dwellers comes from the farmers.

HOW THE UTOPIANS TRAVEL

If someone wants to visit friends who live in another city or is simply taken with a desire to see the place, he easily gets the permission of his syphogrant and tranibor unless a necessary job keeps him from going. He is sent out as part of a group, with a letter from the ruler which grants them permission and sets the day they must be back. They are provided with a carriage and a public slave to drive the oxen and take care of them. But unless there are women in the group, they leave the carriage behind as more of a hindrance than a help. Throughout the whole journey they carry nothing with them; yet they lack for nothing and are at home everywhere. If they stay anywhere longer than one day, each of them works at his trade and is treated very kindly by his fellow craftsmen.

If someone takes it upon himself to wander outside his territory, when he is caught without the ruler's passport, he is treated with contempt, brought back as a runaway, and severely punished. If he dares to repeat the offense, he is punished with slavery. But if someone is taken with a longing to wander through the fields belonging to his own city, he is not prohibited from doing so, as long as he gets his father's permission and his wife's consent. But wherever he goes in the countryside, he is not given any food until he has done the work allotted to the morning or however much work is usually done there before dinner.[31] Under this regulation he is allowed to go anywhere within the boundaries of his city's territory, for he will be no less useful to the city than if he were in it.

So you see that nowhere is there any chance to be idle; there is no excuse for laziness, no wine taverns, no alehouses, no brothels, no occasion to be corrupted,

O holy commonwealth, worthy to be imitated even by Christians

no hideouts, no hangouts. With the eyes of everyone upon them, they have no choice but to do their customary work or to enjoy pastimes which are not dishonorable. Such behavior on the part of the people is bound to produce an abundance of everything. And when it is distributed

Equality ensures that there is enough for everyone

equitably to everyone, it follows that no one can be reduced to poverty or forced to beg.

In the senate at Amaurot (to which, as I said before, three representatives come every year from each city), once they have determined what surpluses are at hand in each place and what places have shortages, they immediately make up the deficiencies of the one with the excess supplies of the other, and they provide them as a free gift, receiving nothing in return from those to whom they gave them. But if they gave something to a city and

31 Cf. 2 Thes 3:10.

received nothing in return, they also get what they need from some other city and pay nothing for it. Thus the whole island is like one household.

A commonwealth is nothing else than a kind of big family

When they have enough provisions for themselves (which they do not think they do unless they have provided for two years, since the next year's outcome is uncertain), they export to other countries vast quantities of grain, honey, wool, linen, timber, red and purple dye, fleece, wax, tallow, leather, and also livestock. They give one-seventh of all this to the poor in that country and sell the rest at a moderate price. In exchange they not only acquire goods they do not have at home (they lack almost nothing except iron) but also they bring back to their homeland enormous quantities of silver and gold. They have continued this practice for such a long time that they now have everywhere a greater supply of those metals than you would think possible. Hence they do not much care whether they are paid in cash or credit, and they accept promissory notes for most of what is owed them, but never from private persons; instead they make the usual legal documents binding on the city government. When the loan comes due, the city requires it to be paid by the private debtors and puts it in the public treasury; then the city enjoys the use of it until the Utopians call it in. For the most part they never do, since they think it is hardly right to claim what is of no use to them from those who have a use for it. But if circumstances require that they lend part of it to another nation they call it in, or when they are obliged to go to war; that is the only reason they keep all of the treasure which they have at home, as protection against extreme danger or sudden emergencies. They use it especially to pay enormous wages to foreign mercenaries, whom they would much rather expose to danger than their own citizens. They are also aware that with large sums of money even the enemies themselves can be bought and set against one another, either through treason or open hostilities.

Utopian business activity

See how they never forget their sense of community

With this method money would be considered worthless

It is enough to avoid war through payment or craft rather than shedding a lot of human blood

This is the reason they reserve such an incalculable treasure, although they do not keep it as treasure but in a form I am really ashamed to tell you. I am afraid you will not believe what I say, and all the more rightly so since I am aware that if I had not seen it in person I would have been reluctant to believe it if someone else told it to me. For in general the more foreign something is to the habits of the listeners, the harder it must be for them to believe it. But actually, a prudent judge of the matter will perhaps be less surprised that they handle silver and gold in their own way rather than ours, since all their arrangements are so different from ours. In fact, since they themselves have no use for money but rather keep it as protection against events which might or might not happen, in the meantime they keep gold and silver (from which money is made) in a form that lets no one place more value on it than it deserves by its nature. And obviously it deserves far less than iron, without which mortals could no more live, by heaven, than they could without fire or water, whereas nature gave to gold and silver no use which we could not easily do without; the folly of mankind gives them value because they are rare, but nature, on the other hand, like a kind and gracious mother, made the most useful elements openly available, like air, water, and earth, but she hid away what is vain and unprofitable in the most remote recesses.

What a clever fellow!

Gold is inferior to iron, when it comes to usefulness

Now if in their society these metals were put away in some tower, the ruler and the senate might be suspected of deceiving the people by some trick and getting some good from it for themselves—such is the foolish anxiety of the mob. And then if they made platters out of them or other vessels made by goldsmiths, if ever the occasion arose to melt them down and use them to pay mercenaries, they realize that once people had begun to delight in them they would be reluctant to give them up. To obviate these difficulties they have thought up a method quite compatible with the rest of their arrangements but very far removed from ours (for we value gold very highly and hide it away quite carefully), a method which is therefore hard to believe unless you have experienced it. Whereas they eat and drink from vessels of earthenware and glass, beautifully crafted but inexpensive, they use gold and silver, not only in the common halls but also in

What a magnificent contempt for gold! private houses, to make all the chamberpots and lowliest containers. Moreover,

the chains and heavy shackles used to restrain the slaves are made of the same metals. Finally, the most notorious criminals wear gold rings in their ears,

Gold the accoutrement for infamy gold rings on their fingers, a gold collar around their necks, and even a gold band

around their heads. By these means they see to it that the same metals which other nations give up with almost as much grief as if their guts were being pulled out have so little value that if circumstances required the Utopians to part with all such metals none of them would think they had lost as much as a single farthing.

Furthermore, they gather pearls on the seashore and even diamonds and rubies on some cliffs; they do not look for them, however, but when they have found some by chance, they polish them. They use them to deck out their infants, who are boastful and

Gems the delight of children proud of such gems in their earliest childhood; but, as they get a little older and

notice that such trinkets are worn only by children, they become ashamed of them of their own accord and, with no urging from their parents, they give them up just as our children discard their baubles, necklaces, and dolls when they grow up.

These arrangements, so different from those of other peoples, have produced quite different feelings and attitudes. That never became clearer to me

A very fine story than in the incident of the Anemolian ambassadors.[32]

They came to Amaurot while I was there and since they had come to discuss important matters, the three citizens chosen by every city had come before they arrived. All the ambassadors from neighboring countries, who had landed there before and were familiar with the customs of the Utopians, knew that they did not revere sumptuous clothing, considered silk contemptible, and even associated gold with disgrace; and so they used to come clothed as modestly as possible. But the Anemolians lived further away and had less contact with them. Hence, when they saw that all the Utopians wore one and the same rough garment, they thought they did so

because they had nothing better to wear and, with more pride than wisdom, they decided to set themselves up as gods by the elegance of their trappings and to dazzle the eyes of the poor Utopians by the splendor of their garb.

And so when the three ambassadors made their entry, their retinue of a hundred retainers was dressed in particolored garments, mostly made of silk, but the ambassadors themselves, who were noblemen in their own country, were garbed in cloth of gold, with large chains and earrings of gold, and also golden rings on their fingers, and on top of that strings of pearls and gems hanging from their hats, and in sum, decked out in everything that the Utopians use to punish slaves, to mark off someone in disgrace, or to make toys for children. And so it was a sight to see how they ruffled their feathers when they compared their finery with the clothing of the Utopians (for the people had poured out onto the streets). On the other hand, it was no less delightful to observe how totally mistaken their hopes and expectations were and how far they were from the consideration they thought they would receive. For in the eyes of all the Utopians, except for the very few who had had some good reason to travel to foreign countries, all their splendid trappings seemed shameful. They greeted all the retainers of the lowest rank reverently as if they were lords. But they considered the ambassadors to be slaves because they wore golden chains, and so they passed over them with no respect whatever. In fact, you could have also seen children there who had thrown away their gems and pearls. When they saw such gems affixed to the hats of the ambassadors, they nudged their mothers and said: "Look, mother, that big lout is still wearing little pearls and gems, as if he were a little boy!" But the mother would reply in all seriousness: "Hush, my son, I think he is one of the am- *O what a craftsman!* bassadors' fools." Others criticized those golden chains as useless because they were so fine that a slave could easily break them and so loosely fastened that a slave could shake them off whenever he wanted and run off anywhere he wanted, footloose and fancy-free.

But after the ambassadors had lived there for a day or two and seen such an enormous amount of gold treated as if it were worthless and contemned

---

32 "Anemolian" is from the Greek word for "windy."

there as much as it was honored in their countries, and when they also noticed that the chains and shackles of only one runaway slave contained more gold and silver than the trappings of all three of them, they were crestfallen and sheepishly put away all the finery which they had so haughtily displayed, especially after they had talked more informally with the Utopians and learned their customs and opinions.

Indeed they are amazed that any mortal can take delight in the dubious sparkle of a tiny gem or precious stone when he can look at a star or even at the sun, or how anyone could be so insane as to imagine that he is nobler because of fine-spun woolen thread, since that wool (however fine-spun) was once worn by a sheep, which was at the same time nothing more than a sheep.[33] They are likewise amazed that gold, which in itself is useless, is now prized so highly everywhere that mankind itself, which gave it value and for whose use it got that value, is valued much less than the gold itself, so much so that some beef-witted blockhead, who has morals to match his folly, nevertheless has many wise and good men in his service, for no better reason than that he has a heap of gold coins. And if some turn of Fortune or trick of the law (which turns things topsy-turvy no less than Fortune herself) should transfer this heap from the heir to the lowest lout in the whole household, the master would shortly enter the service of his servant as if he were a mere adjunct and appendage of the coins. But what they find most amazing and despicable is the insanity of those who all but worship the rich, to whom they owe nothing and who can do them no harm; they do so for no other reason except that they are rich, knowing full well that they are so

He calls it dubious because the gems are fake, or at least because their glitter is scanty and dim

How true and well put!

How much wiser are the Utopians than the general run of Christians!

mean and tightfisted that they will certainly never give them one red cent during their whole lives.

These opinions and others like them they have formed partly from their upbringing, since they were brought up in a commonwealth whose institutions are farthest removed from those kinds of folly, and partly from instruction and books. For though not many in each city are dispensed from physical labor and assigned to do nothing but study (namely those in whom they have perceived from their childhood remarkable talent, extraordinary intelligence, and devotion to learning), nevertheless all children are introduced to good books, and throughout their lives a good many people, both men and women, devote to learning the hours I have mentioned as free from labor.

Study and instruction of the Utopians

They learn the various branches of knowledge in their own language, which has no lack of vocabulary, is not unpleasant to the ear, and is not surpassed by any other in the expression of thought. It has spread throughout most of that part of the world, though everywhere else it is corrupted in various ways.

Of all the philosophers[34] whose names are so famous in this known part of the world, they had not so much as heard of any before our arrival, and yet in music, dialectic, arithmetic, and geometry,[35] they have made almost the same discoveries as our own ancient writers did. But though they measure up to our ancient writers in almost all respects, they are not up to the discoveries of modern dialecticians. In fact, they have not discovered a single one of those rules about restrictions, amplifications, and suppositions which have been so subtly excogitated in the *Parva logicalia* and which are taught to young men everywhere in our world.[36] And then, as for second intentions,[37] they

Music, dialectic, arithmetic

There seems to be some underlying satire in this passage

33 Cf. Lucian, *Demonax* 41; see also *CW* 13: 8. **34** More uses "philosophy" in the older, broader sense of the investigation of all the arts and sciences, including mathematics and the natural sciences (which was often called "natural philosophy"). **35** They have mastered the quadrivium, the second tier of university studies (music, arithmetic, geometry, and astronomy); of the first tier, the trivium

(grammar, logic or dialectic, and rhetoric), dialectic is mentioned here. Grammar and rhetoric they would learn in their literary studies. **36** Peter of Spain's thirteenth-century *Little Logicbook,* with its fine-spun categories and distinctions, was dissected and mocked by More in his *Letter to Dorp,* which he wrote in 1515, near the time he wrote the second book of *Utopia.* On complicated "rules about

restrictions, amplifications, and suppositions," see More's text and Daniel Kinney's introduction to *Letter to Dorp* in *CW* 15: liv–lvii, 29–39. **37** "First intention" refers to the intellect's direct perception of an object; a "second intention" is the intellect's perception of or reflection on a first intention. It has no objective existence outside the mind.

are so far from being able to understand them that none of the Utopians could see man in general,[38] as they say, even when we pointed him out with our finger, though, as you know, he is plainly colossal and bigger than any giant. But they are very expert

Study of stars

in the orbits of stars and the movement of heavenly bodies. In fact, they have devised instruments of various designs which enable them to understand very accurately the movements and positions of the sun and moon and also the other stars which are visible in their hemisphere. But as for the conjunctions and

But nowadays these practitioners rule the roost among Christians

oppositions of the planets and the whole fraud of divination by the stars, they have never so much as dreamed of it.[39] By means of signs that they have perceived from long observation they predict rainstorms, winds, and other changes in the weather. But concerning the causes of those phenomena, and concerning tides and the saltiness of the ocean, and

Natural science the most uncertain study of all

in general concerning the origin and nature of the heavens and the world, they agree on some points with our own ancient philosophers, and on others, just as the ancients disagreed with one another, they also differ from all the ancients and propose new theories, and yet they do not entirely agree among themselves.

Ethics

In that area of philosophy which deals with ethics, they discuss the same issues as we do. They inquire about the goods of the mind and body and external goods, and whether the des-

Order of goods

ignation "good" applies to all of these or only to the gifts of the mind.[40] They discuss virtue and pleasure, but the primary and principal controversy is about what they think human happiness consists in, whether one thing or

many. On this point they seem over-inclined to the position which claims that all or the most important part of human happiness consists of pleasure.[41] And what is even more surprising, they claim support for this self-indulgent view even from religion, which is sober and strict and, indeed, almost gloomy and stern. For they never analyze happiness unless they combine some religious principles with the rational analysis of philosophy, since they think that without such principles reason by itself is too weak and deficient to investigate true happiness.

Ends of goods

The Utopians measure happiness by honorable pleasure

First principles of philosophy should be derived from religion

These principles are of this sort: that the soul is immortal, and by the beneficence of God is born for happiness; that our virtues and good deeds will be rewarded after this life, and our crimes have punishments prepared for them.[42] Though these are religious principles, the Utopians still think that reason leads them to believe and grant them; if they are eliminated, the Utopians have no hesitation in affirming that no one could be so stupid as not to feel that he ought to pursue his own pleasure by hook or crook. He would only be concerned not to sacrifice a greater pleasure for a lesser one and not to pursue one that would be requited by pain. For they think it would be truly insane to pursue virtue, which is harsh and difficult, and not only to banish the pleasures of life but even to seek out pain of your own accord, and to expect to get nothing out of it (for how can you get anything out of it if you get nothing after death, since you have spent your whole life

The theology of the Utopians

The immortality of the soul about which not a few Christians nowadays have doubts

38 That is, the universal concept of man that applies to each man in particular. From the fourteenth century through More's time, scholastic philosophers from the camps of the Realists and the Nominalists quarreled elaborately about whether and how universals had any real existence. **39** More wrote a number of Latin epigrams ridiculing judicial astrology (*CW* 3.2: 101, 118, 169, 182). **40** These three categories of goods (external goods and goods of the mind and of the body) derive primarily from the Aristotelian tradition. Generally the Aristotelians applied "good" to all three categories; the Stoics, only to the goods of the mind. **41** That is, they are inclined to the Epicurean position that pleasure is the highest good. Beginning with Lorenzo Valla's *The True and False Good* (1444–49) and with the help of such thinkers as Ficino, Pico, and Erasmus, Epicurean philosophy had been rehabilitated and shown to consist not in mere hedonism but rather in the calm pleasures of the mind. But the Utopians differ sharply from the Epicureans, who did not believe in immortality and thought the gods were unconcerned about mankind. **42** The fifth Lateran Council (1513) affirmed as dogma the immortality of the soul. The philosopher most closely associated with the dispute concerning the immortality of the soul was Pietro Pomponazzi, whose treatise *On the Immortality of the Soul* (1516) argued that the doctrine could not be proved by reason but has to be derived from revealed religion.

here without pleasure, that is, wretchedly?). But as it is, they think happiness consists not in every sort of pleasure but in pleasure that is good and honorable, for they believe that our nature is drawn to pleasure as the highest good by virtue itself, whereas the opposite faction attributes happiness to virtue alone.[43]

Just as not just any pleasure should be sought after, so too pain should not be pursued except for the sake of virtue

This is a teaching of the Stoics

And then they define virtue as living according to nature; to that end, they say, we were created by God. We follow the guidance of nature when we obey reason in choosing and avoiding things. Furthermore, reason above all inspires mortals to love and revere the majesty of God, to whom we owe our very existence and our capacity to be happy. Secondly, reason admonishes and encourages us to lead lives with as little anxiety and as much joy as possible and, beyond that, to exert ourselves in helping all others achieve the same end because of our natural fellowship. For not even the gloomiest and sternest advocate of virtue, who despises pleasure so much that he would impose toil, vigils, and mortifications on you, would refrain from enjoining you to do as much as you can to alleviate the poverty and distress of others, and he would think it praiseworthy and humane for one human being to rescue and comfort another, since the very essence of humanity (and no virtue is more proper to human beings) is to relieve the distress of others, eliminate sadness from their lives, and restore them to a joyful life, that is, to pleasure. Why should nature not impel us to do the same for ourselves? For either a joyful life, that is, a life of pleasure, is wrong and in that case we should not only not help anyone to achieve it but rather we should do all we can to make everyone avoid it as harmful and deadly, or if you are not only allowed but even required

But nowadays some seek out pain, as if religion consisted in it, whereas pain is only to be borne if it occurs by natural necessity or to someone performing the duties of piety

to obtain it for others, why not do so first of all for yourself? You should be no less well-disposed to yourself than to others. For when nature prompts you to be good to others, she does not require you to turn around and be cruel and merciless to yourself. Nature herself, they say, prescribes as the aim of all our actions a joyful life, that is, pleasure, and they define virtue as following the prescriptions of nature.[44] But when nature invites mortals to help each other to lead cheerful lives (and she is certainly right to do so, since no one is so far above the rank of human beings that nature should care for him alone, whereas in fact she is equally concerned about all those whom she groups together as belonging to the same species), she also, of course, forbids you time after time to seek your own advantages in ways that create disadvantages for others.

Therefore they think that not only private agreements must be kept but also public laws which have either been promulgated by a good ruler or which a people not oppressed by a tyrant or deceived by some trick have laid down by common consent to govern the distribution of vital commodities, that is, the means to pleasure. As long as these laws are not broken, to look out for your own good is prudent; to promote the public good is pious. But to deprive someone else of pleasure to promote your own is wrong; on the other hand, to deprive yourself of something to give it to someone else is a work of humanity and kindness and it always brings you more good than it takes away. For it is counterbalanced by gifts given in return, and also your consciousness of having done a good deed and the thought of the love and good will of those you have benefited will give you mental pleasure that outweighs any loss of bodily comfort. Finally, as religion makes clear to true believers, God will repay the loss of brief and paltry pleasures with enormous and never-ending joy. Following this line of reasoning and having considered

Agreements and laws

Duties toward one another in life

---

43 This is in keeping with the teachings of Epicurus; see Diogenes Laertius 10.130–32. The opposite faction is the Stoics.
44 Seneca, whose Stoicism is often severe and uncompromising, agrees with the Utopians: "Our motto … is 'Live according to Nature'; but it is quite contrary to nature to torture the body, to hate unlabored elegance, to be dirty on purpose, to eat food that is not only plain, but disgusting and forbidding" (*Epistulae morales* 5.4). Unlike some Stoics, Seneca is not entirely unsympathetic with Epicurus: "the teachings of Epicurus are upright and holy and, if you consider them closely, austere; for his famous doctrine of pleasure is reduced to small and narrow proportions, and the rule that we Stoics lay down for virtue, his same rule he lays down for pleasure — he bids that it obey Nature" (*De vita beata* 13.1). The Utopians combine elements of Stoicism and Epicureanism, and add to the blend belief in divine providence, the immortality of the soul, and rewards and punishments in the afterlife — doctrine not specifically Christian but not uniformly held until the advent of Christianity.

the matter long and hard, they think that all our actions, including also our virtuous deeds, are directed toward pleasure as our happiness and final end.[45]

The definition of pleasure They define pleasure as any motion or state of the mind or body which produces delight in accord with the guidance of nature. Not without reason do they add that the impulse must be in accord with nature. For just as not only our senses but also our reason pursues whatever is pleasurable by nature, that is, pleasures not achieved through wrongdoing, or acquired with the loss of a greater pleasure, or followed by hardship, so too they hold that all those *False pleasures* unnatural pleasures which mortals agree to call delightful by the emptiest of fictions (as if it were in their power to change the thing by changing the name) are so far from contributing to happiness that they actually hinder it because, once they have taken over the mind, they occupy it totally and leave no room for true and genuine pleasures. For a great many things are not pleasurable by their very nature and are, in fact, for the most part bitter, but through the perverse enticement of evil desires they are not only thought to be the greatest pleasures but are even included among the primary reasons for living.

Among those who pursue false pleasures they include those whom I mentioned before who think *The error of those who please themselves by their dress* that the finer the gown they wear the better they are. On this one point they are wrong twice over. They are no less deceived in thinking the gown is better than in imagining they themselves are. For if you consider the usefulness of a garment, why is wool woven with fine thread better than wool woven with coarser thread? But they think they excel in fact, not merely in their illusions. They ruffle their feathers; they believe that they are more valuable because of their clothes. And on that basis, honors they would not have dared hope for in cheaper clothes they demand as rightly due to their elegant gown, and they are outraged if someone passes them by without due deference.

And then isn't it equally stupid to be much taken with empty and worthless honors? For what natural pleasure is there in someone's baring his head to you *Foolish honors* or bending his knee? Will that relieve the pain in your own knee or cure the delirium in your head? It is amazing how some are caught up in this imaginary, specious pleasure: delightfully insane, they flatter themselves and take pride in their imagined nobility simply because they happen to be descended from a long series *Empty nobility* of ancestors who are considered to be rich, above all rich landlords (for nowadays there is no other source of nobility except wealth), and yet they think they are not a whit the less noble even if their ancestors have left them no wealth or they themselves have squandered it.

With these they group the persons I mentioned before who are enthralled by gems and precious stones and almost think *The most foolish pleasure is from gems* they have been deified if they ever get a fine specimen, especially if it is the sort most highly valued in their own times; for not all sorts are highly regarded by all persons and at all times. But they do not buy such a stone unless it is removed from its gold setting and exposed, and even then not unless the seller *The opinion of human beings increases or decreases the value of gems* swears and guarantees that it is a genuine jewel and a true gemstone; so afraid are they that their eyes may be deceived by a counterfeit substituted for a real stone. For why should your eyes be any less delighted by a counterfeit since they cannot distinguish it from a real one? To you each of them should have equal value, no less so, by heaven, than they would to a blind man.

What about people who keep superfluous wealth under lock and key, taking delight not in using the amassed treasure but merely in contemplating it? Do they feel any real delight or rather are they not deluded by a false pleasure? How about those who are subject to a different vice and hide away their gold, intending not only never to use it but perhaps never even to see it any more; in their anxiety not to lose it, they lose it. For surely it is lost if it is buried in the ground so as to be of no use to you and perhaps not to any other mortal. But still, when the

---

45 An Epicurean (not a Stoic) teaching; see Diogenes Laertius 10.138.

treasure is hidden away, you feel carefree and happy.

A remarkable hypothesis, and a very apt one

If a thief took it away and you died ten years later without knowing of the theft, in all those years that you lived after the money was stolen, what difference did it make to you whether it was removed or remained safe? In either case its usefulness to you was the same.

To these categories of absurd enjoyment they add gambling (a sort of madness they know of only through hearsay, not experience) and also hunting and falconry. For what pleasure can there be, they

Dicing

say, in throwing dice on a gaming table? Even if there were any pleasure in it, you have done it so often that mere repetition should have made you sick of it. How can it be delightful to hear the barking and howling of dogs?—isn't that a disgusting noise? Why do hunters feel more pleasure when a dog

Hunting

chases a hare than when a dog chases a dog?[46] For in either case the action is the same, that is, running, if that is what pleases you. Or if you are attracted by the hope of carnage and the expectation of seeing the slaughter with your own eyes, you ought instead to be moved to compassion when you see a little hare torn to pieces by a dog, a weak creature tormented by a stronger one, a timid creature fleeing from a ferocious beast, a harmless creature from a cruel hound. And so the Utopians have assigned the whole business of hunting to the butchers, whose trade (as I said before) is conducted entirely by

But nowadays this is the craft practiced by godlike courtiers

slaves, considering it beneath the dignity of free men. They consider it the lowest function of the trade. The other activities of butchers are more useful and honorable, since they contribute much more and destroy animals only out of necessity, whereas the hunter seeks nothing but pleasure from the slaughter and butchering of some poor little creature. Even in beasts themselves,[47] according to the Utopians, such an eagerness to view carnage springs from a cruel disposition, or else the continual indulgence in such brutal pleasure finally degenerates into cruelty.

Though the herd of mortals consider such pursuits as these and others like them (for there is no

end to them) to be pleasures, the Utopians firmly hold that they have nothing to do with pleasure, since there is no natural sweetness in them. Though they ordinarily produce sensual joy (which seems to be the function of pleasure), the Utopians are unwilling to change their minds. The reason they seem pleasant is not the nature of the things themselves but the perverse habits of their devotees, whose vicious attitudes cause them to embrace what is bitter as sweet, just as the defective tastebuds of pregnant women make them think

Pica in pregnant women

that pitch and tallow are sweeter than honey. And yet no one's judgment, if it is vitiated by disease or habit, can change the nature of pleasure, or of anything else for that matter.

True pleasures they divide into various classes, assigning some to the mind, others to the body. To the

Types of true pleasures

mind they attribute understanding and the sweetness which springs from the contemplation of the truth. To these they add the pleasure of looking back on a lifetime of good deeds and the sure hope of happiness to come.

They divide bodily pleasure into two kinds: one

Bodily pleasures

is the sweetness which pervades the senses, either when the supplies our natural heat has used up are replenished (as they are by food and drink) or else when the excessive elements overburdening our bodies are discharged. This happens when we purge our intestines of excrement, or go about generating children or when the itching in some part of the body is alleviated by rubbing or scratching. But sometimes pleasure results not from the replenishment sought by our bodily members nor from relieving them of excess but from some secret but remarkable power which tickles, excites, and attracts our senses to itself, such as the pleasure arising from music.

They claim that there is another kind of bodily pleasure which consists in the balanced and quiet condition of the body, that is, when a person's health is not disturbed by any disease. Such health, as long as it is not interrupted by any pain, is delightful in itself, even though it is not affected by any external pleasure. Though it is less obvious and affects the senses less grossly than the insistent desire for food

---

46 See More's Latin epigram against the cruelty of hunters; *CW* 3.2: 37.

47 More is probably thinking of hunting dogs.

and drink, nevertheless many Utopians hold it to be the greatest pleasure of all. Almost all of them believe that it is a great pleasure and the foundation and basis, as it were, of all the others, since it is the only one which keeps our lives peaceful and desirable; and, if you take it away, there is no room left for any pleasure at all. For the mere absence of pain without health they regard as insensibility, certainly not as pleasure.

It is fitting that the possessor be in good health

They have long since rejected the position of those who think that stable and undisturbed health should not be considered to be a pleasure because, they say, its presence can be felt only through some external stimulus (for they, too, have debated this question intensely). But now they are in almost complete agreement with the opposite position, that health is actually essential to pleasure. For according to them, disease brings pain, which is unalterably opposed to pleasure, in the same way as disease is opposed to health. Why not conclude, in turn, that there is pleasure in undisturbed health? On this point they do not think it makes any difference whether the disease is a pain or the pain comes from the disease; in either case the effect is the same. Thus, if health itself is a pleasure or if it necessarily brings pleasure with it as fire brings heat, the result in either case is that, wherever health is, stable pleasure cannot be lacking.

Moreover, when we eat, they say, what happens is that health, which has begun to fail, now has food as its ally in the battle against hunger. As it gradually becomes stronger, the very progress toward its ordinary vigor brings with it the pleasure of being reinvigorated. And so if health finds joy in the struggle, will it not rejoice when the victory is won? But when it has at last happily recovered its former strength, which was the sole object of the whole struggle, will it immediately become insensible and fail to recognize and embrace its own good? The idea that health is not perceived they consider to be very far from the truth. For when we are awake, who does not perceive that he is healthy—except someone who is not? Who can be so constricted by dullness and lethargy that he does not admit that health is delightful and enjoyable? And what is enjoyment but another name for pleasure?

Above all they embrace the pleasures of the mind, which they consider the first and foremost of all pleasures. They think that mental pleasure springs primarily from the practice of the virtues and the consciousness of a good life. Of the pleasures supplied by the body they give the first place to health. As for the pleasure of eating and drink and whatever else falls under a similar category of delight, they think they should be sought, but only for the sake of health, for such activities are not enjoyable in themselves but only insofar as they counter the unnoticed encroachments of ill health. And therefore a wise man, they say, should ward off disease rather than seek medicine for it and avoid pain rather than seek relief from it; just so it would be better not to have any need for such pleasure than to be relieved by it.

If anyone thinks that this kind of pleasure makes him happy, he must also confess that his life would be the happiest of all if it could be spent in perpetual hunger, thirst, and itching, followed by eating, drinking, scratching, and rubbing—and who can fail to see that such a life would be not only foul but also miserable? Certainly these are the lowliest of all pleasures, since they are the least unadulterated and never occur except in conjunction with the pain contrary to them. Thus the pleasure of eating is coupled with hunger, and not in equal proportions, for the pain is both longer and more intense. For it begins before the pleasure and never departs until the pleasure also ceases. Therefore they do not place much stock in such pleasures, except insofar as necessity demands them. But they also rejoice in them and gratefully acknowledge the kindness of Mother Nature, who uses the sweetest pleasures to entice her offspring to do what they must always be doing out of necessity. How irksome our lives would be if the daily ailments of hunger and thirst had to be warded off by drugs and bitter medications like the other diseases which afflict us less often?

They gladly cherish beauty, strength, agility as special and enjoyable gifts of nature. Certainly the pleasures which are mediated by our ears, eyes, and noses and which nature assigned as proper and peculiar to the human race (for no other kind of creature admires the design and beauty of the world, or is moved by the beauty of fragrances except to distinguish kinds of food, or recognizes the harmonious or discordant intervals in sounds), these pleasures, I say, they cultivate as adding a certain enjoyable spice to their lives. In all of them, however, they impose the limitation that a lesser should not impede a greater pleasure or that a pleasure should not cause pain at some later time — and they think this will necessarily happen if the pleasure is dishonorable.

They think it is certainly quite mad for someone to despise a beautiful figure, to deplete his strength, to turn agility into torpor, to wear out his body with fasting, to ruin his health, and to scorn the other favors bestowed by nature, unless he neglects his own good so as to work more avidly for the good of others or the public welfare, and in return for his effort he expects greater pleasure from God. Otherwise to inflict pain on oneself without doing anyone any good — simply to gain the empty shadow of virtue or to be able to bear with less distress adversities that may never come — this they consider to be insane and the mark of a mind that is both cruel to itself and ungrateful to nature, rejecting her benefits and not deigning to be beholden to her.

This is their view of virtue and pleasure; and in the absence of religious inspiration from heaven revealing something holier, *This point should be noted with special care* they think human reason can discover no truer doctrine.[48] I do not have time now to examine whether or not their teaching is correct, nor is it necessary, since I undertook to present their principles, not to defend them. But whatever validity their precepts may have, I am fully persuaded that nowhere will *Happiness of the Utopians and a description of them* you find a more extraordinary people or a happier commonwealth.

Physically they are agile and vigorous, stronger than you would expect from their height, though they are not undersized. Though their soil is not uniformly fertile and their weather is not particularly favorable, they protect themselves from the climate by moderation in their diet and they work hard to remedy the defects of the soil, so that nowhere in the world will you find a more abundant supply of crops and cattle or bodies more vigorous and subject to fewer diseases. You can see them there diligently employing the usual agricultural methods of improving infertile soil by skill and effort, but you could also see a forest that they uprooted with their own hands and planted in another place. The reason for doing this was not greater production but transportation: they wanted the timber closer to the sea or rivers or the cities themselves, since it takes less labor to move crops by land over long distances than it does to transport timber.

They are an easy-going people, cheerful and clever. They enjoy their leisure but they endure physical labor well enough as long as it is useful (but otherwise they are hardly fond of it); in intellectual pursuits they are indefatigable. When we told them about the literature and learning of the Greeks (for in Latin there is nothing except the *Usefulness of the Greek language* poets and historians that would be likely to interest them very much) it was amazing how eagerly they pressed us to help them master Greek by giving them instruction. And so *The extraordinary teachableness of the Utopians* we began to read, at first more out of a desire not to seem lazy than from any hope that much good would come of it. But when we had made a little progress, their diligence immediately made us anticipate that ours would not be wasted. They began to imitate the shape of the letters so easily, to pronounce the words so readily, to memorize so quickly, and to recite so accurately that we would have thought it miraculous except that the majority of them had undertaken this study not only on their own initiative but also at the explicit command of the senate, and hence they were selected from the most talented and mature scholars. And so in less than three years there was nothing in that language which they *But nowadays blockheads and dolts are chosen to be educated; the most talented minds are corrupted by pleasures* had not mastered; they read good authors with no hesitation, unless they encountered some textual crux. I tend to think they mastered Greek all the more easily because it is somewhat related to their own language. I suspect that the Utopian people originally sprang from the Greeks because their language, which is otherwise closest to Persian, preserves some vestiges of Greek in the names of cities and magistrates.

On the fourth voyage, instead of trade goods I took on board a fair-sized packet of books because I was fully determined to return only after a

---

48 In *The Confutation of Tyndale's Answer* (1532–33), More argued on religious grounds that "besides the taming of the body, fasting and our pain taken therein pleaseth God done with devotion, and serveth us for obtaining many and great gifts of grace" (*CW* 8.1: 72/20).

long time, if ever. From me they got most of Plato's works, more of Aristotle's, and also Theophrastus's[49] *On Plants,* which was mutilated in several places, I'm sorry to say. During the voyage the book had not been put away properly and a playful monkey came upon it; he mischievously ripped out some pages here and there and tore them up. Of the grammarians they have only Lascaris, for I did not take Theodore with me nor any dictionary except Hesychius and Dioscorides.[50] They are very fond of Plutarch's books and they are also much taken with the wit and elegance of Lucian.[51] Of the poets they have Aristophanes, Homer, and Euripides, and also Sophocles in the small typeface of Aldus.[52] Of the historians they have Thucydides and Herodotus, as well as Herodian.[53]

Furthermore, as for medical books, my companion Tricius Apinatus[54] had brought with him some shorter works of Hippocrates and the *Microtechne* of Galen;[55] for these books they have a high regard. Even though there is hardly a country in the world that has less need of medicine, still it is nowhere more honored, precisely because they consider a knowledge of it as one of the finest and most useful branches of science. When they investigate the secrets of nature using the resources of science, they not only experience wonderful pleasure from doing so but they also think they win the highest approbation from the creator and maker of the world. For they suppose that he, like other workmen, set up the marvelous mechanism of this world for mankind to view and contemplate (and men are the only creatures he made capable of doing so) and that therefore he is fonder of a careful observer and meticulous admirer than he is of some lazy blockhead who ignores such a marvelous spectacle as if he were a mindless brute.

Medicine the most useful craft

The contemplation of nature

And so the natural talent of the Utopians, trained by study, is marvelously effective in inventing techniques which make some contribution to a comfortable life. Two of these they owe to us, printing and papermaking, but even these they owe not only to us but in large part to themselves. For when we had shown them some books printed by Aldus on paper and had spoken a bit about the material for making paper and the technique of printing letters, though we did not really explain it (since none of us was expert in either process), they immediately and most ingeniously figured it out. And whereas before they had written only on vellum, bark, and papyrus, they immediately tried to make paper and to print with type. Though at first they did not get it quite right, by frequent attempts they soon mastered both techniques, and they became so proficient that if they had copies of Greek texts, there could have been no lack of printed editions. But as it is, they have no more than what I have mentioned, but what they have they have disseminated in many thousands of printed copies.

Any sightseers who visit them are especially welcome if they are recommended by unusual intellectual gifts or knowledge of many lands gained by traveling widely (and for that reason they welcomed us warmly when we landed), for they are eager to learn what is happening everywhere in the world. But not very many come there to trade. For what can they bring except iron or gold and silver, which they would prefer to take home than to export? As for their own exports, they think it more advantageous to deliver them themselves than to have others pick them up, for in that way they learn more about foreign countries everywhere and they keep their seamanship and nautical skills from getting rusty.

49 The pupil and successor of Aristotle **50** Constantine Lascaris (d. 1501) and Theodore of Gaza (d. 1475) wrote grammars of Greek. The dictionary of Hesychius (fl. *ca.* AD 400) was first published in 1514; Dioscorides (fl. *ca.* AD 50) wrote a handbook of medical and botanical terms. **51** Plutarch (*ca.* AD 50–120) was a favorite Greek writer among Renaissance humanists, both for his *Moralia* and for his *Parallel Lives* of eminent Greeks and Romans. Several pieces by the satirist Lucian (b. *ca.* AD 120)

were translated by More and Erasmus and first published in 1506; they were reprinted ten times in the sixteenth century. **52** In the early sixteenth century the Venetian printer Aldus Manutius was famous for his compact, elegantly printed editions of classical authors in both Latin and Greek. In 1508 he printed the first enlarged edition of Erasmus's huge and elaborate collection of proverbs, *Adagia,* which brought Erasmus almost instant fame. **53** Thucydides and Herodotus are the leading historians of ancient Greece. Herodian (*ca.*

AD 170–240) wrote a Greek history of the Roman emperors who reigned from AD 180 to 238. **54** A name in keeping with that of Hythloday himself: *tricae apinaeque* became proverbial, meaning "stuff and nonsense" (Erasmus, *Adages* 143, CWE 31: 184). **55** Hippocrates (5th century BC) and Galen (2nd century AD) were the leading Greek writers on medicine. *Microtechne* was a medieval summary of Galen.

SLAVES

The remarkable fairness of this people

Prisoners of war they do not consider to be slaves except those captured in wars they themselves have fought. The children of slaves and the slaves of foreign countries whom they have obtained are not kept in slavery.[56] Their slaves are those who have committed a serious crime in Utopia or foreigners who have been condemned to death for committing some crime (and these are by far the larger number), for the Utopians acquire many of them, sometimes cheaply, more often gratis, and take them away. These kinds of slaves they not only keep constantly at work but also in chains. Utopian slaves, however, they treat more harshly since they consider them baser and deserving of more severe punishment because they had an extraordinary education and the best of moral training, yet still could not be restrained from wrongdoing. Another class of slaves is made up of poor, overworked drudges from other nations who choose of their own accord to be slaves among the Utopians. These they treat decently and, except that they make them work a bit harder (since they are used to it), they are treated not much less kindly than the citizens. If they wish to depart (and that does not happen very often), they are not kept against their will nor are they sent away empty-handed.

The sick

They care for the sick, as I said, with great concern, omitting nothing whatever in the way of medicine or diet that might restore them to health. They sit with those who are suffering from an incurable disease, talk with them, console them, and do what they can to alleviate their pain. But if someone suffers from a disease which is not only incurable but also constantly and excruciatingly painful, then the priests and the magistrates point out that he can no longer live a useful life, that he is a heavy burden to himself and to others, and that he has outlived his own death;

Voluntary death

they encourage him to make a decision not to maintain the sickness and disease any longer and urge him not to hesitate to die, but rather to rely on hope for a better life; since he lives in a prison where he is cruelly tormented on the rack, he should escape from this miserable life on his own or willingly allow others to rescue him from it. This would be a wise act, they say, since death would deprive him of no advantages but would save him from suffering; and since in doing so he would be following the advice of the priests, the interpreters of God's will, it would also be a pious and holy deed.[57]

Those who agree with these arguments voluntarily starve themselves to death or are put to sleep and dispatched with no sensation of dying. But they do not do away with anyone who is unwilling, and they do not in any way diminish their attendance on him. Those who are persuaded and die in this way are treated with honor; but otherwise anyone who commits suicide for reasons not approved by the priests and senate is deemed unworthy of either burial or cremation and is ignominiously thrown into a swamp without a proper funeral.

Marriages

A woman does not marry until she is eighteen, a man not until he is four years older than that.[58] If a man and a woman are convicted of engaging in secret intercourse before marriage, they are both severely reprimanded and they are forbidden ever to marry anyone unless the ruler remits the sentence. But both the master and the mistress of the household where the offense was committed fall into utter disgrace for not doing their duty with sufficient diligence. They punish this offense so severely because they foresee that few would join together in married love, living their whole lives with one person and enduring besides the troubles that come with marriage, if they were not carefully restrained from promiscuous intercourse.

Moreover, in choosing spouses they have a custom which seemed to us absolutely absurd and thoroughly ridiculous, but they observe it strictly and seriously. The bride, whether virgin or widow, is

56 The non-hereditary character of Utopian slavery distinguishes it from both ancient slavery and feudal serfdom. In More's time it was generally agreed that Christians should not be enslaved, but the same was not true of Africans and American Indians. **57** Such euthanasia, naturally, is contrary to Catholic teaching; at Morton's court Hythloday himself had said that God has forbidden us to kill ourselves, but he also told More and Giles earlier that he did not intend to discuss whether or not Utopian moral principles are correct. More has a long psychological analysis of suicide in *A Dialogue of Comfort* (*CW* 12: 129–56). **58** According to canon law in More's time, girls could not marry before the age of twelve and boys not before fourteen. Plato (*Republic* 5.9.460e, *Laws* 4.721a–b) and Aristotle (*Politics* 7.14.6.1335a) set the age of marriage for women at at least twenty and for men over thirty.

presented naked to the groom by a sober and re-

This practice is somewhat immodest, but it is far from imprudent

spected matron, and the groom in turn is shown naked to the bride by some
honorable man.[59] When we
laughed at this custom and criticized it as ridiculous, they in turn were amazed at the extraordinary
folly of all other nations: when they are buying a
colt—a matter of no great expense—they are so
cautious that even if the animal is almost completely exposed they refuse to buy it unless the saddle and saddlecloth are removed so as to reveal any
sores that might be hidden beneath them; yet in
choosing a spouse—a matter which will make them
either happy or miserable for the rest of their lives—
they are so careless that they judge her whole person
by a mere handsbreadth, that is, by her face only,
since the rest of her is wrapped up in her clothes,
and according to that judgment they join themselves to her, not without great danger of not getting along with her if they later find something offensive. For not everyone is so wise as to pay
attention only to character, and even in the marriages of the wise the gifts of the body add something to the virtues of the mind. Certainly some
ugly deformity concealed beneath clothing can
completely alienate a man's mind from his wife
when his body can no longer be separated from her.
If such a deformity should occur after the wedding,
then everyone must put up with his lot; but before
the wedding the laws should see to it that no one is
duped or deceived.

All the more care needs to be taken because, of all
the countries in that part of the world, they are the
only one that is monogamous, and their marriages

Divorce

are almost never dissolved
except by death, though
adultery or unbearably offensive conduct can be
grounds for divorce.[60] The offended party gets permission from the senate to remarry; the offender is
disgraced and can never remarry. Otherwise, it is
absolutely forbidden to put away a wife against her
will and without any blame on her part because of
some bodily disfigurement. They consider it cruel to
desert someone at the very time she is in most need
of comfort and they think it would make her

uncertain and insecure about her old age, which
brings diseases with it and is itself a disease.[61]

But sometimes it happens that two people are
temperamentally incompatible, and if they have
each found someone else with whom they hope
they can live more agreeably, they separate by mutual consent and remarry, but not, however, without the permission of the senate, which does not
permit divorce unless the senators and their wives
have examined the case very carefully. Even then
they do not do it readily because they know that the
expectation of easily remarrying is hardly a means
of strengthening the love of married couples.

Adulterers are punished with the harshest servitude, and if both were married the injured parties
may divorce their spouses and marry each other if
they wish to; otherwise they may marry whomever
they like. But if one of the injured parties continues
to love such an undeserving spouse, the marriage
can remain intact, as long as the innocent party is
willing to accompany the criminal condemned to
hard labor; and it happens sometimes that the affectionate concern of the one and the repentance
of the other move the ruler to mercy so that he sets
them free again. But if the crime is repeated, it is
punished with death.

Their laws do not prescribe punishments for
other crimes, but rather the
senate determines penalties

Magistrates determine the amount of punishment

according to how heinous
or venial each particular offense seems to be. Husbands chastise their wives and parents their children, unless an offense is so serious that open punishment is advisable in order to maintain public
morality. But generally the most serious crimes are
punished with servitude, which they consider no
less grievous to the criminal and much more advantageous to the commonwealth than to execute
wrongdoers and immediately get rid of them altogether. They do more good by their labor than by
their death, and they offer a long-standing example
to deter others from similar crimes. If slaves are rebellious and unruly, then they are finally slaughtered like wild beasts that cannot be restrained by
bars or chains. But if they are patient, they are not
left entirely without hope. If they are tamed by long

---

59 Plato requires similar premarital
inspections in *Laws* 6.771e–772a, 11.925a.
60 In More's time the Church permitted

separation in the case of adultery but did
not allow remarriage. In his commentaries
on 1 Cor 7:10–11 and 39, Erasmus favored

relaxing the prohibition of remarriage.
61 See Erasmus, *Adages* 1537 (*CWE* 33:
309–10).

suffering and show that they regret the sin more than the punishment, their servitude may be either mitigated or revoked, sometimes by the ruler's prerogative, sometimes by popular vote.

The penalty for seduction   Attempted seduction is no less dangerous than seduction itself. In fact, in all sorts of crimes, they equate the clear and deliberate attempt with the completed deed, for they do not think that the mere incompletion of the deed should benefit someone who did everything he could to complete it.

They are very fond of fools: they consider it quite shameful to treat them with *Pleasure from fools* contempt, and they have nothing against finding enjoyment in their foolery,[62] since they think that will do the most good for the fools themselves. If anyone is so strict and gloomy that he never laughs at any word or deed, they do not entrust fools to him, out of fear that he would not treat them kindly enough, since to him they would be not only useless but not even entertaining—and that is the only talent they have.

To mock someone for being disfigured or crippled is considered shameful and disfiguring, not to the person mocked but to the mocker, since it is stupid for him to blame someone for a defect which it is not in his power to avoid.

They consider it lazy and negligent not to keep up natural beauty by grooming, but they consider *Counterfeit beauty* seeking help from cosmetics a disgraceful affectation. They know from experience itself that no physical beauty recommends wives to their husbands as much as respect and an upright character. Some men may be snared by beauty alone, but none can be held except by virtue and compliance.

They not only deter from crime by punishments, but they also foster virtue by rewarding it with honors. And so in the market-*Inspiring citizens to duty even by rewards* place they set up statues of outstanding men who have done extraordinary service to the commonwealth, thus preserving the memory of their good deeds so that posterity may have the glory of their ancestors as a spur and incentive to virtuous deeds.

Anyone who campaigns for public office becomes *Campaigning forbidden* disqualified for holding any office at all. The Utopians live together amiably, since no magistrate is arrogant or terrifying; they *Magistrate's honor* are called fathers and they live up to the name. Honor is willingly paid to them (as is proper); it is not exacted from those unwilling to give it. The ruler is not *The dignity of the ruler* singled out by his clothes or a crown but rather by the sheaf of grain he carries:[63] the sign of the high priest is a wax candle borne before him.

They have very few laws, for very few suffice for per-*Few laws* sons trained as they are. Indeed, one of their primary charges against other nations is that endless volumes of laws and interpretations are not sufficient. But they consider it quite unjust to bind people by laws which are so numerous no one can read through all of them or so obscure that no one can understand them. Moreover, they ban absolutely all lawyers as clever practitioners and sly interpreters *The useless horde of lawyers* of the law.[64] For they think it is practical that everyone should handle his own case and present the facts to the judge as he would to a lawyer; in this way there will be less confusion and the truth will be easier to determine, since he tells his story without having learned any evasion from a lawyer, while the judge weighs all the details carefully and protects simple souls from the false accusations of crafty litigants. In other countries, such straightforwardness is difficult to obtain because there is a mass of incredibly intricate laws. But among them everyone is knowledgeable about the laws. For, as I said, there are very few laws, and as for interpretations, they consider the most obvious the most correct. For though all laws (they say) are promulgated to inform everyone of his duty, a subtle interpretation will inform very few (for few can

---

62 The Latin for "fool" here is *morio,* wordplay on More's name; Erasmus had exploited the same pun in the prefatory letter of his *Encomium Moriae (The Praise of Folly),* which is dedicated to More. Thomas More kept a fool, Henry Patenson, in his household; Patenson appears in Holbein's sketch of More's family and is mentioned by More in his *Confutation of Tyndale's Answer (CW* 8.2: 900–901). **63** More says he dreamed of himself as a Utopian *princeps,* carrying just this symbol of authority; see More's Letter to Erasmus of December 4, 1516 (p. 279).   **64** An error in the 1516 edition is corrected differently in the editions of 1517 and 1518, in both cases probably by More himself. One correction could mean that only crafty lawyers are excluded; the other must mean that all lawyers are excluded because all lawyers are crafty. The latter interpretation seems preferable.

understand it); on the other hand, the simpler and more obvious meaning of the laws is clear to everyone. Otherwise, as far as ordinary people are concerned (and they constitute the largest group that needs to be informed), it would make no difference if you formulated no laws at all or if, after you have formulated them, you interpret them in such a way that no one can understand them without great intelligence and long analysis. The dull judgment of ordinary people is not adequate to that task, and they do not have enough time, occupied as they are in making a living.

Inspired by the virtues of the Utopians, those of their neighbors who are free and can choose as they please (for the Utopians themselves have long since liberated many of them from tyranny) ask for and obtain Utopians to act as their magistrates, some for a year, some for five years; when they have served their term, they bring them back to Utopia with great honor and praise, and take replacements with them back to their own country. And certainly these countries are providing very well and very effectively for the public welfare, which depends, for good or bad, on the character of the magistrates. What persons could they choose more wisely than those whose honesty cannot be undermined by bribes (since they will soon return to a place where money is useless) and who cannot be swayed by some person or faction, since they have no connections among that people? Wherever these two vices, favoritism and greed, get a hold on judicial decisions, all justice, which is the mainstay of the commonwealth, is immediately undermined. The peoples who recruit magistrates from them are called allies by the Utopians; the others on whom they have bestowed benefits are called friends.

Treaties   They do not make treaties with any nation—such treaties as other nations so often make, break, and remake. What good is a treaty, they say, as if nature did not sufficiently bind one human being to another? And if someone scorns nature, do you think he will be concerned with mere words? They are especially drawn to that view because in that part of the world treaties and agreements between princes are not usually observed with very much good faith.

In Europe, of course, and especially in those parts which follow the faith and religion of Christ, the authority of treaties is everywhere holy and inviolable, partly because of the goodness and justice of the princes themselves, partly out of reverence and respect for the popes, who themselves undertake nothing which they do not carry out most scrupulously and likewise command all princes to keep their promises to the letter; if any prince reneges, the pope makes him comply by pastoral censure and sharp reproof.[65] Certainly they are right in thinking that it is quite shameful for those who are specifically called the faithful not to be faithful to their treaties.

But in that new world, which is as far from us in customs and way of life as it is removed from us by the distance the equator puts between us, no one has confidence in treaties: the more ceremoniously and solemnly the knot of a treaty is tied, the more quickly it is untied; it is easy to find some defect in the wording, which they often intentionally devise with some clever loophole, so that the language can never bind them so tightly that they cannot somehow escape, breaking both the treaty and their word. If such craftiness, or rather downright fraud and deceit, occurred in a private transaction it would be contemptuously decried as sacrilegious and deserving of the gallows—and that by the very same persons who are proud of having advised the prince to do the same. Thus it happens that justice seems either to be nothing more than a plebeian and humble virtue, far beneath the exalted dignity of a king, or at least there seem to be two kinds of justice: one is fit for ordinary people, lowly and creeping along the ground, fenced in on all sides, totally encumbered with chains and unable to escape; the other kind is a virtue proper to princes, which is more august than the ordinary virtue and hence much freer—forbidden, in fact, to do only what it does not wish to do.

Such behavior on the part of the princes there, who have so little respect for treaties, is the reason, I think, that the Utopians make no treaties; perhaps they would change their minds if they lived here. But even if treaties were strictly observed, they still think the practice of making them at all is

---

65 The rulers and popes of More's time were notorious for breaking treaties or making them with the deliberate intention of breaking them. This was especially true of the popes Alexander VI and Julius II. Machiavelli said Alexander VI "never did anything, never thought of anything other than to deceive men.... And never was there a man who had greater success in asserting, and with greater oaths in affirming a thing, who observed it less" (*The Prince* 18).

a bad custom because it implies that nations think they are natural-born enemies to each other (just as if there were no natural ties between two peoples separated only by a little distance, a hill or a creek) and that they would rightly try to destroy one another if they were not bound by treaties; and that even if they have entered into a treaty, they are not united in friendship but rather have permission to prey upon each other, insofar as nothing which the treaty forbids is couched with sufficient care because of some oversight in the language. On the other hand, the Utopians think that no one should be considered an enemy if he has done no harm, and that the natural bond which unites us should replace treaties, and that men are more adequately bound to one another by good will than by agreements, more strongly joined by their hearts than by their words.

MILITARY PRACTICES

They loathe war as positively bestial (though no sort of beast engages in it as constantly as mankind), and unlike almost all nations they consider nothing more inglorious than glory won in warfare.[66] Therefore, though they regularly devote themselves to military training on certain appointed days so that they will not be incapable of fighting when circumstances require it—and not only the men do so but also the women—they are reluctant to go to war and do so only to defend their own territory, or to drive an invading enemy from the territory of their friends, or else, out of compassion and humanity, they use their forces to liberate an oppressed people from tyranny and servitude. When they come to the aid of their friends, it is not always to defend them but sometimes also to requite and avenge injuries inflicted on them. But they do this only if they have been consulted before any steps are taken and if, after they have verified the facts, demanded restitution, and been refused, they themselves declare war.[67] They decide to do this not only when an enemy has invaded and plundered one of their friends, but also, and even more fiercely, when their friends' merchants in any part of the world have been unjustly accused under some pretext of justice, either by using unjust laws speciously or by interpreting good laws perversely.

This was the only reason for the war which the Utopians fought a little before our time on behalf of the Nephelogetes against the Alaopolitans:[68] some Nephelogete merchants among the Alaopolitans had been treated unjustly under some pretext of justice (or so the merchants thought). Certainly, whether the cause was just or unjust, it was avenged by a hideous war, in which the surrounding nations also added their energy and resources to the hostile forces of the major opponents so that some prosperous peoples were ravaged, others were badly shaken. One disaster followed upon another until finally the surrender and enslavement of the Alaopolitans put an end to the war. The Utopians, who sought nothing for themselves, subjected the vanquished to the Nephelogetes—a people hardly to be compared with the Alaopolitans in their heyday.

So fierce are the Utopians even when they are punishing only monetary injuries against their friends; but they are not so when the injury is against themselves. If they should be cheated out of their property, as long as they are subjected to no physical force, they set limits to their anger: they merely refrain from trade with that nation until restitution is made, not because they care less for their own citizens than for their allies but rather they are more offended by their friends' loss of money than by their own because their friends' merchants are severely injured by such a loss, since it comes from their own private possessions. But their own citizens lose nothing but public property, goods which were abundant at home, even superfluous, for otherwise they would not have been exported. So the loss is hardly perceived by anyone. Hence they feel that it would be cruel to punish an injury by killing many people when it causes no inconvenience to any of the Utopians in their lives or livelihood. But if any of their citizens is unjustly disabled or killed, wherever it may be, whether it be done by a public decision or by a private citizen, they send ambassadors to ascertain the facts, and if the malefactors are not handed over to them they cannot be put off but declare war immediately. If the guilty persons are

66 A common false etymology derived "bellum" (war) from "belua" (beast)—or the other way around. For a full account of pacifism in More and his humanist contemporaries, see R. P. Adams, *The Better Part* of Valor: More, Erasmus, Colet, and Vives on Humanism, War, and Peace, 1496–1535 (Seattle: University of Washington Press, 1962). 67 One of the key texts giving the rules for fighting a "just" war was Cicero, *De officiis* 1.11.34–1.13–40. 68 Greek compounds meaning "cloud-born" and "citizens of a country without people"

handed over for punishment, they are sentenced to death or servitude.

They are not only grieved by a bloody victory but also ashamed of it, thinking *Victory dearly bought* that it is stupid to pay too much for merchandise, however valuable it may be. But if they conquer and crush an enemy by skill and cunning, they glory mightily in the victory, holding public parades to celebrate it and putting up a monument as if for a hard-won victory. For they boast that they have acted with courage and fortitude only when they have won the victory as no other creature but man is able to win it, that is, by the power of his wits. For bears, lions, boars, wolves, dogs, and other animals (they say) fight with the power of their bodies; and though most of them surpass us in strength and ferocity, we outdo them all in intelligence and reasoning.

Their one and only aim in warfare is to gain the objective which, if they had obtained it beforehand, would have kept them from going to war at all. Or, if circumstances make that impossible, they seek to punish those they consider culpable so severely that fear will keep them from daring to do such a thing in the future. These are the goals they set for their undertaking, and they try to achieve them quickly, but yet in such a way that a concern for avoiding danger takes precedence over winning praise and glory.

And so, immediately after declaring war, they see to it that many notices certified by their official seal are put up secretly and simultaneously in the most conspicuous places in the enemy's territory, promising a huge reward to anyone who does away with the enemy's prince; they also assign lesser, but still very substantial, sums for the deaths of those individuals they list in the same notices. These are the persons who, apart from the prince himself, were responsible for plotting against the Utopians. They double the reward assigned to the assassin if he brings them any of the proscribed persons alive; in fact, they offer the same rewards to the proscribed persons themselves, and throw immunity into the bargain, if they turn against their comrades. Thus their enemies quickly suspect all outsiders and even among themselves they are neither trusting nor trustworthy so that they live in a state of utter panic and no less peril. For it has very often turned out (as is well known) that a good number of them, and among them the prince himself, have often been betrayed by those they trusted the most. So easy is it to get someone to commit any crime whatsoever by means of bribes, and for that reason the Utopians set no limits to their bribes. Keeping in mind the great risks they are urging people to take, they take care to balance the magnitude of the danger with the lavishness of the reward; hence they promise not only enormous quantities of gold but also personal and perpetual title to rich estates in the safe and secure territory of their friends, and they faithfully keep their promises.

Other nations condemn this practice of bidding for and buying off an enemy as a barbarous, degenerate crime, but the Utopians think it does them great credit: it shows them to be wise, since in this way they win great wars without fighting at all, and also humane and compassionate, since by killing a few malefactors they spare the lives of many innocent persons who would have fallen in battle, both their own soldiers and those of the enemy; for they pity the rank-and-file of the enemy's soldiers almost as much as their own citizens because they know they do not go to war of their own accord but are driven to it by the madness of princes.

If this procedure is not successful, they sow and cultivate the seeds of dissension by encouraging the brother of the prince or some nobleman to have hopes of gaining the throne. If such internal factions languish, they stir up neighboring peoples and set them against their enemy by digging up some ancient claim such as is never lacking to kings.

When they have promised resources for war, they supply money lavishly, but their citizens very sparingly. They hold their own people so very dear and value each other so highly that they would not be willing to exchange a single one of their own citizens for the enemy's prince. But they are not at all reluctant to pay out gold and silver, since they keep it only for this purpose and would live no less comfortably if they spent all of it. Then too, apart from the wealth they have at home, they also have a limitless treasure abroad, since many nations, as I said before, owe them money. And so they hire mercenaries from everywhere and send them to war, especially *A people not unlike the Swiss* the Zapoletes.[69]

---

69 from a Greek compound meaning "busy sellers" — that is, sellers and resellers of their military services

These people live five hundred miles to the east of Utopia. Rough, rude, and fierce, they prefer to live in the forests and rugged mountains where they were brought up. They are a hardy people, able to en-
5 dure heat, cold, and hard labor. They have no interest in agriculture, no acquaintance with refinements, no concern about their houses or clothes; they care only about their flocks. They live mostly from hunting and plundering. They are born only for warfare;
10 they zealously seek opportunities to fight and when they find one they embrace it eagerly. They set out in great numbers and offer themselves cheaply to whoever needs soldiers. The only skill they have to live on is one that aims at death.

15 They fight fiercely and with complete loyalty for whoever pays them. But they bind themselves for no fixed period. They sign on with the stipulation that if an enemy offers them higher wages tomorrow they will take his side, and if they are lured with
20 slightly higher pay they will return to the side they abandoned. There are very few wars in which a great many of them are not fighting in both armies. And so it happens every day that blood relatives who were hired by the same side and lived together am-
25 icably are separated a little later in opposing armies and fight each other as enemies. Forgetting both kinship and friendship, they run each other through with violent hostility, trying to kill each other for no other reason than that they were hired for a pit-
30 tance by opposing princes. They reckon their wages so strictly that adding one penny to their daily pay can easily cause them to change sides. They have quickly become greedy through and through, and yet it does them no good for what they gain with
35 their blood they immediately squander on debauchery, and wretched debauchery at that.

These people fight for the Utopians against any mortals whatsoever because they hire their services for more than they can get anywhere else. And
40 just as the Utopians seek good men in order to use them, so too they also enlist these wicked men in order to use them up. When they need to use them, they urge them on with great promises and expose them to the greatest dangers so that most of them
45 do not return to claim what they were promised. To the survivors they faithfully keep their promises so as to make them eager to undertake similar exploits. Nor do they have any qualms about doing away with so many of them, since they believe the hu-
50 man race would owe them a great debt of gratitude

if they could purge the whole world of such loathsome and wicked scum.

Apart from the Zapoletes, they use the forces of those for whom they have taken up arms, and af-
55 ter that the auxiliary troops of other friendly nations. As a last resort they add their own citizens, from whom they choose a man of proven valour to command the whole army. Under him they appoint two men who remain private citizens as long as he
60 is safe, but if he is captured or killed, one of the two succeeds him, and in case of a mishap he himself is succeeded by the third, so that if the commander is in danger (and the fortunes of war are quite various) the whole army does not panic.

65 In each city they choose troops from a list of volunteers. No one is sent out to foreign wars against his will, for they are convinced that if someone is by nature fearful he will not only not fight vigorously himself but he will also inspire fear in his comrades.
70 But if their country is invaded during a war, cowards of this sort, as long as they are physically fit, are dispersed among better troops in the ships or they are spread out here and there on the walls so that they have no place to run away to. Thus shame
75 in the presence of their friends, the confrontation with the enemy, and the absence of any hope of escaping overcome fear, and often they make a virtue out of extreme necessity.

Though no one is sent to a foreign war unwill-
80 ingly, if women are willing to accompany their husbands to battle the Utopians are so far from preventing them that they exhort them to do so and encourage them with praise. Each accompanies her husband to the front and is stationed shoulder to
85 shoulder with him in the battle line. Moreover, each soldier is surrounded by his children and relatives by blood or marriage so that they all have help close by from the persons who are by nature most highly motivated to help one another. It is a great disgrace
90 for one spouse to return without the other or for a son to come back after the loss of a parent. The result is that once it comes to hand-to-hand combat, if the enemy stands his ground, the battle is so long and grim that it ends in a general slaughter.

95 Certainly they take every precaution to avoid having to fight themselves, as long as they can wage war using mercenaries to take their place. But when they can no longer avoid entering the fray, the courage with which they fight matches the prudence with which they avoided fighting as long as they 100

could. They do not give their all in a first furious attack but rather they grow stronger gradually and over a period of time, and they are so resolute that they would rather die than retreat. For one thing, they are certain that everyone at home is provided for, and they do not need to worry about their children (such concern generally breaks the spirits of lofty souls); so their courage is proud and contemptuous of defeat. Moreover, their skill in the arts of war gives them confidence. Finally, sound ideas, instilled in them from childhood on, both by instruction and through the institutions of the commonwealth, give them courage: they hold life neither so cheap as to throw it away recklessly nor so perversely dear as to cling to it greedily and shamefully when honor requires them to give it up.

When the battle is at its fiercest everywhere, a picked group of sworn and dedicated young men seek out the enemy commander. Sometimes they attack him openly; sometimes they try to ambush him. They assail him from close by and from a distance and they attack him in a wide, unbroken phalanx, continuously replacing the exhausted men with fresh troops. And unless he saves himself by running away, it rarely happens that he is not killed or captured alive by his enemies.

Above all the commander should be assailed so as to end the war sooner

If they win a victory, they do not slaughter the defeated; they would rather capture than kill those they have put to flight. And they never pursue retreating troops without keeping in reserve at least one battalion drawn up under its colors. They do this so regularly that if the rest of their own forces have been defeated and they win the victory with their last battalion, they would rather let the whole enemy army escape than get into the habit of pursuing the fugitives with their own forces in disarray. They remember something that happened to them more than once: when the main body of the whole Utopian army had been overwhelmed and put to flight, while the enemy was exulting in the victory and pursuing them as they ran away in all directions, a few of their own troops held in reserve and on the lookout for opportunities suddenly attacked the enemy troops, who were scattered and straggling and careless from overconfidence, and thus changed the whole outcome of the battle; snatching certain and undoubted victory from their enemies' hands, the conquered turned the tables and conquered the conquerors.

It is not easy to say whether they are more clever in laying ambushes or more cautious in avoiding them. You would think they are preparing to flee when that is the last thing they intend; on the other hand, when they do intend to flee, you would imagine that is the last thing they have in mind. For if they feel they are at a disadvantage either in numbers or location, then they either move their camp silently at night, or escape by some stratagem, or withdraw gradually by day, keeping their ranks in such good order that they are no less dangerous in retreat than when they attack. They fortify their camp very carefully with a wide and very deep moat; the earth they dig up is piled up on the inside. In such work they do not use the services of common laborers. It is done by the hands of the soldiers themselves, and the whole army joins in the work except for the armed soldiers outside the rampart who keep watch against sudden attacks. With so many soldiers pitching in, they build massive fortifications around a large area with incredible speed.

They wear armor which is strong enough to ward off blows but does not hinder movement and gestures—so much so that they feel no inconvenience even in swimming. For swimming in armor is one of the ordinary rudiments of their military training. At long range their weapon is the arrow which they shoot with great force and accuracy, not only on foot but also from horseback. At close quarters they strike not with swords but with battle-axes, which are deadly because of their sharp blade and their weight, whether used to hack or thrust. They are very skilled in devising siege engines. Once they are made, they conceal them very carefully, lest they become known before it is time to use them and turn out to be more ridiculous than useful. In designing them their primary concern is to make them easy to move and aim.

Types of arms

When they make a truce with their enemies, they keep it so religiously that they do not violate it even under provocation. They do not lay enemy territory waste or burn their crops; they even do what they can to keep the grain from being trampled by men and horses, for they think it may be of some use to them. They injure no unarmed civilians except for spies. They offer amnesty to cities that surrender and even those taken by siege they do not sack; instead they execute those who prevented the surrender;

Truces

they enslave the rest of the defenders, but the civilian populace they leave unharmed. If they find persons who urged the town to surrender, they grant them a share in the property of the condemned; they divide up the rest and give it to their auxiliaries, for none of the Utopians takes any of the booty.

When the war is over, they assess the costs not *But today the victors pay the greatest share* against the friends for whom they incurred them but against the losers; they demand part of it in money, which they reserve for similar use in warfare, and part in estates within enemy territory, from which they forever enjoy a not inconsiderable income. They now have revenues of this sort in many nations; it accumulated gradually in various ways and now amounts to 700,000 ducats a year.[70] To take care of it they send out collectors of revenue, who live there in grand style and play the part of great lords. But there is plenty left over to put into the treasury,[71] unless they choose to give credit to the nation that owes it, which they often do until they need it, and even then it rarely happens that they demand all of it. They also bestow some of these estates on those whom they have persuaded to place themselves in great danger, as I mentioned before.

If some prince takes up arms against them and is preparing to invade their domain, they immediately confront him with a huge force outside their own boundaries, for they are reluctant to wage war within their own territory and no exigency could ever induce them to allow foreign auxiliaries on their island.

THE RELIGIONS OF THE UTOPIANS

There are various religions not only throughout the island but also within individual cities: some worship the sun as god, others the moon, others a different planet. Others worship some ancient paragon of either virtue or glory, venerating such a person not only as a god but as the supreme god. But the vast majority, and those by far the wiser ones, accept none of those gods and believe there is a certain single deity, unknown, eternal, infinite, inexplicable, diffused throughout this whole universe not physically but by his power, in a manner that is beyond human comprehension; him they call their parent. To him alone they attribute the origin, increase, progress, changes, and goals of all things; him and no other they honor as divine.

Actually, though all the others hold different beliefs on some points, they agree with the monotheists in thinking that there is some one supreme being who made and rules the universe, and in their native language they all agree in calling him Mythras,[72] but they differ in that they identify the supreme power variously, each asserting that whatever he considers to be supreme is in fact that single nature to whose divine majesty, by the consensus of all nations, the whole creation is attributed. But gradually they are all abandoning these superstitious variations and joining together in that one religion which seems more reasonable than the others. And there is no doubt that the other beliefs would have vanished long ago if it were not that, whenever something untoward happened to someone who was considering changing his religion, fear made him think that it was not accidental but was sent from heaven, as if the divinity whose cult he was forsaking were avenging a wicked affront to himself.

But after they had heard from us the name, the teaching, the behavior, and the miracles of Christ, and the no less miraculous constancy of so many martyrs who freely shed their blood and thus brought many peoples, from far and wide, over to their religion, you would not believe how eagerly they also were converted, whether through the secret inspiration of God or because Christianity seemed closest to the sect which is predominant among them, although I think it was a matter of no small moment with them to hear that Christ approved of life in common *Monasteries* for his disciples and that it is still practiced among the most genuine Christian communities.[73] But certainly, whatever the reason, no small number of them were converted to our religion and were washed clean in the sacred waters of baptism.

But because there was, I am sorry to say, no priest among the four of us (for only that number

---

70 A ducat was a gold coin minted primarily by Venice and worth about a quarter of a pound sterling at that time. The 700,000 ducats mentioned here would be worth many hundred times that much today.   **71** The Utopians would not have an ordinary treasury; perhaps deposits owed the Utopians and placed in the treasuries of other countries are what is meant here.   **72** Among the ancient Persians, Mithras was the supreme deity, identified with light.   **73** Communism was practiced by religious orders in More's time, as it still is; on communism among the early Christians, see Acts 2:44–45 and 4:32–37.

remained after two of us had given up the ghost), they received the other sacraments but still lacked those which among us are conferred only by priests.[74] But they know about them and long for them most intensely. In fact, they also earnestly discuss among themselves whether someone chosen from among their number could receive the sacerdotal character[75] without the dispatch of a Christian bishop. And in fact it seemed they were about to choose someone, but when I left they had not yet done so.

Even those who do not agree with the Christian religion still do not frighten anyone away from it; they do not oppose anyone who has embraced it, except that one of our community was repressed while I was there. Shortly after he was baptized, over our objections, he harangued publicly about Christianity with more zeal than prudence, and he began to get so carried away that he not only ranked our religion above all the rest but condemned all the others outright. He cried out against them as profane; he denounced their worshipers as wicked, sacrilegious, and worthy to be punished in eternal fire. When he had preached like this for a long time, they arrested him and tried him, not for despising their religion but for exciting riots among the people. They convicted him and sentenced him to exile, for it is one of their oldest policies that no one should come to any harm because of his religion.

People must be drawn to religion by hearing it praised

For Utopus had learned that before his arrival the inhabitants squabbled incessantly about religion and he had noticed that the sects, which generally disagreed with each other and fought for their country in separate groups, provided the opportunity for him to conquer all of them. Hence, from the very beginning, after he had obtained the victory, he decreed first of all that everyone could practice the religion of his choice and could also strive to convert others to it, but only so long as he advocated it calmly and moderately with rational arguments. And if he could not win others over by persuasion,

he was not to assail their religions bitterly nor use force against them, and he was to refrain from insults. Anyone who quarrels insolently about religion is punished with exile or enslavement.[76]

Utopus laid down these rules not only for the sake of peace, which he saw was completely undermined by constant strife and implacable hatred, but also because he thought such a decree would benefit religion itself. In religious matters he did not venture to dogmatize rashly because he was uncertain whether or not God wishes to have varied and manifold kinds of worship and hence inspires different people with different views. Certainly he thought that to use force and threats to make everyone accept what you believe to be true is both arrogant and absurd. Then too, if one religion should be actually true and the rest false, still he easily foresaw that in the long run the truth would sooner or later emerge and prevail by its own force as long as the matter was handled reasonably and moderately. But if the struggle is conducted with arms and uprisings, since the worst people are always the most headstrong, the best and holiest religion, embroiled among empty superstitions, will be choked like grain among thorns and briars. And so he left the whole matter open and left everyone free to believe whatever he wanted, except that he solemnly and strictly forbade that anyone should sink so far below the dignity of human nature as to think that the soul dies with the body or that the world is ruled by mere chance and not by providence.

And for this reason they believe that after this life punishments are ordained for vices and rewards for virtues. Anyone who thinks otherwise they do not even include in the category of human beings since he has degraded the lofty nature of his soul to the base level of a beast's wretched body. Still less will they count him as one of their citizens, since he would set no store whatever by all their laws and morality if it were not for fear. For who can doubt that someone who has nothing to fear but the law and no hope of anything beyond bodily existence would strive to evade the public laws of his country

---

74 Of the seven sacraments, only baptism and matrimony can be administered by laymen.   75 In sacramental theology "character" is a technical term meaning the indelible quality bestowed on a soul by sacraments that cannot be repeated: baptism, confirmation, and holy orders.

76 In Christian England, More approved of punishing religious dissent or heresy, but that was because the true religion had been revealed there, as it had not in Utopia; as More said in *A Dialogue Concerning Heresies* (*CW* 6: 345–46), "if it were now doubtful and ambiguous whether the

church of Christ were in the right rule of doctrine or not, then were it very necessary to give them all good audience that could and would anything dispute on either party for it or against it, to the end that if we were now in a wrong way, we might leave it and walk in some better."

by secret chicanery or to break them by force in order to satisfy his own personal greed? For that reason they bestow no honors on such a person, they assign him to no office, they put him in charge of no public responsibility. He is universally looked down on as a lazy and spineless character. But he is not subjected to any punishment because they are convinced that it is not within a person's power to believe whatever he wishes; they neither compel him by any threats to mask his opinion nor accept any pretexts or lies, which they utterly despise as next door to deliberate malice. Still they do forbid him to argue for his opinion, but only among the common people. Otherwise, in private, among priests and prudent men, they not only permit him to argue but also encourage it, confident that in the end his madness will yield to reason.

There are also others, and they are by no means few (since their position is not forbidden as completely unreasonable or wicked) who go to the opposite extreme and believe that the souls of brute beasts are also immortal, although not comparable to ours in dignity nor destined for the same happiness.

A remarkable opinion about the souls of animals

Almost all of them are certain and fully persuaded that human happiness will be so boundless that they mourn for everyone who is sick but not for anyone who dies, unless they see that he is torn from life anxiously and unwillingly. For they take this to be a very bad sign, as if such a soul, despairing and conscious of guilt, fears to leave life because of some secret presentiment of future punishment. Moreover, they think God will hardly be well pleased when someone who is summoned does not come running eagerly but is dragged off reluctant and unwilling. Therefore when they see such a death they are dismayed and they carry out the dead persons with grief and in silence; after praying that God in his mercy will kindly forgive the infirmities of such souls, they cover the body with earth. On the other hand, when someone dies joyfully and full of good hope, they do not mourn him, but rather they conduct his funeral with song; commending his soul to God with great affection, they

finally cremate his body with reverence, not grief, and erect on that spot a column inscribed with the virtues of the dead person. After they have returned home, they tell of his character and deeds, and no part of his life is rehearsed more often or more eagerly than his cheerful death.

They think this commemoration of his uprightness is a very strong inducement to virtue for the living and the most acceptable form of veneration to the dead, whom they also believe to be present when they are talked about, though invisible to us because the eyesight of mortals is too dull to see them. For it would not be suitable to the condition of the blessed to lack the liberty of going wherever they want, and it would be ungrateful of them to have no desire whatever to visit their friends, to whom they were united in mutual love and charity while they were alive; such charity they suppose, like other good qualities, is increased, not diminished, in good men after their death.[77] Thus they believe that the dead are present among the living, observing what they say and do, and for that reason they go about their business more confidently because of their trust in such protectors; their belief in the presence of their ancestors also deters them from secret wrongdoing.

They have nothing to do with fortune-telling and other vain, superstitious divinations, which other people take quite seriously but which they consider ridiculous. But miracles which happen apart from any natural cause they revere as works and witnesses which manifest the presence of a deity. They say such miracles often happen there, and sometimes, during great crises, they pray publicly for a miracle with great confidence and they do obtain it.

They think the worship which pleases God is the contemplation of nature and the praise which springs from it. But there are others, and they are by no means few, who neglect learning in the name of religion, who do not strive to attain any knowledge, and who allow themselves no leisure at all. They are *The active life* determined to earn happiness after death solely by keeping busy in the service of others. And so some tend the sick, others repair the roads, clear out

---

77 In *A Dialogue Concerning Heresies* (*cw* 6: 211, 213), More wrote concerning saints: "For if their holy souls live, there will no wise man ween them worse and of less love and charity to men that need their help, when they be now in heaven, than they had when they were here in earth.... When saints were in this world at liberty and might walk the world about, ween we that in heaven they stand tied to a post?"

ditches, rebuild bridges, dig turf, sand, or stones, fell and cut up trees, cart lumber, crops, and other provisions into the cities. They perform their services not only for the public but also for private citizens,
5 and they work even harder than slaves. They willingly and cheerfully undertake any tasks which are rough, difficult, dirty, and shunned by most people because of the toil, disgust, and hopelessness they entail. They see to it that others have leisure, while
10 they themselves are continually engaged in labor and toil, but nevertheless they take no credit for it. They neither censure the lives of others nor extol their own. The more they conduct themselves like slaves the more everyone honors them.

15 They are divided into two sects. The one is celibate and not only abstains from any sexual activity but also eats no meat (and some of them no animal products at all), totally rejecting the pleasures of this life as harmful, longing only for those of
20 the world to come, which they strive to obtain by toil and vigils. Meanwhile, confident that they will soon obtain them, they are cheerful and energetic. The other group, no less devoted to labor, prefers to marry: they do not spurn the consolations of mar-
25 riage, and they think that just as they owe such activity to nature, they owe children to their country. They do not refuse any pleasure which does not interfere with their work. They like to eat the flesh of animals precisely because they think such food gives
30 them the strength to do all kinds of work. The Utopians consider this group more prudent; the other they regard as holier. If they claimed on rational grounds to prefer celibacy to marriage and a hard life to a comfortable one, the Utopians would laugh
35 at them; but since they profess to be motivated by religion, the Utopians respect and revere them. On no other subject are they more cautious about making any rash pronouncements than on matters concerning religion. In their language these persons are
40 given the special title "Buthrescae," which could be translated into Latin as *religiosi*.[78]

Their priests are extremely holy and therefore very few. For each city has no more than thirteen, one for each church, except during wartime, when seven
45 of them set out with the army and are replaced by substitutes for the time being. But when the priests return, each assumes his former position. Until the time when the substitutes, in an orderly succession, replace priests who have died, they become atten-
50 dants of the high priest (for one priest has authority over the others). They are elected by the people in the same way as other magistrates, that is, by secret ballot, in order to avoid partisan strife. Once elected, they are consecrated by their own college
55 of priests.

They preside over divine worship, attend to religious matters, and act as guardians of morality. To be summoned by them and rebuked for dishonorable conduct is considered to be a great disgrace.
60 But their role is to exhort and admonish; to repress and punish wrongdoers is the function of the ruler and other magistrates. The priests, however, do excommunicate those they find to be thoroughly vicious. There is almost no other punishment which
65 they fear more, for such persons are both dejected by their infamy and tormented by a bad conscience. They may not even be physically safe for very long. For unless they quickly convince the priests that they are repentant, they will be seized by the senate
70 and punished for their impiety.

Children and young people are educated by the priests, and they devote no more attention to learning than to character and virtue.[79] They take the greatest pains from the very first to instill in the
75 tender and impressionable minds of children sound opinions conducive to preserving the common good. When such ideas are thoroughly absorbed in childhood, they persist throughout all of manhood and they are extremely useful in protecting the sta-
80 tus of the commonwealth, which decays only because of vices which spring from perverse attitudes.

The wives of the priests are the very finest women in the country, unless the priests themselves are women, for that sex is not *Female priests*
85 excluded; but they are rarely elected and must be widows of advanced years.[80]

No magistrates are held in greater honor among the Utopians, so much so that even if they commit a crime they are not subject to a public tribunal but
90 are left to God and their own consciences. For they

---

78 "Buthrescae" is a Greek word meaning "extraordinarily religious." In More's Europe, the adjective "religious" was applied to members of religious orders, who differed, however, from the Buthrescae in that they combined labor with prayer, study, and contemplation. 79 Hythloday must mean that the priests supervise the education of children, for in each city there are many thousands of children and only thirteen priests. 80 In *The Confutation of Tyndale's Answer* (*CW* 8.1: 260–61), More accepts the traditional view that women may not be ordained as priests.

do not think it is right to lay human hands on any-one, however vicious, who has been dedicated to God in such a special way as a holy offering, so to speak. It is easier for them to observe this custom be-cause priests are so few and are chosen so carefully. For it is very unlikely that someone who is the cream of the crop and is elevated to a position of such dig-nity only because of his vir-tue should degenerate into corruption and vice. And even if that very thing should happen — for human nature is changeable — nevertheless there would certainly be no reason to fear that the public would be in any great danger, be-cause the priests are so few and have no power be-yond what derives from the honor paid them. In fact the very reason they have so few and scattered priests is to keep the dignity of the order, now held in such high esteem, from being cheapened by bestowing the honor on many, espe-cially since they think it is hard to find very many who are equal to the dignity of the office, for which merely mediocre virtues are insufficient.

Excommunication

But what a flock of them we have!

Their reputation at home is no greater than the es-teem in which they are held by foreign nations. This becomes quite clear, I think, if we note the reason for it. When troops are engaged in battle, the priests kneel at a distance but not very far away, dressed in their sacred vestments; lifting up their hands to heaven, they pray first of all for peace, and then for victory for their own forces, but without bloodshed on either side. When their soldiers win they rush into the battle line and re-strain the fury of their forces against the routed troops. Merely to see them and make oneself known to them by calling out is enough to save anyone's life; to touch their flowing garments also protects the remaining goods of fortune from any damage due to the war. Hence they are venerated by the countries all around them, who attribute to them such genuine majesty that oftentimes they provide as much protection for their own citizens as they do for their enemies. For sometimes it has happened that, when their battle line was thrown back in de-spair and had turned to flee, as the enemy was

O these priests are far holier than ours!

rushing in to kill and plunder, the intervention of the priests has stopped the slaughter and separated the two armies so that a peace was devised and es-tablished on equitable terms. For nowhere is there a nation so savage, cruel, and barbarous that they do not hold their persons to be sacrosanct and inviolable.

The first and last days of each month and likewise of each year are celebrated as feastdays; the months are marked off by the orbit of the moon, just as the year is established by the course of the sun. In their language they call all of the first days "cynemerni," the last days "trapemerni,"[81] names that are equivalent to "first-feastday" and "last-feastday." Their churches are remarkable not only for their workmanship but also for their capac-ity to hold immense crowds — which is necessary because there are so few of them.[82] They are all dimly lit, and they say this re-sulted not from lack of skill but from the deliberate policy of the priests, who believe that too much light distracts our thoughts, whereas dim and doubtful lighting concentrates the mind and inten-sifies religious devotion.

Observance of holy days among the Utopians

What their churches are like

Since religion is not the same for everyone there, yet all the forms of it, however varied and differ-ent, converge from various directions on one goal, the worship of the divine nature, nothing is seen or heard in the churches which is not held in com-mon by all the religions. If any denomination has a rite peculiar to it, they provide for it in their own homes. Public worship is conducted according to a ritual which does not at all detract from any of the private devotions. Therefore no images of the gods are seen in churches so that everyone can be free to imagine the form of God as he wishes according to his own religion. They invoke God by no other name than Mythras, a name they all apply to the one divine nature, whatever it may be. No prayers are devised which everyone cannot say without of-fending his own denomination.

And so on the last-feastdays they gather in church in the evening, still fasting and ready to give thanks to God for the success they enjoyed during the year

---

81 The first Greek compound means "dog days" (or perhaps "starting days"); the second means "turning days."   **82** There may be more than one service on every feast day, but even so the churches would have to be very large indeed: only thirteen of them serve about one hundred thousand inhabitants of each city.

or month just coming to an end. On the next day, which is the first-feastday, they flock to church in the morning to pray for success and happiness in the following year or month which begins on that feastday. But on the last-feastdays, at home, before they go to church, wives throw themselves at the feet of their husbands, and children do the same before their parents; they confess that they have sinned either through commission or negligence, and they beg forgiveness for their offenses. In this way if some little cloud of strife has arisen in the household, it is dispelled by such atonement so that they can attend the sacrifices with clear and untroubled minds, for they are too conscientious to worship with a disturbed conscience.[83] Therefore those who feel anger or hatred toward someone do not intrude on the sacrifices unless they are reconciled and purged of such feelings, for fear of some swift and severe punishment.

The confession of the Utopians

But among us the most defiled strive to get closest to the altar

When they get there, the men sit on the right side of the church, the women separately on the left. Then too, they position themselves so that the male members of each household sit in front of the master of that household, and the matron of each household sits in the last row of the women. Thus they see to it that all the actions of everyone are observed in public by the persons whose authority maintains discipline at home. Moreover they are also very careful to intermingle everywhere young persons with their elders; otherwise, if children were entrusted to children, they might spend in childish tomfoolery the time that they should devote to cultivating a religious fear of the heavenly beings,[84] the greatest and practically the only incitement to virtue.[85]

In their sacrifices they do not kill any animals; they do not think that a merciful God, who bestowed life on animals precisely that they might live, takes any pleasure in bloodshed and slaughter. They burn incense and other fragrant substances. They also display many candles, not because they do not know that such things add nothing to God's nature, no more than human prayers do, but they like this harmless mode of worship and people feel that somehow such perfumes, lights, and other ceremonies lift up the human heart and make it rise more eagerly in divine worship.

In church the people wear white garments; the priests are clothed in vestments of various colors, marvelous in both workmanship and design, though the materials are not especially expensive, and they are not woven with gold threads or encrusted with rare gems; rather they are fashioned out of the feathers of various birds, so elegantly and skillfully that the costliest material would not match the value of the workmanship.[86] Moreover, these feathers and plumes of birds and the set patterns in which they are arranged on the priests' garments are said to contain certain secret mysteries which, if rightly understood (and the interpretation is carefully handed down by the priests), remind them of the benefits bestowed on them by God and of the devotion they owe him in return, as well as their duty to each other.

When the priest, dressed in this way, comes out of the sacristy, everyone immediately prostrates himself on the ground out of reverence; on all sides the silence is so profound that the spectacle itself inspires a certain fear, as if in the presence of some divinity. They remain on the ground for a while and then arise at a signal from the priest. Then they sing the praises of God, accompanied by musical instruments, which are mostly shaped differently from those seen in our part of the world. Most of them surpass ours in sweetness of tone, but some of them are incomparably superior to ours. But in one respect their music is undoubtedly far ahead of ours: whether instrumental or vocal, it imitates and expresses natural feelings so well, the sound matches the sense of the words so closely (whether they express supplication or joy, peace or turmoil, sadness or anger), and the shape of the melody matches the meaning so well that it quite wonderfully stirs up, pierces, and inflames the hearts of the hearers.[87] Finally the priest and the people recite together

Music of the Utopians

83 Cf. Mt 5:23–24. 84 Latin *superos*, which includes the one God, the other gods believed in by some of the Utopians, and their ancestors who are in heaven. 85 A startling idea, but perhaps Hythloday (or the Utopians) means that for children this tends to be true. 86 In his *Four Voyages*, Vespucci mentions that the American Indians made vestments of feathers. 87 Fr. Surtz notes that many of More's contemporaries, especially Erasmus, objected to the elaborateness of church music and urged that it be composed so as to emphasize the meaning of the words (*CW* 4: 555–56).

certain customary and fixed forms of prayer, composed in such a way that everyone can apply to himself what they all recite together.

In these prayers each one recognizes God as the creator and ruler of the universe and also the source of all good things. He thanks God for bestowing so many benefits on him, but especially because through God's kindness he was placed in the happiest form of commonwealth and has been allotted the religion which he hopes is the truest. If he is mistaken in this matter or if there is some form of commonwealth or religion which is better and more approved by God, he prays that God in his goodness will cause him to recognize it, for he is prepared to follow wherever God leads him. But if this form of commonwealth is the best and this religion is truest, he asks that God will both make him steadfast and lead other mortals to the same way of life and the same idea of God—unless there is in fact something in this variety of religions which pleases his inscrutable will.

Finally he prays that by an easy death God may take him to himself, how soon or late he certainly does not dare to determine. But, provided that God's majesty is not offended by it, he would much rather go to him by a very difficult death than be kept away from him any longer, even by a prosperous way of life. After saying this prayer they once more prostrate themselves on the ground and after a little while they get up again, go to eat lunch, and spend the rest of the day playing games or doing military exercises.

I have described to you as accurately as I can the plan of their commonwealth, which I certainly consider to be not only the best but also the only kind worthy of the name. For elsewhere they always talk about the public good but they are concerned with their own private welfare; here,[88] where there is no private property, everyone works seriously for the public good. And for good reason in both places, for elsewhere is there anyone who does not know that unless he looks out for his own personal interest he will die of hunger, no matter how flourishing the commonwealth may be; therefore necessity causes him to think he should watch out for his own good, not that of others, that is, of the people. On the other hand, here, where everything belongs to everyone, no one doubts that (as long as care is taken that the public storehouses are full) nothing whatever will be lacking to anyone for his own use. For the distribution of goods is not niggardly; no one is a pauper or a beggar there, and though no one has anything, all are rich.

For what greater wealth can there be than to be completely spared any anxiety and to live with a joyful and tranquil frame of mind, with no worries about making a living, not vexed by a wife's complaints and demands, not fearing a son will end up in poverty, not concerned about a daughter's dowry, but secure about the livelihood and happiness of himself and his own, his wife, children, grandchildren, great-grandchildren, great-great-grandchildren, and however long a line of descendants noblemen presume they will have. Indeed those who worked before but are now disabled are no less provided for than those who are still working.

At this point I wish that someone would venture to compare with this equity the justice to be found in other nations, where I'll be damned if I can find any trace whatever of justice or equity. For what sort of justice is it for some nobleman or goldsmith[89] or moneylender or, in short, any of the others who either do nothing at all or something that is not very necessary for the commonwealth, to live luxuriously and splendidly in complete idleness or doing some superfluous task? And at the same time a laborer, a teamster, a blacksmith or farmer works so long and so hard that a beast of burden could hardly sustain it, performing tasks so necessary that without them no commonwealth could survive at all for even a single year, and yet they earn such a meager living and lead such miserable lives that beasts of burden seem to be better off, since they do not have to work so incessantly, their fodder is not much worse (and to them it tastes better), and in the meantime they are not afraid of what will happen to them. These workers are driven to toil without profit or gain in the present; they are crushed by the thought that they will be poverty-stricken in their old age, for their daily wages are not enough for that very day, much less can they accumulate any surplus which might be put aside every day to provide for their old age.

---

88 Hythloday is so carried away that he speaks as if he is still in Utopia.

89 Goldsmiths often functioned as bankers.

Is a commonwealth not unjust and ungrateful if it lavishes so many benefits on noblemen, as they are called, and goldsmiths, and the rest of that crew who are either idle or else merely flatterers and providers of empty pleasures, but makes no proper provision for farmers, colliers, laborers, teamsters, and blacksmiths, without whom there would be no commonwealth at all; unmindful of their sleepless labors and forgetting their many and great contributions, it first uses up the labors of their flourishing years, and then, when they are worn down by old age and diseases, it is totally ungrateful and rewards them with a miserable death. And how about this: every day the rich scrape away something from the wages of the poor, not only by private chicanery but also by public laws. Before, it seemed unjust that those who deserve the most from the commonwealth should receive the least, but now, by promulgating a law, they have transmuted this perversion into justice. From my observation and experience of all the flourishing nations *Note this, reader!* everywhere, what is taking place, so help me God, is nothing but a conspiracy of the rich, as it were, who look out for themselves under the pretext of serving the commonwealth. They think up and devise all ways and means, first of keeping (and having no fear of losing) what they have heaped up through underhanded deals, and then of taking advantage of the poor by buying their labor and toil as cheaply as possible. Once the rich have decreed in the name of the public (including the poor) that these schemes must be observed, then they become laws.

But after these depraved creatures, in their insatiable greed, have divided among themselves all the goods which would have sufficed for everyone, they are still very far from the happiness of the Utopian commonwealth; there, once the use of money was abolished, and together with it all greed for it, what a mass of troubles was cut away, what a crop of crimes was pulled up by the roots! Is there anyone who does not know that fraud, theft, plunder, strife, turmoil, contention, rebellion, murder, treason, poisoning, crimes which are constantly punished but never held in check, would die away if money were eliminated? And also that at the very instant when money disappeared, so would fear, anxiety, worries, toil, and sleepless nights? Indeed, poverty itself, which seems to be merely the lack of money, would itself immediately fade away if money were everywhere totally abolished.

To make this clearer, imagine some barren year of bad harvests when many thousands of people die of hunger. I maintain it is clear that at the end of this famine, if you examined the barns of the rich, you would find so much grain that if it had been divided among those swept away by starvation and disease, no one would have noticed any effect at all of the failure of weather and soil. It would have been easy to provide food if that blessed money, that invention very clearly designed to open the way to what we need to live, were not the only barrier to keep us from it. I have no doubt that the rich also understand this and are not unaware how much better it would be to lack no necessities than to abound in so many superfluities, to be relieved of so many troubles than to be hemmed in by such great wealth. And in fact I have no doubt that everyone's concern for his own well-being or the authority of our savior Christ (who is so wise that he cannot be unaware of what is best and so good that he would never advise what he knew was not the best) would long since have easily drawn the whole world to adopt the laws of this commonwealth, if it were not held back by one and only one monster, the prince and parent of all plagues, pride.

Pride measures prosperity not by her own advantages but by the disadvantages of others. She would *A striking phrase* not even wish to be a goddess unless there were some wretches left whom she could order about and lord it over, whose misery would make her happiness seem all the more extraordinary, whose poverty can be tormented and exacerbated by a display of her wealth. This infernal serpent, pervading the human heart, keeps men from reforming their lives, holding them back like a suckfish.[90]

Since pride is too firmly fixed in the minds of men to be easily plucked out, I am glad that this form of commonwealth, which I would gladly see adopted by everyone, is at least enjoyed by the Utopians; they have followed ethical principles which

---

90 The remora has a suck-disk on top of its head, by which it attaches itself to larger fish or ships; impressed by its tenacity, the ancients thought it could impede the progress of a ship.

enabled them to lay the foundations of a common-wealth that is not only most happy but also, so far as human prescience can foresee, likely to last forever. For now that they have eradicated factional strife and ambition at home, along with the other vices, there is no danger that they can be disturbed by domestic discord, which has been the sole reason for the downfall of many prosperous and splendidly fortified cities. But as long as their domestic tranquility and wholesome social structure is preserved, the envy of all the surrounding princes cannot shock or unsettle their dominion, though in the past they have often unsuccessfully tried to do so.

When Raphael had ended his tale, there occurred to me quite a few institutions established by the customs and laws of that nation which seemed to me quite absurd, not only in their way of waging war, their religious beliefs and practices, and other institutions as well, but also (and above all) in the very point which is the principal foundation of their whole social structure, namely their common life and subsistence with no exchange of money. That one fact entirely undermines all nobility, magnificence, splendor, and majesty, which are (in the popular view) the true adornments and ornaments of a commonwealth.[91] Nevertheless, I knew that his

talk had worn him out, and I was not sure whether he could endure to listen to an opinion contrary to his own—especially since I remembered that he had reproached some persons precisely because they thought they would not be considered wise unless they could find some way of picking apart the ideas of others—and so, having praised their regimen and his own exposition, I took his hand and led him in to dinner, though first I said we would have another time to consider these matters more thoroughly and to confer more fully. I only wish this would happen someday!

Meanwhile, just as I can hardly agree with all the points he made (even though he is a person of unquestionable learning and wide experience of human affairs), so too I readily confess that in the Utopian commonwealth are very many features which in our societies I would wish rather than expect to see.

THE END OF THE SECOND BOOK

The end of the afternoon discourse
of Raphael Hythloday
about the laws and institutions of the little-known
island of Utopia recorded by the most illustrious
and learned gentleman Master Thomas More
citizen and undersheriff of London

---

91 What "More" says here is in keeping with his earlier Aristotelian arguments against community of property. Aristotle continually associates nobility and the highest virtue with wealth; he defines magnificence as "suitable expenditure on a grand scale" (*Nicomachean Ethics* 4.2.1.1122a). But many readers get the impression that More lets the mask of the character "More" slip to reveal a hint of irony.

JEROME BUSLEYDEN
TO THOMAS MORE, GREETINGS.

It was not enough for you, most distinguished More, to have long devoted all your pains, labor, and energy to the interest and advantage of individuals, but your kindness and generosity have prompted you to bestow them also on the general good. You thought that this service of yours, whatever it might be, deserved the greater popularity, sued the greater favor, and sought the greater glory in proportion as it was likely to profit the greater number when extended more widely and conferred on more recipients. Though you have always aimed at this goal on other occasions, yet you have recently secured your object with wonderful success by putting down in writing that afternoon conversation by which you have given to the world a description of the good and just constitution, which all must desire, in the commonwealth of Utopia.

In your happy description of that most excellent system we cannot miss anything either of consummate learning or of complete knowledge of the world in which we live. Both meet so perfectly on an equality and parity that neither confesses itself beaten but both contend on equal terms for the palm of glory. You are so well equipped with varied learning as well as with wide and unerring experience of the world that whatever you write you assert on the grounds of experience and whatever you have determined to assert you write with the greatest learning. This is truly a wonderful and rare felicity, which is the rarer the more it jealously withholds itself from most and gives itself only to a rare few. The latter are chiefly those men who not only want sincerely to serve the common good but who also have the learning to know how, the trust of others to be able, and the prestige with the corresponding power, and who consequently can serve as loyally and honestly and wisely as you are now nobly doing. Regarding yourself as born not for yourself alone but for the whole world, you have thought it worthwhile by your most glorious merit to lay even the whole world itself under an obligation.

In no other way could you have better or more rightly secured this object than by holding up before reasonable mortals themselves that ideal of a commonwealth, that pattern and perfect model of morality, whose equal has never been seen anywhere in the world for the soundness of its constitution, for its perfection, and for its desirability. It far surpasses and leaves a long way behind the many celebrated and much lauded commonwealths of the Spartans, Athenians, and Romans. If these latter had been founded under the same auspices and regulated by the same institutions, laws, decrees, and customs as this state of yours, assuredly they would not yet lie ruined and leveled to the ground—and now, alas, annihilated beyond any hope of restoration. They would, rather, still be intact, prosperous, happy, and most fortunate—all the while mistresses of the world, sharing their wide dominion by land and sea.

You pitied the pitiable fate of these commonwealths, and you wished to save those which today hold the hegemony from a like vicissitude of fortune by using this perfect commonwealth of yours as a means. The latter has devoted its energies not so much to framing laws as to training the most qualified officials. It has not done so without reason, for otherwise, if we are to believe Plato, even the best laws would all be counted dead. After the likeness of such officials, the pattern of their virtue, the example of their conduct, and the picture of their justice, the whole setup and proper course of a perfect commonwealth should be modeled. Above all else, there should be a combination of wisdom in the administrators, bravery in the soldiers, temperance in individuals, and justice in all.

Since this commonwealth of yours, which you praise so highly, is obviously an excellent blend of these virtues, it is no wonder if on this account it comes to be not only formidable to many nations but also revered by all of them, and likewise worthy to be celebrated through all the centuries. This is the more so because, all wrangling over private possession having been eliminated, no one has any property of his own. Moreover, with a view to the common interest, all men have all things in common so that every object and every action, whether public or private, regards not the greed of the many or the caprice of the few, but, however small it is, is totally directed to the maintenance of one uniform justice, equality, and communion. The necessary result of this absolute singleness of purpose is the complete elimination of everything that causes, promotes, and fosters intrigue, luxury, jealousy, and injustice. Into these evils mortals are sometimes driven, even though reluctant, by the private ownership of property, or the burning thirst for gain, or that most

pitiable of passions, ambition, to their immense and unparalleled loss. From these causes often suddenly arise clashes of minds, military preparations, and wars worse than civil. By the latter misfortunes
5 not only is the prosperous condition of most flourishing commonwealths completely destroyed, but their old renown, their past triumphs, their glorious trophies, and their rich spoils, so often won through the conquest of enemies, are totally blotted out of
10 memory.

If in these points this letter of ours should perhaps win less credit than I should wish, certainly there will be at hand the most reliable witnesses to which I can refer you, to wit, all the great cities laid
15 waste, the states destroyed, the commonwealths overthrown, the villages fired and consumed. Today there are scarcely any remains or ruins to be seen of their great catastrophe. Hardly are their names properly recorded by any history, however old and
20 far-reaching. Such notable disasters, devastations, destructions, and calamities of war our commonwealths one and all will easily escape provided that they organize themselves exactly on the one pattern of the Utopian commonwealth and do not depart
25 from it, as they say, by a hair's breadth. By doing so, they will at last most fully recognize by the successful reality how greatly they have benefited by the service you have rendered them. Especially will they have learned thereby how to keep their own com-
30 monwealth safe, unharmed, and triumphant. Accordingly these states will owe you a great debt for saving them in their hour of need—a debt such as is rightly merited by one who has reserved not an individual member of the commonwealth but the en-
35 tire commonwealth itself.

Meanwhile, farewell, and continue successfully to devise, execute, and perfect ever fresh benefits for the commonwealth. They will make the commonwealth eternal and you immortal. Farewell, most
40 learned and most beneficent More, glory of your Britain and of this world of ours.

From our house at Mechlin, 1516

GERHARD GELDENHAUER
OF NIJMEGEN ABOUT UTOPIA

Reader, do you like what is pleasant? In this book 45 is everything that is pleasant. Do you hunt what is profitable? You can read nothing more profitable. If you wish both the pleasant and the profitable, this island abounds in both. By them you may polish your expression and improve your mind. In this 50 book the very sources of right and wrong are revealed by the eloquent More, the chief glory of his native London.

CORNELIS DE SCHRIJVER
TO THE READER 55

Do you want to see new marvels now that a new world has been discovered not long ago? Do you want to learn ways of living different in nature from our own? Do you want to know the sources of the virtues? Do you want to uncover the original causes 60 of the world's evils and to experience the great emptiness lying concealed at the heart of things? Read these pages which the celebrated More has given us in variegated color—More, the honor of London's famous men. 65

JOHN DESMARAIS[1]
OF CASSEL TO MASTER
PETER GILES, GREETINGS.

I have read the *Utopia* of your friend More, together with his *Epigrams*, whether with greater pleasure or 70 greater admiration I cannot decide. O happy Britain which now flourishes with men of such talent as to be able to contend with antiquity itself! O we dullards, nay, more than blockheads, if precedents so close to us cannot rouse us to strive for like 75 praise. "It is disgraceful to keep silent," said Aristotle, "if Isocrates still speaks." We should be ashamed to have time only for lucrative transactions and for pleasures when among the British at the ends of the earth learning flourishes highly on account of the 80 favor and kindness of kings.

---

1 Public Rhetor at the University of Louvain

Although praise for learning has belonged almost exclusively to Greece and Italy, nevertheless Spain, too, has some shining names among the ancients to boast of. Savage Scythia has her Anacharsides, Denmark has her Saxo, France has her Budé. Germany has numerous figures famous for learning. England has very many and these pre-eminent. What conjectures should we make about all the rest if More is so outstanding—in spite of the fact that he is, first, still a young man; next, much distracted by public and domestic affairs; and, finally, professing any activity other than scholarship as his calling.

We alone seem in our own eyes sufficiently happy if proper provision has been made for our bodily pleasure and our money coffer. Indeed, even we, shaking off our lethargy, are girding ourselves for this most noble contest. To be conquered in it is not shameful, and to conquer is most glorious.

Countless examples on all sides summon us to the contest. Charles,[2] the best of princes, who rewards nothing more highly than learned virtue, summons us to it. The one and only Maecenas or patron of every noble pursuit, Jean le Sauvage, Chancellor of Burgundy, summons us.

With greater urgency, I beg you, most learned Peter Giles, to see, as soon as feasible, to the publication of *Utopia*. Whatever pertains to the good constitution of a commonwealth may be seen in it as in a mirror. Would that, just as the Utopians have begun to receive our religion, so we might borrow from them their system of public administration! This perhaps might happen easily if a number of distinguished and invincible theologians would betake themselves to the island. They would promote the faith of Christ already sprouting there and at the same time bring home to us the customs and laws of the Utopian people.

Utopia owes much to Hythloday who has made known a country unworthy of remaining unknown. Its debt is even greater to the very learned More whose pencil has very skillfully drawn it for us. In turn, not the least part of the thanks which are due to both must be shared with you: it is you who will bring into public view both Hythloday's discourse and More's written account. It will serve as a great delight for all—and bring even greater profit if they weigh all its elements carefully.

Utopia has so stirred my soul that, although unaccustomed to their company for a long time, I have again summoned the muses—how happily, you must judge.

Farewell, most honest Peter Giles, you who are both votary and patron of the fine arts.

From our house in Louvain, December 1.

POEM ON THE NEW ISLAND
OF UTOPIA BY THE SAME AUTHOR,
JOHN DESMARAIS,
ORATOR OF THE UNIVERSITY OF
LOUVAIN

Brave men were the gift of Rome, eloquent men
the gift of lauded Greece,
frugal men the gift of famous Sparta, uncorrupted
men the gift of Marseilles,
hardy men of Germany. Courteous and witty men
were the gift of the land of Attica.
Pious men were once the gift of renowned France,
wary men of Africa.
Munificent men were once the gift of the land of
Britain.
Examples of the different virtues are sought in
different peoples,
and what is lacking in one abounds in another.
The total sum of all virtue
once for all is the gift of the island of Utopia to
earth-born men.

THOMAS MORE
TO HIS FRIEND PETER GILES,
WARMEST GREETINGS.

My dear Peter, I was thoroughly delighted with the judgment you know about, delivered by that very sharp fellow in the form of a dilemma directed against my *Utopia:* if the story is being presented as true, I find some things in it rather absurd; if it is a fiction, then I think that More's usual good judgment is lacking on some points. I am very grateful to this man, my dear Peter, whoever he may be, who

2 the future Emperor Charles V

I suspect is learned and whom I see as a friendly critic. I do not know whether any other critique since the book came out has pleased me as much as this one. For, first of all, motivated either by his regard for me or for the work itself, it seems that he did not begrudge the effort of reading it all the way through, and that not cursorily and hastily the way priests read the divine office (if they do so at all) but deliberately and carefully so as to weigh the details thoughtfully. And then, after criticizing some points, and not very many at that, he declares that he approves of the rest, not thoughtlessly but judiciously. Finally, even in the language with which he castigates me he praises me more highly than those who deliberately set out to praise me. For he gives a clear indication what a splendid opinion he has of me when he complains that he is disappointed when he reads a passage that is not as precise as it should be, whereas I myself exceed my own hopes if I happen to be able to publish something in the whole lot that is at least not absolutely absurd.

But in fact, to deal with him no less frankly in turn, I do not see why he should consider himself so eagle-eyed and, as the Greeks say, sharp-sighted, if he discovers some things rather absurd in the institutions of the Utopians or finds that in setting up a commonwealth I have not thought through some matters in a sufficiently practical way, as if there were no absurdities elsewhere in the world, or as if any of all the philosophers everywhere had so devised a commonwealth, a ruler, or a household so perfectly as to propound nothing that could not be improved. On that point, if it were not that I consider as sacred the memory of the most extraordinary men who have been hallowed from ancient times, I could certainly point out features from each of them which everyone would undoubtedly agree in condemning.

But when he is in doubt whether the work is true or fictitious, on this point I think his own usual good judgment is lacking. Nevertheless, I do not deny that if I had decided to write about the commonwealth and a story such as this had occurred to me, I would not have shrunk from a fictional presentation which would make the truth slip more pleasantly into the mind like medicine smeared with honey. But certainly I would have managed it so that, even though I might have wanted to deceive the ignorant mob, I would at least have inserted some pointed hints which would have let the more learned discover what I was about. Thus even if I had done nothing more than assign to the ruler, river, city, and island such names as would have informed learned readers that the island is nowhere, the city is a phantom, the river has no water, the ruler no people—which would not have been hard to do and would have been much more elegant than what I actually did, for if I had not been forced by historical accuracy, I am not so stupid as to use those barbarous and meaningless names Utopia, Anyder, Amaurot, and Ademus.[3]

But my dear Giles, since I see that some people are so cautious, wary, and sagacious that they can hardly be induced to believe what we simple and credulous souls wrote down at Hythloday's dictation, lest such persons should mistrust not only the accuracy of the story but also my own credibility, I am glad that I can say for my brainchild what Mysis in Terence says to keep Glycerius's boy from being considered a changeling: "By heaven, I thank goodness that there were some freeborn matrons present at the birth."[4] For luckily for me it so happens that Raphael told his tale not only to you and me but also to many very respectable and upstanding men. I do not know whether he related more numerous or notable details but I am sure he told them no fewer and no less remarkable matters than he did to us.

But if these incredulous persons will not take even their word for it, they can visit Hythloday himself, for he has not yet died. I just heard from some persons who recently returned from Portugal that on the first day of last March he was healthy and vigorous as ever. Therefore let them ask him for the truth or question him to ferret it out, as long as they understand that I am responsible only for my own work, not for the trustworthiness of others.

Farewell, dearest Peter, to you and your charming wife and pretty little daughter, to whom my wife wishes long life and good health.

3 This sentence is incomplete in the Latin and has been left so in the translation.   **4** *Andria* 4.4.770–71

This illustration by Hans Holbein the Younger is the last page in the 1518 editions of Thomas More's *Utopia*. The Greek at top and bottom is Matthew 10:16: "so be wise as serpents and innocent as doves." The Latin at the left is from Martial 10.47 (regarding what constitutes a happy life): "shrewd simplicity and love of doing right." The Hebrew at the right is from Psalm 125:4: "Do good, O Lord, to those who are good, to those who are upright in their hearts."

216

Epigrams

More wrote almost all his Latin poetry from 1500 to 1520. With the help of Erasmus, the *Epigrams* were first published in March 1518 by Froben in a volume that contained More's *Utopia*, his epigrams, and Erasmus's epigrams as well. Another edition followed from Froben in December 1518, and in 1520 the *Epigrams* were printed as their own volume, with More himself involved in the editing (*CW* 3.2: 7). The *Epigrams* were also later printed in the 1563 *Lucubrationes* and the 1565, 1566, and 1689 *Opera omnia*. As their correspondence indicates, More and Erasmus discussed the publication of the *Epigrams* before June 1516 (see Letters 19 [*EE* 424: 81], 20, 87, 90).

More's major source for his *Epigrams* is the Planudean Anthology, a collection of 2,400 Greek epigrams. At least 106 of More's poems are translations from this source; other sources for his *Epigrams* include Aesop, Plutarch, Seneca, Cicero, Aristotle, Martial, and Lucian, along with proverbs, English songs, and the work of a few contemporaries such as Bebel and Poggio (*CW* 3.2: 12). The prefatory letter from Beatus Rhenanus explains that good epigrams must display "wit combined with brevity," and must "end promptly with a witty point," to the delight of the reader. More's epigrams, Rhenanus observes, are seasoned by the author's mirth and sharp wit, displaying his learning and keen judgment as well.

More's *Epigrams* opens with the "Progymnasmata," preparatory exercises composed by Thomas More and William Lily, who was appointed high master of St. Paul's School in 1510. As the Yale editors observe, "More and Lily may be credited with the invention of the variorum translation of selected Greek epigrams that was to have a brilliant history in the schools and beyond" (*CW* 3.2: 13). These exercises were likely composed before 1510.

The rest of the poems in *Epigrams* address a rich array of subjects and human experiences, in a variety of tones and forms. There are poems on friendship, folly, family, law, philosophy, theology, politics, social life, death, and tyranny; there are personal poems on More's children, and on his meeting with an older woman, now a mother, with whom he had been infatuated as a young man; there is the "Coronation Ode," through which More addresses England and the newly crowned Henry VIII in the fashion of a friendly, yet challenging, orator; there are poems on animals and other earthy subjects, which kindled More's comic muse throughout his life, to the occasional dismay of friends and readers.

More's international quarrel with Germanus Brixius began with the publication of More's satirical epigrams in 1518. These poems occasioned Brixius's counterblast, the *Antimorus*, which in turn prompted additional epigrams from More, as well as his "Letter to Brixius," printed in the "Humanist Letters" section below. The quarrel ended only through the intercessions of Erasmus, and More agreed to recall and destroy copies of his letter.

Among More's writings, few provide as many angles on the author, or reveal as much of his complex mind, as this collection of his poetry. Yale editors Leicester Bradner and Charles Lynch see More's work as "incomparably the best book of Latin epigrams in the sixteenth century," displaying a poetic style that is "never inflated or pompous, and almost always endowed with the virtues of his prose—logical energy, muscular realism, and penetrating intelligence" (*CW* 3.2: 63, 41). Regarding More's style and rhetoric in the *Epigrams*, Elizabeth McCutcheon points out that "More characteristically subverts, questions, or reopens an initial claim, inverts an old proverb, or otherwise renders an epigram open-ended, by juxtaposition, by ambiguity of language and allusion, by exploiting different points of view and incongruities of situation, and by innumerable other rhetorical strategies" (*Moreana* nos. 201–2: 219–20).

Among the groups of poems in the *Epigrams*, the political poems are particularly striking and reveal something of More's mature political philosophy. Bradner and Lynch see these political poems as a uniquely Morean contribution to the epigram genre (*CW* 3.2: 62).

Much work remains to be done studying these poems and relating them to More's other works, especially their companion piece in the early editions, *Utopia*, the Latin vocabulary of which connects to the *Epigrams* in rich and mutually illuminating ways.

The translations provided are from Yale *CW* 3.2; they are prose translations of the Latin poetry.

EPIGRAMMATA CLARISSIMI DISERTISSIMIQVE VIRI THOMAE MORI BRITANNI, PLERAQVE E GRAECIS VERSA.

This title page appeared in the first publication of More's *Epigrams* (in the March 1518 edition of *Utopia*) and again in a 1520 edition of More's *Epigrams* alone. At the bottom, left, is pictured the Roman hero Gaius Mucius Scaevola holding his right hand in the fire while defiantly opposing King Porsenna, who is invading Rome. (See Livy 2.12.)

The Epigrams
of the very famous and learned Englishman
THOMAS MORE printed to agree with
the author's own corrected copy

Beatus Rhenanus[1] greets Willibald Pirckheimer,[2] councilor to the Emperor Maximilian and member of the Nuremberg Senate.

It has seemed to me, most renowned Willibald, exquisitely fitting to inscribe to you in particular this book that our friend Erasmus of Rotterdam recently sent to me, the *Epigrams* of Thomas More, that ornament of Britain, since you and More resemble each other in so many respects. You are both skilled in the law, both learned in Greek as well as Latin. Not only are you both occupied in the public duties of your respective states, but, because of your unusual skill in resolving problems and your wisdom in council, you are both very dear to your rulers, the one to the very powerful King Henry of England, the other to the most holy Emperor Maximilian. Why mention wealth, which you both have in great plenty, so that neither of you lacks whatever distinction is thought to accrue from riches, or rather so that you both have the means in plentiful abundance for setting examples of good deeds, particularly deeds of generosity. Both of you had fathers noted no less for their learning than for their distinguished birth. And so, since likeness and equality are the source of friendship, I have decided that it is very appropriate to dedicate this work of More's to you so that, although for many other reasons you already honor the author with your affection, you may as a result of these *Epigrams* embrace, love, and esteem him even more. And furthermore, there is no one to whom these most delightful diversions can be sent more fittingly than to one who has himself been wont from time to time to descend, as they say, into the same arena. That is to say, if anyone has himself at one time or another tried out his ingenuity at this kind of composition, he is the very man who will know how remarkable a thing is a learned epigram. Truly an epigram, as you know, must have wit combined with brevity; it must be lighthearted, and then it must end promptly with a witty point which the Greeks call ἐπιφώνημα. Surely one may find all these properties in these *Epigrams* of More, especially in those which he himself composed; in the others, which are translated from the Greek, the credit for originality belongs to the ancients. Still, here too, More deserves to be rated as high for translating well from a foreign tongue as for his own work. Undoubtedly the labor of a translator is often greater. This is so because the author is unfettered and freely at liberty to use whatever occurs to him, but the translator is required to keep something else continually in sight; that is, of course, what he has chosen to translate. Whenever this is the case, his skill is much more severely taxed than when he produces something of his own.

In both these fields Thomas More is very remarkable, for he composes most tastefully and translates most happily. How pleasantly his poetry flows! How utterly unforced is his work! How adroit it all is! Here is nothing harsh, nothing rough, nothing obscure. He is bright, sharp, a master of Latin. Furthermore, he seasons all his work with a certain very delightful humor so that I have never seen anything more charming. I could believe that the Muses conferred upon him all there is anywhere of mirth, charm, and wit. How gracefully he pokes fun at Sabinus[3] for bringing up another's children as his own. How wittily he ridicules Lalus,[4] who went to such lengths in his desire to seem French. And yet his witticisms are by no means ill-natured, but rather are honest, sweet, mild, anything but bitter. He provokes laughter, but in every case without pain; he ridicules, but without abuse.

---

1 Rhenanus (1485–1547), also known as Beatus Bild, was a German humanist and editor of Seneca, Tacitus, and Livy.

2 Pirckheimer (1470–1530) was a humanist and city councilor of Nuremberg before he was appointed imperial councilor to

Emperor Maximilian I in 1499. **3** See Epigrams 196, 205, 220. **4** See Epigram 95.

80 At present Italy admires Pontanus and Marullus[5] more than most epigrammatists, but I would wager my life that there is just as much inherent skill in this author of ours and more profit, unless it is possible that someone think it very profitable when Marullus celebrates his Neaera and in many
85 places speaks in riddles, acting like another Heraclitus, or when Johannes Pontanus revives for us the lewdness of the ancient epigrammatists; and nothing could be more uninteresting or less worth reading for a man of principles, not to mention a man
90 of Christian principles. Of course, they longed to imitate antiquity. To preserve the appearance of antiquity untainted, they avoided what was Christian just as Pomponius Laetus, a man excessively Roman, avoided what was Greek, lest he destroy the
95 purity of the Latin language.

Well, just as these amusing trifles of More's demonstrate his natural gifts and his unusual learning, so the very keen judgment he has in politics will be quite apparent from his *Utopia*. Of that I shall
100 make only brief mention in passing because it was praised in a magnificent preface, as well it might be, by a most exacting scholar, Budé,[6] that supreme master of the nobler learning, that great and even unmatched glory of France. The *Utopia* contains
105 such principles as cannot be found in Plato, in Aristotle, or even in the *Pandects*[7] of your Justinian. Its lessons are less philosophical, perhaps, than theirs but more Christian. And yet (listen, by the Muses, to a good story) when the *Utopia* was mentioned
110 here recently at a certain gathering of a few responsible men and when I praised it, a certain dolt insisted that no more thanks were due to More than to any secretary who merely records the opinions of others at a council, sitting in after the fashion
115 of an "extra," as they say, and without expressing any opinions of his own, because all More said was taken from the mouth of Hythloday and merely written down by More. Therefore, he said, More deserved praise only because he had recorded these
120 matters well. And there were some present who approved the fellow's opinion as that of a man of very

sound perception. *Do you not, then, welcome this elegant wit of More, who can impose upon such men as these, no ordinary men, but widely respected and theologians at that?*[8]
125

Finally, in case you would like to know this too, William Lily,[9] More's companion with whom he contended in the translation from the Greek of the epigrams included in this volume under the title *Progymnasmata*,[10] is an Englishman, learned in ev
130 ery way, intimately familiar not only with the Greek authors, but also with the customs native to that people, in that he spent some years on the island of Rhodes. He now conducts with great success a grammar school founded by Colet[11] in London.
135

I have only this left to say: when you have the opportunity, amid the duties which keep you so very busy conferring with embassies and administering the state, pick up this book, read it, and become an admirer of More, whose face, I think, you have not
140 yet seen; but you have known him a long time from his writings. Farewell, most illustrious sir.

Basel, 23 February 1518.

PROGYMNASMATA
EXERCISES BY THE FRIENDLY RIVALS
THOMAS MORE AND WILLIAM LILY

1
THOMAS MORE'S, ON A MISER
When Asclepiades the miser saw a mouse in his house, he said, "Friend mouse, what are you doing in my home?" The mouse, with a pleasant smile, replied, "Lay aside your fear, my friend; it is not board
5 but lodging I want here."

WILLIAM LILY'S
Asclepiades the miser saw a mouse in his house and said, "Friend mouse, what are you doing in here with me?" The mouse smiled and said, "Have no
10 fear, friend; what I want of you is not board but room."

5 Jovianus Pontanus (*ca.* 1426–1503) and Michael Marullus (*ca.* 1458–1500) were Italian poets.   **6** William, or Guillaume, Budé (1467–1530) was a leading humanist scholar in France.   **7** The *Pandects* (or *Digest*), commissioned by Emperor

Justinian I, is a collection of writings by Roman jurists.   **8** This italicized sentence was originally written in Greek.   **9** Lily (*ca.* 1468–1522) was a classical scholar and the first headmaster of Colet's grammar school at St. Paul's in London.

10 a classical form of rhetorical exercise (literally "before-exercises")   **11** John Colet (1467–1519), dean of St. Paul's Cathedral, was a spiritual influence on More and Erasmus.

2
WILLIAM LILY'S, ON A MISER
You have the wealth of a rich man, but a pauper's spirit—you who are wealthy in your heir's behalf, but poor for yourself alone.

THOMAS MORE'S
You have the wealth of a rich man, but yours is a poor man's mind, unhappy man, rich for your heir and poor for yourself.

3
WILLIAM LILY'S, ON THE
UNCERTAINTY OF PROPERTY
We fields recently belonged to Achaemenides, but now Menippus owns us. And we fall now to this one and then again to another, for not long ago that fellow thought he owned us, and now another thinks he does. We are composed of nothing but Chance.

THOMAS MORE'S
Not long ago I belonged to Achaemenides; now, presto, I belong to Menippus. And I shall pass again from one to another. This one thinks he owns me, that one thought he did. But really I am only Luck's field.

4
THOMAS MORE'S, ON EXTRAVAGANCE
To build many residences and to feed many people is surely the direct road to poverty.

WILLIAM LILY'S
To support many persons and to establish numerous residences—that is the road to extreme poverty.

5
WILLIAM LILY'S, ON REASONABLE
EXPENDITURE
May you make use of your wealth as if you were marked for death, and conserve your wealth as if you were destined to live. Truly, he is the wise man who, by pondering both these attitudes, conserves his wealth and sets a limit to his spending.

THOMAS MORE'S
As though death were at hand, enjoy the wealth you have acquired. And again, spare your wealth as if you were certain to live. The wise man is he who, by a proper consideration of these alternatives, is both frugal and generous in due measure.

6
THOMAS MORE'S, ON SCORNING LUCK
Now I have reached port; Hope and Luck, farewell. You have nothing to do with me. Now make sport of others.

WILLIAM LILY'S
I have reached port; Hope and Luck, farewell. You have nothing to do with me. Now make sport of others.

7
WILLIAM LILY'S, ON DEATH
Naked I arrive on earth, naked, too, I leave. Why do I strive in vain, knowing as I do that death is naked?[12]

THOMAS MORE'S
Just as surely as I came on earth naked, so surely naked shall I quit it. Why do I struggle in vain, knowing as I do that death is naked?

8
THOMAS MORE'S,
ON SELF-INDULGENCE AND LUST
If anyone is in haste to join the shades of the dead below, then baths and wine and the pleasures of love shorten the journey thither.

WILLIAM LILY'S
It is baths and wine and the pleasures of love which drag us in headlong haste to the domain of the prince of darkness.

9
THOMAS MORE'S, ON A FALSE FRIEND
The man who admits his hatred does less harm than he who pretends unqualified affection. When I am warned, I avoid the man who hates me, but how can I avoid one who pretends to be my friend? Undoubtedly, one's worst enemy is he who in the guise

12 See Jb 1:21; Eccl 5:14; Propertius 3.5.14.

of friend deceitfully works mischief by unsuspected guile.

WILLIAM LILY'S

The man who frankly says, "I hate you," does less damage than the man who pretends innocent friendship. Obviously, you will avoid the one you know is dangerous, but not the one who says, "I am your friend." I say that he is a deadly enemy who delights to do secret injury and still enjoys the confidence of friendship.

10
THOMAS MORE'S,
ON A SPARTAN SOLDIER

A cruel Spartan mother saw her son as he was hurrying home after losing his weapons. She snatched up a spear, confronted him, and thrust him through. Then over her murdered son she spoke these unwomanly words: "Unnatural son of Sparta, go now at last to the abode of the dead. Go, you are a disgrace to Sparta and to your family."

WILLIAM LILY'S

When a Spartan mother saw her son, stripped of his arms in battle, returning in haste to his father's house, she leaped upon him and pierced his breast with a spear. Then in a hair-raising speech the maddened creature, more like a man than a woman, addressed the corpse: "Since you have belied your native land of Sparta and your forebears, unnatural son, depart at last to join the dead."

11
THOMAS MORE'S, ON A MAN
BOTH LAME AND STUPID

Your mind is as lame as your leg, and your external condition gives sure signs of your inner state.

WILLIAM LILY'S

You are as slow in your wits as you are afoot, for your outward appearance gives a sample of what lies hidden within.

12
THOMAS MORE'S, THE DILEMMA OF
THEOPHRASTUS, FROM AULUS GELLIUS

If by merely knowing your appointed troubles you could avoid them, then surely it would be a fine thing to know what troubles you would encounter. But if you do not have the power to avoid the troubles which you know are coming, what help is it to learn in advance of the suffering you must endure in any case?

WILLIAM LILY'S

If it were possible for you to see misfortunes approaching and, with your foresight, to avoid them, then it would be pleasant to know them. But if you must inevitably suffer the misfortunes you seek to discover, what good is foresight, for you must endure them in any case.

A POEM IN IAMBIC TRIMETER
BY THOMAS MORE

If you could discover in advance what suffering you must endure, and if you could avoid it, then it would be good for you to know. But if, despite your knowledge, suffer you must, what advantage is there in knowing, for the suffering is inevitable.

13
THOMAS MORE'S, ON TWO BROTHERS
WHO WERE BORN AND DIED
ON THE SAME DAY

This tomb contains four brothers. Two of them a single day brought to birth and to death.

WILLIAM LILY'S

This tomb contains four brothers. Two of them were born on the same day and on the same day died.

14
THOMAS MORE'S, ON JUPITER
TRANSFORMED

Jupiter was a bull, a swan, a satyr, and gold, for love of Europa, Leda, Antiope, Danae.[13]

---

13 Europa became Crete's first queen and mother of Minos and Rhadamanthus. Leda, queen of Sparta and wife of Tyndareus, was the mother of Castor, Pollux, Helen, and Clytemnestra. Antiope was the mother of twin brothers, Amphion and Zethus, who built the walls of Thebes. Danae's father imprisoned her in a tower, on account of a prophecy that her son would kill him. However, Zeus visited her in a shower of gold, and she gave birth to Perseus.

WILLIAM LILY'S

Jupiter became a bull, a swan, a satyr, gold, for love of Europa, Leda, Antiope, Danae.

15

THOMAS MORE'S, ON SAPPHO

They say there are nine Muses. Clearly they are mistaken. Now Sappho of Lesbos is the tenth daughter of Pierus.[14]

WILLIAM LILY'S

How rashly some have said that the sisters are nine! Lo, here is Lesbian Sappho the tenth of the Muses.

16

WILLIAM LILY'S, ON A BRONZE
IMAGE OF A SATYR

Either a satyr was applied to the bronze or, induced by artistry, that same bronze was applied to a satyr.

THOMAS MORE'S

This bronze, while it was being worked with thoroughly admirable skill, either coated a satyr or was inclosed by a satyr.

ANOTHER VERSION BY MORE

Either a satyr is fitted to that bronze statue, or a satyr is fitted with that bronze statue.

17

WILLIAM LILY'S,
ON A STATUE OF NIOBE

The gods deprived me of life and turned me to stone. But it was Praxiteles who from stone restored me to life.

THOMAS MORE'S

The gods changed me from a living creature to stone; but when I was stone, Praxiteles made me live again.

18

THOMAS MORE'S, ON A STATUE
OF NEOPTOLEMUS

The entire city of Cecrops honors you, Neoptolemus, with this statue. It is in part your devotion and in part your loyalty which cause the city to do you this honor.

WILLIAM LILY'S

The people of Athens, Neoptolemus, have honored you with this statue because of your devotion and loyalty.

END OF THE PREPARATORY EXERCISES
WRITTEN IN FRIENDLY COLLABORATION BY
THOMAS MORE AND WILLIAM LILY

---

14 Sappho was a Greek lyric poet (*ca.* 610–570 BC). Although the Muses are often called the "Pierides," the daughters of Pierus were maidens who challenged the Muses in song, and were changed into magpies for their presumption.

Epigrams
of the very famous and learned Englishman
THOMAS MORE in large part translated from the Greek

I fear, most glorious prince, that while I was trying to win favor for my awkward verses by the
addition of color (like maidens who have insufficient confidence in their beauty), I may have robbed
them of that characteristic by which they could
have given you the greatest pleasure—I mean time-
liness. For when I had finished writing them at the
time of your coronation and had handed them over
to an illuminator for decoration, an attack of the
gout, no less, by which the illuminator was most inopportunely afflicted immediately upon undertaking the task, has caused me to present my verses to
you only now, considerably later than the circumstances seemed to require. And so (if, in accord with
your inherent kindness, you give me leave to deal
informally with the matter) I do not know whether
greater charm was given to my verses by the illuminator's hands or taken from them by his feet. In any
case it is because of his feet that I am constrained to
fear that my expression of joy may seem to you no
less late, no less untimely, than, in antiquity, the famous expression of sorrow by the citizens of Troy
seemed to the Emperor Tiberius. The Trojans com-
miserated with the Emperor on the loss of a son
who had been dead for a long time. The Emperor
with ready wit made fun of their condolences by
saying that he too sympathized with them in their
loss of that noble warrior Hector.[1] But their effort,
directed at a grief that was not merely fading but
had wholly passed away, could not be anything but
ridiculous. Mine, however, is preserved from this
defect by the immeasurable rejoicing occasioned
by your thronged coronation; for since that joy has
filled the hearts of all with an emotion so strong
and lasting that it cannot fade even in a whole lifetime, the result is that this offering of mine seems to
have arrived, not late and when the event was past
and forgotten, but in time and while the event is

still with us. Farewell, most glorious and (although
this title is strange and rare for kings) most beloved
prince.

19
ON THE CORONATION DAY OF HENRY VIII, MOST GLORIOUS AND BLESSED KING OF THE BRITISH ISLES, AND OF CATHERINE HIS MOST HAPPY QUEEN, A POETICAL EXPRESSION OF GOOD WISHES BY THOMAS MORE OF LONDON

If ever there was a day, England, if ever there was a
time for you to give thanks to those above, this is
that happy day, one to be marked with a pure white
stone and put in your calendar. This day is the limit
of our slavery, the beginning of our freedom, the end
of sadness, the source of joy, for this day consecrates
a young man who is the everlasting glory of our time
and makes him your king—a king who is worthy not
merely to govern a single people but singly to rule
the whole world—such a king as will wipe the tears
from every eye and put joy in the place of our long
distress.[2] Every heart smiles to see its cares dispelled,
as the day shines bright when clouds are scattered.
Now the people, freed, run before their king with
bright faces. Their joy is almost beyond their own
comprehension. They rejoice, they exult, they leap
for joy and celebrate their having such a king. "The
King" is all that any mouth can say.

The nobility, long since at the mercy of the dregs
of the population, the nobility, whose title has too
long been without meaning, now lifts its head, now
rejoices in such a king, and has proper reason for rejoicing. The merchant, heretofore deterred by numerous taxes, now once again plows seas grown
unfamiliar. Laws, heretofore powerless—yes, even
laws put to unjust end—now happily have regained
their proper authority. All are equally happy. All
weigh their earlier losses against the advantages to
come. Now each man happily does not hesitate to
show the possessions which in the past his fear kept

1 See Suetonius, *Tiberius* 52.2.   2 See Rv 21:14; Is 25:8.

hidden in dark seclusion. Now there is enjoyment in any profit which managed to escape the many sly clutching hands of the many thieves. No longer is it a criminal offense to own property which was honestly acquired (formerly it was a serious offense). No longer does fear hiss whispered secrets in one's ear, for no one has secrets either to keep or to whisper. Now it is a delight to ignore informers. Only ex-informers fear informers now.

The people gather together, every age, both sexes, and all ranks. There is no reason why they should lurk in their homes and not take part while the king, after completion of the proper ceremonies, undertakes, amid happy auspices, the rule of Britain. Wherever he goes, the dense crowd in their desire to look upon him leaves hardly a narrow lane for his passage. The houses are filled to overflowing, the rooftops strain to support the weight of spectators. On all sides there arises a shout of new good will. Nor are the people satisfied to see the king just once; they change their vantage points time and time again in the hope that, from one place or another, they may see him again. Three times they delight to see him — and why not? This king, than whom Nature has created nothing more deserving of love.

Among a thousand noble companions he stands out taller than any. And he has strength worthy of his regal person. His hand, too, is as skilled as his heart is brave, whether there is an issue to be settled by the naked sword, or an eager charge with leveled lances, or an arrow aimed to strike a target. There is fiery power in his eyes, beauty in his face, and such color in his cheeks as is typical of twin roses. In fact, that face, admirable for its animated strength, could belong to either a young girl or a man. Thus Achilles looked when he pretended to be a maiden,[3] thus he looked when he dragged Hector behind his Thessalian steeds.[4]

Ah, if only nature would permit that, like his body, the outstanding excellence of his mind be visible to the eye. Nay but in fact his virtue does shine forth from his very face; his countenance bears the open message of a good heart, revealing how ripe the wisdom that dwells in his judicious mind, how profound the calm of his untroubled breast, how he bears his lot and manages it whether it be good or bad, how great his care for modest chastity. How serene the clemency that warms his gentle heart, how far removed from arrogance his mind, of these the noble countenance of our prince itself displays the indubitable signs, signs that admit no counterfeit. But his justice, the skill he has in the art of ruling, his sense of responsibility in the treatment of his people — these can easily be discerned from our faces, these must be perceived from the prosperity we enjoy. In that we are treated thus and are gaining our liberty, in that fear, harm, danger, grief have vanished, while peace, ease, joy, and laughter have returned — therein is revealed the excellence of our distinguished prince.

Unlimited power has a tendency to weaken good minds, and that even in the case of very gifted men. But howsoever dutiful he was before, his crown has brought our prince a character which deserves to rule, for he has provided promptly on his first day such advantages as few rulers have granted in extreme old age. He has instantly arrested and imprisoned anyone who by plots had harmed the realm. Whoever was an informer is closely fettered and confined, so that he himself suffers the woes which he imposed on many. Our prince opened the sea for trade. If any overharsh duties were required of the merchants, he lightened their load. And the long-scorned nobility recovered on our prince's first day the ancient rights of nobles. He now gives to good men the honors and public offices which used to be sold to evil men. By a happy reversal of circumstances, learned men now have the prerogatives which ignoramuses carried off in the past. Our prince without delay has restored to the laws their ancient force and dignity (for they had been perverted so as to subvert the realm). And although formerly each rank in the state was changing character completely, now at once every rank is restored. What if, in the hope of being kind to his people, he decided to retract certain provisions of the law which he knew his father had approved? In this he placed, as he should, his country before his father. This preference does not surprise me; what could lie beyond the powers of a prince whose natural gifts have been enhanced by a liberal education, a prince bathed by the nine sisters in the Castalian fount and steeped in philosophy's own precepts? The whole people used to be, on many counts, in debt to the king, and this in particular was the evil

---

3 See Statius, *Achilles* 1.335–37; Ovid, *Metamorphoses* 13.162–70. **4** See *Iliad* 22.395–404.

they feared. But our king, though he could have in-spired fear in this way and could have gathered from this source immense riches, if he had wished to do so, has forgiven the debts of all, and rendered all se-cure, removing all the evil of distressing fear. Hence it is that, while other kings have been feared by their subjects, this king is loved, since now through his ac-tion they have no cause for fear.

O prince, terror to your proud enemies but not to your own people, it is your enemies who fear you; we revere and love you. Our love for you will prove the reason for their fear. And thus it is that, in the absence of sycophants, your subjects' love and your enemies' fear will hedge you round in peace and safety. As for wars beyond the borders—if the French, for instance, join with the Scots—no one is afraid, provided that England is not divided. And internal strife there will not be, for what cause, what reason, is there to provoke it? Most important, con-cerning your right and title to the crown, there is no opposition, nor can there be. You, all by yourself, represent both sides of the quarrel which usually arises; the fact that both your parents were high-born disposes of this problem. And anyway the an-ger of the people, a wicked thing, common source of civil disturbance, is even more remote from you. To all your subjects you are so dear that no man could be dearer to himself. But if perchance wrath were to bring powerful chieftains to war, your nod will promptly put an end to that wrath, such rever-ence for your sacred majesty have your virtues justly created. And whatever virtues your ancestors had, these are yours too, not excelled in ages past. For you, sire, have your father's wisdom, you have your mother's kindly strength, the devout intelligence of your paternal grandmother, the noble heart of your mother's father. What wonder, then, if England re-joices in a fashion heretofore unknown, since she has such a king as she never had before?

And then there is the fact that this joy, appar-ently as great as it could be, was increased by your marriage—a marriage which the kindly powers above arranged and in which they planned well for you and yours. In her you have as wife one whom your people have been happy to see shar-ing your power, one for whom the powers above

care so much that they distinguish her and honor her by marriage with you. She it is who could van-quish the ancient Sabine women in devotion, and in dignity the holy, half-divine heroines of Greece.[5] She could equal the unselfish love of Alcestis[6] or, in her unfailing judgment, outdo Tanaquil.[7] In her expression, in her countenance, there is a remark-able beauty uniquely appropriate for one so great and good. The well-spoken Cornelia[8] would yield to her in eloquence; she is like Penelope[9] in loy-alty to a husband. This lady, prince, vowed to you for many years, through a long time of waiting re-mained alone for love of you. Neither her own sis-ter nor her native land could win her from her way; neither her mother nor her father could dissuade her. It was you, none other, whom she preferred to her mother, sister, native land, and beloved father. This blessed lady has joined in lasting alliance two nations, each of them powerful. She is descended from great kings, to be sure; and she will be the mother of kings as great as her ancestors. Until now one anchor has protected your ship of state—a strong one, yet only one. But your queen, fruitful in male offspring, will render it on all sides stable and everlasting. Great advantage is yours because of her, and similarly is hers because of you. There has been no other woman, surely, worthy to have you as hus-band, nor any other man worthy to have her as wife.

England! bring incense, and an offering more potent than all incense—loyal hearts and inno-cent hands, that heaven, as it has made this mar-riage, may bless it, that the scepter may be swayed with the help of heaven that gave it, and that these crowns may long be worn by these two, and may at length be worn by their son's son and their descen-dants thereafter.

20

ON A SUDDEN RAIN-STORM WHICH FORMED
DURING THE ROYAL PROCESSION BUT
NEITHER OBSCURED THE SUN NOR
LASTED LONG, BY THOMAS MORE

While the king and queen, in as beautiful a proces-sion as there ever was, made their way to receive their sacred crowns, a golden sun shone all around, and the day, like the hearts of the people, was

---

5 The Sabine women ended the war between the Sabines and the Romans. See Livy 1.13.1–4. **6** Best known from Euripides's *Alcestis*, she chose to die in the place of her husband. **7** Through her sagacity and foresight, Tanaquil helped her husband Tarquinius Priscus become the king of Rome. See Livy 1.34, 1.39. **8** Cicero admired the letters of Cornelia, mother of the two Gracchi. See *Brutus* 58.211. **9** See Ovid, *Tristia* 5.14.35–36, for praise of Penelope's loyalty.

cheerful. But as soon as the great procession reached
midtown, the whole procession was drenched with
rain. No cloud, however, obscured the sun's light,
and the storm itself lingered only a very short time.
It was a lucky relief from the heat; whether one regards the phenomenon itself, or the omen, it could
not have been better. To our rulers, days of abundance are promised by Phoebus with his sunshine
and by Jove's wife with her rains.

21

TO THE KING, BY THOMAS MORE

Plato foretold that everything which any particular
time can produce had often existed and would often exist again some time in the future.[10] "As spring
is banished and returns with the swift passage of
the year, as winter at regular intervals returns as it
was before, just so,"[11] he said, "after many revolutions of the speeding sky all things in countless alternations will be again." The golden age came first,
then the silver; after that the bronze, and recently
the iron age. In your reign, sire, the golden age has
returned. Ah, that Plato should be able to foresee
as far as this!

22

TO THE KING ON THE TOURNAMENT
HELD BY HIM, AN IAMBIC EPODE
BY THOMAS MORE

All the tournaments kings have held until now
have been marked by some sad mishap or by disaster thrust among the festivities by ill luck. Sometimes the ground has been drenched with the life-
blood of a stricken knight; sometimes commoners
have been struck by lances or have been trampled by
the pounding hoofs of the maddened steeds; sometimes a scaffolding has collapsed and crushed the
wretched spectators. But this tournament of yours,
sire, the most beautiful we have ever seen, is disfigured by no misfortune; rather it is conspicuous for
such freedom from trouble as is appropriate to your
character.

23

ON TWO ROSES WHICH BECAME ONE[12]
BY THOMAS MORE

A white rose grew near a red one, and in their struggle to demonstrate superiority each crowded the
other. But both roses are combined to become one
flower, and the contest ends the only way it can.
Now only one rosebush grows and buds, but this
one has all the qualities of both. In other words, this
one rose has the beauty, grace, loveliness, color, and
strength which used to belong to both. Therefore,
if anyone loved either one of these roses, let him
love this one in which is found whatever he loved.
But if anyone is so fierce that he will not love this
rose, then he will fear it, for this flower has its own
thorns, too.

24

ON AN IGNORANT RHETORICIAN,
FROM THE GREEK

I presented the rhetorician Flaccus with five solecisms; promptly he repaid me with fifty. Said he, "Be
content now to have these few, reckoned by number; you will receive them by the bushel when I get
back from Cyprus."

25

ON SUSPICION, FROM THE GREEK

The impression one creates has great influence,
great weight, in the affairs of men. You have no desire to do any harm; but, if you seem to have, you
are done for. Thus in Crotona they killed Philolaus
long ago in the mistaken belief that he wanted to
play the tyrant.

26

ON A SKILFULLY MADE PICTURE
OF A SPEECHLESS RHETORICIAN,
FROM THE GREEK

Sextus himself is silent; the picture of Sextus exercises his art. The picture itself is the rhetorician; by
means of the picture the rhetorician has become a
picture.

---

10 Although Plato does not directly
propose a doctrine of eternal recurrence,
he does discuss political cycles in *Republic*
8.3, 546a–47c. **11** See Horace, *Carmina*
4.7.9–12. **12** The Wars of the Roses
(1455–85), between the Houses of Lancaster and York, ended when Henry VII
took the throne. Henry VIII adopted the
Tudor Rose, which united the red and
white, because his father was Lancastrian
and his mother Yorkist.

27

ON TWO BEGGARS, ONE LAME, ONE BLIND

A blind neighbor carries a lame man about; by a skilful combination he borrows eyes and lends feet.

28

ANOTHER VERSION

A blind man carries a lame man around. They manage the situation with skill; the latter lends his eyes, the former his feet.

29

ANOTHER VERSION

A blind man carries a lame man; and so, by a combined effort, one borrows eyes, the other feet.

30

ANOTHER VERSION

A blind man carries a lame man, a heavy but a useful load: he looks ahead and with his eyes he guides the other's feet.

31

THE SAME TOPIC AT GREATER LENGTH

Very sad misfortune overtook two unhappy men and cruelly deprived the one of his eyes, the other of his feet. Their common misery united them. The lame man rides upon the other. Thus by cooperation they mitigate each other's handicaps. The lame man goes anywhere with the help of the other's feet, the blind man travels a path determined by the other's eyes.

32

ANOTHER VERSION OF THE SAME TOPIC

There can be nothing more helpful than a loyal friend, who by his own efforts assuages your hurts. Two beggars formed an alliance[13] of firm friendship—a blind man and a lame one. The blind man said to the lame one, "You must ride upon my shoulders." The latter answered, "You, blind friend, must find your way by means of my eyes." The love which unites shuns the castles of proud kings and prevails in the humble hut.

33

ANOTHER VERSION

A blind man made with a lame man a mutually helpful arrangement[14] by which the one carried his partner on his shoulders and the other by his own eyes directed his partner's feet.

34

A PINE TREE BLOWN DOWN BY THE
WIND AND DESTINED FOR SERVICE
AT SEA SPEAKS, FROM THE GREEK

I am a pine tree, easy victim of the winds. And so why, stupid man, are you making me into a ship to roam the seas? Aren't you afraid of the omen? If Boreas[15] hunts me down on land, how will I escape him at sea?

35

ANOTHER VERSION OF THE SAME TOPIC

Why am I, a pine tree laid low by the winds, being sent to sea? I was shipwrecked before I was afloat.

36

ON A SHIP WHICH BURNED UP

A cargo ship had escaped the waves of the sea, but perished on the bosom of her mother, the land. She caught fire, and, as she burned, she wished for help from that which she had escaped—the hostile waters of the sea.

37

COMMENTS OF A RABBIT WHICH,
AFTER ELUDING A WEASEL,
FELL INTO NETS SPREAD BY HUNTERS

The weasel I did escape by darting through an opening off to one side, but—alas for me, miserable creature—then I rushed into the hunting nets of men. Now I cannot save my life or win quick death. They are saving me, alas, only to throw me to the ravening hounds. Now, while the hounds tear my flesh to pieces with their wicked teeth, a man looks on and smiles at the bloodshed. Insensate breed, more savage than any beast, to find cruel amusement in bitter slaughter!

---

13 *formed an alliance:* "foedera contraxere" is a legal phrase commonly used in formal treaties or alliances. See *Utopia*, especially the section on "Treaties" [*De foederibus*] on p. 198. **14** The Latin is *lege paciscitur aequa.* This sequence begins with terms of barter in Epigrams 27–29 and ends with terms of law in Epigrams 32–33. **15** the north wind

38
INNOCENCE INVITES INJURY,
FROM THE GREEK

"Even a mouse will dare to bite an evil man," the old proverb says, but the fact of the matter is utterly dif-
5 ferent. It is the harmless folk whom even the mouse dares to bite. To touch a criminal even a serpent is afraid.

39
ON BREAKING WIND, FROM THE GREEK

A fart, if you keep it too long in your belly, kills you; on the other hand, it can save your life if it is promptly let out. If a fart can save or destroy you,
5 then is it not as powerful as dreaded kings?

40
ON EQUALITY IN DEATH,
FROM THE GREEK

Though you conquer the world even to the pillars of Hercules,[16] still the amount of earth which ulti-
5 mately will be yours is the same as any man's. You will die as Irus's[17] equal, not a penny richer; and your land (yours no longer) will consume you.

41
ON A MEAN MAN, FROM THE GREEK

Everyone calls you rich; I say you are downright poor, for use makes wealth, Apollophanes, witness as you are. If you use what you have, it is yours; but
5 if you save it for your heir, then you are even now giving it away.

42
THE HUNTING OF A SPIDER

A lurking spider caught a stray fly and entangled it, to its terror, in a sticky web. The spider's mouth was open for a bite; but, as the old proverb says, much
5 can happen between the mouth and the morsel. Fate, taking pity on the fly and opposing the spider, allotted destruction not to the victim but to the aggressor. Now you, starling, in hungry haste attack both creatures. The web collapses, the fly escapes,
10 the spider perishes. Thus for the wretch under the very blade of the axe there is often some hope, and

for the evildoer, even among a thousand armed guards, there is reason to fear.

43
ON A CYNIC WHO PRACTICED RESTRAINT
IN FOOLISH FASHION, FROM THE GREEK

At a dinner we observed the great wisdom of an un-shaven Cynic who wandered about with his poor man's staff. Now this Cynic began by refusing rad-
5 ishes and pulse, lest—he said—his virtue become his belly's slave. But when he had glimpsed a snow-white onion, he shed his character of unyielding wisdom, asked for it, and with unexpected relish gobbled it all up. "Onions," he said, "do virtue no
10 harm."

44
PHYSICIAN'S EPITAPH, FROM THE GREEK

Hippocrates, of Coan descent, who lived in Thes-saly and belonged to immortal Phoebus's line, re-poses in this urn. Often he routed disease by the force of his healing art. Great glory was his, not be-
5 cause of his luck, but because of his skill.

45
ON A DEAD SLAVE, FROM THE GREEK

While he lived, this man was a slave. But now, in death, he wields no less power than you, mighty Darius.

46
ON A DEAD SERVING-WOMAN

Before Sosima was a slave only in body. Now even that part of her has been freed by death.

47
ON A BELOVED FISHERMAN,
FROM THE GREEK

While a fisherman was catching fish, the daugh-ter of a rich man saw him and fell violently in love with him. Then she was married to the man. Thus in
5 place of a life of poverty he acquired great store of proud wealth. Venus said, "This is my doing." Mis-tress Fortune, throwing back these words, replied, "It is my doing."

16 i.e., the Strait of Gibraltar   17 a beggar who appears in Homer's *Odyssey* 18

48

ON A MAN WHOSE FORTUNE CHANGED
SUDDENLY FROM BAD TO GOOD,
FROM THE GREEK

It is not because Fortune loves you that she has
5 raised you so high. She merely wishes to demonstrate even in your case how great is her power.

49

ON AVOIDING EXTREMES,
FROM THE GREEK

Pity is worse than envy, Pindar says.[18] The successful man's luxurious life causes envy, but we pity those
5 who are exceedingly unfortunate. May the powers above grant that I be neither too successful nor an object of pity. Obviously, the life that lies between is far preferable to either of the extremes. What is at the bottom is trodden upon; what is at the top,
10 falls suddenly.

50

THAT THERE IS NO POINT IN
WORRYING ABOUT FUTURE TROUBLES,
FROM THE GREEK

Fools that we are, why do we permit — our folly lies
5 in permitting — fear unmastered to sear our hearts? Either the trouble is not going to come, in which case we suffer now from needless fear, or if it is going to come, we are making fear itself a further trouble.

51

ONE LINE IN PRAISE OF HOMER'S POEM,
FROM THE GREEK

It was I who composed the poem, but divine Homer wrote it out.

52

ON A COMICAL TRIAL, FROM THE GREEK

A case was being tried. The defendant was deaf, the plaintiff was deaf, and the judge himself was deafer than either. The plaintiff demanded five months'
5 rent for a house. The defendant replied, "My mill was running all night." The judge looked up at them and said, "What is your quarrel? She is the mother of both of you, isn't she? Both of you, support her."

53

TO A LAMP BURNING AT NIGHT

Thrice my mistress swore by you, lamp, that she would return. She has not come. Mete out your punishment, if you are a god. Some night when she finds you pleasant for her dalliance, go out and de- 5
prive her cursed eyes of your blessed light.

54

LAIS, AS AN OLD WOMAN, AT HER MIRROR,
FROM THE GREEK

I am Lais, who not long ago laughed wantonly at you, Greece, when I had at my doors a throng of youthful lovers. But now I dedicate to Venus this 5
mirror, for the woman I am I do not wish to see, the woman I was I cannot.

55

ON THE DAY OF DEATH,
UNKNOWN TO ALL MEN

The dead I do not mourn; I mourn the living, vexed by the lasting fear of death still to come.

56

ANOTHER VERSION

You would be weeping if you knew you had one month to live; you laugh, although you may not have a day.

57

ON THE DILIGENCE OF BEES,
FROM THE GREEK

The bees themselves make their own streams of honey in the air, make the chambers where they dwell. The bee is generous to men, and its fruit is 5
most accessible to the life of men. There is no need for the help of ox or hooked reaping knife. All that is needed here is a jar into which it pours generously sweet cups of honey from its little vessel. Holy creatures, go your way happily; feed upon the variegated 10
flowers, you winged makers of ethereal nectar.

58

ON AN OLD WOMAN WHO
USES DYE IN VAIN

You keep dyeing your hair, but you will never dye old age or smooth the wrinkles of your cheeks. Now stop sprinkling your whole face with powder, lest 5

---

18 Pythian 1.85

you end up with a mask, not a face. Since you will get nowhere with paint and powder, madwoman, what are you about? These devices will never make a Helen of a Hecuba.[19]

59
ON THE BIRTH OF MEN, FROM THE GREEK
Look here, mortal, if you recall what your father did in engendering you, then pride will vanish from your spirit. Plato, on the other hand, in his dream,
5 puffs you up with vain pride and says your seed is everlasting and celestial.[20] Observe, you are fashioned of mire. What reason have you for high aspirations? But that is what one will say who decks you out in a lofty fiction. Rather, if you want to hear the
10 truth, you were born of coition amid shameful lust and of a pitiful droplet.

60
ON A FOOLISH ASTROLOGER
The prophetess of Cumae in the grip of her sacred frenzy does not with her inspired vision see more clearly the events to come than my astrologer, fa-
5 mous in the art of soothsaying, foresees, after a look at the stars, the events of the past.

61
ANOTHER ON AN ASTROLOGER WHOSE WIFE WAS LEWD
All the stars explain themselves to you, the prophet of the skies, and inform you of the destiny of every-one. But the fact that your wife gives herself to
5 everyone—of that fact the stars, though they see everything, have not informed you.

62
IAMBICS ON THE SAME MAN
Observer of the stars above, beloved of us heavenly bodies, I myself, Phoebus,[21] would be very glad now to tell you a little secret, most emphatically your
5 concern, which I learned as I passed over the world the day before you came home recently from court. But Venus frightens me off and threatens me with a new love affair that will be no more successful than my earlier one with Daphne if I report to anyone
10 at all such information as I once reported to her

husband about her. Therefore, this fact you will not learn. Of all other changes in fortune I shall keep you informed, but as concerns your wife, if any-thing turns up contrary to your wishes, the whole world will know it before you do.   15

63
ANOTHER VERSION ON THE SAME MAN
Foolish fellow, why do you search the stars for the character of your wife? Your wife is on the ground. Why do you peer on high? What you are fearful about is down here. While you are asking the heav-   5 ens what she is doing, she meanwhile managed to do what she liked upon the ground.

64
ANOTHER VERSION ON THE SAME ASTROLOGER
Why, madman, are you always searching among the stars, with suspicious mind, to discover what your wife is up to? If you do not know what kind of wife   5 you have, believe that she is chaste. If you persuade yourself thoroughly that she is, you are well off. Why do you seek to learn what does not hurt you until you learn it? Why do you seek to make your-self miserable by your own persistence? This is mad-   10 ness, and no doubt of it, since you can stop right now anxiously seeking what you fear to find.

65
ANOTHER VERSION ON THE ASTROLOGER
Saturn is far away and long since blind, they say; un-able he is to distinguish at close range between a boy and a stone.[22] The lovely moon, as she journeys, is   5 too shy to look and, maiden that she is, can see only the chaste. Jupiter is busy with Europa, Venus with Mars, Mars with Venus, the Sun with Daphne, and Mercury with Hyrce.[23] That is why, astrologer, when your wife takes lovers, the stars give you no hint of   10 the matter.

66
THE DILEMMA OF BEAUTY, IN SCAZONS[24]
I do not know, by Hercules, what beauty contrib-utes. If you are passionately in love, then presto!

19 Hecuba was King Priam of Troy's aged wife, while Helen was "the face that launched a thousand ships" when she ran away with Paris.   20 See Plato, Timaeus 90a.   21 Apollo, the sun god   22 See Hesiod, Theogony 485–91.   23 See Ovid, Metamorphoses 1.452–567, 2.708–51, 2.846–75, 4.171–89.   24 a modification of the iambic tetrameter, in which a spondee or trochee takes the place of the final iambus

the ugly woman is beautiful; if you are unmoved, then even the beautiful woman may be repulsive. I do not know, by Hercules, what beauty contributes.

67

ON THE ASTROLOGER MENTIONED ABOVE

Candidus — what a prophet he is — after examining the stars, proclaimed his wife's goodness to everyone. When his wife left him for a lover, the prophet took another look at the stars and predicted her badness to everyone.

68

EXHORTATION TO TRUE VIRTUE

Alas, whatever in this miserable world attracts miserable man withers at once and dies like the spring rose. Fortune has never yet taken anyone into her comforting arms without squeezing him uncomfortably somewhere. Drink in the virtues; abstain from vain joys. True joys are the companions of the noble spirit.

69

ON SCORNING THIS LIFE

As every wind strikes and bends ears of grain, so hope and grief and wrath and fear drive us where they will. In the affairs of mortals nothing has real weight. You should be ashamed if you are moved by a light touch.

70

THAT ONE OUGHT NOT TO FEAR DEATH
SINCE IT IS THE END OF SUFFERING,
FROM THE GREEK

Is it not stupid to fear death, which is the mother of peace? which banishes disease and dismal poverty? Death alone visits miserable mortals only once; there is none to whom death has come a second time. But other afflictions, many and varied, take their turns, attacking now this victim and now that, time and time again.

71

ON A CERTAIN MEAN AND STINGY BISHOP

If I were to live as long as the Sibyl, I should never forget the kindness of the bishop. He is proprietor of many acres of rented land, possesses large cities, and travels with a retinue of a hundred attendants. And yet, when recently I approached him, although I am a man of very small property, still he received me and addressed me in really agreeable fashion. As a matter of fact, in order that I might taste a cup of his port before leaving, he himself extracted his key from his own purse.

72

ON FICKLE FORTUNE, FROM THE GREEK

Slippery Fortune observes no definite method but continually, unseeing, turns her restless wheel. She delights to strike down the highest, to raise the lowest, and, without principle, to produce alternations of man's lot. When your prosperity is greatest, then trouble is closest at hand; contrariwise, when your troubles are at their height, prosperity is nearest. Endure your troubles with brave heart; do not by grieving be twice unhappy lest you hurry yourself into the grave just before prosperity comes.

73

LIFE IS SHORT

Is it not madness for you to count upon an active old age? — since not even an hour of life is guaranteed. Come, imagine you will live to be as old as Nestor[25] — then your long life will teem with numerous woes. Though you outlive all the troubles of your vigorous years, bent old age will bring you lasting wearisome burdens. And even so, though you live untroubled (as never happens) to a ripe old age, this too is a trifle. Where are Nestor's many years now? Of a life so long there remains not a single day.

74

ENDURANCE

Sufferer, endure; Chance will end your sorrow. And what Chance does not do for you Death will do.

75

LIFE ITSELF IS A JOURNEY TOWARD DEATH

We waste our time and think that death is far, far away. But it lies hidden deep in our entrails. In fact, from the very hour of our birth, life and death steal forward together, step by step. An hour, in the process of measuring itself out, secretly steals that very measure from your life. Little by little we die, but in

---

25 the oldest of the Achaean kings in Homer's *Iliad* and *Odyssey*

a single instant we cease to exist; thus a lamp goes
out when its oil is gone. Even when it does not kill,
10 death is present in time itself. Why, even now, while
we are talking, we are dying.

76
THE GREEDY RICH MAN IS POOR
FOR HIMSELF, FROM THE GREEK

The only true riches, in my judgment, are those of
the mind which values itself above its possessions.
5 The man we rightly call rich, the man we rightly call
wealthy is one who sees how to use his great wealth.
But if anyone is always wretchedly heaping up
riches, wretchedly consumed by the need to count
money, this man toils like the bee in its little many-
10 celled hive. Others eat the honey.

77
THE DILEMMA OF EPICURUS

Let no trouble drive you to misery. If the trouble is
lasting, it is easy to bear; if it is hard to bear, it does
not last long.

78
THE OPPOSITE OPINION

Alas, both kinds of sorrow drive us to misery and
break our hearts: a long sorrow is never light and a
heavy sorrow is never brief.

79
ON DEATH

He is dreaming who thinks that in this life he is
rich; and when death wakes him up, he sees at once
how poor he is.

80
DEATH UNASSISTED KILLS TYRANTS

You who have been cruelly persecuted at the hands
of unjust men, no matter who you are, take hope.
Let kindly hope alleviate your sufferings. A turn of
5 fortune will improve your state — like the sun shining through scattered clouds — or the defender of
liberty. Death, touched by pity, will put forth her
hand, while the tyrant rages, and rescue you. Death
will snatch him away too (the more to please you)
10 and will lay him right before your feet. He who was
so carried away by his great wealth and his empty
pride, he who once upon a time amid his thronging

courtiers was so bold, O, he will not be fierce, will
not wear an expression of pride. He will be an object
of pity, cast down from his high place, abandoned, 15
helpless, penniless. What gift has life ever given you
to compare with this gift? The tables are turned: the
man once so fearsome deserves only a laugh.

81
A POEM TRANSLATED FROM
AN ENGLISH SONG

Break, sad heart, pitiably engulfed in deepest woe.
Let this be the end of your punishment. Show your
mistress your bloody wounds. It is she only who will 5
presently part us two. Alas, how long shall I in my
misery thus weep and complain? Come, dreaded
death, and release me from such monstrous woes.

82
A JESTING POEM TO A FAITHLESS
MISTRESS, TRANSLATED FROM
AN ENGLISH SONG

May the gods preserve us! What dreams I had last
night! The whole universe was overturned and fell 5
to ruin. The sun's light did not survive, nor the
moon's; and the swollen deep overwhelmed the
land. Even more remarkable — you hear? — a voice
seemed to say, "Just look, your mistress has broken
the promise she made." 10

83
ON A RABBIT TWICE CAUGHT

They were lifting me out of the net; out of their
hands I slipped — back into the net again. Alas, alas,
poor me! Escaping once only means captured twice.

84
ON A MAID WITH UNMAIDENLY HABITS

If this maid, who is a seductive, wanton, saucy, footloose, talkative flirt, is a maiden, then so is a woman
who has twice borne children.

85
ON WIVES

This is what every man says: "Nature has not produced anything in this life more troublesome, more
burdensome, to man than these wives of ours." That
is what he says; but still he marries. Yes, when his 5
sixth wife dies, he marries a seventh.

86

ON THE SAME

A wife is a burden, but she could be useful — if she dies betimes[26] and leaves you all she owns.

87

ON A POOR PORTRAIT, FROM THE GREEK

This painting of you which Diodorus recently painted, Menodotus, is anyone's portrait rather than yours.

88

ON THE SAME PORTRAIT

In that portrait of you it is himself the painter has revealed, and so thoroughly that it resembles nobody as little as it resembles you.

89

CHORIAMBICS ON THE PLEASANT LIFE, FROM THE GREEK

I care nothing about Gyges, king of Sardis. My search is not for gold; I do not make myself mis-
5　erable by competing with kings. My ambition is to have my beard well anointed with agreeable perfumes, my brow wreathed with fragrant blossoms. I am concerned with today, for who can know tomorrow? Now, Vulcan, make me a well-rounded sil-
10　ver cup, make it deep and as inexhaustible as you can. And have it decorated round about, not with chariots, constellations, or doleful Orion[27] — instead make green vines and grapes to charm me, and add a handsome figure of Dionysus.

90

ON A DISHONEST PHYSICIAN WHO SOLD A MERE DROP OF PRETENDED MEDICINE FOR A HIGH PRICE

A physician said to a patient who was suffering
5　from a fever, "If anything will help you, balm will. But only I have it, and I have very little. The price is not less than ten pounds a drop. You give me five now, and the other five when you are well, with the understanding that if you die I shall never try
10　to collect the second five. You will win no advantage in this great crisis if you try to settle for half of the very expensive drop." They agreed, and a drop from a tiny linen-wrapped vial was dropped from a

dagger-point into wine. The patient asked the physician to rinse off the point in the wine. But he said,
15　"By no means; the point still holds twice the value of your ten pounds. One drop is enough." And it was enough. Just one drop did it. The patient had hardly drunk the single drop when he died. O, what a very unlucky arrangement! One participant lost
20　half his drop, the other half his life.

91

ON A WOMAN ARTIFICIALLY BEAUTIFIED, FROM THE GREEK

Madam, you dye your hair; but you ask, "How do you know?" Well, your hair was black when you brought it home from the marketplace.　　　　　5

92

ON A FAULTY PORTRAIT

In this portrait of yours the artist tried to show how unlike you he could make it.

93

ON AN ACCURATE PORTRAIT

Your likeness is so truly portrayed in this picture that it is not your picture, but your mirror.

94

ON THE SAME PORTRAIT

I marvel at the great skill with which the artist painted the portrait of you which you showed me, Posthumus. If anyone who has ever seen you looks at this picture, unless he is prejudiced by envy of the　5
artist, he will confess that the similarity between one egg and another is not so great as the discrepancy between you and your portrait.

95

ON AN ENGLISHMAN WHO AFFECTED TO SPEAK FRENCH

My friend and companion, Lalus,[28] was born in Britain and brought up on our island. Nevertheless, although a mighty sea, their languages, and　5
their customs separate Englishmen and the inhabitants of France, Lalus still is scornful of all things English. All things French he admires and wants. He struts about in French dress; he is very fond of little French capes. He is happy with his belt, his　10

---

26 early　27 *Vulcan . . . Orion:* an allusion to Achilles' shield, forged by Hephaestus　in Homer's *Iliad* 18.480–89　28 "Lalus" suggests λάλος, "talkative, babbling."

purse, his sword—if they are French; with his hat, his beret, his cap—if they are French. He delights in French shoes, French underclothes, and, to put it briefly, in an outfit French from head to toe. Why, he even has one servant, and he is a Frenchman. But France herself, I think, could not, if she tried, treat him in more French a fashion: he pays the servant nothing, like a Frenchman; he clothes him in worn-out rags, in the French manner; he feeds him little and that little poor, as the French do; he works him hard, like the French; he strikes him often, like a Frenchman; at social gatherings, and on the street, and in the market-place, and in public he quarrels with him and abuses him always in the French fashion. What! Have I said that he does this in French fashion? I should say rather in half-French fashion. For, unless I am mistaken, he is as familiar with the French language in general as a parrot is with Latin. Still he swells with pride and is, naturally, pleased with himself if he gets off three words in French. If there is anything he cannot say in French, then he tries to say it—granted the words are not French—at least with a French accent, with open palate, a shrill sort of sound, effeminate, like women's chatter, but lisping prettily you may be sure, as though his mouth were full of beans, and pronouncing with emphasis the letters which the foolish French avoid as the cock avoids the fox or the sailor the cliffs. And so it is with this kind of French accent that he speaks Latin, English, Italian, Spanish, German, and every language except only French; for French is the one language he speaks with an English accent. But if any native of Britain in this haughty way scorns his native land in an apelike effort to feign and counterfeit the follies of the French, I think that such a man is intoxicated from drinking of the River Gallus. Therefore, since he is trying to change from Englishman to Frenchman, order him, ye gods, to change from cock to capon.

96

ON NICOLAUS, A WICKED PHYSICIAN

Now I understand that names not only of things but also of people are acquired in no haphazard way but with some reason. There is a physician named Nicolaus. You say, "In what way is that appropriate? It would make a better name for a general." Well, it is by arms that a general conquers nations, but by his poisonous potions this physician lays low the nation and brave generals on every hand. A general's enemies often fight a second battle with him, but no one encounters this physician twice. He is truly named, is Nicolaus.[29]

97

ON THE HANDSOME PORTRAIT
OF A VERY UGLY MAN

That picture of you which I saw recently was, in my opinion, superior to the Venus of Apelles.[30] The painter used up all his skill in that one picture; he wanted to show in that one picture what he could do. What beauty of face! that nose! such lips! what eyes! such color everywhere! Just as surely as the picture was in every respect by far the most beautiful of portraits, so surely did it fail to look like you in any respect.

98

ON AN UNSUCCESSFUL PORTRAIT

When I happened recently to enter an artist's studio, your portrait met my eyes. While the painter thus reproduced all your characteristics, you, I am sure, kept your expression unchanged for a long time. A look at the portrait brought you so completely before me that I knew whose portrait it was the instant the artist told me it was yours.

99

ON A DYING MISER

Alas, rich Chrysalus is dying. He mourns; he groans; no one ever died more reluctantly. He is mourning not because he is parting with his life—there is nothing he holds cheaper than himself—but because he is parting with four coins for a grave.

100

ON A ROTTEN GRAMMARIAN

When I think of the grammarian Heliodorus, my tongue immediately begins to dread solecisms.

101

ON A SILLY SEER

A renowned astrologer predicted, "That noble ruler, the king of the French, this year will be at peace in

---

29 Nicolaus is derived from the Greek νίκη, "victory," and λαός, "people."

30 famous painter of ancient Greece (*ca.* 4th century BC)

his realm." The year had hardly begun when the king died. The seer was defenseless. Someone undertook jokingly to explain the matter by saying, "The prophecy is true; is not the king at peace?" The story spread and spread; and the people on every hand laughingly said, "Is not the king at peace?" When the seer heard this comment from the people, then he said in earnest, "The prophecy is true; is not the king at peace?"

102

ON A MAN WITH A HUGE NOSE,
FROM THE GREEK

Proclus, you could never wipe your nose by hand, for your hand, large as it is, is smaller than your nose. When do you cry "Jupiter" upon sneezing? For obviously you do not hear anything, since your nose extends out so very far away from your ears.

103

ON A MAD POET, FROM THE GREEK

Even among the Muses there are Furies, and it is they who make you the poet you are and inspire you to write many poems without thought. Come now, I entreat you, write ever so many poems, for I find no greater fury to entreat for you than that.

104

ON A TINY MAN, FROM THE GREEK

To be safe, stay well within the city if you are wise, so that no crane—they love the blood of pygmies[31]— may grab you.

105

COMMON GOSSIP OUGHT TO BE
IGNORED, FROM THE GREEK

Just please yourself and scorn the comments of the chattering mob. One among them will praise, another defame you.

106

ON A FOOL, FROM THE GREEK

When the fleas bite Morio, he puts out his light and says, "These fleas will not see me now."

107

ON SLEEP, FROM THE GREEK,
AN ARISTOTELIAN PROVERB

Almost half of life is sleep. During that period the rich and the poor lie equal. And so, Croesus, wealthiest of kings, for almost half a lifetime Irus the beggar was your equal.

108

ANOTHER VERSION

While you are sleeping and do not perceive that you are alive, you are not happy; but if sleep does not come, you are miserable. And so any happy man, proud of his good luck, haughty, and swollen by fleeting prosperity, must, every night, either cease to be happy or begin to be miserable.

109

THE DIFFERENCE BETWEEN A
TYRANT AND A KING[32]

A king who respects the law differs from cruel tyrants thus: a tyrant rules his subjects as slaves; a king thinks of his as his own children.[33]

110

THAT THE TYRANT'S LIFE IS TROUBLED

Great anxiety wears away the waking hours of the mighty tyrant; peace comes at night if it comes at all. But the tyrant does not rest more comfortably on any soft bed than the poor man does on the hard ground. Therefore, tyrant, the happiest part of your life is that in which you willingly become no better than a beggar.

---

31 See *Iliad* 3.2–7. **32** The Latin term used here is *princeps*. Etymologically, it means "capturing first [place]," from *primus* and *-ceps*, a form of *capio*. Here and in Epigrams 111 and 115, a general definition is suggested. For its importance in *Utopia*, see n. 1 on p. 156. When Erasmus writes his *Education of a Christian Prince* in 1516, he defines the *princeps* in Ciceronian terms as the "embodiment of the laws," ideally selected by the vote of a free and willing people. The custom of having a *princeps* "born to the office, not elected," Erasmus comments, "was the custom among some barbarian peoples in the past (according to Aristotle) and is also the practice almost everywhere in our own time" (*CWE* 27: 206). **33** The term for "children" is *liberos*, which also means "freemen."

111
THAT THE GOOD KING IS A FATHER
NOT A MASTER, IAMBICS
A devoted king[34] will never lack children;[35] he is father to the whole kingdom. And so it is that a true king is abundantly blessed in having as many children as he has citizens.

112
ON THE GOOD KING AND HIS PEOPLE
A kingdom in all its parts is like a man; it is held together by natural affection. The king is the head; the people form the other parts. Every citizen the king has he considers a part of his own body (that is why he grieves at the loss of a single one). The people risk themselves to save the king and everyone thinks of him as the head of his own body.

113
THAT OUR ADVANTAGES ARE RECOGNIZED
ONLY WHEN THEY VANISH
Almost all of us recognize our advantages by losing them. While we have them, we ignore them. In this way, also, an evil successor frequently, but too late, enhances the people's memory of a good ruler.

114
THAT THE TYRANT WHILE HE SLEEPS
IS NO DIFFERENT FROM THE COMMONER
Well then, you madman, it is pride which makes you carry your head so high—because the throng bows to you on bended knee, because the people rise and uncover for you, because you have in your power the life and death of many. But whenever sleep secures your body in inactivity, then, tell me, where is this glory of yours? Then you lie, useless creature, like a lifeless log or like a recent corpse. But if you were not lying protected, like a coward, unseen indoors, your own life would be at the disposal of any man.

115
ON KINGS,[36] GOOD AND BAD
What is a good king? He is a watchdog, guardian of the flock, who by barking keeps the wolves from the sheep. What is the bad king? He is the wolf.

116
ON A RAPIST AND HIS LAWYER
A girl charged that she had been raped. There was no denying the accusation. The rapist was doomed. But his clever lawyer suddenly opened the defendant's clothing and took out his male organ. Said the lawyer, "My girl, is this the organ that was in your belly?" The girl was so ashamed that she said, "No." The lawyer cried, "Your honor, we have won this case. She is the one, she herself denies the very thing in the absence of which she also denies she was raped."

117
ON A THIEF AND HIS LAWYER
While Snatch was afraid that he would be convicted of theft, he consulted a lawyer—at a considerable price. When the lawyer had pondered, frequently and long, his mighty tomes, he said, "Snatch, you will get off, I hope, if you take off."

118
ON AN ASTROLOGER WHO PROPHESIED
AFTER THE EVENT, FROM THE GREEK
Astrologers frequently and unanimously told father that his brother was bound to survive him. Now, only Hermoclides said the brother would die first, but he said it after seeing that he was dead.

119
ON THE VANITY OF THIS LIFE
We are all shut up in the prison of this world under sentence of death. In this prison none escapes death. The land within the prison is divided into many sections, and men build their dwellings in different sections. As if the prison were a kingdom, the inmates struggle for position. The avaricious man hoards up wealth within the dark prison. One man wanders freely in the prison, another lies shackled in his cave; this man serves, that one rules; this one sings, that one groans. And then, while we are still in love with the prison as if it were no prison, we are escorted out of it, one way or another, by death.

---

34 The Latin phrase is actually *pius princeps*, reminiscent of Vergil's famous hero *pius Aeneas*. **35** Here More again plans on the dual meaning of *liberos*: "children" and "freemen." **36** Here and in the first sentence, More uses *princeps*.

120

A KING IS PROTECTED, NOT BY A CORPS OF GUARDS, BUT BY HIS OWN GOOD QUALITIES

Not fear (accompanied by hatred), not towering
5 palaces, not wealth wrung from a plundered people protects a king. The stern bodyguard, hired for
a pittance, offers no protection, for the guard will
serve a new master as he served the old. He will be
safe who so rules his people that they judge none
10 other would promote their interests better.

121

THE CONSENT OF THE PEOPLE BOTH BESTOWS AND WITHDRAWS SOVEREIGNTY

Any one man who has command of many men
5 owes his authority to those whom he commands;
he ought to have command not one instant longer
than his subjects wish. Why are impotent kings[37] so
proud? Because they rule merely on sufferance?[38]

122

ON A TINY MAN, FROM THE GREEK

Epicurus constructed the whole world out of atoms, Alchimus, since he believed that there was
nothing smaller than atoms. If you, Diophantus,
5 had been alive at that time, he would have made the
world out of you, for surely you, Diophantus, are
much smaller than an atom. Or perhaps in that case
he would have taught that everything else is made
of atoms, but that the atoms themselves are made
10 out of you.

123

ON LOVE, CHASTE AND UNCHASTE, FROM THE GREEK

These two conflicting emotions, one sinful and one
ennobling, lust on one side and modesty on the
5 other, brought death to two people. A consuming
passion for Hippolytus destroyed Phaedra; and as
for Hippolytus, alas, his holy chastity killed him.[39]

124

ON THE CITY OF ROME, FROM THE GREEK

Hail, Hector, descendant of Mars; if you can hear
at all beneath the earth, breathe again and take
pride in the name of your native land. A city of Il-
ium lives, inhabited now by a glorious race—a race
5 less powerful in battle than you, but still beloved of
Mars. The Myrmidons have perished. Come, Hector, and tell Achilles that all Thessaly is subject to
the descendants of Aeneas.

125

ON AVOIDING EXTREMES, FROM THE GREEK

Too much of anything is unpleasant. Thus even
honey, as the old adage says, is always bitter if there
is too much of it.

126

ON AN EXTREMELY UNHAPPY MAN, FROM THE GREEK

You have never lived, poor man, and you will never
die, for, although you seem alive, in your misery you
are dead. But death at last does make an end of life
5 for those who have untold success and great wealth.

127

ON PYTHAGORAS'S TACITURNITY, FROM THE GREEK

In human affairs silence is great wisdom. On this
point the wiseman Pythagoras[40] will be my witness:
himself a learned speaker, he taught others to keep
quiet, since he found this was a potent drug to promote tranquillity.

128

A JOKE ON GELLIA

Why should we marvel only at the wonders of ages
past—that a bull spoke or a stone fell in a rain-
storm? There is a new wonder greater than the old.
Just look, Gellia rose from her bed yesterday before
5 the shadowy dusk. I was going to tell you more, but
you would think I was joking. Well, just the same,
she did get up before midday. Although ages past

---

37 *principes* **38** As More phrases this same
view in the Latin version of his *History
of King Richard III:* "the title and profit
and the ownership [of England is] totally
[their] own—as a genuine commonwealth"
(*CW* 15: 480); "absolute and supreme
potestas in England is Parliament" (*CW*
15: 320). **39** See Euripides' *Hippolytus.*

40 For the concept of silence attributed to
this famous Greek philosopher (*ca.* 570–
495 BC), see Plutarch's *Life of Numa* 8.6;
see also Diogenes Laertius 8.10.

often saw those old marvels, though future ages
10 will perhaps be able to see them as often, still, until yesterday no one had ever seen the miracle I describe, and after today no one will be able to see it
ever again.

129

ON PALLAS[41] AND VENUS,
FROM THE GREEK

O Tritonian virgin, why do you wrong me, Venus,
so? Why do you clutch my prize in your fingers?
5 Remember that on the rocky side of Ida, if I may
remind you, it was I, not you, whom Paris judged
beautiful. The spear is yours, and the sword; but I
claim the apple. Let the ancient contest suffice for
the apple.

130

THAT HUMAN LIFE IS NOTHING

Breathing the unsubstantial air through narrow
openings in our bodies, we live and look upon Phoebus's light. We are, every man alive, mere instru-
5 ments—but such instruments as drafts of thin air
endow with the breath of life. But if your hand
should interrupt the delicate process of breathing,
then you will tear out a living soul and send it to the
underworld. This, then, is why we are nothing. We
10 are all fattened up for Death; and what nourishes us
is little breaths of thin air.

131

ON A DULLARD'S DULL DAGGER,
FROM THE GREEK

This leaden point of yours is blunt and dull. The
point is as sharp as your wits.

132

ON FAME AND POPULAR OPINION

Most men congratulate themselves if they attain
to fame, empty though it is; and, because they are
light-minded, they are lifted to the stars by the
5 fickle wind of opinion. Why do you derive satisfaction from the comments of the populace? In their
blindness they often interpret what is best as a failing and thoughtlessly approve what is very reprehensible. You hang everlastingly upon a stranger's

opinion for fear that some cobbler will retract the 10
praise he has conferred. Perhaps the man whose
praise makes you proud is mocking you. Though he
praise you from his heart, that praise is ephemeral.
What does fame do for you? You may be praised by
the whole world, but if you have an aching joint, 15
what does fame do for you?

133

JOKE ABOUT A WAITER

A certain guest at a banquet removed some flies
from the mixing-bowl before he drank. When
he had had his drink he put the flies back. He explained, "I do not like flies; but then, I do not 5
know—some of you may like them."

134

ON A HUNTING DOG

One duck was in the dog's mouth when he opened
it to catch another. He missed it, and the one he
had already caught escaped from his mouth. In this
way, miser, while you wretchedly strive to ensnare 5
the property of another, you more often than not
lose your own; and it serves you right.

135

THE MISER IS A DOG IN THE MANGER

The dog in the manger[42] does not himself eat the
hay, nor does he let the horse, who wants hay, take
any. The miser guards his wealth, does not use it
himself. And those who want to put it to some use 5
he keeps at a distance.

136

TO ORESTES, ABOUT TO KILL HIS
MOTHER, FROM THE GREEK

Where will you thrust the sword, through the
womb or through the breast? The womb bore you,
the breasts gave you suck. 5

137

WHAT WE SHOULD ASK FROM GOD,
IN FEW WORDS

Give us, God, what is good, whether you are asked
or not; and, asked or not, withhold what is evil.

---

41 epithet for Athene   **42** See Aesop's "Dog in the Manger;" Whit H565; Til D513.

138

ON MEN TWICE MARRIED,
FROM THE GREEK

The widower who marries again is a shipwrecked
sailor who a second time sails the stormy sea.

139

ON SLEEP, WHICH MAKES THE POOR
MAN THE RICH MAN'S EQUAL

O sleep, peaceful part of life, hope and comfort of
the poor, whom by night you make equal to the
rich, you soothe sad hearts with the gentle dew of
forgetfulness and drive away all awareness of woe.
Generously in happy dreams you confer wealth
upon the poor man. Why do you, rich man, scorn
the poor man's fancied wealth? Real wealth brings
to the rich worry, pain, and grief; imagined wealth
brings the poor real joy.

140

ON AN UGLY, WICKED MAN,
FROM THE GREEK

It is difficult to represent a soul, easy to portray a
body. In your case the opposite is true, for your appearance so reveals your vicious habits that they are
easily discernible all over you. But who would paint
your ugly bodily parts, the omens of your inner
form, since no one would willingly look at them?

141

ON A POISONOUS CAPPADOCIAN,
FROM THE GREEK

A deadly viper bit a Cappadocian: having imbibed
the corrosive blood of the Cappadocian, it died at
once.

142

ON AN IRON STATUE, FROM THE GREEK

To you, the king who ravaged the world, they set up
a statue of iron—as far cheaper than bronze. This
economy was the result of starvation, slaughter,
wrath, and cruel poverty. These are the instruments
by which your greed has ravaged all.

143

TO CANDIDUS: HOW TO CHOOSE A WIFE,
A POEM IN IAMBIC DIMETER
BRACHYCATALECTIC

Your time of life, Candidus, is now reaching a point
where it suggests that at last you reject temporary

attachments, that you cease at last to pursue haphazard love affairs, and that you find a girl to take
as wife formally and in mutual devotion. Let her be
fruitful and add sweet children to your most splendid line. Your father did as much for you. Hand on
with increase to your descendants what you have already received from your ancestors.

Still, do not let your primary concern be how
much dowry she brings or how beautiful she is.
Weakness marks any love which arises either from a
blind impulse roused by mere beauty or from a base
love of money.

The man who loves for money's sake loves only
money. As soon as he acquires the money, his fleeting love is gone and dies almost before it is born.
And the money, which in his miserable selfishness
he had coveted earlier, cannot help him in the least
later on when he is required, however unwilling, to
keep the wife he does not love.

What is beauty? Does it not fail in sickness, perish with time? Like a flower in the sun. Then, when
the bloom leaves her cheek, a love secured only by
such ties as these breaks free and is gone forever.
Only a man of intelligence and foresight, with reason for his guide, can enter upon true love. True
love is inspired, with happy promise, by respect for
a woman's glorious virtue, a noble gift which endures, does not fail in sickness, does not perish with
the years. And so, my friend, if you desire to marry,
first observe what kind of parents the lady has. See
to it that her mother is revered for the excellence of
her character which is sucked in and pressed by her
tender and impressionable little girl.

Next see to this: what sort of personality she has;
how agreeable she is. Let her maidenly countenance
be calm and without severity. But let her modesty
bring blushes to her cheeks; let her glance not be
provocative. Let her be mild-mannered, not throwing her slender arms wantonly around men's necks.
Let her glances be restrained; let her have no roving
eye. Let her pretty lips always be free of pointless
garrulity and also of boorish taciturnity. Let her be
either just finishing her education or ready to begin
it immediately. Happy is the woman whose education permits her to derive from the best of ancient
works the principles which confer a blessing on life.
Armed with this learning, she would not yield to
pride in prosperity, nor to grief in distress—even
though misfortune strike her down. For this reason your lifetime companion will be ever agreeable,

never a trouble or a burden. If she is well instructed herself, then some day she will teach your little grandsons, at an early age, to read.

60 You will be glad to leave the company of men and to seek repose in the bosom of your accomplished wife, the while she attends to your comfort, and while under her dexterous touch the plucked strings resound, while in a sweet voice (as sweet, Procne, as your sister's) she sings delightful songs
65 such as Apollo would be glad to hear. Then you will be glad to spend days and nights in pleasant and intelligent conversation, listening to the sweet words which ever most charmingly flow from her honeyed mouth. By her comments she would re-
70 strain you if ever vain success should exalt you and would comfort you if grievous sorrow should cast you down. When she speaks, it will be difficult to choose between her perfect power of expression and her thoughtful understanding of all kinds of
75 affairs.

I should think that the wife of the bard Orpheus[43] long ago was such a woman; he would never have devoted such enormous effort to recovering from the underworld an uncultivated woman.

80 Such a woman, I believe, was Ovid's famous daughter,[44] who could rival in poetical composition even her own father.

Such a woman, I suspect, was Tullia[45]—never was daughter more beloved by a father, himself in learn-
85 ing second to none.

Such a woman was the mother[46] of the two Gracchi. She taught her sons right principles; she accomplished no less as their teacher than she did as their mother.

90 Why do I continue to contemplate ancient times? After all, our age, however rude it may be, does have one maiden, though it has only one, whom it may set above almost all others and compare with any of those women whose stories come down to us from
95 ages past. Borne high upon the soaring wings of fame, she now gives warning even to remotest Britain, the one and only boast and glory of the whole world, not merely the Cassandra[47] of her own country.

100 Say Candidus, if you were to marry a woman such as those I have mentioned above, could you, even if she were not beautiful, find her wanting or complain that you gain too little by her dowry? This is the truth of the matter: whatever her looks, she is beautiful enough if her looks give pleasure; and 105 no man possesses more than he who is content with what he has.

May my own wife cease to love me if I am not telling you the truth, my friend. If Nature has denied the gift of beauty to a girl, yes, though she be 110 blacker than coal, still, if she has this virtuous disposition, she would be in my eyes fairer than the swan. If fickle Fortune has denied her a dowry, yes, though she be poorer than Irus, still, if she has this virtuous disposition, she would be in my eyes richer, 115 Croesus, than you.

144
A FUNNY STORY ABOUT A SWAGGERER
While Thraso[48] the soldier was away, a rough herdsman seduced his wife. When the soldier came home and heard the story, he picked up his sword and rushed in savage pursuit. When at length he 5 found the rustic alone in a field, he shouted, "You, say, you there, you rascal." The herdsman stopped and picked up an armful of stones. The soldier, with drawn sword, shouted, "Did you lay hand on my wife, you scoundrel?" The herdsman calmly an- 10 swered, "I did." "You confess it," said the soldier. "By all the gods and goddesses, you villain, I swear that I would plunge this sword hilt-deep into your heart if you had not confessed."

145
ON AVOIDING EXTREMES,
FROM THE GREEK
I have no desire for more spacious fields; I do not want the golden bliss of Gyges. Living enough to sustain life is living enough for me. That saying 5 "Avoid excess" suits me excessively.

146
HECTOR DYING, FROM THE GREEK
Get rid of my body when I am dead, you Greeks, for hares fear the carcass of a lion.

---

43 Eurydice. See Ovid, *Metamorphoses* 10.
44 Perilla, whom Ovid addresses in *Tristia* 3.7 45 Cicero's daughter 46 Cornelia Africana 47 Cassandra, a prophetess and the daughter of King Priam and Hecuba of Troy, was cursed by Apollo with the fate that no one would believe her prophecies. 48 the soldier in Terence's *Eunuchus*, proverbial for his self-assurance

147
ON A STUPID POET
The poet who is second to none wrote long ago that in piety Aeneas was second to none.[49] And so a certain fellow who wanted to praise the king said—
5 in elegant imitation of Vergil, of course—"Here is a king to whom no one is second." The king does not deserve such praise as this; but the poet himself richly deserves it. So let us give each the praise which is his due: here is a poet, then, to whom no
10 one is second; here is a king who is second to none.

148
ON A CERTAIN AUTHOR WHO IN UNLEARNED STYLE WROTE HYMNS IN HONOR OF THE SAINTS, EXPLAINING IN HIS PREFACE THAT HE WROTE
5 THEM IN AN OFFHAND WAY WITHOUT OBSERVING THE RULES OF METER AND THAT HIS SUBJECT MATTER REQUIRED NO ELOQUENCE[50]
This sacred book of André's contains within marvel-
10 ously small compass all the feast days of the year in chronological order. It is credible that all the saints celebrated here took counsel for their poet when he wrote; for he wrote in haste, but even so with all the time in the world he could not have written better.
15 His subject matter is religious, and his style was untouched by the ancients and kept in reserve by fate for the present work. If he does not anxiously restrict himself to all the usual quantities, this too is not done by mistake but for a reason. The majesty of
20 the work refuses to be subjected to metrical rule. Assuredly, where the Spirit is, there also is liberty.[51] For the unlearned reader the piety of the book alone suffices; but you who are one accustomed to drink from the Castalian spring will receive such pleasure from
25 this book, if you examine it closely, as you have never had before from any other.

149
ON STRATOPHON, A WORTHLESS PRIZEFIGHTER, FROM THE GREEK
Ulysses, warrior-king of Ithaca, was away from home for twenty years; when he returned, he was
5 still recognized by his swift dog.[52] Well, prizefighter Stratophon, now that you have fought for four hours, your dog and your fellow citizens alike could no longer recognize you. As a matter of fact, Stratophon, if you looked at yourself in a mirror, you would yourself under oath deny that you are 10
Stratophon.

150
ON A WORTHLESS PRIZEFIGHTER, FROM THE GREEK
Here is Nesimus, a prizefighter, who asks the prophet Olympus if advanced old age is to be his lot. The prophet answers, "Perhaps you will live if 5 you retire; but, as long as you continue fighting, the god who brings the chill of death threatens you with his scythe."

151
ON A PARASITE, FROM THE GREEK
When Eutychides runs a race in the stadium, you would think he was standing still; but when he runs to dinner, you would think he was flying.

152
ON A DRINKER, FROM THE GREEK
Do not offer wreaths and unguents at my tomb. To buy wine and warmth for a stone will be a useless expense. Give me these things while I am alive, for throwing good wine on my ashes gives me no wine; 5 it just makes mud.

153
ON A DRINKER, FROM THE GREEK
I was born of earth; when I die, I shall be restored to earth. Therefore, come to me full, earthen bottle.

154
ON AN UGLY WOMAN, FROM THE GREEK
Your looking glass deceives you, Gellia, for, if you once looked into a true looking glass, you would never look again.

155
ON AN UGLY WOMAN, FROM THE GREEK
Antipatra would run to Parthia or to the pillars of Hercules if anyone caught a glimpse of her naked.

---

49 See *Aeneid* 1.544–45. **50** This poem was first published as a laudatory poem in the front of a book of hymns for the liturgical year by Bernard André. **51** 2 Cor 3:17 **52** Homer, *Odyssey* 17.292–310

156
ON AN UGLY WOMAN, FROM THE GREEK
The unhappy man who has an ugly wife will still have darkness when the lamps are lighted in the evening.

157
ON A MAN WHO WAS A PHILOSOPHER
ONLY BY REASON OF HIS BEARD,
FROM THE GREEK
If an untrimmed beard makes a philosopher, why
5 could not a bearded goat be a Plato?

158
ON GRANTING LIBERTIES
Freedom, if unrestrained, exceeds quickly and irrevocably its proper bounds. If you let your wife stamp on your foot tonight, tomorrow upon rising
5 she will stamp on your head.

159
EPITAPH OF ABINGDON, THE SINGER[53]
Let the famed singer, Henry Abingdon, draw your eyes hither; there was a time when he drew your ears with his music. Not long ago he sang in a voice
5 marvelous beyond compare and played the organ with incomparable skill. At first he was the pride of the church at Wells; then the king decided that he should lend his fame to the Chapel Royal. Now God has taken him away from the king and in-
10 stalled him among the stars to add glory to the very inhabitants of heaven.

160
ANOTHER EPITAPH ON THE SAME MAN
Here lies Henry, the constant friend of piety. Abingdon was his family name, if anyone should want his full name. He was once succentor of the
5 kindly church at Wells; and later he became chanter in the beautiful Chapel Royal. He was the best singer among a million. And besides this he was the best of organists. And so now, Christ, since he served you always on earth, admit him to the King-
10 dom of Heaven.

161
ON JANUS, ABINGDON'S HEIR
I wrote a poem in elegiac couplets to mark the tomb of Henry Abingdon at the request of his heir, Janus. Janus did not like it—and it might well have failed to please learned men. But Janus disliked only its
5 better parts. "These verses of yours do not rhyme," he said. I realized at once what kind of inferior food such lips as his like. With a laugh I blurted out some laughable verses. He clapped his hands with delight and gobbled them up. These are the verses
10 he had inscribed on the tomb. He deserves to be thrust forthwith into the same tomb and to be distinguished by the same epitaph. The two-faced god, Janus, sees everything in front of him and behind him. This barefaced Janus, like a faceless mole, sees
15 nothing before or behind.

162
TO A COURTIER
You often boast to me that you have the king's ear and often have fun with him, freely and according to your own whims. This is like having fun with tamed lions—often it is harmless, but just as often
5 there is the fear of harm. Often he roars in rage for no known reason, and suddenly the fun becomes fatal. The pleasure you get is not safe enough to relieve you of anxiety. For you it is a great pleasure. As for me, let my pleasure be less great—and safe.
10

163
TO TYNDAL, HIS DEBTOR
Before I lent you the money, Tyndal, I had the pleasure of your company as often as I liked. But now, if you happen to see me around some corner, you
5 run from me in terror like a man who has just seen a snake. I had no intention of asking for my money back. I had none, but rather than be forced to lose you, I shall. To keep you I am willing to lose the money; but I am not willing to lose both—one or
10 the other is loss enough for me. Therefore, either keep the money and give me back your friendship, or give me back your friendship and the money too. But if neither way pleases you, then at least see that I do not lose my money. And you, lost friend,
15 farewell.

---

53 Abingdon (*ca.* 1418–*ca.* 1497) was a composer, organist, singer, and choirmaster of the Chapel Royal.

164
ON A BEGGAR WHO PRETENDS
HE IS A PHYSICIAN

You pass yourself off as a physician; we grant you
that and more. You are one letter more [*mendicus*]
than physician [*medicus*].

165
ON AN UNFAITHFUL WIFE

Fruitful, how very fruitful is the wife of my friend
Aratus. Yes, three times she has conceived and
borne fruit with no help from her husband.

166
ON A TINY MAN, FROM THE GREEK

To escape the dull grind of his miserable life, Diophantus used a spider's thread, used it for a noose.

167
ON A GIRL WHO FEIGNED RAPE

When a young man saw a girl all by herself and
thought that this was his chance, the rascal put his
eager arms around her—unwilling as she was—and
was prepared to give her kisses, and more than kisses
too. She struggled against him and angrily cited the
law which condemns wretched rapists to have their
heads cut off. But still, with a young man's eagerness, the shameless fellow did his best to win her
over either by coaxing or threatening. She resisted
both coaxing and threats; she screamed. She kicked
him, bit him, struck him. The young man's anger
grew almost as great as his lust. Savagely he said,
"You wildcat, so that's the way it is. I swear to you
by this sword"—and he drew his weapon—"if you
do not lie down nice and easy, and shut up, I'll go
away." Terrified by so dire a threat she lay down at
once and said, "Go ahead and do it, but what you do
you do by force."

168
ON CHRYSALUS

When Chrysalus was burying his treasure chest in
the forest, he stopped to think what sure marks he
could find to locate the spot. And when he saw a
noisy crow in the top of a tree he said, "Here is an

outstanding landmark," and went away. When he
came back, the mere supersufficiency of the sight-
ing he had taken baffled him, for he saw his marks
in every tree.

169
ON AN ASTROLOGER

While astrologers (who, through our own mistake,
are honored as prophets) are producing your destiny in accordance with the position of a star, while
this star is promising and that one threatening, your
mind swings back and forth between hope and fear.
If good fortune is to come, it will come, though the
astrologers keep silent; and unexpected good luck
usually gives more pleasure. If, on the other hand,
bad luck is to come, then it is better to know nothing of it as long as possible and to enjoy the time until it arrives. In fact, this is what I advise, in the very
teeth of the fates themselves: keep your equanimity
and spend your days in good spirits.

170
ON A MAN WHO OUGHT TO BE CRUCIFIED,
FROM THE GREEK

Take away the first two letters of your *Mastauron*;
no one can more richly deserve what is left[54] than
you do.

171
AN EPITAPH, FROM THE GREEK

This tomb contains four brothers. To two of them,
alas, a single day brought life and death.

172
FROM THE GREEK

Timocritus was brave in battle. That is why he lies
here. It is not the brave, but the cowardly whom you
spare, brutal Mars.

173
FROM THE GREEK

That urn you see there contains a pair—both sons
of Neoclides; one freed his fatherland from slavery,
the other from vice.

---

54 That is, the Greek word for "crosses" is left after taking away the first two letters of *Mastauron*.

174

ON A MAN WHO HAS
A SHREWISH WIFE AT HOME

My friend, your wife is always bad. When you treat her badly, she gets worse, but when you treat her
5   well, she becomes worst of all. But if she dies, she will be a good wife; better if she dies while you are alive; and best of all if she dies soon.

175

ON SOME SAILORS WHO MADE
THEIR CONFESSIONS TO A MONK
DURING A STORM AND THEN
THREW HIM OVERBOARD

5   When the heaving sea in a roaring storm was ris- ing high and the anger of the waves was raging against the struggling ship, the frightened sailors were overcome by religious scruples. They cried, "Our ill-spent lives have brought on these ills."
10   There was a monk among the passengers. Into his ear they hastily unloaded their sins. But when they observed that the sea had not in the least calmed down, that, rather, the ship was just barely afloat on the rushing waters, one of them cried out, "No
15   wonder our ship is barely afloat! All this time it has been weighed down by our cargo of sin. Why not throw overboard this monk on whom we emp- tied out all our guilt, and let him take our sins away with him?" The sailors approve of what he said;
20   they lay hold of the man; they heave him into the sea. And—so they say—the ship sailed lighter than before. Now the moral of this story: learn from it how heavy is a load of sin, since a ship cannot sus- tain its weight.

176

TO CANDIDUS, A PASTOR WHO
LED AN EVIL LIFE

My dear Candidus, you have been made pastor of a large congregation. Therefore, I heartily congrat-
5   ulate you and your flock. Either partiality has dam- aged my judgment, or it is not possible that your flock ever before had such a priest. You do not have knowledge of vain disciplines to make you proud; clearly, such knowledge is of no use to your congre-
10   gation. Moreover, yours are rare virtues; just as rare, I believe, were men like you among the ancient fa- thers. Your life can function as a conspicuous model

by which your people can decide what to do and what to avoid. All that is needed is to advise them to observe you closely, avoid what you do, and do   15 what you avoid.

177

FROM THE GREEK

In this urn reposes a sailor, in that a farmer. By land or by sea the journey is the same; it ends at the Styx.

178

ON BISHOP POSTHUMUS

You are now a bishop, Posthumus, and it is only proper that you have this extraordinary authority, for in the whole world there never was a more ex- traordinary man than you. I rejoice that, at last, so   5 important and inviolable an office is no longer con- ferred at random, as it used to be. I say this because a random impulse is likely to be wrong; but, as for you, it is plain that you were selected with great care. Actually, when just one man is taken from   10 among many, he often turns out, by chance, to be bad or, by deliberate choice, to be the very worst. But in your case, if one is to be taken from many thousands, he could hardly match you in stupidity and wickedness.   15

179

ON BOLLANUS

Just before Bollanus lay down, his companions strewed his whole bed with stinging nettles. Yet he said he had not been stung; even so, he did not deny that he did find them when he was undressed and   5 in the dark. Therefore it must be that they avoided his flesh and came in contact only with his nails or his bared teeth. And yet, since he encountered the leaves in the dark without being stung, how did he discover that they were nettles?   10

180

FABLE OF THE SICK FOX AND THE LION

While a fox lay sick in his narrow den, a smooth- tongued lion took his stand at the entrance. Said he, "Tell me, my friend, don't you feel well? You will soon get well if you let me lick you. You just do not   5 know the power of my tongue." "Your tongue," said the fox, "has healing powers; but the trouble is that such a good tongue has bad neighbors."

181

ON A LION AND LYSIMACHUS

While a tamed lion harmlessly licked his trainer, the trainer invited one and all to put themselves in his place. After a long time, when no one among the large crowd of spectators had come forward, brave-hearted Lysimachus leaped up. Said he, "I am brave enough to endure the touch of the lion's tongue, but his teeth are so close to his tongue that I shall not do it."

182

ON FABIAN, THE ASTROLOGER

Now that credulous people, in great numbers, every day, are buying from you great quantities of predictions, if among the many lies you tell there is, by chance, a single truth, then, Fabian, right off, you want me to think you a prophet. But make your predictions invariably wrong. If you can keep this up, Fabian, I might think you a prophet.

183

ON THE KING OF SCOTLAND, WHO ATTACKED NORHAM CASTLE WHICH HAD ALREADY BEEN BETRAYED TO HIM, PRETENDING THAT IT HAD NOT

Scot,[55] why do you launch an armed attack on Norham Castle, which had already been treacherously betrayed into your hands? Are you ashamed of your deceitfulness? Your vices are so many and so notorious that this one should cause you no shame. Your pleasure in taking the castle by artful deception may have been great, but it was short. Within a few days, after the wretched but richly deserved destruction of you and yours, the captured castle was recaptured. And when the betrayer asked for his reward in your realm, he received the wages worthy of his crime, death. It is the destiny of that invincible castle that not only the man who betrays it should perish but also the man to whom he betrays it.

184

AN EPITAPH FOR JAMES KING OF THE SCOTS

It is I, James, King of the Scots, brave and ill-starred enemy of a friendly kingdom, who am interred beneath this sod. Would that my loyalty had been equal to my courage. The sequel with its shame for me would not have happened. But, alas, it is shameful to boast and repugnant to complain — therefore, I shall say no more. And I hope, O chattering Infamy, that you may be willing to keep silent. You kings (I was once a king myself) I warn you not to let loyalty become, as it often does, a meaningless word.

185

ON A BAD PAINTER

A painter admired for his extraordinary skill showed in a picture how a frightened hare flees a dog's cruel jaws. After pondering the innermost secrets of nature, he represented the hare as looking backward in terror during its flight. I hope that the painter who succeeded thus in showing a fleeing hare may himself become a hare and, during his effort to escape, look back.

186

ON THE SAME PAINTER

A hare and a dog were painted in such fashion that no one could determine which was the dog and which the hare. When the artist learned that this was so, with marvelous ingenuity he supplied what his insufficient skill had left out. To make the matter plain and banish ambiguity, he merely wrote at the bottom, "This is the dog; that, the hare."

187

ON TYNDARUS

While Tyndarus happened to be kissing a girl whose outstanding characteristic was not the smallness of her nose, he felt a sudden impulse to be witty about it. Said he, "I cannot make my lips reach yours, for your nose keeps my mouth at a distance." The girl immediately blushed and burned with repressed anger, stung by his not very witty witticism. "If my nose keeps your kisses from my mouth," she said, "then you can kiss me here, where I have no nose."

---

55 James IV of Scotland besieged Norham Castle in August 1513 and held in until he was defeated at Flodden Field in September.

188

ON GERMAN BRIXIUS, WHO WRITES FALSEHOODS ABOUT THE FRENCH SHIP *CORDELIÈRE* AND HER CAPTAIN, HERVÉ

Brixius, while you try to win fame for Hervé,[56]
you defeat the purpose of your poetry, for with
bad faith you have recorded his good deeds. In the
poem, Germanus, you promise us a history, but
since it is not at all true, it is not history either. Let
historians begin to show either prejudice or favoritism, and who will there be to lend any credence at
all to histories? Now this very Hervé of yours has
lost his praise because of you, for what praise can he
have without belief in the facts?

189

ON THE SAME AUTHOR DEALING WITH THE SAME HERVÉ AND THE SAME SHIP (WHICH WAS BURNED UP IN A NAVAL BATTLE)

I am not at all surprised that Brixius has conferred
upon Hervé praise which he did not earn, and has
deprived the opposing captain of his due honor,
and has celebrated, in his poem on the ship *Cordelière*, a thousand lies which are the very opposite
of the facts. Still I don't believe he deliberately set
out to write falsehoods because of a perverse prejudice. Rather, it was simply that no survivor has yet
been able to come back to tell the bard the truth
about the *Cordelière*. But for him to learn the whole
truth, the right thing would have been for him to be
aboard himself—amidships.

190

VERSES TAKEN FROM BRIXIUS'S *CHORDIGERA* BECAUSE SOME OF THE FOLLOWING EPIGRAMS MAKE FUN OF THEM

Left and right the Britons surround Hervé as he
stands alone. Shaft upon shaft flies in a wintry hail-
storm toward the head of Hervé alone, but the hero
boldly shakes them off with his shield and turns
them back against the other side.

A LATER INCIDENT FROM THE SAME POEM *CHORDIGERA*

Hervé spurs his comrades on and himself presses
forward. In the front ranks of a mighty attack, he
drives boldly into the enemy. Some he strikes down
with a javelin through the temples; through another's ribs he thrusts his sword; he lays open the guts
of another; with axe-blows to the neck he cuts off
the heads of some, or wounds a flank or shoulder
with his sharp spear.

MORE'S EPIGRAM MOCKING THE VERSES ABOVE

As for the statements that Hervé struck some enemies down with javelins through their temples,
thrust his sword through the guts or ribs of others, severed the heads of some with axe-blows to
the neck, pierced the shoulders and flanks of others, and as for his bravely fending off with his shield
the hurtled missiles of the enemy and returning
them to their source—all this is beyond the reach
of understanding, how one man could fight with
so many weapons, and that while one arm was burdened with a shield. Unyielding nature herself contradicts this battle. I think that in this passage you
omitted something. For when you represented heroic Hervé fighting with four weapons and a shield
all at the same time, perhaps the fact slipped your
mind, but your reader ought to have been informed
in advance that Hervé had five hands.

191

ANOTHER ON THE SAME SUBJECT

You wonder how Hervé could carry shield, sword,
spear, javelins, and axe and fight with them, too.
Well, his right hand is armed with the merciless
battle-ax, his dire left is equipped with a sword all
its own. At the same time he boldly holds (with
clenched teeth) in his mouth the javelin, and the
spear to take the javelin's place. And because missiles thicker than wintry hail fly toward his head, on
his head he wears his shield. A dragon would not
have so hard a head, nor Celaeno[57] such claws; thus
the elephant with his tusks could not equal him.
And so, as he rushed against the enemy, he was a

---

56 Germain de Brie (1490–1538), also known as Germanus Brixius, published *Chordigerae Navis Conflagratio* in 1513 (see *CW* 3.2: 429–65). The poem commem- orated an engagement with the English on August 10, 1512, honored the French commander, and attacked the English. That same year, More wrote the following epigrams in response. Years later, despite Erasmus's protest, Brixius wrote *Antimorus*, a satire and in-depth critique of More's epigrams, published in 1519. See Letter to Brixius (pp. 456–72) for More's reply, and Letter 87 to Erasmus (pp. 292–303). **57** one of the harpies in *Aeneid* 3.211–17

strange monster, inspiring terror with both his arm
15 and his grin.

192
THE FIRST LINE IN THIS POEM IS
BY BRIXIUS WHO PRESENTS A
PROPHECY ABOUT HIMSELF MADE BY
HERVÉ, WHO WAS SOON TO DIE

5 One not to be despised among the disciples of Phoebus, the poet Brixius celebrated the mighty deeds of
Captain Hervé.

One not to be despised among the disciples of
Phoebus burned up Hervé, his enemies, his com-
10 panions, and the ships.

How, then, did this poet not to be despised among
the disciples of Phoebus—how did he learn what his
poem tells?

The only conclusion is that one not to be despised
15 among the disciples of Phoebus heard it from the
tripod of Phoebus.

193
ON THE SAME WRITER'S THEFT OF
LINES FROM THE POETS

No one cultivates the ancient poets more than you
or culls from them more diligently, for there is not
5 one among the ancient poets from whose lines, here
and there, you have not culled little blossoms and
buds by the handful; and you immediately repay
the poet by the great honor of being slipped in with
what you write. And you do bestow a blessing on
10 the bard, for what you gather proclaims its origin
and shines out among your lines more brightly than
the stars gleaming in the night sky.

So great an honor you never begrudge to any
bard, a friend to them all, so that no one of them,
15 once the glory of an age that is past, now needs to
weep at your neglect. Therefore, lest the hallowed
measures of the poets perish of long disuse, you
save them from the injuries of time and adorn them
with new luster. This is by art to give new life to
20 what is old—there is no happier gift than this. O
blessed art!—and yet whoever, employing your artistic method, shall insert his antique borrowings in
a new context, will by no effort of art, however long
he sweats about it, succeed in imparting their antiq-
25 uity to his own new verses.

194
A MOCKING COMMENT ON THE
CENOTAPH OF HERVÉ

According to your judgment, Brixius, our age can
match the two Decii[58] in the single person of Hervé.
And yet there is this difference: the Decii died of   5
their own free will; Hervé, because he could not run
away.

195
PHOEBUS ADDRESSES BRIXIUS

Do you want to know what I think of that grandil-
oquent little book which recounts the derring-do
and the death of Hervé, mighty in battle? Well,
then, poet sacred to Phoebus, hear these sacred or-   5
acles delivered by Phoebus's tripod. In the whole
work one syllable is missing; there are a thousand
to spare. The work is full up, for what could be less
than what you omitted? The syllable I mean can be
picked out of only one month (though it has not   10
been picked out for you) and it contains more than
half of *mensis*[59] [month].

196
TO SABINUS, WHOSE WIFE BECAME
PREGNANT IN HIS ABSENCE

Sabinus, hurry home; to you is born a child, the support of your existence, the only hope of your extreme old age. Hurry; you must greet your fruitful   5
wife, see the beloved offspring—hurry home, Sabinus. Hurry, I say, and waste no time about it; and,
hurry as you may, you will seem too slow. Hurry
home, Sabinus. Now your wife is complaining about
you, the baby is crying for you; Sabinus, hurry home. 10
Because you are an ungrateful fellow, you are never
there, not at the birth, not even at the conception;
hurry home, Sabinus. Hurry to be in time at least for
the boy's baptism. Sabinus, hurry home.

197
TO CANDIDUS, WHO PRAISED HOLY MEN
ALTHOUGH HE HIMSELF WAS EVIL

You often praise good men; you never, Candidus,
imitate them. You say, "I, Candidus, praise them
without envy, for whoever imitates good men also   5
envies them." O Candidus, ingenuous innocent,
whiter than milk or snow.[60]

58 See Livy 8.6.8–13, 8.9.1–2, 10.28.13–18
for the account of Publius Decius (d.
340 BC) and his son (d. 295 BC) of the

same name, consuls who both chose
death in defense of Rome.   **59** *mens*
(intelligence)

60 See Gn 49:12; Ps 50(51):9; Lam 4:7;
Dan 7:9; Mk 9:3; and Rv 1:14.

198

WHAT IS THE BEST FORM
OF GOVERNMENT

You ask which governs better, a king or a senate.
Neither, if (as is frequently the case) both are bad.
But if both are good, then I think that the senate,
because of its numbers, is the better and that the
greater good lies in numerous good men. Perhaps it
is difficult to find a group of good men; even more
frequently it is easy for a monarch to be bad. A senate would occupy a position between good and bad;
but hardly ever will you have a king who is not either good or bad. An evil senator is influenced by
advice from better men than he; but a king is himself the ruler of his advisers. A senator is elected by
the people to rule; a king attains this end by being
born. In the one case blind chance is supreme; in
the other, a reasonable agreement. The one feels
that he was made senator by the people; the other
feels that the people were created for him so that, of
course, he may have subjects to rule.

A king in his first year is always very mild indeed,
and so every year the consul will be like a new king.
Over a long time a greedy king will gnaw away at his
people. If a consul is evil, there is hope of improvement. I am not swayed by the well-known fable
which recommends that one endure the well-fed
fly lest a hungry one take its place.[61] It is a mistake
to believe that a greedy king can be satisfied; such a
leech never leaves flesh until it is drained.

But, you say, a serious disagreement impedes a
senate's decisions, while no one disagrees with a
king. But that is the worse evil of the two, for when
there is a difference of opinion about important
matters—but say, what started you on this inquiry
anyway? Is there anywhere a people upon whom
you yourself, by your own decision, can impose either a king or a senate?[62] If this does lie within your
power, you are king. Stop considering to whom you
may give power. The more basic question is whether
it would do any good if you could.[63]

199

ON FUSCUS, THE DRINKER

His physician told Fuscus that drinking would destroy his eyes. When Fuscus had considered the
matter, he said, "I would rather destroy my eyes by
drinking than preserve them to be gnawed out by
crawling worms."

200

TO A FRIEND

I gather from what you write that my letter will
come too late. But it won't be too late for you—
no more than weapons which arrive after the war is
over can be said to arrive too late, if those weapons
would have been of no use anyway.

201

ON THE KING AND THE PEASANT

A forest-bred peasant, more naive than Faunus or a
satyr, came to town. See there! the inhabitants have
taken places on either side to fill the avenue, and
throughout the city all one could hear was the cry,
"The king is coming." The peasant was roused by
the strange news and longed to see what the crowd
was watching for so eagerly. Suddenly the king rode
by, in full view, resplendent with gold, escorted by
a large company, and astride a tall horse. Then the
crowd really did roar: "Long live the king"; and
with rapt expressions they gazed up at the king. The
peasant cried out, "Where is the king? Where is the
king?" And one of the bystanders replied, "There he
is, the one mounted high on that horse over there."
The peasant said, "Is that the king? I think you are
making fun of me. To me he looks like a man in
fancy dress."

202

ON THE ILLITERATE BISHOP TO WHOM
AN EARLIER EPIGRAM REFERRED UNDER
THE NAME OF POSTHUMUS

You, mighty father, exclaim, "The letter kills." This
single phrase "The letter kills" you have always in
your mouth. You have taken good care that no letter
may kill you; you do not know any letter. And not
idle is your fear that the letter may kill; you know
that you do not have the spirit which will give you
life.[64]

---

61 See Aesop's "The Fox and the Hedge-hog" and Aristotle's *Rhetoric* 2.20.6–7, 1393b. **62** See Sallust, *Catiline* 6.6–7, where Sallust reports how the Romans did so, choosing a republic with consuls over a monarchy. **63** These last sentences are Clarence Miller's translation; see *CW* 3.2, p. 50. **64** See 2 Cor 3:6.

203

ON THE PRIEST WHO FOOLISHLY WARNED HIS PARISHIONERS OF A FAST DAY WHEN THE DAY HAD ALREADY PASSED

When our priest, as it happened, was advising his
parishioners of the saints' calendar for the coming week, he said, "The feast of Saint Andrew the
Martyr is a great and memorable feast; you know
how dear to God Andrew was. Let austere fasting
mortify the wayward flesh; this is the custom, established by the holy fathers. Therefore I forewarn you
all that in honor of this martyr you ought to have
fasted yesterday."

204

ON A MAN WHO SANG BADLY AND READ WELL

You sang so badly that you could be a bishop, but
you read so well that you could not. Let no one
imagine that it is enough to avoid success in the one
or the other. No, if you want to become a bishop be
careful on both counts.

205

TO SABINUS

Look here, Sabinus, the four children whom your
wife has borne up to now do not in the least resemble you; you yourself do not consider them yours.
But, in preference to the four, you take to your
heart the little fellow she has most recently borne,
the only one who is very like you. You call the four
illegitimate, you keep them at a distance, you dis-
own them. You have appointed this youngest one,
as the only legitimate son, to be your heir; and, like
an ape carrying her young, you carry him in your
arms all over town for everyone to kiss and cod-
dle. And yet weighty scholars who direct all their
efforts at uncovering the secret effects of nature —
weighty scholars, I say, tell us that whatever image
dominates the mother's mind when the child is begotten, secretly in some mysterious way imposes accurate and indelible traces of itself upon the seed;
these marks penetrate deeply and grow with the
embryo, and thus the child reflects the image inbred
in it from the mother's mind. When your wife conceived the four children she was quite unconcerned
about you because you were so many miles away.
That is why she bore children who do not resemble

you. But this son, of all your children, looks like
you because at his conception his mother was very
much concerned about you and had you completely
on her mind; she was worried for fear you, Sabinus,
might inconveniently arrive on the scene, as we say
"speak of the devil."

206

A FUNNY STORY ABOUT A PRINCE AND A PEASANT FROM ZEELAND

A prince, as he gazed at the water, sat down on a
bridge, and his nobles stood respectfully about. A
peasant sat down, too, but not near by, and thought
himself polite because of the distance he kept. A
certain courtier got him up and said, "Peasant, do
you dare to sit on the same bridge with the prince?
Aren't you ashamed?" The peasant answered, "Is it
wrong to sit on the same bridge? What if the bridge
were ten miles long?"

207

A FUNNY STORY ABOUT A COURTIER

A courtier, dismounting from his horse, said to one
of the bystanders, "You — whoever you are — hold
this horse." The bystander, because he was frightened, said, "My lord, I ask you, is one man enough
then to hold this savage horse?" The courtier said,
"One man can hold him." The bystander rejoined,
"If one man can, then you can hold your horse
yourself."

208

TO A SOLDIER WHO RAN AWAY AND WHO WAS WEARING A RING

Soldier, why does that golden ring of yours decorate
your hands? It would more properly decorate your
feet. In that recent fierce battle either one of your
feet was more helpful and more successful than
both your hands.

209

TO THE POET BRIXIUS

Brixius, such an enigma arises in your book as might
be proposed by the Sphinx to Oedipus: you have
the whole word *Chordigera* time and time again,
but nowhere in your whole book do you have the
first syllable of *Cordigera*.[65]

65 *cor* (heart)

210

ON TUSCUS THE DRINKER

"You are ruining your eyes with wine," said the physician to Tuscus. Therefore, Tuscus took thought what course to follow. He observed, "Sky, land, sea, whatever people usually see, I have seen again and again. And yet many a wine remains to be tasted when the new year brings its many new vintages." Then he made his decision and said with firm resolve, "Farewell, eyes, for I have seen enough, but to date enough I have not drunk."

211

TO A PERJURER

Arnus, you have been swearing oaths long enough; you have finally reached such a point that hereafter you need not swear. By this time, you outstanding oathtaker, there is no place where your word is not as good as your oath.

212

TO THE SAME PERJURER

You are always swearing oaths, Arnus, and threatening everyone. Do you want to know what advantage you win by such conduct? The result of your swearing is that now in the end no one believes you; the result of your threats, that they frighten no one.

213

ON THE SAME ARNUS

All this time no one has been better equipped with feet than Arnus, but some time ago he lost the use of his hands as the result of frostbite. Still he wants to fight. I suppose you know what a man will accomplish in a fight if his feet are swift and both his hands disabled. But if a man's tongue is shameless and his hand inactive, then this man's shameless tongue ought to be cut out by an active hand.

214

ON MARULLUS

His physician warned blear-eyed Marullus, Theodore, not to drink any wine unless he was willing to be blind. To obey his doctor (though reluctantly), for two whole days, mark you, he endured to go without. Thereafter, he grew thirsty at the memory of his accustomed wine and then rushed out of doors despite the truth of the physician's warning.

He had made his way to the wine when he gloomily addressed his eyes (destined to perish now that his wine was before him). "Here my journey ends; here you, my faithful eyes, have led me. Now drink, and, sweet guides, farewell." The taste and the bouquet remained; he stared at the vanishing color as his sight vanished in utter darkness. He mitigated his misfortune with the comforting thought that it was the least of the wine's benefits which he must forgo.

215

ON RISCUS, AN UNWARLIKE KNIGHT

Riscus, a prudent knight, skilled by long experience, keeps horses of different kinds, and not without reason. For he keeps two, one swifter than a bird, the other slower than a plodding ass. And so the latter mount delivers him, in no haste, to battle; the former, before the trumpet sounds, brings him back.

216

TO GELLIA

Gellia, my dear, he lies who says you are dark; in my estimation, Gellia, you are not dark, you are black.

217

TO THE SAME GELLIA

"I am fair," you say. I agree. But since you are fair, why does a dark skin conceal this fairness of yours?

218

TO EUPARIPHUS, WHO MORTGAGED HIS FARM TO BUY CLOTHING

I do not wonder that you sweat under the weight of your clothing; this costume of yours contains four acres of land. Not even a man in his grave has so great a mound of earth over him as you will have laid upon yourself, wherever you may be, while still alive.

219

ON GAREMANUS, WHO WAS POOR AFTER SELLING HIS LANDS

Recently Garemanus sold his ancestral estate; now, all of a sudden, rumor says he is living in poverty. It is not that he lacks skill or effort; rather I think that a hostile fate is doing him a bad turn, for he cleverly exchanged his moldy earth for yellow gold, and even so he never makes a profit.

220

TO SABINUS

Two wives are dead; a third wife now is yours. And
yet not one of the three has been faithful to you.
Hence, Sabinus, in your angry heart you wickedly
5 condemn not only your own wives but the whole
female sex. But if you are willing to weigh this problem on the scales of justice, you will be less severe
even on your own wives. For, since all three of your
wives treated you the same way, it must be that the
10 stars at your birth imposed this fate upon you. If
your destiny requires that you be forever a cuckold,
can it be that you expect your wife to control the
stars? She would have been faithful to some other
man. That with you she is an adultress she rightly
15 attributes to your fate.

221

ON A SHIPWRECKED SAILOR BITTEN BY
A SNAKE WHEN HE REACHED SHORE,
FROM THE GREEK

A shipwrecked sailor escaped the raging waters
5 of the sea; the sands of Africa provided him with
ground more cruel than the sea. While he lay there
on the shore, sound asleep, naked, worn out, far
from the hostile sea, a deadly snake killed him. In
vain poor fellow, in vain did you escape the deep;
10 your allotted fate awaited you on land.

222

A PHYSICIAN AND AN OLD WOMAN

A physician applied ointment to an old woman's
ailing eyes, bandaged them, and assured her that five
days of such treatment would be effective. Mean-
5 while, he stole her napkins, bowls, basins, dishes,
and whatever was not protected by its own weight.
When she was cured and looked about without the
bandage, she perceived that the furnishings of her
home were missing. Therefore, when she was asked
10 to pay her bill, she said, "The agreement between us
requires that my sight be improved by your efforts.
Actually, I see less than before, at least of the utensils in my house. I saw many of them before; now I
see none."

223

TO AN UNIDENTIFIED PERSON

If you were as light on your feet as you are in the
head, you could outrun a hare on level ground.

224

ON HEROD AND HERODIAS

While the daughter of Herodias was dancing for
Herod and pleasing him in a way which ought
to have displeased him, King Herod, inebriated
with love for his wife, inebriated by his excess of 5
good fortune, and drunk besides with wine, said,
"State your wish, maiden; it shall be yours, by my
oath, even if it is your pleasure to ask for half this
realm." The wicked girl, at the prompting of her evil
mother, replied, "In that case give me, please, the 10
head of John the Baptist."[66]

The favor you ask, maiden (if such dancing girls
as you are maidens) — the favor you ask is such a favor as you can hardly bear to look upon. O deadly
parent, O cruel stepmother to your own daugh- 15
ter, for you teach her to be a dancer and to cut the
throats of men.

The king regrets his promise; reluctantly he
yields, forced no doubt by a scrupulous regard for
his oath. Here is a king true to his word, but true 20
to it only when to be true is a worse crime than to
be false to it.

225

TO AN UNNAMED DRUNKARD

Because I did not make greater haste to arrive for
my conversation with you, you rebuke my tardiness
and complain. Truly, I confess, I did not meet you
at the proper time. I ought to have chosen an hour 5
either later or earlier. Would that I had arrived either early the same day or early on the next. Now we
have started to do business when the day is too far
advanced, and because you are drunk it has come
to nothing. 10

226

ON A PICTURE OF HEROD'S TABLE

By the blood of man Herod's table was polluted;
polluted, too, the table of Flaminius.[67] These two
murders, so much alike, were brought about by two

---

66 See Mk 6:17–28.   **67** See Cicero,
De senectate 12.42, for his account of the   Roman consul Lucius Quinctius Flaminius,
who executed a prisoner at a harlot's   request, similar to the story of John the
Baptist's execution.

young women of similar characters. A dancing girl accomplished the one, a prostitute the other. But there was this difference: the prostitute's pay was the life of a criminal; that of the dancer, the life of an innocent man.

227
ON THE SAME PICTURE

The king's table bears a severed head and a saint's countenance dripping with hideous gore. So too King Atreus, King Thyestes's brother, served as food to Thyestes the bodies of his two sons.[68] Similarly, to the Thracian king his queen, a loyal sister but a treacherous mother, served their murdered son, Itys.[69] Such delicacies as these mark the tables of kings; I assure you this is not a poor man's fare.

228
TO A MAN WITH AN EXTREMELY LONG
NOSE, FROM THE GREEK

If your nose should be pointed up toward the sun and your mouth kept open, you could show the time of day on your teeth.

229
TO A MAN COSMETICALLY BEAUTIFIED,
FROM THE GREEK

Why do you buy rouge, hair, teeth, honey, and wax when at less expense you could buy a complete mask?

230
TO AN ACTOR, FROM THE GREEK

Your dancing in all respects but one was in harmony with the stories, but in one way—and that an important one—it was contrary to the story. While you played the part of Niobe, you stood as though made of stone; when you were Capaneus, you fell suddenly; but when you played Canace with the sword and came away alive, that was dancing contrary to the story.

231
ON AN ACTOR, FROM THE GREEK

Memphis danced the parts of Niobe and of Daphne. Daphne he played as though he were made of wood, Niobe as though made of stone.

232
THAT SOBER MEN ARE VERY SURLY,
FROM THE GREEK

In the evening, when we are drinking, we are human beings, and kind ones; but in the morning a man who gets up with a thirst is a savage beast to his fellow man.

233
TO ANDREW AS HE VOMITED
INTO THE SEA

You are a grateful and well-deserving person, Andrew, for you pay back the fish, which have so often fed you, by feeding them.

234
ON THE SAME ANDREW

You have eaten the fish which belong to the sea; the sea is angry and demands from your mouth her progeny.

235
TO A GIRL WHO RODE HER
HORSE ASTRIDE

Well, my girl, no one could deny that you can take a man, since your legs can straddle so large a horse.

236
TO A FRENCHMAN WHO APPROPRIATED
THE POETRY OF THE ANCIENTS

Frenchman, the same insight and even the very same inspiration the ancient poets had now belongs to you. For the poems they wrote, and often the lines too, are the same as what you write.

237
ON A POVERTY-STRICKEN JOKESTER

When a jokester saw burglars searching his whole house with great care in the dark of night, he laughed and said, "I wonder what you see here in the middle of the night: I can see nothing in the middle of the day."

238
ON THE ANXIOUS LIFE OF RULERS

Immense power always brings miserable worries, tormented as it is by ever-present fears. Such a

---

68 See Seneca, *Thyestes* 691–1006.   69 See Ovid, *Metamorphoses* 6.620–60.

person does not venture out unless surrounded by a large armed guard, does not eat food which has not been tasted in advance. Certainly these precautions are aids to safety; yet they show that a man is not safe if he cannot be safe without them. Thus a bodyguard reveals fear of an assassin's sword. A food-taster manifests fear of poison. And so what place is without fear in such a life? — where even the very means of repelling what is to be feared themselves engender fear.

239

TO A STEPSON, CRUSHED BY THE FALL
OF HIS STEPMOTHER'S STATUE,
FROM THE GREEK

Putting wreaths of flowers on your stepmother's monument, you think that her death has put an end to her malicious behavior. But suddenly the column topples and crushes you. Stepson, if you are wise, flee even the tomb of your stepmother.

240

TO A CERTAIN POET WHO WROTE
EXTEMPORE

Why do you inform us that you wrote these verses extempore? Your book, you see, apart from any explanation from you, tells us as much.

241

ON STEPMOTHERS, FROM THE GREEK

Even a loving stepmother is a misfortune to her stepson. Phaedra, so grievous to Hippolytus, proves the point.

242

TO ONE WHO SAID THAT HIS POEMS
WOULD NOT LACK GENIUS

A witty epigram of the Spanish poet contains this thought: "To live, a book must have genius."[70] Having read this verse, you set your whole mind on writing poetry yourself, but it turns out to be mindless. The subject and style of your song are matters beneath your notice, such is your confidence that whatever you sing is sure to live by its own genius. For you have no doubt, O man of genius, that presently some sort of genius from somewhere or other will settle on your Muse. Instead you ought to hope

(this hope will be fulfilled) that this book of yours may have no genius, since it has no genuine talent. Any genius which might prolong the life of this book will be one of those evil geniuses which you have about you by the thousand. But, even so, your book will not live — if you can take the word of the same poet — for life does not mean merely living; it means living with health and strength. Still, if, for a book, to live is to languish in unending infamy, then may yours also live in eternal death.

243

ON LUST FOR POWER

Among many kings there will be scarcely one, if there is really one, who is satisfied to have one kingdom. And yet among many kings there will be scarcely one, if there is really one, who rules a single kingdom well.

244

ON THE SURRENDER OF TOURNAI TO
HENRY VIII, KING OF ENGLAND

Warlike Caesar vanquished you, Tournai, till then unconquered, but not without disaster to both sides. Henry, a king both mightier and better than Caesar, has taken you without bloodshed.[71] The king felt that he had gained honor by taking you, and you yourself felt it no less advantageous to be taken.

245

ON FABULLA AND ATTALUS

Recently when Fabulla was angry for some reason with Attalus and wanted to upset him and show how completely she scorned him, she swore to him that if she had a hundred of the parts which are exclusively a woman's she would not condescend to offer so much as one to Attalus. "Wouldn't you?" said he. "What the devil is this new restraint, this new stinginess of yours? Surely you used to be more generous. You couldn't bring yourself, you stingy broad, to put at my disposal a single one from among a hundred? But once upon a time when you had only one, it was your kindly habit to offer that one to a hundred men a hundred times each. What a pity! I fear this unnatural frugality of yours, after so long a time, may mean you have very bad times ahead of you."

---

70 Martial 6.61(60).10   **71** Henry VIII conquered the French city in September 1513.

246

ON THE FEVERISH PATIENT AND
THE DRINKING PHYSICIAN

When a servant boy of mine was suffering from a
semi-tertian fever, I chanced on that occasion to call
upon the services of a Sarmatian physician. When
he had applied his thumb and felt the boy's leaping
pulse, he said, "His temperature is high, but it will
go down." And so he asked for a cup and drained
it to the last drop, as not even Bitias could have
done. After his drink he urged the patient to a similar dose, and, in an effort to lend some reason to
his conduct, he said, "This man's fever is unusually
high; his drinks therefore must be unusually large.
A large fire cannot be put out by a little liquid."

247

ON HESPERUS AT CONFESSION

When Hesperus was purging himself of his sins
by confessing them to a priest in accordance with
sacred usage, the priest, probing Hesperus's conscience, carefully sought for every kind of sin and,
among many questions, asked if Hesperus had ever
in pagan fashion believed in evil spirits. "What! I
believe in evil spirits, Father?" said he; "I still have
all I can do to believe in God."

248

ON THE GOD OPPORTUNITY,
FROM THE GREEK

From what place did this sculptor come?
    Sicyon.
Well, who was he, tell me.
    Lysippus.
Who are you?
    I am Opportunity, master of all things.
Why are you standing on tiptoe?
    I am always turning about.
But why do you have wings on your feet?
    I move like a fleeting breeze.
Well, why is your right hand armed with a sharp
    razor?
    It is symbolic of the fact that no fine edge
        can be compared with me.
Why does a lock of hair lie upon your brow?
    Because if anyone tries to catch me, he must
        get ahead of me.
Why is the back of your head bald?

Because once I get away in headlong flight on
    my swift wings,
Anyone behind me who wants to bring me back
    will have no success whatever.
Thus the talented hand of the sculptor, as you may
see,
Has displayed me in such form as to permit you to
learn a lesson.

249

ON PHYLLIS AND PRISCUS, WHO LOVED
WITH UNEQUAL FERVOR

The wedding of beautiful Phyllis and impatient
Priscus is as happy as the mixing of foaming wine
and crystal-clear water. Priscus's love for Phyllis is
hotter than searing fire, Phyllis's for Priscus colder
than ice water. Their union will be safe, for, if she
should blaze along with him, what home could
withstand two such flames at once?

250

ON ANCIENT COINS PRESERVED IN THE
HOME OF JEROME BUSLEYDEN

What Rome once upon a time owed to her leaders,
all those leaders, Busleyden,[72] owe to you. Rome was
saved by her leaders; you preserve Rome's leaders,
now that Rome is dead, for with devotion to antiquity you seek out and collect the old coins which
present the features of the emperors or of men famous in imperial times or earlier; and these coins
you reckon your only form of wealth. Now when
thick dust conceals their triumphal arches, you keep
the names and features of the triumphant heroes.
The pyramids are not such memorials to their noble
dead as your coin-box, Busleyden, has now become.

251

ANOTHER TO BUSLEYDEN

Why, my dear Busleyden, do you still keep your
gentle Muse within the confines of your own writing box? Why do you keep her in the dark when she
deserves the light? Why do you deny this favor to
her? Why deny it to humanity? Your Muse ought
to be known all over the world. Why do you refuse
her this glory? And the whole world ought to enjoy your charming Muse. You alone thwart all men;
why? Does it seem to you that the chaste band of
maidens ought to be kept far from the society of

72 Jerome de Busleyden (*ca.* 1470–1517) was a distinguished humanist from the Netherlands. See his letter in *Utopia*, p. 212.

men? This, I grant you, is for maidens a source of
anxiety, but only for such as can be deprived of their
virginity. Have no fear; publish your Muse — she has
an unyielding chastity which is neither awkward nor
ignorant. Just as surely as your charming Muse will
not be inferior to Diana herself in spotless chastity,
so surely will she be not inferior to Minerva herself
in taste, in wit, and in beauty.

252

TO BUSLEYDEN ON HIS SPLENDID
HOUSE AT MECHLIN

While recently I gazed with fascinated eyes at the
tasteful decorations in your house, Busleyden, I was
amazed: by what incantation have you charmed the
fates so as to bring back so many ancient masters?
For I think that only the hands of Daedalus could
have built that famous house of yours with its artfully winding passages.[73] The pictures here Apelles
seems to have painted. The sculptures one might
believe to be the work of Myron. When I looked
upon the works modelled in clay I thought them
the product of Lysippus's art. The statues made me
think of the master Praxiteles. Couplets identify every work of art, but couplets such as Vergil, if he
did not write them, might wish that he had. Only
the organ which imitates such a range of voices with
its pipes is, I think, beyond the powers even of the
ancients. And so your whole house is either a noble work of antiquity or a modern work such as to
surpass antiquity. But may this house, which is now
new, be long and slow to grow old, and even then
may it see its master not yet grown old.

253

ON THE FAITHLESS MARRIAGE OF
PHILOMENUS AND AGNA

Behold in our time such miracles of Venus as I
think were not brought to pass even in the days
of old. Philomenus, flower of the young men, and
Agna, flower of the girls, were formally joined by
the kindness of the Paphian goddess. But he, unfortunately, was vain of his overrated voice, and she
was proud of the praise her gentle disposition had
won. Their marriage, for which they had prayed so
often, they attributed not to Venus but to themselves. Because of their ingratitude, the goddess

changed their shapes, and, lest they come together
after the change, she made them into incompatible
species. Soon Philomenus was changed to the bird
which sings each summer, the cuckoo; and Agna became an insatiable she-wolf.

254

REMEDIES FOR ENDING THE FOUL BREATH
WHICH RESULTS FROM CERTAIN FOODS

So that your chopped leeks may not waft their loathsome odors, take my advice and eat an onion right
after the leeks. Then again if you want to get rid of
the foul smell of the onion, the chewing of garlic will
easily accomplish that for you. But if your breath remains offensive even after the garlic, then either it is
incurable or nothing but shit will remove it.

255

TO THE READER, ON THE TRANSLATION
OF THE NEW TESTAMENT
BY ERASMUS OF ROTTERDAM[74]

A holy work, an immortal achievement of the
learned Erasmus is coming out; and how great
are the advantages it brings to men! for the New
Law was first marred by the ancient translator and
then further damaged by the inaccurate copying of
scribes. Jerome long ago may have removed errors,
but his readings, excellent as they were, have been
lost by long neglect. That is why the whole work has
been corrected and translated anew. And Christ's
New Law shines with new splendor. Erasmus has
not ostentatiously disputed the text word by word;
he has considered inviolable whatever is at least
passable. And so it is that, if anyone skims over this
version in rapid flight, he would perhaps think that
nothing of importance is afoot, but, if he retraces
his steps closely, he will decide that nothing could
be finer or more helpful.

256

TO THE MOST REVEREND, ETC.,
THOMAS, CARDINAL AND ARCHBISHOP
OF YORK, ON THE NEW TESTAMENT
PRESENTED TO HIM BY ERASMUS

Incomparable father and patron of learned men,[75]
you to whose words the Pierian band listens with
admiration, you whose honors, despite the respect

---

73 See Ovid, *Metamorphoses* 8.159–61.
74 Erasmus's New Testament, which con-

tained the Greek text, a Latin translation,
and commentary, was published in 1516.

75 Cardinal Wolsey (ca. 1450–1532)

and esteem of the people, fall far short of your worth — this book of yours has come a long way, from your friend Erasmus. I beg that you receive it in the same spirit which prompted him to send it. Nor have I any doubt that you will do so, for the author will quite rightly win favor for his work, and the work for its author. Erasmus has always been among your admirers; the work itself is the law of Christ, which has ever been your preoccupation. That law provides you with the prudence and the authority which enable you to administer justice even in the face of carping critics. For when disputants engage in intricate quarrels, to the amazement of ordinary people, you sort everything out so well that even the loser cannot complain. It is no mere human adroitness which enables you to do this, but the law of Christ, the sole criterion on which your judgments rest. Therefore, most worthy prelate, accept this book with serenity and favor and continue in the future to cherish the author as you do now.

257

TO THE MOST REVEREND, ETC., ARCHBISHOP OF CANTERBURY

That you were right, devout prelate,[76] in bestowing such numerous and generous gifts on your protégé Erasmus, how far he is from wasting the leisure you provide for him, is shown by many things, but above all by this work. Though he has published many books, and they have exercised a wholesome influence, this new one surpasses all that have preceded it. The advantages which this book brings belong to all, but the honor it confers is shared by you and him. He provided the labor; you, kind bishop, provided the support. Yet wholeheartedly he yields his share of the credit to you; whatever he does, he imputes it to your merits. The fruit that he seeks from his labor, kind father, is this: that by this book you win the love of all men, and that he win yours.

258

EPITAPH ON THE TOMB OF JANE, DECEASED WIFE OF MORE, WHO INTENDS THE SAME TOMB FOR HIMSELF AND ALICE, HIS SECOND WIFE

Here lies Jane, the beloved wife of Thomas More, who intend that this same tomb shall be Alice's and mine, too. One of them, my wife in the years of our

vigorous youth, has made me father of a son and three daughters; the other has been as devoted to her stepchildren (a rare and splendid attainment in a stepmother) as very few mothers are to their own children. The one lived out her life with me, and the other still lives with me on such terms that I cannot decide whether I did love the one or do love the other more. O, how happily we could have lived all three together if fate and religion permitted. But the grave will unite us, and I pray that heaven will unite us too. Thus death will give what life could not.

259

TO HIMSELF AS HE REJOICED AT HAVING ESCAPED FROM A STORM

What good is it to have escaped the raging tempests of the sea? Your joy must be either brief or groundless. It is like the relief which suddenly flashes upon men sick with fever, as the painful fits go away and return in their fixed cycles. How many more troubles await you on the land you yearned for than you would have had to endure on the rushing turmoil of the sea. Your death will be ushered in by the scalpel or various diseases, any one of which is more grievous to bear than death itself. Yes, that same death which you escaped to no purpose on the swelling sea will overwhelm you on your pillow, only more treacherously.

260

TO A CERTAIN FAT PRIEST WHOSE HABIT IT WAS TO SAY "LEARNING PUFFS UP"

According to you, though others are puffed up with learning, as Paul teaches,[77] you avoid it. How is it then, O substantial father, that you are so swollen? You can hardly manage your bloated belly with its flabby paunch, and your mind is puffed up with empty folly.

261

TO CHELONUS

Why is the name of stolid ass so hateful to you? Once upon a time a philosopher was great on this account, Chelonus. Still, lest you be thought not to differ from him at all, he was golden, you are more leaden. He had the mind of a man in the body of an ass; you have, in the body of a man, the mind of an ass.

---

76 William Warham (*ca.* 1450–1532)   **77** See 1 Cor 8:1.

262

ON A CAT AND A MOUSE

When I held out to the cat the mouse I had taken from a trap she did not immediately and ravenously eat her prize. With great restraint she placed her trembling prey on open ground and happily toyed with it in extraordinary fashion. She twitched her tail, watched the mouse with shifty eyes, and playfully turned her head from side to side. Gently, with a paw, she provoked the terrified mouse into moving, and when it started to move she stopped it; and alternately she let it go and caught it again. Soon with her paw she tossed it up high and caught it in her mouth. Then she walked away from it and gave it the false hope of still being able to escape. She lay down to watch at a distance, and, as the mouse made off, she joyfully leaped upon it and immediately returned to the spot from which it had fled. Again she left it, and, with amazing perception, the wicked creature made tests of the poor mouse's intentions. While she was repeating this performance and confidently going farther away, the mouse suddenly found a crack and was gone. The cat rushed to the hole and sat on guard—in vain. The mouse, protected in its hiding place, was safe from its enemy. It would have died in the trap if what ordinarily destroys it had not protected and saved it—a cat.

263

HE EXPRESSES HIS JOY AT FINDING SAFE AND SOUND HER WHOM HE HAD ONCE LOVED AS A MERE BOY

You are really still alive, Elizabeth, dearer to me in my early years than I was myself, and once again my eyes behold you. What bad luck has kept you from me all these many years! When I was just a boy, I saw you first; now when I am almost an old man, I see you again. Sixteen years I had lived—you were about two years younger—when your face inspired me with innocent devotion. That face is now no part of your appearance; where has it gone? When the vision I once loved comes before me, I see, alas, how utterly your actual appearance fails to resemble it. The years, always envious of young beauty, have robbed you of yourself but have not robbed me of you. That beauty of countenance to which my eyes so often clung now occupies my heart. It is natural for a dying fire, though buried in its own cold ashes, to flare up when a gust of air blows on it. And however much you are changed from what you were, you

make the old flame glow by giving me this new reminder. There comes now to my mind that distant day which first revealed you to me as you enjoyed yourself amid a band of dancing maidens. Your yellow hair enhanced the pure white of your neck; your cheeks looked like snow, your lips like roses; your eyes, like two stars, dazed our eyes and through my eyes made their way into my heart: I was helpless, as though stunned by a lightning-stroke, when I gazed and continued to gaze upon your face. Then, too, our comrades and yours laughed at our love, so awkward, so frank and so obvious. Thus did your beauty take me captive. Either yours was perfect beauty, or I lent it more perfection than it had; perhaps the stirrings of adolescence and the ardor which accompanies the approach of manhood were the reason, or perhaps certain stars we shared at birth had influenced both our hearts. For a gossipy companion of yours who was in on the secret revealed that your heart, too, was moved. On this account a chaperon was imposed upon us, and a door strong enough to thwart our very destiny kept apart a pair whom the stars wished to bring together. And then that notable day after so many years brought us together, far separated though we were in the pursuit of our different destinies, that day propitious in my finding you alive and well—seldom in my life have I met a happier day. Once upon a time you innocently stole my heart; now too, and innocently still, you are dear to me. Our love was blameless; if duty could not keep it so, that day itself would be enough to keep love blameless still. Well, I beg the saints above, who, after twenty-five years, have kindly brought us together in good health, that I may be preserved to see you safe and sound again at the end of twenty-five years more.

264

THOMAS MORE SENDS BEST WISHES TO HIS BELOVED CHILDREN, MARGARET, ELIZABETH CECILIA, AND JOHN

I hope that a single letter to all four of you may find my children in good health and that your father's good wishes may keep you so. In the meantime, while I am making a journey, drenched by a soaking rain, and while my mount, too frequently, is bogged down in the mud, I compose these verses for you in the hope that, although unpolished, they may give you pleasure. From these verses you may gather an indication of your father's feelings for

you — how much more than his own eyes he loves
you; for the mud, the miserably stormy weather,
and having to urge a small horse through deep waters have not been able to distract his thoughts from
you or to prevent his proving that, wherever he is, he
thinks of you. For instance, when — and it is often —
his horse stumbles and threatens to fall, your father
is not interrupted in the composition of his verses.
Many people can hardly write poetry even when
their hearts are at ease, but a father's love duly provides verses even when he is in distress. It is not so
strange that I love you with my whole heart, for being a father is not a tie which can be ignored. Nature
in her wisdom has attached the parent to the child
and bound their minds together with a Herculean
knot. Thence comes that tenderness of a loving heart
that accustoms me to take you so often into my
arms. That is why I regularly fed you cake and gave
you ripe apples and fancy pears. That is why I used to
dress you in silken garments and why I never could
endure to hear you cry. You know, for example, how
often I kissed you, how seldom I whipped you. My
whip was never anything but a peacock's tail. Even
this I wielded hesitantly and gently so as not to mark
your tender backsides with painful welts. Ah, brutal and unworthy to be called father is he who does
not himself weep at the tears of his child. How other
fathers act I do not know, but you know well how
soft and kind I am by temperament, for I have always intensely loved the children I begot, and I have
always been (as a father should be) easy to win over.
But now my love has grown so much that it seems
to me I did not love you at all before. This is because
you combine the wise behavior of old age with the
years of childhood, because your hearts have been
informed with genuine learning, because you have
learned to speak with grace and eloquence, weighing each word carefully. These accomplishments tug
at my heart so wonderfully, they bind me to my children so closely, that what, for many fathers, is the
only reason for their affection — I mean the fact that
they begot their children — has almost nothing to do
with my love for you. Therefore, my dear little troop
of children, continue to endear yourselves to your
father and, by those same accomplishments which
make me think that I had not loved you before,
make me think hereafter (for you can do it) that I do
not love you now.

78 See Quintilian 1.10.9.

265

HE APOLOGIZES BECAUSE WHILE CONVERSING WITH A PROMINENT CLERIC HE HAD FAILED TO NOTICE A CERTAIN NOBLE LADY WHO ENTERED THE ROOM AND STOOD BESIDE THEM FOR SOME TIME AS THEY TALKED

Mighty prelate, on that recent occasion when your
Excellency saw fit to pay me a call and to enter my
humble house, while you were conversing with me
so pleasantly that my attention was entirely focused
on your countenance, observe! a lady entered — as
my servants informed me too late, yesterday in fact,
when the matter was many days past. Her splendid attire was eye-catching, but it was outshone by
her beauty, which is in turn surpassed by her virtue. She came right up to our couch and stood very
near me for a long time, right at my elbow. She selected and examined some ancient coins, and famous herself, found pleasure in the famous portraits on them. She deigned to take some sweets
from my scanty table, and their taste grew sweeter
in her own sweet mouth. And yet our eyes failed to
observe even so brilliant a beauty as hers. Alas, for
my inborn dullness, duller than dull! Now I forgive
my servants for not warning me. Surely no one of
them thought his master so dull. O eyes, which used
to be able to perceive from a distance such splendor radiating from any girl! Have I grown old? And
is perception dulled in this body of mine? Or did
an evil spirit attend my rising that morning? Or did
you beguile me with your charming conversation so
that I was unable to be aware of anything but you?
Orpheus, by his skill with the lyre, entranced wild
beasts;[78] I too was cast into a trance by your mellif-
luous speech. But that charm of yours imposed the
great risk that the lady think I had neglected her, a
risk that I be reported to have seen her, standing so
near to me, out of the corner of my eye and then
pretended not to have seen her. But I would that
the earth split open and swallow me rather than
that there be found in my heart a rudeness so brutal
that when a fair nymph, wafted so to speak by some
breath of air, enters my room, I fail to look at her
at least (if the occasion allows no more) and, if it is
permitted, fairly win her favor. How miserable it is
not to be able to speak! For whoever cannot deny
anything because he does not speak the language,

tacitly admits everything. Now, because I have little command of French (my lady speaks only her native French), I shall be innocent in the eyes of all, but 50 not forgiven by the one lady in whose court my plea must stand or fall. He who was wounded long ago by the Haemonian spear, from that same spear won help.[79] Since your gift of charming speech (which 55 made me forget myself and ignore the lady) was the cause of this disgraceful deed, your gift of charming speech ought to wipe away this disgrace and restore me to my lady's good graces.

266
ON THE FOLLOWING HENDECASYLLABIC,
VERSES QUOTED FROM BRIXIUS'S
ANTIMORUS BECAUSE THEY ARE THE
SUBJECT OF THE EPIGRAM BELOW
About my ears as I said these things there hovered 5 all the goddesses of vengeance and the Furies, a troop roused from the nethermost depths: Alecto and Tisiphone, her head surrounded by loathsome snakes, and frightful Megaera, with her savage face.

MORE

10 After Brixius heard that many readers had complained that he wrote only lies, in order to correct this defect he then decided to publish something which would be true, which would be unquestioned, which no one would contradict, 15 even though Brixius was the author. It was difficult for him to find anything which his own lack of truth had not robbed of credibility. But when he had looked about, pondered long, and forced his mind to consider everything, then at last he did find 20 one thing which all mankind unanimously agrees is truer than any truth; and, most charming fellow that he is, he wrote that all the Furies surrounded his charming head.

267
ON THE SHIP *CORDELIÈRE* AND THE
ANTIMORUS, A COLLECTION OF POEMS BY
THE FRENCHMAN GERMANUS BRIXIUS
Behold, Germanus Brixius, rich in resources on both 5 land and sea, has a forest [*sylva*] and a raft. Do you want to know what advantage each affords him? His follies ride his raft, the Furies inhabit his forest.

268
ON THE FOLLOWING HENDECASYLLABIC,
OR RATHER THIRTEEN-SYLLABLE,
VERSE FROM THE *ANTIMORUS* OF THE
FRENCHMAN GERMANUS BRIXIUS

To discover and to offer to the gaze of men.   5

MORE

After being puzzled on frequent occasions over a long period at your writing verses so immoderately long—such verses as no poet, ancient or modern, ever wrote—I set about to discover, Brixius, how 10 this had happened to you. And, finally, I found that it is your custom to measure your verses not by meter or by feet but by the yard.

269
ON THE SAME TOPIC
Reader, forgive Germain for putting thirteen syllables into a poem in hendecasyllabics. He has hardly learned to count well enough to go in order correctly from one to eleven. Let him not count for 5 me the stars or the waves of the sea or—this is a more difficult task—the errors in his own poetry. If he can count the years of the siege of Troy or the nine Muses or the eight legs of Cancer or the seven mouths of the Nile or, Ovid, the immortal books of 10 your *Fasti*; if he can count the regions of the sky or the horses of Phoebus or the three Furies (although he is three times as mad as three Furies could make him); if he can count his own—but I won't gamble without stakes, if I lose I want it to be a big loss—if 15 he can count, I say, his own eyes (though he has just two), then I'll let you gouge out one of his.

THE END

---

79 Alluding to Telephus, who was wounded by Achilles' spear. See Ovid, *Amores* 2.9.7–9; *Metamorphoses* 13.171–72.

POEMS IN THE 1518 EDITION
BUT NOT IN THE 1520 EDITION

270
ON FATE, FROM THE GREEK

If you are being borne along, then be borne along
and bear with it. But if you become angry, then not
only will you do yourself harm but also whatever
5 bears you will continue to do so—yes, will even
drag you.

271

ON JAMES, KING OF THE SCOTS

While loyal Henry with victorious armies was re-
claiming you, France, for the Roman Pontiff, behold! James, King of the Scots, was disloyally try-
5 ing to take by armed force the kingdom of the
Britons. The treaties he had so often sworn to did
not deter him from bearing arms against his own
wife's brother, or from joining the French enemy
as a faithful ally, or from his desire to sink the ship
10 of Peter. It is no wonder that as a man he committed these crimes; before this as a boy he dyed his
young hands in his father's blood. Therefore, in accordance with the will of God, he has perished amid
the slaughter of his men. And the result of wrong-
15 doing was just what it usually is.

POEMS NOT IN THE EDITIONS
OF 1518 OR 1520

272

[VERSES FROM THE LAST OF A SERIES OF
NINE PAGEANTS PAINTED ON CLOTH]
THE POET[80]

If anyone delights in looking at these imaginary fig-
5 ures, but (because of the painter's marvelous skill)
thinks them to be real men, he can feast his mind
on the realities themselves, just as he feasts his eyes
upon the painted images. For he will see that the
elusive goods of this perishable world do not come
10 so readily as they pass away. Pleasures, praise, homage, all things quickly disappear—except the love of
God, which endures forever. Therefore, mortals, put

no confidence hereafter in trivialities, no hope in
transitory advantage; offer your prayers to the everlasting God, who will grant us the gift of eternal life. 15

273

ON THE SCHOLARLY LABORS OF HOLT,
AN EPIGRAM BY THE LEARNED
YOUTH THOMAS MORE

This gentle book of Holt's[81] which you are reading,
these kindly pilferings, whether you are man or boy, 5
you are to call by the name "Milk for Children." In
my judgment this book which gives to boys lessons
like milk has a pleasant name and an appropriate
one, too. Read these lessons, you young men of England; it is for your very great advantage that the 10
book, small though it be, appears. The few rules arranged in a tiny book which you read in a few days
Holt with sleepless effort has sought out and chosen
from countless volumes. He wandered diligently all
over the fields. How well he has performed the task 15
of the honey-gathering bee! In his travels whatever tasty honey he gathered into sweet stores he
has brought to this little hive. Let this work be the
introduction, the door to the rest of grammar, for
the English youth who wish to enter. To be sure, 20
learned men built doors before this one, but each of
them imposed his limits because he used the Latin
language. What good to you is a strong larder if a
door which you cannot open keeps you from the
sumptuous food? English boy, how will you man- 25
age in Latin? You cannot, on the first day, understand Latin words. It is only proper that while you
are young you lie under a protector's wings and that
you learn the foreign language by means of your native speech. A door to grammar in English had been 30
built long before, if we confess the truth. But that
door was old, marked by frequent knocking, such a
door as barely squeaks open to perpetual pounding.
Our door is new and very easy for the young crowd.
How promptly it opens at the slightest tapping of 35
a finger!

274

AN EPIGRAM BY THOMAS MORE

Good boy! Rejoice whoever you are if you have been
nourished, to your delight, by Holt's elegant book.

---

80 An alternate translation of this poem
appears in More's *English Poetry* (see p. 4).

81 John Holt's *Lac puerorum, anglice mylke
for chyldren*, a Latin grammar

He does not offer you meat or the bitter berries of
the arbutus tree. He gives you cups aflow with sweet
milk. Lumps of meat lie heavy on a tender stomach,
and arbutus berries are mere moisture, such as belongs to tasteless water. But milk nourishes without
distress even a child, and the taste of milk is sweet in
the mouth of the young. That is why you have been
fed on this. It was clear that this was the proper
way: your constitution, so undeveloped, could
not bear great burdens. Now that you have been
weaned, we suggest a diet not too bland; take something stouter. That is, dine most elegantly at the untroubled board of Sulpicius[82] or eat your fill of the
helpful nourishment of Phocas; or drink the new
wine of Perotti of Siponto[83] or the potions aged in
the casks of Diomedes.[84] Or choose any other you
may wish to follow, provided that he knows how to
combine what is pleasant with what is useful.[85] But
you who take Holt's advice and you who take mine
will be eager for the teachings of Sulpicius above all.
Holt has left heteroclites and the gender of the various nouns to be learned from Sulpicius. There you
will read what is the right construction, but only
after you have studied the past tenses and the su-
pines which belong to each verb. And if you are industrious, you will learn finally that by far the most
beautiful poems are those which have kept within
their boundaries. Therefore, you young men, when
you have entered the company of the Muses, when,
thanks to Sulpicius, you carry your plectrum and
lyre, then say, "When my right hand could not hold
the lyre, it was Holt who offered a pap welcome to
my lips."

275

THOMAS MORE ON LINACRE'S PROGYMNASMATA

Whoever reads with care these rules by the learned
Linacre[86] will, if he retains what he reads here, want
to say, "After so many huge volumes on grammar,
this book, small as it is, has not come out in vain.
The book is very small, but, like a sparkling jewel,
with its diminutive size it has high value."

276

Verses on a two-part picture, in which Erasmus and
Peter Giles are portrayed together by the outstanding artist Quentin[87] in such a way that near Erasmus, as he begins his *Paraphrase of the Epistle to the
Romans*, the books in the picture reveal their titles,
and Peter holds a letter written to him in More's
hand — even this the painter has put in the picture.[88]

THE PICTURE SPEAKS

I show Erasmus and Giles, friends as dear to each
other as were Castor and Pollux of old. More
grieves to be absent from them in space, since in affection he is united with them so closely that a man
could scarcely be closer to himself. They arranged
to satisfy their absent friend's longing for them: a
loving letter represents their minds, I their bodies.

MORE HIMSELF SPEAKS

I think you recognize from their faces those whom
you see here if you have ever seen them before. If
not, then the letter written to the one will identify
him; and notice, so that you should know the name
of the other, he is writing it himself. To be sure, the
books which bear his name — so well known and
widely read all over the world — could tell you who
he is, even if he himself were not doing so. Quentin,
reviver of an ancient art, not less an artist than great
Apelles, marvelously gifted to lend life by a mixture
of colors to lifeless shapes, alas, why were you satisfied to paint on perishable wood portraits so pains-
takingly, so beautifully, done — portraits of such
men as antiquity produced but seldom, such men
as our own day produces less frequently still, such
men as the future, I suspect, may not produce at all.
These portraits you have done ought to have been
entrusted to a more enduring medium which could
preserve through the years what it had received.
O, if you could only have looked out for your own
fame and the desires of posterity; for if future ages
preserve any love of the fine arts and if savage warfare does not obliterate the arts, then what a price
posterity would pay for this picture!

---

82 Johannes Sulpitius Verulanus, a
fifteenth-century humanist   **83** Niccolo
Perotti (1429–80), Archbishop of Siponto

84 the fourth-century grammarian
85 *pleasant . . . useful:* See Horace, *Ars
Poetica* 343.   **86** Thomas Linacre

(*ca.* 1460–1524). The *Progymnasmata* was
an elementary Latin grammar.   **87** Quentin Metsys   **88** See Letters 46 and 47.

277

[ON A FRIAR WHO OBJECTED TO
COMPARING FRIENDS WITH BROTHERS]

To show that two men were great friends, I recently said in a few lines of verse that they were as great friends as Castor and Pollux were of old. A foolish friar said, "It is foolish to compare friends to brothers." "Why not?" I answered. "Do you think that any man can be a better friend to another than brother is to brother?" He laughed at my extraordinary ignorance—that I should be unaware of so obvious a fact. He said, "We have a large and crowded monastery with more than two hundred brothers, but from among the two hundred I'd wager my life you won't find two brothers who are friends."

278

A QUATRAIN OF SIR THOMAS MORE,
WRITTEN THREE YEARS BEFORE HE DIED

You are playing the fool if you expect to stay long here below. Even a fool, More,[89] can tell you that much. Stop playing the fool and contemplate staying in heaven. Even a fool, More, can tell you that much.

ANOTHER DISTYCH BY
THE SAME AUTHOR WRITTEN
AT THE SAME TIME

You who remember More,[90] may your lifetime be long and your death an open gate to eternal life.

279

A QUATRAIN BY THOMAS MORE

If your taste is for poetry or for prose, if piety or learning delights you, then read these works by Busleyden, who is inspired by Apollo and the Muses, and who is the precious glory of his native land.

280

The things you sent me to read I have read, but I read them with both pleasure and pain, happy to see nothing utterly horrible. The author himself corresponds to these writings of his: a man never good, and always the best, a man truly bad, the best of the bad.

281

[A MATHEMATICAL MNEMONIC]

Subtract more from more. Subtract less from less. Add less to more. Add more to less.

---

89 In Greek, "More" means "fool."
90 The Latin reveals a pun on *memento mori*, an adage meaning "remember death,"
such that *Mori* here means both "More" and "death."

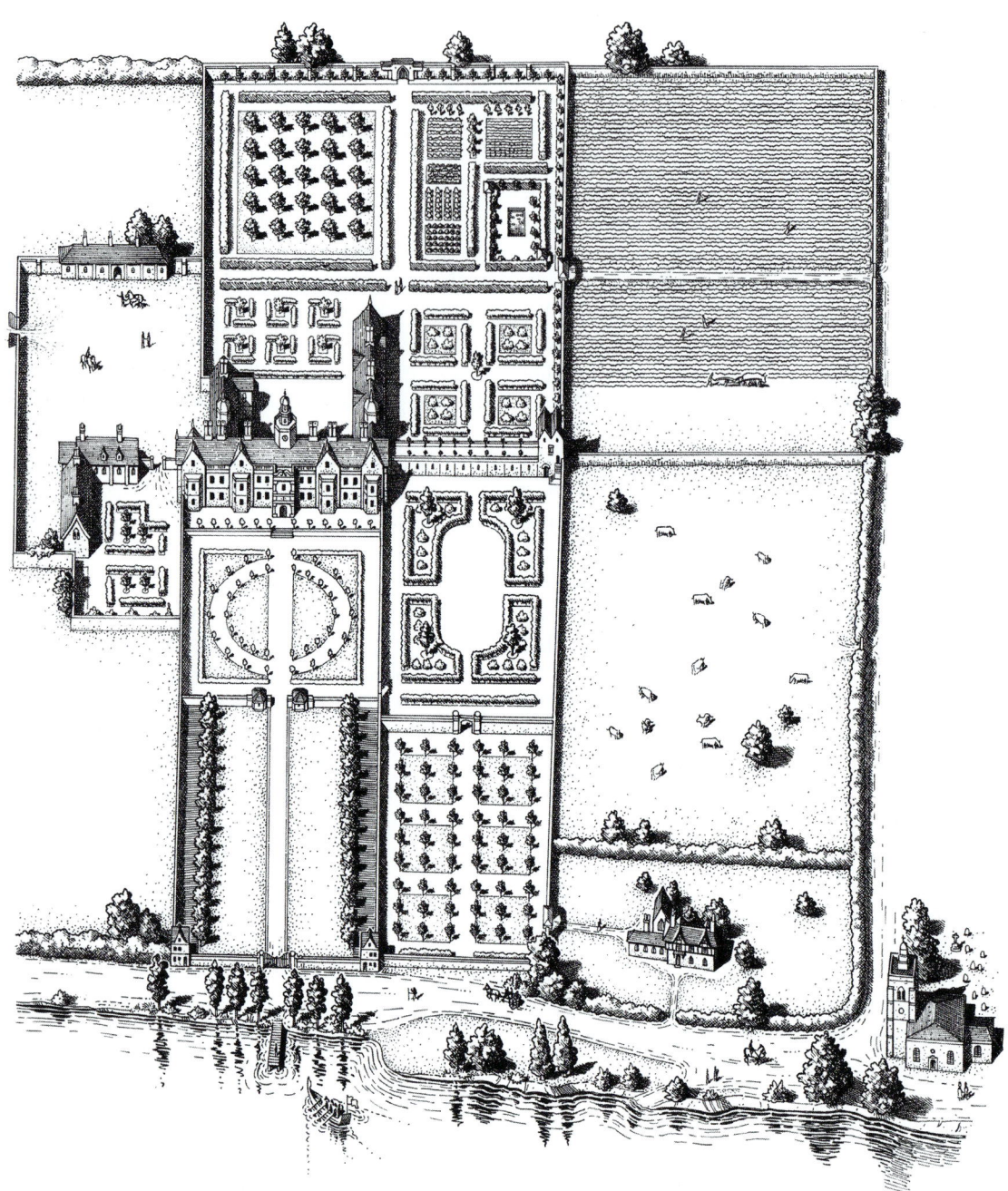

Thomas More's Chelsea Manor, recreated here from existing records by Michael Hall, was a working farm and a place of government that More built in 1525 while serving as Chancellor of the Duchy of Lancaster. Situated on the River Thames, the Manor provided More quickest access downstream to Westminster, London, and Greenwich; upstream to Hampton Court and Windsor. For the "arrangement of the original garden space within the manor's layout," see C. Paul Christianson, *The Riverside Gardens of Thomas More's London* (New Haven: Yale University Press, 2005).

Letters: 1501 to March 1534

Composed in Latin and English, Thomas More's correspondence is divided into three sections in this book: (1) Letters from 1501 to March 1534; (2) Letters on humanism from 1505 to 1520; and (3) Letters from More's imprisonment, from April 1534 to July 5, 1535, the day before his execution on Tower Hill, by nine o'clock in the morning, as the King's order directed.

More's letters display the remarkable range of his many relationships and offices, both public and private, as well as the author's rhetorical art. As Judith Henderson points out in "On Reading the Rhetoric of the Renaissance Letter," Erasmus's *Opus de conscribendis epistolis* "classifies letters under the traditional *causae* of the oration: deliberative, demonstrative, and judicial." The scheme is his own, but it continues the medieval tradition by recognizing the letter as an exercise of persuasion. To this classification, he adds two other classes which might be said to incorporate the special contribution of the humanists: familiar letters and letters discussing issues of scholarship (*Renaissance-Rhetorik*, NY: Gruyter, 1993, p. 150). More writes all five of these types of letters, and ranges, as Elizabeth McCutcheon observes, from "his defensive postures and his commitment to Erasmian humanism" to "the young intellectual, the wit and jokester, the man of letters, the educator, the father and family man, the mature scholar-critic, the patron, the busy administrator, the tenacious opponent of heresy, the man facing his own immanent death" (*Moreana* nos. 201–2 [Dec. 2015]: 382). Addressees of More's letters include King Henry, More's fellow humanists, More's professional colleagues and associates, and More's family.

One common theme informing these letters is friendship in a variety of forms, from civic to intimate. As Erasmus writes in his 1519 letter to Ulrich von Hutten, More "seems born and designed" for friendship, and the record of More's correspondence supports this claim of a life rich in friendship.

Surveying the letters, Elizabeth Rogers writes: "The letters we read may sometimes be disappointingly few or tantalizing in their brevity, but they nevertheless show the wide circle of his friends, not only in England, but also in the Low Countries and in France" (*Corr* xiii). Regarding the preservation of the letters, Rogers remarks that it is primarily "through the deep regard of his friends that More's letters have come down to us," with another source being the State Papers archive (xiv). Of course, friendship is not the only concern in More's letters. The letter to the University of Oxford, for example, addresses liberal education, while other letters address scholarly achievements and theological controversies, and later, the drama of More's arrest, imprisonment, interrogations, and last days.

More's letters remain as varied and complex as the public and private life of Thomas More; they constitute indeed something like a "life in letters" of the author. As *Moreana*'s founding editor, Germain Marc'hadour, wrote in 2004, "No likeness of More can be truer than his own works, especially his letters," texts which disclose "every facet of More's many-sided personality."

Regarding the composition of letters at the time, Elizabeth Rogers explains, "A letter was usually written on a sheet of rag paper about eight by eleven inches. The top of that letter was folded down, and the lower part folded up so that the edges just overlapped. The sides were folded in, deeply overlapping. A pen-knife then cut slits through these folds. A wedge of paper was inserted and its narrow end caught with sealing wax. The wide end of the wedge was wrapped around the letter to prevent its being opened, and that end was sealed with wax. The writer's die (More sometimes used an antique gem) was pressed into the wax. The folded letter was then a rectangle about three by five and a half inches. Even so, letters were often broken open by unauthorized persons, perhaps destroyed, perhaps re-sealed and sent on" (*Corr* xv–xvi).

ABBREVIATIONS

CW	*The Complete Works of St. Thomas More,* followed by volume and page numbers
CWE	*The Collected Works of Erasmus,* followed by volume and page numbers
Corr	*The Correspondence of Sir Thomas More,* followed by page numbers
EE	*Erasmi Epistolae,* followed by letter number
SL	*Selected Letters,* followed by page numbers
Stapleton	Thomas Stapleton's *The Life and Illustrious Martyrdom of Sir Thomas More,* trans. Philip E. Hallett (London: Burns and Oats, 1928), followed by page numbers

CONTENTS

The prefatory number of each letter corresponds to *The Correspondence of Sir Thomas More,* ed. Elizabeth Rogers.

The symbols < > indicate uncertainty about the date or place.

* These letters were written in English; the others, in Latin.

Letters
1501 to March 1534

2. To John Holt
<London, *ca.* November 1501>

Thomas More sends his greetings to John Holt.[1]

I have sent you everything you wanted, except the
5 additions I have made to the comedy about Solomon; those I could not send you at the moment, as
I did not have them with me. I shall arrange for you
to get them next week, along with any other of my
materials you wish.

10 I am glad you have left Smarden, an unhealthy
spot, and have moved to Chichester, which is a
healthier location, with more sunshine. I suppose you will be glad you made the move; the local
bishop, I hear, is very fond of you.

15 As for myself, thanks be to God, I am feeling
quite well; and—something few people can say for
themselves—I am living my life just as I desire; so
please God, may my desires be good. You ask how
I am doing in my studies. Wonderfully, of course;
20 things could not be better. I have shelved my Latin
books, to take up the study of Greek; however,
while dropping the one, I have not as yet completely
caught up with the other. But enough on that point.

Grocyn,[2] my instructor, recently made a very suc-
25 cessful start on his lectures, at Saint Paul's, on the
text of the "Celestial Hierarchies," the famous work
of Saint Dionysius the Areopagite. It would be hard
to tell which is greater—the acclaim for himself, or
the profit for his listeners. His audience includes a
30 group of students, whose numbers, unfortunately,
are more impressive than their learning; but it also
includes very many of the educated class. Several
illiterates too are flocking to the lectures, some
drawn by curiosity, some out of a desire to appear
35 a little erudite. But the majority of self-styled intellectuals are not attending, so as not to give the impression of admitting their ignorance on matters of
which they are ignorant.

Catherine, the illustrious daughter of the King of
40 Spain and bride of our distinguished Prince, lately
made her entry into London, amid a tremendous
ovation; never, to my knowledge, has there been
such a reception anywhere. The magnificent attire
of our nobles aroused cries of admiration. But the
Spanish escort—good heavens!—what a sight! If 45
you had seen it, I am afraid you would have burst
with laughter; they were so ludicrous. Except for
three, or at the most four, of them, they were just too
much to look at: hunchbacked, undersized, barefoot
Pygmies from Ethiopia. If you had been there, you 50
would have thought they were refugees from hell.
Ah, but the lady! take my word for it, she thrilled
the hearts of everyone; she possesses all those qualities that make for beauty in a very charming young
girl. Everywhere she receives the highest of praises; 55
but even that is inadequate. I do hope this highly
publicized union will prove a happy omen for England. Farewell.

3. To John Colet [3]
London, 23 October <1504> 60

Thomas More to his John Colet, greeting.

As I was walking in the law courts the other day,
unbusy where everybody else was busy, I met your
servant. I was delighted to see him, both because
he has always been dear to me, and especially be- 65
cause I thought he would not have come without
you. But when I heard from him not only that you
had not returned, but that you would not return for
a long time, I cannot tell you from what rejoicing
I was cast into what dejection. For what could be 70
more grievous to me than to be deprived of your
most pleasant companionship, whose prudent advice I enjoyed, by whose most delightful intimacy
I was refreshed, by whose powerful sermons I was
stirred, by whose example and life I was guided, in 75
fine, in whose very countenance and nod I was accustomed to find pleasure? And so when encom-
passed by these defenses I felt myself strengthened;

---

1 John Holt (d. *ca.* 1504) was a schoolmaster and grammarian who published
Lac puerorum, the first major Latin

Grammar in English, which More praises
in Epigrams 273–74 (see pp. 261–62).
2 William Grocyn (*ca.* 1446–1519)

3 John Colet (*ca.* 1466–1519), appointed
dean of St. Paul's Cathedral in 1504, was a
spiritual influence on More and Erasmus.

now that I am deprived of them I seem to languish and grow feeble. By following your footsteps I had escaped almost from the very gates of hell, and now, driven by some force and necessity, I am falling back again into gruesome darkness. I am like Eurydice, except that she was lost because Orpheus looked back at her, but I am sinking because you do not look back at me.

For in the city what is there to move one to live well? but rather, when a man is straining in his own power to climb the steep path of virtue, it turns him back by a thousand devices and sucks him back by its thousand enticements. Wherever you betake yourself, on one side nothing but feigned love and the honeyed poisons of smooth flatterers resound; on the other, fierce hatreds, quarrels, the din of the forum murmur against you. Wherever you turn your eyes, what else will you see but confectioners, fishmongers, butchers, cooks, poulterers, fishermen, fowlers, who supply the materials for gluttony and the world and the world's lord, the devil? Nay even houses block out from us I know not how large a measure of the light, and do not permit us to see the heavens. And the round horizon does not limit the air but the lofty roofs. I really cannot blame you if you are not yet tired of the country where you live among simple people, unversed in the deceits of the city; wherever you cast your eyes, the smiling face of the earth greets you, the sweet fresh air invigorates you, the very sight of the heavens charms you. There you see nothing but the generous gifts of nature and the traces of our primeval innocence.

But yet I do not wish you to be so captivated by these delights as to be unwilling to fly back to us as soon as possible. For if the inconveniences of the city so displease you, your country parish of Stepney (of which you should have no less care) will afford you hardly less advantages than where you now dwell, whence you can sometimes turn aside, as to an inn, to the city (where there is so much that needs your service). For in the country, where men are of themselves either almost innocent, or at least not ensnared in great sins, the services of any physician can be useful. But in the city because of the great numbers that congregate there, and because of their long-standing habits of vice, any physician will have come in vain unless he be the most skillful. Certainly there come from time to time

into the pulpit at Saint Paul's preachers who promise health, but although they seem to have spoken very eloquently, their life is in such sharp contrast to their words that they irritate rather than soothe. For they cannot bring men to believe that though they are themselves obviously in direst need of the physician's help, they are yet fit to be entrusted with the cure of other men's ailments. And thus when men see that their diseases are being prescribed for by physicians who are themselves covered with ulcers, they immediately become indignant and obstinate. But if (as observers of human nature assert), he is the best physician in whom the patient has the greatest confidence, who can doubt that you are the one who can do most for the cure of all in the city? Their readiness to allow you to treat their wounds, their trust, their obedience, you have yourself proved in the past, and now the universal desire and anticipation of you proclaim it all again.

Come then, my dear Colet, for Stepney's sake, which mourns your long absence as children their mother's; for the sake of your native place which should be no less dear to you than are your parents. Finally (though this will be a weak force for your return), let regard for me, who am entirely devoted to you and hang anxiously upon your coming, move you. Meanwhile, I shall pass my time with Grocyn, Linacre,[4] and our dear friend Lily,[5] the first as you know the sole guide of my life (in your absence), the second my master in learning, the third the dearest partner of my endeavors. Farewell, and love me ever as now. London, 23 October.

7. From Erasmus
<Paris> 9 June <1510>

This is the prefatory letter to Erasmus's In Praise of Folly.

From Erasmus of Rotterdam, greetings to his friend Thomas More.

Recently, when I was returning to England from Italy,[6] to avoid wasting the whole time that I had to ride on horseback in crude and illiterate talk, I decided to devote some of my attention either to the studies we share with each other or to the pleasure of recalling the most learned and charming friends

---

4 Thomas Linacre (1460–1524)   **5** William Lily (*ca.* 1468–1522)   **6** Erasmus left Rome early in July 1509.

whom I had left in this country. Among them, my dear More, you were one of the first to come to mind, for I have always enjoyed you as much in my memory when we have been apart as I have delighted in your presence when we were together — and rest assured nothing in my whole life could be sweeter than your company. Therefore, since I thought I ought to do something at least, and since that time seemed hardly suited to serious thinking, I chose to amuse myself by composing an encomium of Folly. "How did you ever get that idea?" you will say. First of all, it was suggested to me by your family name "More," which comes as close to the Greek word for folly [*moria*][7] as you yourself are far removed from the fact of folly, and everyone agrees you are far from it indeed. Then too, I suspected that this jeu d'esprit of mine would be especially acceptable to you because you ordinarily take great pleasure in jokes of this sort — that is, those that do not lack learning, if I may say so, and are not utterly deficient in wit — and because you habitually play the role of Democritus[8] by making fun of the ordinary lives of mortals. On the other hand, though your extraordinarily keen intelligence places you worlds apart from the common herd, still the incredible sweetness and gentleness of your character makes you able and willing to be a man for all seasons[9] with all men. And so you will readily accept this little declamation not only as a *memento*[10] of your friend, but also as an object of your patronage and defense,[11] since it is dedicated to you and henceforth is not mine but yours.

For there will probably be no lack of quarrelsome quibblers who will attack it unjustly, some as too light and frivolous for a theologian, some as more biting than is compatible with Christian

moderation. They will cry out that I am reviving the Old Comedy[12] or imitating Lucian,[13] accusing me of ripping everything to shreds. As for those who are offended by the levity and playfulness of the subject matter, they should consider that I am not setting any precedent but following one set long ago by great writers: ages ago Homer amused himself with *The Battle of the Frogs and Mice,* as Vergil did with the Gnat and the Rustic Salad, and Ovid with the Walnut-Tree.[14] So too Polycrates and his corrector Isocrates both wrote encomia of Busiris;[15] Glauco praised injustice;[16] Favorinus, Thersites and the quartan fever;[17] Synesius, baldness;[18] Lucian, the fly and the art of the parasite. Seneca amused himself by writing an *apotheosis* of Claudius.[19] Plutarch wrote a dialogue between Gryllus and Ulysses.[20] Lucian and Apuleius wrote comic tales about an ass, and some writer or other composed the last will and testament of the piglet Grunnius Corrocotta,[21] which is even mentioned by Saint Jerome.[22]

And so, if they wish, they can imagine that I was simply playing with pawns for my own amusement or, if they prefer, that I was riding a hobbyhorse like a child.[23] But surely, since we grant every other state in life its own recreations, it is quite unfair to allow students no amusement at all, especially if trifles lead to serious ideas and if a frivolous subject is handled in such a way that a reader who has any sense at all can profit by it a good deal more than he can from the forbidding and showy subjects undertaken by some writers. Thus, one man praises rhetoric or philosophy in a speech he has patched together for years. Another sings the praises of some prince or other. Another urges war against the Turks. Another predicts future events. Another fabricates some trifling questions like "whether goat's hair may be called

---

7 This pun on More's name was not uncommon.   **8** The philosopher Democritus (5th century BC) was said to have laughed at the follies of mankind (Juvenal 10.28–30; Seneca, *De ira* 2.10.5).   **9** *omnium horarum:* Suetonius, *Tiberius* 42; Erasmus, *Adages* 286 (*CWE* 31: 304–5). In 1520 Richard Whittinton (*Vulgaria,* ed. Beatrice White, London: Early English Text Society, orig. ser. no. 187, 1932, 64–65), applied *omnium horarum homo* to More and translated it "a man for all seasons."   **10** Catullus, *Carmina* 12.13   **11** See More's 1515 Letter to Dorp in defense of the *Folly* and of the humanist program.   **12** Such comedy, represented primarily by Aristophanes,

attacked individuals by name.   **13** Lucian of Samosata (*ca.* 125–90) wrote witty, caustic dialogues, several of which were translated from Greek into Latin by More and Erasmus, working together, in 1505–6 (*CW* 3.1: xxii–xxx).   **14** These four apocryphal poems parody the high style by applying it to low subjects.   **15** These two Greek orators (4th century BC) wrote mock-encomia of the mythical Egyptian tyrant Busiris (Isocrates, *Busiris* 1–4).   **16** according to his brother Plato (*Republic* 357a–62c)   **17** According to Gellius (*Attic Nights* 17.12.2), the rhetorician Favorinus (d. *ca.* AD 135) praised Thersites, the ugliest Greek at Troy (Homer, *Iliad* 2.216–19), and the quartan fever.   **18** This fifth-century

bishop wrote his mock-encomium in reply to Dio Chrysostom's *Praise of Hair.* It was often combined with the *Folly* in early editions. See Genevieve Stenger, "*The Praise of Folly* and Its Parerga," *Medievalia et Humanistica,* N.S., no. 2 (1971): 97–117.   **19** Seneca's *Apocolocyntosis* or "pumpkinification" of Claudius presents the emperor after his death, not deified but banished to the underworld.   **20** Changed to a pig by Circe, Gryllus argues that it is better to remain an animal than to be restored to humanity (Plutarch, *Moralia* 985d–92e).   **21** a school exercise of the third century after Christ   **22** *Commentary in Isaiam,* prol.; *Corpus Christianorum: Series Latina* 73a, 465   **23** Horace, *Sermones* 2.3.248

wool."[24] For just as nothing is more trivial than to treat serious matters in a trivial way, so too nothing is more delightful than to treat trifles in such a way that you do not seem to be trifling at all. Whether I have done so others will judge. But unless I am completely deceived by '*Selflove*,'[25] my praise of Folly is not altogether foolish.

But now, to reply to the false charge that the work is too biting, men of wit have always been free to satirize with impunity the ordinary lives of men, as long as this freedom did not degenerate into furious rage. Hence I am all the more amazed how sensitive ears are nowadays: it seems they can hardly bear to hear anything except solemn titles. Then too, you can see some people so perversely religious that they can tolerate the gravest insults against Christ more easily than the lightest joke aimed at pope or prince, especially when "it concerns the pocketbook."[26] But if someone writes a satire on the lives of men without censuring a single person by name, I ask you, can this be considered scurrilous? Surely it should be taken as judicious and instructive satire. Besides, I beg you to notice on how many counts I indict my own self. Then too, anyone who omits no category of men is clearly not angry at any individual but rather at all vices. Therefore if anyone cries out that he has been injured, he betrays his own bad conscience or at least his fear of exposure. In this sort of writing Saint Jerome took far more liberties and was far more biting; sometimes he did not even refrain from mentioning names. As for me, I not only abstained from mentioning any names at all, but I also moderated my style so that any judicious reader will easily understand that I aimed at giving pleasure, not pain. Moreover, unlike Juvenal, I did not stir up that cesspool of secret vice; I took pains to survey funny rather than filthy vices. And then, if anyone is not satisfied with these explanations, he should at least remember this: it is an honor to be insulted by Folly. Since I made her speak as my persona, I had to preserve decorum by making her speak appropriately. But why am I saying all this to you?—you are such an extraordinary advocate that you can make a strong defense even if the case itself is weak. Farewell, most learned More, and defend vigorously this your *Moria*.

From the country, June 9

8. To John Colet
<London?, *ca.* March 1512?>

I don't much wonder if *they* are bursting with jealousy of your excellent school. For they see that, just as the Greeks who destroyed barbarian Troy came out of the Trojan horse, so from your school come those who reprove and overthrow *their* ignorance.

16. To Erasmus
<London, *ca.* 17 February 1516>

Thomas More to his Erasmus, greetings.

Since your departure,[27] my dearest Erasmus, I have received altogether three letters from you. If I claimed to have answered all of them I do not suppose you would believe me, no matter how solemnly I lied; especially since you know me very well as being a lazy correspondent and not so scrupulously truthful as to shrink from a little white lie as if it were parricide. Our friend Pace[28] is on an embassy in your locality, although not exactly in the same place as you; he is separated from me without being with you. He can converse with me by letter, but not with you face to face. May he come home soon with his business happily concluded, so that at least one half of me can be with me. For I do not know when to expect you,[29] since you intend to move on into Italy, where, I fear, you will meet people who will not let you get away. For the present, I shall be missing one half of me, while he is gone; and the other half, while you are gone. I hope that some excellent fortune, worthy of the man, soon happens to Pace. I am very much aware that it is the intention of the King and the wish of the Cardinal and the endeavor of all good men to honor and promote him.

As for yourself, I would be entertaining even higher hopes if I were not so constantly disappointed; and yet, why can I not have high hopes for you even now? I have not lost hope for the future, just because my previous hopes have not been realized; rather, I am more confident than ever. No man has the same luck indefinitely, and yours cannot continue to be bad, for you are the idol and the admiration of the Pope, of kings, of bishops, of almost all men throughout Christendom. It would

---

24 Horace, *Epistles* 1.18.15; and Erasmus, *Adages* 253 (*CWE* 31: 280–81)   **25** Erasmus, *Adages* 292 (*CWE* 31: 311)   **26** Aristophanes, *Nubes* 648   **27** in May 1515   **28** Richard Pace (*ca.* 1483–1536)   **29** Erasmus, however, did return in July–August 1516.

be a waste of words to mention the attitude toward you among our own bishops, particularly the Archbishop of Canterbury, and the special favor you enjoy with our King. Your previous failures to receive a benefice corresponding to your worth and to the deep love shown you by eminent men have been caused partly by your disregard of the way which others use to solicit support, partly by some accident of fortune, as, for instance, in the recent case of the Tournay canonry, which Lord Mountjoy[30] had reserved for you. Right now, you do not seem averse to it, for, as you say in your letter, you have sent on to him all the documents necessary for its bestowal upon you. However, if you recall, when I was with you at Bruges,[31] I discussed this topic with you; and after listing the advantages and disadvantages of the benefice, you seemed to be uninterested in it; nor did you conceal your attitude from Sampson, who represents the Bishop of York at Tournai.[32] You were forced into that view not only because of your fear that it would not be a permanent position without the further consent of the other bishop,[33] whose authorization you did not expect for this one action of a man whose every act he endeavors to countermand; but also because of the obligation of making a payment of ten English pounds immediately upon receiving the canonry and an additional two hundred nobles or more to redeem the house. Such is the local custom, and if you fail to comply with it, you will barely realize six nobles a year, and not even that much, as I understand, unless you take up permanent residence there. As a result of these considerations, you gave Sampson and me the impression that you would not accept the canonry.

Shortly after your departure, I went to Tournai. There I found out from Lord Mountjoy and also from Sampson that the Archbishop of York had informed the two of them by letter that the benefice was to be given to another party, to whom apparently he had promised it, without knowing it had been intended for you. Upon hearing this and without disclosing my impression that the benefice did not suit your taste, I urged them to send a return letter saying that it had already been conferred

upon you and that the situation was such that no alteration was possible unless some better provision were first made for you. In response, the Archbishop of York said that this post would not at all be suitable for you, as it was not lucrative for one in residence and was totally unproductive for an absentee, and he guaranteed them that he would make you a better offer. So, in my presence and with no dissent on my part, they decided to confer the benefice upon the Archbishop's choice. What happened after that, I do not know. But this I do know: if you are deprived of that benefice, a more profitable one is due to you from the Cardinal, and I hope he makes payment soon. He does often speak of you in very friendly terms.

It was unnecessary for me to ask the Archbishop for your pension. He had thought of it himself, before receiving my letter, and had handled the matter with Maruffo,[34] who, as you know, is regularly employed by him as a broker for such transactions, and at stated times they balance their accounts. The Archbishop was at Otford[35] at the time, and, upon receiving my letter, he wrote again to the fellow urging him to send on to you twenty English pounds with dispatch and promising to make good the payment to Maruffo as soon as he was assured by a receipt from you that the money had been delivered. I had a conference with Maruffo. He said that he would ask you by letter to send back promptly to him a receipt, stating that you had received the money; he would take this receipt to the Archbishop, claim the money, and only then arrange to have it sent on to you. When I learned of that plan, I was afraid there was some danger, if the money were not paid out to him right then, that the delay would also affect you. "This subterfuge is not necessary," I told him; "either send the money immediately, charging it to the account of the Archbishop, or, if it irks you to pay out money without first receiving the equivalent, I shall arrange immediately for you to have the money on hand." "No," he said, "there is nothing to worry about. I shall see to it that Erasmus has the money at once; in fact, it is here right now. For Erasmus has a money draft from

30 William Blount, Lord Mountjoy (d. 1534), was Erasmus's pupil in Paris *ca.* 1496, and invited him to England to visit in 1498. **31** More was a member of an embassy to Prince Charles of Castile, May–October 1515, which had made a treaty renewing the commercial privileges gained in 1495 and 1506. **32** Thomas Wolsey was bishop of Lincoln at the beginning of 1514, received the bishopric of Tournai on the capture of the city, and on the death of Cardinal Bainbridge received the archbishopric of York on August 5, 1514. Richard Sampson (d. 1554) was now at Tournai to further Wolsey's interests, as the French bishop refused to surrender the diocese. **33** the very young French bishop, Louis Guillard **34** the banker who dealt with Erasmus's pension from the Archbishop **35** in Kent, where the archbishops of Canterbury had a manor house

me entitling him to draw, at will, to the amount of one thousand ducats. Whatever amount he draws from this account, must be paid back to me, according to our agreement, out of this pension of his." That is what he says. But I hardly believe that he has given you a draft entitling you to draw from his account, without the money first being put down on his counter. Consequently, if the arrangements are not as he says, inform me quickly.

The Archbishop of Canterbury has finally been relieved of the office of chancellor,[36] a burden, which, as you know, he had tried extremely hard to shake off for several years; at long last he has attained his heart's desire, a life of privacy, and is having wonderful leisure amid his books and his memories of duties well done. He has been replaced, at the appointment of the King, by the Cardinal of York,[37] who as an administrator is far exceeding everyone's expectations, which were very high in virtue of his other qualities; it is no easy thing to be the successor of an extraordinary person, and yet to give complete satisfaction.

Our embassy, which like everything else I do is a matter of interest to you, was quite successful, though it dragged on much longer than I had hoped or wanted. When I left home, I expected to be gone at the most two months; but the embassy lasted more than six. However, those long months were crowned by rather gratifying results. So, when I say that my mission was accomplished and also that further complications were arising which, apparently, would lead to greater delay (as regularly happens with administrators), I wrote to the Cardinal and received permission to return, thanks to the assistance of my friends, especially Pace, who had not as yet gone. But on my return trip I unexpectedly met him at Gravelines; he was in such a hurry that he hardly had time to stop and exchange greetings. Tunstall came back recently, but was here barely ten days, without spending a single one of them pleasantly as he wanted, for his entire stay was squandered on a bothersome, disgusting review of all the details entrusted to him on his mission, and then, without warning, he has been promptly shoved back again on another embassy.[38] It is very much against his will, I am sure, but he cannot refuse.

The office of ambassador has never held a great attraction for me. It does not suit us laymen as it does you clergy, for you either have no wives and children at home, or you find them wherever you travel. Whenever we are away for a short while, our hearts quickly go back to our wives[39] and children. Then too, when a priest goes on an embassy, he can take along with him wherever he wishes, his entire household and, for the time being, can support them at the expense of the king, while at home he would have to support them at his own expense. But when I am on leave, I must support two households, one at home, the other abroad. A rather generous allowance was granted to me by the King for the benefit of my retinue, but no consideration was made for those whom I had to leave at home; and although I am, as you know, a kindly husband and an indulgent father and a gentle master, still I have never had the least success in persuading the members of my family to do without food, for my sake, until I came home. Finally, it is easy for sovereigns, without any cost to themselves, to reimburse clergymen for their work and expenditures by means of ecclesiastical preferments; but no such generous and handy provisions are made for us, though the King, it is true, marked me out, on my return, for an annual pension,[40] which, because of the distinction or the revenue involved, is not to be scorned. However, I have not as yet accepted it, and I do not think I ever shall; for its acceptance would mean that I either would have to leave my present post in London, which I do prefer even to a higher one, or, what is not at all to my liking, I would have to retain it and thereby occasion resentment among the townsfolk. If any dispute over privileges arises between them and the King, as sometimes happens, they would be skeptical about my sincerity and loyalty to them and consider me under obligation to the King as his pensioner.

However, certain aspects of that embassy gave me great pleasure; first of all, the extended and constant association with Tunstall, who is second to none in literary attainments and strictness in life and morals, and yet is a genial companion; secondly, the friendship which I formed with Busleyden,[41] who is extremely wealthy and very generous, and

---

36 Warham resigned December 22, 1515. **37** Wolsey took the oath of office 24 December. **38** Tunstall was "to arrange the treaty lately concluded between England and the Prince of Castile" (*LP* 2:1574). **39** His second wife, Alice Middleton **40** More received a pension in 1518, retroactive from Michaelmas 1517 and charged to the little customs of London (*LP* 2:875, 4247). He then resigned as under-sheriff of London. **41** Jerome de Busleyden (*ca.* 1470–1517)

therefore a magnificent and gracious host. He gave me a tour of his home, which is very artistically decorated and fitted with exquisite appointments; he also showed me his large collection of antiquities, in which, as you know, I am very interested. Finally, he displayed to me his remarkable well stocked library and a mind even more so than any library, so that he completely filled me with amazement. I understand that he will very soon be sent on an embassy to our King. However, the most pleasant experience of my entire trip was my personal relationship with your host, Peter Giles of Antwerp;[42] his learning, his wit, his modesty, his genuine friendliness are such that, bless my soul, I would be happy to pay a good part of my wealth to purchase the companionship of that one man. He sent me your *Apology* and also your commentary on the Psalm *Beatus Vir,* which you dedicated to Beatus Rhenanus, a man truly blessed with this wonderful, lasting memorial of a friend. Dorp[43] has had his letter printed and included as a preface to your *Apology.* I had hoped to meet him, if I had the chance. Since I did not, I sent him my greetings by letter, just a brief laconic note, as I did not have time for a longer one. I could not pass the fellow by without some word of greeting, as I find him curiously attractive because of his extraordinary scholarliness and for many other reasons too, not the least of which is the fact that his criticism of the *Folly* provided you with the opportunity for penning your *Apology.*

I am glad that your works on Jerome and the New Testament are coming along so well. It is remarkable, how eagerly those editions are anticipated by everybody. You can be sure, Erasmus, that Linacre[44] has a very high opinion of you and talks about you everywhere. I recently learned this from some men who were dining with him at the King's table, where he spoke of you in very fond and lavish terms; the King's response, in the course of the conversation, was such as to give my informants the clear impression that you were soon to be the recipient of some unusual bit of good luck. May such be the will of Heaven!

Farewell, my dearest Erasmus, and give my regards to Rhenanus[45] and Lystrius, who, because of your recommendation and their own writings, are dearer and even more intimately known to me than are many of the people with whom I have daily contact. My wife sends you her regards, and so does Clement,[46] whose daily progress in Latin and Greek arouses no little hope in me that one day he will be an honor to his country and to letters.

Again, farewell, and let this one letter satisfy you for several months. In writing this letter, I have tried to mimic a stingy person who seldom entertains, but when he does invite guests to his table, he prepares a banquet that lasts indefinitely, so that the one meal will save him the expense of entertaining every day. For the third time, farewell.

The Bishop of Durham[47] was most gratified by the dedication of your edition of Seneca. Notice how quick I am to copy your habits; this letter has been written to you just as your recent letter to me was, with the help of a secretary; and I copy you so closely, I would not even write these few words in my own hand except that I want to assure you that this letter is from me.

17. To Cuthbert Tunstall[48]
\<London, 1516?\>

What possible gain is it to me to be employed in embassies, for although my Prince is generously inclined toward me, yet far from seeking advancement at Court I turn away from it with loathing?

20. To Erasmus
London, 3 September \<1516\>

More sends his very best greetings to Master Erasmus.

I am sending you my *Nowhere,*[49] which is nowhere well written. I have added a prefatory epistle to my friend, Peter. I know from experience that I do not

---

42 Peter Giles (*ca.* 1486–1533), a humanist friend of More and Erasmus, who figures prominently in Book 1 of *Utopia*   **43** Maarten van Dorp (1485–1525), a humanist theologian   **44** Thomas Linacre (1460–1524)   **45** Gerard Lister of Rhenen in Utrecht, who wrote

a commentary on the *Praise of Folly*   **46** John Clement (*ca.* 1500–72), one of the first students at Colet's humanist school, St. Paul's, became a page and pupil in More's household about 1514; later he became a distinguished physician.   **47** Thomas Ruthall (d. February 4, 1522/3)

48 Cuthbert Tunstall (1474–1559), who became Bishop of London, was a close friend of More.   **49** More's first choice of title for the *Utopia.* The latter comes from Greek *ou* (no) and *topos* (place).

have to tell you to give proper attention to everything else. I have delivered your letter to the Venetian ambassador,[50] who, it appears, was very well disposed to receive your New Testament, which was intercepted by a Carmelite.[51] He is completely devoted to sacred learning and has finished reading almost all the authors who treat of petty questions; he attributes so much importance to them that not even Dorp could outdo him in that. We conferred with one another like candidates campaigning for votes; we tickled one another with set speeches and lengthy encomia. But, to be honest, I like him very much. Apparently, he is very sincere and very competent in the things of man, and now he is completely dedicating himself to learning the things of God; and last, but not least, he is very interested in you.

I have no news as yet from the Archbishop of Canterbury about the situation. Colet has not had a conference with him about that business of yours,[52] but he did have one with the Archbishop of York and says that he found him so much in your favor and so lavish in his praises of you that all he wants now is to have the Archbishop match his brilliant words with deeds. I expect him to do that soon, with openhanded generosity. The money you left with me will be delivered to Giles by my John,[53] at Michaelmas; he will not reach Antwerp before that feast. If you publish my *Epigrams,* give some thought to the propriety of printing my remarks about Brixius,[54] as some of them are rather caustic, although it might well seem that I had provocation from his insulting comments about my country. In any case, as I said, examine those expressions carefully and, in general, anything else that seems to you spiteful. As for any silly remarks, handle them all as you know will be for my own good. Quintilian[55] regrets that Seneca did not follow someone else's judgment in using his own ability as a writer; however, it were better for me, when writing, not only to follow someone else's judgment, but also to use someone else's ability. Farewell, and give my regards to Master Tunstall and Master Busleyden. Hurriedly, from London, September 3.

22. To Erasmus

<London, *ca.* 20 September 1516> 45

More sends his very best greetings to Erasmus.

I received your letter from Calais, and am happy to hear that you had a pleasant voyage. The Provost of Cassel,[56] now on a diplomatic mission to our country, told me that you had arrived safe at Brussels before he left home. Not long ago I encountered Maruffo,[57] who was moaning that, because of some slip, your money was paid, but to his loss. I have also recently sent you another money draft of his, to the amount of twenty English pounds, from the Archbishop. I expect that you will have the same good luck in cashing this draft, if you act quickly before he issues a countermand to his agents, which seems to be exactly what he has in mind. The bearer of this letter will pay to Giles the twenty pounds you left with me, which, at the rate of exchange, amounts to thirty pounds in your money.

Not long ago I talked with Urswick[58] about the horse for you. He says he will arrange for you to have one soon, but right now he does not have any he would care to send to you. Some time ago I sent you my *Nowhere;* I am most anxious to have it published soon and also that it be handsomely set off with the highest of recommendations, if possible, from several people, both intellectuals and distinguished statesmen. I want this principally because of one individual,[59] whose name, I think, will occur to you even without my mentioning it, and who, for some strange motive, which you can also guess, regrets that the work is being published before the lapse of nine years. Handle this matter as you think is for my own good. I am also anxious to know if you have shown it to Tunstall, or at least described it to him, as I think you have done, and which I do prefer. For then he will gain a twofold delight; your account will make the work appear to have a more elegant style than it really has, and also you will save him the job of reading it himself. Farewell.

50 Sebastian Giustinian, ambassador in England from February 1515 to September 1519 51 Peter de Brescia Carmelianus, luteplayer to the King 52 Evidently these sentences refer to hopes of patronage for Erasmus. 53 his brother, who acted as secretary to More 54 Germanus Brixius.

See More's Letter 86, to Brixius, and also More's Epigrams 188–95, 209, 266–69. 55 *Institutia oratoria* 10.1.130 56 George of Theimseke, Provost of Cassel and member of Mechlin Parliament and of the Privy Council, who was often sent on embassies 57 Raffaele Maruffo was a

Genoese merchant and banker in England, who dealt with Erasmus's pension from the Archbishop of Canterbury. 58 Christopher Urswick (1448–1522) 59 Jerome Busleyden

23. To Erasmus
London, <22 September 1516>

Thomas More sends his very best greetings
to Erasmus.

5   Greetings, my dearest Erasmus. The Lord Archbishop of Canterbury has arranged to have twenty
English pounds transmitted to you. So, I have sent
you Maruffo's draft, plus the letter I received from
the Archbishop; thus you can understand that he
10 is generous with his own money and I am by no
means a stingy administrator of other people's
money; you can also promptly inform the Archbishop that you have received the money, so that
Maruffo can be reimbursed. I have written to one of
15 our countrymen who is to receive the money from
me at your exchange market; he can then turn over
thirty Flemish pounds to Giles so that he can vouch,
in your name, for the payment of the twenty English pounds which you had recently left with me.
20   I have forwarded your letter to Latimer,[60] along
with a letter of my own about the Bishop of Rochester;[61] but as yet no word from him, nor from the
Bishop. Colet is working strenuously on his Greek,
with the solicited help of my boy Clement. I do be-
25 lieve he will persevere until he masters the subject,
especially if you keep spurring him on from Louvain; and yet, it might be better to let him follow his
own impulse. As you know, he has the habit of disagreeing with suggestions given him, just to have an
30 argument, even when those suggestions correspond
with his own ideas. I went to see Urswick; he says
he has not forgotten about your horse and will soon
arrange for you to have one. When he does, I shall
let you know, so you will not be taken in by a fraud-
35 ulent exchange.
    Hurriedly, from London, on the morrow of Saint
Matthew the Apostle.

26. To Erasmus
London, 31 October <1516>

40 Thomas More sends greetings to his friend,
Master Erasmus.
    My answer, dear Erasmus, is a little tardy, be-
cause I was anxious to get some definite information to send on to you from Urswick about that

horse for you; but that has been impossible, since 45
he is gone on a business trip several miles from London and has not as yet returned. I expect him any
day now, and as soon as he gets back, the matter will
be taken care of. The money you had left with me, I
am sure, has been paid over to our friend, Giles, as 50
I have received a communication from my agent in
Antwerp, saying that he would make prompt payment. I could not entrust this bearer with the letters from Basel, which you sent me some time ago
to peruse; but I will send them shortly, as soon as I 55
hit upon someone to burden with a large bundle.
Bedill[62] showed me the letter from the Bishop of
Basel to the Archbishop of Canterbury, and also
the Archbishop's response; both were the original
copies. The latter, however, was much too much the 60
original; it was so smeared with words struck out or
written in as to be not at all legible except to the one
who wrote it, and perhaps not even to him.
    Our two letters encouraging Latimer to spend a
month or two with the Bishop of Rochester reached 65
him too late; he had already made up his mind to
go to Oxford and could not possibly be persuaded
to postpone his trip for the time being. You know
how these philosophers regard their own decisions
as immutable laws; I suppose from a love of consis- 70
tency. He does like your rendering of the New Testament very much, although you are too punctilious to suit him. He does not like the fact that you
have retained the word "Sabbath," and other similar points, which you did not think necessary to 75
change, or did not dare to do so. However, he does
not admit of any word at all that would be foreign
to Roman ears. I approved of his criticism insofar as
Hebrew customs and practices would permit. However, I urged him to note down the various words 80
for which he prefers a different rendering and to
send them on to you, along with his criticism; and
I think he will do that. This interest of his, I know,
will make you very happy.
    There are other people, though, my dearest Eras- 85
mus, who have formed a conspiracy here in our
country to read through your writings from quite
a different point of view; and I find their dreadful plot disturbing. Therefore, do not be in a rush
to publish a second edition of your works, as the 90
time is ripe to take stock. Out of my loyalty and my
anxiety for you I urge you, and I beg you to do at

---

60 William Latimer (*ca.* 1460–1545)   **61** John Fisher   **62** Thomas Bedill was secretary to Archbishop Warham.

least this much—to revise and correct everything promptly so as to leave the very least opportunity for slander in any passage. Some very sharp-minded men have set their hearts upon making a careful search for such opportunities and will snap them up greedily. You want to know who these people are? I am reluctant, of course, to mention any names, for fear that your spirit be crushed by the frightening thought of such powerful enemies. However, I shall tell you anyhow, to put you more on your guard. The top-ranking Franciscan theologian, whom you know and to whom you gave honorable mention in your edition of Jerome, has picked a group of men who are of the same Order and made of the same stuff, and has hatched a plot with them, aimed at refuting any errors of yours he can find. To make this operation easier and more effective, they devised a scheme whereby they would divide up your works among themselves, read through each one with a critical eye, and then understand absolutely nothing of it all. So you see what a crisis is hanging over your head! You have got to work hard to condition your troops for facing this monstrous peril. You can be sure, Erasmus, this decision was reached at a council meeting of the elders, late at night, when they were well soaked. But the morning after, as I am told, with the effects of the wine slept off, they forgot, I guess, all about their resolution; since the decree was written in wine, it was now blotted out of their memory, and so they abandoned their proposal, and instead of reading, they went back to their begging, which experience had taught them to be a far more profitable enterprise.

It is worth noting how much everybody enjoys the *Epistolae Obscurorum Virorum;* the educated take it as a joke, while the uneducated take it seriously and think that our laughter is caused by the style alone. While not defending the style, they do maintain that it is offset by the weighty contents, and under the crude scabbard lies a very handsome blade. It is unfortunate that the work does not have a different title! Then not even in a hundred years would the silly fools realize that the authors were sneering at them with a snout more obtrusive than that of a rhinoceros.

I am happy that my *Nowhere* meets the approval of my friend, Peter; if such men like it, I shall begin to like it myself. I am anxious to find out if it meets with the approval of Tunstall, and Busleyden, and your Chancellor;[63] but their approval is more than I could wish for, since they are so fortunate as to be top-ranking officials in their own governments, although they might be won over by the fact that in this commonwealth of mine the ruling class would be completely made up of such men as are distinguished for learning and virtue. No matter how powerful those men are in their present governments—and, true, they are very powerful—still they have some high and mighty clowns as their equals, if not their superiors, in authority and influence. I do not think that men of this caliber are swayed by the fact that they would not have many under them as subjects, as the term is now used by kings to refer to their people, who are really worse off than slaves; for it is a much higher honor to rule over free people; and good men, such as they, are far removed from that spiteful feeling which desires others to suffer while they are well off themselves. I expect, therefore, that those men will also give their approval to my work, and I am very anxious to have it. However, if a deep conviction to the contrary has been implanted in their minds by satisfaction with their present good fortune, then your one vote will be more than adequate to influence my decision. To my way of thinking, we two are a crowd, and I think I could be happy with you in any forsaken spot.

Farewell, dearest Erasmus, more precious to me than my own eyes!

I have succeeded in getting a more favorable letter from Maruffo; that seemed to me to be more convenient and more prudent than to bother the Bishop[64] again about the same matter. Not that he would be unwilling to listen to anything, as long as it concerned you; but I do prefer to approach him with matters of greater import.

Hurriedly, from London, before dawn, All Hallows Eve.

28. To Cuthbert Tunstall
<London, *ca.* November 1516>

Although all the letters I receive from you, my honored friend, are pleasing to me, yet the one you last wrote is the most pleasing; for besides its eloquence and its friendliness—all your letters abound with

63 John le Sauvage (1455–1518)   **64** Warham, Archbishop of Canterbury

these commendations—it gave me especial satisfaction by its praise of my *Commonwealth* (would
that it were as true as it is favorable). I asked our
friend Erasmus to describe to you in conversation
5   its theme, but forbade him to urge you to read the
book. Not that I did not wish you to read it (nothing would have pleased me more) but I was mindful of your wise resolution not to take in hand any
modern authors until you had sated yourself with
10 reading the ancients—a task which, measured by
the profit you have derived from them, is fully accomplished, but, measured by the love you bear
them, will never come to an end. I feared that when
the learned works of so many other authors could
15 not engage your attention, you would never willingly descend to my trifles. Nor would you have
done so, surely, unless you had been moved rather
by your love of me than by the subject of the book.
Wherefore, for having so carefully read through
20 the *Utopia,* for having undertaken so heavy a labor
for friendship's sake, I give you the deepest thanks,
not diminished by your having found pleasure in
the work. For this, too, I attribute to your friendship which has obviously influenced your judgment
25 more than strict rules of criticism. However that
may be, I cannot express my delight that your judgment is so favorable. For I have almost succeeded in
convincing myself that you say what you think, for
I know that you are far from all deceit, and I am not
30 important enough to be flattered, and I love you too
much to deserve mockery. So that if you have objec-
tively seen the truth, I am overjoyed at your verdict;
or if in reading you were blinded by your affection
for me, I am no less delighted with your love, for ve-
35 hement indeed must that love be if it can deprive
Tunstall of his judgment.

29. To Erasmus
<London, *ca.* 4 December 1516>

More sends his special greetings to Erasmus.
40   I have conferred with Urswick about that horse
for you. He insists that he still does not have a horse
which he considers suitable to send to you, but is
definitely going to send you one by the next market day, if not before. I recently dispatched to you
45 Maruffo's money draft, along with his letter con-

taining more favorable terms. At least, so he says;
but I was unable to decipher it; neither could our
friend, Lily,[65] although he knows Italian very well.
The money you had left with me has been in the
hands of our friend Giles for some time now; my   50
agent, who has returned, told me he had made the
payment to him.
    Our friend Master Palsgrave,[66] who, as you are
aware, has long been very much attached to you, is
going to Louvain to study law. But he will retain his   55
devotion to the classics of Latin and Greek literature.
He has heard that you will be living there, and while
he might expect absolutely anything from you since
he is an old friend of yours, still he earnestly begged
me for a letter of recommendation to increase the   60
favor which, he believes, he by himself already enjoys with you. Notice how people think I have great
influence with you; for me this is as much a triumph
as is the friendship of kings, which is the boast of
other men. Palsgrave would like to have your advice   65
and assistance, so as to make progress in his studies.
I realize, my dear Erasmus, that there is no need of
many words when one asks you to help in his studies
a person who has a love for intellectual things, who is
already a well known scholar, with a great future be-   70
fore him, whose great progress is also known to you,
and who, moreover, is your friend and my friend,
which means, he is twice your friend. Years ago, you
took upon yourself the special task of spending the
days and nights of your whole life in advancing the   75
intellectual life of all men. And, if this involves even
a further request, I also ask you to be openhanded
in bestowing upon our friend, Palsgrave, that which
you refuse to no man. I have given him, to deliver
to you, all the letters which you received long ago   80
from your friends in Basel and which I had in my
possession for some time. This is a fortunate coinci-
dence; you could not find a more reliable letter carrier, nor could he want anything that would assure
him a warmer reception than a large bundle of er-   85
udite letters written by dear friends of yours, letters
which you had missed a long time and had almost
despaired of recovering. I have told him, however,
not to hand them over to you until you sign the contract and agree to receive him as if every single one   90
of them were a letter of recommendation for him.
    Each day I stand by, waiting with eager ears, for
news about that business of yours in Sicily. Please

65 William Lily (*ca.* 1468–1522)   **66** John Palsgrave (*ca.* 1485–1554)

God, it may have a happy ending. Master Tunstall recently wrote me a most friendly letter. Bless my soul, but his frank and complimentary criticism of my commonwealth has given me more cheer than would an Attic talent. You have no idea how thrilled I am; I feel so expanded, and I hold my head high. For in my daydreams I have been marked out by my Utopians to be their king forever; I can see myself now marching along, crowned with a diadem of wheat, very striking in my Franciscan frock, carrying a handful of wheat as my sacred scepter, thronged by a distinguished retinue of Amaurotians, and, with this huge entourage, giving audience to foreign ambassadors and sovereigns; wretched creatures they are, in comparison with us, as they stupidly pride themselves on appearing in childish garb and feminine finery, laced with that despicable gold, and ludicrous in their purple and jewels and other empty baubles. Yet, I would not want either you or our friend, Tunstall, to judge me by other men, whose character shifts with fortune. Even if heaven has decreed to waft me from my lowly estate to this soaring pinnacle which, I think, defies comparison with that of kings, still you will never find me forgetful of that old friendship I had with you when I was but a private citizen. And if you do not mind making the short trip to visit me in Utopia, I shall definitely see to it that all mortals governed by my kindly rule will show you the honor due to those who, they know, are very dear to the heart of their king.

I was going to continue with this fascinating vision, but the rising Dawn has shattered my dream — poor me! — and shaken me off my throne and summons me back to the drudgery of the courts. But at least this thought gives me consolation: real kingdoms do not last much longer.

Farewell, dearest Erasmus.

30. To Erasmus

London, 15 December <1516>

Thomas More to Master Erasmus, best greetings.

I am sure, dearest Erasmus, that you have received my letter, which I gave Palsgrave to deliver to you, along with the letters from your friends in Basel.[67] I am glad that Dorp has come back to his senses;[68] obviously, his feelings were salved by stern language, after soothing words had only exasperated him. That is the way some people are; if you show them a little deference, they become bullies; if you treat them somewhat scornfully, they are crushed and flattened. I am desperately anxious to read the correspondence carried on between the two of you, if that can be conveniently arranged.

Lupset[69] has handed over to me several manuscripts of yours, which had been in his possession for some time. Among them are the *Iulii Genius*[70] and two declamations, one on the education of children from infancy, the other a consolation; they are entirely in your own handwriting, but only the first draft, and the text is incomplete. Except for this material, he swears that he has nothing else that belongs to you, which you are trying to recover. If you want these sheets forwarded, please let me know.

Right after Christmas Linacre is going to send his translation of Galen to Paris for printing. Lupset will accompany the manuscript and then stay on to correct the proof. You have no idea how happy you made him by mentioning his books in your recent letter[71] to me; believe me, he is all yours, heart and soul. The Bishop of Winchester,[72] who is, as you are aware, a very discreet person, was present at a large gathering of prominent people when the conversation turned upon you and your laborious publications; he testified, to the approval of all, that your rendering of the New Testament was as valuable for him as ten commentaries, for it shed so much light on the subject; he also said that here was a Latin translation that avoided Greek turns of expression, even apart from any other alteration that had to be made in the text of the Vulgate. Your letter has aroused my hopes, which I greedily seize upon; and from day to day I look forward to my *Utopia* with the feelings of a mother waiting for her son to return from abroad. Farewell, dearest Erasmus.

Hurriedly, from London, December 15.

I have forwarded your letter to Latimer;[73] I am sure he will comply with your wishes, and will be glad to do so. My wife[74] sends you a thousand greetings, and also thanks you for the very thoughtful

---

67 See Letter 29.　68 See Letter 15, which helped to change Dorp's mind, and Letter 82, which congratulated him.　69 Thomas Lupset (*ca.* 1495–1530)　70 Iulii Genius was one of the three characters in the *Iulius exclusus e coelo*, probably written in 1513 or 1514, soon after the death of Pope Julius II.　71 not extant　72 Richard Fox (*ca.* 1446/7–1528)　73 See Letter 26. 74 Dame Alice More

wish that she may enjoy a long life; she craves that all the more, as she says, so as to have a longer time to pester me.

31. To William Warham[75]

<London, January 1517>

I ever judged your Paternity happy in the way you exercised your office of chancellor, but I esteem you much happier now that you have laid it down and entered on that most desirable leisure, in which you can live for yourself and for God. Such leisure, in my opinion, is not only more pleasant than the labors, but more honorable than all your honors. To be a judge is the lot of many, and sometimes of very bad men. But you possessed that supreme office which, when relinquished, is as much exposed to calumny as it formerly conferred authority and independence; and to give this up willingly as your Paternity has with great difficulty obtained permission to do, is what none but a moderate-minded man would wish, and none but an innocent man dare.

I do not know which to admire the most, your modesty in willingly laying down an office of such dignity and power, your unworldliness in being able to despise it, or your integrity in having no fear of resignation; but in any case together with many other men I give to your action my most cordial approval as most excellent and wise. Indeed I can hardly say how heartily I congratulate you on your singular good fortune and how I rejoice in it for your sake, for I see your Paternity retiring far away from secular affairs and the bustle of the courts, and enjoying a rare glory by the honorable repute of your tenure of the Judgeship and your resignation from it. Happy in the consciousness of duty well done, you will pass the rest of your life gently and peacefully in literature and philosophy. This happy state of yours my own wretchedness makes daily more brightly attractive; for although I have no business worth mentioning (yet he was at this time a member of the Royal Council,[76] Under-Treasurer of the realm, and often employed in legations) yet since feeble powers are readily oppressed by paltry affairs,

I am always so distraught that I have not a free moment in which to visit your Paternity or excuse my remissness in writing—indeed I have scarcely been able to get ready this present letter.

Herewith I would beg your lordship to accept a none too witty little book (the *Utopia*). It was written in undue haste, but a friend of mine, a citizen of Antwerp (Peter Giles) allowed his affection to outweigh his judgment, thought it worthy of publication, and without my knowledge had it printed. Although I know it is unworthy of your high rank, your wide experience, or your learning, yet I venture to send it, relying on the generosity with which you habitually encourage all men's literary endeavors, and trusting to the favor I have always experienced from you. Thus I hope that even if the book pleases you but little, yet your good will may be extended to the author.

Farewell, my Lord Archbishop.

32. To a Member of the Royal Court

<London, January 1517>

I had had it in mind to betroth my *Utopia* to Cardinal Wolsey alone (if my friend Peter[77] had not, without my knowledge, as you know, ravished her of the first flower of her maidenhood), if indeed I should betroth her to anyone and not rather keep her with me ever unwed, or perhaps consecrate her to Vesta and initiate her into Vesta's sacred fires.

33. To Erasmus

<London>, 13 January <1517>

More to Erasmus, greeting.

I suppose that draft from Maruffo[78] must be in the same style as this letter of mine, which I shall be surprised if you can read. But you will forgive me, my dearest Erasmus, for I am under such a constant pressure of business, I have neither time to write nor energy to think. But if you have received the money from Maruffo, will you write to the Archbishop, so that Maruffo can recover what he has paid. I have written to thank our friend Busleyden.

---

75 William Warham (*ca.* 1450–1532), Archbishop of Canterbury, resigned as chancellor in 1515. **76** More was called councilor in the pension grant of 1516, but his actual introduction to the Privy Council seems to have been delayed to the summer of 1518. **77** Peter Giles of Antwerp had sent the *Utopia* to Th. Martens of Louvain for publication. **78** See the beginning of Letter 29 above. Raffaele Maruffo was a Genoese merchant and banker in England.

You must thank Desmarez[79] yourself on my behalf no less warmly than Giles, for they wished you
to have the credit of what they wrote. You would
hardly believe how devoted to you Linacre is, and
5   what a keen champion of your studies. Why Grocyn was so anxious to meet you, I have not yet been
able to discover, for he has not yet come to London.
Farewell, dear Erasmus.

   In haste, on St. Hilary's Day.

10 **34. To Antonio <Bonvisi?>**[80]
   <London, January 1517?>

That you have any such esteem of me issues, I suspect, from affection rather than judgment. For love,
generally, when it settles deep in men, spreads dark-
15 ness over their thinking. Which I see has happened
to you, especially since my *Utopia* has pleased you so
much, a book which I think clearly deserves to hide
itself away forever in its own island.

37. To Cuthbert Tunstall
20 <London, 1517?>

That in your letter you thank me so carefully for
my services on behalf of your friends is a mark of
your great courtesy. What I did was quite trifling:
it is only your goodness that exaggerates it. But you
25 scarcely do justice to our friendship, for you seem to
think that what I may do puts you under an obligation, whereas you should rather claim it as your own
and service due you....
   The amber which you sent me,[81] a precious sepul-
30 cher for flies, was most acceptable on many counts.
For the material in color and brilliance can challenge any gem, and the form is all the more excellent in that it represents a heart, a sort of symbol of
your love for me. For thus do I interpret your mean-
35 ing: as the fly, winged like Cupid and as fickle, is so
shut up and entangled in the substance of the amber that it cannot fly away, so embalmed in the ar-
omatic juice that it cannot perish, so your love will
never fly away and always remain unchanged.
40   That I have nothing to give you in return does

not greatly trouble me. For I know you do not look
for an interchange of gifts and I am quite willing to
remain in your debt. But yet I am somewhat distressed that so slender are my small means, I cannot bear myself so dutifully as to appear not unwor-   45
thy of such proofs of your friendship. Wherefore,
since I cannot prove myself to others, I must needs
be content with our joint understanding, yours and
mine.

40. To Erasmus   50
London, 16 July <1517>

Thomas More to Erasmus of Rotterdam, greeting.
   You made me very anxious, dearest Erasmus, by
your latest letters (for I have had two), which give
me to understand that our friend Peter[82] is not yet   55
really restored to health and has something else
hanging over him as well. What sort of thing this
is you guess rather than know, and I could wish
that whatever it is that you guess you had given me
a few oracular hints, for even guesswork is beyond   60
me, and affection being full of fears, I am driven to
be afraid of many things which may be worse than
the truth. Another thing too distresses me, that as
though illness and anxiety were not enough, his
wife's miscarriage has now been as it were piled on   65
the top. O how unfair are the changes of mortal
life! Success creeps on us slowly step by step; adversity descends all at once, and it rarely happens that
any misfortune befalls us in isolation. All the same,
human affairs are always changing; some days play   70
the stepmother, but not all; and so I hope that all
his troubles will be repaid by some great unexpected
good fortune, and that I may see this very soon is
my dearest wish.
   As for that black Carmelite,[83] that he should be   75
so much against you does not surprise me in the
least. Two men could not be more unlike: one ignorant, one very learned; one bad, one very good. But
that he should inveigh against your *Folly* is hardly
credible, for he is entirely made up of folly him-   80
self. The insolence and ingratitude of the man! Is
he so much ashamed of his imperial mistress, who
has given him her charming daughter Self-conceit[84]

79 Jean Desmarez of Cassel (d. 1526)
80 Antonio Bonvisi (d. 1558) was a wealthy
Italian merchant from Lucca and a close
friend of Thomas More.   **81** Tunstall was

abroad in 1517, and would probably have
purchased the amber on the continent.
82 Peter Giles   **83** Jean Briselot (d. 1520),
a suffragan bishop of Cambrai, prior of the

Carmelite house near Valenciennes; in 1507
became abbot of the Benedictine abbey of
Saint-Pierre de Hautmont   **84** a character
in Erasmus's *In Praise of Folly*

"in lasting wedlock bound, to be his wife,"[85] that in her he may take continual delight, for otherwise he could not endure his own company? Does he not realize also how much this bountiful goddess has lately done for him? When he was recently a candidate for so high an office, was it not she alone who wheedled their votes out of the electors? She it was who blinded them by magic arts and "o'er his eyes a godlike splendor spread,"[86] who secured his return with acclamation as worthy holder of that important office by the decisive vote of right honorable men — he being of course "in head and shoulders godlike,"[87] while his rival was cast out in disgrace, for that he skinny was and bald, those depressing marks of a wise man. So this runaway slave with supreme ingratitude now rants at his own mistress; he has donned the lion's skin of wisdom to conceal the fact that he is only Folly's ass. Luckily his ears at any rate stick out, and I hope he will one day be dragged by them away from his parade-harness and back to his panniers.

But that good old man[88] on the other hand — I cannot say how much I wonder what he would be at. Why does a pious and modest man strive so immodestly for reputation, of which he will not have a shred left if he goes on like this? How much better is your own policy! When challenged to a fight, you negotiate for peace and make up your mind so to govern your pen as not to leave the truth defenseless, and yet to mollify your opponent so that things do not issue in frenzy. This means in fact that you abandon your triumph when you have won the day and treat the advantage of all lovers of learning as something more important than your own glory, so that disagreement among the Greeks may not strengthen the barbarians, who turn their dissensions to their own advantage. If Caesar in the olden days had combined this moderate way of thinking with his lofty spirit, he would beyond doubt have won more glory by preserving the republic than he got from all the peoples whom he conquered and subdued. Though personally I think this modesty that you display is more than anything the product of a great and lofty heart. What can be more exalted than the humility which despises and derides fame,

the very patron goddess of the proud? Yet fame follows you and dogs your steps everywhere however much you seek to escape, and you already have your fill and are almost sick of it.

The panel which is to record for me the likeness of you and our dear Peter[89] I await with indescribable impatience and curse the ill-health that so long keeps my hopes unfulfilled. My Lord Cardinal was speaking warmly to me of you lately and clearly seems to have in mind some great benefaction for you. That letter of mine which you say you do not wish to be done out of was so carefully put away by my man William[90] that he cannot find it. None the less, since you so wish, it shall be found wherever it may be, and I will see that it is sent to you. Farewell. From London, in haste, 16 July.

I send you a bundle of letters from the Venetian envoy and his secretary, and also from the Bishop of Rochester.[91]

41. To Erasmus
London, 19 August <1517>

Thomas More to Erasmus, greeting.

The belated and long-postponed departure of my friend Palsgrave,[92] who is daily expected to leave, has meant that you should receive my letter and other people's much later than either I desired or you deserved. For I thought that my answer could most conveniently be carried by the man who had brought me yours. So it proved necessary to add this to my previous letter, to explain the reason for the delay and also to bring you up to date with the news here. If ever we were in trouble before, our distress and danger are at their greatest now, with many deaths on all sides and almost everyone in Oxford and Cambridge and London taking to their beds within a few days and the loss of many of my best and most honorable friends; among them (which I am sorry to think will bring you sorrow too) our dear Andrea Ammonio,[93] who is a very great loss to learning and to all right-thinking men. He saw himself very well protected against the contagion by his modest manner of life, thinking it due to this that,

---

85 Vergil, *Aeneid* 1.73 86 Vergil, *Aeneid* 1.589 87 Erasmus's *Adages* 266 (*CWE* 31: 290) 88 Jacques Lefévre d'Etaples 89 For the two-paneled painting that

Erasmus and Peter Giles sent More, see Plate 9c, Letter 47, and Epigram 276. 90 William Gonell 91 John Fisher 92 John Palsgrave (1468?–1522) returned

from Louvain to London between July 10 and 15. 93 d. August 17, 1517. He was secretary to King Henry VIII and a close friend of Erasmus.

though he rarely met anyone whose whole household had not suffered, the evil has so far attacked none of his own people. Of this he boasted to me himself and to many other men beside, not very many hours before he himself was carried off. For this sweating-sickness is fatal only on the first day.

I and my wife and children are still untouched, and the rest of my household have entirely recovered. But of this I can assure you: one is safer on the battlefield than in the city. It has now begun, I hear, to rage in Calais, at the moment when I am obliged to go there on a mission; as though it was not enough to have lived in the midst of contagion, but I must actually go in search of it. But what can one do? What one's lot brings must be endured. I have prepared my mind to face any outcome. Mind you at least keep well.

In haste, from London, 19 August.

43. To His Daughters and to Margaret Giggs
<1517?>

Thomas More to Margaret, Elizabeth, Cecilia, his darling daughters, and to Margaret Giggs equally dear, best greetings.

I cannot adequately express, my delightful daughters, how greatly pleased I am by your charming letters and no less by the fact, as I notice, that though you are on the road moving from place to place, you yet abandon none of your habit either of dialectic exercises or writing themes or composing verse. This fully convinces me that you love me as you ought, since I observe you feel so much concern in my absence that you practice zealously what you know gives me pleasure when I am with you. When I return I shall make you realize that disposition toward me is as profitable to yourselves as I realize it is pleasurable to me. For believe me truly there is nothing which refreshes me so much in the midst of this bothersome business as reading what comes from you. Whereby I perceive the truth of what your affectionate teacher writes so affectionately that if your own letters did not declare your extraordinary devotion to literature he might appear to have indulged his affection rather than the truth. But now by what you write you win him trust and I credit the truth of his almost incredible

boastings about you, the beauty and discernment of your discourses. And so I long with all my heart to hasten home so as to match my pupil in competitive audition with you; he is a bit too lazy in the matter, because he cannot give up the hope that he may find you fall short of your teacher's promise. But I harbor the hope (knowing that you are persistent) that shortly you will surpass even your teacher, if not in discourse at least in not abandoning the suit. Farewell, my darlings.

46. To Erasmus
Calais, 7 October <1517>

Letters 46 and 47 were sent together to Erasmus and express More's joy on receiving the Metsys diptych.

Thomas More to his Desiderius Erasmus, greeting.

At last, dearest Erasmus, one-eyed Peter has brought the portraits of you and our dear Giles for which I have waited so long,[94] and how delighted I am with them is easier for anyone to gauge from his own feelings than for me to put in words. Here are men whose faces merely sketched in chalk or charcoal might charm anyone who was not wholly dead to all feeling for scholarship and goodness, while I in particular might well be deeply moved by the memory of such dear friends however inadequately recorded; and who can either expound in words or fail to feel in his imagination how I must now be ravished by their pictures, drawn and rendered with such skill that they could easily challenge all the painters of Antiquity? The spectator well might suppose them cast or carved rather than painted, so much do they seem to stand out and project with the proper relief of a man's body. You would hardly believe, my most lovable Erasmus,[95] how my affection for you, which I was convinced would admit of no addition, has been increased by this desire of yours to bind me still closer to you, and how forcibly I exult in the glory of being so highly valued by you; for in this remarkable document you put it on record that there is no one else whose affection you rate so highly. For such is my own interpretation at any rate — conceited it may be, but thus it is: you have sent me this present to remind me of you not merely every day but every hour. You know me well:

---

94 See Plate 9c.   **95** *lovable Erasmus:* More plays on the name Erasmus and the Greek *erasmios*, "charming."

I am sure I need not expend great efforts in proving to you that, although not free from failings in many other ways, at least I am no Thraso;[96] I am entirely free from vainglory. And yet, to tell the truth, this is the one itch in the way of ambition which I find it impossible to shake off, and which tickles me in a most agreeable manner, when it comes into my head that distant posterity will remember me for my friendship with Erasmus, attested in letters and books and pictures and every other way. If only I had some gift that might make it possible to produce something really distinguished, to prove myself not unworthy of such warm affection from a man without peer not only in his own generation but in future ages! But since it lies so far above my meagre capacity to do anything that could make the world understand this, I will at least do all I can[97] to prove myself, on your evidence alone, at any rate not ungrateful.

I have read your *Apologia* right through with close attention, and its effect on me at least was this: never did I perceive your eloquence more clearly or admire it less. What ruled out admiration was the feeling that in such a simple case[98] anyone might shine, not only you who can make the most difficult case look simple. Really I am quite sorry for the man, who has been led on by the applause of his local audience and encouraged to choose for the display of his powers to hold forth on the most chaotic problem that ever was, for the evidence favours now one side and now the other. I hope that your warning will make him see the light. I admired it all very much, but especially the witty way in which you rebuke his conceit, in suggesting that his second edition was prior to your annotations, although it controverts notes which we are asked to believe did not yet exist.

I sent your secretary[99] on to England with ten gros for his journey-money; to Peter[100] I gave a noble, which was very little indeed for the man who brought me that picture, but he seemed content. I hope for a prosperous and happy outcome to the book[101] on the education of a prince which you have sent to our prince as a present. Busleyden's death, heaven knows, was a heavy blow; he was a scholar above the average, a good friend of mine,[102] and fair

and friendly to everybody. As for me, I have to sit here till the beginning of November[103] so continuously that I with difficulty secured two days for a trip to Saint-Omer, especially in hopes of seeing the abbot[104] of Saint Bertin at any rate, whom you described to me long ago. I found him just what you said; he asked me to dinner and gave me a generous welcome. He receives all his visitors at some length, and with me he was positively effusive; but he is a delightful old man and grew young again when he thought of you. Farewell, dearest Erasmus.

Tunstall is back in England. Farewell once more. From Calais, 7 October.

47. To Peter Giles
<Calais> 7 October <1517>

Thomas More to his friend Peter Giles, greeting.

My dearest Peter, greeting. I want passionately to hear whether you are getting strong again, which matters no less to me than any of my own concerns; and so I make careful enquiries and diligently pick up all I can from everybody. A certain number of people have given me a more cheerful account, either (as I hope) because they know it for a fact, or just to give me what they knew I wanted. I have written a letter to our friend Erasmus. This I send you unsealed, and please seal it up yourself, for there is no reason why anything addressed to him need be sealed when it comes to you. I wrote some verses of a sort on that picture; they are as clumsy as it was expert, but I have made a copy for you. If you think them worth it, pass them on to Erasmus; otherwise put them on the fire.

Farewell, this 7 October.

Lines written upon the diptych in which Erasmus and Peter Giles were portrayed together by that excellent artist Quentin,[105] in such a fashion that behind Erasmus, who is beginning his *Paraphrase on the Epistle to the Romans*, his books were painted each with its title, while Peter held a letter addressed to him in More's hand, which was actually imitated by the painter.

96 the soldier in Terence's *Eunuchus*, proverbial for his self-assurance   **97** *all I can:* See Letter 47.   **98** *in such a simple case:* Ovid's *Tristia* 3.11.21   **99** Jan of Friesland   **100** Peter Meghen   **101** a presentation copy of the *Institutio principis christiani* sent to Henry VIII   **102** *friend of mine:* More had met Busleyden during his embassy to the Netherlands in 1515. In Epigrams 250–52, he recalled the refined and hospitable atmosphere of Busleyden's house at Mechelen.   **103** This is a guess by the editors: the Deventer Letter-book gives September.   **104** Antoon van Bergen **105** Quentin Metsys

THE PICTURE SPEAKS[106]

Castor and Pollux were great friends of old:
Erasmus such and Giles you behold.
Far from them, more laments with love so dear
As scarce a man unto himself could bear.
5   Yet letters (making naught of envious space)
Bring near the loved one's mind, and I his face.

NOW I, MORE, SPEAK MYSELF

If you have seen these men before,
10   Their features will be soon detected.
If not, to make all safe and sure,
One holds a note to him directed;
The other writes his name—which yet,
Though he say nought, you'll soon discover,
15   For on the shelf behind are set
Books that are known the wide world over.
Quentin, who giv'st new art for old,
Than great Apelles[107] even greater,
With mingled colours manifold
20   Lending dead shapes the life of nature,
If thou canst paint so well such men
As our forefathers scarce beheld 'em,
In our day rarer still—and then
In future they'll be seen more seldom—
25   This fragile wood why didst thou use
Instead of tablets everlasting,
Such as posterity might choose
To keep thy fame and thee from wasting?
In days to come, if someone cares
30   For liberal arts somewhere on earth,
And brutal Mars Minerva spares,
What will these pictures then be worth?

My dear Peter, marvellously as our Quentin has represented everything, what a wonderful forger above
35   all else it looks as though he might have been! He has
imitated the address on my letter to you so well that I
do not believe I could repeat it myself. And so, unless
he wants it for some purpose of his own, or you are
keeping it for your own ends, do please let me have
40   the letter back: it will double the effect if it is kept
handy alongside the picture. If it has been lost, or
you have a use for it, I will see whether I in my turn
can imitate the man who imitates my hand so well.
Farewell, you and your charming wife.

52. To Erasmus
Calais, 25 October <1517>

Thomas More to Erasmus, greeting.

I have had a letter, my dear Erasmus, from Wentford,[108] which I send straight on to you by the same
courier. You will easily discover from it that the man
is what he always was. I will not ask your pardon
for opening a letter to you, for (as you see) though
written to you it was addressed to me. I make no
doubt that the same mistake has happened and the
letter addressed to you was written to me; but such
was my eagerness to read it that I did not choose
to break the seal. If you find anything in it which
you feel I should wish to know (this I at any rate
consider unlikely), pray tell me. You have, I suppose,
received the letter in which I reported safe arrival
of the picture;[109] for which let me thank you once
again—no, dear Erasmus, again a thousand times.
Of your Peter,[110] since he went to England, I have
no news. That was a present worthy of a king, and
I only hope that in that quarter it will secure you
from the King something worth having. May there
be a blessing on the duties entrusted you by the Emperor, for nothing goes well for him at the moment;
or rather, all is in God's hand. I am sure you are right
to wish not to become immersed in the busy nothings of princes, and you show your affection for me
in hoping that I may be released from them; for you
cannot believe how unwillingly I spend my time
on them, nor could anything be more tedious than
my present mission. For I am exiled to a small seaside town where place and climate are equally unattractive; and as for the litigation, at home I have a
natural distaste for it even when it brings in something, and imagine how tedious it must be here
when accompanied by loss. But my lord makes generous promises that the King will make it all up to
me. When I get it, I will let you know. Till then,
farewell; and I daresay to keep well is all you desire. Give my cordial greetings to Doctor Lee,[111] and
to my friend Palsgrave if he has returned. Farewell
once more.

---

106 See Epigram 276 for an alternate
translation.   107 the most famous painter
of ancient Greece   108 Roger Wentford
was headmaster of St. Anthony's School in
London.   109 See Plate 9c, Letter 46, and
Epigram 276.   110 Peter Meghen, who
brought the Metsys portraits   111 Edward
Lee (*ca.* 1482–1544), who met Erasmus
at Louvain. See Letter 75 (pp. 421–30)
for More's response to Lee's critical
annotations to Erasmus's New Testament
translation.

54. To Erasmus
Calais, 5 November <1517>

Thomas More to his friend Erasmus, greeting.

I had a letter from you today, together with letters for Colet[112] and the Bishop of Rochester,[113] and a pamphlet with them. I will see to it that they are delivered as soon as possible, so that the pamphlet may not lose the charm of novelty. As I read your letter, I wondered why you had not written to my Lord of Canterbury[114] as well, to deal with your business with him yourself, for no one else, if I mistake not, carries such weight with him. Though if you would rather do this through me, and think that someone on the spot can be more effective than any writing of letters, it will give me more pleasure to comply than you to command me. But I shall not have the opportunity to complete it as soon as I should wish to complete any business of yours, for it is the regular practice with us that a man returning from a mission must go straight to the King and not turn aside to see anyone on the way. Besides which, my negotiations proceed so slowly that I fear it may be necessary to stay here longer than I hoped and longer than suits my own interests, unless perhaps I find that there is no hope here which makes it worth while to stay. But for the time being, if you wish, the business can be done by letter; and I have no doubt that that will be your wish. I will proceed therefore on the assumption that this year's annuity is to be deposited with Maruffo[115] and the bill dispatched to you. But as for commuting your annuity I at least think that nothing should be done, both because there is no one who could properly commute it except one man[116] who, they tell me, has no funds to do it from, and because I fear the Archbishop will read this as a sign that you have lost all interest in us. So think again about the commutation; if you decide to go ahead, you will not find me wanting. Meantime I will myself take steps about payment, and I think it would not come amiss if you put in a letter too; he perhaps is waiting for that.

I am delighted that the *Paraphrase*[117] is in the press.

How I envy Louvain! A great blessing has come its way—how great, as far as I can see, it scarcely recognizes. But the man of whom you write,[118] unless I am quite wrong, will never alter. Tunstall[119] just thinks you are too kind-hearted in continuing to trust him after being deceived so often. Pace[120] is still not back, nor can I discover when he will return; for that matter, I cannot imagine what business detains him. At least, as far as I can understand by making inquiries, for a long time there has been nothing afoot either with the Emperor or with the Swiss, yet he is not allowed to pack up and go home, though he has now been stuck in Constance, I believe, for more than a year. I am surprised that he has not returned your book. I will write to him about it to some effect; for there is nothing I would rather achieve, for the cause of good letters or my own sake, perceiving that you intend to set up a monument to our friendship in that work, which I value above all pyramids and mausoleums.

Hermans[121] I must leave to you. For Batt I developed such a penchant long ago from the way you spoke about him that I am almost as keen to see his memory flourish as my own. Only you must consider how you will couple me with him, for he died when I had scarcely reached man's estate, or in fact not even that. But you will contrive all this well enough. Mind you, though: charity begins at home. I insist on a part second only to yours, and no mistake. I am too fond of talking, as you know, to submit to a walking-on part, especially in a comedy from which I promise myself immortality.

Farewell, dearest Erasmus. I am glad you liked my poor lines on the picture.[122] Tunstall thought almost too well of the hendecasyllables, only moderately of the six-line epigram. But a certain friar I could name even had the face to pick a hole in it, because I compared the two of you to Castor and Pollux, and he said you should have been compared to Theseus and Pirithous or Pylades and Orestes, who were friends, as you are, and not brothers. I could not endure the friar, even if he were speaking the truth, and responded to his well-meant interference with an ill-written epigram:

112 John Colet (*ca.* 1466–1519), dean of St. Paul's Cathedral   113 John Fisher 114 William Warham   115 Raffaele Maruffo, a Genoese merchant and banker in England   116 Richard Master, rector of Aldington   117 Erasmus's *Paraphrasis ad Romanos*, published in November 1517   118 probably Maarten van Dorp 119 Cuthbert Tunstall   120 Richard Pace (*ca.* 1482–1536), English diplomat 121 William Hermans and Jacob Batt are interlocutors in the published edition of Erasmus's *Antibarbari*.   122 See Epigram 276.

Quoth I, of two great friends in brief
The affection to declare,
"Such friends they are as once of old
Castor and Pollux were."
5   An owlish brother takes me up,
Of those who wear the cowl:
"Who friends and brothers thus confounds,
Sure, he must be an owl!"
"How so? What can more friendly be
10 Than brother is to brother?"
He laughed at one who did not know
What's known to every other:
"A large and crowded house is ours,
Brothers ten score may be;
15 In those ten score (my life upon't)
Two friends you will not see."[123]

Farewell then once again. From Calais, 5 November,
in haste, the courier being in a great hurry, and under pressure, I dare say, from his driver.

20 **57. To Bishop John Fisher**[124]
    <*ca.* 1517–18>

Much against my will did I come to Court (as everyone knows, and as the King himself in joke
sometimes likes to reproach me). So far I keep my
25 place there as precariously as an unaccustomed rider
in his saddle. But the King (whose special favor I am
far from enjoying) is so courteous and kindly to all
that everyone (who is in any way hopeful) finds a
ground for imagining that he is in the King's good
30 graces, like the London wives who, as they pray before the image of the Virgin Mother of God which
stands near the Tower, gaze upon it so fixedly that
they imagine it smiles upon them. But I am not so
fortunate as to perceive such signs of favor, nor so
35 despondent as to imagine them. But the King has
virtue and learning and makes great progress in
both with almost daily renewed zeal, so that the
more I see his Majesty increase in all the good and
really kingly qualities, the less burdensome do I feel
40 this life of the Court.

62. To Erasmus
<England, *ca.* May 1518>

I have a great affection for Rhenanus and I owe him
much gratitude for his extremely kind preface. I
should long ago have sent him a letter of thanks had   45
not that fatal disease of laziness held me captive.

63. To William Gonell[125]
At Court, 22 May <1518?>

I have received, my dear Gonell, your letter, elegant
and full of affection as always. Your devotion to my   50
children I perceive from your letter, your diligence
from theirs. Everyone's letter pleased me greatly, but
above all that I notice Elizabeth shows a modesty of
character in the absence of her mother, which not
every girl would show in her mother's presence.   55
Let her understand that such conduct delights me
more than all the learning in the world. Though I
prefer learning joined with virtue to all the treasures of kings, yet renown for learning, if you take
away moral probity, brings nothing else but notori-   60
ous and noteworthy infamy, especially in a woman.
Since erudition in women is a new thing and a reproach to the sloth of men, many will gladly assail
it, and impute to learning what is really the fault
of nature, thinking from the vices of the learned to   65
get their own ignorance esteemed as virtue. On the
other hand, if a woman (and this I desire and hope
with you as their teacher for all my daughters) to
eminent virtue of mind should add even moder-
ate skill in learning, I think she will gain more real   70
good than if she obtain the riches of Croesus and
the beauty of Helen. Not because that learning will
be a glory to her, though learning will accompany
virtue as a shadow does a body, but because the reward of wisdom is too solid to be lost with riches or   75
to perish with beauty, since it depends on the inner
knowledge of what is right, not on the talk of men,
than which nothing is more foolish or mischievous.

For as it becomes a good man to avoid infamy, so
to lay oneself out for renown is the sign of a man   80
who is not only arrogant, but ridiculous and miserable. A mind must be uneasy which ever wavers
between joy and sadness because of other men's

---

123 See Epigram 277 for an alternate
translation.   124 John Fisher, Bishop

of Rochester, who, like More, refused to
take the oath to the Act of Succession

125 William Gonell (d. 1560) was a tutor in
More's home.

opinions. Among all the benefits that learning bestows on men, I think there is none more excellent than that by study we are taught to seek in that very study not praise, but utility. Such has been the teaching of the most learned men, especially of philosophers, who are the guides of human life, although some may have abused learning, like other good things, simply to court empty glory and popular renown.

I have written at length on not pursuing glory, my dear Gonell, because of what you say in your letter, that Margaret's lofty and exalted character of mind should not be debased. In this judgment I quite agree with you; but to me, and, no doubt, to you also, that man would seem to debase a generous character of mind who would accustom it to admire what is vain and low. He, on the contrary, raises it who rises to virtue and true goods, and who looks down with contempt from the contemplation of the sublime, on those shadows of good things which almost all mortals, through ignorance of truth, greedily snatch at as if they were true goods.

Therefore, my dearest Gonell, since I thought we must walk by this road, I have often begged not you only, who, out of your exceptional affection for all my family, would do it of your own accord, nor only my wife, who is sufficiently urged by her truly maternal love for them, which has been proved to me in many ways, but absolutely all my friends, continually to warn my children to avoid as it were the precipices of pride and haughtiness, and to walk in the pleasant meadows of modesty: not to be dazzled at the sight of gold; not to lament the lack of what they erroneously admire in others; not to think more of themselves for gaudy trappings, nor less for the want of them; not to deform the beauty that nature has given them by neglect, nor to try to heighten it by artifice; to put virtue in the first place among goods, learning in the second; and in their studies to esteem most whatever may teach them piety toward God, charity to all, and modesty and Christian humility in themselves. By such means they will receive from God the reward of an innocent life, and in the assured expectation of it will view death without dread, and meanwhile possessing solid joy will neither be puffed up by the empty praise of men, nor dejected by evil tongues. These I consider the real and genuine fruits of learning, and though I admit that all literary men do not possess them, I would maintain that those who give

themselves to study with such intent will easily attain their end and become perfect.

Nor do I think that the harvest is much affected whether it is a man or a woman who does the sowing. They both have the name of human being whose nature reason differentiates from that of beasts; both, I say, are equally suited for the knowledge of learning by which reason is cultivated, and, like plowed land, germinates a crop when the seeds of good precepts have been sown. But if the soil of a woman be naturally bad, and apter to bear fern than grain, by which saying many keep women from study, I think, on the contrary, that a woman's wit is the more diligently to be cultivated, so that nature's defect may be redressed by industry. This was the opinion of the ancients, both the wisest and the most saintly. Not to speak of the rest, Jerome and Augustine not only exhorted excellent matrons and honorable virgins to study, but also, in order to assist them, diligently explained the abstruse meanings of the Scriptures, and wrote for tender girls letters replete with so much erudition that nowadays old men who call themselves doctors of sacred literature can scarcely read them correctly, much less understand them. Do you, my learned Gonell, have the kindness to see that my daughters thoroughly learn these works of saintly men. From them they will learn in particular what goal they should set for their studies, and the whole fruit of their endeavors should consist in the testimony of God and a good conscience. Thus they will be inwardly calm and at peace and neither stirred by praise of flatterers nor stung by the follies of unlearned mockers of learning.

But I fancy that I now hear you object that these precepts, though true, are beyond the tender years of my daughters, since you will scarcely find a man, however old and advanced in study, whose mind is so fixed and firm as not to be tickled sometimes with desire of glory. But, dear Gonell, the more do I see the difficulty of getting rid of this pest of pride, the more do I see the necessity of getting to work at it from childhood. For I find no other reason why this inescapable evil so clings to our hearts, than that almost as soon as we are born, it is sown in the tender minds of children by their nurses, it is cultivated by their teachers, it is nourished and brought to maturity by their parents; while no one teaches anything, even the good, without bidding them always to expect praise as the recompense and prize of virtue. Thus long accustomed to magnify praise, they strive to please the greater number (that is, the worse) and end by being ashamed to be good. That this plague of vainglory may be banished far from my children, may you, my dear Gonell, and their mother and all their friends, sing this song to them, and repeat it, and beat it into their heads, that vainglory is despicable, and to be spit upon, and that there is nothing more sublime than that humble modesty so often praised by Christ; and this your prudent charity will so enforce as to teach virtue rather than reprove vice, and make them love good advice instead of hating it. To this purpose nothing will more conduce than to read to them the lessons of the ancient Fathers, who, they know, cannot be angry with them; and, as they honor them for their sanctity, they must needs be much moved by their authority. If you will read something of this sort, besides their reading of Sallust—to Margaret and Elizabeth, who are more mature than John and Cecily—you will bind me and them, already in your debt, still more to you. And besides you will make my children who are dear to me first by the law of nature, and then dearer by learning and virtue, most dear by such advancement in knowledge and good character. Farewell.

From the Court, on the vigil of Pentecost.

65. To William Budé [126]
<*ca.* August 1518>

I never skim any of your works, but study them seriously as works of the first importance. To your treatise, however, on Roman Measures I gave a very special attention such as I have given to no ancient author. For that it cannot be understood in any cursory way, you have provided by your careful choice of words, your well-balanced sentences, the studied gravity of your diction, and not least by the serious and difficult nature of the matters you treat of matters almost lost in antiquity, and requiring the deepest research. But yet if anyone will turn his eyes to what you have written and give it careful and continued attention, he will find that the light you have thrown upon your subject brings the dead past to life again. Whilst he ponders your words, he will live in imagination through all the past ages, and will be able to gaze upon, to count and almost to

take into his hands, the hoarded wealth of all kings, tyrants and nations, which is almost more than any misers have been able to do.

I can hardly enumerate the multitude of reasons for which I am attached to you, my dear Budé. You are so exceedingly good to me: whomsoever I love, you, by good fortune, love also: you possess so many excellent virtues: your temperament, as I judge, hardly differs from mine: you have earned the gratitude of all men for your useful literary labors: though a married man you have happily acquired a degree of learning that was once the exclusive possession of the clergy. Indeed I am hardly content to call you a layman when by your splendid gifts you are so highly raised beyond the level of the laity.

69. To Margaret More
<1518>

I was delighted to receive your letter, my dearest Margaret, informing me of Shaw's[127] condition. Later letters will be even more delightful if they have told me of the studies you and your brother are engaged in, of your daily reading, your pleasant discussions, your essays, of the swift passage of the days made joyous by literary pursuits. For although everything you write gives me pleasure, yet the most exquisite delight of all comes from reading what none but you and your brother could have written. *[And the letter concludes:]*[128] I beg you, Margaret, tell me about the progress you are all making in your studies. For I assure you that, rather than allow my children to be idle and slothful, I would make a sacrifice of wealth, and bid adieu to other cares and business, to attend to my children and my family, amongst whom none is more dear to me than yourself, my beloved daughter. Farewell.

70. To Margaret More
<1518>

You are too bashful and timid in your request for money, from a father who wants to give it and when you have greeted me with a letter such that I would not only repay each line of it with a gold Philippeus

126 William Budé (1467–1540) was a French humanist and friend of More and Erasmus.   **127** *Shai* (genitive). The English form of the name was probably Shaw, but his identity is unknown.   **128** The parenthetical comment is Stapleton's.

(as Alexander did with Choerilos),[129] but, if my means were as great as my desire, I would reward each syllable with two ounces of gold. As it is, I send only what you have asked, but would have added more, except that as I am eager to give, so I like to be asked and coaxed by my daughter, especially by you, whom virtue and learning have made so dear to my heart. So the sooner you spend this money well, as you always do, and the sooner you ask for more, the more will you be sure of pleasing your father. Farewell, my dearest daughter.

71. To Reginald Pole and John Clement[130]
<1518>

I thank you, my dear Clement, for being so keenly solicitous about the health of my famly and myself that although absent you are careful to warn us what food to avoid. I thank you, my dear Pole, doubly for deigning to procure for me the advice of so skilful a physician, and no less for obtaining from your mother[131] — noblest and best of women, and fully worthy of such a son — the remedy prescribed and for getting it made up. Not only do you willingly procure us advice, but equally evident is your willingness to obtain for us the remedy itself. I love and praise both of you for your bounty and fidelity.

72. To Erasmus
<London?, 1518?>

My Clement[132] lectures at Oxford to an audience larger than has ever gathered to any other lecturer. It is astonishing how universal is the approbation and the love he gains. Even those to whom classical literature was almost anathema now show attachment to him, attend his lectures, and gradually modify their opposition. Linacre, who, as you know, never praises anyone extravagantly, cannot contain his admiration for his learning, so that, although I love Clement so much, I am almost tempted to envy him for the high praises heaped upon him.

74. To Bishop John Fisher
<1519?>

I cannot express in words my delight, both for your own sake and for the sake of our country, that your lordship writes in a style that might well pass for Erasmus's. As for the subject-matter, ten Erasmuses could not be more convincing. . . . Farewell, my Lord Bishop, most highly esteemed for virtue and learning.

82. To Martin Dorp[133]
<London, 1519>

I easily foresaw that you would one day think otherwise than then you thought. But really that you would not only become wiser, but even in a most elaborate address testify that you had changed, and that so openly, genuinely, and categorically, this indeed went far beyond not only my expectation, but also the hopes and almost prayers of all, for your action manifested incredible probity and utter self-restraint. For though nothing indeed is more usual than to change one's opinion about a matter, yet nothing is anywhere more rare than, after you have once declared your view and then confirmed it by assertion, and then defended it with vehemence, after all that to reverse course upon realizing the truth and return once again to the harbor from which you sailed, as though your voyage had been vain. Believe me, my dear Dorp, what you have done with such great humility, you would have asked in vain of those whom the world nowadays considers most humble. Men are almost all so foolish in their misdirected shame that they prefer to proclaim that they are fools now, than own that they ever were. How much more virtuously have you acted, my dear Dorp. Although you are so keen-witted, so learned and so eloquent that if you pleased to defend anything, even what appeared improbable or absolutely paradoxical, you could yet prove it to your readers, yet in your love of truth rather than shams you have preferred to declare to all men that you were once deceived, rather than go on deceiving.

129 Choerilos was a worthless Greek poet, whom Alexander thus rewarded beyond his merits. **130** Reginald Pole (1500–1558), a cousin of Henry VIII, later became Archbishop of Canterbury. For his remarks on More's death and appeal to Henry VIII, see p. 1385. John Clement (*ca.* 1500–1572) was a page in More's household and later a distinguished physician. **131** Countess of Salisbury and of royal blood **132** John Clement **133** Maarten van Dorp (1485–1525) was a Latin lecturer at the University of Louvain. Here More is referring to Dorp's retraction of what he wrote against Erasmus. For the context of Dorp's dispute with Erasmus and More's intervention, see the introduction to the *Humanist Letters* (p. 389) and More's "Letter to Dorp" (pp. 391–420).

But what am I to say of the further act of modesty by which you have surpassed that exceptional modesty? Although it was clue to your own happy talent that you saw the truth, yet you chose to ascribe it to the admonitions of others, and even to mine. Thus although the first rank in wisdom is yours by right, and is given to you by all men's votes, yet you alone thrust yourself down to the second rank. Learned men must thrust you back into first rank, with their elbows if necessary. For that letter of mine was wordy rather than convincing; and when I compare it with your address, so eloquent, so full of close-packed and cogent arguments, I see quite clearly, my dear Dorp, and to my shame that my letter had no power to change you, although out of courtesy or modesty you now yield to it praise which belongs to you and which, the more you avoid it, will all the more surely follow you. So, my very dear Dorp, you must consider that the rarer the occurrence of an act like yours, the more it has gained for you of true glory, which will never die.

If they go on boldly in the path they have chosen, attempting to suppress good learning and to drive it from the schools, in a very short time I expect to see a marvelous change. Learned men will arise everywhere. Those teachers in the public academies who now look on such studies with indifference will themselves be accounted but indifferently learned. It vexes me, my dear Dorp, to think of these things, because I cannot help feeling a certain pity for those who by the action of a few bigoted partisans are undeservedly compromised. But the praise that will be your portion is a far more agreeable thought to me than their opprobrium.

87. To Erasmus
<March–April 1520, Greenwich?>

Thomas More to the excellent and most learned man Erasmus of Rotterdam, greeting.

Did you ever, my dear Erasmus, best of men and scholars—did you ever see a more charming character than our friend Brixius? As soon as he takes a fancy to conceal something, he supposes it is hidden from all other mortals too. For the greatest blockhead could not fail to realize how absurd and offensive and discreditable it was to make quarrelsome and scurrilous attacks on anyone unprovoked, and again and again he asserts and repeats and emphasizes that he was provoked by my epigrams and was purely on the defensive throughout, so that though he found himself the target of curses and execrations he hits back at his assailant with nothing but pleasantries and wit and humor. But of the impudence, the falsehoods, and the insults with which he had previously challenged all England, never a word; not a word either of the fact that the difference between us was a live issue long ago in all the confusions of wartime, and had long been dead, until he revives it now after all this time, when peace is fully restored. Our modern Phormio[134] is inspired with such self-confidence that, though he could easily discover that his case is rejected by everyone with a real knowledge of the facts, he behaves all the same as though he had fully and clearly established it before the appropriate tribunal; and now, being I suppose sure of his position, he lets fly at will against me, and bales out (wit and charmer that he is!) all the bilge-water in his bosom. Having decided that two or three epigrams[135] written for fun are to be regarded as invective, as though he only has to say something to carry universal conviction, he convinced himself at the same time that everyone would approve his action, if he were to take a few lines, humorously directed long ago against a very bad-tempered pamphlet of his, and in wartime too, and reply after all these years, when peace is ratified and established in such a spirit of concord as no two peoples have ever shown before, in a book that is simply poisonous. He hopes no doubt that no one will be either sharp-sighted enough to be able to see something he himself is content to wink at or such an unseasonably severe critic that he will ask for evidence other than Brixius's own story, especially as he boasts of the justice of his cause with such self-confidence.

I at least should have found him somewhat less impertinent, if he had dangled all this tinsel only before the eyes of the ordinary public, among whom he might have found some who still knew nothing of the subject, many to whom both of us were strangers, and some who enjoy a quarrel however unjustly, and if this ox were not flaunting his pack-saddles thus in front of you, who are not only

---

134 The proverbial parasite; the hero of Terence's comedy bearing his name

135 *two or three epigrams:* See Epigrams 188–95, 209, 266–69.

familiar with the contest from stem to stern (unless you have failed to read *Chordigera*,[136] for all the rest I know you have read) but also know the contestants themselves under the trappings and through to the skin, as the saying[137] goes. Besides which he knows that quarrels of this kind, even when they arise from just causes, are unpleasant and hateful to a man with your open-hearted and kindly nature. All the more so the very silly, very unjust, and very uncivilized quarrel he is pursuing now, which you have already condemned in a kind of preliminary inquiry, as he could have seen from the letter[138] you sent him, in which you add reasons for your opinion, one of which pays too much respect to us both and was thought up in the interests of courtesy rather than truth, as though he and I were the sort of people whose friendly relations were of any importance to the cause of literature, while the other at least was perfectly justified — that humorous pieces I threw off long ago in the heat of a war ought to be wiped off the slate now that peace is restored. Of your two reasons, the one that was more courteous than true he allows as concerns me with a touch of scorn, but in his own case he is frank and modest and accepts it;[139] the other, the truth of which could not be denied, he has passed over in silence, and once more tries to throw dust in our eyes with this talk of provocation, claiming[140] that I attacked him first and in a hostile spirit.

And indeed if Brixius, devoted as he is to metaphors from comedy, ordains that the action of this play shall start with the second act, that is to say with my epigram, I cannot deny that I did give him provocation. If he follows normal practice and allows the first act to take its proper place, there will, I think, be no doubt that the confused working-out of the plot has nothing comic about it. To begin with, who would not be astonished at the egregious impudence of a man who protests so often that he is the injured party, when he knows all the time that his *Chordigera* is on sale everywhere? Nor should I have pursued it with an epigram, had he not attacked my countrymen as a whole with such abusive falsehoods. In this regard I do not see what he can invent to excuse his calumnies. Can he say that my epigrams preceded his book, when their satire is entirely directed at that book's ignorance, plagiarisms, and falsehoods? Can he maintain, like the sharp little attorney that he is, that his *Chordigera* contains nothing offensive? Let him be as impudent as you like, he will not deny that at the outset of the *Chordigera* he accuses us of breaking treaties and shamelessly calls us perjured.[141] And yet he dares to open with the remark that he carries an olive-branch in the midst of arms, having presumably such an affection for falsehood that he regards perjurer and treaty-breaker as terms of endearment. Does he suppose it no concern of mine if my countrymen are attacked by him with falsehood and calumny, merely because I myself am not mentioned by name? For so he seems to suggest; as though the same reasoning, and indeed the same eloquent assertions, would not justify the footpad in taking the traveler to court who had withstood him perhaps rather uncivilly, on the grounds that he did not attack the man but merely had designs on his purse.

It may be said perhaps that though I did not attack him first, I did at least write with more bitterness; for there are limits even in self-defense. But I, with the barbarity of a Polyphemus,[142] in furious anger pursued Brixius (our modern Ulysses, of course) with curses and execrations. So he maintains, not stopping to think how grossly he lies. He consoles himself with the hope that there must be many people who have not learnt the whole story and can easily be persuaded to believe him, and that thus he will be victorious without a battle; while with you and those who know he is satisfied if he can secure the modified approval of "I should have thought he was speaking the truth if I did not know the facts." But I shall either defend myself with the truth; or alternatively, I would rather lose the day than owe my victory to the ignorance of my judge. And so in this field at any rate, I shall not follow Brixius's example, who right at the end of his crazy collection printed my lines on Abingdon[143] (which I threw

---

136 *Chordigerae navis conflagratio*; see *CW* 3.2: 429–65. It commemorated the French ship *La Cordelière*, which burnt and sank in the Atlantic off Brest on August 10, 1512 together with the English flagship. In particular Brixius celebrated the allegedly heroic death of the French captain, Hervé de Portzmoguer, a Breton. 137 *the saying:* See Erasmus, *Adages* 889 (*CWE* 32: 226). 138 *EE* 620: 34–45. 139 *accepts it:* See *EE* 1045: 11–22; this letter was published with Brixius's *Antimorus*. 140 See *EE* 1045: 82–83. 141 *breaking treaties...perjured:* See *CW* 3.2: 441/18–21. 142 The cyclops of the *Odyssey*, who eats Ulysses' men; see *EE* 1045: 39–46. 143 Henry Abingdon (ca. 1418–97) was a prominent member of the King's Chapel. In his *Antimorus* (*CW* 3.2: 508–11), Brixius took issue with one of More's epigrams (160), a cenotaph rewritten in medieval rhymes and unclassical Latin to satisfy the taste of Abingdon's heir. Brixius chose to ignore the explanation of this mockery given in Epigram 161.

off as a joke to tickle the ass's ears of a certain person whom nothing would satisfy unless it rhymed), omitting two epigrams of mine on the same subject which explained the humorous purpose of the lines.
5   He could hardly do anything more maliciously misleading. I at least will do the opposite. I will get his *Chordigera* reprinted, and add my epigrams at the end. I will also append his collection,[144] so that he cannot complain that anything has been left out;
10 and in this way I hope I shall make it downhill work for all educated men to judge whether Brixius has as good a case as he so pompously maintains.

He calls us perjurers and treaty-breakers; he distorts the whole sequence of events to the credit of
15 his own people and to our discredit by what he himself calls fictions but are really brazen lies; he recounts the lot of it in such absurd terms that nothing so absurd was ever seen before; he dresses it all up in other men's verses, so that you might think you
20 were reading the cento of Valeria Proba,[145] except that she put her material together neatly, and Brixius cobbled his up so ineptly that every seam projects into a kind of knot like a great scar on a wound, or gapes as the ground does in a drought. With all this,
25 I did nothing in those epigrams, by which he claims he was so grievously injured, except to poke fun at the faults I have mentioned, and at any rate there was, I think, no bitterness in it; so that I wonder very much where in my epigrams he can have found the
30 curses and execrations[146] which this witty man, as he prides himself on being, turns into humor. Does he mean by execrations and curses what I say in one of my epigrams,[147] where I produce a humorous excuse for his having to invent, as if no one had returned
35 safe home from the *Chordigera* who could tell him the story of what actually happened?—for I added that Brixius ought to have been in the ship himself, that he might see with his own eyes the events he was to describe, for so he would not be obliged to lie
40 like this so disgracefully and hand falsehood down to posterity as though it were true. Apart from this one point, I am certain that Brixius will never find anything against which he can direct a trumped-up charge of either curses or execrations.
45 Although on this same point either his charges are egregious inventions, or at any rate he shows

himself egregiously ignorant of the meaning of the words execration and curse. There may be someone who also thinks I was rather cutting, though if he were to take a small sample of Brixius's *Chordig-*   50
era I trust he would excuse me without difficulty; but there will be no one to call this execrations or curses, if he knows any Latin at all. That level is not reached even by Martial's remark,[148] which was far more cutting than mine, about the poet Theodorus,   55
who was perhaps as a poet not unlike Brixius; for when Theodorus's house was burnt down, Martial exclaims that it was an outrage, and the gods ought to be ashamed of themselves, that the same fire did not also consume its owner. Whereas I, though I   60
did think Brixius deserved to be well and truly present in the *Chordigera*, so that he could escape the need for such shameless lies, did not wish that that had happened to him; I did not call down upon his head the fire which after all many people escaped   65
who were in the vessel. If one thinks and declares a man worthy of something, one does not in the same breath call that fate down upon his head. For Brixius too, I suppose, thinks thieves deserve to be hanged, and the same of adulterers, and no doubt   70
of perjurers too, though they are not so very many parasangs distant[149] from liars; and yet I cannot think him so heartless as to call down that fate simultaneously on all these classes, who form a large part of the human race. A wish of this kind would   75
be most merciless; it would also perhaps be none too safe for Brixius himself.

But besides that epigram there are nine others, in the first of which—and what I say is perfectly true—I point out in simple language that all writers   80
will lose their credibility if by his example they get the habit of following their emotions rather than the facts. In two I make fun of the way in which he describes Hervé[150] fighting like a prodigy. One is a humorous comment on Brixius's combination of   85
boasting and lack of sense, for besides many other utter absurdities he imagines Hervé prophesying about himself as if he were a nursling of Apollo, and to make this possible he has him deliver a long speech in the midst of the flames, as though he were   90
perfectly at his ease. Furthermore, though there were many survivors from both ships, since several

144 *Antimorus*   **145** Probus, wife of the prefect Adelphus of Rome, composed in hexameters a cento or patchwork of borrowed lines on the subject of sacred history, especially as contained in the gospels.   **146** *curses and execrations:* See EE 1045: 49.   **147** Epigram 189   **148** Martial 11.93.3–4   **149** *many parasangs distant:* A proverbial expression referring to an ancient measure of length comparable to our miles; see *Adages* 1282 (CWE 33: 179).   **150** See Epigrams 190–92.

of our smaller vessels came to the rescue, he chose to burn everybody up rather than leave a survivor from whom he might have been thought to have heard a story which he could write up. In one epigram I referred to the lines invented by Brixius for Hervé's cenotaph.[151] Two of them make play with the fact that Brixius had decorated his *Chordigera* with lines stolen from the poets of Antiquity. In two I showed that I felt a need for more thought and more ingenuity in the *Chordigera* in both invention and arrangement of the subject-matter.

When I wrote these pieces, I was the injured party, public affairs were in turmoil, and I spoke the truth. Even so, I never published them or showed them to anyone by themselves — always joined with other things, so that the reader's attention was either diverted from them as much as possible or at any rate was not monopolized by them; while his *Antimorus* on the other hand offers nothing but abuse of me by name, as crazy as it is offensive. Last but not least, when I heard that moves were on foot to print my epigrams in Basel, you know yourself what steps I took[152] to get what I had written against Brixius, and a few other things, omitted; some of them seemed to me not serious enough, although they are far removed from the indecency which is for some people, I perceive, about the only merit some men's epigrams have to recommend them. And at the same time I had no wish to criticize anyone by name even slightly, however much he might deserve it.

If in this respect my efforts, as far as Brixius is concerned, came to nothing, I am delighted; he makes it very clear that he deserves to have quite different things said about him. Take the places where he asserts, so frequently and so falsely, that I began it, and that I gave mortal offense with a string of insults, calumnies, abuse, curses, and execrations. If he has discovered all the things he lists, although — seeing how things then were, and what he had deserved — I could have defended what I had done on principles which every nation recognizes, yet I will admit forthwith that I am as great a barbarian as the Cyclops Polyphemus, which Brixius maintains. If on the other hand he has not discovered in my work the things that he objects to, I think it only fair that Brixius should acknowledge that he

has wholly invented the passage where he complains of my curses and execrations in order to provide a place where he can drag in Polyphemus, a giant who to be sure needs plenty of room; for he was so much in love with that elegant fiction that, rather than be obliged to leave it out, he preferred to invent a target at which he could discharge some shafts of humor. If Brixius were not more blind than Polyphemus himself, he would easily discern that there is not much credit in this for him, if he passes over criticisms made of him as though they did not exist and raises up other charges against himself which he can easily shoot down.

I had written an epigram on one of my countrymen[153] who made himself ridiculous by going over entirely to French fashions when we were at war with France. In another passage,[154] Brixius having called us treaty-breakers and perjurers, I had touched in passing on the fact that in the war with France we had a religious cause and did our duty toward the church of Christ, whose vicegerent we were aiding, while the French were the other way round, for they encouraged schism and opposed the pope. This precise point I have no wish now to reopen, nor was it at my wish that it was published long ago. And yet, had Brixius pretended (for he is a great hand at fiction) that he was moved to anger by these passages it might perhaps have been easier to forgive him, as a man who seemed to have been imposed on by a false idea of honor, in fact by an inordinate love of his country, which seemed to make him intolerant even of valid criticisms of it, or at least ready to maintain points which have been abandoned in the treaties. And now, like the blockhead that he is, he has chosen to make a case in which he has the same obstacles to surmount as in the other: that it was he who wrote first, he who provided the occasion for it, that his charges are false, that the point at issue has been decided, or rather, has been rendered void and extinguished by international treaties.

There is another most dishonorable thing which I pass over. In public he first gave cause for offense, and in private he poses like this as the injured party. How this can be, he cannot explain; but the curses and execrations piled on him by me he himself

151 *Hervé's cenotaph:* an appendix to the *Chordigerae navis conflagratio* (*CW* 3.2: 464–65), ridiculed in Epigram 194 **152** *what steps I took:* There is no trace of

this in More's surviving correspondence. **153** *an epigram . . . countryman:* Epigram 195 **154** *in another passage:* In Epigram 271 on James IV of Scotland; France and

her allies were laid under an interdict following the schismatic Council of Pisa in 1511.

clearly shows to be his own invention. And so, since he began it by attacking me in print, and falsely too, while my reaction was confined to epigrams (the subject of which was such that, if he denies their truth, he will achieve nothing except to make everyone understand that he has lied twice over), an honorable retreat was not only possible for him, it was his duty. And he would have done so, I am sure, had he not preferred to make his distinguished impudence universally known. His former errors might have been forgiven to his youth, if nothing else, or blamed on the state of things. And now, all these years later, in all this peace and concord, when our two princes are very nearly bound by ties of hospitality (for this is now in preparation), he must needs begin again at the beginning and repay the handful of epigrams I threw off against his book with a poisonous pamphlet in which, as he could think of no answer to make on his own behalf, he has turned entirely against me, pouring out nothing but unmixed calumny and abuse that would disgrace a madman.

In the first place, if at any point Froben's workmen, or even the man, whoever he was, who made the copy for the printer, were perhaps not quite up to the mark, he ascribes it all to me, although he sees that no book ever had such a happy passage through the press that it contains no errors at all, and although he finds in it no list of corrigenda. And yet in their very errors they have generally shown more felicity than Brixius in his corrections. Look at the mischief-making and the falsehood of his charge that I attack the prince's father![155] — though I myself speak only of evils which the prince set right with such incomparable success at the outset of his reign, evils which afflicted the body politic for some years before that, thanks to the perfidy of some men on whom the King's father had relied too heavily at a time when ill health prevented him from managing things himself, though he was in other ways a supremely experienced ruler. And yet Brixius, for all that in his spiteful way he diverts on to the King these evils which came about through other men's villainy, uses this to declaim with astonishing virulence against myself, all whirling fists and buffetings and threats of exile! And as though he felt imprisoned in the constraints of verse and could not range as freely as he wished, he added venomous notes in the margins to direct the reader's attention to these points, in case perhaps he took too little notice of the verses.

And in this fashion, while making it signally clear that he has all he needs for making mischief except power to match his malice, yet the pretty fellow is proud of his witty performance, though his laughter is the laughter of Ajax.[156] Ajax, when the armor was assigned to another man, lost his reason and hung up cattle and belabored them, roaring with laughter all the time and highly delighted with the groans they uttered, madness having convinced him that they were Agamemnon and Ulysses, on whom he longed to wreak vengeance. Brixius is like that: he pursues a vile obstinate invention of his own, hounding it on to destruction, beaming with self-satisfaction because, mindless as he is, he fails to observe that every man — and I mean every single man with any spark either of decency or of common feeling — when he hears this wild Brixius laughter, does not merely scoff at him as a madman but is revolted by this gladiators' spirit of fighting to the death.

And in spite of all this, it is just as though he were writing this stuff for some blockhead Coroebus or Margites[157] and not for Erasmus; as though, with Erasmus ready to overlook the impudence with which he attacked me first, he had so successfully blinded everyone without exception that what he himself did not choose to see became at once invisible to everyone; as though he had now proved his case that I began it, although the facts prove that what I wrote came later; as though wartime conditions were still in force, so that it was proper for him to seek revenge with his venomous inventions for a few heedless words uttered long ago and quite harmless too, at this late date when on both sides princes and peoples alike have so far grown into amity that soldiers actually forget the wounds of which their bodies still bear the scars; as though I myself had assailed him bitterly and rained all sorts of imprecations on him, while he in return had merely sprinkled me with unmixed pleasantries, unmixed humor, unmixed wit, and had not in fact voided over me a flood of crazy invective and ravings for which poisonous would be too mild a word. In the light of all this it is remarkable to see the confidence and

---

155 *prince's father:* See Epigram 19. In his *Antimorus* (*CW* 3.2: 492–93), Brixius had accused More of slandering the memory of Henry VII.   **156** *laughter of Ajax:* See Sophocles, *Ajax*; Erasmus, *Adages* 1646 (*CWE* 34: 24).   **157** *Coroebus or Margites:* See Eramus, *Adages* 1271, 164 (*CWE* 33: 1754, 31: 207).

certainty with which he promises himself not merely forgiveness, as though his reply was unavoidable, but actually praise for his moderation; for when attacked (as we are asked to believe) with curses and execrations (which are non-existent), though he had the right to bear equivalent weapons when he entered the lists he shows his amazingly generous nature and admirably versatile talents by snapping with no fangs (such is his boast),[158] by being humorous without calumny and funny without giving offense and sarcastic but stopping short of personal abuse, by rebukes without severity and instruction that needs no rod; to crown all, in fact, by turning my abuse into joking, my offensive remarks into humor, my insults into witticisms, by making irony out of my execrations and mere scoffing out of my curses.

Would not any casual reader think that Brixius had delivered a pretty peroration, provided he knew nothing at all of the case? For should any reader happen on it who has looked into his *Chordigera* and my epigrams and his idiot *Antimorus*[159] (should anyone have such abundant leisure that he is able to make such a worthless use of his precious time), he will find in those epigrams of mine neither abuse nor insults nor offensive remarks nor curses nor execrations; while in Brixius on the other hand he will find nothing but undiluted scandals and bad language and poisonous picking of quarrels; he will see teeth, but they are broken on the grindstone, and a teacher's rod, but no learning; he will see that the man's criticism consists in foolish attacks on what he does not understand and his teaching in shameless innuendo against anything he does understand;—and then how he will laugh at that laughter of Brixius's that makes Brixius a laughingstock! How he will mock at the mockery which recoils so severely on its author! How humorous he will find Brixius's humor, which reminds one of a camel dancing![160] What a subject for mirth he will find in the mirth of our Germain, in whom he will recognize a true cousin german of Aesop's donkey;[161] for the way the donkey imitated the frisking of that pet dog as he put his muddy feet and claws on his master's shoulders and was chased with sticks back into the kennel was not much less absurd than Brixius's imitations of the poets. With what elegant irony he will outflank Brixius's irony, which is, to be sure, so inelegant that it reminds the reader of that painter who was as much a painter as Brixius is a poet, and having painted a hound and a hare so much alike that no one could tell the difference was careful in the end to make it clear by labeling them which was the hound and which the hare.

Brixius's use of sarcasm is usually such as to fill him with pitiful forebodings that most of the praise he wishes to be taken as ironical will be accepted by many of his readers as serious; and from this danger he saw no escape except to declare that he was being ironical in a marginal note. Being a cautious man, he naturally took precautions to avoid being bound by his own act and deed, as though his praise of me had been seriously meant. There was only one place[162] where he saw no need to warn us in a marginal note that he was being sarcastic, because the elegance of that passage gave him such confidence, although he lists it in the index (as he hopes it will be thought) of my mistakes and (as the facts show) of his own slanderous malice and ignorance. He makes fun of a dialogue in my *Utopia*[163] in which a friar is having a discussion with a jester: "In reporting and developing this dialogue," says Brixius, "More displays with ease the sharp edge of his wit, the vigor of his language, and his incorruptible judgment."[164] For my part, dear Erasmus, my learned friend, I do not think so poorly of Brixius, nor have I such a good opinion of myself, that I would not readily admit I could never have expressed the elegant diction of friars or the keen logic of a jester so prettily as the living truth with which Brixius could have expressed them. It makes such a difference to be familiar with these niceties of style and to approach the jester yourself, not in name alone (as Brixius so courteously and so often concedes that I do) but in nature (for which a wholly justified claim is presented by his *Antimorus*).

And then, when he talks about critical judgment, by which I take it he means that it is absurd to introduce the barbarous diction of friars into a book

158 *his boast:* See EE 1045: 36–39.
159 *his idiot* Antimorus: Latin *moricus eius Antimoros* ("his idiot anti-fool")
160 *camel dancing:* See *Adages* 1666 (CWE 34: 33).   **161** *Aesop's donkey:* See "The Donkey and the Pet Dog."   **162** *one place:*

In his verse treatment of More's epigram on Abingdon, Brixius praised More's mastery of this peculiar genre, but in the prose commentary following the metric part of *Antimorus* he calls this epigram ridiculous, speaking elsewhere of More's inexcusable

offenses against the meter, solecisms, barbarisms, and so on; see CW 3.2: 346–47.
163 See CW 4: 80–85.   **164** See CW 3.2: 534–35.

which you wish to be in Latin (to say nothing for the moment of the fact that the Greeks are thought barbarians by Latin speakers and Latin speakers by Greeks, though all authors so often interlard their
5   Latin with Greek and get praised for it too), I do not foresee, I will not say my own style, in which Brixius detects everywhere such blatant blunders and barbarisms (thanks to his own blatant facility in false accusation and his own blatant ignorance),
10 but Brixius's (which Brixius himself thinks steeped in all the charm of all the Graces) ever reaching the standard of Latinity one finds in Plautus; and yet Plautus thought he was doing nothing absurd and committing no affront on the Latin language
15 when in a Latin comedy he introduced a Carthaginian character from time to time speaking Punic.[165] This precedent, in my opinion, pretty well covers the man who, in a type of composition closely akin to comedy, brings on the stage a friar of this type
20 speaking his own language, which is a sort of pidgin Latin. And yet you yourself know, dear Erasmus, how much I was dissatisfied with that dialogue and how gladly I should have omitted it, had it not given more pleasure than I can say to those persons
25 whom no one with any education and judgment of his own could fail to rate for education and judgment as far above Brixius "as soars man's eye hence to the ethereal heaven."[166]

I would mention some of these people by name
30 here too, but it would be a waste of time, for you know them already, nor have I any wish to expose honorable men, men who indeed deserve honor, to the malignity of this yapping cur, who goes into such a decline when he hears another man well spo-
35 ken of that I really think it would have finished him off had he not vomited some of his mad rage on Beatus Rhenanus,[167] modeling himself for resentment on Aeschines;[168] though he falls as far short of Aeschines in literary gifts as I do of Demosthenes,
40 of whose reputation Aeschines was so jealous that he brought a public prosecution against Ctesiphon too because he had spoken well of Demosthenes,

and was plotting to have him sent into exile, a plot which soon recoiled, and rightly, on his own head. Finding therefore that Beatus Rhenanus has com-
45 mended my epigrams to Willibald,[169] which was one good scholar and good man commending them to another, Brixius flies into an incredible rage, and with passionate virulence and puny muscles draws his leaden sword with its blunt edge to at-
50 tack Rhenanus. A toady he calls him, or, if he won't accept that, he is ignorant, uneducated, and stoneblind for not detecting that my verses are what they seemed to Brixius to be as he examined them through the spectacles that envy provided. But the
55 gnat that attacks the elephant[170] is wasting his time; and what sort of creature Brixius is, he makes clear of his own accord.

To sing Rhenanus's praises I have no desire as things are now, for fear they tell me it is one mule
60 scratching another mule's back,[171] and if I had a mind to it I could not do it properly; everyone knows and they all freely admit that fertile as Germany is in men of creative gifts she has no more elegant stylist if it's style you want, no better scholar
65 if you wish for learning, and if you ask for character, no better man. Indeed I do very much wonder why Brixius chose Rhenanus as the sole target of his fury. Is he the only man who differs from Brixius in his estimate of what I write? — as though I had not
70 been highly praised in print,[172] I will not say by you and Peter Giles, for you might be thought somewhat misled by your affection for me, but by Busleyden, Hutten, Desmarez, Nijmegen, Vives, Grapheus, Zasius, and Budé, with whom I was at that
75 time so far from being linked in friendship that we had not yet exchanged a single line; and the same is true of Rhenanus himself, to say nothing of many other people not unknown as scholars. If Brixius were to imagine that they are all flattering me, I'm
80 sure I am much obliged to him for making me such a great man. If he declares them all blind, ignorant, and uneducated because they disagree with him and credit a man whom he so often calls a fool and labels

---

165 The language of Carthage; see Plautus, *Poenulus* 982–1029. **166** Vergil, *Aeneid* 6.579 **167** See *CW* 3.2: 542–43, where Beatus is censured for his "adulation," although his name is not given. See preface to the epigrams. **168** This Athenian orator and partisan of King Philip of Macedon attacked his rival Demosthenes in public and also attacked Ctesiphon,

who had prepared special honors for Demosthenes (336, 330 BC), but in the end was himself exiled. **169** i.e., Willibald Pirckheimer. See the "Epigrams" section above. **170** See Aesop's "The Lion, Jupiter, and the Elephant." **171** See *Adages* 696 (*CWE* 32: 125–26). **172** *praised in print*: Peter Giles, Jerome de Busleyden, Jean Desmarez, Gerard Geldenhouwer of

Nijmegen, and Cornelius Grapheus had all made complimentary contributions to the first edition of *Utopia*, Guillaume Budé to the second (see *CW* 4: 4–37). Cornelius Grapheus (Schrijveer) of Aalst (*ca.* 1482–1558) was secretary of the town of Antwerp and thus a colleague of Peter Giles, More's good friend.

crazy (not to take the list any further) with somewhat more sense at least than anyone, by what I hear, has yet ascribed to Brixius, himself excepted — even so, no one has invested him with such absolute and dictatorial powers that his personal opinion must be universally accepted without at least some remaining right of appeal to public opinion.

Brixius takes it hard, it seems, that Rhenanus should have preferred my epigrams to those of Marullus and Pontano;[173] but he ought to have looked rather more closely in assessing the value of Rhenanus's praise. It is true that he pays me a much more generous tribute than modesty allows me to accept, but the area where Brixius particularly takes offense he does not praise me so effusively that Brixius was bound to be jealous. Rhenanus does not prefer me to Pontano or Marullus in all respects or think me a match for them. He compares us only in respect of natural gifts, not in knowledge of Greek, so there is no call for Brixius to be so indignant at the sight of an Englishman matched against a Greek. Is there any reason in nature why a man actually as good as any Greek should not see the light "in mist and fog, the home of muttonheads?"[174] Though I myself have neither so much pride nor so little self-knowledge that I can accept the tributes paid me by Beatus Rhenanus, who, as I say, matches me in natural gifts against such men as they, but in usefulness puts me above them, at least to the extent of thinking that anything I contribute in the way of sound principles does my readers more good than all the filth and wickedness with which they defile their pages; and he supposes the benefit they get from my simple and straightforward verses greater than the charm of Marullus's riddling lines. Surely all Rhenanus does in this is to prefer any good there may be in me to the bad there is in them.

Praise of this kind does not preclude that their virtues should exceed mine, as they certainly do, and it ought not therefore to appear so partial as to arouse envy. For that matter take Budé (to say nothing of the others), a man whose experience of public affairs is as great as it is in literature, where he holds some kind of primacy: the things he has written about me are such that though I now know them to be due to the courtesy of a man who loves to think

well of others — which is equally true of the preface contributed to Brixius's *Chordigera* by that excellent scholar Aleandro[175] — all the same I would far rather they should prove to be true than that I should be a better poet than Pontano or Marullus, or better at Latin and Greek than the two of them together. And yet it is surprising how suddenly Brixius turns about and devotes himself (of all people) to the care of my reputation; for it is, he says, only from a devoted concern for it that he has called my attention in such friendly and kindly and loyal fashion to all those errors,[176] so many thousand of them and so disgraceful; the idea being no doubt that with his assistance things should be quietly removed which could not circulate any longer without making me a perfect byword and earning me some sort of indelible black mark for ignorance. And on this score he thinks I owe as great a debt to his well-meaning labors as one man can owe another.

This elegant and graceful attitude so forcibly appealed to Brixius that he now repeats as a serious proposition what moved everyone to mockery who read it in the *Antimorus*, forgetting for the moment those verses[177] in which with astonishing ingenuity he puts forward a scheme by which he now thinks it probable that I could put all this disgrace to rights. And the scheme is that I should arrange to have returned to me from every quarter all the copies of my book which have now been printed anywhere, and having purged them in this way should then reissue them. And yet Brixius is so much frightened of my doing just this, of my dispatching more than five hundred emissaries to every country under the sun and recalling all the copies, that he threatens to take steps to see that uncorrected copies continue to be available in his possession and that of a number of other persons (a result I think he would find difficult to achieve without sending out emissaries for the purpose in his turn), which can demonstrate my errors to the world, those errors which he now urges me to eliminate privately so that no one can hold them against me in future, in such a way that not all the waves of Ocean could wash my record clean.

Here is another example of his long memory or his self-consistency. In that letter to you he says his

173 *Marullus and Pontano:* Michael Marullus, a native Greek, and Giovanni Pontano were authors of well-known collections of Latin epigrams. In his

preface Beatus Rhenanus suggested that their jokes were unsuited to Christian ears.
174 Juvenal 10.50   **175** A complimentary letter by Girolamo Aleandro prefixed to

Brixius's *Chordigera* praises the poem and the dedication to Queen Anne of Britanny; see *CW* 3.2: 440–43.   **176** See *EE* 1045: 56–60.   **177** *CW* 3.2: 508–9

Antimorus has no teeth in it, because he snaps in it without fangs;[178] and yet in his eleven-syllable lines[179] (which he turns off so neatly that he can sometimes squeeze thirteen syllables into one line) he says that his elegiacs steep themselves in my blood. The fact is that when he imitates poets he is as absurd as a monkey imitating a man, and his attempts at concealment are as futile as those of any grey mullet or cony that thinks, as soon as it puts its head into the sand, its whole body is sufficiently concealed; so true is it that no wolf ever had a shorter memory than his and no feather, no puff of wind was ever more consistently inconsistent.

Look now at that place[180] where he says he would have taken your advice had not his book been already in the printer's hands. I am greatly surprised that a man to whom Erasmus's lightest nod is of such importance should give so little weight to your letter[181] of warning that he would rather persist in wrecking his own reputation with such a crazy pamphlet (and particularly in his thirst for glory) than write off a small sum of money. He is after all a man, to use his words,[182] who is well off in respect not only of food and clothing but of servants and a horse to ride and a purse with money always in it; who has a house and garden to which Apollo and all the Muses who would like to move in a body and abandon Parnassus, if Brixius does not bolt the door. And yet I'm surprised if he would have done as you told him, considering that after so much good advice, before the trouble started, he was not willing to listen to Budé or Bérault or Lascaris or Deloynes or to his Eminence the Cardinal[183] who died in France lately. Be that as it may, if he thinks it was your goodness of heart that made you dissuade him from publishing the *Antimorus*, he now thinks all the same that if you do not approve of it now it is published, you are being quite unfair, because you lay down a different set of rules for him in his treatment of me from those you adopted for yourself in dealing with Lefèvre.[184] Nor do I doubt that Brixius regards himself as very sharp and an expert in legal procedure, tying you down as he does with such a weighty precedent that, if you wish to escape the appearance of injustice, you cannot possibly give judgment against him.

For my own part, dear Erasmus—and this I say openly to all comers, but to none more readily than yourself, for I have observed that from this aspect at least your mind is entirely one with mine—I have such respect, such admiration, and veneration for Jacques Lefèvre[185] as I ought to have for a man who by his attainments and character has done more to deserve this than anyone for several centuries; and I doubt whether anyone has worked harder, apart from his devotion to Scriptures, to the exposition of which he has made a useful contribution, to bring over our universities at long last from their foolish waste of words and pointless logic-chopping to a sober and strict devotion to philosophy and to the branches of learning they had so long neglected. This fact is so generally admitted that as a rule he receives the most laudatory tributes even from those who differ from him sometimes very widely indeed on individual statements; and yet nothing arouses them more than Lefèvre's habit (as it seems to many people) of asserting somewhat too absolutely things which would have caused no offense had they been laid down and defended with more moderation, and of making definite statements in an unduly contentious spirit—so easily does a sort of pious enthusiasm often carry a good man too far.

But how little resemblance there is between your defense[186] and that perfectly absurd complaint of Brixius's is beyond all doubt for anybody unless he is quite ignorant of the facts. I do not propose therefore to develop this aspect of it and compare one case with the other and match pamphlet against pamphlet, as though this were the only way to make it clear that at no point, either when it began or as it has gone on ever since, did Brixius's crazy reactions correspond to what you did; so let me not be thought to rouse controversy over a case which is quite clear, or seem to have stirred up sleeping and buried fires from their ashes to no good purpose, or be obliged in any way to give offense to Lefèvre, for whom I have the greatest respect, or be credited with attempting to suborn the judge before whom

178 *EE* 1045: 36; *CW* 3.2: 536–39.
179 *eleven-syllable lines:* "Ad lectorem," *CW* 3.2: 512–13   **180** *EE* 1045: 22–27
181 *EE* 620   **182** See *EE* 1045: 121–27.
183 Antoine Bohlier (*ca.* 1460–1519), Archbishop of Bourges from 1515 and

cardinal from 1517. A member of his household was the young poet Jean Salmon Macrin, who contributed some preliminary verses to Brixius's *Antimorus* and is addressed by Brixius in an answering poem; *CW* 3.2: 482–85.   **184** See *EE* 1045:

66–69.   **185** Jacques Lefèvre d'Étaples (*ca.* 1455–1536) edited St. Paul's Epistles from the Vulgate along with a paraphrase and commentary in 1512.   **186** *Apologia ad Fabrum*

I now plead my case and procure your support by flattery. One thing at least he does say (except that he described himself as light-hearted when he should have said light-headed) which in other ways is not wholly untrue: that you fought at close quarters while he operated at a distance.[187] You went to the heart of the matter, not with a sword as Brixius says (he seems to imagine you as a gladiator) but with the point of a needle, while Brixius is only skirmishing at long range in a lunatic fit, discharging abuse such as any drunken old woman might have poured out at the first comer and most of which was well suited to the man himself, without succeeding in getting anywhere near the target; or if he was sometimes lucky and got close to it, then as often happens on hard ground to a weapon dispatched with insufficient force, it either simply overshot the mark or glanced off it. So his long-range equipment achieved at least this result: it provided evidence that he was a by no means inadequate marksman, granted only that in the kindness of one's heart one was always willing to move the target to the spot where his arrow fell, and a very pretty controversialist, if he could find someone to whom the abuse was applicable which he himself could draw from an unfailing well of scurrilities. And when there is no one on whom this filth will stick, what can he do for the time being except drench himself in it?

But the moment comes when, as though really moved by a letter from you, he begins to take a more pacific line and, if I think fit, now that each of us has come on stage (as he puts it),[188] having donned our tragic masks (as worn by warriors in the olden time when they advanced to do battle) and shown that we can sustain our roles with might and main (I, that is, with a handful of epigrams and Brixius with whole volumes), I as challenger and Brixius as defender (for he is careful to repeat these words lest otherwise someone might not believe them), at long last he does not refuse to clasp hands and, with Erasmus as our *pater patratus* (a practice in ancient times confined of course to the stage), to sign a treaty, especially as you think me a man whom he ought to know and like. At the same time, for fear that peace so easily achieved might be somewhat too lightly valued, or that it might give me too good a conceit of myself, he qualifies his offer, mindful as ever of his own prestige, to the effect that if I prefer to watch the outcome of the tragedy as it now is, he equally has no objections to its running through to the last act. My acting is not brilliant enough to frighten him off the stage, nor am I such a doughty fighter that if I prefer to join battle he must refuse to meet me, provided I descend into the arena to fight in my own armor, not like Patroclus in the arms of Achilles, and give him fair warning with a blast of the trumpet. Look at the astonishing tricks with which Brixius adorns and glorifies this minuscule dispute, in which it is almost true that he is simply sparring with himself! He matches himself and me together as actors both comic and tragic and gymnasts and warriors, and it is wonderful to see what a skillful mixture he makes of these very different things; how neatly he equips fighting men with masks and comic actors with armor, and brings in a *pater patratus* to sign a treaty between actors disguised as army commanders. How he brings fighting men onto the stage and warriors onto the playing-field! And so, with a skilled use of the figure they call *epimonê*,[189] he maintains his simile so elegantly that in about three lines he completes for us a tragical-comical battlepiece.

As for this treaty, dearest Erasmus, you must not put yourself out. Suppose there is a contest between More, that tiny creature, on the one side and on the other Brixius, that noble victor crowned with many a palm[190] and not much more than a palm high himself; this does not threaten the world of letters with such enormous peril that we need Erasmus as our *pater patratus* to achieve a peace, unless anxiety over the outcome of this heroic duel has the same effect on the princes of the literary world as that famous battle of the frogs and the mice had on the anxious gods in Homer,[191] who found it more formidable than their own conflict with the giants. For when you say in your letter that I am exactly the sort of man who ought to be friends with him,[192] I admire your goodness, for you are campaigning for peace at every opportunity. But, dear Erasmus, "of such an honor all unworthy I,"[193] the honor I mean of being counted among the friends of such a mighty nabob,

187 See EE 1045: 71–73. 188 See EE 1045: 85–98. 189 the rhetorical figure of "dwelling on a subject" 190 In the introductory verses "Ad lectorem" of the *Antimorus*, Brixius used the image of the resilient palm tree; see *Adages* 204 (*CWE* 31: 237–38). 191 The *Batrachomyomachia* (Battle of Frogs and Mice), a parody of an epic poem, was in antiquity ascribed to Homer. Zeus intervened in the battle, but his thunderbolts failed to achieve their purpose. 192 See EE 620: 35–37. 193 Vergil, *Aeneid* 1.335

to whose *Antimorus* I have now written an answer for better or worse, which shows perhaps too little reverence for such a great man but in the light of the facts at any rate is perhaps unduly modest, as others judge. And you, dear Erasmus, what do you think? I long to know. It is true that I had what I wrote printed very promptly, and it might perhaps have been safer to take time to polish it, especially as it has to come before a rival with such keen sight that he can descry a fault where no fault is. But I thought it better to leave him many bones on which to try his teeth and weary them or break them in the end than to fill my head for long with all this nonsense. And I should have thought such a crazy pamphlet simply unworthy of any reply, had I not felt it right to follow the advice of some of my friends, who advised me to protect myself against the man's perfectly ludicrous calumnies. This was my sole object; not to exchange abuse and give him as good as I got. Otherwise, had I not decided to consider what was fitting for me to say rather than what he deserved to hear, however lordly Brixius's contempt for my style as unwarlike, effeminate, and limp, I would at least have made him feel the truth of Ovid's line "An easy case makes all men eloquent."[194]

As it is, though he has not merely let fly at my talents and my character but has taken secret steps to secure my undoing so far as it was in his power, and in the literary way has left nothing of mine alone without getting his teeth into it, I on the other hand have touched on nothing of his except just those volumes in which his target is either myself or my native country. On what he is capable of, taking the question as a whole, I pass no judgment and I make no examination. I know how little weight my opinion of him would carry, though even now I take a kinder view of him than many men whom he has done less to offend. All the same, I have never down to this day heard anyone give a truly favorable verdict on Brixius without feeling at the same time that so far he has produced nothing grand enough to correspond to the airs which that boastful little man gives himself; for at one moment he boasts that poetry is his natural field, what the open plain is to a horse,[195] at another he prides himself on competing with antiquity or robbing Hercules[196] himself of his club by force, or threatens with some lack of

modesty that he will breathe forth the thunderbolt. Such are his boasts, and other people who compare them with his poems give as their considered opinion that he is not only insane but incurable.

As for me, although Brixius shows himself in my case a ferocious prophet as well as judge, such that he not only damns everything I have written up to now but asserts that I shall never write[197] anything worth reading hereafter, yet I take a somewhat kinder view of him, basing my judgment mainly on both the *Chordigera* and the *Antimorus*, in which he attacked me in a fit of bad temper — for this very fact still gives me some hopes that that sour talent may one day ripen. Though what he writes is so foolish at the age he is now, he is not, I perceive, one of those men whose talents mature so early that he cannot still continue and ripen in another way. Of course, if I thought he had already reached his full development and vigor, his *acme* (to use the Greek word), I could expect nothing except to see a man whose spring was spent in a coma and his summer in uncontrollable rage enjoy an autumn of unbroken frenzy.

When he says my acting is not brilliant enough to frighten him off the stage,[198] I can at least admit that I neither have nor claim to have anything about me that could frighten anybody. Nor can I deny that Brixius's acting is such a terrifying performance that it might drive from the theatre not only a poor-spirited little creature like myself who am easily frightened by a pale image in its mask[199] but the whole body of spectators, by spectral forms affrighted, if those lines of Brixius's are to be trusted which the silly fool, a second Morychus,[200] inserted in his *Antimorus*:

> As this I wrote, from their infernal marsh;
> The Furies rose; there stood Alecto, there
> Megaera terrible with visage harsh,
> Tisiphone with her snake-knotted hair.[201]

If only Brixius would take off those needlessly tragical masks, the rest of his performance at any rate has nothing about it sufficiently remarkable to make any man stiffen to attention as if he'd seen Medusa's head; nor does my experience suggest that his strength is formidable enough to make

---

194 *Tristia* 3.11.21   **195** See *Adages* 782 (*CWE* 32: 169).   **196** See *Adages* 3095 (*CWE* 35: 498–99).   **197** See *CW* 3.2: 510–11.   **198** *EE* 1045: 94   **199** *pale…mask:* See Juvenal 3.175.   **200** See *Adages* 1801 (*CWE* 34: 89–91). Morychus, the epitome of   foolish behavior, provides another allusion to More's name.   **201** *CW* 3.2: 510–11

Patroclus, or Thersites[202] anyhow, run to Achilles to ask help from his armor against a Hector such as this. But if he has made up his mind to bring on stage with him not those pasteboard Furies but his own fury and rage; if he is resolved to let all his thunders roll, and has decided to brandish that portentous thunderbolt which falls (so he boasts) from his lips whenever, in a private and particular fit of resentment I suppose, he conceives "wrath not of Jove unworthy"[203]—why, then, as far as I am concerned, he can play to empty houses, and the amulet to protect me against such threatening apparitions shall be silence. However, there shall arise perhaps some Hercules, helper of those in need, who has had some practice in subduing monsters like this and will take from Brixius's hands in his turn the club which Brixius forcibly took from him, using as his weapon I fancy a cane or a birch. Brixius's brand of thunder is such that Strepsiades[204] himself would not hesitate to fart in its face. And for this conjuror's trick, this thunderbolt, very figure to suppress it is Cacus,[205] himself no mean exponent of the art of terrifying; or, if his skill is insufficient, the name of Cacus by itself would remind us of the weapons which he had had to use himself against that kind of thunder. Are hapless mortals to perish by that thunderbolt's hot breath? No, no! Into that open mouth, agape with three-cleft bolt, "to piss, or worse, we have the right."[206]

I hope, my dear Erasmus, that we shall see you when the kings meet at Calais, and if you come, both kings, you need not doubt, will make you welcome. Otherwise it would be impertinent for humble friends of yours like me to demand or expect that for our sake you should endure the fatigues of such a journey, when it is more properly our duty to come and see you, as I shall certainly do if the wish to pay your respects to the kings does not bring you there, having asked my prince to allow me a few days leave. Meanwhile, dear Erasmus, farewell; and without any reduction in your usual friendship for Brixius, keep a warm corner as you usually do for More, for you are as dear to me as I could possibly be to myself. Our friend Lupset is lecturing at Oxford to large audiences on the humanities, both Greek and Latin, with great credit to himself and no less profit to his pupils. He has succeeded my friend John Clement,[207] who has devoted himself entirely to medicine, in which one day he will be second to none, unless (which God forbid) the Fates deprive his fellow men of his society.

Farewell once more, and give most cordial greetings in my name to those capital scholars Dorp, Nesen, and Vives.

88. To Erasmus
<Greenwich? End of February–April 1520>

Thomas More to his friend Erasmus, greeting.

Though it was never concealed from me, Erasmus dearest of all my friends, how much better your judgment is than mine, nothing has cast such a bright light on this as the advice we gave you and Lee that that pamphlet of his should be permanently suppressed, while your view on the other hand was that its publication should be allowed at the particular moment when it was so actively expected, so that the whole sad story might one day reach a conclusion, rather than wait till the public interest should have died down and then publish it all the same, stirring up fresh troubles. And so we forced you rather than persuaded you to agree to this truce; but though you say you never broke the agreement, and Lee solemnly swears that he observed it, it was continually broken all the time. Which of you broke it I cannot say for certain, for I was a long way away when it all happened, and you and he were bandying accusations back and forth all the time; I am only bound to regret that my advice carried sufficient weight with the two of you to bring about a truce but would not carry enough to secure that the truce was observed. For I would rather have had the book published then, at a time when feelings were not running so high and its publication would be a milder affair, than that it should come out now after all this time, when resentment has increased and its effect must be exacerbated.

---

202 Thersites is a foul-tongued soldier, silenced by Odysseus with blows; see Homer, *Iliad* 2.212–70. **203** See Ovid, *Metamorphoses* 1.166.   **204** reacting in this manner in Aristophanes's *Clouds* 293   **205** In legend, a brigand who terrorized his neighborhood and was slain by Hercules. More is alluding to the similarity between the name and the verb *cacare*, "to defecate." **206** Juvenal 1.131   **207** Formerly a tutor in More's house and later the husband of his adopted daughter, John Clement had preceded Lupset as Wolsey's reader in the humanities at Oxford. The study of medicine which he had now undertaken would eventually lead him to Louvain.

For it has come out, and is rather more bitter than I might have hoped or than might have been salutary to experts in this field; among whom one looks in vain for the humility which even ignorant men should be ashamed not to display toward one another. But for you surely, my dear Erasmus, it cannot be right—assuming that the complaints he adduces are genuine—to be surprised if he shows a certain bitterness in pouring out his feelings after being so badly hurt; if, on the other hand, he has been misled by some phantom of the truth, you ought to make allowances even so. For what we believe to be true moves us with just as much force as what is proved to be so.

It is, I suppose, hardly necessary to advise or exhort you to display true Christian humility, which in all it undertakes toils solely for Christ's sake, who ought to be the only object before your eyes. The world may be ungrateful and not take the trouble to reward you, it may be grateful but not have the power; so much the more solid the reward you will receive from him. If you have made such sacrifices to secure great advantage for the world, if you have worn out your health by so much toil for the advancement of humane studies, and yet have been repaid evil for good by the jealousy of men who owe you (and you almost alone) what little tincture of a liberal education they may possess, in all this you are made more like unto Christ; and in no way can you more faithfully imitate him than by returning good words for evil, just as it was your good deeds that called them forth. Farewell, Erasmus my heart's dearest friend.

Yours, if he is his own, T. More

90. From Erasmus
Antwerp, 26 April 1520

Erasmus of Rotterdam to Thomas More, greeting.

I was hoping that my letter[208] might have carried some weight with Brixius. But no: his *Antimorus* has come out, and is on sale here. For the author's own sake, to whom I am attached because of his friendly attitude toward both the humanities and myself, as expressed in what he has written, I wish either that the book might have been kept dark forever, or at

least that Brixius might have copied the modest and courteous tone of your epigrams. Yet I could have wished even those had never been published, rather than that this passionate dispute should have arisen between you, from which the cause of the humanities must suffer; for I do not see how they can hold their ground unless they are defended against these obstinate and well-organized barbarians by a band of armed scholars standing shoulder to shoulder.[209] But since what's done can't be undone, my fervent wish, now that this rogue plant has sprung up in an evil hour, is that we may take steps to deal with it, so that if it cannot be pulled out by the roots, at least it may not spread. And this I wish, my dear More, not only for Brixius's sake, to whom I am much attached, but for yours, to whom my attachment is much deeper. Not that I think there is any risk that his *Antimorus* will do any harm to your reputation—I wish it might not have done more harm to his own—but because I am seriously afraid that if you answer and give him tit for tat, the result will be that what they all now think of him they will think in future of you both.

I know how hard it is, when one is answering a book like this which is all prickles, not to be offensive oneself; and yet if you of all people[210] err in that direction, no one who knows you will think it as easy to excuse you as Brixius. To say nothing for the moment of you both as scholars, the position you hold and your standing and your knowledge of the world mean that you must rise above squabbles of this kind, which are as petty as they are spiteful, and not take pains to recompense one insult with another. I hear every day what educated men are saying of Brixius since he published his book; I do not enjoy hearing these things said of him, and much less would I wish to hear them said of you. And so, though I feel the difficulty, when one has been attacked in such a venomous pamphlet, of moderating one's reply so as to give one's passions no play, yet I think the best course would certainly be to neglect and despise the whole affair as it deserves.

Nor would I give you this advice, my excellent More, if there were anything in the *Antimorus* which could have cast any aspersion on you such that it might be worth while trying to wipe it off.

208 *EE* 620, which Brixius claimed did not reach him until his *Antimorus* was   already being printed. See *EE* 1045: 25–29.   **209** *shoulder to shoulder:* See Juvenal 2.46.   **210** See *EE* 999: 254–56.

It is all the kind of thing to which the reader can see the answer for himself as he goes along. Everyone can see that what Brixius objects to is your having so rashly and hastily published your epigrams, though most of them were written over twenty years ago and almost all of them over ten, and even now it was not you who published them. They can see that he is carping at you for mistakes some of which are the copyist's and some the printer's, and most of them such that they cannot be complained of without condemning the greatest writer. They see that your epigram on the *Chordigera* was written long ago in the middle of the war, and that Brixius had no reason to revive a wartime dispute now after so many years when peace has been signed and sealed. They see Brixius poking fun at your epitaph on Abingdon, and with unmistakable ill will concealing what cannot be concealed, that the absurdity of that poem was intentional. Apart from that, the passage where he attacks your poem congratulating the prince on his accession leaves every educated man so aware of Brixius's lack of moderation in both feeling and expression that I, who am, as you know, not too bad as a defender of my friends, can find no way of excusing him except that he wrote in complete ignorance of English affairs; had he understood them, he would not have written that, and would have admitted, angry as he was, that you had paid a splendid tribute to the King in really kingly language.

Everybody thinks this, my dear More, and says so: what reason can remain for you to torment yourself into writing a reply, which is only, as they say, to tell a twice-told tale,[211] and nothing to be got from it except that while no one at the moment is suffering from loss of reputation in the eyes of educated men except Brixius, you run the risk of getting some share of that for yourself, if it should happen (and it is not easy to avoid, if one loses one's temper pen in hand, as sometimes happens) that you write without mercy and repay abuse in the same coin. Not the least part of your enviable reputation is your equable temperament and the unruffled charm of your character, and I should be sorry to see any sacrifice of this. But if you have made up your mind to take a different course (and I hear you have a book against him already in preparation), do be content to defend yourself. Reject the charge that you were offensive and began it all by your spite without casting it back at your opponent; fight with reasons and not abuse, and your moderation will magnify his ill will. All the same, even granted that you took that line, I would certainly much prefer you to keep silent and let the whole thing be buried in oblivion. This may be difficult just now, but it will gradually become possible if, as I hope, it is what you wish.

I had written to Brixius telling him to suppress the *Antimorus*,[212] which I kept hearing at the time that he was planning, and had the courier shown any diligence, I might have succeeded, if Brixius's letter[213] speaks the truth. But, as you can see from his answer, the book was already in the press before he saw my letter. But of you, my dear More, I have far higher hopes than of Brixius; for when I see that I should have persuaded him if my letter had reached him in time, I ought to have no doubt that I shall easily win you over to control your emotions for my sake to the extent of not assailing yet further with fresh pamphlets a man who likes me and whom I like in return. One or the other of you must make the first move to end this controversy, unless you want the contest to go on forever turn and turn about. Your standing and your character demand that the initiative should come from you. Believe me, my dear More, though Brixius has behaved in all this in such a way that even he perhaps is sorry for it by now, and if he could start again he would not do it (no one is so fortunate as to be wise all the time), yet he is a man, if you knew him better, whose character and whose wide reading would delight you, nor would you easily find anyone whom you would be more ready to make friends with. Nor ought you to demand that everyone should keep his emotions under such strict control as we have learnt in view of your record and our long experience of your wisdom to expect without hesitation from you. Brixius had written some things in his *Chordigera* which gave you, as the injured party, the right to reply even more bitterly, especially as things then were; yet once your epigrams, the charm of which made them universally popular, had made him a public laughing-stock, you ought not to be surprised if, as a spirited young man with a thirst for fame, he was diverted by some degree of resentment from thinking over what he had done and concentrated on your verses, thinking himself the injured

211 See *Adages* 370 (*CWE* 31: 365).   **212** See *EE* 620: 30–45.   **213** See *EE* 1045: 4–7, 22–25.

party and not realizing that he had neither the right nor the ideal opportunity to seek revenge.

I know you do not set such a high value on the few epigrams you threw off against him that you could not bear for my sake to suppress them; for unless your instructions had come too late, you were arranging to do this of your own accord some time ago, when you heard to your regret that the book was going to be published entire. I shall therefore secure that with your good will they are omitted in future[214] when the book is reprinted, and in return that the *Antimorus* is given no circulation. Thus it will come about that for want of fuel this fire will gradually die down. If however you have so obstinately resolved to pursue this quarrel, yet in the name of our friendship, which is neither recent nor of any common kind, I beg you again and again to consider very carefully how you propose to treat the business. For my part, if I had the choice, I should prefer, I repeat, for you to say nothing and to despise a topic that really deserves to be despised. If this cannot be, I should hope for the next best thing, that you should do as you have managed to do up to now and continue to show yourself the victor by your scholarship and the goodness of your case, and not by abuse as well. In that way, as I see that one of my two friends has been wounded in this ill-judged engagement, I shall at least be able to preserve the other permanently intact, who is so dear to me that I prefer him alone to all my other friends; though I should be more blest if I might preserve both. For as man can have nothing more precious than a good and faithful friend, it is reasonable to reckon no loss so heavy as the loss of friendship.

I have written this in the midst of the confusion[215] in which you know I live just now. Farewell, most warm-hearted friend.

Antwerp, 26 April 1520.

91. To Erasmus
<Greenwich?, Early May> 1520

Thomas More to Erasmus, that excellent and learned man, greeting.

Brixius's *Antimorus*, dear Erasmus, had been in London for a long time before your letter reached me. I was wondering a little what you had so much at heart that made you so slow in writing about it, unless either the *Antimorus* reached your part of the world rather later, maybe, or you were somewhat slow because, until you heard that I was preparing a pamphlet in answer, you supposed I should despise the book of my own accord, as likely to damage its author more than me and clearly unworthy of a reply. And so I should certainly have done, dear Erasmus, had not certain friends, very good scholars and very wise men too, persuaded me otherwise. They thought Brixius an object for mockery rather than resentment, but they had nothing like the affection for him that I see you have.

It is nearly two years ago now that I heard he was getting something of this kind under way and had the idea of writing to him myself, in the most friendly possible terms, and at the same time of giving him some advice which would have been somewhat more in his own interests than his present intemperate behavior. In the meantime, however, I understood from most reliable news from Paris that the man was so much carried away by his feelings that no persuasion from his friends could restrain him, and even advice from Bérault and Lascaris and Budé — men of the highest standing! — could not make him change his mind, while the authority of a great man like Deloynes or of his Eminence the Cardinal,[216] who has lately died over there, had no effect at all, so fast was he wasting away with a passion for revenge and pitifully consumed like Narcissus with some sort of love of his own verses; though fresh ones were born every day, and he used to carry them round like a new-born babe out of its cradle and dandle them at dinner with Deloynes or the cardinal. Nor was he always quite so happy when he took them home again, hearing sometimes from good scholars and men of judgment criticisms which, had he had any sense, he would have made himself. Much of this I have been told in letters from those parts, but in particular a certain John, a Greek by birth but as learned in Latin as he is in his native tongue, a man of high character and reliable beyond any doubt, told me much by word of mouth; and when I realized from this that Brixius was too much carried away to admit of any overtures, I changed my mind and abandoned my wish to write.

---

214 *omitted in future:* They were not; rather, more were added.   **215** i.e., publishing his replies to Lee   **216** Antoine Bohier

At the same time, "He is letting himself go," I thought, "to the extent of being reluctant to keep quite silent, but he is spending so much effort and so much time on this that it is not unlikely, with the distance and the delay, that the first resentment and a sort of quick reaction that affects us when things happen suddenly are calming down, and he will enjoy himself in wit and humor." Wrangling and abuse and calumny I thought he would entirely refrain from, for fear that his attacks would rightly be considered ill timed, if he assaulted a man more savagely in peacetime than he had himself been assaulted in time of war. And then I had read his *Chordigera* seven years before; though it abounded in faults of invention and arrangement and language yet it did offer a sample of his natural gifts, which I thought would ripen someday with the years (and I saw that the years had passed), and therefore I was in hopes that he would publish something scholarly and well finished, which would give pleasure even to me, at whom the publication was aimed. For I am not as a rule much offended if humor is allowed a certain license.

But when Brixius's famous bantling, the *Antimorus*, appeared, madder than Morychus,[217] more venomous than any poison, and more illiterate even than the *Chordigera*, I could do nothing but laugh, which was reasonable enough, murmuring to myself the old saw, "Seeking gold I found live coals."[218] And indeed, just as the glowing coals of Etna burnt up Empedocles,[219] so did those coals singe Brixius in a similar search for glory, and made him as black as any cinder. And so I had decided to issue no reply at all; but other people whose opinion on my affairs I trusted more than my own took a different view. They admitted that no educated man existed who would not feel sick at the sight of such dull, poisonous, mad stuff; but they gave it as their opinion that his calumnies, absurd and foolish as they were, and besides that, by no means obscure if one attends to the fore and aft of the whole business, would yet not be lucid enough for many people, who might perhaps read his *Antimorus* when they might have no access to the *Chordigera* or to my epigrams. They

persuaded me therefore to put all this together into a single book[220] and set it all before the reader, and then to write something to throw some light on the story, that the reader might need nothing more but his own critical faculty.

You can see, dearest Erasmus, what drove me to a reply. And so I do not feel it necessary to answer your arguments; for unless other people had pushed me in a different direction I should have agreed with you myself all the time. But I see Brixius has persuaded you that it was only through the courier's negligence that you did not succeed in getting him to suppress his *Antimorus* entirely. It greatly surprises me, dear Erasmus, that you should accept this as though you found it proven. "Why should I not believe it," say you, "when he puts Bérault or Budé in the box,[221] both witnesses of the highest probity?" I agree, Erasmus, he produces men of such integrity that either by himself might convince one of anything. "Then why," you ask, "should what Brixius says not win the day?" For this one reason, my dear friend: he produces two witnesses, but both give hearsay evidence and neither is an eyewitness; and "one witness with eyes in his head is worth ten who have but ears."[222] What other evidence can Bérault or Budé possibly give except that on such and such a day they heard from Brixius himself that the *Antimorus* was in the press? That is what Brixius means when he says that he told them of the publication of the *Antimorus* some days before he had read your letter. So you will believe Bérault and Budé; but whom will they believe meanwhile? Surely Brixius himself?

Do you see now, dear Erasmus, how that specious bit of evidence, "Whom saw I brought you yesterday at nightfall?"[223] issued eventually in bundling up Canthara? Not to mention in the meantime that he can never produce any witnesses to prove that he had not read your letter before he saw it in print, when he might have received it and concealed the fact, so that he could use this argument to you afterwards without let or hindrance. Besides which, his *Antimorus* consists of not more than eight quires, which normally take as many days to print, and we

217 More uses a hyperbolic play on words: madder even than the madman (who, he thinks, I am).   **218** See *Adages* 830 (*CWE* 32: 199).   **219** According to a classical legend, the philosopher from Agrigentum (5th century BC) had jumped into the crater, hoping his disappearance would

be taken for an apotheosis.   **220** *a single book:* Initially More considered reprinting the preceding controversial exchanges together with his *Epistola ad Germanum Brixium.* Erasmus's remarks in *EE* 1117: 43–48, 120–23 suggest that the first part of the project was subsequently abandoned.

221 *Bérault and Budé in the box:* See *EE* 1045: 27–31.   **222** See *Adages* 1554 (*CWE* 33: 319–20).   **223** Terence, *Andria* 768–70. Canthara was seen entering the house "with something bundled up under her dress" that turned out to be a baby. Brixius resembles her in his endeavor to conceal the true facts.

cannot infer from Brixius's words that it was half finished when he read your letter; so he compresses into very narrow limits the "some days" in which he says he told Bérault and Budé that the book was being published. "But why," you ask, "should Brixius invent such a thing?" Does it seem to you so surprising if a man of poetic turn invents something to please himself? Though there was also a reason why he should invent. Each of them had often told him not to publish such a foolish book, as full of abuse as any fishwife, and he wanted perhaps to test whether they would receive it, once he had done it, in the same spirit in which they had so often told him not to do it. It sometimes happens that we object strongly to the doing of something as long as the question is open; but when it reaches the point of being too late to put it right, we acquiesce, and gloss over with words what had gone wrong as far as we can.

But I, my dear Erasmus, want you to see in truth how much more truly your friend More is ready to do as you tell him than Brixius is; and so although, when your letter arrived, my book was not actually at press but was entirely printed off (and this I could establish not by a couple of hearsay witnesses who have learnt of it from me, but more than ten with eyes in their heads who have really seen it—in fact on the evidence, I suppose, of your own eyes, for I do not doubt that the book has reached you before this letter), and although the advice of so many friends urged me to publish it, yet when I had had this letter from you, the one man whose opinion weighs more with me than all the votes of everyone else, I did not follow Brixius's example. Though his purse (so he writes) is always heavy with coin,[224] Brixius sets such a high value on your instructions, whose lightest word he obeys (or so he tells us), that he could not face the trifling expense of buying up all those books of his and throwing them on the fire once and for all, so as to conceal from every eye that great nonsense of his by which the great name of Brixius, which the poor dear man so much thirsts to immortalize, will be discredited. Not so I, dear Erasmus: apart from these two, one of which I had already sent to you and the other to Peter Giles, and five more which the printer[225] had sold (for it was just when they were put on sale and had begun to

be in great demand that your letter intervened), I bought up the whole lot and keep them shut up, so that before any fresh steps are taken on my side, we may be able—or rather you may be able after taking counsel with yourself—to decide what you wish me to do.

And so, dear Erasmus, it is now your turn: let me urge you to look closely at your decision, for this is the case of a friend who is determined, whatever you decide, to do as he is told. You recommend that any attack of mine on Brixius should be omitted when my *Epigrammata* are fortunate enough to be reprinted, and that on the other side Brixius's *Antimorus* should be given no further circulation; but for my part, dear Erasmus, I think I have many reasons, so far as Brixius is concerned, for concluding that he is too tender-hearted toward his own verses to endure to be weaned away from a pursuit by which he expects, so far as it can be in his power, to endow his beloved offspring with immortality. My own *Epigrammata* never gave me much satisfaction, as you yourself, Erasmus, can testify; and unless that book had had an appeal for you and certain other people greater than the charm it had for me, perhaps it would not exist anywhere today. As it is, see how things are turned inside out! Suppose you and I had made a compact that you should be authorized to condemn such of my epigrams as you might please, provided you had no power over some few that I might choose to exempt: why, the only lines against which you unsheathe your knife under our agreement would be the only ones I should protect by exemption. Such is the charm they begin to have for me, now that I see many men moved to like them by Brixius's bitter and foolish poetizing. Not that I mean by this to stop you from doing what you please with my verses, who can do what you please even with me.

Now when you say that Brixius is a person whom I should find on closer acquaintance to be the sort of man who more than anyone deserves to be my friend, for my part, dear Erasmus, I do not give myself such airs as to think anyone's position too humble to make friends with him, provided he is not the sort of rascal for whom no one ought to feel any affection; and so I readily agree that Brixius is not unworthy to deserve the friendship of greater

---

224 *EE* 1045: 123–24 **225** Richard Pynson (d. 1530) was a Norman by birth who began printing in London by 1490 and was appointed printer to the King in 1508. In this capacity he printed Henry VIII's *Assertio* of the seven sacraments against Luther.

men than I. He does certainly seem to have rather more — I will not call it pride, but a sort of nobility of spirit and grandeur of attitude — than could ever make him in any way suited to a person of humble and modest gifts like myself, unless I were willing to be as unsuitably coupled in friendship as ill-matched oxen drawing the plough awry.[226] And yet, my dear Erasmus, if this is what you advise, I would not reject his friendship, for I can easily adapt myself even to doing as I am told by better men than myself. At least, so far as his scholarship is concerned, I believe him to be keen to learn and not wholly stupid, and also a man who will one day be made different by experience. All the same, in what he has published hitherto, to tell the truth — and this I could demonstrate — he is not free from bad mistakes and has not kept the rules of meter, and in invention he often sinks further than would be acceptable in a child. And yet, with all his faults, I do not think so well of myself as to suppose that I am comparable to him in erudition, though you, my dear Erasmus, either blinded by affection or (which I think nearer the truth) with a sort of courtesy toward me, set me above him. To speak frankly, so far am I from hating him that, my judgment having now been purged, I can even love him in the cause of literature.

But in the case before us, pray consider rather carefully what you wish to be done before you issue your orders. It comes to this: if I do not reply, many people will think that I provided the reason for this most tedious dispute, and without provocation of any kind attacked him with insults, curses, imprecations; and this would have been no less brutal than I have now shown it to be false, if you will let my book come out. As regards the book, your second precept is that if I am absolutely determined to publish it I must take care that (as you say I have done hitherto) I may be seen to defeat Brixius solely by being a better scholar with a better case, and not by abusing him as well. But, my dear Erasmus, while as far as scholarship goes I am content to be level with Brixius, I have no doubt that my case is far stronger than his, however much Brixius may assert that his is valid and demonstrable and sure to win; that is the opening gambit prescribed by the rules in the defense of a guilty party. In abuse I shall gladly let

myself be beaten, for I am determined never to fight with that sort of weapon. Yet it can easily happen that something which seems to me, as the victim, to have no bitterness in it, might be judged by a man who sees things rather differently to be somewhat offensive. Should this by some chance ever happen, I shall not be so afraid of my readers' sense of justice as to think they will not, even in my case, dear Erasmus, however serious the character your affection disguises me with, making out everything in me to be larger than life, the fact remains that while I still converse with mortal men and am not yet entirely deified, if I may be flippant on this not wholly serious subject, I am not afraid, I repeat, that my humane and human reader will not make some allowances in me too for those human feelings which no human being has entirely thrown off. Farewell, dearest Erasmus.

When we reach Calais, for which the King is preparing to leave shortly, I hope we shall be able to discuss these things more fully face to face. For I fully expect to see you at this meeting of the Kings, and Brixius too; for the Queen[227] of France will be there, and Brixius being her secretary cannot fail, I suppose, to attend. So, as far as I am concerned, you will easily settle things as you think best. For though without any reason he has behaved toward me in such a way as shows that he would have ruined me had he had the power, nonetheless, since I value you, my dear Erasmus, as more than half of myself, I shall be more influenced as regards Brixius by his being your friend than my enemy. Farewell once more. 1520.

93. To Erasmus
Canterbury, 26 May <1520>

Thomas More to Erasmus, greeting.

The young man whose case you recommended to me I had already discussed with his father before you wrote. The boy himself had asked me in a letter some time ago, being convinced that my opinion would have some weight and influence with him. I did all I could; whether I did any good, I am not sure. His father gave me a not entirely inflexible reply; and yet (for I know the man has an eye to the

---

226 *ill-matched . . . awry:* Ovid, *Heroides* 9.29 **227** Claude de France (1499–1524) was the daughter of Louis XII and Anne

of Brittany. In May 1514 she married the future Francis I. Brixius had been her

mother's secretary. It is not known whether he attended the Calais meeting.

main chance) I think his reply was as forthcoming as it was more from a certain reluctance to oppose me than because he said what he really thought. What it came to was that he would follow my advice about his son; but at the same time he made it clear that he would rather see him rich in coin than in culture. But the boy himself, I can see, is resolved to abandon not only his paternal inheritance but his father too, rather than let himself be torn away from liberal studies; clearly, with a mind like that, he deserves the support of everyone and all the help they can give him.

The schoolmaster[228] from Louvain I have found a place for, such that I do not doubt he will be permanently grateful to you. His master is much pleased with his scholarship; and when he heard that it was you who had recommended him, it was his idea to ask me to let him have the young man, and I complied without hesitation, as that was just what on other grounds I had decided to propose. For in my own household there was no place for any more servants.

In those first days, while he was staying with me, he showed me some things by Luis Vives[229] which were as stylish and as scholarly as anything I have seen for a long time. How few people one can find (indeed one can hardly find one anywhere) who at such a tender age (for you tell me in a letter that he is still quite young) have absorbed such encyclopedic learning! I am positively ashamed, my dear Erasmus, of myself and others like me, who make the best of ourselves with two or three slim volumes and those generally not much good, when I see Vives so young and the author of so much that is penetrating and very well written and shows such abstruse reading. It is a great thing to be good in either of the ancient tongues; but he shows himself a past master of both. It is still greater and more fruitful to be well versed in important subjects; but who can show himself to be equipped in more fields and more important fields than Vives single-handed? But much the greatest thing of all is to have imbibed the humanities so well as a learner that you can in turn pass them on to others as a teacher; and who teaches more lucidly, more attractively, more effectively than he? I cannot sufficiently admire the qualities in his *Declamationes* which you detected with such insight and expressed so eloquently; but

most important of all (for in oratory it is the most important thing), he can not only hold the history of those times in a memory more ready than the memory anyone has of his own experience, but he can invest the stories of men who died so many centuries ago with such lively feeling that he seems not to have got what he is presenting out of books, but to have seen it and felt it and been engaged in events as they happened for better or worse; and he can judge their policies not tepidly, on the basis of an account by someone else, but with fire in the light of his own fears and hopes, his perils and successes. If he were as good as this on one side only, he would still deserve our admiration; but as it is, he shows himself such a master on both that you might think him a chameleon, which changes color as its background changes.

How I wish, my dear Erasmus, that certain people who are now too ambitious and hope to be thought good writers would wake up and reorient themselves by the example of your friend Vives!—and I hope it more because they despise everything else than because they either pursue eloquence or properly attain it; for even in their dreams they never conceive any idea of what style is. These men neglect the other arts, and from what subject do they expect to derive their title to distinction? Orator or advocate are not names anyone will rightly confer on a man who neither pleads causes in real life nor declaims on imaginary themes. He will be a very thin and bloodless poet, whose verses are shaped by no philosophical principles, no precepts of the art of rhetoric, no practice in the conduct of discourse. Vives, after distinguishing himself in rhetoric beyond almost all the men who profess nothing else, goes on to leave untouched none of all the other arts which are worth knowing; there is none in which he is not so well versed that you would think he had spent his life on nothing else.

And so, though there is nothing of his that is not universally popular, I take a special kind of pleasure in his *In pseudodialecticos*, not only (though this is certainly one reason) because he makes such elegant fun of their absurd quibbling arguments, opposes them with powerful reasoning, digs them up by the roots, and overturns them with inescapable logic, but also since I see him treat some themes in that book on almost the same lines as I had thought

---

228 possibly Adrianus Aelius Barlandus   **229** Juan Luis Vives

of for myself when I had not yet read anything by
Vives. I approve of them now in Vives's book not
because as my own arguments they had appealed to
me before (for we often approve something that we
see put forward by other people, if we had already
thought of it for ourselves); but it is good for my
self-esteem, when I had previously suspected that
some point was not receiving the expression it deserves and am now confirmed in my belief that it is
by no means foolish, by seeing that Vives too accepts
it. And then it attracts me and gives me satisfaction,
when I see that the same argument has taken possession of the minds and thoughts of both of us and
has been treated by us in such a way that, though he
is fuller and writes better, yet in some things we produce not only the same matter but almost the same
words. And so I readily flatter myself that something
in the way of a kindred star joins our minds with
some sort of secret power and sympathy.

I am glad to think that he has such a good position with his eminent master the cardinal.[230] I hope
the favor of that deity may set right the injustice
of Fortune, who always gives the worst treatment
to those who deserve the best and, as though she
had a grudge against learning and virtue, often lavishes her favors on the exaltation of ignorant and
vicious men. But the Cardinal, for whom it is almost as easy to make any man prosperous as it is for
Fortune herself, is sure to show special generosity
to such a man, whom he has made a member of his
inner circle, and to whom he owes so much of the
distinguished learning for which he is now not a little more illustrious than even for his exalted station;
such is his well-known goodness, such the credit he
will gain with posterity by so doing.

Farewell, dearest Erasmus; I hope we shall soon
greet each other face to face in Calais at this meeting of the monarchs. The Emperor lands today. Tomorrow morning early the King will go to meet
him, perhaps even this same night which now approaches. You would hardly believe the joy with
which not only the King and the nobles but the
people too received the news which made it clear
that the Emperor is due here. Farewell once more,
from Canterbury on Whitsun eve.

There is one point, my dear Erasmus, which I
would mention to Vives if I knew him personally. As
it is, since I am not certain how he would take such

uncalled-for kindness from a stranger, you can tell
him at a suitable opportunity. There are in his *Ae-
des legum* and also in his *Somnium* (which in other
respects far surpasses what many other people have
spent sleepless nights on) some things which are too
abstruse to be clear to any except specialists, though
it would be for the good of the literary world that
everything of his should be as widely understood as
possible. It would be easy enough to remedy this,
either by adding an explanation or by putting very
brief notes in the margin. It will also throw much
light on his *Declamationes*, if he will briefly summarize the story even on a single page at the beginning.

Farewell once more.

96. To William Budé
<Calais, *ca.* June 1520>

If it were not for the vehemence of my desires,
I would not dare to ask you to lessen the pain of
your absence by writing to me. For I fear that engaged as you are in the affairs of the Most Christian King, you will not enjoy much leisure, and for
my part I am only too conscious of my remissness
in this kind of duty, when letters ought to be answered. It is not only my lack of eloquence, my dear
Budé, that keeps me from writing to you, but still
more my respect for your learning. Shame would
even have forbidden me to write this letter, unless
another kind of shame had wrung it from me. This
is the fear lest the letters that you have received
from me should be published along with yours. If
they should go forth to the world alone, their defects would be abundantly clear, but if they were
side by side with yours their shameful poverty
would be exposed as by a light of fierce and unpit-
ying brilliance. For I remember that in our conversation mention was made of the letters that I had
formerly sent you, which you had it in your mind to
publish if you thought I would raise no objection. It
was only a passing suggestion, and I forget what reply I gave. But now, as I think the matter over, I see
that it would be safer if you would wait a while, at
least until I revise my letters. It is not only that I fear
there may be passages where the Latin is faulty, but
also in my remarks upon peace and war, upon morality, marriage, the clergy, the people, etc., perhaps

what I have written has not always been so cautious and guarded that it would be wise to expose it to captious critics.

97. To William Budé
<Calais, *ca.* June 1520>

I doubt, my dear Budé, whether it is good ever to possess things which are pleasing and dear unless you can keep them. For I thought I would be completely happy if I had the good fortune ever to see Budé face to face (of whom reading had drawn me a very beautiful image), and after I got my wish I thought I was happier than happiness itself. But when our duties prevented our meeting often enough to satisfy my longing for conversation with you, and within a few days (as our kings were called away by affairs of state) our association only just begun was at once broken off; and we (who had each to follow his own prince) were drawn in opposite directions, perhaps never to see each other again; the happier our meeting had been, the greater was the sadness which assailed me at our parting. This you can somewhat lighten if you will deign sometimes to visit me by letter, which, however, but that eager longing urges me, I would not dare ask.

101. To His School
At Court, 23 March <1521>

Thomas More to his whole school, greeting.

See what a compendious salutation I have found, to save both time and paper, which would otherwise have been wasted in listing the names of each one of you in salutation, and my labor would have been to no purpose, since, though each of you is dear to me by some special title, of which I could have omitted none in an ingratiating salutation, no one is dearer to me by any title than each of you by that of scholar. Your zeal for knowledge binds me to you almost more closely than the ties of blood. I rejoice that Master Drew[231] has returned safe, for

I was anxious, as you know, about him. If I did not love you so much I should be really envious of your happiness in having so many and such excellent tutors. But I think you have no longer any need of Master Nicholas,[232] since you have learned whatever he had to teach you about astronomy. I hear you are so far advanced in that science that you can not only point out the polar star or the dog star, or any of the ordinary stars, but are able also—which requires the skill of an absolute Astronomer—among the special and principal heavenly bodies, to distinguish the sun from the moon! Onward then in that new and admirable science by which you ascend to the stars! But while you gaze on them assiduously, consider that this holy time of Lent warns you, and that beautiful and holy poem of Boethius[233] keeps singing in your ears, teaching you to raise your mind also to heaven, lest the soul look downwards to the earth, after the manner of brutes, while the body is raised aloft. Farewell, all my dearest. From Court, the 23rd March.

103a. Henry VIII to the Treasurer and Chamberlains of the Exchequer and to More
Windsor, 23 July <1521>

By the King Henry, by the grace of God king of England and of France and lord of Ireland, to the treasurer and chamberlains of our Exchequer and to our trusty and right well-beloved counselor Sir Thomas More, Knight, our undertreasurer, greeting.

We will and command you that for the time ye shall occupy ye do pay and content[234] for costs and expenses which shall behoove[235] us to have and sustain about our household and our great wardrobe out of our treasure[236] and make there assignations to our household and clerk of our great wardrobe according to the act or acts of Parliament, letters, patents,[237] tails,[238] or bills assigned thereof had or made. And that ye also of our said treasure content and pay the fees and rewards of our treasurer, chamberlains, undertreasurer, barons, and chancellor of our Eschequer and to all other officers and ministers of

---

231 Drew is not mentioned in the lists of young tutors given by Roper, Cresacre More, or Erasmus. Perhaps he is the Roger Drew (Drewe or Drewys), B.A. Oxford, 1512, M.A. 1514, Fellow of All Souls from

1512. **232** Nicholas Kratzer (1486/7–August 3, 1550) of Munich B.A. Cologne 1509, and also of Wittenberg, went to England late in 1517, became Astronomer to the King in 1519, and held the office for

many years. **233** Boëthius 5.Metrum 5 **234** satisfy by full payment; compensate **235** be necessary for **236** treasury **237** documents conferring privileges or rights **238** taxes, dues

any of our courts, having fees and rewards accustomed.[239] And also all such wages and fees as is accustomed there to be paid to our servants. And also
that ye do pay for parchment, paper, ink, wax, bags,
canvas, and all other things necessary and behoove-
ful[240] in our said courts as it hath been used and accustomed. And these over[241] letters shall be your sufficient warrant and discharge in this behalf.

Even under our privy seal at our Castle of Windsor, the twenty-third day of July, the thirteenth year
of our reign.

103b. Henry VIII to the Treasurer and Chamberlains of the Exchequer
Windsor, 23 July <1521>

By the King Henry, by the grace of God king of England and of France and lord of Ireland, to the trea-
surers and chamberlains of our Exchequer that now
be and for the time shall be, greeting.

Where before this time we have appointed and
commanded as well diverse lords spiritual and temporal,[242] as[243] other nobles of our Council, to sit
and give their attendance for the hearing, determining, and discussing of many diverse and urgent
causes and matters concerning as well the common
weal and politic[244] rule and order of this our realm
and our subjects of the same, as also our own particular matters and causes by virtue whereof the said
lords and nobles of our said Council, from the twentieth day of April, the twelfth year of our reign ending and the thirteenth year beginning and long before, hitherto truly have given and yet do give their
attendance with their true diligence for the intent
abovesaid. And we in consideration of the premises,[245] the said day and year commanded by our
own mouth our trusty and well-beloved counselor
Thomas More, now knight and our undertreasurer,
to pay and content[246] all manner[247] charges and costs
requisited for the diets[248] of our said Council giving
their attendance for the causes abovesaid as well at
our palace of Westminster and other places, from
the said day and year hitherto and from henceforth
unto such time as he shall have from us otherwise in
commandment by our mouth, according whereunto

the said Thomas More from the said day and year
hitherto hath issued and paid diverse sums of money
for the diets aforesaid, as we certainly know, for the
repayment whereof and also of such sums of money
as the said Thomas More by our said commandment
hereafter shall pay for the cause abovesaid; the said
Thomas hath had of us no sufficient warrant, as we
certainly know, we willing him to be truly contented
and paid as right would.

Therefore will[249] and charge you that of such
our treasure as hath come, is come, and that hereafter shall come to your hands as well of our sub-
sides,[250] quindesinez,[251] and dismes[252] to us heretofore granted and hereafter to be granted, as also
of all other our revenues, whatsoever they be,
and shall be paid at our receipt aforesaid, ye content and pay to the said Thomas More such and as
much money as[253] upon the books of parcels signed
with the hands of the most reverend father in God
Thomas Cardinal and Archbishop of York. And
other[254] our said Council shall be found due to the
said Thomas More unpaid as also from henceforth
upon the showing and delivery of every like book of
parcels signet as is abovesaid. From time to time ye
and our said treasurer content and pay unto the said
Thomas More all manner of sums of money as by
any like book or books of parcels shall appear to be
due to the said Thomas More unpaid upon the delivery of any such book of parcels signed, as abovesaid, unto such time as ye from henceforth shall
have from us otherwise a commandment. And that
ye from time to time receive of the said Thomas
More all and singular such books and book of the
expenses of the said diets and other necessaries incident[255] to the same. And the same book and books
ye do accept from time to time for a true account
and reckoning of the full employment of and every of the said sums of money. And we will that the
said books signed as is aforesaid with these our letters be sufficient warrant and discharge as well unto
you for the payment of every and singular of the
said sums of money as to the said Thomas More for
the employment of the same without any other account thereof to us in any wise[256] to be given and
without prest[257] or any other charge to be set upon
the said Thomas More for the same or by occasion

---

239 customary **240** useful; needful,
due **241** subsequent **242** of the clergy
and laymen **243** as well as **244** prudent
245 aforementioned matters **246** satisfy
by full payment; compensate **247** kind
of **248** sustenance; allowance **249** we
will **250** financial contributions made or
levied to provide assistance, esp. to a lord
or sovereign; subsidies **251** fifteenths
252 tenths; tithes **253** as is **254** other
matters or expenses relating to **255** related
256 way **257** charge; duty, tax

of any the premises. And these our letters shall be
your sufficient warrant and discharge in this behalf.

Given under our privy seal at our Castle of Windsor the twenty-third day of July, the thirteenth year
of our reign.

105. To Bishop John Fisher
<1521>

As to this priest, Reverend Father, of whom you
write that he will soon obtain a prebend if he can
obtain a vigorous advocate with the King's majesty,
I think I have so wrought that our Prince will raise
no obstacle....

Whatever influence I have with the King (it
is certainly very little) but such as it is, is as freely
available to your Paternity and all your scholars as
his own house to any man. I owe your students constant gratitude for the heartfelt affection of which
their letters to me are the token. Farewell, best and
most learned of bishops, and continue your affection for me.

106. To Margaret Roper
<1521?>

Thomas More to his most dear daughter
Margaret.

There was no reason, my darling daughter, why
you should have put off writing me for a single day,
because in your great self-distrust you feared that
your letters would be such that I could not read
them without distaste. Even had they not been perfect, yet the honor of your sex would have gained
you pardon from anyone, while to a father even a
blemish will seem beautiful in the face of a child.
But indeed, my dear Margaret, your letters were so
elegant and polished and gave so little cause for you
to dread the indulgent judgment of a parent, that
you might have despised the censorship of an angry Momus.

You tell me that Nicholas, who is fond of us and
so learned in astronomy, has begun again with you
the system of the heavenly bodies. I am grateful to
him, and I congratulate you on your good fortune;
for in the space of one month, with only slight labor, you will thus learn thoroughly these sublime
wonders of the Eternal Workman, which so many

men of illustrious and almost superhuman intellect have discovered only with hot toil and study, or
rather with cold shiverings and nightly vigils in the
open air in the course of many ages.

I am, therefore, delighted to read that you have
made up your mind to give yourself so diligently to
philosophy as to make up by your earnestness in future what you have lost in the past by neglect. My
darling Margaret, I indeed have never found you
idling—and your unusual learning in almost every
kind of literature shows that you have been making
active progress—so I take your words as an example
of the great modesty that makes you prefer to accuse
yourself falsely of sloth rather than to boast truly of
your diligence; unless your meaning is that you will
give yourself so earnestly to study that your past industry will seem like indolence by comparison. If
this is your meaning, my Margaret, and I think it really is, nothing could be more delightful to me, or
more fortunate, my sweetest daughter, for you.

Though I earnestly hope that you will devote the
rest of your life to medical science and sacred literature, so that you may be well furnished for the
whole scope of human life, (which is to have a
sound mind in a sound body), and I know that you
have already laid the foundations of these studies,
and there will be always opportunity to continue
the building; yet I am of opinion that you may with
great advantage give some years of your yet flourishing youth to humane letters and so-called liberal
studies. And this both because youth is more fitted
for a struggle with difficulties and because it is uncertain whether you will ever in the future have the
benefit of so sedulous, affectionate, and learned a
teacher. I need not say that by such studies a good
judgment is formed or perfected.

It would be a delight, my dear Margaret, to me
to converse long with you on these matters: but I
have just been interrupted and called away by the
servants, who have brought in supper. I must have
regard to others, else to sup is not so sweet as to talk
with you.

Farewell, my dearest child, and salute for me my
beloved son, your husband. I am extremely glad that
he is following the same course of study as yourself.
I am ever wont to persuade you to yield in everything to your husband; now, on the contrary, I give
you full leave to strive to surpass him in the knowledge of the celestial system. Farewell again. Salute
your whole company, but especially your tutor.

106a. To Francis Cranevelt
At Court, 13 February <1521>

Cordial greetings from T. More to his friend
Cranevelt.[258]

I who would not bear that you should be silent
have myself been silent for a long time now, in order to provide something for you to write about, so
that you could take your turn at reproaching me —
which you have a perfect right to do, since for such
a long time I have not repaid the copious letters I received from you. But right after Easter, unless something unforeseen happens, I will be with you and
will repay everything in person with the loquacity
which you have so often and so wearily been forced
to put up with. In the meantime, farewell, together
with your most delightful wife, a lady of the highest
prudence and honor.

From the Court, on the 13th day of February.

Please give some thought to a house, and perhaps
the one that I had before would not be the worst,
but the price was the worst. Find out at what price
it could be rented for two months from May 1 and
thereafter by the week. And also what it would cost
to rent eight or ten beds, together with the rest of
the suitable furnishings. And at your leisure let me
know about these things. You can also discuss the
matter with the friend who is the dearest of all my
friends, Master Nicholas Bonviso.

If the candlesticks have not yet been sent, do not
send them but keep them there till I arrive. Give
my regards to Laurijn, Fevijn, all and our other
friends.

106b. To Francis Cranevelt
London, 9 April <1521>

Greetings from T. More to his friend
Frans Cranevelt.

I have received two letters from you, my dear
Cranevelt. From each of them I have perceived that
most honest heart of yours and a certain, almost incredible love for me, to which if I should not respond with equal good will, I would certainly be an
ungrateful wretch. As for my mistress your wife, or

rather your mistress my wife, since I betrothed myself to her there long since — and seriously she is a
woman of the highest dignity, completely adorned
with the ornaments of all the feminine virtues — I
am delighted that she has been unburdened by giving birth and that your family has been increased
by offspring. I owe you an immense debt of gratitude for the great effort you have made in looking for a house for me. And then, as for your very
friendly offer to me of your own home, I find no
thanks adequate to it. There is many a slip, my dear
Cranevelt, between the cup and the lip, as they say.
Thus it can happen that I myself will not go as a
member of the embassy which will shortly be going there — a journey I could comfortably do without, were it not that I would see you friends of
mine, to see whom I would willingly go anywhere.
But in a few days I will know for certain and once
I know I will write you on the spot. In the meanwhile I have almost made up my mind to stay in
your home immediately after my arrival, not to burden you with my presence very long but in order
to enjoy for a while the spontaneous kindness of
you and my lady, your wife, until I have an opportunity to consider in person what house I could most
conveniently move into. In the meantime, my most
delightful Cranevelt, farewell, together with your
most charming wife, to whom give my warmest regards. London, in haste, April 9. Give my regards to
Master Laurijn, Fevijn.

106c. To Francis Cranevelt
<London, September 1521>

See, my dear Cranevelt [of the leaves there are no
more but] indeed a decent scrap of paper is left.
Even now I am mounting my horse. I am returning your book. Together with it you will receive a
bundle of letters which Erasmus sent me to read.
He neither wants them published nor is there any
need or usefulness in doing so, unless his adversary
continues his insane antics in some way or other.
For which eventuality I deposit them with you for
safekeeping, just as Erasmus himself told me to do.
Share them with Master Laurijn, if he wants to read
any of them. Give my regards to that most excellent

---

258 Francis Cranevelt (1485–1564) was
a legal counselor, and in 1522 he was
a member of the Grand Council of
Mechelen. Erasmus introduced Cranevelt
to More in 1520.

lady, your wife. For her and you and your delightful children I pray for lasting health and happiness.
I am now being called to my horse. Once more,
farewell.

5   Completely at your service, T. M.

106d. To Francis Cranevelt
<Chelsea?,> 12 November <1521>

I recently received a letter from you, my dear
Cranevelt. It is just like you: very fine, most affec-
10   tionate, and thoroughly learned. I got back safe
and sound and found my dear ones safe and sound,
even though the plague is raging everywhere. I pray
that, God willing, they may long remain so. I myself
lapsed into a tertian fever immediately after my re-
15   turn, but now I am beginning to get better and am
almost well again. My whole school sends you their
regards. Give my regards to our mistress and wife.
That warfare of yours, I see, does not do very much
for your welfare. I pray that someday princes will
20   become of sound mind, at least to the point where
some one of them will be willing to be content with
a realm more than sufficient for ten of them. But
the very weariness of war, I hope, will shortly bring
peace. Farewell, my dear Cranevelt — I have never
25   come upon any companion more dear than you. At
my little country place not far from London, the
12th of November.

                         Your servant as much as his own,
                                    Tho. More

30   ### 107. To His Children and Margaret Giggs
At Court, 3 September <1522?>

Thomas More to his dearest children and to
Margaret Giggs, whom he numbers among his
children, greeting.
35   The Bristol merchant brought me your letters the
day after he left you, with which I was extremely delighted. Nothing can come from your workshop,
however rude and unfinished, that will not give me
more pleasure than the most meticulous writing
40   of anyone else. So much does my affection for you
commend whatever you write to me. Indeed, without any recommendation, your letters are capable
of pleasing by their own merits, the charm and pure
Latinity of their style. There has not been one of

your letters that did not please me extremely. But   45
to confess ingenuously what I feel, the letter from
my son John pleased me the best, both because it
was longer than the others and because he seems to
have given it a bit more labor and study. For he not
only put out his matter prettily and composed in   50
fairly polished language, but he plays with me both
pleasantly and cleverly, and turns my jokes on myself wittily enough. And this he does not only merrily, but with due moderation, showing that he does
not forget that he is joking with his father, whom   55
he is eager to delight and yet is cautious not to give
offense.
     Now I expect from each of you a letter almost ev-
ery day. I will not admit excuses (for John makes
none) such as want of time, sudden departure of the   60
letter carrier, or want of something to write about.
No one hinders you from writing, but, on the contrary, all are urging you to it. And that you may not
keep the letter carrier waiting, why not anticipate
his coming, and have your letter written and sealed,   65
ready two days before a carrier is available? How
can a subject be wanting when you write to me, who
am glad to hear of your studies or of your games,
and whom you will please most if, when there is
nothing to write about, you write just that at great   70
length. Nothing can be easier for you, especially for
girls, loquacious by nature and always doing it.
     One thing, however, I admonish you, whether
you write serious matters or the merest trifles, it is
my wish that you write everything diligently and   75
thoughtfully. It will do no harm if you first write
the whole in English, for then you will have much
less trouble and labor in turning it into Latin; not
having to look for the matter, your mind will be intent only on the language. That, however, I leave to   80
your own choice, whereas I strictly enjoin you that
whatever you have composed you carefully examine
before writing it out clean; and in this examination
first scrutinize the whole sentence and then every
part of it. Thus, if any solecisms have escaped you,   85
you will easily detect them. Correct these, write out
the whole letter again, and even then do not grudge
to examine it once more, for sometimes, in rewrit-
ing, faults slip in again that one had expunged. By
this diligence you will soon make your little trifles   90
seem serious matters; for while there is nothing
so neat and witty that will not be made insipid by
silly and careless loquacity, so also there is nothing
in itself so insipid that you cannot season it with

grace and wit if you give a little thought to it. Fare-well, my dearest children. From the Court, the 3rd September.

108. To Margaret <Roper>

At Court, 11 September <1522?>

Thomas More to his dearest daughter Margaret, greeting.

I need not express the extreme pleasure your let-ter gave me, my darling daughter. You will be able to judge better how much it pleased your father when you learn what delight it caused to a stranger. I happened this evening to be in the company of the Reverend Father, John, Bishop of Exeter, a man of deep learning and of a wide reputation for holiness. Whilst we were talking I took out of my pocket a paper that bore on our business and by accident your letter appeared. He took it into his hand with pleasure and began to examine it. When he saw from the signature that it was the letter of a lady, his surprise led him to read it more eagerly. When he had finished, he said he would never have believed it to be your work unless I had assured him of the fact, and he began to praise it in the highest terms (why should I hide what he said?) for its pure Latin-ity, its correctness, its erudition, and its expressions of tender affection. Seeing how delighted he was, I showed him your speech. He read it, as also your poems, with a pleasure so far beyond what he had hoped that although he praised you most effusively, yet his countenance showed that his words were all too poor to express what he felt. He took out at once from his pocket a portague[259] which you will find enclosed in this letter. I tried in every possible way to decline it, but was unable to refuse to take it to send to you as a pledge and token of his good will toward you. This hindered me from showing him the letters of your sisters, for I feared that it would seem as though I had shown them to obtain for the others too a gift which it embarrassed me to have to accept for you. But, as I have said, he is so good that it is a joy to have pleased him. Write him your thanks carefully in the nicest letter you can. You will one day be glad to have given pleasure to such a man. Farewell. From the Court, just before midnight, September 11th.

108a. To Francis Cranevelt

<Chelsea?, March? 1522>

I received your letter, my dearest Cranevelt, which delighted me very much, as everything of yours does. I thank you for taking care of my picture. The Virgin herself will thank you, since at your insis-tence she was finished with greater care. The remain-ing three crowns which were owed to the craftsman upon completion of the work I had thought I left with one of my friends there, but now I have ar-ranged it that he will receive from Jan van Porter a half crown as a gift of my own over and above our agreement, if he shows that his work deserves it. As for the people of Bruges, my dear Cranevelt, I was disturbed by such meanness in the midst of such extravagance: when they have consumed immense wealth in such a way that whatever is spent is lost, they are forced to set things right by bits and pieces, snatching away precisely where it would be appro-priate to add something. But these vices are theirs and let them come to a bad end. But as for you, my dear Cranevelt, your virtue and [diligence] are such that your circumstances will never be found to be anything but honorable. I pray that they may very happily remain so, and if you see anything that could contribute to that on my part I will strive to see to it as if all the resources of all my connections and my own also would be advanced in support of your standing. Farewell, my dearest Cranevelt, to-gether with your wife, the best and most delight-ful of ladies. Regards from my wife and my whole family.

To the most distinguished and most learned gen-tleman Master Francis Cranevelt, Counselor of the city of Bruges.

110. To Cardinal Wolsey

New Hall, 21 September <1522>

It may like your good Grace to be advertised,[260] that yesterday in the morning I received from your Grace your honorable letters written unto myself, dated the nineteenth day of this present month and with the same as well the letters of congratu-lation with the minute[261] of a letter to be written with the King's own hand to the Emperor and the

259 a Portuguese gold coin   **260** informed   **261** note, memorandum

instructions to the King's ambassador there as also those letters which your Grace received from Master Secretary, with the letters by your Grace also devised for the expedition of the gentleman of Spruce.

Which things with diligence I presented forthwith unto the King's Grace the same morning, and to the intent that his Grace should the more perfectly perceive what weighty things they were that your Grace had at that time sent unto him and what diligence was requisite in the expediting of the same, I read unto his Grace the letters which it liked your Grace to write to me. In which it much liked his Grace that your Grace so well allowed and approved his opinion concerning the overtures made by the French King unto the Emperor. After your Grace's said letter read, when he saw of your Grace's own hand that I should diligently solicit the expedition of those other things, forasmuch as your Grace intended and gladly would dispatch the premises this present Sunday, his Grace laughed and said, "Nay by my soul that will not be, for this is my removing day soon at Newhall. I will read the remnant at night."

Whereupon after that his Grace was come home hither and had dined, being six of the clock in the night, I offered myself again to his Grace in his own chamber, at which time he was content to sign the letters to the Emperor and the other letters for the expedition of the gentlemen of Spruce, putting over all the remnant till this day in the morning.

Whereupon at my parting from his Grace yesternight I received from your Grace a letter addressed unto his, with which I forthwith[262] returned unto his Grace in the Queen's chamber, where his Grace read openly my Lord Admiral's letter to the Queen's Grace, which marvelously rejoiced in the good news and especially in that that the French King should be now toward a tutor and his realm to have a governor.

In the communication whereof which lasted about one hour, the King's Grace said that he trusted in God to be their governor himself, and that they should by this means make a way for him as King Richard did for his father. I pray God if it be good for his Grace and for this realm that then it may prove so, and else in the stead thereof I pray God send his Grace one honorable and profitable peace.

This day in the morning, I read unto his Grace as well the instructions most politicly and most prudently devised by your Grace and thereto most eloquently expressed, as all the letters of Master Secretary sent unto your Grace, to whom as well for your speedy advertisement[263] in the one, as for your great labor and pain taken in the other, his Grace giveth his most hearty thanks.

In the reading of the instruction among the incommodities that your Grace there most prudently remembereth if the Emperor should leave the estate of Milan up to the French King, the King's Grace said that the Emperor should besides all those incommodities sustain another great damage, that is to wit[264] the loss of all his friends and favorers in Italy without recovery forever which should be fain[265] to fall wholly to the French King, utterly despairing that ever the Emperor leaving the Duchy when he had it would after labor therefor when he had left it. Which consideration his Grace would have planted into the instructions with his own hand, saving that he said your Grace could, and so he requireth[266] you to do better furnish it or set it forth.

As touching Master Secretary's letters his Grace thinketh, as your Grace most prudently writeth, that they do but seek delays till they may see how the world is, wherein he much alloweth your most prudent opinion that they should be with good round words to their ambassador and other quick ways pricked forth.

And forasmuch as your Grace toucheth an order, that no Venetians should be suffered to ship any of their goods out of the realm, and that it is now showed unto his Grace that one Deodo a Venetian is about to ship, pretending himself to be denizen, which is his pretense whether it be true or not his Grace knoweth not, and also thinketh that he shall under the color[267] of his own send out of the realm the goods of others his countrymen, for which causes his Grace requireth yours to have a respect thereto and cause it to be ordered as to your Grace's wisdom shall seem expedient.

Forasmuch as the King's Grace hath not yet written of his own hand the minute to the Emperor which I delivered his Grace in this morning, therefore I suppose that this letter written this present Sunday the twenty-first day of September in the

---

262 immediately **263** notification **264** say **265** obliged, forced **266** asks **267** pretext, appearance

night cannot be delivered to the post till tomorrow about < >, as knoweth our Lord, who long preserve your Grace in honor and health.

> Your humble orator and most
> bounden beadsman,
> Thomas More

To my Lord Legate's good Grace.

111. From Cuthbert Tunstall
London, <*ca.* October 1522>

Cuthbert Tunstall gives many greetings to Thomas More.[268]

It was some years ago, my dear More, that I was forced to look a little more closely into some calculations that had not been properly handled (I was doing business with some money changers, and when we didn't quite agree on the result, I needed to escape from the fraud I had very much suspected), and I reviewed the art of calculation that I had once had some exposure to as a youth. As a result of doing this, once I had freed myself from the annoyance of those sharp men, I began to think about how it might prove to be no small advantage during the rest of my life, if I were to acquire so ready a knowledge of the art of arithmetic, that I could not be fooled even when tested by the most skilled practitioner.

Consequently, in order to understand the business more thoroughly, I read through all the works of all the writers who wrote on this subject, whether learned or ignorant, both in Latin and in the barbarous tongues that I could proficiently understand (practically every country has some writing on this art, written in the vernacular), and, in order to avoid having often to re-read, tediously, these little books in their entirety, many of which I did not always like reading, I took notes when anything appeared somewhere in them that I liked. And so it came to pass, that from many books, written by many authors, I collected many things myself. I kept them stored privately for a little while, but then it occurred to me that it might be useful if I could make them a little clearer by putting them into Latin; while attempting that, but not succeeding too well, and defeated by tiredness, I often put

aside those little books, and despaired of attaining what I had hoped to accomplish, not only because the matter was difficult in itself, but also because there were so many things that could not go into the Latin tongue, let alone with eloquence. However, I felt ashamed to give up on a task that had seemed so promising at the outset, just because it was becoming too hard a burden for me to bear. So, I tried some more, in the hope that working on it again would bring me more strength. Sometimes I even enjoyed struggling with the difficulties, so that, contrary to what usually happens, the things that were causing me no small annoyance actually made my mind work more stubbornly. I even began to think that, after I proved unable to accomplish what I really wanted to do—that is, to make everything shine with splendor—it would not be a bad thing at least to render less uncouth whatever seemed to be unkempt with barbarity. And so, at last, I conquered my tedium, and struggling through many difficulties, I made all manner of excerpts out of the many possible, and for a long time purposely kept them unpublished, thinking, when I had the leisure, to follow the example of the mother-bear who licks her unformed cubs into shape.

But now, having been designated—as unworthy a man as I am of the honor—to the vacant London bishopric by the kindness of a King who is deserving of the regard of all good men, and by me more than can be expressed, and intending to devote the rest of my days to sacred letters, I have decided that all profane writings should be put aside, and especially these notes on arithmetic that I have been saving and which I now think should be thrown out, as more worthy of the bookcases of Vulcan than of Minerva. They are not worthy to be in the hands of learned men, nor do I think it right, that through taking time to polish them, any part of my life from now on be stolen away from sacred writings. But it came to my mind that these notes might not be without usefulness to those who are intending to study arithmetic, nor that it would make much sense to consign to the flames for destruction what has come into being during so many evenings of study. Nevertheless, I could not convince myself to dedicate this rude and unpolished work to the King, who is learned beyond the typical fortune of

---

268 This dedicatory epistle to *De arte supputandi* was translated by Gerald

Malsbary © CTMS 2018. Tunstall's was the first arithmetic book printed in England.

kings, and deserving of my regard beyond that of all other mortals, lest I delay him even the slightest bit from his public duties while he takes time to read these silly things, and lest I seem to ruin the favor (which I would in vain hope ever to repay), by giving him an unpleasant task.

And so, as I looked about me, to see to whom especially out of my cohort of friends I could dedicate this collection, you (thanks both to our long acquaintance and to the honesty of your mind) seemed the most likely one of all to be ready to be pleased (if anything in it is pleasing), to take it in a good sense (if anything seems inadequate), and to forgive (if anything offends). To whom but you are such acts more fitting? You are now completely involved in computations, as the second in command over the Royal Treasury, and can give them to your children to study, whom you are taking care to be liberally educated, and they would be in a position to make the most out of them, if they are worth reading at all, since the minds of young persons are stimulated by nothing so much as by the discipline of arithmetic.

Farewell.

113. To Conrad Goclenius
London, <*ca.* November 1522>

To the very learned professor of Latin,
Conrad Goclenius, at Louvain.

Some little time ago my good friend Peter Giles sent me Lucian's *Hermotimus,* translated by you, most learned Goclenius, and dedicated to me. When I received it I was indeed very greatly pleased both by your kindness to me and by the charm of the work, together with the elegance of its style; in it you seem to me to compete most happily even with the Greek. So our mutual friend Erasmus was quite right—whose frequent enthusiastic statements of your ability and learning made you dear to me before I knew you. And now really since this additional pledge, so to call it, of your affection and good will toward me in turn, although I loved you so much before that I thought I could not love you more, yet somehow or other, to that earlier love for you I feel a considerable increase has accrued. And so by showing your learned essays also to many

others among us, I have seen to it that you have here many more friends and admirers of your talents. And if there should occur anything in which I can gratify or serve you or any of yours, I shall make clear <by return> how good and kind has been your service to me. Farewell, my very dear friend; all my friends here in London send their most cordial greetings.

Your (in whatever way I may serve you)
Thomas More

117. To Cardinal Wolsey
Woking, 1 September <1523>

It may like your good Grace to be advertised[269] that I have received your Grace's letters directed to myself dated the last day of August with the letters of my Lord Admiral to your Grace sent in post and copies of letters sent between the Queen of Scots and his lordship concerning the matters and affairs of Scotland with the prudent answers of your Grace as well to my said lord in your own name as in the name of the King's Highness to the said Queen of Scots. All which letters and copies I have distinctly read unto his Grace. Who hath in the reading thereof substantially considered as well the Queen his sister's letter with the letters againward devised and sent by my Lord Admiral to her and his letters of advertisement[270] to your Grace as your most politic devices and answers unto all the same among which, the letter which your Grace devised in the name of his Highness to the Queen his sister, his Grace so well liked that I never saw him like thing better, and as help me God in my poor fantasy not causeless, for it is for the quantity one of the best made letters for words, matter, sentence, and couching that ever I read in my life.

His Highness in your Grace's letter directed to my Lord Admiral marked and well liked that your Grace touched my said lord and my Lord Dacre in that that their opinions had been to the let[271] of the great rood, which if it had been ere[272] this time made into Scotland, as by your prudent advice it had, if their opinions with other had not been to the contrary, it should as by the Queen's letter appeareth have been the occasion of some great and good effect.

269 informed   **270** notification   **271** hindrance   **272** before

His Highness also well allowed that your Grace noteth not only remiss dealing but also some suspicion, in that the Lord Dacre so little esteemed the mind and opinion of the King's sister whereof he had by his servant so perfect knowledge.

Finally his Highness is of the mind of your Grace and singularly commendeth your policy in that your Grace determineth for a final way that my Lord Admiral shall set forth his enterprises without any longer tract of time not ceasing to press them with all the annoyance possible till they fall earnestly and effectually to some better train[273] and conformity. And verily[274] his Highness thinketh as your Grace writeth that for any lack of those things, which as he writeth are not yet come to him, he should not have needed to forbear to have done them with smaller roods as the least way some annoyance in the mean season.

I read also to his Highness the letter of Master Doctor Knight written unto your Grace, with your Grace's letter written to myself, by the tenor whereof his Grace well perceiveth your most prudent answer devised and made, as well to his said ambassador as to the ambassador of the Emperor, concerning the disbursing of such money as his Highness should lay out for the *entretènement*[275] of the 10,100 lance knights, wherein his Grace highly well approveth as well your most politic foresight so wisely doubting lest this delay of the declaration might happen to be a device, whereby the Emperor might spare his own charge and *entreteign*[276] the Almains[277] with the only cost of the King's Grace, as also your most prudent order taken therein by which his Highness shall be bound to no charge except the Duke first pass the articles sent by Sir John Russell and that the 10,000 Almains be levied and joined with the Duke and he declared enemy to the French King.

I read also to his Highness the copy of your Grace's letter devised to Master Doctor Sampson and Master Jerningham, wherein his Highness well perceived and marked what labor and pain your Grace had taken as well in substantial advertising his said ambassadors at length of all occurrents here, with the goodly rehearsal[278] of the valiant acquittal of his army on the sea not only there done but also descending on the land with all his preparations and armies set forth and furnished as well toward France as Scotland as also in your good and substantial instructions given unto them for the semblable advancing of the Emperor's army and actual invasion to be made on that side for his part.

His Highness hath also seen and signed the letters by your Grace devised in his name as well to Don Ferdinando and to the Duke of Meckelenburg in answer of their late letters sent unto his Grace as also to the Duke of Ferrara in commendation of the King's orators in case the Duke accept the Order.

In the reading and advising of all which things his Highness said that he perceived well, what labor, study, pain, and travail your Grace had taken in the device and penning of so many, so great things, so high, well dispatched in so brief time, when the only reading thereof held him about two hours; his Highness, therefore, commanded me to write unto your Grace that for your labor, travail, study, pain and diligence, he giveth your Grace his most hearty and not more hearty than highly well-deserved thanks. And thus our Lord long preserve your good Grace in honor and health. At Woking the first day of September.

Your humble orator and most
bounden beadsman,[279]
Thomas More

To my Lord Legate's good Grace.

128. To Margaret Roper
<Woodstock?, Autumn 1523>

I cannot put down on paper, indeed I can hardly express in my own mind, the deep pleasure that I received from your most charming letter, my dearest Margaret. As I read it there was with me a young man of the noblest rank and of the widest attainments in literature—one, too, who is as conspicuous for his virtue as he is for his learning, Reginald Pole. He thought your letter nothing short of marvelous, even before he understood how pressed you were for time and distracted by ill health, while you managed to write so long a letter. I could scarce make him believe that you had not been helped by a teacher until he learned truly that there was no

---

273 order **274** truly **275** upkeep,
maintenance **276** maintain, support **277** Germans **278** account
279 one who prays for another

teacher at our house, and that it would not be possible to find a man who would not need your help in composing letters rather than be able to give any assistance to you.

Meanwhile, something I once said to you in joke came back to my mind, and I realized how true it was. It was to the effect that you were to be pitied, because the incredulity of men would rob you of the praise you so richly deserved for your laborious vigils, as they would never believe, when they read what you had written, that you had not often availed yourself of another's help: whereas of all the writers you least deserved to be thus suspected. Even when a tiny child you could never endure to be decked out in another's finery. But, my sweetest Margaret, you are all the more deserving of praise on this account. Although you cannot hope for an adequate reward for your labor, yet nevertheless you continue to unite to your singular love of virtue the pursuit of literature and art. Content with the profit and pleasure of your conscience, in your modesty you do not seek for the praise of the public, nor value it overmuch even if you receive it, but because of the great love you bear us, you regard us — your husband and myself — as a sufficiently large circle of readers for all that you write.

In your letter you speak of your imminent confinement. We pray most earnestly that all may go happily and successfully with you. May God and our Blessed Lady grant you happily and safely to increase your family by a little one like to his mother in everything except sex. Yet let it by all means be a girl, if only she will make up for the inferiority of her sex by her zeal to imitate her mother's virtue and learning. Such a girl I should prefer to three boys. Goodbye, my dearest child.

133. To the University of Oxford
London, 26 July <1524>

To his very dear friends, the congregation and masters of the University of Oxford.

After the death of the distinguished Sir Thomas Lovell, who was the late High Steward and Agent of your University, your Proctor acting as your representative, most learned Gentlemen, came to me to inform me of your deep regret at the death of that eminent Gentleman, and, furthermore, that, having met to select his successor, you chose me, out of

your friendliness and great love, as the best qualified candidate for that office. This office, conferred upon me with such sincere and friendly approbation, I have very gladly and happily accepted, with the realization that, out of a large group of extremely talented men whose wisdom and prestige could be of great service to you, I was the first choice to whom you would entrust the complete handling of your business affairs and law suits. This appointment has clearly indicated to me your opinion of my devotion to duty and the high value that you have ever set upon my services. Consequently, illustrious Gentlemen, while heretofore I have had from your indulgence the greatest possible pleasure, such that it seemed I could not have greater, while, on my part, I have ever regarded you with such affection that I thought I could not add to it; still, as a result of this recent kindness toward me, I am so moved by affection for you and so filled with new joy by your favor that I seem almost not to have been loved by you before nor to have loved you. For your previous favors were at all times such as can proceed only from the noblest love, and I have welcomed each one of them as such kindnesses should be welcomed by a sincere mind and grateful heart. Your most recent display of good will, however, has placed the crown upon all the rest, and it brought before my mind's eye, in momentary flashes, all your previous favors; and yet the recollection of each of them stirred my heart no less than on the day they were bestowed and made me realize that I should be, as I really was, as grateful as if I were then receiving all of them for the first time. These reflections were caused, not by any desire of mine to occupy this office, but by the recurrent thought that those men before whom I have stood in awe since my youth, and whom I have respected, and whose gratitude I have always endeavored to earn, and whose affection I have prayed to win, were vying with one another in honoring me as if that were their one concern. Therefore, most esteemed and cultured Gentlemen, I extend to you all the sincerest gratitude of which I am capable. And I want you to promise yourselves and to expect from More, who is and will always be yours wholeheartedly, all that you would desire, either as a group from a most devoted patron and friend, or individually, from a very dear comrade or brother. I, for my part, will strive with all zeal, care, and diligence so to prove myself to you — both as a group and individually — that not a single one of you may think that he has been deceived in his expectations. Farewell, most cherished Gentlemen. From London, July 26.

> Entirely yours from the bottom of my heart,
> Thomas More

135. To Francis Cranevelt
London, 10 August <1524>

Cordial greetings! I see and I recognize, my dear Cranevelt, how deeply I am in your debt, so unceasingly do you do what to my mind is the most pleasant thing of all—writing about what is happening with you and our friends. For to Thomas More what either should or could be more agreeable in adversity or more pleasant in prosperity than to receive letters from Cranevelt, *the dearest* of *all men?*[280] Unless someone could provide the opportunity to speak with the man himself in person— although whenever I read what you have written, I am so affected by it that while I am reading I seem to be talking with you face to face. Therefore nothing grieves me more distinctly than that your letter is not longer, although for that defect I could also find a sort of remedy: I read the ones I receive over and over, and slowly at that, so that quick reading does not take away the pleasure too quickly. *So much for that!*

As for what you write about our friend Vives,[281] *and* I say it *in a discussion of bad women*, I agree with your opinion so completely that I think it is not possible to live even with the best of them without any inconvenience at all. *For if you happen to have a wife you will not be free of care*, and, so far as I can tell, Metellus Numidicus told the truth about wives.[282] But I would say it all the more emphatically if we were not to blame for causing many women to become worse. Nevertheless, Vives has such character and prudence, and has acquired such a wife, that he will not only avoid all the vexation of marriage, in so far as that is possible, but he will even find great pleasure from it. In fact everyone's mind is now so totally caught up in concern for the welfare of the public, while everywhere war rages and burns in such a way, that no one is free to pay attention to

private worries. Hence whatever domestic concerns once vexed anyone are obscured by the collective disasters. But enough of such matters.

I come back to you: whenever I think of your kindness and your friendship toward me (and I do so very often), I shake off all sadness. I am grateful for the little book you sent me. And I offer hearty congratulations that your family has been increased by new offspring, and indeed I do so not only for your sake but also on behalf of the commonwealth, to which it is very important which parents enlarge it with the most numerous progeny, for from you only the best can be born. Farewell, and greet your most excellent wife from me most diligently and obligingly. From the bottom of my heart I pray for her a happy state of health and well-being. My wife and children also pray for your well-being, for through my eulogies you are no less known and dear to them than to me myself. Once more, farewell. At London, August 10.

> Yours with all my heart and more,
> Thomas More

136. To Cardinal Wolsey
Hertford, 29 November <1524>

It may like your good Grace to be advertised[283] that yesternight at my coming unto the King's Grace's presence, after that I had made your Grace's recommendations and his Highness showed himself very greatly glad and joyful of your Grace's health; as I was about to declare further to his Grace what letters I had brought, his Highness perceiving letters in my hand, prevented[284] me ere[285] I could begin and said, "Ah! ye have letters now by John Joachim[286] and I trow[287] some resolution what they will do." "Nay verily, sir," quoth I. "My lord hath yet no word by John Joachim nor John Joachim, as far as my lord knew, had yet no word himself this day in the morning when I departed from his Grace." "No had?" quoth he, "I much marvel thereof for John Joachim had a servant come to him two days ago." "Sir," quoth I, "if it like your Grace,[288] this morning my Lord's Grace had nothing heard thereof, for yesterday his Grace at afternoon dispatched me to

---

280 These italicized phrases are in Greek in the original.   281 Juan Luis Vives (1492–1540)   282 See Aulus Gellius, *Noctes Atticae* 1.6.   283 informed   284 anticipated   285 before   286 John Joachim de Passano was secretary to Fregoso, governor of Genoa, and resident at the Court of France.   287 trust   288 *if it like your Grace:* if your Grace like

your Grace with a letter sent from Master Doctor Knight[289] and the same night late his Grace sent a servant of his to my house and commanded me to be with his Grace this morning by eight of the clock, where at my coming he delivered me these other letters and advertisements[290] sent unto him from Master Pace, commanding me that after that your Highness had seen them, I should remit[291] them to him with diligence, as well for that he would show them to other of your Grace's Council as also to John Joachim, for the contents be such as will do him little pleasure." "Marry,"[292] quoth his Grace, "I am well apaid thereof."[293]

And so he fell in merrily to the reading of the letters of Master Pace and all the other abstracts and writings, whereof the contents as highly contented him as any tidings that I have seen come to him, and thanked your Grace most heartily for your good and speedy advertisement; and forthwith he declared the news and every material point, which upon the reading his Grace well noted unto the Queen's Grace and all other about him who were marvelous glad to hear it. And the Queen's Grace said that she was glad that the Spaniards had yet done somewhat in Italy in recompense of[294] their departure out of Provence.

I showed his Highness that your Grace thought that the French King passed the mountains in hope to win all with a visage[295] in Italy and to find there no resistance and his sudden coming upon[296] much abashed the countries, putting each quarter in doubt of other and out of surety[297] who might be well trusted, but now since he findeth it otherwise, missing the help of money, which he hoped to have had in Milan, finding his enemies strong and the fortresses well manned and furnished and at Pavia, by the expugnation[298] whereof he thought to put all the remnant in fear and dread, being now twice rejected[299] with loss and reproach, his estimation[300] shall so decay and his friends fail, his enemies confirmed and encouraged, namely, such aid of the Almaignes[301] of new[302] joining with them, that like as

the French King before wrote and boasted unto his mother[303] that he had of his own mind passed into Italy, so is it likely that she shall have shortly cause to write again to him that it had to be much better and more wisdom for him to abide at home than to put himself there whereas he standeth in great peril whether ever he shall get thence. The King's Grace laughed and said that he thinketh it will be very hard for him to get thence, and that he thinketh the matters going thus the Pope's Holiness will not be hasty neither in peace nor truce.

Upon the reading of Master Knight's letter his Grace said not much, but that if Bewreyne[304] come to his Grace he will be plain with him. And if he do not, but take his dispatch there of your Grace, which thing I perceive his Highness would be well content he did, except he desire to come to his presence, his Grace requireth yours so to talk with him as he may know that his Grace and yours well perceive how the matters be handled by the Emperor's agents in the enterprise.

The King's Grace is very glad that the matters of Scotland be in so good train[305] and would be loath that they were now ruffled[306] by the Earl of Angwishe[307] and much his Highness alloweth the most prudent mind of your Grace, minding to use the Earl of Angwish for an instrument to wring and wrest the matters into better train if they walk awry,[308] and not to wrestle with them and break[309] them when they go right.

It may like your Grace also to be advertised[310] that I moved his Grace concerning the suit of Master Broke in such wise as your Grace declared unto me your pleasure, when Master Broke and I were with your Grace on Sunday. And his Grace answered me that he would take a breath[311] therein and that he would first once speak with the young man and then his Grace departed, but I perceived by his Grace that he had taken the young man's promise not to marry without his advice, because his Grace intended to marry him to some one of the Queen's maidens. If it would like your good Grace in any

289 Dr. William Knight, ambassador at the court of Margaret of Austria-Savoy, the Emperor's aunt and regent in the Netherlands **290** notifications **291** send back **292** originally, the name of the Virgin Mary, but by the sixteenth century a common interjection **293** *apaid thereof:* paid for it **294** *in recompense of:* as an

equivalent for **295** *all with a visage:* merely by showing his face **296** attack **297** uncertain **298** taking by storm **299** repulsed. Pace reported the failure of two assaults on Pavia by Francis I. **300** repute **301** Germans **302** newly **303** Louise of Savoy was regent for Francis I. **304** Florys d'Egmont, Lord of Iselstein, the

Emperor's lieutenant; afterwards Count de Buren **305** order **306** disordered **307** Archibald Douglas, Earl of Angus, second husband of the Queen of Scotland **308** *walk awry:* go perversely **309** ruin **310** informed **311** respite

letter which it should please your Grace hereafter to write hither, to make some mention and remembrance of that matter, I trust it would take good effect. And thus our Lord long preserve your good
5 Grace in honor and health.

> At Hertford the twenty-ninth day of November.
> Your Grace's humble orator[312] and most
> bounden beadsman,[313]
> Thomas More
10 To my Lord Legate's good Grace.

138. To Francis Cranevelt
London, 16 May <1525>

I was pleased, my dear Cranevelt, to receive the quite delightful letter which you sent me from
15 Ghent, from which I understood that both you and all of yours are well, and that news gave me great joy. To let you know in turn about me, I, too, and all of my people are in excellent health, thank heavens.

When I got your letter, our friend Vives had de-
20 parted to rejoin his wife. For some time now we have had the booklet you wrote about, the one published against our friend Erasmus.[314] To me and to many others it seems that it was put out with an assignment to a false author. Hence I would like you
25 to inquire who the real author was, who brought it to the printers, for perhaps it can be learned from them. But if that can be found out, please inform me, so that I too many know who that ass is that has covered himself with the hide of another beast. I
30 am as glad to hear that Fevijn has recovered as I was sorry to learn that he had suffered an illness. Please give him, and your excellent wife, my best regards. As for me there is nothing new. I am sending you and your spouse a number of consecrated rings as
35 a little gift and together with them my best regards. London May 14. Farewell, my good man and dearest friend.

> Yours with all my heart and more,
> Thomas More
40 To the very eminent gentleman, Frans Cranevelt, at Ghent

139. To Francis Cranevelt
London, 6 June <1525>

Greetings, my dear Cranevelt. I received your short letter, to which I am compelled to respond in an
45 even shorter one. What you heard about Luther is true. My arrival was delayed but I hope that I will be with you in August. In the meantime farewell, together with the wife who is mine by day and yours by night but the mistress of us both. London, in
50 haste, June 6.

> Yours, Thomas More
To the most distinguished gentleman Master Frans Cranevelt, at Bruges

142. To Francis Cranevelt
55
London, 22 February <1526>

I was delighted, my dearest Cranevelt, with your letter, which Harst[315] delivered to me. Comparing the pictures of the spouses with your description, I could clearly see (and I was glad to see, precisely
60 for the sake of the mistress) that you are not yet growing old, since you are still such an outstanding judge of beauty. The monarchs have agreed on peace — God knows how long it will last. I wish it would last forever, and I do not entirely despair of
65 that. For they have learned enough of the evils of war to see very well that to enter into it again is not to their advantage. I would hope with more confidence if the terms under which the agreement was concluded were a little gentler than they are said
70 to be (how accurately I do not know). The scoundrels who conspired to produce the trumpery of Taxander,[316] like serpents who have spit out their venom, have hidden themselves in darkness, but the infamy of buffoons comes to light. By the death of
75 Dorp true learning has suffered a great loss indeed. I cannot praise you enough, indeed. I cannot praise you enough, my dear Cranevelt, for the very elegant poem in which you paid your last respects. On my behalf please give best regards to your mistress, and
80 likewise mine. Farewell, Cranevelt, most learned

---

312 suppliant   313 one who prays for another   314 *Apologia in eum librum quem ab anno Eramus Roterodamus de confessione edidit, per Godefridum Ruysium Taxandrum theologum. Eiusdem libellus quo taxatur Delectus Ciborum sive* *Liber de Carnium Esu, ante biennium per Erasmum Roterdamum enixus* (1525), a pamphlet attacking Erasmus's writings on confession. The dedication to "Taxander" was to Edward Lee, but the identities of the authors are uncertain.   315 Karl Harst (1492–1563), Erasmus's messenger   316 See Letter 138 for More's discussion of the pamphlet against Erasmus, which was dedicated to "Taxander," or Edward Lee.

and most dear to my heart. London, February 22, in great haste.

To Master Cranevelt of the Council of Mechelen

142a. From Dr. Johann Eck[317]

Ingolstadt, <*ca.* February 1526>

Johann Eck sends greetings to the most illustrious man Thomas More, Knight.[318]

Perhaps you accuse me of ingratitude because I have not written to you after returning to Germany. I am now writing so that you might not continue to accuse me. Although, we should measure gratitude by the mind, not by epistles. For your humane service toward me will never lose its force.[319] As surety, I am sending you my *Enchiridion*, now enriched. I have entrusted to the printer's press the very agreeable book of William Ross, your countryman (which I think you've seen).

Goodbye, and love me.[320]

In Ingoldstadt, Bavaria

143. To John Bugenhagen[321]

<*ca.* 1526>[322]

As I was returning home from a trip, one of my servants gave me a letter which he said he had gotten from someone he had never seen before. When I opened it, Pomeranus,[323] I found that it was written in your name, but whose hand it was in I do not know. And it was written in such a way as to seem addressed to me neither personally nor generally. For you addressed it, "To the Saints in England." I am, against my will, as far removed from those who truly deserve such a noble title as I am glad to remove myself from the only ones you regard as saints, Pomeranus. For I see that nothing is sacred to you except the Lutheran sect.

And so I was puzzled at first as to how it had come into his head—whoever he was—to want to force such a letter on me, especially me, for I had never got mixed up in the Lutheran business. But

when I thought about it more carefully, I began to suspect that maybe that was it: someone thought I was the right person to try such a letter on precisely because I had not really become involved in the controversy up to that point. When everyone here was crying out everywhere against Luther's foul heresies, I said almost nothing about it. I was not a theologian, and the part I played in the world did not require me to deal with corruption of that kind. I suspect some Lutheran hoped that such a letter—one that seemed on the surface so devout—would easily lure me from my impartial stand and make me take sides with him.

I turned these things over in my mind. Although your letter needed no reply and although I had firmly resolved to avoid all contact with that dangerous disease of yours, I nevertheless decided that it was forced on me against my will. And besides, by keeping quiet, I might perhaps increase the misplaced hope of the person who gave it to me. So I decided to reply to your letter and make it clear to everyone that no matter how ignorant I am of theology I am still too loyal a Christian ever to be a Lutheran. And so I will answer the parts of your epistle one by one, and let you see readily enough what you have accomplished in each. You begin, then, like this:

> Grace be to you and peace from God our Father and our Lord Jesus Christ.[324]

There is nothing wrong with that, but you would have seemed more modest if you had imitated the conduct of the apostle rather than the apostolic style. For this is almost apostolic too:

> We could not but rejoice when we heard that in England, too, the Gospel of the glory of God has been well received by certain persons.[325]

On reading these words are we not reminded of the apostle congratulating the Church when it was still a suckling babe in the cradle? How cleverly you imitate him! Just as the Gospel was first preached to the Corinthians or Galatians in the time of the

317 Translated by Bradley Ritter, © CTMS 2018. **318** The title used here by Eck, *eques auratus*, is for those given an honorary knighthood by the king (see E. E. Reynolds, "Eques Auratus," *Moreana* nos. 65–66: 131). **319** See Cicero, *Epistulae ad familiares* 6.16. **320** A similar valediction is found often in Cicero (see *Epistulae ad familiares* 7.5, 15.19, 16.8, 16.26, and 16.27). **321** a Protestant humanist (1485–1558) from Pomerania, a region near the Baltic Sea in present-day Germany and Poland **322** Although written in 1525–26, this letter was put aside and not published until after More's death, in 1568. **323** Bugenhagen was called Pomeranus because he was born in Pomerania. More addresses him only by this name. **324** *CW* 7: 398; see Eph 1:1. **325** *CW* 7: 398

apostles, so too, now that you are preaching, you would have us believe, the Gospel finally begins to be heard and welcomed by the British. But this is all so new, you say, and occurs so infrequently that the Gospel of God is still not well received in Britain except among a few people.

I do not know what you call the "gospel." But I know this: if you agree that the Gospel is what Christ revealed to the world, and what the four Evangelists—Matthew, Mark, Luke, and John—wrote in the past, and what all the ancient leaders of the Church interpreted as the Gospel, and what the whole Christian world for more than fifteen hundred years has understood and taught as the Gospel—this "gospel," I say, has been well received in England continuously for a thousand years, more or less. In fact the faith of the Gospels was welcomed everywhere in this nation and accepted even by those who were too weak and frail to act in a way that was worthy of the Gospels. But if you want us to take as "gospel" those new, destructive, absurd doctrines that Luther, like another Antichrist, recently introduced among the Saxons—those doctrines that you, Karlstadt, Lambert, and Oecolampadius[326] (Luther's cacangelists)[327] foment and scatter throughout the world—if that is what you mean by the "gospel," then there is hardly anyone in England who welcomes that gospel of yours. And for that we are very glad indeed.

But we have also been told that many weaklings still reject us because of vague rumors reported of us there by those who oppose the gospel of God. This is our glory. I consider it unnecessary to refute the lies told about those who proclaim the gospel. How else could we experience in our own lives the beatitude, "Blessed shall you be when men have reviled you"?[328]

As a matter of fact it is not the weaklings who turn away from you, but those who are much firmer in faith. They turn away not because of any lies told against those who profess the gospel (as you call the Lutherans), but because of the unending sins which you perverters of the Gospel all too truly perpetrate. I ask you, what lies are you talking about? Or how do you profess the Gospel? Would you call it a lie if someone says your sect has destroyed a good part of Germany in riots, murder, looting, and arson? Do you dare call people liars who testify that your unholy doctrine is the cause of so many crimes, so many injuries, so much desolation? Inciting riots, setting laymen against clergy, arming the people against magistrates, inflaming the people against princes, plotting battles, disasters, wars, massacres—do you call that preaching the Gospel? Since you are a distinguished preacher of the Gospel, tell us, I beg of you, whether one who destroys the sacraments of Christ, rejects the saints of Christ, blasphemes the mother of Christ, scorns the cross of Christ, makes light of vows made to Christ, renounces celibacy dedicated to Christ, defiles virginity consecrated to Christ, urges marriage (that is to say, everlasting defilement) on monks and virgins veiled for Christ—and who urges these things not just with words, foul as they may be, but who provokes them as well with his filthy example—tell us, I say, you famous preacher of the gospel—or evangelist of Luther, if you like, for Luther himself is your Christ—tell us whether doing and teaching these shameful things is what you call preaching the Gospel.

There is no doubt, then, just as I said: it is not the weaklings who turn away from you, but those who are much firmer in faith. They turn away from you not only because of the truth told about you—I mean the vicious evils your faction is responsible for, which is why God pursues your vicious sect with manifest vengeance—they also turn away from you because they see that your doctrines are opposed to the teaching of Christ in a fight to the finish.

And speaking of doctrines—in almost every instance they have clear scriptural evidence to oppose to your efforts. Still, to be certain they are not deceived about the meaning of Scripture, they have first of all everyone of the fathers to set against your wild yawps. (But of course that is all you want, to prove your points by yelling.) They have all the ancient fathers who were enlightened by God and not only interpreted Scripture, but also provided an example of noble behavior and thus increased the piety of the Christian people. They also have the support of an unshaken consensus of the whole Christian world through all the ages, from the Passion of Christ down to your own time. But perhaps

---

326 Andreas Bodenstein von Karlstadt (*ca.* 1480–1541), François Lambert (*ca.* 1486–1530), and Johannes

Hussgen or Oecolampadius (1482–1531) **327** *Cacangelist* is More's invention, a combination of the Greek χαχός ("bad,

evil") and ἀγγέλλειν ("to announce"). **328** *CW* 7: 398; Mt 5:11

you object that this consensus came about without the help of the Holy Spirit, who makes all men of one mind in his house. Or you may want to pretend that the devil deceived the whole Church through all those centuries and brought it together in a consensus against Christ's Gospel. If that is the case, you are simply denying the possibility of any faith in the Gospel of Christ whatsoever. For unless the Church had shown you the Gospel in the first place, you would have had no way of knowing what it is. You admit that yourselves.

They also score this against you, that almost everything you currently teach was previously taught by men whose errors have long since been condemned by the fathers of the Church. Whenever heretics gather together, the Church has always driven them out, and God has revealed their wickedness by the punishment inflicted on them. But you, on the other hand, have nothing whatsoever to insinuate against the lives of the blessed fathers, whose memory the Church has venerated for so many ages past. All of them fight for our faith and overthrow yours. A person, therefore, would have to be mad to follow the founders of your faith down where their errors have drowned them. Anyone would prefer to join himself to those who reign with Christ, and you have no doubt that they do reign with him, even though out of hatred and envy you do whatever you can to disparage them. At first you wrongly persuaded yourselves somehow that you were the only ones who knew anything and that learned men among orthodox Christians never read anything except scholastic controversies. And so, relying on the ignorance of others (as it seemed to you), you stated that you would take your stand on the opinions of the holy fathers. Afterward, however, you saw that your hope and expectations were all wrong. The testimony of those saintly men refuted all your basic principles. Then in truth your pride led you to such monstrous hatred that, since you are ashamed to submit to heaven, you have decided to damn everything to hell. And so, you gave birth to this ungodly and completely insane blasphemy: "I care not for ten Jeromes, I care not for a hundred Cyprians, I care not for a thousand Augustines, nor for ten thousand Chrysostoms."[329]

And finally, for fear the glorious majesty and splendor of the saints who reign with Christ will dim your lights, you have begun to destroy the received opinion about them. You attack their reputation, disparage their authority, and take away as much of their veneration and honor as you possibly can. But they are powerful and invulnerable, Pomeranus. They stand at this moment on a lofty rock and laugh at your feeble attacks as at the arrows of children.[330] For the friends of God are accorded honor and they always will be.[331] Their memory will live forever. But the memory of all those will perish together with the sound of their words,[332] all those who created the labyrinths of your deceptions, from the time of the very first heretic, whoever that was, through all the ages. Although thousands of orthodox books have been preserved over the centuries, increasing in value with age, the works of all the heretics have disappeared shortly after their deaths. No work of any ancient heretic exists today. And yet when those heretical works disappeared in ages past, there was no law that said they had to be consigned to the flames. It was thus clearly demonstrated that God destroyed them himself by his own hand so that the snares of heretics might give way like spiderwebs and disappear completely, neglected like dirt and filth. No doubt just as quick a destruction threatens and overhangs your labors, for they constitute a far greater danger to Christian piety. Envy may well bare its teeth and snarl, but the memory of those holy fathers will be revered, their works will grow in popularity, and the faithful will ever draw from them an antidote against the poisons with which you infect the life-giving wellspring of Scripture. The fathers of the Church stand firmly in consensus against you, but you also stand just as firmly in opposition to yourselves because of your own internal dissension. You not only contend against one another, but each of you also disagrees with himself, over and over again. No doubt Catholics turn away from you because of the things I have mentioned and many others like them. I also have no doubt that you alienate thoughtful people by the unspeakably wicked crimes your faction commits.

God love me, I am amazed, time and again, at this: how you can have the gall to write that people are lying about you and that that is all your glory? Have you no shame? How can you stand yourself

---

329 See Luther's *Contra Henricum* (WA 10.2: 215).
330 *arrows of children:* See Ps 63:8(64:7).
331 *the friends . . . be:* See Ps 138(139):17.
332 *memory . . . words:* See Ps 9:7.

when you say that the murderers belonging to your sect are falsely accused when you know yourself they are guilty as charged, witness the uprisings all over Germany and the slaughter of so many thousands. Unbridled license rages to such an extent under pretext of freedom of the Gospel that there is hardly a city in most of Germany, hardly a town, countryseat, house, or farm where your sect has not left bitter reminders of looting, rape, bloodshed, sacrilege, slaughter, fire, ruin, and devastation. When your sect commits such monstrous, sacrilegious crimes, Pomeranus, how can you chant to us so evangelically that *this is our glory*? You do not bother to make a rebuttal, you simply proclaim that you are blessed when men curse you. And you would be right if people were making up lies about you. You would be right if you were cursed because you did what was right. But no one could possibly invent anything about you worse than what you already teach and do, and so your argument is completely beside the point. How splendidly you preen yourself! You put it, of course, that you are blessed because men curse you for the sake of righteousness, when in fact both man and God curse you with perfect justice because of your iniquities, because of your crimes, your sedition, slaughter, pillaging, heresies, and pernicious schisms.

You are obviously encouraged because such things do not happen at Wittenberg, for it is remarkable how you seem to qualify your language by immediately adding:

> But we make no defense if men elsewhere perform unchristian acts under the pretext of Christian liberty, since not everyone who claims for himself the name of Christ has put on Christ.[333]

How discreetly, how cautiously you put all that, Pomeranus — "if anyone" … "if anything" … "if elsewhere" … "if unchristian" — when you are well aware that it is almost everywhere and everything and everyone — everyone, that is, who belongs to your sect. You do things that are not only unchristian, but absolutely diabolic. If Wittenberg refrains from participating in those crimes, do you think that is sufficient reason for people to attribute any authority to your beliefs? After all, we can see that your beliefs stir up, endanger, and destroy all the

rest of Germany. Who could believe that Wittenberg is pure and innocent when he sees that it is the fountain from which flows all the sewage and filthy muck that carries foul corruption and broadens out through all the earth?

But of course Wittenberg is innocent. It is simply the place where Luther pitched his camp — Luther, captain of evildoing, architect and artificer of evil, leader of an army of savages. In council with you and his other lieutenants he makes plans hour by hour, devising nothing but how to incite rebellions, subvert the faith, uproot religion, profane holy things, corrupt morals, prostitute virgins, and destroy virtue. Just as if it were a council of war, the signal is given, passwords devised, commands issued, and reinforcements dispatched. You hurled a burning torch on all of Germany. You lit the wildfire that is now consuming the world, and you keep on fanning the wicked flames with your poisonous breath. All this is too well known to be concealed, too widely circulated to be denied, and too destructive to be tolerated. So how can you write so sanctimoniously, Pomeranus, and say:

> What surprises us is this: why is it that some people there are afraid to receive the holy Gospel of Christ because evil is spoken of us, not remembering that it behooves the Son of Man to be reproved by the world and the preaching of the cross to be esteemed foolishness?[334]

Stop wondering, Pomeranus. All of you, stop being so immensely and mistakenly pleased with yourselves. Do not be so insane as to want to form an opinion of all the people in Britain from two or three apostates and deserters of the faith of Christ. You know little about the common people. If you did, you would think differently. You know little about the bishops. If you understood what sort of men they are, you would abandon your audacious hopes. And because of his learning, you should at least have known that you could not take over and corrupt the authority of the King of this glorious realm. For he is as devout as he is invincible — completely invincible. He defeated your master long ago when Luther was warring against the sacraments. He defeated him by using overt scriptural evidence and irrefutable logic. So how can you be so confident as to hope to seduce his people? Is it because you dare to claim for yourself the title of Bishop of Wittenberg without the laying on of hands—which is contrary to Sacred Scripture, contrary to the teaching of the saints, contrary to the custom of the entire Church through all the ages? Besides bringing in other heresies, you dared to instruct the people of Wittenberg to ignore vows made to God, acting as if your instruction were wholesome and suited to your holy office. For although you were a priest and had taken the vow of chastity, you joined yourself to a female companion in lust. Did you think that opened the door and cleared the way for you to assume the office of Pope of the English, and to do it so grandly too! You speak as though every success the Gospels enjoy here depends completely on you. You would have us believe that the Gospel prospers when you are well received here, and that when you fall in disgrace, the cause of the Gospel is likewise set back.

You certainly are wrong about that! For the Gospel is not taken so lightly here, nor are you so highly regarded that it is either accepted or rejected because of you. Nor is the Son of Man reproved by us and the preaching of the cross esteemed as foolishness. In fact the cross of Christ is glorious to us Christians, though a stumbling block to the Jews and foolishness to the gentiles. It is utterly ridiculous to hear the Lutherans speak so highly of the cross when their christ (that is, Luther—a man deserving a few crosses himself) vomits such ungodly blasphemies against the cross of Christ, which bore his holy and venerable body during his Passion—or rather, our redemption. If anyone thinks I am inventing all this, he has only to read Luther's detestable sermon on the cross,[335] which is on sale almost everywhere, along with other still more sinful tracts by the same author and others, exuding their foul odor and hellish stench. But you act as if all your books fluttered down from heaven smelling of pure nectar, pure ambrosia, and so you are not ashamed to write:

> What if the lies that men tell about us for Christ's sake were true? Would they therefore not accept the Gospel of salvation offered to them by God? What could be more foolish than to be more concerned with my wickedness than with your own

salvation! Will you therefore be no Christian because I am a sinner?

Wonderful! You put that so well and so cleverly! Is it a lie to say that although you were a priest and had vowed to God never to marry, you have nevertheless taken a wife? Or to say that, although you want to be regarded as a bishop, you are a common fornicator every day of your life? Or is it a lie to say the same thing about your friend Lambert, who was a Franciscan, and many other Lutherans as well? Or is it a lie to say that Luther himself, when he was an Augustinian monk, engaged in whoredom, not marriage, with a nun dedicated to God for many years and then stolen from him? Or is it a lie to say that all of you introduce wicked, crazy heresies or to proclaim that your sect commits many disgraceful things throughout the world? Would that the miserable devastation of so many places and the pitiful destruction of so many thousands of people seduced by your teaching did not prove how true all these statements are.

But these manifold sins of yours should not be an obstacle to our receiving the Gospel of salvation from you. Would you have us believe that through you God first offered us the Gospel of salvation? The Gospel of Christ, the Gospel that the Evangelists wrote, the apostles preached, and the holy fathers of the Church interpreted, was not that the Gospel of salvation? Was no one saved from the time of Christ's Passion until this present moment, when God finally chose you to save the world and preach the Gospel of salvation to wretched mortals, corrupted and led astray until now by the apostles and Evangelists? You lie, Pomeranus, when you say that we lie about you and that the things we say are not true, for they are true indeed. Is it so odd, then, considering your wickedness, that we do not trust you enough or think you are the right sort of people to bring others health and salvation when you yourselves suffer from such horrible running sores? For if after all these years Christians still did not possess the true Gospel of Christ and if the whole Church were mistaken about the faith of Christ for so many generations, God would have undoubtedly chosen some good, holy men for his work of recalling the world from the flesh to a renewal of the spirit. In something as important as that God

335 See *WA* 10.3: 332–34, 369–71.

would undoubtedly also have performed miracles to encourage belief in what was being preached. He would not have been so careless as to choose to preach his faith those very men, and only those men, to whom he had already forbidden that right. For through the prophet God spoke to the sinner: "What right have you to speak of my laws and take my covenant upon your lips?"[336] Since God wanted all men to believe his holy preachers, why would he be so careless as not to do anything whereby people could or should believe them?

Luther claims it is a miracle that in such a short time so many Christians deserted the faith of Christ and went over to his heresies. To be sure, his heresies are absurd and crazy enough to make it seem like a portent of some sort that anyone with a spark of human intelligence would entertain such wild beliefs. As for people rushing headfirst into the life of freedom and sensual gratification he offers them — that seems about as much like a miracle as rocks falling downhill.

Now as for that question of yours, Pomeranus, why people do not follow Paul's rule: "Test all things, and hold fast to what is good."[337] That one sentence of Paul's subverts everything you say. When we test all things, we discover that what you write is the worst, and we hold fast to the good. And the good we hold fast to is the writings of those men whose life and faith God indicates were pleasing to him. We reject your writings because they are contrary to the deeds and teaching of the holy fathers and, what is even more important, because they are contrary to the faith of the people of the whole Church through so many centuries. If God did not guide the faith of his Church, the authority of the Gospel would waver, and there would truly be no truth in the words whereby Truth promises he will be with her even to the end of the world.[338]

It would be useful now to consider a bit how carefully and tenderly you touch the sore spot in your teaching.

But, the less educated will say (you assert), "Who is able to understand all these different arguments? Men dispute about free will, about vows and monastic orders, about works of satisfaction, abuse of the holy Eucharist, the worship of saints, the whereabouts of the dead, and purgatory."

Others say, "We are afraid that poison is hidden under all this disagreement."[339]

You do not have it right, Pomeranus. No one is afraid that poison is hidden under all this disagreement. On the contrary, we see and we know that the poison is there, very real and apparent. You do not bother to discuss it soberly and rationally. You simply pontificate about it impudently and arrogantly. You always mock scholastic theology on the pretext that it is dangerous because it brings truth into doubt. But you assert that falsehood is absolutely true, even against the truth. The only thing you accept as truth is what theology proposes in the schools merely for the sake of argument.

In the schools men raise such questions as whether the will has any freedom, whether all things occur at random, whether they are ruled by fate, whether the unchanging will of the divine majesty has decreed all things from eternity in such a way that in the whole natural order he allows no possibility for anything to follow one alternative rather than the other, whether man's free will and God's foreknowledge contradict one another, whether Adam's sin removed our free will, or whether it is removed by Christ's grace. When these questions and others like them are proposed in the schools and are discussed calmly and for a pious purpose, the debate produces results that are quite useful. For theologians enter into debate together with no doubt as to the final outcome. They always carry around in their heads firm and unshakable conclusions about everything they discuss — the same conclusions that are impressed on the hearts of all the faithful by the teachings of the Christian faith, and many of them also by some public pronouncement of the the ordinary belief. Take people who have some shred of human intelligence. They are convinced that God, who makes all things, foresees all things. At the same time they also know from experience that they do what they do by their own free will and not from some external compulsion. Now when theologians bring reason or Scripture to bear on what they hold to be true and infallible, then they use their talents to advantage. They solve many problems by the inspiration of God, who assists devout endeavors, for which they give him thanks. They not only take an intellectual pleasure in this — one that is

336 Ps 49(50):16   **337** 1 Thes 5:21   **338** Mt 28:20   **339** *CW* 7: 398

most pleasant, most honest, and I might even add most holy—they also give others the fruits of their teachings, which are not only sound, but well worth knowing. They shed light on passages of Scripture by comparing those that seem contrary to truth with other passages that are more easily understood. But suppose someone thinks a particular text in Sacred Scripture is so hard and difficult that no one, neither ancient nor modern, can interpret it satisfactorily so as to make it seem not contradictory to some common article of the Catholic faith. Then all of a sudden he recalls the advice of the holy father Augustine that there is either a mistake in the text or he hasn't followed the sense of the passage well enough. For no passage in Sacred Scripture ought to disturb me like that. If it seems to contradict what the Catholic Church of Christ has embraced as sure and undoubted articles of faith, I should not allow it to separate me and drive me away from the genuine, legitimate teachings of the Christian faith, since I am convinced that these teachings were written in the hearts of the faithful by the same Spirit who was present to the Evangelists as they wrote. And so whatever they wrote is consistent with the faith of the Church so long as it remains as it was written and can be understood in the same sense in which it was written. Even if there is a corrupt reading in the text or if the text itself is somewhat obscure, there is no reason to believe less firmly in what Christ taught his Church. Through the Holy Spirit he instructed the Church in all truth[340] and promised that he would be with her even to the end of time.[341] Christ will certainly see to it that the faith of the Church will not falter. This was a promise he obtained from the Father through prayer.[342] It will not falter through errors in the text, for he corrects these day after day through the devout labor of dedicated men; nor through ambiguities in the literal sense, for he explains these, at such times as he finds appropriate, through the pens of learned men; nor through the persecutions of tyrants, for he has subdued them through the victories of his martyrs; nor through the endeavors of heretics, for he has stopped their mouths through the books of the orthodox fathers; nor from the machinations of the devil, for on the cross he laid him low.

Reverence is not lost if in the course of a dispute reason seems to run counter to truth, for it is absolutely certain that since faith is sustained by divine revelation, it far surpasses the reason of mortal men. The less we are able to understand the nature and causes of things, the more pleasure we take in observing them. And so it is with the divine majesty: we are all the more caught up in sweet wonder at it, the more some things seem to disagree and conflict with one another, at the same time as we realize that they undoubtedly agree with one another and come together in harmony. So you see, Pomeranus, the schools are capable of examining these things harmlessly and not without profitable results. But you attack scholastic disputation as something that opposes truth and violates mystery. At the same time, however, you command everyone to believe without any serious discussion your own absurd conclusions and crazy heresies in opposition to all men and to God himself. And you demand that whatever foolishness Luther chooses to utter be considered irrefutable, and as the Greeks say, ἀκίνητον.[343] If anyone asks why you believe the dogmas of this crazy, impious man, he has to be satisfied with the answer αὐτὸς ἔφα,[344] and no wonder either, since Luther proclaims he is certain he got his dogmas from heaven. And though you have nothing to bring to bear against the judgment of the entire Church through all the ages except Luther's own inane inventions, nevertheless, Pomeranus, to make it seem that you have neatly built up your conclusions, you pretend that you have proved them all by the indisputable evidence of Sacred Scripture.

As if (you say) we deal in the enticing words of human wisdom and not the palpable evidence of Scripture, against which even the gates of hell have not yet been able to prevail. Or as if our adversaries brought forth anything against us except human statutes and traditions, which the Lord condemns in Isaiah 29 and Christ in Matthew 15.[345] What poison, then, are you afraid of, since we do nothing in secret and set all our works before the whole world to be judged?[346]

You put that very nicely, Pomeranus. As if there were no traditions of God, on which the Church of God relies in the sacraments and articles of faith.

---

340 See Jn 16:13. **341** See Mt 28:20. **342** See Jn 14:16. **343** "immovable, steadfast" **344** "He himself said it" is a proverbial expression, attributed to the disciples of Pythagoras when asked to give a reason for their beliefs. See Quintilian 11.1.27; Cicero, *De natura deorum* 1.5.10. **345** Is 29:14; Mt 15:8–9 **346** *CW* 7: 398–400

Or as if the most illustrious King of England and other learned men as well had not proved this clearly to you by reason, Scripture, and the universal opinion of the orthodox fathers, to which no man among you as yet has uttered one word of reply. Or as if you proved everything by Scripture and not by your own fantastic glosses, twisting the authority of Sacred Scripture into your own sacrilegious dogmas against the opinions of all the most learned and most holy ancients. Or as if all heretics had not always done the same thing you do now: they administered their poison to the whole world and openly handed around the cup anointed with the honey of Scripture, which they proclaimed, just as boldly as you do now, to be perfectly clear.[347] For the Arians[348] once proclaimed the same thing the Lutherans do now: that Scripture was clearly with them, while their opponents depended only on human statutes which the Lord condemned. And all the other heretics proclaimed the same thing, especially the Pelagians.[349] You Lutherans are so stupid that when you try to avoid their Scylla, your error snatches you straight off to Charybdis.[350] You do not even try to understand that the Church relies in matters of faith on the traditions of God, not on the traditions of men. And so I am not certain I understand you well enough when you write that you deal in the palpable evidence of Scripture against which the gates of hell have not yet been able to prevail. When you say that you do not deal in the enticing words of human wisdom, that I understand quite well and confess it is absolutely true. But I am not certain how you want the rest of the statement to be taken. Do you mean that the gates of hell have not yet been able to prevail against the Scriptures themselves? Or do you mean that they have not yet been able to prevail against your propositions, which you trick out and clothe in Scripture so that they will be regarded as the Gospel of salvation, which is now first offered by you from on high, rejoicing that it is well received by some people even in Britain?

Actually it does not matter a great deal which one you mean, since it amounts to the same thing either way. The Church of Christ has never yet believed what you teach. It has always rejected it, cursed it, destroyed it by fire. If, then, your doctrines are true and confirmed by clear texts in Scripture, you have to admit that the gates of hell have continuously prevailed against God's Scripture. But if, on the other hand, what you say is true, that the gates of hell have never prevailed against the Scripture of God, then you admit that the faith of the Church has always been in agreement with God's Scripture.

But the faith of the Church has always been opposed to the sort of things you teach. And so, Pomeranus, you see, do you not, it follows that your famous beliefs are contrary to Scripture. Moreover, if you argue that the Church has always thought and believed the same thing you now believe (or rather what you now preach, for so help me God, I cannot imagine you believe what you preach) — tell me, I beg of you, what Church are you talking about? When did it exist before you came along? Where on earth was it located? Tell me that, and I will take you for great Apollo himself. For although some of your heresies had various champions at different times and different places, no one — no one people and no one individual — was ever so fundamentally irreligious and so stupid as to believe so many different, completely absurd heresies as you do. No one, that is, until Luther.

But perhaps you argue that there was always a scattered remnant who, though dispersed, nevertheless constituted the true Church even though they were so few as to be hidden from the world, so scattered as never to meet, so illiterate as never to write, and so dumb as never to speak. If so, you have to admit that the fathers, whom the Church of Christ venerates among the saints, always wrote against this Church of yours.

Or do you hope, Pomeranus, that all Christians are such clods that you can convince them of anything? In the Jewish synagogue God saw to it that the holiest men among them were held in esteem after their death so that the people would not be left in doubt about what models to imitate. That being so, would you have us believe that now, in the Church of his Son, God would allow all his holy and faithful people to lie in dishonor while he saw to it that those who were worshiped as saints should be men

---

347 See Hilary, *De Trinitate* 4, and *Liber ad Constantium Augustum* 1.3 (*PL* 10, 559) 348 The heresy of Arianism, which maintained that Christ was created by the Father, was condemned at the Council of Constantinople in 381. 349 Pelagianism, which arose in the fifth century, promoted the belief that human will is capable of a sinless life without divine aid, minimizing man's need for Christ's sacrifice. 350 *Scylla . . . Charybdis:* a mythological monster living on one side of a narrow channel and a whirlpool on the other side of the same narrow channel. See Homer, *Odyssey* Book 12.

who were heretics and fundamentally irreligious, who had seduced the whole world with their writings, who had drawn it away from the true meaning of the Gospel by their false preaching? Would you have us believe that he adorned some of these men with martyrdom, distinguished them all with integrity of life, and never failed to render them illustrious through miracles, demonstrating their piety to the world through wholesome signs and tokens so that no one could doubt that their faith was pleasing to God? Tell me, do you really think God purposely did all this to deceive his own Church? Like it or not, Pomeranus, you have to admit that this is God's Church and that it had within it and as its teachers the holy fathers whom we venerate. If you argue that they were all mistaken in matters of faith, then you have to admit what you denied before, that the gates of hell have prevailed against the Scriptures for more than a thousand years. But if you think you have to stick with what you said before, that the gates of hell have never been able to prevail against the Gospel, then you must also admit that the holy fathers were right in matters of faith. Once you have granted that, then no matter how much you squirm about, you are going to have to admit that what you bullheadedly force on us as the Gospel is completely wrong. For you are unable to deny that the fathers of the Church have already condemned what you teach.

It may be worth our while to learn how you rake up the diverse and far flung rubbish of your teachings in a neat little pile. For you go on to say:

> And lest you plead as an excuse the variety of our teaching, let me say briefly that we teach but one article of faith no matter how much we preach every day, no matter how much we write against our opponents so that they too may be saved. And this is that one article: Christ is our righteousness. For God made him our wisdom, righteousness, satisfaction, redemption. Whoever does not grant us this is no Christian; whoever agrees with us in this will soon give over all righteousness of man.[351]

The soul of brevity! You do not write anything, then, you do not teach anything except that Christ is our righteousness? Does this one holy pronouncement encompass all your dogmas, varied as they are, discordant with one another, absurd, and impious? If one were to grant you this, that Christ is our righteousness, does he also have to admit that the bread in the Eucharist remains bread? That the Mass is of no use to anyone? That the whole Church has performed the sacrifice incorrectly up till now? That up to now it has used an impious and sacrilegious canon, and that the sacrament of ordination is an empty lie? And will this follow logically: Christ is our righteousness, therefore a woman is fit to hear sins in the sacrament of confession? And a woman can consecrate the Body of Christ? And this: Christ is our righteousness, therefore there is no purgatory? And no free will? And no human law a Christian has to obey? Christ is our righteousness, therefore faith alone is sufficient for salvation, and there is no need for good works? And nothing can damn a Christian except his lack of faith alone? Christ is our righteousness, therefore a monk ought to take a wife? Do all these beliefs and many others just as absurd necessarily follow from the fact that Christ is our righteousness? Why not? For if God made Christ your righteousness, what need have you to seek out and follow righteousness? If he was made your wisdom, what need have you to be as cunning as a serpent?[352] If he was made your satisfaction, what need have you to deliver your limbs as servants to righteousness unto holiness as you delivered your limbs as servants to uncleanliness unto iniquity?[353] If he was made your redemption, what need have men to ransom their souls by using their wealth?[354] After mentioning this article of faith, you explained it so well, believing you had proved it to the judges' satisfaction, that you immediately add:

> Whoever agrees with us in this will soon give over all righteousness of man. There will be no trace left here of the Pelagian heresy, by which (although the words are changed) they have been infected who boast that they are the only ones who are Christians. The sects that exist today will count for nothing, nor will all their trust in good works, which our self-justifiers have thrust upon us, rejecting the stumbling block of Christ's cross, peddling works instead of Christ. Against them and against the entire kingdom of Satan we bring forth with Paul this most powerful argument: If

---

351 *CW* 7: 400   **352** *cunning…serpent:* Mt 10:16   **353** Rom 6:19   **354** Prv 13:8

we are made righteous by works and by our own free will, then Christ died in vain.[355] This righteousness which is Christ is testified to by the law and the prophets (Romans 3).[356] A man who follows his own righteousness, will, like the Jews, not arrive at true righteousness (Romans 9).[357] They are not able to submit to God's righteousness (Romans 10).[358] This righteousness of God is yours when you receive Christ through faith. For he did not die for his own sake or for his own sins, but for your sake and for your sins. Whatever else, therefore, you have tried in order to arrive at righteousness — that is, to become righteous and free from the judgment of God, from sin, death, and hell — will be hypocrisy, lies, and wickedness, no matter how it shines with a semblance of piety. For it will strive against the grace of God and deny Christ.[359]

I have no doubt, Pomeranus, that you think you put that extremely well. But you fail to see that all this brilliant discussion of yours is based on two fundamental lies. You use them shamelessly to slander the Church and make that sacrosanct preaching of yours seem like the true Gospel. In the first place you are absolutely incorrect to imply that we are infected by the Pelagian heresy, though our terminology is different.

You also lie when you say that we refused the stumbling block of Christ's cross, introduced a reliance on works and sects, and peddle works instead of Christ. To amuse yourself you call us at times self-justifiers and at other times braggarts who boast that they alone are Christians. Although nothing is more opposed to the teaching of the Church than to attribute anything to oneself, nevertheless Catholic Christians are permitted in the name of the whole Church in general to claim justifiably with a kind of holy pride that they are the only ones who are righteous, that they are the only ones who are Christian. For among men there is no holiness outside the Church, nor any Christian either.

But let me return to the subject at hand. The Church does not hold with Pelagius when he says that the strength and power of nature, along with some general influx of grace, are enough to enable a man to do good. The Church holds instead that special grace is needed for every good act. Similarly, the Church disagrees with you even more when you cunningly try to exalt the grace of God in order to destroy completely the force of man's free will. You say nothing about the freedom of the will except that "it exists only in name,"[360] to use your own words, that it accomplishes nothing, but is simply passive, that it is shaped by God in the same way wax is shaped by the hand of an artist. The Pelagians were completely wrong about all this, but you Lutherans are even more perniciously mistaken. Although the Pelagians attributed too much to nature, they nevertheless attributed the ultimate honor to God since they recognized him as the creator of nature. Moreover, they kept the need to pray for grace since they admitted that it is extremely difficult for nature to function alone and that it works more smoothly supported by grace. But you, on the contrary, leave no reason why we should give thanks to God for the gift of our nature. Our nature is such (if we were to believe you) that we would be better off without it, even after the gift of grace in baptism. For although our nature is such that we constantly slip and fall, it is not capable of rousing itself sufficiently to rise to God's offer of grace. It is not even able to make the effort. Then too, since you preach that our will is merely passive and does nothing whatsoever on its own, do you not destroy the possibility of all human endeavor and all attempts at virtue? Are you not obviously ascribing everything to fate? According to your sect, the will is not only evil in itself, it is not even able to turn toward the good. It is simply God's will that fashions one person for good while another remains evil. There is no reason other than that of one's nature, which one receives through no fault of his own. One who is elected to be good is so shaped and formed by grace that he does not do anything himself, not even cooperate. Just as a tree produces leaves and fruit, so when God works within the elect and nature, which is also his creation, works within the reprobates, the elect bring forth good and the reprobates evil. Now anyone can see that it follows according to your line of reasoning that free will is not free will. With no freedom of choice a man is no different from a tree. No evil can be imputed to man but rather God is necessarily the cause of all deeds, evil as well

355 See Gal 2:21.   **356** Rom 3:21   **359** *CW* 7: 400   **360** See Luther's Heidel-
357 Rom 9:31   **358** Rom 10:3   berg theses of 1518 (*WA* 1: 354, 7: 142).

as good. God's most merciful nature is thought to punish the very sins it has committed. This concept of God is so wicked and so sacrilegious that I'll be damned if I would not rather be Pelagius ten times over than believe for a moment what Luther teaches. But the Church you condemn avoids the errors of both these heresies and condemns them both in turn. The Church believes that without grace man's will is incapable of performing good acts, but that grace is available to all like the light of the sun. Evil men neglect it when it is offered, good men embrace it, and both do what they do according to their own free will. Thus a man who is saved is saved by grace, and yet free will is not inoperative. I do not see anything except by light, and yet I assist the light to some extent when I open my eyes and focus them. If someone lowers a rope in a well and pulls out a man who could not get out by himself, would it not be true that the man in the well did not get out through his own power? And yet he contributed something of his own by hanging onto the rope and not letting it get away. The freedom of the will is similar to that. It can do nothing without grace. But when the divine goodness bestows grace liberally, the free will of a good man clings to it and cooperates with it properly. The free will of an evil man does not accept it and wears itself out in malice. This is what we believe, Pomeranus, and not the lie you tell of us, that we believe Pelagius, nor do we believe you, who are worse than Pelagius. We preserve the respect owed to divine grace and cut off the opportunity you afford vicious men to blame the stubborn malice of their own will on the unavoidable necessity of the divine will.

Now we will treat good works for a while. You are wicked and wrong on this point, and you wantonly, falsely slander the Church. You lie and say that she has given up the stumbling block of Christ crucified and teaches that one should have confidence in sects and good works, peddling works instead of Christ. First, concerning the religious orders, which you call sects and schisms, I do not think it a major crime if under Christ, as under a single general, different men serve under different leaders — military tribunes, as it were. While all of them lead a good life according to the rule and precepts of the Gospel, different religious orders nevertheless spend their time differently. Each in its own way is rich

in various kinds of virtue, especially when one realizes that those rules of life which you condemn were discovered and handed down by saintly men. Religious orders have produced a great many men of extraordinary sanctity. Although some monks have not always lived up to their order and some orders have degenerated to the behavior of the world around them, nevertheless the purest segment of the Christian people have always been found in religious orders. The members of these orders are far from following anyone other than Christ, for they are the ones primarily who sell what they have and give it to the poor and take up the cross and follow Christ. Dedicating their entire lives to vigils, fasts, and prayer, and following the Lamb in chastity, they crucify the vices and desires of the flesh.

If this kind of life is contrary to the Gospel, as you would have it, then the life according to the Gospel would have to be contrary to it — a life, that is, in which one tenderly takes care of himself, eats well, drinks well, sleeps well, satisfies his lust, and melts with pleasure. If that is living the life of the Gospel, we certainly agree that your people lead a most Gospel-like life, except that they add to those splendid virtues a tyrannical violence and brutality worse than that of a wild beast. They rage against Christian friars dedicated to God more ferociously than any pagan tyrant ever did.

But now, as I said, let us come to good works. You put it that we peddle them instead of Christ. You are not embarrassed to write such things even when you know that we believe and teach that our works are not made good without God's mercy and bring no merit without the faith of Christ. And even then they are not in themselves deserving of heaven. (For the sufferings of this present time are not worth comparing with the glory that is to be revealed to us.)[361] It pleased the great kindness of the Creator, however, to place such a high value on our good works, which are cheap in themselves. Even when we have done everything, we are still unprofitable servants and have not done anything other than what we ought to do.[362] And yet he hires our labors at a high salary.

If, moreover, our works have no value at all — no matter if performed in faith, imbued with charity, aided by grace (for you know full well we admit that otherwise they are nothing) — if even so our works have no value, then why does the owner of the estate hire idle men to work in the vineyard for one denarius a day?[363] If works are of no help in freeing man from wrath, judgment, sin, death, and hell, why did the Baptist say, "Generation of vipers, who showed you how to flee the wrath to come? Bring forth fruits worthy of repentance"?[364] Why did the wise man say, "As water puts out fire, almsgiving puts out sin"?[365] Why did the apostle say, "If we judge ourselves, surely we would not be judged"?[366] And again, "As you have yielded your limbs to serve uncleanliness and iniquity, so now yield your limbs to serve justice"?[367] Why did Christ say, "Do this and you will live"?[368] And finally, at the last judgment why will he reward those who performed works of mercy with heaven and reproach the wicked for omitting and neglecting them?[369]

If these things are not lies, Pomeranus (and I do not think they are if the Gospel is true), then you cannot escape the fact that what you write is a lie: you call it hypocrisy, untruth, impiety, a struggle against the grace of God, and an utter denial of Christ, no matter how it shines with the semblance of sanctity, if anyone makes any effort beyond faith — that is, if he joins to faith the works of charity, without which faith is dead, and if through both faith and works together he attempts to live a life of righteousness. A person who acknowledges that he cannot do good works without grace does not struggle against grace in trying to do good works. He does not, like the Pharisee, rely on works, for he knows they are worthless without faith and purchase no reward except through God's sheer generosity. Those who are clearly opposed to grace and utterly deny Christ are the ones who exalt grace and trust in the faith of Christ only to make men lukewarm in doing good. They completely deny that good works have any goodness or merit in them whatsoever, whereas we condemn only the sinful reliance on works. When men are slow to do good, they quickly lose both faith and grace, especially in the present state of the world, when men have to be urged to see the value in good works almost more than in faith, without which works are of no avail. For you find far more who would rather believe well than do well.

But your complete inconsistency is enough to indicate what an evil cause you support. You speak in such confusion that you seem intentionally to guard against anyone's understanding you. Each succeeding word contradicts the one before. For after a bit you go on to say:

> But perhaps you will ask what we think and teach about morals, the worship of God, the sacraments, and things of that sort. I answer that Christ is our righteousness and also became our teacher. Whatever he has revealed to us with his own mouth, this we teach, even as he commanded [in the] last chapter of Matthew.[370]

So do we, Pomeranus. We profess that and teach it too. But tell me, is that all you will teach? I mean, will you unteach everything except what Christ taught with his own mouth? Will you unteach whatever God taught before the birth of Christ through Moses and the prophets except for those portions Christ taught again with his own mouth? Will you unteach whatever Christ taught the Church through so many holy fathers, evangelists, martyrs, and apostles unless he taught it with his own mouth?

But tell me, where did Christ with his own mouth teach you that we should believe only what he taught with his own mouth? Tell me, where did he teach with his own mouth the beliefs you teach to the whole world? Tell me where he taught with his own mouth that man has no free will. Where did he teach with his own mouth that one who has sworn a vow of chastity has to take a wife? Where did he teach with his own mouth that Luther's girlfriend is equal to the mother of Christ? Where did he teach with his own mouth that the Mass is of no use to the dead? Where did he teach with his own mouth that there is no purgatory, but that the souls of the dead sleep until the day of the last judgment? Where did he teach with his own mouth that his cross should be taken down and hidden away in the shadows somewhere lest gold be wasted in adorning it — gold which otherwise, of course, would go directly to the poor?

I think Christ did not teach these things to Luther with his own mouth when he said, "The poor you will always have with you."[371] But Brother Judas, Luther's brother, taught it with his own mouth

363 See Mt 20:1–16.   364 Lk 3:7–8   367 Rom 6:19   368 Lk 10:28   370 *CW* 7: 402; see Mt 28:20.
365 Ecclus 3:33(30)   366 1 Cor 11:31   369 See Mt 25:31–46.   371 Mt 26:11

when he said, "What is the sense in all this waste? It could have been sold for a lot of money and given to the poor."[372]

See here, Pomeranus, when you insist that people believe only what Christ taught with his own mouth, you take away everything else God taught the Church through the Holy Spirit and you end up teaching things Christ never taught, things no decent man can tolerate.

For you go on to say, "First of all Christ taught that this is the work of God, that we believe in him whom the Father sent us."[373] We allow that that is perfectly true. But we do not allow the truth of the conclusion which you draw from it and which is the only reason you bring it up. For you mention it in order to persuade people covertly that faith alone is sufficient. You touch it timidly, concealing the greater part of your mystic teaching. You conceal it in vain, however, since it has been spread abroad through the whole world in the books of your master. Luther treats this opinion of your school more openly and explains it somewhat more boldly. He writes plainly that no sin can damn a Christian except the sin of unbelief. According to the promise of God, we will be saved by faith, and if faith remains or if faith returns, all sins are immediately swallowed up by faith. It is not necessary to confess one's sins or be sorry for one's transgressions or compensate for evil by doing good, for Luther has obviously done away with all these things. As I said, you touch on this more timidly than Luther and shrewdly try to avoid the odium of such an assertion. You hide the fact that you preach the doctrine of faith so as to lure people to vice and unteach virtue. When you say that faith alone is sufficient, you want it to seem as though you mean that if one has faith he will naturally shun vice and embrace virtue.

Even if that were the case, this uproar of yours and this raging against good works would still be extremely stupid. If faith necessarily produces works that are good, what do you think you are doing when you argue against good works? Are you not running on at the mouth against the product of faith? But if there is no possibility of good works — a position your faction obviously holds — then you are not consistent when you say that one who has

faith is like a good tree that necessarily bears good fruit in its season.

But if it is so true that one who has faith will necessarily produce good works, why does the apostle say, "If I have such faith as will move mountains but have not charity, I am as nothing"? Why did he say, "If I have such faith as to deliver my body to be burned but have not charity, I gain nothing"?[374] All that would have been said in vain if faith did not exist apart from charity. Thus, "Faith without works is dead" and "Demons believe, and shudder"[375] . . . but there is no sense in my quoting from the Epistle of James. Since it inconveniences you, you no longer consider it to be apostolic. But Adam, I suppose, believed in God, for as the apostle said, "Adam was not deceived,"[376] and yet he sinned. If it is consistent with faith to do evil, it is no doubt consistent with faith not to do good.

But perhaps you do not believe the apostle, since you believe only what Christ said with his own mouth. Very well then. Did Christ not say with his own mouth that many people would come to him someday and say, "Lord, Lord, did we not prophesy in your name and in your name cast out demons and do many mighty deeds in your name?" "And then I will declare to them," he said, "I never knew you. Depart from me, all you evildoers."[377] Is it not clear from this passage that faith — even a faith great enough to perform miracles — does not bring forth good fruit in certain people? Such people are not through their great faith good trees. They are fig trees, utterly dry, ready to be cut down to the root and cast in the fire. Thus, Pomeranus, it is not true that faith alone is sufficient and that whoever has faith will necessarily bring forth the fruit of good works.

But why do I quote Christ to you? Why not quote Luther to a Lutheran? Since you think his authority is infallible, listen to what he says: "Nothing can condemn a man to hell except the sin of unbelief. If faith remains or if faith returns, all other sins, he says, will be swallowed up by faith."[378]

If he had thought about it for ten years, I do not see how he could have explained it more clearly. He believes that as long as faith remains whole and unharmed, one can commit any sort of sin he wants to. I certainly do not see what words he could have used to explain this more clearly. For you cannot

372 Jn 12:1–8   **373** *CW* 7: 402; Jn 6:29   **376** 1 Tm 2:14   **377** Mt 7:22–23
374 1 Cor 13:2–3   **375** Js 2:26, 19   **378** *De captivitate Babylonica* (*WA* 6: 529)

twist these words — if faith remains — to mean anything other than that he thinks a man can commit
sins and still have faith. And you can easily see how
it follows that faith does not necessarily produce
good works, since it is capable of existing side by
side with evil.

Get out of here, then, with your pretexts, Pomeranus, trying to trick out your ungodly beliefs so
that it seems as though when you command faith
alone you are issuing a command to perform all the
good in the world, as though you believed that faith
necessarily not only prevents sin but also produces
virtue. As you heard, Luther quite openly teaches
that a person can commit sin and still have his faith
remain unharmed. Not only that, but he himself remains unharmed because of the inherent merit of
his faith. "For if faith remains," Luther says, "all sins
will be swallowed up by faith."

Perhaps now you are embarrassed by your teacher
when you see his evil belief stripped bare of its cover
and revealed for what it is. Perhaps you want to appear to believe something more pious than that. If
so, Pomeranus, you have certainly not expressed it
cleverly enough, for it is clear as day that you are at
least equal to him in impiety, if you do not surpass
him. For first you run on at the mouth against good
works, using some statements from Scripture, such
as: "If we are made righteous by works and by our
own free will, Christ died for us in vain." You used
a little free will of your own in that verse when you
added the business about free will. After all, you had
to keep up your role as a sacrilegious forger of Sacred Scripture. Anyone can see that that particular
passage does not denigrate the value of good works.
It simply means that Christ would have died in vain
if we were made righteous by works without faith.
For Christ did not die in vain if works avail nothing without faith, even if they are worth a great deal
when united with faith. I need not mention that the
apostle said this about the works of the Mosaic Law.

Then you went on to add that "a man who follows his own righteousness, will, like the Jews, not
arrive at true righteousness." And this: "they are not
able to submit to God's righteousness." You added
the phrase "like the Jews" on your own hook once
again for fear of quoting Scripture more truthfully
than a Jew. Now, the words of Paul apply to those
who believe that righteousness comes only from the
works of the law without the faith of Christ, or to
those who are lifted up by vain pride in their own
works. But what do these words matter to Christians, who believe that no works, no matter how
good or how many, can make a person partaker of
heaven unless those works are performed in faith?
Even so, good works cannot be performed without
grace, and they cannot earn eternal happiness in
and of themselves. It is God's generosity alone that
grants the immense reward of heaven, which is so
far beyond what men deserve. He freely agrees to
give it and he bestows it on us.

Now that you have attacked good works with
such skillful weapons, thinking you have overwhelmed what you have not even touched, you pass
on to the righteousness of God, which is Christ.
You collect testimony from the law and the prophets, as if anyone ever denied it. And why do you do
that? Just to get rid of and destroy the concept of
good works and lure everyone over to your doctrine
of faith alone.

"This righteousness of God," you say, "is yours
when you receive Christ through faith." Very true.
There is nothing wrong with what you say except
that you reject good works just as earnestly as you
commend faith.

Now we admit that what you set down after that
is absolutely true: "For he did not die for his own
sake or for his own sins, but for your sake and for
your sins." In your case, though, we are afraid that
you bring it up only to encourage, by reliance on
faith alone, man's freedom to sin and the desire to
avoid the sanctity of a more disciplined life. I do not
deny that I would seem eager to interpret you incorrectly, were it not that what you write immediately
following suggests something more than a slight
hint of this suspicion. You make it perfectly obvious. For you say:

> Whatever else, therefore, you have tried in or-
> der to arrive at righteousness — that is, to become
> righteous and free from the judgment of God,
> from sin, death, and hell — will be hypocrisy, lies,
> and wickedness, no matter how much it shines
> with a semblance of piety. For it will strive against
> the justice of God and deny Christ.[379]

Those words make it obvious that you teach faith in order to unteach good works. On this point I shall make it perfectly clear that although Luther alone exceeds everyone else in impiety, you alone surpass him by far. As I said before, for fear that people would think there was anything to care about except lustful living, he wrote that faith swallows up all sins.

You vote for that notion by mentioning some virtues you claim to teach (which I will deal with a little later on and show how false your claim really is), and then immediately adding:

> And because we are still in the flesh, whatever good we do not do or do not do well enough, whatever sins we still commit, we teach with Christ that one should pray constantly that his sins will be forgiven, just as he taught us to pray: forgive us our trespasses.[380] And because of this trust in God, we teach that whatever sin still remains in the flesh will not be imputed to us. For I discover in me—that is, in my flesh—no good thing. But I give thanks to God that Christ came not for the righteous, but for sinners. And publicans and prostitutes will enter into the kingdom of heaven before self-righteous Pharisees.[381]

You say the same thing Luther did, Pomeranus: that a man cannot be damned except through unbelief, since faith alone swallows up all other sins. You explain the same thing another way by saying that a person's sins are not imputed to him if he has such trust in God that he believes that because of his faith alone his sins will not be imputed to him. But you also say you teach that prayer is united with faith, namely this prayer: Forgive us our trespasses.

And so by these two things, by faith alone along with the briefest possible prayer, you have established that the sum total of all sin will either not be imputed to you or else will be absolved. And so you have opened up for mortals a wonderful shortcut to heaven by means of a completely debauched life on earth. In fact you are such compassionate people that you take away all need for men to weep with sorrow for their sins or endure the irksomeness of confession and the unpleasantness of satisfaction. I am not distorting any of this or twisting its interpretation. That is clear from your own words and

the words of your master when he writes about the sacrament of penance in his *Babylonian Captivity*.[382] You both prove what I say plainer than day.

It is clear to everyone, then, that in Luther's opinion and in yours also, Pomeranus, faith alone is sufficient for salvation not only without good works, but even when accompanied by immorality and sin. But as I began to say a little before, you were not satisfied with that amount of impiety. You decided you had to go on and not stop until you taught not only that good works were completely negligible, but also that they should be carefully avoided because they would be harmful and would alienate us from God. Here are your words, which I have already referred to:

> This righteousness of God is yours when you receive Christ through faith. For he did not die for his own sake or for his own sins, but for your sake and for your sins. Whatever else, therefore, you have tried in order to arrive at righteousness—that is, to become righteous and free from the judgment of God, from sin, death, and hell—will be hypocrisy, lies, and wickedness, no matter how it shines with a semblance of piety. For it will strive against the grace of God and deny Christ.[383]

I will not use rhetoric to attack the wickedness of your words. For there is no need for rhetoric to make a good man hate someone who is so full of the breath, so full of the hissing of the ancient serpent, so full of the raging fury of hell that he would not hesitate to blaspheme openly, shamelessly, and maliciously against all other virtues except faith alone by designating and calling them hypocrisy and wickedness, no matter how much they shine like piety, and by contending that they not only oppose Christ's grace but completely deny Christ himself.

I ask you, Pomeranus, when you say these things, are you not simply telling us that God the Father sent his only begotten son to earth to teach men that he came to free them from all work and worry about virtue? That he came to grant them permission and complete freedom to give themselves up to all kinds of debauchery? And then, after they had led that sort of life on earth, he would give them eternal happiness in heaven, only demanding in

380 Mt 6:12   **381** *CW* 7: 402   **382** See *WA* 6: 543–49.   **383** *CW* 7: 400

return that no one hesitate to trust that promise of his, for fear perhaps that if anyone trusted less, he might become either a better or a less bad person?

These beliefs of yours, Pomeranus, are not only wicked, they are absurd. If you had not expressed your opinion explicitly, no one would believe you could be so beastly, since you are, after all, a man, not a beast. I actually put in a good bit of thought and effort trying to find anything that would make it at least seem as though you believe something different, something neither good nor honest but still a good deal less destructive and sacrilegious.

I applied myself to it diligently, for your sake as well as my own: for your sake, because I was extremely ashamed for you and because I pitied you; for mine, because I wanted to make it perfectly clear to everyone that I still have the same disposition I have always had — I would like to interpret everyone's writings in the best and kindest light possible. But I could neither discover nor imagine anything to mitigate what is not in fact merely an opinion about your absurd impiety but rather positive knowledge of it fixed in men's minds by your own explicit language.

While I was trying everything I could, leaving no stone unturned, I thought to myself, what about this? When Pomeranus says, "it is hypocrisy to seek anything other than faith," suppose he does not mean that it is hypocrisy to possess other virtues besides faith. Suppose he means it is hypocrisy to put some other virtue in the place of faith, some virtue in which an individual places his trust and reposes his hope without the faith of Christ.

But right away this interpretation seemed to me so shameless that I could never bear the shame of defending it. I saw that everyone would immediately contradict me and say that I had wasted my time in thinking up a dishonest and ridiculous way of explaining it. They would want to know right away, Pomeranus, how you could mean that when you know that everyone you criticize believes the same thing.

For they would say, of all the people he writes against, whom he calls self-justifiers, whom he criticizes as Pharisees, is there anyone who believes that virtue is of value without faith? And so, whether we want to or not, we have to admit, Pomeranus, that that is the last thing you believe.

But perhaps you will want it to seem as though this is what you meant: you did not forbid anyone to pursue any virtues other than faith alone. You simply wanted to warn people against convincing themselves that any of all the other virtues or any work of man, however well performed, however shaped and formed by faith, will be of any importance at all in attaining salvation or avoiding the punishment of hell. On the contrary, if someone decides to do good with the idea that it will help him either obtain heaven or avoid the flames of hell, he not only undoes himself and deceives himself completely, but he will also lose felicity and fling himself headlong into hell precisely because of that belief. For it is as though he had denied Christ.

If that is what you want us to think, Pomeranus, are you not leaping, as they say, from the frying pan into the fire?[384] For I ask you straight off, Pomeranus, if someone fails to do good works and commits sin, does that not close the gates of heaven and open to him the gates of hell? If you deny this, you leave no one in doubt (though you would very much like to conceal it) that you are the one who beckons the whole world to vice by leaving sins unpunished. If you grant that, as you must, then you will never be able to deny that if the wickedness of our actions plunges us down into hell, then the goodness of our actions, which we perform with the assistance of God, helps us out of hell and makes us more or less suitable for the reward of heaven promised to us. For it would be completely absurd to persuade yourself that God, whose nature is so merciful, would punish sin but offer no reward for virtue.

But we have already shown how foolish this heresy is and how it overtly contradicts several passages of Holy Scripture. We admit that no one should be proud of his virtue. He should recognize that good works are rewarded not in and of themselves because of their own nature, but because of the value God generously places on them. For no one is able to perform good works through his own nature alone without a special gift of grace. Even then one should fear that what he does may be infected by some secret vice. We can, however, be hopeful about our good works, and we ought always to try not to be saved by faith alone, but to avoid evil and do good and in that way to come to life eternal.

God did not promise that infinite and inconceivable reward to anyone lacking faith, and by the same token he did not promise it to anyone who has faith alone. There are more places than one where more than one apostle states that faith alone (no matter how great) is of no use, and that without good works it must be considered completely dead.

Moreover, does not the following passage of Scripture show clearly that when good works are performed in faith they receive an eternal reward? For it is written, "the ransom of a man's soul is his wealth."[385] And what about this passage from the gospels, "Give alms and all things are clean unto you"?[386] What about Christ's words concerning the judgment to come, where he says he will give the wages and reward of eternal bliss for acts of generosity to the poor?[387]

You see, Pomeranus, the witness of Holy Scripture is so self-evident that no matter how you twist it, you will never be able to find anything to contradict it. But perhaps you are such a holy person that you cannot bear to hear the words "wages" and "reward." You would prefer man to serve God freely and expect no reward in return. Otherwise one would be a hireling and not a son. For hirelings do not willingly work for nothing. They render service only for a price.

Who would not confound heaven and earth, sea and sky when he sees a Lutheran bishop—a man who has broken his vow, shattered his faith, violated the chastity of his priesthood, who wallows in continual incest, which he prefers to call marriage, who shakes his ass as he preaches about virtue—suddenly pontificate about the grave and weighty rules and regulations concerning the worship of God as if he were sent down to us from heaven? No one, he says, should expect or look for any reward for his good deeds. If anyone desires or hopes for reward, he should not be regarded by Christ as a Christian because he is a hireling and not a son.

Pomeranus is such a holy little saint, far beyond the ordinary measure of saintliness! I see that he is ashamed to be included among those hired hands the house-holder pays a denarius to work in his vineyard.[388] His spirit is so truly highborn that he would rather die on the gallows outside the vineyard than work inside it for one denarius. See how he looks down from his perch and despises the prophet for having the ignoble mentality of a slave because he was not ashamed to say in public that he served God for what he hoped to receive in return.[389]

Meanwhile our foresighted father does not see what a tight place he has squeezed himself into and gotten himself stuck. For he either hopes for no reward and expects no return for his faith, thus proclaiming that faith is just as unprofitable and unrewarding as the good works he spoke about earlier, or else he expects a reward for his faith and thus falls into the same danger that made him shudder at the idea of a reward for good works—the fear, that is, of putting his faith out to hire.

Pomeranus, perhaps, would reply that the reward of heaven is not granted even to faith in its own nature, but proceeds entirely from the generosity of God: since God has so ordained and promised, there is no doubt that heaven awaits us. Nevertheless one should not believe in God merely to seek the reward he has promised to those who believe in him. We should approach him with the idea that even if we were to obtain no advantage we would still have faith in his Word and worship his ineffable majesty. If this is what Pomeranus were to answer, I would have to admit that his reply was as truthful and reverent as it was completely beside the point.

I imagine, however, he is not such a fool as not to understand that nothing he said in this discourse about faith would not apply equally as well to works. For we do not say that works are capable of laying claim to heaven in and of themselves, but rather that God has generously promised the same thing for our works that he has promised for our faith. That is to say, he will give the gift of heaven to those who have the capacity for both faith and good works and in whom both are joined together.

On the other hand, those who are assisted by God's grace and have the capacity for both, but rely on only one or the other—that is, either faith alone or works alone—do not proceed on the path of life. They have lost their way and go backward.

Besides, Pomeranus, it does not hurt someone to busy himself with fasting, chastity, prayer, and the other virtues which you and your friend Luther try to demolish and destroy. There is no reason why that should prevent him from reaching, at times,

385 Prv 13:8   **386** Lk 11:41   **387** See Mt 25:31–46.   **388** See Mt 20:1–16.   **389** Ps 118(119):112

such piety that it seems as though he would do all those things even if he knew God would not reward his constant efforts.

That is certainly a pious attitude. I confess that such thoughts are holy and greatly to be desired. And I not only contend that they apply both to faith and good works, I also claim that anyone who preaches as you do, Pomeranus, that good works are of no avail, that good works are not rewarded, that good works are of no help in avoiding hell, and that they obstruct grace and utterly deny Christ — anyone who preaches that, I say, not only tries to make people cold and slack toward good works, regarding them as useless and sterile. He also cuts the desire to do good out of men's hearts and casts it away as if it were deadly, diseased tissue. And in order to seduce the common people to his beliefs, he panders to them with lust and licentiousness, allowing them a safe berth and easy opportunity to perform all sorts of shameful things.

That is evidently what you have in mind, Pomeranus. But since you saw yourself bringing it out in the open by the language you use, quoted above, you began to be afraid. Your intentions were becoming too transparent and perhaps too odious. You were afraid that even the wicked and evil might think it unbearable that an absurd, good-for-nothing wretch like you has finally appeared on the scene and has dared, against the common understanding of all these many centuries, to promote vice and assault virtue so violently. So you have been forced to contradict yourself by teaching that, in addition to your obvious persuasions to vice and dissuasions from virtue, you Lutherans have some virtues of your own. You do this to hide your poisoned sting, though it sticks out now clearly enough for everyone to see.

Your falsehoods will become even more obvious as soon as we have had a chance to winnow your words, but they are clear enough from the doctrines of your sect. Your own words, which we have examined above, permit no ambiguity. At the moment it may be worthwhile to see how you clothe with a handsome, beautiful rind the rotten, totally decayed flesh of your fruit. For you speak thus:

Whoever believes in him is a good tree, and cannot fail to bear good fruit in its season: not the fruit imagined by hypocrisy, but the fruit which

the spirit of Christ produces there of its own accord.[390] For those who are moved by the spirit of Christ are the sons of God.[391] Such a one will adore God soberly, piously, and justly, in spirit and truth, not in the elements of this world, in food, clothing, and other hypocrisy. About the sacraments he will believe what Christ taught and established. He will influence his neighbors with instruction, advice, prayer, material possessions, even at the cost of his life. And this not only for friends, but also for enemies. Such are the things Christ taught us; the nature of the spirit draws the hearts of believers to these things; and these are the things we teach must be performed. And because we are still in the flesh, whatever of these we do not do or do not do well enough, and whatever sins we still commit, we teach with Christ that one should pray constantly that his sins will be forgiven, just as he taught us to pray: forgive us our trespasses. And because of this trust in God, we teach that whatever sin still remains in the flesh will not be imputed to us. For I discover in me — that is, in my flesh — no good thing. But I give thanks to God that Christ came not for the righteous, but for sinners. And publicans and prostitutes will enter into the kingdom of heaven before self-righteous Pharisees, despite the fact that wicked backbiters grumble that we teach otherwise. God says through Moses, "Whoever will not hear that prophet (meaning Christ), I will take vengeance on him."[392] Let the enemies of the Gospel hear this judgment of God against them. And the Father cries aloud over Christ, "Hear him."[393] And Christ, "My sheep will hear my voice and not the voices of strangers."[394]

We will see a little further on whether these words that seem so saintly are in fact as saintly as they seem. That one must pray for forgiveness for his sins — it amazes me that you bring that up as part of this new teaching of yours. You insult us quite often by calling us Pharisees and self-justifiers. You sound as though we never said the Lord's Prayer or admitted that we are sinners. But it amazes me even more that you advise people to pray and do the sort of things you mention when you say, "And these are the things we teach must be performed."

390 Mt 7:16–20   **391** Rom 8:14   **392** Dt 18:19   **393** Mt 17:5   **394** *CW* 7: 402; Jn 10:4–5

Why do you persuade people to do anything if there is no free will? Why do you urge me to pray, to give my neighbor good advice, enlarge his mind with learning, assist him with material goods, and not spare my own life if I can be of help to others? Why recommend all this if I am not able to do any of it? You simply ought to pray to God to perform all this in me. You should not even ask me to try to do these things, for according to you, even with the help of grace, I do not cooperate. I simply accept it all passively.

Who urges a stone to shape itself into a statue, the clouds to rain, or the earth to bear crops? If everything is caused by fate and nothing accomplished by man himself, as you Lutherans firmly hold, then there is no reason at all for you to rouse men to virtue and castigate wrongdoing. You also have no grounds for objecting to your opponents, since they have no free will and are driven by fate to do what they have to do. But perhaps you would reply that what you write is not voluntary but dictated by the promptings of fate.

I am also amazed, Pomeranus, that you urge people to do so many of the same things that we urge them to do. If you really do what you claim to, you recommend that they perform good works. So why pick out good works as your specific target to babble on about? If you despise them, why recommend them? If you recommend them, why despise them?

But perhaps you permit people to do good works, but forbid them to call them that. If so, why disallow the term when even God uses it? "This woman," he says, "has performed a good work for me."395 Or perhaps you object because it is called the work of man, even though it is good. Let us call Christ to witness, since you write that you believe only what he says. Did he not say, "the woman has done a good work"? Did he not say the same to the Jews, whom you resemble: "If you are the children of Abraham, do the works of Abraham"?396

You require clear evidence from the Scripture for all your beliefs; so why do you keep shifting ground in the face of these perfectly plain passages of Scripture? How often does Christ command and forbid? What good are these passages if we do nothing? "I was hungry," he says, "and you gave me to eat. I was thirsty, and you gave me to drink. I was a stranger, and you welcomed me."397

Christ says people gave him these things and welcomed him. But you deny it. You say God did it all, and the people simply permitted God to work in them. Christ reproached cruel people for their harshness, saying they did not feed the hungry, disregarded the thirsty, and despised the stranger under the open sky. How stern Christ is to make those charges if they are not able to do any of these things even when assisted by grace or when, through no fault of their own, grace is withheld.

What do you Lutherans say to that? Nothing at all. You simply collect certain passages of Scripture, whatever seems to strip man of freedom and imply that God is the source of our sins! Then, either misquoting the verses or misunderstanding them, you trumpet your victory over the Pharisees and the self-justifiers. At the same time, you dishonestly ignore all the other passages of Scripture that overwhelm your order of battle and destroy it, constantly chanting about the places that support what you believe. You have nothing at all to say about the scriptural quotations that either explain the ones you gathered or are cited in opposition to them. A person would have to be crazy to think that Luther did a good job in responding to the passages cited by the author of the *Treatise in Favor of Free Will*—an extremely learned man398 who deserves much thanks from the Church of Christ. Luther's reply, in the book entitled *The Slavery of the Will,* did no more than reveal clearly how his own will was enslaved to a raving demon when he wrote that book.

For what does Luther say in reply to this perfectly obvious passage in Scripture, "If you would enter into life, keep the commandments"?399 Or what does he say about other passages everywhere in Scripture, perfectly transparent in meaning, that testify to the freedom of the will? Only that they were all said ironically. That God commanded man to do something precisely because he knew man could not do it is such a crazy idea that you would be hard put to find someone who would not laugh at a stupid answer like that. The only ones who could possibly take it seriously are those who want to be free to seek their own destruction, gladly embracing the idea of fate to defend their sinfulness. Anyone else would mock and scorn that vain man's insane boasting. And all the while he runs around with a sardonian laugh trumpeting victory, trophies, triumphs, claiming his reply is so perfect that neither devil nor angel could talk him down. It is easy for a wretch who babbles insane nonsense to shout in his madness that he has argued so brilliantly that no one could possibly refute him.

What he replies to the *Treatise* seems absurd even to Luther himself. He knows ahead of time that it will be condemned. He knows it is capable of provoking only laughter or anger in anyone other than the partisans of his own heresy. He demonstrates this most clearly when he admits in his reply to the *Treatise* that no one can be won over or persuaded of anything unless he has drunk in the Spirit by reading his books.[400] What is that if not admitting that to all others his reply will clearly appear to be what it is in fact, namely absurd, insane, sacrilegious? Only those who have had the wool pulled over their eyes by their love and affection for the Lutheran heresy will find anything very pretty about it. By reading Luther's books they become possessed by the same spirit that makes him tremble with raging madness and, once they have rejected the faith of Christ, drives them mad too.

So you see, Pomeranus, how well you handle the passages of Scripture cited against you in favor of free will. You either dissemble completely or reply to them in the craziest way, while citing other passages that support you against the Church. Some of these are hyperbolical, but all of them taken together (as the holy fathers of the Church persistently attest in their interpretation) simply indicate that certain people are finally deprived of grace because of some enormous depravity of the will. God is said to make these people hard because he has decided never again to offer them grace, which softens hearts of stone. The Scripture you cite also means that no mortal is capable of anything without God—all of which we obviously agree with.

For who would deny what truth itself affirms when it says, "Without me you can do nothing,"[401] and "No one can come to me unless the Father who sent me draws him."[402] But you are so far gone into madness that you contend that man is capable of absolutely nothing, even with God's help. You contend that man does not come to the Father by being drawn to him, but only by being dragged involuntarily. You say that man does not even make an effort to rise up with the one who draws him. Christ,

on the other hand, clearly states that he is always ready to draw men to him, but not someone who is not willing to be drawn. "How often would I have gathered your children together," he says, "as a hen gathers her chicks under her wings, and you would not."[403]

But even where Christ seems to make the least of human activity, so as to put a check on human arrogance—even there he indicates the strength and freedom of our will. "When," he says, "you have done all that is commanded of you, then say, 'We are unworthy servants. We have done only what was our duty.'"[404] See, you brag that you believe in Christ alone, and now you do not even believe in him. He tells us that we act, and you on the contrary deny what he says and assert that we are merely passive.

Go and brag now, Pomeranus, that you teach whatever Christ said with his own mouth. But this is what really puzzles me. You teach that a person should influence his neighbors with prayer and advice, that he should assist them with material possessions and even at the cost of his own life. But what do you mean by this teaching if everything you mention is not only completely worthless so far as judgment, sin, death, and hell are concerned, but leads straight down to hell? For that is what you wrote a little above: "It is hypocrisy, lying, and wickedness, and a striving against grace, and a denial of Christ for a man to attempt anything to free himself from sin, death, and hell except faith alone."

If that is how things are, why not teach the doctrine of faith alone? If faith alone is sufficient or if good works necessarily proceed from faith, why bother to teach good works at all? Take a man standing in the sunlight. Who would urge him to cast a shadow, since he will cast one whether he wants to or not as long as he stands in the sun?

So you see, Pomeranus, this teaching of yours is in many ways so horribly at odds with itself that one part contradicts the other. But you want it to seem harmonious so as to be accepted unconditionally as the new gospel. The problem is you are teaching one thing from the heart while wanting to seem as though you are really saying something else.

You seriously preach and contend as strongly as you can that everyone should be convinced the only true freedom is in reliance on faith alone—freedom

400 See Luther's letter to Erasmus in *De servo arbitrio* (*WA* 18: 601–2). **401** Jn 15:5 **402** Jn 6:44 **403** Mt 23:37; Lk 13:34–35 **404** Lk 17:10

from every care and worry about all the other virtues, safe and sure of heaven despite a life of license and sin. Still, in order to deflect a little of the hatred inspired by such insane teaching, you insert in passing now and then something contrary to what you wrote before, thus raising the question of whether your true beliefs are as crazy as what you write. But you have not handled it all that cleverly, Pomeranus. The cosmetic coating of virtue you carefully applied can easily be wiped off. To let you see that this is no sooner said than done, we will consider right now what kind of fruit the people of your faction cannot but bring forth, for they are, as you say, such good trees.

Whoever believes in Christ (you say) is a good tree and cannot fail to bear good fruit in its season. Not the fruit imagined by hypocrisy, but the fruit which the spirit of Christ produces there of its own accord. For those who are moved by the spirit of Christ are the sons of God.

Many of these are Christ's own words, Pomeranus, and if they were published by someone of orthodox faith, they would be wholesome enough. But since you mix them all up with your own opinions and turn everything to your own advantage by twisting them into Lutheran doctrine, we are properly led to suspect even honey itself when offered by a Lutheran for fear it is poisoned. Take, for example, what you say about the spirit of Christ producing good fruit of its own accord in those who believe.

Although we agree that what you say is true, we do not agree that it is true in the sense in which you seem to take it. For Christ does not of his own accord produce good fruit in a man of faith without the individual's own will and volition. But that is precisely what you think, as is clear from your heretical denial of free will.

Now what you say next shows what fruit you are thinking about. "He will adore God," you say, "soberly, piously, and justly, in spirit and truth." That much is perfectly all right. But go on a little farther, and see what happens. "Not in the elements of this world, in food, clothing, and other hypocrisy. About the sacraments he will believe what Christ taught and established."

That is the place; that is where it really hurts. For you spiritual men have decided to obey the counsel Christ set forth when he said, "One who desires to worship God must worship him in spirit and in truth,"[405] in such a way as to destroy completely the obedience of the flesh to God. But this, Pomeranus, is to worship in spirit and not in truth. One who fools himself with talk of the spirit and fails to subdue and tame the wantonness of the flesh with fasting does not truly worship God.

You think all obedience of the body offered to God is hypocrisy. But it was not hypocrisy to Mary, who washed Christ's feet with her tears and dried them with the hair of her head.[406] Coarse clothing is hypocrisy to you, but it was not hypocrisy to John the Baptist, who dressed in the skin of camels. Abstinence from food is hypocrisy to you, but it was not hypocrisy to John, who ate only locusts.[407] And it was not hypocrisy even to Paul, who wanted to be able to fast all day. It is hypocrisy to you when the faithful pour out their devotion to God in the churches. But the prophet did not believe it was. The dignity of his kingship did not keep him from singing and dancing with the people before the ark of the covenant. And that proud and foolish woman did not go unpunished when she reproached him for worshiping God in that fashion.[408] But now you Lutherans — no less foolish and more proud than she — jeer at the Christian flock for doing the same thing.

Actually, Pomeranus, the true hypocrite is one whose piety is so lukewarm that he does not feel his flesh grow warm when he worships God, and yet he says that he still adores God ardently in spirit.

"About the sacraments he will think," you say, "what Christ taught and established." Short enough, certainly, but not very clear. For you bring into question what Christ taught. We do not doubt that Christ taught whatever the Church of Christ believes, since it cannot err without injury to Christ. Otherwise Christ would have deceived us in promising that he would be with the Church even to the end of time.[409]

You deny everything except what is clearly mentioned in Scripture, and what is clearly mentioned there you call obscure, or, more boldly, you shout that what is obviously against you is obviously for

405 John 4:24   **406** See Lk 7:38; Jn 12:3.
407 See Mt 3:4; Mk 1:6.   **408** David

dances before the ark in 2 Sm 6:14–15. His wife Michal, the daughter of Saul, rebukes

him and as a result bears no children.
409 Mt 28:20

you. And then you wrangle about what constitutes the Church, and you make it so ambiguous that you come to the conclusion that there is no Church at all on earth. Finally, you manage it so that either you would have to be fundamentally irreligious (which is most likely) or else all those would have to be so, who from the time of Christ's Passion until this very day were believed to be devout.

What good man ever believed that the sacrament of orders[410] is a mere fiction? Who ever babbled against contrition? Who, in fact, ever urged us not to feel sorrow for our sins? Who allowed women to hear confession? Who argued against good works? Who belittled fasting? Who held the prayers of the Church in contempt? Who pulled down the decorations in churches? Who has envied the saints their worship? Who denied the fire of purgatory? Who failed to believe that in the Mass the Eucharist is a sacrifice? Who believed that bread remains bread along with Christ's flesh?

Some of the important leaders of your faction, however, have recanted that last statement—Lutheran fashion. For Luther always changes his beliefs for the worse, as he did with indulgences, the power of the pope, and the Eucharist itself. And now Karlstadt, Zwingli,[411] and Oecolampadius, who finally joined the rest, have completely removed Christ's flesh from the Host and left only bread. Luther was already working on the idea and no doubt would have carried it off himself if Karlstadt and Zwingli had not beaten him to it.

That is where it was tending when he permitted people to believe without danger that the Eucharist consists of both, bread and Christ's body. At that point Luther did not condemn those who believed that the bread was turned into flesh. But after a while he considered anyone who held that belief a heretic.

Where do you think Luther was heading when he changed the canon of the Mass, forbidding it to be termed a sacrifice or offering? Or when he pulled down ritual and ceremony, allowed laymen to handle the Host, permitted women to consecrate it, and refused to allow it to be kept in the tabernacle and venerated in the church? He said that Christ did not institute the Eucharist for it to be venerated, but only for it to be received. In fact, it should not even be received, as Luther says in the *Babylonian Captivity*, except once, when a person is leaving this life, just as he receives baptism only once, when he is entering it.[412]

All this proceeded step by step until eventually Luther would have undoubtedly taken the body of Christ right out of the Eucharist. He had smoothed the way and was obviously about to proceed with it. But just as he was about to start, one sin kept him from committing another. It was only envy that restrained him from going ahead and preaching that ungodly heresy in public. For he envied Karlstadt and Zwingli the honor of seeming more irreligious than he. And afterward he envied Oecolampadius too. He preferred to dismantle what he had formerly built up (as anyone could see he was doing) rather than allow anyone else to become the heresiarch of any godless sect.

But what does it really matter what Luther thinks about the Eucharist when his writings show clearly enough the sacrilegious ideas he has about Christ? How can anyone doubt how he feels about Christ when he blasphemes Christ's saints, defiles Christ's cross, and equates Christ's venerable mother with his own whore? But what does it really matter what he thinks about Christ when his filthy heresy testifies to the revolting ideas he has about the sublimity of the divine nature? When he did away with the freedom of the will, Luther made our all-good, all-merciful God not the avenger, but the originator of sin. One can hardly imagine a more impious and sacrilegious heresy against God's holy majesty and a more deadly temptation to commit all sorts of disgraceful acts. At the same time you go about teaching these absurd, ungodly things, you are not embarrassed by speaking as though Lutherans only had a right to influence their neighbors by teaching. The reason you think so, I suppose, is that Luther teaches that all Christians are above all law. And you are well advised to think so, since he advises, in his holy, austere fashion, that one who has taken a vow of celibacy can forget all about it and snatch up a wife. He also very obligingly advises that if a husband is impotent he should hire some man to commit adultery with his wife.[413]

Now as for the Lutherans helping their neighbors at the cost of their own lives, and this not only for friends, but also for enemies—who could listen to that and not burst out laughing, even though the

---

410 ordination to the priesthood   **411** Ulrich Zwingli (1484–1531)   **412** See *WA* 6: 572, 11: 445.   **413** See *WA* 11: 250–51, 6: 555–58.

thought of it is very sad and depressing? One sees the savage troops of your sect massing together on every side, destroying beautiful homes, burning sacred buildings, plundering holy churches, casting out the pitiful and innocent friars, stripped of all their goods and fortune, bereft of all means of support, and many of them with serious bodily injuries. Is that what you call helping your neighbors even at the cost of your own life? And this not only for friends, but also for enemies? I suppose so. No doubt you always treat the best people the worst.

For you take in with open arms any flea-brained, shifty wretch who is willing to cast off the rigors of a disciplined life. He is your holy brother in Christ, and thus another godless soldier is added to the godless troop. But take someone who is truly pious and pursues his purpose without wavering and despises the freedom enjoyed by criminals, you immediately regard him as a Pharisee and self-justifier. He is scorned as a hypocrite by the Lutherans. He is abused, driven off, and harassed just as the innocent martyrs were by pagan tyrants. And yet, so help me God, you speak as though you are the only Christians and gravely rebuke the Church as if she had never heard of Christ. You yelp like a dog the Father's words about God the Son, "Hear him"—out of context. Note, however, that God did not say, "Hear Pomeranus" or "Hear Luther."

For the passage you quote from Moses threatens to ruin you: "Whoever will not hear that prophet, I will take vengeance on him, says the Lord."[414] The Church hears Christ's voice speaking from within itself and thus maintains the same faith that from the time of Christ's death through the apostles, martyrs, and holy confessors even to this present age flowed without interruption from Christ's own breath, and it will endure despite all heretics and all the demons allied to them even to the end of time.

But you condemn the Church of Christ, and thus Christ commands us to regard you as pagans and publicans.[415] At one time or another you will experience the vengeance of God for rejecting Christ in his Church and refusing to listen to Christ speaking to his Church.

The divine goodness uses at times such agents of demons to test the patience of good men in the Church or to punish the sins of the faithful. But God will be true to his word and along with the temptation provide a way out,[416] and eventually he will wipe away every tear from the eyes of those who have mended their ways.[417] But his wrath and indignation, you—you, I say, you ungodly, cruel slayers of the faithful—with the breath of his anger he will blow you to ashes and drive you like dust from the face of the earth.[418]

God recently gave a horrifying instance of this vengeance when those pitiful wretches, the peasants who were led astray by your teaching, destroyed so many monasteries and roamed about aimlessly for a while killing and looting wherever they wanted.[419] When they believed they had achieved almost unlimited and unrestricted license to commit all kinds of crime, behold, the God of glory thundered and destruction suddenly came over them.[420] A sea of misery overwhelmed them like sheep.[421] All told, more than seventy thousand perished. And the rest, whatever the number, were all reduced to bitter servitude.

Are you not disgraced by the part Luther played in this? He was your general and changed from the wickedest commander in the world to the most dishonorable deserter. He was the one who inflamed the peasants to every crime they committed; he armed them and egged them on. Then, when he saw that fortune had deserted them, he grimly cut them down by writing his vicious pamphlets against them. He outlawed them and turned them over to the nobles to be hacked to pieces. And that unspeakable politician did all this in order to extinguish with the blood of those pitiful wretches the fires of hatred directed against himself. He first stirred them up, and then he sacrificed them.

If Luther had a drop of human blood in his heart, he would have preferred to die ten times over rather than by such filthy maneuvering and horrible cringing live a life loathsome to God and man. But perhaps he will find that the nobles are not stupid enough to be softened up with one letter and forget that he was the one who brought them to the brink of destruction. As for the peasants, I suspect they will never forget the man who destroyed them twice over. Godless and blind as he is to divine vengeance,

---

414 Dt 18:19   **415** Mt 18:17   **416** 1 Cor 10:13   **417** Rv 7:17   **418** 2 Thes 2:8; Ps 1:4   **419** More is referring to the Peasants'   Revolt of 1524–25.   **420** Ps 28(29):3   **421** 1 Thes 5:3

Luther worked to ingratiate himself with both parties. But he failed to gain the one, and he obviously lost the other.

Yet it is my sincere hope that the nobles and peasants will forgive him, provided that he decides to act in such a way that God above all can forgive him. I mean, if he recovers from heresy, if without deception he recants his evil beliefs, if he seeks Christ's glory through his own disgrace and does not allow his insatiable pride to keep him from confessing his insanity for the honor of God.

But if Luther has fallen into such despair that he pays no attention to his own salvation, you, Pomeranus, must consider yours. Abandon that ungodly sect, the most shameful that ever existed on earth. Return and rejoin the Catholic Church. Then, in every way you can, correct what you corrupted for so many years with your preaching. Give up your illegitimate bishopric. Send away that unfortunate girl you whore with in the name of marriage. And spend the rest of your life in repentance for what you have done.

If you do these things, Pomeranus — and I pray to God you will — then will you truly joy in us, and instead of feeling sorrow that you are lost, we in turn will rejoice that you are found.

148. To Erasmus
Greenwich, 18 December <1526>

Best greetings: I have received two letters[422] from you, dearest Erasmus, and have also read the one you addressed to the Reverend Father, the Bishop of London.[423] We, who are your dear little friends, are very much disturbed to hear that the stone disorder which gave you terrible pains for so long has now been followed by the disease which proved fatal to Linacre; though God's goodness and your own virtue are turning such evils into good for you, still our joy at your spiritual blessings does not preclude all concern, on our part, for the human frailty of your body; our uneasiness is caused not only by concern for you personally — for whom as for ourselves we do hope and pray for every blessing — but also, and more especially, by concern for all of Christendom; we are afraid that this illness will interrupt the brilliant works you have been writing to promote Christian piety. I pray God that you may bring them to a speedy and happy conclusion, especially the remaining part of the *Hyperaspistes;*[424] for you could have no other work in mind that would be more profitable for others, more satisfying to your friends, and more notable or more urgent for your own self. You would find it hard to believe the eagerness with which all good men are looking forward to that work; there are, on the other hand, some wicked persons, either partisans of Luther or your jealous rivals, who apparently are gleeful and growing in numbers as a result of your delayed response. However, I can sympathize with your delay, if the interruption has been caused by your desire to complete other writings first — as, for instance, your work on *Christian Marriage,*[425] which her Majesty the Queen correctly regards as being of supreme importance — and I hope that fact will shortly be brought home to you in a concrete way. And I am very contented, too, if the delay has been caused by your desire to handle the subject in a leisurely, thoughtful fashion; for I am anxious to see that part handled with the utmost care. But if, according to some reports, the delay is due to the fact that you have been terrorized, and have lost all interest in the work, and have no courage to go on with it, then I am thoroughly bewildered and unable to restrain my grief. You have endured, dearest Erasmus, many, many struggles and perils and Herculean labors; you have spent all the best years of your life on exhausting work, through sleepless nights, for the profit of all the world; and God forbid that now you should so unhappily become enamored of your declining years as to be willing to abandon the cause of God rather than lose a decision.

I am not afraid that you will now throw up to me that quotation from the comic poet: "When we are well, everybody," etc., or, "If you were here, you might think differently."[426] Indeed, I am incapable of making any such promises, nor is anybody else capable of offering such prospects as the whole world is waiting with expectation to receive from you, because you have given extraordinary proof of a heart that is valiant and trusting in God. It is impossible for me to doubt that you will continue bravely to exhibit such strength of spirit right up to your dying breath, even if there were a disastrous

---

422 not now extant   423 Cuthbert Tunstall   424 *Defender of the Diatribe against Martin Luther's The Unfree Will.* It was finished *ca.* August 1527 and published in time for the Frankfort Fair.   425 *The Institution of Christian Marriage,* August 1526, dedicated to Queen Catherine of Aragon   426 Terence, *Andria* 309–10

catastrophe. For you could never fail to trust that God in his merciful kindness would intervene to calm the disturbance. Right now, as far as I can see, you are far from being terrorized; in fact, there is little cause for fear at all. If the Lutherans planned to make any threatening moves, very likely they would have made them before your reply. Then they might have forestalled any answer from you; or if they wanted to gain vengeance on you for your writings, they would have given vent to their rage at the time you published your first volume; for, in that work, you drew such a vivid description of the monster, and you pointed out so accurately the spirit that goads it on, that you displayed, for all the world to see, that fuming, hellish demon, as if you had dragged Cerberus up from the infernal regions.

At present I certainly fail to see any peril beyond that which would threaten you even if you did not write another line. You have replied to the false charges he made against you; you have stabbed him with the point of your pen; all that remains for you is a discussion of Scripture, and, by issuing, like so many promissory notes, a thousand copies of the first volume, you have solemnly promised the whole world that you would faithfully go through with the second volume. Therefore, not even Luther is such a fool as to hope, or such a wretch as to dare to demand, that you would now not carry out God's cause, having accomplished your own, or that you would not fulfill the promise you made publicly, especially since that would be so easy for you to do. Luther, I am sure, would rather have you say nothing, even though, in his letter to you, he pretends to have a supreme contempt for you; it is hard to tell whether that letter is marked more by boastful exaggeration or stupidity. In any case, he is fully conscious that his worthless comments, which laboriously obscure the most obvious passages of Scripture while being frigid enough in themselves, would become, under your criticism, a mass of sheer ice.

Since you, however, are present at the scene of action, while I am some distance away, if you notice that your reply involves some danger which you cannot elude and which I cannot foresee, then, please, do at least this much: write me a confidential note and have it delivered to me by a reliable carrier.

Not only the Bishop of London, an absolutely honest person, as you know, and extremely devoted to you, but also I myself will conscientiously see to it that the note will never be made public, unless that can be done safely.

Your painter,[427] dearest Erasmus, is a remarkable artist; but I am afraid he will not find England as fertile and fruitful as he expected. Still, I shall do my best to see that he does not find it altogether barren. Your pamphlet was a very neat refutation of the rumor spread abroad by some malicious persons that you favored the heresy of Carlstadt;[428] you thus foiled the sly attempts of the clown who had planted that story in some German work. If God ever grants you the free time, I would like eventually to see a treatise in support of our Faith flow from that heart of yours, so perfect an instrument for defending the truth; however, right now I am very much concerned about the *Hyperaspistes* and I would not want you to become absorbed in anything that might turn your interests elsewhere and thus prevent you from completing this work at the earliest possible date.

Farewell, Erasmus, dearest of all men. From the Court at Greenwich, December 18.

Sincerely and more than wholeheartedly yours,
    Thomas More
To the excellent and most learned Master Erasmus of Rotterdam.

150. To the University of Oxford
Richmond, 11 March <1527?>

Right worshipful[429] sir, in my most hearty wise[430] I recommend me[431] unto you.

Signifying unto you the King's pleasure is that for certain considerations moving his Highness, ye shall forthwith upon the sight of these my letters send up to me one Henry the manciple[432] of White Hall, in so sure keeping that he do not escape, and that ye shall by your wisdom handle the matter so closely that there be of his apprehension[433] and sending up as little knowledge abroad as may be. And this his Grace's commandment, his high pleasure is that ye shall with all diligence and dexterity

---

427 Hans Holbein the Younger, who painted the portrait of More, a picture of the whole family, and drawings of the group and of each

member **428** Andrew Bodenstein von Carlstadt (1480–1541) **429** distinguished, honorable **430** manner **431** *recommend me:* commend myself to your benevolent

remembrance or regard **432** an officer or servant chiefly concerned with provisioning **433** arrest

put in execution, as ye intend the continuance of his gracious favor toward you and that his University, the privileges whereof, his Grace of his blessed mind intendeth to see conserved. And for that intent his Highness hath ordered that ye shall send up the said Henry to me, being Steward[434] of this his University. And thus heartily fare ye well, at Richmond the eleventh day of March.

Assuredly your own,
Thomas More

155. To Francis Cranevelt
Calais, 14 July <1527>

Cordial greeting from T. More to his very charming friend Cranevelt.

Indeed I would be utterly heartless, my very dear friend Cranevelt, if I refused to repay the many letters I have received from you with a single letter in return, especially at this time when I have obtained such a reliable letter-carrier that I am completely deprived of the excuse I usually take as a pretext for my laziness, namely that I lack someone to carry my letter. This carrier is a servant of Erasmus, now returning directly to him, highly commended by him as very loyal and close-mouthed. If you want to communicate to Erasmus anything that you do not wish to commit to a letter, you can very safely entrust it to this man. If there is anything else I wish you to know, you will learn it from this letter-carrier. Calais, in haste, July 14.

Give a thousand greetings from me to that pre-eminent lady, your mistress-wife. Farewell, my good man, most distinguished and most dear to your friend More.

To the most illustrious gentleman Francis Cranevelt, Councilor to his Imperial Majesty, at Mechelin

160. From Bishop Cuthbert Tunstall
<London> 7 March 1527/8

Cuthbert, by divine permission bishop of London, sends greetings and blessings in the Lord to that most illustrious and excellent man, his brother and dearest friend, Lord Thomas More.[435]

Now that the Church of God has been assailed throughout Germany by heretics, not a few sons of iniquity have been discovered trying to import into our land the old and condemned Wyclifite heresy as well as its foster child, the Lutheran heresy, by translating into our vernacular language all their corrupt works and publishing them in great numbers; they are striving with huge efforts to defile and stain our country with what are clearly most pestilent teachings, opposed to the truth of the Catholic faith. It is greatly to be feared that the Catholic truth will be completely at risk unless good and erudite men strenuously counter the malignancy of such incorrigible persons. This can be done in no more fitting and excellent way than if truth — in the Catholic language and totally defeating these crazy teachings — be published (and thus brought to light) at the same time as those. This will make it possible for people who, untrained in the Sacred Scriptures but having, alongside these new heretical books, other Catholic books as well which refute them, will now be able either to discern the truth themselves or be rightly advised and instructed by others whose judgment is more insightful.

And, since, dearest brother, you are able to play the part of a Demosthenes in both our native vernacular and in the Latin tongue, and have become a most experienced and keen assertor of Catholic truth in every arena, you will have no better way to spend your excess hours — if you can manage to steal some time from your occupations — than if you were to compose something in our own language that could lay bare the hidden malice of heretics for simple, non-expert individuals, and make them better instructed against such impious supplanters of the Church. You have a most outstanding example to imitate in our most illustrious Lord King Henry VIII, who, undertaking to assert the sacraments of the Church against Luther who was subverting them with all his might, earned therewith the immortal name of Defender of the Church to all eternity.

And so, lest you fight with these specters without knowing what you fight against (like the *Andabatae*, those blindfolded gladiators of antiquity), I am sending you the insane dirges they have written in our language, and, along with that, some books

434 at Oxford and Cambridge a judicial officer, in whom is vested the jurisdiction   belonging to the university in cases of treason and felony   **435** Translated by Gerald Malsbary, © CTMS 2017.

of Luther, from which these monstrous opinions have come forth. Once you have diligently read them through, you will the more easily understand the twisty places where the snakes hide themselves, and the intricate paths by which they seek to escape once they have been caught. For it is a great boost to victory to know thoroughly the enemy's plans, to be deeply acquainted with what they believe and where they are aiming. If you prepare to tear apart what they will claim they do not believe, you waste all your efforts. So then, blessings be upon you for undertaking such a holy labor, by which you both come to the aid of the Church and secure eternal glory in heaven for yourself; we greatly beseech you in the Lord, and we grant and concede you, to this end, the right and the license to keep and read books of this kind.

Given the seventh day of March, the year of our Lord 1527,[436] and the sixth year of our consecration.

162. To John Cochlaeus[437]
\<1528?\>

It is impossible, most honored sir, to express my feelings of debt to you for your kindness in keeping me informed on the incidents occurring in your locale. Germany has become our breeding ground for such things; its brood is as numerous as that once produced by Africa, and much more monstrous. The past centuries have not seen anything more monstrous than the Anabaptists, or more numerous than such baneful curses. Indeed, my dear Cochlaeus, when I view the present situation with its rapid deterioration, from day to day, I imagine that, in the near future, someone will rear his head and preach the utter rejection of Christ. And if some senseless clown does rear his head, with the present frenzied state of the masses, there will be no lack of supporters. I have never laid eyes on anything more foolish or more malicious than the Edict of Bern.[438] And, I am told, they have so dignified the disputation as to put it almost on the same level with their Edict. I wish, my dear Cochlaeus, I had the requisite knowledge in Scripture

and theology to be able to write an effective rejoinder to those baneful curses. Thanks to the goodness of God, most distinguished sir, you do possess that knowledge, with a fullness as few other men do. Nor has God's favor proved ineffectual in your case; you have ever used the talent entrusted to you so that one day you could return it, with abundant interest.[439] This makes me very happy, and God, in his turn, has begun to manifest his pleasure with your loyal services. After all your misfortunes, including a severe personal disaster, he has begun to look upon your sorrows with sympathy. Through his inspiration, your most illustrious Prince has attached you to his service, to the great advantage of our religion and to your own financial profit, and thereby he has chosen a replacement who is the perfect image of your excellent and scholarly predecessor.[440] I extend my congratulations to both of you — to your Prince for his good judgment, to you for having so noble a patron.

163. To Francis Cranevelt
Chelsea, 10 June 1528

As surely as I hope God loves me, your enormous kindness toward me, my dear Cranevelt, makes me ashamed of myself, for you send me such frequent, loving, and elaborate greetings, though I reply so rarely, especially since you have no fewer occupations than I do which you could since you have no fewer occupations than I do which you could give as pretexts, nay rather as genuine reasons. But you are so open-minded, so steadfast that, though you forgive everything in your friends, you yourself are always so persevering in pursuing your undertakings that you have no faults to be forgiven. But be sure of this, my dear Cranevelt, if something should happen which would seriously require that the services of a friend should be manifested, in that matter you would never find me at fault. Please give my regards to my mistress, your wife (for I do not dare to reverse the order again) and also to your whole household, to which mine sends heartfelt greetings. From my little country place, June 10, 1528.

---

436 1528 since, by old-style dating, the "new year" did not begin until March 25.   438 The disputation at Bern was held January 7–26, 1528.   439 1 Cor 15:10,   Mt 25:14 ff.   440 Hieronymus Emser (1477–1527)
437 John Dobneck (1479–1552)

163a. To Francis Cranevelt
London, 8 November <1528>

That most eminent gentleman Master Hacket, our
most serene King's ambassador to your country, has
5 sent me your letter, which was as pleasant to me as
is proper for a letter from someone who is so dear to
my heart that no one else could be dearer. I congratulate you heartily on the peace which has been restored among you, and would that someday I could
10 offer congratulations on a general peace, for which
Christendom has so long been miserably yearning. I
am delighted you have become so Homeric that you
can command such fitting verses from him for any
occasion, which you have also translated into Latin
15 that is in no way inferior to the Greek. I pray that
your spouse, a lady of the highest dignity, will have a
happy journey, complete her business exactly as she
wishes, and swiftly return, though I remember that
you once wrote to me that the most pleasant sleep
20 is in a bed without a wife, but these are the words
of husbands on the first nights after their wives have
been sent away, for on the remaining nights desire
comes creeping back and, unless the wife has left a
proxy, it makes sleep unpleasant. As for your wife,
25 I think she is so prudent that she has taken away all
her maidservants with her. Farewell, most delightful
of all men. London, November 8
　　　　　Such as he is, yours with all his heart,
　　　　　Thomas More, Knight
30 To a gentleman very distinguised for his character
and learning, Master Frans Cranevelt, Counselor to
his Imperial Majesty, at Mechelen

174. To Lady More
Woodstock, 3 September <1529>

35 *Sir Thomas More was made lord chancellor of En-*
gland in Michaelmas[441] *term in the year of our Lord*
1529, and in the twenty-first year of King Henry the
VIII. And in the latter end of the harvest then next be-
fore, Sir Thomas More then chancellor of the Duchy of
40 *Lancaster being returned from Cambrai in Flanders*
(where he had been Ambassador for the King) rode
immediately to the King to the Court at Woodstock.

And while he was there with the King, part of his
own dwelling house at Chelsea and all his barns there
full of corn[442] *suddenly fell on fire and were burnt*
45 *and all the corn therein by the negligence of one of*
his neighbors' carts that carried the corn, and by occa-
sion thereof were diverse of his next neighbor's barns
burned also. Upon which news brought unto him to
the Court, he wrote to the lady his wife this letter fol-
50 *lowing.* [Workes 1418-1419]

Mistress Alice, in my most hearty wise[443]
I recommend me[444] to you.

　　And whereas I am informed by my son Heron of
the loss of our barns and our neighbors' also with
55 all the corn that was therein, albeit[445] (saving God's
pleasure) it were great pity of so much good corn
lost, yet since it hath liked him[446] to send us such
a chance, we must and are bounden not only to be
content but also to be glad of his visitation. He sent
60 us all that we have lost and, since he hath by such
a chance taken it away, again his pleasure be fulfilled; let us never grudge[447] thereat but take in good
worth[448] and heartily thank him as well for adversity as for prosperity and peradventure[449] we have
65 more cause to thank him for our loss than for our
winning, for his wisdom better seeth what is good
for us than we do ourselves. Therefore I pray you
be of good cheer and take all the household with
you to church and there thank God both for that
70 he hath given us and for that he hath taken from us
and for that he hath left us, which if it please him
he can increase when he will and if it please him to
leave us yet less, at his pleasure be it.

　　I pray you to make some good ensearch[450] what
75 my poor neighbors have lost and bid them take no
thought therefor, for and[451] I should not leave myself a spoon there shall no poor neighbor of mine
bear no loss by any chance happened in my house.
I pray you be with my children and your house-
80 hold merry in God and devise somewhat with your
friends what way were the best to take for provision
to be made for corn for our household and for seed
this year coming, if ye think it good that we keep
the ground still in our hands, and whether ye think
85 it good that we so shall do or not, yet I think it were
not best suddenly thus to leave it all up and to put

---

441 the fall term beginning September 29　　remembrance or regard　**445** although　　**447** be unwilling　**448** part　**449** per-
442 grain　**443** manner　**444** *recommend*　　**446** *it hath liked him:* it has pleased God　　haps　**450** search　**451** even if
me: commend myself to your benevolent

away our folk off our farm, till we have somewhat advised us thereon; howbeit[452] if we have more now than ye shall need and which can get them other masters, ye may then discharge us of them, but I would not that any man were suddenly sent away he wot nere whither.[453] At my coming hither I perceived none other but that I should tarry still with the King's Grace but now I shall, I think, because of this chance get leave this next week to come home and see you, and then shall we further devise together upon all things what order shall be best to take.

And thus as heartily fare you well with all our children as ye can wish, at Woodstock the third day of September by the hand of

Your loving husband,
Thomas More, Kg.

174a. From Bishop Cuthbert Tunstall[454]
<London, 1529>

When I looked round to see to whom, from among all my friends, I might dedicate this composition, you seemed to me the most fitting of all both on account of our intimacy and on account of your frankness; for I know that you will be pleased at whatever good it may contain, warn me of whatever is imperfect, and forgive whatever is amiss.

178. To Erasmus
<Chelsea>, 28 October <1529>

Best Greetings. My thoughts and heart had long been set upon a life of retirement, when suddenly, without any warning, I was tossed into a mass of vital business affairs.[455] The nature of these affairs you will discover from your man Quirinus.[456] Some people here, friends of mine, are jubilant and heap congratulations upon me. But you are usually a prudent and shrewd judge of human affairs; perhaps you will sympathize with my lot. I am adapting myself to circumstances, and I am very happy at the extraordinary favor and kindness shown me by our excellent King; lacking the talent and other gifts required for this position, I intend to try seriously to meet his optimistic expectations by making every effort I am capable of, by complete loyalty, and by utter devotedness.

The rest of the details you will get from Quirinus, as I have given him thorough instructions. The more I realize that this post involves the interests of Christendom, my dearest Erasmus, the more I hope it all turns out successfully, for your sake rather than my own. Farewell, dearest Erasmus, more than half of my soul. From my country home, October 28.

More than wholeheartedly yours,
Thomas More

To the excellent and most learned Master Erasmus of Rotterdam, at Freiburg.

182. To Sir John Arundel
Chelsea, 5 April <1530>

Master Arundel, in my right hearty wise[457] I recommend me[458] unto you. And whereas I understand that ye be one of the coparishioners of the manor of Sharshell Barton in the parish of Steeple Barton in the county of Oxford and the farm of Darneton in the same county, and that your part of the same manor and farm amounteth by year to four marks[459] or thereabout, so it is that a servant of mine, one Edward Jones, a man right honest and whom I especially favor, hath obtained of my Lord South and other your partners their good wills and grants for a lease of their parts in the same. Wherefore and forasmuch as the said manor and farm cannot be well occupied but by one tenant without great unquietness of either part if it were occupied by diverse, I therefore heartily require[460] you to be good unto my said servant, which shall be as good a tenant unto you as any other shall, and as much to your profit, of which I will not for any friend of mine require any part of your loss. And in being thus good unto my said servant for my sake, ye shall bind him to pray for you, and me to do for any friend of yours

---

452 however   **453** *wot nere whither:* knows not where   **454** As Stapleton explains in his biography, this short letter is from the mathematics book Cuthbert Tunstall wrote and then dedicated to More.

455 More was appointed lord chancellor on October 25, 1529.   **456** Quirinus Talesius (1505–73) of Haarlem was educated in Cologne and became servant-pupil to Erasmus *ca.* 1524.   **457** *right hearty wise:*

most hearty manner   **458** *recommend me:* commend myself to your benevolent remembrance or regard   **459** In England a mark was equivalent in value to two-thirds of a pound sterling.   **460** ask

any such lawful pleasure as shall lie in my power. And thus heartily fare you well.

   At Chelsea the 5th day of April.

               Your assured lover,

                     Thom. More, Kg, Chancellor

To the right worshipful[461] Sir John Arundel, Knight

182a. To George Guildford
Westminster, 8 July <1530>

I commend me unto you. And whereas a commission was dutied[462] unto you and to others for the examination and hearing of a matter in variance between Richard Bramble and others of Cranbrook, complainants, and Richard Barr of Cranbrook, aforesaid defendant. So it is that the said Richard Bramble hath made petition to me and to others of the King's Council that ye and the other commissioners should make your certificate here unto us what ye with the others do find or perceive therein. Wherefore it is ordered that ye and others of the said commissioners do certify[463] me and others of the said Council what ye with the others have done therein. Or else that ye the said commissioners according to the said commission call before you the said parties, and further to take such order and direction[464] with them, as[465] they or any of them have no further cause to trouble me and others of the said Council concerning the same matter. And if so be that ye the said commissioners can make none end nor determination between the said parties, that then ye with the others to[466] certify me and others of the said Council in the first day of the next term ensuing, certifying us what ye have done about the premises.[467]

   From Westminster, the eighth day of July

               Your lover and friend,

                  Tho. More, Kg

                        Chancellor

To Master George Guildford be this delivered in haste.

183a. From Emperor Charles V to the Chancellor of England[468]
Brussels, 11 March 1531

My Cousin,[469]

   Besides the good, honest, and virtuous desire which I know you have always had toward me and my subjects, of entertaining all good neighborly and friendly relationships between them and the subjects of the King of England, my dearest uncle, cousin, and good brother, I have been acquainted by my ambassador Doctor Eustace Chapuys, overseas resident, of the good office that you daily, constantly, and cleverly provide toward my said subjects regarding things and business they have with the said Lord King my uncle, for which I would like to thank you with very good words, and to inform you that, concerning whatever may please you, you will find me very agreeable and affectionate. I have ordered that my ambassador should give you what you desire. Written in Brussels on the 11th day of March, in the year 1531.

   From the Emperor to the Chancellor of England.

188. To Erasmus
Chelsea, 14 June 1532

Thomas More sends his greetings to Erasmus of Rotterdam.

   It has been my constant wish almost since boyhood, dearest Desiderius, that some day I might enjoy the opportunity which, to my happiness, you have always had, namely, of being relieved of all public duties and eventually being able to devote some time to God alone and myself; at long last this wish has come true,[470] Erasmus, thanks to the goodness of the supreme and almighty God and to the graciousness of a very understanding Sovereign. I have not, however, attained exactly what I had wished for. My prayer had been to reach the crowning point of my life healthy and vigorous, no matter how old, or at least without sickness and suffering,

---

461 honorable, distinguished   462 put under an obligation to take a certain action   463 inform; attest to   464 *take … with them:* arrange matters regarding them in such a way   465 so that   466 are to

467 aforementioned matters   468 The manuscript of this letter is in the Vienna State Archives, *England Varia, Fz. 2.* The translation is by Marie-Claire Phélippeau.   469 Kings and emperors often used the

term "cousin" in a symbolic sense as a sign of respect in addressing noblemen, lords, heads of state, cardinals, etc.   470 More had resigned May 16, 1532.

as far as one could expect at that age. Perhaps that was a little too bold; in any case, the answer to that prayer is at present in God's hands. For some sort of chest ailment has laid hold of me; and the discomfort and pain it causes do not bother me as much as the worry and fear over the possible consequences. After being troubled with this ailment continually for several months, I consulted the doctors, who said that such a lingering disease could be dangerous; in their view there was no speedy cure possible; healing would be a long, slow process, requiring proper diet, medicines, and rest. They did not predict the length of convalescence, nor did they even give me assurance of a complete cure.

So, while turning these thoughts over in my mind, I realized that I would either have to resign my office or be inefficient in discharging it, as I would be unable to carry out the responsibilities which my position entailed, except at the risk of my life; and in the case of death, I would have to give up office as well as life. Therefore I decided to do without the one rather than without both. Out of concern, then, for affairs of state, as well as for my own health, I humbly prevailed upon the generosity of our most noble and excellent Sovereign to condescend to have pity on me and to relieve me of the overwhelming burden of that office, the highest in the realm, with which, as you know, he had shown favor for me and marked me with a distinction far beyond any merit or even ambition or wish on my part. My prayer, then, to all the saints of Heaven is that God, who alone has the power, may repay adequately these acts of fond affection shown me by our most noble King, and, to prevent me from spending whatever time he will add to my life in idleness and inactivity, that God may also grant me both the spirit to employ those good hours well and, in addition, strength of body to do so. For when my health is weak, I am so listless that I accomplish nothing at all.

My dear Erasmus, we are not all Erasmuses; the gracious gift which God has granted to you, practically alone of all mankind, that gift all of us must wait to receive. With the exception of yourself, who would dare to promise what you produce? Though burdened by the weight of your years and constantly suffering from illnesses that would prove exhausting and overwhelming for a healthy young man, still never all through the years of your entire life have you failed to give an account to all the world with outstanding publications, as if neither the weight of years nor ill health could in any way diminish that record. While this one fact alone is, in the judgment of all men, like a miracle, still, amazingly, the miracle is magnified by the fact that the host of brawling critics surrounding and attacking you have in no way deterred you from publishing, though apparently they had the power to crush the heart of a Hercules. Such men are constantly stirred up against you, because they are envious of your unparalleled gifts and also of your learning, which outmatches even those gifts; they readily realize that such unique qualities of native talent and hard work are far beyond their reach; still, almost bursting with envy, they cannot endure being far inferior to you; therefore, of course, they contrive together and strive with might and main by incessant personal abuse to see if they can drag your high honor down to their own shameful level.

However, all during the many years that they have been shouldering this rock of Sisyphus, what have they accomplished by their fruitless and wicked efforts except to have the rock come tumbling down again and again upon their own heads? Meanwhile you have kept surging ever upwards. And does it really matter that on occasion even good men, with a certain amount of learning, have been unsettled because, in their view, you perhaps handled some point with too little restraint? After all, every author has been guilty of that, including your own critics, who, while branding your works, could not refrain from committing the same defect—a defect, in this instance, that was too obvious for men of their rank, and of too frequent occurrence for any type of writing. There is much less reason for excusing them, as they are surely aware of the open confession you made before the outbreak of these pestilential heresies, which are now spreading like wildfire and wreaking utter havoc; you admitted that you had handled some points with too little restraint, but, had you been able to foresee the eventual cropping up of these treacherous enemies of religion, you would have treated those same points more gently and more delicately. The rather strong statements you made in those days were evoked by the defects of certain people—defects which were quite the opposite of your own, and which those people hugged to their bosoms as if they were virtues. Anyone who would consider your vigorous spirit a defect will have a

difficult time trying to justify the holiest of the ancient doctors of the Church; if those doctors had
had the same view of the modern age as they had
of their own, I am absolutely sure that some of the
5 statements they made in their day would have been
more guarded and more carefully modified. But
they did not do that, because they were trying to
cure current evils and did not have in mind future
ones. To be sure, they suffered the same experience
10 as you now are suffering, in being the target for the
slanderous charges of those fellows, for the heretics that mushroomed in a later age have boasted of
their borrowings from the works of the ancients;
this experience you have in common not only with
15 those very holy Fathers and most ancient guardians of the orthodox Faith, but also with the apostles and evangelists, and even with our own Savior,
for their words have been used by all heretics as the
chief, or almost the sole, basis upon which they
20 have attempted to lay the foundation of teachings
utterly false.

Congratulations, then, my dear Erasmus, on your
outstanding virtuous qualities; however, if on occasion some good person is unsettled and disturbed
25 by some point, even without a sufficiently serious
reason, still do not be chagrined at making accom-
modations for the pious dispositions of such men.
But as for those snapping, growling, malicious fellows, ignore them and, without faltering, quietly
30 continue to devote yourself to the promotion of intellectual things and the advancement of virtue.

Concerning the person[471] whom you recommended to me for scholarly reasons, not for religious ones, I have been very prudently and politely
35 warned by friends to be on my guard so as not to
be taken in by him. I shall certainly do all I can to
handle the situation. I am keenly aware of the risk
involved in an open-door policy toward these newfangled erroneous sects. Even though they have
40 been held in check up to now in our country, thanks
to the vigilance of the bishops and the influence of
our Sovereign, still it is remarkable what tricks they
use in their first attempts to sneak into a place, and
then the pertinacity with which they try to crash
45 their way through. And one or two of our own

fellow countrymen, with a steady stream of books
written in our vernacular and containing mistrans-
lations, and worse, misinterpretations of Scripture,
have been sending into our land every brand of heresy from Belgium, where they have sought refuge. 50
I have written replies to several of these books, not
however out of any great worry for one who would
examine the works of both men thoroughly, but because some people like to give an approving eye to
novel ideas, out of superficial curiosity, and to dan- 55
gerous ideas, out of deviltry; and in so doing, they
assent to what they read, not because they believe
it is true, but because they want it to be true. However, one will never in any way succeed in satisfying
that breed of humans who have a passion for wick- 60
edness. All my efforts are directed toward the protection of those men who do not deliberately desert the truth, but are seduced by the enticements
of clever fellows. Farewell, most learned Erasmus,
you who have been of great service to genuine in- 65
tellectual life.

From my home at Chelsea. June 14, 1532.

189. To John Cochlaeus
Chelsea, 14 June <1532>

My excellent and most affectionate Cochlaeus— 70
our man George[472] has returned with your letter,
also with a bundle of books including, among other
things, your polemical works in which, as a valiant
champion of the Gospel and religion, you do battle with that mighty opponent of the Church, Lu- 75
ther; your learning and piety are the equal of your
fighting heart. Since George's return to England, I
have received several letters from you dated at various times. The latest of them contained the information about Zwingli and Oecolampadius,[473] and 80
I was glad to hear the news of their deaths. Unfortunately, however, they have left in their wake
many very real reasons for being sad, which I cannot mention without a shudder and which are
known to everybody and which pious men ought 85
not hear without a heavy sigh. Still, it is right for us
to rejoice that such savage enemies of the Christian

---

471 Simon Gryner (Grynaeus) (*ca.* 1494–
1541) **472** not identified **473** Zwingli
as chaplain was killed in the battle of

Kappel, October 11, 1531, and his body, as
a heretic's, was burned. Oecolampadius,

the first Protestant pastor at the Minster in
Basel, died November 24, 1531.

faith have been removed from our midst, enemies that were so fully equipped for the destruction of the Church and so eager for every opportunity to uproot piety.

For the past several months the condition of my health has aroused strong feelings of fear within me, although outwardly I have not appeared very ill. Not even since my release from all public duties have I succeeded in shaking off this ailment. It was a fact that I was incapable of carrying out my duties as chancellor effectively without aggravating the malady, and the doctor held out no hope for my recovery unless I retired to private life. Not even then could he give me any definite assurance. My decision, then, was influenced by a desire to regain my health, but much more so by my regard for the common good, which I would hinder in many ways if, while handicapped by bad health, I would myself be a handicap to affairs of state. I have resolved to devote to intellectual things and to God the leisure graciously granted to me, at my request, by the sympathetic kindness of our Most Illustrious Sovereign. Give me your help, dearest Cochlaeus, by praying to God that this plan may turn out successfully for me. Good luck and farewell; from my home at Chelsea, June 14.

190. Against John Frith[474]
Chelsea, 7 December <1532>

In my most hearty wise[475] I recommend me[476] to you,[477] and send you by this bringer the writing again[478] which I received from you, whereof I have been offered since a couple of copies more in the meanwhile as late[479] as you wot[480] well it was, whereby men may see how greedily that these new-named brethren write it[481] out, and secretly spread it abroad. So that whereas the King's gracious Highness like a most faithful Catholic prince, for the avoiding of such pestilent books as sow such poisoned heresies among his people, hath by his open[482] proclamations utterly forbidden all English printed books to be brought into this land from beyond the sea, lest our English heretics that are lurking there might there print their heresies among other matters, and so send them hither unsuspected, and therefore unperceived till more harm were[483] felt than after were well remediable, the devil hath now taught his disciples, the devisers of these heresies, to make many short treatises, whereof their scholars may shortly[484] write out copies, but in their treatises to put as much poison in one written leaf as they printed before in fifteen, as it well appeareth in this one writing of this young man's making, which[485] hath, I here say, lately made diverse other things, that yet run in huggermugger[486] so close among the brethren, that there cometh no copies abroad.

And would God for his mercy that since there can nothing refrain[487] their study from the device and compassing[488] of evil and ungracious[489] writing, that they could and would keep it so secret, that never man should see it but such as are already so far corrupted, as never would be[490] cured of their canker. For less harm were it if only they that are already bemired were as the Scripture saith mired on more and more,[491] than that they should cast their dirt abroad upon other folks' clean clothes. But alack this will not be. For as Saint Paul saith, the contagion of heresy creepeth on like a canker.[492] For as the canker corrupteth the body further and further, and turneth the whole parts into the same deadly sickness, so do these heretics creep forth among good simple souls, and under a vain hope of some high secret learning, which other men abroad either willingly did keep from them, or else could not teach them, they daily with such abominable books corrupt and destroy in corners[493] very many before those writings come unto light, till at the last the smoke of that secret fire beginneth to reke[494] out at some corner, and sometimes the whole fire so flameth out at once, that it burneth up whole towns, and wasteth whole countries, ere[495] ever it can be mastered, and yet never after so well and clearly[496] quenched, but that it lieth lurking still in

---

474 Thomas More is responding to *A Christen Sentence* (CW 7: 427–33) by John Frith (1503–33), a Cambridge scholar, English priest, and follower of William Tyndale. **475** manner **476** *recommend me:* commend myself to your benevolent remembrance or regard **477** The person addressed here is unknown. **478** back **479** recent **480** know **481** Frith's book **482** public **483** would be **484** quickly **485** who **486** secret **487** *there can nothing refrain:* nothing can keep **488** *device and compassing:* devising and contriving **489** wicked, graceless **490** *would be:* wish to be **491** See Rv 22:11. **492** See 2 Tm 2:17. **493** secret **494** shoot **495** before **496** completely

some old rotten timber under cellars and ceilings, that if it be not well waited on and marked, will not fail at length to fall on an open fire again, as it hath fared in late[497] years at more places than one, both the one fire and the other. And therefore I am both sure, and sorry too, that those other books as well as this is now of this young man's will once come unto light, and then shall it appear wherefore[498] they be kept so close.[499] Howbeit, a worse[500] than this is, though the words be smooth and fair, the devil, I trow,[501] cannot make. For herein he runneth a great way beyond Luther, and teacheth in few leaves[502] shortly, all the poison that Wycliffe,[503] Hussgen,[504] Tyndale,[505] and Zwingli[506] have taught in all their long books before, concerning the Blessed Sacrament of the altar, affirming it to be not only very[507] bread still as Luther doth, but also, as those other beasts do, saith it is nothing else, and that there is neither the blessed body of Christ, nor his blood, but for a remembrance of Christ's Passion only bare[508] bread and wine. And therein goeth he so far in conclusion that he saith it is all one unto us in a manner[509] whether it be consecrated or unconsecrated. And so that Blessed Sacrament, that is and ever hath in all Christendom been held of all sacraments the chief, and not only a sacrament but the very self[510] thing also which other sacraments betoken,[511] and whereof all other sacraments take their effect and strength, he maketh in manner (taking the consecration so slight and so light) no manner[512] sacrament at all, wherein he runneth yet beyond Tyndale and all the heretics that ever I remember before.

And now the matter being of such a marvelous weight, it is a great wonder to see upon how light and slight occasions he is fallen unto these abominable heinous heresies.

For he denieth not nor cannot say nay but that our Savior said himself, "My flesh is verily[513] meat, and my blood is verily drink."[514]

He denieth not also that Christ himself at his Last Supper, taking the bread into his blessed hands, after that he had blessed it said unto his disciples, "Take you this and eat it; this is my body that shall be given for you." And in like wise gave them the chalice after his blessing and consecration, and said unto them, "This is the chalice of my blood of the New Testament, which shall be shed out for many; do you this in remembrance of me."[515]

The young man denieth not nor can deny but that our Savior here himself said that it was his own body, and said that it was his own blood, and there ordained that it should be in remembrance of him continually consecrated. So that he must needs confess that all they which believe that it is his very body and his very blood indeed, have the plain words of our Savior himself upon their side, for the ground and foundation of their faith.

But now saith this young man against all this that our Savior in other places of Scripture, called himself a very vine, and his disciples very branches.[516] And he calleth himself a door also,[517] not for that[518] he was any of these things indeed but for certain properties for which he likened himself to those things. As a man for some properties saith of his neighbor's horse, "This horse is mine up and down," meaning that it is in everything so like. And like[519] as Jacob built an altar, and called it the God of Israel,[520] and as Jacob called the place where he wrestled with the angel the face of God,[521] and that the paschal lamb was called the passing by of the Lord,[522] with infinite such other phrases as he saith, not for that they were so indeed, but for certain similitudes in the properties; so saith this young man that Christ, though he said by his plain words, "This is my body," and "This is my blood," yet for all that he meant not that it was his body and his blood indeed no more than that he meant that himself was a very door or a very vine indeed though for certain properties he called himself both. And he saith that

497 *fared in late:* happened in recent **498** why **499** secret **500** *Howbeit… worse:* However, a worse book **501** believe **502** pages **503** John Wycliffe (*ca.* 1320–1384), best known for translating the Vulgate into Middle English, was declared a heretic posthumously at the Council of Constance (1415). For his views on the Eucharist, see *Tractatus de apostasia* and *De eucharista tractatus.* **504** better known as Johannes Oecolampadius (1482–1531), a prominent German Protestant **505** William Tyndale (*ca.* 1494–1536), known for his translation of the English Bible from Hebrew and Greek, maintained a close friendship and collaboration with Frith during their exile from England. Tyndale was executed for heresy one year after More's death. **506** Ulrich Zwingli (1484–1531), leader of the Swiss Reformation, denied the real physical presence of Christ in the Eucharist in *De vera et falsa religione commentarius.* **507** actual, true **508** mere **509** *in a manner:* so to speak **510** same **511** typify, symbolize **512** kind of **513** truly **514** Jn 6:56 **515** Mt 26:26–28; Mk 14:22–24; Lk 22:19–20; 1 Cor 11:23–25 **516** Jn 15:1–6 **517** Jn 10:7 **518** *for that:* because **519** just **520** Gn 33:20 **521** Gn 32:30 **522** Ex 12:11, 21

Christ meant in like wise here, not that it was or should be his own body and his blood indeed but that it should be to them and us as a remembrance of him in his absence, as verily as though it were his very body and his very blood indeed as the Paschal lamb was a token and a remembrance of the passing by of the Lord, and as a bridegroom giveth his bride a ring if he hap to go into a far country from her, for a remembrance of him in his absence, and as a sure[523] sign that he will keep her his faith and not break her his promise.

In good faith it grieveth me very sore[524] to see this young man so circumvented[525] and beguiled by certain old lines of the devil, as we now see that he is, when he is fain,[526] for the defense of this error, to flit in conclusion[527] from the faith of plain and open Scripture and so far fall to the new-fangled fantasies of foolish heretics that he will for the allegory destroy the true sense of the letter, in maintenance[528] of a new false sect, against the holy true Catholic faith so fully confirmed and continued in Christ's whole Catholic Church this fifteen hundred years together. For these dregs hath he drunken of[529] Wycliffe and Oecolampadius, Tyndale and Zwingli and so hath he all that he argueth here besides; which four what manner folk they be, is meetly[530] well-perceived and known, and God hath in part with his open vengeance declared.[531] And ever hath God and ever will, by some way, declare his wrath and indignation against as many as fall into such damnable opinions against the blessed body and blood of his only begotten Son. From which perilous opinion and all his other errors, the great mercy of our sweet Savior call home again, and save this young man in time.

As for his allegories I am not offended with, nor with similitudes neither where they may have place, though[532] he take one of his neighbor's horses as he doth, and another if he list[533] of his own cows — provided always for a thing[534] which he list to call like he misconstrue not the Scripture, and take away the very thing indeed as he doth here.

Now his example also of his bridegroom's ring I very well allow.[535] For, I take the Blessed Sacrament

to be left with us for a very token and a memorial of Christ indeed. But I say that whole substance of the same token and memorial is his own blessed body, whereas this man would make it only bread.

And so I say that Christ hath left us a better token than this man would have us take it for, and therein fareth[536] like a man to whom a bridegroom had delivered a goodly gold ring with a rich ruby therein, to deliver over to his bride for a token, and then he would, like a false shrew,[537] keep away that gold ring, and give the bride in the stead thereof a proper[538] ring of a rush and tell her that the bridegroom would send her no better; or else like one that, when the bridegroom had given such a gold ring to his bride for a token, would tell her plain and make her believe that the ring were but copper or brass, to diminish the bridegroom's thanks.[539]

If he said that the words of Christ might besides the literal sense be understood in an allegory, I would well agree with him. For so may every word almost through the whole Scripture, calling an allegory every sense, whereby the words be translated unto some other spiritual understanding, besides the true plain open sense that the letter first intended. But on the other side, because that[540] in some words of Scripture is there none other thing intended but an allegory, to go therefore and in another place of Scripture to take away with an allegory the very true literal sense as he doth here — this is the fault that we find in him, which if it may be suffered,[541] must needs make all the Scripture, as touching[542] any point of our faith, of none effect or force at all. I marvel me[543] therefore much that he is not afraid to affirm that these words of Christ, of his body and his blood, must needs be understood only by way of a similitude or an allegory as the words be of the vine and the door.

Now this he wotteth[544] well, that though some words spoken by the mouth of Christ written in Scripture be[545] to be understood only by way of a similitude or an allegory, it followeth not thereupon that of necessity every like word of Christ in other places was none other but an allegory. For, such kind of sophistication[546] in arguing was the

523 certain; secure   524 greatly
525 entrapped   526 obliged, forced; inclined   527 the end   528 support
529 from   530 fairly   531 Zwingli had died in battle in 1531.   532 even if

533 desires   534 *provided...thing:* provided that given any thing
535 approve   536 acts   537 *false shrew:* deceitful villain   538 attractive
539 credit; gratitude owed (to the

bridegroom)   540 *because that:* because
541 allowed, permitted   542 *as touching:* that touches upon   543 *marvel me:* am amazed   544 knows   545 are
546 sophistry

very cavillation and shift[547] that the wicked Arians[548] used, which like as this young man taketh away now from the Blessed Sacrament the very[549] body and blood of Christ, by expounding his plain words with an allegory under color[550] of some other places where such allegories must needs have place, and were none otherwise meant, so did they take from Christ's blessed person his omnipotent Godhead, and would not grant him to be equal with almighty God his Father, but the plain texts of Scripture which proved his Godhead they expound wrong and frowardly,[551] not only by some other texts that seemed to say otherwise, but also as this young man doth here by some allegories, affirming that he was called God and the Son of God in Holy Scripture, by such manner of speaking, or as this young man calleth it, by such a manner of phrase as the Scripture for some property calleth certain other persons gods and God's sons in other places, as where God saith to Moses, "I shall make thee the god of Pharaoh";[552] and where he saith, "thou shalt not backbite the gods";[553] and where he saith, "I say you be gods and the sons of the high God be you all."[554]

And thus against that — that Christ was God and the Son of God — such cavillations these Arians lay[555] in expounding the plain places with false allegories, resembling[556] them to other places in which like allegories must needs have place, as this young man by the necessary allegories of Christ's words, used in the vine and in the door, would in like wise with like cavillations as the Arians used against Christ's Godhead, pull away the true literal sense of Christ's words concerning the truth of his very body and blood in the Blessed Sacrament.

And surely if this manner of handling of Scripture may be received and brought in ure[557] — that because of allegories used in some places every man may at his pleasure draw every place to an allegory, and say the letter meaneth nothing else — there is not any text in all the Scripture but a wilful person may find other texts against it, that may serve him to trifle out[558] the truth of God's words, with cavillations grounded upon God's other words, in some other place, wherein if he may be heard as long as he list[559] to talk — be it but a woman — yet shall she find chat[560] enough for all a whole year. And so did those old Arians, of whom God forbade that this young man should follow that evil example.

If every man that can find out a new-found fantasy upon a text of Holy Scripture may have his own mind[561] taken, and his own exposition believed, against the expositions of the old holy cunning doctors[562] and saints, then may you surely see that no article of the Christian faith can stand and endure long. For, as holy Saint Jerome saith of himself,[563] if the exposition of other interpreters and the consent[564] of the common[565] Catholic Church, were of no more strength but that every new man might be believed that could bring some texts of Scripture for him, expounded as it pleased himself, then could I, saith this holy man, bring up a new sect also, and say by Scripture that no man were a true Christian man nor a member of the Church that keepeth two coats. And in good faith if that way were allowed, I were able myself to find out fifteen new sects in one forenoon, that should have as much probable hold of Scripture as this heresy hath. Against which, besides the common faith of all Catholic Christian regions, the expositions of the old holy doctors and saints be clear[566] against this young man's mind in this matter, as whole[567] as against any heresy that ever was hitherto heard of. For, as for the words of Christ of which we speak touching[568] the Blessed Sacrament, though he may find some old holy men that besides the literal sense doth expound them in an allegory, yet shall he never find any of them that did as he doth now, after[569] Wycliffe, Oecolampadius, Tyndale, and Zwingli, deny the literal sense, and say that Christ meant not that it was his very body and his very blood indeed; but the old holy doctors and expositors besides all such allegories, do plainly declare and expound that in those words our Savior, as he expressly spoke, so did also well and plainly mean that the thing, which he there gave to his disciples

---

547 *cavillation and shift:* frivolous quibble and fraudulent stratagem **548** Arianism, which subordinates Christ to the Father, was condemned as heresy by the Council of Nicaea in 325. **549** true **550** pretext **551** perversely **552** Ex 7:1 **553** Ex 22:28 **554** Ps 81(82):6 **555** alleged **556** likening **557** *in ure:* into use, practice **558** *trifle out:* dismiss with mockery **559** wants **560** idle prattle **561** opinion; judgment **562** *cunning doctors:* learned theologians **563** *Dialogus adversus Luciferianos* 28 (PL 23: 181–82), referring to Mt 10:10 **564** consensus **565** belonging to all mankind alike **566** entirely **567** completely **568** touching upon, concerning **569** following

in the Sacrament, were in very deed his very flesh and blood. And so did never any of the old expositors of Scripture expound any of those other places in which Christ is called a vine or a door. And therefore it appeareth well that the manner of speaking was not like.[570] For, if it had,[571] then would not the old expositors have used such so far unlike fashion in the expounding of them.

And over[572] this, the very circumstances of the places in the Gospel, in which our Savior speaketh of that Sacrament, may well make open the difference of his speech in this matter and of all those others, and that as he spoke all those but in an allegory so spoke he this, plainly meaning that he spoke of his very body and his very blood besides all allegories. For, neither when our Lord said he was a very vine, nor when he said he was the door, there was none that heard him that anything[573] marveled thereof. And why? For because they perceived well that he meant not that he was a material vine indeed, nor a material door neither. But when he said that his flesh was very meat, and his blood was very drink,[574] and that they should not be saved but if[575] they did eat his flesh and drink his blood, then were they all in such a wonder thereof, that they could not abide.[576] And wherefore?[577] But because they perceived well by his words and his manner of circumstances used in the speaking of them, that Christ spoke of his very flesh and his very blood indeed. For else[578] the strangeness of the words would have made them to have taken it as well for an allegory as either his words of the vine or of the door. And then would they have no more marveled at the one than they did at the other. But now whereas at the vine and the door they marveled nothing,[579] yet at the eating of his flesh and drinking of his blood, they so sore[580] marveled, and were so sore moved, and thought the matter so hard, and the wonder so great, that they asked, how could that be, and went almost all their way, whereby we may well see that he spoke these words in such wise[581] as the hearers perceived that he meant it not in a parable nor an allegory, but spoke of his very flesh and his very blood indeed.

Many other plain proofs[582] might a man gather upon the circumstances of the very texts, where this thing is spoken of in the Scripture, but that it is not my purpose now to stick[583] in argument of this matter, that is of itself so clear[584] out of all question, but only a little to touch it, that ye may see how little pith[585] and substance for his matter is in all those examples of allegory, which Wycliffe, Oecolampadius, Tyndale, and Zwingli have brought out against the Blessed Sacrament, and wherewith those old shrews[586] have with their false similitudes piteously deceived either the simplicity[587] or the lightness of this seely[588] young man, which might if he had not either of lightness[589] overrun himself, or of simpleness been deceived, or of pride and high mind in putting forth heresies willingly beguiled and blinded, easily have perceived himself that the more such allegories that he found in the Scripture in like manner of phrases or speech the worse is his part, and the more clear is it that these places speaking of the Blessed Sacrament were plainly meant as they were spoken, besides all such allegories. For else had never both the hearers at the time and the expositors since, and all Christian people besides this fifteen hundred years, taken only in this one matter the plain literal sense being so strange and marvelous that it might seem impossible, and decline from the letter[590] for allegories in all such other things, being as he saith and as indeed they be, so many far in number more.

Howbeit,[591] as for this point—that an allegory used in some place is not a cause sufficient to make men leave the proper significations of God's Word in every other place, and seek an allegory and forsake the plain common sense and understanding of the letter—this perceived the young man well enough himself. For, he confesseth that he would not so do save[592] for necessity, because he seeth as he saith that the common literal sense is impossible. For, the thing he saith that is meant thereby cannot be true: that is to wit,[593] that the very body of Christ cannot be in the Sacrament, because the Sacrament is in many diverse places at once, and was at the Maundy[594]—that is to wit, in the hands of

---

570 similar 571 had been 572 in addition to 573 at all 574 Jn 6:54–56 575 *but if:* unless 576 remain there 577 why? 578 otherwise 579 not 580 greatly; grievously 581 a manner 582 evidence 583 persist 584 completely 585 force 586 villains 587 ignorance; foolishness 588 pitiable 589 frivolity, unsteadiness 590 literal meaning 591 However 592 except 593 say 594 Last Supper

Christ and in every of his apostles' mouths, and at that time it was not glorified. And then he saith that Christ's body, not being glorified, could no more be in two places at once than his own can. And yet he goeth after further, and saith that no more it can neither when it is glorified too. And that he proveth by the saying of Saint Augustine, whose words be, as he saith, that the body with which Christ rose must be in one place, and that it continueth in heaven, and shall do till he shall come to judge both quick[595] and dead. And yet at the last he proveth that the body of Christ cannot be in many places at once. For if it might be in many places at once, then it might, he saith, be in all places at once. But in all places at once he saith it cannot be, and thereof he concludeth that it cannot be in many places at once. And thus for this impossibility of the thing that riseth upon the common literal sense of Christ's words, he is, he saith, of necessity driven to fall from it unto some allegory, which he confesseth that he would not do, if the plain literal sense were possible. But alas for the dear mercy of God if we should leave the letter and seek an allegory with the destruction of the literal sense, in every place where we find a thing that reason cannot reach unto, nor see which way it were possible, and therefore would take it for impossible; fain[596] would I wit[597] what one article of all our faith this young man could assign me spoken of in the Scripture, from which his reason shall not drive away the strength of his proof in making him leave the literal sense, wherein his proof should stand and send him to seek an allegory that may stand with reason and drive away the faith, where he should believe the letter and make his reason obedient unto faith.

I marvel me very much why the consideration of this impossibility should of necessity drive this young man from the plain open literal sense of Christ's words spoken of the Blessed Sacrament, since so many good and holy men so long together this fifteen hundred years together have believed the literal sense well and firmly, and could not be driven from it for any such consideration of such impossibility, and yet being as natural men, as wise men, as well-learned men, as studious in the matter, and men of more age, and more sure, sad,[598]

and substantial judgment than this young man is yet, and men at the least as likely to see what were possible and what were impossible as this good young man is. And therefore as for all his reasons grounded upon impossibility, since I may be bold to think as all those old holy men have thought, and as all wise men I ween yet[599] think, that nothing is impossible to God,[600] I esteem all those reasons very little worth.

Howbeit, one thing he bringeth in by the way that I would[601] he had showed in what place we might find it—that is to wit, the saying of Saint Augustine. For why[602] to seek out one line in all his books were to go look a needle in a meadow. But surely if we may see the place where the young man found it, we shall I doubt not make a clear answer to it. And yet even as himself hath rehearsed[603] it, that saying maketh nothing for the proof of his purpose. For Saint Augustine saith[604] no more but that the body in which Christ arose must be in one place, and that it continueth in heaven, and shall do till the Day of Doom.[605] As help me God, except[606] this young man in these words of Saint Augustine see further with his young sight than I can see with mine old eyes and my spectacles, I marvel me much that ever he would for his purpose once bring them in. For when Saint Augustine saith that the body in which Christ arose, must needs be in one place, he might mean by those words, for anything that here appeareth to the contrary, not that his body might not be in two diverse places at once, but that it must be in one place—that is to say, in some place one or other, or that he must have one place for his special place, and that place must be heaven, as we say God must be in heaven, and angels must be in heaven. He speaketh nothing of the Sacrament, nor saith not his body with which he rose must needs be so in one place that it can by no possibility be in any more.

Also this word "must" which is in the Latin tongue called *oportet,* which word Saint Augustine here useth as this young man rehearseth him, doth not always signify such a necessity, as excludeth all possibility of the contrary. For, our Savior said himself to the two disciples, *Nonne haec oportuit pati Christum, et ita intrare in gloriam suam?*[607] Was it

---

595 living   **596** gladly, willingly
597 know   **598** serious   **599** *ween yet:*
believe still   **600** Lk 1:37   **601** wish

602 because   **603** related   **604** See
Augustine's *Tractatus in Iohannem* 30.1.
605 *Day of Doom:* Judgment Day

606 unless   **607** "Was it not necessary
that the Christ should suffer these things
and enter into his glory?" (Lk 24:26).

not so that Christ must die, and so enter into his glory? And yet himself said also that he might for all that have chosen whether he would have died or no.[608] For, himself saith that to depart with his soul and to take his soul again, both twain[609] were things put in his own power. And the prophet Isaiah saith of him, "He was offered up because he so would himself."[610] And therefore this Latin word *oportet*, which Saint Augustine hath in that place, is many times in the Latin tongue taken not for full and precise necessity, but for expedient and convenient.[611] And therefore it is translated also into English, not only by this word "must" which yet signifieth not always an impossibility of the contrary, but oftentimes by this word "it behooveth" which word signifieth that it is to be done for our behalf and commodity,[612] and not that it can in no wise[613] be avoided, but that it must needs be. And therefore since all that driveth this young man from the literal sense is as he saith the impossibility of Christ's body to be at once in diverse places, and proveth that thing impossible by the words of Saint Augustine, that saith no more but that it must be in one place, and saith not that it may be in no more but one, nor speaketh not of any such necessity whereof he putteth the contrary for impossible, nor speaketh no word at all there of the Sacrament; since Saint Augustine I say saith no further than this, I marvel much in my heart, what thing this young man seeth in his words worthy the bringing in for any proof of his purpose.

And that ye may the more clearly see that Saint Augustine speaketh here of no necessity, he not only saith that the body of Christ with which he rose must be in one place, but also he determineth that one place in which he must be, if this young man rehearse him right—that is to say, in heaven, there to continue still unto the Day of Doom.

But now I trow[614] this young man thinketh not that Saint Augustine for all his determining that Christ's body in which he rose must be still in the one place—that is to wit, in heaven until the Day of Doom—he meaneth, for all that, that it is so fast bound to abide[615] only there, but that he may when it pleaseth him, in the selfsame body, be beneath here in earth a hundred times before the Day of Doom. And good stories are there, testifying that he so hath been diverse times ere[616] this, since the time of his ascension.[617]

And therefore this young man may perceive plainly that Saint Augustine in those words, though he say that Christ's body with which he rose must be in one place—that is to wit, in heaven—yet he meant no such precise necessity as should drive this young man from the literal sense of Christ's words unto the allegory. He meant not by this word, it must be in one place—that is to say in heaven— that it must so be in that one place till Doomsday, that it might in the meanwhile be in none other beside, and that it must be so of an immutable necessity by no power changeable, whereof the contrary were by no power possible. And therefore as for these words of Saint Augustine to this purpose here, I marvel much in good faith, but if[618] he show more hereafter, that ever this young man would speak of them.

Now as for his natural reasons be[619] not worth the reasoning. For first, that the body of Christ unglorified could no more be in two places at once than his own can, because he is a natural body as Christ's was, and Christ's body a natural body as his is, I will not examine any comparisons between their two bodies. But if Christ would tell me that he would make each of both their bodies to be in fifteen places at once, I would believe him I, that he were able to make his word true in the bodies of both twain, and never would I so much as ask him whether he would glorify them both first or not. But I am sure, glorified or unglorified, if he said it, he is able to do it. When our Savior said that it was as possible for a camel or a great cable-rope to enter through a needle's eye as for a rich man to enter into the kingdom of heaven, and after told his apostles that though those two things were both impossible to men, yet all things were possible to God,[620] I think that he meant that neither the example nor the matter was to God impossible. Now since then at the leastwise that it is not impossible for him to convey the camel or the cable-rope through the needle's eye, what shall me need to study now whether he can bring them through such as they be, or else must of fine force be fain[621] to glorify the camel or

608 Jn 10:18 **609** together **610** Is 53:7 **611** appropriate **612** advantage **613** way **614** believe **615** remain **616** before

617 See Acts 7:54–56, 9:3–15; 1 Cor 15:8. **618** *but if:* unless **619** they be **620** Mk

10:25; Mt 19:24; Lk 18:25 **621** *fine…* *fain:* simple necessity be forced the cable first, as this young man saith of his body that it were impossible for God to bring about to have it in two places at once such as it is now, because it is yet somewhat gross[622] and unglorified, and then by the comparison of his own, he argueth the like of the blessed body of Christ, being like his at his Maundy no more glorified than he. But I say yet again of their bodies both twain, if he said that he would do it, I would not doubt but he could do it. And if he could not do it but if he glorified them first, then were I sure that he would glorify them both. And therefore if it were true that he could not make his own body to be in two places at once at Maundy but if[623] it were then glorified, then since I am sure that he there did it, I am thereby sure also that he then for the time glorified it. For that thing was in his own power to do as oft as he would, as well before his death as at his resurrection, and yet to keep his glorification from perceiving,[624] as he did from his two disciples, which for all his glorified body took him but for a pilgrim.[625] And therefore as I say, if Christ said unto me that he would make both his body, and this young man's too, each of them to be in a thousand places at once, I would put no doubt therein, but that by some manner[626] means he were able enough to do it.

But here would this young man peradventure[627] say, "Ye say very well if God so said, and by his so saying so meant indeed. But ye wot[628] well I deny that he so meant though[629] he so said. For I say that in so saying he meant but by an allegory, as he did when he called himself a vine and a door." But now must this young man consider again that himself confesseth that the cause for which himself saith that Christ in so saying did not so mean is because that if he should have meant so, it was impossible for God to bring his meaning about — that is to say, that Christ's body might be in two places at once. And therefore but if[630] he prove that thing impossible for God to do, else[631] he confesseth that God not only said it, but also meant it indeed.

And yet over[632] this, if Christ had never said it, yet doubt I nothing but that he is able to do it, or else were there somewhat[633] that he could not do, and then were God not almighty.

Now if this young man will say that to make one body to be in two places doth imply repugnance,[634] and that God can do no such thing, I dare be bold to tell him again that many things may seem repugnant both to him and me, which things God seeth how to make them stand together well enough.

Such blind reasons of repugnance induceth many men into great error, some ascribing all things to destiny without any power of man's free will at all, and some giving all to man's own will, and no foresight at all unto the providence of God, and all because the poor blind reason of man cannot see so far as to perceive how God's presence and man's free will can stand and agree together, but seem to them clearly repugnant.

And surely if the seeming of our own feeble reason may drive us once to think that one man to be at once in two places is a thing so hard and so repugnant, and therefore so impossible, that God himself can never bring it about, the devil will within a while set us upon such a trust unto our own reason, that he will make us take it for a thing repugnant and impossible that ever one God should be three persons.

I wot well that many good folk have used in this matter many good fruitful examples of God's other works — not only miracles written in Scripture, but also done by the common course of nature here in earth, and some things made also by man's hand, as one face beholden in diverse glasses, and in every piece of one glass broken into twenty, and the marvel of the making of the glass itself such matter as it is made of, and of one word coming whole to a hundred years at once, and the sight of one little eye present and beholding a whole great country at once, with a thousand such other marvels more — such as those that see them daily done and therefore marvel not at them shall yet never be able (no, not this young man himself) to give such reason by what means they may be done, but that he may have such repugnance laid against it that he shall be fain[635] in conclusion for the chief and the most evident reason to say that the cause of all those things is because God that hath caused them so to be done is almighty of himself and can do what him list.[636]

---

622 material; solid **623** *but if:* unless
624 being perceived **625** Mk 16:12;
Lk 24:18 **626** kind of **627** perhaps
628 know **629** even if **630** *but if:*
unless **631** otherwise **632** in addition to
633 something **634** contradiction;
incompatibility **635** forced **636** *him
list:* he wishes

And also I cannot see why it should be more repugnant that one body may be by the power of God in two places at once than that two bodies may be together in one place at once. And that point I think this young man denieth not. And I verily[637] think there is unto man's reason neither more semblance of difficulty nor of repugnance, neither in the being of one body, be it never so gross and unglorified in twenty diverse places at once, than in the making of all that whole world, in which all the bodies both glorified and unglorified have all their rooms[638] and places — to make, I say, all that whole world of right nought.[639] Which article of our faith we shall find folk within a while not greatly force[640] to deny, if men fall to[641] this point, that for impossibilities of nature, they think the things impossible also to God that is the master and the maker of nature, and that they will upon that imagination do as this young man doth: flee from the literal sense of the Scripture, and seek some allegory in the stead, and say they be driven thereto by necessity, by cause of the impossibility of the matter. For thus shall, as ye may well see, by this means none article of our faith stand.

Now his last argument with which he proveth it impossible for one body of Christ to be in two places at once is this. You can, saith he, show no reason, why he should be in many places at once and not in all. But in all places he cannot be, wherefore we must conclude that he cannot be in many places at once. This is a marvelous concluded argument. I am sure a very child may soon see that this consequent can never follow upon those two premises of his antecedent. For he can no further conclude upon them but that we can show no reason why he should be in many places at once. Now if I should grant him that no man could show a reason why he should be in many places at once, what had he won by that? Might he then conclude thereupon that he could not be in many places at once, as though that it were not possible for God to make his body in two places at once but if[642] we were able to tell how, and why, and whereby, and show the reason? Now in this argument he beginneth with "should" in the major, and then in the minor and the conclusion turneth into "can" and so varyeth his extremities

that the argument can never be good if it were but for that. If he would induce the conclusion which he concludeth here, he must rather have argued thus. If it might be in many places at once, then might it be in all places at once. But in all places at once it cannot be, and therefore it cannot be in many places at once. Thus or in some such manner must he argue, if he will aught[643] prove. But here now both the parts of his antecedent be very weak. The first is this, that if the body of our Savior may be in many places at once, it may be in all places at once. Though I would grant this causal proposition for the truth of the second part, yet would I deny it him for the form. For though I grant it to be true, yet the first part is not the proof of the second, but rather contrariwise the second inferreth well the first. For the reason is good: he may be in all places, ergo he may be in many. But argue the contrariwise as this young man argueth, and then is the form very faint. For this hath little strength — he may be in many places, ergo he may be in all; many men run, ergo all men run; men run in many places, ergo men run in all places — but if[644] the matter maintain the argument, either by the possibility of the antecedent or by the necessity of the consequent; as one man is a stone, ergo all men be stones, one man is a living creature, ergo all men be living creatures. But let this first proposition pass and come now to the second, upon which all his argument hangeth: that is, that the body of Christ cannot be at once in all places. This he saith, but how doth he prove it? If he will bid me prove the affirmative, I may answer that I need not, for it is not the thing that we have in hand. For, we do not say that he is in all places, for the Sacrament is not at once in all places. And we be not bound for this matter to go any further, and that point for[645] so far I prove by the Gospel that saith it is so. And therefore this young man that saith it cannot be, let him prove that it may not be. For if it may be, he then confesseth that the words of Christ do prove that it must be. But because it cannot be, saith he, therefore he is driven to construe these words by an allegory. And now that it cannot be in many places, he proveth by that that he cannot be in all places, and therefore must he prove that, or else give over the argument.

---

637 truly   **638** offices   **639** *of right nought:* out of completely nothing   **640** hesitate   **641** *fall to:* take to, start in with   **642** *but if:* unless   **643** anything   **644** unless   **645** in

Howbeit,[646] as for me, though I be not bound to it, I am content yet to prove that God may make the body of Christ to be in all places at once. And because this young man coupleth that proposition with the other, so will I do too. And I prove therefore that God can make his body be both in many places, at once, and in all places at once, by that that he is almighty, and therefore can do all things. And now must this young man tell us either that this is nothing, or else deny that God can do all things. And then must he limit God's power how far he will give God leave to stretch it. But when this young man shall come to that point, every wise man will, I ween,[647] suppose and think in themselves that this young man hath yet in his youth gone too little while to school, to know all that God can do, but if he bring good witness that he hath learned up the uttermost of all God's cunning, which thing the apostle Paul for all that he was ravished up into the third heaven, reckoned yet so far above his reach that he cried out, "Oh, the altitude of the riches of the wisdom and the cunning[648] of God."[649]

But yet this young man goeth about to prove that point by Scripture. For except[650] we grant him that point to be true, he saith that else[651] we make the angel a liar that said, "He is not here,"[652] and also that else we make as though Christ's body in his ascension did not go up in the cloud into heaven from the earth,[653] but only hid himself in the cloud, and played bo-peep and tarried beneath still.

I am in good faith sorry to see this young man presume so far upon his wit[654] so soon ere[655] it be full ripe. For surely such liking of themselves maketh many wits wax[656] rotten ere they wax ripe. And verily[657] if it do decrease and go backward in this fashion, it may not last long. For even here in the end he forgetteth himself so foul that when he was a young sophist, he would, I dare say, have been full sore[658] ashamed so to have overseen[659] himself at Oxford at a parvis.[660] For, ye wot[661] well that thing which he saith, and which he must therefore prove, is that the body of Christ cannot be in every place at once, by no means that God could make. And the texts that he bringeth in for the proof say no further but that he was not in all places at once,

and say not that by no possible power of his Godhead it could not be in every place at once. And therefore this point is as ye see well of this young man very youngly handled. And therefore ought every man abhor as a plain pestilence all such unreasonable reasons made for nature by more than natural follies, against the possibility of God's almighty power. For we may know it verily that against these follies hath specially a place the good ghostly[662] counsel of Saint Paul, where he warneth us and saith, "Beware that no man beguile you by vain philosophy."[663]

God forbid that any man should be the more prone and ready to believe this young man in this great matter, because he saith in the beginning that he will bring all men to a concord and a quietness of conscience. For, he bringeth men to the worst kind of quietness that can be devised, when he telleth us, as he doth, that every man may in this matter without peril believe which way he list.[664] Every man may in every matter, without any counsel of his, soon set himself at rest, if he list to take that way to believe as he list himself and care not how. But and if that way had been sure, Saint Paul would never have showed that many were in peril of sickness and death too, for lack of discerning reverently the body of our Lord in that sacrament, when they came to receive him.[665]

And against this doctrine of this young brother is the plain doctrine of the old holy Fathers, interpreters of the Scripture. And what fashion is this to say that we may believe if we list that there is the very body of our Lord indeed, and then to tell us for a truth that such a faith is impossible to be true, for God himself can never bring it about to make his body be there?

I am very sure that the old holy doctors which believed Christ's body and his blood to be there, and so taught others to believe, as by their books plainly doth appear, if they had thought either that it could not be there, or that it was not there indeed, they would not for all the good in this world have written as they have done. For, would those holy men, ween you, have taught that men be bound to believe that the very body and blood of Christ is there, if

---

646 However   **647** believe   **648** wisdom; knowledge   **649** 2 Cor 12:2; Rom 11:33   **650** unless   **651** otherwise   **652** Mk 16:6   **653** Acts 1:9

654 intelligence, reason   **655** before   **656** become, grow   **657** truly   **658** greatly   **659** deluded, mistaken   **660** public disputation   **661** know

662 spiritual   **663** Col 2:8   **664** wishes   **665** 1 Cor 11:29–30

themselves thought they were not bound thereto? Or would they make men honor and worship that thing as the very body and blood of Christ, which themselves thought were not it? This gere[666] is too childish to speak of.

Yet one great pleasure he doth us, in that he putteth us all at liberty, that we may without peril of damnation believe as we believed before: that is to wit,[667] that in the Blessed Sacrament the whole substance of the bread and the wine is transmuted and changed into the very body and blood of Christ. For, if we may without peril of damnation believe thus as himself granteth that we may, then granteth he that we may also without any peril of damnation believe that himself lieth, where he saith the truth of that belief is impossible.

And therefore I shall therein conclude with him, as our sovereign Lord the King's Highness in his most famous book of assertion of the Sacrament[668] concludeth in one place against Luther, which in his *Babylonica* confessed that though men in the Sacrament of the altar believed after[669] the common faith as they did before, there was no peril therein. Well then said the King's Grace, ye do yourself grant that in our belief is no peril. But all the Church believeth that in your way is undoubted damnation. And therefore if ye will, as wisdom would ye should, deal surely[670] for yourself, ye should rather leave your unsure way which ye believe, and come yourself and counsel all others whom ye would did well, to believe as we do. Lo, this reason of the King's Grace clearly concludeth this young man upon his own confession, and plainly proveth that except[671] he leave his belief which all good Christian folk hold for damnable, and come home again to his old faith, the common faith of all the Church, in which as himself agreeth there is no peril, I will not for courtesy say he is stark mad, but surely I will say that for his own soul the young man playeth a very young wanton pageant.[672]

Now whereas for another quietness of every man's conscience, this young man biddeth every man be bold, and whether the Blessed Sacrament be consecrated or unconsecrated (for though he most specially speaketh for the wine yet he speaketh it of both) and biddeth care not but take it for all that, unblessed as it is, because the priest, he saith, cannot deceive us nor take from us the profit of God's institution, whether he alter the words or leave them all unsaid — is not this a wonderful doctrine of this young man? We wot well all that the priest cannot hurt us by his oversight or malice, if there be no fault upon our own part. For, that perfection that lacketh upon the priest's part, the great mercy of God doth, as we trust, of his own goodness supply. And therefore as holy Saint Chrysostom saith, no man can take harm but of himself.[673] But now if we see the thing disordered our own selves by the priest, and Christ's institution broken, if we then wittingly[674] receive it unblessed and unconsecrated, and care not whether Christ's institution be kept and observed or no, but reckon it is as good without it as with it, then make we ourselves partners of the fault, and lose the profit of the Sacrament, and receive it with damnation, not for the priest's fault but for our own. Howbeit,[675] as for his belief that taketh it no better but for bare bread and wine, it maketh him little matter consecrated or not, saving that the better it is consecrated the more is it ever noyous[676] unto him that receiveth it, having his conscience cumbered[677] with such an execrable heresy, by which well appeareth that he putteth no difference between the body of our Lord in the Blessed Sacrament, and the common bread that he eateth at his dinner,[678] but rather he esteemeth it less: for the one yet, I think ere he begin, if he lack a priest he will bless it himself; the other he careth not, as he saith, whether it be blessed or no. From which abominable heresy and all his other, our Lord for his great mercy deliver him, and help to stop every good man's ears from such ungracious incantations[679] as this man's reasons be, which are unto such simple people as will be with the wind of every new doctrine[680] blown about like a weathercock much more contagious a great deal than was that evil doctrine which Saint Paul so sore reproveth, with which the false prophets had bewitched the Galatians.[681] But as for those that are

---

666 transient fancy **667** say **668** *Assertio septem sacramentorum* (*Defense of the Seven Sacraments*) **669** according to **670** securely; certainly **671** unless **672** *wanton pageant:* reckless performance

673 See *In Johannem homiliae, PG* 59: 268. **674** knowingly **675** However **676** harmful **677** burdened; vexed **678** 1 Cor 11:29–30 **679** an allusion to Odysseus, who seals his men's ears with wax

to block out the song of the Sirens (Homer, *Odyssey* 12.165–200) **680** See Eph 4:14. **681** See Gal 3.

good and fast faithful folk, and have any grace or any spark of any reason in their heads, will (I verily think) never be so far overseen[682] as in this article (the truth whereof God hath himself testified by as many open miracles as ever he testified any one) to believe this one young man upon his barren reasons, against the faith and reason both of all old holy writers, and all good Christian people this fifteen hundred years, all which, without any doubt or question, believed against his doctrine in this Blessed Sacrament, until Berengarius[683] began to fall first unto this error, which when he better considered he fell from it again and forsook it utterly, and for because he had once holden it, the good man did, of his own good mind uncompelled, great penance willingly all his life after, as ye may read in *Cronica cronicarum* the 190th leaf. And also Friar Barnes,[684] albeit that,[685] as ye wot well, he is in many other things a brother of this young man's sect, yet in this heresy he sore abhorreth his heresy, or else he lieth himself. For at his last being here, he wrote a letter to me of his own hand, wherein he writeth that I lay that heresy wrongfully to his charge, and therein he taketh witness of God and his conscience and showeth himself so sore grieved therewith that any man should so repute him by my writing that he saith he will in my reproach make a book against me, wherein he will profess and protest his faith concerning this Blessed Sacrament, by which book it shall, he saith, appear that I have said untruly of him, and that he abhorreth this abominable heresy, which letter of his I forbear to answer till the book come. By which we may see, since he forsaketh this heresy, what faith he will profess, whether the true faith or some other kind of heresy. For, if he will profess the very[686] Catholic faith, he and I shall in that point be very soon agreed, and I shall then make him such answer therein as he shall have cause to be well contented with.

But in the meantime, it well contenteth me that Friar Barnes, being a man of more age, and more ripe discretion and a doctor of divinity, and in these things better learned than this young man is, abhorreth this young man's heresy in this point as well as he liketh him in many others.

And so I trust will every wise man, and not be so enchanted with such childish reasons as his be that they would thereby do as the hearers of Christ did, that[687] for marvel of this matter, as this young man doth now, refused our Savior and went their way from him,[688] but will rather let them go that will go, and abide themselves with our Savior still, as with him that hath, in the stead of this young man's vain childish foolosophy, not false apparent sophistry but the very words of eternal life. Which words I beseech our Lord give this young man the grace, against his own froward[689] fantasies to believe, and to the same life bring him and us both, where we shall, without the veil or covering of any manner[690] sacrament, behold our blessed Savior face to face, and in the bright mirror of truth the very one Godhead of the three like mighty and each almighty persons; clearly behold and perceive both that it may and indeed is, and also how it may be, that Christ's one body may be in many places at once. Which thing many that will not come there of foolish frowardness affirm to be plain impossible.

Lo, instead of a letter have you almost a book, longer than I trust good Christian folk shall need in so clear an article of the faith, and to all fast faithful people so far out of all doubt, saving that in sending you your copy again, methought I must needs write you somewhat what I myself thought of his writing. In which when I once began, albeit not very well at ease, the abomination yet of that pestilent heresy and the peril of his colorable[691] handling drew me forth further and further, and scant[692] could suffer[693] me now to make an end, but that I was half in mind to have touched also the schism of the Bohemians which he setteth forth here in his writing,[694] saving that it requireth some length, and that I am in mind to make answer once in that matter unto Friar Barnes, which hath made therein, ye wot[695] well, a whole treatise, wherein I wonder if himself ween[696] he have said well.

And as for that holy prayer that this devout young man, as a new Christ, teacheth to make at the receiving of the Blessed Sacrament all his congregation, I would not give the paring of a pear for his prayer though[697] it were better than it is, pulling

---

682 mistaken 683 Berengarius of Tours (*ca.* 1000–1088) 684 Robert Barnes (1495–1540), an Augustinian friar and prior in Cambridge who became a reformer and was executed for heresy in 1540 685 *albeit that:* although 686 true 687 who 688 Jn 6:66–68 689 unruly, perverse; untoward 690 kind of 691 having an appearance of truth 692 scarcely 693 allow 694 See Frith's *A Christian Sentence* (CW 7: 432/14–20). 695 know 696 thinks 697 even if

away the true faith therefore as he doth. Howbeit,[698] his prayer there is such devised, and penned, and painted, with leisure and study, that I trust every good Christian woman maketh a much better prayer at the time of her housel,[699] by faithful affection and God's good inspiration suddenly. For she, besides God's other goodness, thanketh him, I think, for his high singular benefit there presently given her, in that it liketh him to accept and receive her so simple and so far unworthy of herself to sit at his own blessed board,[700] and there, for a remembrance of his bitter Passion suffered for her sin, to suffer her receive and eat not bread though it seem bread, but his own very precious body in form of bread, both his very flesh, blood and bones, the self-same with which he died and with which he rose again, and appeared again to his apostles, and ate among his disciples, and with which he ascended into heaven, and with which he shall descend again to judgment, and with which he shall reign in heaven with his Father and their Holy Spirit in eternal glory, and all his true faithful believing and loving people with him, whom as the mystical members of his glorious body he shall then, and from thenceforth forever, pleasantly nourish and feed and satiate their insatiable hunger with the beholding of his glorious Godhead, whose hunger to heavenward he comforteth and feedeth here by hope, and by the sure[701] token and sign of salvation, the giving of his own very blessed body under the sign and likeness of bread to be eaten and received into our bodies, that our souls by the faith thereof, and our bodies by the receiving thereof, may be spiritually and bodily joined and knit unto his here in earth, and with his holy soul and his blessed body, and his Godhead both with his Father and their Holy Spirit gloriously live after in heaven.

This lo, in effect though not in words, can Christian women pray, and some of them peradventure[702] express it much better too. For God can, as the prophet saith, make not only women that have age, faith, and wit,[703] but the mouths also of infants and young sucking children to pronounce his laud and praise,[704] so that we need not this young man now to come teach us how and what we shall pray, as

Christ taught his disciples the Paternoster.[705] Frith is an unmeet[706] master to teach us what we should pray at the receiving of the Blessed Sacrament, when he will not acknowledge it as it is, but take Christ's blessed body for nothing but bare bread, and so little esteem the receiving of the Blessed Sacrament that he forceth[707] little whether it be blessed or not. I pray God bless these poisoned errors out of his blind heart, and make him his faithful servant, and send you heartily well to fare. At Chelsea the seventh day of December by the hand of

more than all your own,
Tho. More, Knight

191. To Erasmus
Chelsea, <June? 1533>

Thomas More sends his greetings to Erasmus of Rotterdam.

I have received two letters[708] from you; the one was dated February 7th last; the other was delivered by Quirinus, who beside the letters also brought me some valuable information about the happenings in your locale. Many thanks for wanting me to have this information.

You can learn all details about your affairs from Quirinus, who strikes me as being honest and devoted. I am happy for your sake, and, since I love you, also for my own, that the present Archbishop of Canterbury[709] manifests as much affection for you as did Warham in days gone by; no man ever showed you greater affection, and if he appeared somewhat niggardly in his gifts toward the end of his life, it was evidently due to lack of money, not lack of heart; for he died unbelievably poor, leaving enough to cover his debts; he did not owe very much, but when all the funeral expenses were paid, there was not very much left. The Bishop of Durham[710] is surely being impoverished by this war, or rather, by the raids carried on by ourselves and the Scots; his diocese borders on Scotland and is such a distance from us that I hear as rarely from him as I do from you. There was a rumor afloat here that N.[711] and Melanchthon had held a lengthy clandestine conference here through the arrangements of some unnamed persons and that later they secretly parted; this rumor, however, has gradually faded away, and it has been found out that the story was absolutely false. The King appears to be more antagonistic toward heretics than even the bishops are.

The heretic Tyndale, a fellow Englishman, who is nowhere and yet everywhere an exile, wrote here recently that Melanchthon was a guest of the King of France and, on the direct word of an eyewitness, had been welcomed in Paris with a cavalcade of one hundred and fifty horses; Tyndale further expressed his fear that, if the French were to receive the word of God from Melanchthon, they would be confirmed in their belief in the Eucharist in opposition to the teaching of the Wycliffites. How those people fret over this matter, as if God had commissioned them to give the whole world its fundamental instructions in the faith!

Concerning the remark in your earlier letter that you were hesitant about publishing my letter[712] in spite of motives for wanting to have it published, there is no reason, my dear Erasmus, for hesitation on your part. Some chatterboxes around here began to spread the rumor that I had resigned my office[713] unwillingly and that I had kept that detail a secret. So, after making arrangements for the construction of my tomb, I did not hesitate to make, on my Epitaph, a public declaration of the actual facts, to allow anyone a chance to refute them, if he could. As soon as those fellows noted the Epitaph, since they were unable to deny its truth, they charged it with being boastful. However, I preferred this charge rather than allow the other rumor take hold, not for any selfish reason, since I do not have a high regard for what men may say, provided I have the approval of God; but having written several pamphlets in English in defense of the Faith against some fellow countrymen who had championed rather perverse doctrines, I considered it my duty to protect the integrity of my reputation; and so that you can find out how boastful I was, you will receive a copy of my Epitaph; you will notice, in reading it, that, out of confidence in my own position, I do not bait those fellows at all, so as to prevent them from making whimsical remarks about me. After resigning my office, I waited until the opening of the new term, and, so far, no one has advanced a complaint against my integrity. Either my life has been so spotless or, at any rate, I have been so circumspect that, if my rivals oppose my boasting of the one, they are forced to let me boast of the other. As a matter of fact, the King himself has pronounced on this situation at various times, frequently in private, and twice in public. It is embarrassing for me to relate — but on the occasion of the installation of my most distinguished successor, the King used as his mouthpiece the most illustrious Duke, I mean the Duke of Norfolk, who is the Lord High Treasurer of England, and he respectfully ordered the Duke to proclaim publicly that he had unwillingly yielded to my request for resignation; the King, however, was not satisfied even with that extraordinary manifestation of good will toward me; at a much later date, he had the same pronouncement repeated, in his presence, at a solemn session of the Lords and Commons, this time using my successor as his mouthpiece, on the formal occasion of his opening address to that assembly which, as you know, we call Parliament. Therefore, if you agree, there is no good reason for holding back the publication of my letter. As to the statement in my Epitaph that I was a source of trouble for heretics — I wrote that with deep feeling. I find that breed of men absolutely loathsome, so much so that, unless they regain their senses, I want to be as hateful to them as anyone can possibly be; for my increasing experience with those men frightens me with the thought of what the world will suffer at their hands. I shall follow your advice and make no reply to the person about whom you wrote, although I have held a lengthy letter in readiness for some time now. My reason for holding back is not that I have any regard for what he, or all of his coworkers, may think or write about me, but because I do not want to be burdened with the obligations of writing replies to outsiders, when I feel the more immediate responsibility of answering our own associates. Best wishes, my dear Erasmus, and a long farewell; the best of luck always.

From my rural home at Chelsea.

---

712 See Letter 188. In *EE* 2750, Erasmus enclosed a copy of More's Letter 188 and explained that it had arrived to him after a delay of some months.   **713** His successor was Sir Thomas Audley.

INSCRIPTION ON THE TOMB
OF THOMAS MORE.[714]

Thomas More was born in London of respectable, though not distinguished, ancestry; he engaged to some extent in literary matters, and after spending several years of his youth as a pleader in the law courts and after having held the office of judge as an under-sheriff in his native city, he was admitted to the Court by the Unconquerable Henry the Eighth, who is the only King to have ever received the unique distinction of meriting the title "Defender of the Faith," a title earned by deeds of sword and pen; he was received at Court, chosen member of the King's Council, knighted, appointed under-treasurer and then chancellor of Lancaster, and finally chancellor of England by the special favor of his Sovereign. Meanwhile he was elected speaker of the House of Commons; furthermore, he served as the King's ambassador at various times and in various places, last of all at Cambrai, as an associate and colleague of Cuthbert Tunstall, then bishop of London and shortly after bishop of Durham, a man whose equal in learning, wisdom, and virtue is seldom seen in the world today. In that place he witnessed, in the capacity of ambassador, to his great joy, the renewal of a peace treaty between the supreme monarchs of Christendom and the restoration of a long-desired peace to the world:

May heaven confirm this peace
and make it a lasting one.

He so conducted himself all through this series of high offices or honors that his excellent Sovereign found no fault with his service, neither did he make himself odious to the nobles nor unpleasant to the populace, but he was a source of trouble to thieves, murderers, and heretics. His father, John More, was a knight and chosen by the King as member of the group of judges known as the King's Bench; he was an affable man, charming, irreproachable, gentle, sympathetic, honest, and upright; though venerable in age, he was vigorous for a man of his years; after he had lived to see the day when his son was chancellor of England, he deemed his sojourn upon earth complete and gladly departed for heaven. The son, all through his father's lifetime, had been compared with him, and was commonly known as the young More, and so he considered himself to be; but now he felt the loss of his father, and as he looked upon the four children he had reared and his eleven grandchildren, he began, in his own mind, to grow old. This feeling was increased by a serious chest ailment, that developed soon after, as an indication of approaching old age. Now sated with the passing things of this life, he resigned office and, through the unparalleled graciousness of a most indulgent Sovereign (may God smile favorably upon his enterprises), he at length reached the goal which almost since boyhood had been the object of his longing—to have the last years of his life all to himself, so that he could gradually retire from the affairs of this world and contemplate the eternity of the life to come. Then he arranged for the construction of this tomb for himself, to be a constant reminder of the unrelenting advance of death, and had the remains of his first wife transferred to this place. That he may not have erected this tomb in vain while still alive, and that he may not shudder with fear at the thought of encroaching death, but may go to meet it gladly, with longing for Christ, and that he may find death not completely a death for himself but rather the gateway to a happier life, I beg you, kind reader, attend him with your prayers while he still lives and also when he has done with life.

My beloved wife, Jane, lies here.
I, Thomas More, intend that this same
tomb shall be Alice's and mine, too. One
of these ladies, my wife in the days of my
youth, has made me father of a son and three
daughters; the other has been as devoted
to her stepchildren (a rare attainment in
a stepmother) as very few mothers are to
their own children. The one lived out her
life with me, and the other still lives with
me on such terms that I cannot decide
whether I did love the one or do love the
other more. O, how happily we could
have lived all three together if fate and
morality permitted. Well, I pray that the
grave, that heaven, will bring us together.
Thus death will give what life could not.

---

714 The monument was much damaged in the bombing of Chelsea Old Church, but has been carefully restored.

This tomb, with epitaph, Thomas More had erected in 1532 at his parish church in Chelsea within months of his May 16 retirement from royal service. He sent the text to Erasmus for publication, as seen here in Letter 191.

192. To Elizabeth Barton[715]
Chelsea, Tuesday <1533?>

Good Madam, and my right dearly beloved sister in our Lord God.

5   After my most hearty recommendation,[716] I shall beseech you to take my good mind[717] in good worth, and pardon me that I am so homely[718] as of myself unrequired,[719] and also without necessity, to give counsel to you, of whom for the good inspirations, 10 and great revelations that it liketh almighty God of his goodness to give and show, as many wise, well learned, and very virtuous folk testify, I myself have need, for the comfort of my soul, to require and ask advice, for surely, good Madam, since it pleaseth God 15 sometime to suffer[720] such as are far under and of little estimation, to give yet fruitful advertisement[721] to other as are in the light of the Spirit, so far above them, that there were between them no comparison; as he suffered his high prophet Moses to be in some things advised and counseled by Jethro,[722] I cannot 20 for the love that in our Lord I bear you refrain to put you in remembrance of one thing, which in my poor mind I think highly necessary to be by your wisdom considered, referring the end and order thereof, to 25 God and his Holy Spirit to direct you.

Good Madam, I doubt not, but that you remember that in the beginning of my communication with you, I showed you that I neither was, nor would be, curious of any knowledge of other 30 men's matters, and least of all any matter of princes or of the realm, in case it so were that God had, as to many good folks before time he hath, any things revealed unto you, such things, I said unto your ladyship, that I was not only not desirous to hear 35 of, but also would not hear of. Now, Madam, I consider well that many folk desire to speak with you, which are not all peradventure[723] of my mind in this point, but some hap to be curious and inquisitive of things that little pertain unto their parts; and 40 some might peradventure happen to talk of such things as might peradventure after turn to much harm, as I think you have heard how the late Duke of Buckingham[724] moved with the fame of one that was reported for a holy monk and had such talking with him as after was a great part of his destruction 45 and disheriting[725] of his blood, and great slander and infamy of religion. It sufficeth me, good Madam, to put you in remembrance of such thing, as I nothing doubt your wisdom and the spirit of God shall keep you from talking with any persons, specially with 50 lay persons, of any such manner things[726] as pertain to princes' affairs, or the state of the realm, but only to commune[727] and talk with any person high and low, of such manner things as may to the soul be profitable for you to show and for them to know. 55

And thus my good Lady, and dearly beloved sister in our Lord, I make an end of this my needless advertisement unto you, whom the blessed Trinity preserve and increase in grace, and put in your mind to recommend me and mine unto him in your devout 60 prayers. At Chelsea this Tuesday by the hand of
    Your hearty loving brother and beadsman,[728]
    Thomas More, Kt.

192a. To John Harris[729]
Willesden, Sunday, <January–April 1534>   65

Neomenia,[730] the first day of the new moon next after the equinoctial in *Vere,*[731] that is to wit after the entering of the sun into *Aries,*[732] which is the eleventh or twelfth day of March, the day of next change of the moon after that, is the first day of the year 70 with the Jews. And the fourteenth day after, which is *Quartadecima Luna,*[733] is the eating of their paschal lamb at night, and that day is not holy day till night. And on the morrow is their great feast day, that is to wit,[734] the first day of the unleavened bread, 75 but it beginneth in the evening before, and so do all their feasts, and their Sabbath days begin in the evening, and endure to the evening following, *A vespere ad vesperum servabitis sabbata vestra: Levitici 23.*[735] The year in which our Savior was crucified, *Quar-* 80 *tadecima Luna* fell in *feria quinta,*[736] that is to wit upon the Thursday. And therefore in the evening

---

715 Elizabeth Barton (*ca.* 1506–34) was a maidservant who claimed to have visions and denounced the King's divorce. In 1534, she was arrested, required to do public penance, and hanged.   **716** commendation of myself to your benevolent remembrance or regard   **717** opinion; judgment   **718** familiar, rude   **719** unasked   **720** allow; permit   **721** admonition   **722** Ex 18:12–27   **723** possibly   **724** Edward Stafford, 3rd Duke of Buckingham, was executed for treason in 1521.   **725** disinheriting   **726** *any such manner things:* any things of such kind   **727** converse   **728** one who prays for another   **729** More's secretary, who married Dorothy Coly, Margaret Roper's maid   **730** new moon   **731** spring   **732** the ram, a sign of the zodiac   **733** fourteenth day (of the moon)   **734** say   **735** From evening to evening ye shall keep your sabbaths.   **736** the fifth ferial day

that Thursday Christ made his Maundy, and so did all the Jews, for that was the very day appointed by the Scripture in Exodus.[737] And on the morrow (which was Good Friday, and which was *Quinta-decima Luna*)[738] was the first day and the chief day of the unleavened bread, which feast began in the evening before, that is to wit, on Shere[739] Thursday, when the eating of the paschal lamb was, and therefore was eaten with unleavened bread. And so consequently Christ did consecrate in unleavened bread, for in that evening began *Primus dies Azimorum,*[740] as appeareth plainly by Saint Matthew, Saint Mark, and Saint Luke. But the posterior Greeks say that Christ did not eat his paschal lamb in the day appointed by the law, that is to wit, *in vespere quartae-decimae Lunae,*[741] but they say he did prevent[742] the time by a day, and did eat it *in vespere decimae tertiae Lunae.*[743] But yet they said not that he ate it on the Wednesday, for in that I mistook them. But they say that the Thursday was *decimatertia Luna,*[744] and that *Quartadecima Luna* (in which the paschal[745] should be eaten by the law) was on Good Friday, and that the Jews did eat it then, and that in that evening upon Good Friday (in which day Christ died) the Jews did eat the paschal lamb, and that on the morrow (which was the Sabbath day) was *Quinta-decima Luna,* and so therefore on that day was their great feast, that is to wit the first day of the unleavened bread, which began they say on Good Friday in the evening at the rising of the moon. And for that cause they say that Christ did consecrate in leavened bread, because he consecrated on the Thursday, which was they say not *Quartadecima Luna,* but *decima tertia,* and that the unleavened bread came not in until the evening in *Quartadecima Luna,* that was, they say, not till Good Friday in the evening, which they prove by the words of Saint John cap. 13. *Ante diem festum paschae,*[746] and they say *festum paschae* was the feast of eating of the paschal lamb. And so our Lord, say they, made his Maundy before the feast of the eating of the paschal lamb, that is to wit,

the day before *Quartadecima Luna.* And so Shere Thursday they say was *decima tertia Luna.* And therefore say they that the very day thereof (that is to wit, *Quartadecima Luna*) was they say on Good Friday. And the Jews they say did eat that day after Christ's death, and that therefore they would not come *in praetorium, ut non contaminarentur, sed ut manducarent pascha.*[747] And that Christ (because he knew that he should that day be crucified) did prevent the day, and did eat it the day before, and therefore they had no one unleavened bread.

I put you in remembrance of this because I have mistaken it in the paper that you have, and have said that the Greeks held that Christ held his Maundy on Tenebrae Wednesday. I pray you, gentle John Harris, amend that fault of mine. *Ante diem festum Paschae,*[748] is meant by the first day of the feast of the unleavened loaves which was on Good Friday, that was *Quinta decima Luna,* and the feast was called *festum Paschae,*[749] because it began in the evening on Shere Thursday, wherein the paschal lamb was eaten. *Quod abstinebant a praetorio* (*ut mundi manducarent Pascha*)[750] upon Good Friday, was for the unleavened bread which was also called by the name of Pascha, and continued seven days.

Burgensis[751] maketh another manner of reckoning, with which we shall not need to meddle; thus much is perplex enough.

From Willesden[752] this present Sunday, by Your lover Thomas More, Knight

194. To Thomas Cromwell
Chelsea, 1 February <1533/4>

A letter written by Sir Thomas More to Master Thomas Cromwell (then one of the King's Privy Council) the first day of February in the year of our Lord God 1533, after the computation of the Church of England and in the twenty-fifth year of the reign of King Henry the VIII. [Workes 1422]

---

737 Ex 12:43 ff.   **738** the fifteenth of the month   **739** Sheer ("Shere") was applied to Maundy Thursday, alluding to the purification of the soul by confession, and perhaps also to the practice of washing the altars on that day. The usual name Maundy Thursday comes from the Latin *mandatum,* referring to the new "commandment," Jn 13:11–14.   **740** first day of unleavened bread   **741** in the

evening of the fourteenth of the month   **742** act in anticipation of   **743** in the evening of the thirteenth of the month   **744** the thirteenth   **745** the paschal lamb   **746** before the day of the feast of the Passover   **747** "and they themselves entered not into the Praetorium, that they might not be defiled, but might eat the Passover" (Jn 18:28)   **748** before the feast of the Passover   **749** the feast of the

Passover   **750** Because they kept away from the Praetorium so that they might eat the Passover undefiled.   **751** Paul de Santa Maria, born in Burgos, *ca.* 1351.   **752** A parish adjoining the county of London on the northwest. More may have gone there to visit the pilgrimage church of Our Lady of Willesden. His wife's son-in-law, Sir Giles Alington, had a country home in Willesden.

Right Worshipful,[753] in my most hearty wise[754] I recommend me[755] unto you.

Sir, my cousin William Rastell hath informed me that your Mastership of your goodness showed him that it hath been reported that I have against the book of certain articles (which was late put forth in print by the King's honorable Council) made an answer, and delivered it unto my said cousin to print. And albeit that[756] he for his part truly denied it, yet because he somewhat remained in doubt, whether your Mastership gave him therein full credence or not, he desired me for his farther discharge[757] to declare you the very truth, sir, as help me God neither my said cousin nor any man else, never had any book of mine to print, one or other, since the said book of the King's Council came forth. For of truth the last book that he printed of mine was that book that I made against an unknown heretic which hath sent over a work that walketh in over many men's hands[758] named the *Supper of the Lord,* against the Blessed Sacrament of the altar. My answer whereunto, albeit that the printer (unaware to me)[759] dated it anno 1534, by which it seemeth to be printed since the Feast of the Circumcision, yet was it of very truth both made and printed and many of them gone before Christmas. And myself never espied the printer's oversight in the date, in more than three weeks after. And this was in good faith the last book that my cousin[760] had of mine. Which being true as of truth it shall be found, sufficeth[761] for his declaration in this behalf.

As touching mine own self, I shall say thus much farther, that on my faith I never made any such book nor ever thought to do. I read the said book once over and never more. But I am for once reading[762] very far off from many things, whereof I would have meetly[763] sure knowledge, ere[764] ever I would make an answer, though the matter and the book both, concerned the poorest man in a town, and were of the simplest man's making too. For of many things which in that book be touched, in some I know not the law, and in some I know not the fact. And therefore would I never be so childish nor so play the proud arrogant fool, by whomsoever

the book had been made, and to whomsoever the matter had belonged, as to presume to make an answer to the book, concerning the matter whereof I never were sufficiently learned in the laws, nor fully instructed in the facts. And then while the matter pertained unto the King's Highness, and the book professeth openly that it was made by his honorable Council, and by them put in print with his Grace's license obtained thereunto I verily[765] trust in good faith that of your good mind toward me, though I never wrote you word thereof, yourself will both think and say so much for me, that it were a thing far unlikely, that an answer should be made thereunto by me. I will by the grace of almighty God, as long as it shall please him to lend me life in this world, in all such places (as I am of my duty to God and the King's Grace bounden) truly say my mind, and discharge[766] my conscience, as becometh a poor honest true man, wheresoever I shall be by his Grace commanded. Yet surely if it should happen any book to come abroad in the name of his Grace or his honorable Council, if the book to me seemed such as myself would not have given mine own advice to the making, yet I know my bounden duty, to bear more honor to my prince, and more reverence to his honorable Council, than that it could become me for many causes, to make an answer unto such a book, or to counsel and advise any man else to do it. And therefore as it is a thing that I never did nor intended, so I heartily beseech you if you shall happen to perceive any man, either of evil will or of lightness,[767] any such thing report by[768] me, be so good master to me, as help to bring us both together. And then never take me for honest after, but if you find his honesty somewhat impaired in the matter.

Thus am I bold upon your goodness to encumber you with my long rude[769] letter, in the contents whereof, I eftsoons[770] heartily beseech you to be in manner aforesaid good master and friend unto me, whereby you shall bind me to be your beadsman[771] while I live, as knoweth our Lord, whose especial grace both bodily and ghostly[772] long preserve and keep you.

---

753 Distinguished, Honorable 754 manner 755 *recommend me:* commend myself to your benevolent remembrance or regard 756 *albeit that:* although 757 acquittal 758 *walketh … hands:* is in the hands of too many men 759 *unaware to me:* without my knowledge 760 Rastell was the son of John Rastell by his wife Elizabeth, More's sister. 761 is adequate 762 *But… reading:* Because I read the book only once 763 suitably 764 before 765 truly 766 clear 767 inconstancy 768 of 769 inelegant 770 a second time 771 to be one to pray for him 772 spiritually

At Chelsea in the Vigil of the Purification of our Blessed Lady by the hand of

Assuredly all your own,

Thomas More, Knight

195. To Thomas Cromwell

Chelsea, Saturday, <February–March> 1533/4

Another letter written by Sir Thomas More to Master Thomas Cromwell in February or in March in the year of our Lord God 1533, after the computation[773] of the Church of England, and in the twenty-fifth year of the reign of King Henry the Eighth. [Workes 1423]

Right Worshipful.[774]

After right hearty recommendation,[775] so it is that I am informed, that there is a bill[776] put in against me into the higher house before the Lords, concerning my communication with the Nun of Canterbury,[777] and my writing unto her, whereof I not a little marvel, the truth of the matter being such as God and I know it is, and as I have plainly declared unto you by my former letters, wherein I found you then so good, that I am now bold eftsoons[778] upon your goodness to desire you to show me that favor, as that I might the rather by your good means, have a copy of the bill. Which seen, if I find any untrue surmise[779] therein as of likelihood there is, I may make mine humble suit unto the King's good Grace, and declare the truth, either to his Grace or by his Grace's commandment, wheresoever the matter shall require. I am so sure of my truth toward his Grace, that I cannot mistrust his gracious favor toward me, upon the truth known, nor the judgment of any honest man. Nor never shall there loss in this matter grieve me, being myself so innocent as God and I know me, whatsoever should happen me therein, by the grace of almighty God, who both bodily and ghostly[780] preserve you. At Chelsea this present Saturday by the hand of

Heartily all your own,

Tho. More, Knight

197. To Thomas Cromwell

<March? 1534>

Right Worshipful.

After my most hearty recommendation, with like thanks for your goodness in the accepting of my rude[781] long letter, I perceive that of your further goodness and favor toward me, it liked[782] your Mastership to break with[783] my son Roper of that, that I had had communication, not only with diverse that were of acquaintance with the lewd[784] Nun of Canterbury, but also with herself; and had, over[785] that, by my writing, declaring favor toward her, given her advice and counsel; of which my demeanor,[786] that it liketh you to be content to take the labor and the pain, to hear, by mine own writing, the truth, I very heartily thank you, and reckon myself therein right deeply beholden[787] to you.

It is, I suppose, about eight or nine years ago since I heard of that huswife[788] first; at which time the Bishop of Canterbury that then was, God assoil[789] his soul, sent unto the King's Grace a roll of paper in which were written certain words of hers, that she had, as report was then made, at sundry times spoken in her trances; whereupon it pleased the King's Grace to deliver me the roll, commanding me to look thereon and afterward show him what I thought therein. Whereunto, at another time, when his Highness asked me, I told him, that in good faith I found nothing in these words that I could anything regard or esteem, for saving that some part fell in rhyme, and that, God wot,[790] full rude, else for any reason, God wot, that I saw therein, a right simple[791] woman might, in my mind, speak it of her own wit[792] well enough; howbeit, I said, that because it was constantly reported for a truth, that God wrought in her, and that a miracle was showed upon her, I durst not nor would not, be bold in judging the matter. And the King's Grace, as methought, esteemed the matter as light as it after proved lewd.[793]

From that time till about Christmas was twelve-month,[794] albeit that continually, there was much talking of her, and of her holiness, yet never heard I any talk rehearsed,[795] either of revelation of hers,

---

773 reckoning   **774** Distinguished, Honorable   **775** commendation of myself to your benevolent remembrance or regard   **776** A Bill of Attainder, February 21, 1534, against the Nun of Kent and her colleagues, included More and Fisher, but

for misprision not for treason.   **777** Elizabeth Barton. See Letter 192.   **778** again   **779** suspicion   **780** spiritually   **781** unskilled   **782** pleased   **783** *break with:* reveal to   **784** villainous or ignorant   **785** in addition to   **786** conduct

787 obliged   **788** worthless or pert woman   **789** absolve   **790** knows   **791** unlearned   **792** intellect   **793** evil   **794** *Christmas was twelvemonth:* Christmas a year ago   **795** recounted

or miracle, saving that I had heard some times in my Lord Cardinal's days, that she had been both with his lordship and with the King's Grace, but what she said either to the one or to the other, upon my faith, I had never heard any one word.

Now, as I was about to tell you, about Christmas was twelvemonth, Father Resby, Friar Observant, then of Canterbury, lodged one night at mine house; where after supper, a little before he went to his chamber, he fell in communication with me of the Nun, giving her high commendation of holiness, and that it was wonderful to see and understand the works that God wrought in her; which thing, I answered, that I was very glad to hear it, and thanked God thereof. Then he told me, that she had been with my Lord Legate in his life and with the King's Grace, too, and that she had told my Lord Legate a revelation of hers, of three swords that God hath put in my Lord Legate's hand, which if he ordered not well, God would lay it sore[796] to his charge, the first he said was the ordering of the spiritualty[797] under the Pope, as Legate, the second the rule that he bore in order of the temporalty[798] under the King, as his chancellor. And the third, she said, was the meddling[799] he was put in trust with by the King, concerning the great matter of his marriage. And therewithal I said unto him that any revelation of the King's matters I would not hear of, I doubt not but the goodness of God should direct his Highness with his grace and wisdom, that the thing should take such end, as God should be pleased with, to the King's honor and surety[800] of the realm. When he heard me say these words or the like, he said unto me, that God had specially commanded her to pray for the King; and forthwith[801] he broke again[802] into her revelations, concerning the Cardinal that his soul was saved by her mediation;[803] and without any other communication went into his chamber. And he and I never talked any more of any such manner of matter, nor since his departing on the morrow, I never saw him after to my remembrance, till I saw him at Paul's Cross.[804]

After this, about Shrovetide,[805] there came unto me, a little before supper, Father Rich,[806] Friar Observant of Richmond. And as we fell in talking, I asked him of Father Resby, how he did? and upon that occasion, he asked me whether Father Resby had anything showed me of the Holy Nun of Kent? and I said yea, and that I was very glad to hear of her virtue. I would not, quoth he, tell you again that you have heard of him already, but I have heard and known many great graces that God hath wrought in her, and in other folk, by her, which I would gladly tell you if I thought you had not heard them already. And therewith he asked me, whether Father Resby had told me anything of her being with my Lord Cardinal? and I said yea. Then he told you, quoth he, of the three swords; yea verily,[807] quod I. Did he tell you, quoth he, of the revelations that she had concerning the King's Grace? Nay, forsooth, quoth I, nor if he would have done I would not have given him the hearing; nor verily no more I would in deed, for since she hath been with the King's Grace herself, and told him, methought it a thing needless to tell the matter to me, or any man else. And when Father Rich perceived that I would not hear her revelations concerning the King's Grace he talked on a little of her virtue and let her revelations alone; and therewith my supper was set upon the board[808] where I required[809] him to sit with me, but he would in no wise tarry but departed to London. After that night I talked with him twice, once in mine own house, another time in his own garden at the Friars, at every time a great space, but not of any revelation touching the King's Grace, but only of other mean[810] folk, I knew not whom, of which things some were very strange and some were very childish. But albeit that he said that he had seen her lie in her trance in great pains and that he had at other times taken great spiritual comfort in her communication, yet did he never tell me she had told him those tales herself; for if he had I would, for the tale of Mary Magdalene[811] which he told me, and for the tale of the Host, with which, as I heard, she

796 grievously   **797** the clergy
798 temporality   **799** action   **800** security   **801** immediately   **802** *broke again:* began to speak again of   **803** intercession on behalf of. This the nun claimed in 1531. **804** The nun and the clergy who had helped her were forced to read their confessions in public penance before St. Paul's Cathedral, November 1533.   **805** days of shriving

just before Lent   **806** Hugh Rich was included in the Act of Attainder but was not executed at Tyburn. We do not know whether he had died or had been pardoned. He had been Warden at Canterbury, in which post Resby had succeeded him.   **807** truly   **808** table   **809** asked **810** of low degree   **811** Dr. Bocking, a Benedictine monk at Canterbury, kept a

book, in his own handwriting, of the nun's revelations. In 1534 the nun "confessed that the letter purporting to have been written by Mary Magdalene in Heaven, and sent to a widow in London, was written by a monk of St. Augustine's in Canterbury, named Hawkeherst" (*LP 7.72*).

said she was houseled,[812] at the King's Mass at Calais;[813] if I had heard it of him as told unto himself by her mouth for a revelation, I would have both liked him and her the worse. But whether ever I heard that same tale of Rich or of Resby or of neither of them both, but of some other man since she was in hold,[814] in good faith I cannot tell. But I wot[815] well when or where so ever I heard it, methought it a tale too marvelous to be true, and very likely that she had told some man her dream, which told it out for a revelation. And in effect, I little doubted but that some of these tales that were told of her were untrue; but yet since I never heard them reported, as spoken by her own mouth, I thought nevertheless that many of them might be true, and she a very virtuous woman too; as some lies peradventure[816] written of some that be saints in heaven, and yet many miracles in deed done by them for all that.

After this I being upon a day at Syon talking with diverse of the Fathers together at the grate, they showed me that she had been with them, and showed me diverse things that some of them misliked in her and in this talking, they wished that I had spoken with her and said they would fain see how I should like her; whereupon, afterward, when I heard that she was there again, I came thither to see her and to speak with her myself. At which communication had, in a little chapel, there were none present but we two. In the beginning whereof I showed that my coming to her was not of any curious mind, anything to know of such things as folk talked, that it pleased God to reveal and show unto her, but for the great virtue that I had heard for so many years, every day more and more spoken and reported of her, I therefore had a great mind to see her, and be acquainted with her, that she might have somewhat the more occasion to remember me to God in her devotion and prayers; whereunto she gave me a very good virtuous answer that as God did of his goodness far better by her than such a poor wretch was worthy, so she feared that many folk yet beside that spoke of their own favorable minds many things for her, far above the truth, and that of me she had many such things heard, that already she prayed for me and ever would, whereof I heartily thanked her.

I said unto her, "Madam, one Helen, a maiden dwelling about Totnam, of whose trances and revelations there hath been much talking, she hath been with me late[817] and showed me that she was with you, and that after the rehearsal of such visions as she had seen, you showed her that they were no revelations, but plain illusions of the devil and advised her to cast them out of her mind, and verily she gave therein good credence unto you and thereupon hath left to lean[818] any longer unto such visions of her own, whereupon she saith, she findeth your words true, for ever since she hath been the less visited with such things as she was wont to be before." To this she answered me, "Forsooth, sir, there is in this point no praise unto me, but the goodness of God, as it appeareth, hath wrought much meekness in her soul, which hath taken my rude warning so well and not grudged to hear her spirit and her visions reproved." I liked her in good faith better for this answer than for many of those things that I heard reported by[819] her. Afterward she told me, upon that occasion how great need folk have, that are visited with such visions, to take heed and prove well of what spirit they come of, and in the communication she told me that of late the devil, in likeness of a bird, was fleeing[820] and flickering about her in a chamber, and suffered himself to be taken; and being in hands suddenly changed, in their sight that were present, into such a strange ugly fashioned bird, that they were all afraid, and threw him out at a window.

For conclusion, we talked no word of the King's Grace or any great personage else, nor in effect, of any man or woman, but of herself, and myself, but after no long communication had for or ever we met,[821] my time came to go home, I gave her a double ducat,[822] and prayed her to pray for me and mine, and so departed from her and never spoke with her after. Howbeit,[823] of truth I had a great good opinion of her, and had her in great estimation as you shall perceive by the letter that I wrote unto her. For afterward because I had often heard, that many right worshipful folks as well men as women used to have much communication with her, and many folk are of nature inquisitive and curious, whereby

812 communicated   813 "When the King was at Calais, she saw the Host taken from the priest with the blessed blood, and angels brought it to her to receive"   (LP 6.1466).   814 custody   815 know   816 perhaps   817 lately   818 left to lean: stopped leaning   819 of   820 flying   821 but…met: i.e., we did not talk for   very long because I had to leave shortly after we met.   822 Venetian gold coin   823 However

they fall sometime into such talking, as better were to forbear, of which thing I nothing thought while I talked with her of charity, therefore I wrote her a letter thereof, which since it may be peradventure, that she brake[824] or lost, I shall insert the very copy thereof in this present letter.

Good Madam and my right dearly beloved Sister in our Lord God. — [*Here More inserted a copy of his letter to Elizabeth Barton, Letter 192.*]

At the receipt of this letter she answered my servant that she heartily thanked me. Soon after this there came to mine house the proctor[825] of the Charterhouse at Sheen and one brother William with him, which nothing talked with me but of her and of the great joy that they took in her virtue, but of any of her revelations they had no communication. But at another time brother William came to me, and told me a long tale of her, being at the house of a Knight in Kent, that was sore troubled with temptation to destroy himself; and none other thing we talked of nor should have done of likelihood, though we had tarried together much longer. He took so great pleasure, good man, to tell that tale with all the circumstances at length. When I came again another time to Syon, on a day in which there was a profession,[826] some of the fathers asked me how I liked the Nun? And I answered that, in good faith, I liked her very well in her talking; "howbeit," quoth I, "she is never the nearer tried by that, for I assure you she were likely to be very bad, if she seemed good, ere I should think her other, till she happed to be proved naught;"[827] and in good faith, that is my manner indeed, except I were set to search and examine the truth upon likelihood of some cloaked evil; for in that case, although I nothing suspected the person myself, yet no less than if I suspected him sore,[828] I would as far as my wit would serve me, search to find out the truth as yourself hath done very prudently in this matter; wherein you have done, in my mind, to your great laud and praise, a very meritorious deed in bringing forth to light such detestable hypocrisy, whereby every other wretch may take warning, and be feared[829] to set forth their own devilish dissimuled[830] falsehood, under the manner

and color of the wonderful work of God; for verily, this woman so handled herself, with help of the evil spirit that inspired her, that after her own confession declared at Paul's cross, when I sent word by my servant unto the Proctor of the Charterhouse, that she was undoubtedly proved a false deceiving hypocrite; the good man had had so good opinion of her so long that he could at the first scantly[831] believe me therein. Howbeit it was not he alone that thought her so very good, but many another right good man beside, as little marvel was upon so good report, till she was proved naught.

I remember me further, that in communication between Father Rich and me, I counseled him, that in such strange things as concerned such folk as had come unto her, to whom, as she said, she had told the causes of their coming ere themselves spoke thereof; and such good fruit as they said that many men had received by her prayer he and such other as so reported it, and thought that the knowledge thereof should much pertain to the glory of God, should first cause the things to be well and surely examined by the ordinaries,[832] and such as had authority thereunto; so that it might be surely known whether the things were true or not, and that there were no lies intermingled among them or else the lies might after hap to away[833] the credence of those things that were true. And when he told me the tale of Mary Magdalene, I said unto him, "Father Rich, that she is a good virtuous woman, in good faith, I hear so many good folk so report her, that I verily think it true; and think it well likely that God worketh some good and great things by her. But yet are, you wot well, these strange tales no part of our creed; and therefore before you see them surely proved, you shall have my poor counsel not to wed[834] yourself so far forth to the credence of them, as to report them very surely for true, lest that if it should hap that they were afterward proved false, it might diminish your estimation in your preaching, whereof might grow great loss." To this he thanked me for my counsel, but how he used it after that, I cannot tell.

Thus have I, good Master Cromwell, fully declared you, as far as myself can call to remembrance, all that ever I have done or said in this matter

---

824 destroyed **825** Henry Man, professed and proctor at Sheen, which was renamed Richmond by Henry VII **826** day of   taking vows **827** bad, wicked **828** grievously **829** afraid **830** dissembled **831** hardly **832** one who has immediate   ecclesiastical jurisdiction — archbishop, bishop or bishop's deputy **833** (take) away **834** be obstinately attached to

wherein I am sure that never one of them all shall tell you any farther thing of effect,[835] for if any of them, or any man else, report of me as I trust verily no man will, and I wot well truly no man can, any word or deed by me spoken or done, touching any breach of my loyal troth[836] and duty toward my most redoubted[837] sovereign and natural liege[838] lord, I will come to mine answer, and make it good in such wise as becometh a poor true man to do; that whosoever any such thing shall say, shall therein say untrue; for I neither have in this matter done evil nor said evil, nor so much as any evil thing thought, but only have been glad, and rejoiced of them that were reported for good; which condition I shall nevertheless keep toward all other good folk, for the false cloaked hypocrisy of any of these, no more than I shall esteem[839] Judas the true apostle, for Judas the false traitor.

But so purpose I to bear myself in every man's company, while I live, that neither good man nor bad, neither monk, friar nor nun, nor other man or woman in this world shall make me digress from my troth and faith, either toward God, or toward my natural prince, by the grace of almighty God; and as you therein find me true, so I heartily therein pray you to continue toward me your favor and good will, as you shall be sure of my poor daily prayer, for other pleasure can I none do you. And thus the blessed Trinity, both bodily and ghostly,[840] long preserve and prosper you.

I pray you pardon me, that I write not unto you of mine own hand, for verily I am compelled to forbear writing for a while by reason of this disease of mine, whereof the chief occasion is grown, as it is thought, by the stooping and leaning on my breast, that I have used in writing. And this, eftsoons,[841] I beseech our Lord long to preserve you.

198. To Henry VIII
Chelsea, 5 March <1534>

It may like your Highness[842] to call to your gracious remembrance, that at such time as of that great weighty room and office of your chancellor (with which so far above my merits or qualities able and meet[843] therefor, your Highness had of your incomparable goodness honored and exalted me), ye were so good and gracious unto me as at my poor humble suit to discharge and disburden me, giving me the license with your gracious favor, to bestow the residue of my life in mine age now to come, about the provision for my soul in the service of God, and to be your Grace's beadsman[844] and pray for you; it pleased your Highness further to say unto me, that for the service which I before had done you (which it then liked your goodness far above my deserving to commend), that in any suit that I should after have unto your Highness, which either should concern mine honor (that word it liked your Highness to use unto me) or that should pertain unto my profit, I should find your Highness good and gracious lord unto me. So is it now, gracious Sovereign, that worldly honor is the thing whereof I have resigned both the possession and the desire, in the resignation of your most honorable office. And worldly profit I trust experience proveth, and daily more and more shall prove, that I never was very greedy thereon.

But now is my most humble suit unto your excellent Highness, partly to beseech the same somewhat to tender[845] my poor honesty, but principally that of your accustomed goodness no sinister[846] information move your noble Grace, to have any more distrust of my truth and devotion toward you, than I have or shall during my life give the cause. For in this matter of the wicked woman of Canterbury[847] I have unto your trusty counselor Master Thomas Cromwell, by my writing, as plainly declared the truth as I possibly can, which my declaration of his duty toward your Grace and his goodness toward me he hath, I understand, declared unto your Grace. In any part of all which my dealing, whether any other man may peradventure[848] put any doubt, or move any scruple of suspicion, that can I neither tell, nor lieth in mine hand to let,[849] but unto myself is it not possible any part of my said demeanor[850] to seem evil, the very clearness of mine own conscience knoweth in all the matter my mind and intent[851] so good.

835 essential importance   **836** loyalty
837 feared   **838** entitled to feudal allegiance   **839** hold   **840** spiritually
841 again   **842** *It may like your Highness:* Your Highness may like   **843** fit

844 one who prays for another   **845** to offer formally for acceptance; to treat with affectionate care   **846** darkly suspicious
847 Elizabeth Barton. See above, Letter 192. Rastell changed "wicked woman of

Canterbury" to "nun of Canterbury" when he printed this letter in the 1557 *Works.*
848 possibly   **849** prevent   **850** conduct
851 intention, purpose

Wherefore most gracious Sovereign, I neither will nor well it can become[852] me with your Highness to reason and argue the matter, but in my most humble manner prostrate at your gracious feet, I only beseech your Majesty with your own high prudence and your accustomed goodness consider and weigh the matter. And then if in your so doing, your own virtuous mind shall give you, that notwithstanding the manifold excellent goodness that your gracious Highness hath by so many manner ways used unto me, I be a wretch[853] of such monstrous ingratitude as could with any of them all, or with any other person living, digress from my bounden duty of allegiance toward your good Grace, then desire I no further favor at your gracious hand, than the loss of all that ever I may lose in this world, goods, lands, and liberty and finally my life withal,[854] whereof the keeping of any part unto my self could never do me pennyworth of pleasure, but only should then my recomfort[855] be, that after my short life and your long, which with continual prosperity to God's pleasure[856] our Lord for his mercy send you I should once meet with your Grace again in heaven, and there be merry with you, where among mine other pleasures this should yet be one, that your Grace should surely see there then, that (howsoever you take me) I am your true beadsman now and ever have been, and will be till I die, howsoever your pleasure be to do by me.[857]

Howbeit,[858] if in the considering of my cause your high wisdom and gracious goodness perceive (as I verily trust in God you shall) that I none otherwise have demeaned[859] myself, than well may stand with my bounden duty of faithfulness toward your royal Majesty, then in my most humble wise[860] I beseech your most noble Grace that the knowledge of your true gracious persuasion in that behalf may relieve the torment of my present heaviness,[861] conceived of the dread and fear (by that I hear such a grievous bill put by your learned Council into your high Court of Parliament[862] against me) lest your Grace might by some sinister information be moved anything to think the contrary, which if your Highness do not (as I trust in God and your great goodness the matter by your own high prudence examined and considered, you will not) then in my most humble manner I beseech your Highness further (albeit that[863] in respect of my former request this other thing is very slight) yet since your Highness hath herebefore[864] of your mere[865] abundant goodness heaped and accumulated upon me (though I was thereto very far unworthy) from time to time both worship[866] and great honor, too, and since I now have left off all such things and nothing seek or desire but the life to come and in the meanwhile pray for your Grace, it may like your Highness of your accustomed benignity[867] somewhat to tender[868] my poor honesty and never suffer by the means of such a bill put forth against me any man to take occasion hereafter against the truth to slander me; which thing should yet by the peril of their own souls do themselves more hurt than me, which shall, I trust, settle mine heart, with your gracious favor, to depend upon the comfort of the truth and hope of heaven, and not upon the fallible opinion or soon spoken words of light[869] and soon changeable people.

And thus, most dread[870] and most dear sovereign Lord, I beseech the blessed Trinity preserve your most noble Grace, both in body and soul, and all that are your well willers,[871] and amend all the contrary, among whom if ever I be or ever have been one, then pray I God that he may with mine open shame and destruction declare it. At my poor[872] house in Chelsea, the fifth day of March, by the known rude hand of

> Your most humble and most heavy[873]
> faithful subject and beadsman,
> Tho. More, Kg.

199. To Thomas Cromwell
Chelsea, 5 March <1534>

Right Worshipful.[874]

After my most hearty recommendation,[875] it may please you to understand that I have perceived by the relation[876] of my son[877] Roper (for which I

852 be fitting for   **853** despicable person   **854** besides   **855** comfort, consolation   **856** service   **857** *your pleasure be to do by me:* it please you to do by me   **858** However   **859** conducted   **860** way, manner   **861** sadness, grief   **862** Parliament as a court of law or administration   **863** *albeit that:* although   **864** in time past   **865** pure, unmixed   **866** distinction   **867** kindness of disposition   **868** esteem   **869** irresponsible   **870** held in awe, revered   **871** *well willers:* well-wishers   **872** of little worth   **873** sad, grieved   **874** Distinguished, Honorable   **875** commendation of myself to your benevolent remembrance or regard   **876** report   **877** the son-in-law who had married Margaret More

beseech almighty God reward you) your most charitable labor taken for me toward the King's gracious
Highness, in the procuring at his most gracious
hand, the relief and comfort of this woeful heavi-
5 ness[878] in which mine heart standeth, neither for the
loss of goods, lands, or liberty, nor for any respect
either, of this kind of honesty[879] that standeth in the
opinion of people and worldly reputation, all which
manner things (I thank our Lord), I so little esteem
10 for any affection[880] therein toward myself that I can
well be content to jeopard,[881] lose, and forgo them
all and my life therewith, without any further respite than even this same present day, either for the
pleasure of God or of my prince.

15   But surely good Master Cromwell, as I by mouth
declared unto you, some part (for all could I neither then say nor now write) it thoroughly pierceth
my poor heart, that the King's Highness (whose
gracious favor toward me far above all the things
20 of this world I have evermore desired, and whereof
both for the conscience of mine own true faithful
heart and devotion toward him, and for the manifold benefits of his high goodness continually bestowed upon me, I thought myself always sure),
25 should conceive any such mind or opinion of me, as
to think that in my communication either with the
nun or the friars, or in my letter written unto the
nun, I had any other manner mind,[882] than might
well stand with the duty of a tender loving subject
30 toward his natural prince, or that his Grace should
reckon in me any manner of obstinate heart against
his pleasure in any thing that ever I said or did concerning his great matter of his marriage or concerning the primacy of the Pope. Never would I wish
35 other thing in this world more lief,[883] than that his
Highness in these things all three, as perfectly knew
my dealing, and as thoroughly saw my mind, as I
do myself, or as God himself, whose sight pierceth
deeper into my heart, than mine own.

40   For, sir, as for the first matter, that is to wit[884] my
letter or communication with the Nun (the whole
discourse whereof in my former letter I have as

plainly declared unto you as I possibly can), so pray
I God to withdraw that scruple[885] and doubt of my
good mind, out of the King's noble breast and none   45
other wise, but as I not only thought none harm,
but also purposed good, and in that thing most,
in which (as I perceive) his Grace conceiveth most
grief and suspicion, that is to wit in my letter which
I wrote unto her. And therefore sir, since I have by   50
my writing declared the truth of my deed, and am
ready by mine oath to declare the truth of mine intent,[886] I can devise[887] no further thing by me to be
done in that matter, but only beseech almighty God
to put into the King's gracious mind, that as God   55
knoweth the thing is indeed, so his noble Grace
may take it. Now touching the second point concerning his Grace's great matter of his marriage, to
the intent that you may see cause with the better
conscience to make suit unto his Highness for me,   60
I shall as plainly declare you my demeanor[888] in that
matter as I have already declared you in the other,
for more plainly can I not.

Sir, upon a time at my coming from beyond the
sea,[889] where I had been in the King's business, I re-   65
paired as my duty was unto the King's Grace being
at that time at Hampton Court. At which time suddenly his Highness walking in the gallery,[890] broke
with me of[891] his great matter,[892] and showed me
that it was now perceived, that his marriage was not   70
only against the positive laws of the Church and the
written law of God, but also in such wise against
the law of nature, that it could in no wise by the
Church be dispensable.[893] Now so was it that before
my going over the sea, I had heard certain things   75
moved against the bull of the dispensation concerning the words of the Law Levitical and the Law
Deuteronomical to prove the prohibition to be *de
iure diuino,* but yet perceived I not at that time but
that the greater hope of the matter stood in certain   80
faults that were founden in the bull, whereby the
bull should by the law not be sufficient. And such
comfort was there in that point as far as I perceived
a good season,[894] that the Council on the other part

---

878 sadness   **879** honorable position
880 good disposition   **881** risk
882 *manner mind:* kind of intention
883 dearly   **884** *that is to wit:* namely
885 hesitation   **886** intention   **887** contrive   **888** conduct   **889** from Calais,
late September 1527   **890** now called

the Haunted Gallery   **891** *broke with
me of:* disclosed to me   **892** The divorce
was commonly spoken of as the "King's
matter." There was much controversy over
two passages: Lv 20:21 and Dt 25:5. Queen
Catherine said that there was a papal brief
in Spain granting dispensation for the

marriage with Henry, even if the marriage
with Arthur had been consummated. The
latter point, in any case, Catherine denied.
893 subject to dispensation, the granting
of a license by a pope, archbishop or bishop
to do what is forbidden by ecclesiastical
law   **894** *a good season:* for a good while

were fain[895] to bring forth a brief,[896] by which they pretended those defaults[897] to be supplied, the truth of which brief was by the King's Council suspected, and much diligence was thereafter done for the trial of that point, wherein what was finally founden either I never knew or else I not remember.

But I rehearse[898] you this to the intent you shall know that the first time that ever I heard that point moved, that it should be in such high degree against the law of nature, was the time in which as I began to tell you the King's Grace showed it me himself, and laid the Bible open before me, and there read me the words that moved his Highness and diverse other erudite[899] persons so to think, and asked me further what myself thought thereon. At which time not presuming to look[900] that his Highness should anything take that point for the more proved or unproved for my poor mind in so great a matter, I showed nevertheless as my duty was at his commandment what thing I thought upon the words which I there read. Whereupon his Highness accepting benignly[901] my sudden unadvised answer commanded me to commune[902] further with Master Fox, now his Grace's Almoner,[903] and to read a book[904] with him that then was in making[905] for that matter. After which book read, and my poor opinion eftsoons[906] declared unto his Highness thereupon, his Highness like a prudent and a virtuous prince assembled at another time at Hampton Court a good number of very well learned men, at which time as far as ever I heard there were (as was in so great a matter most likely to be) diverse opinions among them. Howbeit[907] I never heard but that they agreed at that time upon a certain form in which the book should be made, which book was afterward at York Place in my Lord Cardinal's chamber read in the presence of diverse bishops and many learned men. And they all thought that there appeared in the book good and reasonable causes that might well move the King's Highness, being so virtuous a prince, to conceive in his mind a scruple against his marriage, which, while he could not

otherwise avoid, he did well and virtuously for the acquieting[908] of his conscience to sue[909] and procure[910] to have his doubt decided by judgment of the Church.

After this the suit began, and the Legates sat upon the matter,[911] during all which time I never meddled therein, nor was a man meet to do,[912] for the matter was in hand by an ordinary process of the spiritual law, whereof I could little skill. And yet while the Legates were sitting upon the matter, it pleased the King's Highness to send me in the company of my Lord of London now of Durham[913] in embassiate[914] about the peace that at our being there was concluded at Cambrai, between his Highness and the Emperor and the French King. And after my coming home his Highness of his only goodness (as far unworthy as I was thereto) made me, as you well know, his chancellor of this realm, soon after which time his Grace moved me again yet eftsoons, to look and consider his great matter, and well and indifferently[915] to ponder such things as I should find therein. And if it so were that thereupon it should hap me to see such things as should persuade me to that part, he would gladly use me among other of his councilors in that matter, and nevertheless he graciously declared unto me that he would in no wise that I should other thing do or say therein, than upon that that I should perceive mine own conscience should serve me, and that I should first look unto God and after God unto him, which most gracious words was the first lesson also that ever his Grace gave me at my first coming into his noble service. This motion was to me very comfortable and much I longed beside anything that myself either had seen, or by further search should hap to find for the one part or the other, yet specially to have some conference in the matter with some such of his Grace's learned Council as most for his part had labored and most have found in the matter.

Whereupon his Highness assigned unto me the now most reverend fathers Archbishops of

895 glad   **896** short letter from the pope on matters of discipline   **897** defects   **898** tell   **899** well-instructed, learned   **900** expect   **901** graciously   **902** converse   **903** an official to a prince or a bishop, who distributes his alms   **904** *The Determinations of the most famous and most excellent universities of Italy and France,*

that it is unlawful for a man to marry his brother's wife, that the pope hath no power to dispense therewith (London, 1531), by Stokesley, Bishop of London, Edward Fox, the King's Almoner, and Dr. Nicholas de Burgo, an Italian Augustinian friar.   **905** *in making:* in course of being written   **906** again   **907** However

908 quieting   **909** put in suit   **910** cause   **911** Cardinals Campeggio and Wolsey held a legatine court from May 31 to July 23, 1529.   **912** *nor…do:* nor was it fitting for a man to do so   **913** Cuthbert Tunstall, at the head of the embassy to negotiate the Treaty of Cambrai, 1529   **914** embassy   **915** without prejudice

Canterbury and York with Master Doctor Fox, now his Grace's Almoner and Master Doctor Nicholas the Italian friar,[916] whereupon I not only sought and read, and as far-forth as my poor wit and learning served me, well weighed and considered every such thing as I could find myself, or read in any other man's labor that I could get, which anything had written therein, but had also diligent conference with his Grace's councilors aforesaid, whose honors and worships[917] I nothing mistrust in this point, but that they both have and will report unto his Highness that they never found obstinate manner or fashion in me, but a mind as toward[918] and as conformable[919] as reason could in a matter disputable require.

Whereupon the King's Highness being further advertised[920] both by them and myself of my poor opinion in the matter (wherein to have been able and meet to do him service I would as I then showed his Highness have been more glad than of all such worldly commodities[921] as I either then had or ever should come to) his Highness graciously taking in gre[922] my good mind in that behalf used of his blessed disposition in the prosecuting of his great matter only those (of whom his Grace had good number) whose conscience his Grace perceived well and fully persuaded upon that part, and as well myself as any other to whom his Highness thought the thing to seem otherwise, he used in his other business, abiding (of his abundant goodness) nevertheless gracious lord unto any man, nor never was willing to put any man in ruffle[923] or trouble[924] of his conscience.

After this did I never nothing more therein, nor never any word wrote I therein to the impairing[925] of his Grace's part neither before nor after, nor any man else by my procurement,[926] but settling my mind in quiet to serve his Grace in other things, I would not so much as look nor wittingly[927] let lie by me any book of the other part, albeit that I gladly read afterward diverse books that were made on his part yet, nor never would I read the book that Master Abell[928] made on the other side, nor other book which were as I heard say made in Latin beyond the sea, nor never give ear to the Pope's proceedings in the matter.

Moreover, whereas I had founden in my study a book that I had before borrowed of my Lord of Bath,[929] which book he had made of the matter at such time as the Legates sat here thereupon, which book had been by me merely gently cast aside, and that I showed him I would send him home his book again, he told me that in good faith he had long time before discharged his mind of that matter,[930] and having forgotten that copy to remain in my hands, had burned his own copy that he had thereof at home, and because he no more minded[931] to meddle anything in the matter, he desired me to burn the same book too. And upon my faith so did I.

Besides this, diverse other ways have I so used myself that if I rehearsed[932] them all, it should well appear that I never have had against his Grace's marriage any manner demeanor[933] whereby his Highness might have any manner cause or occasion of displeasure toward me, for likewise as I am not he which either can, or whom it could become,[934] to take upon him the determination or decision of such a weighty matter, nor boldly to affirm this thing or that therein, whereof diverse points a great way pass my learning, so am I he that among other his Grace's faithful subjects, his Highness being in possession of his marriage[935] and this noble woman really[936] anointed Queen, neither murmur at it nor dispute upon it, nor never did nor will, but without any other manner meddling of the matter among his other faithful subjects faithfully pray to God for his Grace and hers both, long to live and well and their noble issue too, in such wise as may be to the pleasure of God, honor and surety to themselves, rest, peace, wealth, and profit unto this noble realm.

916 Thomas Cranmer, Edward Lee, Edward Fox, Nicholas de Burgo **917** formal titles for holders of certain offices **918** favorable **919** compliant **920** informed **921** profits, interests **922** *in gre:* in good part **923** confusion **924** perplexity **925** impairment **926** instigation **927** knowingly **928** Thomas Abell, Queen Catherine's chaplain, was sent to Spain to procure the papal brief, but secretly showed the Emperor that the Queen most earnestly desired the original should not be sent, lest it be destroyed. Abell was imprisoned in the Tower as if he had been an accomplice of Elizabeth Barton and after six years' confinement was hanged as a traitor in July 1540. The book was his *Invicta Veritas,* 1532. **929** John Clerk, Bishop of Bath and Wells, 1523, became one of Catherine's counselors in 1528, but later joined in pronouncing the King's divorce. **930** *discharged... matter:* dismissed that matter from his mind **931** intended **932** recounted **933** *manner demeanor:* kind of conduct **934** *whom it could become:* to whom it could be fitting **935** Rastell omitted everything from here to the end of the paragraph. **936** Perhaps More wrote "rially," i.e., royally, to be ambiguous.

As touching the third point, the primacy of the Pope, I nothing meddle in the matter. Truth it is, that as I told you, when you desired me to show you what I thought therein, I was myself sometime not of the mind that the primacy of that see should be begun by the institution of God, until that I read in that matter those things that the King's Highness had written in his most famous book[937] against the heresies of Martin Luther, at the first reading whereof I moved the King's Highness either to leave out that point, or else to touch it more slenderly[938] for doubt of such things as after might hap to fall in question between his Highness and some pope as between princes and popes diverse times have done. Whereunto his Highness answered me that he would in no wise anything diminish of that matter, of which thing his Highness showed me a secret cause[939] whereof I never had anything heard before. But surely after that I had read his Grace's book therein, and so many other things as I have seen in that point by this continuance of these ten year since and more have found in effect the substance of all the holy doctors from Saint Ignatius,[940] disciple to Saint John the Evangelist, unto our own days both Latins and Greeks so consonant and agreeing in that point, and the thing by such general councils so confirmed also, that in good faith I never neither read nor heard anything of such effect on the other side, that ever could lead me to think that my conscience were well discharged, but rather in right great peril if I should follow the other side and deny the primacy to be provided by God, which if we did, yet can I nothing (as I showed you) perceive any commodity that ever could come by that denial, for that primacy is at the leastwise instituted by the corps[941] of Christendom and for a great urgent cause in avoiding of schisms[942] and corroborate[943] by continual succession[944] more than the space of a thousand year at the least, for there are passed almost a thousand year since the time of holy Saint Gregory.[945]

And therefore since all Christendom is one corps, I cannot perceive how any member thereof may without the common assent of the body depart from the common head. And then if we may not lawfully leave it by ourself, I cannot perceive (but if the thing were a treating[946] in a general council) what the question could avail whether the primacy were instituted by God or ordained by the Church. As for the general councils assembled lawfully, I never could perceive but that in the declaration of the truths to be believed and to be stood to,[947] the authority thereof ought to be taken for undoubtable, or else were there in nothing no certainty, but through Christendom upon every man's affectionate reason, all thing might be brought from day to day to continual ruffle[948] and confusion, from which by the general councils, the spirit of God assisting, every such council well assembled keepeth and ever shall keep the corps of his Catholic Church.

And verily since the King's Highness hath (as by the book of his honorable council appeareth) appealed to the general council from the Pope, in which council I beseech our Lord send his Grace comfortable speed, methinketh in my poor mind it could be no furtherance there unto his Grace's cause if his Highness should in his own realm before, either by laws making or books putting forth, seem to derogate and deny not only the primacy of the see apostolic,[949] but also the authority of the general councils too, which I verily trust his Highness intendeth not, for in the next general council it may well happen that this Pope may be deposed and another substituted in his room[950] with whom the King's Highness may be very well content; for albeit that[951] I have for mine own part such opinion of the pope's primacy as I have showed you, yet never thought I the Pope above the general council nor never have in any book of mine put forth among the King's subjects in our vulgar tongue, advanced greatly the Pope's authority. For albeit that a man may peradventure[952] somewhat find therein that after the common manner of all Christian realms

937 *Assertio septem sacramentorum,* 1521
938 *more slenderly:* less emphatically
939 Full papal power was necessary for the dispensation that had allowed his marriage. Perhaps the "secret cause" was that the King thought he had evidence that the marriage of Arthur and Catherine had been consummated. If it were a marriage only in name, dispensation would have

been more readily granted. **940** Ignatius, Bishop of Antioch, martyred in Rome *ca.* AD 115 **941** body **942** breaches of the unity of the church not due, according to Augustine and other Fathers, to heretical belief **943** corroborated, strengthened **944** *continual succession:* succeeding to the episcopate by authority in an unbroken line from St. Peter, the first pope **945** Gregory

the Great, Pope 590–604 **946** *a treating:* to be discussed **947** *stood to:* obeyed **948** disorder **949** *see apostolic:* Rome, the see of the apostle St. Peter **950** place. Stapleton omitted "yet never thought I the Pope above the general council."
951 *albeit that:* although **952** possibly

I speak of him as primate, yet never do I stick[953] thereon with reasoning and proving of that point. And in my book against the Masker,[954] I wrote not I wot[955] well five lines, and yet of no more but only St. Peter himself, from whose person many take not the primacy,[956] even of those that grant it none of his successors, and yet was that book made, printed, and put forth of very truth before that any of the books of the council was either printed or spoken of. But where as I had written thereof at length in my confutation[957] before, and for the proof thereof had compiled together all that I could find therefor, at such time as I little looked[958] that there should fall between the King's Highness and the Pope such a breach as is fallen since, when I after that saw the thing likely to draw toward such displeasure between them, I suppressed it utterly and never put word thereof into my book, but put out the remnant without it, which thing well declareth that I never intended anything to meddle in that matter against the King's gracious pleasure, whatsoever mine own opinion were therein.

And thus have I, good Master Cromwell, long troubled your Mastership with a long process[959] of these matters, with which I neither durst[960] nor it could become me[961] to encumber the King's noble Grace, but I beseech you for our Lord's love, that you be not so weary of my most cumbrous[962] suit but that it may like you[963] at such opportune time or times as your wisdom may find to help that his Highness may by your goodness be fully informed of my true faithful mind, and that in the matter of that wicked woman there never was on my part any other mind[964] than good, nor yet in any other thing else never was there nor never shall there be any further fault found in me, than that I cannot in everything think the same way that some other men of more wisdom and deeper learning do, nor can find in mine heart otherwise to say than as mine own conscience giveth[965] me, which condition hath never grown in anything that ever might touch his gracious pleasure of any obstinate mind or misaffectionate[966] appetite, but of a timorous conscience rising haply[967] for lack of better perceiving,[968] and yet not without tender[969] respect unto my most bounden duty toward his noble Grace, whose only favor I so much esteem that I nothing have of mine own in all this world, except only my soul, but that I will with better will forgo it than abide of his Highness, one heavy displeasant[970] look. And thus I make an end of my long, troublous process, beseeching the blessed Trinity for the great goodness ye show me, and the great comfort ye do me, both bodily and ghostly[971] to prosper[972] you, and in heaven to reward you. At Chelsea the fifth day of March by

Your deeply bounden,
Tho. More, Kg.

953 dwell 954 *The Answer to a Poisoned Book,* 1533 955 know 956 *from… primacy:* not many take the primacy away from St. Peter 957 More's *Confutation of Tyndale's Answer,* 1532–33 958 expected 959 discussion 960 dared 961 *become me:* be fitting for me 962 distressing 963 it may please you 964 intention 965 prompts 966 evil-disposed 967 perhaps, by chance 968 understanding 969 careful 970 displeased, angry 971 spiritually 972 *to prosper:* to be propitious to

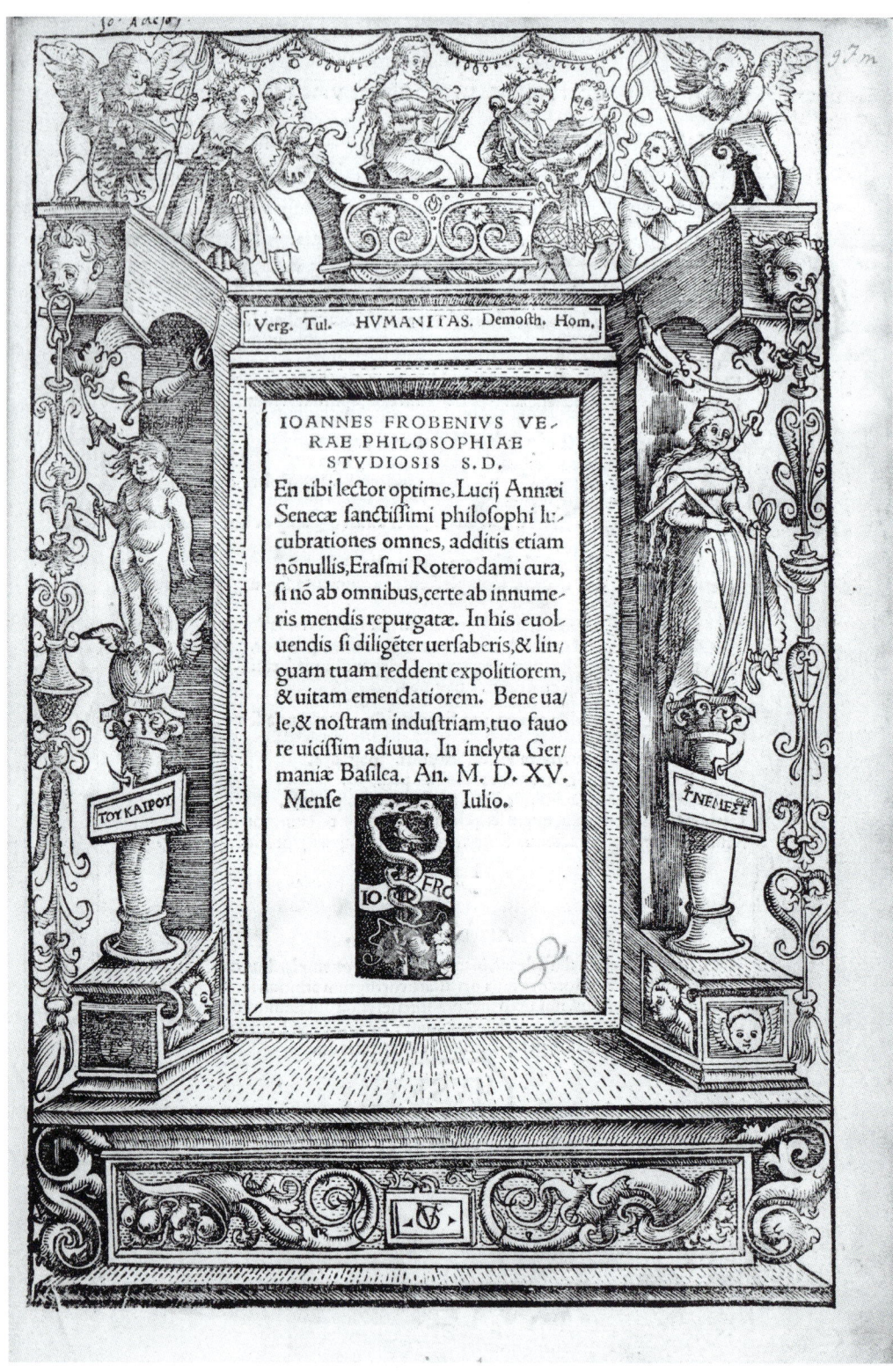

Humanitas reads serenely in her triumphal chariot, pushed by Vergil and Cicero (Tully) and pulled by Demosthenes and Homer. Below on the left is Time; on the right is Fate; the Greek plaques indicate that "Humanitas triumphs over Time & Fate." This is the frontispiece of the 1515 edition of Seneca that Erasmus edited while living in Thomas More's home in London.

Letters: On Humanism, 1505–20

Thomas More, throughout the first half of his career, publicly addressed and defended what we now call the new humanism, especially Erasmian humanism. The letters included in this section—those to Dorp, Oxford University, Edward Lee, a Monk (John Batmanson), and Germanius Brixius—are examples of what Daniel Kinney calls "the Renaissance 'public letter' or letter-essay," works notable for their rhetorical character, even as they manifest "constant attentiveness to a personal addressee" (*CW* 15: xciii). Subjects addressed here include the controversies over new approaches to theology, the relationship between Christianity and learning, and the nature and function of poetry. In Kinney's judgment, "these bold and ambitious" letters are "a singularly valuable resource for any reader who seeks to gain a balanced and reasonably complete understanding of More's life and works" (xvii).

Composed around the same time as *Utopia,* the "Letter to Dorp" is More's intervention in the dispute between Martin Dorp (1485–1525), a theologian at Louvain, and Erasmus. More's letter, addressing both Dorp's criticisms of Erasmus and Dorp's rhetoric, succeeded in persuading Dorp, who "returned to his senses," according to Erasmus, with More's help, something Dorp also acknowledged in later writings (xxiv–xxv). The letter is a public example of More's approach to important contemporary controversies and his commitment to working for peace, even among occasionally warring intellectuals.

In "The Letter to Oxford University," More addresses the "Trojan War" of wits that had broken out in Oxford between critics of the new learning, especially the study of Greek and its supporters. In Erasmus's account, a young English scholar had been teaching Greek with good success when "some barbarian or other in a public sermon began to inveigh against Greek studies with monstrous great falsehoods" (xxix). In the course of addressing the tense situation, More articulates his understanding of the relationship between theology and secular learning that in More's judgment "prepares the soul for virtue." Appealing to the prudence of his addressees throughout, More ends the letter by revealing that King Henry supports the new learning as well. More would later became Chancellor of Oxford, where he had studied as a young man.

More's "Letter to Edward Lee" defends Erasmus's Greek New Testament against one of its English critics. Educated in Oxford, Cambridge, and Louvain, Edward Lee (*ca.* 1482–1544) wrote and eventually circulated a manuscript detailing over 300 problems with Erasmus's first edition, and he attacked the Dutch humanist for being "too proud" to accept counsel and correction (xxxiii–xxxiv). More's attempt to stop Lee's war on Erasmus succeeded—at least publicly—and the two scholars eventually made peace at Calais in 1520, in the company of their fellow humanists (xxxvi). Lee would go on to become Archbishop of York. More's "Letter to a Monk" is another defense of Erasmus's New Testament, and the anonymous addressee has been identified as John Batmanson, a London Carthusian (xli).

The last letter in this section, More's "Letter to Brixius," was published in 1520. Earlier, while England and France were at war, More had satirized Brixius's poem *Chordigera* in his epigrams; later, in peacetime, Brixius responded with his *Antimorus,* which among other things dangerously criticized More's "Coronation Ode," particularly the section where More praises the young King Henry VIII, and daringly finds fault with King Henry VII—a criticism so dangerous that More's friends counseled a strong response. Regarding this fiery exchange, More wrote in a letter to Erasmus that he hoped "humane readers will exhibit some tolerance for those human emotions which no man has ever been able to banish entirely." In his letter to Brixius, More blames Brixius for the quarrel, gives a rather weak defense of his treatment of Henry VII, and makes his own critiques of the French poet's work. In doing so, he also shares his understanding of poetry and rhetoric, leading scholars such as Richard Sylvester and Germain Marc'hadour to call this letter More's *ars poetica* (*CW* 3.2: 551–52). At Erasmus's urging, and to end this strife between poets prudently, More bought all unsold copies of the letter soon after its publication.

CONTENTS

The prefatory number of each letter corresponds to *The Correspondence of Sir Thomas More,* ed. Elizabeth Rogers.
The symbols < > indicate uncertainty about the date or place.

Letters on Humanism

15. To Martin Dorp[1]
Bruges, 21 October <1515>

Thomas More sends his heartiest greetings to Martin Dorp.

If I were at liberty to visit you, my dear Dorp, as I very much wish that I could, first of all I would discuss with you personally in a more fitting way all that I now entrust in a less fitting way to a letter. I would also have liked nothing better than to get to know you face to face, since Erasmus, who feels great affection for both of us, and who is, I hope, equally dear to us both, has instilled in my heart a remarkable longing to see you, to make your acquaintance, and to show you my love. In fact nothing gives him more pleasure than to praise absent friends to friends present, and since his learning and his delightful disposition have endeared him to so many people in various parts of the world, he is constantly trying to make all of them share with each other the same special attachment which binds them to him. Thus he never stops mentioning each of his friends one by one to the rest or describing the gifts for which each merits love, so that each gains a share in the friendship of all. Though he regularly commends all his friends in this way, he commends none more often, more lavishly, or more heartily than he commends you, my dear Dorp, whom he has been celebrating for so long in England that there is no learned man in that country who does not know and honor the name Dorp the same way that the scholars of Louvain themselves do; and they, as they should, honor it very greatly indeed. He has portrayed you so well to me personally that my mind's eye has long since conceived a most flattering image of your mind,[2] the same image, in fact, that I found to illuminate your elegant minor works after I arrived here.

For this reason, as soon as I learned from our most invincible king that I was to serve on an embassy here, believe me, my Dorp, one of the main compensations to which I looked forward in making so lengthy a journey was that I thought it would offer me some opportunity to meet with you. But the nature of the business assigned to us has detained me in Bruges and prevented me from visiting you as I had hoped, for it had previously been agreed that our negotiations with your magnificent prince's most distinguished ambassadors would be conducted here. Thus I deeply regret that though I have enjoyed many other aspects of this embassy I have been disappointed by fortune precisely where I had most hoped for her favor.

But let me finally get down to the issue that has induced me to write this letter. During my stay here I happened to meet several people who to me seemed no strangers to literature. I started a conversation with them about Erasmus and also about you. They knew him from his writings and reputation, but they knew you in other ways as well. They told me something that was as unpleasant as it was incredible, namely that you do not feel any too friendly toward Erasmus and that your letters to him confirm the fact. They promised to bring me the letters the next day, since they saw I was hardly convinced.

They came back the next day, bringing three letters with them.[3] One of these you had written to Erasmus, even though I infer from his answer that he had not received the original of your letter, but rather, like me, he had read it when someone else showed him a copy. In this letter you criticize the *Folly* and exhort him to a *Praise of Wisdom*. You show so little approval and advise such repressive constraints for his project of emending the New Testament from Greek that you virtually oppose the whole enterprise. The second of these letters was written by Erasmus while he was still weary with traveling, and indeed still engaged in his journey, as a cursory response to your criticisms; he also promised to write a fuller response when he had reached Basel. Then there was the third letter, your answer to that of Erasmus.

---

1 Maarten van Dorp (1485–1525), initially a humanist and Latin lecturer at the University of Louvain, turned primarily to scholastic theology. Between 1514 and 1515, he wrote letters to Erasmus in which he criticized the *Praise of Folly*, as well as Erasmus's plans to publish discrepancies between the Vulgate and the Greek New Testament.
2 *mind's eye ... mind:* See Erasmus, *Praise of Folly* (ASD 4/3: 74); *Adages* 550 (CWE 32: 36–37). **3** For the contents of each letter, see EE 2: 10–16, 90–114, 126–36.

When I read these letters in the presence of those men, although none of your statements convinced me, at any rate, that you were an enemy to Erasmus (for what would suffice to convince me of that?), there were nonetheless some which convinced me that you were somewhat more agitated than I had expected. But as I wished rather to banish this thought from their minds than to reinforce it, I asserted that I had read nothing in your letters which did not seem to me to be written with the friendliest intentions.

"But," said one of them, "even discounting what he wrote, it was no friendly gesture on his part to write in the first place. For suppose that anyone was so terribly upset by the *Folly* — and I have never heard anyone anywhere say so, not even in Louvain, a place where I have spent many long periods of time since the *Folly* was published, apart from one or two infantile old grumblers[4] that even the boys there make fun of, whereas otherwise both here and there everybody takes such delight in the *Folly* that many people have learned many passages from it by heart — but as I started to say, suppose that anyone was so terribly upset by the *Folly* that it actually seemed necessary to ask for a palinode from Erasmus. Even so, since, as Dorp himself writes,[5] he had recently been summoned for a private visit with Erasmus, what was the purpose of writing to him? If he thought that some matter required his advice, why not give the advice face to face? As the scene goes in Terence, why not give his instructions in person instead of waiting to step out the door and then shouting them up from the street,[6] when Erasmus was so far away that, though he should have been either the first or even the only person to hear the advice, he was not only the last to find out about it but he learned of it only through others? Consider how candidly Dorp is conducting this business: first of all he pretends that he is defending against everyone a person whom no one accuses, and then, though I am not sure that anyone listens to the arguments that he offers in Erasmus's defense, everyone is reading publicly (except for the one man who ought to) the things Dorp alleges against him."

After he had said this and the others had said various other things which I think it as well to omit here, I answered them and then I dismissed them

in such a way as to make it quite clear that I do not want to hear any slighting remarks about you and that I am almost as fond of you as I am of Erasmus, of whom I am so fond that I could not be fonder of anyone. Indeed, whatever motives you had for writing to Erasmus when you could have talked over the matter in person, they were certainly not bad ones; of this, my dear Dorp, my esteem for you makes me quite sure, while Erasmus, secure in his notion of your feelings toward him, has no doubt about it.

But as for that second letter of yours, a very poor second, which is being read everywhere, I could easily believe that you had no intention at all of releasing it to the public but that it got out completely by accident. The main reason that drives me to think so is that there are some passages in your letter which I am convinced you would have changed had you chosen to publish it, passages unworthy of being written either to him or by you. For you would not have written in certain passages so acerbically to such a great friend or so shoddily to such a great scholar; indeed I am sure that you would have written more mercifully in accordance with your modest character and more carefully in accordance with your uncommon learning. Furthermore, as for the jokes and the taunts that are too much in evidence throughout your composition, I have no doubt that you would have introduced them either somewhat more sparingly or at any rate, my dear Dorp, more wittily.

I am not particularly troubled by the way that you carp at the *Folly*, inveigh at the poets, snarl at all the grammarians, disapprove of his annotations on Scripture, or judge that a training in Greek literature is simply irrelevant.[7] In these matters, without offending anyone, everyone has a right to his own point of view. Besides, you have so far presented your case on these topics in such a way that I have no doubt that many arguments occur to everyone while reading your letter which ought to be stated for the opposite viewpoint. In fact, far from considering that you have said too much on any of these topics, on a number I find a good deal left unsaid, with which I would have liked to see your composition come forth better armed so that Erasmus would have had greater occasion to fortify his opposing position with more massive fieldworks.

4 *infantile old grumblers:* See Erasmus, *Praise of Folly* (ASD 4/3: 82–85); *Adages* 436 (*CWE* 31: 414–15). **5** See *EE* 2: 11. **6** See Terence, *Andria* 490–96. **7** See *EE* 2: 127–29, 133.

On the other hand, it certainly disturbed me a
good deal that you seem to handle Erasmus in a
way that is worthy of neither of you. You treat him
sometimes as if you despise him, sometimes as if
you regard him with haughty derision,[8] sometimes
as if you are not so much offering advice as chastis-
ing him like a stern uncle[9] or humorless censor, and
lastly as if you are deliberately twisting the meaning of his words to get all the theologians and even
all the universities, as they are called, up in arms
against him.

I do not want you to regard this composition
of mine as if it were directed against you, for I do
not believe you have done any of this out of ill will
toward him, or as if I, who could use a defender
myself, plan to mount a defense for a man whom
I know to be too great in all men's esteem and in
actual fact to be relegated to the ranks of the accused. But since I love you and cherish your fame, I
did want to advise you about certain things which
those persons who fail to appreciate fully the modesty and the veritably swanlike candor of your nature are making a pretext for thinking that you are
too keen to enhance your own fame and are treacherously attacking another's.

Would that, just as Aeneas in Vergil stood hidden
by a cloud in the midst of the Carthaginians and
there looked at himself and his deeds represented
in tapestries,[10] would that you too could stand by
unobserved and observe the expressions with which
people read this last letter of yours. I am sure you
would conclude that you owe me a good deal more
gratitude for advising you to change what you wrote
(for by changing it you can make everyone judge, as
I do, that you did not issue this letter but let it slip
forth) than you owe to your flatterers, since even
they themselves criticize in your absence the very
things that they praise to your face.

Yet I wonder indeed if anyone is so bent on flattery that he can praise some of your flourishes even
in your presence; as I started to say, would that
you could observe through a lattice[11] the faces, the
voices, the feelings with which people read your
expressions as you harp away more than once at
Erasmus, "Our theologians, Erasmus, and your

grammarians,"[12] as if you yourself, sitting on high in
the ranks of the theologians, cast him down among
grammar-school tyros. You do indeed rightfully
sit among the theologians, nor do you merely sit;
you preside. Nonetheless he is not to be banished
from the theologian's throne to the grammarian's
footstool.

Yet I suspect that Erasmus will by no means spurn
the title "grammarian" which you ridicule more frequently than cleverly. Or rather, modest as he is,
even though he deserves it more than anyone, he
may still hesitate to accept it, since he knows that
"grammarian" means precisely the same thing as
"man of letters," whose area of study extends across
every variety of literature, that is, every discipline.
For this reason, though anyone who has studied
dialectic may be called a dialectician, anyone who
has studied arithmetic may be called an arithmeti-
cian, and so on in the rest of the arts, no one, in my
opinion at least, may be styled a man of letters who
has not pored through each and every one of the
sciences;[13] otherwise you could confer the title of
grammarian even upon infants who know merely
the letters of the alphabet. But if you claim that
there are no grammarians besides the ones who, as
you put it, play king in low dives where the air rings
with blows, wielding hickory sticks for their scepters, and who, even though they are more foolish
than Self-Love[14] and Folly, suppose that they know
every science just because they have mastered the
mere words and syntax,[15] on my honor, my dear
Dorp, though I admit that grammarians of that sort
are far from being learned, I believe even they come
considerably closer to learning than those theologians who have not even mastered the syntax and
mere words. I myself know of several who fit this
description, and you know (I suspect) of still more,
though we each do our best to conceal the fact.[16]
Erasmus is certainly not one of those grammarians
who have mastered no more than mere words, nor
is he one of those theologians who know nothing at
all outside a tangled labyrinth of petty problems.[17]
He is a grammarian of the same stamp as Varro[18]
and Aristarchus[19] and a theologian of the same
stamp as you, Dorp, that is, of the best. For he is not

8 *haughty derision:* See *Adages* 180 (CWE
31: 215). 9 *stern uncle:* See *Adages* 1339
(CWE 33: 210). 10 See *Aeneid* 1.439–40,
488–89. 11 *observe…lattice:* See *Adages*
2049 (CWE 34: 199–200). 12 EE 2: 128

13 *no one…sciences:* See Cicero, *De
oratore* 1.6.20. 14 Self-Love is a favorite
attendant of Folly; see *Praise of Folly* (ASD
4/3: 78). 15 See EE 2: 131. 16 *though…
fact:* See *Praise of Folly* (ASD 4/3: 82).

17 *tangled…problems:* See *Praise of Folly*
(ASD 4/3: 144, 148); EE 2: 101; *Adages* 1951
(CWE 34: 147–48). 18 Roman scholar
(116–27 BC) 19 Greek grammarian
(ca. 220–143 BC)

ignorant of those petty problems, and he has gone on to do what you too have done in such depth; he has gained something vastly more useful, a general command of sound literature, which means sacred letters especially but not at the expense of the rest.

But I will proceed with your letter, in which this innuendo is pretty much more of the same, "If you should ever see the *Decretals,* Erasmus,"[20] as if he might never get a glimpse of the decretal epistles which you indicate you have seen. So is this slur against him: "Herons muddy the water wherever they go, and beginners too muddle up everything whenever they enter the arena of debate."[21] So is this one: "You cannot figure out what distinguishes a dialectician from a sophist if you know nothing about either of those arts."[22] And then a little later, "Unless you think that everyone is a sophist who shows more skill in disputing than you do, that is, every dialectician."[23] Do you honestly think, Dorp, that Erasmus muddles up everything whenever he disputes, that he has not an inkling of what dialectic is or even what a sophist is, or that he alone is ignorant of something that is known to almost every schoolboy?[24]

But I believe that even you grant him an uncommon and virtually unique skill in rhetoric.[25] If you do give him that, then I fail to see how you can deny him any dialectical skill whatsoever. After all, not the least of philosophers had reason to think dialectic and rhetoric as closely akin as a fist and a palm,[26] since dialectic infers more concisely what rhetoric sets out more elaborately, and where dialectic strikes home with its dagger-like point rhetoric throws down and overwhelms the opponent with its very weight.

But suppose dialectic has nothing in common with rhetoric. Just because he does not dispute in the schools, just because he does not brawl for an audience of boys, just because he now dispenses with those petty problems (as you too will hereafter), do you think that he never learned them, and do you imagine that he has less skill in disputing than any dialectician? On this point see how thoroughly we differ: by my reckoning not even a typical illiterate of average intelligence, but far less intelligent than Erasmus, not even an illiterate, I say, will prove less skilled than every dialectician in any

dispute where both parties are familiar with the subject of the argument and where intelligence can make up for what is lacking in artifice. For what else are the very precepts of dialectic but a particular product of intelligence, that is, the particular formulas of rational conjecture which reason perceives to be useful in learning about the real world? So unlikely it is that Erasmus, whose intellect and learning are admired by everyone, should prove less skilled at disputing than every dialectician, mere schoolboys included.

But I will leave these points alone; they are relatively minor affairs, since they merely involve disagreement about the importance of literature. But that other slur is certainly much more offensive, where you recklessly drag in the names of the Hussite Jerome[27] and the grammarian Cresconius,[28] both heretics, of course; for you seem to be trying to link them with those in whose company you name them. What of this, that you treat several points so invidiously that it seems you would like nothing more than to turn first the Louvain theologians, then all the other theologians in the world, and finally all the universities against him by twisting the meaning of some of his words in the most irresponsible way?[29]

To begin with the last point: he said that not all theologians find fault with the *Folly,* but only the ones who resent the rebirth of sound learning, and then, since you had written that his new edition of Jerome pleased the theologians, he said that the ones who found fault with the *Folly* would dislike the edition as well.[30] Here you snatch up this elegant theme for a joke and exclaim, "What a novel achievement, to edit a text few will like,"[31] as if there remain only a few who will like it once we eliminate from the great crowd of legitimate theologians one or two grumbling old men who have not the slightest legitimate claim to the title they profess. And yet, pressing ahead with the same charming joke, you say,

> Well, then, theologians will not like it (doubtless those were his words); then please tell us, who will? lawyers, or doctors, or even philosophers, so that they can encroach on an alien field? No, you are preparing that text for grammarians.

---

20 *EE* 2: 132; the *Epistolae decretals* is a text of canon law.   **21** *EE* 2: 133   **22** *EE* 2: 134   **23** *EE* 3: 135   **24** *that . . . schoolboy:* See *Adages* 1042 (*CWE* 33: 40).   **25** See

EE 2: 127.   **26** See Cicero, *De oratore* 32.113–14; *De finibus* 2.6; *Brutus* 309.   **27** Jerome of Prague (*ca.* 1365–1416), a follower of John Hus   **28** a Donatist

opponent of Augustine   **29** See *EE* 2: 102–3.   **30** See *EE* 2: 108.   **31** *EE* 2: 130

Then make ready a throne for the grammarians to be arbiters of all the sciences; let them breed us a new kind of theology which will finally be born like a ludicrous mouse. Nor do we need to worry lest scholars refuse to bow down to their scepters. For scepters they have hickory sticks, and with these they play king in low dives where the air rings with blows, and though they are more foolish than Self-Love and Folly, they suppose that they know every science just because they have mastered the mere words and syntax. And so there is no need for universities: schools like Zwolle and Deventer[32] will suffice us. And certainly this is the opinion of that great man, the Hussite Jerome, that God's church derives as much benefit from universities as it does from the devil; nor does it worry the grammarians in the least that this opinion was condemned in the Council of Constance,[33] since it was surely attended by no one who was not quite uncultured and ignorant of Greek.[34]

It would be wrong of me, Dorp, to break in on your joking too often, although it is amazing how long it has kept you so very amused. But if you have finished your joking, now, Dorp, it is your turn to listen.

No one reading your own words could fail to perceive that you had no occasion at all for this tangential comment about universities or that no matter how copiously or eloquently you declaimed your set-piece it has nothing to do with the argument and does not require any answer. Nonetheless I think there should be no room for doubt as to how Erasmus feels about universities, in which he has both studied and taught, and not only what you label grammar, but also (along with much else of considerably more use to all Christians) even those petty problems you presently value so much and will ultimately value so little. Everyone knows how long and how highly regarded he was at Paris, and then later at Bologna as well, to say nothing of Rome for the moment, even though I consider it the foremost of all universities. Oxford and Cambridge now cherish Erasmus, as they clearly should,

for he was active for long periods in both, winning praise for himself as immense as the good he conferred on their scholars. They both urge him to join them, and since he was awarded his doctorate in theology elsewhere, they both seek to adopt him as one of their own theologians.

Yet I am not at all sure that you have much respect for our universities, since you confer so much importance on Louvain and Paris that it seems you leave nothing at all for the rest of mankind, especially in dialectic. You say, after all, that if the theologians of Louvain and Paris were not dialecticians there would be no dialectic on earth nor would there have been any for these many centuries.[35] I was in both universities seven years ago; not long, to be sure, but while there I tried hard to learn what things are taught in each university and what method of teaching is used there. And indeed, though I honor them both, I have so far discovered no reason, either in what I heard while I was there or in what I have learned since I left, why, even for dialectic, I ought to prefer either one of them to Oxford or Cambridge for the education of my own children, for whom I want strictly the best.

And yet I will admit (for I would not like to deny anyone his fair share of praise) that we Englishmen owe a great debt to the Parisian, Jacques Lefèvre d'Etaples.[36] All of our better minds and sounder judgments acknowledge in him a restorer of true dialectic and true philosophy, especially Aristotelian. Through this man it seems Paris is paying us back, in a way, for a benefit received long ago, since through him they restore to our country the same sciences we originally taught them. This last point is so generally acknowledged that even Gaguin,[37] no belittler of France's prestige and no patron of England's, includes it in his *Annals*. And would that the scholars of Louvain and Paris alike would accept Lefèvre's commentaries on Aristotle's dialectic. Unless I am mistaken, in both universities that science would then be less contentious and not quite so corrupt.

But I wonder why you linked the scholars of Louvain and Paris in your comment about dialectic: they are so thoroughly at odds with each other that they do not even agree on a name, since the former

---

32 considered the best schools in the Low Countries at the time   **33** Jerome was condemned as a heretic and executed at the Council of Constance (1414–18) for maintaining the teachings of Wycliffe

and Hus.   **34** *EE* 2: 130; *uncultured... Greek:* See *Adages* 1518 (*CWE* 33: 299–300).   **35** See *EE* 2: 134.   **36** Jacques Lefèvre d'Étaples (*ca.* 1455–1536) edited St. Paul's Epistles from the Vulgate along with

a paraphrase and commentary in 1512.   **37** Robert Gaguin (1433–1501), a French humanist

affect the name "realists," the latter the name "nominalists." But suppose that they both accept Aristotle, that both are engaged in interpreting him, and that all their contentions concern nothing else but his meaning; since the scholars of Louvain and Paris interpret him in two different, or rather in two contradictory senses, how do you know which party you ought to join? On the other hand, if this sort of quarrel is actually relevant to dialectic but not at all relevant to Aristotle, either one party or both are professing not only the logic of Aristotle, as you say they do, but some other, as well. But if the points which give rise to such controversy are not even relevant to dialectic (which they certainly are not, if you hold that he taught dialectic perfectly and if they have no relevance to him), it would be highly absurd to endeavor to learn dialectic by feuding for so many years over things which have nothing to do with it.

Indeed, Dorp, I am tempted to think that many of the theories over which battles are constantly raging as if home and hearth were at stake either have little to do with logic or are not very useful for learning it well. In the study of grammar, for instance, it should be enough to learn those empirical precepts which prepare you to speak Latin yourself and to read it intelligently, but not anxiously to seek out innumerable rules of speech or to squander your life over letters and syllables. In dialectic, by the same token, I should have thought it sufficient to master the nature of words, the force of propositions, and the forms of syllogisms, and at once to apply dialectic as a tool to the other branches of learning. With this very thing in mind Aristotle restricted his own dialectic to the ten ultimate classes of real entities or of predicables, to a treatise on propositions, and to the forms of the syllogism, the demonstrative, the probable, and the captious. To these Porphyry added a kind of entrance or introduction in his five universals, which may be construed either as entities or as words. Certainly neither propounded, and Porphyry flatly refused to propound, those sophistical problems that do more to stunt than to foster young intellects in need of more wholesome instruction.[38]

But there have sprung up of late certain monstrous absurdities, the bane of sound learning in general, which have muddled up subjects which were clearly distinguished by the ancients and have corrupted all subjects by sullying the oldest and purest traditions with their foul accretions. In grammar, for instance, to say nothing of Alexander[39] and others like him (for they did teach grammar somehow, no matter how crudely), a certain Albert, professing to expound grammar, has presented us instead with some sort of logic or metaphysics, or rather with out-and-out drivel and nonsense;[40] yet this unsurpassed trifling is not only accepted in the universities but is even admired so much by some that according to them no one who has not earned the title of Albertist is worth anything as a grammarian.[41] So great is the power of a conviction to pervert even sound minds and judgments once it has been planted by incompetent teachers and reinforced by the passage of time.

For this reason I am not so astonished that the same kind of supersophistical trifling has crept in to supplant dialectic; this trifling affords such delight to its votaries, because of its "subtlety," that in a talk which I recently had on this topic with a certain dialectician who passes for very learned, he claimed (I will use his own words; I cannot see how else to achieve the same brilliant perfection of eloquence) that "how Aristotle wrote was real vulgar," and "these days," he said, "schoolboys get so wonderfully grounded in their *Little Logic* that I am pretty well certain that if Aristotle rose again out of his grave and picked an argument with them they would shut him up good, not only in sophistry but in his logic, too." I was as sorry as I could be to take leave of the fellow, but as things stood just then I was rather too busy for play.

But as for that book, *Little Logic,* so called probably because it contains little logic, it is worth having a look at its chapters on so-called suppositions, on ampliations, restrictions, and appellations, and everywhere else, to see all of the pointless and even false little precepts it does contain, such as those which oblige one to draw a distinction between these propositions (and other ones like them): "The lion than an animal is stronger" and "The lion is stronger than an animal," as if they did not mean the same thing; and admittedly both are so pointless that each of them means almost nothing,

38 See Porphyry's introduction to his *Commentaria in Aristotlem Graeca.*
39 Alexander de Villa Dei (fl. 1200), author of *Doctrinale,* a Latin grammar **40** *out… nonsense:* See *Praise of Folly* (ASD 4/3: 138). **41** More is referring to *Grammatica speculativa,* now attributed to Thomas of Erfurt.

though if anything, then doubtless the same. There is just as much difference between "Wine I drank twice" and "Twice I drank wine"; that is to say, a great difference according to those logic-choppers, but in actual fact none at all. Now if anyone eats meat which is not just well-done, but half-charred, they insist he is telling the truth if he asserts, "Raw meat I ate"; not, however, if he asserts, "I ate raw meat." Then if someone leaves one part for me but appropriates the rest of my money for himself, I will supposedly be lying if I say, "He has robbed me of cash," but lest I should lack words to file my accusation in court I can say, "Of cash he has robbed me." And in one hypothetical instance, which they call a "posited possible," the statement "The pope I have beaten" will be true, while the statement "I have beaten the pope" will be false for the same hypothetical instance, namely, given that whoever is now pope long ago as a boy took a beating from me. By Jove, those who teach this sort of thing as old men should be given a beating themselves for every lesson that they teach to boys.[42]

What about this? They say that the statement "Every man is a father who has a son" is false unless all men already have sons, since of course it amounts to the same thing as saying "Every man is a father, and every man has a son." But at the same time, they affirm that this statement is true, "A father will Socrates be when Socrates will not be a father," and this one, "A father will John go on being when John will not go on being a father." Who can listen to that without thinking that what he is hearing is a riddle?

But the words "AM" and "CAN" simply rule the world, and because, as the saying goes, they are "expansive," they extend their domain far and wide beyond nature's own bounds. Indeed, those men maintain that this statement is true: "Everything which will be, is." But, of course, they interpret it shrewdly. For according to them, "Everything that will be, is," means "Everything that is something that will be, is"; and in this way they see to it that Antichrist, who will be eventually, may not be just yet. For even though "Everything that will be, is," and even though "Antichrist will be," it still does not follow that "Antichrist is," since of course "Antichrist is not a being-that-will-be." And had we not been furnished with this hyperacute exposition of that proposition by theologians adept in dialectical subtleties,

Antichrist would doubtless have invaded Christendom long ago, not without immense danger for everyone else. For I fail to see how the theologians themselves could feel threatened at all, since they hold that these too are true statements: "Antichrist is lovable" and "Antichrist is receptive to love."

But indeed neither Antichrist nor the final day of judgment itself could upset nature's order as thoroughly as this dialectic, which teaches that these propositions are true: "The living was dead"; "The future was past"; whence of course it results that the resurrection of the dead seems to be (as they themselves say) not just "in progress," but rather "in fact." And there are others which are no less remarkable, but these are delightful, besides, and appealing as well as undoubtedly true: "The virgin was a whore" and "The whore will be a virgin" and "The whore is potentially a virgin." It is hard to say which of the two, virgins or whores, owe more thanks to such generous dialecticians; certainly both of them owe a great deal. So the poets are busy with trifles, dialecticians with serious affairs. Poets feign and tell lies; dialecticians speak only the truth, even when they affirm this proposition to be indisputably true: "A dead man is able to celebrate Mass." But although I dare not disbelieve this when the dialecticians assert it, and indeed almost swear to it, for to controvert such an assembly of incontrovertible doctors is out of the question, nonetheless to this day, to the best of my memory, I have never met anyone who professed to have served a Mass said by a dead celebrant. Is this really the same dialectic that Aristotle teaches? That Jerome recommends? That Augustine esteems?[43] Dialectic that even "mad Orestes," in Persius's phrasing, "would swear was the work of a madman"?[44]

I wonder, by Jove, how these petty adepts ever reached the conclusion that those propositions should be understood in a way that no one on earth but themselves understands them. Those words are not technical terms on which these men can claim a monopoly, as it were, so that anyone wishing to use them must go and ask them for a loan. Such expressions are actually common language, though these men do return some of them in a worse state than they were in when they were appropriated from ordinary craftsmen. They have borrowed their words from the public domain; they abuse public property.

---

42 Plato makes a similar joke in *Euthydemus* 298c–299a.   **43** This answers a passage in Dorp's second letter (*EE* 2: 133).   **44** Persius 3.118

But the so-called rule of logic teaches that this is the right way to construe propositions like those. Damn it, since when can some rule slapped together in some corner[45] by men who themselves barely know how to speak impose new laws of speech on the entire world? Grammar teaches the right way to speak, and yet it invents no laws of speech in defiance of custom; instead, it simply sees which constructions appear the most often in speech and points these out to those who are unschooled in speech so that their speech will not flout common usage.[46] Nor does sane dialectic, at least, do its work any differently. For example, this syllogism, "Every animal runs; man is an animal; therefore man runs," is a syllogism not because it is duly set up in accordance with the norm of dialectic and constructed in the figure of "barbara," but because reason teaches that the last statement follows from the premises; and this is precisely why reason made the rule as it did. Otherwise, should it set out to make that rule differently, it would swerve off in every direction from the structure of nature itself. By the same token, let those men also stop insisting that we must interpret the proposition "The whore will be a virgin" as "The whore (who is still or was once a virgin)..." just because a rule orders that it should be so; let them bring us a reason from the fact of the matter why such a rule should have been made. For if that interpretation is right then it must emerge either from the fact of the matter being stated or from the particular force of the idiom employed.

Now, then, since so many of those who spoke Latin long ago lacked neither intelligence nor erudition, nor were they, I think, any less versed in their idiom than these fellows are, how does it happen that none of the ancients could understand this statement to be true, "The whore will be a virgin," or distinguish between these two, "Not a penny have I"[47] and "I have not a penny"? Although no one would deny that transpositions of words often produce different meanings, nor does "Drink before you go" mean the same thing as "Go before you drink." But I do affirm this, that when meanings do vary in this way, all mortals agree on the fact; for they are guided to do so by reason and not coerced rather than persuaded by the rule of the

dialecticians, whose real task is to press us along with true reasoning, to any conclusion, by using the same language we do; to lure us along with insidious trumpery to the point that we wonder how we ever got there is a task, not for them, but for sophists. For this is the dullest kind of acumen and the most foolish finesse in the world, for these men to declare themselves champion debaters and crown themselves victors just because we do not know in what sense, against all common sense, they have secretly agreed to construe our own words.

Yet these quibbles, which do not even merit the label "sophistic," are not seen as sophistical trifles; instead, they are numbered among the most recondite treasures of dialectic. They are not learned by boys as things to be unlearned later on; instead, they are introduced even by old men into the innermost shrine of theology. Some of them use these quibbles to pad out perplexed theological inquiries; from these quibbles they contrive such ridiculous propositions that nowhere on earth could you find such a rich crop of laughing matter, although I would much rather see those who talk this sort of drivel converted to sanity than take pleasure myself in the drivel they talk while insane. And yet why am I saying this to you, Dorp, since I know you would approve of this nonsense as little as I do if you were able to change it? And with the help of men like you, perhaps you can do so, unless you have resolved to be ruled by the driveling of people who should in all fairness defer to your judgment.

But I will return to your letter to show that Erasmus's words gave you no pretext for saying (as you do say) that he charges the Louvain theologians with ignorance, much less all the other theologians in the world. He said he could dispense, not with all theologians, of course—he had already said in the same letter that many of them were outstandingly qualified—but only with those theologians (if some happen to fit the description, and some certainly do) who have never learned anything but sophistical trifles. Here you interject, "I think 'those theologians' refers to the ones in Louvain."[48] Why so, Dorp? As if it were hard to find some theologians of this stamp, or rather this stripe,[49] anywhere in the world? You certainly do have a pretty impression of those in Louvain if you think that they all,

45 *in some corner: Adages* 3467 (*CWE* 36: 187–88). **46** *Grammar...usage:* See Quintilian 1.6.16. **47** See Plautus, *Pseudolus* 365. **48** See *EE* 2: 133. **49** *of this...stripe:* See *Adages* 2444 (*CWE* 35: 94).

and they alone, fit this sort of description, whereas he neither says so nor thinks so.

But a bit further along you construe what he said as if it were said not just against those in Louvain but against all the theologians found anywhere in the world, whereas he spoke it neither against all the rest nor against the Louvain theologians themselves. And yet then, as if you were not listening to him, or even to yourself, you seem not so much to proceed to the following words as to burst out with them, carried away in a violent explosion of feeling:

Do we not see the humblest artisans, or even the basest servants, endowed with the most splendid intellects? Then what is the meaning of those epithets you misapply to all theologians, "stupid," "ignorant," "pestilential," and "senseless"? It takes no skill to throw insults at whomever you please, but it is neither an honorable practice nor something a good man would do, if we take careful note of our Savior's stern sentence: "A man who says 'Racha' to his brother will be liable to the Council, but a man who says 'fool' will be liable to the fire of Gehenna."[50] Here Jerome writes, "If we are to give an accounting for each idle word, how much more must we give for an insult! A man who says 'fool' to a believer in God shows contempt for religion."[51]

Here, at any rate, your words are replete with both gravity and sanctity, and truly worthy of a stern theologian; if only they were spoken in their proper place! They are certainly too good to waste, and if they were hurled down at the people from high in the pulpit, they would never go so far astray as to fail to hit someone or other in whom their points might seem to stick. As things are, though, it pains me to see you declaim all these things at Erasmus alone when he alone is a quite inappropriate target for each of the things you declaim. For the verse that you cite from the Gospel, "A man who says 'fool' to his brother will be liable to Gehenna," has nothing to do with a man who names no names but merely asserts that in a great number of men there are one or two fools. Otherwise, ten hells would not be enough for the man who said, "Infinite is the number of fools."[52]

Furthermore, as for you asking him, "What is the meaning of these epithets that you misapply to all theologians?" I am going to have to ask you the same question, Dorp. For you alone have misapplied to them all what he said about only a few. But I find it completely amazing that you sought to do so, for if—as you say—it takes no skill to throw insults at whomever you please, it certainly requires no skill to pervert things well said by reporting them badly, as you yourself do when you try to make fair criticism seem unfair by deflecting it from those who deserve it to those who do not. Just how easy it is to do this in any circumstances at all you can easily see for yourself.

Honestly, suppose someone subjected your writings to this kind of scrutiny; not a one of your written productions, meticulous as they all are, is meticulous enough to be wholly immune to misrepresentation, not even your latest, most polished epistle, written as an editor's preface for the *Quodlibetica* of that most worthy man, Adriaan Floriszoon of Utrecht.[53] Even though your epistle confers fine and copious praise on that work and its author, praise which I, at least, think to be equally earnest and truthful, nonetheless if a slightly more unsympathetic interpreter came along he might feel you were holding out bread in one hand and a stone in the other.[54] First of all, no enthusiasm on your part, indeed nothing but the prayers and the tearful entreaties of others could induce you to take on the project of editing that work, as if you yourself did not think much of it and accepted the task just to gratify others who liked it. Secondly, you write that you set aside your serious studies for the short time it took you to correct those *Quodlibetica,* as if they had no place among serious studies, even though Master John of Ath,[55] a man as learned as he is judicious, freely lavished his attention on that work, often, as you say, even in the dead of night; for as midwives are commonly summoned by night to help women give birth, it seems that that work could not be emended by day. And then what about this? You praise Adriaan for being unbiased, yet you seem to suggest he is no more unbiased than a Lesbian rule, a rule made out of lead which, as Aristotle reminds us, is not always unbiased, since it bends to fit uneven shapes.[56] My dear Dorp, you must not think that I

50 Mt 5:22   **51** *EE* 2: 134; Jerome, *PL* 26: 37a   **52** Eccl 1:15   **53** future Pope Adrian VI   **54** *holding . . . other:* See *Adages* 729 (*CWE* 32: 139); Mt 7:9.   **55** John Briart of Ath (d. 1520), an influential Louvain professor   **56** See Aristotle, *Nichomachean Ethics* 5.10.7; *Adages* 493 (*CWE* 31: 465).

say these things because I think you meant anything of the sort or were actually joking around in this way when you praised such a man and such a work. For I hear that the man has won much splendid praise for his manifold accomplishments, and I judge that, at least in its genre, the work is a masterpiece. I say all these things merely to prove that not even sheer trifles are immune to misrepresentation, since even your own meticulous and carefully polished writings require that we read them indulgently.

But it seems that Erasmus took care to give no one the slightest excuse to say he spoke of all theologians when he said the things you hold against him, even when he declares, "Every day I find out by experience just how senseless those men are who have never learned anything else but sophistical trifles." He does not say "how senseless all theologians are," or even "those who have learned sophistry," but "those who have learned nothing else." And so when you write, "Moreover, Erasmus, when you make the assumption that our theologians are busy with nothing but studying sophisms you are far off the mark,"[57] here you are the one, my dear Dorp, who is far off the mark, since you make the assumption that Erasmus made such an assumption about all of your theologians when he actually makes it about only one or two, and says nothing which has to be taken to include all theologians.

Thus the next point you added is equally irrelevant: "So tell me then—what is to prevent even those who know nothing at all about poetry from perusing the Gospels, the letters of Paul, and the whole of the Bible?"[58] Nothing at all, Dorp, if they did not prevent themselves, as some do who devote their whole lives to those petty problems but certainly never deign to examine the Bible, as if it were simply irrelevant.[59] And Erasmus thinks some to be like this, not all. Thus, you see, you had no cause to tack on that other point, either: "I can produce many theologians from here who will put aside their books and then, strictly from memory, debate with whomever you please on the text of Scripture. Do not make the mistake of believing that theologians are sleeping the sleep of Endymion[60] while you are awake studying literature or that all are deficient in intellect who do not play the poet or orator."[61]

No one denies, Dorp, that there are some who

can put aside their books and debate on the text of Scripture. Indeed, you can everywhere find all too many who not only have put aside their books but have never examined them, men prepared to debate very stubbornly with true Scripture scholars on any text from Scripture at all, not from memory but rather from folly. Neither will I deny that there are some in Louvain, as indeed there are everywhere, who have memorized many passages from Scripture, and of these men whoever has focused his energies not only on memorizing—even illiterate monks and friars do as much—but far more on absorbing the meaning, and has gained sufficient linguistic ability to measure up to the challenge of fully understanding the works of Jerome, Augustine, Ambrose, and other men like them, such a man, in my view, has an unsurpassed right to be registered among theologians, even if he has never written a verse; yes, and even if he has not spent a whole century on those petty disputes or has even ignored them completely.

But you, too, if you wish to acknowledge the truth, will admit that among those who are called theologians there are also some men who put aside the books of Scripture in such a way that they never take them up again; men who give themselves up so completely to this disputatious theology that not only do they not "play the poet or orator," they apparently care next to nothing about all the holiest fathers and most ancient interpreters of Scripture, and (this much is quite obvious) they definitely neglect both the fathers' expositions of Scripture and the study of Scripture itself; finally, men who shrug off as mere "positive" doctrine whatever is most valuable, most pious, most Christian, and most worthy of true theologians, although these men think none of it worthy of any exertion on their part;[62] they are born to debate petty problems, as matters of much greater import, though the problems that these men pursue most of all are the ones that pertain least of all to sustaining the faith or encouraging virtue.

Now then, just as I revere and admire that first kind of theologian, even so I have really very little respect for the second, against whom, nonetheless, I myself do not plan to defend either poetry or rhetoric, since I am almost as far removed from

57 *EE* 2: 133 **58** *EE* 2: 133 **59** See *Praise of Folly* (*ASD* 4/3: 154). **60** *sleep of* *Endymion: Adages* 863 (*CWE* 32: 216–17) **61** *EE* 2: 133–34 **62** *worthy…part:* See Terence, *Eunuchus* 312.

poetry and rhetoric as they are themselves. But they are almost as far removed from those arts as they are from theology proper; and from nothing, apart from ordinary common sense, are they further removed than from that. The main reason for this is precisely that on top of their blatant and general ignorance they are perversely convinced of their total omniscience, on which they flatter themselves to the point that whatever they hear being cited, in whatever context, without ever reading the passage or seeing the book it appears in, without knowing what has preceded or what is to follow the words of the quotation, and without even knowing whether or not the text quoted appears in the quoted location, they think they alone can interpret the writings of all men, and even Sacred Scripture itself, in whatever sense happens to suit them.[63] Having run across many of this kind, I will not hesitate to describe at least one, using him as a sample to show what we can expect from the rest.

I recently dined with a certain Italian merchant[64] as learned as he is rich (and he certainly is rich). There also happened to be a theologian at dinner, a member of a religious order; a distinguished disputant, he had recently come from the Continent to London in order to dispute various problems which he had prepared and brought with him. In that arena of disputation he intended to test at first hand what the English could show for themselves and to make his name generally acclaimed among our theologians as it was already renowned among those at home. Though it would take a while, I would certainly not hesitate to tell you what theses he posted and how smartly the whole disputation came off for the fellow if it were as pertinent as it was amusing. Anyway, nothing anyone said at that dinner was guarded well enough or supported meticulously enough to keep that man from toppling it over with one of his syllogisms as soon as the speaker had uttered it, even when the topic of the discussion had nothing to do with theology and as little to do with philosophy, indeed even when it had not the slightest connection with that man's profession. At the start of the dinner, however, he had made it clear that nothing could lack a connection with his profession, for he professed he was ready to dispute *pro* and *contra* upon any topic at all.

Gradually the merchant began to get down to more theological problems. He stated some views about usury, about tithes, and about friars hearing confessions in parishes where they were not authorized. It never made a bit of difference to the theologian which side he was defending, but whatever anyone asserted he himself took to task, and whatever anyone else denied he immediately defended.

Finally, as a joke, the merchant brought up the subject of mistresses. He began to defend the position that it was not so evil to have one woman at home as to run through a number away from home. Here again the theologian closed in and ferociously took him to task, not that he appeared to have any real grudge against mistresses but that he hated agreeing with anyone on anything, or perhaps the man just liked variety. Anyway, he asserted that it was the conclusion of a certain Most Translucent Doctor, who wrote that most singular book entitled *A Directory for Men Who Keep Mistresses*,[65] that a man who has one mistress at home is more sinful than a man who has ten whores away from home, not only because of the evil example it sets but also because there are more opportunities to sin with a woman at home.

Though the merchant's responses were certainly learned and acute, it would be time-consuming and idle to list them for you. But as soon as he noticed that the theologian was not such an expert in Scripture as in those petty problems, he started to play with the fellow and draw various arguments from authority. As he went along, he made up various brief texts which appeared to support his position, and even though he had arbitrarily contrived them all out of thin air he would quote one as if from some epistle of Saint Paul, another as if it were from an epistle of Peter, and still another as if it were straight from the Gospel. Indeed he was so diligent in doing so that he always included a chapter citation for what he was quoting, except that if a book was divided into sixteen chapters he would purposely quote from the twentieth.

Meanwhile what of that good theologian? He made brisk work of the other points, certainly, and wrapped himself up like a hedgehog in prickly retorts, but on my word, for all his evasions he barely escaped those fictitious authorities. Yet he did escape; such is the efficacy of art and experience in

63 See Cicero, *De oratore* 2.4.18, 2.18.76; Erasmus, *Praise of Folly* (ASD 4/3: 184).　　**64** most likely Antonio Bonvisi (d. 1558), a wealthy Italian merchant from Lucca and close friend of Thomas More　　**65** anonymous, published in 1508

discourse. For even though he knew nothing at all about the contents of Sacred Scripture, and though he did not doubt that the words being quoted from Scripture were actually there, and though he thought
5 it wrong to oppose or defy the authority of Scripture but at the same time considered it shameful to give up the field in defeat, even when he was caught in such desperate straits, please observe with what cunning that Proteus[66] slipped out of the net. As
10 soon as some supposedly scriptural text was quoted against him right out of thin air, "You quote well, sir," he said, "but I understand that text as follows." And then he would interpret it, not without some bipartite distinction in which he would first say that
15 one meaning supported his opponent and then he would evade it by finding another. But whenever the merchant closed in too intently and claimed that the theologian was not giving the true sense of the text, then the fellow would swear so devoutly that anyone
20 could have believed him that Nicolas de Lyra[67] interpreted that text the same way. Honestly, my dear Dorp, at that one dinner, over the drinks, and indeed from the drinks, just like those earthborn[68] brothers who sprang from the teeth of the serpent, more than
25 twenty of these drunken texts and as many drunken glosses sprang up and at once passed away.

Now, Dorp, what do you say? Do you really think fellows of this sort with their meager knowledge of Sacred Scripture, however puffed up they may
30 be with those theological problems, deserve to be called theologians? I suppose not, but I must say that these comments of yours leave me not at all sure what you think:

35 Do not let yourself be persuaded, Erasmus, that anyone with a literal understanding of the text of the Bible or even someone with Origen's knack for discovering a moral significance is already a perfect theologian. There are many things yet to be learned which are not only more difficult to
40 understand but also more useful to the flock for whom Christ died. How else are we to know how we ought to administer the sacraments, what their forms are, when we ought to absolve and when we

ought to refuse absolution to a sinner, how much restitution we must make and how much we can
45 keep, and innumerable things of that sort? Unless I am very mistaken you can learn a good deal of the Bible by heart much more easily than you can learn to unravel even one of those perplexities which crop up by the score every day, in which
50 even four words can detain one indefinitely— unless what you call theological trifles includes all that pertains to the sacraments, though without them, according to God's Holy Catholic Church, man's salvation is endangered.[69]
55

Believe me, Dorp, if you had not written this yourself nothing in the world could have made me believe that you held this opinion. So those problems made up by the moderns (for those are the real issue) are not only more difficult to understand
60 but also more useful to the flock for whom Christ died? My word, what a huge elephant you make out of such a small gnat![70] For at first you consider that subject so difficult that Erasmus could learn a good deal of the Bible by heart more easily than he
65 could learn to unravel even one of those perplexities they contrive by the score every day,[71] in which four words as sticky and squalid as mud can detain you so long that in the same length of time you could have read the whole Bible and strolled through its
70 delightful and life-giving meadows step by step from one side to the other.[72] So then, the danger thus far was that he had not learned those problems. Now I see there is something still worse to be feared, that they may so transcend his capacity that he will not
75 even be able to grasp them. I do not raise the question of what he can do. But of this I am sure: I know some who in other matters are absolute blockheads, as dull as the dullest of pestles,[73] while in this sort of subtlety they have not only been quick to prog-
80 ress but have also outstripped—at a gallop,[74] as they say—their own far more intelligent and no less industrious comrades in the art of disputing. Indeed, reckless and impudent folly will always leap in where good character and sound judgment will generally
85 hold back out of shame at the prospect of trifling.[75]

66 See *Adages* 1174 (*CWE* 33: 113–14); Proteus is also known as the Old Man of the Sea in Homer (*Odyssey* 4.365–480). **67** Nicolas de Lyra (1270–1340) was a Franciscan known for his *Postillae perpetuae in universam Sacram Scripturam*, an

exposition on the literal sense of Scripture. **68** See Ovid, *Metamorphoses* 3.102–3, 115–25. **69** *EE* 2: 135 **70** *huge…gnat:* See *Adages* 869, 2027 (*CWE* 32: 219, 34: 191–92). **71** *unravel…day: Adages* 1376 (*CWE* 33: 229) **72** *step…other: Adages*

137 (*CWE* 31: 178–79) **73** *dull…pestles: Adages* 2521 (*CWE* 35: 135); Jerome, *Epistolae* 69.4 (*PL* 22: 657) **74** *Adages* 321 (*CWE* 31: 335–36) **75** *reckless…trifling:* See *Praise of Folly* (*ASD* 4/3: 102–4); *Adages* 3454 (*CWE* 36: 178–79).

Dorp, you honestly ought to rejoice in this rare gift of yours, which you owe not to your personal powers but to God, the bestower of every good thing;[76] for it is through his unusual kindness to you that everything in Scripture should strike you as so easy. For you would scarcely have found everything openly expressed in this book, which has been closed by seven seals,[77] if it had not been unsealed for you by that same Lamb who "opens the book, and none closes it, who closes the book, and none opens it."[78] Mind you, Dorp, this same book which strikes you as so easy struck Jerome as exceedingly difficult.[79] Augustine considered it impenetrable.[80] Not one of the ancients, indeed, dared to claim that he understood it, for they thought that God, in his unfathomable wisdom, deliberately hid its meaning far from the surface precisely in order to challenge the sharpest eye and to stimulate minds with the promise of buried and hard-to-reach treasure which their very assurance might otherwise render indifferent to riches set plainly in view.

I will not dwell just now on what uncommon learning and what rare intelligence are needed to take texts which at first may seem quite incompatible with morality and to reconcile them with morality so neatly and skillfully that they seem to be made for the purpose and not dragged in from elsewhere to serve it. Some now practice this art so ineptly that since they get no further than dragging a text from its previous context without fitting it into their own and since there is no sense in their matter or charm in their words, it naturally turns out that their moralization (as they call it), devoid of all spirit and grace, leaves us perfectly cold. I will not dwell on this, as I said. But in any case, even the literal sense is in my view a matter of such immense difficulty that I am not sure any mortal can quite comprehend it. For example, I think no one comprehends the literal sense of the words, "The Lord said to my Lord, 'Sit at my right hand,'"[81] unless he understands that in these words the prophet is making a mystical prediction about Christ himself. And apart from the prophets, not one of the Jews, even though they were constantly studying these books, understood those words thus before Christ revealed this as their literal meaning. And even if he did interpret the Scriptures for his apostles and disciples

(for so far as I know he never disputed those petty problems with them), I would still hesitate to affirm that he either taught them the whole meaning of Scripture in person or conveyed it to them by the Holy Spirit after his ascension. For just as the meaning of many of the things that the prophets had foretold about Christ escaped everyone else until all was made plain by Christ's life, Passion, and resurrection, even so I think that the powers of mortals are not equal to settling the question of whether there may still lie hidden in Scripture mysterious truths about either the Last Judgment or other things we cannot even imagine, mysterious truths none has discerned before now or will ever discern before they are unfolded in actual events at a date and a time foreseen only by God[82] in his inscrutable providence.

But so be it, Dorp: Scripture is easy, petty problems are difficult. That by no means keeps a knowledge of Scripture from being more worthwhile than a training in problems. So, too, vaulting and tying one's body in knots the way certain acrobats and mountebanks do are more difficult feats than to walk, and it is easier to chew bread than to grind up potsherds with your teeth, but I think no one would be willing to trade these normal and commonplace functions for such vain displays. Hence it does not matter much to me which of the two is more difficult. But that you should pretend that those problems are even more useful than a knowledge of Scripture to the flock for whom Christ died, this I honestly cannot endure. For if you claimed that those problems were worth knowing, I would certainly not disagree; if you set them alongside the works of the ancients, I would say you were going too far; since in fact you rank those kitchen-maids of yours not just as high as but indeed even higher than the Bible itself, holy queen of all genres of literature, you must pardon me, Dorp, but by Jove I cannot keep from sending them packing with that line from Terence, "Get lost, you tramps, and take those grand airs with you!"[83]

Indeed, I am dumbfounded when I read the passage where you make such grand claims for those problems, as if the whole weight of the Church were sustained by perplexed problems of this sort—that is, by a reed—just as the poets say heaven is

76 *gift…thing:* See Js 1:17.   77 See Rv 5:1–6.   78 Is 22:22   79 See Jerome, *Epistolae* 49.4, 53; 105.5 (PL 22: 512, 540–49, 836).   80 See Augustine, *De doctrina Christiana* 2.67 (PL 34: 38).   81 Ps 109(110):1; Mt 22:41–46; Mk 12:35–37; Lk 20:41–44   82 See Mt 24:36; Acts 1:7.   83 Terence, *Phormio* 930–32

sustained on the shoulders of Atlas,[84] as if the Church would be in immediate danger of collapsing into a heap of ashes if it lacked such a prop. For you ask, "How else are we to know how we ought to administer the sacraments, what their forms are, when we ought to absolve and when we ought to refuse absolution to a sinner, how much restitution we must make and how much we can keep?"[85] Dorp, do you really think all the old holy fathers, who were as learned as they were devout, were completely ignorant of all those points which you suppose to be found only in modern compilers of problems? Were Jerome, Ambrose, and Augustine stark blind when it came to the form and matter of the sacraments? And so for more than a thousand years — note that more than a thousand years separate the Passion of Christ and the time of Peter Lombard, whose *Sentences*,[86] like the Trojan horse,[87] poured forth this entire army of problems — for so many years, no, for so many centuries, was the Church without sacraments? Did it not have the same ones? Was it so long unknown when we ought to absolve a sinner and when we ought to refuse absolution? Were they ignorant, too, of how much restitution we are taught to make? For I will concede that the ancients were not so acute as those men in disputing how much we can keep. Rather, just as Zaccheus, afraid of returning too little of his ill-gotten gains, publicly promised to make a fourfold restitution,[88] just so those ancient fathers urged everyone to repay even more than enough. In this area they were not, I confess, as precise as the moderns in defining and hair-splitting. Still, as Terence puts it, I would rather emulate the negligence of the former than the pedantic diligence of the latter,[89] who dispute the case over-intently and ask rather what we can keep than what we should give back, rather how close we can get to a sin without sinning than how wide a berth we should give it. And indeed, when one of them gives a thief advice about restitution, like a careful steward of someone else's money, he takes more care to prevent him from going a finger's breadth too far,[90] as they say, than from stopping too short by a mile.

I myself would contend, as I think even you would concede, my dear Dorp, that whatever is necessary for salvation — that is, the things without which we cannot be saved — have been abundantly transmitted to us, first of all through Sacred Scriptures themselves, then through their first interpreters, then too by the customs transmitted to us from hand to hand,[91] as it were, by the ancient fathers, and finally through the sacred decrees of the Church. And if those acute moderns have subjoined any more precise precepts to those which make up this tradition, I will grant that a number of these innovations are advantageous and useful, but I certainly think not a one is so vital that people cannot live without it.

But perhaps you will say that not everything in the works of the ancients is as easy to find or as neatly classified as it is in the works of these moderns, who have assembled all sorts of related and seemingly parallel passages into chapters as if splitting them up into their proper clans. On this point, Dorp, perhaps I concur with you, and I grant that there is some advantage in having the contents of written works, like domestic supplies, thoroughly sorted and clearly distinguished so that you can immediately put your hand on whatever you want without any mistake. This is indeed, as I said, an advantage. But some use this considerable advantage to such disadvantage that it almost appears that, advantage or not, we would be better off without it. For I think that the principal reason that all of the most ancient interpreters of Scripture have been neglected for so long by so many is simply that the corrupt judgments of less gifted intellects persuaded first themselves and then others as well that no honey remains to be found beyond what is amassed in the beehives of those compilations, and therefore, content with the hives alone, they neglect and scorn everything else.

Long ago I myself met a man with this attitude in a certain bookseller's shop. He was an old man, with one foot in the grave,[92] as they say, and both feet before long, I am certain. He had been awarded the distinction of a doctorate, as they call it, more than thirty years before. I happened to say in his presence that Saint Augustine once thought that all demons

---

84 See *Adages* 67, 3493 (*CWE* 31:110, 36: 204); *EE* 2: 11; *Praise of Folly* (*ASD* 4/3: 154). 85 *EE* 2: 135 86 Peter Lombard (*ca.* 1100–60), Bishop of Paris and author of the scholastic textbook *Sententiarum libri quatuor* 87 For the simile, see Cicero, *De oratore* 2.22.94. 88 See Lk 19:2–10. 89 *Andria* 18–21 90 *finger's* … *far: Adages* 406 (*CWE* 31: 390–91) 91 *transmitted … hand: Adages* 3428 (*CWE* 36: 160–61) 92 See *Adages* 1052 (*CWE* 33: 47–48); *Praise of Folly* (*ASD* 4/3: 108).

were corporeal substances,[93] whereupon he at once wrinkled his forehead and checked my temerity with his furrowed brow.[94] Then I said, "I myself do not say this is so, father, nor do I defend Augustine for saying so. Being a man, he could make a mistake. I take his word as seriously as anyone's, but I take no one man's word unconditionally." Now the man really started to seethe, most of all because I had tried to foist so great a misrepresentation on so great a father. For "You think," he exclaimed, "I have not read Augustine? Quite the contrary," he said, "before you were born." His sharp words would have put me to flight had there not been a counterproof ready and waiting. For since all this occurred in a bookshop, I picked up Augustine's tract *On the Divination of Demons,* turned to the passage, and showed it to him. When he had read the passage once, and then once more, and at last, on the third reading, with me to assist him, he had begun to understand what he read, he finally said in bewilderment, "I certainly am amazed that Augustine puts it that way in this book when he certainly does not put it that way in the *Master of the Sentences,* which is a more masterly book than this one."

Men of this motley crew, men who never read any of the ancients or anything out of the Scriptures except in the *Sentences* and their commentaries, seem to me to be acting like someone who neglects all the authors who actually wrote Latin, takes his syntactical precepts from Alexander,[95] and then tries to learn the rest of the Latin language from Perotti's *Cornucopia*[96] and Calepino[97] since he thinks he will find all the words of that language contained in their books. And indeed he will find a great many, and choice ones, at that; and just as one can read sayings of earlier theologians introduced as authorities in the works of more recent ones, so too in these glossaries one can read various ancient poets and orators, including a few who are not even extant today. But these scraps can no more make a Latin-speaker than those alone can make a theologian, not even if he is armed with ten thousand of the prickliest problems on earth; and when I see a theologian of this sort, I wonder just what useful service such problems can ever equip him to do for the Church.

Perhaps to dispute against heretics; for this is their principal selling point. But the heretics are either learned or unlearned. If they are unlearned, as the great majority of them are, then they would understand neither those subtleties which are his only weapon nor the outlandish words which are his only means of expression. Necessarily, then, this sort of disputation would be just as productive as if someone delivered an elaborate oration in French (for the French think no other tongue elegant) exhorting some Turk versed in no other language but Turkish to convert to our faith. But if the heretics are learned, indeed learned in those very problems (for they are almost never heretics with reference to anything else), when will they be refuted? Will there be any end to disputing? For the very problems with which they are assaulted afford them no end of material with which to strike back, so that the plight of both parties is very much like that of men fighting naked between heaps of stones: neither one lacks the means to strike out; neither one has the means to defend himself. Indeed, some of the principal authors they read in the schools — authors fully as subtle as they are reported to be — not to mention that they have dreamt up certain problems about God so ridiculous you might think they were raising a laugh and so blasphemous you might feel they were laughing directly at him, they are certainly so zealous in raising objections to the faith and so backward in answering them that they seem to be in collusion with the opposition, defending the faith in jest and assaulting it in earnest. Now then, pitted against the sort of theologians I have mentioned, how soon are the heretics going to succumb, since they have been trained in the same school of tactics?[98] Not very soon, to be sure, in my view, were they not more intimidated by one little bundle of faggots than daunted by many large bundles of syllogisms.

But he will at least be well suited to preach to the people. Good lord, talk about drafting an ox as a boxer! For since the man has learned nothing but problems which are totally unfamiliar and extremely ill suited to the ears of the people, naturally he must learn some sermon by heart out of *The Disciple's Sermons, The Preacher's Companion,* or *The Sleep-Well;* those sermons are silly affairs in themselves, and

93 See *De divinatione daemonum* (PL 40: 584–86). **94** *furrowed brow:* See *Adages* 748, 2471 (CWE 32: 150–51, 35: 107–8). **95** Alexander de Villa Dei (fl. 1200) **96** Niccolo Perotti (1430–80) **97** Ambrogio Calepino (1430–1510) **98** *trained…tactics: Adages* 1750 (CWE 34: 68)

when the man who delivers them is sillier still, having never prepared for that task and declaiming that whole mass of words from another man's stomach, the whole sermon perforce leaves us cold.

5 Therefore I simply fail to see what those problems can do for a man who knows nothing besides but to render him useless for everything else, since if someone advances some topic from those disputations, more subtle than solid, which he has already practiced a thousand times, now he feels right at home, 10 now he ruffles his feathers like a cock riding high on his dunghill,[99] but if he is led a bit further away from his native preserve, all at once the unknown look of everything buries him in confusion and darkness. Nor does dialectic, no matter how pow-15 erful and acute, rescue him as he stumbles about in his blindness to actual things: just as dialectic elicits various species and numerous patterns of arguments from the nature of things once it is known, even so when the things themselves remain a mys-20 tery dialectic necessarily falls silent, of no use at all. Furthermore, once this fellow, by now an old man, has for whatever reason made off from the camp of the schoolmen, where those problems are constantly being argued, within two years the same 25 problems which he has explored both intensively and exclusively for so many years, all those subtleties, too many to keep track of, slip easily away into nothing, unrestrained by connections with actual 30 things, and disappear like a cloud of smoke, and predictably he himself suffers in practice what Aristotle is frequently quoted as saying holds true for the soul of a child, namely that his soul finally becomes, as it were, a clean slate,[100] on which nothing 35 at all is depicted, and it turns out, through a wondrous reversal, that he who once thought the sum total of wisdom consisted of argumentative loquacity has become an old man with the tongue of an infant, a man all would laugh at if he did not use 40 haughty silence in place of wisdom to cloak his own folly; but in fact he is all the more laughable precisely because the same man who was lately more clamorous than Stentor[101] has now, by the opposite defect, been rendered more dumb than a fish,[102] 45 and now sits among speakers as if he himself had not a tongue in his head,[103] like "a player without

any lines,"[104] as they say, and "a truncated statue of Hermes."[105]

Finally, so that you may understand once and for all how I feel about this whole affair, I neither crit-50 icize all theologians nor condemn all the problems of the moderns; but the kind that are wholly irrelevant, the sort that contribute nothing to erudition and detract a good deal from piety, this sort I believe should be not merely censured but thrown out 55 entirely. As for those that remain, those that treat human concerns seriously or divine concerns reverently, always using a modest approach which will show that their goal is the truth and not winning a quarrel, given that they must not monopolize any-60 one's attention or take up too much of anyone's time, given that they must acknowledge their own limitations and not rank themselves as high as their betters (let alone even higher), these problems, presented like this, I repeat, I am perfectly glad to em-65 brace, although only so far as to grant that such inquiries do have their use as a method of intellectual exercise even as I deny that they furnish an essential and central support for the salvation of the Church as a whole. 70

Now then, I do not castigate those theologians who have had a good taste of these problems; indeed, I even praise those who have complemented a loftier training in Sacred Scripture and a nobler education in the earliest, holiest, and most learned fa-75 thers with these not contemptible accessory studies. But in all honesty I do not praise the sort of theologians who do not merely squander their youth over problems of every variety, but even expire over them; who, hampered by some intellectual defi-80 ciency or spurred on by the childish applause of the schoolmen, have neglected the writings of all of the ancients, slighted even the very Gospels of which they profess themselves doctors, and learned nothing at all except those petty problems, which are 85 partly barren in their own right and partly barren for those who are barren of everything else; who, still worse, are already old men, given up for dead losses, since they cannot treat Scripture aptly without knowing the works of the ancients, and they 90 cannot come to know those with the poor Latin that they now possess, while to go back to grammar

99 *cock . . . dunghill:* See *Adages* 3325 (*CWE* 36: 76); *Praise of Folly* (*ASD* 4/3: 72)   **100** *clean slate:* See Aristotle, *De anima* 3.4.14.   **101** See *Praise of Folly*

(*ASD* 4/3: 144); *Adages* 1237 (*CWE* 33: 150).   **102** *dumb . . . fish:* See *Adages* 429 (*CWE* 31: 408).   **103** *not . . . head: Adages* 979 (*CWE* 32: 270)   **104** See *Adages* 978 (*CWE* 32:

270).   **105** See *Adages* 1910, 3299 (*CWE* 34: 132, 36: 60).

and learn among boys, indeed from boys, is not merely a disgraceful proposal but also comes too late to do any good. My dear Dorp, I am so far from praising such men that I even think these theologians in name, not in fact, should be forced, as the Romans compelled bad officials to give up their public employments, to resign from the office they occupy so undeservingly.

And yet it is no wonder that there are some like this among so great a number of theologians. For what order of men can be cordoned off so strictly that not even one unworthy person may ambitiously worm his way in with a bribe or a favor or other machinations and then, once he has gained a high standing, raise as many like himself as he can into the same high position by giving them his support? This is why there is no order of men that is not rife with unworthy members. For just as there were men in the Roman senate whose majesty no kings could equal, even so there were several so base and inglorious that they died a miserable death in the course of a festival, crushed by the press of the crowd.[106] And yet even as the lowliness of some senators did not lessen the brilliance of the rest, nor did the senatorial title rescue the baseness of the unworthy from being exposed to contempt, so their title does not exempt unworthy theologians from being reviled, nor does any contempt they provoke derogate in the slightest degree from the honor of true theologians or impair in the slightest the reverend majesty of theologians in general, something which I myself am as keen to protect and enhance as any man that has ever lived. For it would be foolish to make the same claim for Erasmus, since everyone knows that whatever is said or imagined unjustly against the sacred order of theologians is Erasmus's own special and personal concern.

There you have my opinion about this affair, my dear Dorp, and by heaven I am convinced that (if you are the man I imagine you are) there you have your opinion, as well; if it meets your approval, consider it that of Erasmus, as well as my own, but if not, then not even my own any longer than you would so have it. For I do not hold any opinion so stubbornly that I am not ready to change it at the command of a person who will never, I know,

command anything without a good reason. But so much for that.

Concerning the rest of your letter I will be just as brief as, regarding this part, I have been disproportionately verbose — rightly so, on both counts. For Erasmus, who never saw what you have written concerning the points I have so far discussed, has both written and promised to write more precisely concerning the points I am planning to talk about next. Moreover, a number of these bear on issues in which Saint Jerome himself not only sides with Erasmus by way of his personal example, as if in a judicial precedent, but has also in effect published his verdict in writing and ruled on Erasmus's behalf.[107] For everything that you say to prevent any changes in Scripture on the basis of Greek textual authorities was urged long ago against Saint Jerome and very powerfully refuted by him, unless you claim to be making a new point when you say that long ago there were many translations, but that all of these were rejected so that textual variations would not cause the faithful to waver, whereas this one, the same one adopted by the holy fathers, emended by Jerome, and passed on all the way down to us, is the only translation the Church has approved, not in some single council but through an unvarying custom of referring to this text whenever any council has faced some perplexity concerning the faith. For it could not have happened that all the rest should have vanished while this one alone has come down to us unless that was the work, not of chance, but of our forefathers' deliberate planning.

First of all, my dear Dorp, I think everyone knows that this very edition, even before Jerome's time — for why else would he have emended this one in particular? — was both accepted by the Church and approved through the regular practice of quoting its text, which I think was indeed the sole reason why it is the only one that has come down to us. Now then, why did Jerome dare to make any changes? But not only did other most virtuous and holy men give their approval to what he had done; even Augustine himself urged him to do it.[108] And Jerome himself states that the changes he made were at points where the sense of the Latin text differed from that of the Greek.[109] He thought this more useful than that which you counsel Erasmus

106 See Suetonius, *Divus Iulius* 40.4.   *PL* 28–29.   **108** See Jerome, *Epistolae*
107 See Jerome's biblical prefaces in   116.31 (*PL* 22: 95).   **109** See *PL* 29: 528.

to do, namely to annotate only those points where the translator could have rendered the meaning more aptly and pointedly, but to leave the sense just as it is, if the texts ever differ, and not point out an obvious corruption to readers of Latin.[110] What Jerome felt to be barely worth troubling about you think ought to get more attention than anything else; what he judged most important you declare to be most ill advised.

But responding to this, you concede that Jerome was right to do what he did, since there was still a need for such work when the Vulgate had not yet been completely corrected, but now that it has been emended it is pointless to try to emend it again.[111] For if the need were as great now as it was then, there is no reason why anyone who did again now what Jerome did then should get any less credit than he did.

First of all, to speak boldly, I think no human being, not even Jerome, has been so bold or so self-assured as to claim that he never missed anything at all as he translated; indeed, even average translators who come along after their betters will now and then find something on which they can make useful refinements. "Then will there be any end to translating?" you ask; yes, the easiest of ends, once it turns out that someone has translated so aptly or corrected another's imperfect translation so well that as long as his work stays intact no one later will find anything he thinks should be changed.

But meanwhile there is a risk that these differing translations may render the minds of the faithful unsure about which they ought to believe the most trustworthy, and you think that this is precisely why all the rest were deliberately rejected, while this one was saved, so that they would not cause the faithful to waver.[112] On this point I disagree with you so completely that what you attribute to the care of our forefathers I assign to the carelessness of the times, which indeed allowed much else besides those translations to perish. Otherwise, even if our forefathers had required that only one be chanted in the churches, still, why was it necessary to throw out the others? There was no risk that these might cause the faithful to waver; indeed, just as now, through the differing accounts of the evangelists, the real sequence of events comes to be understood

more distinctly, even so by comparing various translations the studious reader would be given the chance to note points where equivocal words or ambivalent syntax or the particular force of an idiom had misled some translator, and then, by consulting the others, to grasp the true sense by conjecture. What a useful procedure this is has been noted by Augustine,[113] learned through personal experience by Origen, and confirmed by Jacques Lefèvre d'Etaples, the editor of the *Quincuplex Psalter*.

I have said this much in order to show that even if Saint Jerome's work were intact to this day there would still be no reason to censure whoever found something Jerome overlooked and then gathered it up like the ears left behind by a reaper. But as things actually stand, who can doubt that the need to correct Latin texts from the Greek is as great as it was in Jerome's day, since those texts are so choked with corruptions again that not even the traces[114] of Jerome's emendation are still to be found? This is so generally acknowledged that even you, who deny it most stoutly, admit it yourself. For though your stoutest argument for claiming that there is no point in attempting to correct what we have is that the great diligence of our forefathers has kept Jerome's emendations intact, in the next line, almost, you go on to say: "Tell me this, now, Erasmus, which edition has the Church's approval, the Greek, which it does not use, or the Latin, which is the only text it quotes every time that it has to resolve some point according to Holy Scripture, not even deferring to Jerome if at times he has a different reading, which indeed often happens?"[115] Rather you tell me this now, Dorp: if, as you rightly say, Jerome often has readings different from those of the Vulgate edition, how can what you said before be right, namely that this edition is still as correct as it was after he had corrected it? For I think no one is going to believe that he would have proposed any reading against his own correction. Thus the need for correction is just as great now as it was in his day. Whether it should still be as permissible has yet to be argued, even though it appears there is no room for argument or doubt as to whether emended texts are as useful today to the Church as they formerly were.

But you say, "Now the Church has approved this edition." But the same Church, as I already said, had

110 See *EE* 2: 14–15.   **111** See *EE* 2: 131–32.   *Christiana* 2.12.17–18, 2.14.21 (*PL* 34: 43,   3832 (*CWE* 36: 439–40).   **115** *EE* 2: 132–33
112 See *EE* 2: 132.   **113** See *De doctrina*   45–46).   **114** *not . . . traces*: See *Adages*

approved the same edition in the same way even before Jerome's corrections. But I will not hesitate to examine your reasoning again, which you find so invincible, lest you think I am glossing over anything. Now then, you seem to be making the following inference: Augustine maintained that the Gospel itself would not merit belief if the Church's authority did not decree that it must be believed.[116] But the Church has approved the position that the true Gospel is in this translation. Thus it follows that if the Greek texts ever differ from ours the true Gospel cannot be in them. As it seems to me, this is the gist of your argument, which to me seems the sort that is not going to be hard to refute. For first of all, the Church believes that the Gospel is contained in the Latin rendering—in such a way, however, that it grants that the Gospel was translated from Greek. Therefore it believes in the translation, but even more in the archetype. It believes that the true Gospel is in the Greek texts; it believes that the Gospel in the Latin texts is actually the true one to the same extent that it has faith in the translator, in whom I suppose it will never have so much blind faith that it forgets that he could have erred through human frailty.

But in councils they quote from the Latin text, not from the Greek. Well, how strange that Latin-speakers should quote from a Latin text, as if they did so in order to lessen our confidence in its Greek archetype! Did not the apostles occasionally set aside the authentic Hebrew text and cite passages from the prophets according to the Septuagint translation while writing for Greeks? Yet Jerome did not think that this set any precedent, as if the Greek translation ought to be judged more reliable than the letter of the Hebrew on the basis of the apostles' authority.

I for one am persuaded (and rightly, I think) that whatever contributes to building the faith has not been translated better by anyone than it was written by the apostles themselves. This is why every time a passage crops up in the Latin that apparently undermines faith or morality, the interpreters of Scripture either tease out the meaning of the dubious passage from various statements found elsewhere or evaluate such dubious phrases according to that living Gospel of faith which has been infused into the hearts of the faithful throughout the whole Church, the same Gospel which, even before it was written by anyone, was preached to the apostles by Christ and by them to the whole of mankind; and then if these interpreters, bringing to bear on such phrases the inflexible standard of truth, cannot make them conform to it properly, they readily grant they have either mistaken the sense or the text is corrupt, for which they think it best (though you think it so dangerous) to solicit a cure from several different translations, like doctors, or else to obtain one direct from the source,[117] so to speak, from the language whence all Latin texts of the Scriptures derive.

But, my dear Dorp, you grant that back then men were right to emend, from the Greek, Latin texts which the Church had already received and approved, yet you claim it is not right to do so today on account of the likelihood that the Greeks' own books were either deliberately tampered with when the Greeks broke away from the Roman church many years ago or have at any rate grown faulty since then out of negligence, since you say it is hard to believe that the texts of the Latins have gradually deteriorated, even though they have never stopped caring for the faith, while the texts of the Greeks still remain uncorrupted though they let their faith itself grow corrupt many years ago.[118] This argument, Dorp, did not keep Jerome from translating the Old Testament from Hebrew, though if it ought to have any weight with Erasmus it should have had much more weight with Jerome, since everyone knows that the Jews are avowedly more bitter enemies to all Christians, with whom they are thoroughly at odds, than the Greeks are to the Latins, with whom they agree in the shared name of Christians even though on some points they think differently. And indeed, in all honesty, I find it simply impossible to believe that any people has ever purposely conspired to tamper with its own books, not to mention that none could have done so. For could they have hoped that no one at all would object to the scheme, or that their plan would go undetected? Could they not all foresee that if it were revealed (and it would be, perforce, since every day some deserted the Jews to join Christ or the Greeks to join the Latins) they would not only not gain by the scheme, they would also discredit their own faction if they showed they supported a cause which

116 See *Contra Faustum Manichaeum* 5 (*PL* 42: 176). **117** See *Adages* 4137 (*CWE* 36: 621–22). **118** See *EE* 2: 15, 128–31.

they knew they could defend only by tampering with texts? But let Jerome deal with the Jews. The Greeks at least have this to clear them from that charge of falsehood: in the texts which gave rise to their controversy with us their books are consistent with ours; there was never any question about the text, but only about what the text means. Although no one can doubt that if they had wanted to change anything they would have changed first — indeed, only — those passages which support our position against theirs, and that if they had falsified those passages there would still be no reason to think they would do the same to others. But in actual fact can you imagine any reason why they might want to falsify others, since they left intact the very passages which are actually the only ones they would have wanted to change?

But one may still believe that their texts have at any rate grown faulty through negligence, especially if our own texts have done so, since it is plausible to assume that we have always devoted more care to the books of the faith just as we have to the faith itself. I could cite for the opposite viewpoint not only Jerome, but Augustine as well, who both think that Greek texts are not as corrupt as the Latin. But I wish to argue my case from reason and not from authority. I certainly maintain that no one cares so little about any book as to order a copy without feeling any concern about whether the copy he gets is a faulty or a sound one, since otherwise he could save himself time and expense by not ordering a copy at all. Therefore I am persuaded that the Greeks, too, took care to have their books copied diligently — which no one will doubt who inspects their books diligently. Furthermore, I assert that their vowel markings, punctuation, and accents make it harder for them to make scribal mistakes, and I will not be deterred from asserting this by the fact that you twisted this argument around for the contrary thesis, since you say it is easier to make a mistake where many things need attention. But I think, to the contrary, that it is harder to make a mistake where it is easy to make a mistake, if I too, like the dialecticians, may here pose a riddle. But I have the impression, or rather I know by experience, that just as we often fall down when we are hastening boldly along level ground, where no one expects

to fall, whereas we do not fall when we climb down a slope very slowly, carefully weighing our steps, even so when a scribe has to copy from a difficult original he copies more accurately because he must copy more carefully, whereas he falls into error from sheer overconfidence when the text he is copying is neat. Another fact also makes it clear that our texts have grown faulty, whereas theirs have remained reliable: in ours one can now find the same faults that Jerome thought required emendation long ago, but in theirs you will still see the same words on which Jerome's emendations were obviously based. Thus, shall we be forbidden today to expel from the same texts the very corruptions Jerome expelled then, and though it is accepted procedure to reform all religious orders (as they are called) as often as vices reappear in them, if corruptions reappear in books which have been corrected once before, shall we think it improper to correct them again?

Next you ask why it is that Latin texts grow corrupt, and you answer yourself, "Is it not the combined negligence and ignorance of the printers?" Then at once you proceed, "Look and see which are rarer, those fit to print Greek or those fit to print Latin, and then you will know which texts you ought to think sounder."[119] I do not understand what you mean by these words, Dorp; I do not believe you can suspect that Erasmus may use printed books in his scriptural annotations, for there is no shortage of manuscript texts, nor in what he is doing could he use printed texts even if he wanted to, since (so far as I know) the New Testament, on which he is working so hard, has never yet been printed by any press in Greek. But if you meant to say that since printers print Greek worse than Latin, ancient scribes of both languages did likewise, Dorp, let us forget about those who print Latin so that it looks more like Greek and print Greek so that it looks more like Arabic; in both areas let us compare those who are competent in both, among whom Aldus Manutius the Roman[120] was one of the greatest, as Johann Froben of Basel[121] is today. I venture to assure you of what I myself know through daily experience: these printers and others like them reproduce Greek more accurately and reliably than they do even Latin.

Your own reading would give you a much better

---

119 *EE* 2: 131   **120** (1450–1515) renowned humanist printer   **121** (*ca.* 1450–1527) humanist printer of many of Erasmus's works

understanding of this fact than hearsay does now, and indeed of much else that pertains to this topic, if someday, of your own accord, you would turn to the serious study of Greek. This is something I very much long for, but I can scarcely hope to persuade you to do so where Erasmus himself has failed,[122] against whom — or rather, against your own interests — you so earnestly defend yourself against having to benefit from the knowledge of Greek. Accordingly, even though, since you have such a stubborn aversion to Greek, it is pointless for me to exhort you to learn it, I continue to long, indeed still dare to hope, for the day, none too far in the future, when the debates on this topic have ceased, when your long winning-streak in the schools has stopped making you loath to give way on this point, and when you will do what I see no one else can do, namely, persuade yourself to learn Greek. For by then you will either use your better judgment and ignore those same generals whose cause you now serve, and whose favor you prize more than such an important department of learning, or else you will persuade even them that your Greek will prove useful for their ends as well as to you, in that it will enable you to rout those Grecophiles with their own weapons[123] and to argue against them with greater authority than you now do by debating an issue about which you know nothing at all.

Even so, when you write on this issue as if you think it is quite pointless to spend time on Greek, you do not persuade me, at least, that you mean what you write. For it is not likely that you, with your good sense, should not see the advantages of that language, or that you, with your zeal for all forms of sound learning, should not wish to acquire it, especially since you yourself all but advance the most excellent reasons for wanting to learn it even as you are arguing that we ought to ignore it. For you said, very truly and wisely indeed, that any language excels and takes precedence over others primarily according to how great a treasure of sound learning it keeps housed in the vaults of its literature.[124] Is not this by itself quite enough to convince anyone that all mortals, and especially Christians, should eagerly embrace Greek, since it is from Greek that the rest of mankind has received every variety of knowledge

and that we have been fortunate enough to receive nearly all the books of the New Testament? Unless you think that Greek is worn out and exhausted at last by this steady outpouring of translations as if by continuous childbearing.

First of all, among those very commentators on Aristotle whom you mentioned in that elegant speech which you wrote to praise Aristotle[125] (or was it to castigate Valla?[126] you are equally vehement about both), among these very commentators, Alexander, I mean, Themistius, Ammonius, Simplicius, Philoponus, and Olympiodorus,[127] how many of them (I say) apart from Themistius and the *Problems* of Alexander (for these have made their way into Latin) are yet read in any language but Greek? Anything by the rest of these authors that can be read in Latin (for I know that we do have some fragments of Alexander and Simplicius) is in such poor Latin that it is almost more obscure to Latin readers than the Greek is. I will say nothing here about poets or orators, nor will I say a word about other philosophers, or even about other commentators on Aristotle, although John the Grammarian,[128] all by himself, displays so much subtlety and learning, particularly in Aristotle, that I know that if you could converse with him in his own language that single grammarian would reconcile you with all the grammarians, toward whom you now seem ill disposed. But then, even among ancient writers of Christian doctrine, the great majority of whom certainly wrote their works in Greek, only a very small fraction of these have been translated, while some have been translated so badly that it seems they have rather been travestied. I will come straight to Aristotle himself, whom I too esteem more than many but along with many others, whereas in the speech I have mentioned you seem to cherish him not only more than many but instead of many, and even instead of all. Now then, not even he will be totally accessible to you if you have not learned Greek. I will overlook the fact that none of his works has been translated so well that it does not make a greater impression when couched in his own words, and also the fact that even today there are Greek works believed to be his of which I do not think that the Latins have even the titles; but certainly out of those

122 *EE* 2: 106–7   **123** *rout ... weapons:* See *Adages* 51 (*CWE* 31: 101).   **124** *EE* 2: 128   **125** More is referring to Dorp's *Oratio in laudem Aristotelis*.   **126** Lorenzo

Valla (1406–57) criticized Aristotle in his *Dialecticae disputationes*.   **127** Themistius (*fl.* 350 BC), Ammonius Hermiae (*fl. ca.* 490 BC), Simplicius (*fl. ca.* 535 BC),

Joannes Philoponos (*fl. ca.* 530 BC), Olympiodorus (*fl. ca.* 550 BC)   **128** sobriquet of Joannes Philoponos

very works that they do have today they have some as if they did not have them at all.

It is as certain as it is regrettable that even the *Meteorologica* of Aristotle belongs to this category, though I do not think that any of his labors can yield more valuable knowledge or that any province of nature itself is more admirable than that which is closest to us and surrounds us, though about it we know so much less than about the position of the stars and the motions of heavenly bodies which are so far away from us. But I hope that this work will be made available shortly in Latin by my country-man Thomas Linacre, physician to our most illustri-ous king,[129] for he has recently finished two books of it and would already have completed and published the work as a whole had not Galen,[130] as leader and prince of physicians, prevailed on him to put Ar-istotle aside for a while and to teach him to speak Latin first. Thus Aristotle will appear somewhat later, but by no means less polished; furthermore, he will not be alone. For Linacre is also translat-ing the commentary on that work by Alexander of Aphrodisias; for all this he will earn lasting thanks from all readers of Latin, whom he will have done no common service by issuing this excellent work by that brilliant philosopher, along with this bril-liant interpreter, so that his efforts will at last make it possible for readers of Latin to understand what I personally suspect no one has understood so far without knowing Greek. For some time ago, while I was studying the Greek text of that work by Aris-totle under the tutelage of Linacre, I myself felt an urge to examine the common translation, as well, to see what it was like. What I read instantly made me recall that philosopher's saying about his own *Phys-ics:* he said that work had been made public, but in such a way that it was not in fact public,[131] whereas this work, it seemed, had been translated in such a way that it was not actually translated at all, to the point that the very ideas I grasped easily in Greek I could not understand in the translation.

Nor is there any help to be had from the Latin in-terpreters, since even Albert,[132] whom they call "the Great" in emulation of Alexander the Great, and who claims to be giving us a paraphrase of Aristotle,

might more truly be said to have given us a parody of this work, for though it is his job to express Aris-totle's meaning in different words, what he actually does is to introduce meanings which are (as they say) diametrically opposed to it.[133] And Gaetano[134] (for he too wrote a commentary) tells us how many handfuls of water we get when we liquefy one hand-ful of earth, and how many handfuls of air when we evaporate one handful of water, and so on, with no end in sight; yet these measureless measures he mea-sures[135] do not add one iota[136] to our understanding of Aristotle.

My dear Dorp, it would take me forever to list all that anyone lacks who lacks Greek. Nonetheless I am not unaware that without any Greek many oth-ers, and you above all, have advanced even higher toward the very citadel of learning than many can climb who do know Greek, however hard they strain and pant. Even so, I would dare to say this much is certain: if you would add Greek to the rest of your attainments you would then surpass even yourself[137] by as much as you now surpass others re-gardless of their skill in Greek.

Since Erasmus, who once put me in charge of de-fending the *Folly,* has now undertaken to defend it himself, I do not need to argue its merits at length, for that task, which was already easy, is easier still now that we have divided the work.[138] Thus, while I have no doubt that what he will say, indeed what he has already said in that short letter of his, ought to satisfy everyone, I also believe that what I have to say, which may not carry much weight with others, must carry at least some weight with you. And first, I wonder what you mean by saying, "And now all of a sudden, like Davus,[139] this inoppor-tune *Folly* is upsetting everything."[140] But in what sense "now all of a sudden," as if the *Folly* had just now appeared, when in fact it has been circulating openly for more than seven years, known and cher-ished by all, going through seven new editions al-ready? Or how is it "inopportune"? Is this not quite enough to show what an auspicious appearance it made, that it could not have been issued so often in so many copies had it not found so many whom it could delight? Nor did these readers come from

129 Linacre (*ca.* 1460–1524) did not publish this translation. **130** Linacre translated Galen's *De sanitate tuenda.* **131** See Aulus Gellius 20.5. **132** Albertus Magnus (*ca.* 1200–1280) **133** See *Adages*

945 (*CWE* 32: 254). **134** Gaetano da Thiene (1387–1465) **135** *measureless… measures:* See *Adages* 344 (*CWE* 31: 354). **136** *one iota:* Adages 703 (*CWE* 32: 129–30). **137** *surpass even yourself:* See *Adages* 158

(*CWE* 31: 198). **138** *easy…work:* See *Adages* 1295 (*CWE* 33: 187) **139** a slave in Terence's *Andria* **140** *EE* 2: 13

the common herd of humanity (for I would not be surprised to see wares easily sold which pleased ignorant people, since there is a crowd of these everywhere)[141] but rather from among the most learned. For one proof that Folly pleases only the learned is simply that only the learned understand her, which indeed was perhaps why those two or three theologians that Folly upset became angry: on the basis of what others told them, they thought she said more than she did, while perhaps if they themselves understood what was actually said they would not feel provoked.

But, my dear Dorp, you think she should not have laughed at any theologians, though you all but acknowledge in earnest that some are as Folly described them in jest when you say, "Biting quips which contain a large element of truth leave a bitter memory behind them."[142] By heaven, what you say is true: those sham theologians would not be so embittered by those quips if they were not as true as they are biting. Now then, if those theologians are what you acknowledge them to be, do you prize them? I think not. Well, then, do you castigate them? I am sure that you do so in private, at least, and would do so in public if you had not made up your mind never to cross anyone and to behave in such a way as to make everyone praise you, of whatever character, learned and unlearned, good men and bad, since you say that you like even puppies to signal their friendship by wagging their tails at you.[143]

Though I grant you are acting more cautiously, Dorp, that does not make it any less just to attack bad men simply and openly, the way Gerard of Nijmegen[144] does, let alone to do what Erasmus does when he jokes about them both more decorously and less violently by assuming the character of Folly. Yet though you cannot tolerate his jokes and witticisms and you want him to issue a palinode, you write that you found nothing in Nijmegen's satires you would want him to change, even though those satires are more cutting at their gentlest than Folly is at her most cutting; and so they might well be. For that is prescribed by the nature of the poetry itself, which is not satire if it is not acerbic. And so it is worth seeing how satirically he always attacks

monks and friars and how he describes their pride, luxury, ignorance, drinking bouts, gluttony, lust, and hypocrisy, in a manner as elegant, and indeed as appropriate, as it is acerbic. For though many may not have deserved those reproaches, there are still some who are open to all of them. Therefore I do not wonder that you found nothing in his satires you would want him to change; in fact, neither did I. But I do wonder why Folly could not get your permission to joke freely about theologians when those satires have your permission to aim such harsh reproaches at members of religious orders and even at the theologians among them.

But, putting aside Gerard's satires, if anyone pored through your letters, my dear Dorp, could he not find any passage in which you score some class of people with some cutting word? Do you think there is no bite at all in the passage from your letter, which I have mentioned already, to the lord abbot Menard, in which you heap scorn on religious superiors? While you praise him, you lament the rest thus: "Oh, alas, alas, for those miserable monks who do not live like monks. Surrounded by horses, they re-stage the triumphs of Caesar, though they would do better to creep on the ground than to gallop on horseback to hell, unless they are afraid they cannot get there as quickly on foot."[145] Cutting as it is, my dear Dorp, this quip seems to have charmed you so much that you seem to have brought up the subject of horses expressly in order to keep that fine saying from going to waste. Otherwise, I think you are aware that it is not such a terrible outrage for abbots to ride and use animals as they were designed to be used. Besides, I have heard that not all other religious superiors ride about all the time, and that Abbot Menard rides occasionally, so that your joke very nearly recoils on the very man you wish to spare when you aim it at others. But so charming does everyone find his own notions,[146] so fragrant does everyone find his own farts,[147] that while we wrinkle our foreheads at other men's jokes and condemn them as bitter we cherish our own even when they are not as amusing and more bitter still.

But you will deny you were joking about religious superiors and will say you were rather lamenting them, especially since you start out under the

141 See *EE* 4: 190.   **142** *EE* 2: 13; Tacitus, *Annales* 15.68.4   **143** See *EE* 2: 13; *Adages* 3032 (*CWE* 35: 460–61).   **144** Gerard   Geldenhouwer (*ca.* 1482–1542)   **145** See De Vocht, *Monumenta* 118–19.   **146** *so charming . . . notions:* See *Adages* 2902 (*CWE*   35: 357–58); *Praise of Folly* (*ASD* 4/3: 94).   **147** *so fragrant . . . farts:* Adages 2302 (*CWE* 35: 4)

auspices of that inauspicious interjection, "Alas." I personally regard anything as a joke—in whatever figure of speech it is couched—which is said in such a way that no one can help laughing who hears it.
5 Although what difference does it make if you are being cutting in jest or in earnest? Or rather, it does make a difference: virtually no one refuses to laugh at a jocular saying aimed at him; no one stands for a serious one.¹⁴⁸ Otherwise, if you think it all right
10 to lament, but forbidden to joke, it will be easy for Folly to preface her whole joking discourse with one interjection of woe and thus, changing the figure of speech, use the same words again to lament the very theologians that she originally ridiculed. Nor
15 indeed could you easily tell whether they are more lamentable or laughable.

But perhaps we should think it permissible to say anything we like against religious superiors, even average ones, but forbidden to say even a word against
20 any theologians, no matter how bad. After all, you write words to almost that effect in your most recent letter to Erasmus. For you say, "You are surprised that your Folly, who pleases so many, not only theologians but also bishops, has provoked
25 such an angry reaction. But Erasmus, I myself am amazed that you value the judgment of bishops in this regard more highly than that of theologians, since you are well acquainted with the life-style, the character, and the learning (or should I call it the
30 ignorance?) of the bishops of today; for although there are certainly some who are worthy of such a high place there are actually amazingly few."¹⁴⁹ Here, Dorp, even as you refuse to let theologians be touched with the most harmless joke, you your-
35 self pour down open abuse on the bishops, with all your authority; for you not only find them deficient in learning and carp at their ignorance, but you furthermore savagely criticize their life-style and character. But you say it is very important that the au-
40 thority of theologians should not be impaired in the eyes of the people, as if it is not at all important how bishops are looked on by the people, even though you are not unaware what position they hold in Christ's church or how much higher than
45 your theologians they stand, since you know very well that bishops are the successors of the apostles themselves. Nor should you think you have made

yourself any safer just because you acknowledge that there are some bishops who are worthy of such a high station, since not even you believe that Folly 50 is imputing the defects of unworthy theologians to worthy ones. Indeed, Folly outdoes you in tact: nothing she says denies that there are many worthy theologians, whereas you say not merely that there are few good bishops but even that there are amaz- 55 ingly few.

But suppose that we grant you that there is no harm in attacking bishops with either mockery or slander provided that you do not aim one word at the sacrosanct office of theologians. How will 60 you answer this, that you yourself treat those very theologians so cuttingly that you practically tear them apart—not by name, I concede, but by describing them so plainly that, even by name, they could not have been indicated more clearly—in the 65 elegant prologue you wrote for Plautus's play, the *Pyrgopolynices?*

But meanwhile Plautus's name has reminded me of the words you excerpt from Saint Augustine¹⁵⁰ and turn against poets a number of times in your 70 letter.¹⁵¹ This subject calls for a more thorough discussion, and I will not debate it in this letter. Still, I will ask you this: does it seem to you that by these words Augustine himself meant that Christians ought not to read Terence? For if he is not warn- 75 ing us against making a thorough study of Terence, then that passage affords no support for an argument against reading poets. But if you think that Augustine was trying to make Christians abandon the study of poetry, my next question is this: do you 80 personally feel that Terence still ought to be taught? If you feel that he should, why keep quoting a warning which you do not think we ought to obey? But if, following Augustine's advice, of course, you maintain that Terence ought not to be taught, then 85 I certainly do wonder why it took you so long to accept his advice, which you doubtless had read long before, even though in the meantime you did not refrain from the reading, the teaching, or the public production and staging of Plautus, a poet no chaster 90 than Terence, or rather, not even as chaste. What of this, that you furnished the *Miles gloriosus* with a most charming prologue and supplied for the *Aulularia* not only a prologue but also that comedy's

---

148 *virtually . . . one:* See *Praise of Folly* (*ASD* 4/3: 116), *EE* 2: 96.   **149** *EE* 2: 127   **150** See *Confessions* 1.16.26.   **151** See *EE* 2: 129–30.

missing ending, a supplement which seems to me not inferior to any other part of the comedy for either its elegant language or its true Plautine wit?

What I mean may be illustrated by those very verses in which, as I said, you provide such a handsome description of those uncultured theologians, whom now you defend, that no one could mock them more wittily and no one could attack them more forcefully. For what could be more charming or elegant than the verses which I shall now quote?

> To start with, all of those uncultured louts
> Whose erudition ends with uncouth books
> Can beat it, Plautus says, and go to hell[152]
> Should they, malicious snarlers that they are,
> Do any more of what they do continually,
> Bellowing out their windy disapproval,
> Venting the poison of their chronic envy,
> Bad-mouthing, snapping, sinking grisly fangs
> In everything, and, just the way that dogs do,
> Barking like mad at everyone they meet.
> This sort of men (if they are really men,
> Illiterates and bumpkins that they are)
> Plautus told me to drive away on sight;
> Should any stay to hoot and interfere,
> He promised them a beating for a greeting
> When they become his fellow guests in Hades.[153]

Observe, my dear Dorp, just how little you thought about shunning the poets and just how well you painted those uncultured theologians in their natural colors. But if you deny that you were a theologian yourself then, since you wrote these lines seven years ago, certainly no more than a year and a half has elapsed since you published them in a new collection; and by then you were certainly a theologian, four years after you gave your brilliant speech on the assumption of the Virgin Mother of God. Now, then, what difference does it make if you wrote these lines as a theologian or if, having become one, you gave your blessing to lines written earlier by choosing to publish them?

Well, then, my dear Dorp, when you found nothing you thought should be changed in Gerard's mordant satires describing the filthiest vices of the religious orders, when you yourself mocked as you pitied religious superiors and mocked in a way that

would wound, when you acerbically castigated the ignorance, life-style, and character of all but "amazingly few" bishops, when you yourself called the very theologians whose folly you think it improper for Folly to joke about "uncultured louts," "malicious snarlers," men "whose erudition ends with uncouth books," who "bellow out their windy disapproval," who "vent the livid poisons of their envy," who "bad-mouth, snap, and sink their grisly fangs in everything," who "bark like dogs at everyone they meet," and who, "illiterate bumpkins," barely men, at last you said should simply go to hell, when you did all this, my dear Dorp, just how was it that you never thought of the same cautious counsels on which you now base your most friendly and prudent advice to Erasmus? What had become of that saying from Jerome, "It is totally insane to work hard just to make people hate you"?[154] What had become of the one from Cornelius Tacitus, "Biting quips which contain a good deal of truth leave a bitter memory behind them"?[155] What had happened to the one from Epictetus, "Do not suppose everyone will enjoy hearing what you enjoy saying"?[156]

Indeed, my dearest Dorp, we are naturally prone to require self-restraint from other people as a matter of course while we give ourselves license to do as we please. I myself know of some who could simply not stand it when Reuchlin[157] (good lord, what a man he is!), confronting his personal detractors, that is, a most learned, most prudent, most honorable person confronting the most ignorant, most fatuous, most worthless wretches alive, who had done him so great an injustice that not even a physical act of revenge on his part would have seemed altogether excessive, I know of some, I repeat, who though they actually favored his cause could not stand it when freely, but still no more freely than truthfully, he vented his anger against his detractors in writing. I know, too, that before long the same men who could not stand for Reuchlin's response themselves grew much more violently irate over things which both had less intrinsic importance and did not affect them so directly. So much easier it is to prescribe self-control for the anger of others than it is for our own. "Did I not have the right, then," you ask, "either to approve of Gerard's satires or to speak against uncultured theologians, and religious

152 *Casina* 611; *Menaechmi* 66   **153** prologue to Plautus's *Miles gloriosus*   **154** *EE* 2: 12; Jerome, *PL* 28: 1403   **155** Tacitus, *Annales* 15.68.4   **156** *EE* 2: 127; Epictetus, *Enchiridion* 33.14   **157** Johann Reuchlin (1455–1522)

superiors and bishops, too, either in jest or in earnest, provided that I spoke the truth and did not mention anyone's name?" Quite the contrary, my dear Dorp, I think that you had so much right to
5 do what you did that it seems to me you have never done anything better in your life, provided that you will also be fair enough not to find fault with others for something you praise in yourself.[158]

To conclude, my dear Dorp, in my view none
10 of all your advice on the *Folly* has any real point: no advice is in order, and even if it were, after so many years your advice comes too late. For honestly, I could not keep from chuckling when I read what you wrote at the end of your earlier letter to
15 the effect that Erasmus could pacify those theologians whom the *Folly* upset if he would counter his praises of Folly with a praise of Wisdom. They certainly are wise if they think this encomium of Folly by Folly affords her such exemplary praise that
20 they want Wisdom also to be praised in this mode of address. If this is how they feel, why are they so aroused, since they themselves have been praised at such length by this Folly who gets so much praise?[159] Furthermore, I do not see how Erasmus could ease
25 their resentment against him by writing true praises of Wisdom or how he could even avoid making them resent him all the more, whether he wanted to or not,[160] since he would then feel just as compelled to exclude them from the company of Wisdom as he now does to give them a place in the first
30 rank of Folly's initiates.

As I was writing these last words a letter arrived from my prince summoning me to return to him. His letter has forced me to stop writing at last,
35 though I do not want to stop, and makes me finish this letter, however unwillingly; even though it is already so long that an "interminable *Orestes,* spilling off the page,"[161] might well be shorter, I was somehow so eager to speak with you that it wanted to
40 keep right on growing. But though I do not find it unpleasant to have to fold up my letter at this point, since I am afraid it is already so long that you may find it tedious, even so it does not make me happy that I will not have any chance to refine it
45 or to lick this ungainly and amorphous offspring of mine into shape by degrees. I was certainly planning to do so in order to make it seem somewhat more

polished when it got to you, learned Dorp, since I want you to look with approval on me and on all that is mine. You will pardon my letter's ungainli- 50
ness not only because in my haste to depart I could not even stop to reread it, but also because I had no store of books, indeed virtually no books at all, to consult as I wrote it.

Still, I hope, even such as it is, you will not find 55
my letter displeasing, for although I rely first of all on your humane indulgence I also rely on the thoroughness of my own effort to guard against writing one word in this letter that might give you just cause for offense, unless through human weakness 60
esteem for my own works misleads me. If this does ever happen, and I am advised of it, I will freely acknowledge my fault and not try to defend it. Indeed, just as I am not slow to advise those I love, should it be in their interest, so too, on my honor, 65
I am delighted to have my friends advise me. Nor am I unaware that on a number of points you are not leveling your own charges at Erasmus but rather reporting what you heard from others, so that you too should understand that at a number of points in 70
this letter I have rather been answering those men through you than addressing you personally, whom I not only prize as an excellent friend and respect as an excellent scholar but also revere as an excellent man. Farewell, my dearest Dorp, and be assured 75
that no one, not even in your own Holland, regards you more highly than More does in the land of the faraway Britons,[162] since you are no less dear to him than you are to Erasmus. Than that you can never be dearer, not even to me. Once more, farewell. Bru- 80
ges, 21 October.

Farewell. Bruges, 21 October. Once more, farewell.

60. To the University of Oxford
Abingdon, 29 March <1518>

Thomas More sends his heartiest greetings to 85
the Reverend Fathers, the Vice-Chancellor, the Proctors, and the other members of the Masters' Guild of the University of Oxford.

Learned gentlemen, I felt some misgivings about whether it would be proper for me to address you 90
concerning the issues I presently mean to discuss. My

---

158 *fair . . . yourself: Adages* 2833 (CWE 35:   69, 76). **160** *wanted to or not: Adages*   **162** *land . . . Britons:* Vergil, *Ecologues* 1.6.6
330). **159** See *Praise of Folly* (ASD 4/3:   245 (CWE 31: 274) **161** Juvenal 1.6

misgivings arose not so much from concern about my style (although I am embarrassed about that, too, in the face of so eloquent an assembly) as from fear of appearing presumptuous if an insignificant person like myself, with little prudence, less experience, and only a modicum of learning, were so brash and so bold as to offer my personal advice about anything, but especially about anything literary, to a group of men each of whom is sufficiently learned and prudent to advise many thousands of men. But on the other hand, reverend fathers, this same singular wisdom of yours, which intimidated me so at first glance, reassured me on closer examination, for it occurred to me that whereas foolish and arrogant ignorance refuses to listen to anyone, the wisest and most learned men are the least self-assured and the least prone to scorn anyone's advice. Something else that encouraged me greatly was the thought that fair judges like you never think any less of a man, and indeed always honor and thank him, for offering even imprudent advice which is heartfelt and friendly. Finally, when I consider that next after God this university of yours should be given the credit for whatever learning I do have, since it was there that I came by its rudiments, I seem bound by my duty and loyalty to you not to pass over anything in silence that I think you would do well to hear. And so when I saw that the only risk in my writing was that some people might think me arrogant, whereas my silence could make many people condemn my ingratitude, I was more willing to let all mortals call me a little too bold than to let anyone call me ungrateful, especially toward this school of yours—for I feel very strongly obliged to stand up for its honor—and particularly since I believe that the matter at hand is so crucial that no other problem has arisen in quite a long time which deserves more of your serious attention than this one if you wish to safeguard the honor and welfare of your university.

Let me tell you what matter I mean. I have recently heard it reported by a number of people in London that certain scholars of your university, prompted either by hatred of Greek learning, by a misguided devotion to some other sort, or (as I think more likely) by a shameless addiction to joking and trifling, have formed a deliberate conspiracy to call themselves Trojans. One of them, who

is said to be riper in years than in wisdom, has assumed the name "Priam," another the name "Hector," another the name "Paris" or else that of some other ancient Trojan, and the rest have been doing the same, for the sole purpose of jokingly setting themselves up as a faction opposed to the Greeks to make fun of the students of Greek learning. And so, they say, these men have seen to it that no one who has even a passing acquaintance with that language is allowed to appear either at home or in public without being pointed at, laughed at, and scoffed at by one of those laughable Trojans, who are not laughing at anything but what they know nothing about, namely sound learning in general. Thus it seems that these Trojans are eminent witnesses to the aptness of that ancient adage, "Trojans grow wise too late."[163]

Though I continually heard many different reports on this matter from many different people, and although it irked everyone and upset me especially that some of your scholars were wasting their time and disrupting the sound studies of others with this sort of impertinence, nonetheless, since I saw that no measures, however elaborate, could ever ensure that every member of such a large group of people would sensibly mind his own business I began to think light of the matter. But after I arrived here in Abingdon in the company of our invincible king, I was further informed that this impertinence had started to turn into sheer lunacy. For I learned that one of those Trojans, to show off what he views as his wisdom, what his partisans excuse as his humor and wit, and what others who look at his actions condemn as his madness, chose this holy season of fasting[164] and the medium of a public sermon to blather all too liberally not only against Greek learning and stylistic refinement in Latin but also against all the liberal arts. To avoid any inconsistency in his performance and to make sure that the heading of his sermon was as mad as its body was stolid, he did not expound either a whole chapter of Scripture, as the ancients used to do, or a single short passage from Sacred Scripture, which is the prevalent practice among moderns. Instead, he took as his text various old wives' proverbs in English.[165] And so I have no doubt that so trifling a sermon was very offensive to those who were actually present,

---

163 *Adages* 28 (*CWE* 31: 76–77)   **164** Lent   **165** *old wives' proverbs:* See 1 Tm 4:7; *Adages* 2616 (*CWE* 35: 226).

since I see how it outrages everyone who has heard even a scrap of it. For could anyone with the least spark of Christian devotion in his heart not lament how the majesty of the sacrosanct office of preaching, which won the world over to Christ, is now being violated by the very men who are officially most responsible for upholding the authority of that function? Could anyone imagine a more blatant affront to the office of preaching than for a person who styles himself a preacher to step forth in the holiest season of the year and before a large audience of Christians, in the very temple of God, in the loftiest pulpit — in Christ's very throne, as it were — and in sight of Christ's venerable body, to turn his Lenten sermon into a bacchanalian travesty? How do you think those who stood listening received it when they saw their preacher, from whom they had come to hear lessons of spiritual wisdom, cavorting, guffawing, and monkeying around in the pulpit, and when those who had gathered there piously expecting to hear the words of life went away not recalling that they had heard anything but slurs against literature and impertinent preaching which had dishonored the office of preacher?

But as for his tirade against all types of secular learning, if that good man had withdrawn from the world altogether and had lived many years as a hermit, and if he then abruptly stepped forth and declared that we ought to concentrate on vigils, prayer, and fasting, that this is the right way to get to heaven, and that all other things are mere trifles, or even that study and learning are actually a hindrance, since simple and unlearned people have an easier time rising heavenward, such a sermon might perhaps have been tolerated from a person like this, whose simplicity would earn him indulgence; for his generous hearers would construe it as saintliness and even the most critical hearers as an ignorance which was at any rate pious and devout. But as it is, when they see a man climb to the pulpit clad in an academic gown, with a furred hood on his shoulders — dressed, that is, as a man of learning — and there, in the middle of the university, a place no one frequents except for the sake of learning, they see him rage openly against virtually all branches of learning, certainly no one who sees this considers it anything but blind and egregious malice and proud envy directed at his betters.

In fact many are utterly amazed how the man got it into his head that he ought to be preaching either about the Latin language, of which he understands only a little, or about liberal studies, of which he understands even less, or especially about the Greek language, of which he understands not one iota, when he had such a rich, handy store of material in the seven deadly sins, an appropriate topic for sermons and one with which he seems to be not at all unfamiliar. For he feels more inclined to condemn anything he knows nothing about than to learn it; if this is not sloth, then what is? And he openly slanders anyone he has found to know anything he himself has omitted to learn, whether through laziness or through sheer despair of his own intellectual powers; is this not clearly envy? Finally, he tries to deny any value to any aspect of knowledge but the one he is falsely convinced he has mastered, and he arrogantly lays claim to more praise for his ignorance than the modesty of some will accept for their knowledge; is this not the summit of pride?

Now then, as for secular learning, no one denies that a person can be saved without it, and indeed without learning of any sort. But even secular learning, as he calls it, prepares the soul for virtue. And however that may be, certainly no one disputes that learning is virtually the one and only incentive that draws people to Oxford, inasmuch as that rude and illiterate virtue is something which any good woman can teach well enough to her children at home. Furthermore, not everyone who comes to Oxford comes just to learn theology; some must also learn law. They must also learn prudence in human affairs, something which is so far from being useless to a theologian that without it he may be able to sing well enough for his own pleasure,[166] but his singing will certainly be ill suited for the people. And I doubt that any study contributes as richly to this practical skill as the study of poets, orators, and histories. Indeed, some plot their course, as it were, to the contemplation of celestial realities through the study of nature, and progress to theology by way of philosophy and the liberal arts (all of which he condemns under the name "secular literature"), thus despoiling the women of Egypt[167] to grace their own queen. But since theology is the only subject he seems to allow (if he actually allows even this), I do not see how he can

---

166 *sing…pleasure:* See *Adages* 1030, 2480 (*CWE* 33: 33–34, 35: 113–14).   **167** *despoiling…Egypt:* See Ex 3:22, 11:2, 12:36.

pursue it without any skill in either Hebrew or Greek or Latin, unless perhaps the fine fellow has convinced himself that there are enough books on that subject in English, or unless he thinks that all of theology falls within the confines of those problems which they dispute about so assiduously, for I grant that one needs little Latin to learn those. But I certainly deny that theology, that venerable heavenly queen, is so pent up in those narrow limits that she does not also inhabit and dwell in Holy Scripture as her proper home, from which she makes her pilgrimage through all the cells of the oldest and holiest fathers, Augustine, I mean, Jerome, Ambrose, Cyprian, Chrysostom, Gregory, Basil, and other men like them, whose "positive" writings, as they are now called with contempt, were the mainstay of theological studies for more than a thousand years after the Passion of Christ, before those subtle problems which now command almost exclusive attention were even invented. But whoever boasts of understanding the works of the fathers without considerable skill in the language of each of them will be making that unskillful boast a long time before those who are skilled will believe him.

But if that preacher now tries to cover up for his impertinence by pretending that what he condemned was not secular learning but rather the immoderate study thereof, I do not see that that vice is so widespread that the whole populace needed to be chided or warned about it in a public sermon as if they were all falling head-over-heels over the brink. For I do not see that many have made so much progress in this branch of learning that they might not advance somewhat further while still stopping short of the mean. Furthermore, that fine fellow made it perfectly clear he was far from conveying such a moderate message: he openly called everyone a heretic who wished to pursue Greek learning, and he went on to brand lecturers in Greek as "archdevils," and students of Greek (in a more modest and wittier vein, as he thought) as "underdevils." And in the heat of this passion, or rather this frenzy, that holy man used the term "devil" to label a man who, as everyone knows, is the sort of man who would cause the real devil a great deal of grief by becoming a preacher; and though he did not actually name the man, he referred to him in such an obvious way that everyone was as quick to discern who was meant by that label as they were to label the man who had labeled him that way a madman.

Learned gentlemen, I am hardly so foolish as to take it upon myself to defend Greek learning before prudent judges like yourselves, since I am well aware that you must have already perceived and acknowledged its usefulness. For can anyone fail to perceive that not only in all other arts, but in theology as well, the most original thinkers and the most diligent interpreters of their thoughts were Greek? For in philosophy, apart from the works left by Cicero and Seneca, the schools of the Latins have nothing to offer that is not either Greek or translated from Greek. I will say nothing about the New Testament, which was first written almost entirely in Greek. I will say nothing of the fact that all the most ancient and most skilled interpreters of Sacred Scripture were Greeks and wrote in Greek. But I will say this much, not without the agreement of all learned men: though some works were translated long ago, and though many have recently been translated better, not even half of the volumes in Greek have been translated into Latin, and virtually none has been translated so well that the Greek text is not less corrupt or at least more expressive. And for this reason all the ancient doctors of the Latin church, Jerome, Augustine, Bede, and many others besides, made a strenuous effort to learn the Greek language, doing so at a time when more books had already been translated than many men of today who consider themselves very learned would normally read; nor did they merely learn it, they also advised later scholars, especially those who were going to become theologians, to do the same thing.[168]

Therefore, as I have said, my intention is not to defend the study of Greek before prudent judges like yourselves, but rather to do as my own sense of duty directs me: to urge you to let none be deterred from the pursuit of Greek learning in your university whether by public sermons or by private impertinence, since that language is one which the Church has decreed should be taught in all universities. Hence men of your prudence will easily discern that not everyone in your community who has devoted his energies to Greek is completely obtuse; indeed, some of these men have distinguished themselves so highly that their own fame for learning has won a good deal of real glory for your school

168 See Augustine, *De doctrina Christiana* 2.11.16 (*PL* 34: 42–43); Jerome, *Epistolae* 39.1, 85.3 (*PL* 22: 465, 753).

not only in this realm but also abroad. You will also discern that a large number of people, whose precedent others will follow, have lately begun to make large contributions to your university with the aim of promoting both literary studies in general and, most recently, Greek in particular.[169] But their present enthusiasm for you will undoubtedly wane if they find that their pious intentions are mocked there in Oxford, particularly since in Cambridge, which you have always been wont to outshine, even those who are not learning Greek are each moved by a common devotion to their school to make a handsome personal contribution for the salary of a lecturer to teach others Greek. You will discern all these arguments, I repeat, and a number of others, as well, which my own humble intellect is too weak to discover. But my purpose is rather to tell you what others are saying and thinking than to give you advice about what you should do. You perceive much more sharply than I do that unless you suppress such unsavory factions at once as they arise, more and more will contract this disease until the worse party may grow to outnumber the better, so that others will be forced to step in and help those of you who are virtuous and sensible. For I certainly think that no one who has ever belonged to your number feels any less personal concern for the status of your university than you yourselves do who live there today.

There is no room for doubt that the most reverend father in Christ, the Archbishop of Canterbury,[170] who is the primate of all our clergy as well as your chancellor, will do all that he can in this matter, both for the clergy's sake and for your own, since he realizes how important it is both for the clergy and for you that your system of studies should not go to ruin. But it will go to ruin if the university is racked by contention and if the foolish and slothful are allowed to flout sound learning everywhere with impunity. And what about the most reverend father in Christ, the Cardinal of York,[171] both a patron of learning and a most learned bishop in his own right? Is he going to stand by and permit sound learning and the study of languages to be mocked among you with impunity? Or is he not more likely

to launch all the darts of his learning, his virtue, and his authority to punish those witlings who are treating sound learning with contempt? Finally, what of our most Christian Prince? His sacred majesty has shown as much favor for all sound learning as any prince ever did, while in erudition and judgment he is more than a match for any previous prince. With his limitless prudence and great piety toward God he will undoubtedly never permit the endeavors of wicked and slothful individuals to abolish the pursuit of sound learning in a place where his own most illustrious forebears established a most illustrious university, which is not only one of the oldest, with a long roll of learned alumni who have been ornaments not only to England but to the entire Church, but can also boast so many colleges with perpetual endowments for the support of students that in this one respect there is no foreign university which can compete or compare with your own. And the sole purpose of all of these colleges and the one reason for which you have all those endowments is so that a great number of scholars, free from having to worry about earning a living, can study the liberal arts there.

But I have no doubt that prudent men like yourselves will easily devise your own plan to suppress those disturbances and impertinent factions and that you will make sure that all types of sound learning will not only be safe from derision and mockery but will also be valued and honored. By your diligence in this regard you will do a great service to sound studies at Oxford, and it is hard to express how much thanks you will earn both from our most illustrious Prince and from those reverend fathers in Christ I have named. And although the great love that I bear you already is what led me to write all these things at this time, and with this my own hand, you will also endear yourselves more intensely than ever to me personally, whose devotion and energies your whole assembly and each of its members will perceive to be always at your service. May God keep and preserve this illustrious university of yours and may he grant it perpetual increase of all honest learning and virtue. Abingdon. 29 March.

                 Thomas More

---

169 More is referring to the 1516 founding of Corpus Christi College, Oxford, by Richard Pace. **170** William Warham (*ca.* 1450–1532), chancellor of England from 1504 to 1515 and chancellor of Oxford University from 1506 until his death **171** Thomas Wolsey (1472/73–1530)

75. To Edward Lee
1 May 1519

Thomas More sends his heartiest greetings to Edward Lee.[172]

My dearest Lee, I have received two letters through your brother Wilfred,[173] a most virtuous and amiable young man; both were written in Louvain, one on the tenth day of April and the other on the twentieth. The first one contains three main points, which are these. First of all, you have heard a report which is being spread everywhere by certain Erasmians to the effect that I was more than a little upset by your having prepared a work challenging Erasmus, and that this had turned me against you to the point that I had not only struck you from my list of friends but was also preparing to do you a bad turn. And if you were quite certain of this you would either resolve, if your feelings would bear it, to spurn such a friend altogether,[174] or if you could not bring yourself to do that you would freely indulge your own grief, since nothing grieves you as much as ingratitude, while to you death itself would be preferable to the loss of so great a friend, whom you have loved with an uncommon fervor and constantly praised to the skies[175] with your utmost devotion; thus, it is not surprising that you would consider it an intolerable hardship if I were in turn so ungrateful and even so unfair as to pass hasty judgment on my friend before even hearing him out. Therefore you write that you neither can nor will believe that I have done so, even though the Erasmians steadily insist that I have, before you receive definite news of the fact in a letter directly from me.

Secondly, you try to prove to me that you are not to blame for anything that has happened in this controversy and that all the credit for this tragedy should go to Erasmus. You rehearse the whole course of events more completely and circumstantially and you detail the origins of the entire quarrel from birth to full growth, claiming first that you would never have undertaken that project of annotation if you had not been prevailed upon by your love and his persistent requests, that he then rejected your annotations as hairsplitting trifles, that he nonetheless had your scribe copy them out for him secretly and took from them any corrections he made in his second edition, and that now, not content with this, he has made your name infamous throughout Europe as if you gathered nothing but trifles and as if you supported them with the doctrines of modern thinkers and refused to let him see your work so that he could either retract any errors or defend himself.[176]

Thirdly, you add that even though you could have disgraced him by publishing your annotations you have so far suppressed them, having resolved not to go any further in this controversy until you had delivered them to the reverend father in Christ, the Bishop of Rochester,[177] to weigh and examine, who would allow me to see them too, if I wanted to do so. Here you beg me to give your behavior a fair, balanced assessment, confident that if I do so I will see how straightforwardly you are dealing with him, how unaffectedly, how unobsequiously, how inoffensively, only noting what he writes and in what respect you disagree. But if you ever criticize him more sharply and freely, you ask me also to be fair in weighing the question of whether he deserves it. You assert that (unless your opinion completely misleads you) I will then find that he has made serious and shameful mistakes.

I think this is the gist of your first letter; now on to your second, written just ten days later, which suggests you have gone through a sudden and complete transformation. For in this one you write that now is the time for me to prove myself the sort of man you always supposed I was, namely a fair one, a man whom, in your words, "no partisan feelings have ever deceived." For though you—even after Erasmus had treated you badly—had left it to your common friends to remedy the situation for as long as that policy might safeguard your honor, and though you had already sent the book to the reverend father of Rochester, whose judgment you had decided to stand by, and though even Erasmus himself had approved of this plan when you mentioned it to him, his actual intentions were totally different

172 Edward Lee (ca. 1482–1544), future Archbishop of York, met Erasmus while he was studying Greek and Hebrew in Louvain. Shortly afterwards, Lee began to circulate a manuscript of abusive annotations to the first edition of Erasmus's New Testament. 173 These letters are not extant. 174 spurn . . . altogether: Adages 706 (CWE 32: 131) 175 constantly . . . skies: See Adages 550 (CWE 31: 570). 176 See Lee, Annotationes in Annotationes Novi Testamenti Desiderii Erasmi (Paris: 1520); EE 3: 424, 471; 4: 160. Erasmus answered in his Apologia qua respondet (Erasmi opuscula, ed. Wallace K. Ferguson, The Hague: 1933). 177 Erasmus and Lee agreed to let John Fisher (1459–1535), Bishop of Rochester, arbitrate their dispute.

from those he professed, and within a few days of agreeing to your plan he suddenly spewed out a barrage of utterly insane abuse, wantonly and inappropriately and with no provocation from you, in his *Apology against Latomus*,[178] in which even if he did avoid mentioning your name he was still not discreet enough to keep everyone from shouting immediately that that shot had been aimed straight at you.[179] And so even if your name does not appear in the passage, and even if what he said there does not match your character at all, nevertheless, since all of Europe has been interpreting it this way, you take it as if you had been mentioned expressly by name, especially since he refused your request to relieve you of this suspicion with any apology. Thus, since he has behaved in this way and the business has now gone so far, you feel you would be doing me an injustice if you did not think me fair enough that I would not merely allow you but actually urge you to make every effort to protect your own honor; and since you cannot safeguard it except by publishing your annotations, this is the way you will have to proceed. Finally, you are so firmly persuaded of this that you feel no good or prudent person will try to dissuade you. And you beg me again and again to be your steadfast friend in this matter as you have always been and will always be mine.

Even though, my dear Lee, the subject matter of your letters is so varied and complex that I can make no brief response, I will still respond as briefly as I possibly can, since I do not wish to occupy much of your time and I myself have too little to spare to spend much of it writing a letter of this sort. And besides, as the matter now stands, there might seem to be no point at all in my doing so, since you have already fixed on your own plan of action with Stygian[180] finality, not delaying at all for your brother's return and thus forestalling all the advice of every one of your friends. I do not know what they are going to say now; perhaps some of them will take the old advice, "Make the most of what cannot be changed."[181] But I would venture to give you my strongest assurance that, if you had asked their advice beforehand instead of deciding the point by yourself, you would have found very few here who would not have thought you would do better to put away those annotations forever than ever to publish

them. And yet these men, who are anxious to stop you from putting your plan into action, can swear with a clear conscience (and I certainly believe, Lee, that you too believe it) that they are no less sincerely[182] and truly yours, just as several of them are (I hope) no less wise, than the most prudent of those over there who are goading you on so insistently to rush into publication.

As for myself, though I would defer to almost any of your friends in a contest of learning and prudence, when it comes to goodwill and good faith there is none with whom I would not confidently compete, so that you will not think I am thrown for a loss at the point where you write about how much you love and extol me. I can name various eminent men who will testify that I have responded in kind, and two others whose testimony you cannot reject and must have already heard frequently, namely each of your very dear brothers. And yet even if they are your brothers, I would not concede even to them that they feel more sincere good will for you than I myself do. I confess that I am very fond of Erasmus, for practically no other reason than that for which all of Christendom cherishes him, namely that this one man's unceasing exertions have done more to advance all students of sound intellectual disciplines everywhere in both secular and sacred learning than virtually anyone else's exertions for the last several centuries, though on this basis he should be less dear to me than to you, who have derived not a little more profit from him, as your letters show clearly. On the other hand, Lee, I see more than one reason why I should be linked to you personally by a bond of uncommon affection; not to mention the rest, there is devotion to our common fatherland and the friendly, enduring connection between our respective parents, through which I first came to embrace you many years ago, a precocious boy ten years my junior; and I have remained an admirer of yours ever since. Yet meanwhile I have been more of a friend than an intimate colleague, though I would certainly have been happy to be as intimate as possible if our separate professions and stations in life had not drawn us widely apart. And yet they never drew us so widely apart that I ever lost sight of that fine intellect, so well trained and well cultivated for learning, that insatiable thirst

178 Jacobus Latomus (*ca.* 1475–1544)   **179** See *EE* 4: 1–2 for Erasmus's denial of targeting Lee.   **180** The river Styx is where   the gods swore binding oaths; see Homer, *Iliad* 15.37, and Ovid, *Metamorphoses* 1.188–89, 2.45–46, 101.   **181** See *Adages*   214 (*CWE* 31: 246–47).   **182** *no less sincerely: Adages* 946 (*CWE* 32: 254–55)

for knowledge, that fervent passion for studies, or that intense and unwearying drive, traits which easily held my attention and led me to love you more and more by the day, most of all in the hope that, as I very joyfully promised myself, a time would eventually come when your endeavors would make this Britain of ours famous throughout the rest of the world.

My own feelings for you until now have been just as I have described them, and not even now will I take back my love or abandon my hope; that is how far I am from designing or threatening to harm you. But assuredly, my dear Lee, the more vehemently I have loved you, and the greater the glory I thought you would bring us, the more deeply it hurts me to see you so stubbornly set on a plan which I am not alone in expecting will neither advance your own interests nor add to our country's prestige, since it will be seen as an invidious action on your part when you alone make such a hostile attack on the very work that another man elaborated for the common benefit of all mortals at no small expense to his personal fortunes and health. Indeed, there is a danger that if you go on as you have begun, all will judge that you harbor a general hostility toward all of mankind, and not just toward Erasmus, since it is their interests that you will be trying to hurt; you cannot obstruct his. He is not to be cheated of his due reward at God's hand, who requites all good deeds, even if mortal men should either reject his work or allow it to perish completely as their envy or carelessness has allowed many very profitable volumes to perish before now, though their authors have still reaped the same profit in heaven that they tried to bestow on the earth.

But I see that I must now respond to that part of your letter in which you see me as both ungrateful and unjust if I pass a hasty and disparaging judgment on your labor before reading it through. My dear Lee, I certainly do not have so high an opinion of myself as to presume to pass judgment on anyone's works; I have always thought it a sure enough way to avoid accusations of temerity if I voted the way other men vote, particularly if they were men of manifest virtue and undoubted learning. And when I observed that this class of men was unanimous in acclaiming this one work—the one you assail—more than all of his other works combined,

although there is not one of his works they do not applaud enthusiastically, I certainly did not think that I would be charged with precipitate judgment or found guilty of ingratitude toward you if before reading even one line of your book I felt I ought to place more trust in all of those men than in you. For if I should have been so fair for your sake as to assume that your judgment in condemning Erasmus's translation was rigorous and irrefutable, I would have had to deliver a very severe and very unfair verdict on all of those men, whom I must have supposed to be either so lazy that they had neglected an issue as important as you contend this one to be, or so stupid that they had not understood something which was so obvious to you, or finally so impious that they had refused to resist for Christ's sake the same man against whom you have pitted yourself, like a David opposing Goliath for Israel's sake,[183] on an issue they knew would contribute directly to what you describe as "the ruin of the church." My dear Lee, you will have to forgive me for preferring to be somewhat tentative in the way I accepted your judgment so that I would not be driven to the ruthless condemnation of so many others in my heart, especially when they are such great men that I am sure you would consider it an ample distinction for anyone if he were believed even to approximate the virtue and learning of men such as these, though he might still fall several leagues short of them.

You may answer that some learned men side with you. That should not be considered to weigh against me, since I have heard of barely one or two who are not altogether unlearned; and if you heard them blathering their nonsense over here, I am sure, my dear Lee, you would be quite ashamed to be chosen to lead camp followers of this sort instead of real soldiers, unless Caesar's ambition inspires you, which I hope it does not, to prefer the first rank in Mutina (unless that is not the right name) to the second in Rome.[184] But learned civility and unlearned arrogance being what they are, I suspect that the learned will grant you the first rank before the unlearned will grant you the second or third. But if you are actually being encouraged by certain men over there, they are the very ones who make me still more reluctant to trust you regarding this issue, since I would have trusted you singly considerably more than I do now that witnesses like these have

183 See 1 Sm 17:4–7.   **184** See Plutarch, *Iulius* 11.2.

joined you. It is not that I particularly doubt or, for that matter, acknowledge their learning, since I suspect they are the sort of men who could be black or white for all we know;[185] it is rather that these men are reported to be unequivocally unfair to Erasmus, whether they are egged on by plain human jealousy (for we are all human) or whether, as I think more likely, some demon gave rise to this plague by inciting them, secretly instigating those minions of his to deter the man whom no material expense and no physical illness or danger could tear from the virtuous labors which he was performing for the good of the entire world. With a pretense of holiness they claim to be furthering Christ's work, but they are actually hindering Christ's work as they create work with their irksome slanders for the man who is really pursuing Christ's work and divert him from writing about Sacred Scripture, out of which, as if out of an inexhaustible storehouse, he used to bring something new almost daily for the advancement of scholarship, to writing apologies which are not so much useful to us as compulsory for him.

It is reported that these men get others to run back and forth between you and Erasmus, patching together lies and reporting falsely what each of you has been saying about the other, so that this vile deception will set you at odds and those fellows can serve their own partisan feelings at your peril.[186] They themselves deserve to endure all the hatred which will inevitably be directed against anyone who sets out to do what these men are now urging you to do, not to select just a passage or two in which you can show either that he has made a mistake (which is certainly possible) or that you miss the point (which is also quite possible), but rather to launch an all-out attack[187] on his project by claiming that he ought not to have made the translation at all and ought not to have told us about the discrepancies between the Greek texts and the Latin, and that even if this were worth doing he was not at all competent to do it. Not only do all learned men both in Louvain and here disagree with you on each of these points, but the Pope, best and greatest of primates, who ought to take precedence over all learned men's votes, disagrees with you, too. For at his pious urging Erasmus obediently undertook this task, which with God's help he has now performed

twice with success, and thereby he has twice earned the Pope's special thanks and approval, as his solemn missives acknowledge.[188]

Therefore, given that this book contains the teaching of Christ, if I trusted the vicar of Christ to assess it, who has twice now declared the book useful, if I trusted the pope, I repeat, even though you oppose him and write that the book is pernicious, I judge that I have done nothing rash or unjust to you, even if your own book were completely unknown to me. But in fact it is not so totally unknown to me that I have not at least sampled enough of it to guess what the rest is like. For though it never reached me, it did reach certain people through the friendly solicitude of your close associates when they were surveying the judgments of others lest you might be placing inordinate trust in your own. When these people had read and considered the book thoroughly, and had judged the whole matter in such a way that they urged those who had submitted it that, if they wished to protect your reputation, they should write to you, urging you to abandon this task (and no doubt those same friends faithfully relayed this message to you), they then indicated a few of your principal points to me, too, as examples, the very points on which you seemed to feel that your victory was certain. As I said, my dear Lee, I am not presumptuous enough to hand down a verdict in disputes about theological topics lest anyone should rightly admonish me, "Let the cobbler stick to his last."[189] But even so, the notes which they showed me, which they clearly did as if these were the best ones, were mostly the kind that I feel even I can refute without any great effort. Consequently, when I found most of your principal notes were of this sort, I thought that I could fairly size up the rest on the basis of these, like a lion from his claw,[190] as the saying goes. For if a lion's claws do you no harm, there is no point in fearing his whiskers.

Certainly that argument about the term *proprium* [one's own] which you included in your letter to me, and which seems so substantial to you that in more than one letter you testify that you are amazed at Erasmus's impudence in daring to defend his own views when the truth is so obvious, seems to me, and to others as well, to be such a tenuous bit

---

185 *black ... know: Adages* 599 (*CWE* 32: 65–66)   186 See *EE* 4.169.   187 *launch*

an all-out attack: See *Adages* 3472 (*CWE* 36: 190).   188 See *EE* 2: 114–15, 436–38,

3: 387–88.   189 *Adages* 516 (*CWE* 32: 14)   190 *lion ... claw: Adages* 834 (*CWE* 32: 200)

of sophistry that we on the contrary are thoroughly amazed at your willingness to use it against him. For if you hold all mortals to Porphyry's *Eisagōgē* with such adamantine strictness[191] that, just because he defines *proprium* as that which is exclusively mine and not common to anyone else, therefore no one should use the same word in the way that all peoples everywhere openly do use it, it will then be a crime every time someone calls the country in which he was born his own country, or the parish in which he resides his own parish, or the father by whom he was sired his own father if he happens to have any brothers who have the same father in common with him. Although not even Porphyry is as troublesome on this point as you are, since he mentions many acceptable ways of employing that term. Nor would I have said anything at all about that term in the present letter if you yourself had not mentioned it in yours, since I indicated some time ago how I felt about this entire matter to your brothers and your closest friends, and I know that they passed on my feelings to you long ago, as I meant for them to, so that there would be no need for you to find out about my feelings now, for the first time, through a rumor being spread by Erasmians.

Now I come to your exposition, in which you rehearse the affair from the outset in an effort to show that Erasmus is wholly to blame for the birth and growth of this tragedy. But when it comes to this topic it is certainly worth seeing how you yourself show off the one and only kind of skill you concede to Erasmus and how you play the orator here, heaping up many words to exaggerate things which are basically petty. If anyone removed that mass of words and assembled the things by themselves, I think he would find nothing which ought to make you feel so mortally offended by Erasmus that for a chance to hurt him you would not even balk at subverting the common good of all men. For if anyone gathered up everything you have mentioned in your letters to me or to anyone else in which you magnify his affronts to you, the upshot of these things amounts to the fact that he has neglected your annotations. And to tell you the truth, many feel that this is not a sufficiently compelling reason for you, a man of Christian modesty, to make such a hostile attack on a work that you grant that you would

have promoted if—this is the way they interpret your conduct—his praise of you had met your expectations, though in fact you considered it stingy because of the small number of passages he granted that you had explained to him.[192] But you actually should have considered it an honor for such a great man in all fields of learning to grant he had learned anything at all from you, whether he was telling the truth or simply granted it out of politeness. And yet it is amazing how uncivil you are in denying him any competence at all in Sacred Scripture, whereas you claim a great deal for yourself: you go so far as to predict openly that even in his second edition, on which once again he lavished so much study and effort and for which he compared so many manuscripts, pored through so many authors, and also consulted so many great scholars, he would still have left many glaring errors if he had not corrected it according to your annotations, as if he could not have tracked down for himself, or with anyone else's assistance but yours, the things which you discovered.

My dear Lee, I value your intellect and learning as highly as anyone does; indeed I not infrequently boast of you. But I am sure you consider it a fine enough tribute to your intelligence if anyone merely compares it to that of Erasmus, and I think you do not expect anyone to prefer it to his, whereas it is well known that Erasmus's industriousness and devotion to study since boyhood have been unsurpassed. Thus I think my opinion of you is remarkably high if I do not despair of your one day hereafter becoming a man of the sort that Erasmus is now, but not before you have lived as many years as he has already, nor will I justly be thought to be doing you any injustice if meanwhile I think that he excels you as much in learning as he does in years, since indeed he has spent almost as many years on theology alone as you have spent on your entire literary education since boyhood.

And yet no one is further from the arrogance of which you accuse him. Who makes fewer definitive claims? Who makes rigid assertions more timidly, something many men do all too boldly? He merely points out what the books say. Letting everyone judge for himself, he does not require anyone to agree with him. And if he ever reveals his

---

191 *adamantaine strictness:* See *Adages* 643, 1241 (*CWE* 32: 94–94, 33: 151–52).

192 See Erasmus, *Apologia qua respondet* 146–47, 260–61; *EE* 4:142.

own views and takes issue with those who hold different ones, is he doing anything but what writers of all eras have been free to do as a matter of course? And yet he submits all of his views to the judgment of the church. He repeatedly grants that, being human, he may misconstrue many points in that work; whereas you, who fault him for immodesty, profess with a tone of great authority that you have perfected that work, with regard to theology at least (for I think that is what you mean by "your own province"), to the point that no one could find anything else in it that deserved to be criticized if only Erasmus corrected whatever you note. But when you profess this, you claim more for yourself alone than Erasmus's own modesty would let him accept, even if others freely bestowed it on him, or than I personally would concede to you both put together, even though I concede you a great deal and everyone concedes him almost everything. And though he needs advice less than anyone, no one appreciates advice more than he does. This is quite clear even in the letters he wrote, both to England and to many other countries, to the people whose judgment he trusted the most, some of whom told him what they themselves thought. He thanked them all and accepted the advice some had given, while his written responses led others to see their mistakes so that they themselves thanked him for teaching them even as they were trying to teach him. Certainly I recall no one who created an uproar because not all his counsels were accepted as if they were gospel. For I have no idea what you mean when you write that he would not even let More advise him, since I have never considered myself such a great man that Erasmus should need my advice, whether about any aspect of learning or in his decisions about matters of general importance.

Now as for what you write about the ungracious way he received Dorp's advice, I have no idea whether there might have been some secret feuding between them, but certainly in the apology in which he replied to Dorp publicly[193] he replied with such modesty and indeed with such reverence, despite being provoked and to some extent rudely berated, that nothing else will ever win so much honor for Dorp as the fact that, even after being offended by him, Erasmus conceded him so much authority. This in itself makes it difficult to convince me that

Dorp, having forgotten that favor, would wish to injure once more a friend so honorably disposed toward him. I am confirmed in that opinion by this in particular: that when his feelings cooled down he decided to suppress that harsh letter which he had dictated in the heat of the moment; and on this basis I, too, suppressed mine in turn, since I am always more eager to silence and bury such quarrels, which can do little good and a great deal of harm, than to foster them. Since that time I have loved and esteemed Dorp so much that when you were about to depart for Louvain I urged you to form an especially close tie with him out of all the Louvain academics. I would certainly never have done so if I had not assumed that he was definitely the right man to make you start loving Erasmus (for to be truthful with you, my dear Lee, we knew you were not any too fair in your view of Erasmus even then), since Erasmus has such love for him. And by nature Erasmus is certainly so quick to forgive that I doubt you could find anyone anywhere who would have shown so much patience in bearing so many conspicuous affronts if he had had the same power to retaliate or who would have refrained from indulging his grief now and then by repaying abuse with abuse.[194] For not even when some selected various passages from his minor works as a basis for slander, so that there could be no doubt about whom they were attacking, and then slandered his reputation with all sorts of shameless abuse, not even then did Erasmus repay them with the insults that such men deserve, but dissembling their malice he thought it enough to defend his own writings. He was so generous in sparing their honor that he not only left it unimpaired but to some extent actually enhanced it. And yet this same immoderate modesty of his is undoubtedly the main reason that this hydra is constantly growing new heads[195] after losing so many already. Otherwise I am sure some would not have attacked him so wantonly if they had seen others like them repulsed now and then with a bit more asperity.

Now I come to the end of your first letter, where you indicate that, with the agreement or professed agreement of Erasmus, you have submitted this entire quarrel to the judgment of the reverend father, the bishop of Rochester, to whom you have forwarded the volume of your annotations. This is one

193 See *EE* 2: 90–114.   **194** *abuse with abuse:* See 1 Pt 2:23.   **195** *hydra . . . heads:* See *Adages* 290 (*CWE* 32: 238).

action that everyone praises greatly, whether you acted with Erasmus or alone, both because you have turned your attention to peace and because you have chosen a peacemaker who is not only a partic-
5 ularly well-qualified judge because of his singular learning, which he now has the world to attest, but is also unlikely, because of his extraordinary piety, to let anything good in either book go to waste; a man who moreover loves both of you so much that
10 he will devote all his energies[196] to concord, and a man of such skill and resourcefulness that he will easily find a way to satisfy both of you.

But indeed (to move on to your second letter) to the extent that this wholesome proposal of yours
15 was a holy idea in the first place, whether it was a mutual plan or—as you write—entirely your own, to this same extent whichever of you is to blame for subverting the plan deserves serious reproach. I my-self neither blame nor exonerate either one of you. I
20 will merely state how the affair looks to others, who begin by observing that while you want it to look as if you were alone in soliciting the bishop's judgment it looks as if you were the first to decline it again, indeed first to the point of being virtually alone in
25 declining it. For it is still unconfirmed that Erasmus has rejected it, since he sent his book first and has written no letter recalling it from a judge he could not shun in any case, since by publishing the book he had made everyone his judge. On the other hand,
30 some time ago you sent the book over here secretly to others, but you completely concealed the affair from the bishop; and only now, when he offers you fatherly advice not to get involved with this work, you appoint him your judge. But you do so in such
35 a way that he did not learn that he had been given this office before learning that it had been taken away. For your book did not reach him, and neither did your letter declaring him judge, before another letter arrived to deprive him of his judgeship and
40 to announce your independent decision to publish without waiting for anyone's judgment. When peo-ple compare these and other observations, they cer-tainly begin to suspect you were never sincere about that plan of choosing a judge.
45 This suspicion is certainly strengthened by your own defense, among other things, a defense many view as exceedingly weak, in which you want to

make it appear that you were the target of a passage in Erasmus's *Apology* which no one considers has anything to do with you. For you do not find your
50 name in the passage, nor do you acknowledge the characteristics described there. Furthermore, there are many other people who have done him some wrong and who are more intimate colleagues of La-tomus; indeed there are some whom those who fre-
55 quently travel here from there describe in a hardly more flattering light[197] than the person in that pas-sage, whoever he may be. Thus though there is no pretext for linking the passage to you, there may be certain traces which might lead the reader to any of
60 those men who are cunningly dissembling the mat-ter and exploiting your own credulity to dissociate themselves from that role by conferring it on you, who so gladly accept it. And in this mask they lead you onstage and dishonor you publicly with their
65 applause while your friends pity you, your enemies laugh, and these men feel especially pleased with themselves and rejoice in having been wily enough to trick you into acting their part as a stand-in.

"But," you say, "I have caught him red-handed.
70 For when I complained to him through my brother about this injury, even though he denied he had written those statements against me, he refused when I asked him to testify to that effect with at least an apology."[198] My dear Lee, what you de-
75 manded would not have been easy for him or ben-eficial to you. For then when one person after an-other made such a demand of him, he would either have had to hurt someone by turning him down and provoke open hostility against himself in the
80 place of a secret feud, or else he would have had to damage his own cause by praising someone pub-licly whom he might soon be forced to attack in an explicit way. But you think it will safeguard your honor if he testifies in writing that not one of those
85 statements he wrote was directed against you, as if otherwise they might seem to fit you. Would it not be a fine way to clear you indeed if he promptly ap-pended a note to that passage saying, "I hereby ad-monish everyone not to let undue suspicion cause
90 him to suspect that these statements were written or intended against Lee"? How much better you would have safeguarded yourself by not applying to yourself statements that had nothing to do with

196 *all his energies: Adages* 326 (*CWE* 31: 328)   **197** *describe . . . light:* See *Adages* 306   (*CWE* 31: 323–24).   **198** See *EE* 4: 161, 4: 200; *Apologia qua respondet* 262–63.

you, and by rejecting as a malicious and spiteful interpreter anyone who attempted to transfer them to you, than by taking the matter upon yourself in such a way that you either appear to confess to the statements he wrote or you lack anything to complain about!

Even though, my dear Lee, I see you shutting out my opinion before it is offered, since you think that whoever does not urge the immediate release of those annotations of yours either has scant concern for your honor or certainly does not watch out for it well enough, I myself will not hesitate to endanger my own reputation in your eyes on both counts before I would withhold the advice that I think most expedient for your reputation, and that means, above all, the advice to refrain from the publication of this volume, which will do you no good and earn you much ill will. For when you yourself suppose that this step will make everyone recognize either that you deserve all the credit if Erasmus has corrected any errors or that his stubbornness is to blame if he failed to correct them even after you warned him, you are taking something for granted that you will probably have a hard time making others believe, namely that he bought off your scribes and thus found out about all his errors from you. For you undercut your own assertion by deciding to publish your book before you have even seen his second edition; this is something that many believe you would never have done unless you had some hope that he might still have overlooked some of his errors through his ignorance of your annotations. For if you thought that he had already gained access to your annotations, you could have no doubt that either he would already have emended those passages or at least he would see a good way to defend himself: if he does see one, there would be no reason for you to anticipate winning much glory; on the other hand, if he has emended, you could scarcely avoid disrepute for attempting to win glory perversely, as if, backwardly angling for praise, you were uselessly going to point out not the book's present faults but its past ones.

"But," you say, "I must vindicate my honor, which he has damaged severely by claiming not only that my annotations are trifles but that I support them with the pronouncements of the moderns." By the way, my dear Lee, I do not see how this is consistent with your other views, since you indict Erasmus—as if it were a capital crime—for conceding the moderns too little authority, though he certainly concedes them enough, whereas I doubt that anyone detracts from them more than you do in considering that it dishonors you if he says you support your annotations with the pronouncements of moderns. But if your honor had been sullied so thoroughly that it had to be vindicated, and if there were no other way to cleanse it but to publish this book of yours at once, even though it is more respectable to bear even some loss of renown than to show such an inordinate regard for our own welfare that it drives us to injure the welfare of many,[199] even so I can easily forgive you, today's morals being what they are,[200] if you care more about your own good than about anyone else's.[201] But in my view your honor has not been so terribly slighted, and even if it had, it could scarcely be salvaged with this publication. For that passage in his *Apology* has nothing at all to do with you, and in the letters he has written to England the last thing he appeared to be doing, or indeed even thinking of doing, was injuring your reputation. On the other hand, people here have been whispering for almost a whole year about what you have written against him, though I have not yet seen any good man who is pleased with your plan, nor have I yet perceived any signs of his feeling offended with you, unless we count his recent expressions of some grief at your actions against him, though he certainly writes much more temperately about you than you do about him.[202] And if anyone weighs both your stories I am certainly afraid he will convict you rather than Erasmus of being unjust, unless anyone thinks that the tales he has heard about you are untrue. I myself am as eager to think so as you should be to think that those tales which the same scandalmongers tell you about him are untrue, for if you think that these men are liars, which you will if you want other men to absolve you, you will likewise absolve him of the injustice with which you now charge him.

But you talk about some letter or other in which he has attacked you severely. I do not know if you can produce it, but one thing I do know, my dear Lee, is that there is a letter from you—and an autograph

199 *regard…many:* See Terence, *Andria* 125–28; Cicero, *De legibus* 1.18.49.

200 *today…are:* Terence, *Phormio* 55

201 *more…else's:* See *Adages* 291 (*CWE* 31: 310–11).   **202** See *EE* 3: 459–60.

letter, at that, which you cannot disclaim—from which one may deduce that you yourself both entered upon and proceeded with those annotations in a far different spirit from the one you profess now, calling on your own conscience so often to vouch for it, and that you actually entered upon them in such a way that before you set out, as they say, you had already come to a verdict,[203] prejudging the whole crop to be worthless before you had even seen the shoots, even though all good men everywhere who knew anything of the farmer were confident that it would come to an excellent and beautiful harvest.

But as I started to say, even if you were called on to vindicate your honor I scarcely think you will achieve that objective with this publication, and I fear that while trying to cleanse it in this way you will actually cover it with more mire and filth.[204] For first of all, I see that you are simply mistaken in a number of passages, and it is not unlikely that you are equally mistaken in several which I have not seen. Furthermore, a number of your points are not very important, as not even you will deny; a number of points, even if they do not openly contradict you, certainly do not afford you much support; and a sizable number are points which have long been controversial and on which the judge has yet to rule.[205] And if you subtract these from your total, the rest of the reckoning will be minuscule, and at any rate not large enough to justify your drawing up a new ledger—not to mention one thing which other people are mentioning, who consider it very untimely to point out mistakes which have already been emended.

This is how your case would stand even if you had found a mute adversary, which you know very well yours is not. As it is, since the case against you will be argued by a consummate master in arguing all kinds of cases, who has also devoted more labor and study to this case than to all the others he has ever prepared, certainly, my dear Lee, you will not believe how many things you will hear that you never expected, and if you could have conceived of them before now you would undoubtedly have chosen to have nothing to do with those ill-omened labors of yours—would that you could simply dispense with them! For any trifles you note he will reduce altogether to nothing; anything that is not very helpful to you he will treat in a way that will even make it hurt you; anything that has so far seemed ambiguous he will clearly resolve against you; and if he has altered anything for the better he will not only not thank you on that account, he will even arraign you for insolence, and a thoroughly ludicrous specimen of it at that, as if you not only glory in playing Epimetheus[206] after the fact and in giving us warnings we no longer need, warning us to shun rough spots and holes which have already been evened out, but you also seek praise which should go to the diligence of others, copying whole in your own annotations every note you could find made by him or by others and presenting the offspring of these other men as if they were your own, some of which you continue to find handsome even though their true parents have thrown them away as amorphous and misbegotten monstrosities. But when he finally comes to the points about which he can clearly prove you are mistaken, you have no cause to expect the same sort of kindness he has always displayed until now in sparing others. Since he sees that this trait has provoked many men to be bold in attacking him, he will undoubtedly alter his tactics,[207] and I fear he will make an example of you so that others will not make more trouble for him in the hope of encountering his usual politeness.

Such a reaction is one for which even your judgment should pardon him. For you feel you have cause for a bitter attack on him, whether because you think it wrong to keep silent about anything he left uncorrected or because, even if he left nothing of the sort, you still need to redeem and restore your own honor, which would be totally ruined if all of Europe—as if common folk care for such things[208]—thought that your annotations were trifles. How much more justly you ought to forgive him for answering your freedom with similar freedom, whether his work as it has now been revised retains none of the things that you criticized or the things you reprove as his errors are things that his conscience assures him are perfectly correct (and without any lapse into arrogance he can trust his own judgment no less surely than you can trust yours). Not to mention that all of this agitation

---

203 *before . . . verdict:* See Quintilian 4.5.4; *Adages* 1206 (*CWE* 33: 133–34). **204** *cleanse . . . filth:* See *Adages* 967 (*CWE* 32: 263). **205** *the judge . . . rule:* Horace, *Ars poetica* 78. **206** See *Adages* 31 (*CWE* 31: 78–80); Epimetheus was a Titan and Prometheus's brother; true to his name, Epimetheus lacked his brother's foresight. **207** *alter his tactics: Adages* 860 (*CWE* 32: 213) **208** *as if . . . things:* Terence, *Andria* 185

Letters: On Humanism, 1505–20

on your part is intended to keep him from making people think that any minor points you had annotated were either not right or not very significant, whereas he has to contend against you to escape major notoriety, which he could not escape if your notes on major points were correct, as if he had done something that everyone thinks to be wrong, namely handled holy matters in an unholy way.[209] This being the case, believe me, if you rouse him by publishing those annotations, you can only expect him to forget his customary gentleness and to defend his own rights with all possible rigor.

And so I am very afraid you may seem to impair your own honor in a tactless endeavor to vindicate it at a point when, as far as I can see, he has not yet impugned it. I have seen others suffer the same fate before. Though the outcome must tell whether they were less safe than you are, they were certainly no less convinced of their safety than you are until they had heard his response. Only then did they find out that without the host, as it is said, they had reckoned the cost of their dinner in vain, since whoever does this has to reckon again; for the host generally adds some expense to the bill that they either forgot or conveniently omitted in order to spare themselves.

Therefore, my dearest Lee, I implore you again and again not to stake too much on your self-confidence. Since you implored me in the name of friendship, a name I hold especially sacred, to be fair to you in this episode, may I be as assured, my dear Lee, of retaining your friendship forever as I am convinced that I have no way of showing more fairness than by imploring you in return, as I fervently do, by whatever is even more sacred than friendship, to dispense with these odious reproaches, to resume friendly relations with Erasmus (for I would venture to give you my word that he would not reject them), and to give up the idea of accepting a province[210] which you could not resign once you had entered it, and in which for the rest of your life — which I hope is much less than half finished — amid tumult, reviling, contention, and vexations more vexing than vestments of pitch, my dear Lee, you will feel more as if you are burning than actually living. Recover your own Christian charity instead, and retrieve your serenity. Live this life in contentment and peace. Scorn the loss of one ill-omened

book which would even draw down some ill will on your offspring to come, and seek out a more promising theme for yourself to write up in an elegant way, so that when it eventually appears it will benefit and please everyone, it will both endear your fame to your contemporaries and commend it very favorably to posterity, and above all it will be the sort of work for which you can hope God will provide the supreme recompense, for that kind of reward is much richer than all mortal goods. I have no objection, if there happens to be some point germane to that theme where Erasmus or any other writer has made a particularly serious mistake, and it seems clear that the world should be warned of it so that no one else will trip up over the same obstacle[211] — I have no objection, I repeat, if you too let us know of the stumbling blocks we should avoid; nor could any fair person object to it, provided that the point was discussed with enough moderation to prove that the need for a warning had simply presented itself and that you had not sought out a pretext for fault-finding. But who does not see how that other course deviates from this limitation when book is deliberately pitted against book like enemy against enemy? To deter you from starting a fight of this sort, my dear Lee, once again I beseech and implore you with all the force I can muster, by your honor, which is practically dearer to me than my own; by my hopes for you, which are as great as I have ever conceived for any of my countrymen; by your love for your country, which you are about to embarrass by clouding the bright reputation you owe it; and by the solicitude of your friends, who are all apprehensively joining their own prayers to mine: spare yourself and your country alike, and let no one say either that Lee or that anyone English envies Christendom its present advances. But if you are completely obsessed with so noble a passion for glory that you would rather break your own jaw-tooth[212] than pass up a fight with Erasmus, I can do nothing but pity your plight, but for my country's sake I will do everything in my power to establish that this action of yours, which I see invites so much ill will from all virtuous and learned men, is the act of a Briton, not of Britain, though I will always maintain our friendship to whatever extent you permit me to do so. Farewell. 1 May 1519.

209 *as if . . . way:* See *Adages* 855 (CWE 32: 211–12).   **210** *accepting a province:* See   *Adages* 1341 (CWE 33: 210–11).   **211** *no one . . . obstacle: Adages* 408 (CWE 31: 302)   **212** *break . . . jaw-tooth: Adages* 1159 (CWE 33: 104–5)

83. To a Monk[213]

<1519–20>

A learned epistle from a man of renown, Master
Thomas More, in response to a certain monk's
ignorant and virulent letter, a senseless invective,
belaboring, among other issues, Erasmus's
translation, "In the beginning was Speech, etc."

Dearest brother in Christ, I have received your long
letter, fraught with various remarkable tokens of
how much you love me. For could any affection be
stronger than the one which makes you so inordinately concerned for my well-being as to fear even
imaginary dangers? For you fear that I cherish Erasmus so much that his contact is going to corrupt
me, that I adore the man's writings so much that (in
your words) his new and unorthodox teaching is going to infect me. And lest this should happen, first
you fill up a number of pages with an all-out polemic, one might say, against the man's learning and
character, and then at length, in the holiest of tones,
you pray, plead, and indeed all but conjure me in
the name of God's mercy to take care to shun him.
First you quote the apostle's reminder that "Bad
company corrupts a good character."[214] Then you
cite, from Erasmus's *Adagia,* "A person who lives
with a lame man will learn how to limp."[215] Finally
you draw on the testimony of a poet as well, doubtless so as to make up a triad: "When we look on another's affliction, our eyes are afflicted, as well."[216]
With these arguments and others like them, although there is no danger of the sort that you fear,
you have tried hard to drive me away from the place
where you think (or at least claim to think) that the
danger resides.

Thus, of course, I could rightly be seen as an ingrate for failing to greet such a gracious concern
for my welfare with unbounded gratitude. I would
be even more of an ingrate, in view of the way that
your own fervid transports of love made you fear I
would stumble when you saw me walking on even
terrain, if I looked on without the least qualm as you
ran on the rim of a precipice or if I did not shout
you a warning that you ought to watch your own
step and begin your own wary and cautious descent

from where you are in danger of falling. Thus I will
start by going over my own position, showing everything here to be safe, and then I will go on to show
you that that lofty stronghold of yours from which,
smug and secure, you look down upon our friend
Erasmus is dangerously shaky.

For, first of all, how is it dangerous for me to believe that Erasmus has translated many New Testament passages better than the old translator, or
for me to believe that Erasmus knows more about
Greek and Latin literature than he did? Nor do I
just believe it, I see it and know it for a fact; nor
could anyone doubt it who has any command of
both languages. How is it dangerous for me to enjoy reading those books which the most learned
and most pious people are virtually unanimous in
praising, and which the Pope, best and greatest of
primates, has twice now declared to be useful to
scholars?[217] How can I learn such dangerous doctrines from a teacher who himself never takes a definitive position, who presents both his own views
and those of others in such a way that the reader remains free to judge them?[218] And even if he made assertions which were utterly false, I am not so stupid
that I cannot tell what will square with true faith or
with soundness of morals, nor am I so committed
to anyone's opinions that I will not freely disagree
with him where I have good cause.

As I said, then, Erasmus's opinions are no threat
to me, even if (as you write) there were some un-
sound opinions in what he has written. But you, on
the other hand, as I see to my sorrow, are sadly in
danger, through some trick of fortune, of having
his numerous volumes, replete with both learning
and true piety, more such volumes than anyone else
has produced for the last several centuries, transformed by some wily magician from a health-giving
cure to a poison. Believe me, for the love that I bear
you I was unable to read without profound sorrow
your shockingly heated attack, in which you so in-
temperately vomit abuse by the wagonload[219] onto
a man who has done you no wrong and has publicly
done all a service, whereas you belittle his learning,
rave against his life-style, call him "vagrant" and
"pseudo-theologian," cry "slanderer" at him, and
brand him with charges of heresy and schism, going

---

213 The anonymous addressee has been
identified as John Batmanson, a London
Carthusian.   **214** 1 Cor 15:33   **215** *Adages*
973 (*CWE* 32: 266–67)   **216** Ovid,
Remedia amoris 615   **217** See *EE* 3: 387–88,
2: 436–38.   **218** See *EE* 3: 324.   **219** *abuse*
by the wagonload: See *Adages* 673–74 (*CWE*
32: 110–11).

so far in your scurrility that you even proclaim him a "herald of Antichrist," even though you do hedge that insult very tactfully indeed: as you make such an outrageous accusation, you say you do not want to make it.

My old, dear friend, tell me, what sly, crafty demon has managed to plant so much guile and insidious subterfuge in a heart as sincere and as candid as yours was while you were still a layman, in the heart of a monk and (a word which deserves much more reverence) a priest of so many years' standing, to the point where you are able to say, "I do not call him a heretic, but whoever acts thus is a heretic. I do not proclaim him schismatic, but whoever acts thus is schismatic. I do not pronounce him a herald of Antichrist, but what if this very assertion concerning Erasmus had come straight from God? But I will forbear, lest your hopes for me should surpass what you see me or hear me to be." By all that is sacred in this world and the next, what do I hear you saying? At this point I appeal to your conscience: does it not make you blush, does it not make you tremble all over, when you trick out such an impious charge with such monstrous extravagance, when you take up some nobody's criminal lie and recite it to us with such sanctimony, as if by divine revelation, and when you take defamation of character, the manifest work of the devil, and call God its author? Now as for your saying, as if out of modesty, that you would forbear lest I look for great things from you, would to God it were as certain that each of us felt truly humble as it is that your tale would not have raised my opinion of you in the least, even if you had openly stated that it was your own revelation, even if you had mentioned the name of the angel or demon who brought you the message, it being one I would not have believed even from a sworn witness.[220] Rather, I would have warned you against being too quick to believe every spirit,[221] especially that one, for however brightly he had shone with false light he would still have betrayed himself as an angel of darkness by his buzz of detraction and slander, a sure mark of Satan. I would rather have countered by echoing that verse from Paul, "In the latter times some shall depart from the faith, hearkening unto spirits of error and the doctrines of devils who speak lies in hypocrisy and have consciences seared with a hot iron,"[222] and

also that other verse of his, "Let no man lead you astray in a voluntary humility and worshiping of angels, intruding vainly into things he has not seen, puffed up by his carnal conceit."[223] For these verses would be more to the point than the one which you foolishly transfer to yourself from the apostle. As it is, though, since you indicate that this revelation was not yours but some other fellow's, I am even less impressed. For though I do not doubt that God does now and then bestow some revelations on mortals, I am nonetheless not so foolishly credulous as to be frightened out of my wits by whatever some madman dreams up, some impostor invents, or else some evil spirit suggests to the man he possesses.

I do not doubt that your other informant owes his inspiration to similar unholy rituals, the one who you write warned you as follows: "Be assured that Erasmus, who has such a fine train of words to attend him, has unorthodox opinions regarding the Catholic faith and Holy Scripture. He frequently shows this is so whenever he can get a private hearing. I speak from repeated experience." So much for that fine fellow's report to you about Erasmus, though you say that, whoever he is, he has also thought up a distinguished apology against Erasmus; then you warn me not to suspect that the fellow is Lee. Rest assured, I do not suspect Lee, since I feel quite convinced that though he has been carried away by some passion or other to the point that he now feels ashamed to retreat, his own mind is endowed with such virtue and shaped with such learning that even though he may quarrel about scholarly issues he will not break out into abuse. But some people describe this informant of yours as a man very different from Lee. For though you call him a man of good faith, a man clearly both serious and (using your own pretty phrase) genial-mannered, honorable by the standards of secular dignity, and as conspicuous for personal integrity as for his illustrious learning, he is drawn in a quite different light by the people who know him the best: not a man of good faith, far from genial in character, and actually churlish, though honored by some — honored rather than honorable. But the extent of his learning is shown in the apology you praise, whereas some learned men who have seen it and wish the man well, and for that reason urged

220 See *Adages* 3461 (*CWE* 36: 183–84).   **221** See 1 Jn 4:1.   **222** 1 Tm 4:1   **223** Col 2:18

him to burn it or suppress it forever, insist that the man is deranged to the point of sheer lunacy, though he does have a few lucid intervals. And as they were sketching him thus I could not get them to say who he was; they themselves did not want to disgrace him by name before that illustrious apology came forth to provide a definitive sample of his wit and learning.

But if you please, let us ponder a little just how much good faith that perfidious fellow can claim whose good faith makes you think that Erasmus's opinions regarding the faith are unorthodox, a fellow who goes on to say (lest you doubt the good faith of so faithless a man) that Erasmus repeatedly shows this is so, whenever he can get a private hearing, and that he himself speaks from experience, and repeated experience at that, so that you could be sure that he heard the fact frequently from none other than Erasmus himself. How the truth never fails to assert itself! How contrivers of falsehoods are either exposed through some chance event, balked by the facts of the matter, or given away by their own indiscretion, like shrew-mice![224] For supposing Erasmus did have wrong opinions regarding the faith, how likely is it that he would be too stupid to see how dangerous this would be for him, and how likely is it that he would always be looking for people, or begging them even, to let him inform them in private that he was a heretic? For as that good-faith witness attests, a private hearing was all the inducement he needed.

But how long did Erasmus live with Colet?[225] How long with the reverend father, the bishop of Rochester?[226] How long with the most reverend primate of Canterbury?[227] Not to mention Mountjoy, Tunstall, Pace, and Grocyn,[228] with whom he has associated long and often. I would rightly look silly if I tried to put into words any part of the praise that is due to these men, since everyone knows that no one can praise any one of them richly enough. Which of them has not spoken with him in the most perfect privacy a hundred times? Which of them, even once, has heard anything which could foster the slightest suspicion that Erasmus's opinions regarding the faith are not perfectly orthodox?

For if they had detected the least indication of any such fault, they are certainly too good to have concealed such a monstrous discovery. But which one of them all has not always cherished Erasmus and yet come to love him all the more upon longer and deeper acquaintance?

But I suppose he did not dare trust men such as these, having too much respect for their piety. Naturally, then, he was looking for someone whose conscience he need not respect, and from whom he need not fear betrayal, a person whose face, words, and lifestyle plainly showed him to be an initiate of the same cult. Such a one must your much-praised informant have been — yes, that man of good faith, serious, genial, honorable, learned, and full of integrity, to whom you now see that Erasmus would never have confided his secret so often unless, besides all the remarkable gifts you assign him, he were also a heretic. Though he says that he speaks from repeated experience, if we ask him to prove that he had even one such experience I think he will confess that it cannot be proved, since he maintains that the secret was vouchsafed him only in private. But whoever accuses a man of a crime yet confesses that he cannot prove it is undoubtedly either a slanderer[229] or something close to it. But then too, since he speaks from repeated experience, let us ask where they talked over their heresies or when they had any dealings with each other at all. It must have been some time ago, since Erasmus has long been away. Now then, why did the man hold his tongue when Erasmus was here and when it would have done much more good to expose him, so that we would have shunned the offender, than it can do now, when Erasmus is gone and when we are not in as much danger? For in books no secret is buried too deep for sharp eyes to uncover it. But I am taking more time than I should in refuting this sham revelation and exposing this singular witness, accuser, and self-declared suspect all rolled into one, who you now see is either a fraud and a criminal liar or, if he were telling the truth, a still worse sort of criminal, namely a long-standing partner in crime and a tardy informant — in sum, whether lying or telling the truth, a man wholly perfidious. There

224 See *Adages* 265 (*CWE* 31: 289).
225 John Colet (*ca.* 1466–1519), dean of St. Paul's Cathedral, was a spiritual influence on More and Erasmus. **226** John Fisher, Bishop of Rochester (1459–1535)

227 William Warham (*ca.* 1450–1535), Archbishop of Canterbury **228** William Blount, Lord Mountjoy (1478–1534), Erasmus's patron; Cuthbert Tunstall (1474–1559), Bishop of London; Richard

Pace (*ca.* 1483–1536); William Grocyn (*ca.* 1446–1519) **229** *Adages* 1281 (*CWE* 33: 178–79)

can certainly be nothing obscure about Erasmus's own faith, which has been brightly illuminated by the many exertions and vigils, the many dangers and material and physical hardships that he has sus-
5 tained for Sacred Scripture, the very supply-house of faith, nor indeed is there anything new in fabricating a charge of heresy, something that can be done against every good man. Long ago Satan's followers launched the same charge at the saintliest of
10 men with such violence and craft that the same men whose labors had made the faith flourish were compelled to give an account of their faith by publishing their own creeds.

Now I will turn away from the testimony of that
15 good-faith witness of yours, and from those dreams which were sent down from heaven through the gate of horn mentioned by Homer,[230] and I will proceed to the points in Erasmus's own books which you use as a pretext to charge him with blatant im-
20 piety. The most serious of your indictments is this, that "that impudent fellow Erasmus does not hesitate to make the outrageous assertion in many places in his writings that even the holiest and most learned fathers, those illustrious instruments of the
25 Holy Spirit, Jerome, Ambrose, Hilary, Augustine, and others like them, whose light has illuminated the Catholic church well enough that it has no need of this obscure fellow to darken and stain it anew, were occasionally wrong." Does it really strike you
30 as outrageous for anyone to say that the very men you singled out were occasionally wrong? What if those very men, whose unbidden defender you are, should agree with Erasmus? Will it not make a joke of your vehemence on their behalf if they scorn
35 your support?

Now then, you deny that any of these men was ever wrong. Tell me this: when Augustine maintains that Jerome has mistranslated some places in Scripture, while Jerome vindicates his performance, is
40 neither one wrong?[231] When Augustine asserts that the fidelity of the Septuagint version should not be

impugned, while Jerome denies this and contends that the Septuagint translators made mistakes, is neither one wrong?[232] When Augustine adduces
45 that tale of their perfect consensus according to which all of them were guided by the Holy Spirit to produce the same version in their separate cells, while Jerome derides that silly fiction, is neither one wrong, though their viewpoints are diametrically
50 opposed?[233] When Jerome interprets the letter to the Galatians as if Paul were only pretending to rebuke Peter, while Augustine denies this, is neither one wrong?[234] When Jerome disapproves of Augustine's work on the Psalms, while Augustine ap-
55 proves of it, is neither one wrong?[235] When Augustine regards every lie as a sin, while Jerome praises an opportune lie, is neither one wrong?[236] When Augustine denies that a man who divorced his first wife for fornication can marry again in her lifetime,
60 while Ambrose affirms he can do so, is neither one wrong?[237] Jerome maintained that to marry one wife before baptism and another thereafter does not count as two marriages; the Church now maintains he was mistaken. Augustine asserts that all de-
65 mons, and all angels too, are corporeal substances; no doubt you deny it.[238] He asserts that infants who die without baptism are condemned to an eternity of physical suffering; how many believe that today besides Luther, who they say clings fast to the teach-
70 ings of Augustine, and is reviving this obsolete notion?[239] Did not most of the ancient saints believe that the Blessed Virgin was conceived in original sin?[240] But some recent writers sprang up to deny it, and most of Christendom has sided with these men
75 against all the ancients.

There would be no end to it if I tried to list all the points on which it is quite clear that the most learned and holiest men had mistaken ideas, and if you read their books you could not overlook their
80 mistakes if you understood what you were reading. Thus though you call him impudent, you prove to be not a little more reckless than he is when you

230 See Homer, *Odyssey* 19.562–67.
231 See Jerome, *Epistolae* 104.45, 112.21–22 (*PL* 22: 833–34, 929–31). **232** See Augustine, *De doctrina Christiana* 2.15.22 (*PL* 34: 46); *De civitate dei* 18.42 (*PL* 41: 602–3); Jerome, *Praefatio in Pentateuchum* (*PL* 28: 150). **233** *diametrically opposed: Adagia* 945 (*CWE* 32: 254) **234** See Jerome, *Epistolae* 56.3–4, 67.3–7, 112.4–7, 116.4–30 (*PL* 22: 566–67, 648–50, 917–27, 937–50).

235 See Jerome, *Epistolae* 105.5, 112.20 (*PL* 22: 836–37, 928–29). **236** See Augustine, *De mendacio* (*PL* 40: 505–16); Jerome, *Commentarii in epistolam ad Galatas* 1.2 (*PL* 26: 339–40). **237** See Mt 5:32, 19:9; Mk 10:11; Lk 16:18; 1 Cor 7:11–15; Augustine, *De sermone Domini in monte* 1.14 (*PL* 34: 1248–49), *De coniugiis adulterinis* 1.1 (*PL* 40: 451); Ambrose, *Commentaria in epistolam ad Corinthios primam* 7 (*PL*

17: 218C). **238** See Jerome, *Epistolae* 69 (*PL* 22: 653–59). **239** See Augustine, *De divinatione daemonum* 4 (*PL* 40: 584–86). **240** See Augustine, *Sermones* 294.2–3 (*PL* 38: 1336–37); *Enchiridion* 93 (*PL* 40: 275); *De peccatorum meritis et remissione* 1.16 (*PL* 44: 120–21); *Opus imperfectum contra Iulianum* 2.117, 3.199 (*PL* 45: 1191, 1333); Luther, *Sermon von dem sakrament der Taufe* (*WA* 2: 727–37).

make the reckless assertion that those men were never wrong, an assertion you cannot defend without showing that you either did not read their books or did not understand them. Worse yet, how can you be so brazen as to rebuke him for saying just what you say? For no doubt you yourself say Augustine was wrong in asserting that demons have bodies and in damning infants, Jerome was wrong about double marriages, and almost all the ancients were wrong about the Virgin's conception. And yet, even though this is so, and though those holy fathers disagreed with each other so often in interpreting Sacred Scripture, and though this is too obvious for anyone to deny it, it is amazing how childishly you storm and turn heaven and earth upside down[241] every time someone detects either error in Hugh of Saint Cher[242] or delirium in Nicolas de Lyra.[243] Augustine was not afraid to say he granted no man besides the apostles so much authority that he would accord an unquestioning faith to what he said except insofar as he could prove it clearly either from Scripture or from reason.[244] You think you put all the saints forever in your debt by protesting that they were never wrong. But they either laugh at your ignorance or deplore your misguided devotion. Nor do they want defenders like you, since their charity has more regard for the diligence of those who warn others about it if the saints ever made a mistake than it does for the superstitious piety of those whose misguided defensiveness propagates such mistakes to the peril of others.

But when you go so far as to pit your style against his, you will have to forgive me, I simply cannot keep from laughing. For when you say he lacks that facility of speech which is intelligible to any reader and you censure and mock him for the way he at times mixes Greek words with Latin, you are so very clever that you never notice that this stricture of yours applies equally well to Jerome, on whom, whether you like it or not, those fine quips of yours also reflect, since he too intersperses Greek words in his Latin, while some of what he wrote for virgins is too learned for many theology professors to understand it today. What if Erasmus had written some treatise entirely in Greek? Would you not

then have much better reason to mock him than now, when he merely throws in some Greek words here and there? But our women could give the same reason for mocking all those who have written in Latin. What of this, that of all those who have in fact written in Latin, not one has ever written more plainly than he or perfected an easier style, to the point that Budé, a most learned man with regard to most things, did not hesitate to criticize Erasmus for an excessively easy style?[245] No one is more careful to shun far-fetched terms, though you charge he affects them, whereas those men who you say use a more modest style make up virtually every third word, men from whom I imagine you yourself must have learned those pet phrases of yours, "genial-mannered," "vagabond life-style," "tenebrosity," "identity," and other such gems.

But look here, though you make many other unjustified charges against Erasmus besides affectation of eloquence, he will confess to them all if he has ever affected as much eloquence in an entire volume as you sometimes affect in one line, when you ask, for example, "Then how will they answer these points, they who spend all their years on such short-lived, quick-withering, prettified flowerlets of rhetoric?" Out of all you profess to have read in the works of Erasmus, produce anything you have read as pretentious as this line of yours, which is ungrammatical as well. Nor am I mentioning this because I think you ought to be blamed for a solecism. I neither expect nor demand pure speech from you; I am not unaware that you never had free time to learn it, and even if you had had the time, you would still have lacked teachers to instruct you in it. I am mentioning these points to show that, since you think it is seemly for you to engage in such a strained affectation of eloquence before you even master your grammar, you should not take Erasmus to task for refusing to spurn the refinement which he made his own long ago and which waits on him now uninvited.

When you argue against studying languages it is not unamusing to hear you lament that in learning Greek and Hebrew we tend to lose the purity of our Latin, when you have just finished your merciless tirade against graceful Latin, as if there were such a

---

241 *turn … down: Adages* 281 (*CWE* 31: 300)   **242** Cardinal Hugh of St. Cher (1200–1263), author of *Concordantia*. **243** Nicolas de Lyra (1270–1340), author

of *Postillae perpetuae in universam Sacram Scripturam* **244** See Augustine, *Contra Faustam Manichaeum* 11.5 (*PL* 42: 249). **245** See *EE* 2.396–401, 464–70. Guillame

Budé (1467–1540) was a French humanist and friend of More and Erasmus.

vast difference between pure and graceful speech.[246] Besides, in the passage you cite, Jerome really complains of the harm done to the gracefulness of his speech, and he does so with no other aim than to recommend even more strongly his own study of Hebrew writings, since he thought them worth mastering even at the expense of Latin. But Greek writings are patently more useful still, whether we consider the New Testament (for it takes the same precedence over the Old that a substance has over a shadow or a reality over a figure), or the interpreters of Sacred Scripture (for almost all the finest and holiest of them wrote in Greek), or finally those arts we call liberal, as well as philosophy (for on these topics speakers of Latin wrote practically nothing). Furthermore you can scarcely deny that those Latins who knew the most Greek were also the most fluent in their own tongue, and that this was not only the general rule in the past but is still so today. Nor did Jerome himself write less gracefully after he mastered Hebrew than he did before, as his later works prove, even though he saw fit to apologize for his own style, whether for the reason I mentioned or else because he continually strives to sustain the impression that he never courted the eloquence which now attends him.

This is surely your most splendid touch: you finally come to the point of saying that you approve of a moderate acquaintance with languages and merely condemn too much study of them, as if the study of them had already been pushed well past the mean, while in fact it is still stopped well short of it. You profess that we ought to embrace pure speech with open arms,[247] as they say, yet you thunder with tragic extravagance against a graceful and elegant style, and you lament most pathetically that now a large portion of Christendom has been pitifully ensnared by its charms, though they once appealed only to heathens, as if all of the most ancient holy fathers had not been illustrious for their graceful style, whereas those who discuss Sacred Scripture today virtually desecrate the venerable majesty of that noble office with their impure speech.

But you think you have spoken so well on this topic that even later on, having bravely concluded the fight for that viewpoint, you crow like a victor, demanding, "So what is the point of adorning the verity of Sacred Scripture with flowerlets of speech, which both the apostles and the other doctors completely avoided as wholly absurd, especially since such ornaments seemed to be altogether at odds with the humble capacities of the modestly learned?" Finally, after staging this marvelous display of your rhetoric, you tie up your whole epilogue, ever so wittily, by borrowing a tag from the Gospels: "Older is better."[248] (One touch in these words is especially splendid: you link the apostles and those fathers of the early Church as if both groups employed the same style.) Augustine ventured to attribute eloquence also to the apostles[249]—an eloquence so proper to them that it cannot suit anyone else, nor can anyone else's suit them, though their own eloquence also teems with all sorts of rhetorical figures. Certainly those holy fathers—Jerome, I mean, Cyprian, and Ambrose—were a match for the most fluent speakers of their times.

Nor is eloquence an obstacle to lucidity of style. To the contrary, no obscure speaker is eloquent:[250] one of the cardinal precepts of rhetoric is that we should express ourselves clearly. If the apostles avoided refined speech especially because, as you put it, it seemed to be especially at odds with the humble capacities of the modestly learned, why are they still so obscure that neither the modestly learned nor the very learned understand them without making a great effort, and occasionally not even then? The most ancient and holiest fathers wrote both eloquently and clearly, and yet they are not clear to many theology professors today. Why is this so? Because no light, of course, can shine brightly enough to illuminate even the blind. For those fellows are not (as you put it) modestly learned, but rather, not learned at all. For one fact makes it quite clear that what keeps them from understanding the holy fathers is blindness on their part and not any darkness in what they are reading: young girls once understood what today's proud professors cannot.

I have already said that the style of the fathers is very refined; it is perfectly open, as well, to whoever knows Latin. For they reasonably thought that whoever wanted to understand them would either learn Latin or have their works translated into the vernacular, nor indeed could they guess that such monsters would ever ascend to the chairs of theology, men who to cover up for their own sloth would condemn as obscure every text not in Latino-Gothic. Now then, since you tie up your "stitchwork" from the Gospel (for that is your word for it) with "older is better," I admit that the eloquence of the earliest fathers is better than the stammering of the moderns; so you see that this "stitchwork" of yours, which I see you were marvelously proud of, emphatically strengthens Erasmus's position and recoils on you.[251]

Of the same stripe is what you regard as a cute little joke aimed at his work on Jerome: "You have spoiled the wine for us by watering it down."[252] When he purifies Jerome's works of so many corruptions, when he restores the true reading in so many passages, is this spoiling the wine for you by watering it down? Then why drink it diluted, since you can still get your old vinegar which, to a sick palate, tastes like pure wine? But as for determining what is genuine in that author's works, since the matter depends largely on considerations of style, I will certainly not hold it against you if you fail to see the reasons for Erasmus's verdict even when he points them out with his finger.

But then, since you wanted to show that Greek learning is not as necessary for the true understanding of Scripture as some think it is and that there was no need for the work that Erasmus devoted to retranslating the New Testament from Greek, you propose as a solid foundation the thesis that "those holy fathers," in your words, "Hilary and Augustine, asserted that the Septuagint version was sufficient[253] according to every criterion of scriptural truth; and indeed, if that were not sufficient," you say, "we also have the edition of Jerome, which all tongues rightly ought to acclaim, and we have many others which are both famous and likewise learned, and yet for some reason all these are supposed to be useless unless we add such a rendering as this one by an upstart translator."

See here, from the moment I saw you take up this particular task, since I knew you could never have learned what you needed to know to support your own case, I had no doubt that, even if you could blurt out a few general arguments, just as soon as you got down to the specific ones that you ought

to use to defend your own claims and refute the opposing ones, you would show how inadequately prepared you were for the business at hand. In the name of your faith I beseech you: since you have so many both famous and learned editions and so many translations of the New Testament that there is no need for the one by Erasmus, why are you keeping this priceless treasure all to yourself? I for one am not unaware that there were many of them long ago, and that Augustine professes that they were most useful, and yet I do not find anyone today who professes to have ever seen any apart from the Vulgate. Valla made useful notes on some passages, but he did not translate. Erasmus published those notes; someone else who himself had decided to discuss the same subject might well not have done so. Lefèvre d'Etaples has translated the Pauline epistles and not the whole Testament. Thus you have yet to exhibit those other translations besides the Septuagint and that of Jerome which are so famous and learned that we should accept them and throw away that of Erasmus.

Now Jerome, whose translation you say that you have, never made one, if you take his word for it; rather, he took what he saw was at that time the most current version and emended it according to trustworthy Greek texts. This is adequately established by his letter, "You compel me to make a new work out of an old one,"[254] for whoever can understand that letter adequately. Jerome's work was spoiled by the same agents of blight that now threaten that of Erasmus, the ignorance and the envy of those he endeavored to benefit. Certainly in the edition which is now chanted in churches there is hardly a trace of Jerome's work; indeed, you can still see the very corruptions that he thought should be emended, some of which Erasmus has mentioned in passing in his notes. I am very surprised you never noticed this fact; if you had, then your judgment concerning these facts might have been somewhat sounder. Do not cry out about how the whole Church has sanctioned this translation for so many centuries. It read this one only because this was either the best one it had or (which I think more likely) the first — once this version was generally adopted it would certainly not have been easy to replace it even if someone submitted a better one — but the Church

251 *recoils on you:* See *Adages* 3588 (*CWE* 36: 272–73).   **252** *Adages* 1196 (*CWE* 33: 126–27)   **253** See Hilary, *Tractatus in II Psalmum* 2 (*PL* 9: 262–63).   **254** *PL* 29: 528

never sanctioned this version: to read and to sanction are not the same thing. On the other hand, it is
quite certain that virtually every student of Sacred
Scripture who has achieved any competence in both
Latin and Greek has found many inadequacies in
that translator. And yet he deserves pardon for failing to do what he could not do, even as he deserves
thanks for doing all that he could, the same thanks
that we owe to whoever adds something that this
translator lacks or restores something that someone
else garbled. But meanwhile you see that the edition
prepared by Jerome which you say that you have,
the edition "which all tongues rightly ought to acclaim," is a version which no tongue reads today.

But you write that the Septuagint version, at
least, is sufficient according to every criterion of
scriptural truth, and lest anyone should dare to oppose that assertion you bring in as its champions
the opinions of the holy fathers Hilary and Augustine. What shall I do? Where shall I turn?[255] I
dare not deny what the holiest fathers affirm, but as
soon as I grant that whatever Erasmus has recently
translated was translated well enough long ago
by the Septuagint translators, I must also confess
that it was far less useful for Erasmus to translate
it again. What if I stall for the time being by denying that those fathers make the assertion you assert
that they made? And I will certainly do so until you
show me where they have made it. Look to it, then:
bring me a passage where they say that the Septuagint translators produced a satisfactory Latin version of the New Testament. But for the time being, while you look around for that passage, I can
assume that on this point, at least, you will leave
me in peace. And that passage, I think, will not be
at all easy to find, since I hear that the Septuagint
translators made only one version — in Greek. Now
if that is the case, how can their version be sufficient for Latin speakers? And indeed you must also
look around for an explanation of how the Septuagint translators could produce a sufficient version
of the New Testament when we know that they all
died approximately two hundred years before the
birth of Christ.[256] When you discover that these
are the facts, I am sure you will also discover that
the people whose word you have taken up to now

concerning these issues have not, up to now, discovered one bit of the truth.

Now I come to what you call his petty and futile
remarks, those you thought were uncommonly trifling and therefore transcribed as examples to make
it clear to everyone that Erasmus is wasting his energies and filling "whole sheaves," in your words, with
sheer nonsense. First you criticize his objection to
the reading *sagena*[257] in Matthew 13, where he would
prefer to read *verriculum*, even though, as you put
it, "*sagena* and *verriculum* signify the same thing." I
am sure you think you have said something very impressive, but first prove that Erasmus objected to the
term *sagena*. He does not criticize this term, though
he prefers the other one; he merely says that the
translator left the Greek expression. "But *verriculum* and *sagena* mean the same thing," you say. Who
denies it? Who needs to be told? But as you could
have learned from Erasmus's note, *sagena* is a Greek
expression while *verriculum* is Latin; they are as distinct as *decretum* and *psephisma* ["decree"]. Even
you cannot automatically think that whoever prefers to use Latin terms rather than Greek in a Latin
translation from Greek is just trifling. But perhaps
you will assert that the term *sagena* is also found
in Latin authors. What of it? A Greek term does
not stop being Greek and immediately start being
Latin as soon as some speaker of Latin employs it
among Latin terms. No one has the power to confer
Roman citizenship on all terms, by Jove, any more
than on all human beings. Nor is *psephisma* a Latin
word, even though Cicero himself employed it once
or twice,[258] nor does *energia* [force or import] stop
being Greek even if Jerome did employ it occasionally in Latin,[259] whether because he was writing to
people he knew to have been trained in Greek or
perhaps because he could find no Latin expression
that conveyed well enough (if I may say so) τὴν τῆς
ἐνεργείας ἐνέργειαν [the import of import]. But in
clumsy imitation of Jerome you repeatedly employ
that word with an incorrect meaning. So you see
that when you try to fish up something to criticize
as you haul in *sagena* and seize on *verriculum*, this
sweep of the net nets you nothing at all.

You go on to find fault with his opinion that
Nuptiae impletae sunt discumbentium [The wed-

---

255 *What . . . turn?*: See Terence, *Hecyra*
516. **256** According to tradition, Ptolemy
II of Egypt commissioned seventy Jewish
scholars to translate the Hebrew Old

Testament into Greek for his library
of Alexandria in the third century BC.
257 "fishnet" **258** See Cicero, *Oratorio
pro L. Flacco* 6.15, 7.17, 8.19, 10.23.

259 See Jerome, *Epistolae* 53.2 (PL 22: 541),
Dialogus contra Pelagiones 1.8 (PL 23: 524c).

ding feast was full of guests] is not very good Latin, where he asserts we should read *discumbentibus* [filled with guests], and then (by all that is holy!) you set out to lecture Erasmus on grammar. Then you drag in Calepino, as if Erasmus were not ten times as trustworthy as Calepino on matters of good Latin speech. And then it is especially funny that after citing Calepino you produce nothing but what you have borrowed from Erasmus himself. You left out just one point, though that one should have taught you that all you had said comes to nothing at all. For after he briefly indicated that *impleor* is used with both the genitive and the ablative and provided the same examples that you do, he sums up the matter by saying that though it is possible to say in good Latin *implentur vini* [They are full of wine], this phrase is not good Latin: *domus impletur hominum* [The house is full of people]. Now go out and look for examples which contradict that.

Now when he judged that the translation of the Lord's prayer in Matthew 6 should read *remitte nobis debita nostra* [forgive us our debts] instead of *dimitte* [pardon], you judge this to be such an obvious instance of trifling that none can deny it, and you think you infer this from Erasmus's own words. For "if ἄφες [pardon] has multiple meanings, as Erasmus himself noted," you say, "how can he prefer the translation *remitte* to *dimitte* when that Greek expression serves for both, while indeed *dimitto*, which according to ancient authors means *do* or *dono* [I give or I present], conveys well enough the same meaning?" Here you ought to produce those ancient authors according to whom you found that *dimittere* is the same thing as *dare*. For unless you produce them, and I think you will not, you yourself are obviously trifling. I for one do not think it is good Latin to say *dimitte mihi vestem* [pardon me a coat] for *da mihi vestem* [give me a coat]. Further, even if *dimittere* did mean the same thing as *dare*, I still do not concede that the phrase *dimitte nobis debita nostra* is good Latin, any more than this other one on the basis of which you defend it: *da nobis debita nostra* [give us our debts]. If to your ears *dare debita* sounds the same as *remittere debita*, your disease is one I cannot cure. "But," you say, "what difference does it make? For the sense is as clear with that translator's *dimitte* as with this one's *remitte*."

Who denies we can guess what sense he has in mind? Even so, it does not follow that his phrasing is sufficiently good Latin, nor is it trifling for someone to indicate what he got wrong; but it is trifling to contradict someone who is indicating the truth. And if Erasmus is trifling, he is certainly trifling in a more decent way since he does so in the company of Cyprian, one of the holiest doctors of the Church, who preferred to say *remitte nobis debita* instead of *dimitte*.[260]

You say, "It showed enormous and dangerous temerity for this fellow to go against the judgment of all the ancient fathers in changing such a well-established word in the first chapter of John, where he puts *sermo* [Speech] in place of *verbum* [the Word]." Here you assume, as if it could be taken for granted, the utterly false thesis that none of the ancients dared to say *sermo* in place of *verbum*. But meanwhile you admit that, according to Jerome, λόγος has other meanings besides *verbum*[261] which are quite appropriate for the Son of God, testimony confirmed by Gregory of Nazianzus, who goes so far as to assert that the Son of God was called λόγος not only because he is Speech and the Word but also because he is Reason and Wisdom,[262] not to mention the other meanings of λόγος, as if the evangelist, according to God's own intention, chose that word because it embraced many meanings each of which can appropriately be applied to the Son of almighty God. I myself would go so far as to say that if any word should be so revered as to be kept in its original form, as we have done with χύριε ἐλέησον, "Alleluia," "Amen," and "Osanna," words which we have retained in their original unaltered form, then this utterance *logos* would seem to have had the best possible claim to such reverence. And since it is wonderfully rich in holy meanings, out of which it is not at all easy to choose which you ought to prefer to the others, it would have been not imprudent to retain that very word, without setting a tendentious precedent, and indeed to include many of Christ's epithets in one two-syllable word. But since translators have actually thought it best to do otherwise, I for one think that the next-best procedure is for them to translate it variously so that none of the meanings of λόγος appropriate for Christ goes unknown or falls into disuse.

260 See Cyprian, *De oratione dominica* 22–23 (*PL* 4: 552–53). **261** See Jerome, *Epistolae* 53.4 (*PL* 22: 543). **262** See Gregory of Nazianzus, *Orationes* 30.20 (*PG* 36: 130).

But Jerome did not dare to change *verbum*: how very surprising that he did not change it when he had no occasion to do so! For I ask you, why would he have changed it, since he was not making an entirely new translation but correcting one that already existed? But if he had taken it upon himself to translate the Gospel all over again, he would not have felt so constrained by the precedent of the ancient translator as to think he could not take the liberty of translating differently, provided that he translated well, even if his predecessor did not translate badly. It was for this very reason that he indicated that λόγος has other meanings besides *verbum* which could rightly be referred to the Son of God: he wanted to demonstrate just what you deny, namely that λόγος could rightly have been translated in other ways than "verbum." For the translations *sermo* and *verbum* are used almost interchangeably in Scripture wherever the Greek text has λόγος, although no one who knows any Greek does not know that *sermo* is the meaning of λόγος much more often than *verbum*.

But you bring up a reason (good lord, what a reason!) for saying that the Son of God is more rightly called *verbum* than *sermo*. For *sermo*, you say, "properly speaking, is rather that which is expressed with the voice, whereas *verbum* is that which is inwardly conceived by the mind, namely the thought which is still confined in the silence of the soul, in the privacy of personal knowledge; and if it is ever released to the world, it still becomes public in such a way as to remain permanently closed up within." I ask you, who taught you this distinction between *sermo* and *verbum*? For the author from whom you have excerpted the remarks you adduce about *verbum* does not deny that the same may be said about *sermo*, and no one fails to see that there is internal mental speech by the same reasoning according to which there is an internal word, or that *verbum* properly means that which is expressed with the voice, just as *sermo* does, since those who examine the origins of words hold that *verbum* is derived from *aere verberando* [striking the air]. But if *sermo* as well as *verbum* can mean an unspoken conception of the mind, whereas *verbum* as well as *sermo* can mean conceptions expressed with the voice, you see how that

remarkable reasoning collapses which you thought gave you such fine support.

And yet I myself certainly do not assign much importance to reasoning in these matters, which cannot be known except by divine revelation. I am certain that the Son of God is rightly called λόγος, whether it is understood to mean *verbum* or *sermo* or *ratio* or *causa* or anything else λόγος means, or indeed all it means. Once again, I am certain that he is rightly called λόγος, for I learned this from him who reclined on the breast of the Lord at the Supper,[263] and I know that the Son of God is rightly called *sermo* and *verbum*, for the whole Catholic Church addresses him by these names. Several learned and holy fathers call him *ratio*, as well, but the whole Roman Church calls him *verbum* and *sermo*, without any exception. For when it celebrates the birth of Christ with this solemn chant, "When all things dwelt in the midst of silence and the night was in the midst of her course, your almighty Speech, O Lord, leapt forth from heaven and came from its royal throne,"[264] the Son of God is unambiguously called "Speech"; and where we read in the psalm, "By the Word of God the heavens were made firm,"[265] whereas others read, and among them Augustine, "By the Speech of God the heavens were made solid,"[266] the Son of God is undoubtedly what is meant by both readings. For Ambrose contradicts you when he says, "For the evangelist did not say, 'In the beginning the Word came to be,' but 'In the beginning,' he said, 'was the Word.' Anyone who would attempt to assign a beginning to the Word will be checked by this precedent, since he said, 'In the beginning it was'; not that we should speak of two principles arising from a difference of substance, but because Speech the Son is always with the Father and was born of the Father."[267] Hilary makes the same point when he says, "This Word was in the beginning with God, because the speech of thought is eternal when the thinker is eternal."[268] Lactantius makes the same point in these words: "Then how did he beget him? First of all, no man can either understand or explain the works of God. Nonetheless Sacred Scripture teaches us this much; in them it is explicitly stated that that Son of God is the Speech of God." He also says elsewhere, "But the Greek term λόγος is more suitable than our 'word' or 'speech.'

263 St. John the Evangelist; see Jn 13:23–25, 21:20. **264** an introit based on Ws 18:15 **265** Ps 32(33):6 **266** Augustine, *Enarratio in Psalmum* 32 (*PL* 36: 286) **267** Ambrose, *De fide orthodoxa contra Arianos* (*PL* 17: 554) **268** Hilary, *De Trinitate* 2.15 (*PL* 10: 61)

For λόγος means both 'speech' and 'reason.'"[269] Cyprian makes the same point in these words from the chapter he entitled "That this same Christ is the Speech of God," which he proves with the following words:

> In Psalm 44, "My heart has brought forth a good Speech; I will tell of my works to the King."[270] Likewise in the psalm, "By the Speech of God the heavens were made firm, and all their strength by the breath of his mouth."[271] Likewise in Isaiah, "ratifying and consummating his Word in justice, for God will consummate his Speech throughout the earth." Likewise in the psalm, "He sent forth his Speech and it healed them."[272] Likewise in the Gospel according to John, "In the beginning was the Word, and the Word was with God, and God was the Word; this was in the beginning with God. All things were made by him, and of the things that were made nothing was made without him. In him was life, and the life was the light of men, and the light shines in the darkness, and the darkness comprehended it not."[273] Likewise in the Apocalypse, "And I saw heaven opened, and behold! a white horse; and he that sat upon him was called faithful and true, in fairness and justice judging and making war. And he was clothed in a garment besprinkled with blood; and his name is called the speech of God."[274]

Augustine makes the same point when he takes as the principal basis for his commentary that translation of the Psalter which reads, "By the Speech of God the heavens were made solid." Nor does he disapprove of that reading; instead, he asserts that it has the same import as our reading, "By the Word of God the heavens were made firm," while he manifestly thinks that both *verbum* in this translation and *sermo* in that one are the Son of God. There is also, in the fourth chapter of Hebrews, "For the Speech of God is alive,"[275] a passage in which not only the *Glossa interlinearis* but also the *Glossa ordinaria* declare plainly that Speech is the Son. Indeed, even de Lyra, who proposed to explain the literal sense of Scripture, clearly teaches that *sermo* means the same thing as *verbum* and that in this passage Speech is nothing else but the Son of God, and in this way he

himself expounds the passage not according to any allegory but quite "literally" as we use that term.

But since you must acknowledge those proof-texts, and you cannot refute them, it is worth seeing the fine way you attempt to evade them. For you say, "There is a great deal of difference between what is fitting in various contexts: what is suitable in one is less appropriate in another. But I do not want to spend too much time on this subject lest you think I am drafting a book, not a letter." What a graceful retreat! Under pretext of brevity you refuse to support your own statement, indeed that very statement on which your whole argument depends, and yet not even then do you actually finish your letter. Instead, you go on to waste more paper still on matters that are not at all to the point. I am certain about this much: even if you rack your brains for a year you will never find any support for your case besides that single point you have already mentioned — indeed, barely touched on, as if you yourself found it flimsy — namely, that *sermo* means that which is expressed with the voice and not an unspoken conception of the mind. But if you had any sense you would not have touched this point at all, since it is just as inimical to *verbum* as it is to *sermo*. For *verbum*, too, properly speaking, means a concept expressed with the voice. But there can be no other support for your case. For if both *sermo* and *verbum* can mean the Son of God not only as he was after his mother gave birth to him but also as he was in the bosom of the Father[276] before he took on fleshly form, before the world was even created, what rationale can you make up for saying that any consideration of what you call contextual appropriateness prevents us from calling the Son of God *sermo* in this passage as well as in others? When Cyprian proves against the Jews that the Son of God is the Speech of God, not only from other texts but also from that very text "In the beginning was the Word," do you not see that he would not be proving anything at all unless Speech and the Word were the same thing in that very passage? But to silence you once and for all, Cyprian not only cites the passage in this way; a bit later he cites it in these very words: "In the beginning was Speech, and Speech was with God, and God was Speech."[277] Now go on and call Erasmus an innovator of words, since you hear that

269 Lactantius, *Divinae institutionem* 4.8, 9 (*PL* 6: 467, 469)   **270** Ps 44(45):1   **271** Ps 32(33):6   **272** Ps 106(107):20

273 Jn 1:1–5   **274** Cyprian, *Testimonia adversus Iudaeus* 2.3 (*PL* 4: 726); Rv 19:11–13   **275** Heb 4:12   **276** Jn 1:18

277 Jn 1:11; Cyprian, *Testimonia adversus Iudaeus* 2.3 (*PL* 4: 726, 730)

a most learned father and a most holy champion of Christ read and used the name *sermo* for the Word of God, for whom he shed his blood, more than a thousand years before Erasmus was born. And on this point Saint Augustine in his commentary on John very plainly concurs with Saint Cyprian.[278]

Now you say it suffices to confirm your own case that for so many centuries, with the consensus of all the saints, Holy Mother Church has religiously used the term *verbum*, but you must figure out for yourself how that fact can confirm your position. It certainly does not hurt Erasmus; more than that, it even supports and defends what he has done. For he is not criticizing *verbum* when he translates *sermo*, any more than the old translator is condemning and censuring *sermo* when he translates *verbum*, or indeed any more than the Church condemned *sermo* when it retained *verbum* in regular usage, in which it retained and still does retain *sermo*, as well. Thus when he translates *sermo* Erasmus neither contradicts the Church nor finds fault with the old translator. Then again, when he translates *sermo* as a way of referring to Christ, why should it not also suffice to confirm his case that—as you yourself wrote about *verbum*—for so many centuries, with the consensus of all the saints and doctors, Holy Mother Church has religiously used the term *sermo*? Will anyone forbid a translator to employ whichever he likes of two terms which denote the same thing? Can anyone justly indict a new translator for rendering as "wife" what the previous one called a "spouse"?

"Yes indeed," you say, "since he disturbs the simple common folk with the less familiar term. And so you see where the work of this fellow Erasmus is headed—at starting a schism and fostering vain quarrels." Pray tell, is it really he who disturbs the simple common folk, who would never give a thought to what he writes if it were not for the envy inciting a few? For like another Cain, these men, their countenances falling when they see how the smoke from their brother's burnt offering rises while theirs is brought low,[279] try their hardest to murder a man who is innocent. They use impious slanders to combat the recognized truth and seditious outcries to provoke simple people, whom they either could have kept calm just by not speaking out or at least should have soothed with the truth after stirring them up with their falsehoods. Otherwise, if those

fellows see that they cannot defend their position to intelligent people and so cry out to the unlearned crowd against works that Erasmus addressed to the learned, if they tactlessly force literary debates on illiterate hearers and court the applause of the crowd because they cannot please the discerning, it is they who are stirring up schism. Otherwise, had they either said nothing of these matters to the crowd or at any rate spoken the truth, there would be no schism. For why should it start a schism if different translators employ different words when the words mean the same? On this point I can use against you the very saying you borrowed from Ambrose to hurl at Erasmus: "In my view there is no difference in wording where there is no difference in sense."[280]

But you are afraid that on this basis we will soon have innumerable editions, since you say that "the world contains not a few people who are equal or indeed superior to Erasmus in their knowledge of Greek." I do not know what number makes more than a few by your reckoning, but I have no doubt that if you start to count them by name you will find that his equals number less than a few and his superiors perhaps less than one. If you add the study of Sacred Scripture, without which even the greatest linguistic expertise will be unequal to this undertaking, I for one have no doubt that the work of Erasmus will easily ensure that not many hereafter will translate the same texts again. For though some people may well appear who believe that in one or two passages, perhaps, they have understood something more clearly than he did, I do not expect that there will ever be anyone either learned or reckless enough to hope he could do something worthwhile by retranslating a whole work that Erasmus had already translated.

But suppose that there were many editions; what harm would there be in that? Saint Augustine regards as exceedingly useful the very thing you are afraid of, for though not all of the translators could be equally good, there are places where each of them translates more aptly. "But meanwhile," you say, "the reader will be rendered uncertain as to which one of so many translations he ought to trust most." That is undoubtedly true if the reader is simply a blockhead without any intelligence or judgment of his own. Otherwise, if he does have a mind, he will find it much easier to elicit the true sense out of

278 See *In Iohannis evangelium tractatus* 108.3 (*PL* 35: 1915–16)   **279** See Gn 4:4–8.   **280** Ambrose, *Expositio evangelii secundum Lucam* 2.42 (*PL* 15: 1568)

a variety of translations, as Augustine says.[281] I ask you, why do you fear so much danger from variety and diversity of translations when you do not take any offense as you read such a heterogeneous assortment of commentators who can reach no consensus at all on the sense of the letter where the letter does not vary at all? And yet their disagreements are frequently useful, since they offer the studious a good opportunity to exercise their thought and judgment. Finally, the extent to which various versions are actually a help to the Church, and by no means a source of confusion, is established at least by the Psalms, which are read in translations that vary considerably, nor does anything else prove as helpful to those who endeavor to study them thoroughly, unless anyone is senseless enough to suppose that the commentary of Vienne is sufficient.

I had almost omitted one argument which you think is your strongest, though I think it so flimsy and weak that just one breath could blow it down. But since I see that you regard it as the best fortified of all your defenses, I have decided to quote your own words so that you could not blame my report for corrupting your logic. Now then, you say,

> I simply never stop marveling at the blindness of the many who think that it is a fine feat to collate any work at all with Greek or Hebrew texts, although anyone can infer from the perfidy of the Jews and the various errors of the Greeks that those very texts of theirs must be shockingly corrupt and laden with all sorts of foul errors. Furthermore, from their excessive antiquity it follows that their texts must be more corrupt than our own, not to mention here Saint Jerome's testimony that even in his day the Latin texts were less corrupt than the Greek, and the Greek than the Hebrew.

I am simply amazed that you never stop marveling at this, since you can easily discern that Saint Jerome met with these same objections long ago and completely refuted them. For first of all, he thinks it is foolish for anyone to believe that a whole people would conspire to tamper with all of the books owned by everyone. For not to mention the other difficulties in this scheme, they could have no hope at all of concealing their actions for good, nor could

they doubt that as soon as the scheme was revealed they would seem to have lost their case[282] through their own testimony, since it would be clear that the position that they had supported was one they confessed they could defend only by corrupting their texts. But I think even you see that something done publicly by a whole people could not be kept secret. Indeed, I think you also see that, since every day some people defected from the Hebrews to the Christians, and as many from the Greeks to the Latins, that falsification of books would have been brought to light immediately. Furthermore, since books in both languages were not only in the possession of the unfaithful but also at large in the hands of the orthodox, either the orthodox too would have had to corrupt their own texts as a favor to the unfaithful or else the trustworthy texts of the orthodox would have clearly established the falseness of the others. What of this? On the points we dispute with the Greeks or with the Hebrews, their texts agree with the Latin; the debate never turned on the letter but always on its sense and significance. Thus you can easily conclude that they did not try to alter their books in other passages where it would not matter, since they left them intact even where it would have been most advantageous to alter them.

But "our texts are more trustworthy than Greek ones," you say. Then why does Augustine advise that wherever you have any doubt about the Latin texts you should turn to the Greek? But you would rather side with Jerome, who according to you writes that even in his time the Greek texts were more trustworthy than the Hebrew, and the Latin than the Greek.

The rest of the arguments you had gathered certainly looked very easy to deal with, but I confess that in reading this one I felt somewhat perturbed. For Jerome is an author I always take seriously, and on this point I properly take him most seriously of all. And if he confessed that the books of the Greeks were less corrupt than those of the Hebrews and also that Latin books were less corrupt than the Greek, others might well have found some way out;[283] I myself saw no way to escape.

But then, as I reflected, it started to strike me as perfectly amazing that Jerome should have held such an opinion. For I knew he could not have said anything more opposed to his own undertaking.

281 See *De doctrina Christiana* 2.12.17–18, 2.14.21 (*PL* 34: 43, 45–46). **282** *lost their*   *case:* See Cicero, *De oratore* 1.36.166–67. **283** *found…out: Adages* 2175 (*CWE* 34: 253)

No passage occurred to me where he said this, and I thought it more likely that he would never have said it anywhere. Thinking harder about it, I finally began to remember, as if through a fog,[284] that I had once read something of the sort in the book of pontifical decretals. I snatched up the book in the hope I could prove you mistaken, since I was practically sure that that book was the source of your quotation, and I hoped you had got it wrong.

When I found the passage, I simply lost heart, indeed I practically abandoned all hope, since I found that a gloss in that work said the same thing that you do. For although I was not so intimidated by the learning of whoever produced this commentary that I had no hope of his stumbling occasionally in citing Jerome, I was still overawed by the great diligence that I was convinced must have been brought to bear to ensure that that holy volume of decretals, which inexorably lays down the law for the whole world, would not include anything at all that had not been correctly understood. Nonetheless, I was drawn toward a different conclusion by my respect for Jerome's prudence, since I simply knew he could not be so stupid that even after he had noted the faults of the Greek texts and had chosen to correct the Old Testament according to the true Hebrew readings, and even after he had chosen to emend the corruptions that had appeared in Latin texts of the New Testament on the basis of their Greek originals, he would still admit that the Greek texts are more trustworthy than the Hebrew, and the Latin than the Greek. For what could be said or conceived to undermine his own project more thoroughly?

As I thought these things over I eventually started to feel more dubious about the diligence that went into the gloss than about Jerome's prudence. So I turned to the passage, which is at the end of the letter that begins with the words *Desiderii mei.* Good lord, what a disgraceful mistake I saw that the author of that gloss had made! For in Jerome the passage reads thus: "It is another matter if as against their own position they have accepted the forms of the text which are subsequently attested by the apostles, and if Latin texts are less corrupt than the Greek and the Greek than the Hebrew."[285] For after anticipating the objections that he thought his opponents would make, he finally indicated that if anyone were so signally foolish as to think the Greek texts more trustworthy than the Hebrew, and the Latin than the Greek, he would not deserve any response. But that author of yours, not understanding this figure of speech, lopped off a few words which establish the whole point of the sentence and then cited the rest as a basis for saying that Jerome himself said what he actually thought no one foolish enough to say, namely just what this author of yours says. Now go on and rely on those summary textbooks of yours, on which most now rely so heavily that the authors despoiled by your modern compilers to fill out their summas are regarded as almost superfluous.

Having bravely concluded your siege of his translation and notes — his acropolis, as it were — you attack several of his smaller towns, as if greedy for plunder. You strike hardest of all at his *Moria* ["Folly"], an ample and populous city, but one which you hope can be taken without difficulty since it has a woman in charge,[286] and since she is not one to defer to her generals but always directs things according to whim and caprice. But listen here, you, I predict that in this undertaking her bastions will not be as easy to take as you think. For first of all, as Solomon says, "The number of fools is infinite,"[287] and then what they are lacking in intelligence they make up for in recklessness.[288] Though they would gladly admit you as a citizen if you yearn to become one, they will certainly never agree to have you as a conqueror, for they will fight to the death before they will take orders from anyone.

But joking aside, even Folly herself has less folly to offer,[289] as well as more piety, than some of your — I will restrain myself, and yet I will dare to say this much — than some of the rhythmical prayers with which some of your brethren suppose they put all of the saints in their debt every time that they honor their memory with such foolish jingles that not even a rogue trying his hardest to mock them could muster more foolish ones. And yet some of this trifling stuff has now found a place in our churches, and each day it acquires more authority, particularly when it is provided with a musical accompaniment, so that by now we are much less attentive to the sober and serious prayers holy fathers prescribed long ago. In fact it would be a

---

284 *through a fog: Adages* 263 (*cwe* 31: 287–88)   **285** *pl* 28: 152   **286** *a woman*   *in charge: Adages* 1481 (*cwe* 33: 176–77)   **287** Eccl 1:15   **288** See *Praise of Folly* (*asd*   4/3: 96).   **289** See *Praise of Folly* (*asd* 4/3: 68).

considerable advantage for Christendom if bishops would utterly ban all such silliness, as I am sure they eventually will, so that our subtle foe cannot cause Christ's flock, whom he meant to be not only sim-ple but prudent as well, to slip gradually into the habit of embracing folly in place of piety.

I will not undertake the defense of the *Folly,* since there is no need. For the book has long had the ap-proval of all the best judges, and it was defended long ago against the aspersions of envious people in Erasmus's apology to Dorp, a man of great learn-ing in both secular and sacred disciplines, who had taken the part of those critics by gathering up ev-ery objection that they could contrive and had even gone on to develop them eloquently in an effort to show that he meant what he said, so that you would now be hard pressed to raise any objection that has not been confuted already, though you have found one charge that is utterly new when you say that Erasmus in the *Folly* is acting like someone called Moscus. This reproach I confess I for one cannot answer, since I have no idea what it means, or who that Moscus was, and I am not such an arrogant fool as to make a deliberate pretense of being more learned than I am. I have often heard of someone called Momus,[290] who might have had Moscus as a surname, but I personally cannot confirm it.

I have never been particularly keen to learn who wrote the dialogue *Julius*[291] or what sort of produc-tion it is, though I have heard various opinions on both points. I do know that right after Julius's death the affair was the subject of public skits in Paris. Many know that the Reverend Father Poncher,[292] bishop of the city of Paris, declared, when he came here as an ambassador, that the book was by Fausto.[293] But this theory, should it be true, by no means rules out the possibility that Erasmus also had the book in his possession before it was in print, since Fausto is not a complete stranger to him. But when you base your argument on the style, which you claim is dis-tinctly and purely Erasmian, I cannot refrain from a laugh at the thought that, while you will not let Erasmus base any of his judgments concerning the works of Jerome on their style, even though every-one knows that Erasmus is a consummate expert on fine points of language, you yourself are so arrogant that, without even knowing the meaning of style or

of diction, you single things out as his work on the basis of style even though there are so many learned people intent upon writing just like him. Now sup-pose that he did write the book. Suppose that a man who was fed up with war and provoked by the tur-bulent times did let some passion carry him further than he might have wished after peace was achieved and emotions were soothed. First, most of the blame should then go to the people responsible for the un-timely publication of a once timely book. Then I ask you, was this really your job as a monk, to expose a mistake in your brother, when your office enjoins you to sit by yourself and lament your own sins, not denounce other people's? And I think that assigning the book to Erasmus will win you no thanks among those whom it may have offended, since it would be better for them if the work remained anonymous than if it were commended by being ascribed a pres-tigious author.

Those with leisure to do so may assess Luther's writings for themselves, but I have no doubt at all that if Erasmus has written to Luther he wrote in a way that befits a good man. Nor do you your-self claim to have any real proof, and yet you can-not wait till you do to launch into abuse, doubtless simply in order to get all the pleasure you can from that splendid *bon mot,* "The pot matches the lid,"[294] which appears to have furnished your only incentive for mentioning Erasmus together with Luther. For it is remarkable how you never stop trying to pass for a wit. But what I find amazing is the inordinate quantity of leisure you are free to devote to schis-matic and heretical books—if, that is, you are tell-ing the truth—unless a shortage of good ones com-pels you to spend the short time you do have on the worst ones. For if those books are good, why con-demn them? If bad, then why read them? For since you will never be in an appropriate position to lec-ture the world on combating erroneous beliefs, since you even forswore any care for the world when you entered the cloister, what else do you accomplish by reading false doctrines but to learn them?

Nor will you be content, as I see, just to squan-der good hours on bad books; you must go on to fritter away a great deal of time speaking and chat-ting on themes even worse than bad books. For I see every rumor and slander and scandal on earth

290 See *Adages* 473 (*CWE* 31: 448–50).   Poncher (d. 1525) **293** Fausto Andrelini   (*CWE* 32: 265–66)
291 *Iulius exclusus e coelo* **292** Etienne   of Forli (*ca.* 1412–1518) **294** *Adages* 972

is immediately passed on to you in your cell. And yet we read that once there were monks who withdrew from the world so completely that they would not even read letters from their friends so that they would not have to look back on the Sodom[295] which they had abandoned.[296] Now, however, I see that they read both heretical and schismatic books and vast volumes of absolute rubbish. Now our subtle foe thrusts on the fugitives just the sort of vain talk that they feared among secular people and cloistered themselves to escape, and he artfully thrusts it into their very cells. Nor does their splendid regimen serve any purpose but to help them deceive the unwary, nor does their leisure serve but to give them more time to perfect their disparaging speech, nor does their withdrawal from the world serve but to make them shameless because men cannot see what they do, nor does the narrowness of their little cells serve but to lend freer scope to their slander of others. And yet the first thing that anyone does upon entering those cells is to call on God with the Lord's Prayer to ensure that the talk in that place should be holy and wholesome. But what good does it do to say the Lord's Prayer at the outset of scandalous and slanderous gossip? If this is not taking God's name in vain, then what is? This is surely the most fitting context of all for that verse from the Gospel you cite against Erasmus, for certainly not everyone who says "Lord, Lord" to God in this way will enter into the kingdom of heaven.[297]

Consequently, as I look at this letter of yours, so replete with reproach, abuse, slander, and mockery, and as I think back on the candor and the genuinely amiable nature you had as a youth, when you were as free from these faults as it would have been easy to pardon them in one of that age and condition, if I gauged your whole character on the basis of this letter I would certainly be reminded of that poem by Ovid in which Deianira chides Hercules: "Your beginning surpassed your finale; your performance falls short of your promise; the grown man is no match for the boy."[298] But of course I am not so unfair as to judge you entirely on the basis of a single letter. Indeed, I am more willingly inclined to believe that the goodness and holiness of the rest of your character have made some demon especially resentful and envious of your virtues and that, since

you are avoiding the rest of his snares, he is insidiously trying his hardest to trap you and draw you to himself with his last and by far most insidious snare, when he transforms himself into an angel of light,[299] dazzling our vision till we see without seeing and to our deranged eyes black looks white and white black,[300] others' virtue seems tarnished, and our own faults impress us as glamorous and appealing. Then we call defamation of character fraternal advice; we regard anger and envy as fervor and zeal to serve God; we name ignorance simple and saintly rusticity, and call arrogant stubbornness bold and invincible constancy; and in sum, we are never without an altruistic pretext for indulging our own passions, and generally the worst passions at that, just as in this very letter, while pretending to give me advice, you disparage Erasmus.

Yet not one of the bitter reproaches you hurl at him actually strikes home, whereas many of them promptly recoil on you.[301] You protest that his style is affected, when your own solecisms are more labored than his refinements. You attack him for his mordant wit and cry out that he sinks his fangs into everything, when you yourself sink more teeth into him in one letter than he ever sank into anyone. In fact, if someone went through all the books of Erasmus, all his letters, every variety of writing he has ever produced in the course of producing such numerous volumes, and if he then gathered in one pile every unkind thing that Erasmus ever wrote about anyone, characteristically withholding the names of the people to whom he referred although some deserved much harsher treatment, this whole pile would be dwarfed by the mountainous load of explicitly personal abuse which you heap on Erasmus like a second Great Pyramid, although he never did you the slightest injury, although he even furthered your studies with his writings and thus did you a kindness too great to repay.

You accuse him of arrogance because he dared to challenge the errors of others, and of course you think you are being modest when you find fault with the things he gets right, when you criticize works praised by judges whom only an egregiously immodest man would defy. I could list for you many such men from all over the world, all renowned for their virtue and learning, who vie with each other

---

295 *look . . . Sodom:* See Gn 19:17.
296 See John Cassian, *De coenobiorum institutis* 5.32 (PL 49: 248–49).   **297** See

Mt 7:21.   **298** Ovid, *Heroides* 9.23–24
299 *when . . . light:* See 2 Cor 11:14.
300 *black looks . . . black:* See Is 5:20;

Ovid, *Metamorphoses* 11.314; Juvenal 3.30.
301 *promptly . . . you:* See *Adages* 3588 (CWE 36: 272–73).

in thanking Erasmus for all they have gained by his work. But I will omit all his foreign admirers, since you will probably dispute their authority because you do not know who they are. I will name one or two of our countrymen whom it would be outright impudence to contradict. I will name, and most worshipfully I will name, the reverend father in Christ, John the bishop of Rochester, a man as conspicuous for his virtue as he is for his learning and as eminent for both as any man living today. I will name Colet, a man both as learned and as holy as any of our countrymen has been for the last several centuries. Quite apart from the letters that these men have sent to Erasmus,[302] in which they might appear to be flattering him somewhat were it not that such men would never choose to tell anyone flattering lies, and especially lies that might harm someone else, there are letters in which these men exhort other people as strongly as possible to a diligent reading of Erasmus's translation, from which they will learn a great deal. Master John Longland, the dean of Salisbury,[303] whose preaching and pure living would make you suppose he was another Colet (to sum up his praise in a word), never stops testifying that Erasmus's works on the New Testament have done more to enlighten him than virtually all the rest of the commentaries he owns. There is no need to list any others if you will trust these men; there is even less if you will not. For whom will you trust on this point if you will not trust men such as these? Either way you take a great deal on yourself when you attack with such fanfare what those men so earnestly praise.

What of this, that the Pope has twice given his explicit sanction to what you attack? Like a boy-prophet of the almighty[304] you proclaim to be harmful what the vicar of Christ, as if with the authority of a divine oracle,[305] has already declared to be useful. What the supreme prince of Christendom honors with his own testimonial from the citadel of our religion you sully with your filthy tongue from the darkness of your little cell, an unlearned, obscure little monk. At this point you yourself should apply the advice that you offer Erasmus: do not be wise beyond your share of wisdom, but be wise with sobriety.[306] Are you not doing precisely what you also charge him with doing, neglecting God's ordinance

and setting out to establish your own, when you blithely persist in condemning the very work that the Pope has so often recommended with pious good will to all scholars?

You take as a basic assumption in this condemnation the thesis that Erasmus is utterly ignorant of Scripture—just as you, I suppose, are omniscient—when in fact he has spent almost as many years studying Scripture as you have been living. I am not going to dwell on the possibility that you surpass him in intelligence or diligence. I know this much for sure, and can say so without any slight to your honor at all: you do not surpass him by such a wide margin that you could achieve in a much shorter time something he could not in a much longer one. And yet when he is already growing gray in the study of Scripture, you yourself, a self-tutored young man—indeed one who has never had time to be tutored—are actually immodest enough to lecture an old man as if he were a schoolboy;[307] you actually think you are being very clever when you employ arguments which make it quite clear you have just missed the point.

But you think you have done something especially grand every time that you mock him with patchwork citations from various books of the Bible and when you clown around with the words of Holy Scripture the same way comic parasites play around with their quips. This is not only the most inexcusable game in the world, it is also the easiest. As a case in point, there is a mischievous mimic who recently copied the dress, tone of voice, facial expressions, and gestures of a preaching friar. In the middle of his obscene and ridiculous sermon, which was made up entirely of excerpts from Scripture, he also included an anecdote, just as some friars habitually do, but this anecdote was an indecent story of a friar who seduced and corrupted a housewife. The rogue padded even this disgraceful and sordid tale with so many patchwork citations from Scripture that even when the friar was seducing the adulterous wife, and even when she was being polluted, and even when her husband appeared and discovered the matter, and even when upon this discovery the friar was arrested, and even when upon this arrest both his testicles were cut off, not one word was employed that was not taken directly from the

302 See *EE* 2: 257–58, 268, 598.   Lk 1:76.   **305** *with . . . oracle:* See *Adages*   **307** *lecture . . . schoolboy:* See *Adages* 160
303 (1473–1543), also appointed bishop of   3980 (*CWE* 36: 531).   **306** See Rm 12:3.   (*CWE* 31: 199).
Lincoln in 1521   **304** *Like . . . almighty:* See

text of Scripture, and these excerpts were all applied so aptly to this totally incongruous[308] subject matter that no one, no matter how grave, could refrain from a laugh, even as no one, no matter how giddy, did not feel incensed to behold Sacred Scripture being travestied in this sort of burlesque. And yet there were some present who said it was part of God's own secret plan that, since so many friars had made such an inveterate habit of adulterating God's word,[309] friar-mimics should finally spring up who could outfriar the friars, beat them at their own game, and (as the saying goes) use their own weapons to finish them off.[310] But if it is wrong, and it certainly is, to abuse Sacred Scripture for bawdy amusement, it is still more wrong to abuse it for slandering some other person as you do. Nor does it mitigate the offense that you are writing to someone you know is his friend; indeed, that makes it all the worse. For if you had said these things to someone who hated Erasmus you would merely have alienated someone who was alienated already. But in fact you have done all you could to estrange one of his dearest friends.

Thus, as I already said, when I thought back on the mild, modest nature you had as a youth, it gave me no end of grief and amazement to find out that your greater maturity, in a state of life completely committed not just to humility but to self-abnegation as well, could give rise to this sort of immodesty, which could easily be called something worse. As I ponder in silent amazement what caused this distemper, I sense that the blame lies not only with that common foe at whose covert suggestion, as if from a tainted spring,[311] almost all faults arise, and not only with those accomplices of his who have infected your simplicity with the virulence of their envy; at least some of this poison derives from a certain kind of Scripture which is certainly not new or uncommon to mortals but which has afflicted mankind with more serious evils than any other kind. I refer to that Scripture of covert self-indulgence which makes almost everyone so partial to his own order of existence that he can neither see its faults by himself nor let anyone else point them out to him.

You were blinded with this very Scripture, I see, when your misguided zeal and devotion to religious

orders goaded you into speaking ill of a man who deserves very well of everyone in those orders, and never better than when he is doing the very thing you are trying to twist into something hateful and invidious. For you say, "How often he clamors against the holy observances of religious orders, against the devout ceremonies of the religious, against austerity of living, against holy solitude, and, in summary, against everything that is not to be reconciled with his vagabond lifestyle and conduct!" Upon reading these words I could easily tell what sort of spur must be goading you on,[312] namely zeal for your own religious order. I have no doubt at all that there is no good man anywhere who does not feel a great deal of heartfelt esteem for all religious orders, and certainly I myself have always regarded them not only with love but also with the utmost reverence, since it is my custom to honor the poorest man commended by virtue more than anyone distinguished for his riches or admired for an illustrious birth. But even so, just as I want all other mortals to be deeply devoted to you and your orders, as your merits deserve, of course, since I am inclined to believe that the misery of this world is substantially alleviated by your pleading in its behalf (for if one just man's diligent prayer does a great deal of good,[313] how much good must be done by the incessant prayer of so many thousands?), I would similarly hope that not even you would be so inordinately prejudiced in your own favor that if anyone aims any remark at your practices you will try to pervert things well said by the way you report them or to damn things well thought by the tendentious way you construe them.

I do not know how his words taste to your diseased palate, but I know this for sure: I have never met anyone yet who interpreted his writings as if he were condemning the devout ceremonies of the religious and not rather those people who abuse them superstitiously or rely on them too recklessly and thus foolishly turn to their own peril a practice not bad in itself. I think not even you will deny that there are too many people of this sort, no matter how partial you are to your fellows. For nothing in the world is too holy for our cunning foe to attempt to corrupt it by some sort of trickery, for

---

308 *totally incongruous:* See *Adages* 945 (*CWE* 32: 254). **309** *adulterating God's word:* 2 Cor 2:17, 4:2 **310** *their own…*

off: See *Adages* 51 (*CWE* 31: 100–101). **311** *as if … spring: Adages* 56 (*CWE* 31: 103)

312 *spur… on:* See *Adages* 147 (*CWE* 31: 189–90). **313** *one… good:* Js 5:16

since he is God's opposite in everything, he seeks to produce evil from our good in the same way that God procures good from our evil. How many you can find who place far more importance on the ceremonies of their sect than on God's own commandments! Do you not find whole orders doing battle with other orders for the sake of their rituals as each works not to be but to seem holier, each relying on its own private ceremonies which are frequently less than essential, while they all share a common position on serious, more meaningful matters just as surely as some men in orders are not very careful to live by it! Into what a variety of factions and how many sectarian movements one order can split! And then what a commotion, what tragic upheavals ensue on account of a different color, or a differently cinctured robe, or some other trivial ceremony that is possibly not altogether contemptible, but is certainly an unworthy pretext for banishing charity! And worst of all, certainly, how many there are who are encouraged by belonging to a religious order to conceive such a lofty self-image that they think they are walking in the heavens or that they themselves, perched on a sunbeam, look down from the heights on the general populace creeping like ants on the ground, and not only on the laity but also on the whole class of priests who live outside the cloister! So true is it that for many of them, nothing is holy apart from what they do themselves.[314]

God showed great foresight when he instituted all things in common;[315] Christ showed as much when he tried to recall mortals again to what is common from what is private.[316] For he perceived that corrupt mortal nature cannot cherish what is private without detriment to what is common, as experience shows in all aspects of life. For not only does everyone love his own plot of land or his own money, not only does everyone cherish his own family or his own set of colleagues, but to the extent that we call anything our own it absorbs our affections and diverts them from the service of the common good. So, too, we prefer our own fast-days to public ones, and so, after we have selected some saint as our own, we often prize this one more than ten better ones just because he is ours while the other saints belong to everyone. Now if anyone challenges anything of this sort, he is not condemning popular piety but rather warning us not to let impiety creep in under some pious pretext. For, though no one would criticize any nation for fostering the cult of some saint when it had a good reason to do so, some will probably feel that his admirers are carrying their piety too far when as a special favor to their own saint they drag the patron saint of an enemy nation from the church and throw him in the mud. But just as rituals of this sort and private ceremonies sometimes work out badly for us, by the same token, I think, they do not always work out well for you; and among many of you, the more exclusively something is yours, the more value you place on it. For this reason many prize their own ceremonies more than those of their religious house, their own house's ceremonies more than those of their order, and whatever is exclusive to their order more than everything that is common to all religious orders, while they prize all that pertains to the religious somewhat more than they do those lowly and humble concerns that are not only not private to them but are common to the whole Christian people, such as those plebeian virtues of faith, hope, charity, fear of God, humility, and others of similar character. Nor is this a new problem: long ago Christ rebuked his chosen people by saying, "Why do even you transgress God's commandments for the sake of your own traditions?"[317]

I am sure that the very people who do such things will deny that they do them. For who is idiotic enough to admit that he prizes his own ceremonies more than God's precepts when he knows that unless he abides by those precepts his own ceremonies are useless? Doubtless they will supply the right answers if asked, but their actions make their words ring false. Put me down for a liar if there are not some wretched fellows in orders at various locations who are so stubborn about keeping silence that you could not pay them enough to make them whisper even discreetly in their cloister walks, while if they are diverted one foot to either side they are not at all coy about thundering out dire abuse. There are some who are afraid that a demon will swoop down and take them directly to hell if they change any item in their customary dress, whereas they feel no qualms about amassing money, opposing their abbot, and often supplanting him. Do you think there

---

314 *nothing…themselves:* See *Adages* 3616 (*CWE* 36: 289–90); Terence, *Adelphoe* 98–99.   **315** See Lv 19:18.   **316** See Jn 13:34–35, 15: 12–13; Acts 2:44–46, 4:32–35.   **317** Mt 15:3

are only a few who consider it a foul and extremely lamentable sin if they leave out one line in saying their office, but feel not the least scruple of fear when they often befoul themselves with outrageous and slanderous gossip even longer than their longest prayers? Thus they strain at a gnat as they swallow an elephant whole.[318]

Certainly there are many more than I would wish who suppose that the very title "religious" exalts them far beyond mortal constraints. But a good number of these people are mad without being particularly wicked, the ones who are so pleasantly deranged that they take every product of their addled brain as if it were divinely inspired and think they have been carried up into the third heaven[319] when they have actually been carried away into the third stage of lunacy. But some are mad in a vastly more dangerous way, those who are so insolently assured of their own saintliness that they not only contemn but completely condemn other mortals compared with themselves, and for practically no other reason but that they themselves cling to their own rituals excessively and superstitiously and glory in their own trivial observances, by which some of them think they are protected even when they gird themselves with this sort of defensive equipment for all kinds of crime.

Indeed I know of a man who was formally one of the religious, and in fact he belonged to the order which is currently thought (rightly so, in my personal opinion) to be the most religious of all. Although he was no longer a novice but had already spent many years in what they call regular observances, and had advanced so far in them that he had even been chosen the head of his monastery, through paying less attention to God's precepts than to monastic ritual he slipped from one vice to another, finally sinking so low as to plot the most ghastly and unbelievably heinous crime, and indeed not a single crime but one pregnant with many and various crimes, for he planned to join murder and parricide with sacrilege. But since he did not think himself equal to perpetrating all these crimes by himself he recruited some killers and cutthroats to help him. They committed the most monstrous crime of any I have ever seen. They were arrested and thrown into prison. But I do not plan to unfold the whole incident, and I will withhold the names of the guilty to avoid stirring up any forgotten ill will against their guiltless order. To come to the one point that I had in mind in beginning the story, I heard from these villainous killers that whenever they came to the chamber of that would-be man of religion they never discussed plans for their felony before being ushered into his private chapel to kneel in the approved fashion and pray to the Blessed Virgin with a Hail Mary; it was not until these devotions were rightly concluded that they purely and piously rose to commit their unspeakable crime.

And just as the crime I have mentioned was by far the most ghastly of all, so the one I am now going to mention, though it appears to be much more innocuous, actually may have done little less harm, and the harm that it did was undoubtedly much more widespread. There was a certain friar at Coventry who belonged to that group of Franciscans who have not yet been reformed according to the Rule of Saint Francis. This man preached in the city, in the suburbs, and in the neighboring and outlying villages that whoever said the psalter of the Blessed Virgin every day could never be damned. What he said fell upon eager ears[320] and was gladly believed because it opened up such an easy road to heaven.

There was a certain local pastor, a good and learned man, who considered the friar's words to be foolish but nevertheless looked the other way for a while, reasoning that the business would not lead to any real harm, since the more lavish the people's devotion to the cult of the Blessed Virgin the more piety they would imbibe from it. But at length, on inspecting his pastoral fold, he discerned that his flock had been gravely infected with that scabrous error, that the very worst people were those who recited that psalter most religiously, and that they did so precisely in order to secure themselves a license to do anything at all, since they thought it a sin to retain any doubts about heaven when so weighty an authority as that friar had dropped out of heaven[321] to promise it to them with so much conviction. Then the pastor began to admonish the people not to put too much faith in reciting that psalter, even if they did it ten times a day. He said they would certainly be acting virtuously if they said it virtuously and did not say it with that assurance which some

318 _they strain ... whole:_ See Mt 23:24; _Adages_ 869, 2027 (_cwe_ 32: 219, 34: 191–91). **319** _carried ... heaven:_ See 2 Cor 12:2. **320** _eager ears:_ Tacitus, _Historiae_ 1.1 **321** _dropped ... heaven:_ See _Adages_ 500, 786 (_cwe_ 31: 470, 32: 170–71).

had already conceived; otherwise they would do better to omit the prayers themselves if they would only omit along with them the various crimes which were being committed more confidently beneath their protection.

When he spoke these words from his pulpit they fell on completely intolerant ears; he was hissed, shouted down,[322] and reviled on all sides as an enemy of Mary. On another day, the friar ascended the pulpit and took as his text what was obviously a swipe at the rector, "Blessed Virgin, permit me to praise you; give me strength to encounter your foes."[323] For they say that a certain Scotus[324] employed the same theme to begin the debate on the Blessed Virgin's immaculate conception at Paris, to which they falsely claim he was brought in an instant from three hundred miles away, as if she needed Scotus to come to her rescue. What need to say more? The friar easily persuaded his partisan hearers that the minister was both fatuous and impious.

At the most tumultuous stage of the incident I myself happened to set out for Coventry to visit my sister there. I had barely gotten off my horse when the question was put to me, too, whether anyone who said the psalter of the Blessed Virgin every day could be damned. I laughed it off as a laughable problem. I was instantly warned that my answer was rash and that it contradicted the preaching of a certain most holy and most learned father. I scorned the whole business as one which in no way concerned me.

I was promptly invited to dinner, I accepted, I went. Lo and behold, in walked a cadaverous and somber old friar, followed by a boy carrying books. I knew right then that a fight was in store[325] for me. We sat down, and the host, not wasting any time about it, instantly put the question. The friar responded as he had preached earlier. I myself said nothing. For I take no pleasure in getting involved in vexatious and pointless disputes. They finally asked me what I thought, and since they would not let me keep quiet I said what I thought, but in only a few careless words. Then the friar launched into a long, rehearsed speech, and he blurted out over that dinner enough verbiage for nearly two sermons. The whole gist of his reasoning was dependent on

miracles, many of which he rattled off to us from the *Mariale*[326] along with some he had taken from other such books, which he had the boy bring to the table to lend greater authority to his exposition. When he had finished his speech at long last, I modestly answered that, first of all, nothing he had said in that entire sermon would seem really persuasive to anyone who did not accept the miracles that he had reported, a response which would not necessarily contravene Christian faith, and that even if those miracles were true they were hardly an adequate basis for the thesis at hand. For while you might easily find a prince who would sometimes pardon even his enemies at his mother's entreaty, no prince anywhere is foolish enough to promulgate a law which would encourage his own subjects to defy him by promising immunity to every traitor who propitiated his mother with a set form of flattery. After a lengthy exchange,[327] all I finally achieved was that the friar was praised to the skies whereas I was laughed down as a fool. Indeed, through the misguided devotion of people indulging their own vices under a pretext of piety, the affair finally went so far that only the most forceful action on the part of the bishop could put a stop to it at all.

I do not record these incidents out of any desire to implicate the religious life itself in the offenses committed by some men in religious orders, since the same soil produces both wholesome and noxious herbs,[328] or to criticize the devout practice of those who frequently pray to the Blessed Virgin (for that is a most wholesome devotion), but rather to stress that some people place so much reliance on such rituals that these are precisely what gives them the confidence to commit serious sins. It is this sort of thing that Erasmus believes we should challenge, and if anyone feels angry with him, why not also resent Saint Jerome? Why not also resent the other holy fathers who both recorded the faults of the religious at much greater length and attacked them with much greater bitterness? How cunning is that ancient serpent! How he always flavors his toxins with honey so that no one will balk at the poison! How he sickens our taste and arouses our nausea every time we are offered an antidote! Those who admire us and praise what we do, those who hail us

322 *hissed, shouted down:* Cicero, *Paradoxa Stoicorum* 3.26　**323** Anselm, *PL* 158: 962　**324** Johannes Duns Scotus (*ca.* 1266–1308)　**325** *fight . . . store:* Terence, *Phormio* 133, *Adelphoe* 792　**326** The title of several books honoring the Virgin Mary.　**327** *After . . . exchange: Adages* 284 (*CWE* 31: 302)　**328** *since . . . herbs:* See Ovid, *Remedia amoris* 45–46.

as blessed and saintly, in other words those who seduce us and turn us from fools into madmen,[329] these are obviously candid, benevolent fellows, and these we call good, pious men in return. But those who work to do something much more useful for us, to make us see ourselves as we really are, those men are barking dogs, snappish, malicious, and envious, and those words are used against them even when they never attack the vices of anybody by name and when those who describe them this way openly smear their own filth upon others. And so I see that now there is no place where that comic saying does not apply, since not even the cloister is closed to it: "Flattery is the way to make friends, truthfulness to make enemies."[330] Jerome's truthfulness was once held against him by the slanderer Rufinus[331] even though every fair, virtuous reader construed it in a fair, virtuous way. But you take what Erasmus has written not only truthfully but also so very graciously that he has received from all sides written expressions of deep gratitude from members of every religious order, especially your own,[332] and now, of all times, you tastelessly and arrogantly attack it with slander and abuse. Your whole profession rests on humility as its foundation, and in this spirit of humility you not only exalt your own sect with extravagant praise for its sacred traditions, holy solitude, devout ceremonies, vigils, austere living, and fasts, but you kick him around like a dog while you speak of his bark and his vagabond lifestyle. When I read these words flowing from so religious a pen, I almost imagine I am hearing the humble prayer spoken by that holy pharisee: "Lord, I thank you that I am not as other men are, even as this publican."[333]

Even though I think it a bit closer to holiness to dwell on the praise of good men than to slander them, I have no intention at present of writing an encomium of Erasmus. For my own powers are unequal to so great a task, and everywhere on earth the best and most learned men are each vying to do it as well as they possibly can. And even if they remained silent, his own rich benefactions to all mortal men, which commend him to virtuous men now, will commend him to all when his death puts an end to their envy (though I pray it will not happen soon), when at last he will be missed even by those people whose jaundiced, bleared eyes, as if dazzled with his intense brightness, cannot stand to look straight at him now. Since he has no shortage of praise among virtuous judges, I myself will refrain from fueling the envy even of those who have such perverse minds that they feed on all kinds of detraction and pine away at the praises of virtuous men. But without any offense even to them, I think, I may say this at least. If anyone carefully considers the steady stream of massive, excellent, and numerous volumes that Erasmus has produced singlehandedly, so many that you would think that one man would not even be equal to copying them all out, he will readily conclude that even if Erasmus were not totally preoccupied with virtue he would certainly have little time left to devote to vice. Now if you look even closer with an unbiased eye, first considering the fruitfulness of his works and then appraising the testimony of those who have derived from his works either illumination in their studies or fervor in their affections, I for one think you will not find it at all likely that the heart from which such sparks of piety leap forth to kindle the spirits of others is utterly cold in itself.

Such praises are not, I think, generous enough to stir up any envy, nor is anyone grudging enough to deny it. Yet I would have withheld even this except that your impudence keeps me from drawing the line even there, and compels me to push well beyond it to catch up with you. For whose ears are long-suffering enough to endure your shameless insults when you twit Erasmus with being a vagabond just because he occasionally changes his residence, something he rarely does except when his concern for the good of the public directs him to do so? As if it were the essence of holiness to stagnate forever and stay glued to one rock all the time like an oyster or sponge![334] But if that is so, then the Franciscan order was quite ill conceived, though no order (unless I am mistaken) is holier than this one; and yet many of its members, with perfectly good reasons, go wandering all over the world. Jerome did something wrong when he traveled all the way from Rome to Jerusalem. The most holy apostles were much beneath your sort of holiness when

329 See Terence, Eunuchus 254.
330 Terence, Andria 68; Adages 1853 (CWE 34: 110–11) 331 See Apologia contra Hieronymum 2.5 (PL 21: 576); Apologia adversus libros Rufini 1.30 (PL 23: 421). 332 See EE 2: 29, 244. 333 Lk 18:11
334 rock … sponge: Adages 3745 (CWE 36: 385); Praise of Folly (ASD 4/3: 162); EE 3: 267

they journeyed all over the earth while you people sat still, indeed even before you sat still. Nor am I saying this as a way of placing Erasmus on a level with them, so that no one will captiously charge me with meaning to do so, but rather to show you that just as there is often nothing wrong about moving around so there is no special holiness seated in always sitting still.

For to come to Erasmus, whatever the character of the rest of his conduct, which is actually quite irreproachable, I would certainly not hesitate to prefer his kind of wandering, which you run down so shamelessly, to any part of your virtues, however proud you all may be of it. For I think there is not a man living today who loves ease and hates work who would not rather sit still with you than go wandering with him. For if you consider work, he sometimes does more in one day than you do in many months, and if you consider the usefulness of the work, he sometimes does more fruitful work for the Church in one month than you do in several years, unless you think that anyone's fasts or perfunctory prayers do as much or do such widespread good as so many great volumes, through which the whole world is instructed in righteousness, or unless you suppose he is out for sheer fun when he makes light of turbulent seas, inclement skies, and all sorts of trials in order to work for the common good. What a fine sort of fun, to get seasick from being on a ship, to be battered around by its tossing, to be threatened by storms, and to have death and shipwreck continually before one's eyes! When he crawls so often through rugged forests and wild groves, over rough slopes and precipitous mountains, along roads beset with bandits, when he is buffeted by the wind, splashed with mud, drenched with rain, worn out by his travels, and exhausted by overwork, when he frequently lodges in a miserable inn and wishes that he had your bed and board, what a hedonist's life he appears to be leading! Especially since all these hardships, which could easily wear down a vigorous and sturdy young man, are confronted and borne by Erasmus's old body, which is already breaking down with the strain of his study and work, so that it is practically obvious that he must have succumbed long ago to so many hardships if God, who makes his sun rise on both good men and bad,[335] had not protected him

for the benefit even of ingrates. For from each of his voyages he brings home the splendid fruits of his travels for others but for himself nothing more than poor health and the ill words that his good deeds provoke from the worst sort of men. Thus he takes so much pleasure in those expeditions that if they were not required for the sake of his studies, that is, for the public benefit of everyone (something he often buys at the cost of some private disadvantage), he would be very glad to forgo them. But in the meantime he associates only with people who are respected for both learning and character, and he is constantly gestating some new idea which he later brings forth, not without public intellectual profit, during those travels which you so malign. But if he had paid less attention to that public profit and more to his own advantages, he would have today not only a much less debilitated body but also a much richer and more opulent fortune, since all princes and almost all great nobles are vying to draw him to them on the most generous terms. And yet it would surely have been fair and just that Erasmus, who, wherever he lives, spreads his great bounty all over the world as the sun spreads its rays, should receive benefits from all over the world in return.

Thus, since he is devoted entirely to the welfare of others and asks for no reward whatsoever on earth, I certainly ought not to doubt that God will reward him most generously there where it is better to get one's reward. And for this reason, though I anticipate that your own reward will be very great and I wish for it to be as great as possible, when I compare you with the man you despise and I consider your merits side by side, insofar as I can judge on the basis of human conjecture, I firmly expect that when the day finally dawns on you both when your virtues will get their reward, on that day, without any injury to you and indeed with your cheerful assent as your feelings will stand then, God, the impartial assessor of both of you, will not only prefer his wandering to your sitting still, but since all things work together for good[336] in good men, God will also prefer his eloquence to your silence, his silence to your prayers, his food to your fasting, and his sleep to your vigils, and in summary, God will prize all that you so proudly despise in Erasmus above all that you so dearly esteem in your own way of life.

---

335 *God . . . bad:* See Mt 5:45; Lk 6:35.　　**336** *all . . . good:* See Rm 8:28; *Adages* 1860 (*CWE* 34: 113).

For undoubtedly, though you might be ashamed to admit it, you could never have attacked anyone so arrogantly unless you grossly flattered yourself with an amazing assurance of your own holiness. There is absolutely nothing more dangerous than this to the religious life, and nothing that I, for the love that I bear you, want you to avoid more completely. For it could benefit me and those like me, who drift here and there in a miserable world, to look up to you from below, so to speak, and to admire your observances as we would a pattern of angelic life, so that we could be prompted as if by our awe at the virtue of others to hold our own lives in more perfect disdain. But it could do you, on the other hand, no good at all to contemn and condemn others' lives, sometimes even superior ones, in comparison with your own. You should make it your habit instead to look up even to inferior attainments in others and not only to think more modestly of your own attainments but also to hold them all suspect, and live not without hope but yet always in fear, not just of falling hereafter (for which there is the saying, "He who stands, let him take heed of falling"),[337] but of having fallen long before now, in particular when you yourself thought that you were ascending most rapidly, namely when you entered the religious life.

I am not saying this because I doubt in the least that the portion Mary chose was the better one. But since "All mortal justice is as the rag of a menstruating woman,"[338] so that everyone has good reason to hold even his own good qualities suspect, it would probably be not unwholesome for you to feel inwardly doubtful and fearful lest either you do not share Mary's portion or you have chosen Mary's portion mistakenly, since you rank her function not merely above Martha's office, as Christ did, but even above that of the apostles. You should be afraid that, when you view yourself, too indulgently, as one who has retreated into holy solitude to escape harmful pleasures, the deeper scrutiny of God, who observes us with more penetration, who explores our own hearts more profoundly than we do, and whose eyes discern our imperfections, may find that what you have been doing is avoiding responsibility, dodging work, cultivating the pleasure of repose in the shadow of piety, looking for a way out of life's troubles, and wrapping your talent up in a napkin,[339] thus wasting it inside for fear of losing it out-of-doors.

You will gain at least this much by such meditations: they will stop you from using your sect to fuel personal pride, the most dangerous habit there is, and from putting too much faith in private ceremonies, while they will encourage you to place more hope in the Christian religion than you do in your own religious order and to trust less in the things you can do by yourself than in the things you cannot do except with God's help. You can fast by yourself; you can watch by yourself; you can pray by yourself; why, you can even do all this by the devil. But a truly Christian faith, through which Christ Jesus's name is truly uttered in the spirit; a truly Christian hope, which despairs of its own merits and puts all its faith in the generosity of God; and a truly Christian charity, which is not puffed up, which does not become angry, which does not seek its own glory, are not to be had by anyone except through God's grace and gratuitous favor alone.[340] The more confidence you place in these common virtues of Christianity the less faith you will come to place in your own private ceremonies or in those of your order; and the less faith you have in such things, the more good they will do you. For it is when you consider yourself a useless servant that God will consider you a faithful one. And we can certainly find good cause to see ourselves as useless even when we have done all we can, which I pray to God that both of us, and Erasmus as well, will eventually do, yet not only that we will do all we can, but (especially if it turns out we have done a good deal) that we reckon ourselves to have done really nothing at all. For this way is the surest of all to aspire to the place in which neither the virtue of others will cause us distress nor the brilliance of others will draw any tear from our own bleary eyes.

At the end[341] of your letter you write that my modesty ought to prevent me from showing your letter to anyone. I do not see how that can pertain to my modesty at all. Your own modesty, or at least your own prudence, should certainly have stopped you from showing your letter to as many as you did: modesty if your letter had been what you deem it to be; prudence if you had deemed it to be what it is. But in view of the facts, your own notion of modesty is novel indeed: even as you insist on my silence, as if you were either displeased with your letter or loath to accept any praise for it, you yourself, the moment that you start to burn with a prickling desire for ephemeral glory, go out looking for others provoked by the same scabby itch, so that you can scratch each other's backs[342] in a pleasurable medley of chafing. Having heard how those fellows were boasting wherever they went that your elegant letters, dictated by the Holy Spirit, had changed my opinions enough to make me reject Erasmus's writings, I thought it best to declare my position in a letter in order to show up their folly, if they actually believed what they said, or their malice, if they made it up. For I cannot judge how your letter struck them, since an ass's penchant for thistles has even given rise to an adage.[343] I, at any rate, found nothing in it sufficiently splendid or dazzling to make us stop seeing white as white. Thus although I felt I had to state my own views on account of the unfounded boasting which you or your friends have been doing, thus far I have decided to continue to safeguard your own reputation: I have not only not mentioned your name in my letter (a name which I otherwise hold very dear); I have also erased it in yours, or at any rate in the one copy I have ("I am afraid that what I have to say may appear somewhat brash . . ."). These steps will ensure that no matter how men speak or think of your action—and all good, learned men will undoubtedly think and speak ill of it—you yourself will be spared the least blush of embarrassment.

It pleases me greatly that once you have finished your raving you finally return to your senses and grow less implacable, even hinting that you may be willing to settle your feud with Erasmus on quite easy terms. For you write the following: "Even so, I am not such an enemy of Erasmus that I would refuse to make up with him if he would correct his minor mistakes." My word, you have crowned the man's bliss! For without this assurance the poor fellow might well have wasted away from sheer grief had he lost every hope of eventually gaining your favor, great man that you are. But now that you offer him peace with such easy conditions, making such fair demands, I am sure he will rush to oblige, and correct his mistakes just as soon as you point any out; for thus far you have pointed out only your own. And yet even those readings that you call his minor mistakes, where he alters *sagena* to *verriculum*, *dimitte* to *remitte*, *discumbentium* to *discumbentibus*, and so on, wherever he replaces a barbarous word with a Latin one, a solecism with a grammatical phrase, or an ambiguous phrase with a clear one, wherever he either corrects a mistake of the translator or redresses the lapse of a scribe, even these I repeat, he will change for the worse, one and all, to avoid having you as an enemy, and since (as I see) it was sacrilege, not simple theft, for Erasmus to remove all this treasure from the temple, he will retrieve every barbarism, every solecism, each and every obscurity, each careless rendering or faulty transcription, and faithfully put it all back in the sanctuary, not deterred in the least by the thought that this action will look like a quite unforgivable insult to all of the good, learned men he won over with that other service. For at last, by dispensing with all of them—with the mere rank and file—he will be making friends with the mightiest potentates and paired prefects of literacy, namely you and that paltry apologist.

But joking aside, I sincerely and wholly approve of the decent and pious intentions you showed here, at least, in confessing that all that needs to be corrected are some minor mistakes. For thereby you confessed (somewhat bashfully, in keeping with your modesty, but still truthfully enough to disburden yourself of such a criminal lie), you confessed, I repeat, that all the intemperate charges with which you began about heresy, schism, and the heralding of Antichrist were all pure fabrications. For I still do not think you so totally hopeless that you could regard heresy, schism, and the heralding of Antichrist, three crimes which no mass of evils could rival, as minor mistakes. Therefore, since I see you have recanted all your really serious charges, I am not going to argue with you over trifles, so that we can both simply forget what was said, let the whole uproar, which sprang out of nothing, dissolve at long last into nothing again, and thus finish this tragedy as a comedy. Farewell; and if you hope to reap any benefit from secluding yourself in a cloister, find contentment in spiritual repose, not in this sort of quarreling.   THE END

---

342 *you . . . backs:* See *Adages* 699 (*CWE* 32: 126–27).   **343** See *Adages* 971 (*CWE* 32: 264–65).

86. To Germanus Brixius[344]
London, 1520

T. More to Germanus Brixius, greetings.

I myself, Brixius, am not so fastidious or so self-indulgent as to be vexed or hurt because I have not been granted a thing which has never been granted to anyone among mortal men. For who has ever, in any age, lived out his days so untroubled that he not only had friends but never encountered an enemy?[345] Therefore, since I see that the blessing of having no enemy at all is denied me by the common lot of mortals, I am happy, at least, that through fortune's beneficence I have been granted the best sort of friends and an enemy such that no one would want him as a friend or be troubled by him as an enemy, a man who is equally unable to gratify when he means well and to injure when he is irate.[346] And yet I would certainly be angry with myself if I had given even such a person as you cause to hate me. As it is, I bear it with all the more equanimity since I am quite sure no one fails to perceive that this pointless and worse-than-effeminate quarreling of yours has no source but your own morbid feelings. Indeed, I am also less vexed by this strife since, though no good can come of it, I also see that apart from a loss of paper and time (and I choose to waste little of either) no great ill otherwise can befall either one of us. Each of us, in his way, is immune; you can not injure me, nor can anyone injure you, since your sort leaves no room for disparagement.[347]

I see that your confidence in this fact alone has driven you to embrace the expedient of traducing yourself, far and wide, before all learned people (if any, that is, will see fit to read trifles so trifling as these) with so elegant and splendid a specimen of your natural gifts and so sober a testimony to your moral soundness as that latest tract of yours furnishes. Having already established quite clearly just what sort of poet you are, now no doubt you intend to show by publishing this tract what kind of man you are. Indeed you have shown it so distinctively and have portrayed yourself so graphically that I neither would, if I could, nor could, if I would, spatter

you with so many and such grievous slanders as you plaster all over yourself. And yet you display so much eagerness for that sort of praise, it would seem that the one and only way to placate and propitiate you is to savage you with disgraceful slanders.[348] But I am not so ambitious for your amity that I would not rather speak words which may please even one good and honorable man than words which may please three hundred Brixiuses, and therefore I shall not take in hand that illustrious and rich stock of insults in which you take such vaunting and boastful delight; nor, so far as I can stay away from it, will I touch on it at all. Only if there is some slight admixture of amusing insanity which thoughtful observers may laugh at, and need not detest, will I not hesitate to use it to alleviate my reader's disgust, of which he must endure a great deal as he reads through such quarrelsome and utterly fruitless rebukes. But the other slanders with which you pollute yourself more disgracefully I shall either avoid altogether or else, where I am forced to touch on them, I shall touch on them so lightly as to make it clear to everyone that I am no less eager to conceal your slanders, Brixius, than you are to reveal them and wear them about you like a badge of distinction. For the charges which you lay against me are such insipid calumnies that I would not have seen fit to reply if I had not decided to wash away this single charge, which you constantly harp on, but never establish, that I started this quarrel of yours.

But you should have confirmed that, Brixius, and not just affirmed it. And if you thought that my epigrams sufficed to demonstrate that claim, you ought at least to have included them in your tract,[349] so that you would not have appeared impudent even to those who had no access to my poems. And undoubtedly you would have done so if you had not perceived it was not in your interest that my lines be read. For if they are compared closely with yours (even if anyone else thinks, as you do, that my lines should be quite overcome by the splendor of your verses), mine would still benefit to this extent from the luster of their rivals, that the main issue would be made quite clear: my lines have been rather

344 This letter was originally published with this title: "A letter of Thomas More to Germanus Brixius who once attacked England with shameful lies in a tract which More made fun of in some epigrams more than seven years ago, and who now, not a month and a half ago, in a time of the most perfect peace between England and France, on the very eve of the meeting between their princes, published a tract against More which defames its own author with its pointless and virulent rebukes. In the renowned city of London 1520." **345** *so . . . enemy:* See Plutarch, *Moralia* 86c. **346** *enemy . . . irate:* See *Adages* 1709 (*CWE* 34: 52). **347** *nor . . . disparagement:* See Terence, *Hecyra* 233–34. **348** See *CW* 3.2: 488, 538. **349** *Antimorus*

reviled than refuted, and they do not give you an adequate pretext for launching another savage attack at this late date. To make this still clearer, since I see just how eager you are to forget it, I will refresh your memory about the origin of this splendid duel of yours. But I will do so in such a way as to omit certain points which might strengthen my own case whenever I cannot touch on a point in my favor without insult to this or that nation.

During the late disturbance between Louis, your king, and the Roman pontiff, our unvanquished prince Henry, the eighth of that name, at the request of that sacrosanct see, had decided to lend his assistance to the faltering cause of the Church: he ordered several ships to put to sea to blockade and restrain the formidable fleet which Louis had equipped. When these two fleets engaged each other, all the ships on both sides were lucky enough to survive except two which were lost; for these two, at their first encounter, had immediately thrown out grappling hooks and bound themselves together so tightly that when their decks caught fire they could not be parted—a dismal prelude to the war.

When you described this sea battle in verse, you set out not to combine truth with falsehood but to fabricate practically the whole of your story from out-and-out lies, tailoring new facts according to your personal whim.[350] You disparaged the piety of our king by calling it envy. With false maledictions and unsurpassed petulance you assailed all of England as pact-breaking and perjured. With lies which were more than poetic you led out to sea a Hervé who was more than Herculean.[351] Charging in with the *Cordelière*,[352] all by itself, and a small crew of helpers, relying on the doughty Hervé, you dispersed all our vessels, with which you had covered the main, and drove them away like flies[353] in whatever direction you pleased.[354] You sank most of them under the waves, you cruel man, though a merciful Neptune soon sent home the same ships unscathed. You raced with the *Cordelière* like a thoroughbred hound in pursuit of our *Regent*, which fled like a poor little hare. You drove the *Cordelière* on with the strong arms of oarsmen, although made no use of oars, so that you would not lose that laborious half-line, "driven on by strong arms."[355] You puffed up the sails with Hervé's noisy huffing. You silently passed by the commander of the opposing ship,[356] a man of great name and station, and of course thought it artful to do so. You sang of your well-nigh factitious Hervé fighting not merely stoutly but prodigiously to boot. You foisted him, dauntless, into the midst of his enemies on the *Regent*, on which he did not once set foot. Having taken the *Regent*'s crow's nests and staged that abominable massacre, you led her in tow, bound and vanquished. Unguarded as you were, you threw a bolt of blazing fire from the vanquished ship into the vanquisher (not an easy feat for a crew bound and vanquished). By a lapse of memory (a trap liars often slip into)[357] you made Hervé, whom you had left in the *Regent*, turn up suddenly on the burning *Cordelière*, as if he had two bodies, to deliver himself, there in the flames, of a long-winded sermon. You chose to put off his death for no other reason, I suspect, than to have him sing, in the meantime, of your future election as a nursling of Phoebus to sing of Hervé's own demise. You roasted your heroes to ashes one and all, and had good cause to roast them, indeed, since they chose to burn up when they could have moved onto the *Regent*, which they had captured and which they were leading in tow, bound and vanquished, begging heaven for mercy. You described Hervé, who had outlived his comrades, right on the verge of flying off to the heavenly saints (for by then the fire had burned away everything mortal about him, especially the ruinous emotions of mortals, in particular anger and hatred), and right then, of all times, you pretended that he, though thus purified—provoked, I suppose, by Saint Lawrence's example[358] (whom indeed you had made your exemplar in fashioning that valiant man's

350 *combine...whim:* See Horace, *Ars poetica* 151–52, 338–39. **351** Hervé de Porzmoguer was the Breton commander of the *Cordelière*. **352** The *Cordelière* was a French ship that burned up with the *Regent*, a British ship. Germanus Brixius's poem *Chordigerae navis conflagratio*, published in 1513, commemorated this naval battle that took place on August 10, 1512. More wrote sarcastic epigrams in reply; Brixius responded in his 1519 *Antimorus*, despite Erasmus's advice not to do so. More replied to Brixius in this letter, but at Erasmus's request, withdrew the book from circulation. For More's poems in English translation, see Epigrams 188–95, 209, 266–69. More had left it to Erasmus's judgment whether to include these epigrams concerning Brixius in More's 1518 edition of *Epigrams*, first published by Froben in Basel. **353** *drove...flies: Adages* 2660 (*cwe* 35: 251–52) **354** For More's allusions to the poem, see Brixius's *Chordigera* in *cw* 3.2: 429–65. **355** *cw* 3.2: 450 **356** Sir Thomas Knyvet **357** See *Adages* 1274 (*cwe* 33: 175). **358** The battle occurred on August 10, St. Lawrence's feast day.

character) — was induced by pure envy and lust for revenge, having nothing to gain for himself, to cremate the ship which he had captured and all those fine prisoners' physiques along with him. On top of all this you were not content merely to consume men and ships in the fire so completely that (contrary to what usually happens in tragedies) no *deus ex machina* saved even one man to show you the factual foundation for the story you harp at, but with those very flames you then kindled "the stars with the heavens and with all the fish in it, the sea,"[359] and did so not in some brief hyperbole but in numerous lines of impressively painstaking dullness, a fine emulation of Ovid, of course, which in one respect even outdoes him: in his fabrication, the steeds of the sun, gone astray for the want of their driver, burn only the earth,[360] whereas you, with egregious cunning, of course, enflame sky, land, and sea with just one burning boat. Having thus outdone Ovid, you fiercely challenged Vergil as well, and whereas he had imagined a rain sent by Jove to besprinkle and thus save the fleet of Aeneas when it was afire,[361] you delayed till the ships were long gone and consumed by the blaze and then rained down a copious torrent from heaven, as if otherwise the fire which was belched inexhaustibly out of the water (as water perpetually springs from a pumice stone)[362] might launch some of its flames into heaven. When you handled these things in this way, I happened to get a copy of your book, perhaps even before it was printed, and when I observed such portentous monstrosities, such disgraceful, such shameful lies, such absurd fabrications, and those patches of other men's purple you wore stitched[363] all over your ill-woven bardic *surtout* (to make room for which you had arrayed your whole habit in a form which "Orestes himself, though insane, would swear was a form which no sane man would choose"),[364] I indicated in a couple of epigrams that I found your narration wanting in material credibility and your composition wanting in sense, while the hoard you had gathered of other men's corn had exceeded the measure of your granary.

At the same time I had written an epigram making fun of one of my countrymen who was given to affecting French manners both inopportunely and clumsily. If there is anything in this epigram which is too biting, it recoils on the ludicrous fop himself, not on the French, against whom, torture the epigram as you may, you will exact no other accusation than that as masters you are a little too harsh to your servants. And that, I suppose, not even you will deny. Nor do I attack that propensity in you, but rather, since each race has its own code of conduct, it irked me that that countryman of mine should defy our conventions by treating your countryman too harshly.

Since I was writing these epigrams at the time when everything was ablaze with the tumult of war, even if it had occurred to me to write something more biting, I would certainly not have believed that anyone was so inequitable or that you yourself were so outrageously self-indulgent as to demand that we should aim not one line at you Frenchmen, though you had launched book-length attacks against us. Thus, if I wrote against you first, I will be guilty of having challenged you; but if you wrote against us first, then how can you put an honorable face on so dishonorable an action as that? While I myself repaid a book with an epigram, you in turn retaliated against a jesting epigram with an amazingly virulent volume. Further, I wrote these playful pieces of mine right away, before peace had been made; as for you, only now, so many years later, in the most perfect peace, with our princes conjoined by the closest affinity, with our peoples bound together in a wonderful concord, after the most salutary [of peace settlements] has been consecrated on your side and ours by the most sacred rituals, now, of all times, you spring up and renew old and long-buried feuds, tear apart mending wounds,[365] and chafe open the scars drawn across them; now you cast in our faces our men's disgraceful flight, our fleets scattered and sunk, and our envy and pact-breaking perjury, charges which you disgracefully fabricate.[366]

Yet you want it to seem that all this is entirely in order, namely that you should attack me now, vigorously, as you imagine, simply because I fought with you once in the past.[367] But who fails to see how ridiculously any athlete would be acting if he entered the arena and challenged all comers, if one of them happened to overthrow him and the meet was then finally broken up and the contest concluded, and

359 *CW* 3.2: 460   **360** See *Metamorphoses* 2.201–10.   **361** See *Aeneid* 5.687–99.   **362** *as water...stone: Adages* 375 (*CWE* 31: 369–70)   **363** *purple...stitched:* Horace, *Ars poetica* 15–16   **364** Persius, *Satires* 3.118   **365** *tear...wounds:* See *Adages* 580 (*CWE* 32: 53).   **366** See *Antimorus* (*CW* 3.2: 490).   **367** See *CW* 3.2: 486, 512, 536.

if he then showed up once again, some years later, and only then, when everyone had different interests and outlooks and paid no attention to that sort of strife, he pounced in unexpectedly and seized by the waist[368] the antagonist with whom he had fought in the past and proclaimed himself challenged even now, as if a person who answers a challenge could be called a challenger or as if any strife, once begun, lasts forever; who, I ask, fails to see how ridiculously such an athlete would be acting, even if he should happen to win the fight? But what if he jumps in as you do and lashes out in all directions, flailing his arms and legs, bruising some with his outflung fists and others with his heels,[369] and among these perhaps the sponsors of the preceding contest, and what if at last, when he has racked himself for a long time in vain, unable to throw his adversary, lest he seem to have sallied forth wholly in vain he then spits in his opponent's face and throws up all over him, heaving the toxic and distempered vomit from his drunken stomach, and what if then, swelling with pride as if he had given a splendid performance, he goes off to celebrate his extraordinary triumph in low dives and taverns? Does such a wrestler then merit a victory crown? Or does he deserve rather to have his shins and his ankles broken?

Who does not see by now, Brixius, how much like this athlete you are; though you may be unlike him in this one respect, that you did not challenge our entire nation to a sporting competition but provoked us instead with belligerent abuse, unless perhaps you contend that to charge us with perjury ought not to be classed as an insult — in much the same way, you might argue that a donkey ought not be classed as a quadruped. In response to this challenge I took up a couple of darts, of the blunt-tipped variety, and did not so much fight you as sport with you (since it seemed you were not worth the trouble of wounding). Nonetheless, for one reason or another, as a pustule is easily punctured, my stroke left you in such grievous pain that even now, after so many years have elapsed, after peace has so often been made and confirmed, after concord has been established in so many ways, after our princes have been joined in such intimate affinity[370] (although this fact alone should have settled all long-standing feuds between the nations of both princes), all of a sudden you rise up once more against me, as if you had not given the first challenge and the war were still on; and when everyone else is intent upon love, friendship, and now mutual hospitality, you set upon me with the weapons of war and attack me with darts which, although none too sharp, are (despite the fixed martial conventions of all who are not wholly barbarous and savage) envenomed. Meanwhile, you insist, no less stupidly than dishonestly, that you come forth to answer my challenge, as if you were prepared to respond to those darts which we launched against you in responding to your provocation. But those darts of ours were clearly such that, however much you sweat, you cannot escape them by any response. Knowing this to be true, you arranged your own tract so that you need not touch on your personal defense except timidly and in passing but could turn your whole effort toward skewering me; and although this offensive absorbed every ounce of your vigor and virulence, what else did you finally achieve but to blurt out your bumptious urbanities, to spew out your furious venom, and at last, since you could not really wound me, to do something at least by spitting all over me, after which you marched off an egregious victor and triumphant hero?

But how wittily pert you have proven against me we shall see in good time. Meanwhile let us consider how artfully you refute my objections in that toilsome tract of yours, which has cost you more days to perfect than the book contains lines. Now, whereas I arraigned you for purloining some elements of your poem from the ancients, for developing other elements very absurdly, and for narrating everything in such a way that there was neither any truth in your subject matter nor any credit attached to your words, you responded to the first point as if I had charged that your lines smack too much of antiquity,[371] from which charge, lest you strain yourself too much in answering, I freely absolve you. For elsewhere you touch again on this same charge in passing; again you dissemble the theft you are charged with; again you attempt to defend it as if I had accused you of emulating the ancients, and indeed, not content to escape any blame, you even claim praise for your blameworthy deed; you claim you have emulated the ancients, followed

368 *seized … waist:* See *Adages* 396 (*CWE* 31: 381).   **369** *fists … heels:* See *Adages* 2021 (*CWE* 34: 190).   **370** Henry VIII's daughter Mary was supposed to eventually marry the dauphin of France.   **371** See *CW* 3.2: 488.

assiduously in their footsteps,³⁷² and, in a word, wrested the club out of Hercules' hands.³⁷³ But I had to laugh, by Hercules, as I read what grand and glorious claims you had based on so shameful an action. For you have imitated everything in the worst possible way. You do frequently take over either half-lines or whole lines from others as if they were yours, meanwhile making some small and inept alteration. But in my opinion, Brixius, this is not emulating the ancients but contaminating, disgracing, and polluting them; this is not wresting Hercules's club away forcibly but furtively snatching it up when he has laid it down. Still I cannot deny that this is following in the footsteps of the ancients, but assuredly, Brixius, you follow a bit too relentlessly: you follow so closely in their footsteps that you knock off their shoes and then wear them yourself, though your feet hardly fill them.³⁷⁴ It was a poor defense, for you to boast of doing much the same thing that Vergil claimed to have done (not everyone has any business to head for Corinth).³⁷⁵ He was more than able to make good on his claim; you lack any means to make good on your arrogant boast; unless you suppose it is the same sort of achievement for Vergil to engraft the transitory lines of Ennius into his poems, which will live forever, as it is for you to obtrude Vergil's everlasting lines into yours, which are already dying; for him to set off others' verses with better ones, as for you to commingle whatever is finest in ancient writers with your sordid rubbish; for him to compete with the Greeks so that he everywhere proved himself their equal, often even surpassing them, as for you to encounter the Latins not in order to rival or compete with them, but in order to sneak up and pilfer something which you may transfer whole to your store (if you hope that your theft will not be noticed) or else lop off its tail and its ears, as you would treat a stolen horse, since you would rather secure the use of it even by disfiguring it than not have it at all.

In this matter you prove to be such an industrious and indeed thrifty thief that often, rather than let even a single half-line of some other poet escape you if you think it is especially pretty, you import wildly absurd fantasies and the most pointless fabrications, which the context and subject at hand neither call for nor tolerate, fabrications and fantasies ranging from heaven to earth, but without any bearing on heaven or on earth,³⁷⁶ as the saying goes. And if, in setting forth a battle or representing a tempest or anything else of that sort, you choose any one of the ancients to emulate, you obtrude so many of his words and even whole verses into your verses, you so change for the worse all that you alter, that if anyone considers the parts separately, on the one side you look not at all like your model and on the other side you look just like him. But if anyone regards the whole from both sides at once, then indeed it may seem that some angry god, by a wondrous metamorphosis, has changed some very beautiful hero into a ludicrous ape.³⁷⁷

Such was the elegant method—dissimulation, that is—which you used to answer my charge of thievery. And when you come to the shameless lies which swarm throughout your *Chordigera* like worms in a corpse, then you brandish before me, like the shield of Ajax³⁷⁸ or the aegis of Pallas,³⁷⁹ the privilege peculiar to poetry, whereby, you think, she is exempted from the law of history which prescribes truthful reporting. But assuredly, Brixius, while I would not shut up poetry (an august and extremely free goddess,³⁸⁰ to be sure) in such straitened confines as to deny her the license to fabricate not only words but also incidents, provided it not be used shamelessly, even so I will simply not stand for it if she tells some shameless lie and elaborates it absurdly, if she twists and perverts a whole sequence of incidents and even their very outcome. If you have decided, on the contrary, that she is so absolutely free of all the laws of history, without exception, that she is permitted to sing that men fought to the death, though they never came to blows, and that those who lost, won, and that those who fled, routed their enemies, at that point we would not only laugh at the lamentable fate of Dido, which you adduce as a fabrication³⁸¹ (and indeed, although I am not sure it has been altogether confuted, it is certainly called into question by authors whose own credibility is not altogether unquestionable); we would also be brought to believe that those wars were all falsehoods and those

372 See CW 3.2: 510–42.   373 *wrested...hands:* See Adages 3095 (CWE 35: 498–99) for the saying attributed to Vergil.   374 *wear...them:* See Adages 1446 (CWE 33: 262).   375 *head for Corinth:* See Adages 301 (CWE 31: 317–19).   376 *without...earth:* See Adages 444, 1495 (CWE 31: 422, 33: 285).   377 See Horace, *Ars poetica* 1–9; Adages 2409 (CWE 35: 76).   378 See Adages 2737 (CWE 35: 295–96); Homer, *Iliad* 8.267–68.   379 See Homer, *Odyssey* 22.297.   380 *poetry...goddess:* See Adages 2048 (CWE 34: 199); Horace, *Ars poetica* 9–13.   381 See CW 3.2: 488.

nuptials false fabrications, or that Aeneas was certainly overcome by Turnus and Turnus by Pallas,[382] and in short that everything was done just the opposite way from how it is reported by Vergil; that is,
5 we would leave Vergil to join up with you, and then by the same token leave Homer for Dio,[383] a man so inimical to poetry that he argues that the whole Trojan war, and Troy itself, practically, is a Homeric fabrication, sustaining this argument obstinately de-
10 spite countless proofs which refute him. He had no other motive for doing so, it seems, than to bring about with an inimical intent just the thing that you now bring about with a friendly intent. You two differ in just one respect: he was deliberately trying to
15 keep anyone from esteeming the poets; you accomplish the same thing through heedlessness, not as one craftsman envying another[384] but rather as one envying art its own glory, indeed envying yourself your own glory if you were in fact such a great poet
20 as you would be thought; for do you not spoil your own principal source of prestige if, because of you, no one will deign to have his deeds memorialized in the lines of the poets? Certainly no one will do so who has any sense, at least not if he is convinced that
25 everything a poet sings is to be taken for a fabrication, especially when the singer himself testifies to the fact.

    On this point, moreover, if I may talk with you truthfully and freely, you are not the only one to
30 recount your nation's dealings with ours, if not falsely (for I scruple to utter that word in the presence of such fastidious ears), then at least very freely indeed. A short work was issued by one Pilleus of Tours, in sufficiently melodious lines; for I
35 willingly pass by my other objections, lest he too should proclaim himself challenged. In his tract, however, if anyone observes how frequently he employs the Brixian style of poetry in narrating his story, or with what venerable titles he adorns our
40 England, or with what reverend epithets he dignifies glorious Spain, that observer, I think, will assuredly judge that if anyone, either English or Spanish, should snap back at Pilleus with even more than an epigram, Pilleus would have no reason to complain
45 about being offended, since he was the first to offend. And if anyone on earth were so inequitable

as to think otherwise, I myself would not have hesitated to submit to the calumny of that man if the book had come into my hands at some point in the past. But now that new friendship has rendered 50 such feuds obsolete, it is not my intention to stir matters up all over again, and so I will leave out the book and adduce nothing more than the title, both to enable my readers to gauge the whole lion by its claw[385] and to give anyone who is inclined to read 55 the book a name, at least, with which he can track it down. It bears this inscription: *On the Flight of the English from the Territories of France, and the expulsion of the Spanish from Navarre.* Who needs a sieve to guess what stuff the rest of this book must consist 60 of, since the title he reads consists of such chaff and rings as true to the rest of the book as it rings false to history? For who will not laugh at Pilleus when he boasts that in battle the English were driven out of France? It is, I think, amply established (to say 65 nothing further) that the English were certainly not driven out of France; and if he thinks that the English were driven out by the people of Aquitaine, how could they have been put to flight by a people with whom they did not even have an opportu- 70 nity to clash? But it is even more remarkably absurd that he should trumpet the Spaniards' repulse from their holdings in Navarre, for they entered Navarre at that time, held it steadily thereafter, and hold it today. 75

    But yet let us concede all these whimsies to poetry; for in poetry, at least in the province of fabrications, Pilleus's muse recalls your muse so prettily that nowhere on earth is there simian more similar to simian. And indeed, I guess that that other author will 80 also belabor this sanction of poetry, the one who, not so very long ago, printed in Paris a *Short Sheaf of the Times*,[386] a sheaf truly made to be burned, since its author had gathered within it a number of firebrands which might very well have been enough to 85 touch off a new conflagration between our two peoples if our prince's insight had not given him ample assurance that he and his deeds, both so clearly and generally commended, were proof against the barking of envious men. For besides certain other sedi- 90 tious lies which have lately been inserted into that tract, a final flourish[387] has been added, by far the

---

382 See Vergil, *Aeneid* 10.439–509, 12.887–952.   **383** Dio Cocceianus Chrysostomos (*ca.* 40–*ca.* 120 AD), attempted to discredit the legend of Troy   as completely fictitious in his *Eleventh Discourse.*   **384** *not as . . . another:* See *Adages* 125 (*CWE* 31: 170–71); Hesiod, *Works and Days* 25.   **385** *gauge . . . claw:*   *Adages* 834 (*CWE* 32: 200)   **386** by Werner Rolevinck (1425–1502)   **387** *final flourish:* See *Adages* 3520 (*CWE* 36: 223–24).

most seditious avowal of them all, where we read that your prince fully two years ago would have gone out to ward off the Turks if he had not suspected that the English king was untrustworthy.
Who would put up with such stuff if he knows that at that time your people had not planned any such expedition and that no one had been less suspected by your prince than ours, or had done less to merit suspicion? Now what could be said or imagined more shameless than what that other writer[388] asserted in your language: that while our king was in arms in France, James, the King of the Scots, entered Britain and waged a successful campaign and then made his way home with great glory?[389] Nor was this wretched writer at all disconcerted by what was common knowledge everywhere, even though, as he knew, common knowledge had given every mortal more than ample assurance that the Scots had been routed and driven to flight, that the king himself had been slain with almost all his nobles, and that since he had died excommunicate his body had been kept without burial for so many years in accord with a papal injunction.

Although writings like these often make their way over from your shores to ours, nonetheless, now that such a general peace has been achieved we have chosen rather to make no response and to bear with such calumnies, which are growing in bulk by the day, than to throw them back at you with any offense to your feelings; at the same time we hope that hereafter no less a historian than Paulus Aemilius,[390] so strict and impartial in shaping his narrative that one might suppose he was bound by an oath and so elegant that if he did not write of more recent events he would seem not the humblest of ancients, will report for posterity the deeds of both peoples, at least those deeds which concerned both alike, with an unalloyed credibility.

But since your book was set before me when our relations were at their most troubled, I certainly never thought I would have to expiate my offense with a blood-sacrifice if I chastised that book, which was so bitter and shamelessly given up to lies, with a mere epigram penned in play and in jest.
You, on the other hand, marvelously witty as ever, joke about my lordly privilege[391] should I forbid

you to touch me in turn after I had touched you, and yet even though you took the initiative in assailing the whole of my nation with wanton abuse and shameless lies, you were so irked at my touching your sacrosanct majesty with even a jest that for several years, day and night,[392] you spent all of your energy in preparing to combat my casually improvised epigrams with a carefully planned volume. In it you set up two tasks for yourself, first to vindicate your lines and then to inveigh against mine; and you performed the first so magnificently that out of the things with which I had reproached you you dissembled some and misunderstood others, while the one charge which was too great to sidestep, too commonly known to dissemble, and too true to evade, you conveniently deflected with that definition, according to which all that I had exposed as a lie you contended to be not a lie but a sheer fabrication.

Wherefore, since our confrontation brings me to realize that you are so keen as to split fabrication from falsehood with Tenedian[393] precision, which amounts to the same thing as extricating yourself from a mistaken lie by implicating yourself in a deliberate one, I will not make any more difficulties for you about this matter. You can claim the victory provided that we agree on this one point (and if not I will then win the point with sworn witnesses, whom you burned to a crisp, but who live to this day to expose and mock your fabrications); let us agree, I repeat, that apart from this one point, which you could have summed up in one little line — namely, that two ships were burned — all the other things your volume sings of with such tragic clamor are nothing but your fabrications.

Now, then, since you have driven and beaten me back from your camp in this way, I am forced to retreat to defend my own camp; in which I quake with terror lest so fierce an enemy, so rudely challenged, so mortally offended, fired up by so recent a victory, chasing me all the way from his bulwarks, which I had assaulted so feebly and he had defended so stoutly, all the way to my camp, to which I returned in such wild disarray, should now overwhelm me. I quake all the more violently at this prospect because of those siege-engines of yours,

---

388 unknown   **389** James IV of Scotland besieged Norham Castle in August 1513 and held in until he was defeated at Flodden Field in September.   **390** (*ca.* 1460–1529)

known for his history of France, *De rebus francorum*   **391** See *EE* 4: 130.   **392** *day and night:* See *Adages* 324 (*CWE* 31: 337).

393 For the king of Tenedas's axe, see *Adages* 829 (*CWE* 32: 197).

which so forcefully launch against me not those trifling objections which you scarcely deigned to deflect when I cast them at you, namely, that you had engrafted lines stolen from the ancients among 5 your melodious trifles,[394] that you had covered over the imbecility of your talent with a flimsy veneer of words which in no way disguises it, and that you lied with outrageous impudence. You consider that praiseworthy provided it is called fabrication. No, 10 you charge me instead with barbarisms, and solecisms, and syllables which do not scan quite consistently. Good Lord, what atrocious and impious infractions these are! If compared to those others, how monstrous! For those are your only material 15 objections; the rest is mere verbal abuse, as you cry "fool," "madman," or "raving idiot" time and time again. Such name-calling is simply your seasoning of Attic wit, introduced as a condiment to render a book which is insipid in its own right still more 20 insipid. With those syllables and solecisms, on the other hand, you assault and beset me most stoutly.

But yet, Brixius, there is one more way in which you hedge me in more ruthlessly still; and indeed, you are ruthless beyond all equity and justice, 25 since you are not content to have assaulted me but you also insist on prescribing which arms I may use to defend myself. Thus you command imperiously that I must not attribute to Froben any of the errors which you impute to me personally. Observe how 30 uncivil you are on this point, and inequitable, too: though you knew that my work was printed in Basel, while I stayed in England, and though you cannot doubt that I was too busy at that time to be able to cross over to Basel from London twice daily, you 35 still choose to throw up to the author whatever mistakes you discover in that little work and to ascribe none at all to the printer. If the same law which you applied to me ought to apply to you, I am sure that hereafter, if anything of yours is printed in any place 40 where you do not have ready access to the press of your printer, you will furnish us with plenty of darts we can turn against you,[395] much the same as those you now launch at us as if each by itself could transfix us. A clear confirmation of that point is yielded 45 by this very tract, which you did oversee, in which you are so fierce in imputing mistakes generated by others to me that at times you impute to me

even mistakes which you generated: though it was printed with you standing by and continually cor- recting the forms as the sheets were removed from 50 the press, once the volume was finished, if you had not furnished corrections for your publisher's errors or some one had not furnished corrections for yours, then your book would contain neither fewer nor more tolerable faults than the ones which you now 55 so insipidly sneer at in mine. But not even now have you thoroughly emended your book, since you left, here and there, some warts fouler than any tumor.

Indeed, I can defend my own cause on this point even without shifting any of the blame onto Froben, 60 although he himself wrote me a letter[396] confessing that his workers were careless in printing my book and promising to reprint it more diligently. And in any event, even if I saw that certain passages had been corrupted through no fault of mine, none- 65 theless I could not automatically place the blame on him, since I knew that Froben had not received any copy text from me; for the poems in which I celebrated the king's coronation and the poems in which I made fun of you are virtually the only ones 70 which I myself ever published or had ever intended to publish. And if either my friends or my servants made themselves copies of my booklet when it was not guarded carefully enough—either by me or by someone to whom I had lent it (although not 75 for copying)—and if it happened that people who liked my book thought that it should be published, it is not at all surprising that the copyist should have made some mistakes or that the typesetter should have added others, since he had to rely on 80 a copy text which was somewhat corrupt and quite possibly difficult to make out. It is hardly fair for you to blame me for corruptions caused by the er- rors or inattentiveness of others, and to condemn me for ignorance based on someone else's lack of 85 expertise—unless you will automatically declare a man illiterate and decree that he be hooted out of all learned men's company if he has been just a bit careless about keeping his letterboxes shut tightly.

And if there can be no doubt that the book is 90 marred by faults not my own, since it was set up in type and, before that, transcribed by a number of hands, I can scarcely be led to believe that you your- self do not tacitly absolve me in private of the very

---

394 *melodious trifles:* See Horace, *Ars poetica* 322; *Adages* 2598 (*CWE* 35: 177).   **395** *plenty . . . you:* See *Adages* 51 (*CWE* 51: 100–1).   **396** not extant

same errors of which you accuse me in public with such blatant calumny. If, on the contrary, you do have a deep-seated, fixed, obstinate sense that whatever you found uncorrected ought promptly to be blamed on me, I can no more exonerate myself before you than I can wash the clay out of a brick.[397] See, then, how civilly I will deal with you. For although (as you see) I can carry the point, before equitable judges, that many of the faults you impute to me should be assigned to others (unless something occurred in the printing of my book which has never occurred in the printing of any book at all, that is, that neither the typesetter nor the copyist ever made one mistake); although in the very instances which you belabor most exultantly of all as my surest infractions, I can prove with the surest of arguments that your own judgments are either most slanderous or at any rate most ill-conceived, partly by bringing forth authoritative testimonies according to which it will be crystal clear that many expressions which you take to task are correct, partly by bringing forth those very pages in which I once published those few poems I mentioned, which will make it quite clear that what I composed and circulated is different from what Froben printed, whether it happened because of some illegible copy text, or because of inattentiveness, or because some copyist preferred something which I myself changed by cancellations in the first version (for who can adequately divine by how many accidents a flaw may steal in, or by what fortune it happens to almost every author that even among the earliest copies the readings occasionally vary?); although, as I said, I am able to do all these things, nonetheless, Brixius, since you displayed so much civility in defending yourself that you brought to bear almost nothing which had any real bearing on the case (whether some sense of shame struck you dumb, so that you could not utter the things you had thought of, or your hurry to vilify me kept you from it), I have decided to recompense you with a corresponding civility in arguing my own case. With respect to mistakes such as these, I shall simply defer my defense for the present. It would be useless to you, since you can never be satisfied, and unnecessary for others, since I doubt that you will have persuaded anybody at all that the things which you tax are directly ascribable to me. Indeed, I am sure that every

equitable reader would imagine almost any explanation on his own rather than presume me to be so extraordinarily ignorant as to know nothing about either placement in a verse or solecisms in phrasing.

But even if your claim that these errors are mine did prevail, still, since I myself did not publish the book (a fact which is too manifest for even you to be able to sidestep), what right do you have to reproach a writer whose work was snatched away and published while he was still thinking it over, and who can fairly cite that line of Ovid's, "I would have emended if I had been given the chance"?[398] If anyone has a right to use this line, I most certainly do. For apart from those verses which I had already published some time ago, I was going to suppress the whole book permanently, and I would not have published even those unless readers more literate than I had liked them more than I did. To me personally, none of my writings has ever seemed at all savory till now, when I see from your bilious response that there must have been some touch of salt in the mockery with which I have chafed you. But if I had at some point decided to make the book public, I would certainly have changed various things in it; not because I would think a syllabic mistake so important, but because several poems in it were somewhat more frivolous than I would have liked them to be. But if I went astray anywhere in my scansion of syllables, even though I would not have been reluctant to correct them, nonetheless in one or two places perhaps I would not have strained too hard to change them, especially where I could not readily make a change without damaging the sense, for I find that not only those authors who surpass you just as much as you pompously scorn them but also very ancient authors did not always scan the same syllables in just the same way, so that there are many syllables which may be either long or short.

Finally, this circumstance too lessens my grief at the thought that someone should imagine all the faults you carped at were mine: among these very faults I note some which are not mine, and yet I would not be ashamed to avow them; nor do I have any doubt that examples will occur to everyone, as he reads, which will show that many of the things which you called solecisms on our part are actually Latin through and through.[399] Indeed, to sum up, even if you had better cause to criticize some points,

---

397 *wash…brick:* See *Adages* 348 (*CWE* 31: 356).   **398** Ovid, *Tristia* 1.7.40   **399** *through and through:* See *Adages* 3930 (*CWE* 36: 502–3).

you cannot with certainty impute them to me, since I neither took part in the proofreading nor provided a copy text to be used in the printing nor published the book at all; on the other hand, in those instances when your own judgments are either mistaken or wantonly slanderous, which undoubtedly make up more than half of the total, you have convicted yourself of ignorance or slanderous knavery, and in either case, certainly, of egregious shamelessness, since even as you write so insolently and so gratuitously, in phrases you pondered for such a long time and addressed to a man you now challenge a second time, a man whom you rashly and haughtily urge to scrutinize you in the same way, you still criticize so many things with which nothing is wrong, whether ignorance blinds you to what you are doing or envy makes you do it all too clear-sightedly. But even after you have displayed so much vigor of this sort by blowing down all I have written in a single breath, so to speak, smug and breathing an air of sheer glory you urge me to sift through your writings, in turn; doubtless you are quite certain that all of your writings are so finely wrought that not even a Momus can find a single syllable to pick at.[400]

For my part, Brixius, I would much rather sift through books from which I might sift out something good. But still I did read this book of yours, though I neither expected nor found any fruitful material in it; and I read it all the more carefully since it was written against me, and since an angry enemy will often blurt out faults which ought to be remedied, but which love can occasionally endear to one's friends, or which they do not mention lest they injure his feelings. Thus, I did read attentively, but in the following way. While I never paid any heed to the task which you set me — namely, that I should be punctilious in examining your syllables — wherever you had anything substantial to say I assuredly pondered it with no little diligence. And yet, however much I abhor the thought of idling away my energies stalking syllables, certainly that monosyllable "mind," which I had found wanting in the *Chordigera*, also turned out to be so completely absent from the *Antimorus*[401] — though I searched for it conscientiously, and not only I but many others too — that the title of your book, short as it is, still seems to everyone to be longer by a half than

it should be: your work should be called, not *The Anti-Moron*, but *The Moron*. This new title seems all the more fitting in view of the way you witlessly affect a reputation for wit by punning on my name,[402] as if fortune had not made it possible even for total barbarians to joke in this way about Ermolao Barbaro.[403] To joke in this way about Thomas More's name is also possible for Germanus Brixius, a true and germane cousin-german to a work which is truly, germanely named *Moron*. While I inspected that book very attentively indeed, I found nothing else in it but mad allegations which either criticize things written correctly or reproach me with someone else's errors or directly recoil upon your head. Further, many of your abuses suited me so prettily that they appear to be just as well suited for anyone. I hear currish barking, but it is barked out in vain; rabid biting, but it lacerates you alone; viperish virulence, but it harms only you. Since this is the sort of thing you had to say, I do not wonder at all that you fear lest perchance I will not have the patience to read what no one could endure to read to the end unless (here we have Brixius's sole charm) all these things were sweetened with entertaining delusions. They afford me personally such a powerful incentive to smile at that moronic *Antimorus* of yours that as soon as I have the leisure I am going to see to it that it is reprinted, somewhat more carefully than it has been printed already, and maybe even elucidated with commentaries; note how far I am from begrudging you any of that glory which makes you a god in your own eyes when you hiss at the name More, which you find so despicable, and with that book of yours, with so polished, so erudite, so charming, so festive, and finally so inspired a performance, you consecrate the venerable name Brixius to immortal infamy. Lest the admirable gifts of this book should perchance elude the yawning reader, we will point out a few examples to spur him on, as it were, to penetrate more profoundly into the book and observe more attentively what charming jests, witticisms, pleasantries, honey and treacle, and, indeed, what a milky torrent of persuasiveness streams forth from the Gallic headwaters.

I will begin, therefore, where you began, with the hendecasyllables you wrote to Macrin.[404] In these, as if in the frontispiece of your work, you inscribed a

---

400 *Momus . . . pick at:* See *Adages* 474 (*CWE* 31: 448–50). **401** *Antimorus* is the name of the tract Brixius had just issued against Thomas More. **402** See *CW* 3.2: 486, 496–98, 512. **403** (1454–93), an Italian scholar **404** Brixius's friend, Salmonius Macrinus

distinctive announcement of your imbecility. For at first you made Macrin your Homeric Stentor, your Nestor[405] to boot, long established as the finest of poets, but now unexpectedly sallying forth as an or-
5   ator too, and an orator so comely and so vehement that his power of persuasion, which the comely one, Venus, had charged with such numerous graces and charms, could manipulate your feelings however he pleased; you could not stand firm against his insis-
10 tence that the *Antimorus* should come out at once, and therefore you brought out the volume under his auspices, since you had not been able to with-stand his urgings. Then, a little while later, forget-ting yourself, you deny that for all his insistence
15 and his oratory he could ever have compelled you to issue that splendid elephantine offspring before nine full years had elapsed. But so as not to let the comeliness of your invention go to waste by sup-pressing so comely a tract even a little too long—
20 since taunts, unless hurled back at once, never win any acclaim—you were forced to hasten, and, in or-der that your tract against my epigram might come out lightning—quick, in just a few years, you were forced to dash off individual lines in approximately
25 two days apiece. But since in these lines your tal-ent does not even sustain you long enough to make it through your first page with a consistent pace, or without losing your train of thought so prodi-giously and contradicting yourself so flagrantly
30 through a lapse of memory that, although you at first made Macrin out to be a sufficiently power-ful orator to force you to think the way he does, you now in almost the next line say he failed to per-suade you at all; although you wrote at first that
35 he forced you to issue your book, since supposedly you could not withstand so much honeyed persua-sion, you immediately assert that he never could have spoken so deftly as to lure the book from you; thus, Brixius, since you trip up on the very thresh-
40 old,[406] as I was saying, and in lines so long polished and repolished, with such sustained effort on your part, you write the same sort of drivel which mo-rons blurt out on the spur of the moment, who can fail to agree with the lines where you try to win over
45 your reader as if with a bribe of delight, where you promise that he will obtain great delight from your

poem if he reads conscientiously?[407] Obtain great delight he assuredly will, unless he is so stone-faced that he does not even laugh at the kind of perfor-mance, the only kind almost, through which those   50
to whom nature denies any wit raise men's laughter, namely by talking sheer nonsense, in pure contra-dictions and paradoxes, as if they are lost in a day-dream. Though I will not dissemble the fact that some think this is not a foolish caprice but a cun-   55
ning one, as if you had set out to be witty in making a laughingstock out of Macrin, since you make him out to be so sweet and so vehement an orator, and finally so able to sway you with his suave address, that on the one point where his comely persuasion   60
attempts to persuade you, it fails to persuade you. I, at any rate, have no such suspicion. For Macrin, it seems, merits more loving treatment from you than that you should be laughing at him, and the rest of your book approximates a very different kind of fe-   65
licity more nearly than this sort of wiliness. Hence you had no reason for toiling so artfully to disguise how long you had hung on to your book; just as delay detracts from the acclaim which is given to taunts, even so time and labor set off your sort of wit   70
to advantage. For whenever you say something that is egregiously obtuse, the more you travail in prepar-ing it the more acclaim greets your producing it.

And that is another remarkable touch of urban-ity, indeed, when you vindicate the truthfulness of   75
your lies by reiterating a lie, where you once again make Hervé out to be saving his homeland, again take out your trumpet and sound him the victor, again harp on him harrying and troubling our fleet, even though all these claims are as truthful as you   80
are. Now the proof you adduce here is wonderful indeed. For you say that the things you recount are attested by Englishmen's deaths. If you mean any deaths but those of the men who were killed in the *Regent*, those deaths are as truthful as that victory   85
was. If, on the contrary, you are trying to reproach us with the deaths of the men who perished in the burning of the *Regent*, call me fool just as much as you like, I am not such a fool that I fail to perceive that on this point your acumen is as dull as a pes-   90
tle,[408] since you reproach us with the fact that our ship was burned up as if yours felt a chill while ours

---

405 Stentor was the herald of the Greek forces in the Trojan War; see *Adages* 1237 (*CWE* 33: 150). Homer's Nestor was known for his long-winded speeches; see *Adages* 156 (*CWE* 31: 196–97). **406** *trip… threshold:* See *Adages* 477 (*CWE* 31: 452). **407** See *CW* 3.2: 484. **408** *dull as a pestle:* See *Adages* 2521 (*CWE* 35: 125); Jerome, *Epistolae* 69.4 (*PL* 22: 657).

blazed, or as if you could prove Hervé the victor because his ship was first to catch fire. So this is what Brixian acumen is! So this is a Brixian victory!

But it is worthwhile to observe with what artfulness you handle that passage in which I record among the praises of our prince how he had restored and reformed a commonwealth which had previously been deformed by certain men's crimes, avarice, depredations, incrimination, and calumnies. Even though you decided to leave none of my writings untouched by your own inept calumnies, against this passage you stir up the most pointless tumults of all. You worry this passage with wondrous and unalloyed slanders. On this passage you pour all the splendid and admirable virulence your talent affords you. Here I seemed overweening to you for attempting so weighty a theme, one so vastly exceeding my powers, as if I had taken it upon myself to relate all the praises deserved by our prince, and had not done the same thing in offering due homage to princes that everyone does, even toward the saints, without any reproach, in accord with his own inclinations. Others were competing to celebrate such a happy beginning of our prince's reign, so advantageous to us from the very first day, and I did the same to the best of my abilities, in whatever manner of verse I was able to write. In this regard I do not doubt that it could have been praised both more richly, by more expert writers, and more worthily, by more distinguished ones; even so, others' actions would not have absolved me of my personal duty, and my poems kept no one from doing as I did, or claiming at will the same liberty to do so. Most important of all, whoever decrees that our prince ought to be praised by no one who cannot sustain the whole weight of so great a theme envies our king's attainments under a pretext of admiring them: while everyone ought to extol them, he bids everyone to keep permanently silent about them.

But at this point, if the gods will allow it, you summon Apelles[409] back up from the infernal regions, which indeed is no difficult feat for you, if, as you write, you are on such familiar terms with the infernal Furies. Meanwhile you yourself prove to be such a consummate master of portraiture that even though anyone wishing to paint a definitive portrait must take care, above all, to observe what features and what disposition are so characteristic of this or that subject that when these are set forth in a likeness they will render the countenance most recognizable, the way you insist that the king be portrayed prescribes that we simply leave out of the picture the crowning appeal of his reverend face, one so rare and distinctively his, although this alone renders him most recognizable.[410] For to you, a completely blind painter, I clearly seem stupider than a stump since I did not foresee that I ought not to touch on those praises which in our prince's case were preeminently worth mentioning, whether for the people's sake or for his own; for although I concede that these praises are not poetic in the same way as Brixian praises (since you suppose nothing poetic except what is fabricated), even so there was no one in England who failed to sense through some personal benefit that these praises are true, nor is anyone living so senseless that he does not sense them to be truly regal, unless you can invent for us some feat more regal than to remake a realm which is everywhere crumbling and to render it once again prosperous and happy.

Nor does the honor we give to the present prince detract anything from his forebear's acclaim, whose ill health was the cause of his failure for several years before his death to show adequate vigor in either public or domestic matters. Therefore we have no cause to marvel, and certainly no cause to blame him, if through the perfidy of certain men whom he trusted too much the commonwealth declined; as it swayed on the brink of collapse, his own son rose propitiously to right it, and did so with such purposeful haste that he captured and curbed the felons whose crime had produced the calamity, and he immediately reformed the whole realm before letting himself be adorned with the crown. Nor did it seem to him, nor to any sane person, at any rate, that he injured his father in righting his fatherland when it had been bowed down because of his father's ill health and the malice of others, or in dealing severely with those through whose perfidy, mortally threatening his fatherland, his father had been led astray, or in rescinding some of his father's laws, although these were not disadvantageous for the people, for the sake of some greater advantage, changing good for the better. Even to you, does it

---

409 Apelles was a famous painter of ancient Greece (*ca.* 4th century BC).   See *CW* 3.2: 494, 510.   **410** *crowning…recognizable:* See Plato, *Republic* 2.378d.

seem a portentous impiety if the son's regal virtue quickly accomplished what sickness denied to his father's felicity; if, for the good of his fatherland, for the strength of the laws, for the honor of his father, he suppressed the despoilers of his fatherland, the beguilers of his father, the subverters of the laws; or if, finally, the son surpassed even that most prudent father in prudence and showed in one case more discernment in governing the commonwealth? Since our prince's actions respecting these matters not only had beneficial results in the context of current affairs but also afforded the future so wholesome a regal example, and thereby established him prince of all princely attainments, I would certainly not have been deterred from praising these actions of his even if some blame had been thrown back on his father; nor would we ever have deferred so completely to our sense of respect for the father that it could have preempted the praise which was due to the deed of his son, since in no age has any prince ever performed any deed which was worthier of praise or which it could be more in the public interest to memorialize.

Nor would I ever have assigned such importance to fortune, or even to nature, that I could have preferred the vain splendor of either to the true glory of such an illustrious virtue. Who our parents are is theirs to determine; a good man's only true commendation is virtue. "Our race and our forebears, whatever we have not obtained by ourselves, I scarce call those things ours."[411] Neither Vergil nor Homer, whom you set against me,[412] ever said anything either truer or more wholesome than this maxim taken from Ovid. However much I esteem both the writers you mention, they will never prevail on my judgment to such an extent that I will concede as much authority on this point to both put together as I concede Plato alone. He does actually consider it highly desirable, an aim which we ought to pursue with all possible care, that children should have honorable people for parents,[413] since in this way, to speak metaphorically, a seedbed of good nature and virtue is secretly fostered in these children when they are born; nonetheless, while he considers the good offspring of good parents to be somewhat more fortunate than others, even so he supposes the good son of a bad father to deserve

greater praise, and quite rightly. For if a person is all the more dishonorable if he degenerates from an eminent father, does it not hold, in turn, that more praise is due to someone who is drawn in the opposite direction by the example of a bad parent but has nonetheless grown eminent by his virtue and his good deeds? Thus, since these were his own views, undoubtedly the one sort of poet that "Plato should have driven from his state"[414] was the flattering sort, like yourself, who command that we adulate princes according to the endowments of fortune or nature, and will not let us praise them according to virtue, which we ought to praise even if it costs us the windy esteem of the people;[415] even contrary to the ordinary ideas of the masses, whose taste generally runs to the worst things in life, we should little by little instill proper values in men's hearts with the sweetness of verses.

Accordingly, as I have said, even if some blame had come to rest on the father I would not have suppressed the praise due to the son, which indeed he would have earned all the more richly by resolving to remedy the error of his father instead of to imitate it. And I would have proceeded in this way, deferring and hearkening to reason alone, even if I saw that all of the poets and all of the masses saw things just the opposite way. Note how far I am from regretting that I did not keep silent about those deeds the infamy of which falls on those who exploited the father's credulity and served their own profit through public misfortune, while a vast and an undying glory accrues to the son, since he so quickly punished the guilty and restored the commonwealth, and thus redeemed father and fatherland at once, making good his devotion toward both. But you, who are such an egregious praiser, brandish your censor's rod at the principal element of his regal praise, the same one that the whole of our people in public and private avows as the prince of all praises and that which befits England's prince best of all, one so far from detracting from his father's memory that it actually affords him his own crowning honor, since he himself fathered this prince who now governs the realm with the true regal arts, and you command that this praise be expunged, on no other account, I suppose, than because it is true. Indeed, nothing meets with your sanction apart from

---

411 Ovid, *Metamorphoses* 13.140–41   *Republic* 415a–c.   **414** *CW* 3.2: 494; see   **415** *windy…people:* See Horace, *Carmina*
412 See *CW* 3.2: 492.   **413** See Plato,   Plato, *Republic* 2.378d–358e, 10.59a–608a.   3.2.20.

that poetic product of yours which is wholly con-
flated from fabrication and falsehood. For your poetry, as you assure us, "will cease to be poetry at all
if you take that away."[416] But since our prince did
these things not in secret, by night, as if he were
ashamed of his good deeds, but in the brightest daylight, in the sight of everyone, in private and public hearings, in councils, in the amplest assembly of
the entire realm, and in accord with the commons
as well as the nobles; since every age, order, and sex
saw how splendid his policy was, sensed how wholesome it was, and praised to the heavens how noble
it was; should I actually have been the one person to
leave out the one thing which I should extol most
of all? How even the youngsters[417] would laugh at
my not mentioning what Brixius now has attacked
me for mentioning; for to these very youngsters I
would rightly have seemed either the stupidest of
men, if I had not perceived it, or the most malignant of men, if I had not admired it, or the most envious of men, if I had not praised it.

And yet it is hard to tell which is worse in the
way that you worry this passage, your pointlessness
or your invidiousness; you are so head-over-heels
in your blind rushing on that unwittingly you very
nearly brand our prince with ignorance, and indeed,
since you make your prince our prince's equal, you
brand yours with ignorance equally. Nor yet, in the
meantime (though assuredly this is your style all the
time), do your words show the slightest consistency.
For at first you concede to our prince some concern
for the Latian muse, but so little that he may not
know the rules governing versification; soon you
make him so ignorant that he does not even know
what the words mean; and yet you couple your
king with him, so that both kings are equally "filled
with the genius of the Cecropian goddess."[418] These
statements cohere none too handsomely, do they?
But this is nothing new, that in every other line you
should lose your own train of thought.

Yet you call me a thrifty and stingy praiser,[419] even
though you yourself are such an ungenerous praiser
that when you wished to apply to two princes the
same praise that Vergil attributed to shepherds you
pared away something, as if you supposed it too
sumptuous, and (as you generally do to whatever
you imitate) you altered his praise for the worse.

For his verse reads as follows, describing two shepherds, "both being in the flower of their age,"[420]
while your own reads, describing two princes, "both
equal in age."[421] In that way, Vergil aptly expresses
in those shepherds age at its most flourishing; your
praise, even though you appropriate it for princes
like these, who are truly in the flower of their age, is
nonetheless so ambiguous that it could befit two de-
crepit and cadaverous old men. Further, the praise
you tack on about virtue is not at all generous, since
the way you concede each king virtue leaves you free
to revoke it at will. For while you pronounce both
to be "equal in virtues," you never affirm there to
be any virtues in either; in case you have not heard,
men are just as much equals who lack something
equally as men are who equally possess it.

I do not say this because I think that was your
meaning but rather to show just how easy it is to
discover a vulnerable passage if anyone examines
your praises in the same way that you slander mine.
Nor yet do I here invoke any Apelles and Alexander, any Choerilus, beating, or exile, nor do I advance any such tragedies against you as you stir up
against me. But if the action in question were any
less widely appreciated and our prince were as ignorant as you make him out to be, what dire peril
you might have brought down on me! For it is almost impossible for anyone who is involved in political business to forestall the appearance of someone, at some point, who would gladly seize any
occasion for slander if either the action in question
admitted his cavils or he could exploit any ignorance on the part of the prince, especially if there
are some persons who would like the whole state of
affairs to be violently changed for the worse, since
they dislike the way that the present state of affairs
is more prosperous for the public at large than for
them by themselves. But these men, if there are any
such men, themselves saw the way that the action in
question was done and advanced, not with any clandestine machinery, but out in the public domain;
they themselves perceive how much our prince excels them in their favorite arts, he who beat down,
suppressed, and stamped out the vipers time and
time again, every time that they crept out of hiding as if to lie basking in the new sun which follows a winter and to try to pour forth again their

416 *CW* 3.2: 490.   **417** *even the youngsters:*
See *Adages* 1042 (*CWE* 33: 40).   **418** See
CW 3.2: 492, 494, 510; Cecrops was a
mythical king of Athens.   **419** See *CW*
3.2: 494.   **420** Vergil, *Eclogues* 7.4
421 *CW* 3.2: 510

old venom of calumny; hence they themselves are quite aware that their own harmful longings have lost every hope of fulfilment.

And yet, Brixius, even though what you write is not just absurd and pointless, but criminal as well, and indeed as pernicious as you have been able to make it, nonetheless you name Deloynes, Budé, and Lascaris,[422] men revered by the whole world for their learning and virtue (whose names deserved greater respect than that you should contaminate them with such a tract as yours, as if setting jewels in the mire), and force them to enlist, as it were, in your faction; for you claim that these men were brought in to review and to aid in the planning of your ill-planned plans. But though I myself cannot vouch for their feelings regarding those syllables and solecisms with which you reproach me (and even concerning these points I would not shy away from their judgment if they could hear me out), I am fully convinced that those men have such a thorough knowledge of philosophical principle and such a practical mastery of political principles that if you can extort an endorsement from any of them on this issue, at any rate—that is, if you can get him to attest his agreement with you on the subject of praising kings—I will give way to you on all the rest of the issues and freely surrender my praise; though at present I cannot help suspecting what everyone thinks, that those infernal Furies (who you confess stood by you while you were writing) were the ones who inspired such a plan in you; for whether you look at its fury or its virulence, it recalls very clearly indeed its Tartarean[423] origin.

But once, at long last, while emerging from hell by Trophonius's cave,[424] as it seems, you are cheered and break out into jesting, and with the laughter of an angry cur you snarl at my letter, in which I attribute the tardiness of my booklet to the illuminator whose gout had caused it to be given to the king somewhat later than I had intended. You do not like this plea; superstitiously poetic, the man cannot bear that the truth should be told, and outdoes any courtier's refinement in laughing at me for using, as I tell the prince of a thing which is not at all obscene, the same words that the people use. Who will not laugh at whoever laughs thus?

Further, I do not understand what that taunt means, although it seems to smack of some well-hidden wit, in which you indicate that my household concerns interfere with my studies. Perhaps you are advancing this saying as an artful expedient to win precedence for your own studies on the basis that you have no household, but free and untrammeled by cares you roam back and forth between other men's plates like a parasite, and thus your poem must needs be preeminent because it is nourished by leisure and other men's bread. I for one thought more highly of you, and I still do today, even though, to speak truthfully, your tract does recall both Pyrgopolynices and Artotrogos.[425] And I fail to see how it pertains to the matter at hand when you reproach me for having a household unless you have no household, since otherwise that festive jest or that excellent *bon mot*, as one Plautine parasite puts it, would simply recoil on you.

At any rate, even as I persuade myself that you are not an out-and-out parasite (however your book may enforce that impression), I do truly suspect that you are a philosopher of the Cynical sect, not only because of your barking but also because I observe how you everywhere make fun of riches and everywhere applaud beggary and famine. For you joke at my children's expense and you write of their misery if they were to have for their legacy only my lines, and not also my coins, as if yours will be happy with nothing beyond the lines of their father.[426] But for my part I pray that your children, if you have any or ever should have any, may never have any experience of the gallows or beggary, the ills which urbanely, of course, you forebode for my children, and I pray from my heart that some richer fortune may dawn for them from some other source than your lines, since no one is, I think, so demented that he would buy three hundred thousand of those for a threepence, at least not of the sort you have blurted out up to now.

That other jest smacks of similar wit when you liken yourself to a famished wolf, as if you would have swallowed me up all at once, like a wretched lamb, if the two kings had not ratified the peace for my benefit; but now that the peace has been made you consider it wicked to quarrel, and so now, at last, you have published that meek little tract of yours. But that was an utterly heavenly invention when you fabricated all those Baneful Spirits, and those pretty infernal Graces, the Furies, to be — your darling girlfriends, to play with and gladden your leisure.[427] You seem to be imitating certain clever clowns who discern in themselves either physical deformities or moral depravities which are vulnerable either to scoffs or to scandals. These master-buffoons mock their own flaws: since they cannot circumvent disrepute they can at least outstrip their own rivals in seizing a pretext for carping and, rather than give up the game, hold a triumph at their own expense. Similarly, when you saw that the spirit which breathed through your own *Antimorus* was not only moronic but maniacal to boot, since you saw how apparent to everyone it would be from what quarter this furor was loosed, you chose rather to take the initiative by joking about your own Furies, feigning that they had spontaneously offered their services to you, since of course you are such a close friend to them all and the most firmly sworn of their votaries, and that you would then loose them upon me.

There is one thing that I suspect no one is ever going to read without judging that it is an outstanding mark of your ingenuity and a stroke of distinctively Brixian urbanity: after painting me in your own image, in lines which are worthy of you, you were worried that your self-portrait might not do you justice, and so, in a marginal note, you marked "litigious wrangler,"[428] since you wished to say that in my fatherland that is my status. Brixius, I do not say what my status at home is, lest I be like you; I deserve no such glory as you grant yourself, and I crave no such glory as other men grant you. But you have made it possible to recognize, even abroad, what your status at home is: you wish to be styled a queen's secretary,[429] but you rant at a king's privy councilor with more rabid impudence than anyone would rant, even at a wrangler, unless he himself were a wrangler.

And since this is the way you conduct yourself all through your tract, it is worthwhile to observe how you take up the part of an augur, of course,

and divine that henceforth in return for your own friendly service toward me I will act as an enemy toward you, even though you picked out my shameful errors with pious concern for the honor of their author, an ingrate, however, who you think will never repay you except with ill thanks. You handle that marvelous conceit, drawn from rhetoric's innermost shrine, with such zeal that you practically take on a preacher's part, too; you throw in the word "Christian," too often, and frequently harp on the title of "sinner,"[430] as if you were concerned with the health of my soul, and all but insist I do penance for my solecisms, I suppose since the kingdom of God is at hand.[431] I myself, indeed, Brixius, will not be reluctant to render your augury concerning me false, since I never resolved upon being your enemy. Nor am I so inhuman as not to acknowledge such a friendly service toward me on the part of a man so desirous of serving my fame that in defamatory tracts, published and printed against me, he whispers of others' mistakes in my ear[432] as if they were my own; a man so careful of my honor that before he will pass up the chance to inveigh against me with false calumnies he dishonors his own name with truthful disgrace; a man so intent on my welfare that he arraigns my prince for either impiety or ignorance if he does not simply exterminate me. Nor yet am I so stupid as not to sense just how indebted I am for indulgence like this from a man who is so circumspect that he cannot remember what he wants to say from one line to the next, as if he had just drunk up a draught out of Lethe;[433] so noble a palm[434] that he not only stands upright despite other men's maledictions but even weighs himself down with his own; so stout and unvanquished a pugilist that, using the club which he pilfered from Hercules, he is everywhere violently at odds with himself; so keen-sighted and Lynceus-like[435] that he fails to perceive that his own taunts recoil on him; so refined that he counts "madman," "fool," "lunatic," "cur," and "wrangler" among his urbanities; of so placid and tranquil a nature that when he proclaims someone "faith-breaking," "perfidious," and "perjured," he abstains nonetheless from abuse; so great a champion of poetry that he

427 See *CW* 3.2: 510. **428** *CW* 3.2: 512 **429** See *CW* 3.2: 482. **430** See *CW* 3.2: 536. **431** *kingdom . . . hand:* See Mt 3:2. **432** *whispers . . . ear:* See *Adages* 247 (*CWE* 31: 276). **433** *draught out of Lethe:* Lethe

was a river in the Underworld that caused forgetfulness; see *Adages* 1855 (*CWE* 34: 111). **434** *so noble a palm:* The palm was thought to grow higher when a weight was placed on it; see *Adages* 204 (*CWE* 31: 237–38);

Aulus Gellius 3.6. **435** *keen-sighted and Lynceus-like:* See *CW* 3.2: 540; *Adages* 1054 (*CWE* 33: 487); *Praise of Folly* (*ASD* 4/3: 148, 154).

orders that she should be held in contempt, warning all in advance not to covet her praise, since she suffers no one to believe her; so vehement an orator that he upholds the view that a man who responds to a challenge delivers the challenge, while the first to offend is the man who is challenged; so adroit at upholding the olive branch in the midst of hostilities[436] that in the midst of peace he is quarreling about a war; so equitable that he goes mad because his book was truthfully taxed for its lying by a man whose whole people that same book, before then, had falsely indicted for perjury; so wholesome a praiser that he orders us to praise princes for their physical gifts, lets us praise them for fortune's endowments, but does not permit us to praise them for virtue except in a general way which we might use for anyone at all, and imposes a Pythagorean silence[437] whenever men, women, and children, and even the stones, one might say, all praise some worthy deed;[438] so great an Apelles that he would appear to be blackening two princes from virtually the same pot of paint[439] if his canvas is not viewed indulgently; so careful a Christian that if two kings had not secured me his pardon (with prayers, I suppose), Christ could never have stayed the man, ravenous beyond any wolf, from devouring me whole, like a hapless lambling, simply because he had been stung with one word in reprisal for savaging us long ago; so clever, so genial, so artful, and so thoroughly and consummately wise that he himself tells us the infernal Furies are his familiars.

Thus, since that is the company you keep at home, Brixius, someone somewhere who likes to play games with such intimates as yours may well crave your acquaintance. I for one neither quail at your emnity nor covet your friendship. For no one needs to fear lest the Furies will attack your enemy, as you threaten, since they are too deeply attached to you, with the most secure rivets, for anything to tear them away from a head they love so dearly.[440] Your friends and familiars, however, risk hurt by contagion from this sort of plague. Nor will I myself be your enemy, for I cannot hate anyone whom I pity for being thus afflicted; indeed, I would certainly come to love you if I did not fear you would come to love me in return, since I often have heard how annoying and harmful the love of such specters can be.

Accordingly, as far as possible, my feelings about you will remain neutral; in fact I will not so much as try to find out whether you are white or black. But then there is no need to find that out; your own black ink has stained you as black as a coal. Still, lest I should seem to have simply forgotten so gracious a service as yours was in carefully marking the flaws in my lines and refusing to let them be blamed upon anyone but me, at a time when (if you are telling the truth) you yourself were beset by the Banes and the Furies, I humbly pray for whatever shall serve to make each of us whole; that the powers above may be so propitious to me and to you that they remedy both our deficiencies, correcting my uncouth expression as they purge away your uncouth thinking; that they may be so kind as to pluck out the barbarous words from my speech and those barbarous morals of yours from your heart; and, at last, that they may be so good as to grant me sound feet for my verse and you a sound head for your body.[441]

London, in the publishing house of Pynson.

---

436 See *CW* 3.2: 486.   **437** *Pythagorean silence:* See *Adages* 3272 (*CWE* 36: 44).   **438** *even . . . deed:* See Lk 19:14, *Adages* 4117 (*CWE* 36: 610–11).   **439** *blackening . . . paint:* See *Adages* 603 (*CWE* 32: 68).   **440** *head . . . dearly:* See Horace, *Carmina* 1.24.2.   **441** *sound . . . body:* See Juvenal, *Satires* 10.356.

The Four Last Things

The only source for this text is Rastell's 1557 *Workes*. Because its running header is *De quatuor novissimis*, the common title has long been *The Four Last Things*, even though these words are not part of the *Workes'* title, which is *A treatise (unfinished) upon these words of Holy Scripture,* Memorare novissima, et in aeternum non peccabis, *"Remember the last things, and thou shalt never sin"* [Ecclus 7:40]. Rastell states that the work dates from "about the year 1522."

According to Thomas Stapleton's biography of 1588, More began this work as a kind of writing contest with his daughter Meg: "When More wrote his book on the Four Last Things, he gave the same subject to Margaret to treat, and when she had completed her task, he affirmed most solemnly that that treatise of his daughter was in no way inferior to his own" (113). Margaret's treatise, unfortunately, has been lost. But as "More's first extended piece of writing conceived solely in English," *The Four Last Things* is an important example of his rhetorical "ease and lucidity," "stylistic balance and rhythm," "unlabored syntax," and "vivid, well-realized illustration," in Katherine Rodgers's account (*CW* 1: xciii–xciv).

More begins by praising Scripture and placing it above secular literature. Speaking of the single line from Ecclesiasticus that launches *The Four Last Things*, More writes that it "contains more fruitful advice and counsel" in the service of acquiring virtue and avoiding vice than many whole volumes of works of secular literature. The imperative to "remember the last things" is a "sure medicine" for readers' health, More argues, provided they "forsloth not" in receiving this counsel of Scripture.

More utilizes both "the natural light of reason" and the "spiritual light of faith" as he writes about the danger of human blindness and the propensity of human beings to seek limited pleasures over the "profit" of their souls. More explores the nature of pleasure in this treatise, as he did in Book 2 of *Utopia*. Here More argues that the medicine of the four last things does not destroy pleasure, but fosters something more—namely, that "marvelous ghostly pleasure and spiritual gladness" which rises out of "the love of God, and hope of heaven, and inward liking that the godly spirit taketh in the diligent labor of good and virtuous business." The experience of such pleasure, however, requires demanding work, the "busy minding and deep consideration" of the four last things, since "in the things of the soul, knowledge without remembrance profits little."

More was about forty-four years old when he wrote *The Four Last Things*. In good health, he was entering the prime of his public career. As Rodgers argues, More's book has "the whole of life as its purview" (*CW* 1: lxxxiv), and the author's keen interest in the "details of ordinary experience" and the "all-too-natural world" of everyday life are unusual for the genre (lxxvi). *The Four Last Things* is concerned as much with living "this present life" well, as More writes early in the work, as it is with preparing for eternity prudently.

Of the four medicinal "herbs"—death, judgment, heaven, and hell in the traditional phrasing, or "death, doom, pain, and joy" as More writes—the author treats only the first, the remembrance of death, and that is itself incomplete. In the course of this opening section, More also shares his thinking on the seven deadly sins, beginning with pride, the mother of all vices, and envy, the daughter of pride. More's account of the four last things and the deadly sins breaks off with his consideration of spiritual sloth, which human beings do not often perceive as a deadly sin, though More writes that sloth is "able to destroy" half the way to heaven, by undermining the desire to labor and do good in the soul.

CONTENTS

A Treatyce (vnfyny=
shed) vppon these wordes of holye Scripture,

Memorare nouissima, & ineternum non peccabis. Remem=
ber the last thynges, and thou shalt neuer synne.
Made about the yere of our lorde, 1522, by sir Thomas More
than knyghte, and one of the priuye coun=
sayle of Kyng Henry theight, and also
vndertreasorer of Englande.

Eccle. 7.

IF there were anye
questyon amonge
menne, whyther
the woordes of holy
scripture, or the doc
tryne of anye secu=
lar authour, were
of greater force and
effecte to the weale
and profyte of mannes soule, (thoughe
we shold let passe so many short & weigh
ty wordes, spoken by the mouth of oure
sauiour Christ himself, to whose heauē=
ly wisedom, the wit of none earthly cre=
ature can be comparable) yet this onely
text written by the wise mā in the seuēth
chapiter of Ecclesiasticus is suche, that
it conteineth more fruitfull aduise and
counsayle, to the formyng and framing
of mannes maners in vertue, and auoy=
ding of sinne, then many whole & great
volumes of the best of old philosophers,
or anye other that euer wrote in secular
litterature.

Long would it be to take the beste of
theyr wordes and compare it with these
wordes of holy writ: Let vs consider the
frute and profit of this in it selfe: which
thyng wel aduised and pondered, shall
wel declare, that of none whole volume
of seculare litterature, shall aryse so ve=
ry fruitful doctrine. For what would a
mā geue for asure medicin, ī wer of such
strength, ī it should al his life kepe hym
fro sicknes: namely if he mighte by tha=
uoyding of sicknes be sure to contynue
his life one hundred yere: So is it nowe
ī these wordes geueth vs al a sure medi=
cine (yf we forslouth not the receiuyng)
by which we shal kepe from sicknes, not
the body, which none health may longe
kepe fro death (for dye we muste in fewe
yeres liue we neuer so long) but ī soul,
whiche here preserued frō the sicknes of
sin, shal after this eternally liue in ioy,
and be preserued from the deadly lyfe of
euerlastyng payne.

Dye we must

The phisicion sendeth his bill to the
poticary, & therin writeth sommetime a
costlye receite of many straunge herbes
and rootes, set out of far countreis, lōg F
lien drugges, al the strength worn out,
& some none such to be goten. But thys
phisicion sendeth his bil to thy selfe, no
strange thing therin, nothing costly to
bie, nothing farre to set, but to be gathe=
red al times of the yere in the gardeyn of
thyne owne soule.

Let vs heare than what wholesom re=
ceit this is. Remember (saith this byll)
thy last thinges, and thou shalte neuer
sin in this world. Here is first a short me
dicine, conteinyng onely foure herbes,
comen and well knowē, ī is to wit, deth
dome, pain, and ioy.

Eccle. 7.

Death, dome, payn and ioy

This shorte medicine is of a maruey=
lous force, able to kepe vs al our life fro G
sin. The phisicion canne not geue no
one medicine to euery man to kepe him
from sicknes, but to diuers men diuers,
by reson of the diuersity of diuers com=
plexions. This medicine serueth euery
man. The phisicion dothe but gesse & cō=
iecture ī his receit shal do good: but thys
medicine is vndoubtedly sure.

How happeth it than thou wilt happe
ly say, that so few be preserued from sin,
if euery man haue so sure a medicine, so
ready at hand? For folk fare commonly
as he doth that goeth forthfasting amōg
sick folk for slouth, rather than he wyll
take a litle tryacle before.

Thou wilt saye paraduenture ī some H
parte of thys medicine is verye bytter
and paynfull to receyue. Surely there
canne bee nothyng so bitter, but wyse=
dome would brooke it for so gret a pro=
fyte. But yet this medicyne thoughe
thou make a sowre face at it, is not so
bytter as thou makeste for. For well
thou wottest, he byddeth thee not take
neyther deathe, nor dome, nor payne,
but onelye to remember them, and yet
the ioye of heauen therewith to temper
them

Wyll ye see the sample? Looke vppon his holy apostles, whan thei were taken and scourged with whippes foz chzistes sake, did it grieue them thinke ye? Imagine your self in the same case, & I think ye wil think yea. Now see than foz all y paine of their fleshe, what ioy and pleasure they conceiued in their soule. The holy scripture saith, that they reioysed & ioyed that god had accouted thē wozthy foz Chzistes sake, not onely to be scourged, but also which wold be far greater grief to an honest man than the payne it selfe, to bee scourged with dispite and shame, so that the moze theyz payn was, the moze was their ioy. Foz as the holy doctoz saint Chzisostome saith, thoughe pain be grieuous foz the nature of y affliccion, yet is it pleasaunte by the alacritie and quick mind of them that wilyngly suffer it. And therfoze though y nature of the tozmentes make gret grief and payne, yet the prompt and willyng mynde of them that were scourged, passed and ouercame the nature of y thing, that is to wit, mastryng the outewarde fleshlye payne with inwarde spirituall pleasure. And surely this is so trewe, y it may stande foz a very certaine token, that a penitent beginneth to profite and grow in grace and fauour of god, whan he feleth a pleasure and quicknes in his laboz and pain, taken in prayer, almes dede, pilgrimage, fastig, discipline, tribulacion, affliccion, and such other spiritual exercise, by which the soule wyllingly wozketh with the bodye by theyz own punishment, to purge and rub out the rusty cankerd spots, that sinne hath defiled them with, in the sight of God, and to leaue the fewer to be burned out in the fire of purgatozy. And when so euer as I say y a man feleth in this pain a pleasure, he hath a token of gret grace and that his penance is pleasant to god. Foz as the holy scripture saith, our lozd loueth a glad geuer. And on the tother syde wher as one doth such spiritual busines with a dulnes of spirite & werines of minde, he doth twyse as much & therby taketh fouretimes as muche payne, sith his bodily paine is releued with no spiritual reioyce noz comfozt, I wil not say that his labour is lost, but I dare be bold to say, that he profiteth much lesse with much moze payne. Foz certaine it is, y the best soules, and they that haue best trauailed in spiritual busines, find most coumfozt therin. And therfoze yf thei most pleased god, that in the bodily pain of their penance toke lesse spiritual pleasure, it should therof folow, that the farther a manne proceded in the parfeccion of spiritual exercise, in y wozsse case he were. Which can in no wise bee so, sythe that wee see the holye apostles & other holy men and women, the better y they were, the moze pleasure thei parceiued in their fleshly afflicctions, eyther put vnto them by god, oz taken by them selfe foz goddes sake.

Therfoze let euery manne by y labour of his minde and helpe of prayer, eforce himself in all tribulacion and afflicciō labour paine and trauaile, without spot of pzide oz ascribing any pzaise to hiself to conceiue a delite and pleasure in such spiritual exercise, and thereby to ryse in the loue of our lozd, with an hope of heauen, contempt of the wozld, and lōging to be with god. To thattaining of which mynde, by the putting awaye of the malicious pleasures of the deuil, the filthy pleasures of the fleshe, and the vain pleasures of the wozlde, whiche once excluded, there is place made and cleane purged, to receiue the very swete and pure pleasure of the spirite, there is not anye one thyng lightly as I haue sayd, moze accommodate noz moze effectuall, than this thing that I haue begon with, and taken in hand to entreate, that is to wit the remembzance of the foure last thinges, which is as the scripture saythe so effectual, that yf a mā remember it wel, he shall neuer synne.

Thou wilt happely say, that this not ynough that a man do none euyl, but he must also do good. This is verye truth that ye say. But first if ther be but these two steppes to heauen, be y getteth hym on the tone is halfe vp. And ouer y, who so doth none euil, it wilbe very hard but he must nedes do good, syth mans mind is neuer ydle, but occupyed commonly either with good oz euil.

And therfoze whan folke haue fewe wozdes & vse much musyng, likewise as among many wozdes al be not alwaye well and wisely set, so whan the tounge lyeth still, if the mynde be not occupyed well, it were lesse euil saue foz wozldlye rebuke, to blabber on trifles somewhat sottishlye, than whyle they seeme sage, in kepyng silence, secretely paraduenture the meane whyle to fantasye wyth them self, sylthy sinful deuises, whereof theyz tonges if they wer set on babling, could not foz shame vtter and speake the lyke.

Side-glosses: Actes.5. — S.Chrisostō. — Pleasāt pain — A token of gods fauoz. — Pilgrimage. — Purgatozy. — i.Coz.9. — Comfozt. — Pleasure in spiritual exercise. — Two steppes to heauen. — The mynd neuer ydle. — Musing.

De quatuor nouissimis ("Concerning the four last things") is the section heading for each page of the 1557 *Workes*. This elaborate black-letter edition featured side-glosses and, to assist in referencing, letters in the margins.

The Four Last Things

A treatise (unfinished)
upon these words of Holy Scripture,
Memorare novissima, et in aeternum non peccabis,
"Remember the last things, and thou shalt never sin."[1]
Made about the year of our Lord 1522 by Sir Thomas More then
knight, and one of the Privy Council of King Henry VIII,
and also Under-Treasurer of England

If there were any question among men whether the words of Holy Scripture, or the doctrine of any secular author, were of greater force and effect to the weal[2] and profit of man's soul (though we should let pass so many short and weighty words spoken by the mouth of our Savior Christ himself, to whose heavenly wisdom the wit of none earthly creature can be comparable) yet this only text written by the wise man in the seventh chapter of Ecclesiasticus is such that it containeth more fruitful advice and counsel to the forming and framing of man's manners in virtue and avoiding of sin than many whole and great volumes of the best of old philosophers, or any other that ever wrote in secular literature.

Long would it be to take the best of their words and compare it with these words of Holy Writ. Let us consider the fruit and profit of this in itself: which thing, well advised and pondered, shall well declare that of[3] none whole volume of secular literature shall arise so very fruitful doctrine. For what would a man give for a sure medicine that were of such strength that it should all his life keep him from sickness, namely if he might by the avoiding of sickness be sure to continue his life one hundred years? So is it now that these words giveth us all a sure medicine (if we forsloth[4] not the receiving) by which we shall keep from sickness, not the body, which none health may long keep from death (for die we must in few years, live we never so long), but the soul, which here preserved from the sickness of sin, shall after this eternally live in joy and be preserved from the deadly life of everlasting pain.

The physician sendeth his bill[5] to the apothecary,[6] and therein writeth sometimes a costly receipt[7] of many strange herbs and roots, fetched out of far countries, long-lain drugs, all the strength worn out, and some none such to be got. But this physician sendeth his bill to thyself, no strange thing therein, nothing costly to buy, nothing far to fetch, but to be gathered all times of the year in the garden of thine own soul.

Let us hear, then, what wholesome receipt this is. "Remember," saith this bill, "thy last things, and thou shalt never sin in this world." Here is first a short medicine containing only four herbs, common and well known: that is to wit,[8] death, doom, pain, and joy.

This short medicine is of a marvelous force, able to keep us all our life from sin. The physician cannot give no one medicine to every man to keep him from sickness, but to diverse men diverse,[9] by reason of the diversity of diverse complexions.[10] This medicine serveth every man. The physician doth but guess and conjecture that his receipt shall do good; but this medicine is undoubtedly sure.

How happeth it, then, thou wilt haply[11] say, that so few be preserved from sin, if every man have so sure a medicine so ready at hand? For folk fare commonly as he doth that goeth forth fasting among

---

1 Ecclus 7:40   **2** well-being   **3** out of, from   **4** lose, miss, neglect, spoil, or waste through sloth   **5** medical prescription   **6** pharmacy   **7** list of things to be received   **8** say   **9** *to diverse men diverse:* to different men different medicines   **10** physical constitutions   **11** perhaps

sick folk for[12] sloth, rather than he will take a little treacle[13] before.

Thou wilt say, peradventure,[14] that some part of this medicine is very bitter and painful to receive. Surely there can be nothing so bitter but[15] wisdom would brook[16] it for so great a profit. But yet this medicine, though thou make a sour face at it, is not so bitter as thou makest for. For well thou wottest,[17] he biddeth thee not take neither death, nor doom, nor pain, but only to remember them, and yet the joy of heaven therewith to temper them withal. Now if a man be so dainty stomached[18] that going where contagion is he would grudge to take a little treacle, yet were he[19] very nicely wanton[20] if he might not at the leastwise take a little vinegar and rose water in his handkerchief.

Yet wot[21] I well that many ones will say that the bare remembrance of death alone, if a man consider it and advise it well, were able to bereave[22] a man of all the pleasure of his life. How much more, then, should his life be painful and grievous if, to the remembrance and consideration of death, a man should add and set to[23] the deep imagination of the dreadful doom of God, and bitter pains of purgatory or hell, of which every one passeth and exceedeth many deaths. This is the sage saws[24] of such as make this world their heaven, and their lust[25] their God.

Now see the blindness of us worldly folk, how precisely we presume to shoot our foolish bolt[26] in those matters most in which we least can skill. For I little doubt but that among four thousand taken out at adventure,[27] we shall not find four score[28] but they shall boldly affirm it for a thing too painful, busily to remember these four last things. And yet durst I lay a wager that of those four thousand ye shall not find fourteen that hath deeply thought on them four times in all their days.

If men would vouchsafe[29] to put in proof and experience the operation and working of this medicine, the remembrance of these four last things, they should find therein, not the pleasure of their life lost, but so great a pleasure grow thereby that they never felt the like before, nor would have supposed that ever they should have felt any such. For it is to be known that, like as we be made of two far diverse and unlike substances, the body and the soul, so we be apt and able to receive two diverse and unlike pleasures, the one carnal and fleshly, the other ghostly and spiritual. And like as the soul excelleth the body, so doth the sweetness of spiritual pleasure far pass and excel the gross and filthy pleasure of all fleshly delight, which is of truth no very true pleasure, but a false counterfeit image of pleasure. And the cause why men be so mad thereon is only for ignorance and lack of knowledge of the other—as those that lack insight of precious stones hold themselves as well content and satisfied with a beryl[30] or crystal well counterfeited, as with a right natural diamond. But he that by good use and experience hath in his eye the right mark and very true luster of the diamond rejecteth anon[31] and listeth[32] not to look upon the counterfeit, be it never so well-handled, never so craftily polished. And trust it well that, in likewise, if men would well accustom themselves in the taste of spiritual pleasure and of that sweet feeling that virtuous people have of the good hope of heaven, they should shortly set at nought,[33] and at length abhor, the foul delight and filthy liking that riseth of[34] sensual and fleshly pleasure, which is never so pleasantly spiced with delight and liking but that it bringeth therewith such a grudge and grief of conscience that it maketh the stomach wamble[35] and fare as[36] it would vomit. And that notwithstanding, such is our blind custom that we persevere therein without care or cure of the better, as a sow content with draff,[37] dirt, and mire[38] careth neither for better meat nor better bed.

Think not that everything is pleasant that men for madness laugh at. For thou shalt in Bedlam[39] see one laugh at the knocking of his own head against a post, and yet there is little pleasure therein. But ye think peradventure this example as mad as the mad man, and as little to the purpose. I am content ye so think. But what will ye say if ye see men that are taken and reputed wise laugh much more madly than he? Shall ye not see such laugh at their own craft, when they have, as they think, willfully done

12 because of 13 a medical compound, salve 14 perhaps 15 but that 16 make use of 17 know 18 *dainty stomached:* easily upset 19 *were he:* he would be 20 unmanageable 21 know 22 deprive 23 actively involve 24 *sage saws:* wise sayings 25 pleasure; desire 26 arrow 27 *at adventure:* at random, by chance 28 *four score:* eighty 29 agree, choose 30 a transparent, light green precious stone, worth less than an emerald 31 instantly 32 likes, wishes 33 *set at nought:* value as nothing 34 out of, from 35 feel nauseous 36 as if 37 refuse, dregs 38 swampy ground 39 a hospital for the insane in London

their neighbor wrong? Now whoso seeth not that his laughter is more mad than the laughter of the mad man, I hold him madder than they both. For the mad man laughed when he had done himself but little hurt by a knock of his head to the post. This other sage fool laugheth at the casting of his own soul into the fire of hell, for which he hath cause to weep all his life. And it cannot be but the grudge and fear thereof followeth his laughter, and secret sorrow marreth all such outward mirth. For the heart of a wicked wretch is like a stormy sea that cannot rest, except a man be fallen down into the dungeon of wretchedness, and the door shut over his head. For when a sinner is once fallen down into the depth, he waxeth a desperate wretch and setteth all at naught, and he is in the worst kind of all, and farthest from all recovery. For like as in the body his sickness is most incurable that is sick and feeleth it not, but weeneth[40] himself whole (for he that is in that case is commonly mad), so he that by a mischievous custom of sin perceiveth no fault in his evil deed nor hath no remorse thereof hath lost the natural light of reason and the spiritual light of faith — which two lights of knowledge and understanding quenched, what remaineth in him more than the bodily senses and sensual wits common to man and brute beasts?

Now albeit so that the fleshly and worldly pleasure is of truth not pleasant but bitter, and the spiritual pleasure is of truth so sweet that the sweetness thereof many times darkeneth and diminisheth the feeling of bodily pain, by reason whereof good virtuous folk feel more pleasure in the sorrow of their sins and affliction of their penance than wretches feel in the fulfilling of their foul delight, and credible is it that the inward spiritual pleasure and comfort which many of the old holy martyrs had in the hope of heaven darkened and in manner overwhelmed the bodily pains of their torment — yet this notwithstanding, like as a sick man feeleth no sweetness in sugar, and some women with child have such fond lust[41] that they had liefer[42] eat tar than treacle and rather pitch than marmalade, and some whole people love tallow better than butter, and Iceland loveth no butter till it be long barreled, so we gross carnal people — having our taste infected by the sickness of sin and filthy custom of

fleshly lust, find so great liking in the vile and stinking delectation of fleshly delight that we list[43] — not once prove[44] what manner of sweetness good and virtuous folk feel and perceive in spiritual pleasure. And the cause is why? Because we cannot perceive the one but if[45] we forbear the other. For like as the ground that is all forgrown[46] with nettles, briars, and other evil weeds, can bring forth no corn till they be weeded out, so can our soul have no place for the good corn of spiritual pleasure as long as it is overgrown with the barren weeds of carnal delectation. For the pulling out of which weeds by the root, there is not a more meet[47] instrument than of the remembrance of the four last things, which as they shall pull out these weeds of fleshly voluptuousness, so shall they not fail to plant in their places, not only wholesome virtues, but also marvelous ghostly[48] pleasure and spiritual gladness, which in every good soul riseth of the love of God, and hope of heaven, and inward liking that the godly spirit taketh in the diligent labor of good and virtuous business.

I would not so long tarry in this point nor make so many words of the pleasure that men may find by the receipt of this medicine, were it not that I well perceive the world so set upon the seeking of pleasure that they set by[49] pleasure much more than by profit. And therefore to the intent that ye may perceive that it is not a fantasy found of mine own head, that the abandoning and refusing of carnal pleasure and the ensuing of labor, travail, penance and bodily pain, shall bring therewith to a Christian man, not only in the world that is coming but also in this present life, very sweetness, comfort, pleasure, and gladness, I shall prove it to be true by their testimony and witness whose authority, speaking of their own experience, there will, I ween, none honest man mistrust.

Lo, the holy doctor Saint Augustine, exhorting penitents and repentant sinners to sorrow for their offenses, saith unto them: "Sorrow," saith this holy man, "and be glad of thy sorrow."[50] In vain should he bid him be glad of his sorrow, if man in sorrow could not be glad. But this holy father showeth by this counsel, not only that a man may be joyful and glad for all his sorrow, but also that he may be and hath cause to be glad because of his sorrow.

---

40 thinks   **41** *fond lust:* mad desire   **42** *had liefer:* would rather   **43** desire   **44** try, test   **45** *but if:* unless   **46** overgrown   **47** fitting   **48** spiritual   **49** *set by:* value   **50** from the pseudonymous twelfth-century *Liber de vera et falsa poenitentia,* 13.28 (*PL* 40: 1124), attributed to Augustine in the Middle Ages

Long were it to rehearse[51] the places that prove this point among the holy doctors of Christ's Church. But we will, instead of them all, allege you the words of him that is doctor of them all, our Savior Jesus Christ. He saith that the way to heaven is strait and asper[52] or painful. And therefore he saith that few folk find it out or walk therein. And yet saith he for all that, "My yoke is easy and my burden light."[53] How could these two sayings stand together, were it not that as the labor, travail, and affliction of the body is painful and sharp to the flesh, so the comfort and gladness that the soul conceiveth thereof, rising into the love of our Lord and hope of his glory to come, so tempereth and overmastereth the bitterness of the grief, that it maketh the very labor easy, the sourness very sweet, and the very pain pleasant?

Will ye see the example? Look upon his holy apostles — when they were taken and scourged with whips for Christ's sake, did it grieve them, think ye? Imagine yourself in the same case, and I think ye will think yea. Now see, then, for all the pain of their flesh, what joy and pleasure they conceived in their soul. The Holy Scripture saith that they rejoiced and joyed that God had accounted them worthy for Christ's sake, not only to be scourged, but also — which would be far greater grief to an honest man than the pain itself — to be scourged with despite and shame, so that the more their pain was, the more was their joy.[54] For as the holy doctor Saint Chrysostom saith, though pain be grievous for the nature of the affliction, yet is it pleasant by the alacrity and quick mind of them that willingly suffer it.[55] And therefore though the nature of the torments make great grief and pain, yet the prompt and willing mind of them that were scourged passed and overcame the nature of the thing, that is to wit,[56] mastering the outward fleshly pain with inward spiritual pleasure. And surely this is so true that it may stand for a very certain token that a penitent beginneth to profit and grow in grace and favor of God when he feeleth a pleasure and quickness in his labor and pain taken in prayer, almsdeeds, pilgrimage, fasting, discipline, tribulation, affliction, and such other spiritual exercise, by which the soul willingly worketh with the body by their own punishment to purge and rub out the rusty cankered

spots that sin hath defiled them with, in the sight of God, and to leave the fewer to be burned out in the fire of purgatory.

And whensoever, as I say, that a man feeleth in this pain a pleasure, he hath a token of great grace and that his penance is pleasant to God. For as the Holy Scripture saith, our Lord loveth a glad giver.[57] And on the other side, whereas one doth such spiritual business with a dullness of spirit and weariness of mind, he doth twice as much and thereby taketh four times as much pain, since his bodily pain is relieved with no spiritual rejoice nor comfort. I will not say that his labor is lost, but I dare be bold to say that he profiteth much less with much more pain. For certain it is that the best souls, and they that have best travailed[58] in spiritual business, find most comfort therein. And therefore if they most pleased God that in the bodily pain of their penance took less spiritual pleasure, it should thereof follow that the farther a man proceeded in the perfection of spiritual exercise, in the worse case he were. Which can in no wise be so, since that we see the holy apostles and other holy men and women, the better that they were, the more pleasure they perceived in their fleshly afflictions, either put unto them by God, or taken by themselves for God's sake.

Therefore let every man, by the labor of his mind and help of prayer, enforce himself in all tribulation and affliction, labor, pain and travail, without spot of pride or ascribing any praise to himself, to conceive a delight and pleasure in such spiritual exercise, and thereby to rise in the love of our Lord, with a hope of heaven, contempt of the world, and longing to be with God. To the attaining of which mind, by the putting away of the malicious pleasures of the devil, the filthy pleasures of the flesh, and the vain pleasures of the world (which once excluded there is place made and clean purged to receive the very sweet and pure pleasure of the spirit), there is not any one thing lightly,[59] as I have said, more accommodated nor more effectual than this thing that I have begun with and taken in hand to treat, that is to wit, the remembrance of the four last things, which is, as the Scripture saith, so effectual that if a man remember it well, he shall never sin.

Thou wilt haply[60] say that it is not enough that a man do none evil, but he must also do good. This is

51 tell; cite   **52** rough   **53** Mt 11:30   **54** See Acts 5:27–41.   **55** See   Chrysostom's Homily 24 on Matthew (*PG* 57: 314).   **56** say   **57** 2 Cor 9:7   **58** labored   **59** of little weight or difficulty   **60** perhaps

very truth that ye say. But first, if there be but these two steps to heaven, he that getteth him on the one is half up. And over[61] that, whoso doth none evil, it will be very hard but he must needs do good, since man's mind is never idle, but occupied commonly either with good or evil.

And therefore when folk have few words and use much musing, likewise as[62] among many words all be not always well and wisely set, so when the tongue lieth still, if the mind be not occupied well, it were less evil, save for worldly rebuke, to blabber on trifles somewhat sottishly[63] than while they seem sage in keeping silence, secretly peradventure,[64] the meanwhile to fantasy with themselves filthy sinful devices, whereof their tongues, if they were set on babbling, could not for shame utter and speak the like.

I say not this for that[65] I would have folks fall to babbling, well wotting[66] that, as the Scripture saith, in many words lacketh not sin,[67] but that I would have folk in their silence take good heed that their minds be occupied with good thoughts, for unoccupied be they never. For if ever the mind were empty, it would be empty when the body sleepeth. But if it were then all empty, we should have no dreams. Then if the fantasies leave us not sleeping, it is not likely that ever they leave us waking. Wherefore, as I say, let us keep our minds occupied with good thoughts, or else the devil will fill them with evil.

And surely everything hath his mean. There is, as Scripture saith, time to speak and time to keep thy tongue.[68] Whensoever the communication is naught[69] and ungodly, it is better to hold thy tongue and think on some better thing the while than to give ear thereto and underpin[70] the tale. And yet better were it than holding of thy tongue, properly to speak, and with some good grace and pleasant fashion to break into some better matter; by which thy speech and talking, thou shalt not only profit thyself as thou shouldst have done by thy well-minded silence, but also amend the whole audience, which is a thing far better and of much more merit. Howbeit, if thou can find no proper means to break the tale, then except[71] thy bare authority suffice to command silence, it were peradventure good, rather to keep a good silence thyself than blunder forth rudely, and irritate them to anger, which[72] shall haply[73] therefore

not let[74] to talk on, but speak much the more, lest they should seem to leave at thy commandment. And better were it for the while to let one wanton[75] word pass uncontrolled than give occasion of twain.[76] But if the communication be good, then is it better, not only to give ear thereto, but also first well and prudently to devise with thyself upon the same, and then moderately and in good manner, if thou find aught[77] to the purpose, speak thereto and say thy mind therein. So shall it appear to the presence that your mind was well occupied the while, and your thought not wandering forty miles thence while your body was there, as it often happeth that the very face showeth the mind walking a pilgrimage in such wise that, not without some note and reproach of such vagrant mind, other folk suddenly say to them, "A penny for your thoughts." Which[78] manner of wandering mind in company may percase[79] be the more excusable sometimes by some chargeable business of the party, but surely it is never taken for wisdom nor good manners.

But now to return to my purpose, since the remembrance of these four last things is of such force and efficacy that it is able always to keep us from sin, and since we can never be long void of both, it must thereof ensue that we shall consequently do good; and thereof must it needs follow that this only lesson, well-learned and busily put in ure,[80] must needs lead us to heaven.

Yet will ye peradventure say that ye know these four things well enough, and if the knowledge thereof had so great effect as the Scripture speaketh of,[81] there should not be so many naught as there be. For what Christian man is he, that hath wit and discretion, but he hath heard and, having any faith, believeth these four last things?—of which the first, that is to say, death, we need no faith to believe, we know it by daily proof and experience.

I say not nay, but that we know them either by faith or experience—and yet not so very thoroughly as we might, peradventure, and hereafter undoubtedly shall. Which if we knew once thoroughly, and so feelingly perceived as we might, percase, and namely as we surely shall, there would be little doubt but[82] the least of all the four would well keep us from sin. For as for[83] that, though we have heard

61 beyond   **62** *likewise as:* just as   **63** foolishly   **64** perhaps   **65** *for that:* because   **66** knowing   **67** Prv 10:19   **68** Eccl 3:7   **69** wicked   **70** support, corroborate   **71** unless   **72** who   **73** perhaps   **74** hesitate   **75** undisciplined   **76** two   **77** anything   **78** This   **79** perhaps   **80** use, practice   **81** See   1 Cor 8:1.   **82** but that   **83** *For as for:* As regards

of the doom, yet were we never at it. Though we have heard of hell, yet came we never in it. Though we have heard of heaven, yet came we never to it. And though we daily see men die, and thereby know the death, yet ourselves never felt it. For if we knew these things thoroughly, the least of all four were, as I said, enough to keep us from sin.

Howbeit, the aforesaid words of Scripture biddeth thee not know the four last things, but remember thy four last things, and then, he saith, thou shall never sin.

Many things know we that we seldom think on. And in the things of the soul, the knowledge without the remembrance little profiteth. What availeth it to know that there is a God, which thou not only believest by faith, but also knowest by reason? What availeth that thou knowest him, if thou think little of him? The busy minding of thy four last things, and the deep consideration thereof, is the thing that shall keep thee from sin. And if thou put it in assay[84] and make a proof, thou shalt well find, by that thou shalt have no lust[85] to sin for the time that thou deeply thinkest on them, that if our frailty could endure never to remit or slacken in the deep devising of them, we should never have delight or pleasure in any sinful thing.

For the proof whereof, let us first begin at the remembrance of the first of these four last, which is undoubtedly far the least of the four, and thereby shall we make a proof what marvelous effect may grow by the diligent remembrance of all four, toward the avoiding of all the trains,[86] darts, sleights, enticings, and assaults of the three mortal enemies, the devil, the world, and our own flesh.[87]

THE REMEMBRANCE OF DEATH

What profit and commodity[88] cometh unto man's soul by the meditation of death is not only marked of the chosen people of God, but also of such as were the best sort among gentiles and paynims.[89] For some of the old famous philosophers, when they were demanded what faculty[90] philosophy was, answered that it was the meditation or exercise of death. For like as death maketh a severance

of the body and the soul, when they by course of nature must needs depart asunder,[91] so (said they) doth the study of philosophy labor to sever the soul from the love and affections of the body while they be together.

Now if this be the whole study and labor of philosophy, as the best philosopher said that it is,[92] then may we within short time be well-learned in philosophy. For nothing is there that may more effectually withdraw the soul from the wretched affections of the body than may the remembrance of death—if we do not remember it hourly, as one heareth a word and let it pass by his ear, without any receiving of the sentence into his heart. But if we not only hear this word "death," but also let sink into our hearts the very fantasy and deep imagination thereof, we shall perceive thereby that we were never so greatly moved by the beholding of the Dance of Death pictured in Paul's,[93] as we shall feel ourselves stirred and altered by the feeling of that imagination in our hearts. And no marvel. For those pictures express only the loathly[94] figure of our dead bony bodies, bitten away the flesh, which though it be ugly to behold, yet neither the light thereof, nor the sight of all the dead heads in the charnel house,[95] nor the apparition of a very ghost, is half so grisly as the deep-conceived fantasy of death in his nature, by the lively imagination graven in thine own heart. For there seest thou, not one plain grievous sight of the bare bones hanging by the sinews, but thou seest (if thou fantasy thine own death, for so art thou by this counsel advised), thou seest, I say, thyself if thou die no worse death, yet at the leastwise lying in thy bed, thy head shooting,[96] thy back aching, thy veins beating, thine heart panting, thy throat rattling, thy flesh trembling, thy mouth gaping, thy nose sharping,[97] thy legs cooling, thy fingers fumbling, thy breath shortening, all thy strength fainting, thy life vanishing, and thy death drawing on.

If thou couldst now call to thy remembrance some of those sicknesses that have most grieved thee and tormented thee in thy days, as every man hath felt some, and then findest thou that some one disease in some one part of thy body, as percase[98] the stone[99] or the strangury,[100] have put thee (to thine

---

84 *put it in assay:* put it to the test; try it **85** desire **86** deceits, guiles **87** See 1 Jn 2:15–16. **88** benefit **89** pagans **90** special ability or power **91** apart **92** Plato, *Phaedo* 63e–67e, 81e **93** a now-destroyed mural of the *danse macabre* in the north cloister of St. Paul's Cathedral, London **94** hideous, repulsive **95** *charnel house:* a house or vault for bones of the dead **96** having darting pains **97** sharpening **98** perhaps **99** kidney stones **100** a disease of the urinary organs

own mind) to no less torment than thou shouldst have felt if one had put up a knife into the same place, and wouldst, as thee then seemed, have been content with such a change—think what it will be

5 then when thou shalt feel so many such pains in every part of thy body, breaking thy veins and thy life strings, with like pain and grief as though as many knives as thy body might receive should everywhere enter and meet in the midst.

10 A stroke of a staff, a cut of a knife, the flesh singed with fire, the pain of sundry sickness, many men have assayed[101] in themselves. And they, that have not yet, somewhat have heard by them that felt it. But what manner dolor[102] and pain, what manner

15 of grievous pangs, what intolerable torment, the seely[103] creature feeleth in the dissolution and severance of the soul from the body, never was there body that yet could tell the tale.

Some conjecture and token of this point we have

20 of the bitter Passion and piteous departing of our Savior Jesus Christ, of whom we nothing read that ever he cried for any pain, neither for the whips and rods beating his blessed body nor the sharp thorns pricking his holy head, or the great long nails pierc-

25 ing his precious hands and feet. But when the point approached in which his sacred soul should depart out of his blessed body, at that point he cried loud once or twice to his Father in heaven, into whose mighty and merciful hands, at the extreme point,

30 with a great loud cry he gave up the ghost. Now if the death was so painful and rageous[104] to our Savior Christ—whose joy and comfort of his godhead, if he would have suffered it, might in such wise have redounded[105] into his soul, and so forth

35 into his body, that it should not only have supped up[106] all his pain, but also have transformed his holy body into a glorious form and made it impassible— what intolerable torment will death be then to us miserable wretches, of which the more part among

40 the pangs of our passage shall have yet so painful twitches of our own conscience that the fear of hell, the dread of the devil, and sorrow at[107] our heart at the sight of our sins shall pass and exceed the deadly pains of our body.

45 Other things are there, which will peradventure[108] seem no great matter to them that feel them

not, but unto him that shall lie in that case,[109] they shall be tedious out of all measure.

Have ye not ere[110] this, in a sore sickness, felt it very grievous to have folk babble to you, and 50 namely such things as ye should make answer to, when it was a pain to speak? Think ye not now that it will be a gentle pleasure, when we lie dying, all our body in pain, all our mind in trouble, our soul in sorrow, our heart all in dread, while our life walketh 55 awayward,[111] while our death draweth toward, while the devil is busy about us, while we lack stomach and strength to bear any one of so manifold heinous troubles—will it not be, as I was about to say, a pleasant thing to see before thine eyes and hear 60 at thine ear a rabble of fleshly friends, or rather of flesh-flies, skipping about thy bed and thy sick body, like ravens about thy corpse, now almost carrion, crying to thee on every side, "What shall I have? What shall I have?" Then shall come thy children 65 and cry for their parts;[112] then shall come thy sweet wife, and where in thine health haply[113] she spoke thee not one sweet word in six weeks, now shall she call thee sweet husband and weep with much work and ask thee what shall she have. Then shall thine 70 executors ask for the keys, and ask what money is owing thee, ask what substance thou hast, and ask where thy money lieth. And while thou liest in that case, their words shall be so tedious that thou wilt wish all that they ask for upon a red fire, so thou 75 mightest lie one half-hour in rest.

Now is there one thing which a little I touched before, I wot[114] not whether more painful or more perilous—the marvelous intentive[115] business and solicitation of our ghostly[116] enemy the devil, not 80 only in one fashion present, but surely never absent from him that draweth toward death. For since that[117] of his pestilent[118] envy conceived from the beginning of man's creation, by which he lay in wait to take our first mother Eve, in a train,[119] and 85 thereby drawing our former father Adam into the breach of God's behest, found the means, not without the grievous increase of his own damnation, to deprive us of paradise, and bereave us our immortality, making us into subjection not only of tem- 90 poral death but also of his eternal tormentry, were we not by the great bounty of God and Christ's

101 experienced 102 *manner dolor:*
kind of suffering 103 poor, pitiful
104 outrageous, grievous 105 surged up

106 *supped up:* consumed 107 in
108 perhaps 109 condition 110 before
111 away 112 share 113 perhaps

114 know 115 attentive 116 spiritual
117 *since that:* because 118 harmful
119 snare, trap; deceit

painful Passion restored to the possibility of ever-lasting life, he never ceased since to run about like a ramping[120] lion, looking whom he might devour,[121] it can be no doubt but he most busily travaileth[122] in that behalf at the time that he perceiveth us about to depart hence. For well he knoweth that then he either winneth a man forever, or forever loseth him. For have he him never so fast[123] before, yet if he break from him then he can after his death never get him again. Well he may peradventure have him as his jailer in his prison of purgatory for the time of his punishment temporal. But as he would have him for his perpetual slave, shall he never have him after, how sure soever he had him afore, if he get from him at the time of his death. For so lost he suddenly the thief that hung on the right hand of Christ.[124]

And on the other side, if he catch a man fast at the time of his death, he is sure to keep him forever. For as the Scripture saith, "Wheresoever the stone falleth, there shall it abide."[125] And since he knoweth this for very surety and is of malice so venomous and envious that he had liefer[126] double his own pain than suffer us to escape from pain, he, when we draw to death, doth his uttermost devoir[127] to bring us to damnation, never ceasing to minister, by subtle and incogitable[128] means, first unlawful longing to live, horror to go gladly to God at his calling.

Then giveth he some false glade[129] of escaping that sickness, and thereby putteth in our mind a love yet and cleaving to the world, keeping of our goods, loathsomeness of shrift,[130] sloth toward good works. And if we be so far gone that we see we cannot recover, then he casteth in our minds presumption and security of salvation as a thing well won by our own works, of which, if we have any done well, he casteth them into our minds with over-great liking and thereby withdraweth us from the haste of doing any more, as a thing that either needeth not or may be done by our executors. And instead of sorrow for our sins and care of heaven, he putteth us in mind of provision for some honorable burying — so many torches, so many tapers,[131] so many black gowns, so many merry mourners laughing under black hoods, and a gay hearse, with the delight of goodly and honorable funerals, in which the foolish sick man is sometimes occupied as though he thought that he should stand in a window and see how worshipfully he shall be brought to church.

And thus inveigleth[132] he them that either be good, or but meetly[133] bad.

But as for those that he hath known for special wretches, whose whole life hath in effect been all bestowed in his service, whom he hath brought into great and horrible sins by the horror whereof he hath kept them from confession, these folk at their end he handleth on another fashion. For into their minds he bringeth their shameful sins by heap, and by the abominable sight thereof, draweth them into desperation. For the aggrieving whereof our Lord, after their deserving, suffereth him to show himself to them for their more discomfort in some fearful figure and terrible likeness, by the beholding whereof they conceive sometimes despair of salvation, and yield themselves as captives quick,[134] beginning their hell in this world, as hath appeared by the words and wretched behavior of many that of a shameful sinful life have died and departed with heavy[135] desperate death.

Now death being such as I have described, or rather much more horrible than any man can describe, it is not to be doubted but if[136] we busily remembered the terror and grief thereof, it must needs be so bitter to the fleshly mind that it could not fail to take away the vain delight of all worldly vanities. But the thing that letteth[137] us to consider death in his kind,[138] and to take great profit that would arise of[139] the remembrance thereof, is that for by the hope of long life, we look upon death either so far off that we see him not at all, or but a slight and uncertain sight, as a man may see a thing so far off that he wotteth[140] not whether it be a bush or a beast. And surely so fare we by death, looking thereat afar off through a great long space of as many years as we hope to live. And those we imagine many, and perilously and foolishly beguile ourselves. For likewise as wives would their husbands should ween[141] by the example of Sarah that there were no woman so old but she might have a child,[142] so is there none old man so old but that, as Tully saith, he trusteth to live one year yet.[143] And as for

120 rampaging, raging   **121** See 1 Pt 5:8.   **122** labors   **123** securely   **124** See Lk 23:40–43.   **125** Eccl 11:3   **126** *had liefer*: would rather   **127** endeavor   **128** inconceivable   **129** gleam of hope   **130** confession   **131** candles   **132** beguile, cajole   **133** fairly   **134** living   **135** distressing, grievous   **136** *but if*: unless   **137** prevents; hinders   **138** nature   **139** from   **140** knows   **141** believe   **142** See Gn 20–21.   **143** Cicero, *De senectute* 9.68

young folk, they look not how many be dead in their own days younger than themselves, but who is the oldest man in the town, and upon his years they make their reckoning—where the wiser way were to reckon that a young man may die soon, and an old man cannot live long, but within a little while die the one may, the other must. And with this reckoning shall they look upon death much nearer hand, and better perceive him in his own likeness, and thereby take the more fruit of the remembrance and make themselves the more ready thereto.

Thou wouldst somewhat remember death the more effectually, and look upon him somewhat the more nearly, if thou knewest thyself sick and especially of any perilous sickness that would make an end of thee, though thou feltest yet little pain. For commonly when we be sick, then begin we to know ourselves, then pain bringeth us home, then we think how merry a thing it were to be praying in health, which we cannot now do for grief. Then care we little for our gay gear,[144] then desire we no delicate dainties. And as for Lady Lechery, then abhor we to think on. And then we think in ourselves that if ever we recover and mend in body, we will amend in soul, leave all vices and be virtuously occupied the remnant of our life—insomuch that very true we find the words of the epistle that the well-learned man Plinius Secundus, after his sickness, wrote unto his friend, wherein, after the description of men's fantasies in their disease, he closeth up his letter in this wise: "all the philosophers and wise men in this world give us for instruction of virtuous living, all that can I compendiously[145] give to myself and thee in few words: no more, lo, but let us be such when we be whole, as we think we will be when we be sick."[146]

Now then if thou be ever sick, and ever sick of a perilous sickness, wouldst thou not, if thou knewest thyself in such case, have better remembrance of death than thou hast? It would be hard peradventure[147] to make thee believe thyself sick while thou feelest no harm, and yet is that no sure knowledge of health. Trow[148] ye not that many a man is infected with the great sickness a good while ere[149] he perceive it, and the body sore[150] corrupt within ere

he feel the grief? How many men have there been that have gone about with God's marks[151] on their body, never perceiving themselves to be sick, but as merry as ever they were in their lives, till other men gave them warning how near they were their deaths? And therefore never reckon thyself whole, though thou feel no grief.

But thou wilt haply[152] say, "Be it that I cannot surely reckon myself whole, yet ye show me not why I should reckon myself sick." Thou sayest right well, and that shall I show thee now. Tell me, if one were in case[153] that he must be fain[154] once or twice a day to swaddle and plaster[155] his leg and[156] else he could not keep his life, wouldst thou reckon his leg sick or whole? I ween[157] ye will agree that his leg is not well at ease, nor the owner neither. Now if ye felt your belly in such case that ye must be fain all day to tend it with warm clothes or else ye were not able to abide the pain, would ye reckon your belly sick or whole? I ween ye would reckon your belly not in good quart.[158] If thou shouldst see one in such case that he could not hold up his head, that he could not stand on his feet, that he should be fain to lie down along, and there lie speechless as a dead stock[159] an hour or two every day, wouldst thou not say that he were perilously sick and had good cause to remember death, when he lieth every day in such case as though he were dead already?

Now then I pray thee consider me that all our bodies be ever in such case so tender of themselves that except we lapped[160] them continually with warm clothes, we were not able to live one winter week. Consider that our bodies have so sore a sickness and such a continual consumption[161] in themselves that the strongest were not able to endure and continue ten days together, were it not that once or twice a day we be fain to take medicines inward to clout[162] them up withal and keep them as long as we can. For what is our meat and drink but medicines against hunger and thirst, that give us warning of that we daily lose by our inward consumption?[163] And of that consumption shall we die in conclusion, for[164] all the medicines that we use, though never other sickness came at us.

Consider also that all our swaddling and tending

---

144 *gay gear:* showy apparel   **145** concisely, comprehensively   **146** Pliny the Younger, *Epistolae* 7.26   **147** perhaps   **148** Believe   **149** before   **150** greatly   **151** *God's marks:* physical signs of plague, such as the sweating sickness which afflicted England in the summer of 1517   **152** perhaps   **153** the position   **154** obliged   **155** treat medically with a plaster   **156** or   **157** think   **158** well-being   **159** a tree stump   **160** wrapped up   **161** wasting away, decay   **162** patch, mend   **163** See Augustine, *Confessions* 10.31.43–44.   **164** despite

with warm clothes and daily medicines, yet can our bodies not bear themselves but that almost half our time ever in twenty-four hours we be fain[165] to fall in a swoon which we call sleep, and there lie like dead stocks by a long space ere we come to ourselves again, insomuch that among all wise men of old it is agreed that sleep is the very image of death.

Now thou wilt peradventure say that this is but a fantasy. For though we call this hunger sickness, and meat a medicine, yet men know well enough what very sickness is, and what very medicines be, and thereby we know well enough that they be none.

If thou think this, then would I wit[166] of thee what thou callest a sickness. Is not that a sickness that will make an end of thee if it be not helped? If that be so, then I suppose thou bearest ever thy sickness with thee. For very sure art thou that it will make an end of thee if thou be not helped.

What callest thou, then, a medicine? Is it not such a thing as either applied outwardly to thy body, or received inward, shall preserve thee against that sore or sickness that else would put thee or some part of thee in peril? What can be, then, more properly and more verily[167] a medicine than is our meat and drink, by which is resisted the peril and undoubted death that else should in so few days follow, by the inward sickness of our own nature continually consuming us within? For as for[168] that ye reckon that we know which be sickness, that is but a custom of calling, by which we call no sickness by that name but such as be casual and come and go. For that that[169] is common to all men, and never from any man, because we reckon it natural, we give it not the name of sickness, but we name sickness a passion that cometh seldomer and, as we reckon, against nature, whereas the conflict of the diverse qualified elements tempered in our body, continually laboring each to vanquish other and thereby to dissolve the whole, though it be as sore[170] against the continuance of our nature, and as sore laboreth to the dissolution of the whole body as other sickness do, yet we neither call it sickness, nor the meat that resisteth it we call no medicine, and that for none other cause but for the continual familiarity that we have therewith.

But now consider, if it were so that one whole country were born all lepers, which is a sickness rather foul and perilous than painful, or all a whole country born with the falling sickness,[171] so that never any of them had ever in their lives known or heard either themselves or any other void of those diseases, trow[172] ye that, then, that they would ever have reckoned them for sickness? Nay surely, but they would have counted for sickness the colic[173] and the stone,[174] and such other like as come and go. But as for their leprosy and falling evil, they would never account it other than we account hunger or sleep. For as for that thy hunger doth thee pleasure when it is fed, so doth sometimes the itch of a sore leg when thou clawest about the brinks.[175]

And thus mayest thou surely see that all our whole life is but a sickness never curable, but as an incurable canker,[176] with continual swaddling and plastering,[177] botched[178] up to live as long as we may, and in conclusion undoubtedly to die of the same sickness, and though there never came other.

So that if thou consider this well, thou mayest look upon death, not as a stranger, but as a nigh[179] neighbor. For as the flame is next the smoke, so is death next an incurable sickness, and such is all our life.

And yet if this move you little, but that ye think for all this that death is far from you, I will go somewhat near[180] you. Thou reckonest every man near his death when he is dying. Then if thyself be now already dying, how canst thou reckon thyself far from death?

Some man saith merrily to his fellow, "Be merry, man — thou shalt never die as long as thou livest." And albeit he seem to say true, yet saith he more than he can make good. For if that were true, I could make him much merrier, for then he should never die.

Ye will peradventure marvel of this, but it is easy to prove. For I think ye will grant me that there is no time after that a man hath once life but he is either alive or dead. Then will there no man say that one can die either before he get life or after that he hath lost it, and so hath he no time left to die in but while he hath life. Wherefore, if we neither die before our life nor when we be dead already, needs must it follow that we never die but while we live.

It is not all one to die and to be dead. Truth it is that we be never dead while we live; and it is, meseemeth, as true, not only that we die while we

165 obliged   166 know   167 truly
168 *For as for:* As regards   169 which
170 grievously   171 epilepsy   172 believe,   trust   173 severe gripping pains in the
belly   174 kidney stones   175 edges
176 chronic sore or ulcer   177 medically   applying a plaster   178 clumsily patched
179 near   180 nearer

live, but also that we die all the while we live. What thing is dying? Is it any other thing than the passage and going out of this present life?

Now tell me, then, if thou were going out of a house, whether art thou going out only when thy foot is on the uttermost inch of the threshold, thy body half out of the door, or else when thou beginnest to set the first foot forward to go out, in what place of the house soever ye stand when ye buskle[181] forward? I would say that ye be going out of the house, from the first foot ye set forward to go forth. No man will think other, as I suppose, but all is one reason in going hence and coming hither. Now if one were coming hither to this town, he were not only coming hither while he were entering in at the gate, but all the way also from whence he came hitherward. Nor, in likewise, in going hence from this town, a man is not only going from this town while he hath his body in the gate going outward, but also while he setteth his foot out of his host's house to go forward. And therefore if a man met him by the way, far yet within the town, and asked him whither he were going, he should truly answer that he were going out of the town, all were the town[182] so long that he had ten miles to go ere[183] he came at the gate.

And surely methinketh that in likewise, a man is not only dying, that is to say, going in his way out of this life, while he lieth drawing on, but also all the while that he is going toward his end, which is by all the whole time of his life, since the first moment till the last finished, that is to wit, since the first moment in which he began to live, until the last moment of his life, or rather the first in which he is fully dead.

Now if this be thus, as meseemeth that reason proveth, a man is always dying from before his birth, and every hour of our age, as it passeth by, cutteth his own length out of our life, and maketh it shorter by so much, and our death so much the nearer. Which measuring of time and diminishing of life, with approaching toward death, is nothing else but, from our beginning to our ending, one continual dying: so that wake we, sleep we, eat we, drink we, mourn we, sing we, in what wise soever live we, all the same while die we.

So that we never ought to look toward death as a thing far off, considering that although he made

no haste toward us, yet we never cease ourselves to make haste toward him.

Now if thou think this reason but a sophistical subtlety, and thinkest while thou art a young man, thou mayest for all this think thy death far off, that is to wit,[184] as far as thou hast by likelihood of nature many years to live, then will I put thee a homely example, not very pleasant, but none the less very true and very fit for the matter.

If there were two, both condemned to death, both carried out at once toward execution; of which two, the one were sure that the place of his execution were within one mile, the other twenty miles off, yea a hundred, and ye will, he that were in the cart to be carried a hundred miles would not take much more pleasure than his fellow in the length of his way, notwithstanding that it were a hundred times as long as his fellow's and that he had thereby a hundred times as long to live, being sure and out of all question to die at the end.

Reckon me[185] now yourself a young man in your best lust,[186] twenty years of age, if ye will. Let there be another, ninety. Both must ye die, both be ye in the cart carrying forward. His gallows and death standeth within ten miles at the farthest, and yours within eighty. I see not why ye should reckon much less of your death than he, though your way be longer, since ye be sure ye shall never cease riding till ye come at it.

And this is true, although ye were sure that the place of your execution stood so far beyond his.

But what if there were to the place of your execution two ways, of which the one were four score[187] miles farther about than your fellow's, the other nearer by five miles than his; and when ye were put in the cart, had warning of both; and though ye were showed that it were likely that ye should be carried the longer way, yet it might hap ye should go the shorter, and whether ye were carried the one or the other, ye should never know till ye come to the place; I trow ye could not in this case make much longer of your life than of your fellow's.

Now in this case[188] are we all. For our Lord hath not indented us of the time.[189] He hath appointed what we may not pass, but not how soon we shall go, nor where, nor in what wise. And therefore if thou wilt consider how little cause thou hast to reckon

---

181 to set out hastily   **182** *all were the town:* even if the town were   **183** before   **184** say   **185** for me   **186** vigor   **187** *four score:* eighty   **188** situation   **189** *indented . . . time:* entered into   agreement by indentures with us regarding time. See Jb 14:5.

thy death so far off, by reason of thy youth, reckon how many as young as thou have been slain in the selfsame ways in which thou ridest; how many have been drowned in the selfsame waters in which thou rowest. And thus shalt thou well see that thou hast no cause to look upon thy death as a thing far off, but a thing undoubtedly nigh thee, and ever walking with thee. By which[190] — not a false imagination, but a very true contemplation — thou shalt behold him and advise him such as he is, and thereby take occasion to flee vain pleasures of the flesh that keep out the very pleasures of the soul.

OF PRIDE

Now since I have somewhat laid before thy face the bodily pains of death, the troubles and vexations spiritual that come therewith by thy ghostly[191] enemy the devil, the unrestful cumbrance[192] of thy fleshly friends, the uncertainty of thyself how soon this dreadful time shall come, that thou art ever sick of that incurable sickness, by which, if none other come, thou shalt yet in few years undoubtedly die — and yet, moreover, that thou art already dying, and ever hast been since thou first beganst to live — let us now make some proof of this one part of our medicine, how the remembrance of death, in this fashion considered in his kind, will work with us to the preservation of our souls from every kind of sin, beginning at the sin that is the very head and root of all sins — that is to wit, pride, the mischievous mother of all manner vice.

I have seen many vices ere[193] this that at the first seemed far from pride, and yet well considered to the uttermost it would well appear that of that root they sprang. As for wrath and envy, be[194] the known children of pride, as rising of[195] a high estimation of ourselves. But what should seem farther from pride than drunken gluttony? And yet shall ye find more that drink themselves sow-drunk of[196] pride to be called good fellows than for lust of[197] the drink itself. So spreadeth this cursed root of pride his branches into all other kinds, besides his proper[198] malice for his own part, not only in high mind[199] of fortune, rule and authority, beauty, wit, strength,

learning, or such other gifts of God, but also the false pride of hypocrites that[200] feign to have the virtues that they lack, and the perilous pride of them, that for their few spotted virtues, not without the mixture of other mortal vices, take themselves for quick[201] saints on earth, proudly judging the lives of their even[202] Christians, disdaining other men's virtue, envying other men's praise, bearing implacable anger where they perceive themselves not accepted and set by[203] after the worthiness of their own estimation.

Which[204] kind of spiritual pride, and thereupon following envy and wrath, is so much the more pestilent, in that it carrieth with it a blindness almost incurable, save[205] God's great mercy. For the lecher knoweth he doth naught,[206] and hath remorse thereof. The glutton perceiveth his own fault, and sometimes thinketh it beastly. The slothful body misliketh his dullness, and thereby is moved to mend. But this kind of pride, that in his own opinion taketh himself for holy, is farthest from all recovery. For how can he mend his fault that taketh it for none, that weeneth[207] all is well that he doth himself (and nothing that any man doth else), that covereth his purpose with the pretext of some holy purpose that he will never begin while he liveth, taketh his envy for a holy desire to get before his neighbor in virtue, and taketh his wrath and anger for a holy zeal of justice. And thus while he proudly liketh his vices, he is out all the way to mend them, in so far forth that I surely think there be some, who had[208] in good faith made the best merchandise[209] that ever they made in their lives for their own souls, if they had changed those spiritual vices of pride, wrath, and envy for the beastly carnal sins of gluttony, sloth and lechery. Not that these three were good, which be undoubtedly damnable, but for that[210] like as God said in the Apocalypse unto the Church of Laodice, "Thou art neither hot nor cold but lukewarm. I would thou were cold that thou mightst wax[211] warm,"[212] signifying that if he were in open and manifest sins, he would have more occasion to call fervently for grace and help, so if these folk had these carnal sins, they could not be ignorant of their own faults. For, as Saint Paul saith, the fleshly sins be easy to perceive,[213] and so should

190 this **191** spiritual **192** distress, trouble **193** before **194** they be **195** from **196** out of, from **197** *lust of:* desire for **198** own; particular **199** high mind: pride **200** who **201** living **202** fellow **203** *set by:* esteemed, regarded **204** This **205** except for **206** wickedness **207** thinks **208** would have **209** bargain, exchange **210** *for that:* because **211** become, grow **212** Rv 3:14–15 **213** Gal 5:19

they have occasion to call for grace and wax good, where now, by their pride taking themselves for good where they be naught,[214] they be far from all occasion of amendment, saving the knocking of our Lord, which always standeth at the door of man's heart and knocketh,[215] whom I pray God we may give ear unto and let him in. And one of his good and gracious knockings is the putting us in remembrance of death, which remembrance, as I have said, let us see what stead[216] it may stand us in against this cursed sin of pride.

And surely against this last branch of pride, of such as repute themselves for holy with the disdain of others, and an inward liking of all their spiritual vices, which they commend unto themselves, under the cloak and shadow of some kind of virtue, most hard it is to take remedy by the remembrance of death, forasmuch as they reckon themselves thereby ready to go straight to heaven. But yet if they consider the labor and solicitation of our ghostly[217] enemy, the devil, that shall at the time of their death be busy to destroy the merits and good works of all their life before, and that subtlest craft, and most venomous dart, and the most for them to avoid, shall be, under the color[218] of a faithful hope of heaven, as a thing more than due to their own holiness, to send them wretchedly to the fire of hell for their sinful and willful blind presumption, I say, the remembrance and consideration of this perilous point and fearful jeopardy likely to fall on them at the time of their death is a right effectual[219] ointment long before in their life to wear away the web that covereth the eyes of their souls in such wise as they cannot with a sure sight look upon their own conscience.

As for all other kinds of pride, rising of beauty, strength, wit, or cunning, methinketh that the remembrance of death may right easily mend it, since that they be such things as shall shortly by death lose all their gloss, the owners wot nere[220] how soon.

And as lightly may there, by the same consideration, be cured the pride of these foolish proud hypocrites, which are yet more fools than they that plainly follow the ways of the world and pleasure of their body. For they, though they go to the devil therefor,[221] yet somewhat[222] they take therefore. These mad hypocrites be so mad that where they

sink in hell as deep as the others, yet in reward of all their pain taken in this world, they be content to take the vain praise of the people, a blast of wind of their mouths, which yet percase[223] praise them not but call them as they be. And if they do, yet themselves hear it not often. And sure they be that within short time death shall stop their ears, and the clods[224] cover all the mouths that praise them, which, if they well and advisedly considered, they would, I ween,[225] turn their appetites from the laud of seely[226] mortal men, and desire to deserve their thanks and commendation of God only, whose praise can never die.

Now the high mind of proud fortune, rule, and authority, Lord God, how slight a thing it would seem to him that would often and deeply remember that death shall shortly take away all this royalty, and his glory shall, as the Scripture saith, never walk with him into his grave;[227] but he that overlooketh[228] every man, and no man may be so homely to come too near him, but thinketh that he doth much for them whom he vouchsafeth[229] to take by the hand or beck upon, whom so many men dread and fear, so many wait upon—he shall within a few years, and only God knoweth within how few days, when death arresteth him, have his dainty body turned into stinking carrion, be borne out of his princely palace, laid in the ground and there left alone, where every lewd[230] lad will be bold to tread on his head. Would not, ween ye, the deep consideration of this sudden change, so surely to come and so shortly to come, withdraw the wind that puffeth us up in pride upon the solemn sight of worldly worship? If thou shouldst perceive that one were earnestly proud of the wearing of the gay golden gown, while the lorel[231] playeth the lord in a stage play, wouldst thou not laugh at his folly, considering that thou art very sure that when the play is done he shall go walk a knave in his old coat? Now thou thinkest thyself wise enough while thou art proud in thy player's garment, and forgettest that when thy play is done, thou shalt go forth as poor as he. Nor thou remembrest not that thy pageant may happen to be done as soon as his.

We shall leave the example of plays and players, which be too merry for this matter. I shall put thee a more earnest image of our condition, and that not

214 wicked   **215** Rv 3:20   **216** place
217 spiritual   **218** appearance, pretext
219 *right effectual:* powerful in effect

220 *wot nere:* know not   **221** for it
222 something   **223** perhaps   **224** soil
225 think   **226** silly; weak   **227** See

Ps 48(49):18.   **228** watches over
229 grants, wishes   **230** uneducated; rude
231 rogue

a feigned similitude but a very true fashion[232] and figure of our worshipful estate. Mark this well, for of this thing we be very sure, that old and young, man and woman, rich and poor, prince and page, all the while we live in this world we be but prisoners, and be within a sure prison, out of which there can no man escape. And in worse case be we than those that be taken and imprisoned for theft. For they, albeit their heart heavily[233] hearkeneth after[234] the sessions,[235] yet have they some hope either to break prison the while, or to escape there by favor, or after condemnation some hope of pardon. But we stand all in other plight: we be very sure that we be already condemned to death, some one, some other, none of us can tell what death we be doomed to, but surely can we all tell that die we shall. And clearly know we that of this death we get no manner[236] pardon. For the King, by whose high sentence we be condemned to die, would not of this death pardon his own Son. As for escaping, no man can look for. The prison is large and many prisoners in it, but the jailer can lose none; he is so present in every place that we can creep into no corner out of his sight. For as holy David saith to this jailer, "Whither shall I go from thy spirit, and whither shall I flee from thy face?"[237] — as who saith, nowhither. There is no remedy therefore, but as condemned folk and remediless, in this prison of the earth we drive forth awhile, some bounden to a post, some wandering abroad, some in the dungeon, some in the upper ward, some building them bowers[238] and making palaces in the prison, some weeping, some laughing, some laboring, some playing, some singing, some chiding, some fighting, no man, almost, remembering in what case he standeth, till that suddenly, nothing less looking for, young, old, poor and rich, merry and sad, prince, page, pope and poor soul priest, now one, now other, sometimes a great rabble at once, without order, without respect of age or of estate, all stripped stark naked and shifted out in a sheet, be put to death in diverse wise[239] in some corner of the same prison, and even there thrown in a hole, and either worms eat him under ground, or crows above.

Now come forth, ye proud prisoner, for iwis[240] ye be no better, look ye never so high, when ye build in that prison a palace for your blood — is it not a great royalty if it be well considered? Ye build the Tower of Babylon[241] in a corner of the prison, and be very proud thereof; and sometimes the jailer beateth it down again with shame. Ye leave your lodging for your own blood; and the jailer, when ye be dead, setteth a strange prisoner in your building, and thrusteth your blood into some other cabin. Ye be proud of the arms of your ancestors set up in the prison; and all your pride is because ye forget that it is a prison. For if ye took the matter aright — the place a prison, yourself a prisoner condemned to death, from which ye cannot escape — ye would reckon this gear[242] as worshipful as if a gentleman thief, when he should go to Tyburn, would leave for a memorial the arms of his ancestors painted on a post in Newgate.[243] Surely, I suppose that if we took not true figure[244] for a fantasy, but reckoned it as it is indeed, the very express fashion and manner of all our estate,[245] men would bear themselves not much higher in their hearts for any rule or authority that they bear in this world, which they may well perceive to be indeed no better but one prisoner bearing a rule among the remnant, as the tapster[246] doth in the Marshalsea,[247] or at the uttermost, one so put in trust with the jailer that he is half an under-jailer over his fellows, till the sheriff and the cart come for him.

OF ENVY

Now let us see what help we may have of this medicine against the sickness of envy, which is undoubtedly both a sore[248] torment and a very consumption.[249] For surely envy is such a torment, as all the tyrants of Sicily never devised a sorer.[250] And it so drinketh up the moisture of the body, and consumeth the good blood, so discoloreth the face, so defaceth the beauty, so disfigureth the visage,[251] leaving it all bony, lean, pale, and wan, that a person well set a work with envy needeth none other

---

232 making   **233** sorrowfully, with difficulty   **234** *hearkeneth after:* listens to   **235** the periodical sittings of justices of the peace   **236** kind of   **237** Ps 138(139):7   **238** dwellings   **239** ways   **240** certainly   **241** Babel, Gn 1:1–9   **242** business; matter

243 a prison at London's northwest entrance   **244** shape (of the matter)   **245** condition   **246** one who draws beer   **247** another prison, in the borough of Southwark   **248** grievous   **249** disease causing the wasting of the body, specifically

tuberculosis   **250** e.g., Dionysius and Phalaris. Phalaris had created a bronze bull which, with a victim inside, was heated as a torturous method of execution.   **251** face

image of death than his own face in a glass. This vice is not only devilish, but also very foolish. For albeit that envy, where it may over,[252] doth all the hurt it can, yet since the worse most commonly envieth the better, and the feebler the stronger, it happeth, for the more part, that as the fire of the burning hill of Etna[253] burneth only itself, so doth the envious person fret, fume, and burn in his own heart, without ability or power to do the other hurt. And little marvel it is though envy be an ungracious graft,[254] for it cometh of an ungracious stock. It is the first begotten daughter of pride, begotten in bastardy and incest by the devil, father of them both. For as soon as the devil had brought out his daughter pride, without wife, of[255] his own body, like as the venomous spider bringeth forth her cobweb, when this poisoned daughter of his had helped him out of heaven, at the first sight of Adam and Eve in paradise set in the way to such worship, the devil anon took his own unhappy daughter to wife, and upon pride begot envy, by whose enticement he set upon our first parents in Paradise, and by pride supplanted them, and there gave them so great a fall by their own folly that unto this day all their posterity go crooked thereof. And therefore ever since, envy goeth forth mourning at every man's welfare, more sorry of another man's wealth than glad of her own, of which she taketh no pleasure if other folk fare well with her. In so far forth that one Publius, a Roman, when he saw one Publius Mutius sad and heavy, whom he knew for an envious person, "Surely," quoth he, "either Mutius hath a shrewd turn[256] himself, or some man else a good turn,"[257] noting that his envious nature was as sorry of another man's weal[258] as of his own hurt.

I cannot here—albeit I nothing less intend than to meddle much with secular authors in this matter—yet can I not here hold my hand from the putting in remembrance of a certain fable of Aesop;[259] it expresseth so properly the nature, the affection, and the reward of two capital vices, that is to wit, envy and covetousness. Aesop, therefore, as I think ye have heard, feigneth that one of the paynim[260] gods came down into earth, and finding together in a place two men, the one envious, the other covetous, showed himself willing to give each of them a gift, but there should but[261] one of them ask for them both; but look, whatsoever that one that should ask would ask for himself, the other should have the selfsame thing doubled. When this condition was offered, then began there some courtesy between the envious and covetous, whether[262] of them should ask: for that would not the covetous be brought unto for nothing, because himself would have his fellow's request doubled. And when the envious man saw that, he would provide that his fellow should have little good of the doubling of his petition. And forthwith[263] he required, for his part, that he might have one of his eyes put out. By reason of which request, the envious man lost one eye, and the covetous lost both.

Lo, such is the wretched appetite of this cursed envy, ready to run into the fire, so he may draw his neighbor with him. Which[264] envy is, as I have said, and as Saint Augustine saith, the daughter of pride, in so far forth that, as this holy doctor saith, strangle the mother and thou destroyest the daughter.[265] And therefore, look what manner[266] consideration, in the remembrance of death, shall be medicinable against the pestilent swelling sore of pride, the selfsame considerations be the next remedies against the venomous vice of envy. For whosoever envy another, it is for something, whereof himself would be proud if he had it. Then if such considerations of death as we have before spoken of in the repressing of pride should make thee set neither much by those things, nor much the more by thyself for them if thyself hadst them, it must needs follow that the selfsame considerations shall leave thee little cause to envy the selfsame things in any other man. For thou wouldst not, for shame, that men should think thee so mad to envy a poor soul for playing the lord one night in an interlude.[267] And also couldst thou envy a perpetual sick man, a man that carrieth his death's wound with him, a man that is but a prisoner damned to death, a man that is in the cart already carrying forward? For all these things are, as I think, made meetly[268] probable to thee before.

252 overcome, master   **253** a volcano in Sicily   **254** a shoot grafted onto another shoot or tree   **255** out of, from   **256** *shrewd turn:* malicious act   **257** Macrobius, *Saturnalia* 2.8   **258** wealth; well-being   **259** Included by William Caxton in his *Historyes and Fables of Esop*

(1484) as "The xvii fable … of Phebus … the Avarycious and … the envious," this story from which More adapts the following is actually a fable of Avianus, "*De cupido et invido.*"   **260** pagan   **261** only   **262** which   **263** immediately   **264** This   **265** See *Sermones* 303.2, 304.5 (*PL* 39: 1561,

1565); *Enarrationes in Psalmos* 100.9; *De genesi ad litteram* 11.14; *De catechizandis rudibus* 4; *Epistolae* 140.54; *De sancta virginitate* 31.   **266** kind of   **267** a dramatic scene, usually light and comic, commonly introduced between the acts of a more serious play   **268** fairly; suitably

It is also to be considered that since it is so that men commonly envy their betters, the remembrance of death should of reason be a great remedy thereof. For I suppose if there were one right[269] far above thee, yet thou wouldst not greatly envy his estate, if thou thoughtst that thou mightst be his match the next week. And why shouldst thou then envy him now, while thou seest that death may make you both matches the next night, and shall undoubtedly within few years? If it so were that thou knewest a great duke,[270] keeping so great estate and princely port[271] in his house that thou, being a right mean[272] man, hadst in thine heart a great envy thereat, and specially at some special day, in which he keepeth for the marriage of his child a great honorable court above other times; if thou being thereat, and—at the sight of the royalty and honor shown him of all the country about resorting to him, while they kneel and crouch to him and at every word bare-headed begrace him—if thou shouldst suddenly be surely advertised[273] that for secret treason lately detected to the king, he should undoubtedly be taken the morrow, his court all broken up, his goods seized, his wife put out, his children disinherited, himself cast into prison, brought forth and arraigned, the matter out of question,[274] and he should be condemned, his coat armor reversed, his gilt spurs hewn off his heels, himself hanged, drawn, and quartered, how thinkest thou, by thy faith, amid thine envy, shouldst thou not suddenly change into pity?

Surely so is it that if we considered everything aright and esteemed it after the very[275] nature, not after men's false opinion, since we be certain that death shall take away all that we envy any man for, and we be uncertain how soon, and yet very sure that it shall not be long, we should never see cause to envy any man, but rather to pity every man, and those most that most hath to be envied for, since they be those that shortly shall most lose.

OF WRATH

Let us now somewhat see how this part of our medicine (that is to wit,[276] the remembrance of death) may cure us of the fierce rageous[277] fever of wrath. For wrath is undoubtedly another daughter of pride. For albeit that wrath sometimes riseth upon[278] a wrong done us, as[279] harm to our person, or loss in our goods, which is an occasion given us and often sudden, by reason whereof the sin is somewhat less grievous, the rule of reason being letted[280] for the while by the sudden brunt of the injury, not forethought upon, but coming upon us unprovided, yet shall ye find that in them which have so turned an evil custom into nature that they seem now naturally disposed to wrath and waywardness, the very root of that vice is pride, although their manner and behavior be such besides, that folk would little ween[281] it. For go they never so simply, look they never so lowly, yet shall ye see them at every light occasion testy. They cannot abide one merry word that toucheth them, they cannot bear in reasoning to be contraried, but they fret and fume if their opinion be not accepted, and their invention be not magnified.

Whereof riseth this waywardness, but of a secret root of setting much by themselves, by which it goeth to their heart when they see any man less esteem them than they seem worthy to themselves?

Wilt thou also well perceive that the setting by[282] ourselves is more than half the weight of our wrath? We shall prove it by them that would haply[283] say nay. Take me one that reckoneth himself for worshipful, and look whether he shall not be much more wroth with one opprobrious and rebukeful word—as "knave" percase[284] or "beggar" (in which is no great slander), spoken to his face by one that he reckoneth but his match or far under him—than with the selfsame word spoken to him by one that he knoweth and acknowledgeth for a great deal his better.

We see this point confirmed by all the laws made among men, which laws—forasmuch as the actions of trespass be given to revenge men not of the wrongs only done unto them in their bodies or their goods, but also of their contumelies,[285] griefs,

---

269 very   **270** Here More alludes to the fall of the Duke of Buckingham in 1521.   **271** bearing, demeanor   **272** moderate, average   **273** notified   **274** *out*

of question: beyond a doubt   **275** true   **276** say   **277** rage-filled   **278** from   **279** such as   **280** hindered, prevented   **281** think   **282** *setting by:* valuing of

283 perhaps   **284** perhaps   **285** insolent reproaches or rebukes

and despites, whereby they conceive any displeasure at heart, lest in lack of law to do it for them, they should in following their irous[286] affection, revenge themselves immoderately with their own hands—the laws, I say, considereth, pondereth, and punisheth the trespasses done to every man, not only after[287] the hurt that is done or loss that is taken, but and if[288] it be such as the party grieved is like to be wroth withal,[289] the punishment is aggrieved or diminished, made less or more, after the difference in degree of worship and reputation between the parties. And this is the provision of the laws almost in every country, and hath been afore Christ was born, by which it appeareth by a common consent that a man's own estimation—setting by himself, disdaining to take rebuke of one worse than himself—maketh his wrath the sorer.[290]

For the assuaging whereof, the law contenteth him with the larger punishment of his offender.

And this so far forth that in Spain it is sorer taken, and sorer punished, if one give another a dry blow[291] with his fist, than if he draw blood upon him with a sword. The cause is none other but the appeasing of his mind that is so stricken, forasmuch as commonly they take themselves for so very manly men that three strokes with a sword could not anger one of them so much as that it should appear that, by a blow given him with a bare hand, any man should so far reckon him for a boy that he would not vouchsafe to draw any weapon at him.

So that, as I said, it well appeareth by the common confession of the world, expressed and declared by their laws, that the point and readiness that men have to wax[292] angry groweth of the secret pride by which we set overmuch by ourselves. And like as that kind of good anger that we call a good zeal riseth of that we set, as we should do, so much by our Lord God, that we cannot be but wroth[293] with them whom we see set so little by him that they let[294] not to break his high commandments, so riseth of much setting by[295] ourselves that affection of anger, by which we be moved against them with ire[296] and disdain that displease us and show by their behavior that they set less by us than our proud heart looketh for. By which though we mark it not, yet indeed we reckon ourselves worthy more reverence than we do God himself only.

I doubt not but men will say nay, and I verily believe that they think nay, and the cause is for that we perceive not of what root the branches of our sins spring. But will ye see it proved that it is so? Look whether we be not more angry with our servants for the breach of one commandment of our own than for the breach of God's all ten; and whether we be not more wroth with one contumelious[297] or despiteful word spoken against ourselves than with many blasphemous words irreverently spoken of God. And could we, trow[298] ye, be more moved with the diminishing of our own worship than God's, or look to have our own commandments better obeyed than God's, if we did not indeed set more by ourselves than him?

And therefore this deadly sore of wrath, of which so much harm groweth, that maketh men unlike themselves, that maketh us like wood wolves or furies of hell, that driveth us forth headlong upon sword points, that maketh us blindly run forth upon other men's destruction with our own ruin, is but a cursed branch rising and springing out of the secret root of pride.

And like as it is in physic[299] a special thing necessary to know where and in what place of the body lieth the beginning, and, as it were, the fountain of the sore, from which the matter is always ministered[300] unto the place where it appeareth (for the fountain once stopped, the sore shall soon heal of itself, the matter failing that fed it—which continually resorting from the fountain to the place, men may well daily purge and cleanse the sore, but they shall hardly heal it), likewise, I say, fareth it by the sore of the soul: if we perceive once the root and dig up that, we be very sure the branches be surely gone. But while the root remaineth, while we cut off the branches, we let[301] well the growing and keep it somewhat under, but fail they may not always to spring again.

And therefore, since this ungracious branch of wrath springeth out of the cursed root of pride and setting much by ourselves, so secretly lurking in our heart that uneasily we can perceive it ourselves, let us pull up well the root, and surely the branch of wrath shall soon wither away. For taken once away the setting by ourselves, we shall not greatly dote upon that we set little by.

---

286 wrathful   287 according to
288 and if: if   289 wroth withal:
angry besides or thereby   290 worse

291 dry blow: a blow that does not draw
blood   292 become   293 indignant
294 hesitate   295 setting by: esteeming

296 anger   297 reproachful, humiliating
298 trust   299 medical treatment
300 supplied   301 prevent, hinder

So shall there of[302] such humility, contempt and abjection of ourselves shortly follow in us high estimation, honor, and love of God, and every other creature in order for his sake, as they shall appear
5   more or less lief[303] unto him.

And since that by the destruction of pride followeth, as I have said, the destruction of wrath, we shall apply to the repression of wrath the selfsame considerations in the remembrance of death that
10   we before have shown to serve to the repression of pride.

For who could be angry for the loss of goods, if he well remembered how little while he should keep them, how soon death might take them from him?
15   Who could set so much by himself, to take to heart a lewd[304] rebukeful word spoken to his face, if he remembered himself to be as he is, a poor prisoner damned to death; or so very wroth as we be now with some bodily hurt done us upon some one part
20   of the body, if we deeply remembered that we be, as we be indeed, already laid in the cart carrying toward execution.

And if the wretchedness of our own estate[305] nothing moved us — which being such as it is, should,
25   if it were well pondered, make us little regard the causes of our wrath, considering that all the while we live we be but in dying — yet might the state of him that we be wroth withal make us ashamed to be wroth. For who would not disdain to be wroth with
30   a wretched prisoner, with him that is in the cart and in the way to hanging, with him that were a-dying? And of this would a man be the more ashamed, if he considered in how much peril and jeopardy of himself his own life and his own soul is, while he
35   striveth, chideth and fighteth with another, and that oftentimes for how very trifles. First, shame were it for men to be wroth like women, for fantasies and things of nought,[306] if there were no worse therein. And now shall ye see men fall at variance for kissing
40   of the pax,[307] or going before in procession, or setting of their wives' pews in the church. Doubt ye whether this wrath be pride? I doubt not but wise men will agree that it is either foolish pride or proud folly.

How much is it now the more folly, if we con-
45   sider that we be but going in pilgrimage, and have here no dwelling place, then, to chide and fight for such follies by the way.

How much more shame and folly is it yet, when we be going together to our death, as we be indeed.

If we should see two men fighting together for
50   very great things, yet would we reckon them both mad, if they left not off when they should see a ramping[308] lion coming on them both, ready to devour them both. Now when we see surely that the death is coming on us all and shall undoubtedly
55   within short space devour us all, and how soon we know not all, is it not now more than madness to be wroth and bear malice one to another, and for the more part for as very trifles, as children should fall at variance[309] for cherry stones, death coming, as I
60   say, upon us to devour us all?

If these things and such others as they be very true, so[310] they were well and deeply remembered, I little doubt but they would both abate the crooked branch of wrath, and pull up from the bottom of
65   the heart the cankered root of pride.

Of Covetousness

Let us now somewhat see what this part of our medicine may do to the cure of covetousness, which is a sickness wherein men be very sore[311] deceived. For it
70   maketh folk to seem far[312] of another sort than they be indeed. For covetous men seem humble, and yet be they very proud; they seem wise, and yet be they very foolish. They seem Christian, and yet have no trust in Christ. And (which most marvel is of all)
75   they seem rich, and yet be very beggars, and have nought of their own.

As for pride of the possession of their goods, whoso be well acquainted with them shall well perceive it how heartily they rejoice, where they dare
80   speak and call their betters beggars, if money be not so rife with them, because they regard it less and spend it more liberally.

Men ween[313] them wise also, and so they do themselves, because they seem to have providence and be
85   folk of foresight, and not to regard only the time present, but make provision for time to come. But then prove they more fools than they that live from hand to mouth. For they take at the leastwise some time of pleasure with their own, though they fare
90   hard at another. But these covetous niggards,[314]

---

302 from, out of   **303** beloved, dear
304 rude   **305** condition, state   **306** no
importance   **307** a tablet depicting the

crucifixion, kissed by the celebrating
priest and other participants at a Mass
308 rampaging, raging   **309** *fall at*

variance: begin quarreling   **310** so that
311 grievously; greatly   **312** much more
313 believe   **314** misers

while they pass on with pain always the time present, and always spare all for their time to come, thus drive they forth wretchedly, till all their time be past and none to come. And then when they least look therefor, leave all that they have heaped to strangers that shall never can them thank.

If ye will say there be no such fools, I might say that I have seen some such in my time. And if ye believe not me, I could find ye record.[315] But to the intent ye shall not deny me but that there have been such fools of old, ye shall hear what Solomon said seven years ere[316] I was born. "I have seen," saith he, "another plague under the sun, and it is common among men: a man unto whom God hath given riches, substance,[317] and honor, so that he wanteth nothing that his heart can desire, yet God hath not given him leave to eat of it or to enjoy it, but a stranger devoureth."[318] Of such sort of fools also speaketh the Psalmist thus: "A man disquieteth himself in vain, and heapeth up riches, and cannot tell for whom he gathereth them."[319] And in the forty-eighth psalm the Prophet expresseth plainly the folly of such fools: "For," saith he, "both the rich and the poor shall die, and leave their riches unto strangers."[320] And surely where they seem Christian, they have none earthly trust in Christ. For they be ever afraid of lack in time to come, have they already never so much. And methinketh utterly on the other side that albeit[321] every man that hath children is bound by the law of God and of nature to provide for them, till they be able at the least by the labor of their hands to provide for their bellies (for God and nature looketh not, as methinketh, much farther, nor thrust us not out of the paradise of pleasure to make us look and long to be lords in this wretched earth) yet, I say, meseemeth verily[322] that have we never so little, if we be not in spirit merry therewith, but live in puling[323] and whimpering and heaviness of heart, to the discomfort of ourselves and them that are about us, for fear and dread of lack in time to come, it appeareth, I say, plainly, that speak we never so much of faith and of trust in Christ, we have in our hearts neither more belief in his holy words nor trust in his faithful promise than hath a Jew or a Turk.

Doth not Holy Scripture say, "Cast thy thought into God and he shall nourish thee?"[324] Why takest

thou thought now in thyself, and fearest to fail for food?

Saith not our Savior himself, "Have no care for tomorrow," and then furnisheth and enforceth his commandment by example, saying, "reap, nor gather to no barns, and your heavenly Father feedeth them. Are not ye far more excellent than they? Your Father in heaven knoweth that ye have need of all these things. Seek ye first for the kingdom of heaven and the justice of him, and all these things shall be cast unto you besides."[325] Whosoever he be that heareth this, and yet puleth[326] and whimpereth for doubt and fear of lack in time coming, either he believeth not that Christ spoke these words (and then believeth he not the Gospel) or else, if he believe that Christ spoke them and yet feareth lest he will not keep them, how believeth he Christ or trusteth in his promise? Thou wilt haply[327] say that Christ would not for any trust of him that thou shouldst not provide for tomorrow, but look to be fed by miracle. In this thou sayest true; and therefore he said not, "Provide not for tomorrow, nor labor not for tomorrow." In token whereof he sent the Jews double manna, weekly, the day before the sabbath day, to be provided for before the hand.[328] But he said unto us, "Have none anxiety nor care of mind for tomorrow." For the mind would Christ have clean[329] discharged of all earthly care, to the end that we should in heart only care and long for heaven. And therefore he said, "things God shall cast unto us besides," showing thereby that by the hearty longing for heaven we shall have both twain.[330]

And surely the things coming of[331] the earth for the necessary sustenance of man, requireth rather the labor of the body than the care of the mind. But the getting of heaven requireth care, cure and ardent desire of the mind, much more than the labor of the body, saving that the busy desire of the mind can never suffer the body to be idle.

Thou wilt haply say, "What if I cannot labor, or have more small children to find than my labor of three days will suffice to feed for one day? Shall I not then care and take thought how they shall live tomorrow, or tell what other shift I shall find?" First shall I tell thee what shift thou shalt make in such case, and after shall I show thee that if all shift

315 examples **316** before **317** property, possessions **318** Eccl 6:1–2 **319** Ps 38(39):7 **320** Ps 48(49):11 **321** although **322** *meseemeth verily:* it truly seems to me **323** whining **324** Ps 54(55):23 **325** Mt 6:25–6, 32–33; cf. also Lk 12:24, 31–2. **326** whines **327** perhaps **328** Ex 16:4–5 **329** entirely **330** together **331** from

fail thee, yet if thou be a faithful man, thou shalt take no thought. I say, if thou lack, thou shalt labor to thy power, by just and true business, to get that thee and thine behoveth.[332] If thy labor suffice not, thou shalt show thy state — that thou hast little money and much charge[333] — to some such men as have much money and little charge, and they be then bounden of duty to supply of theirs that thee lacketh of thine. What if they will not? Then I say that yet oughtest thou not to take thought and care in heart, or despair of God's promise for thy living, but to make thyself very sure that either God will provide thee and thine meat by putting other men in the mind to relieve thee, or send thee meat by miracle (as he hath in desert wilderness sent some men their meat by a crow),[334] or else his pleasure is that thou and thine shall live no longer but die and depart by famine, as he will that some other die by sickness. In which case thou must willingly without grudge or care (which, care thou never so sore,[335] cannot get thee a penny the more) conform thyself to his ordinance. For though he hath promised to provide us meat, yet hath he not promised it for longer time than him liketh to let us live, to whom we be all debtors of death. And therefore, though he sent Daniel meat enough by Habakkuk the prophet into the lake among lions,[336] yet sent he none at all to but let him die for famine at the rich glutton's gate. There died he without grudge, without anxiety, with good will and glad hope, whereby he went into Abraham's bosom.[337] Now if thou do the like, thou shalt go into a better bosom, into heaven, into the bosom of our Savior Christ.

Now if the poor man, that nought hath, show himself to lack faith and to have no trust in Christ's words, if he fear lack of finding,[338] what faith hath then the covetous wretch, that hath enough for this day, for tomorrow, for this week, for the next, for this month, for the next, for this year, for the next, yea and peradventure[339] for many years, yearly coming in, of lands, offices, or merchandise, or other ways, and yet is ever whining, complaining, mourning, for care and fear of lack many years hereafter for him or his children, as though God either would not, or were not able to keep his promise with us? And (which is the more madness) his care is all for the living of himself and his children, for some such time as neither himself nor his children shall haply live thereto. And so loseth he the commodity[340] of all his whole life, with the fear of lack of living when he is dead.

Now if he hap to have a great loss, in what heaviness[341] falleth he then? For if he had ten thousand pounds, and thereof had eight thousand taken from him, he would weep and ween[342] he were undone. And yet if he had never had but one, he would have thought himself a great rich man, where now for the loss of eight, twain[343] can do him no pleasure.

Whereof riseth this high[344] folly but of the blind covetous affection that he had to that he lost? If he had had it still, yet he would peradventure not have occupied it, for this that is left is more than he will spend or haply shall need to spend. If ye would have spent it well, ye have no cause to be sorry of the loss, for God accepteth your good will. If ye would have kept it covetously or spent it naughtly,[345] ye have a cause to be glad and reckon that ye have won by the loss, in that the matter and occasion of your sin is by God's goodness graciously taken from you.

But ye will say that ye have now lost of your worship,[346] and shall not be set by[347] so much as ye were when ye were known for so rich. Ah well, I say, now ye come home, lo! Methought always that ye covetous niggards,[348] how lowly[349] soever ye looked, would if ye were well searched, prove yourself proud and high-hearted. For surely make they never so meek and humble countenance, they have much pride in the mind, and put their trust in their goods, making their goods their god. Which[350] thing is the cause that our Savior Christ said it were as hard for the rich man to come into heaven as a great cable or a camel to go through a needle's eye.[351] For it is not sin to have riches, but to love riches.

"If riches come to you, set not your heart thereon," saith Holy Scripture.[352] He that setteth not his heart thereon, nor casteth not his love thereon, reckoneth, as it is indeed, himself not the richer by them, nor those goods not his own, but delivered him by God to be faithfully disposed upon himself and others, and that of the disposition he must give the reckoning. And therefore, as he reckoneth himself never the richer, so is he never the prouder.

---

332 need   **333** care   **334** Elijah was fed by a raven; see 1 Kgs 17:6.   **335** greatly   **336** Dn 14:32–38   **337** Lk 16:19–22   **338** material support,

provisions   **339** perhaps   **340** benefit, profit   **341** sadness   **342** think   **343** two   **344** proud   **345** wickedly   **346** honor, distinction   **347** *set by:* valued, esteemed

348 misers   **349** humble   **350** This   **351** Mk 10:25; cf. also Lk 18:25; Mt 19:24   **352** Ps 61(62):11

But he that forgetteth his goods to be the goods of God, and of a disposer[353] reckoneth himself an owner, he taketh himself for rich. And because he reckoneth the riches his own, he casteth a love thereto, and so much is his love the less set unto God. For, as Holy Scripture saith, "Where thy treasure is, there is thine heart";[354] where if thou didst reckon the treasure not thine, but the treasure of God delivered[355] thee to dispose and bestow, thy treasure should be in earth and thy heart in heaven.

But these covetous folk that set their hearts on their hoards, and be proud when they look on their heaps, they reckon themselves rich, and be indeed very wretched beggars—those, I mean, that be full christened in covetousness, that have all the properties belonging to that name: that is to wit, that be as loath to spend aught[356] as they be glad to get all. For they not only part nothing liberally with other folk, but also live wretchedly by sparing from themselves. And so they reckon themselves owners, and be indeed but the bare keepers of other men's goods. For since they find in their heart to spend nothing upon themselves, but keep all for their executors, they make it even now not their own while they use it not, but other men's, for whose use and behoof[357] they keep it. But now let us see, as I said before, how the remembrance of death may quicken[358] men's eyes against this blind folly of covetousness. For surely it is a hard sore to cure; it is so mad that it is much work to make any good counsel sink into the heart. Wilt thou see it proved? Look upon the young man whom Christ himself counseled to sell that he had and give it to poor folk, and come and follow him. He clawed his head and went his way heavily,[359] because he was rich,[360] whereas Saint Peter and other holy apostles at the first call left their nets, which was in effect all that they had, and followed him.[361] They had no great things whereupon they had set their hearts to hold them back. But and if[362] their hearts had been sore set upon right small things, it would have been a great let.[363]

And no marvel though covetousness be hard to heal. For it is not easy to find a good time to give them counsel. As for the glutton, is[364] ready to hear of temperance, yea and to preach also of fasting himself, when his belly is well-filled. The lecherous, after his foul pleasure past, may suffer to hear of continence, and abhorreth almost the other by himself. But the covetous man, because he never ceaseth to dote upon his goods, and is ever alike greedy thereupon, whoso giveth him advice to be liberal seemeth to preach to a glutton for fasting when his belly is empty and gapeth for good meat, or to a lusty lecher when his leman[365] is lately light in his lap. Scantly can death cure them when he cometh.

I remember me of a thief once cast at Newgate, that cut a purse at the bar when he should be hanged on the morrow. And when he was asked why he did so, knowing that he should die so shortly, the desperate wretch said that it did his heart good to be lord of that purse one night yet. And in good faith methinketh as much as we wonder at him, yet see we many that do much like, of whom we nothing wonder at all. I let pass old priests that sue for advowsons[366] of younger priests' benefices. I let pass old men that hove[367] and gape to be executors to some that be younger than themselves, whose goods, if they would fall, they reckon would do them good to have in their keeping yet one year ere[368] they die.

But look if ye see not some wretches that scant can creep for[369] age, his head hanging in his bosom, and his body crooked, walk pit-pat upon a pair of pattens[370] with the staff in the one hand and the paternoster[371] in the other hand, the one foot almost in the grave already, and yet never the more haste to part with anything, nor to restore that[372] he hath evil-gotten, but as greedy to get a groat[373] by the beguiling of his neighbor, as if he had of certainty seven score[374] years to live.

The man that is purblind[375] cannot see far from him. And as to look on death, we be for the most part purblind all the many, for we cannot see him till he come very near us. But these folk be not purblind but stark blind, for they cannot see him when he cometh so near that he putteth almost his finger in their eye.

Sure the cause is for that[376] they willingly wink, and list[377] not to look at him. They be loath to remember death, loath to put this ointment on their eyes. This water is somewhat pricking and would

353 steward 354 Mt 6:21 355 delivered to 356 anything 357 benefit 358 revive spiritually 359 sadly 360 Mt 19:21–22; Mk 10:21–22; Lk 18:22–23 361 Mt 14:18–22; Mk 1:16–20; Lk 5:9–11

362 *and if:* if 363 hindrance 364 he is 365 mistress 366 the rights to benefices or livings 367 wait, linger; hover 368 before 369 because of 370 thick-soled footwear 371 a set of

rosary beads 372 what 373 very small sum of money 374 *seven score:* 140 375 partially or almost blind 376 *for that:* because 377 choose, wish

make their eyes water, and therefore they refuse it. But surely if they would use it, if they would as advisedly remember death as they unadvisedly forget him, they should soon see their folly, and shake off their covetousness. For undoubtedly, if they would consider deeply how soon they may, yea, and how soon they must, lose all that they labor for, they would shortly cease their business, and would never be so mad, greedily to gather together that other men shall merrily soon after scatter abroad.

If they thought how soon in what painful plight they shall lie a-dying, while their executors afore their face ransack up their sacks, they would, I ween, shortly empty their sacks themselves. And if they doubt how far that death is from them, let them hear what Christ saith in the Gospel to the rich covetous gatherer, that thought to make his barns and his warehouses larger to lay in the more, because he reckoned in himself to live and make merry many years, and it was said unto him, "Thou fool! This night shall they take thy soul from thee; and then these things that thou hast gathered, whose shall they be?"[378] And holy Saint Bernard saith that it may be said unto him further, "Thou that hast gathered them, whose shalt thou be?"[379]

If we would well advise us upon this point, and remember the painful peril of death, that we shall so soon come to, and that of all that we gather we shall carry nothing with us, it would cause us to consider that this covetous gathering and niggardous[380] keeping, with all the delight that we take in the beholding of our substance,[381] is in all our life but a very gay golden dream, in which we dream that we have great riches, and in the sleep of this life we be glad and proud thereof. But when death shall once waken us, our gay golden dream shall vanish, and of all the treasure that we so merrily dreamed of, we shall not (as the holy Prophet saith) find one penny left in our hands.[382] Which[383] if we forgot not, but well and effectually remembered, we would in time cast covetousness out of our heads and, leaving little business for our executors after our death, not fail to dispose and distribute our substance with our own hands.

If thou knewest very certainly that, after all thy goods gathered together, thou shouldst be suddenly robbed of all together, thou wouldst, I ween, have little joy to labor and toil for so much, but rather as thou shouldst happen to get it, so wouldst thou wisely bestow it there as need were and where thou mightst have thanks therefor—and on them especially that were likely to help thee with theirs when thine were all gone. But it is so, that thou art of nothing so sure as that death shall bereave[384] thee of all that ever thou heapest, and leave thee scant[385] a sheet. Which thing, if we did as well remember as we well know, we should not fail to labor less for that we shall so lose, and would put into poor men's purses our money to keep, that death, the cruel thief, should not find it about us, but they should relieve us therewith when the remnant were bereft us.

Of Gluttony

Now have we to consider how this part of our medicine (that is to wit, the remembrance of death) may be applied to the cure and help of gluttony, which is a beastly sickness and an old sore. For this was in the beginning joined with pride in our mother Eve, who besides the proud appetite that she had to be by knowledge made in manner[386] a goddess, yet took she such delight also in the beholding of the apple, that she longed to feel the taste. And so entered death at the windows of our own eyes into the house of our heart, and there burned up all the goodly building, that God had wrought therein. And surely so falleth it daily, that the eye is not only the cook and the tapster,[387] to bring the ravenous appetite of delicate meat and drink into the belly (so far forth that men commonly say it were better fill his belly than his eye, and many men mind it not at all till they see the meat on the board), but the eye is also the bawd,[388] to bring the heart to the desire of the foul beastly pleasure beneath the belly. For when the eye immoderately delighteth in long looking of the beauteous face, with the white neck and round paps,[389] and so forth as far as it findeth no let,[390] the devil helpeth the heart to frame and form in the fantasy, by foul imaginations, all that ever the clothes cover. And that in such excellent

378 Lk 12:16–20　**379** See *Sermo de conversione ad clericos* 8.16–17 (*PL* 182: 843).　**380** miserly　**381** possessions　**382** Ps 75(76):6　**383** This　**384** deprive, dispossess　**385** barely, scarcely　**386** *in manner:* very nearly; so to speak　**387** one who draws beer, keeper of a tavern　**388** a procurer of sexual debauchery or prostitution　**389** breasts　**390** hindrance, obstacle

fashion, as the mind is more kindled in the feigned figure of his own device than it should haply be if the eye saw the body, belly-naked such as it is indeed. And therefore saith the holy Prophet, "Turn away thine eyes from the beholding of vanities."[391]

Now, as I began to say, since it is so that this old sore of gluttony was the vice and sin by which our forefathers, eating the forbidden fruit, fell from the felicity of Paradise and from their immortality into death, and into the misery of this wretched world, well ought we to hate and abhor it, although there should now no new harm grow thereof. But so is it now, that so much harm daily growth thereof new, not to the soul only, but to the body also, that if we love either other, we see great cause to have it in hatred and abomination, though it had never done us hurt of old. For hard it is to say whether this vice be more pestilent to the body or to the soul—surely very pestilent to both.

And as to the soul, no man doubteth how deadly it is. For since the body rebelleth always against the spirit, what can be more venomous and mortal to the soul than gorbellied[392] gluttony, which so pampereth the body, that the soul can have no rule thereof, but carrieth it forth like a headstrong horse, till he have cast his master in the mire. And if the corruptible body be (as the wise man saith)[393] burdenous to the soul, with what a burden chargeth he the soul that so pampereth his paunch that he is scant able to bear the burden of his own belly, though it were taken from the place and laid upon his back. If the body be to the soul a prison, how strait a prison maketh he the body that stuffeth it so full of riff-raff that the soul can have no room to stir itself, but as one were so set, hand and foot, in a strait stocks that he can neither stand up nor lie down, so the soul is so stifled in such a stuffed body that it can nothing wield itself in doing of any good spiritual thing that appertaineth unto his part, but is, as it were, enclosed, not in a prison but in a grave, dead in manner already, for any good operation that the unwieldy body can suffer it to do.

And yet is gluttony to the soul not so pernicious and pestilent for the hurt it doth itself, as for the harm and destruction that is done by such other vices as commonly come thereon. For no man doubteth but sloth and lechery be the very daughters of gluttony. And then needs must it be a deadly enemy to the soul, that bringeth forth two such daughters, of which either one killeth the soul eternally—I mean not the substance of the soul, but the wealth and felicity of the soul, without which it were better never to have been born. What good can the great glutton do with his belly standing a-strut like a tabor,[394] and his noll totty[395] with drink, but bolk[396] up his brews in the midst of his matters, or lie down and sleep like a swine. And who doubteth but that the body delicately fed maketh, as the rumor saith, an unchaste bed. Men are wont to write a short riddle on the wall that D. C. hath no P. Read ye this riddle?[397] I cannot, but I have heard say that it toucheth the readiness that woman hath to fleshly filth, if she fall in drunkenness. And if ye find one that can declare it, though it be no great authority, yet have I heard say that it is very true.

Of our glutton feasts followeth not only sloth and lechery, but oftentimes lewd and perilous talking, foolhardiness, backbiting, debate, variance, chiding, wrath, and fighting, with readiness to all manner[398] mischief, running to ruin for lack of circumspection, which can never be without soberness. The Holy Scripture rehearseth[399] that in desert the children of Israel, when they had sat down and well eaten and drunk, then rose they up and played the idolators, whereof by the occasion of gluttony, the wrath of God fell upon them.[400] Holy Job, when his children fell to feasting, feared so greatly that the occasion of gluttony should in their feasts make them fall into foolish talking and blasphemy, that while they were about their feasts, he fell to prayer and sacrifice, that God might at his prayer send them grace so to make good cheer that they fell not in the vices usually coming of gluttony.[401] Now to the body what sin is so noyous?[402] What sin so shameful? Is it not a beastly thing to see a man that hath reason, so to rule himself that his feet may not bear him, but when he cometh out he weeneth[403] that the sky would fall on his head, and there rolleth and reeleth till he fall down the cannel,[404] and there lie down till he be taken up and borne to bed as a corpse were borne in bier? And in good faith, in my mind much wrong is there done

---

391 See Ps 118(119):37.   392 potbellied
393 Wis 9:15   394 drum   395 *noll totty:*
head tipsy   396 belch, vomit   397 See

Til C901 — to the effect that a drunken woman has no porter to protect her.
398 kinds of   399 recounts   400 Ex

32:6   401 Jb 1:4–5   402 vexatious, troublesome   403 believes   404 channel, gutter

him that any man presumeth to take him up, and that he is not suffered[405] to take his ease all night at his pleasure in the king's highway, that is free for every man.

5 Wonder it is that the world is so mad that we had liefer[406] take sin with pain than virtue with pleasure. For, as I said in the beginning and often shall I say, virtue bringeth his pleasure, and vice is not without pain. And yet speak I not of the world to come, but of the life present. If virtue were all painful, and vice all pleasant, yet since death shall shortly finish both the pain of the one and the pleasure of the other, great madness were it if we would not rather take a short pain for the winning of everlasting pleasure than a short pleasure for the winning of everlasting pain. But now, if it be true, as it is indeed, that our sin is painful and our virtue pleasant, how much is it then a more madness to take sinful pain in this world, that shall win us eternal pain in hell, rather than pleasant virtue in this world, that shall win us eternal pleasure in heaven?

If thou ween[407] that I teach thee wrong, when I say that in virtue is pleasure and in sin is pain, I might prove it by many plain texts of Holy Scripture, as by the words of the psalmist, where he saith, "I have had as great pleasure in the way of thy testimonies as in all manner of riches."[408] And Solomon saith of virtue thus: "Her ways are all full of pleasure, and her paths are peaceable."[409] And further he saith, "The way of the wicked is as it were hedged with thorns; but the way of the righteous is without stumbling."[410] "And we be wearied," shall the wretches say, "in the way of wickedness; we have walked in hard and cumbrous ways,"[411] and the wise man saith, "The way of the sinners is set or laid with stones, but in the end is hell darkness and pains."[412]

But to tell us worldly wretches the words of Holy Writ is but a dull proof. For our beastly taste savoreth not the sweetness of heavenly things. And as for experience, we can none get of the one part: that is to wit,[413] the pleasure that is in virtue. The other part we cannot perceive for bitter, for[414] the corruption of our custom, whereby sour seemeth us sweet. But yet if we would consider our sin well, with the dependents thereupon, we should not fail to perceive the painful bitterness of our wallow[415] sweet

sin. For no man is so mad that will reckon that thing for pleasant that hath with little pleasure much pain. For so might we call a man of India white, because of his white teeth. Now if thou shouldst, for a little itch, claw thyself suddenly deep into the flesh, thou wouldst not call thy clawing pleasant, though it liked[416] thee a little in the beginning. But so is it that for the little itching pleasure of sin, we claw ourselves suddenly to the hard bones, and win thereby not a little pain, but an intolerable torment. Which thing I might prove beginning at pride in every kind of sin, saving that the digression would be overlong. For the abridging whereof, let us consider it but in the selfsame sin that we have in hand.

The pleasure that the glutton hath in his viand[417] can be no longer any very pleasure than while it is joined with hunger—that is to say, with pain. For the very pleasure of eating is but the diminishing of his pain in hungering. Now all that ever is eaten after, in which gluttony beginneth, is in effect pain altogether. And then the head acheth, and the stomach gnaweth, and the next meal is eaten without appetite, with gorge upon gorge and grief upon grief, till the gorbelly[418] be compelled to cast up all again, and then fall to a rere-supper.[419]

If God would never punish gluttony, yet bringeth it punishment enough with itself: it disfigureth the face, discoloreth the skin, and disfashioneth the body; it maketh the skin tawny, the body fat and fobby, the face drowsy, the nose dripping, the mouth spitting, the eyes bleared, the teeth rotten, the breath stinking, the hands trembling, the head hanging, and the feet tottering, and finally no part left in right course and frame. And besides the daily dullness and grief that the unwieldly body feeleth by the stuffing of his paunch so full, it bringeth in by leisure the dropsy, the colic, the stone,[420] the strangury,[421] the gout, the cramp, the palsy, the pox, the pestilence, and the apoplexy, diseases and sickness of such kind that either shortly destroy us, or else, that worse is, keep us in such pain and torment that the longer we live the more wretched we be.

Howbeit, very long lasteth no man with the surfeits of gluttony. For undoubtedly nature, which is sustained with right little (as well appeared by the old fathers that so many years lived in desert with

405 permitted   406 *had liefer:* would rather   407 believe   408 Ps 118(119):14   409 Prv 3:17   410 Prv 15:19   411 Wis 5:7   412 Eccl 21:11   413 say   414 due to

415 sickly   416 was pleasant to   417 provisions of food, victuals   418 pot belly   419 a lavish meal taken late at night in addition to the usual evening meal

420 kidney stone   421 a disease of the urinary organs

herbs only and roots) is very sore[422] oppressed, and in manner overwhelmed, with the great weight and burden of much and diverse viands, and so much laboreth to master the meat,[423] and to divide and sunderly[424] to send it into all parts of the body, and there to turn it into the like, and retain it, that she is by the force and great resistance of so much meat as she hath to work upon (of which every part laboreth to conserve and keep his own nature and kind such as it is) forwearied and overcome, and giveth it over, except[425] it be helped by some outward aid. And this driveth us of necessity to have so much recourse to medicines, to pills, potions, plasters, clysters,[426] and suppositories, and yet all too little — our gluttony is so great and therewith so diverse that, while one meat digesteth, another lieth and putrefieth.

And ever we desire to have some help to keep the body in health. But when we be counseled to live temperately, and forbear our delicacies and our gluttony, that will we not hear of, but fain[427] would we have some medicines, as purgations and vomits, to pull down and avoid that we cram in too much. And in this we fare (as the great moral philosopher Plutarch saith) like a lewd[428] master of a ship that goeth not about to see the ship tight and sure, but letteth by his lewdness his ship fall on a leak, and then careth not yet to stop the chinks, but set more men to the pump rather with much travail and great peril to draw it dry, than with little labor and great surety to keep it dry. "Thus fare we," saith Plutarch, "that through intemperate living drive ourselves in sickness, and botch[429] us up with physic,[430] where we might with sober diet and temperance have less need of and keep ourselves in health."[431]

If we see men die some dear[432] year by famine, we thereof make a great matter — we fall to procession, we pray for plenty, and reckon the world at an end. But whereas yearly there dieth in good years great people of gluttony, thereof we take none heed at all, but rather impute the blame to the sickness whereof they die than to the gluttony whereof the sickness cometh.

And if there be a man slain of a stroke,[433] there is, as reason is, much speech made thereof, the coroner sitteth, the quest[434] is charged, the verdict given, the felony found, the doer indicted, the process sued, the felon arraigned, and dieth for the deed. And yet if men would ensearch how many be slain with weapon, and how many eat and drink themselves to death, there should be found (as Solomon saith)[435] more dead of the cup and the kitchen, than of the dent of sword, and thereof is no words made at all.

Now if a man willingly kill himself with a knife, the world wondereth thereupon, and, as well worthy is, he is indicted of his own death, his goods forfeited and his corpse cast out on a dunghill, his body never buried in Christian burial. These gluttons daily kill themselves[436] their own hands, and no man findeth fault, but carrieth his carrion corpse into the choir, and with much solemn service burieth the body boldly at the high altar, when they have all their life (as the Apostle saith)[437] made their belly their god, and liked to know none other, abusing not only the name of Christian men, preferring their belly-joy before all the joys of heaven, but also abusing the part and office of a natural man and reasonable creature. For whereas nature and reason showeth us that we should eat but for to live, these gluttons are so glutted in the beastly pleasure of their taste that they would not wish to live and[438] it were not for to eat.

But surely wisdom were it for these gluttons well and effectually to consider that, as Saint Paul saith, "the meat for the belly and the belly to the meat, but God shall destroy both the meat and the belly."[439]

Now should they remember and think upon the painful time of death, in which the hands shall not be able to feed the mouth, and the mouth that was wont[440] to pour in by the pottle[441] and cram in the flesh by the handfuls, shall scant be able to take in three drops with a spoon, and yet spew it out again.

Often have they had a sick drunken head, and slept themselves sober. But then shall they feel a swimming and aching in their drunken head, when the dazing of death shall keep all sweet sleep out of their watery eyes. Often have they fallen in the mire, and thence borne to bed; but now shall they fall in the bed, and from thence laid and left in the mire till Gabriel blow them up.[442]

Whereas these considerations much ought to move any man, yet specially should it so much the more move those gluttons, in how much that

---

422 grievously   423 food   424 separately
425 unless   426 enemas   427 gladly
428 wicked   429 mend clumsily
430 medicine   431 Plutarch, *De tuenda*

bona sanitate, Moralia 127c–d   432 lean, scarce   433 blow   434 inquest   435 a reworking of Eccl 37:33–34   436 by
437 Phil 3:18–19   438 if   439 1 Cor 6:13

440 used to, accustomed to   441 tankard
442 *blow them up:* blow his horn. See Til G1; Whit G2.

they may well wit[443] that their manner of living must needs accelerate this dreadful day, and draw it shortly to them, albeit that by course of nature it might seem many years off. Which thing if these intemperate would well and advisedly remember, I would ween verily, it would not fail to make them more moderate in their living, and utterly flee such outrageous riot and pestilent excess.

Of Sloth

Of the mortal sin of sloth men make a small matter. Sloth is a sin so common, and no notable act therein that is accounted for heinous and abominable in the estimation of the world, as is in theft, manslaughter, false forswearing,[444] or treason, with any of which every man would be loath to be defamed, for the worldly perils that do depend thereupon, that therefore of sloth there is no man ashamed, but we take it as for a laughing matter and a sport.

But surely, since it is a great capital sin indeed, the less that we set thereby, the more perilous it is: for the less we go about to amend it.

Now to the intent that we do not deadly deceive ourselves, it is necessary that we consider well the weight. Which if we do, we shall find it far greater than we would before have weened.[445]

There are, ye wot[446] well, two points requisite unto salvation: that is to wit, the declining or going aside from evil, and the doing of good. Now whereas in the first part there are all the other six to be eschewed—that is to wit, pride, envy, wrath, gluttony, covetousness, and lechery—the other part, that is, the one half of our way to heaven, even sloth alone is able to destroy.

Sir Thomas More wrote no farther of this work.

---

443 know   **444** *false forswearing:* treacherous perjuring   **445** believed   **446** know

A Response to Luther

In July 1521, King Henry published his *In Defense of the Seven Sacraments* arguing against Martin Luther's *Babylonian Captivity of the Church* (1520). Later in 1521, Pope Leo X awarded King Henry the title "Defender of the Faith." When Luther published in late 1522 his *Contra Henricum Regem Angliae*, a book marked by "extraordinary violence and vulgarity" and "abusive derision" (*CW* 5: 724, 725), King Henry and the Royal Council asked both Thomas More and Bishop John Fisher to respond.

More did so immediately, creating the persona of an emotional and blunt Spanish student named Ferdinand Baravellus, and placing him in a Spanish and international setting. King Henry apparently decided to delay publication, however, possibly for diplomatic reasons, or to allow Bishop Fisher to respond, or to wait for Erasmus's collaboration (which Erasmus promised in September 1523), or in the hopes that Luther would recant. This delay allowed More to revise his approach, and he changed his persona and setting to English ones, with William Ross as an earthy, blunt, and easily angered lawyer, loyal to King Henry and to the Church, outraged by Luther's disrespect for both. More's caustic, occasionally shocking wit in the *Response* may surprise contemporary readers, but More was directed to respond "in kind" to Luther's rhetoric in *Contra Henricum*, and the polemical manners of the age were rather different from our own.

More's method throughout the *Response to Luther* is to cross-examine Luther's own words rigorously, hence the inclusion of passages from Luther, and the general rhythm of quotation and critique across the work. As John Headley argues, More's method manifests his confidence in "the rationality of man," and the book's structure appeals throughout to "right reason" and the reader's own judgment of the theological controversies exploding across the European stage (*CW* 5.2: 808–9). More will continue to employ this method throughout his later controversial writings, including *Dialogue of Sir Thomas More, Knight*; *The Confutation of Tyndale*; and *The Apology*.

More's *Response* is both polemical and apologetic in character: polemic "in that he is defending the King by revealing what he claims to be the lies and inconsistencies of his opponent"; apologetic "in that, by defending the sacraments as presented in the King's *Assertio*, he moves toward a broader defense of the whole Christian order" (*CW* 5.2: 806). Regarding More's handling of Luther's writings, Headley observes that while there are a small number of inaccuracies in More's quotations, "More's record here is truly impressive," a reflection of scholastic and humanistic practice and culture, and his legal experience as well (810, 812). As More explains later in his *Apology*, he is "loath . . . to misrehearse any man's reason against whom I write, or to rehearse him slenderly."

More's *Response* addresses the theological controversies he will return to throughout much of the rest of his working life. After critiquing Luther's authorship and character, particularly his questionable motivations and alleged inconsistencies, More addresses many subjects, including the nature of the Church, the relation of Scripture and tradition, human liberty, law, and the sacraments, especially the Eucharist, holy orders, and matrimony.

As he states in the peroration, More presents his major concern as revealing the "insane" teachings that threaten the "peace" and "harmony" of the world—a concern that Erasmus came to share over time. Though initially sympathetic to Luther's desire for reform, Erasmus concluded by 1526 that Luther's fiery approach had "almost shattered the whole world." At More's encouragement, Erasmus published *Hyperaspistes (The Shield-Bearer)* in two parts (1526–27) as a rebuttal to *The Enslaved Will* (1525), which was Luther's response to Erasmus's *Discourse concerning Free Will* (1524).

What follows are excerpts from this 350-page Latin work. For the complete text and commentary, see *CW* 5. The full text is also available at www.essentialmore.org. More also addresses Luther and his positions in the "Letter to Bugenhagen," and in part four of the *Dialogue of Sir Thomas More, Knight,* both complete in this volume.

CONTENTS

A Response to Luther

The choice, learned, witty, pious work of the
MOST LEARNED William Ross in which he
very admirably exposes and refutes the frantic
calumnies with which that most foul buffoon,
Luther, attacks the invincible King of England
and France, HENRY the Eighth of that name,
the defender of the faith, renowned no less
for his learning than for his royal power.
London 1523

*Luther's mad intention and
design are revealed.*

[Luther] says[1] of all those who acknowledge the pope, that is, all the Italians, Spaniards, French, Germans, and all Christian people everywhere, all of whom he calls Cyclopes, that although they have been fighting so long with Luther alone, a Ulysses indeed of consummate shrewdness,[2] they have their eyes gouged out like Polyphemus so that, despite the many books he has published, they still cannot determine where he is heading. What a difficult matter! It would require, not an eyeless Cyclops, but some many-eyed Argos and Lynceus[3] to trace Luther's paths. It would perhaps be a difficult matter to trace the path of a snake over the ground, except that by its offensive odor breaking out wherever it turns and creeps along and by its loathsome corruption infecting the earth it betrays itself only too well. Neither, then, is any one of these Cyclopes so blind that he cannot detect the tricks and shifts of this fellow, with what a worthless subterfuge he prepares himself for flight from Aetna so that, having escaped from this island of the Cyclopes, as he calls them, he heads straight for hell. But from there no Tiresias[4] may lead him back.

They do not understand, he says. In vain have I published so many books plainly testifying that I seek only that the divine Scriptures should have sole rule, as is meet and just, but that human inventions and traditions should be abolished as most pernicious scandals, or with their poison cut out and their sting removed, that is, with their power of forcing and commanding and ensnaring consciences taken away, they should be tolerated freely as things neither good nor bad, just as with any other plague or misfortune of the world. These people, violently agitated by incessant madness, advance no argument against me but the decrees of men, the glosses of the fathers, and the practices or customs of the ages; in other words, those very things which I reject and impugn, which even they themselves admit are untrustworthy. I argue *de iure*; they answer me *de facto*. I seek a reason; they show me a work. I

---

1 From his hearing at Worms on April 18, 1521, Luther has just been quoted as saying: "With such blindness and madness has our Lord Jesus Christ stricken that whole realm of papist abomination that for three whole years now these innumerable crowds of Cyclopes fighting with Luther alone cannot yet understand why I am at war with them." **2** Earlier, in *Utopia*, Raphael Hythloday is compared to Ulysses. Erasmus presents Homer's portrayal of this Greek as "ingenious, astute, and wily" (*Adages* 1779, *CWE* 34: 81). **3** Argos was the many-eyed guardian of Io slain by Mercury (Ovid, *Metamorphoses* 1.625f), and Lynceus was one of the Argonauts famed for his sharp-sightedness (Horace, *Epistle* 1.1.28; *Satires* 1.2.90). **4** The blind seer of Thebes (Sophocles, *Oedipus Tyrannus* 408–62; Cicero, *Tusculan disputations* 5.115, *De divinatione* 2.19)

ask: "By what power do you do this?" They answer: "Because this is the way we are doing it,
and this is the way we have done it." Let will
take the place of reason, observance the place of
authority, custom the place of law, and that in
matters pertaining to God. These men have in
their schools a most corrupt manner of disputing, which they call "begging the question." This
the wretched men learn and teach even to gray
hairs, even to the grave, with extreme effort and
expense.[5]

And of the King shortly after:

But this god, growing shockingly arrogant in his
new divinity and certain that whatever he has said
ought to happen or has happened, goes further
and explicitly testifies that he wishes to dismiss
my fundamental principle, leaving it for others
to attack, and to overthrow only the superstructure; that is, to fight with straw and hay against
the rock of God's word. You would not know
whether madness itself could be so mad or dullness itself so dull as is our blockhead Henry. Perhaps this is to verify the proverb: "Kings and fools
are born — not made."[6] What fool would say: "I
declare that there are seven sacraments, but I
shall leave untouched the principal argument of
my opponent"? You would think this book were
published by a noted enemy of the King to the
King's lasting disgrace.[7]

A summary of the matter to be treated
in the whole work.

These very words of Luther, reader, on which he so
excessively plumes himself, not only are absolutely
false but contain almost as many errors as there are
words. A little later when I come to what he calls his
general response I will demonstrate this fact according to proofs taken from the King's book, so that
anyone may readily perceive it. Besides this, I will
show not only that the scoundrel does away with all
the traditions of men, even those which he ought to

obey, but also that he does away with the traditions
of God. And nevertheless not content with this, he
attacks by means of every possible stratagem those
very Scriptures of God for the sovereign authority of which he pretends to fight. In that passage I
will make clear how foolishly he ridicules the Royal
Majesty's method of disputing, which consists of
opposing to the authority of a single buffoon the
authority of so many holy fathers, the custom of so
many centuries and the public faith of the whole
Church. At the same time I will also make clear that
the faulty method of disputing by begging the question, which he attributes to others with so much insolence, is his own sole and almost only form of disputing. Moreover, I will show that he falls into this
practice especially in the very passages in which he
most fiercely reproaches and upbraids others for it.
Then, at the point suited to the purpose, we shall
winnow those words in which he boasts of himself
so inordinately that he overwhelms his readers with
darkness, and we shall scatter with the winnowing
wind this chaff that he labors to sell for grain. This
obviously witty and facetious fellow jeers at the
King for explicitly testifying, when about to defend
the sacraments, that he will leave Luther's chief
foundation for others to attack and that he himself
will tear down only the superstructure built on that
foundation. This will be touched on in the only passage which suits it, where Luther keeps repeating
the same argument seasoned always with a similar
salt; that is, where we will treat the argument that
for Luther the Mass cannot be a good work, an oblation, or a sacrifice, because it is, as he says, a testament. There you will see, reader, that the witless
witticisms of this man of such merry humor make
sport of Luther alone. I set down as separate points
these things that I now promise to do for you, so
that you can require each of them from me in its
own place. I put myself in your debt for them, so
that if I do not discharge in this booklet all that I
have promised I may be thought to have discharged
nothing at all, content to have Luther chant over
and over at me these words of Horace: "What will
this braggart produce worthy of such pompous
language?"[8]

---

5 *WA 10/2*: 182: 16–32   **6** Erasmus, *Adages* 201 (*CWE* 31: 227–36)   **7** *WA 10/2*: 183: 21–30   **8** Horace, *Ars poetica* 138

He answers Luther's pretense of not believing that the King's book was written by the King himself, and at the same time he shows what distinguished authors the book of Luther has.

5   Meanwhile I shall briefly run through those incidental objections to Luther from which the wise man makes such efforts to extricate himself that in doing so he more and more implicates and involves himself. But first, the following.

10   He thought he would doubtless exasperate the King exceedingly if he pretended not to believe that the book published by the King was the King's own, but clearly Lee's,[9] or some phlegmatic sophist's, as he calls him—as if anyone were so phleg-
15   matic, Luther, as not to prefer the phlegm of any person whatever who is not completely raving to your raving bile.

This scoundrel is painfully tormented by the fact that the Royal Majesty's learning in almost all disci-
20   plines and especially in theology is too well known and, in other lands besides Britain, too celebrated for the dolt to be able to persuade anyone that the most wise King wished to seek renown through another man's book at the expense of a frenzied friar-
25   let. I think the King would rather consider it inglorious to contend with him than glorious to conquer him, especially in such a contest as, while it would always be intrinsically noteworthy, he yet knew would be rendered notorious by the folly of his op-
30   ponent. Nor, I think, would the Prince have written anything at all against such a buffoon except that for the honor of Christ he considered nothing a dishonor to himself; but just as for the honor of Christ's name he would not decline to fight against
35   the basest of infidels, if that were his fortune, so for the faith of Christ he deigned to fight with his pen against the most foolish of heretics. But I see what Luther wants: he wishes everyone to believe about the King's book what he is aware of with regard to
40   his own, and what everyone knows was done in his own book. For who does not know that this fellow's response was not the labor of any one man? What single head could ever have begotten such a great mass of follies? By heaven, frenzy itself would have
45   been exhausted from giving birth incessantly to so

much crazy nonsense. But, as is quite well known, the lusts of many madly raving scoundrels have engendered this shapeless and monstrous offspring of Luther. As at their drinking bouts each one is ac-
50   customed to pay his scot, so into this book, a farrago of follies, each of the foolish triflers by common design contributed his own foolish expression. When Luther had received the King's book and had tasted some of it, the wholesome food began
55   to grow bitter to his perverted taste. Since he was not able to gulp it down, wishing then to get rid of its bitterness by tippling, he convoked an assembly of his fellow-tipplers. There, although he would have preferred the work to be hidden in ev-
60   erlasting darkness, yet, because it could not be concealed, he reluctantly brought out the book, after strongly fortifying his spirit by draining his cups. Once the reading started, it began to grate on their asinine ears with biting truth.[10] They therefore close
65   the book, and then soon reopen it. Now they leaf through it to see if they may perhaps discover something which they can reasonably carp at. Nothing occurs convenient to cavil. Now, as in situations of crisis, opinions are sought. The assembly began
70   to be dejected, and things began to look desperate[11] for Luther, except that some Bitias[12] skillfully consoled him, saying: What difference did it make to them what the King of England had written, or why did they have to consider honesty at all, since
75   they had no purpose but to agitate a noisy rebellion and become famous as the ringleaders of a faction? Thus they would exact money from the seduction of the simple and pleasure from the provocation of the more learned. Therefore, what did it hurt how
80   truly the King writes or how shrewdly he refutes their heresies? Let Luther just reply and pursue his usual way: let him be quick to rail and mock. It would be enough for them to impose on and dominate the simple folk. How few of these would ei-
85   ther wish to reconsider the whole matter from the beginning or would be able to evaluate it, once reconsidered? So let him not be disheartened nor at any rate so foolish as to decide that the battle must be waged by reason; all that needed to be employed
90   were reproaches and insults on every page, thicker than winter snow, of which an inexhaustible stream

---

9 Edward Lee (1482?–1544), whom Luther suspected to be the author of the King's book   **10** *it began … truth:* Persius, *Saturae* 1.107–8   **11** *things … desperate:* Terence, *Phormio* 4.4.4–5   **12** a distinguished drinker. See Vergil, *Aeneid* 1.738, 9.672, 11.396.

would gush forth from Luther's breast. With these weapons Luther would be safe; with them he could both strike and keep himself from being struck in return. The generous soul of the King would be indignant that such things were said against himself by such men; it would grieve the souls of all honorable men that the scoundrels were allowed to get away with so much unpunished. If anyone should write a stern and severe answer, the common people would contemn it, which would be enough for Luther. If, on the contrary, someone should determine to make a retort that fit Luther, he would act ridiculously; for, spoken against a man whose person is fouler than every kind of reproach, his words will have no effect. But neither would anyone be equal to Luther, who could take on single-handed ten of the most garrulous and brawling whores. And yet his potfellows themselves, each according to his ability, would not fail to help him, and thus the victory would easily be his.

On being given this advice, Luther began to recover his spirit, which had already almost escaped through the rear. But because he saw that he needed more than his usual brawling, since indeed he had not a single other weapon to employ in the disputation, he urged them each to hurry to the place where they could hunt out the greatest possible matter of stupid brawls and scurrilous scoffs. When each had collected a bagful of these, he should bring it immediately to Luther, for from them he would stuff full his own farrago of a response. With this charge he dismisses the assembly. They then go off in different directions, each to the place that his spirit suggests, and they scatter among all the carts, carriages, boats, baths, brothels, barber shops, taverns, whorehouses, mills, privies, and stews. There they diligently observe and set down in their notebooks whatever a coachman spoke ribaldly, or a servant insolently, or a porter lewdly, or a parasite jeeringly, or a whore wantonly, or a pimp indecently, or a bath-keeper filthily, or a shitter obscenely. After hunting for several months, then, finally, all that they had collected from any place whatever, railings, brawlings, scurrilous scoffs, wantonness, obscenities, dirt, filth, muck, shit, all this sewage they stuff into the most foul sewer of Luther's breast. All this he vomited up through that foul mouth into that railers' book of his, like devoured dung. From there, reader, you receive that accumulated mass of indecent brawlings, with which alone the utterly foolish book is filled. When he tries to say anything to the point, just remove that very ornate mosaic of scurrility; immediately you will see, reader, how slight a handful of substance remains from such a great heap of words, and yet even that is corrupted. That this may become clearer to you, come, let us examine, as I was about to do, those errors, briefly objected to in passing, which he volubly strives to disclaim. It will be fairly easy to infer how he behaves in attacking another since he so prettily defends himself. . . .

He censures the wicked folly of Luther, who is of the opinion that all laws should be repealed.

This extraordinary opinion, by which he would wish all human laws abolished, is like a kind of corollary of this heresy. Indeed, he already denies that any one of all those laws binds any Christian. For he writes thus in the *Babylonian Captivity*:

> And so I say: neither pope, nor bishop, nor any man has the right to impose a single syllable on a Christian man, unless this is done by the latter's consent. Whatever is done otherwise, is done in a tyrannical spirit. Therefore, prayers, fasting, donations, and in short whatever the pope has ordained and demanded in the whole body of his decrees, as numerous as they are wicked, he has demanded and ordained with absolutely no right, and he sins against the liberty of the Church as often as he attempts to decree any of these things.[13]

This madness of the rascal the Prince touches on in the following words:

> But I am amazed that the man has so little shame as to be able to think up such absurd things about laws; as if Christians could not sin, but that such a great multitude of believers were so perfect that nothing should be decreed, either for the worship of God or for the avoidance of crimes; but with the same stroke and with the same shrewdness he takes away all the power and authority of princes and prelates. For what should a king or a prelate do if he can neither establish any law nor execute

it once it has been established; but the people without law drifts to and fro like a ship without a rudder. What then becomes of the Apostle's command: "Let every creature be subject to higher authorities"?[14] What about the text: "Obey your superiors, or the king as supreme,"[15] and what follows? Why then does Paul say: "The law is good"?[16] And elsewhere: "The law is the bond of perfection"?[17] Furthermore, why does Augustine say: "Not without reason have there been instituted the power of the king, the right of the judge, the executioner's instruments of torture, the arms of the soldier, the discipline of the ruler, and even the severity of a good father. All these things have their own bounds, their own causes, reasons, usefulness; and when these things are feared, the wicked are restrained, and the good live in quiet among the wicked"?[18]

But I forbear to speak of kings lest I seem to plead my own cause. I ask this: If no one, whether man or angel, can lay down a law for the Christian man, why does the Apostle lay down so many laws about electing bishops, and about widows, and about women's veiling their heads? Why does he decree that the believing wife should not leave an unbelieving husband, unless she be deserted by him? Why does he dare to say: "To the others I, not the Lord, say"?[19] Why did he exercise such great power as to order the fornicator to be delivered over to Satan for the destruction of the flesh? Why did Peter strike down Ananias and Saphira with a like punishment because they had kept back for themselves a little of their own money? If the apostles were used to decreeing many things besides the special precept of the Lord for the Christian people, why may not those who have succeeded to the position of the apostles do the same thing for the welfare of the people? Ambrose, Bishop of Milan, a holy man, and not at all arrogant, did not hesitate to command that throughout his diocese married couples should abstain from marital embraces during Lent; and is Luther indignant if the Roman pontiff, the successor of Peter, the vicar of Christ, to whom as to the chief of the apostles Christ is believed to have given the keys of the Church so that by him others might enter and be excluded,

enjoins fasting and a few prayers? As for his persuading men that one must obey bodily but retain liberty of mind, who is so blind as not to see these tricks? Why does this simple and sanctimonious fellow carry both fire and water?[20] Why does he order us, as though in the words of the Apostle, not to become slaves of men, not to be subject to the decrees of men, and yet order us to obey the unjust tyranny of a pontiff? Does the Apostle preach in this manner: "Kings have no right over you; you should put up with their unjust rule. Masters have no right over you; you should put up with their unjust slavery"? If Luther does not think the people should obey, why does he say that they must obey? If he thinks they should obey, why does he not himself obey? Why does the slippery fellow trifle with such tricks? Why does he rise up with abusive language against a pontiff who he says must be obeyed? Why does he stir up a tumult? Why does he arouse the people against one whose very tyranny, as he calls it, must by his own admission be endured? Indeed, it is for no other reason, I think, than to procure for himself the favor of such wicked men as would desire impunity for their crimes and who would appoint as their chief him who already struggles for their liberty, and who would divide the Church of Christ, founded for so long upon a firm rock, and would erect a new church gathered together from wicked and criminal men, against which the prophet exclaimed: "I have hated the church of the wicked and I will not sit down with the impious."[21]

What does he answer to this? Exactly what he could; that is, absolutely nothing. What excuse can be given or contrived for an opinion so absurd? And yet this utterly stupid fellow is not ashamed to declare it so often with such great arrogance, as if to think otherwise would be a crime. But he thought he had brilliantly handled this very silly opinion when he replied at Worms that the law of the Gospel alone would ultimately be sufficient and human laws useless if magistrates were good and the faith truly preached. As if even the best magistrates could manage either that the whole Christian people would want to live in common or that the wicked

14 Rom 13:1 **15** Heb 13:1; Pt 2:13 **16** 1 Tm 1:8 **17** Col 3:15 **18** Augustine, *Epistle* 153.6.16 **19** See 1 Cor 7:12–15. **20** *carry…water:* Erasmus's *Adages* 3374 (*CWE* 36: 110–11) **21** Ps 25(26):5; Jer 15:17; King Henry VIII, *Assertio septem sacramentorum* (1523), sigs. K₁–K₂

would not want to steal or that any preaching of the faith could procure that no one anywhere would be wicked. If the law of the Gospel does not permit stealing, surely the human law which punishes steal-
5   ing is not useless; and the human law which alone apportions ownership of goods binds Christians; if this ownership is done away with, there cannot indeed be stealing. But if he should say that from this premise the argument is drawn that we would do
10 better to be without that law from which the ownership of goods arises and would do better to live in a certain natural community with the occasion of stealing eliminated, it does not help his case even if someone should grant him this argument. For even
15 if we could live in common with far fewer laws, we still could not live altogether without laws. For the obligation to work would have to be prescribed for certain classes, and laws would be needed to restrain crimes which would run riot even in that kind of
20 life. But now if, with the faith preached most truly as the apostles used to preach it most truly, with, moreover, the best rulers everywhere put in charge of the Christian people, the ownership of property could yet remain, and many wicked men would re-
25 main, he cannot deny that the human law binds Christians so that no one might steal what the law has apportioned to another, nor would the law be useless in punishing anyone who committed theft.

   As for his statement in the *Babylon* that good and
30 prudent magistrates will govern their charge better by the leading of nature than by laws,[22] who does not see how absurd this is? Will the good magistrate be less just in establishing law than in conducting a court of justice, in which many things can occur
35 which may destroy the innocent? To say nothing meantime of the fact that hardly any judgment is rendered justly which is not rendered according to some established law. For the law of the Gospel does not apportion possessions, nor does reason alone
40 prescribe the forms of determining property, unless reason is attended by an agreement, and this a public agreement in the common form of mutual commerce, which agreement, either taking root in usage or expressed in writing, is public law. Therefore,
45 if you take away the laws and leave everything free to the magistrates, either they will command nothing and they will forbid nothing, and then magistrates will be useless; or they will rule by the leading

of their own nature and imperiously prosecute anything they please, and then the people will in no way   50
be freer, but, by reason of a condition of servitude, worse, when they will have to obey, not fixed and definite laws, but indefinite whims changing from day to day. And this is bound to happen even under the best magistrates, whom, although they may en-   55
join the best laws, nevertheless the people will oppose and murmur against as suspect, as though they govern everything, not according to what is just and fair, but according to caprice. But now, since Luther himself admits that no magistrates can be found   60
anywhere who are not men; that is, of whom it is not very certain either to the citizens or to themselves what sort of men they will be within three days, how shrewdly does this wise man advise that laws be omitted and that all things be permitted to   65
the magistrates, as though the people would thus live in liberty!

   Now I ask you, what sort of statement is this which he makes: "Neither pope, nor bishop, nor any man has the right to impose a single syllable on a   70
Christian man without the latter's consent"?[23] I say nothing for the time being about the pope and about those to whom God has given power to impose many syllables by which they may direct the people in the worship of God; let us consider civil laws. If   75
no one has the power to establish a single syllable for the Christian man without his consent, then neither the king nor the whole people can establish any law which is valid against anyone who opposed it at the time it was proposed. Happy, therefore, are thieves   80
and murderers, who will never be so insane as to agree on a law according to which they will pay penalties. Indeed, this farsighted father does not see that according to this reasoning, should everyone unanimously agree, yet the law can have force only until   85
a new citizen is born or someone is enrolled as a citizen. But the fellow thinks that preaching the faith truly is nothing else than preaching it as he himself has often preached it already; namely, that faith alone suffices not only without good works but even   90
with crimes of any kind, which, so he says, can in no way damn any Christian, if only his faith stays firm or returns; that is, of course, if even while he is committing the crime he yet believes that it cannot harm him because of his faith in the promise of God; or,   95
if he has believed this less firmly while committing

the crime and so because of his infirm faith has committed the crime more timidly, let his faith at least
return once the crime is carried through; let him not
be sorry that he has committed it and torture him-
5 self by useless contrition. Surely, if the people had
faith in the preaching of this Lutheran faith, they
would very soon say truly that no laws obliged anyone, but the people without law would rush forth
into every kind of crime.

10   Now you see, reader, how shrewdly the sagacious
fellow strives to remove all human laws and with
how much profit for the Christian people. You see,
likewise, with how much reasoning, with what testimonies of Scripture he has propped up his decree
15 in opposition to the judgment of all learned men,
in opposition to the judgment of all good men, in
opposition to the public agreement of the whole
world. You see how in that matter, in which hardly
any reason could be strong enough, this sagacious
20 fellow brings forward no reason at all, no scriptural
testimony; rather, he, who falsely imputes to others that they demand credence for themselves alone,
himself demands credence for himself alone against
the whole world, against clear reasons, against the
25 testimonies of Sacred Scriptures, and this to the utter and inescapable destruction of all peoples. And
this in human laws which truly are the traditions
of men. For those items which are listed in his catalogue as traditions of men and are therefore, so
30 he judges, to be tolerated like some pests or altogether abolished as most harmful stumbling blocks,
have long ago been proved to be the traditions of
God, partly contained in the Scriptures themselves,
partly handed on by the living word of God. And
35 this has been proved by reason, by the Scriptures,
and by what is the strongest argument against Luther, the admission of Luther himself. Unless he
either denies again his admission that the Church
has from God the power to distinguish the words
40 of God from the words of men,[24] or brings forward
another catholic Church by whose teaching he has
known the Gospel, or proves to us that the Church
has learned nothing without the Scriptures, despite
the evangelist's statement: "Not all things have been
45 written in this book";[25] and likewise the Apostle's
words: "Hold on to what I have commanded you,
whether by word of mouth or by letters";[26] likewise
what was recalled by the same apostle: "I will give

my laws into their hearts and in their minds I will
write them";[27] and likewise those words of Christ: 50
"The Spirit, the Paraclete, when he shall have come,
will lead you into all truth";[28] or unless Luther
proves to us that for so many ages in the times of the
holy fathers Christ abandoned his Church, and that
the faith failed immediately after the apostles, con- 55
trary to the text which says: "Christ prayed that the
faith of the Church would not fail,"[29] and as though
truth itself were a liar like Luther when he said he
would be with the Church even to the consummation of the world; unless Luther overthrows for us 60
all the objections which the Prince has brought up
against him, all of which he so far conceals and dis-
simulates for no other reason than that he is aware
that he has nothing at all to answer to any of all
those arguments; unless, I say, Luther clearly does 65
all these things, then I have made most clear to
you, reader—rather, I have clearly shown you that
the King has done so—that which I initially promised to show you: that this fellow not only abolishes
the traditions of men, even those which he ought 70
to obey, but that he abolishes even the traditions of
God, which the filthy mouth of this utterly insane
rascal with insolent blasphemy calls plagues and
most harmful stumbling blocks.

He shows that Luther does only one thing: 75
destroy the very Scriptures
for which he pretends to fight.

Now let us see whether he does not by every trick
possible attack the very Sacred Scripture for which
he pretends to fight. In the first place, to say nothing 80
of how he everywhere very wickedly, everywhere stupidly twists the Scriptures to the defense of destructive teachings, what can more thoroughly or more
clearly destroy the whole force and fruit of all the
Scriptures than the fact that this fellow strives hand 85
and foot so that no one will believe any learned men
at all concerning the interpretation of Scripture; so
that no one will believe any of the holy fathers at
all, or all men taken together at all; not believe the
whole Church at all, though it has been of one mind 90
from the very origins of the Church until this day;
but that each one will oppose his own interpretation
to everyone? What fruit will the Scriptures bring

forth if anyone whatever claims such authority for himself that in understanding them he relies on his own interpretation in opposition to that of everyone else, so that he is influenced by no authority at all not to measure the Scriptures according to feeling and fancy? Here he clearly opens the window[30] by which the people may plunge into perdition.

Tell me, Luther, by your madness, if you had lived during that tempest in which the Church was thrown into turmoil by Arian storms, would you have urged what you now urge: that anyone of the common people who pleased might consider himself qualified to judge concerning that controversy, and that each one might rely on himself in understanding the Scriptures which he read, and that he might make light of the judgment of the holy fathers who were present at the council sessions in which the heresies were condemned, so that, although you admit that Christ is present wherever two or three are gathered together in his name,[31] you deny that he was present where there were gathered together in that same name six hundred men, and those from every part of the Christian people?

But who is so blind as not to see that in this matter you have no other intention than that, after abolishing completely the authority of public agreement, you may be able to stir up a tumult from the heedless disagreement of private individuals, in which case you may find some men foolish enough to think themselves free to rely with impunity on you, a single scoundrel, in opposition to the faith of everyone else? Lest the authority of Scripture might have any force against you, you work so that each person will drag into doubt the meaning of the sacred writings and defend his own fancy not only against the judgment of all the holy fathers, against the universal judgment of the whole Church, but even against the judgment of blessed Paul the apostle.

Perhaps, reader, you understand this to mean that Luther is showing boldness in not acknowledging Paul's judgment and in saying: In this or that passage Paul does not mean what the Church believes he means. No, the case is far otherwise, reader, although not even that is to be endured; but this fellow does not fear, when Paul teaches that some text or other from Sacred Scripture refers to Christ, he

does not fear, I say, to draw into doubt once more and to render questionable the judgment of the Apostle and to say: Perhaps Paul did not say that from God, but from his own understanding. So then, you rascal, recognize the sacrilegious words with which in the *Babylonian Captivity* you, truly a captive in the service of demons, pervert the Scriptures and blaspheme the Apostle. For thus you blather:

> Paul, in Ephesians 5, either forcibly applies to Christ on his own initiative those words on marriage quoted from Genesis 2, or else, according to the commonly held opinion, he teaches that the spiritual marriage of Christ is taught in that passage.[32]

O Satan, Satan, how much more honestly even you treat the Scripture than does your disciple Luther! For, although you tried to misuse one text through trickery, yet you applied to Christ those words of Scripture which pertained to him. "It is written of you," you said, "'God has given his angels command concerning you.'"[33] "But Luther not only does not apply to Christ the scriptural text which pertains to Christ, but he even belittles, so far as he can, the trustworthiness of the Apostle's application of the text. Exult, Satan; you have the kind of disciple who makes even the word of Christ doubtful. For, although Christ says, "No disciple is above his teacher, but it is enough for him if he be like his teacher,"[34] it is not enough for your disciple Luther if he be a liar and a schemer such as you are, Satan, but he strives to surpass you by far. And so, when he tries first of all to disparage the authority of the sacrament according to the interpretation he wants accepted: that if that passage of Genesis[35] did pertain in any way to Christ and the Church, it would not, at any event, pertain to him except superficially, as if by some commonly held opinion, lest it be thought to pertain properly to that point; yet, conscious that Paul cannot be so understood since he exalts the greatness of that sacrament so explicitly in so many ways on the authority of that passage of Genesis about the union of Adam with Eve, a passage applied so properly, so truly, to the marriage of Christ with the Church, what does the scoundrel do? Why, something more pestilential than

---

30 *opens the window:* See Terence, *Heauton Timorumenos* 3.481, and Erasmus, *Adages*   303 (*CWE* 31: 321).   **31** *wherever . . . name:* See Mt 18:30.   **32** *WA 6:* 552: 19–21;   Eph 5:31–32; Gn 2:24   **33** Ps 90(91):11   **34** Mt 10:24–25   **35** Gn 2:23–24

anything he could have devised for destroying the force of all the Scriptures. Paul, he says, forcibly applies that passage to Christ, possibly on his own initiative. O scoundrel, scoundrel, you suggest a scruple, as if the Apostle would interpret the Scriptures, not according to the spirit of God, but according to his own — that is, a human — spirit, which you so often call deceptive; nor does he only interpret but he even "forcibly applies" them, as if he seizes them by the neck and twists them resisting into a different meaning.[36]

Is this your deference for the Scriptures, you who boast that you believe nothing but the Scriptures? You who accept nothing else but the Scriptures, do you accept the Scriptures in such a way that you do not believe even the apostles concerning the meaning of the Scriptures, although the apostles learned the meaning of the Scriptures from the Lord? But, you say, they speak some things from Christ, some things from their own head, and the former must necessarily be believed, the latter can be doubted. Let your friariry, Reverend Friar, give us, then, a rule by which we may distinguish those passages in Scripture which the apostles interpret according to God's meaning from those which they forcibly apply and twist according to their own personal judgment. I hear, honored doctor, that you give us such a rule: that the interpretation of the apostles and evangelists on the sacred writings must stand firm wherever they add to their interpretations, "Thus says the Lord"; but, as to the other things which they say, that they themselves speak them, or rather they forcibly apply or twist the Scriptures where they please according to their own personal, that is a human, judgment. Nor should they be believed in such cases because all men are liars, as you have earlier blathered in that madly raving book of yours in regard to Jeremiah, Isaiah, Elias, and John the Baptist.[37] A single scoundrel, therefore, renders questionable all the passages which the evangelists so often cite from the prophets or from any passage of Scripture whatever, all those which the apostles so often bring forward in support of Christ, and he opens the way for everyone to say that these passages were not predictions about Christ but that the evangelists and the apostles have on their own judgment forcibly applied to Christ what the prophets have written about other

persons. What is this, reader, if it is not openly to attack the Scriptures?

But come, though; let this, if you will, be nothing; I grant you, Luther, who are so wicked that hardly any vice is a vice to you, I grant you, I say, that it is a trifling matter to contemn all the holy doctors. I grant that it is not a proof of a mind hostile to the Scriptures that you strive and struggle to render all the interpretations of the apostles suspect. This at least not a single person will be too stupid to sense: how openly, how directly your not hesitating impiously to attack an undoubtedly sacred text as profane aims at sweeping away all the Scriptures. Indeed, what is still more hateful: even if you have conceded that a text is canonical and written by the pen of an apostle, yet you dare to say that no faith should be placed in it and, setting your face against heaven,[38] you do not fear to blaspheme an apostle with your abusive tongue. And so, you scoundrel, recognize again the sacrilegious words with which, when you were hard pressed by the apostle James's words on the sacrament of extreme unction,[39] you, as though engaged in hand-to-hand conflict with the apostle, empty out on an apostle of God, you most base buffoon, the privy of your filthy mouth.

I pass over (you say) the fact that many persons assert with great probability that this epistle is not by James and is not worthy of the apostolic spirit, although whosesoever it is, it has acquired authority by custom. Nevertheless (you say) if it were by the apostle James, I would say that no apostle is permitted to institute a sacrament on his own authority; that is, to give a divine promise with a sign accompanying it. This belonged to Christ alone. Thus, Paul says that he received the sacrament of the Eucharist from the Lord and that he was sent not to baptize but to preach the Gospel. Nowhere in the Gospel, however, does one read of this sacrament of extreme unction.[40]

Reader, please reread what the Prince has written against these words. There you will immediately discover in how few words of Luther the Prince has discovered and refuted how many absurdities. For he shows that Luther unjustly censures the Church, that he impiously contradicts an apostle, and that

---

36 *as if…meaning:* Plautus, *Poenulus* 3.790; Erasmus, *Adages* 1019 (*CWE* 33: 27–28)   **37** *But, you say…Baptist:* See *WA*   6: 552: 18–27 and 553: 18–20.   **38** *setting…* *heaven:* a phrase used frequently by Luther.   See *WA* 10/2: 219: 12 and Rv 13:5–6.   **39** Jas 5:14   **40** *WA* 6: 568: 9–16

he is also stupidly inconsistent with himself. And all three of these things in scarcely three lines, so that no man's wisdom has ever been so wonderful as this fellow's folly is bewildering. What will you say here, Luther? What burrow have you provided for yourself by which you can flee? Will you deny that whoever wrote that epistle is clearly describing a sacrament, and will you depart from your definition of a sacrament as such, which you wanted to consist of a sensible sign and a promise of grace clearly included in the sacred writings? Or will you deny, as you have done, that that epistle should be numbered among the sacred writings? But the same Church which numbers the Gospels among the sacred writings, the same Church, I say, numbers among the sacred writings this epistle. In this matter you are lying, whether the Church can be deceived or whether it cannot be deceived. If she can be deceived in discerning the words of God, you lie precisely in saying that she cannot be deceived on this score. If she cannot be deceived, you again lie in saying that this epistle, which the Church has approved as apostolic, is probably not apostolic. What remains then but that you should retract what you have said and instead deny once again that the Church can discern the words of God, and then you would be calling into doubt even the epistles of Paul and the Gospels? And you who contend that nothing is certain except the Sacred Scripture would then be rendering nothing more uncertain than Sacred Scripture itself.

But still more dangerous is the fact that you even dared to contemn the epistle, if you have admitted that it is the apostle's; doubtless, I suppose, because the apostles are ours, not we theirs, according to that text which you cite as foolishly as you do frequently: "For all things are yours, whether Apollo, or Cephas, or Paul."[41] It does not behoove us, then, you will say, to be judged by them but to judge them. How then, Luther, do you say that you are doing this so that the Scriptures alone may be believed, since you do not admit as Scripture a clear scriptural text? But if you rejected no Scripture at all, nevertheless, since you care not a straw for all interpreters taken together, you return to the same spot since you believe nothing at all which is not manifest in evident scriptural texts. For what scriptural text will ever be sufficiently evident if one can,

as you are trying to do, cause the opinion of good men and of learned men to have no force against either the stupid interpretations of ignorant men or the crafty ones of wicked men? Who does not see that by this means it will come about that nothing at all can be proved from Sacred Scripture to a man so senseless that he either cannot or will not understand the sense of Scripture? Indeed, that nothing is so absurd, nothing is so impious but someone like you, a raging madman and a shameless fellow, can argue he proves it by the testimonies of Sacred Scripture. For example, if some scoundrel should deny that Christ descended into hell, he will boast that he admits nothing besides evident Scriptures, and he will deny that this teaching is proved by any sufficiently evident scriptural text. But if someone should cite that verse from the psalm, "My flesh shall rest in hope because you will not leave my soul in hell,"[42] he will cite in his turn whatever fabrication he chooses from the commentaries of the Jews, and he will deny that that text refers in any way to Christ. But if someone objects in turn that the apostle Peter declared that that psalm speaks of Christ,[43] the scoundrel will not hesitate to say of Peter what our scoundrel said of Paul; namely, that Peter forcibly applied that text to Christ on his own initiative. But if some other scoundrel wants good works not to be required for salvation, he will cite that text of the Gospel, "Whoever believes and is baptized shall be saved";[44] nothing else therefore should be required. Then, if someone should deny that this text is to be so understood and should cite the real meaning, together with the testimony of all the doctors, the fellow will scorn all the doctors and will stick to his own interpretation, bawling only that the scriptural text is evident. But if someone keeps bringing up to him some objection or other from Sacred Scripture, the scoundrel will not hesitate to escape immediately by means of some silly trick or other. For example, if someone brings up that text of James, "Faith without works is dead,"[45] the fellow will say the same thing as our rascal has said: that the epistle is not James's, that it is not any apostle's, that it has nothing worthy of the apostolic spirit.[46] Finally, should the epistle be proved to be an apostle's, the fellow will still say that the apostle does not speak correctly, that he has arrogated too much to himself in imposing the law of good works

---

41 1 Cor 3:22   **42** Ps 15(16):9–10   **43** Acts 2:31   **44** Mk 16:16   **45** Jas 2:26   **46** *epistle . . . spirit:* See *WA* 6: 568: 9f.

on Christians whom Christ has made free in faith alone from every yoke of good works. Nor should anyone but Christ alone be able to impose any law or any syllable of the law on any Christian. For the apostles did not have authority enough to judge us, but it is our right to judge them. "For all things are ours, whether Apollo, or Cephas, or Paul."[47] For thus the fellow has been taught by Luther.

If anyone therefore, passing over your disciple, should object to you once more, Luther: "The Church has judged this epistle to be the apostle's, to have been written by the divine Spirit," and should bring up to you your own words: "This power at least has been given by God to the Church, that she can distinguish the words of God from the words of men,"[48] then you will retract this statement immediately and will say that you have now weighed the matter more carefully, that the Church has no power from God but that the Church can be deceived in accepting Scripture. But if someone or other will add that therefore the Gospels themselves are uncertain, you will doubtless concede this also: that the true Gospels are probably not the Scriptures and Gospels which we read but rather some one of those which the Church has rejected. And concerning these matters, each one believes at his own risk.[49]

But if someone should at this point throw up to you your inconsistency, because you are so often at variance with yourself and disagree with your own self, here indeed with how many jeers, how many guffaws and snorts will that man be mocked who is so ignorant, so inexperienced in arguing that he does not know what it means for a man to disagree with himself, or considers capricious and unstable a person who is consistently inconsistent, or demands that a man's words should be bound fast as a bull's horns are bound fast so that if he has ever said anything worthwhile he should not be permitted later to retract it when it would be to his advantage and to turn it into something evil, even as he changes nothing for the better of those things which he has at any time said badly.

You see here clearly, reader, with what good faith this good man proclaims that he proclaims "The Gospel! The Gospel!"—as if anyone has ever been a heretic who did not proclaim the Gospel—while at the same time he devises for himself a way whereby he may raise a doubt as to whether the Gospel be the Gospel, and by false interpretations weakens the Scriptures which, he says, should alone reign, and gives everyone the license of daring the same thing. Whatever Scriptures he pleases he does not acknowledge as sacred; then, if the case presses him hard, he even contemns those which have been acknowledged; so that you cannot have any doubt that he himself has proved for us that which we initially promised we were ready to prove: that he does this only in order to destroy the very Scriptures for which he pretends to fight.

He declares that Luther, who boasts that the papists use a corrupt method of disputation by begging the initial premise, not only makes this objection falsely against others, but also uses this as his own peculiar and perpetual method of disputing. This whole chapter is delightful.

Come now, let us carefully examine that point in which Luther strangely delights and considers himself witty and skillful, when he makes sport of the catholic Church as papistic and thinks everyone in comparison with himself so ignorant that no one understands either what the point in question is or by what method the point ought to be proved. "There is," he says, "among these very men a most corrupt method of disputing which they call 'begging the initial premise.'[50] This they learn and teach even till grey hairs, even till the grave, with so much sweat, with so much waste, the utterly wretched men."[51]

Let us see, then, reader, which of the two sides begs the initial premise more corruptly; for each side begs some initial premise. We beg of him four postulates.

First, we beg that Luther believe the sacred writings. We beg that he believe that some things were said, done, taught by God which are not contained in writing.

We beg that he believe that the Church has been given the power from God to distinguish the words of God from the words of men and the traditions of God from the traditions of men, with Christ clearly governing his Church constantly and the

---

47 See WA 10/2: 194: 33–37 and 1 Cor 3:22.   See Plautus, *Poenulus* 4.878.   **51** WA 10/2: 182: 30–32
48 See WA 6: 561: 3–4.   **49** *each…risk:*   **50** Aristotle, *Prior Analytics* 64b28–65a38

Holy Spirit always directing the agreement of the Church in matters of faith.

We beg finally that in a disputed interpretation of the sacred writings he believe the consistent judgment of the holy fathers and the faith of the whole catholic Church rather than his own opinion.

Although we consider these postulates no less evident to the Christian than the geometrical postulates of Euclid are to the philosopher, nevertheless this fellow postulates reasons for such postulates.

And so we have presented for the last postulate, besides several other reasons, the fact that it is easier and more probable that one man is deceived and out of his mind than that many are so, that a bad man misunderstands rather than good men, that a heretical man errs rather than the catholic Church.

The second last postulate we prove indeed by many and evident testimonies of Sacred Scripture, with many reasons besides, and finally by the confession of Luther himself.

Next, as to the postulate that some things have been said, done, taught by Christ which have not been written, besides other evident reasons, besides other passages of Scripture, we have proved this on the authority of Paul; we have proved it by the Gospel.

As for the first postulate, that the Sacred Scripture must be believed, we had hoped that Luther would not demand any proof at all for this, because he so often proclaims throughout all his books that he demands nothing else than that the Sacred Scripture alone should be believed.

Luther jeers at all these postulates of ours. He considers the last one to be utterly foolish: that anyone should beg him to believe the fathers and the Church rather than himself. Whereas the fathers, so he says, and the judgment of the Church are at times deceived, he himself cannot be deceived, because he is certain, so he says, that he has his teaching from heaven.[52]

The next to last postulate, however, although once granted by himself, he now nevertheless retracts altogether. For he thinks it ridiculous if anyone should think the Church is governed by the Holy Spirit in the faith, since the Turk would ridicule anyone begging such an initial premise. And so, the pious priest will rather be impious toward Christ than be ridiculous to the Turk.

The second postulate he clearly considers worthless, since whatever Christ has said, done or taught which has not been written Luther once and for all considers as of no importance, because — I suppose — if those points had been of importance, Luther did not think that Christ would have been so negligent as not to have taken care that they be included in Scripture.

Next, because of the authority of Scripture, he treats the first postulate ambiguously. For he often cites the Scriptures erroneously, and very often he twists them from a true meaning to a false one when he has no support for himself but his own words, and those almost always contrary to his own conscience. When the words of Scripture express conflicting ideas, the fathers give a consistent interpretation, and the whole Church through so many ages agrees; at such times we inexperienced Thomists beg the initial premise that he believe everyone taken as a whole rather than a single individual. But because this is begging an initial premise, we are repulsed with the ridicule of this fellow, shrewd and quite artful in arguing, and we are overwhelmed by waves of roaring laughter.

But if you present a text of Scripture which is so clear that there can be no question about its meaning, then, driven by necessity, he betrays himself and openly denies the scriptural text. If the situation requires, he says that the epistle of James is not apostolic, or even if it be an apostle's, still the apostle has arrogated too much to himself. And when once Luther has said this, if anyone again insist that Luther yield to the authority of the apostle, then that person will be mocked in a thousand ways as a man ignorant of disputing, one who is not ashamed to use the most corrupt form of disputing and to beg the initial premise; namely, that that be considered Scripture which Luther denies is Scripture, or that the apostle be believed to have written correctly, although Father Tosspot has said once and for all that he has erred. In this way, then, reader, we corruptly beg the initial premise.

Luther, on the contrary, is a little more modest, for he also has established an initial premise, but only one, which he demands to have granted to himself. It is, however, of this kind: that he alone must be believed on all matters.

This initial premise, as a matter known by nature,

---

52 See *WA 10/2*: 184: 27.

he does not hesitate to beg everywhere; in fact, to assume as by his own right. Suppose there is a question about the meaning of a scriptural text; he first presents what he himself either thinks or at least pretends to think; you in turn present whatever has always been the judgment of all Christians; he drives everyone away like flies and begs that he be believed. He denies that human laws are useful; you in turn present whatever has always been the judgment of mortals; he jeers at the whole world and demands that he be believed. He denies the sacrament of extreme unction; you in turn present the apostle James; he contemns the apostle and demands that he be believed. Thus, almost everywhere he begs that this initial premise be granted him: that in all matters he alone be believed.

This postulate of his: although no one does not see that it is apparently very fair, nevertheless because we fear the snares and subtleties of this sophistical fellow, we will be prevailed upon reluctantly and with difficulty to grant him this postulate, especially because we are aware that on this initial premise and brilliant axiom of Luther rests the whole foundation of the marvelous Lutheran doctrine. Once this initial premise is granted, it is amazing to relate the sort and importance of the conclusions he will prove to you in such a way that you simply cannot deny them. But if you deny that axiom, he proves to you absolutely nothing. We therefore put off granting him so subtle and sophistical a premise, and we ask of him: "By what reason, Father, do you prove that you alone must be believed?"

To this he returns this cause: "Because I am certain," he says, "that I have my teachings from heaven."

Again we ask: "By what reason are you certain that you have your teachings from heaven?"

"Because God has seized me unawares," he says, "and carried me into the midst of these turmoils."[53]

Again therefore we demand: "How do you know that God has seized you?"

"Because I am certain," he says, "that my teaching is from God."

"How do you know that?"

"Because God has seized me."

"How do you know this?"

"Because I am certain."

"How are you certain?"

"Because I know."

"But how do you know?"

"Because I am certain."

I ask you, reader, whether that form of disputing does not find a place here, the form by means of which (unless Luther is lying) Amsdorf[54] lyingly says that the theologians of Leipzig[55] dispute, as follows: when the respondent has denied his opponent's assumed initial premise, the opponent proves the same premise as follows: "It must be so." When the former again denies it, then the latter says a second time, "And how can it be otherwise? It must be so."[56]

To this lie Luther has added, as one of his better sayings, the flourish: "Splendidly," he says, "and most Thomistically, or rather, most Leipzigly and most Henricianly."

Now, since the Reverend Father founds all his arguments on this initial premise: "I am certain because I know, and I know because I am certain, and I am certain because I cannot err, and I cannot err because I am certain, and I am certain because I know," may we not re-echo against the Reverend Father the flourish of the Reverend Father: "Splendidly and most Wittenbergly, or rather, most stupidly and most Lutheranly."

You see, then, reader, that in this passage I quote none of his statements in the way that he usually quotes all the statements from the King's book. He quotes nothing honestly, but he either distorts it badly or he cites from the book statements which are nowhere in the book; but while he is recounting them he is fashioning for himself monsters to conquer. But we, as a matter of fact, make clear that the Scriptures are thus presented by him, thus twisted from their own meaning, that this fellow thus prefers his own fancies to the judgments of all the saints, that he thus counts the whole Church as straw in comparison with himself, that he thus openly denies the Sacred Scripture and clearly contemns the acknowledged Scripture, that he thus establishes his own teachings without Scripture and contrary to Scripture, so that you cannot doubt that in very truth this fellow everywhere begs this single initial premise: that against everyone and everything he alone be believed on all matters.

53 *WA 10/2*: 186: 31–32 **54** Nicholas von Amsdorf (1483–1565), Luther's trusted   friend and fellow worker **55** Jerome Emser (1478–1527) and George, Duke of   Saxony (1500–1539) **56** See *WA 10/2*: 191: 10f.

Lest it can seem that he makes up such absurd
things as these about Luther through calumny,
he recalls the very words of Luther and examines
them carefully; from which it is clear that
5 *Luther both said and thought things in*
many ways still more absurd.

Nevertheless, that you may not doubt that this inference was not drawn from ambiguous words of
his but that it was proclaimed by himself in the
10 clearest of words, consider carefully the very words
of the rascal.

I am certain (he says) that I have my teachings
from heaven, I who have triumphed even over
him who has more strength and cunning in his
15 little fingernail than do all the popes and kings
and doctors.[57]

Likewise, shortly after:

The Lord has seized me unawares and carried me
into the midst of these turmoils.[58]

20 And again:

Here I need have no reason for patience, when
the trifling buffoon attacks with his lies, not me
nor my life, but the very doctrine which I am
most certain is not mine but Christ's.[59]

25 And when he has proved this simply by saying it,
then by his own right the rascal rages wildly against
the King, as if to reprove a heretic on behalf of the
faith were in very truth to blaspheme God.

He would have to be forgiven if humanly he
30 erred. Now, since he knowingly and consciously
fabricates lies against the majesty of my King in
heaven, this damnable rottenness and worm, I
will have the right, on behalf of my King, to bespatter his English majesty with muck and shit
35 and to trample underfoot that crown of his
which blasphemes against Christ.[60]

Come, do not rage so violently,[61] good Father;
but if you have raved wildly enough, listen now, you

pimp. You recall that you falsely complained above
that the King has shown no passage in your whole   40
book, even as an example, in which he said that you
contradict yourself. You told this lie shortly before,
although the King has demonstrated to you many
examples of your inconsistency. Suppose that the
King here in turn asks of you why you have not   45
produced even one passage as an example in which
you say he blasphemes God. Your Paternity must
by all means search out and produce this passage.
But meanwhile, for as long as your Reverend Paternity will be determined to tell these shameless lies,   50
others will be permitted, on behalf of his English
Majesty, to throw back into your Paternity's shitty
mouth, truly the shit-pool of all shit, all the muck
and shit which your damnable rottenness has vomited up, and to empty out all the sewers and priv-   55
ies onto your crown divested of the dignity of the
priestly crown, against which no less than against
the kingly crown you have determined to play the
buffoon.

In your sense of fairness, honest reader, you will   60
forgive me that the utterly filthy words of this
scoundrel have forced me to answer such things,
for which I should have begged your leave. Now
I consider truer than truth that saying: "He who
touches pitch will be wholly defiled by it."[62] For I   65
am ashamed even of this necessity, that while I clean
out the fellow's shit-filled mouth I see my own fingers covered with shit. But who can endure such a
scoundrel who shows himself possessed by a thousand vices and tormented by a legion of demons,   70
and yet stupidly boasts thus: "The holy fathers have
all erred. The whole Church has often erred. My
teaching cannot err, because I am most certain that
my teaching is not my own but Christ's," alluding
of course to those words of Christ, "My words are   75
not my own but his who sent me, the Father's"?[63]
What about the following: "The pope shall fall; my
teachings will stand firm"? Does it not seem to vie
with that statement of Christ: "Heaven and earth
shall pass away, not one iota of my words shall per-   80
ish"?[64] For when he says, "The Lord has seized me
unawares and carried me into the midst of these
turmoils,"[65] this is more than, "The devil took him
and placed him on a pinnacle of the temple."[66]

Then, how boastful is that statement: "I have   85

triumphed over him who has more strength and cunning in his little fingernail than do all the popes and kings and doctors"? How much more boastfully this fellow exults than did Christ, who said of himself somewhat more modestly: "I have overcome the world";[67] and likewise: "The prince of this world comes and in me he has nothing"?[68] But what does this fellow say? "Therefore I have triumphed, not over the world, but far more sublimely, over the prince of the world, the devil." Then he trumpets his triumph and tinsels it with pompous bombast: "I have triumphed,"[69] he says, "over him who has more strength and cunning in his little fingernail than do all popes and kings and doctors."

O swelling triumph! But whence have we learned this? What will he say to us here who proves everything by evident Scriptures? What else but the words of Christ (for he tries to vie with him): "I bear witness to myself"?[70] But if someone should answer, "Your testimony is not true," he will have recourse immediately to his new Scripture: "I am certain that I have my teachings from heaven." And there he will stand firm on this initial premise of his as on a most firm foundation that not all the popes, kings, doctors, men, angels will be able to destroy.

Certain, then, indeed most certain that he has his doctrines from heaven, as men who sleep are certain, indeed most certain that everything they dream is true; or rather certain, indeed most certain that he lies with his eyes wide open[71] in saying that his teachings are from heaven, whereas his own conscience murmurs to him that they have been let loose in him by the deceits of demons; he curses any men and angels who contradict his teachings. And he protests that all those who do not fear to reproach his most filthy blasphemies set their face against heaven and besmirch sacred things and blaspheme God. His only cry is: "Let all be anathema who attack my teachings, because I am certain that I have my teachings from heaven."

With this initial premise begged by the Reverend Father and granted by no one, he thus argues further, this reverend friar, Father Tosspot Luther, fugitive extraordinary of Saint Augustine, one of the unskilled masters of Wittenberg, unformed ranter of both kinds of law, and unlearned doctor in sacred theology: "I am certain that I have my teachings

from heaven; therefore my teachings are heavenly." And then further thus: "My teachings are heavenly; therefore whoever contradicts my teachings sets his face against heaven and blasphemes God. Because, therefore, my teachings are indeed contradicted by the Pope, the Emperor, kings, bishops, priests, the laity, and in fine all good men, I will be permitted on behalf of the majesty of my God, to anathematize the Pope, the Emperor, kings, bishops, priests, the laity, in fine all good men, to assail them with curses and insults, and against all their crowns and heads I will be permitted to spew out of my mouth muck, filth, dung, shit."

These are the conclusions of the Reverend Father, deduced by necessity from this same father's initial premise, begged by him: that we should believe him to be certain that his teachings are from heaven.

But come, Reverend Father, suppose I carried out the deduction thus: "I am certain that the Reverend Friar Father is an ass; therefore the Reverend Friar Father is an ass." If the reverend father should here grant me this antecedent premise, how many conclusions I may infer: he will undoubtedly have to eat hay; he will have to bear burdens; and what is most galling, he will have to do without beer: Father Tosspot would be vexed to hear that. But rather than be forced to this conclusion, he would not hesitate to demand that I prove I am certain he is an ass; otherwise, shameless as he is, he will not be ready to grant what everyone nevertheless sees to be evident. But I should not hesitate immediately to prove the antecedent in this way: "I am certain that as no animal laughs but man, so no animal brays but an ass; but I am certain that the reverend friar, Father Tosspot, is some animal and that he brays most brayingly; therefore I am certain the reverend friar, Father Tosspot, is most truly an ass."

See, Reverend Father, I have proved my antecedent, nor would I have demanded that it be granted me had I not proved it. I pray you also, reverend father, prove that assumption of yours: how your Paternity is certain that you have your teachings from heaven, from what messenger you received them. "For no one has ascended into heaven except him who has descended from heaven."[72] But at this point, as I hear, you will reply that your teachings were brought down to you from heaven, not indeed

67 Jn 16:33 **68** See Jn 14:30. **69** *he trumpets… triumphed:* Erasmus, *Adages*   1659 (*CWE* 34: 28–29) **70** Jn 8:18 **71** *who sleep… open:* Erasmus, *Adages* 2281   (*CWE* 34: 308–9). See also Juvenal, *Satires* 1.57. **72** Jn 3:13. See also Lk 10:18.

by him who descended from heaven, but by him who fell like lightning from heaven. You answer well, Reverend Friar. Really, I do not qualify as your teacher, but I leave you with the cacodaemon who inspires your teachings, with whom you will remain in Tartarus for ever and ever.

I am indeed not so prejudiced in my own favor that I will not easily forgive you, reader, if you should at times little approve of this frivolity of mine by which I occasionally intersperse certain things which suit neither the gravity of the matter nor your seriousness. And yet, I think there has never been anyone so severe as not to think it fair either to wink at us occasionally or to forgive us—when he reads everywhere the most filthy insolence of a most stupid scoundrel against a most prudent prince—if we are so stirred by indignation that, even though unwillingly, we are forced in turn to act foolishly and, as Solomon says, "to respond to the fool according to his folly,"[73] especially since the fellow's book, leaving aside completely the subject of concern, idles about entirely in scurrilous trifles.

We may in passing make sport of his madness; nevertheless, at the same time we handle the matter in such a way that everything that we promised at the beginning is made clearly evident to you. For since his general response includes in sum nothing else than that nothing must be held for certain except what is included in evident Scriptures, but that all other things—even if they are not opposed by the sacred writings and are confirmed by the unbroken agreement of the whole Church—either must be wholly rooted out as traditions of men (which policy he indeed thinks best), or at least they are to be tolerated so freely that each of those things is left wholly to each individual to approve, disapprove, change, condemn, reject, wherever, whenever, as often as he pleases. Since he places in this category all human laws, the decrees of the fathers, the councils of the Church, and the sacraments, fear of purgatory, the veneration of the saints and the rite of celebrating Mass, we have made manifest both by most clear Scriptures and most evident reasons that the word of God has been handed down without

Scripture and that this word is of no less authority than is the Scripture itself. We have proved by the authority of Scripture and even by the confession of Luther himself that the Church cannot err at all in distinguishing the word of God in matters of faith. We have proved that the Church which he calls papistic is the true catholic Church of Christ. We have proved that those sacraments which Luther calls the traditions of men are not the traditions of men but of God, and that thus he denies the word of God, not of men. We have proved that he not only stupidly abolishes all human laws but also attacks both secretly and openly the Scriptures themselves. From the latter we have shown more clearly than light that whatever he has presented from the Scripture he cites so stupidly in support of his own case that no fool could cite it more stupidly. And since, on the meaning of any scriptural text, he would want no one to believe all men taken as a whole but every single person to believe himself, we have made clear that he is contriving to weaken the force of all Scripture and to turn all its fruit into destruction. Then, since he does not admit that an uncontested scriptural text is Scripture but denies that it has anything worthy of Scripture, and since the apostate does not hesitate to censure an apostle, we have made it very clear that he not only secretly but even openly destroys the very Scriptures for which he pretends to fight. Finally, aside from his most wicked lies, and his most stupid contradictions, and his thousand follies, which we have exposed from here and there, we also proved that that corrupt method of disputing by begging the initial premise which he thought he had so very wittily cast in the teeth of others; this method, I say, we proved to be his one and only form of disputing.

Thus then, reader, we have discharged more than we promised, and we have done it with proofs drawn from hardly any other source than the book of the King. And since, as you see, Luther's general response has now turned out prettily for him, we next gird ourselves to handle his special answers; you shall not see one of them in which you will not laugh at the singular folly of the fellow....

73 Prv 26:5

The peroration of the work, in which many points are handled piously, cleverly, and learnedly, as well as pleasantly.

I have no fear, good reader, but that your sense of fairness will make allowance for me that in this book you so often read such things as I think your sense of modesty shuns. Indeed, nothing more irksome could have happened to me than to be forced to such a point of necessity that I should inflict on decent ears anything that would offend by indecent words. But there was no way of avoiding it unless I had determined, as I had tried to do with all my strength, not to touch the buffoonish book of Luther at all. Otherwise, if a response absolutely had to be made to a man on the lookout for spreading calumnies, nothing that he had written should have been omitted, nor was it allowable that words be changed when there was no substance to them, nor was it effective to recount decently what had been written indecently. Finally, how can it be that I who undertake to refute his buffoonish tricks should answer purely and cleanly the most impure words of an impure rascal? For he handles the matter in such a way that he clearly declares that he contemplates within himself a certain most absurd kind of immortality and has already begun to enjoy it and wholly to be in, to be engaged in, to live in, this kind of sense and tickling of paltry glory which he presumes will come after yet some myriads of ages, so that men will recall and say that once long ago there was in a former age a certain rascal by the name of Luther who, when he had got the better of cacodaemons in impiety, in order to adorn his sect with fitting emblems, surpassed magpies in chatter, pimps in wickedness, prostitutes in obscenity, all buffoons in buffoonery. This he zealously strove for, took pains about, accomplished so that as the sects of philosophers have names after the philosophers themselves, and Gnatho contemplated that parasites likewise should be called Gnathonites, so the most absurd race of heretics, the dregs of impiety, of crimes, and filth, should be called Lutherans.[74] For I ask you, reader, what race of heretics was ever so absurd as to be compared to this one? It renews every one of those heresies which the Christian world once condemned, overwhelmed, quenched, each one in its own time; the ashes of all of these this firebrand of hell once more enkindles. Since by this very deed he makes a pretext of piety, to pass over the books of most learned men who have ripped this mask and disguise from his wicked face, if you consider the matter itself, reader, you will easily recognize the tree from its fruit.[75] For if you turn over in your memory the ancient leaders of the Church from the very beginnings of Christianity, you will see, reader, how whatever was honored most holily by them is thus held in the utmost contempt by these Lutherans. What was once celebrated with so much veneration as the most holy sacrifice of the Mass? What has been so defiled by these pigs and trodden underfoot and all but abolished? This one thing, indeed, they still preserve sacred in every temple, but this very thing they pollute and profane by their impieties, since they both contend that it is not a sacrifice and preach that it does not profit the people anything; are they not constructing for themselves a way by which they will very soon cast out even that one sacred thing which they have left? Now how much they value prayers you see, since they not only throw out the canonical hours but also those universal prayers which even from the beginning the Church has continually chanted for the support of the deceased. On this point who will not detest such great cruelty? For if, as they falsely argue, it were especially doubtful whether the prayers of the living were profitable to the dead, nevertheless what ill will would it have been to exercise devout affections and to make a trial of prayers by which, though you might be doubtful perhaps whether you were of service, yet you would be certain that you could do no harm? What was once held to be more religious than fasting? What was more exactly observed than Lent? Yet now these men, finally perfected by the spirit, lest they seem to distinguish day from day, dedicate every day to bacchanalian orgies. Who does not know how continence was once prized? How strictly conjugal fidelity was commanded, how esteemed by the ancients the chastity of widows, how zealously, how rightly virginity was praised? And all these things by the authority of Christ himself. Now this Antichrist has taken away almost completely all sense of modesty. Priests, monks, virgins dedicated to God, now by the favor of the devil, in the Church of the wicked, under the title of lawful spouses, with great

---

74 *so that . . . Lutherans:* See Terence, *Eunuchus* 2.263–64.   **75** See Mt 18:33; Lk 6:44.

pomp of demons celebrate nefarious nuptials, and the contract and fidelity which even when ratified by man none except the wicked violate, they do not fear to violate, though it is ratified by God; they are secure of course with Luther condoning their nuptials, who begins to promise also numerous wives at once, which alone he calls the true second marriage. Very soon no doubt he will confirm this promise when he will have sufficiently fortified himself with troops of men against squadrons of women. But meanwhile, so that he may oblige those also, to how many persons, how easily he opens exits in the *Babylon*, by which it is permitted to leave one's spouse if any have not been able to pay their conjugal debt, unless the husband himself is so fair that he brings in a substitute from elsewhere who will in his place faithfully pay the debt to the wife.[76] And these things, which are not only impious but also so silly that they can seem to be distorted by me for the sake of a joke, you will see, reader, in the *Babylon* so seriously confirmed by him that you cannot wonder enough that he ever finds anyone who is not thoroughly ashamed to be called the disciple of so utterly absurd and insane a master.

But a great stimulus to evil is the hope of liberty and license; while it is extended in the one hand, fear is stretched out in the other. For neither is anything more violent than the Lutherans. What wonder is it if Luther's sect advances itself by these same arts, by which it has grown strong and continues to grow strong from day to day, not unlike that sect of the Turks — that is, if the impiety of these men does not surpass even the Turks themselves? For this is plainly evident, that never have the images of the saints been mistreated with such insult as they are mistreated from day to day by the most criminal fingers of these scoundrels, who do not fear not only to tear them away from their most holy shrines, to cast them aside when torn away, to trample them down when cast aside, but also to abuse them trampled down and trodden underfoot by every kind of mockery and insult.

And these things Luther gleefully beholds perpetrated against the images of the saints, all of whose honors and veneration he judges should be abolished as most harmful scandals, while in the meantime he rejoices that his own truly venerable image is carried about and worshipped. But because he sees,

conscious of his guilt, that his impiety is hateful to all the saints, he hates in turn the veneration and honors of all of them. Even the Turks venerate the virgin mother of God, whose name the Lutherans hardly endure. For how can they endure the honors of Mary when these most criminal buffoons bespatter the most holy image of Christ crucified with the most foul excrement of their bodies destined to be burned? These are the spiritual fruits of that sect. To this point at last has grown Luther's piety. A single impiety protects all the crimes of this heresy: according to it, they want themselves to seem to be, and they argue that they are, necessarily such as they are — on the grounds that the certain and destined will of God drives men into every kind of crime. Do you doubt, do you doubt, illustrious Germany, that those who sow such spiritual goods as these are, will one day reap carnal goods?[77] Indeed now, as I hear, the thistles are reproducing their bad fruit, and God is beginning to show how he approves this sect, when he does not allow the priests who take wives to be joined to any other than public strumpets. And in the case of those whom he once forbade to be joined in legitimate wedlock, except to most pure virgins, he does not now allow their incestuous and criminal nuptials to take place except with the most foul prostitutes. What about the fact that everywhere such spouses, exposed at first with wretched infamy, then ruined by illness, poverty and destitution, shortly afterwards slipping into robbery, he finally punishes with public penalty? And would that the vengeance be confined within these dregs, but unless it is speedily resisted, it will spread somewhat farther. For just as very many of the princes look not without pleasure on a degenerating clergy, undoubtedly because they pant for the possessions of those who defect and hope to seize them on the grounds of abandonment, and just as those princes rejoice that obedience is withdrawn from the Roman pontiff with the hope that they will be able to dispose and divide and squander it all for themselves at home, so too there is no reason for them to doubt but that the people look to the time when they may shake off in turn the yoke of the princes and strip them of their possessions; once they have accomplished this, drunk with the blood of princes and revelling in the gore of nobles, enduring not even common rule, with the laws trampled

76 See *WA 6*: 558: 20-32.   77 See Gal 6:8.

underfoot according to Luther's doctrine, rulerless and lawless, without restraint, wanton beyond reason, they will finally turn their hands against themselves and like those earthborn brethren, will mutually run each other through. I pray Christ I may become a false prophet; I shall if men will come to their senses and resist the rising evils. Otherwise, I fear that I will become what I do not wish, a true prophet. But let Germany see to these things.

I return to Luther's book; since it is such as you see, that is, a mere conglomeration of buffoonish words, you will, reader, consider my book worthy of pardon wherever you see what that fellow's filth has infected to be not sufficiently clean. But if at times I seem too long-winded, let your fairness consider that since his words had to be recorded, and those added which the Prince wrote, as well as something added of my own so that the misrepresentation of Luther might become evident, it could not but happen that the work should grow somewhat, not to mention meanwhile the fact that by the custom of all the courts the respondent obtains a longer time to speak. But if you think that you find less of serious matter and matter worthy of approval than is proportionate to the size of the book, not even that can you rightly impute to me, to whom it was not permitted to stray beyond the limits of that man's book, nor to present anything else from it than what was there. And yet I hope that some things have been thrown in by me which so undermine Luther's foundations that together with them the man's impious doctrines stupidly built upon them will necessarily fall into ruin; this I certainly do not doubt, that nothing from the book of the King was carped at by Luther in which I did not clearly refute Luther's shameless deceitfulness. Finally, as I confess my book not to be the kind that demands publication as something that must be read, so I trust it is not the kind which a person ought rightly to contemn who deigns to read Luther's trifles. For if anyone has spurned his chatter, there is no need, nor do I desire, that he waste his time on this book. Indeed, my most earnest prayer is that I may sometime see the day in which all mortals will cast aside both these trifles of mine and all the insane heresies of that fellow, so that, with the pursuit of the worst things consigned to oblivion, with the incitements to railing buried, and the memory of contentions wiped out, the serene light of faith may shine into souls, sincere piety and truly Christian harmony may return; and I pray that he who came into the world to bring peace from heaven, may one day bring back and restore that harmony to the world. The end.

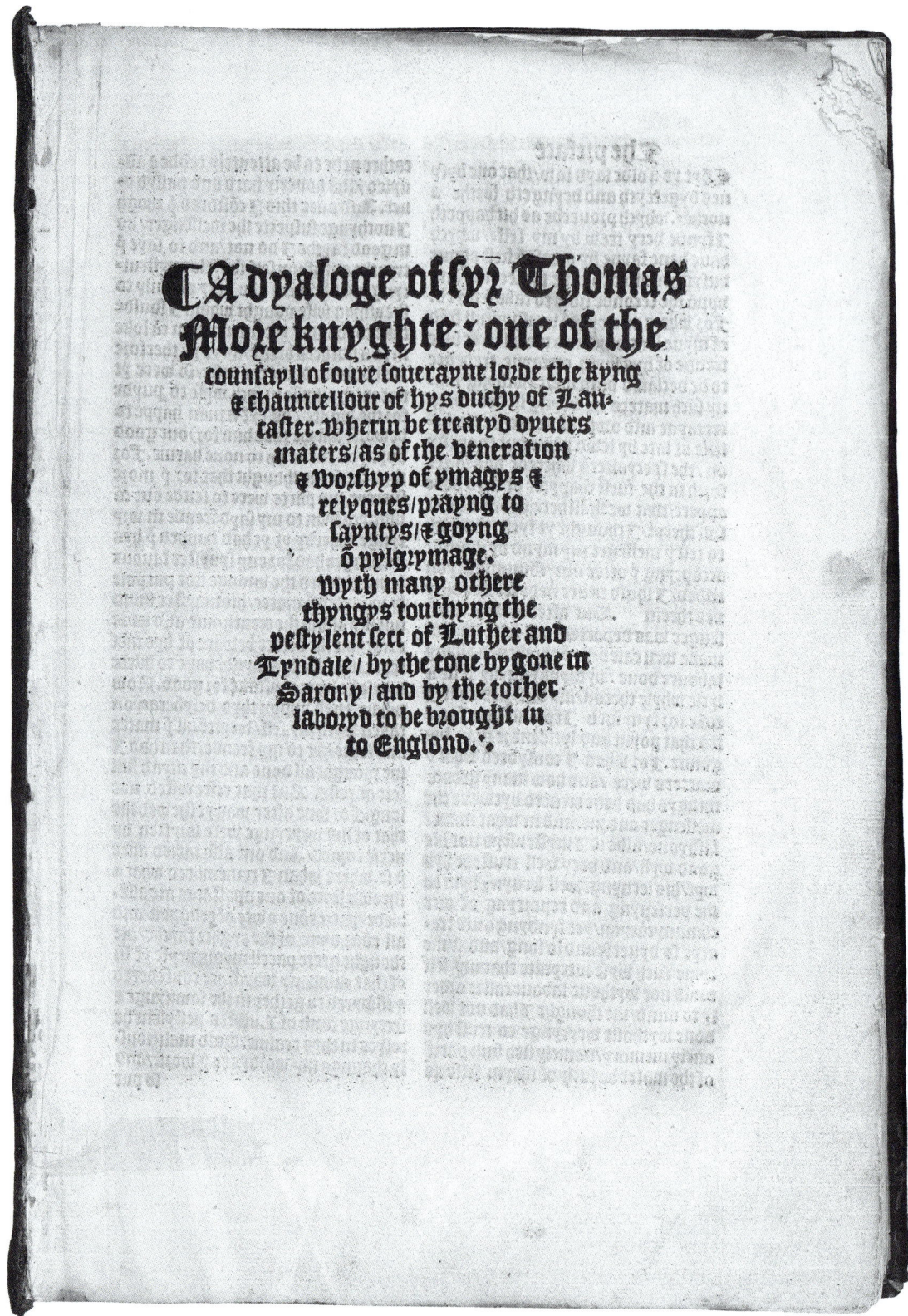

¶A dyaloge of syr Thomas
More knyghte : one of the
counsayll of oure soueranye lorde the kyng
& chauncellour of hys duchy of Lancaster. Wherin be treatyd dyuers
maters / as of the veneration
& worshyp of ymagys &
relyques / prayng to
sayntys / & goyng
õ pylgrymage.
Wyth many othere
thyngys touchyng the
pestylent sect of Luther and
Tyndale / by the tone by gone in
Sarony / and by the tother
laboryd to be brought in
to Englond.

Title page, first edition, *A dyaloge of Syr Thomas More knyght*, 1529; the same wording was used in the 1531 edition. Only in the 1557 *Workes* did editor William Rastell use the title now prevalent: *A Dialogue concerning Heresies*.

A Dialogue of Sir Thomas More, Knight

First published in June 1529, *A Dialogue of Sir Thomas More, Knight,* was composed in response to the request of Cuthbert Tunstall, Bishop of London. A second edition, "newly overseen by the said Sir Thomas More, Chancellor of England," was revised and published in 1531, with additions including More's response to the argument against images in *The Image of Love,* and his updated account of the controversies especially raised by Tyndale's *Answer* in early 1531. A third edition, with the more familiar title, *A Dialogue Concerning Heresies,* was published in the 1557 *Works of Sir Thomas More,* edited by William Rastell. The 1531 text provides the basis for our edition.

Like the earlier *Utopia* and his later Tower work *A Dialogue of Comfort against Tribulation,* this work exhibits More's intellectual commitment to the dialogue genre, as well as his artfulness and skill with this ancient form of writing. Informed by the example of Plato, Cicero, Boethius, and others, More uses the dialogue form for writing and provoking reflection about subjects of fundamental concern. As *A Dialogue* demonstrates, one of More's chief gifts as a writer is his ability to represent human conversation in its variety and reality. The conversation represented is sometimes pithy, sometimes rambling, sometimes funny, sometimes contradictory, sometimes pointed, sometimes urgent—and yet it is always probing and challenging in ways reminiscent of Socrates and his approach, though with a spirit and seasoning distinctly More's own.

Whereas in *Utopia* the dialogue centers on questions such as "What is the best form of a republic?" and "Does a philosophical person have a duty to serve the public?," and while in *A Dialogue of Comfort* the conversation focuses on the question of human suffering and our experience of it, here More represents a long conversation about the "diverse matters of religion" under public debate at the beginning of the Reformation in England. The *Dialogue* has been called by C. S. Lewis the best written Platonic dialogue in English, and the work is marked throughout by More's habitual irony, his flashing and challenging wit, and his distinctive humanism.

Composed in four parts, *A Dialogue* records the serious, merry, and trenchant conversation between More and "the Messenger," a young man sent to More by a friend who is concerned about the Messenger's new opinions as they have grown through the influence of the reformers, or "new men."

The *Dialogue* represents the long conversation of More and the Messenger on the most discussed subjects of religious controversy in the period, including: the nature of the Church and the "common corps" of Christendom; the veneration of saints and the practice of going on pilgrimages; the preeminence of Scripture and the place of liberal education; the respective roles of reason, faith, tradition, and charity; the relationship between grace and nature; the number and nature of the sacraments; the dispute over human liberty and sin; the responsibility of magistrates and the rule of law; and the role of temporal and spiritual authority in political life. The *Dialogue* also contains More's first extended discussion of the handling of seditious heresy by the English authorities, an account that has divided readers of More and his legacy, and yet a text that remains indispensable for those who wish to understand More as he understood himself, his office, and English law.

The *Oxford Dictionary of National Biography* has called More's dialogue the "wittiest" work of the English Reformation, with a "potential to persuade" and "relaxed charm" that are singular. As More writes near the beginning of the work, the questions discussed in this *Dialogue* may be "short," but answering them well is the longer labor, and a necessary one requiring time, conversation, humility, good humor, and courage—More's chosen means for cultivating shared reason and friendship with the Messenger, and the grounds for his hope, stated at the end of the *Dialogue,* that the unity of the Church might be preserved. After centuries of comparative neglect, *A Dialogue of Sir Thomas More, Knight* stands as one of the most comprehensive and valuable resources for the study of the issues involved in the English Reformation and its controversies.

CONTENTS

A Dialogue of
Sir Thomas More, Knight,

one of the Council of our sovereign lord the King,
and Chancellor of his Duchy of Lancaster.
Wherein be treated diverse matters, as of the veneration
and worship of images and relics,
praying to saints, and going on pilgrimage,
with many other things touching the pestilent
sect of Luther and Tyndale,
by the one begun in Saxony, and
by the other labored to be brought into England.

Newly overseen by the said Thomas More,
Chancellor of England.

1530.

THE FIRST BOOK

It is an old-said saw,[1] that one business begetteth and bringeth forth another. Which proverb as it happeth[2] I find very true by[3] myself, which[4] have been fain[5] by occasion first of one business, after to take the second, and upon the second, now to take the third. For whereas a right worshipful[6] friend of mine sent once unto me a secret sure[7] friend of his, with certain credence to be declared unto me, touching many such matters as, being indeed very certain and out of doubt, be nevertheless of late by lewd[8] people put in question (the specialties[9] whereof do so far-forth[10] in the first chapter of this book appear that we shall here need no rehearsal[11] thereof), I thought it first enough to tell the messenger my mind by mouth, accounting that after our communication ended, I should never need further business therein. But after that the messenger was departed, and I felt my stomach[12] well eased—in that I reckoned all my labor done—bethinking myself a little while thereon, my business that I took for finished I found very far from that point, and little more than begun. For when I considered what the matters were, and how many great things had been treated between the messenger and me, and in what manner fashion,[13] albeit[14] I mistrusted not his good will, and very well trusted his wit (his learning well serving him to the perceiving and reporting of our communication)—yet finding our treaty[15] so

---

1 proverb, adage **2** happens **3** of; with regard to **4** who **5** obliged **6** *right worshipful:* very distinguished **7** *secret sure:* confidential and trusted **8** base; vile; uneducated **9** particulars **10** *so far-forth:* to such an extent **11** enumeration; account **12** heart; feelings; spirit **13** *manner fashion:* kind of way **14** although **15** treatment, discussion

diverse and so long, and sometimes such wise intricate that myself could not without labor call it orderly to mind, methought I had not well done, without writing, to trust his only memory, namely[16] since some parts of the matter be such of themselves as rather need to be attentively read and advised[17] than hoverly[18] heard and passed over. And over[19] this I considered that though I nothing suspect the messenger—as in good faith I do not (and, to say the truth, am of myself so little mistrusting that he were like very plainly to show himself naught,[20] whom I should take for bad)—yet since no man can look into another's breast, as it is therefore well done to deem the best, so were it not much amiss in such wise to provide for the worst, as (if a man hap[21] to be worse than we take him for) our good opinion turn us to no harm. For this cause methought that for the more surety,[22] my part were to send our communication to my said friend in writing. Whereby if it had happed that his messenger had, for any sinister favor borne toward the wrong side, purposely mangled the matter, his master should not only know the truth, but also have occasion the better to beware of his messenger—which else might hap to hurt, while he were mistaken for good. Now when I had upon this deliberation taken with myself, written all the matter and sent it to my friend, then had I methought all done, and my mind full set at rest. But that rest rested not long. For soon after it was showed me that of all my writings were written diverse copies, and one also carried over the sea. Where, when I remembered what a shrewd[23] sort of our apostates are assembled—part run out of religion, and all run out of the right faith—methought great peril might arise if some of that company (which[24] are confederated[25] and conspired together in the sowing and setting forth of Luther's pestilent heresies in this realm) should maliciously change my words to the worse, and so put in print my book, framed after their fantasies, which, when I would afterward reprove and show the difference, I might peradventure[26] seem, for the color of my cause,[27] to have amended mine own, upon the sight of theirs. For eschewing[28] whereof, I am now driven, as I say, to this third business of publishing and putting my

book in print myself, whereby their enterprise (if they should any such intend) shall, I trust, be prevented and frustrated. And this have I done not all of mine own head,[29] but after the counsel of others more than one—whose advice and counsel, for their wisdom and learning, I asked in that behalf, and which[30] have at my request vouchsafed[31] to read over the book ere[32] I did put it forth. For albeit that[33] I dare somewhat bold to commune in familiar manner, with such as for their fantasies like to ask me of such matters any question—according to the counsel of Saint Peter bidding us be ready to give a reckoning and to show a reasonable cause to every man of the faith and hope that we have[34]— yet to make and put forth any book (wherein were treated any such things as touch our faith) would I not presume but if[35] better-learned than myself should think it either profitable or at the leastwise harmless. To whose examination and judgment I did the more studiously submit this work for two things in special,[36] among diverse others: the one, for[37] the liberal allegations of the Messenger for the wrong part,[38] so laid out at large that of myself I stood half in a doubt whether it were convenient[39] to rehearse[40] the words of any man so homely,[41] and in manner sometimes unreverently, spoken against God's holy hallows[42] and their reverent memories; the other was certain tales and merry words which he mingled with his matter—and some such on mine own part among[43]—as occasion fell in communication. In which, albeit I saw no harm, yet somewhat doubted I, lest they should unto sad[44] men seem overlight and wanton[45] for the weight and gravity of such an earnest matter. Wherefore, in these two points, though I had already seen some examples of right holy men—which,[46] in their books answering to the objections of heretics in their time have not let to rehearse the very formal words of them whose writings they made answer to, being sometimes of such manner and sort as a good man would not well bear, and have not also let[47] to write a merry word in a right earnest work of which two things I could out of godly men's books and holy saints' works gather a good sort—yet in mine own work I determined that I would nothing allow

16 especially 17 reflected on 18 superficially 19 in addition to 20 wicked 21 happen 22 safety, security; certainty 23 wicked; malicious 24 who 25 confederated 26 perhaps 27 *for the* *color of my cause:* to make my case look better 28 avoiding 29 accord 30 who 31 agreed 32 before 33 *albeit that:* although 34 See 1 Pt 3:15. 35 *but if:* unless 36 particular 37 side 38 because of 39 appropriate 40 repeat 41 plainly; directly 42 saints 43 occasionally 44 serious 45 undisciplined, unruly 46 who 47 hesitated

nor defend that the judgment of other virtuous and cunning[48] men would in any wise[49] mislike. And therefore after that[50] such had read it and severally[51] said their advice, I found (as it often happeth) that
[5] something which one wise and well-learned man would have out, twain[52] of like wisdom and learning specially would have in—neither side lacking good and probable reasons for their part. Wherefore, since it became[53] not me to be judge over the
[10] judgment of them whom I took and chose for my judges—being such, of themselves, as hard were it for any man to say which of them before the others he could in erudition, wit, or prudence anything prefer—I could no further go, but lean to the more[54]
[15] part. Which I so far-forth[55] have followed that, likewise as I diverse things put out or changed by their good advice and counsel, so let I nothing stand in this book but such as twain advised me specially to let stand, against any one that any doubt moved me
[20] to the contrary. And thus much have I thought necessary for my declaration[56] and excuse to advertise[57] you all that shall happen to read this rude simple work, praying you of patience and pardon, whom God, of his especial grace, grant as much profit in
[25] the reading as my poor heart hath meant you and intended in the making.

THE FIRST CHAPTER

[30] *The letter of credence sent from his friend by a trusty secret[58] messenger, with the letter of the author answering the same. The declaration of the credence by the mouth of the messenger; whereupon the matter of all the whole work dependeth.*

The Letter of Credence

Master Chancellor: as heartily as I possibly can,
[35] I recommend me[59] to you, not without a thousand thanks for your good company when we were last together. In which, forasmuch as it liked you to spend some of your time with me in familiar communication—whereof some part I trust so to
[40] remember as myself shall be the better, and some others never the worse, which shall have cause, and

have already, to give you great thanks therefor[60]—I am bold at this time to send you my special secret friend, this bearer, to break with[61] you somewhat further, partly of the same matters, partly of some [45] others, such as are happed there since, whereof great speech and rumor runneth here, whereby ye shall have occasion more at length (if your leisure will serve[62]) to touch certain doubts moved[63] since of the matters treated between us before. Wherein were it [50] not for your other business, I would be bold on your goodness to desire you to take good time with him. And yet nevertheless do require[64] you heartily—as your leisure will serve you—to satisfy him at the full. For he shall (how long soever he tarry therefor) give attendance[65] unto you—days and hours, [55] as ye may spare him time, which cannot in these things be but well bestowed, considering that the matters be such, and so touching to God, as they were well worthy to set worldly business aside, specially in such need. For I assure you, some folk here [60] talk very strangely of the things that he shall move you—not only for such words as they tell that come from thence,[66] but also most especially through the occasion of some letters lewdly[67] written hither out of London by a priest or two, whom they take here [65] for honest. But whatsoever any man tell or write, I shall, for the confidence and trust that I have in you, surely take and tell forth for the very truth whatsoever ye shall affirm unto my friend, whom I send unto you not so much because I may not come [70] myself (howbeit,[68] therefor too) as for because I long to have him talk with you. To whom, whatsoever ye say, reckon it said to myself—not only for his troth[69] and secretness, but also for his memory, with whom to commune,[70] I trust shall not mislike [75] you. For either mine affection blindeth me, or ye shall find him wise and, as others say that can better judge it than I, more than meanly[71] learned with one thing added wherewith ye be wont[72] well to be content: a very merry wit. He is of nature nothing [80] tongue-tied. And I have in these matters bidden him be bold, without any straining of[73] courtesy, whereof the ceremonies in disputation[74] marreth much of the matter, while[75] one studieth more how [85] he may behave him than what he shall say. I have,

48 learned   **49** way   **50** *after that:* after   **51** separately   **52** two   **53** suited, befitted   **54** the majority   **55** *so far-forth:* to such an extent   **56** explanation   **57** notify   **58** trusted, confidential   **59** *recommend me:* commend myself to your benevolent remembrance or regard   **60** for it   **61** *break with:* disclose to   **62** allow   **63** *doubts moved:* questions raised   **64** ask   **65** attention   **66** there (i.e., London)   **67** evilly   **68** although   **69** trustworthiness   **70** talk   **71** moderately   **72** accustomed   **73** *straining of:* restraining out of   **74** *ceremonies in disputation:* formalities of academic debate   **75** when

I say, therefore bidden him more to mind his matter than his courtesy, and freely to lay forth not only what he thinketh, but also what him list,[76] giving no foot[77] in disputing unto your authority, but if[78] he be borne back with reason. Thus may ye see I am bold on your goodness, to put you to labor and business, and send one to face you in your own house. But so much am I bolder, for that[79] in such challenges I know you for a ready and sure defender. And of such labor your wisdom well seeth that God is the rewarder, who long preserve you and all yours.

The Letter of the Author
Sent with the Book

Right worshipful[80] sir: after most hearty recommendation, albeit that[81] of late I sent you my poor mind by the mouth of your trusty friend, to whom ye desired[82] me by your letters to give no less credence than to yourself concerning all such things as he broke of[83] and communed with me in your behalf (and that for[84] the confidence that ye have in him, the wit and learning that I found in him, and honesty that I so much the more think him to be of, in that I perceive you, being of such wisdom and virtue, to have him in so special trust), I neither do nor can believe the contrary but that he hath of all our communication made you faithfully plain and full report, yet since I suppose in myself that if we had might[85] conveniently come together, ye would rather have chosen to have heard my mind of mine own mouth than by the means of another, I have since in these few days (in which I have been at home) put the matter in writing, to the end ye may not only hear it by the mouth of your friend, but also (which better is than suddenly once[86] to hear it of mine own mouth) read it (if ye list[87]) more often, at your best leisure advisedly from mine own pen. Which thing I verily thought myself so much the more bound to do, for that[88] it liked you, of your special favor and affection toward me, so greatly to regard and esteem my mind and answer in those matters that no rumor there running, or tales in your country told, or letters thither written, nor reasons or arguments there made to the contrary, should let or withstand,[89] but that ye would, (as ye wrote), take that thing for undoubted truth that I should (by your friend) ascertain you.[90] And surely, sir, in this point, ye may make yourself sure: that I shall never willingly deceive your trust. And lest I might hap to do it of oversight unware,[91] albeit I nothing said unto your friend by mouth but that I was right well informed of the truth, yet forasmuch as I perceived by him that some folk doubted lest many things were laid to the charge, not only of that man ye wrote of, but also of Luther himself, otherwise than could be proved, I did so much therein that I was suffered[92] to see and show him as well the books of the one, as the very acts of the court concerning the other, that we might both by so much the more surely warrant[93] you the truth. Wherein if ye find any man that yet doubteth whether he told you and I write you the truth or not, I shall, if he understand the Latin tongue, find the means at your pleasure that he shall so see the books himself, that were he never so full of mistrusting, he shall not fail to be fully content and satisfied. And this warrantize[94] will I make you as far-forth as concerneth any act done here. But as for things reasoned and disputed between us, the conclusions themselves be so sure truths that they be not disputable. But whether the reasons[95] by me made in them been effectual or insufficient (albeit your friend either for that[96] of truth he thought so, or for that of courtesy he said so, accepted them for good), yet without prejudice of the principal matters ye may yourself be judge. And thus I pray you take in good worth the little labor and great good will of him whom, in anything that may do you pleasure, ye may to the uttermost of his little power well and boldly command. And thus our Lord send you, with my good lady your bedfellow, and all yours, as heartily well to fare as you would all wish.

Your friend first (after your letter read, when I demanded him his credence) showed me that ye had sent him to me not for any doubt[97] that yourself had in many of those things that he should move[98] unto me, but for the doubt that ye perceived in many others, and in some folk plain persuasion to the contrary, whom ye would be glad to answer

---

76 *him list:* he wishes   **77** ground
78 *but if:* unless   **79** *for that:* because
80 honorable   **81** *albeit that:* although
82 asked   **83** *broke of:* disclosed to

84 because of   **85** *had might:* might have
86 *suddenly once:* all at once   **87** want to
88 *for that:* because   **89** *let or withstand:* hinder or prevent (you)   **90** *ascertain you:*

assure you of   **91** unawares; inadvertently
92 allowed   **93** guarantee   **94** guarantee
95 arguments, explanations   **96** *for that:* because   **97** question   **98** raise

with the truth—albeit some things, he said, were also there so talked that ye wist[99] not well yourself which part ye might believe. For it was there not only spoken, but also thither written by diverse honest priests out of London, that the man ye write of was of many things borne wrong in hand,[100] and therein so sore handled[101] that he was forced to forswear and abjure[102] certain heresies, and openly put to penance therefor, where he never held any such. And all this done for malice and envy, partly of some friars (against whose abusions[103] he preached), partly for that he preached boldly against the pomp and pride and other inordinate living (that more men speak of than preach of) used in the clergy. And they take for a great token that he should not mean evil[104] the proof and experience which men have had of him: that he lived well, and was a good, honest, virtuous man, far from ambition and desire of worldly worship[105]—chaste, humble, and charitable, free and liberal in almsdeed—and a very good preacher, in whose devout sermons the people were greatly edified. And therefore the people say that all this gear[106] is done but only to stop men's mouths, and to put every man to silence that would anything speak of the faults of the clergy. And they think that for none other cause was also burned, at Paul's Cross,[107] the New Testament late[108] translated in English by Master William Hutchins, otherwise called Master Tyndale,[109] who was (as men say), well known ere[110] he went over the sea, for a man of right good living, studious and well-learned in Scripture, and in diverse places in England was very well liked and did great good with preaching. And men mutter among themselves that the book was not only faultless, but also very well translated, and was devised to be burned because[111] men should not be able to prove that such faults (as were at Paul's Cross declared to have been found in it) were never found there indeed, but untruly surmised.[112] And yet such as they were (some men say) were no faults at all if they had been so translated indeed, but blame laid and fault found with things nothing blameworthy

only to deface and infame[113] that holy work, to the end that they might seem to have some just cause to burn it.

And that for none other intent but for to keep out of the people's hands all knowledge of Christ's Gospel, and of God's law, except so much only as the clergy themselves list[114] now and then to tell us. And that little as it is and seldom showed, yet as it is feared, not well and truly told, but watered with false glosses, and altered from the truth of the very words and sentence[115] of Scripture, only for the maintenance of their authority.

And the fear—lest this thing should evidently appear to the people if they were suffered[116] to read the Scripture themselves in their own tongue—was (as it is thought) the very cause not only for which the New Testament translated by Tyndale was burned, but also that the clergy of this realm hath before this time, by a constitution provincial,[117] prohibited any book of Scripture to be translated into the English tongue, fearing men with fire as heretics who so should presume to keep them, as though it were heresy for a Christian man to read Christ's Gospel.

"And surely, sir," quoth he, "some folk that think this dealing of the clergy to thus (and good men to be mishandled for declaring the truth, and the Scripture itself to be pulled out of the people's hands, lest they should perceive the truth) be led in their minds to doubt whether Luther himself (of whose opinions—or, at the least, of whose works—all these businesses began) wrote indeed so evil as he is borne in hand.[118] And many men there be that think he never meant such things. But that because he wrote against the abusions of pardons,[119] and spoke somewhat liberally against the court of Rome, and generally against the vices of the clergy, therefore he was brought in hatred,[120] and first cited[121] to Rome. And when that for fear of bodily harm with wrong[122]—whereof[123] it would have been too late to look for remedy after, if he had once been burned up before—he durst[124] not come thither,[125] then was he accursed,[126] and his books damned,[127] and under

99 knew   **100** *borne wrong in hand:* falsely accused   **101** *sore handled:* badly treated   **102** publicly renounce   **103** corrupt practices   **104** badly   **105** honor   **106** matter   **107** *Paul's Cross:* the outdoor pulpit in front of Old St. Paul's Cathedral in London   **108** lately, recently   **109** *New Testament…Tyndale:* Tyndale (1494–1536) published his English translation of the New Testament in 1526 in Worms; it was declared illegal in England.   **110** before   **111** so that   **112** formally alleged; charged   **113** bring into infamy   **114** want   **115** meaning   **116** allowed   **117** *constitution provincial:* decree made by the bishops of the national synod   **118** *borne in hand:* accused of having done   **119** *abusions of pardons:* corrupt practices   concerning services held for the granting of indulgences   **120** *brought in hatred:* made to be hated   **121** summoned   **122** *with wrong:* unjustly inflicted   **123** by reason of which   **124** dared   **125** *come thither:* go there (i.e., to Rome)   **126** excommunicated   **127** condemned

great pains forbidden to be read. And that thing done because it should not be known what wrong he had, and that he neither meaneth nor saith such odious and abominable heresies as the people be borne in hand[128] to induce them to hatred of him — as it would peradventure[129] appear if his books were suffered to be read.

"And they say that it were no mastery[130] to make it seem that a man should be a heretic, if he may be borne in hand that he saith the thing which he never said, or peradventure one line taken out among many — and misconstrued — not suffering the remnant to be seen, whereby it might more clearly appear what he meaneth. By which manner of dealing a man, they say, might lay heresy to Saint Paul, and find a fault in Saint John's Gospel.

"And yet, they say, the worst of all is this: that the clergy cease not hereby,[131] nor hold themselves content with the condemning of Luther and forbidding of his books, but further abuse[132] the hatred of his name against every man that is, in preaching of the Word of God, anything such as should be — that is to wit,[133] plain and bold, without gloss or flattering — where if they find a man faulty, let them lay his fault to his charge. What needeth to call him a 'Lutheran'? Though[134] Luther were a devil, yet might a man percase[135] say as he saith in something, and say true enough. For never was there heretic that said all false. Nor the devil himself lied not when he called Christ God's Son.[136] And therefore men think that this name of a Lutheran serveth the clergy for a common cloak of[137] a false crime: that where they lack special matter[138] to charge one with by judgment,[139] they labor to bring him first in the infamy of that name, that compriseth (as they make it seem) a confused heap of heresies, no man can tell what.

"And yet in such dealing they wound their own matter[140] another way. For while they defame for Lutherans men that be of known virtue and cunning,[141] what do they thereby but one of the twain:[142] either cause the people (that have, for[143] good living and learning, those men in great reputation) to think that the clergy, for malice and envy, doth untruly defame them, or else that Luther's doctrine is good, while so[144] cunning men, and good men, lean thereto.[145]

"And therefore it were wisdom not to call them Lutherans, but rather, when they teach and hold any such opinions as the people know for Luther's, let it either be dissimuled,[146] or they secretly[147] by fair ways induced to the contrary, if the points that they teach of his be naught.[148] Lest by calling good and cunning men 'Lutherans,' they may peradventure[149] bring themselves in suspicion of malice and envy, and Luther among the people into good opinion — thinking, as they begin to do already, that either Luther said not as evil as is surmised upon[150] him, or else that those things that he saith, as odious as they seem, be good enough in deed."[151]

He said also that it seemed unto many men a sore[152] thing, and far unreasonable, that poor, simple, and unlearned men — although they fell into errors, and were led out of the right way by that they leaned to, the authority of such men as they believed to be virtuous and cunning — should instead of teaching be beaten cruelly, with abjurations[153] and open shame, with peril of burning also, if a few false witnesses shall, after such abjuration, depose[154] that they have heard him fall in relapse.

Finally he said that many good and well-learned men thought plainly that the clergy seemeth far out of all good order of charity — and that they do contrary to the mildness and merciful mind of their Master, and against the example of all the old holy fathers[155] — in that they cause, for any error or wrong opinion in the faith, any man, one or other, to be put to death.

"For they say that the old holy fathers used only to dispute with heretics, teaching them, and convicting them by Scripture, and not by faggots.[156] And that, by that way, the faith went well toward,[157] and one heretic so turned[158] did turn many others, whereas now men abhor this cruelty in the Church. And they that seem turned think still the things that they dare not say. And of the ashes of one heretic springeth up many. And that now we make the fashion of Christendom to seem all turned quite upside down. For whereas Christ made infidels the

---

128 *borne in hand:* led to believe he does   129 perhaps   130 superiority   131 in connection with this   132 take advantage of, misuse   133 say   134 Even if   135 perhaps   136 See Mk 3:11.   137 *cloak of:* cover for   138 *special matter:* specific grounds   139 *by judgment:* in a trial   140 position   141 learning   142 two   143 because of (those men's)   144 such   145 *lean thereto:* subscribe to it   146 ignored   147 privately   148 bad   149 perhaps   150 *surmised*   *upon:* alleged of   151 actuality   152 terrible   153 formal renunciations on oath   154 testify   155 *old holy fathers:* early fathers of the Church   156 bundles of sticks   157 forward   158 converted

persecutors and his Christian people the sufferers, we make the Christian men the persecutors and the infidels the sufferers, whereby men think that secretly Christ's order yet standeth still, though it be not so taken and so perceived. For the people take it that still those that persecute be the miscreants,[159] and those poor people that suffer it be (under the false name of 'heretics') the true-believing men, and very[160] Christian martyrs.

"Christ also, they say, would never have any man compelled by force and violence to believe upon[161] his faith, nor would that men should[162] fight for him or his matters. In so far-forth[163] that he would not suffer[164] Saint Peter to fight for his own self, but reproved him for striking Malchus.[165] Nor would not defend himself, but, healing the ear again of Malchus his persecutor, which Peter had smitten off, and giving all his holy body to the patient sufferance of all the painful torments that his cruel enemies would put to it, showed us, as well by his effectual[166] example of his death as by his godly counsel in his life (and after that, confirmed by the continual passion[167] and martyrdoms of his holy martyrs) that his will and pleasure is that we should not so much as defend ourselves against heretics and infidels, were they pagans, Turks, or Saracens. And much less then should we fight against them and kill them, but that we should persevere in setting forth his faith against miscreants and infidels by such ways as himself began it, keep it and increase it as it was gotten. And that was by patience and sufferance,[168] by which the faith was divulgated[169] and spread almost through the world in little while. Not by war and fighting; which way hath (as they say) well near already lost all that the other way won."

When your friend had thus declared his credence, he desired[170] me, both on your behalf and on his own, in such things as were percase[171] not well said, to take them as they were in deed:[172] the mind[173] of others, whom ye would fain[174] answer and satisfy with reason—which ye trusted to be the better able to do by mine answer—and neither the mind and opinion of you nor him, which did and would in all things stand and abide by the faith and belief of Christ's Catholic Church. But as for such parts of this matter as concerned not any part of our belief, but the dealing of this world—as[175] the justice or injustice of some spiritual persons[176] in the pursuing and condemning men for heretics, or their works for heresies—he thought, he said (as of himself) that men might without any peril of heresy, for their own part, notwithstanding any man's judgment given, yet well and reasonably doubt[177] therein. For though he thought it heresy to think the opinions of any man to be good and Catholic which been heresies indeed, yet might a man (he thought) without any peril of heresy, doubt whether he were a heretic or no, that were by man's judgment condemned for one, since it might well happen that he never held those opinions that were put upon him, but that he was either by false depositions of wrongful witnesses or by the error or malice of unjust judges condemned. And that sometime percase the ignorance of some judges would condemn for heresy such articles as wiser and better-learned would in point of judgment allow for good and Catholic, and of the other judgment discern and judge the contrary.

Howbeit,[178] he said that ye had in me and my learning so special trust and confidence that in any of all these things—whatsoever ye had heard or should hear elsewhere—ye were fully determined to give full credence to me, and take for the truth such answer as he should bring you from me, wherein ye right heartily desired me to take some pain, that ye might in these matters by his mouth know my mind at large.

After this, ere[179] I made any answer to his words, I demanded[180] him what manner acquaintance was between him and you. And thereupon perceiving him to have your sons at school, inquiring further of him to what faculty[181] he had most given his study, I understood him to have given diligence to the Latin tongue. As for other faculties, he rought nought of.[182] For he told me merrily that logic he reckoned but babbling; music, to serve for singers; arithmetic, meet[183] for merchants; geometry, for masons; astronomy, good for no man; and as for philosophy, the most vanity of all, and that it and logic had lost[184] all good divinity[185] with the subtleties of their questions and babbling of their dispicions,[186]

---

159 unbelievers; infidels, heretics
160 true 161 in 162 *would . . . should:* would want men to 163 *In so far-forth:* To such an extent 164 allow 165 See Mt 26:51–54; Jn 18:10. 166 effective

167 suffering 168 tolerance 169 proclaimed 170 asked 171 perhaps
172 actuality 173 opinion 174 willingly
175 such as 176 *spiritual persons:* members of the clergy 177 question

178 However 179 before 180 asked
181 branch of knowledge 182 *rought nought of:* thought nothing of 183 suitable 184 ruined 185 theology
186 disputations

building all upon reason, which rather giveth blindness than any light. "For man," he said, "hath no light but of Holy Scripture." And therefore he said that besides the Latin tongue, he had been (which I much commend) studious in Holy Scripture, which was, he said, "learning enough for a Christian man, with which the apostles held themselves content." And therein, he said, he labored not only to can[187] many texts thereof by heart, but also to ensearch[188] the sentence[189] and understanding thereof, as far as he might perceive by himself. For as for interpreters, he told me that neither his time would well serve him to read, and also he found so great sweetness in the text itself that he could not find in his heart to lose any time in the glosses. And as touching any difficulty, he said that he found by experience that the best and surest interpretation was to lay and confer[190] one text with another, which fail not among them well and sufficiently to declare[191] themselves. And this way he said that he used, which he found sufficient and surest. For so should it most surely tarry,[192] when it were found out and learned by a man's own labor. And that, he said, every man was able enough to do with help of God, which[193] never faileth them that faithfully trust in his promise. And he hath promised that if we seek, we shall find, and if we knock, we shall have it opened to us.[194] And what shall be opened, but that book which, as Saint John saith in the Apocalypse is so shut with seven clasps that it cannot be opened but by the Lamb: that when he shutteth, then can no man open it, and when he openeth it, then can no man shut it."[195]

Upon these words and other like, when I considered that your friend was studious of Scripture, and although I now have a very good opinion of him, nor at that time had not all the contrary— yet to be plain with you and him both, by reason that he set the matter so well and lustily[196] forward, he put me somewhat in doubt whether he were (as young scholars be sometimes prone to new fantasies) fallen into Luther's sect. And that ye peradventure[197] somewhat fearing the same, did of good mind the rather send him to me with such a message, for that[198] ye trusted he should be somewhat answered and satisfied by me. I therefore thought

it not meetly,[199] in so many matters and weighty, to make him an unadvised answer, but with good words welcoming him for the time (pretending lack of leisure for[200] other present business) required[201] him to return on the morrow. Against[202] which time I would so order mine affairs that we would have conference together of all his errand at length. And he in this wise[203] being departed, I began to gather in mind the whole effect, as my remembrance would serve me, of all that he had purposed. And because I would have it the more ready at mine eye, so that I might the more fully and effectually answer it, leaving no part untouched, in such order as he had purposed it—that is to wit,[204] after the manner that I have above rehearsed[205]—I briefly committed it to writing.

THE SECOND CHAPTER
Here summarily is declared what order the author intendeth to treat of the matters purposed unto him. Whereof, because the first was an opinion conceived in some men's heads that a certain person late[206] abjured of heresy for preaching against pilgrimages and images and prayers made to saints was therein greatly wronged, the author briefly declareth his mind concerning the confutation of those perilous and pernicious opinions.

On the morrow, when he was comen again somewhat before seven of the clock (for so I appointed him), taking him with me into my study—and my servants warned that if any others should happen to desire to speak with me (certain except of whom I gave them knowledge), they should defer them till another leisure—I set him down with me at a little table. And then I showed unto him that, where[207] he had purposed on your behalf in short words many long things, whereof the rehearsal[208] were loss of time to him that so well knew them already, I would—all superfluous recapitulation set apart, as briefly as I conveniently could—show him my mind in them all. And first begin where he began: at the abjuration[209] of the man he spoke of. Secondly would I touch the condemnation and burning of the New Testament translated by Tyndale.

---

187 learn   **188** investigate; scrutinize   **189** meaning   **190** *lay and confer:* compare   **191** make clear   **192** remain   **193** who   **194** See Mt 7:7–8.   **195** Rv 3:7, 5:1–7

196 forcefully, energetically   **197** perhaps   **198** *for that:* because   **199** proper   **200** on account of   **201** asked   **202** In anticipation of   **203** way   **204** say

205 related   **206** recently   **207** whereas, given that   **208** enumeration   **209** formal renunciation on oath

Thirdly somewhat would I speak of Luther and his sect in general. Fourthly and finally, the thing that he touched last: that is to wit, the war and fighting against infidels, with the condemnation of heretics unto death, which two points himself had combined and knit together.

And first, as touching the matter of the man's abjuration, where it is reported that the spiritualty[210] did him wrong, and for to make that seem likely, there is laid[211] in them displeasure, malice, and envy toward him, for preaching (as ye say, quoth I) against their vicious living, and in him is on the other side alleged much cunning,[212] virtue, and goodness. I will neither enter into the praise of them nor into the dispraise of him, wherein standeth nothing the effect[213] of this matter. For if there did, I would not pass over some part thereof so shortly.

"But now for this matter: although[214] the whole spiritualty (wherein no man doubteth to be many a right virtuous and godly man) were in their living far worse than devils, yet if they did that man no wrong, there hath for this matter no man against them any cause to complain. And over[215] this, if that man were in all his other living as innocent as a saint, yet if he were infected and faulty in these heresies, he had then in this matter no wrong. And yet besides all this, if he not only were in all other things very virtuous, but also were in all these heresies (whereof he was detected[216]) utterly clean and faultless, yet if it were by sufficient witnesses (were they never so false in deed, seeming honest and likely to say true) proved in open court that he was faulty therein, albeit[217] in such case his witnesses had wronged him, yet had his judges done him but right. And therefore letting pass, as I say, the praise or dispraise of either his judges or him, as things impertinent to the point, I will show you that they not only did him no wrong, but also showed him in my mind the greatest favor, and used toward him the most charitable mercy that ever I wist[218] used to any man in such case.

"And first, as for any wrong that his judges did him, I marvel me much wherein they that report it could assign it. For if any were done him, it must needs have been in one of the two things: either in that he was untruly judged to have preached such articles as he was detected of, where he preached none such indeed; or else in that some such articles as he preached were judged and condemned for heresies where they were none indeed. Except that any man would say that though he were proved and convicted of heresy, yet he should have been put to no penance at all, or else to no such as he was. And of that point if any man so think, I shall speak in the Fourth Part, where we shall touch in general the order that the Church taketh in the condemnation of heretics. But as for the other points: first, if any priest wrote out of London into your country that any such article of his preaching was by his judges declared for heresy as were indeed good and not against the faith of Christ's Church, let him name what article. And either ye shall find that he shall name you such as the man was not charged withal,[219] or else shall ye find that such as he shall name you, were such indeed as yourself shall perceive for heresies at your ear.[220] For the articles wherewith he was charged were that we should do no worship to any images, nor pray to any saints, or go on pilgrimages, which things I suppose every good Christian man will agree for heresies. And therefore we shall let that point pass, and so resort to the second, to see whether it were well proved that he preached them or no."

"Sir," quoth your friend, "I would for my part well agree them for heresies, but yet have I heard some ere[221] this that would not do so. And therefore when we call them heresies, it were well done to tell why, since some men would—I ween[222] if they might be heard—stiffly say nay, which now hold their peace, and bear themselves full coldly that would take the matter more hot, save for burning of their lips."[223]

"Now forsooth,"[224] quoth I, "whosoever will say that these be no heresies, he shall not have me to dispute it, which have no cunning[225] in such matters, but as it best becometh a layman to do in all things, lean and cleave to the common faith and belief of Christ's Church. And thereby do I plainly know it for a heresy—if a heresy be a sect, and a side way (taken by any party of such as been baptized and bear the name of Christian men) from the common faith and belief of the whole Church besides. For this am I very sure and perceive it well—not only by experience of mine own time, and the places where myself hath been, with common report of other

---

210 clergy　211 alleged to be　212 learning　213 *wherein…effect:* which concerns not at all the substance　214 even if

215 beyond　216 accused　217 although　218 knew　219 with　220 *at your ear:* as soon as you hear them　221 before

222 believe　223 *save…lips:* i.e., except that they would be burnt at the stake　224 truly, in truth　225 expertise

honest men from all other places of Christendom, but by books also, and remembrances, left of long time, with writing of the old holy fathers and now saints in heaven — that from the apostles' time hitherto,[226] this manner hath been used, taught, and allowed, and the contrary commonly condemned, through the whole flock of all good Christian people.

"And as touching such texts as these heretics allege against the worshipping of images, praying to saints, and going on pilgrimages — as they lay[227] the law given to the Jews, *Non facies tibi sculptile* ('Thou shalt carve thee none image'),[228] and the psalm *In exitu Israel de Aegypto*,[229] and *Soli Deo honor et gloria* ('Only to God be honor and glory'),[230] and *Maledictus qui confidit in homine* ('Accursed is he that putteth his trust in man'),[231] with many such other like, which heretics have of old ever barked against Christ's Catholic Church — very sure am I that Saint Augustine, Saint Jerome, Saint Basil, Saint Gregory, with so many a godly cunning[232] man as hath been in Christ's Church from the beginning hitherto, understood those texts as well as did those heretics: namely having as good wits, being far better learned, using in study more diligence, being a heap to a handful, and (which most is of all) having (as God by many miracles beareth witness) besides their learning, the light and clearness of his especial grace, by which they were inwardly taught of his only Spirit to perceive that the words spoken in the old law to the Jewish people, prone to idolatry — and yet not to all them neither, for the priests then had the images of the angel cherubim in the secret place of the Temple[233] — should have no place to forbid images among his Christian flock, where his pleasure would be to have the image of his blessed body hanging on his holy cross had[234] in honor and reverent remembrance, where he would vouchsafe[235] to send unto the king Abgar[236] the image of his own face, where he liked to leave the holy vernicle,[237] the express image also of his blessed visage, as a token to remain in honor among such as loved him from the time of his bitter Passion hitherto. Which,[238] as it was by the miracle of his blessed

holy hand expressed[239] and left in the sudary,[240] so hath it been, by like miracle, in that thin, corruptible cloth kept and preserved uncorrupted this fifteen hundred years, fresh and well perceived, to the inward comfort, spiritual rejoicing, and great increase of fervor and devotion in the hearts of good Christian people. Christ also taught his holy evangelist Saint Luke to have another manner[241] mind toward images than have these heretics, when he put in his mind to counterfeit[242] and express in a table[243] the lovely visage of our blessed Lady, his mother.[244] He taught also Saint Amphibalus, the master and teacher of the holy first martyr of England, Saint Alban, to bear about and worship the crucifix. Who showed also Saint Alban himself, in a vision, the image of the crucifix, but God? Which thing wrought in that holy man so strongly, that he with few words of Saint Amphibalus, at the sight of that blessed image (which our Lord had before showed him in his sleep) was clean turned[245] to Christendom. And in the worshipping of the same image was taken and brought forth to judgment, and afterward to martyrdom.

"I would also fain wit,[246] whether these heretics will be content that the blessed name of Jesus be had in honor and reverence or not. If not, then need we no more to show what wretches they be, which dare despise that holy name that the devil trembleth to hear of.[247] And on the other side if they agree that the name of Jesus is to be reverenced and had in honor,[248] then since that name of Jesus is nothing else but a word, which, by writing or by voice, representeth unto the hearer the person of our Savior Christ, fain would I wit of these heretics — if they give honor to the name of our Lord, which name is but an image representing his person to man's mind and imagination — why and with what reason can they despise a figure of him, carved or painted, which representeth him and his acts, far more plain and more expressly?"

"Sir," quoth he, "as touching the cost done upon the Ark and the Temple and the priests' apparel by the commandment of God, there is a proper book, and a very contemplative, written in English — and

---

226 until now	227 adduce; cite	228 Ex 20:4	229 "When Israel went forth from Egypt," Ps 113(114):1	230 1 Tm 1:17	231 Jer 17:5	232 learned	233 See 1 Kgs 6:23–29.	234 held	235 be willing	236 King of Edessa, d. *ca.* AD 50.

The cloth portrait of Christ was called the Image of Edessa.	237 the handkerchief with which St. Veronica wiped the face of Jesus	238 This (vernicle)	239 imprinted	240 vernicle	241 kind of	242 portray	243 painting	244 *Luke…mother:* A

picture of St. Mary ascribed to St. Luke hangs in the Basilica of St. Mary Major in Rome.	245 *clean turned:* completely converted	246 *fain wit:* gladly know	247 See Jas 2:19.	248 See Phil 2:9–11.

entitled *The Image of Love*[249]—which was made as it seemeth by some very virtuous man, contemplative and well-learned. In which book that reason of yours is not only well answered, but also turned again[250] against you. For therein that good holy man layeth sore[251] against these carved and painted images, giving them little praise, and specially least commending such as be most costly, curiously,[252] and most workmanly wrought. And he showeth full well that images be but laymen's books, and therefore that religious men[253] and folk of more perfect life, and more instruct in spiritual wisdom, should let all such dead images pass, and labor only for the lively quick[254] image of love and charity. And very sore he speaketh there against all these costly ornaments[255] of the Church, whereof the money were (as he saith) better bestowed upon poor folk. And he showeth that the saints and holy doctors[256] of old time would suffer no such superfluity in the paraments[257] of the Church, but only see that they were clean and pure, and not costly. And therefore he saith that in their time they had treen[258] chalices and golden priests, and now have we golden chalices and treen priests."

"Surely," quoth I, "that book have I seen, whereof who was the maker, I know not. But the man might peradventure[259] mean well and run up so high in his contemplation spiritual that while he thought he sat in God almighty his[260] bosom up on high in heaven, he contemned[261] and set at nought[262] all earthly things, and all temporal service done to God here beneath, among poor seely[263] men in earth. And verily[264] of his intent and purpose I will not much meddle. For a right good man may hap at a time, in a fervent[265] undiscreet, to say something, and write it too, which when he considereth after[266] more advisedly, he would be very fain[267] to change; but this dare I be bold to say: that his words go somewhat further than he is able to defend. For I doubt it not but that in the days of those holy saints, ornaments[268] in churches of Christ were not only pure and clean, but also very costly. And it might well be—and so have I read that it

hath been in some great dearth of corn and famine of people—that some good, holy bishops have relieved poor people with the sale of some of the vessels and plate[269] of the Church. But I suppose he shall never find (except in some such great, urgent cause chancing upon some occasion) that ever those holy men refused to have God served in his churches with the best and most precious of such metals as his goodness giveth unto man, of which it is very right and good reason that man serve him again with the best, and not do as Cain did: keep all that aught is[270] for himself, and serve his Master and his Maker with the worst.[271] And because he nameth Saint Ambrose,[272] I ween[273] there will no man doubt of the emperor Theodosius,[274] a man so devout unto God as he was, that he would be served himself in cups of gold, and suffer[275] his and our Savior Christ in the church of Milan—where himself resorted, and Saint Ambrose was bishop—to be served in chalices of tree.[276] Nor verily I can scant[277] believe that any Christian people, all were they very poor, would at this day suffer the precious blood of our Lord to be consecrated and received in tree, where it should cleave to the chalice and sink in and not be clean[278] received out by the priest. But that word I ween he set in for the pleasure that he had in that proper comparison between treen chalices and golden priests of old, and now golden chalices and treen priests. But of truth I think he saith not truth—that the chalices were made of treen when the priests were made of gold—and shall find that then were, of old time, many more chalices made of gold than he findeth now priests made of tree. If he look well in Platina's *De vitis pontificum*,[279] I ween he shall well perceive that Christ was served with silver and gold in the vessels, utensils, and ornaments of his Church, long time ere[280] Saint Ambrose was born, or the eldest of those old doctors that he speaketh of. And I dare make me bold to warrant that they themselves used not to say Mass in chalices of tree. And methinketh that the pleasure of God cannot in this point better appear than by his own words written in Holy Scripture: as in

249 *The Image of Love:* published 1525   **250** back   **251** severely   **252** elaborately   **253** *religious men:* members of religious orders   **254** living   **255** furnishings used in worship   **256** theologians   **257** decorations   **258** wooden   **259** perhaps   **260** *almighty his:* almighty's   **261** disdained, scorned   **262** no value   **263** pitiful; poor   **264** truly   **265** fervor   **266** afterwards   **267** pleased   **268** furnishings used in worship   **269** utensils made of precious metals   **270** *aught is:* is worth anything   **271** See Gn 4:2–7; 1 Jn 3:12.   **272** Bishop of Milan (339–97 AD)   **273** suppose   **274** Emperor Theodosius I (347–95 AD), who established the Nicaean Creed against the heresy of Arianism   **275** allow   **276** wood   **277** scarcely   **278** completely   **279** *Platina's… pontificum:* Bartolomeo Platina (1421–81), Italian humanist, published his *Lives of the Popes* in 1479.   **280** before

the Ark of the Testament[281] and the ornaments of the priest, and the cost and richesse[282] bestowed about the Temple of Solomon."[283]

"Marry,"[284] quoth he, "that is the thing that is in the book of *The Images of Love*—as I was about to tell you—very well and clearly answered."

"In what wise?"[285] quoth I.

"Marry," quoth he, "for first, when the Ark was made, there were no poor men to bestow that richesse upon, for while the children of Israel were in desert, they were fed with manna, and their clothes never wasted,[286] nor were the worse, in all that forty years.[287] And as for the richesse of the Temple made by Solomon, could[288] make no matter to the people, for there was then no poor folk neither. For as the very words of the Scripture showeth, there was in his days so great plenty of gold that 'silver was not set by.'"[289]

"Forsooth,"[290] quoth I, "the man maketh a proper[291] answer for the Ark. But I would fain wit[292] of him: though there were no poor folk among them at the time of the making, was there never none among them after the time of the keeping? I ween he will not say nay. And then if there were—since God would by his reason rather have commanded to give that gold to poor men if there had been such, than to make it in the Ark—he would by the same reason after, when there were such, have commanded then to break it again and give it them, rather than to keep it in the Ark. And as for the richesse bestowed upon the Temple of Solomon—where he said that there were then no poor men, because there were so great plenty of gold that 'silver was not set by': every man may well wit[293] that if every man had in his time been rich, he had not had so many workmen. But weeneth[294] he that because there was in his days so much gold, that therefore all the people had enough thereof? I rather fear me that, because he was so rich, his people were the poorer. For albeit[295] he had great gifts sent him, and also used not his own people, of the children of Israel, for bondmen and slaves, yet it is likely that he set great and sore impositions[296] upon them, whereby he gathered great richesse, and they grew in great poverty. And if any man think the contrary, let him

then look after Solomon's death, in the beginning of his son's reign, whether all the people did not so sore complain thereof, that (because they could not get a promise of amendment as sad[297] men advised the king, but by the lewd[298] counsel of young lads that then then led the young king to folly were with a proud rigorous[299] answer put in fear of worse) of the twelve tribes of Israel, ten fell clearly from him, and left him no more but twain.[300] And therefore by the richesse and royalty of the prince to prove that there was no poor people in his royalme[301] is a very poor proof. For so may it hap that the prince may be most rich when his people be most poor, and the richesse of the one causing the poverty of the other, if the people's substance[302] be gathered into the prince's purse. And for conclusion it is little doubt but Solomon might have found poor folk enough to have given his gold unto that he bestowed upon the Temple of God. And therefore that answer answereth not well the matter."

"Well," quoth your friend, "yet hath that book one answer that assoileth[303] all the whole matter. For as it is said there, all those things that were used in the Old Law were but gross and carnal, and were all as a shadow of the law of Christ; and therefore the worshipping of God with gold and silver and such other corporal things ought not to be used among Christian people, but leaving all that shadow, we should draw us to the spiritual things, and serve our Lord only in spirit and spiritual things. For so he saith himself: that God as himself is spiritual, so seeketh he such worshippers as shall worship him "in spirit and in truth"[304]—that is, in faith, hope, and charity of heart—not in the hypocrisy and ostentation of outward observance, bodily service, gay and costly ornaments, fair images, goodly song, fleshly fasting, and all the rabble of such unsavory ceremonies, all which are now gone as a shadow. And our Savior himself, whose faith is our justification,[305] calleth upon our soul, and our good faithful mind, and setteth all those carnal things at nought."[306]

"The book," quoth I, "saith not fully so far as ye rehearse,[307] howbeit[308] indeed many other men do. But these men that make themselves so spiritual,

---

281 Covenant   **282** wealth, riches
283 See Ex 25–28.   **284** an exclamation, from "by Mary"; indeed   **285** way
286 wore out   **287** See Dt 8:2–4.
288 that could   **289** *set by:* valued. See Ex

16:15; Dt 8:2–4; 1 Kgs 10:21.   **290** Truly, In truth   **291** good, correct   **292** *fain wit:* gladly know   **293** say   **294** thinks
295 although   **296** *sore impositions:* harsh taxes   **297** sober, serious   **298** bad

299 harsh   **300** two. See 1 Kgs 12:4–20.
301 realm   **302** wealth   **303** resolves
304 Jn 4:24   **305** See Rom 5:1–2.
306 *setteth at nought:* values as nothing
307 relate   **308** although

God send grace that some evil spirit inspire not to their hearts a devilish device,[309] which under a cloak of special zeal to spiritual service, go first about to destroy all such devotion as ever hath hitherto showed itself, and uttered the good affection of the soul by good and holy works, unto God's honor wrought with the body. These men be comen into so high point of perfection that they pass all the good men that served God in old time. For as for that good godly man Moses, he thought that to pray not only in mind, but with mouth also, was a good way.[310] The good king David thought it pleasant to God not only to pray with his mouth, but also to sing and dance too, to God's honor, and blamed his foolish wife, which did at that time as these foolish heretics do now: mocking that bodily service.[311] Holy Saint John the Baptist not only baptized and preached, but also fasted, watched,[312] prayed, and wore hair.[313] Christ our Savior himself not only prayed in mind, but also with mouth[314]—which kind of prayer these holy spiritual heretics now call 'lip labor' in mockage. And the fasting which they set at nought,[315] our Savior himself set so much by that he continued it forty days together.[316] Now, as for the images, which ye call one of the shadows—"

"Nay, by Saint Mary," quoth he, "I called gay ornaments[317] of the Church, and such other outward observances and bodily ceremonies, as *The Image of Love* calleth them; such things I called, as the book doth, 'shadows of the Old Law.' But as for images, the book adviseth men either clean let pass and leave off or (if we will needs have any) care not how simple it be made—for as well may the most rude[318] image, and most simply wrought, put us in mind[319] of Christ, and our Lady, and any other saint, as may the most costly and most curious[320] that any painter or carver can devise.

"And verily to say the truth, as for images they be no shadows of the old law, but things therein plainly and clearly forbidden, as well in diverse other places of Scripture as in the texts lately remembered by yourself: *Non facies tibi sculptile* ('Thou shalt carve thee, nor grave[321] thee, none image').[322] And by all the whole psalm *In exitu Israel de Aegypto*[323] is it with great execration and malediction[324] prohibited."

"First," quoth I, "ye may not take those words for such a precise prohibition as should forbid utterly any images to be made; for as I showed you before, they had in the Temple the images of cherubim. But it was prohibited to make such images as the Egyptians and other paynims[325] did—that is to wit,[326] the idols of false gods—for that appeareth in the psalm itself, where he layeth for the cause of the prohibition, *Quoniam omnes dii gentium daemonia; Dominus, autem, caelos fecit* ('For all the gods of the paynims be devils; but our Lord hath made the heavens').[327] Doth it not by these words well appear what images were in that psalm forbidden: that is to wit, the images and idols only of those paynim gods? For else,[328] I pray you tell me what reason[329] were this, if one would say, 'Make none image of Christ, nor of our Lady, nor of any Christian saint in no wise;[330] for all the gods of the paynims be but devils'? Were not this a wise reason well concluded?

"There is also in these prohibitions intended that no man shall worship any image as God. For if he should, then should he fall in the contempt of the precept of God, by which we be commanded to worship only one God, and forbidden to worship any false gods. And therefore where it is written *Non facies tibi sculptile* ('Thou shalt grave thee none image'), it goeth next before, *Non habebis deos alienos* ('Thou shalt have no false gods').[331] And it is also written, *Nolite converti ad idola, neque deos conflatiles faciatis vobis* ('Turn not to idols, nor make not for yourselves any gods of metal cast in a mold').[332] And where it is forbidden to worship any image, there is the word that signifieth the honor and service[333] only pertaining to God. And therefore neither may we do any worship to any image and idol of any false paynim, nor with honor and service done as to God may we neither worship image of any saint, nor yet the saint itself. But I suppose neither Scripture nor natural reason doth forbid that a man may do some reverence to an image—not fixing his final intent in the image, but referring it further to the honor of the person that the image

---

309 scheme, contrivance   310 See Ex 15:1–18.   311 See 2 Sm 6:14–23. 312 kept vigils   313 a hair shirt; Mt 3:4   314 See Mt 6:9–13; Jn 17:1–26. 315 *set at nought:* value as nothing 316 See Lk 4:2.   317 *gay ornaments:*

showy furnishings   318 least skillfully made; roughest   319 remembrance 320 elaborate   321 engrave   322 Ex 20:4   323 "Israel went forth from Egypt," Ps 113(114):1   324 *execration and malediction:* condemnation and curse

325 pagans   326 say   327 Ps 95(96):5 328 otherwise   329 argument   330 way 331 Ex 20:3   332 Lv 19:4. See also Ex 34:17.   333 homage, worship

representeth—since that in such reverence done unto the image, there is none honor withdrawn neither from God nor good man, but both the saint honored in his image, and God in his saint. When a mean[334] man, an ambassador to a great king, hath much honor done him, to whom doth that honor redound—to the ambassador, or to the king?

"When a man at the receipt of his prince's letter putteth off his cap and kisseth it, doth he this reverence to the paper, or to his prince?

"In good faith, to say the truth, these heretics rather trifle than reason in this matter. For where they say that images be but laymen's books, they cannot yet say nay but[335] that they be necessary if they were but so. Howbeit, methinketh that they be good books both for laymen and for the learned, too. For as I somewhat said unto you before, all the words that be either written or spoken, be but images representing the things that the writer or speaker conceiveth in his mind, likewise[336] as the figure of the thing framed with imagination and so conceived in the mind is but an image representing the very thing itself that a man thinketh on. As, for example, if I tell you a tale of my good friend your master, the imagination that I have of him in my mind is not your master himself, but an image that representeth him. And when I name you him, his name is neither himself nor yet the figure of him—which figure is in mine imagination—but only an image representing to you the imagination of my mind. Now if I be too far from you to tell it you, then is the writing not the name itself, but an image representing the name. And yet all these names spoken, and all these words written, be no natural signs or images, but only made by consent and agreement of men to betoken and signify such things, whereas images painted, graven, or carved may be so wellwrought, and so near to the quick[337] and to the truth, that they shall naturally and much more effectually represent the thing than shall the name either spoken or written. For he that never heard the name of your master shall, if ever he saw him, be brought in a right full remembrance of him by his image wellwrought and touched to the quick. And surely saving[338] that men cannot do it, else[339] if it might commodiously be done, there were not in this world so

effectual writing as were to express all things in imagery. And now likewise as a book well-made and well-written better expresseth the matter than doth a book made by a rude[340] man that cannot well tell his tale, and written with an evil hand,[341] so doth an image well workmanly wrought[342] better express the thing than doth a thing rudely made, but if[343] it move a man for some other special cause, as peradventure[344] for some great antiquity, or the great virtue of the workman, or for that God showeth at the place some special assistance of his favor and grace. But now as I began to say, since all names spoken or written be but images, if ye set aught by[345] the name of Jesus spoken or written, why should ye set nought[346] by his image painted or carven, that representeth his holy person to your remembrance, as much and more too, as doth his name written? Nor these two words *Christus crucifixus* do not so lively represent us the remembrance of his bitter Passion as doth a blessed image of the crucifix—neither to layman nor unto a learned. And this perceive these heretics themselves well enough. Nor they speak not against images for any furtherance of devotion, but plainly for[347] a malicious mind, to diminish and quench men's devotions. For they see well enough that there is no man but if he love another, but he delighteth in his image or any thing of his. And these heretics that be so sore[348] against the images of God and his holy saints would be yet right[349] angry with him that would dishonestly[350] handle an image made in remembrance of one of themselves, where the wretches forbear not villainously to handle and cast dirt in despite[351] upon the holy crucifix—an image made in remembrance of our Savior himself—and not only of his most blessed Person, but also of his most bitter Passion.

"Now as touching prayer made unto the saints, and worship done unto them, much marvel is it what cause of malice these heretics have to them. We see it common in the wretched condition of this world, that one man of a pride in himself hath envy at another, or for displeasure done, beareth to some other malice and evil will. But this must needs be a devilish hatred: to hate him whom thou never knewest, which[352] never did thee harm, which, if he could now do thee no good where he is, yet either

---

334 common, average   **335** *say nay but:* deny   **336** just   **337** life-like quality **338** except   **339** otherwise   **340** uneducated   **341** *evil hand:* bad handwriting

342 *well workmanly wrought:* very skillfully made   **343** *but if:* unless **344** perhaps   **345** *set aught by:* place any value on   **346** no value   **347** because of

348 strongly   **349** very   **350** disrespectfully   **351** contempt   **352** who

with his good example gone before thee, or his good doctrine left behind him, doth thee, but if[353] thou be very naught[354] of thyself, great good in this world for thy journey toward heaven. And this must needs be an envy coming of a high devilish pride, and far passing the envy of the devil himself, for he never envied but such as he saw and was conversant with, as when he saw man and the glory of God. But these heretics envy them whom they never saw nor never shall see, but when they shall be sorry and ashamed in themselves of that glorious sight.

"For where they pretend the zeal of God's honor himself—as though God, 'to whom only all honor and glory is to be given,'[355] were dishonored in that some honor is done to his holy saints—they be not so mad nor so childish as they make themselves.[356] For if all honor were so to be given only to God that we should give none to no creature, where were then God's precept of honor to be given to our father and mother; to princes, governors, and rulers here in earth; and, as Saint Paul saith, every man to other?[357]

"And well they wot[358] that the Church worshippeth not saints as God, but as God's good servants; and therefore the honor that is done to them redoundeth principally to the honor of their Master, like[359] as in common custom of people we do reverence sometimes and make great cheer to some men for their master's sake, whom else we would not haply[360] bid once 'Good morrow.'

"And surely if any benefit or alms done to one of Christ's poor folk for his sake be, by his high goodness, reputed and accepted as done unto himself, and that whoso receiveth one of his apostles or disciples receiveth himself,[361] every wise man may well consider that in like wise, whoso doth honor his holy saints for his sake doth honor himself. Except these heretics ween[362] that God were as envious as they be themselves, and that he would be wroth[363] to have any honor done to any other, though it thereby redounded unto himself. Whereof our Savior Christ well declareth the contrary, for he showeth himself so well content that his holy saints shall be partners of his honor that he promiseth his apostles that at the dreadful Doom[364]—when

he shall come in his high majesty—they shall have their honorable seats, and sit with himself upon the judgment of the world.[365]

"Christ also promised that Saint Mary Magdalene should be worshipped through the world, and have here an honorable remembrance for that[366] she bestowed that precious ointment upon his holy head.[367] Which thing, when I consider it, maketh me marvel of the madness of these heretics that bark against the old ancient customs of Christ's Church, mocking the setting up of candles, and with foolish, facetious, and blasphemous mockery demand[368] whether God and his saints lack light, or whether it be night with them, that they cannot see without candle. They might as well ask what good did that ointment to Christ's head. But the heretics grudge at[369] the cost now, as their brother Judas did then,[370] and say it were better spent in alms upon poor folk. And this say many of them which can neither find in their heart to spend upon the one nor the other. And some spend sometimes upon the one for none other intent, but to the end that they may the more boldly rebuke and rail against the other. But let them all by that example of that holy woman, and by these words of our Savior, learn that God delighteth to see the fervent heat of the heart's devotion boil out by the body, and to do him service with all such goods of fortune as God hath given a man.

"What riches devised our Lord God himself in the making and garnishing of the Temple, and in the ornaments of the altar, and the priests' apparel? What was himself the better for all this? What for the beasts that himself commanded to be offered him in sacrifice? What for the sweet odors and frankincense?[371] Why do these heretics more mock at the manner of Christ's Church than they do at the manner of the Jews' synagogue, but if[372] they be better Jews than Christian men?

"If men will say that the money were better spent among poor folk—by whom he more setteth,[373] being the quick[374] temples of the Holy Ghost,[375] made by his own hand, than by the temples of stone, made by the hand of man—this would be percase[376] very true, if there were so little to do it with that we

---

353 *but if:* unless   **354** wicked   **355** See 1 Tm 1:17.   **356** themselves to be **357** another. See Mk 7:10; 1 Pt 2:13–17; Rom 12:10.   **358** know   **359** just **360** perhaps   **361** See Mt 25:34–40,

10:40–42.   **362** suppose   **363** very angry, stirred to wrath   **364** Last Judgment **365** See Mt 19:28.   **366** *for that:* because **367** See Mt 26:13.   **368** ask   **369** *grudge at:* complain about   **370** See Jn 12:4.

371 See Ex 25–29.   **372** *but if:* unless **373** values   **374** living   **375** See 1 Cor 3:16.   **376** perhaps

should be driven of necessity to leave the one undone. But God giveth enough for both, and giveth
diverse men diverse kinds of devotion—and all to
his pleasure. In which, as the apostle Paul saith, let
every man for his part abound and be plenteous in
that kind of virtue that the Spirit of God guideth
him to,[377] and not to be of the foolish mind that
Luther is, which wisheth, in a sermon of his, that he
had in his hand all the pieces of the holy cross, and
saith that if he so had, he would throw them there
as[378] never sun should shine on them. And for what
worshipful[379] reason would the wretch do such villainy to the cross of Christ? Because (as he saith)
that there is so much gold now bestowed about the
garnishing[380] of the pieces of the cross, that there is
none left for poor folk. Is not this a high reason?[381]
As though all the gold that is now bestowed about
the pieces of the holy cross would not have failed to
have been given to poor men if they had not been
bestowed about the garnishing of the cross. And as
though there were nothing lost but that is bestowed
about Christ's cross.

"Take all the gold that is spent about[382] all the
pieces of Christ's cross through Christendom. Albeit[383] many a good Christian prince, and other
godly people, hath honorably garnished many
pieces thereof, yet if all that gold were gathered together, it would appear a poor portion in comparison of the gold that is bestowed upon cups. What[384]
speak we of cups?—in which the gold, albeit that
it be not given to poor men, yet is it saved, and
may be given in alms when men will, which they
never will. How small a portion, ween[385] we, were
the gold about all the pieces of Christ's cross, if it
were compared with the gold that is quite cast away
about the gilding of knives, swords, spurs, arras,[386]
and painted cloths—and (as though these things
could not consume gold fast enough) the gilding
of posts and whole roofs, not only in the palaces
of princes and great prelates, but also many right
mean[387] men's houses! And yet among all these
things could Luther spy no gold that grievously
glittered in his bleared eyes but only about the
Cross of Christ. For that gold, if it were thence[388]
the wise man weeneth it would be straight given

to poor men—and that where he daily seeth that
such as have their purse full of gold give to the poor
not one piece thereof, but if they give aught,[389] they
ransack the bottom, among all the gold, to seek out
here a halfpenny,[390] or in his country, a brass penny,
whereof four make a farthing.[391] Such goodly
causes find they that pretend holiness for the color
of[392] their cloaked heresies."

THE THIRD CHAPTER

*The objections of the messenger made against
praying to saints, worshipping of images, and going
on pilgrimages, with the answer of the author unto
the same. And incidentally is it by the messenger
moved[393] that there should seem no necessity for
Christian folk to resort to any churches, but that all
were one to pray thence or there. And that opinion
by the author answered and confuted.[394]*

At this point your friend, desiring me that whatsoever he should say, I should not reckon it as spoken
of his own opinion, but that he would partly show
me what he had heard some others say therein, to
the end that he might the better answer them with
that[395] he should hear of me. This protestation and
prefation[396] made, he said that albeit no good man
would agree that it were well done to do unto saints
or their images despite[397] or dishonor, yet to go in
pilgrimages to them, or to pray to them, not only
seemed in vain (considering that all they, if they
can anything do, can yet do no more for us among
them all than Christ can himself alone, that can do
all; nor be not so ready at our hand to hear us—if
they hear us at all—as Christ, that is everywhere;
nor bear us half the love and longing to help us that
doth our Savior, that died for us; whom, as Saint
Paul saith, we have for advocate afore the Father),[398]
but, over this, it seemeth to smell of idolatry when
we go on pilgrimage to this place and that place,
as though God were not like[399] strong, or not like
present, in every place. But as the devils were of old,
under the false name of "gods," present and assistant[400] in the idols and mammets[401] of the pagans,
so would we make it seem that God and his saints

---

377 See Rom 12:6–8; 2 Cor 9:6–15.
378 where   **379** honorable; pious
380 adorning   **381** argument   **382** on
383 Although   **384** Why   **385** think
386 tapestries   **387** *right mean:* quite

ordinary   **388** not there   **389** anything
390 *here a halfpenny:* In England, half-
pennies were then made of silver.   **391** a
quarter of a penny   **392** *for the color of:* as
a pretext for   **393** proposed   **394** refuted

395 what   **396** introductory statement
397 contempt   **398** See 1 Jn 2:1.   **399** as
400 ready to help   **401** images of false
gods

stood in this place and that place, bound to this post and that post, cut out and carved in images. For when we reckon ourselves to be better heard with our Lord in Kent than at Cambridge, at the north door of Paul's[402] than at the south door, at one image of our Lady than at another, is it not an evident token—and in manner[403] a plain proof—that we put our trust and confidence in the image itself, and not in God or our Lady, which[404] is as good in the one place as in the other, and the one image no more like her than the other, nor cause why she should favor the one before the other. But we blind people, instead of God and his holy saints themselves, cast our affections to the images themselves, and thereto make our prayers, thereto make our offerings, and ween these images were the very saints themselves, of whom our help and health should grow, putting our full trust in this place and that place, as necromancers put their trust in their circles, within which they think themselves sure against all the devils in hell, and ween if they were one inch without, that then the devil would pull them in pieces, but as for the circle he dare not, for his ears, once put over his nose.

"And men reckon that the clergy is glad to favor these ways, and to nourish this superstition under the name and color[405] of devotion, to the peril of the people's souls, for the lucre and temporal advantage that themselves receive of the offerings."

When I had heard him say what him liked, I demanded[406] if he minded ever to be priest, whereunto he answered: "Nay, verily;[407] for methinketh," quoth he, "that there be priests too many already but if[408] they were better. And therefore when God shall send time I purpose," he said, "to marry."

"Well," said I, "then since I am already married twice, and therefore never can be priest, and ye be so set in mind of marriage that ye never will be priest, we two be not the most meetly[409] to ponder what might be said in this matter for the priests' part.

"Howbeit,[410] when I consider it, methinketh surely that if the thing were such as ye say—so far from all frame[411] of right religion, and so perilous to men's souls—I cannot perceive why that the clergy would, for the gain they get thereby, suffer such abusion[412] to continue. For first, if it were true that

no pilgrimage ought to be used, none image offered unto, nor worship done, nor prayer made unto any saint, then if none of all these things had ever been in ure,[413] or now were all undone—if that were the right way, as I wot[414] well it were wrong—then were it to me little question but Christian people, being in the true faith, and in the right way to Godward, would thereby nothing slake[415] their good minds toward the ministers of his Church, but their devotion should toward them more and more increase. So that if they now get by this way one penny, they should (if this be wrong and the other right) not fail, instead of a penny now, then to receive a groat.[416] And so should no lucre give them cause to favor this way and[417] it be wrong, while they could not fail to win more by the right.

"Moreover look me through Christendom, and I suppose ye shall find the fruit of those offerings a right[418] small part of the living of the clergy. And such as, though some few places would be glad to retain, yet the whole body might without any notable loss easily forbear.

"Let us consider our own country here, and we shall find of these pilgrimages far the most part in the hands of such religious persons, or such poor parishes, as bear no great rule in the convocations.[419] And besides this ye shall not find, I suppose, that any bishop in England hath the profit of one groat of any such offering within his diocese. Now standeth then the continuance or the breaking of this manner and custom, specially in them, which take no profit thereby. Which,[420] if they believed it to be (such as ye call it) superstitious and wicked, would never suffer it[421] continue to the perishing of men's souls, whereby themselves should destroy their own souls, and neither in body nor goods take any commodity.[422] And over this we see that the bishops and prelates themselves visit those holy places and pilgrimages with as large offerings, and as great cost in coming and going, as other people do, so that they not only take no temporal advantage thereof, but also bestow of their own therein.

"And surely I believe this devotion so planted by God's own hand in the hearts of the whole Church—that is to wit,[423] not the clergy only, but the whole congregation of all Christian people—that if the

---

402 *Paul's:* Old St. Paul's Cathedral
403 *in manner:* as it were   **404** who
405 guise   **406** asked (him)   **407** truly
408 *but if:* unless   **409** appropriate

410 However   **411** established order
412 wrongdoing   **413** customary use
414 know   **415** *nothing slake:* not at all diminish   **416** fourpence   **417** if

418 very   **419** provincial synods. England had two: Canterbury and York.
420 Who   **421** *suffer it:* allow it to
422 benefit   **423** say

spiritualty[424] were of the mind to leave it, yet would not the temporalty[425] suffer it.

"Nor if it so were that pilgrimages hanged only upon the covetise[426] of evil priests—for evil must they be that would for covetise help the people forward to idolatry—then would not good priests and good bishops have used them themselves. But I am very sure that many a holy bishop, and therewith excellently well-learned in Scripture and the law of God, have had high devotion thereto.

"For whereas ye say men reckon that it smelleth of idolatry to visit this place and that place—as though that God were more mighty, or more present in one place than in another, or that God or his saints had bounden themselves to stand at this image or that image, and that by men's demeanor[427] thereby should appear that the pilgrims put their trust in the place or the image itself, taking that for very God, or for the very saint, of whom they seek for help, and so fare like necromancers that put their trust in their circle—surely, sir, holy Saint Augustine, in an epistle of his (which he wrote to the clergy and the people), taketh pilgrimages for a more earnest and a far more godly thing. And saith that though the cause be to us unknown why God doth in some place miracles, and in some place none, yet is it no doubt but he so doth. And therein had that good holy doctor so great confidence, that as he saith himself, he sent two of his priests in pilgrimage, for the trial of the truth of a great matter in contention and debate between them, out of Hippo in Africa unto Saint Stephen's Church in Milan—where many miracles were wont to be showed—to the end that God might there, by some means, cause the truth to be declared and made open by his power, which by no means known to man he could well find out.[428]

"Nor they that go on pilgrimage do nothing like to those necromancers to whom ye resemble[429] them, that put their confidence in the roundel[430] and circle on the ground, for a special belief that they have in the compass of that ground, by reason of foolish characts[431] and figures about it, with invocations of evil spirits and familiarity with devils, being enemies to God, and the craft and ways of all that work by God himself prohibited and forbidden,

and that upon the pain of death.[432] What likeness hath that unto the going of good men unto holy places, not by enchantment dedicated to the devil, but by God's holy ordinance, with his holy words consecrated unto himself? Which two things if ye would resemble together, so might ye blaspheme and have in derision all the devout rites and ceremonies of the Church, both in the divine service (as incensing, hallowing[433] of the fire, of the font, of the paschal lamb) and over that the exorcisms, benedictions, and holy strange[434] gestures used in consecration or ministration of the blessed sacraments, all which holy things—great part whereof was from hand to hand left in the Church from the time of Christ's apostles, and by them left unto us, as it was by God taught unto them—men might now, by that means, follily[435] misliken unto the superstitious demeanor and fond[436] fashion of jugglery.[437] Nor the flock of Christ is not so foolish as those heretics bear them in hand:[438] that whereas there is no dog so mad but he knoweth a very cony[439] from a cony carved and painted, Christian people that have reason in their heads, and thereto[440] the light of faith in their souls, should ween[441] that the images of our Lady were our Lady herself. Nay they be not, I trust, so mad, but they do reverence to the image for the honor of the person whom it representeth, as every man delighteth in the image and remembrance of his friend. And albeit that[442] every good Christian man hath a remembrance of Christ's Passion in his mind, and conceiveth by devout meditation a form and fashion thereof in his heart, yet is there no man (I ween) so good, nor so well-learned, nor in meditation so well-accustomed, but that he findeth himself more moved to pity and compassion upon the beholding of the holy crucifix than when he lacketh it. And if there be any that for the maintenance of his opinion will peradventure[443] say that he findeth it otherwise in himself, he should give me cause to fear that he hath, of Christ's Passion, neither the one way nor the other but a very faint feeling, since that the holy fathers before us did, and all devout people about us do, find and feel in themselves the contrary.

"Now for the reason[444] that you allege," quoth I, "where ye say that in resorting to this place and that place, this image and that image, we seem to reckon

424 clergy   **425** laity   **426** greed
427 behavior   **428** See *PL* 33: 267–72.
429 liken   **430** ring; circle   **431** magical symbols   **432** See Jer 27:9; Ex 22:18.

433 blessing   **434** unfamiliar, unusual
435 foolishly   **436** foolish   **437** magic
438 *bear them in hand:* make them out to be   **439** rabbit   **440** in addition to that

441 think   **442** *albeit that:* although
443 perhaps   **444** argument

as though God were not in every place like mighty, or not like present, this reason proceedeth no more against pilgrimages than against all the churches in Christendom. For God is as mighty in the stable as in the temple. And as he is not comprehensible nor circumscribed nowhere, so is he present everywhere. But this letteth[445] not heaven, be it a corporal thing or not, to be the place of a special manner and kind of his presence, in which it liketh him to show his glorious majesty to his blessed heavenly company, which he showeth not unto damned wretches in hell; and yet is he never thence.[446] So liked it his goodness to go with his chosen people through the desert in the cloud by day, and the pillar of fire by night;[447] yet was he not bounden, as ye resemble[448] it, like the damned spirits to the old idols of the paynims.[449]

"It liked him also to choose the Ark that was carried with his people; at[450] which Ark specially, by miracle, he diverse times declared[451] his especial assistance, the Ark being translated[452] from place to place.[453]

"Was it not also his pleasure to be specially present in his temple of Jerusalem, till he suffered[454] it to be destroyed for their sin? And instead of that one place of prayer (to which he would[455] before that all his people should come), he hath vouchsafed to spread himself abroad into many temples, and in more acceptable wise to be worshipped in many temples throughout his Christian flock."

Here said your friend, that the temple of Christ is (as Saint Paul saith) man's heart,[456] and that God is not included[457] nor shut in any place. And so himself said to the woman of Samaria that very worshippers should worship in spirit, and in truth, not in the hill[458] or in Jerusalem, or any other temple of stone.[459]

Whereunto I showed him that I would well agree that no temple of stone was unto God so pleasant as the temple of man's heart, but yet that nothing letteth[460] or withstandeth but that God will[461] that his Christian people have in sundry places, sundry temples and churches, to which they should, besides

their private prayers, assemble solemnly, and resort in company to worship him together, such as dwell so near together that they may conveniently resort to one place.

"For albeit[462] our Savior said," quoth I, "unto the woman of whom ye spoke, that the time should come in which they should neither worship God in that hill of Gerizim nor in Jerusalem neither—which places were after destroyed and desolate,[463] and the pagan manner of worshipping of the one, and the Jewish manner of worshipping in the other, turned both into the manner of worshipping of Christian faith and religion—yet said he not to her that they should never after worship God in none other temple. But he said that the time should come, and then was comen already, when the very true worshippers should worship God in spirit and truth.[464] And that, as God is a spiritual substance, so looked he for worshippers that should in such wise worship him. In which words our Savior reproved all false worship as was used after[465] paganism in that hill in Samaria, and all such worship as was done in any place with opinion that God might not be worshipped elsewhere. Those that so believe, they be such as bind God to a place, which[466] our Lord reproveth, showing that God may in heart truly and spiritually be worshipped everywhere. But this excludeth not that besides that, he will be worshipped in his holy temple, no more than when he gave counsel that for avoiding of vainglory, a man shall not stand and pray in the street to gather worldly praise, but rather secretly pray in his chamber.[467] This counsel forbade not the Jews, to whom he gave it, that they should never after come into the Temple and pray.

"And surely albeit that some good man here and there, one among ten thousand—as Saint Paul and Saint Anthony,[468] and a few such other like—do live all heavenly, far out of all fleshly company, as far from all occasion of worldly wretchedness as from the common temple or parish church; yet if churches and congregations of Christian people resorting together to God's service were once

445 prevents   **446** not there   **447** See Ps 77(78):14; Ex 13:21–22; Nm 14:14; Dt 1:33; Neh 9:12, 19.   **448** interpret   **449** pagans   **450** about   **451** made manifest   **452** transported   **453** See Jo 3:14–17; 1 Kgs (1 Sm) 4–6.   **454** allowed   **455** wanted   **456** See 1 Cor 3:16.

457 enclosed   **458** *in the hill:* on the mountain (Mt. Gerizim)   **459** See Jn 4:21, 23.   **460** prevents   **461** wants   **462** although   **463** *which…desolate:* Gerizim was destroyed by the Jews in AD 65; the Temple in Jerusalem was destroyed by the Romans in AD 79.   **464** See

Jn 4:24.   **465** *used after:* practiced in the manner of   **466** whom   **467** See Mt 6:5–6.   **468** *Saint Paul and Saint Anthony:* St. Paul the Hermit (*ca.* 228–343) and St. Anthony of the Desert (*ca.* 251–356), ascetics of Egypt

abolished and put away, we were like[469] to have few good temples of God in men's souls, but all would within a while wear away clean and clearly[470] fall to naught.[471] And this prove we by experience:
5 that those which be the best temples of God in their souls, they most use[472] to come to the temple of stone. And those that least come, there be well known for very ribalds and unthrifts,[473] and openly perceived for temples of the devil. And
10 this not in our days only, but so hath been from Christ's days hither.[474] I trow[475] no man doubteth but that Christ's apostles were holy temples of God in their souls, and as well understood the words of their Master, spoken to the woman of Samaria, as
15 the thing which their Master after told them himself, or else how could some of them have written that communication, which none of them heard, as appeareth by the Gospel?[476] But they—not in their Master's days only, but also after his resur-
20 rection and after that they had received the Holy Ghost, and were by him instructed of every truth belonging to the necessity of their salvation[477]— were not content only to pray secretly[478] by themselves in their chambers, but also resorted to the
25 Temple to make their prayers. And in that place as a place pleasant to God did they pray "in spirit and in truth,"[479] as well appeareth in the book of Saint Luke written of the acts of Christ's holy apostles.[480] So that no doubt is there but that yet unto this day,
30 and so forth to the world's end, it is and shall be pleasant unto God that his chosen people pray to him and call upon him in temple and church, whereof himself witnesseth with the prophet: *Domus mea domus orationis vocabitur* ('My house shall
35 be called a house of prayer').[481]

"Now maketh your reason,[482] as I said, no more against pilgrimages than against every church. For as God is not bounden to the place, nor our confidence bounden to the place, but unto God (though
40 we reckon our prayer more pleasant to God in the church than without, because his high goodness accepteth it so), in like wise do not we reckon our Lord bounden to the place or image where the pilgrimage is, though we worship God there because
45 himself liketh so to have it."

The author declareth in the comprobation[483] of pilgrimages that it is the pleasure of God to be specially sought and worshipped in some one place before another. And albeit that[484] we cannot attain 50 *to the knowledge of the cause why God doth so, yet the author proveth by great authority that God by miracle testifieth it is so.*

With this, your friend asked me what reason were there that God would set more by[485] one place than 55 by another, or how know we that he so doth, namely if the one be a church as well as the other?

Whereunto I answered that why God would do it, I could make him no answer, no more than Saint Augustine saith that he could. I was never so near of 60 his counsel, nor dare not be so bold to ask him. But that he so doth indeed that I am sure enough, yet not for that[486] he setteth more by that place for the soil and pavement of that place, but that his pleasure in some place is to show more his assistance, 65 and to be more specially sought unto, than in some other.

Then he asked me whereby was I so sure of that, whereupon I demanded[487] him that if it so were that, the thing standing in debate and question, it 70 would like our Lord to show a miracle for the proof of the one part, "Would ye not," quoth I, "reckon then the question were decided, and the doubt assoiled,[488] and that part sufficiently proved?"

"Yes, marry,"[489] quoth he, "that would I." 75

"Well," quoth I, "then is this matter out of doubt long ago; for God hath proved my part in diverse pilgrimages by the working of many more than a thousand miracles, one time and other. In the Gospel of John, the fifth chapter, where we read that 80 the angel moved the water, and whoso next went in was cured of his disease[490]—was it not a sufficient proof that God would they should come thither for their health, albeit no man can tell why he sent the angel rather thither, and there did his miracles, than 85 in another water? But whensoever our Lord hath in any place wrought a miracle—although he nothing do it for the place, but for the honor of that saint whom he will have honored in that place; or for the

---

469 likely **470** *clean and clearly:* entirely and completely **471** wickedness **472** are accustomed **473** *ribalds and unthrifts:* good-for-nothings and spendthrifts **474** up until now **475** trust;

think **476** See Jn 4:8. **477** See Jn 16:13. **478** privately **479** Jn 4:23 **480** See Acts 2:46–47. **481** Is 56:7; Mt 21:13; Mk 11:17 **482** argument **483** argument in favor of something, using evidence

484 *albeit that:* although **485** *set more by:* value more **486** *for that:* because **487** asked **488** resolved **489** indeed **490** See Jn 5:4.

faith that he findeth with some that prayeth in that place; or for the increase of faith, which he findeth falling and decayed in that place, needing the show of some miracles for the reviving—whatsoever the cause be, yet I think the affection[491] is to be commended of men and women that with good devotion run thither, where they see or hear that our Lord showeth a demonstration of his special assistance. And when he showeth many in one place, it is a good token that he would be sought upon and worshipped there. Many Jews were there that came to Jerusalem to see the miracle that Christ had wrought upon Lazarus, as the Gospel rehearseth.[492] And surely we were worse than Jews if we would be so negligent that where God worketh miracles we list[493] not once go move our foot thitherward. We marvel much that God showeth no more miracles nowadays, when it is much more marvel that he doth vouchsafe[494] to show any at all among such unkind[495] slothful deadly people, as list not once lift up their heads to look thereon, or that our incredulity can suffer[496] him nowadays to work any."[497]

THE FIFTH CHAPTER
Because pilgrimages be, among other proofs, testified by miracles, the messenger doth make objection against those miracles, partly lest they be feigned and untrue, partly lest they be done by the devil if they be done at all.

Then said your friend, "Well I perceive then the force and effect of all the proof standeth all in miracles. Which I will agree to be a strong proof, if I saw them done, and were sure that God or good saints did them. But first since that men may, and haply[498] do, of miracles make many a lie, we must not prove this matter by the miracles, but if[499] we first prove that the miracles were true. And over this, if they were done indeed, yet, since the angel of darkness may transform and transfigure himself into an angel of light,[500] how shall we know whether the miracle were done by God, to the increase of Christian devotion, or done by the craft of the devil, to the advancement of misbelief and idolatry, in setting men's hearts upon stocks and stones[501] instead of saints—or upon saints themselves that are but creatures, instead of God himself?"

I answered him that the force of my tale was not the miracles, but the thing that I hold stronger than any miracles, which, as I said in the beginning, I reckon so sure and fast,[502] and therewith so plain and evident unto every Christian man, that it needeth none other proof. And that thing is, as I said afore, the faith of Christ's Church, by the common consent whereof these matters be decided and well known: that the worship of saints and images been[503] allowed, approbated,[504] and accustomed for good, Christian, and meritorious virtues, and the contrary opinion not only reproved by many holy doctors,[505] but also condemned for heresies by sundry general councils.

"And this in the beginning I told you," quoth I, "was and should be the force and strength of my tale; albeit[506] of truth I said unto you besides that methought that the miracles wrought by God were sufficient proof and authority therefor,[507] although[508] there were none other, which thing since ye seem to impugn,[509] I shall as I can make you answer thereunto."

"Nay, sir," said he, "I pray you take me not so, as though that I did impugn it, but as I showed you before, I rehearsed[510] you what I have heard some others say."

"In good time," quoth I. "Then because they be not here, I pray you defend and bear out[511] their part, with all that ye have heard them say; and set thereto also all that ever your own mind giveth you that they may more hereafter say, lest you return not fully furnished[512] for your purpose."

THE SIXTH CHAPTER
Because the messenger thinketh that he may well mistrust and deny the miracles because reason and nature tell him that they cannot be done, therefore first the author showeth what unreasonableness would ensue if folk would stand so stiff against all credence to be given to any such thing as reason and nature should seem to gainsay.[513]

---

491 disposition; attitude   **492** tells. See Jn 11:45.   **493** wish to   **494** readily agree   **495** ungrateful   **496** allow   **497** See Mt 13:58.   **498** perhaps   **499** *but if:* unless   **500** See 2 Cor 11:14–15.   **501** *stocks and stones:* statues, idols from blocks of wood and stone   **502** secure   **503** have been   **504** officially approved   **505** theologians   **506** although   **507** for it   **508** even if   **509** dispute   **510** told   **511** *bear out:* be responsible for   **512** equipped   **513** contradict

"And first where ye say—"

"Nay," quoth he, "where 'they' say."

"Well," quoth I, "so be it: where 'they' say. For here ever my tongue trippeth. But now therefore, first, where they say that they never saw any of these miracles themselves, and therefore the miracles be no proof to them—which, while they never saw them, are not bounden to believe them, they seem either very negligent if they nothing inquire when they mistrust and doubt of the truth in such a weighty matter, or if they have diligently made ensearch,[514] then must it needs be that they have heard of so many, told and rehearsed by the mouths and the writing of so good and credible persons that they seem unreasonably suspicious if they think altogether lies that so many true men, or men like to be true, so faithfully do report. If these men were judges, few matters would take end at their hand—or at the least the plaintiff should have evil speed[515]—if they would believe nothing but that[516] were proved, nor reckon nothing proved but that they see themselves.

"Thus may every man reckon himself unsure of his own father, if he believe no man, or because all the proof thereof standeth but upon one woman, and that upon her which, though she can tell best, yet if it be wrong hath greatest cause to lie. Let the knowledge of the father alone, therefore, among our wives' mysteries. And let us see, if we believe nothing but that we see ourselves, who can reckon himself sure of his own mother; for possible it were that he were changed[517] in the cradle, and a rich man's nurse bring home her own child for her master's, and keep her master's for her own, to make her own a gentleman good cheap.[518] And this were no great mastery[519] while the mother hath of her own child no earmark."

"Sir," quoth your friend, "if I should answer them thus, and by these examples prove them that they were of reason bounden to believe such miracles as were reported, because many credible men tell them—forasmuch as else[520] we should believe nothing but that we see ourselves, and then were all the world full of confusion, nor no judgment could be given but upon things done in the judge's sight—I should, I fear me, very feebly satisfy them. For they would soon say that the examples be nothing like the matter. But as it is reason that I should believe honest men in all such things as may be true, and wherein I see no cause why they should lie, so were it against all reason to believe men—be they never so many, seem they never so credible—whereas reason and nature (of which twain[521] every one is alone more credible than they all) showeth me plainly that their tale is untrue, as it must needs, if the matter be impossible, as it is in all these miracles. And in such case, though I can perceive no profit that they can receive thereby, yet when I well see that it could not be true, I must well see that it was not true. And thereby must I needs know that if they can take no profit by lying, they lie not for any covetise,[522] but even only for their special pleasure."

"Forsooth,"[523] quoth I, "this is right merrily answered. And to say the truth, as far as we be yet gone in the matter of these miracles, not much amiss, nor very far from the point. But since this thing is much material,[524] as whereupon many great things do depend, we shall not so shortly shake it off, but we shall come one step or twain nearer to the matter. And first I will say to them that it were hard for them, and not very sure,[525] to believe that every man lieth which telleth them a tale for true that reason and nature seemeth to show them to be false and impossible. For in this wise[526] shall they in many things err and clearly deceive themselves, and sometimes while they make themselves sure of the wrong side if they would with wagers contend and strive therein, they should, upon the boldness of[527] nature and reason, lose all that ever they were able to lay[528] thereon. If there were a man of India[529] that never came out of his country, nor never had seen any white man or woman in his life, and since he seeth innumerable people black, he might ween[530] that it were against the nature of man to be white. Now if he shall—because nature seemeth to show him so—believe therefore that all the world lied if they would say the contrary, who were in the wrong: he that believeth his reason and nature, or they that against his persuasion of reason and nature shall tell him as it is of truth?"

Your friend answered that reason and nature told not the man of India that all men should be black, but he believed so against reason and against nature; for he had nothing to lead him to it but because himself saw no white, which was no reason.

And he might by nature perceive, if he had learning, that the heat maketh his country black. And that of like reason, the cold of other countries must make the people white.

"Well," quoth I, "and yet he cometh to his persuasion by a syllogism and reasoning almost as formal as is the argument, by which ye prove the kind of man[531] reasonable, whereof what other collection[532] have you that brought you first to perceive it, than that this man is reasonable, and this man, and this man, and this man, and so forth, all whom ye see? By example whereof, by them whom ye know, presuming thereby no man to be otherwise, ye conclude that every man is reasonable. And he thinketh himself surer[533] in his argument than he thinketh you in yours. For he saw never other but black people, whereas ye see many men fools. As for that[534] he heareth of others that there be white men elsewhere, this serveth nothing for your purpose if ye believe no witness against the thing that your reason and experience showeth you. And whereas ye say, if the man of India had learning he should perceive that it is not against nature, but rather consonant with nature that some other men should in other countries be white, though all his countrymen be black — so peradventure[535] those whose part[536] ye do sustain, if they had some learning that they lack, should well perceive that of[537] reason they should give credence to credible persons, reporting them things that seem far against reason because they be far above reason, whereof we may peradventure have more perceiving in our communication hereafter, ere[538] ever we finish that[539] we have in hand. But in the meanwhile, to show you further what necessity there is to believe other men in things not only unknown, but also seeming impossible: the man of India that we speak of can by no learning know the course of the sun, whereby he should perceive the cause of his blackness, but if[540] it be by astronomy, which cunning[541] who can learn that nothing will believe that seemeth to himself impossible? Or who would not ween[542] it impossible but if experience had proved it that the whole earth hangeth in the air, and men walk foot against foot, and ships

sail bottom against bottom — a thing so strange, and seeming so far against nature and reason, that Lactantius, a man right wise and well-learned, in his work which he writeth, *De divinis institutionibus*, reckoneth it for impossible, and letteth[543] not to laugh at the philosophers for affirming of that point,[544] which is yet now founden true by experience of them that have in less than two years sailed the world roundabout.[545] Who would ween it possible that glass were made of fern roots?[546] Now if those that ween it impossible by reason, and never saw it done, believe no man that tell it them, albeit that[547] it be no peril to their soul, yet so much have they knowledge the less, and unreasonably stand in their error through the mistrusting of the truth.

"It is not yet fifty years ago since the first man, as far as men have heard, came to London that ever parted the gilt from the silver, consuming shortly[548] the silver into dust with a very fair water.[549] In so far-forth[550] that when the finers[551] and goldsmiths of London heard first thereof, they nothing wondered thereof, but laughed thereat as at an impossible lie, in which persuasions, if they had continued still, they had yet at this day lacked all that cunning.

"Yet will I not say nay but[552] that a man may be too light in belief,[553] and be by such examples brought into belief too far, as a good fellow and friend of mine late,[554] in talking of this matter of marvels and miracles, intending merrily to make me believe for a truth a thing that could never be, first brought in[555] what a force the fire hath that will make two pieces of iron able to be joined and cleave together, and with the help of the hammer be made both one, which no hammering could do without the fire; which thing, because I daily see, I assented. Then said he further, that yet was more marvel that the fire shall make iron to run as silver or lead doth, and make it take a print.[556] Which thing I told him I had never seen, but because he said he had seen it, I thought it to be true. Soon after this, he would have me to believe that he had seen a piece of silver — of two or three inches about, and in length less than a foot — drawn by man's hand through strait[557] holes made in an[558] iron, till it was brought in thickness

---

531 *the kind of man:* mankind   **532** line of reasoning   **533** more certain   **534** the fact that   **535** perhaps   **536** side of the argument   **537** from   **538** before   **539** what   **540** *but if:* unless   **541** science   **542** think   **543** hesitates   **544** See *Divine Institutes* 3.24 of Lactantius (ca.

250–325).   **545** Magellan's famous voyage departed Spain in September 1519 and returned in September 1522.   **546** In Venice at this time, the alkali necessary for glass manufacturing was derived from native ferns.   **547** *albeit that:* although   **548** *consuming shortly:* reducing quickly

549 *fair water:* pure liquid (nitric acid)   **550** *In so far-forth:* This was so (unreasonable)   **551** refiners   **552** *say not but:* deny   **553** *light in belief:* credulous   **554** lately, recently   **555** up   **556** *make…print:* allow it to be cast in a mold   **557** narrow   **558** a piece of

not half an inch about, and in length drawn out I cannot tell how many yards. And when I heard him say that he saw this himself, then I wist[559] well he was merrily disposed."

5 "Marry,[560] sir," quoth your friend, "it was high time to give him over,[561] when he came to that!"

"Well," said I, "what if I should tell you now that I had seen the same?"

"By my faith," quoth he merrily, "I would believe 10 it at leisure,[562] when I had seen the same; and in the meanwhile, I could not let[563] you to say your pleasure in your own house, but I would think that ye were disposed merrily to make me a fool."

"Well," said I, "what if there would—besides 15 me—ten or twenty good honest men tell you the same tale, and that they had all seen the thing done themselves?"

"In faith," quoth he, "since I am sent hither to believe you, I would in that point believe yourself 20 alone, as well as them all."

"Well," quoth I, "ye mean ye would believe us all alike. But what would you then say if one or twain[564] of them would say more?"

"Marry," quoth he, "then would I believe them 25 less."

"What if they would," quoth I, "show you that they have seen that the piece of silver was overgilt,[565] and, the same piece being still drawn through the holes, the gilt not rubbed off, but still go forth in 30 length with the silver, so that all the length of many yards was gilded of the gilding of the first piece not a foot long?"

"Surely, sir," quoth he, "those twain that would tell me so much more, I would say were not so cun-35 ning[566] in the maintenance of a lie as was the pilgrim's companion, which,[567] when his fellow had told at York that he had seen of late at London a bird that covered all Paul's Churchyard[568] with his wings, coming to the same place on the morrow, said that 40 he saw not that bird (but he heard much speech thereof), but he saw in Paul's Churchyard an egg so great that ten men could scant move it with levers. This fellow could help it forth[569] with a proper sideway.[570] But he were no proper underpropper of a lie

that would diminish his credence with affirming all 45 the first[571] and setting a louder[572] lie thereto."

"Well," said I, "then I have espied[573] if ten should tell you so ye would not believe them."

"No," quoth he, "not if twenty should."

"What if a hundred would," quoth I, "that 50 seemed good and credible?"

"If they were," quoth he, "ten thousand, they were worn[574] out of credence with me when they should tell me that they saw the thing that myself knoweth by nature and reason impossible. For when I know 55 it could not be done, I know well that they lie all—be they never so many—that say they saw it done."

"Well," quoth I, "since I see well ye would not in this point believe a whole town, ye have put me to silence, that I dare not now be bold to tell you that 60 I have seen it myself. But surely if witnesses would have served me, I ween[575] I might have brought you a great many good men that would say, and swear too, that they have seen it themselves. But now shall I provide me—tomorrow, peradventure[576]—a cou-65 ple of witnesses, of whom I wot well[577] ye will mistrust neither nother."[578]

"Who be they?" quoth he. "For it were hard to find whom[579] I could better trust than yourself, whom, whatsoever I have merrily said, I could not in 70 good faith but believe, in that[580] you should tell me earnestly upon your own knowledge. But ye use,[581] my master saith, to look so sadly[582] when ye mean merrily,[583] that many times men doubt whether ye speak in sport, when ye mean good earnest." 75

"In good faith," quoth I, "I mean good earnest now; and yet, as well as ye dare trust me, I shall as I said—if ye will go with me—provide a couple of witnesses of whom ye will believe any one better than twain[584] of me; for they be your near friends, 80 and ye have been better acquainted with them, and such as, I dare say for them, be not often wont to lie."

"Who be they," quoth he, "I pray you?"

"Marry," quoth I, "your own two eyes. For I shall, if you will, bring you where ye shall see it, no further 85 hence than even here in London. And as for iron and latten[585] to be so drawn in length, ye shall see it done in twenty shops almost in one street."

---

559 knew   560 Indeed   561 *give him over:* be done with him   562 *at leisure:* after a while   563 prevent   564 two   565 covered with gilding   566 clever; knowledgeable   567 who   568 *Paul's Churchyard:* the churchyard of Old

St. Paul's Cathedral   569 along   570 *proper sideway:* apt change of judgment   571 i.e., first lie   572 more flagrant   573 discerned that   574 *were worn:* would have run   575 think   576 perhaps   577 know   578 *neither nother:* neither

the one nor the other   579 anyone whom   580 that which   581 are accustomed   582 serious   583 jokingly   584 two   585 a metal similar to brass

"Marry, sir," quoth he, "these witnesses indeed will not lie. As the poor man said by the priest—if I may be so homely to tell you a merry tale by the way?"

"A merry tale," quoth I, "cometh never amiss to me."

"The poor man," quoth he, "had found the priest over-familiar with his wife; and because he spoke it abroad[586] and could not prove it, the priest sued him before the bishop's official[587] for defamation, where the poor man, upon pain of cursing,[588] was commanded that in his parish church, he should upon the Sunday, at High Mass time, stand up and say, 'Mouth, thou liest!' Whereupon, for fulfilling of his penance, up was the poor soul set in a pew, that the people might wonder on[589] him, and hear what he said. And there, all aloud (when he had rehearsed[590] what he had reported by the priest) then he set his hands on his mouth, and said, 'Mouth, mouth, thou liest!' And by and by[591] thereupon, he set his hand upon both his eyes and said, 'But eyes, eyes,' quoth he, 'by the Mass, ye lie not a whit!' And so, sir, indeed, and[592] ye bring me those witnesses, they will not lie a whit.

"Howbeit, sir, and though[593] this be true—as in good faith I believe and am sure that it is—yet am I never the more bounden by reason to believe them that would tell me a miracle. For though this thing be incredible to him that heareth it, and strange and marvelous to him that seeth it, yet is it a thing that may be done. But he that telleth me a miracle, telleth me a thing that cannot be done."

"I showed you," quoth I, "this example to put you in mind that in being overhard of belief of things that by reason and nature seem and appear impossible, where they be reported by credible witnesses having no cause to lie, there is as much peril of error as where men be too light of credence.[594] And thus much have I proved you onward:[595] that if ye believe no man in such things as may not be, then must it follow that ye ought to believe no man in many things that may be; for all is one[596] to you, whether they may be or may not be, if it seem to you that they may not be. And of truth ye cannot tell whether they may be or may not be, except[597] they be

two such things as imply contradiction, as one self[598] thing in one self part to be both white and black at once. For else,[599] many things shall seem to you such as all reason will resist, and nature will in no wise[600] admit. And yet they shall be done well enough, and be in some other place in common use and custom. But now, because all your shift[601] standeth in this— that of a miracle told you, ye may with reason believe that all men lie, because reason and nature, being more to be believed than all they, telleth you that they say wrong, in that the thing reported for a miracle cannot be done—I have showed you that nature and reason doth show you that many things may not be done which yet indeed be done, so far-forth[602] that when ye see them done, ye may right well account them as miracles for anything that reason or nature can show you by what natural order and cause it could be done, but that ye shall still see reason stand quite against it, as in the drawing of the silver or iron."

THE SEVENTH CHAPTER
The author showeth that neither nature nor reason do deny the miracles to be true, nor do not gainsay[603] but that they may be well and easily done.

"Sir," saith he, "yet hit we not the point, for albeit that[604] many things be well done, and by nature, in which neither my wit, nor haply[605] no man's else, can attain so near to nature's counsel that we can therein perceive her craft—but like as some rude[606] people muse upon a clock that hath the spring (which is the cause of his[607] moving) secretly conveyed and closed[608] in the barrel,[609] so marvel we and wonder on her[610] work—yet always all those things differ and be unlike to miracles. In that yourself will agree with me: that when I believe that reason and nature teacheth me surely that miracles be things that cannot be done, I am not in this deceived, though I may be in such other things deceived as seem impossible and yet may be done. And therefore as concerning miracles—in which yourself will agree that I am not (by any mistaking of reason and nature)

---

586 in public **587** *the bishop's official:* i.e., the diocesan judge **588** excommunication **589** about **590** repeated **591** *by and by:* immediately **592** if **593** *and though:* even if **594** *be too light of credence:* believe too readily **595** beyond that **596** the same **597** unless **598** same **599** otherwise **600** *in no wise:* by no means **601** contrived argument **602** *so far-forth:* to such an extent **603** deny; contradict **604** *albeit that:* although **605** perhaps **606** uneducated **607** the clock's **608** enclosed **609** cylindrical case **610** Nature's

deceived — ye may not yourself (methinketh) say nay but[611] that I may well with reason believe them twain,[612] against all them that will tell me they have seen such things done, as yourself doth agree, that they twain (that is to wit,[613] nature and reason) doth verily and truly show me cannot be done."

"What manner of things be those?" quoth I.

"Marry,[614] miracles," quoth he, "such as yourself will agree to be done against nature."

"Give us thereof," quoth I, "some example."

"As if men," quoth he, "would now come tell me that at Our Lady of Rouncivalle[615] there were a dead child restored again to life."

"Let that," quoth I, "be one, and let another be that a bishop, in the building of his church, finding one beam cut a great deal too short for his work, drew it forth between another man and him four feet (and[616] ye will) longer than it was, and so made it serve."

"Be it, by my troth,"[617] quoth he.

"Will we," quoth I, "take for the third that a man was, by miracle in a Pater Noster while,[618] conveyed a mile off from one place to another?"

"Be it so," quoth he. "Now they that should tell me," quoth he, "that they had seen these three miracles — were I bound to believe them?"

"Whether ye were bounden," quoth I, "or no, we shall see further after. But now why should ye not of reason trust them, if the men be credible, and earnestly report it, and peradventure[619] on their oaths depose[620] it, having no cause to feign it, nor likely to lie and be forsworn for nought?"[621]

"I will," quoth he, "not believe them because that nature and reason are two records[622] more to be believed than all they that bear witness against them."

"Why," quoth I, "what doth reason and nature tell you?"

"They twain tell me," quoth he, "that those three things cannot be done which those men say they saw done."

"Wot[623] you well," quoth I, "that reason and nature tell you so?"

"Yea marry," quoth he, "that I wot well they do, and I think yourself will agree that they tell me so."

"Nay, by Saint Mary, sir," quoth I, "that will I not.

For I think that neither reason nor nature telleth you so, but rather both two tell you clean[624] the contrary: that is to wit,[625] that they both bear witness that those three things, and such other like, be things that may be well and easily done."

"Yea?" quoth he. "Marry, this is another way. Then have we walked wrong a while, if ye prove that."

"Methinketh," quoth I, "nothing more easy to prove than that. For I pray you tell me," quoth I, "doth reason and nature show you that there is a God or not?"

"Faith showeth me that surely," quoth he, "but whether nature and reason show it me or no, that I doubt, since great-reasoned men and philosophers have doubted thereof. And some of them have been plainly persuaded and in belief that there was none at all, and the whole people of the world, in effect, fallen from knowledge or belief of God into idolatry and worship of mammets."[626]

"Nay," quoth I, "there is little doubt, I trow,[627] but that nature and reason giveth us good knowledge that there is a God. For albeit[628] the Gentiles worshipped among them a thousand false gods, yet all that proveth that there was and is in all men's heads a secret consent[629] of nature, that God there is — or else they would have worshipped none at all. Now as for the philosophers, though a very few doubted, and one or twain thought there was none, yet as one swallow maketh not summer, so the folly of so few maketh no change of the matter, against all the whole number of the old philosophers. Which,[630] as Saint Paul confesseth, found out by nature and reason that there was a God — either Maker or Governor or both — of all this whole engine[631] of the world. The marvelous beauty and constant course whereof showeth well that it neither was made nor governed by chance.[632] But when they had by these visible things knowledge of his invisible majesty, then did they as we do: fall from the worship of him to the worship of idols, as now do Christian men — not as heretics lay to the charge of good people in doing reverence to saints or honor to their images, but in doing as do those heretics themselves: making our belly or beneath our belly, or our goods, or

---

611 *say nay but:* deny   **612** both   **613** say
614 Indeed   **615** *Our . . . Rouncivalle:* a
shrine and hospital near Charing Cross
616 if   **617** trustworthiness; faithfulness
618 *a Pater Noster while:* the time it

takes to say an Our Father   **619** perhaps
620 swear   **621** *be . . . nought:* commit
perjury for nothing   **622** witnesses
623 Know   **624** completely   **625** say
626 statues of false gods   **627** feel sure

628 although   **629** agreement
630 Who   **631** design   **632** See Acts
17:22–29; Rom 1:19–20.

our own blind affection toward other creatures, or our own proud affection and dotage toward ourselves, our mammets and idols and very false gods. But surely both nature and reason will declare and teach us that a God there is."

"Well," quoth he, "I will not stick[633] in this, since Saint Paul saith so."

"Then," quoth I, "if reason and nature show you that there is a God, doth not reason and nature show you also that he is almighty and may do what he will?"

"Yes," quoth he, "that is both natural to his Godhead, and by reason it may well be perceived."

"Then followeth it," said I, "that reason and nature doth not show you that those three miracles (that we were agreed should stand for examples) precisely could not be done, but they taught you only that they could not be done by nature. But ye may, as ye now see, perceive that they themselves teach that they may be done by God, since they teach you that there is a God, and that he is almighty. And therefore when ye will in no wise[634] believe them that tell you they have seen such miracles done, ye refuse not to believe such things as cannot be done, but ye mistrust causeless the credence and faith[635] of honest men in the report of such things as, by him that they said did it, may well and easily be done."

THE EIGHTH CHAPTER

The messenger allegeth that God may nothing do against the course of nature. Of which the author declareth the contrary, and over[636] that, showeth that our Lord in working of miracles doth nothing against nature.

"Sir," quoth he, "ye come indeed somewhat near me now. But yet seemeth me that reason and nature teach me still that I shall in no wise believe them that tell me, they have seen such miracles done. For first, if ye will grant me that they teach me that, if they should be done, they must be done by God against the course of nature, so is it then that reason showeth me that God hath set all things, already from the first creation, to go forth in a certain order and course, which order and course men call

nature, and that hath he of his infinite wisdom done so well, and provided that course to go forth in such a manner and fashion, that it cannot be mended. And therefore seemeth it that reason showeth me that God never will anything do against the course which his high wisdom, power, and goodness hath made so good that it could never be broken to the better. For if it might, then had our Lord not made his order and course perfect in the beginning. And therefore doth, as I say, reason and nature yet bear record[637] against them that shall say they see such miracles, since God will never work against the course of nature, which himself hath already set in so goodly an order that it were not possible to be better, and the goodness of God will make no change to the worse."

"Surely," quoth I, "ye go now very far wide.[638] For neither doth reason prove you that God (although it cannot otherwise be but that anything of the making of his goodness must needs be good) hath made therefore everything to be of sovereign perfection — for then must every creature be equal — nor also that the whole work of his creation, though it have in itself sufficient and right wonderful perfection, that therefore it is wrought to the utterest point of sovereign goodness that his almighty Majesty could have made it of. For since he wrought it not naturally but willingly, he wrought it not to the uttermost of his power, but with such degrees of goodness as his high pleasure liked to limit,[639] for else were his work of as infinite perfection as himself. And of such infinite, equal perfection was there by God brought forth nothing but only the two Persons of the Trinity: that is to wit,[640] the Son and the Holy Ghost. Of which two, the Son was first by the Father begotten, and after the Holy Ghost by the Father and the Son — 'after,' I say, in order of beginning, but not in time — produced and brought forth. And in this high generation and production did the doers work both willingly and naturally, and after the utterest perfection of themselves, which they did only therein and in none other thing. And therefore God might break up the whole world, if he would, and make a better by and by,[641] and not only change in the natural course of this world some things to the better. Howbeit,[642] God in working of miracles doth nothing against nature, but[643] some special benefit above nature. And he doth nought[644] against you that doth another a good turn which ye be not able to do. And therefore since God may do what he will, being almighty, and in doing of miracles he doth for the better, neither reason nor nature showeth you that they which[645] say they saw such miracles do tell you a thing that cannot be done, since ye have no reason to prove that God either cannot do it, or will not do it. For since he can do it, and it may be that he will do it, why should we mistrust good and honest men that say they saw him do it?"

THE NINTH CHAPTER

The author showeth that albeit men may mistrust some of the particular miracles, yet can there no reasonable man neither deny nor doubt but that many miracles hath there been done and wrought.

"Forsooth,"[646] quoth he, "and yet as for miracles, I were not for all this bounden to believe any. For I spoke never yet with any man that could tell me that ever he saw any."

"It may," quoth I, "fortune you to live so long that ye shall find no man that was by at your christening, nor when ye were bishoped[647] neither."

"Marry," quoth he, "for aught I wot,[648] I have lived so long already."

"Why doubt ye not then," quoth I, "whether ye were ever christened or not?"

"For every man," quoth he, "presumeth and believeth that I am christened, as a thing so commonly done that we reckon ourselves sure that no man leaveth it undone."

"If the common presumption," quoth I, "sufficiently serve you to set your mind in surety, then albeit miracles be nothing commonly and customably[649] done, nor that no presumption can sufficiently serve for the proof of this miracle or that, yet hath there ever from the beginning of the world — in every nation, Christian and heathen, and almost every town at sundry times — so many miracles and marvels been[650] wrought besides the common course of nature that I think through the world it is

as well believed universally that miracles and marvels there be as anything is believed that men look upon. So that if common presumption serve you, ye may (as I said) as well believe that miracles be done as that yourself was ever christened. For I dare well say that there are a thousand that believe there hath been miracles done against one that[651] believeth that ye were ever christened — or ever wist[652] whether ye were born or not.

"Nor the doctors of Christ's Church did never mistrust the wonders and marvels that the paynims[653] tell and write to have been done by their false gods, but assigneth[654] them to have been done by the devil through God's sufferance,[655] for the illusion[656] of them that with idolatry had deserved to be deluded. And whether they be miracles — by which name we commonly call the wonders wrought by God — or marvels done by the devil, it forceth[657] not for this purpose of ours. For if ye grant that the devil may do any by God's sufferance, ye cannot say nay but[658] God may much more easily do them himself.

"And since ye be a Christian man and receive Scripture, I might in this matter," quoth I, "have choked[659] you long ago with the manifold miracles and marvels that be showed there."

THE TENTH CHAPTER

The author proveth that many things daily done by nature or craft,[660] whereof we nothing marvel at all, be more marvelous and more wonderful indeed than be the miracles that we most marvel of and repute most incredible.

"Nay," quoth he, "surely, though it hath done me good to hear what ye would say, yet I neither doubt, nor I suppose no good man else, but that God hath, beside the common course of nature, wrought many miracles.

"But yet of those that men tell of as done in your time — by which ye would it should[661] seem that it were well-proved that the praying to saints, going on pilgrimages, and worshiping of images were well and sufficiently proved, although[662] there were

---

644 nothing **645** *they which:* those who everyone who **652** knew **653** pagans **661** *would it should:* would have it; want
646 In truth **647** confirmed **648** *aught* **654** account **655** allowing it it to **662** even though
I wot: all I know **649** customarily **656** deluding **657** matters **658** *say nay*
650 have been **651** *against one that:* for *but:* deny that **659** silenced **660** skill

none other proof thereupon — of these miracles did I mean, in the report of which methinketh I need not believe a common fame of this miracle and that, begun by some seely[663] woman seeking Saint Zita when she sigheth for miscasting[664] of her keys.[665] Of these miracles I speak, and all such as men say nowadays be done at diverse pilgrimages by diverse saints or diverse images, in which methinketh that such as be told to be done, which nature and reason saith be impossible, I may well mistrust the tellers. Or else how many of them shall make me a sufficient proof of an impossible matter? One or two or three — either seemeth me too few to trust their credence in a thing so incredible. And if I shall not believe them till I find many records,[666] I ween I were fain[667] to wander the world about ere[668] I proved many miracles sufficiently, of such, I say, as ye prove your pilgrimages by."

"Your few words," quoth I, "have wrapped in them many things that seem somewhat as they be couched[669] together, which, when we see them unfolded, and consider each part asunder, then may we better examine them and better see whereof they serve.

"First ye speak of seeking[670] to saints for slight causes, as for the loss or miscasting of Kit's keys.[671] Then ye would wit[672] how many ye must hear say they saw a miracle ere ye should of reason believe it. Thirdly, ye think ye were like[673] to go long ere ye should find any proved true. Finally, when ye say that ye mean only those miracles that men tell of as done at pilgrimages, ye seem to put still a difference between those miracles wrought in pilgrimages and such as are wrought by God otherwise. The cause whereof I must further ask you after, for I perceive not well what ye mean by that.

"But first, whereas ye speak still as though ye might mistrust them, were they never so many, because they tell you a thing that reason and nature saith is impossible — methinketh that ye should now change that word. For I have already proved that reason and nature say not that a miracle is impossible, but only that it is impossible to nature. And they confess both that miracles be possible to

God; and they that report them do report them for things done by God. And therefore they do report you none impossible tale.

"For the clearer consideration whereof, let us resort to the miracles which we were agreed should stand for examples. And first, if men should tell you that they saw, before an image of the crucifix, a dead man raised to life, ye would much marvel thereof, and so might ye well. Yet could I tell you somewhat[674] that I have seen myself that methinketh as great a marvel, but I have no lust[675] to tell you, because that ye be so circumspect and wary in belief of any miracles that ye would not believe it for me, but mistrust me for it."

"Nay, sir," quoth he, "in good faith, if a thing seemed me never so far unlikely, yet if ye would earnestly say that yourself have seen it, I neither would nor could mistrust it."

"Well," quoth I, "then ye make me the bolder to tell you. And yet will I tell you nothing but that I would, if need were, find you good witnesses to prove it."

"It shall not need,[676] sir," quoth he, "but I beseech you, let me hear it."

"Forsooth,"[677] quoth I, "because we speak of a man raised from death to life. There was in the parish of Saint Stephen's in Walbrook in London (where I dwelled before I came to Chelsea) a man and a woman — which are yet quick and queathing[678] — and young were they both. The eldest, I am sure, passed not twenty-four. It happed them, as doth among young folk, the one to cast the mind[679] to the other. And after many lets,[680] for the maiden's mother was much against it, at last they came together and were married in Saint Stephen's Church, which is not greatly famous for any miracles, but yet yearly, on Saint Stephen's Day, it is somewhat sought unto and visited with folks' devotion. But now short tale to make, this young woman (as manner is in brides, ye wot[681] well) was at night brought to bed with honest women. And then after that went the bridegroom to bed; and everybody went their ways, and left them twain[682] there alone. And the same night — yet abide,[683] let me not lie now, in faith, to

---

663 pitiable; foolish; helpless   664 misplacing   665 *Saint Zita . . . keys:* St. Zita (1212–72) is the patron saint of domestic servants, and traditionally her intercession is sought for lost keys.   666 *many records:* much evidence   667 *ween I were fain:*

think I would be obliged   668 before 669 concealed   670 going   671 *Kit's keys:* Til K109; Whit K70.   672 *would wit:* want to know   673 likely 674 something   675 desire   676 *It shall not need:* That will not be necessary

677 In truth   678 *quick and queathing:* alive and able to talk   679 *cast the mind:* take a fancy   680 obstacles   681 know 682 both   683 wait a minute

say the truth, I am not very sure of the time—but surely, as it appeared afterward, it was of likelihood the same night, or some other time soon after, except it happened a little afore."

5   "No force for the time,"[684] quoth he.

"Truth," quoth I, "and as for the matter, all the parish will testify for truth: the woman was known for so honest.[685] But for the conclusion, the seed of them twain turned in the woman's body, first into

10   blood, and after into shape of man-child. And then waxed quick,[686] and she great therewith. And was within the year delivered of a fair boy; and forsooth, it was not then (for I saw it myself) passing the length of a foot. And I am sure he is grown now

15   an inch longer than I."

"How long is it ago?" quoth he.

"By my faith," quoth I, "about twenty-one years."

"Tush," quoth he, "this is a worthy miracle!"

"In good faith," quoth I, "never wist[687] I that any

20   man could tell that he had any other beginning. And methinketh that this is as great a miracle as the raising of a dead man."

"If it seem so," quoth he, "to you, then have you a marvelous seeming,[688] for I ween[689] it seemeth so

25   to no man else."

"No?" quoth I. "Can ye tell what is the cause? None other surely but that the acquaintance and daily beholding taketh away the wondering, as we nothing wonder at the ebbing and flowing of the

30   sea or the Thames because we daily see it. But he that had never seen it, nor heard thereof, would at the first sight wonder sore[690] thereat: to see that great water come wallowing up against the wind, keeping a common course to and fro, no cause per-

35   ceived that driveth him. If a man born blind had suddenly his sight, what wonder would he make to see the sun, the moon, and the stars, whereas one that hath seen them sixteen years together marveleth not so much of them all as he would wonder

40   at the first sight of a peacock's tail. And very cause can I see none why we should of reason more marvel of the reviving of a dead man than of the breeding, bringing forth, and growing of a child unto the state of a man. No more marvelous is a cuckoo

45   than a cock, though the one be seen but in summer

and the other all the year. And I am sure if ye saw dead men as commonly called again[691] by miracle as ye see men brought forth by nature, ye would reckon it less marvel to bring the soul again into the body, keeping yet still his shape, and his organs

50   not much perished, than of a little seed to make all that gear[692] new, and make a new soul thereto.[693] Now if ye never had seen any gun in your days, nor heard of any before, if two men should tell you— the one that he had wist a man in a Pater Noster

55   while[694] conveyed and carried a mile off, from one place to another, by miracle, and the other should tell you that he had seen a stone more than a man's weight carried more than a mile in as little space[695] by craft—which of these would you by your faith

60   take for the more incredible?"

"Surely," quoth he, "both twain were very strange. But yet I could not choose but think it were rather true that God did the one than that any craft of man could do the other."

65   "Well," quoth I, "let us then to our third example. If it were showed you that Saint Erkenwald[696] or his sister[697] drew out a piece of timber that was cut too short for the roof in making Barking Abbey,[698] should this be so incredible to you to believe—that

70   they drew in length a piece of wood by the power and help of God's hand—when we see daily a great piece of silver, brass, latten,[699] or iron drawn alength into small wire as wonderfully by man's hand?"

THE ELEVENTH CHAPTER
75
The author showeth that a miracle is not to be mistrusted though it be done in a small matter and seemeth upon a slight occasion.

"Now, though ye would peradventure (as ye seem to do) reckon this cause very slight for God to show

80   such a high miracle—since there might have been without miracle a longer piece of timber gotten, and so ye would haply mistrust it for the slender occasion, resembling[700] it to the miscasting[701] of some good housewife's keys—God hath, I ween, so much

85   wit of himself[702] that he needeth not our advice to inform him what thing were sufficient occasion to

684 *No . . . time:* No matter the time
685 *so honest:* such an honest person
686 *waxed quick:* became alive   **687** knew
688 way of seeing   **689** think, suppose
690 greatly   **691** back   **692** matter

693 as well   **694** *a Pater Noster while:* the time it takes to say an Our Father
695 time   **696** Bishop of London, d. 693; founder of Barking Abbey   **697** St. Ethelburga, first Abbess of Barking

698 *Barking Abbey:* a Benedictine convent near London   **699** a metal similar to brass
700 likening   **701** misplacing   **702** *wit of himself:* sense of his own

work his wonders for. But and if ye read in the books of Cassian,[703] Saint Gregory, Saint Augustine, Saint Jerome, and many other holy virtuous men, ye shall (except[704] ye believe them not) learn and know that God hath for his servants done many a great miracle in very small matters. And so much the more are we bounden to his goodness in that he vouchsafeth[705] so familiarly in small things to show us so great a token of his mighty Godhead. And no reason were it to withdraw[706] his thank and honor because of his familiar goodness. And if ye peradventure would not believe their[707] writings, go to Christ's Gospel and look on his first miracle, whether he might not have provided for wine without miracle. But such was his pleasure in a small matter to do a great miracle for some show of his Godhead among them whom he vouchsafed; where on the other side afore Herod, that would fain[708] have seen some miracle — where it stood upon his life, and might have delivered him from the Jews — yet would he not vouchsafe either to show the proud curious king one miracle, or speak one word.[709] So the times, places, and occasions, reason is that we suffer[710] to rest in his arbitrament,[711] and not look to prescribe and appoint at our pleasure where, when, and wherefore[712] God shall work his miracles, and else blaspheme them and say we will not believe them."

THE TWELFTH CHAPTER
The author somewhat noteth the froward[713] minds of many folk that would be very hard to believe a man in[714] a miracle upon his oath, and very light in a shrewd tale to believe a woman on her word.

"Now where ye require[715] how many witnesses should be requisite and suffice to make you think yourself in reason, to have good cause to believe so strange a thing, methinketh that right few were sufficient of them that would say they saw a great good thing done by the power and goodness of God, except it be hard for us to believe, either that God is so mighty that he may do it, or so good that he would do it.

"But because ye would wit of[716] me how many records[717] were requisite, that thing standeth not so much in number as in weight. Some twain be more credible than some ten. And albeit that I see not greatly why I should mistrust anyone that seemeth honest and telleth a good tale of God in which there appeareth no special cause of lying,[718] yet if any witnesses will serve you, then would I wit of you: how many yourself would agree? For I now put case[719] that there came ten diverse honest men of good substance[720] out of ten diverse parts of the realm, each of them with an offering, at one pilgrimage (as for example at Our Lady of Ipswich), and each one of them affirming upon their oath a miracle done upon themselves, in some great sudden help, well appearing to pass[721] the power of craft or nature. Would you not believe that among them all at the leastwise twain of those ten said true?"

"No, by our Lady," quoth he, "not and[722] there were ten and twenty."

"Why so?" quoth I.

"Marry," quoth he, "for were they never so many, having none other witness, but each man telling his tale for himself, they be but single all and less than single. For every miracle hath but one record,[723] and yet he not credible in his own cause. And so never a miracle well proved."

"Well," said I, "I like well your wisdom: that ye be so circumspect that ye will nothing believe without good, sufficient, and full proof.

"I put you then," quoth I, "another case: that ten young women not very specially known for good, but taken out at adventure,[724] dwelling all in one town, would report and tell that a friar of good fame, hearing their confessions at a pardon,[725] would have given them all in a penance to let him lie with them. On your faith, would ye not believe that among so many, some of them said true?"

"Yes, that I would," quoth he, "by the Mary Mass[726] believe they said true all ten — and durst[727] well swear for them and[728] they were but two."

"Why so?" quoth I. "They be as single witnesses as the others, of whom I told you before. For none of them can tell what was said to another, and yet

---

703 St. John Cassian (360–435)
704 unless **705** is willing **706** withhold (from God) **707** the Church fathers'
708 gladly **709** See Jn 2:8–11; Lk 23:8–9. **710** allow **711** control
712 why **713** perverse **714** about

715 ask **716** *would wit of:* want to know from **717** witnesses **718** *special cause of lying:* particular reason to lie **719** *put case:* propose as a hypothetical instance (a customary legal practice) **720** wealth
721 surpass **722** (even) if **723** witness

724 random **725** a Church festival where indulgence is granted **726** *Mary Mass:* Mass in honor of Mary, mother of Jesus
727 would dare **728** if

they be unsworn also; and therewith[729] be they but women, which[730] be more light and less to be regarded, dwelling all in one town also and thereby might they the more easily conspire a false tale."

"They be," quoth he, "witnesses good enough for such a matter, the thing is so likely of itself—that a friar will be womanish,[731] look the holy whoreson never so saintly."

"Ye deny not," quoth I, "but God may as easily do a good turn by miracle as any man may do an evil by nature."

"That is true," quoth he, "and he list."[732]

"Well," quoth I, "see now what a good way ye be in, that are of your own good godly mind, more ready to believe two simple women that a man will do naught,[733] than ten or twenty men that God will do good."

THE THIRTEENTH CHAPTER
*The author showeth the untoward[734] mind of
many men, which[735] in miracles so highly touching
the honor of God and weal[736] of their own souls,
will neither believe other folk that tell them,
nor themselves vouchsafe to go prove them.*

"But since that this kind of proof will not suffice you, I dare say, if ye would seek and inquire, ye should find many done in your days in the presence of much people."

"Where should I see that?" quoth he.

"Ye might," quoth I, "upon Good Friday, every year this two hundred years (till within this five year that[737] the Turks have taken the town),[738] have seen one of the thorns that was in Christ's crown bud and bring forth flowers in the service time,[739] if ye would have gone to the Rhodes."

"So far?" quoth he. "Nay, yet had I liefer[740] have God's blessing to believe that I see not, than go so far therefor."

"I am well apaid,"[741] quoth I, "thereof, for if ye had liefer believe than take the pain[742] of a long pilgrimage, ye will never be so stiff in any opinion that ye will put yourself in jeopardy for pertinacy[743] and stubborn standing by your part."

"Nay marry,"[744] quoth he, "I warrant[745] you that I will never be so mad to hold till it wax[746] too hot. For I have such a fond[747] fantasy of mine own, that I had liefer shiver and shake for cold in the mids of summer, than be burned in the midst of winter."

"Merrily said," quoth I. "But yet in earnest, where such a solemn yearly miracle is wrought, so wondrously in the face of the world, before so great a multitude, it is a great untowardness in a thing so highly touching the honor of God and health of our own soul, both to mistrust all them that say they have seen it, and either of sloth or incredulity, not vouchsafe himself to prove it."

"If I should have gone," quoth he, "and found it a lie, then had I walked a wise journey! And on the other side, if I should have seen there such a thing myself, yet could I scantly reckon myself sure."

"No?" quoth I. "That were a strange case."

"Not very strange," quoth he. "For where ye speak of miracles done before a multitude, a man may be deceived therein right well."

THE FOURTEENTH CHAPTER
*The messenger maketh objection that miracles
showed before a multitude may be feigned;[748] and
by the author showed how the goodness of God
bringeth shortly the truth of such falsehood to light
(with examples thereof, one or two rehearsed);[749]
and further showed that many miracles there be
which no good Christian man may deny to be true.*

"Some priest, to bring up[750] a pilgrimage in his parish, may devise some false fellow feigning himself to come seek a saint in his church, and there suddenly say that he hath gotten his sight. Then shall ye have the bells rung for a miracle, and the fond[751] folk of the country soon made fools. Then women coming thither with their candles. And the parson, buying of some lame beggar three or four pairs of their old crutches, with twelve pennies spent in men and women of wax thrust through diverse places, some with arrows and some with rusty knives, will make his offerings for one seven-year[752] worth twice his tithes."

---

729 additionally   **730** who   **731** having a great inclination for women   **732** *and he list:* if he wishes or pleases   **733** evil **734** perverse, obstinate   **735** who **736** good; well-being   **737** since

738 *within . . . years:* Rhodes fell to Suleiman the Magnificent in 1522. **739** *in . . . time:* during Mass   **740** rather **741** pleased   **742** trouble   **743** perverse obstinacy   **744** indeed   **745** guarantee

746 grew   **747** foolish   **748** faked **749** related   **750** *bring up:* attract **751** foolish; gullible   **752** seven-year period

"This is," quoth I, "very truth, that such things may be, and sometimes peradventure so be indeed. As I remember me that I have heard my father tell of a beggar that in King Henry his[753] days the Sixth came with his wife to Saint Alban's, and there was walking about the town begging a[754] five or six days before the King's coming thither, saying that he was born blind and never saw in his life, and was warned in his dream that he should come out of Berwick (where he said he had ever dwelled) to seek Saint Alban, and that he had been at his shrine, and had not been helped. And therefore he would go seek him at some other place, for he had heard some say since he came that Saint Alban's body should be at Cologne, and indeed such a contention hath there been. But of truth as I am surely informed, he lieth here at Saint Alban's, saving some relics of him which they there show shrined. But to tell you forth: when the King was comen, and the town full, suddenly this blind man at Saint Alban's shrine had his sight again, and a miracle solemnly rung, and *Te Deum*[755] sung, so that nothing was talked of in all the town but this miracle. So happened it then that Duke Humphrey of Gloucester—a great wise man and very well-learned—having great joy to see such a miracle, called the poor man unto him. And first showing himself joyous of God's glory so showed in the getting of his sight, and exhorting him to meekness, and to none ascribing of any part the worship[756] to himself, nor to be proud of the people's praise, which[757] would call him a good and a godly man thereby, at last he looked well upon his eyes, and asked whether he could never see nothing at all, in all his life before. And when as well his wife as himself affirmed fastly[758] no, then he looked advisedly upon[759] his eyes again, and said, 'I believe you very well; for methinketh that ye cannot see well yet.'

"'Yes, sir,' quoth he, 'I thank God and his holy martyr, I can see now as well as any man.'

"'Ye can?' quoth the Duke. 'What color is my gown?' Then anon[760] the beggar told him.

"'What color,' quoth he, 'is this man's gown?' He told him also; and so forth, without any sticking, he told him the names of all the colors that could be showed him. And when my lord saw that, he bade him walk faitour,[761] and made him be set openly in the stocks. For though he could have seen suddenly, by miracle, the difference between diverse colors, yet could he not, by the sight, so suddenly tell the names of all these colors but if[762] he had known them before, no more than the names of all the men that he should suddenly see."

"Lo, therefore I say," quoth your friend, "who may be sure of such things, when such pageants be played before all the town? I remember me now what a work I have heard of that was at Leominster in the King's father's[763] days, where the prior brought privily[764] a strange wench into the church that said she was sent thither[765] by God, and would not lie out of the church. And after, she was grated within iron grates above in the rood loft,[766] where it was believed she lived without any meat[767] or drink—only by angels' food. And diverse times she was houseled[768] in sight of the people with a host unconsecrated; and, all the people looking upon, there was a device with a small hair[769] that conveyed the host from the paten of the chalice out of the prior's hands into her mouth, as though it came alone, so that all the people—not of the town only, but also of the country about—took her for a very quick[770] saint, and daily sought so thick to see her that many that could not come near to her, cried out aloud, 'Holy maiden Elizabeth, help me!' and were fain[771] to throw their offering over their fellows' heads, for press.[772] Now lay the prior with holy maiden Elizabeth nightly in the rood loft till she was after taken out and tried in the keeping[773] by my lady the King's mother. And by the longing for meat, with voidance of that[774] she had eaten (which had no saintly savor), she was perceived for no saint, and confessed all the matter."

"In faith," quoth I, "it had been great alms[775] the prior and she had been burned together at one stake. What came of the prior?"

Quoth he, "That can I not tell; but I ween he was put to such punishment as the poor nun was, that[776] had given her in penance to say this verse—*Miserere*

753 *Henry his:* Henry's **754** about him as an impostor **762** *but if:* unless
755 *Te Deum:* a traditional hymn of praise **763** *the King's father's:* i.e., Henry VII's
to God **756** *the worship:* (of) the honor **764** secretly **765** there **766** *rood loft:*
757 who **758** steadfastly **759** *advisedly* choir loft **767** food **768** given Communion
upon: intently at **760** immediately **769** *small hair:* thin filament
761 *bade him walk faitour:* i.e., dismissed **770** living **771** obliged **772** *for press:*
because of the crowd **773** *tried in the keeping:* tested in confinement **774** that which **775** *had been great alms:* would have been a very good deed if **776** who

mei, Deus, quoniam conculcavit me homo[777] — with a great threat that and[778] she did so anymore, she should say the whole psalm. But as for holy Elizabeth, I heard say she lived and fared well, and was a common harlot at Calais many a fair day after, where she laughed at the matter full merrily."

"The more pity," quoth I, "that she was so let pass."

"That is truth," quoth he. "But now what say you? What trust can we have — or at least way, what surety can we have — in such things, when we see them feigned so shamefully in the face of the world, so openly, and so much people abused so far, that they would not have letted[779] to swear, and some to jeopard[780] their lives thereon, that all this work was wrought by God's own hand, till the truth came to light, and the drab[781] driven out of the church in the devil's name?"

"Verily,"[782] said I, "there was abusion[783] in the one side and great folly in the other side. And as that noble duke Humphrey wisely found out the falsehood of that blyson[784] beggar, so did that noble lady the King's mother prudently decipher,[785] and found out that beastly filth. And to say the truth there was cause enough in both these parties, whereof the people might reasonably gather so much suspicion, that if they had made thereupon sufficient inquisition and search, they could never have been so far abused.[786] For both might they well mistrust a beggar's word, whom they had but newly known — and well likely to lie for to win first favor, and after money — and also men might well think that a young she-saint was not meetly[787] to be shrined quick[788] in a monastery among a meinie[789] of monks. And yet in conclusion, because no such feigned wonders should infame[790] God's very miracles, his goodness shortly brought them both to knowledge. And so doth his especial cure[791] and providence bring ever shortly such falsehood and faitery[792] to light, to their shame and confusion,[793] and, as he did in Bern (a great city in Almain)[794] bring to knowledge the false miracles whereby certain friars abused the people, for which they were

openly[795] burned.[796] And so God always bringeth such false miracles to light."

"Nay, nay," quoth he, "there be many such, I warrant[797] you, that never come to light, and are still taken for very good."

"Ye cannot very well warrant it," quoth I. "For since God brought to light the false, feigned miracle of the priests of the idol Bel in the old time (as appeareth in the fourteenth chapter of the prophet Daniel), it is more likely that among Christian men he will suffer[798] no such things long lie hid. And also, how can ye warrant that many of those miracles be false? For while there is no doubt but[799] many be true, and ye know not any which ye precisely know for false, ye be not sure whether any be such or not."

"Marry," quoth he, "that reason holdeth as well on the other side. For since I know not any which I precisely know for true, I know not whether any be true or not."

"Nay," quoth I, "that argument will not serve you so. For though no man bindeth you to believe that every thing is true that is told for a miracle, yet some there be of which ye must needs reckon yourself sure, and of which ye cannot — if ye be a Christian man — have any scruple or doubt."

"Yea?" quoth he. "Fain[800] would I wit[801] which were one of those."

"Marry,"[802] quoth I, "all that are written in the Gospel."

"Marry," quoth he, "that wot[803] I well; but them we speak not of, for they were done by God himself."

"Why,"[804] quoth I, "be they not so all? If ye will not agree that ye be sure of any which be told by saints, what say you by[805] the miracles of the apostles written by Saint Luke?"[806]

"Nay," quoth he, "ye mistake me yet,[807] for I do not mean any mistrust in the miracles done of old time by God for his apostles or holy martyrs in corroboration and setting forth of the faith. I mean only these miracles that men tell and talk of nowadays to be done at those images where these pilgrimages be, and where we see some of them ourselves

---

777 "Have mercy on me, God, for man has trampled me," Ps 55(56):1 778 if 779 hesitated 780 jeopardize 781 whore (was) 782 Truly 783 deception 784 possibly More's coinage combining *bisson* (blind) and *blysne* (shining, blushing) or

blissom (lustful) 785 discover, reveal 786 deceived 787 suitable 788 *shrined quick:* enshrined alive 789 bunch 790 defame, make infamous 791 care 792 fakery 793 confounding; overthrow 794 Germany (The inhabitants of Bern spoke German.) 795 publicly 796 Four

Dominicans were burned at the stake in Bern on May 31, 1509, for a similar deception. 797 guarantee 798 allow 799 that 800 Gladly 801 know 802 Indeed 803 know 804 Well 805 about 806 See Acts 2:22; 4:30; 6:8; 7:36; 14:3; 15:2. 807 still proved plainly false, and yet told for so true—and so many false shrews[808] to affirm it, so many simple souls trust it, so much foolish folk believe it—that a man may well with reason mistrust all the remnant."

"Ye have," quoth I, "more oft than once spoken of a difference between the miracles done by God in old time and these miracles that are done, or told to be done, nowadays at pilgrimages. But surely if ye grant the miracles done of old time, we need no more for the proof of all our matter. For I trow[809] that pilgrimages, and miracles done at them, be very old things, and not things newly begun nowadays, except[810] ye call a thousand years ago, or fourteen hundred years ago, 'nowadays.' For I am very sure that so long ago, and yet longer too, did good Christian people pray to saints, and go in pilgrimage to their holy relics, and had[811] images in great veneration; and many wonderful miracles did our Lord work for the comprobation[812] of his high pleasure, to the conservation and increase of the devotion of his Christian people therein, as we find largely written and reported in the godly books of holy Saint Gregory, Saint Augustine, Saint Jerome, Saint Eusebius,[813] Saint Basil, Saint Chrysostom, and many another old holy doctor of Christ's Church whose books were not unwritten this thousand years. And whereas ye say that of miracles many be nowadays feigned, so may it be that some were then also, but neither then nor now neither, were—nor be—all feigned. And any being true, all were they right few,[814] sufficed for our purpose. For if God had but with one miracle declared that the thing contenteth and pleaseth him in his Church, it must needs suffice for the Church against all the heretics in the world that ever would bark against the Church therein. And therefore there can be no doubt in the matter, where God hath declared his pleasure by so many a thousand, and that in every time, not only nowadays, but also a thousand years, or fourteen hundred years, and yet more too before our days. And as for feigned miracles, of which ye speak so much, albeit that some such hath been, yet I verily think that, neither of old time nor now, Christ among Christian people suffereth[815] not such things to happen oft, nor such delusion to last long, but

shortly (to their shame as it hath appeared in some) doth utter[816] and make open their falsehood, as himself said of all such: 'That[817] ye whisper one in another's ear shall be preached out aloud upon the ridge of the house roof.'"[818]

THE FIFTEENTH CHAPTER
The author showeth that if of[819] those miracles that are told and written to be done at diverse pilgrimages and commonly believed for very true, we certainly knew some falsely feigned, yet were that no cause to mistrust the remnant.

"But be it that among so many miracles as be daily told and written done at diverse pilgrimages, between which miracles and others why ye put a difference, we shall, as I said before, know further your mind hereafter. And be it also that of such as long have been reputed and still taken for true, yourself undoubtedly knew some for very false: Would ye therefore think that among all the remnant, there were never one true? What if ye find some fair woman painted, whose color ye had weened were natural? Will ye never after believe that any woman in the world hath a fair color of herself? If ye find some false flatterers that long seemed friendly, will ye take ever after all the world for such? If some prove stark hypocrites whom the world would have sworn for good and godly men, shall we therefore mistrust all others for their sake, and ween there were none good at all?"

"By my troth,"[820] quoth he, "I rode once in good company—and, to say the truth, for good company—to Walsingham in pilgrimage, where a good fellow's horse so fell in halting[821] that he was fain[822] to hire another and let him go loose, which was so lean and so poor, and halted so sore,[823] that empty[824] as he was, he could scant keep foot[825] with us. And when we had went we should have left him behind, suddenly he spied a mare; and forth he limped on three legs so lustily[826] that his master's horse with four feet could scant overtake him. But when he caught him and came again,[827] he swore in great anger all the oaths he might swear that he would trust 'halting Sir Thomas' the worse while he lived."

808 scoundrels 809 trust 810 unless
811 held 812 approval 813 of Caesarea
(*ca.* 260–340) 814 *all . . . few:* even
if they had been very few (they would

have) 815 allows 816 reveal 817 That
which; What 818 Lk 12:3 819 out
of 820 truth, trustworthiness 821 *fell
in halting:* started hobbling or limping

822 obliged 823 badly 824 unladen
825 *scant keep foot:* barely keep pace
826 vigorously 827 back

"What was that 'halting Sir Thomas'?" quoth I.

"Marry," quoth he, "their parish priest, as he told us, 'as lean and as poor and as halting as his horse — and as holy too.' But since he would, while he lived,
5   mistrust the halting[828] priest for his halting horse, if I find a holy whoreson halt in hypocrisy, I shall not fail, while I live, to trust all his fellows the worse."

"Well," quoth I, "ye speak merrily, but I wot well ye will do better, whatsoever ye say. Nor, I am sure,
10   though ye see some white sapphire or beryl so well counterfeited, and so set in a ring that a right good jeweler will take it for a diamond, yet will ye not doubt, for all that, but that there be in many other rings already set right diamonds indeed. Nor ye will
15   not mistrust Saint Peter for Judas. Nor though the Jews were many so naughty[829] that they put Christ to death, yet ye be wiser, I wot well, than the gentlewoman was, which in talking once with my father, when she heard say that our Lady was a Jew,
20   first could not believe it, but said, 'What? Ye mock, iwis![830] I pray you, tell truth.' And when it was so fully affirmed that she at last believed it, 'And was she[831] a Jew,' quoth she, 'so help me God and halidom,[832] I shall love her the worse while I live!' I am
25   sure ye will not do so, nor mistrust all for some, neither men nor miracles."

THE SIXTEENTH CHAPTER

The author showeth that whoso[833] would inquire
should soon find that at pilgrimages been[834] daily
30   *many great and undoubted miracles wrought and*
well known. And specially he speaketh of the
great and open miracle showed at Our Lady
of Ipswich of late upon the daughter of
Sir Roger Wentworth, Knight.

35   "And as for the point that we spoke of concerning miracles done in our days at diverse images where these pilgrimages be, yet could I tell you some such done so openly, so far from all cause of suspicion, and thereto[835] testified in such sufficient wise, that
40   he might seem almost mad that, hearing the whole matter, will mistrust the miracles. Among which I durst[836] boldly tell you, for one, the wonderful work of God that was within these few years wrought in the house of a right worshipful[837] knight, Sir Roger Wentworth, upon diverse of his children, and spe-   45
cially one of his daughters, a very fair young gentle-woman of twelve years of age, in marvelous manner vexed and tormented by our ghostly[838] enemy the devil, her mind alienated[839] and raving, with despis-
ing and blasphemy of God, and hatred of all hal-   50
lowed[840] things, with knowledge and perceiving[841] of the hallowed from the unhallowed, all were she nothing warned thereof,[842] and after that, moved in her own mind, and admonished by the will of God, to go to Our Lady of Ipswich. In[843] the way   55
of which pilgrimage, she prophesied and told many things done and said at the same time in other places which were proved true; and many things said, ly-ing in her trance, of such wisdom and learning that right cunning[844] men highly marveled to hear of so   60
young an unlearned maiden — when herself wist[845] not what she said — such things uttered and spoken as well-learned men might have missed with a long study; and finally, being brought and laid before the image of our blessed Lady, was there, in the sight of   65
many worshipful people, so grievously tormented, and in face, eyes, look, and countenance so grisly changed, with her mouth drawn aside, and her eyes laid out upon her cheeks, that it was a terrible sight to behold.   70

"And after many marvelous things at the same time showed upon diverse persons by the devil, through God's sufferance,[846] as well all the remnant as the maiden herself, in the presence of all the com-pany, restored to their good state, perfectly cured   75
and suddenly.

"And in this matter no pretext of begging, no sus-picion of feigning, no possibility of counterfeiting, no simpleness[847] in the seers; her father and mother, right honorable and rich, sore abashed[848] to see such   80
chances[849] in their children; the witnesses, great number, and many of great worship,[850] wisdom, and good experience; the maid herself too young to feign, and the fashion[851] itself too strange for any man to feign, and the end of the matter virtuous: 85

---

a pun on two archaic meanings: limp-ing and deceiving **829** wicked **830** truly **831** *And was she:* If she was **832** all things holy **833** whoever **834** have been **835** in addition; also **836** dared

837 *right worshipful:* very distinguished **838** spiritual **839** estranged **840** blessed **841** distinguishing **842** *all . . . thereof:* although she had not been informed about them (i.e., not been told which

was which) **843** Along **844** learned **845** knew **846** consent **847** gullibility; ignorance **848** *sore abashed:* greatly shamed **849** happenings **850** distinc-tion **851** appearance

the virgin so moved in her mind with the miracle that she forthwith,[852] for aught[853] her father could do, forsook the world and professed religion in a very good and godly company at the Minoress,[854] where she hath lived well and graciously ever since."

THE SEVENTEENTH CHAPTER

The messenger layeth forth objections against miracles done at pilgrimages, of which he confesseth many to be true. But he layeth causes and reasons whereby he saith that many men be moved to believe and think that those miracles that be done there be done by the devil, to set our hearts upon idolatry by the worshipping of images instead of God.

"But now albeit, as I said, that I might allege[855] you this miracle, and prove it you in such wise that I wot well ye would be as far out of all doubt thereof as ye would be deep in the marvel of the miracle—and peradventure diverse others could I show you done of late at diverse pilgrimages, and prove them well, too—yet would I fain[856] first hear of you what distinction and difference is that that[857] ye make, and wherefore[858] ye make it, between the miracles done of old time and these that be nowadays done at these pilgrimages."

"Sir," quoth he, "somewhat a little I touched it in the beginning, and made in manner a glance thereat. But loath were I to hit it with a full shot and a sharp, as I have seen some with such reasons cleave the prick in twain,[859] that they seemed to bear over the butt[860] and all. Which reasons I would be loath in so sore[861] manner to allege,[862] lest I might haply[863] give you some occasion to think that either I set to somewhat[864] of mine own, or else at the leastwise, liked well that side and were a favorer of that faction."

"Nay, nay," quoth I, "fear not that hardily,[865] for neither am I so suspicious to mistrust that one thinketh evil because he defendeth the worse part[866] well by way of argument and reasoning. And also, I trust that all their shots shall be so far too feeble to bear over the butt, that few of them shall touch the mark—many too faint to pierce the paper. And some too high, and some too short. And some walk too wide of the butt by a bow.[867] And therefore I require[868] you spare not to bring forth all that ever ye have heard, or that ye think may be said, in the matter."

"Sir," quoth he, "since ye can hear it so indifferently,[869] I shall not spare to speak it. And surely to begin with: all that I think true, I will not fail to confess. For albeit that I have long sticked with[870] you to withstand any credence to be given to miracles done nowadays—in which I have much the longer sticked because of some, whom I have known ere this so far from the belief of any miracles at all that, in good faith, they put me half in doubt whether they believe that there were any God at all, if they durst for dread and shame have said all that they seemed to think, yet to say the truth I never heard anything said so sore[871] therein that ever moved me to think that any reason would bear the importune[872] mistrust of them, that among so many an open miracle as is daily in diverse places done, would ween that none at all were true. But verily, as I began a little to touch in the beginning, whether these miracles be made by God and for good saints, or by the devil for our deceit and delusion—albeit I believe, and ever will, as the Church doth—yet some men among[873] some such things say therein[874] that I am driven to do as I do in other articles of the faith: lean fast unto belief, for any reason that I find to make them answer with. For first, they take for a ground[875] that the devil may do miracles. Or if we list[876] not to suffer them called by that name, the matter shall be thereby nothing amended, for if we will have only called by the name of 'miracles' things by God done above nature, yet will we not deny but that God suffereth[877] the devil to work wonders which the people cannot discern from miracles. And therefore when they see them, 'miracles' shall they call them, and for miracles shall they take them. Now since it so is, that the devil may do such things, whereby shall we be sure that God doth them? And since the devil may do them, and we be

---

852 immediately **853** *for aught:* in spite of anything **854** a cloistered convent of the Poor Clares just outside London **855** cite **856** gladly **857** *that that:* that which **858** why **859** *cleave…twain:* split the target in two **860** *bear…butt:* knock over the support or stand on which the target is mounted **861** harsh (a) **862** argue **863** perhaps **864** *to somewhat:* forth something **865** by no means **866** *worse part:* bad side (of the debate) **867** *walk…bow:* miss the target by the length of a bow **868** ask that **869** impartially **870** *sticked with:* persisted in arguing with **871** grievous **872** *bear the importune:* suffer the troublesome **873** now and then; occasionally **874** on that subject **875** basis **876** wish **877** allows

not sure that God doth them, why may not we as well believe that the devil doth them?"

"Marry," said I, "ye told me that ye set nought by[878] logic, but now ye play the logician outright. Howbeit,[879] that argument men may turn on the other side and say that, since God may do them much better than the devil and we be not sure that the devil doth them, why should we not rather believe that God doth them, which[880] may do them better? And much more reason it is, where a wonderful work is wrought, there to ascribe it to God, the Master of all masteries,[881] rather than the devil, that can do nothing but by sufferance, except[882] we see some cause that cannot suffer that work to be reckoned God's."

"Well," quoth he, "then is it reason that we show you some such cause. It is," quoth he, "cause enough, in that we see that God hath in Scripture forbidden such imagery—and that under great malediction, as in the law which yourself spoke of before, *Non facies tibi sculptile*,[883] and in the psalm *In exitu Israel de Aegypto*,[884] where he first by the mouth of the prophet describeth the folly of such as worshippeth those images, that 'hath ears and cannot hear, hands and cannot feel, feet and cannot go, mouth and cannot speak.'[885] All which absurdities and unreasonable follies appeareth as well in the worship of our images as in the paynims'[886] idols. And after, he showeth the maledictions that shall thereupon, saying, 'Like might they be to them all such as make them, and all such as putteth their trust in them.'[887] And forthwith he declareth in whom good men have their trust, and the profit that proceedeth thereupon, saying: *Domus Israel speravit in Domino; adiutor eorum et protector eorum est* ('The house of Israel hath put their trust in our Lord; the helper and defender of them is he').[888] Now when the words of God be clear, open and plain upon this side, what reason is it to believe the comments and glosses of men such as ye brought forth right now, wherewith ye would wind out[889] against the true texts of God? What, should we give credence to the example of men's doings against the plain commandment of God's writings? And when[890] that only Christ is our Savior and our mediator to bring our nature again[891] to God, and our only proctor and advocate[892] afore his Father,[893] and may help us best and will help us most, what[894] shall we make either our Lady or any other creature our advocate, or pray to them—which of likelihood hear us not? For there can none of them be present at so many places at once as they be called upon. And if they were, yet are they no nearer us than God himself, nor so fain[895] would that we did well as he that died for us. And therefore when we not only do them reverence (which I were content were done them, for God's sake, as ye said before), but also pray to them, we do Christ and God great injury. For if we pray to them as mediators and advocates for us, we take from Christ his office and give it them. If we ask help and health of them, then make we them plain gods, and betake[896] to them the power of the Godhead. For only God is it that giveth all good, as witnesseth Saint James: 'Every good and very perfect gift cometh from above, descending from the Father of lights.'[897] And surely if we consider how we behave us to them, though ye say that all the honor given to saints redoundeth unto God—since it is done, as ye say, not for their own sakes, but for his—yet would not I ween God be well content that we should for his sake do to any creature like honor as to himself. For Scripture saith that he will not give his glory from him, nor to any other creature like honor as to himself.[898] And therefore the schools, as I hear say, devise a treble[899] difference in worshipping, calling the one *dulia*, the reverence or worship that man doth to man, as the bondman to the lord; the second, *hyperdulia*, that a man doth to a more excellent creature, as to angels or saints; the third, *latria*, the veneration, honor, and adoration that creatures doth only to God. In which of these parts ye put the worshipping of images, I am neither so well seen[900] therein to tell nor so curious greatly to care. But this I see well: if any of all these three kinds of worship be better than other, the images hath it. For they have all that ever we can do. For what do we to God when we do worship him in that fashion that they call *latria*, but we do the same to saints and images both? If it stand[901] in kneeling, we kneel to

---

878 *set nought by:* value as nothing **879** However **880** who **881** great accomplishments **882** unless **883** "You shall not make for yourself a carved image," Ex 20:4 **884** "When Israel went forth from Egypt," Ps 113(114):1

885 Ps 113:13–15 (115:5–7) **886** pagans' **887** Ps 113:16 (115:8) **888** Ps 113:17 (115:9) **889** *wind out:* circuitously argue **890** given **891** back **892** *proctor and advocate:* two words for a representative, attorney, or defender in court **893** See

1 Jn 2:1. **894** why **895** willingly **896** give; assign **897** Jas 1:17 **898** See Is 42:8. **899** threefold **900** versed **901** consists

saints and their images; if in praying, we pray as bit-terly[902] to them as to God; if incensing and setting up of candles, we cense them also—and set some saint seven candles against God's one, so that what-soever fashion of worshipping *latria* be, the same is as largely done to saints and images as to God. And this not unto images only—which though they have no life, have yet some shape and fashion after man—but, as men ween, unto pigs' bones also sometimes. For what reverent honor is there daily done, under the name and opinion of a saint's relic, to some old rotten bone that was haply[903] sometime, as Chaucer saith, a bone of some 'holy Jew's sheep'![904] See we not that some one saint's head is showed in three places? And some one whole saint's body lieth in diverse countries, if we believe the lies of the peo-ple. And in both the places is the one body wor-shipped, where the one or the other is false, and one body mistaken for another—an evil man haply for a good. And yet will the priests of both places take of-ferings and toll[905] men thither with miracles too. In which case, either must ye say that the miracles of the one place be false and feigned, or else that mir-acles make not your matter good,[906] nor prove your pilgrimages true; and yet might all this gear[907] be much the better borne if it were true that ye defend the things withal, when ye say that in worshipping of saints and images, men worship neither the one nor the other as gods, but the images for the saints, and the saints for God. But now, as it seemeth, the matter is indeed far otherwise. For the people pray to the saints for their necessities, putting thereto trust for their petitions in the saints themselves, as though God gave it not, but they. And in the images put the people their trust instead of the saints them-selves. For albeit that it might stand with reason (as ye have answered me) that presupposed the miracles in these pilgrimages to be done by God, the people might then with reason go seek and visit such places as God by miracle declared that he would have him-self or his holy saints sought and honored in, yet now this answer toucheth the point but in part and matcheth not the whole matter. For the people do not only visit these places and there do all the wor-ship to the saints that they can possibly do to God (with hope of their help from the saints themselves,

which they should well wit[908] only to be given by God—and thus by this demeanor make the saints God's fellows—that is to say, the servants matches with their Master and the creatures mates[909] to the Maker), but also use themselves in as religious fash-ion, and as fervent affection, to the images of stone or tree,[910] as either to saint or God, and plainly take these images for the saints themselves and for God himself, and put in these images of their pilgrim-ages their full hope and whole trust that they should put in God.

"Which, besides that[911] I have said before, ap-peareth well in this: that they will make compari-sons between Our Lady of Ipswich and Our Lady of Walsingham, as weening that one image more of power than the other, which they would never do but if[912] instead of our Lady they put their trust in the image itself. And the people, in speaking of our Lady, 'Of all our Ladies,' saith one, 'I love best our Lady of Walsingham.' 'And I,' saith the other, 'Our Lady of Ipswich.' In which words, what mean-eth she but her love and affection to the stock[913] that standeth in the chapel of Walsingham or Ipswich?

"What say you when the people speak of this fashion in their pains and perils: 'Help, holy cross of Bradman!' 'Help, our dear Lady of Walsingham!' Doth it not plainly appear that either they trust in the images in Christ's stead and our Lady's—letting Christ and our Lady go—or take at the leastwise those images so, that they ween they were verily the one Christ, the other our Lady herself? And so ev-ery way the faith and devotion withdrawn[914] from God that[915] should have it, and our hearts by these images blinded and set upon the dead stocks and stones. Now see the good fruit also that followeth thereupon. I let pass over the faitery[916] and false-hood that is therein used among[917]—sometimes by the priests, sometimes by beggars—in feigning of false miracles. Look what devotion men come thither with. With the most come they that most abuse themselves—such, I mean, as most trust have, and blind faith, in these blind images. But the most part that cometh, cometh for no devotion at all, but only for good company to babble thitherward[918] and drink[919] drunk there, and dance and reel home-ward. And yet here is not all. For I tell you nothing

---

902 intensely, with strong emotion
903 perhaps   **904** See the prologue to the *Pardoner's Tale* 347–51.   **905** summon
906 *make…good:* do not substantiate

your contention   **907** matter, business
908 know   **909** equals   **910** wood
911 what   **912** *but if:* unless   **913** statue
914 are withdrawn   **915** who   **916** fraud

917 on occasion   **918** on the way there
919 drink themselves

now of many a naughty[920] pack, many a fleck and his make,[921] that maketh their images meetings[922] at these wholesome hallows.[923] And many that seemeth an honest housewife at home hath help of a bawd[924] to bring her to mischief as she walketh abroad about her pilgrimages. I heard once, when I was a child, the good Scottish friar Father Donald, whom I reckon surely for a saint if there be any in heaven. I heard him preach at Paul's Cross[925] that our Lady was a virgin, and yet at her pilgrimages be made many a foul meeting. And loud he cried out, 'Ye men of London, gang[926] on yourselves with your wives to Willesden,[927] in the devil's name, or else keep them at heme[928] with you—with sorrow.' And surely so many good men ween it were best, considering that those voyages[929] be but wandering about vanity or superstitious devotion, and the next door to idolatry, when men have their affections instead of God bound to blocks and stones. And now, since that this gear[930] is such, what marvel is it though[931] (as I said before) the devil be glad to give attendance thereon, and do for his part what he may to help his own devices forward? Or what marvel is it though God, in this cursed world, when we fall from him to others, and from the honor of himself to his saints, when we do as the paynims[932] did—instead of God, worship mammets[933]—and all this by falling[934] to follow men's glosses before his own texts, what wonder is it though God again[935] serve us as he served[936] them, and suffer[937] the devil delude us as he did them, and make us lean to false miracles as we fall willfully to false gods? Thus say they," quoth he, "that speak on that side, and yet much more than I can call to mind. But surely since ye willed me to forbear[938] nothing, I have as I could rather set to somewhat[939] (not of mine own opinion, but of mine own invention) than anything left out that I could remember which I had ever heard any man lay,[940] to prove the miracles done at pilgrimages to be uncertain by whom they be wrought—or rather to prove that they should not be God's miracles, but the devil's wonders."

THE EIGHTEENTH CHAPTER

The author deferreth the answer to the aforesaid objections; and first by Scripture he proveth that the Church of Christ cannot err in any necessary article of Christ's faith. And in this chapter be those words of Christ specially touched, Super cathedram Moysi sederunt etc. Quae dicunt vobis, facite; quae autem faciunt nolite facere,[941] *concerning the authority of the Church.*

"Surely," quoth I, "for my part I can you very good thank; for ye have not faintly defended your part as though it were a corrupted advocate,[942] that would by collusion handle his client's matter feebly for the pleasure of his adversary, but ye have said therein, I cannot tell whether as much as any man may say, but certainly I suppose as much as ye either have heard any man say or can yourself say, and at the leastwise much more than I have heard of any man else, or could have said of myself. And undoubted as ye spoke of shooting in the beginning, this gear[943] how near it goeth to the prick[944] we shall see after. But this I promise you, it would fain bear over the butt[945] and all. For if it might hold and be bidden by,[946] and were as well able to be proved true as I trust to prove it false, the butt we shot at were quite[947] gone for any surety that we could reckon of our faith and Christendom. But now to come to the point: since it is agreed already between us that at these images and pilgrimages miracles been[948] there—either showed by God for the comprobation[949] of his pleasure therein, or wonders wrought by the devil for our delusion and damnation—if it may either appear to us that they be not done by the devil, then will it well follow that they be done by God; or if it be proved to be done by God for the good of his Church, then will it be clear enough that they be no wonders wrought by the devil to the deceit of Christian people. And since that either other[950] of these parts proved implieth the reproof[951] of your purpose, I will assay[952] to show, and trust right well to prove you the truth of our side by

---

920 wicked   **921** *fleck and his make:* worthless person and his illicit lover **922** *images meetings:* representations (of their illicit liaisons) of licit gatherings or assemblies   **923** shrines   **924** someone who arranges illicit sexual encounters **925** *Paul's Cross:* the outdoor pulpit at Old St. Paul's Cathedral, in London **926** go (Scottish accent)   **927** Our

Lady of Willesden was a shrine near London.   **928** home (Scottish accent) **929** pilgrimages   **930** matter, business **931** if   **932** pagans   **933** statues of idols **934** starting   **935** in return   **936** treated **937** let   **938** withhold   **939** *set to somewhat:* added in a little   **940** put forward   **941** "They sit on the chair of Moses.... What they say, do; however,

what they do, don't do" (Mt 23:2–3). **942** defense attorney   **943** business; matter   **944** bull's eye   **945** *fain... butt:* have to knock over the archery target   **946** *bidden by:* questioned, investigated   **947** entirely   **948** have been   **949** approval   **950** the one or the other   **951** disproof   **952** attempt some one of these ways, or peradventure by both: that is to wit, as well in proving that God doth these miracles as in reproving[953] and confuting[954] that they should be done by the devil. And first would I fain[955] meet with your objections and answer them forthwith,[956] while they be fresh, saving that meseemeth better for the while to defer them, forasmuch as some things there be whereupon it will be requisite that we first be both agreed, without which we were like to walk wide[957] in words and run all at riot, so loose that our matter could neither have ground, order, nor end.

"Now if I were in this matter to dispute with a paynim, that[958] would make the question between their miracles and ours, albeit I should have a clear matter in the end, yet must it needs be a long matter and much entriked,[959] ere it should come at the end. And whole books would it hold, both the confuting of theirs, and unto them the assertation[960] of our own, specially for that they receive not our Scripture, and between them and us nothing common to ground upon but reason. And if we should dispute with a Jew, less labor should we have, since that we should have with him, though he deny the New Testament, yet reason and the Old Testament agreed upon—wherein we should not vary for the text, but for the sentence[961] and understanding. For therein we should have him stiffly withstand[962] us.

"But now since we shall in our matter dispute and reason with those that agree themselves for[963] Christian men, our dispicions[964] are so much the shorter, in that we must needs agree together in more things. For we must agree in reason, where faith refuseth[965] it not. And over[966] that, we shall agree upon the whole corpus of Scripture, as well the New Testament as the Old. But in the interpretation we may peradventure stick.[967] Is it not so?"

"Yes," quoth he.

"Well," quoth I, "is there any other thing wherein ye think that we shall vary but the interpretation of the Scripture?"

"Not that I remember," quoth he, "except the conclusion itself whereupon we talk—as of the worshipping of images or praying to saints—in which men think there can be no great question, if the Scripture be well interpreted."

"Ye do," quoth I, "agree that such things as are mentioned in the Gospel, spoken by Christ unto Saint Peter and other his apostles and disciples, were not only said to themselves, nor only for themselves, but to them for their successors in Christ's flock, and by them to us all—that is to wit, every man as shall appertain[968] to his part?"

"Whereby mean you that?"[969] quoth he.

"I mean," quoth I, "as for example when he said, *Nisi abundaverit iusticia vestra plus quam scribarum et Pharisaeorum, non intrabitis in regnum caelorum* ('Except your justice abound and exceed the justice of the scribes and Pharisees, ye shall never come in heaven'),[970] and where he saith, 'If thou wilt enter into the kingdom of heaven, keep the commandments.'[971] Did not he say such things to them for all Christian men that should come after?"

"I think yes," quoth he, "for the second word concerning the commandments. But as for the first, that their justice should be better than the justice of the scribes and Pharisees, peradventure he spoke specially to his apostles themselves, that they should not be like the scribes and Pharisees, which[972] commanded others many things, and did nothing themselves."

"That is, in my mind," quoth I, "well taken, and so doth holy Saint Augustine[973] expound it. But since ye think he said that word to his apostles specially, rather than to all his whole flock, whether[974] think you: that he said it only to them, or else to all others also that should after come in their places and succeed them in office?"

"Nay 'fore God," quoth he, "to all the bishops he said it, and prelates and spiritual rulers of his Church, that ever shall be in the Church, forbidding them to bind and lay upon other poor men's backs importunable[975] burdens, to the bearing whereof themselves will not once put forth a finger."

"Very well said," quoth I. "What think you then of that he said: 'Do ye such things as they bid you do, but do not as ye see them do'?"[976]

"In that would our Lord," quoth he, "that all the

---

953 disproving   **954** refuting   **955** gladly
956 right away   **957** astray   **958** who
959 *much entriked:* very complicated
960 making   **961** meaning   **962** oppose
963 to be   **964** discussions   **965** forbids

966 beyond   **967** *peradventure stick:* perhaps be unable to agree   **968** belong
969 *Whereby mean you that:* What do you mean by that   **970** Mt 5:20   **971** Mt 19:17–23   **972** who   **973** See *Tractates on*

the Gospel of John, 122.9; *Answer to Petilian the Donatist,* 2.61.   **974** which of these
975 grievous   **976** Mt 23:3

people should do all that the prelates should command as far as was commanded in the law by God, but he meant no further. And therefore he said that they sat 'upon the chair of Moses,' and he willed that they should for that cause be obeyed.[977] And therein he meant in such things only as they should command that were by God commanded the people, in the law given to Moses, and that Christian men in like wise obey the bishops and prelates commanding only such things as himself hath commanded his people in his Gospel and his own law."

"And in nothing else?" quoth I. "What meaneth it then that our Lord, in the parable of the Samaritan bearing the wounded man into the inn of his Church, and delivering him to the host after that himself had dressed his wounds with wine and oil and left with the host the two groats[978] of the two Testaments, promised the host besides that whatsoever the host would bestow upon him more, he would, when he came again, recompense him therefor?[979] And also in that place that we spoke of, our Savior said that the scribes and Pharisees, besides the Law of Moses on whose seat they sat, did lay great fardels[980] and fast bound them on other men's backs, to the bearing whereof they would not move a finger themselves.[981] And yet, for all that, he bade the people do what their prelates would bid them, though[982] the burden were heavy, and let[983] not to do it though they should see the bidders[984] do clean the contrary. For which he added, 'But as they do, do not you.'"

"By our Lady," quoth he, "I like not this gloss.[985] For it maketh all for the bonds by which the laws of the Church bind us to more ado[986] than the Jews were almost with Moses' law. And I wot well Christ said, 'Come to me, ye that be overcharged, and I shall refresh you.'[987] And his apostles said that the bare[988] law of Moses — besides the ceremonies that were set to[989] by the scribes and the Pharisees — were more than ever they were able to bear and fulfill. And therefore Christ came to call us into a law of liberty and that was in taking away the band[990]

of those weary ceremonial laws.[991] And therefore saith our Savior of the law that he calleth us unto: 'My yoke,' saith he, 'is fit and easy, and my burden but light.'[992] Whereby it appeareth that he meant to take away the strait yoke and put on a more easy, and to take off the heavy burden and lay on a lighter. Which he had not done if he would load us with a fardel full of men's laws, more than a cart can carry away."

"The laws of Christ's Church," quoth I, "be made by himself and his Holy Spirit for the governance of his people, and be not, in hardness and difficulty of keeping, anything like to the laws of Moses. And thereof durst I for need make yourself judge. For if ye bethink you well, I ween if ye were at this age now to choose, you would rather be bounden to many of the laws of Christ's Church than to the circumcision alone. Nor to as much ease as we ween that Christ called us, yet be not the laws that have been made by his Church of half the pain — nor half the difficulty — that his own be, which himself putteth in the Gospel, though[993] we set aside the counsels[994] It is, I trow,[995] more hard not to swear at all, than not to forswear;[996] to forbear[997] each angry word than not to kill; continual watch[998] and prayer than a few days appointed.[999] Then what an anxiety and solicitude is there in the forbearing of every idle word? What a hard threat, after the worldly count,[1] for a small matter? Never was there almost so sore[2] a word said unto the Jews by Moses as is to us by Christ in that word alone where he saith that we shall of every idle word give account at the Day of Judgment.[3] What say ye then by divorces restrained,[4] and liberty of diverse wives withdrawn, where they had liberty to wed for their pleasure, if they cast a fantasy[5] to any that they took in the war?"

"One of that ware[6] is enough," quoth he, "to make any one man warre."[7]

"Now that is merrily said," quoth I, "but though one eye were enough for a fletcher,[8] yet is he for store[9] content to keep twain, and would though[10]

---

977 See Mt 23:2–3. **978** coins **979** for that. See Lk 10:33–35. **980** burdens **981** See Mt 23:3–4. **982** even if **983** hesitate **984** leaders, superiors **985** interpretation **986** trouble, work **987** Mt 11:28 **988** mere **989** added **990** restraint **991** See Acts 15:10; Gal 5:13; Rom 8:21; Jas 2:12. **992** Mt 11:30 **993** even if **994** *the counsels:*

The "counsels of perfection" are poverty (see Mt 19:21), chastity (see Mt 19:12), and obedience (for those who take vows and enter religious life: to a religious superior such as an abbot). **995** think **996** commit perjury **997** refrain from **998** vigil-keeping **999** See Mt 5:33–37, 21–22; Lk 18:1. **1** reckoning **2** harsh; severe **3** See Mt 12:36–37. **4** (being)

prohibited. See Mt 5:31–32, 19:3–9; Lk 16:18. **5** *cast a fantasy:* took a liking **6** articles of merchandise; sexual organ **7** *war … ware … warre:* an elaborate pun. All three words were originally spelled "ware." The latter two both also have double meanings. *warre:* worse; wary **8** arrow-maker **9** reserve **10** even if they were sometime sore both, and should put him to some pain. What ease also call you this: that we be bounden to abide all sorrow and shameful death, and all martyrdom, upon pain of perpetual damnation, for the profession of our faith? Trow ye that these easy words of his 'easy yoke' and 'light burden' were not as well spoken to his apostles as to you? And yet what ease called he them to? Called he not them to watching, fasting, praying, preaching, walking, hunger, thirst, cold, and heat, beating, scourging, prisonment, painful and shameful death? The ease of his yoke standeth not in bodily ease, nor the lightness of his burden standeth not in the slackness of any bodily pain (except[11] we be so wanton[12] that where himself had not heaven without pain, we look to come thither with play), but it standeth in the sweetness of hope, whereby we feel in our pain a pleasant taste of heaven. This is the thing, as holy Saint Gregory Nazianzen[13] declareth, that refresheth men that are laden and maketh our yoke easy and our burden light, not any delivering from the laws of the Church — or from any good temporal laws either — into a lewd[14] liberty of slothful rest. For that were not an easy yoke, but a pulling of the head out of the yoke. Nor it were not a light burden, but all the burden discharged, contrary to the words of Saint Paul and Saint Peter both, which[15] as well understood the words of their Master as these men do. And as a thing consonant and well agreeable therewith, do command us obedience to our superiors and rulers, one and other,[16] in things by God not forbidden, although they be hard and sore.[17]

"But see for God's sake how we be run a great way further than I thought to go when I began, and have left that[18] we should go forth withal."[19]

"It is no loss," quoth he, "for there is a good thing well touched by[20] the way."

"Well," quoth I, "let us go back again where we left. Since ye agree that Christ spoke his words not to his apostles only for their own time, but such things as he said to them, he meant to all that should follow them — and thereof somewhat he spoke to them for the priests and bishops only (as when he said, *Vos estis sal terrae*; 'Ye be the salt of the earth'),[21] and somewhat to the whole flock (as when he said, *Mandatum novum do vobis: ut diligatis invicem sicut ego dilexi vos*; 'I give you a new commandment: that you love together as I have loved you').[22] Tell me then, I require[23] you: when Christ said to Saint Peter, 'Satan hath desired to sift ye as men sift corn;[24] but I have prayed for thee, that thy faith shall not fail,'[25] said he this to him as a promise of the faith to be by God's help perpetually kept and preserved in Saint Peter only, or else in the whole Church — that is to wit, the whole congregation of Christian people professing his name and his faith, and abiding in the body of the same, not being precided[26] and cut off — meaning that his faith should never so utterly fail in his Church, but that it should whole and entire abide and remain therein?"

"Marry," quoth he, "this is good to be advised of. For though Christ, for the more part, such things as he spoke to one spoke to all, according to his own words, *Quod uni dico, omnibus dico* ('That I say to one, I say to all'),[27] yet some things he said and meant particularly as he spoke it. As when he bade Saint Peter come upon the water to him,[28] he bade not the remnant come so. And so may it peradventure be that this word was spoken and meant toward Peter alone."

"That will be," quoth I, "very hard to hold, for his faith after failed.[29] But since that[30] upon his first confession of the right faith, that Christ was God's Son, our Lord made him his universal vicar and under him head of his Church, and that for his successor he should be the first upon whom and whose firm confessed faith he would build his Church, and of any that[31] was only man make him the first and chief head and ruler thereof — therefore he showed him that his faith (that is to wit, the faith by him confessed) should never fail in his Church,[32] nor never did it, notwithstanding his denying. For yet stood still the light of faith in our Lady, of whom we read in the Gospel continual assistance to her sweetest Son, without fleeing or flitting.[33] And in all others we find either fleeing from him one time or other, or else doubt of his resurrection after his death, his dear mother only except.[34] For the signification and remembrance whereof the Church

---

11 unless 12 self-indulgent; spoiled
13 See Gregory's oration *De Pace.*
14 evil 15 who 16 *one and other:* both
17 grievous. See Eph 6:5; Ti 2:9–3:1;
Heb 13:17; 1 Pt 2:13–21. 18 that which

19 with 20 along 21 Mt 5:13 22 Jn
13:34 23 ask of 24 wheat 25 Lk
22:31–32 26 excommunicated 27 Mk
13:37 28 See Mk 14:28. 29 See Lk
22:55–62. 30 *since that:* because 31 *any*

that: anyone who 32 See Mt 16:16–19.
33 See Jn 19:25. 34 See Jn 19:26–27;
Mt 26:31.

yearly, in the Tenebrae[35] lessons,[36] leaveth her candle burning still when all the remnant, that signifieth his apostles and disciples, be one by one put out. And since his faith in effect failed, and yet the faith that he professed abode still in our Lady, the promise that God made was, as it seemeth, meant not to him but as head of the Church. And therefore our Lord added thereto, 'And thou being one of these days converted, confirm and strengthen thy brethren.'[37] In which, by these words, our Savior meant and promised that the faith should stand forever, so that 'the gates of hell should not prevail there against.'[38] Or else might ye say that these words spoken to Saint Peter—'Feed my sheep'[39]—was meant but for himself, and no commandment to any successor of his, or any bishop or prelate. And by that means might ye say also that these words of Christ's promise made unto his disciples—that the Holy Ghost should instruct them of all things[40]—were only meant for themselves in their own persons, and not that ever he should instruct his Church after their days. And when he said, 'Wheresoever be two or three gathered together in my name, there am I myself among them,'[41] we shall say by this means that he meant but of[42] his own disciples in his own time, while he was here with them, and not that he would be likewise present with such other congregations in his Church after. And finally, then were these words frustrate[43]—where he said, 'Lo, I am with you all the days to the world's end'[44]—if he should mean it but with them that heard him speak it. Then should it appear that he had intended a Church only of them and for their time. And then from their death hither,[45] all were done."

"Verily, sir," quoth he, "I can well agree that all such things was spoken by Christ to make them sure that the faith should never fail in his Church. Howbeit if I durst doubt in[46] that point, one thing is there that somewhat sticketh in my mind."

"Doubt on," quoth I, "between us twain and spare not, nor let[47] not to tell me what moveth you."

"Sir," quoth he, "I think that God setteth no more by faith than he doth by charity. But as for charity and good works, with virtuous living, shall[48] cool and decay in the Church, as our Savior saith in the

twenty-fourth chapter of Matthew: 'Because iniquity shall abound, the charity of many men shall cool.'[49] And surely methinketh it is well near all gone already."

"God forbid," quoth I. "For albeit that it greatly day by day decayeth, and much people naught,[50] yet be there many good men about, and shall be always, though they be few in comparison of the multitude. And yet is it not all one of other virtues and of faith—that is to wit, of knowledge and belief of the articles of our faith—I mean of such articles as we be of necessity bounden to believe. For albeit that the flock of Christ shall never lack good and devout virtuous people, yet shall both the best be sinners, and also much more the multitude shall ever have the faith that I speak of, than shall have the goodness of living."

"Why so?" quoth he.

"For two causes," quoth I. "One, the malice of the people, whereby they will not be so ready to live well as to believe well. For the people themselves will better keep the faith than other virtues, since it is a thing of less labor to know what they should believe—and to believe it also when they know it—than it is to work well. For though the knowledge and belief bring many men to the labor of good works, yet the world commonly and the frailty of our flesh, with the enticement of our ghostly[51] enemies, make us willingly and wittingly,[52] well knowing and believing the good, yet to walk in the worse—as doth sometimes the sick man that, believing his physician, and having had also right often good proof by his own experience to his pain before, that some certain meat or drink shall do him harm, doth yet of an importune[53] appetite fall for his little pleasure to his great pain and hurt.

"Another cause is," quoth I, "the goodness of God, which[54] how far soever his people fall from the use[55] of virtue, shall not yet (as himself hath promised) suffer[56] them to fall from the knowledge of virtue, not only for the manifestation of his justice—that their own conscience may condemn them in doing the things that themselves know to be naught—but also to the intent they may still have among them a perpetual occasion of amendment. For if the faith

---

35 *Tenebrae:* "Darkness," a liturgical ritual conducted during Holy Week to mark Christ's time in the tomb   **36** readings (from the Bible); a major part of the ceremony   **37** Lk 22:32   **38** Mt 16:18

39 Jn 21:17   **40** See Jn 14:26.   **41** Mt 18:20   **42** *meant but of:* meant this to apply only to   **43** meaningless; pointless   **44** Mt 28:20   **45** to this day   **46** *durst doubt in:* dare question   **47** hesitate

48 they shall   **49** Mt 24:12   **50** (are) bad, wicked   **51** spiritual   **52** consciously   **53** inopportune   **54** who   **55** practice   **56** permit

were once gone, and the Church of Christ fallen in that error—that they believed vice to be virtue, and idolatry to be the right way of God's worship—then had they no rule to guide them to better. And therefore while we be not in error of understanding and faith, howsoever we fall or how often soever we sin, we see the way to turn again by grace to God's mercy. But if faith were gone, all were gone, and then had God here no Church at all."

THE NINETEENTH CHAPTER

The author proveth that if the worship of images were idolatry, then the Church, believing it to be lawful and pleasant to God, were in a misbelief and in a deadly error. And then were the faith failed in the Church, whereof Christ hath promised the contrary, as is proved in the chapter before.

"Surely, sir," quoth he, "that God made not his Church for a while, but to endure till the world's end, that is there no Christian man but he will well agree. And since his Church cannot stand without faith, which is the entry into Christendom—for as Saint Paul saith, *Accedentem ad Deum oportet credere* ('Whoso will come to God must needs believe')[57]—no man will deny but that faith is, and always shall be, in his Church, and that his Church—not in faith only, and the knowledge of the truths necessary to be known for our souls' health, but also to the doing of good works and avoiding of evil—is, hath been, and ever shall be specially guided and governed by God and the secret inspiration of his Holy Spirit."

"Well," quoth I, "then if the Church have faith, it erreth not in belief."

"That is truth," quoth he.

"It should err," quoth I, "if it believed not all the truths that we be bound to believe."

"What else?" quoth he.

"What and[58] we believed," quoth I, "all that is true, and over that some other thing not only false, but also displeasant to God—did we not then err in our necessary belief?"

"Whereby[59] mean you that?" quoth he.

"As thus," quoth I, "if that one believed in all the three Persons of the Trinity—the Father, the Son, and the Holy Ghost—and therewith[60] were persuaded that there were a fourth Person besides, equal and one God with them."

"He must," quoth he, "needs err in his necessary belief, by which he is bounden to believe in the Trinity. And that fellow believeth in a Quaternity!"

"That is," quoth I, "the whole Trinity and one more."

"But we be not only not bounden," quoth he, "to believe in any more, but also bounden not to believe in any more."

"Very well," quoth I, "then erreth he as much, and as far lacketh his right belief, that[61] believeth too much, as he that believeth too little, and he that believeth something that he should not, as he that believeth not something that he should."

"What else?" quoth he. "And what then?"

"Marry[62] this," quoth I: "If we believe that it were lawful and well done to pray to saints, and to reverence their images, and do honor to their relics and visit pilgrimages; and then where we do these things they were indeed not well done, but were displeasant to God, and by him reputed as a diminishment and a withdrawing of the honor due to himself, and therefore afore his Majesty reproved and odious and taken as idolatry—were not this opinion a deadly pestilent error in us, and a plain lack of right faith?"

"Yes, 'fore God," quoth he.

"But ye grant," quoth I, "that the Church cannot err in the right faith necessary to be believed, which is given and always kept in the Church by God."

"Truth," quoth he.

"Then followeth it," quoth I, "that the Church—in that it believeth saints to be prayed unto, relics and images to be worshipped, and pilgrimages to be visited and sought—is not deceived nor doth not err, but that the belief of the Church is true therein. And thereupon also followeth that the wonderful works done above nature at such images and pilgrimages, at holy relics, by prayers made unto saints, be not done by the devil to delude the Church of Christ therewith, since the thing that the Church doth is well done and not idolatry. But by the great honor done unto saints, God himself the more highly honored,[63] in that his servants have so much honor for his sake. And thereof followeth it that himself maketh the miracles, in comprobation[64] thereof.

"Also if it be true that ye have granted—that God keepeth and ever shall keep in his Church the right faith and right belief by the help of his own hand that hath planted it—then can it not be that he shall suffer the devil to work wonders like unto his own miracles to bring his whole Church into a wrong faith. And then if those things be not done by the devil, I trow[65] ye will not then deny but they be done by God. And so is yet again our purpose doubly proved. First, in that ye grant that God will not suffer his Church to err in his right faith; secondly (which pursueth thereupon), by that he hath by many a visible miracle declared that this faith and manner of observance is very pleasant and acceptable unto him; which miracles, since they been[66] proved to be done upon good ground and cause, appear well to be done by God, and not by our ghostly[67] enemy."

THE TWENTIETH CHAPTER

The messenger allegeth that the perpetual being and
assistance of Christ with his Church to keep it out
of all damnable errors is nothing else but his
being with his Church in Holy Scripture,
whereof the author declareth the contrary.

"How think you?" quoth I. "Is there anything in this matter amiss?"

"I cannot well tell," quoth he, "what I might answer thereto. But yet methink that I come to this point by some oversight in granting."[68]

"Well," quoth I, "men say sometimes—when they would say or do a thing and cannot well come thereon, but miss and oversee themselves[69] in the assay[70]—'It maketh no matter,' they say. 'Ye may begin again and mend it, for it is neither Mass nor Matins.'[71] And albeit in this matter ye have nothing granted but that[72] is in my mind as true as the Matins or the Mass either, yet if ye reckon yourself overswift in granting, I give you leave to go back and call again what ye will."

"In good faith," quoth he, "full hard were it in mine own mind otherwise to think but that God shall always keep the right belief in his Church. But yet since we come to this conclusion by the granting thereof, let us look once again thereupon. And what if men would say (as I heard once one say myself) that God doth peradventure not keep always faith in his Church, to give them warning with when they do well, and when the contrary. But since he hath given them, and left with them, the Scripture—in which they may sufficiently see both what they should believe and what they should do—he letteth them alone therewith, without any other special cure[73] of his, upon their faith and belief. For therein they may see all that them needeth, if they will look and labor therein. And if they will not, the fault is their own sloth and folly. And whoso be willing to mend and be better may always have light to see how, by recourse to the reading of Holy Scripture, which shall stand him in like stead[74] as ye said before, that God kept the faith for, by his special means in his Church."

"If this," quoth I, "were thus, whereof should Christ's promise serve, *Ego vobiscum sum omnibus diebus usque ad finem saeculi* ('I am with you all the days till the end of the world')?[75] Wherefore[76] should he be here with his Church, if his being here should not keep his right faith and belief in his Church?"

"Marry," quoth he, "these words well agreeth withal. For God is, and shall be until the world's end, with his Church in his Holy Scripture, as Abraham answered the rich man in hell, saying, 'They have Moses and the prophets,'[77] not meaning that they had them all at that time present with them, but only that they had their books. And so Christ, forasmuch as the Scripture hath his faith comprehended[78] therein according to his own words, *Scrutamini scripturas, quia scripturae sunt quae testimonium perhibent de me* ('Search you the Scriptures, for they bear witness of me'),[79] therefore he said, *Ego vobiscum sum usque ad finem saeculi* ('I am with you to the end of the world'), because his Holy Scripture shall never fail, as long as the world endureth. 'Heaven and earth,' saith he, 'shall pass away, but my words shall never pass away.'[80]

"And therefore in his Holy Writing is he with us still;[81] and therein he keepeth and teacheth us his right faith if we list[82] to look for it; and else, as I said, our own fault and folly it is."

"If God," quoth I, "be none otherwise with us but in Holy Scripture, then be those words of Christ 'I

---

65 trust   66 have been   67 spiritual
68 conceding (as in a debate)   69 *oversee*
themselves: fail to see their error

70 attempt   71 formal morning prayer
72 what   73 concern, care   74 *stand...*
stead: be of use to him in the same way

75 Mt 28:20   76 Why   77 Lk 16:29
78 included, comprised   79 Jn 5:39
80 Mt 24:35   81 See Mt 28:20.   82 want

am with you to the world's end' somewhat strangely spoken, and unlike the words of Abraham whereunto ye resemble them. For Christ left never a book behind him of his own making, as Moses did, and the prophets. And in their books was he spoken of, as he was in the Gospel. Wherefore if he had spoken and meant of Scripture, he would have said that they should have with them still his evangelists and writers of his Gospels, as Abraham said, 'They have Moses and the prophets,' which were the writers of the books that the Jews had. Christ also said 'I am with you till the end of the world'[83] — not 'I shall be,' but 'I am,' which is the word appropred[84] to his Godhead.[85] And therefore that word 'am' is the name by which our Lord would, as he told Moses, be named unto Pharaoh,[86] as a name which from all creatures (since they be all subject to time) clearly discerneth[87] his Godhead, which is ever being and present, without difference of time past or to come. In which wise, he was not in his Holy Scripture, for that had beginning. And at those words spoken, was not yet all written. For of the chief part, which is the New Testament, there was yet at that time never one word written. And also we be not sure by any promise made, that the Scripture shall endure to the world's end, albeit I think verily the substance shall. But yet, as I say, promise have we none thereof. For where our Lord saith that his 'words shall not pass away,' nor one iota thereof be lost,[88] he spoke of his promises made indeed, as his faith and doctrine taught[89] by mouth and inspiration. He meant not that of his Holy Scripture in writing there should never an iota be lost, of which some parts be already lost — more peradventure than we can tell of — and of that[90] we have, the books in some part corrupted with miswriting.[91] And yet the substance of those words that he meant be known, where some part of the writing is unknown. He saith also that his Father and he should send the Holy Ghost, and also that he would come himself[92] — whereto all this if he meant no more but to leave the books behind them and go their way? Christ is also present among us bodily, in the Holy Sacrament. And is he there present with us for nothing? The Holy Ghost taught many things, I think, unwritten, and whereof some part was never comprised in[93] the

Scripture yet unto this day, as[94] the article which no good Christian man will doubt of: that our blessed Lady was a perpetual virgin as well after the birth of Christ as afore.

"Our Savior also said unto his apostles that when they should be accused and brought in judgment, they should not need to care for answer; it should even then be put in their minds.[95] And that he meant not only the remembrance of Holy Scripture (which before the paynim judges were but a cold and bare alleging), but such words new given them by God, inspired in their hearts, so effectual and confirmed with miracles that their adversaries, though they were angry thereat, yet should not be able to resist it.[96] And thus with secret help and inspiration is Christ with his Church, and will be to the world's end, present and assistant — not only spoken of in writing."

THE TWENTY-FIRST CHAPTER
The author showeth that if it so were indeed as the messenger said — that is to wit, that Christ continued with his Church none other wise[97] but only by the leaving of his Holy Scripture to them, and that all the faith also were only therein — then should it yet follow that, as far as the necessity of our salvation requireth, God giveth the Church the right understanding thereof. And thereupon followeth further that the Church cannot err in the right faith. Whereupon is inferred eftsoon[98] all that the messenger would have fled from before. And thereon also specially followeth that all the texts of Holy Scripture which heretics allege against images, or any point of the common belief of Christ's Catholic Church, can nothing serve their purpose.

"But now would I wit,[99] since ye reckon[100] him none other wise present than in Holy Scripture, whether then doth he give his Church the right understanding of Holy Scripture or not?"

"What if he do not?" quoth he.

"Marry,"[101] quoth I, "then yourself seeth well that they were as well without. And so should the Scripture stand them in as good stead as a pair of spectacles should stand a blind friar."

83 Mt 28:20 **84** appropriate **85** Jn 8:58 **86** See Ex 3:9–15. **87** distinguishes **88** See Mt 5:18, 24:35. **89** were taught **90** that which **91** miscopying **92** See Jn 14:16–18, 15:28. **93** *compromised in:* incorporated into **94** such as **95** See Mt 10:19. **96** See Lk 21:12–15. **97** *none other wise:* in no other way **98** for a second time **99** *would I wit:* I would like to know **100** suppose **101** Indeed

"That is very truth," quoth he. "But therefore hath his wisdom and goodness provided it so to be written that it may be well understood by the collation[102] and consideration of one text with another."

5 "May it not also be," quoth I, "that some of them which do read it diligently, and diligently compare and consider every text, how it may stand with others, may yet, for all that, mistake and misunderstand it?"

10 "Yes," quoth he, "it may be so. For else had there not been so many heretics as there hath been."

"Very truth," quoth I. "But now if all the faith be in Holy Scripture, and no part thereof anywhere else, but that it must be therein altogether learned, were 15 it then sufficient to understand some part aright, and some other part wrong, in the necessary points of our faith? Or must we, as far-forth[103] as concerneth the necessity thereof, misunderstand no part?"

"We must," quoth he, "mistake no part, as far as 20 necessarily concerneth our faith. But we must have so the right understanding of all together, that we conceive no damnable error."

"Well said," quoth I. "Then if we must, we may. For if we may not, we must not. For our Lord bind-25 eth no man to an impossibility."

"We may," quoth he.

"If we may," quoth I, "then may we either by good hap[104] fall into the right understanding, or else by natural reason come to it, or else by supernatural 30 grace be led into it."

"That is truth," quoth he. "Needs must it be one of these ways."

"Well," quoth I, "we will not yet ensearch[105] which. But I would first wit whether Christ have 35 a church in the world continually, and so shall have to the world's end, or else hath one sometimes, and sometimes none at all. As we might think that he had one while he was here himself, and peradventure a while after, and haply[106] none at all never 40 since, nor shall not again — we wot nere[107] when."

"Nay," quoth he, "that cannot be in no wise,[108] but that he must needs have his Church continue still somewhere; for else how could he be with them continually to the world's end — in Scripture 45 or otherwise — if they (with whom he promised to be, and continue to the world's end) should not continually so long endure? Or how could those

words of Christ be true, 'Lo, I am with you all the days to the world's end,' if before the world's end he were away some days — as he were indeed from 50 the Church some days, if in some days he had no church?"

"Well," quoth I, "yet would I wit one thing more: Can he have a church without faith?"

"Nay," quoth he, "that were impossible." 55

"Forsooth,"[109] quoth I, "so were it. For his Church is a congregation of people gathered into his faith. And faith is the first substantial difference discerning Christian men from heathen, as reason is the difference dividing man from all the kinds of brute 60 beasts. Now then if his Church be and ever shall be continual, without any times between in which there shall be none;[110] and without faith it may never be; and no part of the faith is, as ye say, elsewhere had but in Holy Scripture, and all it must be 65 had; and also, as we were agreed a little while afore, there must be none error adjoined thereto; and therefore, as far as toucheth the necessity of faith, no part of Scripture may be mistaken, but all must be understood right, and may be right understood 70 either by hap, reason, or help of grace — it necessarily followeth that by one or other of these ways the Church of Christ hath always, and never faileth,[111] the right understanding of Scripture, as far as longeth for[112] our necessity." 75

"That followeth indeed," quoth he.

"Well," quoth I, "let pass for the while what followeth further. And since the Church so hath,[113] let us first agree by which of these three ways the Church hath it: whether by hap, reason, or grace." 80

"By hap," quoth he, "were a poor having. For so might it hap to have and hap to fail."

"Then," quoth I, "since it hath it ever, it cannot be by hap. What think you then of reason?"

"As little," quoth he, "as any man thinketh. For I 85 take reason for plain enemy to faith."

"Ye take peradventure[114] wrong," quoth I. "But thereof shall we see further after. But now since ye so think, ye leave but the third way, which is the help of grace." 90

"No surely," quoth he.

"Verily," quoth I, "where reason may between diverse texts stand in great doubt which way to lean, I think that God with his Holy Spirit leadeth his

Church into the consent of the truth, as himself said that the Holy Ghost (whom he would send) should lead them into all truth.[115] He said not that the Holy Ghost should at his coming write them all truth, nor tell them all the whole truth by mouth, but that he should by secret inspiration lead them into all truth. And therefore surely for a true conclusion in[116] such means — by God himself, by the help of his grace (as yourself granteth) — the right understanding of Scripture is ever preserved in his Church from all such mistaking whereof might follow any damnable error concerning the faith. And thereof doth there first follow, that besides the Scripture itself, there is another present assistance and special cure of[117] God perpetual with his Church to keep it in the right faith, that it err not by misunderstanding of Holy Scripture — contrary to the opinion that ye purposed when ye said that Christ's being with his Church was only the leaving of his Holy Scripture to us. And over[118] this, if God were no other wise present than ye speak of, yet since it is proved that his Church, for all that, ever hath the right understanding of Scripture, we be comen to the same point again that ye would so fain flit[119] from. For if the Scripture — and nothing but the Scripture — doth contain all things that we be bounden to believe, and to do, and to forbear,[120] and that God also therefore provideth for his Church the right understanding thereof concerning everything necessary for us that is contained in Scripture, then must there needs follow thereupon the thing that ye feared lest ye had wrong and unadvisedly granted: that is to wit, that God always keepeth the right faith in his Church. And thereupon followeth further the remnant of all that is in question between us: that the faith of the Church in the worship that it believeth to be well given unto saints, relics, and images is not erroneous, but right. And thereupon followeth also that the miracles done at such places be none illusions of damned spirits, but the mighty hand of God, to show his pleasure in the corroboration thereof, and in the excitation of our devotion thereto."

"Indeed," quoth he, "we be come back here with going forward, as men walk in a maze."

"Ye have not yet," quoth I, "lost all that labor. For though ye have half a check[121] in this point, yet have ye (if ye perceive it) mated[122] me in another point, by one thing that is agreed between us now."

"What is that?" quoth he.

"This," quoth I, "that I have agreed as well as you: that God hath given his Church the right understanding of Scripture in as far-forth[123] as longeth[124] to the necessity of salvation."

"In what point," quoth he, "hath that mated you?"

"Why," quoth I, "see you not that? Nay, then will I not tell you, but if[125] ye hire me;[126] or if I tell you, yet shall ye not win the game thereby. For since ye see it not yourself, it is but a blind mate."[127]

"Let me know it yet," quoth he, "and I am agreed to take none advantage thereof."

"On that bargain be it," quoth I.

"Ye wot well," quoth I, "that against the worshipping of images and praying to saints, ye laid[128] certain texts of Scripture to prove it forbidden and reputed of God for[129] idolatry. For answer whereof, when I laid that men must lean to the sentence[130] that the Church and holy doctors[131] of the Church give to those texts, ye said they were but men's false glosses against God's true texts. And now since ye grant, and I also, that the Church cannot misunderstand the Scripture to the hindrance of the right faith in things of necessity, and that ye also acknowledge this matter to be such that it must either be the right belief, and acceptable service to God, or else a wrong and erroneous opinion and plain idolatry, it followeth of necessity that the Church doth not misunderstand those texts that ye or any other can allege and bring forth for that purpose, but that all these texts be so to be taken and understood as they nothing make against the Church, but all against your own opinion in this matter.

"And thus have ye suddenly answered yourself, to all those texts, out of hand, with a gloss[132] of your own, as true as any text in the Bible, and which all the world will never avoid,[133] except they would make the Scripture serve the Church of nought,[134] or rather to their hindrance than furtherance in the faith. For so were it, if it might be, that God giveth them not the good understanding thereof,

115 See Jn 16:13.   **116** by   **117** *cure of:* care given by   **118** besides   **119** *fain flit:* gladly flee   **120** refrain from doing   **121** a pun which introduces a chess metaphor: a reversal or rebuff; a threat to one's kin in chess

122 checkmated   **123** *in as far-forth:* to the extent   **124** pertains   **125** *but if:* unless   **126** *hire me:* pay me to; raise the stakes we're playing for   **127** *blind mate:* when one player in chess has checkmated

the other without realizing it   **128** cited   **129** *reputed of God for:* regarded by God as   **130** meaning(s)   **131** theologians   **132** interpretation, commentary   **133** disprove   **134** *of nought:* for nothing but suffereth[135] them to be deceived and deluded in errors, by the mistaking of the letter."[136]

"Marry," quoth he, "this is a blind mate indeed."

"Surely," quoth I, "these two things seem to me two as true points, and as plain, to a Christian man as any petition[137] of Euclid's geometry is to a reasonable man. For as true as it is that every whole thing is more than his[138] own half,[139] as true is it indeed, and to every Christian man, faith maketh it as certain: first, that Christ's Church cannot err in any such article as God upon pain of loss of heaven will that we believe; and thereupon necessarily followeth that there is no text of Scripture well understood by which Christian people are commanded to do the thing which the Church believeth that they may lawfully leave undone, nor any text whereby we be forbidden anything which the Church believeth that they may lawfully do."

THE TWENTY-SECOND CHAPTER

Because the messenger had in the beginning showed himself desirous and greedy upon[140] the text of Scripture, with little force[141] of the old fathers' glosses,[142] and with dispraise of philosophy and almost all the seven liberal sciences,[143] the author therefore incidentally showeth what harm hath happed sometimes to fall to diverse of those young men whom he hath known to give their study to the Scripture only, with contempt of logic and other secular science, and little regard of the old interpreters. Wherefore the author showeth that in the study of Scripture, the sure way is—with virtue and prayer—first to use the judgment of natural reason, whereunto secular literature helpeth much, and secondly, the comments[144] of holy doctors, and thirdly, above all things, the articles of the Catholic faith, received and believed through the Church of Christ.

"And for because we speak of Scripture now, and that the Church, in things needly[145] requisite to salvation, hath the right understanding of Holy Scripture, wherein I perceive ye be studious of the text alone, without great force of the old fathers' interpretations, or any other science—of which ye reckon all seven, save grammar, almost to serve for nought[146]—I have of you so good opinion that I trust all your study shall turn you to good. But surely I have seen to some folk so much harm to grow thereof that I never would advise any man else in the study of Scripture to take that way."

"Why so?" quoth he.

"For I have known," quoth I, "right good wits[147] that hath set all other learning aside—partly for sloth, refusing the labor and pain to be sustained in that learning, partly for pride, by which they could not endure the redargution[148] that should sometimes fall to their part in dispicions.[149] Which affections their inward secret favor toward themselves covered and cloaked under the pretext of simplicity and good Christian devotion borne to the love of Holy Scripture alone. But in little while after, the damnable spirit of pride that, unware[150] to themselves, lurked in their hearts hath begun to put out his horns and show himself. For then have they longed, under the praise of Holy Scripture, to set out to show[151] their own study. Which,[152] because they would have seem[153] the more to be set by,[154] they have first fallen to the dispraise and derision of all other disciplines. And because in speaking or preaching of such common things as all Christian men know, they could not seem excellent, nor make it appear and seem that in their study they had done any great mastery, to show themselves therefore marvelous, they set out paradoxes and strange[155] opinions against the common faith of Christ's whole Church. And because they have therein the old holy doctors against them, they fall to the contempt and dispraise of them, either preferring their own fond[156] glosses against the old cunning[157] and blessed fathers' interpretations, or else lean to some words of Holy Scripture that seem to say for[158] them, against many more texts that plainly make against them, without receiving or ear giving to any reason or authority of any man, quick[159] or dead— or of the whole Church of Christ to the contrary. And thus once proudly persuaded a wrong way,

---

135 allows   136 literal meaning of the text
137 axiom   138 its   139 Euclid's fifth
axiom. See *Elements*, Book 1.   140 *greedy upon:* eager for   141 regard   142 explanations; interpretations   143 arts. The seven liberal arts are grammar, logic,

rhetoric, arithmetic, geometry, music, and astronomy.   144 commentaries
145 necessarily   146 nothing   147 minds, intellects   148 refutation; rebuke
149 debates   150 unknown   151 display; show off   152 Who   153 *would have*

seem: want to have it seem (that they are)
154 *set by:* valued; esteemed   155 unfamiliar   156 foolish   157 wise   158 *say for:* support   159 living

they take the bridle in the teeth and run forth like a headstrong horse, that all the world cannot pluck them back. But with sowing sedition, setting forth of errors and heresies, and spicing their preaching with rebuking of priesthood and prelacy for the people's pleasure, they turn many a man to ruin and themselves also. And then the devil deceiveth them in their blind affections.[160]

"They take for good zeal to the people their malicious envy, and for a great virtue, their ardent appetite to preach — wherein they have so great pride for the people's praise, that preach I ween they would, though God would his own mouth command them the contrary."

"Why should ye ween so," quoth he, "or whereby can ye be sure that ye do not now misconstrue their good mind? Hard is it oft-times to judge another man's deed that hath some appearance of evil, because the purpose and intent may make it good. And what peril is it then where the deed appeareth good, there to judge the mind and intent for naught,[161] which who can see but God? As the Scripture saith, *Dominus autem intuetur cor* ('Only God beholdeth the heart').[162] And therefore saith our Savior, 'Judge not before the time.'"[163]

"I judge not," quoth I, "but upon open things and well apparent. For I speak but of those whose erroneous opinions in their preaching, and their obstinate pride in the defense of their worldly worship,[164] well declareth their minds. And some have I seen which,[165] when they have for their perilous preaching been by their prelates prohibited to preach, have (that notwithstanding) proceeded on still; and, for the maintenance[166] of their disobedience, have amended the matter with a heresy, boldly and stubbornly defending that, since they had cunning to preach, they were by God bounden to preach, and that no man, nor no law that was made or could be made, had any authority to forbid them. And this they thought sufficiently proved by the words of the Apostle, *Oportet magis oboedire Deo quam hominibus*.[167] As though these men were apostles now specially sent by God to preach heresies and sow sedition among Christian men, as the

very apostles were indeed sent and commanded by God to preach his very faith to the Jews. One of this sort, of this new kind of preachers, being demanded why that he used to say in his sermons about, that nowadays men preached not well the Gospel, answered that he thought so because he saw not the preachers persecuted, nor no strife nor business[168] arise upon their preaching. Which things, he said and wrote, was the fruit of the Gospel, because Christ said, *Non veni pacem mittere, sed gladium* ('I am not come to send peace into the world, but the sword').[169] Was not this a worshipful[170] understanding, that because Christ would make a division among infidels, from the remnant of them to win some, therefore these apostles would sow some cockle[171] of dissension among the Christian people,[172] whereby Christ might lose some of them? For the fruit of strife among the hearers and persecution of the preacher cannot lightly[173] grow among Christian men but by the preaching of some strange novelties and bringing up of some newfangled heresies, to the infection of our old faith.

"One wist[174] I that was for his pertinacy[175] in that opinion — that he would and might and was bounden to preach, any prohibition notwithstanding — when he was, after diverse bold and open defenses thereof, at last before folk honorable and few, reasoned withal, and not only the law showed him to the contrary of his opinion (which law was made at a general council),[176] but also by plain authority of Holy Scripture[177] proved that his opinion was erroneous, he so perceived himself satisfied that he meekly acknowledged his error, and offered to abjure[178] it and to submit himself to penance. But on the morrow, when he came forth in open presence of the people, and there saw many that had oft heard him preach, of his secret[179] pride he fell in such an open[180] passion of shame that those should hear him go back with[181] his word which had before had[182] his sermons in great estimation, that at the first sight of the people he revoked his revocation, and said out aloud, that[183] he might well be heard, that his opinion was true, and that he was the day before deceived in that he had confessed

160 passions   161 evil   162 1 Kgs (1 Sm) 16:7   163 1 Cor 4:5. See also Mt 7:1. 164 reputation   165 who   166 defense 167 "We must obey God rather than men" (Acts 5:29).   168 trouble   169 Mt 10:34   170 pious; respectable   171 weed 172 See Mt 13:25.   173 easily; readily 174 knew   175 stubbornness   176 The Fourth Lateran Council (1215) taught that no one could preach after being forbidden.   177 See Rom 10:15. 178 publicly renounce   179 *of his secret:* from his private   180 public; shameless (a pun)   181 on   182 *which had before had:* who before had held   183 so that

it for false. And thus he held his own stubbornly, without reason, till the books were showed him again, and himself read them before all the people, so that he perceived the audience that stood about him to feel and understand his proud folly in the defense of his indefensible error, and thereupon, at the last, yielded himself again. Such secret pride had our ghostly[184] enemy conveyed into the heart of him, which,[185] I ensure[186] you, seemed in all his other outward manner as meek a simple soul as a man should have seen in a summer's day. And some of them let[187] not with lies and perjury to defend themselves, and some to stand in defense of their errors, or false denying of their own deed, to their great peril of the fire, if their judges were not more merciful than their malice[188] deserveth. And all this done because (as themselves doth at last confess) they think if they abjure they shall after be suffered[189] to preach again. Such a scabbed[190] itch of vainglory catch they in their preaching that, though all the world were the worse for it, and their own life lie thereon, yet would they long to be pulpited. And this, I say, hath come[191] of some that have, with contempt of all other learning, given them[192] to Scripture alone. Whose affections of[193] pride and sloth hath not in the beginning been perceived to themselves, but have[194] accounted their vices for devotion."

"Would ye then," quoth he, "condemn that manner of study by which a man hath so great affection to the Scripture alone that he, for the delight thereof, feeleth little savor in anything else, but that we should lose time in philosophy—the mother of heresies—and let Scripture alone?"

"Nay," quoth I, "that mind am I not of. There was never thing written in this world that can in any wise be comparable with any part of Holy Scripture. And yet I think other liberal sciences a gift of God also, and not to be cast away, but worthy to wait and as handmaids to give attendance upon divinity.[195] And in this point I think not thus alone. For ye shall find Saint Jerome, Saint Augustine, Saint Basil, and many of the old holy doctors, open and plain of the same opinion. And of divinity reckon I the best part

to be contained in Holy Scripture. And this I say for him that shall have time thereto,[196] and from youth intendeth to the churchward, and to make himself, with God's help, meet[197] for the office of a preacher. Howbeit, if any man either happen to begin so late that he shall peradventure have no time thereto, or else any man of youth to have that fervent appetite unto Scripture that he cannot find in his heart to read anything else (which affection whoso[198] happeth to have given him is very fortunate, if he with grace and meekness guide it well), then would I counsel him specially to study for the virtuous framing[199] of his own affections,[200] and using great moderation and temperance in the preaching to other men. And in all things to flee the desire of praise and show of cunning, ever mistrusting his own inclinations, and live in dread and fear of the devil's subtle sleight and inventions.[201] Who though he lie in continual await upon every preacher to catch him into pride if he can, yet his highest enterprise and proudest triumph standeth in the bringing of a man to the most abuse[202] of that thing, that is of his own nature the best. And therefore great labor maketh he, and great boast if he bring it about, that a good wit may abuse his labor bestowed upon the study of Holy Scripture.

"For the sure avoiding whereof, my poor advice were—in the study thereof—to have a special regard to the writings and comments[203] of old holy fathers. And yet ere he fall in hand[204] with the one or the other, next[205] grace and help of God (to be gotten with abstinence and prayer and cleanness of living), afore all things were it necessary to come well and surely instructed in all such points and articles as the Church believeth. Which things once firmly had, and fastly[206] for undoubted truths presupposed, then shall reason and they be two good rules to examine and expound all doubtful texts by, since the reader shall be sure that no text is so to be understood as it standeth against them both, or against any point of the Catholic faith of Christ's Church. And, therefore, if it seem to stand against any of them, either shall the light of natural reason, with the collation[207] of other texts, help to

---

184 spiritual **185** who **186** assure
187 hesitate **188** Intention or desire to
do evil or injure another person; active
ill will and hatred; in legal thinking,
state of mind required for a person to be
found guilty of certain criminal offenses

189 *after be suffered:* afterward be allowed
190 diseased **191** *hath come:* is what has
become **192** themselves **193** *affections
of:* inclinations toward, attachments to
194 they have **195** theology **196** for it
197 suitable **198** whoever **199** ordering

200 dispositions **201** *sleight and
inventions:* trickery and schemes
202 *most abuse:* worst misuse **203** commentaries **204** *ere…hand:* before he
proceeds **205** next to **206** steadfastly
207 comparison

find out the truth, or else (which is the surest way) he shall perceive the truth in the comments of the good holy doctors of old, to whom God hath given the grace of understanding. Or finally, if all that he can either find in other men's works, or invent[208] by God's aid of his own study, cannot suffice to satisfy, but that any text yet seem unto him contrary to any point of the Church's faith and belief, let him then, as Saint Augustine saith, make himself very sure that there is some fault either in the translator, or in the writer (or nowadays in the printer), or finally that for some one let[209] or other, he understandeth it not aright. And so let him reverently acknowledge his ignorance, lean and cleave to the faith of the Church as to an undoubted truth, leaving that text to be better perceived when it shall please our Lord with his light to reveal and disclose it. And in this wise shall he take a sure way, by which he shall be sure of one of two things: that is to wit, either to perceive and understand the Scripture right, or else at the leastwise never in such wise to take it wrong, that ever may turn his soul to peril."

THE TWENTY-THIRD CHAPTER
The messenger objecteth against the counsel of the author, in that he would that the student of Scripture should[210] lean to[211] the commenters[212] and unto natural reason, which he calleth enemy to faith. And thereupon the answer of the author to those objections, specially proving that reason is servant to faith, and not enemy, and must with faith and interpretation of Scripture needs be concurrent.[213]

"Sir," quoth he, "I will not say nay but[214] this way will do well. Howbeit, I fear me that we were likely to build up many errors if we square our timber and stones by these three rules: men's glosses, reason, and faith, not that we find in Scripture, but that we bring with us to Scripture. For first, as for the commenters that ye speak of, either their comments tell us the same tale that the text doth, or else another. If they tell me the same, I believe them only because the text saith the same. And if they tell me another, then believe I them not at all, nor

nought[215] I should, except[216] I should believe men better than God. And as for reason, what greater enemy can ye find to faith than reason is, which counterpleadeth[217] faith in every point? And would ye then send them twain forth to school together, that can never agree together, but be ready to fight together and either scratch out other's eyes by[218] the way? It seemeth also somewhat strange that when God hath left us in his Holy Scripture well and sufficiently his doctrine, whereby he would we should have warning of all such things as he would we should believe and do, or leave undone, and hath left us the Scripture for none other cause but for that it should stand unto us for the witness of his will declared us by writing, that we should not say nay but we were warned, and none other cause why the Scripture should be given us but to tell us his pleasure and stir us to fulfill it, we shall now not shape our faith after[219] the Scripture, but first frame us a faith ourselves, and then shape the Scripture of God thereby, and make it agree thereto. This were indeed a good easy way for a slothful mason that were an evil workman: to make him a square and a ruler of lead, that when he list[220] not to take the labor to hew the stone to the square, he may bend the square to the stone, and so shall he yet bring them together at the leastways."

"As for the old commenters," quoth I, "they tell you the same tale that the text doth, but they tell it you more plain, as we shall more talk of after. But surely ye beguiled me now, in that ye set reason so short; for verily, I would never have weened that ye would in Scripture like worse a wise man than an unreasonable reader. Nor I cannot see why ye should reckon reason for an enemy to faith, except ye reckon every man for your enemy that is your better and hurteth you not. Thus were one of your five wits[221] enemy to another, and our feeling should abhor our sight, because we may see farther by four miles than we may feel. How can reason — but if[222] reason be unreasonable — have more disdain to hear the truth of any point of faith than to see the proof of many things natural whereof reason can no more attain to the cause than it can in the articles of the faith? But still for any power that reason hath to perceive the cause, she shall judge it impossible after

---

208 discover   209 hindrance
210 *would…should:* wants the student
of Scripture to   211 *lean to:* rely on
212 commentators   213 compatible

214 *say nay but:* deny   215 not at
all   216 unless   217 contradicts
218 on   219 according to   220 wishes
221 interior senses (memory, imagination,

apprehension, reasoning, will)   222 *but
if:* unless

she prove it true, but if she believe her eye better than her wit.

"When ye see the adamant stone[223] draw iron to it, it grieveth not reason to look thereon, but reason hath a pleasure to behold the thing that passeth[224] her power to perceive. For it is as plain against the rule of reason that a heavy body should move alone any other motion than downward, or that any bodily thing should draw another without touching, as is any article of the faith. Nor never was there yet cause by reason assigned that men may perceive for probable, but only that it is a secret property of the stone — which is as much to say as 'I wot nere[225] what.' And yet, as I say, reason can believe that thing well enough, and be not angry therewith nor strive against it. And yet all the rules that ever she learned tell her still that it may not be."

"Yea," quoth he, "but a man's own eyes tell him that it may be. And that must needs content him."

"May a man then better trust his eyes," quoth I, "than his wit?"[226]

"Yea, marry!"[227] quoth he. "What may he better trust than his eyes?"

"His eyes may," quoth I, "be deceived and ween they see that they see not, if reason give over his hold, except ye think the juggler blow his galls[228] through the goblet's bottom, or cut your girdle afore your face in twenty pieces and make it whole again, and put a knife into his eye and see never the worse, and turn a plum into a dog's turd in a boy's mouth."

Now happened it madly that even with this word came one of my folk and asked whether they should make ready for dinner.

"Abide," quoth I, "let us have better meat[229] first." And therewith your friend and I began to laugh.

"Well," quoth I, "make none haste yet for a little while." And so went he his way, half out of countenance,[230] weening that he had done or said somewhat like a fool, as he was one that was not very wise indeed, and wont[231] so to do. And then said I to your friend, "Now ye see that reason is not so proud a dame as ye take her for. She seeth done indeed by nature that she cannot perceive how, and is well contented therewith. She seeth a fond[232] fellow

deceive her sight and her wit therewith, and taketh it well and merrily, and is not angry that the juggler will not teach every man his craft. And ween ye then that she will take it so highly that God himself, her Master and Maker, should do what him list,[233] and then tell her what, and tell her not how? I pray[234] you," quoth I, "that our Lord was born of a virgin, how know you?"

"Marry," quoth he, "by Scripture."

"How know you," quoth I, "that ye should believe the Scripture?"

"Marry," quoth he, "by faith."

"Why," quoth I, "what doth faith tell you therein?"

"Faith," quoth he, "telleth me that Holy Scripture is things of truth written by the secret teaching of God."

"And whereby know you," quoth I, "that ye should believe God?"

"Whereby?" quoth he. "This is a strange question. Every man," quoth he, "may well wot that."

"That is truth," quoth I. "But is there any horse, or any ass, that wotteth that?"

"None," quoth he, "that I wot of, but if[235] Balaam's ass anything understood thereof.[236] For he spoke like a good reasonable ass."

"If no brute beast can wit[237] that," quoth I, "and every man may, what is the cause why that man may and other beasts may not?"

"Marry," quoth he, "for man hath reason and they have none."

"Ah well then," quoth I, "reason must he needs have, then, that shall perceive what he should believe. And so must reason not resist faith, but walk with her, and as her handmaid so wait upon her that — as contrary as ye take her, yet of a truth — faith goeth never without her. But likewise as if a maid be suffered[238] to run on the bridle,[239] or be cup-shotten,[240] or wax too proud, she will then wax copious and chop[241] logic with her mistress, and fare[242] sometimes as[243] she were frantic, so if reason be suffered to run out at riot, and wax over-high-hearted and proud, she will not fail to fall in rebellion toward her mistress, faith. But on the other side, if she be well brought up and well guided and kept in good temper,[244] she shall never disobey faith, being in her right mind. And therefore let reason be well guided, for surely faith goeth never without her.

"Now, in the study of Scripture—in devising upon the sentence,[245] in considering what ye read, in pondering the purpose of diverse comments,[246] in comparing together diverse texts that seem contrary and be not—albeit I deny not but that grace and God's especial help is the great thing therein, yet useth he for an instrument man's reason thereto.[247] God helpeth us to eat, also, but yet not without our mouth. Now as the hand is[248] the more nimble by the use of some feats,[249] and the legs and feet more swift and sure by custom of going and running, and the whole body the more wieldy and lusty[250] by some kind of exercise, so is it no doubt but that reason is by study, labor, and exercise of logic, philosophy, and other liberal arts, corroborated and quickened,[251] and the judgment—both in them and also in orators, laws, and stories[252]—much riped.[253] And albeit poets be with many men taken but for painted words, yet do they much help the judgment, and make a man, among other things, well furnished of one special thing, without which all learning is half lame."

"What is that?" quoth he.

"Marry," quoth I, "a good mother wit.[254] And therefore are, in mine opinion, these Lutherans in a mad mind, that would now have all learning save Scripture only clean[255] cast away, which things (if the time will serve) be as methinketh to be taken and had,[256] and with reason brought, as I said before, into the service of divinity.[257] And as holy Saint Jerome saith, the Hebrews well 'despoil the Egyptians'[258] when Christ's learned men take out of the pagan writers the riches and learning and wisdom that God gave unto them, and employ the same in the service of divinity about[259] the profit of God's chosen children of Israel, the Church of Christ, which he hath, of the hard stony paynims,[260] made the children of Abraham."[261]

THE TWENTY-FOURTH CHAPTER

The messenger maketh objections against the author, in that he counseled the student of Scripture to bring the articles of our faith with him for a special rule to construe the Scripture by. And the author confirmeth his counsel given in that behalf,[262] declaring that without that rule, men may soon fall into great errors in the study of Holy Scripture.

With this your friend held, as he said, himself somewhat content that reason was not so great an enemy to faith as she seemed. But yet he thought that she should have need rather to be well bridled than to bear much rule in the interpretation of Scripture. But as for the other point—that we should needs bring the faith with us already, as a rule to learn the Scripture by, when we come to the Scripture to learn the faith by—that thing he thought in no wise convenient,[263] but a thing, he said, much like as if we would go make the cart to draw the horse.

"Well," quoth I, "we shall see anon[264] whether the cart draw the horse or the horse the cart, or whether we be yet haply[265] so blind that we see not well which is the cart, which is the horse."

"First," quoth I, "tell me, how old would ye that one were ere he come to the study of Scripture?"

"By my faith," quoth he, "I would have a Christian man's child begin therein very young, and therein continue all his life."

"In good faith," quoth I, "that like I not amiss, so that[266] ye do not mean that ye would have him all his life learn nothing else. And yet that could I suffer too, and allow right well in some. But yet if he did never in his life learn aught[267] else, how old think ye that he should be ere he learned the articles of his belief in the Bible?"

"I cannot readily tell," quoth he, "for I have not seen it assayed."[268]

"Well," quoth I, "since we be not sure how long it would be in learning there, were it not best then that for that while he were taught his creed before, in his own mother tongue?"

---

244 composure   **245** *devising…sentence:* interpreting the meaning   **246** commentaries   **247** also   **248** becomes   **249** *use of some feats:* practice of some exercises   **250** *wieldy and lusty:* agile and healthy   **251** *corroborated and quickened:* strengthened and invigorated

252 histories, historical writings   **253** matured   **254** shrewd intelligence; common sense   **255** completely   **256** held; possessed   **257** theology   **258** See Ex 3:22.   **259** for   **260** pagans   **261** See Mt 3:9; Lk 3:8; Jerome, Letter 10 (*PL* 22: 664–65); Augustine, *De doctrina*

Christiana 2.40.60–61 (*PL* 34: 63).   **262** *in that behalf:* regarding that aspect of the matter   **263** *in no wise convenient:* by no means proper   **264** soon   **265** perhaps   **266** *so that:* so long as   **267** anything   **268** tried; tested

"I deny not that," quoth he, "that he should con[269] his creed before, because every Christian man's child, by the law, should know his faith as soon as he could, but I say he should not therewith take upon him to judge and examine Holy Scripture thereby."

"Well," quoth I, "let this Christian child of ours alone for a while. And let us consider if there were a good old idolater that never had heard in all his life anything of our belief, or of other god than only the man in the moon, whom he had watched and worshipped every frosty night. If this man might suddenly have the whole Bible turned into his own tongue, and read it over, think ye that he should thereby learn all the articles of the faith?"

"I think," quoth he, "that he might."

"Think ye so?" quoth I. "I put case[270] that he believed that all the book were lies."

"Marry," quoth he, "that may he, by the book himself,[271] learn the contrary. For the book in telling his tale affirmeth his tale and teacheth it to be true."

"Ye say very truth," quoth I, "if it were all one to read a thing and learn a thing. But now might there be another book made also, with lesser wonders and fewer, and thereby less unlikely, and yet all untrue. And how should his mind give him then that this book telling so incredible wonders should be true?"

"Nay," quoth he, "that thing must he needs believe, or else he can perceive nothing."

"Well," quoth I, "then is there one point of faith, one great lesson, to be learned without the book, that must be learned somewhere, either by God or man, or else the whole book will do us little service. And of whom we shall learn that, we shall see hereafter. But now suppose that this old idolater were thoroughly persuaded in his mind that all the book were true. Think you then that he should find out therein all the articles of our faith?"

"I think," quoth he, "that he should."

"Think ye so?" quoth I. "Be it so then. But think ye that he shall find them out all in a week?"

"Nay," quoth he, "that can he not do."

"Well," quoth I, "then since he shall not, at the leastwise, find them out all on a day, let us leave him a little while in seeking, and we shall return again after to him, and look what he shall have founden. And in the mean season[272] we shall go look again upon our good little godson, the boy, pardie,[273] that we christened right now and taught him his creed and set him to Scripture. Were it need that this child knew no more of his faith but his creed before he go to Scripture?"

"Methinketh," quoth he, "that it were enough."

"Be it so then," quoth I.

"What if it should fortune him to find some text of Scripture that should seem to him to be contrary to his creed? As, for example, if he happened upon the reading of these words: *Dii estis, et filii Excelsi omnes* ('Gods be ye all, and the children of the High God').[274] What if he would ween that, since in these words it is said all good men be the children of God, our Savior Christ were not God's only-begotten Son, but his son in such wise as God, by the prophet, calleth all good men?"

"That could he not think," quoth he. "For he should in other parts of Scripture find many places that should show him well the contrary."

"Well said," quoth I, "and very truth. But now in the meantime, will ye that he shall believe as that text shall seem to sound[275] to him against his creed, till he have found another text in Scripture that answereth it and seemeth to him to say more plainly the contrary?"

"Nay," quoth he, "not one hour. For he seeth that though other good men be called 'God's children' and 'gods,' yet as they be not very gods, so be they not God's very natural children by generation, but by acceptation; whereas the creed saith of our Savior that he is God's only-begotten Son, that signifieth him to be his son by generation."

"That is," quoth I, "very true, and well and reasonably considered, and according unto the very right faith. But now consider that ye make him by and by[276] fall to the squaring of his stones, like that slothful mason that ye spoke of, with his leaden rule.[277] For now ye make him to examine the truth of this text of the psalm by the article of the faith which he brought with him — and by a collection[278] and discourse[279] of reason. And so, forthwith,[280] ye find both these rules necessary to the discussion of Scripture. Of which twain ye would in the beginning admit neither nother.[281]

"But now go further. What if he would upon this

---

269 learn by heart   **270** *put case:* propose hypothetically (a common legal practice)
271 itself   **272** *mean season:* meantime
273 an exclamation; "by God" (from French)   **274** Ps 81(82):6   **275** mean
276 *by and by:* immediately   **277** *leaden rule:* ruler made of lead   **278** deduction
279 process; argument   **280** right away
281 *neither nother:* neither the one nor the other

text—*Homines et iumenta salvabis, Deus* ('God, thou shalt save both man and beasts')[282]—ween that beasts had immortal souls as men have, and that man and beast should[283] be both saved at last, and so, that no deadly sin should be punished with everlasting pain, till he came to other texts that should prove well the contrary—were that best? Or else were it better that besides his creed he had knowledge before of these articles of our faith—that only our souls be immortal, and not beasts' also, and that the pain of hell shall be for sinners everlasting—and that he may thereby, with reason joined thereto, perceive that this text, 'thou shalt save both men and beasts,' is meant by some other kind of saving and preserving here in this world, and not of bringing both to heaven?"

"All this may he know," quoth he, "by Scripture itself well enough."

"That wot I well," quoth I. "And yet as plain as Christ speaketh of hell in the Gospel, Origen for all that—which[284] neither was a naughty[285] man nor unlearned in Scripture—could not so clearly see it but that he said the contrary, and took the words of Christ in a wrong sense, and would peradventure[286] with one that would stick only upon the words of Scripture (leaving the right sense thereof, which God and his Holy Spirit hath taught his Church), bring him to a bay[287] therein, that he should be fain[288]—not our child only, but also a well elderly man and in Scripture well forward[289]—to take him in conclusion to the faith of Christ's Church.

"Now if our child should read on[290] the text of Scripture, without care of the comments, and without any further instruction of the points of our faith than be specified in our common creed, made in the beginning as a brief remembrance by the apostles, not setting out (in so short a thing) and clearly declaring all that we be bounden to believe, albeit that he should well find in Scripture many plain and open[291] texts whereby the Godhead of our Savior and his equality with his Father may well and sufficiently be proved, yet were he not unlikely, by such other texts as seem to show him to be less than his Father, to fall into the sect and heresy of the Arians, and, against those other texts proving his equal Godhead, to devise such false glosses as they did. Whereas, being before taught and confirmed by the faith of the Church that our Savior is one God and one equal substance with his Father, he shall well perceive and understand thereby that all the texts that seem to make him less be nothing to be understood of his Godhead, but of his manhood only, as when we commonly speak of ourselves and of our own nature, and say we shall die, and worms eat us up and turn all to dust, we mean all this by[292] our body only, and nothing intend thereby to deny the immortality of our soul.

"We may not dine today if I should reckon[293] you the tenth part of such things as we must needs (upon loss of heaven) believe—which neither our child with his only creed (and much less our old idolater without creed) should so find out by Scripture but that they were both well likely to take the Scripture to the wrong part—except[294] we take with us, for a rule of interpretation, the articles of our faith."

THE TWENTY-FIFTH CHAPTER

The author, taking occasion upon certain words of the messenger, declareth[295] the preeminence, necessity, and profit of Holy Scripture, showing nevertheless that many things have been taught by God without writing. And many great things so remain, yet unwritten of truths necessary to be believed. And that the New Law of Christ is the law so written in the heart that it shall never out of his Church. And that the law there written by God is a right rule to interpret the words written in his Holy Scripture. Which rule, with reason and the old interpreters, the author showeth to be the very sure way to wade with in the great stream of Holy Scripture.

"Why then," quoth he, "this were as much to say as that God had not well written his Holy Scripture, if he have caused it to be written so as men may be so soon deceived therein that they were as likely—and as it seemeth by you, more likely—to fall into a false way than find out the true. And better were it then that God had not given us the Scripture at all, than to give us a way to walk wherein we were more likely to sink than save ourselves."

"Holy Scripture," quoth I, "both is such as I have

said, and yet nothing followeth it thereupon that God hath not caused it to be written well, or that it had been better to have kept it from us. And albeit that in this point were a great occasion of a long tale—in declaring and making open that God hath, in that writing of Holy Scripture, used so high wisdom, and showed such a wonderful temperance, that the very strange familiar fashion thereof may, to good men and wise, well declare that, as it was written by men, so was it indited[296] by God—yet passing over the praise, I will speak one word or twain for the answer of such blame as ye lay thereto. For it is almost a common thing among men to speak sometimes as though they could amend the works of God. And few men be there, I ween, but they think that if they had been of God's counsel in the making of the world, though they dare not be so bold to say that they could have made it better, yet if they might have ruled it, he should have made many things of another fashion. And for all that, if he would yet call us all to counsel, and change nothing till we were upon everything all agreed, the world were well likely till Doomsday[297] to go forth on as it goeth already—saving that I wot nere[298] whether we would all agree to be winged.

"But as for the Scripture, shortly: God hath so devised it that he hath given the world therein an inestimable treasure as the case standeth. And yet we should haply[299] nothing have needed thereof if the wounds of our own folly had not, of our great necessity and God's great goodness, required it. For at our creation he gave but two precepts or three by his own holy mouth to our first parents. And as for all that was for them to do besides, the reason which he had planted in their souls gave them sufficient warning. Whereof the whole sum stood, in effect, in the honor of God and God's friends, with love of each to the other, and to their offspring and lineage. But the precepts that he gave by mouth was three: twain commanding generation and eating,[300] the third forbidding the Tree of Knowledge.[301] And that was for them continual, where the other twain, albeit they were thereto bounden by the precept, yet were not they and their posterity bounden thereto at all hours and all places. But need was it in the beginning to give them knowledge thereof,

forasmuch as[302] they had no hunger to warn them of the one, nor sensual, rebellious appetite to warn them of the other. But after that they were by God once admonished thereof, then did reason interpret the remnant, whereby they wist[303] that they should eat for conservation of their bodies, and engender for propagation of their kind. And since they perceived that these two things was the end and intent of those commandments, they thereby consequently knew when it was time and place and occasion convenient[304] to fulfill them. But when they had once, at the subtle suasion of the devil, broken the third commandment in tasting the forbidden fruit, being then expelled out of Paradise,[305] then concerning their food and engendering, not only reason oft showed them what was honest and profitable, but also sensuality, what was beastly and pleasant, which sensuality labored so busily to cause man to set by[306] delight above good and convenient that, for the resistance thereof, it then became to be the spiritual business and occupation of man so to preserve and bring up the body that it were not suffered[307] to master the soul, and so to rule and bridle sensuality that it were subject and obedient unto reason, as God willed the woman to be subject and obediencer of man. Wherein God would that we were learned rather to suffer our sensual parts plain[308] and mourn than to follow their own hurt and ours too, as it had been better for our father Adam, and us all, that he had suffered his wife, our mother Eve, to be sad and angry both, and like a woman to weep too, than to have eaten the apple for fellowship, to please her withal.

"Now did all the sin anon[309] spring up, for the more part, upon the occasion of feeding and engendering, whereof sprung covetise,[310] gluttony, sloth, wrath, and lechery. And many times pride and envy, as one perceiving himself in these things in better condition or worse than another, so began to conceive a setting by[311] himself with contempt of other, or envy and hatred to some other (saving[312] that pride sometimes also sprang out of the soul), and so liked itself that it envied the better, as Cain did Abel;[313] and for to be the more set by, pride longed superfluously[314] to get by covetise and greediness many folks' livings in his own hands, to make other

296 dictated; composed   **297** Judgment Day. See Mt 10:15.   **298** *wot nere:* know not   **299** perhaps   **300** See Gn 1:28–30.   **301** See Gn 2:15–16.
   302 *forasmuch as:* seeing that   **303** knew   **304** appropriate   **305** See Gn 3:4–6, 23.   **306** *set by:* value   **307** allowed   **308** to complain   **309** immediately
   310 covetousness   **311** *setting by:* (high) valuing of   **312** except   **313** See Gn 4:5.   **314** inordinately

folks serve him, and honor and hang upon him for necessity.

"And, of all these mischiefs, was always sensuality ready to minister[315] matter, and by all the doors and windows of the body—by feeling, tasting, smelling, sight, and hearing—ceased never to send in occasions to the soul; nor the devil never ceased, for his part, diligently to put forward. Against whom did reason resist, with good counsel given to the soul; and good spirits appointed by God gave their help also; and God assisted with his aid and grace, where he found the person willing to work therewith. And in this manner continued man long time, not without revelation of Christ once to come. Which faith, delivered to the father, went by the mouth to the son, and so, from child to child, heard and believed among them. And whatso[316] were God's pleasure besides (that nature and reason could not plainly show them), God of his goodness by special message gave them undoubted knowledge—as he did to Noah, Lot, and Abraham, and diverse others, whereof some be since written and comprised in Scripture, and of likelihood not all. For well probable is it that the patriarchs, in diverse things that they did—as in their diverse marriages, and some such other things as then were by them well done for the time—were to them appointed specially by God for causes well known to himself and unknown to us, and the things now forbidden us and therefore to us unlawful, except[317] God's like ordinance or dispensation should hereafter, in general or particular, be revealed to the contrary.

"But so was it after that, the world waxing worse, right good and virtuous lineages declined and decayed. And by the lewd[318] conversation of evil people fell by disorder in such a blindness that, albeit some were there always that perceived well their duty, yet were the common people of the children of Israel by custom of sin so darked in their natural knowledge that they lacked in many things the right perceiving, that reason—had it not been by evil custom corrupted—might verily well have showed them.

"For the remedy whereof God of his endless mercy, by the law written with his own finger unto Moses in the tables of stone,[319] by the Ten Commandments,[320] put in remembrance again certain conclusions of the law of nature which their reason—overwhelmed with sensuality—had then forgotten. And to the end that they should keep his behests the better, he gave them a great heap of the laws, and ceremonies more, to keep them in straitly, for[321] straying abroad in riot. And wrought great wonders that they should well see that those things were his own deed, whereby they might have the more dread to transgress them. And there in writing he gave a warning also of Christ: that God would once send them one springing of themselves, to whom they should give hearing in stead of Moses.[322] Of whom also—as well before as after—by patriarchs and prophets, by figures and prophecies, God ceased not in such wise to foreshow his coming, his cause, his living, his dying, his resurrection, and his holy acts that, if pride and envy had not letted[323] it, the figures and prophecies, set and compared with his coming, conversation, and doings, might well have made all the Jews to know him. And for the perceiving and good understanding of the law written, he sent always some good men whose words, well living—and sometimes also manifest miracles showed therewith—never left them destitute of sufficient knowledge that[324] longed to learn the Law, not to plead[325] it, and for glory to dispute it, but to teach it again meekly, and, as man's frailty could suffer[326] it, specially to fulfill and keep it.

"Yet after all this—when the world was in a more decay and ruin of all virtue—then came our Savior Christ to redeem us with his death and leave us his New Law, whereof was long before prophesied by the prophet Jeremiah. 'Lo, the days be coming, said our Lord, when I shall order and dispose to the house of Israel and the house of Judah a new covenant' (or 'testament'). 'I shall give my law in their minds. And I shall write it in their heart. And I will be their Lord, and they shall be my people.'[327] This law written in men's hearts was, according to the words of the prophet, first brought by our Savior to the house of Israel and the house of Judah, to whom, as himself saith, he was specially sent. 'I am not sent,' saith our Lord, 'but unto the sheep that are perished of the house of Israel.'[328] And also he said, 'It is not good to take the bread from the board[329] of the children and cast it to dogs.'[330] But yet not only the ready towardness[331] of some paynims[332] caused

---

315 supply   **316** whatever   **317** unless
318 wicked   **319** See Ex 31:18.   **320** See
Ex 20:1–17; Dt 5:6–21.   **321** to hinder

322 See Dt 18:15–19.   **323** prevented
324 who   **325** debate   **326** endure
327 Jer 31:31–33; Heb 10:16   **328** Mt

15:24   **329** table   **330** Mt 15:26
331 inclination   **332** pagans

them to be partakers of that bread, but also soon after the stubbornness and obstinate infidelity[333] of the Jews caused Saint Paul and the apostles to say unto their face: 'The Gospel of Christ was ordained by God to be first preached unto you. But since that ye refuse it, lo, we depart from you to the gentiles.'[334] And so was, in their stead, the Church gathered of all the world abroad.[335] All which notwithstanding, both were there at that time out of the Jews converted and made many a good Christian man, and many of the same people turned unto Christ since; and in conclusion, the time shall come when the remnant that shall be then left shall save themselves by the same faith.[336]

"This is called the law of Christ's faith, the law of his holy Gospel. I mean not only the words written in the books of his evangelists, but much more specially the substance of our faith itself, which our Lord said he would write in men's hearts, not only because of the secret operation of God and his Holy Spirit in justifying the good Christian — either by the working with man's good will to the perfection of faith in his soul, or with the good intent of the offerers,[337] to the secret infusion of that virtue into the soul of an innocent infant — but also for that[338] he first, without writing, revealed those heavenly mysteries by his blessed mouth through the ears of his apostles and disciples into their holy hearts; or rather, as it seemeth, it was inwardly infused into Saint Peter his[339] heart by the secret inspiration of God, without either writing or any outward word.

"For which cause when he had, upon Christ's question demanding,[340] 'Of whom say you that I am?' answered and said, 'Thou art Christ, the Son of the living God, which art comen into this world.'

"Our Savior said again[341] unto him, 'Thou art blessed, Simon, the son of John, for neither flesh nor blood hath revealed and showed this to thee, but my Father that is in heaven.'[342] And thus it appeareth that the faith came into Saint Peter his heart — as to the prince of the apostles — without hearing, by secret inspiration, and into the remnant by his confession and Christ's holy mouth. And by them in like manner — first without writing, by only words and preaching — so was it spread abroad in the world that his faith was by the mouths of his

holy messengers put into men's ears, and by his holy hand written in men's hearts, ere ever any word thereof almost was written in the Book.[343] And so was it convenient[344] for the law of life rather to be written in the lively[345] minds of men than in the dead skins of beasts. And I nothing doubt but all had it so been[346] that never Gospel had been written, yet should the substance of this faith never have fallen out of Christian folks' hearts, but the same Spirit that planted it, the same should have watered it, the same should have kept[347] it, the same should have increased it.

"But so hath it liked our Lord, after his high wisdom, to provide that some of his disciples have written many things of his holy life, doctrine, and faith, and yet far from all — which, as Saint John saith, the world could not have comprehended.[348]

"These books are tempered,[349] by the secret counsel of the Holy Ghost, so plain and simple that every man may find in them that he may perceive, and yet so high again, and so hard, that no man is there so cunning[350] but he may find in them things far above his reach, far too profound to pierce unto. Now were to the Christian people the points of Christ's faith (with which points our Lord would have them charged) known, as I say, and planted before; and by reason thereof, they far the better understood those books. And although there might haply[351] be some texts which were not yet of necessity for them to perceive, yet by the points of their faith were they warned, that no text might there be construed contrary to their faith.

"And none evangelist was there, nor none apostle, that by writing ever sent the faith to any nation but if[352] they were first informed by word, and that God had begun his Church in that place.

"And for my part, I would little doubt but that the evangelists and apostles both, of many great and secret mysteries spoke much more openly, and much more plainly by mouth among the people, than ever they put it in writing, forasmuch as their writings were likely enough at that time to come into the hands of pagans and paynims, such hogs and dogs as were not meetly[353] to have those precious pearls put upon their noses, nor that holy food to be dashed[354] in their teeth.[355] For which cause Saint Peter, in his

---

333 lack of belief **334** Acts 13:46 **335** at large **336** See Rom 11:15. **337** baptismal sponsors **338** *for that:* because **339** *Peter his:* Peter's **340** asking **341** in

342 Mt 16:15–17 **343** i.e., Bible **344** fitting **345** living **346** *but... so been:* that even if it had been **347** tended **348** contained. See Jn 21:25.

349 composed **350** learned **351** perhaps **352** *but if:* unless **353** fit **354** thrown, thrust **355** See Mt 7:6.

first sermon unto the Jews,[356] abstained from the declaration of Christ's Godhead and equality with his Father, as our Savior himself, when the Jews that were unworthy to hear it were offended with that[357] he told them plainly that he was the Son of God, withdrew the doctrine from them again and covered it with the verse of the prophet: 'I have said ye be gods, and sons of the high God, all,'[358] as though he would say, 'What grieveth it you that name in me, which name "god" by the prophet, hath given to all good men?'[359] In which demeanor[360] he denied not the truth that he had said of himself, but he blinded their willfully winking eyes, in hiding and putting up again the jewel that he began to bring forth and show them, the bright luster whereof their bleared eyes might not endure to behold.

"And what marvel though the apostles thus did in their speech afore infidels, or writing that might come into pagans' hands, when it appeareth upon the epistles of Saint Paul that among the Christian flock, where he taught them by mouth, he told them not all the truths at one tale[361] — not only for that[362] it were too long, but also for that in the beginning they could not, haply, well have abidden it.[363] And therefore, as Christ said to his disciples, 'I have more to say to you, but ye be not able to bear it yet'[364] (which once appeared, what[365] time that upon the disclosing of the great mystery of the Holy Sacrament, the holy flesh of his body, the hearers said, 'Who can abide this hard word?'[366] and therewith went, almost all, their way), so did Saint Paul, I say, by the Corinthians, not teach them all at once. And therefore he saith in his epistle to them, 'I have given you hitherto but milk, and not strong meat.'[367] And, 'Wisdom speak we,' saith he, 'among folk that be perfect.'[368] Nor I mean not this — that there were any points of the substance of the faith which he showed to the clergy that he kept from the lay people, or showed unto one man that he kept from another — but that to no man lightly[369] he showed all at once. But because some came from the Jews and some came of the Gentiles, therefore, as they were, so were they handled, not only by grace, but also by wisdom, and not only in the points of the faith, but also in the rites and ceremonies, either

of the Church or of Moses' Law — whereof some ceremonies were forthwith[370] abolished, some not by and by,[371] and some taken into the Church of Christ and observed still. But in conclusion, when they were meet therefor,[372] they were all taught, all that God would have them bounden to believe. And then doubt I nothing but that many things that now be very dark in Holy Scripture were, by the apostles (to whom our Lord opened their wits that they might understand Scripture), so plainly declared[373] that they were by the people well and clearly understood. I say not all the whole Scripture, in which it may be that many a secret mystery lieth yet covered concerning the coming of Antichrist, and the day, manner, and fashion of the Final Judgment, which shall never be fully disclosed till the times appointed by God's high Providence meet and convenient[374] for them. And from time to time, as it liketh his Majesty to have things known or done in his Church, so is it no doubt but he tempereth his revelations, and in such wise doth insinuate and inspire them into the breasts of his Christian people that, by the secret instinct of the Holy Ghost, they consent and agree together in[375] one, except heretics that rebel and refuse to be obedient to God and his Church, who be thereby cut off from the lively[376] tree of that vine, and — waxing[377] withered branches — be kept but for the fire first here, and after in hell, except[378] they repent and call for grace, that may graft them into the stock again.[379] But as it may be that many things be there not all at once revealed and understood in the Scripture, but by sundry times and ages more things and more by God unto his Church disclosed and that as it shall like his high goodness and wisdom to dispense and dispose, and as it may be also in things to be done, may fall in his Church variety, mutation, and change, so am I very sure that the Holy Ghost that God sent into his Church — and Christ himself that hath promised unto the end of the world to persevere and abide in his Church[380] — shall never suffer[381] his Catholic Church neither to agree to the making of any law that shall be to God damnably displeasant, nor of any truth that God would were believed, to determine or believe the contrary. For then had

---

356 See Acts 2:22–42.   **357** *with that:* by that which   **358** Jn 10:28–38   **359** See Ps 81(82):6; Jn 10:34.   **360** conduct   **361** *at one tale:* in the same statement   **362** *for that:* because   **363** See 1 Cor 3:1–2.

364 Jn 16:12   **365** that   **366** See Jn 6:61, 67.   **367** 1 Cor 3:2   **368** 1 Cor 2:6   **369** easily; readily   **370** immediately   **371** immediately   **372** *meet therefor:* fit for it   **373** explained   **374** *meet*

and convenient: fit and suitable   **375** as   **376** living   **377** becoming   **378** unless   **379** See Jn 15:6; Rom 11:22–23.   **380** See Mt 28:20.   **381** allow

Christ, which is all truth, broken his promise, and (which were blasphemy and abominable to think) were waxen[382] untrue. And therefore over[383] this as it may be that, as I said before, some things in Holy Scripture be not yet fully perceived and understood, so am I very sure that the Church neither doth nor can do damnably construe it wrong, which it should if they should construe it so as it should make an article of misbelief and of a false, erroneous faith—as if they should by misconstruction[384] of the Scripture bring up and believe that Christ were one God and equal with his Father and with the Holy Ghost, if the truth were otherwise indeed. And therefore, since the Church (in which Christ is assistant[385] and his Holy Spirit) cannot to God's displeasure and their damnation fall in any false belief, in any such substantial point of the faith, it must needs be therefore that Arius and all other heretics be drowned in damnable errors. The contrary opinion of whose execrable heresies the Church was in the beginning taught by the mouth of Christ himself, and after, of his blessed apostles, which[386] read and declared the Scriptures among the people in their time, showing them in what wise[387] the words of Holy Scripture proved the truth of such articles of the faith as they taught them by mouth, and how such texts as seemed the contrary were not contrary indeed, and therewith declared them of those texts the right understanding.

"And albeit that our Savior showed and plainly proved that in the Scripture was given good tokens and sufficient knowledge of him, yet to the intent we should well know that his own word and ordinance needeth none other authority but himself, but is to be believed and obeyed, be it written or not written, some things did he therefore bid to be done, and some things also to be believed, whereof we have in Holy Scripture no writing in the world. Saint Paul commandeth the people of Thessalonica in his epistle[388] to keep the traditions that he took them either by his writing or by his bare[389] word. For the words that he said among them, our Lord had told them him[390] for them. And therefore he writeth unto the Corinthians that of the holy Housel,[391] the Sacrament of the altar, he had showed

them the matter and the manner by mouth, as our Lord had himself taught it to him.[392] And therefore no doubt is there but that by the apostles was the Church more fully taught of that matter than ever was written in all the Scripture. There was learned the manner and form of consecration. There was learned much of the mystical gestures and ceremonies used in the Mass. And if any man doubt thereof, let him consider where should we else have the beginning of[393] the water put with the wine into the chalice. For well we wot that the Scripture biddeth it not. And every wise man may well wit[394] then when the Gospel speaketh only of wine, there durst no man in this world have been so bold to put anything else thereto. For when the Gospel speaketh of wine only turned into his Precious Blood, what man would adventure[395] to make any mixture of[396] water? And now is the Church so well ascertained of God's pleasure therein, without any Scripture, that they not only dare put in water, but also dare not leave it out. And whereby knew the Church this thing, but by God and his holy apostles, which[397] taught it in their time? And so went it forth from age to age, continued in the Church until this day, begun by God in the beginning, without any mention made in Holy Scripture.

"Howbeit, Luther saith because it is not commanded by Scripture, we may choose therefore whether we will do it or leave it. For this one point is the very fond[398] foundation and ground of all his great heresies: that a man is not bounden to believe anything but if[399] it may be proved evidently by Scripture. And thereupon goeth he so far-forth[400] that no Scripture can be evident to prove[401] anything that he list[402] to deny. For he will not agree it for evident, be it never so plain. And he will call evident for him that text that is evident against him. And sometimes, if it be too plain against him, then will he call it no Scripture, as he playeth with the epistle of Saint James. And because the old holy doctors be full and whole against him, he setteth them all at nought.[403] And with these worshipful[404] wise ways he proclaimeth himself a conqueror, where, besides all the remnant—wherein every child may see his proud, frantic[405] folly—he is

382 *were waxen:* would have become
383 beyond   **384** misinterpretation
385 present   **386** who   **387** way(s)
388 See 2 Thes 2:15.   **389** mere (i.e.,
spoken)   **390** to him   **391** Eucharist

392 See 1 Cor 11:23.   **393** *beginning of:*
source for   **394** know   **395** venture
396 *make any mixture of:* mix in any
397 who   **398** foolish   **399** *but if:*
unless   **400** *so far-forth:* to such an extent

401 conclusive, certain   **402** wishes
403 *setteth . . . nought:* values as nothing
404 honorable   **405** insane

shamefully put to flight in the first point: that is to wit,[406] that nothing is to be believed for a sure truth but if it appear proved and evident in Holy Writ. And yet had that point at the first face[407] some visage[408] of probability. Howbeit, to say the truth, he were a lewd lorel[409] that would nothing do that his master would bid him, nor nothing believe that his master would tell him, but if he take it him in writing, as Luther playeth with Christ. Of whose words or acts he will believe nothing except he find it in Scripture—and that plain and evident. Now must he by that means condemn the Church of Christ for that[410] they sanctify not the Saturday, which was the Sabbath day instituted by God among the Jews, commanding the Sabbath day to be kept holy.[411] And albeit the matter of the precept is moral, and the day legal (so that it may be changed), yet will there, I ween, no man think that ever the Church would take upon themselves to change it without special ordinance of God. Whereof we find no remembrance at all in Holy Scripture. By what Scripture is evidently known that every man and woman hath power to minister[412] the sacrament of baptism? Let it be showed either by commandment, counsel, license, or example expressed in Scripture.

"Many things are there like,[413] which, as holy doctors agree, were taught the apostles by Christ, and the Church by the apostles, and so comen down to our days by continual succession from theirs. But I will let all others pass over, and speak but of one.

"Every good Christian man, I doubt not, believeth that our Blessed Lady was a perpetual virgin, as well after the birth of Christ as before. For it were a strange thing that she should, after that blessed birth, be less minded to cleanness and purity, and set less by her holy purpose and promise of chastity, vowed and dedicated unto God, than she did before. For surely whoso considereth the words of the Gospel in Saint Luke shall well perceive that she had vowed virginity. For when the angel had said unto her, 'Lo, thou shalt conceive in thy womb and bring forth a child, and thou shalt call his name Jesus,' she answered him, 'How may this be? For as for man, I know none,'[414] which, though it be spoken but for the time then present, yet must it needs signify that she never would know none, after[415] the manner of speaking.

By which a nun might say, 'As for man, there meddleth none with me,' signifying that never there shall. And in common speech is that figure much in use by which a woman saith of one whom she is determined never to marry, 'We may well talk together, but we wed not together,' meaning that they never shall wed together. And in such wise meant our Lady when she said, 'How may this be? For I know no man,' meaning that she never would meddle with man—or else had her answer nothing been to purpose. For the angel said not, 'Lo, thou art conceived,' which if he had said, she might well have marveled only for that[416] she knew no man already. But when he said, 'Thou shalt conceive,' this could be no marvel unto her for that she knew no man already. And therefore, since she marveled how it might be that ever she should conceive and have a child, it must needs be that her answer meant that she never would meddle with man. And therefore she marveled—because he said it should be, and she knew not how it could be, but that[417] ways by which she was at full point[418] with herself that it should never be—so that then he showed her how it should come about: by the Holy Ghost coming into her, and the power of God on high shadowing[419] her. And then she assented, and said, 'Lo, here the handmaid of God; be it done to me after thy word, as thou tellest me.'[420] And thus appeareth it evidently that she had then a fully determined purpose of virginity—and that, as it seemeth, such as she thought not lawful to change. For else when the angel did the message, she might have inclined thereto though she had before been in another mind. Now, when she had then so full and fast[421] a purpose of perpetual virginity before the birth of her blessed Child—which[422] came, among his other heavenly doctrines, to call and exhort the world from all pleasure of the flesh to the purity and cleanness of the body and soul, and from the desire of carnal generation to a ghostly[423] regeneration in grace—more were it then wonder if she should have then more regard of fleshly delight or cure of[424] worldly procreation than ever she had before her celestial conception of her Maker, made man in her blessed womb. Or what man could think it—that ever God would suffer[425] any earthly man after to be conceived in that holy closet[426] taken up

---

406 say **407** sight **408** semblance **409** *lewd lorel:* wicked rogue **410** *for that:* because **411** See Ex 20:8–11; 23:12; 31:12–17; Dt 5:12–15. **412** administer

413 similar **414** Lk 1:31–34 **415** according to **416** *for that:* because **417** *but that:* except for **418** resolution **419** overshadowing **420** Lk 1:25–38

421 steadfast **422** who **423** spiritual **424** *cure of:* concern for **425** allow **426** private place

and consecrated so specially to God? This reverent article of our Lady's perpetual virginity, the Church of Christ, being taught the truth by Christ, perpetually hath believed since the time of Christ. And yet is there no word thereof in Christ's Gospel written, but rather, diverse texts so sounding to the contrary that by the wrong understanding of them, the heretic Helvidius[427] took the occasion of his heresy by which he would that our Lady after the birth of Christ had other children by Joseph. How can we then say that we could, without the learning of the faith before, find out all the points in the Scripture, when there be some that all Christendom believe—and believe themselves bounden to believe—whereof the Scripture giveth no plain doctrine, but rather seemeth to say the contrary?

"But, as I began to say, the holy apostles, being taught by their great master Christ, did teach unto the Church as well the articles of the faith as the understanding of such texts of Scripture as was meet and convenient[428] for the matter. Whereby it is not unlikely that the Gospel of Saint John and the epistles of Saint Paul were then better understood among the common people than they be peradventure now with some that take themselves for great clerks.[429] And as the apostles at that time taught the people, so did ever some of them that heard them teach forth, and leave their doctrine and traditions to others that came after. By reason whereof, not only came the rites and sacraments and the articles of our faith from hand to hand, from Christ and his apostles unto our days, but also the great part of the right understanding of Holy Scripture, by good and godly writers of sundry times. By whose good and wholesome doctrine, set forth by their virtue with God's good inspiration, grace, and help of the Holy Ghost, we have also the knowledge and perceiving what was the faith of Christ's Church in every time since. And thereby perceive we that these heretics be not only barkers against the faith that now is, but also that hath been ever since Christ died.

"And therefore is Holy Scripture, as I said, the highest and the best learning that any man can have, if one take the right way in the learning.

"It is (as a good, holy saint saith) so marvelously tempered that a mouse may wade therein, and an elephant be drowned therein.[430] For there is no man so low, but if he will seek his way with the staff of his faith in his hand, and hold that fast and search the way therewith, and have the old holy fathers also for his guides, going on with a good purpose and a lowly heart, using reason and refusing no good learning, with calling of God for wisdom, grace, and help that he may well keep his way and follow his good guides—then shall he never fall in peril, but well and surely wade through, and come to such end of his journey as himself would well wish. But surely, if he be as long as Longinus,[431] and have a high[432] heart and trust upon his own wit—as he doth (look he never so lowly) that setteth all the old holy fathers at nought[433]—that fellow shall not fail to sink over the ears and drown. And of all wretches, worst shall he walk that,[434] forcing little of[435] the faith of Christ's Church, cometh to the Scripture of God to look and try therein whether the Church believe aright or not. For either doubteth he whether Christ teach his Church true, or else whether Christ teacheth it at all or not. And then he doubteth whether Christ in his words did say true when he said he would be with his Church till the end of the world. And surely the thing that made Arius, Pelagius, Faustus, Manichaeus, Donatus, Helvidius, and all the rabble of the old heretics to drown themselves in those damnable heresies was nothing but high pride of their learning in Scripture—wherein they followed their own wits and left the common faith of the Catholic Church, preferring their own gay[436] glosses before the right catholic faith of all Christ's Church, which can never err in any substantial point that God would have us bounden to believe. And therefore, to end where we began, whoso will not, unto the study of Scripture, take the points of the Catholic faith as a rule of interpretation, but of diffidence and mistrust study to seek in Scripture whether the faith of the Church be true or not, he cannot fail to fall in worse errors, and far more jeopardous,[437] than any man can do by philosophy, whereof the reasons and arguments in matters of our faith have nothing in like[438] authority."

---

427 Jerome answered him by a treatise written in 383.   428 *meet and convenient:* fitting and appropriate   429 scholars   430 See Gregory the Great, *Commentary on Job.*   431 the name traditionally given to the soldier who pierced Jesus's side with a lance. See Jn 19:34.   432 haughty   433 *setteth at nought:* values as nothing   434 who   435 *forcing little of:* attaching little importance to   436 specious; attractive; ornate   437 dangerous   438 *in like:* like the same

THE TWENTY-SIXTH CHAPTER

*The messenger saying that him seemed he[439] should
not believe the Church if he saw the Church say
one thing and the Holy Scripture another thing,
because the Scripture is the Word of God, the
author showeth that the faith of the Church is
the Word of God as well as the Scripture, and
therefore as well to be believed, and that the
faith and the Scripture well understood be never
contrary, and further showeth that upon all
doubts rising upon Holy Scripture concerning
any necessary article of the faith, he that cannot,
upon all that he can hear in the matter on both
the sides, perceive the better and truer part, hath a
sure and undoubtable refuge provided him by the
goodness of God to bring him out of all perplexity,
in that God hath commanded him in all
such doubts to believe his Church.*

"Truly, sir," quoth he, "methinketh it is well said,
that[440] ye have said. And in good faith, to say the
truth, I see not what I should answer it withal.[441]
And yet, when I look back again upon Holy Scripture,
and consider that it is God's own words—
which I wot[442] well ye will grant—I find it hard
in mine heart to believe all the men in the whole
world, if they would say anything whereof I should
see that the Holy Scripture saith the contrary, since
it is reason[443] that I believe God alone far better
than them all."

"In that," quoth I, "ye say very truth. But now
I put case[444] that God would tell you two things:
whether[445] of them would ye believe best?"

"Neither other,"[446] quoth he, "but I would believe
them both firmly and both alike."

"What if neither other," quoth I, "were likely to
be true, but seemed, both twain, impossible?"

"That should," quoth he, "make little force[447]
to me. For that once known—that God telleth
them—seemed they never so far[448] unlikely, nor
never so far impossible, I neither should nor could
have any doubt but that they were both twain true."

"That is well said," quoth I. "But now and[449] it so
were that those two things seemed the one to the
other clean[450] contrary, what would ye then think,
and which would ye then believe?"

"Yet could I not," quoth he, "doubt anything but
that they were very true both, but I would verily
think that I did not well understand the one[451] of
them."

"What would ye then do," quoth I, "if he bade
you believe them both?"

"Marry," quoth he, "then would I pray him tell
me first how he understandeth them both. For
though I believe that they be both true in that sense
and purpose[452] that he taketh[453] his own words, and
may, in that manner understood, well stand and
agree together,[454] yet can I not believe them both
in that sense and understanding wherein they repugn[455] and be directly contrary each to other."

"That is," quoth I, "so well said that, in my mind,
no man can amend[456] it."

"But now would I wit,"[457] quoth I, "whether that
the faith of the Church be the Word of God, and by
God spoken to the Church or not?"

"Yes," quoth he, "God speaketh to his Church in
the Scripture."

"And is nothing God's words," quoth I, "but
Scripture? The words that God spoke to Moses—
were they not God's words all, till they were written?
And the words of Christ to his apostles—were
they not his words till they were written?"

"Yes, then," quoth he. "But now, since he hath
perfected and finished the corpus of Holy Scripture,
all things that he would Christian people
should[458] believe, and all that he would the Church
should do, and all that he would the Church should
eschew—all this hath he left them his mind sufficiently
in Holy Scripture."

"And none otherwise," quoth I, "besides? I had
weened we had been at another point,[459] in that ye
see the Sabbath day changed into Sunday without
any word of Scripture giving any commandment of
the change in the New Testament from the commandment
given for the Saturday in the Old,[460]
and also for the point that we spoke of touching
the perpetual virginity of our Lady, whereof is no
word written in Scripture. But since I perceive that

---

439 *him seemed he:* to him it seemed that
he **440** what **441** with **442** know
443 reasonable **444** *put case:* propose
hypothetically a case **445** which
446 *Neither other:* Neither the one nor
the other **447** difference **448** *never*

so far: no matter how extremely **449** if
450 completely **451** *the one:* the one
or the other **452** (according to the)
intention **453** understands **454** *well...
together:* be quite consistent and compatible with each other **455** contradict

456 improve upon **457** *would I wit:*
I want to know **458** *would...should:*
wants the Church to **459** point of
agreement **460** See Acts 20:7.

the great affection and reverence that ye bear to the Scripture of God—not without great cause, but without any measure—maketh you in the case that ye take all authority and credence from every word of God spoken beside the Scripture, I would ask you therefore this question: if God in Holy Scripture tell you two things that seem the one contrary to the other—as, for example, if he tell you in one place that he is less than his Father[461] and in another place that he and his Father be all one[462]—which of these will you believe?"

"Marry," quoth he, "both twain. For they may stand together well enough. For he was less as man, and was all one and equal as God."

"Very truth it is," quoth I, "that ye say. But now if ye had been born in the days of Arius the heretic, he would not have received nor held himself content with this answer. But he would have agreed[463] you the first part and put you[464] further to prove the second part. And unto that text he would have made you a gloss that 'his Father and he were one, not in substance, but in will.' And that gloss he would have fortified and made somewhat seemly with another word of Christ, in which he prayed his Father saying, 'As thou and I be both one, so make thou that they and we may be made one,'[465] meaning by[466] his Christian people, which shall never be one with him in substance. So that for the inequality of Christ by reason of his manhood, ye must agree with him; but for unity of Godhead, he will not agree with you, but put you always to prove it."

"Well," quoth he, "and though[467] he so did, yet if I were provided therefor,[468] there be texts enough that plainly prove it."

"That is," quoth I, "very truth. But yet is there none but he shall always set you another against it, and a gloss as fast[469] for yours as ye shall have an answer for his, in such wise as he may abuse[470] a right wise and well-learned man—as he did in his own days, and many days after, many a thousand. Then if it so were that in that dispicion[471] ye could not make your audience to discern the truth, nor peradventure persuade them to believe the truth, because the false part might hap to have, to the minds

of many, a more face[472] of truth, as it had at that time to many that then were of that sect—what way would ye wind out?"[473]

"Marry," quoth he, "I would believe well myself the truth, and go to God, and let them that would believe the false part go to the devil."

"Ye should," quoth I, "have taken therein a good, sure way. But now, if ye had been in that time (albeit ye be now fast and sure in the truth), ye might have happed—while the matter was in question, and many great clerks[474] and well-Scriptured men, and some seeming right holy, set on the wrong side— ye might have happed, I say, so to have been moved with the reasons on both the sides that ye should not have wist[475] on which part to determine your belief. And what would ye then have done?"

Quoth he, "Ye put me now to a pinch; and I shall answer you as I have heard say that Doctor Mayew,[476] sometime Almoner[477] to King Henry the Seventh, answered once the King at his table. It happed that there was fallen in communication[478] the story of Joseph, how his master's (Potiphar's) wife, a great man with the King of Egypt, would have pulled him to bed, and he fled away.[479]

"'Now, Master Mayew,' quoth the King's Grace, 'ye be a tall, strong man on the one side, and a cunning[480] doctor on the other side: What would ye have done if ye had been, not Joseph, but in Joseph's stead?'

"'By my troth,[481] sir,' quoth he, 'and[482] it like Your Grace, I cannot tell you what I would have done, but I can tell you well what I should have done.'

"'By my troth,' quoth the King, 'that was very well answered.' And since that answer served him well there, I shall make the same serve me here. For surely, if I had been in Arius's days, in the point that ye spoke of, what I would have done, that wot I nere.[483] But what I should have done, that can I well tell you, and surely trust I would have done so too."

"What is that?" quoth I.

"Marry, I would have believed the best," quoth he.

"The best?" quoth I. "That were best indeed, if ye wist which it were. But the case is put that the reasons[484] grounded upon Scripture seemed unto you

461 See Jn 14:28.   **462** See Jn 10:30.
463 granted   **464** *put you:* made you go
465 Jn 17:22–23   **466** by that   **467** *and though:* even if   **468** *provided therefor:* prepared for that   **469** firm   **470** delude
471 debate   **472** *more face:* greater semblance   **473** *wind out:* get yourself

out (of that situation)   **474** scholars
475 known   **476** *Doctor Mayew:* Richard Mayew (1439–1516), Bishop of Herefor, who held several academic offices, including chancellor of Oxford   **477** The Lord High Almoner was a royal official in charge of distribution to the poor.

478 *was fallen in communication:* came up in conversation   **479** See Gn 39:4–12.
480 learned   **481** trustworthiness; faithfulness   **482** if   **483** *wot I nere:* know I not   **484** arguments

in such wise each to impugn and answer other[485] that ye stood in such a doubt that ye could in no wise discern whether[486] side said best."

"By God," quoth he, "I had forgotten that. Well, then were it best," quoth he, "and so would I have done, I think, kneel me down and make my special prayer to God that it might please his goodness in so great a peril not to leave me perplexed, but vouchsafe[487] to incline mine assent unto that side that he knew were true, and would I should[488] believe to be true. And then would I boldly believe the one which God should have put in my mind. Had not this been the best way?"

"If it were not," quoth I, "the best, it might peradventure serve for a second."

"A second?" quoth he. "Then ye take it for nought."[489]

"Nay," quoth I. "There be two seconds, after two manner countings:[490] one next unto the worst, another next unto the best. And your way is surely far from the worst. But yet dare I not assent that it were the best till I understand it better. And therefore I pray you tell me this: if, after your special prayers made, ye wrote the one part in one paper and the other part in another, and laid them both on the ground, and then set up a staff between them both — would ye be then indifferent to take the one side or the other after, as it should hap your staff to fall?"

"Why not?" quoth he. "Or else put it upon two lots, and then at adventure[491] draw the one and take it. For when I have done as much as mine own wit[492] will serve, and have heard thereto all that I can of other men, and yet by neither can perceive the better opinion, what should I do, or what could I do, further than pray for grace to guide my choice, and so at adventure boldly take the one and hold it fast, doubting nothing but God assisted my choice, if I have a firm faith in his promise, by which he promiseth that if we ask, we shall have — asking, as Saint James saith, without any doubt?[493] And why should not I, in such perplexed case, after help called for of God, take the one part at adventure by lot, as did the apostles in the choosing of a new, to fulfill the place of the traitor Judas?"[494]

"Lots," quoth I, "be well lawful in the choice of such two things as be both so good that we be likely to choose well enough whethersoever we take. But now, if ye were in the case that I have heard my father merrily say every man is at the choice of his wife — that ye should put your hand into a blind bag[495] full of snakes and eels together, seven snakes for one eel — ye would, I ween, reckon it a perilous choice to take up one at adventure though[496] ye had made your special prayer to speed[497] well. Nor ye ought not in such case to adventure it upon your prayer and trust in God without necessity."

"That is peradventure truth," quoth he. "But in our case there is necessity. For there were none other way to avoid the perplexity but even[498] take the one by prayer and firm trust in God, which[499] never deceived them that trust in him."

"If there were," quoth I, "none other way, somewhat were it then that ye say. But now consider your case again. And when it so were that ye could not, upon that ye heard the Arians and the Catholic party argue together, perceive whether[500] party were the better. And therefore, of those two tales told you by God in many texts of Holy Scripture — some seeming plainly to say that Christ was not equal with his Father, some seeming as plainly to say the contrary — ye could in no wise find any reason whereby ye could find yourself moved to take the one part for more probable than the other. I put case, then, that God would himself say to you, 'I have showed the truth of this matter to such a man, and how my Scripture is to be understood concerning the same. Go thy ways, therefore, to him; and that thing that he shall tell thee, that thing believe thou.' Would ye say, 'Nay, good Lord, I will ask no man but thyself; and therefore tell me thine[501] own mouth, or else I will take the one part at all adventures,[502] and think that thou would have it so'? Or else would ye think that God were your good Lord, and had done much for you, in that it liked him so graciously for your surety[503] to bring you out of such a great perplexity, whereby ye should for your own mind have remained in an insoluble doubt in a matter of the faith, wherein it is damnable to dwell in doubt, or (which yet much worse were) have declined peradventure into an invincible error?"

---

485 *impugn and answer other:* contradict and refute each other **486** which **487** be willing **488** *would I should:* wanted me to **489** nothing; something bad; worthless **490** *after two manner*

countings: according to two ways of counting **491** random **492** mind, intellect **493** See Jn 16:24; Jas 1:6–8. **494** See Acts 1:24–26. **495** *blind bag:* bag that one cannot see into

496 *adventure though:* risk even if **497** success **498** *but even:* except just to **499** who **500** which **501** with your **502** *at all adventures:* completely by fortune **503** certainty; safety

"Verily," quoth he, "great cause should I have had highly to thank God."

"Ye would not, then," quoth I, "first make your prayer and then with good hope (that grace shall guide your fortune) take the one part at adventure by lot, but ye would in your prayer thank God for that provision. And then would ye get you to that man as fast as ye could."

"Very truth," quoth he.

"Then if that man should tell you that Arius and his company were heretics all, and took texts of Scripture wrong, ye would believe him?"

"Yea, verily," quoth he, "that would I."

"I put case," quoth I, "that ye had not doubted before, but had been in yourself at clear point that the Arians's opinion were the truth. Yet ye would, against Arius and all his, and against your own mind also, lean unto his word whom God had bidden you believe?"

"What else?" quoth he.

"What if ye asked him," quoth I, "whether God have sufficiently showed that point in Scripture, so that it may by the words of Holy Writ well and evidently be proved, and that he told you, 'Yea?' And that thereupon he would bring in all the texts that ye had well in remembrance already, and that ye laid against them all that you could lay for the contrary, so far-forth[504] that, when each of you had laid all your texts and all your glosses that either of you both could bring forth, till ye both confessed that neither of ye both could any further thing find therein—he saying still that his way were the truth, and that he had by Scripture well proved it unto you, and yourself, on the other side, for all that ever ye had heard him say, perceiving in your own mind none other but that ye had by Scripture better proved the other part—which would ye now believe? That way that, as far as ye see, God saith himself in Holy Scripture? Or else that man whom God sent you to and bade you believe?"

"Nay verily," quoth he, "I would believe him."

"Well said," quoth I. "But whether would[505] ye only believe him that the truth of the matter were against the Arians, or else would you believe him further, in that he said he had so proved it unto you by Scripture?"

"I would," quoth he, "believe him therein also.

For since God so had commanded me, and had showed me that he had himself instructed that man in what sense the Scripture were to be understood, I could none otherwise think but that were true, and though[506] it appeared to mine own reason the contrary."

"Very well said," quoth I. "Now, if God had said unto you that ye should believe that man concerning the matter itself, and of Scripture had nothing spoken, then would ye have believed him yet in the matter? Would ye not, although he should have told you that he understood no Scripture at all?"

"That is true," quoth he.

"Now, if he should then have told you that the Arians were heretics in that point, and their opinion erroneous and false, ye would have believed him?"

"What else?" quoth he.

"What if he had told you therewith,"[507] quoth I, "that he wist nere[508] whether it might be well proved by Scripture or not?"

"Yet would I," quoth he, "nevertheless believe to be true the matter itself that he had told me."

"What would you then think," quoth I, "of those texts that ye did reckon before well and plainly to prove the contrary?"

"I would," quoth he, "then reckon that they were meant some other ways than I could understand. For I could not doubt but being truly understood, they could never witness against the truth."

"In good faith," quoth I, "ye say marvelously well. Do ye not," quoth I, "take it for all one, whether God bid you do a thing by his own mouth or by Holy Scripture?"

"Yes," quoth he, "saving that I take the bidding by Scripture for the more sure. For there wot I well God speaketh and I cannot be illuded."[509]

"Now," quoth I, "this man that God biddeth you go to and in all things believe him—will it make any change in the matter whether it be man or woman?"

"No change at all," quoth he.

"What if it were a certain known company of men and women together?" quoth I. "Would that make any difference?"

"Never a whit,"[510] quoth he.

"Then," quoth I, "in case it appear unto you (as I suppose it doth to you and to every Christian man

---

504 *so far-forth:* to such an extent   *though:* even if   **507** in addition; also   **510** *Never a whit:* Not in the least
505 *whether would:* would   **506** *and*   **508** *wist nere:* knew not   **509** deluded

else) that in all points of faith, both in things to be believed above nature, and in things also that are of necessity to be known and believed which may be perceived by reason given us with nature, God giveth us in commandment that we shall believe his Church, then are ye fully answered. For then have ye the man that ye must needs resort unto for your final answer and solution of all points and doubts in any wise concerning the salvation of your soul. Of which points no man can deny, but one of the most especial points is to take in Holy Scripture always the right sense. Or else, if we cannot attain the right understanding, yet then at the leastwise to be sure that we shall avoid and eschew[511] all such mistaking as might bring us into any damnable error."

THE TWENTY-SEVENTH CHAPTER
The author proveth that God hath commanded us in all things necessary to salvation to give firm credence and full obedience unto his Church. And a cause why God will have us bounden to believe.

"That is truth," quoth he, "if this may appear. But where shall it appear that God commandeth us in all such things to believe the Church? For first, methinketh that were a very strange manner of commanding. For of the Church be all we that should (as ye say) be by God commanded to believe the Church; and all we together make the whole Church. And what reason were it, then, to command us to believe the Church, which were no more, in effect, but to bid us all believe us all, or each of us to believe other?[512] And then if we fell at diverse opinions, why should the one party more believe the other, than be believed of[513] the other, since both the parties be of the Church and make the Church among them, saving[514] that always that party seemeth to be believed which best and most clearly can allege[515] the Scripture for their opinion? For the words of God must break the strife. He is only to be believed, and his only Son, of whom himself commanded: *Ipsum audite*, 'Hear him,' said the Father at the time of his baptism.[516] And therefore the man that ye speak of, whom God sendeth me

to, and whom he biddeth me hear and believe, is our Savior Christ only, and not any congregation of men. Whose words if we believe before the words of God, and, in the stead of the Scripture of God put our trust and confidence in the doctrine and ordinance of the Church, it were haply[517] to be feared lest we fall in the reproof that is touched in the Gospel, where is said, 'In vain worship they me with the doctrine of men;'[518] and where our Savior also reproveth the scribes and the Pharisees, saying unto them, 'Wherefore[519] do you break and transgress the commandment of God for your traditions?'"[520]

"I trust," quoth I, "yet at last[521] we shall agree. But much ado,[522] methinketh, it is to come to it. But since we must, as ye say—and truth it is—hear our Savior Christ and believe him, is it enough to hear him and believe him? Or be we, besides that, also bounden to obey him?"

"To obey him also," quoth he. "For else were he better unheard."

"Well said," quoth I. "But whether are[523] we bounden to hear him and obey him in some things, or in all things?"

"In all things," quoth he, "without exception, that he commandeth us to do."

"Then if Christ," quoth I, "bid us believe and obey his Church, be we not bounden so to do?"

"Yes," quoth he.

"Then may we," quoth I, "no more doubt to be true whatso[524] the Church biddeth us believe than the thing that our Savior himself biddeth us believe, if he bid us hear his Church as his Father bade us hear him."

"That is truth," quoth he, "if he so do; but methinketh it were a strange bidding, as I said, to bid each of us believe other."

"It seemeth not," quoth I, "so strange a thing to Saint Paul. For he marvelous effectually beseecheth Christian people to 'agree together all in one mind,' and in the faith to tell one tale, suffering[525] no sects or schisms among them.[526] Which agreement and consent[527] can never be where no man giveth credence to other. But among Christian people it will soon be, if every man give credence to the Church."

"But yet," quoth he, "since all be of the Church, of diverse parties which shall believe which?"

---

511 shun 512 the other 513 by 514 except 515 cite 516 These words were spoken by the Father at the Transfig-uration rather than at Jesus's baptism. See Mt 3:17; 17:5. 517 perhaps 518 Mt 15:9 519 Why 520 Mt 15:3 521 *yet at last:* in the end 522 work; trouble 523 *whether are:* are 524 whatever 525 allowing 526 See 1 Cor 1:10. 527 consensus

"Ye take that," quoth I, "for a great doubt and a thing very perplex, which seemeth me very plain. For either first the Church hath the truth and believe all one way till some one or some few begin the change, and then, though all be yet of the Church till some by their obstinacy be gone out or put out, yet is it no doubt but[528] if I will believe the Church, I must believe them that still believe that way which all the whole believed before.

"Or else if there were anything that was peradventure such that in the Church sometime[529] was doubted and reputed for unrevealed and unknown, if after that the whole Church fall in one consent upon the one side, either by common determination at a general council, or by a perfect persuasion and belief so received through Christendom that the Christian people think it a damnable error to believe the contrary, then if any would after that take the contrary way—were it one or more, were it few or many, were they learned or unlearned, were they lay people or of the clergy—yet can I nothing doubt which party to believe if I will believe the Church."

"That is truth," quoth he, "but ye prove me not yet that God hath bidden me believe the Church."

"Ye somewhat interrupted me," quoth I, "with your other subtlety, by which ye would it should[530] seem an absurdity to bid us believe the Church. Forasmuch as thereby, ye said, it should seem that we were commanded nothing else but each to believe other, and then in diverse opinions taken, we could not wit[531] which party should believe which. Whereof[532] since I have showed you the contrary, and removed that block out of the way for stumbling, we shall, I think, soon see the other point: that Christ commandeth us to believe his Church. For as his Father said of himself, 'Hear him,' so said he of his Church when he sent it abroad to be spread forth.

"For when he had gathered his Church of his apostles and his disciples, and thereupon sent them forth to preach, said he not unto them, 'He that heareth you heareth me'? Did he not also command that whoso would not hear the Church should be reputed and taken as paynims[533] and publicans?"[534]

"That was," quoth he, "where men would not amend their living."

"Was it not," quoth I, "general,[535] where a man would not amend any damnable fault?"

"Yes," quoth he.

"Is misbelief," quoth I, "none such?"

"Yes, marry," quoth he.

"Then is," quoth I, "the Church his judge upon his belief, to show him whether it be true or false?"

"So it seemeth," quoth he.

"Hath his living," quoth I, "nothing ado[536] with faith?"

"How mean you that?" quoth he.

"Thus," quoth I, "as if Luther, late[537] a friar and having now wedded a nun,[538] were commanded to amend his lewd living and put away that harlot whom he abuseth in continual incest[539] and sacrilege under the name of a wife, and he would say that he did well enough, and that their vows could not bind them—were he not bounden to believe the Church and obey thereto as well concerning his belief as his living?"

"Yes, verily," quoth he.

"Then appeareth it," quoth I, "that we be by Christ commanded to hear, believe, and obey the Church as well in matters of faith as of manners.[540] Which thing well appeareth also by that our Lord would that whoso were disobedient 'should be taken as a paynim or a publican.'[541] Of which two, the one offended in misbelief, the other in lewd[542] living. And thus it appeareth that not only Christ is the man that ye be sent unto and commanded by God to believe and obey, but also the Church is the person whom ye be by Christ commanded to hear and believe and obey. And therefore, if ye will—in faith, or living, or avoiding of all damnable error (that ye might fall in by misunderstanding of Scripture)— take a sure and infallible way, ye must in all these things hear, believe, and obey the Church, which is, as I say, the person whom Christ sendeth you to for the sure solution of all such doubts, as to the man in whose mouth he speaketh himself, and the Holy Spirit of his Father in heaven.

"And surely this is much to be marked. For it is the perpetual order which our Lord hath continued

528 that   **529** at one time   **530** *would it should:* want to have   **531** know   **532** Concerning which   **533** pagans   **534** Lk 10:16. See also Mt 18:17.   **535** common (belief)   **536** to do

537 formerly   **538** Martin Luther became an Augustinian monk in 1505 and took a vow of celibacy; he later taught that such vows were not binding and in 1523 married Katharina von Bora, a former Cistercian

nun.   **539** so considered because in canon law monks and nuns are regarded as siblings   **540** morals   **541** Mt 18:17   **542** evil in the governance of good men from the beginning: that, like[543] as our nature first fell by pride to the disobedience of God with inordinate desire of knowledge like unto God, so hath God ever kept man in humility, straining[544] him with the knowledge and confession of his ignorance and binding him to the obedience of belief of certain things whereof his own wit would verily ween[545] the contrary. And therefore are we bounden not only to believe, against our own reason, the points that God showeth us in Scripture, but also that God teacheth his Church without Scripture, and against our own mind also, to give diligent hearing, firm credence, and faithful obedience to the Church of Christ concerning the sense and understanding of Holy Scripture, not doubting but[546] since he hath commanded his sheep to be fed, he hath provided for them wholesome meat[547] and true doctrine, and that he hath therefore so far inspired the old holy doctors of his Church with the light of his grace for our instruction that the doctrine wherein they have agreed, and by many ages consented, is the very true faith and right way to heaven, being put in their minds by the holy hand of him *qui facit unanimes in domo* ('that maketh the Church of Christ all of one mind')."[548]

THE TWENTY-EIGHTH CHAPTER

The messenger eftsoon[549] objected against this — that we should believe the Church in anything where we find the words of Scripture seeming plainly to say the contrary, or believe the old doctors' interpretations in any necessary article, where they seem to us to say contrary to the text — showing that we may perceive the Scripture as well as they might. And the answer of the author, proving the authority of the old interpreters and the infallible authority of the Church, in that God teacheth it every truth requisite to the necessity of man's salvation. Which he proveth by a deduction partly depending upon natural reason.

"It seemeth me," quoth he, "that all this goeth well — that we should believe the Church as Christ — as long as they say as Christ saith, for so methinketh meant our Lord.

"But now if they tell me tales of their own, whereof Christ never spoke word, nor mention made thereof in Holy Scripture, I may then say with the prophet Jeremiah, *Non mittebam prophetas, et ipsi currebant; non loquebar ad eos, et ipsi prophetabant* ('Those prophets,' quoth our Lord, 'ran forth of their own heads,[550] and I sent them not, and prophesied of their own heads, when I spoke nothing to them').[551] And then how much may I more say so if they say me a thing whereof Christ or Holy Scripture saith the contrary? Shall I believe the Church above Christ? Were that a good humility, to be obedient more to men than to God? More ought I, methinketh, to believe God alone speaking in his Holy Scripture himself, than all the old fathers if they make a gloss against the text. Nor they do not themselves, for their opinions, say and write that they have them by inspiration, or by revelation, or by miracle, but by wisdom, study, diligence, and collation[552] of one text with another. By all which means men may now perceive the sentence[553] of Scripture as well as they might then. And if ye will peradventure say that grace helped them — which I will well agree — then will I say again that God's grace is not so far worn out yet but that it may as well help us as it helped them, and so may we be, for the right understanding of Scripture, equal with them, and peradventure one ace[554] above them. Whereby when we perceive that they went wrong and others after them, shall we then call it humility so to captive[555] and subdue our understanding, whereby God hath haply given us light to perceive their errors, that without thank[556] given him therefor,[557] we shall so set his gift at nought[558] that we shall believe them before himself, and tell him that himself bade so? And therefore methink where the old doctors or the whole Church telleth me the tale that God doth, there he biddeth me believe them. But where God saith one thing in Scripture, and they tell me another, it thinketh me that I should in no wise believe them."

"Well," quoth I, "then in somewhat[559] ye say, ye will believe the Church, but not in all. In anything beside Scripture ye will not, nor in the interpretation of Scripture ye will not; and so, whereas ye said that ye believe the Church in somewhat, in very deed ye believe the Church in right nought.[560] For

543 just   **544** constraining   **545** *verily ween:* truly think   **546** that   **547** food   **548** Ps 67(68):7   **549** for a second time   **550** accord   **551** Jer 23:21

552 comparison   **553** meaning   **554** *peradventure one ace:* perhaps a little (a reference to dice or cards)   **555** enslave   **556** credit   **557** for it   **558** set at

nought: value as nothing   **559** something   **560** *right nought:* absolutely nothing

wherein will ye believe it if ye believe it not in the interpretation of Scripture? For as touching the text, ye believe the Scripture itself, and not the Church."

"Methinketh," quoth he, "the text is good enough and plain enough, needing no gloss, if it be well considered and every part compared with other."

"Hard it were," quoth I, "to find anything so plain that it should need no gloss at all."

"In faith," quoth he, "they make a gloss to some texts that be as plain as it is that twice two make four."

"Why," quoth I, "needeth that no gloss at all?"

"I trow[561] so," quoth he. "Or else the devil is on[562] it."

"Iwis,"[563] quoth I. "And yet, though ye would believe one that would tell you that twice two ganders made always four geese, yet ye would be advised ere ye believed him that would tell you that twice two geese made always four ganders. For therein might ye be deceived. And him would ye not believe at all that would tell you that twice two geese would always make four horses."

"Tut," quoth he, "this is a merry matter. They must be, all the twice twain, always of one kind. But geese and horses be of diverse."

"Well," quoth I, "then every man that is neither goose nor horse seeth well that there is one gloss yet."

"But now," quoth I, "the geese and the ganders be both of one kind, and yet twice two geese make not always four ganders."

"A sweet matter,"[564] quoth he. "Ye wot what I mean well enough."

"I think I do," quoth I. "But I think if ye bring it forth, it will make another gloss to your text, as plain as your text is; and ye will in all Holy Scripture have no gloss at all. And yet will ye have collation[565] made of one text with another, and show how they may be agreed together, as though all that were no gloss."

"Yea," quoth he, "but would you that we should[566] believe the Church if it set a gloss that will in no wise agree with the text, but that it appeareth plainly that the text well considered saith clean the contrary?"

"To whom doth that appear," quoth I, "so plainly, when it appeareth one[567] to you — and to the whole Church another?"

"Yet if I see it so," quoth he, "though holy doctors and all the whole Church would tell me the contrary, methinketh I were no more bounden to believe them all that the Scripture meaneth as they take it than if they would all tell me that a thing were white which I see myself is black."

"Of late," quoth I, "ye would believe the Church in something. And now not only ye would believe it in nothing, but also, whereas God would the Church should be your judge, ye would now be judge over the Church. And ye will by your wit be judge whether the Church in the understanding of Holy Scripture — that God hath written to his Church — do judge aright or err. As for your white and black, never shall it be that ye shall see the thing black that all others shall see white. But ye may be sure that if all others see it white and ye take it for black, your eyes be sore[568] deceived. For the Church will not, I think, agree to call it other than it seemeth to them. And much marvel were it if ye should in Holy Scripture see better than the old holy doctors and Christ's whole Church.

"But first," quoth I, "ye must consider that ye and I do not talk of one doctor or twain, but of the consent and common agreement of the old holy fathers. Nor that we speak not of the doctrine of one man or two in the Church, but of the common consent of the Church. We speak not also of any sentence taken in any text of Holy Scripture whereby riseth no doubt or question of any necessary article of our faith or rule of our living (for in other by-matters[569] may there be taken of one text ten senses peradventure and all good enough, without warrantize of[570] the best), but we speak of such two diverse and contrary senses taken, as if the one be true the other must needs be false — and that, as I say, concerning some necessary point of our faith or rule of our living, which is also depending upon faith and reducible thereto. As if one would boldly break his vow for that[571] he thought that no man were bounden to keep any. Such points, I say, let us consider; they be that we speak of. And this remembered between us, then will we somewhat see what your saying doth prove.

"I shall not much need," quoth I, "to stick[572] with you in disputing by what means the Scripture is understood, since ye be agreed with nature and

561 believe **562** in on **563** Indeed   *we should:* want us to **567** one way   **571** *for that:* because **572** persist in
564 *A sweet matter:* an ironic expression; **568** greatly **569** incidentals **570** *war-*   arguing
Oh, very cute **565** comparison **566** *that*   *rantize of:* any guarantee as to which is

diligence the grace of God must needs go, or else no diligence or help of nature can prevail. Nor I will nothing deny you but that God may, and will also, give his grace now to us as he gave of old to his holy doctors, if there be as much towardness[573] and no more let[574] or impediment in ourselves than was in them. I will also grant you that we may now, by the same means by which they might then, understand the Scripture as well as they did then; and I will not much stick with you for one ace better. And were it not for the sins that we sink in, we might percase[575] understand it better by cater-trey-deuce,[576] having their labors therein and our own therewith. But since I am so genteel to grant you so many things, I trust ye will grant me this one: that if in any such point of our faith as God would have men bounden to believe, they did understand the Scripture one way and we another, being the one to the other so clean contrary that if the one were true, the other must needs be false, ye will then grant, I say, that either they err or we."

"That must needs be," quoth he.

"Ye will also grant," quoth I, "that in such points as we speak of, the error were damnable. For we speak of those points only to the belief whereof God will have us bounden."

"I grant," quoth he, "for damnable were it in such case to believe wrong. And wrong should they or we believe, if they or we believed a wrong article, because they or we thought that the Scripture affirmed it. And as damnable were it and yet much more, if we believed a thing whereof we believed that the Scripture affirmeth the contrary. For then believed we that the Scripture were false."

"This is," quoth I, "very well said. But for the more plainness, let us put one example or twain. And what point rather than the article touching the equality in Godhead of our Savior Christ with his Father? For if the contrary belief were true, then were this always damnable and plain idolatry."

"Very truth," quoth he.

"May not," quoth I, "the other example be the matter that we have in hand, concerning saints' relics, images, and pilgrimages? Which things, if it[577] be (as ye say many reckon it) idolatry, then is it yet worse to do therein as we do than if our belief were wrong in the other point—and that as much worse

as the saints, or the images either, be worse than the holy manhood of Christ."

"That is," quoth he, "very true."

"Then," quoth I, "let the first point alone, because therein we be all agreed, and speak of the second: if the old fathers took the Scriptures one way and we the contrary. Though it might be that we were able to understand the Scriptures as well as they, yet if they so understood them that they thought this kind of worship not forbidden but commanded and pleasant to God, and we new men on the other side thought it utterly forbidden and holden for idolatry, the one party did not indeed understand the Scripture right, but were in a damnable error."

"That will no man deny," quoth he.

"I doubt not now," quoth I, "but that yourself seeth very well how many things I might here lay[578] for them to prove you that they erred not so: first, their wits as[579] much as our new men's; their diligence as great; their erudition greater; their study as fervent; their devotion hotter; their number far greater; their time continued longer by[580] many ages persevering; the contrary opinions in few, and those always soon faded; they taken always for Catholic, the contrary part for heretics. Here might I lay you the holiness of their life, and the plenty of their grace well appearing thereby, and that our Lord therefore opened their eyes and suffered[581] and caused them to see the truth. And albeit he used therein none open miracle nor sensible[582] revelation (whereof, as ye say, they none allege or pretend[583] for the proof of their opinions in their interpretations of Holy Scripture), yet used he the secret supernatural means by which his grace, assistant[584] with good men that labor therefor, by motions insensible to themselves, inclineth their assent unto the true side; and that thus the old holy fathers did, in the point that we speak of and in such others, perceive the right sense of Holy Scripture so far-forth at the leastwise as they well knew that it was not contrary to their belief. And here might I lay you also that if it had been otherwise, and that they had therein damnably been deceived, then, living and dying in damnable error, they could not have been saints—as God hath showed them to be, by many a thousand miracles both in their lives and after their deaths. With this might I also lay, and very well conclude,

---

573 inclination   **574** hindrance
575 perhaps   **576** four, three, or two
times better (continuing the "ace" or

dice metaphor)   **577** i.e., honor given
to these things   **578** submit as evidence
579 are as   **580** through   **581** allowed

582 perceptible to the senses   **583** claim
584 present to help

that since those holy doctors and the Church be (as by their books plainly appeareth) all of one faith in this point and such others, that thereby well appeareth that the Church is in the truth, and is not, in the understanding of the Scripture that speaketh of the matter, anything deceived, but they clearly deceived that do understand those texts of Holy Scripture to the contrary. These things, as I say—and yet many others more—might I lay. But since ye did yourself put the Church and them both in one case, and so they be indeed, I will rather prove you the truth of them by the truth of the Church, than the truth of the Church by the truth of them. And so seemeth me good reason. For surely, since they were but members of his Church, God had his special cure[585] upon them most especially for the profit of his Church, by whose whole corps he more setteth[586] than by any member thereof—saint, apostle, evangelist, or other. And therefore must I yet ask you again whether the Church may have any damnable error in the faith, by mistaking of Scripture or otherwise."

"That is," quoth he, "somewhat hard to tell."

"Now," quoth I, "somewhat I marvel that ye remember not that yourself hath agreed already that these words of Christ spoken unto Peter—'I have prayed that thy faith shall never fail'[587]—were not only meant by the faith in Peter his own person, but also by the faith of the Church. For to him was it spoken as head of the Church."

"Yes, I remember," quoth he, "right well that I agreed it. But I remember also that, notwithstanding mine agreement, ye were content that we should ensearch[588] again and again the matter otherwise besides, wherein mine agreement should not bind me."

"Lo," quoth I, "that had I forgotten again. But let it then alone for the while, and tell me this: Did not Christ intend to gather a flock and congregation of people that should serve God and be his special people?"

"Yes," quoth he, "that is very truth. For so saith plain Scripture of Christ in sundry places, as where the Father of heaven saith unto Christ in the psalm, *Postula a me, et dabo tibi gentes hereditatem tuam* ('Ask of me, and I shall give thee paynim people for thine inheritance'),[589] and many other places. And

else[590] undoubtedly his whole coming had been, in manner,[591] frustrate and in vain."

"That people," quoth I, "which should be an inheritance, did he intend should endure for his own days only, while he lived here, or else that it should go forth and continue long after?"

"Nay," quoth he, "that shall continue while the world lasteth here, till Doomsday, and after in heaven eternally."

"Shall this people," quoth I, "have among them the knowledge and understanding what he would they should[592] do to please God withal?"

"Yea," quoth he.

"Whether shall they," quoth I, "have this knowledge for a while, in the beginning, and then lose it; or shall they have it still as long as they continue?"

Here he began a little to stagger.

"Why," quoth I, "can ye call them his people any longer if they lose the knowledge how to serve him and please him? If they forsloth[593] to do their duty, as slack servants sometimes do, yet may they mend and do better another time. But if they lose the knowledge of their duty, then wot they nere[594] which way to amend, as he that knoweth fornication for sin may fall by frailty to fornication; but since he knoweth it for naught,[595] though he sinned more in the doing than if he had not known the prohibition, yet doth the knowledge give him warning, and occasion of repentance and amendment, which must needs lack if he had lost the knowledge."

Upon this, he granted that it must needs be that this people must needs have always the knowledge how to serve and please our Lord, or else they ceased to be his people.

"Is not this people," quoth I, "called the Church?"

"Yes," quoth he.

"Then the Church," quoth I, "always hath—and always shall by your reason—have the knowledge and understanding how God may be served and pleased."

"Truth," quoth he.

"Is," quoth I, "that knowledge fully had without the knowledge of such things as God bindeth us to believe?"

"Nay," quoth he.

"What if we knew them in such wise," quoth I, "as we could rehearse[596] them on our fingers' ends,

585 care **586** values **587** Lk 22:32 **588** investigate **589** Ps 2:8   **590** otherwise **591** *in manner:* so to speak **592** *would they should:* wants them   to **593** neglect **594** *wot they nere:* know they not **595** wickedness **596** recite

and yet believed them not to be true? Would this knowledge serve?"

"In no wise," quoth he. "For if ye believed them to be false, though ye so knew them that ye could rehearse them by row,[597] ye could take no warning by them to please and serve God with them, which is the cause wherefore the Church should of necessity know them."

"This is," quoth I, "very well said. Then since ye grant that the Church shall ever endure, and that it could not endure without the knowledge of such things as please God, nor those things can be all known if knowledge lacked of those things that God bindeth us to believe, nor the knowledge of them anything serve to the knowledge and warning given us of God's pleasure, but if[598] we not only can tell them, but also believe them—which belief ye grant is called 'faith'—of this it consequently followeth that the Church always hath, and always shall have, the knowledge and belief of such things as God will have it bounden to believe."

"That is truth," quoth he, "because God hath left Holy Scripture to the Church; and therein is all, and the Church believeth that to be true. And therefore therein and thereby hath the Church all that warning and learning of God's pleasure that ye speak of, without which it cannot endure."

"Are ye there yet again?" quoth I. "We have sundry ways proved and agreed between us that this knowledge and faith was before Scripture and writing, and many things of necessity to be both believed and done that are not in Holy Scripture. And yet after all this (too long to be repeated), ye return again to the first point—so often confuted—that nothing is learned nor known but by Holy Scripture. But now go to and suppose it were so. What should ye win thereby? For what if God," quoth I, "had left the Scripture to the Church locked up in a close[599] chest, and that no man should look therein? Would that have served?"

"Nay, pardie,"[600] quoth he.

"What if he had left it open, and written in such wise that no man could read it?"

"That were all one," quoth he.

"What if every man," quoth I, "could read it, and no man understand it?"

"As little would it serve," quoth he, "as the other."

"Then," quoth I, "since it serveth the Church to learn God's pleasure therein, and that can it not, as ye grant yourself, but if[601] the Church understand it, it followeth of this that the Church understandeth it. And thus every way for the faith and knowledge of God's pleasure—if it be, as ye say, all known by the Scripture and no part otherwise—yet always to this point ye bring it in the end: that the Church hath the sure knowledge thereof. And then, if that be so, ye shall not (as ye lately said ye should) in any diverse texts of Scripture seeming to make a doubtous[602] article of our faith and to bring in question what we be bounden to believe, after ye have read in Scripture all that can be read, and heard on both sides all that can be said, then take which part seemeth to yourself most probable. Nor if ye stand still, for all that, in a doubt, then after your bitter[603] prayers made to God for his grace and guide in the choice, go take you the one part at adventure[604] and cleave thereto, as though ye were sure by your confidence in God that his grace had inclined your assent to the surer side. But since I have showed you plainly by reason that he hath given his Church in all such things knowledge of the truth, ye shall take the sure way and put yourself out of all perplexity, if in the point itself and the Scriptures that touch it, ye take for the truth that way that the Church teacheth you therein, howsoever the matter seem beside[605] unto yourself or to any man else."

THE TWENTY-NINTH CHAPTER
The author proveth by Scripture that God instructeth the Church of Christ in every truth necessarily requisite for our salvation.

"Truly," quoth he, "ye wind it well about.[606] But yet ye made as though ye would have showed that God had in Scripture told me that he had and ever would tell his Church the truth in all such matters. And now ye bring it to the point: not the Holy Scripture telleth me the tale, but man's reason. And surely, as I showed you before, I dare not well trust reason in matters of faith and of Holy Scripture."

"I began," quoth I, "to prove it you by Scripture,

and ye then put me out[607] in the beginning. Howbeit,[608] this reason hath Scripture for his[609] foundation and ground. And though it somewhat build further thereon, yet is not reason always to be mistrusted, where faith standeth not against it, nor God saith not the contrary—except[610] reason be so far out of credence with you that ye will not now believe him if he tell you that twice twain make four. I ween ye will fare by[611] reason as one did once by a false shrew.[612] He swore that he would not for twenty pounds hear him say his creed. For he knew him for such a liar that he thought he should never believe his creed after, if he heard it once of his mouth.

"Howbeit," quoth I, "let us yet see whether God himself in Scripture tell you the same tale or no. God telleth you in Scripture that he would be with his Church to the end of the world. I think ye doubt not thereof but those words he spoke to the whole Church that then was, and ever shall be, from the apostles' days continued till the end of the world."

"That, in good faith," quoth he, "must needs be so."

"Then were this in good faith enough," quoth I, "for our purpose, since no man doubteth wherefore he will be with his Church—except[613] we should think that he would be therewith for nothing, wherefore should he be with it but to keep it and preserve it, with the assistance of his gracious presence, from spiritual mischief specially, and of all other, specially from infidelity and from idolatry? Which was the special thing from which he called his Church out of the Gentiles, which else[614]—as for moral virtues and political—if they had not lacked the right cause and end of referring their acts to God, were many of them not far under many of us? Let us go further. Doth he not in the fourteenth, fifteenth, and sixteenth chapters of Saint John again and again repeat that after his going he will come again to them, and saith he 'will not leave them orphans,'[615] as fatherless children, but will come again to them himself? Let us add now thereunto the words before rehearsed—that he will be with them till the world's end—and it appeareth plain that he meant all this by his whole Church that should be to the world's end.

"When he said unto them, 'I call you friends, for all that I have heard of my Father I have made known to you,'[616] he spoke as to his perpetual Church and not to the apostles alone, but if[617] he said to them alone these words also—'I command that ye love each other'[618]—so that none should love each other after but only they. Now lest the things that he taught them should by the Church after be forgotten (which was more to be doubted[619] than of themselves that[620] heard it), he said unto them also: 'These things,' quoth he, 'have I spoken to you abiding here with you. But the Comforter—which is the Holy Ghost, whom my Father shall send in my name—he shall teach you all things, and he shall put you in mind and remembrance of all things that I shall have said unto you.'[621] So that here ye see that he shall again always teach the Church of new,[622] the old lessons of Christ. And he said also to them that this Comforter, the Holy Ghost, the 'Spirit of truth,' should be sent to abide with them 'forever,'[623] which cannot be meant but of the whole Church. For the Holy Ghost was not sent hither into the earth here to dwell with the apostles forever, for they dwelled not so long here. Now if the Spirit of truth shall dwell in the Church forever, how can the Church err in perceiving of the truth—in such things, I mean, as God will bind them to know, or shall be necessary for them to know? For only of such things meant our Lord when he said that the Holy Ghost shall teach them all things. For as Saint Paul saith, 'the manifestation and showing of the Spirit is to the utility and profit.'[624] This Holy Spirit also was not promised by our Savior Christ that he should only tell his Church again his words, but he said further: 'I have,' quoth he, 'besides all this, many things to say to you; but ye be not able to bear them now. But when he shall come that is the Spirit of truth, he shall lead you into all truth.'[625] Lo, our Lord said not that the Holy Ghost should write unto his Church all truth, but that he should lead them, by secret inspiration and inclination of their hearts, into all truth—in which must needs be conceived both information and right belief of every necessary article, and of the right and true sense of Holy Scripture, as far as shall be requisite to conserve the Church from any damnable error.

---

607 *put me out:* distracted me   **608** However   **609** its   **610** unless   **611** *fare by:* treat   **612** *false shrew:* dishonest scoundrel   **613** unless   **614** *which else:* who otherwise

615 See Jn 14:18, 23, 28; 16:16, 22.   **616** Jn 15:15   **617** *but if:* unless   **618** Jn 15:12   **619** feared, apprehensive   **620** *themselves that:* they themselves who   **621** Jn

14:25–26   **622** *of new:* anew   **623** Jn 14:16–17   **624** 1 Cor 12:7   **625** Jn 16:12–13

"Now when the Holy Ghost shall, by God's promise, be for this purpose abiding in the Church forever; and Christ himself hath also said that he will not leave his Church as orphans, but will come himself, and be with it unto the end of the world, and saith also that his Father is in him and he is in his Father, and that his Father and he be both one thing[626]—not both one person, but both one substance—and, with the Holy Ghost, both one God, then must it needs follow that to the world's end there is with the Church resident the whole Trinity. Whose assistance, being to the Church perpetual, how can it at any time fall from true faith to false errors and heresies?"

THE THIRTIETH CHAPTER
Whereas the messenger had thought before that it were hard to believe anything certainly save Holy Scripture, though[627] the Church did agree therein and command it, the author showeth that saving[628] for the authority of the Church, men could not know what Scripture they should believe. And here is it showed that God will not suffer[629] the Church to be deceived in the choice of the very[630] Scripture of God from any counterfeit.

"Now is it, I suppose, well and clearly proved by Scripture the thing that I promised: that is to wit, that the Church cannot err in any such substantial article as God will have us bounden to believe.

"But yet forasmuch as ye regard nothing but Scripture only, this would I fain wit of[631] you: whether ye believe that Christ was born of a virgin."

"What else?" quoth he.

"Why believe you that?" quoth I.

"The Gospel showeth me so," quoth he.

"What if it did not?" quoth I. "Were then your creed out of credence, but if[632] he bring witness with him?"[633]

"The creed," quoth he, "is a thing by itself."

"Yet is it," quoth I, "no part of the Gospel, as the Pater Noster is.[634] And yet I think if Gospel had never been written, ye would have believed your creed."

"So think I too," quoth he.

"And wherefore,"[635] quoth I, "but for[636] because the Church should have showed you so? But let our creed alone a while, and go we to the Gospel itself. Which Gospel telleth you that Christ was born of a virgin?"

"The Gospel of Saint Luke,"[637] quoth he.

"How know you that?" quoth I.

"For I read it so," quoth he, "in the book."

"Ye read," quoth I, "such a book. But how know you that Saint Luke made it?"

"How know I," quoth he, "other books, but by that they bear the names of their authors written upon them?"

"Know you it well thereby?" quoth I. "Many books be there that have false inscriptions, and are not the books of them that they be named by."[638]

"That is truth," quoth he. "But yet though men did peradventure err and fail in[639] the name, as if he should repute a book of stories[640] to be made by Titus Livius[641] which he never made, but some other honest cunning[642] man, yet were the books neither less elegant nor less true therefor. Nor in like wise if the Church did mistake the very name of some evangelist and Gospel, yet were the Gospel nevertheless true."

"That is," quoth I, "well said. But how be ye sure that the matter of the book is true?"

"Marry," quoth he, "for I am."

"That is," quoth I, "the reason that a maiden layeth[643] for her own knowledge of her maidenhead. But she could tell another how she knoweth she hath it, saving that she is loath to come so near[644] as to be acknown[645] that she could tell how she might lose it. But here is no such fear. Tell me, therefore, whereby wot ye[646] that the matter of that book is true?"

"I think," quoth he, "that God showeth me so."

"That is well thought," quoth I. "But he told it you not mouth to mouth."[647]

"No," quoth he. "But he hath told it to others in the beginning, or else it was well known in the beginning when he wrote it. And he[648] was known and believed by his living, and the miracles that God did for him. And after that it was once known,

---

626 See Jn 17:21.   **627** even if
628 except   **629** allow   **630** true
631 *fain wit of:* like to know from   **632** *but if:* unless   **633** it   **634** See Mt 6:9–13.

635 why   **636** *but for:* except   **637** See Lk 1:26–37.   **638** *named by:* attributed to
639 concerning   **640** histories   **641** Livy (59 BC–AD 17)   **642** learned   **643** gives

644 *come so near:* become so intimate
645 i.e., known to still have her virginity
646 *whereby wot ye:* how do you know
647 *mouth to mouth:* in person   **648** Luke

the knowledge went forth from man to man. And God hath so wrought with[649] us that we believe it because the whole Church hath always done so before our days."

5   "Now come you," quoth I, "to the very point. For many things hath been true that in process after hath left[650] to be believed. And many a thing hath in the beginning been known for false, and yet hath after happed to be believed. But the Gospels and Holy
10   Scripture, God provideth that, though percase[651] some of it may perish and be lost, whereby they might have harm, but not fall in error (for the faith should stand though the Scriptures were all gone), yet shall he never suffer[652] his Church to be deceived
15   in that point: that they shall take for Holy Scripture any book that is not. And therefore saith holy Saint Augustine, 'I should not believe the Gospel but if it were[653] for the Church.'[654] And he saith good reason. For were it not for the Spirit of God keeping
20   the truth thereof in his Church, who could be sure which were the very Gospels? There were many that wrote the Gospel. And yet hath the Church, by secret instinct of God, rejected the remnant and chosen out these four for the sure, undoubted true."

25   "That is," quoth he, "sure so."

"This is," quoth I, "so sure so, that Luther himself is driven of necessity to grant this; or else he perceiveth that there were none hold nor surety[655] in Scripture itself, if the Church might be suffered
30   by God to be deceived in that point, and to take for Holy Scripture that writing that indeed were not. And therefore he confesseth that this must needs be a sure infallible ground, that God hath given this gift unto his Church: that his Church can always
35   discern the word of God from the word of men."[656]

"In good faith," quoth he, "that must needs be so, or else all would fail."

Quoth I, "Then ye that would believe the Church in nothing, nor give sure credence to the tradition
40   of the Church but if[657] it were proved by Scripture, now see it proved to you that ye could not believe the Scripture but if it were proved to be Scripture by the judgment and tradition of the Church."

"No," quoth he, "but when I have learned once
45   of the Church that it is Holy Scripture and the Word of God, then I believe it better than I believe all the Church. I might by a light[658] person sometime know a much more substantial man. And yet when I know him, I will believe him much better
50   than him by whom I know him, if they varied in a tale and were contrary."

"Good reason," quoth I. "But the Church biddeth you not believe the contrary of that[659] the Scripture saith. But he[660] telleth you that in such places as ye would better believe the Scripture than
55   the Church, there ye understand not the Scripture. For whatsoever words it speaketh, yet it meaneth not the contrary of that the Church teacheth you. And the Church cannot be deceived in any such weighty point."
60
"Whereby shall I know?" quoth he.

"Why be we at that point yet?" quoth I. "Have we so soon forgotten the perpetual assistance of the Trinity in his Church, and the prayer of Christ to keep the faith of his Church from failing, and the
65   Holy Ghost sent of purpose to keep in the Church the remembrance of Christ's words and to lead them into all truth? What would it have profited to have put you in the remembrance of the assistance of God with the children of Israel—walking with
70   them in the cloud by day, and in the pillar of fire by night, in their earthly voyage[661]—and thereby to have proved you the much more special assistance of God with his Christian Church in their spiritual voyage, wherein his especial goodness well declareth
75   his tender diligence by that he doth vouchsafe to assist and comfort us with the continual presence of his Precious Body in the Holy Sacrament? All this would not help if manifest reason that I made you, and evident Scripture that I rehearsed[662] you, can-
80   not yet print in your heart a perceiving that the assistance of God in his Church must needs preserve his Church from all damnable errors in the faith, and give his Church so far-forth the understanding of Scripture that they may well perceive that no
85   part thereof, well understood, standeth against any article that the Church believeth as parcel of their Christian faith."

"Nay," quoth he, "I perceive it well when I remember it; but it was not ready in remembrance."
90

649 *wrought with:* brought about in
650 ceased   **651** perhaps   **652** allow
653 *but if it were:* were it not   **654** *Against*
the Fundamental Epistle of Manichaeus 5
655 security; certainty   **656** See Luther's
Babylonian Captivity of the Church 7.2.
657 *but if:* unless   **658** of little account
659 what   **660** i.e., the Church   **661** See
Ex 13:21–22.   **662** quoted (to)

THE THIRTY-FIRST CHAPTER

In that the Church cannot err in the choice of the true Scripture, the author proveth by the reason which the King's Highness,[663] in his noble and most famous book,[664] objecteth against Luther: that the Church cannot err in the necessary understanding of Scripture. And finally the author in this chapter doth briefly recapitle[665] certain of the principal points that be before proved. And therewith endeth the First Book.

"Yet would I," quoth I, "ask you one thing: Wherefore,[666] think you, will not Christ suffer[667] his Church to be deceived in the discerning of Holy Scripture from other writing, and suffer them to take a book of Holy Scripture that were none indeed?"

"Lest men might," quoth he, "of some false book reputed of Holy Scripture, have great occasion given them to conceive the wrong doctrine and wrong opinions of the faith, if God would suffer his Church to take a false devised book for Holy Scripture and for his own holy words."

"Ye say," quoth I, "very truth. Now what if in the very[668] Scripture he should suffer his Church mistake the very sentence,[669] in a matter substantial of our faith? Were they not in like peril to fall by misunderstanding into like errors as they might by false writings?"

"Yes, that they were," quoth he.

"Forsooth,"[670] quoth I, "so were they—and in much more.[671] For in a false book mistaken for Scripture, though they had[672] it in never so high reverence for some good things that they found in it, and thereby should have great occasion to believe the false errors written in the same, yet having— as the Church always shall have, the true faith first in heart—they should find many shifts[673] to keep out the errors. But now if they falsely should understand the true Scripture, there were no way to escape from damnable errors. And therefore may I say to you as the King's Highness most prudently laid[674] unto Luther: since God will not suffer his Church to mistake a book of Scripture, for[675] peril of damnable errors that might ensue thereon, and like peril may there ensue by the misconstruing of the sentence as by the mistaking of the book, it must needs follow that God will, in things of our faith, no more suffer them to take a false sentence for true than to take a false book for Scripture. And with this reason his Highness concluded[676] him so clearly that he durst[677] never since, for shame, touch that point again, nor any color could lay,[678] but that upon his own confession in all substantial points concerning the faith or knowledge of virtue pleasant to God, the Church hath so right understanding of Scripture that it well and truly perceiveth that no text therein can be right understood against any article that the Church believeth for thing to be believed of necessity. And this point durst he never since touch, nor make answer thereto, albeit that the King's Highness with this one point alone plainly turneth up and destroyeth the ground and foundation of all the heresies that Luther would have believed. And therefore of all things had Luther greatest cause to answer this point earnestly— and would undoubtedly if he had wist[679] how."

"Surely," quoth your friend, "I marvel not though he did not. For this point is so clear he could not, and I am herein fully satisfied."

"Then be you," quoth I, "satisfied in this also: that the faith of the Church is a right rule to carry with you to the study of Scripture, to shape you the understanding of the texts by, and so to take them as they may always agree therewithal?"[680]

"Be it,"[681] quoth he.

"Then are ye," quoth I, "also fully answered in this: that where[682] ye said ye should not believe the Church telling a tale of their own, but only telling you Scripture, ye now perceive that in such things as we speak of—that is to wit, necessary points of our faith—if they[683] tell you a tale which if it were false were damnable, ye must believe and may be sure that, since the Church cannot in such things err, it is very true all that the Church in such things telleth you. And that it is not their own word, but the word of God, though it be not in Scripture."

"That appeareth well," quoth he.

"Then are ye," quoth I, "as fully satisfied that, where ye lately said that it were a disobedience to God and preferring of the Church before himself

---

663 *so far-forth:* to such an extent
664 *King's Highness:* Henry VIII's *Defense of the Seven Sacraments,* published in 1521
665 summarize 666 Why 667 allow

668 true 669 meaning 670 truly, in truth 671 more peril 672 *though they had:* even if they held 673 means; tactics
674 put forward as evidence 675 because

of the 676 refuted 677 dared
678 *color could lay:* pretense could offer
679 known 680 with it 681 *Be it:* Yes
682 whereas 683 the Church

if ye shall believe the Church in such things as God in his Holy Scripture saith himself the contrary, ye now perceive it can in no wise be so. But since his Church, in such things as we speak of, cannot err, it is impossible that the Scripture of God can be contrary to the faith of the Church."

"That is very true," quoth he.

"Then it is as true," quoth I, "that ye be further fully answered in the principal point: that the Scriptures laid[684] against images and pilgrimages and worship of saints make nothing against them. And also that those things — images, I mean, and pilgrimages and praying to saints — are things good and to be had[685] in honor in Christ's Church, since the Church believeth so. Which, as ye grant, and see cause why ye so should grant, can in such points not be suffered,[686] for the special assistance of God and instruction of the Holy Ghost, to fall in error. And so be we for this matter at last with much work, comen to an end. And therefore will we now to dinner. And your other objections that ye have laid, by which ye would prove those things reprovable[687] and make them seem idolatry, which we deferred afore, those will we talk of after dinner."

"By my troth," quoth he, "I have another tale to tell you that, all this gear[688] granted, turneth us yet into as much uncertainty as we were in before."

"Yea?" quoth I. "Then have we well walked after the ballad,[689] 'The further I go, the more behind.' I pray you, what thing is that? For that long I to hear yet ere we go."

"Nay," quoth he, "it were better ye dine first. My lady will, I ween, be angry with me that I keep you so long therefrom. For I hold[690] it now well toward twelve. And yet more angry would wax with me, if I should make you sit and muse at your meat[691] — as ye would, I wot well, muse on the matter if ye wist what it were."

"If I were," quoth I, "like my wife, I should muse more thereon now, and eat no meat for longing to know. But come on then and let us dine first, and ye shall tell us after."

The end of the First Book

---

684 cited   **685** held   **686** allowed   **689** *well … ballad:* truly borne out that
687 reprehensible   **688** matter   saying   **690** believe   **691** meal

THE SECOND BOOK

THE FIRST CHAPTER

The messenger—recapitiling[1] certain things before
proved, and for his part agreeing that the Church
of Christ cannot in any necessary article of the faith
fall in any damnable error—doth put in doubt
and question which is the very[2] Church of Christ,
alleging that they peradventure[3] whom we call
heretics will say that themselves is the Church, and
we not. Whereof the author showeth the contrary,
declaring[4] whereby we may know that
they cannot be the Church.

After dinner we walked into the garden. And there shortly, sitting in an arbor, began to go forth in our matter, desiring him to show what thing might that be that made our long forenoon process[5] frustrate and left us as uncertain as we began.

"Sir," quoth he, "that shall I shortly show you. Whereas there was principally in question whether worshipping of images and relics, and praying to saints, and going on pilgrimages were lawful or not, and that I put you in mind that men laid[6] against themselves certain texts of Holy Scripture, and also said unto you that it seemed the texts themselves, which be the words of God, were of more authority against them than the glosses of men, that in such wise expound the texts as they may seem to make for them, ye laid on the other side the consent, and agreement, and common Catholic faith of the Church; which ye said—and indeed, to say the truth, both by reason and by Scripture ye proved—that it could not be erroneous, and that the Church could not err in the faith that God would have known and believed. Ye proved the matter also by miracles, in which, when I laid diverse things moving men to doubt—partly lest they were not true, but specially lest they were not done by God, for corroboration of the faith, but were percase[7] by God's sufferance,[8] done by the devil for our delusion, deserving so to be served by our falling from the worship of God himself to the worship of his creatures—ye proved me yet again that the miracles were true, and that they must needs be done by God. And that ye proved me by this: that it

should else follow that the Church had a wrong belief and a damnable, which eftsoons[9] ye proved well and substantially to be impossible. And forasmuch as there fell in the way occasion to speak of the contrariety that seemed sometimes to fall between the texts of Holy Scripture itself and the common persuasion and faith of the Church, where I said that it was thought reasonable to believe the Scripture, being God's own words, rather than the words of men, ye therein proved that the common faith of the Church was as well God's own words as was Holy Scripture itself, and of as great authority; and that no student in Scripture should presume to try, examine, and judge the Catholic faith of Christ's Church by the Scripture, but by the Catholic faith of Christ's Church should examine and expound the texts of Scripture; and that in the study of Scripture this were the sure way, wherein should give (ye said) great light the writing of the old holy doctors,[10] whereby we be ascertained[11] that the faith that the Church hath now is the same faith, and the same points, that they had then of old, in every age and every time. And in this part ye proved yet again, by reason and Holy Scripture, that the Church hath, by the teaching of God and the Holy Ghost, the right understanding of Scripture in all points that are of necessity to be known. And thereupon eftsoons ye deduced and proved that no text of the Scripture—well understood—could stand against the worshipping of images and relics and the seeking of pilgrimages, but that all these things be well proved good and pleasant to God, and the miracles done in such places, done by God, since his special assistance so informeth and instructeth his Church in so great and so substantial an article, so highly touching the honor or dishonor of God, that it cannot be suffered to fall to superstition and idolatry instead of faith and honor done to God.

"And this is," quoth he, "as far as I remember, the whole sum and effect of all that hath hitherto been proved between us."

"Very true," quoth I. "And this is of you very well remembered, and well and summarily rehearsed."[12]

---

1 summarizing; recapitulating **2** true **3** perhaps **4** explaining **5** reasoned discussion **6** cited **7** perhaps **8** allowing **9** once again **10** theologians **11** assured **12** recounted

"But now," quoth he, "all this gear[13] granted, we be never the near."[14]

"Why so?" quoth I.

"Marry,"[15] quoth he, "for a man that believed the worship of images to be wrong and unlawful might grant that—that 'the Church doth not err,' and that 'the Church hath the right faith,' and that 'the Church doth not mistake the Scripture'—and when all this were agreed, he might say that the Church peradventure doth not believe as ye say it doth. For he might haply[16] deny the Church to be that people that ye take it for, and say that it is the people that believeth as he believeth: that is to wit,[17] all these kinds of worship to be wrong, and that believeth them whom ye take for the Church to believe wrong."

"If he and his company," quoth I, "be the Church, he must tell where his fellows be."

"Why so?" quoth he. "If men should ask you and me where the Church is, we could tell no one place, but many diverse countries."

"Let him," quoth I, "in like wise assign some companies that be known for congregations together in diverse countries."

"Why," quoth he, "in the beginning, and a good while after, the Church of Christ in every place hid itself, that men could not tell in any country where they were, nor durst[18] not come out and show themselves."

"That was in the beginning," quoth I, "while the persecution lasted. But when the persecution ceased once, it was soon known in every country where the Church was."

"Marry," quoth he, "if I should take that part,[19] I would haply say that in that case it is still, and that the Church is that company peradventure that ye (which[20] call yourselves the Church) do use to[21] call heretics—which now do know one another well enough, and call themselves and their fellows about the world the very Church, though they dare not profess it openly, because that ye (that call yourselves the Church and them heretics) do persecute them as the church of the paynims[22] did in the beginning. And therefore they do hide themselves as the Church did in the beginning. But and if[23] ye would cease your persecution once, and let them live in rest, ye should see them flock together so fast that they should soon show you the Church with a wet finger."[24]

"They might," quoth I, "peradventure show a shrewd[25] sort within a while, if they were suffered, and the church that the prophet David speaketh of: *Odi ecclesiam malignantium* ('I hate the church of malicious men').[26] But they shall never show themselves the Church of Christ.

"The Church of Christ, wheresoever it was in all the persecution, used to come together to the preaching and prayer, though it were privily in woods or secret houses. They used also the sacraments among themselves—as baptism, confirmation, matrimony, holy orders—priests and bishops among them, fastings, vigils kept, the Sundays hallowed, the Mass said, holy service[27] sung, and their people houseled,[28] as well appeareth not only by the stories[29] of the Church, but also of the paynims, and partly well appeareth by an epistle of Pliny written to the Emperor Trajan.[30] And such things must there be therein, if it be any church or congregation of Christ. Now these people that ye speak of use[31] no such things among themselves, and therefore they cannot be the Church of Christ."

"They preach," quoth he, "privily among themselves; and all the remnant they do in our churches."

"This," quoth I, "plainly proveth that they cannot be the Church of Christ. For the Church of Christ ever fled and forbore the temples in which idols and mammets[32] were. And it was a plain renaying[33] of Christ's faith to do any observance thereto, though they did it only with their body, for fear, and thought the contrary with their heart. For our Lord saith, 'He that denieth me before the world, I will deny him before my Father in heaven.'[34] And Holy Scripture saith, *Spiritus Sanctus effugiet fictum* ('The Holy Ghost fleeth from feigning').[35] But these men, whom you call the Church, come to the churches where the images be which they take for idols, and there they come to service with us, whom they take for idolaters. And where they teach

---

13 discourse 14 *never the near:* no nearer
15 Indeed 16 haply 17 say 18 dared
19 side 20 who 21 *use to:* customarily
22 pagans 23 *and if:* if 24 *with a wet finger:* with the greatest of ease 25 bad

26 Ps 25(26):5 27 *holy service:* the Divine Office or Prayers of the Hours 28 given Communion 29 historical writings
30 Pliny the Younger (61–113), while governor of Bithynia (modern Turkey),

wrote to Emperor Trajan (53–117) about 111 to ask advice on how to conduct trials against Christians. See Epistle 10.96.
31 practice 32 false gods 33 renouncing
34 Mt 10:33 35 Ws 1:5

among themselves that we do naught,[36] they come to our church, as I say, and in face[37] of the world they do the same: kneel to images as we do, set up candles as we do, pray to saints as we do—and haply more loud with their mouths while they mock them with their hearts. And over[38] this, many mock also the sacraments which they receive.

"And this putteth me in mind also that besides all this, ye cannot say that these be the Church, whom we call heretics, but ye must tell which kind of them is the Church. For all cannot be, since the Church is, and must be, all of one belief, and have all one faith. And, as it was written in the Acts of the Apostles, *Erat multitudo credentium anima una et cor unum* ('The multitude of faithful, believing men were all of one mind and of one heart').[39] And in the Church is the Holy Ghost, *qui facit unanimes in domo* ('which[40] maketh all of one mind in the house of God'—that is, in the Church).[41] But as for among heretics, there be as many diverse minds, almost, as there be men.

"The Church of Christ also is a thing that always hath stood and continued. But the sects of heretics and their churches never continued, but ever shortly decayed and vanished quite away, so far-forth[42] that of all the old heretics, the books also be gone and lost, when there was no law made yet to burn them, so that it is easy to see that God himself destroyed them, and the world clean[43] gave them up at some time, though new heretics now, long after, take them up again. For if their opinions had anywhere continually endured, there would their books have been continually reserved, which be now quite gone many years ago. And thus may ye well see that there can no such folk be the Church, that[44] in so many years have no church, nor come to none, but to theirs in which they say themselves that they worship idols."

"Well," quoth he, "peradventure they will not stick much to assign you a place and show you a company and congregation which they will say is the very[45] Church. For what if they will show you Bohemia,[46] and now in Saxony, where Luther is, and peradventure in a good part of Germany?"

"Marry," quoth I, "if they say so, then leap they like a flounder out of a frying pan into the fire. For in Saxony, first, and among all the Lutherans, there be as many heads, as many wits—and all as wise as wild geese. And as late as they began, yet be there not only as many sects almost as men, but also the masters themselves change their minds and their opinions every day, and wot nere[47] where to hold them. Bohemia is also in the same case: one faith in the town, another in the field; one in Prague, another in the next town; and yet in Prague itself, one faith in one street, another in the next, so that if ye assign it in Bohemia, ye must tell in what town. And if ye name a town, yet must ye tell in what street. And yet all they acknowledge that they cannot have the sacraments ministered[48] but by such priests as be made by authority derived and conveyed from the Pope, which[49] is—under Christ—vicar and the head of our Church."

THE SECOND CHAPTER
The author showeth that no sect of such as the Church taketh for heretics can be the Church, forasmuch as[50] the Church was before all them, as the tree from which all those withered branches be fallen.

"That none of all these can be the Church shall well appear also by another means. Whether[51] will ye say: that the very Church and congregation of Christ was before all the churches and congregations of heretics, or some church of heretics before the Church of Christ?"

"Marry," quoth he, "there might be some church of heretics before the Church of Christ. For there might be some among the Jews, before the birth of Christ. And such, I suppose, were the Sadducees, that believed not the resurrection, nor the immortality of the soul."[52]

"If we should go," quoth I, "to that reckoning, we might fetch the Church of Christ far above, and begin it at Adam. For from the first good man to the last, all shall in conclusion be his Church triumphant in heaven. But I speak of Christ's Church now as of that congregation that, bearing his name, and having his right faith, and being begun to be gathered by himself and spread abroad by his

---

36 evil   **37** sight   **38** beyond   **39** Acts 4:32   **40** who   **41** Ps 67(68):7   **42** *so far-forth:* to such an extent   **43** completely   **44** who   **45** true   **46** modern Czech

Republic, at that time controlled by followers of John Hus   **47** *wot nere:* know not   **48** administered   **49** who   **50** *forasmuch as:* seeing that   **51** Which (of

these two)   **52** See Mt 22:23; Mk 12:18; Lk 20:27; Acts 23:8.

apostles, hath and doth and shall, till his coming to the dreadful Doom,[53] continue still in this world. Whether was this Church before all the churches and congregations of heretics, or some one of them before it?"

"Nay," quoth he, "I think it was before them all."

"Whereby may we," quoth I, "be sure of that?"

"Marry," quoth he, "for always the heretics came out of it."

"That is," quoth I, "true. For they could be none heretics, but by being first therein, and after[54] coming out. And it appeareth by the Gospel, in which the good husbandman 'went forth to sow his seed, and when he had sowed good seed, then the enemy sowed his evil after, and they grew up together.'[55] It appeareth also by the words of the apostle and holy evangelist Saint John, where he said of heretics, *Ex nobis profecti sunt, sed non erant ex nobis* ('They be gone,' he said, 'out of us, but they were none of us"),[56] meaning that ere[57] ever they professed themselves openly for heretics—yet being such indeed, since the Church of Christ is a people of one faith—these folk, that have another special faith by themselves, varying and gainsaying[58] the other, be not perfectly of the Church though they be for the while[59] in it. So it is now that any member of that body, till it be cut off for fear of corruption of the remnant, hangeth on it in a manner, and some little light or life hath by the Spirit of God, that[60] upholdeth the body of his Church, being ever in case[61] to take occasion of amendment by some vein of that wholesome moisture of God's grace that specially spreadeth throughout that holy body. But those that, by the profession of heresies and infidelity,[62] fall off from that body, or—for fear of corrupting the remnant—be by curse[63] cast out of the body, they plainly dry up and wither away. Our Savior saith himself: 'I am,' saith he, 'a very vine, and my Father is a gardener. I am the vine, and ye be the branches. And every branch that beareth in me no fruit, my Father taketh it away. And every branch that beareth fruit, he purgeth it to make it bring the more fruit. And as the branch can do no good being taken from the tree, right[64] so can ye do no good, nor serve for nought[65] but for the fire, except[66] ye abide in me.'[67] By these words of our Savior and many more there spoken at length, though

it appeareth that whoso keep the faith, yet except he work well therewith, God will pluck him out, and whoso by faith abiding in the stock doth work good works, the more he doth, the more grace and help shall have of God to grow the better and to do the more, yet appeareth it also that all the good works that may be done will not serve if we be out of the stock. And out of the stock of the vine be all that be not grafted in by faith, or fallen off by open profession of heresy, or cut off and cast out for infidelity. For faith is the gate into God's Church, as misbelief is the gate into the devil's church. For as the Apostle saith, *Accedentem ad Deum oportet credere* ('A man cannot come to God without faith').[68] And therefore whoso professeth a false belief, let him be sure that he is gone out of the gate of God's Church before actual excommunication, and fallen off the body of the vineyard. And if they be secret— neither professing their heresies nor actually being accursed and cast out—they be in the Church, but not perfectly of it. But in such wise, in manner,[69] thereof be they as a dead hand is rather a burden in the body than verily[70] any member, organ, or instrument thereof. And therefore saith Saint John, as I said before, that the heretics 'be gone out of us, but they were not of us; for if they had been of us, they would have tarried with us,'[71] meaning thereby not, as some would have it seem, that a good man is not of the Church, nor in God's favor while he is good, because he happeth to wax[72] worse afterward. But he meaneth that in that they went their way from us, they showed that they were naught[73] indeed while they were with us. And so though they were with us, yet were they not of us. For though heretics and infidels be among faithful and well-believing people, yet be they, pardie,[74] none of them. And so it appeareth, as ye said before, that the Church of Christ is before all the churches of heretics, and that all congregations of heretics have comen out of the Church of Christ."

"That is very true," quoth he.

"Well," quoth I, "if that be true, as it is indeed, then can no sect in Bohemia be the right church. For the church which we call 'the Church,' that believeth as we believe, was there before them all. And never a church had any church of heretics yet, but it was built by our Church to their hands,

---

53 Last Judgment   54 afterwards   55 Mt
13:24–30   56 1 Jn 2:19   57 before
58 going against   59 time   60 who

61 a position   62 unbelief   63 excommunication   64 even; just   65 nothing
66 unless   67 Jn 15:1–6   68 Heb 11:6

69 *in manner:* so to speak   70 truly
71 1 Jn 2:19   72 become   73 wicked
74 indeed

so that it is evident that none of all them can be Christ's Church; but Christ's Church must needs be that church that was before all them, and out of which all they have sprungen, and since severed themselves—which is the Church that all they deny not to believe against them the points which we believe and they reprove."

THE THIRD CHAPTER
The messenger moveth[75] *that the very Church peradventure is not the people that we take for it, but a secret unknown sort of such only as be by God predestinate*[76] *to be saved. Whereunto the author answereth, and declareth*[77] *that it cannot be so.*

"Peradventure," quoth he, "there might be said that it needeth not to assign[78] any place where the very Church and true Christian congregation is. But since every place is indifferent thereunto, it may be that all the good men and chosen people of God that be predestinate to be saved—in what part soever they be, and howsoever they be scattered, here one and there one, here two and there two—that these be the very Church of Christ, and be in this world unknown as yet, while the Church doth but wander in the pilgrimage of this short life."

"Marry," quoth I, "this gear[79] groweth from worse to worse. And in very deed, yet is this point their sheet-anchor.[80] For first, they see plainly that they must needs grant that the very Church can neither be deceived in the right faith, nor mistake Holy Scripture, or misunderstand it, to the introduction of infidelity and false belief. And this ground find all the heretics themselves so sure and fast[81] that they perceive well except[82] they would openly and utterly deny Christ altogether, it cannot be undermined. And since they manifestly see that, and as evidently see therewith that the Church (which is the very Church indeed) damneth all their ways—whereof, since the Church cannot err in discerning the truth, it must needs follow that they mistake themselves all the whole matter, and be quite in a wrong way—therefore be they driven to deny for the Church the people that be known for the Church, and go seek another, they neither know what nor where, and build up in the air a church all so spiritual that they

leave therein at length neither God nor good man. And first, where they say that there be none therein but they that be predestinate to be saved, if the question were of the Church triumphant in heaven, then said they well. But we speak of the Church of Christ militant here in earth; and therefore goeth their frame as far wide from the place they should set it on as heaven and earth stand asunder. For first would I wit,[83] if the Church be none but those that be predestinate, whether all that been predestinate be members thereof."

"Why not?" quoth he.

"Then," quoth I, "he that is predestinate to be saved, whether may he or not be diverse times a sinner in his days?"

"What if he may?" quoth he.

"May he not," quoth I, "be also diverse times in his days in a wrong belief and a false heresy, and after turn, repent, and amend, and so be saved at last, as God hath predestinate him to be?"

"What then?" quoth he.

"Marry," quoth I, "for then shall it follow that he shall be a member of the very Church, and so still continue, and never can be cast out, being a stark[84] heretic."

"Yet," quoth he, "is he all that while a quick[85] member of the Church by reason of God's predestination, since, though he be not sure, yet it is indeed sure that he is and ever shall be one of the very Church."

"It is," quoth I, "sure indeed, and well known to God, that he so shall be. But as sure is it that for the while, he is not, except that all things that ever shall be, is already present indeed as it is present to God's knowledge. And then were Saint Paul as good while he was a persecutor as when he was apostle, and as verily a member of Christ's Church ere he was born as he is now in heaven."

"Well," quoth he, "though that peradventure all those that be living and predestinate to be saved be not in it, yet may it be that there be none others in it than predestinates."

"But it may be," quoth I, "that, as men be changeable, he that is predestinate may be many times in his life naught.[86] And he that will at last fall to sin and wretchedness and so finally cast himself away, shall in some time of his life be good, and therefore for the time in God's favor. For God blameth nor hateth no man for that he shall will, but for that malicious will that he hath, or hath had already. And thus shall there by this reason be good men out of Christ's Church and naughty men therein, faithful men out of it and heretics in it, and both the one and the other without reason or good cause why."

THE FOURTH CHAPTER
The messenger moveth that though the Church be not the number of folk only predestinate to bliss, yet may it peradventure be the number of good and well-believing folk here and there unknown— which may be peradventure those whom we condemn for heretics for holding opinion against images. Whereof the author proveth the contrary.

"Well," quoth he, "yet may it be that the very Church of Christ is all such as believe aright and live well wheresoever they be—though the world know them not, and though few of them know each other. For God, as Saint Paul saith, 'knoweth who be his.'[87] And Christ saith that against his Church 'the gates of hell shall not prevail;'[88] but the gates of hell do prevail against sinners. And therefore it appeareth well that there can be no sinners in his Church, nor that there be none of his Church but good folk. And unto them our Lord is present, and keepeth them from errors, and giveth them right understanding of his Holy Scriptures. And where they be forceth not;[89] how few they be together maketh no matter. For our Savior saith, 'Wheresoever be two or three gathered together in my name, there am I also among them.'[90] And so is his very Church—here and there—of only good men to the world unknown, and to himself well known. And though they be few in comparison, yet make they about in all the world a good many among them. As God said when the children of Israel were fallen in idolatry and worshiped the idol Baal so far-forth[91] that it seemed all were in the case,[92] and men knew not who were otherwise, yet said our Lord (as appeareth in the nineteenth chapter, the Third Book of the Kings), 'I shall reserve for myself seven thousand that have not bended their knee before Baal,'[93] so that where the synagogue and church was then,

it was unknown to man, but it was well known to God. And they were not his Church that[94] seemed to be, but a company ungathered, that no man was aware of, nor would have weened.[95] And so may it be peradventure now, that the very Church of Christ is not, nor many days hath not been, the people that seemeth to be the Church, but some good men scattered here and there unknown, till God gather them together and make them known—and haply[96] those that believe against images, and whom we now call heretics."

"This is," quoth I, "a reason that Luther maketh himself, by which he would bring the very Church of Christ out of knowledge, and would put it in doubt whether the saints that the Church honoreth were good men or not, and would that it might seem peradventure nay, but that they were haply not good, but the good men, and saints indeed, were some others whom the world, for their open lewd[97] living, reputed for naught. But where he saith that the church or synagogue of the right belief was then unknown, that is not true. For it was well known in Jerusalem and Judaea, though it had been unknown who were faithful in Samaria. And the Scripture also saith not that these seven thousand whom he would leave yet in Israel, that[98] had not bowed their knees before Baal, were secret and unknown; but he saith only that such a number of such folk he would leave. But now, for our purpose, since ye will have the very Church a secret unknown—not company and congregation, but a disparkled[99] number of only good men—will you that those good men, which[100] after your reckoning make the very Church, shall have the same faith and none other than we have, which be now reputed for the Church, or else a faith and belief different?"

"What if they have the same?" quoth he.

"Marry," quoth I, "then will your new-built Church nothing help your purpose. But they shall as fast[101] confirm the worship of images, praying to saints, and seeking to pilgrimages as we, and as deeply condemn for heresy your opinion to the contrary."

"That is very truth," quoth he. "But it may be that of that very Church, the faith and belief shall be that all this gear[102] is erroneous and as plain idolatry as was the worshipping of Baal."

87 2 Tm 2:19   88 Mt 16:18   89 *forceth not*: makes no difference   90 Mt 18:20   91 *so far-forth*: to such an extent   92 *the case*: that state   93 3 Kgs (1 Kgs) 19:18   94 who   95 thought   96 perhaps   97 wicked   98 who   99 scattered;   dispersed   100 who   101 steadfastly   102 matter

"If it were so," quoth I, "then had Christ not kept him seven thousand from the worship of Baal in all the regions that bear the name of Christendom, except these new folk of Saxony and Bohemia which yourself grant to be the heretics, as sects comen out of the Church. And more than wonder were it if all the Church of Christ should be clean[103] among infidels and heretics, and no part at all thereof among the great unchangeable Christian countries which have kept their faith in one constant fashion derived from the beginning. For this am I sure: that in all those regions, as I say, if any have any such opinion against images and saints, yet cometh he to the church among his neighbors, and there boweth his knees to Baal (if the images be Baal) as his neighbors do — but go to,[104] let us forth on a little further. And supposing that there were some such secret good folk as ye speak of, that had the right belief, and were the right Church, and that they were so dispersed asunder that they were to the world unknown, hath not God set an order in his Church that some shall preach to the remnant for exhortation of good living, and information wherein good living standeth[105] — as in faith and good works?"

"Yes," quoth he.

"Bade not Christ," quoth I, "sacraments also to be ministered in his Church, by the priests of the same?"

"Yes," quoth he.

"Now," quoth I, "if some infidels, as Turks or Saracens, having heard of Christ's name, did long to know his Scripture and his faith, and hearing that there were many people that professed themselves for Christian men, whole nations, but they were all open idolaters and in a misbelief, and clearly deceived and beguiled (and that specially by the clergy that teacheth them), howbeit[106] there were yet a few good folk, and right-believing, which[107] were not deceived, which among them be the very true Church, but who they be, or where they be, or how to ask for them, or if he happen on them, yet whereby to know them, that can no man tell him — how should these infidels come to the faith, and of whom should they hear it? For they — being warned before that there were many sects of heretics, and but one true Church — would never be so mad[108] to

learn of them that[109] they might ween were wrong. And how should they now come to the right, when the true Church is unknown?"

"They might," quoth he, "take the Scripture."

"They should," quoth I, "be therein like[110] to Eunuchus,[111] that[112] could not understand without a reader.[113] And then if they took a wrong reader of a wrong church, all were marred. And also they would not trust the Scriptures, nor reckon that they had the right books of Scripture, among false sects, but would look to receive the true Scripture of the right and true Church. And thus here it appeareth if it were thus, God had left none ordinary way for his Gospel and faith to be taught. But let go these infidels and speak of ourselves, which are (if this way were true) as false as they. Where be then preachers of this very Church that should preach and teach us better? For it is no church if it have no preachers."

"It hath," quoth he, "some that preach sometimes, but ye will not suffer[114] them. Ye punish them and burn them."

"Nay," quoth I, "they be wiser than so. They will not be burned for us; for they will rather swear on a book that they never said so — or else[115] that they will no more say so. And in this appeareth that there is no such secret unknown Church of Christ that, having such opinions, is the very Church. For the very Church hath ever had some that hath abidden by their faith and their preaching, and would never go back with[116] God's Word, to die therefor.[117] And this Church that we be of, that take your church for heretics, have had many such martyrs therein that believed as we do against your opinions — as appeareth by the histories and by many of their books — whereas of your secret Church I never yet found, or heard of, anyone in all my life but he would forswear[118] your faith to save his life. Where be also your priests and your bishops? For such must they have if they be the Church of Christ. Now such can your Church have none; ye be each to other unknown. And though some of such churches have a false opinion that every man is a priest, and every woman too, yet this heresy — false as it is — will not serve this unknown Church. For the holders of that opinion do put[119] that no man

103 completely   104 *go to:* come; never mind   105 consists   106 although   107 foolish, irrational   108 whom   109 who   110 similar   111 taken here as a   proper name, but usually translated today as "a eunuch"   112 who   113 interpreter. See Acts 8:27–39.   114 allow   115 otherwise   116 *go back with:* go back on, deny   117 *to die therefor:* to the point of dying for it   118 renounce under oath   119 propose

may, for all that, take upon him to preach or meddle as priest, till he be chosen by the congregation. And where can that be in this imaginary Church, of which no man knoweth other? And whereas our Lord saith, 'Wheresoever be two or three gathered together in my name, there am I with them,'[120] he spoke not as though every two or three, whatsoever they were, should make his Church; but that wheresoever there came together two or three in his name that be of his Church, there is he with them. And so doth the one[121] text of the Scripture in the Gospel plainly declare, as it is well set out and opened[122] by the holy doctor and glorious martyr Saint Cyprian, in his epistle against Novatian.[123]

"When our Savior saith also that he which would not amend by his fault showed him before two or three witnesses should be complained upon unto the Church, did he mean a secret Church, which no man wist[124] where to find?[125] Now when the Apostle[126] writeth unto the Corinthians that rather than they should plead[127] and strive in the law before the infidels, they should set such as[128] were in the Church little set by[129] to be judges in their temporal[130] suits, of what Church did he speak? Of such one as no man wist where to seek it?[131] This unknown church, which they be driven to seek that be loath to know the Church, will never serve. But the Church of Christ is a church well known. And his pleasure was to have it known, and not hid. And it is builded upon so high a hill of that holy stone—I mean upon Christ himself—that it cannot be hid. *Non potest abscondi civitas supra montem posita* ('The city cannot be hid that is set on a hill').[132] And he would have his faith divulged and spread abroad openly, not always whispered in hugger-mugger.[133] And therefore he bound his preachers to stand thereby, and not to revoke his word for no pain. For he said that he did not light that candle to put it and hide it under a bushel[134]—for so would no man do—but he had kindled a fire which he would not should[135] lie and smolder as coals doth in quench, but he would it should burn and give light.[136] And therefore folly were it to say that Christ, which[137] would have his Church spread through the world, and everywhere gathered in company, would have it turned to a secret unknown single sort, severed asunder and scattered about in corners, unknown to all the world and to themselves too. Now, where they say that there is none of[138] the Church but only those that be good folk, this would make the Church clearly unknown, were the people never so many and the place never so large. For who can know, of the multitude, who be good indeed and who be naught,[139] since the bad may suddenly be amended, unware[140] to the world, and the good as suddenly waxen[141] worse? Now lay they for the proof of that opinion the words of Christ which Luther allegeth[142] also, for the same intent, in his book that he made against Ambrosius Catharinus[143]—that is to wit, the words wherein our Lord said unto Saint Peter that against his Church 'the gates of hell should not prevail,' by which words Luther doth (as he thinketh, and saith himself) marvelous gaily prove that there can be no man of the Church but he that sinneth not. For this argument he maketh: Christ saith that the 'gates of hell' shall not prevail against the Church; but the 'gates of hell' is nothing but the devil, and he prevaileth against all folk that sin; ergo, no folk that sin be the Church.[144] And by this worshipful[145] argument, it is a world[146] to see what boast the madman maketh: that he hath clearly proved that the Church is not these people whom we take for the Church, because they be sinners—which argument hath so many follies and faults therein, and so much inconvenience[147] and absurdity following thereupon, that it is more than marvel that a child of one week's study in sophistry could, for shame, find in his heart to bring it in place for[148] any earnest[149] argument. For first, if men deny him that the 'gates of hell' do in that place signify the devil, then he can never prove it; and then is all his reason wiped quite away. Now do there indeed diverse old commenters[150] and doctors of the Church take in that place, for the 'gates of hell,' the great tyrants and heretics by whose persecutions and heresies (as it were, by two gates) many a man hath gone into hell; and our Savior promiseth in that place that neither of those two gates—that is to wit, neither

---

120 Mt 18:20   **121** *the one:* that same   **122** explained   **123** St. Cyprian (200–258) opposed the antipope Novation and his followers. See Cyprian's *The Unity of the Church*, ch. 12 (PL 4: 524–25).   **124** knew   **125** See Mt 8:15–17.   **126** St. Paul   **127** enter pleas   **128** *set such as:* appoint

those who   **129** *set by:* valued   **130** civil   **131** See 1 Cor 6:4.   **132** Mt 5:14   **133** secret   **134** bushel basket   **135** *would not should:* did not want to   **136** See Lk 11:13, 12:49.   **137** who   **138** *none of:* no one (who is) in   **139** bad   **140** unknown   **141** become   **142** cites   **143** He lived

from 1483 to 1553, was baptized Lancelotto Politi, changing his name when he became a Dominican monk. Luther's book was published in 1521.   **144** See Luther, *WA* 7: 710–12.   **145** distinctive   **146** great thing, marvel   **147** inconsistency   **148** of   **149** serious   **150** commentators

paynim tyrant nor christened heretic—should prevail against the Church. For though they have destroyed and shall destroy many of the Church, yet shall they not be able to destroy the Church; but the Church shall stand and be by God preserved in despite of all their teeth.[151] And thus ye see how soon Luther's special arguments were overthrown with truth. But if a man would grant him that the 'gates of hell' did here signify the devil, yet should we not need to grant him that the devil, as he is called of God by the name of 'the gates' (which is not done for nought),[152] doth prevail against every man that sinneth. For he that sinneth and riseth again out of sin (and so cometh within the gates as yet the gates cannot hold him, but that he breaketh out of the gates), the gates do not prevail against him; but he prevaileth against the gates. And thus is Luther's wise argument which he groundeth upon the text avoided[153] again. It appeareth also that it is a very frantic[154] argument. For where he saith that against the Church of Christ the gates of hell prevail not, but they prevail against our Church—that is to wit, all the Christian people whom we call the Church, under obedience of the Pope, ergo they be not the Church—this argument proveth that there is in earth no Church at all. For what Church can he find or imagine in earth that doth not sin? And specially if that were true that himself saith, among his other heresies, where he holdeth stiffly that all the good works of good men be sins, and that men sin in that they do good. And thus he would both have the Church to be only a secret unknown sort of folk that do not sin, and yet he confesseth that there be none such. And so, as he goeth about to take away the very Church that is well known—making as though he would find out a better—he leaveth in conclusion no church at all. And to such a fond[155] and false end must they needs bring it all, that will make it a number of only such as be good men and do not sin. For if he should be in it always when he is out of sin, and out of it when he is in sin, then should a man peradventure[156] be in it in the morning, and out of it at noon, and in again at night, so that who were in it, or when, or where it were, who could tell? And of that uncertainty must needs grow all such inconveniences[157] and

contradiction unto Scripture as is before rehearsed. The Church, therefore, must needs be the common known multitude of Christian men, good and bad together, while the Church is here in earth. For this net of Christ hath for the while good fishes and bad.[158] And this field of Christ beareth for the while good corn[159] and cockle, till it shall at the Day of Doom be purified, and all the bad cast out, and the only good remain.[160] And therefore when the Apostle[161] wrote unto the Corinthians of him that had lain with his mother-in-law,[162] he commanded that he should be separated out of the Church. Which he never was, after the deed done, till the excommunication denounced,[163] but was still, for all his sin, one of the Church, though he was naught,[164] and out of God's favor. Christ himself said to his apostles, 'Now be you clean, but not all'[165]—and yet were they all of his Church, albeit that[166] one of them was, as our Savior said himself, a devil. 'Did I not,' said he, 'choose twelve of you, and one of you is a devil?'[167] And if there were none of the Church but good men as long as they were good, then had Saint Peter been once no part of the Church after that Christ had appointed him for chief.

"But our Lord, in this his mystical body of his Church, carrieth his members[168]—some sick, some whole,[169] and all sickly. Nor they be not for every sin clean[170] cast off from the body but if[171] they be, for fear of infection, cut off, or else willingly do depart and separate themselves, as do these heretics that either refuse the Church willfully themselves, or else for their obstinacy be put out. For till their stubborn hearts do show them incurable, the body beareth them yet about—sick, and naughty, and key-cold[172] as they be—to prove whether the warmness of grace going through this whole mystical body of Christ's Church might get yet,[173] and keep, some life in them. But when the time shall come that this Church shall wholly change her place and have heaven for her dwelling instead of earth, after the final judgment pronounced and given, when God shall, with his Spouse, this Church of Christ, enter into the pleasant wedding chamber to the bed of eternal rest, then shall all these scaldy[174] and scabbed pieces scale[175] clean off, and the whole body of Christ's holy Church remain pure, clean, and

---

151 opposition 152 nothing 153 disproved 154 frantic; foolish 155 foolish 156 perhaps 157 inconsistencies 158 See Mt 13:47–50. 159 grain 160 See

Mt 13:24–30. 161 St. Paul 162 See 1 Cor 5:1–5. 163 (was) pronounced 164 wicked 165 Jn 13:10 166 *albeit that:* although 167 Jn 6:70 168 See

Eph 5:23. 169 healthy 170 completely 171 *but if:* unless 172 cold as a key; i.e., without heat or fervor 173 still 174 blistered 175 flake; peel

glorious, without wem,[176] wrinkle, or spot;[177] which is (and for the while, I ween, will be, as long as she is here) as scabbed as ever was Job,[178] and yet her loving Spouse leaveth her not, but continually goeth about by many manner medicines—some bitter, some sweet; some easy, some grievous; some pleasant, some painful—to cure her."

THE FIFTH CHAPTER
The author showeth and concludeth that this common known multitude of Christian nations, not cut off nor fallen off by heresies, be the very Church of Christ—good men and bad together.

"And finally, to put out of question which is Christ's very Church, since it is agreed between us, and granted through Christendom, and a conclusion very true, that by the Church we know the Scripture—which Church is that by which ye know the Scripture? Is it not this company and congregation of all these nations that, without factions taken and precision[179] from the remnant, profess the name and faith of Christ? By this Church know we the Scripture; and this is the very Church; and this hath begun at Christ, and hath had him for their head, and Saint Peter, his vicar after him, the head under him, and always since, the successors of him continually, and have had his holy faith and his blessed sacraments and his Holy Scriptures delivered, kept, and conserved therein by God and his Holy Spirit. And albeit some nations fall away, yet likewise as how many boughs soever fall from the tree, though they fall more than be left thereon, yet they make no doubt which is the very tree, although each of them were planted again in another place and grew to a greater than the stock he came first of, right so, while we see and well know that all the companies and sects of heretics and schismatics, how great soever they grow, came out of this Church that I spoke of, we know evermore that the heretics be they that be severed, and the Church, the stock that all they came out of. And since that only the Church of Christ is the vine that Christ spoke of in the Gospel, which he taketh for his body mystical, and that every branch severed from that tree loseth his lively nourishing,[180] we must needs well know

that all these branches of heretics fallen from the Church, the vine of Christ's mystical body—seem they never so fresh and green—be yet indeed but witherlings[181] that wither, and shall dry up, able to serve for nothing but for the fire."

THE SIXTH CHAPTER
The messenger moveth that since the Church is this known multitude of good men and bad together, of whom no man knoweth which be the one sort and which be the other, that it may be peradventure that the good sort of the Church be they that believe the worship of images to be idolatry, and the bad sort they that believe the contrary. Which objection the author doth answer and confute.[182]

When I had said,

"Sir," quoth he, "ye have, in good faith, fully satisfied me concerning the sure and undoubted knowledge of the very Church here in earth. But yet thinketh me that one little doubt remaineth for our principal matter."

"What is that?" quoth I.

"Marry, sir," quoth he, "it is this: that though the very faith be in the Church, and the Church cannot err therein; nor the Church cannot be deceived, against the faith, in any text of Scripture; nor no Scripture is there that (being well understood) doth or can do stand against the faith of the Church; and that also the Church is none other but, as ye say, and as I see it is indeed, but this whole common congregation of Christian people good and bad, not separating themselves for frowardness,[183] nor being put out for their obstinate faults; yet—since it appeareth well that, though the right faith be in the Church, it is not in every man of the Church, and though the Church cannot err in such things, yet some of the Church may—now seemeth it to some men that it may well peradventure happen that the good men, well-believing and undeceived, be those that believe the worship of images and praying to saints to be idolatry, and on the other side, that those which believe the contrary be that part of the Church that be the naughty men, misbelievers and foully deceived."

"That were a very strange work," quoth I. "Ye

---

176 blemish; scar   **177** See Eph 5:27.
178 See Job 2:7.   **179** separation

180 See Jn 15:1–6.   **181** shriveled up branches; enemies (pun)

182 disprove; refute   **183** perversity

would right now,"[184] quoth I, "that in the Church we should think that there were none other but good men. Will ye now agree that there be therein some good men?"

5 "Yea," quoth he, "that must needs be."

"Well," quoth I, "whether be[185] they good men that do naught?"[186]

"Nay," quoth he.

"Do they well," quoth I, "that do idolatry indeed, 10 though it be against their hearts?"

"Nay," quoth he.

"But all," quoth I, "come to church and worship images; and all pray to saints. Wherefore, if that be idolatry, then the Church of Christ is all naught. 15 For thus do they that be of the contrary side, for fear of being perceived. Also, if one do well or preach well, is he a good man if he deny it for fear?"

"Nay," quoth he.

"But now," quoth I, "all that are of that sort, if 20 they happen to adventure[187] somewhat and be spied, they will first perjure themselves, and after abjure[188] their opinion; so that if their opinion were good, yet were themselves naught."[189]

"But yet," quoth he, "if their opinions be good, 25 then be not they so evil in hiding their intents for fear as they that[190] against their true opinions do and preach openly, and pursue them for saying truth, as some that fainted[191] and fled from martyrdom were not so evil as they that pursued them."

30 "Very truth," quoth I, "if these men's opinions were true. But yet, though[192] they were true, yet were these men naught."

"And the others worse," quoth he.

"That is well said," quoth I. "But they and the oth-35 ers be the whole Church. And if yours be naught — as ye grant and must needs grant they be — if the others were naught too, then were in the Church none good. But yourself deny not but in the Church it must needs be that there be some good. And there 40 can be none but either your party or the other. Ergo, since yours be naught, those that be good must needs be the other. But none of those that be of the other could be good men if they were idolaters, and pursued your party for saying the truth, and com-45 pelled them to deny the truth; ergo, the other party be not idolaters, nor the opinion of your party, for which they pursue your party, be not true. And thus

it appeareth, as meseemeth, that good men of the Church be against you, and the naughty with you."

THE SEVENTH CHAPTER　　50
The author somewhat doth corroborate the truth
against the heresies holding against images,
and recapituling[193] somewhat briefly what hath
been proved, so finisheth and endeth
the proof of his part.[194]　　55

"And yet speak I nothing of all the good men, and well known for good men, and holy men, and now saints in heaven, that have condemned your party and written against you. And your party therefore be so sore[195] against saints again because they see 60 their heresies impugned and condemned by their holy writings. Nor besides this have I nothing spoken of the general councils condemning your party by good and substantial authority comprobated[196] and corroborated by the whole body of Christen-65 dom, led thereunto, both long before and ever since, through the secret operation of the Holy Ghost, who could never suffer[197] (as yourself agreeth) the Church of Christ to continue so wholly and so long in so damnable idolatry, as this were if it were su-70 perstition, and not a part of very faith and true devout religion. Wherefore, since I have proved you that the Church cannot err in so great a point, nor against the right faith mistake the sentence[198] of Holy Scripture; and also that these people that be-75 lieve images to be worshipped be the very Church of Christ; and that of his Church the good and bad both doth use it, and the good men doth it truly, and the bad falsely; and that all the good men of old hath allowed and used this way, and condemned 80 the contrary, which hath also been declared for false heresy by the whole general council of Christendom, approved by the faith and custom of all the people, besides growing into such consent by God's Holy Spirit, that governeth his Church — I never 85 need to go further or touch your texts or arguments to the contrary. For this side thus proved good, it must needs follow that the other side is naught — except ye have against this any further thing to say. Which if ye have, never let[199] to bring it forth. 90 For I will for none haste leave any corner of the

---

184 *would right now:* were wanting just now　**185** *whether be:* are　**186** evil　**187** risk themselves　**188** renounce

189 bad　**190** who　**191** lost courage　**192** even if　**193** summarizing; recapitulating　**194** side (of the argument)

195 greatly　**196** confirmed　**197** allow　**198** meaning　**199** hesitate

matter unransacked, as far as we can any doubt find therein."

"In good faith, sir," quoth he, "I am in this matter even at the hard wall, and see not how to go further."

"Now I assure you," quoth I, "if I could myself find any further objection, I would not fail to bring it in. But in good faith, I suppose we be waded in this matter as far as we can both find. And, I am sure, as far as ever Luther found, or any that ever I have seen that anything have said or written on that side."

THE EIGHTH CHAPTER

The author entereth the answer to the objections that had been before laid by the messenger against the worship of images, and praying to saints, and going on pilgrimages. And first he answereth, in this chapter, the objections made against praying to saints.

"Now therefore, as I say, further need I not to go. But yet will I somewhat touch the things which, as ye say, do move many men to take the worship of images for idolatry. And it so taken, and their opinion so reputed,[200] they reckon it a ground to think the miracles done at the images, or by invocations of saints, to be illusions of the devil. And first will we begin at the saints themselves. And by the way shall we speak of their relics, images, and pilgrimages, as there shall occasion rise in our matter. And for the first: in good faith, saving that the books and writings of holy doctors condemn these men's heresies, the displeasure and anger whereof setteth them on a fire to study for the diminishing of their estimation that so stand in their light, else would I much wonder what these heretics mean, to impugn the worship of saints and forbid us to pray to them. And albeit I now see the cause of their malice, yet can I not much the less marvel of their madness, that show their evil will so openly that they neither have reason nor good color[201] to cloak or cover it with. First they put in doubt whether saints can hear us. And if they do, yet whether they can help us. And finally if they could, yet would they we should[202] think it folly to desire them,[203] because God can do it better

and will do it sooner himself than they all. Now where they doubt whether saints hear us, I marvel whereof that doubt ariseth, but if they think them dead as well in soul as body. For if their holy souls live, there will no wise man ween them worse, and of less love and charity to men that need their help, when they be now in heaven, than they had when they were here in earth. For all that while, were they never so good, yet the best was worse than the worst is now, as our Savior said by Saint John the Baptist: that there was no woman's son greater than he, yet the least that was already in heaven was his better.[204] We see that the nearer that folk draw thitherward,[205] the more good mind bear they to men here. And therefore Saint Stephen, when he saw heaven open for him, he began to pray for them that maliciously killed him.[206] And think we then that being in heaven, he will not vouchsafe[207] to pray for them that devoutly honor him, but hath less love and charity being there than he had going thitherward? If the rich man that lay in hell had,[208] yet not only for fear of increase of his own punishment by his brothers' damnation growing of his evil example in sin, but also of carnal love and fleshly favor toward his kin (which fleshly affection, being without grace or virtue may peradventure stand with the state of damnation) had a cure[209] and care of his five brethren, were it likely that saints then being so full of blessed charity in heaven, will nothing care for their brethren in Christ, whom they see here in this wretched world? Now if there be no doubt (as I trow[210] none there is) but their holy souls be alive, they would we did well. And as little doubt but that they be alive if God be their God, as he is indeed— and he not the God of dead men but of living, as our Savior saith in the Gospel,[211] for all men live still, and ever shall, that he hath taken to him and once given life unto—there resteth then no further to see but whether they can do us any good or no, either for that[212] they cannot hear us, or for that they cannot help us. And first, I marvel much if they think they cannot help us. For while they were here they could, as appeareth in the Acts of the Apostles.[213] And since imbecility[214] and lack of power is here part of our misery, and strength and plenty of power is one great part of wealth,[215] they were well furthered in that point if they were now less able to do good to them whom they fain[216] would were helped than they were before. For whether they be able there to do it themselves, or only by their intercession made unto God, this maketh no force[217] for our matter, so that by their means, the one way or the other, we take help by our devotion toward them, and prayer made unto them."

"I think," quoth he, "they may do indeed much more than they might, both by power and prayer. But it is hard somewhat to think that they should hear us and see us—and specially in so many places at once. For though they be not circumscribed in place (for lack of bodily dimension and measuring), yet are they, and angels also, definitively so placed where they be for the time that they be not at one time in diverse places at once—as saints be in sundry countries, and very far asunder, called upon at once."

"Ye marvel," quoth I, "and think it hard to be believed that saints hear us. And I (while we see that the things we pray for, we obtain) marvel much more how men can doubt whether the prayers be heard or not. When saints were in this world at liberty and might walk the world about, ween[218] we that in heaven they stand tied to a post? But the wonder is how they may see and hear in sundry places at once. If we could no more but feel, and neither see nor hear, we would as well wonder. Or if we could not wonder thereof, because we could not hear thereof, yet should we be far from any conceiving in our mind that it were possible for man to see or hear further than he can feel. For we that prove it, and do see and hear indeed, cannot yet see the cause, nor in no wise[219] cease to wonder by what reason and means it may be that I should see two churches, or two towns, each of them two a mile asunder—and both twain[220] as far from me as each of them from other—and measure so great quantities[221] with so small a measure as is the little apple[222] of mine eye. And of hearing many men's voices, or any man's words coming at once into many men's ears, standing far asunder, hath like[223] difficulty to conceive. And when all the reasons be made—either of beams sent out from our eyes to the things that we behold, or the figure of the things seen multiplied in the air from the thing to our eye, or of the air stricken with the breath of the speaker,

and equally rolling forth in roundels[224] to the ears of the hearers—when all the reasons be heard, yet shall we rather delight to search than be able to find anything in these matters that were able to make us perceive it. Now, when we may with our fleshly eye and ear in this gross body see and hear things far distant from us and from sundry places far distant asunder, marvel we so much that blessed angels and holy souls—being mere[225] spiritual substances, uncharged[226] of all burdenous flesh and bones—may in doing the same, as far pass[227] and exceed us and our powers natural as the lively[228] soul itself exceedeth our deadly body, nor cannot believe they hear us, though we find they help us, but if[229] we perceived by what means they do it (as whether they see and hear us coming hither to us, or our voice coming hence to them; or whether God hear and see all, and show it them; or whether they behold it in him, as one doth in a book the thing that he readeth; or whether God by some other way doth utter it unto them as one doth in speaking)—except[230] we may know the means, we will not else[231] believe the matter? As wise as were he that would not believe he can see, because he cannot perceive by what means he may see."

"Yet see I," quoth he, "no cause or need why we should pray to them, since God can as well, and will as gladly, both hear us and help us, as any saint in heaven."

"What need you," quoth I, "to pray[232] any physician to help your fever, or pray and pay any surgeon to heal your sore leg, since God can hear you and help you both, as well as the best, and loveth you better and can do it sooner, and may afford his plasters better cheap,[233] and give you more for your words than they for your money?"

"But this is his pleasure," quoth he, "that I shall be helped by the means of them as his instruments, though indeed all this he doth himself, since he giveth the nature to the things that they do it with."

"So hath it," quoth I, "pleased God in like wise that we shall ask help of his holy saints, and pray for help to them. Nor that is not a making of them equal unto God himself, though they do it by his will and power, or he at their intercession. Though God will (as reason is) be chief and have no match, yet forbiddeth he not one man to pray for help

216 gladly   **217** difference   **218** think   **219** way   **220** of the two   **221** amounts of space   **222** pupil   **223** similar

224 circles   **225** wholly   **226** unencumbered   **227** surpass   **228** living   **229** *but if:* unless   **230** unless   **231** otherwise

232 ask   **233** *afford…cheap:* provide his medicinal dressings at a lower cost

of another. And though the Father hath given all the judgment to his Son,[234] yet doth he delight to have his holy saints partners of that honor, and at the Day of Judgment to have them sit with him.[235] Was Elisha made equal to God because the widow prayed him to revive her dead son?[236] Were the apostles equal to Christ because that they were prayed unto for help after his death — and in his life also?[237] And many things did they at folks' prayer.[238] And sometimes they were prayed unto and assayed[239] it also, and yet could not do it, but the parties were fain[240] to go from them to their Master therefor.[241] And yet was he content that they were prayed unto. And for proof thereof suffered[242] them at men's devout instance[243] and prayer, to do many miracles. And sometimes were they prayed to be intercessors to their Master, as where they came to Christ and said, *Dimitte illam, quia clamat post nos* ('Dispatch this woman, for she crieth upon us').[244] And think you then that he being content and giving men occasion to pray to them while they were with him in earth, he will be angry if we do them as much worship[245] when they be with him in heaven? Nay, but I think on the other side, since his pleasure is to have his saints had[246] in honor and prayed unto, that they may be for us intercessors to his high Majesty, whereunto, ere we presume to approach, it becometh[247] us and well behooveth us to make friends of such as he hath in favor. He will disdain once[248] to look on us if we be so presumptuous and malapert[249] fellows that, upon boldness of familiarity with himself, we disdain to make our intercessors his especial beloved friends. And where Saint Paul exhorteth us each to pray for other,[250] and we be glad to think it well done to pray every poor man to pray for us, should we think it evil done to pray holy saints in heaven to the same?"

"Why," quoth he, "by that reason I might pray not only to saints, but also to every other dead man."

"So may ye," quoth I, "with good reason, if ye see none other likelihood but that he died a good man. And so find we, as I remember, in the *Dialogues* of Saint Gregory, that one had help by prayer made unto a holy man late[251] deceased which[252] was

himself yet in purgatory.[253] So liked it our Lord to let the world know that he was in his special favor, though he were yet in pain of his purgation. For our Lord loved him nevertheless, though he left not for him the order of his merciful justice. And therefore let no man take his trouble or sickness as a token of God's hatred, but if[254] he feel himself grudge[255] and be impatient and evil content with it. For then is it a token of wrath and vengeance, and is to the sufferer as fruitless as painful, and in effect nothing else but the beginning of his hell, even here. But on the other side,[256] if he take it patiently, it purgeth; if gladly, it greatly meriteth; and glad may he be that is, with meekness, glad of God's punishment. Saint Augustine (as is written by Possidius), lying sore[257] sick himself of an access,[258] cured another with his prayer, and yet he died of his sickness himself.[259] Wherein there was to him more mercy and favor showed than if himself had been cured too. For now, instead of health, he had heaven, where he should nevermore be sick again."

"Marry," quoth he, "but I have ever heard it said that we should not pray to any dead man but with this condition: 'If thou be a saint, then pray for me.'"

"Why so," quoth I, "more than praying to a quick[260] man, where I am not bound to say, 'If thou be a good man, pray for me'? But since I may reasonably think him good while I know him not the contrary, so may I think him that is dead."

"Why," quoth he, "whereof serveth[261] canonizing then? If this be true, I am never advised to be canonized while I live."

"Ye do the better," quoth I, "nor seven years after, neither. For it would be but a business[262] for you."

"But why be they canonized then?" quoth he.

"Those," quoth I, "that be not canonized, ye may for the more part both pray for them and pray to them, as ye may for and to them that be yet alive. But one that is canonized, ye may pray to him to pray for you, but ye may not pray for him. For, as I remember, Saint Augustine saith that 'he that prayeth for a martyr doth the martyr injury.'[263] And of every man ye may trust well and be seldom certain, but of the canonized ye may reckon you sure."

234 See Jn 5:22.   **235** See Mt 19:28.
236 See 4 Kgs (2 Kgs) 4:28–35.   **237** See
Mt 10:1, 8; Mk 6:7, 13; Lk 9:1–2, 6; Lk 10:9,
17, 19; Acts 3:43; 5:12–13, 15–16; Acts 6:7.
238 request   **239** tried   **240** obliged
241 for it. See Mk 9:14–29.   **242** allowed

243 persistent entreaty   **244** Mt 15:23
245 honor   **246** held   **247** befits
248 on any occasion   **249** impudent
250 See Jas 5:16; 1 Tm 2:1; Eph 6:18.
251 recently   **252** who   **253** See
Dialogues 4.40 (PL 32: 59–64).   **254** but

if: unless   **255** discontented   **256** hand
257 grievously   **258** attack of fever or
disease   **259** See St. Possidius, *Life of Saint
Augustine* 29.   **260** living   **261** *whereof
serveth:* of what use is   **262** anxious care
263 Sermon 159.30 (PL 38: 868)

THE NINTH CHAPTER

*The messenger yet again objecteth against relics,
and putteth great doubt in canonizing.
Whereunto the author maketh answer.*

"How can I," quoth he, "be sure thereof? May the taking up of a man's bones, and setting his carcass in a gay[264] shrine, and then kissing his bare scalp, make a man a saint? And yet are there some unshrined, for no man wotteth[265] where they lie, and some that men doubt whether ever they had any body at all or not. But marry, to recompense that withal, there be some again that have two bodies, to lend one to some good fellow that lacketh. For as I said before, some one body lieth whole in two places far asunder, or else the monks of the one be beguiled. For both the places plainly affirm that it lieth there. And at either place they show the shrine. And in the shrine they show a body, which they say is the body, and boldly bide[266] thereby that it is it, alleging[267] old writing and miracles also for the proof. Now must we confess that either the miracles at the one place be false, or done by the devil, or else that the same saint had two bodies indeed. And then were that, in my mind, as great a miracle as the greatest of them all. And therefore is it likely somewhere a bone worshipped for a relic of some holy saint that was peradventure a bone, as Chaucer saith, of some holy Jew's sheep.[268] Our Savior also seemeth in the Gospel to blame and reprove the Pharisees for making fresh the sepulchres of holy prophets, and making shrines of their graves.[269] Whereby it appeareth that he would not have the dead bodies worshipped and set in gay golden shrines. And yet besides this ye shall find many more worshipped, I ween, than shrined, many shrined that ye find not canonized, though ye seek up[270] all the registries in Rome. And when they be shrined and canonized too, yet since the Church in the canonization useth a means that may beguile them — for they stand to the record[271] of men both of their lives and of their miracles, which men may peradventure lie — why may it not then be that the Church be deceived in the canonization? And that they may — for lack of true knowledge believing untrue men — canonize for saints such folk sometimes

as be full far therefrom? I dare not say so much as saith Saint Augustine. For he letteth[272] not to say plainly that many bodies be worshipped for saints here in earth whose souls be buried in hell."[273]

"Ye have," quoth I, "said many things very stoutly.[274] But yet let us first consider whereunto altogether[275] weigheth. For it stretcheth no further, if it were all true, but that we might be deceived in some that we should take for saints. And it neither proveth that there be no saints (which I wot well no wise man will say) nor that if any be, they should not be worshipped nor prayed unto. Except[276] ye would say that if we might by possibility mistake some, therefore we should worship none. And then should you, by that reason never take[277] any physician, since ye might happen upon a dog-leech[278] for lack of knowledge, of the cunning.[279] For in records[280] of men, ye might be as well deceived there as here. Now suppose then, first, that of saints and of relics, some were true and some were false; yet the worship that ye would we should[281] do to them all should be because (that standing as they do unknown and undiscerned) ye reckoned them all true, and all for God's well-beloved servants. For if ye knew of them which were true and which false, then would ye worship the true, and tread the false underfoot."

"That is no doubt," quoth he.

"Then," quoth I, "if we were beguiled in some, I see no great peril grow toward us thereby. For if there came a great many of the King's friends into your country, and ye for his sake made them all great cheer; if there came among them, unware[282] to you, some spies that were his mortal enemies — wearing his badge, and seeming to you, and so reported, as his familiar friends — whether would he blame you for the good cheer ye made his enemies, or thank you for the good cheer ye made his friends?"

"He would, I think," quoth he, "thank me for the good entreating of them both, since both seemed good to me and both had of me their cheer but for[283] they seemed his friends, and for his sake."

"Ye say," quoth I, "good reason.[284] But I put case[285] now that ye had an inkling, or else a plain warning, that some of them were his enemies that seemed his

---

264 ornate **265** knows **266** maintain **267** citing **268** See "The Prologue," line 351, of *The Pardoner's Tale*. **269** See Mt 23:29–31. **270** *seek up:* go look in **271** *stand to the record:* go by the testimony **272** hesitates **273** See Augustine's *On Care to Be Had for the Dead*, 4–5. **274** firmly, boldly **275** all of them together **276** Unless **277** have recourse to **278** quack **279** craft **280** testimonies **281** *would we should:* want us to **282** unknown **283** *but for:* only because **284** *Ye say good reason:* You speak good sense **285** *put case:* propose

best friends—but which they were, no man can tell you. What would you now do? Make them all cheer, and honorably entreat them all? Or else, showing them that ye hear say plainly that some of them be naught,[286] therefore bid them be walking all with sorrow?"[287]

"Nay," quoth he, "no doubt were it, but that I should look for thanks if I cherished his enemies for his friends, rather than despitefully to handle his friends for his enemies."

"Very well," quoth I. "And this were true although ye had warning that some of them were his enemies. But what thanks would ye then deserve if ye should shake off both where ye had no such warning at all, but would say that ye durst not make any of them cheer because ye thought that peradventure it might be that some were worse than they were taken for? For in such case be you here: ye know not that any man worshipped for a saint is none, but only ye think that ye be not sure whether all be or some not."

"Yes," quoth he, "Saint Augustine, as I told you, giveth me warning that many be none."

"Ye be," quoth I, "deceived[288] therein, as I shall tell you after. But in the meanwhile, mark me well this, and let it stand for a sure ground: that all your objection, if it were true, serveth not against worshipping of saints or saints' relics, but against the worshipping of such as were no saints, nor no saints' relics—and that after it were proved. And now this thing that is in question being first confessed and agreed between us for a thing nothing able to hurt our principal matter, let us go further therein, and search whether we find any such cause of doubt in any, or have good cause to reckon ourselves sure that all be saints indeed, whom the Church of Christ hath in honor and veneration for saints. First, as for the authority that ye allege of Saint Augustine, I have heard it often alleged in like wise for the same purpose. But surely they that so take Saint Augustine been foully deceived. I durst[289] be bold to say that Saint Augustine did never write such words, but it is a word run in many men's mouths, begun by mistaking, and believed without examination. For surely the words whereof they took the

occasion, which he writeth in the First Book *De civitate Dei*,[290] and repeateth again in his book of that cure[291] and care that men should have for them that be dead[292]—those words, I say, go far wide from all such purpose. For there he speaketh only of costly burying, and making of sumptuous sepulchres, and doing the dead corpses of rich men worldly worship in the carrying forth and interring of the body, as it plainly and evidently appeareth by the matter that he writeth of.

"And surely since our Lord never would among his chosen people give the glory of his name to another,[293] nor never so suffer[294] idolatry among the Jews, but that either he forthwith[295] punished and purged it, or so severed the flock of idolaters that it might well appear where his faithful flock remained (as it did when that, Samaria falling to idolatry, the right synagogue of the Jews remained in Jerusalem and in Judaea),[296] this were full unlikely: that this Holy Spirit being sent unto his Church here to remain and instruct it, and himself also therewith being and giving his special assistance unto the end of the world, should either suffer his Church to be unknown or in such wise to err and be deceived as to give honor to the devil instead of himself, or to his enemies instead of his friends. And therefore when the Church, by diligent ensearch,[297] findeth the life of a man holy; and that thereto[298] it is well witnessed that God by his miracles testifieth the man's blessedness and the favor in which he standeth with him in heaven, declaring by the boot[299] and profit which he doth to many men for his sake that he will have him honored and had for hallowed[300] in his Church here in earth; and this thing (either by them that hath the cure[301] of his Church, after such diligence used, being by the canonization declared unto the people, or peradventure without canonization growing thereof, by the holiness well known, and miracles many seen) so sure a common persuasion through the whole people of Christendom that the person is accepted and reputed for an undoubted saint, be the bones translated[302] or not, his body founden or not, albeit by possibility of nature it might be that men were in such things deceived, as ye have said, yet we boldly may, and well

286 bad; wicked   287 *bid…sorrow:* tell them all to leave or they'll be sorry   288 mistaken   289 dare   290 *The City of God* 1.12–13   291 concern   292 On

Care to Be Had for the Dead, 4–5   293 See Is 42:8.   294 allow   295 right away   296 See 3 Kgs (1 Kgs) 16:24.   297 investigation   298 also   299 advantage

300 *had for hallowed:* held as sainted   301 charge; care   302 transported; relocated

we ought, in this case, to trust that the grace and aid of God and his Holy Spirit assisting his Church hath governed the judgment of his ministers and inclined the minds of his people to such consent, and that he hath not suffered them to err in a thing so nearly touching his honor and worship, either truly to be applied, where his will were it should[303] (upon himself, or his holy saints for his sake) or to be withdrawn thence, and by erroneous mistaking of truth—necessary, meet, and convenient[304] to be perceived of the Church for God's honor (which kind of truth God sent the Holy Ghost to teach his Church)—the same worship to be bestowed upon them whom he would in no wise should[305] have it, but whom he reserveth for eternal shame. For the body shrined or not maketh no doubt of the saint. No man doubteth of our Lady; no man doubteth of Saint John the Evangelist, though their bodies be not founden. And yet if they were, then were there, I think, no good Christian man but he would be contented they were shrined and had[306] in honor.

"For whereas ye would take the reverence from all relics because that some be doubtful—in that some saint's head is, as ye say, and of some the whole body, showed at two sundry places—it may fortune, for all this, that of one head there may be sundry parts, and either part, in the common speech of people, called 'the head.' For at Amiens is 'Saint John's head' (the Baptist), as men call it in talking—even they that have been there and seen it. But then if they be asked further question thereof, they tell that the nether jaw lacketh.[307] This may well happen also, and so doth it hap indeed, by some saint of whom in two diverse countries be diverse shrines. And there be reckoned and reported that in either of them be laid the whole body, and the pilgrims at neither place do look into the coffin of that shrine to see whether it be all or part. In some place peradventure lay the body, and by some occasion the body translated[308] thence of old,[309] and yet the shrine showed still with some of the relics remaining therein. It may well hap also that there were two good holy men in diverse countries, both of one name. And percase[310] in some place may there be some very[311] relics unknown and misnamed. For in old time, when men at the incursion of infidels

did hide holy saints' relics, at the finding again, the names haply[312] decayed, some relics might rest unknown, or some peradventure lost or mistaken. As myself saw at the Abbey of Barking (besides London), to my remembrance about thirty years past, in the setting an old image[313] in a new tabernacle, the back of the image, being all painted over and of long time before laid with beaten gold, happened to crease in one place, and out there fell a pretty[314] little door, at which fell out also many relics that had lain unknown in that image, God wot how long— and as long had been likely to lie again, if God by that chance had not brought them to light. The Bishop of London came then thither, to see there were no deceit therein. And I, among others, was present there while he looked thereon and examined the matter. And in good faith, it was to me a marvel to behold the manner of it. I have forgotten much thereof, but I remember a little piece of wood there was, rudely shapen in cross, with thread wrapped about it. Writing had it none; and what it was we could not tell; but it seemed as new-cut as if it had been done within one day before. And diverse relics had old writings on them, and some had none; but among others were there certain small kerchers[315] which were named there our Lady's, and of her own working. Coarse were they not, nor they were not large, but served, as it seemed, to cast[316] in a plain and simple manner upon her head. But surely they were as clean seams, to my seeming, as ever I saw in my life, and were therewith as white for all the long lying, as if they had been washed and laid up within one hour. And how long that image had stood in that old tabernacle, that could no man tell; but there had in all the Church none, as they thought, stood longer untouched. And they guessed that four or five hundred years ago, that image was hidden when the abbey was burned by infidels, and those relics hidden therein, and after the image founden and set up—many years after, when they were gone that had hidden it. And so the relics remained, unknown, therein till now that God gave that chance that opened it. And thus, as I say, may it peradventure happen, some names to be forgotten, or haply to be mistaken, and yet God well content that the relics be had in reverence, since he specially

303 *were it should:* wants it to be
304 *meet, and convenient:* appropriate and fitting   305 *would…should:* did

not in any way want to   306 held
307 *nether jaw lacketh:* lower jaw is missing   308 was removed   309 *of*

old: long ago   310 perhaps   311 true
312 perhaps   313 statue   314 cleverly made   315 kerchiefs   316 be put

favoreth their persons, and needeth nothing their names to know them by, as he shall once so fully restore again many a glorious body that they shall not lose the least hair of their head that may serve to their beauty, of whom the names, haply, the whole world hath long ago forgotten. And the name is not so very requisite but that we may mistake it without peril, so that we nevertheless have the relics of holy men in reverence. But as for pigs' bones for holy relics, or damned wretches to be worshipped for saints, albeit that if it happened, yet it nothing hurted the souls of them that mistake it, no more than if we worship a host in the Mass which percase the negligence or malice of some lewd[317] priest hath left unconsecrated, yet is it never to be thought, though such a thing might happen suddenly, that ever God will suffer[318] such a thing to last and endure in his Church.

"For albeit that his Church useth one means that might, as ye say, beguile them—which is the record[319] and witness of men—yet hath it in such things, as Saint Thomas and other holy doctors write, another means besides, which never can beguile them. And that is the assistance of God and the Holy Ghost. For else might the Church be most easily beguiled in the receiving of the very Scripture, wherein they take outwardly but the testimonies of men, from mouth to mouth and hand to hand, without other examination. But that secret means that inclineth their credulity to consent in the believing all in one point, which is the secret instinct of God, this is the sure means that never can in any necessary point fail here in Christ's Church. For if it might, all were quite at large.[320] And that point once taken away, Scripture and all walketh with it. And in this mind, as it seemeth, was very sure and fastly[321] confirmed the holy apostle Saint Paul, which[322] in his First Epistle to the Corinthians writeth in this wise: *Obsecro vos, fratres, per nomen Domini nostri Iesu Christi, ut idipsum dicatis omnes, et non sint in vobis schismata, sed sitis integrum corpus, eadem mente et eadem sententia* ('I beseech you, my brethren, by the name of our Lord Jesus Christ, that you say all one[323] thing; and let there be no schisms'[324]—or several sects—'among you, but be ye one whole, entire body, of one mind and one sentence').[325] Truth is it that he taught them and others the right way—so far-forth[326] that he boldly forbade an angel of heaven to be believed, if any would come and preach another Gospel. But yet in this place I note much that he called upon them only for agreement, bidding them only to agree all upon one thing, and maketh no mention of agreement upon 'the best' and upon 'the truth,' but only to avoid all discord and division, and by common consent exhorteth them to agree all in one, meaning thereby, as methinketh, that if the Church of Christ, intending well, do all agree upon any one thing concerning God's honor or man's soul, it cannot be but that thing must needs be true. For God's Holy Spirit, that animateth his Church and giveth it life, will never suffer it[327] all consent and agree together upon any damnable error. And therefore would he never suffer the Church so fully to consent in the worship of saints and reverence of relics if it were a thing such as some men would have it seem: that is to wit, a thing damnable, false, and feigned.

"Wherein as much as ye lay[328] to diminish their credence, that it might seem, as ye say well enough, that some of them were feigned, yet wist I never[329] proved that any such so taken,[330] and by the Church approved, was ever yet hitherto reproved,[331] either here in Christ's Church or among the Jews in their synagogue before Christ's days; and yet saints they had in honor, as patriarchs and prophets, and their bodies and relics in reverence. Now if of such as seemed good men we never had founden any for hypocrites, albeit it might be that some were such, yet would we not, I think, suppose that there were any so in deed,[332] if we never had known it tried and proved so. And why shall we then of saints or relics have doubt and mistrust? Of whom, being received by the Church for true, we never, that I could wit,[333] since God wrought[334] the world, tried and proved any of both sorts untrue—neither, as I say, in the Church of Christ nor synagogue of the Jews, which two sorts only were God's chosen people. And yet had as well the Jews as we both saints, as I said, in honor and their relics in great reverence, as appeareth as well by the Gospel as by the Old Testament.

317 bad   **318** allow   **319** testimony   **325** Gal 1:8   **326** *so far-forth:* to such an   I never knew it to be   **330** *such so taken:*
320 *at large:* unsettled   **321** steadfastly   extent   **327** *suffer it:* allow (the Church)   of those taken to be saints   **331** disproved
322 who   **323** the same   **324** 1 Cor 1:10   to   **328** cite as evidence   **329** *wist I never:*   **332** truth   **333** know of   **334** created

Jacob, that holy patriarch, commanded his children in[335] his deathbed to carry his body to the
burial out of that country of Egypt; and so they
did.[336] And Joseph also required his brethren that
when they should after depart out of Egypt, they
should carry his bones with them.[337] The dead
bones of the prophet Elisha, as the Bible mention-
eth, raised a dead body to life.[338] And think you
then that those bones were not there honored for
holy relics?

"Nor our Savior Christ blameth not the Jews in
the Gospel for that they garnished[339] the sepulchres
of the old prophets—with whose honor he was well
content—but for that they condemned themselves
in following the condition of them that slew them,
intending to kill Christ as their forefathers did his
holy prophets.[340] For as for the dead bodies of the
holy prophets, that God would have them had in
honor and reverence he declared well by that he
raised a dead body by the touch of the dead bones
of the prophet Elisha, as I said to you before.

"Did not our Lord, in the finding of that holy
relic his holy cross, declare by miracle and make
his own cross known from the crosses of the two
thieves by the raising of a dead man with the touch
thereof?[341] Wherein is to be noted, by the way, that
there was between his and theirs no notable difference, but they[342] nailed as he was; or else had it
been no doubt upon the first sight which of them
was his. Was not the body of Saint Stephen found
out by miracle, and the head of Saint John Baptist
also? Yes, of surety,[343] and many another holy martyr more, that else had lain unknown. Whereby well
appeared that God would have not their souls only,
but also their bodies—and in a manner the very
soles of their shoes—set by[344] for their sakes, and
themselves for his. Was not the woman healed by
the touch of our Lord's garments?[345] Hath there
not, both among the Jews and Christian people
also, many men marvelously been helped by the
only touch of holy saints' vestures? And doubt we
then whether God would we should worship[346]
them, when he so well and above nature rewardeth
us for the worship we do them?"

THE TENTH CHAPTER

*The messenger objecteth many things against
pilgrimages and relics and worshipping of saints,
because of much superstitious manner used therein,
and unlawful petitions asked of them,
and harm growing thereupon.*

"Sir," quoth he, "ye have in my mind very well
touched the matter concerning that it is not in vain
to pray to saints, nor to worship them and to have[347]
their relics in some reverence. But, sir, all this is far
from the great sore;[348] for though saints may hear
us, and help us too, and are glad and willing so to
do, and God also contented that they and their relics and images also be had in honor, yet can neither
he nor they be content with the manner of the worship: first, taking away his own worship in that we
do them the same worship, in every point, that we
do to God. And secondly, taking their worship from
them then also, in that we do to their images the
same that we do to themselves—taking their images
for themselves—and so make not themselves only,
but also their images, fellows and matches to God;
wherewith[349] as I have said before, neither God nor
good saint can, nor good man ought to, be content
and pleased."

"In faith," quoth I, "therein if it so be, ye say very
true."

"What say we then," quoth he, "of the harm that
goeth by going of pilgrimages—roiling[350] about in
idleness, with the riot, reveling, and ribaldry, gluttony, wantonness, waste, and lechery? Trow ye[351]
that God and his holy saints had not liefer[352] they sit
still at home than thus to come seek them with such
worshipful service?"

"Yes, surely," quoth I.

"What say we then," quoth he, "to that I spoke
not of yet, in which we do them little worship while
we set every saint to his office and assign him a craft
such as pleaseth us? Saint Loye[353] we make a horse-
leech,[354] and must let our horse rather run unshod
and mar his hoof than to shoe him on his day[355]—
which we must, for that point, more religiously
keep high and holy than Easter Day. And because

---

335 on   **336** See Gn 49:29, 50:14.
337 See Gn 50:25.   **338** See 4 Kgs (2 Kgs)
13:21.   **339** *for that they garnished:* because
they adorned   **340** See Mt 23:29–31.
341 See Jacobus de Voragine, *The Golden*

Legend, "The Invention of the Holy
Cross."   **342** they were   **343** certainty
344 *set by:* valued   **345** See Lk 8:44–46;
Mk 5:25–29.   **346** *would we should
worship:* wants us to venerate   **347** hold

348 difficulty   **349** with that   **350** wandering   **351** *Trow ye:* Do you believe
352 rather   **353** *Saint Loye:* also called
St. Eligius   **354** doctor   **355** i.e., on St.
Loye's feast day

one smith is too few at a forge, we set Saint Hippolytus to help him. And on Saint Stephen's Day we must let[356] all our horses' blood with a knife, because Saint Stephen was killed with stones. Saint Apollonia we make a tooth-drawer,[357] and may speak to her of nothing but of sore teeth. Saint Zita women set to seek their keys. Saint Roch we set to see to the great sickness, because he had a sore. And with him they join Saint Sebastian, because he was martyred with arrows. Some serve for the eye only, and some for a sore breast. Saint Germanus only for children. And yet will he not once look at them but if[358] the mothers bring with them a white loaf and a pot of good ale. And yet is he wiser than Saint Wilgefortis; for she, good soul, is (as they say) served and content with oats. Whereof I cannot perceive the reason, but if it be because she should provide a horse for an evil husband to ride to the devil upon. For that is the thing that she is so sought for, as they say, in so much that women hath therefore changed her name, and instead of Saint Wilgefortis call her Saint Uncumber, because they reckon that for a peck of oats she will not fail to uncumber[359] them of their husbands. Long work were it to rehearse[360] you the diverse manners of many pretty pilgrimages, but one or two will I tell you. The one, Pontano[361] speaketh of in his *Dialogues*:[362] how Saint Martin is worshipped. I have forgot the town, but the manner[363] I cannot forget, it is so strange. His image[364] is on his day borne in procession about all the streets. And if it be a fair day, then use they[365] as he cometh by to cast rose water and all things of pleasant savor upon his image. But and[366] it happen to rain, out pour they piss-pots upon his head, at every door and every window. Is not this a sweet service and a worshipful worship? And this, as I say, Pontano writeth, and telleth where it is. But this that I shall now tell you, I dare as boldly make you sure of as if I had seen it myself. At Saint Valery's, here in Picardy, there is a fair abbey, where Saint Valery was monk. And upon a furlong[367] off or two, up in a wood, is there a chapel in which the saint is specially sought unto for the stone,[368] not only in those parts, but also out of England. Now was there a young gentleman which[369] had married

a merchant's wife.[370] And having a little wanton[371] money, which him thought burned out the bottom of his purse, in the first year of his wedding took his wife with him and went over the sea for none other errand but to see Flanders and France, and ride out one summer in those countries. And having one in his company that told by the way many strange things of that pilgrimage, he thought he would go somewhat out of his way, either to see it if it were true, or laugh at his man[372] if he found it false, as he verily thought he should have done indeed. But when they came into the chapel, they found it all true. And to behold, they found it fonder[373] than he had told. For like[374] as in other pilgrimages ye see hanged up legs of wax, or arms, or such other parts, so was in that chapel all their offerings that hung about the walls none other thing but men's gear,[375] and women's gear, made in wax. Then was there, besides these, two round rings of silver, the one much larger than the other, through which every man did put his privy members, at the altar's end, not every man through both, but some through the one and some through the other. For they were not both of a bigness, but the one larger than the other. Then was there yet[376] a monk, standing at the altar, that hallowed[377] certain threads of Venice gold. And them he delivered to the pilgrims, teaching them in what wise themselves, or their friends, should use those threads against[378] the stone: that they should knit it about their gear, and say I cannot tell you what prayers. And when the monk had declared the manner, the gentleman had a servant that was a married man and yet a merry fellow; and he, thanking the monk for the thread, desired him to teach him how he should knit it about his wife's gear. Which (except[379] the monk had some special craft in knitting) he thought would be cumbrous, because her gear was somewhat short. It need not to tell you that every man laughed then, save the monk, that cast up his rings and threads in a great anger and went his way; was not this—abide,[380] by God, I had almost forgotten one thing, that would not be left for a groat.[381] As this gentleman and his wife were kneeling in the chapel, there came a good sad[382] woman to him, showing[383] him that one special point

---

356 draw, drain   **357** dentist   **358** *but if:* unless   **359** unburden; disencumber   **360** tell   **361** Giovanni Pontano (1426–1503) was an Italian humanist and poet.   **362** See the dialogue *Charon*.   **363** custom

364 statue   **365** *use they:* it's their practice   **366** if   **367** 220 yards   **368** *for the stone:* relief from kidney stones   **369** who   **370** widow   **371** surplus   **372** servant   **373** more foolish   **374** just   **375** genitals

376 besides   **377** blessed   **378** to prevent or cure   **379** unless   **380** wait a minute   **381** *a groat:* for anything   **382** serious; somber   **383** telling

used[384] in that pilgrimage—and the surest against the stone—she wist nere[385] whether he were yet advertised[386] of. Which, if it were done, she durst lay[387] her life he should never have the stone in his life. And that was, she would have the length of his gear, and that should she make in a wax candle, which should burn up in the chapel, and certain prayers should there be said the while. And this was against the stone the very sheet-anchor.[388] When he had heard her (and he was one that in earnest feared the stone), he went and asked his wife counsel. But she, like a good faithful Christian woman, loved no such superstitions. She could abide the remnant well enough; but when she heard once of burning up the candle, she knit the brows and earnestly (blessing herself): 'Beware, in the virtue of God, what ye do,' quoth she. 'Burn up?' quoth a.[389] 'Marry, God forbid! It would waste up your gear, upon pain of my life. I pray you beware of such witchcraft!' Is this kind of service and worship acceptable and pleasant unto God and his saints? Now, when people worship saints in such wise that they make them fellows to God, and images in such wise that they take them for the saints themselves; and then again, on the other side, honor them with such superstitious ways that the paynim[390] gods were worshipped with no worse; finally, that worst is of all, pray to them for unlawful things, as thieves pray to the thief that hung on the right side of Christ[391] to speed[392] them well in their robbery—and have found him a name also, calling him 'Dismas,' I ween, and his fellow 'Gismas,' to rhyme withal—think you not that this gear[393] is such among the people as rather were likely so to provoke God and his saints to displeasure that the devil should have license and liberty therefore to work his wonders in delusion of our superstitious idolatry, than so to like and content our Lord that he should show miracles for the comprobation[394] of that manner of worshipping which—we may well perceive—all reason, religion, and virtue reproveth?"[395]

THE ELEVENTH CHAPTER
*The author answereth all the objections proponed[396]
by the messenger in the tenth chapter, and some of
them touched by the messenger more
at large in other parts before.*

"Your whole tale, in effect," quoth I, "containeth three things: one, that the people worship the saints, and their images also, with like honor as they do God himself; another, that they take the images for the things themselves (which points do sound to[397] idolatry); the third is the superstitious fashion of worship, with desire of unlawful things. And since the worship that the people do to the saints and the images be such, ye conclude the thing displeasant to God and to all hallows,[398] and that it may thereby well appear that the miracles also be not the works of God, but the delusion of the devil. The first point, which ye have now twice touched, is at once soon and shortly answered, for it is not true. For though men kneel to saints and images, and incense them also, yet it is not true that therefore they worship them in every point like unto God."

"What point lack they?" quoth he.

"Marry, the chief of all," quoth I. "That is, that they worship God with the mind[399] that he is God—which mind in worship is the only thing that maketh it *latria*,[400] and no certain gesture nor bodily observance. Not and[401] we would wallow upon the ground unto Christ, having therewith a mind that he were the best man that we could devise and thinking him not God. For if the lowly manner of bodily observance were the thing that would make *latria*, then were we much in peril of idolatry in our courtesy used to princes, prelates, and popes, to whom we kneel as low as to God Almighty, and kiss some their hands—and some our own, ere ever we presume to touch them—and in the pope, his feet. And as for incensing, the poor priests in every choir be as well incensed as the Sacrament,[402] so that if *latria*—that is, the special honor due to God—stood in such things, then were we great idolaters, not in our worship done to saints only, and their images, but also to men—one to another—among ourselves. But albeit

384 *point used:* thing customarily done
385 *wist nere:* knew not   386 informed
387 *durst lay:* dared bet   388 the largest
anchor   389 he (dialectical pronoun)
390 pagan   391 See Mt 27:38, 44; Mk

15:27; Lk 23:33, 39; Jacobus de Voragine,
The Golden Legend, "The Passion of
Our Lord."   392 assist   393 affair
394 proof; attesting   395 condemns;
denounces   396 proposed   397 *sound to:*

seem to suggest   398 saints   399 thought
400 the worship given only to God
401 even if   402 Eucharist

that God ought of duty to have with our body the most humble and lowly reverence that we can possibly devise, yet is not that bodily worship *latria* but if we so do it that in our mind we consider and acknowledge him for God, and with that consideration and intent do him that worship. And so doth, as I think, no Christian man to image or saint either. And so is avoided the peril of idolatry, for the first point ye spoke of.

"Now, as touching[403] the second—that the people take the images for the saints themselves—I trust there be no man so mad, nor woman neither, but that they know quick men from dead stones, and tree[404] from flesh and bone. And when they prefer, as ye spoke of, our Lady at one pilgrimage before our Lady at another, or one rood[405] before another, or make their invocations and vows some to the one and some to the other, I ween it easy to perceive that they mean none other but that our Lord and our Lady—or our Lord for our Lady—showeth more miracles at the one than at the other, and that they intend, in their pilgrimage, to visit some of them one place and some another, as their devotion leadeth them, or partly sometimes as the place lieth for[406] them—and yet not for the place, but for that[407] it liketh our Lord by manifest miracles to provoke men to seek upon him or his blessed Mother, or some other holy saint of his, in those places more specially than in some others.

"The thing itself also showeth that they take not the images for our Lady herself. For if they so did, how could they possibly in any manner wise[408] have more mind to the one than to the other? For they can have no more mind to our Lady than to our Lady. Moreover, if they thought that the image at Walsingham were our Lady herself, then must they needs think that our Lady herself were that image. Then if in like wise they thought that the image at Ipswich were our Lady herself, and (as they must therewith[409] needs think) that our Lady herself were that image at Ipswich, then must they needs think therewithal, that all those three were one thing. And then every two of them were one thing. And so must they, by that reason, suppose that the image of Ipswich were the selfsame image that is at Walsingham. Which, if ye ask any of them whom ye take for the simplest, except a natural fool, I dare hold

you a wager she will tell you nay. Besides this, take the simplest fool that ye can choose, and she will tell you that our Lady herself is in heaven. She will also call an image an image, and she will tell you a difference between an image of a horse and a horse in deed.[410] And then appeareth it well, whatsoever her words be of her pilgrimage—by a common manner of speech to call the image of our Lady 'our Lady,' as men say, 'Go to the King's Head for wine,' not meaning his head in deed, but the sign—so meaneth she none other in that image but our Lady's image, howsoever she call it. And if ye will well prove that she neither taketh our Lady for that image, nor that image for our Lady (as both must she take if she take the one), talk with her of our Lady; and she will tell you that our Lady was saluted with[411] Gabriel, and that our Lady fled unto Egypt with Joseph;[412] and yet will she not in the telling say that our Lady of Walsingham, or of Ipswich, was saluted of Gabriel or fled into Egypt. Nor if ye would ask her whether it were our Lady of Ipswich or our Lady of Walsingham that stood by the cross at Christ's Passion, she will, I warrant[413] you, make answer that neither of both. And if ye demand[414] her further, 'Which Lady, then?' she will name you none image, but our Lady that is in heaven. And this have I proved often, and ye may, when ye will, and shall find it true, except it be in one so very a fool that God will give her leave to believe what she list.[415] And surely for this point, I think in my mind that all those heretics that make as though they found so much peril of idolatry among the people for mistaking of images do but devise that fear to have some cloak to cover their heresy, wherein they bark against the saints themselves, and when they be marked, then say they mean but the misbelief that women have in images. Now, as touching the third point, of superstitious manner of worshipping, or unlawful petitions desired[416] of saints, as one example may serve both: if women offer oats to Saint Wilgefortis to have her uncumber[417] them of their husbands, somewhat is it indeed that ye say,[418] and yet not all things to be blamed that ye seem to blame. For as to pray to Saint Apollonia for the help of our teeth is no witchcraft, considering that she had her teeth pulled out for Christ's sake, nor there is no superstition in such other things like.[419] And peradventure

---

403 regards   **404** wood   **405** cross; crucifix   **406** near   **407** *for that:* because   **408** *manner wise:* kind of way   **409** also   **410** reality   **411** by   **412** See Lk 1:28; Mt 2:13–14.   **413** guarantee   **414** ask   **415** pleases   **416** asked   **417** unburden   **418** *somewhat . . . say:* there is indeed something in what you say   **419** similar

since Saint Loye was a farrier,[420] it is no great fault to pray to him for the help of our horse."

"Well then," quoth he, "since Saint Crispin and Saint Crispinian[421] were shoemakers, it were well done in like wise to pray them sit down and mend our shoes, and pray to Saint Dorothy[422] for some flowers, because she beareth always a basketful."

"Nay," quoth I, "the things be nothing like. For the one thing pertaineth nothing to our necessity; the other we may do ourselves, or soon find who shall. But as for your horse, is a thing wherein as well as in our own bodies, a right good leech[423] may fail of[424] his craft, and is to many a man a greater loss than he may well recover. And albeit that God commanded that we should chiefly seek for heaven, and promiseth that if we so do, all other things that we need shall be cast unto us,[425] and would that we should[426] in no wise live in anxiety and trouble of mind for any fear of lack, considering that our Father in heaven provideth meat[427] for the very birds of the air, by whom he setteth nothing so much as he doth by us,[428] yet willed not he the contrary but we should with our bodies labor therefor, having our hearts all the while in heaven, and willed also that we should ask it of him, without whose help our labor will not serve. And therefore is our daily food one of the petitions of the Pater Noster, the prayer that himself taught his disciples.[429] And the horse he set not so little by but that—rather than it should perish—he reckoned it no breach of the Sabbath day to pull him out of a pit.[430] And therefore indeed meseemeth the devotion to run somewhat too far if the smiths will not for any necessity set on a shoe upon Saint Loye's Day, and yet lawful enough to pray for the help of a poor man's horse. But as for your teeth, I ween if they ached well, ye would yourself think it a thing worthy, and not too simple, to ask help of Saint Apollonia and of God too."

"Yea, marry," quoth he, "and of the devil too, rather than fail,[431] as the Lombard[432] did for the gout. That,[433] when he had long called upon God and our Lady and all the holy company of heaven, and yet felt himself never the better, he began at last to call as fast[434] for help unto the devil. And when

his wife and his friends, sore[435] abashed and astonied,[436] rebuked him for calling on the devil—which he wist[437] well was naught,[438] and if that he helped him it should be for no good—he cried out as loud as he could again,[439] *Ogni aiuto é bono!* ('All is good that helpeth!').[440]

"And so, I ween, would I," quoth he, "call on the devil and all, rather than abide in pain."

"Nay," quoth I, "whatsoever ye say, I cannot think ye would believe in the devil as that Lombard did. Ye would rather fare like another that,[441] when the friar apposed[442] him in confession whether he meddled anything with witchcraft or necromancy, or had any belief in the devil, he answered him, *Credere en le diable? Messire, no; Io grand fatigue a credere in Dio.* ('Believe in the devil?' quoth he. 'Nay, nay, sir, I have work enough to believe in God I.')[443] And so would I ween that ye were far from all believing in the devil; ye have so much work to believe in God himself, that ye be loath methink to meddle much with his saints."

When we had laughed a while at our merry tales, "In good faith," quoth I, "as I was about to tell you, somewhat[444] indeed it is, that ye say. For evil it is, and evil it is suffered[445] that superstitious manner of worship. And as for that ye told of Saint Martin, if it be true, it hath none excuse, but that it nothing toucheth our matter: for it is not worshipping, but despiting[446] and disworshipping, of saints. Touching the offering of bread and ale to Saint Germanus, I see nothing much amiss therein. Where ye have seen it used,[447] I cannot tell. But I have myself seen it oftentimes, and yet am I not remembered that ever I saw priest or clerk[448] fare the better therefor, or once drink thereof; but it is given to children or poor folk to pray for the sick child. And I would ween it were none offense in such fashion to offer up a whole ox and distribute it among poor people. But now, as for our merry matters of Saint Valery, because the place is in France we shall leave the matter to the University of Paris to defend. And we will come home here to Paul's[449] and put[450] one example of both, that is to say, the superstitious manner and unlawful petitions, if women there offer oats

---

420 person who shoes horses **421** *Saint Crispin and Saint Crispinian:* brothers martyred in 286 **422** *Saint Dorothy:* martyred about 311 **423** doctor **424** at **425** See Mt 6:33. **426** *would…should:* wanted us to **427** food **428** *by whom…by us:* whom he values less than he values us. See

Mt 6:25–26. **429** See Mt 6:11. **430** See Lk 14:5; Mt 12:11. **431** lack; go without (being helped) **432** Italian (Lombardy is a region in northern Italy) **433** who **434** steadfastly **435** greatly **436** astonished, stunned **437** knew **438** wicked **439** in reply **440** The Lombard dialogue

(here and below) has close ties to the Italian. **441** who **442** asked **443** myself **444** something **445** allowed, permitted **446** insulting **447** practiced **448** a man in one of the minor orders below deacon, such as acolyte or lector **449** St. Paul's Cathedral **450** give

unto Saint Wilgefortis, in trust that she shall uncumber them of their husbands, yet can neither the priests perceive till they find it there that the foolish women bring oats thither, nor it is not, I think, so often done, nor so much brought at once, that the Church may make much money of it above the finding[451] of the canons'[452] horses."

"Nay," quoth he, "all the oats of a whole year's offering will not find three geese and a gander a week together."[453]

"Well," quoth I, "then the priests maintain not the matter for any great covetise;[454] and also what the peevish[455] women pray, they cannot hear. Howbeit, if they pray but to be uncumbered, meseemeth no great harm, nor unlawfulness therein. For that may they by more ways than one. They may be uncumbered if their husbands change their cumbrous conditions,[456] or if themselves peradventure change their cumbrous tongues, which is haply[457] the cause of all their cumbrance. And, finally, if they cannot be uncumbered but by death, yet it may be by their own, and so their husbands safe enough."

"Nay, nay," quoth he, "ye find them not such fools, I warrant you. They make their covenants[458] in their bitter[459] prayers as surely as they were penned, and will not cast away their oats for nought."[460]

"Well," quoth I, "to all these matters is one evident easy answer—that they nothing touch[461] the effect of our matter, which standeth in this: whether the thing that we speak of (as praying to saints, going in pilgrimage, and worshipping relics and images) may be done well, not whether it may be done evil. For if it may be well done, then though many would misuse it, yet doth all that nothing diminish the goodness of the thing itself. For if we should, for the misuse of a good thing, and for the evils that grow sometimes in the abuse thereof, not amend the misuse, but utterly put the whole use[462] away, we should then make marvelous changes in the world. In some countries they go on hunting commonly on Good Friday in the morning, for a common custom. Will ye break that evil custom, or cast away Good Friday? There be cathedral churches into which the country[463] cometh with procession at Whitsuntide,[464]

and the women following the cross with many an unwomanly song—and that, such honest[465] wives as out of the procession ye could not hire to speak one such foul ribaldry word as they there sing, for God's sake, whole ribaldrous songs as loud as their throat can cry. Will you mend that lewd manner, or put away Whitsuntide?

"Ye speak of lewdness used[466] at pilgrimages. Is there, trow ye,[467] none used on holy days? And why do you not then advise us to put them clean[468] away, Sundays and all? Some wax[469] drunk in Lent of wigs and cracknels;[470] and yet ye would not, I trust, that Lent were fordone.[471] Christmas, if we consider how commonly men abuse it, we may think that they take it for a time of liberty for all manner of lewdness. And yet is not Christmas to be cast away among Christian men, but men rather admonished to amend their manners, and use themselves in Christmas more Christianly. Go me to[472] Christ's own coming and giving us our faith and his holy Gospel and sacraments. Be there not ten the worse therefor, against one the better? Be not all the paynims, all the Jews, all the Turks, all the Saracens, all the heretics, all the evil-living people in Christendom, the worse—by their own fault— for the coming of Christ? I trow they be. And yet would no wise man wish that Christ had not comen here. Nor it had been no right that God should have left the occasion of merit and reward that good folk would, with his help, deserve by his coming, for the harm that wretches would take thereof by their own sloth and malice. Nor, in like wise, right were it none that all worship of saints, and reverence of holy relics, and honor of saints' images— by which good devout folk do much merit—we should abolish and put away because some folk do abuse it. Now touching the evil petitions, though[473] they that ask them were (as I trust they be not) a great[474] people, they be not yet so many that ask evil petitions of saints as there be that ask the same of God himself. For whatsoever they will ask of any good saint, they will ask of God also. And commonly in the wild Irish—and some in Wales, too, as men say—when they go forth in robbing, they bless

451 feeding, supplying provision for **452** laymen who have taken vows **453** *a week together:* seven days in a row **454** greed **455** silly **456** *cumbrous conditions:* burdensome dispositions, behaviors **457** perhaps

458 stipulations, promises **459** grievous; pitiable **460** nothing **461** pertain to **462** custom, practice **463** i.e., the people of the region **464** the week beginning with Pentecost Sunday **465** honorable; respectable **466** engaged in **467** *trow*

ye: do you suppose **468** completely **469** become **470** *wigs and cracknels:* wine-dipped buns and biscuits **471** done away with **472** *Go me to:* Consider **473** even if **474** great many

themselves and pray God send them good speed,[475] that they may meet with a good purse, and do harm, and take none. Shall we therefore find a fault with every man's prayer, because thieves pray for speed in robbery? This hath, as I say, no reason although[476] they were a great people that abused a good thing. And whereas the worst that ye assign in our matter is that, as ye say, the people do idolatry, in that ye say, they take the images for the saints themselves, or the rood[477] for Christ himself—which, as I said, I think none doth (for some rood hath no crucifix[478] thereon; and they believe not that the cross which they see was ever at Jerusalem, nor that it was the holy cross itself; and much less think they then that the image that hangeth thereon is the body of Christ himself)—and although some were so mad so to think, yet were it not, as ye call it, 'the people.' For a few doting[479] dames make not the people. And over[480] this, if it were—as ye would have it seem—a whole people indeed, yet were not a good thing to be put away for the misuse of bad folk."

THE TWELFTH CHAPTER
The author confirmeth the truth of our faith and usage in the worship of images by the consent of the old holy doctors of the Church approving the same (as appeareth well in their writings), whom God hath by many miracles testified to be saints. The messenger eftsoon[481] doubteth whether we can be sure that the miracles told by them were true or not, or themselves saints or not. Whereupon the author proveth that, of any miracles told by any saints, we may be most sure of theirs, and consequently by their miracles most sure of them that they be surely saints. And in this chapter also proveth that the miracles and consent of those holy doctors do prove that this must needs be the very true Church, in which they have written, and miracles have been done. Whereupon is finally concluded eftsoons the truth of the principal question; and therewith finisheth the Second Book.

"And we be very sure that the thing is good, and our way good therein, and our belief therein right, not only by reasons and authority (by which I have proved it you more than once already), but also by that[482] all the old holy saints and doctors of Christ's Church—as Saint Jerome, Saint Augustine, Saint Basil, Saint Chrysostom, Saint Gregory, with all such others as plainly we read in their books—did as we do therein, and believed thereof as we believe. And since we see what they believed, we need not to doubt what is best that we believe. For if any sect believed better than other, we be sure of the best were they, that so well believed, and lived therewith, that God hath accepted them for saints, and by miracles openly declared that their faith and living liked[483] him. Whereas on the other side of such as believed otherwise—as were these manifold sects of obstinate heretics—we see not one a saint among them, nor one miracle showed for them."

"I wot nere,"[484] quoth he, "whether this reason that ye make would surely satisfy the other side or no. For men may peradventure answer you that there is many a glorious saint in heaven of whom we see no miracles in earth, nor haply[485] never heard of their name."

"That may well be," quoth I, "and I suppose it very true."

"May it not also be," quoth he, "that though it were hard to think but that of miracles some among so many must needs be true, yet, since some also may be feigned, may it not be that those been[486] feigned which been told to have been done by them whom ye rehearsed?—them, I mean, that of old have written for your party; I mean those whom ye call the old doctors of the Church, and whom the Church taketh for saints."

"This," quoth I, "were worse than anything that we spoke of yet tofore.[487] The worst was, before, that we should pray to no saints. And now ye would either that we should have none—or at the least that we should know none."

"Yes," quoth he, "ye may have saints, and know for saints, and many one since the apostles' time, though those be none whose writing ye would authorize by their sanctifying."

"Then fall you," quoth I, "to that point again that ye think it may be that the Church may take for saints, and worship as saints, them that be none."

"Surely," quoth he, "the proof that ye have laid[488]

---

475 success   **476** even if   **477** cross
478 figure of the crucified Christ
479 foolish   **480** beyond   **481** once

again   **482** *by that:* because   **483** pleased
484 *wot nere:* know not   **485** perhaps

486 have been   **487** *yet tofore:* before this
488 presented

unto me contrary, though it be somewhat probable, yet seemeth me not very strong, nor able and sufficient to strain[489] a man to consent thereto. For though the assistance of God and his Holy Spirit will not suffer[490] his whole Church to agree and consent together in any damnable error, yet may he suffer them well to err in the knowledge and worship of a saint, and mistake for a saint one that were a damnable wretch. For therein were no more danger to man's soul, nor no more honor taken from God, than when the people do worship a host unconsecrated, mistaking it, through the default of an evil priest, for the sacred body of our Lord himself. And this ye doubt not but it is sometimes done."

"Forget not now, by the way," quoth I, "that ye still agree that God will not suffer his whole Church to agree in any damnable error and fall in a false faith. And therewith remember that though it were no damnable error to take one for a saint that were none, or a bone for a relic that were none, yet were it a damnable error to worship any, if we should worship none at all. And therefore, since the Church believeth that we should worship them, that kind of belief can be none error, but must needs be true. Nor that kind of worship can be none idolatry, but must needs be good and acceptable to God. And so, our principal matter standing still sure and fast, we shall see somewhat further whereto your words will weigh and amount. Ye deny not," quoth I, "but there be some saints and some miracles."

"No," quoth he.

"To what purpose," quoth I, "were miracles specially wrought by God? Was it not to the intent to make his messengers known, and the truth of his message, as when he sent Moses to Pharaoh, were not the miracles done by God to make Pharaoh to perceive thereby the truth of his word?"

"Yes," quoth he.

"When Christ," quoth I, "sent his disciples to preach, the power that he gave them to do miracles, was it not for the proof of the doctrine that they taught, as is well witnessed in the Gospel?"[491]

"Yes," quoth he.

"If this be thus," quoth I, "as indeed it is, ye have most cause to believe, of all miracles, those that are told and reported as done for the doctors of Christ's Church, since miracles were specially devised by God for a knowledge of his true messengers and a proof of their message, so that where ye would we should[492] not utterly be deceived in saints and miracles, but yet we might be deceived in doctors whom we take for saints, and in their miracles, now it seemeth on the other side that of all others we be of them and of theirs most sure."

"This is well said," quoth he. "But yet always it runneth in men's minds that miracles may be feigned."

"Be it so," quoth I, "so that it run again in men's minds that all be not feigned. And then, if ye think any true, this reason abideth still: that since miracles were specially given by God for the knowledge of his doctors and declaration of his doctrine, those miracles be specially to be taken for true that be reported to be done by his doctors. For they serve for the comprobation[493] of his holy doctrine. And for because ye say that miracles may be feigned, that[494] we spoke of Moses and Christ's disciples putteth me now in mind: there were of old time also false doctors and miracles falsely feigned, were there not?"

"Yes, marry," quoth he.

"By whom were those miracles feigned?" quoth I.

"Marry," quoth he, "some by men, as there be now, and some by the devil, and haply so there be now too."

"Well, be it," quoth I, "both twain, and[495] ye will. But were there not in the old time both twain found out and vanquished by the true doctors sent by God and true miracles for them wrought by God, as when the serpent of Moses devoured all the serpents made by the witchcraft of the Egyptian jugglers,[496] and when the prophet Daniel did by the steps[497] of the false priests' feet find out the means whereby the meat[498] was eaten that they feigned to be eaten by the idol Bel,[499] and when the prophet Elijah vanquished by miracle the false prophets of Baal?[500] And the holy apostles and disciples of Christ did, at their word, all-to[501] break in pieces the false idols in sight of the paynim people, so that always God hath prepared his true doctors to destroy, by plain miracle, the false miracles whereby men were and might be deceived. Is not this thus?" quoth I.

"Yes," quoth he.

"Well then," quoth I, "if our old holy doctors were false, and their doctrine untrue, and their miracles feigned, it is not enough now to say so. But if any of them that so say be sent by God to re-prove[502] it, then must they prove that they be sent so — and that not in words only, but let some of them come forth and at their word break our im-ages, as Christ's doctors did the paynims'. And to prove our miracles feigned, let them do some very miracles themselves."

"As for miracles," quoth he, "be none[503] article in any man's creed. And there is not so simple a sect of heretics but they might, if they were set thereon, soon match you with miracles — whereof they might feign fifteen in a forenoon. And then, as we said now, it would be thought that though some were untrue, yet all were not lies."

"It were easy indeed," quoth I, "if men were mad among whom they should report them, and would nothing do for the trial."[504]

"Iwis;[505] yet if they did," quoth he, "yet might a few mean-witted[506] men devise and feign a thing of such a fashion that it would be believed, and hard to try[507] the truth out."

"Let it be so," quoth I. "But yet would it not long hold among good Christian people. But God would either bring the falsehood to light, or soon cast it out of credence. What labor took Philostra-tus to make a book full of lies, whereby he would have had Apollonius Tianius in miracles match unto Christ?[508] And when he had all done, he never found one old wife so fond[509] to believe him. But I pray you tell me," quoth I, "be there not of heresies many sects?"

"Yes," quoth he.

"Is there," quoth I, "any more very[510] churches of Christ than one?"

"No more," quoth he.

"Is not that it," quoth I, "that is true?"

"Yes," quoth he.

"Be not," quoth I, "then all the sects of heresies false?"

"Yes," quoth he.

"Who is likely," quoth I, "to feign and lie: that company that is the true party, or some of them that be false?"

"It is," quoth he, "more likely that they should all

lie that be false, than that company that is the true party."

"Then false and feigned miracles," quoth I, "be they lies, or not?"

"What else?" quoth he.

"Then," quoth I, "by your argument it seemeth that they were much more likely to be among every sect of heretics than in the Church."

"So seemeth it," quoth he.

"How happeth it then," quoth I, "if miracles be feigned ware,[511] that among all the false sects of heretics — where such false stuff should be by all rea-son most rife — is none at all spoken of, but miracles told only in the Church of Christ, which is only,[512] as ye agree, the true party?"

"There be," quoth he, "peradventure some done — either miracles or marvels — but they dare not speak of them, for fear of persecution."

"If they were," quoth I, "false marvels only done by the devil, it would not help your matter. For then must you grant very miracles of God only done in Christ's Church. And if there had been very mira-cles of God done for any sect whom we call here-tics, that sect had been no sect of heretics, but the very Church. Or else had God by miracles testified the truth of a false faith, and that is impossible. And thereof should have followed that, except[513] there were of Christ two churches of two con-trary faiths, and both true — which were impossi-ble, else[514] not some, but all the miracles done, told, and wrought in one church had been either feigned or done by the devil — whereby[515] should it follow that our church were not the very Church, but a false sect of heretics, which were, as I have already proved you diverse ways, as far impossible. But now for the more clearness of our party therein, and for the further proof that ours is the sure Church, and only the doctors and the doctrine of our Church approved by miracles, never hath there been any done for the doctors of any sects of heretics. For if there hath any true miracles been done by God, and then that sect not a false sect but the true Church, all the persecution that could have been could never have quenched the fame thereof, as well ap-peareth by the miracles done in our Church in all

502 disprove   **503** *be none*: (they) are not an   **504** *nothing…trial*: not attempt an examination   **505** Certainly   **506** i.e., of average intelligence   **507** test   **508** Lucius Flavius Pilostratus (*ca.*

170–250) wrote *The Life of Apollonius of Tyana* about 220. Apollonius (*ca.* 40–120), a Pythagorean philosopher, is described as performing miracles including healing the sick, raising the dead, and ascending

into heaven.   **509** foolish   **510** true   **511** *feigned ware*: counterfeit goods   **512** alone   **513** unless   **514** otherwise   **515** and thus

such time as both the Jews and the paynims pursued it. Now since there be so many false sects, and but one Church true, and miracles not spoken of in any but in one, it is a good token that the matter and substance of them is true. For else they were as likely to be spoken of in more, since of false and lying sects be so many. And then also, miracles being true, and being done, but in one of all those many companies each calling himself the Church, it is a good proof that the same one in which only[516] they be done is only the very true Church of Christ, to which his Holy Spirit and marvelous Majesty giveth his special assistance. And surely of all miracles that ever God hath wrought for his Church, I see not, in my mind, lightly[517] a more marvelous than that, as many sects of heretics as hath sprungen and parted out of Christ's Church, and each of them laboring to be taken for the very Church, yet hath our Lord hitherto never suffered[518] neither the devil to do any wonder for them that might have the color and face[519] of a miracle, nor—as false as they be themselves—yet hath he not suffered them hitherto not so much to do as feign a miracle for their party. Which is, to my mind, not only great wonder, but also their confessed falsehood considered, a very clear proof that they could never have been kept from it but by the especial providence of God and his tender cure upon[520] his chosen Church, by which it hath liked him hitherto[521] that miracles, among other things, have been one good and sure mark[522] between his Church and all those erroneous sects that been sprungen[523] out thereof and be not his Church, but would seem to be. For as for paynims[524]—Turks and Saracens, which[525] by open profession are of another flock, and bear not the name of Christ, nor look for him[526]—he suffereth the devil sometimes to delude with wonders and marvels. But the Jews that still gape after[527] him, their miracles, as far as I can hear, be gone, to the intent they may know that he hath left them and given them up which was wont[528] to work all those wonders for them. Now as for heretics which falsely feign themselves to be his own flock, and presume to bear and profess his name, he keepeth them from the honor of any miracles doing, to the end that the lack thereof among all their sects, and the

doing thereof in his only Church, may be among many other things one good mark and sure token whereby all these false sects of them may be discerned and known from his very true Church— that is to say, from the whole congregation of true Christian people in this world which,[529] without intermixtion of obstinate heresies, profess the right, Catholic faith.

"Now is it not only true that miracles be wrought only in the Church, and thereby do show which is the very Church, but also they do show that those holy doctors for whom God hath showed them were good men and of the right belief. For if it were as ye would of late have had it seem—that it might peradventure be so that the holy doctors of our faith (whom we take for saints) were indeed no saints, nor saved souls, but haply[530] those were saved souls and saints in heaven (though it were unknown here in earth) which did teach the doctrines here that we now call heresies—then were it a wondrous change, that whereas God among the Jews provided that in every age there were some good men by their good living and his high miracles so notable and well known to the people that men had them always like bright lively[531] stars, whose doctrine they might boldly believe, and whose living they might surely follow, he would now in his special Church of Christ, not only do nothing like, but also do clean the contrary. For if he should take that way that ye say—to leave,[532] ever since the apostles' days, all the true interpreters of his and their holy writing, and doctors of the very true faith, lie to the world unknown, and then, on the other side, set forth with miracles, or suffer[533] so to be set forth with marvels, that his Church should take and accept for saints such evil persons or hypocrites as construed the Scripture wrong, and ever since his apostles' days have taught false errors, and led his flock out of the right way in a bypath to hellward with wicked heresies and idolatry—then hath not God sent the Holy Ghost, and himself also tarried still therein, to teach his Church the truth as he said he would. But he then had helped to beguile them himself, which were impossible for God to do, and more than blasphemy for any man to think. For this were not like the sufferance[534] of an unconsecrated host, whereof

---

516 alone   **517** easily   **518** allowed   **519** *color and face:* semblance and appearance   **520** *cure upon:* concern for; care for   **521** *liked him hitherto:*

pleased him up to this time   **522** i.e., of the distinction   **523** *been sprungen:* have sprung   **524** pagans   **525** who   **526** *look for him:* expect him (to return)   **527** *gape*

after: look longingly for   **528** *which was wont:* who made it his practice   **529** who   **530** perhaps   **531** living   **532** let   **533** allow   **534** permitting

ye put the example, wherein the people's invincible ignorance[535] with their devout affection may, without harm to their souls, be suffered in the thing that seldom happeth, and endureth for so short a while. But if God would leave all good doctors unknown, and suffer his Church to be deceived with miracles and marvels done by them that taught heresies and set forth idolatry, then should himself, as I say, not only suffer his honor and right faith and religion to be perpetually lost, but help also himself to destroy it—which, whoso could think possible were worse than Judas, and more mad than any man in Bedlam. And therefore can it not in no wise be that the Church can be deceived in that they take for saints these holy doctors of the Church. Nor, they so being, can it in any wise be that the doctrines wherein they consent and agree can be false or untrue. Among which doctrines, since the things whereof we speak—I mean the praying to saints, the worship of images, reverencing of relics, and going in pilgrimages—is a part, as by their books plainly doth appear, we may well and surely conclude that none of these things be damnable or displeasant to God, but things highly to his contentation[536] and pleasure. And since we further perceive that their books be written in diverse regions and sundry ages, we thereby well perceive that these things be parcel of the rites, usages, and belief of Christ's Church, not only now and of late, but continually from the beginning hitherto. And since it is plainly proved

you that the Church can in no wise be suffered of God to fall into any damnable error thereby, it is yet most surely concluded that these things be none such, and consequently proved that no text of Scripture seeming to sound to the contrary can be so taken or understood, nor that the Church cannot in prejudice of the faith misunderstand the Scripture. And that the substantial points of the faith therefore learned of the Church is one of the surest rules that can be founden for the right interpretation of Holy Scripture. And that no sect of heretics can be the Church of Christ, but that our church is the very[537] Church. And it is also clearly proved that the matter of miracles therein daily done is neither feigned by men, nor done by the devil, but only by the mighty hand of God. And such objections as ye laid unto the contrary of any point aforesaid be, as far as I can see, sufficiently answered, except that ye have any further objection to lay therein. Which if ye have, ye get no thanks to spare."

Whereunto he said—and swore therewith—that he so fully felt himself answered and contented therein that he thought himself able therewith to content and satisfy any man that he should happen to meet with that would hold the contrary. Whereupon for that day we departed till another time, in which we appointed to peruse the remnant of the things that he had in the beginning purposed.[538]

The end of the Second Book

535 *invincible ignorance:* a kind of ignorance that would excuse an otherwise sinful act. See Aquinas, *Summa theologica* 1-2, q. 76, art 3.   **536** satisfaction   **537** actual   **538** proposed

THE THIRD BOOK

THE FIRST CHAPTER

The messenger, having in the meanwhile been at the university, showeth unto the author an objection
5 *which he learned there against one point proved in the First Book: that is to wit,[1] that in the necessary points of the faith, equal credence is to be given to the Church and to the Scripture. Which objection the author answereth and dissolveth.[2]*

10 About fortnight after, your friend came again in a morning, new comen from the university, where he was, as ye wot,[3] at learning ere he came at[4] you. And there had he now, as he said, visited some of his old acquaintances. And, upon occasion rising
15 in communication, had again repeated with some of them—very fresh learned men—good part of our former disceptation[5] and reasoning had between us before his departing. Which, as he said, they took great pleasure in, and much wished to
20 have been present thereat. But surely he said that some of them seemed to take very sore[6] to heart the hard handling[7] of the man that ye write of,[8] and the burning of the New Testament, and the forbidding of Luther's books to be read, which were, as
25 some of them thought, not all things[9] so bad as they were made for.[10] And finally, touching the burning of heretics, there were some that thought the clergy therein far out of right order of charity.

"I am," quoth I, "very glad that it hath been your
30 hap[11] to be there, not so much for anything that ye have showed them of our communication had already, concerning the praying of[12] saints, worshipping of images and relics, and going in[13] pilgrimage (wherein I think ye told them no novelty, for I
35 doubt not but they could have told you more of the matters themselves than ye have heard or could hear of me), as for that I think that among them, being, as ye say, so well-learned, ye have either heard somewhat[14] whereby ye be in some part of these matters
40 (that we shall speak of) already satisfied, whereby our business therein may be the shorter, or else ye be the more strongly instructed for the other part,[15]

whereby our disputation shall be the fuller, and the matters the more plainly touched, for the more ample satisfaction of such as yourself or your master 45
shall hereafter happen to find in any doubt of[16] these things that we shall now touch and treat of."

"Indeed," quoth he, "somewhat have they showed me their minds therein, as in some part of the matters ye shall hear when we hap to come to them." 50

"That shall I gladly hear," quoth I, "and shape you such answer as my poor wit[17] will serve me. But yet I pray you be plain with me in one thing: Were they satisfied, and held themselves content, in those things that were at last with much work agreed be- 55
tween us?"

"In good faith," quoth he, "to say the truth, all were save[18] one, and he in all things save one. And to your great praise and high commendation, they said that in these matters—" 60

"Nay," quoth I, "let their praise pass, lest ye make me too proud. But I pray you tell me, not which one misliked one thing, but what one thing it was, and why he misliked it."

"Surely," quoth he. "For aught[19] that I could 65
bend[20] upon him, he could never agree that the faith of the Church out of[21] Scripture should be as sure[22] and bind us to the belief thereof as the words of Holy Scripture."

"Why," quoth I, "if ye remembered well what we 70
said, ye had enough to prove him that."

"Truth is it," quoth he, "so had I, and so did I— and in such wise[23] that diverse ways I brought him to the bay[24] that he wist[25] not how to void.[26] But then said he to me that he would not do with me as 75
I had done with you. 'Nor it was,' he said, 'no wisdom for a man against his adversary to use always the buckler hand.[27] For so must all the peril be his, and his adversary stand in surety.[28] But, on the other side, if he use the sword therewith,[29] and strike 80
among,[30] and drive the other to his defense, so may he hap to put him in half the peril.' And likewise he said that if I proved my part[31] so clearly to him that he could not say nay, yet if I would again answer

---

1 say **2** resolves **3** know **4** *ere… at:* before he came to **5** disputation
6 grievously **7** *hard handling:* harsh treatment **8** Thomas Bilney (*ca.* 1495–1531)
9 *all things:* altogether **10** out to be

11 fortune **12** to **13** on **14** something
15 side **16** about **17** intellect **18** except
19 all; anything **20** bring to bear **21** *out of:* apart from **22** certain; trustworthy
23 (a) manner **24** *brought… bay:* backed

him into a corner **25** knew **26** escape
27 *use… hand:* use always the hand that holds the shield; i.e., be always on the defensive **28** safety **29** also **30** now and then **31** side

him another while,[32] he might peradventure[33] bring me to the same point on the other side; and then should the matter stand yet at large.[34] For of two contraries, if both the parts be proved, then stand they both unproved. 'And therefore,' quoth he, 'I pray you answer me this a little: When you believe the Church, wherefore[35] do you believe the Church? Do you not believe it because it saith truth?'

"'Yes, marry,'[36] quoth I. 'What else?'

"'And how know you,' quoth he, 'that the Church saith truth? Know ye that any other wise than by Scripture?'

"'Nay, marry,' quoth I, 'but then by plain Scripture I know it very well. For the Scripture telleth me that God hath fully taught and teacheth his Church, and biddeth me believe his Church.'

"'Lo,' quoth he, 'for all your long process,[37] see whereto ye be brought now. Ye would in any wise before — and ye seemed to prove it, too, all the while that ye argued and I answered — that the Church was, in all necessary points of our faith, as much to be believed as the Scripture, and that we should not have believed the Scripture but for the authority of the Church, as ye say Saint Augustine saith. And now, when I argue and ye answer, I have driven you to the wall in three words,[38] and proved unto you that the Church is not to be believed, nor that yourself believeth it not, but for the authority of the Scripture.' And after that he had thus said, the remnant that were present allowed it much;[39] and I was therewith astonied,[40] and said I would advise me[41] further thereon. But he laughed and said he would lend me this,[42] and not to be hasty on[43] me; for he would give me respite of payment till I had spoken with you again."

When your friend had told, "Forsooth,"[44] quoth I, "he dealt with you like a courteous creditor. And since he hath given you so long day,[45] you shall not need — I trust — to die in his debt. And, to say the truth, ye owe him not much. For ye may bear him his own again[46] and tell him his money is nought.[47] But I espied[48] it is, as he saith, a great advantage for him to oppose.[49] For he hath such craft in arguing that he will soon bring the answerer to a perilous point, if he happen on one that will answer him handsomely,[50] as he would have him. But on the other side, if he had happened on one that had answered him as frowardly[51] as the boy answered one Caius, a poet at Cambridge, then had he, by his opposing part,[52] won nothing at all. For Caius, for his pleasure playing with the boy, being a young sophister,[53] said that he would prove the boy an ass. Which, when the boy denied, 'Well,' quoth Caius, 'thou wilt grant me this first: that everything that hath two ears is an ass.'

"'Nay, marry,[54] Master, will I not!' quoth the boy.

"'No wilt thou?' quoth Caius. 'Ah, wily boy, there thou wentest beyond me. For and[55] thou wouldst have granted me that, I would have proved thee an ass anon.'[56]

"'Marry, Master,' quoth the boy, 'ye might well; and so might every fool do.'

"'Well,' quoth Caius, 'I will go now another way to work with thee. Thou wilt grant me that every ass hath two ears.'

"'Nay, marry, will I not, Master!' quoth the boy.

"'Why so, boy?' quoth he.

"'Marry, Master,' quoth he, 'for some ass may hap to have never one; for they may be cut off both.'

"'Nay,' quoth Caius, 'I give thee over;[57] for thou art too froward a boy for me.' And so, if ye had not granted what he would,[58] he had[59] nothing won at your hand."

"Why," quoth your friend, "what thing did I grant him that I should not?"

"Forsooth," quoth I, "no more but all that ever ye granted. For first, when he asked you whether the cause why we believe the Church be not because it is true that[60] the Church telleth you, though your answer which ye made therein was not the cause of your redargution,[61] nor the thing whereby ye were concluded,[62] yet answered ye not well thereto when ye granted it."

"Why," quoth he, "wherefore[63] should I believe the Church — or any man else — but because they tell me true?"

"Sometimes," quoth I, "it happeth so; but sometimes it happeth otherwise. For if a known liar tell

---

32 *another while:* in turn   33 perhaps
34 *yet at large:* still unsettled   35 why
36 an exclamation, from "by Mary"; indeed
37 argument   38 *in three words:* with a
few words; in short order   39 approved
40 astonished, bewildered   41 *advise me:*
deliberate   42 this one   43 *not to be hasty*

on: would not demand quick repayment
from   44 In truth   45 *so long day:* such
a long time before the due date   46 *may
bear… again:* can take him back what
he lent you   47 of no value, worthless
48 noted that   49 be the one on the offensive   50 suitably; helpfully   51 contrarily

52 *had he… part:* he would have, by being
on the offensive   53 sophist   54 indeed
55 if   56 right away   57 *give thee over:*
give up on you   58 wanted (you to grant)
59 would have   60 what   61 *redargution:*
being disproved   62 refuted   63 *Why…
wherefore:* Well … why

you a known-true tale, ye will believe him because he telleth you truth. But, now, if a known-true man tell you an unknown truth,[64] ye believe not him because the thing is truth, but ye believe the thing to be truth because ye believe the man to be true. And so believe you the Church, not because it is truth that the Church telleth you, but ye believe the truth of the thing because the Church telleth it. But yet was not that answer of his, as I say, the thing that confounded[65] you. For now if ye so should have answered him as I have showed you, though ye should have somewhat blenched him[66] therewith, yet he might — and would, of likelihood — have gone further with you, and have asked you whereby ye know that ye should believe the Church. And what answer would ye then have made thereunto?"

"Marry," quoth he, "then might I have said that I believe the Church because that in such necessary points of faith the Church cannot err."

"That had[67] been very well said," quoth I. "But he would have asked how ye know that."

"Then must I," quoth he, "have said the same that I did: that I know it by plain and evident Scripture that the Church in such things cannot say but true. And then would I have laid[68] him the texts that ye alleged[69] unto me for the same purpose before."

"If ye so had said," quoth I, "ye had answered him truly, but yet not with your most[70] advantage."

"Why so?" quoth he.

"For," quoth I, "your next answer were[71] to say, as truth is, that ye believe that the Church in such things cannot err, because ye believe that God hath taught and told the same things to his Church."

"Then would he have asked me further," quoth your friend, "what thing maketh me believe that God hath taught and told the Church those things."

"So would he have asked you," quoth I, "and so might he well."

"Then were we comen," quoth your friend, "unto the same point again, that he should have concluded[72] me as he did before."

"Nay," quoth I, "not if ye answered thereto well."

"Why," quoth he, "what could I answer else, but clearly grant him that I believe that thing for none other cause but only because the Scripture so showeth me?"

"No could ye?"[73] quoth I. "What if never Scripture had been written in this world? Should there never have been any church or congregation of faithful and right-believing people?"

"That wot I nere,"[74] quoth he.

"No do ye?"[75] quoth I. "Were there never any folk that believed in God, and had a true faith, between Adam and Noah — of such as never heard God speak themselves?"

"Yes," quoth he, "I suppose there were some; but it should seem there were very few. For there were few saved in Noah's ship."

"The world was at that time," quoth I, "waxen[76] worse and worse, as it waxeth now. But it is not unlikely that there were many right-believing people in the meantime."

"That is," quoth he, "likely enough."

"Now as for the days," quoth I, "of Noah himself, though there were few saved alive, yet proveth not that the people to be all miscreants[77] and without faith. For it fared by[78] them as it fareth now by us: that there were many that believed the truth and had a faith, but they followed the flesh and sank for their sin. For there appeareth no further upon the story in Genesis but that the world was washed with the water of the great flood for the filth of their fleshly living.[79] And albeit that[80] in the First Epistle of Saint Peter it might seem some incredulity[81] in them,[82] yet may it be that it stretched no further than to the lack of fear in the credence of God's commination,[83] and overmuch hope and boldness[84] of God's further favor and sufferance — whereof they repented after, too late for this present life, and yet many, through God's mercy, not too late for the final salvation of their souls (as appeareth by the good and great clerk Nicholas de Lyra, upon[85] the same place),[86] which could in no wise[87] have been so if they had lacked faith. Which faith — what Scripture had they to teach them, or all the men in effect that any faith had from Adam thitherto?[88]

---

64 *an unknown truth:* something you don't already know is the truth **65** defeated **66** *blenched him:* made him flinch; disconcerted him **67** would have **68** cited **69** quoted **70** *with your most:* to your best **71** would be **72** *that he should have concluded:* so that

he would have refuted **73** *No could ye?:* You could not answer otherwise? **74** *wot I nere:* know I not **75** *No do ye?:* You don't? **76** growing **77** unbelievers **78** *fared by:* happened with **79** See Gn 6:4–8:22. **80** although **81** seem there was some unbelief **82** See 1 Pt 3:19–20.

83 punishment **84** presumption **85** in his commentary on **86** See Nicholas de Lyra (1270–1349), *Postillae perpetuae in universam S. Scripturam.* **87** way **88** until then

Was there also no faithful folk at all from Noah to Moses — nor himself neither till he had the Law delivered him in writing? Did Abraham never believe more but those things that we find in Scripture specially to have been told him by God? Was his father and all his friends[89] infidels? Were there no people besides, in all that long time, that had a right faith?"

"Yes," quoth your friend, "that I think verily there was."

"That may ye," quoth I, "be sure there was. And why did any man then believe the Church — that is to wit, the number and congregation of good and right-believing folk, of whose mouth and tradition he heard the true belief — against the wrong and misbelief that was in all the world among infidels and idolaters besides? Why did any man this, but because they believed that God hath taught those things to good men before, and that it was and would be still[90] the good lesson of God? And then what thing made them to believe that God had taught them so? It was not the Scripture that made them believe that, as ye would[91] that nothing can tell us that belief but the Scripture. I pray you tell me what Scripture hath taught the Church to know which books be the very[92] Scripture, and to reject many others that were written of the same matters — and that in such wise written, and in the names of such men, as, saving[93] for the Spirit of God given to his Church, a natural wise man had[94] been likely enough either to have taken both for Holy Scripture, or to have rejected both as none Holy Scripture. And surely in the receipt of the one and rejection of the other, there would have been at the leastways such diverse opinions that the whole Church had never taken all the one sort and rejected all the other, had not that Holy Spirit inspired that consent,[95] *qui facit unanimes in domo* ('which maketh the Church all of one mind and accord').[96] And therefore, albeit that against them that[97] nothing will believe but Scripture, we prove the authority of the Church by Scripture, and in such wise prove it them by Scripture that they shall be fain[98] either further to grant that they be bounden to believe the Church in things not specified in Scripture, and as fully as they believe the Scripture itself,

or else they shall deny the Scripture and all, yet should we have believed the Church if never Scripture had been written, as those good faithful folk did that believed well before the Scripture was written. And now the Scripture itself maketh us not believe the Scripture, but the Church maketh us to know the Scripture. And God without[99] Scripture hath taught his Church the knowledge of his very Scripture from all counterfeit Scripture. For it is not, as I say, the Scripture that maketh us to believe the Word of God written in the Scripture — for a man might (as haply[100] many doth) read it altogether and believe thereof never a whit[101] — but it is the Spirit of God that, with our own towardness[102] and good endeavor, worketh in His Church, and in every good member thereof, the credulity and belief whereby we believe as well the Church concerning God's words taught us by the Church, and by God graved[103] in men's hearts, without Scripture, as his holy words written in his Holy Scripture. And thus ye perceive that where ye granted him that so did oppose you that we believe the Church by none other way but by the Scripture, there did ye not answer him well. For we beside the Scripture do believe the Church, because that God himself, by secret inspiration of his Holy Spirit, doth (if we be willing to learn) teach us to believe his Church, and also, if we will walk with him, leadeth us into the belief thereof by the selfsame means by which he teacheth us and leadeth us into the belief of his Holy Scripture. For likewise as when we hear the Scripture or read it, if we be not rebellious but endeavor ourselves to believe, and captive[104] and subdue our understanding to serve and follow faith, praying for his gracious aid and help, he then worketh with us, and inwardly doth incline our heart into the assent of that[105] we read, and after a little spark of our faith, increaseth the credence in our incredulity — so doth his goodness in like wise incline and move the mind of every like toward and like well-willing body[106] to the giving of fast[107] and firm credence to the faith that the Church teacheth him in such things as be not in the Scripture, and to believe that God hath taught his Church those points by his holy word without writing. And now

---

89 relatives   **90** always   **91** would have it   **92** true; actual   **93** except   **94** *a natural wise man had:* a man wise from natural reason would have   **95** consensus   **96** Ps 67(68):7   **97** who   **98** obliged   **99** outside of; apart from   **100** unfortunately   **101** *never a whit:* not a bit; not in the least   **102** receptivity; cooperativeness   **103** engraved   **104** restrain   **105** what   **106** *like … body:* similarly cooperative and well-meaning person   **107** steadfast

if ye had answered him thus, I believe surely that ye had clearly[108] disarmed him and broken his gay sword in twain.[109] Which in my mind, I promise you, how gaily soever it glitter in one's eye for a flourish,[110] yet who[111] fight therewith shall find it neither sharp nor sure, if it fall on a good buckler,[112] and not on a naked[113] man."

"By my troth,"[114] quoth your friend, "so seemeth me now too. And though the brightness bleared mine eye at that time, yet I trust he shall win no worship thereof[115] when we meet again."

THE SECOND CHAPTER

Incidentally somewhat is there touched the superstitious fear and scrupulosity that the person abjured[116] did, as it is said, begin with. The weariness whereof drove him to the delight of such liberty as brought him to the contempt of the good devout[117] things used commonly in Christ's Church. And in this chapter is somewhat touched the good mean manner[118] between scrupulous superstition and reckless negligence that would[119] be used in the singing or saying of divine service.[120]

"But surely, sir, concerning the man's abjuration[121] that we spoke of, they be marvelously persuaded that he had much wrong. Not in that the opinions were Catholic which were laid to his charge[122] (for therein have ye said enough), but in that he was wrong borne in hand that he had[123] preached them, where he did not so. And thus be they very credibly informed, both by word and writing of such as were present thereat. And therefore long I sore,[124] and would be very glad, to hear how those matters[125] were proved."

"Now and[126] I am," quoth I, "for my part very sorry, so help me God, to lose time therein, as a thing in effect fruitless, saving[127] that it may be peradventure a fruitful example that no man be light[128] to believe such things hereafter as he shall hap to hear

spoken against the Church in the favor of any man condemned[129] of heresy, while[130] he seeth as much said against the judgment[131] of this man—wherein, so to say, they can have no more hold[132] than if they would say the crow were white. And in good faith, to say the truth, there cannot in my mind be a more meet[133] example to match their words withal. For likewise[134] as he that would say the crow were white must, if he will be believed, go tell the tale to a blind man, and may percase[135] with him be as well believed as one that will say the contrary, till that he be—either by more men or men of more honesty[136]—put after[137] out of credence, so must these folk that thus talk and write of him seek (as they do indeed) such hearers as be blind in the matter and know nothing thereof, whom they persuade, with false suggestions, to conceive an evil opinion of the judges, to incline their hearts first, for pity, to the favor of the man, and after to the favor of the matters that he was abjured for. I have myself seen a letter written out of London by a priest reputed honest—howbeit indeed,[138] as I saw it proved after, a plain pestilent heretic—in which letter he wrote that the man we now talk of did no more abjure any heresy than he had done himself, or the man that he wrote unto. And yet was his writing as false as God is true. Wherewith he labored covertly to make the man believe that the opinions were none heresies, and that he which was pretended[139] to have abjured them had not so done indeed, but had well avowed them and stiffly abidden[140] by them. Lo, thus do such as are of that sect set forth their matters[141] with lies. And reason is it that they so do. For since their sects be false, lies be for them most meet.[142] And yet is it a mad thing of them to boast of him. For he forthwith[143] forsook them, and ever before his judges he confessed from the beginning that the matters were plain, false heresies—and the holders therewith[144] heretics—saying for himself that he never preached them. And so had they no cause to be proud of him, which[145] in open audience, at the first word, refused[146] and condemned them. But they—haply[147]

---

108 *had clearly:* would have completely 109 two 110 *for a flourish:* when being flourished 111 whoever 112 shield 113 unarmored 114 truth; trustworthiness 115 *worship thereof:* honor by it 116 who renounced under oath his heresies 117 devotional 118 *mean manner:* middle way 119 should 120 the Divine Office

or Prayers of the Hours 121 formal renunciation under oath 122 *which… charge:* with which he was charged 123 *wrong… had:* unjustly characterized as having 124 greatly 125 charges 126 even if 127 except 128 *be light:* should be quick 129 convicted 130 when 131 trial 132 basis, relevance

133 fitting 134 just 135 perhaps 136 respectability 137 afterwards 138 *howbeit indeed:* although in fact 139 alleged 140 stood 141 contentions; ideas 142 fitting 143 immediately 144 besides; also 145 who 146 repudiated 147 maybe

thinking that for all his denying with his mouth, he favored still indeed them and their heresies in his mind—pardoned therefore those words, which they thought spoken but of infirmity, for fear and faint heart. And therefore would they be glad yet, among men that knew not the matter, to maintain and uphold his authority against[148] a better time. And surely this that I shall tell you have I heard reported, howbeit[149] I will not warrant[150] it for truth. But yet have I, as I say, heard it reported right credibly that the man we speak of, which[151] was abjured, used among some of that sect to say, 'Let us preach and set forth our way. And if we be accused, let us say we said not so; and yet some of them shall we win always the while.'[152] And albeit I will not, as I say, warrant you that he thus said, yet I assure you, to my mind his manner in his matter before his judges was as consonant as could be to that intent and purpose. For surely the effect[153] of his defense was nothing else but, against a well and plainly proved matter, an obstinate shameless nay."

"By my troth," quoth your friend, "I marvel me much thereof. For he was called a good man and a very devout."

"I will not," quoth I, "as I told you in the beginning, go about to reprove his living, since the question standeth not but in[154] his teaching; and yet may I be bold with you to tell you what I have heard. He was (as it was said) after that he fell[155] from the study of the law (wherein he was a proctor[156] and partly well-learned) unto the study of Scripture— he was, as I say, very fearful and scrupulous, and began at the first to fall into such a scrupulous holiness that he reckoned himself bounden so straitly[157] to keep and observe the words of Christ after[158] the very letter that, because our Lord biddeth us when we will pray, enter into our chamber and shut the door to us,[159] he thought it therefore sin to say his service[160] abroad,[161] and always would be sure to have his chamber door shut unto him while he said his Matins.[162] Which thing I indeed heard him once deny in an honorable presence.[163]

"But I heard again another man—more credible than twain of him (and if I had said than such ten, I think I lied[164] not), and one of his best-proved friends—avow it in his face for truth. Howbeit,[165] I tell you not this thing for any great hurt in the man. For it was more peevish[166] and painful than evil and sinful. But surely men say that in conclusion,[167] with the weariness of that superstitious fear and servile dread, he fell as far to the contrary, and under pretext of love and liberty waxed so drunk of the new must[168] of lewd[169] lightness of mind and vain gladness of heart, which he took for spiritual consolation, that whatsoever himself listed[170] to take for good, that thought he forthwith[171] approved by God, and so framed himself a faith, framed himself a conscience, framed himself a devotion wherein him list;[172] and wherein him liked, he set himself at liberty."

"And if it so were," quoth your friend, "then ye see, lo, what cometh of this saying of service."

"Of saying service?" quoth I. "This is much like as at Beverley[173] late,[174] when much of the people being at a bear-baiting, the church fell suddenly down at Evensong[175] time and overwhelmed[176] some that then were in it. A good fellow that after heard the tale told, 'Lo,' quoth he, 'now may you see what it is to be at Evensong when ye should be at the bear-baiting.' Howbeit, the hurt was not therein—being at Evensong—but in that the church was falsely[177] wrought. So was in him or any man else no harm but good in saying of divine service; but the occasion of harm is in the superstitious fashion that their own folly joineth thereunto, as some think they say it not but if[178] they say every psalm twice."

"In faith," quoth your friend, "then if I were as he, I would mumble it up apace[179] or else say none at all."

"That were as evil," quoth I, "on the other side. There is a mean may serve between both."

"Yea," quoth he, "but wot[180] ye what the wife said, that complained to her gossip[181] of her husband's frowardness?[182] She said her husband was so wayward[183]

---

148 in anticipation of 149 although
150 guarantee 151 who 152 *the
while:* in the meantime 153 sum or
substance 154 *standeth … in:* concerns
nothing except 155 *after that he fell:*
after he turned 156 advocate; defense
attorney 157 *straitly:* strictly; rigorously
158 according to 159 See Mt 6:6.

160 prayers called the Divine Office
161 outside that room 162 morning
prayers 163 *an honorable presence:*
the presence of a high-class person
164 would have lied 165 However
166 silly 167 *in conclusion:* finally
168 wine 169 wicked 170 wished,
desired 171 immediately 172 wished

173 a town in Yorkshire, in northeastern
England, and a major pilgrimage destination 174 recently 175 Vespers; Evening
Prayers 176 crushed 177 improperly
178 *but if:* unless 179 quickly
180 know 181 female friend 182 bad
disposition 183 capricious; self-willed

that he would never be pleased. 'For if his bread,' quoth she, 'be dough-baken,[184] then is he angry.' 'Marry, no marvel,' quoth her gossip. 'Marry, and wot ye what, gossip?' quoth she. 'And if[185] I bake it all to hard coals, yet is he not content neither, by Saint James.' 'No,' quoth her gossip, 'ye should bake it in a mean.' 'In a mean?'[186] quoth she. 'Marry, I cannot happen on it.' And so in a pair of Matins it is much work to happen on the mean. And then to say them too short[187] is lack of devotion, and to say them too seriously is somewhat superstitious. And therefore the best way were, in my mind, to say none at all."

"Yea," quoth I, "but then is God as wayward a husband as ye spoke of, that will neither be content with his bread burned to coals nor dough-baken neither."

"By our Lady," quoth he, "but be he content or not, I ween[188] he hath much dough-baken bread among.[189] For the Matins, I tell you, be in some places sung faster than I can say them."

"Peradventure,"[190] quoth I, "so were it need.[191] For if they should sing Matins no faster than ye say them, they should, I ween, sing very few Matins in a year."

"In faith," quoth he. "And[192] some that say them make me to doubt[193] much whether the bees in their hives use[194] to say Matins among them. For even such another buzzing they make."

"Surely," quoth I, "that is as true as it is evil done. For as it is a vice and some fault to be, in the service of God, superstitious instead of religious — over-dreadful[195] and scrupulous instead of devout and diligent — so is it a much more fault to be therein reckless and negligent. 'For accursed is he,' as Holy Scripture saith, 'that doth the work of God negligently.'[196] The peril thereof appeareth by Eutychus, the young stripling that is spoken of by Saint Luke in the Acts of the Apostles, who, falling in sleep while the apostles and the disciples were occupied in reading, preaching, and prayer, fell out of a high window down unto the ground, and there had[197] died — God wot in what case[198] — if the merits of Saint Paul had not recovered him.[199] And now, if

he be of[200] God accursed that negligently doth his work, how much is he more accursed that casteth his work away and leaveth it quite undone — such work, I say, as they be bound to do? But in this matter we spend more time than needeth.[201] For it is not much to our present purpose, saving[202] that if it be truth that the man whom we talk of fell first in such superstition, it is the more likely that the devil did cast him therein for none other intent but that he might after, for very weariness thereof, bring him into a contempt of all the things that he was waxen[203] weary of, and set him in a delight of liberty, whereby, with leaning to[204] his own wit,[205] he might reckon everything good or bad as himself would account it, which was the ready way to bring him to these heresies wherein he was now fallen."

THE THIRD CHAPTER
The author showeth that men ought not to be light[206] in mistrusting of any judgment given in the court, and that much less ought any man to be bold in the reproving[207] of a common law. And he showeth also the cause why that the law admitteth more slight[208] witnesses in heinous criminal causes[209] than in slighter matters of covenants or contracts.

"Fallen?" quoth your friend. "What? Abide[210] — we be now gone over the stile[211] ere we come at[212] it. We be yet in question whether it were righteously judged that he was fallen in them or not. For I think it no sin to doubt thereof yet till I hear how the matter[213] was proved."

"Indeed," quoth I, "that is, as ye say, the matter whereof we first have to talk. And yet if ye never heard further therein but that he was judged faulty,[214] although[215] ye had ever accounted the man in your own mind for very virtuous and of right belief, yet since he cannot be good except[216] more men than he be naught,[217] whom ye ought no more to misdeem[218] than him — and specially his judges, which[219] are elected and chosen for indifferent,[220]

---

184 doughy; underdone **185** *And if:* Even if **186** middle way **187** quickly **188** think **189** sometimes; here and there **190** Perhaps **191** *so were it need:* that would be necessary **192** But **193** question **194** are accustomed **195** overly fearful **196** Jer 48:10 **197** would

198 state (of soul) **199** See Acts 20:9-12. **200** by **201** is necessary **202** except **203** grown **204** on **205** mind **206** quick **207** criticizing **208** unreliable **209** *heinous criminal causes:* trials for the most serious crimes **210** Wait **211** steps or the like allowing

passage over or through a fence **212** *ere... at:* before we get to **213** subject of litigation **214** guilty **215** even if **216** unless **217** bad; wicked **218** think ill of **219** who **220** (being) impartial

and which without likelihood of lucre[221] or loss be set to consider, examine, and by their judgment order the cause[222] of another man, whereas the parties may reasonably be more mistrusted themselves, both the accuser, which[223] may speak of[224] malice, and specially the party that is accused, which is well likely to lie for his defense in a matter of peril if he were proved guilty—ye therefore ought not to mistrust the judgment except[225] ye knew the matter untruly judged indeed, or by[226] very good and substantial folk that were present and indifferent had plain and sure information thereof."

"Marry," quoth he, "men think that if any such information may serve, they have had enough thereof by men of wisdom, learning, and honesty, both by mouth and by writing, that were present at all the handling of the matter."

"Well," quoth I, "we shall let their wisdom and their learning alone. But as for their honesty, shall[227] somewhat show itself upon the truth or untruth of their report. Wherein first I pray you, could they say that he was not convicted by as many witnesses, and as good and as credible, as the law requireth?"

"So many," quoth he, "and such, as the law requireth? Would God," quoth he, "that we could as easily find good men and true as we may find so many such.[228] For the law doth, as I hear say, require but twain,[229] and yet in cause[230] of heresy careth not much how bad they be—not though[231] they be heretics themselves. And is not this a wondrous case, that whereas in a matter of a little money, no law receiveth[232] any witnesses but honest and credible, the law made by the Church should in so great a matter—so highly touching[233] the utter destruction of a man in body and goods, with a death the most painful that can be devised—admit and receive a person infamed,[234] and give faith and credence to an infidel, whom they have proved and re-proved false in his faith to God? Nor methinketh the excuse but very slender[235] that I have ere this heard in this point alleged for the Church: that such simple witnesses are admitted in heresy because the crime is so great and so odious that therefore it is worthy to be handled with the more rigor and the less favor.

And this thing will I well agree for good reason[236] in the punishment of the crime, when it is proved, but—'fore God—not in hatred and persecution[237] of the person ere the crime be proved.

"But now, whereas they receive the witness of so slight[238] and false fellows for a proof, they pursue the person and not the crime. Whereas methinketh, on the other side, the more heinous, odious, and abominable that the crime is, the more slow should we be to believe it, and the more sure and plain proof should we have ere we should judge any man for so evil to commit it."

"There is," quoth I, "no doubt but that the world is so bad that there be many so naughty that they will be ready enough to bear false witness. And yet God forbid that it were so bad as ye say: that a man might sooner find such than good men and true. And also, though[239] the witnesses were false and would lie, yet when they be wisely and severally[240] examined, they can seldom so well make their tale before[241] but that their untruth shall in some part appear. And finally, the law bindeth not the judge so precisely[242] to the words of the witness but that it leaveth many things to be pondered and weighed by his wisdom. For it is in[243] a judge as it is in a physician, to whom there be many good books written able to give good light and instruction. And yet whoso[244] would so precisely bind him to his book that he should nothing[245] use the discretion of his brain, he should sometimes do full evil service.[246]

"And yet is it, as Aristotle saith, well done indeed to make the laws so sufficient that as few things as may shall remain and be left to the discretion of the judge, since that the common laws be commonly made by many more[247] than are the particular judges, and also many such as are as wise as judges.[248] And over[249] that, the laws be to the judges a sure and substantial shield, to defend and keep them from the hatred and obloquy[250] that else would follow their sentence on the one side or the other, were their judgments never so just. For men be so partial always to themselves that our heart ever thinketh the judgment wrong that wringeth[251] us to the worse. For be

---

221 gain   222 *order the cause:* settle the case   223 who   224 out of   225 unless   226 from   227 that will   228 such as the law requires   229 two   230 a case   231 even if   232 accepts   233 concerning   234 *person infamed:* convicted felon   235 flimsy   236 *for good reason:* to make good sense   237 prosecution   238 unreliable   239 even if   240 *wisely and severally:* astutely and separately   241 beforehand   242 strictly   243 with   244 whoever   245 not at all   246 *do full evil service:* do him a disservice   247 more in number   248 See *Rhetoric* 1.1.7; *Politics* 3.16   249 besides   250 reproach   251 distresses

it never so right, all reckon we wrong whereof we feel harm.

"But yet of all things specially the law should best content us, for that[252] it is furthest out of all cause of suspicion. For whereas a judge meddleth with a matter present, and persons whom he seeth and knoweth—whereby there may percase[253] favor, hatred, hope, or dread, pity, cruelty, meed,[254] request, or some other affection incline him to misorder himself in the matter—the laws always be made for the punishment of things only that are yet to come; and who shall fall in peril, the makers cannot tell. Haply[255] their foes; haply their friends; and (as men's manners[256] be mutable) peradventure themselves—for which cause, the makers of the law made by[257] the people in causes criminal can be but indifferent. And therefore I marvel the more, since that fault ye find now is not in the judges, but in the laws themselves, wherein ye think it evil[258] provided that, for[259] the hatred of a heinous crime, the person peradventure innocent should fall in peril of a painful death by the taking of more slight[260] witness than would be taken for sufficient in a far slighter matter. Somewhat ye said[261] indeed if the hatred of the crime were all the cause. But therein ye go far wide.[262] For the chief cause why that in heinous criminal cases—as[263] theft, murder, treason, and heresy—the law taketh such for witnesses as it will not accept in a matter of money or other contract made between two parties, is for that else[264] all such crimes should pass forth unpunished—and thereby should the world swarm full of such mischievous[265] people—for lack of proof and trial in the matter, by cause that[266] those which go about such a heinous deed as coming once to knowledge would bring them to a shameful death, do not use[267] commonly to take a notary and honest witness with them to make an instrument[268] thereof (as many men do, and all men may do, in a contract or covenant), but use to[269] do it by stealth, as covertly as they can. By reason whereof, reason moveth and necessity compelleth (except[270] ye would have all go to nought)[271] to receive such records[272] as they be wont[273] to make of their counsel,[274] which[275] be, as ye wot well, none but such as they be themselves. And yet sometimes, which may seem more strange, we be content, and reason would we so were, with the witness of the parties themselves. For if that ten thieves robbed four men at once in a wood, though all the goods that they take away were one common purse of all four—and would[276] all ten, when they were taken, well and stiffly say nay[277]—yet were I their judge (since all witness serveth but only to induce a credence or credulity in the judges' minds), I would not let[278] (except some other circumstance withstood[279] it) to believe the four complainants,[280] in their own matter,[281] against all ten defendants. And albeit that percase a judge might be, in a contract made between two parties, induced in his own mind, without any doubt to the contrary, to give credence in such a point to the one party against the other for the well-known troth[282] and honesty of the one and in the other party the contrary, yet doth the law, through[283] the world almost, prohibit him so to proceed in a civil case, lest they should bring that form of judgment in custom[284] wherein, for lucre ensuing to the party, there were occasion to corrupt the judge—and also forasmuch as that fashion were, in a civil case, clean[285] without necessity, since the parties may if they list[286] for the surety of their bargains,[287] have writing[288] or good witnesses thereat. Which if they list not for to do—either for folly, sloth, or trust—good reason is[289] that it rather turn themselves to loss than, for the redressing of their oversight, to bring in place that form and fashion of judgment that may be the cause of other men's wrongful trouble. Whereas in heinous criminal causes neither is there always such cause of corruption—specially toward the condemnation[290] upon which side only falleth the fault and peril that ye speak of—and is also, as ye see, inevitable necessity for lack of possibility of other record and witness,[291] till ye provide that thieves and murderers will be content to take honest witnesses with them that may bear witness against them."

---

252 *for that*: because   253 perhaps
254 bribery   255 maybe   256 morals
257 about   258 wrongly   259 on account
of   260 unreliable   261 *Somewhat ye said*: i.e., There would be something to what you said   262 astray   263 such as   264 *for that else*: because otherwise
265 evil   266 *by cause that*: because
267 make it their practice   268 official

written record   269 *use to*: usually
270 unless   271 *go to nought*: come to nothing   272 witnesses   273 accustomed
274 *make of their counsel*: take into their confidence   275 who   276 even if
277 *say nay*: deny it   278 hesitate
279 argued against   280 plaintiffs
281 suit   282 integrity; trustworthiness
283 throughout   284 *in custom*: into

common practice   285 completely
286 wish   287 *surety of their bargains*: security of their contracts   288 *have writing*: have them put in writing
289 *good reason is*: it makes good sense
290 *toward the condemnation*: favoring the conviction   291 *record and witness*: witness and testimony

THE FOURTH CHAPTER

The author showeth upon what ground and cause the man was convicted, and also diverse other things not then brought in judgment,[292] whereby it may well appear that he was greatly guilty. And so he showeth incidentally wherefore it were not reason,[293] in a detection[294] of heresy, to suffer,[295] after the witnesses published[296] and the crime well proved, any new witnesses to be received for the party that is accused.

"Howbeit,[297] though this serve for such matters in general, yet for this one matter that we now speak of, we stand far in another case.[298] For this man was not convicted by the words of one or twain, but by the oaths of one or twain above twenty, not such men as we now speak of—Lollards[299] and heretics—but honest men, and almost of all sorts: of religious folk, husbandmen, and gentlemen."[300]

"Indeed," quoth he, "to say the truth, I heard say there were many witnesses. But I heard, again, that he offered to bring twice as many and that of such as were present as well as they, and stood as near as they, and understood as well as they, and slept no more at his preaching than a parson doth at his offering, and would depose[301] plainly for him."

"Whether he said so or not," quoth I, "that can I not tell you, but this I wot well: himself was well-learned in the law, and never could say that he was denied any favor that the law would grant. And many a witness was there to whom he laid none exception,[302] nor could say the contrary but that they were at his sermons and heard him. And then, when he was so clearly convicted by so many, so honest, and so far from all suspicion of corruption, it were peradventure a thing not convenient,[303] after those witnesses published, to bring proofs[304] afresh upon the principal matter. For if it so should be, then should either the new proofs depose the same that the others did before, or else they should depose the contrary, or finally say such thing as neither could make nor mar.[305] Now, if they did the first—that is to say, depose as the first did—then were we no further than we were before, and that time lost and the matter[306] delayed in vain. If they did the third—deposing percase that themselves were not present, or asleep, or not well understood or not well remembered the matter—yet were we still at one stay.[307] Put now the second point (which were, in manner, the only thing that might seem to have any color[308] for him): that the new proofs would depose that they were at the same time present, and stood near him, marked him well, and were also well remembered[309] that he said not so—yea, and peradventure that he said the contrary. This case were possible; but surely it were so seldom likely that it were not worth to change a law therefor.[310] But now if it so should happen, here were a great confusion. And how could any sentence[311] be given if they should believe the second as well as the first?"

"That maketh," quoth he, "no matter. For if the matter appear upon his side thereby—either clear or doubtful[312]—then may the judges acquit and assoil[313] the defendant. And better were it the faulty[314] to be quit[315] than the faultless to be punished."

"It were a strange thing," quoth I, "if the law should, in such a matter as this is, after the witnesses once published,[316] and thereby the matter well proved, then examine other witnesses afresh upon the principal point. This were in my mind perilous, not only for fear of subornation[317] and false instruction of witnesses (a thing easy to be done upon the sight of that that is deposed[318] already before), but also for that[319] if the affirmative be proved—especially in this case of heresy, being by so many sufficiently proved, that one taught and preached such things in his open[320] sermons—if others that were present at the same sermons would now depose the contrary, it may be that the first heard the thing which the second marked not, as many times it happeth. And more likely is it also that one may forget the thing that he heard, than that another should remember that thing that he heard not. And if they would peradventure add thereto that he said the contrary of such things as was proved[321] against him, then can it at the best be no better taken than

---

292 *brought in judgment:* considered during the trial   293 reasonable   294 accusation   295 allow   296 publicly named   297 However   298 situation   299 followers of John Wycliffe (*ca.* 1324–84)   300 *religious…gentlemen:* members of religious orders, farmers, and persons of rank   301 testify   302 *laid none exception:* made no objection   303 appropriate   304 witnesses   305 *make nor mar:* help nor hurt   306 trial   307 *one stay:* the same impasse   308 allegeable ground   309 *were also well remembered:* also clearly remembered   310 for that   311 verdict   312 *clear or doubtful:* clearly or possibly   313 clear; exonerate; acquit   314 guilty   315 acquitted   316 *once published:* have already publicly testified   317 procuring for the purpose of giving false testimony   318 *that that is deposed:* what is testified   319 *for that:* because   320 public   321 established; demonstrated

that he in one sermon said, taught, and preached both twain:[322] that is to wit,[323] the truth and the heresies. In which case, he well were worthy in judgment to acknowledge his fault[324] and be corrected therefor."[325]

"By my troth," quoth he, "yet methinketh ever that it ought to be heard, all that any man will say, and take all to the best for him that is accused—and specially in heresy pretended[326] to be preached where so many be present."

"Surely," quoth I, "what were best, God wotteth, for I cannot tell. But this wot I well: that the wit[327] of the whole world, in effect, agreeth that in all such heinous crimes, reason is clear[328] to the contrary and quite against your mind.[329] And where ye think your mind worthy to take special place in the proof and examination of heresies, surely meseemeth that of all crimes, in heresy might it least be suffered.[330] For well ye wot that heresies be false belief and factious ways full of business.[331] And such as give themselves thereto be sturdy[332] and studious[333] about the furtherance of their seditious sect. And since they be fallen from God and his true faith, they have no great care of truth, nor be very scrupulous in the lending of an oath till they need in like case[334] to be paid again.[335] So that if their 'nay' may stand against other good men's 'yea,' and where the heresy is proved to have been preached, there men may be heard and believed in deposing[336] the contrary, the false preacher may be bold to say what him list.[337] For he shall never fail to have his records[338] ready."

"Yea," quoth he, "but this way would not serve him. For men might take exception to them if they were heretics."

"Nay," quoth I, "not if they be so, but if they be proved so. And that shall they never be if your way were received.[339] For each of their witnesses shall always serve other."

"Forsooth,"[340] quoth he, "it seemeth somewhat perilous, as ye say, if men should, against the affirmative proved, lean to[341] the contrary witnesses for the negative in any crime that is seditious and hath daily folk of evil conscience fervently fall in

thereto. But yet I much marvel of one thing. For I have heard it credibly reported that there were twain, and both beneficed[342] men, both very cunning[343] men, both twain very virtuous men, which[344] heard him preach as well as they did that had deposed against him. And those twain affirmed, and offered to depose, that he preached not the things which he was accused of. And surely, had I been judge, I would have believed those twain above other twenty, except witnesses be taken only by number and not by weight."

"Surely," quoth I, "my mind and yours be not far asunder. For since all witnesses serve to induce the judge's mind to conceive a credence and an opinion—or rather a certain persuasion—on the one side,[345] I could not myself but believe some twain better than some twenty, and would not fail to weigh them, rather than take them by tale.[346] Howbeit," quoth I, "of those twain that ye speak of, the one was indeed such as ye say. But as for the other, was neither then holden very clear,[347] and since that time proved clearly naught.[348] But though[349] the one was, as he was indeed, a very good man, yet for the man's excuse[350] he was no very good witness; nor the other neither, although[351] he had been as good a man as he; nor if they had been forty men more, as good as the better of them both, saying as they did."

"Why?" quoth he, "Said they not well for him?"

"Yes," quoth I, "for as far as they went; but they went not far enough."

"Ah," quoth he, "their words were of likelihood narrowly taken."

"They were," quoth I, "taken as large[352] as they were spoken, which was that he preached not such heresies in a place where they heard him in London. But then was his detection,[353] and the proof made thereupon, of[354] those heresies preached at sundry places out[355] of London—whereby their words went as wide for his excuse[356] as if one that were arraigned for a felony done at Salisbury on Shrove Tuesday[357] brought in good witnesses to the bar that would depose[358] and swear for him that he did no such felony at Shrewsbury on Sheer Thursday,[359] for

322 of them two   **323** say   **324** guilt   **325** *corrected therefor:* punished for it   **326** alleged   **327** mind; intellect, reason   **328** completely   **329** opinion   **330** allowed   **331** trouble   **332** strong; hard to manage; impetuously brave; violent   **333** eager; intent   **334** situation   **335** back   **336** testifying   **337** *what him list:* whatever

he wishes   **338** witnesses   **339** accepted   **340** In truth   **341** *lean to:* side with; believe   **342** in possession of a paid church position   **343** intelligent   **344** who   **345** *on the one side:* on the one side or the other   **346** count   **347** *holden very clear:* considered very convincing   **348** bad   **349** even if   **350** exoneration   **351** even if

352 broadly   **353** *his detection:* the accusation made against him   **354** about   **355** outside   **356** *wide for his excuse:* far astray for the purpose of exonerating him   **357** *Shrove Tuesday:* the day before Ash Wednesday   **358** testify   **359** *Sheer Thursday:* Holy Thursday

they were with him there all that day themselves. But for conclusion he was convicted by more than twenty, and excused by never one. And therefore if his judges wronged him, there was never man had right.[360] And yet were there, besides the witnesses, some letters written of his own hand unto one of his judges — which letters I have since seen — sounding, in mine ears, to[361] as evil heresies as those were that he was detected[362] of. Which letters were never laid into the Court[363] till that, after the proofs published[364] and read, he appeared obstinate, standing still in the denial and proudly refusing to submit himself to his abjuration.[365] For then said his judge, to whom they were written, that since he refused to be reconciled to the Church, he would keep no counsel of his, and therewith brought in those letters and filed them among the records of the Court.

"This man had also been, before that, accused unto the greatest prelate[366] in this realm, who, for his tender favor borne to the university, did not proceed far in the matter[367] against him. But accepting his denial, with a corporal oath[368] that he should, from that time forth, be no setter-forth of heresies, but in his preachings and readings[369] impugn them, dismissed him very benignly, and of his liberal bounty gave him also money for his costs. And yet was none of all these matters laid unto his charge. Which if they had been, would peradventure have put him to peril.

"I was also myself, since his abjuration, present (as it happed) with an honorable prelate at such time as one that was an ancient[370] heretic had been examined, and there had confessed that he had held, taught, and in diverse countries spread about almost all the heresies that any lewd[371] heretic holdeth."

"May ye not tell his name?" quoth he.

"Which of them?" quoth I. "For he had more names than half a leaf can hold."

"Where dwelled he?" quoth your friend.

"Everywhere and nowhere," quoth I. "For he walked about, as an apostle of the devil, from shire to shire and town to town through the realm, and had in every diocese a diverse name. By reason whereof

he did many years much harm ere he could be found out. This heretic, touching[372] all his other heresies, he acknowledged them in conclusion to be naught,[373] and offered to abjure them. But as for despising of images, relics, and pilgrimages, those things, he said, were none heresies, but very good and true points;[374] for he heard them preached, he said, of[375] the 'great doctor,' naming the man we speak of, and told where, confessing also that he liked so well his sermons that he letted[376] not to go twenty miles to hear him. And yet was there since that another heretic that confessed for his own part the like. So that ye may see that good Christian folk were offended with his preaching, and heretics liked his preaching, and grounded their heresies upon his preaching. And then look you what manner of preaching it was likely to be.

"I told you also, right now, that one of those two that ye took for so good and cunning[377] men was after founden worse than many men would have weened.[378] Sir, so was it indeed that he was detected for buying of many books of Luther, Lambert,[379] and Zwingli, with others of that sort — and well proved, and by himself also confessed, that he had bought of those books very many — which he brought forth at last, where he had laid them up no less suspiciously than secretly, and so secretly that all the town should have sought them long ere they should have found them out.

"He had also set a priest of his, and a secular servant of his besides, to buy many of the same suit,[380] and double and treble of one sort,[381] which were by them uttered[382] to diverse young scholars such as they found properly witted,[383] featly[384] learned, and newfangly minded, and thus labored to corrupt the realm. Another parish priest had he before, that kept his cure[385] also, as this other did, which[386] was after proved a very pernicious heretic."

"But what was," quoth he, "done to the master?"[387]

"Forsooth," quoth I, "great favor had he — and as some men said, great wrong too — that he was not openly declared.[388] Howbeit, because he was in good estimation,[389] there was of[390] pity much regard had

---

360 justice 361 to describe 362 accused
363 *laid into the Court:* entered into Court
records 364 *proofs published:* testimonies
(had been) publicly announced 365 formal renunciation on oath 366 *greatest
prelate:* highest-ranking clergyman
367 case 368 *corporal oath:* an oath
made solemn by touching a sacred object,

like a Bible or a relic 369 scriptural
expositions 370 longtime 371 evil
372 regarding 373 wicked 374 *true
points:* valid positions 375 by 376 hesitated 377 intelligent 378 thought
379 Francis Lambert (1486–1530),
Professor at the University of Marburg
380 kind 381 *double and treble of one sort:*

two and three sets of one same collection
382 sold; given out 383 intelligent
384 suitably 385 *kept his cure:* fulfilled
his pastoral responsibilities 386 who
387 leader 388 *openly declared:* publicly
charged 389 *in good estimation:* held in
high esteem 390 out of

to the conservation of his honesty.[391] And nothing was there, in effect, exacted of him but his amendment, with the acknowledging of his fault. For surely that man was of such a poor spirit in Christ that, for any oath that could be given[392] him, long it was ere pride would, for shame, suffer[393] him to say the truth. After which, once confessed with his handwriting then—as far as I have heard, without any other abjuration—there was secretly[394] his solemn oath taken in judgment[395] that he should do no such thing anymore, upon pain of a relapse,[396] and so with certain secret penance dismissed. But the thing that I tell you my tale for is this. This man—besides that all the books in effect which he had bought of this Lutheran sect were diligently read over and studied, and with such manner of notes marked in the margin, and words written of his own hand where the worst matters were, that he left no man in doubt that read them what fervent affection he bore unto them—he had, I say, besides all this, diverse epistles (I wot nere[397] whose, but written were they with his own hand) wherein were plenty of pestilent heresies, and a sermon also, worse than they all, written with his own hand also, ready to be preached, as it seemed, if the world would so change that the time would serve[398] it. And when he was in his examination sore[399] pressed upon to tell for what intent he made such a sermon ready and laid it up so secretly, destitute at last of all excuses that might bear any color[400] of any good cause, 'Well,' quoth he, 'I see well I must tell all. I am loath to hurt anybody.' And thereupon he told how it was made, the most part, by the man that was abjured of whom we specially speak. So that, now setting all this gear[401] together— this man's confession, his secret[402] friend and companion in such matters, his old accusations of like matters, the heretics' confessions that[403] founded their heresies in the same matters upon the authority of his sermon, and besides all this, more than twenty witnesses plainly proving the matter against him—I would fain wit[404] who had right if he had wrong, although[405] there had been used to[406] him more rigor[407] a great deal than there was."

THE FIFTH CHAPTER

The author proveth that the spiritual[408] judges did the man marvelous favor—and almost more than lawful—in that they admitted him to such an abjuration[409] as they did, and that they did not rather leave him to the secular hands.[410]

"Why," quoth he, "what devil rigor could they more have showed for the first time[411] than make him abjure and bear a faggot?"[412]

"Yes," quoth I, "some man had liefer[413] bear twain cold in[414] his neck than have one bear him hot, on a fire at his feet."

"In faith," quoth he, "they could not have done that to him at the first time."[415]

"No," quoth I, "not if he willingly returned to the Church, acknowledging his fault, and ready to abjure all heresies, and penitently submitted himself to penance. And else[416] if he prove himself obstinate and impenitent, the Church neither is bounden nor ought to receive him,[417] but utterly may forsake him and leave him to the secular hands. But now was he so obstinate that he would not abjure of[418] long time. And diverse days were his judges fain,[419] of their favor, to give him—with sufferance of[420] some his best friends, and whom he most trusted, to resort unto[421] him. And yet scantly[422] could all this make him submit himself to make his abjuration. And finally were they fain, for saving of his life, to devise a form of abjuration whereof I never saw the like—nor in so plain a case never would, were I the judge, suffer the like hereafter."

"What manner of abjuration was that?" quoth he.

"Marry," quoth I, "his abjuration was such that he therein abjured and forswore[423] all heresies, acknowledging himself lawfully convicted. But whereas they be wont[424] to confess in their own abjuration that they have holden such heresies, and be guilty thereof, that would he do in no wise; but, as clearly as his fault was proved, and by as many, yet would he not—to die therefor[425]—confess himself faulty, but

---

391 good name; reputation   392 administered to   393 allow   394 privately   395 adjudication   396 i.e., into heresy (with the resultant punishment)   397 *wot nere:* know not   398 be right for   399 greatly   400 semblance   401 matter   402 close   403 who   404 *fain wit:* like to know   405 even if

406 on   407 severity   408 ecclesiastical   409 renunciation of his heresy   410 authorities   411 offense   412 bundle of sticks (Those who renounced heresy carried the wood in public that would have been used to burn them if they had not abjured.)   413 *had liefer:* would rather   414 around   415 *the*

first time: a first offense   416 otherwise   417 *receive him:* take him back   418 for a   419 willing   420 *sufferance of:* permission for   421 *resort unto:* visit   422 scarcely   423 renounced   424 accustomed   425 *to die therefor:* even if the refusal would mean his death

always stood still upon it,[426] in virtue of his oath,[427] that all they belied[428] him."

"It might happen," quoth he, "that he had forgotten that he so had preached."

"That were," quoth I, "great wonder. For I am sure, when he had preached so in so many places, he had not done it of a sudden adventure,[429] but of a deliberate purpose — which, except[430] he fell mad, it were not well possible for him in so great a matter to forget. And besides this, it was also deposed[431] that in a place where he preached, he was after the sermon reasoned withal forthwith,[432] and by an honest layman had it laid unto his charge[433] that he had perilously preached, showing him wherein. Whereunto he made answer, not that he had not said so, nor that he had not meant so, or that they had mistaken and wrongly understood his words, but that he would preach there again soon after, and prove his preaching true by the old doctors[434] of the Church. And this happed[435] him not long before that he was accused. Was it now possible, by your faith,[436] that he could have forgot this?"

"It was," quoth he, "possible enough that altogether[437] was false, and that they lied all. For so might they do by possibility, being but men, and though[438] they had been more than they were. And then he, peradventure knowing that they so did, why should he falsely confess a fault in himself for[439] the falsehood of other folk?"

"That is," quoth I, "true if he so knew it. But how could that be so, against so many proofs[440] sworn and deposing the matter upon their oaths, being, though they were but men, yet men of wit[441] and honesty; and some well-learned also; and men that bore him no displeasure for any other matter than his evil preaching; men almost all such as could have none other matter to[442] him; folk that never had other matter with him; and many of them of little acquaintance, or none, the one with the other, so that there was no fear of conspiring together in one tale?"

"Yet," quoth he, "were it possible that they might lie all."

"And what,"[443] quoth I, "that he had been accused in other places before — as he was indeed not only to the most honorable prelate that I told you,[444] but besides him unto two other bishops too?"

"Well," quoth he, "and yet they that so accused him might happen to lie too."

"And what," quoth I, "that his own secret[445] acquaintance confessed that he made the first draft of that ungracious[446] sermon that I told you?"

"Heard you that yourself?" quoth he.

"Myself," quoth I, "nay; but such as I heard it of were men of more worship[447] and truth thereto than that any man, I ween, would mistrust their tale."

"As worshipful as they were," quoth he, "and as trusty, too, I could mistrust their tale well enough sometimes for lack of indifferency,[448] peradventure as they stood unsworn.[449] And yet though I mistrusted not them all, it might be that they said true, and that the other lied, which[450] for his own excuse[451] laid the first making of that sermon to the other man."

"The laying thereof to him," quoth I, "could not excuse himself. For he confessed that himself liked it and allowed[452] it, and therefore wrote it out, and added also many things more thereto."

"Well," quoth he, "and yet all this might be."

"And what," quoth I, "of the heretics that grounded their opinions upon his sermons?"

"May it not be," quoth he, "that they lied?"

"And what," quoth I, "of them that accused him to other prelates before?"

"By God," quoth he, "even as I told you before, it might be that they lied, well enough."

"And what then," quoth I, "of all those twenty that deposed against him now?"

"Marry," quoth he, "as I told you now, it might be that they did even the same."

"This is," quoth I, "a strange thing to me."

"Why," quoth he, "should this be strange to you? Methinketh it should be strange to no man, but very plain to every man, that it might be so. For I pray[453] you, might it not so be? Were it not possible that they might all lie, and though[454] they were as many more?"

426 *stood still upon it:* kept maintaining   **427** *in virtue of his oath:* under oath   **428** slandered   **429** chance   **430** unless   **431** testified   **432** immediately   **433** *laid unto his charge:* charged against him   **434** *old doctors:* early theologians

435 happened to   **436** *by your faith:* do you truly believe   **437** the whole thing   **438** even if   **439** on account of   **440** witnesses   **441** intelligence   **442** with   **443** what about the fact   **444** *told you:* told you about   **445** personal, close

446 devoid of grace; wicked   **447** reputation   **448** impartiality   **449** *peradventure…stood unsworn:* perhaps as they were not under oath   **450** who   **451** exoneration   **452** approved of   **453** ask   **454** *and though:* even if

"Possible?" quoth I. "That[455] I say not nay, but that it were possible though they were a thousand times as many."

"Well," quoth he, "since it might be so, then put case[456] it was so. Did not he right then in that he still said[457] so? And if he had died therein, had he not died for the truth? For knowing in himself that all they belied him, he was not bound to belie himself with them, and confess against himself an untruth, but had been in great sin if he so should have done. What say ye to this?"

"I say," quoth I, "to this that all the force and effect of your conclusion hangeth upon the case which ye put: that all that ever aught[458] said or deposed against him lied, all the many. Which case ye would needs have granted because it was possible. And then, that case once granted, ye deduce your conclusion very surely. And in good faith, ye bring me therewith so to my wit's end that I wot not well which way to answer you, admitting your case. But ever my mind giveth me that your case, though it be possible, were rather to be granted at a school[459] in argument than at a court in judgment.[460] And I pray you for the proof thereof let me put you another case, which, in good faith, I am half ashamed to put you, saving that ye drive me to seek a shift.[461] And yet shall not my case, in my mind, be much unlike to yours. If it so were that Wilkins had laid a wager with Simkins that in a certain way named[462] between them (usual enough for men and horses both) there had gone of late a horse or two, and that he would so clearly prove it that it could not be the contrary. If Simkins said and laid his wager the contrary, and then they both should choose us for judges, and we coming all four into the way,[463] Wilkins would show us on the ground, part in the clay and part peradventure in the snow, the prints of horse-feet, and of men's feet also, by a long way (ten miles together, and[464] ye will), till they come at[465] a water whereas[466] went away by ship, no man can tell who nor whither (it forceth[467] not for our wise case). But now, if Wilkins would say that he

had won his wager — 'For lo, here ye see the prints of the horse-feet all this way shown, and all with the very nails in them, so that it may be none otherwise but horse hath gone here' — if Simkins, after all this, would say the wager were his — 'For it is not proved that any horse had gone there; for it might be that they were geldings, or mares' — here were we fallen in a great question of the law: whether the gray mare may be the better horse or not, or whether he have a wise face or not that looketh as like a fool as a ewe looketh like a sheep. And in this question, if the parties demurred in[468] our judgment, we might ask advice further of learned men and judges."

"We might," quoth he, "by suit,[469] to be sure of the matter, make it a Chequer Chamber[470] case. Or, saving the Praemunire,[471] we might have it tried in the Rota[472] at Rome."

"Very well," quoth I, "so that I see well by your wit[473] and mine together, one shift or other we should find for a final end therein, if the doubt were in that point. But now if[474] Simkins sticked not thereto,[475] but would say thus: 'Lo, here ye see the men have gone this way; and how can ye then be sure that any horse went here? For I put case,' saith he, 'that these men which went here had horseshoes in their hands, made fast upon long steels,[476] and always as they went pricked them down hard in the ground.'"

"Tut," quoth he, "this were a wise invention."

"Verily," quoth I, "to me it would not seem very gay.[477] But now if Simkins were contentious and would say the wager were his except[478] it be so proved that it can be none otherwise but that horses have of late gone there, and then will say to us, 'Lo, sirs, as ye see it, it may be otherwise. For men might make with their hands all the prints of horseshoes in the ground.' And then if we would say that was never so, he would ask us how can we be sure thereof, while we cannot say nay but[479] it might be so, and then would still press upon us with this question: 'May it not be so?'"

"It may," quoth he, "by possibility be so."

455 to that   **456** *put case:* suppose (for the sake of argument that)   **457** *still said:* continued to say   **458** *that ever aught:* who ever anything   **459** university   **460** a trial   **461** strategem   **462** *in… named:* along a certain path specified   **463** *into the way:* onto the path   **464** if   **465** to   **466** at which   **467** matters   **468** *demurred in:* took exception

to   **469** bringing suit   **470** *Chequer Chamber:* The Court of Exchequer Chamber was the highest regular court in England. Its decisions could be appealed only to the House of Lords.   **471** *saving the Praemunire:* except that it would violate the Statute of Praemunire (1393). This statute forbade British subjects from appealing any legal decisions to any foreign

person or body. It specifically applied to appeals made to Church courts in Rome.   **472** highest court of the Catholic Church   **473** intelligence   **474** what if   **475** *sticked not thereto:* did not make an issue of that   **476** *made fast upon long steels:* fastened to long steel poles   **477** humorous   **478** unless   **479** *say nay but:* deny that

"Then," quoth I, "when we grant him once that it may be so, then will he by and by put case[480] that it were so. And then, if we grant him his case once for the possibility, then will he shortly conclude that the other part[481] is not so surely proved as it must be if Wilkins should[482] win the wager. What should we say to him now? To whom should we give the wager?"

"In faith," quoth he, "I wot nere[483] what to say to him. And the matter is so mad that, as for the wager, what I would give Wilkins I wot nere, but as for Simkins, except[484] he better impugned the proof, if the wager were but a butterfly, I would never award him one wing."

"Surely," quoth I, "and you shall rule the matter for me. For if ye give him nought,[485] he getteth as little of me. But now what if he wax[486] angry that his proper invention were no more set by,[487] nor his wit no more regarded, and would thereupon help forth his part with his oath, and swear upon a book[488] that himself saw when the men made those prints in the ground with horseshoes holden in their hands? What would ye then say?"

"Marry" quoth he, "then would I say—and swear too—that besides the loss of his wager, he had like a false foolish knave lost his honesty[489] and his soul too."

"In good faith," quoth I, "and for aught[490] I see yet, I durst be bold to swear with you. And then, letting Wilkins alone with Simkins disputing their sophism themselves, let us return home again to our own matter. In which, while there were so many so clear and open proofs[491] against the man of whom we speak all this while, though it were possible that all they might be false, yet could there none indifferent[492] judge so think, except[493] it were so proved— and that by other means than the only[494] oath of the party that is accused, swearing alone against them all."

"Yet," quoth he, "for all that, if he know indeed that he did it not, he doth but well to abide by the truth."

"Very sooth[495] ye say," quoth I. "Nor Simkins, neither, if he saw the men print the horseshoes in the highway, though it seemed us never so unlikely, yet had he done well enough to say it, and swear it too, and stiffly to stick thereby. And yet ye remember, pardie,[496] that if he so would have sworn, ye and I both durst[497] right now right boldly have believed that he lied. And might we not well believe the same in our case too?"

"Yes," quoth he, "that will I well.[498] And therefore the judges did him but right to reckon him as convicted, and therefore to compel him to abjure.[499] But yet they showed him therein no such favor as ye speak of, in that they admitted him to his abjuration without confessing of the fault.[500] For if they had forced him thereto, they had in my mind done him plain and open wrong, because it might be that he said and swore true. And then should they have forced him, against his conscience, to say of himself untrue. And that should they do, not only clean[501] against right, but also without necessity, considering that they might—as in conclusion they did— abjure him otherwise. And therefore they took the best way, both for him and for themselves also. But since they did therein none otherwise than as they were of duty bounden, it well appeareth he had therein no such favor as ye would make it seem that they showed him."

"Well," quoth I, "since yourself agreeth that he had no wrong, albeit[502] no favor had been showed him, yet were your errand[503] answered as far as toucheth his abjuration. And now if I should prove you that his judges showed him such favor, I fear me lest I should therewith somewhat seem to charge them that they had done, though not wrong, yet very near wrong—the favor appearing to be showed if not against the law, yet at the leastways, the law for[504] favor so far stretched forth that the leather could scant[505] hold. But yet choose they for me. For since I have said it, I will tell you why—and so much the more boldly between us twain, for that[506] I perceive not in you any such manner of mind toward them that ye would blow abroad[507] any fault of unlawful favor founden in them."

---

480 *by and by put case*: immediately postulate   **481** side (of the argument)   **482** *if Wilkins should*: for Wilkins to   **483** *wot nere*: know not   **484** unless   **485** nothing   **486** grows   **487** *proper…by*: excellent contrivance was no more valued   **488** i.e.,

Bible   **489** reputation   **490** anything   **491** testimonies   **492** impartial   **493** unless   **494** *the only*: only the   **495** truth   **496** certainly; "by God" (from the French)   **497** dared   **498** well believe   **499** renounce under oath   **500** guilt

501 completely   **502** even if   **503** *were your errand*: would your relayed message   **504** because of   **505** hardly   **506** *for that*: because   **507** *blow abroad*: publicize

"Ah, well said," quoth he, and laughed. "Ye ween I were more ready to report their rigor[508] than any point of their favor."

"Well taken of you," quoth I. "I see well a man cannot have a good opinion of you but your conscience construeth it to the contrary. But now for the matter, I trow[509] we be agreed both, that all were it[510] so that the man had been faultless indeed, yet were the proofs against him so many, so good, so clear and evident, and so much more than sufficient, that neither his judges nor ourselves neither—nor, I think, his own father neither if he had heard them—could have thought him other than very greatly guilty."

"Surely," quoth he, "that is true."

"Now," quoth I, "that being true that they could none otherwise reckon in[511] him though he still swore the contrary, must it not needs be that in his denying, in virtue of his oath,[512] the things which they could not but believe true, they must needs therewith believe him all that while to lie and be perjured?"

"That followeth," quoth he.

"Now," quoth I, "when one is accused and convicted of heresy, what thing will[513] the law that the Church shall receive him to?"

"What thing?" quoth he. "Marry, to mercy."

"Nay," quoth I, "mercy is the thing, as it seemeth, that they receive him by, not the thing that they receive him to."

"Then is it," quoth he, "to penance."

"That seemeth well said," quoth I. "For the Church, by mercy, receiveth him to penance."

"But now," quoth I, "doth the Church openly[514] receive to penance any person appearing and proving himself still impenitent?"

"Nay," quoth he.

"Appeareth not he still impenitent," quoth I, "that still appeareth perjured, and still standing in perjury? And where[515] the first part of penance is confession and humble acknowledging of the fault, can the Church reckon him penitent that still refuseth to confess his fault, that lieth falsely still, and falsely forsweareth[516] himself?"

"The Church," quoth he, "cannot surely[517] know whether he swear true or false, and therefore they cannot surely judge him forsworn. For it may be, by possibility, that all the witnesses lied."

"It may be, too," quoth I, "by possibility, if we go this way to work, that all the men lied that ever have said they came from Rome, and that all the briefs and bulls were feigned[518] that ever were supposed to be brought from thence, for aught[519] that he can tell that never came there himself. For some one man might lie, and some one bull or brief might be feigned, and so some other and one by one—and so forth—of all the remnant. For like possibility is there in every one as is in any one. And peradventure,[520] as for your own self, have never yet talked with twenty that have told you they have been at Rome."

"No, no," quoth he, "nor, I ween, with ten neither."

"And how many bulls," quoth I, "and briefs have ye seen that came thence?"

"By our Lady," quoth he, "bulls very few, and briefs never none; for I never ask after them."

"Then," quoth I, "might you by your own reason as well doubt whether there were any Rome or no, as whether that man lied and were forsworn or no. But in this point I will not long stick[521] with you. For surely, standing the matter in such case[522] that his judges could not otherwise think of him but that he was faulty of things which he still in virtue of his oath denied—all were it[523] so that they might think therewith[524] that by possibility they might be in that mind deceived, yet while[525] they could not think, nor they could have none other mind,[526] but that he (though it might by possibility be true that[527] he swore) yet was forsworn in deed,[528] and in very deed persevered in perjury. Now the matter, I say, standing in such case, since he that with so plain appearing perjury standeth[529] in the denial of his fault and false defense of himself cannot be reckoned of his fault penitent, and unto penance ought none impenitent person to be admitted, I will not say that his judges did wrong. But surely methinketh I may well say that they showed him great favor in that they received him to penance without the confession of his fault. And I think verily it was a favorable[530] fashion of abjuration, and so strange

---

508 severity   **509** trust   **510** *all were it:* even if it were   **511** regarding   **512** *in virtue of his oath:* under oath   **513** commands   **514** publicly   **515** given that   **516** perjures   **517** with certainty   **518** forged

519 all   **520** perhaps   **521** keep arguing   **522** *standing…case:* the situation being such   **523** *all were it:* even if it were   **524** also   **525** as long as   **526** opinion   **527** what   **528** *was forsworn indeed:* had lied under oath in truth   **529** persists   **530** beneficial (to him); showing partiality (on their part)

that the like hath been very seldom seen, if ever it were seen before. And that did they in hope that God shall send him more grace in time to come, and so I beseech him to do. For, I promise you, for my part I never can conceive good hope of his amendment all the while that I see that pride abide still in his heart that cannot suffer[531] him for shame to confess his fault."

THE SIXTH CHAPTER

The author showeth that the person abjured for his own worldly honesty,[532] and for the more fruit of his preaching—if he be suffered to preach in time to come—it were much better for him openly[533] and willingly to confess the truth. And that now by the standing still in the denial, he both shameth himself, and should, if he preached, slander the Word of God.

"It is," quoth he, "peradventure better thus. For then should he slander himself—and the Word of God also, if he should hereafter preach again."

"Nay, marry," quoth I, "then should he rather deliver himself from slander, and the Word of God also. For then should every man see the devil cast clean[534] out of his heart, and hope that he should be from thenceforth a very good man. Where now, thinking him to persevere in a proud perjury, we can none other think but that he must needs be very naught[535] still, though we should hereafter hear him preach never so well. And that were a sore[536] slander to the Word of God, that men should see him, whom they hear preach well, so proud a hypocrite, and therewith so foolish too, that for a false hope of his own estimation[537] preserved, he laboreth as much as in him is[538] to make the world ween that twenty true men were forsworn[539] against him. Wherein while[540] there is no man so mad[541] to believe him, he loseth (if he preach in this plight)[542] all his whole purpose, and winneth nothing but the contrary: that is, double shame of his proud perjury and high malicious mind, instead of the praise that he looketh and preacheth for."

THE SEVENTH CHAPTER

The messenger moveth a question: if a man be sworn by a judge to say the truth of himself in a crime whereof he is had[543] suspect, whether he may not lawfully[544] on his oath swear untruth, where he thinketh the truth cannot be proved against him. Whereunto the author answereth that he is bounden upon peril of perjury to say and confess truth. And the much more sin and folly both was it, then, for the man that thus was abjured to forswear himself in the thing that he wist[545] well would be proved, and a shameless folly to stand still by his perjury when he saw the matter so clearly proved indeed. And with this finisheth he the matter of his abjuration.

"In good faith," quoth he, "I begin in this matter to be of your mind. For the matter being so plain and clearly proved, it was and is both sin and folly to stand in the denying. But there cometh a thing in my mind, though it be somewhat out of our matter,[546] wherein I would be glad to hear what ye think."

"What thing is that?" quoth I.

"Marry," quoth he, "I have heard some well-learned men say if a man were accused of a fault that were true indeed, yet if it be secret[547] and cannot be proved, in an oath put unto him he may, and ought, to swear nay, because that[548] of secret and unknown things no man can be his judge. For only God is judge of man's heart. And if he should confess it where he needeth not, before no competent judge—that is to wit,[549] his secret fault openly before men, whereof only God is judge—then should he defame himself; and that were great sin. For Holy Scripture saith, *Curam habe de bono nomine* ('Take heed of thy good name.')[550] *Et melior est nomen bonum quam divitie multe* ('Better is a good name than much riches').[551] And it saith also, *Maledictus homo qui negligit famam suam* ('Accursed is that man that careth not what men say of him').[552] And therefore I have heard some well-learned men say that in this case a man may boldly deny the matter[553] upon his oath, be it never so true, so that[554] it be so secret as it be not able to be proved by witnesses."

---

531 allow **532** reputation **533** publicly **534** completely **535** wicked **536** serious **537** reputation **538** *as much . . . him is:* as hard as he can **539** *were forsworn:* committed perjury **540** *Wherein*

while: About which since **541** *so mad:* so insane as **542** state **543** held **544** morally **545** knew **546** *out of our matter:* outside our subject matter **547** hidden; private **548** *because that:*

because **549** say **550** Ecclus 41:15 **551** Prv 22:1 **552** This verse is not in the Vulgate. **553** charge **554** *so that:* as long as

"Forsooth," quoth I, "it is a large and a long matter to speak of perjury. But as for this point, I hold it in my mind little question. For I hold this once[555] for a sure and an infallible conclusion: that a man may never lawfully be forsworn.[556] Marry, truth it is that a man's oath receiveth[557] interpretation, and is not always bounden precisely to the words, as if a judge would swear me generally[558] in a court to make true answer to such things as should be asked of me, and after mine oath given, he would ask me certain questions of matters nothing belonging to him,[559] I were not by mine oath bounden to make him answer, forasmuch as no such thing was in mine oath intended. And therefore if a priest that had heard a man's confession were called before a judge and sworn for a witness, he might boldly swear he knew nothing of the matter — not for[560] the common gloss[561] (that the confession was not made to him as to himself, but as to God's minister), but for that the law dischargeth him of showing any such thing, no less than if his oath were given[562] him in this manner: 'What know ye of this matter out of[563] confession?' For else if there were a tyrant that would compel him by express words to swear[564] what he knew by[565] the man's confession, the confessor had[566] in my mind no remedy but to tell him plainly, 'Sir, I will not swear for you, nor in such matter make you any answer to die therefor, not for anything that I know in the man for[567] this matter though[568] I told you all his whole confession anon,[569] but for the evil that should grow by such a precedent. For if I should now excuse[570] an innocent, swearing truly that I heard no such things in his confession, I should in some other cause[571] either be forsworn, or by my refusing to swear I should make the man the more suspect, in that I refuse to swear as much for him as I did for another. And therefore will I not make any answer in this, for the peril that may fall in other.'[572] And with this answer, or such other, must he plainly refuse to swear, what pain soever he should endure therefor. And in like wise, if any judge would give[573] an oath to any person to tell him the truth of any crime which were so secret as that judge had never heard anything thereof, but would for his only pleasure[574] know by the man's oath whether there were peradventure any such thing or not, the party may deny[575] to swear or to make him answer therein. But on the other side, if he be denounced or detected[576] unto him, either by common fame[577] or other information, with such conjectures and likelihoods as the law giveth the judge authority to give the party an oath for the further search[578] of the matter, there is he plainly bounden upon pain of eternal damnation, without covering or cautel,[579] to show and disclose the plain truth, and to have more respect[580] to his soul than to his shame. For as for those texts which ye alleged,[581] be far from this point.[582] For they none other mean but that a man should in his living avoid not only sin, but also all occasions whereby men might have reasonable cause falsely to defame him. And it was never meant of[583] the shame that a man taketh of his own confession for his sin committed in deed. For by that he loseth not his good name, but getteth his good name, among good folk. And as for of evil men's words,[584] there is no reckoning. But surely, as I say, if a man had been all ill[585] as a devil, and after repenting his sin would, for part of his penance, willingly offer himself to the sufferance of open[586] shame, there were no good Christian man that would after that like the man the worse, but a great deal the better. And if all such open confession were sin, there was much sin used[587] among good folk many day[588] in Christ's Church when it was much better than it is now.

"Lo, Achan, that had committed sacrilege, whereof is written in Joshua,[589] was exhorted by Joshua to confess his fault openly, and give glory to God, that had detected him by lots.[590] And so did he, and meekly suffered for his sin as well the shame and wonder[591] of the world as the pain and bitterness of death. And therefore I no more doubt of that thief but that he is a glorious saint in heaven than I doubt of that thief that Christ promised

555 once and for all   **556** *lawfully be forsworn:* morally commit perjury   **557** admits of   **558** *swear me generally:* put me under a general oath   **559** *nothing belonging to him:* not at all under his jurisdiction   **560** because of   **561** interpretation   **562** administered to   **563** *out of:* outside of   **564** tell under oath   **565** from   **566** would have

567 concerning   **568** even if   **569** right now   **570** help acquit   **571** court case   **572** other cases   **573** wanted to administer   **574** *his only pleasure:* his pleasure alone   **575** refuse   **576** *denounced or detected:* publicly charged or accused   **577** *common fame:* public report   **578** investigation   **579** *covering or cautel:* concealment or crafty deceit   **580** *respect to:* regard for

581 cited   **582** *be far ... point:* they are far from relevant here   **583** about   **584** *of ... words:* what evil men say   **585** evil   **586** *sufferance of open:* endurance of public   **587** practiced   **588** *many day:* at many times   **589** See Jo 7:10–26.   **590** *that ... lots:* who had found him out through drawings of lots   **591** stares, gapes

paradise hanging on the cross.[592] And surely if men's old faults were still their infamy after their amendment, then was Saint Peter little beholden to Saint Matthew and others of his fellows that have slandered him in their gospels, telling how shamefully, after all his crakes,[593] he forsook his Master and forswore[594] him both.[595] If a good man wax naught,[596] the better he was, the more sin it is, and the more shame also. And is it not then in reason,[597] on the other side, if a naughty man wax good, the worse he was, the better is for him, and the more worship[598] also? Our Lord saith himself that for one sinner coming again to grace there is more joy in heaven than upon almost an hundred good folk that never sinned.[599] And reckon we then that man shamed by the knowledge of his sin here among sinful men, whose humble confession and meek amendment winneth him so much worship in heaven? Trust me truly when a man hath done evil, if he be duly sworn, it is a worshipful shame and a joyful sorrow to confess the truth. And good folk, though they abhor the sin, yet love they and commend the man, as one that was naught and is good. And the shame that he conceiveth in his heart afore the world getteth him great honor afore God; and the short glowing heat in his cheeks speedily burneth up and wasteth the never-wasting[600] fire of hell, standing him further in stead[601] of great part of his purgatory. And therefore to the point that we speak of, without long process[602] I tell you plainly my mind: that no man can be excused from the peril of endless damnation that would—upon boldness of any doctor's[603] opinion—hide or cover his fault by any cautel[604] after a lawful oath given[605] him to tell the plain truth therein. And whoso will say the contrary, he must needs hold plain against the law, and say that no judge may lawfully give an oath to the party. For whereof should the oath serve,[606] if the party might lawfully forswear[607] himself? And also if the judge may not lawfully give him the oath, then may he refuse to swear, and[608] may not first swear and then say false, which every man must upon damnation

eschew[609] though he follily[610] take an oath, where he lawfully might refuse it."

"Forsooth," quoth he, "methinketh ye take the sure way."

"Well," quoth I, "if this be so in one that[611] is sworn where the matter,[612] as he thinketh, cannot be well proved, how far wrong went the man that we spoke of, to forswear himself in a matter of preaching that he wist[613] well was so open[614] that it would be plainly proved what sin was therein? And what sin, and folly thereto,[615] was there to stick still in his perjury, when he saw the matter already proved so clearly, and by so many, so good, so honest, and so indifferent,[616] that he could nothing now win by the denying but evil opinion[617] and almost a despair of his amendment in all that ever heard him?"

"In good faith," quoth he, "all this is very truth, and therefore we shall let him alone till God send him better mind."[618]

THE EIGHTH CHAPTER
The author showeth why the New Testament of Tyndale's translation[619] was burned, and showeth for example certain words evil,[620] and of evil purpose,[621] changed.

"But now I pray you let me know your mind concerning the burning of the New Testament in English, which Tyndale lately translated, and (as men say) right well, which maketh men much marvel of the burning."

"It is," quoth I, "to me great marvel that any good Christian man having any drop of wit in his head would anything marvel or complain of the burning of that book if he know the matter.[622] Which whoso calleth 'the New Testament' calleth it by a wrong name, except[623] they will call it 'Tyndale's Testament,' or 'Luther's Testament.' For so had Tyndale, after[624] Luther's counsel, corrupted and changed it from the good and wholesome doctrine of Christ to

592 See Lk 23:39–43. **593** brags; boasts **594** denied under oath **595** See Mt 26:33–35, 69–74. **596** *wax naught:* grows evil **597** *is it . . . reason:* does it not then stand to reason **598** honor **599** See Lk 15:7. **600** *wasteth the never-wasting:* put an end to the never-ending **601** *standing . . . stead:* benefiting him even more

by taking the place **602** argument **603** scholar's **604** crafty deceit **605** administered to **606** *whereof . . . serve:* what would be the point of the oath **607** perjure **608** but **609** avoid **610** *though . . . follily:* even if foolishly **611** who **612** case (against him) **613** knew **614** public **615** as well

616 impartial **617** *evil opinion:* a bad reputation **618** judgment **619** *the . . . translation:* Tyndale's translation of the New Testament **620** badly **621** *of evil purpose:* with a bad intent **622** content; situation **623** unless **624** in accord with the devilish heresies of their own, that it was clean[625] a contrary thing."

"That were marvel," quoth your friend, "that it should be so clean contrary. For to some that read it, it seemed very like."

"It is," quoth I, "nevertheless contrary—and yet the more perilous. For like[626] as to a true silver groat,[627] a false copper groat is nevertheless contrary though it be quicksilvered over, but so much the more false in how much it is counterfeited the more like to the truth, so was the translation so much the more contrary in how much it was craftily devised like, and so much the more perilous in how much it was, to folk unlearned, more hard to be discerned."

"Why," quoth your friend, "what faults were there in it?"

"To tell you all that," quoth I, "were in a manner to rehearse you[628] all the whole book, wherein there were founden and noted wrong and falsely translated above a thousand texts by tale."[629]

"I would," quoth he, "fain[630] hear some one."

"He that should," quoth I, "study for that should study where to find water in the sea. But I will show you for example two or three such as every one of the three is more than thrice three in one."

"That were," quoth he, "very strange except[631] ye mean more in weight. For one can be but one in number."

"Surely," quoth I, "as weighty be they as any lightly[632] can be. But I mean that every one of them is more than thrice three in number."

"That were," quoth he, "somewhat like a riddle."

"This riddle," quoth I, "will soon be read.[633] For he hath mistranslated three words of great weight, and every one of them is, as I suppose, more than thrice three times repeated and rehearsed in the book."

"Ah, that may well be," quoth he, "but that was not well done. But I pray you, what words be they?"

"The one is," quoth I, "this word, 'priests'; the other, 'the Church'; the third, 'charity.' For priests, wheresoever he speaketh of the priests of Christ's Church, he never calleth them 'priests,' but always 'seigniors'; the Church he calleth always 'the congregation'; and charity he calleth always 'love.' Now do these names in our English tongue neither express the things that be meant by them, and also

there appeareth (the circumstances well considered) that he had a mischievous mind in the change. For first, as for priests and priesthood, though that of old they used commonly to choose well elderly men to be priests, and therefore in the Greek tongue priests were called *presbyteri* (as we might say, 'elder men'), yet neither were all priests chosen old—as appeareth by Saint Paul writing to Timothy, *Nemo iuventutem tuam contemnat* ('Let no man contemn[634] thy youth')[635]—nor every elder man is not a priest. And in our English tongue, this word 'seignior' signifieth nothing at all, but is a French word used in English more than half in mockage, when one will call another 'my lord' in scorn. And if he mean to take the Latin word *senior*, that word in the Latin tongue never signified a priest, but only an elder man. By which name of 'elder men,' if he would call the priests Englishly, then should he rather signify their age than their office. And yet the name doth in English plainly signify the aldermen of the cities, and nothing the priests of the Church. And thus may we perceive that rather than he would call a priest by the name of 'a priest,' he would seek a new word, he neither wist[636] nor cared what.

"Now, where he calleth the Church always 'the congregation,' what reason had he therein? For every man well seeth that though the Church be indeed a congregation, yet is not every congregation the Church, but a congregation of Christian people; which congregation of Christian people hath been in England always called and known by the name of the Church; which name, what good cause or color[637] could he find to turn into the name of 'congregation,' which word is common to a company of Christian men or a company of Turks?

"Like wisdom was there in the change of this word 'charity' into 'love.' For though charity be always love, yet is not—ye wot well—love always charity."

"The more pity, by my faith," quoth your friend, "that ever love was sin. And yet it would not be so much so taken if the world were no more suspicious than they say that good Saint Francis was, which,[638] when he saw a young man kiss a girl once in way of good company,[639] kneeled down and held up his hands into heaven, highly thanking God

---

625 completely   **626** just   **627** fourpence coin   **628** relate to you; read aloud   **629** *above . . . tale:* over a thousand passages   by number   **630** like to   **631** unless   **632** probably   **633** solved   **634** despise   **635** 1 Tm 4:12   **636** knew   **637** pretext   **638** who   **639** *in way . . . company:* in an erotic way

that charity was not yet gone out of this wretched world."

"He had," quoth I, "a good mind,[640] and did like a good man, that deemed all things to the best."[641]

"So say I too," quoth he. "But how far be folk fallen from the good mind now. Men be nowadays waxen so full of mistrust that some man would, in faith, ween his wife were naught[642] if he should but find her in bed with a poor friar."

"Forsooth, ye be a wanton!"[643] quoth I. "But yet, in earnest, how like you the change of these words?"

"Surely," quoth he, "very naught. And that it was not well nor wisely done, there will, I trow,[644] no good wise man deny. But yet whether Hutchins[645] had, in the translation thereof, any malicious purpose or not, therein will I, till I see further, play Saint Francis's part, and judge the man no worse than the matter requireth."

"First," quoth I, "would ye that the book should go forth and be read still in that fashion?"[646]

"Nay, in good faith," quoth he, "that would I not, if he use it so very often."

"With that word," quoth I, "ye hit the nail on the head. For surely, if he changed the common known word into the better, I would well allow[647] it. If he changed it into as good, I would suffer[648] it. If somewhat into worse, so[649] he did it seldom, I would wink at it. But now, when he changeth the known, usual names of so great things into so far the worse, and that not repeateth seldom, but so often and so continually inculketh[650] that almost in the whole book his lewd[651] change he never changeth, in this manner could no man deem other but that the man meant mischievously[652]—scant[653] such a good seely[654] soul as would ween all were well when he found his wife where ye said right now. If he called charity sometimes by the bare[655] name of 'love,' I would not stick thereat.[656] But now, whereas 'charity' signifieth in Englishmen's ears not every common love, but a good, virtuous, and well-ordered love, he that will studiously flee from that name of good love, and always speak of 'love' and always leave out 'good,' I would surely say that he meaneth naught."[657]

"In good faith," quoth he, "so is it not unlikely."

"Then," quoth I, "when ye see more, ye shall say it is much more than likely.

"For now it is to be considered that at the time of this translation Hutchins was with Luther in Wittenberg, and set certain glosses in the margent,[658] framed[659] for the setting forth of the ungracious[660] sect."

"By Saint John," quoth your friend, "if that be true—that Hutchins were at that time with Luther—it is a plain token[661] that he wrought somewhat after his counsel, and was willing to help his matters forward here. But whether Luther's matters be so mad as they be made for,[662] that shall we see hereafter."

"Very true," quoth I. "But as touching the confederacy[663] between Luther and him, is[664] a thing well known and plainly confessed by such as have been taken[665] and convicted here of heresy, coming from thence—and some of them sent hither to sow that seed about here, and to send word thither from time to time how it sprang.[666]

"But now, the cause why he changed the name of 'charity,' and of 'the Church,' and of 'priesthood,' is no very great difficulty to perceive. For since Luther and his fellows, among other their damnable heresies, have one that all our salvation standeth[667] in faith alone, and toward our salvation nothing force of good works,[668] therefore it seemeth that he laboreth of purpose to diminish the reverent mind that men bear to charity, and therefore he changeth that name of holy, virtuous affection into the bare name of 'love,' common to the virtuous love that man beareth to God and to the lewd love that is between fleck and his make.[669] And for because that Luther utterly denieth the very[670] Catholic Church in earth, and saith that the Church of Christ is but an unknown congregation of some folk, here two and there three, no man wot where, having 'the right faith' (which he calleth only his own new-forged faith), therefore Hutchins in the New Testament cannot abide the name of 'the Church,' but turneth it into the name of 'congregation,' willing that

---

640 disposition; judgment **641** *that…best:* who judged everything in the best light **642** *ween…naught:* believe that his wife was being immoral **643** rogue; rake **644** trust **645** another surname used by the Tyndale family **646** *in that fashion:* as it is written **647** approve of **648** allow **649** so long as **650** inculcates **651** evil

652 wickedly **653** short of; save for **654** poor; simple; innocent **655** simple; mere **656** *stick thereat:* object to that **657** *meaneth naught:* means "bad" (i.e., a bad kind of love); means badly (i.e., has a bad intention) **658** margin **659** designed **660** wicked **661** indication **662** *made for:* construed

663 conspiracy; collusion **664** it is **665** arrested for **666** *how it sprang:* as to how well it sprouted **667** consists **668** *nothing…works:* i.e., good works count for nothing **669** *fleck…make:* man and his paramour **670** true

it should seem to Englishmen either that Christ in the Gospel had never spoken of the Church, or else that the Church were but such a congregation as they might have occasion to say that a congregation of some such heretics were the Church that God spoke of.

"Now as touching the cause why he changed the name of 'priest' into 'seignior,' ye must understand that Luther and his adherents hold this heresy: that all holy orders[671] is nothing, and that a priest is nothing else but a man chosen among the people to preach, and that by that choice[672] to that office he is priest by and by,[673] without any more ado[674]—and no priest again whensoever the people choose another in his place—and that a priest's office is nothing but to preach. For as for saying Mass and hearing of confession, and absolution thereupon to be given—all this he saith that every man, woman, and child may do as well as any priest. Now doth Hutchins therefore—to set forth this opinion withal—after[675] his master's heresy put away the name of 'priest' in his translation, as though priesthood were nothing. Wheresoever the Scripture speaketh of the priests that were among the Jews, there doth he in his translation call them still[676] by the name of 'priests.' But wheresoever the Scripture speaketh of the priests of Christ's Church, there doth he put away the name of 'priest' in his translation, because he would make it seem that the Scripture did never speak of any priests different from laymen among Christian people. And he saith plainly in his book of *Obedience* that priesthood and all holy orders among Christian people be but feigned inventions, and that priests be nothing but officers chosen to preach, and that all the consecration whereby they be consecrated is nothing worth. And for this cause in all his translation wheresoever he speaketh of them, the name of 'priest'— which to us, in our own tongue, hath always signified an anointed person and with holy orders consecrated unto God—he hath changed into the name of 'seignior': no word of our language, but either used half in mockage, when we speak French in sport (*Dieu vous garde, Seignior*),[677] or at the furthest, nothing betokening but 'elder.' So that it is

easy to see what he meant in the turning[678] of these names."

"In good faith," quoth your friend, "it seemeth verily that he meant not well."

"Surely," quoth I, "ye would well say so if ye saw all the places which I shall cause you to see when ye will,[679] and ye shall soon[680] judge them yourself. For it were too long to rehearse them all now. Nor these have I not rehearsed you as for[681] the chief, but for that they came first to mind. For else I might shortly rehearse you many things more as far out of tune as these be. For he changeth commonly the name of 'grace' into this word, 'favor,' whereas every favor is not grace in English; for in some favor is there little grace. 'Confession' he translateth into 'acknowledging,' 'penance' into 'repentance.' A 'contrite' heart he changeth into a 'troubled' heart, and many more things like, and many texts untruly translated for the maintenance[682] of heresy, as I shall show you some when we look in the book. Which things we shall not now reason upon, for they be not worthy to be brought in question.[683] But I tell you this much only for this cause: that ye may perceive that he hath thus used[684] himself in his translation to the intent that he would set forth Luther's heresies and his own thereby. For first he would make the people believe that we should believe nothing but plain Scripture, in which point he teacheth a plain, pestilent heresy. And then would he, with his false translation, make the people ween[685] further that such articles of our faith as he laboreth to destroy, and which be well proved by Holy Scripture, were in Holy Scripture nothing spoken of, but that the preachers have all this fifteen hundred years misreported the Gospel, and Englished the Scripture wrong, to lead the people purposely out of the right way."

THE NINTH CHAPTER
The author showeth another great token[686]
that the translation was perilous,
and made for an evil purpose.

"But to the intent ye shall yet the less doubt what good fruit was intended by this translation, and

---

671 *holy orders:* the sacrament of ordination   672 election   673 *by and by:* immediately   674 labor   675 following   676 always   677 *Dieu*

vous garde, Seignior: "God keep you, sir."   678 changing   679 want   680 quickly; readily   681 *as for:* because they are   682 support   683 *in question:* into debate

684 habitually conducted   685 believe, suppose   686 indication

easily judge yourself whether it was well worthy to be burned or not, ye shall understand that there hath been since that time another book made in English, and imprinted, as it saith, in Almain[687] — a foolish railing book against the clergy, and much part made in rhyme, but the effect thereof was all against the Mass and the holy sacraments. In this book, the maker raileth[688] upon all them that caused Tyndale's translation of the New Testament to be burned, saying that they burned it because that it destroyed the Mass. Whereby ye may see that he reckoned that translation very good for their purpose toward the destruction of the Mass."

"By Saint Mary Mass,"[689] quoth your friend, "that book is a shrewd gloss[690] for the other. For it showed a cause for which it was well worthy to be burned — and the maker with it — if it were made to destroy the Mass. But who made that second book?"

"Forsooth," quoth I, "it appeareth not in the book. For the book is put forth nameless,[691] and was in the beginning reckoned to be made by Tyndale. And whether it so were or not, we be not yet very sure. Howbeit, since that time Tyndale hath put out in his own name another book, entitled *Mammona*,[692] which book is very *mammona iniquitatis* (a very "treasury and wellspring of wickedness").[693] And yet hath he since put forth a worse also, named *The Obedience of a Christian Man*,[694] a book able to make a Christian man — that would believe it — leave off all good Christian virtues and lose the merit of his Christendom.[695] In the preface of his first book, called *Mammona*, he saith that one Friar Jerome made the other book that we talk of; which Friar Jerome, giving up his order (of the Friar Observants),[696] came to him where he was, showing him that he would cast off his habit and leave his religion,[697] and 'assay[698] now to serve God,' and that afterward he left him and went unto Roye[699] — which is, as I think ye know, another apostate — by whose counsel Tyndale saith that the friar Jerome made the book, wherein Tyndale saith that he misliketh his rhymes and his overmuch

railing, and saith also that he feareth lest Friar Jerome shall not well prove all that he promiseth in that book."

"Why," quoth your friend, "is that all the fear that he findeth in himself, and all the fault that he findeth in the friar and his book?"

"Yea, in good faith," quoth I, "every whit."[700]

"Then findeth he," quoth your friend, "no fault in his apostasy?"

"No more," quoth I, "than I show you."

"Nor findeth he," quoth your friend, "no fault in that the friar's book saith that the New Testament of Tyndale was burned because it destroyed the Mass?"

"Never a whit," quoth I, "more than you hear."

"And feareth he," quoth your friend, "nothing else but lest the friar should fail of performing of somewhat[701] that his book promiseth?"

"That is all," quoth I. "And what he promiseth therein, in faith I remember not. But it seemeth whatsoever it be, Tyndale would it were well performed."

"He had," quoth your friend, "much more cause, as methinketh, to fear lest men should reckon high default[702] in his translation, in that he nothing answereth to those words of the friar's book, wherein he saith that the New Testament that was burned did destroy the Mass."

"Ye say," quoth I, "very truth, in my mind; and so would he of likelihood if himself had not meant as the friar said. But surely, for[703] the translation, I shall show you so many texts in such wise corrupted that ye shall not, I suppose, greatly doubt what he meant in his doing." And therewithal I showed your friend a book with the places ready noted — which book I had, by license,[704] a little before lent unto me for the nonce.[705] Wherein he saw so many corruptions, and of such manner sort,[706] that albeit upon some we somewhat reasoned in[707] the way, yet at the last himself said ho,[708] and verily confessed that the book in such wise translated was very naught[709] and nothing meetly[710] to be read.

687 Germany   **688** rants abusively
689 *Saint Mary Mass:* the Mass in honor of Mary   **690** *shrewd gloss:* sinister interpretation   **691** anonymously   **692** *The Parable of the Wicked Mammon* (1528) contains a translation into English of Luther's sermon on Lk 16:1–13.   **693** Lk

16:9   **694** *The Obedience of a Christian Man:* also published 1528   **695** Christianity   **696** Franciscans   **697** religious order   **698** try   **699** William Roye, who helped Tyndale publish his New Testament   **700** *every whit:* entirely; every little bit   **701** something   **702** defects   **703** as for

704 *by license:* with permission   **705** *the nonce:* that express purpose   **706** *manner sort:* a kind   **707** *reasoned in:* argued along   **708** enough   **709** bad   **710** *nothing meetly:* not at all fit

THE TENTH CHAPTER

The author showeth that the translation of
Tyndale was too bad to be mended.

But yet he said that the faults might be by some
good men amended, and then the book printed
again, if nothing letted[711] but that.

"Surely," quoth I, "if we go thereto, the faults be —
as ye see — so many, and so spread through the whole
book, that likewise as it were as soon done to weave
a new web of cloth as to sew up every hole in a net,
so were it almost as little labor, and less, to translate
the whole book all new as to make in his translation
so many changes as need must be ere it were made
good. Besides this, that there would no wise man, I
trow,[712] take the bread which he well wist was of[713]
his enemy's hand once poisoned, though he saw his
friend after scrape it never so clean."

THE ELEVENTH CHAPTER

The messenger findeth fault with the clergy, in that
he saith they have made a constitution provincial[714]
that no Bible in English should be suffered.[715] And
in this chapter incidentally[716] the messenger much
reproveth the living of the clergy. Whereunto[717] the
author somewhat showeth his mind, deferring for
the while[718] his answer to the objection
made against the constitution.

"Sir," quoth your friend, "I will not greatly stick[719]
with you in that point. But surely the thing that
maketh in this matter the clergy most suspect, and
wherein, as it seemeth, it would be full hard to excuse them, is this: that they not only damn[720] Tyndale's translation (wherein there is good cause), but
over[721] that do damn all others, and, as though a layman were no Christian man, will suffer no layman
have any at all. But when they find any in his keeping, they lay heresy to him therefor.[722] And thereupon they burn up the book, and sometimes the
good man withal, alleging, for the defense of their
doing, a law of their own making: a constitution

provincial, whereby they have prohibited that any   40
man shall have any, upon pain of heresy. And this is
a law very provincial;[723] for it holdeth but here. For
in all other countries of Christendom, the people
have the Scripture translated into their own tongue,
and the clergy there findeth no such fault therein;   45
wherefore either our people be worst of all people,
or else our clergy is worst of all clergies. But, by my
troth, for aught[724] that I can see here or perceive
by[725] them that have been elsewhere, our lay people be as good and as honest as be anywhere. And if   50
any be otherwise, the occasion and example cometh
of the clergy, among whom we see much more vice
than among ourselves.

"Whereas they should give us example of virtue
and the light of learning, now their examples —   55
what they be — we see. And as for learning, they
neither will teach us but seldom — and that shall be
but such things as pleaseth them, some glosses[726] of
their own making — nor suffer us to learn by ourselves, but by their constitution pull Christ's Gos-   60
pel out of Christian people's hands. I cannot well
see why, but lest we should see the truth. The Jews
be not letted to read[727] their law — both learned and
lewd.[728] And yet are there in the Old Testament
things for unlearned folk far more strange and per-   65
ilous than in the New. And why should, then, our
laymen be forbidden the Gospel, but if they[729] will
make us worse than Jews?[730] Wherein I can, in good
faith, see no excuse they can find. For the Scripture
is to good folk the nourisher of virtue, and to them   70
that be naught, it is the means of amendment. And
therefore while[731] the clergy doth withdraw it[732] us,
if our souls be in good health, they take away our
food; if our souls be sick, they take away the medicine. And therefore, as I said, the fault is not in the   75
damning of Tyndale's translation, but in that they
have by an express law forbidden that we should
have any at all."

"Your words," quoth I, "be somewhat pugnant[733]
and sharp. But surely they prick somewhat more the   80
men than the matter. For where ye touch in effect
two things — one, the constitution provincial by

711 hindered **712** trust **713** by
714 *constitution provincial:* ecclesiastical
law enacted by the bishops of a province
of the Church (in this case, the province
of England). The decree in question was
one of many passed by a synod at Oxford
in 1407 presided over by the Archbishop
of Canterbury, Thomas Arundel, and

thus sometimes known as the Arundel
Constitutions. **715** allowed **716** in
passing **717** about which **718** time
being **719** persist in arguing **720** condemn **721** in addition to **722** *lay...*
therefor: charge him with heresy for it
723 local **724** anything **725** *perceive*
by: understand from **726** interpretations

727 *letted to read:* hindered from reading
728 *learned and lewd:* the educated and
the uneducated **729** *but if they:* unless
the clergy **730** *worse...than:* inferior to
Jewish readers **731** as long as **732** *with-*
draw it: withhold it from **733** hostile

which ye think the clergy of this realm have evil[734] prohibited all translations of Scripture into our tongue; another, the vice of the clergy in general — the first point, which indeed toucheth our matter, I can and will with few words answer you. But as for the other, which toucheth the men, as[735] where ye accuse the clergy in their persons of very vicious living, as[736] men much worse than ye say that we be — and yet, as though their own faults were too few, charge them with ours too, whereof ye call them the cause — in this point will I keep no schools[737] with you, nor enter into dispicions[738] thereof, nor gladly meddle with the matter. For as I told you in the beginning, since we talk but of men's learning, I will not meddle of men's living, nor, in that treating of this matter, either praise or dispraise any man's manner, except some such as are, for their heresies and evil doctrine, cast out of Christ's Church, and through all Christendom damned and defamed already by their own obstinate malice. But yet where ye speak of other countries, making an argument that our clergy is the worst of all others, I wot[739] well the whole world is so wretched that spiritual and temporal[740] everywhere all be bad enough; God make us all better! But yet for that[741] I have myself seen, and by credible folk have heard, like[742] as ye say by our temporalty[743] that we be as good and as honest as anywhere else, so dare I boldly say that the spiritualty[744] of England, and specially that part in which ye find most fault — that is to wit, that part which we commonly call the secular clergy[745] — is, in learning and honest living, well able to match (and, saving the comparisons be odious, I would say further) far able to overmatch, number for number, the spiritualty of any nation Christian. I wot well there be therein many very lewd and naught.[746] And surely wheresoever there is a multitude, it is not, without miracle, well possible to be[747] otherwise. But now if the bishops would once take unto priesthood better laymen and fewer (for of us be they made), all the matter were more than half amended. Now where ye say that ye see more vice in them than in ourselves, truth it is that everything in them is greater, because they be more bounden

to be better. But else[748] the things that they misdo be the selfsame that we sin in ourselves; which vices that, as ye say, we see more in them than in ourselves, the cause is, as I suppose, for[749] we look more upon theirs than on our own, and fare as Aesop saith in a fable — that every man carrieth a double wallet[750] on his shoulder, and into the one that hangeth at his breast he putteth other folks' faults, and therein he tooteth and poreth[751] often. In the other he layeth up all his own, and swingeth it at his back, which himself never listeth[752] to look in, but others that come after him cast an eye into it among.[753] Would God[754] we were all of the mind that every man thought no man so bad as himself! For that were the way to mend both them and us. Now they blame us, and we blame them, and both blameworthy, and either party more ready to find other's faults than to mend their own. For in reproach of them we be so studious that neither good nor bad passeth unreproved. If they be familiar,[755] we call them light.[756] If they be solitary, we call them fantastic. If they be sad,[757] we call them solemn. If they be merry, we call them mad. If they be companable,[758] we call them vicious.[759] If they be holy, we call them hypocrites. If they keep few servants, we call them niggards.[760] If they keep many, we call them pompous. If a lewd[761] priest do a lewd deed, then we say, 'Lo, see what example the clergy giveth us!' — as though that priest were the clergy. But then forget we to look what good men be therein, and what good counsel they give us, and what good example they show us. But we fare as do the ravens and the carrion crows, that never meddle with any quick[762] flesh, but where they may find a dead dog in a ditch, thereto they flee, and thereon they feed apace.[763] So where we see a good man, and hear or see a good thing, there we take little heed. But when we see once an evil deed, thereon we gape, thereof we talk, and feed ourselves all day with the filthy delight of evil communication. Let a good man preach a short tale[764] shall serve us thereof, and we shall neither much regard his exhortation nor his good example. But let a lewd friar be taken[765] with a wench, we will jest and rail upon the whole order[766] all the

734 wrongly **735** such as **736** being **737** *keep no schools:* not engage in any academic discussion **738** debates **739** know **740** *spiritual and temporal:* clerics and lay people **741** what **742** just **743** *by our temporalty:* about our laity **744** clergy **745** *secular clergy:* priests who are not members of religious orders **746** *lewd and naught:* uneducated or rude and wicked **747** *to be:* for it to be **748** otherwise **749** because **750** *double wallet:* knapsack with two pockets **751** *tooteth and poreth:* looks and peers **752** wishes **753** now and then **754** *Would God:* I wish to God **755** friendly **756** frivolous **757** serious **758** sociable **759** corrupt **760** misers **761** bad **762** living **763** quickly **764** sermon **765** caught **766** *the whole order:* i.e., all the clergy

year after, and say, 'Lo what example they give us!' And yet, when we have said,[767] we will follow the same, and then say that we learned it of them, forgetting that we list[768] not to hear and follow some other, whose word and deed would give us light to do better if we listed as well to learn the better as to follow the worse."

"Indeed," quoth he, "because ye speak[769] of light, they say that if a woman be fair, then is she young, and if a priest be good, then is he old. But yet have I seen a priest give light to the people that was but very young."

"Marry," quoth I, "God forbid else. Ye may see that often and ye will."[770]

"Truly," quoth he, "it is pity that we see such light so seldom, being this wretched world in such darkness as it is. For I never saw it but once. Nor, as it seemed, few of the people neither. For in faith they wondered as fast thereon[771] as though they had never seen it before."

"How happed that?" quoth I.

"Marry," quoth he, "it happed that a young priest very devoutly, in a procession, bore a candle before the cross for lying with a wench, and bore it lighted all the long way. Wherein the people took such spiritual pleasure and inward solace that they laughed apace. And one merry merchant said unto the priests that followed him, *Sic luceat lux vestra coram hominibus* ('Thus let your light shine afore the people')."[772]

"Forsooth," quoth I, "it were pity but that an evil priest were punished.[773] But yet it is as much pity that we take such a wretched pleasure in the hearing of their sin, and in the sight of their shame. Good is it for them to look on their faults, but for us were it better to look less to theirs and more unto our own. But surely many of us have such delight to hear of their harm[774] that it seemeth we be glad when one of them doth any such thing as we may have occasion to see them punished or had[775] in derision. Which wretched appetite and sinful affection yet is much worse, and much more worthy the curse of God, than the lewd mind of Ham, which fell into[776] the curse of his father, Noah, for that[777] he made a

gaud[778] and showed forth in scorn the secret members[779] of his father, that of adventure[780] lay and slept uncovered, which parts Shem and Japheth, the blessed children, reverently covered, going backward to him because they would not[781] see him.[782] And surely we have little cause to laugh at their lewdness. For undoubtedly, if the clergy be naught, we must needs be worse, as I heard once Master Colet,[783] the good dean of Paul's,[784] preach. For he said that it can be none other but that we must ever be one degree under them. For surely as he said, it can be no lie that[785] our Savior saith himself, which[786] saith of them that they 'be salt of the earth.' And if the salt once appall,[787] the world must needs wax unsavory.[788] And he saith that they 'be the light of the world. And then if the light,' saith he, 'be darkened, how dark will then the darkness be!'[789] — that is to wit, all the world besides, whereof he called the clergy, only, the light. Howbeit,[790] though there be both among us and them many very naught — whose faults be neither the faults of the temporalty nor of the spiritualty, but of those lewd persons themselves — yet are, I trust, neither their party nor ours come to that point but that there be many good men among us, and as for among them, I wot nere[791] whether I may say many more or not, but surely I think many better."

"I fear me," quoth your friend, "that those 'many' be very few in comparison of the multitude."

"I cannot," quoth I, "look into their hearts to see who is good and who is bad, nor have the leisure, if they were all known, to go about and tell them by the polls,[792] to see which side were the more. And therefore, in the meanwhile, I trust in God the better part is the greater. Howbeit, if there were indeed among them very few, yet think I verily that for those few all the world fareth the better, and is in their virtue and prayer, by God's great mercy, maintained and upholden — as we find in Scripture places more than one declaring plainly the profit that a whole sinful city, or sometimes a whole region, taketh by the prayer of a few godly men.[793] And no doubt is there but, likewise[794] as he that is in the clergy naught is far the worse because he is

---

767 finished speaking   **768** desire
769 *because ye speak:* i.e., speaking
770 *and ye will:* if you want to   **771** *wondered . . . thereon:* stared as intently at it
772 Mt 5:16   **773** *were pity . . . punished:* would be a pity if a bad priest were not punished   **774** pain   **775** held   **776** *fell*

into: incurred   **777** *for that:* because
778 mockery   **779** *secret members:* private parts   **780** *that of adventure:* who by chance   **781** *would not:* did not want to   **782** See Gn 9:21–23.   **783** John Colet (1467–1519) was a noted scholar and humanist.   **784** St. Paul's Church in

London   **785** what   **786** who   **787** *once appall:* ever loses its flavor   **788** *wax unsavory:* grow insipid, lose its flavor
789 See Mt 5:13, 14; 6:23.   **790** However
791 *wot nere:* know not   **792** *tell . . . polls:* do a head count   **793** See Gn 18:23–32; 19:20–21.   **794** just

therein, so he that therein is good is for his clergy[795] very far the better — and his prayer to God for himself and all others far the more available."[796]

THE TWELFTH CHAPTER
The author toucheth one special prerogative that we have by[797] a priest, be he never so bad, in that his naughtiness cannot take from us the profit of his Mass. Whereupon is by the messenger moved a doubt:[798] whether it were better to have fewer priests and better, with fewer Masses, or more and worse for[799] to have the more Masses. Whereunto the author answereth.

"And be a priest never so naught, albeit that he do some way[800] much harm both to himself and others, yet this advantage take we by the privilege and prerogative of his priesthood, besides the ministration of the sacraments unto us, the goodness whereof his naughtiness cannot appair:[801] that, be he never so vicious, and therewith so impenitent and so far from all purpose of amendment that his prayers were afore the face of God rejected and abhorred, yet that sacred sacrifice and sweet oblation of Christ's holy Body offered up by his office can take none impairing[802] by the filth of his sin, but highly helpeth to the upholding of this wretched world from the vengeance of the wrath of God, and is to God as acceptable, and to us as available, for the thing itself, as though it were offered by a better man, though percase[803] his prayers joined therewith neither much profit others, nor the oblation himself, as with whom[804] God is the more greatly grieved, in that, being so bad, he durst presume to touch it."

"Marry," quoth your friend, "if this be thus I marvel then why ye said right now that it were good to make fewer priests, that[805] they might be taken only of the better, and the worse refused. For if their Masses be so good for us, be themselves never so naught, then seemeth it better for us to make yet more, though[806] they were yet worse, that we might have more Masses."

"That reason,"[807] quoth I, "will not hold. For

though God of his goodness — how bad soever the priest be — well accepteth the oblation of Christ's holy Body for other folk, yet is he with that priest's presumption highly discontented. And we never ought to seek our own commodity[808] with our neighbor's harm. And also we should, of[809] our duty to God, rather forbear the profit that ourselves might attain by a Mass than to see his majesty disreverenced by the bold presumption of such an odious minister as he hath forbidden to come about him. Like[810] as if ye sent a present unto a prince which were very pleasant unto him, though the messenger much misliked him, so far that he had been forbidden[811] the court, yet if ye were not aware thereof, your gift could not lose his thank,[812] but his malapert[813] boldness might peradventure[814] be punished, and well were worthy to be. But, on the other side, if ye knew the messenger for such as the prince would not have come at[815] him, ye would rather keep your present at home and forbear the thank, than wittingly[816] to send it by such a messenger; or else, though your present were very great, your thank would be very little. And surely, in like manner wise,[817] whoso surely knoweth a priest to be naught, vicious, and in deadly displeasure of God,[818] should get, I think, little thank if he made him say Mass. And therefore well shall the prelates do, as much as they may, to provide that God shall rather be more seldom presented with the pleasant present of the Mass than more often offended with a displeasant messenger. And verily, were all the bishops of my mind (as I know some that be), ye should not of priests have the plenty that ye have. The time hath been when there were very few in a great city, and in a monastery of five hundred in one house scantly[819] would there four monks be bold[820] to be priests. Then was all holy orders in high honor. Then find we that the degree[821] of a deacon was a great thing, and of such dignity that when one of them went sometimes in[822] pilgrimage, he would not be acknown of his order,[823] because he would not that folk should do him worship[824] in the way. But as for nowadays if he be deacon and priest too, he shall need to fear no such pride, but rather rebuke and

795 *for his clergy:* because of his being a member of the clergy   **796** effectual, efficacious   **797** *have by:* get with   **798** *is...moved a doubt:* is...raised a question   **799** in order   **800** *some way:* in some way   **801** diminish   **802** *can... impairing:* can in no way be lessened

803 perhaps   **804** *as with whom:* since he is someone with whom   **805** so that   **806** even if   **807** argument   **808** benefit; profit   **809** out of; from   **810** just   **811** forbidden admission to   **812** value; credit   **813** *his malapert:* its presumptuous   **814** perhaps   **815** to;

near   **816** knowingly   **817** *in...wise:* in the same way   **818** *in...God:* mortally displeasing to God   **819** scarcely   **820** *be bold:* venture   **821** rank   **822** on a   **823** *be...order:* let it be known that he was ordained   **824** reverence villainy.[825] Which though it have[826] happened by the lack of virtue among them, and decay of devotion among us, yet hath much of all this gear[827] grown by the means of so great a number of priests, and so familiar among us. Which thing needs must diminish on our part reverence and estimation[828] toward them, which we never have but in things rare and scarce. Gold would we not set by[829] if it were as common as chalk or clay. And whereof is there now such plenty as of priests?"

"In faith," quoth he, "there is more plenty of priests than of good men, and there be too many but if[830] they were better chosen."

"Doubtless," quoth I, "there would[831] be more diligence used in the choice, not of their learning only, but much more specially of their living. For without virtue, the better they be learned, the worse they be—saving[832] that learning is good store against God send[833] them grace to mend. Which else[834] it would be then haply[835] too late to look for, specially if the proverb were true that ye spoke of, that 'if a priest be good, then he is old.' But this is a very surety:[836] that it is not well possible to be without many very naught of that company[837] whereof there is such a main multitude.[838] The time was, as I say, when few men durst[839] presume to take upon them the high office of a priest—not even when they were chosen and called thereunto. Now runneth every rascal and boldly offereth himself for able.[840] And where the dignity passeth[841] all princes, and they that lewd[842] be desireth it for worldly winning,[843] yet cometh that sort thereto with such a mad mind that they reckon almost God much bounden[844] to them, that they vouchsafe[845] to take it. But were I pope—"

"By my soul," quoth he, "I would ye were, and my lady your wife popess too!"

"Well," quoth I, "then should she devise[846] for nuns. And as for me, touching the choice of priests, I could not well devise better provisions than are by the laws of the Church provided already, if they were as well kept as they be well made. But for the number, I would surely see such a way therein that we should not have such a rabble[847] that every mean[848] man must have a priest in his house to wait upon his wife—which no man almost lacketh now, to the contempt of priesthood in as vile office as his horse-keeper."[849]

"That is," quoth he, "truth indeed and in worse too—for they keep hawks and dogs. And yet meseemeth surely a more honest service to wait on a horse than on a dog!"

"And yet I suppose," quoth I, "if the laws of the Church, which Luther and Tyndale would have all broken, were all well observed and kept, this gear[850] should not be thus, but the number of priests would be much diminished and the remnant much the better. For it is by the laws of the Church provided—to the intent no priest should, unto the slander of priesthood, be driven to live in such lewd manner or worse—there should none be admitted unto priesthood until he have a title of[851] a sufficient yearly living, either of his own patrimony or otherwise. Nor at this day they be none otherwise accepted."

"Why," quoth he, "wherefore[852] go there, then, so many of them a-begging?"

"Marry," quoth I, "for[853] they delude[854] the law—and themselves also. For they never have grant of a living that may serve them in sight[855] for that purpose, but they secretly discharge[856] it ere they have it, or else they could not get it. And thus the bishop is blinded by the sight of the writing;[857] and the priest goeth a-begging, for all his grant of a good living; and the law is deluded; and the order is rebuked[858] by the priest's begging and lewd living, which either is fain to walk at rovers[859] (and live upon trentals[860] or worse) or else to serve in a secular man's house, which should not need[861] if this gap were stopped.[862] For ye should have priests few enough if the law were truly observed that none were made but he that were, without collusion, sure of a living already."

"Then might it hap," quoth he, "that ye might

---

825 insult   826 *though it have:* even if it has   827 matter   828 esteem   829 *set by:* value   830 *but if:* unless   831 should   832 except   833 *good . . . send:* a good provision toward such time as God may send   834 *Which else:* And if it were otherwise   835 perhaps   836 *very surety:* real certainty   837 *to . . . company:* for there not to be many very bad people in any group   838 huge number   839 dared   840 qualified   841 surpasses that of   842 lowborn   843 advancement; gain   844 obliged   845 agree graciously   846 *should she devise:* would she make the arrangements   847 mob   848 common   849 *to the . . . horse-keeper:* with the result that priesthood is scorned as being as low-status an office as that of a man's horse-keeper   850 matter   851 *a title of:* an entitlement to   852 *Why . . . wherefore:* Well . . . why   853 because   854 elude or evade the purpose of (with pun)   855 *in sight:* publicly   856 waive   857 document   858 *order is rebuked:* priesthood is brought into contempt   859 *which . . . rovers:* who is made either to wander with no home or destination   860 payments for sets of thirty Masses said for the soul of a deceased person   861 be necessary   862 *gap were stopped:* deficiency were corrected

have too few to serve[863] the rooms and livings[864] that be provided for them, except[865] the prelates would provide that orders[866] were not so commonly given, but always receive into orders as rooms and livings fall void to bestow[867] them in, and no faster."

"Surely," quoth I, "for aught[868] I see suddenly,[869] that would not be much amiss. For so should they need no such titles[870] at all, nor should need neither run at rovers nor live in laymen's houses — by reason whereof there groweth among[871] no little corruption in the priests' manners,[872] by the conversation of[873] lay people and company of women in their houses."

"Nay, by our Lady," quoth he, "I will not agree with you therein. For I think they cannot lightly[874] meet with much worse company than themselves, and that they rather corrupt us than we them."

THE THIRTEENTH CHAPTER
*The messenger moveth[875] that it would do well
that priests should have wives.
Whereunto the author maketh answer.*

"But I would ween it would amend much part of this matter if they might have wives of their own."

"Marry," quoth I, "so saith Luther and Tyndale also, saving that they go somewhat further forth. For Tyndale (whose books be nothing else, in effect, but the worst heresies picked out of Luther's works, and Luther's worst words translated by Tyndale, and put forth in Tyndale's own name) doth, in his frantic[876] book of *Obedience* — wherein he raileth at large[877] against all popes, against all kings, against all prelates, all priests, all religious, all the laws, all the saints, against the sacraments of Christ's Church, against all virtuous works, against all Divine Service,[878] and, finally, against all-thing,[879] in effect, that good is — in that book, I say, Tyndale holdeth that priests must have wives. And that he groundeth wisely upon the words of Saint Paul, where he writeth to Timothy, *Oportet episcopum esse irreprehensibilem, unius uxoris virum* ('that a bishop must

be a man unreprovable,[880] and the husband of one wife'),[881] and that it must be considered whether he have well brought up his children, and well governed his household. By these words doth Tyndale, after[882] Luther, conclude for a plain matter that priests must needs have wives, and that Saint Paul would there should[883] in no wise be none other priests but married folk. Is it not now a wonder with what spectacles Luther and Tyndale have spied this thing now in these words of Saint Paul? In which, of so many great cunning[884] fathers and holy saints as have often read, and deeply considered, those words before, there was never none that had either the wit[885] or the grace to perceive that great special commandment these fifteen hundred years, till now that God hath at last by revelation showed this high secret mystery to these two goodly creatures Luther and Tyndale, lest that holy friar should have lost[886] his marriage of[887] that holy nun, and Tyndale some good marriage that I think him toward.[888] Tyndale nothing answereth in his book to that point, but runneth and raileth over without reason, and saith that the Scripture is plain therein for him.

And ever he passeth over, as though he heard it not, that all the holy doctors that ever were in Christ's Church said that the Scripture which he allegeth to be very plain for him is very plain against him — as it is indeed. For Saint Paul in that place,[889] forasmuch as[890] yet at that time, except[891] none but young men should have been priests (which he thought not commonly convenient),[892] else could they make no priests then but such as either were or had been married; therefore the Apostle,[893] having in the choice of priests a special respect to chastity,[894] and willing to go as near to 'no wife' as might be, did ordain, as God had instructed him, that whosoever should be admitted to priesthood should be 'the husband of one wife,' meaning such as then had, or before had had, no more but one, and that never had had twain. He meant not, as mad Luther and Tyndale would now make the world so mad to believe, that a priest must needs have one, nor that he may never lack one, nor that

863 fill   **864** *rooms and livings*: positions and benefices   **865** unless   **866** holy orders   **867** *fall void to bestow*: become vacant to place   **868** anything   **869** at the moment   **870** entitlements **871** *groweth among*: comes about now and then   **872** morals   **873** *conversation of*: consorting with   **874** easily   **875** proposes   **876** insane   **877** *raileth at large*: rant abusively at length   **878** *all Divine Service*: praying the Mass and the Prayers of Hours   **879** everything   **880** irreproachable   **881** 1 Tm 3:2–4   **882** following   **883** *would…should*: wants there to   **884** learned; wise   **885** intelligence   **886** missed out on   **887** to   **888** inclined toward   **889** passage   **890** *forasmuch as*: seeing that   **891** unless   **892** *commonly convenient*: ordinarily appropriate   **893** *the Apostle*: Saint Paul   **894** *respect to chastity*: regard for celibacy

he may have one after another, nor the only[895] forbidding of twain at once; but he meant only that none should be admitted to priesthood but only such a man as never had had, nor should have, but only one, which is the thing that ever was and hath been by those words understood. And not only where Saint Paul taught, but also through Christendom, where the other apostles planted the faith, hath it ever been so observed. Which is a plain proof that, concerning the prohibition of any more wives than one, and the forbidding of bigamy by the wedding of one wife after another, was the special ordinance of God, and not of Saint Paul, whose epistles wherein he writeth anything of this matter, was peradventure not comen to the hands of other apostles when they took yet the same order by[896] the same Spirit that taught it him. For this is certain: that ever and everywhere in Christendom, the bigamy of two wives each after other hath been a let[897] and impediment against the taking of holy orders, and hath of long time been a let though the one wife had been married and buried before the man's baptism. And now these two wise men, against the old holy fathers and cunning doctors, and against the continual custom of Christ's Church so many hundred years begun and continued by the Spirit of God, have spied at last that Saint Paul saith and meaneth that a priest may marry twice, and have one wife after another—and that he must so have. For by[898] Tyndale, a priest must ever have one wife at the least. And surely if we leave the true understanding of Saint Paul's words, and believe Tyndale that it is there meant and commanded, because of this word *oportet*,[899] that a priest must have one, then may Tyndale, as for that place,[900] tell us that a priest is at liberty to have twain at once—or twenty and[901] he will—because Saint Paul saith no more but that the bishop must be 'the husband of one wife.' Which words Tyndale may tell us be verified if he be the husband of ten wives. For the husband of ten wives were the husband of one, as the father of ten children is the father of one—if the wives were as compatible[902] as the children be—as it is no doubt but Luther and Tyndale would soon make them by Scripture, if their own interpretation

may be taken for authority against the perceiving[903] that God hath given to all good Christian people this fifteen hundred years. Now, as I say, upon Tyndale's taking, Saint Paul should mean not that a priest should have but one wife (for that 'but' is not in Saint Paul's words), but he should mean that a priest must have one at the least—as though Saint Paul had liefer[904] that the priest had twenty, save for overcharging.[905] Yet it seemeth that Tyndale so take it indeed, and that a priest might have diverse wives at once, specially for the great reason[906] that he setteth thereto. For whereas[907] Saint Paul, since there was at that time little choice to make priests of but married men, willed therefore that in the choice of the bishop there should be considered how he had governed his own household, because he that had mistetched[908] his wife and his children were unmeet for a great cure,[909] therefore saith Tyndale that never should there any priest be made but such as hath a wife and children and by the governance of them showed that he is meet to bear a rule.[910] As though we never saw any man that never had wife govern a household better than many that have had wife. And if the having and good ruling of a wife be so special a proof of a man meet to be a priest as Tyndale taketh it, then—since Saint Paul, after[911] Tyndale's interpretation, cannot appear to forbid the having of diverse together[912]—best were it, after Tyndale, specially to make that man a priest that had many wives, and all at once, and many children by each of them, if he guide them all well. For more proof is it of a wise governor to rule well five wives than one, and forty children than four.

But now that every child may see the wisdom of Tyndale and his master Luther in the construction[913] of Holy Scripture—whereof he speaketh so much and understandeth so little—I beseech you consider like words of Saint Paul in a much like matter. Saint Paul, as he writeth to Timothy that a bishop must be 'the husband of one wife,' so writeth he also to him that no widow should be specially chosen and taken in to be founden of[914] the goods of the Church that were 'younger than sixty years,' and that she should be one that 'had been the wife of one husband.'[915] Now set these two texts together, of the bishop and

895 *the only:* only the **896** *took…
by:* adopted yet the same arrangement
897 hindrance **898** according to
899 "it is necessary; it is becoming"
900 *as for that place:* on the basis of that

text **901** if **902** agreeable **903** understanding **904** rather **905** the excessive
expense **906** argument **907** because
908 taught bad habits to **909** *unmeet for
a great cure:* unfit for spiritual responsibility

910 position of authority **911** according
to **912** concurrently **913** construing;
interpreting **914** *founden of:* provided for
out of **915** 1 Tm 5:9

the widow, and consider the words of 'one wife' in the one, and 'one husband' in the other. If we shall, after Tyndale, take the one words for the bishop, that Saint Paul should mean not that he have, or have had, but one wife, but that he must needs have one wife, then must we likewise take the words spoken by Saint Paul of the widow as though Saint Paul should mean not a widow which[916] had never had more than one husband, but a widow that had had one husband, as though Saint Paul had nothing feared nor forbidden but lest Timothy should take in such a widow as never had no husband at all. Were not this wisely construed?[917] Now if Tyndale will agree, as he needs must but if[918] he be mad, that Saint Paul, in giving commandment that the widow should be such as had had 'one husband,' meant thereby such one as never had had more than one, then must he needs grant—and his master Luther too—that Saint Paul, in like wise, where he said that a bishop must be a good man and the husband of 'one wife' meant that he must never have, nor have had, any more than one, and not that he must needs have one, or that he must have one at the least, and might have many more than one, either each after other, or all together, and he list.[919] And in this matter hath Tyndale no shift.[920] For since this word 'one' in 'one wife' and 'one husband' was not by Saint Paul set in for nought,[921] it must needs signify either that there should be no more but one, or that there should be one at the least. If he should mean that a bishop should have one wife at the least, and that the widow should have had one husband at the least, then would he rather that they should have more than so few; which every man seeth how foolish that construction is. Now if Tyndale will say that by this word 'one' Saint Paul meant there should be but one wife at once and one husband at once, then did Saint Paul so speak of the bishop as though he had said, 'A bishop must be a good man and have but one wife at once.' In which words, Tyndale had lost his purpose.[922] For so were[923] only a prohibition for any more than one—and no commandment—but a bare[924] permission for one. And yet were it little to purpose; for in Saint Paul's days, a layman had but one wife at once.

And the folly of this construction appeareth in the words spoken of Saint Paul in[925] the choice of the widow, wherein Tyndale would, by this way, make Saint Paul to say thus: 'Take and choose in but such a widow as hath had but one husband at once'— as though the guise[926] were in his days that wives might have two husbands at once."

"In faith," quoth your friend, "I think Saint Paul meant not so. For then had wives been in his time little better than grass widows[927] be now. For they be yet as several[928] as a barber's chair, and never take but one at once."

"In faith," quoth I, "the folly of such folk doth well appear that seek in the Scripture of God such new constructions against the very[929] sense that God hath this fifteen hundred years so taught his whole Church that never was there pope so covetous yet that durst dispense in[930] this point, seeing the consent[931] of Christ's Church so full and whole therein, and the mind of Saint Paul so clear to suffer[932] only one, with utter exclusion of any more than one, that whosoever would construe him otherwise must needs fall into such open follies as Tyndale and Luther do. And thus ye see how substantially[933] Tyndale and his master construe the Scripture, and with what authority they confirm this noble new doctrine of theirs, by which they would condemn all Christendom as breakers of the Law of God as long as they suffer not any priest take a wife—or rather as long as they suffer him to be without a wife. For wives they must needs have, by Tyndale's tale,[934] whether they will or no."

"By my troth," quoth your friend, "if Tyndale and Luther have none other hold[935] than that place of Saint Paul, they be likely to take a fall. But I think they say more than that."

"Surely," quoth I. "Tyndale hath another reason[936] indeed. He saith that chastity is an exceeding seldom[937] gift, and unchastity exceeding perilous for that estate.[938] And thereon he concludeth that priests must needs have wives. But now what if a man would deny him—though chastity be a great gift, that yet it is a seldom gift? For though it be rare and seldom in respect of the remnant of the people that have it not, yet is it not seldom indeed; for

---

916 who   917 interpreted; constructed
918 but if: unless   919 and he list: if he desires   920 means out   921 nothing
922 argument   923 there would be
924 mere   925 about   926 custom

927 grass widows: women who cohabit with men, but never marry   928 exclusive
929 true   930 durst dispense in: dared give a dispensation on   931 consensus
932 allow   933 soundly   934 telling;

meaning   935 support; leg to stand on
936 argument   937 rare   938 state of life (the priesthood)

many men have it. And Christ saith that all men take[939] it not, but he saith not that no man taketh it, nor that few men take it. And highly he commendeth them that for his sake do take it. What inconvenience[940] is it, then, to take into his special service men of that sort that he most specially commendeth? Or if we granted to Tyndale that few men can live chaste—which is plainly false, for many hath done and doth—but now if we did, I say, grant him that thing, though he might peradventure thereupon conclude that there should not be so many priests made and bounden to chastity as could not live chaste, yet could he not conclude as he now concludeth: that no priest should be suffered to live chaste, but that every priest must needs have a wife. For this is his argument: few men can live chaste; ergo, every priest must take a wife. If we should impugn the form of this argument, Tyndale would rail and say we meddle with sophistry; and wise men would say we were idly occupied, to labor to show that folly that so evidently showeth itself. And therefore we shall let his wise argument alone, since it sufficeth us that every man that any wit hath may well see that upon his unreasonable reason one of two things must needs follow: either that Christ, in commending perpetual chastity, did commend a thing not commendable, or else, if every priest must needs have a wife, then were it not lawful[941] to make a priest of that sort that is of God's own mouth commended."

"Surely," quoth your friend, "methink they go far[942] therein, to say that priests must needs have wives. But methink that this they might well say, and I too: that it is not well done to bind them with a law that they shall have none, but it may be well done to suffer them have wives that would, as they have in Wales. And I hear say that in Almain[943] they find great ease[944] therein. For like as here the goodwife keepeth her husband from her maids, so there the parson's wife keepeth her husband from all the wives in the parish."

"As for Wales," quoth I, "ye be wrong informed; for wives have they not. But truth it is that incontinence is there in some places little looked unto, whereof much harm groweth in the country. And as for Almain, such part thereof as that is used[945] in—which is only where Luther's sect is received—whoso consider well what commodity[946] hath comen to them by such ungodly ways, I think shall have no great fantasy[947] to follow them."

"Well," quoth he, "let Wales and Almain go; yet priests had wives of old, when they were better than they be now, and yet have in Greece, where they be better than they be here."

"As for the priests of Greece, I will not dispraise[948] them," quoth I, "for I know them not. But somewhat[949] was not well there, that God hath suffered all that empire to fall into heathen men's hands.[950] And yet be they there not so loose[951] as ye reckon them. For though a wedded man taken there into the clergy be not, nor cannot be, put[952] from his wife, but is there suffered to minister in the office of a priest notwithstanding his marriage, yet if he be unmarried at the time that he taketh priesthood, he then professeth perpetual continence and never marrieth after, as I have learned by such as have comen from thence.

"Now where ye speak of old time, surely ye shall understand that there married not so many as ye would haply ween."[953]

"Peradventure," quoth he, "no more there would now. Some of them would have no wives though[954] that law were set at large.[955] For as a good fellow said once to his friends—that marveled why he married not, and thought him unnatural if he cared not for the company of a woman—he said unto them that he had liefer[956] lose a finger than lack a woman; but he had liefer lack the whole hand than have a wife. So if the priests were at liberty, some of the worst sort would yet, I ween, rather have women than wives. But others that would[957] be more honest would, I suppose, be married. And yet would some peradventure live in perpetual continence, as few do now."

"God forbid," quoth I.

"Well," quoth he, "they that would were not restrained. But if I shall be bold to say what I think, it seemeth me surely a very hard thing that the Church should make a law to bind a man to chastity—maugre his teeth[958]—to which God would never bind any man."

939 receive   **940** impropriety; offense; trouble   **941** ethical   **942** too far   **943** Germany   **944** convenience   **945** practiced   **946** profit   **947** inclination   **948** criticize   **949** something

950 *empire . . . hands:* Constantinople, the capital of the Greek (Byzantine) Empire, fell to the Turks in 1453. The last island holdouts fell in 1475, and the Greeks were under Muslim rule at More's time.

951 free   **952** separated   **953** *haply ween:* perhaps imagine   **954** even if   **955** *set at large:* relaxed   **956** rather   **957** wanted to   **958** *maugre his teeth:* against his will

"The Church," quoth I, "bindeth no man to chastity."

"That is truth," quoth he, "except[959] a priest be a man."

"Ye mistake the matter," quoth I, "as I shall show you after."

"There would," quoth he, "many harms be avoided, and much good would there grow thereof, if they might have wives that would."

"What good or harm," quoth I, "would come thereof, the proof[960] would show, wherein we might be the more bold to trust well, were it not that we now find it naught[961] in Saxony, where we newly see it assayed.[962] And as for that ye spoke of 'old time when the priests were better' — surely as I would, if ye had not stopped me, have said further before — we perceive well by writers of old time that, of those good men, very few were married, and none in effect after that office taken. And many such as had wives before, willingly with the assent of their wives forbore the carnal use of them. And since the good or harm growing of the matter best appeareth by the proof, besides the experience that we have now in Saxony where this change is begun with an infinite heap of heresies, it is easy to see that the good fathers which[963] gave their advice to the making of that law, with the thing almost received in general custom before, and with the consent[964] of all Christendom in effect that ratified and received it after, had a good proof thereof, and found this the best way before the law made;[965] and therefore I will not dispute with you thereupon. But forasmuch as ye lay unreasonableness to their charge that made it,[966] because they bind men as ye reckon against their will to chastity, somewhat were it that ye say,[967] if the Church compelled any man to be priest. But now when every man is at his liberty not to be priest but at his pleasure, how can any man say that the Church layeth a bond[968] of chastity in any man's neck against his will? The Church doth, in effect, no further but provide that — whereas men will of their own minds some live chaste and some will not — the ministers of the Sacrament shall be taken of[969] that sort only that will be content to profess chastity.

Wherewith whoso findeth fault blameth not only the clergy, but also the temporalty,[970] which be, and have been all this while, partners in the authority of the making and conservation of this law. Whereof there can no man blame the provision[971] but if[972] he be either in that heresy that he think that the cleanness of chastity is no more pleasant to God than the carnal use of matrimony, or else that he think it evil done to provide that the priests which shall serve God in his holy sacraments should be taken of the purest and most pleasant sort. Whereunto the very paynims[973] had such respect that their priests durst not presume to the sacrifice of their maumets but[974] after certain time of corporal cleanness,[975] kept from their wives, and some of them bounden[976] to perpetual chastity with the loss of that part of their body wherewith they might do the contrary."

"Yea, marry," quoth he, "that was a good sure way."

"It was," quoth I, "sure indeed, but not so good as this. For therein would be lost the merit that good men have in resisting of the devil, and the refraining[977] of their fleshly motion.[978] But as I would and was about to say, in the Old Law given to Moses, the priests of the Temple, for the time of their ministration, forbore their own house and the company of their wives. And therefore they served the Temple by course,[979] as it well appeareth in the beginning of Saint Luke's Gospel. So that[980] chastity was thought, both to[981] God and man, a thing meet and convenient[982] for priests among them[983] which most magnified[984] carnal generation. And then how much more specially now to[985] the priests of Christ, which[986] was both born of a virgin, and lived and died a virgin himself, and exhorted all his to the same? Whose counsel in that point, since some be content to follow and some to live otherwise, what way were,[987] I say, more meetly than to take into Christ's temple, to serve about the Sacrament, only such as be of that sort that are content and minded to live after the cleanness[988] of Christ's holy counsel?"

"Truth — if they so would,"[989] quoth he.

"They say," quoth I, "that they will when they come thereto, being already warned[990] of the law.

959 unless **960** result **961** bad
962 tried **963** who **964** consensus
965 was made **966** *lay…made it:* accuse
those who made it of being unreasonable
967 *somewhat…say:* there would be
something to what you say **968** chain
969 from **970** laity **971** *blame…*

provision: fault the law **972** *but if:*
unless **973** pagans **974** *durst…but:*
dared not to offer sacrifice to their idols
except **975** abstinence **976** were
bound **977** restraining **978** desires
979 taking turns **980** *So that:* So
981 by **982** *meet and convenient:*

fitting and appropriate **983** the Jewish
people **984** honored **985** with regard
to **986** who **987** would be **988** *after
the cleanness:* in accord with the purity
989 desired **990** informed

And to the intent that fewer should break it, therefore would I (as I said) have the better respect taken to the choosing.[991] And since it is hard to have so many so good, I would have the fewer made. But to say that the Church bindeth men to chastity against their will—because they take not a priest but if[992] he first professed chastity—is as far against reason as if he would say that they bind men to chastity against their will because they will make no monks but such as will promise to live chaste. Which promise every man well wotteth they make of their own minds, though the Church will neither make monks nor priests but such as so will. And as touching whether the order[993] of the Church therein be better than the contrary, good men and wise men both had the proof of both[994] before the law made, and it[995] well allowed through Christendom long time since. Which, ere I would assent to change, I would see a better author thereof than such a heretic as Luther and Tyndale, and a better example than the seditious and schismatic priests of Saxony."

"Surely," quoth he, "ye have well declared[996] the Church touching that law. But whatsoever the cause be, by my troth naught[997] they be, and as far worse than we as they be bounden to be better—and yet be we the worse for them."

"There be," quoth I, "many right good among them, and else were it[998] wrong with us. And many be there bad also, and some the worse for us. But whether[999] party is the better or the worse will I not dispute. But this will I say: that it were best that they thought themselves the worse, and we ourselves—and every man himself—worst.

"I would that we were all in case[1] with our own faults as my father saith that we be with our wives. For when he heareth folk blame wives and say that there be so many of them shrews, he saith that they defame them falsely. For he saith plainly that there is but one shrewd[2] wife in the world; but he saith indeed that every man weeneth he hath her, and that one is his own. So would I fain[3] that every man would ween there were but one man naught in all the whole world, and that one were himself, and

that he would thereupon go about to mend that one, and thus would all wax[4] well. Which thing we should shortly do, if we would once turn our wallet[5] that I told you of, and the bag with other folks' faults cast at our back, and cast the bag that beareth our own faults—cast it once before us—at our breast. It would be a goodly broach[6] for us to look on our own faults another[7] while. And I dare boldly say, both they and we should much the better amend if we were so ready each to pray for other as we be ready to seek each other's reproach and rebuke."

"In faith," quoth he, "I trow[8] that be true, and pray God we so may."

THE FOURTEENTH CHAPTER
The author answereth the doubt moved[9]
before (in the eleventh chapter) concerning the
constitution provincial,[10] and that the clergy is
therein far from the fault that is imputed to them
in that point, showing also that the clergy hath
not forbidden the Bible to be made
and read in English.

"But now to the matter we were in hand with:[11] ye said ye would make answer for the law whereby the clergy of this realm hath forbidden all the people to have any Scripture translated into our tongue—which is, as I said, in my mind an evil-made law."

"Marry," quoth I, "that is soon answered. Lay the charge[12] to them that made it."

"Marry," quoth he, "so I do. For who made that constitution but they?"

"Surely," quoth I, "nobody else—nor they neither."

"No?" quoth he. "What? Every man knoweth it."

"Verily," quoth I, "many men talk of it; but no man knoweth it. For there is none such indeed. There is of truth a constitution that speaketh of such matter, but nothing of such fashion. For ye shall understand that the great arch-heretic Wycliffe[13]—whereas the whole Bible was, long before his days, by virtuous and well-learned men translated into the English

991 *respect taken to the choosing:* consideration used in the selection   **992** *but if:* unless   **993** arrangement; rule   **994** both approaches   **995** priestly celibacy   **996** clarified   **997** bad   **998** *else were it:* otherwise it would be   **999** which   **1** the same position   **2** shrewish;

bad-tempered   **3** wish   **4** grow   **5** *once turn our wallet:* for once turn around our knapsack   **6** goad; brooch   **7** once in a   **8** believe   **9** *doubt moved:* question raised   **10** *constitution provincial:* decree of the synod   **11** *were in hand with:* had in hand   **12** *Lay the charge:* Impute the fault

13 John Wycliffe (1324–84) was a priest and scholar who translated the Vulgate into English near the end of his life. His teachings were declared heretical by synods in England in 1377, 1382, and 1407, and by the Ecumenical Council of Constance in 1415.

tongue, and by good and godly people with devotion and soberness well and reverently read—took upon him, of a malicious purpose, to translate it of new.[14] In which translation, he purposely corrupted that holy text, maliciously planting therein such words as might in the readers' ears serve to the proof of such heresies as he went about to sow, which he not only set forth with his own translation of the Bible, but also with certain prologues and glosses which he made thereupon. And these things he so handled (which was no great mastery),[15] with reasons probable[16] and likely to lay people and unlearned, that he corrupted in his time many folk in this realm. And by other ill books which he made in Latin, being after borne into Bohemia and there taught by John Hus and others, he was the occasion of the utter subversion of that whole realm, both in faith and good living, with the loss also of many a thousand lives. And as he began again the old heresies of those ancient heretics whom, and whose errors, the Church of Christ had condemned and subdued many diverse ages[17] before, so doth Luther again begin to set up his.[18] For all that he hath, in effect, he hath of him—saving that, lest he should seem to say nothing of his own, he added some things of himself of such manner sort[19] as there was never heretic before his days neither so wicked that he would for[20] sin nor so foolish that he durst for shame write, say, or, I trow, think the like."

"I long," quoth he, "to hear some of them; for the man is taken for wiser than to mean so madly as men bear him in hand."[21]

"Well," quoth I, "that shall we see soon, when we come thereto. But for our present purpose, after that it was perceived what harm the people took by the translation, prologues, and glosses of Wycliffe, and also of some others that after him helped to set forth his sect, then, for that cause—and 'forasmuch as it is dangerous to translate the text of Scripture out of one tongue into another, as holy Saint Jerome testifieth, forasmuch as in translation it is

hard always to keep the same sentence whole'[22]— it was, I say, for these causes at a council held at Oxford, provided upon great pain[23] that 'no man should from thenceforth translate into the English tongue (or any other language) of his own authority, by way of book, libel,[24] or treatise,[25] nor no man, openly or secretly,[26] any such book, libel, or treatise read, newly made in the time of the said John Wycliffe or since, or that should be made any time after, till the same translation were by the diocesan[27]—or, if need should require, by a provincial council— approved.'[28] And this is a law that so many so long have spoken of, and so few have, in all this while, rought[29] to seek whether they say truth or no. For I trow that in this law ye see nothing unreasonable. For it neither forbiddeth the translations to be read that were already well done of old, before Wycliffe's days; nor damneth[30] his because it was new, but because it was naught; nor prohibiteth new to be made, but provideth that they shall not be read if they be mismade, till they be by good examination amended, except[31] they be such translations as Wycliffe made, and Tyndale, that the malicious mind of the translator had in such wise handled it as it were[32] labor lost to go about to mend them."

"I long, by my troth," quoth he, "and even sit on thorns,[33] till I see that constitution. For not myself only, but every man else hath ever taken it far otherwise, that ever I have heard spoken thereof[34] till now. But surely I will see it myself ere I sleep."

"Ye shall be sooner eased," quoth I. "For I cannot suffer[35] to see you sit so long on thorns. And therefore ye shall see it by and by."[36]

And therewith I fetched him forth the constitutions provincial with Lyndwood thereupon,[37] and turned him to the place in the title *De magistris*.[38] Which, when himself had read, he said he marveled much how it happened that in so plain a matter men be so far abused[39] to report it so far wrong.

"This groweth," quoth I, "partly by malice, partly by sloth and negligence, in that folk be more glad to

---

14 *of new:* anew   15 achievement 16 *reasons probable:* arguments that sounded plausible   17 *diverse ages:* different times   18 Wycliffe's   19 *manner sort:* a kind   20 on account of   21 *bear him in hand:* make him out (to mean) 22 *sentence whole:* full sense. More quotes the opening words of the seventh constitution of the 1407 Synod of Oxford. The synod is not directly quoting Jerome.

They seem to have had in mind his letter to Pammachius (#57), where Jerome addresses criticism about his "sense for sense" (rather than word for word) method of translation.   23 *provided upon great pain:* stipulated on pain of severe punishment 24 pamphlet   25 tract   26 *openly or secretly:* publicly or privately   27 bishop of the diocese   28 *no man…approved:* another literally translated quote from

the seventh constitution   29 cared 30 condemns   31 unless   32 *as it were:* that it would be   33 *on thorns:* in painful suspense   34 *spoken thereof:* speak of it   35 bear   36 *by and by:* right now 37 *constitutions…thereupon:* the edition of the synodal decrees published with Bishop William Lyndwood's (1375-1446) commentary   38 *De magistris:* "On teachers"   39 misled

believe and tell forth a thing that may sound to the dispraise of the clergy than to search and be sure whether they say true or no."

THE FIFTEENTH CHAPTER

The messenger moveth against the clergy that, though they have made no law thereof, yet they will indeed suffer none English Bible in no man's hand, but use⁴⁰ to burn them where they find them—and sometimes to burn the man too. And for example he layeth⁴¹ one Richard Hunne, showing that the Chancellor of London murdered him in prison and after hanged him—feigning⁴² that he hanged himself—and after condemned him of heresy, because he had an English Bible, and so burned the Bible and him together. Whereunto the author answereth.

"I suppose," quoth he, "that this opinion is rather grown another way: that is to wit, by the reason that the clergy—though the law serve them not therefor⁴³—do yet indeed take all translations out of every layman's hand. And sometimes with those that be burned or convicted of heresy, they burn the English Bible without respect, be the translation old or new, bad or good."

"Forsooth," quoth I, "if this were so, then were it in my mind not well done. But I believe ye mistake it. Howbeit,⁴⁴ what ye have seen I cannot say. But myself have seen, and can show you, Bibles fair and old, written in English, which have been known and seen by the bishop of the diocese, and left in laymen's hands—and women's too—such as he knew for good and Catholic folk, that used it with devotion and soberness. But of truth all such as are founden in the hands of heretics they use⁴⁵ to take away. But they do cause none to be burned, as far as ever I could wit,⁴⁶ but only such as be founden faulty. Whereof many be set forth with evil prologues or glosses maliciously made by Wycliffe and other heretics. For no good man would, I ween, be so mad to

burn up the Bible wherein they found no fault, nor any law that letted it to be⁴⁷ looked on and read."

"Marry," quoth he, "but I have heard good men say that even here in London, not many years ago, in the days of the bishop that last died, they burned up as fair Bibles in English as any man hath lightly⁴⁸ seen—and thereto⁴⁹ as faultless, for aught⁵⁰ that any man could find, as any Bible is in Latin. And yet, besides this, they burned up the dead body of the man himself whom themselves had hanged in the bishop's prison before, making as though the man had hanged himself. And of the burning of his body had they no color but⁵¹ only because they found English Bibles in his house. Wherein they never found other fault but because they were English."

"Who told you this tale?" quoth I.

"Forsooth,⁵² diverse honest men," quoth he, "that saw it, and specially one that saw the man hanging in the bishop's prison ere he was cut down. And he told me that it was well and clearly proved that the Chancellor and his keepers⁵³ had killed the man first, and then hanged him after, and that they had laid heresy to him⁵⁴ only for hatred that he sued a Praemunire⁵⁵ against diverse persons for a suit taken about a mortuary⁵⁶ in the Audience⁵⁷ of the Archbishop of Canterbury.⁵⁸ And then they proved the heresy by nothing else but by the possession of a good English Bible. And upon heresy so proved against him whom they had hanged, lest he should say for⁵⁹ himself, they burned up the Holy Scripture of God, and the body of a good man therewith. For I have heard him called a very honest person and of a good substance."⁶⁰

"Forsooth," quoth I, "of good substance; he was, I think, well worth a thousand marks. And of his worldly conversation⁶¹ among the people, I have heard none harm. But surely as touching his faith toward Christ, methinketh I may be bold to say that he was not honest. And as touching truth in words, he that hath told you this tale was not so honest indeed as methinketh ye take him for."

"Why," quoth he, "do ye know the matter well?"

40 are accustomed **41** cites **42** alleging falsely **43** *serve them not therefor:* does not help them in this **44** However **45** are accustomed **46** ascertain **47** *letted...to be:* is there any law which prevents it from being **48** readily **49** also **50** anything **51** excuse; pretext **52** In truth **53** guards **54** *laid heresy to him:* charged him with heresy **55** The Statute

of Praemunire (1393) forbade British subjects from appealing any legal decisions to any foreign person or body. It specifically targeted appeals made to Church courts in Rome. **56** fee paid to the priest presiding at a funeral **57** The Court of Audience heard civil suits filed under canon law. **58** *sued...Canterbury:* Hunne refused to pay the customary fee for burying his

infant son. A year later, after a real estate dispute, the priest sued Hunne, ostensibly to recover the fee. In response, Hunne filed the Praemunire suit, alleging that he could not be sued in the Archbishop's court, because that court derived its authority from Rome. **59** *say for:* speak in defense of **60** wealth **61** conduct

"Forsooth," quoth I, "so well I know it, from top to toe, that I suppose there be not very many men that knoweth it much better. For I have not only been diverse times present myself at certain examinations thereof, but have also diverse and many times sunderly[62] talked with almost all such, except the dead man himself, as most knew of the matter. Which matter was many times in sundry places examined. But especially at Baynard's Castle one day was it examined at great length, and by[63] a long time, every man being sent for before, and ready there all that could be found that anything could tell, or that had said they could anything tell, in the matter. And this examination was had before diverse great lords, spiritual and temporal,[64] and others of the King's honorable Council, sent thither by his Highness for the nonce,[65] of his blessed zeal and princely desire borne to the searching of the truth. Whereunto his gracious mind was much inclined, and had been by a right honorable man informed that there was one[66] had showed a friend of his that he 'could go take him by the sleeve that killed Hunne'—for Richard Hunne was his name, whom ye speak of. I was also myself present at the judgment given[67] in Paul's, whereupon[68] his books and his body were burned. And by all these things I very well know that he of[69] whom ye have heard this matter hath told you tales far from the truth."

"In good faith," quoth your friend, "he told me one thing that ye speak of now: that there was one that said he 'could go take him by the sleeve that killed Richard Hunne,' and that he did so indeed, before the lords, and came even there to the Chancellor,[70] and said, 'My lords, this is he.' But when he was asked how he knew it, he confessed that it was by such an unlawful[71] craft as was not taken for a proof. For it was, they say, by necromancy. And the bishops that were there would have had that man burned, too, for witchcraft. And told[72] me also that there was another which[73] had seen many men that had hanged themselves: a man that had been long in office under diverse of the King's almoners[74]—to

whom the goods of such men as kill themselves be appointed by the law, and his office, as deodands[75] to be given in alms. This man, as I have heard say, showed unto the lords, by such experience as he had, good and plain tokens by which they perceived well that Hunne did never hang himself. I have heard also that a spiritual[76] man—and one that loved well the Chancellor, and was a laborer for that party—yet could not deny before all the lords but that he had told a temporal man,[77] and a friend of his, that Hunne had never[78] been accused of heresy if he had never sued the Praemunire.[79] And by Saint Mary, that was a shrewd word. Howbeit, indeed it went not so near the matter[80] as the other two things did."

"Yes, in good faith," quoth I, "all three like near, when they were all heard. But of truth, many other things were there laid[81] that, upon the hearing, seemed much more suspicious than these, which yet, when they were answered, always lost more than half their strength. But as for these three matters, I promise you, proved[82] very trifles—and such as, if ye had heard them, ye would have laughed at them seven years after."

"I beseech you," quoth he, "let me hear how they proved."

"I am loath," quoth I, "to let you, and lose your time in such trifles. Howbeit, since ye long so sore therefor,[83] rather than ye should lose your child for them, ye shall have them all three, as shortly[84] as I can. First ye must understand that because[85] the coming together of the lords from Greenwich to Baynard's Castle for the trying out of[86] the matter should not be frustrate, there was such diligence done before that every man that aught had said therein[87] was ready there against their coming,[88] where they began with the first point that ye spoke of, as the special motion[89] whereupon the King's Highness had sent them thither. Wherefore, after the rehearsal[90] made of the cause of their coming, the greatest temporal lord there present said unto a certain servant of his own standing there beside,[91]

---

62 separately　**63** for　**64** *spiritual and temporal:* ecclesiastical and secular
65 particular purpose　**66** someone
67 *judgment given:* trial held　**68** after which　**69** from　**70** of the diocese of London　**71** wicked　**72** my informant told　**73** who　**74** officers who distribute alms to the poor　**75** things forfeited to

the Crown for charitable use　**76** ecclesiastical　**77** *temporal man:* layman
78 *had never:* would never have　**79** *sued the praemunire:* filed the praemunire suit　**80** *went . . . matter:* had not so much relevance to the case　**81** alleged　**82** they proved　**83** *sore therefor:* greatly for it
84 quickly　**85** in order that　**86** *trying*

out of: judicial inquiry into　**87** *aught . . . therein:* anything had said about the matter
88 *against their coming:* in advance of the lords' arrival　**89** *as the special motion:* it being the specific reason　**90** recounting, report　**91** beside him

'Sir, ye told me that one showed you that he could go take him by the sleeve that killed Hunne. Have ye brought him hither?'

"'Sir,' quoth he, 'if it like[92] your Lordship, this man it was that told me so'—pointing to one that he had caused to come thither. Then my lord asked that man, 'How say ye, sir? Can ye do as ye said ye could?'

"'Forsooth, my lord,' quoth he, 'and[93] it like your Lordship, I said not so much; this gentleman did somewhat mistake me. But, indeed, I told him that I had a neighbor that told me that he could do it.'

"'Where is that neighbor?' quoth my lord.

"'This man, sir,' quoth he, bringing forth one which had also been warned[94] to be there. Then was he asked whether he had said that he could do it.

"'Nay, forsooth,' quoth he, 'my lord, I said not that I could do it myself, but I said that one told me that he could do it.'

"'Well,' quoth my lord, 'who told you so?'

"'Forsooth, my lord,' quoth he, 'my neighbor here.'

"Then was that man asked, 'Sir, know you one that can tell who killed Richard Hunne?'

"'Forsooth,' quoth he, 'and it like your lordship, I said not that I knew one surely[95] that could tell who had killed him; but I said, indeed, that I know one which I thought verily[96] could tell who killed him.'

"'Well,' quoth the lords, 'at the last—yet with much work—we come to somewhat.[97] But whereby[98] think you that he can tell?'

"'Nay, forsooth, my lord,' quoth he, 'it is a woman. I would she were here with your lordships now.'

"'Well,' quoth my lord, 'woman or man, all is one; she shall be had, wheresoever she be.'

"'By my faith, my lords,' quoth he, 'and[99] she were with you, she would tell you wonders. For, by God, I have wist her tell[100] many marvelous things ere now.'

"'Why,' quoth the lords, 'what have you heard her told?'[101]

"'Forsooth, my lords,' quoth he, 'if a thing had been stolen, she would have told who had it. And therefore I think she could as well tell who killed Hunne as who stole a horse.'

"'Surely,' said the lords, 'so think all we too, I trow.[102] But how could she tell it? By the devil?'

"'Nay, by my troth, I trow,' quoth he, 'for I could never see her use any worse way than looking in one's hand.'

"Therewith the lords laughed, and asked, 'What is she?'

"'Forsooth, my lords,' quoth he, 'an Egyptian;[103] and she was lodged here at Lambeth,[104] but she is gone overseas now. Howbeit, I trow she be not in her own country yet; for they say it is a great way hence, and she went over little more than a month ago.'"

"Now, forsooth," quoth your friend, "this process came to a wise purpose.[105] Here was a great post well thwitted to a pudding prick.[106] But I pray you, to what point came the second matter: of him that had been in office under so many of the King's almoners that he knew by his own experience, and proved, that Richard Hunne had not hanged himself?"

"Forsooth," quoth I, "he was called in next. And then was he asked whereby he knew it. But would God ye had seen his countenance. The man had of likelihood said somewhat too far, and was much amazed,[107] and looked as though his eyes would have fallen out of his head into the lords' laps. But to the question he answered and said that he saw that very well, for he saw him both ere he was taken down and after."

"'What then?' quoth the lords. 'So did there many more, which[108] yet upon the sight could not tell that.'

"'No, my lords,' quoth he, 'but I have another insight in such things than other men have.'

"'What insight?' quoth they.

"'Forsooth,' quoth he, 'it is not unknown that I have occupied[109] a great while under diverse of the King's almoners, and have seen and considered many that have hanged themselves; and thereby, if I see one hang, I can tell anon[110] whether he hanged himself or not.'

"'By what token can you tell?' quoth the lords.

"'Forsooth,' quoth he, 'I cannot tell the tokens; but I perceive it well enough by mine own sight.'

"But when they heard him speak of his own sight, and therewith saw what sight he had, looking as though his eyes would have fallen in their laps, there

---

92 please **93** if **94** informed; notified **95** certainly **96** truly **97** *come to somewhat:* are getting somewhere **98** *whereby think you:* for what reason do you think **99** if **100** *wist her tell:* known her to tell

101 tell **102** trust **103** *an Egyptian:* a Gypsy **104** a place near Westminster; Lambeth Palace was the residence of the Archbishop of Canterbury **105** *this... purpose:* this discussion came to a sensible

end **106** *thwitted to a pudding prick:* whittled to a toothpick **107** terrified **108** who **109** been employed **110** at once could few forbear[111] laughing, and said, 'We see well, surely, that ye have a sight by yourself.'[112] And then said one lord merrily, 'Peradventure as[113] some man is so cunning by[114] experience of jewels that he can perceive by his own eyes whether a stone be right[115] or counterfeit, though he cannot well make another man to perceive the tokens, so this good fellow, though he cannot tell us the marks,[116] yet he hath such an experience in hanging that himself perceiveth upon the sight whether the man hanged himself or no.'

"'Yea forsooth, my lord,' quoth he, 'even as[117] your lordship saith. For I know it well enough myself, I have seen so many by reason of mine office.'

"'Why,' quoth another lord merrily, 'your office hath no more experience in hanging than hath a hangman. And yet he cannot tell.'

"'Nay, sir,' quoth he, 'and it like[118] your lordship, he meddleth not with them that hang themselves, as I do.'

"'Well,' quoth one of the lords, 'how many of them have ye meddled with in your days?'

"'With many, my lord,' quoth he, 'for I have been officer under two almoners, and therefore I have seen many.'

"'How many?' quoth one of the lords.

"'I cannot tell,' quoth he, 'how many, but I wot[119] well I have seen many.'

"'Have ye seen,' quoth one, 'a hundred?'

"'Nay,' quoth he, 'not a hundred.'

"'Have ye seen fourscore and ten?'[120] Thereat a little he studied,[121] as one standing in a doubt and that were loath to lie; and at last he said that he thought nay, not fully fourscore and ten. Then was he asked whether he hath seen twenty. And thereto, without any sticking,[122] he answered, 'Nay, not twenty.' Thereat the lords laughed well, to see that he was so sure that he had not seen twenty, and was in doubt whether he had seen fourscore and ten. Then was he asked whether he had seen fifteen. And thereto he said shortly nay. And in like wise of ten. At last they came to five, and from five to four. And there he began to study again. Then came they to three, and then—for shame—he was fain[123] to say that he had

seen so many, and more too. But when he was asked when, whom, and in what place, necessity drove him at last unto the truth; whereby it appeared that he never had seen but one in all his life. And that was an Irish fellow called Crookshank, whom he had seen hanging in an old barn. And when all his cunning[124] was come to this, he was bid walk like[125] himself. And one said unto him that because he was not yet cunning enough in the craft of hanging, it was pity that he had no more experience thereof by one more.'

"Forsooth," quoth your friend, "this was a mad fellow. Came the third tale to as wise a point?"

"Ye shall hear," quoth I. "The temporal man that had reported it upon the mouth of[126] the spiritual man was a good worshipful[127] man, and for his troth[128] and worship was in great credit. And surely the spiritual man was a man of worship also, and well known both for cunning and virtuous. And therefore the lords much marveled, knowing them both for such as they were, that they should be like[129] to find either the one or the other either make an untrue report or untruly deny the truth. And first the temporal man—before the lords, in the hearing of the spiritual person standing by—said:

"'My lords all, as[130] help me God and halidom,[131] Master Doctor here said unto me his[132] own mouth that if Hunne had not sued the Praemunire, he should never have been accused of heresy.'

"'How say you, Master Doctor?' quoth the lords. 'Was that true? Or else why said you so?'

"'Surely, my lords,' quoth he, 'I said not all things so; but marry, this I said indeed: that if Hunne had not been accused of heresy, he would never have sued the Praemunire.'

"'Lo, my lords,' quoth the other, 'I am glad ye find me a true man. Will ye command me any more service?'

"'Nay, by my troth,' quoth one of the lords, 'not in this matter; by my will, ye may go when ye will. For I have espied, good man, so[133] the words be all one,[134] it maketh no matter to you which way they stand,[135] but all is one to you: a horse mill and a mill horse, "Drink ere ye go" and "Go ere you drink."'"

---

111 keep from   112 *by yourself:* all your own   113 *Peradventure as:* Perhaps just as   114 *cunning by:* knowledgeable on account of his   115 genuine   116 signs; criteria   117 *even as:* (it is) just as   118 *and it like:* if it please   119 know   120 ninety

121 reflected   122 hesitating   123 obliged; forced   124 knowledge, cleverness   125 *walk like:* do the same   126 *upon the mouth of:* as having been said by   127 distinguished; honorable   128 integrity; truth; trustworthiness   129 likely   130 so

131 all things holy   132 with his   133 as long as   134 the same   135 *which way they stand:* what order they are in

"'Nay, my lords,' quoth he, 'I will not drink, God yield[136] you.' And therewith he made courtesy[137] and went his way, leaving some of the lords laughing to see the good plain old honest man, how that, as contrary as their two tales were, yet when he heard them both again, he marked no difference between them, but took them both for one because the words were one."

"By my troth," quoth your friend, "these three things came merrily to pass, and I would not for a good thing but I had heard them. For here may a man see that misunderstanding maketh misreporting. And a tale that flieth through many mouths catcheth many new feathers, which, when they be pulled away again,[138] leave him as pilled as a coot[139]—and sometimes as bare as a bird's ass. But I think verily, for all this, there was great evidence given against the Chancellor;[140] for he was at length indicted of[141] Hunne's death, and was a great while in prison, and in conclusion never durst abide the trial of[142] twelve men for his acquittal, but was fain[143] by friendship to get a pardon. But I beseech you, for my mind's sake, show me what thought yourself therein."

"Of truth," quoth I, "there were diverse suspicious things laid against him, and all those well and substantially answered again for him.[144] Howbeit, upon the telling of a tale oftentimes happeth[145] that when all is heard that can be said therein, yet shall the hearers some think one way and some another. And therefore, though I cannot think but that the jury, which were right honest men, found[146] the verdict as themselves thought in their own conscience to be truth, yet in mine own mind, for aught that ever I heard thereof in my life—as help me God—I could never think it."[147]

"If he had not been guilty," quoth your friend, "he would never have sued[148] his pardon."

"Yes," quoth I, "right wise men have I heard say ere this that they will never refuse neither God's pardon nor the King's. It were no wisdom in a matter of many suspicious tales, be they never so false, to stand[149] on twelve men's mouths where one may find a surer[150] way. But I think verily that if he had been guilty, he should never have gotten his pardon. For albeit that there was never, I trow, brought in this world a prince of more benign nature, nor of more merciful mind, than is our sovereign lord that now reigneth (and long mote[151] reign) upon us, whereby never king[152] could find in his heart more freely to forgive and forget offenses done and committed unto[153] himself, yet hath his Highness such a fervent affection to right and justice in other men's causes, and such a tender zeal to the conservation of his subjects (of whose lives his high wisdom considereth many to stand in peril by the giving of pardon to a few willful murderers), that never was there king, I believe, that ever wore the crown in this realm, which[154] hath in so many years given unto such folk so few. And therefore I make myself sure that in such a willful, purposed,[155] heinous, cruel deed as this had been if it had been true, all the friends that could have been founden for the Chancellor in this world could never have gotten his pardon to pass in such wise,[156] had it not been that upon the report of all the circumstances, the King's high prudence—which, without flattery, pierceth as deep into the bottom of a doubtful matter as ever I saw man in my life—had well perceived his innocence. And since I verily believe that if he had been guilty, he never could have gotten, in such a heinous murder, any pardon of the King's Highness, I dare make myself much more bold[157] of his innocence now. For ye shall understand that he never sued pardon therefor.[158] But after long examination of the matter, as well the Chancellor as the others,[159] being indicted of[160] the deed, and arraigned upon the indictment in the King's Bench,[161] pleaded that they were not guilty. And thereupon the King's Grace—being well and sufficiently informed of the truth, and, of[162] his blessed disposition, not willing that there should in his name any false matter be maintained[163]—gave in commandment to his attorney to confess their pleas to be true without any further trouble. Which thing, in so faithful a prince, is a clear declaration that the matter laid to the Chancellor was untrue.

---

136 reward   **137** obeisance (to the lords)   **138** *away again:* back off   **139** *pilled as a coot:* bald as a guillemnot, a seabird with a black head   **140** William Horsey, who was indicted by the coroner's jury for Hunne's murder, and eventually pardoned by Henry VIII, thereby avoiding a trial   **141** *at length indicted of:*

eventually indicted for   **142** *durst... of:* dared to stand trial by   **143** glad; obliged   **144** *substantially answered again for him:* solidly answered in response in his favor   **145** it happens   **146** gave; returned   **147** it was true   **148** petitioned for   **149** rely on   **150** safer   **151** may (he)   **152** *whereby never king:* because of which

(merciful mind) there was never a king who   **153** against   **154** who   **155** premeditated   **156** *pass... wise:* come about in such a way   **157** confident   **158** for it   **159** i.e., the Chancellor's guards   **160** for   **161** *King's Bench:* a civil court   **162** on account of   **163** *matter... maintained:* charge be sustained

"And as for myself, in good faith as I told you before, I never heard in my life (and yet have I heard all, I ween, that well could be said) therein anything that moved me, after both the parties heard,[164] to think that he should be guilty.

"And besides all this, considering that Hunne was (as they that well know him say he was indeed), though he were a fair dealer among his neighbors, yet a man high-minded and set on the glory of a victory which he hoped to have in the Praemunire—whereof he much boasted, as they said, among his familiar[165] friends, that he trusted to be spoken of long after his days, and have his matter[166] in the Years and Terms[167] called 'Hunne's Case'—which, when he perceived would go against his purpose, and that in the temporal law[168] he should not win his spurs, and over[169] that in the spiritual law[170] perceived so much of his secret sores unwrapped and discovered that he began to fall in[171] fear of worldly shame, it is to me much more likely that for[172] weariness of his life he rid himself out thereof; which manner of affection[173] we see not seldom happen, specially since the devil might peradventure join therewith a marvelous hope of that which after happed: that the suspicion of his death might be laid to the charge and peril of the Chancellor. This is, I say, much more likely to me than the thing whereof I never heard the like before: that the Bishop's Chancellor should kill in the Lollards' Tower[174] a man so sore[175] suspected and convicted of heresy, whereby he might bring himself in business,[176] whereas if he hated the man (for kill him he would not, ye wot well, if he loved him), he might easily bring him to shame and peradventure to shameful death also."

"In good faith," quoth your friend, "wist I that it were[177] true that he was a heretic indeed, and in peril to be so proved, I would well think that in malice and despair he hanged himself."

"God," quoth I, "knoweth of all things the truth. But what I have heard therein, that shall I show you.

"Myself was present in Paul's[178] when the Bishop, in the presence of the Mayor and the aldermen of the city, condemned him for a heretic after his death. And then were there read openly the depositions, by which it was well proved that he was convicted as well of diverse other heresies as of misbelief toward the Holy Sacrament of the altar. And thereupon was the judgment given that his body should be burned; and so was it.

"Now this is," quoth I, "to me a full proof. For I assure you, the Bishop was a very wise man, a virtuous and a cunning."

"By Saint Mary," quoth he, "the proof is the better by so much."

"I shall tell you," quoth I, "another thing, which, when ye hear, ye shall peradventure believe it yet the better."

"That would I gladly know," quoth he. "For as far as I can hear, never man had[179] him suspect of any such thing before."

"Forsooth," quoth I, "that can I not tell. But so it happed that—as I remember, six or seven years after that Hunne was thus hanged and his body burned for a heretic—there was one in Essex, a carpenter that used to make pumps, which had intended, with others such as he was himself, to do great robbery; and thereupon was he brought unto the Court, where by the commandment of the King's Grace, a great honorable estate[180] of this realm and myself had him in examination. Wherein, among other things, he confessed that he had long held diverse heresies, which he said that his brother, being a clerk[181] of a church, had taught both his father and him. And I promise you, those heresies were of a height.[182] Then he showed us what other cunning masters[183] of that school he had heard read,[184] and specially in a place which he named us in London, where he said that such heretics were wont to resort[185] to their readings in a chamber at midnight. And when we asked him the names of them that were wont to haunt those midnight lectures, he rehearsed[186] us diverse; and among others he named Richard Hunne. Whereof we somewhat marveled in our minds; but nothing said we thereto, but let him rehearse on all such as he could call to mind. And when he stopped and could remember no more, then asked we of[187] them that he had named,

---

164 were heard   165 close   166 lawsuit
167 *Years and Terms:* The set of books covering all the court proceedings in England.   168 *temporal law:* civil court
169 besides   170 *spiritual law:* ecclesiastical court   171 into   172 because of

173 *manner of affection:* kind of mental disposition   174 *Lollards' Tower:* a part of Lambeth Palace used as a prison for heretics   175 strongly   176 *in business:* into trouble   177 *wist I that it were:* if I knew that it was   178 St. Paul's Church

179 held   180 nobleman   181 someone in minor orders (not a priest); scholar
182 serious nature   183 *cunning masters:* learned teachers   184 give lectures
185 *wont to resort:* accustomed to go
186 named   187 about

what they were and where they dwelled. And he told us of some of them that were convicted, and some that were fled, and some that were yet at that time dwelling still in the town. And in[188] the way, when we asked him what man was that 'Hunne' that he spoke of, he told us his person[189] and his house. 'And where is he now?' said we. 'Marry,' quoth he, 'I went to Tournai,[190] and when I came thence again, then heard I say[191] that he was hanged in the Lollards' Tower, and his body burned for a heretic.' And thus there learned we, long after, that Hunne had haunted heretics' lectures by night long before, which we declared unto the King's Highness as he[192] had confessed. And his Highness, though he was sorry that any man should be so lewd,[193] yet highly did rejoice that the goodness of God brought such hid mischief[194] more and more to light. So after[195] had we (by the King's commandment) that man's brother in examination, which[196] did indeed confess nothing, neither of the felonies[197] nor of the heresies. But yet his brother did abide[198] by them and avowed them in[199] his face, with such marks and tokens as it might well appear that he said truth. And surely marvel were it[200] if he would falsely have feigned such heinous things against his own brother, his own father, and himself, being thereto nothing compelled, nor put either in pain or fear. Now was the father dead; and others could we not come by, whom we might further examine of[201] that night school, saving[202] that he which, as I told you, confessed this matter, showed us also, at the first time, of one man in London, taken for good and honest, which[203] was (as he said) a scholar[204] also of his brother in those heresies—which man, for his honesty,[205] we forbore to meddle with till we should have the other brother. Whom, as soon as we had in hands, and that he was committed to the Marshalsea,[206] this other man, which was, as I told you, detected[207] unto us for a heretic and a scholar of his, came to me to labor and sue[208] for him, pretending that he did it for charity. And forasmuch as we thought we could not fail of him when we would have him,[209] we forbore therefore to examine

him till we should have examined the other whom he labored for. But then were we not aware in what wise we should be disappointed of him. For so mishapped it indeed that, after his being at[210] me to labor for him whose scholar in heresy he was detected to be, he was in his own house suddenly stricken and slain. And that wretched end had he. What conscience he died with, God knoweth; for I can tell you no further."

"By Saint John," quoth your friend, "but, upon the whole tale, it seemeth to me very clear that Hunne was himself not clear of the matter."

"Surely," quoth I, "so seemed it, as far as I could wit,[211] unto as many as ever heard it, and would yet, I ween,[212] have seemed so more clearly if they had been present at the examinations, and seen under what manner the man came forth therewith."

"But yet," quoth your friend, "as for his English Bible, though Hunne were himself a heretic, yet might the book be good enough. And no good reason is there why a good book should be burned with an evil man."

"Ye call me well home,"[213] quoth I, "and put me well in mind.[214] For that was the thing whereby ye took occasion to talk of Hunne, of whom we talked so long that at last I had forgotten wherefore and whereupon[215] we entered into that communication. And yet make those books not a little[216] to the matter that we had in hand—I mean toward the perceiving what opinion that Hunne was of. For surely at such time as he was denounced for a heretic, there lay his English Bible open (and some other English books of his), that every man might see the places noted with his own hand:[217] such words, and in such wise, that there would no wise man that good were have any great doubt, after the sight thereof, what naughty[218] minds the men had, both he that so noted them and he that so made them. I remember not now the specialties of the matter,[219] nor the formal[220] words as they were written. But this I remember well: that besides other things framed for the favor of diverse other heresies, there were in the prologue of that Bible such

---

188 along   **189** *his person:* what he looked like   **190** a French town captured by England in 1513 and returned to the French in 1518   **191** *heard I say:* I heard it said   **192** that thief   **193** wicked   **194** evil   **195** afterward   **196** who   **197** *the felonies:* their crimes of grand larceny   **198** stand firm   **199** to   **200** *were it:* would it be

201 concerning   **202** except   **203** who   **204** pupil; student   **205** *for his honesty:* because of his reputation   **206** a famous prison near London   **207** informed on; accused   **208** *labor and sue:* advocate and petition   **209** *fail . . . have him:* fail to get hold of him whenever we wanted to   **210** *being at:* coming to

211 know; discern   **212** think   **213** *to the point*   **214** *put . . . mind:* i.e., remind me   **215** *wherefore and whereupon:* why and on what basis   **216** *make . . . little:* those Bibles have no little relevance   **217** *with . . . hand:* in his own handwriting   **218** wicked   **219** *specialties of the matter:* particulars of the content   **220** exact

words touching the Blessed Sacrament as good Christian men did much abhor to hear, and which gave the readers undoubted occasion to think that the book was written after Wycliffe's copy,[221] and by him translated into our tongue. And yet whether the book be burned or secretly kept, I cannot surely say. But truly—were the clergy of my mind—it should be somewhere reserved for the perpetual proof of the matter, there hath gone so much suspicious rumor thereof. Which, as I believe, were[222] all well answered and the mind fully satisfied of any man that wise were and good therewith, that once had overlooked,[223] read, and advisedly[224] considered that book."

THE SIXTEENTH CHAPTER

The messenger rehearseth[225] some causes which he hath heard laid[226] by some of the clergy wherefore the Scripture should not be suffered[227] in English. And the author showeth his mind: that it were convenient[228] to have the Bible in English. And therewith endeth the Third Book.

"Sir," quoth your friend, "yet for all this can I see no cause why the clergy should keep the Bible out of laymen's hands, that can[229] no more but their mother tongue."

"I had weened," quoth I, "that I had proved you plainly that they keep it not from them. For I have showed you that they keep none from them but such translation as be either not yet approved for good, or such as be already reproved for naught,[230] as Wycliffe's was, and Tyndale's. For as for other old ones, that were before Wycliffe's days, remain[231] lawful, and be in some folks' hands had and read."

"Ye say well," quoth he. "But yet, as women say, somewhat it was always that the cat winked when her eye was out.[232] Surely so is it not for nought[233] that the English Bible is in so few men's hands, when so many would so fain[234] have it."

"That is very truth," quoth I. "For I think that, though the favorers of a sect of heretics be so fervent in the setting forth of their sect that they let[235] not to lay their money together and make a purse[236] among them for the printing of an evil-made or evil-translated book (which, though it hap to be forbidden and burned, yet some be sold ere they be spied,[237] and each of them lose but their part),[238] yet I think there will no printer lightly[239] be so hot to put any Bible in print at his own charge—whereof the loss should lie wholly in[240] his own neck—and then hang[241] upon a doubtful trial[242] whether the first copy of his translation was made before Wycliffe's days or since. For if it were made since, it must be approved before the printing. And surely how it hath happed that in all this while, God hath either not suffered or not provided that any good virtuous man hath had the mind in faithful wise[243] to translate it, and thereupon either the clergy or at the leastwise some one bishop to approve it, this can I nothing tell. But howsoever it be, I have heard and hear so much spoken in[244] the matter, and so much doubt made therein,[245] that peradventure it would let and withdraw[246] any one bishop from the admitting thereof without the assent of the remnant. And whereas[247] many things be laid against it, yet is there in my mind not one thing that more putteth good men of the clergy in doubt to suffer it than this: that they see sometimes much of the worse sort more fervent in the calling for it than them whom we find far better, which maketh them to fear lest such men desire it for no good, and lest if it were had in every man's hand, there would great peril arise, and that seditious people should do more harm therewith than good and honest folk should take fruit thereby. Which fear, I promise you, nothing feareth me;[248] but that[249] whosoever would of their malice or folly take harm of that thing that is of itself ordained to do all men good, I would never, for the avoiding of their harm, take from others the profit which they might take and nothing deserve to lose. For else,[250] if the abuse of a good thing should cause the taking away thereof from others that would use it well, Christ should himself never have been born, nor

---

221 *written . . . copy:* copied from Wycliffe's edition   222 would be   223 examined; inspected   224 carefully   225 relates   226 alleged   227 allowed   228 appropriate   229 can speak   230 *reproved for naught:* condemned as bad   231 they remain   232 *the cat . . . out:* Proverbial: a one-eyed cat has no choice but to wink (the bishops have no choice but to say they approve of some English translations, but they don't really approve)   233 nothing   234 gladly   235 hesitate   236 fund   237 noticed   238 own share (of the cost)   239 likely   240 on   241 depend   242 investigation   243 *faithful wise:* an accurate way   244 about   245 *doubt made therein:* question expressed about it   246 *let and withdraw:* prevent and deter   247 while   248 *nothing feareth me:* does not at all frighten me   249 *but that:* rather   250 otherwise

brought his faith into the world, nor God should never have made it[251] neither, if he should — for[252] the loss of those that would be damned wretches — have kept away the occasion of reward from them that would, with help of his grace, endeavor them to deserve it."[253]

"I am sure," quoth your friend, "ye doubt not but that I am full and wholly of your mind in this matter, that the Bible should be in our English tongue. But yet that the clergy is of the contrary, and would not have it so, that appeareth well in that they suffer it not to be so. And over that, I hear in every place almost where I find any learned man of them,[254] their minds all set thereon to keep the Scripture from us. And they seek out for that part[255] every rotten reason that they can find, and set them forth solemnly to the show,[256] though five of those reasons be not worth a fig. For they begin as far[257] as our first father, Adam, and show us that his wife and he fell out of Paradise with desire of knowledge and cunning.[258] Now if this would serve, it must from the knowledge and study of Scripture drive every man — priest and other — lest it drive all out of Paradise. Then say they that God taught his disciples many things apart because the people should not hear it. And therefore they would[259] the people should not now be suffered to read all. Yet they say further that it is hard to translate the Scripture out of one tongue into another — and specially, they say, into ours, which they call a tongue vulgar and barbarous. But of all things specially they say that Scripture is the food of the soul, and that the common people be as infants that must be fed but with milk and pap.[260] And if we have any stronger meat, it must be chammed[261] afore by the nurse and so put into the baby's mouth. But methink though they make us all[262] infants, they shall find many a shrewd brain among us that can perceive chalk from cheese well enough, and if[263] they would once take[264] us our meat in our own hand. We be not so evil-toothed[265] but that within a while they shall see us cham it ourselves as well as they. For let them call us young babies and[266] they will — yet by God they

shall, for all that, well find in some of us that an old knave is no child!"

"Surely," quoth I, "such things as ye speak, is the thing that, as I somewhat said before, putteth good folk in fear to suffer the Scripture in our English tongue: not for the reading and receiving,[267] but for the busy chamming thereof, and for much meddling with such parts thereof as least will agree with their capacities. For undoubtedly, as ye spoke of our mother Eve, inordinate appetite of knowledge is a means to drive any man out of Paradise. And inordinate is the appetite when men unlearned, though they read it in their language, will be busy to ensearch and dispute the great secret mysteries of Scripture, which though they hear they be not able to perceive. This thing is plainly forbidden us that[268] be not appointed nor instructed thereto. And therefore holy Saint Gregory Nazianzen — that great solemn doctor — sore toucheth and reproveth[269] all such bold busy[270] meddlers in the Scripture, and showeth that it is in Exodus (by Moses ascending up upon the hill, where he spoke with God, and the people tarrying beneath) signified that the people be forbidden to presume to meddle with the high mysteries of Holy Scripture, but ought to be content to tarry beneath and meddle none higher[271] than is meet[272] for them, but receiving from the height of the hill by Moses that that[273] is delivered them — that is to wit, the laws and precepts that they must keep, and the points they must believe, look well thereupon, and often, and meddle well therewith, not to dispute it but to fulfill it.[274] And as for the high secret mysteries of God, and hard texts of his Holy Scripture, let us know that we be so unable to ascend up so high on that hill that it shall become[275] us to say to the preachers appointed thereto as the people said unto Moses: 'Hear you God, and let us hear you.'[276] And surely the blessed holy doctor Saint Jerome greatly complaineth[277] and rebuketh that lewd[278] homely manner[279] that the common lay people — men and women — were in his days so bold in the meddling, disputing, and expounding of Holy Scripture, and showeth plainly that they shall have

---

251 the world   252 on account of
253 *endeavor . . . deserve it:* exert themselves
to earn it   254 *of them:* among the clergy
255 side; cause   256 view   257 that
far back   258 learning   259 desire
that   260 See Heb 5:12–14; 1 Cor 3:1–3.
261 chewed   262 all out to be   263 *and*

if: if   264 give   265 ill-toothed; poorly
equipped with teeth   266 if   267 accepting   268 who   269 *sore toucheth and
reproveth:* strongly rebukes and criticizes
270 prying   271 *none higher:* with no
higher things   272 appropriate; fitting
273 which   274 St. Gregory (329–90)

was Archbishop of Constantinople; see
his *Defense of his Flight to Pontus* (*PG* 35:
495–96).   275 be proper for   276 Ex
20:19   277 laments; deplores   278 uneducated; vulgar; bad   279 practice; custom

evil proof[280] therein, that will reckon themselves to understand it by themselves without a reader.[281] For it is a thing that requireth good help, and long time, and a whole mind given greatly thereto. And surely since as the holy apostle Saint Paul in diverse of his epistles saith, God hath by his Holy Spirit so instituted and ordained his Church that he will have some readers and some hearers, some teachers and some learners,[282] we do plainly pervert and turn upside down the right order of Christ's Church when the one party meddleth with the other's office. Plato, the great philosopher, specially forbiddeth such as be not admitted thereunto, nor men meet therefor,[283] to meddle much and embusy[284] themselves in reasoning and disputing upon the temporal laws of the city, which would[285] not be reasoned upon but by folk meet therefor and in place convenient.[286] For else they that cannot very well attain to perceive[287] them begin to mislike, dispraise, and contemn[288] them. Whereof followeth the breach of the laws and disorder of the people. For till a law be changed by authority, it rather ought to be observed than contemned. Or else the example of one law boldly broken and set at nought[289] waxeth a precedent for the remnant to be used like.[290] And commonly the best laws shall worst like[291] much of the common people, which most long (if they might be heard and followed) to live all at liberty under none at all. Now if Plato, so wise a man, so thought good[292] in temporal laws—things of men's making—how much is it less meet for every man boldly to meddle with the exposition of Holy Scripture, so devised and indited[293] by the high wisdom of God that it far exceedeth, in many places, the capacity and perceiving[294] of man. It was also provided by the Emperor,[295] in the law civil, that the common people should never be so bold to keep dispicions[296] upon the faith or Holy Scripture, nor that any such thing should be used[297] among them or before them.[298] And therefore, as I said before, the special fear in this matter is lest we would be too busy in chamming of the Scripture ourselves—which ye say we were[299] able enough to

do—which undoubtedly the wisest and the best-learned, and he that therein hath by[300] many years bestowed his whole mind, is yet unable to do. And then far more unable must he needs be that boldly will, upon the first reading, because he knoweth the words, take upon him therefore to teach other men the sentence,[301] with peril of his own soul and other men's too, by the bringing men into mad ways, sects, and heresies, such as heretics have of old brought up and the Church hath condemned. And thus in these matters, if the common people might be bold to cham it, as ye say, and to dispute it, then should ye have the more blind, the more bold; the more ignorant, the more busy;[302] the less wit,[303] the more inquisitive; the more fool, the more talkative of great doubts[304] and high questions of Holy Scripture and of God's great and secret mysteries—and this not soberly, of any good affection,[305] but presumptuously and unreverently, at meat and at meal. And there when the wine were in and the wit out, would they take upon them with foolish words and blasphemy to handle Holy Scripture in more homely[306] manner than a song of Robin Hood. And some would, as I said, solemnly take upon them, like as[307] they were ordinary readers,[308] to interpret the text at their pleasure, and therewith[309] fall themselves, and draw down others with them into seditious sects and heresies, whereby the Scripture of God should lose his[310] honor and reverence, and be, by such unreverent and unsitting demeanor,[311] among much people quite and clean abused,[312] unto the contrary of that holy purpose that God ordained it for. Whereas if we would no further meddle therewith but well and devoutly read it; and in that that is plain and evident (as[313] God's commandments and his holy counsels) endeavor ourselves to follow, with help of his grace asked thereunto; and in his great and marvelous miracles consider his Godhead;[314] and in his lowly birth, his godly life, and his bitter Passion, exercise ourselves in such meditations, prayer, and virtues as the matter shall minister[315] us occasion; acknowledging our own ignorance where we find a

---

280 outcome 281 *a reader:* an interpreter
282 See 1 Cor 12:28–30; Eph 4:11.
283 *meet therefor:* suitable for it 284 busy
285 should 286 appropriate. See *Laws*
(Book 1). 287 *attain to perceive:* manage
to understand 288 disregard 289 *set at nought:* values as nothing 290 *used like:* treated the same way 291 please

292 *so thought good:* thought this way
good 293 inspired; composed; dictated
294 understanding 295 Justinian
(482–565) 296 *keep dispicions:* engage in
disputations 297 practiced; engaged in
298 See the *Code of Justinian*, 1.1.4.
299 would be 300 for 301 meaning
302 meddlesome 303 intellect;

sense 304 difficulties 305 inclination
306 rough 307 *like as:* as if 308 *ordinary readers:* ordained lectors trained to
read the Scripture 309 by that 310 its
311 *unsitting demeanor:* unbecoming
behavior 312 *quite…abused:* utterly
and completely misused 313 such as
314 divinity 315 supply

doubt, and, therein leaning to[316] the faith of the Church, wrestle with no such text as might bring us in a doubt and weresty of[317] any of those articles wherein every good Christian man is clear—by this manner of reading can no man nor woman take hurt in Holy Scripture. Now then, the things on the other side that unlearned people can never by themselves attain[318]—as in the Psalms and the prophets and diverse parts of the Gospel, where the words be sometimes spoken as in the person of the prophet himself, sometimes as in the person of God, sometimes of some others, as angels, devils, or men, and sometimes of our Savior Christ (not always of one fashion,[319] but sometimes as God, sometimes as man, sometimes as head of this mystical body his Church militant here in earth, sometimes as head of his Church triumphant in heaven, sometimes as in the person of his sensual[320] parts of his own body, otherwhile[321] in the person of some particular part of his body mystical), and these things, with many others, oftentimes interchanged,[322] and suddenly sundry things of diverse matters diversely mingled together—all these things which is not possible for unlearned men to attain unto, it were more than madness for them to meddle withal, but leave all these things to them whose whole study is beset[323] thereupon, and to the preachers appointed thereunto, which[324] may show them such things in time and place convenient,[325] with reverence and authority, the sermon so tempered[326] as may be meet[327] and convenient always for the present audience. Whereunto it appeareth that our Savior himself, and his apostles after him, had ever special respect.[328]

"And therefore, as I say, forsooth, I can in no wise agree with you that it were meet for men unlearned to be busy with the chamming[329] of Holy Scripture, but to have it chammed unto them. For that is the preachers' part, and theirs that after long study are admitted to read[330] and expound it. And to this intent weigh all the words, as far as I perceive, of all holy doctors that anything have written in this matter. But never meant they, as I suppose, the forbidding of the Bible to be read in any vulgar tongue.

Nor I never yet heard any reason laid[331] why it were not convenient to have the Bible translated into the English tongue, but all those reasons, seemed they never so gay[332] and glorious at the first sight, yet when they were well examined, they might, in effect, for aught that I can see, as well be laid against the holy writers that wrote the Scripture in the Hebrew tongue, and against the blessed evangelists that wrote the Scripture in Greek, and against all those in like wise that translated it out of every of those tongues into Latin, as to their charge that[333] would well and faithfully translate it out of Latin into our English tongue. For as for that our tongue is called barbarous, is[334] but a fantasy. For so is, as every learned man knoweth, every strange[335] language to other.[336] And if they would call it barren of words, there is no doubt but it is plenteous enough to express our minds in anything whereof one man hath used[337] to speak with another.

"Now as touching the difficulty which a translator findeth in expressing well and lively[338] the sentence[339] of his author—which is hard always to do so, surely, but that he shall sometimes diminish either of the sentence or of the grace that it beareth in the former tongue—that point hath lain in their light that[340] have translated the Scripture already, either out of Greek into Latin or out of Hebrew into any[341] of them both, as by many translations which we read already (to them that be learned) appeareth. Now as touching the harm that may grow by such blind bayards[342] as will, when they read the Bible in English, be more busy[343] than will become them: they that touch that point harp upon the right string, and touch truly the great harm that were likely to grow[344] to some folk—howbeit, not by the occasion yet of the English translation, but by the occasion of their own lewdness and folly, which yet were not, in my mind, a sufficient cause to exclude the translation and to put other folk from[345] the benefit thereof, but rather to make provision against such abuse, and let a good thing go forth. No wise man were there that would put all weapons away because manquellers[346] misuse them.

316 *leaning to:* relying on   317 *weresty of:* uncertainty about   318 come to understand   319 *of one fashion:* in the same way   320 physical   321 other times   322 alternated   323 spent   324 who   325 suitable; appropriate   326 properly constituted   327 fitting

328 regard; consideration   329 chewing   330 *admitted to read:* officially authorized to interpret   331 alleged   332 *never so gay:* no matter how brilliant   333 who   334 that is   335 foreign   336 another   337 been accustomed   338 vividly   339 meaning   340 *in . . . that:* in the full

view of those who   341 either   342 *blind bayards:* proverbial for recklessness and self-confident ignorance   343 inquisitive   344 come   345 *put . . . from:* deprive other people of   346 murderers

Nor this letted[347] not, as I said, the Scripture to be first written in a vulgar tongue. For the Scripture, as I said before, was not written but in a vulgar tongue, such as the whole people understood, nor in no secret ciphers, but such common letters as almost every man could read. For neither was the Hebrew, nor the Greek tongue, nor the Latin neither, any other speech than such as all the people spoke. And therefore if we should lay that it were evil done to translate the Scripture into our tongue, because it is vulgar and common to every Englishman, then had it been as evil done to translate it into Greek or into Latin, or to write the New Testament first in Greek or the Old Testament in Hebrew, because both those tongues were as very vulgar as ours. And yet should there, by this reason, also not only the Scripture be kept out of our tongue, but, over that, should the reading thereof be forbidden both all such lay people and all such priests, too, as can[348] no more than their grammar, and very scantly[349] that. All which company, though they can understand the words, be yet as far from the perceiving of the sentence[350] in hard and doubtful texts as were our women if the Scripture were translated to our own language. Howbeit, of truth seldom hath it been seen that any sect of heretics hath begun of such unlearned folk as nothing could[351] else but the language wherein they read the Scripture, but there hath always commonly these sects sprungen of[352] the pride of such folk as had, with the knowledge of the tongue, some high persuasion in themselves of their own learning besides. To whose authority some other folk have soon after—part of malice, part of simpleness, and much part of pleasure and delight in newfangledness—fallen[353] in and increased the faction. But the head hath ever commonly been either some proud learned man, or at the least, besides the language, some proud smatterer[354] in learning, so that if we should, for fear of heretics that might hap to grow thereby, keep the Scripture out of any tongue, or out of unlearned men's hands, we should for like fear be fain[355] to keep it out of all tongues—and out of learned men's hands too—and wot not whom we might trust therewith. Wherefore there

is, as methinketh, no remedy but if any good thing shall go forward, somewhat must needs be adventured.[356] And some folk will not fail to be naught.[357] Against which things provision must be made, that as much good may grow, and as little harm come, as can be devised, and not to keep the whole commodity[358] from any whole people because of harm that—by their own folly and fault—may come to some part. As though a lewd[359] surgeon would cut off the leg by the knee to keep the toe from the gout, or cut off a man's head by the shoulders to keep him from the toothache. There is no treatise[360] of Scripture so hard but that a good virtuous man, or woman either, shall somewhat find therein that shall delight and increase their devotion—besides this, that every preaching shall be the more pleasant and fruitful unto them when they have in their mind the place of Scripture that they shall there hear expounded. For though it be, as it is indeed, great wisdom for a preacher to use discretion in his preaching, and to have a respect unto the qualities[361] and capacities of his audience, yet letteth that nothing but[362] that the whole audience may without harm have read and have already the Scripture in mind that he shall in his preaching declare[363] and expound. For no doubt is there but that God and his Holy Spirit hath so prudently tempered their speech through the whole corpus of Scripture that every man may take good thereby and no man harm, but he that will in the study thereof lean proudly to the folly of his own wit.[364] For albeit that Christ did speak to the people in parables and expounded them secretly[365] to his especial disciples[366]—and sometimes forbore to tell some things to them also, because they were not as yet able to bear them,[367] and the apostles in like wise did sometimes spare to speak[368] to some people the things that they did not let[369] plainly to speak to some others[370]—yet letteth[371] all this nothing the translation of the Scripture into our own tongue, no more than in[372] the Latin. Nor it is no cause to keep the corpus of Scripture out of the hands of any Christian people, so many years fastly[373] confirmed in faith, because Christ and his apostles used such provision[374] in their utterance of so strange and

347 prevented 348 know 349 hardly, barely 350 meaning 351 knew 352 from 353 joined 354 dabbler 355 obliged 356 *somewhat…adventured:* something must be risked 357 bad 358 benefit 359 ignorant, unskillful;

wicked 360 book 361 *respect unto the qualities:* consideration of the dispositions or characters 362 *letteth that nothing but:* this in no way prevents 363 explain 364 intellect 365 in private 366 See Mk 4:33–34. 367 See Jn 16:12.

368 *spare to speak*: refrain from saying 369 hesitate 370 See 1 Cor 3:1–3. 371 prevents 372 into 373 steadfastly; solidly 374 foresight

unheard mysteries either unto Jews, paynims,[375] or newly christened folk — except[376] we would say that all the expositions which Christ made himself upon his own parables unto his secret[377] servants and disciples, withdrawn from the people, should now at this day be kept in like wise from the commons, and no man suffered[378] to read or hear them but those that in his Church represent the state[379] and office of his apostles. Which there will, I wot well, no wise man say, considering that those things which were then commonly most kept from the people be now most necessary for the people to know, as it well appeareth by all such things, in effect, as our Savior at the time taught his apostles apart. Whereof I would not for my mind withhold the profit that one good, devout, unlearned layman might take by the reading — not for the harm that a hundred heretics would fall in by their own willful abusion[380] — no more than our Savior letted,[381] for the weal[382] of such as would be with his grace of his little chosen flock, to come into this world and be *lapis offensionis, et petra scandali* ('the stone of stumbling, and the stone of falling')[383] and ruin to all the willful wretches in the world besides. Finally, methinketh that the constitution provincial[384] of which we spoke right now hath determined this question already. For when the clergy therein agreed that the English Bibles should remain which were translated afore Wycliffe's days, they consequently did agree that to have the Bible in English was none hurt.[385] And in that they forbade any new translation to be read till it were approved by the bishops, it appeareth well thereby that their intent was that the bishop should approve it if he found it faultless,[386] and also of reason amend it where it were faulty, but if the man were a heretic that made it, or the faults such and so many as it were more easy to make it all new than mend it — as it happed for both points in the translation of Tyndale.

"Now if it so be that it would haply[387] be thought not a thing meetly to be adventured[388] to set all on a flush[389] at once, and dash rashly out Holy Scripture in every lewd fellow's teeth,[390] yet thinketh me there might such a moderation be taken therein as neither good virtuous lay folk should lack it, nor rude and rash brains abuse it. For it might be with diligence well and truly translated by some good, Catholic, and well-learned man, or by diverse, dividing the labor among them, and after,[391] conferring[392] their several parts together, each with other. And after that might the work be allowed and approved by the ordinaries,[393] and by their authorities so put unto print as all the copies should come whole unto the bishop's hand. Which he may, after[394] his discretion and wisdom, deliver to such as he perceiveth honest, sad,[395] and virtuous, with a good monition and fatherly counsel to use it reverently, with humble heart and lowly mind, rather seeking therein occasion of devotion than of dispicion,[396] and providing as much as may be that the book be, after the decease of the party, brought again[397] and reverently restored[398] unto the ordinary, so that, as near as may be devised, no man have it but of the ordinary's hand, and by him thought and reputed for such as shall be likely to use it to God's honor and merit of his own soul. Among whom, if any be proved after to have abused it, then the use thereof to be forbidden him, either forever or till he be waxen[399] wiser."

"By our Lady," quoth your friend, "this way misliketh[400] not me. But who should set the price of the book?"

"Forsooth," quoth I, "that reckon I a thing of little force.[401] For neither were it a great matter for any man in manner to give a groat or twain[402] above the mean[403] price for a book of so great profit, nor for the bishop to give them all free, wherein he might serve his diocese with the cost of ten pounds (I think) or twenty marks. Which sum, I dare say, there is no bishop but he would be glad to bestow about[404] a thing that might do his whole diocese so special a pleasure with such a spiritual profit."

"By my troth," quoth he, "yet ween I that the people would grudge[405] to have it on this wise[406] delivered them at the bishop's hand, and had liefer pay for it to the printer[407] than have it of the bishop free."

---

375 pagans   376 unless   377 trusted; confidential   378 allowed   379 status; rank   380 misuse; perversion   381 refrained; hesitated   382 well-being   383 1 Pt 2:8   384 *constitution provincial:* decree of the synod   385 *none hurt:* not at all harmful   386 free of error   387 perhaps   388 *meetly to be adventured:* suitably to be risked   389 *set all on a flush:* suddenly increase the number (of Bibles) all   390 *dash…teeth:* rashly throw a Bible into every bum's face   391 afterward   392 collecting and comparing   393 bishops   394 according to   395 soberminded; serious   396 debate   397 back   398 returned   399 *be waxen:* grows, becomes   400 displeases   401 importance   402 *groat or twain:* fourpence or two   403 average   404 *bestow about:* spend on   405 complain   406 *on this wise:* in this way   407 *had…printer:* would rather pay the printer for it

"It might so happen with some," quoth I. "But yet, in mine opinion, there were in that manner more willfulness than wisdom, or any good mind, in such as would not be content so to receive them. And therefore I would think, in good faith, that it would so fortune⁴⁰⁸ in few. But, 'fore God, the more doubt⁴⁰⁹ would be lest they would grudge and hold themselves sore grieved⁴¹⁰ that would require⁴¹¹ it and were haply denied it. Which I suppose would not often happen unto any honest householder, to be⁴¹² by his discretion reverently read in his house. But though⁴¹³ it were not taken to every lewd⁴¹⁴ lad in his own hands, to read a little rudely⁴¹⁵ when he list,⁴¹⁶ and then cast the book at his heels—or, among others such as himself, to keep a quodlibet⁴¹⁷ and a pot parliament⁴¹⁸ upon—I trow there will no wise man find a fault therein. Ye spoke right now of the Jews, among whom the whole people have, ye say, the Scripture in their hands. And ye thought it no reason⁴¹⁹ that we should reckon Christian men less worthy thereto than them. Wherein I am, as ye see, of your own opinion. But yet would God we had the like reverence to the Scripture of God that they have. For I assure you, I have heard very worshipful⁴²⁰ folk say, which⁴²¹ have been in their houses, that a man could not hire⁴²² a Jew to sit down upon his Bible of the Old Testament; but he taketh it with great reverence in hand when he will read, and reverently layeth it up again when he hath done. Whereas we, God forgive us, take little regard⁴²³ to sit down on our Bible with the Old Testament and the New too. Which homely⁴²⁴ handling, as it proceedeth of⁴²⁵ little reverence, so doth it more and more engender in the mind a negligence and contempt of God's holy words. We find also that among the Jews, though all their whole Bible was written in their vulgar tongue, and those books thereof wherein their laws were written were usual⁴²⁶ in every man's hands, as things that God would⁴²⁷ have commonly known, repeated, and kept in remembrance, yet were there, again,⁴²⁸ certain parts thereof which the common people of the Jews of old time, both of reverence and for the

difficulty, did forbear to meddle with. But now since the veil of the Temple is broken asunder that divided, among the Jews, the people from the sight of the secrets,⁴²⁹ and that God had sent his Holy Spirit to be assistant⁴³⁰ with his whole Church to teach all necessary truth, though it may therefore be the better suffered⁴³¹ that no part of Holy Scripture were kept out of honest laymen's hands, yet would I that no part thereof should come in theirs which,⁴³² to their own harm and haply their neighbors' too, would handle it over-homely, and be too bold and busy⁴³³ therewith. And also, though Holy Scripture be, as ye said while ere,⁴³⁴ a medicine for him that is sick, and food for him that is whole,⁴³⁵ yet since there is many a body sore⁴³⁶ soul-sick that taketh himself for whole, and in Holy Scripture is a whole feast of so much diverse viand⁴³⁷ that, after the affection⁴³⁸ and state of sundry stomachs, one may take harm by the selfsame that shall do another good—and sick folk often have such a corrupt tallage in their taste⁴³⁹ that they most like the meat that is most unwholesome for them—it were not, therefore, as methinketh, unreasonable that the ordinary (whom God hath in the diocese appointed for the chief physician, to discern between the whole and the sick and between disease and disease) should, after his wisdom and discretion, appoint everybody their part, as he should perceive to be good and wholesome for them. And therefore as he should not fail to find many a man to whom he might commit all the whole,⁴⁴⁰ so, to say the truth, I can see none harm therein though⁴⁴¹ he should commit unto some man the Gospel of Matthew, Mark, or Luke, whom he should yet forbid the Gospel of Saint John, and suffer⁴⁴² some to read the Acts of the Apostles whom he would not suffer to meddle with the Apocalypse.⁴⁴³ Many were there, I think, that should take much profit by Saint Paul's epistle *Ad Ephesios*,⁴⁴⁴ wherein he giveth good counsel to every kind of people, and yet should find little fruit for their understanding in his epistle *Ad Romanos*,⁴⁴⁵ containing such high difficulties as very few learned men can very well attain.⁴⁴⁶ And in like

---

408 happen   409 *more doubt:* greater fear or danger   410 *sore grieved:* severely offended or incensed   411 request   412 *to be:* i.e., who wanted it in order for it to be   413 even if   414 ignorant; base; immoral   415 roughly; unskillfully   416 desires   417 academic disputation   418 *pot parliament:* drinkers' assembly   419 *no*

reason: not reasonable   420 respectable   421 who   422 pay   423 *take little regard:* give no care   424 rough   425 from   426 ordinarily   427 wanted to   428 on the other hand   429 mysteries. See Mt 27:51.   430 present to help   431 allowed   432 who   433 prying; inquisitive   434 *while ere:* a while earlier   435 healthy

436 grievously   437 food, fare   438 *after the affection:* according to the disposition   439 *corrupt . . . taste:* distorted sense of taste   440 *commit . . . whole:* entrust the whole Bible   441 even if   442 allow   443 Book of Revelation   444 *Ad Ephesios:* to the Ephesians   445 *Ad Romanos:* to the Romans   446 come to understand

wise would it be in diverse other parts of the Bible, as well in the Old Testament as the New, so that, as I say, though the bishop might unto some layman betake[447] and commit, with good advice and instruction, the whole Bible to read, yet might he to some man, well and with reason, restrain the reading of some part, and from some busybody, the meddling with any part at all more than he shall hear in sermons set out and declared[448] unto him — and in like wise, too, take the Bible away from such folk again as be proved by their blind presumption to abuse the occasion of their profit unto their own hurt and harm. And thus may the bishop order[449] the Scripture in our hands, with as good reason as the father doth by his discretion appoint which of his children may for his sadness[450] keep a knife to cut his meat, and which shall for his wantonness[451] have his knife taken from him, for cutting off[452] his fingers. And thus am I bold, without prejudice of[453] other men's judgment, to show you my mind in this matter: how the Scripture might, without great peril and not without great profit, be brought into our tongue and taken to lay men and women both, not yet meaning thereby but that the whole Bible might,[454] for my mind, be suffered to be spread abroad in English. But if that were so much doubted[455] that percase[456] all might thereby be letted,[457] then would I rather have used such moderation as I speak of, or some such other as wiser men can better devise. Howbeit, upon that[458] I read late in the epistle that the King's Highness translated into English, of his own,[459] which his Grace made in Latin, answering to the letter of Luther,[460] my mind giveth me that his Majesty is of his blessed zeal so minded to move[461] this matter unto the prelates of the clergy — among whom I have perceived some of the greatest and of the best of their own minds well inclinable thereto already — that we lay people shall, in this matter, ere long time pass, except the fault be found in ourselves, be well and fully satisfied and content."

"In good faith," quoth he, "that will, in my mind, be very well done. And now am I, for my mind, in all this matter fully content and satisfied."

"Well," quoth I, "then will we to dinner, and the remnant will we finish after." And therewith went we to meat.[462]

The end of the Third Book

---

447 entrust   448 explained   449 arrange
450 *for his sadness:* because of his maturity
451 playfulness   452 *for cutting off:*
lest he cut off   453 to   454 *not yet . . .*

might: not, however, meaning by this that
the whole Bible might not   455 feared
456 perhaps   457 prevented   458 *upon
that:* from what   459 *of his own:* by

himself   460 *read . . . Luther:* the King's
letter was published in Latin in 1526 and
1527, and in English in 1526 and 1528.
461 propose   462 (our) meal

THE FOURTH BOOK

THE FIRST CHAPTER

The author showeth wherefore[1] it were not well done to suffer[2] Luther's books — or any other heretic's — to go abroad and be read among the people, though there were some good things in them among the bad.

When we had after dinner a little paused, your friend and I drew ourselves aside into the garden. And there, sitting down in an arbor, he began to enter forth into the matter, saying that he had well perceived that, not in his country[3] only, but also in the university where he had been, there were that[4] had none evil opinion of Luther, but thought that his books were by the clergy forbidden of[5] malice and evil will, to the end that folk should not surely see and perfectly perceive what he saith — or, at the least, what thing he meaneth by his words. Which will not appear, they think, by a line taken out in the mids of a leaf,[6] but by the diligent consideration of the whole matter. Without which, men might impute a wrong blame, they say, to the best writers that ever wrote in this world. But they think that the clergy will not have his books read because that in them laymen may read the priests' faults, which was, they say, the very[7] cause of the condemnation. For else[8] whether he had written well or evil, yet they say his books had[9] been kept in men's hands and read. For there is, they think, therein, though some part were naught,[10] many things yet well said, whereof there was no reason that men should lose the profit for[11] the bad. And also, reason men think it were[12] that all were heard that can be said touching the truth to be known concerning the matters of our salvation, to the intent that, all heard and perceived,[13] men may for their own surety[14] the better choose and hold the right way.

"Forsooth,"[15] quoth I, "if it were now doubtful and ambiguous whether the Church of Christ were in the right rule of doctrine or not, then were it very necessary to give them all good audience that[16] could and would anything dispute on either part,[17] for it or against it, to the end that if we were now in a wrong way, we might leave it and walk in some better. But now, on the other side, if it so be — as indeed it is — that Christ's Church hath the true doctrine already, and the selfsame that Saint Paul would not give an angel of heaven audience to the contrary,[18] what wisdom were it[19] now therein to show ourselves so mistrustful and wavering that, for to search whether our faith were false or true, we should give hearing, not to an angel of heaven, but to a fond[20] friar, to an apostate, to an open incestuous[21] lecher, a plain limb[22] of the devil, and a manifest messenger of hell? In which words, if ye would haply[23] think that I use myself too sore[24] to call him by such odious names, ye must consider that he spareth not — both untruly and without necessity — in his railing[25] books to call, by as evil,[26] them whom his duty were highly to reverence, whereas I do between us twain[27] call him but as himself hath showed him,[28] in his writing, in his living, and in his mad marriage. And yet I neither do it, nor would, were it not that the matter itself of reason doth require it. For my part is it of necessity to tell how naught[29] he is, because that the worse the man is, the more madness were it for wise men to give his false fables hearkening against God's undoubted truth, by his Holy Spirit taught unto his Church, and — by such multitude of miracles, by so much blood of holy martyrs, by the virtuous living of so many blessed confessors,[30] by the purity and cleanness of so many chaste widows[31] and undefiled virgins, by the wholesome doctrine of so many holy doctors,[32] and, finally, by the whole consent and agreement of all Christian people this fifteen hundred years — confirmed. And, therefore, not any respect unto[33] his railing against the clergy is, as some would have it seem, the cause of his condemnation and suppression of his books. For the good men of the clergy be not so sore grieved with[34] them that

---

1 why   **2** *were…suffer:* would not be good to allow   **3** part of the country   **4** those who   **5** out of   **6** *mids of a leaf:* middle of a page   **7** true   **8** otherwise   **9** would have   **10** bad   **11** on account of   **12** *reason…were:* people think it reasonable   **13** understood   **14** safety; certainty   **15** Indeed   **16** who   **17** side

18 *to the contrary:* if it spoke against. See Gal 1:8.   **19** *were it:* would it be   **20** foolish   **21** because he married a nun, Katharina von Bora. In canon law monks and nuns are regarded as siblings.   **22** agent   **23** perhaps   **24** *use myself too sore:* am being too severe   **25** ranting   **26** bad words   **27** both   **28** *showed him:*

presented himself   **29** bad   **30** saints who gave heroic witness but were not martyred   **31** *chaste widows:* widows who remained celibate for the rest of their lives   **32** theologians   **33** *respect unto:* regard for   **34** *grieved with:* offended by

touch the faults of the bad, nor the bad themselves be not so tender-eared that for the only[35] talking of their faults they would banish the books that were good in other things besides. For else could not the books of many old holy fathers have endured so long, wherein the vices of them that in the clergy be naught[36] be very vehemently rebuked.

"But the very cause why his books be not suffered[37] to be read is because his heresies be so many, and so abominable, and the proofs wherewith he pretendeth[38] to make them probable[39] be so far from reason and truth, and so far against the right understanding of Holy Scripture—whereof, under color[40] of great zeal and affection, he laboreth to destroy the credence and good use—and, finally, so far stretcheth all things against good manner and virtue, provoking the world to wrong opinions of God and boldness in sin and wretchedness, that there can no good, but much harm grow by the reading. For if there were the substance good, and of[41] error or oversight some cockle among the corn which might be sifted out and the remnant stand in stead,[42] men would have been content therewith, as they be with such others. But now is his not besprent[43] with a few spots, but, with more than half venom, poisoned the whole wine—and that right rotten of itself—and this done of purpose and malice,[44] not without an evil spirit in such wise[45] walking with his words that the contagion thereof were likely to infect a feeble soul, as the savor[46] of a sickness sore[47] infecteth a whole body. Nor the truth is not to be learned of[48] every man's mouth. For as Christ was not content that the devil should call him God's Son, though it were true, so is he not content that a devil's limb,[49] as Luther is, or Tyndale, should teach his flock the truth, for infecting them with their false devilish heresies besides. For likewise as the Holy Scripture of God, because of the good Spirit that made it, is of his own nature apt to purge and amend the reader, though some that read it, of their invincible malice, turn it to their harm, so do such writings as Luther's is—in the making whereof the devil is of counsel[50] and giveth therewith a breath of his assistance— though the goodness of some men master the malice

thereof, walking harmless[51] with God's help, as the prophet saith, upon the serpent and the cockatrice,[52] and treading upon the lion and the dragon,[53] yet be such works of themselves always right unwholesome to meddle with, meet[54] and apt to corrupt and infect the reader. For the proof whereof, we need none other example than this that we be in hand withal,[55] if we consider what good the reading of his books hath done in Saxony. And this find we more than too much proved here among us: that of ten that use[56] to read his books, ye shall scantly find twain[57] but that they not only cast off prayer, and fasting, and all such godly virtues as Holy Scripture commendeth, and the Church commandeth, and virtuous people have ever had in great price,[58] but also fall in[59] plain contempt and hatred thereof, so that what fruit should grow of the reading ye may soon guess."

THE SECOND CHAPTER
The author showeth many of Luther's heresies to be so abominable, and some part also so peevish,[60] that the very bare rehearsal[61] is enough, without any further dispicion[62] thereupon, to cause any good man abhor them, and to be ashamed also to seem so foolish as to hold them. And for an example the author rehearseth diverse, whereof some be new set forth by Tyndale in his English books, worse yet in some part than his master Luther is himself.

"And in good faith, I would ween[63] that any good man, except[64] some reasonable necessity should compel him thereto, else would, if he heard but his opinions once rehearsed, be very loath to lose his time in the reading, either of his fond[65] proof, or of the very titles and names thereof again."

"If they be such indeed," quoth your friend, "and that they be not mistaken or misreported."

"Methinketh," quoth I, "that the fruit which ye see spring of them should suffice to make you perceive them for naught. And iwis[66] a friar's living[67] that weddeth a nun—when his living is such— should make it easy to wit[68] that his teaching is not very good."

---

35 *the only:* only the 36 bad 37 allowed
38 professes 39 believable 40 pretext
41 by 42 See Mt 13:24–30. 43 sprinkled 44 *of...malice:* on purpose and out of malice 45 (a) way 46 stench
47 greatly; grievously 48 from

49 agent 50 *of counsel:* one of the advisors 51 unharmed 52 a two-legged dragon with a rooster's head 53 See Ps 90(91):13. 54 suitable 55 with 56 are accustomed 57 two 58 *had in great price:* held in great esteem 59 into

60 foolish 61 recounting 62 disputation 63 think 64 unless 65 foolish
66 certainly 67 state of life; manner of life or conduct 68 know

"Surely," quoth he, "I cannot say nay but[69] that these be shrewd tokens."[70]

"I shall," quoth I, "do more for you. For I shall find the means that ye shall see his own books, and therein perceive yourself that men belie[71] him not."

"I pray[72] you," quoth he, "let me hear some of his opinions by mouth the while, and for[73] the seeing of them in his own books, I shall bethink me after."

"First he began," quoth I, "with pardons[74] and with the Pope's power, denying finally any of both to be of any effect at all.

"And soon after—to show what good spirit moved him—he denied all the seven sacraments except baptism, penance, and the Sacrament of the altar, saying plainly that all the remnant be but feigned[75] things and of none effect.

"Now, these that he leaveth for good, it is good to see how he handleth them. For in penance, he saith that there neither needeth[76] contrition nor satisfaction. Also he saith that there needeth no priest for the hearing of confession, but that every man, and every woman too, is as sufficient to hear confession and assoil[77] and do all that longeth[78] to a confessor, as is a priest."

"Marry,[79] sir," quoth your friend, "this were an easy way for one thing.[80] For the sorest[81] thing that I find in confession is that when I see many confessors at a pardon,[82] yet can I scant[83] like one of them so well upon the sight that I would tell any such tales to, once in seven years, and[84] I might choose. But now, if I might—after[85] Luther's way—be confessed to a fair woman, I would not let[86] to be confessed weekly."

"Ye would," quoth I, "peradventure[87] tell her a tale that ye would not tell every man. But yet if some men told some tales to a fair woman that they tell in confession to a foul friar, they would wish, I ween, among[88] that they had kept their counsel in their own breast."

"Marry," quoth he, "that may happen also in the confession that is made unto a priest."

"Possible it were indeed," quoth I. "And Tyndale, in his book of *Obedience*—or rather disobedience— saith that the curates[89] do go and show the bishops the confessions of such as be rich in their parishes, and that the bishops thereupon do cite[90] them, and lay their secret sins to their charge,[91] and either put them to open[92] shameful penance, or compel them to pay at the bishop's pleasure. Now, dare I be bold to say—and I suppose all the honest men in this realm will say and swear the same—that this is a very foolish falsehood imagined of his own mind, whereof he never saw the example in his life. We see in some rather the contrary fault: that not only the rich, but the poor also, keep open queans,[93] and live in open adultery, without payment or penance or anything almost once said unto them. But therewith findeth Tyndale no fault in the bishops. For he saith plainly that the bishop hath none authority to punish any such thing at all. But he letteth not, on the other side, to belie the bishops and the curates too, feigning[94] that the one doth utter folks' confessions to the other. And when he hath so belied them, then forthwith,[95] as though he had proved his tale true, he taketh the same false, feigned[96] lie for a ground thereupon to build the destruction of that holy sacrament of penance. For upon that lie and such others like,[97] he saith plainly that confession to the priest is the worst thing that ever was found. Now if that were true as it is as false as he that said it, how happed it then—which question Luther and he be asked often, and always make as[98] they heard it not—how happed it, I say, that of so many virtuous, wise, and cunning[99] fathers as have been in Christ's Church in so many hundred years, never none had the wit[100] nor the grace to spy this great thing, but all teach confession, till now that Tyndale came, which yet in this point passeth[101] his master, Luther? For he saith he would in any wise[102] have confession stand, but he would have it made at liberty as well to women as men. But Tyndale will have none at all, because he listeth[103] to belie both the bishops and the curates, feigning that they should between them disclose our confessions."

"In faith," quoth your friend, "that is a thing that I never heard to have happened."

"Nor he neither," quoth I, "that dare I boldly say. And yet, I wot[104] well, as ye said right now, that priests

69 *say nay but:* deny **70** *shrewd tokens:* malicious signs **71** slander **72** ask **73** as for **74** indulgences **75** invented **76** is required **77** pardoned; give absolution **78** belongs **79** from "by Mary," indeed **80** *for . . . thing:* in one respect **81** most grievous **82** a service making the sacrament of confession available, in which indulgences would be granted **83** hardly, barely **84** if **85** according to **86** hesitate **87** perhaps **88** from time to time **89** parish priests **90** formally summon **91** blame **92** public **93** prostitutes **94** pretending **95** immediately **96** fabricated **97** similar **98** as if **99** learned **100** intelligence **101** surpasses **102** *in any wise:* by all means **103** chooses **104** know

should utter folks' confession were well possible—and in[105] many of them nothing in this world more likely neither—if God and his Holy Spirit were not, as it is, assistant[106] and working with his holy sacra-
5 ment. But surely whereas there be many things that well and clearly prove the sacrament of confession to be a thing instituted and devised by God, yet if all the remnant lacked,[107] this one thing were unto me a plain persuasion and a full proof, which thing
10 I find in the noble book that the King's Highness made against Luther: that is to wit,[108] that in so common a custom of confession, ofter than once in the year—where no man letteth[109] boldly to tell such his secrets as upon the discovering[110] or close[111] keeping
15 thereof his honesty[112] commonly, and oftentimes his life also, dependeth, so many simple[113] as be of that sort that hear them, and in all other things so light and lavish of their tongue,[114] and some therewith so lewd[115] in all their living that for money they force[116]
20 little to steal, rob, and murder too, and might many times with the disclosing of some such things get so much as some of them would kill a man for less—yet find we never any man take harm by his confession, or cause given of complaint, through any such se-
25 crets uttered and showed by the confessor."

"In good faith," quoth he, "this is very truth, and a great thing in mine opinion. But undoubtedly if confession came once to women's ears, there would be a sore[117] change. For it would be hard for God
30 and the devil too to keep their tongues."

"Yes, yes," quoth I, "a woman can keep a counsel[118] well enough. For though she tell a gossip, she telleth it but in counsel yet, nor that gossip to her gossip neither; and so, when all the gossips in the town
35 know it, yet is it but counsel still. And therefore I say it not for any harm that would come by them, but for the novelty thereof."

"Now, in earnest," quoth your friend, "this was a much merry mad invention of Luther; and Lu-
40 ther is in a manner as mad as Tyndale. For it were as good, almost, to have no confession at all as to set women to hear it."

"Forsooth," quoth I, "if it had been wisdom and not against God's will, it would of likelihood have
45 been founden by some good men before these days, in this long time of so many hundred years.

Howbeit,[119] he goeth near enough to take it all away. And diverse of his scholars[120]—besides Tyndale—do now deny it utterly. And himself leaveth little substance and little fruit therein. For he would that 50 we should[121] not care much for any full confession of all deadly[122] sins, nor be very studious in the gathering of our faults to mind, nor pondering the circumstances, nor the weight and gravity thereof, nor taking any sorrow therefor.[123] Now these things 55 taken away, and the sacrament of penance left such as he would have it, consider in yourself what fruit were a man likely to find in it. He that taketh a confessor he forceth[124] not whom, and then confesseth he forceth not what, disposing him to repentance 60 he forceth not how, good works in satisfaction accounteth for nought:[125] what manner of amendment shall this man come to? And specially if, besides all this, he may take to[126] his confessor a fair woman such as a young man would have a lust to 65 break his mind unto. Doth it not plainly appear that this fond[127] fellow so playeth with this holy sacrament of penance that he goeth about utterly to destroy it? And yet is this one of the three he leaveth, taking four away expressly." 70

"Surely," quoth your friend, "so doth he this too as thinketh me."

"Forsooth," quoth I, "and he handleth the sacrament of baptism not much better. For he magnifieth baptism but to the suppression of penance and 75 of all good living. For therein he teacheth that the sacrament itself hath no virtue[128] at all, but the faith only.

"Item: he teacheth that only faith[129] sufficeth to our salvation with our baptism—without good 80 works. He saith also that it is sacrilege to go about to please God with any works, and not with faith only.

"Item: that no man can do any good work.

"Item: that the good and righteous man always 85 sinneth in doing well.

"Item: that no sin can damn any Christian man, but only lack of belief. For he saith that our faith suppeth[130] up all our sins, how great soever they be.

"Item: he teacheth that no man hath no free 90 will, nor can anything do therewith—not though[131] the help of grace be joined thereunto—but that

---

105 with   106 present to help   107 were lacking   108 say   109 refrains   110 disclosing   111 secret   112 reputation   113 poor; deficient   114 *light* …   *tongue:* prone to speaking easily and too much   115 wicked   116 care   117 great   118 secret   119 However   120 students; disciples   121 *would* … *should:* wants us to   122 mortal. See Jn 5:16–17.   123 for them   124 cares   125 nothing   126 for   127 foolish   128 power   129 *only faith:* faith alone   130 swallows   131 even if

everything that we do, good and bad, we do nothing at all therein ourselves, but only suffer[132] God to do all things in us, good and bad, as wax is wrought into an image or a candle by the man's hand, without anything doing thereto itself.

"Item: he saith that God is as verily[133] the author and cause of the evil will of Judas in betraying of Christ as of the good will of Christ in suffering of his Passion.

"In[134] matrimony, he saith plainly that it is no sacrament; and so saith Tyndale too.

"Item: that if a man be not able to do his duty to his wife, he is bounden secretly without slander[135] to provide another to do it for him."

"Forsooth," quoth your friend, "this was courteously considered of him—he is a very gentleman, I warrant[136] you. It is no marvel though his wife be well teeming,[137] if he make her such provision."

"Surely," quoth I, "this wise device[138] hath he. And much other beastliness he saith in[139] such things, and his disciple after him, of such sort as honest ears could scant abide the hearing.

"In the sacrament of orders, he saith that priesthood and all holy orders[140] be but a feigned[141] invention.

"Item: that every Christian man and every Christian woman is a priest.

"Item: that every man may consecrate the body of Christ."

"This is a shameful saying, in good faith," quoth your friend.

"Abide[142] ye," quoth I, "and ye shall hear worse yet. For he saith further that every woman and child may consecrate the body of our Lord."

"Surely," quoth he, "then is the man mad outright."

"He saith," quoth I, "further yet, that the Canon[143] of the Mass is false.

"Item: that the Host[144] in the Mass is none oblation nor sacrifice.

"Item: that the Mass with its canon—after[145] the form that is and ever hath been used in Christ's Church—is sacrilege and abomination.

"And though much of this concerneth his damnable heresies touching the Blessed Sacrament of the altar, yet saith he thereof many lewd[146] doctrines more. And among others, he teacheth that it is heresy to believe that there is not very[147] bread and very wine in the Sacrament of the altar joined with the body and blood of our Lord.

"Item: Zwingli and Oecolampadius,[148] scholars[149] of Luther, have builded further upon this ungracious[150] ground of their master, and teach that the Sacrament of the altar is not the very body nor blood of our Lord at all. And Luther himself, albeit[151] he now writeth against them therein, yet (as it by many things appeareth) minded and intended to put forth by[152] leisure the same heresy himself, till he changed his mind for envy that he bare toward them, when he saw that they would be heads of a sect themselves—for that could he suffer no man to be but himself. But before, as I say, he did intend it himself. And therefore he made a way toward it by these other heresies that I have rehearsed[153] you, and by diverse others more.

"For he teacheth also that the Mass availeth no man, quick[154] nor dead, but only to the priest himself.

"Item: he teacheth that men should go to Mass as well after supper as before breakfast,[155] and in his common clothes, as he goeth all day, without light[156] or any other honorable rite used therein.

"Item: he saith it were best that men should never be houseled[157] but once in their life—and that never till they lie a-dying, as they be but once christened, and that at their beginning.

"Item: he teacheth that every man and woman should take the Holy Sacrament, and spare not to touch it and handle it as much as them list.[158]

"Item: he saith that the Blessed Sacrament of the altar is ordained of God to be received, but not to be worshipped."

"In faith," quoth your friend, "these things be far out of course."[159]

"Ye see," quoth I, "now how he handleth all the blessed sacraments.

"But now hath he other wild heresies at large.[160]

---

132 allow　**133** truly　**134** Concerning
135 causing discredit or scandal　**136** guarantee　**137** pregnant　**138** scheme; invention　**139** about　**140** *holy orders:* the diaconate, subdiaconate, and so forth　**141** fictitiously devised
142 Wait　**143** prayer of consecration
144 the consecrated body of Christ

145 in　**146** wicked　**147** true; actual
148 *Zwingli and Oecolampadius:* Ulrich Zwingli (1484–1531) and Johannes Oecolampadius (1482–1531) were prominent Protestant theologians in Switzerland and Germany, respectively.　**149** pupils
150 without grace; wicked　**151** although
152 at (his)　**153** recounted to　**154** living

155 *go . . . breakfast:* Church law at the time required fasting from at least midnight before receiving Communion at Mass.
156 candlelight　**157** given Communion
158 wish　**159** *out of course:* unorthodox
160 *at large:* freely circulating; written of at great length

For he teacheth, against Scripture and all reason, that no Christian man is or can be bounden by any law made among men, nor is not bounden to observe or keep any.

"Item: he teacheth that there is no purgatory.

"Item: that all men's souls lie still and sleep till the Day of Doom.[161]

"Item: that no man should pray to saints nor set by[162] any holy relics nor pilgrimages,[163] nor do any reverence to any images."

"By my troth,"[164] quoth your friend, "I had forgotten that when I was now in the university,[165] in the communication that I had with my friends there in that matter, one of them objected against me that the worship of images hath been, ere this, condemned by a great council in Greece."

"There was indeed," quoth I, "a council once in Greece gathered by an emperor that then was a heretic[166] there, which was after—in the eighth synod by the general council[167]—damned[168] and annulled. But this no more doth to[169] the matter than if there would now, in Saxony and Switzerland and such other places, such people as be swerved from the faith gather themselves together and keep, as they would call it, a 'general council', wherein they might determine what they would. And yet were all that no prejudice to the right belief of the Catholic Church, which is always that known people that still persevere as one body with our Savior Christ in their former fast-confirmed[170] faith, from which faithful body these other withering branches[171] be blown away by the devil. And therefore, as a council of Lutherans assembling themselves in Saxony could make none authority against the true faith of the Church, so could that council in Greece nothing prove their purpose, which[172] made none interruption of the right belief and godly custom of worship[173] done to saints and images, that yet did for all that continue still in all the Catholic Church of Christ, and ever since hath done."

"Forsooth," quoth he, "that is truth.

"But yet," quoth he, "was there one at our communication learned in the law, and in his chamber were we, which[174] said that if he list,[175] he could show a fair law, incorporated in the decrees[176] of the Church, which law, if it were laid in their light that[177] would take upon them the defense of any worship to be done to images, would make all their eyes daze. Then longed not only I but all the remnant also, very sore[178] to see that law. In bringing forth whereof, he made[179] a while somewhat strange,[180] as of a thing kept for a secret mystery.

"But in conclusion, he set forth a book of the decrees; and therein he read us, in good faith, a plain text (as methought and all that were present) by which Saint Gregory[181] writeth unto a certain bishop[182] that had broken down the images[183] in his church; and there Saint Gregory, albeit that he blameth[184] him for breaking them, yet for all that, he commendeth him for that[185] he would not suffer them to be worshipped."

"Did you," quoth I, "read that law yourself?"

"In good faith," quoth he, "I stood by and looked on that book while he read it."

"Did he," quoth I, "or you either, read the next law following in the book?"

"Nay, verily," quoth he, "for methought this was enough."

"So was it, verily," quoth I, "and too much too—without more. But and if[186] ye had either read the next law following or the gloss upon the selfsame law that ye read, ye should then have seen that the law which he showed you made little for[187] his purpose."

"By my troth, as for the gloss," quoth he, "neither I nor any man else that there was had list once to look on,[188] considering that the text was plain and easy to understand. And as for the law next following, we looked not after, for we thought to find it contrary. And if we should, then should we not yet have wist[189] which we should believe."

"Yes, yes," quoth I. "Ye would not much have

---

161 *the Day of Doom:* Judgment Day
162 *set by:* value   163 shrines   164 trustworthiness; faithfulness   165 *now in the university:* at the university this last time
166 *worship ... heretic:* The Council of Hieria was called by Byzantine Emperor Constantine V (an iconoclast) in 753.
167 *eighth ... general council:* This was the Second Ecumenical Council of Nicaea, held in 787. It was the seventh, not the

eighth Ecumenical Council, but he may be referring to the eighth (and last) session of that council, at which the new Empress, Irene, signed the statement of faith issued by the Council.   168 condemned   169 *no more doth to:* has no more to do with
170 steadfastly or certainly confirmed
171 See Jn 15:4–6.   172 which council
173 honoring; veneration   174 who
175 wished   176 canon-law decrees

177 *laid ... light:* given them to understand
178 greatly   179 acted   180 strangely, peculiarly   181 *Saint Gregory:* Pope Saint Gregory the Great (540–604)   182 *a certain bishop:* Serenus   183 representations of saints or the divinity (e.g., icons, statues, sculptures)   184 rebukes   185 *for that:* because   186 *and if:* even if   187 *made little for:* gave little support to   188 at it
189 *not yet have wist:* still not have known

doubted if ye had read the law that followeth; for it is a law synodal, made in the sixth synod,[190] in which there is well and plainly showed that images be to be worshipped among Christian men, and well declareth in what wise we worship them, and owe to do: that is to wit, none image to be worshipped as God; nor the hope of our health[191] to be beset[192] upon the image; nor to look[193] that the image shall be he which shall judge our souls in time to come; but we worship the image, and reverence[194]—and well owe to do—for the remembrance of the thing that the image representeth. And yet though we do the image honor and reverence, yet for divine honor, and service[195] only done to God, that kind of worship called *latria* we neither do nor may do, neither to image nor any creature in all the whole world, either in heaven or earth.[196] And this should ye have seen if ye had either read, as I say, the law next following or the gloss of that law that ye read."

"Marry," quoth he, "but in the law itself that we read, good Saint Gregory saith plain the contrary. For he commendeth the bishop there because he would not suffer the images to be worshipped at all."

"That word 'at all,'" quoth I, "ye set to[197] yourself, more than ye find in the book. For indeed the book saith no more but that they 'should not be worshipped,' by this Latin word: *adorare*. By which word, he understood the divine worship called *latria*."

"Whereby know we," quoth he, "he understood it so? For I believe not much the gloss."

"Ye may," quoth I, "perceive[198] it by the law that followeth. Wherein, albeit that there be the same word, *adorare*, yet is it there showed how we may *adorare*— that is to wit, how we may worship—images."

"Why," quoth he, "if that law say *quod possumus adorare*[199] and Saint Gregory saith *quod non licet adorare*,[200] be not they twain[201] plain repugnant?"[202]

"Yes," quoth I, "if they both took that word *adorare* in one[203] sense. But when the synod used that word for such worship as we may do to a creature, and Saint Gregory useth it for such worship

only as may not be done but only to the Creator, then they be nothing repugnant at all."

"But yet," quoth he, "whereby shall I be sure that Saint Gregory took it so? For it appeareth by the law, as yourself saith, that the word may be taken otherwise. For the same law itself taketh it otherwise; and then peradventure[204] so did he, and thereby forbade all manner worship to be done unto images."

"That were very unlikely," quoth I, "that Saint Gregory were of one mind and the whole synod of the contrary.

"But now, since ye make the matter so clear upon the words of Saint Gregory incorporated in the decrees, and will not believe the gloss—which appeareth plainly that he meant only to forbid us to do such worship to images as is only due to God— will ye be content therein to believe Saint Gregory himself if he tell you himself that he meant none other?"

"Yea, fore God," quoth he, "that will I well."

"Then," quoth I, "we shall agree well enough." And therewith I took down of[205] a shelf, among my books, the *Register*[206] of Saint Gregory's epistles, and therein turned to the very words which are by Gratian taken out of his second epistle *ad Serenum, episcopum Massiliensem*,[207] and incorporated in the decrees. And then caused I him to read the formal[208] words as they be couched in the decree. And by the collation[209] of the one with the other, I caused him to see that Gratian had taken but a part of the epistle, and that by other words of the epistle itself, it appeareth evidently that Saint Gregory spoke of none other worship to be withdrawn from images but only divine worship and observance due to God, as by diverse other things in the epistle appeareth plain, as in that he saith that it is not lawful to worship anything wrought by hand, because it is written, *Dominum Deum tuum adorabis, et illi soli servies* ('Thou shalt worship thy Lord God, and only him shalt thou serve').

"Now is it in this place of Scripture meant none other worship nor service than divine honor and service called *latria*, as is to learned men well

---

190 *the sixth synod:* The law following Gregory's letter is from the Second Ecumenical Council of Nicaea, which was the seventh, not the sixth, Ecumenical Council. **191** soundness or well-being; salvation **192** set **193** expect **194** reverence it

195 worship **196** *none . . . earth:* More closely paraphrases ch. 28 of *Distinctio* III. **197** *set to:* add in **198** understand **199** *quod . . . adorare:* "which we are able to adore" **200** *quod . . . adorare:* "which it is not permitted to adore"

201 both **202** contradictory **203** the same **204** perhaps **205** from **206** a published collection of his letters **207** *ad Serenum, episcopum Massiliensem:* "to Serenus, Bishop of Marseille" **208** exact **209** comparison

known. And he that will affirm the contrary and say that in Scripture is forbidden from images all manner of worship, he must affirm also that all manner worship, and all manner service, is forbidden by Scripture from all manner creatures. For the Scripture saith there, 'Thou shalt worship and serve only God,' and so should we, by that construction,[210] neither worship nor serve father nor mother, master nor prince, nor king. And in the same place Saint Gregory saith that we do worship only the Holy Trinity; which showeth that he speaketh only of divine worship called *latria*, which is done with a mind that reputeth[211] the thing worshipped to be very God. For else by those words, if he forbade any manner worship for to be done to anything, saving the Trinity, then did he forbid any worship to be done to any saint, or to our blessed Lady either. And every man well wotteth how reverently himself worshipped both our Lady and all saints, as well by many books and epistles of his as by the litany which (as his epistles well showeth) he ordained to be, with great devotion, used in honor of God, our Lady, and all holy saints—and over[212] that, by the great honor that he did to saints in churches specially dedicated unto them, and also great honor and reverence used[213] unto their holy relics, as in his own books and epistles appeareth. And finally if his epistles had been lost out of which the decree is taken, yet the words of the decree itself would well enough suffice. For therein is it specified that images be 'the books of lay people, wherein they read the life of Christ.' And then if it be, as it is indeed, well and virtuously done devoutly to kiss a book in which Christ's life and his death is expressed by writing, why should it be evil done reverently to kiss the images by which Christ's life and his Passion be represented by scripture[214] or painting?"

"In good faith," quoth he, "I am well satisfied in this matter. And so would they that then were with me, if they had seen all that I see now."

"They may," quoth I, "soon see as much whensoever they list to look therefor.[215]

"But now, to turn again to the matter, neither the bishop of Marseilles that broke the images that they speak of, nor the council of Greece neither, schismatical as it was, went never yet so far as Luther and Tyndale and their company do, which[216] not only set at nought[217] images, but also leave no saint unblasphemed—nor Christ's own mother neither.

"For Luther cannot abide the common anthem of our Lady and the most devout *Salve Regina* because we therein call that blessed virgin our advocate.

"Item: he saith that every other woman now living, if she have the same faith, may be prayed unto as well as our Lady, and with her prayer as much profit us.

"Item: he teacheth that men should do no worship to the holy cross that Christ died on, saying that if he had it whole, or all the pieces thereof, he would cast it in such a place as no sun should shine thereon, to the end it should never be founden to be worshipped more.

"Item: of all feasts, he saith that he hateth the Feast of the Holy Cross and the Feast of Corpus Christi.

"He teacheth also that no man or woman is bounden to keep and observe any vow that he hath made to God of virginity, or widowhood, or other chastity out of marriage, but that they may marry at their liberty, their vow notwithstanding."

"And how proveth he that?" quoth your friend.

"Marry," quoth I, "by the breaking of his own, when he married the nun. And now he raileth against all chastity, and saith that if a priest live chaste, he is like to the priests of the idol Cybele.[218]

"Long would it be to write you all the abominable heresies of this new sect. But some of them have I rehearsed, that ye may thereby consider whether he that teacheth such things go not about utterly to destroy the whole faith, religion, and virtue of Christendom. And that he is not in any of these points belied,[219] I shall find the means that ye shall see it in his own books. And there shall ye see how madly he laboreth to prove them."

"Prove them?" quoth your friend. "The substance of these matters be too abominable to be reasoned. And to make him hated of all good folk, is[220] enough to hear them rehearsed. But I marvel me much how he fell into such a heap of heresies."

---

210 interpretation   211 regards
212 besides   213 i.e., customarily shown
214 This may be an error for "sculpture."

215 *list to look therefor:* wish to look for it   216 who   217 *set at nought:* value as nothing   218 a Phrygian mother

goddess whose priests castrated themselves
219 slandered   220 it is

THE THIRD CHAPTER

The author showeth by what occasion that Luther
first fell to the devising of these heresies; and that
the occasion was such as well declareth[221] that he
was pricked[222] thereto by malice, and ever proceeded
from evil to worse, not witting where to hold him;[223]
and that he refuseth to stand to the judgment
of any folk earthly concerning the truth or
falsehood of his opinions save[224] only himself.

"Now, that is," quoth I, "somewhat worth to consider: how this lewd[225] friar began to fall in these mischievous matters. Ye shall understand that there was a pardon[226] obtained[227] in Saxony, for which pardon, as the manner[228] is there, Luther was the preacher, and preached to the people, exhorting them thereto and advancing the authority thereof all that he possibly might—not without his great advantage[229] therefor. So happed it then, soon after, that the setting forth of the pardon[230]—with the advantage thereof—was taken from him and set to another. For anger whereof, he fell into such a fury that forthwith he began to write against all pardons.[231] Howbeit, because the matter[232] was new and strange,[233] he began first by way of doubts and questions only, submitting himself and his writing to the judgment of the Pope, and desiring[234] to be informed of the truth. Whereupon when he was by writing answered by the master of the Pope's palace, then waxed he more wood[235] and fell to railing against him, and made also another book against the power of the Pope, affirming that his power upon the Church was never instituted of[236] God, but ordained only by the common consent of Christian people, for avoiding of schisms. But yet he said that all Christian men were bounden to stand[237] and obey thereunto, and that the Bohemians were damnable heretics for doing the contrary. But soon after, when he was in such wise answered by good and cunning[238] men that he perceived himself unable to defend that[239] he had affirmed, then fell he from reasoning to railing, and utterly denied that he had before affirmed, and then began

to write that the Pope had no power at all, neither by[240] God nor man, and that the Bohemians, whom he had in his writings before called damnable heretics, were good Christian men, and all their opinions good and Catholic. Then when he was cited[241] by the Pope's Holiness to appear, he appealed to the next general council which should be gathered in the Holy Ghost, so that whatsoever general council were after assembled, he might jest and rail thereon, and say it was not it that he appealed unto, for it was not assembled in the Holy Ghost."

"He took," quoth your friend, "a good wily way."

"As wily as it was," quoth I, "yet would he not stand thereby,[242] but fled from that to another. For now shall ye understand that yet soon after this, in the book by which he not answereth but raileth against that book wherein our sovereign lord the King—like a most faithful, virtuous, and most erudite prince—evidently and effectually revinced and confuted[243] the most venomous and pestilent book of Luther, entitled *The Captivity of Babylon*, in which he laboreth to destroy the holy sacraments of Christ's Church: in that book, I say, Luther, which[244] had before appealed to the next general council, utterly denieth the authority of all general councils, and setteth them all at nought."[245]

"By my troth," quoth your friend, "either was the man very negligent before—or very naught[246] after—when he changeth so often, and writeth ever the longer the more contrary,[247] not to his adversary only, but also to himself. But I pray you, how excuseth he his inconstancy?"

"Marry," quoth I, "he saith that he seeth further than he saw before. Whereunto the King's Grace showeth him that it were unlikely that he should see better through a pair of evil spectacles of ire and envy."

"Very true," quoth your friend, "by my troth. But yet I hear say that he hath offered to stand at[248] the judgment of learned men in all his matters, if his offer had been taken in time."

"Indeed," quoth I, "once he promised to stand to the judgment of the University of Paris; and

---

221 clarifies 222 spurred, incited; stung 223 *not witting where to hold him:* not knowing where to stop himself 224 except 225 wicked 226 a service making the sacrament of confession available, in which indulgences would be granted 227 held 228 custom 229 benefit; profit 230 *setting*

forth of the pardon: officiating at the service 231 indulgences 232 *the matter:* this doctrine 233 unfamiliar 234 requesting 235 *waxed he more wood:* grew he more angry 236 by 237 submit to 238 learned 239 what 240 from 241 summoned 242 *stand thereby:* remain firm in it 243 *revinced*

and confuted: refuted and disproved 244 who 245 *setteth … nought:* values them all as nothing 246 bad; wicked 247 *writeth … contrary:* his writing is more and more contradictory as time goes by 248 *stand at:* submit to

thereupon was there open dispicions kept,[249] and the very words written by notaries sworn for both the parties. But when his opinions were after at Paris by the University condemned, then he refused to stand to their judgment, and fell again to his old craft of railing.

"He appeared also at Worms, before the Emperor and the princes of the Empire,[250] by a safe-conduct, and there recognized and acknowledged as well the said pestilent book written against the sacraments as many others of like sort, to be his own, and offered to abide by them.[251] Which he might boldly do, being by the safe-conduct in good surety of[252] himself that he could take none harm. Then was he moved to dispicions upon the articles, so that he should[253] agree upon some persons, virtuous and well-learned, that should be judges of that disputations, and that he should be content to stand to their judgment upon the same. Whereupon he agreed to come to dispicions; but he would in no wise agree to make any men living judges upon it, nor stand to no man's judgment earthly."

THE FOURTH CHAPTER
The author showeth how that Luther, in the book that himself made of his own acts at the city of Worms in Almain,[254] doth so madly oversee[255] himself that he discloseth unaware certain follies of[256] himself which a man will well laugh at, and marvel much to see it.

"And that these things be true, it well appeareth to all the world in the book that he made himself of his demeanor[257] and his acts at the city called Worms,[258] in Almain. Which book, whoso readeth shall have a great pleasure to see therein both the frantic[259] vainglory of that fond[260] friar and yet therewithal[261] to see him carried out[262] with folly so far from himself that in a line or twain he discovereth[263] all that he went about to hide in all the book beside. For ye shall understand that, albeit he made that book himself, yet he made it so that he would it should[264] seem to have been of some other man's making, and not of his own, to the intent that such worshipful[265] words as he speaketh of himself might make him, in the ears of the reader, seem some honorable person. Which words else,[266] he wist[267] well, spoken of his own mouth, all the world would wonder on. Now in this book—besides that he leaveth out some things there said and spoken where the words written in could do him no worship, and some things reciteth with advantage for his part, rehearsing the other side nakedly and barely,[268] and some part pared off too to make it seem the more slender[269]—one thing he observeth diligently: that whereas speaking of the Emperor he calleth him never but simply and singly 'Charles,' he never speaketh of himself but he setteth forth his name in great capital letters and solemn titles—'The Man of God Luther.' And whereas they that spoke against his errors, he writeth that they 'burst out' in 'virulent' and venomous words, when he cometh to his own answer, then he writeth in this wise: 'But then Doctor Martin, for his incredible humanity and bounty, answered in this wise benignly.' And sometimes with these words: 'The most benign Father most mildly made answer.' And finally, he finisheth and endeth his book, as it were, with a *Gloria Patri* to the whole psalm, in this wise: 'This holy, devout man, therefore, even born to teach and preserve the Gospel of God, our Lord long preserve for his Church, with his holy Word also, Amen.'[270] Now, who was there ever born so suspicious that ever would have suspected that he which wrote such glorious words of Luther should be Luther himself? For where should a man find so very a vainglorious fool that would not in himself be ashamed of himself to think such things?

"But now, ye that read this, I pray you, for God's sake see how utterly this itch and tickling of vanity and vainglory had cast him clean beside[271] his mind and memory. For whereas all the book beside[272] was so devised and handled that it should seem some other to have made it and not himself, suddenly the fond fellow bewrayed[273] himself unaware. For in one place, forgetting himself, he speaketh in this wise:

249 *open dispicions kept:* public disputations held   **250** the Holy Roman Empire   **251** i.e., (the judgment of) the Emperor and princes   **252** *surety of:* security about   **253** *moved…should:* invited to disputations on his claim, provided he would   **254** Germany   **255** fail to see; misjudge   **256** about   **257** conduct   **258** *book…Worms: Acta et res gestae, D. Martini Lutheri, in comitiis principum uuormaciae* (May 1521)   **259** insane   **260** foolish   **261** also; in addition   **262** away   **263** reveals   **264** *would… should:* wanted it to   **265** honorable   **266** otherwise   **267** knew   **268** *nakedly and barely:* in isolation (i.e., out of context) and poorly or scantily   **269** deficient, inadequate   **270** *WA* 7: 857   **271** *clean beside:* completely out of   **272** *book beside:* rest of the book   **273** exposed

'When this was spoken, then the orator of the Empire, in a chiding manner, said that I had not answered to the purpose, and that those things which had been damned[274] and determined in General Councils of old ought not now of new[275] to be brought again in question by me; and therefore I should give a plain answer whether I would revoke mine errors or not. Then unto this I answered in this wise: "Since that it is so," etc.'[276]

Lo, here may ye see the incredible humility and lowly mind of this 'most benign father,' which[277] under the visor of a strange[278] herald bloweth out himself his own boast. Then may ye see therewith his marvelous, profound prudence, that had not the wit[279] to beware that himself bewrayed not[280] his own so foolish a device, in the vain avaunting[281] of his own false boast and praise, that though the words had been true, yet would almost a very natural[282] fool have been ashamed of himself to write them."

"By my troth," quoth your friend, "this device was madly minded of[283] Luther, and madly handled, and madly overseen,[284] to show himself so fond,[285] but if[286] pride, as the proverb is, must needs have a shame."

THE FIFTH CHAPTER
The author showeth the perpetual inconstancy of Luther and his contrariety and repugnance[287] against himself.

"Now, as for his constancy, appeareth,"[288] quoth I, "by that[289] I have before rehearsed of his continual change in his heresies from day to day, from worse to worse, which course he kept not only in the matters above rehearsed, but almost in all the remnant. For as concerning purgatory, he wrote first that, although it could not be proved by evident Scripture (as he affirmed), yet was there no doubt but that there is purgatory; and that thing, he said, was of all Christian men firmly to be believed. And then he wrote that he wondered of[290] the madness of such false and foolish heretics as were born within one hundred years past and are not ashamed to deny purgatory, which the whole Church of Christ hath believed this fifteen hundred years. Now, what constancy is there in this friar, that wrote this of heretics that deny purgatory, and within a while after denieth it himself, saying, in the sermon that he wrote of the rich man and Lazarus, that all men's souls 'lie still and sleep till Doomsday?'"[291]

"Marry," quoth your friend, "then hath some man had a sleep of a fair length. They will, I ween, when they wake forget some of their dreams."

"By my faith," quoth I, "he that believeth Luther that his soul shall sleep so long shall when he dieth sleep in shrewd[292] rest."

"I much marvel," quoth your friend, "what evil ailed him to find out this fond folly."

"To this opinion," quoth I, "or rather to the feigning of this opinion—for I verily think that himself thinketh not as he writeth—he fell for envy and hatred that he bore to priesthood; by the malice of which his ungracious mind, he rather were content that all the world lay in the fire of purgatory till Doomsday than that there were one penny given to a priest to pray for any soul."

"This is," quoth your friend, "very likely."

"Like constancy," quoth I, "hath he used[293] in the matter of holy vows. For in his book of *The Captivity of Babylon*, he writeth that 'neither man nor angel' is able to dispense with the vow made by man to God.[294] And soon after, he wrote that no vow could bind any man, but that every man may boldly break them of his own head.[295] But it well appeareth that he wrote the first of[296] anger and malice toward the Pope, and then changed to the second of a lecherous lust to the nun that he minded to marry."

THE SIXTH CHAPTER
The author showeth how that Luther hath been fain,[297] for the defense of his undefensible errors, to go back and forsake all the manner of proof and trial which he first promised to stand[298] to, and now, like a man shameful and shameless, hath no proof in the world but his own word, and calleth that the Word of God.

274 condemned　**275** *of new:* anew　**276** *WA* 7: 835–38　**277** who　**278** *visor of a strange:* guise of an unknown　**279** understanding, intelligence　**280** *bewrayed not:* did not expose　unintentionally　**281** bragging　**282** born　**283** *minded of:* conceived by　**284** overlooked　**285** foolish　**286** *but if:* unless　**287** contradiction, inconsistency　**288** this is shown　**289** what　**290** at　**291** See　*WA* 10.3: 192, 195.　**292** evil; undesirable; malicious　**293** exercised　**294** *WA* 6: 542　**295** accord, i.e., on the basis of his own mind or invention　**296** out of　**297** obliged　**298** submit

"His inconstant wit[299] and very devilish intent specially showed itself by this also, which I shall now rehearse[300] you. In the beginning the man had the mind that commonly such fools have: he reckoned all the world wild geese save[301] himself, and all the wit and learning to stand[302] in his own head. And then, weening that he should find no match, but that he should—as he list[303]—be able to prove the moon made of green cheese, he professed in his books that he would, for the proof or reproof[304] of his opinions, stand[305] to natural reason, to the authority of the old holy fathers, the laws and canons of Christ's Church, and to the Holy Scripture of God, with the interpretations of the old holy doctors. But soon after, when he perceived himself in his opinion deceived,[306] and that he saw himself confuted and concluded[307] evidently, both by Scripture, natural reason, the laws and determinations of the Church, and the whole consent of the holy fathers, interpreters of Holy Scripture, then began he to sing another song. For then, as for reason, he refused to stand to, saying that the matters of our faith be things above reason, and that reason hindereth us in our faith, and is unto faith an enemy. And as for the laws of the Church, he with other blasphemous heretics burned up openly at Wittenberg, singing in derision a dirge about[308] the fire for the law's soul. And then would he stand to nothing but only Scripture—nor to that neither, but if[309] it were very plain and evident. But now, if it were in question whether the Scripture were evident for him or against him, therein would he stand to no man's judgment but his own. For as for the whole faith of Christ's Church—continued by[310] so many hundred years—he set utterly at nought,[311] calling it men's devices.[312] And in Scripture, the interpretation of Saint Jerome, Saint Augustine, Saint Ambrose, and all the old holy fathers of so many years past, he nothing would esteem, but with blasphemous words letted[313] not to write, 'I care not for Augustine; I care not for a hundred Cyprians; I care not for a thousand Jeromes; I care not but for Scripture alone; and that is plainly on my part.'[314] As though none of these old holy cunning[315] men had understood any Scripture till he came. Now was he by this unreasonable manner[316] driven to another devilish device against saints. For to the intent that their authority should not, by the devotion and reverence that all good men bear them, diminish his credence, he was forced to labor to bring men in[317] that heresy that they should pray to no saints, but would have their images drawn down, all their pilgrimages left up,[318] all their relics cast out, all their honor and men's devotion toward them withdrawn—so far-forth[319] that he could neither abide the honor of our blessed Lady, nor the holy cross, nor Christ's blessed body—as plainly declareth his abominable books."

THE SEVENTH CHAPTER
The author showeth what things caused the people to fall into Luther's fond and furious[320] sect. And he showeth also what mischief the followers of that sect have done in Almain,[321] Lombardy, and Rome.

"It is," quoth your friend, "a wonder to me that the people, being before brought up in the right belief, could find in their hearts to give him audience in some such heresies as these be."

"Ye must understand, and may perceive," quoth I, "that he did not set forth all at once. But as Tyndale hath begun here in England with the thing that had a good visage[322] (though he had corrupted it and meant naught[323] indeed), putting forth first the New Testament in such wise handled that unlearned folk were likely to take harm and conceive diverse heresies in their hearts ere they could perceive his falsehood, and then hath since, by two other books, openly showed himself to lack nothing of Luther but that he hath not yet married a nun, so did Luther also put forth, in the beginning, no more but the matter of pardons,[324] as I told you, and therein nothing affirmed neither against the determination of the Church, but submitted himself thereto. Now with this demeanor was there no man offended. But yet did he that time intend a further mischief, which he little and little pursued and brought to pass. And one special thing with which he spiced all the poison was the liberty that

---

299 mind **300** relate to **301** except
302 reside **303** wished **304** refutation
305 submit **306** to be mistaken; to
be in error **307** refuted **308** around
309 *but if:* unless **310** for **311** *set . . .*

nought: valued it as absolutely nothing
312 inventions **313** hesitated **314** side
315 learned **316** habitual mode, fashion
317 into **318** *pilgrimages left up:* shrines
abandoned **319** *so far-forth:* to such an

extent **320** *fond and furious:* foolish and
irrational **321** Germany **322** appearance
323 evil **324** indulgences

he so highly commended unto the people, bringing them in belief that, having faith, they needed nothing else. For as for fasting, prayer, and such other things, he taught them to neglect and set at nought as vain and unfruitful ceremonies, teaching them also that, being faithful Christians, they were so near cousins to Christ that they be in a full freedom and liberty: discharged of all governors and all manner laws, spiritual or temporal, except the Gospel only. And albeit he said that of a special perfection it should be well done to suffer[325] and bear the rule and authority of popes, princes, and other governors—which rule and authority he calleth but only[326] tyranny—yet he saith that the people be so free by faith that they be no more bounden thereto than they be bounden to suffer wrong. And this doctrine also teacheth Tyndale, as the special matter[327] of his holy book of disobedience. Now was this doctrine in Almain, of[328] the common uplandish[329] people, so pleasantly heard that it blinded them in the looking upon the remnant, and could not suffer them to consider and see what end the same would in conclusion come to. The temporal[330] lords were glad, also, to hear this gear[331] against the clergy—and the people as glad to hear it against the clergy and against the lords too and against all their governors of every good town and city. And finally, so far went it forward that, at the last, it began to burst out and fall to open force and violence. For, intending to begin at the feeblest, there gathered them together, for the setting forth of these ungracious[332] heresies, a boistous[333] company of that unhappy[334] sect, and first rebelled against an abbot, and after against a bishop, wherewith the temporal lords had good game and sport, and dissembled the matter—gaping after[335] the lands of the spiritualty[336]—till they had almost played as Aesop telleth of the dog, which, to snatch at the shadow of the cheese in the water, let fall and lost the cheese that he bore in his mouth. For so was it shortly after that those uplandish Lutherans took so great boldness, and so began to grow strong, that they set also upon the temporal lords. Which had they not set hand thereto the sooner, while they looked

for other men's lands, had been like[337] shortly to lose their own. But so quit[338] they themselves that they slew upon the point of[339] seventy thousand Lutherans in one summer, and subdued the remnant in that part of Almain to a right miserable servitude. Howbeit, in the meanwhile many mischievous[340] deeds they did.

"And yet in diverse other parts of Almain and Switzerland, this ungracious sect, by the negligence of the governors in great cities, is so far-forth grown that finally the common people have compelled the rulers to follow them, whom, if they had taken heed in time, they might have ruled and led.

"And now is it too piteous a sight to see the despiteous despites[341] done there in many places to God and all good men, with the marvelous[342] change from all face and fashion[343] of Christendom into a very tyrannous persecution, not only of all good Christian people, quick[344] and dead, but also of Christ himself. For there shall ye see now the goodly monasteries destroyed, the places burned up, the religious people[345] put out and sent to seek their living—or in many cities the places yet standing, with more despite to God than if they were burned up to ashes. For the religious people—monks, friars, and nuns—be clean[346] drawn and driven out, except such as would agree to forsake their vows of chastity and be wedded, and the places dedicated to cleanness and chastity left only to these apostates and brothels,[347] to live there in lechery. Now the parish churches, in many places, not only defaced, all ornaments withdrawn,[348] the holy images pulled down and either broken or burned, but also the Holy Sacrament cast out, and the abominable beasts (which abhorreth[349] me to think on) not abhorred in despite to file in the pyxes,[350] and use, in many places continually, the churches for a common siege.[351] And that in so despiteful wise that when a stranger of[352] other places, where Christ is worshipped, resorteth to[353] these cities, some of those unhappy wretched citizens fail not, as[354] it were for courtesy and kindness, to accompany them in walking abroad, to show them the pleasures and commodities[355] of the town, and then bring them to no place

---

325 allow   **326** *but only:* nothing but   **327** *special matter:* particular subject   **328** by   **329** rustic, uncultivated   **330** secular   **331** discourse; business   **332** graceless; wicked   **333** violent; rough   **334** troublesome   **335** longing for   **336** clergy   **337** likely   **338** acted, acquitted   **339** *upon the point of:* nearly   **340** evil   **341** *despiteous despites:* cruel outrages   **342** terrible; amazing   **343** *face and fashion:* appearance and semblance   **344** living   **345** *religious people:* those in religious orders   **346** completely   **347** prostitutes   **348** removed   **349** horrifies   **350** *file…pyxes:* defecate in the boxes that held the Eucharist   **351** *common siege:* communal privy   **352** from   **353** *resorteth to:* visits   **354** as if   **355** *pleasures and commodities:* pleasing sights and goods

lightly³⁵⁶ but only the churches, to show them in derision what uses the churches serve for.

"Of this sect was the great part of those ungracious people also which late entered into Rome with the Duke of Bourbon³⁵⁷—not only robbing and spoiling³⁵⁸ the city (as well their own friends as the contrary party), but, like very beasts, did also violate the wives in the sight of their husbands, slew the children in the sight of the fathers. And to extort the discovering³⁵⁹ of more money, when men had brought out all that ever they had, to save themselves from death or further pain, and were at pacts and promises of rest³⁶⁰ without further business,³⁶¹ then the wretched tyrants and cruel tormentors, as though all that stood³⁶² for nothing, ceased not to put them eftsoons³⁶³ to intolerable torments. And old ancient honorable men, those fierce heretics letted³⁶⁴ not to hang up by the privy members,³⁶⁵ and from many they pulled them off and cast them in the street. And some³⁶⁶ brought out naked, with his hands bounden behind him and a cord tied fast unto his privy members. Then would they set before him, in his way, others of those tyrants with their Moorish pikes, the points toward the breasts of these poor naked men. And then one or two of those wretches would stand behind those Moorish pikes and draw the poor souls by the members toward them. Now, then was all their cruel sport and laughter either to see the seely³⁶⁷ naked men, in shrinking from the pikes, to tear off their members, or, for pain of that pulling, to run their naked bodies in deep upon the pikes. Too piteous and too abominable were it to rehearse the villainous pain and torments that they devised on the seely women—to whom, after that they had beastily abused them (wives in the sight of their husbands, and the maidens in the sight of their fathers), they were reckoned for piteous³⁶⁸ that did no more but cut their throats. And very certain is it that not in Rome only, but also in the country³⁶⁹ of Milan that they kept and oppressed, after torments used³⁷⁰ and money fetched out that way, then some³⁷¹ calling himself a gentleman in Almain or Spain would feign himself fallen in love of his host's daughter,

and that he would marry her in any wise,³⁷² and then make much earnest business for to have some money with³⁷³ her. And whether he got aught or got nought by that device, he letted not soon after to put the father, the mother, the fair daughter, and all the whole house to new torments, to make them tell where any more money were—were there any or none. And some failed not to take the child and bind it to a broach,³⁷⁴ and lay it to the fire to roast—the father and mother looking on—and then begin to common of³⁷⁵ a price for the sparing of the child, asking first a hundred ducats, then fifty, then forty, then twenty, then ten, then five, then twain, when the seely father had not one left, but these tyrants had all before. Then would they let the child roast to death. And yet in derision, as though they pitied the child, they would say to the father and the mother, 'Ah, fie, fie, for shame. What marvel is it though³⁷⁶ God sent a vengeance among you. What unnatural people be you, that can find in your hearts to see your own child roasted afore your face, rather than ye would out with one ducat to deliver it from death.'

"Thus devised these cursed wretches so many diverse fashions of exquisite cruelties that I ween they have taught the devil new torments in hell that he never knew before, and will not fail to prove himself a good scholar and surely render them his lesson when they come there, where it is to be feared that many of them be by this.³⁷⁷ For soon after that they had in Rome exercised a while this fierce and cruel tyranny, and entered into the holy churches, spoiled³⁷⁸ the holy relics, cast out the Blessed Sacrament, pulled the chalice from the altar at Mass, slain priests in the church—left no kind of cruelty or spite undone, but from hour to hour imbruing³⁷⁹ their hands in blood, and that in such wise as any Turk or Saracen would have pitied or abhorred—our Lord sent, soon after, such a pestilence among them that he left not of them the third part alive. For this purpose I rehearse you this their heavy mischievous³⁸⁰ dealing: that ye may perceive by their deeds what good cometh of their sect. For as our Savior saith, ye shall know the tree by the fruit."³⁸¹

---

356 swiftly **357** *late . . . Bourbon:* Rome was sacked May 6, 1527, by troops under Duke Charles, who had died in the battle. **358** despoiling **359** revealing **360** freedom from further violence or trouble **361** trouble **362** counted **363** soon

afterwards **364** hesitated **365** *privy members:* private parts **366** someone would be **367** helpless, defenseless, pitiable **368** merciful **369** province **370** practiced **371** someone **372** *in any wise:* by any means **373** *have . . . with:*

get some money along with **374** spit **375** *common of:* discuss **376** that **377** this time; now **378** despoiled **379** staining **380** evil **381** Mt 7:16–20

THE EIGHTH CHAPTER

*The messenger saith that the malice of the men is
not to be imputed to the sect, since that of every sect,
some be naught.[382] And the author showeth that
in the Lutherans, the sect itself is the cause
of the malice that the men fall to.*

"Sir," quoth your friend, "in good faith, I neither can nor will defend that sect. But yet reason it is to take everything as it is. And if it be naught, it hath the less need to be made worse. But as for the malicious cruel dealing of men of war, is[383] not, in my mind, to be imputed to the sect of Luther. For there is no sect so saintly but they fall in cruelty when they fall to war. And of every sect, also, be some bad. And therefore the malice of the men is not, as meseemeth, to be imputed unto the sect."

"It is not," quoth I, "all one to be some naught and all naught. But they that fall in this sect wax[384] naught, all the whole meinie.[385] For forthwith upon this sect once begun, the whole flocks of such as were infected therewith fell unto those mischievous deeds that I before rehearsed you. And also though men in war wax furious and cruel, yet was there never none that went therein so far — and specially in such kind of cruelty as hath been among Christian men in their wars always forborne,[386] as is the despites done to the Blessed Sacrament, wherein these beasts were more hot and more busy than would[387] the great Turk — and that because their sect is yet, in manner, worse than his. Moreover, the unhappy[388] deeds of that sect must needs be imputed to the sect itself while the doctrine thereof teacheth and giveth occasion to their evil deeds. A Christian man's evil living cannot be imputed to his Christendom.[389] For his living is contrary to the doctrine and living of Christ. But as for the doctrine of this unhappy sect, and the living[390] also of the beginners of the same, is[391] such as every wise man well perceiveth doth teach and give occasion of their evil deeds. For what good deed shall he study or labor to do, that[392] believeth Luther that he hath no free will of his own, by which he can with help of grace either work or pray? Shall he not say to himself that he may sit still and let God alone?

"What harm shall they care to forbear, that believe Luther that God alone, without their will, worketh all the mischief that they do themselves?

"What shall he care how long he live in sin, that believeth Luther that he shall, after this life, neither feel well nor ill in body nor soul till the Day of Doom? Will not he, trow[393] you, say as the Welshman said? 'If thou give her[394] that day, by God, Davy will have thy coat too!'[395] And this thing I say but for an example. For look his opinions through, and ye shall find that they plainly set forth[396] all the world to wretched living. If they would say that we misconstrue their words, their books be open,[397] and the words plain, and inculked[398] again and again so often and so openly that men cannot err therein, nor they by any cloak or color[399] defend them.

"And besides that, not only the commonalty[400] of their sect show the effect and fruit of their doctrine by their abominable dealing, as I have rehearsed you, but also the doctors[401] and the archheretics themselves well declare[402] the holiness of their doctrine by their own living. For as they live, they teach; and as they teach, they live."

THE NINTH CHAPTER

*The author showeth that it is a great token that
the world is near at an end while[403] we see
the people so far fallen from God that they
can abide it to be content with this pestilent
frantic[404] sect, which no people —
Christian or heathen — could have
suffered[405] afore our days.*

"If the world were not near at an end, and the fervor of devotion so sore[406] cooled that it were almost quenched among Christian people, it could never have comen to pass that so many people should fall to the following of such a beastly sect. For albeit that[407] the Muhammadans, being a sensual and filthy sect, did in few years draw the great part of the world unto it by the selfsame ways which now the Lutherans use — that is to wit, voluptuous living and violence, offering delight unto the receivers and death to the refusers — yet was there before

---

382 bad   383 it is   384 grow   385 group
386 refrained from, avoided   387 *more . . .
would:* more active than would be
388 objectionable   389 Christianity
390 conduct   391 it is   392 who

393 believe, suppose   394 a Welsh idiom
for "him" (Davy)   395 *If . . . too:* i.e., If
he can wait that long to pay back or be
punished, he'll take your coat in addition
to your money.   396 *set forth:* direct

397 public   398 repeated   399 pretext
400 general body of followers   401 theologians   402 make manifest   403 when
404 insane   405 tolerated   406 greatly
407 *albeit that:* although

this abominable sect never any sect so shameless that would still avow themselves for Christian folk, granting the Scripture to be true, and therewithal so enemiously[408] blaspheme and oppugn[409] the Church of Christ, the sacraments of Christ, the saints of Christ, the cross of Christ, the mother of Christ, and the holy body of Christ: so shamefully living, and openly professing a bestial manner of living, clean[410] contrary to the doctrine and life of Christ. The Arians, the Pelagians, the Manichaeans, and so forth — every sort of heretics — began of such as, though they wickedly erred in substantial articles of the faith, yet was their outward fashion of living so honest and spiritual in appearance that men thought themselves bounden the better to believe their doctrine as Christian, for[411] some spiritual form and fashion of their Christian living. But now, the chieftains of these execrable heresies both teach and use[412] more sensual and licentious living than ever did Muhammad. Which, though he license men to[413] many wives, yet he never taught nor suffered his folk to break their chastity promised once and solemnly dedicated to God. Whereas Luther not only teacheth monks, friars, and nuns to marriage, but also, being a friar, hath married a nun himself, and with her liveth, under the name of wedlock, in open incestuous[414] lechery, without care or shame, because he hath procured and gotten so many shameful and shameless companions.

"Who could have bidden[415] to look any man in the face that should have done thus in Saint Jerome's and Saint Augustine's days? What[416] speak we of Saint Jerome and Saint Augustine? Who durst have done it for shame any time since Christ's birth until our wretched days? Or who since Adam's time, among the chosen people of God? What speak we of the chosen people of God? The very paynims[417] and pagans — idolaters — kept their chastity vowed once to their false gods, and rather chose to cut off the members with which they might break it than to stand in the jeopardy to break it. And in Rome of old time, when they were pagans, if any vestal virgin (for so called they their nuns) were violated, they not only beat the man to death with rods in the marketplace, and buried the woman quick,[418] but also reckoned it for a wonderful monster,[419] and a token of wrath and indignation of their gods toward their city and empire — putting thereupon themselves in devoir[420] with open[421] processions, and prayers, and sacrifice, to procure the recovery of their gods' favor. Is it not, then, now a wondrous case to see — since that the chastity[422] promised once to God, and also to the false idols under the name of 'god,' hath always been, since the world began, among Christian and heathen so highly esteemed that the breakers thereof have always been, by the common consent of the whole world, as a thing taught by God unto good men, and by nature to all men, taken, reputed, and punished as abominable, wicked wretches — is it not, I say, now a wondrous thing to see, that in the flock of Christian people, which by Christ himself, by all his apostles, by all his holy martyrs, confessors, and doctors, by all his whole Church, all the whole time of these fifteen hundred years past, chastity hath been more highly praised and esteemed than ever it was of any other sect since the world began, we should see now a lewd[423] friar so bold and so shameless to marry a nun and bide thereby,[424] and be taken still for a Christian man, and, over that, for a man meet[425] to be the beginner of a sect whom any honest man should vouchsafe[426] to follow? If our Lord God — whose wisdom is infinite — should have sat and studied to devise a way whereby he might cast in our face the confusion of our folly, how might he have founden a more effectual openly to show us the shame of our sin than to suffer us that call ourselves Christian folk to see such a rabble spring up among us as, professing the faith and religion of Christ, let not to set at nought[427] all the doctors of Christ's Church and lean to the only[428] authority of Friar Tuck and mad[429] Marian?"

408 hostilely, spitefully   409 attack
410 completely   411 on account of
412 practice   413 to have   414 Under
canon law, monks and nuns were considered brothers and sisters.   415 endured
416 why   417 heathens   418 alive
419 marvel; something unnatural
420 duty   421 public   422 celibacy
423 bad; lascivious   424 *bide thereby:*
stick by this   425 fit   426 be willing
427 *let … nought:* do not hesitate to value as nothing   428 *lean to the only:* rely alone on   429 changed to "maid" in 1557 *Workes*

THE TENTH CHAPTER

The author inveigheth against this detestable article of this ungracious[430] sect whereby they take away the liberty of man's free will and ascribe all things to destiny.

"Surely, as I say, this world is either, after the words of Saint John, *totus positus in maligno* ('all set in malice'),[431] that we be so prone wittingly[432] to take so wrong a way, or else is it in a marvelous blindness, if we can neither perceive by the naughty living of the persons that their sect is naught, nor can perceive by their doctrine that their sect must make their persons naught, their heresies being such as ye have heard. Whereby every man that any faith hath, and any manner knowledge of Christian belief, may well and surely perceive that Luther and all his offspring, with all those that favor and set forth his sect, be very limbs[433] of the devil and open enemies to the faith of Christ. And not only to the faith and manhood of our Savior Christ, but also against the Holy Ghost, and the Father himself, and utterly against all goodness of the Godhead—as those that wretchedly lay all the weight and blame of our sin to the necessity and constraint of God's ordinance, affirming that we do no sin of ourselves by any power of our own will, but by the compulsion and handiwork of God, and that we do not the sin ourselves, but that God doth the sin in us himself. And thus these wretched heretics, with this blasphemous heresy alone, lay more villainous rebuke[434] to the great majesty of God than ever any one ribald laid unto[435] another. For who was there ever that laid unto another all the particular evil deeds of any one other man, where these ribalds lay to the charge and blame of God all the malice and mischief, from the first fault to the last, that ever was wrought or thought by man, woman, or devil. And by this give they wretches great boldness to follow their foul affections, as things—after[436] their opinion—more verily wrought in them by God than the best minds be in good men, and that it were therefore in vain for them to resist their sinful appetites. And if they shall be damned, yet they say it shall be long ere they feel it. For Luther saith that all souls shall sleep, and feel neither good nor bad after this life till Doomsday.[437] And then they that shall be damned, shall be damned, he saith, for no deserving of their own deeds, but for such evil deeds as God only forced and constrained them unto, and wrought in them himself, using them in all those evil deeds but as a dead instrument, as a man heweth with a hatchet. And that God shall damn all that shall be damned for his own deeds only, which himself shall have done in them, and finally for his only pleasure,[438] because it liked[439] him not to choose them as he did his chosen people, whom they say that he chose in such wise, before the beginning of the world, that they can never sin."

THE ELEVENTH CHAPTER

The messenger saith that howsoever Luther and his followers in Almain believe, yet he cannot think that such as be Lutherans in England—of whom some, he saith, have seemed good and honest—be so mad and unhappy to believe that all hangeth upon destiny. Whereupon the author showeth the contrary, and that they be naught[440] indeed, seem they never so good. And for proof that howsoever they color their words, they mean that all dependeth upon only destiny, he rehearseth a certain dispicion[441] had with a heretic detected[442] to the bishop and examined— the author being present—where the heretic, being learned and a preacher, made many shifts[443] to make it seem that in his evil words he meant but well.

When your friend had heard all this, he said at last that albeit the words of Luther seemed very plain toward the affirming of such opinions, yet were the things so far out of all frame[444] that it gave him occasion to doubt lest Luther meant not all things so evil as his words seem to weigh[445] to. And if he so meant himself, with others of his flock and affinity[446] in Almain, yet thought your friend that such as here favor and follow his sect, in England—of whom some seem right honest, and far from his manner of living—do not so take his words, nor understand them that way, but construe them to some better sense.

---

430 graceless, wicked   431 1 Jn 5:19
432 knowingly   433 agents   434 insult,
disgrace   435 *ribald laid unto:* scoundrel
attributed to   436 according to

437 Judgment Day   438 *only pleasure:*
pleasure only   439 pleased   440 bad
441 disputation   442 reported;
accused   443 evasions; fraudulent devices

444 established order   445 amount
446 association

"Forsooth," quoth I, "they cannot but know his open living in lechery with his lewd leman[447] the nun, and that all the captains of that sort—some late[448] Carthusians, some Observants,[449] some of other religions,[450] and all now apostates and wedded—live in like manner and teach others the same. And by this can they not doubt but that their doctrine is naught, except themselves allow[451] that way for good. Now as for their own goodness, ye find few that fall to that sect but that soon after they fall into the contempt of prayer, and fasting, and of all good works, under the name of 'ceremonies.' And if any do otherwise, it is for some purpose for the while to blind the people and keep themselves in favor till they may find the time, by leisure, to fashion and frame them better to their purpose, which[452] in the beginning—if they showed themselves plainly—could haply[453] not abide to hear them. Of which their demeanor,[454] and that in these heresies they mean here no better than Luther doth himself, I have had good experience, and among many other things, this that I shall show you. It happed me to be lately present whereas[455] one in the Lutheran books deeply learned—and of truth neither in Holy Scripture nor in secular literature unlearned (as I perceive not only by the testimony of other men and the degrees that he had taken in the university, but also by his words and his writing)—was, in the presence of right honorable, virtuous, and very cunning[456] persons, examined. For he was at that time in ward[457] for heresy, because that, being learned, and using to hear[458] confessions, and among many folk meetly well allowed[459] in preaching, and thereby growing in good opinion and favor of many good, simple people, abused all these open and apparent good things to the secret sowing and setting forth of Luther's heresies. And had for that intent not only taught and written and covertly corrupted diverse light and lewd[460] persons, but also had bought great number of the books of Luther, and Wycliffe, Hus, and Zwingli, and such other heretics—and of many one sort[461] diverse books—to be delivered, as he could find occasion, unto young scholars of the universities, such as he thought, of[462] youth and lightness,

most likely to be soon corrupted. This man, I say, being examined and long keeping himself close[463] from disclosing of the matter, and more ready to go straight to the devil with lying and false forswearing[464] than to be acknown of[465] his evil demeanor and confess the truth, at the last perceiving the matters (partly by the confession of other folk, partly by his own handwriting) so far-forth comen to light that they could in no wise be cloaked, then began he somewhat plainly to confess and declare, not only what he had done for the setting forth of that sect, but also partly what opinions he and others, his fellows, had holden[466] and were of. Setting,[467] nevertheless, all the colors[468] he could to make it seem that though[469] the words which they spoke or wrote were strange and contrary to right belief, yet the effect of their meaning was not much discrepant[470] from the true faith of Christ's Church. Howbeit, when he was reasoned withal,[471] and saw that he could not so shift it off, but that, for any color he could find, one part of his tale ever contraried[472] another, at last he showed plainly their opinions, and laid forth (as in part for his own excuse, as things inducing him thereto) all the texts of Scripture by which they pretend[473] to prove their opinions true. Among which opinions, when he came to the opinion by which they hold that only faith alone is sufficient, without good works, unto that he said in the beginning that they meant nothing else thereby but that men should put their faith in God's promises and hope to be saved thereby, and that they should not put their trust in their works, for that would turn them to pride.

"Then was it answered him that he and his fellows could not mean so. For if they did, then could they not blame the Church as they do, making as though the Church had all this while hid the true faith from the people, and that themselves were now shent[474] for preaching the Gospel truly. For if this were their meaning, they then meant none other than every common preacher of the Church hath always preached before Luther's days. For what preacher hath not told the people the parable of the poor publican ashamed of his sins and

447 *lewd leman:* lascivious beloved
448 former   **449** Observant Franciscans   **450** religious orders   **451** *except themselves allow:* unless they approve
452 who   **453** perhaps   **454** conduct
455 where   **456** intelligent   **457** custody

458 *using to hear:* accustomed to hearing
459 approved   **460** *light and lewd:* gullible and ignorant   **461** kind of
462 on account of   **463** shut up, concealed   **464** denying under oath
465 *be acknown of:* acknowledge

466 held   **467** Showing   **468** pretexts
469 even if   **470** different than
471 with   **472** contradicted   **473** allege
474 disgraced, ruined

the proud Pharisee boasting of his virtues?[475] Who hath not bidden them do well, and, albeit that God will reward them for their good deeds, yet put not their trust in themselves and their own deeds, but in God's goodness? Who hath not told them that they should, as God biddeth them in the Gospel, that when they have done all they can do, yet say to themselves, 'We be but unprofitable servants; we have done but our duty'?[476] These things and such others the Church hath always taught against the putting of a proud trust in our own deeds, because that we cannot always surely[477] judge our own deeds, for the blind favor[478] that we bear toward ourselves. And therefore was it said to him, 'If ye meant but thus, as the Church meaneth, then would ye preach but as the Church preacheth, and not blaspheme the Church in your sermons, as though ye began true preaching of the Gospel and that the Church had hitherto preached false. And also ye must needs mean some other thing. For Luther, whose sect ye confess that ye have leaned unto, writeth in this matter far otherwise. For he saith plain that faith alone, without any good works, doth justify us and sufficeth for our salvation.' Then answered he that therein they meant none other but that faith is sufficient alone if one happen, after he have faith and baptism, to die ere he have time to do any good works. Then was it said unto him, if they should teach this opinion, under such words, for a great, secret mystery new founden out, and thereby blame the Church for misteaching the people—as though the Church taught them to put less trust in God and in faith of[479] Christ than they should do, and induced them to put their trust in themselves and their own good works—they used themselves marvelously,[480] considering that if they meant none other, the Church and they meant all one thing. But they could not mean so. For then why should they blame the Church, that[481] saith not the contrary? And also, if they meant none other thing, few[482] words would serve them. They should not need so often to speak thereof. For then that tale can do little good here or anywhere else where folk be christened in their cradles. For either they die ere they have time to do good works, and then they be too young to hear that sermon, or else they

live and have time to do good works. And then that sermon were not wholesome for them: that good works need not,[483] but only faith is sufficient, without them. 'And when the people take it as ye speak it—that faith alone is enough for them—then is it now a bare gloss[484] for you to say that ye meant not so, but only that faith alone had been enough for them if they had died in their swaddling clothes.'

"To this he said that they thought also that faith alone doth justify a man without any good works, not only in children, but also in every age. 'For whensoever a man that hath been a sinner doth repent and amend in his mind with a full faith in the promises of God, he is justified ere ever he do any of these good works: alms, fasting, or any such other. For he cannot work well till he be good already. For as Christ saith, *Arbor mala non potest bonum fructum facere* ("An evil tree cannot bring forth good fruit");[485] and therefore, since good works be good fruit, an evil man cannot work them. Whereby it appeareth well that the man is justified before by his faith alone, without the works, and then out of that faith groweth the good fruit of good works. But faith did justify the man before, and the man was as good before the works as he is after. For his faith did justify him. And as for the works, be[486] but things that the faith in the man, or the man by the faith, bringeth forth, as the tree bringeth forth his[487] leaves and can do none other, faith being in the heart.'

"Then was it said unto him that in this tale he seemed to make the good works to be much like a shadow that the body maketh of necessity while it standeth in the sun, and is never the better therefor.[488] And then was it asked him whether a man must not, if his faith shall serve him, have charity therewith, and a purpose to do good works. 'Yes,' quoth he, 'that he must, if he have age and discretion thereto.'[489] Then was it answered him that then was all gone that himself had said before. For then did not faith alone justify the man; but the charity, with the purpose of good works, must—by his own granting—needs go therewith, or else would his faith justify nothing at all. For if he had never so great a faith and never so sure a belief in God's promises, yet if he purposed to do no good deeds

475 See Lk 18:9–14.   **476** Lk 17:10   **477** with certainty   **478** *for the blind favor:* because of the blind partiality   **479** in   **480** *used themselves marvelously:* conducted themselves wondrously   **481** which   **482** a few   **483** *need not:* are not necessary   **484** *bare gloss:* worthless commentary   **485** Mt 7:18; see also Lk 6:43.   **486** they are   **487** its   **488** for it   **489** sufficient for that (purpose)

therewith, but peradventure harm, he should have little justification by his only faith. And therefore it was false that[490] he had said—'a man is never the better for his good works'—while[491] his good works be so taken and reputed with[492] God that the purpose of them, yet undone, so far-forth worketh to his justification that without that purpose he cannot be justified. And that it is also false that[493] he said—that 'faith alone justifies a man'—when himself is fain[494] to grant that faith without charity and purpose of good works cannot justify, which is as much to say as faith alone cannot justify.

"To this he answered that he had said that faith only was sufficient, and that faith alone doth justify, because that if a man had faith, it could not be but that he should work good works. 'For faith,' he said, 'could never be idle, as the fire must needs burn and give heat. And therefore, as a man may say, "The fire is enough to burn a tree," though he speak nothing of heat, and yet the fire doth it by heat; and a man may say "The fire maketh me see by night," and yet the fire doth it but by the light, so may a man say that faith doth save us, though faith do it not without hope, and charity, and other virtuous works, because that faith hath always good hope and charity with it, and cannot but work well—no more than the fire can be without heat and light and burn all combustible things that it may touch and tarry with.'

"Then was it said unto him that albeit a man might so speak by[495] the fire, yet would not this thing serve their sect. 'For he that saith fire alone is enough to burn would not say nay to[496] him that would say the fire could not burn but if[497] it had heat. But your sect scorneth and blameth the Church because the Church saith that faith will not suffice but if it have charity and good works. For else[498] ye had no cause in this matter to preach contrary to the Church. Moreover, where ye say that faith hath always good hope with it, that seemeth not always true. For he that hopeth that by faith alone he shall be saved, without any good works—as Lutherans do believe indeed—he hath an evil hope, and a damnable. Now where ye say that ye preach faith alone to be sufficient because that faith hath always charity joined therewith—if this were true, why preach ye not as well that charity alone is sufficient, which were as near the truth as the other? Now, where ye make all the ground upon

this—that faith hath ever charity therewith, and that it cannot be but that charity, which is indeed the thing that specially bringeth forth good works, much more properly than faith, for faith bringeth them forth by charity when it is joined therewith, as the Apostle saith, *Fides quae per dilectionem operatur* ("Faith worketh by charity")[499]—where ye say it cannot be but that this charity is always joined unto faith, this ground will fail you, and make your foundation false, and all your building fall. The apostle Paul in many places of his epistles saith the contrary thereof. For he saith that if a man have so great faith that he might by the force of his faith work miracles, and also such fervent affection to the faith that he would give his body to the fire for the defense thereof, yet if he lacked charity, all his faith sufficed not.'"[500]

"In good faith," quoth your friend, "he was well and properly answered. But yet methinketh he might have replied a little again[501] to those words of Saint Paul, and might have avoided[502] them well with other words of his own.[503] For where he writeth also to the Galatians that if any angel would come down from heaven and preach a contrary gospel to that that he had preached already, 'accursed should he be,' and not to be believed,[504] he did not in these words affirm nor intend thereby that ever it should so be, or could so be, that any angel so should do indeed. For he knew right well it was impossible that any angel of heaven should come down and tell a false tale. But he said it only by a manner of speaking (which is among learned men called 'hyperbole') for the more vehement expressing of a matter, nothing meaning else but that the gospel which he had preached was the plain, sure, and undoubtable truth, against which no man were to be believed. And in like wise methinketh the man that ye speak of might have said that though Saint Paul said 'If he had so great faith that he were able thereby to remove hills, except[505] he had charity therewith' it would not serve him, he meant thereby no more but to show the great need that men have to[506] charity, and not that it were possible that faith could be without charity, no more than he meant that an angel may come down from heaven to preach a false faith. And therefore might it yet stand right well with all those words of Saint Paul that faith cannot

490 what, that which   491 since   *to:* disagree with; contradict   497 *but*
492 *reputed with:* regarded by   493 what   *if:* unless   498 otherwise   499 Gal
494 obliged   495 about   496 *say nay*   5:6   500 See 1 Cor 13:2.   501 back   502 refuted   503 *his own:* Saint Paul's
504 See Gal 1:8.   505 unless   506 for

fail of salvation, since it cannot fail of charity. And of truth, meseemeth as that man said: that faith cannot be idle, but it must needs work well."

"Forsooth," quoth I, "the man lacked⁵⁰⁷ you there; for he found not that gloss, which though⁵⁰⁸ he had, yet would it not have served him. For between those two places of Saint Paul is there great difference. For in the one is there an impossible excess and hyperbole; in the other is there not so. For angels of heaven never can come down and teach a false faith, but faith may be severed from charity. And in the one place he none other thing intended than (as ye say) to show, by that great exceeding word, the undoubted truth of the faith which himself had preached. But in the other place his special purpose was to teach the Corinthians that they should neither trust that any gift of nature, or gift of God above nature, or any manner virtue — alms-deed, faith, or other — were able to stand them in stead⁵⁰⁹ without charity. And this did he specially for that he would⁵¹⁰ that no man should be in such error as to reckon that either excellent gift of cunning,⁵¹¹ great labor spent in preaching, great alms spent on poor people, or a very fervent faith might suffice to their salvation if charity lacked.⁵¹² Against which error, he doth in such wise exhort them to charity, in avoiding the rancor which by occasion of schisms did arise among them, that he showed them precisely that without charity they lost clearly⁵¹³ the merit of all their other virtues and graces that God had given them — cunning, alms-deed, faith, and all — putting the example by his own self, which, though he were a chosen servant and apostle, yet if he were in language equal with all the whole world and with angels too and had all the cunning that possibly could be had, and the spirit of all prophecy therewith, and would give all his goods in alms, and had also all the full faith so great that it sufficed to work wonders with, and so fervent that he would abide to be burned for it, yet if he lacked charity, all this would not serve him. So that ye may see now that your gloss would not have relieved⁵¹⁴ this man. For though none angel could come down and teach an untruth, and therefore the words that ye allege⁵¹⁵ can be none otherwise taken than, as ye say, by way of excess and hyperbole, to declare the vehemence

of his mind in the matter of faith which he then spoke of, yet this other place of Saint Paul, that was laid⁵¹⁶ against that heretic that I speak of, as great and vehement as the words be, yet do they plainly prove that the Apostle showeth that faith may be without charity — and that both so great that it may suffice to the doing of great wonders and so fervent that it may suffer a painful death, and yet, for fault⁵¹⁷ of charity, not sufficient to salvation, and that this may hap as well in faith as in alms-deed, which the Apostle putteth in the same case.⁵¹⁸ And therefore, where that man said, and ye seem to confirm the same — that faith cannot be idle from the working of good works — the Apostle, to show the contrary, and that all the works of faith, though they seem never so good, be yet naught⁵¹⁹ indeed if they be not wrought with charity, commendeth only the faith that worketh by charity, signifying that all other works of faith be not available.⁵²⁰ And surely faith alone, without charity, may be besides this not only idle, without the busyness of good works, but also, for lack of good works, it may be utterly dead. And therefore, as it was there objected unto that man, the holy apostle James saith to them that reckon faith sufficient for salvation without good works that they be worse than devils.⁵²¹ For he saith that the devils do believe, and tremble for the fear of God, and that men which by the hope and boldness of their belief think their faith without good works sufficient be worse than devils, because they stand out of dread⁵²² of God, that menaceth⁵²³ unto them the pains of hell except⁵²⁴ they do good works. Without which, Saint James, for a final conclusion, saith that the faith is but dead.

"But here was it also said unto him, yet again, that though Saint James do say that 'faith without good works is dead,'⁵²⁵ he should not thereby run to his old gloss and say that therefore he and other Lutherans meant that faith sufficeth to salvation because they think it cannot be but that it shall needs bring forth good works, and that therefore, on the contrary side, if one have no good works, he hath no faith, because a dead faith is no faith, as a dead man is no man. It was told him that this gloss would not serve him. For Saint James meant not that the faith that he calleth dead for lack of good works is no faith — no more than Saint Paul meant that a widow living in delight and pleasure is no woman, though he said that she 'is dead even as she goeth alive'[526] — but Saint James meant only that such faith shall not stand them in stead.[527] For Saint James denieth not but that such a dead faith as he calleth dead because it is unprofitable is yet a very faith indeed, though it be not quick[528] in good works. And therefore he resembleth[529] such a faith in a man unto the unprofitable faith that is in a devil. For he saith that where such a man is bold of[530] his faith, the devil hath faith as well as he; for the devil doth believe such things as we believe. To this the man answered that some 'right well-learned men' were of the mind that without[531] a man wrought good works, it was a good proof that he had no faith at all; for very faith could not but work, and that the devil had no faith but by equivocation of this word 'faith.' For the very faith, indeed, is a faith in the promises of God. And the devil is desperate,[532] and hath not nor cannot have faith and trust in God's promises.

"Then was it answered him that those 'right well-learned men' were Luther and Tyndale and their fellows, that take themselves for better learned than Christ's blessed apostles Saint Paul or Saint James, which[533] in their holy writing affirm fully the contrary. And where they say that the devil hath no faith, but hath the knowledge of the things that we believe, and so he hath not faith, they affirm therein more than they may make good.[534] For Saint James saith they 'believe,' and saith not they 'know.' And he, when he wrote it, knew much better than Luther, and Tyndale too, what manner[535] perceiving the devils have in the articles of our faith. In which, as there be some whereof the devils have peradventure not a belief, but a certain and sure knowledge — as of Christ's descension into hell, and spoiling[536] of their possession — so are they of likelihood in[537] any other articles of our faith whereof they have only belief and persuasion, without the very knowledge and science.[538] And where those 'well-learned men' Luther and Tyndale say that the devil hath not faith but by the equivocation of the word 'faith' — being indeed (as ye say) a faith in the promises of God, whereby Christian men hope to come to heaven,

whereas the devils be desperate and can have no such faith in God's promises, nor hope or look for heaven — these 'well-learned men' that so say go about to set Saint James to school.[539] For they would we should ween[540] that Saint James did speak of faith like one that wist[541] not what faith meant, but were deceived by equivocation of the word, calling faith the thing that is not faith indeed; whereas indeed Saint James speaketh of it as he should, and useth the word in his[542] right signification, and these Lutherans abuse the word of[543] a malicious mind to deceive unlearned people with equivocation. For whereas faith signifieth the belief and firm credence given, not only to such things as God promiseth, but also to every truth that he telleth his Church, by writing or without, which thing he will have us bounden to believe; and whereas of truth, the devils, as Saint James saith, do believe such things and have[544] them in a reverent dread: now would these heretics blind us with their equivocation by which they not only restrain[545] the faith unto the promises alone, from all other articles of the faith — of which many be no promises, as[546] to believe that there is a God, and that there be three Persons, and many such other articles — but also abuse the word 'faith' altogether, turning it slyly from belief into trust, confidence, and hope, and would have it seem as though our faith were nothing else but a sure trust and a faithful hope that we have in God's promises. And this sophistical handling of 'faith' is the thing that, as appeareth by Tyndale in his book of *Obedience*, these Lutherans ween to deceive all the world withal,[547] and to make men ween that 'faith' betokeneth not belief, but hope and trust; and so to make men ween that Saint James wist not what 'faith' meant when he laid[548] against them that put their trust, as these Lutherans teach us, in their only faith,[549] the comparison between them and devils, which believe as surely as they. And therefore to reprove[550] Saint James, they would make us believe that our faith were nothing but hope, whereas every man wotteth[551] that faith and hope be two distinct virtues, and that hope is not faith, but followeth faith, in him that hath hope. For no man can hope for heaven if he believe it not. But on the other side,

---

526 1 Tm 5:6   **527** *stand them in stead:* do them any good   **528** alive   **529** compares   **530** *is bold of:* presumes upon   **531** unless   **532** in despair   **533** who   **534** *make good:* prove   **535** kind of, custom of

536 despoiling   **537** with regard to   **538** understanding   **539** *set … to school:* correct   **540** *would … ween:* want us to think   **541** knew   **542** its   **543** *abuse the word of:* misuse the word out of   **544** hold

545 restrict, limit   **546** such as   **547** with   **548** alleged, set forth   **549** faith alone   **550** refute   **551** knows

he may as the devil doth, though he believe it, and know it too, yet fall far from all hope thereof. And if these Lutherans will defend their heresy by that sophistical gloss, they must then change their article and say no more that faith alone is sufficient, but they must say that hope alone is sufficient. And yet shall they then lie as loud[552] as they do now. For hope without charity will but beguile[553] them.'

"After such reasoning, the man said that he and the other Lutherans, when they spoke that 'only faith was sufficient,' they mean not of a dead faith, that is without charity and good works, but a very[554] faith, that is quick[555] and worketh by charity, and that such faith, he thought, was sufficient. But then was it answered that neither they nor he could mean so. For how could they call that thing 'faith only' that is joined with charity and good works? Or how can it stand[556] that they mean that faith which by charity worketh good works, when they say that it is sufficient alone without good works, and that it is, as Luther saith, 'great sin and sacrilege' to go about to please God by good works, and not by only faith? How could they say that 'only faith' sufficeth, if they should mean that without charity and good works, no faith sufficeth? For it were a mad thing to say that faith alone sufficeth, without good works, and therewith to say that without good works, faith sufficeth nothing. And so was it said unto him that therefore, though they color[557] their matters when they be examined, yet it cannot be but that he and other Lutherans, where they sow their heresy, mean plainly as they speak: that folk need no more but believe, and then howsoever they live shall make no matter. For nothing, as Luther saith, 'can damn a Christian man save only lack of belief.' For all other sins — if belief and faith stand fast — be quite absorbed and 'supped up,'[558] he saith, in that faith.

"When this man was, with such reasoning and much better than I do or can rehearse you, somewhat sore[559] pressed upon, then brought he forth another gloss, and said that they meant not but that faith, if it should suffice for salvation, must needs have with it charity and good works, or else it were no very faith, as a dead man is no very man. Howbeit, he said that though it be nothing without good works, yet when it is joined with good works, all the merit cometh of our faith only, and no part thereof for our works, so that God giveth us heaven for our faith only, and nothing for our works. For though he give it not for our faith if we lack good works, yet if we have both, he regardeth not in his reward our works anything,[560] but only our faith. And he said that for this cause they say that only faith causeth our salvation.

"To this, it was answered that, if this opinion were true, yet it well appeared that this is not the thing that they mean. For the words of Luther and Pomeranus[561] and all the archheretics of that sect be very plain. For they say that it is sacrilege to go about to please God by any good works but faith only. And then why should good works be joined to faith? Or why should God exact good works of us? Whereof should they serve, if they be nothing pleasant to God? And when Luther saith that nothing can damn any Christian man but only lack of belief, he showeth manifestly that we not only need no good works with our faith, but also that, so[562] we have faith, none evil works can hurt us. And so he meaneth plainly that faith only, without any good works joined thereto — and also with all kind of evil works joined thereto — is sufficient to save us. 'And therefore, if ye be of his sect,' was it said to the man, 'ye cannot avoid but that this is your very doctrine, howsoever ye color it.'

"Then was it further asked him: If their meaning should be such as he had said, what should move him and others, his fellows, so to think that in faith and good works joined together, the good works were nothing worth, but that all the merit should be in the faith, and all the thank[563] and reward should be given to the faith, and right nought[564] to the good works?

"Whereunto he answered that many texts of Scripture induced them thereto, and special texts of Saint Paul: *Fides iustificat* ('Faith justifies');[565] and *Credidit Abraham Deo, et reputatum est ei ad iustitiam* ('Abraham believed God, and it was accounted in him for justice');[566] *Si ex operibus, habet quidem gloriam, sed non apud Deum* ('If he were justified by the works, then had he glory, but not with God');[567] *Si ex operibus, Christus pro nobis gratis mortuus est* ('If we be justified by the works, then did Christ die

552 openly, palpably   **553** disappoint, cheat, delude   **554** true   **555** alive
556 be consistent   **557** disguise, cloak
558 *supped up:* swallowed up; consumed

559 strongly   **560** at all   **561** John Bugenhagen (1485–1558), a Protestant humanist from Pomerania, a region near the Baltic Sea in present-day Germany

and Poland   **562** so long as   **563** credit
564 nothing   **565** Rom 5:1. See also Gal 3:24.   **566** Rom 4:3   **567** Rom 4:2

for us for nought');⁵⁶⁸ *Gratis redempti estis* ('Ye be redeemed freely').⁵⁶⁹ And thereby may we see that our
works were no part of the cause. And yet specially
these words of Our Savior Christ, he said, much
moved them to be of that mind, where he saith, *Qui
crediderit et baptizatus fuerit salvus erit* ('He that
believeth and is baptized shall be saved'),⁵⁷⁰ where
Christ requireth nothing but only faith.'

"By all these texts, he said, it plainly appeared that
all our salvation came of faith, as Abraham was justified by faith and not by his works, and that if our
good works should be the cause of our salvation,
then, as Saint Paul saith, Christ died for nought.
For he needed not to die for us if our own works
might save us. Nor we were not⁵⁷¹ redeemed freely
if we should redeem ourselves with the payment of
our own works.

"To this was it answered that those texts, and
all others alleged⁵⁷² for that purpose, signify none
other but that after the faith of Christ brought⁵⁷³
into the world by the Incarnation and Passion of
our blessed Savior, men are no longer bounden to
the observance of Moses' law. Nor that all the law of
Moses, nor all the good works of man, were not able
to save one man of⁵⁷⁴ themselves, nor without faith,
and that Christ freely redeemed us. For neither had
he, or ever shall have, any reward of us for the bitter
pains taken in his blessed Passion for us. Nor never
deserved we unto⁵⁷⁵ him that he should so much
do for us. Nor the first faith, nor the preaching
thereof, nor the first justification of man thereby,
nor the sacrament and fruit of our baptism, was not
given to the world for any good works that ever the
world had wrought, but only of God's mere⁵⁷⁶ liberal goodness. But yet there is never a text of them,
nor any other in all Scripture, so meant that after the baptism, the faith only shall save us without good works, if we live and have reason⁵⁷⁷ to do
them. For though it be said by the mouth of our
Savior, 'He that believeth shall be saved,' where he
nothing speaketh of any good works, yet meaneth
he not that he that believeth shall be saved without good works if he live to do them. For else why
should ye not as well say that men shall be saved for
keeping of the commandments without faith, since
Christ saith, 'If thou wilt enter into the kingdom of

heaven, keep the commandments,'⁵⁷⁸ and saith also,
'Do that and thou shalt have life'?⁵⁷⁹ At which time,
he spoke no word of⁵⁸⁰ any faith. he saith also in
Holy Scripture, *Date elemosinam, et omnia munda
sunt vobis* ('Give alms, and all is clean in you').⁵⁸¹
Which words, if men should as largely⁵⁸² construe
for the preeminence of alms-deed⁵⁸³ as ye that are of
Luther's sect construe the texts that speak of faith,
they might take a false gloss⁵⁸⁴ and color to say that
without faith, or penance either, or any other virtue, alms-deed alone sufficeth for salvation, how
wretchedly soever we lead our life besides. But if we
should so say of alms-deed, we should say wrong, as
ye do when ye say so of faith. For likewise as it is understood that faith must needs go with good works
if they shall be fruitful, though it be not spoken of
in those texts that speak of good works, so is it understood that in them which after baptism have
time and reason to work well, good works must
walk with faith, and sorrow at heart for fault⁵⁸⁵ of
good works, if the faith shall aught⁵⁸⁶ avail them.
For if both good works and final repentance of the
lack of good works do fail us, having time and reason to them,⁵⁸⁷ we be like to fare much the worse for
our faith. And that this is thus, we may well know
by the texts of Holy Scripture if we set them together, and take not one text for our part⁵⁸⁸ and set
another at nought.⁵⁸⁹

"To this answered he that albeit that these texts set
together do prove that faith alone doth not suffice
without good works (which thing he said that himself denied not), yet he said that none of those texts
prove anything the contrary, but that when faith and
good works be joined together, all the merit cometh
yet of our faith only, and nothing of our works.

"Whereunto he was answered that though it so
were indeed that no texts of Scripture proved the
contrary, yet since there is none that saith so, and
the whole Church saith and believeth the contrary,
what reason have ye to say so, and to give the whole
merit unto faith, and no part of the reward to good
works? And now have ye much less reason so to do,
when the plain words of Holy Writ be openly to
the contrary. For did not God say to Cain, 'If thou
do well, thou shalt have well'?⁵⁹⁰ Saith not Christ
of them that doth alms, 'A good measure, shaken

---

568 Gal 2:21   **569** Rom 3:24   **570** Mk
16:16   **571** *were not:* would not have been
572 cited   **573** was brought   **574** by
575 from   **576** sheer   **577** sufficient

reason   **578** Mt 19:17   **579** Lk 10:28
580 about   **581** Lk 11:41   **582** fully;
widely; without restraint   **583** almsgiving   **584** interpretation   **585** lack

586 anything   **587** to perform them
588 side   **589** *set another at nought:* value
another as nothing   **590** Gn 4:7

together, heaped and running over shall they give into your bosom'?⁵⁹¹ Doth not our Lord show that in the Day of Judgment he will give the kingdom of heaven to them that have done alms — in meat,⁵⁹² drink, clothes, and lodging — because of their charity used⁵⁹³ in those deeds?⁵⁹⁴ Which deeds, though he will not reward with heaven except⁵⁹⁵ faith went with them, yet if they were wrought in faith, he promiseth to reward those works, and not their faith only; and that so far-forth,⁵⁹⁶ that it appeareth by the words of our Savior in the same places, and by his words in which he said he would in the Day of Judgment speak to them that had by faith wrought wonders in his name without good works and charity, whom he would then bid walk⁵⁹⁷ workers of wickedness, and tell them that he knoweth them not⁵⁹⁸ — by these things, I say, it well appeareth, that be a man's faith never so great, yet if those good works fail him, his faith shall fail of heaven.'

"Then said he yet again that faith can never be without good works — but and if⁵⁹⁹ a man have faith, his faith shall not fail nor cease to bring forth the fruit of good works, as the tree bringeth forth his leaves.

"Then was it answered him that he was driven from that point before, as well by the authority of Saint Paul as of Saint James, and also that he wist well that faith or belief is not contrary to every sin, but only to infidelity and lack of belief, so that with other sins it may stand. Then said he that if men believed surely,⁶⁰⁰ he thought they would not sin. 'For who would sin,' said he, 'if he believed verily and surely that sin should bring him to hell?' Whereunto it was answered, 'Whoso believed after⁶⁰¹ your Lutheran faith should never let⁶⁰² to sin, since Lutherans believe that no sin could damn them but only lack of belief, and that no good work needeth⁶⁰³ them, but that they shall be saved howsoever they live, for their only faith. Whereby it well appeareth that ye Lutherans have but half a faith. For ye believe God only in his promises, and in his threats ye believe him not at all. Howbeit, if one believed indeed surely, as ye would now seem to believe, truth is it that it would let⁶⁰⁴ many a man from sin, but

yet not every man. For albeit that many men there be, either the more bold in sin or the more negligent in good virtues, because their faith is very faint and feeble, which⁶⁰⁵ would, if they had a sure and an undoubted faith, be in such dread of God — and love also — that it would withdraw them from sin and set them in the way of virtue, yet many men be there, on the other side, that, were their faith never so strong, yet should it not master the frowardness⁶⁰⁶ of their malicious appetites. And this would happen sometimes — and daily doth — in men not deeply drowned in malice, nor folk out of the faith neither, which⁶⁰⁷ yet fall into the breach of God's commandment by the subtle suggestion of the devil, or by the frailty of their own flesh. Whereof it seemeth that the holy Apostle was himself so sore afraid — for all his faith — that he thrice prayed God to take the temptation away.⁶⁰⁸ I cannot see but that Adam believed the words of God, and yet he broke his commandment. And I think that King David fell not from his faith, though he fell first in adultery and eft⁶⁰⁹ in manslaughter.⁶¹⁰ And some examples have we seen of them that have sought the revenging of⁶¹¹ their own malicious minds⁶¹² by such ways as they saw, when they went about it, their own undoubted death before their eyes. And therefore it is but a tale⁶¹³ to say that faith draweth always good works with it, and that ye Lutherans, in that ye say that faith is sufficient alone, without good works, should say so because it bringeth always good works with it. For this were a very vain⁶¹⁴ doctrine — that faith is alone sufficient to save them that have the use of reason, without good works — if in such as have the use of reason, faith be never without good works.'

"After such objections, then fell he to another point, and said that if our good works and faith be joined, yet might it well appear by Scripture that all the merit was in our faith, and nothing in man's works. 'For all the works of man,' he said, 'be stark naught,⁶¹⁵ as things all spotted with sin.' And for that he laid⁶¹⁶ diverse texts of Scripture, but specially, as the most plain proof, the words of the prophet, *Omnis iustitia nostra velut pannus menstruatae.*⁶¹⁷ 'And since that all our works,' he said,

---

591 Lk 6:38 **592** food **593** exercised **594** See Mt 25:34–36. **595** unless **596** *so far-forth:* to such an extent **597** depart as **598** See Mt 7:22–23. **599** *and if:* if **600** securely; certainly **601** in accordance with **602** hesitate

603 is necessary for **604** hinder **605** who **606** perversity **607** who **608** See 2 Cor 12:7–9. **609** soon afterwards **610** See 2 Kgs (2 Sm) 11:2–15. **611** *the revenging of:* vengeance in accord with **612** intentions, thinking, judgment

613 falsehood **614** useless, futile **615** wicked **616** cited **617** *Omnis… menstruatae:* "All our justice is like the rag of a menstruating woman" (Is 64:6).

'be spotted and sinful and naught, how good soever they seem, it must needs follow that all the merit cometh of our faith.'

"To this was answered him: 'Lo, now by this ye have somewhat opened yourself unware,[618] and declared[619] your opinion in this matter to be far other than ye said before. For in the glosses that ye have used before, ye have always said that ye—and all the sect of Luther, as far as ye knew and thought—believed that faith could not save us, if we had reason, without good works. But ye said that faith was enough alone because it brought of necessity good works with it. And yet all the merit and reward due to the faith only, and not to the good works that it bringeth forth. And now ye say that there be no good works at all, but all our works be stark naught. Now if ye think that there be no good works, how can ye say, as ye said before, that ye think that faith always bringeth forth good works? Moreover, the words of the prophet, though it be generally spoken, may be well understood to be verified in far the most part of mankind, though not of all; or of the justice of man, if it were compared with the sovereign justice of God; or that justice of right good men is yet sore spotted with sin, for that[620] the frailty of our nature seldom constantly standeth any while together in good works, but that the perseverance is interrupted, often spotted and besprent[621] with sin. And thereof is it said, *Septies in die cadit iustus, et resurget* ("Seven times in the day falleth the righteous man, and riseth again").[622] It may be also understood of all the righteousness of a man alone wrought of himself and his pure[623] natural powers, without the aid and help of special grace. For surely all such justice of ours—as is only ours—is all spotted, and, in effect, all one foul spot, for any beauty that it hath in the glorious eye of God. But surely the holy prophet never meant, as Luther and his fellows would have seem, that the grace of God is in all his people so feeble of itself, and of so little force and effect, that no man may with the help thereof be able to do one good virtuous deed. For Luther saith plainly that no man, though[624] he have the help of God's grace thereto, is able to keep and observe the commandments of God. Which blasphemous words seem

to signify that both Saint John the Baptist and our blessed Lady also were sinners, and over[625] all this that God were not able, by the aid and help of his grace, to make a man keep his commandments, and keep him out of sin, though he would.[626]

"'All the old fathers that wrote against Pelagius[627] —which[628] held opinion that man is of[629] nature, or, at the leastwise with the general influence of grace, able and sufficient to do good and meritorious works without help of any special grace toward every good deed itself—misliked and condemned his doctrine, for that it diminished the necessity of man's recourse unto God for calling help of his grace. But ye that hold all men's deeds for utterly naught, though grace wrought with them, be double and treble[630] more enemies to grace than they. For where they said we might do good sometimes without it, ye say we can at no time do no good with it. And then were grace, by your tale, a very void thing. Was then all the labor and the pain that the apostles took in preaching all naught and sinful? All the torments that the martyrs suffered in their passion altogether sin? All the deeds of charity that Christ shall (as himself saith) reward with everlasting life at the general judgment—be they sin altogether?[631] Saint Paul reckoned it otherwise. For he said boldly of himself, *Bonum certamen certavi, cursum consummavi, et nunc super est mihi corona iustitiae* ("I have labored and striven a good strife;[632] I have performed[633] my course; now lacketh me no more for me but the crown of justice").'[634]

"Thereunto he answered that Saint Paul would not say that our deeds were sufficient of themselves, but that all our sufficiency is of God. Whereunto it was answered that this was little to the matter.[635] For no more is our faith sufficient of itself, but the sufficiency thereof is also of God, in that our Lord, with our endeavor, giveth us grace to believe, and in that it liketh[636] our Lord, of his goodness so highly to reward it. For surely as it is very true that[637] Saint Paul saith, that *non sunt condignae passiones huius vitae ad futuram gloriam quae revelabitur in nobis* ("all that ever we can suffer in this world is not worthy the glory to come that shall be showed in us")[638]—for what thing could a seely[639]

---

618 *opened yourself unware:* revealed yourself without realizing   **619** shown   **620** *for that:* because   **621** besprinkled   **622** Prv 24:16   **623** mere   **624** even if   **625** beyond   **626** *though he would:*

even if he wanted to   **627** British monk (354–418) who denied original sin and emphasized free will   **628** who   **629** by   **630** *double and treble:* two or three times   **631** See Mt 25:34–36.   **632** *striven a good*

strife: fought a good fight   **633** accomplished   **634** 2 Tm 4:7–8   **635** point   **636** pleases   **637** what   **638** Rom 8:18   **639** poor; pitiable

wretched creature do or suffer for God in the brief time of this short life that might of right[640] require to be rewarded everlastingly, with such inestimable joy as neither eye hath seen nor tongue can express, nor heart can imagine or conceive?[641] — so is it also as true that all the faith we have or can have, can of his[642] own nature as little or much less deserve heaven, as our other good deeds. For what great thing do we to God, or what great thing could we ask him of right, because we believe him? As though he were much beholden unto us, in that we vouchsafe[643] to trust him! As though his worship[644] hung in our hands, and his estimation lost if he were out of credence with[645] us. And therefore, among many foolish words of Luther — as foolish as ever heretic spoke — he never spoke a more frantic[646] than in that he saith that God hath need of our faith. For he saith that God hath no need of our good works, but he hath need of our faith, and hath need that we should believe him. Truth is it that he needeth neither our faith nor our works. But since that he hath determined that he will not save us without both, if we be of discretion[647] to have both, therefore have we need of both. And yet neither is there the one nor the other, nor they both together between them, that be of their own nature worthy the reward of heaven. But as we see that one ounce of gold — whereof ten pounds' weight were not of his[648] own nature toward[649] man worth one ounce of wheat, nor one hundred pounds' weight thereof of the nature itself[650] worth one seely[651] sheep — is yet among men, by a price appointed and agreed, worth many whole[652] sheep, and many a pound's weight of bread, so hath it liked the liberal goodness of God to set as well our faith as our deeds (which were else, both twain, of their own nature right little in value) at so high a price as none is able to buy them and pay for them but himself, because[653] we should work them only to[654] him, and have none other paymaster, nor none other chapman[655] to sell our ware and work unto but only him, except[656] we would be so mad, and toward him so unkind, that we would sell it to another for less rather than to

him for more, as some do that had liefer[657] travel far off and sell for less than they would for more sell to their neighbors at home, and as do these foolish hypocrites, which rather than they would sell their work to God for everlasting joy of heaven, sell it all to the world for the peevish[658] pleasure of the vain praise puffed out of poor mortal men's mouths with a blast of wind.'

"Unto this he said that very true it was that all our works took their value and price after the acceptation[659] of God, and as he list to allow[660] them. But he said that God rejected, disallowed,[661] and set at nought[662] all the works of infidels wrought without faith — for *sine fide impossibile est placere Deo* ('without faith it is impossible to please God')[663] — and that of his faithful chosen people, that believe and trust in him, he accepteth and alloweth all the deeds. 'And that is,' said he, 'well proved by the words of Saint Paul: *Nihil damnationis est iis qui sunt in Christo Iesu.*'[664] And albeit that in the rehearsing of the communication had with this man, it may well be that my remembrance may partly miss the order[665] — partly peradventure add or diminish in some part of the matter — yet in this point, I assure you faithfully, there is no manner change or variance from his opinion, but that, after many shifts,[666] he brought it plainly to this point at last, that he and his fellows that were of Luther's sect were firmly of this opinion: that they believed that only God worketh all in every man, good works and bad. Howbeit, such as he foreknoweth to be damned, no manner works be profitable to them. For God taketh them for naught,[667] be they never so good. But on the other side, in those he hath chosen from the beginning and predestinate to glory, all works be good enough. For God accepteth and taketh them well a-worth[668] be they never so bad.

"It was asked him then whether that the forsaking of Christ by Peter[669] was allowed[670] and well approved by Christ, and whether the adultery and manslaughter was by God well allowed in David.[671]

"Whereunto he said that because they were chosen and predestinate, therefore those sins were not — nor

---

640 justice   **641** See 1 Cor 2:9; Is 64:4.
642 its   **643** deign   **644** honor   **645** *out of credence with:* not believed by   **646** mad
647 i.e., at the age of reason and so capable of good judgment   **648** its   **649** to;
for   **650** *the nature itself:* its own nature
651 feeble   **652** healthy   **653** in order

that; so that   **654** for   **655** customer
656 unless   **657** *had liefer:* would rather
658 silly   **659** acceptance, approval
660 *list to allow:* pleases to permit or count   **661** refused to reward   **662** *set at nought:* valued as nothing   **663** Heb 11:16   **664** *Nihil…Iesu:* "There is no

condemnation for those who are in Christ Jesus" (Rom 8:1).   **665** *miss the order:* have the order wrong   **666** evasions   **667** bad
668 in esteem or honor, or at their worth
669 See Mt 26:69–75; Mk 14:66–72; Lk 22:54–62; Jn 18:15–27.   **670** permitted
671 See 2 Kgs (2 Sm) 11:2–17.

the sins of any such men be not—imputed unto them. But God, because he hath from the beginning chosen them to everlasting bliss, therefore he arrecteth[672] no blame of their deeds unto them; but all the works of a just man—'that is to say,' quoth he, 'of a person by God predestinate to glory'—turn him to good, how evil soever they be. And this for conclusion he declared to be their very plain mind and opinion, for all the cloaks that he had set upon the matter before, to make it seem that they meant in their words none harm. And there it clearly appeared that he and his fellows, which[673] in their preaching do covertly and craftily set out[674] the damnable sect of Luther, hope and gape[675] always for some other time in which they trust openly and boldly to play the ravenous wolves and devour the sheep and mar the whole flock. And in the mean season[676] be content to play the wily foxes and worry[677] simple souls and poor lambs as they may catch them straggling from the fold—or rather like a false shepherd's-dog that would but bark in sight, and seem to fetch in the sheep, and yet kill a lamb in a corner. Men speak of some that bear two faces in one hood. I never saw any that more verily play that pageant than do this kind of such preachers. For in preaching to the people, they make a visage as though they came straight from heaven to teach them a new better way—and more true than the Church teacheth, or hath taught this many hundred years. And then to the Church, in examination, they show themselves as poor men of middle earth,[678] and as though they taught none other wise than the Church doth. But in conclusion, when they be well examined, and, with much work, that falsehood of their cloaked collusion is pulled off, then appeareth there all the malicious treachery, and what poison they put forth under the cloak of honey. As this man that I tell you of, laboring all that he might, by many means, to make it seem that, in preaching that faith alone was sufficient for our salvation and that good works were nothing worth, had nothing intended but well and according to the doctrine of the Church, and that he and his fellows never meant otherwise than the Church meaneth, yet in conclusion he plainly showed himself, that he and his fellows intend thereby to bring

the people to this point at last: that all things hangeth only upon destiny; and that the liberty of man's will should serve of right nought,[679] nor men's deeds, good or bad, made no difference afore God; but that in his chosen people, nothing misliketh him, be it never so bad, and in the other sort, nothing pleaseth him, be it never so good—the very worst and most mischievous[680] heresy that ever was thought upon, and thereto[681] the most mad. For, as it was said unto him, if this were true, whereto preach they at all, and counsel any man one thing or other? What fruit could come of their exhortation, if all should hang upon destiny? There were showed unto him many things for the reproof[682] of that unreasonable and detestable heresy, and that the texts which he alleged[683] nothing made for his purpose.[684] For as for that he alleged of Saint Paul—that 'there is no damnation[685] to them that be in Christ Jesus'[686]—was meant of good faithful folk that live virtuously; and therefore where he saith that 'there is no damnation to them that be in Christ Jesus,' it followeth forthwith[687] in the text, 'those that walk not after the flesh,'[688] meaning, plainly, that there is no man so planted in Christ Jesus but and[689] if he follow the fleshly ways of his sensual appetites, he shall be damned, for all his faith in Christ. For else it should follow, upon this false opinion—if God accept well all the works of them that are predestinate—then is sin no sin in them, but in the other sort only, whom God hath not predestinate. And then is it as much to say as no man may lawfully be naught[690]—no man lawfully do theft or adultery, nor lawfully be a manqueller,[691] nor lawfully forswear[692] himself—but God's good sons and his special chosen children.

"Now, where he alleged the words of Saint Paul, *Quod iustis omnia cooperantur in bonum* ('To a just man all things work together to his weal'),[693] it was said that it meant that all the evils that men did unto them, turn them to good, and be to good men occasion of their merit, as was to Job all the torments by which the devil assaulted his patience, and all the pains that pagan tyrants did unto the holy martyrs. And sometimes the sin in which a good man is, by God's sufferance,[694] permitted to fall is an occasion to him of a greater good, or of the avoiding

672 imputes   673 who   674 *set out:* propagate   675 long   676 *mean season:* meantime   677 strangle, choke   678 *middle earth:* the world, understood as a middle region between hell and heaven   679 *serve of right nought:* deserve or merit nothing   680 evil; harmful   681 also   682 refutation   683 cited   684 contention, argument   685 condemnation   686 Rom 8:1   687 immediately   688 Rom 8:4   689 *but and:* that   690 wicked   691 murderer   692 perjure   693 well-being; Rom 8:28   694 allowance

of a greater sin, as the eschewing[695] of a high spiritual pride, into which peradventure[696] the continual course of his virtuous life might, by the devil's subtle suggestion, have brought him, whereas one foul act of lechery hath showed him his frailty, and instead of pride brought him into penance and humility, and make him run the faster forward in virtue because he hath letted[697] and sat still awhile in sin; and therefore will he run forth to win again in his way that[698] he before cast himself behind.[699] But it was not meant that ever their sins so turned them to good that they were accepted[700] the more, and rewarded the better, for their evil deeds. Nor God remitteth not the sins of his chosen people, nor forbeareth not to impute the blame thereof unto them, because they be his chosen people. For he accepteth not folk for their persons, but for their merits. But whereas they have sinned, he punisheth as well them as others, and sometimes more, because their former good living somewhat of congruence[701] deserved that they should by punishment be called again to grace, and not be for their fault so soon cast clean away, as some others, obdurate in malice and evil custom[702] of sin, deserve to have the grace of God and his calling-on nevermore offered unto them, and unto some it is offered that will not receive[703] it. God called on David by the prophet Nathan, and yet punished his offense. Christ looked on Peter after he had forsaken and forsworn him, and Peter therewith took repentance. God looked on Judas, and kissed him too and he turned to none amendment.[704] Now God from the beginning, before the world was created, foreseeing in his divine prescience—or rather in the eternity of his Godhead presently[705] beholding—that Peter would repent and Judas would despair, and that the one would take hold of his grace and the other would reject it, accepted and chose the one and not the other, as he would have made the contrary choice if he had foreseen in them the contrary change."

The author inveigheth against[706] the most pestilent sect of these Lutherans, which ascribe our salvation and damnation, and all our deeds, to destiny.

"But now, for to say (as that heretic said after all his shifts,[707] at last) that all that shall be saved shall be saved only because that God from the beginning hath chosen them; and because of that choice all their deeds be good, or, if they be evil, yet God, for cause[708] of his eternal choice, taketh them well in worth[709] and imputeth no blame unto them; and that all other people whom God hath created shall be damned only because he would not choose them; and that all their deeds either be naught,[710] or not well accepted, because God list[711] not in the beginning to choose them; and that he worketh, both in the one sort and in the other, all their deeds himself alone, and they do nothing therein themselves; and so that God, whose goodness is inestimable, doth damn so huge a number of people to intolerable and interminable torments only for his pleasure, and for his own deeds wrought in them only by himself— this false opinion is, as the King's Highness most virtuously writeth in his epistle to Luther, the most abominable heresy that ever was. And surely it is so far against all Holy Scripture well understood, so far against all natural reason, so utterly subverting all virtue and all good order in the world, so highly blaspheming the goodness and majesty of almighty God in heaven, that it is more than wonder how any man earthly that hath either one spark of wit[712] in his head, or toward God or man one drop of good will in his heart, should not abhor to hear it. For this execrable heresy maketh God the cause of all evil; and such cruel appetite as never tyrant and tormentor had, ascribe they to the benign nature of almighty God. For whereas Our Savior Christ took upon himself all our sin, and of his endless pity bore the pain of them for our sake, this damnable heresy holdeth that God should be, first, so untrue that he should lay unto us the wite[713] and blame of his own faults—that is to wit, the evil works which (as they say) be not wrought by us but in us by God—and thereunto they make him so despiteous[714] and cruel

---

695 avoiding   **696** perhaps   **697** hesitated   **698** *that which*   **699** *himself behind:* behind himself   **700** approved   **701** *of congruence:* fittingly, reasonably, rightly   **702** habit   **703** accept   **704** See

Mt 26:49–50; 27:3–5; Lk 22:47–48.   **705** instantly, now   **706** *inveigheth against:* denounces   **707** evasions   **708** *for cause:* because   **709** *well in worth:* as acceptable and good   **710** bad

711 wished   **712** intelligence   **713** punishment; torments of hell   **714** spiteful; malevolent

that for his own deeds so done he shall have a perpetual delight and pleasure to torment us.

"Now turn they the treacle[715] of Holy Scripture quite into poison. For this false error once taken for truth, whereof should all Scripture serve? Whereof should serve the exhortations to good works, if men neither any do, nor any can do, neither of themselves nor with help of grace? Or if any be done by them which[716] be not chosen, their deeds be not accepted of God, because he hath not chosen their persons, whereof shall serve the preachings and exhortations to the faith, if the hearers have no liberty of their own will by which they may, together with God's grace, labor to submit and subdue the rebellion of their reason to the obedience of faith and credence of the Word of God? Whereof shall serve all the dehortations and comminations[717] and threats in Scripture by which God calleth men from sin and evil works, if the world were once of mind that they believed after Luther: that no man doth any evil deed himself, but God doth them all himself; and that every man is either chosen or unchosen; and if we be of the chosen sort, none evil deed can damn us; and if we be of the unchosen sort, no good deed can avail us? He that thus believeth, what careth he what he doth, except for the fear of temporal laws of this world? And yet if his false faith be strong, he forceth little of[718] them also. For he shall think dying in his bed or on the gallows cometh not after[719] his deserving, but hangeth all upon destiny. And therefore all laws they set at nought. And they hold that no man is bounden to obey any, but would be at liberty to believe what they list, and do what they list—as they say that God doth with us not what we deserve, but what himself list.

"Whereof shall reason serve, if man had no power of himself toward the direction of his own works, but that all our works were brought forth of us without our will, worse than the works be indeed out of a brute beast by the appetite of his sensual motion?[720] For ours should be, by this opinion, brought forth as the leaves come out of the tree, or as a stone falleth downward and the smoke upward by the power of nature—so should, I say, all our deeds good or bad, ascend or descend by the violent hand of God, maugre our minds.[721] And thus the beasts be not ashamed to say, when they prove hourly by their own experience in themselves that when they will do a thing, they do it, and when they list,[722] they leave it. I say not by themselves alone, without God. But his assistance is always at hand, if we be willing to work therewith, as the light is present with the sun, if we list not willfully to shut our eyes and wink.

"Whereof should serve all laws, and where were become[723] all good order among men, if every misordered wretch might allege that his mischievous[724] deed was his destiny?

"If free will serve for nought, and every man's deed is his destiny, why do these men complain upon[725] any man, except[726] they will say they do it because it is their destiny to do so? And why will they then be angry with them that punish heretics, except they will say because it is their destiny to be so? For if they will hold them to their own sect, and say men do them wrong to burn them for their heresies because it was their destiny to be heretics, they may be then well answered with their own words, as one of their sect was served in a good town in Almain—which, when he had robbed a man and was brought before the judges, he could not deny the deed, but he said it was his destiny to do it, and therefore they might not blame him. They answered him, after[727] his own doctrine, that if it were his destiny to steal, and that therefore they must hold him excused, then it was also their destiny to hang him, and therefore he must as well hold them excused again.[728] And undoubtedly among men these takers-away of free will may never avoid[729] that answer by reason. But then fall the wretches to the desperate ways of devils and damned souls. Then fall they to railing and reproving[730] the justice of God, and say that himself hath wrought their evil works, and wrongfully punished them, and cruelly created them to wretchedness. Our mother Eve laid the wite[731] of her sin to the serpent, and God was offended that she took not her own part[732] to herself.[733] But these wretches excuse themselves, and the devils and all, and lay both their own faults and the devils' too, to the blame of almighty God. But

715 antidote, remedy   **716** who
717 *dehortations and comminations:*
dissuasions and warnings of punishment   **718** *forceth little of:* cares little
about   **719** according to   **720** impulses

721 *maugre our minds:* regardless of our
intentions   **722** choose   **723** *where were
become:* what would become of   **724** evil
725 about; against   **726** unless   **727** in
accord with   **728** in turn   **729** refute

730 *railing and reproving:* complaining
vehemently about and reproaching
731 blame   **732** share   **733** See Gn
3:13, 16.

surely whatso they say, they little care indeed of hell or of heaven, but would in this world live in lewd[734] liberty, and have all run to riot. And since they see that they cannot so be suffered,[735] nor their sect allowed in judgment,[736] they devise by all the ways they can to get so many to fall into their sort that they may be able to turn the world upside down, and defend their folly and false heresy by force. And this they call 'the liberty of the Gospel'—to be discharged of all order and of all laws, and do what they list—which be it good, be it bad, is (as they say) nothing but the works of God wrought in them. But they hope that by this means God shall for the while work in them many merry pastimes. Wherein if their heresy were once received, and the world changed thereby, they should find themselves sore[737] deceived. For the laws and orders among men with fear of punishment once taken away, there were no man so strong that could keep his pleasure long, but that he should find a stronger take it from him. But after that it were once come to that point, and the world once ruffled[738] and fallen in a wildness, how long would it be, and what heaps of heavy mischiefs would there fall, ere that way were founden to set the world in order and peace again?"

THE THIRTEENTH CHAPTER

The author showeth his opinion concerning the burning of heretics, and that it is lawful, necessary, and well done, and showeth also that the clergy doth not procure it, but only the good and politic[739] provision of the temporalty.[740]

"The fear of these outrages and mischiefs to follow upon such sects and heresies, with the proof[741] that men have had in some countries thereof, have been the cause that princes and people have been constrained to punish heresies by terrible death, whereas else more easy ways had[742] been taken with them. And therefore here will I somewhat," said I to your friend, "answer the points which ye moved at our first meeting, when ye said that many men thought it a hard[743] and an uncharitable way taken by the clergy, to put men convicted

of heresy sometimes to shame, sometimes to death, and that Christ so far abhorred all such violence that he would not any of his flock should[744] fight in any wise, neither in the defense of themselves or any others—not so much as in the defense of Christ himself, for which he blamed Saint Peter— but that we should all live after him in sufferance[745] and patience, so far-forth[746] that folk thought, as ye said, that we should not fight in defense of ourselves against the Turks and infidels. These objections be soon answered. For neither doth the clergy therein any such thing as is laid[747] and imputed unto them, nor the temporalty neither. For albeit with good reason they might, yet had they never indeed fallen so sore to force and violence against heretics if the violent cruelty first used by the heretics themselves against good Catholic folk had not driven good princes thereto for preservation, not of the faith only, but also of the peace among their people. For albeit that forthwith upon the death of Christ, in the beginning of the Church, many sects and heresies began (as well appeareth by the Apocalypse of Saint John the Evangelist and the epistles of the apostle Paul), and after, almost continually diverse heresies sprang in diverse places (as we plainly see by the story[748] of the Church by the books of Saint Jerome, Saint Augustine, Saint Eusebius, Saint Basil, Saint Ambrose, Saint Gregory Nazianzen, Saint Chrysostom, and many other doctors of the Church), yet in all this time, by a long space of many years, was there never other punishment done upon them, in effect, but only redargution and reproving by dispicions[749] (either in words[750] or writing), or condemnations of their opinions in synods and councils, or finally excommunications and putting out of Christ's flock, saving that they were put sometimes to silence upon pain of forfeiture of certain[751] money. But, as I said before, if the heretics had never begun with violence, though[752] they had used all the ways they could to allect[753] the people by preaching, though they had therewith done as Luther doth now, and as Muhammad did before—bring up opinions pleasant to the people, giving them liberty to lewdness[754]—yet if they had set violence aside, good Christian people had

---

734 wicked **735** allowed **736** *allowed in judgment:* approved in court **737** greatly **738** thrown into confusion **739** prudent **740** secular authorities **741** experience **742** *easy ways had:* moderate ways would

have **743** harsh, cruel **744** *would... should:* would not want any of his flock to **745** *after him in sufferance:* following him in endurance **746** *so far-forth:* to such an extent **747** (being) attributed

748 history **749** *redargution... dispicions:* rebuking and refuting (them) by disputations **750** spoken words **751** a certain amount of **752** even if **753** allure **754** *liberty to lewdness:* license for evil

peradventure[755] yet unto this day used less violence toward them than they do now. And yet were heresy well worthy to be as sore punished as any other fault, since there is no fault that more offendeth God. Howbeit, while[756] they forbore violence, there was little violence done to them. And surely though God be able, against all persecution, to preserve and increase his faith among the people—as he did in the beginning for[757] all the persecution of the paynims[758] and the Jews—yet is it no reason to look[759] that Christian princes should suffer[760] the Catholic Christian people to be oppressed by Turks, or by heretics worse than Turks."

"By my soul," quoth your friend, "I would all the world were all agreed to take all violence and compulsion away upon all sides, Christian and heathen, and that no man were constrained to believe but as he could be by grace, wisdom, and good words induced, and then he that would go to God, go on a[761] God's name, and he that will go to the devil, the devil go with him."

"Forsooth," quoth I, "and if it so were, yet would I little doubt but that the good seed, being sown among the people, should as well come up and be as strong to save itself as the cockle,[762] and God should always be stronger than the devil. But yet be heretics and heathen men in two diverse cases. For in case[763] the Turks, Saracens, and paynims would suffer the faith of Christ to be peaceably preached among them, and that we Christian men should therefore suffer, in like wise, all their sects to be preached among us, and violence taken away by assent on both the sides, I nothing mistrust that the faith of Christ should much more increase than decay. And albeit that we should find among us that would,[764] for the lewd liberty of these sects, draw to the devil, yet so should we find, I doubt not, among them also many a thousand that should be content to leave that beastly pleasure and come to the faith of Christ, as came in the beginning to Christendom out of the paynims, that lived as voluptuously[765] as the Turks do now. But since violence is used on that part,[766] and Christ's faith not there suffered to be preached and taken, he that would now suffer

that sect to be preached or taught among Christian men, and not punish and destroy the doers,[767] were a plain enemy to Christ as he that were[768] content to suffer Christ lose his worship in many souls on this side without any one won in their stead on the other side. But now if violence were withdrawn on that side, then this way that ye speak of were peradventure between Christendom and Turkey or pagans—if the world were assented thereunto and could hold[769] it—none evil way. For since we should nothing so much regard as the honor of God, and increasing of the Christian faith, and winning of men's souls to heaven, we should seem to dishonor God if we mistrusted[770] that his faith preached among others indifferently,[771] without disturbance, should not be able to prosper. And believing that it were, we should hinder the profit if we would refuse the condition, where there be many more to be won to Christ on that side than to be lost from him on this side. But yet, as for heretics rising among ourselves, and springing of ourselves, be[772] in no wise to be suffered, but to be oppressed[773] and overwhelmed in the beginning. For by any covenant with them, Christendom can nothing win. For as many as we suffer to fall to them, we lose from Christ. And by all them we cannot win to Christ one the more, though we won them all home again; for they were our own before. And yet, as I said, for all that, in the beginning never were they by any temporal punishment of their bodies anything[774] sharply handled, till that they began to be violent themselves.

"We read that in the time of Saint Augustine, the great doctor of the Church, the heretics of Africa called the Donatists[775] fell to force and violence: robbing, beating, tormenting, and killing such as they took of the true Christian flock, as the Lutherans have done in Almain.[776] For avoiding whereof, that holy man Saint Augustine, which[777] long had with great patience borne and suffered their malice, only writing and preaching in the reproof[778] of their errors—and had not only done them no temporal harm, but also had letted[779] and resisted others that would have done it—did yet at the last, for the peace of good people, both suffer[780] and exhort

---

755 *had peradventure:* would perhaps have
756 as long as   **757** despite   **758** *of the paynims:* inflicted (on Christians) by pagans   **759** *no reason to look:* not reasonable to expect   **760** allow   **761** in **762** See Mt 13:24–30.   **763** the case that

764 those who would   **765** sensually; indulgently   **766** side   **767** preachers **768** *that were:* who would be   **769** stick to   **770** doubted   **771** equally **772** be they   **773** suppressed   **774** at all **775** They believed that sacraments could

not be conferred by priests who had at one time fallen away from the faith.   **776** Germany   **777** who   **778** *the reproof:* refutation   **779** hindered; prevented **780** allow the Count Boniface[781] and others to repress them with force and fear[782] them with bodily punishment.[783] Which manner of doing, holy Saint Jerome and other virtuous fathers have in other places allowed.[784] And since that time hath there upon necessity—perceived by great outrages committed against the peace and quiet of the people in sundry places of Christendom, by heretics rising of a small beginning to a high and unruly multitude—many sore[785] punishments been devised for them, and specially by fire, not only in Italy and Almain, but also in Spain, and in effect in every part of Christendom. Among which in England, as a good Catholic realm, it hath been long punished by death in the fire. And specially forasmuch as in the time of that noble prince of most famous memory, King Henry the Fifth,[786] while the Lord Cobham[787] maintained certain heresies—and that by the means thereof the number so grew and increased that, within a while, though himself was fled into Wales, yet they assembled themselves together in a field near unto London in such wise and such number that the King with his nobles were fain to put harness[788] on their backs for the repression of them, whereupon they were distressed[789] and many put to execution, and after that, the Lord Cobham taken in Wales and burned in London—the king, his nobles, and his people, thereupon considering the great peril and jeopardy that the realm was like to have fallen in by those heresies, made at a Parliament[790] very good and substantial provisions (besides all such as were made before) as well for the withstanding as the repressing and grievous punishment of any such as should be founden faulty[791] thereof, and by the clergy left unto the secular hands.[792]

"For here ye shall understand that it is not the clergy that laboreth to have them punished by death. Well may it be that as we be all men and not angels, some of them may have sometimes either over-fervent mind[793] or indiscreet zeal, or percase[794] an angry and a cruel heart, by which they may offend God in the selfsame deed whereof they should else[795] greatly merit. But surely the order of the spiritual[796] law therein is both good, reasonable, piteous,

and charitable, and nothing desiring the death of any man therein. For at the first fault,[797] he is abjured,[798] forsweareth all heresies, doth such penance for his fault as the bishop assigneth him, and is in such wise graciously received again into the favor and suffrages[799] of Christ's Church. But and if[800] he be taken eftsoons[801] with the same crime again, then is he put out of the Christian flock by excommunication. And because that, being such, his conversation[802] were perilous among Christian men, the Church refuseth[803] him, and thereof the clergy giveth knowledge to the temporalty[804]—not exhorting the prince, or any man else, either to kill him or punish him; but only in the presence of the temporal officer, the spiritualty[805] not delivereth him but leaveth him to the secular hand, and forsaketh him as one excommunicated and removed out of the Christian flock. And though the Church be not light and sudden in receiving him again, yet at the time of his death, upon his request with tokens[806] of repentance, he is absolved and received again."

THE FOURTEENTH CHAPTER
The author somewhat showeth that the clergy doth no wrong in leaving heretics to secular hand, though their death follow thereon. And he showeth also that it is lawful to resist the Turk and such other infidels, and that princes be bounden thereto.[807]

"Marry," quoth your friend, "but as methinketh, the bishop doth as much as though he killeth him, when he leaveth him to the secular hand in such time and place as he wotteth[808] well he shall soon be burned."

"I will not here enter into the question," quoth I, "whether a priest might for any cause—and if for any, whether, then, for heresy—without blame of irregularity,[809] put or command any man to death, either by express words or under the general name of right and justice. In which matter, I could not lack both reason, authority, and example of holy men. But in this matter that we have in hand, it is

---

781 last Roman governor of Africa, d. 432
782 threaten   **783** See Augustine's
Letter 185.   **784** approved   **785** severe
786 Henry V reigned 1413–22.   **787** John
Oldcastle (executed 1417), a follower
of Wycliffe   **788** *fain to put harness:*
obliged to put on armor   **789** subjected

to penalties   **790** in 1401, under
Henry IV   **791** guilty   **792** authorities
793 purpose   **794** perhaps   **795** otherwise   **796** *order…law:* procedure of
the canon law   **797** offense   **798** made
to renounce the heresy under oath
799 prayers; approval; rights   **800** *and*

if: if   **801** afterwards   **802** company
803 rejects   **804** civil authorities
805 ecclesiastical authorities   **806** signs
807 to do so   **808** knows   **809** action
incompatible with holy orders

sufficient that the bishop neither doth it nor commandeth it. For I think there will no reason bear[810] it that, when the heretic if he went abroad[811] would with the spreading of his error infect other folk, the bishop should have such pity upon him that he should, rather than other men should punish his body, suffer[812] him to kill other men's souls.

"Indeed," quoth I, "there be some, as ye say, that either of high[813] pretended pity, or of a feigned observance of the counsels of Christ, would[814] that no man should punish any heretic or infidel either — not though[815] they invaded us and did us all the harm they possibly could. And in this opinion is Luther, and his followers, which among their other heresies hold for a plain conclusion that it is not lawful to any Christian man to fight against the Turk, or to make against him any resistance, though he come into Christendom with a great army and labor to destroy all. For they say that all Christian men are bounden to the counsels of Christ, by which they say that we be forbidden to defend ourselves, and that Saint Peter was, as ye rehearsed, reproved of[816] Our Savior when he struck off Malchus's ear, albeit that he did it in the defense of his own master, and the most innocent man that ever was.[817] And unto this they lay,[818] as ye said in the beginning, that since the time that Christian men first fell to fighting, it[819] hath never increased, but always diminished and decayed — so that at this day the Turk hath estraited us very near,[820] and brought it in within a right narrow compass, and narrower shall do, say they, as long as we go about to defend Christendom by the sword. Which, they say, should be as it was in the beginning increased, so be continued and preserved: only by patience and martyrdom. Thus holily speak these godly fathers of Luther's sect, laboring to procure that no man should withstand the Turk, but let him win all. And when it should come to that, then would they, as it seemeth, win all again[821] by their patience, high virtues, and martyrdom, by which now they cannot suffer[822] to resist their beastly voluptuousness, but break their vows, and take them harlots under

the name of wives. And where they may not fight against the Turk, arise[823] up in great plumps[824] to fight against their even[825] Christian. It is, I trow,[826] no great mastery to perceive whom they labor to please, that have that opinion. And if the Turk happen to come in, it is little doubt whose part[827] they will take, and that Christian people be like to find none so cruel Turks as them. It is a gentle[828] holiness to abstain for[829] devotion from resisting the Turk, and in the meanwhile to rise up in routs[830] and fight against Christian men, and destroy — as that sect hath done — many a good religious house; spoiled,[831] maimed, and slain many a good virtuous man; robbed, polluted,[832] and pulled down many a goodly church of Christ.

"And now where they lay[833] for a proof, that God were not contented with battle made against infidels, the loss and diminishment of Christendom since that guise[834] began, they fare[835] as did once an old sage father-fool in Kent at such time as diverse men of worship[836] assembled old folk of the country[837] to common and devise[838] about the amendment of Sandwich haven.[839] At which time, as they began first to ensearch[840] by reason, and by the report of old men thereabout, what thing had been the occasion that so good a haven was in so few years so sore[841] decayed, and such sands risen, and such shallow flats[842] made therewith, that right small vessels had now much work to come in at diverse tides, where great ships were within few years past accustomed to ride without difficulty — and some laying the fault to Goodwin Sands,[843] some to the lands inned[844] by diverse owners in the Isle of Thanet out of the Channel, in which the sea was wont to compass the Isle and bring the vessels round about it, whose course at the ebb was wont to scour the haven, which now the sea, excluded thence for lack of such course and scouring, is choked up with sand — as they thus alleged (diverse men, diverse causes). There started up one good old father and said, 'Ye masters, say every man what he will, 'cha[845] marked this matter well as some other. And by God, I wot how it waxed naught[846] well enough. For I knew it

---

810 support **811** free; wandering about **812** allow **813** proud **814** wish **815** even if **816** by **817** See Mt 26:51–42; Lk 22:49–51; Jn 18:10–11. **818** *unto this they lay:* in addition to this they allege **819** Christendom **820** *estraited us very near:* enclosed us very tightly **821** back **822** endure **823** they

arise **824** bands **825** fellow **826** trust **827** side **828** courteous **829** because of **830** rabbles; mobs **831** despoiled **832** desecrated, profaned **833** put forth; cite **834** practice **835** act; behave **836** repute **837** area **838** *common and devise:* discuss and figure something out **839** *amendment of Sandwich*

haven: improvement of Sandwich harbor **840** inquire; investigate **841** greatly **842** sandbars **843** a ten-mile-long sandbar lying about six miles off the coast **844** reclaimed **845** I've (*'ch* is a contracted form of *Ich,* the form of *I* still used in Kent at that time) **846** *waxed naught:* became bad

good, and have marked — so ch'ave[847] — when it began to wax worse.' 'And what hath hurt it, good father?' quoth these gentlemen. 'By my faith, masters,' quoth he, 'yonder same Tenterden[848] steeple, and nothing else. That, by the Mass, ch'ould[849] 'twere a fair fish pole!'

"'Why[850] hath the steeple hurt the haven, good father?' quoth they. 'Nay, by'r Lady, masters,' quoth he, 'ich cannot tell you well why; but ch'ot[851] well it hath. For, by God, I knew it a good haven till that steeple was builded. And by the Mary Mass[852] — 'cha marked it well — it never throve since!'

"And thus wisely speak these holy Lutherans, which, sowing schisms and seditions among Christian people, lay the loss thereof to the withstanding of the Turk's invasion and the resisting of his malice, where they should rather, if they had any reason in their heads, lay it to the contrary. For when Christian princes did their devoir[853] against miscreants[854] and infidels, there be stories[855] and monuments enough that witness the manifest aid and help of God in great victories given to good Christian princes by his almighty hand. But, on the other side, since that the ambition of Christian rulers desiring each other's dominion have set them at war and deadly dissension among themselves — whereby while each hath aspired to the enhancing of his own, they have little forced[856] what came of the common corps of Christendom — God, for the revenging[857] of their inordinate appetites, hath withdrawn his help and showed that he careth as little: suffering,[858] while each of them laboreth to eat up other, the Turk to prosper and so far-forth to proceed that, if their blind affections[859] look not thereto the sooner, he shall not fail (which our Lord forbid) within short process[860] to swallow them all.

"And albeit Christ forbade Saint Peter (being a priest, and under himself prince of his priests) to fight with the temporal sword toward the impeachment[861] and resistance of his fruitful Passion, whereupon depended the salvation of mankind — which affection our Savior had before that time so sore reproved and rebuked in him that he called him therefor Satan[862] — yet is it nothing to the purpose to allege that by that example temporal princes should, without the let[863] of such spiritual profit, and the sufferance[864] of much spiritual harm, suffer their people to be invaded and oppressed by infidels, to their utter undoing not only temporal, but also of a great part perpetual, which were like of[865] their frailty for fear of worldly grief and incommodity,[866] to fall from the faith and renay[867] their baptism.

"In which peril, since our Lord would[868] not that any man should willfully put himself — and for that cause advised his disciples that if they were pursued[869] in one city, they should not come forth and foolhardily put themselves in peril of renaying Christ by impatience of[870] some intolerable torments, but rather flee thence into some other place where they might serve him in quiet,[871] till he should suffer them to fall in such point[872] that there were no way to escape; and then would he have them abide by their tackling[873] like mighty champions, wherein they shall not, in such case, fail of his help — now, albeit so[874] that Christ and his holy apostles exhort every man to patience and sufferance, without requiting of an evil deed or making any defense, but using[875] further sufferance, and doing also good for evil, yet neither doth this counsel bind a man that he shall of necessity, against the common[876] nature, suffer another man causeless to kill him, nor letteth[877] not any man from the defense of another, whom he seeth innocent and invaded[878] and oppressed by malice. In which case, both nature, reason, and God's behest bindeth first the prince, to the safeguard of his people with the peril[879] of himself as he taught Moses to know himself bounden to kill the Egyptians in the defense of Hebrew;[880] and after, he bindeth every man to the help and defense of his good and harmless neighbor against the malice and cruelty of the wrongdoer. For as the Holy Scripture saith, *Unicuique dedit Deus curam de proximo suo* ('God hath given every man charge of his neighbor'),[881] to keep him

---

847 I have   848 a nearby village   849 I wish   850 How   851 I know   852 *Mary Mass:* Mass in honor of Mary   853 duty; utmost   854 misbelievers   855 historical records   856 cared   857 punishing   858 allowing   859 passions   860 course of time   861 hindrance   862 *therefor*

Satan: Satan for it; see Mt 16:23.   863 prevention   864 allowance   865 *like of:* likely because of   866 *grief and incommodity:* hardship and discomfort   867 renounce   868 wants   869 persecuted   870 *impatience of:* inability to endure   871 peace. See Mt 10:23.

872 state   873 *abide by their tackling:* maintain their position; hold their ground   874 *albeit so:* although it is true   875 practicing   876 *the common:* shared human   877 prevents   878 attacked   879 *with the peril:* at the risk   880 See Ex 2:11–12.   881 Ecclus (Sir) 17:14

from harm of body and soul as much as may lie in his power.[882]

"And by this reason[883] is not only excusable, but also commendable, the common[884] war which every people taketh in the defense of their country against enemies that would invade it, since that every man fighteth, not for the defense of himself of a private affection to[885] himself, but of a Christian charity, for the safeguard and preservation of all others. Which reason, as it hath place in all battle of defense, so hath it most especially in the battle by which we defend the Christian countries against the Turks, in that we defend each other from far the more peril and loss, both of worldly substance,[886] bodily hurt, and perdition of men's souls. And now if this be lawful, and enjoined[887] also to every private person,[888] how much more belongeth it to princes and rulers? Which if they may not, upon the peril of their souls, wittingly suffer[889] among the people whom they have in governance anyone to take away another's horse, how may they, without eternal damnation, suffer other people, and specially infidels, to come in, spoil[890] and rob, and captive[891] them all? And if they be bounden to the defense and may not do it alone, what madness were it to say that the people may not help them."

THE FIFTEENTH CHAPTER
That princes be bounden to punish heretics,
and that fair[892] handling helpeth little
with many of them.

"And surely, as the princes be bounden that they shall not suffer their people by infidels to be invaded, so be they as deeply bounden that they shall not suffer their people to be seduced and corrupted by heretics, since the peril shall in short while grow to as great, both with men's souls withdrawn from God, and their goods lost and their bodies destroyed by common[893] sedition, insurrection, and open war within the bowels of their own land. All which may

in the beginning be right easily avoided by punishment of those few that be the first. Which few well repressed, or if need so require utterly pulled up,[894] there shall far the fewer have lust[895] to follow. For if they were handled in a contrary manner, and, as ye seemed to mean in the beginning of our matter,[896] instead of punishment, entreated, favored, and by fair words and rewards brought home again, I fear me then that you should find little fruit in that fashion. For first, whereas they fall into heresy by pride, that way should make them prouder, and set the more by[897] themselves. And then would many more fall thereto, of purpose to be hired[898] again therefrom. So that, as Mamelukes[899] and Janissaries[900] about[901] the Turk and sultan have used to christen their children of purpose,[902] that by the renaying of their faith after,[903] they might be made Mamelukes or Janissaries as their fathers were, and may be had the more in estimation and favor about the great Turk, even likewise within a while, if we take that way with heretics, we shall have young fresh fellows first become heretics, that they may be prayed and hired after to come to Christ's faith again. I would not they were over-hastily handled, but little rigor and much mercy showed where simpleness appeared, and not high[904] heart or malice. For of such as be proud and malicious, much proof hath been made[905] already. For of some sort, many full fair handled, little change themselves or come to good amendment. I told you myself, and very true it was, of twain that were detected[906] of heresy unto the most honorable prelate of this realm, and in what benign, fatherly manner — and liberal[907] also — he dealt with them. And yet what amendment made his genteel and courteous entreaty in their stubborn stomach?[908] Were they not after worse than they were before, and so used[909] themselves that after much harm done by them, they came in short space after to their open[910] conviction? They be, ye wot well, at the first customably received to grace;[911] and verily for such merits, forgiveness is reward enough. And if they cannot by that warning be

---

882 See Lv 19:18; Lk 10:27–37; Rom 15:2.   883 reasoning   884 shared; public 885 *of a private affection to:* because of a private regard for   886 wealth; goods 887 prescribed as a duty   888 citizen 889 allow   890 despoil   891 enslave 892 kind; mild   893 public   894 *pulled up:* rooted out   895 desire   896 discussion   897 *set the more by:* value more

highly   898 bribed   899 an army unit in Egypt formed by drafting the children of slaves, mostly Christians   900 an elite military force of the Ottoman Empire consisting entirely of boys taken from Christian families at around the age of six, raised as Muslims, and trained to fight Christians   901 around   902 *used… purpose:* made a practice of having

their children baptized for the purpose 903 afterward   904 proud   905 *proof hath been made:* experience has been had   906 accused   907 generous 908 heart(s)   909 conducted   910 public   911 *at…grace:* after a first offense customably allowed to confess their sin warned, surely, as Saint Paul saith, he is not to be trusted often, but rather of all good Christian people to be eschewed and avoided[912] from the flock. For they be so far waxen crooked that seldom can they be righted again."[913]

"Forsooth," quoth your friend. "yet, as I said at my first coming to you, were I worthy to be of counsel with[914] the clergy when there were a man founden faulty[915] therein whom the people have in good estimation for some great opinion[916] of learning and virtue, they should be secretly[917] and soberly admonished, and not the matter published among the people. And finally, if they so should needs be openly convicted and corrected[918] in face of the world, then would I not yet have them called 'Lutherans,' lest the people which had good opinion of them may peradventure like Luther the better for them; or if they happen to perceive them for naught and so take them, then shall they peradventure give the less credence to all good men, and set the less by all good preachers after."

"Surely," quoth I, "certain rule that were always best were hard to give in such case. Sometimes there may peradventure such honesty be joined with such repentance that it would not be much amiss to preserve the man's estimation among the people, to whom his perfect change may percase[919] more than recompense his former error and oversight. But whereas[920] the contrary shall seem convenient,[921] there can I not see why we should forbear to call them 'Lutherans,' since it is both an old usage to call heretics after the name of him whom they follow in their heresy, and also—as Luther's sect is, in effect, the whole heap of all heresies gathered together—it is now all one to call him a 'Lutheran' or to call him a 'heretic,' those two words being in manner equivalent, Luther teaching almost nothing but heresies, nor none heresies founden anywhere almost that the Lutherans have not among them. And since it so is, reason doth (in my mind) require that the name of 'Lutherans' should be customably[922] brought in men's ears[923] as odious as the name of 'heretics.' Nor I see not so great fear that either folk shall, for opinion of any man's virtue in[924] whom they see

themselves deceived, withdraw their favor and affection from such as are good indeed, or fall into the favor of Luther's sect for the estimation[925] of the man whom they now see proved naught. For this will no man do but such as either be so foolish that they would hate all Christ's apostles for the falsehood[926] of Judas, or so naughty that they would fain[927] have all the world fall to the same sect and be of their own suit."[928]

THE SIXTEENTH CHAPTER
Of simple unlearned folk that are deceived by the great good opinion that they have percase in the learning and living of some that teach them errors.

"Forsooth," quoth your friend. "yet would there, methinketh, be much pity used in those matters among.[929] For many a man unlearned, when he heareth one that he taketh for cunning,[930] and seeth such a man as he taketh for virtuous, commend Luther's way, he is of simpleness and good mind moved to follow the same."

"Surely," quoth I, "therein I say not nay but[931] that these things being such, great pity it is to see many good simple souls deceived and led out of the right way by the authority of such as they reckon for good men and cunning, whom they have, either by open[932] sermons or secret[933] communication, perceived to be favorers of that ungracious[934] sect, thinking that men of such cunning and knowledge in Scripture, being therewith of such virtuous behavior as they seem to be, would never lean to[935] that way but if[936] they knew it for good. And surely where it so happeneth that any simple soul is, by the good opinion that he hath in[937] his master, led out of the right belief of the faith, weening that were the very faith which he seeth his master (whom he reckoneth good and cunning) follow and lean unto, it is a very piteous thing. And as that person is less in blame and more easily cured, so is that master doubly damned, as the cause both of his own sin and his that[938] followeth him; and very hard is he to mend. Howbeit, sometimes we deserve with our sin that God, for the

912 *eschewed and avoided:* shunned and expelled   **913** See Tit 3:10–11.   **914** *of counsel with:* consulted by   **915** guilty   **916** *for some great opinion of:* because they have a high opinion of (his)   **917** privately   **918** punished   **919** perhaps   **920** wherever   **921** appropriate   **922** customarily, habitually   **923** *brought . . . ears:* made to sound   **924** about   **925** *for . . . of:* because of the regard for   **926** *for the falsehood:* because of the treachery   **927** gladly   **928** kind; group   **929** from   **930** learned   **931** *say not nay but:* do not deny   **932** public   **933** private   **934** without grace; wicked   **935** *lean to:* favor   **936** *but if:* unless   **937** of   **938** who

punishment thereof, suffereth[939] us to have lewd[940] leaders and evil teachers. And surely for the more part, such as be led out of the right way do rather fall thereto of a lewd lightness[941] of their own mind than
5 for any great thing that moveth them in their master that teacheth them. For we see them as ready to believe a purser,[942] a glover,[943] or a weaver, that nothing can do but scantly[944] read English, as they would be to believe the wisest and the best-learned doctor[945]
10 in a realm. Howbeit, be a man never so well-learned, and seem he never so virtuous, yet can we with no reason excuse ourselves if we leave the right belief for the trust that we have in any man earthly. For our belief is taught us by God surely planted in the
15 Church of Christ, and the articles thereof not new begun, but now continued many a hundred years in the great congregation of Christian people as things certain, sure, and stable, and out of[946] all question — which none heretic doth or can deny — and in the
20 hearts of this congregation be they written by the holy handiwork of God. And therefore accursed is he that, through his trust put in any man, believeth the contrary of any point that the Church of Christ is taught to believe by God.
25   "This faith was taught by Christ, preached by his apostles; of this, wrote his evangelists, and many more things were taught than are written.[947] And this faith should have been taught and firmly stood although[948] nothing had been written. And the ar-
30 ticles of this faith had in men's hearts be the just and sure rules of construction[949] by which we construe and understand the Holy Scripture that is written. For very sure are we that whoso would construe any text of Holy Scripture in such wise as he
35 would make it seem contrary to any point of this Catholic faith which God hath taught his Church, he giveth the Scripture a wrong sentence,[950] and thereby teacheth a wrong belief. And as Saint Paul saith, cursed be he, and though[951] he were an angel
40 of heaven. And therefore be we not excusable if we believe any man to the contrary of the faith, how good or how cunning soever he seem, while[952] we see that he teacheth us a wrong way — which we may soon know if we be good Christians and know the
45 belief already.

"And we may have also a great guess threat, if he teach us secretly, as a privy[953] mystery, the doctrine that he would not were[954] uttered and showed openly. For such things be they, commonly, that these heretics teach in hugger-mugger[955] against the
50 faith that all the Church believeth. Now would I give this counsel to every unlearned man: When any man so teacheth thee whom thou hast in great estimation for virtue or cunning, then consider in thyself that he neither hath more virtue nor more
55 cunning than had Saint Augustine, Saint Jerome, Saint Ambrose, Saint Gregory, Saint Cyprian, Saint Chrysostom, with many old fathers and holy doctors, which[956] believed all their days — and died in — the belief that thou believest already, whereof he
60 teacheth the contrary. And so say boldly to him. But then if he would beguile thee, and say that those holy doctors believed not as thou dost, but as he saith, bring him to the reckoning before some other good and well-learned men. And I dare be bold to
65 warrant[957] that thou shalt find him doubly false. For neither shalt thou find it true that[958] he told thee, and, besides that, he shall not let to belie[959] thee, saying — and swearing too — that thou sayest wrong on him, and that he never told thee so."
70
"Marry, sir," quoth your friend, "he will haply say that he were peradventure in that point to be pardoned, because of the jeopardy that he might fall into by the maintenance of his opinion."

"Pardon him if ye will," quoth I. "But yet is he
75 not then so good as were those good fathers. For either is his way naught — and then doth he naught to teach it — or, if it be good, then is he naught that for any fear forsaketh[960] it. For he that forsaketh any truth of Christ's faith, forsaketh Christ. And then
80 saith our Savior that whoso doth shall be forsaken of[961] him.[962] And he that so doth is not to be believed like those holy fathers which[963] have taught us far the contrary. For they did abide by the right faith that they taught, which is, as by their books
85 appeareth, the selfsame faith that we believe. And so far-forth abide they thereby, that diverse of them sustained great persecution therefor,[964] and some of them death and martyrdom. So that we were more than mad if we had not liefer[965] send our souls to
90

---

939 allows **940** evil **941** *lewd lightness:* wicked thoughtlessness **942** pursemaker **943** glovemaker **944** barely **945** scholar **946** *out of:* beyond **947** See Jn 21:25. **948** even if

949 interpretation **950** meaning **951** *and though:* even if **952** when **953** private, secret **954** *would not were:* does not want to be **955** a secret way **956** who **957** guarantee **958** what

959 *let to belie:* hesitate to slander **960** denies **961** by **962** See Lk 12:9. **963** who **964** for it **965** *had not liefer:* would not rather

the souls of those holy fathers—of whose cunning, virtue, and salvation we be sure—than to cast them away with these folk, which, how holy soever they seem, yet show themselves naught in that they teach the contrary of such things as those undoubted holy doctors taught."

"I marvel, then," quoth your friend, "why they live so virtuously—fasting, and giving their goods in alms, with other virtuous exercises, both in forbearing[966] the pleasure of the world, and also taking pain in their bodies?"

"To this matter," quoth I, "our Savior himself answereth where he saith (in the Gospel of Matthew), *Attendite a falsis prophetis, qui veniunt ad vos in vestimentis ovium, intrinsecus autem sunt lupi rapaces* ('Beware of the false prophets, that come to you in the clothing of sheep and yet withinforth[967] be ravenous wolves').[968] For since that they by false doctrine labor to devour and destroy men's souls, we be sure enough that wolves they be indeed, how sheepishly soever they look. And hypocrites must they needs be, since they be so denounced by God's own mouth. And well may we perceive that he meaneth not well, when he teacheth evil. And that evil he teacheth we may well wit,[969] when we see him teach the contrary of that which God hath already taught his whole Church. In which hath been so many holy fathers, so many cunning doctors, and so many blessed martyrs—that so have bidden[970] by the faith to the death—that it were a frenzy[971] if we would now, against so many such, believe any false heretic and feigning hypocrite teaching us the contrary.

"Of those holy fathers of our faith, whom their books showeth to have believed as we believe, we have seen and known their virtuous life well proved by their blessed end, in which our Lord hath testified by many a miracle that their faith and their lives hath liked[972] him. But never have we yet seen any such thing by[973] any of these heretics. Nor yet so much as any constancy in their doctrine; but and if[974] they were once found out and examined, we see them always first ready to lie and forswear[975] themselves, if that will serve. And when that will not help, but their falsehood and perjury proved

in their faces, then ready be they to abjure and forsake[976] it, as long as that may save their lives. Nor never yet found I anyone but he would once[977] abjure though he never intended to keep his oath. So holy would he be, and so wise therewith, that he would with perjury kill his soul forever, to save his body for a while. For commonly soon after, such as so do, show themselves again—God, of his righteousness, not suffering[978] that their false forswearing[979] should stand them long in stead."[980]

THE SEVENTEENTH CHAPTER

The author showeth that some which be Lutherans and seem to live holily, and therefore be believed and had in estimation,[981] intend a further purpose than they pretend, which they will well show if they may once find their time.[982]

"And as for their living, the good appearance whereof is the thing that most blindeth us. As much surety as we have of the godly life of our old holy fathers—whereof the world hath written, and God hath borne witness by many great miracles showed for their sakes—as uncertain be we of these men, with whom we neither be always present, and little also can tell what abominations they may do too some of them secretly. Nor yet can know their intent and purpose that they appoint[983] upon, and the cause for which they be for the while content to take all the pain.

"Very certain is it that pride is one cause wherefore[984] they take the pain. For pride is, as Saint Augustine saith, the very mother of all heresies.[985] For of a high[986] mind to be in the liking of the people hath comen into many men so mad a mind, and so frantic,[987] that they have not rought[988] what pain they took without any other recompense or reward but only the fond[989] pleasure and delight that themselves conceive in their heart when they think what worship[990] that people talketh of them. And they be the devil's martyrs, taking much pain for his pleasure, and his very apes,[991] whom he maketh to tumble through the hoop of that 'holiness' that putteth

966 abstaining from **967** inwardly **968** Mt 7:15 **969** know **970** stood **971** craziness, wild folly **972** pleased **973** concerning **974** *and if:* if **975** perjure **976** *abjure and forsake:* renounce

under oath and repudiate **977** at some point **978** permitting **979** *false forswearing:* deceitful renouncing under oath **980** *stand...stead:* benefit them for long **981** *had in estimation:* held in

high regard **982** opportunity **983** agree **984** why **985** See Sermon 46, ch. 18. **986** proud **987** insane; wild and ungovernable **988** cared **989** foolish **990** honor **991** dupes

them to pain without fruit, and yet oftentimes maketh them miss of[992] the vain praise whereof only they be so proud. For while they delight to think how they be taken for holy, they be many times well perceived and taken for hypocrites, as they be.

"But such is this cursed affection[993] of pride, and so deep setteth in the claws where it catcheth, that hard it is to pull them out. This pride hath ere this made some learned men to devise new fantasies in[994] our faith because they would be singular among the people, as did Arius, Faustus,[995] Pelagius, and diverse other old heretics, whose false opinions have been, long time past, openly[996] condemned by many holy synods and General Councils — and now, God be thanked, not only their opinions quenched, but also all their books clean[997] gone and vanished quite away, ere ever any law was made for such books' burning, so that it well appeareth to have been the only work of God that hath destroyed those works, which wrought in their times much harm in his Church. This affection of pride hath not only made some learned men to bring forth new fantasies, but maketh also many men of much less than mean[998] learning so sore[999] to long to seem far better learned than they be that, to make the people have[1] them in authority, they devise new sects and schisms to the pleasure of newfangled folk, sparing no pain, for the while, to set forth their sect withal, rewarding their labor with only delight of beholding what pleasure the people have in their preaching.

"And albeit that this frantic pleasure with which the devil inwardly feedeth them be the only thing that satisfieth and contenteth some, yet many are there, of those that evil teacheth and appear holy, which[2] are both secretly more loose and voluptuous[3] than they seem. And some also, which warily keep[4] themselves for the while, intend toward more liberal lewdness at length.[5] Will ye see example thereof? Look on Tyndale, that translated the New Testament, which[6] was indeed (as ye said in the beginning) before his going over[7] taken for a man of sober[8] and honest living, and looked and preached holily, saving that yet sometimes it savored so shrewdly[9] that he

was once or twice examined thereof. But yet because he glossed then his words with a better sense, and said and swore that he meant none harm, folk were glad to take all to the best. But yet ye see that though he dissembled himself[10] to be a Lutheran or to bear any favor to his sect while he was here, yet as soon as he got him[11] hence, he got him to Luther straight. And whereas in the translation of the New Testament he covered and dissimuled[12] himself as much as he could, yet when he perceived his cloaked heresies espied and destroyed, then showed he shortly himself in his own likeness, sending forth first his wicked book of *Mammona*, and after, his malicious book of *Obedience*. In which books he showeth himself so puffed up with the poison of pride, malice, and envy, that it is more than marvel that the skin can hold together. For he hath not only sucked out the most poison that he could find through all Luther's books or take of[13] him by mouth[14] — and all that hath spit out in these books — but hath also in many things far passed his master, running forth so mad for malice, that he fareth as though he heard not his own voice. He barketh against the sacraments much more than Luther. For whereas Luther left yet some confession, and reckoned his secret[15] confession necessary and profitable, though he set a lewd[16] liberty therein, Tyndale taketh it away quite,[17] and raileth thereon, and saith it was begun by the devil. Which thing had undoubtedly never been obtained[18] among the people — that folk should show themselves[19] their secret sins to another man — if God had not brought it up[20] himself. Nor never could it have continued so many hundred years without great harm grown by disclosing of many men's offenses, if the Holy Spirit of God had not assisted his holy sacrament, as the King's Highness most prudently writeth. Luther also sometimes affirmeth purgatory, sometimes doubteth, and sometimes denieth. But Tyndale putteth[21] no doubt at all, but denieth it as utterly, as foolishly, without ground, cause, or color laid wherefore.[22] Concerning the holy Mass, Luther, as mad as he is, was never yet as mad as Tyndale is, which like himself[23] so raileth thereupon in his frantic book of

---

992 *miss of:* fail to obtain   **993** inclination; disposition   **994** regarding   **995** a contemporary of Augustine and a Manichean   **996** publicly   **997** completely   **998** average   **999** greatly   **1** hold   **2** who   **3** sensual   **4** restrain   **5** *at length:* eventually   **6** who   **7** overseas

8 serious, temperate   **9** *savored so shrewdly:* smelled so badly   **10** *dissembled himself:* pretended not   **11** himself   **12** *covered and dissimuled:* concealed and disguised   **13** from   **14** word of mouth   **15** private   **16** wicked   **17** completely   **18** *been obtained:* become established and

customary   **19** *show themselves:* themselves reveal   **20** *brought it up:* introduced it   **21** expresses   **22** *color laid wherefore:* pretext given why   **23** *which like himself:* who, in his habitual manner

Obedience that any good Christian man would abhor to read it. And yet writing as he doth, he is not ashamed to say that the Church will not believe holy Saint Jerome, Saint Augustine, and such others—as though these holy doctors were on his side. Among all whom he shall scant read one leaf wherein he shall not find one or other of his abominable heresies reproved.[24] Luther himself was never so shameless to say that these holy fathers held[25] on his side. But because they were against him, he rejected the authority of them all. But what conscience hath this Tyndale, that thus can write to blind unlearned people with, when himself well knoweth that they do all, with one voice, prove that shrift[26] and confession is of necessity requisite to our salvation, and that they lay for them[27] the Holy Scripture plenteously for the further proof of this part[28]—which Tyndale would wickedly, with only railing and jesting against all their wholesome doctrine, drive away clean and[29] he could? He knoweth also himself that all they with one voice teach, and prove by Scripture too that there is the fire of purgatory, which I marvel why Tyndale feareth so little, but if he be at a plain point with himself[30] to go straight to hell. They teach also all with one voice the great profit of the Mass and honor that ought to be done thereto—which Tyndale teacheth to dishonor.

"They teach all[31] the worshipping of images and relics, and praying to saints, going on pilgrimages, and credence to be given to miracles, of all which Tyndale teacheth the contrary.

"All they teach also chastity,[32] and preach high preeminence of virginity and widowhood[33] above wedding, and ever have had[34] in abomination the breach of any vow of chastity, whereas Tyndale, against them all teaching the contrary, is therein so shameless, and so little respect hath of his own conscience, that—seeing all them to write against him and himself against them all, and that every man that learned is must needs perceive his shameless boldness therein—letteth[35] not yet both to rail against Christ's Church for saying as these old holy saints said before, and also to say that the Church will not hear them, whereas himself seeth that the Church and they say all one thing, and as well they

as the Church abhor and condemn his deadly damnable heresies.

"Now ween I that we need little to doubt how he liveth that thus writeth. He liveth of likelihood as evil as he teacheth—and worse he cannot. But, as I began to say, this Tyndale in the beginning bore forth a fair face, and seemed unto the people peradventure an honest man, as some others haply do now whom ye speak of, which,[36] when they see their time,[37] shall, if they may be suffered,[38] cast off their visors[39] of hypocrisy and show themselves at length in their own likeness, as he doth now.

"I pray you look on Luther himself. If he should in the beginning have said all that he hath said since, who could have suffered him? If he should in the beginning have married a nun, would not the people have burned him? And yet now, by little and little, he hath brought them to be content therewith. And let us not think the contrary but that of those heretics that here seem so good (if there be any such), we see not yet their stomachs,[40] but shall, if they be upholden[41] a while, see them follow their author[42] in lewd living—Doctor Luther with his leman[43]—and shall, by the devil's help, induce good and simple souls so far into wrong ways that they shall at length well like and commend the things which now their uncorrupted conscience abhorreth.

"And therefore let all good Christian people knock and break, as Holy Scripture counseleth, the young children's heads of Babylon against the stone:[44] that is to say, let good Christian folk suspect, abhor, and pursue[45] in the beginning all such evil doctrine as is contrary to the faith and teaching of Christ's Catholic Church, which God and his Holy Spirit, both by writing and without writing, hath taught his Church, and which hath in his Church continued from Christ's days hitherto, as it well appeareth by the good and godly books of all our forefathers, holy doctors of Christ's Church Militant here in earth, and now glorious saints in his Church Triumphant in heaven. From whose firm faith joined with good works (which as two wings carried them up to heaven) there shall, but[46] we be more than mad, no fond[47] heretic lead us, seem he never so saintish with any new construction[48] of Christ's Holy Gospel or

---

24 refuted   **25** believed   **26** penance   **27** *lay for them:* cite for themselves   **28** side of the argument   **29** *clean and:* completely if   **30** *but…himself:* unless he is resolved, determined   **31** *teach all:* all teach   **32** celibacy   **33** remaining in widowhood   **34** held   **35** hesitates   **36** who   **37** opportunity   **38** allowed   **39** masks   **40** hearts   **41** supported   **42** creator; founder; instigator   **43** mistress; beloved   **44** See Ps 136(137):8–9.   **45** attack   **46** unless   **47** foolish   **48** interpretation

other part of Holy Scripture — which no wise man will doubt but that those holy cunning⁴⁹ men, illumined with the grace of God, much better understood than all the rabble of these lewd heretics. Of all which that ever sprang in Christ's Church, the very worst and the most beastly be these Lutherans, as their opinions and their lewd living showeth.

"And let us never doubt but all that be of that sect, if any seem good (as very few do), yet will they in conclusion decline to the like lewd living as their master and their fellows do, if they might once⁵⁰ (as by God's grace they never shall) frame⁵¹ the people to their own frantic fantasy. Which dissolute living, they be driven to dissemble because their audience is not yet brought to the point to bear it; which they surely trust to bring about, and to frame this realm after the fashion of Switzerland, or Saxony and some other parts of Germany, where their sect hath already fordone⁵² the faith, pulled down the churches, polluted⁵³ the temples, put out and spoiled⁵⁴ all good religious folk,⁵⁵ joined friars and nuns together in lechery, despited⁵⁶ all saints, blasphemed our blessed Lady, cast down Christ's cross, thrown out the blessed Sacrament, refused all good laws, abhorred all good governance, rebelled against all rulers, fallen to fight among themselves (and so many thousands slain, that the land lieth in many places in manner deserted and desolate), and finally — that most abominable is of all — of⁵⁷ all their own ungracious⁵⁸ deeds lay the fault in God, taking away the liberty of man's will, ascribing all our deeds to destiny, with all reward or punishment pursuing upon all our doings, whereby they take away all diligence and good endeavor to virtue, all withstanding and striving against vice, all care of heaven, all fear of hell, all cause of prayer, all desire of devotion, all exhortation to good, all dehortation⁵⁹ from evil, all praise of well-doing, all rebuke of sin, all the laws of the world, all reason among men; set all wretchedness abroach,⁶⁰ no man at liberty, and yet every man do what he will, calling it not his will but his destiny, laying their sin to God's ordinance, and their punishment to God's cruelty, and finally turning the nature of man into worse than a beast, and the goodness of God into worse than the devil. And all this good fruit would a few mischievous⁶¹ persons — some for desire of a large liberty to an unbridled lewdness, and some of a high, devilish pride cloaked under pretext of good zeal and simpleness — undoubtedly bring into this realm, if the prince and prelates, and the good faithful people, did not in the beginning meet with⁶² their malice."

THE EIGHTEENTH CHAPTER

The author showeth that in the condemnation of heretics the clergy might lawfully do much more sharply⁶³ than they do, and that indeed the clergy doth now no more against heretics than the Apostle⁶⁴ counseleth, and the old holy doctors did.

"For as for the clergy — whom they labor to bring in hatred under the false accusation of cruelty — do⁶⁵ no more therein than Saint Augustine, Saint Jerome, and other holy fathers have been wont⁶⁶ to do before, nor no further than the Apostle adviseth himself. For they do no more but — when one heretic, after warning, will not amend but waxeth⁶⁷ worse — eschew him then, and avoid⁶⁸ him out of Christ's flock. Which is the very thing that Saint Paul counseleth where he writeth to Titus, *Haereticum hominem post primam et secundam correctionem devita.*⁶⁹ And this is much less that the clergy doth to heretics, than Saint Peter did unto Ananias and Sapphira for a far smaller matter: that is to wit, for their untrue saying,⁷⁰ and keeping aside a portion of their own money, when they made semblance as though they brought to the apostles altogether.⁷¹ For though they were not killed by his own hand, yet appeareth it well that God killed them both twain by Saint Peter — his means as governor of his Church — to the fearful example of all such as would after that break their promise and vow to God, willingly made, of themselves or their own goods. Which thing Luther and Tyndale would have all men do now. Did not Saint Paul write unto the Corinthians that they should deliver to the devil him that had defouled his father's wife, 'to the punishment of his body, that the spirit

49 learned   50 ever   51 shape, form
52 abolished   53 desecrated, profaned
54 robbed   55 *religious folk:* members
of religious orders   56 shown contempt
for   57 for   58 graceless; wicked

59 dissuasion   60 abroad; flowing freely
as from a broached cask   61 evil   62 *meet
with:* grapple with, take precautions against
63 harshly   64 St. Paul   65 they do
66 accustomed   67 grows   68 expel

69 *Haereticum . . . devita:* "Shun the
heretical person after the first and second
reproof" (Tit 3:10).   70 *untrue saying:*
speaking untruthfully   71 all of it; Acts
5:1–10

might be saved in the Day of Judgment'?[72] What say we of Hymenaeus and Alexander, of whom he writeth (unto the Corinthians also),[73] *Hymenaeum et Alexandrum tradidi Satanae, ut discant non blasphemare* ('I have,' quoth he, 'betaken[74] Hymenaeus and Alexander to the devil, to teach them to leave their blasphemy.')?[75] In which words we may well learn that Saint Paul, as apostle and spiritual governor in that country, finding them twain fallen from the faith of Christ into the blasphemy of that[76] they were bounden to worship, did cause the devil to torment and punish their bodies, which every man may well wit[77] was no small pain, and peradventure not without death also. For we find nothing of their amendment. And this bodily punishment did Saint Paul, as it appeareth, upon heretics, so that if the clergy did, unto much more blasphemous heretics than I ween they twain were, much more sorrow[78] than Saint Paul did to them, they should neither do it without good cause nor without great authority and evident example of Christ's blessed apostles. And surely when our Savior himself calleth such heretics 'wolves cloaked in sheep's skins,'[79] and would[80] that his shepherds, the governors of his flock, should in such wise avoid[81] them as very shepherds would avoid very wolves, there is little doubt but (as an honorable prelate of this realm, in his most erudite book, answereth unto Luther)[82] the prelates of Christ's Church rather ought temporally to destroy those ravenous wolves than suffer[83] them to worry[84] and devour everlastingly the flock that Christ hath committed unto their cure,[85] and the flock that himself died for to save it from the wolves' mouth.[86] But now, though it well appear (as methinketh it doth) that the clergy might in this case right sore procure[87] against heretics, yet do they indeed no further than the old holy fathers did in their time, and the blessed Apostle[88] counseleth them to do. But all the sore[89] punishment of heretics wherewith such folk as favor them would fain[90] defame the clergy, is and hath been — for the great outrages and temporal harms that such heretics have been always wont to do, and seditious commotions that they be wont to make, besides the far passing[91] spiritual hurts that they do to men's souls — devised and executed against them of necessity by good Christian princes and politic[92] rulers of the temporalty,[93] forasmuch as their wisdoms well perceived that the people should not fail to fall into many sore and intolerable troubles if such seditious sects of heretics were not by grievous punishment repressed[94] in the beginning, and the spark well quenched ere it were suffered to grow to over-great a fire."

"Forsooth," quoth your friend, "it appeareth well that the clergy is not in this matter to be blamed, as many men reckon. For it seemeth that the sore punishment of heretics is devised, not by the clergy, but by temporal princes and good lay people — and not without great cause."

"Well," quoth I, "and to the intent that ye shall perceive it much the better — and over that believe your own eyes, and not my words, in many things that ye have heard of my mouth — we will not part this night but I shall deliver into your hands here more books than ye will read over till[95] tomorrow. But for[96] that ye shall neither need to read all, nor lose time in seeking for that ye should see, I have laid you the places ready with rushes[97] between the leaves, and notes marked in the margents,[98] where the matter is touched."

So caused I to be borne into his chamber a book of decrees,[99] and certain works of Saint Cyprian, Saint Augustine, and some other holy doctors, and therewithal, a work or twain of Luther, and as many of Tyndale. And in this wise went we to supper; and on the morrow forbore I to speak with him till near dinnertime. At which our meeting, he showed me that in the decrees where the rushes lay — namely in *Causa XXII quaestione quinta*[100] and diverse others of the questions consequently[101] following — he had seen at full that the clergy doth at this day no further for the punishment of heretics than did the old fathers and holy doctors and saints in time past, as by their own words there alleged[102] doth open and plain appear, and that as well the clergy in the

72 1 Cor 5:5   **73** *unto the Corinthians also:* actually not to them, but to Timothy   **74** handed over   **75** 1 Tm 1:20   **76** that which   **77** know   **78** physical pain   **79** Mt 7:15   **80** wants   **81** expel. See Acts 20:28–31.   **82** *as . . . Luther:* St. John Fisher (1469–1535), Bishop of Rochester; his book is *Assertionis Lutheranae confutatio* (1523).   **83** allow   **84** struggle, choke   **85** care. See 1 Pt 5:2; see also Jn 21:15–17; Acts 20:28.   **86** See Jn 10:11–16.   **87** *right sore procure:* very strongly act   **88** St. Paul   **89** severe   **90** like to   **91** surpassing   **92** prudent   **93** temporal estate of the realm   **94** suppressed   **95** *read over till:* i.e., be able to read through before   **96** so   **97** plant stems used as bookmarks   **98** margins   **99** *Decretals* of Gratian   **100** *quaestione quinta:* question five; in fact *Causa* 23, not 22   **101** consecutively; sequentially   **102** quoted

persecution[103] of heretics lawfully may do, as the temporal princes in war against infidels be deeply bounden to do, much more than they now do, or of long time have done—or yet, as it seemeth, go about to do. And over[104] this he said that he had seen of Luther's own words worse than he had ever heard rehearsed,[105] and in Tyndale worse yet in many things than he saw in Luther himself. And in Tyndale's book of *Obedience* he said that he had founden what things Tyndale saith against miracles and against the praying to saints.

"Marry," quoth I, "and these two matters made us two much business[106] before your going to the university. I would it had happed you and me to have read over that book of his before. Howbeit, in good faith if ye will, we shall yet peruse over his reasons in those points, and consider what weight is in them."

"Nay, by my troth," quoth your friend, "we shall need now to lose no time therein. For as for miracles, he saith nothing in effect but that which I laid against them before—that the miracles were the works of the devil—saving that where I said that it might peradventure be said so, he saith that indeed it is so, and proveth it yet less than I did. And therefore, as for that word[107] of his, without better proof is[108] of little weight."

"Forsooth," quoth I, "Tyndale's word alone ascribing all the miracles to the devil ought not to weigh much among Christian men against the writing of holy Saint Augustine, Saint Jerome, Saint Ambrose, Saint Chrysostom, Saint Gregory, and many another holy doctor, writing[109] many a great miracle done at holy pilgrimages[110] and saints' relics—done in open presence of many substantial folk, and diverse done in their own sight. All which miracles all those blessed saints do ascribe unto the work of God, and to the honor of those holy saints that were worshipped at those pilgrimages. Against all whom, when Tyndale ascribeth them all to the devil, he plainly showeth himself as faithful as he would seem: very near sib[111] to the infidelity of those Jews that ascribed Christ's miracles to the devil, saying that he did 'cast out devils by the power of Beelzebub, prince of devils.'"[112]

"Surely," quoth your friend. "And as for that he reasoneth against praying to saints, is very bare."[113]

"It must needs," quoth I, "be bare, except he well avoid[114] the miracles. Whereto, when he hath nothing to say but to ascribe God's works to the devil, he showeth himself driven to a narrow strait.[115] For he and his fellows, as touching miracles, neither have God willing, nor the devil able, to show any for the proof of their part[116]—nor, I trust in God, never they shall."

"In faith," quoth your friend, "as for reasoning the matter[117] of praying to saints, he is not worth the reading now. For all the substance, in effect, that ye prove it by, is by him clean[118] untouched."

"That is," quoth I, "no marvel, for he hath not heard it."

"In faith," quoth your friend. "And of his own making he layeth[119] arguments for it, such as he list,[120] which he layeth forth faintly, and then doth answer them so slenderly[121]—and all his whole matter,[122] in those points and others, so plainly confuted by the old holy fathers—that if I had seen so much before, it had been likely to have shorted much part of our long communication.

"For by my troth," quoth he, "when I consider both the parts[123] well, and read Luther's words and Tyndale's in some places where ye laid me the rushes, I cannot but wonder that either any Almain could like the one, or any Englishman the other."

"I cannot much marvel," quoth I, "though many like them well. For since there is no country wherein there lacketh plenty of such as be naught,[124] what wonder is it that vicious folk fall to the favor of their like? And then, as for such, when their hearts are once fixed upon their blind affections,[125] a man may with as much fruit preach to a post as reason with them to the contrary. For they nothing ponder what is reasonably spoken to them; but whereto their fond[126] affection inclineth, that thing they lean to, and that they believe; or, at the leastwise, that way they walk and say they believe it. For in good faith, that they so believe indeed, their matters[127] be so mad that I believe it not. And yet make they semblance as though they believed that

---

103 prosecution   104 beyond
105 related   106 trouble, difficulty
107 statement   108 it is   109 writing
of   110 shrines   111 akin   112 See Lk
11:15.   113 *is very bare:* it is paltry or

poor in quality   114 *except he well avoid:* unless he disprove   115 *to a narrow strait:* into a tight spot   116 side   117 *as for . . . matter:* i.e., as for the purpose of discussing the issue   118 completely   119 presents

120 pleases   121 inadequately   122 case
123 sides   124 wicked   125 passions;
inclinations   126 foolish   127 beliefs

no man were able to confute Luther or Tyndale, where methinketh, for these matters of their heresies that they so set forth, if the audience were indifferent,[128] there were not in this world a man more meet[129] to match them both twain in dispicions[130] than were mad Collins[131] alone, if he were not of the same sect. For he lasheth out[132] Scripture in Bedlam as fast as they both in Almain. And, in good faith, they both expound it as madly as he. And so help me God, as methinketh that man is as mad as any of all three, which,[133] when he seeth the right faith of Christ continued in his Catholic Church so many hundred years; and on that side so many glorious martyrs, so many blessed confessors, so many godly virgins. And in all that time, virtue had[134] in honor; fasting, prayer, and alms had in price;[135] God and his saints worshipped; his sacraments had in reverence; Christian souls tenderly prayed for; holy vows kept and observed; virginity preached and praised; pilgrimages devoutly visited; every kind of good works commended. And seeth now suddenly start up a new sect setting forth clean the contrary: destroying Christ's holy sacraments; pulling down Christ's cross; blaspheming his blessed saints; destroying all devotion; forbidding men to pray for their fathers' souls; contemning fasting days; setting at nought[136] the holy days; pulling down the churches; railing against the Mass; villainously demeaning the Blessed Sacrament of the altar, the sacred body of our Savior Christ. And seeth the one side, and the continuance thereof, so clearly proved by many a thousand miracles, so clearly testified[137] by the virtuous and erudite books of all the old holy doctors from the apostles' time to our days; and seeth on the other side a fond friar and his fellows without wit[138] or grace bear us in hand[139] that all those holy fathers never understood the Scripture, but only these beasts that teach us vice as fast[140] as ever the others taught us virtue. And that seeth on the one side Saint Cyprian, Saint Jerome, Saint Ambrose, Saint Augustine, Saint Basil, Saint Chrysostom, Saint Gregory, and all the virtuous and cunning[141] doctors,

by row,[142] from the death of Christ and the time of his apostles till now, and seeth among all these neither priest, monk, nor friar that ever did, after his profession made, marry and take a wife, or any suffered[143] to break their vowed chastity,[144] in all their time; and seeth on the other side none other doctors of this new sect but Friar Luther and his wife, priest Pomeranus[145] and his wife, Friar Hussgen[146] and his wife, priest Karlstadt[147] and his wife, Dan Otho,[148] monk, and his wife, Friar Lambert[149] and his wife, frantic[150] Collins, and more frantic Tyndale, that saith all priests, monks, and friars must needs have wives — that man were, I say, as frantic as they both, that would rather send his soul with such a sort as these be than with all those holy saints that ever since Christ's days have testified by their holy handwriting that they died in the same faith that the Church believeth yet, and all this fifteen hundred years hath done, and shall do till the world's end. Go there never so many heretics out thereof, and leave it never so little, yet shall it remain and be well known always by the profession of that faith and those holy sacraments that have continued therein from the beginning thereof, and the holy doctors thereof ever had[151] in honor and reverence, and their acceptation with[152] God incessantly testified by miracles, which never one sort of so many sects of heretics could yet allege for any doctor of theirs, nor never shall, I think, till the great indignation of God, provoked by our sin and wretchedness, shall suffer[153] the head of all heretics, Antichrist (of whom these folk be the forewalkers),[154] to come into this wretched world, and therein to work such wonders that the sight thereof shall be able to put right wise men and good men in great doubt of the truth, seeing false Antichrist proving his preaching by miracles;[155] whereas now neither good man nor wise man can have any color[156] of excuse, if men were so mad to believe these mad masters of whom they see the principal archheretics, and first authors of the sect, neither show miracle for the proof of their doctrine, and yet their teaching and their living all

---

128 impartial; unbiased   **129** fit, proper   **130** debates   **131** an English gentleman whose wife's infidelity drove him mad. He was eventually executed for heresy after mocking the Eucharist.   **132** *lasheth out:* pours forth impetuously   **133** who   **134** held   **135** esteem   **136** *setting at nought:* valuing as nothing   **137** attested   **138** intelligence   **139** *bear us in hand:*

try to make us believe   **140** steadfastly   **141** learned   **142** *by row:* one after the other   **143** allowed   **144** celibacy   **145** John Bugenhagen married in 1522.   **146** the original surname of Johannes Oecolampadius, who married in 1528   **147** Andreas Bodenstein (1486–1541) married in 1522.   **148** Otho Brunfels (1488–1534), a former Carthusian

monk, married in 1524.   **149** Francis Lambert (1486–1530), a former Observant Franciscan, married in 1523.   **150** insane   **151** held   **152** *acceptation with:* approval by   **153** allow   **154** forerunners   **155** See Mt 24:24; Mk 13:22; 1 Jn 2:18–22; 4:2–3; 2 Jn 1:7; Rv 13: 1–4, 11–18; 16:13–14; 19:20; 2 Thes 2:3–12.   **156** pretext

set upon sin and beastly concupiscence — and so,[157] clean contrary to the doctrine of all the old holy doctors, for whom God hath and doth show so many miracles in his Church. Which, as I said, shall not fail to be conserved, and his right faith therein to be preserved, in despite of all the heretics that ever shall spring — Antichrist and all — and in spite of the devil, the great master of them all, whom Christ shall at the last restrain, and destroy his idol Antichrist, 'with the Spirit of his holy mouth,'[158] repairing and dilating[159] his Church again, and, gathering thereinto as well the remnant of the Jews[160] as all other sects abroad about the world, shall make all folk one flock under himself the Shepherd,[161] and shall deliver a glorious kingdom to his Father[162] of all the saved people from our former father Adam to the last day, from thenceforth to reign in heaven, in joy and bliss incogitable,[163] one everlasting day with his Father, himself, and the Holy Ghost[164] — which[165] send these seditious sects the grace to cease, and the favorers of those factions to amend, and us the grace that, stopping our ears from[166] the false enchantments[167] of all these heretics, we may, by the very faith of Christ's Catholic Church, so walk with charity in the way of good works in this wretched world that we may be partners of the heavenly bliss which the blood of God's own Son hath bought us unto.[168] And this prayer," quoth I, "serving us for grace, let us now sit down to dinner." Which we did.

And after dinner, departed he home toward you, and I to the Court.

Finis

Cum privilegio regali[169]
Anno Domini 1531 mense Maii[170]

---

157 so thus   158 2 Thes 2:8   159 expanding   160 See Rom 11:14–26.   161 See Jn 10:16.   162 See 1 Cor 15:24.   163 unthinkable, inconceivable   164 See Ps 144(145):13; Dn 2:44; 7:27; 1 Pt 2:11.   165 whom may it please to   166 against   167 See Ps 57(58):5.   168 See 1 Pt 1:18–19; Acts 20:28; 1 Cor 6:20; 7:23; Rv 5:9.   169 *Cum privilegio regali:* "With royal privilege"; i.e., published with royal permission   170 *Anno…Maii:* "In the month of May in the year of our Lord 1531"

ADDENDA TO BOOK 3, CHAPTER 7[1]

Every act of perjury is (as it seems to me) a mortal sin without any exception whatsoever.

But I think that perjury is a violation of a lawful oath. Otherwise, he who swears to kill someone would sin if he did not kill. If anything secret is entrusted to someone, he is bound by the divine law to conceal it: unless it be such a misdeed that, even if he is not called upon to do so, he is bound to reveal it—of which sort are plots of treason, or homicide and the like, unless such things are revealed in sacramental confession, where the seal of secrecy has another prerogative from divine law beyond the seal of secrecy born of natural law. If therefore any lawful secret is entrusted to anyone outside of confession, and if it is of such a kind that the revelation of it might harm the person who entrusted it, then he is bound by a double bond to conceal it: both because the thing was entrusted to him for safekeeping as a deposit, and because he is bound to conceal every-thing which, if it were not concealed, would harm his neighbor, no matter how it came to his knowledge, provided it is not a misdeed which it would benefit the state to reveal. No one has the power to tender an oath to anyone else binding him to reveal such a secret as can and should be kept hidden. If a general oath is tendered, it is always understood that it applies to misdeeds, the knowledge of which was acquired by the swearer in such a way that he can lawfully reveal them. If a particular kind of oath is tendered, even with the express clause saying: "whether you can lawfully or cannot lawfully, you will swear that you will indeed reveal," he ought to refuse this oath as unlawful, no less unlawful than if he were constrained to swear to kill a man. If, overcome by force, he swears, nevertheless he is not only not bound to discharge what he has sworn, but on the contrary he is bound not to discharge it. So where are we then? Will it be lawful for him to lie? I shall deny this if I follow Augustine's opinion; if I follow Jerome's, I won't deny it; for their opinions regarding the "officious" lie do not agree. But in the meanwhile I decide as follows: should he lie, he is not guilty of perjury because he is not violating a lawful oath. In Augustine's opinion, he must also, once he has taken the oath, stand fast on this point—that he will say that, even if he knew anything secret, he is unwilling to reveal it. And I say "according to Augustine," not because I remember that he said this in so many words, but because it seems to me clearly to follow from the way his thought develops. For I have satisfied myself that Augustine, even though he is unwilling that anyone should lie to preserve either his own or another's life, does not, nevertheless, want anyone, rather than he should lie, either to kill himself or someone else, or to bring that killing about by what he had said. Neither could he, therefore, betray a lawful secret, entrusted to him, if the revelation of it might harm whoever entrusted it to him.

I have treated this subject in the fourth[2] book of my *Dialogue*, not thoroughly enough, I think, but I don't remember.

---

1 This discussion of perjury "appears to have been composed by More as a brief note to himself during his incarceration in the Tower," as editor and translator Richard Sylvester notes (*CW* 6: 768).   **2** Actually, in the third book, chapter 7.

Sir Thomas More, bronze statue by L. Cubitt Bevis, on the banks of the Thames in front of Old Chelsea Church, London. This statue was unveiled in 1969 by the Speaker of the House of Commons. On the three other sides of the pedestal are inscribed: SCHOLAR, STATESMAN, SAINT. More's head is turned slightly to the left looking downstream toward his last journey. Beneath the statue is a reproduction of his signature, the signature that would have saved his life if he had taken the oath. The face, cross, hands, and chain are in gold leaf.

Sir Thomas More, by Hans Holbein the Younger, 1526–27. This early charcoal sketch, so different from Plate 2, is described in K. T. Parker's catalogue as agreeing "essentially with the head of More in the Basel drawing (fifth figure from the left) and presumably [having] preceded it" (see Plate 4a).

Plate 1

Tho: Moor L.ᵈ Chancelour

This life-size drawing in colored chalks indicates the careful preparation Holbein took before painting his famous oil portrait of More (facing page). As can be seen above, the outlines of More's face, nose, eyes, and neck have been pricked with a needle; the reverse of this drawing shows that charcoal was "pounced" through these holes for transfer to another preparatory cartoon or to Holbein's main canvas.

Plate 2

The rich, opulent colors of the clothing contrast with More's apparent disregard for appearances, as indicated by the facial stubble and the hair sticking out from his cap. Holbein portrays More with work in hand, thoughtfully gazing outward. He wears a chain of office as Chancellor of the Duchy of Lancaster. At the lower left, the year M.D.XXVII (i.e., 1527) appears, the year Holbein painted this portrait, More's fiftieth year.

Plate 3

(a) In this preparatory sketch from 1526–27 for his *More Family Portrait*, Hans Holbein the Younger depicts from left to right: Elizabeth (age 21), Margaret Giggs (22), Judge John More (76), Anne Cresacre (15), Sir Thomas (50), John (18), Henry Pattenson ("fool," 50), Cecily (20), Margaret (22), Lady Alice (57), and the family monkey. The names and ages are in the hand of Nicholas Kratzer. Emendation notes are in brown ink.

(b) *The Family of Sir Thomas More, ca.* 1530. The canvas and painting were likely begun by Hans Holbein the Younger and then completed by Rowland Lockey *ca.* 1593. The emendations indicated in the sketch above have been added (musical instruments, family monkey, classical books and not just small psalters, Lady Alice sitting, daughters shown pregnant…). The two dogs were added generations later. The life-size watercolor original of 1527 was destroyed in a fire in the eighteenth century.

Plate 4

(a–b) Details of Plate 4(b): The book identified on the shelf is Boethius's *Consolationis Philosophiae*, and under Elizabeth's arm is Seneca's *Epistulae,* which comprises 124 letters addressed to young Lucilius about the quest for wisdom. On the right, Margaret is shown deeply in thought, pointing to the word *demens* ("mad") in the chorus of the fourth act of Seneca's *Oedipus.* Lines 893–898 are shown on the right-hand page: "...while mad, the lad [Icarus] sought the stars, in strange arts trusting, and strove to vanquish true birds in flight." The opposite page of her book gives another approach to the troubles that "fate" seems to bring. Using terms from sailing, the Chorus of the play advises: "Were it mine to shape fate at my will, I would trim my sails to gentle winds, lest my yards tremble, bent 'neath a heavy blast."

(c) With the garden of More's Chelsea estate in the background and London in the far distance, Thomas More II (1531–1606) is seated with his wife Maria Scrope (1534–1607). Between them is their youngest son and heir Cresacre More (1572–1649), great-grandson and biographer of Sir Thomas More. More's love for gardens is seen in the settings of *Utopia* and of his 1529 *Dialogue,* in this "fair garden" of Chelsea (see pp. 1396, 1408), and in his wife's final plea to him in prison (p. 1411). For his imagery of the "garden of [the] soul," see pp. 477, 610, 1095, and 1116. An artistic rendition of his gardens at Chelsea is on page 264.

Plate 5

(a) Sir John More (1451–1530), 76, became a judge of the King's Bench in 1520, and was married for the fourth time when this sketch was done. His promotion to sergeant-at-law in 1503 may have been the occasion for his son's "Merry Jest" (p. 7).

(b) Elizabeth More (1506–64) married William Dauncey, son of Sir John Dauncey, Knight of the Body to Henry VIII. Like others in the More clan, he was imprisoned and found guilty of treason, but he was pardoned in 1544.

(c) John More (1508–47) married Anne Cresacre in 1529, signed the Oath of Supremacy in 1534, moved to Anne's Barnborough estate in Yorkshire, and was imprisoned in connection with the Plot of Prebendaries in 1543. He was convicted of treason but pardoned in 1544 upon signing again the Oath of Supremacy.

(d) Cecily More (1507–?) in 1525 married Giles Heron, wealthy heir of Sir John Heron, Treasurer of the Chamber of Henry VIII. Giles was attainted by Parliament for treason in 1540 and was hung, drawn, and quartered. No records exist about her life after 1540. Her eldest son, Thomas, regained the family lands in 1554.

Plate 6

(a) Adopted as a ward by the More family in 1524, Anne (1510–77) married John More in 1529; their son Thomas More II was born in 1531 and grandson Cresacre wrote a biography of his grandfather, published in 1630. Anne's estate became the family homestead.

(b) Margaret Giggs (1508–70), an adopted daughter, was a scholar of Greek, mathematics, and medicine. In 1526 she married John Clement (present but silent in *Utopia*). The only family member at More's execution in 1535, Giggs later escaped to Louvain in 1547 and helped with More's 1557 *Workes*.

(c) Lady Alice More (*ca.* 1474–*ca.* 1551) had been married to the wealthy London merchant John Middleton, who died in 1509. She married Thomas More in 1511, and Erasmus marveled at how well the two, with quite different temperaments, worked and lived together.

(d) Hans Holbein the Younger (*ca.* 1497–1543) painted this self-portrait in 1542–43, when he had long established his reputation in England. He first came to England in late 1526, stayed at More's home, and received his first commissions from and through More.

Plate 7

(a) Margaret Roper (1505–44), "Meg," was the oldest of More's children and the most intellectually accomplished. Above she is depicted at "30 years," which would be the year of her father's death in 1535. She holds her Book of Hours and is wearing a medallion on which St. Michael grapples with Lucifer. She was the first non-royal woman to publish a book in England, and she was proficient in Greek, Latin, medicine, and liberal learning. Her daughter Mary Basset was also exceptionally learned, translating books from Greek and Latin, including her grandfather's *De tristitia*.

(b) William Roper (1496–1578) lived in the More household from *ca.* 1518 to 1534. He married Margaret More in 1521, served as a member of four Parliaments, and kept his office of prothonotary of the Court of King's Bench for fifty-four years. In 1543 he was imprisoned for four months, allegedly for plotting to discredit Cranmer. He was later released with a severe reprimand, a fine of £100, and the requirement to sign again the Oath of Succession. In 1568, he was called before the Privy Council for helping finance Catholic exiles. He wrote his *Life of More ca.* 1555, but it was not printed until 1626. Here he is depicted at "42 years." This is the only known portrait of Roper.

(c) The title page of Margaret's *Devout Treatise,* published in 1524; it shows a young teacher sitting at her lectern.

(d) Richard III, last of the kings of York, reigned from 1483 until he was defeated and killed at Bosworth Field by Henry Tudor in 1485. Shakespeare's first tetralogy is on the Wars of the Roses, based largely on Thomas More's *History of King Richard III*.

Plate 8

(a) Queen Elizabeth of York (1465–1503) is featured in More's early poem "Rueful Lamentation." Elizabeth is holding a white rose of the Yorks, but having married Henry VII, a red rose Lancastrian, she wears a pendant in the shape of the famous "Tudor rose," uniting red and white.

(b) Henry Tudor (1457–1509), holding a red rose, defeated Richard III in 1485 and ended the Wars of the Roses; he assumed the throne as Henry VII. Thomas More's "Coronation Ode" for Henry VIII does not speak favorably of Henry VII and his approach to government.

(c–d) Thomas More wrote Epigram 276 to thank Erasmus and Peter Giles for the gift of this diptych they had commissioned Quentin Metsys to paint in 1517. In his portrait, Erasmus wears a ring given to him by More; among the books identified on his shelf are Lucian and *Mor[iae] Encomium,* the latter having been written in More's house, at More's suggestion, and playing upon More's name. Other books identified are Erasmus's edition of Saint Jerome and his Greek edition of the New Testament. See the detail of this painting on p. 1368. Giles is holding in his hand a letter from More; the books identified on his shelves are Plutarch, Seneca, Suetonius, and Erasmus's *Education of a Christian Prince.*

Plate 9

(a) Both Thomas More and Thomas Cromwell began their careers at Court by working closely with Thomas Wolsey (1473–1530), here depicted *ca.* 1520, when serving as Lord Chancellor, Archbishop of York, Cardinal, and Papal Legate.

(b) On the outside of the letter on Cromwell's table is written, "To our trusty and right well beloved Counsaillor Thomas Cromwell, Maister of o[u]r Jewell House." Holbein painted this portrait in 1532–33. Cromwell was arrested and executed in 1540.

(c) Praised in the opening of *Utopia* and a longtime friend of More, Cuthbert Tunstall (1474–1559), skilled diplomat and humanist, became bishop of London and then of Durham, living during the reigns of four Tudor monarchs and dying under house arrest for refusing the Oath of Supremacy in 1559 under Elizabeth I.

(d) In 1532, octogenarian William Warham (*ca.* 1450–1532), Archbishop of Canterbury, incurred the wrath of Henry VIII in February by formally protesting anticlerical legislation; in May, Warham and leaders of Convocation accepted Henry's Supremacy; in August, Warham died writing a legal defense repeatedly invoking St. Thomas Becket.

Plate 10

(a) John Fisher (*ca.* 1469–1535), Bishop of Rochester, promoted education at both Oxford and Cambridge, became Queen Catherine's major defender, and was imprisoned in the Tower and then attainted and executed like More.

(b) In 1522, Henry VIII asked his counselor Thomas More to respond "in kind" to Martin Luther's strident and scatological *Against Henry*, written in reply to Henry's 1521 *Defense of the Seven Sacraments*. Erasmus strongly opposed Luther's alleged denial of free will, and More encouraged Erasmus to write *Hyperaspistes I & II.*

(c) William Tyndale (1494–1536) and Thomas More had extensive exchanges. More's *Confutation of Tyndale* is over 1,000 pages in *CW* 8. The couplet beneath Tyndale's hand has been translated: "To scatter Roman darkness by this light / The loss of land and life I'll reckon slight."

(d) Thomas Cranmer (1489–1556) became Archbishop of Canterbury in October 1532, annulled Henry's marriage to Catherine May 23, 1533, validated Henry's marriage to Anne on May 28, and anointed Anne queen on June 1. He compiled the first two editions of *The Book of Common Prayer* during Edward VI's reign.

Plate 11

The Field of the Cloth of Gold, artist unknown, *ca.* 1545, Hampton Court. In this spectacular display of wealth and power, Henry VIII brought 6,000 in his English entourage and 2,000 horses to a field outside of Guisnes, France, in addition to the 6,000 workmen from England and Flanders who had been sent ahead to build the temporary palace, the city of tents, and the tournament fields. The occasion was peace talks with King Francis I on June 7–24, 1520. The painting is a composite of several major events: on the left, Henry's procession to meet Francis on June 7; on the right, the feasting, meetings, and jousts of the days following.

Plate 12

Directly in back of the temporary palace is the King's gold dining tent; further back in another tent of gold can be seen the wrestling match between King Henry (who lost) and King Francis. In front of the two-story temporary palace is a fountain that flowed with red and white wines. In the upper left is a flying dragon, part of the celebratory display. In the distant left is Calais; in the distant right is the French town of Ardres, where the French contingent stayed. Queen Catherine, Thomas More, Erasmus, and William Budé were among the many who attended.

Plate 13

At the bottom, center, Thomas More as Speaker of the House stands behind the bar with members of the Commons. This is the earliest known depiction of More. In watercolor and goldleaf, this elaborate seating plan depicts the 1523 Parliament. On King Henry's immediate right are seated Archbishops Warham and Wolsey; standing behind the bench is Bishop of London Tunstall holding the roll of his opening speech. To the King's left, behind the bench, are the Treasurer and Comptroller of the Royal Household. Three earls stand on the carpet decorated with lilies; one holds the cap of maintenance; one, the upraised sword of state; another, the white wand of office. Between the throng of eldest sons of peers and the front temporal bench is the Garter King of Arms, Thomas Wriothesley. At the top of the front temporal bench are the Duke of Norfolk (with gold baton as Earl Marshall) and Duke of Suffolk wearing coronets and four ducal bars of white miniver. Below them are seven earls (with three ducal bars), behind whom and on the cross bench are sixteen barons (with two ducal bars) and the prior of St. John's in black. Ten bishops in red and seventeen abbots in black are seated to the King's right. Seated in the middle on wool sacks are ten judges (the two chief judges on the top bench; More's father, Judge John More, among the others) and four sergeants of law, behind whom are two recording clerks.

Plate 14

This painting is one of eight depicting "The Building of Britain" in St. Stephen's Hall, the main entrance to Great Britain's Parliament in the Palace of Westminster. The caption below this mural reads: "Sir Thomas More as Speaker of the Commons in spite of Cardinal Wolsey's imperious demand refuses to grant King Henry the Eighth a subsidy without due debate by the House, 1523." At the beginning of that same Parliament of 1523, More made the first recorded petition and defense for freedom of speech (see Roper's *Life* and Edward Hall's *Chronicles* for accounts of both events, pp. 1387, 1393–94). In this 10′ × 14.5′ painting, More calmly points to the mace and the book of laws that are on the table, symbols of an authority greater than either Cardinal and Lord Chancellor Thomas Wolsey or himself. Wolsey's youthful attendants carry the instruments of Wolsey's royal and ecclesiastical power: "his maces, his pillars, his pole-axes, his crosses, his hat, and the Great Seal, too" (p. 1395). Behind More are the older and serious faces of the burgesses and knights of the shire. Thomas Cromwell is standing behind Speaker More's chair.

Plate 15

This 1667 copy of the original 1537 mural (9′ × 12′) shows a triumphant King Henry VIII, his father King Henry VII, his mother Queen Elizabeth of York, and his wife Jane Seymour, mother of Prince Edward. The poem in the middle is "couched in the forcefully panegyric language of an imperial conquerer, neatly complementing the visual symbolism of the 'imperial Roman' bust in the roundel above the central plinth" (catalogue, London: Walker Museum, 2003). Gerald Malsbary's translation of the poem is: "If it pleases you to gaze upon the glorious figures of heroes, / Behold these: no painting ever brought any greater to view. / The contest, the dispute, the question is great: / Who is the greater, father or son? Well, both win the prize: / The former put down his enemies, and often stopped the destructive / Fires of his country, so as finally to restore peace to his citizens. / The son, born to greater things, removed unworthy priests / From the altars, and replaced them with good ones. / The arrogance of popes has yielded to sure virtue, / Now that Henry the Eighth holds the scepter in his hand. / Religion has been restored, now that he is king, / And the teachings of God are beginning to be held in their proper honor."

Plate 16

Hans Holbein's *The Ambassadors* commemorates these two French diplomats' involvement in a London event that took place at 10:30 a.m. on April 11, 1533 (see pillar dial and sundials) — Good Friday (see crucifix in upper left), the day and time when Archbishop Thomas Cranmer asked to hear Henry VIII's case for annulling the marriage to Catherine of Aragon. On the left is Jean de Dinteville, 29, the resident ambassador from France; his estate, "Policy," is identified on the terrestrial globe. On the right is bishop-elect and French ambassador-at-large George de Selve, 25. The mosaic on the floor replicates the one around Edward the Confessor's tomb in the sanctuary of Westminster Abbey, the spot where Anne Boleyn would be crowned queen on June 1, 1533. The death's head or skull in the middle of the floor is clearly visible only when viewed from a particular angle and is a famous example of anamorphism. The broken string on the lute, the open book of division, the Lutheran hymnal, and the instruments of navigation all contribute to the puzzling assortment of elements in this painting.

Plate 17

(a) Catherine of Aragon (1485–1536) often said
"More alone was worthy of the position and the
name" of counselor (Stapleton 76). She was married
to Prince Arthur 1501–02. In 1509, she married
Henry VIII and was divorced in 1533. Mary was
born in 1516.

(b) Anne Boleyn (1501–36) married Henry VIII
secretly in January 1533. Thomas More refused to
attend her coronation in June 1533. Elizabeth
was born September 7. Anne was accused of high
treason in April 1536 and executed May 19 for
incest, adultery, and plotting to kill the King.

(c) John Colet (1467–1519) was a leading humanist,
dean of St. Paul's, and founder of St. Paul's School.
Young Thomas More chose him as his spiritual
guide (see Letters 3 and 8), and Colet is probably
the one who introduced More to Pico della
Mirandola's writings.

(d) John Houghton was prior of the London Charterhouse,
which More had frequented during and after his law-school
days. Houghton was one of four monks whom Thomas
More and Margaret saw from his prison window being
dragged to Tyburn on May 4, 1535 for execution.

Plate 18

(a) John Morton (*ca.* 1420–1500), Archbishop of Canterbury and Lord Chancellor of England, persuaded More's father to send More to Oxford. At twelve, More served as a page in Morton's palace at Lambeth. Morton has a prominent place in More's *Richard III* and *Utopia*.

(b) Thomas Howard (1473–1554), Duke of Norfolk, is shown here with gold baton as Earl Marshal, white wand as Lord Treasurer, and collar of the Order of the Garter with the St. George pendant. He was one of the nineteen commissioners appointed to preside at More's trial.

(c) William Grocyn (*ca.* 1446–1519), one of More's most learned teachers, invited the twenty-three-year-old More to give lectures on Augustine's *City of God* at his church in London. The six medallions cite these features of his life: Born 1446, died 1519; Educated at New College, Oxford; Divinity Reader at Magdalen; Prebendary of Lincoln; Taught Greek at Oxford; Rector of St. Lawrence Jewry, 1496.

(d) Thomas Linacre (ca. 1460–1524) studied Greek and medicine in Italy. He achieved fame as a physician and translator of Aristotle and Galen, became the King's physician, and was a founder and first president of the Royal College of Physicians in London. He was a mentor to young Thomas More and part of the "More circle."

Plate 19

More was imprisoned on the first floor of the Bell Tower (*upper left*). He expected to be hung, drawn, and quartered on July 6, but the day before was informed that King Henry remitted his execution to beheading. The 1555 engraving (*bottom*) shows the 1535 hanging and quartering of the Carthusians. More (*upper right*) on his way to execution.

Plate 20

The Supplication of Souls

In February 1529 Simon Fish smuggled into England his sixteen-page anticlerical pamphlet entitled *A Supplication for the Beggars*, published in Antwerp and dedicated to King Henry VIII. The pamphlet described the helpless condition of England's poor and blamed the English clergy for their ravenous greed in requiring that the poor pay for the clergy's prayers for those souls of relatives and friends who were supposedly in purgatory. In October 1529, More published his response, over ten times longer than Fish's pamphlet, defending the clergy and the existence of purgatory. Addressed "to all good Christian people," this refutation takes the form of a letter from the souls suffering in purgatory, writing to their relatives and friends in England for "help, comfort, and relief."

The three main motives More identifies for Fish's attack in *A Supplication of Beggars* are: the hatred of the clergy; the desire to confiscate the clergy's property; and the desire to spread the teachings of Luther and Tyndale. Germain Marc'hadour explains the power and danger of Fish's appeal, given the broader political context in which his pamphlet first appeared: "Since Henry was already aware of the plea for royal supremacy over the Church contained in Tyndale's *Obedience of a Christian Man*, Fish's tirade against the clergy, accusing them of every abomination from extortion to adultery, and his plea for confiscation of all their properties and income, made a potentially dangerous appeal to a king already impatient of clerical delays in the great matter of his divorce" (*CW* 7: lxvii). More also manifests concern that the author has used "a very wise fashion of flattery" in addressing his pamphlet to the King. More's rapid and lengthy response to Fish's pamphlet is explained in part by More's identification here of the strategy that eventually prevailed against the clergy and their liberty: begin with known abuses of some clergy; extend and exaggerate those abuses to all clergy, while inventing new crimes worthy of removing the clergy's traditional independence in matters of spiritual jurisdiction. As the purgatorial souls strongly put it, *A Supplication of Beggars* "is much grounded upon many great lies"—slanders they repeatedly call "malicious" and "seditious," with the intent to bring the clergy "in displeasure of the King and hatred of the people" and thus to "destroy the Church" and its long-standing "spiritual jurisdiction" in England.

More responds to Fish in Book 1 by arguing that Fish's claims are marred by dissimulation, false calculations, and railing rhetoric, as well as numerous lies and foolish assertions about the clergy. More contends that Fish's arguments really aim to support the "new gospel" of Luther and Tyndale, which promises "Christian freedom" while "spurring forward the devilish unbridled appetite of lewd, seditious, and rebellious liberty." More fears that this new theology will "infect and corrupt the people," who do not perceive its character and motivation clearly, and will ultimately lead them to adopt an "obstinate, rebellious mind against all laws, rule, and governance." More's emphasis on the appeal of reformers to a new doctrine of liberty links his thinking here in the *Supplication* to his other polemical books such as *The Response to Luther*, *The Dialogue of Sir Thomas More*, and *Confutation of Tyndale*, which also address free will and the "spice" of the new theology's rhetoric about liberty.

Book 2 of *The Supplication of Souls* is More's defense of purgatory, beginning with reason and proceeding through arguments based on Scripture, the Church fathers, and Church tradition. The Yale edition includes an account of the teaching about purgatory, conciliar definitions of purgatory, and disputes between More, Fisher, Luther, and John Frith (*CW* 7: lxxxvii–cxvii).

CONTENTS

The Supplication of Souls

made by Sir Thomas More — Knight, Councilor to our Sovereign Lord the King, and Chancellor of his Duchy of Lancaster — against *The Supplication of Beggars*

To all good Christian people.

In most piteous wise[1] continually calleth and crieth upon your devout charity and most tender pity, for help, comfort, and relief, your late[2] acquaintance — kindred, spouses, companions, playfellows, and friends — and now your humble and unacquainted and half-forgotten suppliants, poor prisoners of God, the seely[3] souls in purgatory, here abiding and enduring the grievous pains and hot cleansing fire that fretteth[4] and burneth out the rusty and filthy spots of our sin till the mercy of almighty God, the rather[5] by your good and charitable means, vouchsafe[6] to deliver us hence.

From whence if ye marvel why we more now molest[7] and trouble you with our writing than ever we were wont[8] before, it may like you to wit[9] and understand that hitherto, though we have been with many folk much forgotten of[10] negligence, yet hath always good folk remembered us; and we have been recommended unto God and eased, helped, and relieved both by the private prayers of good virtuous people, and specially by the daily Masses and other ghostly suffrages[11] of priests, religious, and folk of Holy Church. But now since that of late there are sprungen up certain seditious persons, which[12] not only travail and labor to destroy them by whom we be much helped, but also to sow and set forth such a pestilent opinion against ourselves as, once received and believed among the people, must needs take from us the relief and comfort that ever should come to us by the charitable alms, prayer, and good works of the world, ye may take it for no wonder though[13] we seely souls that have long lain and cried so far from you that we seldom break your sleep, do now in this our great fear of our utter loss forever of your loving remembrance and relief, not yet importunately bereave[14] you of your rest with crying at your ears at unseasonable time when ye would (as we do never) repose yourselves and take ease, but only procure[15] to be presented unto you this poor book, this humble supplication of ours, which it may please you parcelmeal[16] at your leisure to look over for all seely souls' sake, that it may be as a wholesome treacle[17] at your heart against the deadly poison of their pestilent persuasion that would bring you in that error to ween[18] there were no purgatory.

Of all which cruel persons so procuring,[19] not the diminishment of your mercy toward us but the utter spoil and robbery of our whole help and comfort that should come from you, the very worst and thereby the most deadly deviser of our pains and heaviness[20] (God forgive him) is that dispiteous and despiteful[21] person which[22] of late, under pretext of pity, made and put forth among you a book that he named *The Supplication for the Beggars*: a book indeed nothing less intending than the pity that it pretendeth, nothing minding the weal[23] of any man, but, as we shall hereafter show you, much harm and mischief to all men, and among other great sorrow, discomfort, and heaviness unto us, your even-Christian and nigh kin,[24] your late neighbors and pleasant companions upon earth, and now poor prisoners here.

And albeit that[25] his unhappy book doth for our own part touch us very near, yet we be much more moved to give the world warning of his venomous writing for the dear love and charity that we bear to you than for the respect[26] of our own relief. For as for us, albeit that the gracious help of your prayer, alms-deeds, and other good works for us may be

---

1 ways **2** former; recent **3** pitiable, poor; helpless **4** consumes; chafes **5** sooner **6** grant **7** disturb **8** accustomed **9** know **10** out of, due to **11** *ghostly suffrages:* spiritual prayers for the dead

12 who **13** if **14** *importunately bereave:* in an untimely way deprive **15** endeavor; ask **16** piecemeal; a little at a time **17** antidote **18** believe **19** endeavoring **20** sadness, grief **21** *dispiteous and*

despiteful: pitiless and cruel **22** who **23** well-being **24** *even-christian . . . kin:* fellow Christians and close relatives **25** *albeit that:* although **26** consideration; regard

the means of relieving and releasing of our present pains, yet such is the merciful goodness of God that, though the whole world would clean forget us, yet would his mercy so remember us, that, after temporal punishment and purging here, he will not finally forget to take us hence, and wiping all the tears out of our eyes, translate[27] us at sundry times, as his high wisdom seeth convenient,[28] into that eternal heavenly bliss to which his holy blessed blood hath bought us. But surely to you worldly people living there upon earth — not only for this present time, but also for as long as this world shall endure — the wretched maker of that ungracious[29] book (whom God give once the grace to repent and amend), if folk were so fond[30] to follow him, should not fail to work as well much worldly trouble to every kind of people as, over[31] that (which most loss were of all) to bring many a good simple soul, for lack of belief of purgatory, the very straight way to hell.

And the case so standing, there would, we think, no man doubt but though[32] the man that made the book were well known among you, and in hold[33] also — whereby, his heinous treason to God and the world disclosed and declared by us, he might be in peril of exquisite[34] painful punishment — yet we both might and ought, rather to put him in the danger of his own demeanor,[35] than for the sparing of his just correction, to suffer him abuse[36] the people with his pestilent writing, to the inestimable harm of the whole world in goods, body, and soul. And since we so might of reason, and so should of charity, though the man were known and taken,[37] how much may we now more frankly tell you all, and nothing[38] shall need to spare him, since his book is nameless,[39] and so himself among you unknown and thereby out of the peril of any punishment for his unhappy deed?

But for[40] that both ye and he shall well perceive that we desire but your weal[41] and ours by giving you warning of his malice, and nothing intend to procure his punishment — which we rather beseech our Lord of his mercy to remit — ye shall understand that neither is his name nor person unknown among us, and therefore we might well discover him if we were so minded. For there is not only some of his acquaintance and counsel, whom God gave at their death the grace to repent, come hither to purgatory — nothing more now lamenting among us than their cruel unkindness toward us, in giving counsel against us to the making of that ungracious book, with infidelity and lack of belief of the purging fire which they now find and feel — but he is also named and boasted among us by that evil angel of his, our and your ghostly[42] enemy, the devil. Which[43] as soon as he had set him awork with that pernicious book, ceased not to come hither and boast it among us; but, with his enemious and envious laughter, gnashing the teeth and grinning, he told us that his people had by the advice and counsel of him and of some heretics almost as evil as he, made such a book for beggars that it should make us beg long ere we get aught,[44] whereby he trusted that some of us should not so soon creep out of our pain as we had hoped.

Wit[45] ye well, these words were heavy tidings to us. But yet because the devil is wont[46] to lie, we took some comfort in that we could not believe him, specially telling a thing so far incredible. For who could ever have thought that any Christian man could for very pity have founden in his heart to seek and study the means whereby a Christian man should think it labor lost to pray for all Christian souls?

But alack the while,[47] we found soon after that the falsehood and malice of the man proved the devil true. For by some that died soon after the book put forth, we have heard and perceived the wretched contents thereof, well and plainly declaring what evil spirit inspired him while it was in making. For albeit that[48] it is so contrived and the words so couched that, by the secret inward working of the devil that helped to devise it, a simple reader might by delight in the reading be deadly corrupted and venomed, yet if a wise man well warned advisedly will weigh the sentence,[49] he shall find the whole book nothing else but falsehood under pretext of plainness, cruelty under the cloak of pity, sedition under the color[50] of counsel, proud arrogance under the name of supplication, and under the pretense of favor unto poor folk, a devilish desire of noyance[51] both to poor and rich, priest, religious,

---

27 transport **28** appropriate; suitable
29 devoid of grace; wicked **30** foolish
as **31** beyond **32** even if **33** custody
34 excruciating **35** behavior **36** *suffer him abuse:* allow him to deceive

37 arrested **38** not at all **39** published anonymously **40** so **41** well-being
42 spiritual **43** Who **44** *ere … aught:* before we get anything **45** Know
46 accustomed **47** *alack the while:*

alas the times **48** *albeit that:* although
49 meaning, sense **50** appearance, pretext
51 harm

and layman, prince, lord, and people, as well quick[52] as dead.

He deviseth a piteous bill of complaint and supplication, feigned to be by the poor, sick, and sore[53] beggars put up to the King, lamenting therein their number "so sore[54] increased" that, good folks' alms "not half" sufficing to find them meat,[55] they be constrained heavily to "die for hunger."[56] Then layeth[57] he the cause of all these poor beggars—both their increase in number and their default in finding[58]— all this he layeth to the only[59] fault of the clergy, naming them in his bead-roll:[60] "bishops, abbots, priors,[61] deacons, archdeacons,[62] suffragans,[63] priests, monks, canons,[64] friars, pardoners,[65] and summoners."[66] All these he calleth mighty, sturdy[67] beggars and "idle holy thieves," which, he saith, hath "begged so importunately that they have gotten into their hands" the "third part"[68] of all the realm of England, besides tithes, privy tithes,[69] probates of testaments[70] and offerings, with mass-pennies[71] and mortuaries,[72] blessing and cursing, citing,[73] suspending, and soiling.[74] Then cometh he particularly to friars, to whom he maketh, as he thinketh, a plain and open reckoning[75] that they receive by begging through the realm yearly 43,333 pounds, six shillings, eight pence sterling. Then showeth he that all this cast[76] together amounteth yearly far above the half of the whole substance[77] of the realm.

After this, presupposing as though he had proved it that the clergy hath the half, he then, to prove the two-hundredth part of that[78] they have were more than sufficient for them, taketh for his ground that if the number of them be compared with the number of laymen, the clergy be not the hundredth part; and that if they be compared with the lay men, women, and children, the clergy is not then the four-hundredth person of that number. And then intendeth he thereby to prove and conclude that since they have, as he saith, more than the half of altogether,[79] and be themselves not fully the four-hundredth part, therefore if that better half that they have were divided into two hundred parts, then were yet one part of those two hundred parts, as he thinketh, too much for them—specially because they labor not. After this, he gathereth a great heap of evils wherewith he belieth[80] the clergy to bring them in displeasure of the King and hatred of the people.

And lest men should anything[81] esteem the clergy for the suffrages of their prayer in relief of us seely[82] Christian souls in purgatory, to take away that good mind out of good Christian men's hearts, he laboreth to make the world ween[83] that there were no purgatory at all. Wherein, when he hath done what he can, then laboreth he to the King for a license to rail upon the clergy—saying that there is none other effectual remedy against them but[84] that it might please the King to give him and such others free license and liberty to defame the clergy at their pleasure among the people. For he saith that if any of them be punished anything in the temporal[85] laws, then they sore[86] trouble the laborers thereof by the spiritual[87] law, and then the heads of the clergy do so highly more than recompense the loss of their fellows[88] that they may be bold to do the like offense again at their pleasure.

And for to prove that it is always so, he layeth that it hath been so thrice, and as it shall after be showed, he lieth in all three. The first he layeth that the Bishop of London was in a great rage "for indicting of certain curates[89] of extortion and incontinency[90] the last year, in the wardmote quests."[91] And for the second he layeth that Doctor Alen,[92] after that he was punished by Praemunire[93] for his contempt committed against the King's temporal law, was therefor[94] by the bishops highly recompensed

---

52 living   **53** physically suffering
54 greatly   **55** *find them meat:* provide
them with food   **56** *He … hunger:* See
A Supplication for the Beggars in *CW* 7:
412/3–10. The quotation here, as well as
the quotations and paraphrases below,
is from *CW* 7: 412–22.   **57** ascribes;
alleges   **58** *default in finding:* lack of being
provided for   **59** *to the only:* solely to the
60 prayer-list, but here ironic since a bead-
roll is normally a list of people to be prayed
for, rather than blamed   **61** assistants to
the abbots in monasteries   **62** assistants to
the bishops   **63** bishops not in charge of

dioceses   **64** members of religious orders
who are not as strictly bound as monks, but
more so than friars   **65** priests authorized
to collect money donated to obtain papal
indulgences   **66** ecclesiastical officers who
summoned people to appear in the bishop's
or archdeacon's court   **67** violent; strong
68 *the "third part":* one-third   **69** *privy
tithes:* tithes levied on eggs, fowl, and
fruit   **70** wills   **71** an offering given for
having a Mass said for a person who has
died   **72** payments to priests for funerals
73 *cursing, citing:* excommunicating, summoning to appear before an ecclesiastical

court   **74** absolving (either from sin or
from ecclesiastical censure)   **75** *open
reckoning:* public calculation   **76** put
77 wealth   **78** what   **79** everything
80 slanders   **81** at all   **82** poor; helpless
83 think   **84** except   **85** civil   **86** grievously   **87** ecclesiastical   **88** fellow
clergymen   **89** parish priests   **90** unchastity   **91** *wardmote quests:* the inquests
held in each ward in London   **92** John
Alen (1476–1534), at that time Cardinal
Wolsey's commissary   **93** a statute that
forbade appealing to any foreign court or
authority, e.g., Rome   **94** for that

in benefices.⁹⁵ And for the third he layeth that Richard Hunne,⁹⁶ because he had sued a Praemunire against a priest for suing him in the spiritual court in a matter determinable in the King's court, was accused of heresy and committed to Bishop's Prison, where he saith that "all the world knoweth" that he was murdered by Doctor Horsey with his accomplices, then the Bishop's Chancellor, and that the same Doctor Horsey (he saith upon other men's mouths) "paid six hundred pounds for him and his accomplices," and after obtained the King's "most gracious pardon." Whereupon he saith the "captains" of the spiritualty,⁹⁷ because he had "foughten so manfully against the King's crown and dignity," "promoted" him forth "with benefice upon benefice, to the value of four times as much." And by these examples he concludeth there will no such punishment serve against the spiritualty, and also who that⁹⁸ justly punish a priest by the temporal law is unjustly troubled again⁹⁹ in the spiritual law. Whereof he would conclude that of necessity, for a special remedy, the King must needs grant a license to such lewd¹⁰⁰ fellows to rail upon them.

Then cometh he at last unto the device¹⁰¹ of some remedy for the poor beggars—wherein he would in no wise have none hospitals made, because he saith that therein the profit goeth to the priests. What remedy then for the poor beggars? He deviseth nor desireth nothing to be given them, nor none other alms or help requireth¹⁰² for them, but only that the King's Highness would first take from the whole clergy all their whole living, and then set them "abroad in the world to get them wives" and "to get their living with the labor" of their hands and "in the sweat of their faces," as he saith it is "the commandment of God" in the first chapter of Genesis,¹⁰³ and finally to tie them "to the carts to be whipped naked about every market town till they fall to labor."¹⁰⁴ And then if these petitions were once granted and performed, he showeth many great commodities¹⁰⁵ that would, as he saith, ensue thereupon, both to the King and the people, and

to the poor beggars. Which things we shall, ere¹⁰⁶ we leave, in such wise repeat and ponder that your wisdoms¹⁰⁷ may consider and perceive in yourselves what good fruit would follow the speed¹⁰⁸ of his goodly supplication, whereof we have rehearsed¹⁰⁹ you the whole sum and effect.

Truth it is that many things wherewith he flourisheth¹¹⁰ his matters to make them seem gay¹¹¹ to the readers at a sudden show, we leave out for the while¹¹² because we would,¹¹³ ere we come thereto, that ye should first have the matter itself in short set forth before your eyes. And then shall we peruse his proofs and in such wise consider everything apart¹¹⁴ that we nothing doubt but whoso¹¹⁵ shall read his worshipful¹¹⁶ writing after shall soon perceive therein flourishing without fruit, subtlety without substance, rhetoric without reason, bold babbling without learning, and wiliness without wit.¹¹⁷ And finally, for the foundation and ground of all his proofs, ye shall find in his book not half so many leaves¹¹⁸ as lies, but almost as many lies as lines.

And albeit¹¹⁹ we lie here in that case¹²⁰ that about the examination and answering of such a mad malicious book we have neither lust¹²¹ nor leisure to bestow the time, whereof misspent in our life we give now a hard and a heavy reckoning, yet not only the necessity of our cause driveth us to declare unto you the feebleness of his reasons wherewith he would bring you in the case to care nothing for us, believing that there were no purgatory, but also most specially doth our charity toward you stir us to show you the mischief that he mindeth¹²² to yourselves as well in that point of infidelity as in all the remnant of his seditious book. In answering whereof, we would gladly let his folly and lack of learning pass if it were not more than necessary that all folk should perceive his little learning and less wit, lest simple folk, weening¹²³ him wise and well-learned, might unto their harm esteem his evil writing the better for their wrong opinion of his wit and learning. As for his malicious mind and untruth, there can no

95 gifts; ecclesiastical livings **96** *Richard Hunne:* He was a merchant tailor in London who in 1511 refused to pay the funeral fee for burying his infant son. After Hunne filed a lawsuit against another priest over a real estate dispute, his own parish priest sued him for the funeral fee. After the Church court ruled against Hunne, he filed a Praemunire suit challenging the jurisdiction of that court. There were other lawsuits filed on both sides. Eventually, Hunne's home was raided, heretical materials were found, and he was imprisoned on the charge of heresy. He died in prison under suspicious circumstances in December 1514. **97** clergy **98** *who that:* whoever **99** in return **100** evil **101** devising **102** requests **103** See Gn 3:19. **104** *fall to labor:* start doing manual labor **105** advantages; benefits **106** before **107** *your wisdoms:* you wise people **108** success **109** told **110** embellishes **111** fine, beautiful; enjoyable **112** time **113** desire **114** *everything apart:* each thing by itself **115** *nothing…whoso:* have no doubt that whoever **116** honorable **117** intelligence **118** pages **119** although **120** condition, state **121** desire **122** intends **123** thinking

man look[124] that we should leave untouched but he that would rather the man were believed than answered, and would wish his bill sped[125] were it never so malicious and false.

For where he so deviseth his introduction as[126] all his purpose should have a great face of charity, by that he speaketh all in the name of the poor beggars, this is nothing else but the devil's drift,[127] always covering his poison under some taste of sugar.

As for us, we trust there will no wise man doubt what favor we bear to beggars as folk of their own fellowship and faculty,[128] and of all whom there be nowhere in the world neither so needy nor so sore[129] and so sick, nor so impotent and so sore[130] in pains, as we and that so far-forth[131] that if ye might see them all on the one side and but one of us on the other side, we be very sure that the world would pity one of us more than them all. But although we be more beggars than your beggars be, as folk daily begging our alms of you and them both, yet envy we not them as one of them doth another, but we pray and require[132] you to give[133] them for our sakes, whereby your gift greatly comforteth us both. And they be also our proctors[134] and beg in our name, and in our name receive your money, whereof we receive both your devotion and their prayers, so that ye may be well assured there could be put no bill nor supplication forth for their advantage which we would in any wise hinder, but very gladly further in all that ever we might.

But in good faith, as our poor brethren the beggars be for many causes greatly to be pitied for their disease and sickness, sorrow, pain, and poverty, so do we much in this case sorrow their mishap that they have not had at the leastwise so much fortune as to fall upon a wiser scrivener[135] to make their supplication; but upon such a one as under his great wiliness showeth so little wit that, beginning with a cloak of charity, doth by and by[136] no less disclose his hatred and malice than if he nothing else had intended but to cast off the cloak and set out his malice naked to the show. Wherein like a beggars' proctor he goeth forth so nakedly that no beggar is there so bare of cloth or money as he showeth

himself bare of faith, learning, troth,[137] wit, or charity. Which thing, as it already well appeareth to wise men, so will we make it evident to all men, taking our beginning at the declaration of his untruth, which one thing well perceived will be sufficient to answer and overturn all his whole enterprise. Howbeit,[138] we neither shall need nor do purpose to cumber[139] you with rehearsal and reproof[140] of all his lies, for that were too long a work, whereof we fear ye should be weary to abide the hearing. But of so many we shall pray you take patience while we show you some, and such as for the matter be requisite to be known, forasmuch as all his proofs be specially[141] grounded upon them.

And first, to begin where he beginneth, when he saith that the number of such beggars as he pretendeth to speak for—that is, as himself calleth them, "the wretched, hideous monsters, on whom," he saith, "scarcely any eye dare look, the foul unhappy sort of lepers and other sore people, needy, impotent, blind, lame, and sick, living only of alms"[142]— have their number now "so sore increased that all the alms of all the well-disposed people of the realm is not half enough to sustain them, but that for very constraint they die for hunger"—unto all those words of his, were it not that, though we well wist[143] ourselves he said untrue, yet would we be loath so to lay as a lie to his charge anything whereof the untruth were not so plainly perceived but that[144] he might find some favorers which[145] might say he said true, else would we peradventure not let[146] to tell him that, for a beginning, in these few words he had written two lies at once.

If we should tell you what number there was of poor sick folk in days passed long before your time, ye were at liberty not to believe us. Howbeit, he cannot yet on the other side,[147] for his part neither, bring you forth a bead-roll[148] of their names, wherefore we must for both our parts be fain to remit[149] you to your own time, and yet not from your childhood (whereof many things men forget when they come to far greater age), but unto the days of your good remembrance. And so doing, we suppose if the sorry sights that men have seen

124 expect   **125** to meet with success   **126** as if   **127** scheme; device   **128** occupation; power   **129** physically suffering   **130** grievously   **131** *so far-forth:* to such an extent   **132** *pray and require:* beg and ask   **133** give to   **134** representatives; alms-collectors   **135** scribe   **136** *by and by:* immediately   **137** trustworthiness; truth   **138** However   **139** burden   **140** *rehearsal and reproof:* recounting and rebuttal   **141** particularly   **142** *of alms:* from charity   **143** knew   **144** *but that:* unless   **145** who   **146** *peradventure not let:* perhaps not hesitate   **147** hand   **148** prayer list   **149** *fain to remit:* obliged to refer

had left as great impression still remaining in their hearts as the sight maketh of the present sorrow that they see, men should think and say that they have in days past seen as many sick beggars as they see now. For as for other sicknesses, they reign not, God be thanked, but after such rate as they have done in times past. And then of the French pox, thirty years ago went there about sick, five against one that beggeth with them now. Whereof, whoso list[150] to say that he seeth it otherwise, we will hold no great dispicions[151] with him thereupon, because we lack the names of both the sides to make the trial with. But surely whoso shall say the contrary, shall as we suppose either say so for his pleasure, or else shall it fare by his sight as folks fare with their feeling; which what they feel they whine at, but what they have felt they have more than half forgotten, though they felt it right late.[152] Which maketh one that hath but a poor boil upon his finger think the grief more great than was the pain of a great botch[153] that grieved his whole hand little more than a month afore.[154] So that in this point of the number of sick beggars so sore[155] increased so late, albeit we will forbear so to say to him as we might well say, yet will we be so bold to deny it him till he bring in some better thing than his bare word for the proof.

And in good faith, if he be put to the proof of the other point also—that is to wit,[156] that "for very constraint" those poor sick folk "die for hunger"— we verily[157] trust and think he shall seek far and find very few if he find any at all, for albeit that[158] poor householders have these dear years[159] made right hard shift[160] for corn, yet, our Lord be thanked, men have not been so far from all pity as to suffer[161] poor impotent persons die at their doors for hunger.

Now whereas he saith that "the alms of all well-disposed people of this realm is not half enough to sustain them," and the "well-disposed people" he calleth in this matter all them that giveth them alms, and he speaketh not of one year nor twain[162] but of these many years now passed, for neither be the number of the clergy nor their possessions nor the friars' alms, in which things he layeth[163] the cause why the alms of good people is not half

sufficient to keep and sustain the poor and sick beggars from famishing, any great thing increased in these ten or twelve or twenty years last past, and therefore if that[164] he said were true, then by all these ten years at the least, the alms of good people hath not been half able to sustain the poor and sick beggars from famishing. And surely if that were so—that in four or five years in which was plenty of corn,[165] the poor and sick beggars, for lack of men's alms, died so fast for hunger—though many should fall sick never so fast again, yet had they in the last two dear years died up of likelihood almost every one. And whether this be true or not we purpose not to dispute, but to refer and report ourselves to every man's eyes and ears, whether any man hear of so many dead or see so many the fewer.

When he hath laid these sure stones to begin the ground and foundation of his building with—that sore and sick beggars be so "sore increased" that the alms of all the good people of this realm "is not half enough to sustain them," and that therefore by "very constraint" they daily "die for hunger"—upon them he layeth another stone: that the cause of all this evil is the great possessions of the spiritualty,[166] and the great alms given to the friars.

But herein first he layeth that—besides tithes and all such other profits as rise unto the Church by reason of the spiritual[167] law or of men's devotion— that they have "the third part of all" the temporal[168] lands of the realm. Which, whoso[169] can tell as much of the revenues of the realm as he can tell little that made the book, doth well know that though they have much, yet is the "third part of all" far another thing, and that he saith in this point untrue.

Then goeth he to the poor friars. And there, as we told you, he showeth that the alms given them of certainty amounteth yearly unto 43,333 pounds, six shillings, eight pence, sterling. Peradventure[170] men would ween[171] the man were some apostate and that he never could be so privy to the friars' reckoning but if[172] he had been long their limiter[173] and seen some general view of all their whole accounts. But surely since the man is bad enough besides, we would be loath folk should reckon him for apostate, for surely he was never friar for aught[174]

150 *whoso list*: whoever chooses, desires
151 debates 152 *right late*: very recently
153 swelling 154 before 155 greatly
156 say 157 truly 158 *albeit that:*
although 159 *dear years:* years of

scarcity 160 *right hard shift:* every
effort 161 allow 162 two 163 alleges
164 what 165 grain 166 clergy
167 ecclesiastical; canon 168 secular
169 whoever 170 perhaps 171 suppose

172 *but if:* unless 173 friar licensed to beg within certain boundaries 174 anything

that we know, for we never wist[175] that ever in his life he was half so well disposed. And also when ye hear the ground of his reckoning, ye will yourselves think that he neither knoweth much of their matters, and of all the realm beside make as though he knew many things for true which many men know for false.

For first he putteth for the ground of his reckoning that there are in the realm two-and-fifty thousand parish churches, which is one plain lie to begin with. Then he putteth that every parish, one with another,[176] hath ten households in it — meaning besides such poor houses as rather ask alms than give; for of such, ye wot[177] well, the friars get no quarterage.[178] And that point, albeit that the ground be not sure, yet because it may to many men seem likely, therefore we let it pass. But then he showeth further for a sure truth a thing that all men know surely for a great lie: that is to say, that of every household in every parish, "every of[179] the five orders of friars" hath every quarter a penny. For we know full well, and so do many of you too, first, that the common people speak but of four orders — the White,[180] the Black,[181] the Augustinian, and the Grey[182] — and which is the fifth, in many parts of the realm few folk can tell you.

For if the question were asked about, there would be peradventure[183] founden many more, the more pity it is, that could name you the Green friars[184] than the Crutched.[185] Ye know right well also that in many a parish in England, of forty households ye shall not find four pay neither five pence a quarter nor four neither, and many a parish never a penny. And as for the five pence quarterly, we dare boldly say that ye shall find it paid in very few parishes through the realm, if ye find it paid in any. And yet this thing, being such a stark lie, as many men already knoweth and every man shortly may find it, he putteth as a plain well-known truth for a special post[186] to bear up his reckoning.

For upon these grounds now maketh he a clear reckoning in this manner ensuing, which is good also to be known for folk that will learn to cast account:[187]

There be 52,000 parishes; and in each of them ten households. So have ye the whole sum of the households, five hundred thousand and twenty thousand. Even just.[188] Go now to the money, then. Every order of the five orders of friars hath of[189] every of these households a penny a quarter. *Summa*:[190] for every house among all the five orders, every quarter, five pence; and hereby may ye learn that five times one maketh five. Now this is, he showeth you, among the five orders of every house for the whole year twenty pence, and so learn ye there that four times five maketh twenty.

"*Summa*," saith he: "five hundred thousand and twenty thousand quarters of angels."[191] Here we would[192] not that because the realm hath no coin called the "quarter angel," ye should therefore so far mistake the man as to ween[193] that he meant so many quarter sacks of angels. For indeed (as we take him), by the naming and counting of so many "quarters of angels," he meaneth nothing else but to teach you a point of reckoning and to make you perceive and know that twenty pence is the fourth part[194] of six shillings, eight pence. For after that rate it seemeth that he valueth the angel noble.[195] Then goeth he forth with his reckoning and showeth you that "five hundred thousand and twenty thousand quarters of angels maketh two hundred threescore[196] thousand half angels." And by this, lo, ye may perceive clearly that he meant not quarter sacks of angels, for then they would have held, ye wot[197] well, many more pieces of forty pence than forty times this whole sum cometh to. Then he showeth you further that "260,000 half angels amount just[198] unto 130,000 angels," wherein every man may learn that the half of sixty is thirty and that the half of twain[199] is one. Finally then he casteth it all together and bringeth it into pounds. "*Summa totalis*:[200] forty-three thousand pounds, three hundred and thirty-three pounds, six shillings, eight pence."

But here, to continue the plainness of his reckoning, he forgot to tell you that three nobles make twenty shillings, and that twenty shillings make a pound. But who can now doubt of this reckoning

---

175 knew   **176** *one with another:* on average   **177** know   **178** quarterly payment   **179** *every of:* each of; every one of   **180** Whitefriars; Carmelites   **181** Blackfriars; Dominicans   **182** Greyfriars; Franciscans   **183** perhaps   **184** *Green friars:* Reformed Franciscans at Greenwich   **185** Friars of the Holy Cross   **186** pillar   **187** *cast account:* do accounting   **188** *Even just:* Just so   **189** from   **190** Total   **191** *angels:* The angel, or angel noble (see below), was a gold coin with St. Michael the Archangel engraved on it.   **192** wish   **193** think   **194** *the fourth part:* one-fourth   (there were 12 pennies to a shilling and 20 nobles to a pound)   **195** *For… noble:* The angel had been revalued by the King in 1526, going from 6 shillings, 8 pence, to 7 shillings, 6 pence.   **196** sixty   **197** know   **198** exactly   **199** two   **200** *Summa totalis:* Grand total

when it cometh so round that of so great a sum he leaveth not out the odd noble?

But now since all this reckoning is grounded upon two false grounds—one, upon 52,000 par-5 ish churches; the other, that every of the five orders hath every quarter, of every household, a penny— this reckoning of 43,333 pounds, six shillings, eight pence, seemeth to come much like to pass as if he would make a reckoning with you that every ass 10 hath eight ears. And for to prove it with, bear you first in hand[201] that every ass hath four heads, and then make *Summa*: four heads. Then might he boldly tell you further that every ass head hath two ears, for that is commonly true except[202] any be cut 15 off. *Summa* then: two ears, and so *summa totalis*: eight ears. At this account of eight ears of one ass, ye make a lip[203] and think it so mad that no man would make no such. Surely it were a mad count indeed; and yet, as mad as it were, it were not so mad by half 20 as is his sad[204] and earnest count that he maketh you now so solemnly of the friars' quarterage.[205]

For this should he ground but upon one lie, where he groundeth the other upon twain[206] as open lies as this and as great. Now might we, and we would, 25 say that all his reckoning were nought,[207] because he reckoneth twenty pence for the quarter of the angel, and all the remnant of his reckoning followeth forth upon the same rate. But we would be loath to put him in the fault that he deserve not. For surely 30 it might be that he was not ware[208] of the new valuation, for he ran away[209] before the valuation changed.

But now upon this great sum of 43,333 pounds, six shillings, eight pence—upon these good grounds heaped up together, he bringeth in his ragman's 35 roll[210] of his rude[211] rhetoric against the poor friars, beginning with such a great exclamation that we heard him hither,[212] and suddenly were all afraid when we heard him cry out so loud, "O grievous and painful exactions thus yearly to be paid, from 40 the which the people of your noble progenitors, ancient Britons, ever stood free." And so goeth he forth against the poor friars with "Danes" and "Saxons" and "noble King Arthur," and "Lucius the Emperor," the Romans, the Greeks, and the great Turk, 45 showing that all these had been utterly marred and

never had been able to do nothing in the war, if their people had given their alms to friars.

After his railing rhetoric ended against the friars, then this sum of 43,333 pounds, six shillings, eight pence he addeth unto all the others that he 50 said before that all the clergy hath besides; which he summeth not, but saith that this and that together amount unto more between them "than half of the whole substance[213] of the realm." And this he affirmeth as boldly as though he could reckon 55 the whole revenues and substance of all England, as readily as make the reckoning of his beggar's purse.

Then showeth he that this better half of the whole substance is shifted[214] among fewer than the four-hundredth part of the people. Which he proveth 60 by that he saith that all the clergy compared unto the remnant of the men only, be "not the hundredth person;"[215] and if they be compared unto the remnant of "men, women, and children," so "are they not," he saith, "the four-hundredth person." But now 65 some folk that have not very long ago, upon great occasions, taken the reckoning of priests and religious places in every diocese, and on the other side, the reckoning and the number of the temporal men[216] in every county, know well that this man's mad reckon-70 ing goeth very far wide,[217] and seemeth that he hath heard these wise reckonings at some congregation of beggars. And yet, as though because he hath said it he had therefore proved it, he runneth forth in his railing rhetoric against the whole clergy and that in 75 such a sort and fashion that very hard it were to discern whether it be more false or more foolish.

For first, all the faults that any lewd[218] priest or friar doth, all that layeth he to the whole clergy, as well and as wisely as though he would lay the 80 faults of some lewd lay people to the default[219] and blame of all the whole temporalty.[220] But this way liketh him so well that thus laying to the whole clergy the faults of such as be simple[221] and faulty therein, and yet not only laying to their charge the 85 breach of chastity and abuse in fleshly living of such as be naught,[222] but also madly, like a fond[223] fellow, laying much more to their charge and much more earnestly reproving the good and honest living of those that be good, whom he rebuketh and 90

201 *bear you first in hand:* tries first to make you believe **202** unless **203** face **204** serious **205** quarterly payment **206** two **207** nothing; worthless **208** aware **209** *ran away:* i.e., from England **210** *ragman's roll:* list of complaints **211** unskilled; ignorant; harsh **212** here (in purgatory) **213** wealth **214** apportioned **215** i.e., not even 1 percent **216** *temporal men:* lay people **217** *goeth very far wide:* is far from accurate **218** wicked **219** fault **220** laity **221** ignorant; deficient **222** wicked **223** foolish

abhorreth because they keep their vows and persevere in chastity—for he saith that they be the marrers and destroyers of the realm, bringing the land into wilderness for lack of generation by their abstaining from wedding—then aggrieveth[224] he his great crimes with heinous words, gay repetitions, and grievous exclamations, calling them "blood-suppers" and "drunken in the blood" of holy martyrs and saints, which he meaneth for the condemning of holy heretics. "Greedy golofers"[225] he calleth them, and "insatiable whirlpools," because the temporalty hath given them possessions, and give to the friars their alms. And all virtuous good priests and religious folk he calleth "idle holy thieves" because they spend their time in preaching and prayer.

And then saith he:

> These be they that make so many sick and sore[226] beggars. These be they that make these whores and bawds. These be they that make these thieves. These be they that make so many idle persons. These be they that corrupt the generations. And these be they that with the abstaining from wedding hinder so the generation of the people that the realm shall at length fall in wilderness but if[227] they wed the sooner.

And now upon these heinous crimes laid unto the whole clergy—and laid, as every wise man seeth, some very falsely, and some very foolishly—after his goodly repetitions he falleth to his great and grievous exclamations, crying out upon the "great, broad, bottomless ocean sea of evils," and upon the "grievous shipwreck of the commonwealth," the translating[228] of the King's kingdom, and the "ruin of the King's crown." And therewith rolling in his rhetoric from figure to figure, he falleth to a vehement invocation of the King, and giveth him warning of his great loss, asking him fervently, "Where is your sword, power, crown, and dignity become?" As though the King's Grace had clean lost his realm specially for lack of people to reign upon, because that priests have no wives. And surely the man cannot fail of such eloquence, for he hath gathered these goodly flowers out of Luther's garden almost word for word, without any more labor but only the translating out of the Latin into the English tongue.

But to inflame the King's Highness against the Church, he saith that the clergy laboreth nothing else but to make the King's subjects "fall into disobedience and rebellion" against his Grace.

This tale is a very likely thing. As though the clergy knew not that there is nothing earthly that so much keepeth themselves in quiet, rest, and surety,[229] as doth the due obedience of the people to the virtuous mind of the prince, whose high goodness must needs have much more difficulty to defend the clergy and keep the Church in peace if the people fell to disobedience and rebellion against their prince. And therefore every child may see that the clergy would never be so mad as to be glad to bring the people to disobedience and rebellion against the prince, by whose goodness they be preserved in peace, and were, in such rebellion of the people, likely to be the first that should fall in peril. But neither is there desired by the clergy, nor never shall by God's grace happen, any such rebellion as the beggars' proctor[230] and his fellows, whatsoever they say, long full sore[231] to see.

But this man against the clergy fetcheth forth old fern[232] years and runneth up[233] to King John's days,[234] spending much labor about the praise and commendation of that good gracious king, and crying out upon the pope that then was, and the clergy of England, and all the lords and all the commons[235] of the realm, because King John, as he saith, made the realm "tributary" to the Pope; wherein he meaneth, peradventure,[236] the Peter Pence.[237] But surely therein is all his hot accusation a very cold tale when the truth is known. For so is it indeed that, albeit there be writers that say the Peter Pence were granted by King John for the release of the interdiction, yet were they paid indeed ere[238] ever King John's great-grandfather was born, and thereof is there proof enough. Now if he say, as indeed some writers say, that King John made England and Ireland tributary to the Pope and the See Apostolic by the grant of a thousand marks,[239] we dare surely say again[240] that it is untrue, and that all Rome neither can show such a grant nor never could, and if they could, it were right nought

224 aggravates   **225** gluttons   **226** physically suffering   **227** *but if:* unless   **228** transferring, removing   **229** safety, security   **230** representative; agent; alms-collector   **231** *full sore:* very greatly   **232** *fern years:* far bygone times   **233** *runneth up:* goes back   **234** *King John's days:* He reigned 1199–1216.   **235** commoners   **236** perhaps   **237** *Peter Pence:* a collection taken in every parish and sent to Rome   **238** before   **239** A mark was half of a pound.   **240** in reply

worth.[241] For never could any king of England give away the realm to the pope, or make the land tributary, though he would;[242] nor no such money is there paid, nor never was. And as for the Peter Pence, if he mean them, neither was the realm tributary by them, nor King John never granted them. For they were paid before the Conquest[243] to the Apostolic See toward the maintenance thereof, but only by way of gratitude and alms.

Now, as for the Archbishop Stephen,[244] whom, he saith, being a traitor to the King, the Pope[245] made Archbishop of Canterbury against the King's will, therein be there, as we suppose, two lies at once. For neither was that Stephen ever traitor against the King, as far as ever we have heard, nor the Pope none otherwise made him Archbishop than he made all others at that time. But the same Stephen was well and canonically chosen Archbishop of Canterbury by the convent of the monks at Christ's Church in Canterbury, to whom, as the King well knew and denied it not, the election of the Archbishop at that time belonged. Nor the King resisted not his election because of any treason that was laid[246] against him, but was discontented therewith;[247] and after that his election was passed and confirmed by the Pope, he would not of long season suffer[248] him to enjoy the bishopric because himself had recommended another unto the monks, whom they rejected, and preferred Stephen. And that this is as we tell you, and not as the beggars' proctor writeth for a false foundation of his railing, ye shall mow[249] perceive not only by diverse chronicles but also by diverse monuments[250] yet remaining as well of the election and confirmation of the said Archbishop as of the long suit and process[251] that after followed thereupon.

Now showeth he himself very wroth[252] with the spiritual[253] jurisdiction, which he would[254] in any wise[255] were clean taken away, saying that it must needs destroy the jurisdiction temporal.[256] Whereas the good princes past have granted, and the nobles in their times and the people too have by plain

Parliaments confirmed them,[257] and yet hitherto,[258] blessed be God, they[259] agree better together than to fall at variance for the wild words of such a malicious makebate[260]—which, for[261] to bring the spiritualty into hatred, saith that they call their jurisdiction a "kingdom." In which word he may say his pleasure, but of truth, he seldom seeth any spiritual man[262] at this day that so calleth any spiritual jurisdiction that he useth.[263]

Now where this man useth as a proof thereof that the spiritualty nameth themselves always before the temporalty, this manner of naming cometh not of them but of the good mind[264] and devotion of the temporalty—so far-forth[265] that at the Parliament, when that any acts be conceived, the words be commonly so couched that the bill saith it is enacted first by our Sovereign Lord the King, and by the Lords Spiritual and Temporal, and the Commons,[266] in that present Parliament assembled. And these bills be often drawn, put forth, and passed first in the Common House, where there is not one spiritual man present.

But such truth as the man useth in this point, such useth he where he calleth the poor friars' alms an "exaction," surmising that it is exacted by force and the people compelled to pay it, where every man well wotteth[267] that they have, poor men, no way to compel no man to give them aught,[268] not though[269] they should die for default.[270] But this good honest true man saith that whoso will not pay the friars their quarterage, they will make him be taken[271] as a heretic. We be well content that ye take this for no lie, as many as ever have known it true. But who heard ever yet that any man taken for a heretic did so much as once say that he thought it conveyed[272] by the malice of any friar for refusing to pay the friar's quarterage? This lie, lo, is a little too loud[273] for any man that were not waxen[274] shameless.

Like truth is there in this that he saith: if any man trouble a priest for any temporal suit, the clergy forthwith[275] will make him a heretic and burn him but if he be content[276] to "bear a fagot[277]

---

241 *were right nought worth:* would be altogether worthless   **242** *though he would:* even if he wanted to   **243** the Norman Conquest of 1066   **244** Stephen Langton (ca. 1155–1228)   **245** Pope Innocent III (1161–1216)   **246** alleged   **247** i.e., with the monks' choosing of Langton   **248** *of long season suffer:* for a long time allow   **249** be able to   **250** official records

251 *suit and process:* legal proceedings   **252** angry   **253** ecclesiastical   **254** wishes   **255** way   **256** civil   **257** the legal rights of the Church   **258** *yet hitherto:* still to this day   **259** the clergy and the lay people   **260** troublemaker   **261** in order to   **262** *spiritual man:* clergyman   **263** exercises   **264** disposition; judgment   **265** *so far-forth:* to such an extent   **266** House of

Commons   **267** knows   **268** anything   **269** even if   **270** lack   **271** arrested and taken into custody   **272** brought about   **273** flagrant   **274** become   **275** immediately   **276** *but if he be content:* unless he is willing   **277** *bear a fagot:* carry a bundle of sticks

for their pleasure." The falsehood of this cannot be unknown. For men know well in many a shire how often that many folk indict priests of rape at the sessions.[278] And as there is sometimes a rape committed indeed, so is there ever a rape surmised,[279] were the women never so willing, and oftentimes where there was nothing done at all. And yet of any such that so procured priests to be indicted, how many have men heard taken and accused for heretics? Ye see not very many sessions pass, but in one shire or other this pageant[280] is played; whereas through[281] the realm, such as be put to penance for heresy be not so many in many years as there be priests indicted in few years. And yet of all such so taken for heresy, he shall not find four this fourscore[282] years, peradventure[283] not this four hundred years, that ever pretended themselves so troubled for indicting of a priest, so that his lie is herein too large to get any cloak to cover it.

Now where he saith that the captains of Doctor Alen's kingdom have heaped him up benefice[284] upon benefice, and have rewarded him ten times as much as the five hundred pounds which he paid for a fine by the Praemunire, and that thus hath the spiritualty[285] rewarded him because he fought so manfully against the King's crown and his dignity—all that know the matter do well perceive that the man doth in this matter as he doth in others: either lieth for his pleasure or else little wotteth how that the matter stood. For it is well known that Doctor Alen was in the Praemunire pursued[286] only by spiritual men and had much less favor and much more rigor showed him therein by the greatest of the clergy than by any temporal men.

He saith also to the King's Highness, "Your Grace may see what a work there is in London, how the Bishop rageth for indicting of certain curates[287] of extortion and incontinency[288] the last year in the wardmote quest."[289] Would not upon these words every stranger ween[290] that there had been in London many curates indicted of extortion and rape, and that the Bishop would labor sore[291] to defend their faults, and that there were about that matter a great commotion in all the city? How shameless is he that can tell this tale in writing to the King's Highness, for a truth, whereof neither bishop nor curate nor mayor nor alderman nor any man else ever heard word spoken? It were hard to say whether we should take it for wiliness or lack of wit[292] that he saith all this work was in the city "the last year," and then his book neither was put up[293] to the King, nor beareth any date, so that a man would ween he were a fool that so writeth of "the last year" that the reader cannot wit[294] which year it was. But yet ween we he doth it for a wiliness. For since he knoweth his tale false, it is wisdom to leave the time unknown, that his lie may be uncontrolled.[295] For he would that men should[296] ween always that it was in one year or other.

But finally for a special point he bringeth in Richard Hunne, and saith that if he had not "commenced an action of Praemunire against a priest, he had been yet alive and none heretic at all." Now is it of truth well known that he was detected[297] of heresy before the Praemunire sued or thought upon. And he began that suit to help to stop the other withal,[298] as indeed it did for the while. For albeit that[299] he that was sued in the Praemunire was nothing belonging to[300] the Bishop of London, before whom Richard Hunne was detected of heresy, yet, lest such as would be glad sinisterly to misconstrue everything toward the blame of the clergy might have occasion to say that the matter were hotly handled against him to force him to forbear his suit of the Praemunire, the Bishop therefore did the more forbear till it appeared clearly to the temporal judges and all that were anything[301] learned in the temporal law that his suit of the Praemunire was nothing worth in the King's Law, forasmuch as by plain statute the matter was out of question that the pleas to be held upon mortuaries[302] belong unto the spiritual court. After which thing well appearing, the matter went forth afore[303] the Bishop,[304] and he[305] there well proved naught,[306] and his books after brought forth, such, and so noted with his own hand in the margins, as every wise man well saw what he was, and was full sorry to see that he was such as they there saw him proved.

278 court sessions 279 alleged 280 show 281 throughout 282 eighty 283 perhaps 284 gift; ecclesiastical living 285 ecclesiastical authorities 286 prosecuted 287 parish priests 288 unchastity 289 *wardmote quest:* an inquest held in each ward in London

290 *stranger ween:* foreigner think 291 hard 292 intelligence 293 *put up:* submitted (since all books in England were legally required to obtain a license from the King) 294 know 295 untested for accuracy 296 *would...should:* wants men to 297 accused 298 with

it; thereby 299 *albeit that:* although 300 *nothing belonging to:* not at all under the jurisdiction of 301 at all 302 *upon mortuaries:* about payments to priests for funerals 303 before 304 Cuthbert Tunstall 305 Hunne (was) 306 wicked

Now goeth he further and asketh the King,

> Did not Doctor Horsey and his accomplices most
> heinously, as all the world knoweth, murder in
> prison that honest merchant Richard Hunne, for
> that[307] he sued your writ of Praemunire against a
> priest that wrongfully held him in plea in a spir-
> itual court, for a matter whereof the knowledge
> belonged unto your high courts? And what pun-
> ishment hath he for it? After that he had paid,
> as it is said, six hundred pounds for him and his
> accomplices, as soon as he had obtained your
> most gracious pardon, he was immediately pro-
> moted by the captains of his kingdom with ben-
> efice upon benefice, to the value of four times as
> much. Who is he of their kingdom that will not
> rather take courage to commit like offense, seeing
> the promotions that fell to such men for their so
> offending? — so weak and blunt is your sword to
> strike at one of the offenders of this crooked and
> perverse generation!

We have here somewhat cumbered[308] you with a
piece of his own words, because ye should have a
show of his vehement eloquence, with which the
bold beggars' proctor so arrogantly presumeth in
his bill to ask the King a question, and to bind his
Highness to answer as[309] his Mastership appointed
him. For if his Grace say nay, then he telleth him
before that "all the world" wotteth yes. But surely
if he call "all the world" all that ever God made,
then is there three parts[310] that knoweth the contrary. For we dare be bold to warrant you that in
heaven, hell, and here among us in purgatory, of all
that this man so boldly affirmeth, the contrary is
well and clearly known. And if he call "the world"
but only men among you there living upon middle
earth,[311] yet so shall he peradventure[312] find in some
part of the world, if he seek it well, more than four
or five good honest men that never heard speak of
the matter. And of such as have heard of the matter and known it well, he shall find enough — and
specially, we think, the King's Grace himself (whose
Highness he is so homely[313] to ask the question and
appoint him his answer himself) — that of all five

things which he hath here in so few lines affirmed,
there is not one true, but lies every one.

For first, to begin where he leaveth, when he saith
that the clergy have, since the death of Richard
Hunne, "promoted" Doctor Horsey with "benefice
upon benefice," "four times as much" as "six hundred pounds" — the plain untruth of this point may
every man soon know that will soon inquire. For he
liveth yet at Exeter, and there liveth upon such as
he had before, without that new heap of benefices
given him by the "captains of his kingdom" for killing of Richard Hunne — or thanks, either, save only
of[314] God for his long patience in his undeserved
trouble. But to the end that ye may see how little
this man forceth[315] how loud the lie, consider that
he saith that the clergy gave unto Doctor Horsey,
after he came out of prison, "benefice upon benefice, to the value of four times as much" as "six hundred pounds." Now, if this be true, then hath Doctor Horsey had in benefices — besides all such as he
had before his trouble — the value of two thousand
four hundred pounds. We trust that the man, his
substance,[316] and his livelihood is so well known
that we need not to tell that the beggars' proctor[317]
in this point hath made one loud lie.

Another is that he saith that Hunne was kept in
plea in the spiritual[318] law for a matter determinable
in the King's court; for the matter was for a mortuary,[319] which by plain statute is declared to pertain to the spiritual law. The third is that Hunne
was "honest" — except[320] heresy be honest. The
fourth is that "Doctor Horsey and his accomplices"
murdered him in prison; for thereof is the contrary well known, and that the man hanged himself for despair, despite,[321] and for lack of grace. We
might, and we would, lay for the fifth the payment
which he speaketh of: the "six hundred pounds,"
with which money he would men should ween[322]
that he bought his pardon. Wherein he layeth[323] a
good great sum, to the end that folk, well witting[324]
that Doctor Horsey was not like[325] to have so much
money of his own, should ween therewith that the
clergy laid[326] out the money among them, and then
gave him benefices whereof he might pay them
again.[327] But this[328] layeth he from[329] himself, and

---

307 *for that:* because   308 burdened
309 as if   310 *three parts:* three-fourths
of it   311 *middle earth:* so called because
it is a place between the high region
(heaven) and the lower regions (hell and

purgatory)   312 perhaps   313 familiar;
direct   314 from   315 cares   316 wealth
317 advocate; representative; alms-collector
318 ecclesiastical   319 payment to a priest
for a funeral   320 unless   321 spite;

malice   322 *would . . . ween:* wants people
to think   323 asserts; alleges   324 knowing   325 likely   326 paid   327 back
328 i.e., this supposition   329 away from

showeth not to whom;[330] for he saith "it is said" so. And yet were it no wrong that it were accounted his own, till he put it better from[331] him, and prove of whom he heard it.

5   Howbeit,[332] since there is other store enough, we shall leave this lie in question between him and we wot nere[333] whom else, and we shall for the fifth lay you that lie that he layeth forth himself: that is to wit,[334] where he saith that the Chancellor purchased the King's "most gracious pardon" for the murdering of Hunne. For this is the truth: that he never sued[335] any pardon therefor;[336] but after that the matter[337] had been by long time and great diligence so far-forth[338] examined that the King's Highness at length (as time always trieth[339] out the truth) well perceived his innocency, and theirs also that were accused and indicted with him, his noble Grace, when they were arraigned upon that indictment, and thereto pleaded that they were not guilty, commanded his attorney general to confess their plea to be true; which is the thing that his Highness, as a most virtuous prince, useth for[340] to do when the matter is not only just, but also known for just, upon the part of the party defendant. Because that, like[341] as where the matter appeareth doubtful, he doth, as reason is,[342] suffer[343] it to go forth and letteth the truth be tried, so where he seeth and perceiveth the right to be on the other side, his Highness will in no wise[344] have the wrong set forth or maintained in his name. Now when it was then thus indeed—that neither the Chancellor nor any man else ever sued any charter of pardon for the matter—this is then the fifth lie that this man hath made in so few lines. Which things, whoso well consider cannot but marvel of the sore pithy[345] point wherewith he knitteth up all his heavy matter, saying to the King, "Who is there of their kingdom that will not take courage to commit like offense, seeing the promotions that fall to such men for their offending?—so weak and so blunt is your sword to strike at one of the offenders of this crooked and perverse generation!"

Lo, how this great zelator of the commonwealth crieth out upon the King, that his sword is not strong and sharp to strike off innocents' heads! He hath of likelihood ransacked up all Dame Rhetoric's rolls to find out this goodly figure—to call upon the King and ask his Highness, "Where is your sword?" and tell him his sword is too dull—as though he would bid him bear it to the cutler's to grind,[346] that he might strike off Doctor Horsey's head, whom his Grace had found faultless, and testified him himself for an innocent. If this man were here matched with some such as he is himself—that hath the eloquence that he hath, that could find out such comely[347] figures of rhetoric as he findeth, set forth and furnished with such vehement words as he thundereth out like thunder blasts, that hath no less matters in his mouth than the "great, broad, bottomless ocean sea full of evils," the weakness and dullness of the King's sword, the translation[348] of the King's kingdom, the "ruin of the King's crown," with great exclamations ("O grievous and painful exactions!" "O case most horrible!" "O grievous shipwreck of the commonwealth!")—what might one that had such like eloquence say here to him? Surely so much, and in such wise, as we seely poor puling[349] souls neither can devise nor utter.

But verily,[350] two or three things we see and may well say: that neither be these great matters meet[351] for the mouth of the beggars' proctor; nor such preaching of reformation and amendment of the world meet matters for him to meddle with, which,[352] with open heresies and plain pestilent errors busily goeth about to poison and infect the world; nor very convenient[353] for him to take upon him[354] to give counsel to a king, when he showeth himself to have so much presumption and so little wit[355] as to ask the King a question and appoint him his answer—and therein to tell him that "all the world" knoweth that thing to be true which the King hath himself already, by his attorney and his judges in open judgment[356] and in his high court of record, testified and confessed[357] for false. If that man were not for malice as mad, not as a March hare but as a mad dog that runneth forth and snatcheth he seeth not at whom, the fellow could never else[358] with such open folly so suddenly oversee[359] himself.

---

330 *showeth not to whom:* says not to whom (he ascribes this allegation)   **331** away from   **332** However   **333** *wot nere:* know not   **334** say   **335** petitioned; sought to obtain   **336** for that   **337** case   **338** *so far-forth:* to such an extent

339 sifts   **340** *useth for:* makes it his practice   **341** just   **342** *as reason is:* as stands to reason   **343** allow   **344** way   **345** *sore pithy:* very small   **346** sharpen   **347** pretty   **348** transference, removal   **349** *seely poor puling:* poor pitiful crying

350 truly   **351** appropriate   **352** who   **353** appropriate   **354** himself   **355** sense   **356** *open judgment:* a public trial   **357** *testified and confessed:* attested and acknowledged   **358** otherwise   **359** fail to perceive

But it were wrong with the world if malice had as much wit, circumspection, and providence[360] in the pursuit of an ungracious[361] purpose, as it hath haste, evil will, and wiliness in the first enterprising.[362] For as an ape hath some similitude of a man, and as a fox hath a certain wiliness somewhat resembling an unperfect wit, so fareth this fellow, that beginneth, as one would ween, at[363] good zeal and charity borne toward the poor beggars, but forthwith[364] he showeth himself that he nothing else intendeth but openly to destroy the clergy first, and after that, covertly, as many as have aught[365] above the state of beggars. And whereas he would in the beginning, by the touching[366] of great matters, fain[367] seem very wise, within a while in the progress he proveth himself a very stark fool. And where he would seem to show many notable things which no man had marked but he, he provideth wisely that no man may believe him, he maketh so many lies; and all that ever he doth further, he buildeth upon the same.

He layeth[368] that the living which the clergy hath is the only cause that there be so many beggars that be sick and sore.[369] Very well and wisely—as though the clergy by their substance[370] made men blind and lame! The clergy also is the cause, he saith, why they "die for hunger"—as though every layman gave to beggars all that ever he could, and the clergy give them never a groat;[371] and as though there would not more beggars walk abroad if the clergy left off[372] such laymen as they find.[373]

But he proveth you that the clergy must needs be the cause why there be so many poor men and beggars. For he saith that before the clergy came in, there were but few poor people—and yet they begged not neither, but men, he saith, gave them "enough unasked." But now, where sat he when he saw the people give poor folk so fast their alms unasked that no man needed to beg, before the clergy began? This man of likelihood is of great age, and, or ere[374] the clergy began, was wont[375] to sit at Saint Savior's with a sore leg; but he begged not, men gave him so much unasked. For whereas he allegeth[376] the Bible for him, in the Acts of the Apostles,[377] verily we marvel much what the man meaneth. For there

he may see that the apostles and the deacons, which were then the clergy, had altogether in their own hands, and distributed to every man as themselves thought good. And therefore we wonder what he meaneth, to speak of that book. For we think that he meaneth not to hurt the clergy so now as to put all into their hands. And surely but if[378] he mean so, else[379] is this place nothing for his purpose.

Now herein he showeth also a high point of his wit: where he saith that the great living that the clergy hath, which he layeth[380] and lieth to be more than half of the whole revenues and substance[381] of the realm, is shifted[382] among fewer than the four-hundredth part of the people. As though that of the clergy's part there had[383] no lay people their living—no servant any wages, none artificer[384] any money for working, no carpenter, no mason any money for building—but all the money that ever cometh in their hands, they put it by and by[385] in their own bellies, and no layman hath any relief thereof. And therefore this point was wisely written, ye see as well as we.

Now for the truth thereof: If it were true that[386] he saith, that the clergy compared to the residue of the men only be not one to a hundred, then shall ye not need to fear the great Turk and[387] he came tomorrow—except ye suffer[388] among you to grow in great number these Lutherans that favor him. For we dare make you the warrantise[389] that if his lie be true, there be more men a great many in London and within four shires next adjoining than the great Turk bringeth into Hungary.

But in this ye must hold him excused, for he meddleth not much with algorism,[390] to see to what sum the number of men ariseth that is multiplied by a hundred. All his practice in multiplication meddleth with nothing but lies; and therein match him with whom ye will, he will give you a hundred for one. Whereof if ye lack, let this be the example: that he saith, "If the Abbot of Westminster should sing every day as many Masses for his founders as he is bounden to do by his foundation,[391] a thousand monks were too few." Ye doubt not, we think, but he can tell you who hath bound them to how

---

360 prudent foresight   **361** devoid of spiritual grace; wicked   **362** attempt   **363** with   **364** immediately   **365** anything   **366** treating   **367** desire to   **368** alleges   **369** physically suffering   **370** wealth   **371** a coin worth four pence

372 *left off*: abandoned   **373** provide a living for (by employing them)   **374** *or ere*: before   **375** accustomed   **376** *allegeth … him*: cites the Bible to support him   **377** See Acts 4:34–35.   **378** *but if*: unless   **379** otherwise   **380** alleges   **381** wealth

382 distributed   **383** received   **384** craftsman   **385** *by and by*: directly   **386** what   **387** if   **388** allow   **389** guarantee   **390** arithmetic   **391** founding charter

many, and so can make ye the plain reckoning that the Abbot is bound in the year to no fewer Masses than 365,000. He knoweth what is every man's duty save[392] his own. He is meet[393] to be a beggars' proctor,[394] that can so prowl about and can tell all things.

But now were all his painted process,[395] ye wot well, nothing worth but if[396] he devised against all these mischiefs some good and wholesome help. It is therefore a world[397] to see what politic[398] devices he findeth against the "great, broad, bottomless ocean sea of evils"—what remedies to repair the ruin of the King's crown, to restore and uphold his honor and dignity, to make his sword sharp and strong, and, finally, to save all the "shipwreck of the commonwealth." Ye would peradventure ween[399] that the man would now devise some good wholesome laws for help of all these matters. Nay, he will none thereof. For he saith he doubteth that the King is not able to make any law against them. For he saith that the clergy is stronger in the Parliament than the King himself. For in the higher House, he reckoneth that the spiritualty[400] is more in number and stronger than the temporalty.[401] And in the Common House he saith that "all the learned men of the realm" except the King's "learned council" be feed with[402] the Church to speak against the King's crown and dignity in the Parliament for them, and therefore he thinketh the King unable to make any law against the faults of the clergy.

This beggars' proctor would fain[403] show himself a man of great experience, and one that had great knowledge of the manner[404] and order used in the King's Parliaments. But then he speaketh so savorly[405] thereof that it well appeareth, of his wise words, he neither canneth any skill[406] thereof, nor never came in the House. For as for the higher House, first, the King's own royal person alone more than counterpoiseth[407] all the lords spiritual present with him and the temporal too. And over[408] this, the spiritual lords can never in number exceed the lords temporal, but must needs be far underneath them if it please the King. For his Highness may call thither by his writ many more temporal lords at his own pleasure.

And being as they be, there was never yet seen that the spiritual lords banded themselves there as a party against the temporal lords. But it hath been seen that the thing which the spiritual lords have moved and thought reasonable, the temporal lords have denied and refused, as appeareth upon the motion made for legitimation of the children born before the marriage of their parents. Wherein, albeit that[409] the reformation which the lords spiritual moved was a thing that nothing pertained to their own commodity,[410] and albeit that they laid[411] also for their part[412] the constitution and ordinance of the Church and the laws of other Christian countries, yet could they not obtain[413] against the lords temporal that[414] nothing alleged[415] to the contrary but their own wills. And therefore in the higher House the spiritual party never appeared yet so strong that they might overmatch the temporal lords. And then how much are they too feeble for them and the King too—whose Highness alone is over-strong for them both, and may by his writ call to his Parliament more temporal lords when he will.

Now where he saith that in the Common House "all the learned men" of the realm are feed[416] to speak for the clergy except the King's "learned council," there be two follies at once. For neither be all the learned men of the realm knights or burgesses in the Common House, and the King's "learned council" is not there at all. And therefore it seemeth that he hath heard somewhat of[417] some men that had seen as little as himself. And surely if he had been in the Common House (as some of us have been), he should have seen the spiritualty not gladly spoken for. And we little doubt but that ye remember acts and statutes passed at sundry Parliaments such, and in such wise and some of them so late,[418] as yourselves may see that either the clergy is not the stronger party in the King's Parliament, or else have no mind[419] to strive.

And for the further proof that the King's Highness is not so weak and unable in his own Parliament as this beggars' proctor so presumptuously telleth him, his Grace well knoweth, and all his people too, that in their own convocations his Grace

---

392 except   393 fit   394 representative; advocate; alms-collector   395 *painted process:* deceptive line of argument   396 *but if:* unless   397 wonder   398 scheming, crafty; prudent   399 *peradventure ween:* perhaps think   400 clergy   401 laity

402 *feed with:* hired by   403 gladly   404 custom   405 wisely   406 *canneth ... skill:* has any knowledge in power, counterbalances   408 beyond   409 *albeit that:* although   410 advantage   411 cited   412 side (in the debate)

413 prevail   414 who   415 cited as evidence   416 hired for a fee   417 *somewhat of:* something from   418 recently   419 intention

never devised nor desired anything in his life that ever was denied him. And therefore this gay[420] invention of this beggars' proctor—that he feigneth the King's Highness to be in his high court of Parliament more weak and feeble than the clergy—is a very feeble device.[421]

But now since he will have no law devised for the remedy of his great complaints, what help hath he devised else?[422] The help of all this gear[423] is, he saith, none other thing but to let him and such royal railers rail and jest upon the Church, and tell the people the priests' faults—and for the lewdness[424] of part, bring the whole clergy in contempt and hatred among all the temporal folk. Which thing, he saith, the King must needs suffer[425] if he "will eschew[426] the ruin of his crown and dignity." And this thing, he saith, shall be more "speedful"[427] and effectual "in the matter than all the laws that ever can be made, be they never so strong."

Lo, good Lords and Masters,[428] then shall ye need no more Parliaments! For here is, God be thanked, an easy way wisely founden to remedy with railing the "great, broad, bottomless ocean sea of evils," and to save the commonwealth from shipwreck, and the King's crown from ruin.

But now to the poor beggars. What remedy findeth their proctor for them? To make hospitals? Nay, wary of that; thereof he will none in no wise.[429] For thereof he saith "the more the worse," because they be profitable to priests. What remedy then? Give them any money? Nay, nay, not a groat.[430] What other thing then? Nothing in the world will serve but this: that "if the King's Grace will build a sure[431] hospital that never shall fail to relieve" all the sick beggars forever, let him give nothing to them, but look what the clergy hath, and take all that from them.

Is not here a goodly mischief for a remedy? Is not this a royal feast, to leave these beggars meatless,[432] and then send more to dinner to them?[433] Oh, the wise! Here want[434] we voice and eloquence to set out an exclamation in the praise and commendation of this special high provision. This bill putteth he forth in the poor beggars' name. But we verily[435] think if themselves have as much wit as their proctor lacketh, they had liefer[436] see their bill-maker burned than their supplication sped.[437] For they may soon perceive that he mindeth not[438] their alms, but only the spoil[439] of the clergy. For so that[440] the clergy lose it, he neither deviseth further, nor further forceth[441] who have it.

But it is easy to see whereof springeth all his displeasure. He is angry and fretteth at the spiritual jurisdiction for the punishment of heretics and burning of their erroneous books, for ever upon that string he harpeth: very angry with the burning of Tyndale's testament.[442] For these matters he calleth them "blood-suppers[443] drunken in the blood of holy saints and martyrs." Ye marvel peradventure[444] which "holy saints and martyrs" he meaneth. Surely by his "holy saints and martyrs" he meaneth their holy schismatics and heretics, for[445] whose just punishment these folk that are of the same sect fume, fret, froth, and foam, as fierce and as angrily as a new-hunted sow. And for the rancor conceived upon this displeasure cometh up all his complaint of the possessions of the clergy. Wherein he spareth and forbeareth[446] the nuns yet,[447] because they have no jurisdiction upon[448] heretics; for else he would have cried out upon their possessions too.

But this is now no new thing, nor the first time that heretics have been in hand with[449] the matter. For first was there, in the eleventh year of King Henry the Fourth, one John Badby[450] burned for heresy. And forthwith[451] thereupon was there at the next Parliament, held the same year, a bill put in declaring how much temporal land was in the Church, which reckoning the maker thereof guessed at by the number of knights' fees, of which he had weened[452] he had made a very just account. And in this bill was it devised to take their possessions out again.[453] Howbeit,[454] by the bill it appeared well unto them which well understood the matter that the maker of the bill neither wist[455] what land there was, nor how many knights' fees there was in the Church, nor well what thing a knight's fee

---

420 brilliant; excellent   **421** plan; scheme   **422** instead   **423** matter   **424** wickedness   **425** allow   **426** avoid   **427** successful   **428** *Lords and Masters:* titles of the members of the upper and lower houses of Parliament, respectively   **429** way   **430** a coin worth four

pence   **431** safe, secure   **432** without food   **433** *to them:* in addition to them   **434** lack   **435** truly   **436** *had liefer:* would rather   **437** succeed   **438** *mindeth not:* cares not for   **439** despoiling; plundering   **440** *so that:* so long as   **441** cares   **442** translation of the New

Testament   **443** bloodsuckers   **444** perhaps   **445** on account of   **446** leaves alone   **447** still   **448** over   **449** *been … with:* taken up   **450** a follower of Wycliffe executed in 1410   **451** immediately   **452** thought   **453** *out again:* back out   **454** However   **455** knew is; but the bill devised of[456] rancor and evil will by some such as favored Badby, that[457] was burned, and would have his heresies fain[458] go forward.

And so that bill, such as it was, such was it esteemed and set aside for nought.[459] So happed it then, soon after, that in the first year of the King's most noble progenitor King Henry the Fifth, those heresies secretly creeping on still among the people, a great number of them had first covertly conspired and after openly gathered and assembled themselves, purposing by open war and battle to destroy the King and his nobles and subvert the realm, whose traitorous malice that good Catholic king prevented,[460] withstood, overthrew, and punished by many of them taken in the field,[461] and after, for their traitorous heresies, both hanged and burned. Whereupon, forthwith, at the Parliament held the same year, likewise[462] as that royal prince, his virtuous nobles, and his good Christian commons[463] devised good laws against heretics, so did some of such as favored them eftsoons[464] put in the bill against the spiritualty. Which, eftsoons considered for such as it was, and coming of such malicious purpose as it came, was again rejected and set aside for nought.

Then was there long after that one Richard Hundon[465] burned for heresy. And then forthwith were there a rabble of heretics gathered themselves together at Abingdon, which[466] not intended to lose any more labor by putting up of bills in the Parliaments, but to make an open insurrection and subvert all the realm, and then to kill up[467] the clergy and sell priests' heads as good cheap[468] as sheep's heads — three for a penny, buy who would. But God saved the Church and the realm both, and turned their malice upon their own heads. And yet after their punishment, then were there some that renewed the bill again.

And yet long after this was there one John Goose roasted at the Tower Hill.[469] And thereupon, forthwith, some other john-goose[470] began to bear that bill abroad again, and made some gaggling a while, but it availed him not. And now because some

heretics have been of late abjured,[471] this gosling therefore hath made this beggars' bill, and gaggleth again upon the same matter — and that, as he thinketh, by a proper[472] invention likely to speed now (because he maketh his bill in the name of the beggars), and his bill couched as full of lies as any beggar swarmeth full of lice.

We neither will nor shall need to make much business about this matter. We trust much better in the goodness of good men than that we should need for this thing to reason against an unreasonable body. We be sure enough that good men were they that gave this gear[473] into the Church, and therefore naught[474] should they be of likelihood that would pull it out thence again. To which ravin[475] and sacrilege, our Lord, we trust, shall never suffer[476] this realm to fall.

Holy Saint Augustine in his days, when he perceived that some evil people murmured at the possessions that then were given into his church, did, in an open[477] sermon among all the people, offer them their lands again,[478] and that his church and he would forsake them,[479] and bade them take them who would. And yet was there not founden in all the town — albeit that[480] the people were (as these Africans be) very barbarous, fierce, and boistous[481] — yet was there none, as we say, founden anyone so bad that his heart would serve him to enter into one foot.[482]

When Pharaoh, the king of Egypt, bought up in the dear years[483] all the lands that were in every man's hand, so that all the people were fain[484] to sell their inheritance for hunger, yet, idolater as he was, he would never suffer, for any need, the possessions of the priests to be sold, but made provision for them beside,[485] and suffered them to keep their lands still, as the Bible beareth witness.[486] And we verily trust that the good Christian princes of the Christian realm of England shall never fail of more favor toward the clergy of Christ than had that prince idolater to the priests of his idols. Yet is it not enough to the cruel mind of this man to take from the whole clergy all that ever they have,

---

456 *devised of:* was made out of   457 who
458 gladly   459 *for nought:* as nothing
460 anticipated   461 *taken in the field:*
taken captive on the battlefield   462 just
463 members of the House of Commons
464 for a second time   465 *Richard
Hundon:* executed 1430   466 who

467 off   468 *as good cheap:* for as cheap
a price   469 *And yet … Hill:* executed
1474   470 a male goose   471 *of
late abjured:* recently made to recant
472 fine   473 stuff, matter   474 bad
475 pillage   476 allow   477 public
478 back   479 *forsake them:* give them up

480 *albeit that:* although   481 savage
482 i.e., a measure of any of those
properties   483 *dear years:* years of dearth
or famine   484 obliged   485 separately
486 See Gn 47:13, 20–22.

but that he would further have them bounden unto carts and whipped, to drive them to labor.[487]

Of all thieves is this one of the worst and most cruel kind. For of all thieves men most abhor them that,[488] when they have taken a man's money from him, then take and bind him and beat him too. But yet is this wretch much worse. For he fareth[489] as a cruel thief that would, without respect of his own commodity,[490] take a man's money from him and cast it he care not where, and then bind the man to a tree and beat him for his pleasure. O, the charity!

But he saith he would have them whipped to compel them to labor and "get their living in the sweat of their faces." And this would he not, good man, but for fulfilling of God's commandment. For he saith that it is commanded them in the first chapter of Genesis. And therefore is he therein so indifferent that he excepteth none, but calleth the best but idle holy thieves, and so would have them all robbed and spoiled, bounden and beaten, to compel them to work with their hands, to "get their living in the sweat of their faces" for the fulfilling of God's commandment. Among this company that he would suddenly send forth new-robbed, with right nought[491] left them, is there many a good man that hath lived full godly many a fair day, and duly served God and prayed for us (which we have well found), many an old man, many a sore[492] sick man, and many blind and many lame too. All which, as soon as they be driven out of their own doors, this charitable man would be very well content to see them bounden and beaten too, because they be of the clergy. For exception maketh he none in this world.

He layeth unto the charge of the clergy that they live idle all, and that they be all bound to labor and get their living in the sweat of their faces by the precept that God gave to Adam in the first chapter of Genesis. Here this man showeth his cunning. For if this be so, then were the priests in the Old Law bound thereto as well as is the clergy now. And then how happed it that of this point there was no mention made by Moses? How happed it that God in that law provided them much larger living than he did the lay people? And that, such kind of living as declared that his pleasure was that

they should live out of labor and upon the labor of other men's hands?[493] The holy apostle Saint Paul, although himself in some places forbore to take his living freely, but rather chose to live of his own labor than to be in their danger which would haply[494] have said that he preached because he would live at ease thereby—and this did he specially to put such false apostles to silence as for such desire of idle living fell somewhere[495] to false preaching—yet neither did he so in every place, and also confessed and said that he might well and lawfully have done the contrary, affirming it for good reason that he that serveth the altar should live of the altar, and saying also, "If we sow unto you spiritual things, is it a great thing if we reap your carnal things?"[496] Now, Christ his own mouth said unto the people that they should not leave their duties unpaid unto the priests.[497] And this good Christian man would have them all clean taken from them, and yet the priests well beaten too.

He reckoneth all the clergy idle because they labor not with their hands till their faces sweat. But our Savior Christ reckoned far otherwise in blessed Mary Magdalene, whose idle sitting at her ease and hearkening[498] he accounted and declared for better business than the busy stirring and walking about of his good hostess Martha, which was yet of all worldly business occupied about the best, for she was busy about alms and hospitality, and the guesting[499] of the best poor man and most gracious guest that ever was guested in this world.[500]

Now if this cannot yet content this good man because of God's commandment given unto Adam that he should eat his bread in the sweat of his face, then would we fain wit[501] whether himself never go to meat[502] till he have wrought so sore[503] with his hands that his face sweateth. Surely we believe he laboreth not so sore before every meal. But yet it were not good to trust his answer, for he will haply say yes, and not let for[504] one lie among so many. Howbeit,[505] he thinketh it peradventure[506] enough for him that he sitteth and studieth till he sweat in seeking out old heresies and devising new. And verily if he look[507] that such business should serve him for a discharge of hand labor,[508] much better may we

---

487 i.e., manual labor **488** who **489** acts **490** profit **491** *right nought:* absolutely nothing **492** grievously **493** See Lv 7:32–36; Nm 5:9–10; 18:20–21, 35:2–8; Dt 18:1–4. **494** perhaps

495 *fell somewhere:* resorted in some places **496** 1 Cor 9:11 **497** See Mt 8:4; Mk 1:44; Lk 5:14. **498** listening carefully **499** hosting **500** See Lk 10:38–42. **501** *fain wit:* like to

know **502** dinner **503** *wrought so sore:* worked so hard **504** *let for:* refrain from **505** However **506** perhaps **507** expects **508** *discharge … labor:* exemption from manual labor

think discharged thereof many good men whom he would have beaten thereto, living their lives in fasting, prayer, and preaching, and studying about the truth.

5   But it is good to look betimes[509] what this beggars' proctor meaneth by this commandment of hand labor that he speaketh of. For if he confess that it bindeth not every man, then is it laid to no purpose against the clergy. For there was a small clergy when 10 that word was said to our first father, Adam. But now, if he call it a precept, as he doth, and then will that it extend unto all the whole kind[510] of man, as a thing by God commanded unto Adam and all his offspring, then, though he say little now, he mean- 15 eth to go further hereafter than he speaketh of yet. For if he might first have the clergy put out of their living, and all that they have clean taken from them, and might have them joined to these beggars that be now, and, over[511] that, added unto them and sent 20 a-begging too, all those that the clergy find[512] now full honestly—this pageant[513] once played, and his beggars' bill so well sped[514]—then, when the beggars should have so much less living and be so many more in multitude, surely likewise[515] as for the beg- 25 gars he now maketh his bill to the King's Highness against bishops, abbots, priors, prelates, and priests, so would he then, within a while after, make another bill to the people against merchants, gentlemen, kings, lords, and princes, and complain that 30 they have all, and say that they do nothing for it but live idle, and that they be commanded in Genesis to live by the labor of their hands in the sweat of their faces, as he saith by[516] the clergy now. Wherein if they ween[517] that they shall stand in other case than 35 the clergy doth now, they may peradventure sore[518] deceive themselves. For if they will think that their case shall not be called all one because they have lands and goods to live upon, they must consider so hath the clergy too. But that is the thing that 40 this beggars' proctor complaineth upon, and would have them taken away.

Now if the landed men[519] suppose that their case shall not seem one with the case of the clergy because they shall haply think that the Church hath 45 their possessions given them for causes which they fulfill not, and that if their possessions happen to be taken from them, it shall be done upon that ground, and so the lay landed men out of that fear[520] because they think that such like occasion and ground and consideration faileth and cannot be found in them 50 and their inheritance, surely if any man, clerk or lay, have lands in the gift whereof hath been any condition adjoined which he fulfilleth not, the giver may well with reason use therein such advantage as the law giveth him. But on the other side,[521] whoso will 55 advise princes or lay people to take from the clergy their possessions, alleging matters at large[522]—as laying to their charge that they live not as they should, nor use not well their possessions, and that therefore it were well done to take them from them by 60 force and dispose them better—we dare boldly say whoso giveth this device,[523] as now doth this beggars' proctor, we would give you counsel to look well what will follow. For he shall not fail, as we said before, if this bill of his were sped, to find you 65 soon after in a new supplication new bald[524] reasons enough that should please the people's ears, wherewith he would labor to have lords' lands and all honest men's goods to be pulled from them by force and distributed among beggars. Of which there 70 should, in this wise that he deviseth, increase and grow so many that they should be able for a sudden shift[525] to make a strong party. And surely as the fire ever creepeth forward and laboreth to turn all into fire, so will such bold beggars as this is never cease 75 to solicit and procure all that they can, the spoil[526] and robbery of all that aught[527] have, and to make all beggars as they be themselves.

We be content that ye believe us not but if it have[528] so proved already by those uplandish[529] Lu- 80 therans that rose up in Almain.[530] Which,[531] being once raised by such seditious books as is this *Beggars' Supplication*, and such seditious heretics as is he that made it, set first upon spiritual prelates. But shortly thereupon they so stretched unto the tem- 85 poral princes that they were fain[532] to join, in aid of themselves, with those whom they laughed at first to see them put in the peril—hoping to have had the profit of their loss, till they saw that they were likely to lose their own with them. And for all the 90

---

509 next   510 race   511 in addition to   512 employ   513 scene on a stage   514 met with success   515 just   516 about   517 think   518 greatly   519 *landed men:* men possessed of land   520 *out of that fear:* are not afraid   521 hand   522 *alleging matters at large:* making general allegations   523 advice   524 meager, paltry   525 *for a shift:* for want of something better   526 despoiling, plundering   527 anything   528 *but if it have:* except that it has been   529 rustic   530 Germany (a reference to the Peasants' Revolt of 1525)   531 Who   532 obliged

punishment that they pursued[533] upon those rebellious persons—of whom there were in one summer slain above sixty thousand—yet is that fire rather covered than quenched, because they suffered[534] it creep forth so far at first that dissension grew thereby among the lords themselves, as there can never lack some needy ravenous landed men that shall be ready to be captains in all such rebellions, as was the Lord Cobham called Oldcastle, sometime a captain of heretics in England in the days of King Henry the Fifth.[535] And surely there would soon follow some sore change in the temporalty if this beggars' proctor have his malicious supplication sped against the spiritualty.

But yet, lest folk should abhor his hard heart and cruelty, the man tempereth his matter with a goodly visage of the sore inward sorrow that he taketh for the diminishment of mankind, and with the great zeal that he beareth to generation[536] for the good increase of Christian people in the land. For he would for that cause in any wise that all the clergy should have wives. For he asketh the King's Highness (as the man hath caught a great pleasure to appose[537] the King, wherein he useth a figure of rhetoric that men call "sauce malapert"[538]), "what an infinite number of people might have been increased to have peopled your realm, if this sort of folk had been married like other men."

This matter that priests must needs have wives he bringeth in diversely in three or four places. And among others he hath one wherein he showeth, in railing against the clergy, a principal part of his excellent eloquence. For there he useth his royal figure of rhetoric called "repetition," repeating often, by[539] the whole clergy, "these be they" in the beginning of his clause: "These be they that have made a hundred thousand idle whores in your realm;" "These be they that corrupt the generation of mankind in your realm;" "These be they" that draw men's wives into incontinency in your realm. And after diverse of such "these be theys," he concludeth and knitteth up the matter with his accustomed vehemence fetched out of Luther's volumes, asking, "Who is able to number the great broad bottomless ocean sea full of evils that this mischievous and sinful

generation bringeth up upon us?" As though all the whole clergy were of this condition and no man else but they! But among all his "these be theys," this is one which, as the sorest[540] and the most vehement, he setteth in the forefront of them all: "These be they that by their abstaining from marriage do let[541] the generation of the people, whereby all the realm at length,[542] if it should be continued, shall be made desert and unhabitable."

Lo, the deep insight that this beggars' proctor hath in the "broad bottomless ocean sea full of evils" to save the "grievous shipwreck of the commonwealth." He seeth far farther than ever Christ was aware of, or any of his blessed apostles, or any of the old holy fathers of Christ's faith and religion since his holy ascension hitherto, till now that Luther came of late and Tyndale after him, and spied out this great secret mystery that neither God nor good man could espy. If their abstaining from marriage should make all the land "desert" and "unhabitable," how happeth it that habitation endureth therein so long? For the land hath lasted since the beginning of their abstaining from marriage, ye wot[543] well, many a fair day. And now if, their abstaining from marriage notwithstanding, the land hath been upholden with the generation of you that are the temporalty so long, ye shall likewise hereafter, by God's grace and the help of good prayers for keeping the land from wilderness, be able to get children still yourselves, and shall not need to call neither monks nor friars to help you.

Now if it be so that the clergy be, as he saith, but the hundredth part of the men, and yet not so much neither, there is not then so great peril of the land to fall to wilderness, but that the ninety-nine parts may maintain it populous, though the hundredth part abstain. But he, for to show that he hath not left his anxious favor toward his native country though he be run away from it for heresy, feareth sore[544] lest the hundredth part forbearing marriage, all the ninety-nine parts shall not be able so to preserve it with generation, but that it shall wax,[545] not only deserted, but also (whereof we most wonder) unhabitable: that is to say, such as of itself shall not be able[546] for man's habitation. But

---

533 inflicted **534** allowed **535** *as was . . . Fifth:* Sir John Oldcastle, a Lollard, was imprisoned for heresy in 1413, but escaped. He then raised a rebel army and was involved in several plots to overthrow the King. He was captured in 1417, and executed on December 14 that year. **536** procreation **537** interrogate **538** *sauce malapert:* impudent sauciness **539** about **540** worst **541** prevent, hinder **542** *at length:* eventually **543** know **544** greatly **545** become **546** suitable

he peradventure[547] taketh "unhabitable" for desert, desolate, and not inhabited, because[548] men should see that he can so roll in his rhetoric that he wotteth not what his own words mean.

And somewhat yet is it to be considered that in such part of his book that he would have it appear that their living[549] is too much, there he would make it seem that they were very few. And where he would have them take wives, he would have them seem so many that their abstaining from marriage were able to bring all the land into desolation and wilderness. And thus he handleth either part so wisely that there lacketh him nothing earthly therein but even a pennyweight of wit. For fault whereof, his wily folly foreseeth not that one part of his process[550] ever impugneth[551] another. For they that were right now so small a part of people that a little would suffice for their living be now suddenly so many that if they were married, "infinite number of people," he saith to the King, would increase to people his realm with.

Now if that be true—that of them alone, if they were married, so infinite number of people would increase that it would make the realm populous— then either are they, contrary to his count, more than the hundredth part (for one out of a hundred is no very perceivable miss, nor one added to a hundred no very perceivable increase), or else, if they be but the hundredth part, as he made his reckoning right now, yet if it be then true that[552] he saith since—that of the hundredth part married, so infinite number of people might increase to people the realm—then can he not deny but that of the ninety-nine parts there may grow ninety-nine times "infinite number of people." And then, that being so, though the clergy, being (as he saith) but the hundredth part, never marry, yet shall the poor fool not need to wake and wax lean[553] for fear of the realm falling to wilderness. In which, he seeth that there may of the ninety-nine parts residue[554] grow and increase ninety-nine times "infinite number of people" to make the land populous.

Yet marvel we much of one thing: that in all his fear that generation should fail because the clergy marrieth not, he seeth no man unmarried in all the realm but them. How many servants? How many tall serving men are there in the realm that might, if men saw such a sudden necessity, rather marry than the clergy that have vowed to God the contrary? But he forceth[555] not so much for the matter that he maketh his pretext as he doth indeed to have all vows void, that he might get Luther some lewd companions in England.

But now what if this good man had the rule of this matter, and would put out all the clergy and bid them go wed? He should peradventure find some that would not much stick[556] thereat; but they should be of the worst sort, and such as now be slander of their order, and whom it were most need to keep from generation, lest evil crows bring you forth evil birds. But as for the good priests and good religious whose children were like[557] to be best and to be best brought up, they would not marry for breach of their vows. And thus should ye have the naughty[558] generations increase, whereof there be too many already, and of the better never the more.

What would this good man do now with good folk of the clergy, that would not marry? He would of likelihood bind them to carts and beat them, and make them wed in the waniand.[559] But now, what if women will not wed them, namely since he sendeth them out with right nought,[560] saving[561] slander, shame, and villainy? What remedy will he find therefor?[562] He will of likelihood compel the women to wed them; and if the wench be nice and play the wanton[563] and make the matter strange,[564] then will he beat her to bed too.

Surely we cannot but here confess the truth: These nice[565] and wanton words do not very well[566] with us; but we must pray God and you to pardon us. For in good faith, his matter of monks' marriages is so merry and so mad that it were able to make one laugh that lieth in the fire, and so much the more in how much he more earnestly presseth upon the King in this point, to have in any wise the clergy robbed, spoiled, bounden, beaten, and wedded. Whereby what opinion he hath of wedding ye may soon perceive, for ye see well that if he thought it good, he would not wish it them.[567]

547 perhaps   **548** so that   **549** income
550 line of argument   **551** contradicts
552 what   **553** *wake . . . lean:* lose sleep and become thin   **554** remainder   **555** cares

556 hesitate   **557** likely   **558** wicked
559 *in the waniand:* with a vengeance
560 *right nought:* absolutely nothing
561 except   **562** for that   **563** *nice . . .*

wanton: coy and dally   **564** *make . . .
strange:* make difficulties; seem unwilling
565 loose-mannered   **566** *do . . . well:* are not appropriate   **567** for them

Many that read his words ween[568] that he were some merry mad guest, but he seemeth us far otherwise. For except[569] he were a wondrous sad[570] man of himself, he could never speak so earnestly in so mad a matter.

Yet one thing would we very fain wit[571] of him: When he had robbed, spoiled, bounden, beaten, and wedded all the clergy, what would he then? Should any of them be curates of men's souls and preach and minister the sacraments to the people or not?

If they should, it were a very strange fashion to rob him, bind him, and beat him on the one day, and then kneel to him, and confess to him, and receive the Sacrament of his hand on the other day— reverently hear him preach in the pulpit, and then bid him go get him home and clout[572] shoes. Either he must mean to have it thus (which none honest man could endure to see) or else (of which twain[573] we wot nere well whether[574] is the worse) he intendeth to have all holy orders[575] accounted as nothing, and to have no more sacraments ministered at all, but whereas soon after Christ's ascension his Church buried the ceremonies of the Jews' synagogue with honor and reverence, so would he now that Christian people should kill and cast out on a dunghill the blessed sacraments of Christ with villainy, rebuke, and shame. And surely to tell you the truth, this is his very[576] final intent and purpose, and the very mark that he shooteth at, as a special point and foundation of all Luther's heresies, whereof this man is one of the banner bearers.

And therefore here would his own high sore words have good place against himself. For this mischievous device[577] of his is indeed a "great broad bottomless ocean sea full of evils" wherein would not fail the "grievous shipwreck of the commonwealth," which God would soon forsake if the people once forsook his faith and contemned his holy sacraments, as this beggars' proctor laboreth to bring about. Which thing his device and conveyance[578] well declareth, although he forbear[579] expressly to say so far, because of the good and gracious Catholic mind that he well knoweth, and by his Grace's excellent writings perceiveth, to be borne by the King's Highness to the Catholic faith. For which, he covereth his malicious intent and purpose toward the faith under the cloak of many temporal benefits that he saith should succeed and follow to the King's Highness and his realm if these his high politic devices were once by his Grace agreed.

For in the end of all his bill, he gathereth his high commodities[580] together, saying that if the King take all from the clergy, set them abroad at the wide world with right nought to wed and take wives, and make them labor for their living till they sweat; bind them to carts and beat them well—he saith to the King in the beggars' names:

Then shall as well the number of our foresaid monstrous sort, as of the bawds, whores, thieves, and idle people, decrease. Then shall these great yearly exactions cease. Then shall not your sword, power, crown, dignity, and obedience of your people be translated[581] from you. Then shall you have full obedience of your people. Then shall the idle people be set awork. Then shall matrimony be much better kept. Then shall the generation[582] of your people be increased. Then shall your commons[583] increase in riches. Then shall none take our alms from us. Then shall the gospel be preached. Then shall we have enough and more. Then shall be the best hospital that ever was founded for us. Then shall we pray to God for your noble estate long to endure.

Lo, here hear ye heaped up many great commodities, if they were all true. But we showed you before, and have also proved you, that his bill is much grounded upon many great lies, whereof he by and by[584] began with some and after went forth with more. And now to the intent that the end should be somewhat suitly[585] to the remnant, as he began with lies and went forth with lies, so will he with lies likewise make an end—saving[586] that in the beginning he gave them out by tale,[587] and in the end he bringeth them in by heaps.

For first he saith that then shall the number of sore[588] and sick beggars decrease. How so? Shall there by the robbing, wedding, binding, and beating of the clergy, blind beggars get their sight again, or lame beggars their legs? Is there no man in all the clergy sick and sore that shall be by this way sent unto them? Should there not many, that now be in good health, wax shortly[589] sick and sore and sit and beg with them? Were this a diminishment of sick and sore beggars: to make more and send to them?[590]

"Then shall," he saith, "bawds and whores, thieves, and idle people decrease." This man weeneth[591] he were cousin to God and could do as he did: *Dixit et facta sunt.*[592] For as soon as he hath devised it, now weeneth he that if they were all put out and so served by and by, then were all forthwith[593] in good order. As soon as he saith "Let them wed," now he weeneth that forthwith every priest, monk, and friar hath a wife. As soon as he hath said "Bind them and beat them to work," forthwith, he weeneth, every man is at his work. And all this he reckoneth sure ere[594] ever he provide work for them, or where they shall dwell, or who shall take so many to work[595] at once that never were wont[596] to work before—and this where he seeth many walk idle already, that either no beating can drive to work, or else no man will take to work.

First, we trust that among the clergy there be many men of that goodness and virtue that scant[597] a devil could find in his heart to handle them in such dispiteous and despiteful[598] manner. But go to,[599] let their honest living and virtue lie still in question, yet at the leastwise he will grant they be good or naught.[600] Now then if they be good, he is too very[601] a villain that would serve good men so. And on the other side if they be all as he would have them all seem—unthrifty, lewd, and naught—how can it be that by the reason of so many so naughty, so suddenly set out at large, ye should have bawds, harlots, thieves, and idle people decrease? Except[602] he think that those whom he calleth naught already—being, as they now be, kept in, and in honest fashion refrained,[603] and many kept up in cloisters—will be better ruled abroad, running at the wild world as bucks broken out of a park. Over[604] this, how can there, by the marriages of priests, monks, and friars, be fewer whores and bawds, when by the very marriage itself—being as it were incestuous[605] and abominable—all were stark harlots that married

them, and all stark bawds that should help to bring them together?

"Then shall," he saith, "these great yearly exactions cease." How can such things cease as never yet began? Ye remember what things he called exactions: the friars' quarterage,[606] which he said that they exact of every household, and compel them to pay it upon pain of heresy—bearing of a fagot or burning. Can he, among so many as payeth it not, lay[607] you one example that ever any said he was so served this seven years, this seven-score[608] years, this seven hundred years? Can he say that ever it was exacted of himself? We know where he dwelled, and that if he had had none other cause to run away, surely for any fear of friars that ever exacted of him quarterage, he would not have been afraid to dwell by the best of their beards.[609]

"Then shall idle folk," he saith, "be set awork." By what means? Whom hath he devised more to set idle men awork?—but if he look[610] that idle men shall be set awork by them whom he sendeth out of their own houses without money or ware,[611] neither he nor they wot whither.[612]

"Then shall matrimony be much better kept." Why so? Because there be more men unmarried sent out abroad to break it? Who (if they be such as he calleth them) were, if they went all abroad, well likely to break many another man's marriage ere they made all their own.

"Then shall the generation of your people be increased." Is that the greatest fault he findeth, the lack of generation? If he saw as far as he would seem to see, then should he spy that it were first more need to provide houses to dwell in, with land laid[613] thereto for tillage; or else experience teacheth that there is generation enough for the corn[614] that the ground beareth. And that thing once well provided for, there will enough be founden to multiply more generation of such as may lawfully wed and would wed, if they wist[615] where after wedding their wife and their children should dwell.

"Then shall not your sword, power, crown, and dignity, and obedience of your people, be taken

589 *wax shortly:* become soon   **590** *send to them:* i.e., send them to join the others   **591** thinks   **592** "He spoke and they were made" (Ps 32(33):9, 147(148):5).   **593** immediately   **594** before   **595** *take . . . work:* employ so many   **596** accustomed

597 scarcely   **598** insulting; vicious   **599** *go to:* come now   **600** bad; wicked   **601** truly   **602** Unless   **603** restrained   **604** Beyond   **605** In canon law, monks and nuns are regarded as siblings.   **606** quarterly payment   **607** cite   **608** A score is twenty.   **609** *by . . . beards:*

Friars and the poor wore beards. See Whiting B112.   **610** *but . . . look:* unless he expects   **611** goods   **612** *wot whither:* know to where   **613** adjoined   **614** grain   **615** knew

from you." Who hath taken it away now? Who hath his sword borne but his Highness himself, or such his deputies as he appointeth it unto? His crown no man weareth but himself, as far as ever any of us heard. And yet if his Highness have any crowned kings under him, his "sword, power, crown, and dignity" is nothing defaced[616] nor diminished, but honored and enhanced by that. But all the mischief is that the spiritual court hath examination of heretics; this is all the grief. For as for obedience of the King's people, his Highness findeth none taken from him. Was there ever king in this realm better obeyed than he? Hath his Highness of any part of his realm been better obeyed or more humbly served than of his clergy? Was there ever any king in the realm that had his crown translated[617] from him because the clergy had lands given them, or because men gave alms to the poor friars? In good faith, ye may trust us, we never knew none such. When the beggars' proctor proveth any such, ye may then believe him; and in the meantime, ye may well believe he lieth.

"Then shall ye have obedience of your people." Yet again? Till he find in the King's realm some that dare disobey him, it were not much against reason that, harping so much upon that string, that every man's ear perceiveth so false and so far out of tune, he should confess himself a fool.

"Then shall your people increase in riches." Wherefore the rather?[618] Not one halfpenny for aught[619] that he hath spoken yet, except[620] he mean, when he taketh the land from the clergy, then to divide it among the people and make a dole of the friars' alms too. And if he mean so, when he saith it out plainly, then will we tell you what he meaneth more. But in the mean season[621] to prove him both false and foolish, it is enough to tell him that the people cannot wax rich by their coming to them that are sent out naked and bring nought with them.

"Then shall none beg our alms from us." No, pardie[622]—none but all they that ye will have sent out naked to you—which would be more than ye would be glad to see sit and beg with you, and see them ask your alms from you that were wont to give alms to you.

"Then shall the gospel be preached." Yea, marry,[623]

that, that.[624] There is the great matter that all this gaping[625] is for. For undoubtedly all the gaping is for a new gospel. Men have been wont this many years to preach the gospel of Christ in such wise as Saint Matthew, Saint Mark, Saint Luke, and Saint John hath written it, and in such wise as the old holy doctors[626]—Saint Jerome, Saint Augustine, Saint Ambrose, Saint Gregory,[627] Saint Chrysostom, Saint Basil, Saint Cyprian, Saint Bernard, Saint Thomas, and all the old holy fathers since Christ's days until your own days—have understood it. This gospel hath been, as we say, always thus preached. Why saith he now that if the clergy were cast out for nought,[628] that then the gospel should be preached? Who should then be these preachers? He meaneth not that the clergy shall; ye may see that well. Who, then? Who but some lay Lutherans? And what gospel shall they preach? Not your old Gospel of Christ, for that is it which was wont to be preached unto you. And he would ye should[629] now think that the gospel shall begin to be preached—and yet not begin to be preached among you till the clergy be cast out. What gospel shall that be then that shall then be preached? What gospel but Luther's gospel and Tyndale's gospel?—telling you that only faith[630] sufficeth you for salvation, and that there needeth no good works, but that it were sacrilege and abomination to go about to please God with any good works, and that there is no purgatory, nor that the sacraments be nothing worth, nor that no law can be made by man to bind you, but that by your only faith ye may do what ye will—and that if ye obey any law or governor, all is of your own courtesy and not of any duty at all; faith hath set you in such a lewd[631] liberty.

This and many a mad frantic folly shall be the gospel that then shall be preached, whereof he boasteth now as of one of the most special commodities[632] that shall succeed upon his goodly and godly devices.[633]

Will ye plainly perceive that he meaneth thus? After all his mischiefs rehearsed[634] against the Church, he hath another matter in his mind, which he dare not yet speak of, but he maketh thereof a secret overture, leaving it in such wise at large[635] as he would

616 *nothing defaced:* not at all discredited
617 transferred, removed **618** *Wherefore the rather?:* Why more? **619** anything
620 unless **621** *mean season:* meantime
622 an exclamation (from "by God,"

French); certainly **623** an exclamation (from "by Mary"); indeed **624** i.e., that that is the point **625** eager longing
626 theologians **627** Pope Saint Gregory the Great (Pope Gregory I) **628** nothing

629 *would ye should:* wants you to
630 *only faith:* faith alone **631** licentious
632 benefits; improvements **633** plans; schemes **634** recounted **635** *at large:* unspecified

that men should guess what he meant, and yet he reserveth himself some refuge to flit therefrom when
he list.[636] For if he should see that men should mislike it, he would in such case say that he meant some
other thing. And therefore he purposeth[637] it under
these words:

> Here leave we out the greatest matter of all, lest
> we, declaring such a horrible carrion of evil against
> the ministers of iniquity, should seem to declare
> the one only fault—or rather, the ignorance—of
> our best-beloved minister of righteousness, which
> is to be hid till he may be learned,[638] by these small
> enormities[639] that we have spoken of, to know it
> plainly himself.

This thing put forth like a riddle—hard to read
what it should signify—we have had since (by such
as we before showed you, that died and came hither)
plainly declared unto us. And surely whoso well adviseth[640] his words, and well pondereth his whole
purpose, and the summary effect of his book, shall
mow soon[641] perceive what he meaneth in that place.
For what should that thing be that he leaveth out,
that should be the "greatest of all," and that should
be laid[642] against the "ministers of iniquity" (which
he meaneth and calleth the whole clergy), and that
should be "such a horrible carrion of evil" that it
should pass[643] and exceed any mischievous matter
that he had already spoken against before? What
manner of mischievous matter should this be?

This "horrible carrion of evil" that he "leaveth
out" since it is, he saith, the "greatest matter of all,"
must needs, ye wot[644] well, be greater against the
clergy than all that "great broad bottomless ocean
sea of evils"; more than all his "these be theys"; more
than the making of such great number of beggars,
of idle men, bawds, whores, and thieves; more than
the hindering of matrimony, corrupting of generation; more than translating[645] the King's kingdom;
more than bringing the King's crown to ruin; more
than bringing the commonweal to shipwreck, and
all the realm to wilderness.

What thing can this "horrible carrion" be that the
clergy doth, that he "leaveth out" for the while, that
so far exceedeth these mischievous matters before
remembered,[646] that in comparison of it he calleth
them all "small enormities" and, as a man would say,
little pretty peccadilloes?[647] Verily,[648] by this thing
meaneth he none other but the preaching of the very
whole corps and body of the blessed faith of Christ,
and the ministering of the blessed sacraments of our
Savior Christ—and of all those, in especial the consecrating of the Sacred Body, the flesh and blood,
of our Savior Christ. For the teaching and preaching of all which things, this beggars' proctor—or
rather, the devil's proctor—with other beggars that
lack grace and neither beg nor look for none, bear all
this their malice and wrath to the Church of Christ.

And seeing there is no way for attaining their intent but one of the twain[649]—that is to wit,[650] either
plainly to write against the faith and the sacraments
(wherein if they got themselves credence and obtained,[651] they then see well the Church must needs
fall therewith), or else to labor against the Church
alone, and get the clergy destroyed (whereupon
they perceive well that the faith and sacraments
would not fail to decay)—they, perceiving this,
have therefore first assayed[652] the first way already,
sending forth Tyndale's translation of the New Testament in such wise handled as it should have been
the fountain and wellspring of all their whole heresies. For he had corrupted and purposely changed in
many places the text, with such words as he might
make it seem to the unlearned people that the
Scripture affirmed their heresies itself. Then came,
soon after, out in print the dialogue of Friar Roy
and Friar Jerome, between the father and the son,
against the Sacrament of the altar,[653] and the blasphemous book entitled *The Burying of the Mass*.[654]
Then came forth, after, Tyndale's wicked book of
Mammona,[655] and after that, his more wicked book
of *Obedience*.[656] In which books afore specified,
they go forth plainly against the faith and holy sacraments of Christ's Church—and most especially
against the Blessed Sacrament of the altar with as
villainous words as the wretches could devise.

But when they have perceived by experience that

---

636 wants   637 proposes   638 taught
639 transgressions   640 considers
641 *mow soon:* be able easily to
642 alleged   643 surpass   644 know
645 transferred, removed   646 *before
remembered:* above-mentioned
647 minor faults   648 Truly   649 two

650 say   651 succeeded   652 tried
out   653 *the dialogue . . . altar:* Friar
William Roy's English adaptation (*A Brief
Dialogue between a Christian Father and
His Stubborn Son*) of a book by Wolfgang
Capito   654 *The Burying of the Mass:*
Better known as *Read Me and Be Not

Wroth, this book is an adaptation (by Friar
Jerome Barlowe, published in 1528) of
Niklaus Manuel's *Die Krankheit der Messe*
(*The Illness of the Mass*).   655 *The Parable
of the Wicked Mammon* (1528)   656 *The
Obedience of a Christian Man* (1528)

good people abhorred their abominable books, then they, being thereby learned that the first way was not the best for the furtherance of their purpose, have now determined themselves to assay the second way: that is to wit, that forbearing to write so openly and directly against all the faith and the sacraments as good Christian men could not abide the reading, they would, with little touching of their other heresies, make one book specially against the Church, and look how that would prove. Which, if it succeeded after their appetites—that they might with false crimes laid unto some, or with the very faults of some, bring the whole Church in hatred and have the clergy destroyed—then should they more easily win their purpose that way. For when the preachers of the faith and very gospel were destroyed or far out of credence with the people, then should they have their own false gospels preached, as ye may perceive that this man meaneth where he saith that "then shall the gospel be preached."

And therefore this is the thing which this man as yet "leaveth out" against them: that is to wit, the preaching of the right faith and the sacraments, which thing he reckoneth in the clergy a more horrible carrion than all the crimes wherein he hath belied[657] them before. And therefore saith he that he leaveth it out lest he should "seem to declare the one and only fault" of the King's Highness. Which[658] "one only fault" he meaneth his Grace's most famous and most gracious book that his Highness, as a prince of excellent erudition, virtue, and devotion toward the Catholic faith of Christ, made—of *The Assertion of the Sacraments*—against the furious book of Martin Luther. This godly deed done by his Highness, with the acceptation of his godly well-deserved title of Defensor of the Faith, given his Grace by the See Apostolic—this calleth this beggars' proctor the King's "one and only fault," and "ignorance" of their false faith (in estimation of these heretics), which this beggars' proctor saith that he will for the while hide and cover under his cloak of silence, till the King may by these "enormities" wherewith he belieth the Church in his beggars' bill (which enormities he calleth "small enormities" in comparison of the preaching of the Catholic faith and the sacraments) be learned. What lesson, trow ye?[659] None other surely but that they hope that as well his Highness as his people may by such beggars' bills be first allured and brought in to contemn, hate, and destroy the Church, and then thereby learn the other lesson which he now "leaveth out" for the while: that is to wit, to set at nought[660] the Catholic faith and all the blessed sacraments, after[661] the teaching of Luther's and Tyndale's gospel. And therefore saith he, as we told you before, that "then shall the gospel be preached."

And in the meantime the man useth, as he weeneth[662] himself, toward the King's Grace a very wise fashion of flattery, calling him their "best-beloved minister of righteousness," yet be they not only run away for fear of the righteousness of their "best-beloved minister of righteousness," but also would it should seem that his Highness were such a minister of righteousness as either set so little by righteousness that he would wittingly suffer,[663] or else had so little insight in[664] righteousness that he could not perceive so great a matter and "such a horrible carrion of evil" committed by the Church, as were so heinous, so huge, and so great, that in comparison thereof, the translating of his kingdom, the ruin of his crown, the shipwreck of his commonwealth, the dispeopling of his realm, and bringing all his land into desolation and wilderness were but slight matters and "small enormities." And that his Highness should, toward this great horrible and intolerable mischievous demeanor of the Church, be aiding and assistant, either of evil mind or of "ignorance," till that, by their beggarly bill, being turned into the hatred and the destruction of the Church, he might thereby be illumined to learn and perceive that the faith which his Grace had before both learned and taught, and whereof himself is the Defensor, is false and feigned, and that the sacraments be but men's inventions, and that thereupon he should be content to learn the gospel of Luther and the testament of Tyndale. And thus ye may see what the beggars' proctor meant by his proper invented riddle; by which, as ye see, under a fond[665] face of flattery he useth toward his prince and sovereign lord (whose Majesty, both by the law of God and the duty of his allegiance, he were highly bounden to reverence) an open plain despite and contumely.[666]

Now to the intent that ye may yet further perceive and see that they, by the destruction of the

---

657 slandered **658** By which **659** *trow ye:* do you think **660** *set at nought:* regard as nothing **661** following **662** believes **663** *wittingly suffer:* knowingly allow **664** into **665** foolish **666** *despite and contumely:* contempt and insolence

clergy, mean the clear abolition of Christ's faith, it may like you to confer and compare together two places of his beggars' bill. In one place, after that he hath heaped up together all his lies against the whole clergy (and thereto adjoined his grievous exclamation, "O the grievous shipwreck of the commonweal!"), he saith that "in ancient time, before the coming of" the clergy, "there were but few poor people, and yet they did not beg, but there was given them enough unasked," because "at that time," he saith, there was no clergy—whom he calleth always "ravenous wolves"—"to ask it from them"; and this, saith he, "appeareth in the book of the Acts of the Apostles."

In this place we let pass his threefold folly: one, that he would, by that[667] there were no beggars in one place, prove thereby that there were none in all the world beside. For as he, for lack of wit and understanding, mistaketh the book, he weeneth[668] that there were none that begged in Jerusalem. Which if it were true, yet might there be enough in other places.

Another of his follies is in that he allegeth[669] a book for him that nothing proveth his purpose. For in all that whole book shall he neither find that there was at that time few poor people, nor that poor people at that time begged not. For of truth, there were poor people and beggars, idle people, and thieves too, good plenty, both then and always before, since almost as long as Noah's flood—and yet peradventure[670] seven years afore that too. And so were there, indeed, in Jerusalem also, among them all, till Christendom came in, and yet remained then among such people there as turned not to the faith of Christ.

The third folly is, he layeth[671] that book for him which indeed proveth plain against him. For where he saith it appeareth there that the clergy was not then come, we cannot in the world devise[672] of what people he speaketh: paynims,[673] Jews, or Christian men. If he mean among paynims, his folly and his falsehood both is too evident. For who knoweth not that among the paynims they had always their priests—whose living was well and plenteously provided for, as ye may perceive not only by many other stories, but also by many places in the Bible,

and specially in the forty-seventh chapter of Genesis? If he speak of the Jews, every man wotteth[674] well that they had a clergy thousands of years before the book that he allegeth—and their living far more largely provided for than any part of the people beside, and that by God's own ordinance. Now if he speak of the Christian people that was at that time in Jerusalem, where the faith began, his book maketh sore[675] against him. For there was a clergy as soon as there was any Christian people—for the clergy began then. And that clergy had,[676] not a part of the Christian people's substance,[677] but had it altogether, and did distribute it as they saw need[678]— which no man doubteth but that the parties showed them,[679] or else in some needs they must needs have lacked. So that here were many poor men, if they be poor that have nought[680] left, and all they beggars if they be beggars that be fain[681] to show their need and ask, and the clergy had altogether.[682] And yet layeth this wise man this book for him, being such as, if he should have sitten and studied therefor,[683] he could not have found a book that made more against him.

But as we said before, we shall let his false folly pass, and pray[684] you to consider what he would have you believe. He saith, and would ye should ween, that there were few poor folk—and no beggars nowhere—before the clergy of Christendom came in, but that all the poverty and beggary came into the world with the Christian clergy. Now knoweth every man that the Christian clergy and the Christian faith came in to the Christian people together, so that in effect his words weigh to this: that all poverty and beggary came into the world with the Christian faith.

Set now to this place the other place of his, in the end and conclusion of his book, where he saith that after the clergy spoiled[685] once and cast out, "then shall the gospel be preached," and "then shall we beggars have enough and more." Lo, like as in the one place he showeth that all beggary came in with the clergy that brought in the faith, so showeth he in the other that there should with the clergy all beggary go forth again, if they were so clean cast out that—Christ's gospel being cast out with them, and the faith which came in with them—they might

---

667 *by that:* because **668** thinks
669 cites **670** *yet peradventure:*
perhaps even **671** cites **672** *in the
world devise:* for all the world figure out

673 pagans **674** knows **675** *maketh
sore:* counts greatly **676** held; controlled
677 wealth **678** See Acts 4:34–35.
679 *showed them:* i.e., declared when they

had needs **680** nothing **681** obliged
682 everything **683** for it **684** ask
685 are despoiled

have that gospel preached as they say they should, and as indeed they should, which they call the gospel: that is to wit,[686] Luther's gospel and Tyndale's testament, preaching the destruction of Christ's very[687] faith and his holy sacraments, advancing and setting forth all boldness of sin and wretchedness, and, under the false name of "Christian freedom," spurring forward the devilish unbridled appetite of lewd[688] seditious and rebellious liberty that slew in one summer, as we showed you before, above sixty thousand of the poor uplandish[689] Lutherans in Almain.[690] And this is all that these heretics look for as the fruit of their seditious books and beggars' bills — trusting by some such ways to be eased of their beggary which they now sustain, being run out of the realm for heresy. For if they might (as they fain[691] would) have the clergy cast out, and Christ's gospel cast off, and their own gospel preached, then hope they to find that word true where he saith, "Then shall we have enough and more."

For of all that ever he hath said, he hath not, almost, said one true word save this. And surely this word would, after their gospel once preached and received, be founden over-true. For then should the beggars — not such beggars as he seemeth to speak for, that be sick, sore, and lame, but such bold presumptuous beggars as he is indeed, whole and strong in body, but weak and sick in soul, that have their bodies clean from scabs and their soul foul infect with ugly great pocks and leprosy — these beggars would hope to have, and except[692] good men take good heed would not fail to have, enough and a great deal more. For after that they might, the clergy first destroyed, bring in once[693] after that the preaching of Luther's gospel and Tyndale's testament, and might with their heresies and false faith infect and corrupt the people, causing them to set the blessed sacraments aside; to set holy days and fasting days at nought; to contemn all good works; to jest and rail against holy vowed chastity; to blaspheme the old holy fathers and doctors of Christ's Church; to mock and scorn the blessed saints and martyrs that died for Christ's faith; to reject and refuse the faith that those holy martyrs lived — and died for — and in the stead of the true faith of Christ continued this fifteen hundred years, to take

now the false faith of a fond[694] friar, of old condemned and of new reforged within so few days, with contempt of God and all good men, and obstinate rebellious mind against all laws, rule, and governance, with arrogant presumption to meddle with every man's substance, with every man's land, and every man's matter,[695] nothing pertaining to them — it is, we say, no doubt but that such bold presumptuous beggars will, if ye look not well to their hands, not fail to have, as he writeth, enough and more too. For they shall gather together at last, and assemble themselves in plumps[696] and in great routs,[697] and from asking fall to the taking of their alms themselves, and under pretext of reformation (bearing every man that aught hath in hand[698] that he hath too much) shall assay[699] to make new division of every man's land and substance — never ceasing, if ye suffer[700] them, till they make all beggars as they be themselves, and at last bring all the realm to ruin — and this not without butchery and foul bloody hands.

And therefore this beggars' proctor, or rather the proctor of hell, should have concluded his supplication not under the manner that he hath done: that after the clergy cast out, then shall the gospel be preached; then shall beggars and bawds decrease; then shall idle folk and thieves be fewer; then shall the realm increase in riches, and so forth. But he should have said: "After that the clergy is thus destroyed and cast out, then shall Luther's gospel come in; then shall Tyndale's testament be taken up; then shall false heresies be preached; then shall the sacraments be set at nought; then shall fasting and prayer be neglected; then shall holy saints be blasphemed; then shall Almighty God be displeased; then shall he withdraw his grace and let all run to ruin; then shall all virtue be had[701] in derision; then shall all vice reign and run forth unbridled; then shall youth leave labor and all occupation; then shall folk wax[702] idle and fall to unthriftiness;[703] then shall whores and thieves, beggars and bawds, increase; then shall unthrifts flock together and swarm about, and each bear him bold of other;[704] then shall all laws be laughed to scorn; then shall the servants set nought by their masters, and unruly people rebel against their rulers; then will rise up rifling and

---

686 say   687 true   688 licentious
689 rustic; rural   690 Germany
691 gladly   692 unless   693 at
some time   694 foolish   695 affair;

business   696 bands   697 mobs
698 *bearing . . . hand:* falsely telling every
man that has anything   699 attempt
700 allow   701 held   702 become

703 wastefulness; dissoluteness
704 *each . . . other:* behave aggressively
toward the other

robbery, murder and mischief, and plain insurrection, whereof what would be the end, or when you should see it, only God knoweth."

All which mischief may yet be withstood easily, and with God's grace so shall it if ye suffer no such bold beggars to seduce you with seditious bills. But well perceiving that their malicious purpose is to bring you to destruction, ye, like good Christian people, avoiding their false trains and grins,[705] give none ear to their heinous heresies, nor walk their seditious ways, but, persevering in your old faith of Christ, and observing his laws with good and godly works and obedience of your most gracious king and governor, go forth in goodness and virtue, whereby ye cannot fail to flower and prosper in riches and worldly substance, which, well employed, with help of God's grace, about charitable deeds to the needy—and the rather[706] in remembrance and relief of us, whose need is relieved by your charity showed for our sake to your neighbor—be able to purchase you much pardon of the bitter pain of this painful place, and bring you to the joyful bliss to which God hath with his blessed blood bought you and with his holy sacraments ensigned[707] you.

And thus will we leave the man's malicious folly, tending to the destruction, first of the clergy and after of yourselves, wherein his mad reckoning hath constrained us to trouble you with many trifles, God wot,[708] full unmeet[709] for us; and now will we turn us to the treating of that one point which, though it specially pertaineth to ourselves, yet much more specially pertaineth it unto you: that is to wit, the impugnation[710] of that uncharitable heresy wherewith he would make you, to our great harm and much more your own, believe that we need none help, and that there were no purgatory.

The end of the First Book

---

705 *false trains and grins:* treacherous lures and snares   **706** *the rather:* all   the more   **707** marked   **708** knows   **709** *full unmeet:* highly inappropriate   **710** refutation

THE SECOND BOOK

When we consider in ourselves, dear brethren and sistren in our Savior Christ, the present painful pangs that we feel, and therewith ponder upon the other part the perilous estate[1] of you that are our friends there living in that wretched world, wit[2] you very surely that this pestilent opinion begun against purgatory, not so much grieveth us for the lack that we should find thereby in the relief of our own intolerable torments, as doth — for the love that we bear you — the fear and heaviness[3] that we take for[4] that peril and jeopardy that should everlastingly fall to your own souls thereby. Nor of all the heavy tidings that ever we heard here was there never none so sore[5] smote us to the heart as to hear the world wax[6] so faint in the faith of Christ that any man should need now to prove purgatory to Christian men, or that any man could be founden which[7] would in so great a thing, so fully and fastly[8] believed for an undoubted article this fifteen hundred year, begin now to stagger and stand in doubt, for[9] the unwise words of any such malicious person as is he that made *The Beggars' Supplication*. For whose answer and full confutation it seemeth us[10] sufficient that ye may clearly perceive his words to be of little weight while[11] ye see that the man hath neither learning, wisdom, nor good intent, but all his bill utterly grounded upon error, evil will, and untruth. And surely this were[12] to us great wonder, if Christian men should need any other proof in this world to reprove[13] such seditious folk withal[14] than the only[15] token of the devil's badge which themselves bear ever about them — the badge, we mean, of malice and of a very deadly devilish hate.

For whereas our Savior Christ hath so left love and charity for the badge of his Christian people, that he commandeth every man so largely to love others that his love should extend and stretch unto his enemy, nor there is no natural man, neither paynim,[16] Jew, Turk, nor Saracen, but he will rather spare his foe than hurt his friend; this kind of folk is so far fallen not only from all Christian charity but also from all humanity and feeling of any good affection[17] natural, and so changed into a wild fierce cruel appetite more than brutish and bestial that they first, without ground or cause, take their friends for their foes, hating the Church deadly[18] because it willeth their weal[19] and laboreth to amend them, and after to do the Church hurt, whom they take for their enemies; they labor to do us much more hurt whom they call still for their friends. For they, to get pulled from the clergy the frail commodities[20] of a little worldly living, labor to have us — their fathers, their mothers, their friends, and all their kin — left lying in the fire here helpless and forgotten — they little force[21] how long. And in this they show their affection much more unnatural and abominable than he that would with his sword thrust his friend through the whole body to the hard haft,[22] to give his enemy behind him a little prick with the point.

This way of theirs were very naught[23] and detestable, although[24] they truly meant indeed as much good as they falsely pretend. For whereas they cloak their cruel purpose and intent under color[25] of a great zeal toward the commonwealth, which they lay[26] to be sore impaired by great pomp and inordinate living used[27] in the Church, we be so far from the mind of defending any such spiritual vice, carnal uncleanness, or worldly pomp and vanity used in the clergy that we would to God it were much less than it is, not in them only but also in the temporalty.[28] And there is none of neither sort but if he were here with us but one half hour, he would set little by[29] all such worldly vanities all his life after, and little would he force or reck[30] whether he wore silk or sackcloth.

But surely this man, if he meant well, the faults of evil folk he would lay[31] to themselves, and not unto the whole clergy. He would also labor for amendment and bettering, not for destruction and undoing finally. He would hold himself within his bounds, only devising against men's vices, and not start out therewith into plain and open heresies. But surely so hath it ever hitherto proved that never

1 state 2 know 3 grief, sadness 4 on account of 5 *so sore:* that so greatly 6 become 7 who 8 steadfastly; firmly 9 on account of 10 to us 11 when 12 would be 13 refute 14 with

15 mere 16 pagan 17 disposition; inclination 18 implacably; excessively 19 well-being 20 benefits 21 care 22 handle 23 *were very naught:* would be very wicked 24 even if 25 appearance,

pretense 26 allege 27 practiced 28 laity 29 *set little by:* value little 30 *force or reck:* care or mind 31 attribute 32 *never... while:* as hidden as possible for the time

was there any that showed himself an enemy to the Church but, though he covered it never so close for the while,[32] yet at the last always he proved himself in some part of his works so very[33] an enemy to the Catholic faith of Christ that men might well perceive that his malice toward the clergy grew first and sprang of[34] infidelity and lack of right belief. And of this point was there never a clearer example than this beggars' proctor,[35] which was so far-forth farced,[36] stuffed, and swollen with such venomous heresies that, albeit[37] he longed sore[38] to keep them in for the season,[39] and only to rail against the clergy and hide his enemious intent toward the faith, yet was he not able to contain and hold, but was fain,[40] for[41] bursting, to puff out one blast of his poisoned sect against us seely[42] souls, the goodness of God driving him to the disclosing and discovering of his malicious heresy, to the intent ye should thereby perceive out of what ungracious[43] ground his enmity sprang that he bore against the Church. Which[44] things once perceived and considered must needs diminish and bereave him[45] his credence among all such as are not affectionate toward his errors and infected and envenomed with his mortal[46] heresies, and of such folk we trust he shall find very few.

For surely not only among Christian people and Jews — of whom the one hath, the other hath had, the perceiving and light of faith — but also among the very miscreant[47] and idolaters (Turks, Saracens, and paynims),[48] except only such as have so far fallen from the nature of man into a brutish beastly persuasion as to believe that soul and body die both at once — else[49] hath always the remnant commonly thought and believed that after the bodies dead and deceased, the souls of such as were neither deadly[50] damned wretches forever, nor on the other side, so good but that their offenses done in this world hath deserved more punishment than they had suffered and sustained there, were punished and purged by pain after the death ere[51] ever they were admitted unto their wealth[52] and rest.

This faith hath always not only faithful people had, but also, as we say, very miscreants and idolaters have ever had a certain opinion and persuasion of the same, whether that, of[53] the first light and revelation given of such things to our former fathers, there hath always remained a glimmering that hath gone forth from man to man, from one generation to another, and so continued and kept among all people, or else that nature and reason have taught men everywhere to perceive it. For surely that they have such belief not only by such as have been traveled in many countries among sundry sects, but also by the old and ancient writers that have been among them, we may well and evidently perceive.

And in good faith, if never had there been revelation given thereof nor other light than reason, yet — presupposed the immortality of man's soul, which no reasonable man distrusted, and thereto agreed the righteousness of God and his goodness, which scant[54] the devil himself denieth — purgatory must needs appear. For since that God of his righteousness will not leave sin unpunished, nor his goodness will[55] perpetually punish the fault after the man's conversion, it followeth that the punishment shall be temporal. And now, since the man often dieth before such punishment had, either at God's hand by some affliction sent him or at his own by due penance done, which the most part of people wantonly[56] doth forsloth,[57] a very child almost may see the consequent: that the punishment at the death remaining due and undone is to be endured and sustained after. Which, since his Majesty is so excellent whom we have offended, cannot of right and justice be but heavy and sore.[58]

Now if they would, peradventure[59] as in magnifying of God's high goodness, say that after a man's conversion once to God again, not only all his sin is forgiven but all the whole pain also, or that they will under color[60] of enhancing the merit and goodness of Christ's Passion tell us that his pain suffered for us standeth in stead[61] of all our pain and penance, so that neither purgatory can have place nor any penance need to be done by ourselves for our own sin — these folk that so shall say shall, under pretext of magnifying his mercy, not only sore diminish his virtue of justice, but also much hinder the opinion and persuasion that men have of his goodness. For albeit that God of his great mercy may forthwith[62] forgive some folk freely their sin

---

33 truly 34 from 35 representative; agent; alms-collector 36 *so far-forth farced:* to such an extent crammed 37 although 38 greatly 39 time 40 forced 41 to keep from 42 poor 43 devoid of grace;

wicked 44 These 45 *bereave him:* deprive him of 46 lethal; mortally sinful 47 unbelieving 48 pagans 49 otherwise 50 fatally; implacably 51 before 52 well-being 53 from 54 scarcely

55 *his goodness will:* will his goodness 56 light-heartedly; recklessly 57 neglect 58 grievous; severe; intense 59 perhaps 60 the appearance, the pretext 61 the place 62 immediately

and pain both, without prejudice of his righteousness, either of his liberal bounty or for some respect had[63] unto the fervent sorrowful heart that fear and love, with help of special grace, have brought into the penitent at the time of his return to God, and also that the bitter Passion of our Savior, besides the remission of the perpetuity of our pain, do also lessen our purgatory and stand us here in marvelous high stead, yet if he should use this point for a general rule — that at every conversion from sin with purpose of amendment and recourse to confession, he shall forthwith fully forgive without the party's pain or any other recompense for the sins committed save only Christ's Passion paid for them all — then should he give great occasion of lightness[64] and bold courage to sin.

For when men were once persuaded that be their sins never so sore,[65] never so many, never so mischievous, never so long-continued, yet they shall never bear pain therefor,[66] but by their only faith[67] and their baptism, with a short return again to God, shall have all their sin and pain also clean[68] forgiven and forgotten — nothing else but only to cry him mercy as one woman would that treadeth on another's train — this way would, as we said, give the world great occasion and courage not only to fall boldly to sin and wretchedness, but also careless to continue therein, presuming upon that thing that such heretics have persuaded unto some men already: that three or four words ere they die shall sufficiently serve them to bring them straight to heaven.

Whereas, besides the fear that they should have, lest they shall lack at last the grace to turn at all, and so for fault of those three or four words fall to the fire of hell, if they believe therewith the thing that truth is besides — that is to wit,[69] that though[70] they hap to have the grace to repent and be forgiven the sin and so to be delivered of the endless pain of hell, yet they shall not so freely be delivered of purgatory, but that, besides the general relief of Christ's holy Passion extended unto every man not after[71] the value thereof but after the stint[72] and rate appointed by God's wisdom, great and long pain abideth[73] them here among us, whereof their willingly taken penance in the world, and affliction

there put unto them by God, and there patiently borne and suffered with other good deeds there in their life done by them, and finally the merits and prayers of other good folks for them, may diminish and abridge the pain which will else hold them here with us in fire and torments intolerable only God knoweth how long — this thing, we say, as it is true indeed, so if the world well and firmly for a sure truth believe it, cannot fail to be to many folk a good bridle and a sharp bit to refrain[74] them from sin. And on the other side, the contrary belief would send many folk forward to sin, and thereby, instead of purgatory, into everlasting pain.

And therefore is this place of our temporal pain of purgatory not only consonant unto his righteous justice, but also the thing that highly declareth his great mercy and goodness, not only for that[75] the pain thereof, huge and sore as it is, is yet less than our own sin deserveth, but also most especially, in that by the fear of pain to be suffered and sustained here, his goodness refraineth men from the boldness of sin and negligence of penance, and thereby keepeth and preserveth them from pain everlasting, whereas the light forgiveness of all together would give occasion, by boldness of sin and presumption of easy remission, much people to run down headlong thither. And therefore were, as we said, that way very far contrary not only to God's justice and righteousness, but also to his goodness and mercy. Whereupon, as we said before, it must needs follow that since the pain is always due to sin, and is not always clean forgiven without convenient[76] penance done or other recompense made, nor pain is not always done, nor any recompense made in the man's life, and yet the man discharged of hell by his conversion, all the pain that remaineth must needs be sustained here with us in purgatory.

But now, if these heretics, as they be very selfwilled and willful, will set at nought[77] the common opinion and belief and persuasion of almost all the world, and, as they be very unreasonable, make little force[78] of reason and ever ask for Scripture, as though they believed Holy Scripture, and yet when it maketh against them, they then with false and fond[79] glosses of their own making do but mock and shift over[80] in such a trifling manner that it may

---

63 *respect had:* consideration taken
64 frivolity, thoughtlessness 65 grievous; severe 66 on that account 67 *only faith:* faith alone 68 completely 69 say

70 even if 71 according to 72 measure
73 awaits 74 restrain 75 *for that:* because 76 appropriate 77 *set at nought:* value as nothing 78 make

little force of: attach little importance to
79 foolish 80 *shift over:* change positions

well appear they believe not Scripture neither —
yet since they make as[81] they believed Scripture
and nothing else, let us therefore see whether that
purgatory do not appear opened and revealed unto
Christian people in Holy Scripture itself.

And first it seemeth very probable and likely
that the good king Hezekiah for none other cause
wept at the warning of his death given him by the
Prophet,[82] but only for the fear of purgatory.[83] For
albeit that[84] diverse doctors[85] allege diverse causes of
his heaviness[86] and loathness at that time to depart
and die, yet seemeth there none so likely as the cause
that ancient doctors allege: that is to wit, that he
was loath to die for the fear of his estate[87] after his
death, forasmuch as he had offended God by overmuch liking of himself, wherewith he wist[88] that
God was displeased with him, and gave him warning, by the Prophet, that he should live no longer.

Now considered he so the weight of his offense
that he thought and esteemed the only[89] loss of this
present life far under the just and condign[90] punishment thereof, and therefore fell in great dread of far
sorer punishment after. But being as he was a good
faithful king, he could not lack sure[91] hope, through
his repentance, of such forgiveness as should preserve him from hell. But since his time should be so
short that he should have no leisure to do penance
for his fault, he therefore feared that the remnant
of his righteous punishment should be performed
in purgatory. And therefore wept he tenderly and
longed to live longer, that his satisfaction done there
in the world, in prayer and other good virtuous
deeds, might abolish and wear out all the pain that
else were toward[92] him here among us. To which his
fervent boon[93] and desire, at the contemplation of
his penitent heart, our Lord of his high pity condescended and granted him the lengthening of his life
for fifteen years, making him for his further comfort sure thereof by the show of a manifest miracle.

But whereto[94] granted our Lord that longer life?
To be bestowed upon worldly delight and pleasure?
Nay, nay verily.[95] But to the intent it might appear
that it was of God's great mercy granted for the redeeming of his purgatory by good works for his satisfaction, he was promised by the Prophet not only

that he should within three days be recovered and
whole, but also that he should go into the Temple
to pray. So that it may thereby appear for what end
and intent he longed so sore[96] for a longer life.

Now if the beggars' proctor,[97] or Tyndale or Luther either, list[98] to say that in this point we do but
guess at that good king's mind, and therefore purgatory thereby rather somewhat reasoned than well
and surely proved, thereto may we well answer and
say that, the circumstance of the matter considered,
with the virtuous holiness and cunning[99] of such
as so long ago have taken the Scripture thus, that
place alone is a far better proof for purgatory than
ever any of them could hitherto lay against it yet.
For albeit this beggars' proctor saith that right wise
and cunning men will say that there is no purgatory
at all — by which wise men he meaneth Luther and
Tyndale and himself — yet was there never any of
them all that yet laid any substantial thing, either
reason or authority, for them, but only jest and rail,
and say that purgatory is a thing of the pope's own
making, and that souls do nothing till Doomsday[100]
but lie still and sleep.

And thus telling such wise tales for their own
part,[101] and making mocks and mows[102] at everything that maketh against their folly for our part,
they go forth in their evil will and obstinacy and,
with murmur and grudge[103] of their own conscience, content themselves with the only[104] feeding of their malicious minds by the increase of their
faction of such as fall into their fellowship rather of
a light mind and lewd pleasure to take a part than
of any great credence that they give unto them or
greatly force[105] which way they believe. For surely
if these folk were reasonable and indifferent,[106] as
it is not well possible for them to be after that they
refuse once to believe the Catholic Church, and in
the understanding of Scripture lean only to their
own wits — but else, as we say, if they could with
an equal and indifferent mind consider and weigh
what they hear, they should soon see their heresy reproved[107] and purgatory surely confirmed, not only
by probable reason taken of the Scripture, as in the
place that we rehearsed[108] you of Hezekiah, but also
by plain and evident texts.

81 *make as:* act as if   **82** Isaiah   **83** See Is
38, 2 Kgs 20, and 2 Chr 32.   **84** *albeit that:*
although   **85** theologians   **86** sadness
87 condition, state   **88** knew   **89** mere
90 deserved   **91** secure; certain

92 approaching   **93** request   **94** to what
end   **95** truly   **96** greatly; intensely
97 representative; agent; alms-collector
98 wishes   **99** knowledge, cleverness
100 Judgment Day. See Mt 10:15.

101 side   **102** derisive grimaces   **103** *murmur and grudge:* muttered complaints
and discontent   **104** mere   **105** care
106 impartial   **107** refuted   **108** cited

For have ye not the words of Scripture, written in the book of the Kings, *Dominus deducit ad inferos et reducit* ("Our Lord bringeth folk down into hell and bringeth them thence again")?[109] But they that be in that hell where the damned souls be— they be never delivered thence again. Wherefore it appeareth well that they whom God delivereth and bringeth thence again be in that part of hell that is called purgatory.

What say they to the words of the prophet Zechariah, *Tu quoque in sanguine testamenti tui eduxisti vinctos tuos de lacu in quo non erat aqua* ("Thou hast in the blood of thy testament[110] brought out thy bounden prisoners out of the pit," or "lake," "in which there was no water")?[111] In that they whom the prophet there speaketh of were "bounden," we may well perceive that they were in a prison of punishment. And in that he calleth them the prisoners of God, it is easy to perceive that he meaneth not any that were taken and imprisoned by any other than the damned spirits, the very jailers of God. And in that he saith that there is in that lake no water, we may well perceive that he spoke it in description of that dry pit of fire, wherein there is no refreshing, for as hot are we here as they are in hell. And what heat is in the pit where there lacketh water our Savior himself declareth by the words of the rich glutton lying in such a lake from whence, at sight of poor Lazarus in Abraham's bosom, he desired heavily to have him sent unto him with one drop of water to refresh his tongue, that after all the delicates that it had tasted in his life, lay there then sore burning, and never set half so much by[112] twenty tons of wine as he set by one poor drop of water.[113] So that, as we show you, these words of the prophet Zechariah, "Thou hast brought out thy bounden prisoners out of the lake wherein is no water," do right well appear to be spoken of these poor imprisoned souls whom Christ, after his bitter Passion, by his precious blood wherewith he consecrated his Church in his new testament, delivered out of the lake of fire wherein they lay bounden for their sins. But now is there no man that doubteth whether Christ delivered the damned souls out of hell or not. For in that hell is there no redemption, and in *limbo patrum*[114] the souls were in rest.

Wherefore it appeareth clearly that those prisoners whom he brought out of their pain he brought only out of purgatory. And so see these heretics purgatory clearly proved by the plain words of this holy prophet.

Another place is there also in the Old Testament that putteth purgatory quite out of question. For what is plainer than the places which in the book of the Maccabees make mention of the devout remembrance, prayer, alms, and sacrifice to be done for souls when the good and holy man Judas Maccabeus gathered money among the people to buy sacrifice withal to be offered up for the souls of them that were dead in the battle?[115] Doth not this place of Scripture so openly declare the need that we souls have in purgatory, and the relief that we find by the prayer and suffrages[116] of good people upon earth, that all the heretics that bark so fast against us can find neither gloss nor color[117] to the contrary?

What shift[118] find they here? Surely a very shameless shift, and are fain[119] to take them to that tackling that is their sheet-anchor always when they find the storm so great that they see their ship goeth all to wreck. For first they use[120] to set some false gloss to the text that is laid against them, and deny the right sense.

But now if the text be so plain that they can have no such color, then when they can have no more hold, but see that their part goeth all to nought,[121] they fall to a shameless boldness and let[122] not to deny the Scripture and all, and say the Holy Scripture which is laid against them is none Holy Scripture at all, as Luther playeth with the godly epistle of Christ's blessed apostle Saint James. And even the same do those heretics with the authority of this holy book of Maccabees: they be not ashamed to say that it is not Scripture.

But upon what ground do they deny it for Scripture? Because it is not founden and accounted for Holy Scripture among the Jews? They neither do nor can deny but that it is taken for Holy Scripture by the Church of Christ. For if they would deny that—both the whole Church beareth witness against them at this day, and it also appeareth plainly by Saint Jerome, Saint Augustine, and other

109 1 Sm 2:6 **110** covenant **111** Zec 9:11 **112** *set half so much by:* valued half as much **113** See Lk 16:19–31. **114** *limbo patrum:* the limbo of the fathers; the place in which good departed souls were detained until Jesus ascended into heaven **115** See 2 Mc 12:38–45. **116** intercessory prayers for the dead **117** *gloss nor color:* interpretation nor ground **118** stratagem **119** obliged, forced **120** are accustomed **121** nothing **122** hesitate

old holy doctors that the Church so took it also in their days and before—then would we gladly wit[123] of these new men (these enemies, we mean, of ours) whether the Church of Christ be not of as great authority and as much to be believed in the choice and election of Holy Scripture as the Jews. If they will say yes, then answer they themselves, for then is the book of the Maccabees by the choice of the Church proved Holy Scripture, though the Jews never accounted it so. Now if they will say no and will contend that it cannot be accounted Holy Scripture, though the Church of Christ so take it, but if[124] the Jews so took it too, then go they near to put out Saint John's Gospel out of Scripture too, for the Jews never took it for none. And surely if they admit for Scripture that book that the Jews admitted, and deny that book to be Scripture which the Church of Christ receiveth for Scripture, then do they say that the Spirit of God was more effectually present and assistant unto the synagogue of the Jews in the law of his prophet Moses than unto the Church of his own only-begotten Son in the law of Christ's Gospel.

If they consider well the books of the Maccabees, they shall find such things therein as may give them good occasion to put little doubt but that it should be of great and undeniable authority. For they shall find there that the great good and godly valiant captain of God's people did institute and ordain the great feast of the Dedication of the Temple of Jerusalem called *Festum encaeniorum*,[125] of the annual institution of which feast we read nowhere else but in the book of the Maccabees. And yet find we that feast ever after continued and had in honor until Christ's own days, and our Savior himself went to the celebration of that same feast, as appeareth in the Gospel of Saint John.[126] So that it may well appear that the books of that noble history, whereof remaineth so noble a monument and remembrance, continually kept and reserved[127] so long after, and honored by Christ's own precious person, and testified by his holy Evangelist in the book of his holy Gospel, cannot be but undoubted truth and of divine authority.

And surely if they deny the book of the Maccabees for Holy Scripture because the Jews account it not for such, then shall they by the same reason refuse the authority of the book of Sapience,[128] and prove themselves insipients.[129] And likewise if they take all Scripture besides the New Testament to be of none other force and authority than it is accounted in the rule and canon of the Jews, then shall the whole Psalter of David (the very sum[130] of clear and lightsome prophecies) lose among them great part of his authority, since it is not taken in like force and strength among the Jews as it is in Christ's Church.

Finally for the book of the Maccabees, since the Church of Christ accounteth it for Holy Scripture, there can no man doubt thereof but he that will take away all credence and authority from the whole Scripture of God—the very Gospels and all. For if these heretics deny for Holy Scripture any book that the Church of Christ accounteth for Holy Scripture, then deny they one of the greatest foundations of all Christian faith, and the thing which their master Martin Luther himself hath already confessed for true. For he affirmeth himself that God hath given unto the Church of Christ that gift—that the Church cannot fail surely and certainly to discern between the words of God and the words of men, and that it cannot be deceived in the choice of Holy Scripture and rejecting of the contrary—so far-forth[131] that he confesseth (as he needs must, of necessity) that the noble doctor and glorious confessor Saint Augustine said very well when he said that he should not have believed the Gospel but for the authority of the Church.[132] For he had not known which had been the very[133] book of the Gospels and which not, among so many as were written, but by the authority of the Church, whom the Spirit of God assisted as it ever doth and ever shall, in the choice and receiving of Holy Scripture and rejection of the counterfeit and false. Whereby it appeareth clearly not only by that holy doctor Saint Augustine, but also by the confession of the arch-heretic Luther himself, that the Church cannot be deceived in the choice of Holy Scripture and rejection of the contrary, so far-forth that it neither can receive as Holy Scripture any book that is none, nor reject for other than Holy Scripture any book that is Holy Scripture indeed. And surely

123 know   124 *but if*: unless   125 *Festum encaeniorum*: the Feast of Lights, Hanukkah   126 See Jn 10:22–23.   127 preserved   128 Wisdom   129 unwise persons   130 summit   131 *so far-forth*: to such an extent   132 See Luther, *De captivitate Babylonica* (WA 6: 561); St. Augustine, *Against the Fundamental Epistle of Manichaeus* 1.5 (PL 42: 176).   133 true

if the Church might so be deceived in the choice of Holy Scripture that they might take and approve for Holy Scripture any book that were none, then stood all Christendom in doubt and unsurety[134] whether Saint John's Gospel were Holy Scripture or not, and so forth of all the New Testament.

And therefore since, as we have showed you by the heretics' own confessions, the Church of Christ cannot be deceived in the choice and election of Holy Scripture, by which their confession they must needs abide and not flit therefrom—as they daily do change and vary from their own words in many other things, except that they will in the falling from that point refuse the strength and authority of the New Testament of Christ—and since, as yourselves well perceiveth also, the Church of Christ receiveth and taketh and (as ye see by Saint Jerome and other old holy doctors this thousand year) hath approved and firmly believed the holy book of the Maccabees to be one of the volumes of Holy Scripture, and then in that book ye see so manifestly purgatory proved that none heretic, as shameless as they be, can yet for shame say the contrary, but are by the plain and open words of that holy book so driven up to the hard wall that they can no farther but are fain[135] to say that the book is no part of Scripture, which shift[136] they must needs forsake again or else revoke their own words and therewith also the authority of all Christ's Gospel, there shall, if either reason or shame can hold, never need any further thing for the proof of purgatory to stop the mouths of all the heretics that are or shall be to the world's end.

But yet, since they be so shameless and unreasonable that the thing which they can in no wise[137] defend they cannot yet find in their proud heart to give over, but when it is proved by diverse plain texts of the Old Testament, then having no probable reason for their part, they never the more give place to truth, but stick to their obstinate nay, let us see whether our purpose be not proved by good and substantial authority in the New Testament also.

And first let us consider the words of the blessed apostle and evangelist Saint John, where he saith, *Est peccatum usque ad mortem; non dico ut pro eo roget quis.* "There is," saith he, "some sin that is unto the death; I bid not that any man shall pray for that."[138] This sin, as the interpreters agree, is understood of[139] desperation and impenitence, as though Saint John would say that whoso depart out of this world impenitent or in despair, any prayer after made can never stand him in stead.[140] Then appeareth it clearly that Saint John meaneth that there be others which die not in such case, for whom he would men should pray, because that prayer to such souls may be profitable. But that profit can no man take neither being in heaven where it needeth[141] not, nor being in hell where it booteth[142] not. Wherefore it appeareth plain that such prayer helpeth only for purgatory, which they must therefore needs grant except[143] they deny Saint John.

What say they to the words of Saint John in the fifth chapter of the Apocalypse? "I have heard," saith he, "every creature that is in heaven and upon the earth and under the earth and that be in the sea and all things that be in them—all these have I heard say, 'Benediction and honor and glory and power forever be to him that is sitting in the throne, and unto the Lamb."[144]

Now wotteth[145] every man well that in hell among damned souls is there none that giveth glory to Christ for the redemption of man. For they, for anger that by their own default[146] they have lost their part thereof, and cannot, for proud heart, take their fault to themselves, fall to blasphemy as the devil doth himself, and impute their sin to the fault of God's grace, and their damnation to the blame of his creation. So that the praise and glory that is given by creatures in hell unto the Lamb for man's redemption is only by the souls in purgatory, that be and shall be partners of that redemption, as the creatures walking upon earth or sailing in the sea that give the honor to Christ for man's redemption be only the Christian people, which look and hope to be partners thereof, and not infidels, that believe it not. But the blessed creatures in heaven give honor to Christ for man's redemption, for that joy and pleasure that their charity taketh in the society and fellowship of saved souls.

And in this place it is a world[147] to see the folly of some heretics, what evasion they seek to void[148] from this place of Scripture. They say that it is no more to be understood by[149] souls here in purgatory, nor Christian men living upon earth, than by fishes in the sea and the devil and damned souls in

---

134 uncertainty **135** obliged, forced **139** as **140** *stand him in stead:* benefit him **144** Rv 5:13 **145** knows **146** fault
136 stratagem **137** way **138** 1 Jn 5:16 **141** is needed **142** helps **143** unless **147** wonder **148** escape **149** as

hell, because the text saith that every creature in the sea and in hell spoke that laud and honor to the Lamb. But by this wise way might they prove that when ye pray for "all" Christian souls, ye mean to pray for our Lady's soul, and for Judas's too, and that our Savior, when he sent his apostles and bade them preach his Gospel to "every creature,"[150] they may bear you in hand[151] that he bade them preach to oxen and kine[152] and their calves too, because all they be creatures. But as they were sent to none other creature than such as he meant of, though he spoke of all, nor ye mean to pray for no souls but such as have need and may have help, though ye speak of "all," so though Saint John spoke of every creature in hell giving honor to Christ for man's redemption, yet meant he but such as be in that hell in which they rejoice therein and shall be partners thereof, which be only we in purgatory, and not the devils and damned souls that blaspheme him, though their just punishment redound[153] against their will to the glory of God's righteousness.

If all this will not satisfy them, will ye see yet another clear place, and such as none heretic can avoid? Doth not the blessed apostle Saint Peter, as appeareth in the second chapter of the Apostles' Acts, say of our Savior Christ in this wise,[154] *Quem Deus suscitavit, solutis doloribus inferni*?[155] In these words he showeth that pains of hell were loosed.[156] But these pains were neither pains of that hell in which the damned souls be pained—which neither were loosed then nor never be loosed, but be and shall be, as our Savior saith himself, everlasting— nor these pains that were then loosed were not the pains in *limbo patrum*,[157] for there were none to be loosed, for the good souls were there, as our Savior showeth himself, in quiet comfort and rest.[158] And so appeareth it evidently that the pains of hell that were loosed were only the pains of purgatory, which is also called "hell," by occasion of the Latin word and the Greek word both.

For in these tongues (forasmuch as before the resurrection of our Savior Christ there was never none that ascended up into heaven) there was no people that any otherwise spoke of souls than that they were gone down "beneath," into the "low place." And therefore in the words of the common[159] Creed

is it said of our Savior Christ after his Passion, *Descendit ad inferna* (that is to say, "He descended down beneath, into the low places"), instead of which "low places" the English tongue hath ever used this word "hell." And certain is it and very sure that Christ descended not into all these low places, nor into every place of hell, but only into *limbus patrum* and purgatory. Which two places, because they be parts of habitations of souls beneath (all which habitations beneath have in English been always called "hell"), therefore are these two places, among others, taken and comprehended under the name of "hell." Which word "hell" nothing else signifieth unto us in his general signification but the habitations of souls beneath or under us, in the low places under the ground. Albeit, because *limbus patrum* and purgatory be called in English also by their special names besides, therefore is most commonly this word "hell" restrained to the special signification of that low place beneath in which the damned souls be punished.

This much have we showed you of this word "hell," because we would not that the common taking thereof might bring you into any error. So that by this place ye see proved, by the plain words of Saint Peter, that Christ at his resurrection did loose and unbind pains in hell, which, as we have showed you, could be nowhere there but in purgatory. For in the special hell of damned souls the pains were not loosed. And in *limbus patrum* was no pains to be loosed. And therefore, except they deny Saint Peter, they cannot deny purgatory.

And yet if they deny Saint Peter, we shall then allege[160] them Saint Paul, whom they be best content to hear of, because that of the difficulty of his writing, they catch sometimes some matter of contention for the defense of their false exposition. This blessed apostle in his First Epistle to the Corinthians, the third chapter, speaking of our Savior Christ, the very foundation and the only foundation of all our faith and salvation, saith,

If any man build upon this foundation gold, silver, precious stones, wood, hay, or straw, every man's work shall be made open, for the Day of our Lord[161] shall declare it, for in the fire it shall be

---

150 See Mt 28:19–20. 151 *bear you in hand:* assert against you 152 cattle 153 contributes 154 way 155 *Quem… inferni:* "Whom God has raised up, having

loosed the sorrows of hell" (Acts 2:24). 156 dissolved 157 *limbus patrum:* the limbo of the fathers; the place in which good departed souls were detained until

Jesus ascended into heaven 158 See Lk 16:20–22, 25. 159 i.e., Apostles' 160 quote 161 Doomsday

showed, and the fire shall prove what manner of thing every man's work is. If any man's work that he hath builded thereon do abide,[162] he shall have a reward. If any man's work burn, he shall suffer harm, but he shall be safe, but yet as by fire.[163]

In these words the Apostle showeth that likewise as some men abiding upon Christ and his very lively[164] faith build up thereupon such good works as are so good and so pure that they be like fine gold, fine silver, or such fine precious stones as when they be cast in the fire it can find no filth to fetch out of them, and therefore they remain in the fire safe and undiminished, so are there some on the other side which, though they do not (as many others do), with mortal sins and lack of good works, wound their faith unto the death and fall from Christ, the foundation that they must build upon, yet do they, abiding upon that foundation, build up thereupon many such simple and frail and corruptible works as can never enter heaven. And such be venial sins, as[165] idle words, vain and wanton[166] mirth, and such other things like, which be but like wood, hay, or straw. Which works, when the soul after his departing out of the world bringeth hither into purgatory, he cannot so get through it as doth the soul whose works were wrought clean, or fully purged by penance ere he died.

For that soul in the fire can feel no harm, like[167] as fine gold can in the fire nothing lose of its weight. But this soul that bringeth with him such frail works, either wrought by themselves or inserted peradventure[168] and mixed amidst of some good and virtuous work—as, for example, some lack peradventure sufficient attention and heed, taken by some sudden wavering of the mind, in time of prayer, or some surreption[169] and creeping in of vainglory and liking of their own praise in their alms given or other good deed done, not forthwith[170] resisted and cast out, but kept and fed upon too long, and yet neither so long peradventure nor so great as our Lord will for that thought deprive him the merit and reward of his work—lo, in such cases, as the Apostle saith, the Day of our Lord, which is to the whole world the day of the general judgment, and to every man particular the day of his own judgment after his death, shall show his work; what manner thing it is the fire shall prove and declare.

For here in purgatory, like as the fire can in the clean souls take none hold, but they shall be therein without any manner[171] pain or grief, so shall it in the souls that are uncleansed and have their works imperfect, unclean, and spotted hastily catch, hold, and keep them fast and burn them with incessant pain, till the filthiness of their sins be clean[172] purged and gone, and that shall be in some sooner, in some later, as their sins or the spots remaining thereof be more easy or more hard to get out. And that is the thing that Paul signifieth by the "wood," "hay," and "straw," of which the one is a light flame, soon ended; the other smoldereth much longer, and the third is hottest and endureth longest. But yet hath it an end, and so shall have, at length, all the pains of them that shall be purged here. But whatsoever soul mishap to die in deadly[173] sin and impenitent, since he is thereby fallen off forever from our Savior Christ that was his foundation, and hath builded up wretched works upon your ghostly[174] enemy the devil, wherewith he hath so thoroughly poisoned himself that he can never be purged, the fire shall therefore lie burning upon him forever, and his pain never lessed, nor his filthy spots never the more diminished.

And forasmuch as ye never can conceive a very right imagination of these things which ye never felt, nor it is not possible to find you any example in the world very like unto the pains that seely[175] souls feel when they be departed thence, we shall therefore put you in remembrance of one kind of pain, which though it be nothing like for[176] the quantity of the matter, yet may it somewhat be resembled by reason of the fashion and manner. If there were embarked many people at once to be by ship conveyed a long journey by sea, of such as never came thereon before, and should hap[177] all the way to have the seas rise high and sore wrought,[178] and sometime soon upon a storm to lie long after wallowing at an anchor, there should ye find diverse fashions of folk. Some peradventure (but of them very few) so clean from all evil humors and so well attempered[179] of themselves that they shall be all that long voyage by sea as lusty[180] and as jocund as if they were on land. But far the most part shall ye see sore[181] sick, and

162 remain 163 1 Cor 3:12–15
164 *very lively:* true living 165 such
as 166 lustful; unruly, unrestrained
167 just 168 perhaps 169 surprise
attack 170 immediately 171 kind
of 172 completely 173 mortal
174 spiritual 175 poor 176 in terms of
177 happen 178 *sore wrought:* severely
rough 179 balanced 180 healthy
181 greatly; grievously

yet in many sundry manners: some more, some less, some longer time diseased, and some much sooner amended. And diverse that a while had weened[182] they should have died for pain, yet after one vomit or twain[183] so clean rid of their grief that they never feel displeasure of it after. And this happeth after as[184] the body is more or less disposed in itself thereto. But then shall ye sometimes see there some other whose body is so incurably corrupted that they shall walter and tolter,[185] and wring their hands, and gnash the teeth, and their eyes water, their head ache, their body fret, their stomach wamble,[186] and all their body shiver for pain, and yet shall never vomit at all, or if they vomit, yet shall they vomit still and never find ease thereof.

Lo, thus fareth it, as a small thing may be resembled to a great, by[187] the souls deceased and departed the world, that such as be clean and unspotted can in the fire feel no disease[188] at all, and on the other side, such as come thence so deadly poisoned with sin that their spots be indelible and their filthiness unpurgeable lie fretting and frying in the fire forever. And only such as neither be fully cleansed nor yet sore defiled but that the fire may fret out[189] the spots of their sin — of this sort only be we that here lie in purgatory, which these cruel heretics would make you believe that we feel none harm at all, whereof the blessed Apostle, as we have showed you, writeth unto the Corinthians the contrary.

Now if they would bear you in hand[190] that because some doctors do construe those words of the Apostle in diverse other senses — as they do construe in diverse senses almost every text in Scripture, sometimes after the letter,[191] sometimes moral,[192] and sometimes otherwise, and all to the profit and edifying of the hearers — if these heretics would therefore pretend that Saint Paul in that place meant nothing of purgatory but the fire that shall be sent before the Doom,[193] or worldly tribulation, or some such other thing, ye shall well understand that though his words may be verified and well and profitably applied unto such things also, yet letteth that nothing[194] these words to be properly by Saint Paul spoken of purgatory, no more than it letteth these words to be

properly spoken by[195] Christ, *Ego in flagella paratus sum*,[196] and many another verse in the Psalter also, though the same words may be well applied and verified of[197] many another man offering himself patiently to the sufferance of unjust punishment.

And therefore, lest these heretics should with any such inventions beguile you and make you believe that we, for the furtherance of our own cause, expound the Apostle's words wrong and so make them seem to say for our part, ye shall understand that those words have been expounded and understood of purgatory this thousand year and more by the ancient holy doctors of Christ's Church, as well Greeks as Latins. And among others the great clerk[198] Origen, in more places of his works than one, declareth plainly that the afore-remembered[199] words of the Apostle are spoken by[200] the pains of purgatory. The holy confessor and great pillar of Christ's Church Saint Augustine, in diverse of his godly and erudite books, expoundeth that place of Saint Paul to be clearly spoken of purgatory. And over this,[201] the blessed pope Saint Gregory,[202] in the fourth book of his godly *Dialogues*, beareth witness that the Apostle in the place aforesaid wrote those words of purgatory.[203] So that ye may plainly perceive that this exposition is neither our device[204] nor any new-founden fantasy, but a very truth well perceived and witnessed by great cunning[205] men and holy blessed saints more than a thousand years ago.

Now if these heretics will be so mad to flit in this case from Saint Paul, and say they be bounden to believe nothing but only the Gospel, let us then yet see further whether we may not plainly prove you purgatory by the very words of the Gospel itself. Doth not our blessed Savior himself say that there is a certain sin which a man may so commit "against the Holy Ghost" that it shall never be remitted nor forgiven "neither in this world nor in the world to come"?[206] Now as for to dispute what manner sin that should be, both the matter were very hard,[207] and also we shall here nothing[208] need to touch it. But of one thing both ye and we may make us very sure: that there is nor can be any sin committed in the world so sore,[209] so grievous, nor so abominable

---

182 thought   **183** two   **184** *after as:* according to how   **185** *walter and tolter:* toss and turn   **186** feel nausea   **187** with   **188** discomfort   **189** *fret out:* eat away   **190** *bear you in hand:* assert to you   **191** *after the letter:* according to the literal sense   **192** allegorical   **193** Last

Judgment   **194** *letteth that nothing:* hinders that not at all   **195** about   **196** "I am ready for scourges," Ps 37(38):18. **197** *applied and verified of:* applied to and borne out by   **198** scholar   **199** abovecited   **200** with reference to   **201** in addition to   **202** Gregory the Great

(*ca.* 540–604)   **203** See *Dialogorum libri quatuor* 4.39 (*PL* 77: 396).   **204** invention   **205** intelligent; learned   **206** See Mt 12:31–32.   **207** *were very hard:* would be very difficult   **208** not at all   **209** great; severe

but that if a man work with God's grace by contrition and heaviness of heart, with humble confession of mouth and good endeavor of penance and satisfaction in deed, against his thought, word, and deed by which God was offended, he shall obtain of God's goodness remission, forgiveness, and pardon.

But it may peradventure[210] so befall that by some kind of unkindness[211] used toward God extending to the blasphemy of his Holy Spirit, the committer of that sin may so far offend that he shall, for his desert and demerit, have the grace of almighty God so clearly[212] withdrawn from him that our Lord shall never offer his grace after, nor nevermore call upon him. And then his grace once clearly withdrawn from a man, he can never be able to repent and return again to God. For grace is the light wherewith men see the way to walk out of sin, and grace is the staff without help whereof no man is able to rise out of sin, according to the words of Holy Writ spoken to man in the person of our Lord God, *Ex te perditio tua, ex me salvatio tua* ("Thy perdition cometh of thyself, but thy salvation cometh of me by the aid and help of my grace.")[213] Which grace, as we tell you, being from some man utterly withdrawn for some manner[214] unkind behavior toward God and blasphemy against the Holy Ghost, that sin, for lack of repentance, which can never come where grace is clean gone, shall "never be forgiven in this world nor in the world to come." And in such a manner kind of unkindness toward God and blasphemy toward the Holy Ghost fall also all such wretches as have the grace of God ever calling and knocking upon them for repentance all the days of their life, and yet all that notwithstanding, will not use it, nor work therewith, nor turn to God, but willingly will die desperate and impenitent wretches.

This kind of blasphemers of God's goodness and his Holy Spirit have in the miserable passing of their sinful souls out of their sensual bodies the grace of God so fully and so finally withdrawn from them forever that they be thereby fixed and confirmed in an unchangeable malice, which, eternally dwelling with them, is the very special[215] cause of their everlasting torment. But in this matter, as we said, we wade out of our purpose, saving[216] that it seemed us yet necessary, since our Savior in the place that we speak of doth himself show that there is a certain sin so touching the Holy Ghost that it shall "never be forgiven, neither in this world nor in the world to come" — it seemed, as we say, somewhat necessary to say somewhat therein, lest some that read it might conceive a wrong opinion and a false fear drawing them toward despair, that if they mishappened (which our Lord forbid) to fall into blasphemy against the Holy Ghost, they could never after be forgiven how sore[217] soever they repented, or how heartily and how busily soever they should pray therefor.[218]

In which thing, since we have showed you what we take for truth, we shall leave that matter and show you how those words of Christ prove you our principal purpose: that is to say, that there is a purgatory. Howbeit,[219] we shall scantly[220] need to show you that, for the very words be plain and evident of themselves. For when our Lord saith that the "blasphemy against the Holy Ghost" shall not be forgiven "neither in this world nor in the world to come," he giveth us clear knowledge that of other sins, some shall be forgiven in this world and some in the world to come.

Now are there in this world every sin forgiven in such as shall be saved souls, except such venial sins and such temporal pain as yet due to the deadly[221] sins rest and remain to be purged here in purgatory. For none other place is there than this in the world to come after man's life, in which either sin or pain due to any sin shall be remitted. For into heaven shall neither sin nor pain enter, and in hell shall never none be released. And therefore when Christ, by showing that some kind of sin shall not be remitted in the world to come, doth give men knowledge that, on the other side, some sins shall in the world to come be remitted and forgiven, and then since no man doubteth but that neither in hell shall any sins be forgiven nor in heaven, very reason teacheth that the place in which some sins shall be forgiven after this life can be none other but purgatory.

There is, as we suppose, no Christian man living but he will think that any one place of Holy Scripture is enough to the proof of any truth. Now have we proved you purgatory by the plain texts of more places than one, two, or three. And yet shall we give you another so plain, as we suppose, and so evident for the proof of purgatory, as none heretic

210 perhaps   **211** unnaturalness; ingratitude; absence of natural affection or   consideration; hostility   **212** completely   **213** Hos 13:9   **214** kind of   **215** particular   **216** except   **217** greatly   **218** for it   **219** However   **220** scarcely   **221** mortal shall find any good color[222] of escape. For our Savior Christ saith, as it is rehearsed[223] in the twelfth chapter of Matthew, that men shall "yield a reckoning of every idle word,"[224] and that shall be after this present life. Then wotteth[225] every man that by that "reckoning" is understood a punishment therefor, which shall not be in hell, and much less in heaven. And therefore can it be nowhere else but in purgatory.

Lo, thus may ye see purgatory clearly proved by the very Scripture itself—by the book of the Kings, by the prophet Zechariah, by the holy book of the Maccabees, by the words of Saint John, by the apostle Saint Peter, by the writing of[226] our Savior Christ himself[227]—so that we not a little marvel either of[228] the ignorance or shameless boldness of all such as having any learning dare call themselves Christian men and yet deny purgatory. For if they have learning and perceive not these clear and open texts, we marvel of their ignorance. With which, while they join a proud pretense of learning, they fall into the reproof that Saint Paul spoke of the paynim[229] philosophers: *Dicentes se esse sapientes, stulti facti sunt* ("While they called themselves wise, they proved stark fools").[230] Now if they perceive well these texts of Holy Scripture so plainly proving purgatory, and yet themselves stick stiff in the denying, we then marvel much more that they dare for shame call themselves Christian men, and then deny the thing which the blessed apostles of Christ, the sacred majesty of our Savior himself, in the Holy Scripture, in his holy Gospels, so manifestly and so plainly affirmeth.

And yet many another plain text is there in Holy Scripture that, as the old holy doctors bear witness, well proveth our purpose[231] for purgatory, which we speak here nothing of, since fewer texts than we have already showed you both might and ought to suffice you. For any one plain text of Scripture sufficeth for the proof of any truth, except[232] any man be of the mind that he will have God tell his tale twice ere[233] he believe him.

Now if these heretics fall to their accustomed frowardness[234] and, as they be wont[235] to do, will rather deny that the swan is white and the crow black than agree that any text in Holy Scripture hath any other sense than themselves list[236] to say, and will in this point, for the maintenance of their heresy, set at nought[237] Saint Augustine, Saint Jerome, Saint Ambrose, Saint Gregory, Saint Chrysostom, Saint Basil, Saint Cyprian,[238] and finally all the old holy fathers and blessed saints that anything say against them, yet can they neither deny that the Catholic Church of Christ hath always believed purgatory, condemning for heretics all such as would hold the contrary. Nor if they grant that, can they then by any manner means avoid it but that[239] the thing is true that all the Church so full and whole so long hath in such wise believed, although[240] there were not founden in all Holy Scripture one text that so plainly proved it, as they might find many that seemed to say the contrary, except[241] they will not only say that our blessed Lady lost her virginity after the birth of Christ, but over[242] that be driven further to diminish the strength and authority of the very Gospel itself, which, if the Church may err in the right faith, had[243] clearly lost its credence.

And therefore, as we say, whereas we by plain Scripture have proved you purgatory, yet if there were therein not one text that anything seemed to say for it, but diverse and many texts which as far seemed unto the misunderstanders to speak against purgatory, as many diverse texts of the Gospel appeared unto the great heretic Helvidius[244] to speak against the perpetual virginity of Christ's blessed mother, yet since the Catholic Church of Christ hath always so firmly believed it for a plain truth that they have always taken the obstinate affirmers of the contrary for plain erroneous heretics, it is a proof full and sufficient for purgatory to any man that will be taken for a member of Christ's Church, and is alone a thing sufficient in any good Christian audience to stop the mouths of all the proud highhearted[245] malicious heretics that anything would bark against us.

But when they be so confuted and concluded[246] that they have nothing to say, yet can they not hold their peace, but fall to blasphemy and ask why there

222 appearance; pretext   **223** related   **224** Mt 12:36   **225** knows   **226** about   **227** See 1 Sm 2:6; Zec 9:11; 2 Mc 12:38–45; 1 Jn 5:16; Acts 2:24; Mt 12:31–32.   **228** at   **229** pagan   **230** Rom 1:22   **231** case   **232** unless   **233** before   **234** willful obstinacy   **235** accustomed

236 wish; choose   **237** *set at nought:* regard as nothing   **238** St. Ambrose, Bishop of Milan (d. 397 AD); St. Chrysostom, Archbishop of Constantinople (347–407 AD); St. Basil the Great (329–79 AD); St. Cyprian, Bishop of Carthage (200–58 AD)   **239** *but that:* that

240 even if   **241** unless   **242** in addition to   **243** would have   **244** Helvidius's non-extant work against the perpetual virginity of Mary was answered by Jerome's treatise *The Perpetual Virginity of Blessed Mary* in the fourth century.   **245** haughty, proud   **246** overcome

cometh none of us out of purgatory and speak with them. By which blasphemous question they may as well deny hell and heaven too, as they deny purgatory. For there cometh as many to them out of purgatory as out of either of the other twain. And surely if there came one out of any of them all three, unto folk of such incredulity as those heretics be, yet would they be never the better. For if they believe not now them whom they should believe, no more would they believe him neither that should come out of purgatory to tell it them, as Abraham answered the rich man that required[247] the same in hell,[248] and as it well appeared also by the miscreant[249] Jews, which were so little amended by the coming again of Lazarus out of *limbus patrum*[250] that, lest others should believe him, they devised to destroy him.[251] And yet if the thing that they require would content them, it hath not lacked. For there hath in every country and in every age apparitions been had, and well known and testified, by which men have had sufficient revelation and proof of purgatory, except such as list[252] not to believe them, and they be such as would be never the better if they saw them.

For whoso listeth to believe that altogether is lies that he heareth so much people speak of and so many good men write of—for no country is there in Christendom in which he shall not hear credibly reported of such apparitions diverse times there seen and appearing, and in the books of many a holy saint's writing shall he find such apparitions in such wise told and testified, as no good man could in any wise mistrust them, and over this, when the apostles at Christ's appearing to the eleven in the house took him at the first for a spirit,[253] it well appeareth that apparitions of spirits was no new thing among the Jews, which ye may well perceive also by that the better sort of them said in excusing[254] of Saint Paul, "What if some angel or some spirit have spoken to him?" (as is mentioned in the Apostles' Acts)[255]—so that, as we say, whoso list to take all this for lies, and is so faithless and so proudly curious[256] that he looketh ere he believe them to have such apparitions specially showed unto himself and miracles wrought in his presence, would

wax[257] the worse and[258] he saw them, and would ascribe it either to some fantasy or to the devil's work, as did those Jews that ascribed Christ's miracles to Beelzebub.[259]

For surely if such people were in the case of Saint Thomas of India[260]—that they were otherwise very virtuous and good, having in that only point some hardness of belief as he had in Christ's resurrection[261]—our Lord, we doubt not, would of his special goodness provide some special way for their satisfaction to recover them with. But now, since they be plain, carnal, high-hearted, and malicious, longing for miracles as did these crooked-hearted Jews, which said unto Christ that they longed to see him show some miracle, he doth therefore with these folk as Christ did with them. For as he answered them, by the example of Jonah the prophet, that he would none show before that perverse and faithless people till he were dead,[262] so answereth he these perverse and crooked malicious people that he will show them no such apparition till they be dead. And then shall he send them where they shall see it so surely, and to their pain see such a grisly sight as shall so grieve their hearts to look thereon, that they shall say as Christ said to Saint Thomas of India: *Beati qui non viderunt et crediderunt* ("Blessed and happy be they that believed this gear[263] and never saw it").[264]

For surely in this world the goodness of God so tempereth such apparitions as his high wisdom seeth it most profitable for help and relief of the dead and instruction and amendment of the quick,[265] keeping such apparitions, of his great mercy, most commonly from the sight of such as would turn his goodness into their own harm. And surely of his tender favor toward you doth his great goodness provide that such apparitions, revelations, and miracles should not be too copious and common, whereby good men, seeing the thing at eye,[266] should lose the great part of that[267] they now merit by faith, and evil folk, when they were once familiar with it, would then as little regard it as they now little believe it.

Now it is a world[268] to see with what folly they fortify their false belief, and into what fond fan-

247 requested   **248** See Lk 16:27–35. **249** unbelieving   **250** *limbus patrum:* the limbo of the fathers; the place in which good departed souls were detained until Jesus ascended into heaven   **251** See Jn 12:9–11.   **252** choose, wish   **253** See Lk 24:37.   **254** defense   **255** Acts 25:9 **256** cautious; fastidious   **257** become **258** if   **259** See Mt 12:24.   **260** the apostle Thomas, who is believed to have established the Church in modern-day Kerala   **261** See John 20:24–25.   **262** See Mt 12:38–40.   **263** matter   **264** Jn 20:29 **265** living   **266** *at eye:* with their eyes **267** what   **268** marvel

tasies[269] they fall, while they decline[270] from the truth. For while they deny purgatory, they now affirm (and specially Luther himself) that souls unto Doomsday do nothing else but sleep. Woe would they be if they fell into such a sleep as many a soul sleepeth here, and as Judas hath already slept fifteen hundred years in hell.

Then say they that if there were any purgatory out of which the pope might deliver any soul by his pardon, then were he very cruel in that he delivereth them not without money, and also that he riddeth them not hence all together at once. The first is a great folly—that since our Lord sendeth them thither for satisfaction to be made in some manner for their sin, the pope should rather, against God's purpose, deliver them free than change the manner of their satisfaction from pain into prayer, alms-deed, or other good works to be done by their friends for them, in some point profitable and necessary for the whole corps of Christendom or some good member of the same.

Now is there in the second not only much more folly, but it importeth also plain and open blasphemy. For presupposed that the pope may deliver all souls out of purgatory, yet if he were therefore cruel as often as he leaveth any there, this unreasonable reason layeth cruelty to the blame of God, which may undoubtedly deliver all souls thence and yet he leaveth them there. This blasphemy should also touch his high Majesty for keeping any soul in hell, from whence no man doubteth but that he might, if he list,[271] deliver them all forever. But as he will not deliver any thence, so will he not without good order deliver any soul hence. For as of his justice they be worthy to lie there forever, so be we worthy to lie here for the while, and in God no cruelty though he suffer[272] his mercy to be commonly suspended and tempered with the balance of his justice. And though he take us not hence all at once, orderless and at adventure,[273] his high wisdom is praiseworthy and not worthy blame. Our Lord forbid that ever we so should (and such is his grace that we never shall for[274] any pain possible that we can suffer here) hold ourselves content to hear such foolish words as imply so plain blasphemy against God's high merciful Majesty. For surely these folk,

in putting forth of this their unwise argument, make a countenance[275] to throw it against the pope, but in very deed they cast it at God's head.

For as for the pope, whoso consider it well goeth further from the example of God, that is set for Christ's vicar in his Church by giving overliberal pardon than by being therein too scarce and strait.[276] For God remitteth not here at adventure, though he may do his pleasure, but observeth right good and great respect, as[277] the prayers and intercessions made for us or other satisfaction done for us by some other men. And this order useth, and of reason ought to use, his vicar also in the dispensing toward our relief, the precious treasure of our comfort that Christ hath put in his keeping. For else,[278] if either the pope or God should always forthwith[279] deliver every man here—or rather keep every man hence, as these heretics would make men believe that God doth indeed, and would that the world should[280] so take it—then should God or the pope, as we somewhat have said before, give a great occasion to men boldly to fall in sin, and little to care or force[281] how slowly they rise again. Which thing neither were meet[282] for the pope's office nor agreeable to the great wisdom of God, and much less meet for his mercy. For by that means should he give innumerable folk great occasion of damnation, which,[283] presuming upon such easy short remission, would lustily[284] draw to lewdness with little care of amendment.

And so appeareth it that the thing which these wise men would have ye take for cruel is of truth most merciful, and the thing which they would have to seem very benign and piteous is in very deed most rigorous and most cruel, likewise as a sharp master that chastiseth his servant is in that point more favorable than is an easy one that for lack of punishment letteth them run on the bridle[285] and giveth them occasion of hanging. Which thing hath place also between the father and the child. And therefore in Holy Scripture, that father is not accounted for unloving and cruel that beateth his child, but rather he that leaveth it undone. For "he that spareth the rod," saith Holy Writ, "hateth the child."[286] And God therefore, that is of all fathers the most tender, loving, and most benign and merciful, leaveth no child of his uncorrected, but "scourgeth every child that he taketh to him."[287] And therefore neither God remitteth at adventure the pains of purgatory, nor no more must the pope neither, but if that he will,[288] while he laboreth to do good and be piteous to us that are dead, be cruel and do much more harm to them that be quick,[289] and while he will draw us out of purgatory, drive many of them into hell. From desire of which kind of help we so far abhor[290] that we would all rather choose to dwell here long in most bitter pain than by such way to get hence as might give occasion of any man's damnation.

Now where they likewise object in countenance[291] against the clergy—but yet in very deed they strike the stroke at us, whom they would bereave[292] the suffrages of good people—objecting that no man may satisfy for another, nor that the prayer nor alms nor other good deed done by one man may stand another in stead,[293] but that every man must needs all-thing[294] that he will have help of, do it every whit[295] himself, and so that no man's good deed done among you for us in relief of our pain could in any manner serve us—this opinion, as it is toward us very pestilent and pernicious, so is it of itself very false and foolish. For first, if all that ever must avail any man must needs be done by himself, and no man's merit may be applied to the help of another, then were wiped away from all men all the merits of Christ's bitter Passion, in which, though it be true that God died on the cross because of the unity of God and man in person, yet had his tender manhood all the pain for us, and his impassible[296] Godhead felt no pain at all. Whereof[297] serveth also the prayers that every man prayeth for others? Wherefore[298] did Saint Paul pray for all other Christian men, and desire them all to pray for him also and each of them for others, that they might be saved?[299]

And why is there so special a mention made in the Acts of the Apostles, that at the delivery of Saint Peter out of prison the Church made continual prayer and intercession for him but for to show that God the rather[300] delivered him for other men's prayers?[301] And think ye that if God have pity upon one man for another's sake, and delivereth him at another man's petition from a little pain or imprisonment in the world there upon earth, he hath not at other men's humble and hearty prayer much more pity upon such as lie in much more heavy pain and torment here in the hot fire of purgatory?

Then find these folk another knot hard (as they think) to undo. For they say that "if another man's merits may serve me, whereto should I need to do any good myself?" This objection is much like as if they would say, "If other men may take me out of the fire, whereto should I labor to rise myself?" Very truth it is that sometimes the good works of one man, wrought with good affection,[302] may purchase another man grace for to amend and work for himself. But surely, of common course, he that will not himself work with them getteth little good of other men's good deeds. For if thyself do still draw backward while other good men with their prayer labor to pull thee forward, it will be long ere thou make any good day's journey. And therefore that holy doctor Saint Augustine, in the blessed book that he made of the cure[303] and care that men should have of us seely parted[304] souls, toucheth quickly[305] the very point that there can none take profit of other men's good deeds, but only such as have deserved by some good thing in their own deeds that other men's deeds should help them, and that hath every man done, at the leastwise by his final repentance and purpose of amendment, that departeth the world in the state of grace.[306]

For he that is out of that state cannot take the profit of other men's merits done for him. And therefore damned souls cannot by other men's merits be delivered of[307] damnation, nor in like wise he that intendeth to persevere in sin and do no good for himself. But since that we be not in that case, but have with help of God's grace deserved to be partners of such good deeds as ye that are our friends will of your goodness do for us, ye may by your merits highly relieve us here and help to get us hence. And surely great wonder were it if we should not be able to take profit of your prayers. For there will no wise man doubt but that the prayer of any member of Christendom may profit any other that it is made for which hath need and is a member of the same.

---

287 Heb 12:6 **288** *but if … will:* unless he will **289** living **290** recoil **291** appearance **292** deprive of **293** his place **294** everything **295** bit **296** incapable of experiencing suffering

297 To what purpose **298** Why **299** See Rom 10:1; Eph 1:15–18 and 6:18–20; Phil 1:9–10; 2 Thes 1:11–12; and 1 Tm 2:1–4. **300** *the rather:* sooner; all the more **301** See Acts 12:5–12.

302 disposition; inclination **303** concern **304** *seely parted:* poor or helpless departed **305** vigorously; perceptively **306** See Augustine, *De cura pro mortuis* 1.18.22 (*PL* 40: 609). **307** from, out of

But none is there yet living that is more very[308] member of Christ's mystical body—that is, his Church—than we be, nor no man living that hath more need of help than we. For in surety[309] of salvation we be fellows with angels; in need of relief we be yet fellows with you. And therefore being so sure members of one body with angels, holy saints, and you, and having necessity both of their help and yours, there is no doubt but since every member that need hath may take good by others, we stand in the case that both angels' and saints' intercessions and your good prayers and alms-deed done for us, whatsoever these heretics babble, may do us marvelous much good.

How many have by God's most gracious favor appeared unto their friends after the death and showed themselves helped and delivered hence by pilgrimage, alms-deed, and prayer—and special[310] by the sacred oblation of that Holy Sacrament offered for them in the Mass. If these heretics say that all such things be lies, then be they much worse yet than their master was, Luther himself, as long as any spark of shame was in him. For he confesseth in his sermons that many such apparitions be true, and his heart could not for very shame serve[311] him that so many so often told in so many places, so faithfully reported by so many honest folk, and so substantially[312] written by so many blessed saints, should be all false.

Wherein if these men list[313] like lusty[314] scholars to pass and overgo[315] their mad master in this point, and deny these things altogether, yet shall there stick in their teeth the scripture of the Maccabees, whereof we told you that Judas Maccabeus gathered and sent a great offering to Jerusalem for to buy sacrifice to be offered for them that he found slain in the field,[316] and certain things about them taken of the idols forbidden them by the Law, which caused him to fear lest they were for their sins fallen after their death into pain, and therefore made that gathering, that alms and offering (as himself saith), that they might thereby be loosed and delivered of their sins.[317] So that there appeareth plainly by Scripture that such suffrages stand us seely souls in stead.[318] Against which authority, if they will with their master labor to break out and deny that book for Holy Scripture, we have stopped them that gap already with such a bush of thorns as will prick their hands through a pair of hedging gloves ere[319] they pull it out.

And finally, for this point that the suffrages[320] of the Church and the prayers of good Christian people stand us here in relief and comfort, there needeth in this world (as Saint Augustine saith, and Saint Damascene)[321] none other manner[322] proof than that all Christendom hath ever used to do so, and have thought themselves always so bounden to do, damning always for heretics all them that would affirm the contrary.

And in this point may they have a marvelous great thing against them in the judgment of every good man: the great antiquity of the service[323] of Christ's Church, by which the Church hath so[324] long ago customably recommended in their prayers all Christian souls to God. For we trust that though[325] these heretics find many men both glad to hear and light[326] to believe every lewd[327] tale that can be surmised[328] against the Church that now is, yet trust we that they shall find few or none so far out of all frame[329] but that they will at the least believe that there hath been some good and godly men, wise and well learned too, among the clergy in days past one time or other. Go then to the old time and to the good men that then were, and hear what they said, and see what they did, and believe and follow them. There remaineth yet, and books enough thereof, the very Mass in the very form and fashion as Saint Basil, and Saint Chrysostom, and other holy fathers in that virtuous time said it,[330] in which ye shall find that in their daily Masses they prayed ever for all Christian souls.

Ye shall also perceive clearly by Saint Chrysostom in a sermon of his[331] that in his time there were in the funeral service, at the burying of the corpse, the selfsame psalms sung that ye sing now at the Dirge.[332] Whereby it well appeareth that it is no

---

308 truly a **309** security; certainty **310** especially **311** prompt **312** soundly **313** choose; wish **314** vigorous; self-confident **315** *pass and overgo:* surpass and overtake **316** battlefield **317** See 2 Mc 12:38–45. **318** *stand . . . stead:* benefit us poor souls **319** before **320** prayers for the dead **321** See Augustine's *De cura*

pro mortuis (*PL* 40: 593) and *Sermones* 172 (*PL* 38: 936–37). Also see *De iis qui in fide dormierunt* (*PG* 95: 249–50), a work incorrectly attributed to St. John Damascene (*ca.* 675–749) in More's time. **322** kind of **323** liturgy **324** from so **325** even if **326** frivolous, unthinking **327** rude; uneducated; wicked

328 alleged **329** order **330** See *PG* 31: 1641, 1656, 1672, 1675; 63: 905, 917. **331** See Chrysostom's *In epistolam ad Philippenses commentarius* 1.3.4 (*PG* 62: 204). **332** prayer service (taken from the Office for the Dead) which preceded the funeral Mass

new-found thing, for his time was far above a thousand years ago, and yet was that thing long used afore[333] his days. And because[334] ye shall know that the more surely, he saith that the guise[335] and custom to pray for souls was instituted and begun in the Church by the blessed apostles themselves. And so while so good men so long ago began it, and good folk hath ever since continued it, ye may soon guess whether they be good men or no that now provoke you to break it.

Now where they say that if the Mass could do us any good, that then the priests be very cruel that will say none for us but they be waged,[336] this word is as true as their intent is fraudulent and false. For their purpose is in those words to make the world ween[337] that the clergy were so covetous and cruel therewith that there will no priest pray for us poor souls here without[338] he be hired thereto, whereof, our Lord be thanked, we find full well the contrary. For albeit that[339] of Luther's priests we can have none help, since their Masses offer not up the sacrament to God neither for quick[340] nor dead, nor make no very[341] priests among them, since they take priesthood for no sacrament, yet of good Christian priests we find great relief, as well in their Dirges and much other suffrages by old institution of the Church specially said for us, though[342] no man give them one penny through the year. And so may all the world wit[343] that this word of these heretics hath much malice and little effect therein.

But now, though the priests pray for us of their own charity, yet when good people desire them thereto and give them their alms therefor,[344] then are they double bounden, and then riseth there much more good and profit upon all sides. For then take we fruit both of the prayer of the one and the alms of the other. And then taketh the priest benefit of his own prayer made both for the giver and for us. The giver also getteth fruit both of his own merciful alms, and of double prayer also—that is to wit,[345] both the prayer of the priest that prayeth for us, which commonly prayeth for him too, and also the prayer of us, which[346] with great fervor of heart pray for our benefactors incessantly and are so far-forth[347] in God's undoubted favor that very few men living upon earth are so well heard as we—besides that of all kinds of alms that any man can give, the most meritorious is that which is bestowed upon us, as well for that[348] it is unto the most needy and also to them that are absent, and finally for that of all manner alms it is most grounded upon the foundation of all Christian virtues: faith. For as for[349] to poor folk, a natural man will give alms either for pity of some piteous sight, or for weariness of their importunate crying, but as for us poor souls passed the world, whom he that giveth alms neither seeth nor heareth, would never bestow one penny upon us but if[350] he had a faith that we live still, and that he feared that we lie in pain, and hoped of his reward in heaven. Which kind of faith and good hope joined with his gift and good work must needs make it one of the best kinds of alms-deed that any man can do in the world.

And since that it so is (as indeed it is), what uncharitable and what unfaithful folk are these that for hatred which they owe to priested[351] would make you believe that there were no purgatory, and would rather wish by their wills that their own fathers should lie here in fire till the Day of Doom[352] than any man should give a priest one penny to pray for them?

And yet is there here one thing well to be considered: that they rather hate priests for hatred of Christ's faith than speak against purgatory for hatred of priests. Which thing, though it seem you dark[353] at the first hearing, ye shall yet, if ye look well, very well perceive. For if it so were that this kind of people did speak against purgatory only for the hatred of the pope and the clergy, then would they grant that saved souls are yet purged in the fire here for their sins unsatisfied[354] in the world, and it should then suffice them to say for their purpose that neither priest nor pope nor any man else, nor any man's alms or prayer, can in this place of punishment anything relieve us. For this were enough, ye see well, to serve their purpose against the clergy. But yet because they have a far further purpose against all good Christian faith, they be not content therefore to leave at this point, but step them forth farther and deny purgatory utterly, to the end that

333 before　**334** so that　**335** practice
336 *but they be waged:* unless they be
paid　**337** think　**338** unless　**339** *albeit
that:* although　**340** living　**341** true;
proper　**342** even if　**343** know

344 for it　**345** say　**346** who　**347** *so
far-forth:* to such an extent　**348** *for
that:* because　**349** regards　**350** *but if:*
unless　**351** *owe…priested:* bear toward
the ordained (those who have been made

priests)　**352** *Day of Doom:* Judgment
Day　**353** hard to understand or perceive
354 not absolved

men should take boldness to care the less for their sins. And if they might once be believed therein, then would they step yet farther and deny hell and all, and after that heaven too. But as for heaven, albeit that as yet they deny it not, yet pull they many a simple soul thence, which were it not for their mischievous[355] doctrine were else well likely to be there a full bright and glorious saint.

And surely the more that wise men advise themselves upon this matter, the more shall they marvel of the mad mind[356] of them that deny purgatory, or say that the prayers or good works of men living in the world can do us here no good. For every man that any wit[357] hath wotteth[358] well that the surest way were in every doubt best to be taken. Now suppose then that purgatory could in no wise be proved, and that some would yet say plainly that there were one, and some would say plainly nay; let us now see whether[359] sort of these twain[360] might take most harm, if their part[361] were the wrong. First, he that believed there were purgatory, and that his prayer and good works wrought for his friends' souls might relieve them therein, and because thereof used much prayer and alms for them, he could not lose the reward of his good will although his opinion were untrue, and that there were no purgatory at all, no more than he loseth[362] his labor now that prayeth for one whom he feareth to lie in purgatory whereas he is already in heaven. But on the other side, he that believeth there is none, and therefore prayeth for none, if his opinion be false and that there be purgatory indeed (as indeed there is), he loseth much good and getteth him also much harm, for he both feareth much the less to sin and to lie long in purgatory, saving[363] that his heresy shall save him thence and send him down deep into hell.

And it fareth between these two kinds of folk as it fared between a lewd[364] gallant and a poor friar. Whom when the gallant saw going barefoot in a great frost and snow, he asked him why he did take such pain. And he answered that it was very little pain if a man would remember hell. "Yea, Friar," quoth the gallant, "but what and[365] there be none hell? Then art thou a great fool." "Yea, Master," quoth the friar, "but what and there be hell? Then is your Mastership a much more fool."

Moreover, there was never yet any of that sort that could for shame say that any man is in peril for believing that there is purgatory. But they say only that there is none in deed,[366] and that they may without any sin affirm their opinion for truth. But now upon the other side, many a hundred thousand — that is to wit, all the whole Church of Christ that is or ever hath been — affirm that the affirming of their opinion against purgatory is a plain damnable heresy.

Wherefore it well and plainly appeareth, and every wise man well seeth, that it is the far surer[367] way to believe in such wise as both the parties agree to be out of all peril than that way which so far the greater party, and much further the better party, affirm to be undoubted deadly[368] sin. And now, whereas every fool may see that any wise man will take the surest way — which is, as ye see doubly proved, to believe that there is purgatory — yet said the wise proctor[369] of beggars that wise men will say there is none. For he saith that many great lettered men, and right cunning[370] men, will not let[371] to put themselves in jeopardy of shame, and of death also, to show their minds[372] that there is no purgatory. He is loath to say that these be heretics, but he saith these be they that men call heretics. Wherein he speaketh much like as if he would point with his finger to a flock of fat wethers,[373] and say, "These be such beasts as men call sheep."

But now would we fain[374] see which be these wise men and well-lettered, which shall not fail upon their own confession to agree that their adversaries take the sure way and farthest out of peril, and themselves the most dangerous and farthest from all surety. But yet would we for the while fain hear who they be. Surely none other but Luther and Tyndale, and this beggars' proctor, and a few such of that sect — men of such virtue, wisdom, and learning as their lewd[375] writing, and much more their lewd living, showeth.

But now are they far another manner[376] sort, both in number, wisdom, learning, truth, and good living, which affirm and say the contrary. And surely if three or four hundred good and honest men would faithfully come forth and tell one that some of his friends were in a far country for debt kept in prison,

355 wicked 356 disposition; judgment
357 intelligence, sense 358 knows
359 which 360 two 361 side
362 wastes 363 except 364 wicked
365 if 366 truth; fact 367 safer
368 mortal 369 advocate; representative; alms-collector 370 intelligent; learned 371 hesitate 372 judgments;
opinions 373 rams 374 gladly; willingly
375 wicked 376 kind of

and that his charity might relieve[377] them thence, if then three or four fond[378] fellows would come and say the contrary and tell him plain there is no such prison at all, as he is borne in hand[379] that his friends are imprisoned in—if he would now be so light[380] to believe those three or four naughty[381] persons against those three or four hundred good and honest men, he then should well decipher[382] himself, and well declare thereby, that he would gladly catch hold of some small handle[383] to keep his money fast[384] rather than help his friends in their necessity.

Now if ye consider how late[385] this lewd sect began, which among Christian men barketh against purgatory, and how few always, for very shame of their folly, hath hitherto fallen into them, and then if ye consider on the other side how full and whole the great corps[386] of all Christian countries so many hundred years have ever told you the contrary, ye shall, we be very sure, for every person speaking against purgatory find for the other part[387] more than many a hundred.

Now if these men will peradventure[388] say that they care not for such comparison, neither of time with time, number with number, nor company with company, but since some one man is in credence worth some seven score[389]—if they will therefore call us to some other reckoning and will that we compare of the best choice on both sides a certain,[390] and match them man for man, then have we (if we might for shame match such blessed saints with a sort as far unlike) Saint Augustine against Friar Luther, Saint Jerome against Friar Lambert,[391] Saint Ambrose against Friar Hussgen,[392] Saint Gregory against priest Pomeranus,[393] Saint Chrysostom against Tyndale,[394] Saint Basil against the beggars' proctor.

Now if our enemies will, for lack of other choice, help forth their own part with their wives, then have they some advantage indeed, for the other holy saints had none. But yet shall we not lack blessed holy women against these friars' wives. For we shall have Saint Anastasia[395] against Friar Luther's wife,[396] Saint Hildegard[397] against Friar Hussgen's wife, Saint Bridget[398] against Friar Lambert's wife, and Saint Catherine of Siena[399] against priest Pomeranus's wife.

Now if they will have in these matches the qualities of either side considered, then have we wisdom against folly, cunning against ignorance, charity against malice, true faith against heresies, humility against arrogance, revelations against illusions, inspiration of God against inventions of the devil, constancy against wavering, abstinence against gluttony, continence against lechery, and finally every kind of virtue against every kind of vice.

And over[400] this, whereas we be not yet very sure whether that all these naughty persons whom we have rehearsed you of the worse side be fully fallen so mad as utterly to deny purgatory, saving[401] in that we see them in many things all of one sect, yet if there were of them far many such more, they shall not yet find of that simple suit[402] half so many as for our part remaineth holy blessed saints to match them. For likewise as many[403] their holy works, eruditely written and by the help of the Holy Ghost indited,[404] evidently declare that not only Saint Augustine, Saint Jerome, Saint Ambrose, and that holy pope Saint Gregory, with Saint Chrysostom, and Saint Basil afore-remembered,[405] and those holy women also that we have spoken of, but over that, the great solemn doctor Origen, all the three great doctors and holy saints of one name in Greece—Gregory Nazianzen, Gregory Nyssene, Gregory Emissenus[406]—Saint Cyril,[407] Saint Damascene, the famous doctor and holy martyr Saint Cyprian, Saint Hilary,[408] Saint Bede,[409] and Saint Thomas, and finally all such as are of that suit and sort, either Greeks or Latins, have ever taught and testified and exhorted the people to pray for all Christian souls and preached for purgatory, so doth there no man doubt but that all good and devout Christian people, from Christ's days hitherto, hath firm and fast been of the same belief, and with their daily prayers and alms-deed done for us have done us great relief.

---

377 release   **378** foolish   **379** *borne in hand:* being led to believe   **380** unthinking   **381** bad, wicked   **382** reveal   **383** excuse   **384** secure   **385** recently   **386** body; collective   **387** side   **388** perhaps   **389** 140   **390** certain one   **391** Francis Lambert (1486–1530)   **392** Johannes Oecolampadius (1482–1531)   **393** John Bugenhagen (1485–1558)   **394** William Tyndale (1494–1536)

395 St. Anastasia of Sirmium (d. 304), a martyr during the persecutions of Diocletian   **396** Katherine von Bora (1499–1552), a Cistercian nun before her marriage to Luther   **397** St. Hildegard (1098–1179), a German mystic   **398** St. Bridget of Sweden (ca. 1303–73)   **399** St. Catherine of Siena (1347–80), an Italian mystic   **400** in addition to   **401** except   **402** *simple suit:* foolish

company   **403** many of   **404** inspired   **405** aforementioned   **406** St. Gregory of Nazianzus (ca. 330–89), St. Gregory of Nyssa (ca. 335–94), St. Gregory of Neocaesarea (213–70)   **407** St. Cyril of Alexandria (ca. 375–444)   **408** St. Hilary of Poitiers (ca. 315–ca. 367)   **409** St. Bede the Venerable (ca. 672–753)

So that, as we said, both for number of many folk and goodness of chosen folk our enemies are far under us. And yet have we for the vantage,[410] as we have before declared you, the fear of Hezekiah, the book of the Kings, the words of the prophet Zechariah, the faith of Maccabeus, the authority of Saint John, the words of Saint Peter, the sentence[411] of Saint Paul, the testimony of Saint Matthew, and the plain sentence of our Savior Christ.[412]

Now if these heretics be so stiff and stubborn that rather than they will confess themselves concluded[413] they will hold on their old ways and fall from worse to worse, and like as they have already against their former promise first rejected reason, and after law, and then all the doctors and old holy fathers of Christ's Church, and finally the whole Church itself, so if they will at length, as we greatly fear they will, reject all Scripture and cast off Christ and all—now, as we say, if they so do, yet have we left at the worst way[414] Luther against Luther, Hussgen against Hussgen, Tyndale against Tyndale, and finally every heretic against himself. And then when these folk sit in Almaine[415] upon their beer bench in judgment on us and our matters, we may as the knight of King Alexander appealed from Alexander to Alexander—from Alexander the drunk to Alexander the sober—so shall we appeal from Luther to Luther—from Luther the drunken to Luther the sober, from Luther the heretic to Luther the Catholic—and likewise in all the remnant.

For this doth no man doubt but that every one of them all, before they fell drunk of the dregs of old poisoned heresies, in which they fell a-quaffing[416] with the devil, they did full sadly[417] and soberly pray for all Christian souls. But since that they be fallen drunken in wretched and sinful heresies, they neither care for other men's souls nor for their own neither. And on the other side, if ever they work with grace to purge themselves of those poisoned heresies, wherewith they be now so drunk, they will then give sentence[418] on our side, as they did before. It were not evil that we showed you somewhat for example whereby ye may see what soberness they were in before, and in what drunkenness the devil's draught hath brought them. And in whom

should we show it better than in Luther himself, arch-heretic and father abbot of all that drunken fellowship?

First, this man was so fast of[419] our side, while he was well and sober, that yet when he began to be well washed[420] he could not find in his heart utterly to fall from us. But when his head first began to daze of[421] that evil drink, he wrote that purgatory could not be proved by Scripture. And yet that notwithstanding, he wrote in this wise[422] therewith: "I am very sure that there is purgatory, and it little moveth me what heretics babble. Should I believe a heretic born of late, scant[423] fifty years ago, and say the faith were false that hath been held so many hundred years?"[424] Lo, here this man spoke well upon our side. But yet said he therewith one thing or twain[425] that could not stand therewith, and thereby may ye see that he began to reel. For he both affirmed that purgatory could not be proved by Scripture, and affirmed further that nothing could be taken for a sure and certain truth but if[426] it appeared by "clear and evident Scripture." Which two things presupposed, how could any man be sure of purgatory? But the help is that both those points be false. For both is purgatory proved by Scripture, and the Catholic faith of Christ's Church were[427] sufficient to make men sure thereof albeit[428] there were not in all Scripture one text for it, and diverse that seemed against it, as we have showed you before.

But here, as we say, ye see how shamefully he staggered and began to reel, howbeit soon after, being so dowsy[429] drunk that he could neither stand nor reel, but fell down sow-drunk in the mire, then like one that nothing remembered what he had said, nor heard not his own voice, he began to be himself that babbling heretic against whom he had written before, and being not fully fifty years old began to gainsay[430] the faith of almost fifteen hundred years afore his days in the Church of Christ, besides fifteen hundred years three times told among other faithful folk before.[431] For now in his drunken sermon that he wrote upon the Gospel of the rich man and Lazarus, whereas he had in his other books before framed of[432] his own fantasy new fond[433] fashions of purgatory, and told them forth for as plain

---

410 *for the vantage:* in addition **411** passage; insight **412** See Is 38; 1 Sm 2:6; Zec 9:11; 2 Mc 12:38–45; 1 Jn 5:16; Acts 2:24; 1 Cor 3:11–15; Mt 12:31–32, 36. **413** confuted, overcome **414** *at the worst way:* if worst comes to worst **415** Germany **416** into drinking copiously **417** seriously **418** judgment; verdict **419** *fast of:* fixed on **420** soaked in wine **421** from **422** way **423** scarcely **424** *WA* 1: 555–56 **425** two **426** *but if:* unless **427** would be **428** even if **429** stupid **430** deny **431** More is referring to the timeline of 4,500 years between Adam and Christ. **432** from **433** foolish

matters as though he had been here and seen them, now in this mad sermon of his, he saith plainly that there is none at all, but that all souls lie still and sleep, and so sleep shall until the Day of Doom.
O sow-drunken soul, drowned in such an insensible sleep that he lieth and routeth[434] while the apostles, the evangelists, all the doctors of Christ's Church, all the whole Christian people, and among them Christ himself, stand and cry at his ear that we seely[435] Christian souls lie and burn in purgatory, and he cannot hear, but lieth still in the mire and snorteth and there dreameth that we lie still and sleep as he doth.

And thus, whereas the beggars' proctor[436] writeth that wise men say there is no purgatory, ye see now yourself how wise is he whom they take for the wisest of all that sort, as him that is now the very wellspring and arch-heretic of all their sect. Of all which wise men we leave it to your wisdom to consider, whether ye find any whom your wisdoms would in wisdom compare with any of those old holy doctors and saints whom we have rehearsed[437] before. But this man, we wot[438] well, for another of these wise men meaneth William Tyndale. Whose wisdom well appeareth in that matter by that[439] he layeth against it nothing but scoffing, wherein he saith that the pope may be bold in[440] purgatory because it is, he saith, a thing "of his own making,"[441] whereas we have proved you by Scripture that purgatory was perceived and taught, and dead men's souls prayed for, so long ere ever any pope began.

But forasmuch as he saith that wise men will say there is no purgatory—among which wise men we doubt not but the wise man accounteth himself, for he layeth for that part,[442] as himself weeneth,[443] very wise and weighty reasons, the wisdom whereof we have already proved you very plain frantic[444] folly—we will now finish the dispicions[445] of all this debate and question, with the declaration of one or two points of his especial wisdom, and with one of which himself wisely destroyeth all his whole matter.

First, ye see well that albeit[446] indeed he intendeth to go further if his bill were once well sped,[447] yet he pretendeth nothing in visage[448] but only the spoil,[449] wedding, and beating of the clergy, to whom he layeth[450] not all only such faults as ye have heard, and hath proved his purpose[451] with such grounds as we have proved false, but also layeth one great necessity to take all from them: because they break the statute made of mortmain,[452] and purchase more lands still against the provision thereof. And then saith he that any land which once cometh in their hands cometh never out again. For he saith that they have such laws concerning their lands as they may neither give any nor sell. For which cause, lest they should at length have all, he deviseth to let them have nothing.

Now first, where he maketh as though there came yet, for all the statute, daily much land into them,[453] and that there can none at all come from them, neither is the one so much as he would make it seem, and the other is very false. For truly there may come and doth come land from them by escheat,[454] as we be sure many of you have had experience, and also what laws soever they have of their own that prohibit them to sell their lands, yet of this are we very sure, that notwithstanding all the laws they have, they may sell in such wise, if they will, all the lands they have, that they can never recover foot[455] again. And besides all that, albeit there be laws made by the Church against such sales as shrewd husbands[456] would else boldly make of the lands of their monasteries, yet is there not so precise provision made against all sales of their lands, but that they be alienated[457] for cause reasonable, approved by the advice and counsel of their chief head. And many a man is there in the realm that hath lands given or sold out of abbeys and out of bishoprics both, so that this part is a plain lie.

The other part is also neither very certain nor very much to purpose. For truly, though that in the city of London, to which there is granted by authority of Parliament that men may there devise[458] their lands into mortmain by their testaments,[459] there is somewhat among[460] given into the Church—and yet not all to them, but the great part unto the companies and fellowships of the crafts—in other

434 snores **435** poor; helpless **436** advocate; representative; alms-collector **437** cited **438** know **439** *by that:* since **440** regarding **441** Tyndale, *Obedience of a Christian Man* (1528) **442** side of the controversy **443** thinks **444** insane **445** disputations **446** although

447 met with success **448** *pretendeth nothing in visage:* claims nothing in appearance **449** despoiling **450** ascribes **451** case **452** *the statute made of mortmain:* statute forbidding transfer of lands into the inalienable ownership of any entity without license of the Crown **453** their

possession **454** reversion of property to the Crown when there are no legal heirs **455** one square foot **456** *shrewd husbands:* cunning managers **457** parted with; transferred to other ownership **458** bequeath **459** wills **460** *somewhat among:* something now and then places of the realm there is nowadays no great thing given, but if[461] it be sometimes some small thing for the foundation of a chantry.[462] For as for abbeys or such other great foundations, there be not nowadays many made, nor have been of good while, except somewhat done in the universities.

And yet whoso consider those great foundations, that have this great while been made anywhere, shall well perceive that the substance[463] of them be not all founded upon temporal[464] lands newly taken out of the temporal hands into the Church, but of such as the Church had long afore, and now the same translated[465] from one place unto another. And over[466] this shall he find that many an abbey, whose whole living this man weeneth stood all by[467] temporal lands given them in their foundation, have the great part thereof in benefices[468] given in and impropriated[469] unto them. So that if he consider the substance of all the great foundations made this great while, and all that hath into any such these many days been given, and then consider well therewith how cold the charity of Christian people waxeth[470] by the means of such devil's proctors as, under pretext of begging for the poor, intend and labor to quench the fervor of devotion to Godward[471] in simple and soon-led souls, he shall not need to fear that all the temporal land in the realm shall come into the spiritualty.[472] And yet if men went now so fast to give in still to the Church as they did before, while devotion was fervent in the people and virtue plenteous in the Church, yet might it be—and in other countries is provided for well enough—both that men's devotion might be favored, and yet not the Church have all.

But this wise man, lest they should have all, would leave them right nought.[473] For his wisdom weeneth there were no mean[474] way between every whit[475] and never a whit but nothing at all. And surely where that he layeth so sore unto[476] them the new purchasing of more temporal lands, either bought or given them, it appeareth well he would say sore[477] to them if they pulled the land from men by force,

which now layeth so highly to their charge[478] because they take it when men give it them, which thing we suppose himself, as holy as he is, would not much refuse. Nor they be not much to be blamed if they receive men's devotion, but if[479] they bestow it not well.

And yet where he saith there can no statute hold them, but they purchase still and break the statute— wherein he would seem cunning[480] because he had a little smattering in the law—it were good, ere he be so bold to put his ignorance in writing, that he should see the statute better. Which when he list[481] to look upon again and let some wiser man look with him, if he consider well what remedy the statutes provide and for whom, he shall find that the makers of the statute not so much feared the great high point that pricketh him now, lest the whole temporal lands should come into the Church, as they did the loss of their wards, and their unlikelihood of escheats[482] and some other commodities[483] that they lacked when their lands were alienated into the Church—and yet not into the Church only but also into any mortmain.[484] And for this they provided that if any more were alienated[485] into the Church or into any manner of mortmain, the king or any other lord, mediate or immediate,[486] that might take loss thereby might enter thereinto, to the intent that, ere ever the purchase were made, they should be fain in such wise[487] to sue to every one of them for his license and good will that each of them should be arbiter of his own hurt or loss and take his amends at his own hand.[488] And this statute is not made only for the advantage of the temporal lords against the clergy, but it is made indifferently[489] against all mortmain, which is as well temporal folk as spiritual, and for the benefit as well of spiritual men as temporal. For as well shall a bishop or an abbot have the advantage of that statute, if his tenant alienate his lands into any mortmain, as shall an earl or a duke.

And now when the Church pulleth not away the land from the owner by force, but hath it of[490] his

---

461 *but if:* unless   **462** a chapel endowed for the daily singing of Masses for certain souls   **463** subsistence, capital   **464** secular   **465** *the same translated:* i.e., the same capital has been transferred   **466** in addition to   **467** *weeneth stood all by:* thinks depended entirely on   **468** ecclesiastical livings   **469** annexed   **470** is becoming   **471** *to Godward:*

toward God   **472** clergy's possession   **473** nothing   **474** middle   **475** little bit   **476** *layeth so sore unto:* charges so grievously against   **477** *say sore to:* speak harshly   **478** *which . . . charge:* who now so haughtily reproaches them   **479** *but if:* unless   **480** learned   **481** chooses; wishes   **482** reversions of property to the Crown when there are no legal heirs   **483** benefits

484 statute forbidding transfer of lands into inalienable ownership of any entity without license of the Crown   **485** parted with; transferred to other ownership   **486** *mediate or intermediate:* possessing directly or through an intermediary (under feudal law)   **487** *fain . . . wise:* obliged in such a way   **488** discretion   **489** impartially   **490** out of

devotion, and his gift given of his own offer un-asked, and yet not without license of all such as the statute limiteth,[491] where is this great fault of theirs, for which, lest they should take more in the same manner, he would they should[492] lose all that they have already? What wisdom is this, when he lay-eth[493] against them their deed wherein they break no law? And yet, since they cannot take it without[494] the king and the lords, his words, if they weighed aught,[495] should run to the reproach and blame of them whom he would fain[496] flatter, without fault founden in them whom he so sore accuseth.

But now the special high point of his wisdom, for which we be driven to speak of this matter, he specially declareth in this. Ye see well that he would that the temporal men should take from the clergy, not only all these lands purchased since the statute of mortmain, but also all that ever they had before too, and yet over this, all the whole living that ever they have by any manner means besides, because he thinketh that they have too much by altogether.

And when he hath given his advice thereto and said that they have too much, then saith he by and by[497] that if there were any purgatory in deed,[498] it were well done to give them yet more, and that they have then a great deal too little. But now so is it that purgatory there is in deed, nor no good Christian man is there but he will and must believe and con-fess the same. Whereof it plainly followeth that, his own agreement added unto the truth (that is to say, that the Church hath, as he saith, too little if there be a purgatory, added unto the truth that there is a purgatory, and that every true Christian man doth and must confess it), then hath, lo, the wise man brought all his purpose so substantially[499] to pass that, by his own plain agreement added unto the undoubtable truth, no man may do that[500] he would have all men do—spoil and pill[501] the Church—but he that will first plainly profess himself a plain and undoubted heretic.

And therefore, since ye now see the wit[502] of this wise man that laboreth to bring us out of your re-membrance; since ye see the simple[503] ground of his proud *Supplication,* and ye perceive the rancor

and malice that his matter standeth on, for fulfill-ing whereof he would by his will bring all the world in trouble; and since ye see that he hateth the clergy for the faith, and us for the clergy, and in reprov-ing[504] purgatory proveth himself an infidel; since we have made it you clear that your prayers may do us good, and have showed it you so plainly that a child may perceive it, not only by the common opinion of all people and the fast[505] infallible faith of all Chris-tian people from Christ's days until your own time, confirmed by the doctrine of all holy doctors, de-clared by good reason, and proved by the Scripture of God, both apostles and evangelists, and our Sav-ior Christ himself, we will encumber you no further with disputing upon the matter, nor argue the thing as doubtful that is undoubted and questionless.

But letting pass over such heretics as are our ma-licious mortal enemies, praying God of his grace to give them better mind,[506] we shall turn us to you that are faithful folk and our dear loving friends, be-seeching your goodness of your tender pity that we may be remembered with your charitable alms and prayer. And in this part, albeit we stand in such case that it better becometh us to beseech and pray ev-ery man than to find any fault with any man, yet are we somewhat constrained not to make any matter of quarrel or complaint against any man's unkind-ness,[507] but surely to mourn and lament our own hard fortune and chance in the lack of relief and comfort which we miss from our friends, not of evil mind withdrawn us[508] or of unfaithfulness, but of negligence forslothed[509] and foded forth[510] of for-getfulness. If ye that are such (for ye be not all such) might look upon us and behold in what heavy[511] plight we lie, your sloth would soon be quickened,[512] and your oblivion[513] turn to fresh remembrance.

For if your father, your mother, your child, your brother, your sister, your husband, your wife, or a very stranger too, lay in your sight somewhere in fire, and that your means might help him, what heart were so hard, what stomach[514] were so stony, that could sit in rest at supper, or sleep in rest abed, and let a man lie and burn? We find, there-fore, full true that old-said saw,[515] "out of sight, out

491 restricts; prohibits 492 *would they should:* wants them to 493 charges; alleges 494 without the permission of 495 anything 496 desire to 497 *by and by:* immediately 498 truth 499 soundly 500 what 501 *spoil and* *pill:* despoil and pillage 502 intellect; ingenuity 503 foolish 504 rejecting 505 fixed, steadfast 506 disposition; judgment 507 unnatural disposition; absence of natural affection or loyalty 508 *of evil…us:* on account of ill will withdrawn from us 509 neglected 510 *foded forth:* put off; deferred 511 grievous 512 enlivened 513 obliv-iousness 514 disposition; temperament 515 *old-said saw:* old saying

of mind." And yet surely, to say the truth, we cannot therein with reason much complain upon you. For while we were with you there, for wantonness[516] of that wretched world we forgot in like wise our good friends here. And therefore can we not marvel much though[517] the justice of God suffer[518] us to be forgotten of you as others have been before forgotten of us. But we beseech our Lord for both our sakes to give you the grace to mend for your part that common fault of us both, lest when ye come hither hereafter, God of like justice suffer you to be forgotten of them that ye leave there behind you, as ye forget us that are hither afore you.

But albeit that we cannot well, as we say, for the like fault in ourselves, greatly rebuke or blame this negligence and forgetfulness in you, yet would we for the better wish you that ye might, without your pain, once at the leastwise behold, perceive, and see what heaviness of heart and what a sorrowful shame the seely[519] soul hath at his first coming hither to look his old friends in the face here, whom he remembereth himself to have so foul forgotten while he lived there. When albeit that in this place no man can be angry, yet their piteous look and lamentable countenance casteth his unkind forgetfulness into his mind, wit[520] ye well, dear friends, that among the manifold great and grievous pains which he suffereth here (whereof God send you the grace to suffer either none or few) the grudge[521] and grief of his conscience in the consideration of his unkind forgetfulness is not of all them the least.

Therefore, dear friends, let our folly learn you wisdom. Send hither your prayer; send hither your alms before you—so shall we find ease thereof, and yet shall ye find it still. For as he that lighteth another the candle hath never the less light himself, and he that bloweth the fire for another to warm him doth warm himself also therewith, so surely, good friends, the good that ye send hither before you, both greatly refresheth us, and yet is wholly reserved here for you, with our prayers added thereto for your further advantage.

Would God we could have done ourselves as we now counsel you. And God give you the grace which many of us refused, to make better provision while ye live than many of us have done. For much have we left in our executors' hands, which would God we had bestowed upon poor folk for our own souls and our friends' with our own hands. Much have many of us bestowed upon rich men in gold rings and black gowns, much in many tapers[522] and torches, much in worldly pomp and high solemn ceremonies about[523] our funerals, whereof the brotle[524] glory standeth us here, God wot,[525] in very little stead,[526] but hath, on the other side, done us great displeasure. For albeit that the kind solicitude and loving diligence of the quick used about[527] the burying of the dead is well allowed and approved afore the face of God, yet much superfluous charge[528] used for boast and ostentation—namely devised by the dead before his death—is of God greatly misliked, and most especially that kind and fashion thereof wherein some of us have fallen, and many besides us that now lie damned in hell.

For some hath there of us, while we were in health, not so much studied how we might die penitent and in good Christian plight[529] as how we might be solemnly borne out to burying, have gay and goodly funerals with heralds at our hearses,[530] and offering up our helmets, setting up our escutcheon and coat armors[531] on the wall, though there never came harness[532] on our backs, nor never ancestor of ours ever bore arms before. Then devised we some doctor[533] to make a sermon at our Mass in our Month's Mind,[534] and there preach to our praise with some fond fantasy devised of[535] our name, and after Mass, much feasting, riotous and costly, and finally like madmen made men merry at our death, and take our burying for a bridal.[536] For special punishment whereof, some of us have been by our evil angels brought forth full heavily,[537] in full great despite,[538] to behold our own burying, and so stood in great pain invisible among the press,[539] and made to look on our carrion corpse carried out with great pomp, whereof our Lord knoweth we have taken heavy pleasure.

Yet would ye peradventure ween[540] that we were in one thing well eased: in that we were, for the time,

516 unruliness; lustfulness   517 if
518 allow   519 poor   520 know
521 murmur   522 candles   523 connected with; surrounding   524 brittle, fragile   525 knows   526 *standeth … stead:* works very little to our advantage   527 *the quick used about:* the

living customarily practiced concerning
528 expense   529 manner, state
530 pagoda-like structures decorated with banners, heraldic devices, and lighted candles, sometimes bearing complimentary verses attached by loved ones   531 *escutcheon and coat armors:* shield with armorial

bearings and coats of arms   532 armor
533 priest   534 *Month's Mind:* a memorial Mass celebrated a month after the person's death   535 *devised of:* contrived from   536 wedding feast   537 miserably
538 scorn; malice   539 crowd   540 *peradventure ween:* perhaps think

taken hence out of the fire of our purgatory. But in this point if ye so think, ye be far deceived. For likewise as good angels and saved souls in heaven never lose nor lessen their joy by changing of their places, but though[541] there be any special place appointed for heaven farthest from the center of the whole world, or wheresoever it be, be it bodily or above all bodily space, the blessed heavenly spirits, wheresoever they be come, be either still in heaven or in their heavenly joy; nor Gabriel when he came down to our Lady, never forbore any part of his pleasure, but he had it peradventure with some new degree increased by the comfort of his joyful message,[542] but diminished might it never be, not and[543] he had an errand into hell—right so fareth it, on the other side, that neither damned wretches at any time, nor we for the space of our cleansing time, though we have for the generalty[544] our common place of pain appointed us here in purgatory, yet if it please our Lord that at any season our guardians convey some of us to be, for some considerations, any time elsewhere—as some percase[545] to appear to some friend of ours and show him how we stand, and by the sufferance[546] of God's sovereign goodness to tell him with what alms, prayer, pilgrimage, or other good deed done for us he may help us hence, in which thing the devil is loath to walk with us, but he may not choose and can no further withstand us than God will give him leave—but whithersoever he carry us, we carry our pain with us, and like as the body that hath a hot fever as fervently burneth if he ride on horseback as if he lay lapped[547] in his bed, so carry we still about no less heat with us than if we lay bounden here. And yet the despiteful[548] sights that our evil angels bring us to behold abroad so far augmenteth our torment that we would wish to be drowned in the darkness that is here rather than see the sights that they show us there.

For among[549] they convey us into our own houses, and there double us our pain with sight sometimes of the selfsame things which while we lived was half our heaven to behold. There show they us our substance[550] and our bags stuffed with gold, which when we now see, we set much less by them[551] than would an old man that found a bag of cherry stones which he laid up when he was a child. What

a sorrow hath it been to some of us when the devils hath in despiteful mockage cast in our teeth our old love borne to our money, and then showed us our executors as busily rifling and ransacking our houses, as though they were men of war that had taken a town by force.

How heavily hath it, think you, gone unto our heart when our evil angels have grinned and laughed and showed us our late wives, so soon waxen[552] wanton, and forgetting us, their old husbands that have loved them so tenderly and left them so rich, sit and laugh and make merry, and more too sometimes, with their new wooers, while our keepers in despite keep us there in pain to stand still, and look on. Many times would we then speak if we could be suffered,[553] and sore we long to say to her, "Ah, wife, wife, iwis[554] this was not covenant, wife, when ye wept and told me that if I left you to live by,[555] ye would never wed again." We see there our children too, whom we loved so well, pipe, sing, and dance, and no more think on their fathers' souls than on their old shoes, saving that sometimes cometh out, "God have mercy on all Christian souls." But it cometh out so coldly, and with so dull affection, that it lieth but in the lips and never came near the heart. Yet hear we sometimes our wives pray for us more warmly. For in chiding with her second husband to spite him withal,[556] "God have mercy," saith she, "on my first husband's soul, for he was iwis an honest man, far unlike you." And then marvel we much when we hear them say so well by us. For they were ever wont[557] to tell us otherwise.

But when we find in this wise[558] our wives, our children, and friends so soon and so clearly forget us, and see our executors rap and rend[559] unto themselves—catch every man what he can, and hold fast that[560] he catcheth—and care nothing for us, Lord God, what it grieveth us that we left so much behind us, and had not sent hither more of our substance before us by our own hands. For happy find we him among us that sendeth before all that may be forborne. And he that is so loath to part with aught,[561] that hoardeth up his goods and had as lief[562] die almost as to break[563] his heap, and then at last, when there is none other remedy but that he must needs leave it, repenteth himself

---

541 even if   **542** Lk 1:20–37   **543** even if   **544** most part   **545** perhaps **546** allowance; leave   **547** covered up   **548** cruel   **549** on occasion, now

and then   **550** possessions   **551** *set... them:* value them much less   **552** become **553** allowed   **554** indeed   **555** *to live by:* (money) to live on   **556** with

557 accustomed   **558** way   **559** *rap and rend:* snatch and wrench away   **560** what **561** anything   **562** rather   **563** break up, cut into

suddenly and lacketh time to dispose it, and therefore biddeth his friends to bestow it well for him,
our Lord is yet so merciful that, of his goodness,
he accepted the good deeds that his executors do
5   in performing his device.[564] And since that late is
better than never, our Lord somewhat alloweth the
man's mind,[565] by which he would his goods that he
hath immoderately gathered and greedily kept together as long as he might were yet at the leastwise
10 well bestowed at last, when he must needs go from
them. Which mind yet more pleaseth God than
that a man cared not what were done with them.
And therefore, as we say, the goodness of God
somewhat doth accept it.

15   But yet surely, since we might and ought to have
done it ourselves, and of a filthy affection toward
our goods could not find in our heart to part from
any part of them, if our executors now deceive us
and do no more for us than we did for ourselves,
20 our Lord did[566] us no wrong though[567] he never gave
us thank of all our whole testament,[568] but imputed
the frustration and not-performing of our last will
unto our own fault, since the delay of our good
deeds, driven[569] off to our death, grew but of our
25 own sloth and fleshly love to the worldward,[570] with
faintness of devotion to Godward,[571] and of little respect and regard unto our own souls. And over[572]
this, if our executors do these good things indeed
that we do thus at last devise in our testament, yet
30 our default[573] driving all to our death, as we told you
before, though God, as we said, of his high goodness leaveth not all unrewarded, yet this warning
will we give you, that ye deceive not yourselves; we
that have so died have thus found it, that the goods
35 disposed after us get our executors great thank, and
be to usward[574] accounted afore God much less than
half our own, nor our thank nothing like to that[575]
it would have been if we had in our health given
half as much for God's sake with our own hands.
40 Of which we give you this friendly warning not
for that[576] we would discourage you to dispose well
your goods when ye die, but for that we would advise you to dispose them better while ye live.

　　And among all your alms, somewhat remember

us: Our wives there, remember here your husbands.   45
Our children there, remember here your parents.
Our parents there, remember here your children.
Our husbands there, remember here your wives.
Ah, sweet husbands, while we lived there in that
wretched world with you, while ye were glad to   50
please us, ye bestowed much upon us and put yourselves to great cost, and did us great harm therewith. With gay[577] gowns and gay kirtles,[578] and
much waste in apparel, rings and ouches,[579] with
partlets and pastes[580] garnished with pearls, with   55
which proud picking up, both ye took hurt and we
too, many more ways than one, though we told you
not so then. But two things were there special[581] of
which yourselves felt then the one and we feel now
the other. For ye had us the higher-hearted[582] and   60
the more stubborn to you, and God had us in less favor, and that, alack, we feel. For now that gay gear[583]
burneth upon our backs, and those proud pearled
pastes hang hot about our cheeks; those partlets
and those ouches hang heavy about our necks and   65
cleave fast[584] fire-hot—that woe be we there, and
wish that while we lived, ye never had followed our
fantasies, nor never had so cockered[585] us, nor made
us so wanton,[586] nor had given us other ouches than
onions or great garlic heads, nor other pearls for   70
our partlets and our pastes than fair orient[587] peas.
But now forasmuch as that is passed and cannot be
called again,[588] we beseech you, since ye gave them
us, let us have them still; let them hurt none other
woman but help to do us good; sell them for our   75
sakes to set in saints' copes,[589] and send the money
hither by mass-pennies,[590] and by poor men that
may pray for our souls.

　　Our fathers also, which while we lived fostered us
up so tenderly, and could not have endured to see   80
us suffer pain, now open your hearts and fatherly
affection and help us, at the leastwise with a poor
man's alms. Ye would not when we were with you
have letted[591] to lay out much money for a great
marriage. Which if ye meant for our sakes and not   85
for your own worldly worship,[592] give us now some
part thereof and relieve us here with much less cost
than one marriage, and more pleasure than fifteen,

---

564 will, intent　**565** disposition
566 would be doing　**567** even
if　**568** *thank of . . . testament:* credit for
our whole will　**569** put　**570** *to the
worldward:* directed toward the world
571 *to Godward:* directed toward God

572 in addition to　**573** fault　**574** *to
usward:* in relation to us　**575** what
576 *for that:* because　**577** bright, showy
578 outer petticoats　**579** pendants
580 *partlets and pastes:* add-on collars and
decorative headdresses　**581** in particular

582 haughtier　**583** apparel　**584** fixedly
585 pampered　**586** rebellious　**587** precious, lustrous; of the East　**588** back
589 vaults　**590** an offering given for
having a Mass said for a person who has
died　**591** hesitated　**592** prestige

though⁵⁹³ every one were a prince or a princess of a realm.

Finally, all our other friends, and every good Christian man and woman, open your hearts and have some pity upon us. If ye believe not that we need your help, alas the lack of faith. If ye believe our need and care not for us, alas the lack of pity. For whoso pitieth not us, whom can he pity? If ye pity the poor, there is none so poor as we that have not a brat⁵⁹⁴ to put on our backs. If ye pity the blind, there is none so blind as we which are here in the dark, saving⁵⁹⁵ for sights unpleasant and loathsome, till some comfort come. If ye pity the lame, there is none so lame as we, that neither can creep one foot out of the fire, nor have one hand at liberty to defend our face from the flame. Finally, if ye pity any man in pain, never knew ye pain comparable to ours, whose fire as far passeth⁵⁹⁶ in heat all the fires that ever burned upon earth, as the hottest of all those passeth a feigned fire painted on a wall.

If ever ye lay sick and thought the night long, and longed sore⁵⁹⁷ for day while every hour seemed longer than five, bethink you then what a long night we seely⁵⁹⁸ souls endure, that lie sleepless, restless, burning, and broiling in the dark fire one long night of many days, of many weeks, and some of many years together. You walter peradventure and tolter⁵⁹⁹ in sickness from side to side, and find little rest in any part of the bed; we lie bounden to the brands and cannot lift up our heads. You have your physicians with you, that sometimes cure and heal you; no physic⁶⁰⁰ will help our pain, nor no plaster⁶⁰¹ cool our heat. Your keepers do you great ease and put you in good comfort; our keepers are such as God keep you from, cruel damned spirits, odious, envious, and hateful, dispiteous⁶⁰² enemies and despiteful⁶⁰³ tormentors, and their company more horrible and grievous to us than is the pain itself and the intolerable torment that they do us, wherewith from top to toe they cease not continually to tear us.

But now if our other enemies, these heretics almost as cruel as they, procuring to their power⁶⁰⁴ that we should be long left in the devil's hands, will (as their usage⁶⁰⁵ is to rail instead of reasoning)

make a game and a jest now of our heavy pain, and peradventure laugh at our lamentation, because we speak of our heads, our hands, our feet, and such our other gross⁶⁰⁶ bodily members as lie buried in our graves, and of our garments that we did wear, which come not hither with us, we beseech you, for our dear Lady's love, to let their folly go by, and to consider in your own wisdom that it were impossible to make any mortal man living perceive what manner⁶⁰⁷ pain and in what manner wise we bodiless souls do suffer and sustain, or to make any man upon earth perfectly to conceive in his imagination and fantasy what manner of substance we be—much more impossible than to make a born-blind man to perceive in his mind the nature and difference of colors. And therefore, except⁶⁰⁸ we should of our painful state tell you nothing at all (and there would they have it), we must of necessity use⁶⁰⁹ you such words as yourself understand, and use you the similitudes of such things as yourself is in ure⁶¹⁰ with.

For since neither God, angel, nor soul is in such wise blind, dumb, deaf, or lame as be those men that for lack of eyes, legs, hands, tongue, or ears be weak and impotent in the powers that proceed from them, but have in themselves a far more excellent sight, hearing, deliverness,⁶¹¹ and speech, by means uncogitable⁶¹² to man, than any man can have living there on earth, therefore doth Holy Scripture in speaking of such things use to represent them to the people by the names of such powers, instruments, and members⁶¹³ as men in such things use and occupy themselves. Which manner of speaking in such case, whosoever have⁶¹⁴ in derision declareth very well how little faith he hath in Christ's own words, in which our Savior himself, speaking of the souls of the rich glutton and poor needy Lazarus, and of the patriarch Abraham also, speaketh in like manner as we do—of finger and tongue too, whereof they had neither nother⁶¹⁵ there. And therefore whoso maketh a mock at our words in this point, ye may soon see what credence ye should give him, wherein we be content ye give him even as much as ye see yourself that he giveth to God, for more ye ought not, and surely less ye cannot. For he

---

593 even if **594** rag, scrap of clothing **595** except **596** surpasses **597** greatly; intensely **598** poor **599** *walter peradventure and tolter:* toss perhaps and turn **600** medical treatment **601** salve **602** pitiless **603** cruel **604** *procuring to their power:* contriving to the best of their ability **605** wont, habit **606** material **607** kind of **608** unless **609** use with **610** practice **611** agility **612** inconceivable **613** body parts **614** holds **615** *neither nother:* neither the one nor the other

giveth God not a whit,[616] but taketh in his heart that story told by God for a very fantastic fable.

And therefore, as we say, passing over such jesting and railing of those uncharitable heretics, mortal enemies unto us and to themselves both, consider you our pains, and pity them in your hearts, and help us with your prayers, pilgrimages, and other alms-deeds, and of all things in special[617] procure us the suffrages and blessed oblation of the holy Mass, whereof no man living so well can tell the fruit as we that here feel it.

The comfort that we have here, except our continual hope in our Lord God, cometh at seasons from our Lady, with such glorious saints as either ourselves with our own devotion while we lived, or ye with yours for us since our decease and departing, have made intercessors for us. And among others, right especially be we beholden to the blessed spirits, our own proper good angels.[618] Whom when we behold coming with comfort to us, albeit that we take great pleasure and greatly rejoice therein, yet is it not without much confusion and shamefastness[619] to consider how little we regarded our good angels and how seldom we thought upon them while we lived. They carry up our prayers to God and good saints for us, and they bring down from them the comfort and consolation to us. With which when they come and comfort us, only God and we know what joy it is to our hearts, and how heartily we pray for you.

And therefore, if God accept the prayer after[620] his own favor borne toward him that prayeth and the affection that he prayeth with, our prayer must needs be profitable, for we stand sure of his grace. And our prayer is for you so fervent that ye can nowhere find any such affection upon earth. And therefore, since we lie so sore in pains, and have in our great necessity so great need of your help, and that ye may so well do it, whereby shall also rebound upon yourselves an inestimable profit, let never any slothful oblivion[621] erase us out of your remembrance, or malicious enemy of ours cause you to be careless of us, or any greedy mind upon[622] your goods withdraw your gracious alms from us.

Think how soon ye shall come hither to us; think what great grief and rebuke would then your unkindness be to you, what comfort on the contrary part when all we shall thank you, what help ye shall have here of your goods sent hither. Remember what kin ye and we be together, what familiar friendship hath ere this been between us, what sweet words ye have spoken and what promise ye have made us. Let now your words appear and your fair promise be kept.

Now, dear friends, remember how nature and Christendom bindeth you to remember us. If any point of your old favor, any piece of your old love, any kindness of[623] kindred, any care of acquaintance, any favor of old friendship, any spark of charity, any tender point of pity, any regard of nature,[624] any respect of Christendom be left in your breasts, let never the malice of a few fond[625] fellows, a few pestilent persons borne toward priesthood, religion, and your Christian faith, erase out of your hearts the care of your kindred, all force[626] of your old friends, and all remembrance of all Christian souls.

Remember our thirst while ye sit and drink, our hunger while ye be feasting, our restless watch[627] while ye be sleeping, our sore and grievous pain while ye be playing, our hot burning fire while ye be in pleasure and sporting—so mote[628] God make your offspring after remember you; so God keep you hence or not long here, but bring you shortly to that bliss to which, for our Lord's love, help you to bring us, and we shall set hand to help you thither to us.

Finis

Cum privilegio[629]

---

616 bit, jot   **617** particular   **618** i.e., guardian angels   **619** *confusion and shamefastness:* embarrassment and shame   **620** in accord with   **621** obliviousness

622 *mind upon:* disposition toward   **623** *kindness of:* natural disposition toward   **624** *regard of nature:* natural regard   **625** foolish   **626** care   **627** wakefulness

628 may   **629** *Cum privilegio:* With [the King's] permission

Tyndale.

Iudge whyther yt be possible that any good sholde come oute of theyr domme
ceremonyes and sacramentes in to thy soule. Iudge theyr penaunce, pylgry-
mages, pardones, purgatorye, praynge to postes, domme bleſſynges, domme ab
ſolucyons, theyr domme paterynge and halowynge, theyr domme ſtraunge ho
ly geſtures, wyth all theyr domme diſgyſynges, theyr ſatisfaceyons and iuſte-
fyenge. And becauſe thou fyndeſt them falſe in ſo many thynges / truſte theu
in nothynge, but iudge them in all thinges.

More.

Iudge good cryſten reader whyther yt be poſſyble that
he be any better then a beſte / oute of whoſe bꝛutyſhe beſtely
mouth, cōmeth ſuch a fylthye fome of blaſphemyes agaynſt
cryſtes holy ceremonyes and bleſſed ſacramentes, ſent in to
his chyꝛche out of his owne bleſſed bloody ſyde. And foꝛ by=
cauſe ye fynde this felowe ſo frantike and ſo falſe in the rap   B
lynge and ieſtynge agaynſte the ſacramentes of Cryſte : ye
may well iudge that who ſo can delyte oꝛ be cōtent with his
blaſphemouſe rybauldy, hath great cauſe in hym ſelf to fere
that his cryſten fayth begynneth to fayle and faynte.

Tyndale.

Marke at the laſte the practyſe of our fleſhely ſpirytualtye, and theyr wayes
by whyche they haue walked aboue .viij. hondred yeres / how they ſtablyſhe
theyr lyes fyrſt wyth falſyfyenge the ſcrypture, then thorow corruptyng with
theyr ryches wherof they haue infynyte treaſure in ſtory, and laſte of all with
the ſwerde.

More.

ye may marke J pꝛaye you. Foꝛ this is mych to be mar
keth lo, ꝑ Tyndale can not bere the fleſſhelynes of oure ſpy
rytualtye, bycauſe the fleſſhelynes of theyꝛ chyꝛch is ſpyꝛy=
tuall. Foꝛ the fleſſhely wedded harlotes of theyꝛ chyꝛche   C
be theyꝛ chyef holy ſpyꝛytuall fathers, and holy ſpyꝛytuall
mothers, monkes, freres, and nunnes. And bycauſe theyꝛ
holy chyꝛch is but new bygonne / Tyndale wolde we ſhold
wene, that this .viii. hundꝛed yere and moꝛe Criſte hath had
no chyꝛch in the woꝛlde at all. Foꝛ ſo longe ſayth Tyndale
all hath be nought / by the reaſon that all this whyle the cler
gye hath falſyfyed the ſcrypture, and hyꝛed men wyth gyf=
tes, and compelled them wyth the ſwerde to byleue them / &
ſo all this .viii. hundꝛed yeres ſayth Tyndale by theſe meanes all the crpſten nacyons haue in ſtede of true fayth byle-
ued falſe lyes, and ſo haue ben out of the fayth & all nought.
Jf Tyndale dyd not lye now, as blyſſed be god he doth /
here

This page, from the first edition of Thomas More's *Confutation of Tyndale's* Answer (London: Rastell, 1532,
sig. l₄v), shows More's favored style toward the end of his life. As he would do later with St. German and
then with George Joye, More responds here in great detail to William Tyndale's 1531 *Answer* to More's 1529
Dialogue—responding sometimes to a paragraph, sometimes to a sentence. More published three books of
this reply—while serving as Lord Chancellor—in 1532. His full response fills 1,034 pages in *CW* 8.

The Confutation of Tyndale's *Answer*
made by Sir Thomas More, Knight
Lord Chancellor of England

In March 1528, London Bishop Cuthbert Tunstall formally requested Sir Thomas More to "play Demosthenes" in defending the Catholic faith in the vernacular, by "publishing in English for the common man." More responded by first publishing *The Dialogue of Sir Thomas More, Knight* in 1529; William Tyndale published in 1531 his own response, *An Answer unto Sir Thomas More's* Dialogue. More then replied, not with a fictional frame as in the 1529 dialogue, but by quoting Tyndale's words, then analyzing and refuting his claims.

In his essay on More's polemical career, Louis Schuster summarizes More's approach: "More's method of confutation consists in quoting Tyndale's text in gobbets, seldom more than one paragraph at a time and often merely a single sentence, then overwhelming it with a varied barrage of polemical artillery: painstaking logic in isolating and reconstructing premises, copious invention of arguments to bolster the case of the opposition, biblical exegesis, invective, and *ad hominem* barbs, patristic documentation, heckling, legalistic analogy, occasional ribaldry, testimony of saints and martyrs, cautionary reference to past heretics, conciliar pronouncements, theological distinctions, mocking repetition, together with countless variations on these practices" (*CW* 8: 1260). More's practice of quoting a polemical opponent directly and responding in detail continues his practice from the *Response to Luther* (1523) onwards. As Schuster also notes, "so accurate is More's citation of Tyndale's text...that one could reconstruct verbatim the Preface of Tyndale's *Answer* from the first book of the *Confutation*."

Comprising nearly 500 double-columned pages in the 1557 *Workes,* More's *Confutation of Tyndale's* Answer is his longest writing, and was completed in this order: Books 1–3 were published in March 1532, while More was Lord Chancellor; Books 4–8 were published in 1533, after his resignation; the fragmentary Book 9, intended as the conclusion but never published, Rastell printed from the manuscripts he saved, in his 1557 *Workes*. More's rhetorical strategy in the *Confutation*, marked by frequent repetition and recapitulation chapter by chapter of his chief arguments on behalf of the Church, is explained by the author in his *Apology*, published in 1533: "Now have I then considered that they would peradventure wax weary to read over a long book, and therefore have I taken the more pain upon every chapter, to the intent that they shall not read over any chapter but one, and that it shall not force greatly which one throughout the book."

More explains his purposes in the excerpt given here, his "Preface to the Christian Reader" (*CW* 8: 3–41). In this text, More also addresses the case of Robert Barnes, doctor of theology, an Augustinian friar and prior in Cambridge who became a reformer. Barnes had abjured heresy in 1526, but then fled England to Antwerp and Germany, where he met Luther. Barnes had recently been allowed to return to England in 1531. In 1540, Barnes and two other Protestants were executed for heresy at Smithfield; joining them on the scaffold were three Catholics, who were executed for treason. After the opening discussion of the case of Barnes and others, More describes the structure of the *Confutation* as leading to the core issue, "the very breast of all this battle"—the nature of the Church. What is it? Where is the Church found? More understands his long book as providing the reader with the means—scriptural, rational, theological, legal, and historical—of confuting Tyndale and his writings.

The full text of More's *Confutation*, running to over 1,000 pages, is available in volume 8 of *The Complete Works of St. Thomas More* and online at www.essentialmore.org.

CONTENTS*

*These are pages 3–41 of *CW* 8.

The Confutation of Tyndale's *Answer*
made by Sir Thomas More, Knight
Lord Chancellor of England

The Preface to the Christian Reader

5 Our Lord send us now some years as plenteous of good corn[1] as we have had some years of late plenteous of evil books. For they have grown so fast and sprung up so thick, full of pestilent errors and pernicious heresies, that they have infected 10 and killed, I fear me, more seely[2] simple souls than the famine of the dear years[3] have destroyed bodies. And surely no little cause there is to dread that the great abundance and plenty of the one is no little cause and occasion of the great dearth and scarcity 15 of the other. For since that[4] our Lord of his especial[5] providence useth temporally[6] to punish the whole people for the sins of some part to compel the good folk to forbear[7] and abhor the naughty[8] whereby they may bring them to amendment and avoid 20 themselves the contagion of their company, wisdom were it for us to perceive that, like as folk begin now to delight in feeding their souls of the venomous carrion of[9] those poisoned heresies (of which may well be verified the words of Holy Writ "Death 25 is in the pot"),[10] our Lord likewise againward,[11] to revenge[12] it with, beginneth to withdraw his gracious hand from the fruits of the earth, diminishing the fertility both in corn and cattle, and bringing all in[13] dearth, much more than men can remedy or 30 fully find out the cause. And yet besides this, somewhere[14] he sendeth war, sickness, and mortality, to punish in the flesh that odious and hateful sin of the soul that spoileth the fruit from all manner of virtues: I mean unbelief, false faith, and infidelity, 35 and to tell you all at once in plain English, heresy. And, I say, that God now beginneth. For I fear me surely that, except[15] folk begin to reform that fault the sooner, God shall not fail in such wise[16] to go forward that we shall well perceive and feel by the

increase of our grief that all this gear[17] hitherto 40 is but a beginning yet. The prophet Elijah, as it is written in the Third Book of Kings,[18] for the infidelity and idolatry that then was used[19] in Israel, by his hearty prayer made unto God, kept that whole country from rain by[20] the space of three years and 45 a half—not of evil will or malice, but of devotion and pity; by the pain and pinching of the bodies, to compel men to remember their souls, which else were in peril of perishing by false idolatry.

Now albeit that these bold shameless heretics 50 have of long while neither letted[21] nor ceased falsely to insimulate[22] and accuse the Church of God, calling all good Christian people idolaters for honoring of saints and reverent behavior used at[23] their images, yet that have they done so far against their 55 own conscience—by which themselves well wot[24] that the Church useth[25] to saints and images none honor but ordinate, not honoring images but for the saints' sake, nor saints but for the sake of God, and neither image as saint nor saint as God—and this 60 knoweth, I say, Tyndale himself so well, and thereby so far hath railed against his own conscience—that now at the last, in his answer[26] to my book, he retreateth so far back that he revoketh[27] almost all that ever he said before, and is fain[28] now to grant 65 that Christian men may have images, and kneel before them too, as ye shall hereafter see when we shall come to the place.

But we, on the other side,[29] say plainly unto them that the things wherewith they corrupt the world 70 are of infidelity and faithless idolatry, the very most accursed kind. The chief evil in an idol was that it bore the name of God, either itself or the devil that it represented, and, being so reputed and worshipped for God, robbed the reverence and devout 75 honor from God.

1 grain 2 poor 3 *dear years:* years of dearth or scarcity 4 *since that:* since, given that 5 special (as opposed to general) 6 *useth temporally:* is accustomed in the present life 7 avoid 8 wicked 9 by 10 4(2) Kgs 4:40 11 in

response 12 avenge; punish 13 into 14 in some places 15 unless 16 a way 17 matter 18 3(1) Kgs 17–18. In More's day, what are now 1 and 2 Samuel were 1 and 2 Kings. 19 practiced 20 for 21 refrained from 22 charge 23 *used*

at: shown toward 24 know 25 gives 26 Tyndale's *An Answer unto Sir Thomas More's Dialogue* 27 rescinds; retracts 28 obliged 29 hand

Now when Tyndale calleth his heresies by the name of faith, and maketh men serve the devil while they ween[30] to serve God—what abominable idolatry is this?

5   If it be idolatry to put trust in the devil, and serve the devil with faith, it is worse than idolatry to make men ween they serve God with faith while they despite[31] him with a false belief.

And if it be very infidelity to do as the Turks do—bid men believe in Muhammad's Koran—it is more
10 infidelity to do as Tyndale hath done: purposely mistranslate Christ's holy Gospel, to set forth heresies as evil as the Koran.

And if it be idolatry to do as the paynims[32] did—
15 make an idol God—it must needs be much worse idolatry to do as these heretics do, that call God the cause of all evil, and thereby make God not a vain idol but a very devil.

And what can be worse kind of infidelity than to
20 make books of heresies, and call them the right faith?

And what more abominable infidelity than to abuse the Scripture of God to the color[33] of their false belief?

And what can be a worse belief than to believe
25 that the sacraments that God hath ordained by his Holy Spirit be but inventions of man, or as Tyndale saith of confession, but invention of the devil?

And what can be worse belief than to believe that God's word is not to be believed but if[34] it be put in
30 writing? Or what can be a worse belief than to believe that men's good works, be they never so[35] well done, be yet nothing worth, nor the man never the better for them, nor no reward for them coming toward[36] man in heaven?

35 Or what can be a worse belief than to believe that a man doth wrong to pray for his father's soul?

Or what can be a worse belief than to believe that a man may as slightly regard Whitsun[37] Sunday as Hock Monday,[38] and as boldly eat flesh[39] on Good
40 Friday as on Shrove Tuesday?[40]

And what can be a worse belief than to believe that none other sin can damn a man but only lack of belief?

And if it be idolatry to do as the paynims[41] do—
45 give worship unto an idol—how much is it worse

than idolatry to do as Tyndale doth: forbid us to give worship to the very Body and blessed Blood of God in the holy Sacrament of the altar?

These pestilent infidelities, and these abominable kinds of idolatries, far exceed and pass,[42] and incom- 50
parably more offend the majesty of our Lord God than all the setting up of Bel, and Baal, and Beelzebul, and all the devils in hell. Wherefore, like as in other places where these heresies have taken deeper root and been more spread abroad, God hath taken 55
more deep and sore vengeance, not only by dearth[43] and death, but also by battle and sword: so is it to be feared that for the receipt of these pestilent books, our Lord sendeth us some lack of corn[44] and cattle for a beginning, and will not fail but if[45] our fault be 60
amended to send us as sore punishment as he hath sent already into such other places as would not be by like warning amended—according as he saith in the twenty-sixth chapter of Leviticus, where he speaketh in this wise:[46] 65

If ye will not give ear unto me, nor fulfill all my commandments, but set my laws at nought,[47] despise my judgments, and leave those things undone that are by me ordained, and break my pact and covenant, then will I againward[48] do 70
these things following[49] unto you. I will hastily visit you with penury[50] and burning heat (or "fever") which shall sore[51] vex and grieve your eyes, and consume you even to the death. Over[52] this, ye shall sow your seed in vain, for your enemies 75
shall devour it. I shall also set my face against you, and ye shall fall before your adversaries, and be made subjects unto them that hate you. Ye shall flee where no man chaseth you. And if ye will not yet for all this obey me, I shall for your sins add 80
and put[53] to these plagues sevenfold more, and I shall tread down the pride of your stubbornness (and so forth).

And who doth more properly[54] fall in the danger of this commination[55] and threat than they 85
that despise Christ's sacraments, which are his holy ordinances and a great part of Christ's New Law and testament.[56] And who shall less set by his

30 *while they ween:* when they think
31 insult 32 pagans 33 pretext; show of reason 34 *but if:* unless 35 *never so:* to an unlimited degree 36 to 37 Pentecost
38 the second Monday after Easter
39 meat 40 the Tuesday before Ash Wednesday 41 pagans 42 surpass
43 scarcity 44 grain 45 *but if:* unless 46 way 47 no value 48 in turn 49 *things following:* following things
50 destitution 51 terribly 52 In addition to 53 attach 54 particularly
55 denunciation 56 covenant

commandments than they that, upon the boldness of "only faith," set all good works at nought, and little force[57] the danger of their evil deeds, upon the boldness that a bare[58] faith and slight repentance, without shrift[59] or penance, sufficeth, and that no vow made to God can bind a man to live chaste, nor let[60] a monk from marriage—all which things, with many pestilent errors besides, these abominable books of Tyndale and his fellows teach us.

Of these books of heresies there be so many made within these few years—what by Luther himself and by his fellows, and afterward by the new sects sprung out of his, which like the children of the viper would now gnaw out their mother's belly—that the bare names of those books were almost enough to make a book; and of every sort of those books be some brought into this realm, and kept in huggermugger,[61] by some shrewd masters[62] that keep them for no good.

Besides the books of Latin, French, and Deutsch, in which there are of these evil sects an innumerable sort, there are made in the English tongue, first Tyndale's New Testament, father of them all by reason of his false translating. And after that, the Five Books of Moses translated by the same man, we need not doubt in what manner, when we know by what man and for what purpose.

Then have ye his introduction[63] into Saint Paul's epistle, with which he introduceth and bringeth his readers into a false understanding of Saint Paul, making them, among many other heresies, believe that Saint Paul were in[64] the mind that only faith were always sufficient for salvation, and that men's good works were nothing worth, nor could no thank[65] deserve nor no reward in heaven, though[66] they were wrought[67] in grace. And these things teacheth Tyndale as the mind of Saint Paul, whereas Saint Paul saith himself that they which so misconstrue him to the depraving[68] of men's good works be well worthy[69] damnation.

Then have we by Tyndale the *Wicked Mammon*, by which many a man hath been beguiled and brought into many wicked heresies, which thing— saving that the devil is ready to put out men's eyes that[70] are content willingly to wax[71] blind—were else, in good faith, to me no little wonder, for never was there made a more foolish frantic[72] book.

Then have we Tyndale's book of *Obedience*,[73] whereby we be taught to disobey the doctrine of Christ's Catholic Church, and set his holy sacraments at nought.[74]

Then have we from Tyndale the First Epistle of Saint John in such wise expounded that I dare say that blessed apostle, rather than his holy words were in such a sense believed of all Christian people, had liefer[75] his epistle had never been put in writing.

Then have we the *Supplication of Beggars*, a piteous beggarly book wherein he[76] would have all the souls in purgatory beg all about for nought.

Then have we from George Joye, otherwise called clerk,[77] a goodly godly epistle, wherein he teacheth diverse other heresies, but specially that men's vows and promises made of chastity[78] be not lawful nor can bind no man in conscience, but he may wed when he will.

And this man, considering that when a man teacheth one thing and doth himself another, the people set the less by[79] his preaching, determined therefore with himself that he would of his preaching show himself example. And therefore, being priest, he hath beguiled a woman and wedded her— the poor woman, I ween,[80] unaware that he is priest. Howbeit,[81] if it be not done already, it is well likely now that (but if[82] God be her special guide) he shall by leisure[83] work her and win her to his own heresy.

Then have ye an exposition also upon the seventh chapter of Saint Paul's epistle to the Corinthians, by which exposition in like wise[84] priests, friars, monks, and nuns be taught that evangelical liberty that they may run out a caterwauling,[85] and so woo and wed and lawfully live in lechery.

That work hath no name of the maker,[86] but some ween it was Friar Roye,[87] which,[88] when he was fallen in heresy, then found it unlawful to live in chastity,[89] and ran out of his order,[90] and hath since sought many a false unlawful way to live by, wherein he made so many changes that, as Bayfield (another heretic, and lately burned in Smithfield)

---

57 take heed of   **58** mere   **59** confession
60 hinder   **61** secret   **62** *shrewd masters:* wicked teachers   **63** Its full title is *A Compendious Introduction, Prologue, or Preface unto the Epistle to the Roman.*
64 *were in:* was of   **65** grace   **66** even if   **67** done, performed   **68** disparaging

69 deserving of   **70** who   **71** become
72 crazy   **73** *The Obedience of a Christian Man, and How Christian Rulers Ought to Govern*   **74** no value   **75** preferred   **76** the author, Simon Fish   **77** a cleric. George Joye (*ca.* 1490–1533) was ordained in 1515.   **78** celibacy   **79** *set . . . by:*

value   **80** suppose   **81** However   **82** *but if:* unless   **83** *by leisure:* gradually
84 manner   **85** *a caterwauling:* in heat; in animalistic pursuit of sex   **86** author
87 William Roye (d. 1536)   **88** who
89 celibacy   **90** religious order

told unto me, he made a meet[91] end at last and was burned in Portugal.

Then have we the *Examination of Thorpe*, put forth, as it is said, by George Constantine—by whom there hath been, I wot[92] well, of that sort great plenty sent into this realm. In that book the heretic, that[93] made it as a communication between the bishop and his chaplains and himself, maketh all the parties speak as himself liketh, and layeth[94] nothing spoken against his heresies but such as himself would seem solemnly to assoil.[95] Whose book, when any good Christian man readeth that hath either learning or any natural wit, shall not only be well able to perceive him for a foolish heretic, and his arguments easy to answer, but shall also see that he showeth himself a false[96] liar in his rehearsal[97] of the matter, wherein he maketh the other party sometimes speak, for his commodity,[98] such manner things as no man would have done that were not a very[99] wild goose.

Then have we Jonah made out by Tyndale[100]— a book that whoso[101] delight therein shall stand in peril that Jonah was never so swallowed up with[102] the whale, as by the delight of that book a man's soul may be so swallowed up by the devil that he shall never have the grace to get out again.

Then have we, by Tyndale also, the *Answer* to my *Dialogue*, whereof I shall nothing now need to say, because the confutation of that answer is the matter of my present book.

Then have we also the book of Frith[103] against purgatory—the errors of which book I shall hereafter, God willing, declare[104] you.

Then have ye a book of Luther translated into English in[105] the name of Brightwell, but as I am informed, the book was translated by Frith, a book of such sort as Tyndale never made a more foolish, nor more full of false lies. And surely Frith's prologue (if it be his, as it is said) is right suitly[106] and a very meet[107] cover for such a cup, as bringeth the people a draught of deadly poison.

Then have we the *Practice of Prelates*, wherein Tyndale had went[108] to have made a special show of his high worldly wit, and that men should have seen therein that there were nothing done among

princes but that he was fully advertised[109] of all the secrets, and that so far forth that he knew the privy[110] practice made between the King's Highness and the late Lord Cardinal,[111] and the Reverend Father Cuthbert,[112] then bishop of London, and me: that it was devised wilily that the Cardinal should leave the chancellorship to me, and the bishopric of Durham to my said lord of London, for a while, till he list[113] himself to take them both again.[114] Was this not a wily drift,[115] trow[116] you? Which while every man well seeth there was no man so mad to tell Tyndale, no man doubteth but that Tyndale devised it of his own imagination; and then needeth no man to doubt what manner a brain Tyndale hath, that dreameth such frantic drifts.

Then have we now come forth the book of Friar Barnes,[117] sometime doctor in Cambridge, which[118] was for heresy before this time abjured,[119] and is at this day come to the realm by safe-conduct, which at his humble suit the King's Highness of his blessed disposition condescended to grant him to the end that, if there might yet any spark of grace be found in him, it might be kept, kindled, and increased, rather than the man to be cast away. Which manner of Christian zeal and princely benignity his Grace had before used,[120] both to Richard Bayfield and George Constantine, which came over hither without safe-conduct, upon the only[121] trust of his gracious forgiveness, and had it. And thereupon too, by and by,[122] both twain[123] deceitfully did abuse his goodness, and brought in again more of Tyndale's books and false heresies afresh; whereof[124] as God hath of his justice since requited the one, so mote[125] his mercy by grace amend the other.

But to speak of Friar Barnes's book, surely of all their books that yet came abroad[126] in English—of all which was never one wise nor good—was never none yet so bad, so foolish, nor so false as his, as it hath since his coming been plainly proved in his face, and that in such wise that when the books that he citeth and allegeth in his book were brought forth before him, and his ignorance shown him, himself did in diverse things confess his oversight, and clearly acknowledged that he had mistaken and wrongly understood the places.[127] And was in

---

91 fitting   **92** know   **93** who   **94** presents   **95** absolve; acquit or clear of a crime   **96** detestable   **97** recounting   **98** convenience, benefit   **99** true   **100** the Book of Jonah as translated by Tyndale   **101** whoever   **102** by   **103** John

Frith (1503–33)   **104** make known to   **105** under   **106** *right suitly:* quite suitable   **107** fitting   **108** thought   **109** informed   **110** secret   **111** Thomas Wolsey   **112** Cuthbert Tunstall (1474–1559)   **113** wished   **114** back   **115** scheme, plot

116 think   **117** Robert Barnes (d. 1540)   **118** who   **119** put on trial, and did recant   **120** practiced   **121** *the only:* solely the   **122** *by and by:* right away   **123** of the two   **124** for which   **125** might   **126** out   **127** passages

such wise finally confounded with shame that he was in a mammering[128] whether he would return again over the sea, or tarry still here and renounce his heresies again, and turn again to Christ's Catholic Church. And therefore he desired that he might have a learned man then present assigned unto him for the further instruction of his conscience, which his request was granted him, and what will further come thereon, God knoweth. If God give him the grace to amend, every good man will be glad thereof. If he have so far gone against God's truth, and thereby aggrieved God in such wise, that God have already given him over forever — or else that though God offer his grace again, the malice of the man's will withstand it yet and reject it — it is not then to be doubted but God will find a time for him well enough to show his justice on him, as he hath done upon such others, and namely of late, in Switzerland, upon Zwingli, which[129] was the first that brought Barnes's heresy thither,[130] concerning the Sacrament of the altar. But as for hence,[131] he shall, I am sure, have leave to depart safe, according to the King's safe-conduct. And yet hath he so demeaned[132] himself since his coming hither, that he hath clearly broken[133] and forfeited his safe-conduct, and lawfully might be burned for his heresies, if we would lay his heresies and his demeanor since his coming hither, both twain,[134] unto his charge. But let him go this once, for God shall find his time full well.

Then have we further yet, besides Barnes's book, the *ABC for Children*. And because there is no grace therein, lest we should lack prayers, we have the Primer, and the Ploughman's Prayer, and a book of other small devotions, and then the whole Psalter too. After the Psalter, children were wont to go to their donet[135] and their accidence,[136] but now they go straight to Scripture. And thereto have we as a donet the book of the *Pathway to Scripture*; and for an accidence, because[137] we should be good scholars[138] shortly and be soon sped,[139] we have the whole sum of Scripture in a little book; so that after these books well[140] learned, we be meet[141] for Tyndale's Pentateuch, and Tyndale's Testament, and all the other high[142] heresies that he and Joye and Frith and Friar Barnes teach in all their books besides — of all which heresies the seed is sown, and prettily sprung up, in these little books before. For the Primer and Psalter, prayers and all, were translated and made in this manner by none other but heretics.

The Psalter was translated by George Joye the priest, that[143] is wedded now; and, I hear say, the Primer too, wherein the seven psalms[144] be set in without the litany, lest folk should pray to saints. And the Dirge[145] is left out clean,[146] lest a man might hap[147] to pray thereon for his father's soul.

In their calendar before[148] their devout prayers, they have set us a new saint: Sir Thomas Hitton, the heretic that was burned in Kent, of whom I shall tell you more after. Him have they set in on Saint Matthias' Eve, by the name of Saint Thomas the Martyr.

A long work would it be to rehearse[149] you all their books, for there be yet more than I know. Against all which the King's high wisdom politicly[150] provided, in that his Highness by his proclamations forbade any manner English books printed beyond the sea to be brought into this realm, or any to be sold printed within this realm, but if[151] the name of the printer and his dwelling place were set upon the book.

But yet so is it, as I said before, that of these ungracious[152] books full of pestilent poisoned heresies — that have in other realms already killed by schisms and war many thousand bodies, and by sinful errors and abominable heresies, many more thousand souls — have now a few malicious mischievous[153] persons brought into this realm, and labor and enforce[154] themselves, in all that ever they may, to corrupt and infect all good and virtuous people.

Nor no man is there anywhere living more studious and busy to do himself good, than those envious[155] wretches be laborious and fervent to do all other men harm, in body, substance,[156] and soul.

There be fled out of this realm for heresy a few ungracious folk — what manner folk, their writing and their living showeth. For the captains be priests, monks, and friars that neither say Mass nor Matins, nor never come at church; talking still of faith and full of false heresies, would seem Christ's

---

128 state of doubt (as to)   129 who
130 over there   131 his departing
132 behaved   133 violated   134 together
135 introductory textbook   136 first,
elementary catechism   137 so that
138 schoolgoers   139 skilled   140 are

well   141 ready   142 high-level, lofty
143 who   144 penitential psalms: 6,
31(32), 37(38), 50(51), 101(102), 129(130),
142(143)   145 Office of the Dead
146 completely   147 happen   148 at
the front of   149 name   150 prudently

151 *but if:* unless   152 without grace;
wicked   153 destructive, injurious
154 strongly exert   155 malicious
156 goods, possessions

apostles and play the devil's disours;[157] speaking much of the Spirit with no more devotion than dogs—diverse of them, priests, monks, and friars, not let[158] to wed harlots and then call them wives.

5　And when they have once villained[159] the sacrament of matrimony—then would they make us violate the Sacrament of the altar too, telling us, as Tyndale doth, that it is sin to do the blessed Body of Christ in that sacrament any honor or reverence, but only

10　take it for a token.

Now when their chief captains be such, we shall not need to doubt of what sort we shall reckon the remnant. These fellows that nought[160] had here, and therefore nought carried hence,[161] nor nothing find-

15　ing there to live upon, be yet sustained and maintained with money sent them by some evil-disposed persons out of this realm thither—and that for none other intent but to make them sit and seek out heresies, and speedily send them hither.

20　Which books albeit that they neither can be there printed without great cost nor here sold without great adventure[162] and peril—yet cease they not with money sent from hence to print them there and send them hither by the whole vatfuls at once,

25　and in some places, looking for no lucre, cast them abroad by night; so great a pestilent pleasure have some devilish people caught, with the labor, travail, cost, charge, peril, harm, and hurt of themselves to seek the destruction of others. As the devil hath a

30　deadly delight to beguile good people and bring their souls into everlasting torment without any manner winning, and not without final increase of his own eternal pain, so do these heretics, the devil's disciples, beset[163] their whole pleasure and study, to

35　their own final damnation, in the training[164] of simple souls to hell by their devilish heresies.

Much they cry out against the clergy, saying that the priests love to reign in men's consciences. But they themselves show that when they have made the

40　devil reign in a man's conscience, so far forth that he hath no conscience to eat flesh[165] on Good Friday, nor to cast Christ's cross in the cannel,[166] nor to throw his blessed Body out of the pyx—then after that, likewise as the false preachers that were Jews

45　labored to have all Christian people circumcised, to the intent that, as Saint Paul saith, they might

"glory in their flesh,"[167] so be these arch-heretics very glad, and great glory they take, when they may hear that any man is brought to burning through their books. Then they boast that they have done a　50 great mastery,[168] and say they have made a martyr, when their poisoned books have killed the Christian man both in body and soul.

Thus rejoiced Tyndale in the death of Hitton, of whose burning he boasteth in his *Answer* to my　55 *Dialogue*, where he writeth thereof that whereas I said that I had never found nor heard of any of them but that he would forswear[169] to save his life, I had heard, he saith, of Sir Thomas Hitton, whom the bishops of Rochester and Canterbury slew at　60 Maidstone.

Of this man they so highly rejoice that they have, as I said, set his name in the calendar before[170] a book of their English prayers, by the name of Saint Thomas the Martyr, in[171] the vigil of the blessed　65 apostle Saint Matthias, the twenty-third day of February, and have put out for him the holy doctor and glorious martyr Saint Polycarp, the blessed bishop and the disciple of Saint John the Evangelist—for that was his day in deed, and so is it in some calen-　70 dars marked.

Now to the intent that ye may somewhat see what good Christian faith Sir Thomas Hitton was of— this new saint of Tyndale's canonization, in whose burning Tyndale so gaily glorieth, and which[172] hath　75 his holy day so now appointed to him that Saint Polycarp must give him place in the calendar—I shall somewhat show you what wholesome heresies this holy martyr held.

First ye shall understand that he was a priest　80 and, falling to Luther's sect, and after that to the sect of Friar Hussgen, and Zwingli, cast off Matins and Mass and all divine service,[173] and so became an apostle sent to and fro between our English heretics beyond the sea and such as were here at home.　85

Now happed[174] it so that, after he had visited here his holy congregations, in diverse corners and lusks' lanes,[175] and comforted[176] them in the Lord to stand stiff[177] with the devil in their errors and heresies—as he was going back again at Gravesend,　90 God, considering the great labor that he had taken already, and determining to bring his business to its

157 jester　**158** hesitating　**159** debased
160 nothing　**161** (with them) out of here
162 risk　**163** place　**164** luring, deceitful
leading　**165** meat　**166** gutter　**167** Gal

6:13　**168** feat　**169** renounce under oath
his faith　**170** at the front of　**171** on
172 who　**173** *divine service:* liturgical
prayer　**174** happened　**175** *lusks' lanes:*

places where idlers hang out　**176** encouraged, strengthened　**177** firm

well-deserved end, gave him suddenly such a favor, and so great a grace in the visage,[178] that every man that beheld him took him for a thief. For whereas[179] there had been certain linen cloths pilfered away that were hanging on a hedge, and Sir Thomas Hitton was walking not far off, suspiciously in the meditation of his heresies, the people, doubting[180] that the beggarly knave had stolen the cloths, fell in question with him and searched him—and so found they certain letters secretly conveyed in his coat, written from[181] evangelical brethren here unto the evangelical heretics beyond the sea. And upon those letters found, he was with his letters brought before the most reverend father in God the Archbishop of Canterbury, and afterward as well by his Lordship as by the reverend father the Bishop of Rochester examined, and after, for his abominable heresies, delivered to the secular hands and burned.

In his examination he refused to be sworn to say truth, affirming that neither bishop nor pope had authority to compel him to swear. Which point, although it be a false[182] heresy, yet is it likely that he refused the oath rather of frowardness[183] than of any respect[184] that he had either in keeping or breaking. For never could I find heretic yet that any conscience[185] had in any oath. And of truth, Tyndale, in his *Answer* to my *Dialogue*, teacheth them that they may break their oath and be forsworn[186] without any scruple at all.

His father and his mother, he would not be acknown of what[187] they were; they were some so good folk, of likelihood, that he could not abide the glory.

He would not be acknown that himself was priest, but said that he had by the space of nine years been beyond the sea, and there lived by the joiners'[188] craft. Howbeit,[189] he said that he had always, as his leisure would give him leave, and as he could find opportunity in places where he came, taught the Gospel of God after his own mind and his own opinion, not forcing of[190] the determination of the Church, and said that he intended, to his power, so to persevere still.

Of his teaching, these things were part. First, as for baptism, he agreed it for a sacrament necessary to salvation. Howbeit, every layperson, he said, might as well baptize as a priest, were the child in necessity or not, and that the form of baptizing used in the Church were much better if it were spoken in English.

Of matrimony, whether it were a sacrament or not, he said he wist ne'er.[191] But he said yet that it was a thing necessary, and of Christian people to be observed and kept. Howbeit, as for the solemnization of marriage at Church, he agreed it for good, but said it needed not. The man meant by likelihood that it was good enough to wed upon a cushion when the dogs be abed, as their priests wed, I ween,[192] where their persons[193] be known. For else they let[194] not to wed openly at Church, and take the whole parish for witnesses of their beastly bitchery.[195]

The extreme unction or aneling[196] and confirmation, he said be no sacraments of the Church, nor be nothing necessary to the soul.

The sacrament of order,[197] he said, is no sacrament of the Church, nor was never ordained[198] by God in the New Testament, but only by man.

The Mass, he said, should never be said. For he said that to say Mass after the manner of the Church is rather sin than virtue.

As for confession made to a priest, he said nothing profiteth the soul; nor penance enjoined of[199] the priest unto the penitent confessed,[200] is nothing necessary.

Purgatory he denied, and said also that neither prayer nor fasting for the souls departed can do them any good.

To vow and enter into any religion approved by the law, he said availeth not, but he said that all that enter into religion[201] sin in so doing.

He held also that no man hath any free will after that he hath once sinned.

He held that to say any divine service[202] after the ordinance of the Church availeth nothing, and that all divine service may be left unsaid without any sin.

He held that all the images of Christ and his saints should be thrown out of the Church.

He held also that whatsoever the pope or the general council make,[203] beside that that is expressly

178 face **179** given that, since **180** suspecting **181** by **182** detestable; deceitful **183** contrariness, perversity **184** concern **185** qualm of conscience **186** commit perjury **187** *be acknown of what:* admit anything about who **188** woodworkers' **189** However **190** *forcing of:* caring about **191** *wist ne'er:* knew not at all **192** suppose **193** identities **194** hesitate **195** lewdness **196** anointing **197** holy orders **198** established, instituted **199** by **200** after confessing **201** religious life **202** *divine service:* liturgical prayer **203** establishes as a law commanded in Scripture, every man may lawfully break it, without any manner sin at all, mortal or venial either.

He held also that it is not lawful neither for the king of England nor for any other Christian prince to make any law or statute for the punishment of any theft, or any other crime, by which law any man should suffer death. For he said that all such laws be contrary to the Gospel, which wills no man to die.

As touching the Blessed Sacrament of the altar, he said it is a necessary sacrament; but he held that after the consecration there was none other thing therein but only the very substance of material bread and wine; and so, he said, he firmly believed, and that he would hold that opinion to the death.

Finally, holding all these abominable heresies, with yet diverse others more of like suit and sort, he said that he was very certain and sure that he had the grace of God with him, and that the Holy Ghost was within him.

And so was he, after much favor shown him, and much labor charitably taken for the saving of him, delivered in conclusion, for his obstinacy, to the secular hands, and burned up in his false faith and heresies, whereof he learned the great part of[204] Tyndale's holy books, and now the spirit of error and lying hath taken his wretched soul with him straight from the short fire to the fire everlasting.

And this is, lo, Sir Thomas Hitton, the devil's stinking martyr of whose burning Tyndale maketh boast. Wherefore since Tyndale alloweth his cause,[205] he must needs defend his articles.[206] And now wot[207] I well that some of those articles Tyndale hath himself given over[208] at last for shame — as[209] the article against images, and the article against the liberty of man's free will, wherein he beareth me in hand,[210] in his *Answer* to my *Dialogue*, that I belie[211] Luther. But when I shall come to the place, I shall let you see Luther's own words in that point so plain that ye shall not marvel though[212] Tyndale were ashamed of his master.[213] And yet shall ye marvel that Tyndale was so shameless to deny the thing which ye shall see so plainly proved.

But ye see that, of this holy martyr, Tyndale hath not so great cause to glory but that he may scrape

out his name again[214] out of the calendar and restore the blessed bishop Saint Polycarp again into his place.

Then have ye had here burned since at London, of late, Richard Bayfield, late a monk and a priest, which[215] fell to heresy and was abjured,[216] and after that like a dog returning to his vomit, and being fled over the sea, and sending from thence Tyndale's heresies hither with many mischievous[217] sorts of books, had yet the King's gracious forgiveness and, as it was after proved both by other men's and his own confession too, was occupied about two things at once: that is to wit,[218] both in suing[219] for remission and pardon of his offense for bringing in those books, and therewith also in selling them here still secretly, and sending over for more, with which at last he was taken. And to rehearse[220] his heresies needeth little; the books that he brought well showeth them, and his holy life well declareth[221] them when, being both a priest and a monk, he went about[222] two wives, one in Brabant, another in England. What he meant I cannot make you sure — whether he would be sure of the one if the other should hap refuse him, or that he would have them both, the one here, the other there, or else both in one place, the one because he was priest, the other because he was monk.

Of Bayfield's burning hath Tyndale no great cause to glory. For though Tyndale's books brought him to burning, yet was he not so constant in his evangelical doctrine but that after that he was taken,[223] all the while that he was not in utter despair of pardon, he was well content to have forsworn[224] it again, and letted not to utter[225] his evangelical brethren both in England and elsewhere, causing some of them to be taken — as George Constantine, ere[226] he escaped, was ready to have, in word at the leastwise, abjured all that holy doctrine. What his heart was, God and he know, and peradventure[227] the devil too, if he intended otherwise. But surely there was intended toward him somewhat more good than his dealing[228] had before deserved. And so much the more favor was there minded[229] him in that he seemed very penitent of his misusing of himself in falling to Tyndale's heresies again. For which he

---

204 from   **205** cause for canonization as a martyr   **206** articles of his creed   **207** know   **208** *given over:* abandoned   **209** such as   **210** *beareth me in hand:* makes against me the claim

211 misrepresent   **212** that   **213** teacher **214** back   **215** who   **216** required to recant   **217** harmful   **218** say **219** petitioning   **220** relate, recount **221** makes known   **222** *went about:*

sought   **223** arrested, taken into custody **224** repudiated it under oath   **225** *letted…utter:* did not hesitate to expose **226** before   **227** perhaps   **228** conduct **229** extended to; intended toward

acknowledged himself worthy to be hanged — that he had so falsely[230] abused the King's gracious remission and pardon given him before, and had, for all that, in the while both bought and sold of those
[5] heretical books and secretly set forth those heresies. Whereof he showed himself so repentant that he uttered and disclosed diverse of his companions, of whom there are some abjured[231] since, and some that he wist[232] well were abjured before — namely Rich-
[10] ard[233] Necton, which[234] was by Constantine's detection taken[235] and committed to Newgate, where except he hap[236] to die before in prison, he standeth in great peril to be, ere it be long, for his falling again to Tyndale's heresies, burned. And thus it seemed
[15] by the manner of George Constantine while he was here in prison, that he so sore did forthink[237] his errors and heresies, and so perceived the pestilent poison of them, that he thought it better that such as were infected therewith might be by the means
[20] of his detection amended, and with the loss of his body the soul cured, than both twain cast away; or, if the man were peradventure of hard heart and malicious mind incurable, he thought it were then better to send him to the devil alone than let him live
[25] and draw many others with him.

This good mind it seemeth that Constantine had then, and therefore was there good hope of his amendment. And peradventure the man had amended, and stood still in grace, if some evil coun-
[30] sel had not come at him; of which there was left unsought no devilish invention or means to send him — insomuch that one of the letters I fortuned to intercept myself, written unto him by one John Burt, otherwise calling himself Adrian, otherwise
[35] John Bookbinder, and yet otherwise now, I cannot tell you what.

Of truth, George Constantine, after he had confessed unto a faithful servant of mine, to be declared[238] to me, that Necton had of his delivery
[40] many of these heretical books — he sent word forthwith[239] to Necton that he should send the books home to me. Which if he did, and that I might have yet seen sure tokens of amendment in the man, Constantine perceived well that he had been yet
[45] likely to have had favor shown him. But when that

Necton had once made Burt of his counsel, they devised between them that Necton should not do so in no wise,[240] affirming to Constantine that it could not be done; and haply it could not indeed, for peradventure they were all sold already. Howbeit, Nec-
[50] ton now, since he was taken,[241] said that his wife had burned them. But it is well known that Necton had himself, and a man[242] of his also, sold many such books of heresy, both in London and in other shires, since his abjuration. But howsoever the mat-
[55] ter was, Burt by his letter advised Constantine, if he might possibly, to call back his confession again; wherein I think it good that ye hear his very letter itself. Lo, in these words he wrote:

> The grace and peace of our Savior Jesus be with
> [60] you, good brother Constantine. Sir, as for the
> matter that ye would have brought to pass, will[243]
> not be, in no manner wise; the person is not at
> home that should receive the stuff and deliver
> it according unto your mind. Therefore, if ye
> [65] have not spoken so far in the matter that it may
> be none prejudice or hurt unto you, I would ye
> should go no further in the matter, but even,[244] as
> a man armed with faith, go forth in your matter
> boldly and put them to their proofs. As for one
> [70] is none,[245] you know well, by the law of God or
> man.[246] If there be anything that I can do, send
> word and ye shall find me ready to my power,
> even to death, by God's grace, who I pray long to
> preserve you and comfort[247] you in your trouble,
> [75] to the confusion[248] of all tyrants.

Lo, here have ye heard an apostolical epistle counseling the man to go back with[249] the truth and arm himself with faith, and make him strong to lie loud and forswear[250] himself if need were, for Burt wist[251]
[80] well I were not likely to leave and believe him at his bare[252] word.

Here will Burt peradventure[253] preach, and bring us in[254] the midwives of Egypt that saved the children of Israel from Pharaoh, for which God gave
[85] them new houses.[255] Wherein Burt and I will not much dispute. For albeit that God hath given him no house yet, nor it is not all one with a lie to save

230 detestably   231 recanted   232 knew
233 actually Robert   234 who
235 arrested, taken into custody   236 happens   237 *sore did forethink:* seriously did
repent of   238 made known   239 at once

240 manner   241 taken into custody
242 servant   243 it will   244 directly
245 *As . . . none:* As not one of their
claims has any proof   246 2 Cor 13:1
247 encourage   248 ruin; confounding

249 on   250 perjure   251 knew
252 mere   253 perhaps   254 *us in:* up
to us   255 See Ex 1:15–21.

a young innocent babe and with perjury to defend an old pestilent heretic; and though Saint Augustine saith that it is not lawful to lie for no thing, yet I tell not my tale to lay a lie so highly to any such men's charge as these folk be, whose whole sect is nothing else but lies, but I rehearse[256] you his letter because ye should see what truth there is in such folks' words.

Howbeit, as for Constantine—as I said before, seemed in prison here very penitent, and utterly minded to forsake such heresies and heretics forever. In proof whereof he not only detected,[257] as I said, his own deeds and his fellows', but also studied and devised how those devilish books which himself and others of his fellows had brought and shipped might come to the bishop's hands to be burned. And therefore he showed me the shipman's name that had them, and the marks of the fardels[258] by which I have since his escape received them. And it may be, by God's grace, that though the man fled hence for fear of such harm as he wist he had well deserved (and yet was nothing toward him but peradventure more good than he was aware of), he is yet amended in his mind and hath in his heart forsaken all Tyndale's heresies, and so I pray God it be, for I would be sorry that ever Tyndale should glory and boast of his burning. Howbeit, in the meanwhile, till it may well appear that he be surely turned to the Catholic faith again, I will advise all good Christian folk, and especially the King's subjects, to forbear and eschew his company. For that Englishman which shall be found to be familiar with him there, before his conversion here known and proved, may thereby bring himself in suspicion of heresy, and haply[259] hear thereof at his returning hither.

I hear also that Tyndale highly rejoiceth in the burning of Tewkesbury,[260] but I can see no very great cause why but if[261] he reckon it for a great glory that the man did abide still by the stake when he was fast bound to it. For as for the heresies, he would have abjured them again with all his heart, and have accursed Tyndale too, if all that might have saved his life. And so he gave counsel unto one James[262] that was for heresy in prison with him. For as James hath since confessed, Tewkesbury said

unto him, "Save you yourself and abjure. But as for me, because I have abjured before, there is no remedy with me but death." By which words, if he had not been in despair of life, it well appeareth he would with good will have once abjured, and once perjured, again. And yet at his examination he denied that ever he had held any such opinions as he was abjured for—notwithstanding that there were at his examination some persons present of much honesty and worship,[263] two that had been present at his abjuration before, to which also his own hand was subscribed.[264]

And afterward being further examined upon the same, some he denied, and some he defended again. Among other things, he said that he used to pray to saints, and that he believed them to be God's friends, and that their prayers were profitable to us, and well done to pray to them. Whereupon I said unto him myself that I was glad to see him in that point yet amended, and I showed him, as the truth was indeed, that James held the contrary, and that he had so great a trust in Tewkesbury that I doubted not but when he should hear that Tewkesbury had revoked that point, he would revoke it too. As soon as Tewkesbury heard that, he went from it again by and by[265]—and that so far that finally he would not agree that before the Day of Doom there were either any saint in heaven or soul in purgatory, or in hell either. Nor the right faith in the Sacrament of the altar would he not confess, in no wise. For which things and diverse other horrible heresies, he was delivered at last unto the secular hands and burned, as there was never wretch, I ween,[266] better worthy.

Yet is there one thing notable, and well declaring what good and charitable mind the man died in. For after that he was delivered unto the secular hands, neither while he was in prison nor at the time of his death would he by his will be acknown of[267] any of his heresies unto any man that asked him any question, but covered and hid them by all the means he could make, and labored to make every man ween that he had never held any such opinion. And by this dealing[268] every man may see that he rought not so much for[269] his heresies, nor took them not in his own mind for such things as he so greatly forced[270] whether they went forward or backward, as he would fain[271] leave an opinion among the people that his judges had borne him wrong in hand[272] and condemned him for such heresies as he never held. And what conscience he had that died in that mind, there is no good man doubteth.

Now was his examination[273] not secret, but folk enough thereat, both spiritual and temporal, and of either party right worshipful,[274] so that his malicious mind can in that point little take effect. And yet did the same James also confess afterward that Tewkesbury had read unto him Wycliffe's *Wicket* against the blessed Sacrament. And over[275] that was there found about him, by the sheriff's officers in the prison, a book of heresy of his own handwriting: that is to wit,[276] the book of Martin Luther wherein he teacheth men under the name of Christian liberty to run into the devil's bondage. And in his house was found Tyndale's book of *Obedience,* which he well allowed,[277] and his wicked book also of the *Wicked Mammon,* saying at his examination that all the heresies therein were good and Christian faith, being in deed as full of false[278] heresies, and as frantic, as ever heretic made any since Christ was born. And yet, all this notwithstanding, when he was in the sheriff's ward, and at the time of his death, he would not speak of his heresies anything, nor say that he had held and would hold this point and that, but handled himself as covertly as he could, to make the people ween that he had held no manner[279] opinion at all, nor never had, I think, if Tyndale's ungracious[280] books had never come in his hand. For which the poor wretch lieth now in hell and crieth out on him, and Tyndale, if he do not amend in time, he is likely to find him, when they come together, a hot firebrand burning at his back, that all the water in the world will never be able to quench.

Another is there also whom his unhappy books have brought unto the fire: Thomas Bilney, that[281] was before abjured, which[282] was the man of whom without name[283] I spoke so much in my *Dialogue,* which, being convicted by twenty witnesses and above, did yet stick still in his denial, and said they were all forsworn[284] and had utterly belied[285] him.

But God, which is very truth, and bringeth at last always the truth to light, would not suffer[286] such obstinate untruth at length to pass unpunished, but of his endless mercy brought his body to death, and gave him yet the grace to turn and save his soul. For so was it that—after diverse sermons which he had after his abjuration, and against the prohibitions given him upon his abjuration, made in sundry secret corners, and some also openly, whereof the Bishop yet, because he heard of no heresy therein, had forborne to lay the disobedience to his charge—he went unto Norwich, where he had infected diverse of the city before. And being there secretly kept by a certain space,[287] had in the while resort unto an anchoress, and there began secretly to sow his cockle, and brought unto her diverse of Tyndale's books, and was there taken in the doing, and the books after found about[288] another man, that[289] was conveying them thence; and these things, whoso heard the whole process,[290] came in such wise to pass that he could nothing doubt but that it came to light by the very provision of God.

When he came to examination, he waxed[291] stiff and stubborn in his opinions. But yet was God so good and gracious Lord unto him that he was finally so fully converted unto Christ and his true Catholic faith that, not only at the fire, as well in words as writing, but also many days before, he had revoked, abhorred, and detested such heresies as he before had held; which notwithstanding, there lacked not some that were very sorry for it, of whom some said, and some wrote out of Norwich to London, that he had not revoked his heresies at all, but still had abided by them. And such as were not ashamed thus to say and write, being afterward examined thereupon, saw the contrary so plainly proved in their faces, by such as at his execution stood by him while he read his revocation himself, that they had in conclusion nothing else to say but that he read his revocation so softly that they could not hear it. Howbeit, they confessed that he looked upon a bill and read it, but they said that they could not tell whether it were the bill of his revocation or not. And yet rehearsed[292] they themselves certain things spoken by him to the people at the fire, whereby they could not but perceive well that he revoked his errors, albeit that some of them watered

---

270 cared   271 gladly   272 *borne…
hand:* misrepresented him   273 at trial
274 *right worshipful:* very respectable
275 beyond   276 say   277 approved of

278 detestable; deceitful   279 kind of
280 without grace; wicked   281 who
282 who   283 mentioning his name
284 perjured   285 slandered   286 allow

287 *kept by a space:* put up for a length of
time   288 in the possession of   289 who
290 story   291 grew   292 related

his words with additions of their own—as it was well proved before them. They could not also deny but that forthwith[293] upon his judgment[294] and his degradation, he kneeled down before the Bishop's Chancellor,[295] in the presence of all the people, and humbly besought him of[296] absolution from the sentence of excommunication, and with his judgment held himself well content, and acknowledged that he had well deserved to suffer the death that he then wist[297] he should.

They could not say nay but that upon this humble request and prayer, he was there, in the presence of all the people, assoiled,[298] before that he was carried out of the court—which themselves well wist would never have been but if he had revoked.

Yet was there another thing that they could not deny (for albeit they said they were not thereat, yet they had heard it in such wise that, as they said, they believed it to be true), and that thing was such as itself alone must needs make them sure that he had revoked his heresies.

The thing was this. He labored and made great instance[299] certain days after his judgment[300] that he might be suffered[301] to receive the blessed Body of Christ in form of bread. Wherein the Chancellor made a while great sticking and difficulty, to the intent that he would the better and more clearly perceive what devotion the man had thereto. And finally perceiving him to be of a true perfect faith, and his desire to proceed of a fervent mind, it was agreed and granted. And thereupon was he houseled[302] in so true perfect faith, and so great devotion, that every good Christian man hath great cause to rejoice therein. And when his confessor in the end of the Mass, which Bilney full devoutly heard upon his knees, brought unto him the Body of Christ upon the paten of the chalice, with very good and godly exhortation used unto him, that except he were in heart as he was in word and outward semblance, he should else forbear to receive that blessed Body, since he should then undoubtedly receive it on[303] his own damnation—it would have gladdened any good Christian heart to have heard his faithful Christian answer as they report and testify that were at that time by.[304]

Moreover, where, in the presence of that holy Sacrament held yet upon the paten in the priest's hands, Bilney before he received it said the collect[305] *Domine Iesu Christe*—when he came at these words, *ecclesiae tuae pacem et concordiam*,[306] he diverse times repeated those words, with tunsions[307] and knockings upon his breast, and there unto God confessed, and asked his mercy, that he had so grievously erred in that point, and so sore offended him in contemning his Church. And no marvel was it though[308] he had a special remorse of that article. For the contemning of Christ's Catholic known Church, and the framing[309] of a secret unknown church, that he learned of Luther and Tyndale, was the very point that brought him unto all his mischief, as the very foundation whereupon all other heresies are built. And therefore, as the goodness of God gave him grace to cast unto the devil all his other errors, so gave he him his special grace to have of that heresy that was and is the ground of all the remnant, most especial repentance and remorse; whereby we may very well hope and trust that our Lord, whose high goodness gave him such grace so fully to repent and revoke his heresies that he with glad heart was content to suffer the fire for the punishment of his offense, hath of his infinite mercy taken and accepted that pain for so far as he will exact of the poor man's purgatory, and setting the merits of his own painful Passion thereunto, hath forthwith from the fire taken his blessed soul to heaven, where he now prayeth incessantly for the repentance and amendment of all such as have been by his means while he lived, into any such errors induced or confirmed. And I firmly trust that God's grace to that effect with that holy man's prayer will work, and so I pray God it may.

But thus ye see that Tyndale hath no great cause to glory of his martyrs when that their living is openly naught,[310] their opinions such as himself will abhor, they ready to abjure again if it might save their life, their sects so desperate that either they dare not at the fire set forth their opinions, for shame, or else of malice do dissemble them to bring the people in a false opinion of their judges, to ween that they judged wrong. And Bilney, that had learning, and had been accustomed in moral virtues, was by God revoked from Tyndale's heresy ere he

---

293 immediately **294** conviction **295** Thomas Pelles, chancellor of Richard Nix, Bishop of Norwich **296** *besought him of:* begged of him **297** knew **298** absolved **299** *great instance:* earnest entreaty **300** conviction **301** allowed **302** given Holy Communion **303** to **304** nearby **305** Mass prayer **306** *ecclesiae . . . concordiam:* (grant unto) "thy Church peace and concord" **307** strikings **308** that **309** devising **310** evil

died—and that, of likelihood, the rather[311] because God would not have all his good works lost.

And yet glorieth Tyndale ungraciously in their destruction, reckoning that their painful death doth great worship[312] to his books—which are of such sort that never were there worse nor more abominable written.

And yet his books being such, some folk there are that with such foolish favor and such blind affection read them that, their taste infected with the fever of heresies, they not only cannot discern the thing that they read (which if they could, they were in good way toward amendment), but also are discontent and angry with any man that would help them to perceive it, and fain[313] would they have them rather believed than answered.

Of which sort, some have asked what have I to do to meddle with the matter, saying that being a layman, I should leave it to the clergy to write in, and not having professed the study of Holy Scripture, I should leave the matter wholly unto divines. Surely, first, as touching learning, if that these matters were very doubtful and things of great question—or had been so cunningly handled by Tyndale and his fellows as they might seem thereby matters of great doubt and question—then would I peradventure[314] let them alone myself, to be debated by men of more erudition and learning. But now the matters being so plain, evident, and clear—and by the whole Church of Christ so clearly put out of question that it is plain and open heresy earnestly to bring them in question—I never purpose, being in my right mind and a true Christian man, to give a heretic so much authority as to reckon myself unable in so plain points of the Christian faith to answer him; namely since I have gone somewhat to school myself, and bestowed as many years in study, and under as cunning masters, as some of them have, and that I see not hitherto[315] these matters handled in such wise by Tyndale, or the best of them besides that ever have written therein,[316] but that a right mean-learned man,[317] or almost an unlearned woman having natural wit and being sure and fast in the true Catholic faith, were well able to answer them.

For so help me God as I nothing find effectual among them all, but a shameless boldness and unreasonable railing—with Scriptures wrested awry, and made to minister them matter unto their jesting, scoffing, and outrageous ribaldry—not only against every estate[318] here in earth, and that against them most that be most religious in living, but also against all the saints in heaven, and against the blessed Body of Christ in the holy Sacrament of the altar. In which things they fare as folk that trust in nothing else but to weary all writers at last with endless and importunate babbling, and to overwhelm the whole world with words.

Now as for me, the cause is, of my writing, not so much to debate and dispute these things with them—which (though I trust therein to give them no great place) many men may do much better yet than I—as to give men warning what mischief[319] is in their books, because many good simple folk, believing that these men neither say nor mean so evil as they be borne in hand,[320] and longing therefore to read their books and see the thing themselves, be first infected with some heresies that seem not at the first intolerable, ere ever they come at the greatest; and then, being before infected with the less, they fall at last to bear the greater, to which in the beginning they could never have abided.

Now if they will ask, is there nobody to give them warning but I?—yes, there be that be meet[321] thereto, and there be that in deed do so; and yet, among others, that part appertaineth to me. For I well know that the King's Highness—which,[322] as he, for his most faithful mind to God, nothing more effectually desireth than the maintenance of the true Catholic faith (whereof he is, by his no more honorable than well deserved title, Defensor), so nothing more detesteth than these pestilent books that Tyndale and such others send into the realm, to set forth here their abominable heresies with—doth, of his blessed disposition, of all earthly things abhor the necessity to do punishment; and for that cause hath not only by his most erudite famous books, both in English and in Latin, declared his most Catholic purpose and intent, but also by his open[323] proclamations (diverse times iterated and renewed) and finally in his own most royal person, in the Star Chamber, most eloquently, by his own mouth, in great presence of his lords spiritual and temporal, gave monition[324] and warning to all

---

311 sooner   **312** honor   **313** gladly   **314** perhaps   **315** thus far; as yet   **316** on them   **317** *right mean-learned:* very   little educated   **318** state or part of the body politic   **319** harm   **320** *be borne in hand:* are being accused of   **321** *that*   *be meet:* some who are suitable   **322** who   **323** public   **324** admonition; instruction

the justices of peace, of every quarter of his realm, then assembled before his Highness, to be by them in their counties to all his people declared, and did prohibit and forbid, upon great pain, the bringing in, reading, and keeping of any of those pernicious poisoned books, to the intent that every subject of his, by the means of such manifold effectual warning, with his gracious remission of their former offense in his commandment before broken, should from thenceforth avoid and eschew the peril and danger of punishment, and not drive his Highness of necessity to the thing from which the mildness of his benign nature abhorreth.

Now—seeing the King's gracious purpose in this point—I reckon that, being his unworthy chancellor, it appertaineth, as I said, unto my part and duty to follow the example of his noble Grace, and, after my poor wit and learning, with opening to his people the malice and poison of those pernicious books, to help, as much as in me is, that his people, abandoning the contagion of all such pestilent writing, may be far from infection, and thereby from all such punishment as, following thereupon, doth oftentimes rather serve to make others beware that are yet clear, than to cure and heal well those that are already infected; so hard is that carbuncle,[325] catching once a core,[326] to be by any means well and surely cured. Howbeit, God so worketh that sometimes it is. Toward the help whereof—or if it haply[327] be incurable, then to the clean cutting out the part for infection of the remnant—am I by mine office in virtue of mine oath, and every officer of justice through the realm for his rate, right especially bound, not in reason only and good congruence, but also by plain ordinance and statute.

Wherefore I reckon myself of duty deeply bound to show you, good readers, the peril of these books, whereof the makers have such mischievous[328] mind that they boast and glory when their ungracious writing bringeth any man to death. And yet make they semblance as though they were sorry for it. And then Tyndale crieth out upon the prelates and upon the temporal princes, and calleth them murderers and martyr quellers[329]—dissembling that the cruel wretch with his wretched books murdereth the man himself, while he giveth him the poison of his heresies and thereby compelleth princes by

occasion of their incurable and contagious pestilence to punish them according to justice by sore[330] painful death, both for example and for infection of others.

Which thing as sore as these heretics reprove, affirming that it is against the Gospel of Christ that any heretic should be persecuted and punished, and especially by bodily pain or death—and some of them say the same of every manner crime (theft, murder, treason, and all)—yet in Almaine[331] now, contrary to their own evangelical doctrine, those evangelicals themselves cease not to pursue and punish by all the means they may, by purse,[332] by prison, by bodily pain, and death, diverse their evangelical brethren that vary from their sect; as there are of those counterfeit evangelicals more sundry sorts of diabolical sects than a man may well rehearse.

And to this, at the last, be they driven themselves, contrary to their own former doctrine, because they find and prove well by experience that, though their sects be but false[333] heresies all, yet cannot the one sort long dwell with the other, but that if they begin once to be matches, they shall not fail at length to contend and strive together, and by seditions the one drive the other to ruin. For never shall the country long abide without debate and ruffle, where schisms and factious heresies are suffered[334] a while to grow.

Believe me not if any man can reckon a place where ever he found it otherwise. In Africa the Donatists; in Greece the Arians; in Bohemia the Hussites; in England the Wycliffists; and now in Almaine the Lutherans, and after that, the Zwinglians: what business they have made, what destruction and manslaughter they have caused, partly the stories witness,[335] partly men have presently seen. And yet hath God always maintained and continued his true Catholic faith, with the great fall and ruin at length of many schismatical sects, whose fall undoubtedly the remnant will in conclusion follow, with the plain and open wrath of God showed upon their false prophets—as it fell upon the prophets both of Bel and Baal, and now this year upon Zwingli himself, that first brought into Switzerland the abominable heresy against the Blessed Sacrament of the altar, and was, as I say, by the hand of God this year slain in plain battle against the

---

325 skin lesion   326 a hard mass of dead tissue in the center of a boil   327 perhaps   328 harmful   329 killers   330 grievous   331 Germany   332 imposition of fines   333 detestable; deceitful   334 allowed   335 attest

Catholics, with many a thousand of his wretched sect, being in number to the Catholics three against one, and as proudly and with as malicious purpose invading them as ever did the Egyptians pursue the children of Israel.

But now saith Tyndale and Friar Barnes both, that I do them wrong in that I call their books seditious. For they counsel, they say, the people, in their books, to be obedient unto their sovereigns and rulers although they should suffer wrong, "and how can our books then," say they, "be seditious?"

Surely, to make men heretics and then bid them be meek (when heresy springeth, as Saint Augustine saith, of pride) standeth as well with reason, as to make a man drunk, and bid him be sober; make him stark mad, and bid him be well advised; make him a stark thief, and bid him see he steal not.

Howbeit—besides the sedition that every schism and division must needs move and provoke among any people that are of diverse sects, although they were all obedient unto one prince, and cause them thereby, though they rebelled not against his person, yet to break the peace and quiet of his country, and run into the danger and peril of his laws—let us yet further look and consider in what manner and fashion they counsel the people to obey their princes.

They bid the people for a countenance[336] to be obedient. But they say therewith that the laws and precepts of their sovereigns do nothing bind the subjects in their consciences but if[337] the things by them commanded or forbidden were before commanded or forbidden in Scripture. And all the words of Scripture whereby they be commanded to obey their governors would they restrain[338] unto those things only that are expressed already within the corps[339] of Scripture. So that if they can beguile the laws and precepts of their sovereigns unawares to other men, and thereby flee from the peril of outward bodily punishment, their evangelical liberty should serve them sufficiently for discharge of their conscience, and inwardly make them in their souls clear angelical hypocrites.

Now when they falsely tell them that they be not bound to obey their governors' lawful commandments, and then holily counsel them to obey their unlawful tyranny (for by that name call they the laws), what effect ween[340] ye they would that their advice should have? They know themselves well enough, and the manner of the people too, and be not so mad, I warrant[341] you, but that they perceive full well that if they can persuade the people to believe that they be not in their conscience bound to obey the laws and precepts of their governors, themselves be no such precious apostles that folk would forbear their own ease or pleasure for the faint feigned counsel of a few false apostates. And thus is it sure that by their false doctrine they must, if they be believed, bring the people into the secret contempt, and spiritual disobedience, and inward hatred of the law; whereof must after follow the outward breach, and thereupon outward punishment and peril of rebellion—whereby the princes should be driven to sore[342] effusion of their subjects' blood, as hath already mishappened in Almaine[343] and, of old time, in England.

Let us yet consider further a point of their good holy counsel concerning the people's obedience.

Friar Barnes, in his frantic book, biddeth the people that they should not rebel, in no wise.[344] But he biddeth them therewith that, for all the King's commandment, they should not suffer Tyndale's false translation of the Scripture go out of their hand, but rather die than leave it. Now knoweth he well that the false malicious manner that Tyndale hath used in the translating thereof—as I have proved both in my *Dialogue* and since again in this book, and as Tyndale doth himself in his own *Answer* openly confess in the titles of "Penance" and "Priest"—was done to set forth his false heresies with. And therefore it appeareth well that Barnes would have the people rather die than obey their princes in putting away that book that is falsely translated for the maintenance of many pestilent heresies. And thus ye see how fain[345] he would glory in the people's blood. For he wotteth[346] very well that the King's Highness will in no wise—nor in no wise may, if he will save his own soul—suffer[347] that false translation in the hands of unlearned people which is by an open heretic purposely translated false, to the destruction of so many souls.

Now no man doubteth, I think, but that Tyndale himself would no less were done for the maintenance of his false translation of the evangelists than

336 appearance sake   337 *but if:* unless   341 guarantee   342 great   343 Germany   344 way, manner   345 gladly   338 limit   339 collective body   340 think   346 knows   347 allow

would his evangelical brother Barnes, but that folk should against the King's proclamations keep still his books, and rather than leave them, die in the quarrel for the defense of his glory.

5 Whereas I before in my *Dialogue* did say that Luther's books be seditious, as I now say that Tyndale's be too, and moving people to their own undoing to be disobedient and rebellious to their sovereigns, in affirming that they be not, nor cannot be, bound by

10 any law made by men. Tyndale answereth me for[348] Luther that I say untruly. And then saith he further in this wise: "A Christian man is bound to obey tyranny — if it be not against his faith nor the law of God — till God deliver him thereof."

15 Now let I pass much railing[349] that he consequently maketh upon princes, and shall for this time only counsel you to consider these few words of his which he layeth forth for a rule of people's obedience to their prince. For his rule is that they shall

20 obey their tyranny till God deliver them thereof. And in this point will I not be Tyndale's interpreter; he may mean diverse ways, but which way he meaneth indeed, he shall himself declare at his further leisure, for methinketh he meaneth not very well —

25 saving that I will not take him to the worst.

But in the other point, I may be bold to say that no good man may take him well where he saith that a Christian man is bound to obey their prince's tyranny if it "be not against his faith nor the law of

30 God." And yet will I well agree that if these words were spoken of a good faithful man's mouth, and where any need required it, they were very well said; as they were when the apostles said, "We must rather please God than man."[350] But when Tyndale, that is

35 a heretic, putteth for a rule of the people's obedience to a good Christian prince that they be bound to obey his tyranny if it "be not against his faith" — I say that this, his rule of obedience, is a plain exhortation to disobedience and rebellion. For every man

40 well seeth that Tyndale among many other abominable heresies teacheth for the right faith that friars may lawfully wed nuns, and that no man is bound to the keeping of any fasting day or holy day made by the Church, and that no man should pray to any

45 saint, nor pray for all Christian souls, and that it is great sin to do any worship[351] to Christ's precious Body in the blessed Sacrament of the altar — and

would the people should keep his false translation of Scripture for maintenance of these heresies. And

50 therefore if any prince make a law against Tyndale's heresies, in any of these points or such other like, Tyndale here teacheth that the people are not bound to obey it, but may and must withstand such tyranny. Or, at the leastwise, though they be bound

55 peradventure[352] openly to obey their prince's tyranny in forbearing flesh[353] on Good Friday or coming to God's service on Whitsun[354] Sunday, or friars in forbearing open[355] wedding with nuns (in all which things they be yet, by Tyndale's godly Gos-

60 pel, at their evangelical liberty secretly to do what they list[356] themselves, where no peace is broken nor any weak conscience offended); yet, for any law or commandment either of prince or pope, or general council of all Christian nations, or of any angel that

65 would come out of heaven to command in God's name the contrary, every man must keep still Tyndale's false translation of Scripture, and abide by his other false[357] books made for the maintenance of his manifold false heresies. And no man must for no

70 law nor commandment pray to any saint, nor for any soul in purgatory, nor kiss any relic, nor creep to Christ's cross,[358] nor do any worship to Christ's blessed Body and Blood in the holy Sacrament of the altar.

75 But if any prince would by any law or commandment compel his people to any of those things — then Tyndale here plainly teacheth them that they may and must stiffly withstand his tyranny. So that finally concerning obedience, Tyndale's holy doc-

80 trine is that the people should in the defense of his false heresies not let[359] to disobey, but stubbornly too, withstand their prince. Which if any man were so mad to do, and then were therefor in their obstinacy burned, or otherwise in their rebellion slain —

85 there were the triumph, the great feast and glory of Tyndale's devilish proud dispiteous heart, to delight and rejoice in the effusion of such people's blood as his poisoned books had miserably bewitched, and from true Christian folk turned into false wicked

90 wretches.

Now to the intent that ye may the more clearly perceive the malicious mind of these men, and that their pestilent books be both odious to God and deadly contagious to men, and so much the more

---

348 with regard to **349** ranting   **354** Pentecost **355** public **356** please   The reference is to the Good Friday
350 who **351** reverence **352** perhaps   **357** deceitful **358** *creep to Christ's cross:* veneration of the cross. **359** hesitate
353 *forbearing flesh:* abstaining from meat

perilous in that their false heresies wilily walk forth under the counterfeit visage of the true Christian faith — this is the cause and purpose of my present labor whereby, God willing, I shall so pull off their

5 gay painted visors[360] that every man listing[361] to look thereon shall plainly perceive and behold the bare ugly gargoyle faces of their abominable heresy.

And for because the matter is long, and my leisure seldom and short, I cannot, as I fain[362] would,

10 send out all at once, but if[363] I should keep still altogether by me longer than methinketh convenient.

I send out now, therefore, of this present work, these three books first. In the first of which I answer Tyndale's preface made before his *Answer* to

15 my *Dialogue*; which preface of his is, in a manner, an introduction into all his heresies. The second book is against his defense of his translation of the New Testament. The third, against two chapters of Tyndale's *Answer* — the one, "Whether the Word

20 Were before the Church, or the Church before the Word," the other, "Whether the Apostles Left Anything Unwritten Necessary to Salvation" — whereupon great part of all his heresies hang.

Now shall I (God willing) at my next leisure go

25 further in his book, and come to the very breast of all this battle, that is to wit,[364] the question: Which is the Church? For that is the point that all these heretics, by all the means they may, labor to make so dark that by their wills no man should wit[365] what

30 they mean. But I trust to draw the serpent out of his dark den, and as the poets feign that Hercules drew up Cerberus, the mastiff of hell, into the light, where his eyes dazed — so shall I, with the grace of that light "which illumineth every man that cometh

35 into this world,"[366] make you that matter so lightsome, and so clear to every man, that I shall leave Tyndale never a dark corner to creep into, able to hide his head.

Then after that I have so clearly confuted Tyndale

40 concerning that point, and shall have plainly proved you the sure and steadfast authority of Christ's Catholic known Church against all Tyndale's trifling sophistications, which he would should seem so solemn subtle insolubles, which ye shall see

45 proved very frantic follies; after this done, I say, before I go further with Tyndale, I purpose to answer good young Father Frith, which[367] now suddenly

cometh forth so sagely that three old men — my brother Rastell,[368] the bishop of Rochester,[369] and I — matched with Father Frith alone, be now but 50 very babes and, as he calleth us, insipients.[370] But thus goeth the world forth between Frith and us. He increaseth, I see well, as fast as we decay. For once, I ween, the youngest of us three, three days ere Father Frith was born, had learned within a lit- 55 tle as much as Father Frith hath now. Howbeit, I shall leave young Father Frith in his pride and glory for the while. But when Tyndale is once in that article touching the Church confuted, then hath Frith already concerning purgatory clearly lost the field, 60 and all his well-beloved book is not worth a button, though[371] it were all as true as it is false. For then is the faith of the Church in that point infallible, or at the least inculpable, were there Scripture therefor or not. And no Scripture can there prove[372] the 65 very true Church to hold an article as true faith that were in deed damnably false.

And yet shall I, for all that, go further with young Father Frith, and touch, if God will, every part of his fresh painted book; and so shall I pluck off, I 70 trust, the most glorious feathers from his gay peacock's tail that I shall leave him (if he have wit and grace) a little less delight and liking in himself than he seemeth now to have, which thing hath hitherto made him for to stand not a little in his own light. 75

I pray God heartily send that young man the grace to bestow[373] his wit and learning, such as it is, about some better business than Tyndale misbestoweth it now. For now is Frith's wit and learning nothing but Tyndale's instrument whereby he 80 bloweth out his heresy.

Finally after that I shall have answered Frith, I purpose to return again unto Tyndale's book, and answer him in every chapter that he hath impugned in the four books of my *Dialogue*. Wherein I trust 85 to make every child perceive his wily follies and false crafts, with his open shameless lies put in and mingled among them, wherewith he fain[374] would, and weeneth to, blind in such wise the world that folk should not espy the falsehood and folly of his 90 execrable heresies.

I think that no man doubteth but that this work both hath been and will be some pain and labor to me, and of truth, so I find it. But as help me God,

---

360 masks   361 wishing   362 gladly
363 *but if:* unless   364 say   365 know
366 Jn 1:9   367 who   368 *brother*

Rastell: brother-in-law John Rastell
(1475–1536)   369 John Fisher   370 fools

371 even if   372 be that proves
373 employ   374 gladly

I find all my labor in the writing not half so grievous and painful to me as the tedious reading of their blasphemous heresies; that would God, after all my labor done, so that the remembrance of
5 their pestilent errors were erased out of Englishmen's hearts, and their abominable books burned up, mine own were walked³⁷⁵ with them—and the name of these matters utterly put in oblivion. Howbeit, since I see the devil in these days so strong,
10 and these devilish heresies so sore set abroach³⁷⁶ in some unhappy hearts, that they never cease in all that ever they may to spread these books abroad to such as keep them in hugger-mugger,³⁷⁷ and secretly poison themselves, weening the books were
15 very good while³⁷⁸ they read but them alone—and then of those evil books so many daily made by so many idle heretics, and by and by³⁷⁹ sent hither— it were need, as meseemeth, that diverse wise and well-learned men should set their pens to the book,
20 which though they shall not satisfy them that will needs be naught,³⁸⁰ yet shall they do good to such as fall to these folk of oversight, weening that their new ways were well.

Our Savior saith that the children of darkness be
25 more politic in their kind than are the children of light in their kind.³⁸¹ And surely so seemeth it now. For these false³⁸² faithless heretics, whose hearts are in the deep dark dungeon of the devil, are more wily, and more busy therewith, in setting forth of
30 their heresies, than are the faithful learned folk in the defense of the truth.

And as the true disciples of Christ were in slumber and fell in sleep in Christ's company, while Judas the traitor was waking and watching about his
35 detestable treason,³⁸³ so while these Judases watch and study about the making of their ungracious books, good and true-believing men that were meet³⁸⁴ to answer them, and that were able in writing to much more than overmatch them, if they
40 would wake and pray and take the pen in hand, be now so forwearied, with the sorrow and heaviness³⁸⁵ to see the world wax³⁸⁶ so wretched, that they fall even in a slumber therewith and let these wretches alone, saving that yet sometimes some good Peter in
45 a good zeal so smiteth off Malchus's ear³⁸⁷ that God setteth it on better again and giveth it grace to draw

back from the hearkening³⁸⁸ of false heresies, and to give itself to the hearing of Christ's true Catholic faith. And sometimes again some good holy Paul shaketh the poisoned adder into a fair fire,³⁸⁹ that
50 lying and lurking among the dry fruitless faggots³⁹⁰ catcheth good folk by the fingers and so hangeth on their hands with the poison sting of false "only faith," that they would withhold them from setting their hands to any good, virtuous works.
55

But now leaving other men to do as God shall like to put in their minds, I shall for my part perform that I have promised, if God give me life and grace thereto. For as for leisure, shall not, I trust, one time or other lack to suffice, for so much and for much
60 more too. Which when I have, as I before said, altogether performed—I would in good faith wish that never man should need to read any word.

For surely the very best way were neither to read this nor theirs, but rather the people unlearned to
65 occupy themselves, besides their other business, in prayer, good meditation, and reading of such English books as most may nourish and increase devotion—of which kind is Bonaventure of³⁹¹ *The Life of Christ*, Gerson of *The Following*³⁹² *of Christ*,
70 and the devout contemplative book of *Scala Perfectionis*, with such others like—than in the learning what may well be answered unto heretics.

The very treacle³⁹³ were well lost, so that all venom and poison were utterly lost therewith. And better
75 were it not to be sick at all than of a great sickness to be very well healed.

And if it might be provided that every man should be so well tempered that no man should by distemperance fall into disease, then were it better
80 that the physician bestowed all his time about that part of physic that teacheth to preserve our health than to write any word of that part that restoreth it. But since it can never be brought to pass that poison will be forgotten, nor that every man shall use
85 himself so circumspectly but that either of oversight or adventure³⁹⁴ some shall have need of cure, therefore it is necessary that treacle for the one, and other medicines for the other, be provided and had. And therefore, as I would wish that their books
90 were all gone and mine own therewith—so, since I see well that that thing will not be, better it is, I

---

375 gone   376 *sore set abroach:* set greatly
astir   377 *in hugger-mugger:* clandestinely
378 when   379 *by and by:* immediately
380 bad   381 Lk 16:8   382 detestable;
deceitful   383 Mt 26:36–50   384 suitable   385 grief   386 become   387 Jn
18:10–11; Lk 22:49–51   388 listening
389 Acts 28:1–6   390 bundles of
sticks   391 *Bonaventure of:* Bonaventure's
392 *Imitation* (This book was at that time
commonly believed to have been written by
Jean Gerson.)   393 antidote   394 chance

reckon, that there be treacle ready than the poison to tarry and no treacle for it.

Howbeit, though every shop were full of treacle—yet were he not wise, I ween, that would willfully drink poison first to drink treacle after, but rather, cast the poison to the devil and let the treacle stand for some that should hap to need it. And likewise would I counsel every good Christian man, and especially such as are not groundly learned,[395] to cast out the poisoned draught[396] of these heretics' books which when they be drunk down infect the reader and corrupt the soul unto the everlasting death; and therefore neither vouchsafe[397] to read their books nor anything made against them neither, but abhor to hear their heresies so much as named, according to the gracious[398] counsel of the blessed apostle Paul against fornication, where he writeth unto the Ephesians, "Let not fornication be so much as named or spoken of among you."[399] And yet—since that would not be brought to pass that he counseled, and would fain[400] have had observed—he was fain himself to speak thereof and write thereof, to arm the people against it, in more places[401] than one, as both he and other apostles, and all holy doctors since, have been driven to write against heresies, and yet would fain that folk would so clear have cast all heresies out of remembrance that neither themselves should have needed to write thereof nor other folk to read that part of their books.

And therefore, as I would advise any man neither to read these heretics' books nor mine, but occupy their minds better and, standing firmly by the Catholic faith of this fifteen hundred years, never once muse upon these newfangled heresies, so, on the other side, if it mishap any man to fall in such a fond[402] affection and vain curious mind that neither peril temporal in breach of his prince's proclamation and the laws of the realm, nor the peril spiritual in hurting of his own soul, nor they both together by putting himself in danger to burn both here and in hell, can hold his itching fingers from their poisoned books, then would I counsel him in any wise to read therewith such things as are written against them, and weigh them both at the leastwise indifferently, and not to fall suddenly so drunk in the new must[403] of their newfangled novelties that the old wholesome wine with which good folk have lived now this fifteen hundred years offend their drunken taste because it is not so wallow-sweet[404] but drinketh[405] more of the verdure.[406]

Furthermore forasmuch as, according to the words of Christ,[407] it will none otherwise be but that some stumbling blocks will always be by malicious folk laid in good people's way, though best were to stop your ears utterly and give none hearing to any false enchanters that would bewitch you wilily to make you delight in those books, yet since some that be plain and simple may fortune to be secretly misled by false wily shrews[408] except they be well armed before, I doubt not by God's grace but if they read first the things that are written against them, they shall themselves be able to reject and confound[409] any devil that would draw them to them. And therefore—as I am sure that evil and ungracious folk shall ever find the means that such books shall never in some corners lack, whereby good people may be deceived and corrupted—it is more than necessary that men have again at hand such books as may well arm them to resist and confute them. Of which kind of good books, albeit I know well there may, and doubt not but there shall, be many better made than mine—and that some such I see already—yet have I not so slightly seen unto mine own, nor shuffled it up so hastily, nor let it so pass unlooked over by better men and better learned also than myself, but that I trust in God it may among the better stand yet in some good stead. And that it so may to God's honor and the profit of some good folk, I heartily beseech our Lord—without the adspiration[410] and help of whose especial grace no labor of man can profit, and to whom therefore be all thank referred—which[411] liveth and reigneth in eternal glory. To which as he hath already brought many a blessed saint, so mote[412] his mercy bring with speed the souls that are in purgatory—and give us that here live, in this wretched world, aid and help of grace by true faith and good works to follow them, the rather[413] by the intercession and prayers of all his holy saints that are already with him. Amen.

395 solidly educated **396** drink (scriptural) **402** foolish **403** wine sharpness **407** Lk 17:1 **408** scoundrels
397 agree **398** grace-filled; righteous **404** cloyingly sweet **405** savors **409** utterly defeat **410** favor **411** who
399 Eph 5:3 **400** gladly **401** passages **406** the fruit's agreeable freshness and **412** may **413** more readily

A Treatise concernynge the diuision betwene the spiritualtie and temporaltie.

Christopher St. German published anonymously the *Treatise concernynge the Division* in 1532. It was published five times before 1535; the first and at least two others were by Berthelet, the King's printer (*CW* 9: xxxvii; *CW* 10: xxi ff.).

The Apology of
Sir Thomas More, Knight

Thomas More resigned as Lord Chancellor on May 16, 1532, the day after Archbishop Warham and other leaders of the Convocation agreed to the "Submission of the Clergy," which gave the King authority over Church laws in England. Through the Submission, the clergy "promised to make no new canon without royal license, and to submit existing canons to a committee of 32, half lay and half clerical and all to be chosen by the King, for revision" (ODCC 1319). The Submission was officially signed before a group of commissioners, including Thomas Cromwell, on the day of More's resignation; in effect, the Church surrendered its independence and liberties to the King's power through the Submission (Lehmberg 152). King Henry's formal Act of Supremacy would follow in 1534.

Although More resigned from political office, he retained and continued to use his 1528 commission to defend the Church from attack — a commission he had received from London bishop Cuthbert Tunstall, with King Henry's approval. On the whole, More wrote over 1,500 pages in defense of the Church from 1529 to 1533. In June 1529, he published *A Dialogue of Sir Thomas More, Knight*, and in September, *The Supplication of Souls*. In March 1532, he published Books 1–3 of *The Confutation of Tyndale's* Answer, and in December, *A Letter Against Frith*. In early 1533, he finished *The Confutation of Tyndale's* Answer, Books 4–8.

In late 1532, lawyer and legal scholar Christopher St. German (*ca.* 1460–1540/41) published, with the King's printer, his anonymous *A Treatise Concerning the Division Between the Spiritualty and Temporalty* (facing). In this work, St. German accuses the clergy of greed, cruelty, pride, and unjust treatment of heretics; of not treating the laity equally under law; and of being the ones responsible for a dangerous and growing division within the country. St. German's anonymous *Treatise* was printed five times by the end of 1537, at least several by the King's printer.

By spring 1533, More responded to this legal and political attack, staying within his 1528 commission but using a thirty-six chapter "digression" to respond to St. German's most serious charges against the clergy and the Church. Because St. German's book was published anonymously, More gave the author an ironic name, "the Pacifier," used over 160 times, suggesting that St. German's work was ordered to increasing division, not peace, between the spiritual and the temporal orders.

Although More structures his book as an "apology" or defense against seven charges that had been made about him (for example, his alleged mistreatment of heretics), most of the book is a detailed refutation of St. German's *Division* and its arguments. St. German's response to More, the anonymous *Salem and Bizance,* prompted More's *Debellation of Salem and Bizance*, around November 1, 1533.

CONTENTS

This facsimile from the first edition of the *Apology* (reduced) shows More's lawyerly habit of quoting his opponent at length and then refuting in detail.

The Apology
of Sir Thomas More, Knight

**Sir Thomas More, Knight
to the Christian Readers**

5

THE FIRST CHAPTER

So well stand I not (I thank God), good reader, in mine own conceit,[1] and thereby so much in mine own light, but that I can[2] somewhat with equal[3] judgment and an even eye behold and consider both myself and mine own. Nor I use not[4] to follow the condition of Aesop's ape,[5] that thought her own babes so beauteous and so far passing in all goodly feature and favor, nor the crow that accounted her own birds the fairest of all the fowls that flew.[6] But like[7] as some (I see well) there are that can somewhat less than I, that yet for all that put out their works in writing, so am I not so blind, upon the other side, but that I very well perceive very many so far in wit[8] and erudition above me that in such matters as I have anything written, if other men as many would have taken it in hand as could have done it better, it might much better have become me to let the matter alone than by writing to presume anything to meddle therewith.

And therefore, good reader—since I so well know so many men so far excel and pass me in all such things as are required in him that might adventure[9] to put his works abroad, to stand and abide the judgment of all other men—I was never so far overseen[10] as either to look[11] or hope that such faults as in my writing should by mine oversight escape me could by the eyes of all other men pass forth unspied, but shortly should be both by good and well-learned perceived, and among so many bad brethren as I wist[12] well would be wroth[13] with them, should be both sought out and sifted to the uttermost flake of bran, and largely thereupon controlled[14] and reproved.

But yet against all this fear this one thing recomforted[15] me: that since I was of one point very fast[16] and sure—that such things as I write are consonant unto the common Catholic faith and determinations of Christ's Catholic Church, and are clear confutations of false blasphemous heresies by Tyndale[17] and Barnes[18] put forth unto the contrary— any great fault and intolerable should they none find of such manner, sort, and kind as the readers should in their souls perish and be destroyed by, of which poisoned faults mine adversaries' books be full.

Now then, as for other faults of less weight and tolerable, I nothing doubted nor do, but that every good Christian reader will be so reasonable and indifferent[19] as to pardon in me the thing that happeth in all other men, and that no such man will over me be so sore an auditor,[20] and over my books such a sore controller,[21] as to charge me with any great loss by gathering together of many such things as are with very few men aught[22] regarded, and to look for such exact circumspection and sure sight to be by me used in my writing as, except the prophets of God, and Christ and his apostles, hath never, I ween,[23] been founden in any man's else before—that is to wit,[24] to be perfect in every point clean from all manner of faults—but hath always been holden[25] for a thing excusable, though[26] the reader in a long work perceive that the writer have, as Horace saith of Homer,[27] here and there sometimes fallen in a little slumber, in which places, as the reader seeth that

40
45
50
55
60
65

---

1 idea, conception   **2** *but . . . can:* that I cannot   **3** impartial, unbiased   **4** *I use not:* do I make it a practice   **5** See Aesop's "Jupiter and the Monkey."   **6** See Aesop's "The Crow and Its Ugly Fledglings." **7** just   **8** mind, intellect   **9** risk   **10** mistaken   **11** expect   **12** knew   **13** angry **14** criticized   **15** encouraged   **16** certain **17** William Tyndale (*ca.* 1494–1536),

also known as William Hitchins, was a prominent English reformer, known for translating the New Testament into English. He was ultimately executed for heresy near Brussels.   **18** Robert Barnes (1495–1540) took vows as an Augustinian, but later left the order and became a Lutheran. He was imprisoned for heresy in 1526, and after his release

went to the Continent. He won Henry VIII's favor by approving of his divorce, but after associating himself with Thomas Cromwell, Barnes was burned at the stake after Cromwell fell from favor.   **19** impartial, unbiased   **20** *sore an auditor:* severe a listener   **21** critic   **22** at all   **23** suppose **24** say   **25** held   **26** even if   **27** *De arte poetica* 358–59

the writer slept, so useth he of[28] courtesy if he cannot sleep, yet for company at the leastwise to nap and wink with him, and leave his dream unchecked. Which kind of courtesy, if I should show how often I have used with Tyndale and Barnes both, winking at their tolerable faults, and such as I rather thought negligently escaped them of oversight or folly than diligently devised of wily falsehood or malice — if I would add all those faults to their others, then should I double in length all my books, in which the brethren find for the special fault that they be too long already.

But albeit that[29] when I wrote I was (as I have told you) bolded[30] and encouraged by the common custom of all indifferent readers — which[31] would, I wist[32] well, pardon and hold excused such tolerable oversight in my writing as men may find some in any man's, almost, that ever wrote before — yet am I now much more glad and bold when I see that those folk which would fainest[33] find my faults cannot yet happen on them, but after long seeking and searching for them, for all their business[34] taken thereabout, are fain[35] to put for faults in my writing such things as well considered shall appear their own faults for the finding.

For they find first for a great fault that my writing is overlong, and therefore too tedious to read. For which cause, they say, they will never once vouchsafe to look thereon.

But then say they further that such places of them as are looked on by those that are learned and can skill[36] be soon perceived for nought,[37] and my reasons of little force. For they boast much that they hear sometimes diverse parts of my books answered and confuted fully in sundry[38] of some men's sermons, though my name be forborne,[39] and then they wish me there, they say, for that[40] it would do their hearts good to see my cheeks red for shame.

And over[41] this, they find a great fault that I handle Tyndale and Barnes, their two new gospelers, with no fairer words nor in no more courteous manner.

And over this, I write, they say, in such wise[42] that I show myself suspect in the matter and partial toward the clergy.

And then they say that my works were worthy much more credence if I had written more indifferently,[43] and had declared and made open to the people the faults of the clergy.

And in this point they lay for an example the goodly and godly, mild and gentle fashion used by him, whosoever he was, that now lately wrote the book of *The Division between the Temporalty and the Spiritualty*; which charitable mild manner, they say that if I had used, my works would have been read both of[44] many more and with much better will.

And yet they say, besides all this, that I do but pick out pieces at my pleasure, such as I may most easily seem to soil,[45] and leave out what me list,[46] and such as would plainly prove the matter against me. And so they say that I use but craft and fraud against Tyndale. For as for Friar Barnes, I perceive by sundry ways that the brotherhood speak much less of him, either for that they find him in their own minds well and fully answered, or else that they take him in respect of[47] Tyndale, but for a man of a second[48] sort. And that may peradventure[49] be, because he leaveth out somewhat[50] that Tyndale taketh in — that is to wit,[51] the making of mocks and mows[52] against the Mass, and the Blessed Sacrament of the altar.

But finally, they say further yet that I have not fulfilled my promise. For I promised, they say, in my preface of my *Confutation*, that I would prove[53] the Church; and that, they say, I have not done.

THE SECOND CHAPTER

Now will I begin with that point that I most esteem. For of all the remnant make I little count.[54] But surely loath would I be to misrehearse[55] any man's reason against whom I write, or to rehearse him slenderly.[56] And in that point, undoubtedly they see full well themselves that they say not true. For there is no reason that I rehearse of Tyndale's, or of Friar Barnes's either, but that I use the contrary manner therein that Tyndale useth with mine. For he rehearseth mine in every place faintly and falsely too, and leaveth out the pith[57] and the

28 *useth he of:* it is usual for him out of
29 *albeit that:* although   30 emboldened
31 who   32 knew   33 most gladly
34 trouble; pains   35 constrained
36 *can skill:* have expertise   37 nothing

38 several   39 left unmentioned   40 *for
that:* because   41 beyond   42 a way
43 impartially   44 by   45 refute   46 *me
list:* I please   47 *respect of:* comparison
with   48 inferior   49 perhaps

50 something   51 say   52 deridings
53 define and show the authority of; *CW* 8:
34/29–35/8   54 account; consideration
55 relate inaccurately   56 inadequately;
slackly   57 substance; import

strength, and the proof that most maketh for the purpose. And he fareth[58] therein as if there were one that, having day of challenge appointed, in which he should wrestle with his adversary, would find the means by craft to get his adversary before the day into his own hands, and there keep him and diet him with such a thin diet that at the day he bringeth him forth feeble, faint, and famished, and almost hunger-starven,[59] and so lean that he can scant[60] stand on his legs; and then is it easy, ye wot[61] well, to give the seely[62] soul a fall. And yet when Tyndale hath done all this, he taketh the fall himself.

But every man may well see that I never use that way with Tyndale nor with any of these folk, but I rehearse their reason[63] to the best that they can make it themselves, and I rather enforce[64] it and strengthen it of mine own than take any part of theirs therefrom.

And this use I[65] not only in such places as I do not rehearse all their own words (for that is not requisite in every place), but I use it also in such places besides as of all their own words I leave not one syllable out. For such darkness[66] use they purposely, and Tyndale in especial, that except[67] I took some pain to set out their arguments plainly, many that read them should little wit[68] what they mean.

And to the intent every man may see that these good brethren little care how loud they lie, let any man look, whoso will, and he shall find that of Friar Barnes I have left out little, except a leaf[69] or two concerning the General Councils,[70] and I show the cause why; and as for Tyndale, of diverse whole chapters of his I have not wittingly[71] left out one line—and very few, I am sure, of oversight either—but have put in all his chapters whole whereupon any weight of his matter hangeth, except only in the defense of such English words as he hath changed in his translation of the New Testament. And yet therein they can never say but that I have put in all the strength and pith of his proof.

But all the remnant of his chapters, as far as I have gone, have I put in whole, leaving out nought[72] but railing and preaching without proof, and that but in one place or twain,[73] and where I so do, I give the reader warning.

Now that his chapters be whole rehearsed in my book, I suppose it may meetly[74] well appear by the matter consequently pursuing,[75] if the reader leave my words out between, and read but Tyndale's alone. Or if any one word or some few left out of chance put that proof in doubt, yet have the brethren among them, I warrant you, of Tyndale's books enough by which they may try[76] this true.

And well ye wot[77] if this were untrue that I say, some of them could assign[78] at the leastwise some one such place for an example. But that thing neither do they, nor never can while they live.

THE THIRD CHAPTER

Now whereas these good blessed brethren say that my writing is so long and so tedious that they will not once vouchsafe to look thereon, they show themselves that my writing is not so long as their wits be short, and the eyes of their souls very purblind,[79] while they cannot see so far as to perceive that in finding so many faults in that book, which they confess themselves they neither read nor can find in their heart to look upon, they show themselves either of lightness[80] ready to give hasty credence to other folk, or of malice to make many lies themselves.

It is little marvel that it seem long and tedious unto them to read it over within, whom it irketh to do so much as look it over without; and every way seemeth long to him that is weary ere[81] he begin.

But I find some men, again, to whom the reading is so far from tedious that they have read the whole book over thrice—and some that make tables thereof for their own remembrance—and that,[82] such men as have as much wit[83] and learning both, as the best of all this blessed brotherhood that ever I heard of.

Howbeit,[84] glad would I have been if it might have been much more short, for then should my labor have been so much the less.

But they will, if they be reasonable men, consider in themselves that it is a shorter thing and sooner done to write heresies than to answer them. For

---

58 acts **59** starved to death **60** hardly **61** know **62** poor; foolish **63** argument **64** reinforce **65** *use I:* I usually do **66** obscurity **67** unless **68** know **69** page **70** *General Councils:* Ecumenical Councils, to which all the bishops of the world are summoned **71** knowingly **72** nothing **73** two **74** fairly **75** *consequently pursuing:* immediately following **76** test **77** know **78** point out **79** nearsighted; partially blind **80** *of lightness:* out of thoughtlessness **81** before **82** those **83** intelligence **84** However the most foolish heretic in a town may write more false heresies in one leaf than the wisest man in the whole world can well and conveniently[85] by reason and authority soil and confute[86] in forty.

Now when that Tyndale not only teacheth false heresies, but furnisheth his errors also with pretense of reason and Scripture—and instead of reason, sometimes with blunt subtleties and rude riddles too—the making open and lightsome to the reader the dark writing of him that would not by his will be well perceived, hath put me to more labor and length in answering than some man would peradventure[87] have been content to take.

And I sometimes take the pain to rehearse some one thing in diverse fashions in more places than one, because I would that the reader should, in every place where he fortuneth to fall in reading, have at his hand, without remitting over[88] elsewhere, or labor of further seeking for it, as much as shall seem requisite for that matter, that he there hath in hand. And therein the labor of all that length is mine own, for ease and shortening of the reader's pain.

Now on the other side, as for Tyndale and Barnes, I wot nere[89] well whether I may call them long or short.

For sometimes they be short indeed, because they would be dark, and have their false follies pass and repass all unperceived.

Sometimes they can use such a compendious kind of eloquence that they convey and couch up together, with a wonderful brevity, four follies and five lies in less than as many lines.

But yet for all this, I see not in effect any men more long than they. For they preach sometimes a long process[90] to very little purpose. And since that of all their whole purpose they prove in conclusion never a piece at all, were their writing never so short, yet were their whole work at last too long by altogether. But greatly can I not marvel, though these evangelical brethren think my works too long. For everything think they too long that aught is.[91] Our Lady's Psalter[92] think they too long by all the Ave Marias,[93] and some good piece of the Creed too.

Then the Mass think they too long by the secrets,[94] and the canon,[95] and all the collects[96] wherein mention is made either of saints or souls.[97]

Instead of a long portuous,[98] a short primer[99] shall serve them. And yet the primer they think too long by all our Lady Matins.[100]

And the Seven Psalms[101] think they long enough without the litany.[102]

And as for Dirge[103] or commendation for their friends' souls,[104] all that service they think too long by altogether.

But now, good readers, I have, unto these delicate dainty folk that can aweigh[105] with no long reading, provided with mine own pain and labor as much ease as my poor wit could devise.

First, when they were before fast[106] in the Catholic faith, they never needed to have read any of these heretics' books that have brought them into these newfangled fantasies. But now, since they be, by their own folly, fallen first into doubting of the truth, and afterward into the leaning toward a false belief, they be very negligent and unreasonable if they will not, at the leastwise for their own surety,[107] search and see somewhat[108] whereby they may perceive whether these new teachers of theirs be such as they take them for.

Now have I then considered that they would peradventure wax[109] weary to read over a long book, and therefore have I taken the more pain upon every chapter, to the intent that they shall not need to read over any chapter but one, and that it shall not force[110] greatly which one, throughout all the book.

For I dare be bold to say, and am ready to make it good with the best evangelist of all this evangelical brotherhood that will set his pen to the contrary, that there is not one chapter of Tyndale's, or Barnes's either, that I have touched through mine whole work but that I have so clearly and so fully confuted him that whoso read it indifferently may well and clearly see that they handle their matter so falsely, and yet so foolishly therewith, that no man which regardeth either truth or wit should once vouchsafe to read any farther of them.

---

85 appropriately   86 *soil and confute:* refute   87 perhaps   88 *remitting over:* referring   89 *wot nere:* do not know   90 discourse   91 *aught is:* is anything worthwhile   92 *Our Lady's Psalter:* the rosary   93 *Ave Marias:* Hail Marys   94 prayers of the Mass which are not spoken out loud   95 the prayer of Eucharistic consecration   96 prayers of the Mass which change daily   97 i.e., souls in purgatory   98 (portable) breviary, a prayer book   99 a prayer book for lay people   100 *Lady Matins:* evening prayers from "The Little Office of Our Lady"   101 *Seven Psalms:* a recitation of penitential psalms—6, 31(32), 37(38), 50(51), 101(102), 129(130), 142(143)   102 a repeated request to a list of saints to "pray for us"   103 a prayer for the dead   104 *commendation… souls:* a liturgical prayer commending the souls of the dead to God   105 put up   106 steadfast   107 certainty; security   108 something   109 become, grow   110 matter

Now he that will, therefore, read any one chapter — either at adventure,[111] or else some chosen piece in which himself had went[112] that his evangelical father Tyndale had said wonderfully well, or else Friar Barnes either — when he shall in that one chapter, as I am sure he shall, find his holy prophet plainly proved a fool, he may be soon eased of any further labor. For then hath he good cause to cast him quite off and never meddle[113] more with him, and then shall he never need to read more of my book neither, and so shall he make it short enough.

Howbeit,[114] if he list,[115] for all that, to pardon his prophet in that one place, and think that he wrote that piece peradventure while the Spirit was not upon him, and that he saith much better in some other place, and so will read on further to find it, then shall himself make my work long. For he shall, I trust, read it over, and yet shall he never come to it. And thus as for the tedious length of my writing, I have, I trust, without great length given the good brotherhood a sufficient answer.

THE FOURTH CHAPTER

But now will the brethren peradventure[116] say that I may be bold to say very largely of mine own because men may not be bold in these matters to defend Tyndale's part.

It were indeed somewhat better than it is, if they said true. But neither are such things so diligently controlled,[117] nor such folk so feard of such heretical favor,[118] as they should be if every man did his part; nor they lack no wily drifts[119] in such wise also to defend those things, as they may save for themselves some color[120] to say that they meant none harm.

And to prove that they be neither so sore[121] afeard in such things nor lack such inventions[122] of uttering their forbidden ware, besides the bold erroneous talking that is now almost in every lewd[123] lad's mouth, the brethren boast that they hear diverse parts of my book well and plainly in sundry[124] of their sermons confuted, and then they cannot say, ye see well, that they leave me unanswered for fear.

Howbeit,[125] though they be bold upon some parts even now, some parts haply[126] there are whereupon they dare not be so bold yet, but little and little will peradventure hereafter.

Howbeit, some parts that they be already bold upon be meetly[127] well for a beginning, whereof for example I shall remember you one or twain.[128]

Tyndale's false translation of the New Testament was (as ye wot[129] well and as himself confesseth) translated with such changes as he hath made therein purposely, to the intent that by those words changed, the people should be nuzzled[130] in those opinions which himself calleth true Catholic faith, and which things all true Catholic people call very false pestilent heresies.

This translation therefore being by the clergy condemned, and at Paul's Cross[131] openly burned, and by the King's gracious proclamation openly forbidden, I wrote in a place[132] of my *Dialogue*, in the 100th leaf, among other things these words:

> The faults be so many in Tyndale's translation of the New Testament, and so spread through the whole book, that likewise as it were as soon done to weave a new web of cloth as to sew up every hole in a net, so were it almost as little labor and less to translate the whole book all new as to make in his translation so many changes as need must be ere it were made good, besides this: that there would no wise man, I trow,[133] take the bread which he well wist[134] was of his enemy's hand once poisoned, though he saw his friend after scrape it never so clean.[135]

These words of mind were rehearsed[136] in a sermon, and answered in this wise: that though there were bread that were poisoned indeed, yet were poisoned bread better than no bread at all.

Now was this word taken up, and walked about abroad among the brethren and sistren, so highly well liked among them that some of them said that all my reasons were avoided clean[137] with that one word.

Howbeit, indeed one of their own wives yet

---

111 random   **112** thought   **113** deal, concern himself   **114** However
115 chooses; desires   **116** perhaps
117 restrained   **118** appearance   **119** ploys
120 plausible reason; pretext   **121** greatly

122 plans, schemes   **123** uneducated; rude
124 many   **125** However   **126** perhaps
127 suitably   **128** *remember . . . twain:* remind you of one or two   **129** know
130 fed; nurtured   **131** *Paul's Cross:* an

open-air pulpit near St. Paul's cathedral in London   **132** passage   **133** trust
134 knew   **135** *Dialogue of Sir Thomas More, Knight,* p. 525   **136** repeated
137 *avoided clean:* made void completely

told her own husband at home, when she heard him boast it, how jollily it was preached: "Better poisoned bread than no bread." "By our Lakin,[138] Brother Husband," quoth she, "but as properly as that was preached, yet would I rather abide the peril of breeding worms in my belly by eating of flesh without bread than to eat with my meat the bread that I wist well were poisoned."

And of truth, good reader, this word of his was one of the most proud and presumptuous, and therewith the most unwise too, that ever I heard pass the mouth of any man reputed and taken for wise.

For when the thing had been examined, considered, and condemned by such as the judgment and the ordering of the thing did appertain unto, that false poisoned translation was forbidden the people; it was a heinous presumption of one man, upon the trust of his own wit, to give the people courage and boldness to resist their prince and disobey their prelates, and give them no better staff to stand by than such a bald poisoned reason: that poisoned bread is better than no bread.

For first, I pray you, how proveth he that poisoned bread were better than no bread? I would ween[139] it were as good to forbear meat and starve for hunger as to eat ratsbane[140] and die by poison but if[141] the preacher prove me that it were better for a man to kill himself than die.

But now falleth he in double folly; for first, his proper wise word can have no wit therein but if he prove that the people must needs perish for lack of spiritual food except[142] the Scripture be translated into their own tongue.

Now, if he say and affirm that, then every fool almost may feel the man's folly.

For the people may have every necessary truth of Scripture, and everything necessary for them to know concerning the salvation of their souls, truly taught and preached unto them though the corps and body of the Scripture be not translated unto them in their mother tongue. For else had it been wrong with English people from the faith first brought into this realm unto our own days, in all which time before, I am sure that every English man and woman that could read it had not a book by them of the Scripture in English. And yet is there, I doubt not, of those folk many a good saved soul.

And secondly also, if the having of the Scripture in English be a thing so requisite of precise necessity that the people's souls should needs perish but if[143] they have it translated into their own tongue, then must there the most part perish for all that, except the preacher make farther provision besides that all the people shall be able to read it when they have it; of which people, far more than four parts of all the whole divided into ten, could never read English yet, and many now too old to begin to go to school, and shall, with God's grace, though they never read word of Scripture, come as well to heaven, and as soon too as himself peradventure that preached that wise word. Many have thought it a thing very good and profitable that the Scripture well and truly translated should be in the English tongue. And albeit that many right wise and well-learned both, and very virtuous folk also, both have been and yet be in a far other mind, yet for mine own part, I both have been and yet am also of the same opinion still, as I have in my *Dialogue* declared, if the men were amended and the time meet[144] therefor. But that it were a thing of such precise necessity that the people's souls must needs perish but if that be had, and that therefore we should suffer[145] rather such a poisoned translation than none, and willfully kill ourselves with poison rather than we would take wholesome meat in at our mouth but if we may first have it in our own hands: this heard I never any wise man say, no, nor fool neither till Tyndale came forth with his new-translated Scripture, translating the truth of Christ into false Luther's heresies.

And yet when the brethren have heard such a wise word in a sermon, that word use they to[146] take solemnly for a sure authority, and say that all the long reasons of Sir Thomas More is here answered shortly with one word.

But now have I, with more words than one, made you plain and open the folly of that wise word.

And whensoever he that preached it can hereafter again, with many more words than I have here written, prove his word wisely spoken, let him keep one copy thereof with himself for losing,[147] and send another to me; and then that copy that I receive, I will be bounden to eat it though the book be bounden in boards.

---

138 colloquial variant of "our Lady"   *if:* unless   **142** unless   **143** *but if:* unless   **146** *use they to:* they usually   **147** *for*
139 think, suppose   **140** arsenic   **141** *but*   **144** suitable, appropriate   **145** allow   *losing:* in the case of loss

THE FIFTH CHAPTER

Another example of such kind of answering have I seen made unto the first chapter of my third book of *Tyndale's Confutation*, of which answer the brethren boast greatly and say that I am answered even[148] to the point.

For this word was said unto a friend of mine in great boast by a special sure secret brother of this new-broached[149] brotherhood; whereupon, when I had heard it, I longed sore[150] to see that answer. For in good faith, I had myself thought that I had so fully answered that chapter of Tyndale's, which is "Whether the Church Were before the Word or the Word before the Church," that he should never without his shame be able to reply while he lived. And therefore, longing sore to see how I was answered now therein, I required[151] my friend to find the means, if he might, that I might see the book, weening that some new work of Tyndale's had been of late come over. But afterward he brought me word that it was answered, not beyond the sea, but here within the realm—not by any book specially made against it, but in a sermon once or twice openly preached. Howbeit,[152] not of a sudden brayed,[153] but forestudied and penned; whereof the book, as a spirit in close,[154] goeth about secretly *velut negotium perambulans in tenebris*[155] among this blessed brotherhood; but I trust to turn it into *daemonium meridianum*,[156] that every man may see him somewhat more plainly appear, and show himself in his own likeness.

Now is it so, indeed, that in that chapter of Tyndale's there be certain lines left out in mine answer. Howbeit, they were of truth left out by oversight in the printing, which may well appear by this: For in mine answer I so touch those words that the leaving out of them maketh mine own more dark and less perceived. And therefore are they content to find no fault at the leaving out of them, but make as though all were in, and also because that[157] mine answer is, as they boast, by that sermon so well and substantially confuted.

But now, because I would be loath to be judged by the only[158] brethren and sisters of the false fraternity—and to the intent they shall all well see that I fear not the judgment of indifferent[159] folk—I shall put abroad, that all folk may see, those words of that solemn sermon by which they boast that mine answer unto that chapter of Tyndale's chapter is so goodly confuted.

The very formal[160] words, lo, good readers, of that sermon, for as far as pertain to this matter, after[161] the copy that was delivered me (which copy I reserve and keep for my declaration),[162] therein be these words that hereafter follow:

Now it followeth in the epistle, *Voluntarie enim genuit nos verbo veritatis.*[163]

This text may be expounded after this manner: "He made us by the truth of his word"; he made us first (ye know) of nothing; and he made us as the chief and principal of all his creatures. For he gave unto us wit[164] and reason, the which he gave unto no creature living in the earth but only to us. But to come more near the matter, we may say that God willingly begot us by the word of his truth, and hath put us here into this world, and here to be as the lord and ruler of all his creatures, the which he made for our comfort and succor.[165] But yet we may go more near you, and say how that he hath begotten us by the word of his truth. Mark, I pray you here, how that Saint James saith that God "hath begotten us through his word of truth." Here it appeareth that we be not true of ourselves, for we are made true by God through his word. And whereas of ourselves we were none other but liars, God of his infinite goodness hath made us by his word the children of truth and of salvation, whereas before we were but liars, and such as worketh none other thing but even the very displeasure of God.

Now God of his merciful goodness by his holy word of truth hath made us his children—that is to say, the children of his truth—"even as it pleased him," saith Saint James, "He hath begotten us by the word of his truth." Mark how that he saith "even as it pleased him" he begot us. If we were begotten and made as it pleased him, then was it not done as it pleased us. And again, and if

148 right   149 newly introduced
150 greatly   151 asked   152 However
153 cried out (as by an ass, but also a pun on braid, "an extemporaneous attack")
154 secret   155 *velum . . . tenebris:* "like a pestilence walking in the darkness"
156 *daemonium meridianum:* "a noonday devil"   157 *because that:* because   158 *by the only:* only by the   159 unbiased, impartial   160 exact   161 according to
162 evidence   163 *Voluntarie . . . veritatis:* "For by his will he begot us by the word of truth" (Jas 1:18).   164 intellect
165 assistance

we were begotten by him, then could not we give him none occasion to love us, for why[166] we came of him, and not we of us. Here may you perceive also that this text maketh against them that will say the Church was before the Gospel.

It is plain enough that the Church was not before the Word; for Saint James saith that God begot us through the Word of his truth. If we were begotten by the Word, then needs must the Word be before we were gotten — or else how should we be begotten by the Word? — and "by the Word," he saith, we were begotten. If God begot us through the Word, we must needs grant that he that begot us was before that we were begotten; and he that begot us begot us by the Word; then needs must the Word be before that we were begotten. Now then, if this Word were before we were begotten, how can we say that the Church was before this Word? If we mean by "the Church" the church of lime and stone, then it is plain enough that the Word was before any such church was made. For we find that it was many a day after man was made ere[167] ever there were any such churches made.

If ye mean by "the Church" the Universal Church of God, the which is the congregation of all Christian people, if you mean this Church, and say how this Church was before the Word, then Saint James maketh you an answer to that, saying how that by the Word this Church was begotten. Then needs must we grant that the Word of God was before any Church was.

Yea, but some will not be content with this answer, but they will say that the Church was before that this Word was written of any man, and it was admitted and allowed by the Church, and so was the Church before his Word. Yea, but yet I will say to you again[168] how that this Word was written before the Church was; yea, and it was not written by men, but it was written by God our Savior afore the beginning of the world, as witness Saint Paul, where he saith to the Hebrews, *Dabo leges meas*,[169] etc. "I will give my laws, saith God, into their hearts, and in their minds shall I write it." Behold how God gave it them at the beginning in their hearts, and writ it in their minds,

and they exercise his law written in their hearts in deed and in effect.

Thus may ye see that at the beginning God wrote his laws in their hearts, and therefore must we needs grant that the Word of God was taught to them long ere ever the Congregation taught it. For you see that by the Word we were begotten; therefore the Word must needs be before we were begotten; or else how could the Word beget us?

Some peradventure[170] will say that the Church was before this Word was written in books of paper and parchment and such other things, and that the Church did admit them to be read of them which[171] they thought necessary to look on them. They will say that the Church was before this was done. Yea, but what thing is this to the purpose, or what shall we need to stand arguing of this matter?

It is plain enough to all men that hath eyes to see and ears to hear how the Word of God was before any Church was, and how the Word of God was written afore it was written in any books or tables; and therefore what shall we need to dispute this matter? But good Lord, if it had not been written by the evangelists in those days, how should we do in these days, the which bring forth the Scripture for them indeed? — and yet they will bear them in hand[172] that it is no Scripture and if[173] it had not been written in books then. Notwithstanding, ye may perceive how the Word was ere ever the Church was, and the Word begot us, and not we the Word; and also it was written ere ever the Church allowed it to be written.

Now, good readers, to the intent ye may the better perceive for what purpose the brotherhood boasteth these words, ye shall understand that whereas Luther first, and Tyndale after him, tell us for a foundation of all their abominable heresies that there is nothing that ought to be taken for a sure[174] and undoubted truth of the Christian belief but if[175] it may be proved by plain and evident Scripture, the King's Highness, in his most famous book of *Assertion of the Sacraments*, laid[176] against Luther — and I, out of the same book of my said sovereign lord, took and laid against Tyndale and all

166 the reason that **167** before **168** in reply **169** *Dabo…meas:* "I will give my laws" (Heb 10:16). **170** perhaps **171** whom **172** *bear them in hand:* lead them to believe **173** *and if:* if **174** secure; certain **175** *but if:* unless **176** argued such—that the Word of God is part written in the Scripture, and part unwritten that appeareth not proved therein, as, for example, the perpetual virginity of our Lady and other diverse points which were only taught by Christ to his apostles, and by them forth to the Church, and so, by tradition of the Church, beside the Scripture and without writing, taught and delivered unto Christian people from age to age, and so the faith and belief of those things kept and continued from the apostles' days unto our own time, and that if the Church were nothing bounden to believe but only the things plainly written in Scripture, then had all folk before Moses's days been left at liberty to leave all God's words unbelieved. And then had Christ's Church in the beginning been at liberty to leave a great part of Christ's own words unbelieved. For the Church was gathered, and the faith believed, before any part of the New Testament was put in writing. And which writing was or is the true Scripture, neither Luther nor Tyndale knoweth but by the credence that they give to the Church.

And therefore, since the Word of God is as strong unwritten as written, and which is his Word written Tyndale cannot tell but by the Church, which hath, by the assistance of the Spirit of God therein, the gift of discretion to know it, and since that that gift is given (as Saint Augustine saith and Luther himself confesseth) to this common-known Catholic Church, why should not Luther and Tyndale as well believe the Church in that it telleth them this thing did Christ and his apostles say as they must believe the Church (or else believe nothing) in that it telleth them this thing did Christ's evangelists and apostles write?

Now, good readers, Tyndale, seeing how sore[177] this reason of the King's Highness doth touch and turn up the very foundation and great part of his heresies, he doth in his book against me, of which book he maketh the title *Which Is the Church, and Whether It May Err or Not*, put this chapter: "Whether the Church were before the Gospel, or the Gospel before the Church." Which chapter, to the end ye may the more clearly perceive the matter, I shall rehearse[178] you whole, and after that, some part of mine answer thereto. And then if ye read again the words of this sermon that I have here inserted before, every child almost shall be well able

to judge whether this preacher have in his sermon avoided[179] well mine answer or no. These are Tyndale's words:

Another doubt there is: whether the Church, or Congregation, be before the Gospel, or the Gospel before the Church. Which question is as hard to solve as whether the father be elder than the son or the son elder than his father. For the whole Scripture and all believing hearts testify that we are begotten through the Word. Wherefore,[180] if the Word beget the Congregation, and he that begetteth is before him that is begotten, then is the Gospel before the Church. Paul also, *Romano* 9,[181] saith, "How shall they call on whom they believe not? And how shall they believe without a preacher?"

That is, Christ must first be preached ere men can believe in him. And then it followeth that the word of the preacher must be before the faith of the believer.

And therefore, inasmuch as the Word is before the faith, and faith maketh the Congregation, therefore is the Word or Gospel before the Congregation.

And again, as the air is dark of itself, and receiveth all her light of the sun, even so are all men's hearts of themselves dark with lies and receive all their truth of God's Word, in that they consent thereto.

And moreover, as the dark air giveth the sun no light, but contrariwise, the light of the sun in respect of[182] the air is of itself and lighteneth the air and purgeth it from darkness, even so the lying heart of man can give the Word of God no truth; but contrariwise, the truth of God's Word is of herself and lighteneth the hearts of the believers, and maketh them true, and cleanseth them from lies, as thou readest, John 1[:3], "Ye be clean by reason of the Word." Which is to be understood in that the Word had purged their hearts from lies, from false opinions, and from thinking evil good, and therefore from consenting to sin. And, John 17[:17], "Sanctify them, O Father, through thy truth. And thy Word is truth." And thus thou seest that God's truth dependeth not of man. It is not true because man so saith or admitteth it for true. But man is true

---

177 greatly   **178** tell   **179** refuted   **180** Therefore   **181** "In Romans" (actually Rom 10:14)   **182** *respect of:* comparison with

because he believeth it, testifieth, and giveth witness in his heart that it is true. And Christ also saith himself, John 5[:34], "I receive no witness of man." For if the multitude of man's witness might make aught[183] true, then were the doctrine of Muhammad truer than Christ's.

Lo, good readers, here have ye heard Tyndale's chapter, the matter whereof the brethren boast that the words of that sermon do so well and substantially maintain against mine answer made unto this chapter.

But now, to the intent ye may yourself judge whether that sermon may bear out their boast or not, I shall rehearse you some part of mine answer. Lo, thus beginneth mine answer unto Tyndale's chapter:

Lo, he that readeth this and heareth not the answer—except himself be well-riped[184] in the matter—may ween[185] that Tyndale in these words had quit[186] himself like a man, and borne me over quite:[187] he solveth the objection so plainly, and playeth therewith so pleasantly. But now, when ye shall understand that never man was so mad to make this objection to Tyndale but himself, then shall ye laugh to see that he wrestleth all alone and giveth himself a fall, and in his merry solution mocketh also no man but himself.

I said in my *Dialogue* that the Church was before the Gospel was written, and that the faith was taught, and men were baptized, and Masses said and the other sacraments ministered among Christian people before any part of the New Testament was put in writing, and that this was done by the Word of God unwritten. And I said also there—and yet say here again—that the right faith which Adam had, and such as in the same faith succeeded him long ere writing began, was taught by the Word of God unwritten, and so went from man to man, from the father to the son, by mouth. And I said that this Word of God unwritten is of as great authority as is the Word of God written.

I showed also that the Church of Christ hath been, is, and ever shall be taught and instructed by God and his Holy Spirit with his holy word of

either kind—that is to wit,[188] both with his Word written and his Word unwritten—and that they which will not believe God's Word but if[189] he put it in writing be as plain infidels as they that will not believe it written, since God's Word taketh his[190] authority of God that speaketh it, and not of man that writeth it.

And there is like surety and like certain knowledge of the Word of God unwritten as there is of the Word of God written, since ye know neither the one nor the other to be the Word of God but by the tradition of the Church.

Which Church—as all Christian men believe, and the Scripture showeth, and Saint Augustine declareth, and Luther himself confesseth, and the devil himself saith not nay—the blessed Spirit of God hath inwardly taught, teacheth, and ever shall teach to know, judge, and discern the Word of God from the word of man, and shall keep the Church from error, "leading it into every truth,"[191] as Christ saith himself in the sixteenth chapter of Saint John's Gospel. Which he did not if he suffered[192] the Church to be damnably deceived in taking the word of man for the Word of God; whereby it should, instead of service to be done to God, fall in unfaithfulness and with idolatry do service to the devil.

And therefore I showed in my said *Dialogue*[193]— and yet the King's Highness much more plainly showed in his most erudite famous book against Luther, out of which I took it—that the Word of God unwritten is of as great authority, as certain, and as sure as is his Word written in the Scripture. Which point is so fast and sure pitched upon the Rock—Our Savior Christ himself— that neither Luther, Tyndale, nor Hussgen,[194] nor all the hellhounds that the devil hath in his kennel never hitherto could, nor while God liveth in heaven and the devil lieth in hell never hereafter shall (bark they, bawl they, never so fast) be able to wrest it out.

And that they be all, as I tell you, so feeble in this point whereupon the effect of all their whole heresies hangeth (for but if[195] they vanquish this one point, all their heresies fully be burned up and fall as flat to ashen as it were alms[196] all obstinate heretics did), ye may see a clear proof

---

183 anything 184 well-educated
185 think, suppose 186 conducted
187 *borne . . . quite:* refuted me entirely

188 say 189 *but if:* unless 190 its
191 Jn 16:13 192 allowed 193 i.e.,
A Dialogue of Sir Thomas More, Knight

194 better known as Johannes Oecolampadius (1482–1531) 195 *but if:* unless
196 a mercy

by these words of Tyndale which he hath set so gloriously forth in the forefront of his battle, as though they were able to win the whole field. For whereas I said that the Gospel and the Word of God unwritten was before the Church, and by it was the Church begun, gathered, and taught, and that the Church was before that the Gospel that now is written was written — that is to wit, before any part of the Gospel was written; for as for all the whole Gospel (that is to wit, all the words of God that he would have known, believed, and kept) was yet never written — this being the thing that I said, Tyndale, with all the help he hath had of all the heretics in Almain[197] this two or three years together, is yet in such despair to be able to match therewith that he is, with shame enough, fain[198] to forget that I said the Church was before the Gospel written. Which thing himself cannot deny, and is fain to frame the doubt and make the objection as though I had said that the Church had been before the Gospel and the Word of God unwritten; whereof himself knoweth well that I said clean the contrary. And therefore, good readers, having this thing in your remembrance, take now the pain to read Tyndale's words again, and ye shall have a pleasure to see how fondly[199] he juggleth afore you. For now, his craft opened and declared unto you, ye shall perceive that he playeth nothing clean, but fareth[200] like a juggler that conveyeth his galls[201] so craftily that all the table spieth them.

Lo, good readers, here have I now rehearsed you but a piece of mine answer unto that chapter of Tyndale; and yet by this one piece alone may ye clearly perceive that all those words of that sermon go so far wide from the point that they not only do nothing help Tyndale (for all the labor that they take about it), but also the preacher of them taketh a fouler fall than Tyndale, in that the preacher stumbleth at the same stock,[202] and falleth into the same puddle, that Tyndale did — and that after that he was warned by mine answer made to Tyndale afore.

For this here ye see: that this preacher in the first part of his words toucheth not the matter; but little and little he descendeth thereto by the expounding of these words of Saint James: *Voluntarie enim*

genuit nos verbo veritatis — that is in English, "He hath willingly begotten us by the Word of truth."[203]

Howbeit,[204] the preacher Englisheth it thus: "He made us," or "begot us," "by the truth of his Word." Which words, after that he hath expounded after diverse manners, he cometh at last to that exposition by which he expoundeth those words in this wise:[205] that "God hath willingly by his Word made us the children of truth and of salvation." And after a thing or two noted and marked therein (which I shall haply[206] make you to mark well and see somewhat more therein hereafter than the preacher showeth you there), he cometh to the point with which we be now in hand;[207] and therein thus he beginneth:

Here may you perceive also that this text maketh against them that will say the Church was before the Gospel.

But now do you, good readers, clearly perceive and see that this preacher saith wrong. For while they against whom he preacheth — that is to wit, they that say the Church was before the Gospel written — do both mean and plainly write that the Church was not before that the Gospel was in God's mind, nor before it was preached and taught by mouth, but only before it was written in books, and that the cause why they so say and write and put men in mind of that point is because that the heretics would make men ween[208] that God's Word were of none authority nor worthy to be believed but if[209] it were written in the books, now I say that since ye know, good readers, that they against whom this preacher thus preacheth do mean and say and write as ye now see they do, ye cannot but clearly perceive and see that this preacher doth in this point but labor to blind his audience, and meeteth nothing with the matter.

For now, this thing had in mind and considered, all his reason after, which he taketh out of Tyndale's chapter, waxeth even[210] dead for cold.

For what heat or what one spark of life, after this thing considered, have all his words that follow, wherein he saith:

It is plain enough that the Church was not before the Word; for Saint James saith that God begot us through the Word of his truth. If we were begotten by the Word, then needs must the Word be before we were gotten—or else how should we be begotten by the Word?—and by the Word, he saith, we were begotten. If God begot us through the Word, we must needs grant that he that begot us was before that we were begotten; and he that begot us begot us by the Word; then needs must the Word be before that we were begotten. Now then, if this Word were before we were begotten, how can we say that the Church was before this Word?

If we mean by "the Church" the church of lime and stone, then it is plain enough that the Word was before any such church was made. For we find that it was many a day after man was made ere ever there were any such churches made. If ye mean by "the Church" the Universal Church of God—the which is the congregation of all Christian people—if you mean this Church, and say how this Church was before the Word, then Saint James maketh you an answer to that, saying how that by the Word this Church was begotten. Then needs must we grant that the Word of God was before any Church was.

All this childish reason, ye wot[211] well, which Tyndale hath begotten him, and which he bringeth out of Tyndale's chapter and fathereth it upon Saint James, be it never so quick[212] in another matter, is yet in this, as touching them against whom he preacheth it, clean quailed in the travail[213] and utterly born dead while[214] they against whom he preacheth say not precisely that the Church was before the Gospel, nor before God's Word, but only say that the Church was before the Gospel and God's Word was put in writing.

And that his reason is dead, as I say it is, himself that preached it perceiveth; and therefore he goeth farther and draweth nearer to the matter, and saith:

Yea, but some will not be content with this answer, but they will say that the Church was before that this Word was written of any man, and it was admitted and allowed by the Church, and so was the Church before his Word. Yea, but yet I will say to you again how that this Word was written before the Church was; yea, and it was not written by men, but it was written by God our Savior afore the beginning of the world, as witness Saint Paul, where he saith to the Hebrews, *Dabo leges meas,*[215] etc. "I will give my laws, saith God, into their hearts, and in their minds shall I write it." Behold how God gave it them at the beginning in their hearts, and writ it in their minds, and they exercise his law written in their hearts indeed and in effect.

Thus may ye see that at the beginning God wrote his laws in their hearts, and therefore must we needs grant that the Word of God was taught to them long ere ever the Congregation taught it. For you see that by the Word we were begotten; therefore the Word must needs be before we were begotten; or else how could the Word beget us?

By these words, good readers, ye see that himself perceiveth that all his other words were not worth a rush,[216] because they came not near the purpose,[217] nor anything toucheth[218] them against whom he preacheth them. And therefore, seeing that Tyndale is by mine answer therein proved a fool, he goeth, as ye see, farther than Tyndale went. But therein, the nearer he cometh to the point, the more he proveth himself to go the farther from reason. For what reason hath he that, in arguing against others, saith but the same that they say?

Now all that ever he saith in these words say we, against whom he preacheth them.

And we not only say the things that he saith now—that is to wit, that God's Word was ere ever it was written, and that it was written in hearts ere ever it was written in books—but these be also the things that we specially lay[219] against him whose said chapter this preacher would with these words defend. For since the Gospel of Christ and the words of God that are now written in books were all written in hearts before they were written in books, and yet were at that time of the same strength and authority that they be now, we say to Luther and Tyndale and all such other heretics that they say false in that[220] they preach and teach—that men are bounden to believe nothing but if it be written in books—since

God is at his liberty to give his Word into his Church even yet at this day by his own mouth, through the inspiration of his Holy Spirit sent thereunto, and by himself abiding ever therein, and, at the preaching of the Church, write it in the hearts of the hearers, as well and as surely as ever he gave his Word to his Church by his apostles, and wrote it in the people's hearts at their preaching, at such time as it was yet unwritten in any of the apostles' books.

And over²²¹ this, we tell them that the same Church—by only which Church they now know which books be those that have the Word of God in them that the apostles and evangelists have written—the same Church, I say, doth tell them that the words of God which God will have us believe be not all written in those books, but some part still remain only written in hearts, as before the books written they did altogether. And we tell them that Tyndale must as well believe the Church in telling him which be those words of God that yet remain unwritten as he doth and must believe it in telling him which be those books in which the words of God are written.

And therefore, good readers, what things in this world could this preacher have devised worse to bring forth against me for Tyndale's defense than those with which, as ye see, Tyndale is most clearly confounded?

But now shall ye see that this preacher perceiveth it well enough himself. And therefore, after that he hath set forth Tyndale's reason, and dissimuled²²² mine answer that I have made to it, and so, before his audience, wrestled a while in the dark, where, for lack of sight of the matter, they might not see how he fell, he waxed²²³ yet half weary thereof at last, and somewhat ashamed too, lest he were peradventure spied, and fain²²⁴ would he therefore have shaken off the matter and rid himself out honestly; and therefore in conclusion he cometh down to this:

Some peradventure will say that the Church was before this word was written in books of paper and parchment and such other things, and that the Church did admit them to be read of them which they thought necessary to look on them. They will say that the Church was before this was

done. Yea, but what thing is this to the purpose, or what shall we need to stand arguing of this matter?

It is plain enough to all men that hath eyes to see and ears to hear how the Word of God was before any church was, and how the Word of God was written afore it was written in any books or tables, and therefore what shall we need to dispute this matter? But good Lord, if it had not been written by the evangelists in those days, how should we do in these days, the which bring forth the Scripture for them indeed? And yet they will bear them in hand²²⁵ that it is no Scripture and if²²⁶ it had not been written in books then. Notwithstanding, ye may perceive how the Word was ere²²⁷ ever the Church was, and the Word begot us, and not we the Word; and also it was written ere ever the Church allowed it to be written.

Here have ye seen, good readers, after long wrestling with me, what shift this preacher maketh to shake the matter off. For seeing that he can in no wise defend Tyndale's reason, he would at last fain²²⁸ shake off the question. And indeed the question, as Tyndale frameth it of his own fashion for his own advantage, is very frivolous and foolish. And therefore this preacher goeth, as I say, somewhat farther and cometh nearer to the point in which the matter of the question lieth. But then, because he cannot defend Tyndale and avoid²²⁹ mine answer, after the time driven forth²³⁰ in furnishing of Tyndale's reason, when he cometh to the point he leaveth mine answer untouched, and would shake off the question for nought.²³¹

But that thing now, good readers, will not well be for him. For the necessity of this question you see now yourself. For since Luther and Tyndale and other such heretics do teach that no Word of God is now to be believed, nor to be taken for God's Word by the teaching of the Catholic Church, but if²³² it be written in Scripture, they drive us of necessity to tell them again²³³ that the Church was before the Scripture, and before that any of God's words were written therein; and that all his words that he will have believed were never written, and that he is not so tongue-tied but that he is at liberty to speak yet more words when he will, and may bind us as well

to believe them as ever he bound us to believe any word that ever he spoke before, be it unwritten or written; and that in all such things Luther and Tyndale both, and Friar Barnes too, and all the here-
5 tics of them, must, as I said, of reason believe the Church as well when it telleth them "these things Christ hath by his own Spirit or by the mouth of his apostles taught us" as when it telleth them "these things hath Christ by the pen of his apostles writ-
10 ten us." Now is this knot so sure that it can never be loosed but if these heretics, or this preacher for them, can by plain Scripture prove us that God hath caused all such things to be written in Scripture already—and, over that, made a promise, either
15 that he will never speak any such word more, or that if he do, he will at the leastwise take no displeasure with us though we tell him plainly that since it is not in Scripture already, he shall write it in if he will, or else will we not believe him.

20   THE SIXTH CHAPTER

A nd this preacher himself so well perceiveth that this point is true that I tell you that he would fain, if he could prove it, say that all such things are written already in Scripture. And therefore, though
25 because he seeth that I have, in the last chapter of my first part of *Tyndale's Confutation*, overthrown Tyndale therein, he forbore to affirm it forth out in plain and open words, yet he giveth his audience a proper insinuation thereof, and maketh a pretty[234]
30 glance thereat, in those words where he saith in the last end:

But good Lord, if it had not been written by the evangelists in those days, how should we do in these days, the which bring forth the Scripture
35 for them indeed? And yet they will bear them in hand that it is no Scripture and if it had not been written in books then. Notwithstanding, ye may perceive how the Word was ere ever the

Church was, and the Word begot us, and not we the Word; and also it was written ere ever the 40 Church allowed it to be written.

By these words would he, lo—though he say it not plain out—that folk should ween[235] that, of anything which we be bounden to believe, the evangelists and apostles left in their days nought[236] un- 45 written. Which point, if it could be proved, would help some heresies well forth, but yet not so many as heretics would make men ween. For many things that they say be not in Scripture are yet in Scripture indeed, as is for the sacrament of confirmation, 50 and aneling,[237] and holy orders, and matrimony, and the very[238] blessed Body and Blood of Christ in the holy Sacrament of the altar, and for good works against[239] faith alone, and for holy vows of chastity against the abominable bitchery[240] of friars 55 that wed nuns, and many such other things. And in all such matters, the question is not of the Word written or unwritten, but upon the interpretation and the right understanding of God's Word already written. 60

And therein is, in effect, the question also no more but whether that in the construction and exposition of Holy Scripture we should of reason better believe holy Saint Augustine, holy Saint Ambrose, holy Saint Jerome, holy Saint Cyprian, holy 65 Saint Chrysostom, holy Saint Basil, holy Saint Cyril, and the three Gregorys of Greece,[241] holy saints all three, and holy Saint Gregory the pope,[242] with all the other old holy doctors and fathers of the faithful doctrine, on the one side, or else, on the other 70 side, lewd Luther, and Lambert,[243] Barnes, Hussgen, and Zwingli, Schwarzerdt,[244] Tyndale, George Joye,[245] and Denck,[246] Bainham,[247] Bayfield,[248] Hitton,[249] and Tewkesbury,[250] with Brother Burt,[251] and young Father Frith.[252] 75

There would be now between these two sorts no great doubt in the choice (as methinketh) if he that should choose have wit.

And in such matters this is the great question

---

234 clever   235 think   236 nothing
237 anointing (of the sick)   238 true,
actual   239 as opposed to   240 lewdness,
harlotry   241 *three ... Greece:* St.
Gregory of Neocaesarea (*ca.* 213–70), St.
Gregory Nazianzus (329–90), and St.
Gregory of Nyssa (*ca.* 335–95)   242 *Saint Gregory the Pope:* Gregory the Great
(*ca.* 540–604)   243 Francois Lambert

(1486–1530)   244 better known as Philip
Melancthon (1497–1560)   245 an English
Protestant known for his Bible translations
(*ca.* 1495–1553)   246 Hans Denck
(*ca.* 1495–1527), an Anabaptist   247 James
Bainham, an English lawyer burned for
heresy in 1532   248 Richard Bayfield,
an English Benedictine who embraced
Protestant theology and was burned for

heresy in 1531   249 Thomas Hitton, an
English priest who became a follower of
Tyndale and was burned for heresy in 1530
250 John Tewkesbury, a leather merchant
of London, who was burned for heresy
in 1531   251 John Burt, an otherwise
unknown bookbinder charged with heresy
252 John Frith (1503–33), an English priest
burned for heresy in 1533

indeed—which thing, if any of their favorers dare deny, and will affirm that in the construction of the Scripture they have the old holy doctors on their side, let all these heretics and all that bear them favor find out among them all so much as one of all the old holy saints that so did construe the Scripture as now these new heretics do, for wedding of monks, friars, and nuns, which the whole Catholic Church, all this fifteen hundred years before these late lewd heresies began, have evermore abhorred and holden for abominable—let these new brethren, I say, now find out, among them all, any one of the old holy saints that said the breach of their vows was no sin; and then am I content they say that all the remnant be whole upon their part in all the remnant of all their poisoned heresies.

But on the other side, if they cannot among them all find out so much as one old holy man for their part in this point in which we can bring many against them, then must they needs confess that in the construction of the Scripture (forasmuch, at the leastwise, as appertaineth to this point), saving for the undoubted faith of the whole Catholic Church full fifteen hundred years together against these vow-breaking brethren (which thing alone sufficeth for their full condemnation), else standeth all the question but in this: whether of the twain[253] should, in the exposition of Holy Scripture, be by reason among the unlearned people better believed—the old holy, gracious[254] doctors and saints, or these new-wedded monks and friars, graceless[255] apostates and heretics.

And then, since no good Christian man can doubt whether part is the better of these twain, no good man can there doubt, ye see well, but that these new doctors—Luther, Lambert, Tyndale, Hussgen, and Zwingli, with all their adherents—be plain abominable heretics in this one point at the least. Which point, while[256] it is so shameful and full of filthy beastliness, I dare be bold to say that neither hath that man nor that woman any respect or regard of any cleanness or honesty that can with favor vouchsafe[257] to read their books or hear them till they first forswear and abjure the defense and maintenance of that incestuous[258] sacrilege and very beastly bitchery.[259]

THE SEVENTH CHAPTER

But now to return to the point which this preacher would covertly color[260] in his said words, and would make it seem that the apostles and evangelists had written all things that God bindeth us to believe, where he saith:

> But good Lord, if it had not been written by the evangelists in those days, how should we do in these days, the which bring forth the Scripture for them indeed? And yet they will bear them in hand[261] that it is no Scripture and if it had not been written in books then.

These words seem to be miswritten, either in the principal book or in the copy. For I think it would be, "if it had not been written by the evangelists in those days, how should we do in these days, in which we bring forth the Scripture for us indeed? And yet they bear us in hand that it is no Scripture." Howbeit,[262] howsoever his words were indeed, he meaneth by them, as ye see, to show that there was a necessity wherefore God caused all necessary things to be put in writing. But unto that point, as I have already made answer unto Tyndale in the *Confutation*, all the things that the Church teacheth for necessary, and saith they were God's words—all those, I mean, which these heretics say be not specified in Scripture and that therefore they be not God's words nor any necessary truths, but false inventions of Satan (as Tyndale saith) and damnable dreams of men (as Barnes saith)—this preacher yet cannot deny but kept have such things been in remembrance and observed this thousand years, yea, twelve or thirteen hundred, among Christian people, yea, and as long as the Gospels of Christ hath been written, and haply[263] somewhat before too, as may be gathered of old ancient writings.

Howbeit, though[264] it were somewhat less shall little force[265] for the matter. For if they may abide by any means in remembrance a thousand years, by the selfsame means may they abide in remembrance another thousand too. Then since these folks say that these things, being so long preserved and kept in remembrance, be out of the Scripture, now would I

---

253 *whether … two:* which of the two
254 godly; grace-filled   **255** ungodly;
devoid of grace   **256** when, since   **257** be
willing   **258** because monks and nuns
were regarded in canon law as brothers
and sisters   **259** lewdness; harlotry
260 dissemble; camouflage   **261** *bear …
hand:* lead them to believe   **262** However
263 perhaps   **264** even if   **265** *little force:*
make little difference

wit[266] of this preacher whether they have been so long kept and preserved by God, or by man, or by the devil. If he say by God, then be they of likelihood good things, and not falsehoods but truths. And if he say that they be false, and that yet God hath kept them, then followeth it at the least that he could have kept them as well all this long while though they had been true, and that without[267] the Scripture, as he hath kept them hitherto.

And thereof followeth it also that he had no necessity to cause every necessary truth that he would have kept in remembrance to be put in the Scripture, as this preacher would have it seem.

But now if this preacher will say on the other side that these things have not been preserved by God among Christian people, but be false things, and have all this long while been kept either by man or devil, yet since God is as strong and as mighty as man and devil both, it followeth, ye see well, that the thing which they have done in keeping of false things God could as well do in the keeping of true things, and needed to[268] the keeping no more Scripture than they.

And thus, good readers, every way ye see that this reason of this preacher which Tyndale laid against me before him—that God did cause all necessary things to be written in Scripture, because that else they could not have continued in remembrance—this reason, I say, ye see cannot hold. For those things have continued as long in remembrance, which things themselves say be not in the Scripture.

For where this preacher protesteth the necessity of the putting of all things in Scripture with a figure of apostrophe, and turning his tale to God, crying out,

> O good Lord, if it had not been written by the evangelists in those days, how should we do in these days, the which bring forth the Scripture for them indeed? And yet they will bear them in hand that it is no Scripture.

These words, lo, prove plainly for my part: that there is as great surety[269] in the Word of God unwritten and taught unto the Church by the Spirit without the Scripture as in his word written in the Scripture. For whoso believe the Church will

grant both, and whoso believe not the Church will deny both, as this preacher here saith himself. For he knoweth not which is the Scripture but by the Church. And therefore where he saith that men nowadays, if we lay them forth the Scripture indeed, "they will bear them in hand that it is no Scripture," verily,[270] if it hap (as it happeth often) that the preachers of these new sects do lay forth for them[271] very Scripture indeed, which Scripture maketh not for them indeed, but some false glosses[272] that they give the Scripture indeed, there will the true Catholic preachers say that they abuse the Scripture indeed. But they will never say that the Scripture which they brought forth is no Scripture indeed. For that way doth none use but these heretics only; nor they cannot all say that there is any leaf or line that ever themselves have taken for Scripture hitherto but the Catholic Church, of whom they learned it, doth affirm the same. But on the other side, there are some parts of Scripture which the whole Catholic Church affirmeth for Scripture, which parts yet these heretics affirm for none. As, for example, the selfsame epistle of Saint James which this preacher made that sermon upon; which epistle Friar Luther and Friar Barnes both let[273] not boldly to deny for Scripture, because in many places it destroyeth their heresies. And yet is there never a heretic of them, for all that, but where it may serve to seem to prove his purpose, there will he bring it forth for Saint James' own, and find no fault therewith.

And thus, good Christian readers, here have I somewhat showed you how little cause the brethren have to boast that piece of that sermon, and say that it hath well defended Tyndale's said chapter and clearly confounded me in that part of my *Confutation*. And this have I showed you somewhat the more at length because it toucheth a point that is, either for the maintaining or confounding of many great heresies, a very special key.

THE EIGHTH CHAPTER

For as for the preacher's other pieces in the beginning of those words, I have let pass untouched, where he saith,

266 know   267 outside, apart from   268 for   269 security; certainty   270 truly   271 *lay forth for them:* cite as being on their side   272 interpretations   273 hesitate

"He hath begotten us by the word of his truth, even as it pleased him." Mark that Saint James saith "even as it pleased him." If we were begotten and made even as it pleased him, then was it not done as it pleased us. And again, and if we were begotten by him, then could not we give him none occasion to love us. For why we came of him, and not we of us.

These words, good readers, have no great harm in them at the first face.[274] But they allude unto certain words of Tyndale with which he argueth against me because I say in my *Dialogue* that man may, with his free will, by good endeavor of himself, be a worker with God toward the attaining of faith. Against which saying of mine, Tyndale (as I have showed in my second part of *Tyndale's Confutation*), in mockage of man's endeavor toward the belief, and in scorning that man should captive his understanding and subdue his reason into the service of faith, answereth me with a hideous exclamation, and crying out upon my fleshliness and folly, foameth out his high spiritual sentence[275] after this fashion:

O how beetle-blind[276] is fleshly reason! The will hath none operation at all in the working of faith in my soul, no more than the child hath in the begetting of his own father. For, saith Paul, it is the gift of God, and not of us. My wit must show me a true cause or an apparent cause why, ere my will have any working at all.

To this piece of Tyndale's tale, it seemeth that this preacher doth allude. And he covertly layeth,[277] as ye see, the reason that Tyndale layeth for it: of the begetter and him that is begotten. But he layeth not the authority of Saint Paul, as Tyndale doth; but he layeth the words of Saint James which he hath here in hand — "God hath willingly begotten us with the word of his truth" — and sticketh for this purpose upon this word "willingly," and argueth thus: "God begot us 'willingly,' saith here Saint James — that is to wit,[278] after his own will, and as it pleased him — ergo he did not beget us after our own will, nor as it pleased us."

This argument hath this preacher underpropped and enforced[279] with interpreting of the word "willingly," for that is the word of Saint James. Which word the preacher strengtheneth here with "after his own will, and as it pleased himself." And yet neither that word "willingly" of itself nor strengthened with all these others can make but a bare form of arguing if it were in another matter. For if I desired a man to give me a thing, and labored much to him therefor, and much endeavored myself in many things to please him, to the intent that he should give it me, and that he thereupon so did, this were then but a poor argument, to say thus: "This man willingly gave me this thing, and after his own will, and as it pleased him; ergo, he gave it me not after mine own will and as it pleased me." For as ye see, it both pleased him to give it me and also it pleased me that he so should, or else I would never have desired it, nor never have labored therefor.

And thus ye see that the authority of Saint James nothing helpeth this preacher in his purpose against all occasion and all endeavor of man toward the getting of faith, by which we be begotten.

But Tyndale layeth that text of Saint James against the sacrament of baptism, to prove that "the word of the promise" doth all the work in the regendering[280] of the soul by faith, and that the water, toward the infusion of grace or washing of the soul, is none instrument of God, nor nothing else but a bare graceless token, because Saint James saith that God hath cleansed us "by the word of truth," which Tyndale there expoundeth "by the word of his promise," as though never a word of God were true but only his promise. Now of truth, the Word of God that a preacher preacheth, by which the points of the faith be learned, be signs and tokens that signify the things in the mind which are by those words brought unto the hearer's ear and from the ear to the heart, as the water signifieth and betokeneth the inward washing of the soul in that sacrament. And as God useth the one token of the Word to the washing and cleansing of the soul through the means of obedience of the will, in captiving of his reason and understanding into the service of faith, by credence and assent given unto the word of faith — in which, whatsoever Tyndale say, and this preacher too, man having age and use of reason may be a willing worker with God; or else whereto should any man advise and bid another come unto the true faith?—so may God use the other token, of the water, as an instrument also to the same purpose, by the like means of obedience on the man's part, in submitting himself to that ablution for the fulfilling of God's commandment and ordinance.

Howbeit,[281] what I further answer Tyndale to these words of Saint James, whoso list[282] to see, let him read in my first part of *Tyndale's Confutation*, in the answer unto Tyndale's preface, the number 53, and then set this to it; and he shall see that neither Tyndale there, nor this preacher here, hath by their manner of expounding these words of Saint James won themselves much worship. Howbeit, of truth the thing that goeth nearer to their purpose against all the work of free will, and all endeavor of man toward the attaining of faith, is the authority of Saint Paul that Tyndale bringeth forth; which yet proveth it not. And the reason that he layeth by example of the father and the son—which reason this preacher, though somewhat faintly, since he seeth it will not serve, yet somewhat repeateth here by these words, where he saith,

> And again, if we were begotten by him, then
> could not we give him none occasion to love us,
> for why we came of him and not we of us

—by these words he meaneth the thing that Tyndale allegeth where he saith,

> The will hath none operation at all in the working
> of faith in my soul, no more than the child hath
> in the begetting of his father.

And of truth, Tyndale and this preacher said somewhat, if in the spiritual generation the man that is regendered were evermore as far from all work of will at such time as God goeth about to beget him by faith as is the child at such time as his grandfather goeth about by nature to beget his father.

But now on the other side, if in the generation at the begetting of his father, the son be not yet so much as a child, nor hath no will at all, and at the time of the spiritual regeneration of himself, he that is regendered hap to be more than a child, and have the freedom of his own will, and hath the choice thereby put in his own hand whether he will, at God's calling to faith—by reading, preaching, miracle, and such other occasions, with good inward motions added also thereto—follow the Spirit, and walk and work with God by captiving of his own understanding and subduing of his own reason into the assent and belief of the things that he shall be moved unto, and by calling upon the continuance of God's gracious help thereunto, and thereby come into the service of faith, or whether he will else reject God's good and gracious motion and resist it, and so flee from the getting of the gift of faith—if the man, I say, be at the time of his spiritual begetting in this case, as every man that hath, at the time, age and use of reason is, then is this example that Tyndale doth there put, and that this preacher doth here repeat, of the child at the carnal birth of his father, much less like the man at the spiritual birth of himself than is an apple like unto an oyster.

Howbeit, good readers, because the brethren blame my books for the length, I will make no longer argument of this matter here, for in these few words it appeareth meetly[283] well.

But if any man think himself with this not yet fully satisfied, then hath he need for his contentation[284] to see the matter handled somewhat more at length. And whoso therefore listeth[285] so to do, let him read in my fourth book of *Tyndale's Confutation* (which is in the first book of the second part), in the chapter of "The Manner and Order of Our Election," beginning, if he list, in the leaf that is marked with the number of 112, and then will his own reason serve him to see how far the matter goeth; which if he read out, I dare boldly promise that he shall there find such things as, against Tyndale and this preacher both, shall as for this point in all reason be sufficient to satisfy him.

But now if this preacher will peradventure[286] say that of his words in both these matters I have misrehearsed[287] him, I am ready to bring forth my copy and the man of whom I had it too. Or else I shall make him a much fairer offer: because he may peradventure say that he never wrote that sermon himself, but that some of his audience, which of[288] devotion wrote as much as they bore away upon the hearing, did write it diminute[289] and mangled for lack of good remembrance, let him upon this answer of mine seen (if it happen to come into his hands) write his own words himself, not only as well as he then suddenly spoke them, but as well also as he can with long leisure make them. And when he hath done in them the best that ever he can, and take whose help he will too, if he make it so as he may therewith avoid and refel[290] my confuting of Tyndale in those two points that those words of his sermon touch, then dare I be bounden to forswear[291] this land and live in Antwerp and be Tyndale's man.

Howbeit, if in the matter of man's endeavor toward the attaining of faith by walking on with God willingly after that God hath prevented[292] him with his grace by calling on him and giving him occasion to come forward, if any brother think to escape and avoid my proof in the place aforeremembered,[293] by the distinction that Tyndale hath learned of Philip Schwarzerdt[294] and bringeth forth against me, of historical faith and feeling faith (which distinction diverse of the brethren and sistren have in their mouths now, and therewith suddenly cast a mist before unlearned men's eyes, and make them a-dazed, for the time, that[295] never heard of it before), he that would wind[296] away with this distinction shall nothing avoid my confuting of Tyndale in that place. For if his distinction be true, yet upon God's gracious prevention[297] and first calling upon, I say, and there prove, that the willing endeavor of man in following helpeth to the attaining of every manner kind of faith, and procureth the progress and increase of grace to the perfecting of that virtue in man and with man, which God first began in man by God's own prevention without man—but in them that have age and discretion,[298] useth not to[299] finish and fulfill it without man, but when man refuseth, except[300] he mend and turn; else[301] God leaveth finally his own good-begun work unfinished. And therefore saith Saint Augustine to every man that hath use of reason: "He that hath created thee without thee, doth not justify thee without thee."

And yet for further conclusion, because I hear say that the same distinction of historical faith and feeling faith glittereth now so gaily in the brethren's eyes, let them read my *Confutation* through. Or because they call that too long, let them read but the seventh book, which is entitled "The Defense of the Second Reason against Tyndale." Or if they think that book alone too long, let them leave a great part of the book, and begin in that leaf and that side of the leaf that is marked with the number of 340. And then if they can for heart-burning abide and endure to read it up to the end, I dare be bold to warrant that they shall find the same gay golden distinction of historical faith and feeling faith founden first by Philipp Schwarzerdt—which, like as Friar Hussgen hath named himself Oecolampadius, hath made his name now Melanchthon. This distinction, I say, so made by Melanchthon, shall they see so brought in there by Tyndale, and so set forth and furnished by the learning and labor of them both, that it cometh to such pass in conclusion that no part of all Tyndale's tale is brought to more shameful confusion.

But now the brethren will (when any good Catholic man provoketh them to read the place in my book) answer as diverse of them have done ere this to such good Catholic folk as provoked them thereto and offered to read it with them, and thereupon to try between them whether Tyndale or I had better reason on our part: the brethren have upon this offer shrunken at last therefrom, after great crakes[302] made of Tyndale's part, with great contempt of mine answer before, and have answered that they will not misspend their time in reading of mine answer, they see Tyndale's tale so sure.

Now of truth this had been a good answer and a reasonable if when they were fast[303] in the true Catholic faith they would thus have answered any such as would have advised them to read in Tyndale, and search whether the faith of all the holy saints and of all the whole corps of Christendom this fifteen hundred years together were true or false. For that were a thing whereof it were a very frenzy to doubt.

But now they that are fled from the faith of all them of whose faith there was no cause to doubt, and are fallen to the faith of a few faithless folk—false apostates, wild wedded monks and friars, and their fond[304] disciples—if they make themselves so sure of their devilish doctrine that they refuse to read the things that are written for the confutation of their errors, every good Catholic man that so

---

290 *avoid and refel:* refute and disprove
291 renounce, abandon   **292** *prevented him:* come to him first   **293** aforementioned   **294** better known as Melancthon

(1497–1560)   **295** who   **296** escape
297 coming (to someone) beforehand
298 use of reason   **299** *useth not to:* (God) does not usually   **300** unless

301 otherwise   **302** crowings; boasts, brags   **303** steadfast   **304** foolish

seeth them do may with good reason tell them that they do not cleave to these foolish heretics for anything that they think them to say truth, but because they would fain[305] it were truth whether it be or no, and that they show their frowardness[306] therein very plainly while their hearts abhor and cannot abide to read any book by which their own conscience giveth them that they shall find their opinions plainly proved false, and their arch-heretics plainly proved fools. For if they hoped the contrary, they would, I warrant you, be themselves the first that would call others thereto.

And thus much for this time sufficeth for this point.

THE NINTH CHAPTER

Now come I to them that say I handle Tyndale and Frith and Barnes ungoodly and with uncomely[307] words, calling them by the name of heretics and fools, and so use[308] them in words as though the men had neither wit nor learning, whereas it cannot be denied, they say, that they be such as every man knoweth well have both.

As for wit and learning, I nowhere say that any of them have none, nor I mean no further but for the matters of their heresies. And in the treating of those, they show so little wit, or learning either, that the more they have, the more appeareth the feebleness of their part and the falsehood of their heresies, if they have any great wit or any great learning indeed, and then, for all that, in the defending of those matters with such foolish handling so shamefully confound themselves.

Howbeit, of very truth, God, upon such folk as, having wit and learning, fall willfully from faith to false heresy, showeth his wrath and indignation with a more vengeance in some part than, as some doctors[309] say, he doth upon the devil himself.

For, as diverse doctors hold opinion, the fiends be fallen from grace, and therefore have lost their glory, yet God hath suffered[310] them to keep their gifts of nature still, as wit, beauty, strength, agility, and such other like.

And Father Alphonse, the Spanish friar, told me that the devils be no such deformed evil-favored creatures as men imagine them, but they be in mind proud, envious, and cruel. And he bade[311] me that if I would see a very right[312] image of a fiend, I should no more but even[313] look upon a very fair woman that hath a very shrewd fell[314] cursed mind. And when I showed him that I never saw none such, nor wist[315] not where I might any such find, he said he could find four or five, but I cannot believe him. Nor verily,[316] no more can I believe that the fiends be like fair shrewd women if there were any such. Nor as the world is, it were not good that young men should ween[317] so. For they be so full of courage that, were the fiends never so cursed, if they thought them like fair women, they would never fear to adventure[318] upon them once. Nor, to say the truth, no more can I believe, neither, that the damned spirits have all their natural gifts as whole and as perfect as they had before their fall.

But surely, if they have, then, as I said before, God hath on Tyndale, Barnes, and Frith, and those other heretics, more showed his vengeance, in some part, than he did upon the devil. For in good faith, God hath, as it seemeth, from these folk taken away the best part of their wits.

For likewise as they that would have builded up the Tower of Babylon[319] for themselves against God had such a stop thrown upon them that suddenly none understood what another said, surely so God upon these heretics of our time, that go busily about to heap up to the sky their foul filthy dunghill of all old and new false stinking heresies, gathered up together against the true Catholic faith of Christ that himself hath ever hitherto taught his true Catholic Church—God, I say, which,[320] when the apostles went about to preach the true faith, sent down his own Holy Spirit of unity, concord, and truth unto them, with the gift of speech and understanding, so that they understood every man and every man understood them,[321] hath reared up and sent among these heretics the spirit of error and lying, of discord and of division, the damned devil of hell, which so entangleth their tongues and so distempereth their brains that they neither understand well one of them another, nor any of them well himself.

305 wish   306 perversity   307 unbecoming, unseemly   308 treat; act toward   309 theologians   310 allowed   311 told   312 accurate   313 just   314 *shrewd fell:* wicked cruel   315 knew   316 truly   317 think   318 take a chance   319 Babel, Gn 11:1–9   320 who   321 Acts 2:1–12

And this that I here say, whoso list[322] to read my books shall find it so true and so plainly proved in many places that he shall well see and say that this is the thing which in my writing grieveth this blessed brotherhood a little more than the length.

And therefore, where they find the fault that I handle these folk so foul, how could I other do? For while I declare and show their writing to be such (as I needs must, or leave the most necessary points of all the matter untouched), it were very hard for me to handle it in such wise as when I plainly prove them abominable heretics, and against God and his sacraments and saints very blasphemous fools, they should ween that I speak them fair.

But then they say that the Pacifier, which writeth of the division[323] between the spiritualty[324] and the temporalty,[325] calleth no man by no such names, but speak he never so evil of any, he can yet use his words in fair manner, and speak to each man genteelly.

I cannot say nay but[326] it is very truth. Howbeit, every man hath not like wit[327] nor like invention in writing. For he findeth many proper[328] ways of uttering evil matter in good words, which I never thought upon, but am a simple plain body much like the Macedonians for whom Plutarch writeth that King Philip, their master, made a reasonable excuse. For when they were in the war, some of their enemies fled from their own king and came into King Philip's service against their own country; with whom, when the Macedonians fell sometimes at words (as it often happeth among soldiers), the Macedonians in spite would call them traitors. Whereupon they complained to King Philip, and made the matter sore and grievous that whereas they had not only left their own native country, but did also fight against it and help to destroy it, for the love and service that they bore toward him, his own people letted[329] not in anger and in despite[330] to call them false traitors. Whereupon King Philip answered them, "Good fellows, I pray you be not angry with my people, but have patience. I am sorry that their manner is no better. But iwis,[331] ye know them well enough: their nature is so plain, and their utterance so rude, that they cannot call a horse but a horse, they."[332] And in good faith, like those good folk am I. For though Tyndale and Frith in their writing call me a poet, it is but of their own courtesy, undeserved on my part. For I can neither so much poetry, nor so much rhetoric neither, as to find good names for evil things; but even as the Macedonians could not call a traitor but a traitor, so can I not call a fool but a fool, nor a heretic but a heretic. Some of the brethren said that I should at the leastwise call Friar Barnes by the name of "Doctor," because he was authorized and made a doctor of divinity by the university. But one answered for me to that, and said that name was given to serve for the time in which he was meet[333] to teach, and not now, when he is not meet to teach, but is by the Church for false teaching forbidden to teach. But then, unto that, one of them answered again and asked, "Why should I then call him 'Friar' still while he is now no longer a friar no more than a doctor?"

But unto this I could between them tell some reason of difference. Howbeit, rather than to make this book overlong by holding a problem upon every trifle, I shall be content, like[334] as instead of "Doctor" men call him heretic, so instead of "Friar" to call him the other name that every man calleth all those that be run out of religion. Lo, there have I fallen on a fair figure unware[335] (that is, I trow,[336] called periphrasis), to avoid the foul name of apostate.

But now these good brethren that find the fault with me that I speak no fairer unto these holy prophets of theirs be so equal and indifferent[337] that in them they find no fault at all for their abominable railing against so many other honest, honorable, good, and virtuous folk, nor for condemning for damned heretics the whole Catholic Church of all Christian people except heretics, both spiritual and temporal,[338] secular and religious too.

But then the good brethren excuse them and say that they write against none but only them that are naught,[339] and write but against their vices.

But this will evil[340] defend them, when Barnes writeth against the whole clergy, and Tyndale saith expressly that of them all there is never one good.

And also they write not so much against pomp and pride and gluttony as against watching[341] and praying, fasting and willful[342] poverty; and all these things in good religious people[343] the heretics abhor, and call it but hypocrisy.

---

322 *whoso list:* whoever wishes   323 dissension   324 clergy   325 laity   326 *say nay but:* deny   327 intellect   328 clever, artful   329 refrained   330 contempt

331 indeed   332 *Macedonians...they:* See Plutarch, *Moralia* 178b.   333 fit   334 just   335 unawares   336 believe   337 impartial   338 *spiritual and temporal:*

of the clergy and of the laity   339 bad, immoral   340 ill; badly   341 keeping vigil   342 voluntary   343 *religious people:* monks and nuns

Then rail[344] they not so sore[345] in words against the lay people, but as fair as they flatter them to make them enemies to the clergy, yet they damn them all to the devil—both themselves and their fathers, and their grandfathers, and their grandfathers' great-grandfathers too. For they say that this eight hundred years all the corps of Christendom hath been led out of the right way from God, and have lived all in idolatry, and died in service of the devil because they have done honor to Christ's cross, and prayed unto saints and reverenced their relics and honored their images, and been baptized in Latin, and taken matrimony for a sacrament, and used confession, and done penance for sins, and prayed for all Christian souls, and been aneled[346] in their deathbed, and have taken their housel[347] after the rite and usage of the Church, and have set more by[348] the Mass than they should do, and believed that it was a sacrifice, a Host,[349] and an oblation, and that it should do them good, and have believed that there was neither bread nor wine in the Blessed Sacrament of the altar, but instead of bread and wine, the very Body and Blood of Christ. All these things, say Tyndale and Barnes, both be very false belief and great, damnable sin in the doing; and so damn they to the devil the whole Catholic Church both temporal and spiritual, and (except heretics) leave not one man for God's party this eight hundred years past, by their own limitation; and of truth, if their false heresies were true, not in the other seven hundred before that neither.

Now when that against all the whole Catholic Church (both that now is and that ever before hath been from the apostles' days hitherto, both temporal and spiritual, laymen and religious), and against all that good is (saints, ceremonies, service of God, the very sacraments and all), and most against the best (that is to wit,[350] the precious Body and Blood of our Savior himself in the Holy Sacrament of the altar), these blasphemous heretics in their ungracious[351] books so villainously jest and rail, were not a man, ween[352] you, very far overseen[353] and worthy to be counted uncourteous that would, in writing against their heresies, presume without great reverence to rehearse their worshipful[354] names?

If any of them use their words at their pleasure, as evil and as villainous as they list[355] against myself, I am content to forbear any requiting thereof, and give them no worse words again[356] than if they speak me fair; nor, using[357] themselves toward all other folk as they do, fairer words will I not give them than if they spoke me foul. For all shall be one to me; or rather, the worse, the better. For the pleasant oil of heretics cast upon my head can do my mind no pleasure; but contrariwise, the worse that such folk write of me for hatred that they bear to the Catholic Church and faith, the greater pleasure (as for mine own part) they do me. But surely their railing against all others I purpose not to bear so patiently as to forbear to let them hear some part of like language as they speak. Howbeit,[358] utterly to match them therein I neither can though I would, nor will neither though I could, but am content (as I needs must) to give them therein the mastery, wherein to match them were more rebuke than honesty.

Now, if they excuse themselves and say they speak evil but of evil things (for so call they good works of penance, and so call they the ceremonies and sacraments of Christ's Church), I answer them plainly that they lie; wherein every true Christian man will testify that I say truth, for those things be good and holy which they rebuke and call naught.[359] And I say further, also, that by that excuse of theirs they make mine excuse too, in the thing wherewith they be worst content: that is to wit, where I somewhat sharply rebuke wedding of friars and nuns; which thing is, as all the world wotteth,[360] beastly and abominable indeed.

And also if they will excuse themselves and say that, as touching men, they rail against none but such as be lewd[361] and naught, to this I answer, first, that in this thing they lie. For they rail against all. And some they call naught by name whose special goodness shall have record and witness of all good folk that know them. Secondly, I say further that by this excuse of theirs they must needs excuse me too, when I rebuke themselves. For they be well and openly known and convicted for heretics, which is, ye wot well, the worst crime that can be—and that, for heretics of such a manner sort as is the worst kind of that crime that ever came out of Christendom.

---

344 abuse   **345** grievously; greatly
346 anointed   **347** Holy Communion; Eucharist   **348** *set more by:* more

highly valued   **349** victim   **350** say
351 wicked   **352** suppose   **353** out of line
354 illustrious   **355** wish   **356** in return

357 behaving   **358** However   **359** evil
360 knows   **361** wicked

Howbeit, I am yet content, for all this, to fall at[362] some reasonable composition[363] with them. Let us take this way between us from hence forth, if they list: Like[364] as I do not allow,[365] but abhor, incontinence in sacred professed persons that have vowed chastity, so let them confess that themselves abhor also the beastly bitcherly[366] marriages of monks, friars, and nuns, and of all such as have unto God promised and vowed the contrary. And then since all our matter is only of the faith, let them forbear, instead of reasoning, to fall to railing upon other men's living. For thereby fleeing from the matter of faith, they furnish out their process[367] with lying, while the faults of some they lewdly lay[368] to all.

If they will not (which were the best) revoke their false heresies, nor will not (which were the next) be heretics alone themselves, and hold their tongues and be still, but will needs be babbling and corrupt whom they can, let them yet at the leastwise be reasonable heretics and honest, and write reason and leave railing; and then let the brethren find the fault with me if I use[369] them not after that in words as fair and as mild as the matter may suffer[370] and bear.

But this way will they never take, I ween. For then they see well that their disciples will never have half the lust to look upon their books, wherein they should then find but a poor feast and an evil-dressed[371] dinner. For in their only railing standeth all their revel;[372] with only railing is all their roast meat basted, and all their pot seasoned, and all their pie meat spiced, and all their manchets,[373] and all their wafers, and all their hippocras[374] made.

THE TENTH CHAPTER

Now, passing over this point, I come to this that these good brethren say: that they list[375] not to read my books, for I am suspect in these matters, and partial toward the spiritualty.

As for suspect, if I be now suspect, the world waxeth[376] all of a new kind. For men were wont to call those folk suspect that were suspect of heresy. And this is now a new kind of suspects, if men be now

"suspected" of the Catholic faith. Howbeit, in that suspicion am I glad to be fallen, and purpose never to purge it.

Now as touching partiality upon my part toward the spiritualty, I marvel whereof they gather it. Myself am, pardie,[377] a temporal man, and by twice wedding am come in the case[378] that I can never be priest. And as for all the lands and fees[379] that I have in all England, besides such lands and fees as I have of the gift of the King's most noble Grace, is not at this day, nor shall be while my mother-in-law[380] liveth (whose life and good health I pray God long keep and continue), worth yearly to my living the sum of full fifty pounds. And thereof have I some by my wife, and some by my father (whose soul our Lord assoil[381]), and some have I also purchased myself; and some fees have I of some temporal men. And then may every man well guess that I have no very great part of my living by the clergy, to make me very partial to them.

And over[382] that, this shall I truly say: that of all the yearly living that I have of the King's gracious gift, I have not one groat[383] by the means of any spiritual man, to my knowledge, but, far above my deserving, have had it only by his own singular bounty and goodness and special favor toward me.

And verily,[384] of any such yearly fees as I have to my living at this day of any other,[385] I have not had one groat granted me since I first wrote, or went about to write, my *Dialogue*; and that was, ye wot[386] well, the first work that I wrote in these matters.

But then say the brethren (as their holy father writeth, and telleth also diverse whom he talketh with) that I have taken great rewards in ready money of diverse of the clergy for making of my books.

In good faith, I will not say nay but that[387] some good and honorable men of them would, in reward of my good will and my labor against these heretics, have given me much more than ever I did, or could, deserve. But I dare take God and them also to record[388] that all they could never feoff me with[389] one penny thereof, but (as I plainly told them) I would rather have cast their money into the Thames than take it. For albeit they were, as indeed they were,

---

362 *fall at:* come to **363** agreement prepared **372** entertainment **373** rolls or small loaves made of the finest wheat **374** spiced wine **375** want **376** is becoming **377** certainly; "by God" (from French) **378** position **379** inheritable lands **380** stepmother **381** absolve from sin **382** beyond **383** a coin worth four pence **384** truly **385** *of any other:* from anyone else **386** know **387** *say nay but that:* deny that **388** *to record:* as sworn witnesses **389** *feoff me with:* put me in possession of

364 Just **365** approve of **366** lewd; wanton **367** *furnish out their process:* supply what is lacking in their argument **368** *lewdly lay:* wickedly attribute **369** treat **370** allow **371** badly

both good men and honorable, yet look I for my thanks of God, that is their better, and for whose sake I take the labor, and not for theirs.

And if any of the brethren, believing their holy fathers, think, as some of them say, that I have more advantage of these matters than I make for,[390] and that I set not so little by money as to refuse it when it were offered, I will not much dispute with them longer upon the matter. But let them believe as they list,[391] yet this will I be bold to say for myself, although they should call me Pharisee for the boast and Pelagian[392] for my labor too: that how bad soever they reckon me, I am not yet fully so virtuous but that of mine own natural disposition, without any special peculiar[393] help of grace thereto, I am both overproud and over-slothful also, to be hired for money to take half the labor and business[394] in writing that I have taken in this gear[395] since I began.

And therefore, cause of partial favor to the priests' persons have I none more than hath every good Christian man and woman which[396] is of duty bounden to give honor and reverence unto that holy sacrament of Order with which the clergy is specially consecrated and dedicated unto God.

But whereas the brethren say that I am not indifferent[397] in the matter, therein do they the thing that they seldom do: that is to wit,[398] say the truth. For if they call the matter either the vice or virtue of the persons — which I take not for the matter — yet therein am I not indifferent indeed between a temporal man and a spiritual. For as for vice, I hold it much more damnable in a spiritual person than in a temporal man. And as for virtue, equal virtue, I hold it yet much more if it happen in the temporal man than in the spiritual, because, though the thing be equal, they be not both equally bound thereto. And therefore if they take this for the matter, in this wise[399] I am not indifferent.

Now if they take for the matter the thing that I take for the matter — that is to wit, the true faith and false heresies — then am I much less indifferent. For God keep me from being indifferent between those two sorts. For every good man is bounden between truth and falsehood, the Catholic Church

and heretics, between God and the devil, to be partial, and plainly to declare himself to be full and whole upon the one side and clear against the other.

But else as for any partial favor that I bear to the clergy, whereby do these brethren prove it? I never said that they were all faultless, nor I never excused their faults. And if ever I did, let them rehearse of[400] my writing some one place at the least; let them tell where I commend pomp and pride, where I praise avarice, where lechery, or such other thing.

Those that be spiritual persons by profession, and are therewith carnal and wretched in their condition, have never been favored by me.

When I was first of the King's Council, and after, his Undertreasurer, and in that time while I was Chancellor of his Duchy of Lancaster, and when I was his Chancellor of this realm, it was meetly[401] well known what manner of favor I bore toward the clergy, and that as I loved and honored the good, so was not remiss nor slack in providing for the correction of those that were naught, noyous[402] to good people, and slanderous to their own order. Which sort of priests and religious, running out of religion[403] and falling to theft and murder, had at my hand so little favor that there was no man that any meddling had with them into whose hands they were more loath to come.

And in this point found I their ordinaries[404] so well minded to their amendment and correction that they gave me great thanks therefor.

And I found those priests rather content to remain in the King's prisons a month than in the Bishop's a week, saving for hope of deliverance by the common course of their purgation.

And yet as far as my poor wit could give me, saving that the danger of escapes is to the ordinary so chargeable that the fear thereof maketh them fain[405] of their deliverance, else were they likely to be waxen[406] better ere they got thence,[407] or else to tarry there as long as ever they lived.

But I perceive well that these good brethren look that I should rebuke the clergy, and seek out their faults, and lay them to their faces, and write some work to their shame, or else they cannot call me but partial to the priests. Howbeit, by this reason they

---

390 *make for:* pretend   391 want   396 who   397 impartial   398 say   usually bishops   405 desirous   406 *be*
392 one who believes salvation can come   399 way   400 *rehearse of:* quote from   *waxen:* become   407 out of there
through works alone, without grace   401 quite   402 troublesome   403 i.e., a
393 particular   394 trouble   395 stuff   religious order   404 ecclesiastical judges,

may call me partial to the laymen too. For I never used that way neither toward the one nor the other. I find not yet such plenty and store of virtue in myself as to think it a meetly[408] part and convenient[409] for me to play, to rebuke as abominable vicious folk, any one honest company either spiritual or temporal, and much less meet to rebuke and reproach either the whole spiritualty or temporalty because of such as are very stark naught[410] in both.

I dare be bold to say that proud folk be naught, that covetous folk be naught, that lecherous folk be naught, and to speak against open-known thieves, open-known murderers, open-known perjured persons, open-known apostates, open-known professed or convicted heretics. But surely my guise[411] is not to lay the faults of the naughty to the charge of any whole company, and rail upon merchants and call them usurers, nor to rail upon franklins[412] and call them false jurors,[413] nor to rail upon sheriffs and call them raveners,[414] nor to rail upon escheators[415] and call them extortioners, nor upon all officers and call them bribers, nor upon gentlemen and call them oppressors, nor so forth up higher, to call every degree[416] by such odious names as men might find some of that sort.

And of all degrees, specially for my part I have ever accounted my duty to forbear all such manner of unmannerly behavior toward those two most eminent orders that God hath here ordained in earth: the two great orders, I mean, of special consecrated persons—the sacred princes and priests. Against any of which two reverent orders, whoso be so lewd[417] unreverently to speak, and malapertly[418] to jest and rail, shall play that part alone for me.[419] And rather will I that these brethren call me partial than for such ill fashion indifferent.

And over[420] this, I cannot see what need there were that I should rail upon the clergy and reckon up all their faults. For that part hath Tyndale played and Friar Barnes both already, and left nothing for me to say therein, not though my mind were sore[421] set thereon.

They have with truth and lies together laid[422] the living[423] of bad to bad and good both, in such a vile villainous fashion that it would make a good stomach to vomit to hear their ribaldous railing. And yet not against the sacred persons only, but against the blessed sacraments also.

And now would their disciples that I should not speak against their execrable heresies and their despiteful[424] dealing but if[425] I should by the way[426] do as they do, and help them forth in the same.

And herein fare[427] they much like as if there were a sort of villain[428] wretched heretics that—meeting the priests and clerics (religious[429] and other) going with banners, copes, crosses, and censers,[430] and the Sacrament[431] borne about with them upon a Corpus Christi[432] Day—would pick quarrels to them, and first call them all that could come in their villain mouths, and haply say true by[433] some, and then catch them all by the heads and throw them in the mire, surplices, copes, censers, crosses, relics, Sacrament, and all. And then if any man rebuked their villainous dealing, and would step unto the priests, and pull them up, and help to wipe the copes, and reverently take up the crosses, the relics, and the Blessed Sacrament, were it not now well and wisely spoken if one would reprove him that thus did, and say he should not meddle himself in the matter, hot nor cold, but if[434] he would be indifferent and do somewhat[435] on the both sides, and therefore he should, to show himself indifferent, either revile and rebuke the priests (or at the leastwise some of them), and souse them somewhat in the mire for the pleasure of them that so served them, or else go by about his other business and let the matter alone, and neither take up good man out of the mire, nor surplice, cope, nor censer, nor relic, but let them lay the Sacrament in the dirt again: were not this a goodly way? Surely, for my part, I am not so ambitious of such folk's praise as to be called indifferent, nor will, in writing against their heresies, help them forth in their railing.

---

408 fitting **409** appropriate **410** *stark naught:* boldly bad **411** way; approach **412** landowners of free but not noble birth **413** *false jurors:* perjurers **414** plunderers **415** tax collectors **416** social class **417** wicked (as)

418 impudently **419** *for me:* as far as I am concerned **420** beyond **421** strongly **422** attributed; imputed **423** manner of life **424** contemptuous **425** *but if:* unless **426** *by the way:* in the process **427** behave **428** *sort of villain:* group

of wicked **429** members of religious orders **430** incense burners **431** i.e., Holy Communion **432** *Corpus Christi:* the feast of the Body of Christ **433** about **434** *but if:* unless **435** something

THE ELEVENTH CHAPTER

But now, whereas the brethren lay a blame in me that I had not used such a goodly mild manner, and such an indifferent fashion, as they find used by him that made the book of *The Division between the Spiritualty and the Temporalty*, I am not greatly blameworthy therein. For his book was put out since; and therefore could I, when I wrote, take none example thereof; and every man is not like[436] inventive of his own wit. For surely he hath founden some certain proper invented figures[437] in that book in which I am so far from finding the like of myself that, being, as they now be, founden to mine hand already, hard were it for me in the like matter to follow them.

And yet though my books be very far under his, they may be, for all that, ye wot well, meetly[438] good, if his be so far excellent as the brethren boast it. In which book yet, as much as they boast it, he declareth and expressly testifieth, like a true Christian man (howsoever the matters go between the temporalty and the spiritualty), that yet their opinions are heresies.

But they take, as it seemeth, all those words of his well in worth, because they reckon themselves recompensed in another part, in that they falsely persuade unto themselves either that he dissimuleth[439] for the while and believeth as they do, or else that, believe he never so well himself, yet, either of pity or some other affection, he could be content to help that they should themselves with their evil belief be let alone and live in rest, and be suffered[440] to believe as they list.[441]

But I trust in God that in that point they lean too much to the letter of his words and, of their own favor to themselves, misconstrue the good man's mind. For God forbid that any Christian man should mean so.

Howbeit, as touching the matter wherewith we be now in hand[442] — that is to wit, the manner of mild and indifferent writing by me or by him concerning the spiritualty and the temporalty — therein am I very sure that his mild indifferent book of the *Division* neither is more mild nor more indifferent than any book of mine.

For first, as for mine own part, look my *Dialogue*, my *Supplication of Souls*, and both the parts of the *Confutation*, and ye shall clearly see that I neither have used toward the clergy nor toward the temporalty any warm[443] displeasant word, but have forborne to touch in special[444] either the faults of the one or of the other. But yet have I confessed the thing that truth is: neither party to be faultless. But then which is the thing that offendeth these blessed brethren, I have not letted[445] furthermore to say the thing which I take also for very true: that as this realm of England hath had hitherto, God be thanked, as good and as laudable a temporalty, number for number, as hath had any other Christian region of the quantity,[446] so hath it had also, number for number, compared with any realm christened[447] of no greater quantity, as good and as commendable a clergy, though there have never lacked, in any of both the parties, plenty of such as have always been naught, whose faults have ever been their own, and not to be imputed to the whole body neither of spiritualty nor temporalty, saving that there have been peradventure[448] on either part, in some such as by their offices ought to look thereto, some lack of the labor and diligence that in the reforming of it should have belonged unto them; which I declare always that I would wish amended, and every man specially labor to mend himself, and rather accustom himself to look upon his own faults than upon other men's, and against such as are in either sort founden open[449] evil, and naught, and noyous[450] unto the commonweal — as thieves, murderers, and heretics, and such other wretches — the whole corps of the spiritualty and temporalty both, each with other lovingly to accord and agree and, according to the good ancient laws and commendable usages[451] long continued in this noble realm, either party endeavor themselves diligently to repress and keep under those evil and ungracious folk that, like sores, scabs, and cankers, trouble and vex the body, and of all them to cure such as may be cured and, for health of the whole body, cut and cast off the incurable cankered parts therefrom, observed in the doing evermore such order and fashion as may stand and agree with reason and justice, the King's laws

436 similarly   437 i.e., figures of speech   442 *in hand:* dealing   443 heated; angry   448 perhaps   449 publicly   450 harmful
438 fairly; somewhat   439 disguises;   444 *touch in special:* discuss in particular   451 customs
falsifies   440 allowed   441 wish   445 hesitated   446 size   447 baptized

of the realm, the Scripture of God, and the laws of Christ's Church, ever keeping love and concord between the two principal parties, the spiritualty and temporalty, lest the dregs of both sorts conspiring together and increasing, may little and little grow too strong for both; whereto they might have a fair[452] gap and a broad gate to enter if they might find the means by craft to sever and set asunder the temporalty against the clergy to strive, and so let, as it were, the soul and the body brabble[453] and strive together, and while they study nothing else but the one to grieve[454] the other, the naughty then conspire and agree together, and set upon the good people of both.

This hath been hitherto the whole sum of my writing, without any displeasant word used either toward temporalty or spiritualty. And more mild manner than this toward all good folk hath not this other book, of *Division*, nor yet a more indifferent, as far as I can see, but if[455] he be reckoned more mild because he setteth his words much more mild and cold when he speaketh aught[456] of heretics and showeth himself therein more temperate and thereby more discreet than I, and but if he be reckoned for more indifferent because his words in rehearsing the faults of the spiritualty be not in the worst things partially[457] pointed toward such as be naught, but indifferently directed and pointed toward the whole body.

THE TWELFTH CHAPTER

Howbeit, as touching the manner of his handling, to tell you the very truth, it seemeth to me somewhat strange for one that would go about the purpose that he pretendeth:[458] that is to wit, to pacify and appease two parties being at so sore[459] a dissension and "division," as he saith, that the temporalty is in grudge against the spiritualty, not here and there but everywhere noted—as he saith, "in a manner universally"[460]—through this whole realm. Howbeit, I trust in God very far from so. And yet not fully so far but that it may by misfortune, for abundance of sin and lack of grace, in time grow and come to it.

For truth it is that murmur and dissension (God knoweth how it began) against the clergy is a great way gone onward in his[461] unhappy journey, and may by such manner and means of pacifying within short process[462] be conveyed round about the realm, and leave no place in peace. Not that I would think the man that made that book to be of such malicious mind as willingly to sow dissension, but that, as meseemeth, he taketh at the leastwise unware a wrong way toward the contrary, and that the manner of his handling is far from such indifference as he should use that would make a loveday[463] and appease any murmur and grudge of the lay people against the priests.

For he showeth, in the progress of all his process,[464] that the grudge is borne by the temporalty, and the causes and occasions thereof grown and given, in effect, all by the spiritualty. Which handling is not, as methinketh, very much indifferent.

I let pass that he which verily[465] would intend to pacify, assuage, and appease a grudge would (as much as he conveniently[466] might) extenuate the causes and occasions of the grudge. But and if[467] he would needs walk plainly forth and take no such byways, he would not yet, at the leastwise, not accumulate and exaggerate the griefs, and, by all the means he might, make the griefs appear many, great, and most odious. Or finally if, for hatred of their faults, no favor of their persons could cause him to forbear that, yet would he forbear at the leastwise to seek up and rehearse causes of grudge before unknown unto the party whose displeasure he would assuage and pacify. But now this appeaser, contrariwise, not only doth in all these things the contrary, but bringeth forth also, besides all this, some such faults more as, if they were true, were of the greatest weight, and telleth them as though they were true, where they be very plain false indeed.

But now the good brethren, that boast it, lay forth for a great token of temperance and good mind toward the spiritualty that he forbeareth to speak anything of the great open faults that many priests be openly taken in, as theft, robbery, sacrilege, and murder, whereof in sundry shires of the realm there are at every sessions openly founden some.

---

452 unobstructed   **453** quarrel; squabble   **454** harm   **455** *but if:* unless   **456** anything   **457** with bias; particularly   **458** claims to have   **459** great; intense   **460** *CW* 9: 179/35   **461** its   **462** length of time   **463** agreement to reconcile   **464** discourse   **465** truly   **466** appropriately   **467** *and if:* if

And yet the most part of such faults as he speaketh of, he saith them not as of himself, nor affirmeth them not for true, nor as things neither spoken by the mouths of very many, but to mitigate the matter with, he saith no more but that "thus by[468] the clergy some say," and some find this fault with them, and some find that, and though that many small sums make a great, what can he do thereto?[469] Can he let[470] men to speak? Or is he bound to stop his ears and hear them not? Or may he not tell what he heareth some others say?

And yet say they further that he telleth indifferently[471] the faults as well of the temporalty as of the spiritualty, and would there should[472] not be between the temporalty and the spiritualty[473] so much as any one angry word. And therefore they say that it cannot be possible that he wrote of any evil intent, since no man can use himself neither more mildly, nor with more indifference, nor finally with more tender charity.

But now to these excuses, some other men answer again[474] that the leaving out of felony, sacrilege, and murder is rather a token of wiliness than any forbearing or favor. For since he saw well that every wise man would answer in himself that those great, horrible, open evils of such desperate naughty wretches were not to be laid[475] against the clergy (as the like in temporal wretches are not to be laid against the temporalty), he would therefore rather seek out and heap up a sort of those things that might, by his manner of handling, sound in the readers' ears to be such as the temporalty might ascribe and impute unto (and therefore bear a grudge unto) the main multitude of the whole clergy, and extend in substance unto every part.

And as touching that he saith not the things as of himself, but bringeth them in with a figure of "some say," to that point some others say that for that courtesy no man hath any cause to can[476] him any thanks. For under his fair figure of "some say," he may, ye wot well—and some say that he so doth—devise to bring in all the mischief that any man can say. And yet over this, without his masker of "some say," he saith open-faced some of the worst himself, and that in some things that are, as some true men say, not true.

Then as touching his indifferency in telling the faults of the temporalty too, of truth, among a great heap of shrewd[477] faults rehearsed against the clergy, for which the temporalty might, if the things were all true, seem to have great cause of grudge, he rehearseth also some faults of the temporalty too, as that they be to blame because they use the priests over-familiarly, and give them overly gay gowns or light-colored liveries,[478] and one or two such things more as, though they might be mended, yet were of no such kind as the priests that so be dealt withal have been wont to find any cause of great grudge.[479]

Howbeit, yet in one place, to show his farther indifference, he layeth against them both that the priests against lay people, and lay people against priests, have used to have evil language, and either against other to speak unsitting[480] words. And thereupon he showeth his tender charity, and saith, "If all these words were prohibited on both sides upon great pains, I think it would do great good in this behalf."

THE THIRTEENTH CHAPTER

But now, good readers, if that it so were that one found two men standing together, and would come step in between them, and bear them in hand[481] they were about to fight, and would, with that word, put the one prettily[482] back with his hand, and all-to[483] buffet the other about the face, and then go forth and say that he had parted a fray[484] and pacified the parties, some men would say again[485] (as I suppose) that he had as lief[486] his enemy were let alone with him, and thereof abide the adventure,[487] as have such a friend step in between to part them.

Howbeit, if this Pacifier of this *Division* will say that this is nothing like the present matter because he striketh neither party, but only telleth the one the other's faults, or else (as he will say) telleth them their faults both, if it so happeth, good readers, he found a man that were angry with his wife (and haply[488] not all without cause), if this maker of the book of *Division* would take upon him to go and reconcile them again together, and help to make them at one, and therein would use this way—that

468 about 469 about it 470 prevent 471 impartially 472 *would there should:* wants there to 473 *temporalty… spiritualty:* laity and the clergy 474 back 475 alleged 476 give 477 vile; wicked 478 garments; distinctive dress 479 resentment 480 unfitting; inappropriate 481 *bear them in hand:* lead them to believe 482 gently 483 soundly 484 *parted a fray:* put an end to the fight 485 in reply 486 gladly 487 *abide the adventure:* take the risk 488 perhaps

when he had them both before him, and before all their neighbors too, then saving for some change to make it meet[489] for their persons, else he would begin holily with the same words, in effect, with which he beginneth his indifferent[490] mild book of *Division*, and for an entry into his matter first would say thus unto them —

Who may remember the state that ye stand in without great heaviness[491] and sorrow of heart? For whereas in times past hath reigned between you charity, meekness, concord, and peace, there reigneth now anger and malice, debate, division, and strife. Which thing, to see so misfortune between any two Christian folk, is a thing much to be lamented, and then much more to be lamented when it mishappeth to fall between a man and his wife. And many good neighbors greatly marvel, iwis,[492] upon what causes this great grudge[493] is grown. And therefore, to the intent that ye may remove the causes and amend these matters, and thereby then by the grace of God agree,[494] I will tell you what I hear men say that the causes be.[495]

And now, after this holy prologue made, go forth and tell them that some folk say the wife hath this evil condition, and some others say that she hath that evil condition, and yet others some say that she hath another evil condition, and so, with twenty diverse "some says" of other men, say there himself by[496] the poor woman all the mischief that any man could devise to say, and among those, some things, peradventure true, which yet her husband had never heard of before. And some things false also, whereof because the Pacifier would be put unto no proof, he would not say them as of himself but bring them forth under the fair figure of "some say." And when he had all said, then yet at the last say thus much of himself:

As for these things here and there I have heard some others say, whether they say true or no, the charge[497] be theirs for me.[498] But yet in good faith, good sister, since ye know that the displeasure and grudge that your husband hath to you is grown upon these causes, I marvel much myself that you do use the same conditions still. Iwis,[499] till you meek[500] yourself and amend them, this anger of your husband will never be well appeased.

Lo, with such words he voideth the color[501] of his fair figure of "some say," either by forgetfulness or else by the plain figure of folly. For when he saith of himself that she keepeth those evil conditions still and amendeth them not, he showeth that all his "some says" be of his own saying, though he might haply in some of them hear some others say so too besides.

But then if among all these faults so mildly rehearsed[502] against her, he would, to show somewhat[503] of his indifference, tell her husband his parseverse[504] too, and say, "But yet, forsooth,[505] your wife hath not given you so many causes of displeasure for nought.[506] For I will be plain with you and indifferent between you both: You have in some things toward her not dealt very well nor like a good husband yourself. For this I know myself: that ye have used to make her too homely[507] with you, and have suffered[508] her to be too much idle, and suffered her to be too much conversant among her gossips, and you have given her overly gay gear and too much money in her purse; and surely, till you amend all this gear for your part, I cannot much marvel though she do you displeasure. And sometimes evil words between you causeth debate on both sides. For you call her (as I hear say) cursed quean[509] and shrew;[510] and some say that she behind your back calleth you knave and cuckold. And iwis,[511] such words were well done to be left[512] on both sides, for surely they do no good. And therefore "if all these words were prohibited on both sides upon great pains, I think it would do great good in this behalf."

"Now get you hence as wise as a calf,"[513] would, I ween, the good wife say to this good ghostly[514] Pacifier. For spoke he never so mildly, and would seem never so indifferent, though he looked therewith right simply, and held up also both his hands holily, and would therewith swear to the woman full deeply that his intent were good, and that he nothing meant but to bring her husband and her at one,

---

489 suitable   490 impartial   491 sadness
492 indeed   493 ill will   494 reconcile
495 See *CW* 9: 177/19–25.   496 about
497 responsibility   498 *for me:* as
far as I'm concerned   499 Certainly

500 humble; subdue   501 *voideth the*
color: nullifies the disguise   502 told
503 something   504 school lesson
505 truly   506 nothing   507 familiar;
casual   508 allowed   509 harlot; hussy

510 an ill-tempered woman   511 indeed
512 avoided; abandoned   513 dolt; idiot
514 spiritual

would she, think you, for all that believe him? I suppose verily nay, nor her husband neither if he were
wise, although he saw some part of his tale true, as
none is so foolish to say all false that would win him
credence. But believe the husband as he list,[515] I durst
be bold to swear for the wife that he should never
make her such a fool as to believe that he meant to
mend the matter, with rehearsing her faults more
than ever her husband had heard of, and some of
them false too, and then color all his tale with his
proper invention[516] of "some say." But she would for
his "some say" shortly say to him, "I pray you, Goodman 'Some Say,' get you shortly hence. For my husband and I shall agree much the sooner if no such
Brother 'Some Say' come within our door."

Now of very truth this Pacifier, as some say, goeth
yet worse to work in his book of *Division* than this
"Some Say" that we put for an example between
the man and his wife. For he gathereth first all the
causes of displeasures that he can find out or devise, and diverse of them such as few lay people
unlearned — yea, and few of the learned too — had
anything heard of before, as are diverse of those
which he gathereth out of Jean Gerson.[517]

If he say that he meant as Gerson did — that he
maketh mention of them because he would have the
clergy mend them — surely whoso, for such good will
telleth a man his faults, useth[518] to tell it him secretly;
and so did Jean Gerson himself when he wrote them
in Latin, and not in the vulgar tongue.[519]

But this Pacifier, contrariwise, because he would
have the lay people, both men and women, look on
them, doth translate them into English, whereas
Jean Gerson would[520] not that a man should reproach and rebuke the prelates before the people.

Also, this Pacifier aggrieveth[521] — as much as in
him lieth — the clergy of England for use of the laws
not made by themselves, but be the common laws
of all Christendom.

If he will say that he blameth but their abuses
thereof,[522] the truth appeareth in some place otherwise in his book. And yet since he proveth that
point but by a "some say," he might with the same
figure lay[523] like faults in the temporalty concerning
the laws of this realm, and prove it in like wise with
a great "some say" too. And therein he showeth

himself not indifferent when he bringeth in the one
and leaveth the other out. And on the other side, if
he bring in the other too, then shall he make two
faults for one. For if he handle them as truly as he
handleth these, then shall he make two lies for one.

And yet besides all the faults that he bringeth in
under "some say" and "they say," some that himself
saith without any "some say" be such as some say
that he can never prove, and some, they say, be plain
and open false.

By all which manner of handling, it appeareth
that if the man mean well himself (as by God's grace
he doth), then hath some other subtle shrew[524] that
is of his counsel[525] deceived him, not only in the
misframing of his matter more toward division
than unity, but also by causing him to plant in here
and there some such word as might make his best
friends to fear that he greatly forced not[526] for the
furtherance of the Catholic faith.

THE FOURTEENTH CHAPTER

But forasmuch as[527] the touching[528] of the book is
here not my principal purpose, I will therefore
not peruse it over and touch every point thereof.
Which if I would, I could (I think), well make men
see that very few parts thereof had either such charity or such indifference therein as not only the new
naughty brotherhood boasteth, but some good folk
also take it at a superficial reading.

And yet because the brethren's boast hath made
it an incident unto my matter, and that some things
therein are such as it is more than necessary that
men be well advised of them, and well foresee what
they do in them, and lest a better opinion of the
book than the matter may bear, if it be pondered
right, may be occasion to move men in some great
things to do no little wrong, and to the intent also
that ye may see that in all that I have said, I belie[529]
him not, I shall, for an example of handling, touch
by the way one or two places[530] of his.

And lest folk should think that I pick out here
and there two or three lines of the worst, I will take
his first chapter whole. In which, though all be not
naught,[531] nor all false (for a very fool were he that

515 wants　**516** *proper invention:* fine
device　**517** Jean Charlier of Gerson
(1363–1429), theologian and Chancellor of
the University of Paris　**518** is accustomed

519 *vulgar tongue:* vernacular　**520** wished
521 makes grievances with　**522** of
the laws　**523** allege　**524** scoundrel
525 *that … counsel:* who gives him advice

526 *greatly forced not:* did not care much
527 *forasmuch as:* seeing that　**528** discussing　**529** misrepresent; misquote
530 passages　**531** bad

would put forth a book and make all naught and all false, even in the very forefront that shall come first to hand), yet if it be considered and advised[532] well, there will, I ween, even in the very first chapter appear less good, and less truth too, than men at a sudden shift,[533] in the first reading over, do thoroughly perceive. Lo, thus it beginneth:

Who may remember the state of this realm now in these days without great heaviness and sorrow of heart? For thereas[534] in times past hath reigned charity, meekness, concord, and peace, reigneth now envy, pride, division, and strife—and that not only between laymen and laymen, but also between religious and religious, and also between priests and religious, and, that is yet more to be lamented, also between priests and priests.[535]

Some say that a man might here a little lament this man's wit,[536] that weeneth it less to be lamented that debate and strife should be between priests and religious persons, or between those that are, both the parties, religious folk, than between those that are, both the parties, priests. For some say that many religious folk be priests. And they that so say do say also that as many priests be religious folk. And some say, therefore, that except[537] this man mean here by religious folk either women or children, with whose variance[538] the temporalty is not very greatly cumbered,[539] or else the lay brethren that are in some places of religion, which[540] are neither so many nor so much esteemed that ever the temporalty was much troubled with their strife, else besides these, there falleth no variance lightly between religious and religious wherewith the temporalty have been offended but it falleth of necessity between priests and priests; and then the variance, namely[541] such a variance as this book speaketh of—that is so notable that the temporalty so much marketh it, and hath so great cause to lament it when it falleth between religious and religious—is a thing no less lamentable than if it fell between as many priests when themselves be both priests.

And then if he mean here by "priests" those that

are secular priests,[542] as by his other words he seemeth to do, and so taketh it for a thing more to be lamented if variance fall between secular priests than between those priests that are in religion, then say some men that he saith somewhat worse. And then they that so say seem to me to say true. For albeit[543] great pity it is to see strife and variance fall between any secular priests, yet is it more pity to see it fall between those priests that have also vowed and professed further somewhat a more strait[544] renouncing of all such manner[545] things as matter of debate and strife do commonly spring upon. And therefore this manner of increase and growing of this man's oration is but a counterfeited figure of rhetoric, as some men say.

And in good faith as for myself, I see not the reason that moved him. For it were a very cold[546] excuse to a man learned that will weigh the whole periodus[547] together, if he would hereafter say that he meant by these words "between priests and priests" the priests that are in religion. For besides that a man may by diverse things well perceive the contrary, he had, if he so had meant, left then no lamentation for any strife that happeth between secular priests among themselves. I cannot therefore, in good faith, divine what he should by that increase[548] ending in "priests" after all the religious, but if[549] he meant to signify that the state of priests professing religion were a state of less perfection, by reason of the profession, than is the state of those secular priests that have temporal lands of their own purchase or inheritance, or that else serve some chantry[550] or live upon trentals[551] abroad.

And surely if the man thus meant indeed, besides that he should have set out his sentence more plainly, his meaning will, but if he declare[552] it the better, mislike better men and better learned too, than I and he be both. And saving for that point—which is no small matter—else, as for his rules of rhetoric or grammatical congruity either, or oversight in reasoning, as things of no great weight, I would not much vouchsafe[553] to touch. For they be such offenses as a man may fall in and yet be a saved soul, as well as though he never wrote any work at all.

532 thought over   533 glance
534 whereas   535 CW 9: 177   536 intellect   537 unless   538 disagreement
539 burdened; vexed   540 who
541 especially   542 secular priests: priest
for the diocese, rather than religious orders   543 although   544 strict; rigorous   545 kind of   546 unconvincing   547 sentence   548 additional clause   549 but if: unless   550 a chapel endowed
for the daily singing of Masses for certain souls   551 sets of thirty Masses said for the soul of a deceased person   552 clarify   553 be willing

THE FIFTEENTH CHAPTER

Which division hath been so universal that it hath
been a great unquietness and a great breach of
charity through all the realm; and part of it hath
risen by reason of a great singularity that religious
persons and priests have had to[554] their state of
living, whereby many of them have thought their
state most perfect before all others. And some
of them have thereby exalted themselves in their
own sight so high that they have risen into such
a ghostly[555] pride that they have in manner disdained and despised others that have not lived in
such perfection as they think they do. And of this
hath followed that some of them have had unsitting[556] words of the others, calling them flatterers, dissimulers,[557] and hypocrites; and they have
called the others again[558] proud persons, covetous,
vainglorious, and lovers of worldly delights, and
such other.[559]

Of some particular variance among diverse persons of the clergy have I diverse times heard,
as sometimes one parson against another for his
tithes, or a parson against a religious place for meddling within his parish, or one place of religion with
another upon some suchlike occasion, or sometimes
some one religion have had some question and disputed, as it were, a problem upon the antiquity or
seniority of their institution, as by which the Carmelites claim to fetch their original from Elijah and
Elisha. And some question hath arisen in the order
of Saint Francis between the Observants and the
Conventuals. For as for the third company — that
is to wit, the Coletans[560] — there are in this realm
none. But yet of all these matters was there never,
as far as I read or remember, in this realm either so
very great or so many such things all in hand at once
that ever it was at the time noted through the realm
and spoken of for a great notable fault of the whole
clergy. And as for the faults of some particular parties, either persons or places, is nothing that ought
of reason be reckoned for the cause of this division
and of this displeasure and grudge of the temporalty against the clergy — no more than many more
variances growing daily, in diverse times and places,

with unlawful assemblies and great riots also, cause
the clergy to grudge against the temporalty. And as
it is not reason that it so were, so that it is not indeed
may well be perceived by this: For if it were, then
must this grudge of ours against them have been a
very old thing; whereas it is indeed neither so great
as this man maketh it, and grown to so great as it is,
but even of late,[561] since Tyndale's books and Frith's
and Friar Barnes's began to go abroad. And yet —
although that it appeareth well in his words afterward that those variances can be no part or cause of
this division whereof he maketh his book — yet hath
it delighted either himself or some subtle shrews[562]
that so have set him awork to bring them in too, of a
good mind and a favorable, to lay these faults to the
clergy's face, besides the matter of this division that
he taketh in hand to treat of.

Now, the remnant (whereby somewhat appeareth
also that by the increase of his oration, with putting
in the end — "and, that is yet more to be lamented,
also between priests and priests" — he meant to
put for the more lamentable strife that variance
which falleth between secular priests than that
that falleth between those that, besides their order of priesthood, have by their holy vows entered
into religion) he handleth here in such wise that he
first reproacheth both the parties of "great singularity which both religious persons and also priests
have had to their states of living," by which words
he showeth that each of them contend with other
upon the perfection of their two states whether[563]
should have preeminence — these priests that are
secular or those that are religious — and which of
the both himself taketh for the chief appeareth by
the piteous increase and growing of his lamentable
oration.

Then rebuketh he, of the religious, some that
have appearance to be the most perfect and best,
and saith that through the

     great singularity that they have to their state of
     living, they have exalted themselves in their own
     sight so high that they have risen into such a
     ghostly pride that they have in manner disdained
     and despised others that have not lived in such
     perfection as they think they do.

---

554 in   **555** spiritual   **556** unfitting;
inappropriate   **557** dissemblers   **558** in
turn   **559** *CW* 9: 177–178   **560** a group

of Franciscans tracing their origin to St.
Colette of Corbie (1381–1447)   **561** *even*

of late: only recently   **562** scoundrels
563 which of the two

This is a great thing spoken by guess, because among many good virtuous folk, there may fall some by the devil's means into some great ghostly pride, as Lucifer did in the good company of angels. But this chance of such change is so old that these words will nothing serve his lamentable beginning, which standeth, ye wot well, in lamenting the change from the old virtues of times passed into the new vices of this time present. And this vice is very old, and reigned most when religious folk lived best. And verily the clergy is not all-thing[564] so evil as he maketh it, if the religious folk live now so holily as the temporalty may note that through perfectness of living the devil bring so many to such a high spice[565] of pride.

But then goeth he forth and setteth them to chide together. Howbeit, his words be so confounded with "they" and "them" and "other," and in the two verses of their chiding his words be so unsuitly[566] sorted, that I cannot perceive which of the two parties calleth which, nor who calleth whom, by those names that he saith the one sort calleth the other, nor himself I suppose neither, as the thing that he never knew for true, but thinketh he may boldly tell everything for true that any man perceiveth possible.

THE SIXTEENTH CHAPTER

And another part of this division hath risen by diversities of opinions that have been upon the authorities, powers, and jurisdiction of spiritual men among themselves. And upon these divisions some laymen have in time past favored the one party, and some the other; whereby the people have greatly been inquieted.[567]

Diverse opinions upon powers, authorities, and jurisdictions of spiritual men among themselves, there happeneth I think now and then to rise, while in such cases either party hath his opinion upon his own side. But of any great inquietation that the people hath had by any such division risen within this realm, or of any laymen bearing their favor some to the one party and some to the other, I ween the people of this realm that felt it have

forgotten it, if any such were, it is so long ago. And surely myself remember none, nor I trow[568] no man else for the time of this twenty years; within which time, or ten fewer, all this gear[569] is begun whereof he maketh his division. And therefore this piece of his is, to my feeling, very cold.[570]

THE SEVENTEENTH CHAPTER

But I wot not fully by what occasion it is that now of late the great multitude of all the lay people have found default[571] as well at[572] priests as religious, so far-forth that it is now in manner noted through all the realm that there is a great division between the spiritualty and the temporalty. And verily it is great pity that such a noise should spring and go abroad.[573]

In the beginning he said that division reigneth now between spiritual men and spiritual men. And then saith he here, "But it reigneth now between spiritual men and temporal men."

I am content to let his but[574] alone, and will not shoot thereat for this once. Howbeit, surely his but, being a preposition adversative, standeth more properly to shoot at between his two nows than it would if it were turned into some conjunction copulative.

But whereas he cannot fully tell by what occasion "the great multitude have found default as well at priests as religious," a man needeth never to study for occasions thereof; but if he be so curious as to seek for faults, he may soon find enough, not only in priests and in religious, but in every sort and kind of temporal people too, and ever might yet, in every age since Christendom began, and may peradventure, if he search well, find some in himself too. So that if there be no other cause of variance than that, they may, both spiritualty and temporalty, take each other by the hand like good fellows, and agree together well enough.

But yet happeth it well that this good Pacifier hath so great pity that the noise of this division should spring and go abroad. For he, to remedy that matter withal, and to pull back the noise thereof,

---

564 altogether   **565** kind; sort
566 unfittingly   **567** *inquieted:* disturbed;
CW 9: 178/5–9   **568** believe   **569** stuff
570 unpersuasive   **571** fault   **572** with
573 *CW* 9: 178/9–15   **574** a pun on "butt"
(a target for archery practice)

and to stop up clearly the spring, because all should be hushed and never more words made thereof, hath, as ye see, put it out abroad in print.

THE EIGHTEENTH CHAPTER

5 And some allege diverse causes why it should be so noised.[575]

A very few folk may soon begin a noise[576] of evil will and malice. And a noise may soon be borne abroad, whatsoever the matter be, with some 10 of simplicity, some of light-giving credence, and some of a lust unto[577] talking.

First they say that neither priests nor religious keep the perfection of their order to the honor of God and good example of the people, as they 15 should do.[578]

Verily they that so say peradventure say not much untrue. For I think that every man's duty toward God is so great that very few folk serve him as they should do. And therefore whoso pry upon every 20 man's deed so narrowly as to spy that fault and fall at variance of great zeal with every man that doth not to the very point and perfection, even all that he should do, shall wax[579] within a while at variance with every man and every man with him. But I sup- 25 pose they keep it now at this day muchwhat[580] af- ter such a good meetly mean[581] manner as they did many of those years before in which this division was never dreamed on. And therefore they that say this is the cause have need to go seek some other.

30 But that some of them procure their own honor, and call it the honor of God, and rather covet to have rule over the people than to profit the people.[582]

Were there never none of these till now so late[583] 35 as about the beginning of this division? Or be they all such now? Among Christ's own apostles was some desire of prelacy,[584] and that with some con- tention too. There are of our prelates some such at

this day now, as I pray God that when there shall any new come, they may prove no worse. For of these, 40 when they die (if they wax not worse before), whoso shall live after them may, in my mind, be bold to say that England had not their better any day this forty years; and I durst go a good way above too. But this is more by twenty years and ten set thereto, than this 45 division hath anything been spoken of.

And that some covet their bodily ease and worldly wealth,[585] in meat and drink and such other, more than commonly any temporal man doth.[586]

This is a very cold[587] cause of this new division, 50 to say that there be not now "commonly" so bad men in the temporalty as there be "some" in the spiritualty. For when was it otherwise? Not even in Christ's own days. For Judas, that was one of his own apostles, was not only worse than the com- 55 mon sort of all those that loved their bellies and their ease among Christ's disciples, were they men or women, but worse also than the very worst in all the world beside. But what cause were this that the temporalty should (nor, though this man say thus, 60 I think them not so unreasonable that they would) be at debate and division with the whole body of the clergy: because that some of them were worse than those are that are in a mean[588] common sort of naughtiness[589] among themselves? 65

And that some serve God for a worldly laud[590] and to be magnified therefor, more than for the pure love of God.[591]

That same some that so do be some of the most foolish apes that the devil hath to tumble afore him 70 and to make him laugh, when he seeth them take so much labor and pain for the reward of the blast of a few men's mouths.

Howbeit, there may be some such for all that, and yet nothing to the purpose of this matter. For as for 75 the speech of fools is not to be counted for a proof of division. And among wise men the guess and conjecture that in the clergy there be secretly some very naught before God, whom yet in the sight of the world men take for very good, can by no reason 80

---

575 CW 9: 178/15 576 rumor 577 *lust
unto:* desire for 578 CW 9: 178/15–18
579 become 580 pretty much
581 *meetly mean:* appropriately moderate 582 CW 9: 178/18–20 583 recent
584 authority; primacy; Lk 22:24
585 well-being 586 CW 9: 178/20–22
587 unconvincing 588 average 589 wickedness 590 praise 591 CW 9:
178/22–23

be the cause of any grudge toward the spiritualty, wherein may be, besides them that are such (and so there are indeed), many very virtuous holy men indeed, whose holiness and prayer hath been, I verily think, one great special cause that God hath so long holden his hand from giving of some sorer[592] stroke upon the necks of them that are naught and care not, in the spiritualty and the temporalty both.

And yet this fault that this Pacifier assigneth — of serving God for laud — is, I suppose, somewhat amended of late, and will within a while, if some gear[593] go forward, wear away quite[594] by the help and means of another fault.

For if these heresies that rail upon religions,[595] and call all their prayer pattering, and all their fasting folly, and all their holy vows of chastity worse than Friar Luther's lechery — if these heresies, I say, may grow and go forward, as they begin to grow now and prosper full prettily in some places, and then if those that be of the same sect and of policy dissimule[596] it for a season may in the meantime spread abroad an opinion in the minds of men, that of themselves mean none harm, that the religious people do fast and pray but for laud, they shall well perceive within a while that they shall have so little laud thereof that if there would remain none other cause of this division but because they serve God for laud, ye shall have it soon changed of likelihood, and then shall we shortly agree together very well.

But now good readers, consider, I beseech you, that if these causes which this Pacifier allegeth under the color[597] of "some say" be causes that might move the temporalty to be in division and grudge against the clergy — that is to wit, because they serve not God as they should do, but some of them love authority and some love their ease, and some serve God of vainglory, for laud and praise of men — then should this division not have so late begun, but must have been ever before, and can never be remedied hereafter, but as long as the world lasteth must this division ever continue still.

For how could this Pacifier find the means that in the whole clergy, so many as are therein, none should be naught when of Christ's apostles there was yet one naught in the small number of twelve? And verily, in this declination[598] of the world and by this great fall of faith, the old fervor of charity so beginning to cool, it is to be feared at length that, if it thus go forth and continue, both the spiritualty from the apostles and the temporalty from the other disciples may fall so far down, down, down, down, that as there was then one naught among twelve, so may there in time coming, if these heresies go forward, among twelve spiritual, or peradventure twenty temporal either, be founden at last in some whole country scant any one good. But that world is not, I thank God, in England yet, nor never shall, I trust, come.

Howbeit, that all may be good, that will be hard for this Pacifier to devise the means. So that if the being of some naught may be a good cause of division, division may be, by sometimes fewer naught, made sometimes somewhat less, but end can it never have while the world standeth.

But if this Pacifier, to cease and quench this division, could find the means to make all the whole clergy good, yet for all that — since he layeth for causes of this division that some men say this by[599] the clergy, and some men say by them that — were all the clergy never so good indeed, and served God never so well, this division, by his own tale, yet could not for all that cease except he could provide farther that no piteous Pacifier should, in lamenting of division, put forth a book and say that some laymen say that some of the clergy be naught, and love their ease and their wealth, and that some say that those that seem best and take most labor and pain be but hypocrites for all that, and serve God but for vainglory to get themselves laud and praise among the people.

THE NINETEENTH CHAPTER

And some laymen say further that though religious men have varied[600] with religious, and that some priests have varied also with religious in some points concerning the preeminence of their perfection, as is said before, that yet in such things as pertain to the maintenance of the worldly honor of the Church and of spiritual men, which they call the honor of God, and in such things as pertain to the increase of the riches of spiritual men, religious or secular, they say they agree all in one.[601]

---

592 more grievous; greater   **593** things   **596** *policy dissimule:* expediency disguise   **600** quarreled; been at odds   **601** *CW* 9:
594 entirely   **595** religious orders   **597** guise   **598** decline   **599** about   178/23–30

As for calling the worldly honor of the Church, and of spiritual men, the honor of God, I wot nere[602] whether I perceive well what this man meaneth thereby. But by the first of those two things — that is to wit, by the worldly honor done to the Church and taken as honor done to God — he seemeth to mean the honor that Christian people here in the world use to[603] do to the Church, as in building of the churches fair and goodly, and in apparelling[604] the churches for the use of God's service honorably.

And then in the second point — that is to wit, the honor of spiritual persons — he meaneth, I suppose, such honor as good Christian people do and are bounden to do to their prelates and their curates, and to priests and religious persons, for the respect and regard that they bear both of devotion and very bounden duty to the holy sacrament of their sacred orders, and holy profession of their godly state of living.

Then, as for the third point — that is, the things that he saith pertain to the increase of riches in spiritual men — himself declareth soon after that he meaneth trentals,[605] chantries,[606] obits,[607] pardons,[608] and pilgrimages.

Now saith he that some laymen lay[609] this for a further thing: that all the clergy do use to agree together in all these things, howsoever they happen to vary among themselves for some other things. And verily therein I think he saith true, for so must they do or displease God, and so doth every good layman agree with them therein too. And I have seen it proved by experience that in some of these things, when the laymen have moved[610] some things sometimes whereby should be restrained some such things as the clergy might win by — yea, and also no little somewhat taken from them, to that that lawfully was their own before — the clergy have not striven with the temporalty therefor, but rather than to stick in contention have suffered and let it pass, albeit the cantles[611] that have been cut off have been somewhat broader than a bridecake,[612] and greater than a Christmas loaf in a right good husband's[613] house.

And yet where this Pacifier saith that some laymen say that in all such things all the clergy, both secular and religious, agree and hold together, himself can, if he will, tell the same "some laymen" that so told him so that some other laymen say nay. For they say that they see very well, that in all those things there are now some such of the clergy, such as it is pity that ever they were thereof, either secular priests or religious persons. And yet are there some such of both which now cast off their favor from both twain, and from the Christian faith also, and therefore agree not to these things (as those "some men" told this man that the whole clergy doth), but do both speak and write against all these things every whit:[614] both honor to prelates, building of churches, buying of bells and ornaments, and against pilgrimages, trentals, chantries, obits, and pardons, and finally purgatory too.

THE TWENTIETH CHAPTER

And therefore they say that all spiritual men, as to the multitude,[615] be more diligent to induce the people to such things as shall bring riches to the Church (as to give money to trentals, and to found chantries and obits, and to obtain pardons, and to go upon pilgrimages, and such other) than they be to induce them to the payment of their debts, to make restitutions for such wrongs as they have done, or to do the works of mercy to their neighbors that be poor and needy, and that sometimes be also in right extreme necessity.[616]

Now in good faith for aught[617] that I see, such as so murmur against chantries, trentals, obits, pardons, and pilgrimages, as would have them all fordone,[618] have an inward hatred unto the profit of men's souls, besides the envy that they bear to priests. For some of these things be such that they make not the priests so very rich that all the clergy should, for the great lucre, so sore[619] bend unto the setting forth thereof.

For as for chantries, though there be many, no one man can have any great living thereby; and that a priest should have some living of such a mean[620] thing as commonly the chantries be, there will, I ween, no good man find great fault that all the

---

602 *wot nere:* do not know   603 *use to:* usually   604 furnishing   605 sets of requiem Masses   606 donations for Masses sung for the dead   607 annual memorial Masses for the souls of the dead   608 church festivals at which indulgences are granted   609 cite   610 proposed   611 sections; portions   612 wedding cake   613 farmer's   614 little bit   615 majority   616 *CW* 9: 178/30–38   617 anything   618 done away with   619 strongly   620 lowly

clergy would have it so; for so would, I suppose, every good layman too.

And as for pilgrimages, though the shrines be well garnished, and the chapel well hung with wax,[621] few men, I fear me, need much at this day to grudge and complain of very chargeable[622] offerings, but those men make most ado that offer nothing at all.

And pardons[623] have been purchased not only by the spiritualty, but in diverse places by the good faithful devotion of virtuous temporal princes, as was to Westminster,[624] and unto the Savoy,[625] great pardon purchased by the most noble prince of famous memory King Henry the Seventh, father to our most dear sovereign lord the King that now is. And in good faith, I never yet perceived the people make so great offerings at a pardon that we should either pity greatly their cost or envy the priests that profit.

But then the trentals, lo, they be the things, ye wot well, whereby the multitude of the clergy, and specially the prelates get, every man among them, an infinite treasure in a year, so that it is no marvel though the whole clergy, secular and religious, what variance soever they have among themselves beside[626] (concerning the preeminence of their perfection, as this Pacifier saith), agree together, for all that, in this point: to keep and hold fast the trentals, because of the great increase of the riches that they bring in by heaps unto every man among them. I, that nothing can get by them, beseech God to keep in men's devotions toward trentals and toward obits too. For as much as he saith that secular and religious both stick to these profits, yet if religious Lutherans may proceed and prosper—that cast off their habits and walk out and wed nuns and preach against purgatory, and make mocks of the Mass—many men shall care little for obits within a while and set no more by a trental than a ruffian[627] at Rome setteth by a trentune.[628]

Howbeit, where this Pacifier saith that some say that "all spiritual men as to the multitude" do rather induce the people to pilgrimages, pardons, chantries, obits, and trentals than to the payment of their debts, or to restitution of their wrongs, or to the deeds of alms and mercy to their neighbors that are poor and needy, and sometimes too in right

extreme necessity, for my part, I thank God, I never heard yet of any one that ever would give that counsel; nor no more hath, I see well, this Pacifier himself, for he saith it but under his common figure of "some say." But therefore this would I say: that either he believed those some that so said unto him, or else he believed them not. If he believed them not, it had been well done to have left their tale untold till he had believed them better. And on the other side, if he believed them well, he might as well with conscience have been less light of belief,[629] or boldly might have believed that they lied, rather than lightly believe the lewd[630] words of some, and upon the malicious mouths of some, blow abroad in books so false a tale himself against not a small sum, but, as himself saith, "as to the multitude," against all spiritual men.

THE TWENTY-FIRST CHAPTER

And forasmuch as it is most commonly seen that among a great multitude there be many that work rather upon will than upon reason, and that though they have good zeal, yet many times they lack good order and discretion, which is the mother of all virtue, therefore some persons, thinking that worldly honor and riches letteth[631] greatly devotion—so much that, as they think, they cannot stand together—have holden opinion that it is not lawful to the Church to have any possessions. And some, taking a more mean[632] way therein, have said that (as they think) it is lawful and also expedient that the Church have possessions; but they think that the great abundance that is in the Church doth great hurt, and induceth in many of them a love to worldly things, and letteth and in manner strangleth the love of God. And therefore they think that it were good to take away that is too much, and to leave that is sufficient. And some also, as of a policy to pull riches from the Church, have inveighed against all such things as bring riches to the Church. And because great riches have come to the Church for praying for souls in purgatory, have by words affirmed that

---

621 i.e., votive candles   **622** expensive
623 indulgences   **624** Westminster
Abbey   **625** Savoy Hospital, founded 1512

626 otherwise   **627** pimp   **628** (literally
"thirty-one" in Italian): gang rape of a
prostitute by thirty-one men   **629** *light*

of belief: ready to believe   **630** wicked
631 hinders   **632** moderate

there is no purgatory, and that granting of pardons riseth of covetise of the Church, and profiteth not the people, and that pilgrimages be of no effect, and that the Church may make no laws and such other things as founding of chantries, making of brotherhoods, and many more. Wherein they show outwardly to rise against all the things before rehearsed, and to despise them, and yet they know and believe in their hearts that all these things be of themselves right good and profitable, as they be indeed if they were ordered as they should be. And some persons there be that through grace find default only at the abusion and misorder of such things, and speak nothing against the things themselves, neither of purgatory, pilgrimages, setting up of images, or such other. For they know well they be ordained of God, and that the misorder riseth only of man for covetise, singularity, or some other suchlike default, through persuasion and deceit of the ghostly enemy.[633]

Here is, good readers, a special fruitful piece of three manner of "some says," or three manner of thinkings. The first is of those that think and say that it is not lawful that the Church should have any possessions, but that all their livelihood, and all such things as any riches cometh into the Church by, should be taken away, every whit.

And these men, in the judgment of this piteous Pacifier, be not "discreet," but yet they have, he saith, a "good zeal" though. And this good zeal had, ye wot well, Simon Fish when he made the supplication of beggars.[634] But God gave him such grace afterward that he was sorry for that good zeal, and repented himself and came into the Church again, and forsook and forswore all the whole hill of those heresies out of which the fountain of that same good zeal sprang.

And of truth, some such are there yet that have the same good zeal still that Simon Fish had when he was at the worst. And God sendeth some of them such good speed[635] as they have good zeal. For some such have I known that have engrossed[636]

into their hands much other men's goods, and for a while flowered, and were accounted thrifty,[637] and held their own and other men's too, but in conclusion wasted away both twain, and fain[638] to find a place to hide their heads, or to keep them from prison find some other shift.[639]

Of these sort was there one, not very long ago, which[640] went about to make a good bargain, and was not then known but for his own man,[641] and yet is now, God be thanked, his own man again, for any other man that he hath to wait upon him. But so happed it then that as he sat in a tavern in Lombard Street with an honest merchant with whom he should[642] have bargained, the other had heard an inkling, which yet he believed not, that this man was not much aforehand.[643] And as they fell in talking of the world, they talked at last of the clergy, wherein, when he was fallen, he waxed so warm with the wine, and so full of good zeal, that he swore by the Mass he trusted shortly to see them lose all, and that "the King should put them all forever out of his protection!" And with that word, he clapped his fist upon the board[644] with such a fervent zeal that his own protection[645] fell out of his sleeve. Which, when the other perceived, "Brother," quoth he, "you be not a thief, I think, and therefore I trust it is no pardon[646] that ye have purchased there. You trust, you say, to see the clergy put out of the King's protection; and I purpose to see you out of the King's protection ere[647] you and I bargain anymore together."

And such bankrupts be these men of that good zeal, that gape after the spoil of the spiritualty, which, when they have wasted and misspent their own, would then very fain,[648] save for hanging, rob spiritual and temporal too.

THE TWENTY-SECOND CHAPTER

The second sort that this Pacifier speaketh of be they that think and say that it were good to take away from the clergy all that is too much, and leave that is sufficient, because that great abundance

633 *CW 9*: 178/39-179/30   **634** Simon Fish, a follower of Tyndale who died in 1531. His *Supplication for the Beggars* was a pamphlet published about 1529, arguing in strong terms against purgatory and urged King Henry VIII to confiscate the Church's lands.   **635** success   **636** amassed   **637** thriving, prosperous   **638** (were) forced   **639** manner of livelihood   **640** who   **641** *his own man*: a financially independent man (not a debtor)   **642** wanted to   **643** solvent, i.e., able to pay his debts   **644** table   **645** a legal document guaranteeing immunity from debt collection   **646** indulgence   **647** before   **648** gladly letteth,[649] they say, and in manner strangleth the love of God. And these that thus say, this Pacifier alloweth[650] for folk wise and discreet. But by what right men may take away from any man, spiritual or temporal, against his will, the land that is already lawfully his own, that thing this Pacifier telleth us not yet. But he will peradventure at another time tell us of some men that lay[651] this reason and that reason for it. But I have heard some good and wise and well-learned men say that all the world can never bring the reason that ever can prove it right. And as for mine own part, like[652] as I have somewhat more largely said in my book of the *Supplication of the Souls*, if any man would give the counsel to take any man's land or goods from him, pretending[653] that he hath too much, or that he useth it not well, or that it might be better used if some other had it, he giveth such a counsel as he may, when he list[654]—and will peradventure after—stretch a great deal farther than the goods or possessions of only spiritual men.

And where he saith that some say that great abundance doth let and in manner strangle the love of God, that is many times very true: that many men in plenty forget God which[655] in penury run unto him. But this reason runneth out[656] against every kind of men, spiritual and temporal too; and yet are there in both twain some in whom the love of God is neither letted nor strangled therewith, but it is made, by the good use thereof, the matter and occasion of merit. Which, if it might not be, but must needs let and strangle the love of God, then were the reason so strong against all men that no man might without deadly[657] sin keep any abundance in his hands. And then if, to withdraw that inevitable necessity of damnable deadly sin, it were lawful to take as much away from any one man as the remnant that were left him should be but even sufficient, the same reason would, as I say, serve with one little wrench[658] farther, to take in like wise away from every other man were he spiritual or temporal, in whom there might be laid appearance of so much abundance that it letted[659] him to love God. For that is, ye wot well, every man bound to do, spiritual and temporal both.

And on the other side, if there be taken from no man anything but from him that hath so much as

no man that hath so much may so love God as he may come to heaven, then shall there be from no man taken anything. For I doubt not but that there are at this day holy saints in heaven, of such as were spiritual and of such as were temporal too, that had while they lived here as great possessions as hath either spiritual or temporal within the realm of England now.

Moreover since this Pacifier accounteth them for "discreet" that, leaving the clergy sufficient, would that all the remnant were taken away from them, because the great abundance letteth them, they say, to love God, it had been well done that he had somewhat declared his mind how little he calleth sufficient, lest that some of his discreet folk would undiscreetly misconstrue that word, and for lack of such favor and pity as himself, ye see well, beareth to the clergy, would leave them too little and call it enough. For if this Pacifier would moderate and measure his sufficiency by the words of Saint Paul, where he saith, "Having meat and drink and wherewith to be covered, let us be content,"[660] except[661] himself that loveth them go farther therein and appoint them their fare[662] and their apparel too, some others haply[663] that love them not so well will devise them a diet as thin as Galen deviseth for him that hath an obstruction in his liver,[664] and because Saint Paul speaketh but of covering, will devise them clothes that shall only cover them and not keep them warm.

Besides this, it seemeth that yet his discreet folk should not, under the name of abundance, take all from the Church that they would take from every man to whom they would leave bare sufficient, but that they rather should, such as they would take from one that hath more than sufficient, divide it among such others of the Church that have less than sufficient. Now, if they should yet besides this (which I ween they should not) find yet a great sum remaining after all the spiritual folk sufficiently provided for, then had it been good that he had yet farther devised how it would please him that his discreets should order the remnant. For though they be, as he taketh them, discreet persons of themselves because they would take away but the great abundance and leave but the bare sufficient, yet their discretion shall do a great deal the better if

649 hinders; prevents **650** takes
651 cite; allege **652** just **653** claiming
654 wants **655** who **656** *runneth*

out: applies; goes **657** mortal. See 1
Jn 5:16–17. **658** trick; cunning device
659 prevented, hindered **660** 1 Tm 6:8

661 unless **662** food **663** perhaps
664 *as thin … liver:* See Galen's *Ars medica*
34.

it like him to give them his discreet counsel too. When it should come to this point, here might peradventure himself and his discreets make us many devices,[665] and ever the more the more indiscreet.

I have been within these four or five years—for before, I heard little talking of such manner of devices—but within this four or five years, I have been at such devices in diverse good merry companies, never earnestly talking thereof (for as yet I thank God that of this matter I never heard any such), but for pastime, by way of familiar talking, have I heard diverse, both in hand[666] with prelates and secular priests and religious persons, and talked of their living, and of their learning, and of their livelihood too, and whether themselves were such as it were better to have them or lack them, and then, touching their livelihood, whether it might be lawfully taken from them or not, and if it might, whether it were expedient so to be, and if it so were, then to what use. And in many such merry talkings I have always remembered—and because our communication came sometimes to a much like point, sometimes have I told and rehearsed—the story that Titus Livy[667] telleth of one Pacuvius Calavius the Capuan, in the third book of his third decade[668] that treateth of the Romans' war with Hannibal and the city of Carthage. This Capua was of all Italy the chief city, and of the greatest power save only the city of Rome. In which city, so happed it that the commonalty[669] were fallen in grudge and murmur and at division with the Senate, as this Pacifier saith that the temporalty is here at these days against the clergy. Whereupon this Calavius, being a senator, and nonetheless leaning all unto the people (because he saw them, by sufferance[670] and oversight of the Senate, grown into an unbridled liberty, and, as they must be when they conspire whole together, waxen[671] the more mighty part), studied and bethought himself what means he might invent first to bring the Senate in his danger,[672] and then by some benefit win all their good wills, and yet therewith increase his favor with the people besides. Upon this—being, as it happened, the chief governor of the city for the time—he broke[673] upon a day suddenly to the Senate, and told them that themselves wist[674] well enough what grudge

the people had to them, but the peril and danger that they then presently stood in, that, he said, wist they not. But he knew well that the people intended now after the great overthrow which the Romans had late had at Cannae, to kill up all the senators, and break their league with the Romans, and fall into the party of Hannibal. "Howbeit," quoth he, "if ye dare put yourselves in my hands, I have devised a way whereby ye shall see me shortly not only save all your lives, but also preserve your state."[675] And when the senators in that sudden fear agreed to put him whole in trust to order all the matter as he would, he commanded them all suddenly to be locked fast in their council chamber; and, setting armed men at the gate to see that neither any other man should enter in unto them nor any of them come out, he called suddenly to an assembly the whole people of the city, and there said in this wise[676] unto them:

The thing that ye have, dear friends, these many days much desired—that ye might once be revenged upon this unhappy Senate, and remove them from the room[677] that by their covetous and cruel dealing have well showed themselves full unmeet[678] to bear the name of fathers unto the people—this thing have I now, by policy,[679] for your sakes peaceably brought into your hands—and that in such wise as ye shall not need to fight therefor, or assault particularly their houses. In expugnation[680] whereof, being, as they would be, fenced with[681] their servants and their friends, yourselves might stand in peril. But I have shut them up yonder together alone by themselves, clean out of armor without aid or any manner[682] defense, where you shall have them all without any man's death or stroke.[683]

At this word, glad was all the people, and, giving him high thanks, would forthwith fain[684] have been upon them. "Sirs, there needeth in this point none haste," quoth he,

but one thing is there that, if ye thought thereon, ye would, I dare say, do first. For they be the while safe enough, thereas[685] they escape not from you.

665 plans; schemes   **666** concert
667 *History of Rome* 23.2–3, but modified
(*CW 9*: 345–46)   **668** set of ten; the
"third book…" is book 23.   **669** common

people   **670** allowance   **671** become
672 power   **673** burst in   **674** knew
675 social position   **676** way   **677** office
678 unfit   **679** stratagem   **680** attacking

681 *fenced with:* defended by   **682** kind of
683 injury   **684** gladly   **685** there where

But I have ever known you so wise that ye will not, I wot well, set your short present pleasure before your perpetual wealth,[686] which, ye see well, ye should do if ye should live lawless and without a rule; nor no law can serve except there be some governors.[687] And therefore two things must ye do at once: that is to wit, both remove these and also set of yourselves some better men in their places. Wherefore I have brought here their names in a pot. Let them be drawn out, and as they come unto hand, determine your pleasure of[688] their persons, and substitute therewith their successors.

This motion of Calavius was such that either of reason they could not mislike it, or else for shame they would not refuse it. And thereupon out was there drawn a name, at the hearing whereof they cried out, all the company, "An evil and a naughty man!" and bade away with him. "Very well," quoth Calavius, "whom will you now name to put in his place?" At that they paused a little and began to bethink them.[689] But shortly some named one, and some named another. But with perusing,[690] after this fashion, of a few, there was none that one man named and advanced for good but five for that one rejected him, as either very naught[691] or at the least more unmeet to take in than he whom they would put out. So that long ere they had perused half, as much as they misliked many of their old, yet found they it so hard a thing to find out the better new that they waxed[692] weary of the seeking. So that Calavius, perceiving them begin in the matter somewhat to stacker and stay,[693] persuaded them easily to concord with those that they had before; and thereupon they left off their election, and let the new-chosen pass, and kept their old senate still.

And surely somewhat like,[694] but not all after this fashion, hath it fared in such good company as it hath happed me to be at communication upon these matters of the clergy. For in conclusion, after many faults laid against the spiritualty that is now, and many new devices[695] for their lands, when we came at last unto Calavius's pageant,[696] and those that found the faults in the body at large in such a large fashion laid forth by them as though there were not one

good man among them, when they had the names of this prelate and that prelate recited and rehearsed unto them by row,[697] and were asked, "What say you by[698] him?" and "What by him?" albeit that they did by some of them say they were naught, and that if, like[699] as the Capuans should have changed a senator for a commoner, so if they should for every one of the spiritualty take into his place by choice and election some good temporal man, they might for this prelate or that, concerning some of them, shortly make a good change. For some of them thought they such as, for one point or other, they could not lightly find a worse. Yet on the other side again, at some of them they stayed and stackered, and with much work brought forth some at last with whom they might, as they thought, match them, and yet by their own confession no more than match them, and in my mind not so much neither; but like as in some they and I somewhat varied, so in diverse others we were agreed both, that for to make the change, neither could they find their better nor their match neither.

Now whereas we went thus no farther than the prelates, if we should have perused over the whole clergy both religious and seculars, though we might have found out some that both might and gladly would have been changed for the prelates (for I have heard many laymen that would be bishops with a good will), and though we might have also founden enough of those that would match them that are evil and naughty secular priests, and them that are run out of religion too, and that would and were able to match them in their own ways were they never so bad, yet of those that would match the good, as few as some folk would have them seem, it would not, I ween, as the world goeth now, be very easy to find out so many. But as wealthy, and as easy, and as glorious as some say to this Pacifier that religion[700] is, yet if some others should say to them, "Lo, sirs, these folk that are in religion shall out; come you into religion in their steads, and live there better than they do, and you shall have heaven," they would answer, I fear me, that they be not yet weary of this world.

Then if they were invited into religion on the other fashion, and it were said unto them thus — "Sirs, we

---

686 well-being **687** More leaves out "You must either have a king — what an abomination! — or else a senate, the only deliberative body in a free state" (Livy 23.3.5). **688** *your pleasure of:* what you want done with **689** *bethink them:* think it over **690** examining **691** bad **692** became **693** *stacker and stay:* waver and hesitate **694** similarly **695** plans **696** stageplay **697** rank **698** about **699** just **700** life in a religious order

will not bid you live so strait[701] in religion as these men should have done; come on and enter, and do but even as they did, and then shall you there have a good easy life and a wealthy, and much worldly praise therewith"—I ween a man should not yet, for all that, get them to go to it. But as easy as we call it, and as wealthy too, and now peradventure when our wives are angry, wish ourselves therein, yet if it were thus offered, we would play as Aesop telleth a fable of a poor old man, which, bearing up a hill a burden of bushes in his neck, for help of his necessity, panting for weariness, in the midway laid down his burden and sat him down and sighed, and waxed so weary of his life that he wished and called for death. Whereupon Death came anon[702] readily toward him, and asked him, "What wilt thou with me?" But when the poor fellow saw him, the lean whoreson, there so ready, "I called you, sir," quoth he, "to pray you do so much for me as help me up again with this bitched[703] burden, and lay it in my neck." So ween I that for all our words, if that easy life and wealthy that is in religion were offered us, as weary as we be of wedding, we would rather abide all our old pain abroad than in a cloister take a religious man's life for ease. So that in conclusion we should be fain[704] either to put worse in their stead or keep our old still, till, as they little and little die and depart, God in like wise little and little, as he hath ever hitherto provided, shall inspire his grace into the breasts of others, and make them fall in devotion and enter into religion, and so succeed in their places.

Now as it fared in our communication by[705] the spiritual persons, so fared it in a manner by the spiritual men's possessions. Not for that[706] we might not always find others enough content to enter into their possessions, though we could not always find other men enough content to enter in their religions,[707] but for that in devising what way they should be better bestowed, such ways as at the first face seemed very good, and for the comfort and help of poor folk very charitable, appeared after, upon reasoning, more likely within a while to make many beggars more than to relieve them that are already. And some way that appeared at the first to more stand the realm in great stead, and be an increase of the King's honor, with a great strength for the land and a great surety[708] for the Prince, and a great sparing of the people's charge,[709] well appeared after, upon further reasoning, to be the clean contrary, and of all other ways the worst.

And to say the truth, much marvel have I to see some folk now so much and so boldly speak of taking away any possessions of the clergy. For albeit that once in the time of the famous prince King Henry the Fourth, about the time of a great rumble that the heretics made, when they would have destroyed not the clergy only, but the King also and his nobility too, there was a foolish bill and a false put into a Parliament or twain,[710] and sped[711] as they were worthy, yet had I never founden in all my time while I was conversant[712] in the Court, of all the nobility of this land, above the number of seven (of which seven there are now three dead) that ever I perceived to be of the mind that it were either right or reasonable, or could be to the realm profitable, without lawful cause to take any possessions away from the clergy which good and holy princes and other devout virtuous people, of whom there be now many blessed saints in heaven, have of devotion toward God given to the clergy to serve God and pray for all Christian souls. And therefore, as for such folk as this Pacifier calleth "discreet" for their discreet invention of taking from the clergy the abundance of their possessions, I never look to see them so discreet as were those men both discreet and devout that gave them.

THE TWENTY-THIRD CHAPTER

Yet putteth this Pacifier a third kind of thinkers, such a kind as I never to my remembrance have heard of before: that is to wit, of such as purposely say evil and openly speak heresy, and for all that think well. And those, he saith, are "politic"[713] which, to pull away riches from the Church, speak against all things that anything bring into it, as against praying for souls in purgatory, granting of pardons,[714] pilgrimages, making of laws, founding of chantries,[715] making of brotherhoods, and many more.

And though they speak against all these things, yet, he saith, they know well enough that all these things be good and may be well used. But because they bring riches into the Church, therefore, he

---

701 strictly; rigorously   702 at once
703 accursed   704 forced   705 with
regard to   706 *for that:* because

707 religious orders   708 safety; security
709 monetary burden   710 two
711 fared   712 occupied   713 prudent;

shrewd; crafty   714 indulgences
715 chapels for saying Masses for the dead

saith, though they know them for good and think them good, yet they speak against them all, of policy—not against the abuses only, but also against the very things themselves. For of those that speak against the abuses only, he putteth another sort beside these men whom he calleth, for this point, so politic. And he saith that those that only speak against the abuses do better and have more grace, but yet that excludeth not, ye wot well, but that the others may be good enough, and have grace enough too, though not so much.

Thus hath this Pacifier put three kinds of folk that would have the goods taken from the Church:

The first, of those that would take all and leave nothing. And those men, he saith, have a good "zeal."

The second, of those that would leave sufficient and take away the remnant. And those men have, he saith, good "discretion."

The third kind he calleth those which, rather than the Church should have anything, let[716] not to speak against good things. And those men, though they speak openly plat[717] and plain heresy, yet he denieth not to be wise men and use a good "policy."

But now, whereas they deny purgatory, this is, as methinketh, an evil policy: for withdrawing of offerings from the clergy, to withdraw therewith our alms from the poor lay people too, and yet, that worst is of all, from the seely[718] souls themselves that lie there and piteously cry in pain.

By this policy, we wot well that these politic folk might impugn in general the affection of giving anything in alms. For that affection, ye wot well, bringeth in the year somewhat into some part of the clergy. And well ye wot that since the belief of purgatory and others of those things against which these politic men so speak be plain and open truths revealed by God, and the contrary belief is by the whole Catholic Church plainly determined for heresy; and since men cannot know that a man believeth the truth in his heart if he hold against it openly with his mouth, and those therefore that speak heresies, every good man that heareth them is bounden to denounce or accuse them, and the bishops are bounden upon their words proved to put them to penance and reform them, which if they refuse or fall in relapse, the bishop is bound to deliver them, and all good temporal governors are then bounden to punish them, if every other man

did on all sides the part of a good Christian man, it appeareth that the policy of those whom this Pacifier calleth so politic would within a while prove a poor policy.

Howbeit, what mind this Pacifier hath himself concerning these points, himself declareth that he believeth the right way and the true. Which I am very glad to hear, and for my part, as help me God, I verily[719] trust he feigneth not therein, but as a true Christian man verily saith as he thinketh. And yet is not every man therein of my mind. And therefore it would be wrong if every "some say" and every "some think" should serve to bring a man in hatred or obloquy. For surely some say that they think that, if some men may, as he saith, of policy feign themselves heretics and yet believe full truly, for all that, in their hearts, some one man may much better feign himself, for policy, full Catholic, and yet in his heart believe the while full falsely. But whatsoever some men say or some men think, in that matter I never will think that a man believeth otherwise than he saith he doth but if[720] himself should, by some other words or deeds of his own, declare of his mind the contrary. And as I will not, against a man's words spoken according to the right faith, think that he believeth wrong, surely so can I not think that he which in his words openly inveigheth against good and faithful things, and despiseth true points of the common-known Catholic faith, doth in his heart secretly think and believe right, but if he were among paynims[721] that would for fear of pain compel him to renay[722] his faith—which were yet in that case damnable to his soul—and therefore is here among Christian men, where no such force compelleth him, but upon his peril forbiddeth him, of very good reason damnable to his body.

THE TWENTY-FOURTH CHAPTER

Howbeit, what this good Pacifier, though he believe right himself and plainly protesteth the truth of his belief, yet what he would should be done either with those that against their own wrong words he believeth to believe right in their minds, or with those, either, whom he believeth to believe wrong indeed, I cannot very well gather of his words here. For here he saith of them thus:

---

716 hesitate   **717** blunt   **718** poor; helpless   **719** truly   **720** *but if:* unless   **721** pagans   **722** deny; renounce

And though some men have mistaken themselves in the said articles, yet diverse others have said that if they had been well and charitably handled, they might have been reformed, and peradventure saved in body and in soul.[723]

In these words I find again, good readers, a plain open declaration as, in my mind, that this man believeth in these articles like a true Catholic man. For he confesseth in these words that all those that have died in the contrary belief been perished in body and soul. For he saith that some men say that with good handling "they might have been reformed, and peradventure saved in body and soul." So that it appeareth by these words that neither himself thinketh, nor hath heard so much as any other men say, but that they be now plainly lost and perished for those heresies. Which is yet another good token that he not only believeth well himself, but also talketh not much, nor hath no such conversation with heretics that they dare well and plainly put him in full trust. For if he were, he should hear them undoubtedly say that those folk be saved souls and holy saints, as Bainham, that was late burned, said by[724] Bayfield, both a heretic and an apostate, that was burned about a year before him.

Howbeit, though they call them saved souls and saints, yet will they say that they be not in heaven. For there is no soul, they say, but in some place of rest they lie still and sleep full soundly, and sleep shall, they say, till Gabriel's trump awake them and call them up early to rise and record their appearance before our Savior at the general Day of Doom.[725]

But in good faith this one thing am I sorry to see: that since himself seemeth to me so faithful, and that therefore I cannot persuade unto myself but that in his own heart he loveth and favoreth the clergy—which no man can, as I think, heartily hate but he that hateth also the faith—some of these wily heretics, like the angels of Satan transfiguring themselves into the likeness of angels of light,[726] should so deceive this good man, and so abuse his good gentle nature and simplicity, as to make him with their wily invented figure of "some say," under a pity pretended[727] toward those heretics that are in their obstinacy perished, set his words in such wise as though his mind were to aggrieve[728] and bring

in hatred among the people the name and body of the clergy, by making the people ween that their ordinaries had, with evil and uncharitable handling, been the occasion that those heretics are both in soul and body destroyed, since they might, as is here said under the figure of "some say," by good and charitable handling of the clergy, have been better reformed, and peradventure in soul and body saved.

Would God these same "some folk" that so have said unto this Pacifier had named him at the leastwise some one that was so evil and so uncharitably handled that the lack of better and more charitable handling hath been the loss of his body and soul. For then might the clergy declare their demeanor toward that man, and then should they perceive by this Pacifier in which part of their dealing good charitable manner lacked. But verily, whomsoever they should have named, I doubt not but those that were the ordinaries in the cause could easily prove that they had used no rigor to him against the law, nor omitted no charitable means unto him that came to their minds while the man lived and the matter in their hands, nor in providing for good exhortation toward his conversion again and his salvation, even till the life left his body.

But now forasmuch as some so say by[729] them concerning some of them that are gone, the clergy would, I ween, be yet glad to hear in what wise manner of charitable fashion this piteous Pacifier would have them handle other heretics hereafter, such as shall be denounced and *ex officio* brought before them. For albeit that this Pacifier in another place somewhat seemeth to mislike that order, yet I fear me there would, as I shall after show you, many a place in the realm swarm very full ere ever they were brought before the ordinary[730] by the means of accusation.

Howbeit, let us put the example by[731] someone that is likely to be brought and delivered unto the ordinary by the means of the King's Grace and his Council. I mean John Frith. For he is in prison in the Tower already, taken by the Bishop's servants, by the aid of the King's officers at commandment of his Grace and his Council, and so by the King's officers brought into the Tower, where he remaineth yet; and therefore he shall, I doubt not, be brought, as I said, and delivered unto the ordinary.[732]

723 *CW* 9: 179/30–33 **724** about **725** *Day of Doom:* Judgment Day **726** See 2 Cor 11:14. **727** claimed **728** discredit **729** about **730** ecclesiastical judge **731** concerning **732** *John . . . ordinary:* Frith was arrested

Now then, if the ordinary knew this good piteous Pacifier, and would, because he seeth his good and charitable mind, desire[733] him of his good advice and counsel, in what wise he might best and most charitably handle him for the saving of his soul and body, the laws of Christ's Church observed, that the saving of him, if he would stick stiff in his obstinacy, should not be the occasion of corrupting and destroying the souls of other men, what counsel would this man give him?

First, if no man would profess himself for his accuser, and yet there would twenty be ready, when they were by commandment of the Court compelled, not to let but depose[734] the truth—that he hath, since he came in the Tower, written afresh against purgatory, and a book that he calleth *The Mirror*,[735] against religious, advising every man to give none of them nothing, though they be of that religion[736] that nothing have of their own; and twice hath he there in like wise written against the Catholic faith of Christ concerning the Blessed Sacrament of the altar—whether[737] would now this Pacifier: that the ordinary, having good proofs and yet none accuser, should proceed against him *ex officio*, or else for lack of an accuser let him fair go? If he would he should[738] proceed *ex officio*—as I think he would think it reason—what should he then do, since all cannot be done in a day? Whether should he let him walk abroad upon his promise to appear again, which Frith were likely to break and get him overseas, or else take sureties bounden for his appearance, as John Purser and some such others were bounden for John Burt, and force[739] not to forfeit their bond for brotherhood, but let him slip aside and never bring him forth, and keep him close[740] among the brethren as the other was kept, till the apostle may make some bishops among the new brethren, and after his new Titus and Timothy stablished, each in his own see, then the new Paul, this apostle Frith, take shipping[741] at Sandwich and sail into Friesland. Would this Pacifier advise the ordinary thus, or else to keep him in prison, where he should do no hurt, and let the walls and the locks be his sureties for his forthcoming?

Thus far yet, as I suppose, this Pacifier would advise the ordinary to keep Frith fast. But now, when his heresies were laid unto his charge, as for to give counsel to the ordinary to exhort Frith to leave them, this Pacifier, I dare say, shall not need, nor to take him to grace neither, nor to show him great favor upon good tokens of his repentance and amendment. But now if he were one of this Pacifier's politiques, and would say that he believed ever the right way in his own heart contrary to the words that his own hand wrote, but, after the manner that this Pacifier speaketh, he wrote all these heresies of policy, because that by the belief of purgatory, and of the Sacrament of the altar, and of miracles in so many places so plainly showed thereon, he saw that offering and riches came into the clergy, and therefore would say that he must not be taken for a heretic, but for a man wise and politic, what advice would here this Pacifier give his ordinary?

What counsel would he give the ordinary if Frith would make none excuse by policy, but say that he wrote against purgatory, and all religious orders, and the Sacrament of the altar too, for love that he beareth to the truth, and that those heresies be very[742] faith, by which he will abide unto the death? What advice will this Pacifier give the Bishop then? What good and charitable handling will he devise to save his body and soul—specially when he shall see certain letters which some of the brethren let fall of late, and lost them, of likelihood, as some good Kit[743] loseth her keys, by which letters both Tyndale and George Joye write unto Frith and counsel him to stick fast, and Tyndale showeth him that all the brethren look what shall become of him, and that upon his speed[744] hangeth all their hope? I cannot tell what good and charitable handling this Pacifier can devise, but I dare say that there is neither ordinary nor other honest man, spiritual nor temporal, but that he is as sorry as this Pacifier himself to see that young man, or any other, so stubbornly set in such heresies that no man can show him the favor that every man fain[745] would without the displeasure of God and peril of their own souls and many other men's too.

in October 1532. More published the *Apology* just before Easter in 1533. Frith was indeed subsequently tried and convicted of heresy, and burned at the stake on July 4, 1533.   **733** ask   **734** *let but depose:* hinder but testify to   **735** *The Mirror: A Mirror, or Glass, Where You May Know Thyself*   **736** religious order   **737** which of these   **738** *would he should:* wants him to   **739** care   **740** concealed   **741** *take shipping:* board a ship   **742** true; authentic   **743** woman   **744** success   **745** gladly

THE TWENTY-FIFTH CHAPTER

And upon all these matters there is risen a great opinion in the people, in manner universally, that in punishing and corrections all these persons before rehearsed should have like punishment if spiritual men might have free liberty in that behalf, and that spiritual men would, if they could, as well put them to silence that speak against the abusion or disorder of such things as be before rehearsed as them that speak against the thing itself.[746]

Those words be not very well spoken of this Pacifier by the people. For if he have spoken with many more than the one-half, and felt their opinions himself, else is it not only against the spiritualty spoken very shamefully, but also to the false contrived rebuke of the whole people in manner universally. For since that neither this Pacifier nor any man else can bring forth any one of these heretics that have been by their ordinaries delivered for their obstinacy in the secular hands[747] and burned that have had any wrong done them, or been therein otherwise handled than charity with justice, according to the common laws of all Christ's Catholic Church, and the laws of this realm have required, there is no good man nor reasonable that hath any cause thereby to conceive by[748] the clergy such a malicious foolish suspicion as this Pacifier here untruly layeth unto the whole people of this realm in manner universally when he maketh as though the whole people in manner universally were so malicious and so foolish as—because the clergy, which hath toward many heretics been overmuch favorable, have of necessity been driven to deliver them to the secular hands and therein have done them right—he maketh as the whole people were in manner universally so mad and malicious as thereupon to take an opinion that to those which are none heretics the clergy would do wrong.

Surely in this one point is this book of his the most indifferent that it is in any part that I see therein. For there is no point in all the book wherein it more defameth the spiritualty than in this one it defameth in manner all the whole people universally.

But now if he say the people in manner universally think that those which are, as he saith, for lack of good and charitable handling lost and perished in body and soul, had wrong and ought not have been by the clergy delivered to the secular hands, and that therefore the whole people in manner universally do, and well may, think in their minds that the clergy would in like wise do wrong to others, and bring to like punishment all those persons that anything speak against only the abusions of such things as bring riches into the Church, now cannot this Pacifier thus excuse his words. For he confesseth in his own words that they which thus have been lost and perished, that might, as he saith, with good and charitable handling have been saved, be of those that have mistaken themselves in those articles of purgatory, trentals,[749] obits,[750] and pilgrimages, and have, as himself saith before, spoken against them and despised them; and then had they no wrong. For I am sure there was none of them but that he was either relapsed or else did of obstinacy stand still in them. And then appeareth it yet again that, in going about to defame the clergy, he doth indeed greatly defame the people, when he saith that because the clergy hath punished them that have so far mistaken themselves in those articles that they have spoken against those holy things and despised the things themselves, the people would be so far unreasonable as therefore to think that they would punish in like wise all those that would only speak against the abuses and not against the things. For all the people see, pardie,[751] that the clergy punisheth those that speak against the sacrament of matrimony, and yet they punish not those that speak against the abuses thereof, as adultery, or against those that under the name of matrimony live in sacrilege and incestuous lechery, as Friar Luther doth, and Friar Lambert, and Friar Hussgen, and Otho the Monk, and such others.

And yet if he will go from his own words again, and say now that some of them, that be for lack of good and charitable handling in body and soul so perished, did not mistake themselves at all, nor did not speak against any of the things, but did only speak against the abuses, and that therefore he may, without reproach of the people, well say that the people have an opinion that the clergy would, if

---

746 CW 9: 179 **747** *in the secular hands:* to the civil authorities **748** about **749** sets of requiem Masses **750** annual memorial Masses for the souls of the dead **751** certainly; "by God" (from French)

they might, have free liberty in like manner to punish all others that would in like manner speak—that
is to wit, not against the good and holy things, but
against the abuses of them—to this I say yet once
5 again that he still defameth the people of a great intolerable fault (that is to wit, an unjust and unreasonable judgment) while[752] he saith that they think
and believe that the clergy hath done to those men
in so great a matter so great wrong, and hitherto not
10 one such wrong proved.

But I shall in this point go yet a little nearer him.
Since he speaketh of those that might with charitable handling have been in body and soul saved, it appeareth well, as I have said, that in this piece of his
15 tale he speaketh of those that have not been saved,
but in earth here condemned and burned, and in
hell damned and there burning still. Now as for any
time so late[753] before this brabbling[754] or speech of
any division between the spiritualty and the tem-
20 poralty that this Pacifier might seem to mean of, I
remember none delivered to the secular hands but
Sir Thomas Hitton at Maidstone, and Sir Thomas
Bilney at Norwich, and one of late at Exeter, and
one of late in Lincoln Diocese; and in London here,
25 Bayfield the Monk, and Tewkesbury the Pouch-
maker, and Bainham. Now this will I say: let this
Pacifier come forth or, if he be any religious recluse
that cannot come abroad, let him appear by attorney. Howbeit,[755] it appeareth that he can be none
30 such, but must needs be of likelihood some such
as goeth much abroad, for else he could not surely
tell us of so many "some says," nor what opinion the
whole people of the realm hath in manner universally; and therefore let him come forth and appear
35 in his own proper person before the King's Grace
and his Council, or in what place he list,[756] and there
prove, calling me thereto, that any one of all these
had wrong, but if[757] it were for that[758] they were
burned no sooner; and because he shall not say that
40 I bid him trot about for nought,[759] this shall I prof-
fer him: that I will bind myself for surety and find
him other twain[760] besides, of better substance[761]
than myself, that for every one of these whom he
proveth wronged, his ordinary, or his other offi-
45 cer by whom the wrong was done, shall give this
Pacifier all his costs done about the proof, and a

reasonable reward besides. And yet now though no
man would give him nothing, it were his part pardie to prove it for his own honesty, since he hath
said so far. And this dare I be bold to offer, to see   50
the truth openly proved. After which well proved
once to be as he saith, men may be bold to say the
thing that they see proved true; and thereupon if
they list to cast and suspect some further fear of
the like—yea, or of worse, if they will—I will not   55
let[762] them. But without any such thing proved before, there will no reason nor good conscience bear
it that we should suspect that our prelates and ordinaries in their judgments against heretics use[763]
to do them wrong, since all the laws, both spiritual   60
of the whole Church and temporal of this realm,
have ordained full faith and credence to be given to
them therein. Which laws, to contrary now there
appeareth little cause, considering that the King
our sovereign lord that now is, and long mote[764] be,   65
hath in his time as prudently and as virtuously provided for this realm that it should have such prelates and ordinaries as should, in learning, wisdom,
justice, and living, be meet and convenient[765] therefor, as any prince hath (number for number) that   70
hath reigned over this realm, I dare boldly say this
hundred years, and should in my mind keep myself
a great way within my bounds although I would set
another hundred to it. But now letting this piece
pass, wherein I might say many things more than I   75
do—and would, save that the brethren would then
call me long, and will yet peradventure say that I am
scant[766] short enough—let us go farther and speed
up this one chapter of his.

THE TWENTY-SIXTH CHAPTER   80

And many other murmurs and grudges besides these that be before rehearsed be among
the people, more than I can rehearse now, but
yet above all others methinketh that it is most
to be lamented and sorrowed that spiritual   85
men, knowing these grudges and murmura-
tions among the people, and knowing also that
many laymen have opinion that a great occasion
thereof riseth by spiritual men, and that they do

---

752 when   **753** recently   **754** quarreling   **759** nothing   **760** two   **761** wealth   **764** may (he)   **765** *meet and convenient:*
755 However   **756** chooses   **757** *but*   **762** prevent   **763** are accustomed   fit and suitable   **766** scarcely
if: unless   **758** *for that:* because

no more to appease them, ne[767] to order themselves in no other manner for the appeasing of
them, than they do. For all that they do therein,
most commonly, is this: they take it that they
that find default at[768] such abusions and disorder love no priests; and therefore they esteem
that they do of malice all that they do, to destroy
the Church, and to have their goods and possessions themselves; and therefore they think it
a good deed to see them punished, so that they
shall not be able to bring their malice to effect.
And therefore have they punished many persons, which much people have judged them to do
upon will,[769] and of no love unto the people. And
though spiritual men are bound in this case — for
appeasing of these opinions in the people which
be so dangerous, as well to spiritual men as to
temporal men, that many souls stand in great
peril thereby — not only to reform themselves,
and to leave and avoid all things that give occasion to the people so to offend that may by charity be omitted and left, but also to fast, pray, wear
the hair,[770] give alms, and to do other good deeds
for themselves and for the people, crying continually to our Lord that these divisions may cease,
and that peace and concord may come again
into the world, yet it appeareth not that they do
so, but that they rather continue still after the
old course, pretending[771] by confederacies and
worldly policies and strait corrections[772] to rule
the people; and that is greatly to be lamented,
and it will be hard for them to bring it so about.
But if they would a little meeken themselves, and
withdraw such things as have brought the people into this murmur and grudge, they should
anon[773] bring a new light of grace into the world,
and bring the people to perfect love and obedience to their superiors.

And here methinketh I might say farther in
one thing, and that is this: that as long as spiritual rulers will either pretend that their authority is so high and so immediately derived of God
that the people are bound to obey them, and to
accept all that they do and teach without arguments, resistance, or grudging[774] against them,

or that they will pretend that no default[775] is
in them, but in the people — and will yet continue still in the same manner, and after the same
worldly countenance,[776] as they do now, and have
done late time past[777] — the light of grace that is
spoken of before will not appear, but that both
parties shall walk in this darkness of malice and
division, as they have done in time past.[778]

His other murmurs and grudges that he saith
he cannot now rehearse, he rehearseth after[779] many of them in his other chapters, which I
will pass over untouched, both for that[780] the more
part of them be such as every wise man will, I suppose, answer them himself in the reading, and satisfy his own mind without any need of mine help
therein, and for that some things are there also
therein that are very well said, and some also that,
be they good or bad, I purpose not to meddle much
withal, as[781] are the things that touch any laws or
statutes already made, be they of the Church or
of the realm; defend them I am content to do, if I
think them good. But on the other side, if I think
them naught,[782] albeit that in place and time convenient[783] I would give mine advice and counsel to
the change, yet to put out books in writing abroad
among the people against them, that would I neither do myself nor in the so doing commend any
man that doth. For if the law were such as were so
far against the law of God that it were not possible
to stand with man's salvation, then in that case the
secret advice and counsel may become every man,
but the open reproof and redargution[784] thereof
may not, in my mind, well become those that are
no more spiritual than I. And surely if the laws
may be kept and observed without peril of soul,
though the change might be to the better, yet, out
of time and place convenient to put the defaults of
the laws abroad among the people in writing and
without any surety of the change, give the people
occasion to have the laws in derision under which
they live — namely[785] since he that so shall use[786] to
do may sometimes mistake the matter and think
the thing not good whereof the change would be
worse — that way will I not, as thus advised, neither

---

767 nor   768 *default at:* fault with
769 *upon will:* voluntarily   770 hair-
shirt   771 claiming; professing
772 *strait corrections:* harsh punishments

773 immediately   774 murmuring
775 fault; defect   776 behavior; conduct
777 *late time past:* in recent times
778 *CW* 9: 179/40–180/42   779 later

780 *for that:* because   781 such as
782 bad   783 appropriate   784 rebuke;
criticism   785 especially   786 be
accustomed

use myself nor advise no friend of mine to do. And therefore I will, as I say, leave some things of his book untouched, whether he say well or evil. And finally for that[787] the touching of this matter is no part of my principal intent, but happeneth as an incident to fall in my way—wherein it sufficeth by the consideration of one piece or twain to give men an occasion to look well to the remnant, and let it not overlightly sink deep down into the breast till it be well chammed[788] and chewed in the mouth, and not only see what he saith, but also, by the wisdom of the reader, consider what may be said against it—and whoso hath wit and readeth it in that wise,[789] shall, I warrant you, soon perceive that mild indifferent[790] book to bear more shrewd[791] store of evil stuff therein than the brethren that boast it would that such good folk should see, as of a good mind meaning none harm ween everything were well meant that they see fair set out to the show, and soft and smoothly spoken.

THE TWENTY-SEVENTH CHAPTER

I will not also stick[792] much upon his high solemn divination wherein he prophesieth that

as long as the spiritual rulers will either pretend that their authority is so high and so immediately derived from God that the people are bound to obey them, and accept all that they do and teach, without argument, resistance, or grudge, and that they will pretend that no default is in them, but will yet continue still in the same manner, and the same worldly countenance as they do now and have done in late time past, the light of grace that is spoken of before,[793]

be with you now and evermore, amen.

The end of this holy sermon is to little purpose. For first as for worldly countenance is among the clergy within these few years not a little abated. Which thing, whoso list[794] with an even eye to look upon it and indifferently consider it shall not fail to perceive. And so there is good hope, if that may help the matter, that then the light of the grace that this gracious Pacifier spoke of before is not now very far

behind. And verily for aught[795] that I can see, a great part of the proud and pompous apparel that many priests in years not long past were, by the pride and oversight[796] of some few, forced in a manner against their own wills to wear, was, before his goodly counsel so by this pretty printed book privily given them in their ear, much more, I trow,[797] than the one-half spent, and in manner well worn out. And I wot well it is worn out with many which intend hereafter to buy no more such again. And for the residue of the countenance, I dare be bold to warrant that I can find of those that most may spend, which,[798] were they sure that it should in this matter do any good, would be well content to withdraw from all their other countenance the chief part of their movables, and of their yearly livelihood too, and out of hand bestow the one, and with their own hand yearly bestow the other openly among the poor. And I durst again be bold to warrant that if they so did, even the selfsame folk that now grudge and call them proud for their countenance would then find as great a grudge and call them hypocrites for their alms, and say that they spend upon naughty beggars the good that was wont to keep good yeomen, and that thereby they both enfeeble and also dishonor the realm.

Now as for the other part of his prophecy, concerning that the light of grace that he spoke of before will not appear "as long as spiritual rulers will pretend that their authority is so high, and so immediately derived of God that the people are bounden to obey them and to accept all that they do and teach, without arguments, resistance, or grudging against them"—in this part he must first declare whether he mean in these words "their authority" all their whole authority, or their authority in some part. If he mean that they say thus of all their whole authority in everything that they may now at this time lawfully do or say, I answer that they neither pretend, nor never did, all that authority to be given them immediately by God, but have authority now to do diverse things by the grant of kings and princes, as have also many temporal men, and by those grants have such right in those as temporal men have by the like grants in theirs. And therefore in that part the Pacifier is answered.

And then if he mean that the light of his grace

787 *for that:* because **788** chomped **789** way **790** impartial **791** malignant **792** linger **793** *CW* 9: 180/32–40 **794** chooses **795** all; anything **796** negligence **797** trust **798** some who

that he spoke of before will not appear as long as
the prelates pretend that any part of their authority
is so high that it is immediately given them of God,
then hath this Pacifier lost the light of truth. For the
greatest, and highest, and most excellent authority
that they have, either God hath given them himself,
or else they be very presumptuous and usurp many
things far above all good reason. For I have never
read, or at the leastwise I remember not that I have
read, that ever any king granted them the authority that now not only prelates but other poor plain
priests also daily do take upon them, in ministering
the sacraments and consecrating the Blessed Body
of Christ, with diverse other authorities besides.

But it seemeth to him peradventure that in one
point at the leastwise the spiritualty is too proud.
For he saith they pretend[799] to be obeyed, and have
their ordinances and their teachings observed,
without resistance, grudge, or arguments to the
contrary. Surely in such things as the whole clergy
of Christendom teacheth and ordereth in spiritual things—as be diverse of those laws which this
Pacifier in some places of this book toucheth, being made against heretics, and albeit that they be
and long have been through the whole corps of
Christendom, both temporalty and spiritualty, by
long usage and custom ratified, agreed, and confirmed, yet he layeth[800] some lack in them, calling
them very sore[801]—in those things I say that, since
I nothing doubt in my mind but in that congregation to God's honor graciously gathered together,
the good assistance of the Spirit of God is according to Christ's promise as verily present and assistant as it was with his blessed apostles, men ought,
with reverence, and without resistance, grudge, or
arguments, to receive them.[802] And if a provincial
council err, there are in Christ's Church ordinary
ways to reform it. But in such things as any spiritual governors, after[803] a lawful order and form, devise for the spiritual weal[804] of their souls that are in
their charge, and which things are such as good folk
may soon perceive them for good, in these things
at the leastwise should the good not give ear to the
bad folk and froward,[805] that against the best thing
that can be devised can never lack a fond[806] froward
argument. And therefore not only the apostles, being diverse assembled together with the Church in

their Council holden at Jerusalem, did in those laws
that they there devised and promulgated among the
gentiles that were in diverse countries far off converted unto Christ, did with authority write unto
them, "These things have seemed both to us and to
the Spirit of God necessary for you to keep,"[807] lest
some stubborn fools would peradventure be bold
with froward arguments and reasoning to resist it,
but Saint Paul also by himself when he devised unto
the Corinthians certain good laws and orders concerning their order that he would have them keep in
the church in time of God's service[808]—lest such as
would fain[809] with disputing against good order be
taken and reputed for wise should, with some problem pulled out of a penny pitcher, inveigle[810] and
corrupt the company, whom far the feebler reason
may draw to the worse part for affection unto lewd
liberty—he finally, besides the reasons that he laid
for his law, did put them to silence with his authority and, forbidding them to reason or dispute thereagainst but obey it, said, against all such arguments
and such chop-logics[811] against good rules, "If any
man will be contentious in this matter, let him well
know that we have no such guise[812] or custom, nor
the churches of God."[813]

But now will this Pacifier peradventure say that
he neither speaketh nor meaneth of such things as
the spiritualty doth or saith that is good, but that
the light of grace will not appear

> as long as the prelates pretend that their author-
> ity is so high and so immediate of God, that the
> people are bound to obey them and to accept all
> that they do and teach, without arguments, resis-
> tance, or grudging,

so that he hath circumspectly for the nonce[814] qualified and moderated his tale with this word "all":
that the prelates should not pretend to be obeyed in
things as well bad as good. Who heard ever the prelates of this realm pretend this, that they should be
obeyed in all things were the things bad or good? I
am very sure that ever hitherto they have professed
the contrary, and not letted[815] to say that if ever any
prelate of this realm—yea or the most part of them,
yea, or all the whole many—were so far fallen from
God as to preach the contrary of our old known

799 claim 800 alleges 801 grievous
802 See Acts 15:28. 803 according to
804 well-being 805 perverse; contrary
806 foolish 807 Acts 15:28 808 See
1 Cor 11:1–16. 809 gladly 810 deceive
811 sophistical arguments 812 practice
813 1 Cor 11:16 814 *for the nonce:* on
purpose; explicitly 815 hesitated

Catholic faith—as, for example, that there were no purgatory after this world; or that it were not lawful to pray to our blessed Lady or other holy saints; or to preach that there is yet never a saint in heaven, but that all souls lie still and sleep; or to preach against penance, as Tyndale doth, that is as loath, good tender pernel,[816] to take a little penance of the priest as the lady was to come anymore to disciplining[817] that wept, even for tender heart two days after when she talked of it, that the priest had on Good Friday with the disciplining rod beaten her hard upon her lily-white hands—whoso would, I say, preach any of these heresies, or that in the Blessed Sacrament of the altar were not the very Body and very Blood of Christ, but as Frith teacheth nothing but wine and bread, or else as Tyndale jesteth, starch instead of bread, though there would hereafter (which shall, I trust, never happen) all the prelates in this realm fall thereto and preach the same, yet all the prelates hitherto plainly do preach and teach that no layman should then believe them.

And therefore like[818] as if the prelates did pretend[819] the thing that this Pacifier speaketh of, then were his aforesaid words well and wisely tempered and circumspectly spoken, so while they neither pretend that thing now, nor never herebefore did, there is little wit in those words. For now doth all his tale amount unto no more but that the light of grace will never appear as long as the prelates do the thing that they neither do nor never did. Is not this therefore, good readers, by this good Pacifier brought unto a wise conclusion?

THE TWENTY-EIGHTH CHAPTER

Now where he most lamenteth that the clergy doth no more to appease these grudges of the temporalty toward them, and after, he preacheth to them holily what things they should do that they do not—that is to wit, forbear such things as he spoke of before, whereby he specially meaneth, as both before and in diverse places after appeareth, the evil and uncharitable handling of heretics, whereof the man hath nothing proved—but also that they should do things which, he saith, men see them not do (that is

to say, give alms, and wear hair,[820] and fast, and pray, that this division may cease), now that all the spiritual men do not so, that is very true. And it is as true, I trow,[821] that this thousand years was never the time that all so did. And therefore if that thing cause and keep in[822] this division, it must have been a thing of a thousand years old. But I think that many of them do all these things which this Pacifier preacheth to have done. For I am sure that though some do not their part therein, yet among the spiritualty there is both giving of great alms, and wearing of hair, and fasting, and praying for peace. But whether they take this division to be so great and so universal as this Pacifier speaketh of, that can I not tell; and peradventure they do not. And whether they do or no, surely I do not. Nor whether they pray for the pacification of this division in all such manner wise[823] as the thing requireth, that I cannot tell, but there may be peradventure therein some oversight upon their part. For if they leave nothing unprayed-for that may pertain to the pacification of this division, then must they peradventure put into their service (both Matins,[824] Mass, and Evensong)[825] some special collect,[826] and therein pray God that it may please him that the people may perceive the subtle sleights of the devil, and some others of his limes,[827] in many parts of this book of this pacification; which things peradventure the compiler perceived not himself, but was therein of simplicity by some subtle shrew[828] deceived.

THE TWENTY-NINTH CHAPTER

But this Pacifier, perceiving that what one man doth in secretness, another cannot see, is therefore bold to say they do not all those things which he would have them do: that is to wit, fast, and pray, wear hair, and give alms. For, he saith, "that they do all these things it appeareth not."

As for praying, it appeareth pardie[829] they do. And that so much they daily pray as some of us laymen think it a pain once in a week to rise so soon from sleep, and some to tarry so long fasting as on the Sunday to come and hear out their Matins. And yet is not the Matins in every parish, neither,

---

816 weak or wanton person **817** a voluntary public penance service **818** just **819** claim **820** hair-shirts **821** trust **822** *keep in:* make continue **823** *manner wise:* kinds of ways **824** morning prayer **825** evening prayer **826** a type of prayer **827** traps **828** scoundrel **829** indeed

all-thing[830] so early begun nor fully so long in doing as it is in the Charterhouse,[831] ye wot well. And yet at our sloth and gluttony that are lay people, this Pacifier can wink and feign himself asleep. But that the clergy prayeth not, that can he shortly spy, as soon as their lips leave stirring.

Howbeit, because he is peradventure of the clergy himself, therefore lest he should seem partial to his own party, he rather speaketh of their defaults than ours, wherein I will not much strive with him. But surely as he may be bold to preach, being a priest, so if I were a priest too, I would be bold to preach thus much again to him: that for any winning of the gloss[832] and fame of indifferency,[833] though he leave the faults of us lay people untouched, yet of his own party, the clergy, for no laymen's pleasure he never should say more than truth.

For now as touching of alms, is there none given, troweth he, by the spirituality? If he say, as he saith here, that it appeareth not that they do give alms, I might answer again that they follow therein the counsel of Christ, which saith, "Let not thy left hand see what thy right hand doth,"[834] as I might in praying have laid[835] those other words of Christ: "Thou, when thou wilt pray, enter into thy chamber and shut the door, and pray to thy Father privily."[836] But likewise as God, for all that counsel, was content that men should both pray and give to the needy, and do other works, both of penance and of charity, openly abroad in company where there be no desire of vainglory, but that the people, by the sight thereof, may have occasion to give therefor laud and glory to God,[837] so dare I boldly say that, as they both secretly and openly too, do use and accustom to[838] pray so do they both secretly and openly too, give no little alms in the year, whatsoever this Pacifier say. And I somewhat marvel that since this Pacifier goeth so busily abroad that there is no "some say" anywhere almost in all the whole realm but that he heareth it and can rehearse it — I marvel, I say, not a little that he neither seeth nor heareth any "some say" that there is in the spirituality given anything in alms. I use not much myself to go very far abroad, and yet I hear some say that there is; and I see sometimes myself so many poor folk at Westminster at the doles, of whom, as far as ever I heard, the monks use not to send away many unserved, that myself for the press of them have been fain[839] to ride another way.

But one answered me to this once, and said that it was no thanks to them, for it was lands that good princes have given them. But as I then told him again,[840] it were then much less thanks to them that would now give good princes evil counsel for to take it from them.

And also if we call it no giving of alms by them because the lands whereof they give it other good men have given them, whereof will you have them give alms? For they have none other.

THE THIRTIETH CHAPTER

Another thing also which this Pacifier seemeth to dispraise under the name of proud worldly countenance,[841] if men were as ready in a deed of his[842] own nature indifferent to construe the mind and intent of the doer to the better part as they be of their own inward goodness to construe and report it to the worse, then might I say that the same thing which they call the proud worldly countenance, they might and would call a full charitable alms: that is to wit, the right honest finding[843] and good bringing up of so many temporal men in their service, which,[844] though they be no beggars, yet might peradventure the great part of them go beg if they found[845] them not, but sent them abroad to seek themselves a service.[846]

And like as if you would give a poor man some money because he needeth and yet would make him work therefor in your garden lest he should by your alms live idle and wax[847] a loiterer, the labor that he doth taketh not away the nature and merit of your alms, no more it maketh the finding[848] of servants none alms though they wait on the finder and do him service in his house. And of all alms, the chief is to see them well brought up, and well and honestly guided. In which point, though neither party do fully their duty, yet I suppose in good faith that the spirituality goeth in that point, which is no small alms, rather somewhat afore us than anything drag behind us.

---

830 entirely   831 Carthusian monastery
832 superficial luster   833 impartiality
834 Mt 6:3   835 cited   836 Mt
6:6   837 See Mt 5:16.   838 *use and*

accustom to: practice and are accustomed to
839 forced   840 in reply   841 appearance   842 its   843 supporting; providing
with food and clothing   844 who

845 supported   846 position; job
847 become   848 supporting; providing
food and clothing

THE THIRTY-FIRST CHAPTER

Then followeth their fasting, which thing the spiritualty doth, as I suppose—all such as keep still the old Christian faith, and fall not unto these new heresies.

But this Pacifier findeth a fault, and rehearseth out of Jean Gerson, that the clergy keepeth not now the law by which it was ordained that the clergy should keep a longer Lent than they now do. And would God, as Saint Paul saith,[849] that both they and we could and would every day. But this Pacifier, that is so well seen in the laws of the Church, seeth well enough that the universal custom to the contrary dischargeth the bond[850] of that law, though peradventure it discharged not them that first began the breach whereby the custom grew. For as for fasting, the custom of the country may—either to the bond or to the discharge and interpretation of the laws made therefor—the custom, I say, may do much, as Saint Augustine showeth in more places than one. For if it were otherwise, then fasted almost no man any fast at all at this day while we dine at noon. For the very[851] fast was of old, as both by the Scripture[852] and holy writers appeareth, to forbear their meal till night, which is, as ye see, all changed. And the Church, to condescend unto our infirmity, hath been fain[853] therefore to say in Lent their Evensong before noon, and besides the natural days, to devise us new days *ex fictione juris*,[854] that we should at the least have Evensong in the Lenten fast before we fall to meat.[855] And yet we keep not that neither. But as an Almain[856] of mine acquaintance, when I blamed[857] him lately for not fasting upon a certain day, answered me, "Fareto[858] sould te laymen fasten? Let te priester fasten,"[859] so we begin, God wot, to fast full little for our own part, but bid the priester go fasten. And where[860] ourselves would for our own part be fain[861] that the Lent two weeks less, yet would we that for the clergy the Lent were one week longer. But some of them toss it from themselves as fast, and send it to the friars. And verily religious[862] folk use, I trow,[863] both long Lents and Advent too, and some of them diverse other fasts besides, and they be pardie[864] a great part of the spiritualty.

THE THIRTY-SECOND CHAPTER

Then preacheth this Pacifier yet farther, that the clergy should wear hair. He is surely somewhat sore[865] if he bind them all thereto, but among them I think that many do already—and some whole religion[866] doth. But yet saith this Pacifier that it doth not appear that they do so. Ah, well said. But now if all the lack stand in that point, that such holiness is hid, so that men may not see it, it shall be from henceforth well done for them, and so they will do, if they be wise, upon this advertisement[867] and preaching of this good Pacifier, come out of their cloisters, every man into the marketplace, and there kneel down in the cannel[868] and make their prayers in the open streets, and wear their shirts of hair in sight upon their cowls;[869] and then shall it appear, and men shall see it. And surely for their shirts of hair in this way were there none hypocrisy, and yet were there also good policy, for then should it not prick them.

THE THIRTY-THIRD CHAPTER

But as for all this Pacifier's preaching, the spiritualty may be content to take in good worth.[870] For peradventure if he were known, he were such one as to preach to all the spiritualty might well become his personage; and yet[871] if he be but a simple parson indeed, yet the spiritualty may meeken themselves according to his good counsel, and admit his wholesome admonitions. But surely this one thing, though the spiritualty bear it and take it well in worth, methinketh yet that every good temporal man may very much mislike: that this Pacifier, in the beginning of this his holy preaching, preacheth upon them to their sore[872] slander, first with an

849 See 1 Cor 6:12–13; 9:24–27; Rom 14:17–21. **850** obligation **851** true **852** See Jgs 20:26; 2 Sm 1:12; 3:35. **853** *been fain:* found it necessary **854** "by a fiction of law" **855** *fall to meat:* start eating. Canon law changed the Lenten days to last from noon to noon, rather

than from midnight to midnight, and thus the evening prayer was just before noon, at the end of these days. **856** German **857** reproved **858** Whereto; Why **859** *Fareto … priester fasten:* a rendering of a German accent **860** whereas **861** glad **862** i.e., members of religious

orders **863** trust; believe **864** certainly; "by God" (from French) **865** harsh **866** religious order **867** admonishment **868** gutter **869** monk's garment with a hood **870** *in good worth:* as valuable **871** even **872** great; grievous

untrue surmise grounded upon imagination, and after with a very plain open lie, neither an idle lie nor of any good purpose (of which two kinds of lying Saint Augustine admitteth neither nother[873] in folk of the perfection that this Pacifier, by his preaching used with such authority toward all the spiritualty, should seem to be), but a lie very pernicious, which is one of the things that least can become any good Christian man.

For first he saith that

> all that the spiritualty doth to the appeasing of the people is most commonly this: that they take it that they that find default at abusions and disorder of the spiritualty love no priests, and therefore they esteem that they do it of malice, all that they do, to destroy the Church.[874]

This is a goodly false surmise, grounded, as I said, upon a charitable imagination. But for all this, though good temporal men be evil-content with such as are in the spiritualty naught,[875] with whom the good folk of the spiritualty be as evil-content[876] as they, yet I verily trust for all this, as I say, that not the temporalty nor any one good temporal man, is, for them that are naught among the spiritualty, so displeased and angry against the spiritualty — that is to wit, against the corps and body thereof — that they should greatly need to be appeased, nor do not lay the faults of naughty spiritual persons to the rebuke of the whole spiritualty, no more than they would think it reason that the strangers of other realms so should lay the faults of evil temporal folk here to the rebuke of the whole temporalty, that they should grudge and say shrewdly by us for them.[877]

Now if this Pacifier will say that it is not like, and will say that we be not suitly[878] the temporalty and spiritualty of this realm, but that we be much better for our part than the spiritualty be for theirs: the temporalty shall not be dispraised for[879] me. For I trust that, though in respect of[880] the goodness that God's benefits unto man requireth of men again,[881] and in respect of the constancy and perseverance in virtue that men should hold fast and keep, there are few or none good in neither nother party, yet in such kind of goodness as the frailty of our nature suffereth[882] in this world — now up, now down, now falling by sin and now rising again by grace — the temporalty is good, I trust, and the spiritualty both, for all that there lacketh not a sort of some such as are very desperate devilish wretches in both, as no man doubteth but there was a very good Church of Christ in his blessed apostles' days, and yet were there even then many full very naught and stark heretics too therein.

And as for the difference in goodness between them and us, God knoweth the better and the worse both. But strangers of other countries that come hither and see both — saving some that have come both out of France and Flanders, and have here been put in trouble by the spiritualty for bringing in of Luther's Gospel — other strangers else, I say, when they have considered the spiritualty of this realm, and compared them in their minds not only with the temporalty of the same, but also with the spiritualty of their own countries, have said that our spiritualty may without any special reproach show their faces among other folk. And therefore, that the whole body of the spiritualty of this realm is so far fallen in the grudge and indignation of the whole temporalty, as this Pacifier speaketh, I neither see cause why it should[883] so nor yet believe that it is so, nor think it either good or honorable for this realm that other realms should ween it were so.

But whereas this Pacifier speaketh of appeasing, I pray God that some of the spiritualty have not in some things gone about overmuch to appease that sort of people by whose means they have thought that all their disease[884] hath come — those folk, I say, of whom by good information they have had detected[885] unto them for very stark[886] heretics indeed; whom, if, for any fear of such other folk's false suspicion springing upon such slanderous lies as this Pacifier speaketh of and groundeth his conclusions upon, the clergy begin to spare, and for any such causes begin to slack, and be the more remiss in the calling, attaching,[887] and examining, and of the further ordering[888] of heretics, God will not fail to make fall in[889] their necks the double slander of that from which they flee. For when they wax[890] so fainthearted in his great cause of repressing of

---

873 *neither nother:* neither one nor the other   **874** *CW* 9: 180/8–11   **875** bad   **876** discontent   **877** *shrewdly . . . them:* harshly of us on account of them   **878** accordingly   **879** by   **880** *respect of:* comparison with   **881** in return   **882** allows for   **883** should be   **884** trouble   **885** denounced   **886** complete   **887** *calling, attaching:* summoning to court, taking legal custody of   **888** correcting; punishing   **889** on   **890** become

heresies and maintaining of his faith that they forbear their duty for fear of false slanderous words,
God will then make them fall into the more slander by the selfsame means by which they flee from
5 the less. For instead of the false slander of evil men
and heretics that they fear in the pursuing, God will
send them a true slander, and make them be defamed among good men and Catholics, for their
slack and remiss handling. And further, if they
10 fall into the folly that the prophet reproveth, and
cease to call upon God for strength, and then tremble for dread where there is no peril,[891] and for any
dread of men (which, if they not only would slander them, but beat them and kill them too, can yet
15 kill but the body and then have spit all their poison)
would forget the fear, God (which, when he hath
slain the body, may send the soul into everlasting
fire), if (which our Lord forbid) any bishop fall in
this fear and cowardice of faint heart that, for any
20 worldly fear, they suffer[892] to be blown out the light
of his lantern of faith, he will not fail to make fall
upon them the terrible communication and threat
that the Spirit speaketh of in the Apocalypse unto
the Bishop of Ephesus: "I will come and remove thy
25 candlestick out of his place."[893]

THE THIRTY-FOURTH CHAPTER

Now where this Pacifier here surmiseth that the
spiritualty doth most commonly nothing else
but maliciously misconstrue the minds, and there-
30 fore maliciously persecute and pursue the bodies of
all them that find default at their disorder and abusions, the untruth of this surmise well and plainly
appeareth by this that every man daily heareth: that
there is not in all the clergy any man that useth[894] to
35 preach the Word of God but that, as he toucheth
the faults of the temporalty, such as he seeth in that
audience meetly[895] to be spoken of, so toucheth he
in like wise the faults of the spiritualty, and is for
his so doing not hated of[896] the spiritualty no more
40 than of the temporalty, but well commended of[897]
both. But of truth, he that would either upon the
spiritualty alone or upon the temporalty alone, or
upon any one part of either the one or the other—as

of only kings, or only dukes, or only lords, or only
gentlemen, or only men of law, or only merchants— 45
make his whole sermon when that one part only
were not his whole audience, and would by[898] that
part among all folk say many shrewd[899] things by
manner of exhortation to the amending, though
evil folk and malicious would have a pleasure to 50
hear it, yet would no good folk and indifferent[900]
think that he did well, and specially if he would use
that manner where himself pretended[901] that all the
remnant of his audience were in grudge and division already against that one part whose faults and 55
vices all his whole sermon holily putteth in all the
people's ears to mitigate their hatred with, and with
such preaching so to make the peace in like manner wise[902] as if he found a corner of his neighbor's
house burning, he would of great love and policy 60
lay on faggots[903] and gunpowder to put out the fire.

THE THIRTY-FIFTH CHAPTER

Now where this Pacifier, upon that misimag-
ined surmise, goeth on farther and saith that
because the clergy so misconstrueth the minds of all 65
those that find fault at their misorder and abusions,

therefore they think it a good deed to see them
punished, and they have therefore punished
many persons, which much people have judged
them to do upon will[904] and not of no love to the 70
people[905]

—in these words how charitably this Pacifier meant,
I cannot tell; but either by malice or oversight, either by default[906] of himself or craft of some subtle shrew, these words are as evil and as maliciously 75
written as anyone that would fain[907] falsely defame
the clergy could imagine or devise.

For here he saith that because they have (as himself beareth them in hand)[908] conceived a false suspicion against all those that find fault at their mis- 80
order and abusions, therefore they not only have
persecuted and punished many persons, but also
think their wrongful persecution and unrighteous
punishment well done. What can be worse done

---

891 See Ps 13(14):4–5; 52(53):4–5.
892 allow   893 Rv 2:5   894 be accustomed   895 appropriately   896 by
897 by   898 about   899 bad

900 impartial, unbiased   901 claimed
902 *like manner wise:* the same way
903 bundles of wood   904 *upon will:*
voluntarily   905 CW 9: 180/12–15

906 fault   907 gladly   908 *beareth them
in hand:* leads them to believe

than this? And therefore, as this doing were the worst that could be, if it were true, so is this saying the very worst that can be since it is very false.

And in these words the figure of "some say" will not well serve him; and yet in it cometh here also, much augmented and increased, in that he saith not that "some men" so "say," but that "much people" so "judgeth." Howbeit, as I said, this figure will not serve him here. But he playeth like a wily thief that, because he would not be known, would wear a visor, and yet, forgetting himself, would first come forth barefaced, and when every man had seen him and marked him well, would then put on his visor apace,[909] and cover his visage to walk away unknown. Even thus wisely, lo, playeth this Pacifier here. For first he saith as of himself that the clergy hath punished many persons "therefor": that is to wit, for the evil and false suspicion that they have conceived against all those that find fault in their misorder and abusions. And when he hath thus said as of himself, and thereby well showed himself, then, to cover and color[910] it with, he saith that "much people" "judgeth" so. And therefore his whole tale amounteth unto no more but that himself first affirmeth it, and after confirmeth his affirmation by the pretense[911] that much people judgeth the same; of which "much people" he nameth yet never one, nor proveth that much people so doth, nor showeth cause wherefore either much people or little people, or any one person, so should, but bringeth forth a bare surmise in such wise imagined against the clergy as every man that list[912] to lie may soon imagine in some other matter against any temporal men.

But as for his "much people," I set not much by.[913] For much people may sometimes believe some one man's lie. And against his much people—if there were much of them that so judge before the proof, and fish before the net, and set the cart before the horse, as I ween[914] there is not—yet is there against them much other people more wise in that point, and more circumspect, which,[915] till they see such an evil tale proved true, will either of indifferency keep themselves in a stay and suspend their sentence[916] for the season, or else, of a good mind, rather for the while think and believe the contrary.

Letting therefore for this time his much people

pass, I would now demand of him how he proveth this abominable fault that he layeth here to[917] the spiritualty himself, where he saith plainly that they have punished many persons "therefor"—that is to wit, for the thing that he there hath rehearsed—which is, ye wot well, because they have, he saith, conceived a false suspicion against them for finding default at their misorder and abusions, and take it as though they loved not the clergy, but of malice would destroy the Church and have their goods and possessions themselves. Now if the clergy have therefor punished many persons—because the same persons have only spoken against their misorder and abusions, and that the clergy have therefore misconstrued their minds and imagined that they would destroy the clergy for their possessions (which those other folk that spoke against their misorder went about with those words to get from the clergy to themselves)—if the clergy did, I say, for this cause of their own false imagined suspicion, punish those many persons that this Pacifier speaketh of, what thing in this world could they do that were worse? And therefore since that saying against the clergy is an intolerable defamation but if[918] that be true, I ask this Pacifier by what means he proveth it true.

And first to show that in some part at the least his words appear false, every man knoweth that some of those that have been punished have been such as neither, if the clergy lost their lands, should have any part thereof themselves, and were of such well-known naughtiness and lewd living besides that no good man could think it likely that such folk as they were should do it for any devotion—as was Sir Thomas Hitton, that was waxen a joiner,[919] and in many a day neither said Matins nor Mass, but raged and railed against the Blessed Sacrament; and Blomfield,[920] the apostate that was abjured[921] in London, and after railed against all religions[922] at Ipswich, and thereupon taken and imprisoned at Norwich; and Bayfield, the monk and apostate that was, as an abjured, and after perjured and relapsed heretic, well and worthily[923] burned in Smithfield. These, with diverse such others as have been punished for heresy, have been none such as the clergy needed to punish them for fear that they should get from them any part of their lands to themselves, nor

909 in a hurry   **910** disguise   **911** claim   **912** wants   **913** *set not much by:* value that little   **914** think   **915** who

916 judgment   **917** *layeth here to:* alleges here against   **918** *but if:* unless   **919** *that . . . joiner:* who had become a

cabinet maker   **920** William Blomfield, a Benedictine monk   **921** caused to recant   **922** religious orders   **923** deservedly

were of such wisdom, learning, nor virtue neither that the clergy could fear that any men of wit or of authority would anything regard their words, but only that⁹²⁴ the clergy feared: that by their means might grow the loss and destruction of many light persons' souls.

For if this Pacifier will say that the clergy feared lest those folk, and many such other like, should conspire and gather together, and pull all away from them by force, I cannot say nay but⁹²⁵ such a thing might indeed by long sufferance⁹²⁶ come about as well in this land as it hath in others. But then if the clergy feared that thing, they feared for more than themselves. For surely if such thing should fortune, as I trust it never shall, those folk would not take only from the clergy, but, among others from some of their own lay brethren too, such as have aught⁹²⁷ to lose.

But this Pacifier will peradventure say that though such manner folk as evil priests and apostates that the clergy have punished be none of those that they punished for that cause, but because they were heretics indeed, yet many others have they punished for that cause: that is to wit, because they misconstrued their minds and reckoned them for enemies to the clergy, for only finding of faults at the misorder and abusions of the clergy. And he will say, as he saith, that not only himself saith that the clergy have punished many persons therefor, but that also much people (though they say not so far as he saith—that is to wit, that they punished them "therefor") will yet say that they punished them rather of will⁹²⁸ than of love to the people. Well, yet the same much people, if this Pacifier have heard them so say, though their so saying be grounded but upon imagination and guessing at the secrets of other men's minds (as his own imagination is), yet judge they not so evil⁹²⁹ as himself doth. For if they judge in that punishment no more but less love to the people than desire to punishment, they judge not yet that the punishers did the parties wrong, as this Pacifier doth himself, that saith the clergy misconstrued their minds and, upon such mistaking of their minds for only speaking against their misorder and abusions, did therefore punish them.

And therefore letting, as I said before, his much

people pass by about their other business, I ask this Pacifier himself, since he saith that the clergy hath for that cause "punished many," what number is the least that he calleth many? For though very few be overmany to be so wrongfully mishandled and punished for only speaking against misorder and abusions, yet evermore this word "many" must needs import and signify some greater number pardie⁹³⁰ than one or two or three.

And over⁹³¹ this, because the matter whereupon this Pacifier bringeth it in is for a cause of a great and "in manner universal" grudge and division now of late (as he saith) sprungen up and grown between the spiritualty and the temporalty, these "many" persons that he speaketh of, which⁹³² have been so late,⁹³³ for only speaking against misorder and abusions, punished, must needs be so many as that there have been some such so punished almost in every diocese. For else he plain reproveth his own process,⁹³⁴ and excuseth the clergy himself unware, and layeth no little fault in the temporalty, if for the wrongful demeanor of one bishop or twain in one person or twain, they would bear a universal grudge against all the remnant.

Now to prove to what pass⁹³⁵ this Pacifier could bring his process of his many persons so sore⁹³⁶ mishandled and punished for only speaking against misorder and abusions of the clergy, let this Pacifier peruse and rehearse⁹³⁷ by name all the dioceses of England and Wales therewith, and I ween verily⁹³⁸ that, except London and Lincoln, he shall scant⁹³⁹ in any one of all the remnant find punished for heresy four persons in five years, and in the more part of them, not five in fifteen years, nor delivered into the secular hands, in the most part of them, any one in twenty years. And then if this be thus, although⁹⁴⁰ (which I trow⁹⁴¹ no man thinketh) of all those that in all the other dioceses have been punished were wronged, every one, yet were not so few likely to have made so great a universal grudge as this Pacifier speaketh of. For I suppose no man doubteth but that, by one occasion and other, more men than so many have mishapped to be in less space⁹⁴² mispunished in so much space of the land by temporal men; and yet hath there not grown any universal grudge or division against any part of the people thereby.

924 what   **925** *say nay but:* deny that
926 allowance   **927** anything   **928** *of will:* voluntarily; determinedly   **929** badly
930 indeed   **931** beyond   **932** who

933 recently   **934** *reproveth . . . process:* disproves his own argument   **935** result
936 terribly   **937** *peruse and rehearse:* examine one by one and list   **938** *ween*

verily: believe truly   **939** hardly
940 even if   **941** trust   **942** length of time

Let us now then come to those two dioceses of London and Lincoln, and of those twain, first to speak of Lincoln. As great a diocese as it is, and as many shires as it hath within it, yet have I not heard of late many punished for heresy among them all. But about a ten-year ago, to my remembrance, there were in that diocese about twelve or fourteen abjured in one town, and at that time every man that I heard speak thereof, either in the Court or elsewhere, appeared very glad that such a bed of snakes was so found out and broken. For then were there at that time no pacifiers to put forth books and lament such divisions, with laying for a cause of the grudge that many persons were mishandled and punished for only speaking against the misorder and abusions of the clergy. But now every one that is punished anywhere is enough for a matter of a lamentable book of *Division*, that may, to pacify the grudge ere it begin, use a figure of "some say," and "they say," and "many say," and "much people saith," and "many men think," and such other, and therewith inveigle[943] the reader, and make some good folk ween that right were wrong and every one man a hundred.

But now come I to the Diocese of London, in which, though there have been somewhat more ado in these matters, there is no great marvel, since unto this diocese there is so great resort and confluence, not only from other parts of this realm, but also from other lands. And yet even here, of all that hath been punished in this diocese, either in the County of Essex (for as for in Middlesex, I remember none) or in the City itself, either of residents therein or of resorters[944] thereto, Englishmen or strangers,[945] since this Pacifier affirmeth that "many persons" be punished by the clergy for the only speaking against their abusions and misorder, and of those that have been punished, either right or wrong, far the most part have been here (double and treble, I trow, to all the remnant of the whole realm), and this is here next at hand, whereby the proofs[946] of all such mishandling may here with least labor and charge[947] be brought forth, and the truth most easily tried, let this Pacifier, of those many mishandled and wrong-punished persons that he speaketh of, come forth and here prove us some. Let him prove twenty, let him prove twelve, let him prove ten, let him prove six, let him prove twain; or, for very shame, after

such a great word of "so many," let him prove some one at the least. But surely I suppose he shall never be able to do that.

THE THIRTY-SIXTH CHAPTER

But I suppose in good faith that this Pacifier hath, of some facility[948] of his own good nature, been easy to believe some such as have told him lies, and hath been thereby persuaded to think that many other folk said and knew the thing that some few told him for very truth. And surely they that are of this new brotherhood be so bold and so shameless in lying that whoso shall hear them speak and knoweth not what sect they be of shall be very sore abused[949] by them.

Myself have good experience of them. For the lies are neither few nor small that many of the blessed brethren have made, and daily yet make, by[950] me.

Diverse of them have said that of such as were in my house while I was Chancellor, I used to examine them with torments, causing them to be bounden to a tree in my garden, and there piteously beaten.

And this tale had some of those good brethren so caused to be blown about that a right worshipful[951] friend of mine did of late, within less than this fortnight, tell unto another near friend of mine that he had of late heard much speaking thereof.

What cannot these brethren say, that can be so shameless to say thus? For of very truth, albeit that for a great robbery, or an heinous murder, or sacrilege in a church (with carrying away the pyx with the Blessed Sacrament, or villainously casting it out), I caused sometimes such things to be done by some officers of the Marshalsea,[952] or of some other prisons, with which ordering[953] of them by their well-deserved pain, and without any great hurt that afterward should stick by them, I found out and repressed many such desperate wretches as else had not failed to have gone farther abroad, and to have done to many good folk a great deal much more harm; yet though I so did in thieves, murderers, and robbers of churches—and notwithstanding also that heretics be yet much worse than all they—yet, saving only their sure keeping, I never did else[954] cause any such thing to be done to

---

943 deceive   944 visitors   945 for-
eigners   946 witnesses   947 expense   948 pliancy   949 misled; deceived
950 about   951 distinguished   952 a prison near London   953 correcting
954 otherwise

any of them all in all my life, except only twain; of which the one was a child and a servant of mine in mine own house, whom his father had, ere ever he came with me, nuzzled up[955] in such matters, and had set him to attend upon George Joye or Gee, otherwise called Clerk, which is a priest and is now, for all that, wedded in Antwerp; into whose house there, the two nuns were brought which John Burt, otherwise called Adrian, stole out of their cloister to make them harlots. This George Joye did teach this child his ungracious heresy against the Blessed Sacrament of the altar, which heresy this child afterward, being in service with me, began to teach another child in my house, which uttered his counsel. And upon that point perceived and known, I caused a servant of mine to stripe[956] him like a child before mine household, for amendment of himself and example of such others.

Another was one which, after that he had fallen into the frantic[957] heresies, fell soon after into plain open frenzy besides. And albeit that he had therefore been put up in Bedlam, and afterward by beating and correction, gathered his remembrance to him and began to come again to himself, being thereupon set at liberty and walking about abroad, his old fancies began to fall again in his head. And I was from diverse good holy places advertised[958] that he used, in his wandering about, to come into the church and there make many mad toys and trifles,[959] to the trouble of good people, in the divine service; and specially would he be most busy in the time of most silence, while the priest was at the secrets[960] of the Mass, about the elevation.[961] And if he spied any woman kneeling at a form,[962] if her head hung anything[963] low in her meditations, then would he steal behind her and, if he were not letted,[964] would labor to lift up all her clothes and cast them quite over her head. Whereupon I, being advertised of these pageants,[965] and being sent unto and required[966] by very devout religious folk to take some other order with him, caused him, as he came wandering by my door, to be taken by the constables and bounden to a tree in the street, before the whole town, and there they striped him with rods therefor till he waxed[967]

weary, and somewhat longer. And it appeared well that his remembrance was good enough, save that it went about in grazing till it was beaten home. For he could then very well rehearse his faults himself and speak and treat[968] very well, and promise to do afterward as well. And verily, God be thanked, I hear none harm of him now.

And of all that ever came in my hand for heresy, as help me God, saving, as I said, the sure keeping of them—and yet not so sure, neither, but that George Constantine could steal away[969]—else had never any of them any stripe or stroke given them, so much as a fillip[970] on the forehead.

And some have said that when Constantine was gotten away, I was fallen for[971] anger in a wonderful rage. But surely though I would not have suffered[972] him go if it would have pleased him to have tarried still in the stocks, yet when he was neither so feeble for lack of meat but that he was strong enough to break the stocks, nor waxen so lame of his legs with lying but that he was light enough to leap the walls, nor by any mishandling of his head so dulled or dazed in his brain but that he had wit enough, when he was once out, wisely to walk his way; neither was I then so heavy[973] for the loss but that I had youth enough left me to wear it out,[974] nor so angry with any man of mine that I spoke them any evil word for the matter, more than to my porter that he should see the stocks mended and locked fast, that the prisoner steal not in again. And as for Constantine himself, I could[975] him in good faith good thanks. For never will I for my part be so unreasonable as to be angry with any man that riseth if he can, when he findeth himself that he sitteth not at his ease.

But now tell the brethren many marvelous lies of much cruel tormenting that heretics had in my house—so far-forth that one Sygar,[976] a bookseller of Cambridge which was in mine house about four or five days, and never had either bodily harm done him or foul word spoken him while he was in mine house, hath reported since, as I hear say, to diverse that he was bounden to a tree in my garden, and thereto too[977] piteously beaten, and yet besides that,

955 *nuzzled up:* nurtured   **956** lash, whip   **957** insane   **958** informed   **959** *toys and trifles:* tricks and pranks   **960** silent prayers   **961** lifting up of the Host for the adoration of the people   **962** bench   **963** at all   **964** prevented   **965** scenes   **966** asked   **967** became   **968** handle, discuss   **969** Constantine (*ca.* 1500–1560), a priest who became a follower of Tyndale, fled to Antwerp in the 1520s, but then returned to England, where he was arrested by More. He escaped from   More's custody in November 1531.   **970** a small tap with the finger   **971** because of   **972** let   **973** sad   **974** *wear it out:* endure it   **975** gave   **976** Sygar Nicholson   **977** also

bounden about the head with a cord and wrungen, that he fell down dead in a swoon.

And this tale of his beating did Tyndale tell to an old acquaintance of his own, and to a good lover of mine, with one piece farther yet: that while the man was in beating, I spied a little purse of his hanging at his doublet, wherein the poor man had (as he said) five marks; and that caught I quickly to me and pulled it from his doublet, and put it in my bosom, and that Sygar never saw it after; and therein, I trow, he said true; for no more did I neither nor before neither nor, I trow, no more did Sygar himself neither in good faith.

But now when I can come to goods by such goodly ways, it is no great marvel though I be so suddenly grown to so great substance of riches, as Tyndale told his acquaintance and my friend; to whom he said that he wist[978] well that I was no less worth, in money and plate[979] and other movables, than twenty thousand marks. And as much as that have diverse of the good brethren affirmed here nearer home.

And surely this will I confess: that if I have heaped up so much goods together, then have I not gotten the one half by right. And yet by all the thieves, murderers, and heretics that ever came in my hands am I not, I thank God, the richer of one groat,[980] and yet have they spent me twain.[981] Howbeit, if either any of them, or of any kind of people else, that any cause[982] have had before me, or otherwise any meddling with me, find himself so sore grieved with anything that I have taken of his, he had some time to speak thereof. And now since no man cometh forth to ask any restitution yet, but hold their peace and slack[983] their time so long, I give them all plain peremptory warning now, that[984] they drive it off no longer. For if they tarry till yesterday, and then come and ask so great sums among them as shall amount to twenty thousand marks, I purpose to purchase such a protection[985] for them that I will leave myself less than the fourth part, even of shrewdness, rather than ever I will pay them.

And now dare I say that if this Pacifier had by experience known the troth[986] of that kind of people, he would not have given so much credence to their lamentable complaining as it seemeth me by some of his "some says" he doth.

Howbeit, what faith my words will have with him in these mine own causes, I cannot very surely say, nor yet very greatly care. And yet stand I not in so much doubt of myself but that I trust well that among many good and honest men, among which sort of folk I trust I may reckon him, mine own word would alone, even in mine own cause, be somewhat better believed than would the oaths of some twain of this new brotherhood in a matter of another man.

THE THIRTY-SEVENTH CHAPTER

But now to come to some spiritual men's causes against whom there are laid like lies, one Simonds, a long well-known heretic walking about the realm, was taken not long ago by the officers of the right reverend father my lord Bishop of Winchester, and, being put in a chamber to keep and breaking out at a window, hath told many of his brethren since that he was marvelously tormented by the Bishop's officers in prison, and should have been murdered therein too, and that else he would never have run his way. But he would never since complain of his harms to the King or his Council, but will rather of perfection suffer them all patiently than to pursue and prove them with his forthcoming again.

Would God this Pacifier might have the examination of that matter. It would peradventure do him great good hereafter to find out the truth of such a false heretic's tale.

And now notwithstanding that the brethren boast much of his happy escape, yet if he happed to die or be hanged somewhere, thereas[987] no man wist where but they, they would not let[988] for a need to say that he escaped not at all, but was privily killed in prison, and privily cast away. For so said some of them by[989] George Constantine, not only upon his first flight out of my keeping, but also even now of late, notwithstanding that they well know that many merchants of our own had seen him since laugh and make merry at Antwerp.

---

978 knew   **979** articles made of or plated with a precious metal   **980** a silver coin worth four pence   **981** *spent me twain:* ... cost me two   **982** court case   **983** allow to slip by   **984** so that   **985** guarantee of ... immunity   **986** faithfulness; truthfulness   **987** in a place   **988** hesitate   **989** about

Such lust have these blessed brethren, that ever talk of faith and Spirit and troth and verity, continually to devise and imagine lies of malice and hatred against all those that labor to make them good.

And such a pleasure hath either Frith himself or else some other false foolish brethren of his sect. For he told one or twain, and caused the brethren to blow it farther about, that word was sent him into the Tower that the Chancellor of London said it[990] should cost him the best blood in his body.

Now whether Frith lied or his fellows, let them draw cut[991] between them. For surely where they tell it under such manner—as though Master Chancellor should rejoice and have a cruel desire of the man's death—I know him so well that I dare well say they falsely belie him therein.

Howbeit, some truth they might hap to hear whereupon they might build their lie. For so was it that on a time one came and showed me that Frith labored so sore that he sweat again, in studying and writing against the Blessed Sacrament. And I was of truth very heavy[992] to hear that the young foolish fellow should bestow such labor about such a devilish work, and, wishing that the man had some good Christian friend to whom he would give ear, that might withdraw him from giving and inclining all his heart to the following of that frantic[993] heresy, wherewith he were in peril to perish both body and soul, said in the communication[994] these words, or others of like effect: "For if that Frith," quoth I, "sweat in laboring to quench the faith that all true Christian people have in Christ's Blessed Body and Blood, which all Christian folk verily, and all good folk fruitfully, receive in the form of bread, he shall labor more than in vain. For I am sure that Frith and all his fellows, with all the friends that are of their affinity, shall neither be able to quench and put out that faith. And over that, if Frith labor about the quenching thereof till he sweat, I would some good friend of his should show him that I fear me sore[995] that Christ will kindle a fire of faggots[996] for him, and make him therein sweat the blood out of his body here, and straight from hence send his soul forever into the fire of hell."

Now in these words I neither meant nor mean that I would it were so. For so help me God and none otherwise, but as I would be glad to take more labor, loss, and bodily pain also than peradventure many a man would ween to win that young man to Christ and his true faith again, and thereby to preserve and keep him from the loss and peril of soul and body both.

Now might it peradventure be that I told Master Chancellor this tale; and so, I ween, I did; and he might thereupon happen to report it again, or say some suchlike words of like purpose[997] to some other man, and that thereupon these brethren build up their tower of lies. Or else, which were not impossible, Frith, if he heard the tale told by[998] me, might, withdrawing the best, and making it seem such as himself list,[999] tell it out by Master Chancellor to bring him among the people in opinion of malice and cruelty. But his mild mind and very tender dealing in such matters is among all the people by good experience so plainly proved and so clearly known that it will be hard to bring any such sinister opinion of him in any good honest man's head, for the words of a great many such manner folk as Frith is, which not only speaketh lies against honest men, but also writeth false lies and heresies against the Blessed Sacrament of the altar.

Some man will yet peradventure say that this is a thing far unlikely: that either Frith or any man else would wittingly[1] take a burden from one man and lay it in another man's neck, and namely to lay it to the Chancellor from me, since that all such folk reckon in themselves that they have more cause of grief against me than him.

Surely if they were wise and intended to be good, they should neither think themselves to have cause of grief or grudge against me nor him neither. For of myself I wot well, and of him I believe the same: that we nothing intend unto them but their own wealth,[2] which, without their amendment by change of their heresies into the true faith again, is impossible to be gotten.

But for the point that I spoke of—that it were not so far unlikely as it would haply[3] seem that Frith would turn that tale from me to Master Chancellor—ye shall perceive partly by his own deed, and partly by the dealing of some other such in suchlike manner of matter. For ye shall understand that after that Frith had written a false foolish treatise against the Blessed Sacrament of the

---

990 i.e., his stay in the Tower　**991** *draw cut:* draw straws, cast lots　**992** saddened　**993** insane　**994** conversation　**995** greatly　**996** bundles of wood　**997** effect　**998** about　**999** wants　**1** knowingly　**2** well-being　**3** perhaps

altar,[4] I, having a copy thereof sent unto me, made shortly an answer thereto.[5] And for because that his book was not put abroad in print, I would not therefore let mine run abroad in men's hands. For, as I have often said, I would wish that the common people should of such heresies never hear so much as the name. But forasmuch as that thing is impossible to provide but that heretics will be doing, therefore are other folk sometimes driven of necessity to speak of those matters also, and to make answer unto them.

And therefore when heretics abjure and do their penance, the preacher is fain to rehearse[6] their opinions in the pulpit, and there answer those devilish arguments openly with which those heretics first deceive men and women in corners secretly and after spread them abroad in audience by defense of those heresies in their examination openly.

And also if their books be once put abroad in print, it is a thing very hard to get them well in again. But as for me, I used therein this provision for the remedy on both parts: that though I would not put mine answer abroad into every man's hands at adventure[7] (because Frith's book was not put out abroad in print), yet I caused mine answer to be printed under mine own name, to the intent I might, as indeed I have, give out some to such as I perceived had seen his book before.

Now happed it that, upon a time, the right reverend father my lord Bishop of Winchester sent for Frith unto his own place, of very[8] fatherly favor toward the young man's amendment, which he sore desired, both for other causes and, among other causes, partly also for this: because he was, not many years ago, a young boy waiting upon him and a scholar of his. In that communication, what words were between them were now too long to rehearse. But such they were as I would wish that all such as be wise, and ween that Frith were wise (which be peradventure some that hear the brethren speak of him, and weigh not themselves his words), had there stood by and heard. For they should, I am sure, have taken Frith ever after for such as he plainly, before good record,[9] proved himself then—which was not a heretic only, but besides that a proud unlearned fool.

But as I was about to tell you, in that communication my said lord of Winchester among other things communed[10] with Frith against his afore-remembered[11] heresy that he so sweateth in to impugn the true Christian faith concerning the Sacrament of the altar. And when Frith there stood in his heresy as stiffly as he defended it foolishly secretly between them twain, my lord, longing that the fellow's folly might appear, called good and worshipful[12] witnesses unto them. And then, because his Lordship perceived Frith loath to have it known abroad, out[13] of the brotherhood, as yet at that time that he went about to poison the realm with that pestilent heresy against the Sacrament, my lord, I say, said unto him that it was now too late for him to think that he could keep close:[14] "Revoke it, Frith," quoth his Lordship, "ye may, and repent it, and so were it well done ye did; but keep it from knowledge you cannot, ye be gone now so far. For your books of this matter have been seen abroad in many men's hands, and that so long that, lo, here is an answer already made unto it"—and showed him my book in print; but of troth, he delivered it not unto him. Howbeit, soon after, he got mine answer—I cannot tell of whom—and since have I heard of late that he sweateth about that matter afresh, and hath, I hear say, the devilish books of Wycliffe, Zwingli, and Friar Hussgen secretly conveyed unto him into the Tower, and hath begun and gone on a great way in a new book against the Sacrament.

But the thing that I tell you this tale for is this: I am well informed that he knoweth very well that I made that answer; and it is not very likely but that, by one or another, he hath the book in print; and of likelihood he never had it otherwise. For that was as easy a way, ye wot well, as one to write it out that had it in print already; and before it was printed, I know very well he could never get it. And at the leastwise I know it well that he knoweth well enough that the answer was made by me; and yet he dissimuleth that, and, feigning himself not to know who made it, but to think it rather that my said lord of Winchester made it than any man else, maketh his new book, as I am very certainly informed, not against me by name, but all against my said lord, of a solemn pride that he would have his book seem a disputation between the boy and the Bishop.

But there shall not greatly need such a bishop so learned as my said lord is to dispute with any such as Frith is, for five such books as that is, if it be no wiser than was his other, or than this his new is either, if it be no wiser than one telleth me that both can[15] good skill and hath heard a great part read; nor, howsoever he have handled it, wise will it never be while the matter thereof is so false. And therefore when the book shall hereafter be finished and happeth to come to mine hands, I trust to make almost every boy able to perceive the false folly thereof, though he cover his rotten fruit as close[16] and as comely[17] as ever any costermonger[18] covered his basket.

But this, as I said, ye may, good readers, see: that as Frith taketh mine answer from me, which himself and every man else knoweth well for mine, and imputeth it to the Bishop of Winchester, it were not much unlikely that he would, when he had heard of a thing that I had said, and when himself had made it worse, then change it from me and impute it unto Master Chancellor of London.

THE THIRTY-EIGHTH CHAPTER

Which if he do, he doth it not alone. For this point played also Thomas Philips of London, leather-seller, now prisoner in the Tower. Whom, when I was Chancellor, upon certain things that I found out by[19] him, by the examination of diverse heretics whom I had spoken with, upon the occasion of the heretics' forbidden books, I sent for; and when I had spoken with him, and honestly entreated him one day or twain in mine house, and labored about his amendment in as hearty loving manner as I could, when I perceived finally the person such that I could find no troth[20] neither in his word nor his oath, and saw the likelihood that he was, in the setting forth of such heresies closely, a man meet[21] and likely to do many folk much harm, I by indenture[22] delivered him to his ordinary.[23] And yet, for because I perceived in him a great vainglorious liking of himself, and a great spice[24] of the same spirit of pride that I perceived before in Richard Hunne[25] when I talked with him, and feared that if he were in the Bishop's prison, his ghostly[26] enemy

the devil might make him there destroy himself, and then might such a new business arise against Master Chancellor that now is as at that time arose upon the Chancellor that was then — which thing I feared in Thomas Philips somewhat also the more because a cousin of his, a barber in Paternoster Row called Holy John, after that he was suspected of heresy and spoken to thereof, fearing the shame of the world, drowned himself in a well — I for these causes advised, and by my means helped, that Thomas Philips (which, albeit that he said that the clergy loved him not, seemed not yet very loath to go to the Bishop's prison) was received prisoner into the Tower of London. And yet after that he complained thereupon, not against me, but against the ordinary. Whereupon the King's Highness commanded certain of the greatest lords of his Council to know how the matter stood. Which, known and reported to the King's Grace, his Highness, as a most virtuous Catholic prince, gave unto Thomas Philips such answer as, if he had been either half so good as I would he were, or half so wise as himself weeneth he were, he would forthwith[27] have followed, and not stand still in his obstinacy so long as he hath now put himself thereby in another deeper peril.

Others have besides this complained that they have been untruly and unjustly handled; and this have they not letted[28] to do after that they have been convicted and abjured, and their just condemnations, after their open examinations and plain and clear proofs, so well and openly known that they have, by their shameless clamor, nothing gotten but rebuke and shame. And yet were some of them, if their ordinaries had been so sore[29] and so cruel as this book of this Pacifier maketh them, fallen again in the danger and peril of relapse.

And some hath been heard upon importunate clamor, and the cause and handling examined by the greatest lords temporal of the King's most honorable Council — and that since that I left the office — and the complainer founden in his complaining so very shamelessly false that he hath been answered that he was too easily dealt with, and had wrong that he was no worse served.

And such have these folk ever been founden and ever shall. For when they fall to a false faith in

---

15 have   16 secretly   17 attractively
18 apple-seller   19 about   20 truth;
fidelity   21 fit   22 official written
agreement   23 bishop   24 admixture

25 He was a merchant tailor in London, who was imprisoned on the charge of heresy. He died in prison under suspicious circumstances in December 1514. More

thought it was suicide, but many accused the authorities of murder.   26 spiritual
27 immediately   28 hesitated   29 strict

heart, their words cannot be true. And therefore if this Pacifier well and thoroughly knew them, I dare say he would less believe their lamentable tales than I fear me that he hath believed some in complaining upon their ordinaries, against whom he seemeth, upon such folk's false complaining, to have conceived this opinion that his book of *Division* showeth: that is to wit, that the clergy think that every man that speaketh against their misorder and abusions loveth no priests, and that therefore they have punished many men—which God forbid were true. For if it were, surely they that so punished any one man for that cause—that is to wit, because themselves conceive a false suspicion against him— it were pity that they lived. But I think in good faith that the prelates will never desire to live longer than till this Pacifier prove that same false tale true.

THE THIRTY-NINTH CHAPTER

I said before that I would touch of this book, and so have I touched his first chapter whole, because it hath, for the first setting forth, the chief countenance[30] of mildness and charity. And yet what charity there is therein, when it is considered, I suppose you see. For no part is there of the clergy that can please him—neither prelates nor mean[31] secular priests, nor religious[32] persons, not so much as any one man—as you may plainly perceive by other words of his in other places of his loving book. And yet among all these faults, I see him find none with them that run out in apostasy, but all the faults be assigned in[33] them that abide in their profession still. Nor I find not in his book any cause of his division to be founden in the sowing and setting forth of these new-sprungen heresies. And yet do they make, and needs must make, wheresoever they come, the greatest division that can be: first in opinions and contrarious minds, and afterward in fervor of language and contentious words, and finally, if it go forth long, in plain sedition, manslaughter, and open war.

And this fault of these heresies he might as well have laid unto the clergy as some of the others that he sore[34] speaketh of, if he take heresies for any. For like as naughty priests and naughty

religious persons have always been they that do those other faults which, under the figure of "some say," this book layeth to the charge of the spirituality, so have naughty priests and naughty religious folk (being among the clergy as Judas was among Christ's apostles) betrayed the faith of Christ and begun and set forth these ungracious heresies as fast[35] and as fervently for their part as naughty lay folk for theirs; and both twain first corrupt some of their company at home, and after run out in apostasy and put abroad their heresies in writing. And some men say that some prelates have not done all their parts in the repressing and due punishment of them. And yet as great faults as these be, and such as all the temporalty should be most grieved with and grudge at, and therefore should be most cause of this division, if there be such a division, and that every default that is in any naughty persons of the spirituality be a cause of almost a universal division and grudge of the whole corps of the temporalty against the whole body of the spirituality, yet, I say, for all this, the book of this Pacifier layeth no piece of this fault unto the spirituality, but rather findeth fault and cause of grudge and division in the spirituality for oversore handling of them that are heretics indeed, and laboreth to abash the ordinaries with obloquy, and put them in dread with fear of infamy, and falsely beareth them in hand[36] that they have punished many persons for a wrong suspicion falsely conceived in their own minds against those whom they punished.

And thus far hath he gone in his first chapter. In which manner, albeit I trust in God the man meant himself but well, yet I fear me some wily shrew hath somewhat set him awry in the tempering of his words.

THE FORTIETH CHAPTER

And verily albeit, as I said before, I purpose not to meddle with every part of his book that I think were well done for him to amend, yet in his seventh chapter and his eighth—which twain treat all of these matters of heresies—for the great weight of the matter, I shall not forbear to show you some difference and diversity between his mind and mine.

30 appearance   **31** ordinary   **32** i.e.,   attributed to   **34** strongly   **35** steadfastly
of religious orders   **33** *assigned in:*   **36** *beareth . . . hand:* leads us to believe

Another occasion of the said division hath been, by reason of diverse suits that have been taken in the spiritual courts of office (that is called in Latin, *ex officio*),[37] so that the parties have not known who hath accused them, and thereupon they have sometimes been caused to abjure in causes of heresies—sometimes to do penance, or to pay great sums of money for redeeming thereof—which vexation and charges the parties have thought have come to them by the judges and the officers of the spiritual court (for they have known none other accusers), and that hath caused much people in diverse parts of this realm to think great malice and partiality in the spiritual judges. And if a man be *ex officio* brought before the ordinary for heresy, if he be notably suspected of heresy, he must purge himself after the will of the ordinary or be accursed;[38] and that is by the law *Extravagant de hereticis, cap. Ad abolendam.*[39] And that is thought by many to be a very hard law, for a man may be suspected and not guilty, and so be driven to a purgation without proof or without offense in him, or be accursed.[40]

I will, in this point of conventing[41] *ex officio*, no farther speak at this time than concerning the crime of heresy. For I am in good faith loath to meddle with this book of his at all. For loath am I anything to meddle against any other man's writing that is a Catholic man, saving that it seemeth me verily[42] that, be this man never so good, yet if his mind were followed in this matter, it would work this realm great harm and no good.

For surely if the conventing of heretics *ex officio* were left, and changed into another order by which no man should be called, be he never so sore suspected nor by never so many men detected but if[43] some man make himself party against him as his accuser, the streets were likely to swarm full of heretics before that right few were accused, or peradventure any one, either.

For, whatsoever the cause be, it is not unknown, I am sure, that many a man will give unto a judge secret information of such things as, though they be true, yet gladly he will not, or peradventure dare

not, be openly aknown that the matter came out by him. And yet shall he sometimes give the names of diverse others, which, being called by the judge, and examined as witnesses against their wills, both know and will also depose[44] the truth—and he that first gave information also; and yet will never one of them willingly make himself an open accuser of the party, nor dare peradventure for his ears.[45]

And this find we not only in heresy, but in many temporal matters among ourselves, whereof I have had experience many a time and oft, both in the disclosing of felonies, and sometimes of much other oppression used by some one man or twain in a shire, whereby all their neighbors sore smarted, and yet not one durst openly complain.

Howbeit, it cometh in heresies sometimes to much worse point. For I have wist[46] where those that have been in the company at the time, being folk of good substance[47] and such as were taken for worshipful,[48] being called in for witnesses, have first made many delays, and afterward, being examined on their oaths, have sworn that they heard it not, or remembered it not, and took no heed to the matter at the time, whereas it well appeared, by the depositions of diverse others being with them at the time, that in every man's conscience they lied. When would these folk become a heretic's accuser, against whom they would rather be forsworn[49] than of the truth to bear witness?

And this thing maketh that it may be sometimes (albeit very seldom it happeth) that in heresy, upon other vehement suspicions without witnesses, a man may be put to his purgation[50] and to penance also if he fail thereof. Which thing, why so many should now think so hard a law as this Pacifier saith they do, I cannot see, nor those wise men neither that made the law. And yet were they many wise men, and not only as wise, but peradventure many more also in number, than those that this Pacifier calleth "many" now, that, as he saith, find now the fault. For though it be alleged in the *Extravagant de hereticis cap. Ad abolendam,*[51] yet was that law made in a General Council.

And verily methinketh that he which cannot be proved guilty in heresy, and yet useth such manner

---

37 "by (virtue of) his office"   38 excommunicated   39 *Decretals* of Gregory IX, Book 5, title 7 ("On Heretics"), chapter 9   40 *CW* 9: 188/36–189/13   41 summoning

to appear before a tribunal   42 truly   43 *but if:* unless   44 testify to   45 *for his ears:* for fear of his safety   46 known   47 wealth   48 distinguished; of good

repute   49 *be forsworn:* commit perjury   50 *put…purgation:* required to clear himself   51 *Decretals* of Gregory IX, Book 5, title 7 ("On Heretics"), chapter 9

of ways that all his honest neighbors ween[52] he were one, and therefore dare not swear that in their conscience they think him any other, is well worthy, methinketh, to do some penance for that manner
5　of behavior whereby he giveth all other folk occasion to take him for so naughty.

　　And by the common law of this realm, many times upon suspicion the judges award a writ to inquire of what fame and behavior the man is in his
10　county; and himself lieth sometimes still in prison till the return; and if he be returned good—that is to wit, if he be in a manner purged—then is he delivered; and yet he payeth his fees ere he go. And if he be returned naught,[53] then use[54] the judges to
15　bind him for his good abearing,[55] and sometimes sureties[56] with him too, such as their discretion will allow. And then to lie still till he find them is sometimes as much penance to the one as the spiritual judge enjoineth to the other. For the one cometh
20　to the bar as openly as the other to the consistory;[57] and sometimes his fetters weigh a good piece of a faggot, besides that they lie longer on the one man's legs than the faggot on the other's shoulder. And yet is there no remedy but both these must be done,
25　both in the one court and in the other; or else instead of one harm (which to him that deserveth it not happeth seldom, and as seldom, I am sure, in heresy as in theft, and much more seldom too), ye shall have ten times more harm happen daily to folk
30　as innocent as they—and of innocents many made nocents,[58] to the destruction of themselves and others too, both in goods, body, and soul.

　　And because this Pacifier taketh it for so sore a thing in the spiritual law that a man shall be called
35　*ex officio*[59] for heresy, where he shall not know his accuser, if we should change the spiritual law for that cause, then had we need to change the temporal too, in some such points as, change it when ye will, and ye shall change it into the worse for aught[60] that
40　I can see, but if[61] it be better to have more thieves than fewer.

　　For now if a man be indicted at a sessions, and none evidence given openly at the bar (as many be, and many may well be; for the indicters may have
45　evidence given them apart, or have heard of the

matter ere they came there, and of whom be they not bounden to tell, but be, rather, bounden to keep it close,[62] for they be sworn to keep the King's counsel and their own), shall then the party that is indicted be put unto no business[63] about his acquit-　50
tal? And who shall tell him there the names of his accusers, to entitle him to his writ of conspiracy?[64] This Pacifier will peradventure say that the same twelve men that are his indicters are his accusers, and therefore he may know them. But what helpeth　55
that his undeserved vexation if he were faultless? For amends the law giveth him none against any of them, nor it were not well done he should, but may, when he is after by other twelve acquitted, go get him home and be merry that he hath had so fair a　60
day, as a man getteth him to the fire and shaketh his hat after a shower of rain. And now as it often happeth that a man cometh into a shower by his own oversight, though sometimes of chance and of adventure,[65] so surely though sometimes it hap that a　65
man be accused or indicted of[66] malice, or of some likelihood which happed him of chance and not his fault therein, yet happeth it in comparison very seldom but that the party by some demeanor of himself giveth occasion that folk have him so suspected.　70

　　Now if this Pacifier say that yet here is at the leastwise in a temporal judge an open cause[67] appearing, whereupon men may see that the judge calleth him not but upon a matter brought unto him, whereas the spiritual judge may call a man upon his own　75
pleasure if he bear the party displeasure, this is very well said as for the temporal judge. But what saith he now for the temporal twelve men? For ye wot well they may do the same if they were so disposed, and then had I as lief[68] the judge might do it as they.　80
For in good faith I never saw the day yet but that I durst as well trust the troth[69] of one judge as of two juries. But the judges be so wise men that for the avoiding of obloquy[70] they will not be put in the trust.[71]　85

　　And I dare say the ordinaries be not so foolish neither, but that they would as fain[72] avoid it too if they might, saving that very necessity, lest all should fall to nought,[73] compelleth them to take this way, which necessity sometimes causeth also both the　90

---

52 think　**53** bad　**54** it is usual for　**55** conduct; behavior　**56** bail　**57** Church tribunal　**58** guilty people　**59** "by (virtue of) his office"　**60** all; anything　**61** *but if:* unless　**62** secret

63 trouble　**64** *writ of conspiracy:* a legal mechanism by which someone could accuse others of falsely testifying against him　**65** accident　**66** out of　**67** *open cause:* public trial　**68** gladly　**69** integrity;

truthfulness　**70** disrepute, infamy　**71** position of responsibility　**72** *as fain:* rather　**73** nothing

temporal judges and the King's Council to put some folk to business,[74] or dishonesty[75] sometimes, without either jury or bringing of the accuser to the proof of the matter in the party's presence.

For if the judge know by sure information that some one man is of such evil demeanor among his neighbors that they may not bear it, and yet that the man is, besides, so violent and so jeopardous that none of them dare be aknown to speak of it, will there no judges, upon many secret complaints made unto them, without making the party privy who told him the tale, bind that busy troublous man to good abearing?[76] I suppose yes, and have seen it so too; and wrong would it be sometimes with good poor peaceable folk in the county but if[77] it were so done among.[78] And myself when I was Chancellor, upon such secret information have put some out of commission and office of justice of the peace which else for much money I would not have done; and yet if I were in the one room[79] still and they in the other again, but if they be amended (whereof I neither then saw nor yet hear any likelihood), I would put them out again, and never tell them who told me the tales that made me so to do.

But yet will peradventure this Pacifier say that sometimes, in some very special case, he could be content that the spiritual judge should upon his discretion call one[80] for suspicion of heresy *ex officio*; but he would not have men commonly called but either by accusation or presentment in their senes[81] or indictments at the common law. I had as lief,[82] for anything that I see, that this Pacifier should say thus: "By this way that they be called, I would not have them called; but I would have them called after such an order as they might be sure that then should they never be called." For as for accuse folk openly for heresy, every man hath experience enough that ye shall seldom find any man that will but if[83] the judge should set an officer of the Court thereto, without any peril of expenses; and then were this way and that way all of one effect. And as for presentments and indictments, what effect would come of them concerning heresy, ye see the proof, I trow,[84] meetly[85] well already.

For this is a thing well known unto every man: that in every sene, every session of peace, every session of jail delivery,[86] every leet[87] through the realm, the first thing that the jury have given them in charge is heresy. And for all this, through the whole realm how many presentments be there made in the whole year? I ween in some seven years not one. And I suppose no man doubteth but that in the meantime some there be. I will not be curious about the searching out of the cause, why it is either never or so very seldom presented, not five in fifteen years. But this I say: that since some will not, some cannot, and none doth, if he should put away the process *ex officio*, the thing should be left undone; and then should soon after, with heretics increased and multiplied, the faith be undone; and after that, through the stroke of God revenging their malice and our negligence, should by sedition, and trouble, and dearth,[88] and death, in this realm many men both good and bad be undone. And therefore for conclusion of this piece, my poor advice and counsel shall be that for heresy — and specially now, this time — men shall suffer the processes *ex officio* stand, and for as many other sins also as are only reformable by the spiritual law, except there be any such sins of them as ye think were good to grow.

THE FORTY-FIRST CHAPTER

And it appeareth (*De hereticis li.vi.*, in the chapter "*In fidei favorem*") that they that be accursed and also parties to the same offense may be witnesses in heresy; and in the chapter "*Accusatus*," parag. *Licit*, it appeareth that if a man be sworn to say the truth concerning heresy, as well of himself as of others, and he first confesseth nothing, and after, contrary to his first saying, he appealeth[89] both himself and others — if it appear by manifest tokens that he doth it not of lightness of mind, ne[90] of hatred, nor for corruption of money — that then his witness in favor of the faith shall stand as well against himself as against others; and yet it appeareth evidently in the same court, and in the same matter, that he is a perjured person. This is a dangerous law, and more like[91] to cause untrue and unlawful men to condemn innocents

---

74 trouble   **75** disgrace; a bad reputation
76 *good abearing:* legally acceptable
conduct   **77** *but if:* unless   **78** now
and then   **79** office; position   **80** *call*

one: summon someone   **81** ecclesiastical
meetings; synods   **82** gladly   **83** *but
if:* unless   **84** trust   **85** moderately
86 *sene . . . delivery:* three types of court

sessions   **87** a special kind of court
held once or twice a year   **88** famine
89 accuses   **90** nor   **91** likely

than to condemn offenders. And it helpeth little that if there be tokens that it is not done of hatred, nor for corruption of money, that it should be taken; for sometimes a wolf may show himself in the apparel of a lamb. And if the judge be partial, such tokens may be sooner accepted than truly showed.[92]

This piece, concerning the testimony of known evil persons to be received and taken in heresy, I have somewhat touched in the third chapter of the third book of my *Dialogue*,[93] where, since they may read it that will, I will make here no long tale again thereof. But well he wotteth[94] that heresy, whereby a Christian man becometh a false traitor to God, is in all laws, spiritual and temporal both, accounted as great a crime as is the treason committed against any worldly man. And then why should we find so great a fault that such witnesses should be received in a cause of heresy as are received not only in a cause of treason, but of murder also, and of other more single[95] felony, not only in favor of the Prince, and detestation of such odious crimes, but also for the necessity which the nature of the matter worketh[96] in the proof. For since evil folk use not to[97] make good folk of their counsel in doing of their evil deeds, those that are done should pass unpunished, and more like be committed afresh, but if[98] they were received for records[99] to their condemning that were of their counsel and partners to the doing. Which kind of folk will not let[100] to swear twice nay before they confess once yea; and yet their one "yea" more true upon their bare[101] word than their twice "nay" upon a solemn oath; and yet confess they not so simply but that it is commonly helped with some such circumstances as make the matter more clear.

Now see you well that, as himself showeth, the law provideth well against all light receiving of such confession. And yet this Pacifier saith that all that helpeth little, because the judge may be partial, and the witness may be a wolf, showing himself appareled in the apparel of a lamb; which appearing in apparel, poor men that cannot apparel their speech with apparel of rhetoric, use commonly to call a wolf in a lamb's skin.

But what order[102] may serve against such objections? What place is there in this world, spiritual or temporal, of which the judge may not have some say that he is, or at the leastwise (as he saith here) may be, partial? And therefore not only such witnesses should be, by this reason of his, rejected in heresy, treason, murder, or felony, but also, by his other reason of a wolf in a lamb's skin, all manner of witnesses in every matter. For in every matter may it happen that he that seemeth a lamb may be indeed a wolf, and be naught[103] where he seemeth good, and swear false where he seemeth to say true. And therefore this patch[104] of this Pacifier concerning witnesses, every wise man may bear witness that there is little wit[105] therein; and less good would grow thereof if folk would follow his invention and make of the laws a change.

THE FORTY-SECOND CHAPTER

And in that chapter there, that beginneth *Statuta quaedam*, it is decreed that if the bishop or other inquirers of heresy see that any great danger might come to the accusers or witnesses of heresy by the great power of them that be accused, that then they may command that the names of the accusers or witnesses shall not be showed but to the bishop or inquirers, or such other learned men as be called to them, and that shall suffice, though they be not showed to the party. And for the more indemnity of the said accusers and witnesses it is there decreed that the bishop or inquirers may enjoin such as they have showed the names of such witnesses unto to keep them close,[106] upon pain of excommunication, for disclosing that secret without their license. And surely this is a sore[107] law: that a man shall be condemned, and not know the names of them that be causers thereof.

And though the said law seem to be made upon a good consideration for the indemnity of the accusers and witnesses, yet it seemeth that that consideration cannot suffice to prove the law reasonable. For it seemeth that the accusers and witnesses might be saved from danger

---

92 *CW* 9: 189/13–29   **93** pp. 642–44   *if:* unless   **99** witnesses   **100** hesitate   **104** part of the argument   **105** sense
94 knows   **95** singular   **96** brings about   **101** mere   **102** procedure   **103** evil   **106** secret   **107** oppressive
97 *use not to:* usually do not   **98** *but*

by another way, and that is by this way: if the bishop or inquirers dread that the accusers and witnesses might take hurt, as is said before, then might they show it to the King and to his Council, beseeching his Grace of help in that behalf, to save and defend the accusers and witnesses from the extort[108] power of them that be accused. And if they would do so, it is not to suppose but that the King would sufficiently provide for their safeguard. But forasmuch as it should seem that spiritual men somewhat pretend[109] to punish heresies only of their own power, without calling for any assistance of the temporal power, therefore they make such laws as may help forth their purpose, as they think. But surely that is not the charitable way—to put the knowledge of the names of the accusers and witnesses from him that is accused—for if he knew them, he might percase[110] allege and prove so great and so vehement cause of rancor and malice in them that accuse him that their sayings by no law ought not to stand against him. And that spiritual men pretend that they only should have the whole inquiry and punishment of heresy, it appeareth *Extravagant de hereticis li. vi. cap. Ut inquisitionis*, parag. *Prohibemus*, where all powers, and all lords temporal and rulers, be prohibited that they shall not in any manner take knowledge[111] or judge upon heresy, since it is mere[112] spiritual; and he that inquireth of heresy taketh knowledge of heresy. And so the summa[113] called *Summa rosella* taketh it, *titulo*[114] "*Ex communicatio*," parag. iiii. And if that be true, it seemeth, then, that all justices of peace in this realm be excommunicated: for they, by authority of the King's commissions and also by statute, inquire of heresies. And I think it is not in the Church to prohibit that: for though it were so that the temporal men may not judge what is heresy and what not, yet they may, as it seemeth, by their own authority inquire of it, and inform the ordinary what they have found. And also if a metropolitan[115] with all his clergy and people of his diocese fell into heresy, it would be hard to redress it without temporal power. And therefore temporal men be ready and are bound to be ready to

oppress heresies when they rise, as spiritual men be. And therefore spiritual men may not take all the thanks to themselves when heresies be punished, as though their charity and power only did it; for they have the favor and help of temporal men to do it, or else many times it would not be brought about.[116]

The provision of the law that he speaketh of was made, as appeareth, upon a great cause, in the avoiding of the great danger that might in some special case happen to those by whose means heresies were detected and convicted. But this law this Pacifier accounteth sore and uncharitable, and deviseth, as he thinketh, a better. But his device peradventure,[117] though it would serve in some one land, would yet not serve in some other; and they that made that law made it as it might serve most generally through Christendom; whereas this device, though it might serve in England, might not have served well in many places of Almain[118] that are perverted since, not even while the matter was in a mammering[119] before the change was made.

But surely that law and others of old made against heresies, if they had been in Almain duly followed in the beginning, the matter had not there gone out at length to such an ungracious ending. And undoubtedly, if the Prince, and prelates, and the noblemen of this realm, and the good people of the same, had not been diligent in the time of the Prince of famous memory King Henry the IV both to have against heresies those laws of the Church kept with which this Pacifier findeth now these faults, and also to make great provisions against it besides, it was then very likely and coming to the point as utterly to have subverted the faith in this realm here as it hath done since in any part of Switzerland or Saxony.

And also the doubt that this Pacifier putteth in exceptions[120] to be laid by the party against the accusers or witnesses, since the knowledge of the party lacketh, must be supplied the more effectually by the judges, to inquire and ensearch by their wisdoms whether any suspicion of evil will or other corruption might lead the witnesses or accusers anything to depose or do in the matter. Wherein if diligence be by the judges used, it will be very hard

---

108 wrongfully obtained; overwhelming **109** claim **110** perhaps **111** *take knowledge:* open formal proceedings **112** purely **113** treatise **114** "under the title" **115** archbishop **116** *CW* 9: 189/29–190/40 **117** perhaps **118** Germany **119** *a mammering:* an unsettled state; confusion **120** objections

that any such thing should be of any weight but they shall hear thereof, and may consider the matter according.

And on the other side, the remedy that he deviseth for the surety[121] of the witnesses should not peradventure make the men so bold as in a cause of heresy to meddle in the matter against some manner of man, but that they rather would, for their own surety, keep their own tongues still than, with all the surety that could be founden[122] them besides, have their persons disclosed unto the party.

And as touching the conjecture of this Pacifier that the spiritualty pretend that no layman should have the inquiry and punishment of heresies, the laws of this realm and the laws of the whole Church may well stand together, for aught[123] that I see in them both; and so have they in these matters of heresy, God be thanked, hitherto full well. And therefore this Pacifier seemeth me to bring in this matter to no great purpose now but if[124] it be either to set[125] some division, or else to fill up the leaf.[126] And therefore since, as I said before, I purpose not in any open[127] English book to ransack[128] and rebuke either the one law or the other, I shall let him with that matter alone.

THE FORTY-THIRD CHAPTER

Nevertheless mine intent is not to prove the said laws all wholly to be cruel and unreasonable; for I know well that it is right expedient that strait[129] laws be made for punishment of heresies that be heresies indeed—more rather than any other offense—and that the discretion of the judges spiritual may right well assuage the rigor of the said laws, and use them more favorably against them that be innocents than against them that be willful offenders, if they will charitably search for the truth. But surely if the said laws should be put into the handling of cruel judges, it might happen that they should many times punish innocents as well as offenders, but I trust in God it is not so. Nevertheless whether it be so or not, certain it is that there is a great rumor among the people that it is so, and that spiritual men punish not

heresy only for zeal of the faith, and of a love and a zeal to the people, with a fatherly pity to them that so offend (as they ought to do, how great offenders soever they be), but that they do it rather to oppress them that speak anything against the worldly power or riches of spiritual men, or against the great confederacy that (as many men say) is in them to maintain it.[130]

Now his intent is not, he saith, to prove the said laws of the Church against heresies wholly cruel and unreasonable, but so much of them as it standeth not with his pleasure to approve. And now he is content that strait laws be made for punishment of heresies such as be heresies indeed; wherein, in this book of his, he meaneth two things: one, that he is content they be sore[131] punished if they be condemned. But first he would have them called[132] by such means as he seeth well they never should be sent for. And then he would exclude all such witnesses as were likely to bewray them.[133] And when that no man shall accuse them, nor no man be received that can prove it against them, then when the judge can lawfully convict them, he would, I trow,[134] be content that they were burned twice; and so would, I ween, themselves be content too; for they shall be safe enough, I warrant you, then.

Yet another mystery he meaneth, whatsoever it be, in those words "the punishment of heresies that be heresies indeed." Here would he peradventure have every heresy, when these new brethren were taken therein, be brought in question again, and stand in controversy whether it were heresy or not; and that were another good help for them—as though the Church used to lay to their charges the speaking against some false faith, or at the leastwise would prove them heretics in speaking against some such things as they had never heard of before.

But now he showeth why he doth not wholly condemn these laws of the Church. But then the cause he showeth to be such as he by and by[135] taketh it away. For he layeth[136] the cause to be for that[137] the judges (if they be good and charitable) may by their wisdom and goodness moderate and temper the rigor of the laws; but on the other side, the evil judges may do by those laws, he saith, much harm. But now what laws are there or may there be, by the abuse of which none evil judge may do harm?

But then to show that by these laws of the Church much harm and little good or none could come, he handleth it so that he would make men ween there were not a good indifferent judge in all the whole clergy. For when he hath showed what hurt an evil judge and a cruel should do by those laws, he saith that himself trusteth the spiritual judges be not such. Howbeit, lest we should take him at that word and believe him, he showeth us yet that the common people with a great rumor say the contrary. And the thing that he saith here under the name of "the people" and "great rumor," that saith he in his first chapter under the name of "many men." And yet immediately before that, he saith much worse as of himself, affirming that "many persons" have been punished by the spiritualty for an evil suspicion and a false of their own imagination, because those many persons so punished had before spoken only against spiritual men's misorder and abusions; which point, honesty would he should[138] have proved first, and then write it after.

And now cometh he and covertly goeth about to make men ween that no spiritual judges be indifferent. For thus he saith:

And though many spiritual men may be found that have right many great virtues and great gifts of God, as chastity, liberality, patience, soberness, temperance, cunning, and such others, yet it will be hard to find any one spiritual man that is not infected with the said desire and affection to have the worldly honor of priests exalted and preferred; and therefore if any layman report any evil of a priest, though it be openly known that it is as he saith, yet they will be more diligent to cause the layman to cease of that saying than to do that in them is to reform that[139] is amiss in the priest that it is spoken of, taking, as it were, an occasion to do the less in such reformations because laymen speak so much against them. But surely that will be none excuse to spiritual rulers afore God, when he shall ask account of his people that were committed unto their keeping.[140]

If the best spiritual men be such as this Pacifier here saith they be, then be they a very shrewd[141] sort indeed, if they be all so bad that it be hard to find any one but that, though any priest be so naughty that his lewdness[142] is openly known, yet if any layman report it, the best spiritual men will, he saith, be more diligent to cause the layman cease of his saying than to do their devoir[143] to reform the priest; yea, and yet more than this, he saith they will do the less toward the amendment of the priest because laymen speak so much of it. And this saith this Pacifier himself, showing forth boldly therein his own open face without any visor of "some say." And therefore since he saith this even by[144] the best, till he prove it somewhat better, this shameful tale is somewhat shameless, dare I say; and somewhat is it foolish too, since he saith therewith that those which thus will do have yet, among many other great gifts of God, patience, soberness, temperance, and cunning too. For I am sure if they have that condition—that they be so affectionate unto every priest that they can so evil bear the dispraise of his open-known unthriftiness[145] that they will do the less toward his amendment because laymen much abhor his lewdness—this Pacifier may be patient, I will not say nay, and may peradventure have much cunning too; but surely either is this Pacifier not very sober, or hath his brain otherwise somewhat out of temper, if he take them (as he calleth them) for patient folk or for temperate either.

THE FORTY-FOURTH CHAPTER

And yet to bring the spiritualty in the more hatred, and to make the name of the spiritualty the more odious among the people, this piteous Pacifier in diverse places of his book, to appease this division withal, allegeth against them that they make great confederacies among them to make and maintain a party against the temporalty, and by such confederacies, and worldly policies, and strait corrections, to rule the people and punish them, and keep them under. And this point he bringeth in here and there in diverse places, sometimes with a "some say," and sometimes with a "they say," and sometimes he saith it himself. And I wot not well if he hated the spiritualty indeed (as some say he doth, and yet I trust he doth not) what more odious thing he might say.

What any one kind or sort of people is there in this realm—husbandmen,[146] artificers, merchants, men of law, judges, knights, lords, or other—but that evil-disposed people might begin against them a seditious murmur, casting abroad a suspicious babbling of gathering, and assembling, and rounding,[147] and talking, and finally confedering[148] together? And yet all such suspicious babbling not worth a feather altogether, when it were well considered.

But in sundry places much he harpeth upon the laws of the Church, as though the spiritual laws which the spiritualty here have made were a great cause of this division. And then diverse of the laws that he speaketh of be laws not provincial, made by the clergy here, but the laws usual through the whole Church of Christ, whereof the making may not be laid[149] to them; nor men are not therefore so unreasonable (though[150] those laws were less good than the great wisdom of this Pacifier could devise) as to be angry for them with our clergy that made them not, but have been bound to keep them.

And as for defaming them with the abuse of those laws toward[151] cruelty, as he doth in his book, there is no great cunning in the making of that lie. For every fool that list[152] may devise and lay the like to some other folk when he will.

Now as for their assemblies and coming together to the making of their laws and constitutions provincial, this Pacifier to lay those for any confederacies that should be now a cause of this so sudden a late[153] grudge and division were a very far-fetched invention. For, setting aside the disputation whether those constitutions be so unreasonable as this Pacifier would have them seem, this thing sufficeth against him: that there is not, I think verily, any one provincial constitution that he speaketh of that was made, or to any man's grief or grudge put in execution, in the time of any of all the prelates that are now living. And how could then any of them be any such confederacy or cause of this late-sprungen division?

But I suppose he calleth those assemblings at their convocations by the name of confederacies. For but if[154] he so do, I wot nere[155] what he meaneth by that

word. And on the other side, if he so do, for aught[156] that I see, he giveth a good thing and a wholesome an odious heinous name. For if they did assemble ofter, and there did the things for which such assemblies of the clergy in every province through all Christendom from the beginning were instituted and devised, much more good might have grown thereof than the long disuse can suffer[157] us now to perceive.

But as for my days, as far as I have heard, nor, as I suppose, a good part of my father's neither, they came never together to convocation but at the request of the King, and at their such assemblies, concerning spiritual things, have very little done. Wherefore—that they have been in that great necessary point of their duty so negligent—whether God suffer to grow to a secret unperceived cause of division and grudge against them, God, whom their such negligence hath, I fear me, sore offended, knoweth. But surely this hath in my mind been somewhat a greater fault in the spiritualty than diverse of those faults which under his figure of "some say" this Pacifier hath made very great in his book.

But surely if this Pacifier call those assemblies confederacies, I would not greatly wish to be confederated with them and their associates in any such confederacies. For I could never wit them yet[158] assemble for any great winning, but come up to their travail, labor, cost, and pain, and tarry and talk, etc., and so get them home again. And therefore men need not greatly to grudge or envy them for any such confederacies.

THE FORTY-FIFTH CHAPTER

But what faults soever this Pacifier find in the spiritualty, yet of his tender pity he hath ever a special eye to see that they should not rigorously mishandle such good men as are suspected or detected of heresy. And therefore, whereas in other places he hath showed before that they have punished many men of[159] malice, for only speaking against their misorder and abusions, now he cometh in the eighth chapter and, lest besides their malice they might happen to punish them also for their own ignorance, therefore he teacheth the spiritual judges one great point concerning heresy, and saith:

It is a common opinion among doctors that none is a heretic for that only[160] he erreth, but for that he defendeth opinatively[161] his error. And therefore he that erreth of simplicity may in no wise be said a heretic. And *Summa rosella*, in the title "*Hereticus in principio*," saith that a man may err and merit thereby; and he putteth this example: if a simple unlearned man hear the preaching of his bishop that preacheth haply[162] against the faith, and he believeth it with a ready mind to obey, this man meriteth, and yet he erreth, but that is to be understood where ignorance excuseth. Then it seemeth that it is not enough to prove that a man is a heretic for that he hath holden opinions against that the Church teacheth — ne[163] that he ought not to make any purgation nor abjuration for it — for that that[164] he held in such case was not his faith, but the faith of the Church was his faith, though haply he were not then fully advised of it. And therefore Saint Aidan,[165] when he held the wrong part of keeping of Easter, was no heretic, and some say that Saint Chad[166] was of the same opinion as Saint Aidan was, which in like wise was no heretic; for their desire was to know the truth, and therefore it is not read that they made either purgation or abjuration. Nor yet the Abbot Joachim,[167] which nevertheless erred, for he was ready to submit himself to the determination of the Church, and therefore he was neither holden as a heretic ne compelled to abjure. Then if this be sooth,[168] it were great pity if it should be true, as is reported, that there should be so great a desire in some spiritual men to have men abjured or have the extreme punishment for heresy, as it is said there is. For as some have reported, if any will witness that a man hath spoken anything that is heresy — though he speak it only of an ignorance, or of a passion — or if he can by interrogatories and questions be driven to confess anything that is prohibited by the Church, anon[169] they will drive him to abjure, or hold him attainted[170] without examining the intent or cause of his saying or whether he had a mind to be reformed or not. And that is a very sore way; our Lord be more merciful to our souls than so grievously to punish us for every light default.[171]

This process[172] were a pretty piece, and somewhat also to the purpose, if this Pacifier's doctoring[173] were a good proof that the spiritual judges knew not this tale before, nor wist[174] what appertained unto their part in this matter until this Pacifier taught them this great secret mystery sought out in *Summa rosella*: so strange a book to find and so hard to understand that very few men had meddled with it before.

But the tale is not so much told of[175] any pride to teach them, as of charity to teach us to take and believe for true every false feigned tale with which any man list to belie[176] them. For upon this lesson he bringeth in, as you see, his charitable infamation[177] of the clergy's cruelty, making men ween it were so, under his fair figure of lamentation "and great pity that it were, if it should be so, but yet it is," he saith, "reported so, and some say that it is so."

But surely some say again[178] that like as there is nothing so evil but that some may hap to do it, so is there nothing so false but some may hap to say it. And some others say also that like as there is nothing so false but some man may hap to say it, so can no man say anything so false but some man under pretext of pacifying may hap to repeat and report it.

For as for all that gay reported tale — that some laymen say that some spiritual men have

so great desire to have men abjured, or to have extreme punishment for heresy that if any will witness that a man have spoken anything that is heresy, though he speak it but of ignorance or of a passion, or if he can be driven by interrogatories and questions to confess anything that is prohibited by the Church, anon they will drive him to abjure, or hold him attainted, without any farther consideration of his intent or cause or whether he would be reformed or not[179]

— all this tale, though he tell it but, as it were, by[180] "some" spiritual men, yet is it told to make all laymen ween that those "some" spiritual men were so great a sum that it were some great cause of all this

---

160 *for that only:* only because   **161** opinionatedly; obstinately   **162** perhaps   **163** nor   **164** *for that that:* because what   **165** Bishop of Lindisfarne (d. 651)   **166** Bishop of Mercia (d. 672) and a disciple of St. Aidan   **167** Joachim of Fiore (*ca.* 1135–1202)   **168** true   **169** right away   **170** convicted   **171** *CW* 9: 191/38–192/31   **172** argument   **173** theologizing   **174** knew   **175** out of   **176** *list to belie:* wishes to defame   **177** defamation   **178** in reply   **179** See *CW* 9: 192/21–29.   **180** about

great grudge and division which he saith that the temporalty now hath in this realm against the spiritualty "in manner universally." Wherein he maketh yet, as I trust, in manner a universal lie, since I can yet see no such universal cause, and least cause of all in this point specially which most specially, as the sorest and the most cruel heinous point, in sundry places of his book this Pacifier preacheth and presseth upon—that is to wit,[181] the mishandling of men in the cause of heresy—making men ween, with his heinous handling, that the spiritual judges in this realm handled that thing so cruelly that all the world had cause to wonder and grudge thereat.

But when all his wholesome holy babbling is done, every man may see these three things true: First, that since in punishing of heresies there is, and a good while hath been, so little business in all the shires of England and Wales, both about examination and punition[182] of heretics, except only London and Essex, and those are both in one diocese, his "some spiritual men" that he would have seem so great a sum are yet of truth so few that he seemeth in manner to point them with his finger, and might as well in manner rehearse[183] them even by name.

Secondly, of those same "some," so few, yet is there some so learned to whom the matter most specially pertaineth that if this Pacifier keep no more cunning in his breast than he putteth out in his book (as cunning as he weeneth it were), he is no more able to teach some one of those the lessons that belong to the matter than he that learned to spell is able and meet[184] to teach a good master in grammar to read.

Thirdly, that all his whole tale of their great desire of men's shame or harm, and of their mishandling of men, and of uncharitable dealing, is a very false feigned tale, and so hath been already proved and founden in those that have had their surmise[185] brought forth unto the trial, and so shall be proved again, I doubt it not, whensoever this Pacifier will fall from that babbling of a generality (wherein he may point and spice a false tale with suspicious words) and come to the naming of any one person special, and before any folk indifferent[186] offer himself to the proof.

For let him come forth and name any one whom he will, and I warrant you the deed shall show itself

that the spiritual judges which had the matter in hand were neither such as needed of this Pacifier to be taught what belonged unto right, nor were so malicious and cruel but that they would be as loath as himself to do them rigor or wrong.

And he shall find, whomsoever he will name that hath been either punished or abjured, that the matters which have been laid[187] unto them they have not been by any subtle questions induced to confess them; but they have been both well proved against them, and neither have been slight, nor light, nor so strange articles and unknown as they might therein of ignorance or simplicity so sore overshoot themselves.

But where this Pacifier speaketh of passions and of willing to be reformed, surely if he will so lightly pardon all passions that he will have no man punished for anything done or said in a passion, then shall his piteous affection many times do much harm, by the taking away of the punishment whereof the fear is ordained to refrain the passion and to make others also forbear the like for any such manner[188] passion.

For well ye wot, men fall in adultery through such damnable passions. And by the passion of ire and anger men fall into manslaughter. And by a passion of pride many a man falleth to treason. And by the same passion also, men fall into heresy, and sometimes, ye wot well, fall in a plain frenzy too. And in their passions of heresy, they speak ungraciously, and contend against the sacraments, and blaspheme our blessed Lady, and our Savior himself also, and horribly despise the holy housel,[189] and make mocks and mows[190] of the Mass, and rail on Christ's own Blessed Body and Blood in the Blessed Sacrament. Will this Pacifier[191] that all these blasphemous damnable heretics shall be spared, for such desperate damnable passions? If that way were allowed, then were that heretic most sure[192] that against all the faith most could rail and rage. For then might it be said that the man was in a great passion.

Now as for willing to be reformed, I dare say that the spiritual judges would gladly see every man, and therein would gladly show them all the favor they could; but sometimes they cannot show all the favor that they fain[193] would. For though they may receive him and save his life at the first time, yet are they straited[194] by the plain law that they may not so do at the second, when the man is relapsed.

And the laws have determined who shall be taken and reputed for a heretic, and who not, as well as this Pacifier can teach us, and a little better too. And they have both had a respect and a sure eye to provide that neither innocents or plain simple folk should be for any slight offense sore handled or untruly circumvented[195] and punished, nor that wily false wretched heretics should by craft and sophisms be suffered[196] to seem wise among unlearned people, and feign simplicity and say they repent, and so be sent away lightly to go teach their heresies and sow their poison into men's souls again.

For if that way were taken which it seemeth that this Pacifier would have—that every man might be held excused that would say he spoke heresy of ignorance, or of oversight, or of simplicity, or of a passion, or which[197] as often as he would not defend his heresy and stubbornly stick thereto, or though he did for the while would afterward yet offer to be reformed and promise that he would amend—if all these, I say, should always pass unpunished, the Church of Christ at the making of the laws foresaw, and all Christendom should shortly find, how little fruit would grow thereof.

And when this Pacifier hath told thus much mishandling and cruelty of the clergy, wherein if he said true it touched yet very few, and hath proved it by a "some say" of as few, and findeth some such things for faults as, if they were changed after the fashion of his book, would of heretics in many places for a very few make a very great many, and the lies that heretics of malice blow about against their judges, laboreth to make men believe them for true, by his repeating and reporting under a pretext of charity, then endeth he that painted process[198] with his devout prayer full holily and saith:

This is a very sore[199] way; our Lord be more merciful to our souls than so grievously to punish us for every light default.

When he hath proved those evil devices good, and those false lies true, then let this good Sir John "Some Say" take his portuous[200] and his beads and pray. But in the meanwhile those good men, whom by such figures and such holy pretexts he goeth about ungodly to defame, do earnestly pray God for him, to give him the grace to change this evil fashion and this very sore way. And they pray God heartily to be more merciful to this Pacifier's poor soul than this Pacifier is to other men's, whose souls (believe himself never so well, and mean he never so well therewith) yet his book goeth about, by sowing of dissension and embolding of heretics, to infect and envenom with a grudge and hatred against the spiritualty, and with the canker of pestilent poisoned heresies, and all against their own salvation.

THE FORTY-SIXTH CHAPTER

For here shall ye see to the further encouraging of heretics what another goodly "some say" this good Sir John "Some Say" findeth. Lo, thus he saith:

And here some say that because there is so great a desire in spiritual men to have men abjure, and to be noted with heresy—and that some, as it were of a policy, do noise it that the realm is full of heretics, more than it is indeed—that it is very perilous that spiritual men should have authority to arrest a man for every light suspicion or complaint of heresy till that desire of punishment in spiritual men be ceased and gone; but that they should make process against them to bring them in upon pain of cursing;[201] and then, if they tarry forty days, the King's laws to bring them in by a writ *De excommunicato capiendo*,[202] and so to be brought forth out of the King's jail to answer. But surely, as it is somewhat touched before in the seventh chapter, it seemeth that the Church in time past hath done what they could to bring about that they might punish heresy of themselves, without calling for any help therein of the secular power.

And therefore they have made laws that heretics might be arrested and put in prison, and stocks if need were, as appeareth *Clementinis de hereticis (Capi. Multorum querela)*. And after, at the special calling on of the spiritualty, it was enacted by Parliament that ordinaries[203] might arrest men for heresy, for some men think that the

---

194 constrained   195 *untruly circum-vented:* deceitfully entrapped   196 allowed   197 who   198 *painted process:* pretended proceeding   199 harsh, oppressive   200 breviary   201 excommunication   202 "Of seizing an excommunicated (person)"   203 bishops

said Clementine was not of effect in the King's law to arrest any man for heresy. But if a man were openly and notably suspected of heresy, and that there were sufficient record and witness against him, and there were also a doubt[204] that he would flee and not appear, whereby he might infect others, it seemeth convenient[205] that he be arrested by the body,[206] but not upon every light complaint that full lightly may be untrue. And it will be right expedient that the King's Highness and his Council look specially upon this matter, and not to cease till it be brought to more quietness than it is yet, and to see with great diligence that pride, covetise, nor worldly love be no judges, nor innocents be punished, ne[207] yet that willful offenders go not without due correction.[208]

In this process,[209] lo, good readers, this Pacifier declareth that he would have the King's Highness and his Council so specially look upon this matter that neither innocents should be punished nor yet willful offenders go without due correction. Who could end and conclude all his matter more fruitfully?

But now the special ways whereby he deviseth that the King's Highness and his Council should bring this thing about be twain:

The one is if they provide that neither men that be proud, nor covetous, nor have any love to the world, be suffered[210] to be judges in any cause of heresy.

The other is that the bishops shall arrest no man for heresy till the desire that spiritual men have to cause men [to] abjure heresies, and to punish them for heresies, be ceased and gone.

And surely I think that his two devices will serve sufficiently for the one part: that is to wit, that none innocents shall be punished. But I fear me very sore that they will not serve half so sufficiently for the other part: that is to wit, that willful offenders go not without correction.

For now to begin with his first device (that none be suffered to be judges in cause of heresy that are proud, or covetous, or have love to the world), if he mean of such as have none of these affections with notable enormity, then till he prove them that are already[211] worse than he proveth them yet—that

is to say, till he prove it otherwise by some of their outrageous deeds in the dealing and mishandling of men for heresy that he here defameth them of, than he hath yet proved, and that he prove their cruel wrongful dealing otherwise than by "some says," or by his own saying—the King's Highness and his Council can see, for all his wholesome counsel, no cause to change those judges that are already, but to leave them still, and then serveth that device of nought.[212]

And on the other side, if he mean that the King's Highness shall suffer none to be judges in cause of heresy that hath any spice[213] at all either of pride, or of covetise, or any love at all unto this world, heretics may sit still and make merry for a little season, while men walk about and seek for such judges. For it will not be less than one whole week's work, I ween, both to find such, and to be sure that they be such.

And it will be somewhat the more hard because that whereas[214] men would have weened soonest to have found them, there this Pacifier hath put us out of doubt that there shall it be marvelous hard to find any one of them: that is to wit, in any part of the spiritualty—prelates, secular priests, or religious persons—any one or other. For he saith plainly that have they never so many virtues beside, yet it will be hard to find any one spiritual man but that he is so infected with desire and affection to have the worldly honor of priests exalted that he is through such pride far from such indifference and equity as ought and must be in those judges that this Pacifier assigneth, which must have no spice of pride, covetise, nor love toward the world. And then since in all the spiritualty it will be, as he saith, hard to find any one, it will be, ye wot well, twice as hard to find twain; and yet be they too few for all the realm, though they were made justices of eyre.[215]

Now if it will be so hard to find any one such in the spiritualty, I can scant believe but that it would be somewhat ado[216] to find many such in the temporalty either, and specially not only such but those also that the King might be sure to be such, besides that there must be then many changes and many new devices of laws for the matter, because few temporal men be sufficiently learned in those laws of the Church by which that matter hath been accustomed to be ordered before. And haply²¹⁷ if any such men be so sufficiently learned, yet is it possible that those men which are so learned are not those that are so pure and clean from every spice of pride, covetise, and worldly love. And therefore were the heretics likely thus to make merry a good while before there should be founden good judges for them.

Now as for the other point — that bishops should not arrest them — this would also help to the surety²¹⁸ of innocents as from any trouble of suit; and so will it also further, if neither bishop nor king arrest them. And in like wise will it save innocents from the trouble of all false indictments if no man should be neither for no felony arrested nor indicted neither.

But then this way would not well serve for the other side, that willful offenders should not pass unpunished. And thereby since it would help willful offenders to pass without punishment, it might hap to punish innocents more sore than should the trouble of suit and wrongful arresting do.

But yet is this Pacifier not so favorable toward folk suspected of heresy as to take away the power of the bishop forever of arresting them, and to drive the ordinaries forever to sue citations against heretics and process of excommunication, but will have, he saith, the bishop's power of arresting no longer suspended than as long as spiritual men have that great desire to cause men abjure or to have them punished for heresy — as though he had well proved that they have so, because he saith that some men say so.

But now if "some say" be no sufficient proof, then is his tale lost. For then he showeth no cause why that power of theirs should in any cause be more suspended now than in any time herebefore. And on the other side, if "some say" be a good proof, then the suspending will be as long as a depriving forever, since there shall never be any time in which there shall lack one or other "some say" to say more than truth.

Yet is he content at the last, lest every man might spy the peril of his device,²¹⁹ to temper his device in such wise that till the spiritualty have left their cruel desire of abjuring and punishing folk for heresy, they should not be suffered²²⁰ to arrest folk for every light suspicion or every complaint of heresy.

Howbeit, he granteth that where one is openly and notably suspected of heresy, and sufficient record and witness against him, and besides all that, a doubt²²¹ that he would flee, whereby he might infect others, then he granteth it convenient²²² that he should be arrested by the body.²²³ And therein he bringeth in the Clementine and the statute by which the ordinaries have power to arrest folk for suspicion of heresy; and would, as far as I perceive, have the King reform them after his device.²²⁴ But yet, since which is a light suspicion and which is a heavy, and which is a light complaint and which is a heavy, and which is an open²²⁵ suspicion and which but a privy,²²⁶ and which suspicion is notable and which is not notable, and which witnesses be sufficient and which be not sufficient, be things that must be weighed by the spiritual judges, and upon their weighing of the matter for light or heavy must follow the arresting of the party or the leaving of the arrest, we be come again, as in a maze, to the point where we began: that, be the matter great or small, lest all the while they be cruel they should judge light heavy and small great, their arresting of any at all must be suspended from them, and send them to sue by citation till men see that same mind of theirs of desiring men's abjuration and punishment utterly changed and cease — that is to say, till there be no man left that will so much as say that some men say that they have not left that mind yet, and make a lie again of them then as those some have done that have so said already to Sir John "Some Say" now. And long will it be, I warrant you, ere ever all such folk fail.

And therefore — since in the mean season,²²⁷ by this Pacifier's good device, heretics may go unarrested — I cannot believe that if his way were followed, it would be any good means to make that willful offenders in heresy should not pass unpunished as fast²²⁸ as, both in the end of this chapter and the other before also, he calleth upon the King's Highness, and his Council, and his Parliament, to look upon this matter after his good advertisement,²²⁹ and never cease till they bring it to effect.

I little doubt but that if the King's Highness do as I doubt not but his Highness will do — maintain and assist the spiritualty in executing of the laws, even those that are already made against heresies,

---

217 perhaps   **218** safety   **219** plan
220 allowed   **221** fear   **222** (to be)
appropriate   **223** *by the body:* bodily

224 *after his device:* in accord with his plan
225 public   **226** private   **227** *mean
season:* meantime   **228** earnestly

229 *after his good advertisement:* following
his good warning

and command every temporal officer under him to do the same for his part—though there were never more new laws made therefor, yet shall both innocents be saved harmless well enough, and offenders
5   punished too.

THE FORTY-SEVENTH CHAPTER

Now whereas this Pacifier saith that some of the spiritualty as of policy do noise it that the realm is full of heretics more than it is indeed,
10 I think there is no politic[230] man of the spiritualty that will make that noise, whereby the heretics might be the more bold, and the Catholics more inclinable to the worse party, and the more faint and feeble in the faith.
15   But I know this very well: that heretics have made that noise, both for the cause aforesaid and also to fear the ordinaries therewith, and to put their officers in dread from doing of their office. And peradventure upon such noise some officers have been
20 afeard. And at the leastwise, I wot well, some heretics have been so bold that they have not feared to flock together—not all at the first for heresy, but some fall in among them for good company, to do some shrewd turn[231] they cared not greatly what, but
25 afterward with a little more acquaintance and communication, have fallen into their heresies also. And such noises be sometimes for the advantage and furtherance of them that intend unhappiness, to make folk ween they were very many, be they never so few.
30   I remember many times that even here in London, after the great business that was there on a May Day in the morning, by a rising[232] made against strangers[233]—for which diverse of the apprentices and journeymen suffered execution of[234] treason by
35 an old statute made long before, against all such as would violate the King's safe-conduct—I was appointed among others to search out and inquire by diligent examination in what wise and by what persons that privy confederacy began. And in good
40 faith after great time taken, and much diligence used therein, we perfectly tried out[235] at last that all that business of any rising to be made for the matter

began only by the conspiracy of two young lads that were apprentices in Cheap.[236] Which,[237] after the thing devised first and compassed[238] between them 45
twain, perused[239] privily the journeymen first, and after the apprentices, of many of the mean[240] crafts in the city, bearing the first that they spoke with in hand[241] that they had secretly spoken with many other occupations already, and that they were all 50
agreed thereunto, and that besides them there were two or three hundred of serving men of diverse lords' houses, and some of the King's too, which would not be named nor known, that would yet in the night be at hand, and when they were once up, 55
would not fail to fall in with them and take their part.

Now this ungracious invention and these words of those two lewd[242] lads (which yet in the business fled away themselves, and never came again after) 60
did put some others, by their oversight and lightness,[243] in such a courage and boldness that they weened themselves able to avenge their displeasure in the night, and after either never to be known, or to be strong enough to bear it out and go farther. 65

And the like ungracious policy devise now these heretics that call themselves evangelical brethren: some pot-headed[244] apostles they have, that wander about the realm into sundry shires, of whom every one hath in every shire a diverse name; and some 70
peradventure in corners here and there, they bring into the brotherhood. But whether they get any or none, they let[245] not to lie when they come home, and say that more than half of every shire is of their own sect. And the same boast Bayfield, the apostate 75
which was after burned in Smithfield, made unto mine own self. But blessed be God, when he came to the fire, he found none very ready to pull him from it.

Howbeit, there was in one place of the Diocese of 80
London, but late,[246] a company that by such means, each encouraging other, took such heart and boldness, and openly by day they ensembled themselves together to the number of a hundred or above, to rescue a well-known open heretic out of the ordi- 85
nary's hands. Howbeit, as many as they were, they sped[247] not, and some of them punished after.

---

230 prudent   **231** *shrewd turn:* bad deed   **232** uprising; riot   **233** *great . . . strangers:* On May 1, 1517, a riot broke out in London protesting the presence of foreigners in the city, dramatized in *The Book of Sir*

Thomas More.   **234** for   **235** *perfectly tried out:* completely ascertained   **236** Cheapside   **237** Who   **238** plotted   **239** approached one by one   **240** humble; lowly   **241** *bearing in hand:* leading to

believe   **242** wicked   **243** *oversight and lightness:* negligence and credulity   **244** thickheaded; stupid   **245** hesitate   **246** recently   **247** succeeded

And in that same diocese also, when there was
a priest taken for heresy, and in the commissary's
hands,[248] word was brought him that except he delivered the priest and let him go, he should within
5 two hours have two or three hundred come fetch
him that would pluck down his house or burn it
over his head. Whereupon the commissary, worse
afraid than hurt, delivered out the priest; whom, if
he had kept still, there would peradventure for all
10 the crakes,[249] not one heretic of them all have been
so bold to come fetch him. But yet that could I not
well have warranted him.

And in some place of the same diocese also, they
have made a great face[250] and said that though the
15 King sent his commission under his great seal therefor, they would not suffer[251] a sore-suspected priest
of theirs for heresy to be taken thence. Howbeit,
when that after I sealed a commission and sent it
upon the assay,[252] it made their hearts (God be
20 thanked) faint and were so well come down that
they laid all the wite[253] to a few lewd fellows and
women in the town.

And therefore boast and brag these blessed brethren never so fast,[254] they feel full well themselves
25 that they be too feeble in what county soever they
be strongest. For if they thought themselves able to
mete[255] and match the Catholics, they would not, I
ween, lie still in rest three days.

For in all places where heresies have sprungen
30 hitherto, so hath it ever proved yet. And surely so
negligently might it be handled, and the matter so
long forslothed,[256] that at length, in time, so might it
hap here too. And verily that they look once therefor[257] (as far as they be yet from the power), some
35 of them have not let[258] to say, nor some to write it
neither. For I read the letter myself which was cast
into the palace of the right reverend father in God
Cuthbert, now Bishop of Durham and at that time
Bishop of London,[259] in which, among many other
40 bragging words, meet whatsoever[260] they were for
those heretic brethren that made it, were these
words contained: "There will once come a day."

And out of question[261] that day they not only

long for, but also daily look for, and would, if they
were not too weak, not fail to find it, and in some 45
morning early, like good thriving husbands,[262] arise
by themselves uncalled, as they suddenly did in
Basel.

And the greater hope have they because in places
where they fall in company, men use them not now- 50
adays as the time was when they did. For they see
that it beginneth almost to grow in custom[263] that
among good Catholic folk, yet be they suffered
boldly to talk unchecked. Which thing, albeit far
from commendable, yet with many folk it happeth 55
upon a good surety[264] that good men in their own
mind conceive of the strength and fastness of the
Catholic faith, which they verily think so strong
that heretics, for all their babbling, shall never be
able to vanquish. And therein undoubtedly their 60
mind is not only good, but also very true. But they
think not far enough. For as the sea shall never surround and overwhelm all the land, and yet hath it
eaten many places in, and swallowed whole countries up, and made many places now sea that some- 65
time were well-inhabited lands, and hath lost part
of his[265] own possession in other parts again, so
though the faith of Christ shall never be overflown
with heresies, nor the gates of hell prevail against
Christ's Church, yet as in some places it winneth in 70
new people, so may there in some places by negligence be lost the old.

For if that we, because we know our cause so good,
bear ourselves thereupon so bold that we make light
and slight of our adversaries, it may happen to fare 75
between the Catholics and heretics at length[266] as it
fareth sometimes in a suit at the law by some good
man against whom a subtle wily shrew beginneth a
false action,[267] and asketh from him all the land he
hath. This good man sometimes that knoweth his 80
matter[268] so true, persuadeth to himself that it were
not possible for him to lose it by the law. And when
his counsel talketh with him, and asketh him how he
can prove this point or that for himself, answereth
again, "Fear ye not for that, sir, I warrant you; all the 85
whole county knoweth it, the matter is so true, and

248 commissary's hands: custody of the bishop's representative 249 crowings; boasts, brags 250 show 251 allow 252 upon the assay: as an experiment; to try that out 253 blame 254 stead-fastly 255 equal 256 neglected through sloth 257 look once therefor: expect it to happen at some future time 258 hesitated 259 Cuthbert Tunstall (1474–1549) 260 meet whatsoever: however fitting 261 out of question: undoubtedly 262 farmers 263 grow in custom: become customary 264 confi-dence; certainty 265 its 266 at length: eventually 267 false action: frivolous lawsuit 268 case

my part so plain, that I care not what judges, what arbiters, what twelve men go thereon. I will challenge no man, for any labor that mine adversary can make therein." And with such good hope, the good man goeth him home, and there sitteth still and putteth no doubt in the matter. But in the meanwhile his adversary (which for lack of truth of his cause must needs put all his trust in craft) goeth about his matter busily and, by all the false means he may, maketh him friends, some with good fellowship, some with rewards, findeth a fellow to forge him false evidence, maketh means to[269] the sheriff, getteth a partial[270] panel, laboreth the jury, and when they come to the bar, he hath all his trinkets ready, whereas good Tom Truth cometh forth upon the other side, and because he weeneth all the world knoweth how true his matter is, bringeth never a witness with him, and all his evidence unsorted. And one wist[271] I once that brought unto the bar (when the jury was sworn), and openly delivered his counsel, his tinder box with his flint and his matches, instead of his box of evidence, for that had he left at home. So negligent are good folk sometimes, when the known truth of their matter maketh them overbold.

And surely muchwhat after this fashion in many places play these heretics and we. For like as a few birds always chirking[272] and flying from bush to bush many times seem a great many, so these heretics be so busily walking that in every alehouse, in every tavern, in every barge, and almost every boat, as few as they be, a man shall always find some; and there be they so busy with their talking, and in better places also where they may be heard, so fervent and importune in putting forth of anything which may serve for the furtherance of their purpose that, between their importune pressing and the diligence or rather the negligence of good Catholic men, appeareth oftentimes as great a difference as between frost and fire.

And surely between the true Catholic folk and the false heretics, it fareth also much like as it fared between false Judas and Christ's faithful apostles. For while they, for all Christ's calling upon them to wake and pray, fell first in a slumber and after in a dead sleep, the traitor neither slept nor slumbered, but went about full busily to betray his Master, and bring himself to mischief.[273]

But yet when he came with his company, they escaped not all scot-free; nor Peter, well-awaked out of his sleep, was not so slothful but that he could cut off one knave's ear,[274] nor all the wretches of them, with all their weapons, able to stand against Christ's bare word, when he said, "I am he whom ye seek," but to ground they fell forthwith,[275] upright upon their backs.[276] Whereby we be sure that neither heretics nor devils can anything do but by God's special sufferance,[277] and that they shall, between them both, never be able to destroy the Catholic faith, nor to prevail against the Catholic Church; and all the mischief shall be their own at length, though God for our sin suffer them for a scourge to prevail in some places here and there for a while; whom, upon men's amendment he will not fail to serve at the last as doth the tender mother which, when she hath beaten her child for his wantonness,[278] wipeth his eyes and kisseth him, and casteth the rod in the fire.

Howbeit, if ever it should (as God forbid it should, and I trust it never shall), by such cold[279] sloth and negligence on the Catholic part, and such hot fervent labor of the heretics, that the heretics' party should hap to grow so strong as they should conspire to give the adventure[280] by feat of hands,[281] I nothing doubt of good men's good hearts, nor of the present aid and help of God, but that the presence of peril raising men out of this dull sleep would cause them then so to wax warm and diligent in the matter that the heretics should have such speed[282] as they have before this time had in this realm when they have attempted the like.

But yet though the heretics' party should (as I verily trust they should) have evermore the worst, yet very sure it is that neither party should have the better; but that it would then well appear that it had been much more wisdom for all good Catholic men to have waxen warmer before, and to have repressed those heretics in time, before they grew to so many.

And this thing was perceived very well both before the making of that statute of King Henry the IV, which statute this Pacifier would have now reformed, and also at the time of the making, and yet much better soon after, in the reign of the Prince of famous memory, King Henry the V. For before this statute made, the Parliament, in the fifth year of King Richard the II, complained of heretics, and

269 *maketh means to:* intercedes with; makes overtures to **270** biased **271** knew **272** chirping **273** See Mt 26:38–50. **274** See Jn 18:10. **275** immediately **276** Jn 18:6 **277** permission **278** waywardness **279** apathetic **280** *give the adventure:* try their luck **281** *feat of hands:* combat **282** success

found great harm grow that they were not arrested, but without arrest, in contempt of the censures of Holy Church, spread their heresies about from shire to shire and from diocese to diocese. Whereof the realm feared, as the statute expresseth, that thereof would at length grow some great commotion and peril. And therefore it was then provided that at the request of the ordinary, the Chancellor should from time to time award out commissions to attach[283] such heretics and keep them in strong prison till they were justified and ordered[284] according to the laws of the Church. And yet was it afterward well perceived that this provision could not suffice. For the heretics would commonly be gone before the commission could come, and do as much hurt in another place. And therefore the Parliament, in the second year of King Henry the IV, both being informed by the clergy and also by themselves perceiving that those heretics increased still, and would at length do some great mischief but if[285] they were better repressed, did, among other good things, provide that the ordinaries might arrest the heretics and imprison them themselves. And yet was all that too little too. For in some places the heretics waxed too strong, and would not be arrested for[286] them. And therefore at last it came to that point that men long had looked for. For those heresies begun by Wycliffe in the time of the noble prince King Richard the II, and being then by some folk maintained, and by many men winked at, and almost by all folk forslothed, the peril was so long neglected that the heretics were grown unto such number, courage, and boldness that afterward, in the time of the said famous prince King Henry the Fifth, they conspired among them not only the abolition of the faith and spoiling[287] of the spiritualty, but also the destruction of the King and all his nobility, with a plain subversion and overturning of the state of his whole realm. Upon which their false conspiracy disclosed, when they were by the policy of the noble Prince and his Council disappointed and secretly prevented,[288] and the field taken up before in which they had intended to gather together by night and from thence to have made their invasion, then, after due punishment done upon many of them, it was well perceived what great need it

was ever after to repress and subdue such seditious heresies forthwith, at the first springing. And therefore was there by and by[289] thereupon, by the full Parliament, not only that law confirmed, which law this Pacifier here speaketh of in this chapter, but also more made thereunto: as that they that were delivered to the secular hands should forfeit both goods and lands, and that the great officers of the realm should be solemnly sworn to repress heretics and assist the ordinaries. And therefore undoubtedly the good Christian zeal of the Prince, the nobles, and the commons toward the maintenance of the faith, and their high wisdom in providing for the conservation of the peace, rest, and surety[290] of the realm, were the authors and very doers in the making and passing of that very virtuous and very prudent act. Which act, that ever this Pacifier, or a great many such, shall be able to induce this prudent Parliament to change, that will I see ere I believe. Which I trust I never shall in this time, namely[291] in which, though there be not the fifteenth part of so many[292] heretics as these that be would very fain[293] there were, and while there be not, yet would have them seem to be, yet are there of troth[294] many more than there were within these few years past; and thereby the cause for which the statute was made not only standeth still, but is, over[295] that, of late very greatly increased, and so more need to let those laws stand, and make more such to them besides, than by the assuaging and mitigation of any part of them to bring these heretics into such courage and surety as the goodly devices of this Pacifier could not fail, if they were followed, to bring them.

THE FORTY-EIGHTH CHAPTER

Which,[296] whereas he useth to the setting forth of his purpose a surmised suspicion against the spiritualty, making men believe under his figure of "some say" that the spiritual judges mishandle those matters and use[297] themselves therein cruelly, I dare be bound to warrant that right good witnesses and worshipful[298] shall record and testify that they have been present and seen the judges handle

283 seize   284 *justified and ordered:* tried and punished   285 *but if:* unless   286 despite   287 robbing   288 *disappointed and secretly prevented:* thwarted and secretly anticipated   289 *by and by:* immediately   290 safety, security   291 especially   292 *the fifteenth part of so many:* one-fifteenth as many   293 *very* *fain:* very much wish   294 in truth   295 beyond   296 Who, i.e., "These heretics"   297 conduct   298 respectable

them with very great favor always, and sometimes, to say the truth, too tenderly.

Whereof, for the meanwhile, methink I may take to record, for all his "some says," this Pacifier himself and his own words which in this piteous book of *Division* himself saith. For in his first chapter he saith (as I showed you) that some men, to pull riches from the Church, have not only spoken and by plain words affirmed heresy, but have also despised pilgrimages and purgatory, and plain inveighed[299] against them of[300] policy.

Now seeth every man that any eyes hath that if the ordinaries and the spiritual judges were so fierce and so cruel as this Pacifier speaketh of, then would not those other men think that openly to speak and affirm false heresies were, for any manner purpose, any proper policy. And therefore as for such cruelty and mishandling of innocents, that this Pacifier's tale is untrue, both other good folk can testify, and his own words also bear witness.

And therefore need we no such change of the laws for that purpose. But on the other side, what harm would come of his mitigations, and what increase of heretics, the whole sum and sequel of his devices do more than manifestly show.

For suppose me, now, that a tinker[301] or a tiler[302] which could (as some there can) read English, and being instructed and taught by some old cunning weaver in Wycliffe's *Wicket* and Tyndale's books, and Frith's, and Friar Barnes's, were now become himself an usher[303] or, after his master's decease, a doctor,[304] and that were such a one as Frith writeth resorted to him, which, though he was but Frith's disciple and scholar, was yet (he saith) more meetly[305] to be bishop than many that wear the mitre; now if this tinker or tiler lurking about and teaching his Gospel in corners were secretly detected[306] to his ordinary, and thereupon sent for, and came, he should—by the device of this Pacifier—for the first shift[307] say, "Bring me forth mine accuser," and then, since the calling *ex officio*[308] were gone, home goeth the tinker again merrily for that time, and taketh forth his scholars a new lesson.

Then if the Court will appoint an officer of their own for an accuser, as an officer of a temporal court may give information for the King, the tinker yet,

when he were called again, would cry out upon that. And whoso holdeth against the process *ex officio* would take the tinker's part therein too, and call those twain but both one, and so home goeth the tinker again.

Then if some man (which would be long erst,[309] I ween) could yet at the last be founden that would offer himself as an accuser against this tinker when he were called again and his heresies were laid unto his charge, yet if the witnesses were peradventure some scholars of his own, and, lacking the wily shifts that himself had, first had denied their heresies upon their oaths, and after yet confessed them again—both upon themselves and their master tinker too—then, were there never so many of them, yet by the device of this Pacifier all their witness were nought worth,[310] because they were naughty men, heretics themselves, and first forsworn[311] also, so that yet home goeth the tinker again.

Now if there were, after other good honest proofs,[312] one that would come in and prove plainly the heresies that he held, when the tinker were thereto called, he would say he said it all of ignorance. Then if the matter were such as he must needs have heard of and known the true faith before, as pilgrimage, purgatory, or the Sacrament of the altar, he will not yet stick[313] much to say, "Bring in somebody here that will swear that ever he did teach it me." And yet when that answer in such an open matter[314] will not serve, he will say that he said it of simplicity, and that he believeth as the Church believeth, he. And when he is asked how the Church believeth, he will say he wotteth nere.[315] And if his words be rehearsed unto him clean contrary to the common-known Catholic faith of the Church, he will say he was not aware that the Church believed so, and will say that they should not speak of such high matters, that serve for doctors, to such a poor tinker that meddleth with brass and not with Latin. And there shall he then have some of his other faculty[316] gather and stand about, and say it is pity indeed that such a poor simple soul should have any such questions asked him. But they will put it for no pity at all that such an unlearned fool shall, among such others as are less learned than himself, teach boldly the false part, and there brag and boast that

---

299 spoke vehemently   **300** out of; for the sake of   **301** a repairer of pots and kettles   **302** a layer or maker of tiles   **303** assistant teacher   **304** theologian

305 fit   **306** reported   **307** tactic; ploy   **308** "by (virtue of) his office"   **309** before (it happened)   **310** *nought worth:* not worth a thing   **311** perjured   **312** *honest*

proofs: respectable witnesses   **313** hesitate   **314** *open matter:* matter of common knowledge   **315** *wotteth nere:* has never known   **316** trade; profession

he better understandeth the matter than all the doctors in the town.

Yet if it appear that by sore[317] words he despised and inveighed against pilgrimages, and purgatory, and such other things so that he did it not of simplicity when he spoke therein so shrewdly, then hath this Pacifier taught him to say that he did it of policy to pull away riches from the Church, and therefore can that be no heresy.

Now if the judges be so sore and so cruel that they will not allow that policy, yet hath this Pacifier taught him farther to say that he did but speak it affirmatively, and will not hold it opinionatively; and then, ye wot well, it is by this Pacifier no heresy.

And therefore must his judges, when they have all done, send this tinker yet once home again, and not keep him too long away, lest his scholars should play the truants and lack their learning the while.

And yet if he said as much after again, and thereupon were called again, he might say again that he were overseen[318] in that saying, of a lightness of wit and slipperiness of tongue. But he will not hold it opinionatively, and therefore yet again it may be no heresy, so that home must the tinker again.

And now if it should happen him to say and do so far as he were afraid to bide any further reckoning — namely where spiritual men so fierce and so cruel should be his judges — the bishop might not arrest him yet, till proofs be brought in first that the spiritualty have left their great desire to abjure and punish heretics; but must all the meanwhile cite him, suspend him, and accurse[319] him, and fetch him in by the King's writ when he is run out far off into another country, and there hath changed his name and set up a new school, whereas men can neither find him nor yet[320] wot where to seek him.

When should there by these means willful offenders be punished? Which, though this Pacifier pretend[321] that he would have done, yet consider these three chapters of his which I have rehearsed you — the first, the seventh, and the eighth — and ye shall find his devices come to little better effect than after this fashion that I have here described you.

And then if such good provisions may be made for them that they may never be brought in to answer, and that they may have so many shifts[322] whensoever they come, it will little fear them what pain ye set after conviction. Burn them twice, if ye will, after judgment; they will with good will agree, providing first such good acts for them as they shall never come so far.

And therefore, good Christian readers, would God the world were such as every man were so good — spiritual, temporal, and all — that neither party could find any fault in other, and all these heretics so clean gone and forgotten, and all those that are infected were so clean turned and changed that no man needed either abjuration or punishment. But since that this is more easy to wish than likely to look for, therefore is it wisdom that spiritual and temporal both, albeit men be not all saints, yet if their conditions be tolerable, either party labor to make himself better, and charitably somewhat either party bear with other. And those extreme vices which neither the one nor the other ought in any wise to suffer — as theft, adultery, sacrilege, murder, incest, and perjury, sedition, insurrection, treason, and heresy — both parties in one agreeing, to the honor of God and peace of Christ's Church, with rest, wealth, and surety[323] of the Prince and the realm, diligently reform and amend in such as are mendable, and those whose corrupt canker no cure can heal, cut off in season for corrupting farther.

THE FORTY-NINTH CHAPTER

And thus, good Christian readers, I make an end of this matter — the book, I mean, of this division; wherein I have nothing touched nor intended but only that I would not the temporalty bear the spiritualty the worse mind or affection for any such subtle invented ways that lay the faults of the bad to the whole body (wherein be many good) and under a figure of "some say" say some things false themselves, nor that men should causeless, upon such surmised and unproved cruelty, change the good laws before made against heretics, whereby, to the displeasure of God and provoking of his indignation, we were likely to have the faith decay, and more harm grow thereon than any man yet can tell.

The whole sum and effect therefore of my mind in this matter is that, as touching the spiritualty, I bear a tender mind of truth toward, I say, the body,

---

317 strong, harsh   **318** mistaken   **322** ploys   **323** *rest, wealth, and surety:*
319 excommunicate   **320** even   **321** claim   tranquility, well-being, and safety

not toward those that are naught[324] therein. And this mind is every man bound to bear; and I trust so doth this Pacifier too, and will of himself, I ween, do well enough, if he use to the contrary none evil counsel.

As touching heretics, I hate that vice of theirs and not their persons, and very fain[325] would I that the one were destroyed and the other saved. And that I have toward no man any other mind than this (how loudly soever these blessed new brethren, the professors and preachers of verity, belie me), if all the favor and pity that I have used among them to their amendment were known, it would, I warrant you, well and plain appear; whereof, if it were requisite, I could bring forth witnesses more than men would ween.

And sure this one thing will I be bold to say: that I never found any yet but had he been never so bad, nor done never so much harm before, yet after that I found him once changed and in good mind to mend, I have been so glad thereof that I have used him from thenceforth not as an evil man or an abject,[326] nor as a stranger neither, but as a good man and my very friend.

Howbeit, because it were neither right nor honesty that any man should look for more thanks than he deserveth, I will that all the world wit[327] it, on the other side, that whoso be so deeply grounded in malice, to the harm of his own soul and other men's too, and so set upon the sowing of seditious heresies that no good means that men may use unto him can pull that malicious folly out of his poisoned proud obstinate heart, I would rather be content that he were gone in time than overlong to tarry to the destruction of others.

Finally as for the author of the book of *Division*, because he professeth these heretics' opinions for heresies, as they be, I trust in all his other things himself meaneth but well, but partly may be by some pitiful affection[328] led. And some things he saith but upon report, and some things affirmeth peradventure as of himself because of the firm credence that he therein hath given to some that were not so credible as he took them for. But in conclusion, whatsoever he be, for anything that I perceive in his book, he shall, I trust, in conclusion be founden no such manner of man as folk should of

reason reckon to bear unto the weal[329] of the Prince and the realm any better mind than I. Howbeit, if his wit[330] and his learning find a better way than not only I (which am but a plain soul and can invent no novelties, but am content to stand to the old order and laws), but also than all they which for this realm in special, and for the whole Church of Christ in general, have made those provisions of old, I neither can nor will forbid any man to follow him.

But this will I be bold to counsel every man to whose part soever any such change shall pertain: first, that they have, as I doubt not but they will, a good Christian mind to the maintenance of Christ's Catholic faith, and that they therein stand by the old, without the contrary change of any point of our old belief for anything brought up for new, not only by Luther, Tyndale, Frith, or Friar Barnes, but also if there would (as there never will) an angel, as Saint Paul saith, come out of heaven and preach a contrary new.[331]

Secondly, forasmuch as these new fathers of these new brethren, like[332] as they make falsehood truth and truth falsehood, and faith heresies and heresies faith, so do call also the new old and the old new—not letting[333] to call in their books that faith but new which themselves confess in the same books to be more old than the age of eight hundred years—I will advise you therefore, good readers, for the true taking of the old faith, and for the discerning thereof from all new, to stand to the common well-known belief of the common-known Catholic Church of all Christian people: such faith as by yourselves, and your fathers, and your grandfathers, you have known to be believed, and have, over that, heard by them that the contrary was in the times of their fathers, and their grandfathers also, taken evermore for heresy. And also ye that read but even in English books shall in many things perceive the same by stories five times as far afore that.

We must also, for the perceiving of the old faith from new, stand to[334] the writings of the old holy doctors and saints, by whose expositions we see what points are expressed in the Scripture, and what points the Catholic Church of Christ hath, beside the Scripture, received and kept by the Spirit of God and tradition of his apostles.

And specially must we also stand, in this matter

---

324 bad   **325** gladly   **326** outcast   emotion   **329** well-being   **330** intellect   **334** *stand to:* abide by
327 knows   **328** disposition; inclination;   **331** See Gal 1:8.   **332** just   **333** hesitating

of faith, to the determinations of Christ's Catholic Church.

Now if any man will bear other in hand[335] that this point or that point is not determined, or that the holy doctors of the Church write not in such wise but the contrary, then whosoever is not of such learning as to perceive by himself whether of those two say true that hold therein contrary parts, then, except the article be a plain open-known thing of itself not doubted before, let him not be light of credence in the believing either the one disputer or the other, though they would both preach high praises of their own cunning, and say that besides all their much worldly business they had spent many years about the study of Scripture, and boast that their books of divinity were worth never so much money, or that by the Spirit they were inspired and with the celestial dew suddenly sprungen up divines, as lusty, fresh, and green as after any shower of rain ever sprung any bed of leeks. Let no man, I say, be light in believing them for all that, but let him by my poor counsel pray God inspire himself to believe and follow the thing that may be his high pleasure, and let him thereupon appoint with himself[336] to live well and, forthwith[337] to begin well, get himself a good ghostly[338] father, and shrive[339] him of his sins, and then, concerning the question, ask advice and counsel of those whom himself thinketh, between God and his new-cleansed conscience, for learning and virtue most likely, without any partial leaning, indifferently to tell him truth.

And thus far I say for the faith itself, because I hear some men much speak and boast that they will labor for declarations[340] of heresy, which, as meseemeth, is a thing that little needeth. For I never wist[341] any man in my life put in trouble for any point of heresy but such points as were for heresy well and openly known among the common people. And Saint Paul saith that heresies be manifest and open, so that he thought, as it seemeth, that there needed none other declaration than the common-received faith of the Christian people to the contrary.

But now as touching any new order[342] concerning heresies, with the change of laws before devised for the repression of them, I have no more to say therein, but advise every good man endeavor himself to keep well the laws already made of old, except he see the cause of the making changed, or some other great necessity, and that he see that point by more ordinary means proved than either by "some say" or "they say," or "many say," or else that he perceive well, at the least, that those folk which would labor to change them be better and wiser both than ever were those that made them. And thus finish I this matter concerning heresies, beseeching our Lord and Savior for his bitter Passion that, as his holy sacraments thereof took their strength, so by the prayer of all those holy saints that have both by their holy doctrine and example of living, some of them planted the faith and some of them in sundry times well watered the plants,[343] so himself will of his goodness specially now vouchsafe as the warm sun (the very eternal only-begotten Son of his eternal Father) to spread his beams upon us, and aspire[344] his breath into us, and in our hearts, as Saint Paul saith, give his faith strength and increase.

THE FIFTIETH CHAPTER

Now come I to the last fault that the brethren find in my books. For as for one more that was showed me within this seven-night, I not so much esteem as to vouchsafe to answer: that is to wit, where they reprove that I bring in, among the most earnest matters, fancies and sports and merry tales. For as Horace saith, a man may sometimes say full sooth in game.[345] And one that is but a layman, as I am, it may better haply[346] become him merrily to tell his mind than seriously and solemnly to preach. And over this, I can scant[347] believe that the brethren find any mirth in my books. For I have not much heard that they very merrily read them.

But as to the last fault that they find, which I was about now to speak of, whereas they say that as concerning the Church, I have not fulfilled my promise, I shall here first put you in remembrance what my promise was.

In the end of my preface before *Tyndale's Confutation*, these are my very words:

---

335 *bear . . . hand:* lead others to believe   **336** *appoint with himself:* resolve   **337** immediately   **338** spiritual   **339** absolve   **340** explanations; clarifications   **341** knew   **342** procedure   **343** See 1 Cor 3:6.   **344** breathe   **345** *sooth in game:* truth in jest. See Satires, 1.1.24–25.   **346** perhaps   **347** scarcely

Now shall I (God willing) at my next leisure go farther in his book, and come to the very breast[348] of all this battle: that is to wit, the question, Which is the Church? For that is the point that all these heretics, by all the means they may, labor to make so dark that by their wills no man should wit[349] what they mean. But I trust to draw the serpent out of his dark den, and as the poets feign that Hercules drew up Cerberus, the mastiff of hell, into the light where his eyes dazed,[350] so shall I, with the grace of that light which illumineth every man that cometh into this world,[351] make you that matter so lightsome and so clear to every man that I shall leave Tyndale never a dark corner to creep into, able to hide his head. Then after that I have so clearly confuted Tyndale concerning that point, and shall have plainly proved you the sure and steadfast authority of Christ's Catholic known Church, against all Tyndale's trifling sophistications—which he would should[352] seem so solemn subtle insolubles,[353] which ye shall see proved very frantic follies—after this done, I say, before I go farther with Tyndale, I purpose to answer good young Father Frith.[354]

Now good readers, whoso list[355] to say that I have not fulfilled this promise, if he read not my book, I cannot make him see the thing that he list not to look on.

If he have read it, and think himself not satisfied, I cannot make him perceive more than his wit will serve him.

If he understand it well, and yet will say my promise is not fulfilled, I cannot let him for his pleasure to lie. But let him, whatsoever he be, put in writing what moveth him so to say, and I shall then, I doubt not, make other folk perceive that all my promise in that point I have fully performed and more: that is to wit, by as much more at the least as all mine eight books amounteth. For like as in the others I have fully confuted Tyndale's church, so have I in that book confuted, as for this world, the church that Friar Barnes had falsely framed here also, whereof I promised nothing. So that, as touching the certainty of the Church and of the infallible doctrine thereof, whoso read and advise[356] well this work of mine made for the confutation of Tyndale, and therewith read and consider the seven first chapters and the last of my second book of my *Dialogue*, whereupon Tyndale made all his work, I doubt not but he that thus will do shall find himself fully satisfied.

And therefore, good Christian readers, as for such further things as I have in my said preface promised, I purpose to pursue at some other, further leisure. But first I think it better to bestow some time upon another thing, and leaving for a while both defense of mine own faults and finding of other men's in writing, think better to bestow some time about the mending of mine own in living, which is a thing now for many men more necessary than is writing. For of new bookmakers there are now more than enough.

Wherefore, that all such as will write may have the grace to write well or, at the leastwise, none other purpose than to mean well, and as well writers as others to amend our own faults and live well, I beseech Almighty God to grant us; and that all folk spiritual and temporal in this world living, and all good Christian souls departed hence and yet not out of pain, may for grace every party pray for other; and all the blessed holy saints in heaven, both here for grace and there for glory, pray to God for us all. Amen.

Printed by W. Rastell in
Fleet Street in Saint
Bride's Churchyard.
1533
Cum privilegio.[357]

348 heart   **349** understand   **350** *as the poets … dazed:* This was the twelfth and final labor of Hercules   **351** See Jn 1:9.   **352** *would should:* wants to   **353** irrefutable arguments   **354** *CW* 8: 34/29–35/11   **355** wishes   **356** consider   **357** *Cum privilegio:* With [the King's] permission

The Debellation of Salem and Bizance

The intensity and importance of More's final contest with Christopher St. German (and therefore with Henry VIII and Cromwell) are indicated by the rapid-fire publications between these two legal scholars. In December 1532 St. German published anonymously, with the King's printer, his thirty-five-page *Treatise Concerning the Division Between the Spiritualty and the Temporalty*. In April 1533, More's 172-page response was already in print, somewhat disguised, as his *Apology*. More's reply, laced with satire and humor, prompted St. German to publish his seventy-page response in September, *Salem and Bizance: A Dialogue Between Two English Men* — again anonymously and again with the King's printer. By November, More's detailed reply of 230 pages was published — having been written, More says, "in a few days." Within three months, Henry VIII was insisting upon More's imprisonment. What would follow was legislation, not debate.

At stake, More argues in his *Debellation*, are "the very good, old, and long-approved laws both of this realm and of the whole corps of Christendom, which laws this Pacifier in his book of *Division*" attacks with "warm words and cold reasons." The "Pacifier" claims that he writes to achieve peace but, as More argued in *The Apology*, the *Division*'s effect was quite the contrary.

As in his *Apology*, More again challenges the Pacifier to give even one example of his accusations that English bishops used unjust procedures in their ecclesiastical courts. Nowhere either in *Division* or in *Salem and Bizance* did St. German give such an example. Instead, he offered what "some say," thus giving rise to More's second satirical name for this opponent: "Sir John Some Say." Despite More's sharp satire, St. German would give no examples in his mid-1534 *New Additions of Salem and Bizance*. As legal scholar H. A. Kelly observes, More explains in both *The Apology* and with even greater detail in *The Debellation* that the legal procedures of the English ecclesiastical courts were "very workable and reasonable" and "already contained the procedures and safeguards that [St. German] required" — while

St. German's own proposals were "unworkable because there were too many disadvantages and dangers" involved ("Thomas More on Inquisitorial Due Process," *English Historical Review*, vol. 123 [2008]: 893–94). In Tudor historian John Guy's summary: "Throughout the five closing chapters of the *Debellation*, More emphasized what he had said before, that the King's Council had investigated the critics' complaints and had vindicated the spiritual judges" (*CW* 10: lxxx–ix). The Pacifier went still further, however, accusing the clergy of acting as a "confederacy ... against the King's laws and the old customs of the realm," even when, More argued, their procedures were recently and long approved by Parliament and custom and the international Church.

St. German's importance in Cromwell's and Henry's political program is particularly clear, John Guy explains, "because St. German was at work in 1531 on a program of parliamentary reform and propaganda designed to purchase peace between church and state at the expense of the clergy's traditional privileges and jurisdictional independence" (*CW* 10: xxxix). In More's mind, "St. German was a dangerous man because his general theory of English law and institutions denied the independent legislative and jurisdictional powers of the church" (xxix). Guy further notes that St. German "was the first Englishman to articulate the theory of the sovereignty of the king in parliament — the theory that grounded the English Reformation and finally prevailed" (xxxix–xl).

The danger More personally faced in this legal contest was great, and in the Preface of the *Debellation*, More draws attention to the anger caused by his *Apology*. More reports: "heard I shortly that thick and threefold the pens went to work, and answers were a-making, diverse, by diverse very great cunning men." More responds with *Debellation*, however, because he is sure that the "shrewd, malicious intent that was purposed in [the] first book, of *Division*," is still at work, the same strategy More had already pointed out in his *Supplication of Souls* — the intent of "deadly defamation of the whole spiritualty." In *Debellation*, More calls Sir John Some Say's writings "seditious slanderous books" designed to increase division "under color of reformation" (*CW* 10: 15/5–9).

Only the beginning and end of More's *Debellation* are given here because, as More explains, his basic argument is the same as in his *Apology*, and More quotes long sections of that work again in *Debellation*. So why write another book about the same topic? More asks that question himself, and the most pressing reason he gives in his Preface is that Sir John Some Say, in responding, "for the most part used a pretty craft: to misrehearse my matter and leave my words out. Yea, and besides this, the man hath in some places left out some of his own, and misrehearsed them to make the reader ween that, in the reproving them, I had written wrong." As a result, More decides it is necessary to respond to *Salem and Bizance* in a detailed and orderly way, replying, as he explains in his conclusion, "to every chapter of his book by row [in order]." The result is More's side of the argument, expressed with urgency and vigor, about the nature of law and England's legal future.

For the full text of *The Debellation of Salem and Bizance*, see www.essentialmore.org.

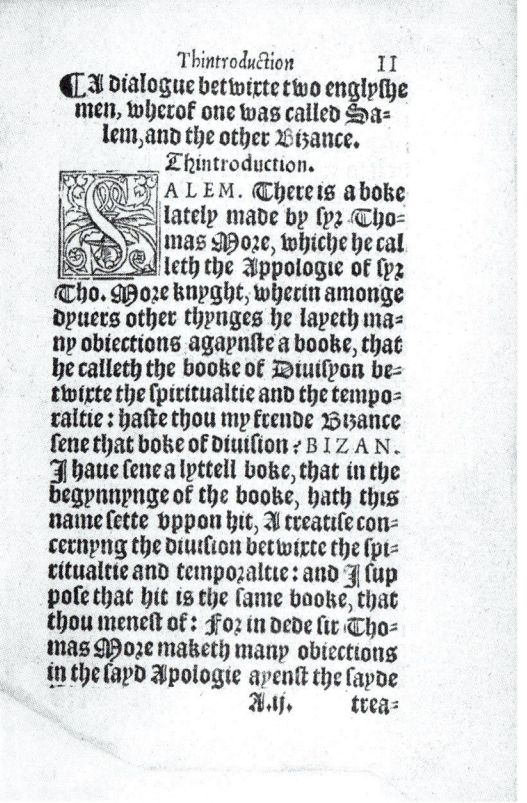

This response by Christopher St. German to Thomas More's *Apology* was published anonymously in September 1533 by the King's printer, Thomas Berthelet. The book's full title (given above on page ii), is *A dialogue between two Englishmen, whereof one was called Salem, and the other Bizance*. After More's 270-page reply published in November, *The Debellation of Salem and Bizance*, St. German responded again anonymously in mid-1534 with *New Additions of Salem and Bizance*.

The Debellation of Salem and Bizance
by Sir Thomas More

The Declaration[1] of the Title

5 The *Debellation*[2] *of Salem and Bizance*[3] — sometime[4] two great towns, which, being under the great Turk, were between Easter and Michaelmas[5] last past (this present year of our Lord, 1533) with a marvelous metamorphosis enchanted and turned into two Englishmen by the wonderful in-

10 ventive wit and witchcraft of Sir John Some Say, the Pacifier and so by him conveyed hither in a dialogue,[6] to defend his *Division*[7] against *The Apology*[8] *of Sir Thomas More, Knight*. But now — being thus, between the said Michaelmas and Halloweentide

15 next ensuing, in this debellation vanquished — they be fled hence and vanished, and are become two towns again, with those old names changed, "Salem" into "Jerusalem" and "Bizance" into "Constantinople," the one in Greece, the other in Syria, where

20 they may see them that will,[9] and win them that can. And if the Pacifier convey them hither again, and ten such other towns with them, embattled in such dialogues, Sir Thomas More hath undertaken to put himself in the adventure alone against them all. But

25 and if[10] he let them tarry still there, he will not utterly forswear[11] it, but he is not much minded as yet, age now so coming on and waxing all unwieldy,[12] to go thither and give the assault to such well-walled towns, without some such lusty[13] company as shall

30 be somewhat likely to leap up a little more lightly.[14]

The Preface
Sir Thomas More to the Christian Readers

If any man marvel (as I ween some wise men will) that ever I would vouchsafe to bestow any time
35 about making answer to the Pacifier's *Dialogue*, considering his faint and his feeble reasoning: I cannot,

in good faith, well excuse myself therein.[15] For as I suddenly went in hand therewith[16] and made it in a breyde:[17] so when I since considered how little need
40 it was, I marveled mine own self, and repented too, that I had not regarded the book as it was worthy, and without any one word let it even[18] alone. Howbeit,[19] good readers, what one thing or twain[20] specially moved me to make answer to it, and how it
45 happed me to fall in hand therewith and to spend and lose a little time about it, to make the matter the more plain unto you, that thing shall I show you.

As soon as mine *Apology* was once come out abroad, anon[21] heard I word that some were very
50 wroth[22] therewith. And yet in my mind had there no man cause, neither preacher nor pacifier, no, nor no heretic neither. For I had but spoken for myself, and for good folk, and for the Catholic faith — without reproach or reproof to any man's person,
55 or willing any man any harm that were willing to amend. And whoso[23] were willing to be naught[24] still, had cause to be wroth with himself, you wot[25] well, and not with me.

But all this would not serve me, for very wroth
60 were they with me. Howbeit, their causeless anger did not greatly grieve me. For I was not so far unreasonable as to look for reasonable minds in unreasonable men.

But then heard I shortly that thick and threefold
65 the pens went to work, and answers were a-making, diverse, by diverse very great cunning[26] men. And of this travail of such great mountainous hills, I heard much speech made almost every week — so far forth that at last it was told me for truth that unto one
70 little piece one great cunning man had made a long answer of twelve whole sheets of paper, written near together and with a small hand.[27]

But in good faith, I could but laugh at that. For as for that piece, I was very sure that the cunningest

1 Explanation **2** Conquest **3** Byzantium **4** formerly **5** the feast of St. Michael the Archangel (September 29) **6** *A Dialogue between two Englyshe men, whereof one was called Salem, and the other Bizance*, by Christopher St. German **7** *A Treatise Concerning the Division between the Spiritualty and the Temporalty*, by St. German **8** defense **9** wish to **10** *and if:* if **11** renounce **12** *waxing… unwieldy:* growing all feeble **13** vigorous **14** easily, nimbly **15** in that **16** *in hand therewith:* engaged with that **17** short span of time **18** untroubled **19** However **20** two **21** immediately **22** angry **23** whoever **24** wicked **25** know **26** learned, clever **27** handwriting of St. German, noted for its "compact lines and minute characters" (*CW* 10, xxiv)

man that could come thereto, neither in twelve sheets nor in twelve quires[28] neither, write as near as he could, should never answer it well.

For that piece was the answer that in mine *Apology* I make, as you see there, unto certain sermons wherein my *Dialogue*[29] was touched[30] for writing against Tyndale's false translation; and wherein was also defended, against my *Confutation*,[31] Tyndale's wise[32] chapter in which, against my *Dialogue*, he laboreth to prove that the Word was before the Church—and in all his chapter never toucheth the point; and the sermon that defended him walketh as wide as he.

It was told me, as I say, that answer was made to that place, and what shift[33] there was found to the remnant, that could I not hear. But to the first point I heard say that there was devised that whereas I rehearse that the preacher spoke of "poisoned bread," I rehearsed him wrong, for he spoke but of "moldy bread." And this piece, it was told me that in that new answer it was reasoned at length, and set forth very lustily.

But come the book abroad once, I shall soon abate that courage.[34] For first, since he taketh record that he said but "moldy bread," if I bring witness also that he said "poisoned bread," then can his witness stand him in none other stead but for to prove for him that he said both.

Secondly shall I prove that he said "poisoned bread" by such means that men shall see by reason that though the other were possible—yet was it far unlikely.

Finally shall I further prove that though the man had said not "poisoned bread" but only "moldy bread"—yet shall I prove, I say, that as the case stood, that same not "poisoned bread" but "moldy bread" was yet, for all that, a very poisoned word.

Hearing, therefore, that this gay book was made of the twelve sheets of paper, and lacked but overlooking,[35] and that many more were in hand that shortly should come out, like as a husband whose wife were in her travail hearkeneth every handwhile[36] and fain[37] would hear good tidings—so since I so much heard of so sore[38] travail of so many, so cunning, about diverse answers, I longed of their long labor to see some good speed,[39] and some of those fair babes born that they travailed on.

And when these great hills had thus travailed long, from the week after Easter till as much before Michaelmas, the good hour came on as God would, that one was brought abed, with sore labor at last delivered of a dead mouse. The mother is yet but green, good soul, and hath need of good keeping; women wot what caudle[40] serveth against her afterthroes.[41]

Now after that the book was out and came into my hands and that I saw the manner and the fashion thereof two things only moved me to write and meddle with it. One, that I saw therein followed and pursued the selfsame shrewd[42] malicious intent that was purposed in his first book, of *Division*: that is to wit, to make the ordinaries,[43] with fear of slander and obloquy,[44] leave their duties undone and let heretics alone, and over[45] that, with an evil new change of good old laws, labor to put heretics in courage, and thereby decay the faith.

This was indeed the very special point that made me write yet again. And yet found I so little reason in his reasoning that methought it should not need.[46] For this wist[47] I very well: that whosoever had wit, and would confer[48] and compare together the words of his answer with the words of mine *Apology*, should soon perceive that his answers were even[49] very dull and dead.

But then was there another thing that I considered in it—which point, unprovided for, might soon deceive the reader. For albeit the Pacifier hath in some places put in mine own words where it pleased him, yet hath he for the most part used a pretty craft: to misrehearse my matter and leave my words out. Yea, and besides this, the man hath in some places left out some of his own, and misrehearsed them to make the reader ween[50] that, in the reproving[51] them, I had written wrong.

Now had I supposed to remedy those things, and make him an answer, in three or four leaves, with only pointing the reader to the places,[52] with writing in what leaf he should find the matter. For the words once read—the trouble should show itself.

28 sets of four sheets, each sheet yielding twelve leaves   **29** *Dialogue of Sir Thomas More, Knight*   **30** mentioned; criticized   **31** *Confutation of Tyndale's* Answer   **32** clever   **33** tactic   **34** *abate … courage:* put an end to that confidence   **35** proofreading   **36** *hearkeneth every handwhile:* is on the alert at every moment   **37** gladly   **38** great   **39** success   **40** medicinal drink   **41** pain following childbirth   **42** wicked   **43** bishops; Church authorities   **44** ill repute   **45** beyond   **46** be necessary   **47** knew   **48** put side by side   **49** fully   **50** think   **51** refuting   **52** the passages in the *Apology*

But while I was thus minded and went thereabout—his answer in his *Dialogue* had found such a way, with walking to and fro, keeping no manner order, and therewith making me seek so long for some one place, that I saw well I should sooner answer him all anew than find out for many things the place that I should seek for. I made, therefore, in few days, this answer that you see. And some such places yet as I had happed to find, I have remitted[53] the reader unto in mine *Apology*, where for his ready finding, I have numbered him the leaf. And yet have I for some folk done somewhat more too. For I see well, surely many men are nowadays so delicate[54] in reading, and so loath to labor, that they fare in other books as women fare with their primer,[55] which though they be content to say sometimes the Fifteen Psalms,[56] and over that, the Psalms of the Passion[57] too, if they find them all fair set out in order at length—yet will they rather leave them all unsaid than turn back to seek them out in other parts of their primer.

And therefore, lest some readers might hap in this book to do the same, some places of the *Apology* much necessary and not long, that with much seeking I fortuned to find out, to ease the reader's labor and make all open unto him, I have put in also into mine answer here. Yea and yet over this, in the things of most weight, I have put into this book his own words too. And so shall you, good readers, without any pain of seeking, have all the matter plain and open before your eyes, that ye shall well see that I love the light no less than this Pacifier would fain walk in the dark. For, as the dark is in this matter all his advantage, even so is verily the light in like wise mine. And whereas there are some that commend his answer for the compendious brevity thereof and shortness, I nothing therein envy the man's praise. For like as no man can make a shorter course than he that lacketh both his legs, so can no man make a shorter book than he that lacketh as well words as matter. And yet when, by the places conferred so well together, the feebleness of his answer shall appear, then shall he lose the praise of shortness too. For when it shall well be seen that he saith nothing to the purpose, then

shall every wise man think his book too long by all together. And that you may well perceive that so it is in deed, let us now leave of the preface and fall into the matter.

. . . .

THE TWENTY-FIRST CHAPTER
[Conclusion]

In his twenty-first chapter (beginning in the 84th leaf), because I said in mine *Apology*[58] that there be few parts in his book of *Division* that shall, if they be well considered, appear so good at length as they seem to some men at the first sight and at superficial reading, he provoketh[59] me to show what other faults I find therein. And then, to prick me forward, he bringeth forth two or three things which he saith it seemeth most likely that I should mean. But wherefore[60] it should be most likely that I should mean those things—thereof showeth he nothing—but leaveth folk occasion to think that his own mind misgiveth him in those things. For me hath he never heard make any business of them.

And afterward, in the leaf 91, again he provoketh me to the same. And there he reciteth how many chapters of his I meddle[61] not with; wherein he might have made a shorter work if he would have let them stand that I touched[62] not and have spoken of them only that I touched—for they were very few—as he that was very unwilling to have touched any one at all, save for the much evil that covertly was cloaked in them. And for the withdrawing of that cloak, that men might the better see what it meant, I touched the first chapter for a show,[63] and the seventh and the eighth for that[64] they labored, to the great decay of the Catholic faith, to put away or change into worse the most especially good laws, both of the whole Church and of this realm, that have been made and observed long for the preservation thereof.[65] And the first chapter was in effect nothing else but by false slanderous surmises against the ordinaries (as though they mishandled men for heresy) a shrewd[66] preparative to it. And therefore, leaving his other trifles alone—I answered in effect

---

53 referred　**54** fastidious, particular
55 prayer book　**56** *the Fifteen Psalms:*
the Gradual Psalms, or Songs of Ascents;
Psalms 119–33(120–34)　**57** *Psalms of the*

Passion: the Penitential Psalms; Psalms 6,
32(33), 38(39), 51(52), 102(103), 130(131),
and 143(144)　**58** See pp. 845–46 and
901–3.　**59** challenges　**60** why　**61** deal

62 discussed　**63** example　**64** *for that:*
because　**65** See *CW* 9: 177–80, 188–93.
66 cunning; malicious

only these, of which so much harm might grow. Which things if they had been out of his book, all the remnant, good and bad together, should have gone forth for me, and therefore yet so shall they. For I purpose not to embusy myself with confuting of every fault that I find in every man's book. I should have then overmuch ado.

Nor I will not dispraise or deprave[67] anything that I think good either in his book or in any man's else. And therefore I have in mine *Apology* said expressly that he saith some things well. But forasmuch as there be many things naught[68] too, I give therefore the reader warning not to walk away with them over-hastily, but read them with judgment and advise them well—and not believe every spirit, but prove whether it be of God or not—and that that is good, take; and that that is evil, let it go to the devil.

I well allow,[69] therefore, and like not a little, the great good mind of Salem toward the vanquishing of the great Turk and conquering of the Holy Land, wherein he spendeth the other three chapters of his book. But I mislike much, again, that as he would dilate the faith by force of sword in far countries hence—so he laboreth to change and take away the good and wholesome laws whereby the faith is preserved here at home. I like also marvelously well that such points of the Catholic faith as heretics now labor to destroy, as praying to saints, pilgrimage, and purgatory, and the sacraments, and especially the Blessed Sacrament of the altar, whereof in the 86th leaf he speaketh so well that, as help me God, it did me good to read it—this, I say, liketh me marvelously well: that the right faith of[70] these points, he confesseth so well and so fully for his own person. But the better opinion that I have of his own person therein, the more sorry am I to see that his books are, by some shrewd counsel, handled in such wise as, if they were followed, would make the faith decay and perish in many other folk. This is the great thing that in his books grieveth me.

For as for the point that he speaketh of in the leaf 91, of that the priests should eat no flesh from Quinquagesima[71] to Easter, I take it for a matter as small as he doth. But then he asketh me wherefore in the thirty-first chapter of mine *Apology*,

beginning in the 175th leaf,[72] I make so great a matter of it. Whoso list[73] to read the chapter shall see that I wrote it not all in vain, nor show myself unwilling that the priests should do it neither, though they be not bound to it. But the less that the weight of the matter was, the more cause this man gave me to speak thereof. For the more was he to blame to put that, and other such small matters as that is, for causes of so great a division as he surmiseth[74] that this is. This was, lo, the cause that made me to speak thereof. Which cause this man gave himself and therefore needeth not to marvel as he doth, wherefore I spoke thereof.

And therefore thus have I, good readers, now replied to every chapter of his book by row,[75] save only the last three, which go about a good voyage into the Holy Land, a great way far off from me. And I have not leaped to and fro, now forward, now backward, in such manner as he playeth in his answer made unto me, without either order kept or cause appearing wherefore, save only the cause that every man may spy: that he would not have it seen what places[76] he left untouched.[77] Which is, in a manner,[78] the most part of altogether[79] that in my book is touched of the three chapters of his. And I have, on the other side,[80] not left any one piece unproved[81] that myself spoke of before, or that anything pertained unto me.

And therefore whereas, in the beginning of the twenty-second chapter, Simkin[82] Salem giveth his sentence[83] upon the said answer to the said *Apology*, and alloweth[84] the said answer well, methinketh that if he considered, not only how much he hath left unanswered, and how much of his own words undefended which he nothing hath touched at all, but over that, how feebly he hath defended those things that he hath touched here—Salem being indifferent[85] had been like to have allowed it but a little.

For, setting aside for the while all the remnant, if he go but to the very principal point alone—wherein he laboreth to change and put away those good laws, the change whereof (such as he deviseth) the decay of the Catholic faith and the increase of heresies would follow—in that point alone, I say we lay against him the common consent of this

---

67 disparage   **68** bad   **69** approve of   whoever cares   **74** alleges   **75** *by row:*   were   **79** all   **80** hand   **81** unexamined
70 concerning   **71** the Sunday before Ash   in order, one after another   **76** passages   **82** Fool   **83** opinion   **84** accepts
Wednesday   **72** See p. 871.   **73** *whoso list:*   **77** unmentioned   **78** *in a manner:* as it   **85** impartial, unbiased

realm. And he layeth his own reason against it. We lay against him the consent of the general council. And against this he layeth his own reason. We lay against him the general approbation of all Christian realms. And against this he layeth his own reason. And what is his own irrefragable[86] reason that he layeth against all this? Surely no more, as you see, but that by those laws an innocent may sometime take wrong.[87] Against this reason we lay him that if this reason should stand, then against malefactors there could no law stand. We lay against it also that by his devices, if they were followed, by the increase of heresies many innocents must needs take much more wrong.

To this answereth he that he will not answer that. And now, when Salem seeth that he cannot answer that, and seeth that all the weight of the matter hangeth upon that, then Sim Salem giveth sentence that he hath answered very well. But surely if such answering be well, I wot[88] not which way a man might answer ill.

And therefore whereas Simkin Salem saith that if this good man will, he will cause a friend of his answer all the remnant — he may do this good man a much more friendly turn if he make his friend answer this better first, that this good man hath answered already. Howbeit,[89] if they list[90] thus to give over this, and assay[91] what they can say better to any other piece — let them in God's name hardily go to, for me. And if they say anything meetly[92] to the matter, I will put no friend to pain to make them answer, but at leisure convenient shall answer them myself. And where they say well, I will not let[93] to say so. And where they say wrong, I will not let to tell them. But on the other side, if they go no better to work, nor no nearer to the matter, than this man hath done — I shall peradventure[94] let them even alone, and let them like their writing themselves, and no man else. But now letting pass all the special points — I shall answer the generalities that this good man speaketh of. For in the leaf 90 these are his words:

And now shall I say somewhat further in a generality, as Master More hath done, and that is this: that all that I speak in the said treatise was

to appease[95] this division, and not to begin any, nor to continue it. And therefore how they can salve their conscience that say I did rather intend a division than agreement, I cannot tell; their own conscience shall be judge. And I intended also somewhat to move[96] that might be occasion to put away abusions,[97] evil examples, and heresies — and not to increase them or maintain them, I dare boldly say.

To this I answer that it neither was nor is my mind that men should think that he meant evil himself, as I have in many places of mine *Apology* testified. But verily I thought, and yet think, that by some wily shrews[98] his book was so mishandled that it meant naught[99] though he meant well. For whereas he saith that with his book of *Division* all his purpose was to appease division — I will not contend with him upon his own mind. But surely this will I say: that if I had been of the mind to sow and set forth division, I would have used even the selfsame ways to kindle it that he used (as he saith) to quench it.

Then goeth he further and saith:

And further, as Master More knoweth better than I, *Mentire est contra mentem ire*; that is to say, "To lie is when a man saith against his own mind." And in good faith, in all that treatise, I speak nothing but that I thought was true.

To this I answer that indeed such a thing I have read, and, as I remember, in Aulus Gellius. Which thing though I have now no leisure to look for, yet two points I remember thereof. One, that it is there *mentiri*, and not *mentire* — which infinitive mode in what book of grammar this good man hath found, I cannot tell. I was afeard it had been overseen[100] in the printing. But I have looked[101] the corrections, and there find I no fault found therein.

The other point I remember: that there is a difference put between *mentiri* and *mendacium dicere*; that is, as we might say, between him that wittingly[102] lieth and him that telleth a lie weening[103] that it were true. And there it is said, "Wittingly not to tell a lie pertaineth to a good man. And not to tell

---

86 irrefutable   **87** *take wrong:* suffer injustice   **88** know   **89** know **90** choose   **91** try   **92** appropriately

93 refrain   **94** perhaps   **95** settle **96** propose   **97** abuses   **98** scoundrels

99 badly   **100** overlooked   **101** examined **102** knowingly   **103** thinking

a lie unawares is the part of a wise man." And surely, since the Scripture saith that he that shortly[104] believeth is over light,[105] this good man to believe so many lies so soon and with so many "some says" to set them forth in print, to the rebuke and slander of the spiritual[106] judges and make men ween they mishandled men for heresies, though the man's innocent mind made the sin the less, yet was the thing at the least no less than a very great lightness; yea, and also a great proof toward the reproof[107] of his words that follow next, where he goeth further thus:

> And further, I will ascertain[108] Master More, as far as in me is, that I neither had any "subtle shrews' counsel" nor any evil counsel at the making of the said treatise which he calleth the "book of *Division*" (as is said before).

To this I answer that albeit this good man and I be at much variance[109] here in diverse things—yet for the good and plain profession of the Catholic faith that I find in him, in good faith I much better love him than in that point to believe him. For if he said therein true, then were all the faults only his own, in which, as I have often said, I much rather think that some subtle shrews have deceived him.

And besides sundry other things that lead me so to think, one very strong thing is this, that every man may well see by his book: that all such as have resorted[110] to him to tell him any such things as under "some says" he put out again, have always told him evil, and never told him good. And of mishandling for heresies have ever told him lies, and never told him true. For whereas the punishment for heresies hath been very little anywhere, save even here at hand[111]—and here but right done to them, and that with much favor too—they have made him, good seely[112] soul, believe that ordinaries mishandle men for heresy in manner[113] throughout the realm.

Also, whereas such slanderous clamor hath been sundry times of late, in all that ever complained, plainly proved false before the King's most honorable Council, not one man came to tell him nothing thereof, nor not one "some say" thereof written in all his book; and over[114] this, whereas mine own self have plainly told him the same things in mine *Apology* by writing—yet (which most marvel were of all, save for such wily shrews) every man may well see that he never read it. For he saith not one word thereto. And therefore it is easy to perceive, whatsoever himself say, which is loath of his goodness to put other folk in fault, that there be some wily shrews so much about him that they neither suffer[115] him anything to hear but that themselves list[116] to tell him, nor yet[117] anything to read but where themselves list to turn him.

And now, since I have here answered these generalities of his—I will not long encumber you with any generalities of mine own, but generally I would that all were well. And so help me, my Savior, and none otherwise, but as I would wish no heretic one halpworth[118] harm, that had clearly[119] left his heresy and were well turned to God. But on the other side, whoso stick still therein, rather would I wish him sorrow to[120] his sin, whereby there are many folk many times amended, than prosperously to proceed in his mischief[121] to the loss of his own soul and other men's too. And toward that point, against all malefactors in the spirualty[122] and the temporalty[123] too, would I wish all good folk of both parties to agree, and each love other well, and stick fast to the faith, which were likely sore to decay by the change of these good laws that this good man goeth about to destroy. For whose unreasonableness therein the better to be perceived, with the danger and peril that would ensue thereon, I will desire[124] you, good readers, to resort[125] to mine *Apology*, and beginning at the leaf 270, read unto the leaf 287,[126] wherein you shall, I trust, be well and fully satisfied. And unto all that ever is in all that spoken—this man hath nothing said.

And whereas in confuting the faults that this man findeth in the suit *ex officio*[127] and the laws made against heretics, I have used some examples of the common law, which this man hath labored to prove unlike, and I have therein clearly confuted him afresh; it may peradventure happen that he will now take another way therein, and say that in such points those spiritual[128] laws may be reformed, and those temporal[129] too.

---

104 quickly   105 See Prv 14:15; 2 Thes 2:1–3; 1 Jn 4:1.   106 ecclesiastical   107 refutation   108 assure   109 disagreement   110 gone   111 *at hand*: close by   112 pitiable; helpless; foolish   113 *in manner*: nearly   114 besides   115 allow   116 wish   117 even   118 halfpenny's worth (of)   119 entirely   120 for   121 evildoing   122 clergy   123 laity   124 ask   125 refer   126 See pp. 899–904.   127 *ex officio*: in discharge of one's office   128 ecclesiastical   129 civil

Howbeit,[130] if he so say, but if[131] men forget what hath been said before, else shall they see that his saying will not serve him.

For first, as I have said ofter than once already, the same things in the common law be not to be changed. For if they be, there shall come thereof more harm than good. And if it happen one innocent to take harm by the law, there shall five for one take more harm by the change.

Moreover, if we should for that cause change those temporal laws—that is to wit, because some innocent may sometime take harm by them—we must change, by the same reason, all that old-used law that a man may be arrested, and remain in prison till he find sureties[132] for the peace, upon the bare[133] oath of his enemy that saith he is afeard of him. For by that law may sometime an innocent take harm too. And yet must that law stand if we do well. For else shall there, by the change, more innocents take more harm.

What trouble have there many men in Wales by that they be compelled to be bound[134] to the peace, both for themselves and for their servants and other friends too? And yet is the order[135] there so necessary that in many lordships it may not be forborne.[136]

And surely if we fall to changing laws upon that simple ground—we must then change so many that it would not be well.

Besides this, if men should reform and change a law because that an innocent may sometime take[137] harm thereby, then must they when they have changed it, change it yet again, and after that change, yet change it again, and so forth, change after change, and never cease changing till the world be all changed at the Day of Doom.[138] For never can all the wits that are in it make any one penal law such that none innocent may take harm thereby.

Howbeit, if a new law were drawn and put forth to be made against any such mischief as would else do much harm, good reason it were to take an exception to the bill, and show that innocents might be much harmed by this point or that, and therewith provide the remedy and put it in the law, and stop as many such gaps as then could be spied. Yea and if, after the law made,[139] men found notable harm that good folk were much wronged by it and the law such that it either might be forborne or else the means found to be changed to the better, good reason would it to make provision for it.

But surely to come forth as this man cometh here, against so good laws, so well made, and by so great authority, so long approved through the whole corps of Christendom, in this realm ratified specially by Parliament (and that upon a proof not without great ground and cause), ever since found so profitable for preservation of the faith and proved so necessary, upon this man's own devices, that without great increase of heresies they cannot be forborne nor never can be changed but either to the straiter[140] or else to the worse—to come now forth and, for appeasing[141] of division, sow first a slander that may make division; and then labor to change those laws, upon none other ground but only that an innocent may hap to take harm by means of false judges; and then prove not any wrong done, but by false "some says" only, against which false "some says" the truth is proved contrary, both by just examination before the King's Council and, over that, plainly by this one point also, which no man can deny, that there is no law provided against so great a crime,[142] by which lawless people have in this realm been punished—therefore to come now thus, as this good man doth, and procure the change of these laws so old, so good, and so necessary, and to make them more easy, wherewith heretics would wax[143] bold, which thing himself (as you see) denieth not in the end, what is this, good Christian readers, but to procure that the Catholic Christian faith might fade and fall away?

And yet as for this man himself, to tell you for conclusion what I think, albeit there are, as you see, right evil and perilous things in his books with devices that would make heresies increase, yet since he professeth so plainly the Catholic Christian faith and by his exhortation also toward the conquest of the Holy Land declareth his mind zealous and fervent toward it, I rather believe, though himself thereto say nay, that in those things which he writeth so perilous and so naught, some wily shrews beguile the good innocent man, than that himself in his own mind mean all that harm.

But yet, forasmuch as in this point, without sight

---

130 However   131 *but if:* unless
132 pledges, securities   133 mere
134 legally constrained   135 established
procedure   136 dispensed with
137 suffer   138 *Day of Doom:* Judgment
Day   139 was made   140 more
severe   141 settling   142 that of making
slanderous allegations   143 grow

of man's heart, we can but go by guess, and whoso goeth by guess may be deceived (for, as himself saith, a wolf may look simply, lapped[144] in a sheep's skin), I shall therefore trust the best, and leave the truth to God. And concerning such evil writings, since it must needs be that he wrote them either deceived by some shrews or else but of himself, I can no more do for him but heartily pray for him thus. If shrews deceive him, God send them shortly from him. If he wrote them of his own mind, then since the things be naught, he wrote them either of evil will or of oversight. If he wrote them of malice, God give the evil man more grace. If he wrote them of folly, God give the good man more wit.

And thus I beseech our Lord send us every one, both the spiritual and the temporal too, both wit and grace to agree together in goodness, and each to love other, and each for other to pray, and for those that of both parties are passed into purgatory, and there pray for us as we pray here for them, that they and we both, through the merits of Christ's bitter Passion, may both with our own prayers and the intercession of all holy saints in heaven, avoiding the eternal fire of hell, have pity poured upon us in the very fire of purgatory, which in those two places verily burneth souls. And finally, for our faith and good works, which his grace (working with the wills of those that wit have) giveth each good man here, God give us in heaven, together, everlasting glory.

Printed by W. Rastell in
Fleet Street in Saint
Bride's Churchyard, the
year of our Lord 1533.
Cum privilegio[145]

144 wrapped　**145** *Cum privilegio:* With [the King's] permission

The Answer to a Poisoned Book

Written in the summer of 1533, this defense of the Eucharist would be the last book More published in his lifetime. More's five-part treatise responds to the first part of *The Supper of the Lord,* an exposition of John 6 regarding the Eucharist, written by George Joye (*ca.* 1495–1553) but published anonymously. At the beginning of *The Answer,* More announces his intent to leave for later *The Supper*'s second part dealing with the institution narrative and the definition of the sacrament. According to scholars such as Germain Marc'hadeur, More's *Treatise on the Passion* answers that second part, with its extended yet "unpolemical" theological discussion of the Eucharist (*CW* 11: lix–lx). In any case, More writes in the Preface to *The Answer* that this book "might suffice for the whole matter" because it provides readers with what is needed for "perceiving of the truth" in the contested matter of the Eucharist, which More had also addressed in the "Letter to Frith" and elsewhere. The central question at issue is whether the Eucharist is the real presence of Christ, or "only bare bread and wine."

As Clarence Miller explains, More "returned *ad fontes*" in making his *Answer,* by selecting and translating passages from the Church fathers, as his opponents had also done (*CW* 11: lix). In doing so, More was part of a larger polemical exchange that, while tremendously detailed and often bitterly intense, nevertheless "helped to recover and restore the great and varied treasure of patristic thought and eloquence" (lxi). More's three major sources in *The Answer* are Cyril of Alexandria, John Chystostom, and Theophylactus.

The "problem of language and interpretation" is of central importance as More develops his argument (*CW* 11: lxxix). Throughout the *Answer,* More levels his fundamental charge that the then-anonymous author of *The Supper* dissembles and deliberately misinterprets matters; More argues that this author hides himself "behind the false mask of flamboyant and impudent anonymity," and deploys lies that amount to serving poisonous dishes at an unsavory supper (lxxx). More calls this anonymous author the "Masker" throughout, as he had called Christopher St. German the "Pacifier" in the *Apology,* and King Richard "the Protector" in *History of Richard the Third.* More's rhetorical approach throughout the work — including such leveling jests as terming his opponent a "foolosopher" — is deliberately tuned to a lay audience, to "the everyday Londoner" in the streets, and appeals to common sense with effect and humor, as Stephen Foley argues (lxxxiv–lxxxvi). More's rhetoric aims to persuade the everyday Londoner that Christ's "body and blood are as real to them as the streets they walk on when they leave their churches and stroll past the wrestlers at Clerkenwell or pause to give a penny to a lame beggar by Savygate" (lxxxvi).

In the pivotal year of 1533, part of the urgency that compels More to write is certainly an appeal to King Henry VIII's well-known veneration of the Eucharist. Throughout the *Answer,* More appeals to the "known Catholic Church," the unity of "all the corps of Christendom of this 1500 year," right up to the book's concluding prayer for "one Church." More would be imprisoned in the spring of the following year, 1534, and his Tower works would follow.

CONTENTS

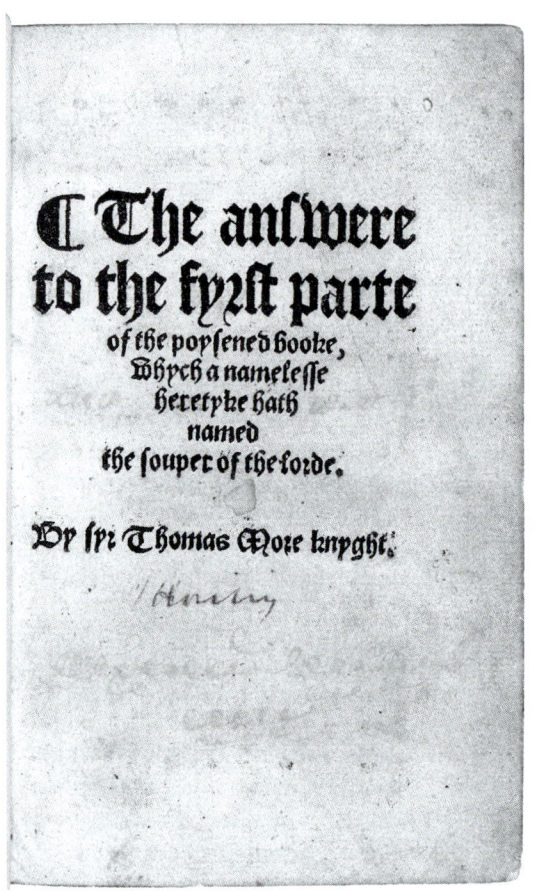

Title page, *The Answer to a Poisoned Book*

The Answer to a Poisoned Book, sig. E₃

The page on the right shows clearly More's preferred polemical style of quoting at length and then refuting in detail. More explained the rationale for this method in his *Apology*: "But surely loath would I be to misrehearse any man's reason against whom I write, or rehearse him slenderly" (820 above). Then, responding to the objection that his writing was too long and tedious, More went on to write:

But I find some men, again, to whom the reading is so far from tedious that they have to read the whole book over thrice — and some that make table thereof for their own remembrance — and

that, such men as have as much wit and learning both, as the best of all this blessed brotherhood that ever I heard of.

Howbeit, glad would I have been if it might have been much more short, for then should my labor have been so much the less.

But they will, if they be reasonable men, consider in themselves that it is a shorter thing and sooner done to write heresies than to answer them. For the most foolish heretic in a town may write more false heresies in one leaf than the wisest man in the whole world can well and conveniently by reason and authority soil and confute in forty. (821–22 above)

The Answer to the First Part of the Poisoned Book,

which a nameless
heretic hath
named
The Supper of the Lord

By Sir Thomas More, Knight

THE PREFACE
**Sir Thomas More, Knight,
to the Christian reader**

Would God, good Christian readers, as I have often said, that every good Christian man, yea man and woman both, which are of that inward good and gracious mind that they would not for all this world forsake the true faith themselves, had as much burning zeal and fervor in their hearts to see it outwardly kept and preserved among all others, as these that are fallen in false heresies and have forsaken the faith have a hot fire of hell in their hearts, that never can suffer[1] them to rest or cease, but maketh them both day and night busily labor and work to subvert and destroy the Catholic Christian faith, with all the means that ever they can devise.

For surely if all such as believe well themselves were as loath to hear any word spoken wrong against the faith as they would be to speak it themselves, there should neither fellowship of their matches,[2] nor fear of any such as are after[3] the worldly count accounted for their betters, anything let[4] or withstand them both by word and countenance to show themselves plainly to hate and detest and abhor utterly the pestilent contagion of all such smoky communication.

The time hath been ere[5] this when honest Christian people would walk so far off from all lecherous living that they would not come so much toward it as to abide the talking, but followed the Apostle's precept that saith, "Let not fornication or any uncleanness be so much as named among you."[6]

In that while[7] was there much honest cleanness, and by shamefastness[8] much was chastity conserved. But after time that in words folk fell unto more liberty, and such as would forbear the doing would yet be well content to fall in the fellowship of foul and filthy talking, then began cleanness greatly to decay. For as the Apostle also rehearseth,[9] "Evil communication marreth and corrupteth good manners."[10]

But this decay from chastity, by declination[11] into foul and filthy talking, hath begun a great while ago and is very far grown on. But the time hath been even until now very late[12] that, albeit of[13] fleshly wantonness men have not letted to use[14] themselves in words both lewd and very large,[15] yet of one thing ever would every good man be well aware: that heresy would he no man suffer to talk at his table, but would both rebuke it and detect it too, although[16] the thing touched his own born brother. Such hath been till of late the common Christian zeal toward the Catholic faith.

And albeit that I doubt not but that (God be thanked) the faith is itself as fast[17] rooted in this realm still as ever it was before (except some very few places, and yet even in those few, the very faithful folk many more than are the faithless too), yet since good men have of late not letted to hear the evil talk, and uncontrolled to speak blasphemous words in their company, the courage thereof hath out of all question much given occasion that heretics have spread their errors much the more abroad. For it is

---

1 allow **2** equals **3** according to
4 *anything let:* at all hinder **5** before
6 Eph 5:3 **7** time **8** modesty **9** tells,

relates **10** 1 Cor 15:33 **11** turning aside;
falling away **12** recently **13** *albeit of:*
although from **14** *letted to use:* hesitated

to conduct **15** unrestrained; vulgar
16 even if **17** firmly; securely

not only lechery that the Apostle's words are verified of where he saith that evil company corrupteth
good manners, albeit thereof be they verified too,
but specially be they verified of heresy. And against
the communication of heretics did Saint Paul specially speak them in his First Epistle to the Corinthians, among whom some began homely[18] then to
talk against the general resurrection,[19] as some begin
among us now to talk against the blessed sacraments.

And such communication it is therefore that the
Apostle speaketh against, of which he saith also
that the contagion creepeth forth and corrupteth
further, after the manner of a corrupt canker.[20]

And therefore he biddeth us that we should have
none other communication with heretics, but only
of reproving their heresy and giving them warning to leave. And yet not every man be bold to talk
too long with them, not even thereof neither, nor
over-often to meddle with them, lest as the pestilence catcheth sometimes the leech[21] that, fasting,
cometh very near and long sitteth by the sick man,
busy about to cure him, so some folk faint and feeble in the faith, matched with a fellow stubborn and
strong in heresy, may sooner himself take hurt than
do the other good.

Saint Paul therefore, inspired with the Spirit of
God, compendiously toucheth, in very few words,
both these two points at once, where he writeth
unto Titus, "That man that is a heretic, after once
or twice warning" (lo, hear the communication that
he would we should[22] have with him), "void and eschew him."[23] So here ye see, lo, that after once or
twice warning of them, the bishop should as folk incorrigible expel them, and we should, if we well did,
keep no more company nor no more communication with them—no, saith Saint John, not so much
as bid them good speed or good morrow when we
meet them.[24]

These biddings of these blessed apostles, if all
Catholic folk would follow—which either of[25] negligence or fear or for sinful civility, while we follow
not, we never discharge well our conscience toward
God—there would, without any great suit[26] or
trouble, be shortly far fewer heretics than there be.
And they that are should shortly perceive in every

place where they ween[27] themselves many how very
few they be, which as few as they be, would God
yet[28] they were yet[29] far fewer than they be. For albeit[30] there are of heretics far fewer than those that
are would have it seem there were, yet are there undoubtedly, by such dissimuling sufferance,[31] many
more than else[32] there should have been.

And this is also the cause that of these heretics'
books there be so many now brought in as there be.
For while men may so boldly speak out their heresies, even among them whom they know none heretics, this maketh many folk, that else durst[33] not
meddle with such books, to buy them and look on
them and long to see what they say.

But some there are, that first begin but of such a
vain[34] curious mind, whom the devil driveth after
forward, and first maketh them doubt of the truth,
and after bringeth them out of doubt to a full belief of heresy.

And thus of such books, as sore[35] as they be forbidden, yet are there many bought. Nor the peril refraineth[36] not much people from the buying, since
there is none house lightly[37] that hath so little room
that lacketh the room to hide a book therein.

But when they had the books, if men would abhor their talking, gone were all the pleasure that
they take therein. But now while men control them
not, but laugh and let them babble, pride maketh
them proceed, and they procure more, and spread
the books more abroad, and draw more brethren to
them.

There is no small number of such erroneous English books printed, of which if few were bought,
there would not of likelihood so many be put in
print, saving[38] that some brethren there are in this
realm that of their zeal to their sects, being of such
substance[39] that they may forbear it,[40] give some
money thereto beforehand, content to abide the
adventure[41] of the sale, or give the books about for
nought[42] to bring men to the devil.

And in this wise[43] is there sent over to be printed
the book that Frith made last against the Blessed
Sacrament, answering to my letter, wherewith I
confuted the pestilent treatise that he had made
against it before.[44] And the brethren looked for it

18 plainly, directly   **19** See 1 Cor 15:12.
20 sore; ulcer; 2 Tm 2:17   **21** physician   **22** *would we should:* wants us to
23 *void and eschew:* avoid and shun; Ti
3:10–11   **24** 2 Jn 10–11   **25** on account

of   **26** pursuit; prosecution   **27** think,
suppose   **28** moreover   **29** hereafter
30 although   **31** *dissimuling sufferance:*
feigned forbearance   **32** otherwise
33 dare   **34** idle   **35** greatly   **36** restrains

37 in all probability   **38** except
39 wealth   **40** *forbear it:* spare, dispense
with   **41** risk   **42** nothing   **43** way
44 John Frith (1503–33) was a Cambridge
scholar, English priest, and follower of

now at this Bartholomew-tide[45] last passed and yet look every day, except[46] it be come already and secretly run among them.

But in the meanwhile, there is come over another book against the Blessed Sacrament, a book of that sort,[47] that Frith's book the brethren may now forbear.[48] For more blasphemous, and more bedlam-ripe[49] than this book is, were that book hard to be, which is yet mad enough, as men say that have seen it.

This book is entitled *The Supper of Our Lord*.[50] But I beshrew[51] such a sewer,[52] as so serveth in the supper that he conveyeth away the best dish, and bringeth it not to the board,[53] as this man would if he could convey from the Blessed Sacrament Christ's own blessed flesh and blood, and leave us nothing therein but, for a memorial only, bare bread and wine.

But his hands are too lumpish and this mess also too great for him to convey clean,[54] especially since the dish is so dear and so dainty that every Christian man hath his heart bent thereto and therefore his eye set thereon to see where it becometh.[55]

The man hath not set his name unto his book, nor whose it is I cannot surely say. But some reckon it to be made by William Tyndale, for that[56] in an epistle of his unto Frith, he writeth that, in anything that he can do, he would not fail to help him forth.

Howbeit,[57] some of the brethren report that the book was made by George Jay.[58] And of truth, Tyndale wrote unto Frith that George Jay had made a book against the Sacrament, which was as yet, partly by his means, partly for lack of money, retained and kept from the print. Howbeit, what George Joye would do therein afterward when his money were come—that could he not, he saith, assure him.

Now of truth, George Joye hath long had in hand, and ready lying by him, his book against the Sacrament. And now if this be it, he hath somewhat enlengthened it of late by a piece that he hath patched in against me, wherein he would seem to soil[59] mine arguments, which in my letter I made in that matter against the devilish treatise of Frith.

And in very deed, diverse that are learned and have read the book reckon it verily[60] to be the book of George Jay, whereof Tyndale wrote unto Frith, especially by certain words that were in that letter. For therein writeth Tyndale that if George Jaye did put forth his book, there should be founden in it many reasons and very few to the purpose.

Howbeit, methinketh, by that mark, that this book should not be that. For in this book be there very few reasons, and of them all never one to the purpose.

The maker of the book, in the end of his book, for one cause why he putteth not his name thereto, writeth in this wise: "Master Mock, whom the verity most offendeth and doth but mock it out when he cannot soil it, he knoweth me well enough."[61]

This sad[62] and sage earnest man that, mocking at mine name, calleth me Master Mock, doth in these wise words nothing but mock the readers of his book, save[63] that his reason is so rude and foolish that the mock returneth to himself.

For since he writeth not his book to me, nor sendeth me none of them, but the brethren keep them from me as closely as they can, what if I wist[64] never so well who he were that wrote it, what were this to the brethren that read it? Know they thereby who it is to?

Now for myself also, though I know Tyndale by name, and George Jay or George Joy by name also, and twenty such other fond[65] fellows of the same sect more, yet if ten of those would make ten such foolish treatises and set their names to none, could I know thereby which of those mad fools made which foolish book?

Diverse there are indeed of those that are learned and have read the book that think, for the lack of learning and of wit[66] also that they find everywhere therein, the book should neither be made by Tyndale nor by George Jay neither, but rather by some young unlearned fool.

Howbeit, as for me, I think the book might be for all that made by Tyndale or by George Jay either. For the matter being devised against the Blessed Sacrament, the wisest or the most fool, the most learned or the least, is all in manner one, and in that

William Tyndale. The treatise is Frith's *A Christen Sentence* (*CW* 7: 427–33), which More answered in Letter 190: Against John Frith, 7 December <1532> (see pp. 358–70).   **45** festival on August 24   **46** unless   **47** *of that sort:* such   **48** do without   **49** ready for the insane asylum.

The hospital of St. Mary Bethlehem in London was used as an asylum for the treatment of the mentally ill.   **50** For the full text, see *CW* 11: 303–40.   **51** curse   **52** superintendent of the meal   **53** table   **54** completely   **55** *where it becometh:* what becomes of it   **56** *for that:* because

57 However   **58** George Joye (also Jay or Jaye, *ca.* 1495–1553), a biblical translator, fled to the Continent to escape charges of heresy in 1527.   **59** refute   **60** truly   **61** *CW* 7: 339   **62** serious   **63** except   **64** knew   **65** foolish   **66** intellect; ingenuity

matter maketh little difference. For I never found yet any man so well-learned and so naturally well-witted withal,[67] but after that he fell once to the defense of heresies, and especially of this abominable
5 heresy against the Blessed Sacrament, neither learning nor wit never well served him after.

For as for Tyndale, the captain of our English heretics, who before he fell to these frenzies, men had weened[68] had had some wit and was taken for
10 full prettily learned too, ye see, good Christian readers, plainly tried by his books, that an unlettered man might be ashamed to write so unlearnedly, and a mad man would almost wax[69] red for shame to write in some things so frantically.[70]
15 As touching Friar Barnes[71] and George Jay, the brethren and sistren themselves see their wits so wasted, and their learning waxen so slender, that the brotherhood hath little list[72] to read them.

And some of the brethren that say this new work
20 was made by George Jay think that the cause why he set not his name thereto was because he wist[73] well the brethren did not regard him. And Tyndale had in his letter also declared him for a fool, by reason whereof he thought that if it came under his name,
25 the estimation thereof were but lost.

Frith was, lo, a proper young man and a toward,[74] till he fell unto these fools, after which to what decay both his wit and his learning came every wise man much marveled, that in his open[75] examination
30 heard and considered his answers.

For albeit that[76] in the book that the brethren that are here have sent over to print, Tyndale and his fellows, to beguile the world withal,[77] purpose to make many changes and amend and advance his
35 part, underpropping it with their own proper lies, yet shall the means be meetly[78] well founden to control their falsehood, I trust, and to take away their cloaks and leave his folly bare. And then shall men plainly see that of one whom the brethren boast for
40 so wise, there never died in England before any false heretic so foolish.

But now as touching this new[79] come-over book, which the maker hath entitled *The Supper of the Lord*, though the man hath named it *The Supper*
45 *of Our Savior Christ*, yet hath the man made it the supper of the devil.

The special effect of all his whole purpose is to

feed us with the most poisoned heresy that laboreth to kill the Catholic Christian faith, concerning the Blessed Sacrament of the altar, albeit by the way he 50 putteth forth diverse other heresies besides.

This unsavory supper of his, without any corn[80] of salt and spiced all with poison, he divideth, as it were, into two courses—that is to wit,[81] into the treating and declaring of two special things speci- 55 fied in the Gospel of Christ, whereby Christian people plainly perceive that in the Blessed Sacrament of the altar is the very blessed body of Christ, his very flesh and his blood.

In the first part, which I call here his first course, 60 occupying the one half of his book, he treateth the words of Christ spoken in the sixth chapter of Saint John, which words our Savior speaketh of the eating of his flesh and drinking of his blood.

In his second part, which I call his second course, 65 he treateth the Maundy of Christ with his apostles upon Sheer Thursday, wherein our Savior actually did institute the Blessed Sacrament and therein verily[82] gave his own very flesh and blood to his twelve apostles himself. 70

I shall therefore divide this work of mine into two parts in like wise, of which twain[83] this shall be the first, wherein I shall detect and make every man perceive this man's evil cookery in his first course, concerning the treating of Christ's words in the 75 sixth chapter of Saint John.

And albeit that I shall afterward send you forth my second part also, against his second course, yet shall I so handle this man's mischievous heresy in this first part that though[84] I never wrote word 80 more hereafter of the matter, yet to the perceiving of the truth and detection of his falsehood this first part might suffice for all the whole matter.

In his first part, he first expoundeth the latter part of the sixth chapter of Saint John, and by his decla- 85 ration laboreth to draw men from the perceiving of the truth, and setteth forth also both his principle heresy, and over[85] that diverse others.

Also in the same part he argueth against all men in general that expound any of those words of 90 Christ there spoken to be meant by Christ of the very eating of his flesh, as the Catholic Church believeth, in the Blessed Sacrament.

In that first part also he argueth against me by

67 moreover **68** thought he **69** become **70** insanely **71** Robert Barnes (*ca.* 1495–1540) **72** desire **73** knew **74** promising; apt **75** public **76** *albeit that:* although **77** thereby **78** fittingly **79** recently **80** grain **81** say **82** truly **83** two **84** even if **85** besides

name in special,[86] and pretendeth to soil[87] such arguments as I made in my letter against the poisoned treatise, that John Frith had before made in that matter against the Blessed Sacrament.

In that part also the man bringeth in two places all in great,[88] which he hath picked out by long leisure among all my books, in either of which two places, he showeth that I have notably contraried mine own writing that I have written myself in other places before, and showeth also the places where.

I shall therefore, good readers, in this first part of mine give you five books, and some of them very short.

In the first will I give you the exposition of the selfsame words of Christ, mentioned in the sixth chapter of Saint John, by which, whoso confer them and consider them together shall, I trust, perceive well the falsehood of his exposition, and not be deceived thereby. And for mine exposition ye shall give me the thanks. For I have but picked it out here and there out of the writings of diverse old holy men.

The second shall show you, for an example, some of the faults both in follies and errors that the man hath made us in his exposition.

The third shall answer and soil his wise reasons, with which he would make all men fools that have expounded that place before, contrary to his heresy now—that is to wit, all the old holy doctors[89] and saints from the apostles' days unto our own time.

In the fourth shall ye see what wit[90] and what learning he showeth in soiling of mine arguments made before in that matter against his fellow John Frith.

The fifth shall declare you the diligence that the man hath done in seeking out my negligence, leaving some places in my writing repugnant[91] and contrary the one place to the other. And of such places ye shall (as I said) see him with diligent search of three years at last bring you forth twain.[92] And there shall you see, good Christian readers, that in those twain my negligence shall, for all his diligence, prove him twice a fool.

But in the treating of this matter with him, I shall lack somewhat of the commodity[93] that the man hath in disputing with me. For he hath a great pleasure oftentimes, now in one manner, now in another, now to talk of me, and now to speak to me by name, with "thus saith More," and "lo, Master More," and sometimes "Master Mock," and "let More mock on and lie too," and many such goodly garnishings more. But he will be for his own part sure that I shall not dispute with him by name, and therefore he keepeth it away.

And therefore what folly and what falsehood be founden in his book he forceth[94] very little. For shame he thinketh he can none take thereby, while folk know not his name.

Wherein he fareth much like to some beastly body, that would not care to sit down with his face to the wallward and ease himself in the open street, and though all the town at once toot in[95] his tail, take it for no shame at all, because they see not his face.

And verily, as we see sometimes that such as walk in visors have much the less fear and shame, both what[96] they do and what they say, because they think themselves unknown, so do these folk oftentimes little force what they write, that use[97] to put out their books, and set not their names unto them. They think themselves unseen while their name is unknown, and therefore they fear not the shame of their folly, as some have I seen ere[98] this full boldly come dance in a masque, whose dancing became them so well that if their visors had been off their faces, shame would not have suffered[99] them to set forth a foot.

And Master Mummer under his masker's face forceth not much to shift a false cast among,[100] with a pair of false dice.

And therefore since this man, by withdrawing his name from his book, hath donned on a visor of dissimulation, dissimuling[101] his person to avoid the shame of his falsehood, and speaketh too much to be called Master Mummer, which name he were else[102] well worthy for his false dice, I shall in this dispicion[103] between him and me be content for this once (since by some name must I call him) for lack of his other name to call him Master Masker. And thus finishing this preface, we shall begin the matter.

---

86 particular **87** refute **88** *all in great:* in total; in all **89** theologians **90** intellect; ingenuity **91** contradictory, inconsistent **92** two **93** advantage

94 cares **95** *toot in:* look at **96** in what **97** are accustomed **98** before **99** allowed **100** *shift … cast among:* substitute a false throw of the dice from time to time **101** dissembling **102** otherwise **103** debate

THE FIRST BOOK

THE FIRST CHAPTER

Master Masker hath in this his poisoned treatise against Christ's wholesome supper thirty-two leaves,[1] in the first fourteen whereof he expoundeth us the latter part of the sixth chapter of Saint John. And incidentally by the way, the man maketh as though he answered the reasons[2] which I made in my letter against the pestilent treatise that Frith made first against the Blessed Sacrament. And in the same fourteen leaves also, he bringeth forth two things for special notable, wherein he saith I have openly contraried mine own writing.

I will, good reader, peruse the remnant of his book after this first part answered, in which, containing these three things that I have rehearsed[3] you, the first hath he so handled that all were there[4] not (as there are indeed) diverse false heresies interlaced therein, yet it were for the matter of very slight effect. For in his exposition he nothing toucheth nor cometh near to the thing wherein the point of all the matter standeth.

The second point hath he so well treated in his argumentation that, the reasons which I lay against Frith, Master Masker first falsely rehearseth and after so foolishly soileth[5] that he leaveth them more stronger against him when he hath done than he found them when he began.

And as for the third point concerning his notable notice of such things as he layeth to mine oversight, them he so garnisheth and setteth out so seemly to the show that I would no man should[6] ever after this day trust any word that I shall write but if[7] ye see Master Masker plainly proved therein either so foolish as no man should trust his wit, or so false that no man should trust his troth.[8] Let us therefore now come to the first point—that is to wit,[9] his exposition.

THE SECOND CHAPTER

The whole sum of his exposition is that our Savior in all those words, taking occasion of the miracle that he so late[10] before had wrought among them, in feeding five thousand of them with five barley loaves and two fishes,[11] did in those words, upon their new resort unto him when they followed him to Capernaum, first rebuke and blame them because they sought him not for the miracles that they had seen him work, but because they had been fed by him and filled their bellies, and that therefore our Savior exhorted them to labor rather to get that meat[12] that never should perish.[13] Upon which exhortation, when the Jews asked him what they should do whereby they should work the works of God, Christ said unto them that the work of God was to believe and trust in him whom the Father had sent.[14]

Then goeth he further and showeth that upon the words of the Jews asking our Lord what token he showed for which they should believe in him, since their forefathers had given them the bread of manna in desert,[15] of which it was written, "He gave them bread from above,"[16] our Lord showed them that Moses gave them not that bread from heaven, but his own Father had given them the very[17] bread that was descended from heaven,[18] and that our Lord there, by all the remnant of those words in the said sixth chapter of Saint John, declareth that himself is that very bread, and is to be eaten by the faith and the belief that Christ's flesh and body was broken and his blood shed for our sins. And so expoundeth he forth all these words of Christ, applying them only to the declaration of his Passion to be suffered for our redemption, and that our Savior would have them believe that point, and that the belief of that point was meant by the eating, and that that faith and belief is the meat of our souls.

The whole sum of his exposition is this in all his said fourteen leaves. I mean not that this is all that ever he saith therein, for I leave out his circumstances, his garnishings, his notes, his argumentations, his contentions with me, his mocks, his

---

1 pages   **2** arguments   **3** told   **4** *all were there:* even if there were   **5** refutes   **6** *would no man should:* want no man to   **7** *but if:* unless   **8** truthfulness; integrity   **9** say   **10** recently   **11** See Jn 6:1–15.   **12** food   **13** See Jn 6:25–27.   **14** See   Jn 6:28–29.   **15** See Ex 16.   **16** Jn 6:31   **17** true; full   **18** See Jn 6:30–32.

taunts against all Catholic folk, and his manifold heresies also, withal[19] which here and there he furnisheth all the progress of his painted process,[20] all which things I shall after touch by themselves. But the sum, the substance, and the end whereto all the whole process of his exposition cometh is this that I have rehearsed you.

THE THIRD CHAPTER

But now, good Christian readers, all this exposition, were it never so true, never so comely,[21] nor never so cunningly handled, yet were it (as I told you before) very far from the purpose. For this exposition might be good enough, and yet might Christ in those words teach the thing that we speak of besides: that is to wit, besides the teaching them that himself was the very bread that was descended from heaven to give life to the world,[22] and that he should suffer death for the sins of the world, and that they should believe these things, and so eat him here by faith; he might, I say, teach in those words also that he would give unto men his very body and his very flesh to eat and his very blood to drink, and that he would that they should[23] believe that lesson also, and with the spiritual eating thereof, by faith receive and eat also his very Blessed Body, flesh and blood, by the mouth, not in his own fleshly form as the fleshly Jews mistook it,[24] but—as himself then meant it and part there expounded it, and by his institution did after more clearly declare it—in form of bread and wine in the Blessed Sacrament of the altar.

It is, I trow,[25] good readers, to no man almost unknown that the Holy Scripture of God is in such marvelous manner, by the profound wisdom of his Holy Spirit, for the more plenteous profit of his Church, devised, indited,[26] and written that it hath not only that one sense true which we call the literal sense (that is to wit, that sense which, for the first lesson thereof, God would we should perceive and learn), but also diverse other senses spiritual, pertaining to the profit of our manners, and instructions in sundry virtues, by means of allegories, opening of mysteries, and lifting up of the soul into the lively light and inward high sight of God. And all those manifold senses (diverse in the way and all tending to one end) may be convenient[27] and true, and all by one Spirit provided, and into diverse spirits by the same one Spirit inspired, for spiritual profit to be by many means multiplied and increased in his Church.

But never hath any good man been accustomed to play the pageant[28] that Master Masker playeth us here, with a spiritual exposition of allegories or parables, to take away the very first sense that God would we should learn of the letter and, because of some allegories, turn all the plain words from the first right understanding into a secondary sense of allegories.

Of this manner[29] handling of Scripture I make mention in my letter against Frith's false handling of this same place of Saint John.[30] And there I showed in what wise[31] the false heretics, the Arians, used by the same means to take the Godhead from Christ's person, as Frith and these fellows, by the selfsame manner of expounding the Scripture, do take away Christ's manhood from Christ's Blessed Sacrament.

In that epistle I showed also that I would in allegorical expositions find no fault, but be well content with them, so that men misuse them not, to the taking away of the true literal sense besides.

This thing I there showed, good readers, in the selfsame epistle, that Master Masker maketh here as though he could and would answer. And yet as though he had never heard my words but slept while he read them, he playeth here the selfsame pageant himself, while with his allegorical exposition of spiritual eating of Christ's Godhead and of his body by belief of his Passion, he goeth about to take away from us the very literal truth of the very eating and bodily receiving of Christ's own very flesh and blood.

Now will I not lay any manner blame at all to any man that will expound all the whole process of Genesis by allegories, and teach us certain convenient[32] virtues understood by the four floods[33] of Paradise, and tell us that Paradise is grace, out of which all the floods of all virtues flow and water the earth, calling the earth mankind, that was made thereof, being barren and fruitless but if[34] it be watered with the floods of virtue, and so forth in some such manner expound us all the remnant. He, lo, that thus

---

19 with, by   **20** *painted process:* deceptive line of argument   **21** appropriate, seemly   **22** See Jn 6:30–32.   **23** *would that they*   *should:* wants them to   **24** See Jn 6:52.   **25** trust   **26** composed   **27** suitable, proper   **28** performance   **29** kind of   **30** See Letter 190, pp. 358–70.   **31** way   **32** appropriate, suitable   **33** rivers; Gn 2:10–14   **34** *but if:* unless

doth, doth in my mind right well. But, marry,[35] if he would do it in the manner and with the mind that Master Masker expoundeth us Christ's words all in allegories here, and would teach us such a spiritual sense to make us believe that those words were to be none otherwise understood besides, but that there were no such floods flowing forth of paradise, nor no such Paradise at all, I would ween verily[36] that he were a very heretic.

I find no fault also with them that expound the story of Sampson tying the foxes together by the tails, and setting a fire in them, and sending them so into the field of the Philistines to burn up the corn;[37] in those, I say, that expound that story by[38] the devil sending his heretics into the cornfield of God, the Catholic Church of Christ, with the fire of false words to destroy the corn both of true faith and good works, tied together by the tails in token that all their heresies, be their heads never so far asunder, yet are their tails tied together in that it all tend toward one end—that is to wit, to the destruction of all manner grace and goodness—and that the tying of the fire and their tails together signifieth also that for their foxly falsehood, finally in the end, the hot fire of hell shall be so fast[39] tied in all their tails, wrabbling[40] there together, that never shall they get the fire from their tails, nor from the bands of hell be severed or break asunder—with this allegory of those good men that thus expound that story, I find no fault at all. But on the other side, if any man would expound it so by that spiritual allegory against these heretics, that he would therewith enforce himself to take away the literal sense, and say the text signified nothing else, and that there was no such thing done indeed, him would I reckon for a heretic too.

And in like wise, good readers, if Master Masker here did only expound all those words of Christ as things spoken of spiritual eating by way of allegory, that way would I well allow, for so doth not only such as he is, but also good faithful folk too. But now when he draweth all Christ's words to those allegories, of[41] a false wily purpose, to make men ween (and so saith himself, for his part) that they signify none other thing, this is the point that proveth Master Masker a heretic.

And therefore, as I said, all his exposition is far off from the purpose and approacheth not to the point. For the question is not whether those words may be well verified and expounded of spiritual eating by way of an allegory, but whether it may, besides all that, be truly expounded of the very bodily eating of Christ's Blessed Body indeed. For if it so may, then is there no man of so slender wit, but he may well see that all Master Masker's allegorical exposition of his only spiritual eating flitteth[42] from the purpose quite, and dare not come near the point.

Wherefore, to the intent that ye may clearly see that in this exposition of his (as holy as he would have it seem) he doth but clearly mock, saving[43] that it is much worse than mocking to make men fall from the faith, I shall give you of the same words of Christ, written in the sixth chapter of Saint John, another exposition myself, in which I shall, besides all such spiritual expositions, as this man useth therein by way of allegories or parables, declare you the very literal sense of those words, "My flesh is verily meat[44] and my blood verily drink,"[45] so that ye may see thereby that our Savior verily spoke and meant, not only such a spiritual eating as Master Masker saith he only meant, but also the very bodily eating and drinking of his very flesh and blood indeed, which exposition of mine, if it be in that point true, then must it needs follow (ye see well) that his exposition is far from the purpose. For although[46] there were not one false word therein, yet were it in dissembling of the truth very lewd[47] and falsely handled.

And now that mine exposition shall be true indeed, that shall you, ere[48] I leave you, so clearly perceive and see that I trust there shall never any such heretic, as this is, be able to blind any man after that[49] readeth it, except some such as willingly list[50] to wink, or while he put out their eyes, will hold their heads to him themselves.

Now to the intent ye may the better perceive and mark whether mine exposition agrees with the text, and whether I leave anything untouched, I shall first give you the words of the text itself in English altogether, and then expound it you[51] piece by piece after. And yet had it not been evil to begin somewhat before, at Christ's disciples going into the ship in the evening, and Christ's own walking after upon the sea, and after that on the morrow the people coming after to seek him in other ships,[52] which

---

35 indeed; from "by Mary" **36** *ween verily*: believe truly **37** Jgs 15:4–5 **38** as **39** securely; firmly **40** wriggling **41** out **42** flees **43** except **44** food **45** Jn 6:56 **46** even if **47** villainously; ignorantly **48** before **49** who **50** choose **51** to you **52** See Jn 6:16–24.

piece Master Masker left out and would not meddle with, because it hath a hard allegory declared by holy doctors, which show that the ship in which the disciples went betokened the Church, which was but one, and the other diverse ships that came after betokened the diverse churches of heretics.[53] And yet in that one ship that signified the Church, there were, as appeared after, both good and bad together. But let this piece pass for this once; I will begin the text but there as Master Masker beginneth himself. Lo, good Christian readers, these be the words.

THE FOURTH CHAPTER

"Verily, verily, I say to you, you seek me, not because ye have seen miracles, but because ye have eaten of the loaves and are filled. Work you not[54] the meat that perisheth, but that abideth into everlasting life, which the Son of Man shall give you, for him hath God the Father sealed." They said therefore unto him, "What shall we do that we may work the works of God?" Jesus answered and said unto them, "This is the work of God: that ye believe in him whom he hath sent." Then they said unto him, "What token showest thou, therefore, that we may see and believe thee? What workest thou? Our fathers have eaten manna in the desert, as it is written, 'He gave them bread from heaven to eat.'" Then said Jesus to them, "Verily, verily, I say to you, Moses hath not given you the bread from the heaven, but my Father giveth you the very[55] bread from the heaven. For the very bread is that that is descended from heaven and giveth life to the world." Then said they to him, "Lord, give us always this bread." Then said Jesus to them, "I am the bread of life; he that cometh to me shall not hunger, and he that believeth in me shall never thirst. But I have said unto you that ye have both seen me and have not believed. All that my Father giveth me shall come to me, and he that cometh to me, I shall not cast him out. For I am descended from heaven, not to do mine own will, but the will of him that hath sent me. This is verily the will of him that hath sent me — that is to

wit,[56] the Father — that all that he hath given me I should not lose anything thereof, but should raise it again in the last day. This is verily the will of my Father that hath sent me: that every man that seeth the Son and believeth in him should have everlasting life, and shall raise him again in the last day." The Jews murmured[57] therefore of that that he had said: "I am the lively[58] bread that am descended from heaven." And they said, "Is not this man the son of Joseph, whose father and mother we have known? How saith he therefore, 'I am descended from heaven'?" Jesus therefore answered and said unto them, "Murmur not among yourselves. There can no man come to me but if[59] the Father that sent me draw him, and I shall raise him again in the last day. It is written in the prophets, 'And they shall be all taught of God.' Every man that hath heard of the Father and hath learned cometh to me, not because any man hath seen the Father, but he that is of God hath seen the Father. Verily, verily, I tell you, he that believeth in me hath life everlasting. I am the bread of the life. Your fathers have eaten manna in the desert and be dead. This is the bread descending from the heaven, that if any man eat thereof, he should not die. I am the living bread that am descended from the heaven. If a man eat of this bread, he shall live forever, and the bread which I shall give is my flesh, which I shall give for the life of the world." The Jews therefore strove among themselves, saying, "How can this man give us his flesh to eat?" Then said Jesus to them, "Verily, verily, I say to you, but if ye eat the flesh of the Son of Man and drink his blood, ye shall not have life in you. He that eateth my flesh and drinketh my blood hath life everlasting, and I shall raise him in the last day. My flesh is verily meat and my blood is verily drink. He that eateth my flesh and drinketh my blood dwelleth in me and I in him. As the living Father sent me, I also live for the Father. And he that eateth me, he shall also live for me. This is the bread that hath descended from heaven, not as your fathers have eaten manna and are dead. He that eateth this bread shall live forever." These things said he in the synagogue, teaching in Capernaum. Many therefore of his disciples, hearing said, "This is

---

53 See Alcuin, *PL* 100: 827. **54** not for **55** true; actual **56** say **57** muttered complaints **58** living **59** *but if:* unless

a hard saying, and who may hear him?" Jesus therefore, knowing in himself that his disciples murmured at this, said unto them, "Doth this offend you: if ye shall then see the Son of Man ascending up where he was before? The spirit it is that giveth life; the flesh availeth nothing. The words which I have spoken to you be spirit and life. But there be some of you that believe not." For Jesus knew from the beginning who should be the believers and who should betray him, and he said, "Therefore I have said unto you that no man can come to me but if[60] it be given him of my Father." From that time, many of his disciples went back, and now walked no more with him. Then said Jesus to the twelve, "Will you go your ways too?" Then answered unto him Simon Peter, "Lord, to whom shall we go? Thou hast the words of everlasting life, and we believe and have known that thou art Christ, the Son of God." Jesus answered unto him, "Have not I chosen you twelve, and one of you is a devil?" He said that by[61] Judas Iscariot, the son of Simon. For he it was that should betray him, being one of the twelve.[62]

The exposition of the said text
THE FIFTH CHAPTER

Whoso read and consider well, good Christian readers, the doctrine and the doings of our Savior Christ shall by sundry places of Holy Scripture perceive that of his heavenly wisdom his wholesome usage[63] was in many great things that he purposed to do, before the doing of the same (besides the figures of the Old Testament fore-figuring the same, and besides the prophecies of the old prophets fore-prophesying the same), for men's more readiness toward the things when he would execute them by his deed, to give them some warning and information thereof before by his words.

Thus before he made Saint Peter his chief shepherd over his flock, three times at once, specially bidding him to feed his sheep,[64] he first said unto

him, "Thou shalt be called stone," and after said also to him, when he confessed him to be Christ, "Thou art stone and upon the same stone shall I build my Church, and the gates of hell shall not prevail against it."[65]

Thus, before he made him his general vicar, he gave him the name of stone, which stone he said after he would build his Church upon.

Thus he gave his apostles and disciples warning of his betraying, of his taking, of his death, of his resurrection, of his ascension, by his word, before the things were done in deed. And of his coming again to the Doom[66] also at the general resurrection,[67] which things surely shall be and are not yet done indeed. And always the more strange the things were, the more he opened them with words. And yet had he, for all that, some of those things for that while[68] not very well believed, not even of[69] some of his own disciples.[70] But yet neither were his words fully fruitless at the time, but that they took some hold in some folk, and wrought in some souls, though not a full faith, yet an inclination and a disposition toward it, and now serve, and ever since have served, and ever while the world lasteth shall serve to the planting, rooting, and watering of the faith, in all Christian nations all the world about.

Now as our Lord did in many things, so did he specially in the two great sacraments: the sacrament of baptism, and in this high Blessed Sacrament of the altar.

Of the one he talked with Nicodemus that came to him by night and durst[71] not be seen with him by day for dread of the Jews.[72]

And of the other—that is to wit,[73] of the Sacrament of the altar—he talked here, and taught the very thing but not the very form thereof unto the Jews and his disciples among them.

And as he found Nicodemus far off from the perceiving of the spiritual fruit that riseth in the sensible[74] ablution and faithful washing of baptism, so found he the substance[75] of these folk very far from the perceiving of the spiritual fruit that groweth of the bodily receiving of Christ's own Blessed Body to them that faithfully receive it in the Blessed Sacrament under the sensible form of bread.

60 *but if:* unless   **61** about   **62** Jn 6:26-71   **63** custom   **64** See Jn 21:15-17.   **65** Mt 16:16-19   **66** Last Judgment   **67** See Mt 16:21, 27; 17:21-22; 20:18-19; 25:31-33; Mk 8:31, 38; 9:30; 10:32-34; Lk 9:22, 26, 44; 18:31-33.   **68** time   **69** by   **70** See Mk 9:31; Lk 9:45; 12:40; 18:34.   **71** dared   **72** See Jn 3.   **73** say   **74** perceptible to the senses   **75** majority

Our Savior also, good reader, because the thing that he now went about to tell them was a marvelous high thing and a strange, used in the proponing[76] thereof unto them, diverse ways devised of[77] his divine wisdom.

First, to make them the more meet[78] to receive the doctrine of that point and to perceive it, he did two miracles, before he began to speak thereof: one (which though they were not at it, yet they perceived well as the Gospel showeth, in going over the water without a vessel;[79] and another that he did not only in their presence, but also made them all partners of the profit, that is to wit, when he fed them all, being five thousand in number, of two fishes and five loaves, and yet when all their bellies were full, gathered and filled twelve baskets of the fragments.[80]

Upon the occasion of this miracle, good reader, of these five loaves by such a miracle so multiplied as a thing very convenient,[81] he took his beginning to induce[82] thereupon the feast that he would in this world leave perpetually with his Church, by feeding of innumerable thousands with that one loaf that is his Blessed Body in the form of bread. Not for that[83] the miracle of that feeding of the Jews and this feeding of Christ's Church is in everything like,[84] between which twain[85] there are incomparable differences, but because the less[86] miracle and in some part like, is a convenient thing for an entry and a beginning wherewith to draw them further. And unto his apostles at that time, so was it, and yet unto this time unto all good Christian people, so is it.

Our Savior also to induce them the better to the belief of his great kindness, in that he would vouchsafe[87] to give them his own body to be received and eaten into theirs, he did tell them two other things: the one that he was very[88] God, the other that he would die for their sakes. Of these two points, the one might make them sure that he would do it, and the other that he could do it. For what could he not do that was God Almighty? Or what would he disdain to do for us, that would not disdain to die for us?

Now, good readers, remembering well these things, mark what our Savior hath said in this Gospel, and consider well what he meant.

THE SIXTH CHAPTER

When that after the miracle of the feeding so many people with so few loaves, our Lord had, as it followeth in the Gospel,[89] withdrawn himself aside into the hill, because he saw the people were minded to make him their king, the disciples had entered in the evening after into a ship, and Christ appearing to them, walking upon the sea, and calming the tempest, when they would have taken him into their ship, the ship was suddenly comen to the land. The people on the morrow, longing to find our Lord again, took other little ships that came thither after, and followed his disciples, from whom they thought he would not long be, although they knew that Christ went not in the ship with them. And when they came on the other side of the sea to Capernaum, and found not only them there, but him too, then marveling much thereof, they said unto him, "Master, when camest thou hither?" Our Lord answered again and said unto them, "Sirs, I tell you very truth, the cause that you seek me now is not the miracles that you have seen, but it is because that of the loaves that I gave you; you have well eaten and well filled your bellies."[90]

In these words, our Savior well declared his Godhead, in that he told them their minds and thoughts, which is a property belonging only to God, for as the Scripture saith, "Our Lord beholdeth the heart,"[91] and specially since he told them, their minds being such as reason would have weened[92] their minds had been the contrary. For since that after that God had so fed and filled them of that bread, and that they had seen so much left yet besides, they did upon the sight of that miracle say, "This is the very prophet that shall come into the world," and by those words declared clearly that they thought he was Christ— that is to wit, Messiah—whom they looked for by the prophecy of Moses[93] and other prophets, that should come to save the world, and that thereupon they would have made him king, who could have weened that they could have had so soon upon the morrow so cold a mind toward him as to go assail and seek him for none other devotion but for the feeding of their bellies? But our Savior, whose deep sight entered into their hearts and labored not upon any fallible conjectures, both saw the sickness

76 proposing   **77** from, by   **78** fit
79 See Jn 6:16–21; Mt 14:22–32.   **80** See
Mt 14:13–21.   **81** appropriate, suitable

82 introduce   **83** *for that:* because
84 similar   **85** two   **86** lesser   **87** deign,
be willing   **88** truly; fully   **89** See Jn 6.

90 Jn 6:26   **91** 1 Sm 16:7; 1 Kgs 8:39;
1 Chr 28:9; Ps 7:10; Jer 17:10   **92** supposed, thought   **93** See Dt 18:15–22.

928 *Answer to a Poisoned Book* [*CW* 11: 27–29]

of their unperfect minds, and as a perfect physician against their disease, devised them a good and perfect medicine, saying unto them thus: "Work, sirs, and labor for the meat,[94] not the meat that perisheth, but for the meat that abideth into everlasting life, which meat the Son of Man shall give you, for him hath God the Father sealed." As though he would say, "Ye labor hither and seek me for such meat as I fed you with the other day, but that meat is soon gone and perisheth. Labor and work, and make you meet[95] that you may eat the meat that shall never be gone nor never perish, but shall last with you forever in everlasting life."

By these words of the meat everlasting our Savior did, as the old holy doctors declare, insinuate and secretly signify to them the meat of his own blessed person, both the spiritual eating of his Godhead by fruition in heaven and the bodily eating of his very body here in earth, of which both meats he more declareth after.

For the better perceiving whereof, ye shall understand that the material meat that men eat here hath two manner of perishings, one by which through the natural operation of the body that receiveth it, it is altered and changed and loseth its own form, shape, nature, and substance, and is turned into the nature and substance of the body which it nourisheth. And in this manner of perishing, perisheth all the meat that every man eateth, or else it nothing nourisheth.

The other manner of perishing, by which the meat perisheth, is that perishing by which the meat that is taken through gluttony is, for the inordinate appetite and use thereof, destroyed and punished by God, and the gluttonous belly too, of which manner of perishing Saint Paul saith, "The meat for the belly, and the belly for the meat, and God shall destroy both the one and the other."[96] This is spoken against those that eat not for the conservation of their life and their health to preserve themselves to the service of God, but eat and drink only for the voluptuous pleasure of their body.

Now taught our Lord the Jews in these few words a doctrine short and compendious, that they should neither be gluttons in laboring for the meat that perisheth of that second fashion, nor so very highly esteem the meat that perisheth of the first fashion—that is to wit,[97] any manner of meat that only nourisheth the body—but that they should labor and work and endeavor themselves, that they might be meet to receive and eat that meat that shall abide and endure with them in everlasting life, that is to say, that as themselves were both bodies and souls, so spiritually to receive and eat of his own Godhead, with the fruition whereof they should after this life be everlastingly fed among his angels in heaven, and for the meanwhile in this world bodily to receive and eat his own Blessed Body into theirs, as an earnest penny[98] of their perpetual conjunction and incorporation with him afterward in the kingdom of his eternal glory, where our bodies shall also be fed forever with the far passing[99] pleasure of the bodily beholding of his glorious body there in his own beautiful form, which we now verily[100] receive here, hid in the Blessed Sacrament in likeness and form of bread.

This is the meat that Christ in those words meant, and would they should[101] labor to make themselves meet for. For this meat will in no wise[102] perish. But whereas the bodily meat that the man eateth of the sheep in the nourishing of the man perisheth and loseth his own nature, not turning the flesh of the man into the flesh of the sheep, but being turned from the own proper nature of sheep's flesh into the natural flesh of the man, this meat is of such vigor and strength that in the nourishing of the man it abideth whole and unchanged, not being turned into the flesh of the man, but altering, turning, and transforming, as holy Saint Augustine saith,[103] the fleshly man from his gross fleshliness into a certain manner of the pure nature of itself, by participation of that holy blessed flesh and immortal, that is with his lively spirit immediately joined and unseparably knit unto the eternal flowing fountain of all life, the Godhead. This meat therefore Christ biddeth them labor and work for in those words: "Work you not the meat that perisheth but that abideth into everlasting life."

But yet, though Christ commanded them that they should not be idle sluggards and slothful of themselves, but that they should work and labor for their own part to get this meat and make themselves meet therefor,[104] yet he let them know that no man could by his own only power attain it. And

---

94 food **95** fit **96** 1 Cor 6:13–14 **97** say **98** *earnest penny:* pledge, foretaste **99** surpassing **100** truly **101** *would they should:* wanted them to **102** way **103** See *City of God* 21.15. **104** for it therefore he added these words, "which meat the Son of Man shall give you," telling them thereby that himself, which had fed them before with that other meat which was perishable, would also, if themselves would work and labor for it, give them the other meat, that is permanent into life everlasting too.

And therefore, as diverse holy doctors say, when the priest ministereth[105] us this meat, let us not think that it is he that giveth it us — not the priest, I say, whom we see — but the Son of Man, Christ himself, whose own flesh not the priest there giveth us, but as Christ's minister delivereth us. But the very giver thereof is our blessed Savior himself, as himself in these words witnesseth where he saith, *quem filius hominis dabit vobis* ("which meat the Son of Man shall give you").

Now lest the Jews might have cause to mistrust that he that were the Son of Man could not give them that meat that were free from all perishing and permanent into everlasting life, he taketh away that objection, and showeth them that he is not only the Son of Man but also the Son of God, and no more verily man, by that that he is the Son of Man (that is to wit, not of Joseph but of our forefather Adam, the first man) than he is verily God, in that he is the Son of God, as verily and as naturally begotten of God the Father by generation, as he was verily and naturally descended of our forefather Adam by lineal descent and propagation, which thing our Savior showed them in these words: *Hunc enim pater signavit Deus* ("For him hath God the Father sealed"). This is to say, that him hath God the Father specially sequestered and severed and set aside out of the number of all creatures, and hath sent him into the world, anointed, signed, and marked with the very print of his own seal. For (as the old holy doctors declare, and among others, Saint Cyril and Saint Hilary)[106] the seal of the Father with which he sealed his Son is nothing else but himself, his own very nature and substance. And therefore hath God caused these words to be written in Holy Scripture: that God the Father hath sealed his Son, as our Savior said here to the Jews, and that Christ is the image, print, and character of the Father,[107] as saith Saint Paul, because we thereby should learn and understand that as a true seal truly printed leaveth in

the other the very whole express thing that it is itself, not as it is iron, steel, or copper, silver, brass, or gold, but as it is a seal — that is to wit, this fashioned figure or that — and yet keepeth it whole still never the less itself, so did God the Father in the sealing of God the Son — that is to wit, in his eternal begetting — give him all that ever was in himself, all his whole will, all his whole wisdom, all his whole might and power, and finally all his whole nature, substance, and Godhead, and yet keep never the less all the same still himself.

And thus the Son of God so sealed by his Father, and not only expressly representing, but also verily being one equal God, in nature, substance, wisdom, will, might, and power, with Almighty God his Father, being sent into the world by his Father and himself and their both Holy Spirit, equal God with them both, took upon him the manhood, the very flesh, and the very soul of our Savior Christ, anointed above all other creatures[108] with fullness of all graces, by the conjunction of his manhood in wonderful unity with his omnipotent Godhead, marvelously making one perfect person and one far passing[109] perfect person of God and man together.

Thus hath our Savior not only showed them the great gift of everlasting lively[110] meat that, if they would work for it, he would give them, but hath also showed them that himself is equal God with his almighty Father, and thereby well able to give it them, and also sent into the world for the nonce,[111] because he should, to such folk as would be well willing to labor and work therefor,[112] work with their good will and willingly give it them.

THE SEVENTH CHAPTER

When that the Jews had heard our Savior speak of such a meat that would not perish but should abide and endure with them into everlasting life, glad men were they. For yet they hoped to have some meat that so should fill their bellies and so satisfy them that they should never need to labor for any more.

Now were those Jews yet somewhat less gluttons than are many Christian people nowadays. For they could have been content, so that they should never

have felt hunger more, to have forborne[113] eating forever, as the woman of Samaria, so that she might have had of our Savior one draught of such water as might have quenched her thirst forever, was well
5   contented in her own mind to have forborne drink forever.[114] But many Christian men there are that would not, I ween,[115] be content to take either such meat or such drink, though[116] God would offer it them. For many men have such a pleasure in eat-
10   ing and drinking that they would not gladly live but even to eat and drink. And for the pleasure thereof, they love better hunger and thirst than the harmless lack of them both, though God would give it them. For we see that they seek means to make their
15   appetite greedy. And some will eat salt meat purposely to give them a courage to the cup. These folk do not long to eat and drink to live the longer, but long to live to eat and drink the longer. These be those therefore of whom the Apostle saith, *Esca*
20   *ventri et venter escis, Deus et hunc et illam destruet.* ("The meat for the belly and the belly for the meat; God shall destroy both the one and the other").[117]

And surely besides the punishment of God in another world, and besides all the pains that even
25   in this world through sickness and sores arise and spring of such gluttony, they that gladly would endure a grief perpetually to have the pleasure of the continual 'swaging[118] have in their best wealth[119] but a displeasant pleasure, except[120] men be so mad as to
30   think that he were well at ease that might be ever ahungered and ever eating, ever athirst and ever drinking, ever lousy and ever clawing, ever scurvy[121] and ever scratching.

These Jews, I say therefore, and the woman of Sa-
35   maria, were not of this mind, but so that they might have lacked the grief of hunger and thirst they would have been content, as it seemeth, to have forborne meat and drink.

Howbeit,[122] to say the truth, their words well
40   weighed, it seemeth that their affections were worse than they seem at the first sight. For as methinketh, they were not so glad to put away their fault as to make a change of one fault for another, not so glad to lose the pleasure of the meat that is the mainte-
45   nance of gluttony as to get them to rest and idleness

that is the maintenance of sloth. And our Lord touched[123] the appetite of sloth in these Jews when he bade them, *Operamini non cibum qui perit,* etc. ("Work you for the meat, not that that perisheth but that that abideth into everlasting life"), not-   50 ing therein, as saith Saint Chrysostom, the slothful appetite by which they would fain[124] have had him feed them still by miracle, without any labor of their own.[125] And the woman of Samaria said unto him, "Lord, give me of that water that I need no   55 more to labor hither, and draw up water here at this deep well."[126]

But surely, whoso put not away his vice but make a change may soon hap[127] to take as evil as he leaveth, and not a worse lightly[128] than sloth, which vice God   60 saw so noyous[129] unto mankind that even when he set him in paradise, he bade him be occupied in the keeping of that pleasant garden. And afterward, when he should be driven thence into the earth, he gave him a necessity to labor, making the earth to be   65 such as without man's labor should not bring him forth his living.[130]

And therefore an evil and a perilous life live they that will in this world not labor and work, but live either in idleness or in idle business, driving forth all   70 their days in gaming for their pastime, as though that else[131] their time could never pass, but the sun would ever stand even still over their heads and never draw to night, but if[132] they drove away the day with dancing or some such other goodly gaming.   75

God sent men hither to wake and work, and as for sleep and gaming (if any gaming be good in this vale of misery in this time of tears), it must serve but for a refreshing of the weary and forwatched[133] body, to renew it unto watch and labor again — not   80 all men in bodily labor, but as the circumstances of the persons be — so to be busied in one good business or other. For rest and recreation should be but as a sauce. And sauce should, ye wot[134] well, serve for a faint and weak stomach to get it the more appe-   85 tite to the meat, and not for increase of voluptuous pleasure in every greedy glutton that hath in himself sauce malapert[135] already enough. And therefore, likewise as[136] it were a fond[137] feast that had all the table full of sauce, and so little meat therewith   90

---

113 abstained from 114 See Jn 4:5–26.
115 think, believe 116 even if 117 1 Cor 6:13 118 assuaging; alleviation
119 well-being 120 unless 121 scabby

122 However 123 discussed 124 willingly 125 See Chrysostom, *PG* 59: 249.
126 Jn 4:15. 127 happen 128 probably 129 harmful 130 See Gn 2:15,

3:19. 131 otherwise 132 *but if:* unless
133 weary from staying awake 134 know
135 presumptuous, impudent, saucy
136 *likewise as:* just as if 137 foolish, silly

that the guests should go thence as empty as they came thither, so is it surely a very mad-ordered life that hath but little time bestowed in any fruitful business, and all the substance idly spent in play.

And therefore, to the end that the Jews should know that he would not nourish them in their sloth and idleness, he bade them work. And yet lest they might ween that he would have all their work about worldly business, he bade them work, not for the meat that perisheth, but for the meat that abideth into everlasting life, whereby he meant not to forbid them to labor for the one, but to teach them to labor much more for the other.

THE EIGHTH CHAPTER

But they, as I told you, their mind set upon their belly-joy, and therefore not understanding his words, hoped by that word to have their bellies so well filled once that they should never need more to labor for their living after. And therefore they said again unto him, "What shall we do that we may work the works of God?" For they thought, as it seemeth, that some things there were that Christ would have them do, after which once done, then should they have that merry feast of that meat that he spoke of, and therefore would they fain wit[138] what work that were, that they might shortly rid it out of hand[139] that they were[140] at dinner, for they waxed[141] ahungered. Our Savior then, upon that question of theirs, showed them what work it was that he would have them do for that meat, and said unto them, "This is the work of God, that you should believe in him whom he hath sent."[142] As though he would say, "This is the work that God will ye shall work, before he will I shall give you this lively meat that I told you of; he will ye shall first believe in me whom he hath sent unto you."

Christ here, for the getting of that spiritual meat, setteth them about a spiritual work, bidding them labor to believe. Why is it any labor to believe? Yea, verily,[143] good readers, to believe well is no little work, and so great a work that no man can do it of his own strength without the special help of God.

But here shall you see clearly that Christ truly told them their thought, when he said unto them that they sought him not for his miracles but for their bellies. For when our Savior here had showed them that if they would have that lively meat, they must first believe in him, their minds were so set upon their bellies that they thought they would make him by craft come off and give them some meat apace[144] for their dinner. And therefore they said unto him, "What miracle then showest thou that we may see it and thereby believe thee? What thing workest thou? Our fathers did eat manna in desert, as it is writ, 'He gave them bread from heaven to eat.'"[145]

Here you may see that whereas Christ told them they must believe in him before they should have that lively meat that he told them of, they thought they would by craft, before they would work toward the belief, cause him to give them some other meat in the meanwhile; and therefore they not only said that it were reason[146] he should work some miracle before them ere he should look[147] that they should believe him, but also they assigned him, in manner,[148] what manner a miracle they would have him do: that is to wit, give them some meat by miracle by and by[149] one or other without any work or labor of theirs. And therefore they put him in mind of the meat of manna that their forefathers had from heaven while they were in wilderness and worked nothing therefor.[150]

But against this our Lord told them again that the bread that they did eat in desert was not given them by Moses, nor given them verily from heaven neither. For though that Moses was their prophet and their guide, yet was that bread of manna given them by God. And it came not also verily down from heaven, but from a far lower place of the air. But he showed them that God his own Father, that gave them that bread then out of the air, giveth them now verily down from heaven that bread that is for spiritual sustenance and lively nourishing, such manner of very bread that, in comparison and respect thereof, the other bread of manna might seem no bread at all. For "Verily, verily," said our Lord unto them, "not Moses gave you that bread from heaven, but my Father giveth you the very bread from heaven. For the very bread is that that cometh down from heaven, and giveth life to the world."

138 *fain wit:* gladly know   **139** *rid…hand:* clear it away   **140** *that they were:* so that they would be   **141** became   **142** Jn 6:29   **143** truly   **144** quickly   **145** See Ex 15:16; Ps 77(78):24.   **146** *it were reason:* it would be reasonable   **147** *ere*   **148** a way   **149** *by and by:* immediately   **150** *nothing therefor:* not at all for it   *he should look:* before he should expect

Now when they heard this, weening yet[151] that Christ spoke of some such bread as manna was, that God would at his request give them down from heaven, as manna was given down in Moses's days, and that this bread should feed the body as manna did, and yet be far better too, they prayed him and said, "Lord give us this bread always," as though they would say, "Good Lord, give us this very bread that thou speakest of that thy Father sendeth down from heaven, that we need not to labor and toil for bread in tilling of the earth, and give it us, good Lord, always, not for a season, as our fathers had the other in desert, but give it us forever, and let us never lack it nor need no more to work and labor for it."

THE NINTH CHAPTER

Then was our Lord plain with them and said, "I am the bread of life; he that cometh to me shall not hunger, and he that believeth in me shall never thirst."

"Lo," saith our Lord, "the bread of life that I speak of is myself, whom my Father giveth down from heaven to give not only nourishing, but also life to the world.

"The common bread doth but help to keep and conserve the life that the man hath already. But my Father hath sent me down—me I say, the very bread whereof angels feed, not only to conserve and keep the life of the body (albeit that[152] do I too, and heal of your sick folks full many), but also to quicken them that are dead, many in body and all the whole world in soul, whereof none can have life but by me.

"And therefore he that cometh to me—that is to wit, whoso will work the work of God that I told you, that is to wit, come by faith unto me and believe in him whom the Father hath sent, that is to wit, in myself—his hunger and thirst shall I take away forever."

Good is it, good readers, to consider well these words, lest by these words wrong understood some men might ween—as these heretics teach, that nowadays renew that old heresy that both Saint James and Saint Paul by plain express words reprove[153]— that our Lord would ask no more of any Christian man but only bare faith alone, which heresy, whereof they so much boasted a while, these heretics now feel so fully confuted that, though they live still like those that believe it, yet in their words and writing they are fain[154] to retreat for shame, and to seek such glosses to save their old writing, as might make unwise men ween that they never meant otherwise than the whole Catholic Church commonly teacheth and preacheth, which, if they had meant none other indeed (as indeed they meant and yet mean far other still), then had they, ye wot[155] well, made much business about nought.[156]

But letting these heretics pass, ye shall, good Christian readers, understand that like as if[157] a man would teach a child to read, he must first begin at his ABCs (for without the knowledge of his letters he can never go forward), so forasmuch[158] as no man can come unto Christ without faith, but faith must needs be the first entry toward all Christian virtues, since no man can either hope in him or love him whom he knoweth not, and Christ can no man Christianly know but by faith (for, as Saint Paul saith, he that cometh unto God, he must needs believe),[159] so did our Savior therefore, as a good and a wise master of his Christian school, begin there with the Jews that there offered themselves as his scholars; he began, I say, with faith. But yet he meant not that to salvation they should need nothing else but only bare faith, so that if they would believe all things that he should tell them, they should thereby be surely saved, though[160] they would do nothing that he would bid them.

But then what say we to these words of our Savior, "He that believeth in me shall never thirst"?[161] By this word of never thirsting, he meaneth everlasting salvation, which he promiseth here to all those that believe in him, wherefore it may seem that whosoever believe, though he do nothing else, shall by this promise of our Savior be saved.

Saint John the Baptist, at such time as people came to him, and asked what they should do whereby they might avoid damnation, he bade them give alms. And when the publicans asked him what they should do to avoid damnation, he bade them forbear[162] bribes, and take no more than the due customs and toll. And to the soldiers asking him the same question for their part, he answered that they should pick no quarrels, nor do no man no violence, nor take nothing by force, but hold themselves content with their wages.[163] Yet did he not mean that any of all these lessons was enough to save them without any more, but he told them, for the while, each of them the thing that should be most meetly[164] for them, and most properly pertain to their persons, and therefore most meetly for them to learn first, and the remnant should each of them after learn, little and[165] little at length, so that at last they should each of them do that one thing with all other things necessary also, and without which that one thing could not save them.

Thus did our Savior also because the Jews were full of infidelity and full of incredulity, which unbelief enduring, they could not enter into the way of salvation. He therefore first taught them the lesson of belief and faith, which once had, they should be meet to learn on the remnant, and increase both in hope and in well-working charity, so that faith once had, he told them they should not perish. For if they once believed his word, it was a means to make them hope in him and love him both, and those three things would make them obey him and work in such other virtues as he would for their own weal[166] command them.

There are also, good readers, diverse holy doctors that say that in these words by which our Savior said unto the Jews, "He that believeth in me shall never thirst," he meant not him that had a bare faith alone, which is, as Saint James saith, but a dead faith,[167] but him that had faith well-formed with hope and charity.

And therefore saith holy Saint Augustine thus:

Christ saith not "believe him," but "believe in him." For it followeth not by and by[168] that whoso believe him, believeth in him. For the devils believed him, but they believed not in him. And we believe Saint Paul, but we believe not in Saint Paul. To believe therefore in him is with believing to go into him, and to be incorporated in his members. This is the faith that God requireth and exacteth of us: that is to wit, the faith that by love will work well. Yet is faith discerned and severed from works; as the Apostle saith, a man is justified by faith without the works of the law.[169] And there are works that seem good without the faith of Christ, but they be not, for they be not referred[170] unto that end of which all good things come. For the end of the law is Christ unto justice unto all that believe.[171] And therefore our Savior would not discern and divide faith from the work but saith that the faith itself was the work of God: that is to wit, the faith that by love worketh.[172]

Here ye perceive, good readers, that to believe meritoriously, so as it shall be rewarded with salvation, may not be faith alone, but faith with a working love. Nor it may not be a bare believing of Christ, but it must be a believing in Christ, that is, as Saint Augustine saith, not an idle dead-standing belief, but a belief lively, quick,[173] and stirring, and by charity and good works ever walking and going into Christ. And then they that so believe in him, not with the bare only faith that these heretics preach, but with the well-working faith that the Catholic Church teacheth, they shall be saved, saith our Savior, from eternal hunger and thirst.

THE TENTH CHAPTER

But then goeth Christ further and showeth them that they lack this meat,[174] though it stand before them, and showeth them also by what means they may get it. Lo, thus he said unto them, "But I have told you that both you have seen me, and you have not believed," as though he would say, "You have seen me do miracles, and yet it hath not made you believe."

He bade them before that they should work to get the lively meat, and he told them after that the work which they should work to get it with was faith and belief. And he wrought miracles, which they saw, to make them believe. And now he showeth them that for all this they have not the belief yet, but yet must work and labor to have it.

Then might they have asked him, "Which way may we come to it?" But because they asked him not, he of his high goodness told them the means

163 See Lk 3:10-14. 164 fit 165 by
166 well-being 167 See Js 2:20.
168 immediately 169 Rom 3:28
170 directed 171 Rom 10:4
172 *faith … worketh:* Gal 5:6; Augustine,
Corpus Christianorum: Series Latina 36:
254 173 living 174 food

unasked and said, "All that my Father giveth me shall come to me," as though he would say, "Though my Father has sent me down to call you to me, and though I preach to you and tell you the truth at your ear, and work miracles before you that you may see them at your eyes, yea, and feed you by miracles, and put them even in your belly, yet can you never come to me by faith but if[175] my Father bring you. Never can you be mine by faith, but if my Father give you me. Now if ye know of any good guide that could bring you to the place whither ye would fain[176] go, where you should find the thing that ye would fain have, what would you do? Would you not labor to him? Would you not pray and entreat him to go with you and guide you thither? Now have I told you who can bring you to me by faith: that is to wit, God my Father; and therefore labor to him to guide you to me, pray him to give you to me, without whose help ye can never come to me. It is, I tell you, no small thing to believe in me. For but if the grace of my Father first prevent[177] you, ye can never begin to think thereon. But he hath now prevented you by sending me to call upon you. Howbeit,[178] yet for all that, but if he go forth with you and help to lead you forward, you may faint and fall and lie still by the way, and come no further forth toward me. But now he helpeth you forward by mine outward miracles, which himself worketh with me. But yet except[179] he work with you inwardly, with his inward help to draw you, you can for all this never come at me. Call well upon him therefore, and pray him to draw you and bring you and give you to me, which if you do and endeavor yourself for your own part, as I bade you before to work and walk with him toward me, he shall surely bring you into faith, and by faith into hope and into charity both, and so give you graciously to me. And then shall I give you the lively meat that I spoke of if ye will abide with me. 'For him that cometh to me will I not cast out.' Let him look that he cast not himself out; for surely I will not if himself will abide. For it is my Father's will that I should not, 'and I am descended from heaven not to do my will, but to do the will of him that hath sent me. And this is verily[180] the will of the Father that sent me: that all that he hath given me I should lose nothing thereof, but that I should raise up that again in the last day.'"

THE ELEVENTH CHAPTER

These words might, good readers, seem to an unchristian man, or to a false-christened Arian,[181] to signify that our Savior were not equal God with his Father, in that he speaketh so often (as in many more places of Scripture he speaketh more often) that he is obedient to his Father, and that his Father sent him, and that he is less than his Father, and many such other places, by which the old Arian heretics defended their heresy against the Godhead of Christ in his person, as these Lutheran heretics and these Hussgenians,[182] Zwinglians, and Tyndaleans draw now diverse other texts to the maintenance of their false heresies, against the precious body and blood of Christ in his Blessed Sacrament.

But as good Christian men well know that these new heretics are falsely now deceived in the one, so know they too that those old heretics were falsely then deceived in the other.

For all the minority and the obedience that the Scripture speaketh of in Christ is all meant of his manhood (which was less indeed) and not of his Godhead, for they were both equal.

For how could they be in Godhead unequal, when that in Godhead they were both one, though in persons diverse? And therefore our Savior by his Godhead hath the selfsame will that his Father hath, and none other, as he hath the same wit,[183] and the same might, the same nature, the same substance, and finally, the same Godhead and none other. And therefore whatsoever the one doth, the other doth, and as the Son was sent by the Father, so was he also sent both by himself and by the Holy Ghost too. And when the Holy Ghost was sent, he was sent both by the Father and the Son and by himself also. But incarnate was there no more but the Son alone, who, as he had by his Godhead none other will but the very selfsame that his Father had and the Holy Ghost, so had he by his manhood another several will and proper unto the person of his manhood itself, as every man hath his own. And of that will is it that he saith, "I am descended from heaven, not to do my will but the will of him that sent me,"[184] for in the will of his manhood he obeyed the Godhead.

But now if this obedience be understood of his manhood, how can it stand with these words of

---

175 *but if:* unless   **176** gladly   **177** anticipate, i.e., assist   **178** However   **179** unless
180 truly   **181** Arianism, a heresy

condemned at the Council of Nicaea in
325, denied the divine nature of Christ.
182 followers of Hussgen (German

surname) or Johannes Oecolampadius
183 mind   **184** Jn 6:38

his: "I am descended from heaven not to do my will but the will of him that sent me"? With that point, good reader, shall no man need to be moved. For since both the Godhead and manhood were joined and uned[185] together both in the one person of Christ, that whole person might say of itself such things as were verified and true in any of the both natures. For like[186] as a man may say of himself, "I shall die and return into the earth," and yet that shall not his soul do but his body only, and "I shall after my death go forthwith[187] to joy or to pain," and yet that shall not his body do by and by[188] but his soul, so might Christ say of himself, "I am descended from heaven," because his Godhead descended from thence, though his body did not, and he might say, "I shall suffer and die," because his manhood so should, and yet was his Godhead neither mortal nor passible.[189] And, for all that, might it be said of Christ, "God died for us," because he died that then was God. And of Christ might it well be said, "This man made heaven and earth," and yet his manhood made it not, but was made by his Godhead as other creatures were. But those words are well verified by the reason that he, which of the person of Christ saith, "this man," signifieth and meaneth not his only manhood but his whole person, which is not only man but very[190] God also.

This thing and this manner of speaking expressed our Savior very plain himself, when he said unto Nicodemus in talking with him of the sacrament of baptism, "No man hath ascended into heaven but he that descended from heaven, the Son of Man that is in heaven."[191] In these words he showeth unto Nicodemus that there was more credence to be given unto himself alone than unto all the prophets that ever were before. For himself more perfectly knew all things than all they did. For never man had there been in heaven but he. "For never man," said our Lord, "hath ascended into heaven but he that descended from heaven, the Son of Man, that is to wit, I myself that am in heaven."

Here he said that the Son of Man had been in heaven, and had descended from heaven, and was yet in heaven still. Now was not his Godhead the Son of Man but the Son of God, nor his manhood the Son of God but the Son of Man. But now, though the Godhead and the manhood were not both one but two distinct natures still, yet since the Son of God and the Son of Man were both one—that is to wit, both twain[192] one person, Christ—Christ therefore might well say then of himself, "I the Son of God am the Son of Man, and I the Son of Man am the Son of God, and I the Son of God am walking among men on earth, and I the Son of Man am sitting with my Father in heaven."

Now that ye may, good readers, the better conceive this matter and more easily perceive the sentence[193] of these words of Christ, "All that my Father giveth me, etc." I shall expound you these words of his in order, as[194] it were in his own person, speaking the words of this exposition himself.

"No man can come to me by his own labor alone. But all that my Father giveth me shall come to me. Labor therefore to my Father and pray him to give you to me, giving you occasion and helping you and, with your own will working with him, making you believe me; and so shall you, working with him by your own good will in subduing of your reason to the obedience of faith, by belief come to me, and with good will of well-working also with the belief, shall not only believe me, but also believe in me, and go into me by being a member of mine and incorporating yourself in me; and I shall, by the gift of mine own body to be eaten and received of yours, incorporate myself in you, and I will not cast you out from me but be still incorporated with you, but if[195] you cast me out from you, and so by sin cast yourself away from me; else[196] of all that cometh to me by my Father's bringing, I will cast none out. For if ye came to me by my Father through faith, and that I would not then suffer death for your salvation, then did I cast you out. For none can come into my bliss of heaven but by his ransom paid by my death and Passion. But I will not refuse that, but I will suffer and die for the world to give the dead world life by my death. For I am descended from heaven, sent by my Father not to do mine own will, but the will of him that hath sent me. But I mean not by these words that I will die against mine own will, but that albeit[197] the sensual part of my manhood would of the nature of man abhor, shrink, and withdraw from the grievous pain of such an intolerable Passion, yet shall my will both of my Godhead be all one with the will of my Father, and thereby in such

---

185 united   **186** just   **187** immediately, at once   **188** *by and by:* immediately   **189** capable of suffering   **190** true   **191** Jn 3:13   **192** together   **193** meaning   **194** as if   **195** *but if:* unless   **196** otherwise   **197** although

manner obedient unto his Father, as we say a man is obedient unto his own reason, and yet is not his own reason another power superior above himself. And my will of my manhood shall also be so con-
5 formable to the will of my Father, the will of the Holy Ghost, and the will of mine own Godhead— all which three wills are indeed one will, as all our three persons are in Godhead one God—that I will willingly die for them all that so come to me by my
10 Father's bringing, through the well-working faith, and will abide and persevere. And likewise as I will by mine own body, given unto them by eating into their own, give them an earnest penny[198] of our incorporation together, and a memorial of that death
15 and Passion, by which I will willingly give myself for them by being slain and sacrificed for their sin, and made the ransom of their redemption, when God shall for this obedience of my manhood unto the death, the vile death of the cross, lift me up and
20 exalt me, and give me the name that is above all names,[199] then shall I by my resurrection again to life give them an example and make them sure that I shall in like wise at the last day leave none of them to be lost, no more in body than in soul, but shall so
25 resuscitate and raise again their bodies that like as I shall myself ascend into heaven again from whence I came, so shall they as members of my body ascend thither with me, and there be fed of this everlasting lively bread that I tell you of: that is to wit, of
30 the fruition of my Godhead and beholding also of my glorious manhood forever, each of you that have use of reason after the analogy and proportion of the well-formed faith, with hope and well-working charity that you shall have had in this life herebe-
35 fore. For this is, as I before told you, the will of my Father that sent me: that every man that seeth his Son as you do, and not only seeth him as you do, but also believeth in him as you do not, shall have, if he persevere in that well-working belief, the meat that
40 I speak of that shall not perish but abide into everlasting life. For though ye see every man die here for the while, yet I shall, as I told you, being of equal power with my Father, raise them all up again myself at the last day, and then shall my faithful folk be
45 fed with this everlasting lively bread of mine own person, both God and man, forever. And lo, now have I plainly told you what bread I mean."

Whereas I have, good reader, in the exposition of these words of our Savior, inserted the incorpora-
50 tion of him and us together, by the receiving and eating of his own Body into ours, I have not done it to make any man ween[200] that that point appeared and were proved by any part of those words, but because it is a very truth indeed, and not only touched
55 and signified in other words of his before, but also plainly expressed and declared by other words of his own after, as you shall hereafter see. Therefore so plain a truth, and so necessary, and so necessarily pertaining to that place of the matter, methought it
60 not meetly[201] for to be left out.

THE TWELFTH CHAPTER

But now shall you hear how Christ's audience that came to seek him were affectionate to this everlasting lively bread when they had heard him declare it.
65 All the while that he spoke those other words before, they were yet in good hope that whatsoever he meant besides, he would give them some meat for their bellies. And as they were gross,[202] so had they
70 at the first weened. And so had they liefer[203] that he would have given them some such gross bread made of earthly corn[204] for their earthly bellies, such as he gave them and multiplied for them before, than any manna that came down from the air. But after-
75 ward, when they heard him tell them of far better bread that should come from heaven than manna was, which their fathers did eat in desert, then were they better apaid,[205] and prayed him that they might have of that. But then when they perceived in conclusion that he meant all of such bread as should
80 feed their souls, and gave them no good comfort after their gross minds of any gross feeding for their gross bodies, then like as some of their forefathers murmured[206] in desert against Moses for manna, and said that their stomach wambled[207] against that
85 light meat, and wished their old bondage again,[208] of which they were before so weary while they were in Egypt, yet thought they now that they were well then, because they might then sit over the pots that had the sodden[209] flesh in them, of such flesh yet
90 some of such bond slaves had haply[210] then but the

---

198 *earnest penny:* pledge; foretaste
199 See Phil 2:8–9. 200 think, believe
201 fitting 202 material; fleshly; dull

203 rather 204 grain 205 pleased
206 grumbled 207 rolled about

208 See Ex 16:2–8; Nm 21:5. 209 boiled, cooked 210 perhaps

savor. When these had heard him now speak all of such spiritual food, their hearts so sore[211] arose against him that their affections were clean[212] fallen from him suddenly. For a day before they had him in high estimation, and called him the prophet that should come and redeem the world, and would have made him king,[213] because they thought he would feed them by miracle without their labor, where their other kings used to pill them and poll[214] them and keep them under tribute so bare that with great labor they could scant[215] find themselves meat. And therefore would they, as I say, after that feeding that he fed them so by miracle, so fain[216] have made him king that he was fain[217] to withdraw himself aside and flee from them, till that mind of theirs were gone. And that was not long, as ye see. For now that after their great hope of such another feast for their bodies, they heard him turn all to the feeding of their souls, and that for the feeding of their bellies he went not about to give them so much as one loaf among them all to their breakfast, they murmured against that that[218] he had said of himself, "I am the quick[219] bread that am descended from heaven." And then they said: "Is not this Joseph's son? Know not we his father and his mother both? How saith he then of himself, 'I am descended from heaven'?"

Lo, here they called him a carpenter's son, and therein they belied[220] him unaware, but far were they now fallen from the making him a king.

Then said our Savior to them, "Murmur not among yourselves; no man cometh to me, but if[221] my Father draw him," as though he would say, "Leave your murmuring and fall to prayer, and work and walk with my Father in coming to me by faith. Men are so weak of themselves in the walking of this way that there can no man come to me but if my Father not only come to him and take him by the hand and lead him, but also draw him too. And therefore, since he must do so much for you or else you cannot come, so much have you the more need to leave your murmuring, and apply yourself to pray him (if he draw you not) to draw you, and, as the Prophet saith, to pray him strain your jaws with a bit and a bridle[222] and draw you by the cheeks, maugre your teeth,[223] and make you turn your wills from your belly-joy to come to the soul food with me. For

whereas your belly meat shall perish, belly and all, he that thus shall come to my feast, he shall not perish. For I shall raise him up again in the last day unto everlasting life. And if ye marvel at this that I say, that my Father must bring you and draw you — that is, that he must, besides all outward teaching, teach you within by leading and drawing you into the truth of faith, by his inward operation joined with the towardness[224] of your wills, prevented, moved, and set awork with occasions of his former grace — if ye marvel of this manner of drawing and of my Father's inward teaching, remember that your own prophets say that 'all folk shall be taught of God.'[225] And now God teacheth you, for I teach you, which am, as I told you, the bread of life that am descended from heaven. And surely there shall no man be taught the faith but if[226] God teach him. Nor every man is not full taught that heareth it but he that heareth it and learneth it, which no man can do by any outward voice without God working within. And he will not work, nor his wisdom will not enter into an evil-willed heart.[227] And therefore leave your murmuring, and pray my Father to teach you, not only outwardly as he teacheth you now by me, but inwardly also, that you may be learned by his working to faith with you and within you. But why do I tell you so often that you cannot come to his gift of faith (without which you cannot come at me) but if my Father give it you? Verily, because I would you should[228] pray him for it. For though he prevent you and give you occasions toward the getting of that gift, yet setteth he not so little by this great gift of learning and faith that he list[229] to cast it away upon them that, when it is showed them, set not so much thereby as to desire it and pray therefor.[230]

And therefore I would have you desire it of him that may give it you, and yet is not that my Father only but myself also. Howbeit,[231] if I should bid you ask it of me, and pray me give you this grace, you be so far from the belief in me that ye would not do it.

And therefore, not speaking of mine own power, I tell you all of the power of the Father, that without him ye cannot come to me, because I would have you pray to him that he would give you the grace that, as ye know by faith and knowledge

211 greatly; violently   **212** completely
213 See Jn 6:15.   **214** *pill and poll:* rob and extort   **215** hardly, barely   **216** gladly, willingly   **217** obliged, forced   **218** *that*

that: that which   **219** living   **220** slandered   **221** *but if:* unless   **222** See Ps 31(32):9.   **223** *maugre your teeth:* despite your resistance   **224** inclination   **225** Is

54:13   **226** *but if:* unless   **227** Wis 1:4   **228** *would you should:* want you to   **229** chooses   **230** for it   **231** However

him already for God, so ye may know by faith and knowledge him for my Father too, and then shall you, by the same faith, know and acknowledge me also for his Son. And then shall you not murmur at my words, but humbly come to me as to the Son, not of Joseph but of God, and acknowledge me for the quick bread that is descended from heaven: 'For every man that hath heard this lesson of my Father, and hath not only heard it but also learned it, he cometh (as I have told you) to me. But yet this will I tell you, that never man saw my Father yet. But he that is of God—that is to wit,[232] myself that am his own Son—he hath seen the Father, and so hath no man else.'[233] And therefore the lesson that any man heareth and learneth of my Father, he must hear of him by me and learn it by the inward work of my Father, with whose work I work also. And so shall he come to me through perfect well-working faith in me. And I tell you very truth, he that so believeth in me and persevereth at his death in that perfect belief is sure of eternal life. For I am (as I diverse times now have told you) the very bread of life. 'Your fathers that murmured as you do now did eat the bread of manna in desert, and they be dead and perished.' Leave therefore that wrong way of your forefathers, leave your grudge and your murmur, and labor to my Father that he may bring you to me by such faith as ye may eat this bread that is myself. For this bread is bread descending from heaven, for the nonce[234] that whoso may eat and be fed of that shall not perish by everlasting death. For I tell you yet again that 'I am the quick bread that am descended from heaven.' Whosoever come to me by my Father's bringing, so that by perfect perseverance and well-working faith he may eat and be fed of this bread—that is to wit, attain the fruition of my glorious Godhead, with the glorious sight whereof the angels are fed in heaven—he shall be sure of everlasting life."

THE THIRTEENTH CHAPTER

Whereas our Savior, good readers, in the beginning, upon occasion of his miracle wrought upon the multiplication of the bread, touched both the bread of his Godhead and also of the giving them of his own body to be eaten in form of bread, and that he somewhat did insinuate and set forth the same in those words, "Work you not the bread that perisheth, but the bread that abideth into everlasting life, which the Son of Man shall give you," as I somewhat told you before, not of mine own mind, but of the mind of diverse holy doctors, Alcuin, Saint Thomas, Theophylactus, and Saint Cyril,[235] ye see that our Savior in many words, which I have now declared you, hath opened and showed unto them the bread of his Godhead.

And now, good readers, take heed how in those words that now follow, he declareth unto them the bread of his own very body, which he giveth us verily to eat in the Blessed Sacrament, wherein that exposition that I shall give you shall be none invention of mine, but the clear faith and sentence[236] of all the holy doctors of Christ's Church, old and new both, from Christ's death to this day, of whom I shall for an example give you, ere[237] I make an end, the names and the sentences of some such as yourselves shall well see and perceive for other manner[238] men than I am or Master Masker either, and that if they were good men and true, ye shall then yourself say that Master Masker is naught[239] and false, and that his exposition, though[240] it were true as it is both foolish and false, yet since it cometh not near the purpose, is (as I told you before) very falsely handled.

Let us hear now therefore of the giving of Christ's own blessed body verily to us, to eat in the Blessed Sacrament, what Christ himself saith.

After his declaration of the bread of his glorious Godhead, these are his words: "And the bread that I shall give you is my flesh which I shall give for the life of the world."

Whereas before they murmured at the light[241] spiritual bread of his Godhead, he telleth them now that he will not only give them that bread to feed upon, by fruition of the beholding face to face when the time shall come, as he hath also given it them in one manner already by his incarnation, to feed them spiritually in the meanwhile by spiritual doctrine, but that the bread that he will give them to feed upon shall besides that be his own flesh, even the very same that he will give for the life of the world,[242] meaning that he would verily give men the same very flesh to eat and feed upon, both

232 say   233 Jn 6:46   234 particular purpose   235 Alcuin of York (*ca.* 735–804), Saint Thomas Aquinas (1225–74), Theophylactus of Ohrid (d. *ca.* 1110), Saint Cyril of Alexandria (*ca.* 376–444)   236 meaning; sense   237 before   238 kinds of   239 bad, wicked   240 even if   241 insubstantial   242 See 1 Cor 11:24.

bodily and spiritually in remembrance of his death, that he would for man's redemption verily give to death, and verily for a sacrifice offer up to God by death.

But now saith Master Masker, the adversary of the Blessed Sacrament, that our Savior meant no more in those words, "And the bread that I shall give you is my flesh, which I shall give for the life of the world,"[243] but that he would give it for the life of the world by his death, and meant nothing at all of the giving of his flesh before his death, or after his death, nor nothing in these words or any that in the same chapter follow intended to speak of any such manner of giving his body to eat, as he is received and eaten in the Blessed Sacrament, nor nothing meant in this chapter anything to speak of that matter.

Thus would Master Masker that all men should ween,[244] as it appeareth plainly by his exposition. And thus also saith Luther,[245] and thus saith Frith also, and affirmeth this saying so boldly that he saith it twice in his one book wherein he answereth me. Therein saith he twice that all learned men are full and whole agreed in that point.

And therefore will these adversaries of the Sacrament say that in this exposition of mine, all that ever I say, whereby it may appear that our Savior in these words written in this sixth chapter of Saint John anything spoke or meant of the giving of his body to be eaten in the Blessed Sacrament, is an imagination of mine own head, as Master Masker argueth and speaketh always of "Master More his faith," as though it were no man's else but mine.

But to the intent, good readers, that ye may clearly perceive Master Masker's malicious falsehood therein, I shall in diverse places of this exposition, concerning specially this point of Christ's speaking and meaning of the giving of his own very body in the Blessed Sacrament, rehearse[246] you the names of some of those whom I follow therein, and some of their words too, by which ye shall see that I deceive you not as Master Masker doth, that through all his exposition flitteth all from the point and dissimuleth[247] all the words of those old holy men that expounded it in such wise[248] as he would we should ween that no good man ever did.

Upon these words therefore of our Savior, "And the bread that I shall give you is my flesh that I shall give for the life of the world," thus saith Theophylactus:

Consider that that bread that we eat in the Sacrament is not only a figure of the flesh of our Lord, but it is also the flesh of our Lord itself. For he said not, 'The bread that I shall give is a figure of my flesh,' but he said, 'It is my flesh.' For the same bread by secret words, through the mystical benediction, and by the coming also of the Holy Spirit thereunto, is transformed and changed into the flesh of our Lord. And lest that any man should be troubled in his mind, weening that it were not to be believed that bread should be flesh, this is well known that while our Lord walked in his flesh, and of bread received his nourishing, that bread which he then ate was then changed into his body, and was made such as his holy flesh was, and did sustain and increase his flesh after the common manner of men. And therefore now also is the bread changed into the flesh of our Lord. And how is it then (will some man say) that it appeareth not to us flesh but bread? That hath Christ provided, to the intent we should not abhor[249] from the eating of it. For if it were given us in likeness of flesh, we should be displeasantly disposed toward the receiving of our Housel.[250] But now, by the goodness of God condescending to our infirmity, this sacramental meat appeareth unto us such as we have at other times been accustomed with.[251]

These are not my words, lo, good Christian reader, but the words of that old holy cunning[252] doctor Theophylactus, which was also no Latin man but a Greek, because Master Masker speaketh so much of papists, as though the Catholic faith, whereby the Catholic Church believeth that in the Blessed Sacrament is the very blessed body of Christ, were a thing but made and imagined by some pope of Rome.

Now if Master Masker will say that mine exposition is in this point false, here you see, good readers, that mine exposition is not mine but the exposition of Theophylactus. And therefore let him leave dancing with me, and dance another while with him.

243 Jn 6:51 **244** *would . . . ween:* Master Masker wants all men to believe **245** See *WA* 23: 205, 33: 209–10. **246** tell **247** pretends not to see **248** a way **249** recoil; shrink **250** the consecrated elements of the Eucharist **251** *PG* 123: 1308 **252** learned

But mark well two things now, good reader, in these words: One, that this good holy doctor calleth the Blessed Sacrament bread as Saint Paul doth,[253] and our Savior himself also, in these words of his in this sixth chapter of Saint John, and so doth also every doctor of the Church almost, upon which calling of it bread, Friar Luther, and Melanchthon, and their fellows take their hold to say and affirm that it is very bread still, as well after the consecration as afore. And Friar Hussgen, with Zwingli, George Joye, John Frith, and Tyndale, turn forth further to the devil and not only say that it is very bread still, but also that it is nothing else.

But now consider therefore, as I say, that Theophylactus here calleth it bread as well as they, saying the bread that we receive in the mysteries or Sacrament is not only a certain figure of the flesh of our Lord, but it is also the flesh of our Lord itself. But then expresseth he plainly that though he calleth it bread, he meaneth not that it is very material bread still as it was, but that the bread is transformed, gone, and changed into the very flesh of Christ. And he setteth it out also with an example of the bread that is eaten and turned into the flesh of the man whom it nourisheth, which every man well wotteth[254] that any wit hath that it is no longer bread then.

And therefore Theophylactus calleth it bread, because it was bread, as in the Scripture the serpent into which Aaron's rod was turned is called a rod still, while it was no rod but a serpent. For there is it thus written: "The rod of Aaron did devour the rods of the magicians."[255] And as the Scripture calleth the serpent there a rod, so calleth it the Sacrament bread. And as Theophylactus calleth here the Blessed Sacrament by the name of bread, and yet declareth that it is no bread, even so do all holy doctors that call it by that name of bread both mean indeed, and also do clearly declare, that though they call it bread, they know well it is no bread but in likeness and form of bread under the sacramental sign the very Blessed Body of Christ, flesh, blood, bones and all, and neither without the soul nor the Godhead neither.

Mark also, good reader, that Theophylactus saith, "The bread which we eat in the mysteries or Sacrament is not only a figure of the flesh of our Lord, but it is also the flesh of our Lord itself."

In these words, good readers, mark well that he saith it is a figure and yet for all that the very flesh of Christ.

This thing I specially desire you to note, because that by the marking of this one point, ye may avoid almost all the craft with which Master Masker, Frith, and Tyndale, and all these heretics labor to deceive you in the writings of all the old holy doctors.

For wheresoever any of them call the Blessed Sacrament a figure, there would these fellows make us ween that he meant it were nothing else. But here you see that Theophylactus saith it is a figure, as it is indeed, but he telleth us that it is also (as indeed it is) the very flesh of our Lord.

And therefore mark well these two points in this one place, that[256] when these heretics prove that the Blessed Sacrament is called bread, they prove nothing against us. For they that call it bread declare yet that indeed it is not bread but the body of Christ. And when they prove that it is called a figure, they prove nothing against us. For they that say it is a figure say it is not only a figure, but also the flesh of Christ. But when we prove that the Blessed Sacrament is not only called the Body and Blood of Christ, but also that the old holy doctors and the expositions of Holy Scripture do plainly declare that it is so, then prove we plain against them. For we deny none of the other two points, but this point do they deny.

THE FOURTEENTH CHAPTER

Yet to the intent that ye may see that Master Masker in his exposition doth but plainly mock you, consider yet again these words well, *Et panis quem ego dabo caro mea est, quam ego dabo pro mundi vita*, which text, albeit that[257] in the Latin it be somewhat otherwise — that is to wit, *Et panis quem ego dabo caro mea est pro mundi vita*, without these words, *quam ego dabo* in the second place, which Latin text were yet more for my purpose — yet since not only the Greek text is as I rehearsed you first, which was the language wherein the Evangelist wrote, but that also both the Greek expositors, and many of the Latin expositors too, do so expound it, and that though those words were out, yet they be such as the sentence[258] would well require to repeat

---

253 See 1 Cor 11:26.   **254** knows   **255** Ex 7:9–13   **256** so that   **257** *albeit that:* although   **258** sense, meaning

and understand, and finally because I find that Master Masker himself doth in his exposition take that text in the first fashion, only changing one word in the second place, that is to wit, this word "give" into this word "pay," which change he maketh as for an exposition, I am content to take the text as himself doth — that is to wit, after the first manner thus: "And the bread that I shall give you is my flesh, which I shall give for the life of the world."

Consider now, good reader, that in these words, our Savior here speaketh of giving his flesh twice, by which he meaneth that in the one giving, he would give it to them, and in the other giving, he would give it for them. The one giving was in the Blessed Sacrament; the other was on the cross.

And look now whether the very words of Christ agree with this exposition or not; the words, ye wot well, be these: "And the bread that I shall give you is my flesh." Here is, lo, the one giving, by which he shall, saith he, give his flesh to them. Then saith he further, "which I shall give for the life of the world." Lo, here he telleth them of the other giving, by which he should give it for them. And because his giving to them should be a memorial of his giving for them, therefore he spoke of them both together. But yet because his principle purpose was to speak in that place, not of his giving of his flesh for them, but of his giving it unto them, therefore of his giving it to them he maketh after a very plain and express declaration in many plain open words, but of his giving it for them, he spoke but a little, and as[259] it were but for a declaration of the other giving. For when he had said, "And the bread which I shall give you shall be my flesh," then to declare that he meant to give them his very flesh, he added thereto these words, "which I shall give for the life of the world," as though he would say, "Will you wit[260] what flesh this bread is that I will give to you? Verily the selfsame that I will give for you, and not only for you but for the life of the whole world too — that is to wit, for as many of the world as when they hear it preached, will refuse to take it. And therefore when ye know hereafter which flesh of mine I shall have given for you upon the cross, then shall you not need to doubt which flesh of mine I shall give you in the bread of the Sacrament, except you list[261] not to believe me.

For now I tell you as plain as I can that it shall be the same flesh."

This exposition, good readers, ye see is evident, open, and plain. But now see, good readers, for God's sake, the falsehood of Master Masker in his exposition upon the same words. Whereas our Savior, as you see, speaketh in these few words of these two givings — the giving to eat and the giving to die, the giving in the Sacrament and the giving on the cross — cometh me now Master Masker, and expoundeth Christ's words altogether of the one giving — that is to wit, the giving by death on the cross — and letteth the other giving go by, as though he saw it not, albeit that Christ speaketh of that giving both first and most.

Now if Master Masker will say that I do but feign these two givings and say, as he saith often, that Christ meant there but one giving — that is to wit, by his death — and will say that Christ speaketh there no word of the Sacrament,[262] I shall tell him again that so might Master Masker mar all his own exposition utterly. For Christ when he saith, "Which I shall give for the life of the world," speaketh no word in the world neither of his cross nor of his death. If he say that they be understood, then must he give me leave to say the like for my part, that as death and the cross are understood in the one giving, so eating and the Sacrament is understood in the other giving. Howbeit,[263] for my part yet touching the first giving, I may say that Christ speaketh of the Sacrament, and signifieth his meaning in this word "bread," when he saith, "The bread that I shall give you is my flesh." And of the eating thereof he speaketh expressly after. And therefore shall Master Masker never wade out thereof, but that I have the words of the Scripture much more clear for the first giving than he for the second. And ye may see that of the two givings Master Masker, to mock us with, hath in his exposition of a foolish wiliness winked and dissembled the one.

But yet if Master Masker strive with me still upon this point — whether our Savior speak of two givings of his flesh, or but of one — albeit that I have proved my part therein meetly[264] plain myself, yet am I content that a better than we both shall break the strife between us. I shall therefore name you that holy cunning[265] doctor Saint Bede, whose words I trust

---

259 as if   **260** know   **261** *except you list:* unless you choose or desire   **262** See *CW* 11: 309–10.   **263** However   **264** suitably   **265** learned

every wise man will believe a little better than either Master Masker's or mine. Lo, thus saith Saint Bede upon these words of Christ, "And the bread which I shall give is my body, which I shall give for the life of the world." "This bread," saith Saint Bede, "did our Lord give when he gave the Sacrament of his body and his blood unto his disciples and when he offered up himself to God his Father upon the altar of the cross."[266]

Here you see, good readers, that Saint Bede telleth you plain the same tale that I tell you: that is to wit, that our Savior in those words speaketh of two givings of himself, the one to his disciples in the Sacrament, the other to death for his disciples on the cross. And therefore, while Master Masker with his heresy doth utterly deny the one, and by his exposition affirmeth that Christ in this place did speak but of the other, Saint Bede beareth me record that Master Masker lieth, and hath made his exposition false. And the further ye go in the words of this Gospel, the more shall Master Masker's false dice appear.

THE FIFTEENTH CHAPTER

When the Jews heard our Lord say that, besides the spiritual meat of the bread of his Godhead, the bread that he would give them should be his own flesh, then began they to contend and dispute among them upon that word, as one of the most marvelous and strange words that ever they had heard before. And therefore they said, "How can this man give us his flesh to eat?"[267]

Saint Bede saith here, and so saith Saint Augustine both, that they had conceived a false opinion that our Lord would cut out his own body in gobbets, and make them eat it so, in such manner of dead pieces, as men buy beef or mutton out of the butchers' shops.[268] This thing they thought that he neither could do, and also that though[269] he could, yet would they not eat it as a thing foul and loathsome.

We find, good readers, of one or two more, besides these Jews here, that at the word of God asked how. For both our Lady asked how, and Nicodemus also asked how.[270]

Our blessed Lady, when the angel told her that she should conceive and bring forth a child, asked this question, "How shall that be? For man I know none,"[271] not for that[272] she anything doubted of the truth of God's word sent her by God's messenger, but because she would know the means, forasmuch as she had determined herself upon perpetual virginity, and thereof a promise had passed and a vow was made, and Joseph well agreed therewith, as it may well be gathered upon the Gospel.

For the angel said not, "Thou hast conceived," but, "Thou shalt conceive."[273] And therefore when she answered, "How shall that be, since I know no man?" this answer had not been to the purpose if she had meant no more but that she knew none yet, for he said not that she was conceived yet but should conceive after, which she might after do by the knowledge of her husband after, though she knew no man yet. And therefore we may well gather of his words and hers together, as I have showed in my *Dialogue*,[274] that when she said, "How shall this be, for I know no man?" she meant therein not only that she knew none already, but also that she had promised and vowed that she never would know man afterward, using therein such a manner of speaking as a maid might say by[275] one whom she would never have, "We may well talk together, but we wed not together."

Now that her determination was not with herself only, but confirmed also with the consent of her spouse, it may well appear. For without his agreement she could not reckon herself to be sure to keep it.

And that her determination of perpetual virginity was a promise and a vow to God, it may well appear by this: that else[276] when she had word from God by the angel that she should conceive and bear a child, she had had no cause to ask the question how. For if she were at liberty to lie with a man, then had that revelation been a commandment unto her to labor for the conception, while there were upon her part no let[277] or impediment, neither of nature nor conscience.

And very like[278] it is that if she had been in that point at her liberty, then though she had minded perpetual virginity, yet since she had intended it

266 passage not identified **267** Jn 6:52 **268** Bede, *In S. Ioannis evangelium expositio* 6 (*PL* 92: 720); Augustine, *In Ioannis evangelium tractatus* 27.2 (*CCSL* 36: 270) **269** even if **270** Lk 1:26–38; Jn 3:1–20 **271** Lk 1:34 **272** *for that:* because **273** Lk 1:31 **274** *Dialogue of Sir Thomas More*, pp. 589–90 **275** about **276** otherwise **277** hindrance **278** likely

neither for avoiding of the bodily pain of the birth, nor for any abomination of God's natural ordinance for procreation[279] (for such respects be both unnatural and sinful), but only for God's pleasure and of[280] devotion, it is well likely that, hearing by the messenger of God what manner of child that was that God would she should[281] have, she would have made no question of the matter, but gladly gone about the getting.

But here may some man haply[282] say that this reason by which I prove her vow will serve well enough to soil[283] itself, and prove that it appeareth not that she had made any vow at all, but had only some mind and desire of perpetual virginity, but yet still at her liberty, without any promise or bond. For since she had now by revelation from God that his pleasure was she should have a child, a bare purpose of virginity and a vow of virginity were all of one weight. For God was able as well to dispense with her vow as to bid her leave off her unvowed purpose.

Of truth, if our Lady had weighed her vow as light as haply some light vowess would, this mind she might have had. Yea, and some vowesses peradventure[284] there are, which as yet never intend to break their vow but think they would not with the breaking of their vow fall in the displeasure of God, though they wist[285] to win therewith all this whole wretched world, which yet would be peradventure well content that God would send them word and bid them go wed and get children.

And those vowesses, lo, that happen to have any such mind,[286] let them at the first thought make a cross on their breast and bless it away. For though it be no breaking of their vow, yet is it a way well toward it, and driveth (if it be not sin) very near the piteous brink of sin when they would be glad that God would send them their pleasure without any sin.

And surely, if upon the delight in such a naughty[287] mind God would suffer[288] the devil to illude[289] such a vowess, and transfigure himself into the likeness of an angel of light, and call himself Gabriel, and tell her that God greeteth her well and sendeth her word that she shall have a child, though he therewith went his way and never told her more whether it should be good or bad, her secret inward affection toward her fleshly lust—lurking in her heart

unknown unto herself, covered and hid under the cloak of that mind that she would not for all the world take her own pleasure without God's will— would make her understand this message for a dispensation of her vow, and for a commandment to break it, and so go forth and follow it without any further question, and go get a child, and make the devil a prophet.

But this blessed Virgin Mary was so surely set upon the keeping of her vowed virginity that she never neither longed nor looked for any messenger from God that should bid her break it. And therefore was she so discreet and circumspect that she would not only consider who spoke to her to discern whether it were man or spirit, and also whether it were a good spirit or an evil, but she would also weigh well the words (were the spirit never so good) lest her own mistaking by negligence might mar the revelation. And therefore at Gabriel's first appearance, because he was goodly, and his words were fair and pleasantly set and spoken somewhat like a wooer, she was somewhat abashed and troubled in her mind at the manner of his salutation. But after, upon his further words when she advised[290] him and his message well, then perceiving him to be, not a man but an angel, not an evil angel but a good, and specially sent from God, and his matter no worldly wooing but a heavenly message, she was not a little joyful in her heart. And as I said, had she not vowed virginity, but had been at her liberty, she had, as meseemeth, had no cause to doubt what God would have her do, namely having a husband already. Nor never would she have thought that it had been better for her to live still in virginity than to go about that generation whereof God had sent her word. But now forasmuch as she was by her vow bound to virginity, whereof she wist well she might not dispense with herself, and the angel bade not her go about to conceive, but only told her, as by way of prophecy, that she should conceive, and well she wist God, from whom the message came, could make her conceive without man if he would, therefore she neither would tempt God in desiring him to do that miracle, nor by mistaking of his message for haste and oversight offend his master by the breaking of her vow, but discreetly did ask the messenger how and in what wise[291] she should conceive,

279 See Gn 1:28. **280** out of **281** *would she should:* wanted her to **282** perhaps **283** refute **284** perhaps **285** *though they wist:* even if they knew **286** intention **287** bad, wicked **288** allow **289** trick, deceive **290** considered **291** way

whereupon he showed her that she should be conceived[292] by the Holy Ghost.

Here you see, good readers, that the cause of her question in her asking how rose of no diffidence,[293] but of very sure faith, because she surely believed that he could make her conceive and her virginity saved. For else had she not had firmly that faith, she had had no cause to ask the question, but might have reckoned clearly that he would have her conceived by her husband.

And therefore was her question far from the question of Zechariah, the father of Saint John, which asked not the angel how, but what token he should have that he said true,[294] for else it seemed that, for all his word, because of their both ages, he was minded no more to meddle with his wife, since he thought possibility of generation passed. And for that diffidence was he punished by loss of his speech till the birth of the child.

And her question was also very far from this question of the Jews here, and from their asking how, while the cause of her question was faith, and the cause of their question diffidence.

Nicodemus also when our Lord began to tell him of the sacrament of baptism and said unto him, "Verily, verily, I tell thee, but if[295] a man be born again he cannot see the kingdom of God," answered our Savior and said, "How may a man be born again when he is old? May he enter again into his mother's belly and be born again?"[296]

Lo, here the man was deceived in that he thought upon a bodily birth, whereas our Savior meant of a spiritual birth by faith and by the sacrament of baptism. And therefore our Lord told him forthwith[297] that he meant not that a man should be bodily born again of his mother, but meant of a spiritual regeneration in soul by the water and the Holy Ghost.

Howbeit,[298] he told him not for all that all the form and manner of that sacrament, but what the substance should be, and by whose power, and whereof it should take effect.

Now these Jews here, to whom Christ preached of the giving of his body to them for meat, were not fully in the case of Nicodemus, but in some point they were nearer the truth than he was at the beginning. For they took our Savior's words right in that they understood that he spoke of his own very

flesh, and that he would give it them to eat, whereas Nicodemus understood no part of the generation and birth that Christ spoke of. But they mistook the manner how he would give it them, and ran forth in the device[299] and imagination of their own fantasy. But in diffidence and distrust they were like Nicodemus, which said, "How may a man be born again when he is old?" and peradventure the further off from endeavor toward believing. For in Nicodemus, though I find no consent of faith in conclusion, yet the Gospel speaketh not of any final contradiction[300] in him, nor of any desperate[301] departing, as these Jews and these disciples did. And Nicodemus spoke in his cause after, but these disciples never walked after with him.[302]

Now Christ there unto Nicodemus, because he was clean[303] from the matter, told him that it should be no bodily birth but a spiritual, and bade him marvel not thereof no more than of the spiring[304] or moving of the Spirit or of the wind (for that word diverse doctors take diversely), whose voice though he heard, he neither wist from whence it came nor whither he would go. But now when that Nicodemus, perceiving what the thing was, did yet wonder on still and said, "How may these things be?" then our Lord did no more but leave him with the same tale still, and bid him believe, and tell him why he so should, since himself that so told him came from heaven, and therefore could tell it, and gave him a signification of his death, whereby that sacrament should take the strength.[305] But as for his question, "How this might be?" otherwise than that it was by the power of God, that question Christ left unsoiled.[306]

Now did he likewise with these Jews here. Since it was so that they perceived already that he spoke of his very flesh, and yet for all that would not believe he could give it them, but thought the thing so strange and wonderful that they thought he could not do it, and therefore asked how he could do it, he did no more but still tell them that he would do it, and that he verily would give them his flesh to eat and his very blood to drink, and told them the profit that they should have if they believed him and did it, and what loss they should have if for lack of belief they would leave it undone, and that he was come from heaven, and therefore they

292 made pregnant **293** lack of faith **294** See Lk 1:18–20. **295** *but if:* unless **296** Jn 3:3–4 **297** immediately, at once **298** However **299** contrivance **300** opposition, denial **301** in despair **302** See Jn 7:50–51. **303** entirely **304** blowing **305** Jn 3:8–21 **306** unresolved; unanswered ought neither to mistrust his word nor his power to perform his word. And as for otherwise how and in what manner he could or would do it, he left their question and their how unsoiled.

But now, lest Master Masker might make men ween[307] that I make all this matter of[308] mine own head, ye shall hear, good readers, upon this question of the Jews what Saint Cyril saith:

The Jews (saith he) with great wickedness cry out and say against God, "How may he give us his flesh?" And they forget that there is nothing impossible to God. For while they were fleshly, they could not, as Saint Paul saith, understand spiritual things,[309] but this great Sacrament and mystery seemed unto them but folly. But let us, I beseech you, take profit of their sins, and let us give firm faith unto the sacraments, and let us never in such high things either speak or think that same how. For it is a Jew's word that same, and a cause of extreme punishment. And Nicodemus therefore, when he said, "How may these things be?" was answered as he well was worthy: "Art thou the master in Israel and knowest not these things?"[310] Let us therefore, as I said, be taught by other folks' faults, in God's work not to ask how, but leave unto himself the science and the way of his own work. For likewise as though no man knoweth what thing God is in his own nature and substance, yet a man is justified by faith when he believeth that they that seek him shall be royally rewarded by him, so though a man know not the reason of God's works, yet when through faith he doubteth not but that God is able to do all things, he shall have for this good mind great reward. And that we should be of this mind, our Lord himself exhorteth us by the prophet Isaiah, where he saith thus unto men:

My devices[311] be not as your devices be nor my ways such as your ways be, saith our Lord, but as the heaven is exalted from the earth, so be my ways exalted above yours and my devices above your devices.[312]

Christ therefore, which excelleth in wisdom and power by his Godhead, how can it be but that he shall work so wonderfully that the reason and cause of his works shall so far pass and excel the capacity of man's wit that our mind shall never be possible to perceive it? Dost thou not see oftentimes what things men of handicraft do? They tell us sometimes that they can do some things wherein their words seem of themselves incredible. But yet because we have seen them sometimes done such other things like,[313] we thereby believe them that they can do those things too. How can it be therefore but that they be worthy extreme torment that so contemn almighty God, the worker of all things, that they dare be so bold as in his works to speak of how, while he is he, whom they know to be the giver of all wisdom, and which (as the Scripture teacheth us) is able to do all things? But now, thou Jew, if thou wilt yet cry out and ask how, then will I be content to play the fool as thou dost, and ask how too. Then will I gladly ask thee how thou camest out of Egypt, how Moses's rod was turned into the serpent,[314] how the hand stricken with leprosy was in a moment restored to his former state again,[315] how the waters turned into blood,[316] how thy forefathers went through the mid-seas as though they had walked on dry ground,[317] how the bitter waters were changed sweet by the tree,[318] how the fountain of water flowed out of the stone,[319] how the running river of Jordan stood still,[320] how the inexpugnable[321] walls of Jericho were overthrown with the bare noise and clamor of the trumpets?[322] Innumerable things there are in which if thou ask how, thou must needs subvert and set at nought[323] all the whole Scripture, the doctrine of the prophets, and Moses's own writing too, whereupon you Jews, ye should have believed Christ, and if there seemed you then any hard thing in his words, humbly then have asked him. Thus should ye rather have done, than like drunken folk to cry out, "How can he give us his flesh?" Do ye not perceive that when ye say such things, there appeareth anon[324] a great arrogance in your words?[325]

Here you see, good readers, that Saint Cyril in these words plainly showed that Christ here in these

307 think, suppose, believe 308 out of, from 309 See 1 Cor 2:14. 310 Jn 3:9–10 311 plans 312 Is 55:8–9 313 similar 314 See Ex 4:2–4. 315 See Ex 4:6–7. 316 See Ex 7:20. 317 See Ex 14:21–22. 318 See Ex 15:25. 319 See Ex 17:5–6. 320 See Jo 3:16–17. 321 impregnable 322 See Jo 6:20. 323 set at nought: regard as nothing 324 at once, straightaway 325 Cyril, In Iohannis evangelium 4.2 (PG 73: 573–76)

words, "The bread that I shall give you is my flesh which I shall give for the life of the world," meant of the giving of his flesh in the Sacrament, and that the Jews wondered that he said he would give them
5 his flesh, and asked how he could do it, because they thought it impossible. And in reproof of their incredulity and that foolish mind of theirs, by which they could not believe that God could give them his own flesh to eat, Saint Cyril both showeth that many
10 handicrafted men do things, such as those that never saw the like would ween impossible, and also that in any work of God, it is a madness to put any doubt and ask how he can do it, since he is almighty and able to do all things. And to the intent that no
15 Christian man should doubt of the change and conversion of the bread into Christ's blessed body in the Sacrament, Saint Cyril here, by way of objection against the Jews, putteth us in remembrance — for us he teacheth, though he spoke to them — among
20 other miracles, he putteth us, I say, in remembrance of diverse conversions and changes out of one nature into another that God wrought in the Old Law, as how the hand was turned from whole to sore, and from sore to whole again suddenly, how the waters
25 were suddenly turned from bitter into sweet, and how the waters were turned from water to blood, and how the dead rod of Moses was turned into a quick³²⁶ serpent.

THE SIXTEENTH CHAPTER

30 But yet shall ye see that upon the words of Christ following, Saint Cyril always more and more declareth that Christ spoke there of his very body that he would give men to eat in the Blessed Sacrament. For it followeth in the text of the Gospel:
35 "Then said Jesus unto the Jews, 'Verily, verily, I say unto you, but if³²⁷ ye eat the flesh of the Son of Man, ye shall not have life in you. He that eateth my flesh and drinketh my blood hath everlasting life.'"
Upon those words thus saith Saint Cyril:

40 Christ is very merciful and mild, as the thing itself showeth. For he answereth not here sharply to their hot words, nor falleth at no contention with them, but goeth about to imprint in their

minds the lively³²⁸ knowledge of this Sacrament or mystery. And as for how (that is to wit,³²⁹ in 45 what manner) he shall give them his flesh to eat, he teacheth them not. For they could not understand it. But how great good they should get by the eating if they eat it with faith, that thing again and again he declareth them to drive them 50 to faith by the desire of eternal life, and faith first once had, they should be then the more easy to be taught. For the prophet Isaiah saith, "But if³³⁰ ye believe, ye shall not understand."³³¹ Therefore it was of necessity requisite that they should first 55 fasten the roots of faith in their mind, and then ask such things as were meetly³³² for a man to ask. But they, before they would believe, would out of season ask their importune questions first. And for this cause our Savior declared not unto them 60 how it might be done, but exhorteth them to seek the thing by faith. So on the other side, to his disciples that believed he gave the pieces of the bread, saying, "Take you and eat; this is my body." And in like wise he gave them the cup about, say- 65 ing, "Drink you of this all; this is the cup of my blood, which shall be shed for many, for remission of sins."³³³ Here thou seest that to them that asked without faith he opened not the manner of this mystery or Sacrament. But to them that be- 70 lieved, he expounded it though they asked not. Therefore let them hear this, those folk, I say, that of arrogance and pride will not believe the faith of Christ.³³⁴

Here ye see, good readers, that Saint Cyril plainly 75 declareth you that our Savior would not teach them at that time the manner of the eating, because of their infidelity for all their asking, but afterward he told and taught it his faithful disciples at his Last Supper and Maundy when he took them the bread 80 and bade them eat it, and told them that the same was his body, and the cup and bade them drink thereof, and showed them that that was his blood. And thus you see well by Saint Cyril that Master Masker here, which by his exposition would make 85 us ween that our Savior in all his words here to the Jews meant only to tell them of the giving of his flesh to the death, and that he meant nothing of the giving of his flesh to eat in the Blessed Sacrament, doth in all his exposition but play with false dice to deceive you.

Now as for that[335] Saint Cyril here calleth it by the name of bread, that is, I trow,[336] the thing that can nothing trouble you. For I have showed you before, by the words of that great holy doctor Theophylactus that it is called bread because it was bread, and because of the form of bread that remaineth, and yet is no bread indeed, but is the very Blessed Body of Christ, his very flesh and his blood. As you see also by Saint Cyril here, which of this Blessed Sacrament so often rehearseth[337] and inculcateth the miracle, exhorting all folk that no man be moved to mistrust it, though the thing be marvelous, nor ask as the Jews did how such a wonderful work can be wrought, but meekly believe it, since he is God that saith it, and therefore as he saith it, so doubt not but he can do it, as he doth other like things and did ere[338] he were born into this world, of which things Saint Cyril hath here rehearsed some, as[339] the turning of the water into blood,[340] as he turneth in the Sacrament the wine into blood, and the turning of Aaron's rod into a serpent, and that into such a serpent as devoured up all the serpents of the Egyptian witches,[341] like as our Savior in the Blessed Sacrament turneth the bread into his own body, that holy wholesome serpent that devoureth all the poisoned serpents of hell, and was therefore figured by the brazen serpent that Moses did set up in the manner of a cross in the desert, the beholding whereof devoured and destroyed the venom of all the poison serpents that had stung any man there.[342]

THE SEVENTEENTH CHAPTER

And albeit that[343] I show you, good Christian readers, Saint Cyril's words and his exposition upon the place, because Master Masker shall not make men ween[344] that I make all the matter of mine own head, yet seemeth me that our Savior declareth this matter with plain words himself. For what can be plainer words than are his own, when that upon their wondering and their murmuring question, "How can he give us his flesh to eat?" he said unto them, "Verily, verily, I say to you, but if you eat the flesh of the Son of Man and drink his blood, ye shall not have life in you. He that eateth my flesh and drinketh my blood hath life everlasting, and I shall raise him up again in the last day. For my flesh is verily meat, and my blood is verily drink. He that eateth my flesh and drinketh my blood dwelleth in me and I in him."

In these words ye see, good readers, how plainly that our Lord showeth them both the profit of the receiving and the peril of the refusing, and also both that he not only speaketh of his very body and blood, which thing Master Masker agreeth, but over[345] that, also that he more plainly and more precisely saith, that they should verily eat it and drink it, which thing Master Masker denieth, and yet is that the thing that our Savior in these words most specially laboreth to make them believe. For that he spoke of his very flesh they perceived well enough. But that he would have them verily eat it—that they thought such a manner[346] thing that they neither would do nor could believe, because they mistook the manner thereof, weening that they should eat it in dead pieces, cut out as the butchers cut the beasts in the shambles.[347]

And Christ therefore would at this time for their arrogant infidelity, as Saint Cyril hath told you, nothing declare them of the manner of his giving it to be verily eaten, not in the proper form of flesh, as they fleshly imagined, but in the form of bread in the Blessed Sacrament because, as Theophylactus declared you, men should not abhor to eat it. But leaving that untaught till the time of his Maundy supper (whereas Saint Cyril hath also showed you he taught it his faithful disciples at the institution of that Blessed Sacrament), he laboreth, as I say, in these words here most special,[348] with as plain words as can be devised, to tell them and make them believe that they shall verily eat his flesh, which thing, for anything that he could say to them, they were so hard-hearted that they would not believe him.

And yet is Master Masker here much more obdurate now, and much more faithless too, than all they were then. For he, both having heard what Christ said to those infidels then, and also what he taught his faithful disciples at his Maundy after, and what all holy doctors and saints have said thereon and believed ever since, yet will he, with a few fond[349] heretics, take a foolish froward[350] way and believe

---

335 *as for that:* the fact that   336 trust
337 tells   338 before   339 such as
340 See Ex 7:20.   341 See Ex 4:3.

342 See Nm 21:8–9.   343 *albeit that:* although   344 think, believe
345 besides   346 kind of   347 butchers'

stalls   348 particular   349 foolish
350 unruly, perverse

the contrary, or at the leastwise, say that he believeth the contrary. But, in good faith, that they verily believe as they say—that can I not believe, except[351] that of the Scripture and the Christian faith these folk believe nothing at all. And so, upon my faith, I fear me that you shall see it proved at last, as appeareth by some of them that so begin already, and have in some places put forth such poison in writing.

But surely though[352] neither any man had ever written upon these words of Christ, nor our Savior himself never spoken word thereof after, that ever had in writing comen into men's hands, yet are these words here spoken so plain and so full that they must needs make any man that were willing to believe him clearly perceive and know that in one manner or other he would give us his own very flesh verily to be received and eaten. For when the Jews said, "How can he give us his flesh to eat?" he answered them with no sophisms, but with a very plain open tale told them they should neither distrust that he could on his part give them his flesh to eat, nor yet refuse upon their part to eat it, if ever they would be saved—as though he would say, "Marvel you and mistrust you my word? And ask how I can give you mine own flesh to eat? I will not tell you how I can give it, nor in what form or fashion ye shall eat it, but this I will tell you, neither in tropes, allegories, nor parables, but even for a very plain truth, that eat ye shall my very flesh indeed if ever ye purpose to be saved, yea, and drink my very blood too. For but if[353] you be content to eat and with a true faith to eat the flesh of the Son of Man and drink his blood, ye shall not have life in you. But whoso with a true well-working faith eateth my flesh and drinketh my blood, he hath everlasting life," not only because he is as sure to have it when the time shall come as though he had it already, by reason of the promise that Christ here maketh, where he saith, "And I shall resuscitate and raise him up at the last day," but also for that[354] the very Body of Christ that he receiveth is very life everlasting of itself, and such a life as to them that well will receive it in true faith, and purpose of good living, it is the thing that is able to give life and quickness[355] everlasting. For as the Godhead is of his own nature everlasting life, so is the flesh joined in

unity of person to the Godhead, by that immediate conjunction and unity, made both everlasting and lively in itself, and also everlasting life to the giving of life everlastingly to all others that well and worthily receive him, and will persevere and abide with him. For though every man here naturally die for the while, yet shall Christ, as he promiseth here, raise and resuscitate him again to everlasting life in the last day.

THE EIGHTEENTH CHAPTER

And to show more and more that he meaneth plainly of very eating and very drinking, he saith, "My flesh is verily meat and my blood is verily drink." Upon these words saith Saint Cyril thus:

> Christ here declareth the difference again between the mystical benediction—that is to wit, the Blessed Sacrament and manna—and between the water flowing out of the stone and the Communion of the holy blood. And this he repeateth again, to the intent they should no more marvel of the miracle of manna, but that they should rather receive him which is the heavenly bread and the giver of eternal life. "Your fathers," said our Savior, "did eat manna in the desert, and they be dead. But this bread is descended from heaven that a man should eat thereof and not die." For the meat of manna brought not eternal life, but a short remedy against hunger. And therefore manna was not the very meat—that is to wit, manna was not the bread from heaven, but the holy body of Christ that is the meat that nourisheth to immortality and eternal life. "Yea," saith some man, "but they drank water out of the stone." But what won they by that, for dead they be, and therefore that was not the very drink, but the very drink is the blood of Christ, by which death is utterly turned up and destroyed. For it is not the blood of him that is only man, but the blood of that man, which being joined to the natural life (that is to wit, the Godhead), is made also life himself. Therefore we be the body and the members of Christ. For by this Blessed Sacrament we receive the very Son of God himself.[356]

---

351 unless   **352** even if   **353** *but if:* unless   **354** *for that:* because   **355** vitality   **356** *In Iohannis evangelium* 4.2 (*PG* 73: 581–84)

Here you see, good readers, that Saint Cyril plainly declareth here that these words of Christ, "My flesh is verily meat, etc." are spoken and meant of his holy flesh in the Blessed Sacrament, of which Master Masker, in all his exposition and in all his whole wise work, telleth us plainly the contrary. But Saint Cyril is here open and plain, both for that point and for the whole matter. For who can more plainly declare anything than that holy doctor declareth in these words that in the Blessed Sacrament is verily eaten and drunken the very blessed body and holy blood of Christ? And yet doth not Saint Cyril say it more openly than doth our Savior in his own words himself.

And now further to show that it must needs be so, that he which eateth his flesh and drinketh his blood must needs be resuscitated and raised again in body to everlasting life, our Savior addeth thereunto and saith, "He that eateth my flesh and drinketh my blood dwelleth in me and I in him." Upon which words also, thus saith holy Saint Cyril: "Like as if a man unto molten wax put other wax, it cannot be but that he shall throughout mingle the one with the other, so if a man receive the flesh and the blood of our Lord worthily and as he should, it cannot be but that he shall be so joined with Christ, as Christ shall be with him and he with Christ."[357]

Thus may you, good readers, see how verily a man eateth in the Sacrament the Blessed Body of Christ, and by that eating how each of them is in other. And then if he so persevere, how can it be that that body shall have everlasting death in which there is dwelling everlasting life? For as ye have heard, the body of Christ is by the conjunction with his Godhead made everlasting life.

But this is meant, as I say (and all the holy doctors do declare the same), of them that receive the Sacrament, not only sacramentally, but also effectually: that is to wit, of them that not only receive the body of our Savior by the Sacrament into their bodies, but also by true faith and true repentance and purpose of good living receive his Holy Spirit therewith into their souls, and be made thereby very lively[358] members of that thing that the Blessed Sacrament signifieth and betokeneth — that is to wit, of the mystical body of Christ, the Church, and congregation of saints.

For as you have heard by Theophylactus before, this Blessed Sacrament is not only the very flesh of Christ, but is also a figure. And that is it in diverse wise,[359] as I shall further declare you in my book against Frith's answer to my epistle, with which book (were his once come in print, which is already sent over to be printed) I shall, God willing, well make all his English brethren see and perceive his folly, that list[360] not willingly to continue fools and wink.

But as I was about to say, they that receive our Lord by the Sacrament only, and not by faith and purpose of amendment, though they receive him, yet they receive him not, and though they eat him, they eat him not. For though his Blessed Body be received into their bodies, yet his Holy Spirit is not received into their souls, and therefore he dwelleth not in them nor they in him, but they eat and drink their judgment, and receive him to their damnation, for that[361] they receive him without faith and due reverence, and therefore do not, as saith Saint Paul, discern the body of our Lord.[362]

And therefore saith Saint Augustine, as Prosper rehearseth[363] in *Liber sententiarum Prosperi*, "He receiveth the meat of life, he drinketh the draught of eternity that dwelleth in Christ and in whom Christ dwelleth. For he that discordeth from Christ neither eateth the flesh of Christ nor drinketh his blood, though he receive every day indifferently the Sacrament of that great thing to the judgment and damnation of his presumption."[364]

This text of Saint Augustine alleged[365] Frith for his purpose in a certain communication, willing to prove thereby that the very body of Christ was not always verily received and eaten in the Sacrament, as the Church saith. For here, said Frith, Saint Augustine saith plain that evil men, though they receive the Sacrament, eat not the body of Christ.

But here Frith either had not learned or else had forgotten that Saint Augustine meant of the effectual receiving, by which a man not only receiveth Christ's Blessed Body into his own sacramentally, but also virtually[366] and effectually so receiveth therewith the Spirit of God into his soul that he is incorporated thereby with our Savior, in such wise that he is made a lively member of his mystical body, that is, the congregation of saints, by receiving it

357 *In Iohannis evangelium* 4.2 (PG 73: 584)   **358** living   **359** ways   **360** *that list:* who wish   **361** *for that:* because

362 See 1 Cor 11:29.   **363** tells, relates   **364** *Liber sententiarum ex operibus S. Augustini delibatarum* 343 (PL 51: 481)

365 cited   **366** as far as essential qualities are concerned

worthily, which evil folk do not that receive it to their damnation.

For that Saint Augustine meant not to deny that the Blessed Body of Christ is verily received and eaten in the Blessed Sacrament, both of evil folk and good, it appeareth plain by that that,[367] in more places than one, he speaketh of the traitor Judas. For albeit that in some places he putteth it in doubt and question whether Judas received the Sacrament among the apostles at Christ's Maundy, or else that the morsel that he received were not it, yet in diverse places he affirmeth that he did.[368] And in those places, he affirmeth plainly that in the Sacrament he received Christ's Blessed Body, as evil and as false as the traitor was, as in his fifth book *De baptismo* he clearly declareth in these words:

> Like as Judas to whom our Lord gave the morsel, not by receiving any evil thing but by evil receiving of a good thing, gave the devil a place to enter into himself, so every man that unworthily receiveth the Sacrament of Christ maketh not the Sacrament evil because he is evil, nor maketh not thereby that he receiveth nothing because he receiveth it not to his salvation. For it was nevertheless the body of our Lord and the blood of our Lord, even unto them of whom the Apostle said, "He that eateth it and drinketh it unworthily, he eateth and drinketh damnation to himself."[369]

Here Saint Augustine, good readers, expressly declareth that not only good folk, but evil folk also, receive and eat in the Sacrament the very body and blood of Christ, though the one to salvation, the other to damnation. And therefore you see that Saint Augustine here plainly reproveth Frith.

And that ye may plainly see also that Saint Augustine, in calling the Blessed Sacrament the body of Christ, meaneth not to call it only a figure or a memorial (besides his other plain words in many sundry places), he writeth in an epistle unto Eleusius, Glorius, and Felix, declaring the great excellent goodness that Christ showed to the false traitor Judas, he writeth, I say, that Christ gave unto Judas at his Last Supper the price of our redemption. And

what was the price of our redemption, but his own very blessed body?[370]

Howbeit, Frith was on every side deceived in the perceiving of Saint Augustine's mind, which mishapped him, as I suppose, for lack of reading any further in Saint Augustine's works than those places that he found falsely drawn out into Friar Hussgen's book.[371]

For Saint Augustine in very many places plainly declareth that every man, good and bad both, receiveth and eateth in the Sacrament the very body and blood of Christ. And also those words in which he saith that evil folk eat it not, he meaneth that they eat it not so as they receive the effect thereof — that is to wit, to be by the receiving and eating thereof incorporate spiritually with him, as a lively member of his mystical body, the society of saints, so that he may dwell in Christ and Christ in him — but lacketh that spiritual effect of his eating because he is evil and eateth not Christ's flesh in such manner as he should do: that is to wit, worthily in true faith and purpose of clean and innocent life, as Saint Augustine, in his book *De blasphemia Spiritus Sancti*, declareth well in these words:

> This also that Christ saith, "He that eateth my flesh and drinketh my blood, dwelleth in me and I in him" — how shall we understand it? May we understand those folk therein too, of whom the Apostle saith that they eat and drink their judgment when they eat the same flesh and drink the same blood?[372] Did Judas the traitor and wicked seller of his master? Though he first with the other apostles, as Saint Luke the Evangelist very clearly declareth, did eat and drink the same Sacrament of his Flesh and his Blood made with his own hands,[373] did he abide yet in Christ and Christ in him? Finally, many men which with a feigned heart eat that flesh and drink that blood, or else when they have eaten and drunken it, become apostates after, do they dwell in Christ and Christ in them? But there is undoubtedly a certain manner of eating that flesh and drinking that blood, in which manner he that eateth it and drinketh it dwelleth in Christ and Christ in him. And therefore not whosoever eat the flesh

---

367 *by that that:* by the fact that **368** See *Epistolae* 44.5 (PL 33: 178); *Enarrationes in Psalmos* 3.1, 10.6; *Sermones* 71.11 (PL 38: 453); *In Iohannis evangelium tractatus* 62.3. **369** *De baptismo contra Donatistas* 5.8 (PL 43: 181); 1 Cor 11:29 **370** See Augustine, *Epistolae* 43.8, 44.5 (PL 33: 171, 178). **371** Johannes Oecolampadius's *Quid veteres* senserint **372** See 1 Cor 11:29. **373** See Mt 26:27; Mk 14:23; Lk 22:21.

of Christ and drink his blood dwelleth in Christ and Christ in him, but he that eateth it and drinketh it after a certain manner, which manner Christ saw when he spoke the words.[374]

Here you see, good readers, that Saint Augustine showeth that Judas in the Sacrament received and did eat the body of Christ, and declareth also the very whole thing that he meaneth concerning the understanding of this word of Christ, "He that eateth my flesh and drinketh my blood dwelleth in me and I in him"—that is to wit, they that eat it in a certain manner, by which he meaneth they that eat it well and in the state of grace, as he plainly declareth both in his exposition upon Saint John's Gospel, and many sundry places besides.[375]

And those that receive him otherwise, with a feigned heart and in purpose of deadly sin, they follow Judas and shortly show themselves. For such as they were wont[376] to be, such will they be still, or yet rather much worse if they were before very naught.[377] And therefore saith Saint Augustine that a man to eat the flesh of Christ is to dwell in Christ, and to have Christ dwelling in him. For he that dwelleth not in Christ well declareth that though he have received and eaten his flesh into his body by the Sacrament, yet hath he not received and eaten his Spirit, as I said, into his soul, and therefore hath not received and eaten his flesh effectually, but without the effect of the Spirit and life, which is the thing whereby the flesh giveth the life, and without which, as our Savior saith, his flesh availeth us nothing. And so for lack of the spiritual eating, the fleshly eater of his flesh, though he receive the Sacrament, receiveth not the effect of the Sacrament, the thing that the Sacrament signifieth, that is the participation of the mystical body of Christ: that is to wit, the Church and congregation of all saints, which Church and congregation is gathered together as many members into one body Christ, as the bread which our Lord in the Sacrament changeth into his blessed body is one loaf made of many grains of wheat, and the wine which he changeth into his blood is one cup of wine made of many grapes, as the Apostle declareth.

And verily to be a quick[378] lively member of that body doth no man attain that receiveth the Sacrament without faith and purpose of good life, but waxeth[379] a more weak member and a more lame, more astonied,[380] and more loosely hanging thereon than he did before, and by such often receiving so rotteth more and more that finally it falleth quite off, and is cast out into the dunghill of hell, and shall never be resuscitated and raised again to be made a member of that body in glory.

But as Saint Augustine saith, if a man after the receiving of the Sacrament do dwell still in God—that is to wit, abide and persevere in true faith and good works—then is it a good sign and token that he hath effectually eaten the flesh of Christ in the Blessed Sacrament. And thereupon must it needs, good Christian reader, follow that he that receiveth the Blessed Sacrament well, and eateth therein the flesh of Christ not only verily, which every man doth good and bad, but also—which only the good folk do—effectually, and so dwelleth in Christ and Christ in him perseverantly, that man or woman without doubt, it must needs be that they can never everlastingly die, but Christ dwelling in them shall conserve their souls and resuscitate again their bodies that so dwell in him, into everlasting life.

THE NINETEENTH CHAPTER

For the surety and infallible proof whereof, our Savior said forthwith[381] upon his words aforeremembered[382] further unto the Jews, "As the living Father sent me, so also do I live for my Father. And he that eateth me shall live also for me."

The Father of heaven, being the original substance of life, before all beginning begot his coeternal Son, and gave unto him his own whole substance, and therefore his own whole life, as to him whom he begot one equal God with himself, in nothing different but in only person.

The Father, I say, gave all his own whole life to his Son, and yet none thereof from himself. And therefore saith our Savior Christ that himself liveth for or by his Father. And so that man, saith he, that eateth me shall live through me. For since that by the very eating of his very Blessed Body the eater (but if[383] himself be the let[384]) is joined with the flesh of Christ, as holy Saint Cyril hath declared,[385]

374 *Sermones* 71 (*PL* 38: 453)   375 See *In Iohannis evangelium tractatus* 26.17 (*CCSL* 36: 268).   376 accustomed   377 bad,   wicked   378 active; productive   379 becomes   380 paralyzed; powerless   381 immediately   382 aforementioned   383 *but if:* unless   384 hindrance   385 See *In Iohannis evangelium* 4.3 (*PG* 73: 586).

and thereby with that Holy Spirit of his also, which from that holy flesh is unseparable, and so joined unto the very substance of life, that is life and giveth life too, he cannot but live through Christ.

Upon this our Savior finally for conclusion telleth them that this bread also is come from heaven, saying, "This is the bread that is descended from heaven," not meaning that his flesh was first in heaven, and so sent down from thence, as some heretics have ere[386] this held an opinion, but that his body was in the Blessed Virgin his mother by the heavenly obumbration[387] of the Holy Ghost. And also since his Godhead and his manhood were joined and knit together in very unity of person, our Savior used that manner of speaking by the one that he used by the other. And therefore, as he said unto Nicodemus, "The Son of Man descended from heaven," so saith he here of his flesh, "This is the bread that is descended from heaven."

And because that the Jews had in the beginning of this communication boasted unto him the bread of manna, bringing forth for the praise thereof the words of the Prophet, "Thou hast given them bread from heaven,"[388] our Lord here showed them that this bread that he would give them to eat — that is to wit, his own very flesh, as himself very plainly declared them, is of another manner descended down from heaven than the manna whose descending from heaven they in the beginning boasted so. And therefore he said, "This is the bread that is descended from heaven, not as your fathers did eat manna and are dead. He that eateth this bread shall live forever," as though he would say, "This is another manner of bread, otherwise come from heaven, than manna was that ye boast of so. For that bread was given you but for the sustenance of the life in this world, but this bread that is mine own body, conceived by the Holy Ghost, and in unity of person joined with my Godhead as verily as it is joined with mine own soul, is another manner of heavenly bread, and shall be given you to eat for another manner of purpose. For manna that was given your fathers to eat for the only sustenance of their temporal life was but a figure of this bread thus given you to eat, as I shall begin to give it at my Maundy supper, the manner whereof I will not tell you now. And therefore, as the figure or the shadow

of a thing is far from the property of the thing itself, so was the bread of manna far from the property of this bread that is my flesh. For likewise[389] as because it was a figure of this bread that is very life, it served for the sustenance of life, so because it was but a figure and not the very life itself, it served therefore not to give life, but to sustain life, not forever but for a while. But this bread that is my flesh, which I shall give you as verily to eat as ever your fathers did eat manna, because it is not the figure only of the thing that is life, but is also, by conjunction with the Godhead, the very life itself that was figured, I shall give it you to eat in such a manner that it shall not only maintain, feed, and sustain the body of the eater in this present life, but it shall also give life, yea, and that everlasting life in glory, not only to the soul, but also to the body too, in time meet and convenient,[390] raising it up again from death, and setting it with the soul in eternal life of everlasting bliss."

THE TWENTIETH CHAPTER

This communication with the Jews had our Lord, teaching in the synagogue at Capernaum. "And many therefore of his disciples, hearing these things said, 'This word is hard, and who can hear him?'" The more and more that our Savior plainly told them that he would give them his very flesh to eat, the more and more marvelous hard they thought his saying, and reckoned that it was impossible for any man to believe it. And therefore for lack of belief they lost the profit. And these that thus thought this matter so marvelous hard and strange that they would not believe, but for lack of belief lost the profit, were not only such Jews as were his enemies, but many of those also that were his own disciples.

But our Savior, knowing in himself (as he that was God and needed no man to tell him) that his disciples murmured at his words, because he told them so often and so plainly that men should have no life but if[391] they would be content verily to eat his own flesh, he said unto them, "Doth this offend you? Do you stumble at this? What then if you shall see the Son of Man ascend up whereas[392] he was before? The Spirit is that that quickeneth;[393] the flesh availeth nothing. The words that I have spoken to you be spirit and life."

In these words our Lord shortly toucheth all their objections growing upon their infidelity, and also confuteth[394] their infidelity, and in his words after following, putteth them yet again in mind of the medicine that might remove their unfaithfulness and give them the very fast[395] faith.

The Jews had before murmured against that that[396] he had said—that he was descended from heaven— against which they said, "Is not he the son of Joseph, whose father and mother we know? And how saith he then that he is descended from heaven?"[397] And a great piece of their murmur therein arose, as ye see, upon that point that they had misconceived, ween-ing[398] that Joseph had been his father. For had they believed that his manhood had been conceived by the Holy Ghost, they would have murmured the less. And had they believed that his Godhead had descended into it from heaven, they would not have murmured at all.

In like wise they murmured at the second point, in that he showed them so plainly that he would give them his very flesh to be their very meat, and said, "How can he give us his flesh to eat?" And many of his disciples said also, "This is a hard word, and who may hear him?" And a great part of their murmur was because they thought that they should have eaten his flesh in the self[399] fleshly form, and because (as Saint Augustine saith in sundry trea-tises)[400] that they thought they should have eaten his flesh in dead gobbets, cut out piecemeal as the meat is cut out in the shambles,[401] and also because they knew him not to be God. For had they known that the manner in which he would give them his very flesh to eat should not be in the selfsame fleshly form, but in the pleasant form of bread, though they would yet have marveled, because they would have thought it wonderful, yet would they have murmured the less, because they would not have thought it loathly. But then had they further known that he had been God, then would they not, I suppose, have murmured at the matter at all. For I ween verily that there were neither of those dis-ciples, nor of those Jews neither, anyone so evil as

now be Master Masker, and Frith, and his fellows, that seeing the receiving nothing loathsome, and believing that Christ was God (if they believe it), will not yet believe he can do it, but murmur and grudge[402] against it still.

For though Master Masker say that if Christ said he would do it, then himself would believe he could do it,[403] yet it shall appear ere we part, both that Christ saith it, and he will not believe that Christ, though he say it, meaneth it, and also that the cause why he will not believe that Christ meaneth it is be-cause he believeth that God cannot do it.

But now said our Savior unto them in answer-ing all this gear,[404] "Do you stumble at this? What if ye see the Son of Man ascend up where he was be-fore? What will you then say?" For then could they have no cause to distrust that he descended down, when they should see him ascend up. For that thing seemeth in men's mad eyes, such as they were that would not take him but for a man, far the greater mastery of the both.

Also when they should see him ascend up to heaven whole, then should they well perceive that they mistook him by a false imagination of their own device,[405] when they construed the giving of his flesh to eat as though he meant to give it them in such wise as himself should lose all that they should eat.

And when he said they should see the Son of Man ascend up there as he was before, he gave them again a signification that himself, the Son of Man, was the Son of God also, and thereby himself God also, and into the world come and descended from heaven.

In these words, our Savior showeth that his ascen-sion should be a sufficient cause to make them know his power and leave their murmuring. And therefore they that leave not murmuring at his Blessed Sacra-ment yet[406] show a great token that they believe not his wonderful ascension neither. For if they believed well that he had power of himself to ascend up in body and sit in heaven, one equal God with his Fa-ther and the Holy Ghost, then would they never ween, as they do, that God lacked power to make his own body to be in diverse places at once, and be both in heaven and earth.

393 *that quickeneth:* which gives life   **398** thinking   **399** selfsame   **400** See   **402** complain   **403** See *CW* 11: 309, 317.
394 refutes   **395** steadfast, firm; certain   *In Iohannis evangelium tractatus* 27.2–4,   **404** matter   **405** contrivance   **406** also;
396 *that that:* that which   **397** Jn 6:42   27.5 (*CCSL* 36: 272).   **401** butchers' stalls   moreover

THE TWENTY-FIRST CHAPTER

But now forasmuch as a great part of these folks' diffidence[407] and distrust rose of that—that the respect of the loathsomeness made them the less willing to believe, in that they thought that he meant to give them his flesh to eat in gobbets, cut out dead without life or spirit—our Savior answered them to that point. And though he would not at that time tell them the manner how he would give it them to eat, yet he told them that he would not give it them so. And therefore he said unto them, "The spirit is it that quickeneth or giveth life, the flesh availeth nothing. The words which I have spoken to you be spirit and life."

As though he would say unto them, "I told you before that whoso would eat my flesh should have everlasting life. And therefore why be you so mad as to ween that I mean my flesh cut out in gobbets dead without life or spirit? It is the spirit that giveth life. And therefore without the spirit, the flesh should avail you nought.[408] But being knit with the spirit of my Godhead, which is the substance and very fountain of life, so it shall (to them that worthily eat it) give everlasting life. And therefore the words that I speak be not only flesh, for that will no more give life alone than will faith alone give life that is dead without the will of good works. But my words therefore that I have spoken to you of my flesh to be eaten be not flesh alone, but spirit also and life. Therefore you must understand them not so fleshly as you do, that I would give you my flesh in gobbets dead, but you must understand them spiritually, that you shall eat it in another manner, animated with my soul, and joined with the spirit of my Godhead, by which my flesh is itself made not only lively but also giving life."

Thus meant our Lord in those words, wherein lest Master Masker might make men ween that I run all at riot upon mine own invention, holy Saint Augustine showeth that in these words,

"The spirit it is that quickeneth, the flesh availeth nothing," our Savior meaneth that his flesh dead and without the spirit availeth nothing, as cunning[409] nothing availeth without charity, without which, as Saint Paul saith, it doth but puff up a man in pride.[410] But on the other side, like[411] as cunning much edifieth and profiteth joined with charity, so the flesh of our Savior much availeth joined with his Holy Spirit.[412]

Saint Cyril also upon the same words, declaring them by a long process to the purpose that I have showed you, saith among many other things in this manner, as[413] it were in the person of Christ speaking to those Jews, and to those disciples of his that said his words were so hard that no man could abide to hear him, which they said, as saith Saint Chrysostom, for their own excuse, because themselves were about to walk their way.[414] To them therefore saith our Savior thus in Saint Cyril's exposition:

Ween you when I said that whoso eat my flesh shall have everlasting life, that I meant therein that this earthly body of mine doth give life of its own proper nature? Nay, verily. But I did speak to you of the Spirit and of eternal life. But it is not the nature of the flesh that maketh the Spirit give life, but the power of the Spirit maketh the flesh give life. The words therefore that I have spoken to you be spirit and life: that is to wit,[415] they be spiritual and spoken of the spirit and life: that is to wit, of that spirit that is the natural life that giveth life. But yet the thing that we have already said, it shall do no harm though we repeat it again. The thing that I have said is this. The nature of the flesh cannot of itself give life. For what had then the nature of the Godhead more? But then, on the other side, there is not in Christ only flesh, but he hath the Son of God joined with it which[416] is the equal substance of life with his Father. And therefore, when Christ calleth his flesh a giver of life, that power of giving life he doth not attribute unto his flesh and unto his Holy Spirit both of one fashion. For the Spirit giveth life by itself and of his own nature. But the flesh ascendeth unto that power of giving life by reason of the conjunction and unity that it hath with that Holy Spirit. Howbeit,[417] how and by what means that thing is done, we neither are able with tongue to tell, nor with mind to imagine, but with silence and firm faith we receive it.[418]

---

407 lack of faith **408** nothing **409** intelligence **410** 1 Cor 8:1; 2 Cor 13:1–13 **411** just **412** Augustine, *In* *Iohannis evangelium tractatus* 27.5 (*CCSL* 36: 272). **413** as if **414** See *In Ioannem homiliae* 47(46).2 (*PG* 59: 264). **415** say **416** who **417** However **418** Cyril, *In Iohannis evangelium* 4.3 (*PG* 73: 604)

Thus have you heard, good readers, that the thing that I say, do not only I say, but Saint Augustine also and Saint Cyril both, which is enough to you to perceive that I devise not mine exposition all of mine own head,[419] and may be enough to any good Christian man also to perceive clearly that our Savior in these words did speak, not only of a spiritual eating of his flesh by belief and remembrance of his death and Passion, as Master Masker and Frith and these fond[420] fellows stiffly bear us in hand,[421] but spoke also and meant it of the remembering of his death and Passion, by the very eating of his very blessed body as it is eaten in the Blessed Sacrament.

THE TWENTY-SECOND CHAPTER

But these heretics are so set upon mischief and willfulness that they will not in any wise[422] understand the truth. And how could they understand the truth, when they will not believe? For as the prophet Isaiah saith, but if[423] you believe you shall not understand.[424] And therefore these heretics cannot understand. For they be in the case now that those disciples and those Jews were, with whom our Savior found that fault then, in his words next ensuing, and said, "But there be some of you that believe not," as though he would say, "As plainly as I have told it you and as often, yet are there some of you that believe it not." But he knew from the beginning who should believe, and who also should betray him.

And so knoweth he likewise now too who be good and who be naught,[425] and who shall amend and who shall never amend—not that his foreknowledge forceth them to be naught, but for it is impossible for them to be naught but that his infinite foresight must needs from the beginning foresee it. And yet when he foreseeth that it so shall be, it shall so be in deed, and cannot otherwise be but that it shall so be if he foresee that it shall so be. For he should not foresee that it shall so be, if it so were that in deed it should otherwise be. But likewise as if I see one sit, it must needs be that he sitteth, for else[426] should I not see him sit; and that therefore it well followeth I see him sit, ergo it must needs be that he sitteth. And yet my sight forceth him not to

sit, nor of that argument the consequent proposition of his nature necessary but contingent, though of the one proposition inferred upon the other, the consequency or consecution[427] be necessary. So being presupposed that God foreseeth such a thing which he should not foresee but if[428] the thing should be, yet his foresight no more forceth the person that doth it in the thing that is yet to come than my sight forceth him to sit whom I see sit, of whom no man can say but that he must needs sit in the while in which he will presuppose that I see him sit.

And therefore because his prescience and his providence forced them not to continue in their willfulness to their damnation, he putteth them once again in remembrance of the means whereby they may avoid that willful ignorance and infidelity, and thus he saith unto them, "Therefore I have told you already that no man can come to me but if it be given of my Father."

"Think not," saith Saint Chrysostom upon these words, "that every man to whom the Father giveth it hath it as by way of a special privilege, so that they that have not given them lack it only, therefore, because God will not give it them. God, saith Saint Chrysostom, will gladly give it them, if they would not by their own dealing make themselves unworthy to receive it."[429] And therefore saith Saint Cyril upon the same words that "those that among the Jews lived well and were of good conditions had the faith given them and came to Christ. But they that were stubborn, arrogant, malicious, and willful, as were the scribes and the Pharisees and the stiff-necked bishops, they letted[430] themselves from the gift of faith."[431]

This gift of faith without the help of God cannot be had, nor no man can come to the Son but if[432] the Father draw him. And whom he draweth, and whom he draweth not, and why him, and why not him, let us not seek nor search, as Saint Augustine saith, if we will not err.[433]

But yet that he rejecteth no man that will seek for his soul health, but rather calleth upon to be sought upon, that doth the Scripture well witness, where God said himself, "Lo, I stand at the door knocking; if any man hear my voice and open me the door, I will go in to him and sup with him

419 accord **420** foolish, ignorant
421 *bear us in hand:* assert against us
422 way **423** *but if:* unless **424** See Is
7:9. **425** bad, wicked **426** otherwise

427 *consequency or consecution:* conclusion
of the argument or sequence of reasoning
428 *but if:* unless **429** Chrysostom, *In
Ioannem homiliae* 47(46) (PG 59: 266)

430 hindered **431** Cyril, *In Iohannis
evangelium* 4.3 (PG 73: 608) **432** *but if:*
unless **433** See *In Iohannis evangelium
tractatus* (PL 35: 1619).

and he with me."[434] And the prophet Isaiah saith, "Seek you our Lord while he may be founden. Call you upon him while he is near. Let the wicked man leave his way, and the unrighteous man leave his devices, and let him turn to our Lord, and he will have pity upon him. For he is great in forgiveness."[435] Our Savior saith himself also, "Ask and you shall have. Seek and you shall find. Knock and you shall be let in."[436] And finally that no man should take these words of our Savior—that no man can come to him but if it be given him of the Father, and these words of his also, "No man can come to me but if my Father draw him"[437]—that no man, I say, should so take these words in such a presumptuous way of election[438] that weening he were drawn into such a feeling faith that could never fail and so should, as Tyndale teacheth, make himself so sure of his own salvation by his sure and infallible election that he should stand out of all fear and wax[439] slothful, the Scripture crieth, "Let him that thinketh he standeth beware lest he fall."[440] And, on the other side, that no man should upon these words take that imagination that these heretics also teach of desperate inevitable destiny of damnation, and sit still and do no good himself, weening that his own devoir[441] were in vain, because he feeleth not God anything[442] draw him, holy Saint Augustine, whose words these heretics for election and destiny against the devoir of man's free will most lay for them,[443] biddeth every man for all their babbling, "If thou be not drawn, pray God to draw thee."[444]

And therefore, to that intent did our Savior Christ put them again in mind of that[445] he had said before, that they could not come to him but if[446] it were given them by his Father, because he would that they should[447] for their part labor to remove the lets[448] that, on their own part, letted[449] his Father to give them that gift. And that is that they should have less cure[450] and care of their bellies, the desire of whose fleshly filling with perishable meat made them angry to hear of the spiritual food of his own holy flesh, by the well-eating whereof they might have everlasting life.

He taught them also by those words to perceive (if they would) that Joseph was not his father. For when he said that they could not have that great gift but of his Father, nor could not come to him but if his Father drew them, they might well wit[451] he meant not Joseph, but his Father of heaven. And therefore would he by those words give them warning that they should leave their murmuring, and pray his Father give them the grace to believe him.

THE TWENTY-THIRD CHAPTER

But whereas they should have taken this way and walked forward with him, they took the contrary way, not only the other Jews but many also of his own disciples, and went away backward from him, and as the Gospel saith, walked no more with him.

But though that many of his disciples went away from him, because his Father brought them not unto him, yet as himself said before, "All that my Father giveth me shall come to me,"[452] all went not away. His apostles tarried. And yet among those twelve tarried one false shrew.[453] And in the stead[454] of those disciples that went away, which were, as Saint Augustine saith, about three score[455] and ten, he chose soon after other three score and ten, whom he sent to preach about as he had sent his twelve apostles before.[456]

But then seeing there were at that time so few left and so many gone, he said unto his twelve apostles, "Will you be gone too?"[457] He neither bade them go as though he would be glad of their going, nor yet bade them abide as though he had need of their abiding, but only asked them whether they would go or not, signifying that for all their election they were, in the liberty of their own free will, either to go after the others or to abide still with him. Then answered Simon Peter and said, "Lord, to whom shall we go? Thou hast the words of everlasting life. And we believe and know that thou art Christ, the Son of God"[458]—as though he would say, "If we love life, to whom should we go from thee? For only thou hast the words not of life only but also of life everlasting, for all thy words and thy doctrine draw men thereto. And we believe, and by belief we

434 Rv 3:20　**435** Is 55:6–7　**436** Mt 7:7　**437** Jn 6:44, 46　**438** special choice by God　**439** become　**440** 1 Cor 10:12　**441** best effort　**442** at all, in any way　**443** *lay for them:* cite for their cause

444 *In Iohannis evangelium tractatus* 26.4 (*CCSL* 36: 261–62)　**445** what **446** *but if:* unless　**447** *would . . . should:* wanted them to　**448** hindrances, obstacles　**449** hindered　**450** concern

451 know　**452** Jn 6:37　**453** rascal, villain　**454** place　**455** A score is twenty. See *Enarrationes in Psalmos* 98.6 (*CCSL* 39: 1385).　**456** See Lk 10:1.　**457** Jn 6:67 **458** Jn 6:68

know, that thou art Christ, the very Son of God. And thereby we know that thou art not only very man, but also very God. And we perceive well therefore that thou art the bread that is descended from heaven, and that thou shalt ascend thither again, and that therefore thou art able and of power to give us that marvelous meat of thine own holy flesh to eat. And that thou so wilt do we believe and wot[459] well, because thou so dost promise. And we perceive well that thou wilt not give it us in dead gobbets that could not avail us, but alive and with thine Holy Spirit, the fountain of life, whereby thy flesh shall give us, if we will eat it, everlasting life, when thou shalt resuscitate our bodies in the last day. But in what marvelous manner thou wilt give it us to eat — that hast thou not yet declared us, nor we will not be too boldly curious or inquisitive of thy marvelous mystery, but therein abide[460] the time of thine own determination, as to whose high heavenly wisdom the season meet and convenient[461] is open and known, and unknown to mortal men. And we will therefore obediently receive it and eat it, at what time and in what wise[462] that thy gracious pleasure shall be to command us."

When Saint Peter, as head under Christ of that company, had made this answer, not only for himself but also for them all, not saying "I" but "we," our Lord to let him see that he was somewhat deceived, and had said more than he could make good — for one false shrew was there yet still remaining among the twelve, whereof eleven were not aware — our Savior therefore said, "Have not I chosen you twelve, and of you twelve yet is there one a devil?" This he spoke by[463] Judas Iscariot, the son of Simon, for he it was that should betray him, being one of the twelve.

Our Lord here, good readers, showed himself not deceived. For though Judas's falsehood was unknown to his fellows, yet was it not unknown to his master, which though he showed himself not ignorant of his servant's evil mind, and traitorous purpose toward his own person (toward which purpose, as it seemeth, Judas's heart had at this time conceived some inclination), yet had he patience with him, and continually did use the ways to reform and amend him, never casting him out till he clearly cast

out himself, according to the saying of our Savior, "He that cometh to me I will not cast him out."

THE TWENTY-FOURTH CHAPTER

But here do many men marvel not only that our Savior would keep him so long, knowing him so false, but also that he would take him to him for his apostle in the beginning, foreknowing by his Godhead from the beginning that he would after be false. And diverse holy doctors hold also that he was never true nor good, but naught[464] and false from the beginning. And in this matter whereof God hath not so fully revealed unto men the certainty that we be precisely bounden to the belief of either other part, every man is at liberty to believe whether[465] part that himself thinketh most likely by natural reason and Scripture.

And therefore, though some good holy men and saints have thought that Judas was never good, but that our Savior took him to[466] his apostle and so kept him in all his malice still, for the accomplishment of the great mystery of his Passion, well using thereby the evil of man, as man evil useth the goodness of God, yet thinketh me that, as Theophylactus saith, and Saint Cyril, and Saint Chrysostom too, Judas was once very good when our Lord did chose him for his apostle, and was at that time given unto Christ by his Father.[467] For proof whereof that godly cunning[468] doctor Master Lyra[469] well bringeth in the words of our Savior himself, saying to his Father a little after his Maundy finished, "Them that thou hast given unto me I have kept, and none of them hath perished but the son of perdition,"[470] which he meant by Judas, being then yet alive in body by nature, but dead in soul by deadly sin. Him our Lord took unto him for his apostle while he was good, and not of the common sort of good men but also very special good, as these holy doctors do divine and guess.

And though Christ foresaw the wretchedness that he would after fall to, yet would he not forbear the right order of justice, but take him in such degree for the time as his present goodness of good congruence[471] deserved. For being at that time more

---

459 know **460** await **461** *meet and convenient:* fitting and appropriate **462** *way* **463** about **464** bad, evil **465** which **466** as **467** See Theophylactus,

Enarratio in evangelium Marci 14 (PG 123: 649); Chrysostom, *In Ioannem homiliae* 47 (PG 59: 267–68); Cyril, *In Iohannis evangelium* 4.4 (PG 73: 632). **468** learned

469 Nicholas de Lyra (*ca.* 1270–1340) **470** Jn 17:12 **471** *of good congruence:* as was fitting or reasonable

meet for the office of an apostle than another man, if Christ should have rejected him as unworthy and unmeet for the fault that himself knew he would after do, toward which fault he was at that time nothing minded,[472] then should he have reproached him at such time as he was not worthy to be reproached. And then were it somewhat like as if a man, because he maketh himself very sure that his wife and his children will one time or other not fail to displease him afterward at some one time or other, be angry therefore with them all and chide them and beat them before. Our Savior therefore, when Judas was very good, after such rate[473] of goodness as is in mortal men, took him and promoted him to the office and dignity of his own apostle after that order of justice by which he rewardeth one man above another after the rate of their merits, and yet every man of them all far above all his merits.

Now when he was afterward through covetise waxed naught,[474] yet our Lord kept him still, and would not by taking his office from him disclose his secret falsehood, and put him to shame, but used many other means to mend him, and keep therewith the honesty of his name, not letting[475] to procure his amendment on his part, though he well knew the wretch would never amend upon his part.

But likewise as though a man have an incurable sickness, it yet becometh[476] the physician all the time that he liveth therewith to do his part still toward the curing thereof, so became it our Savior to do it as he did, and not to leave off or slake[477] his goodness toward the cure and amendment of the man's incurable malice.

For though Judas was, with all that goodness of Christ used unto him, not only nothing the better, but also very far the worse, and fell far the deeper into death and damnation, yet since there came of his traitorous dealing none harm but unto Christ, whose goodness was for our weal[478] very glad to suffer it, and unto the traitor himself and such others as willfully would deserve it, it had been neither right nor reason[479] that for to save them from hell that needs would walk into it, he should have left any of his goodness and sufferance undone, whereby he procured the salvation of so many thousands as should be saved by his bitter Passion.

And much more reason it was that our Savior should have respect and regard to procure the bliss of those that should be saved than to care for the pain of those that should be damned. For it had been, as it seemeth, not consonant unto right, if our Lord should for avoiding of their pain, that[480] for all his calling back to the contrary would yet willingly run forth into damnation, have kept away the reward of bliss from them that would with his help deserve it.

And therefore our Lord, as I say, took Judas and made him his apostle, being very good, and after had long patience with him while he was very naught, till that through his immedicable[481] malice he fell of[482] himself, and so was cast out and perished. But by his perishing our Savior lost not but won. For of his evil came there much more good, and his own place of apostleship was afterward fulfilled with Saint Matthias.[483]

And in like wise, the other disciples that departed now—which were (as Saint Chrysostom saith and as the Gospel seemeth also to say)[484] all that then were present, save[485] only his twelve apostles, and were, as Saint Augustine saith, in number above three score and ten—all they lost themselves when they willingly lost their Savior. And he found better to succeed in their places. For soon after, in the stead of those three score and ten, he chose other three score and ten disciples, as I before showed you, whom he sent about to preach as he had sent his twelve apostles before.

And unto Judas yet at this present time he gave a secret warning[486] that he might well wit[487] that his naughtiness was known, which thing might make him the less bold to sin; and yet he disclosed him not openly, because he would not shame him, and thereby make him haply[488] shameless, as many such wretches wax, and after that, sin the more boldly.

THE TWENTY-FIFTH CHAPTER

This word also so spoken to all twelve was (as Saint Chrysostom saith and Saint Cyril both) a marvelous goodly warning for them all. These are, lo, the words of Saint Cyril:

---

472 *nothing minded:* not at all disposed
473 *after such rate:* according to such degree or extent   474 *waxed naught:* become wicked   475 hesitating   476 is
proper for   477 slacken   478 well-being
479 reasonable   480 who   481 irremediable   482 out of, due to   483 See Acts 1:23–26.   484 See *In Ioannem homiliae*
47.3 (*PG* 59: 266).   485 except   486 See Lk 22:21; Jn 6:71–72.   487 know
488 perhaps

Our Lord here with sharp words confirmeth his apostles and maketh them the more diligent, by putting before their eyes the peril of their ruin. For this he seemeth to say unto them: "O my disciples, much need have you to use much watch and great study[489] about your salvation. The way of perdition is very slipper, and not only withdraweth a feeble mind from thinking of their fall by making them to forget themselves, but also sometimes deceiveth them by vain delectation and pleasure that are of mind very firm and strong. And that this tale is true that I now tell you, you may see well proved, not by the example only of them that are gone aback, but among yourselves also that tarry and dwell still with me. For I have, you wot[490] well, chosen you twelve as good, well knowing that indeed you were so. For I was not ignorant, but being God (as I am) very well knew your hearts. Howbeit,[491] the devil hath deceived one of you with avarice, and so pulled him away. For a man is a free creature, and may choose his way as he will, either on the right hand or else on the left if he will."

Our Lord therefore maketh them all the more vigilant, because that[492] who should betray him he doth not express by name. But telling them all in a generalty[493] that one of them should work such wickedness, he made them all stand in fear. And by that horror and dread, lifted them up to more vigilant diligence.[494]

Here have you heard, good readers, the words of Saint Cyril. Now shall ye somewhat hear what saith Saint Chrysostom:

When Saint Peter said, "We believe," our Savior, not causeless, out of the number of them excepted Judas and said, "Have not I chosen you twelve and one of you is a devil." This thing he said to remove the traitor far from his malice. And where he saw that nothing did avail him, yet he went about still to do well for him, and see the wisdom of Christ, for neither would he bewray[495] him, nor let him lurk untouched—the one, lest he should have waxed[496] shameless and swear nay;

the other, lest weening[497] that none were aware, he should be the bolder in mischief.

And afterward, this in effect he saith:

It is not the custom of God by force to make men good whether they will or no, nor in his election he chooseth not folks by violence, but by good advice and motion.[498] And that ye may well perceive that his calling is no constraint of necessity, many whom he calleth do willingly for all his calling perish. And therefore it is evident that in our own will is the power set to choose whether we will be saved or lost. By these admonitions, therefore, let us labor to be sober and vigilant. For if Judas, which was one of the number of that holy company of the apostles, he that had obtained so great a gift, he that had done miracles (for Judas himself was sent, among others, to cure the lepers, and raise up dead men to life), after that he was once fallen into the grievous disease of avarice, neither the benefits, nor the gifts, nor the company of Christ, nor the service, nor the washing of the feet, nor the fellowship of his own board,[499] nor the trust in keeping of the purse anything[500] availed him, but all these things were with him a passage and a way to his punishment.[501]

Lo, good readers, here have ye heard both by Saint Cyril and Saint Chrysostom that our Savior gave that secret warning of Judas's falsehood, and said that one of the twelve was a devil, to the intent that all folk, of what holiness so ever they were, should stand ever in dread and fear, and not do as these heretics teach—upon boldness of any feeling faith or final election, presume themselves so sure of salvation—but that while Judas fell after to naught[502] that was once a holy apostle, there shall no feeling faith nor proud hope upon final election set any man in his own heart so sure, but that with his good hope he shall always couple some fear as a bridle and a bit to refrain and pull him back, lest he fall to mischief, and follow Judas in falsehood, and wax a devil, as Christ called him, which name our Savior gave him not without good cause. For that

---

489 *watch and great study:* vigilance and great effort   **490** know
491 However   **492** the one   **493** *in a generalty:* in general   **494** Cyril, *In*

Iohannis evangelium 4.4 (PG 73: 629–32)
495 expose, reveal   **496** become
497 thinking, supposing   **498** prompting
499 table   **500** at all   **501** Chrysostom,

In Ioannem homiliae 47(46) (PG 59: 267–68)   **502** wickedness

devil's servant, saith Saint Cyril, is a devil too. For likewise as he that is by godly virtues joined unto God is one spirit with God, so he that is with devilish vices joined with the devil is one spirit with him.[503]

And therefore, good readers, he that in such plight receiveth the Blessed Sacrament without purpose of amendment, or without the faith and belief that the very flesh and blood of Christ is in it, he receiveth, as Saint Augustine saith, notwithstanding his naughtiness, the very flesh and blood of Christ, the very price of our redemption. But he receiveth them to his harm, as Judas did, and eateth and drinketh his own judgment and damnation, as saith Saint Paul,[504] because he discerneth not our Lord's body. But whoso doth on the other side (which, I beseech God, we may all do) cast out the devil and his works by the sacrament of penance, and then in the memorial and remembrance of Christ's Passion receive that Blessed Sacrament with true faith and devotion, with all honor and worship, as to the reverence of Christ's blessed person present in it appertaineth — they that so receive the Blessed Sacrament, verily receive and eat the blessed body of Christ, and that not only sacramentally, but also effectually, not only the figure, but the thing also, not only his blessed flesh into their bodies, but also his Holy Spirit into their souls, by participation whereof he is incorporate in them and they in him and be made lively members of his mystical body, the congregation of all saints, of which their souls shall, if they persevere, attain the fruit and fruition clean and pure once purged after this transitory life, and their flesh also shall Christ resuscitate unto the same glory, as himself hath promised, of which his gracious promise, his high grace and goodness vouchsafe to make us all partners through the merits of his bitter Passion. Amen.

And thus end I, good readers, my first book, containing the exposition of those words in the sixth chapter of Saint John, whereby you may both perceive by the minds of holy saints, whose words I bring forth, the truth of our faith concerning the blessed body and blood of Christ verily eaten in the Blessed Sacrament, and may also perceive and control[505] the wily false foolish exposition of Master Masker to the contrary, such as have his book, and they be not a few. And yet that all men may see that I neither blame him for nought[506] nor belie him, I shall in my second book show you, as I promised, some part of his faults both in falsehood and in folly, and his own words therewith.

Here endeth the First Book.

---

503 Cyril, *In Iohannis evangelium* 4.4 (*PG* 73: 632)　**504** See 1 Cor 11:29.　**505** check on　**506** nothing

THE SECOND BOOK

THE FIRST CHAPTER

I have, good readers, in my first book herebefore perused you[1] the exposition of all that part of the sixth chapter of Saint John, which Master Masker hath expounded you before. And in the beginning of this exposition, I have not brought you forth the words of any of the old expositors because that (as I suppose) mine adversaries will not much contend with me for so far. But afterward, concerning those words in which our Savior expressly speaketh of the giving of his very[2] flesh and blood to be verily eaten and drunken, there have I brought you forth such authorities of old holy doctors[3] and saints that ye may well see both that I feign you not the matter but expound it you right, and also ye see thereby clearly that Master Masker expoundeth it wrong. For though a man may diversely expound one text and both well, yet when one expoundeth it in one true manner of[4] a false purpose to exclude another truth that is in that writing by the Spirit of God first and immediately meant, his exposition is false although[5] every word were true, as Master Masker's is not.

And therefore, since you see mine exposition proved you by excellent holy men, and by their plain words ye perceive that the words of our Savior himself do prove against all these heretics the Catholic faith of Christ's Catholic Church very faithful and true, concerning the very flesh of Christ verily eaten in the Blessed Sacrament, of which eating Master Masker would with his exposition make men so mad as to ween[6] that Christ spoke nothing at all, now I say by this exposition of mine ye see his exposition avoided[7] clearly for nought,[8] and all the matter clear upon our part, though no man wrote one word more.

And yet will I for all that, for the further declaration of Master Masker's handling, show you some pieces of his exposition in special,[9] by which ye may clearly see what credence may be given to the man, either for honesty, or learning, virtue, wit, or troth.[10]

THE SECOND CHAPTER

In the beginning of the second leaf[11] of his book, these are Master Masker's words:

> Consider what this meat[12] is which he bade them here prepare and seek for, saying, "Work, take pains, and seek for that meat," etc. and thou shalt see it no other meat than the belief in Christ. Wherefore he concludeth that this meat so often mentioned is faith, of the which meat, saith the prophet, the just liveth.[13] Faith in him is therefore the meat which Christ prepareth and dresseth, so purely powdering and spicing it with spiritual allegories in all this chapter following, to give us everlasting life through it.[14]

I will not lay these words to his charge as heresy, but I will be bold by his license to note in them a little lack of wit,[15] and some good store of folly. For though a man may well and with good reason call faith a meat of man's soul, yet is it great folly to say that the meat that Christ speaketh of here is, as Master Masker saith it is, none other meat but faith.

For Master Masker may plainly see, and is not, I suppose, so purblind,[16] but that he seeth well indeed that the meat which Christ speaketh of here is our Savior Christ himself, which thing he so plainly speaketh that no man can miss to perceive it when he saith, "I am myself the bread of life;" and when he saith, "I am the lively bread that am descended from heaven; he that eateth of this bread shall live forever;" and when he saith also, that the meat should be his own flesh, which promise he performed after at his Maundy, which thing he told them plain in these words, "And the bread which I shall give you is my flesh. And he that eateth my flesh and drinketh my blood hath everlasting life, and I shall resuscitate him in the last day;" and when he said, "My flesh is verily[17] meat."

Thus you see, good readers, how oft and how plainly that he declareth that the meat which he speaketh of here is himself. And now saith Master

---

1 *perused you:* expounded for you   **2** true   **3** theologians   **4** for   **5** even if   **6** think, believe   **7** refuted, invalidated   **8** nothing   **9** particular   **10** truthfulness; integrity   **11** page   **12** food   **13** See Hab 2:4.   **14** *CW* 11: 305   **15** intellect   **16** completely blind; dim-witted   **17** truly

Masker very solemnly, and with authority biddeth every man mark it well and consider it, that the meat that Christ speaketh of here is nothing else but belief.

5 And upon what color[18] saith Master Masker so? Because (saith he) that our Lord bade them labor and work for the meat that would not perish, but abide into everlasting life, and afterward told them that the work of God, by which they should work 10 and labor for that meat, was nothing else but faith and belief in him.

First, in this construction Master Masker lieth very large. For though Christ said that to believe in him was the work of God, he said not, as Master 15 Masker maketh it, that nothing else was the work of God but only belief.

But now suppose that Christ had said as Master Masker would make it seem: that is to wit,[19] that the work of God were nothing else but the belief; yet ye 20 see well, good readers, that Christ, in saying that the belief in him is the work by which they shall work to get the meat, saith that the belief is the means to get the meat, and not that the belief is the meat. But Master Masker, because the belief is the way 25 to this meat, therefore he calleth the belief the meat, as wisely as though he would call the King's Street Westminster Church, because it is the way thitherward if he come from Charing Cross. And because men must spiritually eat this meat with faith, there-30 fore he calleth the faith the meat as wisely as if he would, because he eateth his meat with his mouth, therefore call his mouth his meat. What wit hath this man?

But now will Master Masker wax[20] angry with my 35 words, and call me Master Mock as he doth once or twice in his book.[21]

But now, good readers, I will not adjure you by God's holy names to judge justly, but even only desire you that, in way of good company, that you will 40 say but even indifferently.[22] Were it not, ween[23] you, great pity that a man should mock Master Masker, when every fool may perceive him in so great a matter write so wisely?

And yet you may see that I deal with him very 45 gently. For in this point wherein by contrarying of

Christ's own words he writeth plain heresy, I diminish his burden of that odious crime, and because the matter in this place so serveth me, do cover the botch[24] of his cankered[25] heresy, with this pretty plaster of his pleasant frenzy. 50

And yet I ween the man hath so little honesty that he will never can me thank[26] for my courtesy, specially because that (as far as I can see) the man had liefer[27] confess himself a heretic than be proved a fool. And that appeareth well in this. For this little 55 scab of his folly he laboreth somewhat to hide and cover, so that a man must pull off the clout ere[28] he can spy the botch. But as for the botch of his cankered heresies, without any clout or plaster he layeth out abroad to show, to beg withal,[29] among the 60 blessed brethren, as beggars lay their sore legs out in sight that lie a-begging a Fridays about Saint Savior and at the Savegate.[30]

But as for railing against images, purgatory, and praying to saints, and against the holy Canon of 65 the Mass, all this he taketh for trifles, and would we should[31] reckon all these heresies of his for points well and sufficiently proved by that that[32] he goeth so boldly forth on beyond them, and denieth the blessed body of Christ itself in the Blessed Sacra- 70 ment too. And whereas he not only mocketh and jesteth against the old holy doctors and saints of Christ's Catholic Church, but against our Savior himself in his Holy Sacrament too, yet the sage sad[33] earnest holy man, all made of gravity, sadness, 75 and severity, must himself be reverently reasoned with, and may have no mock of his matched with no merry word of mine in no manner wise.[34]

But yet like as if a right great man would wantonly walk a-mumming,[35] and disguise himself, and 80 with nice apparel dissemble his personage, and with a fond[36] visor hide and cover his visage, he must be content to be taunted of[37] every good fellow that he meeteth, as merrily as himself list[38] to jest with them, so till Master Masker here put off his Mask- 85 er's visor, and show forth his own venerable visage, that I may see him such an honorable personage as it may become him to say to me what he list, and me to requite his mocks with no merry word in this world, but stand still demurely and make him 90

18 pretext   **19** say   **20** become   **21** See *CW* 11: 339.   **22** impartially   **23** think **24** boil, ulcer   **25** festering; malignant; corrupt   **26** *can me thank:* thank me

27 rather   **28** *clout ere:* bandage before **29** with   **30** Savior's Gate at St. Savior's Monastery in Southwark   **31** *would we should:* wants us to   **32** *that that:* that

which   **33** serious   **34** *manner wise:* kind of way   **35** *wantonly walk a-mumming:* frivolously play-act   **36** silly   **37** by **38** wishes; pleases

low courtesy again, I will not let[39] in the meantime, while I wot nere[40] what he is, and while his witless writing maketh men ween he were a wild goose, to be so bold and homely[41] with his mastership (as sorry as I am for him when he playeth the blasphemous beast) to laugh yet and make merry with him where I see him play the fool.

Yet will I now let pass his repugnance,[42] another folly of his. For if ever he defend his folly that I have showed you, then shall he be fain[43] to declare his repugnance himself. And therefore I leave that point for himself, that in defending his folly he may show his repugnance, and so for defense of a single folly prove himself thrice a fool: first in writing folly, secondly in writing repugnance, thirdly to be so foolish as, in defense of that one folly, to bring in the other two.

Making therefore for this time no longer tale of his follies, which would make mine answer overlong to bring them in all, let us see some piece of his fruitful exposition.

THE THIRD CHAPTER

In the second leaf these are his words:

"I am the bread of life, and whoso come to me" (that is to say, whoso is grafted and joined to me by faith) "shall never hunger," (that is, whoso believe in me is satisfied). It is faith therefore that stauncheth his hunger and thirst of the soul. Faith it is therefore in Christ that filleth our hungry hearts, so that we can desire none other if we once thus eat and drink him by faith: that is to say, if we believe his flesh and body to have been broken and his blood shed for our sins, for then are our souls satisfied and we be justified.[44]

The word of Christ, good reader, with which he beginneth, is well and fully fulfilled, if it be understood as I have before declared: that is to wit, that whoso come once by well-working faith, and perseverance therein, unto the meat that is Christ, and attain the possession and fruition of him in bliss, he shall never hunger nor thirst after. And besides this, diverse good holy doctors expound these words of the eating of our Savior in the Blessed Sacrament also.

But surely I believe that it will be very hard for Master Masker to verify the words of his holy exposition, yea, scant[45] of some such piece thereof as seemeth at the first sight well said, as[46] where he saith that faith so filleth our hungry hearts, and so stauncheth[47] the hunger and thirst of our soul, that we be satisfied.

For I suppose that men are not satisfied here, neither with faith alone, nor with faith and hope and charity too, but yet they hunger and thirst still. For as our Savior saith, "He that drinketh me shall yet thirst still, and long sore[48] as he drinketh him in grace, so to drink him in glory."[49]

But then tempereth Master Masker his words of never thirsting with that that[50] he saith: that if we eat and drink God by faith, we shall never hunger nor thirst; but we be satisfied, for the faith so filleth our hungry hearts that we can desire none other thing if we once thus eat him and drink him by faith. And then what it is to eat him and drink him by faith he forthwith[51] declareth as for the whole sum and exposition of faith, and saith: "That is to say, if we believe his flesh and his body to have been broken and his blood shed for our sins, for then are our souls satisfied, and we be justified."

Lo, here you see, good readers, that he saith that whoso believeth this here is all that needeth. For he that thus believeth is justified, and eateth and drinketh Christ, and so his soul satisfied, because he that so eateth him once can never after hunger nor thirst. And why? For he can desire none other thing.

First I ween[52] that all men are not agreed that he that longeth for none other thing is not athirst if he long still for more of the same. For if a man drink a pint of ale, though he found himself so well content therewith that he do not desire neither beer, wine, nor water, yet if his appetite be not so fully satisfied, but that he would fain[53] of the same ale drink a quart more, some man would say he were a dry soul and were athirst again.

But now if this man meant any good in this matter, and would say that whoso so eateth God, as he hath him well incorporated in him shall so have his hunger and his thirst slaked[54] that he shall not hunger and thirst after the pleasure of his body, nor after

39 hesitate   **40** *wot nere:* know not
41 blunt   **42** inconsistency   **43** obliged, forced   **44** *CW* 11: 306   **45** scarce, bare

46 such as   **47** quenches   **48** greatly; intensely   **49** Ecclus 24:29   **50** *that that:* that which   **51** immediately   **52** think

53 gladly, willingly   **54** diminished; satisfied

the goods and riches nor after the pomp and pride of this wretched world, I would have suffered[55] him go forth with his exposition, and not have interrupted it. And yet it could not (ye wot[56] well) have well and
5 fully served for the text, since the text is "he shall never hunger nor thirst," which signifieth a taking away of desire and longing. And by this exposition, though there be taken away the desire and longing for other things, yet remaineth there a desire and
10 longing for more and more of the same.

But yet I would, as I say, have let it pass by and wink thereat, if he meant none harm therein. But now cometh he after and declareth by example what he meaneth by this his saying, that he that eateth
15 and drinketh God by believing that he died for our sins shall thirst and hunger for none other. For he saith, "He shall desire none other; he shall not seek by night to love another before whom he would lay his grief; he shall not run wandering here and there
20 to seek dead stocks and stones."[57]

Lo, good readers, here is the end of all this holy man's purpose, for which he draweth the words of Christ from the very[58] thing that Christ principally spoke of unto another spiritual understanding, in
25 turning the meat that Christ spoke of—that is to wit, the meat of his own blessed person, his God-head and his manhood both—into the meat of faith, to the intent that under the pretext of prais-ing the true faith, he might bring in slyly his very
30 false wretched heresies, by which he would have no prayer made unto saints, nor their pilgrimages sought, nor honor done them at their images.

It is evident and plain that our Savior meant in this place to speak unto the Jews neither against im-
35 ages nor saints, but rather against the sensual appe-tite that they had to the filling of their bellies with bodily meat, the inordinate desire whereof made them the less apt and meet[59] for spiritual food. And therefore he bade them that they should less care
40 for that perishable meat, and labor and work to win faith by prayer, and by faith to come to him. And because they so much hated and feared hunger and thirst, he would give them himself for their meat his very flesh and blood, verily here to eat, not dead
45 but quick,[60] with soul and Godhead therewith in this world, which if they would well eat here with a well-working faith, he would give them the same, so

in another world that then should they never have thirst nor hunger after.

And he meant not that they should never, when 50 they had once received him, thirst nor hunger after in this present world, in which—besides that they must both hunger and thirst, or else be ever eating and drinking to prevent their hunger and thirst— besides this, I say, they shall hunger and thirst still 55 after God, if they be good.

Now if men will say that the pain of that hunger and thirst is taken away with hope, which greatly gladdeth the heart, surely they that neither hun-ger nor thirst for heaven, nor care how long they be 60 thence so that they may make merry here the while, and yet have a hope that they shall have heaven too when they go hence, they feel in their faint hope neither great pleasure nor pain. But he that hopeth well of heaven, and not only hopeth after it, but 65 also sore thirsteth for it, as did Saint Paul when he said, "I long to be dissolved" (that is, to have my soul loosed and departed from my body) "and to be with Christ,"[61] such a man, lo, as he findeth pleasure in his hope, so findeth he pain in the delay of his hope. 70 For as Solomon saith, "The hope that is deferred and delayed, paineth and afflicteth the soul."[62] But when men shall, with well eating of this meat of Christ's blessed person, make them meet to eat it, and shall eat it by very fruition in heaven, then although they 75 shall never be fastidious or weary thereof, but as they shall ever have it so shall ever desire it (so that of that state may be said also, "He that drinketh me shall yet thirst"), yet because they shall not only al-ways desire it, but also always have it, and so by the 80 continual everlasting having thereof their everlast-ing desire everlastingly fulfilled, their desire shall ever be without any grief and pain and ever full of everlasting pleasure, so that of that state only the prophet David saith, "I shall be satiated, or satisfied, 85 when thy glory shall appear."[63]

And this meant here our Savior Christ, and not that a man shall by his faith be fully satisfied in this wretched world, and never hunger nor thirst after here, as Master Masker maketh here by his exposi- 90 tion, in turning the saturity[64] of heaven into a satu-rity in this life, and turning the very meat of Christ's blessed person into the only[65] belief of Christ's bit-ter Passion, and then bringeth all in conclusion to

55 allowed **56** know **57** *CW* 11: 306   **62** Prv 13:12 **63** Ps 16(17):15 **64** satis-
58 true **59** fit **60** living **61** Phil 1:23   faction **65** *the only:* only the

the advancing of his heresy against the blessed saints, as though Christ in those words had meant to speak against the honoring of his saints, wherewith he was so well content that he promised Saint Mary Magdalene a perpetual honor in earth, for her devotion toward him in bestowing her costly glass of ointment upon him,[66] and promised his twelve apostles the honor of twelve seats, to sit with him in judgment upon the world, for the dishonor and penury that they should sustain for him before in the world.[67]

THE FOURTH CHAPTER

And see now, good reader, also how much pestilent poison Master Masker hath in this piece of his exposition put here, by this one syllable, "once."[68]

For it is not enough to him to say that whoso eat Christ by faith shall never hunger (which words he might expound by perseverance and abiding still with him after his once coming to him, as Christ meaneth by his), but he saith, whoso come to him by faith once, he shall never hunger nor thirst. And yet this word "once" is not there in the text of Christ's words, but added by Master Masker in his gloss.

And yet if Master Masker were a good Catholic man, I would not much mark his word "once." But since he showeth himself well that he is of Master Tyndale's sect, or is peradventure[69] Master Tyndale himself, one of whose false heresies is that whoso have once the faith can never after fall therefrom, nor never fall after into deadly sin, therefore I cannot let Master Masker's "once" this once pass unmarked by me, by which he saith that whoso come once to Christ by faith—that is to say, saith he, whoso believe once that Christ suffered his Passion for our sins—he shall never hunger nor thirst, but that is, he saith, to be understood that he shall never after desire none other.

But now would I wit[70] of Master Masker once again, what he meaneth by this word "none other." If he mean that no man that once believeth that Christ suffered Passion for us shall after at any time desire any other savior, besides that he saith one

false heresy in that word "once" (for that[71] faith may be once had and afterward lost again, as testify not only all holy doctors and the Catholic faith, but the plain Scripture too),[72] he hath in those words, I say, besides that false heresy, a very false wily folly. For the Catholic Church of Christendom, which he toucheth in[73] praying to saints and going in pilgrimages, do seek no saint as their savior, but only as them whom their Savior loveth, and whose intercession and prayer for them he will be content to hear, and whom for his sake he would they should[74] honor, and whom, while for his sake they do honor, the honor that is done them for his sake specially redoundeth[75] to himself; as himself saith, he that heareth them, heareth him, and he that despiseth them, despiseth him, and in like wise, he that worshipeth them for his sake, worshipeth him.[76]

Now if Master Masker will say that by these words, "Whoso once believeth that Christ died for us shall never after desire none other," he meaneth that he shall so mind and desire ever after only Christ that he shall not hunger nor thirst nor desire after that any other thing but God. Then since Master Masker in this book of his asketh me so many questions, and saith so often, "I ask Master More this," Master Masker must of reason give Master More leave to ask Master Masker some questions again.[77]

Now might I ask him, ye see well, whether he that hath had once that belief should never after in such wise[78] be ahungered that he should desire his dinner. But then would Master Masker call me Master Mock, and say that it were but a scoffing question. And yet out of all question, that same scoffing question would quite overthrow his earnest exposition. But now because I will not anger him, I will let that scoffing question go, and I will ask him now another manner[79] thing, a thing of that weight and gravity that it weigheth some souls down unto the deep pit of hell. For if Master Masker be Master Tyndale, then will I ask him whether he, being a priest, desired none other thing but only God, when since that he said he had once that belief, he hath, being a priest, broken his promise made once to God and gone ofter than once a-wooing.

And if Master Masker be Master George Joye, then would I ask him whether that after that belief

---

66 See Mt 26:12–13; Mk 14:8–9. **67** See Mt 19:28. **68** *CW* 11: 306 **69** perhaps **70** know **71** *for that:* because **72** See Heb 6:4–6; Rom 11:20–21; 1 Cor 10:12. **73** concerning **74** *would they should:* wants them to **75** returns **76** Lk 10:16 **77** in return **78** a way **79** kind of

once had, he desired nothing but God, when being a priest he broke his promise to God, and wedded a widow, and by such wedding never made her wife, but made her a priest's harlot.

If Master Masker be neither of these twain,[80] yet since whatsoever he be he is a disciple of Luther and Friar Hussgen both (as contrarious as they be both each of them to other), I shall ask him then whether both his masters, being both professed friars, and having both vowed perpetual chastity to God, did after that faith once had, never after desire any other thing but only God, not then when they broke both their solemn vows made unto God, and ran out of religion and wedded, the one a single woman, the other a nun, and made them friars' harlots both? Did not then Friar Luther and Friar Hussgen both, contrary to Master Masker's words, desire another, and each of them go seek by night to love another, before whom he would lay his grief? What answer shall Master Masker make Master More to this? He must either confess, against his own exposition, that after that belief had once, his own masters, the arch-heretics themselves, thirsted in the desire of some other thing besides God, or else must he fall to blasphemy and call a friar's harlot God, or say that for God's sake they wedded, and then for his sake they wedded against his will, or else affirm finally that the masters of his faith had never the faith yet — not the selfsame faith that they teach. And why should any man then be so mad to give ear to such heretics, and believe their faithless tales?

THE FIFTH CHAPTER

Now handling his exposition and his doctrine of faith not only thus falsely but also thus foolishly too, as ye do now perceive, yet as though he had wonderful wisely declared some high heavenly mysteries that never man had heard of before, in the fourth leaf he boasteth his great cunning[81] in comparison of mine and saith:

Had Master More have understood this short sentence, "Whoso believe in me hath life everlasting," and known what Paul with the other apostles preached — especially Paul, being a year and a half among the Corinthians,[82] determining not, neither presuming not, to have known any other thing to be preached them (as himself saith) than Jesus Christ, and that he was crucified[83] — had Master More understood this point, he should never thus have blasphemed Christ and his sufficient Scriptures, neither have so belied his evangelists and holy apostles as to say they wrote not all things necessary for our salvation, but left out things of necessity to be believed, making God's holy Testament insufficient and imperfect, first revealed unto our fathers, written eftsoons[84] by Moses and then by his prophets, and at the last written both by his holy evangelists and apostles too. But turn we to John again, and let More mock still and lie too.[85]

Had Master Masker understood the selfsame short sentence of Christ that he speaketh of, and had Master Masker well understood also the other short sentence of Saint Paul that he now toucheth, and after those two texts well understood, had looked upon his own book again, he would rather have eaten his own book, but if[86] he be shameless, than ever have let any man see his false folly for shame.

For first, as for the first text touching the bread and the belief, his false and foolish handling ye perceive more than plain, in that he saith it is nothing but faith, where Christ saith it is himself.

Now the place that he toucheth of Saint Paul in his First Epistle to the Corinthians, I marvel me much to see the madness of this Masker, that bringeth it forth for his purpose here. For as you see, he meaneth to make men ween[87] that by that place it were proved, against my *Confutation*, that the apostles left no necessary thing unwritten.[88]

Now of any other apostle, ye see well, he bringeth not one word for that purpose of his, nor of Saint Paul neither, but this one place, which place, since he bringeth forth for the proof of their heresy that there is nothing necessarily to be believed but if[89] it may be proved by plain and evident Scripture, it appeareth plain that Master Masker there mistaketh Saint Paul, and weeneth that he preached nothing to them of Christ but only his Passion. For else he might, notwithstanding the words of that place, preach to them diverse things of Christ by mouth, and leave it with them by tradition, without writing too, which neither himself nor none of his fellows never wrote any time after. And of truth, so he did, as I have proved at length in my work of Tyndale's *Confutation*, of which things one is, among diverse others, the putting of the water with the wine in the chalice, which thing Christ did at his Maundy when he did institute the Blessed Sacrament, and after he taught the order thereof to Saint Paul himself by his own holy mouth, and Saint Paul so taught it again to the Corinthians by mouth, and left it them first by tradition without any writing at all. And when he wrote unto them afterward thereof, he wrote it rather, as it well appeareth, upon a certain occasion to put them in remembrance of their duty in doing due reverence to it, because it is the very blessed body of God, than in that place to teach them the matter and the form of consecrating the Sacrament. For he had taught them that much more fully before by mouth than he doth there by that writing. For as ye wot[90] well, though he tell them there what it is when they drink it — that is to wit, the blood of our Lord — yet he telleth them not there whereof they shall consecrate it. For he neither nameth wine nor water. And yet saith in the end that, at his coming to them again, he will set an order in all other things.[91] And where will Master Masker show me all those things written, and prove it to be all those?

But here you see how madly Master Masker understandeth that place of Saint Paul, when he taketh it in that wise[92] that he would thereby prove us that we were bounden to believe no more but that Christ died for us.

And of truth you see that speaking of faith before, this is his very conclusion, in which when I read it and confuted it here now before, yet marked I not therein so much as I do now. For though he said there, "If we once eat him and drink him by faith — that is to say, if we believe his flesh and body to have been broken, and his blood shed for our sins — then are our souls satisfied and we be justified," I marked not, as I say, that he meant so madly as all men may now see he meaneth, that is to wit, that men be bounden to believe nothing else but that Christ was crucified and died for our sins. Master Masker maketh us a pretty short creed now.

But that he thus meaneth indeed he now declareth plainly, when he would prove against me that no necessary thing was left unwritten, by those words of Saint Paul by which he writeth to the Corinthians that he preached nothing among them but Jesus Christ and that he was crucified.

And as Master Masker misunderstandeth those words of Saint Paul so I perceive that long before Master Masker was born, there were some such other fools that mistook those words after the same fond[93] fashion then, and therefore affirmed that adultery was no deadly sin, as these foolish folk affirm now that it is no deadly sin for a friar to wed a nun. And their argument was that if adultery had been deadly sin, Saint Paul would have preached that point unto the Corinthians. But he preached, as himself saith in his epistle, nothing unto them but Christ and him crucified, and thereupon they concluded that adultery was no deadly sin.

But Saint Augustine answereth those fools, and this fool too, that he preached not only Christ's crucifixion. For then had he left his resurrection unpreached, and his ascension too, which both we be bounden as well to believe as his crucifixion, and many other things more besides. And therefore, as Saint Augustine saith, to preach Christ is to preach both everything that we must be bound to believe, and also everything that we must be bounden to do to come to Christ — and not, as those fools and this fool teacheth, that we be justified if we believe no more but only that Christ was crucified and died for our sins.[94]

And when Master Masker saith that by affirming any necessary point to be left unwritten in the Scripture I make God's holy Testament insufficient and unperfect, for all that it was first revealed unto our fathers, and eft[95] written by Moses, and then by his prophets, and at last written both by his holy evangelists and apostles too, to this I say that God's Testament is not insufficient nor imperfect, though some necessary things be left out of the writing. For I say that his Testament is not the writing only, but all the whole thing revealed by God unto his Church, and resting and remaining therein, part in writing and part without writing still, as it was altogether first without writing given. And see now, good readers, the wit[96] of Master Masker in this word of his. For

90 know   **91** See 1 Cor 11:23–34.   Augustine, *De fide et operibus* (PL 40:   **96** intellect
92 way   **93** foolish, silly   **94** See   197, 202–3, 206–7).   **95** afterwards

if I make the Testament of God unperfect and in-sufficient, because I say that some necessary points thereof be not yet written, doth not he, good read-ers, say and affirm thereby that it was altogether
5　unperfect and unsufficient all the while that God taught it himself by his own revelation of Spirit, and that our Savior taught it himself by his own blessed mouth, till Moses and the prophets and the apostles wrote it with the pen?

10　　　And whensoever that Master Masker is able to prove that all these things which we be bounden to believe more than that Christ died for our sins are so fully written by Christ's apostles that they left none of them all unwritten—when he shall
15　have proved this, let him then come hardly[97] and bid Master More mock on and lie on too. But now while he saith so, so far out of season, while my work of Tyndale's *Confutation* hath proved my part so plainly that neither himself nor all the heretics
20　of them all shall well avoid[98] it while they live, now may Master More be bold to bid Master Masker go mock on and lie on too.

　　　And this may I now say to Master Masker the more boldly, since you see that he understandeth
25　not, or else willingly misconstrueth the place of the Apostle that he bringeth forth himself, and Saint John's Gospel too, and would make us ween[99] that it were enough to salvation to believe no more but that Christ was crucified for our sins. And then
30　should we not need indeed to believe that we should do penance for our sins ourselves, nor to believe the presence of Christ in the Blessed Sacrament neither, which point they would have now taken for indif-ferent, and many necessary points more. Whereof
35　Master Masker would take away the necessity, be-cause Saint Paul saith he preached nothing to the Corinthians but Christ and him to be crucified, which argument of Master Masker were not even very strong, although Saint Paul had at that time
40　preached them nothing else, because he might then have begun with that, and preach them many more things after, or send it unto them by writing.

　　　But now would I fain[100] that Master Masker had gone a little further in the same epistle. For even
45　within three lines after it followeth, "My preaching was not among you in persuasible words of man's wisdom."[101]

These words I lay not against Master Masker, for he keepeth himself sure enough for that point, and is aware well enough that he speak no persuasible　50
words of man's wisdom. But then saith Saint Paul further, "But my preaching was among you in show-ing of spirit and of power, to the intent that your faith should not be in the wisdom of men, but in the power of God."[102]　55

Here may Master Masker see that Saint Paul, be-cause he taught strange doctrine, proved his doc-trine not by subtle philosophical reasoning, nor by rhetoric and goodly fresh eloquence, but by mira-cles and the mighty hand of God.　60

Now if Master Masker therefore will be believed, reason is[103] that he do as Saint Paul did, since he teacheth as hard things and as strange to Christian men, and as far against the Christian faith as Saint Paul and the other apostles taught either Jews or　65
paynims[104] things hard and strange and far from the fashion of their false persuasion.

For setting aside all the whole heap of his other heresies, this one that he setteth forth in this pes-tilent book of his against our Savior himself in the　70
Blessed Sacrament is as strange and as execrable in all good Christian ears, and ever hath been since Christ's days, as ever was the preaching of Christ's Godhead among the gentiles or the Jews either. And therefore, if he will look to be believed as Saint Paul　75
was, reason is that he do miracles as Saint Paul did.

If he say that he needeth not, for he proveth his doctrine by Scripture, thereto first we say and say true that in his so saying he lieth. And besides that we say that though he proved his doctrine by Scrip-　80
ture indeed, yet since it seemeth to the whole Chris-tian nations that the Scripture proveth not his part but the contrary, and so have thought so long there-fore as our Savior himself and his apostles after him, which by the Scripture proved their part very truly　85
to the Jews, did yet for all that prove the truth of their such exposition by miracles, so must Master Masker prove his expositions by miracles to be true. For else[105] since our Savior, though he would not work miracles at every man's bidding, said yet of　90
the Jews that if himself had not done among them such works as no man else had done, their infidelity should not have been imputed unto them,[106] we may well be bold to say to Master Masker that, except[107]

he work miracles too, he can of reason blame no man that in the exposition of Holy Scripture believeth better all the old holy doctors and saints, and all the whole Catholic Church, than him.

And therefore while Master Masker would seem to play Saint Paul and be an apostle here to teach English men a new faith, as Saint Paul did the Corinthians, and then teaching things as strange and as incredible to Christian men as his were to the paynims, and cannot do miracles for his doctrine as Saint Paul did for his, but hath against him for our part such a multitude of miracles that for the proof of any one thing there were never showed so many, and when Master Masker, instead of miracles, proveth his expositions of Scripture so foolish himself and so false that to such as mark him well, he may surely seem to mean nothing else but to mock, we may go forth in the matter, and let Master Masker yet again mock on still and lie on too.

THE SIXTH CHAPTER

In the third leaf thus he saith: "And the cause of this your blindness is (I will not say over-hardly[108] to you) that the Father hath not drawn you into the knowledge of me, or else ye had received me. For all that the Father giveth me must come to me."[109]

Master Masker's exposition of these words (I will not say over-hardly to him) is, I promise you, good readers, very bare, and left off so shortly, and handled so slenderly, that his own friends could here scant[110] think any other than that liefer[111] than he would lay hardly to the Jews' charge the fault of their own infidelity, he had liefer lay it in the neck of the Father of heaven, and there leave it.

Those words and all the words of Christ, in which is any hardness,[112] his exposition so smoothly walketh over them that he giveth no light unto the understanding of them no more than if he never touched them.

The brethren cannot bear that my writing is so long. But surely it is no mastery for a man to be short, that can find in his heart to do as Master Masker doth: leave all the hard places undeclared.[113]

For he nowhere sticketh but upon the places in which he falsely laboreth, by the color[114] of his exposition of a spiritual eating by faith, to hide and withdraw the very literal truth and the very faith indeed, by which our Savior teacheth us to believe that the thing which in the Blessed Sacrament we spiritually must eat and bodily both is his own very flesh indeed.

THE SEVENTH CHAPTER

In the end of the fourth leaf, he expoundeth these words of Christ: "And this bread that I shall give you is mine own flesh, which I shall give for the life of the world."[115] And forasmuch as at those words specially beginneth between him and me the way to part in twain,[116] and he to go the one and I the other—he drawing it all to that point as though Christ there began to show them none other thing of his flesh but the giving it upon the cross, and that he nothing in all those words meant to tell them of the giving of his flesh to eat that he giveth in the Blessed Sacrament, and I there expounding it that he there telleth them of both, but specially of the giving of his flesh to be eaten which he giveth in the Blessed Sacrament—therefore at those words, good readers, begin to take special good heed to Master Masker's fingers. For there he specially beginneth to play a mummer's cast[117] with his false dice. And therefore, confer his exposition upon the same words with mine, and then shall ye bid him cast again, for that cast goeth for nought.[118]

THE EIGHTH CHAPTER

In the fifth leaf thus he saith:

No marvel was it though these fleshly Jews abhorred the bodily eating of Christ's flesh, albeit[119] our fleshly papists, being of the Jews' carnal opinion, yet abhor it not.[120]

What thing more false, more foolish, or more blasphemous could any brute beast say than this? For the Jews had an opinion that he would have them eat his flesh in the very[121] form of flesh, and as Saint Augustine saith, they thought they should eat it dead, cut out in gobbets as sheep's flesh is in the shambles.[122] And now is not Master Masker ashamed to rail upon all good Christian people under the name of papists, and say that they be all of the Jews' carnal opinion. Doth any man that receiveth the Blessed Sacrament think, as the Jews thought, that the flesh of Christ that he receiveth is in form of flesh, cut out in gobbets as sheep's flesh is sold in the shambles, and not in form of bread? If Master Masker were now barefaced himself, he were wonderful shameless if he could endure to look any man in the face for shame.

Now as this was, good readers, written (as you see) most falsely—that he saith we be of the Jews' opinion—so where he saith that we abhor not to eat Christ's flesh in the Sacrament, that is yet written, ye see well, as foolishly.

For the wise goodness of God hath, as the old holy doctors declare, given us his flesh not in form of flesh, but in form of bread, because we should not abhor it. And therefore, what horrible sight seeth this fool in the Blessed Sacrament, for which he should abhor to receive it?

But where was there ever a more blasphemous beastly word spoken than this frantic fool speaketh here, that mocketh and raileth upon all good Christian people in this fifteen hundred year because they do not abhor to receive the Blessed Body of Christ, in such wise given us by Christ, that no creature can abhor it but either devils or devils' fellows, heretics.

THE NINTH CHAPTER

Then saith Master Masker further in the same place,

> Neither cease they daily to crucify and offer up Christ again, which was once forever and all offered up, as Paul testifieth (Hebrews 9).[123]

Lo, what lewd[124] boldness it giveth when a man may walk about in a visor unknown. Master Masker careth not what he saith while his visor of dissimulation[125] is on, that men know him not. For who saith that Christ is daily new crucified? Truth it is that the Church saith that Christ is at the altar

every day offered, his own blessed body in the Sacrament. This of truth the Church saith, and that Christ is our daily sacrifice. But no man saith that he is daily crucified of new, and daily put to new pain. But as he was once crucified and killed and offered on the cross, so is that one death, oblation, and sacrifice daily represented by the selfsame body, the only quick[126] sacrifice and oblation that God hath left unto his new Christian Church, instead of all the manifold sacrifices and oblations of his old synagogue the Jews. And that ye may know that I feign you not fantasies, Saint Chrysostom declareth it very plainly, whose words are these:

> What is that then that we do? Do not we offer daily? Yes, forsooth.[127] But we do it in remembrance of his death. And this Host is one Host and not many. How is it one Host and not many? For because that Host was once offered, and was offered into the holiest tabernacle, and this sacrifice is a copy or example of that. We offer always the selfsame. Nor we offer not now one lamb, and tomorrow another, but still the same. This sacrifice therefore is one. For else[128] because it is offered in many places at once, are there many Christs? Nay, verily. For it is but one Christ everywhere, being both here whole, and there whole one body. For in like manner as he that is offered everywhere is but one body and not many bodies, so it is also but one sacrifice. And he is our bishop that offered the Host that cleanseth us. We offer now also the same Host which was then offered, and cannot be consumed. And this that we do is done in remembrance of that that[129] was done. For, he saith, "Do ye this in remembrance of me."[130] It is none other sacrifice, as it is none other bishop, but always we do the same, or rather we make a remembrance of that same sacrifice.[131]

What words can there be clearer to prove Master Masker a very fond[132] blasphemous mocker than these? By which this holy doctor Saint Chrysostom, against Master Masker mocking here the Mass, declareth his false folly clearly, and not only showeth that it is a sacrifice and an oblation, but also showeth that it is the daily representation of the same offering and sacrificing, by which he was sacrificed

---

122 butchers' stalls   **123** i.e., in Heb 9:28; *CW* 11: 309   **124** rude; wicked   **125** dissembling   **126** living   **127** truly   **128** otherwise   **129** *that that:* that which   **130** Lk 22:19   **131** Chrysostom, *Homiliae*   *in Epistolam ad Hebraeos* 17 (*PG* 63: 131)   **132** foolish

and offered up on the cross. And yet to stop Master Masker's mouth in the whole matter, he showeth that this oblation, this blessed sacrifice, the Sacrament of the altar, is all one oblation, all one Host, though it be offered at once in never so many places. And he showeth also that it is the very selfsame body that was offered on the cross. And that in this sacrifice of offering up the selfsame body in the Mass, we follow the example, as a copy is written after a book, and do represent the selfsame sacrifice by which Christ, the very selfsame body, was sacrificed on the cross.

How can Master Masker be more plainly confuted and confounded than Saint Chrysostom here confoundeth him, upon the occasion of this foolish blasphemous jesting of his? — with which he raileth against the Church, and saith that it ceaseth not daily to crucify Christ, as though the Church at this day did put Christ to new pain because his death is represented in the Mass, and of his goodness his very blessed body offered up daily, a sweet sacrifice for our sins.

Gracian also reciteth in the decrees, for our purpose in every point, as effectual words of Saint Ambrose, *De consecratione, Distinctione 2, Cap. In Christo semel.*[133]

Saint Augustine also, in the sixteenth book *De civitate Dei*, saith of the holy Mass in this wise:[134]

That sacrifice is succeeded into the place of all those sacrifices of the Old Law, which sacrifices were offered for a shadow of the thing to come. And for that cause also we know that voice in the thirty-ninth psalm, the prophecy of our mediator Christ, where he saith, "Sacrifice and oblation thou wouldst not have, but the body thou hast perfected me."[135] For in the stead of all those sacrifices and oblations, his body is offered and ministered[136] unto them that will be partakers of it.[137]

What speak I of Saint Chrysostom and Saint Augustine all the old holy doctors and saints of Christ's Church, without any exception, were ever more clear in this point that Master Masker here now denieth and thus jesteth on, that the Blessed Sacrament in the Mass is a sacrifice and an oblation.

And this cannot Master Masker himself deny.

For his own first master, Martin Luther, the late[138] well-spring of all this flood of heresies, in his pestilent book of *Babylonica*, putting forth this heresy that Master Masker toucheth here — that the Blessed Sacrament in the Mass is no sacrifice, nor none oblation — objecteth against himself and saith thus:

Now must we take away another occasion of ruin: that is, that the Mass is everywhere believed to be a sacrifice that is offered unto God. And for that opinion seems to sound the Canon of the Mass, where it is said, "These gifts, these holy sacrifices, this oblation and offering." And therefore is Christ called the Host or Sacrifice of the altar. Then cometh there also on this part the sayings or sentences of the holy fathers and then so many examples.

Against all these things, because they be very fastly[139] received, we must very constantly object[140] the words and example of Christ at his Maundy.

And afterward he saith again,

What shall we say then to the Canon of the Mass and to the sayings of the old holy doctors and saints? I say that if we have nothing else to say, let us yet rather deny them all than grant that the Mass should be any good work or any sacrifice, lest we should deny the word of Christ, and cast down faith and Mass and all.[141]

Thus you see, good readers, that Luther himself confesseth that in this heresy against the sacrifice and oblation of the Mass, which Master Masker, with two other heresies too, bringeth here forth now, the old holy doctors and saints are against him, and then were we wise, if we would ween that Martin Luther and Master Masker, evil Christian heretics, understand Christ's words better than ever did all the holy doctors of Christ's Church before.

And thus you see, good readers, what a compendious writer Master Masker is, that hath in less than three lines compacted up together such three abominable blasphemous heresies, as the devil himself never devised worse.

In the sixth, the seventh, the eighth, the ninth, the tenth leaf,[142] he hath certain arguments against all

133 Gratian, *Decretum, De consecratione* 2.53   **134** way   **135** Ps 39:7(40:6)   **136** given   **137** *De civitate Dei* 17.20   **138** recent   **139** firmly, steadfastly   **140** bring forward   **141** Luther, *De captivitate Babylonica, WA* 6: 523–24   **142** See *CW* 11: 310–15.

men in general that expound those words of Christ in the sixth chapter of John to be spoken and meant of the very eating of his Blessed Body in the Sacrament, and not only of a spiritual eating by belief of his death. And some solutions hath he there, such as they be, against mine argument in special[143] made unto Frith, all which things I will sort into their places apart from his exposition, so that ye may see some of the faults of his exposition by themselves, and his arguments answered by themselves, and his solutions avoided[144] by themselves, and the notable notes that he maketh of my notable repugnances[145] last of all laid open to you by themselves, because I will lay all things in order plain before your eyes, so that when ye see the things in such wise before you without interlacing, ruffle, and confusion, ye shall the more easily judge whether Master Masker in his mummery[146] be an honest man, or else a false hazarder[147] and play with false dice.

THE TENTH CHAPTER

In the eleventh leaf,[148] after that in the other ten before he had spoken many times of faith alone, and that the only belief of far fewer things than we be bounden indeed to believe, when it were once had, should both satisfy the soul and also make us safe forever, it appeareth in that leaf that either his own mind began to misgive him, or else some other wily brother gave him warning, that this manner[149] writing of faith alone would make all the world to wonder on him. For Luther himself, writing first on the same fashion that faith alone was sufficient for salvation, though it pleased idle unthrifts[150] very well, that were glad to be by bare faith discharged of all good works, it was yet so sore[151] abhorred among all honest men that both himself and all his sect were fain[152] to seek some plasters of false glosses to heal the foul mormal[153] of their scabbed shins, that they had gotten by that text of their false faith alone.

And then they said that they meant that manner faith that had always both hope and charity with it. But then could not that gloss serve them. For that manner faith taught ever the common Catholic Church, which they reproved. And also that

gloss marred their text, and was clean[154] contrary to all their tale. For all the text of their preaching had been of faith alone, and their gloss was of faith not alone, but encompanied with two good fellows, pardie,[155] the one called hope and the other charity.

Now therefore either upon this fear of his own mind, or upon this advertisement[156] of some other man, Master Masker, to mend his exposition with and to make all the matter safe, hath at the last, in the end of the eleventh leaf, plastered his mormal of his only faith on[157] this fashion:

"By love, we abide in God and he in us."[158] Love followeth faith in the order of our understanding, and not in order of succession of time, if thou lookest upon the self[159] gifts and not of their fruits, so that principally by faith, whereby we cleave to God's goodness and mercy, we abide in God and God in us, as declare his words following, saying, "As the living Father sent me, so live I by my Father. And even so he that eateth me shall live because of me or for my sake. My Father sent me, whose will in all things I obey, for I am his Son. And even so verily must they that eat me—that is, believe in me—form and fashion them after my example, mortifying their flesh and changing their living, or else they eat me in vain and dissemble their belief. For I am not come to redeem the world only, but also to change their life. They therefore that believe in me, shall transform their lives after[160] mine example and doctrine, and not after any man's traditions."[161]

This plaster, good readers, hath some good ingredients. But it is both too narrow by a great deal to cover his scald[162] shin, and hath also some dead apothecary drugs put in it that can do no good, and something also repugnant to his remedy.

But let us now consider his words. First where he saith that "by love we abide in God and God in us," he saith truth, for so saith the Scripture, but that is to be understood as long as we love him, and dwell so still in him. But when we break his commandments, and thereby declare that we love him not, as the Scripture also saith, against which Scripture Master Tyndale saith that he that hath once a

143 particular   **144** refuted   **145** contradictions, inconsistencies   **146** play-acting   **147** dicer, gamester   **148** See *CW* 11: 315–16.   **149** kind of   **150** spendthrifts; dissolute persons   **151** greatly   **152** forced, obliged   **153** sore, ulcer   **154** completely   **155** certainly; "by God" (French)   **156** admonishment   **157** in   **158** 1 Jn 4:16   **159** same   **160** in accordance with   **161** *CW* 11: 316   **162** scabby

feeling faith can never fall therefrom,[163] and against the same Scripture Master Masker saith that faith once had sufficeth for salvation.

And Master Masker maketh yet his matter much worse than William Tyndale. For Tyndale did yet at the leastwise make some bumbling about a color[164] for the matter, with a long process of historical faith and feeling faith, whose false wily folly therein I have so confuted in my *Confutation* that, though[165] he write again therein, as long as ever he liveth he shall never shake off the shame.

But Master Masker handleth the matter both more wilily than Tyndale doth, and yet much more foolishly too. For seeing that his saying cannot be defended, he ruffleth up all the matter shortly in a few words, both for sparing of labor, and also because he would not have his words well understood, but that his words might stand for a short text, which he would leave for every other good brother to make some good gloss thereto to maintain it with.

For in his next words following where he saith, "Love followeth faith in the order of our understanding, and not in the order of succession of time, if thou lookest upon the self gifts and not upon their fruits," in these few dark[166] words he would both show his clerkliness[167] before unlearned men, and leave them also undeclared, because he would have them ween that his high learning passeth[168] their low capacities.

But yet in these words he juggleth with us, and may with his wiliness beguile them that will take none heed. But whoso look well to his hands shall perceive where his galls[169] go well enough.

For true it is that whensoever God infoundeth[170] either the habit of faith, or the full perfect quick[171] lively faith that is called *fides formata*, he infoundeth in like wise hope and charity both. But this is not the "faith alone." For faith is never such faith, but while he hath his two fellows with him. But faith may begin, and tarry too, before his two fellows come to him, as a man may believe well long ere he will do well. And faith may tarry also when both his fellows be gone from him, as he that hath had all three may by deadly sin fall from the other twain,[172] and have faith alone remain. And faith may come and continue still, and neither of both of his fellows never come at him at all, as where a man believeth truly every article of the faith and yet hath never the will to work well, nor never will be baptized, but after dieth in despair. And in all these cases is it faith alone. And because it neither worketh well, nor hath will to work well, neither in act nor in habit, therefore is it called *fides informis*, and a dead faith—not dead in the nature of faith or belief, but dead as to the attaining of everlasting life.

Now would Master Masker juggle and make us believe that he meaneth the first manner of faith—that is, quick and lively—by the reason that it hath good hope and charity therewith.

But I cannot suffer[173] you, good Christian readers, to be so beguiled by such a fond[174] false juggler. For if ye take heed unto him, ye shall soon perceive that he is even but a very bungler.

For when that he first telleth us what belief is sufficient, and saith that if we once eat and drink Christ by faith, and then expoundeth the whole sum of all that faith saying—that is to say, "if we believe his flesh and his body to have been broken, and his blood shed for our sins, then are our souls satisfied, and we be justified"—and now addeth thereunto that love followeth faith in the order of our understanding and not in the order of succession of time, by which he meaneth that every man hath charity ever more as soon as he hath faith, ye may clearly see that he saith that a man hath charity ever as soon as he hath that faith, so that by him whosoever believeth that Christ died for us, he hath both faith, hope, and charity, though he believe nothing else.

But now is this a very false devilish doctrine. For this is no full faith. For a man may believe this, and yet leave many a thing unbelieved, which we be bounden to believe besides. And therefore you may well see that though the theological virtue of full and perfect faith have always charity together infounded with it, yet Master Masker's faith, that is neither perfect nor full, may be not in the beginning only but also ever after without any charity at all.

Also where he saith that the faith that he describeth, once had, is sufficient, and speaketh of no perseverance, a man may well see that his saying is insufficient. For both that, faith standing, a man may well fall from charity, and then though he had once charity as soon as that faith (if that bare faith without more were possible to have charity with it), yet might it lack charity after. And also that faith might itself fall quite away too. For he that once believeth every article of the faith, and then can fall from any, as Master Masker is fallen from many, may little and little fall from them every one. For I dare well say that Master Masker believeth no point that he believeth most surely anything[175] more surely now than he hath believed ere this, diverse of those points which he now believeth least if he believe as he writeth.

And thus, good readers, you see that whereas his mormal[176] is more than a handful broad, this plaster of his passeth not the breadth of a penny. For I dare say the devil believeth[177] at this day as much as Master Masker saith that is sufficient—that is to wit,[178] that Christ died for our sin—and yet hath he no charity. Nor no more hath no man that will believe no more but that, or though he do believe more than that, will yet think that he believeth all the remnant but of his courtesy,[179] and not one whit more of[180] duty.

THE ELEVENTH CHAPTER

Now where he saith further:

So that principally by faith, whereby we cleave to God's goodness and mercy, we abide in God and God in us, as declare his words following, saying, "As the living Father sent me, so live I by my Father. And even so, he that eateth me shall live because of me or for my sake."

This is a very false naughty[181] declaration of Christ's words. For whereas the holy doctors do declare[182] those words, as I before have showed you, that like[183] as our Savior had his eternal life of his Father before any beginning of time, in that his Father eternally before all time begot him, and his flesh, not of his own nature but by the conjunction

that it had with the Godhead, had now the same life and so lived for the Father, so should he that eateth that flesh according to Christ's institution with due circumstances of faith and good hope, and charity—well-willing[184] to work—attain everlasting life also, by reason of his conjunction and incorporation with his everlasting flesh; so I say always if the eater eat it with all due circumstances requisite, so that like as they receive not his holy flesh dead as the Jews had weened,[185] but quick[186] with Holy Spirit joined thereto, so their souls may join with his spirit as their flesh joineth with his; whereas the holy doctors, I say, do expound these words thus, now cometh Master Masker and saith that in these words Christ teacheth us that we abide in him and he in us, not principally by charity but principally by faith.

Now, good reader, what one word of those words of Christ anything soundeth to the maintenance of Master Masker's exposition that God is in us and we in him principally by faith? The Scripture saith, "God is charity, and he that dwelleth in charity dwelleth in God, and God in him."[187]

Now if Master Masker would have said that by faith a man might eat the flesh of Christ, and by faith might dwell in God, if Master Masker were a good Catholic man, I would for so far find no fault in his exposition. For it might have a meaning good enough, beside the literal sense of Christ's words. But now when he contendeth that this is the literal sense, and therewith would shake off the very[188] eating that our Savior meant in the Blessed Sacrament, and bear us in hand[189] that our Savior meant not so, but meant an only eating of his flesh by a bare belief of his death, and not the very bodily eating at all, and that in those words he meant that though we dwell in God by love, yet not principally by love, but principally by faith, as to which virtue the virtue of charity were but a follower and a perpetual handmaid, where there is in those words of Christ not one syllable sounding toward it, what good Christian man can abide it? Namely while the Scripture by plain words condemneth it, and saith, *Fides, spes, charitas, tria hec maior horum charitas* ("Faith, hope, and charity, these three, but the principal of these is charity").[190]

---

175 to any extent **176** sore, ulcer **177** See Js 2:19. **178** say **179** *of his courtesy:* by his indulgence or good will **180** out of **181** bad, wicked **182** make clear **183** just **184** favorably disposed **185** thought, believed **186** living **187** 1 Jn 4:16 **188** true; full; proper **189** *bear us in hand:* lead us to believe **190** 1 Cor 13:13

THE TWELFTH CHAPTER

Now where he goeth, good reader, further forth yet upon these words, and saith:

My Father sent me, whose will in all things I obey, for I am his Son. And even so verily[191] must they that eat me, that is, believe in me, form and fashion them after my example, mortifying their flesh and changing their living, or else they eat me in vain and dissemble their belief.[192]

Though these words here seem very good, yet while they be all written unto this one intent, that this gay flourish should so glitter in our eyes that we might thereby be blinded and not beware of the perilous pit into which he goeth about to cast us — that is, to make us ween that our Savior in saying that we should eat his flesh meant no very eating thereof in the Blessed Sacrament but only a spiritual eating by believing that he died for our sins, as here he declareth again, "They that eat me, that is, believe in me," etc. — while all draweth, I say, to that end, his tale is naught altogether.

And yet it is a world[193] also to see the blindness that the devil hath driven into him, by which he cannot be suffered[194] to see that by these selfsame words with which he would advance his purpose, he very plainly destroyeth it.

For his purpose is, ye wot[195] well, to make us ween that faith were not only the principal, but also that faith hath ever love waiting upon her, and following her as her unseparable servant, as heat ever followeth the fire. And now you see that he saith here that whoso do not form and fashion them after Christ's example do eat him in vain. And then to eat him, he saith, is but to believe in him. And so he saith, without good living — that is to wit,[196] without charity — the belief is but in vain. Now to believe in vain is, ye wot well, to believe, and yet have his belief fruitless for lack of that love that is the theological virtue called charity.

And thus ye see, good readers, how well and circumspectly Master Masker looketh to his matter, that when he hath told us that faith never lacketh charity, forgetting himself forthwith,[197] telleth us himself, within ten lines after, that faith may lack charity, and therefore be but in vain.

Now where he saith, "or else they dissemble their belief," I will not dissemble with him, but tell him very plain that, as great a dissembler as he is, he wotteth not, as it seemeth, what this word "dissembling" meaneth, or else wot I nere[198] what he meaneth thereby. For a man dissembleth the thing that he hath and will not be acknown[199] thereof, as a man dissembleth his hatred when he hateth one and feigneth himself his friend to cover his hatred with. And so we say that a man dissembleth a thing when he seeth it and will not see it, but maketh as though he saw it not. But no man dissembleth the thing that he seeth not indeed, nor the thing that he hath not indeed, but maketh as though he saw it or had it. For he feigneth or lieth, and not dissembleth, as in the Latin tongue (whereof this English word cometh), *ille simulat non dissimulat.* And therefore, if Master Masker mean here by these words, "or else they dissemble their belief," any other thing than they feign a belief, making as though they believed and do not, let him not dissemble with me, but tell me what other thing he meaneth. And if he mean by those words none other thing than that, then will I not dissemble with him, but tell him the plain truth: that he may peradventure[200] mean wisely enough, but he speaketh but like a fool. For by that word he saith the clear contrary, that is to wit, that they make as though they believed not, but yet they do.

THE THIRTEENTH CHAPTER

But now at last he concludeth all together thus:

For I am not comen to redeem the world only, but also to change their life. They therefore that believe in me, shall transform their life after mine example and doctrine, and not after any man's traditions.

I will not here hold a long dispicion[201] with Master Masker upon man's traditions, by which word he would have all the laws made by men utterly set at nought,[202] and would have man bound but either

---

191 truly   **192** *CW* 11: 316   **193** marvel   **197** immediately, at once   **198** *wot*   **200** perhaps   **201** discussion   **202** *set at*
194 allowed   **195** know   **196** say   *I nere*: know I not   **199** recognized   *nought*: valued as nothing

by the plain word of Scripture, or else by his own express agreement and consent. For Luther saith that neither man nor angel can make the bond of any one syllable upon any Christian man, without his own express consent,[203] so that no law can be made by that wise reason, by the prince and the people, to hang up either thief or murderer, or to burn up a heretic, but if[204] the thieves, murderers, and heretics will consent and agree thereto themselves. Nor no law made this day can bind him that shall be born tomorrow, till he come to good age and agree thereto first himself, as our sovereign lord the King's Grace most prudently laid against Luther.

But I let this folly of Master Masker pass, and this also: that the traditions which these heretics be worst content withal[205] be the traditions of the apostles, which they delivered to the Church, as Christ, not by writing but by tradition, delivered the things to them, for which Saint Paul saith, *Ego enim accepi a domino quod et tradidi vobis* ("For I have received the thing of our Lord by tradition, without writing the which I have also delivered unto you"),[206] as though he would say, "As I have received it by tradition or delivery of our Lord, so without writing I have delivered it by tradition to you."

I will let pass all these advantages (which I might, as ye see, take against Master Masker here), and I will well allow these words of his for this once, so that himself will stick and stand by them stiffly, and confess that they that transform not their life after Christ's example and doctrine have either their belief in vain, or else make as though they believed, and have no belief at all.

This once agreed between him and me, aye, if he will rail upon the priests and prelates of the Catholic Church for doing of the contrary, let him name who they be and wherein they do it, and by my troth,[207] in such evil doing, they shall never be defended for[208] me.

But then of reason must Master Masker give me leave again to put him in remembrance of the priests and prelates of their heretics' sects, and I will speak of none but by name. Friar Luther, I will name him the chief and principal author of their heresies. I will name him Friar Lambert, Dane Othe the Carthusian, Zwingli the priest, and the priest Pomeranus, and Friar Hussgen the friar Brigittine.[209] These be, lo, the very prelates and bishops, metropolitans[210] and apostles of their sects.

Now will I then ask Master Masker what example of Christ or what doctrine of Christ he can show, by which those holy prelates of these new sects, evil Christian caitiffs,[211] that have sowed all this sedition, have broken their holy vows and promises made unto God, and run out of their orders, and to the shame of matrimony and holy orders both speak of the spirit, and fall to the flesh? Which while they have all done, against the doctrine and example as well of Christ as of all holy doctors and saints, and of all good Christian people since the death of Christ unto this their own wretched time, and now teach it forth for a doctrine, reason it is[212] that Master Masker confess that all the prelates of his sundry sects either have but a vain faith, or else make as[213] they had faith and have no faith at all. And then are there no man's traditions so evil as are their own, being themselves so evil men as they be. And why should we then hear Master Masker preach either their faith or traditions either, while their faith is either vain faith or else false and none at all, and their doctrine as devilish doctrine as themselves are devilish men, and more devilish, I ween, is scant[214] the devil himself.

Thus have I, good readers, noted you certain pieces of Master Masker's exposition, by which as by a taste of a draught or twain,[215] ye may see what poisoned drink is in the whole vessel. And now shall I come to his arguments, which he maketh in general against all them that expound this place of Christ's words in the sixth chapter of Saint John to be spoken or meant of that eating, by which we eat Christ's blessed body in the Blessed Sacrament.

Here endeth the Second Book.

203 See *De captivitate Babylonica, WA* 6: 536. **204** *but if:* unless **205** with **206** 1 Cor 11:23 **207** trustworthiness; faithfulness **208** by **209** François Lambert (1486–1530) Otho Brunfels (ca. 1488–1534), Ulrich Zwingli (1484–1531), Johann Bugenhagen (1485–1558), Johannes Oecolampadius (1482–1531) **210** bishops who have the oversight of the bishops of a province **211** wretches **212** *reason it is:* it would be reasonable **213** *make as:* pretend that **214** hardly, scarcely **215** two

THE THIRD BOOK

THE FIRST CHAPTER

In the fifth leaf[1] upon his exposition of these words, "and the bread which I shall give for the life of the world," thus he argueth:

And even here since Christ came to teach to take away all doubt and to break strife, he might (his words otherwise declared than he hath declared and will hereafter expound them) have soluted[2] their question, saying, if he had so meant as More expoundeth, that he would have been conveyed and converted (as our jugglers sleightly[3] can convey him with a few words) into a singing loaf,[4] or else (as the Thomistical papists say) been invisible with all his dimensioned body under the form of bread transubstantiated[5] into it, and after a like Thomistical mystery, the wine transubstantiated too into his blood, so that they should eat his flesh and drink his blood after[6] their own carnal understanding (but yet in another form) to put away all grudge[7] of stomach. Or since Saint John, if he had thus understood his master's mind, and took upon him to write his master's words, would leave this sermon unto the world to be read, he might now have delivered us and them from this doubt. But Christ would not so satisfy their question, but answered, "Verily,[8] verily, I say unto you, except[9] ye eat the flesh of the Son of Man and drink his blood, ye shall not have that life in yourselves. He that eateth my flesh and drinketh my blood hath life everlasting, and I shall stir him up in the last day. For my flesh is very meat and my blood the very drink." He saith not here that bread shall be transubstantiated or converted into his body, nor yet the wine into his blood.[10]

Lo, good Christian readers, this man here in a foolish, jesting, and much blasphemous railing manner, against the conversion of the bread and wine into the blessed body and blood of Christ in the Blessed Sacrament, in conclusion as for a clear confutation of me and of Saint Thomas both, upon which holy doctor and saint he foolishly jesteth by name, he argueth, as you see, that if Christ had intended to have given them his flesh and his blood in the Sacrament, then might he have declared it more openly with more words and more plainly. And then Master Masker deviseth Christ the words that he would have had him say if he had so meant. And therein the blasphemous beast deviseth that he would have had our Savior say that he would play as jugglers do, and slyly convey himself into a singing loaf; and that our Savior so doth, he saith is mine opinion, wherein the man is shameless, and shamefully belieth[11] me. For I say, as the Catholic faith is, that he not conveyeth but converteth the bread into his own body, and changeth it therein too, and neither conveyeth, as he speaketh, his body into the bread (for then were the bread and his blessed body both together still, which false opinion is Luther's heresy, and that knoweth this man well enough, and therefore showeth himself shameless in laying that opinion to me), nor also converteth not his blessed body into bread, for that were yet much worse. For then remaineth there nothing else but bread still, and that is, ye wot[12] well, Master Masker's own heresy for which he writeth against me, and therefore is he double shameless, as you see, to say any such thing of me.

But in conclusion the effect of all his fond[13] argument is that even there in that place, to break strife and to assoil[14] all their doubt, our Lord might and would have done at the self[15] communication, or else at the leastwise, the Evangelist, at the time of his writing, might and would have told them plainly that they should eat it, not in form of flesh but in form of bread. But neither our Savior then told them so, nor the Evangelist hath told us so in the reporting of his words spoken to them; ergo it must needs be that Christ meant not so.

This is Master Masker's argument, which he liketh so specially that afterward, in another place,[16] he harpeth upon the same string again. But surely if the man be in Scripture anything[17] exercised, then hath he a very poor remembrance. And whether

---

1 page **2** solved **3** craftily **4** *singing loaf:* the communion wafer **5** changed. According to the doctrine of the Roman Catholic Church, the whole substance of the bread and wine is converted into the body and blood of Christ, with only the appearances of bread and wine remaining. **6** according to **7** grumbling **8** Truly **9** unless **10** *CW* 11: 309 **11** slanders **12** know **13** foolish **14** refute **15** same **16** See *CW* 11: 317. **17** at all

he be Scriptured or not, he hath a very bare barren wit,[18] when he can ween[19] that this argument were aught.[20]

For first, as for the Scripture, can he find no more places than one, in which our Savior would not tell out plainly all at once?

Could Christ of the sacrament of baptism have told no more to Nicodemus if he had would?[21] Could he to the Jews that asked him a token have told them no more of his death, sepulture,[22] and resurrection but the figure of the prophet Jonah, three days swallowed into the whale's belly?[23]

When his disciples asked him of the restitution of the kingdom of Israel, and mistook his kingdom for a worldly kingdom, did he forthwith[24] declare them all that ever he could have told them? Or all that ever he told them thereof at any other time after? Nay, nor the Evangelist in the rehearsing[25] neither.[26]

Hath this man either never read or else forgotten that albeit[27] our Savior came to be known for Christ and sometimes declared him so himself, yet at some other times, he forbade his disciples to be acknown[28] thereof?[29] So that as for the Scriptures (except[30] he have either little read or little remembered of them) would have made Master Masker to forbear[31] this foolish argument for shame.

But now what wit hath this man that can argue thus, when he should, if he had wit, well perceive his argument answered by the like made against himself upon the very selfsame place?

For Master Masker saith here that our Lord meant nothing else but to tell them of the giving of his flesh to the death for the life of the world, and to make them believe that. Now ask I therefore, Master Masker, whether Christ could not have told them by more plain words than he did there (if it had so been his pleasure) that he should die for the sin of the world, and in what wise[32] also. If Master Masker answer me no, I am sure every wise man will tell him yes. For he spoke there not half so plainly of the giving of his body to be slain as he did of giving it to be eaten. For as for his death, not so much as once named it, but only saith, "And the bread that I shall give you is mine own flesh, which I shall give

for the life of the world," in which words he not once nameth death. But of the eating, he speaketh so expressly by and by,[33] and so spoke before all of eating, and much more afterward too, that he gave them little occasion to think that he meant of his death any word there at all but of the eating only.

And some great holy doctors also construe those whole words, "And the bread that I shall give is my flesh which I shall give for the life of the world," to be spoken only of the giving of his blessed body in the Sacrament, and neither the first part nor the second to be spoken of his death, but that in the first part Christ showeth what he would give them to eat—that is to wit,[34] his own flesh—and in the second part, he showed them why he would give the world his flesh to eat, and what commodity[35] they should have by the eating of it, saying that he would give it men to eat for the life that men should have by the eating of it. And therefore he pursueth forth both upon the eating thereof, and upon the life that they shall lack that will not eat it, and of the life that they shall have that will eat it, so that, as I say, Christ spoke and meant, after[36] the mind of some holy cunning[37] men, but of the eating only, but by[38] all good men of the eating specially, and without any manner[39] question of the eating most plainly, as of which he speaketh by name expressly. And of his death (if he there spoke of it, as diverse holy doctors think he did), yet he spoke it so covertly that he rather meant it than said it, as the thing whereof he nothing named, but only the giving to eat. So that whereas Master Masker argueth that Christ nothing meant of giving of his flesh to be eaten in the Sacrament, but only of his flesh to be crucified because that if he had meant of his flesh to be eaten in the Sacrament, he could and would have told them plainly so, ye see now, good readers, very plain proved by the selfsame place that, since Master Masker cannot say nay but that[40] of his body to be given by death Christ could have spoken much more plainly than he did in that place, as well as he could have spoken more plainly of the giving of his body to be eaten in the Blessed Sacrament, Master Masker's own argument (if it were aught,[41] as it is nought)[42] utterly destroyeth all his own exposition

---

18 mind; intellect　**19** think, believe　**20** anything　**21** wished. See Jn 3:1–20.　**22** burial　**23** See Mt 12:38–41; Lk 11:29–32.　**24** immediately, at once

25 recounting, telling　**26** See Acts 1:6.　**27** although　**28** acknowledged　**29** See Mt 12:16; 16:20.　**30** unless　**31** refrain from　**32** way, manner　**33** *by and*

by: immediately　**34** say　**35** benefit　**36** according to　**37** learned　**38** concerning　**39** kind of　**40** *say nay but that:* deny that　**41** anything　**42** nothing

whole. And therefore ye may see that the man is a wise man and well overseen[43] in arguing.

THE SECOND CHAPTER

In the eleventh leaf he hath another argument, toward which he maketh a blind induction[44] before. And because ye shall see that I will not go about to beguile you, I will rehearse[45] you his induction first, and then his argument after. These are his words:

> When the Jews would not understand this spiritual saying of the eating of Christ's flesh and drinking of his blood, so oft and so plainly declared, he gave them a strong trip, and made them more blind, for they so deserved it (such are the secret judgments of God), adding unto all his sayings thus: "Whoso eat my flesh and drink my blood abideth in me and I in him." These words were spoken unto the unbelievers into their futher obstination,[46] but unto the faithful for their better instruction. Now gather of this the contrary, and say, "Whoso eateth not my flesh and drinketh not my blood abideth not in me nor I in him," and join this to that aforesaid sentence, "Except ye eat the flesh of the Son of Man and drink his blood, ye have no life in you." Let it never fall from thy mind, Christian reader, that faith is the life of the righteous, and that Christ is this living bread whom thou eatest, that is to say, in whom thou believest.[47]

Here is Master Masker fallen to juggling, lo, and as a juggler layeth forth his trinkets upon the table and biddeth men look on this and look on that and blow in his hand, and then with certain strange words to make men muse, whirleth his juggling stick about his fingers to make men look upon that, while he playeth a false cast[48] and conveyeth with the other hand something slyly into his purse or his sleeve or somewhere out of sight, so fareth Master Masker here, that maketh Christ's holy words serve him for his juggling boxes and layeth them forth upon the board[49] afore us, and biddeth us, "lo, look on this text," and then look, "lo, upon this," and when he hath shed forth thus two or three texts

and bid us look upon them, he telleth us not wherefore,[50] nor what we shall find in them. But because they be so plain against him, he letteth them slink away, and then to blear our eyes, and call our mind from the matter, up he taketh his juggling stick, the commendation of faith, and whirleth that about his fingers, and saith:

> Let it never fall from thy mind, Christian reader, that faith is the life of the righteous, and that Christ is this living bread whom thou eatest: that is to say, in whom thou believest.

What are these words, good Christian reader, to the purpose? All this will I pray[51] you remember too. But I will pray you remember therewithal whereabout this juggler goeth that would, with bidding us look up here upon faith, juggle away one great point of faith from us, and make us take no heed of Christ's words plainly spoken here of the very[52] eating of his holy flesh. And therefore let us remember faith, as he biddeth. But let us remember well therewith specially this piece thereof that this juggler, with bidding us remember, would fain[53] have us forget.

But now after this induction, forth he cometh with his wise argument in this wise:

> For if our papists take eating and drinking here bodily as to eat the natural body of Christ under the form of bread, and to drink his blood under the form of wine, then must all young children that never came at God's board departed[54] and all laymen that never drank his blood be damned.[55]

If our Savior Christ, which is the way to truth, and the truth itself, and the very true life also,[56] could and would say false, and break his promise by which he promised his Church to be therewith himself unto the world's end,[57] and to send it also the Spirit of truth, that should teach it and lead it into all truth,[58] then would there of truth both of these words of Christ and these other words of his also, "But if[59] a man be born again of the water and the Holy Ghost, he cannot see the kingdom of God,"[60] and of many other words of his more, many great doubts arise, right hard and inexplicable. But

---

43 versed, skilled　44 introduction
45 quote to　46 obstinacy　47 *CW* 11:
315–16　48 trick　49 table　50 why

51 request　52 true; proper　53 gladly
54 be separated (from God)　55 *CW* 11:
316　56 See Jn 14:6.　57 See Mt 28:20.

58 See Jn 16:13.　59 *But if:* Unless
60 Jn 3:5

now am I very sure, since truth cannot be but true, Christ's promise shall ever stand and be kept, and therefore shall his Church ever more, by the means of his Holy Spirit which maketh men of one manner and mind in the house of his Church,[61] so fall in a concord and agreement together upon the true sense, and so be led into every necessary truth, that by mistaking of any part of Scripture, it shall never be suffered[62] to fall into any damnable error, which thing, what prating soever Master Masker make, I have so often and so surely proved for the common-known Catholic Church of good and bad both, against William Tyndale,[63] that neither he nor all these heretics among them all shall never be able to void[64] it.

Now as for his argument concerning laymen of age, it were[65] a little more strong if the blessed body of our Lord were in the Blessed Sacrament under form of bread without his blood, which while it is not, nor their receiving is not the sacrifice nor oblation, which to the integrity thereof requireth both the forms — that the thing should agree with the figure, the figure, I say, of the bread and wine that was offered by Melchizedek[66] — Master Masker's argument is of a feeble force, of which thing, because I purpose once to touch, God willing, in answering to Doctor Barnes's treatise specially made of that matter,[67] I will hold here Master Masker for this time with no long tale thereof. But to the intent ye may shortly see how little wit[68] is in his wise argument, with which upon Christ's general words, "But if you eat the flesh of the Son of Man and drink his blood ye shall not have life in you," he argueth universally of all men and women and children that die and never eat his flesh or never drink his blood shall be damned by the selfsame form of arguing upon these general words, "But if a man be born of water and the Spirit, he shall never see the kingdom of God," Master Masker may argue generally that whoso die before he be baptized by water and the Spirit shall be damned, and thereupon conclude that many martyrs be damned for lack of baptizing in water, for all their baptizing in their own blood. And thus you see, good readers, how substantial his argument is.

THE THIRD CHAPTER

In the twelfth leaf, to prove that Christ meant nothing[69] to give his body to be eaten, Master Masker upon these words that the disciples which were offended with his words said, "This is a hard word; who may hear him?" bringeth in another wise argument under color[70] of expounding the text, in this wise: "These words did not only offend them that hated Christ, but also some of his disciples. They were offended, saith the text, and not marveled, as More trifleth out of truth." These words, good reader, of "offending" and "marveling," I shall answer anon in a more convenient[71] place. "Which disciples said, 'This is a hard saying; who may hear him?' These disciples stuck no less in Christ's visible flesh, and in the bark[72] of his words, than doth now More, believing him to have spoken of his natural body to be eaten with their teeth."[73]

Here Master Masker maketh as though the Catholic faith in the Blessed Sacrament were but my faith. But likewise, as I do confess that his heresy is not only his, but that he hath fellows in the same falsehood — not only Frith and Tyndale, but Wycliffe[74] also and Zwingli and Friar Hussgen too, besides a lewd[75] sort of wretched heretics more — so must he confess, if he will say true, that my faith is not only my faith, but that I have fellows in the same faith, not only the common whole multitude of all good Christian countries this fifteen hundred year, but specially by name those holy saints whose words I have rehearsed you before upon this same matter, as Theophylactus, and Saint Bede, Saint Irenaeus, and Saint Hilary,[76] and Saint Augustine, Saint Cyril, and Saint Chrysostom, the plain words of every one of all, whom I have here already brought you forth against Master Masker, proving themselves fellows of mine in my faith already, now in this answer of this first part of his. And yet keep I for Master Masker matter enough besides of holy saints' authorities, as well the same saints as others, to fill up the messes[77] at the second course. And where he bringeth forth for him in his second part Augustine, Tertullian, and Saint Chrysostom (for in all this his first course, he bringeth forth never

61 See Ps 67(68):7.　**62** allowed
63 See More's *Confutation*.　**64** refute
65 would be　**66** See Gn 14:18–20.
67 See *Confutation* and Letter 190: Against John Frith, pp. 358–70.　**68** ingenuity;

intellect　**69** not at all　**70** appearance; pretext　**71** appropriate　**72** external part　**73** *CW* 11: 316　**74** John Wycliffe (*ca.* 1330–84)　**75** such as　**76** *Irenaeus… Hilary:* Irenaeus (d. *ca.* 202), Hilary of

Poitiers (*ca.* 310–67); More does not quote either directly here, though he does in *A Treatise on the Passion*.　**77** dishes

one), those three dishes, I warrant you, shall when I come to them but barely furnish his board.[78]

But where Master Masker saith that More sticketh in the visible flesh of Christ, to be eaten as those disciples and those Jews did, he is bold to say what him list[79] because he goeth invisible. For else[80] how could he for shame say that we that are of the Catholic Church think that Christ giveth us his visible flesh to eat, as those disciples and those Jews thought, when every man well wotteth[81] that those disciples and those Jews thought that they should receive his flesh visible cut out, as Saint Augustine declareth, in visible dead pieces, and every man as well knoweth, and Master Masker too, that we think that we do (and so indeed we do) receive and eat his flesh invisible, not in dead pieces, but his quick[82] blessed body whole, under the visible form of bread. And therefore you see, good readers, what truth is in this man.

But now goeth he forth and cometh to his wise worshipful[83] argument and saith:

Which offense Christ seeing, said, "Doth this offend you? What then will you say if you see the Son of Man ascend thither where he was before? If it offend you to eat my flesh while I am here, it shall much more offend you to eat it when it shall be gone out of your sight, ascended into heaven, there sitting on the right hand of my Father, until I come again as I went, that is, to judgment."[84]

The exposition of these words of Christ I have, good readers, showed you before, according to the minds of holy doctors and saints: that by those words of his ascension he gave them warning before that he would by his ascending up to heaven make them a plain proof that they were deceived when they thought it could not be that he was descended down from heaven, and by his ascending up with his body whole and undiminished make them a plain proof that they were deceived, when they thought he would in pieces cut out, and so give his flesh to them as he should give it from himself, and thereby lose it himself. For his whole body ascending should well prove that though his apostles had every one eaten it, yet had he it still whole

himself, that[85] they should thereby not doubt afterward, but that as each of them had it and did eat it, and yet himself had it still, and all at once in thirteen diverse places in earth, and himself ascended after whole therewith into heaven, so should ever after all good Christian folk receive it whole here in earth, and himself nevertheless have it whole still with him in heaven.

This being, good Christian readers, the mind[86] of our Savior in those words, as by the holy doctors and saints well doth appear of old, now cometh this new drunken doctor Master Masker, and with a wise exposition of his own brain, would make us ween that those words with which (as the old doctors testify) Christ confirmed the Sacrament, in declaring his power by which he worketh that wonderful miracle in the Sacrament, our Savior had himself spoken against his miracles in the Sacrament. For thus, lo, doth Master Masker make Christ expound his own words and say, "If it offend you to eat my flesh while I am here, it shall much more offend you to eat it when my body shall be gone out of your sight ascended into heaven, there sitting on the right hand of my Father until I come again as I went."

There were, good readers, two causes for which those Jews and those disciples were offended at the hearing of Christ, when he said they should eat his flesh. One was the strangeness and the impossibility that they thought was therein; the other was the loathsomeness[87] that they had thereto. Now if Master Masker mean here for the impossibility by reason of the difference of his presence and his absence, I cannot see why they should be more offended after his ascension than before. For if it be possible for him to make his body to be in many diverse places at once in earth, then it is as possible for him to make it at once in those two diverse places, earth and heaven. For the marvel standeth not in the far distance of the two places asunder, but in the diversity of the two places having in them both one body, be they never so near together. And as for the difference of his presence here in earth and his absence hence by his ascension into heaven, Master Masker is more than mad to put that for a difference, as a cause after the ascension to make them more offended to hear of the eating of his body. For

78 table. For the Masker's use of the Church fathers, see CW 11: 332–34. See Tertullian, *Adversus Marcionem* 4.40.3 (*CCSL* 1: 656); Augustine, *Contra Adamantum* 12 (*PL* 42: 146); Chrysostom, *Commentarius in S. Mattaeum* 82(83) (*PG* 58: 743). **79** wishes **80** otherwise **81** knows **82** living **83** distinguished **84** *CW* 11: 316–17 **85** so that **86** intention **87** repugnance

if he make (as he can and doth) his body to be as well here in earth as in heaven, then is his body no more absent from hence than from thence as for the verity of his presence in the place, though it be more absent in consideration to us that see not his body here, but in the form of bread. But the blessed angels see that one blessed body of his in heaven and here in the Blessed Sacrament both at once. And thus you see that Master Masker's argument hath no pith or strength if he mean for impossibility.

Now if Master Masker here mean that after Christ's ascension into heaven, it should be a thing that should of reason more offend the Jews to eat his flesh than at the time while he was here, as a thing that would be then a much more loathsome meat, what devil reason hath Master Masker to bear that mad mind[88] withal, and to think that his glorified flesh should be more loathsome to receive than if it were unglorified?

And yet either he meaneth thus, or else he lacketh the way to find the words with which he would express his mind. For these are the words that he maketh Christ to say: "If it offend you to eat my flesh while I am here, it shall much more offend you to eat it when my body shall be gone out of your sight."[89] You see now that he saith it shall more offend you to eat it when it is gone out of your sight into heaven. Now if he had meant in the other manner for the impossibility, he would have said (except[90] he cannot speak) that it should more offend them to hear it told them that they should then eat his flesh, when his flesh were so far absent from them, than to hear it told them that they should eat it while it were present with them, and not say it should then more offend them to eat it. For they shall not be offended with the eating if they eat it not. And therefore, if he can tell how to speak and express his own mind, he meaneth here while he saith, "It shall more offend you to eat it," he meaneth, I say, that they should of reason think his flesh then more loathly to eat after his glorious ascension than it was ere[91] he died. Thus it appeareth that Master Masker meant. And verily[92] if he so mean, he hath a mad meaning. And if he mean not so, then hath he a mad manner of speaking. And yet besides that, his meaning is as mad that way as the other.

For as I have showed you, the thing is no more impossible to Christ to give them his body to eat after his ascension than before, and therefore is Master Masker a fool to say that it should more offend them to hear that they should eat it after his ascension than before. For by their eating he should not lose it, but both men may have his body here in earth with them, and the angels may have it in heaven with them, and himself may have it both in earth and in heaven with him, and all this at once.

Wherein, lest Master Masker might make some ween that I do as he saith I do, and as indeed Master Masker doth himself—that is to wit,[93] mock in this matter and lie—ye shall, good readers, hear what holy Saint Chrysostom saith:

Elijah left unto Elisha his mantle as a very great inheritance. And in very deed, a great inheritance it was, and more precious than any gold. And Elisha was a double Elijah, and there was then Elijah above and Elijah beneath. I know well that you think he was a just and a blessed man, and you would fain[94] each of you be in his case. What will you say then, if I show you a certain other thing: that all we that[95] are seasoned with the holy sacraments have received that[96] far excelleth Elijah's mantle? For Elijah indeed left his disciple his mantle. But the Son of God, ascending up, hath left unto us his flesh. And as for Elijah leaving his mantle to his disciple, left it off from himself. But our Savior Christ hath both left it still with us, and yet in his ascension hath taken it with himself too. Let never therefore our hearts fall for fear, nor let us not lament and bewail, nor dread the difficulties of the troublous times. For he that neither hath refused to shed his blood for us all, and hath also, besides that, given unto us all his flesh to eat, and the same blood again to drink, he will refuse nothing that may serve for our salvation.[97]

How say you now, good Christian readers? Doth not Saint Chrysostom with these words affirm you plainly the substance of that that[98] I say, and as plainly destroy all that Master Masker saith in his heretical exposition of these words of Christ, which he construeth so as he would thereby make a repugnance[99] between the being of Christ's blessed body in the Blessed Sacrament, and the being of his body by his ascension in heaven? For though Master Masker say they cannot stand together, but is utterly repugnant that his body should be here in earth before Doomsday,[100] because that until Doomsday it shall be still in heaven, yet saith Saint Chrysostom plainly that Master Masker in his exposition lieth. For he saith that Christ's blessed body is both in heaven and also in earth in the Blessed Sacrament indeed.

And therefore let Master Masker leave his jesting with me, and go jest and rail against Saint Chrysostom. For he confuteth you, Master Masker, you see well, a little more clearer than I. And then whether of them twain[101] ye shall believe and take for the more credible man, Master Masker or holy Saint Chrysostom, every man's own wit,[102] that any wit hath, will well serve him to see.

THE FOURTH CHAPTER

But Master Masker, to show you a further declaration of his wit, forthwith[103] upon his wise and worshipful[104] exposition of those words of Christ, he repeateth that fond[105] argument again that Christ meant not of eating his flesh in the Sacrament, because that if he had meant it, he could and would have declared his meaning more plainly. And in that matter thus Master Masker saith:

Here might Christ have instructed his disciples the truth of the eating of his flesh in form of bread, had this been his meaning. For he left them never in any perplexity or doubt, but sought all the ways by similitudes and familiar examples, to teach them plainly; he never spoke them so hard a parable, but where he perceived their feeble ignorance, anon[106] he helped them and declared it them. Yea, and sometimes he prevented[107] their asking with his own declaration. And think ye not that he did not so here? Yes, verily. For he came to teach us and not to leave us in any doubt and ignorance, especially the chief point of our salvation, which standeth in the belief in his death for our sins. Wherefore to put them out of all doubt as concerning this eating of his flesh and drinking of his blood that should give everlasting life, where they took it for his very body to be eaten with their teeth, he said, "It is the spirit that giveth this life. My flesh profiteth nothing at all to be eaten as ye mean so carnally; it is spiritual meat that I here speak of. It is my spirit that draweth the hearts of men to me by faith, and so refresheth them ghostly.[108] Ye be therefore carnal to think that I speak of my flesh to be eaten bodily. For so it profiteth you nothing at all. How long will you be without understanding? It is my spirit, I tell you, that giveth life. My flesh profiteth you nothing to eat it, but to believe that it shall be crucified and suffer for the redemption of the world, it profiteth. And when ye thus believe, then eat ye my flesh and drink my blood, that is, ye believe in me to suffer for your sins." The Verity hath spoken these words: "My flesh profiteth nothing at all"; it cannot therefore be false. For both the Jews and his disciples murmured and disputed of his flesh, how it should be eaten, and not of the offering thereof for our sins as Christ meant. This therefore is the sure anchor to hold us by, against all the objections of the papists, for the eating of Christ's body as they say in form of bread. Christ said, "My flesh profiteth nothing," meaning to eat it bodily. This is the key that solveth all their arguments and openeth the way to show us all their false and abominable blasphemous lies upon Christ's words, and uttereth their sleight[109] juggling over the bread to maintain Antichrist's kingdom therewith. And thus when Christ had declared it, and taught them that it was not the bodily eating of his material body, but the eating with the spirit of faith, he added, saying, "The words which I here speak unto you are spirit and life," that is to say, "This matter that I here have spoken of with so many words must be spiritually understood to give ye this life everlasting. Wherefore the cause why ye understand me not is that ye believe not." Here is, lo, the conclusion of all his sermon.[110]

Many a fond process[111] have I read, good Christian readers, but never read I neither a more foolish nor a more false than this is. For the effect and the

---

99 contradiction, inconsistency
100 Judgment Day　　101 *whether of them twain:* which of the two　　102 mind, intellect　　103 immediately　　104 distinguished　　105 foolish　　106 immediately, soon　　107 anticipated　　108 spiritually　　109 crafty　　110 *CW* 11: 317　　111 *fond process:* foolish argument

purpose of all this process is that Christ, in all his words spoken in this sixth chapter of Saint John, meant nothing of the eating of his blessed body in the Blessed Sacrament, but only of an allegorical eating of his body, by which he meant only that they should believe that he should be crucified and shed his blood and die for redemption of the world.

Now that our Savior, besides all such allegories and other spiritual understandings, plainly meant of the very eating of his blessed body in the Blessed Sacrament, you have, good readers, already seen, by so many holy doctors and saints, whose plain words I have rehearsed[112] you, that no man can doubt but that in the whole conclusion of his argument and his exposition Master Masker hath a shameful fall, except[113] any man doubt whether Master Masker be better to be believed alone, or those holy doctors among them all.

But now this false conclusion of his, how feebly and how foolishly he defendeth — that is even a very great pleasure to see.

In this process hath he two points. The first is that Christ could and would have made it open and plain in this place by clear and evident words, if he had meant of the eating of his flesh in the Sacrament. The second is that by these words, "It is the spirit that giveth life; my flesh profiteth nothing at all. The words that I have spoken to you be spirit and life," Christ doth plain and clearly declare both that he meant not the eating of his flesh in the Sacrament, and also that he meant only the belief that he should die for the sin of the world.

Now touching his first foolish point, I have confuted it already, and showed you some examples where Christ could at some time have declared the matter much more openly than he did, and that in great matters of our faith.

For I think the sacrament of baptism is a principal point of our faith. And yet Christ taught not Nicodemus all that he could have told him therein, as I said before.

And longeth[114] it nothing to the faith to believe the remission of mortal sins? I suppose yes. And yet could Christ, if he had would,[115] have declared more clearly those words of his, "Whoso blaspheme the Son of Man, it shall be forgiven him. But he that blasphemeth the Holy Ghost, it shall neither be forgiven him in this world nor in the world to come."[116]

No good Christian man thinketh other but that it is a principal article of the Christian faith to believe that Christ is one equal God with his Father. And yet Christ (albeit that by all places set together, he hath declared it clear enough in conclusion to them that will not be willful and contentious) yet did he not in every place where he spoke thereof declare the matter so clearly as he could have done if he then had would, which appeareth by that that in some other places he declared it more clearly after. And yet in all the places of the Scripture set together, he hath not, nor would not, declare it in so plain words as he could have done. For then should there never have needed any of those comments that all the holy doctors have made upon it since. And surely so saith Luther and these other heretics that there needed none. For all the Scripture (they say) is open and plain enough. And therefore they put every man and woman unlearned in boldness and courage to be in the Scripture sufficiently their own masters themselves. But while they thus teach them, they forget that by their own teaching they should hold their peace themselves. And indeed so were it good they did, but if[117] they taught better.

And thus for his first point, you see, good readers, that Master Masker maketh men perceive him for a double fool when it was not enough for him to come forth with this folly once, but he must, a[118] God's name, bring in this his one folly twice.

THE FIFTH CHAPTER

Now as touching his second point, in that it is a world[119] to see how strongly the man handleth it. For whereas Christ hath, by so many open plain words before, taught and declared that he would give his own flesh to be eaten, and his own blood to be drunken, and so often repeated it, and in such effectual wise[120] inculcated it, and, as who should say,[121] beat it into their heads, that (saving[122] for the form and manner of the eating, which he declared by his word and his deed at his Holy Maundy) else[123] as for to make men sure that verily eat it and drink it they should, there could never more clear words have been of any man desired, nor by Master Masker himself devised, now cometh Master Masker forth with certain words of Christ, by which he saith that Christ clearly declareth that he meant clear the contrary—that is to wit, that his flesh should not be eaten—and also that by this word "eating" of his flesh, he meant nothing else but the belief of his death for men's sins.

Now the words of our Savior that (as Master Masker saith) prove these two things are these: "It is the spirit that giveth life; my flesh profiteth nothing at all. The words that I have spoken to you be spirit and life."

These words have, good readers, in themselves neither anything in disproof of the very eating of his flesh, nor for the proof that he meant the belief of his death. For these words, as Saint Augustine declareth, speak not precisely against the eating of his flesh, as he meant to give it them with the spirit and the life therein, but against the eating of his flesh alone, dead and cut out in gobbets, as they conceived a false opinion that he meant to make them eat it. And as I have showed you before, Saint Cyril expoundeth these words after the same manner, and other holy doctors too. And now if ye read again Master Masker's words here, ye shall find that all that seemeth to prove his purpose is only the words of himself, and nothing the words of Christ, but himself expounding Christ's words in such wise that (as I have showed you) Saint Augustine and Saint Cyril and other holy doctors, expound it clear against him.

If his own argument were aught[124] worth, that he layeth against the interpretation of all that expound those words of Christ to be spoken of the very eating, by which we eat his blessed body in the Sacrament, it would make against[125] no man so sore[126] as against himself even here in this place.

For if it be true that he saith—that if Christ had meant of the eating of his flesh in the Sacrament, he might and would have in this place told it them plainly, and because he told them not that point out plainly, therefore it is clear that he meant it not— then say I that since in these words, which Master Masker saith is the very anchor-hold, Christ doth not so plainly declare that he meaneth by the eating of his flesh the belief that he should die for our sins,

as he could if he had would,[127] and would, as Master Masker saith, if he had so meant. This is therefore a plain proof by Master Masker's argument against Master Masker's mind[128] that our Savior meant not so, and then is all Master Masker's matter gone.

Now that our Savior doth not here declare that point clearly, that he meant nothing but that they should believe that he should die for them, I will have Master Masker's own words to bear me record, which will, I ween, make Master Masker somewhat wroth[129] with himself, for writing them in himself so foolishly against himself.

For where he saith that both the Jews and the disciples murmured and disputed of his flesh, how it should be eaten, and not of the offering thereof for our sins, this declareth and witnesseth well for our part against his own: that our Savior declared more plainly his mind for the eating of his flesh than for the offering thereof to the death for our sins. And of very truth so he did indeed, though Master Masker say "nay" a hundred times. For of the eating of his flesh, as I have before said, he spoke very precisely, and plainly, and often, and of his offering up upon the cross he never spoke plainly so much as one word.

For as for these words which Master Masker calleth the anchor-hold, "It is the spirit that giveth this life; my flesh profiteth nothing at all," hath not one plain word for his purpose at all. For all the uttermost that he could take of these words were no more but that Christ should tell them that the spirit is the thing that giveth his flesh the life, without which of itself it could not profit them at all, and therefore the words that he spoke were spirit and life, and to be understood spiritually—that they should eat his flesh with his spirit), and not carnally (that they should eat his flesh alone without his spirit, cut out in dead pieces of flesh, as they had conceived a fond opinion thereof—out of which he said all this to bring them, but yet not so much as he could have said and he had would,[130] nor would not because of their unworthiness to hear it, and yet that they should eat his flesh he told them clear enough.

But as I say, what one word is there in all these words of his anchor-hold, whereby Master Masker may take one handful hold that Christ here showed them so clearly that he meant the offering of himself for our sins? He speaketh in all these words not one word of offering, nor of crucifying, nor of death. And by Master Masker's own argument, if he had meant that way, as he well could, so he would also have told them plainly thus: "Sirs, I mean not that you shall eat my flesh, but that you shall believe that I shall die for your sins." And since he said not thus, Master Masker's own argument hath cut off his cable-rope, and lost his anchor, and run his ship himself against a rock. For he saith that if he had meant it, he would have told them plain the tale to put them out of all doubt.

And here you see now, good readers, by more means than one, as well by the expositions of old holy doctors and saints, as by the wise argument of Master Masker himself, to what wise worshipful end this rial[131] brag of his is come to pass, in which he triumpheth over the Catholic Church and the Blessed Sacrament, where he boasteth thus:

This therefore is the sure anchor to hold us by, against all the objections of the papists, for the eating of Christ's body, as they say, in form of bread. Christ said, "My flesh profiteth nothing," meaning to eat it bodily. This is the key that solveth all their arguments and openeth the way to show us all their false and abominable, blasphemous lies upon Christ's words, and uttereth their sleight[132] juggling over the bread to maintain Antichrist's kingdom therewith. And thus when Christ had declared it, and taught them that it was not the bodily eating of his material body but the eating with the spirit of faith, he added, saying, "The words which I here speak unto you are spirit and life," that is to say, "This matter that I here have spoken of with so many words must be spiritually understood to give ye this life everlasting. Wherefore the cause why ye understand me not is that ye believe me not." Here is, lo, the conclusion of all his sermon.[133]

Since yourselves have seen, good readers, that in this matter and in this whole exposition, there are against Master Masker not only the Catholic Church of our time, but also all the old holy doctors and saints, which with one voice expound

these words of Christ to be spoken and meant of that eating of Christ's flesh, by which it is eaten in the Blessed Sacrament, against which point Master Masker here rageth in this his furious boast, railing upon them all that so teach or believe, under his spiteful name of papists, I would wit[134] of Master Masker whether Saint Bede, Saint Augustine, and Saint Ambrose, Saint Irenaeus, and Saint Hilary, Theophylactus, Saint Cyril, and Saint Chrysostom, were all papists or not? If he answer yea, and say they were, then shall he make no man (that wise is) ashamed of the name of papists (as odious as he would make it), if he grant us that such good godly men, and such holy doctors and saints were papists.

Now if he answer me "nay," and say that they were no papists, then he maketh it plain and open unto you, good readers, that he playeth but the part of a foolish railer and a jester, and doth but deceive and mock all his own fraternity, when by railing against papists, whom he would have taken for folk of a false faith, he dissembleth the truth that his heresy is not only damned by them that he calleth papists, but by them also whom he confesseth for no papists, and whom he cannot but confess for old holy doctors and saints, nor cannot so blind you, but that you plainly perceive by their own words, which I have rehearsed you, and yet shall hereafter more plainly perceive by more holy doctors and saints of the same sort, and by more plain words also of the same, that they do all with one voice expound these words of Christ mentioned in the sixth chapter of Saint John to be spoken and meant of that eating of his flesh, by which we eat it in the Blessed Sacrament.

And thus have I, good readers, answered you all Master Masker's arguments, by which he reproveth in general, under the name of papists, all those — that is to wit, all the old holy doctors and saints — that contrary to his heresy expound the said words of Christ to be meant of the very eating of his flesh, and not only of the believing of his death for our sin. And now will I come to his subtle disputations, that he maketh against me by name in special to soil[135] such things as I in my letter wrote against John Frith.

Here endeth the Third Book.

THE FOURTH BOOK

In the sixth leaf, thus he saith:

> Here maketh Master More this argument against the young man. Because the Jews marveled at this saying, "My flesh is very meat[1] and my blood drink," and not at this, "I am the door and the very vine,"[2] therefore this text, saith he, "my flesh," etc. must be understood after[3] the literal sense — that is to wit, even as the carnal Jews understood it, murmuring at it, being offended, going their ways from Christ for their so carnal understanding thereof — and the other texts, "I am the door," etc. must be understood in an allegory and a spiritual sense, because his hearers marveled nothing at the manner of speech.[4]

I have, good readers, before this argument that he speaketh of, another argument in that epistle of mine against Frith, which although it went before and was read before this, yet because it would not well be soiled,[5] Master Masker was content to dissemble it. But I shall afterward anon[6] lay it afore him again, and set him to it with a fescue,[7] that[8] he shall not say but he saw it.

But now as for this argument of mine, that he maketh the first, I misfortuned to make so feeble that he taketh even a pleasure to play with it, and therefore he soileth it and soileth it again, and that full wisely ye may be fast[9] and sure, and so shall you say yourself when you see all. But yet though he win himself worship[10] in the soiling, it was no great wisdom to lose his worship in the rehearsing, with false bearing in hand[11] that I say that those words of Christ must be understood after that literal sense that the carnal Jews took therein that murmured and went their way therefore. For they took that of his flesh to be eaten in the selfsame fleshly form and, as holy Saint Augustine saith, that they should have eaten his flesh dead, without life or spirit, as beef or mutton is cut out in butchers' shops. And I am very sure that Master Masker hath no such word in my letter, whereof he may take hold to say that I say that Christ's words should be taken so. But this

is no new fashion of these folks, to rehearse[12] other men's arguments in such manner as themselves list[13] to make them, and then they make them such as themselves may most easily soil them, which while Master Masker hath done with mine, yet hath he little advantage thereby. But to the intent that all things shall be the more open before your eyes, I shall rehearse you first the thing that he would be content you saw not: that is to wit, mine own words as I wrote them, which he rehearseth as[14] himself maketh them new.

These were, good reader, my words:

> And over[15] this the very circumstances of the places in the Gospel, in which our Savior speaketh of that Sacrament, may well make open the difference of his speech in this matter and of all those others, and that as he spoke all those but in an allegory so spoke he this, plainly meaning that he spoke of his very body and his very blood, besides all allegories. For neither when our Lord said he was a very[16] vine, nor when he said he was the door, there was none that heard him that anything[17] marveled thereof. And why? For because they perceived well that he meant not that he was a material vine indeed, nor a material door neither. But when he said that his flesh was very meat, and his blood was very drink, and that they should not have life in them but if[18] they did eat his flesh and drink his blood, then were they almost all in such a wonder thereof that they could not abide. And wherefore?[19] But because they perceived well by his words and his manner of circumstances used in the speaking of them, that Christ spoke of his very flesh and his very blood indeed. For else[20] the strangeness of the words would have made them to have taken it as well for an allegory as either his words of the vine or of the door. And then would they have no more marveled at the one than they did at the other. But now whereas at the vine and the door they marveled nothing,[21] yet at the eating of his flesh and drinking of his blood, they so sore[22] marveled, and were so sore moved, and

---

1 *very meat:* true food   2 Jn 10:9, 15:1   3 according to   4 *CW* 11: 310   5 refuted   6 at once   7 small stick for teaching children the alphabet, pointer   8 so that   9 steadfast; secure; certain   10 distinction; honor   11 *bearing in hand:* assertions; charges   12 quote, relate   13 choose; please   14 as if   15 beyond   16 true;   proper   17 in any way   18 *but if:* unless   19 why   20 otherwise   21 not at all   22 greatly

thought the matter so hard, and the wonder so great, that they asked how could that be, and went almost all their way, whereby we may well see that he spoke these words in such wise[23] as the hearers perceived that he meant it not in a parable nor an allegory, but spoke of his very flesh and his very blood indeed.[24]

Lo, good readers, here I speak of Christ's very flesh and his very blood, as the truth is indeed. But here I say not, as Master Masker saith I say, that Christ meant of his flesh and his blood, in such wise as the Jews thought that forsook him therefor,[25] which[26] thought, as you have heard, that they should eat his flesh in the self[27] fleshly form, and also piecemeal in loathly[28] dead gobbets, without either life or spirit.

And now that you have seen his truth in rehearsing, you shall see a show of his sharp subtle wit in the soiling, wherein first, after his juggling fashion, to carry the reader with wondering from marking well the matter, thus he beginneth with a great gravity, giving all the world warning to beware of me:

Lo, Christian reader, here hast thou not a taste but a great ton[29] full of More's mischief and pernicious perverting of God's Holy Word. And as thou seest him here falsely and pestilently destroy the pure sense of God's Word, so doth he in all other places of his books.[30]

Lo, good readers, now have you a great high tragical warning, with not a little taste but a great ton full at once, of my mischievous pernicious false pestilent perverting and destroying of the pure sense of God's holy words in this one place, which he will shall stand for a plain proof that I do the same in all other places.

Now good readers, albeit that[31] it might mishap me by oversight to mishandle this one place, and yet in some other to write well enough, yet am I content to take the condition at Master Masker's hand that if mine handling of this one place be such a heinous handling as maketh it such a pernicious pestilent, not only perversion, but also destruction of the pure sense of God's Holy Word, never make

examination of any other word of mine further. For I then forthwith[32] confess even here that I have in all other places written wrong every whit.[33] But now on the other side, though you should hap to find that in this place, I have somewhat overseen myself[34] in mistaking of some one word for another, without the effect of the matter changed, then will I require[35] you to take my fault for no greater than it is indeed, nor mistrust all my writing for that one word in this one place mistaken, without the impairing of the matter. For such a manner[36] mistaking of a word is not the destroying of the pure sense of God's Holy Word. And therefore if you find my fault, good readers, no further than such, ye will, I doubt not of your equity, bid Master Masker leave his iniquity, and change his high tragical terms, and turn his great ton full of pernicious pestilent false perverting poison into a little taste of wholesome enough, though somewhat small and rough Rochelle[37] wine. And therefore let us now see wherein he layeth this great high heap of mischievous perverting. Lo, thus good readers, he saith:

First, where More saith they marveled at Christ's saying, "My flesh is very meat, etc.," that is not so. Neither is there any such word in the text, except[38] More will expound *murmurabant id est mirabantur*, "they murmured," that is to say, "they marveled," as he expoundeth *oportet, id est expedit et convenit*, "he must die," or "it behooveth[39] him to die," that is to say, "it was expedient and of good congruence[40] that he should die, etc." This poet may make a man to signify an ass, and black white, to blear the simple eyes.[41]

Now good readers, I wot[42] well that you consider that the cause wherefore I spoke of the marveling that they had, which heard Christ speak of the eating of his flesh, was because that none of those that heard him at other times call himself a vine or a door marveled anything thereat, so that by the great difference of the behavior of the hearers, it might well appear that there was great difference in the speaking, and that the other two were well perceived to be spoken only by way of allegory, and the third to be spoken of his very flesh indeed, whereas

23 a way 24 See Letter 190: Against John Frith, pp. 358–70. 25 for it 26 who 27 same 28 repulsive 29 wine-cask 30 *CW* 11: 310 31 *albeit that:* although 32 immediately 33 bit 34 *overseen myself:* blundered 35 ask, request 36 kind of 37 a seaport in western France 38 unless 39 befits 40 *of* *good congruence:* fitting 41 *CW* 11: 310 42 know

Frith held opinion that this was none otherwise spoken, but only by way of an allegory as the other twain[43] were.

Now good readers, if you read my words again, and in every place of them where I write, "they marveled," it would like[44] you to put out that word, "they marveled," and set in this word, "they murmured," in the stead thereof, ye shall find no change made in the matter by that change made in the words. But you shall see mine argument shall stand as strong with that word, "they murmured," as with this word, "they marveled." For when, at the hearing of Christ's words speaking of the eating of his flesh, the Evangelist showeth that many of the hearers murmured, and neither at the calling of himself a vine, nor at the calling of himself a door, none of his hearers murmured for that manner of speaking, it appeareth as well the difference in Christ's speaking, by the difference of diverse his hearers at the one word "murmuring," and at the other two "not murmuring," as at the one "marveling," and at the other two "not marveling."

Lo, thus you see, good readers, that in this matter in which Master Masker maketh his great outcry upon me for changing of this word "murmuring" into this word "marveling," since there is no change in the matter by the change of the word, but mine argument as strong with the one word as with the other, I neither have done it of any fraud for advantage of mine own part in the matter, nor yet since the change is but in the word without change of the matter, I have not thereby perniciously and pestilently by the whole ton full of falsehood at once perverted and destroyed the pure sense of God's Holy Word. But it appeareth well, on the other side, that Master Masker hath given us here, I will not be so sore[45] to say a ton full, but at the leastwise, a little pretty[46] taste of his little pretty falsehood, with which a little he prettily believeth me.

THE SECOND CHAPTER

But yet shall you now see his wit[47] and his truth both a little better tried, even upon this same place, in which with his huge exclamations he maketh his part so plain.

As for *oportet* of which he speaketh here, we shall talk of after in another place. But now, touching this word "they marveled," Master Masker saith thus: "That is not so, nor there is no such word in the text."[48] So you see, good readers, that he saith two things. One, that it is not so, and another that there is no such word there in the text. As for the word, good reader, I will not greatly strive with him. But where he saith it is not so, and therein affirmeth that they marveled not, I think the words of the text will well maintain my saying. For, good reader, when they said, "How can he give us his flesh to eat?" and when they said, "This word is hard and who can hear it?" do not these words prove that they marveled and thought it strange when they called it so hard that no man might abide to hear it and asked how he could do it, because they thought it impossible?

Now you see, good readers, that the Gospel saith the selfsame thing that I say, though it say not the selfsame word, and therefore lieth Master Masker in saying it is not so.

But by this wise way of Master Masker, if I had written that Absalom was angry with Ammon his brother for violating his sister Tamar,[49] Master Masker would say, "Lo, good reader, here thou hast not a taste but a ton[50] full of More's pernicious perverting of God's Holy Word, and as thou seest him here falsely and pestilently destroy the pure sense of God's Word, so doth he in all other places of his works. For where he saith that Absalom was angry with Ammon, it is not so, neither is there any such word in the text, except[51] More will expound *oderat eum, id est irascebatur ei*, 'he hated him,' that is to say, 'he was angry with him,' as he expoundeth *murmurabant id est mirabantur*, 'they murmured,' that is to say, 'they marveled.' And thus may this poet make a man to signify an ass. For the Bible saith not as More saith, that Absalom was angry with Ammon. For the text saith no more, but that Absalom hated Ammon and caused him to be killed."[52]

How like you now, good readers, this wise solution of Master Masker? This proveth not him a poet that can make a man signify an ass, but proveth him rather instead of a poet, and instead of a man, a very stark ass indeed.

THE THIRD CHAPTER

But of very truth, good reader, not without a good cause and a great, I did rather touch the thing that was the cause of the Jews' murmur and their dissension when they disputed upon the matter than I did their murmur and their dissension. For of truth, where he said of himself that he was a door, there grew dissension among his hearers upon that word of his, and upon other words that he spoke therewith at the same time, so that the Gospel saith, "And there was dissension among the Jews upon these words, some saying that the devil was in him and some saying nay, and that the devil was not wont[53] to make blind men see,"[54] as there was here dissension and disputing upon these words of eating of his flesh. But in the tenth chapter, they nothing[55] marveled of his calling himself a door, for he expounded the parable at length so that they perceived well that he called himself a door, but only by way of an allegory. And therefore of calling himself a door they marveled not of that word when he declared it, for they perceived it for a parable. But they disputed upon that word and upon his other words also, wherein he said that no man could kill him against his will, and that he would die for his sheep, and that he had power to put away his soul and take it again.[56] Of these things they disputed and thought them strange and marvelous too, but not for the words or the manner of speaking, but for the very matter. For all they understood the words meetly[57] well, but many of them believed them not. But not one of them did so take that word, "I am a door," as that they marveled how that could be. And therefore none of them for any such marvel said there, "How can he be door?" as these Jews said here, "How can he give us his flesh to eat?" And therefore, as I say, therein appeareth well that our Savior in the one place called himself a door, by way of a parable, and in the other spoke of the eating of his own very[58] flesh itself, besides all parables, which well appeared, I say, by his audience. For the one word they perceived for a parable, and therefore none of them marveled of the manner of the speaking of that word, though they marveled and murmured and disputed at the thing that the parable meant. But in the other place, many marveled

at the thing by the selfsame name that he gave thereto, saying, "How can he give us his flesh to eat?" whereby it well appeareth that they perceived that he spoke of very eating of his flesh indeed, and in the other place appeareth not that they thought he meant that he was a very door indeed, but the contrary plain appeareth. For Christ by his plain and open exposition of that parable delivered them clean from all occasion of thinking that he meant himself to be a very door indeed. But in these words of eating of his flesh, because he would give his very flesh to be eaten in very deed, therefore he more and more told them still the same, and also told them himself was God, and therefore able to do it, and over[59] that gave them warning that they should not eat it in dead gobbets, but should eat it quick[60] with spirit and life. For his words were spirit and life. For his flesh should else[61] avail nothing. And that though his body should be eaten by many sundry men in many sundry places, yet should it nevertheless be also still whole and sound, wheresoever he would[62] besides, which he declared by his ascension with his body perfect into heaven, notwithstanding that it should be before that eaten of many men in earth.

And thus have I, good readers, as for this solution of Master Masker, made open and plain unto you his falsehood and his folly both, and made it clear, for all his high pernicious pestilent words, both that I have handled this place of the Scripture right, and also taken rather the sentence[63] than the word. And I have also, by occasion of his wise solution, caused you to perceive that in mine argument was and is more pith and more strength than peradventure[64] every man perceived before. And therefore thus much worship[65] hath he won by this his first solemn solution.

THE FOURTH CHAPTER

But in his second solution, he specially showeth his deep insight and cunning,[66] and mine oversight too shamefully. For therein, lo, thus he saith:

But yet for his lordly pleasure, let us grant him that "they murmured" is as much to say as "they

---

53 accustomed   **54** Jn 10:19–21   **55** not at all   **56** See Jn 10:15, 18.   **57** fairly   **58** true; proper   **59** besides   **60** living   **61** otherwise   **62** would go   **63** sense, meaning   **64** perhaps   **65** distinction, honor   **66** learning

marveled," because perchance the one may follow at the other. And then do I ask him whether
Christ's disciples and his apostles heard him not
and understood him not, when he said, "I am the
door and the vine," and when he said, "My flesh,"
etc. If he say no or nay, the Scripture is plain
against him (John 6, 10, and 15).[67] If he say yea
or yes, then yet do I ask him whether his disciples
and apostles, thus hearing and understanding his
words in all these three chapters, wondered and
marveled as Master More saith, or murmured,
as hath the text, at their master's speech. What
think ye More must answer here? Here may you
see whether this old holy upholder of the pope's
Church is brought, even to be taken in his own
trap. For the disciples and his apostles neither
murmured nor marveled, nor yet were not offended with their master Christ's words and manner of speech.[68]

Lo, good readers, here Master Masker, because he
thinketh that not enough for his worship to show
himself once a fool by his first solution, cometh
now farther forth to show himself twice a fool, yea,
thrice a fool, by the second.

And first, for a way to come thereto, he saith he
will grant me, for my lordly pleasure, that "they
murmured" is as much to say as "they marveled,"
in which granting, he doth me no great lordly pleasure. For I have, as you have heard well, proved him
already that I need not his granting therein. But verily in the cause that he addeth thereto, when he saith
because perchance the one may follow at the other,
therein he doth me a very great lordly pleasure. For
it is even a pleasure for a lord and for a king too to
see him play so far the fool as without necessity to
write in that word himself, which helpeth mine argument against himself, and maketh all his wondering that he hath in his first solution upon me fall
in his own neck. For if their murmuring followed
upon their marveling, as himself here saith that peradventure it did, then playeth he first peradventure
the fool, to make such an outcry upon me for saying
that they marveled, where the text saith they murmured, as though I with that word utterly destroyed
the pure sense of God's Holy Word. For that word
doth not so pestilently pervert the sense, if it may

stand with the sentence, as it may indeed, if Master
Masker say true that peradventure the one may follow upon the other—that is to wit,[69] the murmuring upon the marveling, for so he meaneth thereby.
For as mad as he is, he is not, I think, so mad yet
as to mean that the marveling followed upon the
murmuring. For they marveled first and murmured
after. And now since this one word of his therefore overthroweth all his wondering that he hath
made on me, and proveth himself willingly and wittingly[70] in all his high tragical exclamation against
his own conscience, and his own very knowledge to
belie[71] me, he hath therein, as I say, done me a very
special pleasure, to see him so far play the fool as to
bring forth that word himself, specially where there
was no need at all, but even for a garnish of his induction, with a show of his cunning, to make men
know that he had not so little learning, but that he
wist[72] well enough himself that he had shamefully
belied me in all that ever he had cried out against
me, concerning any misconstruing of that place of
Holy Scripture.

THE FIFTH CHAPTER

Now after this his double folly well and wisely
put forth at once, he bringeth me to mine opposition. And therein he handleth me so hardly that
I cannot escape, which way so ever I take, whether
I say that Christ's disciples and apostles heard and
understood their master's words in all the three
places, or that I say that in any one of those three
places they understood him not. For here to be sure,
to hold me in on both sides that I escape not, he
showeth what danger I fall in, which way so ever I
take. For he saith that, on the one side, I deny the
Gospel if I answer no or nay, and on the other side,
I am taken in mine own trap if I say yea or yes.

And surely here he playeth the wisest point, and
the most for his own surety[73] that I saw him play
yet. For ye shall understand that in the first part of
my *Confutation* in the third book, the 180th side,
forasmuch as[74] Tyndale hath been so long out of
England that he could not tell how to use these English adverbs, nay and no, yea and yes, I gave him a
rule and a certain examples of the rule, whereby he

---

67 See Jn 6:53; 10:9; 15:1.   **68** *CW* 11: 310–11   **69** say   **70** knowingly   **71** slander   **72** knew   **73** security   **74** seeing that

might learn where he should answer nay and where no, and where yea and where yes.[75]

Now Master Masker when he wrote his book, neither having my book by him, nor the rule by heart, thought he would be sure that I should find no such fault in him, and therefore on the one side for the answer, assigneth yea and yes both, and on the other side both nay and no, leaving the choice to myself, which he durst[76] not well take upon him, lest he might show therein such congruity[77] in the English tongue as he showeth in some other things wherein he speaketh English as congrue as a man might that had learned his English in another land.

But now must I answer him to his subtle questions. His first question is this.

He asketh me whether Christ's disciples and his apostles heard him not and understood him not, when he said, "I am the door," and when he said, "I am the vine," and when he said, "My flesh is verily meat,"[78] etc.

Master Masker is so wily that I must needs take better heed what I answer him than I should need if I were to answer a good plain man of the country. For Master Masker in the twenty-ninth leaf boasteth himself of his cunning[79] rially[80] and saith, "It is verily the thing that I desire even to be written against in this matter. For I have the solutions of all their objections ready."[81]

Now since therefore this man is so cunning, and hath his answers so ready for all objections that men may lay to him, he cannot be by likelihood but wonderful sure and ready, with subtle replications[82] against all answers that men may make to those oppositions that he deviseth against other men himself. I will therefore be as ware[83] of him as I can. And first I say that his question is captious.[84] For he asketh one answer to three things at once, and in each of the three he asketh me two questions at once. For he asketh of the door, and the vine, and of his flesh, all three at once. And yet of each of these not a double question, as I told you, but a quadruple question at once. For he asketh both of his apostles and the disciples, and not only whether all these heard Christ at all three times, but also whether all these understood him. And all twelve questions Master Masker wilily, to beguile such a simple soul as I am, asketh in one question at once. And

therefore, lest he betrap me, I shall somewhat at the leastwise divide them.

And then I say to the first question—whether Christ's disciples and apostles heard him not and understood him not, when he said, "I am the door"—because the question is yet double and captious, I purpose to make sure work and answer that I cannot tell; I think that some did and some did not, for some of them I ween[85] were not there.

Now if he say that he meaneth only them that were there, so would I too have taken him, if he were a good plain soul, and not such a subtle sophister that longeth to be arguing, and hath all things so ready upon his fingers' ends.

But go to now,[86] though I could yet have other answers for him if I would, yet for his lordly pleasure, I shall be content to grant him that they both heard him and understood him, wherein I grant him more yet, I promise you, than he can precisely bind me to by the text. All this granting for this place giveth him no ground yet. For here I am well content, not only to say all that he saith, that is, that his apostles and his disciples understood that Christ calleth himself the door but by[87] a parable, and therefore marveled not at that manner of speaking. But I say more too, that so did also the Jews that reproved him and repugned[88] against him, and say also that they repugned so much the more against him, and so much the more murmured and disputed against the matter, in how much they more understood the manner of the speaking, and that it was but a parable. For they wist well that word of the door was spoken by a parable, for Christ plainly expounded it. But they murmured much at that, that no man might well come in but by him.

Let us now to the second then. And where he asketh me whether Christ's disciples and his apostles heard him not and understood him not, when he said, "I am the very vine," here I would for mine own surety ask him whether he mean by Christ's disciples and apostles some of both sorts, or else those disciples only that were both disciples and apostles. Howbeit,[89] if I should ask him thus, he would say I did but trifle, and that every man may well wit[90] by the putting of his question that he meaneth of either sort some. For else[91] he would have said no more but apostles, which had been enough if he had

75 See *CW* 8: 231–32.　**76** dared　　**79** learning　**80** royally　**81** *CW* 11:　　　now (interjection)　**87** as　**88** contended
77 grammatical correctness　**78** *verily*　336　**82** replies　**83** wary　**84** fallacious,　**89** However　**90** know　**91** otherwise
meat: truly food. See *CW* 11: 310.　　sophistical　**85** think　**86** *go to now*: come

meant but them. And also it were against his purpose, if Christ's other disciples understood him not, though his apostles did. Well I am content then to take it so. And then unto the question whether his disciples and apostles heard not Christ and understood him not, when he said, "I am the very vine," to this question copulative,⁹² I answer no.

But then Master Masker replieth that the Scripture is plain against me. But unto that replication I say nay. For I say that the Scripture there, with Saint Mark and Saint Luke set unto it,⁹³ proveth mine answer true. For it appeareth well among them three that, besides the apostles, none of his other disciples understood him, for none of his other disciples heard him, for none of his other disciples were there, nor yet all his twelve apostles neither, for Judas was gone before, so that in this part of his first question, Master Masker hath given himself a fall in the subtle proponing⁹⁴ of his question. As to the understanding, I agree that they that were there understood him, which maketh nothing against me.

Now to the third place when he asketh me whether Christ's disciples and his apostles heard him not and understood him not, when he said, "My flesh is very meat," etc. First as for his disciples, I say no, not all. Then saith Master Masker that if I say nay or no, the Scripture is plain against me (John 6). But to that say I again that when I say no, the Scripture is even there with me. For as the Gospel there plainly telleth, many of his disciples, though they heard him well, did understand him amiss. For though they understood him right, in that they perceived that he spoke of the very eating of his very flesh, yet they understood him wrong, in that they took him that they should eat it in the self⁹⁵ fleshly form and in dead pieces without life or spirit, and therefore they went their way from him and left him, and walked no more after with him. Here hath Master Masker another fall in this place too, touching his first question as for the disciples.

But what say we then for the apostles? Did not they understand him? What if I here would say nay? Then except⁹⁶ Master Masker could prove yes, else is not only his first question gone, which he maketh for a way to the second, but his second question is clearly gone too, wherewith he would make me be

taken in mine own trap. And therefore first for argument sake, I deny that the apostles themselves understood Christ's word. How will now Master Masker prove me that they did? Marry,⁹⁷ saith he, for they were well acquainted with such phrases. And answered their master Christ when he asked them, "Will you go hence from me too?" "Lord," said they, "to whom shall we go? Thou hast the words of everlasting life, and we believe that thou art Christ, the Son of the living God."⁹⁸

Now good reader, I think there be some texts in Scripture that Master Masker understandeth not no more than other poor men. But yet if he will not agree that, but say that he understandeth them all, yet if we would put the case that there were some such one text, he would, I think, admit the case for possible. Let us then put him hardly none other, but even the same words of Christ that we be now in hand withal.⁹⁹ For no man understandeth any word worse than he understandeth those, even yet while he writeth on them. If himself had been then of that flock, and had seen all other things in Christ that his apostles saw, and had believed in him, and had not mistrusted Christ, but been ready to do what he would bid him do, and believe what he would bid him believe, but had yet as for those words of eating Christ's flesh thought them hard to perceive what Christ meant by them, but though he fully understood them not as he thought, yet he doubted not but that good they were that God spoke, and that Christ, if he tarried¹⁰⁰ his time, would tell him further of the matter at more leisure, if now when others went their way, Christ would have said unto him, "Wilt thou, Master Masker, go thy way from me too?" Whether would¹⁰¹ then Master Masker have letted¹⁰² to say even the selfsame words that the apostles said with others like, "Whither should I go from the good Lord? Thou hast the words of everlasting life, and I believe and know that thou art Christ, the Son of the living God, and art able to do what thou wilt, and thy words be holy and godly, whether I understand them or no, and thou mayst make me perceive them better at thy further pleasure." Would Master Masker have been contented to say thus, or else would he have said, "Nay, by my faith, good Lord, thou shalt tell me this tale a little more plainly that I may better perceive it by and by,¹⁰³ or else will

I go to the devil with yonder good fellows, and let them dwell with thee that will"?

Now if Master Masker would (as I ween[104] he would but if[105] he were stark mad) have said the same himself that Saint Peter said, or be content at the least that Saint Peter should say it for him, though himself had not well and clearly perceived what Christ meant by those words, how can he now prove by the same words of theirs that the apostles understood his words then?

Thus you see, good readers, that of his two questions, the first have I so answered that it is come to nothing (if I would stick with him still at his answer) till he have better proved me than he hath yet that the apostles in the sixth chapter of Saint John did understand Christ's words. And now therefore till he have better handled his first question, he can against me never use his second, whereby he boasteth that I could make none answer, but such as should take myself in mine own trap, from which, since I am clean[106] escaped already by the answering of his first question, you may, good readers, see that Master Masker goeth as wilily to work to take me as a man might send a child about with salt in his hand, and bid him go catch a bird, by laying a little salt on her tail, and when the bird is flown, comfort him then to go catch another, and tell him he had caught it and it had tarried a little.

THE SIXTH CHAPTER

But yet to see now how craftily he could betrap me if I would let him alone, let us grant him, for his lordly pleasure, that the disciples and apostles understood Christ's words well in all three places, not only when he said he was the door, and when he said he was the vine, but also when he said, "My flesh is verily meat."[107] What now? "Marry then," saith Master Masker,

If More answer yea or yes, then do I ask him further, whether Christ's disciples and apostles, thus hearing and understanding his words in all the three chapters, wondered and marveled (as More saith) or murmured (as hath the text) at their master's speech. What think you More must answer here? Here may you see whether this old holy upholder of the pope's Church is brought even to be taken in his own trap. For the disciples and his apostles neither murmured nor marveled, nor yet were not offended with this their master Christ's words and manner of speaking.[108]

In what trap of mine own, or his either, hath Master Masker caught me here? Mine argument was, ye wot[109] well, that at the hearing Christ say, "I am the door," and "I am the very vine," no man marveled at the manner of speaking because that every man perceived his words for allegories and parables. But in the third place where he said, "My flesh is verily meat and the bread that I shall give you is my flesh. And except[110] you eat the flesh of the Son of Man and drink his blood, you shall not have life in you," so many marveled because they perceived well it was not a parable but that he spoke of very eating of his flesh indeed, that of all his hearers very few could abide it, but murmured and said, "How can he give us his flesh to eat?" And his own disciples said, "This word is hard; who may hear him?" and went almost all their way. Now when the effect of mine argument is that, in this point, many marveled at the thing, as a thing plainly spoken, and not a parable, but a plain tale that men should verily eat his flesh, and that no man marveled at the other two manner of speakings because they perceived them for parables, what maketh it against me that in the third place there were some that marveled not nor murmured not since that though some did not, yet many did, and both marveled and murmured and went their way, and that for the most part, and save[111] the apostles almost everyone? And verily the other disciples, as Saint Chrysostom[112] saith, those that then were present (against Master Masker's saying) went their ways all the many.

Where is now, good readers, this trap of mine own making that I am fallen in? Hath Master Masker cast me down so deep with proving me that some marveled not, where I said many did? Be these two propositions so sore repugnant[113] and so plain contradictory—many marveled, and some marveled not—that because I said the first, and he proveth the

---

104 think, believe   **105** *but if:* unless
106 completely   **107** *verily meat:*
truly food; Jn 6:55, 10:7, 15:1   **108** *CW*

11: 310–11   **109** know   **110** unless
111 except   **112** See *PG* 59: 266.   **113** *sore*

repugnant: greatly inconsistent or
incompatible

second, therefore I am quite cast and caught in mine own trap? This man is a wily shrew[114] in argument, I promise you.

THE SEVENTH CHAPTER

But now that I have, good readers, so fair[115] escaped my trap, I trust, with the help of some holy saint, to catch Master Masker in his own trap, that his mastership hath made for me.

Ye wot well, good readers, that the trap which he made for me were these two wily captious[116] questions of his, with which he thought to catch me: that is to wit,[117] first whether the disciples and apostles heard and understood our Savior in all three places, and then upon mine answer yea or yes, his other question further, whether they marveled or murmured, unto which, while I have answered no, now by the traps of his questions he reckoneth me driven to be caught in mine own, because I said that many marveled, as though many others might not because the apostles did.

Now before I show you how himself is taken in his own trap ye shall hear his own glorious words with which he boasteth that he hath taken me, and would make men ween it were so. Lo, these are his words:

Here may you see whether this old holy upholder of the pope's Church is brought, even to be taken in his own trap. For the disciples and his apostles neither murmured nor marveled, nor yet were not offended with this their master Christ's words and manner of speech. For they were well-acquainted with such phrases, and answered their master Christ when he asked them, "Will ye go hence from me too?" "Lord," said they, "to whom shall we go? Thou hast the words of everlasting life, and we believe that thou art Christ, the Son of the living God." Lo, Master More, they neither marveled nor murmured. And why? For because, as ye say, they understood it in an allegory sense, and perceived well that he meant not of his material body to be eaten with their teeth, but he meant it of himself to be believed to be very God and very man, having flesh and blood as they had, and

yet was he the Son of the living God. This belief gathered they of all his spiritual sayings, as himself expoundeth his own words, saying, "My flesh profiteth nothing," meaning to be eaten, "but it is the spirit that giveth this life. And the words that I speak unto you are spirit and life, so that whoso believe my flesh to be crucified and broken, and my blood to be shed for his sins, he eateth my flesh and drinketh my blood, and hath life everlasting. And this is the life wherewith 'the righteous liveth even by faith'" (Habakkuk 2).[118]

Lo, good reader, here have I rehearsed[119] you his words whole to the end. And yet because you shall see that I will not hide from you any piece of his that may make for any strength of his matter, I shall rehearse you further his other words written in his thirteenth leaf, which I would have touched before, saving that I thought to reserve it for him, to strength withal[120] this place of his, where it might do him best service, where he would prove against me to trap me with, that the cause why the disciples and apostles marveled not, nor murmured not, nor were not offended, was because they understood Christ's words to be spoken not of very[121] eating of his flesh, but only of the belief of his Passion by way of a parable or an allegory, as he spoke those other words when he said, "I am the door," and when he said, "I am the vine."[122] The words, lo, of Master Masker with which he setteth forth the proof of this point in his thirteenth leaf be these, in the end of all his exposition upon the sixth chapter of Saint John:

Here is, lo, the conclusion of all this sermon. Christ, very God and man, had set his flesh before them to be received with faith, that it should be broken and suffer for their sin. But they could not eat it spiritually, because they believed not in him. Wherefore many of his disciples fell from him and walked no more with him. And then he said to the twelve, "Will ye go away too?" And Simon Peter answered, "Lord, to whom shall we go? Thou hast the words of everlasting life, and we believe and are sure that thou art Christ, the Son of the living God." Here it is manifest what Peter and his fellows understood by this eating and drinking of

114 villain, scoundrel   **115** completely   **116** fallacious, sophistical   **117** say   **118** *CW* 11: 310–11; Hb 2:4   **119** quoted to   **120** *strength withal:* strengthen thereby   **121** true   **122** Jn 10:7, 15:1

Christ. For they were perfectly taught that it stood all in the belief in Christ, as their answer here testifieth. If this matter had stood upon so deep a miracle as our papists feign, without any word of God not comprehended under any of their common senses, that they should eat his body under form of bread as long, deep, thick, and as broad as it hangeth upon the cross, they being yet but feeble of faith, not confirmed with the Holy Ghost, must here needs have wondered, stonied and staggered,[123] and have been more inquisitive in and of so strange a matter than they were. But they neither doubted nor marveled nor murmured, nor nothing[124] offended with this manner of speech, as were the others that slipped away, but they answered firmly, "Thou hast the words of everlasting life, and we believe," etc. Now to the exposition of the words of our Lord's Supper.[125]

Lo, good readers, ye will, I trow,[126] now bear me record that I deal plainly with Master Masker here, and hide nothing of his aside that may do him any substantial service toward the proof of his purpose. And I warrant you it shall be long ere[127] you find him, or any of all that sect, deal in such plain manner with me.

But now, good Christian reader, read all these whole words of his in both the places as often as you list,[128] and consider them well, and then shall you perceive in conclusion that he proveth his purpose by none other thing in all this world than only by his own words expounding always the words of Christ, as Master Masker list himself. And upon that that[129] himself saith—that the cause wherefore[130] the disciples and apostles marveled not, nor murmured not at these words of Christ, "The bread that I shall give you is my flesh," etc. was because they perceived that Christ spoke it in a parable (as I say of his other words, "I am the door," and "I am the very vine")— upon these words of Master Masker's own, Master Masker concludeth for his purpose the selfsame thing that he first presupposeth, the thing that he should not presuppose but prove: that is to wit, that Christ spoke it but by way of a parable.

But against Master Masker and his presumptuous presupposing, the matter appeareth plain. For as I have before said, our Savior when he said, "I am the door," and when he said, "I am the very vine," did so prosecute[131] and declare in both the places his own words that there could no man have cause to marvel at the manner of speaking, for his own declaration in prosecuting his own words was such that it must needs make any man (but if[132] he were an idiot or an ass) perceive that Christ spoke in those two places that he was the vine and the door but by way of a parable. And this may every man soon see that list to look on the places. And therefore no man said, "How can he be a vine?" nor "How can he be a door?" as many said in the third place, "How can he give us his flesh to eat?" Which words, if they were so clearly spoken but by way of parable, as the other twain[133] were, it were far unlikely that so many wise men would have taken it so far otherwise ever since, that take the other twain for none other—and namely such holy doctors and saints as are well-acquainted with Christ's phrases and parables, and in the study thereof have spent the great part of all their lives. And therefore Master Masker, against so many wise men and so good, going about now to prove this point but a parable, by none other substantial means than only by the authority of his own worshipful[134] word, proveth us his purpose very faint and slender, for all his "lo, Master More," as though his purpose appeared very clear.

THE EIGHTH CHAPTER

Howbeit, for to furnish his matter with, and to set it the better forth, because he would not have it seem to stand all upon his own only exposition, that is to wit, upon his own only word, he setteth unto his own bare word, his own bare bald reason, and saith:

If this matter had stood upon so deep a miracle as our papists feign, without any word of God, not comprehended under any of their common senses, that they should eat his body being under the form of bread as long, deep, thick, and as broad as it hanged upon the cross, they being yet but feeble of faith, not confirmed with the Holy Ghost, must here needs have wondered, stonied and staggered,[135] and have been more inquisitive

---

123 *stonied and staggered:* been astonished and wavered   **124** were not at all   **125** *CW* 11: 317–18   **126** trust   **127** before   **128** choose; please; wish   **129** *that that:* that which   **130** why   **131** deal with in detail   **132** *but if:* unless   **133** two   **134** honorable   **135** *stonied and staggered:* been astonished and wavered

in and of so strange a matter than they were. But they neither marveled nor murmured, nor nothing offended with this manner of speech, as were the others that slipped away, but they answered firmly, "Thou hast the words of everlasting life, and we believe," etc. Now to the exposition of the words of our Lord's Supper.[136]

Here hath Master Masker given us a major[137] of an argument, and a minor too. His major is his first part unto these words, "But they" etc., and his minor is all the remnant. But we may now ask him ergo what? For conclusion he setteth none unto them. If he think the conclusion follow so clear that he needed not, but every man must needs see what followeth upon his two premises, in good faith for my part, if I should set ergo to it — that is, the common note of the consequent[138] — I see not what would follow any more than the common verse of the compute manual, *Ergo ciphos adrifex*,[139] he hath made his major so foolishly.

In which, that first it pleaseth his mastership to trifle and mock in this great matter, and make us poor people ween that everything that any doctor saith in dispicions,[140] or holdeth by way of problem, were delivered us to believe as a necessary point of our faith, he doth but play the false fool for his pleasure. For as for the manner how the blessed body of Christ is in the Blessed Sacrament, whether with his dimensions as long, thick, and broad as he hanged on the cross, or with his dimensions proportionable to the form of bread, as his blessed body was as verily his body in the first moment of his holy conception as it ever was at his Passion, and yet was it then neither so thick, so long, nor so broad, or whether his body be there in his natural substance, without any dimensions at all, or whether he be there in all his distinctions of the members of his holy body, or there have all his members without any distinction of place at all — these things and such others in which learned men may moderately and reverently dispute and exercise their wit[141] and learning, the Catholic Church in such wise[142] leaveth at large that it bindeth not the people to any such straits[143] in the matter, but only to the points that we be bounden

by certain and sure revelation, to believe: that is to wit, that under what manner so ever it be there, verily there it is, his very flesh and his very blood. And in the form of bread, verily eat his very body there we do when we receive the very Blessed Sacrament. Thus far have we by certain and sure revelation, both by Holy Scripture and by the tradition also, by which Christ taught it to his apostles, and they to the Church, as Saint Paul did to the Corinthians,[144] and the Church to the people by succession from age to age ever since the apostles' days unto our own time.

And therefore, with those mocks and jests, Master Masker mocketh no man but himself, save that under the name of papists, he mocketh all the Catholic Church of this fifteen hundred year, both clergy and temporalty,[145] men and women, and all, and among the remnant, all the old holy doctors and saints that have, without doubt or question, both believed and taught that Christ meant not to speak those words, "My flesh is very meat," by way of a parable, as Master Masker saith he only meant, but that he verily spoke and meant of the very eating of his flesh indeed.

But now shall you see that, as I said, his major is so foolishly made that all the world may wonder where his wit was when he made it. For he saith that if the matter stood indeed upon such a great miracle as the Catholic Church, which he calleth the papists, believe — that is to wit, that his very body should be eaten in form of bread, and that also, which he putteth for a necessary part of our faith, as long, as deep, as thick, and as broad as it was when it hanged on the cross — then the disciples and apostles, because they were yet but feeble in the faith, must needs have wondered, stunned and staggered,[146] and have been more inquisitive therein than they were. Now wotteth[147] well every child, good reader, that Christ did not in that place plainly tell them in what manner that they should eat it: that is to wit, that they should eat it in form of bread. For though he gave them an insinuation and signification thereof, in that he said, "And the bread that I shall give you is my flesh,"[148] which words, coupled with his deed when he did institute it indeed at his

136 *CW* 11: 318　　**137** major premise
138 conclusion of a syllogism　　**139** *Ergo ciphos adrifex:* The compute manual was a set of tables for calculating astronomical occurrences and the movable feasts of the

calendar. The mnemonic *Ergo ciphos adrifex* is part of a nonsense verse.　　**140** disputations, discussions　　**141** intelligence, ingenuity　　**142** a way　　**143** rigorous conditions　　**144** See 1 Cor 11:23–24.

145 lay people　　**146** *stunned and staggered:* been astonished and wavered　　**147** knows
148 Jn 6:51

Maundy,[149] might then make them clearly perceive that they should eat his flesh in form of bread, yet at the time when the word was first spoken, it was not so plain for that matter, but it might seem to them that he used that word "bread" but by manner of allegory to signify there his flesh, because they should verily eat it as men eat bread.

Now see then, good reader, the madness of Master Masker, that saith here that that thing must needs have made the apostles wonder, stunned, and stagger, at the time when Christ spoke those words in the sixth chapter of Saint John, at which time every child knoweth that they, though they well perceived that they should verily eat his flesh, yet they knew not that they should eat it in form of bread. And how could it then have made them wonder (that thing I say that he speaketh of and so sore[150] exaggerateth to increase the wonder), that is to wit, that his flesh should be eaten in form of bread, and that as long, as thick, as deep, and as broad as it was when it hanged on the cross. How could this thing, I say, have made them wonder at that time, at which time they thought not of the eating thereof in the form of bread? Heard ever any man such a mad argument as Master Masker hath made us here?

Now if Christ had there told them indeed all that Master Masker hath here put in so foolishly to make the matter the more wonderful, then would I deny his major. And so will I do if himself put all that out again, and leave no more in his major than Christ said indeed, that is, that they should verily eat his flesh and have life thereby, and that they should not only eat it bodily but also spiritually, nor in dead gobbets without life or spirit, but quick[151] and joined with the lively spirit, by which it should give life, and without which his flesh of his own proper nature to the giving of life could not avail. Now say I that if Master Masker had made his major of this, all this had been no cause for his apostles to wonder, nor to be stunned and stagger, nor to murmur and grudge[152] as they did that slipped away. For as feeble as Master Masker maketh the apostles in the faith of Christ, yet at that time, without any such manner of marvel as might make them stun and stagger and slip away from him, they believed such other things as were as hard to believe as this, and that without any further inquisition at all.

For else[153] why should they not at the same time have marveled of his ascension up to heaven, and been more inquisitive thereof. For that was no little marvel neither, and was one of the things that made the Jews and those disciples to stun and stagger that there slipped away from him.

Also they believed that he was God, and had no such wonder thereof as made them stun and stagger or be more inquisitive thereof, which was as strange a matter as was all the other, and which point once believed, it was easy to believe the other without any such manner of marveling as should make them either stun or stagger thereat.

Now as for being inquisitive thereof, holy Saint Chrysostom saith that as strange as the thing was of eating his flesh (for that men had been risen from death they had heard of in the Scripture before, but that one should eat another's flesh, saith Saint Chrysostom, that had they never heard of), yet they believed Christ's word and followed forth still, and confessed that he had the words of everlasting life, and would not be by and by[154] curious and inquisitive, as Master Masker saith they would, if they had believed him that he meant of eating of his flesh indeed. For Saint Chrysostom saith, "That is the part of a disciple: whatsoever his master affirmeth, not to be curious and inquisitive thereof, nor to make search therein, but to hear and believe, and if they would anything further be informed, abide a convenient[155] time." For they that did otherwise and were inquisitive went away back, and that through their folly. For saith Saint Chrysostom,

Whensoever it cometh in the mind to ask the question how the thing may be done, then cometh there into the mind incredulity therewith. So was Nicodemus troubled and asked, "How may a man be born again when he is old? May a man enter again into his mother's belly and be born again?"[156] And so the Jews said here too, "How can he give us his flesh to eat?" But thou Jew, if thou ask that, why didst thou not ask that in like wise in the miracle of the five loaves? Why didst thou not then ask, "How can he feed so many of us with so little meat?" Why didst thou not ask by what means he would and did increase it so much? The cause was because they cared but for the meat, and not for the miracle. But thou wilt peradventure[157] say the thing at that time declared and showed itself. But then I say again that of that manifest open miracle that they saw him there work, they should have believed that he could do these things too: that is to wit, these things that they now murmured at when they said, "How can he give us his flesh to eat?" For therefore (saith Saint Chrysostom) did our Savior work the other miracle of his five loaves before, because he would therewith induce them that they should not distrust those things that he would tell them after[158]

—that is to wit, good readers, of his Godhead, and of the giving of his flesh to eat.

THE NINTH CHAPTER

Now, good Christian readers, here you see by Saint Chrysostom that though the apostles understood well that Christ spoke of the very eating of his flesh, yet there was no cause why they should either doubtfully wonder, stun or stagger, or be by and by curious and inquisitive thereof, and so destroyeth he plain Master Masker's reason, but if[159] it be to such as are disposed for their pleasure better to believe Master Masker than Saint Chrysostom.

For every man may here well see that Saint Chrysostom meaneth here that Christ in those words, besides all parables and allegories, spoke and meant of the very eating of his very flesh indeed, which thing, lest Master Masker might, as he is shameless, bring yet in question and controversy, I shall rehearse[160] you a few lines further of Saint Chrysostom in this selfsame place. Lo, thus there saith he further:

Those Jews at that time took no commodity,[161] but we have taken the profit of that benefit. And therefore is it necessary to declare how marvelous are these mysteries (that is to wit, of the Blessed Sacrament)[162] and why they be given us, and what is the profit thereof. We be one body and members of Christ's flesh and his bones. And therefore they that are Christian are bound to obey his precepts. But yet that we should be not only by love, but also in very deed turned into that flesh of his, that thing is done by the meat that his liberality hath given us. For while he longed to declare and express his love that he bore toward us, he hath by his own body mingled himself with us, and hath made himself one with us that the body should be united with the head. For that is the greatest thing that lovers long for — that is to wit, to be, if it were possible, made both one. And that thing signified Job of his servants, of whom he was most heartily beloved, which to express the vehement love that they bore toward him said, "Who could give us the gift, that we might have our bodies even fulfilled with his flesh?"[163] — which thing Christ hath done for us indeed, both to the intent to bind us in the more fervent love toward him, and also to declare the fervent love and desire that himself bore toward us. And therefore hath he not only suffered[164] himself to be seen or looked upon by them that desire and long for him, but also to be touched and eaten, and the very teeth to be infixed into his flesh, and all folk to be fulfilled in the desire of him. From God's board[165] therefore let us rise like lions that blew out fire at the mouth, such as the devil may be afeard to behold us, and let us consider Christ our head and what a love he hath showed us. The fathers and the mothers oftentimes put out their children to other folk to nurse. "But I," may our Savior say, "nourish and feed my children with mine own flesh. I give them here mine own self, so favor I them all. And such great hope I give them all against the time that shall come." For he that in such wise giveth us himself in this life here, much more will he give us himself in the life that is to come. "I longed," said our Lord, "to be your brother. And for your sakes I have communicated and made common unto you my flesh and my blood. The things by which I was joined with you, those things have I exhibited again and given to you," (that is to say, the very flesh and blood by which I was made natural man with you, that same have I in the Sacrament exhibited and given again unto you). This blood causeth the King's image to flower in us. This blood will not suffer the beauty and the nobleness of the

---

157 perhaps   **158** Chrysostom, *In Ioannem homiliae* 45 (*PG* 59: 260–61)   **159** *but*   *if*: unless   **160** quote to   **162** The parenthetical statements are   **161** benefit   More's.   **163** Jb 31:31   **164** allowed   **165** table

soul, which it ever watereth and nourisheth, to wither or fade and fall. The blood that is made in us of our other common meat is not by and by[166] blood, but before it be blood, it is somewhat else. But this blood of Christ out of hand[167] watereth the soul and with a certain marvelous might and strength seasoneth it by and by. This mystical or sacramental blood (that is to say, this blood of Christ in the Sacrament) driveth the devils far off and bringeth to us not angels only, but the Lord of all angels too. The devils, when they behold and see the blood of Christ within us, they flee far from us, and the angels run as fast toward us.[168]

And yet Saint Chrysostom ceaseth not with all this, but goeth forth with a longer process, declaring the great benefit of this blood, both by the shedding on the cross, and by the receiving in the Sacrament, which whole process I shall peradventure[169] hereafter in some other place rehearse.

But for this matter, good Christian readers, thus much doth more than suffice. For by less than this ye may more than plainly perceive that this old holy doctor Saint Chrysostom manifestly declareth and showeth that our Savior in those words that he spoke to the Jews, mentioned in the sixth chapter of Saint John, verily[170] spoke and meant of the very eating of his flesh, which thing he promised there, and which promise he performed after at his Maundy when he there instituted the Blessed Sacrament.

THE TENTH CHAPTER

And now, good readers, to finish at last this matter of Master Masker's against my second argument, which he calleth my first, because my first is such as he is loath to look upon, I return once again to Master Masker's two sore captious[171] questions, and likewise as he hath asked them of me, and I have, as you see, so well avoided his gins and his grins,[172] and all his trim-trams[173] that he hath not yet trained[174] me into no trap of mine own, as you see him solemnly boast, so will I now be bold to ask of him first, whether Saint Chrysostom here, yea, and

Saint Augustine too, and Saint Cyril, Saint Bede, Saint Irenaeus, and Saint Hilary, were of the mind that the apostle understood their master Christ's words when he said, "And the bread that I shall give you is my flesh," etc. "And my flesh is very meat," etc. "And I tell you very truth, except you eat the flesh of the Son of Man" etc.

If Master Masker answer me to this question nay or no, then shall he make me bold to answer the same to him. For then shall he not fear[175] me with his own saying, that the Gospel saith contrary in the sixth chapter of Saint John, if he grant and confess himself that all those holy doctors say therein against his own saying, which among them all understood that Gospel as well as himself alone, yea, and though[176] he take Frith and Friar Hussgen to him too. And therefore if he answer nay or no, then is he quite overthrown, as you see, and his second question quite gone too, for then can he never come to it.

Now on the other side, if he answer me yea or yes, then see, good readers, whereto Master Masker bringeth himself even to be taken in his own trap. For then he marreth all his matter. For since you see clearly, good readers, that all these holy doctors and saints openly do declare by their plain words, which yourselves have here already heard, that Christ in those words verily spoke and meant of the very eating of his very flesh indeed, it must needs follow against Master Masker's mind, in the ears and the hearts of all such as believe better all those holy doctors than him, that this is the right understanding of Christ's words, and that the apostles, if they understood his words, understood them after the same fashion: that is to wit, that he spoke and meant of the very eating of his very flesh indeed. And so serveth him his second question of nought.[177] For the cause why they marveled not in any murmuring manner was because they believed it well at their master's word, which Master Masker doth not, and the cause why they were not by and by curious and inquisitive was, as you have heard Saint Chrysostom declare, because they were meek and obedient, and not so presumptuous and malapert[178] as Master Masker would have been.

Lo, Master Masker, here may you see, lo, what worship[179] you have won with your questions, with

166 by and by: immediately   **167** out of hand: immediately   **168** Chrysostom, *In Ioannem homiliae* 45 (PG 59: 260–61)   **169** perhaps   **170** truly   **171** fallacious, sophistical   **172** gins and grins: stratagems and snares   **173** trifles   **174** enticed   **175** frighten   **176** even if   **177** *of nought:* for nothing   **178** impudent, saucy   **179** honor, distinction

which you have not only missed of training me into mine own trap, as you triumph and boast, but are also driven into your own trap yourself, out of which you can never climb up yourself nor all the brotherhood be able to draw you up as long as the devil, the very father of your lying brotherhood, lieth in the deep den of hell.

Thus have I, good readers, my first argument (as he calleth it) that he boasteth to have twice so substantially soiled[180] that he maketh me therein such a feeble babe that I were not able to stand in his strong hand; that argument have I so strongly now defended, and given him in his own turn so many great and foul falls, in every part of his process, that if this great clerk had so many so great falls given him at Clerkenwell[181] at a wrestling, he would have had, I ween, neither rib, nor arm, nor leg left him whole long ago, nor at this last lift,[182] his neck unbroken neither. And now therefore let us look how he soileth my third argument, which himself calleth my second, because he would have the first forgotten.

THE ELEVENTH CHAPTER

Lo, thus good readers, goeth Master Masker forth:

The second argument of More.

After this text thus wisely proved to be understood in the literal sense with the carnal Jews, and not in the allegoric or spiritual sense with Christ and his apostles, the whole sum of More's confutation of the young man standeth upon this argument, *a posse ad esse*: that is to wit, God may do it, ergo it is done. God may make his body in many or in all places at once, ergo it is in many or in all places at once, which manner of argumentation, how false and naught[183] it is, every sophister and every man that hath wit[184] perceiveth. A like argument: God may show More the truth and call him to repentance as he did Paul for persecuting his Church;[185] ergo More is converted to God. Or God may let him run, of an indurate[186] heart, with Pharoah, and at last take an open and

sudden vengeance upon him for persecuting his Word, and burning his poor members; ergo it is done already.[187]

In all this tale, good readers, you see that Master Masker is yet at the leastwise constant and nothing changeth his manners. For as falsely as he rehearsed[188] mine other argument before (wherein what falsehood he used you have yourselves seen) as falsely now rehearseth he this other. For read, good readers, all my letter through yourselves, and when you find that fashioned argument there, then believe Master Masker in this matter, and in the meanwhile believe but as the truth is, that with his lies he mocketh you. And since he maketh us first a loud lie for his foundation and buildeth after his arguments upon the same, wherewith he scoffeth so pleasantly at me that it as properly becometh the man to taunt as it becometh a camel or a bear to dance, I will not with him argue *a posse ad esse*, and say he can lie, ergo he doth lie, but I will turn the fashion, and argue *ab esse ad posse*, and say that he doth lie, ergo he can lie, and so commend his wit. Lo, this form of arguing can he not deny. And the antecedent[189] shall you find as true, when you read over my letter, as himself cannot say nay but[190] that the consecution[191] is formal.

But then goeth Master Masker forth on and saith:

Master More must first prove it us by express words of Holy Scripture, and not by his own unwritten dreams, that Christ's body is in many places or in all places at once. And then though our reason cannot reach it, yet our faith, measured and directed with the word of faith, will both reach it, receive it, and hold it fast too, not because it is possible to God and impossible to reason, but because the written word of our faith saith it. But when we read God's words in more than twenty places contrary, that his body should be here, More must give us leave to believe his unwritten vanities — verities, I would say — at leisure.[192]

Here ye see, good readers, how many things Master Masker hath told us here, and how freshly he flourisheth them forth.

---

180 refuted   **181** a traditional location in London for St. Bartholomew's Day wrestling matches   **182** emergency   **183** bad, evil   **184** intellect   **185** See Acts 9:4–7.   **186** *of an indurate:* on account of an obstinate or hardened   **187** *CW* 11: 311; see Ex 9:12, 10:1, 27; 11:10.   **188** recounted   **189** statement in logic upon which any   consequent statement depends   **190** *say nay but:* deny   **191** sequence of reasoning   **192** *CW* 11: 311

The first is that I must prove it him that the body of Christ is in many places at once, or in all places at once.

The second is that I must prove it by express words of Scripture.

The third is that I may not prove it by mine own unwritten dreams.

The fourth is that if I prove it so by express words of Scripture, then he will both reach it, and receive it, and hold it fast too.

The fifth is that he findeth twenty places of Scripture and more to the contrary, proving that his body is not here.

The sixth is that therefore I must give him leave to believe mine unwritten vanities—verities, he would say—at leisure.

Now for the first, good readers, where Master Masker saith that Master More must first prove it him that Christ's body is in many places at once or in all places at once, I say that as for all places at once, Master More must not prove at all. For, since the Sacrament is not in all places at once, whether his blessed body may be in all places at once is no point of our matter.

Now as touching the being of his blessed body in many places at once, where Master Masker saith that ere[193] he be bound to believe it, I must prove it, he is very far out of reason and out of the right way. For is Master Masker, nor Father Frith before him, bounden to believe no more than Master More were able to prove them? I say again to Father Frith and Master Masker both that if either of them both, or any such other fond[194] fellow as they be, begin to deny now any such plain article of the faith as all good Christian nations are, and long have been full agreed upon, so long and so full as they have been upon this, and so long reckoned the contrary believers for heretics,[195] either Master More or any man else might well with reason reprove them thereof, and rebuke them therefore, and only answer the foolish arguments that they make against the truth, and should not once need to go about the proof of the full received and undoubted truth, as though it were become doubtful upon every proud heretic's blasphemous foolish argument.

For if Master Masker would now bring up the Arians' heresy again against the Godhead of Christ, which he might as well as this frantic heresy of Friar Hussgen and Wycliffe against the Blessed Sacrament, or if he would now begin the other foolish heresy, whereof the Prophet speaketh in the psalter: *Dixit insipiens in corde suo non est deus* ("The fool said in his heart, 'There is no God'"),[196] which he might as well begin as any of the other twain,[197] if he would now, for the furnishing of this heresy, come forth with such unreasonable reasons, as some foolish foolosophers brought in therefore of old, were it not enough for me to confute those foolish arguments wherewith he would blind simple souls? Must I needs besides that go make much ado[198] and prove that there were a God, or else grant this goose that there were no God at all, because himself would say so still, when his fond reasons were soiled?[199]

Now to his second point, where it is not enough for him to say that I must prove it (wherein, as ye see, I have proved him a very fool), but he assigneth me also what manner of proof I must make, and none may serve him but such as himself list[200] assign, and that therefore I must prove it him by express words of Holy Scripture. I ask him then whether he will be content if I prove it him by express words of Christ written in all the four evangelists, Saint Matthew, Saint Mark, Saint Luke, and Saint John. If he say yea, as I suppose he will, then ask I him further wherefore[201] he will believe the writing of them four. Whereto what will he answer, but because that those Gospels of theirs are Holy Scripture? But then shall I further desire him to show me how he knoweth that those four books, or any one of all four, is the book of him whose name it beareth, or is the Holy Scripture of God at all. To this question, lo, but if[202] he can go further than holy Saint Augustine could, or the master captain of his own heresies, Martin Luther, either,[203] he must say that he knoweth those books for Holy Scripture, because the common-known Catholic Church hath so told him. Now when he shall have once answered me thus, every child may soon see what I shall ask him again.[204] For then shall I say, "Tell me then, Master Masker, I beseech you, since you believe this common-known Catholic Church in that one great verity, whereupon by your own saying all the other writers depend, why should you not as well believe it in this other article, which it as plainly telleth you, and yet you do deny it? Why should you not, I say, Master Masker, believe the Church as well, when it telleth you God hath taught his Church that this is his very body, as you believe the same Church when it telleth you God hath taught his Church that this is his very Scripture, namely since there are written in the same Scripture other things to man's reason as hard to conceive and as incredible to believe as that."

Here you see, good readers, to what point I have brought Master Masker. I have set him here so fast[205] in the mire that therein shall he stick and never clean[206] wade out while he liveth.

Moreover, Master Masker cannot deny me this but that the right belief in the Sacrament, and diverse other things more, were once taught and believed, and Christian men bounden to believe them too, without express words of Holy Scripture laid forth for the proof, before any word of the New Testament was written and after peradventure[207] too, where the articles were preached and written Gospels not there. Now if such things were at one time not only believed, but men also bounden to the belief thereof without express words of Scripture for the proof, Master Masker must then, though there be come writing since, yet either prove us by express words of Scripture that of all that God will we shall[208] believe there is nothing left out, but every such thing there written in with express words, or else may he never make himself so sure, and face it out a[209] this fashion with express words that, saving[210] the very plain express words of Scripture, we be no man of us bounden to believe nothing else.

Now this am I sure enough, that such express words shall he never find in Scripture that tell him expressly that all is written in. And then since he cannot prove us this point by Scripture, but that at the leastwise we may be bounden to believe some such things as in Holy Scripture is not expressly written, which things those may be and which not, of whom will God we shall learn but of his known Catholic Church, by which he teacheth us which be the very Scripture?

Now as for the third point that Master Masker toucheth, in which he will allow for no sufficient proof mine own unwritten dreams, he giveth my dreams, I thank him of his courtesy, much more

authority than ever I looked for. For while he rejecteth none of them but such as are unwritten, he showeth himself ready to believe them, if I would vouchsafe[211] to write them.

In the fourth point, he promiseth that if I do by express words of Scripture prove that it is so, then though it be above the reach of his reason, yet will he by belief both reach it, and receive it, and hold it fast too. Would God Master Masker would abide by this word. For now I ask him again, whether he will be content, if I prove it him by express words of some one of the four evangelists. And if he be content with express words of any one, then will I do more for him: prove it by all four.

For Saint John rehearseth[212] that our Savior said himself he would give them his flesh to eat. And that he meant of the Sacrament you see already proved herebefore.

And the other three rehearse that Christ said himself when he gave them the Sacrament, "This is my body that shall be broken for you."[213] What words can there be more plain and express than these?

But here saith Master Masker that these be not express words. For he saith that these words be spoken but by way of allegory. And he proveth it, as Frith doth, by that our Savior said of himself, "I am the door," and "I am the vine."

Now remember, good readers, that Master Masker belied[214] me right now, and said that all my second argument was *a posse ad esse* (it may be so, ergo it is so). But now consider, good Christian readers, yourselves whether this argument of his be not *a posse ad esse* indeed. For by those places, "I am the door," and "I am the vine," and such other, he concludeth that these other places of eating his flesh and giving of his body was spoken by an allegory too. And how concludeth he that it is so? But because it may be so. And thus ye see, good readers, that the selfsame kind of arguing which Master Masker feigneth himself to find with me—and falsely belieth me therein, for I needed there none other thing to do but answer the things that Frith laid forth against the Catholic faith—the selfsame kind of arguing I say Master Masker useth himself, and so doth young Father Frith, his fellow in folly, too.

But then again when they argue thus, "These

---

205 firmly; quickly   **206** completely   us to   **209** *face it out a:* lie boldly in   **213** Lk 22:19   **214** slandered
207 perhaps   **208** *will we shall:* wants   **210** except   **211** be willing   **212** recounts

places may be so understood by an allegory only, as those other places be; ergo they be to be so understood indeed," I have proved already that his intent is false, and that they may not be understood in an allegory only as the other be, but the plain and open difference between the places appear upon the circumstances of the text. This have I proved against Frith already, and that in such wise, as yourselves hath seen here, that Master Masker cannot avoid it, but in going about to defend Frith's folly hath, with his two solutions of mine one argument, ofter than twice overthrown himself and made mine argument more than twice so strong.

But yet good readers, because I say that those words of Christ, "The bread that I shall give you is my flesh, which I shall give for the life of the world," and "My flesh is verily meat, and my blood verily drink," and "But if[215] you eat the flesh of the Son of Man, and drink his blood, you shall not have life in you," and so forth, all such words as our Savior spoke himself, mentioned in the sixth chapter of Saint John, and those words of our Savior at his Maundy written with all the other three evangelists, "This is my body that shall be broken for you," be plain and express words for the Catholic faith, and Master Masker saith that they be not words plain and express, but expoundeth them all another way, therefore to break the strife therein between him and me, I have brought you forth for my part in mine exposition the plain express words of diverse old holy saints, by which you may plain and expressly see that they all said as I say.

And Master Masker also cannot himself say nay but[216] that against other heretics before his days and mine, diverse whole general Councils of Christendom have plainly and expressly determined the same to be true that I say.[217]

And all the countries christened[218] can also testify that God hath himself by manifold open miracles plain and expressly declared for the Blessed Sacrament that this is the true faith, which Master Masker here oppugneth,[219] and that God hath by those miracles expounded his own words himself to be plain and expressly spoken for our part.

And therefore now, good Christian readers, if Master Masker will make any more sticking[220] with us, and not grant Christ's words for plain and express and, according to his promise, reach and receive the true faith and hold it fast too, ye may plain and expressly tell him there shall never true man trust his false promise after.

Now touching the fifth point, where he saith that he findeth twenty places in Scripture and more too, proving that Christ's body is not here in earth, remember this well, good reader, against[221] he bring them forth. For in his second part when we come to the tale, ye shall find his more than twenty far fewer than fifteen, and of all that shall well serve him, ye shall find fewer than one.

Then where he concludeth in the last point upon these five points afore (which five, how well they prove, good Christian readers, you see) that I must give him leave to believe mine unwritten vanities (verities, he would say) at leisure, if the things that he calleth unwritten verities were indeed unwritten and invented also by me, then he might be the bolder to call them mine unwritten vanities, and (as he calleth them before) mine unwritten dreams too. But on the other side, since you see yourselves that I have showed you them written in holy saints' books, and that a thousand years before that I was born, and yourselves seeth it written in the plain Scripture too, proved plain and express for our part against him by the old exposition of all the holy doctors and saints, and by the determinations of diverse general councils of Christ's whole Catholic Church, and proved plain for our part also, by so many plain open miracles, Master Masker must needs be more than mad to call now such written verities mine unwritten vanities, or mine unwritten dreams either, except[222] he prove both all those things to be but an invention of mine, and over[223] that all those writings to be yet unwritten, and that holy doctrine both of holy saints and of Holy Scripture vanities, and also that all the while that all those holy folk were awork therewith, they neither wrote nor studied nor did nothing but dream.

Now while Master More must therefore, upon such considerations, give Master Masker leave to believe this unwritten vanity, which is in all the four evangelists an express written verity, while I must, I say, therefore upon such foolish false considerations, give him leave to believe the true faith at leisure, if he had put it in my choice, I would have

215 *But if*: Unless   **216** *say nay but*: deny   **217** The Fourth Lateran Council (1215) affirmed the real presence, or transubstantiation. The Council of Constance (1414–18) condemned Wycliffe's and Huss's doctrines on the Eucharist.   **218** christianized   **219** attacks   **220** hesitation, delay   **221** against the time at which   **222** unless   **223** beyond

been loath to give him any longer leisure therein, for he hath been too long out of right belief already. But since he saith I must, I may not choose, whereof I am, as help me God, very sorry. For except he take himself that leisure betimes,[224] leaving the business that he daily taketh in writing of pestilent books to the contrary, he shall else not fail to believe the true faith at a long leisure overlate: that is to wit, when he lieth wretchedly in hell, where he shall not write for lack of light and burning up of his paper, but shall have everlasting leisure from all other work to believe there that[225] he would not believe here, and lie still and ever burn there, in everlasting fire, for his former ungracious obstinate infidelity, out of which infidelity I beseech God give him the grace to creep and get out betimes.

And thus you see, good readers, what a goodly piece Master Masker hath made you, which pleased him, I warrant you, very well when he wrote it. But it will not, I ween, please him now very well when he shall after this mine answer read it.

THE TWELFTH CHAPTER

But now goeth he further against me with a special goodly piece wherein thus he saith:

Here mayst thou see, Christian reader, wherefore[226] More would so fain[227] make the belief that the apostles left aught[228] unwritten of necessity to be believed, even to establish the pope's kingdom, which standeth of More's unwritten vanities, as of the presence of Christ's body, and making thereof in the bread, of purgatory, of invocation of saints, worshipping of stones and stocks,[229] pilgrimages, hallowing of boughs[230] and bells,[231] and creeping to the cross,[232] etc. If ye will believe whatsoever More can feign without the Scripture, then can this poet feign ye another Church than Christ's, and that ye must believe it whatsoever it teach you, for he hath feigned too that it cannot err, though ye see it err and fight against itself a thousand times, yea, if it tell you black is white, and good is bad, and the devil is God, yet must ye believe it or else be burned as heretics.[233]

Still ye see the wisdom, good readers, and the truth of Master Masker, in every piece of his matter. For here you see that all these things that he speaketh of, as that the Church cannot err, and the creeping to the cross, with all other ceremonies of the Church, invocation of saints, going on pilgrimage, worshipping of images, believing of purgatory, believing the body of our Savior present in the Blessed Sacrament, all these things he calleth mine unwritten vanities, and maketh as though these things were all of my feigning. Is not this, ween you, wisely feigned of him, that the things commonly used this fourteen hundred year before I was born should now be feigned and imagined by me? But yet shall it be as long after my days, and his too, ere Master Masker and all the many of them shall among them all be able to confute the things that myself have in these matters written. And yet hang not the matters upon my writing, but upon the truth itself, revealed unto Christ's known Catholic Church, both by Christ himself and his apostles after him, by tradition and by writing both, and by many miracles confirmed, and with the secret instinct and inspiration of his Holy Spirit, wrought and brought into a full and whole Catholic agreement and consent, as necessary points of the true Christian faith.

This is also by Master Masker wonderful wisely feigned: that More hath feigned all these things, even to the intent to establish the pope's kingdom. But now what great cause should move me to bear that great affection to the pope as to feign all these things for establishment of his kingdom—that thing Master Masker telleth you not, as the thing that is so plain and evident that he needeth not. For he thinketh that every man knoweth already that the pope is my godfather and goeth about to make me a cardinal.

But now, good Christian readers, they that would, at the counsel of this evil Christian caitiff,[234] cast off all such manner things as all good Christian people have ever taken for good, and now neither creep to the cross, nor set by[235] any hallowed thing, despise pilgrimages, and set holy saints at nought,[236] no more reverence their images than a horse of wax, nor reckon their relics any better than sheep's

224 early; in good time   225 what
226 why   227 gladly; willingly   228 anything   229 blocks of wood   230 a rite of blessing flowers and palm-branches

on Palm Sunday   231 a ceremony that included petitions against evil spirits and storms   232 *creeping to the cross:* the veneration of the cross on Good Friday

233 *CW* 11: 311–12   234 villain   235 *set by:* regard, esteem   236 *set . . . nought:* regard the saints as nothing

bones, scrape clean the litany[237] out of every book, with our Lady Matins[238] and the dirge[239] too, and away with our Lady's Psalter,[240] and cast the beads[241] in the fire, and beware also that we worship not the Sacrament, nor take it for no better thing than unblessed bread, and believe that the Church erreth in every thing that it teacheth, and all that holy saints have taught therein this fourteen hundred year (for all they have taught all these things that this man now despiseth), then would there wax[242] a merry world, the very kingdom of the devil himself.

And verily it seemeth that they would set the people upon mirth. For penance they shake off as a thing not necessary. Satisfaction they call great sin, and confession they call the devil's drift.[243] And of purgatory, by two means they put men out of dread: some by sleeping till Doomsday,[244] and some by sending all straight to heaven, every soul that dieth and is not damned forever. And yet some good comfort give they to the damned too. For till they see some time to deny hell all utterly, they go about in the mean season[245] to put out the fire. And some yet boldly forthwith[246] too say there is none there, that they dread a little, and therefore for the season they bring the matter in question, and dispute it abroad and say they will not utterly affirm and say the contrary, but the thing is, they say, but as *problema neutrum*,[247] wherein they would not force whether[248] part they should take, and yet if they should choose, they would rather hold nay than yea, or though there be fire in either place, that yet it neither burneth soul in hell, nor paineth soul in purgatory. But Christ, I wot[249] well, in many places saith there is fire there,[250] and his holy saints after him affirm and say the same, and with that fire he frayed[251] his own disciples, bidding them fear that fire, that they fell not therein.

Now though that[252] clerks may in schools hold problems upon everything, yet can I not perceive what profit there can come to call it but a problem among unlearned folk, and dispute it out abroad, and bring the people in doubt, and make them rather think that there is none than any, and that this word "fire" is spoken but by parable, as these men make the eating of Christ's blessed body. Thus

shall they make men take both paradise, and heaven, and God, and all together, but for parables at last.

Though fear of hell alone be but a servile dread, yet are there already too many that fear hell too little, even of them that believe the truth and think that in hell there is very fire indeed. How many will there then be that will fear it less, if such words once may make them ween that there were in hell no very fire at all, but that the pain that they shall feel in hell were but after[253] the manner of some heavy mind or of a troublous dream?

If a man believe Christ's word that in hell is fire indeed, and make the fear of that fire one means to keep him thence, then though there were no fire there, yet hath he nothing lost, since good he can get none there, though the fire were thence. But if he believe such words on the other side, and catch thereby such boldness that he set hell at light, and by the means thereof fall boldly to sin, and thereupon finally fall down unto the devil, if he then find fire there as I am sure he shall, then shall he lie there and curse them that told him those false tales, as long as God with his good folk sitteth in the joy of heaven.

And therefore, good Christian readers, wisdom will we believe Christ's own words, and let such unwise words and devilish devices[254] pass.

THE THIRTEENTH CHAPTER

But now after this pleasant discourse of his into the rehearsal[255] of this heap of heresies that you have heard, for which, as for little trifles his heart fretteth sore[256] that any heretic should be burned, he goeth on against me and saith:

But let us return to our propose.[257] To dispute of God's almighty absolute power, what God may do with his body, it is great folly and no less presumption to More, since the pope, which is no whole God but half a God, by their own decrees hath decreed no man to dispute of his power. But Christian reader, be thou content to know that God's will, his word, and his power be all one, and

237 repeated petitions to saints to "pray for us"   238 the first hour in the office of the Blessed Virgin   239 the office for the dead   240 a rosary that corresponds to the number of psalms   241 rosary

beads   242 grow, become   243 scheme   244 Judgment Day   245 time   246 immediately, at once   247 insoluble problem   248 which   249 know   250 Mt 13:42, 50; 18:8–9; 25:41

251 frightened   252 *though that:* though   253 in accordance with   254 contrivances   255 telling   256 greatly   257 subject

repugn²⁵⁸ not. And neither willeth he, nor may not do anything, including repugnance, imperfection, or that should derogate,²⁵⁹ diminish, or hurt his glory and his name. The glory of his Godhead is to be present and to fill all places at once essentially, presently with his almighty power, which glory is denied to any other creature, himself saying by his prophet, "I will not give my glory to any other creature."²⁶⁰ Now therefore, since his manhood is a creature, it cannot have this glory which only is appropried²⁶¹ to the Godhead. To attribute to his manhood that property, which only is appropried to his Godhead, is to confound both the natures in Christ. What thing so ever is everywhere after the said manner, that must needs be infinite, without beginning and end; it must be one alone, and almighty, which properties only are appropried unto the glorious majesty of the Godhead. Wherefore Christ's body may not be in all or in many places at once, Christ himself saying as concerning his manhood he is less than the Father, but as touching his Godhead, "The Father and I be both one thing."²⁶² And Paul, reciting the psalm, affirmeth Christ as concerning his manhood to be less than God, or less than angels, as some text hath it.²⁶³ Here is it plain that all things that More imagineth and feigneth are not possible to God, for it is not possible for God to make a creature equal unto himself, for it includeth repugnance and derogateth his glory.²⁶⁴

Now have you, lo, good Christian readers, heard a very special piece, wherein Master Masker, as you see, solemnly first rebuketh the folly and the presumption of me, for that²⁶⁵ I was so bold in my letter against his fellow Father Frith, to dispute of God's almighty absolute power. But now, good readers, when you shall see by the matter that it was Frith which argued against God's almighty power, denying that Christ could make his own body in many places at once, and that I did in effect nothing else but answer him, and said and affirmed that God was able to do it, and that Frith was but a fool so to strait²⁶⁶ and to limit the power of Almighty God, but if²⁶⁷ he could prove repugnance²⁶⁸ (which against God's own word plain spoken in his holy Gospel Father Frith could never do), when you see

this, good readers, I doubt not but ye will say that it is neither folly nor presumption for the simplest man or woman in a town to maintain that God may do this thing or that, namely the thing that God hath said himself he doth, against him that is so foolish as to presume, against the plain Word of God, to determine by his own blind reason the contrary, and specially since the thing is such indeed as though²⁶⁹ God had not spoken thereof, yet had he none hold²⁷⁰ to say that God could not do it, forasmuch as²⁷¹ it implieth no such repugnance as should make the thing impossible unto God.

But now see further, good readers, the wisdom and the meekness of Master Masker here, which as soon as he hath scant²⁷² finished his high solemn rebuking of me for such disputing of God's almighty power, that I said he was indeed so mighty that he could do the thing that we disputed upon against him that said nay, falleth himself forthwith²⁷³ in the same fault that he findeth, and yet not in the same fault (for the fault that he found was none) but in the fault that he would seem to find. For he disputeth and taketh the part against God's almighty power indeed, and argueth, as you see, that God indeed cannot do it.

And this point he argueth in such manner²⁷⁴ fashion that in my life I never saw so foolish an argument so solemnly set up a²⁷⁵ high. First he maketh his reason thus. It is the glory of the Godhead and appropried²⁷⁶ only thereunto to be present and to fill all places at once, essentially, presently, with his almighty power, and is denied to any creature. But Christ's manhood is a creature. Ergo it cannot have this glory that is appropried to the Godhead.

Here is a wise argument. God hath many glories. And his chief glory standeth not in being present at once essentially in every place. And though he will not give his glory from him, yet of his glory he maketh many creatures in many great parts of it to be partners with him. It is one part of his glory to live and endure in eternal bliss, and though no creature be without beginning, yet maketh he many a thousand possessors of joy without ending.

How proveth Master Masker that to be present at once in all places is such a kind of glory so appropried unto God that God cannot give that gift to any creature? The Scripture seemeth to approprie unto God alone the knowledge of man's secret thought.[277] And yet can I not see but that God might give that knowledge to some creature too and yet abide[278] God still himself.

THE FOURTEENTH CHAPTER

Then maketh Master Masker another argument, wherewith he would, as it seemeth, somewhat strengthen the first, as it hath of truth no little need, being as it is so feeble of itself.

His other argument therefore is, as you have heard, this: What thing so ever is everywhere after[279] the said manner, that must needs be infinite without beginning and end. It must be one, and alone, and almighty, which properties are appropried unto the glorious majesty of the Godhead. But Christ's manhood is not such, as himself witnesseth in Holy Scripture; ergo his manhood cannot be in all or in many places at once.

First, (that we labor not about nought)[280] we must consider what Master Masker meaneth by these words, "after the said manner." He said, you wot well, in the other argument before, that the glory of God is to be present, and to fill all places at once, essentially, presently, with his almighty power. And therefore when he saith now, "Whatsoever thing is everywhere at once after the said manner," he meaneth (you see well) present, and filling all places at once, essentially, presently, with his almighty power.

I let pass here his word "presently," whose presence needeth[281] not in that place for aught[282] that I can see. For when he said before, "present and filling all places at once essentially," his other word "presently" may take his leave and be absent well enough. For how can he be present and essentially fill the place, and not presently? But now when he saith, "by his almighty power," what is this to the matter?[283] For it is enough against him if any creature may be present in every place at once, and essentially fill the place, not by his own almighty power, but by the almighty power of God, and yet not so fill the place neither, but that it may have another with it in the same place. For I trow[284] he will not deny but that there be many creatures in those

places, which God with his own presence essentially filleth full.

Therefore, as for these words, "after the said manner," which he putteth in to make us amazed, Master Masker must put out again. Now that being put out, rehearse[285] and consider well Master Masker's argument. What thing so ever is in every place at once, that thing must needs be infinite without beginning and end, it must be one, and alone, and almighty, which properties are appropried to the glorious majesty of the Godhead. But the manhood of Christ is a creature and not God; ergo Christ's manhood cannot be in all places or in many places at once. And yet consider here that though[286] he leave out that odious word, yet must his conclusion be indeed that God cannot make it so, as you see plain by his beginning, where he showeth that it implieth repugnance, and that therefore God cannot do it.

Now good readers, consider well his first proposition, which we call the major: that is to wit, that God cannot make anything created to be everywhere at once. Let us pray[287] him to prove it, and give him one year's leisure to it. But here he taketh upon him to prove it, and layeth for the reason that God cannot make any creature to be in all places at once because it should then be infinite, and thereby God Almighty's mate and high fellow. Let him, as I say, prove us this in two years that it should then be infinite, without beginning, and without end, and almighty. In good faith, either am I very dull, or else doth Master Masker tell us herein a very mad tale.

I think he will not deny but that God which could make all this world, heaven, and earth, and all the creatures that he created therein, could, if it so had pleased him, have created only one man, and let all the remnant alone uncreated, and have kept him still, and never have made heaven nor earth nor none other thing, but only that one man alone. The soul now that then had been created in that man, had it not then been in all places at once? I suppose yes. For there had been no more places than that man's body, and therein had there been many places in many diverse parts of the man, in all which that soul should have been present at once, and the whole soul in every part of all those places at once. For so is every soul in every man's body now. And yet had that soul not been infinite, no more than every soul is now.

If God would now, as if he would he could, create a new spirit that should fulfill[288] all the whole world, heaven and earth and all, as much as ever is created, that in such wise should be whole present at once in every part of the world, as the soul is in every part of a man, and yet should not be the soul of the world, I will here ask Master Masker, were that new created spirit infinite? If he answer me nay, then hath he soiled[289] his own wise reason himself. For then no more were[290] the manhood of Christ, though it were present in all those places of the whole world at once. If he answer me yea, then since that spirit were no more infinite than the world is, within the limits and bounds whereof it were contained, it would follow thereof that the world were infinite already, which is false. And also, if it were true, then would it follow by Master Masker's reason that God Almighty had a match already, that is to wit, another thing infinite besides himself, which is the inconvenience that maketh Master Masker affirm it for impossible that God could make Christ's manhood to be in all places at once.

Thus you see, good readers, upon what wise ground Master Masker hath here concluded that God cannot make Christ's body to be in all places at once.

But yet is it a world[291] to consider how madly the man concludeth. His conclusion is this, ye wot well, wherefore[292] Christ's body cannot be in all places, or in many places at once. All his reason, ye wot well, goeth upon being in all places at once, because that thereupon would it, by his wise reason, follow that it should be infinite. And now is that point of truth no part of our matter. For we say not that Christ's body is in all places at once, but in heaven, and in such places in earth as the Blessed Sacrament is. And therefore, whereas his reason goeth nothing against being in many places at once, but only against being at once in all places, he concludeth suddenly against being in many places, toward which conclusion no piece of his premises had any manner of motion. And so in all this his high solemn argument, and his far-fetched reason, neither is his major true, nor his argument toucheth not the matter, nor his premises anything[293] prove his conclusion.

And yet after this goodly reasoning of his, he rejoiceth in his heart highly to see how jollily he hath handled it, and saith: "Here it is plain that all things that More imagineth and feigneth are not possible to God. For it is not possible to God to make a creature equal to himself, for it includeth repugnance[294] and derogateth[295] his glory."

Master Masker speaketh much of mine unwritten dreams and vanities. But here have we had a written dream of his, and therein this foolish boast also so full of vainglorious vanity that if I had dreamed it in a fit of a fever, I would, I ween, have been ashamed to have told my dream to my wife when I woke. And now shall you, good readers, have here another piece as proper:[296]

God promised and swore that all nations should be blessed in the death of that promised seed which was Christ; God had determined and decreed it before the world was made,[297] ergo Christ must needs have died, and not to expound this word *oportet*, as More minceth it. For it was so necessary that the contrary was impossible, except[298] More would make God a liar, which is impossible. Paul concludeth that Christ must needs have died, using this Latin term *necesse*, saying wheresoever is a testament, there must the death of the testament-maker go between, or else the testament is not ratified and sure, but righteousness and remission of sins in Christ's blood is his New Testament, whereof he is mediator; ergo the testament-maker must needs have died.[299] Wrest not therefore, Master More, this word *oportet* (though ye find *potest* for *oportet* in some corrupt copy) unto your unsavory sense. But let *oportet* signify "he must," or "it behooveth him" to die. For he took our very mortal nature for the same decreed council, himself saying (John 2 and 12), *Oportet exaltari filium hominis*, etc. ("It behooveth," or "the Son of Man must die, that everyone that believe in him perish not,[300] etc."). Here may ye see also that it is impossible for God to break his promise. It is impossible to God, which is that verity to be found contrary in his deeds and words, as to save them whom he hath damned, or to damn them whom he hath saved. Wherefore all things imagined of More's brain

288 fill   **289** refuted   **290** would be
291 marvel   **292** why   **293** in any way
294 contradiction   **295** diminishes,

lessens   **296** characteristic   **297** See
Gal 3:8, 16, 29; Gn 18:18, 22:18; Acts

3:25.   **298** unless   **299** See Heb 9:15–17.
300 See Jn 3:14; 12:34.

are not possible to God. And when More saith that Christ had power to let[301] his life and to take it again,[302] and therefore not to have died of necessity, I wonder me that his school matter[303] here failed him, so cunning[304] as he maketh himself therein, which granteth and affimeth, as true it is, that with the necessary decreed works of God's foresight and providence standeth right well his free liberty.[305]

THE FIFTEENTH CHAPTER

If this piece were, good readers, anything to the purpose of our principle matter, concerning the Blessed Sacrament, Master Masker had here given me hold enough to give him four or five such foul falls on the back that his bones should all-to[306] burst therewith. But forasmuch as[307] you shall perceive by the reading of my letter that all this gear[308] is but a by-matter, risen upon a certain place of Saint Augustine, which Frith alleged[309] imperfectly, I purpose not to spend the time in vain dispicions[310] with Master Masker, in a thing out of our matter. And namely since the man hath, after his long babbling against me, yet in the end answered himself well and sufficiently for me.

For when he hath said a great while that it was in such wise necessary that Christ must die, that the contrary thereof was impossible, at last, as though he would mock me therewith and show mine ignorance, he bringeth in his own, and showeth that for anything that God hath either foreseen or decreed and determined therein, he had left Christ at his liberty to die or live if he would.[311] And then if he was at his liberty not to die but if[312] he had would, then was it not impossible for him to have lived if he had would. But the keeping of his life was the contrary of his dying; ergo his dying, how necessary so ever it was for man's redemption — that is to wit, so behoveful[313] thereto that without it we should not have been saved — yet Master Masker here to show himself a great schoolman in respect of me confesseth himself, against himself, that Christ to die was not in such wise necessarily constrained, that the contrary thereof — that is to wit, Christ to live was

impossible to him if he had would — while Master Masker cannot say nay, but must needs give place to the Scriptures that I laid[314] him, and therefore must confess, and so he doth, that Christ could by no constraint be compelled to die, but was offered because himself so would.

But the dispicions of this point is, as I say, good reader, all beside our principle matter, and therefore I will let his other follies that I find in this piece pass by.

Then goeth Master Masker forth and saith:

But Master More saith at last, "If God would tell me that he would make each of both their bodies too," (meaning the young man's body and Christ's) "to be in fifteen places at once, I would believe him, ay, that he were able to make his word true in the bodies of both twain,[315] and never would I so much as ask him whether he would glorify them both first or not, but I am sure, glorified or unglorified, if he said it, he is able to do it."[316] Lo, here may ye see what a fervent faith this old man hath, and what an earnest mind to believe Christ's words if he had told him; but I pray ye, Master More, what and if[317] Christ never told it you, nor said it nor never would, would ye not be as hasty to not believe it? If he told it you, I pray ye tell us where ye speak with him, and who was by to bear ye record, and yet if you bring as false a shrew[318] as yourself to testify this thing, yet by your own doctrine must ye make us a miracle to confirm your tale, ere we be bound to believe you, or yet to admit this your argument: God may make his body in many places at once, ergo it is so.[319]

THE SIXTEENTH CHAPTER

Read, good readers, in my letter, the twenty-first leaf, and then consider Master Masker's goodly mock that he maketh here, and you shall find it very foolish. But now Master Masker asketh me, where I spoke with Christ when he told me that he would make his own body in two places at once, as though Christ could not speak to me but if[320] I spoke to him, nor could not tell me the tale but if he appeared to me face to face, as he did after his resurrection to his disciples.[321] This question of Master Masker cometh of a high wit,[322] I warrant you. I answer Master Masker therefore, Christ told it at his Maundy to other good credible folk, and they told it forth to the whole Catholic Church, and the whole Church hath told it unto me, and one of them that was at it, that is to wit, Saint Matthew, hath put it in writing as the same Church telleth me.[323] For else[324] were I not sure whether that Gospel were his or not, nor whether it were any part of Holy Scripture or not. And therefore I can lack no good and honest witness to bear me record in that point that will depose for me that I feign not the matter of mine own head. And I have a testimonial also of many old holy doctors and saints, made afore[325] a good notary, the good man God himself, which hath with his seal of many a hundred miracles, both testified for the truth of those men, and also for the truth of the principle matter itself: that is to wit, that Christ's very body is in the Blessed Sacrament, though[326] the Sacrament be either in two or in ten thousand places at once. And thus Master Masker's questions concerning Christ's blessed body, that Christ hath told me that he would make it be in two places at once is, I trust, sufficiently answered. But now as for Frith's body (which writeth that Christ's body can be no more in two places at once than his), though I would have believed that Christ could have made it in two places at once if Christ had so told me, yet since Christ hath now told me, by his whole Catholic Church, and by writing of the old holy saints of the same, and by his own Holy Scripture too, which Scripture by the same Church and the same holy saints I know, and also see declared and expounded, and over[327] that hath by many wonderful miracles manifestly proved and testified that the opinions in which Frith obstinately and therewith very foolishly died were very pestilent heresies, whereby he is perpetually severed from the lively body of Christ, and made a dead member of the devil, I believe therefore and very surely know as a thing taught me by God that the wretched body of that fellow shall never be in two places at once, but when it shall rise again and be restored to that wretched obstinate

soul, shall therewith lie still ever more in one place, that is to wit, in the everlasting fire of hell, from which I beseech our Lord turn Tyndale and George Jay, with all the whole brotherhood and Master Masker among others (whosoever he be) betimes.[328]

Now upon his aforesaid such a proper-handled mock as you have heard, Master Masker goeth on, and giveth me right wholesome admonition that I meddle no more with such high matters, as is the great absolute almighty power of God, and therein thus he saith unto me: "Sir, you be too busy with God's almighty power, and have taken too great a burden upon your weak shoulders."[329]

THE SEVENTEENTH CHAPTER

Here he should have rehearsed what one word I had said of God's almighty power, in which word I was too busy. Read my letter over, and you shall clearly see that I say nothing else but that God is almighty, and that he therefore may do all things. And yet, as you shall hear Master Masker himself confess, I said not that God could do things that imply repugnance.[330] But I said that some things may seem repugnant unto us, which things God seeth how to set together well enough. Be these words, good reader, over-highly[331] spoken of God's almighty power? May not a poor unlearned man be bold to say that God is able to do so much? And yet for saying thus much, saith Master Masker that I am too busy, and have taken too great a burden upon my weak shoulders, and have overladen myself with mine own harness[332] and weapons, and many gay words more to utter his eloquence withal.[333] But Master Masker on the other side is not himself too busy at all with God's almighty power, in affirming that God hath not the power to make his own blessed body in many places at once. His mighty strong shoulders take not too much weight upon them when instead of omnipotent, he proveth God impotent, and that by such impotent arguments, as you see yourself so shamefully halt, that never lame cripple that lay impotent by the walls in creeping out unto a dole[334] halted half so sore.[335] But then goeth he further for the praise of young David and saith:

321 See Mt 28:16–20; Mk 16:12–17; Lk 24:36–53; Jn 20:19–30; 21:1–25. 322 *high wit:* lofty intellect 323 See Mt 26:26–29. 324 otherwise 325 before, in the presence of 326 even if 327 besides 328 soon 329 *CW* 11: 313 330 contradiction 331 over-proudly 332 armor 333 besides 334 distribution of alms 335 much

You have overladen yourself with your own harness and weapons, and young David is like to prevail against you with his sling and his stone.[336]

As for Master Masker's young Master David, whoso look upon his first treatise and my letter together shall soon see that his sling and his stone be beaten both about his ears. And whensoever his new sling and his new stone (which is, as I now hear say, very lately come over in print) come once into my hands, I shall turn his sling into a cock-stele[337] and his stone into a feather, for any harm that it shall be able to do, but if[338] it be to such as willingly will put out their own eyes, to which they never need neither stone nor sling, but with a feather they may do it and[339] they be so mad.

But a heavy thing it is to hear of his young foolish David, that hath thus, with his stone of stubbornness, stricken out his own brain, and with the sling of his heresies slungen himself to the devil.

Yet Master Masker cannot leave me thus, but on he goeth further in his railing rhetoric and thus he saith:

> God hath infatuated your high subtle wisdom; your crafty conveyance is espied. God hath sent your Church a meet[340] cover for such a cup, even such a defender as you take yourself to be, that shall let all their whole cause fall flat in the mire, unto both your shames and utter confusion. God therefore be praised ever, amen.[341]

THE EIGHTEENTH CHAPTER

As for wisdom, I will not compare with Master Masker therein, nor would wax[342] much the prouder in good faith, though[343] men would say that I had more wit[344] than he. I pray God send us both a little more of his grace, and make us both good.

But whereas he jesteth concerning my defense of the Church, whoso look my books through shall find that the Church, in the truth of whose Catholic faith concerning the Blessed Sacrament I write against Frith and Tyndale and Master Masker, and such false heretics more, is none other Church but the true Catholic Church of Christ, the whole congregation of all true Christian nations, of which Church I take not myself to be any special defender; howbeit,[345] to defend it is indeed every good man's part. And as for hitherto, the things that I have written are (I thank God) strong enough to stand, as it is plainly proved against all these heretics that have wrestled therewith, whereof they could never yet overthrow one line, and no man more shamefully soused[346] in the mire than Master Masker here himself, that boasteth his victory while he lieth in the dirt. But the Catholic Church hath another manner[347] defender than is any earthly man. For it hath God himself therein, and his Holy Spirit, permanent and abiding by Christ's own promise to defend it from falsehood unto the end of the world.[348] And therefore it cannot fall flat in the mire, but God maketh heretics fall flat in the fire.

Yet to the intent, good readers, that you should well see that I left not untouched the point of repugnance, with which Master Masker hath all this while set out his high solemn reason against God's almightiness, himself showeth here at last that of repugnance I did speak myself, howbeit indeed somewhat more moderately than he, as ye shall not only perceive by the words of my letter, but also by the words of Master Masker himself which be these:

> Then saith Master More, though it seemeth repugnant both to him and to me, one body to be in two places at once, yet God seeth how to make them stand together well enough. This man with his old eyes and spectacles seeth far in God's sight, and is of his privy council that knoweth belike[349] by some secret revelation how God seeth one body to be in many places at once includeth no repugnance. For word hath he none for him in all Scripture no more than one body to be in all places at once. It implieth first repugnance to my sight and reason that all this world should be made of nothing, and that a virgin should bring forth a child. But yet when I see it written with the words of my faith, which God spoke, and brought it so to pass, then implieth it no repugnance to me at all. For my faith reacheth it and receiveth it steadfastly. For I know the voice of my

herdsman, which if he said in any place of Scripture that his body should have been contained under the form of bread and so in many places at once here in earth, and also abiding yet still in heaven too, verily I would have believed him, ay, as soon and as firmly as Master More. And therefore even yet, if he can show us but one sentence truly taken for his part, as we can do many for the contrary, we must give place.[350] For as for his unwritten verities and the authority of his antichristian synagogue, unto which (the Scripture forsaken) he is now at last with shame enough compelled to flee, they be proved stark lies and very devilry.[351]

THE NINETEENTH CHAPTER

Is not this a wise invented scoff that Master Masker mocketh me withal,[352] and saith that with mine old eyes and my spectacles I see far in God's sight, and am of God's privy council, and that I know belike, by some secret revelation, how God seeth that one body to be in many places at once includeth no repugnance? It is no council, ye wot well, that is cried at the cross.[353] But Christ hath cried and proclaimed this himself, and sent his heralds, his blessed apostles, to cry it out abroad, and hath caused his evangelists also to write the proclamation, by which all the world was warned that his blessed body, his holy flesh and his blood, is verily eaten and drunken in the Blessed Sacrament. And therefore, either all those places be one in which the Blessed Sacrament is received at once, or else God may do the thing that is repugnant, or else he seeth that his body to be in diverse places at once is not repugnant. For well I wot, he saith he doth it, in all the four evangelists. And well I wot also that he cannot say but sooth.[354] And therefore neither need I to see very far for this point, nor need no secret revelation neither, since it is the point that to the whole world God hath both by word, writing, and miracles revealed and showed so openly. Where is Master Masker now?

For where he saith I have no word of Scripture for Christ's body to be in many places at once no

more than to be in all places at once, if I had not, yet if God had otherwise than by writing revealed the one to his Church and not the other, I would and were bound to believe the one, and would not, nor were bounden to believe, the other, as I believe and am bound to believe now that the Gospel of Saint John is Holy Scripture, and not the gospel of Nicodemus.[355] And if God had revealed both twain[356] unto the Church, I would and were bound to believe both twain, as I believe now that the Gospel of Saint John is Holy Scripture, and the Gospel of Saint Matthew too.

But now of truth, Master Masker abominably belieth[357] the Word of God when he saith that we have not the Word of God, no more for the being of Christ's body in many places at once than in all places at once. For as for the being thereof in all places at once, we find no word plainly written in the Scripture. But for the being thereof in many places at once, Christ's words in his Last Supper, and before that in the sixth chapter of Saint John, be as open, as clear, and as plain as any man well could with any reason require,[358] except[359] any man were so wise as to ween that diverse men's mouths were all one place. And therefore when Master Masker, in his words following, maketh as though he would believe it as well as he believeth the creation of the world, and Christ's birth of a virgin, which seem also to his reason repugnant,[360] if Christ in any plain place of Scripture said it, the truth appeareth otherwise. For unto him that is not with his own frowardness[361] blinded by the devil, the thing that he denieth is as plainly spoken as are the other twain that he saith he believeth. And some other wretches such as himself is, in folly and stubbornness deny both the other twain for the repugnance, as well as he doth this, which thing you have heard him already, with very foolish reasons, declare for so repugnant that he saith that God cannot do it, because it were, as he saith, a giving away of his glory. And therefore his heart once set and fixed on the wrong side, the devil causeth him so to delight in such fond[362] foolish arguments of his own invention that he cannot endure to turn his mind to the truth, but every text, be it never so plain, is dark[363] unto him, through the darkness of his own brain.

---

350 *give place:* yield, give ground   **351** *CW* 11: 314   **352** with   **353** *cried at a cross:* proclaimed at a market cross   **354** truth   **355** an apocryphal gospel   **356** together   **357** slanders   **358** ask   **359** unless   **360** contradictory   **361** perversity   **362** silly   **363** obscure

THE TWENTIETH CHAPTER

But now for because he saith that he will be content and satisfied in this matter with any one text truly taken, while I shall say that the texts that I shall bring him be by me truly taken, and he shall say nay, and shall say that I take them amiss and untruly, while he and I cannot agree upon the taking, but vary upon the exposition and the right understanding of them, by whom will he be judged, whether he or I take those texts truly? If by the congregation of Christian people, the whole Christian nations have this fifteen hundred year judged it against him. For all this while have they believed that Christ, at his Maundy, when he said, "This is my body,"[364] meant that it was his very body indeed, and ever have believed and yet do that it was so indeed. If he will have it judged by a general council, it hath been judged for me against him by more than one already, before his days and mine both. If he will be judged by the writings of the old holy doctors and saints, I have already showed you sufficiently that they have already judged this point against him. If he and I would vary upon the understanding of the old saints' words, besides that you see them yourself so plain that he shall in that point but show himself shameful and shameless, yet the general councils (which himself denieth not) having read and seen those holy doctors themselves, and many of those holy saints being present at those councils themselves, have thereby judged that point against him too. For no wise man will doubt but that among them they understood the doctors then as well as Master Masker doth now. If he say that he will, with his other more than twenty texts of Scripture of which he spoke before, disprove us the texts one or two that I bring for the Blessed Sacrament, then cometh he, you see well, to the selfsame point again, wherein he is overthrown already. For all the corps of Christendom of this fifteen hundred year before us, and all the old holy doctors and saints, and all the general councils, and all the marvelous miracles that God hath showed for the Blessed Sacrament yearly almost, and I ween daily too, what in one place and other, all which things prove the texts that I lay[365] to be meant and understood as I say. All they do thereby declare against him also that none

of his more than twenty texts can in any wise[366] be well and right understood as he saith. For else[367] should it follow that diverse texts of Holy Scripture, not only seemed (which may well be) but also were indeed (which is a thing impossible and cannot be) contrarious and repugnant unto others.

Now good Christian readers, here you see that in his shift[368] that he useth, where he saith that he will believe any one text truly taken, we bring him for the true taking, upon our part, all these things that I have here shortly rehearsed[369] you, of which things himself denieth very few, that is to wit,[370] the old holy doctors to hold on our part, and the people of their time. But therein have I showed you diverse of the best sort against him. And the faith of the people of the diverse times appeareth by their books and by the councils. And then that the general councils and the miracles are on our part, of these two things he denieth neither nother. But since he can deny none of them, he despiseth both. And the holy councils of Christ's Church he calleth the antichristian synagogue. And God's miracles both Frith and he be fain[371] to call the works of the devil. And therefore, good Christian readers, while you see all this, ye see well enough that the texts of the Gospel which we lay for the blessed body of Christ in the Blessed Sacrament be clear and plain for the purpose, and Master Masker will not agree it so, but saith that we take them not truly, only because he will not perceive and confess the truth.

THE TWENTY-FIRST CHAPTER

Now whereas Master Masker saith of me further thus:

"As for his unwritten verities and the authority of his antichristian synagogue, unto which (the Scripture forsaken) he is now at last with shame enough compelled to flee, they be proved stark lies and very devilry."[372] Consider, good Christian readers, that in these words Master Masker telleth you two things: first, that I am, with shame enough, compelled to flee from the Scripture to mine unwritten verities, and to the authority of the antichristian synagogue, by which he meaneth the traditions and the determinations of the Catholic Church; the other that

---

364 See Lk 22:19.   **365** cite   **366** way   **369** told   **370** say   **371** glad; obliged;
367 otherwise   **368** stratagem; sophistry   inclined   **372** *CW* 11: 314

the traditions and determinations of the Church be already proved stark lies and very devilry. For the first point, you see that in this matter of the Blessed Sacrament, which is one of the things that he meaneth, he hath not yet compelled me to flee from the Scripture. For I have well already proved you this point, and very plain and clearly, by the selfsame place of Scripture which Master Masker hath expounded and falsely would wrest it another way: that is to wit, the words of Christ written in the sixth chapter of Saint John. Now if I do for the proof of this point lay the tradition of the whole Catholic Church beside, which thing is also sufficient to prove the matter alone, is that a fleeing from the Scripture? If that be a fleeing from the Scripture, then might the old heretics very well have said the same unto all the old holy doctors that this new heretic saith now to me. For this wotteth[373] well every man that any learning hath: that those old holy doctors and saints laid against those old heretics not the Scripture only, but also the traditions unwritten, believed, and taught by the Church. And if Master Masker, when he shall defend his book, dare deny me that they so did, I shall bring you so many plain proofs thereof that be he never so shameless he shall be ashamed thereof. And if he cannot say nay but[374] that they so did, as I wot well he cannot, then you see well, good readers that by Master Masker's wise reason, those old heretics might have said against each of those old holy doctors and saints, as Master Masker saith against me now, that they had made him with shame enough flee from the Scripture, because he besides the Scripture proved the true faith and reproved their false heresies, by the authority of the Catholic Church. Such strength have always, lo, Master Masker's arguments.

Now touching the second point, where he calleth the Catholic Church the antichristian synagogue, and the unwritten verities stark lies and devilry, he hath already showed and declared partly which things they be that himself meaneth by that name. For he hath before specified purgatory, pilgrimages, and praying to saints, honoring of images, and creeping to the cross, and hallowing of bells against evil spirits in tempests, and boughs on Palm Sunday, and believing in the Blessed Sacrament. And Tyndale, that is either himself or his fellow, mocketh

under the same name the sacrament of aneling,[375] and calleth the sacrament of confirmation the buttering of the boy's forehead, and had as lief[376] have at his christening sand put in his mouth as salt, and mocketh much at fasting.[377] And as for Lent, Father Frith under name of Brightwell,[378] in the revelation of Antichrist calleth it the foolish fast, which jest was undoubtedly revealed Father Frith by the spirit of the devil himself, the spiritual father of Antichrist.

So that you may see, good readers, that to say the litany, or our Lady Matins, and creep to the cross at Easter, or pray for all Christian souls, these things and such others as I have rehearsed you, Master Masker saith are already proved stark lies and very devilry. But he showeth us no such proof yet, neither of lies nor of devilry. But every man may soon see that he which saith so much and nothing proveth maketh many a stark lie, and that thus to rail against God and all good men and holy saints, and helping of good Christian souls, and railing against the blessed body of Christ in the Blessed Sacrament, calling the belief thereof devilry, if such railing in Master Masker be not (as I ween it is) very plain and open devilry, that can be no less yet at the leastwise than very plain and open knavery.

THE TWENTY-SECOND CHAPTER

Master Masker cometh at last to the mocking of those words of my epistle, wherein I show that if men would deny the conversion of the bread and wine into the blessed body and blood of Christ, because that unto his own reason the thing seemeth to imply repugnance,[379] he shall find many other things, both in Scripture, and in nature, and in handicrafts too, of the truth whereof he nothing doubteth, which yet for any solution that his own reason could find, other than the omnipotent power of God, would seem repugnant too, of which manner things other good holy doctors have in the matter of the Blessed Sacrament used some examples before.

Now forasmuch as[380] in these words I speak of the appearing of the face in the glass, and one face in every piece of the glass broken into twenty, Master

---

373 knows   **374** *say nay but:* deny
375 anointing; extreme unction
376 gladly   **377** See *CW* 8: 79.

378 Frith, under the pseudonym Richard Brightwell, wrote a prefatory letter to a translation of Luther's *Revelatio Antichristi.*

379 contradiction   **380** *forasmuch as:* seeing that

1016 *Answer to a Poisoned Book* [*CW* 11: 206–8]

Masker hath caught that glass in hand and mocketh and moweth[381] in that glass, and maketh as many strange faces and as many pretty pots[382] therein, as[383] it were an old rivelled ape. For these are his words, lo:

Then saith he that ye wot well that many good folk have used in this matter many good fruitful examples of God's other works, not only miracles written in Scripture—*unde versus*? ("where one," I pray ye?)—but also done by the common course of nature here in earth (if they be done by the common course of nature, so be they no miracles), and some things made also by man's hand, as one face beholden in diverse glasses, and in every piece of one glass broke into twenty, etc. Lord, how this pontifical poet playeth his part. Because, as he saith, we see many faces in many glasses, therefore may one body be in many places, as though every shadow and similitude representing the body were a bodily substance. But I ask More, when he seeth his own face in so many glasses, whether all those faces that appear in the glasses be his own very face, having bodily substance, skin, flesh, and bone, as hath that face which hath his very mouth, nose, eyes, etc., wherewith he faceth us out[384] the truth thus falsely with lies? And if they be all his very faces, then in very deed there is one body in many places, and he himself beareth as many faces in one hood. But according to his purpose, even as they be no very faces nor those so many voices, sounds, and similitudes, multiplied in the air between the glass or other object and the body (as the philosopher proveth by natural reason) be no very bodies, no more is it Christ's very body, as they would make the belief in the bread in so many places at once.[385]

Now good readers, to the end that you may see the customable[386] manner of Master Masker in rehearsing my matter to his own advantage, since my words in my letter that touch this point be not very long, I shall rehearse them here unto you myself; lo, good readers, thus shall you find it there in the twenty-sixth leaf:

I wot well that many good folk have used in this matter many good fruitful examples of God's

other works, not only miracles written in Scripture, but also done by the common course of nature here in earth and some things made also by man's hand, as[387] one face beholden in diverse glasses and in every piece of one glass broken into twenty and the marvel of the making of the glass itself such matter as it is made of. And of one word coming whole to a hundred ears at once and the sight of one little eye present and beholding a whole great country at once with a thousand such other marvels more, such as those that see them daily done and therefore marvel not at them shall yet never be able, no, not this young man himself, to give such reason by what means they may be done, but that he may have such repugnance laid against it that he shall be fain[388] in conclusion for the chief, and the most evident reason, to say that the cause of all those things is because God that hath caused them so to be done is almighty of himself and can do what him list.[389]

Lo, good Christian readers, here you see yourself that I made none such argument as Master Masker beareth me in hand.[390] Nor no man useth[391] upon a similitude to conclude a necessary consequence in the matter of the Blessed Sacrament, unto which we can bring nothing so like,[392] but that indeed it must be far unlike, saving[393] that it is, as seemeth me,[394] somewhat like in this: that God is as able by his almighty power to make one body be in twenty places at once, as he is by common course of nature, which himself hath made, able to make one face, keeping still his own figure in his own place, cast yet and multiply the same figure of itself, into twenty pieces of one broken glass, of which pieces each hath a several[395] place. And as he is able, by the nature that himself made, to make one self[396] word that the speaker hath breathed out in the speaking to be forthwith[397] in the ears of a whole hundred persons, each of them occupying a several place, and that a good distance asunder, of which two things, as natural and as common as they both be, yet can I never cease to wonder, for all the reasons that ever I read of the philosopher. And likewise as I verily trust that the time shall come, when we shall, in the clear sight of Christ's Godhead, see this great miracle soiled,[398] and well perceive how it is, and how

381 makes grimaces **382** grimaces **383** as if **384** *faceth us out:* disputes with us impudently **385** *CW* 11: 314–15 **386** customary **387** such as **388** forced, obliged **389** wishes **390** *beareth me in hand:* asserts against me **391** is **392** similar **393** except accustomed **394** to me **395** separate **396** same **397** immediately **398** refuted

it may be that his blessed body is both in heaven and in earth, and in so many places at once, so think I verily that in the sight of his Godhead then, we shall also perceive a better cause of those two other things than ever any philosopher hath hitherto showed us yet, or else I ween for my part I shall never perceive them well.

But now whereas Master Masker mocketh mine argument, not which I made, but which himself maketh in my name and maketh it feeble for the nonce[399] that he may, when he hath made it at his own pleasure, soil it, as children make castles of tile shards and then make them their pastime in the throwing down again, yet is it not even so—so feeble as his own, where he argueth in the negative, as I lay the example for the affirmative. For as for the one that he maketh for me, though the argument be nought[400] for lack of form, yet holdeth it somewhat so-so, by the matter in that the consequent[401]—that is to wit, that God may make one body to be at once in many places—is, whatsoever Master Masker babble, a truth without question necessary.

But where he argueth for himself in the negative, by that that the bodily substance of the face is not in the glass, that therefore the bodily substance of our Savior Christ is not in the Blessed Sacrament, that argument hath no manner[402] hold at all. For the antecedent[403] is very true, and except[404] God's word be untrue, else[405] as I have already, by the old holy expositors of the same, well and plainly proved you the consequent is very false.

Now if he will say that he maketh not that argument, but useth only the face in the glass for an example and a similitude, then he showeth himself to play the false shrew,[406] when of my bringing in the selfsame example, he maketh that argument for me. And therefore now when upon those faces in the glass, he maketh and faceth himself that lie upon[407] me, and then scoffeth that I face out the truth with lies, and then proveth never one, he doth but show what pretty words he could speak, and how properly he could scoff, if the matter would serve him.

And yet I pray you, good readers, consider well the words of that argument that he maketh in mine name: "We see many faces in many glasses; therefore may one body be in many places." Now spoke not I, you wot well, of many faces seen in many glasses, as he both falsely and foolishly rehearseth me, but of one face seen at once in many glasses. For that is like to the matter. For like[408] as all those glasses, while only one man looketh in them, he seeth but his own one face in all those places, so be (as Saint Chrysostom declareth) all the Hosts of the Blessed Sacrament being in so far distant several places asunder, all one very body of our blessed Savior himself, and all one host, one sacrifice, and one oblation.

And as properly as Master Masker scoffeth at that example and similitude of the glass, I would not have misliked mine own wit[409] therein if the invention thereof had been mine own. For I find not many examples so meet[410] for the matter, to the capacity of good and unlearned folk, as it is. For as for the point of which Master Masker maketh all the difficulty, that one substance being but a creature might be in many places at once, every man that is learned seeth an example that satisfieth him shortly. For he seeth and perceiveth by good reason that the soul is indivisible and is in every part of the body, and in every part it is whole.[411] And yet is every member a several[412] place. And so is the Blessed Substance of the spiritual Body of Christ's flesh and his bones whole in every part of the Sacrament.

But this example of the soul cannot every man unlearned conceive and imagine right, but of the glass hath for his capacity a more meetly similitude, and that that in one point also doth more resemble the matter. For the soul forsaketh every member that is clean[413] divided from the body. But the blessed body of our Savior abideth still whole in every part of the Blessed Sacrament, though it be broken into never so many parts, as the image and form of the face abideth whole still to him that beholdeth it, in every part of the broken glass. And thus, good readers, as for this example and similitude of the face in the glass, Master Masker may, for his foolish facing it out,[414] be much ashamed, if he have any shame, whensoever he looketh on his own face in the glass.

And for conclusion, this being of the body of Christ in diverse places at once, since the old holy doctors and saints saw and perceived that the soul of every man, which is a very substance, and peradventure[415] yet of less spiritual power than the flesh

---

399 express purpose   400 null, nothing   401 conclusion of the argument   402 kind of   403 statement in logic upon which any consequent statement depends   404 unless   405 otherwise   406 villain   407 *faceth . . . upon:* tells a manifest lie about   408 just   409 intellect; ingenuity   410 appropriate   411 See *Summa theologica* 1, q. 76, a. 8.   412 different, separate   413 completely   414 *facing it out:* impudent lying   415 perhaps

and bones of our Savior Christ be now, and yet very flesh for all that and very bones also still, they reckoned not that the being thereof in diverse places at once would after their days begin to be taken for so strange and hard a thing as these heretics make it now. And therefore they made nothing so great a matter of that point, but the thing that they thought men would most marvel of was the conversion and turning of the bread and the wine into Christ's very flesh and blood. And therefore to make that point well open, and to make it sink into men's breasts, those old holy doctors and saints, as I said in these words which Master Masker mocketh, used many more good examples of things done by nature.

But then were they no miracles, saith Master Masker. And what then, good Master Masker? Might they not serve to prove that God might do as much by miracle as nature by her common course? Those words, lo, were by Master Masker (you see well) very well and wisely put in.

THE TWENTY-THIRD CHAPTER

Over[416] this, toward the perceiving and belief of that point of conversion of the bread and the wine into the very flesh and blood of Christ, I said that those holy doctors and saints used examples of other miracles done by God and written in Holy Scripture.

Now at this word, Master Masker asketh me, *Unde versus?* ("Where one," I pray you?). You have heard already, good readers, in the fifteenth chapter of the first book, the words of that holy doctor Saint Cyril, in which for the credence of that point — that is to wit, the changing of the bread and the wine into Christ's flesh and his blood, he bringeth the miracles that God wrought in the Old Law, as the changing of the water into blood — and the changing of Moses's rod into a serpent,[417] and diverse other changes and mighty miracles more.

You have heard also before how Saint Chrysostom, against them that would doubt how Christ could give them his flesh to eat, layeth forth the miracle of the multiplying of five loaves so suddenly to twelve baskets full more than the sufficient feeding of five thousand folk.[418]

Here be, lo, some verses yet, Master Masker, and more than one miracle, pardie,[419] that those holy doctors and saints have used in this matter of the Blessed Sacrament. And yet such others more shall I bring you at another leisure, ere I have done with your second course, that it shall grieve you to see them. And surely where properly[420] you scoff at me with my many faces in one hood, I have here in this first part already brought you for the true faith of the Catholic Church, against your false heresy, wherewith you would face our Savior out of[421] the Blessed Sacrament, I have brought against you to your face Saint Bede and Theophylactus, Saint Augustine, and Saint Hilary, Saint Irenaeus, Saint Cyril, and Saint Chrysostom, so many such good faces into this one hood that all the shameful lies that your shameless face can make shall never against these faces be able to face out the truth. And thus end I, good readers, my fourth book.

Here endeth the Fourth Book.

---

416 Beyond   **417** See Ex 4:6–7; 7:20.   **418** See Mt 14:13–21; Chrysostom, *In* *Ioannem homiliae* 45 (*PG* 59: 260–61).   **419** certainly; "by God" (French)   **420** excellently   **421** *face…out of*: shamelessly exclude our Savior from

THE FIFTH BOOK
AND THE LAST OF THE
FIRST PART

THE FIRST CHAPTER

Now come I, good Christian readers, to the last point that I spoke of, the two contradictions of mine own that Master Masker hath highly laid unto my charge, whose words I shall, good readers, first rehearse[1] you whole. Lo, these they be, God save them:

At last note, Christian reader, that Master More in the third book of his *Confutation of Tyndale*, the 249th side, to prove Saint John's Gospel unperfect and insufficient for leaving out of so necessary a point of our faith, as he calleth the Last Supper of Christ, his Maundy, saith that John spoke nothing at all of this Sacrament.[2] And now see again in these his letters against Frith, how himself bringeth in John's sixth chapter to impugn Frith's writing, and to make all for the Sacrament, even thus: "My flesh is verily meat and my blood drink." Belike[3] the man had there overshot[4] himself foul, the young man here causing him to put on his spectacles and pore better and more wishly[5] with his old eyes upon Saint John's Gospel to find that thing there now written, which before he would have made one of his unwritten verities. As yet, if he look narrowly, he shall espy that himself hath proved us by Scripture, in the thirty-seventh leaf of his dialogue of "quoth he" and "quoth I," our Lady's perpetual virginity, expounding *non cognosco, id est, non cognoscam*, which now written unwritten verity he numbereth a little before among his unwritten vanities. Thus may ye see how this old holy upholder of the pope's Church, his words fight against themselves into his own confusion, in finding us forth his unwritten written vanities— verities, I should say. But return we unto the exposition of Saint John.[6]

Now have you, good Christian readers, heard his whole tale concerning my two contradictions, of which twain[7] I will first answer the last that concerneth the perpetual virginity of our Lady, which point I have touched toward the end of the twenty-fifth chapter of the first book of my dialogue, wherein Master Masker mocketh me for "quoth I" and "quoth he," and would I see well in no wise[8] that in the rehearsing of a communication had between myself and another man, I should not for shame say "quoth I" and "quoth he," but rather rehearse our two talkings, with "quoth we" and "quoth she."

I have also spoken of that point in more places than one of my work that I wrote of Tyndale's *Confutation*,[9] which places, whoso list[10] to read shall find this point of contradiction answered already, that Master Masker now layeth to my charge,[11] dissimuling[12] such things as I have answered it with.

And of this contradiction I am so sore[13] ashamed that for all Master Masker's words even here before in my first book of this work, I have not letted[14] the best that my wit[15] will serve me this unwritten verity to prove yet again by the selfsame place of Saint Luke's holy writing.

For why,[16] to say the truth, I do not so much force[17] to have that article taken for an unwritten verity with good Catholic folk for the maintenance of my word as to have it for the honor of our Lady, taken and believed for an undoubted truth, with Catholics and those heretics too, that will take it for no such truth but if[18] it be written in Scripture.

Now doth the clear certainty of this article indeed depend upon the tradition of the apostles, continued in the Catholic Church. For albeit that[19] myself think that I find some words written in Scripture that would well prove it, and upon those words let[20] not to write mine own mind,[21] and diverse old holy doctors too, yet while I see that holy Saint Jerome himself, a man far otherwise seen[22] in Scripture than I, arguing for the defense of that article

---

1 quote to   **2** See *CW* 8: 312–14, *CW* 6: 150–51.   **3** Perhaps   **4** overreached   **5** fixedly, intently   **6** *CW* 11: 315   **7** two   **8** way   **9** See *CW* 8: 287–88, 312–14, 472–74, 1005–6.   **10** wishes   **11** *layeth to my charge:* charge me with   **12** dissembling   **13** greatly   **14** refrained from   **15** intellect; ingenuity   **16** which reason   **17** care   **18** *but if:* unless   **19** *albeit that:* although   **20** hesitate   **21** opinion; judgment   **22** versed

against that heretic Helvidius did only soil[23] the Scriptures that Helvidius laid against it, and layeth no Scripture himself for the proof of his part, but resteth therein to the authority of Christ's Catholic Church,[24] which Master Masker here calleth the antichristian synagogue, I neither dare nor will take so much upon myself as to affirm surely that it is proved to be a written verity. And this lack of taking, lo, so much upon myself is the thing that Master Masker calleth so shameful repugnance,[25] to my great confusion.

And therefore in that place of my *Dialogue*,[26] though I upon that word of our Lady, "In what wise shall this thing be done, for I know not a man?"[27] do reason and show my mind that it proveth for this part, as indeed methinketh it doth, yet I am not so bold upon mine own exposition therein as to affirm that the Scripture saith there openly and plainly that she was a perpetual virgin. For if it had been a very precise plain evident open proof of that matter, mine own mind giveth me that Saint Jerome would not have failed to have found it before me.

I shall also for this point have Master Masker himself to say somewhat for me, though he do therein (as he is often wont[28] to do) speak somewhat against himself. For he saith here himself that if a man look narrowly, then he shall espy that I have myself proved our Lady's perpetual virginity. Now since that Master Masker saith that a man cannot spy it but if he look narrowly, he saith, you see well, himself that it is no plain open proof. And then is it no proof to them, you wot[29] well. For they receive no Scripture for proof of any purpose but only plain, open, and evident.

And therefore by Master Masker's own tale, though I proved it sufficiently a written verity unto good Catholics, yet rested it unproved still a written verity unto such heretics, and against them, ye wot well, wrote I. Howbeit,[30] here will I demand of Master Masker, touching the perpetual virginity of our Lady to be plainly written in Holy Scripture, whether I prove that point well or not? If not, then may I well enough, notwithstanding any such proof of mine, say still that it is an unwritten verity. If he will confess that I prove it well, I will be content with that praise of himself to abide his rebuke of

that contradiction. For I set more, as I said, by[31] the profit of his soul in falling from the contrary heresy to the right belief of our Lady's perpetual virginity than I set by mine own praise and commendation of abiding well by my words.

But yet if he will allow my proof made of that point, I marvel me much but if[32] that he allow now my proof made for the blessed body of Christ present in the Blessed Sacrament. For I am very sure I have proved much more clearly, by much more open and plain words of the Scripture, and the sense of those words by diverse old holy doctors, other manner of men than myself, than I have proved or any man else the perpetual virginity of our blessed Lady.

Howbeit, of truth, though I proved well that point of the perpetual virginity of our Lady to be a verity written in Scripture, and that many other also proved it much better than I, as I think there do, and that myself had affirmed it never so strongly for never so clear a written verity, yet since William Tyndale, against whom I specially wrote, taketh it, as in his writing well and plain appeareth, for no written verity, and yet agreeth that it is to be believed, but not of necessity, and yet after upon his own words I prove him that of necessity too, I may, without any contradiction or repugnance at all, lay it against him for an unwritten verity, for as much as himself so taketh it.

Moreover all the proof that I make of our Lady's perpetual virginity is no more but that she was a perpetual virgin except[33] she broke her vow. And surely as I say, it seemeth to myself that I prove this very clearly. And this being proved is indeed enough to good Christian folk for a full proof that she was a perpetual virgin. But yet unto these heretics against whom I wrote, since they set nought by[34] vows of virginity, but say that they that make them do both unlawfully make them, and may, when they will, lawfully break them, and that therefore friars may run out of religion and wed nuns, this proof of mine is to them no manner[35] proof at all. And therefore I may to them, without contradiction or repugnance, lay it for an unwritten verity still.

And thus I trust you see, good readers, that as for this repugnance, turneth to Master Masker's confusion and not mine.

---

23 refute   **24** See *De perpetua virginitate . . . adversus Helvidium* (PL 23: 183–206).   **25** contradiction   **26** See   *CW* 6: 150.   **27** Lk 1:34   **28** accustomed   **29** know   **30** However   **31** *set more . . . by:* value more   **32** *but if:* unless   **33** unless   **34** *set nought by:* value as nothing   **35** kind of

THE SECOND CHAPTER

Now come I then, good readers, to the other contradiction that he layeth against me, his words wherein, before mine answer, I pray you read once again. And lest ye should be loath to turn back and seek them, here shall you have them again; lo, these they be:

At last note, Christian reader, that Master More, in the third book of his *Confutation of Tyndale*, the 249th side, to prove Saint John's Gospel unperfect and insufficient for leaving out of so necessary a point of our faith, as he calleth the Last Supper of Christ, his Maundy, saith that John spoke nothing at all of this Sacrament. And now see again in these his letters against Frith, how himself bringeth in John's sixth chapter to impugn Frith's writing, and to make all for the Sacrament, even thus: "My flesh is verily[36] meat and my blood drink." Belike[37] the man had there overshot[38] himself foul, the young man here causing him to put on his spectacles and pore better and more wishly[39] with his old eyes upon Saint John's Gospel to find that thing there now written, which before he would have made one of his unwritten verities.[40]

When myself, good reader, read first these words of his, albeit that I was sure enough that in the things that I purposed there was no repugnance indeed, yet seeing that he so diligently laid forth the leaf in which my fault should be found, I very plainly thought that I had not so circumspectly seen unto my words as wisdom would I should.[41] And taking therefore mine oversight[42] for a very truth, I never vouchsafed[43] to turn my book and look.

But afterward it happed on a day I said in a certain company that I was somewhat sorry that it had mishapped me to take in this one point no better heed to mine hand, but to write therein two things repugnant and contrary, whereunto some of them made answer that such a chance happeth sometimes ere[44] a man be aware in a long work. "But yet," quoth one of them, a gentlewoman, "have you considered well the place in your book, and seen that he saith truth?" "Nay, by my troth,"[45] quoth I,

"that have I not. For it irketh me to look upon the place again now when it is too late to mend it. For I am sure the man would not be so mad to name the very leaf, but if[46] he were well sure that he said true." "By our Lady," quoth she, "but since you have not looked it yourself, I will, for all the leaf laid out by him, see the thing myself ere I believe his writing, I know these fellows for so false." And therewithal she sent for the book, and turned to the very 249th side, and with that number marked also. And in good faith, good readers, there found we no such manner matter, neither on the one side of the leaf nor on the other.[47]

Howbeit, of truth, I cannot deny but that in a side after mismarked with the number of 249, which should have been marked with the number of 259, there we found the matter in that place. But therein found we the most shameful either folly or falsehood of Master Masker that ever I saw lightly[48] in any man in my life, which because ye shall not seek far to find, I shall rehearse you here the very words of that place. Lo, good readers, these they be:

But now because of Tyndale, let us take some one thing. And what thing rather than the Last Supper of Christ, his Maundy with his apostles, in which he instituted the Blessed Sacrament of the altar, his own blessed body and blood. Is this no necessary point of faith? Tyndale cannot deny it for a necessary point of faith and though[49] it were but of his own false faith, agreeing with Luther, Hussgen, or Zwingli. And he cannot say that Saint John speaketh anything thereof, specially not of the institution. Nor he cannot say that Saint John speaketh anything of the Sacrament at all, since that his sect expressly denieth that Saint John meant the Sacrament in his words where he speaketh expressly thereof in the sixth chapter of his Gospel.[50]

Where have you ever, good Christian readers, seen any fond[51] fellow before this handle a thing so falsely or so foolishly as Master Masker here handleth this? He telleth you that I said here that Saint John spoke nothing of the Sacrament at all. Now you see that Master Masker in that point belieth[52] me. For I said not here that Saint John spoke

---

36 truly   **37** Perhaps   **38** overreached
39 fixedly, intently   **40** *CW* 11: 315
41 *would I should:* wanted me to   **42** error

43 was willing   **44** before   **45** trustworthiness, faithfulness   **46** *but if:* unless
47 See *CW* 8: 313–14.   **48** in all probability

49 even if   **50** *CW* 8: 313   **51** foolish
52 slanders

nothing thereof, but first I said there that Tyndale, against whom I there wrote, could not say that Saint John wrote anything of the Blessed Sacrament, specially not of the institution thereof. And this is very truth. For as touching the institution thereof at Christ's Last Supper and Maundy, neither Tyndale nor no man else can say that Saint John anything wrote thereof in his Gospel.

Then said I further there, as you see, not that Saint John speaketh nothing of the Sacrament, but that Tyndale cannot say that Saint John speaketh of the Sacrament anything at all. And that I meant not in those words, to say mine own self, that Saint John spoke nothing thereof, I declare plainly there forthwith,[53] by that I show the cause why Tyndale cannot say that Saint John spoke anything of the Sacrament at all — that is to wit,[54] because that all his sect expressly denieth that anything was meant of the Sacrament in the words of Christ written in the sixth chapter of Saint John.

By this ye may see plainly, good readers, that Master Masker plainly belieth me. For I said not myself that Saint John spoke nothing of the Sacrament, but that Tyndale, because of the opinion of all his sect in that point, could not say that Saint John spoke anything thereof, which was enough for my purpose, while Tyndale was the man against whom I wrote, though myself would for mine own part say the contrary. For it is that kind of argument that is in the schools called *argumentum ad hominem*.[55] And thus you see, good readers, Master Masker in this thing either shamefully false, or very shamefully foolish: shamefully false, if he perceived and understood my words, and then for all that thus belieth me; shamefully foolish if the thing being spoken by me so plain, his wit[56] would not serve him to perceive it.

But now as clear as ye see the matter already by this, to the intent yet that Master Masker shall have no matter left him in all this world to make any argument of for his excuse therein, read my words again, good readers, and bid Master Masker mark well my words therein, where I say expressly that Saint John spoke expressly thereof in the sixth chapter of his Gospel. For these words are, as you see, there the very last words of all: "Nor Tyndale cannot say that

Saint John speaketh anything of the Sacrament at all, since that his sect expressly denieth that Saint John meant the Sacrament in his words where he speaketh expressly thereof in the sixth chapter of his Gospel."

Whose words are these? Where he speaketh expressly thereof? Are not these words mine? And do I not in these words expressly say that Saint John expressly speaketh of the Blessed Sacrament in the sixth chapter of his Gospel, in which place Tyndale's sect saith expressly that he nothing spoke thereof? And now saith Master Masker that I said there that Saint John spoke nothing thereof at all, and layeth it for a foul repugnance[57] in me that in my letter against Frith, I say thereof the contrary.

But how now, Master Masker? What have you now to say? With what shameful shift[58] will your shameless face face us out[59] this foolish lie of yours, that you make upon me here? If you lied so loud wittingly,[60] how can you look[61] that any man should trust your word? If for lack of understanding, how can you look then for shame that any man should trust your wit? Why should we think that your wit will pierce into the perceiving of hard words in the Holy Scripture of God when it will not serve you to perceive such poor plain words of mine?

Ye write that the young man hath here made me don on my spectacles and look more wishly[62] on the matter, to find now written therein the thing that I said before was not written therein. But now must you look more wishly upon my words, on which you make here so loud a lie, and pore better on them with your spectacles upon your Masker's nose.

I wist[63] once a good fellow, which while he danced in a mask, upon boldness that no man could have known him, when he perceived that he was well espied by his evil-favored[64] dancing, he waxed[65] so ashamed suddenly that he softly said unto his fellow, "I pray you tell me, doth not my visor blush red?" Now surely, good readers, Master Masker here, if he were not utterly past shame, hath cause enough to be in this point so sore[66] ashamed that he might ween[67] the glowing of his visage should even pierce through his visor, and make it red for shame.

Thus have I now, good Christian readers, answered at the full in these five books of my first part,

---

the first part of Master Masker's work, and taken up the first course of Master Masker's Supper, which he falsely calleth the last supper of the Lord, while he hath with his own poisoned cookery made it the supper of the devil. And yet would the devil, I ween, disdain to have his supper dressed of such a rude ruffin,[68] such a scald[69] Colyn cook as under the name of a clerk, so ribaldiously raileth against the blessed body of Christ in the Blessed Sacrament of the altar.

THE THIRD CHAPTER

But one thing will I yet rehearse you that I have hitherto deferred: that is to wit, my first argument against Frith, which, as I showed you before, Master Masker let go by, as he hath done many things more, and made as though he saw them not. That argument, good readers, was this:

In this heresy, besides the common faith of all Catholic Christian regions, the expositions of all the old holy doctors and saints be clear against Frith, as whole as against any heretic that ever was hitherto heard of. For as for the words of Christ of which we speak touching the Blessed Sacrament, though he may find some old holy men that besides the literal sense doth expound them in an allegory, yet he shall never find any of them that did as he doth now, after[70] Wycliffe, Oecolampadius, Tyndale, and Zwingli, deny the literal sense, and say that Christ meant not that it was his very[71] body and his very blood indeed, but the old holy doctors and expositors, besides all such allegories, do plainly declare and expound that in those words, our Savior as he expressly spoke so did also well and plainly mean that the thing which he there gave to his disciples in the Sacrament was in very deed his very flesh and blood. And so did never any of the old expositors of Scripture expound any of those other places in which Christ is called a vine or a door. And therefore it appeareth well that the manner of speaking was not like.[72] For if it had, then would not the old expositors have used such so far unlike fashion in the expounding of them.[73]

This was, lo, good readers, the first argument of mine that Master Masker met with, and which he should first therefore have soiled.[74] But it is such as he listed[75] little to look upon. For whereas he maketh much ado[76] to have it seem that both these words of our Savior at his Last Supper, "This is my body," and his words of eating of his flesh and drinking of his blood, written in the sixth chapter of Saint John, should be spoken in a like phrase and manner of speaking, as were his other words, "I am the door" and "I am the very vine," I showed there unto Frith, whom Master Masker maketh as though he would defend, that by the expositions of all the old holy doctors and saints that have expounded all those four places before, the difference well appeareth, since none of them declare him to be a very material door, nor a natural very vine. This saith no man not so much as a very natural fool. But that in the Sacrament is his very natural body, his very flesh and his blood, this declare clearly all the old holy expositors of the Scripture, which were good men and gracious, wise and well-learned both. And therefore, as I said, the difference may soon be perceived, but if[77] Master Masker list better to believe himself than all them, which if he do, as indeed he doth, then is he much more fool than a natural fool indeed.

For as for his three places of Saint Augustine, Tertullian, and Saint Chrysostom,[78] whom he bringeth in his second part, I shall in my second part in taking up of his second course, when we come to fruit, pare him, I warrant you, those three pears so near that he getteth not a good morsel among them, and yet peradventure ere[79] I come at it too.

For so is it now, good readers, that I very certainly know that that book which Frith made last against the Blessed Sacrament is come over into this realm in print, and secretly sent abroad into the brethren's hands and some good sisters too. And forasmuch as[80] I am surely informed for truth that Frith hath into that book of his taken many texts of old holy doctors, wilily handled by false Friar Hussgen before, to make it falsely seem that the old holy doctors and saints were favorers of their false heresy, therefore will I for the while set Master Masker's second part aside till I have answered that pestilent peevish book of John Frith, about which I purpose to go as soon as I can get one of them, which so

---

68 *rude ruffin:* harsh fiend   **69** scabby   **75** wished   **76** trouble   **77** *but if:* unless   *ere:* perhaps before   **80** *forasmuch as:*
70 in accord with   **71** true   **72** similar   **78** See *CW* 11: 332–34.   **79** *peradventure*   seeing that
73 Letter 190, pp. 361–62   **74** refuted

many being abroad, shall I trust not be long too. And then shall I, by the grace and help of Almighty God, make you the folly and the falsehood of Frith and Friar Hussgen both as open and as clear as I have in this work made open and clear unto you the falsehood and the folly of Master Masker here.

And whereas I, a year now passed and more, wrote and put in print a letter against the pestilent treatise of John Frith,[81] which he then had made and secretly sent abroad among the brethren, against the Blessed Sacrament of the altar, which letter of mine, as I have declared in mine *Apology*, I nevertheless caused to be kept still and would not suffer[82] it to be put out abroad into every man's hands, because Frith's treatise was not yet at that time in print, yet now since I see that there are comen over in print, not only Frith's book,[83] but over[84] that this Masker's book also, and that either of their both books maketh mention of my said letter, and would seem to soil[85] it, and laboreth sore[86] thereabout, I do therefore now suffer the printer to put with this book my said letter also to sale.

And forasmuch also as those authorities of Saint Augustine, Saint Chrysostom, and Tertullian, which Master Masker layeth in his second part,[87] I shall of likelihood find also in Frith's book, and therefore answer them there, and all Master Masker's whole matter too, before I return to his second part, which yet I will after all this, God willing, not leave nor let go, so in the meanwhile, may Master Masker (since it is, as he saith, so great pleasure to him to be written against, having, as he boasteth, all solutions so readily) look and assay[88] whether he can soil these things with which I have in this first part overthrown his whole heresy, and proved him very plain a very false fool already, of whose false wily folly to beware our Lord give us grace, and of all such other like, which with foolish arguments of their own blind reason, wresting the Scripture into a wrong sense, against the very plain words of the text, against the expositions of all the old holy saints, against the determinations of diverse whole general councils, against the full consent of all true Christian nations this fifteen hundred year before their days, and against the plain declaration of almighty God himself, made in every Christian country by so many plain open miracles, labor now to make us so foolishly blind and mad as to forsake the very true Catholic faith, forsake the society of the true Catholic Church, and with sundry sects of heretics fallen out thereof, to set both holy days and fasting days at nought,[89] and for the devil's pleasure to forbear and abstain from all prayer to be made either for souls or to saints, jest on our Blessed Lady the immaculate mother of Christ, make mocks at all pilgrimages, and creeping of Christ's cross, the holy ceremonies of the Church and the sacraments to turn them into trifling, with likening them to wine garlands and ale-poles,[90] and finally, by these ways in the end and conclusion, forsake our Savior himself in the Blessed Sacrament, and instead of his own blessed body and his blood ween there were nothing but bare bread and wine, and call it idolatry there to do him honor. But woe may such wretches be. For this we may be sure: that whoso dishonor God in one place with occasion of a false faith, standing[91] that false belief and infidelity, all the honor that he doth him anywhere besides is odious and despiteful[92] and rejected of[93] God, and never shall save that faithless soul from the fire of hell, from which our Lord give them grace truly to turn in time, so that we and they together in one Catholic Church, knit unto God together in one Catholic faith — faith, I say, not faith alone as they do, but accompanied with good hope, and with her chief sister, well-working charity — may so receive Christ's blessed sacraments here, and specially that we may so receive himself, his very blessed body, very flesh and blood, in the Blessed Sacrament, our holy blessed housel, that we may here be with him incorporated so by grace, that after the short course of this transitory life, with his tender pity poured upon us in purgatory, at the prayer of good people and intercession of holy saints, we may be with them in their holy fellowship, incorporated in Christ in his eternal glory. Amen.

Finis

81 *A Christen sentence* (*CW* 7: 427–33)
82 allow **83** *A book . . . answeringe unto M mores lettur* (Antwerp, 1533) **84** beyond
85 refute **86** intensely **87** See *CW* 11:

332–34; Tertullian, *Adversus Marcionem* 4.40.3 (*CCSL* 1: 656); Augustine, *Contra Adamantum* 12 (*PL* 42: 146); Chrysostom, *Commentarius in S. Mattaeum* 82(83)

(*PG* 58: 743). **88** test **89** *to set at nought:* regard as nothing **90** *wine garlands and ale-poles:* tavern signs **91** continuing in, remaining with **92** insulting **93** by

A Treatise upon the Passion of Christ

Most of Thomas More's unfinished *Treatise on the Passion of Christ* was probably written early in 1534, before his imprisonment on April 17 (*CW* 13: xli). Like the *Sadness of Christ*, this *Treatise* quotes biblical passages from John Gerson's *Monotessaron* (a Gospel harmony from the early 1400s), followed by commentaries that are referred to in this work as "exposition," "lecture," or "homily." Unlike *Sadness*, however, most sections of *Treatise* are followed by a related prayer. The other major source informing More's *Treatise* is the *Catena aurea*, or "Golden Chain," of Thomas Aquinas, which presents the text of the Gospels part by part, link by link, followed by relevant comments from the Church fathers (xliv). As More remarks in the title paragraph, his exposition is "taken for the more part out of the sayings of sundry good old holy doctors," whose writings he had studied since the beginning of his career.

A Treatise on the Passion of Christ is generally considered a continuation of More's doctrinal writings on the Eucharistic controversies of the time, and is possibly the second part of More's *Answer to a Poisoned Book*. Garry Haupt understands the *Treatise* as an expression of More's humanism: "More draws together devotional and exegetical currents in a work of the Christian humanist rhetorician attempting to persuade, to 'move,' rhetorically, his readers" (li). In his *Treatise*, More unites eloquence, piety, and learning in a synthesis that communicates "a feeling of heightened ordinary humanity avoiding extremes of intellectual and religious sensibility, solidly rooted on this earth in a world of common sense and yet looking confidently to heaven" (cxxii). More remarks in the short introduction to the *Treatise* that he writes for himself, and for readers like him, who in their human imprudence and forgetfulness, bestow little consideration on the hereafter, and "so little remember to labor and provide that they may have some house commodious for their ease, and well favoredly trimmed to their pleasure" in heaven.

Though incomplete, More's *Treatise* reflects his lifelong interest in the Passion as an example of Christ's charity and fortitude. As early as the *The Life of Pico* in 1510, for example, he writes of Christ's ascent to heaven "by manly fight / and bitter passion." As late as May 1535, in a letter to Margaret Roper, he shares with his daughter what he had told his interrogators: "I had fully determined with myself neither to study nor meddle with any matter of this world, but that my whole study should be upon the Passion of Christ and mine own passage out of this world." His last book, *The Sadness of Christ*, is a commentary on the example of Christ "the captain," and his experience of suffering in the garden of Gethsemane. Opposite God's love, in More's judgment, stands the sin of pride. *The Treatise* begins with More's account of the fall of the angels, the creation, and the fall of man, and More counsels readers to consider and beware the least "spice" or trace of pride, presented as the "pestilence" through which human beings fall first into "the delight and liking of themselves," and then proceed to neglecting, condemning, and finally forsaking God. "The premise of the *Treatise*," Seymour Baker House contends, "is that we are engaged in a perpetual spiritual war," one in which the Passion emerges as a most useful weapon and "remedy."

The *Treatise* breaks off after More's discussion of the washing of the feet (John 13) and in the midst of his third "lecture" on the Eucharist. As Louis Martz and Garry Haupt have indicated, More's thoughts at the end of the *Treatise on the Passion* are completed by the treatise that was published separately under the title of *A Treatise to Receive the Blessed Body of Our Lord Sacramentally and Virtually Both*. That text immediately follows the *Treatise on the Passion* in this edition.

More's *Treatise* was only published in full for the first time in Rastell's 1557 *Workes*. This edition of the *Treatise* is based on the text in volume 13 of *The Yale Edition of the Complete Works of St. Thomas More*. Garry E. Haupt's abbreviated edition, glossed and with standardized spelling and punctuation (part of Yale's Modernized Series) was published in 1980 and is also used extensively here.

CONTENTS

*As editors Louis Martz and Garry Haupt have indicated, this third lecture is completed by the treatise that was published separately under the title of *A Treatise to Receive the Blessed Body of Our Lord Sacramentally and Virtually Both.* See that *Treatise*, pp. 1101–06.

A Treatise upon the Passion of Christ

A treatise historical, containing the bitter Passion of our Savior Christ, after the course and order of the four evangelists, with an exposition upon their words, taken for the more part out of the sayings of sundry good old holy doctors,[1] and
⁵ beginning at the first assembly of the bishops, the priests, and the seniors[2] of the people about the contriving of Christ's death, written in the twenty-sixth chapter of Saint Matthew, the fourteenth of Saint Mark, and in the twenty-second of Saint Luke. And it endeth in the committing of his blessed body into his sepulchre, with the frustrate[3] provision of the Jews about the keeping thereof
¹⁰ with soldiers appointed thereto, written in the twenty-seventh of Saint Matthew, the fifteenth of Saint Mark, the twenty-third of Saint Luke, and the nineteenth of Saint John.

FIRST: AN INTRODUCTION UNTO THE STORY

¹⁵ *Non habemus hic civitatem manentem, sed futuram inquirimus* ("We have not here a dwelling city, but we seek the city that is to come").[4]

If it be (good Christian reader) true, as out of doubt it is even very true, that (as Saint Paul in the
²⁰ afore-rehearsed words saith) we have not here any city to dwell in, but we be seeking for the city that we shall dwell in hereafter, then seemeth me[5] that many men are very far overseen,[6] such men, I mean, as I am (alack) myself, that so much time and study
²⁵ beset[7] about their night's lodging here in passing by the way, and so little remember to labor and provide[8] that they may have some house commodious for their ease, and well-favoredly trimmed[9] to their pleasure, in that place whither once go we shall, and
³⁰ when we come once there, dwell there we shall and inhabit there forever.

Sir Thomas More wrote no more of this introduction.

The First Point: The Fall of Angels

The glorious blessed Trinity—the Father, the Son, ³⁵ and the Holy Ghost, three distinct and diverse equal and like mighty persons, and all three nevertheless one undivisible and indistinct infinite almighty God, being from before all time eternally stablished in the infinite perfection of their incomprehensible ⁴⁰ and undecayable glory—did when it pleased themselves, not of any necessity nor for increase of any commodity[10] that their full and perfect and not increasable bliss could receive thereby, but only of their mere[11] liberal goodness, create of nothing the ⁴⁵ noble high beautiful nature of angels to make some creatures partners of the Creator's goodness. And albeit that[12] in that excellent company of angels all were not of like perfection, but ordinately[13] divided into diverse orders and degrees, the higher in excel- ⁵⁰ lence of nature far surmounting the lower, yet did the lowest far pass[14] and excel the natural state that mankind afterward had in his[15] creation.

But yet had not the angels forthwith[16] in their creation given unto them the perfect bliss, heaven, ⁵⁵ nor were forthwith endued[17] with the very[18] fruition and plain beholding of the glorious Trinity, but were left in the hand of their own free will and

1 early Church fathers **2** elders **3** ineffectual **4** Heb 13:14 **5** *seemeth me:* I think **6** imprudently mistaken **7** bestow **8** prepare, get ready **9** *well-favoredly trimmed:* handsomely adorned **10** benefit **11** complete, simple **12** *albeit that:* although **13** in ordered sequence **14** surpass **15** its **16** immediately **17** endowed **18** actual

liberty, either with help of God's grace, by turning to God with laud[19] and thanks for that they had already of his gift to be received by grace unto that glory, or else willingly declining from grace and turning themselves from God, as graceless caitiffs frowardly[20] to fall into wretchedness. For if they had once already had the very sight of God at that time, in such wise as the glorious company of angels and saved souls blessedly have it now, the heavenly beholding thereof must needs have been so delectable and so joyful unto them, and so should have pierced and fulfilled them thoroughly with sweetness, that it should not have left any place in them for any contrarious appetite or affection[21] to enter. But now, standing[22] thus in the liberty of themselves, with those excellent beauteous gifts of their nature, and being by grace moved to turn unto God and love him and give him condign[23] thanks for the same, great multitude followed that instinct of grace, and so did, and were of God therefore exalted into the clear sight of the Godhead and by grace confirmed and established in the full surety of joyful perfect bliss and everlasting glory.

Lucifer, on the other side, an angel of excellent brightness, willfully letting slip the grace and aid of God, wherewith he was stirred to look upward unto his Maker, began in such wise[24] to look downward upon himself and so far-forth[25] to delight and dote in the regarding and beholding of his own beauty that, albeit[26] he well wist[27] he had a Maker infinitely far above him, yet thought he himself meet to be his match. And as wise as he was of nature, yet pride made him so frantic[28] that he boasted that he would be God's fellow[29] in deed, saying unto himself, *In caelum conscendam super astra Dei. Exaltabo solium meum et sedebo in monte testamenti in lateribus aquilonis. Ascendam super altitudinem nubium: similis ero altissimo* ("I will ascend into the heaven above the stars of God. I will exalt my seat and will sit in the hill of the testament[30] in the sides of the north. I will ascend above the height of the clouds, and I will be like unto the highest").[31] But as he used this blasphemous presumption in his mind against the great majesty of God, he was suddenly cast out and thrown down with an infinite number of the like traitorous angels, as the prophet Isaiah toucheth[32] him in these words: *Quomodo cecidisti de*

caelo Lucifer, qui mane oriebaris? Corruisti in terram ("How art thou fallen out of the heaven, Lucifer, that sprangest in the morning? Thou art fallen into the earth").[33] And afterward he saith, *Veruntamen ad infernum detraheris in prefundum laci* ("Howbeit thou shalt be drawn down into hell into the depth of the lake").[34] These words, with others, the prophet Isaiah rehearseth in the fourteenth chapter in resembling[35] the fall of Nebuchadnezzar unto the ruin of Lucifer.

And as well of[36] his fall as the fall of his fellows may well be verified the words of Saint John in his Apocalypse, where he saith in the twelfth chapter, *Et factum est praelium magnum in caelo. Michael et angeli eius praeliabantur cum dracone, et draco pugnabat et angeli eius, et non valuerunt, neque locus inventus est eorum amplius in caelo. Et proiectus est draco ille magnus, serpens antiquus qui vocatur diabolus, et Satanas qui seducit universum orbem. Et proiectus est in terram, et angeli eius cum eo missi sunt* ("There was a great battle in heaven. Michael and his angels fought with the dragon. And the dragon and his angels fought and were not able, nor their place was no more found in heaven. And out was thrown that great dragon, the old serpent which is called the devil, and Satan which seduceth and deceiveth the whole world, and he is thrown down into the earth, and his angels be cast down with him").[37]

Thus the inflexible justice of almighty God cast out of heaven Lucifer and all his wicked proud spirits and deprived them from his grace forever, and thereby from all hope and comfort of recovery of any manner attaining to the celestial glory, but forever condemned to pain, howbeit[38] not to the uttermost part of their pain at the first, nor all to pain alike. But as their offenses were not all alike, but some part of them by reason of their more noble nature and greater gifts of God received, their unkindness so much the more, and their sin so much the more grievous, and in diverse angels also diverse degrees of malice, in some the more, in some the less, so did the righteousness of God temper and proportion their punishments, driving the great devil down into the deep dark den of hell, into the very bottom and center of the earth, and others hover about into the air and over part of the earth and

the sea, which with continual recourse and counsel had with their chief prince and ruler Lucifer, that reigneth as king over all the children of pride, do (and shall do till the Day of Doom) persecute, at-
5   tempt,[39] deceive, trouble, vex, and punish such as they can catch into their claws of the seely[40] sin-ful kind[41] of man. And then at the final judgment, they shall all (as they to their further discomfort be surely showed already) lose all their authority and
10 rule over man, and enter with evil men into the self-same infernal fire that was first and principally pre-pared for themselves, and therein shall they, with the sinful souls that have left God and followed them, in torments intolerable burn in hell forever.
15   Let us here now, good readers, before we proceed further, consider well this matter, and ponder well this fearful point: what horrible peril there is in the pestilent sin of pride, what abominable sin it is in the sight of God when any creature falleth into the
20 delight and liking of itself—as the thing, where-upon continued, inevitably faileth not to follow: first the neglecting, and after the contemning, and finally, with disobedience and rebellion, the very full forsaking of God.
25   If God was so wroth with pride that he spared not to drive down into hell for pride the noble high excellent angels of heaven, what state[42] can there be so great in this wretched world that hath not high cause to tremble and quake every joint in his body
30 as soon as he feeleth a high proud thought enter once into his heart, remembering the terrible com-mination[43] and threat of God in Holy Scripture: *Potentes potenter tormenta patientur*[44] ("The mighty men shall mightily suffer torments"). And then if
35 it be so sore[45] a thing and so far unsitting[46] in the sight of God to see the sin of pride in the person of a great estate, that hath yet many occasions of inclination thereunto, how much more abomina-ble is that peevish[47] pride in a lewd unthrifty javel,[48]
40 that hath a purse as penniless as any poor ped-dler, and hath yet a heart as high as many a mighty prince. And if it be odious in the sight of God that a woman beautiful indeed abuse the pride of her beauty to the vainglory of herself, how delectable
45 is that dainty damsel to the devil, that standeth in her own light and taketh herself for fair, weening[49]

herself well-liked for her broad forehead, while the young man that beholdeth her marketh more her crooked nose. And if it be a thing detestable for any creature to rise in pride upon the respect and regard   50
of personage, beauty, strength, wit, or learning, or other such manner[50] thing as by nature and grace are properly their own, how much more foolish abusion[51] is there in that pride by which we worldly folk look up on height[52] and solemnly set by[53] our-   55
selves, with deep disdain of other far better men, only for very vain worldly trifles that properly be not our own? How proud be men of gold and sil-ver, no part of ourselves, but of the earth, and of nature no better than is the poor copper or tin, nor   60
to man's use so profitable as is the poor metal that maketh us the ploughshare, and horseshoes, and horse nails? How proud be many men of these glis-tering stones, of which the very brightest, though he[54] cost thee twenty pounds, shall never shine half   65
so bright nor show thee half so much light as shall a poor halfpenny candle? How proud is many a man over his neighbor because the wool of his gown is finer? And yet as fine as it is, a poor sheep wore it on her back before it came upon his, and all the while   70
she wore it, were her wool never so fine, yet was she pardie[55] but a sheep. And why should he be now bet-ter than she by that wool, that, though it be his, is yet not so verily his as it was verily hers?

But now how many men are there proud of that   75
that[56] is not theirs at all? Is there no man proud of keeping another man's gate? another man's horse? another man's hound or hawk? What a bragging maketh a bearward[57] with his silver-buttoned bal-dric[58] for pride of another man's bear? Howbeit,[59]   80
what speak we of other men's and our own? I can see nothing, the thing well-weighed, that any man may well call his own. But as men may call him a fool that beareth himself proud because he jetteth[60] about in a borrowed gown, so may we be well called   85
very[61] fools all if we bear us proud of anything that we have here. For nothing have we here of our own, not so much as our own bodies, but have borrowed it all of God, and yield it we must again, and send our seely soul out naked no man can tell how soon.   90
"What hast thou," saith Saint Paul, "that thou hast not received? And if thou have received it, whereof

---

39 tempt   **40** poor, pitiable   **41** race
42 person of rank   **43** denunciation
44 Wis 6:7   **45** grievous, great   **46** unfit-ting   **47** foolish   **48** *lewd…javel:* base,

prodigal rascal   **49** thinking   **50** kind of
51 corruption   **52** *up on height:* on
high   **53** *set by:* esteem   **54** it   **55** "by
God" (from French); certainly   **56** which

57 keeper of a bear   **58** belt worn over
one shoulder   **59** However   **60** struts
61 true

gloriest thou, as though thou haddest not received it?"[62] All that ever we have, of God we have received: riches, royalty, lordship, beauty, strength, learning, wit, body, soul, and all. And almost all these things hath he but lent us. For all these must we depart from every whit again, except our soul alone. And yet that must we give God again also, or else shall we keep it still[63] with such sorrow as we were better lose it. And for the misuse thereof and of our bodies therewith, and of all the remnant of that borrowed ware whereof we be now so proud, we shall yield a full strait[64] account and come to a heavy reckoning, and many a thousand, body and soul together, burn in hell eternally, for the peevish[65] pride of that borrowed ware so gloriously boasted before in the transitory time and short soon-passed life of this fond wretched world. For surely this sin of pride, as it is the first of all sins, begun among the angels in heaven, so is it the head and root of all other sins and of them all most pestilent.

But it is not my purpose to declare[66] here, by the manifold branches thereof, all the kinds of mischief that proceedeth upon it (for that would occupy more time than were meet for this present matter), but only will I counsel every man and woman to beware even of the very least spice[67] thereof, which seemeth to be the bare delight and liking of ourselves for anything that either is in us or outwardly belonging to us. Let us every man lie well in await[68] of ourselves, and let us mark well when the devil first casteth any proud vain thought into our mind, and let us forthwith make a cross on our breast and bless it out by and by[69] and cast it at his head again. For if we gladly take in one such guest of his, he shall not fail to bring in two of his[70] fellows soon after, and every one worse than other.[71] This point expresseth well the Spirit of God by the mouth of the prophet, where he noteth the perilous progress of proud folk, in the person of whom he saith in this wise: *Dixerunt linguam nostram magnificabimus, labia nostra a nobis sunt, quis noster dominus est?* ("They have said, 'We will magnify our tongues; our lips be our own; who is our Lord?'")[72] First they begin, lo, but as it were with a vain delight and pride of their eloquent speech, and say they will set it out goodly to the show,[73] wherein yet seemeth

little harm save a fond foolish vanity if they went no farther. But the devil, that bringeth them to that point first, intendeth not to suffer[74] them rest and remain there, but shortly he maketh them think and say farther: *Labia nostra a nobis sunt* ("Our lips be our own, we have them of ourselves"). At what point are they now, lo? Do they not now the thing that God hath lent them take for their own, and will not be aknown[75] that it is his? And thus become they thieves unto God. And yet, lo, the devil will not leave them thus neither, but carrieth them forth farther unto the very worst point of all. For when they say once that their lips be their own and of themselves, then against the truth that they have their lips lent them of our Lord, their proud hearts arise and they ask, *Quis noster dominus est?* ("Who is our Lord?"), and so deny that they have any Lord at all. And thus, lo, beginning but with a vain pride of their own praise, they become secondly thieves unto God, and finally from thieves they fall to be plain rebellious traitors, and refuse to take God for their God, and fall into the detestable pride that Lucifer fell to himself. Let us therefore (as I said, good Christian readers) beware of this horrible vice, and resist well the very first motions thereof; and the first suggestions[76] of the devil, as the young infants of Babylon, let us all-to frush[77] and break in pieces against the stone[78]—that is, our sure strong Savior Christ—with consideration of his great humility, by which he (being as verily God as man) humbled himself for our sake (to redeem us out of the proud devil's dominion) unto the vile death of the cross, which is the matter of his bitter passion, whereof I have taken in hand to treat, and have for the first point toward it told you the sore[79] fall of the proud angels, whereby in part the occasion of our damnation, and consequently for our redemption the occasion of Christ's Passion grew.

A Prayer

O glorious blessed Trinity, whose justice hath damned unto perpetual pain many proud rebellious angels, whom thy goodness had created to be partners of thine eternal glory, for thy tender mercy plant in mine heart such meekness that I so may by thy grace follow the motion[80] of my good angel,

---

62 1 Cor 4:7   **63** always   **64** strict
65 foolish   **66** explain   **67** trace
68 *lie . . . await:* remain very watchful
69 *by and by:* immediately   **70** the

guest's   **71** See Mt 12:45.   **72** Ps 11(12):4
73 *goodly . . . show:* well for display
74 permit   **75** *be aknown:* acknowledge
76 temptations   **77** *all-to frush:* utterly

smash   **78** Ps 136(137):9   **79** grievous
80 prompting

and so resist the proud suggestions[81] of those spiteful spirits that fell, as I may through the merits of thy bitter Passion be partner of thy bliss with those holy spirits that stood and, now confirmed by thy grace, in glory shall stand forever.

The Second Point: The Creation and Fall of Mankind

The glorious majesty of almighty God, after the fore-rehearsed[82] ruin and fall of angels, not willing to suffer[83] the malice of his proud envious enemies make such a diminishment in his glorious court of heaven, determined of his great goodness to create a new kind of creature, wherewith he would make up and fulfill[84] with glorious blessed people the number of all those evil angels that were, through their high malicious pride, thrown out of wealth[85] into wretchedness.

This new kind[86] then, that he would for this purpose create, the deep wisdom of God determined marvelously to mingle[87] and temper.[88] For since it should be able (with help of his grace) to attain unto such high heavenly glory, he would have it spiritual and immortal. And yet, to refrain[89] it from the proud heart that Lucifer had and his fellows in their spiritual and immortal substance, God determined that this new kind of creature should also be bodily gross and mortal. And thus, after this visible world made,[90] and air, earth, and sea furnished with fowl and fish, and beasts, grass, herbs, trees, and fruit, he made the body of man of the slime of the earth, and created of nothing the spiritual substance of the soul after the image and similitude of himself, in that he endued[91] it with the three great gifts, memory, understanding, and will, in a certain manner of resemblance of the glorious blessed Trinity, the Father, the Son, and the Holy Ghost.

This kind of man created God of a marvelous convenience[92] also with all other manner of creatures. For he made it have a being, as hath the dead stone, a life, as hath the insensible tree; a sensible feeling, as hath the unreasonable beast; a reasonable understanding, as hath the celestial angel.

Thus our forefather Adam being created of the earth, and our mother Eve formed and framed out of the rib of his side (as in the first and the second chapter of Genesis is declared), albeit that[93] they were ordained unto the high pleasant palace of heaven, yet lest over-sudden enhancing so high might make such pride spring in their hearts as might be the cause of their driving[94] down again, the great goodness of God measured their state and wealth, setting them not on high in heaven, but beneath in the pleasant garden or orchard of earthly paradise. And for the further safeguard of their persons from pride, he gave them precepts and commandments, whereby they should remember and consider themselves to be but servants. And therefore he both bade them there to be occupied and work in the keeping of that pleasant garden, and also forbade them the eating of the fruit of the tree of knowledge. And yet unto their further acknowledging of subjection and repressing of all occasion of pride, he set upon the breaking of his behest the threat of a very sore[95] pain — that is to wit,[96] that whensoever they did eat of the forbidden tree they should die; that is to wit, that whereas they had now their bodies such as though they might die by their own default,[97] yet such as, without their default should never die, there should, after that his commandment were by them broken, enter into their bodies and into the bodies of all their posterity an inevitable necessity of dying. Thus had God of his high goodness set them in the possession of a right wealthy[98] state, and in the expectation of yet a far passing[99] better, of which they could never fail without their own default. And to keep them from falling into the fault, he was ready to assist them with his grace, and against proud disobedience that might make them fly from his grace, he graciously fenced and hedged in their hearts with fear.

Now stood our father Adam and our mother Eve lords of all the whole earth, had[100] full dominion over all the beasts of the same, out of[101] dread of death or any bodily hurt. And authority they should have had over all their own offspring, with which they were with the blessing of God commanded to increase and multiply and replenish the world. Their palace was the most pleasant place of Paradise. Their apparel was the vesture of

81 temptations **82** aforementioned
83 permit **84** fill to the full **85** well-being **86** race, sort **87** make of more than one element **88** mix **89** restrain

90 had been made **91** endowed
92 *of . . . convenience:* with a marvelous fitness **93** *albeit that:* although
94 being driven **95** grievous, great

96 say **97** fault, misdeed **98** prosperous
99 surpassing **100** and had **101** *out of:* free from

innocency, more glorious than cloth of gold. Their nakedness as far from dishonesty and all cause of shame as their bodies were far from all filthy tokens of sin. Their sensual parts comfortable unto reason. Against their souls no rebellion in their obedient bodies, which for a season should have endured there without age, weariness, or pain, without spot or wem[102] or any decay of nature, preserved continually by the wholesome fruits and help of God's hand, and all their children forever after the same rate.[103] And each at sundry times when God's pleasure were, should have had their bodies changed suddenly into a glorious form, and without death depart out of the earth, carried up with the soul into the bliss of heaven, there to reign in joy and bliss eternally with God, fulfilling[104] the places from which the proud angels fell. This was, lo, the state in which our first father stood, a state full of heavenly hope of eternal joy to come, and a state for the meanwhile full of present wealth.

But oh, woe worth[105] wicked envy, the daughter of pestilent pride. For the proud hateful enemy of God and traitorous wretch, the devil, beholding this new creature of mankind set in so wealthy state, and either conjecturing by his natural understanding, or (to the increase of his grief for his proud envious stomach[106]) having it revealed unto him that of this kind should be restored the ruin that was happed[107] in heaven by the fall of himself and his fellows, conceived so great heart-burning again the kind[108] of man therefor, that he rather would wish his own damnation doubled, so that[109] he might destroy them, than suffer God honored in them, and them so to proceed and prosper that their gross mingled nature, so base in respect of his, should ascend up to that height of heaven that himself was fallen from.

The devil then, devising with himself upon some mischievous means by which he might bring mankind unto destruction, called to mind the means by which he had before wretchedly destroyed himself. And as he saw his own damnation grown by the occasion of pride, so wist[110] he well that if he might by some wily suggestion bring pride into the kind of man and make the first fathers disobey God's commandment, then would God of his justice keep his promise in their punishment and take from the posterity the gift that he promised their forefather for them, if the condition were broken upon which he gave it.

Upon this, this old serpent, the devil, being as the Scripture saith, "wilier than all the beasts of the earth,"[111] would not begin at the man, whom he perceived to be wiser and more hard to beguile, but first began at the woman, as the kind in wisdom more weak, more light[112] of belief, and more easy to be beguiled, whom if he might make on his side, then should he and she together be twain[113] against one. And the wily wretch perceived well also the tender mind that the man had to his make,[114] and thereby guessed (as it there happed[115] and elsewhere happeth oft) that to bring man to woe the woman may do more than with all his craft the devil can do himself. This wily serpent therefore, the devil, devising to entice this woman to this deadly deed, took his time[116] for his wretched wooing when her husband was not with her. And then gan he fall familiar[117] with her and inquisitive of such things as pertained to her husband and her and nothing[118] at all to himself. For there he asked her this question: "Wherefore did God," quoth he, "command you that ye should not eat of every tree of Paradise?" Or as it rather seemeth by the Greek phrase usual in many places of Scripture, he asked her thus: "Why did God command you that you should eat of no tree in Paradise?" And that his question was such appeareth by the manner of her answer.

Howbeit,[119] if she had showed herself unwilling to fall familiar with him and had said again,[120] "What is that for you," or had answered him and said, "My husband shall answer you," all his wretched wooing had been at end and he confounded and gone. But while she was content to be talkative with a stranger and wax a proper[121] entertainer (which property some gentlewomen ween[122] were a goodly praise), mark well what followed thereon. She answered the serpent and said, "Of the fruit of the trees that are in Paradise we eat. But of the fruit of the tree that is in the midst of Paradise, God hath commanded us that we shall not eat and that we should not touch it, lest we may hap to die."[123]

Mark here that, in these words, the contagious

---

102 stain   103 *after . . . rate:* in the same manner   104 filling   105 *woe worth:* cursed be   106 disposition   107 *was happed:* occurred   108 *again the kind:* against the race   109 *so that:* provided that   110 knew   111 Gn 3:1   112 unsteady   113 two   114 mate   115 occurred   116 *took his time:* chose the right time   117 *gan . . . familiar:* he began to become intimate   118 in no way   119 However   120 in reply   121 *wax a proper:* become a perfect   122 suppose   123 Gn 3:2–3

conversation of this wicked serpent, with his questioning and her ear-giving thereto, wrought not as it seemeth, not outwardly only with her eye and her ear, but inwardly also with some subtle suggestion in her heart. For by this answer of hers it appeareth that forthwith upon his questioning she began to stagger and half to doubt of the truth and steadfastness of God's word. For whereas God had precisely promised that if they did eat of the fruit of that tree they should die, she, by the inward leaning to the devil's instigation and not cleaving to the grace of God, by this her answer turned it into a doubt, saying, *Ne forte moriamur* ("Lest peradventure[124] we die"). By reason of which doubting, and thereby but half dreading, she made half the way herself for the devil to walk farther with her. For thereupon he letted[125] not boldly to blaspheme God before her and say, "Nay ye shall not die. But God doth know that whatsoever day you shall eat of that tree, your eyes shall be opened and you shall be as gods, knowing both good and evil."[126] And upon these words, she seeing that it seemed a good tree to eat of, and fair to the eye, and delectable to behold, she by and by[127] plucked off the fruit thereof and ate it, and gave it to her husband, and he ate it too.

O wretched wicked serpent, how much of thy deadly poison hast thou put into the seely[128] soul of this woeful woman at once? For here had he made her believe that of his own devilish conditions[129] God had had twain, that is to wit, falsehood and envy. For he made her think that God had told them a lie, in that he said that whensoever they ate thereof they should die, and also that God were envious and could not for envy suffer[130] it that they should have so high a thing as the knowledge of good and evil.

Then struck he into her heart the poison of proud curious appetite and inordinate desire to know the thing which for her weal[131] God had forbidden her to know. For God would of his goodness she should have known but good. But she by the devil's enticement would needs know evil too. And when her curious mind had made her once set her fair hands unto the feeling of that foul pitch, she could never rub the filth from her fingers after. What should I speak of the other less[132] evils that he allured and

allected[133] her with, as the pleasure of the eye in the beholding of that fruit, with lickerous[134] desire of the delicious taste?—sins not small in themselves, but small in respect of the far passing greater, when he made her desire and long by reason of high knowledge to be like a goddess, and for that cause proudly to disobey God and eat of the forbidden fruit. And she being thus infected and so sore[135] envenomed with so many poison spots, infected her husband forthwith. For at her enticement, and not so much for credence giving to[136] the serpent's words as to content his wife (whose request he could not find in his heart to contrary), he kept her company in her lewdness[137] and letted[138] not to eat with her. But the wallow[139] sweet pleasure of that fruit soon turned to displeasure and pain. For scant[140] was the fruit passed down both their throats, when it so began to wamble[141] in their stomachs that they wished it out again and in his belly that counseled them to eat it. For anon[142] was there such a marvelous change spread through both their bodies, that whereas when they put it in their mouth they were such as it was a great pleasure each of them to behold other and be beholden of the other, as soon as they both had eaten it they felt such filthy sensual motions of concupiscence rise and rebel against reason in their flesh, that their hearts abhorred to be beholden and seen, either of any other or themselves either, and for shame of their nakedness covered their flesh with fig leaves.

Now is there no doubt but that their wicked enemy the serpent (which, as appeareth by the Bible, abode still by them till the sentence given by God upon their all three punishment[143]) in his mischievous[144] manner highly rejoiced to see his devilish device brought unto such pass,[145] and had a great game[146] to behold them come forth so comely, appareled so richly in their royal robes of fig leaves.

O what a confusion was this unto them, to see their feigned friend, their very deadly enemy the devil, first by their own folly so harmfully deceive them, and then so spitefully sit and laugh them to scorn. But they had no long leisure left them to take heed to that ere[147] that great confusion was overwhelmed with a greater. For suddenly, lo, they heard our Lord coming, and therewith for shame they

---

124 perhaps **125** hesitated **126** Gn 3:4–6 **127** *by and by:* immediately **128** poor, pitiable **129** attributes **130** permit **131** well-being **132** lesser

133 enticed **134** greedy **135** grievously **136** *for…to:* because he credited **137** wickedness **138** hesitated **139** cloyingly **140** scarcely **141** roll about

(in nausea) **142** at once **143** *their… punishment:* the punishment of all three **144** wicked **145** completion **146** delight **147** before

fell in a fear and fled and hid themselves from the face of God in the mids of a tree. And our Lord, as though he saw them not, called for Adam and said, "Adam, where art thou?" And he answered, "Lord, I heard thy voice and was afeard[148] to come before thee because I was naked, and therefore I hid me." "Who showed thee," quoth our Lord, "that thou were naked, but because thou hast eaten of the tree of which I commanded thee thou shouldest not?"[149]

Then took Adam a way far awry[150] from forgiveness. For he confessed not his fault, but began to excuse himself and lay the fault from him to his wife and in a manner unto God too. "The woman," quoth he, "that thou gavest me for my companion, she gave it me, and so I ate it." Then said our Lord God unto the woman, "Why didst thou so?" And she in like wise never acknowledged her fault nor asked forgiveness, but excused her by the serpent and said, "The serpent deceived me, and so I ate it."[151]

Then gave God the sentence of punishment upon all three, using like order in declaring of his doom[152] as they did in the doing of their sin. For first he began at the serpent, the first malicious contriver of all this mischief. And unto him he said, "Because thou hast done this, accursed be thou among all the living things and beasts of the earth. Upon thy breast shalt thou creep, and earth shalt thou eat all the days of thy life. Enmity will I put between thee and the woman, and between thy seed and hers, and she shall frush[153] thine head in pieces, and thou shalt lie in await[154] to sting her heel."[155] Then gave he the woman her judgment and said unto her, "I shall multiply thy miseries and thy conceptions, and in sorrow shalt thou bring forth thy children, and thou shalt be under the power of the man, and he shall be lord over thee." Then finally said he to Adam, "Because thou hast given ear unto thy wife's words and hast eaten of the tree of which I forbode thee to eat, accursed be the earth in thy work. With labor shalt thou eat of the earth all the days of thy life. It shall burgeon[156] thorns and briars, and thou shalt eat the herbs of the earth. In the sweat of thy face shalt thou eat thy bread, till thou return again into the earth out of which thou were taken. For dust art thou, and into dust shalt thou return."[157] Then our Lord made them coats of skins, and clothed them

therein, and said, "Lo, Adam is like one of us now, knowing both good and evil."[158] And God with that angry scorn, to keep him from the tree of everlasting life, put them both forthwith[159] out of that pleasant paradise into the wretched earth.

Long were it here, and not of necessity pertaining to this present point—that is to wit,[160] the fall of our forefather—to note and declare such things as in the discourse of this matter men may note and mark upon this part of the Scripture. As for example, that in these words of God with which he scorned Adam, saying, *Ecce Adam factus est sicut unus ex nobis* ("Lo, Adam is now made as one of us"), may be well marked that, like as by all words of the whole text appeareth plain that there is but one God, so is there in that God more persons than one. For else could he not conveniently[161] say, "Lo, Adam is now as one of us," that is to wit, a god as we be, but he would have said, "Lo, Adam is now as I am."

Those words also seem well to declare that though Adam were not so fully deceived by the persuasion of the serpent as Eve was (for which Saint Paul saith, "The man was not seduced but the woman,"[162] whereupon Saint Augustine at good length declareth certain difference between them),[163] yet was Adam by the means of his wife somewhat seduced and brought into a foolish hope, to be through the eating of that fruit, by the knowledge of good and evil, made like a god. For God, speaking to Eve no word of that foolish proud affection, taunted and checked Adam therewith specially by name, saying, *Ecce Adam quasi unus ex nobis factus est, sciens bonum et malum* ("Lo, Adam is now made as one of us, knowing both good and evil"). But this was not by the serpent's persuasion, whom Adam would not have regarded but shortly shaken him off. But the seducing of Adam was by that that[164] the serpent's shrewd[165] words came to his ear out of his wife's mouth, whom he would suffer[166] to speak. And therefore our Lord, in declaring his punishment unto him, laid for the cause: *Quia audisti vocem uxoris tuae, maledicta terra in opere tuo etc.* ("Because thou hast given ear to the words of thy wife, accursed be the earth in thy work, and so forth").[167] And because that the woman's preaching and babbling to her husband did so much harm in the

---

148 afraid   **149** Gn 3:9–11   **150** off course   **151** Gn 3:12–13   **152** judgment   **153** crush   **154** ambush   **155** Gn 3:14–15   **156** bud, sprout   **157** Gn 3:16–19

158 Gn 3:22   **159** immediately   **160** say   **161** suitably   **162** 1 Tm 2:14   **163** See St. Augustine's *De civitate Dei,* 14.11, and *De Genesi ad litteram* (*PL 34,* 453–54).

164 *by that that:* because   **165** malicious   **166** permit   **167** Gn 3:17

beginning and would, if it were suffered to proceed, do always more and more, therefore Saint Paul commandeth that a woman shall not take upon her to teach her husband, but that her husband should teach her and that she should learn of him *in silentio* (that is, in silence), that is to wit, she should sit and hear him and hold herself her tongue.[168] For Saint Paul well foresaw that if the wife may be suffered to speak too, she will have so many words herself that her husband shall have never one.

There may be marked also in the foresaid discourse the marvelous mischievous nature of envy. For the devil so well knew the justice of God, and by his own destruction so sore had assayed[169] it, that he doubted not but that his malicious deceit should not pass unpunished. And yet was he rather content to take harm himself than suffer another take good. And such a devilish delight he took in beholding their harm and shame that he voided[170] not at God's coming, but abode[171] to see the sentence of their damnation till he took his own with him too.

In this discourse is to be considered also that when God punisheth the sinner by and by,[172] he showeth him thereby more favor than when he deferreth it longer. And oftentimes when he delayeth it, he doth it not of favor but of indignation and anger. For if he had here punished Eve as soon as herself had broken his commandment, both had Adam been warned by it and their offspring by her sin alone, as holy doctors[173] declare, had not lost original justice nor fallen in damnation of death. But forasmuch as, though she was created to be Adam's fellow, she was yet of less perfection and more frail and more easy to fall than he, albeit[174] he had as then no dominion given him over her, yet his reason might show him that to give her good counsel he should have kept her company, which if he had done, the serpent had not deceived her. Therefore since he did not, but by wandering another way from her he suffered her to miscarry[175] and be infected, God suffered the contagion of the selfsame infection to stretch unto himself too and thereof to grow his destruction.

And this may be a warning to every man in this world to do the diligence[176] that he possibly can to keep every other man from hurt. For as the Holy Scripture saith, *Et mandavit illis unicuique de proximo suo* ("God hath given every man cure[177] and charge of his neighbor").[178] And harm creepeth from one to another by more means than men beware of. And he that care not though his neighbor's house fall afire may hap[179] to lose his own. Howbeit,[180] as this lesson generally pertaineth to every man for the natural love and Christian charity that every Christian man is bounden to bear other, yet pertaineth it most specially to those that have over other men that special charge given unto them, that our Lord therefore by the mouth of Ezekiel terribly threateneth them in this wise: *Si dicente me ad impium, morte morieris, non annunciaveris ei, neque locutus fueris uti avertatur a via sua impia et vivat, ipse impius in impietate sua morietur, sanguinem autem ejus de manu tua requiram* ("If when I say to the wicked man 'thou shalt die,' thou do not show it him, nor do not speak unto him that he may turn from his wicked way and live, both shall that wicked man die in his wickedness, and yet the blood of him shall I require of thine hands").[181] This is a fearful word, lo, to those that have the cure[182] over other folk and a necessity to take good heed to their flock, to guide them well, call upon them and give them warning of such ways as they may perish in. For else shall the sheep not perish and be punished only, but the scab[183] of the flock shall catch and consume shepherd and all for his negligence.

This is here another thing specially to be marked, that like as the kind of man was not corrupted with original sin nor lost the state of innocency by the fault of Eve alone, which was but the feebler and inferior part, till Adam that was the stronger and superior part made himself partner to the same sin also, so is there no man accounted afore[184] God for an offender in any deadly actual sin[185] by any manner motion[186] or suggestion of the devil unto the sensual part, as long as the will after[187] the judgment of reason resisteth and refuseth to consent. But when reason giveth over to sensuality, whereby the man whole and entire falleth into the consent either to do a deadly sin or to delight in the devising and thinking upon any such sinful act for the

168 1 Tm 2:11–12 **169** *sore…assayed:* greatly had tested **170** departed **171** waited **172** *by and by:* immediately **173** early Church fathers **174** although **175** come to harm **176** utmost **177** care **178** Eccl 17:12 **179** happen **180** However **181** Ez 3:18 **182** care **183** skin disease **184** before **185** *actual sin:* sin derived from one's acts, as opposed to inherited original sin **186** *manner motion:* kind of prompting **187** in accordance with

pleasure that he taketh in that thought, all were it[188] so that he thought therewith he would not do the deed, yet were the full consent to the pleasure of that only thought,[189] full and whole deadly sin.

5 Howbeit,[190] a sudden surreptitious delight cast by the devil into the sensual part is no sin at all, but may be matter of merit, except the will, with reason giving over thereto, either consent to delight therein or else is so negligent in looking to sensuality that he letteth her over-long alone therein, and listeth[191] not to do his diligence in driving that sinful suggestion from her. For surely such manner negligence is afore the face of God accounted for a consent and so for a deadly sin.

15 It is also specially to be marked that the stubborn manner of Adam and Eve, not praying God of forgiveness but excusing their sin, was in manner more displeasure to God than was their sin itself.

This is also notably to be marked, that as tenderly 20 as Adam loved Eve, rather content to displease God than her, yet when he saw that sorrow should come thereon, he would fain[192] have laid it from himself unto her. And thus will it fare by these fleshly wretched lovers here: when they come in hell together, they shall curse each other full fast.[193] Howbeit, letting pass as impertinent to my matter many things that might be marked more, let us not forget to mark this one point well, which is the sum of all the second point: that is to wit,[194] let us consider 30 deeply from what weal[195] into what wretchedness, by the folly of our forefathers, mankind is woefully fallen through the false wily suggestion of our mortal enemy the devil. On which thing when I bethink me, methinketh[196] I may well say the words of Saint 35 John in the Apocalypse, with which he bewaileth this wretched world by reason of that the devil fell out of heaven thereinto: *Vae terrae et mari, quia descendit diabolus ad vos, habens iram magnam, sciens quia modicum tempus habet* ("Woe to the earth and 40 to the sea, for the devil is come down to you, having great anger, knowing that he hath but a little time").[197] This woe well found our forefathers when the devil, full of ire for his own fall and envy that they should succeed him, labored to bring them 45 to the place of his final damnation, from which he saw well he had but a little time left, that is to

wit, the time of this present world, which is transitory and soon shall pass and is a time in all together very short, from the first creation to the final change thereof at the Day of Doom, if all that 50 time be compared with his everlasting fire that followeth. He found them innocents joyful and merry, much in the favor of God, and oft rejoicing[198] his visitation and company, the man and his wife each delighting in other, finding nothing to mislike in 55 themselves, lords of all the world, all beasts obedient unto them, their work without weariness, their meat[199] pleasant at hand, no necessity to die, nor any bodily hurt, high pleasure in hope of heaven, and all their children after them. 60

All this hath this false serpent bereft them by his deceitful train,[200] poisoning them with his own pride, that threw himself out of heaven. For as himself would have been[201] God's fellow, so made he them ween[202] they should. But while they weened 65 to be gods by the knowledge of good and evil both, they lost, alas, the good that they had and got but evil alone. They lost their innocency and became sinful. God's favor they lost and fell in his displeasure; his visitation they rejoiced not but were afeard 70 to come near him, each of them ashamed to behold the other or themselves either. All beasts were at war with them, and each of them with themselves, their own bodies in rebellion and battle against their souls, thrust out of pleasant paradise into 75 the wretched earth, their living gotten with sore[203] sweat, their children born with pain. Then hunger, thirst, heat, cold, sickness sundry and sore. Sure sorry looking, for[204] the unsure time of death, and dread after all this of the fearful fire of hell, with 80 like pain and wretchedness to all their offspring forever.

This is, lo, good readers, the wretched change that our forefathers made with falling into pride at the devil's false suggestion. In honor they were and 85 would not see it. Honor they sought and thereby fell to shame. They would have waxed[205] gods and were turned into beasts, as the Scripture saith, *Homo cum in honore esset non intellexit, comparatus est iumentis insipientibus, et similis factus est il-* 90 *lis* ("When man was in honor, he perceived it not, but he was compared unto the foolish beasts, and to

---

188 *all ... it:* even though it were
189 *only thought:* thought alone
190 However 191 chooses 192 gladly

193 *full fast:* very vigorously 194 say
195 well-being 196 it seems to me
197 Rv 12:12 198 enjoying 199 food

200 snare 201 *would have been:* wished to be 202 think 203 grievous
204 because of 205 thought

them was he made like"),[206] and yet brought indeed into far worse condition. For many beasts live with less labor and less pain too than man, and none of them go to hell. In danger whereof all the kind of man stood by the occasion of their fall if the goodness of God had not by his grace helped with his merciful hand. And unto heaven had no man gone had not our blessed Savior redeemed man and paid his ransom by his bitter painful Passion, whereof the occasion was this wretched fall of man. And thus finish I the second point that I said I would show you before I come to the woeful history of Christ's bitter Passion.

A Prayer

Almighty God, that of thine infinite goodness didst create our first parents in the state of innocency, with present wealth[207] and hope of heaven to come, till through the devil's train[208] their folly fell by sin to wretchedness, for thy tender pity of that Passion that was paid for their and our redemption, assist me so with thy gracious help, that unto the subtle suggestions of the serpent I never so incline the ears of mine heart, but that my reason may resist them and master my sensuality and refrain[209] me from them.

The Third Point: The Determination of the Trinity for the Restoration of Mankind

When the devil has thus guilefully betrapped[210] and thus falsely betrayed our first father and mother by their own oversight and folly, and thereby brought into miserable estate[211] and damnable themselves with all their posterity, neither would the mighty majesty of God endure and suffer[212] his malicious proud enemy the devil to rejoice the withdrawing of the kind of man from doing him honor, nor the marvelous mercy of God abide and sustain to see the frail kind of man eternally destroyed by the deceit and circumvention[213] of the false wily devil. For though his justice was content forever to lose all thankful service (for thankless they serve him still) of those malicious angels, that without other motion than their own malice wilfully turned from him, and that his mercy no cause had to counterplead[214] his justice, in abridging the eternity of the proud spirits' pain, that of obdurate heart would never be sorry for their sin, yet in beholding the wretched decayed kind of man brought into sin not all of himself but by the subtle suggestion of his false envious enemy, and that would after wax[215] meek and repent and pray for pardon, the sharp justice of God and his tender mercy entered into counsel together. And by the deep wisdom of God was the means found that man should so be restored as they should both twain be satisfied: that is to wit, both man by justice for his sin somewhat punished and yet upon repentance by means of mercy should his fault be paid for, and from all eternal bondage man redeemed and saved and, in spite of the devil, enhanced to more honor than ever he was entitled to before he took the fall.

To devise this way, lo, was a wonderful thing, far passing the capacity of all the angels in heaven. For since the amends must needs be made and, in maintenance of the true justice of God, the ransom must needs be paid for the kind of man, that was by sin addicted[216] and adjudged to the devil, as his perpetual thrall never to come in heaven, whosoever should pay this ransom must and was most convenient[217] to be such as would and were able and ought[218] it. Now ought there this ransom no creature but man, and therefore since by him that ought it of reason it should most conveniently be paid, man must he be that should of duty pay it. But now was there no one man able to pay the ransom for the whole kind of man. For since all the whole kind had lost heaven and were all in one damnation, condemned all to bodily death already, any of them all, though he should willingly suffer death in recompense of the sin, it could nothing serve his fellows, nor yet himself neither, for he paid but his debt of death for his own part, in which debt and much more himself was condemned already.

Now as for angels, neither can we know that any would then do so much for man, man being fallen by sin from God's favor, nor any of them all was able, being but a creature, to satisfy for the deadly trespass done unto the Creator. And yet was it over[219] this far from good convenience that any angel should have been suffered to do it. For the redemption of man after his fall was a greater benefit

---

206 Ps 48(49):13, 21   **207** prosperity   **208** deceit   **209** restrain   **210** entrapped   **211** condition   **212** permit   **213** crafty   **214** plead against   **215** grow   **216** delivered over formally by sentence of   outwitting   **217** suitable   **218** owed   **219** in addition to   a judge

unto him than was his creation. For as our mother holy Church singeth in the paschal service, *Quid enim nasci profuit, nisi redimi profuisset?* ("What availeth it man to be born were not the profit of his redemption?")[220] And therefore if angel had, by payment man's ransom and recompense made for his trespass, redeemed him, then would man have thought himself more in a manner beholden to angel than to God. And the occasion[221] thereof had been a very foul disorder.

Thus was as I say, therefore, the device of a means convenient for man's redemption the thing that far passed the wisdom of all the wise angels of heaven. But the deep and infinite high wisdom of almighty God devised the marvelous merciful just means himself, that is to wit,[222] that by the cruel painful death of that innocent person, that[223] should be both God and man, the recompense should be made unto God for man. For that person both, being God, should be of that nature that was able to do it and, being man, should be of that nature that was bounden to do it. And the devil (unware[224] that he were) unrighteously procuring that righteous man's death should righteously lose the power upon man that God had for man's unrighteousness righteously given unto him before.

This excellent means of man's redemption the deep wisdom of God devised, and in time convenient the second Person (the Son of God, the wisdom of the Father, and the Father's express absolute image and brightness of his Father's glory), being sent by his Father and himself and the Holy Ghost down here into the earth (and nevertheless abiding still above in heaven), and in the blessed womb of the pure Virgin Mary taking into unity of person the poor nature of man (by the obumbration[225] of the Holy Ghost, of the pure blood of her body, without man's seed or fleshly delectation,[226] and therefore without original sin conceived and without help of midwife or pain of travail born), living here in pain and labor, fasting, watch,[227] preaching and prayer, and finally, for the truth of his doctrine, by the procurement[228] of the devil, the treason of Judas, the malice of the Jews, and cruel hands of the paynims,[229] through the painful bitter Passion and death of his innocent manhead[230] (not bounden or subject unto death, neither by nature nor sin, but by death for man's sake willingly suffered), that excellent means, I say, of man's redemption so by himself devised, himself most graciously fulfilled; and by the pleasant acceptable sacrifice of himself obediently offered on the cross up to the Father, he pacified the wrath and indignation of God against man, and by his glorious resurrection and marvelous ascension, sitting in the nature of man upon the Father's right hand, hath reduced[231] mankind (in such as will take the benefit) to more joy, more wealth, and far more honor too than ever the fall of our first father lost us.

Now albeit (as I suppose) few men have less lust[232] to move great questions and put manner of dispicions[233] in unlearned laymen's mouths than I, which rather would wish every man to labor for good affections[234] than to long for the knowledge of less necessary learning or delight in debating of sundry superfluous problems, yet of some such demands[235] as I now see many men of much less than mean learning have oft right hot in hand,[236] I shall not let[237] one or twain myself here a little to touch.[238]

A Question

First be they commonly willing to search this thing: wherefore mankind should, more than Adam and Eve themselves, need any redemption at all. For how could it (say they) stand with the justice of God that for the fault of only Adam and Eve all that ever came of them should fall into such miserable fault? This question and many such other like, when they be of a curious bold presumption demanded, be not to be hearkened unto and answered, but with the words of the blessed apostle Paul rather to be rejected and rebuked: *O homo tu quis es qui respondeas Deo? Numquid dicit figmentum ei qui se finxit, quid me fecisti sic?* ("O man, what are thou to take upon thee to dispute with God? Is there any workman's work that asketh the workman, 'Wherefore hast thou made me thus?'")[239] And must almighty God then of his work wrought in man give a reckoning to man that is but his handwork? Howbeit,[240] on the other side, where such

---

220 from the Easter office, specifically the prefatory prayer used on Holy Saturday at the blessing of the Paschal candle 221 result 222 say 223 who 224 unaware 225 overshadowing

226 pleasure 227 vigils 228 contrivance 229 pagans 230 human nature 231 restored 232 desire 233 *manner of dispicions*: various kinds of disputations 234 inclinations 235 questions

236 *have … hand*: are very eager about 237 forbear, hesitate 238 treat of; address 239 Rom 9:20 240 However

questions are not demanded of frowardness,[241] of a vain pride, nor of blasphemous purpose, it is not only no displeasure to God but is also a good occupation of the mind in that a man delighteth to think upon heavenly things rather than upon earthly. And many a holy man hath, of no vain curious mind but of very pure devotion, beset[242] much study upon the foresaid question. And of those holy men hath diverse had diverse opinions. One sort have thought that by the fall of Adam the whole kind[243] of man not only lost original justice,[244] and became subject unto the necessity of temporal death, and therewith lost also the joyful bliss of heaven, but over[245] that, by the filth of original sin (with which every man born into this world by natural propagation is infected in the vicious sinful stock, in that[246] we were all in, of Adam, as the fruit is in the tree, or the ear of corn in the grain that it came of) was also damned unto perpetual pain and sensible[247] torment in hell, although it were a child that died in the cradle, which to the original sin taken of his parents (of which the prophet saith, "Lo, in wickedness was I conceived, and my mother conceived me in sin")[248] never added actual sin[249] of his own. And from this eternal damnation of sensible pain in the fire of hell, they thought that never any of the kind of man should be preserved but by the merits of the Passion of Christ and faith in him comen[250] or to come—faith, I say, actual or habitual,[251] and in infants by the faith of their parents and the faithful Church (with certain sacraments or sacrifices duly referred to God, after[252] the sundry laws and ceremonies of sundry diverse times, wherewith these infants have habitual faith infused).

And as touching the faith of Christ, that he should once come by whom they should be saved, revelation was given to Adam, Noah, Abraham, and all the old fathers and by them to the people of every generation before the law written;[253] and at[254] the law written, revelation given to Moses, and by him to the people; and after to all the prophets, and by them to the people of Jews of every generation, unto the coming of our Savior Christ himself. Now as for such folk, either now or then, as among the paynims[255] lived well according to nature, so

that they lacked nothing to keep them from the perpetual fire of hell but the faith of Christ, some holy doctors have thought that God of his merciful goodness by one means or other failed not to give them the faith, as he that is of so merciful goodness that he will fail no man in thing necessary without the man's own fault.

But then other doctors that were in this point of opinion with them, that original sin damned every man to sensible pain of hell without the faith of Christ, were not in that point agreed with them, that unto all such paynims as in any place lived naturally well and kept themselves from idolatry, God sent the faith of Christ to keep them from hell, as not suffering[256] any man to be perpetually damned to the sensible pain of fire without his own actual fault, since they themselves denied not but that the infants of paynims and of the christened both that deceased without baptism were damned unto perpetual sensible pain in hell, and yet had they none actual sin of their own but only the sin original.

Now whereas this thing might haply[257] seem hard in the hearts of some such as direct their eye to the merciful nature of God and cannot also perceive by any rule of justice taught unto man, either by reason or Scripture, how this thing could agree with the merciful justice of God, these good men answer that hell is the place for sinful folk and that pain is due to sin and that those children and all be sinful in original sin. For all are sinful that are through filthy concupiscence brought by propagation out of that sinful stock of our first sinful father, for in that stock were we all and were infected with sin in the same in such a certain manner as all the sour crabs[258] that ever come of the crab tree do take their sourness of the kernel whereof the tree grew. And if a poor potter may, without reproach and uncontrolled,[259] make (as Saint Paul saith) of one self[260] piece of clay two vessels, the one to serve in honest use, the other in vile and filthy,[261] where the clay whereof he maketh the vile vessel was nothing[262] faulty but good, who should be so bold and so blasphemous as to think that God doth wrong to make and use all those vessels for vile (that is to wit,[263] all the kind of man) whereof the clay that they all

241 perversity **242** bestowed
243 race **244** righteousness before
God **245** besides **246** i.e., which
247 perceptible by the senses **248** Ps
50(51):7 **249** *actual sin:* sin derived from

one's acts, as opposed to inherited original
sin **250** having come **251** *actual or
habitual:* exhibited in deeds or inherent
in the character **252** in accordance with
253 was written **254** at the time when

255 pagans **256** allowing **257** perhaps
258 crabapples **259** unrestrained
260 same **261** Rom 9:21 **262** in no
way **263** say

came of (that is to wit, their first father and mother) were ere[264] they came of them waxen[265] by their sin both twain very vile and naught.[266]

Besides this (say these good holy doctors) the Scripture declareth us that God thus doth indeed. For Saint Paul calleth all the offspring of Adam by nature the children of wrath, saying, *Eramus natura filii irae* ("We were," saith he, "by nature the children of wrath").[267] And that we became such by the corruption of our nature in our first father, Adam, he showeth well where he saith, *Per unum hominem peccatum in hunc mundum introivit, et per peccatum mors, et ita in omnes homines mors pertransit, in quo omnes peccaverunt* ("By one man sin entered into the world, and by sin death, and so passed death through into all men, through that one man in whom all men have sinned").[268]

And after he saith, *Sicut enim unius delicto mors regnavit per unum, multo magis abundantiam gratiae et donationis et iusticiae accipientes in vita regnabunt per unum Iesum Christum. Igitur sicut per unius delictum in omnes homines in condemnationem, sic et per unius iusticiam in omnes homines in iustificationem vitae. Sicut enim per unius hominis inobedientiam peccatores constituti sunt multi, ita et per unius obedientiam iusti constituentur multi. Lex autem subintravit, ut abundaret delictum. Ubi autem abundavit delictum, superabundavit et gratia. Ut sicut regnavit peccatum in mortem, ita et gratia regnet per iustitiam in vitam eternam, per Iesum Christum Dominum nostrum* ("Likewise as by the sin of one man death hath entered by one, much more men, receiving the abundance of grace and of the gift and of justice, shall reign in life by one Jesus Christ. Therefore likewise as by the sin of one man it went into all men unto condemnation, so by the justice of one man also it goeth into all men unto justification[269] of life. For likewise as by the disobedience of one man many be constituted[270] and made sinners, so shall also by the obedience of one many men be constituted and made righteous. The law truly hath entered,[271] that sin should abound. But where sin hath abounded, there hath grace also more abounded, that likewise as sin hath reigned unto death, so grace should also reign by justice unto everlasting life through Jesus Christ our Lord").[272]

By these words of wrath, of sin, of condemnation, of death grown by the sin and disobedience of Adam into all his offspring, that is to wit, into all the kind of man by natural propagation engendered and begotten of him, and by the contrary words of justice, of obedience in Christ, and of justification and righteousness in man through grace growing into everlasting life, it well appeareth (say some doctors) that Saint Paul meant that the death grown to all mankind contracted by original sin from Adam should be the death of everlasting pain. From which Saint Paul well, by all the process[273] of the same words, declareth that no man can be saved but by our Savior Christ. Which thing Saint Peter showeth yet more expressly where he saith, *Non aliud nomen est sub caelo datum hominibus, in quo oporteat nos salvos fieri* ("There is none other name under heaven given to men in which we must be saved").[274] And that no man shall be saved without faith Saint Paul declareth where he saith, *Sine fide impossibile est placere Deo,*[275] that is to wit, either actual or habitual,[276] infounded[277] in the sacrament of baptism, or otherwise if God be so pleased, whose power is at liberty, not so bounden to his holy sacraments but that he may beside them give his grace where he list.[278] But with his sacraments he hath by his promise bound himself to do, and without them he doth unto few men, and with contempt of them to no man. And for this cause say those holy doctors infants be received to baptism to keep them from the peril of eternal damnation and perpetual pain in the fire of hell. And of this opinion was holy Saint Augustine, as in sundry plain places of his works well appeareth.[279]

Now since it is so (say they) that by the Scripture this point so plainly appeareth, what should we dispute the righteousness thereof, as though that man might attain to see the bottom of God's righteousness? How many things be there very well done and righteously by men which yet seem unto children to be no right at all. And infinitely farther asunder be the wisdom of God and the wisdom of the wisest man than is the wisdom of the wisest man above the wisdom of the most foolish child. The prophet in the person of God saith, *Non enim cogitationes meae cogitationes vestrae, neque viae meae viae*

264 before **265** become **266** wicked
267 Eph 2:3 **268** Rom 5:12 **269** being made righteous **270** established
271 i.e., the Mosaic law came into being

272 Rom 5:17–21 **273** *all the process*: the whole tenor **274** Acts 4:12 **275** Heb 11:6 **276** *actual or habitual*: exhibited in deeds or inherent in the character

277 infused **278** wishes **279** See esp. Augustine's *De peccatorum meritis et remissione et de baptismo parvulorum* (*PL* 44, 109–200).

vestrae, quia sicut exaltantur caeli a terra, sic exalta-
tae sunt viae meae a viis vestris, et cogitationes meae,
a cogitationibus vestris ("My thoughts be not like
your thoughts, nor my ways be not like your ways,
for as high as heaven is above earth, so high are my
ways above your ways, and my thoughts above your
thoughts").[280] And therefore saith Saint Paul, *O al-*
titudo divitiarum sapientiae et scientiae Dei, quam
incomprehensibilia sunt iudicia eius, et investigabiles
viae eius? quis enim cognovit sensum Domini? aut quis
consiliarius eius fuit? ("O the altitude (or height) of
the riches of the wisdom and cunning[281] of God.
How incomprehensible (or unable to attain unto)
be his judgments? And how investigable[282] be his
ways?"[283]—that is to wit, how unable to be sought
and found out? Who hath known the mind of our
Lord or who hath been of his counsel?)[284] God hath
no rule of justice to be ruled by but is himself the
rule by whose will all justice must be measured and
shapen.[285] And therefore he can do none injustice.
And when we be discharged once of this gross corruptible body, that aggrieveth and beareth down
the soul and oppresseth the mind that many things
thinketh upon, then shall such folk as shall be saved
behold and see in the glorious Godhead the very
clear solutions of such inexplicable problems.

With such things as this, and many more that
were too long to rehearse[286] here, have those good
fathers answered this matter, those I say that have
thought that by the sin of Adam every man old and
young, though he deceased with none other sin than
original only, was in like wise and in like reason[287]
damned to perpetual sensible[288] pain in the fire of
hell, as by the bondage of the father all his offspring
is in this world bounden unto perpetual thralldom.
Howbeit,[289] to tell you the whole truth, holy Saint
Augustine, which was (among others) of this mind
and opinion, for all the reasons with which he answered other men therein concerning the justice
of God in the damnation of infants unto perpetual sensible pain for that only sin original that they
contracted by the natural propagation of the first
condemned father, with all those reasons, I say, with
which he contented other men, he could never yet
satisfy and content himself. For in a certain epistle
which he writeth unto Saint Jerome[290] he debateth

this matter at length, very substantially and with
great erudition. And in that epistle he confesseth
the defense and maintenance of that opinion for so
hard that, as he there toucheth, some great cunning
men for the defense thereof have been driven to the
devising of a very great perilous error. For they, to
maintain the justice of God in that point, said that
the souls which every man have put in their bodies
by succession of time were all created at once before the seventh day in which God rested. And of
those words, that God in the seventh day rested,
they took a foundation for that error, forgetting the
words of our Savior: *Pater meus usque modo opera-*
tur, et ego operor ("My Father worketh still yet, and
I work still also"),[291] but in the seventh day God
rested from the creating of any new kind of creature. Then said they that the souls offended God before they came into the bodies and that they were
put into the bodies, some to be purged in them,
and some to be damned with them, so that the infants that die with original sin have the bodies worthy damnation because they naturally proceed out
of the damned stock with lack of original justice,[292]
and the soul was worthy to come into that body,
by the society whereof it should be bounden unto
eternal pain. The soul they said was worthy for that
other sin with which it had offended God before it
came into the body. This fantasy[293] were some fain
to find,[294] for maintenance of God's justice, of those
that held the foresaid way in the damnation of infants unto sensible pain in hell.

But this erroneous opinion, as reason is, Saint
Augustine rejected and confuteth. Howbeit,[295] that
yet notwithstanding, he confesseth himself to find
such difficulty in the maintaining of God's justice
to stand with his own opinion of condemning infants to sensible pain in hell, that himself seemeth
to doubt whether God create always every soul of
new,[296] or else that as well the soul as the body be
produced and propagated of the father and the
mother as well as the body. For if they so were, he
thought that then the answer were more easy if the
whole person of the man were taken by natural
propagation of the substance of our first father and
mother, being subject unto that damnation. And
therefore he desireth Saint Jerome to consider well

---

280 Is 55:8–9   **281** knowledge
282 unsearchable   **283** Rom 11:33–34
284 See Prv 8:15–16   **285** formed
286 recount   **287** *in like reason:* for the

same reason   **288** perceptible by the
senses   **289** However   **290** St. Jerome,
Epistola 166 (*PL 33*, 720–33)   **291** Jn
5:17   **292** righteousness   **293** capricious

speculation   **294** *fain to find:* glad to
contrive   **295** However   **296** *of new:*
anew

that point and search whether it might stand with
the Scripture or not. And if it might, he thought it
meet[297] that Saint Jerome should take that way too.
And if not, himself would not hold it neither. Howbeit, if that way would not be maintained, he then
desired Saint Jerome to write unto him by what reason he thought that the justice of God might be
maintained in the damning of infants unto sensible
pain in hell. For he said that himself could not see
how it could stand with justice that God should create a new soul that never offended and put it without any desert of itself into that body, by whose
company it should contract forthwith[298] such an
infelicity that, the body dying and the soul departing therefrom unchristened before it come to discretion, it should be damned to perpetual torment.
And then layeth he forth there certain reasons with
which himself was wont to answer other men in
that point for the time, for lack of better. But there
he requireth Saint Jerome to devise him better. For
he plainly confesseth that those answers which himself was wont to make other folk in the matter never
satisfied nor contented himself. Would God there
remained the answer of Saint Jerome again. But
whether ever he made any or not, we none find.

And thus have I, good readers, showed you the
mind of some good holy doctors which were of the
opinion that original sin, without actual adjoined
thereto, damned the kind of man naturally descended from Adam unto perpetual sensible pain in
the fire of hell. Now shall ye further understand that
there are others which have another manner[299] mind
therein, whereupon there ensueth nothing so great
difficulty concerning the righteousness of God.

Their mind in the matter is this, that God in the
creation of man gave to him two states: one, competent and convenient[300] for his mortal nature;
another, of special grace, a further state of special
prerogative,[301] that is to wit, the possibility of immortality put in his own hand and of the obtaining
of eternal bliss in heaven, of which two things there
was neither nother[302] naturally pertaining to him.
If God had given him only the first, that is to wit,
only natural, his soul yet should have been immortal, for God created the nature such. But unto the
bliss of heaven, the fruition of the Godhead, he did
not create it to attain by nature, nor as it seemeth

angel neither, but by a special gift and prerogative
of his grace. The body, being made of the earth and
mixed with other elements, was of nature dissoluble
and mortal, as the bodies of other beasts be. Howbeit, if God had given Adam no further gift than
competent unto his nature, he had yet had a good
state far above all beasts, and yet a state far under
the state that he stood in by God's further gift. For
first, if man had had but his natural state, albeit he
should have had (as some men think) the rebellion
of his sensuality against his reason, yet had he had
(while he lived) the use of the reasonable soul, and
should have had knowledge of God, and cause to
love him, honor him, and serve him, and had been
bounden to master his sensuality and resist the
devil, and by the doing of the contrary should have
deserved hell, and by doing his duty to God should
have deserved to have after this life not the fruition
of the Godhead (that is the bliss of heaven) but a
life good quiet and restful, with spiritual delight in
such knowledge of God and his wonderful works as
reason at the least, without revelation, might attain
unto. Which should have been a pleasure far above
the pleasure that ever any man had by only natural
means in this world since this world first began, and
such as (I suppose) whosoever might attain it would
not change that state with the state of the greatest
king that ever reigned on earth.

And yet, though they call this the natural state
of man, they mean not (I think) thereby that man
was or should have been able to have lived well after his nature and have attained the end of that
state by his own only[303] natural power, without special aid and help of God, since there is no creature
nother[304] high nor low, but as it could not without
God be created, no more can it without God be
conserved. And man, if he never had had but his
natural state, he should have been in danger to do
sin more than he was with the state of innocency
that God gave him further, and yet in that state he
sinned. And therefore, if not only we, which now
by more means than one have our naturals vitiated,[305] but also Adam, that had more than his naturals in Paradise whole and in good plight, had need
yet of God's grace to help him there to stand, it
must needs be (as I said) that he must have needed
the help of God's grace to maintain him if he had

297 fitting **298** immediately **299** kind
of **300** *competent and convenient:* proper
and appropriate **301** divinely given privilege **302** *neither nother:* neither of the
two **303** solely **304** neither **305** *naturals vitiated:* natural gifts corrupted

had his only natural state. And if any man marvel that God made all his creatures such as they should always need aid of his grace, let him know that God did it of his double goodness: first, to keep them from pride, by causing them perceive[306] their feebleness and to call upon him; and secondly, to do his creatures honor and comfort. For the creature (that wise is) can never think himself in so noble condition, nor should take so great pleasure or so much rejoice that he were made able to do a thing well enough himself, as to remember and consider that he hath the most excellent majesty of God his creator and maker ever more attendant himself at his elbow to help him.

If any man will herein take a contrary part and affirm that man in the state of innocency, and the angels that fell, were able of themselves to have stood[307] in their former state and, by natural liberty of their will without peculiar[308] help of God, to have chosen the better and to have refused the worse; and that their strength therein then, and our feebleness in this state corrupted now, have their differences by reason of their nature then whole and unhurt and ours now sore[309] impaired and wounded; and that the cause why we cannot now without help of grace choose the good, but willingly apply the freedom of our will to the choice of the evil, is the corruption of our nature grown by the sin of Adam; and that therefore (before that sin) Adam was (before that fall) able to choose the good of his own natural power, and angel yet more able than he, before the fall of Lucifer; and thereupon list[310] to conclude that neither angel nor man in the state of their first creation needed unto the resisting of sin none other help of God but only their natural power—to him that this list to reason, mine answer will I temper[311] thus: that they were of nature stronger and better able naturally than we, that will I gladly grant. But that they were so able to resist sin of their own nature then, that they needed for their assistance none help of God at all, that can I full hardly consent.[312] Howbeit, if any man affirm stiffly[313] yes, I will keep no schools[314] upon the matter nor almost in nothing else, but leave off and be content with that that[315] I trust he will grant me: that is to wit, that they were

never so able to withstand sin by their own natural power but that, at the leastwise yet, with God's help (which was ready when they would ask it) they should have been able the better.

Thus have I somewhat showed you of what mind some men be concerning the only[316] natural state given by God unto Adam. And now shall I further somewhat show you, what mind they be of, concerning that state which he had by the reason of the other gifts given him conditionally, by special prerogative, above his natural state, which things he lost by the condition broken.

They say that, above the natural condition and state of his body, God gave him this gift, that his body should never have died. He gave him this gift also, that his sensual parts should never have rebelled against his reason. He gave him also therewith that he should never have had dolor or pain in body, nor heaviness[317] or sorrow of mind, but all things necessary without weariness or grief. He had further given him, above his nature, this excellent high gift very far surmounting all the remnant, that is to wit, undeceivable[318] hope and ability both body and soul through grace to come to glory, the bliss (I say) of heaven, the joyful fruition of the glorious Trinity forever. All these gifts God gave him above his naturals, and not for himself only, but for him and for all his posterity. But all these supernatural gifts he gave him with the knot[319] of this condition, that is to wit, that if he broke his commandment, then should he lose them all. And that was understood[320] by the promise of death, and not only the necessity of temporal death, the dissolution of the soul and the body (by which the man doth indeed but half die, since his far better part, that is to say the soul, by that death dieth not at all) but, by the loss of heaven, the whole entire man hath a very sore death in that he is separate and departed[321] from the fruition of the very fountain of life, almighty glorious God.

Now say there, as I told you, therefore some good men that Adam by his sin lost from himself and all his posterity all those gifts that God gave him above his nature. And therein could his posterity have no wrong nor any cause to complain upon God but upon Adam only. For they were all given unto us

306 to perceive   307 remained   308 special, particular   309 greatly   310 wishes   311 devise   312 *full hardly consent:* scarcely agree with   313 stubbornly   314 *keep no schools:* engage in no academic disputations   315 which   316 merely   317 grief   318 certain   319 obligation   320 signified   321 *separate and departed:* separated and severed

but upon condition hanging on his hand,[322] which condition when he broke, those gifts could by no reason belong or be due unto us. But yet remained there high cause for us to thank God for the remnant. For the gifts only pertaining to the natural state of man (which I showed you before), those gave not God unto the kind of man upon condition to be lost by the sin of Adam, nor no man to be perpetually damned by sensible feeling of the fire of hell for original sin contracted without his witting,[323] but only for actual sin freely committed by his own vicious will. And then if the truth thus be, this matter may partly be resembled unto some great good prince, which, giving to a poor man for him and his heirs of his body forever lands to the yearly value of one hundred pounds, frank and free *simpliciter*[324] and without any condition, would give him farther other lands to the yearly value of ten thousand pounds with the honor of a dukedom also to him and his said heirs forever, restrained nevertheless with this condition, that, if he commit any treason against this prince's majesty, this duchy with all those lands of the yearly ten thousand pounds should be forfeited and lost from him and his said heirs perpetually, and that yet the other lands should still remain in the blood, and that every man of them, if he do either treason or other great crime against the king, should stand unto his personal peril of death or other pains, according to justice for his personal fault, without the loss of the land from the stock[325] for the fault of any their ancestor. If now this man committed treason and lost this duchy from his heirs by his deed and yet left them this hundred pound lands of the king's gift beside, there were (ye wot[326] well) none of his heirs that ever could have cause to blame the king for the loss of the duchy but had yet greater cause to thank him for their living of the yearly hundred pounds, which they still enjoy of his liberal gift, more by every groat[327] than ever the good king ought[328] them.

Lo, thus say they that likewise God took from the posterity of Adam the royal duchy, that is to wit, the joys of heaven with the commodities[329] of those other gifts above man's nature, which he gave Adam for himself, and then upon condition, which condition Adam broke. But yet he left them still the good honest living of the yearly hundred pounds, that is to wit, the commodities of man's competent[330] state natural, which I have before partly showed you, which state also man hath without his desert received, of[331] the only mere liberal goodness of God, and which commodities by affliction of perpetual pain felt in fire God never taketh from any man for the original sin contracted from his forefather without actual deadly sin of himself. Now to that that[332] the whole kind of man are called in Scripture the children of wrath by nature[333] and put under condemnation and death by the sin of Adam, and such other words like, they answer that those words are and well may be meant of the loss and condemnation of mankind in the loss of the inheritance of heaven and of those other gifts that God had conditionally given it, above the competent state of man's nature, for[334] the wrath of the condition broken by the sin of Adam, as it were a great condemnation to lose a duchy with ten thousand pounds and retain only a mean[335] man's living of one hundred pounds.

And they further declare that there are two manner of pains, that is to wit, *poena damni et poena sensus* (pain of loss and pain of feeling), as a man may be pained by loss of money or loss of his hand. Pain of loss may be also by two means, either by the losing of a thing that he hath in possession, or by duty should have come unto him, or by the losing of a thing that should have come unto him, and yet of no duty but of the mere liberality of some other man, which for displeasure given changeth his will and withdraweth it. Now say they that, for actual deadly sin, every man that impenitent dieth therein is damned both to the pain of loss and to the pain of feeling—that is to wit, to the pain of the loss of the joys of heaven, the fruition of the glorious sight of the Godhead forever, and to the perpetual sensible pain of feeling the fire of hell perpetual.

But for only original sin they say that no man is damned unto the pain of feeling, but only unto the pain of the said loss alone. And whereas the same pain of loss of the fruition of the Godhead is yet, unto those Christian people that are damned for actual deadly sin, a greater grief than is their intolerable feeling of the hot fire of hell, because they were by regeneration of their baptism made inheritors

---

322 *hanging…hand:* depending upon his action **323** knowing **324** *frank… simpliciter:* held without obligation of rent or service; unconditionally **325** descendants **326** know **327** coin worth four pence **328** owed **329** benefits **330** suitable **331** out of **332** *that that:* the fact that **333** Eph 2:3 **334** because of **335** average

of heaven and have lost it by their own fault, yet unto those that die unchristened with none other sin than original, the pain of that loss is not grievous, because it was the thing which, though it might have comen to them, yet were they never entitled thereto indeed, nor were not by their own fault the cause of their own loss. And thus say some as I show you, concerning all folk old and young that, never being christened nor nothing hearing of Christ, carry no deadly sin with them out of this world but sin original only. And as for infants dying unbaptized, albeit that[336] in many of these things that I have rehearsed by the way, many men will peradventure[337] think otherwise, yet in the effect and substance of the point whereunto all the matter draweth, that is to wit, that those infants be damned only to the pain of loss of heaven, and not unto the pain of feeling by any sensible pain in the fire of hell, to this point I think the most part of all Christendom both learned and unlearned agree.

Now as for such as die unchristened at man's state and never heard of Christ, some say one and some say another, as I have showed you before. And some say that without the faith of Christ, if they come to discretion,[338] they must besides original sin die of necessity in actual sin and be damned to sensible pain. For they say that all the deeds that ever they do be sin. Which saying meseemeth[339] hard, but I will not dispute it here. Howbeit, well I wot[340] that some texts of Scripture that they lay[341] therefore nothing prove for their purpose. Yet shall I not leave unshowed you one comfortable[342] saying that Master Nicholas de Lyra[343] toucheth upon those words of Saint Paul in the eleventh chapter of his epistle to the Hebrews: *Sine fide autem impossibile est Deo placere quemquam. Credere enim oportet accedentem ad Deum, quia est, et inquirentibus se remunerator sit* ("Without faith," saith Saint Paul, "it is impossible any man to please God. For every man that cometh unto God must believe that God is, and that he is the rewarder of them that seek him").[344] Upon these words saith Master Lyra that, although the people of the Jews to whom the law was given were bounden to the belief of more than this, and the learned men of the Jews to the belief of more than the common people, and we Christian people

and those that are the priests and learned among us be rateably[345] bounden to the belief of more things than were the Jews, or they that were learned among them, yet unto the paynims and gentiles, to whom the law was not given, nor never had heard of Christ, it was sufficient for their salvation to believe those two points only which Saint Paul here rehearseth, that is to wit, that there is one God and that he will reward them that seek him. And those two points be such as every man may attain by natural reason, helped forth with such grace as God keepeth from no man but from him that by his own default[346] either will not receive it or deserveth to have it withdrawn.

So that, if this be true that Master Lyra saith, then is there no man of discretion among the gentiles or paynims unsaved without his own default, and so no color[347] of quarrel against the justice of God in this matter. And it is to be considered that Master Lyra there saith that in the belief of those two points is implied the belief of Christ, which is the means of our salvation, in that that[348] he which believeth that God will reward them that seek him hath therein implied that God hath a respect unto man's salvation and provideth a means thereunto, and so believeth he that there is a means of man's salvation and reward, though he know not that the means is Christ. And there though he believe not on Christ by the name of Christ, yet believeth he and hopeth for the means of salvation, which is indeed Christ. And that belief sufficeth (saith Master Lyra) for his salvation, though he think not on Christ, of whom he never heard.

Thus have I showed you, concerning the necessity of man's redemption, and the manner of man's fall, and the things that he lost thereby, and the justice of God used therein, and as well his justice as his mercy tempered together in the marvelous means of man's redemption, sundry diverse things. And concerning Adam's gifts and his losses for his posterity, I have showed you sundry things of diverse other men's opinions, in which I will bind myself to the defense of neither part. But this thing am I very sure of, that by the fall of Adam every man and child that by natural propagation came of him had so verily lost and forfeited the bliss of heaven that

---

336 *albeit that*: although   **337** perhaps
338 age of reason   **339** seems to
me   **340** know   **341** present, allege

342 consoling   **343** Lyra's *Postillae*
(1322–30) was printed with other biblical
glosses in the glossed Bibles of More's

period.   **344** Heb 11:6   **345** proportionately   **346** misdeed, fault   **347** pretext
348 *in that that*: insomuch as

never should nor never shall any of them all attain again thereto without the means of our mediator and savior, Jesus Christ, the merits of whose bitter Passion hath redeemed us and thereto made us inheritable[349] again — as many of us (I mean) as by his faith, without contempt of his sacraments, use[350] ourselves in such wise[351] as by our own sin we do not willfully and finally fall again from the benefit. And thus upon this first question, without any bold affirmations or opinion that I will hold or maintain, I have somewhat showed you diverse things that diverse doctors say.

Another Question

Then are there many men in hand[352] with another question, and therein demand[353] they this: while our Savior Christ (say they) bestowed upon the redemption of man all the blessed blood of his body to the very following of the water after, and that not only being an innocent sinless man and a good, but also being beside that very God too, by reason whereof the least drop of his blessed blood might have sufficed to recompense and satisfy for the sin of seven whole worlds, wherefore be not all men, by the virtue[354] of his such painful death, either taken up into heaven, glorified in body and beautified in soul, forthwith as soon as they be born, or else at the leastwise restored to the state that Adam by his sin lost them before in Paradise? — That is to wit, that their bodies might be preserved from death, and the reasonable soul from rebellion of the sensual body, and have but the devil alone left him to strive withal,[355] and man discharged of all pain and vexation, and live here in such pleasant plight as we should have lived if Adam had not sinned, and (by serving God in such wise) then in such time or times after as God should think convenient[356] all men to be translated[357] out of earth into the joys of heaven?

In this question are there more things than one. But for the first, we must mark and consider well that Christ willingly would, by the ordinance of the whole Trinity, suffer more pain for our redemption than was of necessity requisite. Howbeit, though he so did without necessity, yet did he it not without a

great good cause. For the pleasure of God was that, by the hideous torment and willingly taken pain of that holy blessed and almighty Person, man should two things consider: one, how much we be bounden and beholden to him that would endure and sustain such horrible affliction for our sake; the other, that we should thereby consider the burden and weight of sin and well remember in ourselves, since that innocent almighty Person willingly suffered so sore[358] bitter pain for the sin of other, how much we very sinful wretches should of reason be well content, every man to suffer for our own. For unto sufferance for our sin, how loath and irksome[359] would we be of ourselves,[360] when we be so scantly[361] stirred yet thereto, for all that wonderful example? And whereas our hard hearts are so dispiteous[362] that many for all the consideration of Christ's bitter Passion and most painful death cannot yet with compassion relent into tears and weep, if he had paid our ransom but with one drop of his blessed blood pricked out with a pin, what doubt is there but that thereat then many a wretch would laugh?

Now as for bringing every man unto heaven forthwith upon his birth without any more ado,[363] why God would[364] not the effect of his Passion to weigh to[365] such purpose, there are more causes than one. First, that thing had been impertinent[366] to the nature of redemption, the nature whereof were at the farthest,[367] but to restore men to the liberty and freedom of their former state. But man in the state of innocency living in Paradise should not have been in that case[368] to have been forthwith translated into heaven, but should first have served God in Paradise, and somewhat have done therefor,[369] and in all that while have stood still[370] upon the winning or losing of heaven after his abearing.[371] For if he had abiden[372] in Paradise untempted many years more than he did and had afterward before his translation,[373] upon the suggestion of the old serpent the devil and of the young serpent the woman, eaten of the fruit as he did, he had in any time of his life had the selfsame fall. And peradventure any of his sons, if he had happed[374] any to beget before his fall, might, for himself and the posterity coming after of his own body, have lost by the like fall

---

349 capable of inheriting 350 behave
351 a way 352 *in hand:* occupied
353 ask 354 efficacy 355 with 356 fitting 357 transported 358 grievously, intensely 359 weary 360 *of ourselves:*
on our own 361 barely 362 pitiless
363 trouble 364 wanted, willed
365 *weigh to:* be sufficient for 366 irrelevant 367 most 368 *in that case:* in such a state as 369 for it (heaven) 370 *stood*
still: relied always 371 *after his abearing:* according to his conduct 372 dwelt
373 *before his translation:* before he was taken (up to heaven) 374 happened

the self-same state. And therefore I say that to bring man to heaven by and by[375] upon his birth was nothing belonging to the nature of redemption, which nature is to restore him only to the freedom of his first estate,[376] which was not (as I show you) man to go forthwith to heaven.

But then why be we not at the leastwise restored unto the same state, the state of innocency that Adam had in Paradise with all the commodities thereunto pertaining? To this I answer you, Christ when he redeemed us, how much pain soever himself took thereabout, was yet at his own liberty to temper the fruit that we should take thereby. And therefore if we took thereby much less fruit than we do, there could no man in reason find any fault therein. Howbeit,[377] as there is no doubt but that God could by the Passion of Christ have redeemed and restored us, not only to the conditional title of inheriting heaven at length, but also to the immediate attaining of heaven forthwith upon our birth or to the state of innocency in Paradise first for the meanwhile, if he had would,[378] so doubt I nothing also but likewise as he restored us not straightways to heaven because his high wisdom wist[379] it was not for God convenient,[380] so restored he us not to the state of innocency because his high wisdom well wist it was for ourselves not best. To be stablished[381] in the possession of eternal wealth, without any manner pain taken or anything done toward the deserving thereof, was and is so proper to God alone (the three persons of the glorious Trinity, the Creator) that God would never communicate[382] that thing with any other person being but a creature, neither man in earth nor yet angel in heaven. And therefore man to look for that point as the effect of his redemption were full unreasonable and far overproud a request.

Now man to be restored to the state of innocency, God saw that for man it was not best. For as the Scripture saith, *Homo cum in honore esset, non intellexit* ("When man was in honor, his understanding failed him; he could not know himself").[383] And therefore to the keeping of him from sin, and specially from pride the root of all sin, a more base estate was better. And better was it also for him to have two enemies, that is to wit,[384] the devil and his own sensuality both, than for to lack the one. For the having of both is a cause of double fear, and therefore of double diligence, to set his reason to keep sure watch to resist them, and for double help to call double so much upon almighty God for grace. And then with his so doing, he is more able and more sure now to subdue them both, than with less looking for God's help he was before the one,[385] and hath yet also thereby for his double victory against his double enemies the occasion of double reward.

Besides this, if God should by his Passion have restored them that came to his faith both in the Old Law and in the New unto the state of innocency, so that the children circumcised or christened should never have died till they were comen to discretion and had done some deadly sin, and that then their nature should change and by the sacrament of penance yet be restored again, then should it (as holy Saint Augustine saith)[386] have been a great occasion to make folk come to the faith and sacraments for the commodities of this present life, whereas God will have heaven so sore[387] desired and sought for that he will have the desirers thereof set by[388] the pleasures of this world not only nothing at all but also seek for the contrary and suffer displeasure and pain.

Moreover, if it so should have been, every person's secret sinful state should by the sudden open change of his nature have been, to his open shame, detected and disclosed in the sight of all the people. And over this, if it should thus have been, then must there have been so many common open miracles continually that man should in manner[389] have been drawn to the faith by force, and by that means have lost more than half the merit, which God would in no wise of his great goodness suffer.[390] And yet besides this, God, that[391] well wist[392] what thing the bliss of heaven is, saw that it was not convenient to give so great a gift to every slothful javel[393] that nothing did set thereby. And he well showeth himself to set nothing by it that can find in his heart to do nothing for it. Finally, God wist that it was nothing meet, the servant to stand in better condition than his master, as our Lord saith himself

---

375 *by and by:* immediately   **376** condition   **377** However   **378** desired   **379** knew   **380** fitting, appropriate   **381** set firmly   **382** share   **383** Ps   48(49):13, 21   **384** say   **385** *he…one:* i.e., he was able before (the fall) to subdue the one (the devil)   **386** *De civitate Dei* 13.4   **387** greatly   **388** *set by:* value   **389** *in manner:* as it were   **390** permit   **391** who   **392** knew   **393** rascal

in the Gospel. And therefore would he not suffer that, while he came to his own kingdom not without travail and pain, his servants should be slothful, and sit and pick their nails, and be carried up to heaven at their ease, but biddeth every man that will be his disciple or servant take up his cross upon his back, and therewith come forth and follow him. And for this cause, lo, though the painful Passion of Christ, paid for all mankind, was of the nature of the thing much more than sufficient for the sins of us all, though we nothing did but sin all our whole life, yet God, not willing to fill heaven with hell hounds, limited of his own wisdom and goodness after what rate and stint the commodity[394] thereof should be employed upon us, and ordinarily[395] devised that the merits of his pain taken for us should make our labor and pain taken for ourselves meritorious, which else, had we taken for our sin never so much and done never so many good deeds toward the attaining of heaven, could not have merited us a rush.[396] And this, I say, ordinarily. For by special privilege his liberal hand is yet nevertheless at liberty to give remission of sin, and to give grace and glory, where and whensoever he list.[397]

And thus have I somewhat touched the answer unto this question: wherefore the painful Passion of Christ restored not man again unto the former state of innocency that Adam before had in Paradise?

Now albeit that sundry other questions both may be moved and are, which might be induced and entreated[398] here, yet (lest I should therewith make this work too tedious and the introduction longer than the principal process[399] of the Passion) we shall be content with these few as those that most properly pertain unto the matter of the redemption; and, beseeching almighty God of his great grace that, all curious appetite of vain problems put apart, we may with meekness give our hearts to the very fruitful learning of those necessary things that we be bound to know, we shall haste us to the matter of the blessed Passion itself.

The Prayer

O holy blessed Savior Jesus Christ, which willingly didst determine to die for man's sake, mollify mine hard heart and supple it so[400] by grace that through tender compassion of thy bitter Passion I may be partner of thine holy redemption.

Whereas I have here before showed you three points, that is to wit, the ruin of angel, the fall of man, and the determination of the Trinity for man's redemption by means of Christ's Passion, as three things that were causes going before, whereupon his bitter Passion followed, I doubt not but that such as are learned will like also that, ere I begin with the lamentable story of the Passion itself, I should first show further some other points, that is to wit, by what means this determination of the Trinity was notified[401] unto man. And also the other causes of Christ's death and Passion, as the malice of the Jews, the treason of Judas, and the obedient will of his own holy manhead.[402] And verily these points might well and conveniently have been declared[403] before, and in the treating of these three other points, somewhat have I made mention of all these points too. But I have not thought it like[404] requisite to declare them before so full as those others, because the words of the Gospel itself give us more occasion to declare these points in the process of the Passion itself than those other three points which I have as a preamble touched more at large[405] before.

A Warning to the Reader

Here I will give the reader warning that I will rehearse the words of the evangelists in this process of the Passion in Latin word by word after my copy as I find it in the work of that worshipful father Master John Gerson, which[406] work he entitled *Monotessaron*[407] (that is to wit, "one of all four") as I have declared you before in my preface, because I will not in any word willingly mangle or mutilate that honorable man's work, but so rehearse it that learned[408] which shall read it here may have

---

394 *after . . . commodity:* according to what estimation and measure the benefit **395** normally, as a rule **396** straw **397** wishes **398** *induced and entreated:* adduced and considered **399** narrative

400 *supple it so:* make it so compliant **401** announced **402** human nature **403** explained **404** equally **405** *at large:* at length **406** whose **407** Here and in *The Sadness of Christ,* More takes

the Gospel texts he expounds from the *Monotessaron,* a Gospel harmony by John Gerson (1363–1429), a French churchman and spiritual writer. **408** learned persons

the selfsame commodity[409] thereby that they may have by the reading of the same among his own other works, as in considering such doubts as he sometimes moveth concerning the context[410] of the story, and in searching (if their pleasure be) every word in his[411] own proper place, where it was gathered and taken out of the four evangelists, and for their own learning list confer[412] the place and use their own judgment in the allowing[413] or in the controlling[414] of any part of his context, in the gathering and compiling of his present work.

But yet will I not fully follow the same fashion in the rehearsing of the same thing in English. For if I should, there neither could any such fruit grow thereof, and also the context of the story should in the eye of the English reader (and yet much more in the ear of the English hearer) seem very far unsavory by reason of the often interposition of the initial letters signifying the names of the four evangelists, and some one sentence[415] with so little change so often repeated, and in some place the context so diversely entricked in his collection,[416] that himself with a note in the margin declareth himself to doubt and stand unsure whether in that place he join and link well in one the sundry words of the evangelists or no. And therefore in the rehearsing of his context in English, nothing will I put in of mine own, but out will I not let[417] to leave any such thing as I shall think to be unto the English reader no furtherance but a hindrance to the clear progress of this holy story, which we shall with help of God in this wise now begin.

THE FIRST CHAPTER

O f the feast of the Unleavened Loaves approaching[418]

There approached near the holy day of the Unleavened Loaves, which feast is called Pascha.[419] *For the Pascha and the Unleavened Loaves was two days after. And so was it that, when Jesus had ended all these sermons, he said unto his disciples, "You know that after two days shall be the Pascha, and the Son of Man shall be delivered*[420] *to be crucified." Then gathered there together the princes of the priests, and the ancients*[421] *of the people into the palace of the prince of the priests which*[422] *is called Caiphas, and took counsel together. And they sought the ways, both the chief priests and the scribes, how they might with some wile*[423] *take him and put him to death. For they were afeard of the people. They said therefore, "Not on the holy day, lest there arise some seditious ruffle*[424] *among the people." But there entered Satan into Judas, whose surname is Iscariot, one of the twelve. Then went he to the princes of the priests and to the chief priests to betray him to them. And he had communication with the princes of the priests and with the rulers, in what manner he should betray him to them. And he said unto them, "What will ye give me and*[425] *I shall deliver him to you," who, when they heard him, were well apaid,*[426] *and promised and covenanted with him to give him money, and appointed to give him thirty groats.*[427] *And he made the promise. And from that time forth he sought opportunity that he might commodiously*[428] *betray him out of the presence of the people. Before the holy day of the Pascha, Jesus, knowing that his hour came on to go out of this world unto his Father, whereas he had loved those that were his, unto the end he loved them.*

A Prayer

Good Lord, give us thy grace, not to read or hear this Gospel of thy bitter Passion with our eyes and our ears in manner of a pastime, but that it may

---

409 benefit, advantage   **410** coherent structure   **411** its   **412** *list confer:* choose to compare   **413** approving **414** calling into question   **415** meaning **416** *entricked . . . collection:* entangled in his arrangement   **417** hesitate   **418** Gerson takes his account from Mt 26:1–5, 14–16; Mk 14:1–2, 10–11; Lk 22:1–6; and Jn

13:1. This section is introduced with the heading "The context of Master Gerson, whereof first the rubric, *De festo azimorum appropinquante. Mt 26, Mk 14, Lk 22, Jn 13.*" — and is followed by Gerson's Latin text in which abbreviations for Matthew, Mark, Luke, and John are used by Gerson to label the sources of words, phrases, and

sentences in his Gospel harmony. In the *Treatise,* More quotes Gerson's Latin here, but Gerson's Latin has been omitted in this edition.   **419** Passover   **420** handed over (to destruction)   **421** elders   **422** who **423** stratagem   **424** tumult   **425** if **426** pleased   **427** coins worth four pence each   **428** opportunely

with compassion so sink into our hearts, that it may stretch to[429] the everlasting profit of our souls.

The First Lecture

There approached near the holy day of the Unleavened Bread, which is called Pascha.[430] *For the Pascha and the Unleavened Loaves was two days after.*

These words, good Christian readers, be the words of Saint Matthew, Saint Luke, and Saint Mark, three of the four evangelists, which, by the mention-making of the Pascha and the Unleavened Bread, give us here in the beginning occasion to speak of the point which I before touched, that is to wit, in what wise the merciful, just, and high devised means of man's redemption, the deep secret mystery of the blessed Trinity (which, till God revealed it unto them, none angel in heaven knew or could think upon) was of God's comfortable[431] goodness signified and declared to man. For which ye shall understand that, albeit our first parents Adam and Eve were disobedient, and thereby broke God's commandment, and were also stubborn in the beginning (whereby they rather excused their default, and each of them put it from himself to some other, than meekly confessed their fault and asked for pardon and mercy) for which demean,[432] besides the sentence of death conditionally pronounced (before mentioned in the second chapter of Genesis, that whatsoever day Adam did eat of the tree of knowledge he should die), God, as is recited in the third chapter, declared after[433] certain other punishments that either of them should have for them and their offspring too (the one with sore[434] travail about the getting of his daily living, the other with sore travail in bringing forth of her children, and either of them some other thing besides, as you have in the second point heard rehearsed before), yet never find we that of God's mercy they fell into despair, as we find of Cain and of Judas.

And therefore after their not desperate[435] but fruitful repentance, taken upon[436] God's inward motion, and thereby calling to God for remission and mercy (with taking great wreak[437] willingly themselves upon themselves, as well with inward heaviness[438] and sorrow as outward labor and pain for their heinous offenses committed against God by the bold breaking of his high commandment), the great goodness of God giving them knowledge of the means of their salvation and of that Mediator by whose death they and their offspring should be redeemed again to bliss, did, in the faith of the said Mediator, remit and forgive them the eternality of the pain due unto their offense, reserving their actual enhancing[439] into heaven until the great mystery of Christ's Passion should be performed, and thereby the ransom paid, in such time as the high foresight and providence of God had from the beginning, before the world wrought,[440] laid up out of sight in the deep treasure of his unsearchable knowledge, little and little[441] at sundry seasons to be signified and insinuate[442] conveniently[443] to man before.

And therefore this great secret mystery did God reveal in diverse wise, that is to wit, partly with inward inspiration, partly with outward means, as well by words as other outward tokens. The first mention that we find made thereof is the third chapter of Genesis, where God unto the serpent said among other things thus: *Inimicitias ponam inter te et mulierem, et semen tuum et semen illius. Ipsum conteret caput tuum, et tu insidiaberis calcaneo illius* ("I shall put enmity," said our Lord to the serpent, "between thee and the woman, and between the seed of thee and the seed of her. That seed shall tread and all-to frush[444] thine head, and thou shalt lie in await[445] for his heel").[446] In these words was there a secret insinuation[447] and (as men might say) a watchword[448] given of Christ, which should be the seed of the woman (and the only seed of only woman without man), which seed should all-to tread and frush in pieces the devil's head and his power upon man, and that all that ever the devil should do again against Christ should not be able to reach his head (that is to wit, his Godhead), but only to fumble about his foot (that is to wit, his manhead), and yet rather lie in await to hurt it than able to hurt it indeed. For all that ever the devil (when with long lying in await therefore, he could nothing prevail by himself) caused by his wily train the Jews and the gentiles to do against his holy manhead, was yet, the thing well weighed and considered, not able to do it hurt,

---

429 *stretch to:* serve for   430 Passover   431 consoling   432 conduct   433 afterward   434 great   435 despairing   436 *taken upon:* derived from   437 punishment   438 grief   439 raising   440 had been wrought   441 *little and little:* little by little   442 imparted to the mind subtly   443 suitably   444 *tread and all-to frush:* trample and completely smash   445 waiting   446 Gn 3:15   447 covert suggestion   448 premonitory sign

but (as the prophet saith) *Sagittae parvulorum factae sunt plagae eorum* ("The wounds that they gave him were like as they had been made with the arrows that are shot out of a little boy's bow").[449] For all the wounds that they gave him in his body could not so take hold, but that within three days after, all his flesh was rid of all manner pain, and in far better health and incomparable better condition after forever than it was five days before.

And here, good reader, marvel not though I rehearse you the text of Genesis otherwise here than I did in the second point before. For whereas I there rehearsed it after the Latin translation, whereof the sentence[450] may stand very well, yet seemeth this letter[451] after the Hebrew text to serve more meet and more proper for the matter, in that by the Latin text the treading down of the devil seemeth applied unto our blessed Lady (which she did indeed by means of her holy seed, our Savior), but by the Hebrew text it is, as you see, referred (as more meet is) unto her holy Son himself.

But now when this mystery of man's redemption was thus there prophesied by God, I doubt it not but that of this watchword[452] the devil gathered somewhat and ever gnawed after upon that bone from that time to the coming of Christ, as a matter of his grief and torment. But yet will I not warrant that he very well understood it. And Adam (would I ween)[453] at the first hearing understood that word yet much less. For though God suffered[454] the serpent, whom he threatened therewith to his grief and displeasure, somewhat to guess thereat, yet while man was at that time nothing yet reconciled, but in his heinous offense stubbornly stood at his defense and his sorrow shortly after thereupon declared unto him, it seemeth me[455] not likely that God gave him the knowledge of his pardon before the full knowledge of his punishment or the acknowledging and repentance of his fault. Howbeit upon his repentance after, I nothing doubt but that God gave him further understanding what was by those words meant. Besides this, he signified this mystery to them by the sacrifice. For by the killing and offering up unto God the innocent beast in sacrifice was betokened the death of our innocent Savior and offering up of his body by the hot fervent pain of the cross.

And thus by diverse ways was there revelation given of this great mystery unto other of the old fathers (as Noah, Abraham, Isaac, and Israel and Joseph) by sundry diverse tokens too long here to rehearse, before the law given[456] in writing. Then was there in the law written express warning given by Moses unto the children of Israel in desert,[457] when he wrote unto them in the eighteenth chapter of the Deuteronomy: *Prophetam de gente tua et de fratribus tuis sicut me, suscitabit tibi Dominus Deus tuus, ipsum audies* ("A prophet of thine own people and of thy brethren, like unto me, shall thy Lord God raise up unto thee, and that prophet shalt thou hear").[458] Here in these words Moses gave them warning of Christ, that he should be a very man coming lineally of one of their own tribes, and that he should be a bringer of a New Law to them, as himself was, and that they should therein, upon the pain of the vengeance of God (as after followeth in the text), be bounden when he should come to hear and obey him. Now to bring them a New Law, as Moses did, God never sent none after but only Christ. And therefore him were they, by those words of their old lawyer[459] Moses, commanded for to hear and obey in those words, *Ipsum audies* ("Him shalt thou hear").

And therefore since they so were commanded of God by the mouth of Moses, though there had been before Christ's coming no word spoken of his Godhead, yet when himself so plainly declared it unto them, they were, I say, by the said commandment of God given them by Moses, bounden to give therein full faith and credence to him. Howbeit, that Christ was the very Son of God, and himself very God, beside the figures[460] and prophecies of the Old Law very plain and plenteous, the Father of heaven himself, present with the Holy Ghost at Christ's baptism, testified and recognized him for his very Son, saying, *Hic est filius meus dilectus, in quo mihi complacui* ("This is my well beloved Son, in whom hath been my delight").[461] Besides this, of his birth, of the place and the time of his doctrine and his miracles, and the malice conceived against him by the Jews, and the false treason of his familiar[462] enemy, of his Passion, his death, his resurrection, and his glorious ascension was warning given by sundry wise, as well by the words of the holy prophets as by tokens

449 Ps 63(64):8   **450** meaning   **451** text   to me   **456** was given   **457** *in desert:*   **459** lawgiver   **460** types   **461** Mt 3:17
452 premonitory notice   **453** think   in the wilderness   **458** Dt 18:15   **462** of his own household
454 allowed   **455** *seemeth me:* seems

and figures of things done among the chosen people (both before the law written[463] and after) and by things also commanded to be done among the children of Israel in their sacraments, rites, ceremonies, and sacrifices, commanded them (I say) by God (by the mouth of Moses) in the law given them by writing. For as saith Saint Paul, *Omnia in figura contingebant illis* ("All things came to them in figures").[464]

But forasmuch as I wot[465] well no wise man would look that I should in this place rehearse all those things, which would make a long book alone, I will therefore (letting all the remnant pass) only with a word or two show you what feast the evangelists here speak of, in these words of theirs which I have rehearsed you, that is to wit, the feast of Pascha and of the Unleavened Bread.

That the children of Israel were in servitude and thralldom in Egypt under the proud prince Pharaoh; and that God conducted them thence in strong and mighty hand and made that high stubborn king, maugre his teeth,[466] fain[467] to let them go; and that when he farther followed them of his heart-burning malice through the Red Sea, the same way where God had sent his own people through safe, this fierce furious king with all his whole main mighty army was—with the waves of the water (which water, while the children of Israel passed through, stood up like high walls of crystal on both sides, leaving a great broad space of dry ground all the mids[468]) suddenly relented[469] and fallen and flowing shortly together again—involved[470] and tossed up, overthrown and tumbled down, overwhelmed and wretchedly drowned: all this process (I say) shall I nothing need to speak of, as things so commonly known that, for the atrocity[471] of the story and the wonderful work of God therein, almost every child hath heard.

And every man almost is (I trust) instructed also that, though these things be no feigned tales told for parables, but were things verily done indeed, yet did they by the provident ordinance of God serve also to signify certain great secret mysteries concerning the redemption of man. As for example, the thralldom of the children of Israel under King Pharaoh and the Egyptians signifieth the bondage of mankind under the prince of this dark world, the devil and his evil spirits. Their delivery[472] thence under the leading of Moses betokeneth the delivery of man from the devil and his evil angels under our captain Christ. The safe passage of the children of Israel through the Red Sea, and all the power of Pharaoh drowned in the same, signifieth mankind passing out of the devil's danger[473] through the water of baptism, the sacrament taking his force of the red blood of Christ that he shed in his bitter Passion, and all the devil's power, usurped upon[474] us before and laboring to keep us still, drowned and destroyed in the water of baptism and the red blood of Christ's passion. And by all the course after of the people conveyed from the Red Sea, by the desert[475] toward the land of behest,[476] and their waywardness and many punishments, with manifold mercy showed again by the space of forty years together ere[477] any of them came there, is there signified and figured[478] the long painful wandering of men in the wild wilderness of this wretched world ere we can get hence to heaven and the frowardness[479] of ourselves that so sore[480] keepeth us from it that, with great help of God's grace, in respect of the multitude that by their evil desert eternally perish in this worldly desert, very few (I fear), and with much work, attain unto it.

But for the perceiving of these words of the Gospel, "There approached near the feastful[481] day of the Unleavened Loaves, which feast is called Pascha,"[482] ye shall understand that the Jews among all their feasts and holy days through the year had one feast the most solemn that was called "Pascha" and "the Feast of the Unleavened Bread" which God specially commanded them to celebrate yearly forever, as appeareth at length in the twelfth chapter of Exodus.[483] For after that the proud stiff-necked Pharaoh, being by Moses in the name of God commanded to suffer[484] the children of Israel to depart out of his land into desert with all their wives and their children and all their cattle,[485] would in no wise suffer it, but albeit that[486] by the force and constraint of sundry sore strokes and plagues (wherewith God wonderfully smote him) he granted their delivery[487] for the time that he stood in dread (the

463 was written　**464** 1 Cor 10:11　**465** know　**466** *maugre his teeth:* in spite of his resistance　**467** willing　**468** *all the mids:* in the middle　**469** broken loose　**470** enveloped　**471** savage enormity

472 deliverance　**473** power, dominion　**474** *usurped upon:* appropriated wrongfully from　**475** wilderness　**476** *land of behest:* promised land　**477** before　**478** symbolized　**479** perversity

480 grievously　**481** festal　**482** Lk 22:1　**483** Ex 12:14, 17　**484** permit　**485** possessions, chattel　**486** *albeit that:* although　**487** deliverance

rod of God laying the lashes upon him), yet, after the rod scant[488] removed, ever more his stubborn pride sprang into his hard heart and made him forbid their passage again and hold them in thralldom still, our Lord at the last commanded Moses that the tenth day of that month they should take every household a lamb without spot, and the fourteenth day of the same month, in the evening, offer it and eat it up all together, head and guts and all, so that they should leave nothing thereof, but if anything were left they should burn it up. And of this lamb should they nothing eat raw nor sod[489] but only roasted at the fire. And they should eat it with wild lettuce and unleavened bread, and should have no leaven, neither that night nor in seven days following, within their house upon pain of death. And they should eat it having their gowns gird[490] or tucked up about the reins[491] of their back, and their shoes upon their feet, and their walking staves in their hands, and so eat it in haste, as folk that had made them ready to be going and therefore might not tarry because they were upon their passage.

And then God showed them of two passages: the one of theirs, the other of his. For he showed them that the twenty-first day of the same month, which should be at the end of the said seven days of the unleavened bread, they should all pass and depart out of Egypt over the Red Sea. And he showed them that in the night of the said fourteenth day, in which they should offer in sacrifice and eat the unspotted lamb, himself would make a passage through Egypt and by his angel kill in that one night all the first begotten of the Egyptians, as well men as cattle in every house, from the first begotten son of Pharaoh that sat in his seat, to the first begotten son of the poorest and most simple slave that lay in prison. And he commanded them that with a bundle of hyssop they should besprinkle the posts and the hance[492] of their doors with the blood of the lamb, which blood should be the mark unto him that should strike these first begottens that should that night be slain, so that upon the sight of that mark the striker should pass by their houses so marked and not enter thereinto to do there any harm; but he warned them that there should that night none of them come out of their doors.

And likewise as God had promised, so performed he that great sore[493] slaughter and vengeance thorough all Egypt in that one night, so that thereupon Pharaoh with all the Egyptians were so sore[494] daunted that both Pharaoh and all his people not only licensed[495] but also required and prayed the children of Israel to get them out of Egypt into the desert about their sacrifice, and, in all that they might, they also hasted them forward, and not only let them carry and convey out with them all their own but lent them also so great substance of theirs that the Hebrews, as the Scripture saith, in their going with that plenteous borrowing, "spoiled the Egyptians,"[496] and that by the special commandment of God—either in recompense of the wrongful oppression that the Egyptians had done them before, or because that, since *Domini est terra et plenitudo eius, orbis terrarum, et universi qui habitant in eo* ("The earth belongeth to our Lord, and all-thing that is therein, the whole roundel[497] of the world and all the people that dwell therein"),[498] God might well with reason take what he would from whom he would, and give it where he would, and make their possession lawful.

But now was this Feast of the Unleavened Bread yearly kept holy the space of the said seven days by the special commandment of God, and called *dies azymorum* in the Greek tongue, that is to say, "the days of the unleavened bread." And the first day of them was the great solemn day. And that first day began always the night before in the evening in the feast of Pascha, wherein was immolate[499] and offered in sacrifice the unspotted lamb. For, as I have showed you, that lamb were they commanded to eat with unleavened bread, and so forth from that time to continue the unleavened bread seven days after. This feast, therefore, of the sacrifice of the unspotted lamb is that feast that is called Pascha, whereof the evangelists here speak. And they call it also the Feast of the Unleavened Bread, because that feast began the same night in which the lamb was sacrificed.

This feast which was in the Greek called *Pascha,* and which name the Latins have taken of the Greeks and continued, was in the Hebrew tongue called *Phase* and (as Saint Jerome saith)[500] *Pascha* too. It was called *Phase* for that[501] *Phase* in the

488 scarcely   **489** boiled   **490** girdled   **491** region of the kidneys   **492** lintel   **493** grievous   **494** greatly   **495** allowed   **496** Ex 12:36   **497** sphere   **498** Ps   23(24):1   **499** sacrificed   **500** More could have based this and the following reference to Jerome on the *Glossa ordinaria,* one of the common biblical glosses found   in Bibles in More's period.   **501** *for that*: because

Hebrew signifieth "passing" or "going" and the feast was (as I have showed you) ordained in remembrance of God's passing through Egypt in doing the vengeance upon the Egyptians by the slaughter of all their first begottens to compel them to suffer the Hebrews pass out of their thralldom. It is also called *Pascha,* for that that (as Saint Jerome saith) *pascha* in the Hebrew signifieth "immolation," and therefore for the immolation of the lamb that feast hath in Hebrew that name. The Greeks, as I have told you, have taken the name *Pascha*—and that peradventure[502] the rather for that that[503] the same Hebrew word signifieth also in their tongue another thing, very consonant and convenient for the season and the matter. For *pascha* in the Greek tongue signifieth "passion." And because that in that night of his Maundy,[504] in which he immolated the lamb, he began his bitter Passion—the immolation of the very unspotted Lamb, his own blessed body, which immolation and passion he finished on the morrow—therefore they took and used the name of *Pascha,* wherein the Latin Church followeth them.

Thus have I somewhat showed you, good Christian readers, the first point that I spoke of rising of the text, that is to wit, in what wise the determination of the Trinity for man's redemption was notified[505] unto man, that is to say, by the inspiration and prophecies in words and writing, and by figures contained as well in other things done among the chosen people as in their rites, sacraments, ceremonies, and sacrifices. I have also showed you somewhat concerning this feast of the Unleavened Loaves and the Pascha. But, as I said before, all these things which then were verily done foresignified in Christ and his Church things after to be done. For that innocent lamb without spot was a figure betokening our Savior Christ, the very innocent Lamb of whom Saint John the Baptist witnessed, *Ecce agnus Dei qui tollit peccata mundi* ("Lo, the Lamb of God, which taketh away the sins of the world"),[506] by whose immolation and sacrifice on the cross, and by his holy body received into ours as that lamb was into theirs, his faithful folk should be delivered out of thralldom of the devil's dominion. And therefore may we to the fruit[507] of our souls consider, in the foresaid figure, by these Egyptians that

in Egypt (which signifieth by interpretation "darkness") do labor to keep in captivity the children of Israel—the people which God calleth from their thralldom into the liberty of his service—we may (I say) understand by the proud King Pharaoh and his chief captains, the great high proud prince, the Soldan[508] of Babylon, the devil. And as two the[509] special bashaws[510] of that proud souterly[511] soldan, may we well consider the world and the flesh. And the whole people of the Egyptians under them may well betoken the devilish people, and the worldly people, and the fleshly people that follow them and willingly be governed by them.

For verily all these labor to draw into their service and to make their thrall servants, bondmen, and slaves, all those whom the goodness of God calleth out of the dark, devilish, worldly, and fleshy subjection into the lightsome[512] liberty of his celestial service. For surely the devil himself, nor the world, nor a man's own flesh do not so much by their own strength to the bringing of good folk into their bondage as they do by the means and help of the devilish, worldly, and fleshly people, by occasions of pride, envy, wrath, and covetise,[513] gluttony, sloth, and lechery (to which one vice of lechery, for an example, how oft hath an old wily wretched bawd brought and betrayed a good simple maid, whom else neither the lust of her own flesh, nor the rewards of all the world, nor the labor of all the devils in hell should never have drawn thereto). By the first-begotten children of the Egyptians we may well understand the first motions of sin, as the subtle inward suggestions of the devil, and the inward incitation[514] of the flesh, and the outward occasions and provocations of the world and evil people, by all which manner of motions good well-disposed folk be many sundry wise solicited unto sin. And surely killed must there be these first-begotten children, not only of the Egyptian people (that is to wit, the first motions unto such vices as have their springing of the soul) but also the first-begotten of their beasts too (that is to wit, the first motions unto such vices as specially spring of the sensual beastly body), or else it will be very hard for the children of Israel, the well-disposed people, to escape well out of bondage of these Egyptians.

But now to destroy those first-begotten children of the Egyptians the children of Israel are of themselves not sufficient,[515] but it must needs be the work of God for them. And yet will God that themselves shall do somewhat too. For he will that they shall make and receive this sacrifice of the Paschal lamb, and then, if they do worthily the one for him, he will do the other for them. And therefore he will that we shall receive the holy Paschal Lamb, his own blessed body, both bodily in the Blessed Sacrament and spiritually — with faith, hope, and charity — receive it worthily,[516] and in such wise also virtually[517] when we receive it not sacramentally. But he will we shall eat it with no leaven bread, that is to wit, with no sour taste of malice or sin, but with the sweet unleavened loaves of sincere love and verity. We must also, with a bundle of the low-growing herb of hyssop that signifieth humility, mark the posts and the hance[518] of the door of our house with the blood of the lamb, that is to wit, have remembrance of his bitter Passion and his blessed blood shed therein. And likewise as with a bundle of hyssop, the bitter eisell[519] and gall was given him to drink in the painful thirst of his Passion, which he so humbly suffered, we should with a bundle of humility (as it were with a painter's pencil[520]) dipped in the red blood of Christ, mark ourselves on every side and in the hance of our forehead with the letter of *Tau*,[521] the sign of Christ's holy cross.

And then will God himself with his holy angels pass by, and kill and destroy for us those first-begotten of the Egyptians, from the first-begotten child of the king that sitteth in his seat (that is to wit of pride, which is of all sin the prince) unto the first-begotten child of the poorest prisoned slave that is covetise,[522] lo, the very caitiff knave. For he is yet of all wretched vices the most base, by setting[523] and binding his affection neither unto God, nor man, nor woman, nor unto himself neither, but only made in the pleasure of possessing a great heap of round metal plates, which while he liveth he loveth better than himself and cannot find in his heart to break his heap to help himself. And when he goeth, he carrieth none hence with him, but is while he liveth in like wise rich (as the prophet

saith) as a poor man is in a dream, which, when he waketh, hath never a penny of all the treasure that he was so glad of in his sleep.[524] And covetise is a very prisoner, for he cannot get away. Pride will away with shame, envy with his enemies' misery, wrath with fair entreating, sloth with hunger and pain, lechery with sickness, gluttony with the belly too full. But covetise can nothing get away — for the more full the more greedy, and the elder the more niggard, and the richer the more needy.

And while God killeth those Egyptians, that mark of Christ's bloody cross upon the posts of our house shall defend us, and be the mark by which we shall be marked from harm, as were the twelve thousand marked with the same sign of the letter *Tau*, mentioned in the seventh chapter of the Apocalypse Saint John.[525] But yet we must remember that in that perilous time we may not walk out abroad, but keep ourselves close (God biddeth us) within our so marked house from all evil outward occasions. We must also have our garments girt, and our walking staff in our hand, and eat apace for token of haste, in consideration of Christ's passage to kill the Egyptians for us by his own bitter Passion, and in remembrance also that we may not tarry here long about our meat, nor take leisure as we list[526] at our meal, but with our gear[527] girt and tucked up (for letting[528] us by the way), and our shoes upon our feet (for filing of[529] our affections with the dirt of sin), and with our walking staff in our hand (the remembrance of Christ's cross, to stay us with and beat from us venomous worms), get us forward apace upon our way out of the Egyptians' danger.[530]

A Prayer

Good Lord, which, upon the sacrifice of the Paschal lamb, didst so clearly destroy the first-begotten children of the Egyptians that Pharaoh was thereby forced to let the children of Israel depart out of his bondage, I beseech thee, give me the grace in such faithful wise to receive the very sweet Paschal lamb, the very[531] blessed Body of our sweet Savior, thy Son, that, the first suggestions of sin by thy power killed in mine heart, I may safe depart out of the danger of the most cruel Pharaoh, the devil.

---

515 able   **516** with a fitting disposition
517 with spiritual effect, even though the Eucharist is not taken bodily   **518** lintel
519 vinegar   **520** paintbrush   **521** The name of the letter *T* in the Greek,

Hebrew, and ancient Semitic alphabets. It has the form of a St. Anthony's cross.   **524** Ps 75(76):6   **525** Rv 7:2–4. The letter *Tau* is not mentioned in this

passage but is in a related passage, Ez 9:4.   **526** wish   **527** clothing   **528** *for letting:* as a precaution against hindering   **529** *for filing of:* as a precaution against defiling   **530** power, dominion   **531** true

The Second Lecture

So was it that, when Jesus had ended all these sermons, he said unto his disciples: "You know that after two days the Pascha shall be, and the Son of man shall be delivered[532] to be crucified."

In these words we may, good Christian people, well perceive the goodness and the prescience of our holy Savior Christ—his prescience in that he foreknew the time of his parting by death out of this world unto his Father in heaven. And how could he but foreknow it, since he was not only man but God also, that foreknoweth all things and not his own Passion only, whereof he gave his disciples warning in this wise: "Two days hereafter not only shall the Paschal Feast be, which thing you know well, but also, which thing you think not on, the Son of Man shall be delivered to be crucified." Christ was by more than one delivered to be crucified. His Father delivered him for pity upon mankind. Judas delivered him for covetise, the priests and the scribes for envy, the people for ignorance and folly. The devil delivered him for fear, lest he might lose mankind by his doctrine, and then lost he mankind after indeed more fully by his death than before by his doctrine.

His high provident goodness appeareth well in these words: *Et factum est cum consummasset Iesus sermones hos omnes, dixit discipulis suis* ("When Jesus had ended all these sermons, then he gave his disciples warning of his death coming so near at hand").[533] What sermons these were appeareth well in the context of the Gospels before: that is to wit, his doctrine (that he taught them as well in the temple as elsewhere) and the revelations of the things to come (as of the destruction of Jerusalem and the Day of Doom), which things of doctrine and revelations he had preached unto them sundry days before that time. For since the cause of his coming into the earth was to bring man into heaven, and since he had also his life and his death in his own hand so that no man could, before himself would, force or compel him to die, he would not take the time for his death till he had first finished and ended those words and those things of heavenly doctrine that he had determined to do; and that done, as the thing finished that he had to do first, then sped he him apace toward his death.

And here is it good to consider that, as our Savior wist[534] when he should die (because he should not nor could not till he would) and yet did nevertheless diligence in those things that he had to do before his death (albeit he might have deferred his death unto what time him list[535] and have done in the meantime everything at ease and leisure), how much need have we—poor wretches that shall die ere[536] we would, and cannot tell the time when, but peradventure[537] this present day—what need have we, I say, to make haste about those things that we must needs do, so that we may have nothing left undone when we be suddenly sent for and must needs go. For when death cometh, the dreadful mighty messenger of God, there can no king command him, there can none authority strain[538] him, there can no riches hire him to tarry past his appointed time one moment of an hour. Therefore let us consider well in time what words we be bounden to speak and what deeds we be bounden to do, and say them and do them apace, and leave unsaid and undone all superfluous things (and much more all damnable things), witting[539] well that we have no void[540] time allowed us thereunto.

For as our Lord saith, "the day of our Lord shall steal on us like a thief,"[541] and "we wot[542] not when he will come, whether in the morning, or in the midday, or in the evening, or at the midnight."[543] And therefore have we need, as our Savior saith, "to watch well that the thief break not in at the walls upon us, ere we be aware, when we be asleep in deadly sin."[544] For then he robbeth us of all together[545] and maketh us poor miserable wretches forever. Let us then evermore make ourselves so ready for death, nothing left undone, that where our Savior said, after all his sermons ended, that after two days he should be delivered to be crucified, we may by help of his grace say to ourselves and our friends every day, "I have done all my business that I am come into this world for. For I shall, I wot nere[546] how soon, but peradventure this day, be delivered by God unto the cross of painful death. From which if I die naught,[547] I depart from death to the devil, as did the blasphemous thief that hung

---

532 handed over (to destruction)   **533** Mt 26:1   **534** knew   **535** *him list:* he chose   **536** before   **537** perhaps   **538** control   **539** knowing   **540** idle   **541** 1 Thes 5:2. See also 2 Pt 3:10 and Rv 3:3.   **542** know   **543** Mk 13:35–36   **544** This passage   perhaps alludes to Mt 24:43 and Lk 12:39.   **545** *all together:* everything   **546** *wot nere:* know not   **547** wicked

on his cross beside Christ. And if I die well, as I trust in God to do, I may with his mercy straight depart into Paradise, as did the penitent thief that hung on his other side."

5   And God give us all the grace so to do all our business in time that we spend not our time in vanities, or worse than vanities, while we be in health, and drive off[548] the things of substance that we should do till we lie in our deathbed, where we shall
10   have so many things to do at once, and everything so unready, that every finger shall be a thumb and we shall fumble it up[549] in haste so unhandsomely[550] that we may hap, but if[551] God help the better, to leave more than half undone.

15   A Prayer

Good Lord, give me the grace so to spend my life that when the day of my death shall come, though I feel pain in my body, I may feel comfort in soul and, with faithful hope of thy mercy, in due love toward
20   thee and charity toward the world, I may through thy grace part hence into thy glory.

The Third Lecture

Then gathered there together the princes of the priests and the ancients[552] into the palace of the prince of the
25   *priests, which[553] is called Caiphas, and took counsel together. And they sought the ways, both the chief priests and the scribes, how they might with some wile[554] take him and put him to death. For they were afeard of the people. They said therefore: "Not on the holy day, lest*
30   *there arise some seditious ruffle[555] among the people."*

Upon these words, good Christian reader, riseth there occasion to speak of another point that I touched also before: that is to wit, the other cause of Christ's death, rising upon the malice of the Jews.
35   For in these words is touched (as you see) their malicious assembly in devising and compassing[556] his death. Howbeit, before this council assembled here (which was the day before his Maundy, that is to wit, the Wednesday before his Passion, and the
40   morrow after the afore-remembered[557] warning of his Passion given unto his disciples), there was

another council gathered together among them for the selfsame purpose, whereof mention is made in the eleventh chapter of Saint John. For whereas our Savior Christ had oftentimes reproved the priests,   45
the scribes, and the Pharisees for their pride and their hypocrisy, their avarice and their evil constitutions[558] (made unto the commodity[559] of themselves in derogation of the law and commandment of God), with which monitions[560] their part had   50
been to have amended their manners[561] and to have given him thanks for his good doctrine, they on the other side took so far the contrary way that for his goodness they so maliciously hated him that, albeit they perceived well by the prophecies fulfilled in   55
his birth and his living and his doctrine — with the manifold marvelous miracles which he continually wrought — that he was Christ, yet so mighty was (I say) their malice that they labored to destroy him. But specially after that he had raised Lazarus from   60
death to life, the thing so well and openly known, and the wonder so far spread and so much in every man's mouth, and the man well-known once for four days dead and buried, and so many men seeing him alive again, and eating and drinking and   65
talking with him (for which the people fell so thick unto Christ that the priests, the scribes, and the Pharisees were afeard to lose their authority), they waxed so wood[562] therewith that they thereupon devised both to have slain Lazarus and also to de-   70
stroy Christ. For without his death they thought it in vain to slay Lazarus, since he that raised him once was able to raise him again.

But because they never read of any man in the Scripture before that ever after his death raised   75
again himself (for of raising other they had read), therefore, if they slew Christ too, they thought they should make all the matter safe. Whereupon as Saint John in the eleventh chapter of his Gospel remembereth,[563] "The bishops and the Pharisees   80
gathered together a council and said: 'What do we? This man doth many miracles, and if we leave him thus, all shall believe in him, and then shall the Romans come and destroy both our town and our people.'"[564] Thus the wily wretches, lo, the mischievous   85
deed that they went about[565] for the maintenance

of their own worldly winning[566] and in revenging
of their own private malice, that would they color
under the pretext of a great zeal unto the common
wealth of all the people. And in this saying, they
very well wist that they lied. For the Romans nothing rought[567] what or on whom the Jews believed,
whose true belief in one God they counted for superstition. And for nothing cared they among the
Jews but that the emperor of Rome should be their
chief temporal governor and have them his tributaries, and that they should have no king but under
him and at his assignment. Now that Christ went
about no temporal authority, nor would take upon
him as king[568] (albeit indeed he was king), was well
enough known unto them by that he not only fled
from being king when the people would have made
him king, but also refused to be so much as a judge
or an arbitror in a temporal matter concerning the
dividing of a private inheritance between two brethren, saying to the one, "Who hath appointed me
judge or divider between you?"[569]

But yet for all this one of that council, called
Caiphas (which was bishop for that year), well allowed[570] their false lying motion and was angry that
it went not farther straight unto Christ's death; and
therefore himself sharply, by the authority of his office, reproved them and said unto them, "You know
nothing"—as though he would say, "You be fools,
you consider not that it is expedient for you that
one man die for the people, and not all the people
to perish." These words, as the evangelist saith, he
spoke not of himself, but like as though[571] he were
an evil bishop, yet he was a bishop, so, though he
meant but to further his malicious purpose, yet God
so framed his words that unware[572] to himself they
should be a very true profitable prophecy, signifying that that one man, our Savior Christ, should die
for all the people, and not only for that people, but
also, as Saint John farther saith, to gather together
in one the children of God that were dispersed
abroad. And from that day did they purpose to kill
our Savior Christ.[573] For which, for a while, our Savior forbore to walk abroad among the Jews, withdrawing himself into the city of Ephraim, with his
disciples, near unto the desert, because the bishops
and the Pharisees had given a commandment that

if any man might wit[574] where he were, he should
show them that they might make him be taken.

But yet for to declare that this withdrawing of
Christ was to give his disciples example, according to his own commandment[575] to fly from persecution when they conveniently can—lest in temerarious[576] and foolhardy offering themselves thereto
their bold pride might turn into cowardice and take
a foul shameful fall—that their instruction was (I
say) the cause of his withdrawing, and not any fear
of himself, he declared well on Palm Sunday after,
when he letted not openly to ride into the city, with
his disciples about him, where, without dread of his
enemies, all the people received him with procession and reverence, where all the people cried out as
he went, *Hosanna filio David, benedictus qui venit in
nomine Domini: Hosanna in altissimis!* ("Hosanna
to the son of David; blessed is he that is come in the
name of our Lord! *Hosanna* in the high places!")[577]
Hosanna in Hebrew signifieth, "I beseech thee save
me."

But when the bishops, the priests, and the scribes,
and the Pharisees heard and saw this, and that the
people came so many with him, and among them so
many of those that had seen Lazarus both quick[578]
and dead and four days buried too, and after yet
now alive again, they thought again upon the killing of Lazarus and our Savior too. And because they
durst[579] at that time not meddle with him for fear of
the people, some of the Pharisees would have had
him cease that voice of the people himself, and said
unto him, "Master, make thy disciples here hold
their peace,"[580] as though that cry were but the cry
of his disciples and not the common voice of the
people. But our Savior soon answered them far of
another fashion and said unto them, "Though these
would hold their peace, the very stones shall cry it
out."[581] And this word proved true upon the Good
Friday following. For when the bishops, the priests,
the scribes, and the Pharisees had made the people leave off crying out of Christ's praise, and also
turned them to the crying out against him to have
him crucified, then, after all their cruelty spent out
upon his death, the very stones in their manner
cried him out for Christ when, as the Gospel saith,
Velum templi scissum est a summo usque deorsum,

566 gain   567 *nothing rought:* cared
not at all   568 *take…king:* undertake
the office of king   569 Lk 12:13–14

570 sanctioned   571 *like as though:* just
as if   572 unknown   573 For the whole
episode, see Jn 11:49–53.   574 know

575 Mt 10:23   576 rash, reckless
577 Mt 21:9   578 living   579 dared
580 Lk 19:39   581 Lk 19:40

et petrae scissae sunt, et monumenta aperta sunt, etc.
("And the veil of the temple rived[582] from the height down unto the ground, and the stones broke, and the graves opened, and after that out of them rose many holy men's bodies").[583] But, as I began to tell you, when Christ came riding into Jerusalem so royally upon Palm Sunday, his enemies said unto themselves, "You see we prevail nothing. Lo, all the world is fallen to him."[584] And upon this arose this new council taken upon the Wednesday after (whereof our present lecture speaketh), in which there were gathered together against Christ the princes of the priests and the ancients of the people into the palace of Caiphas, that was (as you have heard) bishop for that year, to devise and study the means to take and destroy our Savior.

Where the Gospel saith "the princes of the priests" ye shall understand that it was ordained in the law that there should be but one prince of the priests — bishop, or chief priest — and he to continue his office during his life. But afterward, by ambition of the priests, usurpation and covetise of the kings, the right order of the making or choosing of the bishop was changed, and they were put in and put out by the kings, sometimes for pleasure, sometimes for displeasure, and sometimes for money too, so that instead of one, now were they waxen[585] many. The ancients of the people were seventy, which, by Moses at the special commandment of God, were (as it appeareth in the eleventh chapter of Numbers) instituted and ordained to be judges over the people, and, in great causes wherein their sentences varied, to refer the matter unto the chief priest and stand to his determination in the matter.[586] This number was still continued in Jerusalem and these were their ordinary judges upon the people, and these were those whom he calleth here the ancients of the people.

Here was, as you see now, a solemn great assembly, but then consider whereabout: about nothing else but to seek the ways and the means how they might by some wile[587] take and put an innocent unto death. So may we see that every great council is not always a good council, but as two or three be a good council that come together in God's name to commune[588] and counsel about good, and among them

is God (witnessing our Savior[589] where he saith, "Wheresoever are two or three gathered together in my name, there am I too myself in the mids of them"),[590] so when men assemble them together to devise and counsel about mischief and wretchedness, the more that are at it the worse is the council and the less to be regarded, be their personages in the sight of the world never so seemly[591] and their authority never so great as these that here assemble about the death of Christ were the chief heads and rulers of the people, and specially the chief of the spiritualty,[592] so that those to whom it specially belonged to provide for an innocent's surety, they were these, lo, that specially gathered together to compass[593] an innocent's death. Out of such council God keep every good man. For that holy king and prophet David, speaking of blessedness, putteth in the beginning of all his psalter for a principal blessedness: *Beatus vir qui non abit in consilium impiorum* ("Blessed is that man that hath not gone into the council of wicked men"),[594] that is to wit, that unto their wicked council hath not been partner nor given his assent. For likewise as God is in the mids[595] of the good council, so in the middest[596] of an evil council is there undoubtedly the devil.

But why went they about[597] so busily to take him by some wily train rather than boldly by force? The Gospel showeth the cause: "For they were afeard of the people." His living was so holy, his doctrine was so heavenly, his miracles were so many and so marvelous, that — though the priests, the scribes, and the Pharisees that bore the rule deeply desired his death for their malicious anger and envy — yet the people of their own minds so highly did esteem him that, if he had been taken in their company, they would not have failed to fight for him. And therefore agreed this great assembly that they would not take him on the holy day, *ne forte tumultus fiat in populo* ("lest there should arise some seditious business among the people").[598] The people they feared, but God they feared not at all. And as the prophet saith, *Illic trepidaverunt timore, ubi non fuit timor* ("There trembled they for dread, where the dread was not").[599] For as for the people, they might percase[600] by policy have founden the means to master, but God might they never master. The wavering

582 split **583** Mt 27:51–52 **584** Jn 12:19 **585** become **586** Nm 11:16–17 **587** stratagem **588** speak **589** *witnessing…Savior:* as our Savior testifies

590 Mt 18:20 **591** stately **592** clergy **593** contrive **594** Ps 1:1 **595** middle **596** most central part **597** *Went… about:* did they undertake **598** Mt

26:5 and Mk 14:2 **599** Ps 13(14):5 **600** perhaps

people they found the means on the morrow so to turn against Christ, that as fast[601] as they honored him and lauded him within five days before, and not long afore that would fain[602] have made
5   him king, as fast on the morrow they mocked him and cried out to have him crucified. But God, when all this great council had done their uttermost, the Godhead (I say) of Christ himself (for his Father and himself and their Holy Ghost are all three but
10   one God) raised up his dead body again and, maugre[603] their men whom they set to keep his grave, he rose and went out through the hard stone, and after sent such a vengeance upon them all that from their misused liberty they be fallen ever since in ev-
15   ery part of the world into perpetual thralldom.

And on this great assembled council against Christ, that thought themselves so strong and their wily devices so wise that they would, with the provision of that assembled council, utterly destroy
20   the innocent, are also well verified the words of the prophet: *Qui habitat in caelis irridebit eos, et Dominus subsanabit eos* ("He that dwelleth in heaven shall laugh them to scorn, and our Lord shall make them a mow").[604] For soon after was their council
25   dissolved, and their council house drawn down, and all the city destroyed, and he whom they killed with their council in despite of their council liveth and reigneth in heaven, while the foolish wretched wily counselors (such as die in their sin) lie weeping and
30   wailing, the devil's burning prisoners, in the deep dungeon of hell.

The Prayer

Gracious God, give me thy grace so to consider the punishment of that false great council that gathered
35   together against thee, that I be never to thy displeasure partner, nor give mine assent to follow the sinful device of any wicked council.

The Fourth Lecture

But there entered Satan into Judas, whose surname is
40   *Iscariot, one of the twelve. Then went he to the princes of the priests and to the chief priests to betray him to them. And he had communication with the princes of the priests and with the rulers in what manner he* *should betray him to them. And he said unto them:*
"What will you give me, and[605] *I shall deliver him*
45   *to you?" And they, when they heard him, were well apaid*[606] *and promised and covenanted with him to give him money, and appointed to give him thirty groats. And he made them promise, and from that time forth he sought opportunity how that he might*
50   *at most commodity*[607] *betray him out of presence*[608] *of the people.*

Upon these words, good Christian people, is there given us the occasion to speak yet of the third cause of Christ's Passion: that is to wit, upon what occa-
55   sion the false traitor Judas was first moved to fall to this heinous treason. For the perceiving whereof, we must here repeat you one thing that was done a few days before. As it is remembered in the twenty-sixth chapter of Saint Matthew, and in the fourteenth of
60   Saint Mark, and in the twelfth of Saint John, our Savior six days before the feast of Pascha went into Bethany, where he had before raised Lazarus from death to life.[609] There had he supper prepared for him, in the house of Simon, the leper whom Christ
65   had cured. Martha served them, and Lazarus was one of the guests that sat at the supper. Then came there Mary Magdalene, sister unto Lazarus and Martha, and she took a pound-weight of ointment of nard, truly made and very dear,[610] and therewith
70   anointed she Christ's feet, and wiped them with the hairs of her head. And over that she broke the alabaster in which she brought it, and poured all the remnant on his head. And all the house smelled sweet of the savor of that sweet ointment.
75

Then Judas, which after fell to the treason and betrayed his master, grudged[611] therewith and was wroth therewith and said, "Wherefore was not this ointment sold for three hundred pence and given to poor folk? It might have been sold for a great deal,
80   yea, more than for three hundred pence, and given to poor folk." And thus said the thief, not for anything that he cared for poor folk, but, as the Gospel saith, because he was a thief and bore the purse, into which he would fain[612] have had the price of that
85   ointment so that he might thereof, after his customable[613] manner, have stolen out a part. Our Savior mildly answered for Mary Magdalene and said, "Why reprove you this woman? As for poor men you shall have ever with you, but me shall ye not
90

---

601 earnestly   **602** gladly   **603** in spite of   **604** *mow*: derisive grimace. Ps 2:4   **605** if   **606** pleased   **607** advantage   **608** the company   **609** Mt 26:6–15; Mk 14:3–10; Jn 12:1–8   **610** costly; expensive   **611** complained   **612** gladly   **613** usual

ever have." And then opened he the mystery secretly wrought by God in the open work of her good affection, that where she did it to show how glad she was of his presence there, as the manner was that folk at feasts with pleasant sweet odors used to gladden their guests, God wrought therein, as our Savior there declared, the signification of his burying. For the manner then was in that country to anoint the dead corpse with sweet odors, as we dress the winding sheet here with sweet herbs and flowers.

And then whereas the rude grudging words of Judas were spoken to her reproof, and in manner of her rebuke, our Savior on the other side even there openly showed that for that deed should she forever, with the preaching of that Gospel, be renowned and honored throughout all the world—so pleasant is to God the good affection of the heart declared by the frank[614] outward deed. For him must we serve, though specially with the mind (which if it be not good, vitiateth[615] all together), yet are we bound to serve him also with body and goods and all, for all have we received of him. But Judas, the covetous wretch, when he saw that this ointment was not sold so that he might steal a piece of the price, and then saw our Savior allow[616] her devotion in the deed and disallow his finding of that fault, as mildly as his Master touched him, yet could not the proud beast bear it, but beside his covetise fell unto malice too. And the devil took his time[617] and entered into his heart, and thereunto did put the suggestion of his horrible treason, and made him to devise and determine that the money which he lost by the anointing of his Master he would get it up again by the betraying of his Master. And thereupon came he to this assembly that we speak of now, and unsent-for presented himself unto them to help forward their ungracious[618] council.

And therefore, good reader, here we may well consider that when men are in device about mischief,[619] if they bring their purpose properly[620] to pass, cause have they none to be proud and praise their own wits. For the devil it is himself that bringeth their matters about much more, a great deal, than they. There was once a young man fallen in a lewd mind toward a woman, and she was such as he could conceive none hope to get her, and therefore

was falling to a good point[621] in his own mind to let that lewd enterprise pass. He mishapped[622] nevertheless to show his mind to another wretch, which encouraged him to go forward and leave it not. "For begin thou once, man, the matter," quoth he, "and never fear it; let the devil alone with the remnant; he shall bring it to pass in such wise as thyself alone canst not devise how." I trow[623] that wretch had learned that counsel of these priests and these ancients, assembled here together against Christ at this council. For here you see that while they were at their wits' end how to bring their purpose about in the taking of Christ, and were at a point to defer the matter and put it over till some other time, the devil sped them by and by.[624] For he entered into Judas' heart, and brought him to them to betray him forthwith out of hand.[625]

And therefore at his first coming, he went roundly[626] to the matter and said unto them, "What will ye give me and I shall deliver him to you?" Here shall you see Judas play the jolly[627] merchant, I trow. For he knoweth how fain[628] all this great council would be to have him delivered. He knoweth well also that it will be hard for any man to deliver him but one of his own disciples. He knoweth well also that of all the disciples, there would none be so false a traitor to betray his Master but himself alone. And therefore is this ware,[629] Judas, all in thine own hand. Thou hast a monopoly thereof. And while it is so sought for and so sore[630] desired, and that by so many, and them that are also very rich, thou mayest now make the price of thine own ware thyself, even at thine own pleasure; and therefore ye shall, good readers, see Judas wax[631] now a great rich man with this one bargain. But now the priests and these judges were on the other side covetous too; and as glad as they were of this ware, yet while it was offered them to sell,[632] they thought the merchant was needy, and that to such a needy merchant a little money would be welcome, and money they offered him, but not much. For thirty groats they said they will give, which amounteth not much above ten shillings of our English money. Now would we look that the fool would have set up[633] his ware, namely being such ware as it was, so precious in itself that all the money and plate in the whole world were too little

---

614 generous   **615** impairs, corrupts
616 approve   **617** *took his time:* chose
the right time   **618** wicked   **619** *in
device about mischief:* contriving evil

620 completely   **621** resolution   **622** had
the misfortune   **623** believe   **624** *sped
them by and by:* made them succeed
immediately   **625** *out of hand:* at once

626 directly   **627** arrogant   **628** gladly
629 merchandise   **630** greatly
631 become   **632** for sale   **633** *set up:*
raised the price of

to give for it. But now what did the fool? To show himself a substantial merchant and not a huckster, he gently[634] let them have it even at their own price.

I wot[635] it well that, of the value of the money that Judas had, all folk are not of one mind, but whereas the text saith *triginta argenteos*,[636] some men call *argenteus* a coin of one value and some of another. And some put a difference between *argenteus* and *denarius*, and say that *denarius* is but the tenth part of *argenteus*. But I suppose that *argenteus* was the same silver coin which the Romans at that time used stamped in silver, in which they expressed the image of the emperor's visage and the superscription of the emperor's name, and was in Greek called *drachma*, being in weight about the eighth part of an ounce. For of such coin there are yet many remaining both of Augustus' days and Tiberius' and of Nero's too. So that if the coin were that (for greater silver coin I nowhere find that the emperor coined at that time), then was Judas' reward the value of ten shillings of our English money, after the old usual groats used in the time of King Edward the Third, and long before and long after.

The ointment was of nard of the true making, as the Gospel declareth in this word, *nardi pistici*.[637] And that ointment truly made was very costly, which was the cause that the true making was less used, and folk for the great cost thereof used another making thereof that was called counterfeit ointment of nard. But this was of the true making, and was (as the Gospel saith) precious, and that so far-forth[638] that Judas valued it at three hundred deniers, which I take for three hundred pieces of the selfsame coin that was called *argenteus*. For if it were but a coin (as some take it) that were worth but the tenth part of that, then had all the ointment not been much above the value of four groats, which had been no such thing as had been likely that the evangelists would have called precious. And therefore I reckon that ointment to have been esteemed by Judas at a hundred shillings. And now was his reward ten shillings, which is the tenth part of that hundred shillings, as thirty groats is the tenth part of three hundred. And thus hath he by the betraying of his Master's body the tenth part of the value of that ointment whereof he lost his advantage by the anointing of his Master's body.

Now if it be, as some doctors reckon, that he minded to win as much by his treason as he reckoned for his own part lost in that ointment, then seemeth it after this count and reckoning that, of such as came in his keeping, he was after his customable[639] manner wont to steal the tenth. And then was Judas a figure of two false shrews[640] at once: the one the parishen[641] that stealeth his tithe from his curate, to whom his duty were to pay it in God's stead; the other yet the worse thief of them both, the evil curate himself, which, when he receiveth it, misspendeth upon himself such substance thereof as above his own necessary finding[642] God putteth him in trust to bestow upon the poor needy people.

It is a world[643] also to mark and consider how the false wily devil hath, in everything that he doth for his servants, ever more one point of his envious property,[644] that is to wit, to provide (his own purpose obtained) that they shall have of his service for their own part as little commodity as he can, even here in this world. For like as he got here unto[645] Judas no more advantage of his heinous treason (the occasion of his final destruction) but only this poor ten shillings — whereas if his Master Christ had lived, and he still carried his purse, there is no doubt but that he should at sundry times have stolen out for his part far above five times that — so fareth he[646] with all his other servants.

Look for whom he doth most in any kind of filthy fleshly delight, or false wily winning,[647] or wretched worldly worship; let him that attaineth it in his unhappy service make his reckoning in the end of all that feast and count well what is come in and what he hath paid therefore — that is to wit, lay all his pleasures and his displeasures together — and I dare say he shall find in the end that he had been a great winner if he never had had any of them both, so much grief shall he find himself to have felt, far above all his pleasure, even in those days in which his fantasies were in their flowers and prospered, besides the pain and heaviness of heart that now in the end grudgeth[648] and grieveth his conscience, when the time of his pleasure is passed and the fear of hell followeth at hand.

Let us therefore leave the devil's false deceitful service and take nothing at his hand. For he nothing giveth but trifles, nor never giveth half an inch

634 generously; courteously   **635** know   **636** Mt 26:15   **637** Jn 12:3   **638** *so far-forth:* to such an extent   **639** usual, habitual   **640** rascals   **641** parishioner   **642** support   **643** *It . . . world:* It is a marvel   **644** *envious property:* attribute of envy   **645** *like as . . . unto:* just as he obtained here for   **646** *fareth he:* he behaves   **647** gain   **648** troubles of pleasure without a whole ell[649] of pain. And yet had Judas not the wit to disdain their simple niggardous[650] reward, but continued for it in his treason still, till he had wretchedly done it. And from that time of that reward promised him, with which yet (as it seemeth) they would not trust him till they had the ware in their own hand, he studied and sought the time in which he might peaceably deliver our Lord, when the people were out of the way.

In this, as the great clerk[651] Origen declareth, this Judas was a figure also of many other Judases.[652] For in many places when the people be out of the way and gone aside from the faith, then shall there some false wretch that hath been with Christ many a fair day, and hath been his disciple, and among other true disciples hath faithfully preached the truth, come forth in the devil's name among the people and, for wretched worldly winning to be gotten by their favor, shall falsely betray the truth and cause to be spitefully killed the faithful true doctrine of Christ. But woe may that wretch be by whom the truth is betrayed.

A Prayer

O my sweet Savior Christ, whom thine own wicked disciple, entangled with the devil, through vile wretched covetise betrayed, inspire, I beseech thee, the marvel of thy majesty with the love of thy goodness so deep into mine heart that, in respect of the least point of thy pleasure, my mind may set always this whole wretched world at nought.[653]

The Fifth Lecture

Before the feast of the Pascha, Jesus, knowing that his hour came on to go out of this world unto his Father, whereas he had loved those that were his, unto the end he loved them.

In these words the holy evangelist Saint John, whom Christ so tenderly loved that on his breast he leaned in his Last Supper, and to him secretly he uttered[654] the false dissimuled[655] traitor, and into whose custody he commended on the cross his own dear heavy[656] mother, and which is (for the manifold tokens of Christ's special favor) specially called in the Gospel, *discipulus ille quem diligebat Iesus* ("the disciple that Jesus loved"),[657] declareth here what a manner of faithful lover our holy Savior was, of whom himself was so beloved. For unto those words he putteth and forthwith joineth the rehearsing of his bitter Passion, beginning with his Maundy,[658] and therein his humble washing of his disciples' feet, the sending forth of the traitor, and after that his doctrine, his prayer, his taking, his judging, his scourging, his crucifying, and all the whole piteous tragedy of his most bitter Passion. Before all which things he setteth these fore-rehearsed[659] words to declare that all these things that Christ did, in all this he did it for very love. Which love he well declared unto his disciples by many manner means at the time of his Maundy, giving them in charge[660] that in loving each other they should follow the example of himself. For he, those that he loved, he loved unto the end, and so would he that they should. He was not an unconstant lover that doth, as many do, love for a while and then upon a light occasion[661] leave off and turn from a friend to an enemy, as the false traitor Judas did. But he still so persevereth in love unto the very end, that for very love he came to that painful end; and yet not only for his friends that were already his, but for his enemies, to make them friends of his, and that not for his benefit but only for their own.

And here shall we note that, whereas the Gospel saith in this place and diverse others that Christ should go out of this world unto his Father (as where he said, "Poor men shall ye always have, but me shall you not always have"),[662] it is not meant that he shall be no more with his Church here in the world nor come no more here till the Day of Doom. For himself promised and said, "I am with you all the days even unto the end of the world."[663] He is here in his Godhead; he is here in the Blessed Sacrament of the altar, and sundry times hath here, since his ascension, appeared unto diverse holy men. But those other words, as Saint Jerome saith (and Saint Bede too), are understood[664] that he will not be here in corporal conversation[665] among us, as he was

---

649 unit of length, roughly equivalent to a yard   **650** niggardly; miserly   **651** scholar   **652** See Origen's commentary on Mt 26:14–16 (*PG 13*, 1726–27).   **653** *set at nought*: regard as nothing   **654** revealed   **655** dissembling   **656** sorrowful   **657** Jn 19:26. See also Jn 13:23.   **658** Last Supper   **659** already mentioned   **660** *in charge*: as a commandment   **661** *Upon … occasion*: for a trivial reason   **662** Jn 12:8. See also Mk 14:7.   **663** Mt 28:20   **664** interpreted as meaning   **665** *corporal conversation*: bodily presence

before his Passion among his disciples, with whom he commonly did eat and drink and talk.[666]

Let us here deep consider the love of our Savior Christ, which so loved his unto the end, that for their sakes he willingly suffered that painful end, and therein declared the highest point of love that can be. For as himself saith, *Maiorem hac amorem nemo habet, quam ut animam suam ponat quis pro amicis suis* ("A greater love no man hath than to give his life for his friends").[667] This is indeed the greatest love that ever any other man had. But yet had our Savior a greater. For he gave his, and I said before, both for friend and foe.

But what a difference is there now between this faithful love of his and other kinds of false and fickle love used in this wretched world. The flatterer feigneth to love thee, for that he fareth well with thee. But now if adversity so diminish thy substance[668] that he find thy table unlaid, farewell, adieu; thy brother flatterer is gone, and getteth him to some other board,[669] and yet shall turn sometimes to thine enemy too and wait[670] thee with a shrewd[671] word.

Who can in adversity be sure of many of his friends when our Savior himself was at his taking left alone and forsaken of his? When thou shalt go hence, who will go with thee? If thou were a king, will not all thy realm send thee forth alone and forget thee? Shall not thine own flesh let thee walk away, naked seely[672] soul, thou little wottest[673] whither? Howbeit, if thou die in the devil's danger, some fleshly lover of thine may soon after hap to follow thee, some such as in lecherous love hath borne thee filthy company. But if[674] such a lover of thine happen there to come to thee, there will there be no love touches between you, but cursing and banning[675] shall you lie together wretchedly burning forever, where each of you shall be a hot faggot of fire to your filthy fellow.

Let us every man, therefore, in time learn to love, as we should, God above all things and all other things for him. And whatsoever love be not referred to that end, that is to wit, to the pleasure of God, it is a very vain and an unfruitful love. And whatsoever love we bear to any creature whereby we love God the less, that love is a loathsome love and hindereth us from heaven. Love no child of thine own so tenderly but that[676] thou couldest be content so to sacrifice it to God as Abraham was ready with Isaac,[677] if it so were that God would so command thee. And since God will not so do, offer thy child otherwise to God's service. For whatsoever thing we love whereby we break God's commandment, that love we better than God — and that is a love deadly and damnable. Now, since our Lord hath so loved us for our salvation, let us diligently call for his grace that against[678] his great love we be not found unkind.[679]

A Prayer

O my sweet Savior Christ, which, of thine undeserved love toward mankind so kindly wouldest suffer the painful death of the cross, suffer not me to be cold nor lukewarm in love again toward thee.

THE SECOND CHAPTER

Of the sending of Saint Peter and Saint John, the first day of the Unleavened Loaves, specified in the twenty-sixth of Saint Matthew, the fourteenth of Saint Mark, the twenty-second of Saint Luke, and the thirteenth of Saint John[680]

The first day of the Unleavened Loaves, when the Paschal lamb was offered, in which the Paschal lamb must needs be killed, there came the disciples to Jesus and say to him, "Whither wilt thou that we go and make ready for thee, that thou mayest eat the Paschal lamb?" And he sendeth of his disciples Peter and John, saying, "Go you and make ready for us the Paschal lamb that we may eat it." But they said, "Where wilt thou that we shall make it ready?" And he said unto them, "Go you into the city to a certain man. Lo, as you shall be entering into the city, there shall meet you a man bearing a pot of water; follow you him into the house into which he entereth. And ye shall say to the goodman[681] *of the house, 'The Master saith to thee, "My time is near, with thee I make my Paschal.*[682] *Where is my refection,*[683] *where is my place where I may eat*

---

666 The interpretations of St. Jerome and St. Bede can be found in the *Glossa ordinaria,* one of the biblical glosses available in the glossed Bibles of More's period. **667** Jn 15:13 **668** wealth

669 table **670** spy upon **671** abusive **672** pitiable **673** know **674** *But if:* Unless **675** damning **676** *but that:* unless **677** Gn 22 **678** in return for **679** lacking in natural gratitude **680** In

the text that follows, Gerson inserted letters identifying which passages came from which evangelist; those letters have been removed. **681** master **682** Passover **683** place of refreshment

my Paschal with my disciples?"' And he shall show you
a great supping place paved,[684] *and there make you it*
ready." And his disciples went and came into the city.
And, as they went, they found as Jesus had said unto
them. And they made ready the Paschal lamb. When
the evening was come, he came with the twelve. And
when the hour was come, he set down at the table, and
the twelve apostles with him.

The Homily or Lecture
upon the Second Chapter

I have before, good Christian readers, showed
you in the exposition of the first chapter the ordinance[685] and institution of the Feast of the Paschal Lamb and of the Feast of the Unleavened
Bread, and how the offering of that lamb was a figure of the offering up of Christ, the very unspotted lamb, that should be offered up to cleanse and
wash away the spots of our sin with the innocent
blood of himself that had no spot of sin of his own.
The Paschal lamb was commanded to be sacrificed
and eaten after the equinoctial in vere,[686] the fourteenth day of the month. And on the morrow, and
so forth seven days after (that is to wit, beginning
the fifteenth day), was the Feast of the Unleavened
Bread, during which space they were commanded
that they should have no leaven in their house.

Ye must understand also that though the first day
of the Feast of the Unleavened Loaves was the fifteenth day, yet likewise as we begin every feast from
the noon before, so did the Jews begin that first day
of the Feast of the Unleavened Loaves in the evening before, when they might see the moon and
the stars appear in the element.[687] And so, though
the eating of the Paschal lamb was the fourteenth
day of the month, and the first day of the Feast of
the Unleavened Loaves was on the fifteenth day, yet
by reason that the same first day of the feast began
at the evening before (that is to wit, in the evening
of the fourteenth day, in which evening the Paschal lamb was to be sacrificed and eaten), these two
feasts were, as you see, coincident together. For the
one fell in the beginning of the other. And for this
cause were each of them called by the both names,

that is to wit, by the name of "the Feast of the Paschal" and also by the name of "the Feast of the Unleavened Bread." For since the Feast of the Paschal
Lamb was the chief feast and was also the beginning
of the other, all the Feast of the Unleavened Loaves
was called the "Paschal." And again because the first
day of the Feast of the Unleavened Loaves, though
it were the fifteenth day of the month, yet, since it
began (I say) in the evening of the fourteenth day
(at such time as the Paschal lamb was sacrificed and
eaten), the Feast of the Paschal Lamb was also called
the "Feast of the Unleavened Bread" and "the first
day of the Feast of the Unleavened Bread."

And for this cause do both Saint Matthew and
Saint Mark call the Sheer Thursday[688] in which
Christ made his Maundy[689] the first day of the Unleavened Loaves, saying: "The first day of the Unleavened Loaves, in which the Paschal lamb must be
killed and sacrificed, the disciples came to Jesus and
asked him, 'Whither wilt thou that we shall go to
make ready the Paschal lamb?'"[690] And, as I said, the
Jews called also the Feast of the Unleavened Bread
the "Feast of Paschal." And specially they called and
hallowed by that name of "Paschal" the first day of
the Unleavened Bread, which was the morrow after
the eating of the Paschal lamb.

And after that manner of their naming that day
the "Feast of Paschal," Saint John in the thirteenth
chapter of his Gospel: *Ante diem festum Paschae,*
sciens Iesus quia venit hora eius ut transeat ex hoc
mundo ad patrem, etc. ("Before the holy day of Paschal, Jesus, knowing that his time was come that he
should go out of this world unto his Father, and so
forth").[691] Here, lo, Saint John calleth Sheer Thursday, in the evening of which day the Paschal lamb
was eaten, he calleth it (I say) by the name of "the
day before that feastful[692] day of the Paschal," because the Jews did celebrate the morrow (after the
Paschal eaten)[693] very solemnly, and called (as I have
told you) that feast the Feast of the Paschal. And
therefore Saint John here saying *Ante diem festum*
Paschae, and calling Sheer Thursday "the day before the feastful day of Paschal" (because the Jews
so used to call the first day of the Unleavened
Bread that began in the evening before, in which
the Paschal lamb was killed), used such a manner of

---

684 prepared   **685** ordained usage
686 *equinoctial in vere:* equinox in spring-
time   **687** sky   **688** Maundy Thursday

689 Last Supper   **690** The quotation is
an adaptation of Gerson's *Monotessaron,*
composed of passages from Luke as well

as Matthew and Mark.   **691** Jn 13:1
692 festal   **693** was eaten

speaking as we might call "Christmas Even" the day before the feastful day of Christmas.

I would not, good readers, stick so long upon the declaration of this point (as a thing wherein some shall peradventure[694] take little savor),[695] saving that I thought it not a time all lost to let you know that, upon[696] the Scripture in this point mistaken,[697] the Church of Greece fell from the Church of the Latins in a point or twain. For upon their own wrong construing this place of Saint John, they say that Christ did anticipate the time of eating his Paschal lamb with his apostles, and (where the very day was the fourteenth day after their vernal equinoctial[698] in the evening) he did it, say they, the day before.[699]

And you shall understand that this is the cause for which they consecrate the body of Christ in leavened bread, contrary to the Latin Church, which consecrateth in unleavened bread. For they say (and truth it is) that the Feast of the Unleavened Loaves began the fifteenth day. And then (say they) he consecrated his blessed body at his Maundy on the thirteenth day (that was, say they, Sheer Thursday), and therefore he consecrated then with leavened bread. Now to this we have showed you that the first day of that Feast of Unleavened Bread began the feast in the evening before, that is to wit,[700] on Sheer Thursday at night, and that Christ made then his Maundy in the very time that was by the law appointed to the eating the Paschal lamb. And since he intended to fulfill the law, so was it most convenient that he should and most likely that he would — and so of truth he did, as the three evangelists, Saint Matthew, Saint Mark, and Saint Luke, plainly do declare. For they three agree together that it was in the first day of the Unleavened Bread and in which day the Paschal lamb must be killed. And so it appeareth by them that, though the first day of that feast was the fifteenth day, yet the feast of that fifteenth day began in the evening before in which the Paschal lamb was eaten, and eaten (as it appeareth plainly) with unleavened bread.

And verily methinketh that if it so had been (as it was not) that Christ had made his Maundy a day

before the time, yet would not that sufficiently serve for the proof of their purpose[701] that he consecrated in leavened bread. For though it be a good proof that, since he consecrated in the Feast of the Unleavened Loaves, he consecrated not in leavened bread (because the law forbade them to have any leaven in the house), yet if he had consecrated five days before that feast began, it would not prove that he consecrated in leavened bread. For they might then and at all times have unleavened bread, since that was at no time forbidden.

But surely the Church of Greece was far overseen[702] in this point and diverse others, in which they partly acknowledged their errors after and were reformed in general councils,[703] and yet returned of frowardness[704] to their errors again, and in conclusion we see whereto they be comen.[705]

But ye shall understand that, when I speak of the Church of Greece in this error, I speak but of the posteriors.[706] For the old holy doctors of the Greeks were of the contrary mind, as appeareth in this point by the plain words of Saint Eusebius and Saint Chrysostom both.[707] And that you may the more plainly perceive what peril it was unto them to fall to an opinion contrary to the Church by construing the Scripture after[708] a few folks' fantasies, those Greeks that began this opinion were fain[709] in conclusion for the defense of their error to say that Saint Matthew, Saint Mark, and Saint Luke wrote in that point wrong all three, and that therefore Saint John wrote otherwise and corrected them — which untrue saying of theirs is so far out of all frame[710] that it is among Christian men more than shame to say it, that any of the four evangelists should in the story write anything false, for then which of them might we trust, since we can be no more sure of the one than of the other. But now let us proceed forth in the letter.[711]

"When his disciples had asked him where his pleasure was that they should make ready the Paschal for him, he sent two of his apostles, that is to wit, Peter and John, and said unto them: 'Go you and prepare the Paschal lamb for us that we may eat it.'"

---

694 perhaps **695** enjoyment **696** on the basis of **697** wrongly understood **698** equinox **699** A passage concerned with the dating of the Last Supper — added here to the text by Rastell in 1557 on the basis of a letter written by More to his secretary, John Harris — has been omitted in this edition. See *CW* 13:

88/22–90/14, 91/14–22, and notes. **700** say **701** proposition **702** mistaken **703** *general councils:* such as the councils of Lyons (1274) and Florence (1438) **704** unruliness; rebelliousness **705** *be comen:* have come **706** those later in time **707** More may be thinking of quotations from Eusebius and Chrysostom

in the *Catena aurea,* a collection of patristic quotations on the four Gospels made by St. Thomas Aquinas. **708** according to **709** willing **710** *so far . . . frame:* so remote from any kind of established order **711** text

Our Savior, which said of himself, *Non veni solvere legem sed adimplere* ("I am not come to break the law but to fulfill it"),[712] likewise as he would be circumcised first before he changed that sacrament into the more perfect sacrament of baptism, so, for the fulfilling of the Old Law, before he would offer up his own blessed body, the very unspotted lamb, upon the cross, and before also that he would institute the eating of his own blessed body in form of bread and wine in the Blessed Sacrament of the altar, he would first fulfill the precept of the law by the eating of the Paschal lamb in time and manner appointed by the law, and so fulfill and finish the figure, and institute in the stead thereof the sacrament of highest perfection, the Blessed Sacrament of the altar, and offer up for the spots of our sin his own unspotted body as the most sweet sacrifice unto the Father upon the altar of the cross.

It followeth: "Then they said unto him, 'Where wilt thou that we shall make it ready?' And he said unto them: 'Go you into the city to a certain man. Lo, as you be entering into the city, there shall a man meet you bearing a pot of water; follow you him into the house into which he entereth, and you shall say to the goodman[713] of the house: "The Master saith to thee, 'My time is near, with thee I make my Paschal. Where is my place where I may with my disciples eat the Paschal?'" And he shall show you a great supping place on high paved,[714] and there do you make it ready.'"

In these words it appeareth well that our Lord, when he sent Saint Peter and Saint John unto the house where they should prepare his Maundy, he would neither name them the dweller of the house nor tell them any known token of the house, of which thing diverse of the old doctors conject[715] and tell diverse causes. Some say he sent them to a man not named in token that God will come not only to men that are in the world famous and of great name but also to folk of none estimation in the count of the world nor of no name. Some others say (and both twain may well be true) that forasmuch as our Savior (to whom nothing was unknown) knew the promise of the false traitor Judas made unto the Jews upon the day before to betray him, and that he went about ever after that to seek a time fit therefore where he might betray him to

them out of sight of the people, if he should have named the man or the place, the traitor might have caused him and his disciples to be taken before his Maundy made and his holy body consecrated in the Blessed Sacrament. And therefore, albeit that[716] if the traitor had come and all the whole town with him, our Savior could have kept them all off with one word of his mouth or with one thought of his holy heart, yet this way liked his high wisdom as the most meet and convenient by which he would keep the traitor from the accomplishment of his traitorous purpose till the time should come in which himself had determined to suffer it. And therefore our Savior used[717] himself in this point wonderfully. For albeit that the two disciples whom he sent were of all his apostles the most special chosen and most in trust and favor with him, Saint Peter, which (as it appeareth in Scripture and as the doctors say) specially loved him, and Saint John, which (as the Scripture saith and the doctors thereon) specially was beloved of him, yet would he not take them aside and tell them the name of the man, lest he might thereby have given occasion of envy or suspicion to Judas, or peradventure grief to the remnant, if Christ should have seemed to trust them with that errand secretly with which he would trust none of them; he gave them therefore their errand in so strange a fashion that neither themselves nor any of the other ten could wit[718] what to think therein. For he answered them as though he would say, "Where you shall prepare I will not tell you, nor who shall bring you thither I will not show you, but to let you see what I can do when me list,[719] such a token shall I tell you to bring you thither as neither no man knoweth nor no man can know but myself that am able at the time to make it so."

Then it followeth: "And his disciples went forth and came into the city, and they found as Jesus had said unto them and prepared there the Paschal."

Here had his apostles and by them we too a proof of his glorious Godhead, secretly covered and unseen under the cloak of his seeming feeble manhead. And that not in this thing alone, but in this among many more, some of other kind of miracle, and some also like unto this. For as he did here show his disciples where they should meet the man with the water pot and then what he would have

---

712 Mt 5:17   **713** master   **714** *on . . .*
paved: prepared in an upper-level room

715 conjecture   **716** *albeit that:* although   **719** *me list:* it pleases me
717 conducted   **718** know

them do further, and that his bidding should surely be fulfilled and obeyed, so did he on the Palm Sunday before, when he sent his disciples and told them where they should find the ass and the colt tied, and bade them take them boldly without any leave of the owner, and, whosoever would say aught[720] unto them therefor,[721] they should say that their Master must occupy[722] them. A much like manner of message he gave his two apostles now, telling them where they should meet with a strange man and so forth what they should do further.

Now who but God could surely send men on such manner messages in which they should be sure to find such things as are unto all creatures unsure and uncertain, as things accounted to fall under chance and hap?[723] And therefore, while they found everything come to pass as he had before told them, they might (and we may) surely know him for God. For who could tell that the man with his pot of water walking on his errand and the two apostles going forth on theirs, neither party looking for other, should so begin to set forth and in such wise hold on their way that they should, at a place which neither of the both parties appointed, so justly[724] meet together? This could none do but he that not only beheld both parties at once but was able also to put in both their minds to set forth in time such as should serve therefore, and to moderate and measure their paces himself in such wise as themselves wist[725] not why, and by his sure providence (seeming to themselves hap, fortune, or chance) suddenly to meet together. This thing can there of himself none other do but he that hath the acts and the deeds of all creatures in his own hand, that of two sparrows being both not worth a halfpenny, not so much as the one falleth, as our Savior saith, upon the ground without him.[726]

Then it followeth further: "When the evening was come, Christ came with his twelve. And when the hour was come, he sat him down at the table and his twelve apostles with him."

Notwithstanding that the bishops and the Pharisees had before given commandment (as appeareth in the eleventh chapter of the Gospel of Saint John) that if any man wist where Christ were, he should give them knowledge that they might take him,[727] and notwithstanding also that his own disciple Judas had promised them to do that traitorous deed himself, yet our Savior, since his time came on in which he was determined willingly to die, letted[728] not to come into the city and came also not alone but with his twelve apostles waiting upon him, whereby his coming was well likely to be noted. But he wist well enough what would befall, and that upon any marking of that coming he should not be taken. For he would not so be taken, nor would not so prevent[729] his traitor of his purpose, nor so disturb him of his promise, nor so make him lose his reward, but, benignly suffering him and taking patience with him, and yet offering him grace and kindness to win him, brought him to the Maundy with him. And therefore saith Saint Mark, "He came and his twelve with him."[730] Whereby it should seem that Saint Peter and Saint John, after their errand done, resorted unto Christ again and made him report of their speed,[731] and so came in company with the other ten unto the Maundy with him.

Judas the traitor, in such places as the evangelists make mention of his going to the council and assembly of the priests to offer them his service in the treason, both[732] Saint Matthew, Saint Mark, and Saint Luke make specially mention that he was one of the twelve.[733] And here we see therefore by the evangelists not only mention that he came with our Lord but also that he sat at the supper with our Lord, and so for all the treason that the traitor wrought, yet was the traitor Christ's apostle still. And this point the evangelists again and again rehearse, not only to the shame of his traitorous falsehead, in betraying such a Master with whom he was so taken forth[734] to be so near about him, one of that few chosen number and so specially put in trust, but also that we should note well and mark thereby that the vice of a vicious person vitiateth not the company or congregation. For Christ with his twelve apostles were a holy company as a company, though one companion of the company was a very false traitorous wretch. And for all his falsehead, both before that in theft and then in treason too, Christ abode still with him among his other apostles, and his ungraciousness letted[735] not but that of that company (as evil as he was) yet one he

---

was. Nor now likewise the vices of vicious folk in Christ's Church cannot let but that his Catholic Church, of which they be part, is, for all their unholiness, his holy Catholic Church, with which he hath promised to be unto the end of the world.

Upon this chapter among many things that men may take occasion to note, I note specially twain: one, the example that our Savior here giveth us to be diligent and studious in the keeping of his New Law (which he hath ordained to endure in this world as long as the world shall last), while himself was so diligent in the observing of the Old Law (which, given unto Moses, himself came to change into so far the better and to deliver us from the sore yoke thereof). But surely I fear me sore[736] that with a great part of Christian people the law of Christ is worse kept a great deal than was with the Jews the law of Moses at the coming of Christ, when it was kept worst. As for the sovereign points of patience and charity and contempt of the world, wherein our Savior saith in the sixth chapter of Saint Matthew that he would have his new Church far pass and excel the old synagogue,[737] be so far, I fear me, let slip and forgotten that even in the very plain precepts we be more negligent than they. The Jews were in the keeping of the spirit of the law so negligent that God therefore, by the mouths of his prophets David and Isaiah, showed himself to reject and set at nought[738] their outward ceremonies, sacrifices, and observances of their law, wherein he confessed them diligent, and said that with so little as they used of the other, he had of them so much that he was full thereof fastidious[739] and weary. Not that those things misliked[740] him, either done of their private devotion or for the fulfilling of the law, but for that they rested and satisfied their hearts in them, and both left the better things undone and also did much evil too, trusting that those outward works of their ceremonies and sacrifices should recompense it, and afore God bear it out.[741] Which erroneous mind of theirs our Lord by the prophets reproved, declaring that on their fasting days they would, while they fasted from meat, not fast from sin but strive and chide and fight and sharply sue their debtors. He bade them amend those faults and be charitable and forgive and give, and then would he better allow their bare offering and sacrifice by word than now, with these fashions used,[742] he would their sacrifice in offering up of their beasts unto their no little cost. This tale that I tell you doth well appear upon the forty-ninth psalm of David and upon the fifty-eighth chapter of Isaiah, whose words to rehearse here were very long.

But now me think that we Christian folk wax[743] in worse case. For in the deeds of charity we walk, I fear me, nothing afore them. And in those evil things we be nothing behind them. And yet in the outward ceremonies also, I ween[744] we be nothing matches with them. For surely they did much more cost[745] and used more devotion than we do. Of the cost there can no man deny but that their offerings and their sacrifices were besides their tithes far more chargeable[746] and costly to them than the rites and ceremonies of Christendom are unto the Christian people. Of their diligence and devotion therein, we may well perceive, both by the places that I have spoken of (in which our Lord rejecteth their diligence therein because of their negligence of charity and their froward malicious manners[747] besides) and also by many other places in the Old Law where the commendable devotion of their costly ceremonies and sacrifices appear. Their fastings were also very painful and precise,[748] and ours negligent, slack and remiss, and now almost worn away. Their Sabbath days and their feasts kept they very solemn. How slackly we keep ours in many places, and in what manner fashion, I cannot for sorrow and very shame rehearse. As for their faith, from those that among them held on the truth, the Jews were fallen into sects one or twain. But now if we should count and reckon the sundry sects which from the true faith are fallen about in diverse parts of Almayne,[749] I fear me we should find almost as many score. I can no more but pray God therefore that we may have the grace to follow the example of our Savior and observe his New Law, which we be bounden to keep, as he observed the Old Law, which, though he came to change it, yet he would first fulfill it, for all that[750] he was not bound to keep it.

The other thing that I note in this chapter is that

---

736 *I . . . sore:* I am greatly afraid   **737** Mt 6:2–6   **738** *set at nought:* regard as nothing   **739** disgusted   **740** were displeasing to   **741** *bear it out:* make it supportable

742 *with . . . used:* with the practice of these customs   **743** grow   **744** think   **745** *did . . . cost:* expended much more money   **746** expensive   **747** *froward*

malicious manners: perverse moral conduct   **748** strict   **749** Germany   **750** *for . . . that:* even though it appeareth thereupon, as Theophilactus and Saint Bede say and Saint Chrysostom also,[751] that Christ had none house of his own, nor none of his apostles neither, as himself said of himself in the ninth chapter of Saint Luke: *Filius hominis non habet ubi caput suum reclinet* ("The Son of Man hath not where to lay his head").[752] And therefore his apostles asked him in what house he would eat his Paschal. And our Savior again, to let them see that whoso for God's sake is content to lack a house shall not be disappointed when they should need it, sent them to another man's house, they neither wist whose nor where, and yet were they there welcome and well-received.

In this we may take example also, that those that will be the disciples of Christ and followers of his apostles should not long to be great possessioners[753] and build up great palaces in this wretched wilderness of the world, wherein, to show that we have, as Saint Paul saith, "no dwelling city,"[754] our Savior and his apostles would have no dwelling house. One of the most special things to move us to the contempt of this world and to regard much the world to come is to consider that in that world we shall be forever at home and that in this world we be but wayfaring folk. And verily though it be (as indeed it is) easy enough for any man to say the word that he is here but a pilgrim, yet is it hard for many a man to let it fall feelingly and sink down deep into his heart, which (against[755] that word slightly[756] spoken once in a year) useth to rejoice and boast many times in a day, by the space peradventure of many years together, what goodly places in this world he hath of his own, in every of which continually he calleth himself at home. And that such folk reckon themselves not for pilgrims here, they feel full well at such time as our Lord calleth them hence. For then find they themselves much more loath to part from this world than pilgrims to go from their inn.

The Prayer

Almighty Jesus Christ, which wouldest for our example observe the law that thou camest to change, and being maker of the whole earth wouldest have yet no dwelling house therein, give us thy grace so to keep thine holy law and so to reckon ourselves for no dwellers but for pilgrims upon earth, that we may long and make haste, walking with faith in the way of virtuous works, to come to the glorious country wherein thou hast bought us inheritance forever with thine own precious blood.

THE THIRD CHAPTER

Of the washing of the feet, specified[757] in the thirteen chapter of the Gospel of Saint John

And when supper was done, when the devil had put into the heart of Judas, the son of Simon of Iscariot, to betray him, Jesus, knowing that his Father had given him all things into his hands, and that he was come from God and goeth to God, ariseth from supper and putteth off his clothes and took a linen cloth and did gird it about him. Then he did put water into a basin and began to wash the feet of his disciples and wipe them with the linen cloth that he was gird withal.[758] Then cometh he to Simon Peter, and Peter saith unto him, "Lord, washest thou my feet?" Jesus answered and said unto him, "What I do thou knowest not now, but thou shalt know after." Peter saith unto him, "Thou shalt never wash my feet." Jesus answered unto him, "If I wash thee not, thou shalt have no part with[759] me." Simon Peter said unto him, "Lord, not only my feet, but my hands and my head too." Jesus saith unto him, "He that is washed needeth no more but that he wash his feet, but is all clean. And you be clean, but not all." For he knew who he was should betray him. Therefore he said, "You be not clean all." Then, after that he had washed their feet, he took his clothes again. And when he was set down again at the table, he said unto them, "Wot[760] ye what I have done to you? You call me master and lord. And you say well, for so I am. Therefore if I have washed your feet, being your lord and your master, you owe[761] also one to wash another's feet. For I have given you an example that, likewise as I have done to you, so should you do too. Verily, verily, I say to you, the bondman is not more than his lord, nor an apostle greater than he that hath sent him. If you know these things, blessed shall you be if you do these things."

751 More is perhaps alluding to passages quoted in the *Catena aurea* of St. Thomas Aquinas. **752** Lk 9:58 **753** owners   **754** Heb 13:14 **755** in contrast to **756** carelessly **757** related in detail   **758** with **759** *have . . . with:* have nothing to do with **760** Know **761** ought

The Exposition

The holy evangelist Saint John, in the beginning of the thirteenth chapter, beginning to speak of the Last Supper of our Lord, showeth that our Savior, *Cum dilexisset suos qui erant in mundo, in finem dilexit eos* ("Whereas he loved those that were his which were in the world, he loved them into the end"),[762] that is to wit,[763] as some doctors say, "He loved them to the uttermost." For well ye wot the end of everything is the uttermost. And Christ loved his to the very uttermost, that is to wit, unto that extreme point of love beyond which no man could go. For he said himself, *Maiorem amorem nemo habet, quam ut animam suam ponat quis pro amicis suis* ("Greater love can there no man have, than that a man give his life for his friends").[764] This kind of extreme kindness had Christ, not to his friends only, but to his enemies too. For he gave his own life for both twain. And therefore those that he loved he loved unto the end, that is to wit, unto the very uttermost.

Some doctors expound those words, "He loved them to the end," that is to wit, not for a while and then cast them off, as many folk love in this world, but "He loved them to the end" so that when he should part out of this world (by a death so painful that the thinking thereof would make a man forget all his friends for heaviness, dread, and fear), he, the nearer he drew toward that painful terrible death, the more he remembered his twelve apostles whom he had specially loved in the world, and the more tenderly took he thought for them when he was parting out of this world. And for to show that as himself said, *Qui ad me venit non eiiciam foras* ("He that cometh to me, I will not cast him out"),[765] our Savior would not cast out Judas the traitor till he cast out himself, but, for all his traitorous purpose, tenderly went about to mend[766] him and brought him to the supper with him.

Some expound also those words, "He loved them into the end," to signify that the love that he bore them was not such a kind of love as worldly minded folk use to bear each to other—that is to wit, either for their own commodity to take pleasure by them, while that in this passage toward the end (that is to wit, the world to come) they be by the way walking with them, or else to do them some such kind of commodity as may serve them and stand them in some stead for their use in the way. But our Savior, those that he loved in the world, he loved not into the way (that is to wit, not only unto their worldly commodities that are transitory and shall pass from them, which they shall leave behind them in the way) but he loved them into the end, that is to wit, toward the bringing of them to the end that he by his precious blood bought[767] them to.

And thus you see how all these expositions of the old holy doctors are very meet[768] for the matter, which Saint John here beginneth to treat, which in this thirteenth chapter beginneth to enter toward the treating of Christ's Passion, by which our Lord declared well that he loved unto the end, that is to wit, as I told you, to the uttermost. And first he beginneth therein to treat of his Last Supper, wherein he declared by many things, as shall after appear, that he loved his apostles to the end, that is to wit, that the nearer he drew to his death the more tenderly he remembered them. He declared also at that supper that he loved them into the end, that is to wit, into the world to come to the bliss of heaven, the end that he by his death prepared for them. This he declared specially at the Last Supper, both by the institution of the Blessed Sacrament and by the godly doctrine that he taught them to conduit[769] them thitherward, of which the very entry and open gate our Savior showed them in these words of the Gospel that I have here before rehearsed you, as you shall well perceive by the perusing of the letter, which in this wise beginneth: "When the supper was done, when the devil had put into the heart of Judas, the son of Simon of Scariot, to betray him," etc.

In these words, "when the supper was done," it is not to be taken that it was all done. For (as you see here) our Lord and all his apostles, after their feet washed, sat down at the table again. But you shall understand that the supper of the Paschal lamb was done. For that was then eaten before that our Lord rose from the table to go about the washing of the apostles' feet.

"Whereas the devil had put into the heart of Judas, the son of Simon of Scariot, to betray him." By this, that the devil did put that treason in his heart, is meant the secret suggestion of the devil by which he stirred the traitor Judas thereunto. By which we

---

762 Jn 13:1 **763** say **764** Jn 15:13 **765** Jn 6:37 **766** reform **767** redeemed **768** fitting **769** guide

be learned[770] to know and consider that, when an ungracious[771] purpose falleth in our mind, we may well think that the devil is then even busy about[772] us, and not (as it is commonly said) at our elbow, but even at our very heart. For into the fleshly body can the devil enter and cast imagination[773] in our mind and offer us outward occasions also to illect,[774] stir, and draw us to his purpose.

Judas was called not Scariot, but Iscariot, that is to wit, *Iscariotes*, "of a place named Iscariot."

"Jesus, knowing that the Father had given him all things into his hands, and that he was come out from God and goeth to God, riseth from the supper, and putteth off his garments, and took a linen cloth and gird[775] it about him, and then put water into the basin, and began to wash the feet of his disciples, and wipe them with the linen cloth with which he was gird."

We need (I trust) to put no man in remembrance that our Savior Christ was as verily God as man. And therefore where the Evangelist saith that he came out from his Father and goeth again to his Father, it is not meant that his Godhead was at any time departed from the Father; but by his going from the Father was nothing meant but his being incarnate in the world, and his going again to the Father, the taking up of his manhead into heaven with him. For by his coming into the earth he left not heaven but ever was, and ever is, and ever shall be, with his Father and their Holy Spirit both in heaven and in earth, and everywhere else at once. Nor by that he saith his Father had given him all things into his hands is not meant that God the Father giveth anything unto the equal God the Son. But like as he hath been eternally begotten of him, so hath he eternally equal dominion of all things with him. I mean not only as much dominion, but also the selfsame dominion, in like manner[776] as he is equal God with his Father and the Holy Ghost not by being another God as great but by being, albeit another distinct person, yet the selfsame God that they be.

And therefore the Father hath nothing in time given the Son but eternally before all time gave him all (if a man may call it giving) by his only begetting.[777] Howbeit, Christ as man might receive of God's gift in time, as he was created in time. And

therefore is there in these words expressed Christ's marvelous excellent humility, as though the Evangelist had in more words declared it in this manner: our Savior Christ, whereas Judas had by the suggestion of the devil made promise to betray him and continually persevered in that traitorous purpose, notwithstanding that he was very God and descended from heaven to be incarnate and should ascend thither again in the glorious body and soul of his blessed manhood, and that his Godhead had ever had of his Father by his eternal generation, and[778] to his manhood, by the unity of person with his Godhead, belonged also of all-thing the whole dominion, so that with the traitor and all those to whom he should be betrayed he was able to do what him list,[779] yet would he, not only to his other apostles but also to that very traitor too (whereby he should give his high stubborn heart occasion to relent and repent and amend if it would be), so far humble himself that, being their Master, their Lord, and their God, he would vouchsafe to do them lowly service in the washing, not of their heads or their hands, but even of their very feet, and wipe them too his[780] own hands. And therefore he would have nobody help him therein, nor do a piece himself for a countenance[781] and let another do the remnant, but he would put off his overgarments himself, put the water into the basin himself, wash all their feet himself, and wipe their feet all himself.

Then followeth it in the letter: "He came then unto Simon Peter, and Peter saith unto him, 'Lord, washest thou my feet?'" Saint Peter, having our Savior in such estimation and honor, as it well became him to have, thought it in his mind unmeetly[782] that his Lord and Master should wash his feet. And therefore he said unto him, "Lord, washest thou my feet?" To whom our Savior said, "That that I do thou knowest not now. But thou shalt know afterward." As though he would say, "Though thou think it not convenient because thou canst not see for what cause I do it, yet I (all whose deeds are of such perfection that I do nothing for nought) know a great cause necessary and convenient[783] for which I do it, which thou canst not conject.[784] But when we have done, thou shalt know it, and therefore suffer[785] me first to do it."

But Saint Peter had so deep imprinted in his breast the marvelous high majesty of the person of Christ, being the very Son of God, and with his almighty Father and his Holy Ghost equal and one God, and therefore infinitely more in dignity above him than the heaven is in distance above the earth, could not, for all that word of our Savior, find in his heart to suffer him do such simple humble service unto him. And therefore with plain refusing thereof he withdrew his feet and answered our Savior in this wise: "Thou shall never wash my feet in this world." Our Lord, then—as he sometimes did in other things touch[786] and temper the zeal of Peter, through fervor and heat somewhat undiscreet,[787] so to show him here that there could no virtue stand in stead[788] without a humble obedience, but that it would work unto damnation (seemed the thing never so good) if it were joined with disobedience against the will of God—spoke sharply to him and said, "But if[789] I wash thee, thou shalt have no part with[790] me." When Saint Peter heard that word, he cast off his undiscreet courtesy and turned it unto perfect obedience, submitting himself whole unto the will of Christ, and said: "Lord, not only my feet, but also my hands and my head too." As though he would say: "Though I would for mine unworthiness be loath to have thy most excellent person do such simple service unto me, yet since I see that for cause unknown unto me, of which it becometh me not to ask thee a reckoning, thou hast so determined to wash mine unworthy feet, that if I therein obey not thine high pleasure I shall by disobedience fall in thy displeasure and be departed[791] from thee and lose my part of thy glory, I rather will be content to suffer thee not only, Lord, to wash my feet, but over that mine hands and mine head too."

"Jesus answered and said unto him, 'He that is washed needeth not to wash but his feet, but is all clean.'" Forasmuch as Saint Peter offered himself to suffer to be of Christ's holy hands washed, not his feet only that are the lowest part but his hands also that are about the mids[792] and his head too which is the highest part, by which three he signified himself content that Christ should wash all his whole body, Christ answered him that that thing were more than needed. For he that is washed once already by baptism is so clean washed altogether from all sin, both actual and original, that he never needeth to be all washed again, nor never shall be all washed again by baptism. For baptized shall no man be but once; the character and spiritual token by baptism imprinted in the soul is indelible and never can be put out. But in them that, for their unfaithfulness or for their evil living after their baptism, shall finally be damned, that token shall in their soul perpetually remain to their harm and shame, by which it shall evermore appear that they be neither paynims, Jews, nor Saracens, but (which worst is of all) false and unkind[793] Christian men. But there is none washed so clean by baptism but that (if he live) he shall have need to have his feet washed often. For by his feet are meant his affections.[794] For likewise as our feet bear our body hither and thither, so do our affections carry us to good works or bad. For look which way that our affections lead us and that way commonly walk we. And therefore said our Savior to Saint Peter when he offered to be all washed again both[795] feet, hands, and head, "He that is washed is all clean and needeth to have no more washed but his feet," that is to wit, his affections, "and then is he all clean." And with that our Savior, considering the traitor Judas (the filthy feet of whose wretched covetous affection had carried him to the council of the Jews to offer them his Master for money to sell, and from which traitorous affection Christ's great marvelous humanity, washing the traitor's filthy feet, had not cleansed him), he said unto them all, "You be clean, but yet all you be not clean," for he knew who it was that should betray him. And therefore he said, "All you be not clean."

Upon the foresaid words of Christ unto Peter, "He that is washed needeth but to wash his feet," and those words, "You be clean," it appeareth, as the old holy doctors say, that the apostles were before that all baptized and clean. But Judas had by his filthy affection of his wretched covetise[796] defiled himself by his false treason again.

"Then after that he had washed their feet, he took his clothes again, and when he was set at the table again, he said unto them, 'Wot[797] ye what I have done to you?'" Our Savior here giveth us in these words a good occasion to perceive that his outward works had, beside those visible apparent things which every man might behold and see, such secret spiritual mysteries meant and signified, and not only signified but also wrought and done in them, that those spiritual things unseen were so much the more principal parts of his deed that whoso know not them, though they know his outward deed, yet may it be said that they know not what he did.

So where our Savior healed a man in his body outwardly, and inwardly also in his soul—whereof it is said, *Totum hominem sanum fecit in sabbato* ("He made all the man whole in the Sabbath day"),[798] that is to wit, not the body only, for the body alone is not all the man, but the soul too—they that looked on, though they wist[799] what he had outwardly done in the healing of the body, yet was that inward work of his in healing of the soul so far passing[800] that, that it may well be said they wist not what he did. And so was it in his works that he wrought in the Blessed Sacrament: as, when he consecrated his blessed body and blood in the form of bread and wine at this his Last Supper, had he not told them that point himself, who could have told what he did?

And therefore here in the washing of his disciples' feet, albeit that[801] they could not but both see and feel what he did, yet because his outward work therein was not in such a special manner his deed as was the inward mystery that he did and meant therein, he asked them, "Know you what I have done to you?" As though he would say: "I have done more than you know, for by the outward washing of your feet I have given you example of humility," which thing he declared unto them with most effectual words. For first, to the intent that they should consider of what weight and authority both his deed and his word should be with them, he plainly declared, taking occasion upon their own confession, that he was their very lord and their very master. And therefore he said unto them, "You call me master and lord, and you say well. For so I am indeed."

He was very lord of them as of his creatures; he was very master of them as of his disciples. Now putting this first in their remembrance for a foundation, thereupon he builded them a marvelous fruitful lesson with the declaration[802] of his former deed, saying unto them, "Therefore if I have washed your feet, being your lord and your master, you must

also wash one another's feet." Then goeth he farther and declareth wherefore he washed their feet, as he before said to Saint Peter that he should know it afterward. And therefore now he telleth that he did it to give example by his own deed unto them that they should each to other do the like. And therefore he said: "An example have I given you, that likewise as I have done to you, so should you do also, that is to wit, do each of you to other as I have done to you all."

Then goeth our Savior further yet and enforceth[803] his doctrine and his example with a strong mighty reason, saying, "Verily, verily, I tell you, the bondman is not greater than his lord, nor a messenger more[804] than he that hath sent him." As though he would say, "Since the bondman is no better than his lord, and I that am your creator am more highly lord over you that are my creatures than any earthly lord is over his bondman, how should you disdain to wash your fellow's feet, when I your high lord have not disdained to wash yours? And since the messenger is not better than he that hath sent him, and all you be but mine apostles, that is to wit, but my messengers to do my message in preaching my word about the world, since I that send you and therefore so far your better and yet have not disdained to wash your feet, there can none of you without very sinful and shameful pride disdain to wash the feet of his fellow."

And finally Christ knitteth[805] up all the whole matter with a very short substantial lesson: "If you know these things, blessed shall you be if you do these things." In which words our Savior well declareth that the bliss of heaven will not be gotten by knowing of virtue but by the use and doing thereof. For as no man can come at Canterbury by the bare knowledge of the way thither if he will sit still at home, so by knowing the way to heaven we can never the more come there but if[806] we will walk therein. And therefore saith our Lord by the mouth of the prophet: *Beati immaculati qui ambulant in lege Domini. Non enim qui operantur iniquitatem in viis eius ambulaverunt* ("Blessed are they that are undefiled, that walk in the law of our Lord. But they that work wickedness walk not in his ways").[807] And our Savior saith[808] his own mouth that the knowledge without work not only doth no profit but also causeth increase of a man's punishment, in respect that[809] his punishment should be if, without his willful ignorance, his knowledge had been much less. For thus saith our Lord: "The bondman that knoweth not the will of his lord and doth it not shall be beaten with few stripes. But the bondman that knoweth his lord's will and doth it not shall be beaten with many stripes."[810] And therefore with this necessary fruitful doctrine our Lord did knit up all and said, "If you know these things," that is to wit, "that my washing of your feet is done for your example, that since I am indeed (as yourselves do call me) your Lord and your Master, and that the bondman is not better than his lord, nor the messenger more than his master that sent him, you should not be so proud as to disdain to do as lowly service, each of you to other, as I have done to you all. If you know this and do it indeed, then shall you be blessed, or else for the bare knowledge shall you be but the worse."

Upon these words before rehearsed, had between our Savior and Saint Peter, that refused for reverence the thing that our Lord would do to him, holy doctors note that no man lawfully may for any private mind of reverence or devotion to God do the thing that God forbiddeth nor leave the thing undone that God biddeth. For it is an undiscreet[811] devotion, and an unreverent reverence, and no right humility, but an unperceived pride to stand stiff[812] against God's will and disobey his pleasure. For as the Scripture saith, "Better is obedience than sacrifice."[813] Nor never shall God's precepts be obeyed if every man may boldly frame himself[814] a conscience with a gloze[815] of his own making after his own fantasy put unto God's word. For of such manner dealing, whereby folk will of their private devotions, against the commandment of God, follow their own way, may these words of the Scripture be verified: *Est via quae videtur hominibus iusta, et novissima eius tendit ad infernum.* ("There is a way that unto men seemeth just, and the last end thereof leadeth unto hell").[816]

King Saul thought, after his own mind, that he did very well when he kept and spared the goodly oxen for sacrifice. But while he broke, in his so doing, the commandment of God, this false-framed devotion helped him not but that he lost his kingdom therefore. Saint Peter here thought he did well when he for reverence toward Christ would not suffer him wash his feet. But our Savior showed him that, if he would for any such framed reverence of his own stand obstinately disobedient unto God's pleasure, he should have no part with him. And therefore, while Christ was presently conversant[817] with him, he was the interpreter of his own precept. And King Saul should not have followed his own wit, but should have asked the prophet by whom that precept came to him. And in like wise, if a man doubt of the sentence and understanding of anything written in the Scripture, it is no wisdom for him then to take upon him such authority of interpretation himself, as that he shall therein boldly stand unto[818] his own mind, but lean unto the interpretation of the old holy doctors and saints and unto that interpretation that is received and allowed by the universal Church, by which Church the Scripture is comen to our hands and delivered unto us, and without which we could not (as Saint Augustine saith) know which books were Holy Scripture.[819]

Our Savior here saith, "I have given you an example, that, likewise as I have done to you, so should you do also." Would God that all the prelates, and all curates, and all preachers, yea, and fathers and mothers, and all masters of households too, would here of our Savior take example for to give good example. There are many that can be well content to be preaching, some to show their cunning[820] and some to show their authority. But would God they would use the fashion that our Savior used, that is to wit, the things that they bid other men do, do it first themselves. The Scripture saith of our Savior, *Cepit Iesus facere et docere* ("Jesus began to do and to teach"),[821] so that he not only taught men to do this or that, but he gave them also the example and did the thing first himself. To stir us to fast, he not only taught us what fashion we should use in fasting, but also for our example fasted forty days himself. To stir us to wake and pray, he not only taught us by word, but used also by night to go forth into

809 *in respect that:* compared with what   **810** Lk 12:47–48   **811** imprudent   **812** *stand stiff:* remain stubborn   **813** 1 Kgs 15:22   **814** *frame himself:* devise   for himself   **815** gloss, interpretation   **816** Prv 14:12   **817** *presently conversant:* in personal and familiar contact   **818** *stand unto:* persist in   **819** See Augustine,   *Contra epistolam Manichaei* 5 (*PL* 42, 176).   **820** knowledge   **821** Acts 1:1

the Mount of Olivet and there to wake and pray by night himself, by which custom the traitor knew where to find him. To set nought by the royalty[822] of the world he not only taught us by word, but also by his poor birth, and all the course of his poor life, he gave us the example himself. To stir us to patience and suffering of tribulation, he not only taught us and exhorted us by word, but gave us the example by his own cross, his own passion, and his own painful death. And surely, albeit that[823] the best is (for him that hath a good thing taught him by one whom he seeth do the contrary himself) to do as he is well taught and not follow the lewd[824] example of his evil deed, yet is our common condition such that, whereas word and deed both be scant able to draw us to do good, every one of the both is able enough to draw us to naught.[825] And therefore he that biddeth other folk do well and giveth evil example with the contrary deed himself fareth[826] even like a foolish weaver that would weave apace with the one hand and unweave as fast with the other.

The example of Christ in washing the apostles' feet, with his exhortation unto them by his example to do the like, bindeth not men to follow the literal fashion thereof in washing of folks' feet as for a rite or a ceremony or a sacrament of the Church — howbeit much it hath been ever since and yet in every country of Christendom in places of religion used it is, and noble princes and great estates[827] use that godly ceremony very religiously. And none I suppose nowhere more godly than our sovereign lord the King's Grace here of this realm, both in humble manner washing and wiping and kissing also many poor folks' feet after the number of years of his age, and with right liberal and princely alms therewith.

And surely if the interpretation of the Scripture were not by the Spirit of God put in the whole corps[828] of the Catholic Church, he that would upon his own head stick upon the letter of the Gospel and his own exposition thereto might contend that the washing of the feet were a sacrament unto which our Savior bound his Church of necessity. But, as the universal Church believeth, so is it not. Howbeit, in time and place convenient, it is (as Saint Augustine saith) a thing of the more

perfection if we not only do not disdain in our hearts but do it also in deed with our hands as our Lord did with his.[829]

When our Lord said, "You be clean but not all," he meant that the congregation and company of his twelve apostles, as a congregation and a company, was a clean company, though Judas, one of the company, was not clean. For many a right honest company is there that hath yet some not honest among them. And so is the Catholic Church called *Sancta Ecclesia,* "Holy Church," because that out thereof[830] there is none holiness, and for those that are holy therein, which are always many, both priests and laymen too, though there be therein besides many bad of both sorts also.

Finally, where our Savior saith, *Si haec scitis, beati eritis si feceritis ea* ("If you know these things, you shall be blessed if you do them"),[831] two things in those words he giveth us warning of: the one, that without faith there can be no good work that can be meritorious touching[832] the bliss of heaven; the other, that have we the faith never so great, yet if we will not work well our faith shall fail of the bliss. And therefore to give us warning of the necessity that we have of faith, he said not these words alone, "If you do this you shall be blessed," but he began with these words, "If you know these things." Now the knowledge of those things that pertain to such kind of well doing as shall stand us in stead toward[833] salvation, that knowledge have we not but by faith. As the apostles there, though they saw him wash their feet, yet that he did it to give them an example of humility, and that such humility should be requisite to help them to heaven, and to be rewarded there, this knew they not but by the faith that they gave therein unto Christ's word. For, *fides ex auditu, auditus autem per verbum Dei* ("Faith," saith Saint Paul, "cometh of hearing, and the hearing thereof is by the word of God").[834] Therefore, as I say, our Lord began their blessedness with faith. For faith is the very gate and first entry toward heaven: *accedentem ad Deum oportet credere* ("He that is coming to God must give credence and believe").[835] For if a man that believeth not do the selfsame thing either by chance or of some other affection,[836] which thing done by a faithful man in faith were meritorious,

822 magnificence, pomp   **823** *albeit that:* although   **824** wicked   **825** wrongdoing   **826** acts   **827** *great estates:* persons of high social rank   **828** body   **829** See Augustine's *In Iohannis evangelium tractatus* 58.4 (*PL* 35: 1794).   **830** *out thereof:* apart from it   **831** Jn 13:17   **832** as regards   **833** *stand . . . toward:* be of use to us with regard to   **834** Rom 10:17   **835** Heb 11:6   **836** inclination, passion

that deed done by the faithless is not meritorious at all. But yet, though faith be the first gate into heaven, he that standeth still at the gate and will not walk forth in the way of good works shall not come where the reward is. And therefore our Savior left[837] not with these words, *Si haec scitis beati eritis* ("If you know these things you shall be blessed"), but went further and, to make up his tale perfect, he added, *si feceritis ea* ("if you do them").

I fear me there be many folk that, for delight of knowledge or for a foolish vainglory to show and make it known how much themselves know, labor to know the law of God (and know it right well indeed, and can well preach it out again) that shall yet see many a poor simple soul with a gross plain faith (with no learning but good devout affection, walking the way of good works in this world) sit after full high with our Lord in heaven, when those great clerks[838] wandering here in evil works shall, for all their great knowledge and for all gay[839] preaching in the name of Christ, hear our Lord say to them (as in the thirteenth chapter of Saint Luke he saith he will say to such): *Discedite a me operarii iniquitatis* ("Walk you from me you workers of wickedness").[840]

And for conclusion, all the work (with this example of his and all his declaration[841] thereupon) our Savior instructeth and exhorteth his apostles to, is the work of humility. For likewise as pride threw down the devil out of heaven, so shall there never none ascend but with meekness thither. And since the devil that fell himself by pride is ever most busy to tempt every man to the same sin (and specially those that he seeth aspire toward any excellence in spiritual kind of virtue or that he espieth put in prelacy[842] and authority over other men, whereby he hopeth to find a gate open to enter), our Savior therefore to keep against the ghostly[843] enemy that gate well warded[844] and sure, in sundry places again and again giveth his apostles (whom he made prelates and spiritual governors of his flock) special counsel against the prick[845] of pride, and with words and with this example of washing their feet his[846] own hands, exhorteth them by meekness and humility to count[847] and reckon and use[848] themselves as far under others as himself doth in order[849] and authority prefer and enhance[850] them above, and would that we should of

duty for their degree do great honor unto them, and that they should themselves of[851] meekness as fast[852] again put it from them.

The Prayer

Almighty Jesus, my sweet Savior Christ, which wouldest vouchsafe thine[853] own almighty hands to wash the feet of thy twelve apostles, not only of the good but of the very traitor too, vouchsafe, good Lord, of thine excellent goodness, in such wise to wash the foul feet of mine affections that I never have such pride enter into mine heart as to disdain either in friend or foe, with meekness and charity for the love of thee, to file[854] mine hands with washing of their feet.

THE FOURTH CHAPTER

Of the institution of the sacrament, written in the twenty-sixth of Saint Matthew, the fourteenth of Saint Mark, and in the twenty-second of Saint Luke

The First Lecture
upon the Blessed Sacrament

And as they were sitting at the table and eating, Jesus saith, "With desire have I desired to eat the Paschal with you before I suffer. I say to you that from this time I shall not eat it, till it be fulfilled in the kingdom of God." As they were at supper Jesus took bread, gave thanks, and blessed and broke it, and gave it to his disciples, and saith, "Take you and eat you. This is my body, the which for you shall be delivered. This do you for the remembrance of me." Likewise, taking the chalice after that he had supped, gave thanks and gave it them, saying, "Take and divide it among you, and drink of this all. This is my blood of the new testament. This is the chalice, the new testament in my blood, which for you and for many shall be shed for remission of sins. I say verily to you that I shall not drink from henceforth of this generation[855] of the vine, until that day when I shall drink it new[856] with you in the kingdom of my Father God." And they drank all thereof.

837 stopped   838 scholars   839 brilliant   840 Lk 13:27   841 elucidation   842 ecclesiastical power   843 spiritual   844 guarded   845 goad   846 i.e., with his   847 account, consider   848 conduct   849 rank   850 *prefer and enhance:* promote and exalt   851 out of   852 firmly   853 i.e., with thine   854 defile   855 fruit   856 anew

Albeit, good readers, that I have rehearsed you this chapter in such wise as the right famous clerk Master John Gerson rehearseth in his work called *Monotessaron,* gathered of the words of all the three evangelists, Saint Matthew, Saint Mark, and Saint Luke, and in a convenient order, linked and chained ensuingly[857] together, yet seemeth me[858] that for the beginning the thing shall somewhat the better appear if we rehearse the words of Saint Luke somewhat more full, which words he writeth upon the end of the eating of the Paschal lamb and before the institution of the Blessed Sacrament of the altar. For in his twenty-second chapter thus beginneth he this matter: *Et cum facta esset hora, discubuit, et duodecim apostoli cum eo. Et ait illis: Desiderio desideravi hoc Pascha manducare vobiscum antequam patiar. Dico enim vobis, quia ex hoc non manducabo illud, donec impleatur in regno Dei. Et accepto calice gratias egit, et dixit: Accipite et dividite inter vos. Dico enim vobis quod non bibam de generatione vitis donec regnum Dei veniat* ("And when the hour was come, he sat down at the table, and his twelve apostles with him. And he saith unto them, 'With desire have I desired to eat this Paschal lamb with you before I suffer. For I tell you that from this time I shall not eat it till it be fulfilled in the kingdom of God.' And the cup taken, he gave thanks and said, 'Take you and divide you it among you. For I say to you that I shall not drink of the generation of the vine till the kingdom of God come'").[859]

These words hath Saint Luke whole[860] together of the finishing of the old Paschal before he entereth into the rehearsing of the new Paschal, whereof the old was a figure, that is to wit,[861] before he beginneth to rehearse the institution of the Blessed Sacrament of the altar, of which he beginneth to speak forthwith after these words ended.

In the beginning of these words, written in the twenty-second chapter of Saint Luke, our Savior expresseth the great desire that he had to eat the Paschal lamb at that time with his apostles, saying, *Desiderio desideravi hoc Pascha manducare vobiscum antequam patiar* ("With desire have I desired to eat this Paschal lamb with you before my Passion").[862]

These words "with desire have I desired" are spoken after the manner of the Hebrew speech, in which speech our Savior spoke at the time himself. For the Hebrews to express a thing vehemently use oftentimes, as it appeareth in sundry places of Scripture, to double a word, sometimes by the participle and the verb, sometimes by the noun and the verb, as our Savior did here, saying, "with desire have I desired," that is to wit, "very sore[863] have I desired," or "very desirously have I longed for to eat this Paschal lamb with you."

Two causes there were for which our Savior so sore longed at that time to eat the Paschal lamb with his disciples. The one appeareth upon that[864] I have showed you before, that is to wit, because that (as Saint John saith): *Cum dilexisset suos qui erant in mundo, usque in finem dilexit eos* ("Whereas he had loved his that were in the world, he loved them to the end").[865] And therefore, since he was now so near drawing to his Passion, which he had determined to suffer on the morrow, he, like a most tender lover, longed with that Last Supper to make them his farewell at his departing from them.

Wherein, as I before have said, appeared his wonderful loving heart. For had he been after the manner of other men (since himself saw his Passion drawing so near, to which he should be so violently taken so shortly upon[866] his supper, and that Passion so bitter as himself well wist[867] it should, of which he was so feared[868] and for which he was so sorrowful within so few hours after), he would have taken little pleasure or comfort in the company of his apostles nor list[869] to make them a supper at that time.

But he loved them so tenderly that all the pain, sorrow, dread, and fear that was toward[870] him could not so master and overwhelm his kind loving affection toward them, but that the desire and longing to make his Last Supper with them so much increased greater as he surely saw that his bitter Passion drew nearer. And that was therefore (as I say) one of the causes for which he said unto them at the eating thereof, "With desire have I desired," that is to say, "Sore have I longed to eat this Paschal lamb with you before my Passion."

The other cause for which he longed so sore to eat that Paschal lamb with them was because that he longed for the time in which he should, with his bitter Passion, pay the price of our redemption and restore the kind[871] of man unto the inheritance of the kingdom of heaven. And because that he would, before the offering up of his own blessed body (the very lamb, innocent and immaculate) unto the Father, institute the new Paschal (the very eating of the selfsame holy, unspotted lamb, his own blessed body and blood, to be continually sacrificed, offered up unto the Father, and eaten in remembrance of his bitter Passion under the form of bread and wine), he would, as was convenient,[872] before the institution of the new very Paschal, reverently finish the old Paschal that was the figure thereof.

And therefore at the Last Supper, to declare the desire that he had so to do (that is to wit, to institute his new Paschal by the finishing of the old), he said unto them, "With desire have I desired to eat this Paschal lamb with you before my Passion." And for to declare the more clearly that the cause of his desire was to the intent that he would finish it and offer up himself the very lamb, whereof the other was the figure, and would by that pleasant sacrifice bring the nature of man into the kingdom of heaven, he therefore said farther unto them: *Dico enim vobis, quia ex hoc non manducabo illud, donec impleatur in regno Dei* ("I say verily to you, that from this time I shall eat that no more till it be performed[873] in the kingdom of God").[874]

The fulfilling or performing of the sacrifice of the Paschal lamb, being a figure, was the offering of his own blessed body in sacrifice, by which the nature of man was restored unto the kingdom of heaven. And by that new offering up of that innocent lamb so offered (which offering was the verity) was that old offering of the Paschal lamb in Jerusalem (that was the figure) fully performed and thereupon took his full perfection in the kingdom of heaven.

But here must we consider that our Savior, in saying that he would eat the old Paschal lamb no more till it were performed in the kingdom of heaven, did not mean that after that the figure were performed and had his perfection in heaven, he would then use or have used the same figure again in earth, but he meant that he would no more eat it at all. For this word *donec* in Latin (that is to say, "until" in English), when it limiteth[875] a time before which it denieth a certain thing to be done, doth not always mean or imply (though sometimes it do) the doing of the same thing after that time. As when

the Gospel saith, *Non cognovit eam, donec peperit filium suum primogenitum* (Joseph "knew not her till she had brought forth her first-begotten son"),[876] meaneth not that he knew her after. Nor where the prophet speaketh as in the person of the Father unto Christ, *Sede a dextris meis, donec ponam inimicos tuos scabellum pedum tuorum* ("Sit on my right hand till I put thine enemies for a footstool under thy feet"),[877] the prophet there meaneth not that when the enemies of Christ be thrown under his feet he shall then sit on the Father's right hand no longer. Nor here in like wise our Savior meant not that, after the verity fulfilled and perfected in the kingdom of God, he would use or have used the figure here still in earth.

And that appeareth plain by two things. One, by this word *impleatur,* "till it be fulfilled." For, since it was but a figure, and he said he would use it no more till it were fulfilled, he must needs mean that he would use it no more at all. For, being but a figure, it had no cause of use after that it was by the verity fulfilled.

And therefore as touching[878] the Paschal lamb, when our Savior said, "I will from henceforth eat this no more till it be fulfilled in the kingdom of God," was as much as to say, "after this I will never eat it more," after such manner of speaking as one might say that looked for to die or that were entering into the Charterhouse,[879] "I will never eat flesh more in this world," or thus, "I trust to be in heaven ere I eat any more flesh,"—or such other kind of speaking like, not meaning that he would eat flesh in another world, but that he would eat none here, and consequently never eat flesh more.

The other thing, by which it appeareth plain that our Savior intended not to have the figurative old Paschal lamb any longer continue, is that he forthwith instituted the verity thereof, the new sacrifice, his Blessed Body and Blood, the Blessed Sacrament of the altar.

But before the institution of his own Christian sacrament, to the intent it should appear that he would fully finish the old Paschal of the Jews (and as who say wash it away), himself with his apostles, as for a final end thereof, after the eating thereof, drank thereunto. Whereof Saint Luke proceedeth farther and saith, *Accepto calice gratias egit, et*

---

872 fitting   **873** fulfilled   **874** Lk 22:16   **877** Ps 109(110):1   **878** pertaining to   **879** a Carthusian monastery in London,
875 fixes definitely   **876** Mt 1:25   known for its austerity

dixit: accipite et dividite inter vos ("He took the cup and gave thanks and said, 'Take and divide among you'").880

Our Savior as man gave thanks unto God the Father that the old sacrifice of the Paschal lamb was now come to an end and that he was now come to the institution of the new sacrifice, his own blessed body in the Holy Sacrament of the altar.

Then our Lord commanded them to take and divide the cup of wine among them and drink all thereof, as the farewell of the old Paschal. And then said he further unto them, *Dico enim vobis, quod non bibam de generatione vitis, donec regnum Dei veniat* ("I say to you that I shall not drink of the generation of the vine till the kingdom of God come").881

The kingdom of God he calleth here the state of his glory after his resurrection, in which he rose immortal, impassible,882 and glorious. Afore which time he said here unto them that he would drink no wine, as though he would say, "Such drink as I now drink with you to the old sacrifice of the Paschal lamb will I drink no more till I arise again in my glory after my Passion."

But after his resurrection, he did verily eat and drink with them again, as appeareth plain by the evangelists, and as Saint Peter beareth witness where he saith, *Qui manducavimus et bibimus cum illo postquam resurrexit a mortuis* ("We have eaten and drunken with him after that he was arisen from death").883

After this done, our Savior Christ by and by, in the stead of that old sacrifice of the Paschal lamb so ended, did institute the new sacrifice and the only sacrifice to be continued in his Church, the Blessed Sacrament of the altar. Which new sacrifice, instead of that old sacrifice and of all the old sacrifices which among the Jews fore-figured the very fruitful884 sacrifice of Christ's blessed body upon the cross, should, in his own Church of Jews and gentiles together, continually with the selfsame body and blood offered in the Mass under the form of bread and wine, represent that sacrifice in which on Good Friday Christ once forever offered the selfsame body and blood in their proper form to the Father upon the cross.

And therefore, after the old sacrifice of the Paschal lamb clearly finished, as ye have heard, ere ever they rose from the board,885 our Savior forthwith went in hand886 with the instituting of that that should be the new sacrifice, the Blessed Sacrament of the altar, his own holy body and blood under form of bread and wine.

The manner of which institution, in the Gospel of Saint Matthew, Saint Mark, and Saint Luke, is rehearsed in this wise: "Jesus took bread, gave thanks and blessed it, and broke it, and gave it his disciples, saying, 'Take you and eat you. This is my body, which shall be delivered for you.'"

First our Savior, in the beginning of this excellent work, gave thanks and blessed the bread to give us example, as saith Saint Bede, that in the beginning of every good work we should give thanks to God. Then he broke it and gave it unto them himself to signify, saith Saint Bede, that he gave himself to his Passion of his own free will.887 But to the intent they should well understand that this holy sacrament that himself instituted in his own holy person wonderfully far passed the old sacrifice of the Paschal lamb instituted by the ministry of Moses in the Old Law, lest they might peradventure888 take it for a far less thing than it was — as they should have had a great cause to do if it had been none other substance than the substance of bread, as to their eyes it seemed (for then had the lamb, which was a living sensible889 creature, been of the proper nature890 much more excellent than the insensible substance of bread) — our Savior therefore, to give them sure knowledge how great a gift it was that he there gave them and how incomparably far above all the merit of man to receive (that they should thereby consider how deeply they were bounden and beholden to him therefore, and with devout thanks inwardly remember his inestimable bounty therein), he gave them knowledge that though it was bread when he took it in hand and that to their bodily senses seemed yet bread still, yet it was now his own very body indeed. And therefore he said unto them, "Take you and eat you. This is my body." As though he might say, "Think not that for my special new sacrifice, that I institute to represent forever in mine own Church (till I return to the general judgment) my most precious Passion, I give you a thing of more base nature than was the thing that was

880 Lk 22:17   881 Lk 22:18   882 incapable of suffering   883 Acts 10:41   884 beneficial   885 table   886 *went*   *in hand:* proceeded   887 More may have found the references to Bede in the *Catena aurea,* a biblical gloss selected   by St. Thomas Aquinas.   888 perhaps   889 endowed with sensation   890 *of the . . . nature:* of its own nature

wont to be sacrificed to fore-figure it in the short[891] and soon passing synagogue—which you might think if my sacrifice of representation were but insensible bread, where their fore-figuring sacrifice was celebrated in a living creature, a fair unspotted lamb. But I will that you shall understand and know that the thing which I give you here to eat is of a nature above all measure more excellent. For though it seem bread, yet is it flesh. And though it seem dead, yet is it living. The lamb, though it was quick taken to the sacrifice, yet was it eaten dead. But this shall you eat quick, and it shall rest and abide quick in you. And the lamb did feed and nourish your bodies; but this shall feed and nourish your souls. For this is mine own body, and not my dead body, but animated and living with my soul. And mine own body shall never be separated from my Godhead, so that if you receive and eat virtuously the one into your body, you receive the other graciously[892] into your souls."

In these few compendious[893] words of our Savior, "This is my body," is all this long tale included, and many a long holy process more. And albeit that in those words alone he told them the thing plain enough, and notwithstanding that he had also declared them before that he would give them his own body to eat, inculking[894] that point into them with many words at length, mentioned in the sixth chapter of Saint John, yet to make them the more clearly perceive that this was the thing that he then told them of, he said not only, "This is my body," but he farther also added thereunto, "which shall be delivered for you"—as though he would say, "If any would be so far from believing of the truth, that rather than believe this to be my very body, he would seek a gloss[895] against mine own word and say that by this word, 'my body,' I meant but a sign or a figure or a token of my body, to put all such folk out of doubt I say that this which I give you here to receive and eat is that sameself body that shall be delivered for you to the Jews and to gentiles and by them to the cross and to the death."

Now to the intent that it should appear plain that he gave them not his body for that only time, as a special show of kindness to their own persons alone, but that they should perceive that he did it to begin and institute a new sacrament, instead of the old Paschal, which should endure in his Church in the stead of the other there finished, he said unto them, *Hoc facite in meam commemorationem* ("This do you in the remembrance of me")[896]—as though he would say to them, "Likewise as the synagogue of the Jews have hitherto used for a figure of my Passion the old sacrifice of the Paschal lamb, so do you use in my Church from henceforth in remembrance of my Passion this new sacrifice of mine own body, that shall suffer that Passion and be sacrificed once forever upon the cross"—which sentence of our Savior's words is also declared by Saint Paul in the eleventh chapter of his first epistle to the Corinthians, of which we shall speak hereafter.[897] But first shall we peruse the words of our Savior himself.

After that he had thus given them his own blessed body to eat in the form of bread, he gave them likewise his blessed blood to drink in the form of wine, whereof it followeth in the Gospel: "And likewise taking the chalice after supper, he gave thanks and gave it to them, saying, 'Take you and drink all you of this. This is my blood of the new testament. This is the chalice, the new testament in my blood, which for you and for many shall be shed into the remission of sins.'"

Our Savior at the converting and turning of the wine into his own precious blood, which he should so shortly after shed for our sins upon his painful cross, murmured not nor grudged[898] not at the remembrance of his bitter passion, but was glad, and gave God the Father thanks that he vouchsafed to suffer[899] him by his pain to pay our ransom and buy our souls from pain, as say Saint Remigius and Saint Chrysostom. And our Savior in his so doing (saith Saint Chrysostom) teacheth us what pain soever we suffer, to suffer it in such wise as we give God thanks therefore.[900]

"And after his thanks given to God, he gave the chalice to his apostles and commanded them all drink thereof, saying, 'This is my blood of the new testament. This is the chalice, the new testament in my blood.'"

In these words our Savior showed them what thing it was that he gave them to drink in the chalice, that is to wit,[901] that it was his own blood, saying, "This is my blood of the new testament," as Saint Matthew rehearseth[902] it, or, "This is the

891 briefly lasting **892** by means of divine grace **893** succinct, summary **894** inculcating **895** interpretation **896** Lk 22:19 **897** See 1 Cor 11:25. **898** complained **899** *vouchsafed to suffer:* agreed to allow **900** More probably refers to passages by Remigius and Chrysostom in the *Catena aurea* of Aquinas. **901** say **902** recounts, tells

chalice, the new testament in my blood," as Saint Luke rehearseth it, either for that our Savior spoke both the one words and the other, or else for that both of the one words and the other the sentence is all one. For in the twenty-fourth chapter of Exodus is it specified how that Moses in the confirmation of the Old Law put half the blood of the sacrifice into a cup, and the other half he shed upon the altar, and, after the volume of the law read, he besprinkled the blood upon the people and said unto them, *Hic est sanguis foederis, quod pepigit Dominus vobiscum super cunctis sermonibus his* ("This is the blood of the league[903] that our Lord hath made with you upon all these words").[904] And so was the old testament ratified and confirmed with blood. And in like wise was the new testament confirmed with blood, saving that for to declare the great excellency of the new testament brought by the Son of God above the old testament brought by the prophet Moses, whereas the old testament was ratified with the blood of a brute beast, the new testament was ratified with the blood of a reasonable man, and of that man that was also God, that is to wit, with the blessed blood of our holy Savior himself. And the selfsame blood gave our Lord here unto his apostles in this Blessed Sacrament, as he plainly declared himself, saying, *Hic est sanguis meus novi testamenti* ("This is my blood of the new testament"),[905] or, *Hic est calix novum testamentum in meo sanguine, qui pro vobis et pro multis fundetur in remissionem peccatorum* ("This is the chalice, the new testament in my blood, which shall be shed for you and for many for remission of sins").[906]

Here you see that by the words of our Savior rehearsed by Saint Matthew, and upon his words rehearsed by Saint Luke, our Lord very plainly declared unto his apostles that in that cup was the same blood of his own with which he could ratify his new testament, and which blood should be shed upon the altar of the cross for the remission of sins, not of themselves alone but also of many more.

When our Lord said, "This is the cup of the new testament in my blood, which shall be shed for you and for many into remission of sins," he declared therein the efficacy of the New Testament above the old in that the Old Law in the blood of beasts could but promise the remission of sin afterward

to come. For as Saint Paul saith, "It was impossible that sin should be taken away with the blood of brute beasts."[907] But the New Law with the blood of Christ performeth the thing that the Old Law promised, that is to wit, remission of sins. And therefore our Savior said, "This is the chalice, the new testament in my blood," that is to wit, "to be confirmed in my blood, which shall be shed into remission of sins."

His words also declared the wonderful excellence of this new Blessed Sacrament above the sacrifice of the Paschal lamb in these words: *Pro vobis et pro multis* ("For you and for many"). For in these words our Savior spoke (saith Saint Chrysostom) as though he would say, "The blood of the Paschal lamb was shed only for the first-begotten among the children of Israel, but this blood of mine shall be shed for remission of sin of all the whole world." And so was it, according as Saint Chrysostom saith, shed for the sin of the whole world. For sufficient it was for the sin of the whole world and as many more too.

But it was effectually shed for those only that shall take the effect thereof, which are only those that shall be saved thereby, which shall be as Saint Remigius saith, and as the truth is, not the apostles only but also many other of many regions, according to the foresaid words of our Savior: "This is the chalice, the new testament in my blood, which shall be shed for you and for many into remission of sins."

Then likewise as he had before said (as you have heard rehearsed by Saint Luke) that, when he had with his disciples drunken after the Paschal lamb, he would drink no more of the generation[908] of the vine till the kingdom of God were come, so said he here again to them after the institution of his holy Blessed Sacrament: *Dico enim vobis quia non bibam a modo de hoc genimine vitis, usque in diem illum cum illud bibam novum vobiscum in regno Patris mei Dei.*[909]

These words diverse doctors do declare diversely. Some take this saying of our Savior rehearsed by Saint Matthew and Saint Mark to be the selfsame that Saint Luke rehearseth, and that they were spoken only after the institution of the Sacrament, and that Saint Luke observed the verity of the saying and not observed the time. And of this mind seemeth Master Gerson to have been, as appeareth by his rehearsing of the matter.

But diverse other doctors take them as spoken at diverse times, the one after the Paschal finished, the other after that at the institution of the Blessed Sacrament. And so seemeth it most plain to appear upon the words of Saint Luke. And albeit that the first words rehearsed by Saint Luke and these other rehearsed by Saint Matthew and Saint Mark may be both understood in one sentence and as one thing twice said—that is to wit, that in both the times of that saying our Savior meant that he would no more drink with his apostles (after that time in which they should then depart after that supper) until himself were risen again from death, and his body forever immortal and impassible[910] (which glory of his he called the kingdom of his Father), after which entry thereinto by his resurrection, he would both eat and drink with them again, and so would drink with them the wine new[911] in the kingdom of his Father (that is to wit, himself being in the kingdom of his Father should drink the wine with them in a new manner, that is to wit, when he should be forever immortal and impassible), and that he would no more drink of that kind of wine of which he consecrated, and which he turned into his blessed blood, till his Passion were passed and his new life comen—albeit (I say) that I deny not but that thus they may be taken (and by some of the old holy doctors thus are declared indeed), yet are they by diverse others of those old holy doctors expounded diverse other wise, and (as it seemeth) may well be declared thus.

In the words rehearsed by Saint Luke when our Savior said, *Dico enim vobis quod non bibam de generatione vitis, donec regnum Dei veniat* ("I say verily to you that I shall not drink of the generation of the vine till the kingdom of God come"),[912] our Savior meant in these words that not only not after the supper but also not after the time of that draft there drunken to the Paschal lamb, he would drink no more of the generation of the vine till the kingdom of God were come, that is to wit, that he would before his resurrection drink no more wine after that draft of wine which he drank next before those words spoken. And so did he then by those

words also teach them to know and perceive well afterward that the wine, which (before his other words that Saint Matthew and Saint Mark rehearse spoken at the institution of the Blessed Sacrament) was in the chalice, and which wine he there converted into his own precious blood, was, at the time of the drinking thereof, not wine but his own holy blood under the form of wine, which thing they were (I say)—besides his other plain words: "This is my blood of the new testament, which shall be shed for you and for many into remission of sins"—well showed and taught, in that he told them before the drinking of that (of which as I shall after show he drank himself with them) that before his resurrection, which was not then comen, he would drink no wine.

Now in his second words rehearsed by Saint Matthew and Saint Mark—which words he spoke at the institution of the Blessed Sacrament, when that (after the wine turned into his blood and taken to his apostles) he said, *Dico autem vobis, quia non bibam a modo de hoc genimine vitis, usque in diem illum cum illud bibam novum vobiscum in regno Patris mei Dei*[913]—in these words (gathered together in one out of the Gospel of the two foresaid evangelists) our Savior meant that he would after that draught[914] no more drink with them of his own blessed blood, which he drank with them then, until his bitter Passion and his glorious resurrection were performed. For after his glorious resurrection it is very probable, both upon these words and some other places of the Scripture too, that he not only did eat with them common meat but also did consecrate and eat with them the Blessed Sacrament also.

Now that he should call here his own blessed blood by the name of the generation of the vine is nothing to be marveled, while we see it in the common manner of Holy Scripture to call his blessed body and blood by the former names of the thing which he converted into them, as God in the Scripture calleth Adam earth because he was made of the earth, saying, *Terra es et in terram reverteris.*[915] And the Scripture calleth the serpent into which the rod of Aaron was turned by the name of a rod or a yard,[916] while it was not a rod but a serpent: *Virga Aaron devoravit virgas magorum Aegyptiorum.*[917]

---

910 incapable of suffering   **911** anew
912 Lk 22:18   **913** Mt 26:29 and Mk 14:25: "I say verily to you that I shall not drink henceforth from this fruit of the vine

until that day when I will drink it with you new in the kingdom of my Father, God."
914 act of drinking   **915** Gn 3:19. "For dust thou art, and unto dust thou shalt

return."   **916** stick   **917** Ex 7:12. "The rod of Aaron swallowed up the rods of the magicians of Egypt."

And over this our Savior in those second words, as some holy doctors declare, by the vine meant himself, which afterward unto his apostles he declared himself, saying in the fifteenth chapter of Saint John, *Ego sum vitis vera* ("I am the very vine").[918]

And so may every way these words of our Savior (spoken after the conversion of the wine into his blessed blood) be well thus understand:[919] "I say verily to you that I shall not, from this time in which I drink now thereof with you, drink again of the generation of the vine, that is to wit, of my blood which I have here consecrated, and into which I have here converted and turned the generation of the vine (that is to say, the wine that came of the vine and was in the chalice before) until that day when," etc.

Or else, after those other holy doctors that expound the vine to be himself, they may be well understood thus: "I say verily to you that I shall not, from this time in which I drink thereof with you now, drink anymore of this generation of the vine that we now drink of, that is to say, of mine own blood of the new testament (as I have told you), which is the generation of that vine of which these other words of mine are verified, *Ego sum vitis vera,* 'I am the very vine'[920] (for of mine own body is mine own blood) — of this generation of the vine will I no more drink after this time until that day in which I shall drink it with you new, that is to wit, when it shall be new in the kingdom of my Father God (that is to say, that I being in the kingdom of God, my very natural Father,[921] that is to wit, after my resurrection when my body shall be forever immortal and impassible and in eternal glory), until that day will I not after this time drink anymore of this generation of the vine, that is myself, which am the very vine. And then after that will I drink it again with you, at which time it shall be new."

Now that with those words this exposition, by which they be understood not of wine but of his blessed blood, most properly should agree, it appeareth both by diverse other things that well may be gathered upon the circumstance[922] of the matter and also upon this latter saying of our Savior compared with the former. For in the former, he said that he would, after that draft of wine that he drank to the Paschal lamb, drink no more wine till after his resurrection. And now had he drunken wine again after that and before his resurrection, if that which he drank the second time had been wine (as it was not, but was only his own blessed blood). And therefore is it very probable that, in his second saying, by these words, "this generation of the vine," he meant not any wine, but the blessed blood of himself.

Also in the words that he spoke before of the Paschal lamb (when he said he would eat the Paschal lamb after that no more till it were fulfilled and perfected in the kingdom of God) he meant that the Mosaical sacrifice of the Paschal lamb, that was the only figure,[923] he would never eat more. But the very Paschal lamb that was the verity of that figure, that is to wit, his own blessed body and blood, after that the figure were by his new sacrament instituted, and (by his Passion suffered and by his glorious body risen again from death) fulfilled in the kingdom of God, that would he then eat again with them in the Blessed Sacrament under the form of bread, as he now would when he instituted it, and as he did after indeed. And so are these words of the chalice understood in like wise of his blessed blood in the sacrament, which it seemeth that he by those words in like wise promised to drink again with them after his resurrection.

Finally, for this exposition, I note this word *novum,* that is to say, "new." Where our Savior in the said latter saying saith, *Dico autem vobis, quia a modo non bibam de hoc genimine vitis, usque in diem illum cum illud bibam novum vobiscum in regno Patris mei Dei* ("I say verily to you that from henceforth I shall not drink of this generation of the vine, until that day when I shall drink it with you new in the kingdom of my Father God"),[924] in these words, I say, I note and mark this word *novum,* "new." For albeit that diverse doctors expound it, *novum, id est novo modo* ("new," that is to wit, "in a new manner"), because our Lord after his resurrection did both eat and drink with his disciples such common meat and drink as he was before wont to do, but yet in a new manner (that is to wit, now immortal and impassible, and not for the necessary food of the body, but for the proof of that he was risen with his very body), albeit, I say, that some doctors expound that word *novum* thus, yet seemeth me that the other exposition is much more apt and consonant

---

918 Jn 15:1   **919** understood   true Father of my nature   **922** context   **924** Mt 26:29 and Mk 14:25
920 Jn 15:1   **921** *my . . . Father:* the   **923** *the . . . figure:* merely a type

thereunto. For this word *novum* seemeth not there to be put for an adverb, but is a noun adjective, and therefore it signifieth some kind of newness in the drink itself, whereas by that exposition all the newness is in the drinker (that is to wit, in the person of Christ) and in the act of drinking, as done for a new cause, but no manner of newness in the drink itself at all.

For in the common wine that our Savior drank with them after his resurrection was there none other manner of newness than there was therein before. And therefore, as I said, this other exposition that I have here showed seemeth much more agreeable unto the text, that is to wit, that after that time he would no more drink with them his own blessed blood, which he drank with them then in the Blessed Sacrament, until that day when he should in the kingdom of God his Father drink that blood with them new. For after his glorious resurrection that holy blood of his and all his blessed body was waxen new, that is to wit, of a new condition, other than it was at that time in which they received it in the Blessed Sacrament.

For albeit that his body, so delivered them at that time, suffered not, nor by their eating and receiving into their bodies was not pained, yet was it such that afterward it did suffer pain and death upon the cross. But when they received it again sacramentally after his resurrection, then was it in eternal glory so confirmed, and in such wise immortal and impassible, that it should never die nor never suffer pain after. And so, though there were in his blessed body and his blood given them in the sacrament before his Passion such a secret wonderful glory of impassibility for the time (as was in his body for the time a visible, open glory at his marvelous transfiguration), yet in the sacramental receiving after his glorious resurrection it had that point of newness which it had not actually before, that is to wit, without loss, diminishment, or intermission,[925] eternal enduring of impassible and immortal glory.

And so should (as I say) that generation of that vine, that is to wit, the blessed blood of his own holy person which he drank with them, consecrated of the generation of the common vine and in the likeness and form of common wine, be new after his glorious resurrection, before which time he there told them that he would drink no more

thereof after that time, in which at his Maundy in the first institution he and all they did drink thereof together, of which their drinking with him Saint Mark maketh mention, saying, *Et biberunt ex eo omnes* ("and they drank thereof all"),[926] that is to wit, all the twelve apostles.

That all the apostles drank thereof appeareth well by these words, at the leastwise as many as were present at the time, and that were they all twelve. For though some have doubted and some also thought that Judas was gone before, yet is it the most common sentence[927] of all the old holy men, and most received for the truth among all Christian people, that the traitor received it too, whereof we shall have occasion to speak after in other places.

But now that our Savior did receive and eat his own blessed body, and drink his own blessed blood in the Blessed Sacrament at his Maundy with his apostles himself, if any man doubt, it seemeth me[928] that his own holy words afore-rehearsed will well declare it, in which words he said that himself would drink no more thereof till he would drink it with them new in the kingdom of God, that is to wit, in his glory as I have before showed you.

And that he called his glory the kingdom of God appeareth both by other places of Scripture and also by his own words, where, intending to show to some of his disciples (that is to wit, Saint Peter, Saint James, and Saint John) a sight and show of his glory in his transfiguration, he said, *Sunt quidam de hic stantibus qui non gustabunt mortem, donec videbunt regnum Dei* ("There be some here standing that shall not taste the death till they shall see the kingdom of God").[929]

Besides this, likewise as he did himself both eat and drink with them of the old Paschal lamb that was but the figure, so is it none other to be thought but that in the instituting of this new Blessed Sacrament, the verity of that figure, he did himself eat and drink with them too. And that he so did indeed holy Saint Chrysostom declareth, which in an homily upon these words of Christ, *Bibite ex hoc omnes* ("Drink you of this all"), saith thus: *Ne autem hoc audientes turbarentur, primum ipse sanguinem suum bibit, inducens eos sine turbatione in communionem mysteriorum* ("Lest that they hearing that word should be troubled therewith, he drank his blood first himself, inducing them into the communion of

the sacraments without abashment or trouble").[930]
Holy Saint Jerome also in his book against the great
heretic Helvidius writeth in this wise: *Sic igitur Do-*
minus Iesus fuit conviva et convivium, ipse comedens
et qui comeditur ("So therefore was our Lord Jesus
both the guest and the feast. He was both the eater,
and was also he that was eaten").[931]

Now forasmuch as we shall somewhat farther enter into the treating of this Blessed Sacrament, let us
pray him that hath instituted it that we may in such
wise treat thereof that it may both in the writer and
the reader stretch to[932] the fruit of their souls.

The Prayer
Our most dear Savior Christ, which after the finishing of the old Paschal sacrifice hast instituted
the new sacrament of thine own blessed body and
blood for a memorial of thy bitter Passion, give us
such true faith therein and such fervent devotion
thereto that our souls may take fruitful ghostly[933]
food thereby.

The Second Lecture
upon the Blessed Sacrament

So excellent is, good Christian readers, this holy
Blessed Sacrament above all other, that neither is
there any man able to enter, pierce,[934] and perceive
so many great wonderful things as are to be noted
therein, nor those that of the old holy doctors are
already noted, and of all Christian regions already
received and believed, able (as the dignity of the
thing requireth) well to declare or worthily to speak
of. For in this holy sacrament is the very body and
the very blood of him of whom all other sacraments
receive their virtue and strength. For it is (as you
have heard of Christ's own words) the selfsame sacred body of Christ, and the selfsame blessed blood
of his, that was delivered and shed for our sin.

Now albeit that there are in diverse countries of
Christendom some (and hard it is to find any country so fortunate as to be clear and clean without)
that labor in this Blessed Sacrament to subvert the
very true Christian faith—and would make men
ween[935] that those plain words of Christ, "This is my
body" (etc.), were otherwise meant than they were

indeed, and that our Savior in his so saying did not
affirm nor intend that the thing which he gave his
apostles to eat and to drink was his very body and
his very blood, but that they were still bread and
wine which he called then (say they) by the names
of his body and his blood because he would institute them for to stand as tokens of his body and his
blood for perpetual remembrance of his Passion—
albeit there lack not, I say, some that labor to bring
good faithful folk out of the true belief into this erroneous mind, yet is it not my present purpose to
dispute the matter with them but to show and set
forth the truth before the eyes of the reader, that he
may rather of the truth read, increase in faith, and
conceive devotion, than with much time bestowed
in the reading of their erroneous fallacies misoc-
cupy his ears and heap up in his heart a dunghill of
their devilish vanities.

Howbeit, somewhat of theirs is it, good readers,
in my mind necessary that you know, to the intent
you may the better beware of their wiliness. Three
special engines[936] use these manner of folk with
which they busily with all their might oppugn[937]
the inexpugnable[938] person of our Savior Christ, enforcing themselves[939] by force to put out his glorious body out of the Blessed Sacrament.

First, using the name of sacrament of Christ's
body with us, whereby good simple folk would
ween they meant as we do, they misuse the meaning of that word against us, and in corners[940] corrupt some well-minded men before they perceive
the train[941] of their crafty purpose. For they make
them ween that, since we call it all the Blessed Sacrament of Christ's body and blood, therefore it is
none other but a bare sacrament only, that is to wit,
a token, a figure, a sign or memorial of his body and
his blood crucified and shed, and not his own very
body and his blood indeed.

Secondly, they say that those words of Christ may
be well and conveniently expounded in such wise
as they may serve to prove the sacrament a figure.
And upon that they conclude that, since they may
be so expounded conveniently by an allegory, there
is no necessity to expound them otherwise, nor that
those words should not be so taken and declared
as to say that they signify that in the sacrament is
Christ's blessed body indeed.

---

930 More is probably quoting Chrysostom
from the *Catena aurea* of Aquinas.
931 More is probably also quoting Jerome
from the *Catena aurea*.   **932** *stretch to:*
serve for   **933** spiritual   **934** see thoroughly into   **935** think   **936** instruments
of warfare   **937** attack   **938** impregnable
939 *enforcing themselves:* striving   **940** *in*
corners: in secluded places   **941** deceit

Thirdly, they enforce that reason[942] with the expositions of old holy men, which have expounded those words in an allegory[943] sense and have in their writings called this blessed Holy Housel[944] by the name of a sacrament, a sign, a memorial, and a figure. By which words of those old holy saints those new folk labor to blear the unlearned reader's eye and make him therewith ween that those old holy men, in that they called it a sign, a token, or a figure, did well declare that they took it not for the very body indeed, for that body cannot be (they say) by no means a figure of itself.

These three are, I say, good reader, their three special darts. For I deny not but that they use more as the words of Scripture, whereby they would prove Christ's body not in earth because he said before his ascension to heaven that they should not have him here still in earth (but he meant of his corporal conversation[945] as they had him before), and where they would also by the words of Scripture prove the Blessed Sacrament bread (but the custom of the Scripture is so common in that point to call a thing, not as it is, but as it was, or as it seemeth, whereof I have told you an example or two before, that all the hold they can take thereof slippeth out of their hand).

I deny not also but that they lay against[946] the Sacrament and say that Christ's blessed body is not there, because they say it cannot. For it cannot be (they say) in so many places at once. But now since the truth is that himself saith it is there, and in his so saying so meant in very deed (as both before is proved and yet shall hereafter), all that reason of theirs (that it cannot be so) hath to any Christian man (that taketh Christ for God) no manner taste of any reason at all. For it standeth, you see, well upon this ground only, that God is not able to perform his word.

Therefore albeit that (as I say) they say such other things too, yet are those three things that I have rehearsed you[947] the special things, and in effect the only things, with which they have their special hope to deceive unlearned folk.

Now purpose I not yet, in this present treatise upon the Passion, to enter much in dispicions[948] with them upon these three points neither. For that thing would require a whole volume alone (the labor whereof, if God hereafter give me time and opportunity thereto, I purpose not to refuse); but I will in effect, for this while, only rehearse you some of those things that holy cunning[949] men before my days have of this holy Blessed Sacrament, concerning this matter, left us behind them in writing. Which things, if the reader diligently consider, shall (I trust) be able somewhat to serve and suffice him to spy the fallacies and soil[950] the subtleties of all those folks' false arguments and objections by himself.

Consider now, good readers, and remember that — since this excellent high Sacrament, under a form and likeness so common and so simple in sight, covertly containeth in it a wonderful secret treasure, and signifieth and betokeneth also manifold marvelous mysteries — the holy cunning fathers afore our days have had much ado to find names enough and convenient with which they might in any wise insinuate[951] and show so many such manner things of this Blessed Sacrament as are partly contained therein and partly signified thereby. And therefore, by the secret instinct[952] of the Spirit of God, by which the Catholic Church of Christ is in such things led and ruled, the old holy virtuous fathers have not only called (upon effectual causes)[953] this Holy Sacrament by sundry diverse names, to signify thereby sundry singular things thereof, but have also, for the same intent (upon diverse effectual respects that they saw and considered therein), called some two sundry things both by one common name.

For the better perceiving whereof, we must mark and consider that in this Blessed Sacrament there are two things actually and really contained: one that is a very bodily substance and that is the very blessed body and blood of our Savior himself; the other that is not any substance but accidents, that is to wit, those accidents that were before in the bread and wine (which bread and wine are converted by the almighty power of God into the very body and blood of Christ). Those accidents, I say, of whiteness, redness, hardness, softness, weight, savor, and taste, and such other like, remain and abide in the Blessed Sacrament, and by the mighty power of almighty God they remain without the body of which they be the accidents, which — while they be now neither accidents in the bread and wine (since

---

942 *enforce that reason*: reinforce
that explanation   943 allegorical
944 Eucharist   945 *corporal conversation*:

bodily presence   946 *lay against*:
attack   947 *rehearsed you*: mentioned
to you   948 disputations   949 learned

950 refute   951 impart to the mind subtly
952 prompting   953 *upon effectual causes*:
for valid reasons

bread or wine none is there), nor accidents unto the blessed body and blood of Christ (which two things are the only corporal substance that are there) and accidents are not naturally, nor the mind of a living man cannot well imagine how any accident can be but in a bodily substance whereunto it is accident and whereupon it dependeth — much folly were it therefore much to muse thereupon how, and in what wise, and wherein these accidents abide and are conserved. But that question with many such other more — wherewith a proud curious mind hath carried many a man out of faith — let us remit unto God. For as he only can make those miracles, so can he only tell how.

Now albeit that an accident, by a general manner of speaking, is a thing (since it is not nothing), and in such wise I mean by this word "a thing" when I say there are in the Blessed Sacrament two things; yet, forasmuch as the name of "sacrament" properly signifieth a sign or token, which betokeneth a holy thing, the "thing" of a sacrament is properly called that holy thing that the sacrament betokeneth — as in baptism the washing of the body with water, signifying the washing of the soul by grace, is properly the sacrament, and the washing of the soul from sin is called the "thing" of the sacrament, that is to say, the thing that the sacrament or sacramental sign (I mean the washing in the water) betokeneth.

Now in this Holy Sacrament of the altar (which hath, as reason is,[954] above all other sacraments sundry special prerogatives)[955] there are two sacraments or sacramental signs of sundry kinds: the one an outward sacrament or sacramental sign sensible (as baptism hath, and confirmation, and the other four), the other an inward sacrament or sacramental sign unsensible,[956] which none of the remnant[957] have. The outward sensible sacrament or sacramental sign is the form of bread and the form of wine. The inward sacrament and sacramental sign unsensible is the very blessed body of Christ under that form of bread and the very blessed blood of Christ under the form of wine.

Now are there likewise in this Blessed Sacrament (above the nature also of all the other six) two things of the sacrament, or two sacramental things — that is to wit, two things that are by the two sacramental signs betokened. And those two things, though

they be both secret and unsensible, yet are they of diverse sundry kinds too. For the one is both by the sacrament (that is to wit, by the sacramental sign) signified and also in the sacrament contained. The other is only by the sacrament signified, but in the sacrament it is not contained. The thing of the sacrament that is both signified and contained is the very body and the very blood of our Savior himself, therein actually and really present. The thing of this Blessed Sacrament that is signified thereby and not contained therein is the unity or society of all good holy folk in the mystical body of Christ.

For this must we now first understand, that the first kind of sacrament that we spoke of (that is to wit, the outward sacramental signs) be sacraments (that is to wit, signs and tokens) of both these two sacramental things: that is to wit, of the very natural body of Christ that is in the sacrament contained, and also of the society of all saints in the mystical body of Christ that is not contained in it but signified and betokened by it. For the outward sacramental signs (that is to wit, the form of bread and wine) betoken the very natural body and blood of Christ being in the Sacrament. For as the holy doctors declare, likewise as bread specially refresheth and sustaineth the body — whereof the Scripture saith, *Panis confirmat cor hominis*[958] ("Bread strengthens a man's heart") — and wine gladdeth the heart — whereof the Scripture saith also, *Vinum laetificat cor hominis*[959] — so the very blessed body and blood of Christ in the Sacrament, received worthily,[960] doth specially above all other sacraments refresh, make strong, and confirm the soul in grace, and so fulfilleth in some good folk the soul with spiritual consolation that the soul is in a certain manner of a heavenly drunkenness. In proof whereof our Savior saith of his body in the Sacrament, *Panis quem ego dabo caro mea est; qui manducat hunc panem vivet in aeternum* ("The bread that I shall give is my flesh; he that eateth this bread shall live everlastingly").[961] And of his blessed blood in the Sacrament he saith by the mouth of the prophet, *Calix meus inebrians quam praeclarus est?* ("My cup that maketh men drunk, how noble it is?")[962]

These outward sacramental signs (the form of bread and wine) do also signify and betoken unto us the other sacramental thing (or the other thing

---

954 *as reason is:* in conformity to reason   **958** Ps 103(104):15   **959** Ps 103(104):15.   **960** with a fitting disposition   **961** Jn
955 divinely given privileges   **956** imper-   "Wine gladdens the heart of man."   6:52, 59   **962** Ps 22(23):5
ceptible to the senses   **957** others

of the Sacrament), that is to wit, that thing of the sacrament that is signified by the Sacrament but not contained therein—that is to wit, the society of all saints in the mystical body of Christ. For likewise as the bread, which is in this Holy Sacrament turned into Christ's very body (of which bread the form still remaineth), was made of many corns[963] of wheat into one loaf and the wine that is converted into his blessed blood (of which wine the form remaineth) was made of many grapes flowing into one wine, so be all holy saints gathered together in one, into the unity of Christ's holy mystical body, as Saint Paul toucheth in his epistle to the Corinthians, saying, *Unus panis et unum corpus multi sumus; omnes qui de uno pane, et de uno calice participamus* ("We many be one bread and one body, as many as be partakers of one bread and one cup").[964]

The other kind of sacrament or sacramental sign (that is to wit, the sacrament or sacramental sign secret and unsensible)[965] is, I say, the very natural body and blood of our Savior in the form of bread and wine. For his very body and his very blood in these forms so known and seen unto us, not by our senses but by the truth of our faith, do betoken and represent unto us the selfsame body and the selfsame blood crucified and shed upon the cross. For our Savior at his Last Supper, at the institution of the Blessed Sacrament, did ordain, institute, and appoint them to signify, betoken, and represent unto his Church under those forms the selfsame body crucified and the selfsame blood also shed for remission of man's sins at his bitter Passion.

And therefore when our Savior gave his blessed body in form of bread unto his apostles, saying unto them, *Hoc est corpus meum, quod pro vobis tradetur* and *hic est sanguis meus qui pro vobis et multis effundetur in remissionem peccatorum* ("This is my body, which shall be delivered for you;[966] this is my blood, which for you and for many shall be shed into remission of sins"),[967] he said unto them farther, *Hoc facite in meam commemorationem* ("This do ye in the remembrance of me").[968] So that there we may see that he there instituted the same body of his that should be delivered for us unto death and the same blood that should be shed for our sins to be in his Church continually consecrated and celebrated as a monument and a memorial representing to us himself.

Now in what wise those secret invisible sacraments (his own very natural blessed body and blood) under those visible sacraments (those forms of bread and wine) should signify, betoken, and represent unto us himself (that is to say, the same body and blood in their proper form), the apostle explaineth in the eleventh chapter of his first epistle to the Corinthians, saying, *Quotienscumque manducabitis panem hunc et calicem bibetis, mortem Domini annunciabitis donec veniat* ("As often as you shall eat this bread and drink this cup, you shall show the death of our Lord till he come").[969] Here we see that, whereas our Savior in his own words ordained his own very body and blood in the Sacrament to signify, betoken, and represent himself unto our remembrance, Saint Paul showeth here that it is the remembrance of him as in his Passion; and so betoken his body and his blood in the Sacrament the selfsame body in his[970] own likeness hanging on the cross and the selfsame blood in the proper likeness on the same shed for our sin. The selfsame insensible[971] Sacrament also, the natural body of Christ that is under the sensible sacrament of bread, signifieth and betokeneth the other aforesaid sacramental thing, that is to wit, the society of saints. For like as the natural body of Christ is many members in one natural body, so is that society of saints many lively[972] members in the unity of Christ's mystical body.

And thus we see, good Christian readers, that the outward sensible sacraments (the forms of bread and wine) be in such wise figures, tokens, and sacramental signs, that they be only sacramental signs and not sacramental things. And on the other side, the secret sacramental thing which is both by the outward sensible sacraments and by the secret unsensible sacraments signified and not contained (that is to wit, the society of saints in the unity of Christ's body mystical) is only the thing of the sacrament, or the sacramental thing, and not a sacramental sign, neither sensible nor unsensible (for it is signified

963 grains   **964** 1 Cor 10:17. At this point More directed that a passage be inserted from St. Augustine (*In Iohannis evangelium tractatus* 26, *PL* 35, 1614–15) to support the symbolic significance of bread uniting many grains and wine many grapes. Rastell

(*English Workes,* 1557) gave the Latin and translated it (with less skill than one would have expected from More). Both the Latin and the translation are omitted here. **965** imperceptible to the senses   **966** Lk 22:19. See also Mt 26:26; Mk 14:22.

967 Mt 26:28. See also Mk 14:24; Lk 22:20.   **968** Lk 22:19   **969** 1 Cor 11:26 **970** its   **971** imperceptible to senses **972** living only and signifieth not). But the very natural body and blood of Christ, in the form of bread and wine, be both sacramental signs, because they signify, and also sacramental things, because they be signified.

Yet must we further know that, albeit we speak only of the blessed body and blood of Christ, that are verily present in form of bread and wine, yet is there with them the soul of our Savior also. For his blessed body and blood in the Sacrament, though they seem dead — for the more full representation and figuring of the same body and blood remaining dead on the cross after his holy soul given up to the Father, whereby his bitter Passion was fully performed and finished — yet be they not dead in the Sacrament, but quick[973] and animated with his blissful soul, which after the return thereof and copulation[974] again with his immortal and impassible body never departed after from it nor never shall.

There is with it also, beside his blessed soul, his almighty Godhead. For the Godhead from the first time of his incarnation never departed neither from the soul nor from the body. But when they two were by death departed[975] and severed asunder, the Godhead — that is to wit, the almighty natural Son of the almighty Father, the second person in Trinity (of which Father and Son the third almighty person of the coeternal Trinity proceeded) — was still in unity of person, both with the blessed soul delivering the old fathers in hell, and with the body lying dead in the sepulcher too.

Moreover, albeit that the blessed blood is consecrated severally under the form of wine, to signify and represent unto us that in the Passion (of which the Blessed Sacrament is a memorial) the blood was severed from the body, yet is there in the Blessed Sacrament both the blood with the body that is in the form of bread, and the body with the blood that is under form of wine — that is to wit, the body (under the form of bread) immediately, as by the form of bread most specially signified, and the blood by concomitance, because the body is never without it; and likewise, under the form of wine the blessed blood immediately, because there by that form of wine the blood is chiefly signified, and the whole blessed body is there with it by concomitance, because that the blood, since his glorious resurrection,

never was, nor is, nor never shall be separate from his whole blessed body.

If men ask then the question, what we may think of the holy blood of Christ out of the Sacrament, continually kept and honored in diverse places and with many great miracles approved,[976] me thinketh it may be answered in two manner wise without any peril of our faith. For I see no necessity to say that all the blood that Christ had in his body at any time here in earth is in his body now. And so may some part of his very holy blood that hath been sometimes in his blessed body be now remaining in earth. And also, since his blessed body may be where it will, his very glorious blood may be by miracle in sundry places sensible, where it pleaseth himself, and his blessed body invisible also therewith.

In a crucifix striken,[977] God may also create new blood, which is none of his. And over this, the blissful soul of Christ and his almighty Godhead also be both twain,[978] I say, not immediately contained in the Sacrament, because they be neither immediately signified by those sensible sacramental signs (the forms of bread and wine), nor be there as secret unsensible signs appointed to signify any other things (as the blessed body and the blood be), but be therefore there by concomitance, because from the body and the blood neither the soul nor the Godhead is at no time since the resurrection asunder.

And by concomitance are there also both the Father and the Holy Ghost. For since the Godhead of the Son and the Godhead of them both is all one self[979] Godhead, neither of them both can be severed from him, but it must needs be that where he is, there be they both, not only by a general manner of being (by which each of them is ever with any of all the things that they have created), but also by that special manner of being by which (whatsoever manner that be) any of those three persons is with himself, except the only personal distinction.[980] It seemeth also that by concomitance, though not a concomitance following of like necessity (yet by a certain concomitance following of convenient congruity), there is everywhere evermore about this Blessed Sacrament a glorious heavenly company of blessed angels and saints, as diverse holy doctors declare.

973 living   **974** union   **975** separated
976 attested to   **977** pierced, cut
978 together   **979** same   **980** *except…*

distinction: except that the distinction among the persons remains (Thus, the Father is with the Son as the Son is with

himself, except that the Father is a distinct person from the Son, whereas the Son is not personally distinct from himself.)

Now forasmuch as under any of the two outward sensible sacraments (the forms either of the bread or the wine) the whole inward unsensible sacrament (the very body and blood of Christ) is, as I have showed you, verily and fully contained, and also under every part thereof (be it divided into never so many), therefore whosoever worthily do receive his Holy Housel[981] under any one of those two forms only[982] doth verily and sufficiently receive both the blessed body and blood of our Savior and therewith his blessed soul and his Godhead too, yea, and all the whole Trinity together. And albeit that of old time lay people did commonly receive their Housel under both the forms, yet always from the beginning did they sometime receive it some under the one form and some under the other alone, as by the old writings of the old holy saints it doth in diverse places appear. Howbeit,[983] when they received their Housel under the one kind alone, it was most commonly under the form of bread, because that under that form it was most able both to be carried without peril of spilling and longest to be kept without peril of turning.[984]

Upon which thing so long ago begun and used, it came to that point afterward that for diverse inconveniences,[985] which many times mishapped[986] in the blessed blood under the form of wine when the common people were houseled[987] under both the forms, the whole people through[988] Christendom fell in a custom uniform all in one fashion to receive their holy housel (that is to wit, the very whole body of Christ and blood both) under the form of bread only—of which custom no man hath heard or read any beginning, which thing alone may well suffice to make indifferent[989] men perceive that it began even forthwith[990] after Christ's death and that the leefulness[991] thereof was known and taught by the tradition of the apostles themselves. For surely if it had not been known for leeful of old, the whole people of all Christendom would never have taken it up of new,[992] being a thing of neither pleasure nor winning, nor being nothing forced unto it (for law was there none made to command it).

Howbeit, when that the country of Boheme, falling into many heresies, began not only to do the contrary, receiving it under both the forms (wherein the body of Christendom would not have sticked to suffer[993] them as a thing leeful to them that would),[994] but also took upon them farther to reprove and reproach for damnable the common long-continued custom of the whole corps[995] of Christendom—upon this demeanor of theirs, the general Council of Constance[996] condemned in their so doing their over-arrogant error. For upon that point of theirs, if the whole body of Christendom may damnably be deceived in matter concerning our faith or the use of the sacraments, then followeth there an inevitable confusion and nothing can there in the Catholic Church be sure: neither tradition, law, custom, nor Scripture—neither to know how it is to be understood nor yet so much as which the very books be, as holy Saint Augustine (against the great heretics the Manichees) doth very clearly declare.[997]

Now is this custom (and long was, ere their heresies began in Boheme) so universal that neither lay nor priest, man nor woman, good nor bad, either otherwise used[998] in receiving the Holy Housel beside[999] the Mass or anything repugned[1] thereat. Howbeit, though (as I say) this guise[2] and custom was universal both with lay people and priests, in being houseled of[3] another man's hand (as the priests be themselves always, save only when they say Mass), yet did there never priest in the Mass use to consecrate in the one form alone. And the cause is because that in the Mass the Blessed Sacrament is (as the old holy doctors all with one voice agree, and all the corps of Christendom with them from the apostles' days) not only a sacrament but also a sacrifice that by the offering of the body and blood of Christ (under the forms of bread and wine upon the altar) representeth the sacrifice in which the selfsame body and blood in their own proper form was offered upon the cross.

And therefore, albeit that in each of the two forms is the whole sacrament, both for the thing that it signifieth and for the thing that it containeth, yet under the one kind only was it never used to offer that holy sacrifice, but under the both twain together, that the thing should be correspondent unto

---

981 Eucharist   **982** alone   **983** However   **984** spoiling   **985** unfortunate occurrences   **986** happened unfortunately   **987** given Communion   **988** throughout   **989** impartial   **990** immediately

991 lawfulness   **992** *of new:* anew   **993** *sticked to suffer:* been hesitant to allow   **994** wished to   **995** body   **996** The Council of Constance (1415) condemned the Bohemian reformer Jan Huss

(ca. 1372–1415) to death.   **997** Augustine, *Contra epistolam Manichaei*, 5   **998** practiced   **999** outside of   **1** resisted   **2** practice   **3** by

the figure (for this holy sacrifice was forefigured in the offering of Melchizedek,[4] that offered both bread and wine).

Yet is there also put into the wine, before the consecration, a little water always, whereof we find no word written in the Gospel, nor any plain place in all the Scripture for it. And yet may it not be leefully[5] left out, as all the old holy doctors teach us. And diverse causes they lay[6] of that institution,[7] partly for that out of the holy heart of Christ, when it was pierced with the spear, there issued both blood and water.[8] And some allege that it is done for to signify the joining of the people with Christ (for, as it appeareth in the Apocalypse, by water is signified people).[9] And finally, some holy saints say that it is done because that our Savior himself, at his Maundy, tempered his wine with water. And all these may be good causes, with the truth and the will of God well-known. But else I verily believe that no good man (upon any of these considerations or any other), when he should consecrate, would presume or adventure[10] to put water into his wine—where the Gospel of the institution[11] speaketh of no water at all (but only of wine alone)—and therefore it well and clearly appeareth, both by this point and diverse other more (as in the very words and manner of consecration), the rites and the manner of this Holy Sacrament were more at large showed and more fully taught by Christ's apostles by mouth than afterward written by their pen.

And so appeareth it also by Saint Paul, which first taught it the Corinthians without any book written thereof; and, after writing them somewhat thereof, saith yet finally, *Caetera cum venero ipse disponam* ("The remnant I will order when I come myself").[12] And never wrote he those orders after[13] that he took farther at his coming, as far as ever I could hear proved. Origen saith also (and diverse other old holy doctors) that many things of the Mass were taught by the apostles by tradition, without writing, by mouth.[14] Saint Denis also, in his book *De Ecclesiastica hierarchia,* saith that the apostles taught the manner of consecrating in the Mass by mouth.[15]

Now because of these wonderful things, and many other wherein this most Blessed Sacrament so far excelleth all other, as that sacrament that not only signifieth and betokeneth but also verily and really containeth the holy and blessed blood of him of whom all the other sacraments take their strength (for he is, as I have said, not only man but also God, and with his holy body and blood is also his holy soul, and with both his body and soul joined his unseparable Godhead, and of him his Father and their Holy Spirit is all one Godhead and therefore there present all three)—for these causes, I say, for which this Blessed Sacrament so many manner ways differeth from all other, the old holy doctors have accustomed to speak of this Holy Sacrament in diverse wise and, to signify and insinuate thereby the diverse properties thereof, by sundry diverse names have been accustomed to call it.

Whereas the sacrament of baptism is not called "the sacrament" alone but "the sacrament of baptism," nor any of the remnant[16] without the addition of their own proper name (as the sacrament of confirmation, the sacrament of penance, and so forth the remnant), only this Blessed Sacrament is called and known by the name of "Sacrament" alone, signifying and showing thereby that this Blessed Sacrament is the most excellent and of all holy sacraments the chief. And that I see not why it were, if it were not (as it is) the very body of Christ, for the sacrament of baptism is unto salvation of more necessity than it, and the sacrament of penance too.

This Blessed Sacrament of the body and blood of Christ is called also distinctly by the name of either form, *Sacramentum Panis et Sacramentum Vini* ("the Sacrament of Bread and the Sacrament of Wine"), because that the form of bread betokeneth and immediately containeth the one, and the form of wine the other. And albeit that they be indeed two distinct sacraments (that is to wit, both two distinct sacramental outward signs, for neither is the form of bread the form of wine, nor the form of wine the form of bread, and two distinct sacramental inward signs too), and two distinct sacramental things also, of that kind of thing that is contained therein (for neither is the body the blood, nor the blood the body), yet is all together called by the name of "the Blessed Sacrament" in the singular number, *Sacramentum altaris* ("the Sacrament of the altar"); and yet is it never used at the altar but in both the forms. But for because that the very

4 See Gn 14:18. **5** permissibly, lawfully **6** present, allege **7** established rule **8** See Jn 19:34. **9** Rv 17:15 **10** venture **11** founding **12** 1 Cor 11:34 **13** afterward **14** See Origen's fifth homily on the Book of Numbers (*PG* 12: 603). **15** Dionysius (Denis), the pseudo-Areopagite (*PG* 3: 375, 378) **16** others

real thing that is contained under both those forms is one entire body—that is to wit, the very lively, natural, glorious body of our Savior Christ himself, to the integrity whereof the blood of the same per-
5 taineth, and whereof it is now an inseparable part—which blessed body and blood (though they, being in the Sacrament under several forms, severally do signify and therefore be well and with good reason called several sacraments) be yet never severally sep-
10 arate asunder indeed; therefore to give us knowledge that all that is really contained in both these sacramental forms is one very real thing—that is to wit, the very blessed one entire body of Christ—all the whole, under the both forms together, is called
15 by the name of "the Sacrament of the altar" in the singular number.

It is called *Sacramentum Panis* ("the Sacrament of Bread") and it is called also *Panis* (that is to say, "Bread") because that of bread it was consecrated
20 and that, after the bread converted and turned into the body of Christ, the form and accidents of the bread abide and remain (as I before have showed you that in Scripture a man is called "earth" because he was made of the earth, and in the Scrip-
25 ture Moses's yard[17] was called still a "yard" when it was turned from a dead yard into a quick serpent that devoured all the serpents that the witches of Egypt had by their enchantment brought forth before Pharaoh their king). But yet, lest the naming it
30 "Bread" might make some men ween[18] it were but bread indeed, it is called also plainly by the name of the thing that it is indeed, the Body and Blood of our Lord.

It is also called *Sacramentum Communionis* ("the
35 Sacrament of Communion") because that the thing that all the sacraments or sacramental signs (both outward signs and inward, both sensible and unsensible) do signify is, as I showed you, the communion —that is to wit, the union together—of all holy
40 saints in one society, as lively members in the mystical body of Christ. It is also called not only "the Sacrament of Communion" but over that the "Communion" itself, which is called in Latin *Communio* and *Synaxis* in the Greek. And this Blessed Sacra-
45 ment is called the Communion—that is to say, the union or gathering together in one—because that this sacrament doth not only signify that communion but that the very real thing that is in this

Blessed Sacrament (beside the signification thereof) doth also effectually make[19] it. For the blessed per-
50 son of our Savior Christ, being verily both God and man, doth as God, of his almighty power, by his manhead as by his instrument (not an instrument dead and separate as are all his other sacraments, but by his instrument lively, quick, conjoined, unied,[20]
55 and forever unseparable), in special manner—by grace that he giveth with the joining of his own holy body and blood unto them that effectually receive it—doth work, I say, this wonderful work of this communion of men together with God.
60

And over this, our Savior, that is in the Sacrament, is not only the worker of this communion, but, since that this communion is a gathering together of all saints into his own mystical body, this Holy Sacrament therefore, in which his own very
65 body is, may be well called the communion. And so by their calling this Blessed Sacrament by the name of Communion, the old holy doctors and all the congregation of all Christian people have and do put every man and woman of the same congre-
70 gation in remembrance that in that Blessed Sacrament is the very body and blood, and by concomitance (as I have before declared) the very whole person, of our sovereign Lord and almighty Savior Christ, from whom (as I have said) neither his al-
75 mighty Father nor their almighty Spirit either is or can be sundered.

This Blessed Sacrament is also called *Eucharistia,* which in the Greek tongue signifieth "giving of thanks," to put us in remembrance how high hearty
80 thanks we be bounden of duty to give unto God for this inestimable benefit. This Holy Sacrament is also called *Sacrificium* ("the sacrifice") because it is, as I have told you, the only sacrifice betaken[21] by Christ unto his Christian Church, instead of the
85 old Paschal (which was the figure thereof), to be offered up while the world standeth:[22] instead of flesh and blood of beasts, the very flesh and blood of our Savior himself, immortal and impassible under the forms of bread and wine, representing the most ac-
90 ceptable sacrifice of the same flesh and blood offered up, once forever, mortal and passible[23] upon the cross at his bitter Passion.

This Holy Sacrament is also called of the old holy doctors *Cena Dominica* ("the Supper of our Lord"),
95 by which name there are signified unto us two

17 stick   18 think   19 effect   20 united   21 granted   22 continues   23 capable of suffering

things. One is the excellency of this Blessed Sacrament, this new very Paschal lamb, the sacred body of our Savior himself, over and above the old Paschal lamb of the Jews. For that Paschal being but the figure, and this of that figure the verity, the figure passed[24] and finished, this only[25] verity — the blessed body and blood of Christ — beareth now the name alone of the Supper of our Lord to signify the other to be nothing in the respect of[26] this. The other thing which that name signifieth and representeth unto us is the verity of the blessed body and blood of Christ in the Sacrament. For it is called the Supper of our Lord to put us in mind and to let us know that it is not another thing but the selfsame thing that our Lord gave there to his apostles: not another supper, but the selfsame Supper. For his body is the selfsame body now that it was then, and his blessed blood the selfsame in like wise, and that was the supper that he last gave unto them after the Paschal lamb eaten.[27] And that selfsame body and blood is the thing that he giveth us. And therefore is it called the Supper of our Lord, to let us (as I say) perceive that the thing that we receive at God's board now is the very selfsame thing that the apostles received then, and that is not the same bread and the same wine that were then turned but the very selfsame body and blood into which they were then turned.

Finally, beside yet diverse other names diversely signifying the manifold great graces thereof, it is, as I have said, both by the Scripture and all the holy doctors plainly and clearly called by the proper name of the thing that indeed it is, that is to wit, *Corpus Domini et Sanguis Domini* ("the Body and Blood of our Lord").

And likewise as by all these names aforerehearsed, and yet other more, for the cause aboveremembered, this Blessed Sacrament is called by the old holy doctors and all the corps of Christendom, not in Latin only and in Greek, but in other vulgar tongues too, so in our English tongue is it also called the "Holy Housel" — which name of "housel" doth not only signify unto us the blessed body and blood of our Lord in the sacramental form, but also, like as this English word "God" signifieth unto us not only the unity of the Godhead but also the Trinity of the three Persons, and not only their supersubstantial[28]

substance but also every gracious property (as justice, mercy, truth, almightiness, eternity, and every good thing more than we can imagine), so doth unto us English folk this English word "housel" though not express, yet imply and under a reverent devout silence signify both the sacramental signs and the sacramental things, as well the things contained as the things holily signified, with all the secret unsearchable mysteries of the same. All which holy things right many persons — very little learned, but yet in grace godly minded, with heart humble and religious, not arrogant, proud, and curious — under the name of Holy Housel, with inward heavenly comfort, do full devoutly reverence, as many a good, poor, simple, unlearned soul honoreth God full devoutly under the name of God that cannot yet tell such a tale of God as some great clerks can that are yet for lack of like devotion nothing near so much in God's grace and favor.

Here have I, good Christian readers, rehearsed you some of those many names by which, for the manifold mysteries contained therein and signified thereby, this Blessed Sacrament is called. And this have I done to the intent that if it hap[29] you at any time hereafter to hear or read any of these things that are said or written by them that use of some of these names to take occasion of oppugning[30] the truth, you may have ready before, at your hand, the fallacy of their sophism soiled.[31] As for example, because it is called (as it is indeed) the sacrament of Christ's body — that is to wit, a figure, a token, or a representation of his body — they labor to make men ween[32] that it cannot be his very body indeed. But I have here before showed you in what wise it is a sacrament and doth betoken, and in what wise it is the thing of the sacrament and is betokened.

Howbeit, where we say that the very body in the form of bread betokeneth and representeth unto us the selfsame body in his own proper form hanging upon the cross, they say that nothing can be a figure or a token of itself, which thing I marvel much that any man taketh for so strange. For if there were but even in a play or an interlude[33] the personages of two or three known princes represented, if one of them now liked for his pleasure to play his own part himself, did he not there, his own person under the form of a player, represent his own person in form of his own estate? Our Savior (as Saint Augustine saith), walking with his two disciples toward the castle[34] of Emmaus in form of a wayfaring man, betokened and was a figure of himself in form of his own person glorified, going out of the corporal conversation of this world by his wonderful ascension unto heaven.[35] And in like wise our Savior, appearing to Mary Magdalene in the form of a gardener, was a figure of himself in his own proper form, planting the faith and other virtues in the garden of our souls.[36]

Now as you see, good readers, that these folk trifle in this point, so do they (as earnest and as great as the matter is) but in a manner utterly trifle in the remnant. As (for another example) because the Sacrament is called in Scripture "bread," they say it is bread indeed. And surely if that argument be so sure as they would have it seem, the selfsame reason must of reason[37] serve sufficiently (since it is in Scripture as plainly called "flesh") to drive them to grant that it is very flesh indeed. Howbeit indeed, the most part of these that are fallen from the right belief of the Sacrament are not yet in that point fallen fully so foul but that they let[38] not to confess that in the Blessed Sacrament is Christ's very flesh indeed. But then say they that it is very bread too. Howbeit, the custom of Scripture in calling it bread though it be not bread, that have I twice touched before.

But then say the other sort (the far worse sort again) if the calling it bread in Scripture prove it not bread indeed, then by the same reason the calling it flesh in Scripture proveth it not flesh indeed. To that we say that, if it were but a bare word spoken, it might be taken for an allegory or some other trope or figure of common speaking. But in this point so many things in Scripture agree together upon the very thing, that it is very clear and plain that in calling it bread the Scripture meaneth not that it is bread, but calleth it by the name that it did bear before and that it seemeth still. But in calling it the body of Christ, though it useth (as it doth in many places) an allegorical sense besides, yet appeareth it, I say, plain upon[39] the circumstances that the Scripture meaneth that it is the very blessed body of our Savior himself indeed. To this say they again, "Yea, but we can and do conster[40] all those texts another

way with an allegory[41] sense and prove by the old doctors that our exposition is true."

To this we answer them and say, if you conster all those texts diverse other good ways with your allegories—so that[42] you do not with any of those ways take away the true sense of the letter—we will not withstand[43] your allegories but will well allow them, for the old holy doctors did the same. But on the other side, if with any of your allegorical expositions you deny the very literal sense beside, and say that the body of our Savior is not really under the form of bread in the Sacrament, then say we that in your such expounding you plain expound it false. For we say that such manner of your expositions is plain against the very sentence and the meaning of the text. And we say that in this point you report the old holy doctors untruly. For all the holy doctors and saints from the apostles' days to your own declare the Scripture clear against you. I will not here enter into the declaring of all the places of Scripture, by which places (opened and explained with the circumstances of the letter) good Christian people may well and plainly perceive that the very meaning of the Scripture is against these folk and proveth plain for the Catholic Church. For that were both a very long work and also a digression somewhat too long from my present purpose, which is only to declare those words that I have already declared—that is to wit, the words of our Savior himself, rehearsed by the three foresaid evangelists, Saint Matthew, Saint Mark, and Saint Luke, and spoken by our Savior at the institution of this Blessed Sacrament—and not to declare here all his other words that he spoke thereof before—rehearsed in the sixth chapter of Saint John, where he said, *Panis quem ego dabo vobis caro mea est pro mundi vita* ("The bread that I shall give you is my flesh for the life of the world")[44] and *Caro mea vere est cibus, et sanguis meus vere est potus* ("My flesh is verily meat and my blood is verily drink"),[45] with many more plain words further—nor to declare the words of Saint Paul either—where he saith in the eleventh chapter of the first epistle to the Corinthians, *Dominus Iesus in qua nocte tradebatur, accepit panem et gratias agens fregit et dixit: Accipite et manducate; hoc est corpus meum quod pro vobis tradetur* ("Our Lord Jesus in the same night that he

---

34 village   **35** Lk 24:15, 13. See also Augustine's *Sermones* 235–36 (*PL 38*, 1118, 1121).   **36** Jn 20:15. See also Augustine, *In*

Iohannis evangelium tractatus 121 (*PL 35*, 1957).   **37** *of reason:* in accordance with reason   **38** hesitate   **39** on the basis of

40 construe   **41** allegorical   **42** *so that:* provided that   **43** oppose   **44** Jn 6:52   **45** Jn 6:56

was betrayed took bread and giving thanks broke it and said, 'Take and eat; this is my body, which shall be betrayed for you'")[46] and *Quicumque manduca-verit panem hunc, et biberit calicem Domini indigne, reus erit corporis et sanguinis Domini* ("Whosoever eateth this bread and drinketh the cup of our Lord unworthily[47] shall be guilty of the body and blood of our Lord")[48] and, by and by after, he saith also, *Probet autem seipsum homo, et sic de pane illo edat, et de calice bibat; qui enim manducat et bibit indigne, iudicium sibi manducat et bibit, non diiudicans corpus Domini* ("Let a man examine and judge himself and so eat of this bread and drink of the cup; for he that eateth and drinketh unworthily, eateth and drinketh judgment and damnation to himself, not discerning and esteeming the body of our Lord").[49] These places of Scripture, and yet other more, plainly proving the presence of Christ's very body and blood in the Blessed Sacrament, is not, as I say, my present purpose to declare.

But yet to the intent you shall see that in the foresaid exposition of those words of our Savior at the institution of the Blessed Sacrament, where he calleth it his own body and his own blood, I have not told you a tale of mine own head, but that the old holy doctors and saints, contrary to these new men's tale, do plainly declare the same and plainly do affirm that in the Blessed Sacrament is the very body and blood of our Savior Christ himself, I shall rehearse you the plain words of some of them.[50]

Here have you, good Christian readers, heard the very plain open words of diverse of the old holy doctors, by which we may plainly perceive and see that they were of the selfsame belief of old that we be now, and which hath ever been the belief of Christ's whole Church since the institution of the Blessed Sacrament unto this day. And many years was it ere ever any man began to doubt, but that as well Catholics as all other that were yet in sundry other points heretics agreed together all in one that in this Blessed Sacrament is the very body and the very blood of Christ. For like as it was known to the apostles by the teaching of our Savior Christ himself, and so forth[51] unto the primitive Church or congregation of Christian people that were

gathered together in many parts of the world in the apostles' days, so was the selfsame truth taught by the apostles themselves, first fully and thoroughly by mouth and tradition, or delivery without writing, and afterward by writing conveniently also. Of the understanding of which writing there could at that time no doubt or debate arise, forasmuch as the whole people knew the truth of the thing before the writing of the apostles and evangelists, by the faith that the apostles and evangelists had taught them before by mouth.

And so using and teaching the sacraments, and understanding without any difficulty the words of the Scripture therein, by their foretaught[52] and from time to time kept and continued faith, lived in unity and concord of belief concerning this Blessed Sacrament, no man gainsaying[53] the very blessed body and blood to be therein, even after that many folk were fallen in many other points from the true Catholic faith. And this appeareth very plain, by that we see both[54] Saint Irenaeus confound the Valentinians, and Saint Hilarius confound the Arians, and Saint Augustine confound the Manichees, by certain arguments grounded upon the verity of the very body and blood of our blessed Savior in this Holy Sacrament, which had been, you wot[55] well, nothing to the purpose if those three sects of heretics had not agreed with those three holy saints, and with the Catholic Church, that in the Sacrament is the very body and blood of Christ.

Howbeit, after that began there some (among their other heresies) to fall then unto some of these concerning the Blessed Sacrament. For when men began once to take the bridle in the teeth and run forth at rovers[56] out of the common trade[57] of the foretaught and received—and by the whole Catholic Church believed and professed—faith, then could there not, nor yet can, with such manner of folk the letter of Holy Scripture be any bridle to refrain them back. For setting the authority of the whole corps of the known Catholic Church at nought[58] and challenging[59] the Spirit of God from the same, and ascribing that Holy Spirit, some to such a known church of heretics as themselves assigned, and the more part of them ascribing that

---

46 1 Cor 11:23–24   **47** without proper regard   **48** 1 Cor 11:27   **49** 1 Cor 11:28–29   **50** At this point More quotes (in Latin and English) passages from nineteen Latin and Greek Fathers (from St. Ignatius of Antioch to Theophylactus of Bulgaria). They have been omitted here. See *CW* 13: 160–70.   **51** *so forth:* then onward   **52** previously taught [faith]   **53** denying   **54** i.e., all three   **55** know   **56** *at rovers:* at random   **57** track   **58** *setting at nought:* regarding as nothing   **59** laying claim to

Spirit to an only[60] unknown church, and challenging yet nevertheless (contrary to their own position) the truth of understanding and interpreting of Holy Scripture (to which they confessed the inspiration of that Holy Spirit requisite) every man of them to himself — using[61] (I say) themselves in this wise, the Scripture could not hold them. For they would and did (and yet such folk do) deny for Scripture which books of Scripture they list,[62] and such as they list to receive, interpret and conster[63] as they list. By reason whereof at sundry times sundry heresies sprung[64] and spread abroad, and — with great trouble of the good Catholic folk, and great decay of the true Catholic folk, and eternal destruction of their souls that took those wrong ways — flowered for a little while. Howbeit,[65] our Lord (laud and thanks be to him) ever provided with his Holy Spirit that all these heresies were in short space by his Catholic Church condemned and suppressed. And so hath his Catholic faith in his Catholic Church, as well in this article of the Blessed Sacrament as in all the remnant, this fifteen hundred year continued and ever continue shall while this world last, what wrestling soever the infidels shall make with it.

Howbeit, men may gather upon the Scripture that, like as Christendom hath now in some place lost many lands and in some other win[66] many lands again, so shall it be, after the faith spread[67] so full round about it, that there shall be no land in any part thereof (in which part people are dwelling) but that they shall have heard of the name and faith of Christ. Which was not all done (as Saint Augustine saith) in the time of the apostles themselves, but, like these words of Christ (saith Saint Augustine), *Qui vos audit, me audit* ("He that heareth you, heareth me"),[68] though they were spoken only to the apostles, were not yet only meant for the apostles' persons only but spoken to them in the name of the Church as governors for the same — and therefore to those governors of the Church also as to the world's end should succeed in their places — so this prophecy of *In omnem terram exivit sonus eorum, et in fines orbis terrae verba eorum* ("Into all the world is gone out the sound of them, and into the ends of the

roundel[69] of the earth the words of them"),[70] which words were written by the prophet David many years ere the apostles were born (and yet prophesied by the verb of the pretertemps,[71] or time past, to signify that the thing prophesied should as surely succeed and be verified as though it were past already), were not meant that the thing should be fully performed by their own persons, but part in one time, part in other, by such as the governors of the Catholic Church, which should succeed in their places, should in times and opportunity convenient[72] send forth about it and appoint thereunto.

But afterward, when it is all preached round about upon all parts of the earth, the time shall come when it shall so sore decay again, and the Church by persecution so straited[73] into so narrow a corner, that, in respect of[74] the countries into which Christendom hath been and shall be dilated and spread before, it shall seem that there shall be then no Christian countries left at all. Whereof our Savior said, *Quum venerit filius hominis, putas inveniet fidem in terra?* ("When the Son of man shall come — that is to wit, at the day of doom to judge the world — trowest[75] thou that he shall find faith in the earth?")[76] But that time shall be but short, for our Savior saith, *Propter electos breviabuntur dies illi;*[77] and then shall our Lord come soon after, and finish this present world, and reward every good man after his good works wrought in his true Catholic faith: *Reddet unicuique secundum opera sua* ("He shall yield every man according to his works").[78] But yet such works we must understand as are wrought in faith, for as Saint Paul saith, *Sine fide impossibile est placere Deo* ("Without faith it is impossible to please God").[79]

But finally this Catholic faith of the presence of Christ's very body and blood in the Blessed Sacrament hath, as I have showed, been the faith of Christ's whole Catholic Church ever since Christ's first institution thereof until this present time, and ever shall be while the world endureth. Whereagainst[80] whoso wrestleth cannot fail in conclusion to take a very foul fall, as far down — except he repent — as from the place that he walketh on in the earth into the deep pit of hell, from which fall our Lord of his goodness defend every Christian man.

---

60 single 61 behaving 62 wish
63 construe 64 sprang up 65 However
66 won 67 has been spread 68 Lk
10:16. See also Augustine's *De civitate Dei*,

18.50; and *De natura et gratia* (PL 44, 249).
69 sphere 70 Ps 18(19):5 71 past tense
72 suitable 73 constricted 74 *in
respect of*: in comparison with 75 believe

76 Lk 18:8 77 Mt 24:22: "For the
elect's sake those days shall be shortened."
78 Mt 16:27 79 Heb 11:6 80 against
which

The Third Lecture of the Sacrament

I have in the first lecture, good readers, expounded you the words of our Savior at the institution of the Blessed Sacrament. And after have I in the second showed you somewhat of the sacramental signs and of the sacramental things that are either contained therein or signified thereby, and have also somewhat rehearsed you the very words of tlie old holy doctors, whereby we may plainly perceive that the old holy saints believed the presence of the very body and blood of Christ in the Blessed Sacrament in like wise as we do.

Now is it convenient[81] that we somewhat speak in what manner wise we ought to use[82] ourselves in the receiving. We must understand that of this Holy Sacrament there are three manners of receiving. For some folk receive it only sacramentally, and some only spiritually, and some receive it both.

Only sacramentally do they receive it which receive the Blessed Sacrament unworthily. For they verily receive the very body and blood of our blessed Savior into their body in the Blessed Sacrament in form of bread out of[83] the Mass, or in form of bread and wine in the Mass. Fot as holy Saint Augustine saith of the false traitor Judas, though he was naught[84] and received it at the Maundy to his damnation, yet was it our Lord's body that he received.[85] But because they receive it in deadly sin—that is to wit, either in will to commit deadly sin again, or impenitent of that they have committed before—therefore they receive it not spiritually; that is to say, they receive not the spiritual thing of the Sacrament, which (as I before have showed) is the sacramental thing that is signified thereby, that is to wit, the society of holy saints—that is to say, he is not by the spirit of God unied[86] with holy saints as a lively[87] member of Christ's mystical body.

For we must understand that Christ in giving his own very body into the very body of every Christian man, he doth in a certain manner incorporate all Christian folk and his own body together in one corporation mystical. And therefore saith Saint Paul, *Omnes de uno pane manducamus* ("All we eat of one loaf").[88] Not that all the people eat of one material loaf, for there were among them distributed many, but he meaneth that that very thing that is there under the form of that loaf of bread is that one thing that the apostle and all they and all we too eat. And then saith he also, *Unus panis multi sumus* ("We many be of one loaf").[89] And so are we, as I say, by the receiving each of us that loaf that is himself mystically, all incorporate together and all made that one loaf. And therefore when our Lord in giving that loaf at the first institution unto his apostles that there represented his Church said, "This is my body," in giving (I say) to his Church his very body, he not by word but by his deed called (as Saint Cyprian saith in his sermon *De cena Domini*) his Church his body too.[90]

But now, though that every Christian man so receiving is in a certain manner a member of his mystical body, the Church, by this sacramental receiving, yet, for his receiving it in deadly sin, he receiveth it not spiritually; that is to say, though he receive Christ's holy flesh into his body, he receiveth not yet Christ's Holy Spirit into his soul. And therefore this manner of deadly receiving his quick flesh giveth no quickness or life unto the soul. And in such a receiver of Christ's flesh are these words of Christ verified: *Spiritus est qui vivificat, caro non prodest quicquam* ("The flesh availeth nothing; the spirit is it that giveth life").[91]

And therefore I say that, without the spiritual receiving, the sacramental receiving nothing availeth. And not over that it nothing availeth, but over that it sore noyeth[92] and hurteth. For Saint Paul, after that he hath plainly told and showed the Corinthians that the thing which they did eat and drink was the Body and Blood of Christ, he said unto them, *Quicumque manducaverit panem et biberit calicem Domini indigne, reus erit corporis et sanguinis Domini, et iudicium sibi manducat et bibit, non diiudicans corpus Domini* ("Whosoever eat the bread and drink the cup of our Lord unworthily shall be guilty of the Body and Blood of our Lord, and eateth and drinketh judgment unto himself, for that that[93] he discerneth not the body of our Lord, that is to wit, considereth it not and useth it like as he ought to do, it being the body of our Lord as it is").[94]

---

81 appropriate, suitable   82 conduct
83 *out of:* apart from   84 wicked
85 Augustine, *In Iohannis evangelium tractatus 62* (PL 35, 1801)   86 united; formed into one   87 living   88 1 Cor

10:17   89 1 Cor 10:17   90 Ernaldus Abbas Bonaevallis, *Liber de cardinalibus operibus Christi* (PL 189, 1643). Chapter 6 of this work, which was attributed to Cyprian in More's time, is entitled *De cena*

domini, et prima institutione consummantis omnia sacramenta.   91 Jn 6:64   92 *sore noyeth:* grievously harms   93 *that that:* the fact that   94 1 Cor 11:27–29

Here we see that, notwithstanding that he that receiveth the Blessed Sacrament receiveth the very body of our Lord, yet receiving it unworthily (and therefore not spiritually), though he be by the only[95] sacramental receiving of Christ's body incorporate as a member (in a certain manner) in the mystical body of his Catholic Church, yet, for lack of the spiritual receiving by cleanness of spirit, he attaineth not the fruitful thing of the sacrament, that is to wit, the society of saints; that is to say, he is not by the spirit of Christ animated and quickened and made a lively member in the pure mystical body, the fellowship and society of saints.

Some, as I said before, receive this Blessed Sacrament only spiritually and not sacramentally, and so do all they receive it which are in clean life and are at their high Mass devoutly. For there the curate offereth it for him and them too. And although that only himself receive it sacramentally, that is to wit, the very body and blood under the sacramental signs (the forms of bread and wine), yet as many of them as are present at it and are in clean life receive it spiritually, that is to wit, the fruitful thing of the sacrament; that is to say, they receive grace, by which they be by the spirit of Christ more firmly knit and unied quick lively members in the spiritual society of saints.

A Treatise to Receive
the Blessed Body of Our Lord
Sacramentally and Virtually Both

made in the year of our Lord 1534 by Sir Thomas More, Knight, while he was prisoner in the Tower of London[1]

They receive the blessed body of our Lord both sacramentally and virtually[2] which[3] in due manner and worthily receive the Blessed Sacrament. When I say "worthily," I mean not that any man is so good, or can be so good, that his goodness could make him of very right and reason worthy to receive into his vile earthly body that holy blessed glorious flesh and blood of almighty God himself, with his celestial soul therein, and with the majesty of his eternal Godhead, but that he may prepare himself, working with the grace of God, to stand in such a state as the incomparable goodness of God will, of his liberal bounty, vouchsafe[4] to take and accept for worthy to receive his own inestimable precious body into the body of so simple[5] a servant.

Such is the wonderful bounty of almighty God that he not only doth vouchsafe but also doth delight to be with men if they prepare to receive him with honest and clean souls, whereof he saith: *Delitiae meae esse cum filiis hominum* ("My delight and pleasures are to be with the sons of men").[6] And how can we doubt that God delighteth to be with the sons of men when the Son of God, and very almighty God himself, liked not only to become the Son of Man (that is to wit,[7] the son of Adam, the first man) but, over that, in his innocent manhood to suffer his painful Passion for the redemption and restitution[8] of man.

In remembrance and memorial whereof he disdaineth not to take for worthy such men as wilfully make not themselves unworthy to receive the selfsame blessed body into their bodies, to the inestimable wealth[9] of their souls. And yet of his high sovereign patience, he refuseth not to enter bodily into the vile bodies of those whose filthy minds refuse to receive him graciously[10] into their souls. But then do such folk receive him only sacramentally and not virtually, that is to wit, they receive his very blessed body into theirs under the sacramental sign; but they receive not the thing of the sacrament, that is to wit, the virtue and the effect thereof (that is to say, the grace by which they should be lively[11] members incorporate[12] in Christ's holy mystical body), but instead of that lively grace, they receive their judgment and their damnation.

And some such, by the outrageous enormity of their deadly sinful purpose, in which they presume to receive that blessed body, deserve to have the devil (through the sufferance of God) personally so to enter into their breasts that they never have the grace after to cast him out, but like as a man with bridle and spur rideth and ruleth a horse and maketh him go which way he list[13] to guide him, so doth the devil by his inward suggestions govern and guide the man, and bridle him from all good and spur him into all evil, till he finally drive him to all mischief, as he did the false traitor Judas, that sinfully received that holy body, whom the devil did therefore first carry out about the traitorous death of the selfsame blessed body of his most loving Master (which he so late so sinfully received) and, within a few hours after, unto the desperate destruction of himself.

And therefore have we great cause, with great dread and reverence, to consider well the state of

1 As editors Louis Martz and Garry Haupt have indicated, this *Treatise* completes the last lecture of *A Treatise on the Passion*. See *The Tower Works: Devotional Writings,* ed. Garry E. Haupt (New Haven: Yale University Press, 1980), p. xiii, n. 6, and Louis L. Martz, "Thomas More: The Tower Works," *St. Thomas More: Action and Contemplation*, ed. Richard S. Sylvester (New Haven: Yale University Press, 1972), pp. 69–74. **2** with spiritual effect **3** who **4** be willing, deign **5** lowly; of little account **6** Prv 8:31 **7** say **8** restoration **9** well-being **10** through divine grace **11** life-giving; vigorous **12** united, incorporated **13** desires

our own soul when we shall go to the board[14] of God, and as near as we can (with help of his special grace, diligently prayed for before) purge and cleanse our souls by confession, contrition, and penance, with full purpose of forsaking from thenceforth the proud desires of the devil, the greedy covetise[15] of wretched worldly wealth, and the foul affection of the filthy flesh, and be in full mind to persevere and continue in the ways of God and holy cleanness of spirit, lest that (if we presume so unreverently to receive this precious margarite,[16] this pure pearl, the blessed body of our Savior himself, contained in the sacramental sign of bread) that like a sort[17] of swine rooting in the dirt and wallowing in the mire, we tread it under the filthy feet of our foul affections, while we set more by[18] them than by it, intending to walk and wallow in the puddle of foul filthy sin; therewith the legion of devils may get leave of Christ so to enter into us as they got leave of him to enter into the hogs of Genezareth,[19] and, as they ran forth with them and never stinted till they drowned them in the sea, so run on with us (but if[20] God of his great mercy refrain[21] them and give us the grace to repent), else not fail to drown us in the deep sea of everlasting sorrow.

Of this great outrageous peril, the blessed apostle Saint Paul giveth us gracious warning where he saith in his first epistle to the Corinthians: *Quicumque manducaverit panem et biberit calicem Domini indigne, reus erit corporis et sanguinis Domini* ("Whosoever eat the bread and drink the cup of our Lord unworthily, he shall be guilty of the body and blood of our Lord").[22] Here is, good Christian readers, a dreadful and terrible sentence that God here (by the mouth of his holy apostle) giveth against all them that unworthily receive this most Blessed Sacrament, that their part shall be with Pilate and the Jews, and with that false traitor Judas, since God reputeth[23] the unworthy receiving and eating of his blessed body for a like heinous offense against his majesty as he accounts theirs that wrongfully and cruelly killed him.

And therefore to the intent that we may avoid well this importable[24] danger, and in such wise[25] receive the body and blood of our Lord, as God may of his goodness accept us for worthy (and therefore

not only enter with his blessed flesh and blood sacramentally and bodily into our bodies but also with his Holy Spirit graciously[26] and effectually into our souls), Saint Paul, in the place afore-remembered,[27] saith: *Probet seipsum homo, et sic de pane illo edat, et de calice bibat* ("Let a man prove himself, and so eat of that bread and drink of that cup").[28] But then in what wise shall we prove ourselves? We may not go rashly to God's board,[29] but by a convenient[30] time taken before we must (as I began to say) consider well and examine surely what state our soul standeth in.

In which thing it will be not only right hard, but also peradventure impossible, by any possible diligence of ourselves to attain unto the very full undoubted surety thereof, without special revelation of God. For as the Scripture saith: *Nemo vivens scit, utrum odio vel amore dignus sit* ("No man living knoweth whether he be worthy the favor or hatred of God").[31] And in another place: *Etiamsi simplex fuero, hoc ipsum ignorabit anima mea* ("If I be simple,[32] that is to say, without sin, that shall not my mind surely know").[33] But God yet in this point is of his high goodness content if we do the diligence[34] that we can to see that we be not in the purpose[35] of any deadly sin. For though it may be that, for all our diligence, God (whose eye pierceth much more deeper into the bottom of our heart than our own doth) may see therein some such sin as we cannot see there ourselves—for which Saint Paul saith: *Nullius mihi conscius sum, sed non in hoc iustificatus sum* ("In mine own conscience I know nothing, but yet am I not thereby justified")[36]—yet our true diligence done in the search God of his high bounty so far-forth[37] accepteth that he imputeth not any such secret lurking sin unto our charge for an unworthy receiving of this Blessed Sacrament, but rather the strength and virtue thereof purgeth and cleanseth that sin.

In this proving and examination of ourselves which Saint Paul speaketh of, one very special point must be to prove and examine ourselves and see that we be in the right faith and belief concerning that holy Blessed Sacrament itself: that is to wit, that we verily believe that it is, as indeed it is, under the form and likeness of bread, the very blessed body, flesh

---

14 table **15** covetousness **16** any precious stone **17** herd **18** *set more by:* value more highly **19** Mt 8:28–32; Mk 5:11–14; Lk 8:32–33 **20** *but if:* unless **21** restrain **22** 1 Cor 11:27 **23** considers **24** unbearable **25** a way **26** through divine grace **27** mentioned before **28** 1 Cor 11:28 **29** table **30** suitable **31** Eccl 9:1 **32** innocent **33** Jb 9:21 **34** the utmost **35** determined intention or aim **36** 1 Cor 4:4 **37** *so far-forth:* to such an extent

and blood of our holy Savior Christ himself, the very selfsame body and the very selfsame blood that died and was shed upon the cross for our sin, and the third day gloriously did arise again to life and, with the souls of holy saints fetched out of hell, ascended and stied[38] up wonderfully into heaven, and there sitteth on the right hand of the Father, and shall visibly descend in great glory to judge the quick[39] and the dead, and reward all men after[40] their works.

We must, I say, see that we firmly believe that this Blessed Sacrament is not a bare sign, or a figure,[41] or a token of that holy body of Christ, but that it is, in perpetual remembrance of his bitter Passion that he suffered for us, the selfsame precious body of Christ that suffered it by his own almighty power and unspeakable goodness, consecrated and given unto us.

And this point of belief is, in the receiving of this Blessed Sacrament, of such necessity and such weight with them that have years and discretion that, without it, they receive it plainly to their damnation. And that point believed very full and fastly[42] must needs be a great occasion to move any man in all other points to receive it well. For note well the words of Saint Paul therein: *Qui manducat de hoc pane, et bibit de calice indigne, iudicium sibi manducat et bibit, non diiudicans corpus Domini* ("He that eateth of this bread and drinketh of this cup unworthily eateth and drinketh judgment upon himself, in that he discerneth not the body of our Lord").[43] Lo, here this blessed apostle well declareth that he which[44] in any wise unworthily receiveth this most excellent sacrament receiveth it unto his own damnation, in that he well declareth by his evil demeanor toward it, in his unworthy receiving of it, that he discerneth it not, nor judgeth it, nor taketh it for the very body of our Lord, as indeed it is. And verily it is hard, but[45] that this point deeply rooted in our breast should set all our heart in a fervor of devotion toward the worthy receiving of that Blessed Body. But surely there can be no doubt, on the other side, but that, if any man believe that it is Christ's very body and yet is not inflamed to receive him devoutly thereby, that man were likely to receive this Blessed Sacrament very coldly and far from all devotion if he believed that it were not his body, but only a bare token of him instead of his body.

But now, having the full faith of this point fastly grounded in our heart, that the thing which we receive is the very blessed body of Christ, I trust there shall not greatly need any great information further to teach us, or any great exhortation further to stir and excite us, with all humble manner and reverent behavior to receive him. For if we will but consider, if there were a great worldly prince which for special favor that he bore us would come visit us in our own house, what a business we would then make, and what a work it would be for us to see that our house were trimmed up in every point to the best of our possible power, and everything so provided and ordered that he should by his honorable receiving perceive what affection we bear him and in what high estimation we have him, we should soon by the comparing of that worldly prince and this heavenly prince together (between which twain[46] is far less comparison than is between a man and a mouse) inform and teach ourselves with how lowly mind, how tender loving heart, how reverent humble manner we should endeavor ourselves to receive this glorious heavenly king, the king of all kings, almighty God himself, that so lovingly doth vouchsafe[47] to enter not only into our house (to which the noble man Centurio acknowledged himself unworthy)[48] but his precious body into our vile wretched carcass, and his Holy Spirit into our poor simple soul.

What diligence can here suffice us? What solicitude can we think here enough, against[49] the coming of this almighty king, coming for so special gracious favor, not to put us to cost, not to spend of ours, but to enrich us of his, and that after so manifold deadly displeasures done him so unkindly[50] by us, against so many of his incomparable benefits before done unto us? How would we now labor and foresee that the house of our soul (which God were coming to rest in) should neither have any poisoned spider or cobweb of deadly sin hanging in the roof, nor so much as a straw or a feather of any light lewd[51] thought that we might spy in the floor, but we would sweep it away?

But forasmuch, good Christian readers, as we neither can attain this great point of faith, nor any other virtue but by the special grace of God, of whose high goodness every good thing cometh—for as Saint James saith: *Omne datum optimum, et omne donum*

38 rose, ascended   39 living   40 according to   41 type   42 steadfastly, firmly   43 1 Cor 11:27–29   44 who   45 except

46 two   47 deign; agree graciously   48 See Mt 8:8. The Centurion's words preceded the receiving of Communion

in the Mass.   49 in preparation for   50 ungratefully   51 rude; base; bad

perfectum, de sursum est, descendens a Patre luminum ("Every good gift, and every perfect gift, is from above, descending from the Father of lights")[52]—let us therefore pray for his gracious[53] help in the attaining of this faith, and for his help in the cleansing of our soul against[54] his coming, that he may make us worthy to receive him worthily. And ever let us of our own part fear our unworthiness, and on his part trust boldly upon his goodness if we forslow[55] not to work with him for our own part. For if we willingly upon the trust and comfort of his goodness leave our own endeavor undone, then is our hope no hope, but a very foul presumption.

Then when we come unto his holy board, into the presence of his Blessed Body, let us consider his high glorious majesty, which his high goodness there hideth from us and the proper form of his holy flesh covereth under the form of bread—both to keep us from abashment,[56] such as we could not peradventure[57] abide if we (such as we yet be) should see and receive him in his own form such as he is, and also for the increase of the merit of our faith in the obedient belief of that thing (at his commandment) whereof our eyes and our reason seem to show us the contrary.

And yet forasmuch as, although we believe it, yet is there in many of us that belief very faint and far from the point of such vigor and strength as would God it had, let us say unto him with the father that had the dumb son, *Credo Domine, adiuva incredulitatem meam* ("I believe, Lord, but help thou my lack of belief"),[58] and with his blessed apostles, *Domine, adauge nobis fidem* ("Lord, increase faith in us").[59] Let us also with the poor publican, in knowledge of our own unworthiness, say with all meekness of heart, *Deus, propitius esto mihi peccatori* ("Lord God, be merciful to me sinner that I am").[60] And with the Centurion, *Domine, non sum dignus ut intres sub tectum meum* ("Lord, I am not worthy that thou shouldest come into my house").[61]

And yet with all this remembrance of our own unworthiness, and therefore the great reverence, fear, and dread for our own part, let us not forget on the other side to consider his inestimable goodness, which disdaineth not for all our unworthiness to come unto us and to be received of us.

But likewise as at the sight or receiving of this excellent memorial of his death (for in the remembrance thereof doth he thus consecrate and give his own blessed flesh and blood unto us) we must with tender compassion remember and call to mind the bitter pains of his most painful Passion, and yet therewithal rejoice and be glad in the consideration of his incomparable kindness (which in his so suffering for us to our inestimable benefit he showed and declared toward us), so must we be both sore afeard[62] of our own unworthiness, and yet therewith be right glad and in great hope at the consideration of his unmeasurable goodness.

Saint Elizabeth, at the visitation and salutation of our blessed Lady (having by revelation the sure inward knowledge that our Lady was conceived with our Lord), albeit that[63] she was herself such as else (for[64] the diversity between their ages) she well might and would have thought it but convenient and meetly[65] that her young cousin should come visit her, yet now, because she was mother to our Lord, she was sore amarvelled[66] of her visitation and thought herself far unworthy thereto, and therefore said unto her: *Unde hoc, ut veniat mater Domini mei ad me?* ("Whereof is this, that the mother of our Lord should come to me?")[67] But yet for all the abashment of her own unworthiness she conceived throughly[68] such a glad blessed comfort that her holy child Saint John the Baptist hopped in her belly for joy, whereof she said: *Ut facta est vox salutationis tuae in auribus meis, exultavit gaudio infans in utero meo* ("As soon as the voice of thy salutation was in mine ears, the infant in my womb leapt for joy").[69]

Now like as Saint Elizabeth by the Spirit of God had those holy affections,[70] both of reverent considering her own unworthiness in the visitation of the mother of God, and yet for all that so great inward gladness therewith, let us at this great high visitation, in which not the mother of God, as came to Saint Elizabeth, but one incomparably more excelling the mother of God than the mother of God passed Saint Elizabeth doth so vouchsafe to come and visit each of us with his most blessed presence that he cometh not into our house but into ourselves—let us (I say) call for the help of the same

---

52 Jas 1:17   **53** conferring grace; benevolent   **54** in preparation for   **55** neglect, out of laziness; delay   **56** embarrassment   **57** perhaps   **58** Mk 9:23   **59** Lk 17:5

60 Lk 18:13   **61** Mt 8:8   **62** *sore afeard:* greatly afraid   **63** *albeit that:* although   **64** because of   **65** *convenient and meetly:* suitable and appropriate   **66** *sore*

amarvelled: greatly astonished by   **67** Lk 1:43   **68** throughout   **69** Lk 1:44   **70** dispositions

Holy Spirit that then inspired her, and pray him at
this high and holy visitation so to inspire us that
we may both be abashed with the reverent dread of
our own unworthiness and yet therewith conceive
a joyful consolation and comfort in the consideration of God's inestimable goodness, and that each
of us, like as we may well say with great reverent
dread and admiration, *Unde hoc, ut veniat Dominus
meus ad me?* ("Whereof is this, that my Lord should
come unto me?")[71] and not only unto me but also
into me, so we may with glad heart truly say at the
sight of his blessed presence, *Exultavit gaudio infans in utero meo* ("The child in my belly — that is to
wit, the soul in my body, that should be then such a
child in innocency as was that innocent infant Saint
John — leapeth, good Lord, for joy").[72]

Now when we have received our Lord and have
him in our body, let us not then let him alone and
get us forth about other things and look no more
unto him (for little good could he that[73] so would
serve any guest), but let all our business be about
him. Let us by devout prayer talk to him, by devout meditation talk with him. Let us say with the
prophet: *Audiam quid loquatur in me Dominus* ("I
will hear what our Lord will speak within me").[74]

For surely, if we set aside all other things and attend unto him, he will not fail with good inspirations to speak such things to us within us as shall
serve to the great spiritual comfort and profit of our
soul. And therefore let us with Martha provide that
all our outward business may be pertaining to him,
in making cheer to him and to his company for his
sake, that is to wit, to poor folk, of which he taketh
every one not only for his disciple but also as for
himself. For himself saith: *Quamdiu fecistis uni de
his fratribus meis minimis, mihi fecistis* ("That that
you have done to one of the least of these my brethren, you have done it to myself").[75] And let us with
Mary also sit in devout meditation and hearken well
what our Savior, being now our guest, will inwardly
say unto us. Now have we a special time of prayer,
while he that hath made us, he that hath bought[76]
us, he whom we have offended, he that shall judge
us, he that shall either damn us or save us, is of his
great goodness become our guest, and is personally
present within us, and that for none other purpose

but to be sued unto for pardon and so thereby to
save us.

Let us not lose this time, therefore; suffer not this
occasion to slip, which we can little tell whether
ever we shall get in again or never. Let us endeavor
ourselves to keep him still,[77] and let us say with his
two disciples that were going to the castle[78] of Emmaus, *Mane nobiscum Domine* ("Tarry with us,
good Lord"),[79] and then shall we be sure that he will
not go from us, but if[80] we unkindly put him from
us. Let us not play[81] like the people of Genezareth,
which prayed him to depart out of their quarters
because they lost their hogs by him, when instead of
the hogs he saved the man out of whom he cast the
legion of devils that after destroyed the hogs.[82] Let
not us likewise rather put God from us by unlawful
love of worldly winning[83] or foul filthy lust, rather
than for the profit of our soul to forbear it. For sure
may we be that, when we wax[84] such, God will not
tarry with us, but we put him unkindly from us. Nor
let us not do as did the people of Jerusalem which
on Palm Sunday received Christ royally and full devoutly with procession, and on the Friday after put
him to a shameful Passion; on the Sunday cried,
Benedictus qui venit in nomine Domini ("Blessed be
he that cometh in the name of our Lord"),[85] and on
the Friday cried out, *Non hunc, sed Barabbam* ("We
will not have him but Barabbas");[86] on the Sunday cried, *Hosanna in excelsis,*[87] on the Friday, *Tolle,
tolle, crucifige eum.*[88] Sure if we receive him never
so well nor never so devoutly at Easter, yet whensoever we fall after to such wretched sinful living as
casteth our Lord in such wise out of our souls, as his
grace tarrieth not with us, we show ourself to have
received him in such manner as those Jews did. For
we do as much as in us is[89] to crucify Christ again:
Iterum (saith Saint Paul) *crucifigentes filium Dei.*[90]

Let us, good Christian readers, receive him in such
wise as did the good publican Zacchaeus, which,[91]
when he longed to see Christ and because he was
but low of stature did climb up into a tree, our Lord,
seeing his devotion, called unto him and said: "Zacchaeus, come off[92] and come down, for this day must
I dwell with thee."[93] And he made haste and came
down, and very gladly received him into his house.
But not only received him with a joy of a light[94] and

71 Lk 1:43   **72** Lk 1:44   **73** *he that:* he
do who   **74** Ps 84:9(85:8)   **75** Mt 25:40
76 redeemed   **77** always, continually
78 village   **79** Lk 24:29   **80** *but if:*
unless   **81** act   **82** Mt 8:34; Mk 5:17; Lk
8:37   **83** gain   **84** become   **85** Mt 21:9
86 Jn 18:40   **87** Mk 11:10: "Hosanna in
the highest"   **88** Jn 19:15: "Away, away
with him! Crucify him."   **89** *in us is:* is
in our power   **90** Heb 6:6: "Crucifying
the Son of God once more"   **91** who
92 along   **93** Lk 19:5   **94** slight; fickle

soon sliding[95] affection, but that it might well appear that he received him with a sure earnest virtuous mind, he proved it by his virtuous works. For he forthwith was contented to make recompense to all men that he had wronged, and that in a large[96] manner, for every penny a groat,[97] and yet offered to give out also forthwith the one half of all his substance unto the poor men, and that forthwith also, by and by,[98] without any longer delay. And therefore he said not, "Thou shalt hear that I shall give it," but he said, *Ecce dimidium bonorum meorum do pauperibus* ("Lo, look, good Lord, the one half of my goods I do give unto poor men").[99]

With such alacrity, with such quickness of spirit, with such gladness, and such spiritual rejoicing as this man received our Lord into his house, our Lord give us the grace to receive his blessed body and blood, his holy soul, and his almighty Godhead both, into our bodies and into our souls, that the fruit of our good works may bear witness unto our conscience that we receive him worthily, and in such a full faith and such a stable purpose of good living as we be bounden to do. And then shall God give a gracious sentence[100] and say upon our soul, as he said upon Zacchaeus, *Hodie salus facta est huic domui* ("This day is health and salvation come unto this house"),[101] which that holy blessed person of Christ, which we verily in the Blessed Sacrament receive, through the merit of his bitter Passion (whereof he hath ordained his own blessed body in that Blessed Sacrament to be the memorial), vouchsafe,[102] good Christian readers, to grant unto us all.

---

95 passing **96** generous **97** coin worth four pence **98** *by and by:* immediately **99** Lk 19:8 **100** *gracious sentence:* merciful judgment **101** Lk 19:9 **102** be willing; deign

A Dialogue of Comfort against Tribulation

made by a Hungarian in Latin, and translated out of Latin into French, and out of French into English

Written in 1534 while More was imprisoned in the Tower of London, *A Dialogue of Comfort* was first published by Richard Tottel in London, November 1553, eighteen years after More's execution, and five months after Queen Mary's accession. The *Dialogue* was published again in 1557 by William Rastell as part of his 1,458-page folio of *The Workes of Sir Thomas More Knight*. In 1573, John Fowler published a smaller, convenient edition of the *Dialogue* in Antwerp.

In this late work, More again employs the dialogue form, as he did in the earlier *Utopia* and 1529 *Dialogue of Sir Thomas More*. Here the focus is on "comfort" (from the Latin *confortare*, meaning "to strengthen") against "tribulation" (from the Latin *tribulare*, meaning "to oppress or afflict," and *tribulum*, a "threshing-sledge"). The *Dialogue* works to explore the fundamental questions: Is there any credible hope of "comfort" in the face of human "tribulation" and suffering? What is the best way to understand—and respond to—suffering?

The rest of the title is more playful. The details about the work's "Hungarian" authorship and subsequent translation from Latin into French and then into English may be a prudent expedient to protect More. More may also be suggesting the universality of his work on suffering through this witty means (*CW* 12: 331).

In any case, the underlying plot is a thin veil to the situation faced by More and his family during his imprisonment. Set in Vienna on the brink of another Turkish invasion, the *Dialogue* records a conversation between two family members. Old Antony, suffering on his deathbed, has experienced similar terrors twice before. Young Vincent—a wealthy leader concerned for his family, friends, and country—comes to Antony for advice, terrified by the threat of an imminent invasion and death. These

interlocutors are close relatives who share common perspectives. As the reader learns through Antony's Socratic questioning, however, Vincent does not know himself well and has not reflected sufficiently on the pressing issues facing him. Though a leader, Vincent seems unprepared intellectually, imaginatively, and affectively for the trials at hand.

Their conversation takes place in Hungary in 1527–28, before the Turks would attack in 1529, led by Suleiman I. Vincent begins the dialogue overcome by the fear of these invasions, perhaps recalling the battle of Mohács in 1526 and its bloody conclusion. After three long conversations at three different sittings, however, Vincent is presented hopeful of "conquering" (playing upon his name's etymology from *vincens*), equipped and ready to face whatever comes—or so he states at the end of Book 3, as he prays for "the grace to follow your good counsel." For his part, Antony seems to have practiced, across the work, an artful and loving fatherhood toward Vincent and, through Vincent, toward anxious Vienna and its citizens.

The title and the introductory chapters place this work within both the classical tradition of "comfort" books (especially Boethius's *De consolatione philosophiae*, as well as certain writings by Cicero and Seneca) and the biblical tradition. While Antony thinks the classical tradition useful at times, he considers ancient wisdom to be inadequate for dealing with human suffering. Even the keenest reason, he suggests, needs help when it considers—or experiences—a mystery like human suffering.

The *Dialogue* is noted for the number and variety of its "merry tales," and the work is shot through with More's customary mingling of high wit, good humor, and sudden incisive seriousness. The *Dialogue* can seem rambling and digressive—perhaps an imitation of real conversation—and even remarkably simple at times. Old Antony, however, insists that he is highly selective in his approach to the conversation, as shown in his careful delay of Vincent's greatest concern—the fear of violent death and martyrdom—until the end of the work, once the necessary groundwork has been established through friendly conversation.

As Louis Martz has observed, the *Dialogue* is "an ultimate spiritual testament," a work that, composed in solitude and silence—in the shadow of death—"displays all the signs of More's finest literary skill, both in the details of its language and in the total command of its development" (*CW* 12: lxvi).

TIMELINE

16 May 1532	More resigns from his office as Lord Chancellor.
1 June 1533	More does not attend Anne Boleyn's coronation.
21 Feb 1534	Henry VIII demands More's indictment; the House of Lords refuses.
Feb–Mar 1534	More admits great fear (Letter 210).
17 April 1534	More is imprisoned for refusing the oath of the Act of Succession.
Later 1534	Margaret (Letter 211), Wilson (Letters 207–8), and others express great fear. More writes *A Dialogue of Comfort against Tribulation*.

CONTENTS

Iohan. Fouleri Briſtolienſis in D. Th. Mori
effigiem, Hexaſtichon.

Effigiem quamcunque tui ſic fingimus , at non
Tam facile eſt mores fingere , More, tuos.
Quàm vellem Pictor mihi tam perfectus adeſſet,
Pingere qui verè poſſet vtrumque ſimul.
Tum quoque qui vitam totã, mortémque referret.
Ille magis multò doctus Apelle foret.

The ſame in Engliſh Meter.

As Painters Art can ſkill, o Moore;
  Thy face here may we ſee :
Thy manners yet and vertues al
  To ſhew, hard would it be.
Would God ſome Painter might be had
  So perfect in his ſkill,
That truly face and manners both
  Could ſet foorth al at wil.
And then thy whole life, and thy death
  Could draw and make vs ſee.
Apelles learned hand could not
  Be better ſkild, than he.

This octavo edition of *A Dialogue of Comfort* was printed in 1573 by John
Fowler, son-in-law of John Harris, More's last secretary who appears in *The
Family of Sir Thomas More* (Plate 4b). In 1553 Richard Tottel had printed
the first edition of More's *Dialogue of Comfort*, which was also the first
book from Tottel's press. The English translation of the Latin poem reads:

> As painters' art can skill, O More;
>   Thy face here may we see:
> Thy manners yet and virtues all
>   To show, hard would it be.
> Would God some painter might be had
>   So perfect in his skill,
> That truly face and manners both
>   Could set forth all at will.
> And then thy whole life, and thy death
>   Could draw and make us see.
> Appelles' learned hand could not
>   Be better skilled than he.

A Dialogue of Comfort against Tribulation

made by a Hungarian in Latin, and translated out of Latin
into French, and out of French into English

THE FIRST BOOK

PREFACE

VINCENT: Who would have weened,[1] O my good Uncle, afore a few years passed, that such as in this country would visit their friends lying in disease and sickness should come, as I do now, to seek and fetch comfort[2] of them, or in giving comfort to them, use the way that I may well use to you? For albeit that[3] the priests and friars be wont[4] to call upon sick men to remember death, yet we worldly friends, for fear of discomforting them, have ever had a guise[5] in Hungary to lift up their hearts and put them in hope of life. But now, my good Uncle, the world is here waxen[6] such, and so great perils appear here to fall at hand,[7] that methinketh the greatest comfort that a man can have is when he may see that he shall soon be gone. And we that are likely long to live here in wretchedness have need of some comfortable counsel against tribulation[8] to be given us by such as you be, good Uncle, that have so long lived virtuously and are so learned in the law of God, as very few be better in this country here, and have had, of such things as we now do fear, good experience and assay[9] in yourself, as he that[10] hath been taken prisoner in Turkey two times in your days, and now likely to depart hence ere[11] long. But that may be your great comfort, good Uncle, since you depart to God. But us here shall you leave of your kindred a sort of very[12] comfortless orphans, to all whom your good help and counsel and comfort hath long been a great stay,[13] not as an uncle unto some, and to some as one farther of kin,[14] but as though unto us all you had been a natural father.

ANTONY: Mine own good Cousin,[15] I cannot much say nay but that there is indeed, not here in Hungary only, but almost in all places of Christendom, such a customable manner[16] of unchristian comforting, which, albeit that in any sick man it doth more harm than good—withdrawing him, in time of sickness, with the looking and longing for life, from the meditation of death, judgment, heaven, and hell, whereof[17] he should beset[18] much part of his time, even all his whole life in his best health—yet is that manner in my mind more than mad where such kind of comfort is used to a man of mine age: for as we well wot[19] that a young man may die soon, so be we very sure that an old man cannot live long. And yet since there is, as Tully[20] saith, "no man, for all that, so old but that he hopeth yet that he may live one year more"—and of[21] a frail folly delighteth to think thereon, and comfort himself therewith—other men's words of like manner[22] comfort, adding more sticks to that fire, shall in a manner[23] burn up quite[24] the pleasant moisture that most should refresh him: the wholesome dew, I mean, of God's grace, by which he should wish with God's will to be hence,[25] and long to be with him in heaven. Now where[26] you take my departing from you so heavily[27]—as of him of whom ye recognize of your goodness to have had herebefore[28]

---

1 thought   2 strengthening, encouragement, support; from *cum forte*, "with fortitude or courage"   3 *albeit that:* although   4 accustomed   5 custom, habit   6 grown, become   7 *fall at hand:* be imminent   8 great affliction, as from a *tribulum* or "threshing-sledge"   9 test, trial   10 who   11 before   12 truly; exceedingly   13 support   14 *farther of kin:* more distantly related   15 Kinsman (in this case, nephew)   16 *customable manner:* customary practice   17 on which   18 spend   19 know   20 Cicero, *On Old Age* 7.24   21 out of, from   22 *like manner:* the same kind of   23 *in a manner:* as it were; so to speak   24 completely   25 away from here   26 whereas   27 sadly   28 before now, up till now

help and comfort — would God[29] I had, to you and others more, done half so much as myself reckoneth had been my duty to do. But whensoever God take me hence, to reckon yourself then comfortless, as though your chief comfort stood in me, therein make ye, methinketh, a reckoning very much like as though ye would cast away a strong staff and lean upon a rotten reed; for God is and must be your comfort, and not I. And he is a sure[30] comfort that,[31] as he said to his disciples, never leaveth his servants in case[32] of comfortless orphans, not even when he departed from his disciples by death, but both (as he promised) sent them a comforter, the Holy Spirit of his Father and himself, and made them also sure that to the world's end he would ever dwell with them himself.[33] And therefore, if ye be part of his flock and believe his promise, how can ye be comfortless in any tribulation, when Christ and his Holy Spirit, and with them their inseparable Father — if you put full trust and confidence in them — be never one finger-breadth of space, nor one minute of time from you?

VINCENT: O my good Uncle, even these same self[34] words, wherewith ye well prove that because of God's own gracious presence we cannot be left comfortless, make me now feel and perceive what a miss[35] of much comfort we shall have when ye be gone; for albeit, good Uncle, that while[36] ye do tell me this, I cannot but grant it for true, yet if I now had not heard it of you, I had not remembered it, nor it had not fallen in my mind.[37] And over[38] that, like[39] as our tribulations shall in weight and number increase, so shall we need not only one such good word or twain,[40] but a great heap thereof, to stable and strengthen the walls of our hearts against the great surges of the tempestuous sea.

ANTONY: Good Cousin, trust well in God, and he shall provide you teachers abroad,[41] convenient[42] in every time, or else shall himself sufficiently teach you within.

VINCENT: Very well, good Uncle. But yet, if we would leave[43] the seeking of outward learning where we might have it, and look to be inwardly taught only by God, then should we thereby tempt God and displease him. And since that[44] I now see the likelihood that when ye be gone, we shall be sore[45] destitute of any such other like,[46] therefore thinketh me that God of[47] duty bindeth me to sue to[48] you now, good Uncle, in this short time that we have you, that it may like[49] you, against these great storms of tribulations — with which both I and all mine are sore beaten already, and now upon the coming of this cruel Turk, fear to fall in far more — I may learn of you such plenty of good counsel and comfort that I may, with the same laid up in remembrance, govern and stay[50] the ship of our kindred, and keep it afloat from peril of spiritual drowning.

You be not ignorant, good Uncle, what heaps of heaviness[51] hath of late fallen among us already, with which some of our poor family be fallen into such dumps that scantly can any such comfort as my poor wit[52] can give them anything[53] assuage their sorrow. And now, since the tidings have come hither so breme[54] of the great Turk's enterprise into these parts here, we can almost neither talk nor think of any other thing else than of his might and our mischief.[55] There falleth so continually before the eyes of our heart a fearful imagination of this terrible thing: his mighty strength and power, his high malice and hatred, and his incomparable cruelty, with robbing, spoiling,[56] burning, and laying waste all the way that his army cometh, then killing or carrying away the people far hence from home, and there sever the couples and kindred asunder, every one far from the other, some kept in thralldom,[57] and some kept in prison, and some for a triumph[58] tormented and killed in his presence. Then send his people hither, and his false faith therewith, so that such as are here and remain still shall either both lose all, and be lost too, or forced to forsake the faith of our Savior Christ, and fall to the false sect of Muhammad. And yet — which we more fear than all the remnant — no small part of our own folk that

---

29 *would God:* I wish to God   30 secure; certain   31 who   32 the position   33 See Jn 14:16–18, 25–26; Mt 28:20.   34 *same self:* very same   35 lack, loss   36 *albeit... that while:* although   37 *nor...mind:* nor would it have come to mind (More often uses a double negative where modern English uses only one.)   38 beyond   39 just   40 two   41 outside yourself   42 suitable, appropriate; at hand   43 leave off   44 *since that:* because; seeing that   45 grievously; very much   46 *any such other like:* anyone else like you   47 out of   48 *sue to:* ask   49 please   50 steady, support   51 grief, sadness   52 mind, intellect   53 in any way   54 loudly, much spoken of   55 misfortune, evil plight   56 despoiling, plundering   57 servitude; slavery   58 *for a triumph:* during a victory festival

dwell even here about us are, as we hear, fallen to him, or already confedered[59] with him, which if it so be, shall haply[60] keep this quarter from the Turk's incursion; but then shall they that turn to his law leave all their neighbors nothing, but shall have our goods given them and our bodies both, but if[61] we turn as they do, and forsake our Savior too. And then (for there is no born Turk so cruel to Christian folk as is the false Christian that falleth from the faith) we shall stand in peril, if we persevere in the truth, to be more hardly[62] handled and die more cruel death by our own countrymen at home than if we were taken hence and carried into Turkey.

These fearful heaps of peril lie so heavy at our hearts—while we wot[63] not into which we shall fortune[64] to fall, and therefore fear all the worst—that, as our Savior prophesied of the people of Jerusalem, many wish among us already before the peril come that the mountains would overwhelm them, or the valleys open and swallow them up and cover them.[65]

Therefore, good Uncle, against these horrible fears of these terrible tribulations—of which some, you wot well, our house already hath, and the remnant stand[66] in dread of—give us, while God lendeth you us, such plenty of your comfortable[67] counsel as I may write and keep with us, to stay[68] us when God shall call you hence.

ANTONY: Ah, my good Cousin, this is a heavy[69] hearing, and likewise[70] as we that dwell here in this part fear that thing so sore[71] now which[72] few years passed feared it not at all, so doubt I that ere[73] it long be, they shall fear it as much that think themselves now very sure[74] because they dwell further off. Greece feared not the Turk when that[75] I was born, and within a while after, all the whole empire was his.[76] The great Soldan[77] of Syria thought himself more than his match, and long since ye were born

hath he that empire too. Then hath he taken Belgrade, the fortress of this realm.[78] And since[79] hath he destroyed our noble young goodly king.[80] And now strive there twain[81] for us—our Lord send the grace that the third dog[82] carry not away the bone from them both. What should I speak of the noble strong city of Rhodes?[83] The winning thereof he counteth as a victory against the whole corps[84] of Christendom, since all Christendom was not able to defend that strong town against him. Howbeit,[85] if the princes of Christendom everywhere about would, where as need was,[86] have set to their hands[87] in time, the Turk had never[88] taken any one place of all these places; but partly dissensions[89] fallen among ourselves, partly that[90] no man careth what harm other folk feel, but each part suffer[91] other to shift[92] for itself, the Turk is in few years wonderfully increased, and Christendom on the other side very sore decayed. And all this worketh our unkindness,[93] with which God is not content.[94]

But now, whereas you desire[95] of me some plenty of comfortable[96] things, which ye may put in remembrance and comfort therewith your company,[97] verily[98] in the rehearsing[99] and heaping of your manifold fears, myself began to feel that there should much need,[100] against so many troubles, many comfortable counsels; for surely, Cousin, a little before your coming, as I devised[101] with myself upon the Turk's coming, it happed[102] my mind to fall suddenly from that into the devising upon mine own departing, wherein,[103] albeit that I fully put my trust, and hope to be a saved soul, by the great mercy of God, yet since there is here no man so sure that, without revelation,[104] may clean[105] stand out of dread, I bethought me also upon the pains of hell, and after, I bethought me then upon the Turk again. And first methought his terror nothing, when I compared it with the joyful hope of heaven. Then compared I it

---

59 confederated, allied   60 perhaps
61 *but if:* unless   62 roughly, cruelly
63 *while we wot:* since we know   64 happen   65 See Lk 23:28–30.   66 we
stand   67 encouraging, comforting,
strengthening   68 support, sustain;
strengthen   69 distressing, sorrowful,
grievous   70 just   71 grievously; greatly
72 who   73 before   74 safe, secure
75 *when that:* when   76 The Ottoman
Sultan was called "the (Great) Turk." Sultan
Mahomet II sacked Athens in 1452 and
Constantinople (capital of the Byzantine
Empire) in 1453.   77 *The Great Soldan:*
Kansuh Ghuri, Sultan of the Mamelukes of

Syria and Egypt; the Ottomans defeated his
army, and Ghuri died in battle near Aleppo
in 1516.   78 *Then . . . realm:* Suleiman the
Magnificent captured Belgrade (at that
time part of the Kingdom of Hungary)
in 1521.   79 since then   80 Louis II
(1506–26) was killed in the Battle of
Mohács.   81 two. After the death of
Louis, both John Zapolya (Voivode of
Transylvania) and Ferdinand (Archduke of
Austria) claimed the kingship of Hungary.
82 *third dog:* Suleiman the Magnificent;
cf. Aesop's fable "The Dog and his
Shadow."   83 an island fortress that fell
to Suleiman in 1522   84 collective body

85 However   86 *where . . . was:* wherever a
need arose   87 *set to their hands:* actively
involved themselves   88 *had never:* would
never have   89 because of dissensions
90 because   91 allows the   92 manage,
provide   93 *worketh our unkindness:* our
unnatural kinship or disposition produces
94 pleased   95 ask   96 encouraging,
comforting, strengthening   97 household,
companions   98 truly   99 telling,
relating   100 *much need:* be much needed
101 thought   102 happened   103 in
which (devising or thinking)   104 i.e., a
personal revelation   105 completely

on the other side with the fearful dread of hell, and therein casting[106] in my mind those terrible devilish tormentors, with the deep consideration of that furious endless fire, methought that if the Turk with all his whole host, and all trumpets and his timbrels too, were to kill me in my bed, come to my chamber door, in respect of[107] the other reckoning,[108] I regard him not a rush.

And yet when I now heard your lamentable words, laying forth, as it were present before my face, that heap of heavy sorrowful tribulations that, besides those that are already fallen,[109] are in short space like[110] to follow, I waxed therewith[111] myself suddenly somewhat aflight.[112] And therefore I well allow[113] your request in this behalf, that would have store of comfort aforehand ready by you, to resort to and to lay up in your heart, as a treacle[114] against the poison of all desperate[115] dread that might rise of occasion[116] of sore[117] tribulation. And herein shall I be glad (as my poor wit[118] will serve me) to call to mind with you such things as I before have read, heard, or thought upon, that may conveniently[119] serve us to this purpose.

THE FIRST CHAPTER
That the comforts devised by the old paynim[120]
philosophers were insufficient,
and the cause wherefore

ANTONY: First shall ye, good Cousin, understand this: that the natural wise men of this world, the old moral philosophers, labored much in this matter, and many natural reasons[121] have they written, whereby they might encourage men to set little by[122] such goods (or such hurt either), the going and coming whereof are the matter and cause of tribulation — as are the goods of fortune (riches, favor, and friends, fame, worldly worship,[123] and such other things), or of the body (as[124] beauty, strength, agility, quickness, and health). These things, ye wot[125] well, coming to us are matter[126] of worldly wealth, and taken from us by fortune or by force, or the fear of the losing, be matter of adversity or tribulation. For tribulation seemeth generally to signify nothing else but some kind of grief, either pain of the body or heaviness of the mind.

Now the body not to feel that[127] it feeleth, all the wit in the world cannot bring about. But that the mind should not be grieved, neither with the pain that the body feeleth, nor with the occasions of heaviness[128] offered and given unto the soul itself, this thing labored the philosophers very much about, and many goodly sayings have they toward[129] the strength and comfort against tribulation, exhorting men to the full contempt of all worldly loss, and despising[130] of sickness, and all bodily grief, painful death and all. Howbeit,[131] in very deed, for anything that ever I read in them, I never could yet find that ever these natural reasons were able to give sufficient comfort of themselves, for they never stretch so far but that they leave untouched, for lack of necessary knowledge, that special point, which is not only the chief comfort of all, but without which also all other comforts are nothing — that is to wit,[132] the referring the final end of their comfort unto God, and to repute[133] and take for the special cause of comfort that, by the patient sufferance of their tribulation, they shall attain his favor, and for their pain receive reward at his hand in heaven. And for lack of knowledge of this end, they did (as they needs must) leave untouched also the very special[134] means without which we can never attain to this comfort: that is to wit, the gracious help and aid of God to move, stir, and guide us forward in the referring all our ghostly[135] comfort — yea, and our worldly comfort too — all unto that heavenly end. And therefore, as I say, for lack of these things, all their comfortable counsels are very far insufficient. Howbeit, though they be far unable to cure our disease of themselves, and therefore are not sufficient to be taken for our physicians, some good drugs have they yet in their shops, for which they may be suffered[136] to dwell among our apothecaries[137] — if the medicines be not made of their own brains, but after the bills[138] made by the great Physician, God, prescribing the medicines himself and correcting the faults of their erroneous receipts;[139] for without

---

106 considering   107 *in respect of:* in comparison with   108 consideration   109 *are already fallen:* have already occurred   110 likely   111 *waxed therewith:* became at that   112 nervous, afraid   113 approve, accept   114 antidote   115 despairing, stemming from despair   116 *of occasion:*

from an occasion   117 great; grievous   118 ingenuity; intellect   119 suitably, appropriately   120 pagan   121 arguments, explanations   122 *set little by:* put little value on   123 honor, renown, distinction   124 such as   125 know   126 kinds   127 what   128 sadness,

grief   129 concerning   130 disregarding; disdaining   131 However   132 say   133 consider as, reckon   134 particular   135 spiritual   136 allowed   137 pharmacists   138 prescriptions   139 formulas, recipes

this way taken with them, they shall not fail to do as many bold blind apothecaries do, which,[140] either for lucre[141] or of a foolish pride, give sick folk medicines of their own devising, and therewith kill up in corners[142] many such simple folk as they find so foolish to put their lives in such lewd[143] and unlearned blind bayards'[144] hands.

We shall therefore neither fully receive[145] those philosophers' reasons in this matter, nor yet utterly refuse them, but, using them in such order[146] as shall beseem[147] them, the principal and the effectual medicines against these diseases of tribulation shall we fetch from the high, great, and excellent Physician, without whom we could never be healed of our very deadly disease of damnation; for our necessity wherein, the Spirit of God spiritually speaketh of himself to us, and biddeth us of all our health give him the honor, and therein thus saith unto us: *Honora medicum, propter necessitatem enim ordinavit eum Altissimus* ("Honor thou the physician, for him hath the high God ordained for thy necessity").[148]

Therefore, let us require[149] that high Physician, our blessed Savior Christ, whose holy manhood God ordained for our necessity to cure our deadly wounds with the medicine made of the most wholesome blood of his own blessed body, that, likewise as he cured by that incomparable medicine our mortal malady, it may like[150] him to send us and put in our minds such medicines at this time as against the sickness of sorrows and tribulations may so comfort and strengthen us in his grace as our deadly enemy the devil may never have the power, by his poisoned dart of murmur,[151] grudge,[152] and impatience, to turn our short sickness of worldly tribulation into the endless everlasting death of infernal damnation.

THE SECOND CHAPTER
That for a foundation, men must need begin with faith

ANTONY: Since all our principal comfort must come of God, we must first presuppose in him to whom we shall with any ghostly[153] counsel give any effectual comfort, one ground to begin withal,[154] whereupon all that we shall build must be supported and stand: that is to wit,[155] the ground and foundation of faith, without which had ready[156] before, all the spiritual comfort that any man may speak of can never avail[157] a fly. For likewise[158] as it were utterly vain to lay[159] natural reasons of comfort to him that hath no wit,[160] so were it undoubtedly frustrate[161] to lay spiritual causes of comfort to him that hath no faith. For except[162] a man first believe that Holy Scripture is the word of God, and that the word of God is true, how can a man take any comfort of that that[163] the Scripture telleth him therein? Needs must the man take little fruit of the Scripture if he either believe not that it were the word of God, or else ween[164] that though it were, it might yet be, for all that, untrue. This faith, as it is more faint or more strong, so shall the comfortable words of Holy Scripture stand the man in more stead[165] or less. This virtue of faith can neither any man give himself, nor yet any one man another, but though men may with preaching be ministers unto God therein, and the man, with his own free will obeying freely the inward inspiration of God, be a weak worker with almighty God therein, yet is the faith indeed the gracious gift of God himself. For as Saint James saith, *Omne datum optimum et omne donum perfectum de sursum est, descendens a Patre luminum* ("Every good gift, and every perfect gift, is given from above, descending from the Father of lights").[166] Therefore feeling our faith by many tokens very faint, let us pray to him that giveth it, that it may please him to help and increase it. And let us first say with him in the Gospel, *Credo Domine, adiuva incredulitatem meam* ("I believe, good Lord, but help thou the lack of my belief").[167] And after, let us pray with the apostles, *Domine, adauge nobis fidem* ("Lord, increase our faith").[168] And finally, let us consider by Christ's saying unto them that if we would not suffer[169] the strength and fervor of our faith to wax[170] lukewarm — or rather, key-cold[171] — and in manner[172] lose his vigor by scattering our minds abroad about so many trifling things that of the matters of our faith we very seldom think, but

---

140 who (the apothecaries)   **141** money
142 *kill up in corners:* kill off secretly
143 uneducated; bungling; evil   **144** *blind bayard:* proverbial for recklessness and self-confident ignorance   **145** accept
146 manner; arrangement   **147** befit, be appropriate for   **148** Ecclus 38:1

149 request of   **150** please   **151** muttering complaints   **152** grumbling; being discontent   **153** spiritual   **154** with   **155** say
156 *had ready:* had or possessed already
157 profit, benefit   **158** just   **159** present
160 intelligence   **161** useless, fruitless, ineffectual   **162** unless   **163** *that that:*

that which   **164** think, suppose
165 *stand in stead:* profit, benefit, support
166 Jas 1:17   **167** Mk 9:24   **168** Lk 17:5
169 allow   **170** grow, become   **171** cold as a key; i.e., entirely without heat or fervor
172 *in manner:* so to speak

that we would withdraw our thought from the respect[173] and regard of all worldly fantasies,[174] and so gather our faith together into a little narrow room, and, like the little grain of mustard seed (which is of nature hot), set it in the garden of our soul, all weeds pulled out for the better feeding of our faith, then shall it grow, and so spread up in height that the birds (that is to wit,[175] the holy angels of heaven) shall breed in our soul, and bring forth virtues in the branches of our faith; and then, with the faithful trust that, through the true belief of God's word, we shall put in his promise, we shall be well able to command a great mountain of tribulation to void[176] from the place where he stood in our heart, whereas with a very feeble faith and a faint, we shall be scant able to remove a little hillock. And therefore, as for the first conclusion, as we must of necessity before any spiritual comfort presuppose the foundation of faith, so, since no man can give us faith, but only God, let us never cease to call upon God therefor.[177]

VINCENT: Forsooth,[178] good Uncle, methinketh that this foundation of faith, which, as you say, must be laid first, is so necessarily requisite that without it all spiritual comfort were utterly given in vain. And therefore now shall we pray God for a full and a fast[179] faith. And I pray you, good Uncle, proceed you farther in the process[180] of your matter of spiritual comfort against tribulation.

ANTONY: That shall I, Cousin, with good will.

THE THIRD CHAPTER
The first comfort in tribulation may a man take in this: when he feeleth in himself a desire and longing to be comforted by God

ANTONY: I will, in my poor mind, assign for the first comfort the desire and longing to be by God comforted; and not without some reason call I this the first cause of comfort. For like[181] as the cure of that person is in a manner desperate that[182] hath no

will to be cured, so is the discomfort of that person desperate that desireth not his own comfort.

And here shall I note you two kinds of folk that are in tribulation and heaviness:[183] one sort that will seek for no comfort, another sort that will. And yet of these that will not are there also two sorts. For first, one sort there are that are so drowned in sorrow that they fall into a careless deadly dullness, regarding nothing, thinking almost on nothing, no more than if they lay in a lethargy, with which it may so fall that wit and remembrance will wear away, and fall even fair[184] from them. And this comfortless kind of heaviness in tribulation is the highest kind of the deadly sin of sloth. Another sort are there that will seek for no comfort, nor yet none receive, but are in their tribulation (be it loss or sickness) so testy, so fumish,[185] and so far out of all patience, that it booteth[186] no man to speak to them. And these are in a manner[187] with impatience so furious as though they were half in a frenzy, and may, with a custom of such fashioned behavior, fall in thereto full and whole. And this kind of heaviness in tribulation is even a mischievous[188] high branch of the mortal sin of ire. And then is there, as I told you, another kind of folk, which fain[189] would be comforted, and yet are they of two sorts too. One sort are those that in their sorrow seek for worldly comfort, and of them shall we now speak the less, for[190] the diverse occasions that we shall after have to touch[191] them in more places than one. But this will I here say, that I learned of Saint Bernard:[192] he that in tribulation turneth himself unto worldly vanities, to get help and comfort by them, fareth like a man that in peril of drowning catcheth whatsoever cometh next to hand, and that holdeth he fast, be it never so simple a stick; but then that helpeth him not, for that stick he draweth down under the water with him, and there lie they drowned together.[193]

So surely, if we custom[194] ourselves to put our trust of comfort in the delight of these peevish[195] worldly things, God shall for that foul fault suffer[196] our tribulation to grow so great that all the pleasure of this world shall never bear us up, but all our

---

173 consideration; esteem 174 delusive imaginations 175 say 176 leave 177 for it 178 In truth 179 steadfast 180 discussion 181 just 182 i.e., in that person who 183 sadness, grief 184 *even*

fair: quite completely 185 irascible, hot-tempered 186 helps 187 *in a manner:* very nearly, as it were 188 harmful 189 gladly 190 on account of 191 discuss 192 St. Bernard of Clairvaux

(1090–1153) 193 See St. Bernard's *Sermon on the Advent of the Lord* 1.1. 194 accustom 195 foolish; perverse 196 allow

peevish pleasure shall in the depth of tribulation drown with us.

The other sort is, I say, of those that long and desire to be comforted of God. And as I told you before, they have an undoubted great cause of comfort even in that point alone, that they consider themselves to desire and long to be of almighty God comforted.

This mind[197] of theirs may well be cause of great comfort unto them for two great considerations. The one is that they see themselves seek for their comfort where they cannot fail to find it. For God both can give them comfort and will: he can, for he is almighty; he will, for he is all good, and hath promised himself, *Petite et accipietis* ("Ask and you shall have").[198] He that hath faith (as he must needs have that shall take comfort) cannot doubt but God will surely keep this promise, and therefore hath he a great cause to be of good comfort (as I say) in that he considereth that he longeth to be comforted by him which[199] his faith maketh him sure will not fail to comfort him.

But here consider this, that I speak here of him that in tribulation longeth to be comforted by God, and that is he that referreth the manner of his comforting to God, holding himself content whether it be by taking away or diminishment of the tribulation itself, or by the giving of him patience and spiritual consolation therein. For him that only longeth to have God take his trouble from him, we cannot so well warrant[200] that mind for a cause of so great comfort: for both may he desire that that never mindeth[201] to be the better, and may miss also the effect of his desire, because his request is haply[202] not good for himself. And of this kind of longing and requiring[203] we shall have occasion further to speak hereafter. But he that, referring the manner of his comfort unto God, desireth of God to be comforted, asketh a thing so lawful[204] and so pleasant unto God that he cannot fail to speed;[205] and therefore hath he, as I say, great cause to take comfort in the very desire itself. Another cause hath he to take of that desire a very great occasion of comfort, for since his desire is

good, and declareth[206] unto himself that he hath in God a good faith, it is a good token unto him that he is not an abject[207] cast out of God's gracious favor while he perceiveth that God hath put such a virtuous well-ordered appetite[208] in his mind. For as every evil mind cometh of the world and ourselves and the devil, so is every such good mind, either immediately[209] or by the means of our good angel or other gracious occasion, inspired into man's heart by the goodness of God himself. And what a comfort may then this be unto us, when we by that desire perceive a sure undoubted token that toward our final salvation our Savior is himself so graciously busy about us.

THE FOURTH CHAPTER
That tribulation is a means to draw man to that good mind to desire and long for the comfort of God

VINCENT: Forsooth,[210] good Uncle, this good mind of longing for God's comfort is a good cause of great comfort indeed; our Lord in tribulation send it us. But by this I see well that woe may they be which in tribulation lack that mind, and that desireth not to be comforted by God, but are either of[211] sloth or impatience discomfortless,[212] or of folly seek for their chief ease and comfort anywhere else.

ANTONY: That is, good Cousin, very true, as long as they stand in that state; but then must ye consider that tribulation is yet a means to drive him from that state. And that is one of the causes for the which God sendeth it unto man: for albeit that[213] pain was ordained of[214] God for the punishment of sin (for which they that can never now but sin can never be but ever punished in hell), yet in this world, in which his high mercy giveth men space to be better, the punishment by tribulation that he sendeth serveth ordinarily for a means of amendment.

Saint Paul was himself sore[215] against Christ till Christ gave him a great fall, and threw him to the ground and struck him stark blind. And with that tribulation, he turned to him at the first word, and

197 judgment; disposition; intention   **198** Jn 16:24   **199** who   **200** guarantee   **201** *that never mindeth:* who never intends   **202** perhaps   **203** requesting   **204** legitimate   **205** succeed; achieve his end

206 shows, makes clear   **207** wretch; downtrodden person   **208** inclination; desire   **209** directly, without an intermediary   **210** In truth   **211** because of, out of   **212** lacking all comfort

213 *albeit that:* although   **214** *ordained of:* intended by   **215** greatly, very much; grievously

God was his physician and healed him soon after, both in body and soul, by his minister Ananias, and made him his blessed apostle.[216]

Some are in the beginning of tribulation very stubborn and stiff against God, and yet at length tribulation bringeth them home. The proud king Pharaoh did abide[217] and endure two or three of the first plagues, and would not once stoop at them. But then God laid on a sorer lash, that made him cry to him for help, and then sent he for Moses and Aaron, and confessed himself for a sinner and God for good and righteous, and prayed them to pray for him and to withdraw that plague, and he would let them go. But when his tribulation was withdrawn, then was he naught[218] again.[219] So was his tribulation occasion of his profit, and his help again cause of his harm. For his tribulation made him call to God, and his help made hard his heart again.

Many a man that in an easy tribulation falleth[220] to seek his ease in the pastime of worldly fantasies findeth, in a greater pain, all these comforts so feeble that he is fain[221] to fall to the seeking of God's help. And therefore is, as I say, the very tribulation itself many times a means to bring the man to the taking of the aforeremembered[222] comfort therein — that is to wit,[223] to the desire of comfort given by God, which desire of God's comfort is, as I have proved you, great cause of comfort itself.

THE FIFTH CHAPTER
*The special means to get this first comfort
in tribulation*

ANTONY: Howbeit,[224] though the tribulation itself be a means oftentimes to get man this first comfort in it, yet itself sometimes alone bringeth not a man to it. And therefore, since without this comfort first had, there can in tribulation none other good comfort come forth, we must labor[225] the means that[226] this first comfort may come. And thereto seemeth me[227] that if the man — of[228] sloth, or impatience, or hope of worldly comfort — have no mind to desire and seek for comfort of God, those that are his friends that come to visit and comfort him must

afore all things put that point in his mind, and not spend the time (as they commonly do) in trifling and turning him to the fancies of the world. They must also move him to pray God to put this desire in his mind, which, when he getteth once, he then hath the first comfort, and without doubt, if it be well-considered, a comfort marvelous great. His friends also that thus counsel him must, unto the attaining thereof, help to pray for him themselves and cause him to desire good folk to help him to pray therefor. And then if these ways be taken for the getting, I nothing doubt but the goodness of God shall give it.

THE SIXTH CHAPTER
*It sufficeth not that a man have a desire to be
comforted by God only by the taking away
of the tribulation*

VINCENT: Verily[229] methinketh, good Uncle, that this counsel is very good. For except[230] the person have first a desire to be comforted by God, else[231] can I not see what it can avail to give him any further counsel of any spiritual comfort. Howbeit, what if the man have this desire of God's comfort: that is to wit, that it may please God to comfort him in his tribulation by taking that tribulation from him? Is not this a good desire of God's comfort, and a desire sufficient for him that is in tribulation?

ANTONY: No, Cousin, that is it not. I touched before a word of[232] this point, and passed it over because I thought it would fall in our way again; and so wot[233] I well it will, ofter than once. And now am I glad that ye move it me[234] here yourself.

A man may many times well and without sin desire of God the tribulation to be taken from him; but neither may we desire that in every case, nor yet very well in no case (except very few) but under a certain condition either expressed or implied; for tribulations are, ye wot well, of many sundry kinds: some by loss of goods or possessions, and some by the sickness of ourselves, and some by the loss of friends, or by some other pain put unto our bodies,

---

216 See Acts 9:1–20.   217 await defiantly, withstand   218 wicked   219 See Ex 7:14–8:14.   220 turns, begins   221 forced, obliged   222 previously

mentioned   223 say   224 However   225 work for, strive after   226 so that; by which   227 *seemeth me:* it seems to me   228 out of   229 Truly   230 unless

231 otherwise   232 *touched . . . of:* said before a little something on   233 know   234 *move it me:* bring it up to me

some by the dread of the losing of those things that we fain[235] would save — under which fear fall all the same things that we have spoken of before. For we may fear loss of goods or possessions, or the loss of our friends, their grief and trouble, or our own, by sickness, imprisonment, or other bodily pain; we may be troubled with the dread of death, and many a good man is troubled most of all with the fear of that thing which he that most need hath, feareth least of all: that is to wit, the fear of losing through deadly[236] sin the life of his seely[237] soul. And this last kind of tribulation is the sorest[238] tribulation of all; though we touch here and there some pieces thereof before, yet the chief part and principal point will I reserve, to treat apart effectually[239] that matter in the last[240] end.

But now, as I said, where the kinds of tribulation are so diverse, some of these tribulations a man may pray God to take from him, and take some comfort in the trust that God will so do. And therefore, against hunger, sickness, and bodily hurt, and against the loss of either body or soul, men may lawfully many times pray to the goodness of God, either for themselves or for their friend. And toward this purpose are expressly prayed many devout orisons[241] in the common service[242] of our mother, holy Church. And toward our help in some of these things serve some of the petitions in the *Pater Noster*,[243] wherein we pray for our daily food, and to be preserved from the fall in temptation and to be delivered from evil.[244]

But yet may we not always pray for the taking away from us of every kind of temptation. For if a man should in every sickness pray for his health again, when should he show himself content to die and depart unto God? And that mind a man must have, ye wot well, or else it will not be well.

One tribulation is it unto good men to feel in themselves the conflict of the flesh against the soul, the rebellion of sensuality against the rule and governance of reason, the relics that remain in mankind of our old original sin, of which Saint Paul so sore complaineth in his epistle to the Romans.[245] And yet may we not pray while we stand[246] in this life to have this kind of tribulation utterly taken from us. For it is left us by God's ordinance to strive against it and fight withal,[247] and by reason and grace to master it, and use it for the matter of our merit.

For the salvation of our soul may we boldly pray. For grace may we boldly pray — for faith, for hope, and for charity, and for every such virtue as shall serve us to heavenward.[248] But as for all other things before remembered,[249] in which is contained the matter of every kind of tribulation, we may never well make prayer so precisely but[250] that we must express, or imply, a condition therein — that is to wit, that if God see the contrary better for us, we refer it whole[251] to his will, and, instead of our grief taken away, pray that God of his goodness may send us either spiritual comfort to take it gladly, or strength at the leastways to take it patiently. For if we determine with ourselves that we will take no comfort in nothing[252] but in the taking of our tribulation from us, then either prescribe we to God that we will he shall no better turn[253] do us — though he would — than we will ourselves appoint[254] him, or else we declare that what thing is best for us, ourselves can better tell than he.

And therefore, I say, let us in tribulation desire[255] this help and comfort, and let us remit[256] the manner of that comfort unto his own high pleasure; which, when we do, let us nothing doubt but that, like as his high wisdom better seeth what is best for us than we can see ourselves, so shall his sovereign goodness give us the thing that shall indeed be best; for else,[257] if we will presume to stand unto[258] our own choice — except it so be that God offer us the choice himself, as he did to David in the choice of his own punishment after his high pride conceived in the numbering of his people[259] — we may foolishly choose the worse, and by the prescribing unto God ourselves so precisely what we will that he shall do for us, except that of his gracious favor he reject our folly, he shall for indignation grant us our own request, and after shall we well find that it shall turn us to harm. How many men attain health of body, that were better for their soul's health,[260] their body were sick still?

235 gladly　**236** mortal; see 1 Jn 5:16–17.
237 poor, pitiable　**238** most grievous
239 thoroughly　**240** very　**241** prayers
242 *common service:* public prayer
243 *Pater Noster:* Our Father　**244** See
Mt 6:9–13.　**245** See Rom 7:14–25.

246 remain　**247** with it　**248** *serve
us to heavenward:* help us get to heaven
249 *before remembered:* previously mentioned　**250** except　**251** wholly, entirely
252 anything (another typical double
negative)　**253** favor　**254** prescribe for

255 request　**256** leave　**257** otherwise
258 *stand unto:* insist on　**259** See 1 Chr
21:1–13.　**260** *that … health:* who would
be better off spiritually if

How many men get out of prison that hap on[261] such harms abroad as the prison should have kept them from? How many that have been loath to lose their worldly goods have in keeping of them soon after lost their life? So blind is our mortality, and so unware[262] what will fall—so unsure also what manner mind[263] we will ourselves have tomorrow—that God could not lightly[264] do man a more vengeance than in this world to grant him his own foolish wishes.

What wit[265] have we poor fools to wit[266] what will serve[267] us, when the blessed Apostle himself, in his sore tribulation praying thrice unto God to take it away from him, was answered again[268] by God in a manner[269] that he was but a fool in asking that request, but that the help of God's grace in that tribulation to strengthen him was far better for him than to take the tribulation from him.[270] And therefore, by experience perceiving well the truth of that lesson, he giveth us good warning not to be too bold of our own mind when we require aught[271] of God, nor to be precise in our asking, but refer[272] the choice to God at his own pleasure. For his own Holy Spirit so sore[273] desireth our weal[274] that, as man might say, he groaneth for us in such wise[275] as no tongue can tell: *Nos autem*, saith Saint Paul, *quid oremus, ut oportet nescimus; sed ipse Spiritus postulat pro nobis gemitibus inenarrabilibus* ("What may we pray that were behovable[276] for us, cannot ourselves tell; but the Spirit himself desireth for us with unspeakable groanings").[277]

And therefore I say for conclusion of this point, let us never ask of God precisely our own ease by delivery from our tribulation, but pray for his aid and comfort by which ways himself shall best like. And then may we take comfort even of our such request, for both are we sure that this mind cometh of God, and also be we very sure that, as he beginneth to work with us, so, but if[278] ourselves flit from him, he will not fail to tarry with us. And then, he dwelling with us, what trouble can do us harm? *Si Deus nobiscum, quis contra nos?* ("If God be with us," saith Saint Paul, "who can stand against us?")[279]

THE SEVENTH CHAPTER

A great comfort it may be in tribulation, that every tribulation is (if we will ourselves) a thing either medicinable or else more than medicinable

VINCENT: You have, good Uncle, well opened[280] and declared[281] the question that I demanded you: that is to wit,[282] what manner[283] comfort a man might pray for in tribulation. And now proceed forth, good Uncle, and show us yet further some other spiritual comfort in tribulation.

ANTONY: This may be, thinketh me, good Cousin, great comfort in tribulation: that every tribulation which anytime falleth unto us is either sent to be medicinable if men will so take it, or may become medicinable if men will so make it, or is better than medicinable but if[284] we will forsake[285] it.

VINCENT: Surely this is very comfortable if we may well perceive it.

ANTONY: These three things that I tell you, we shall consider thus: every tribulation that we fall in cometh either by our own known deserving deed bringing us thereunto, as[286] the sickness that followeth our intemperate surfeit,[287] or the prisonment or other punishment put upon a man for his heinous crime; or else it is sent us by God without any certain deserving cause open[288] and known unto ourselves, either for punishment of some sins past (we certainly know not for which), or for preserving us from some sins in which we were else like[289] to fall; or finally for no respect[290] of the man's sin at all, but for the profit of his patience and increase of his merit. In all the former cases, tribulation is, if we will, medicinable; in this latter case of all, it is yet better than medicinable.

---

261 *hap on:* happen upon   **262** unaware of; unwary of   **263** *manner mind:* kind of disposition   **264** easily   **265** *what wit:* what mental capacity   **266** know   **267** be good for   **268** in return, in reply   **269** *in a manner:* to the effect   **270** St.

Paul; 2 Cor 12:7–10   **271** *require aught:* ask anything   **272** leave   **273** strongly, greatly   **274** well-being   **275** ways   **276** useful, advantageous   **277** Rom 8:26   **278** *but if:* unless   **279** Rom 8:31   **280** explained   **281** clearly answered

282 say   **283** kind of   **284** *but if:* unless   **285** refuse; renounce   **286** such as   **287** overindulgence   **288** evident, obvious   **289** *else like:* otherwise likely   **290** regard, consideration

THE EIGHTH CHAPTER

The declaration larger²⁹¹ concerning them that fall in tribulation by their own well-known fault, and that yet such tribulation is medicinable

VINCENT: This seemeth me very good, good Uncle, saving²⁹² that it seemeth somewhat brief and short, and thereby methinketh somewhat obscure and dark.

ANTONY: We shall therefore, to give it light withal, touch every member²⁹³ somewhat more at large. One member is, ye wot²⁹⁴ well, of them that fall in tribulation through their own certain well-deserving deed, open and known to themselves, as where we fall in a sickness following upon our own gluttonous feasting, or a man that is punished for his own open fault.

These tribulations, lo, and such other like, albeit that²⁹⁵ they may seem discomfortable,²⁹⁶ in that a man may be sorry²⁹⁷ to think himself the cause of his own harm, yet hath he good cause of comfort in them if he consider that he may make them medicinable for himself, if himself will.

For whereas there was due to that sin, except it were purged here, a far greater punishment after this world in another place, this worldly tribulation of pain and punishment, by God's good provision for him put upon him here in this world before, shall by the means of Christ's Passion (if the man will in true faith and good hope, by meek and patient sufferance of his tribulation, so make it) serve him for a sure medicine to cure him and clearly discharge²⁹⁸ him of all his sickness and disease of those pains that else he should suffer after; for such is the great goodness of almighty God that he punisheth not one thing twice. And albeit so that²⁹⁹ this punishment is put unto the man not of his own election and free choice, but so by force as he would fain³⁰⁰ avoid it, and falleth in it against his will, and therefore seemeth worthy no thanks,³⁰¹ yet so far passeth³⁰² the great goodness of God the poor unperfect³⁰³ goodness of man that, though men make their reckoning one here with another such, God

yet of his bounty in man's account toward him alloweth³⁰⁴ it far otherwise. For though that³⁰⁵ a man fall in his pain by his own fault, and also first against his will, yet as soon as he confesseth his fault, and applieth his will to be content to suffer that pain and punishment for the same, and waxeth³⁰⁶ sorry—not for that only that³⁰⁷ he shall sustain such punishment, but for that also that he hath offended God, and thereby deserved much more—our Lord from that time counteth it not for pain taken against his will, but it shall be a marvelous good medicine and work,³⁰⁸ as a willingly taken pain, the purgation and cleansing of his soul, with gracious remission of his sin, and of the far greater pain that else had been prepared therefor peradventure³⁰⁹ forever in hell.

For many there are undoubtedly that would else³¹⁰ drive forth and die in their deadly sin, which³¹¹ yet in such tribulation—feeling their own frailty so effectually,³¹² and the false flattering world failing them so fully—turn goodly to God and call for mercy, and by grace make virtue of necessity, and make a medicine of their malady, taking their trouble meekly, and make a right godly end.

Consider well the story of Achan, that³¹³ committed sacrilege at the great city of Jericho, whereupon God took a great vengeance upon the children of Israel, and after told them the cause, and bade them go seek the fault³¹⁴ and try it out by lots:³¹⁵ When the lot fell upon the very man that did it—being tried by the falling first upon his tribe, and then upon his family, and then upon his house, and finally upon his person—he might well see that he was deprehended³¹⁶ and taken against his will. But yet, at the good exhortation of Joshua saying unto him, *Fili mi, da gloriam Deo Israel, et confitere et indica mihi quid feceris, et ne abscondas* ("Mine own son, give glory to the God of Israel, and confess and show me what thou hast done, and hide it not"),³¹⁷ he confessed humbly the theft, and meekly took his death therefor, and had, I doubt not, both strength and comfort in his pain, and died a very good man, which,³¹⁸ if he had never comen in the tribulation—had been in peril—never haply³¹⁹ to have had just remorse thereof in all his whole life, but might have

---

291 *declaration larger:* expanded explanation　**292** except　**293** item　**294** know　**295** *albeit that:* although　**296** miserable, distressful, discouraging　**297** sorrowful　**298** *clearly discharge:* entirely relieve or rid　**299** *albeit . . . that:* although　**300** gladly

301 *worthy no thanks:* deserving of no merit　**302** exceeds　**303** incomplete; imperfect　**304** receives; accounts　**305** *though that:* even though　**306** grows, becomes　**307** *for that . . . that:* only because　**308** bring about, accomplish　**309** perhaps

310 otherwise　**311** who　**312** strongly　**313** who　**314** *seek the fault:* find out who had committed what transgression　**315** *try . . . lots:* reveal it by drawings of lots　**316** found out, detected　**317** Josh 7:19　**318** who　**319** perhaps

died wretchedly and gone to the devil eternally. And thus made this thief a good medicine of his well-deserved pain and tribulation.[320] Consider the well-converted thief that hung on Christ's right hand: did not he—by his meek sufferance and humble knowledge[321] of his fault, asking forgiveness of God, and yet content to suffer for his sin—make of his just punishment and well-deserved tribulation a very good special medicine to cure him of all the pain in the other world, and win him eternal salvation?[322] And thus I say that this kind of tribulation, though it seem the most base and the least comfortable, is yet (if the man will so make it) a very marvelous wholesome medicine, and may therefore be, to the man that will so consider it, a great cause of comfort and spiritual consolation.

THE NINTH CHAPTER
The second point: that is to wit, that tribulation that is sent us by God without any open[323] deserving cause known unto ourselves, and that this kind of tribulation is medicinable if men will so take it, and therefore great occasion of comfort

VINCENT: Verily,[324] mine Uncle, this first kind of tribulation have you to my mind opened[325] sufficiently, and therefore I pray you resort[326] now to the second.

ANTONY: The second kind was, ye wot[327] well, of such tribulation as is so sent us by God that we know no certain cause deserving that present trouble: as we certainly know that upon such a surfeit,[328] we fell in such a sickness; or as the thief knoweth that for such a certain theft, he is fallen into such a certain punishment.

But yet since we seldom lack faults against God worthy[329] and well deserving great punishment indeed, we may well think—and wisdom is so to do—that with sin we have deserved it, and that God for some sin sendeth it, though we certainly know not ourselves for which. And therefore as yet, thus farforth[330] is this kind of tribulation (somewhat in effect) in comfort to be taken like unto the other:

for this, as ye see, if we will thus take it well, reckoning it to be sent for our sin and suffering it patiently therefor, is medicinable against the pain in the other world to come, for our sins in this world past, which is, as I showed you, a cause of right great comfort.

But yet may then this kind of tribulation be to some men of more sober living (and thereby of the more clear conscience) somewhat a little more comfortable, for though they may none otherwise reckon themselves than sinners—for as Saint Paul saith, *Nullius mihi conscius sum, sed non in hoc iustificatus sum* ("My conscience grudgeth[331] me not of anything, but yet am I not thereby justified"),[332] and Saint John saith, *Si dixerimus quia peccatum non habemus, ipsi nos seducimus, et veritas in nobis non est* ("If we say that we have no sin in us, we beguile ourselves, and truth is there not in us")[333]—yet forasmuch as[334] the cause is to them not so certain as it is to the other aforeremembered[335] in the first kind, and that it is also certain that God sometimes sendeth tribulation for keeping and preserving a man from such sin as he should else fall in, and sometimes also for exercise of their patience and increase of merit, great cause of increase in comfort have these folk of the clearer conscience in the fervor of their tribulation, in that they may take the comfort of a double medicine, and of a thing also that is of the kind which we shall finally speak of, that I call better than medicinable. But as I have before spoken of this kind of tribulation, how it is medicinable in that it cureth the sin past, and purchaseth remission of the pain due therefor, so let us somewhat consider how this tribulation sent us by God is medicinable in that it preserveth us from the sin into which we were else like[336] to fall.

If that thing be a good medicine that restoreth us our health when we lose it, a good medicine must this needs be that preserveth our health while we have it, and suffereth[337] us not to fall into that painful sickness that must after drive us to a painful plaster.[338]

Now seeth God sometimes that worldly wealth is with one that is yet good coming upon him so fast that, foreseeing how much weight of worldly

---

320 See Josh 7:1–26.   **321** acknowledgement   **322** See Lk 23:32–33, 39–43.   **323** evident   **324** Truly, Indeed   **325** explained   **326** *pray you resort:* ask you

to turn   **327** know   **328** overindulgence   **329** meriting   **330** *thus far-forth:* this far; to this extent   **331** troubles   **332** 1 Cor 4:4   **333** 1 Jn 1:8   **334** *forasmuch as:*

seeing that, inasmuch as   **335** previously mentioned   **336** *else like:* otherwise likely   **337** allows   **338** treatment

wealth the man may bear, and how much will over-charge[339] him and enhance[340] his heart up so high that grace should fall from him low, God of his goodness, I say, preventeth[341] his fall and sendeth him tribulation betime,[342] while he is yet good, to gar him to ken[343] his Maker, and by less liking the false flattering world, set a cross upon the ship of his heart, and bear a low sail thereon, that the bois-tous blast[344] of pride blow him not under the water.

Some young lovely lady, lo, that is yet good enough, God seeth a storm coming toward her that would, if her health and her fat feeding should a lit-tle longer last, strike her into some lecherous love, and instead of her old-acquainted knight, lay her abed with a new-acquainted knave.[345] But God, loving her more tenderly than to suffer[346] her fall into such shameful beastly sin, sendeth her in sea-son[347] a goodly fair fervent[348] fever, that maketh her bones to rattle, and wasteth away her wanton flesh, and beautifieth her fair fell[349] with the color of the kite's claw,[350] and maketh her look so lovely that her lover would have little lust[351] to look upon her, and maketh her also so lusty that if her lover lay in her lap, she should so sore long to break unto him the very bottom of her stomach[352] that she should not be able to refrain[353] it from him, but suddenly lay it all in his neck.

Did not (as I before showed you) the blessed Apostle himself confess that the high revelations that God had given him might have enhanced[354] him into so high pride that he might have caught a foul fall, had not the provident goodness of God provided for his remedy? And what was his remedy but a painful tribulation, so sore[355] that he was fain[356] to call thrice to God to take the tribulation from him? And yet would God not grant his request, but let him lie so long therein till himself, that saw more in Saint Paul than Saint Paul saw in himself, wist[357] well the time was come in which he might well without his harm take it from him.[358]

And thus ye see, good Cousin, that tribulation is double medicine: both a cure for the sin past, and a preservative from the sin that is to come. And therefore in this kind of tribulation is there good occasion of a double comfort; but that is, I say, di-versely to sundry diverse folk, as their own con-science is with sin cumbered[359] or clear.

Howbeit,[360] I will advise no man to be so bold as to think that their tribulation is sent them to keep them from the pride of their holiness: let men leave that kind of comfort hardily[361] to Saint Paul, till their living be like;[362] but of the remnant may men well take great comfort, and good besides.

THE TENTH CHAPTER
Of the third kind of tribulation, which is not sent a man for his sin, but for exercise of his patience and increase of his merit—which is better than medicinable

VINCENT: The third kind, Uncle, that remaineth now behind—that is to wit, which is sent a man by God, and not for his sin (neither committed, nor which would else come), and therefore is not me-dicinable, but sent for exercise of our patience and increase of our merit, and therefore better than medicinable—though[363] it be, as you say (and as in-deed it is), better for the man than any of the other two kinds in another world, where the reward shall be received, yet can I not see by what reason a man may in this world, where the tribulation is suffered, take any more comfort therein than in any of the other twain[364] that are sent a man for his sin, since he cannot here know whether it be sent him for sins before committed, or sin that else should fall,[365] or for increase of merit and reward after to come, namely[366] since every man hath cause enough to fear and to think that his sin already past hath deserved it, and that it is not without peril [for] a man to think otherwise.

ANTONY: This that ye say, Cousin, hath place of truth in far the most part of men, and therefore must they not envy nor disdain[367]—since they may take in their tribulation consolation for their part

---

339 overfill; overpower **340** lift; elevate **341** anticipates **342** in good time, early **343** *gar him to ken:* make him know **344** *boistous blast:* violent wind **345** vil-lain, rogue **346** let **347** *in season:* in time **348** intense; burning **349** *fair fell:* beautiful skin **350** *color of the kite's claw:* yellowish-white (a kite is a kind of hawk) **351** wish; sexual desire **352** *break . . . stomach:* reveal the very depths of her desire; i.e., vomit **353** keep **354** lifted, elevated **355** great, intense; grievous **356** obliged **357** knew **358** See 2 Cor 12:1–10. **359** encumbered, burdened **360** Nevertheless **361** certainly, assuredly **362** similar, the same (as his) **363** even if **364** two **365** *else should happen:* otherwise should happen **366** especially **367** scorn

sufficient—that some other that more be worthy take yet a great deal more. For as I told you, Cousin, though the best man must confess himself a sinner, yet be there many men (though to the multitude,[368] few) that for the kind[369] of their living, and thereby the clearness of their conscience, may well and without sin have a good hope that God sendeth them some great grief for exercise of their patience and for increase of their merit, as it appeareth not only by Saint Paul in the place[370] before remembered, but also by that holy man Job,[371] which in sundry places of his dispicions[372] with his burdenous comforters letted[373] not to say that the clearness of his own conscience declared and showed unto himself that he deserved not the sore tribulation that he then had. Howbeit,[374] as I told you before, I will not advise every man at adventure[375] to be bold upon this manner of comfort. But yet some men know I such as I durst,[376] for their more ease and comfort in their great and grievous pain, put them in right good hope that God sendeth it unto them not so much for their punishment as for exercise of their patience. And some tribulations are there also that grow upon[377] such causes that in these cases I would never let, but always would without any doubt give that counsel and comfort to any man.

VINCENT: What causes, good Uncle, be those?

ANTONY: Marry,[378] Cousin, wheresoever a man falleth in tribulation for the maintenance of justice or for the defense of God's cause. For if I should hap to find a man that had long lived a very virtuous life, and had at last happened to fall into the Turk's hands, and there did abide by the truth of his faith, and with the suffering of all kind of torments taken upon his body, still did teach and testify the truth, if I should in his passion[379] give him a spiritual comfort, might I be bold to tell him no further but that he should take patience in this pain, and that God sendeth it him for his sin, and that he is well worthy to have it although[380] it were yet much more? He might well answer me and such other comforters as Job answered his: *Onerosi consolatores estis vos*

("Burdenous and heavy comforters be you").[381] Nay, I would not fail to bid him boldly (while I should see him in his passion) cast sin and hell and purgatory and all upon the devil's pate,[382] and doubt not but likewise[383] as if he gave over his hold, all his merit were lost and he turned into misery, so if he stand and persevere still in the confession of his faith, all his whole pain shall turn all into glory.

Yet more shall I yet say you than this: that if there were a Christian man that had among those infidels committed a very deadly crime, such as were worthy death not only by their law, but by Christ's too (as manslaughter, adultery, or such other thing like); if, when he were taken, he were offered pardon of his life upon condition that he should forsake the faith of Christ; if this man would now rather suffer death than so do–should I comfort him in his pain but as I would a malefactor?[384] Nay, this man, though he should have died for his sin, dieth now for Christ's sake, while he might live still if he would forsake him. The bare patient taking[385] of his death should have served for the satisfaction of his sin—through the merit of Christ's Passion, I mean, without help of which no pain of our own could be satisfactory.[386] But now shall Christ, for his forsaking[387] of his own life in the honor of his faith, forgive the pain of all his sins of his mere liberality,[388] and accept all the pain of his death for merit of reward in heaven, and shall assign no part thereof to the payment of his debt in purgatory, but shall take it all as an offering, and requite it all with glory. And this man, among Christian men, all had he[389] been before a devil, nothing would I after doubt to take him for a martyr.

VINCENT: Verily,[390] good Uncle, methinketh this is said marvelous well, and it specially delighteth and comforteth me to hear it because of our principal fear that I first spoke of: the Turk's cruel incursion into this country of ours.

ANTONY: Cousin, as for the matter of that fear, I purpose to touch[391] last of all; nor I meant not here to speak thereof, had it not been that the vehemence

---

368 *to the multitude:* compared to the total number of people   **369** *for the kind:* because of the manner   **370** passage (2 Cor 12:7–10)   **371** See Job 16:2.   **372** discussions   **373** hesitated   **374** However   **375** *at adventure:* at

random, recklessly   **376** dare   **377** *grow upon:* come about by   **378** an exclamation, from "by Mary!"; indeed   **379** suffering   **380** even if   **381** Job 16:2   **382** head   **383** just   **384** criminal   **385** *bare patient taking:* mere patient acceptance   **386** be

satisfactory: serve to make satisfaction for sin   **387** renouncing, giving up   **388** *of . . . liberality:* out of his sheer generosity   **389** *all had he:* even if he had   **390** Truly, Indeed   **391** *purpose to touch:* intend to discuss it

of your objection brought it in my way. But rather would I else have put some example for this place of such as suffer tribulation for maintenance of right and justice, and that rather chose to take harm than do wrong in any manner[392] of matter. For surely if a man may, as indeed he may, have great comfort in the clearness of his conscience that[393] hath a false crime put upon him, and by false witness proved upon him, and he falsely punished and put to worldly shame and pain therefor, a hundred times more comfort may he have in his heart that,[394] where white is called black and right is called wrong, abideth by the truth and is persecuted for justice.

VINCENT: Then if a man sue me wrongfully for my land, in which myself have good right, it is a comfort yet to defend it well, since God shall give me thanks therefor?

ANTONY: Nay, nay, Cousin, nay. There walk ye somewhat wide,[395] for there you defend your own right for your temporal avail.[396] And since Saint Paul counseleth, *Non vosmet defendentes carissimi* ("Defend not yourselves, most dear friends"),[397] and our Savior counseleth, *Si qui vult tecum in iudicio contendere et tunicam tuam tollere dimitte ei et pallium* ("If a man will strive with thee at law and take away thy coat, leave him thy gown too"),[398] the defense therefore of our right asketh no[399] reward. Say you speed well if ye get leave;[400] look hardily[401] for no thanks.

But on the other side, if you do as Saint Paul biddeth, *Quaerentes non quae sua sunt sed quae aliorum* ("Seek not for your own profit but for other folks'"),[402] but defend therefore of[403] pity a poor widow, or a poor fatherless child, and rather suffer sorrow by some strong extortion than suffer[404] them take wrong, or if ye be a judge and will have such zeal to justice that ye will rather abide[405] tribulation by the malice of some mighty man than judge wrong for his favor, such tribulations, lo, be those that are better than only medicinable, and every man upon whom they fall may be bold so to reckon them, and in his deep trouble may well say to himself the words that Christ hath taught him for his comfort: *Beati misericordes, quia misericordiam*

consequentur ("Blessed be the merciful men, for they shall have mercy given them"); *Beati qui persecutionem patiuntur propter iustitiam, quoniam ipsorum est regnum caelorum* ("Blessed be they that suffer persecution for justice, for theirs is the kingdom of heaven").[406] Here is a high comfort, lo, for them that are in the case. And in this case their own conscience can show it them, and so may fulfill their hearts with spiritual joy that the pleasure may far surmount the heaviness[407] and the grief of all their temporal trouble. But God's nearer cause of[408] faith against the Turks hath yet a far passing[409] comfort, and by many degrees far excelleth this—which, as I have said, I purpose[410] to treat last. And for this time this sufficeth concerning the special comfort that men may take in the third kind of tribulation.

THE ELEVENTH CHAPTER
Another kind of comfort, yet in the base kind of tribulation, sent for our sin

VINCENT: Of truth, good Uncle, albeit that[411] every of these kinds of tribulation have cause of comfort in them (as ye have well declared), if men will so consider them, yet hath this third kind above all a special prerogative therein.

ANTONY: That is undoubtedly true. But yet is there not, good Cousin, the most base kind of them all but that yet hath more causes of comfort than I have spoken of yet, for I have, ye wot well, in that kind that is sent us for our sin, spoken of none other comfort yet but twain:[412] that is to wit, one that it refraineth us from the sin that else we would fall in, and in that serveth us, through the merit of Christ's Passion, as a means by which God keepeth us from hell, and serveth for the satisfaction of such pain as else[413] we should endure in purgatory.

Howbeit,[414] there is therein another great cause of joy besides this: for surely these pains sent us here for our sins, in whatsoever wise[415] they hap unto us, be our own sin never so sore,[416] nor never so open and evident unto ourselves and all the world too, yet if we pray for grace to take it meekly and

392 kind 393 who 394 who
395 *walk…wide:* miss somewhat the
point 396 advantage, profit 397 Rom
12:19 398 Mt 5:40 399 *asketh no:* does
not call for any 400 *speed…leave:* have

great success if you get the opportunity
401 certainly, assuredly 402 See Phil 2:4;
1 Cor 10:24. 403 out of 404 allow
405 face, endure 406 Mt 5:7, 10
407 sadness 408 *nearer cause of:* more

immediate reason for 409 surpassing
410 intend 411 *albeit that:* although
412 two 413 otherwise 414 However
415 ways, manner 416 great, grievous

patiently, and, confessing to God that it is far over-little for our fault, beseech him yet — nevertheless[417] that since[418] we shall come hence so void of all good works whereof we should have any reward in heaven — to be not only so merciful unto us as to take that (our present tribulation) in release of our pain in purgatory, but also so gracious unto us as to take our patience therein for a matter of merit and reward in heaven, I verily trust and nothing doubt it but God shall, of his high bounty,[419] grant us our boon.[420] For likewise as in hell pain serveth only for punishment without any manner of purging because all possibility of purging is past, and in purgatory punishment serveth for only purging because the place of deserving[421] is past, so while we be yet in this world, in which is our place and our time of merit and well deserving, the tribulation that is sent us here for our sin shall, if we faithfully so desire, besides the cleansing and purging of our pain, serve us also for increase of reward.

And so shall, I suppose (and trust in God's goodness), all such penance and good works as a man willingly performeth enjoined by his ghostly[422] father in confession, or which he willingly further do of his own devotion besides. For though man's penance, with all the good works that he can do, be not able to satisfy of themselves for the least sin that we do, yet the liberal goodness of God through the merit of Christ's bitter Passion — without which all our works could neither satisfy nor deserve,[423] nor yet do not indeed neither merit nor satisfy so much as a spoonful to a great vesselful in comparison of the merit and satisfaction that Christ hath merited and satisfied for us himself — this liberal goodness of God, I say, shall yet, at our faithful instance[424] and request, cause our penance and tribulation patiently taken in this world to serve us in the other world both for release and reward, tempered after such rate[425] as his high goodness and wisdom shall see convenient[426] for us, whereof our blind mortality cannot here imagine nor devise the stint.[427] And thus hath yet even the first kind of tribulation and the most base — though not fully so great as the second, and very far less than the third — far greater cause of comfort yet than I spoke of before.

THE TWELFTH CHAPTER
A certain objection against the things aforesaid

VINCENT: Verily, good Uncle, this liketh[428] me very well; but yet is there, ye wot[429] well, some of these things now brought in question: for as for any pain due for our sins to be diminished in purgatory by the patient sufferance of our tribulation here, there are, ye wot well, many that utterly deny that, and affirm for a sure truth that there is no purgatory at all; and then is (if they say true) the cause of that comfort gone, if the comfort that we shall take be but in vain and need not. They say, ye wot well also, that men merit nothing at all, but God giveth all for faith alone, and that it were sin and sacrilege to look for any reward in heaven, either for our patient and glad suffering for God's sake, or for any other good deed; and then is there gone, if this be thus, the other cause of our further comfort too.

ANTONY: Cousin, if some things were as they be not, then should some things be as they shall not. I cannot indeed say nay but that some men of late have brought up some such opinion, and many more than these besides, and have spread them abroad. And albeit that it is a right heavy thing to see such variance[430] in our belief rise and grow among ourselves — to the great encouraging of the common enemies of us all, whereby they have our faith in derision and catch hope to overwhelm us all — yet do there three things not a little recomfort my mind.

The first is that in some communications had of late together hath appeared good likelihood of some good agreement to grow in one accord of our faith.

The second, that in the meanwhile till this may come to pass, contentions (dispicions[431] with uncharitable behavior) is prohibited and forbidden in effect upon all parties[432] — all such parties, I mean, as fell before to fight for it.

The third is that all Germany, for all their diverse opinions, yet as they agree together in profession of Christ's name, so agree they now together in preparation of a common power in defense of

---

417 notwithstanding   418 subsequently
419 *high bounty:* great generosity
420 request, favor asked   421 meriting
422 spiritual   423 merit   424 urging,

insistence   425 *tempered…rate:* modified
to such a degree   426 suitable, appropriate
427 *devise the stint:* conceive of the
amount or limit   428 pleases   429 know

430 divergence; discord   431 discussions,
disputations   432 sects, sides

Christendom against our common enemy the Turk. And I trust in God that this shall not only help us here to strengthen us in this war, but also that as God hath caused them to agree together in the defense of his name, so shall he graciously bring them to agree together in the truth of his faith.

Therefore will I let God work and leave off contention, and nothing shall I now say but that with which they that are themselves of the contrary mind shall in reason have no cause to be discontent. For first, as for purgatory, though they think there be none, yet since they deny not that all the corps[433] of Christendom by so many hundred years have believed the contrary—and among them, all the old interpreters of Scripture from the Apostles' days down to our own time, of whom they deny not many for holy saints, that I dare not now believe these men against all those—these men must of their courtesy hold my poor fear excused. And I beseech our Lord heartily for them that when they depart out of this wretched world, they find no purgatory at all, so[434] God keep them from hell. And as for the merit of man in his good works, neither are they that deny it full agreed among themselves, nor any man is there almost of them all that, since he began to write, hath not somewhat changed and varied from himself. And far the more part are thus far agreed with us that like as we grant them that no good work is aught worth to heavenward[435] without faith; and that no good work of man is rewardable in heaven of his[436] own nature but through the mere[437] goodness of God, that list[438] to set so high a price upon so poor a thing; and that this price God setteth through Christ's Passion, and for that also that[439] they be his own works with us (for good works to Godward[440] worketh no man without[441] God work with him); and as we grant them also that no man may be proud of his works, for his[442] own unperfect[443] working and for that that[444] in all that man may do, he can do God no good, but is a servant unprofitable and doth but his bare duty[445]—as we, I say, grant unto them these things, so this one thing or twain do they grant us

again:[446] that men are bound to work good works if they have time and power, and that whoso worketh in true faith most shall be most rewarded. But then set they thereto[447] that all his reward shall be given him for his faith alone, and nothing for his works at all, because his faith is the thing, they say, that forceth him to work well. Strive will I not with them for this matter now, but yet this I trust to the great goodness of God: that if the question hang on that narrow point, while Christ saith in the Scripture in so many places that men shall in heaven be rewarded for their works, he shall never suffer our souls—that are but mean-witted men, and can understand his words but as himself hath set them, and as old holy saints hath construed[448] them before, and as all Christian people this thousand years have believed—to be damned for lack of perceiving such a sharp subtle thing, specially since some men that have right good wits, and are besides that right well-learned too, can in no wise[449] perceive for what cause or why these folk that from good works take away the reward, and give the reward all whole to faith alone, give the reward to faith rather than to charity; for this grant they themselves, that faith serveth of nothing, but if[450] she be companied with her sister charity. And then saith the Scripture too, *Fides, spes, caritas; tria haec, maior autem horum, caritas* ("Of the three virtues faith, hope, and charity, of all these three, the greatest is charity")[451]— and therefore as worthy to have the thanks[452] as faith. Howbeit, as I said, I will not strive therefor; nor indeed, as our matter standeth, I shall not greatly need. For if they say that he which suffereth tribulation or martyrdom for the faith shall have his high reward, not for his work, but for his wellworking faith, yet since they grant that have it he shall, the cause of the high comfort in the third kind of tribulation standeth. And that is, ye wot well, the effect of all my purpose.[453]

VINCENT: Verily, good Uncle, this is truly driven[454] and tried out[455] to the uttermost, as it seemeth me. I pray[456] you proceed at your pleasure.

---

433 collective body   **434** so long as, provided that   **435** *aught worth to heavenward:* worth anything toward getting to heaven   **436** its (good work's)   **437** sheer, utter   **438** pleases, chooses   **439** *for that … that:* because   **440** to

Godward: toward God   **441** unless   **442** *for his:* because of his   **443** incomplete; imperfect, flawed   **444** *for that that:* because   **445** See Lk 17:10.   **446** in return   **447** *set they thereto:* they set down against that   **448** interpreted   **449** way

450 *but if:* unless   **451** See 1 Cor 13:13.   **452** credit   **453** *effect … purpose:* point of my whole argument   **454** *truly driven:* correctly deduced   **455** *tried out:* sifted out, ascertained; proved, tested   **456** ask, beseech

THE THIRTEENTH CHAPTER

*That a man ought to be comfortable to himself, and
have good hope, and be joyful also in tribulation
appeareth well by this: that a man hath great cause
of fear and heaviness that continueth always still
in wealth discontinued with no tribulation*

ANTONY: Cousin, it were too long work to peruse
every comfort that a man may well take in tribulation; for as many comforts, ye wot[457] well, may a
man take thereof as there be good commodities[458]
therein, and that be there surely so many that it
would be very long to rehearse and treat of them.
But meseemeth we cannot lightly[459] better perceive
what profit and commodity, and thereby what comfort, they may take of it that[460] have it, than if we
well consider what harm the lack is, and thereby
what discomfort the lack thereof should be, to
them that never have it. So it is now that all holy
men agree, and all the Scripture is full, and our own
experience proveth at our eye,[461] that we be not
come into this wretched world to dwell here, nor
have not, as Saint Paul saith, "our dwelling city here,
but we be seeking for that city that is to come;"[462]
and therefore Saint Paul showeth us that we do
seek for it because he would put us in mind that
we should seek for it, as they that are good folk and
fain[463] would come thither do.

For surely whoso[464] setteth so little thereby[465]
that he lusteth[466] not to seek therefor, it will be, I
fear me, long ere[467] he come thereat, and marvelous
great grace if ever he come thither. *Sic currite*, saith
Saint Paul, *ut comprehendatis* ("Run so that ye may
get it").[468] If it must then be gotten with running,
when shall he come at it that list[469] not once to step
toward it?

Now because this world is, as I tell you, not our
eternal dwelling, but our little while wandering,
God would that we should[470] in such wise use it as
folk that were weary of it, and that we should in this
vale of labor, toil, tears, and misery not look for rest
and ease, game, pleasure, wealth, and felicity, for
they that so do fare like a fond[471] fellow that, going
toward his own house where he should be wealthy,
would for a tapster's[472] pleasure become a hostler[473]
by the way, and die in a stable and never come at
home.

And would God that those that drown themselves in the desire of this world's wretched wealth
were not yet more fools than so, but alas, their folly
as far passeth[474] the foolishness of that other fond
fellow as there is distance between the height of
heaven and the very depth of hell, for as our Savior saith, *Vae vobis qui ridetis nunc, quia lugebitis et
flebitis* ("Woe may you be that laugh now, for you
shall wail and weep").[475] *Est tempus flendi*, saith the
Scripture, *et est tempus ridendi* ("There is time of
weeping, and there is time of laughing");[476] but as
you see, he setteth the weeping time before, for that
is the time of this wretched world, and the laughing
time shall come after in heaven. There is also a time
of sowing, and a time of reaping too.[477] Now must
we in this world sow, that we may in the other world
reap, and in this short sowing time of this weeping
world must we water our seed with the showers of
our tears, and then shall we have in heaven a merry
laughing harvest forever. *Euntes ibant et flebant*,
saith the prophet, *mittentes semina sua* ("They went
forth sowing their seeds weeping") — but what saith
he shall follow thereof? *Venientes autem venient
cum exultatione portantes manipulos suos* ("They
shall come again more than laughing with great joy
and exultation, with their handfuls of corn in their
hands").[478]

Lo, they that in their going home toward heaven
sow their seeds with weeping shall at the Day of
Judgment come to their bodies again with everlasting plentiful laughing. And for to prove that this
life is no laughing time, but rather the time of weeping, we find that our Savior himself wept twice or
thrice,[479] but never find we that he laughed so much
as once. I will not swear that he never did, but at
the leastwise he left us no examples of it. But on the
other side, he left us example of weeping. Of weeping have we matter enough, both for our own sins
and other folks' too — for surely so should we do:
bewail their wretched sins, and not be glad to detract them,[480] nor envy them neither. Alas, seely[481]
souls, what cause is there to envy them that are ever
wealthy in this world and ever out of tribulation,

---

457 know   458 benefits, advantages
459 readily, easily   460 who   461 *at
our eye:* before our eyes; at first glance
462 Heb 13:14   463 gladly, willingly
464 whoever   465 *setteth so little*

thereby: values that so little   466 desires
467 before   468 1 Cor 9:24
469 wishes, desires, chooses   470 *would
that we should:* wants us to   471 foolish
472 tavern keeper's   473 horsekeeper,

stableman   474 surpasses   475 Lk 6:25
476 Eccl 3:4   477 See Eccl 3:2.   478 Ps
125(126):6   479 See Lk 19:41; Jn 11:35.
480 *detract them:* damage their reputations
481 poor, pitiful

which,[482] as Job saith, *ducunt in bonis dies suos et in puncto ad inferna descendunt* ("lead all their days in wealth, and in a moment of an hour descend into their grave and be painfully buried in hell")?[483] Saint Paul saith to the Hebrews that God, "those that he loveth, he chastiseth," *et flagellat omnem filium quem recipit* ("and he scourgeth every son of his that he receiveth").[484] Saint Paul saith also, *Per multas tribulationes oportet nos introire in regnum Dei* ("By many tribulations must we go into the kingdom of God").[485] And no marvel, for as our Savior said of himself unto his two disciples that were going into the castle[486] of Emmaus, *An nesciebatis quia oportebat Christum pati et sic introire in regnum suum?* ("Know you not that Christ must suffer and so go into his kingdom?")[487] And would we that are servants look for more privilege in our Master's house than our Master himself? Would we get into his kingdom with ease, when himself got not into his own but by pain?[488] His kingdom hath he ordained for his disciples, and he saith unto us all, *Qui vult meus esse discipulus, tollat crucem suam et sequatur me* ("If any man will be my disciple, let him learn at[489] me to do as I have done: take his cross of tribulation upon his back and follow me").[490] He saith not here, lo, "Let him laugh and make merry."

Now if heaven serve but[491] for Christ's disciples, and they be those that take their cross of tribulation, when shall these folk come there that[492] never have tribulation? And it be[493] true that Saint Paul saith—that God chastiseth all them that he loveth, and scourgeth every child that he receiveth, and to heaven shall none come but such as he loveth and receiveth—when shall they then come thither whom he never chastiseth, nor never do vouchsafe to file[494] his hands upon them and give them so much as one lash? And if we cannot (as Saint Paul saith we cannot) come to heaven but by many tribulations, how shall they come thither then that never have none at all?

Thus see we well by the very Scripture itself how true the words are of the old holy saints, that with one voice, in a manner,[495] say all one thing: that is to wit, that we shall not have both continual wealth in this world and in the other too. And therefore, since that[496] they that in this world without any tribulation enjoy their long continual course of never-interrupted prosperity have a great cause of fear and of discomfort—lest they be far fallen out of God's favor, and stand deep in his indignation and displeasure while he never send them tribulation, which he is ever wont[497] to send them whom he loveth—they therefore, I say, that are in tribulation have on the other side[498] a great cause to take in their grief great inward comfort and spiritual consolation.

THE FOURTEENTH CHAPTER
A certain objection, and the answer thereto

VINCENT: Verily, good Uncle, this seemeth so indeed, howbeit[499] yet methinketh that you say very sore[500] in something concerning such persons as are in continual prosperity—and they be, ye wot well, not a few. And those are they also that have the rule and authority of this world in their hand; and I wot well that when they talk with such great cunning[501] men as I trow[502] can tell the truth, and when they ask them whether, while they make merry here in earth all their life, they may not yet, for all that, have heaven after too, they do tell them, "Yes, yes, well enough," for I have heard them tell them so myself.

ANTONY: I suppose, good Cousin, that no very wise man, and specially none that very good is therewith,[503] will tell any man fully of[504] that fashion; but surely such as so say to them, I fear me that they flatter them, either for lucre[505] or fear. Some of them think peradventure[506] thus: "This man maketh much of me now, and giveth me money also, to fast and watch[507] and pray for him; but so, I fear me, would he do no more[508] if I should go tell him now that all that I do for him will not serve him but if[509] he go fast and watch and pray for himself too; for if I should set thereto[510] and say further that my diligent intercession for him should, I trust, be the means that God should the sooner give him grace to amend, and fast and watch and pray

482 who   483 Job 21:13   484 Heb 12:6   485 Acts 14:22   486 village   487 Lk 24:26   488 See Mt 10:24–25; Jn 15:18–20.   489 from   490 See Mt 16:24; Lk 14:27.   491 *serve but:* is intended only   492 what   493 *it be:* if

it be   494 *vouchsafe to file:* deign to defile   495 *in a manner:* so to speak   496 *since that:* because; seeing that   497 accustomed   498 hand   499 although   500 severely, oppressively   501 intelligent; learned   502 trust   503 besides

504 *fully of:* precisely in   505 monetary gain   506 perhaps   507 keep vigil   508 longer   509 *but if:* unless   510 *set thereto:* add to that

and take affliction in his own body for the bettering of his sinful soul, he would be wondrous wroth[511] with that, for he would be loath to have any such grace at all as should make him go leave off any of his mirth, and so sit and mourn for his sin." Such mind as this is, lo, have there some of those that are not unlearned and have worldly wit at will, which[512] tell great men such tales as perilously beguile them, rather than the flatterer that so telleth them would with a true tale jeopard[513] to lose his lucre.

Some are there also that such tales tell them for consideration of another fear: for seeing the man so sore[514] set on his pleasure that they despair any amendment of him whatsoever they should show him, and then seeing also besides that the man doth no great harm, but of a gentle nature doth some good men some good, they pray God themselves to send him grace, and so they let him lie lame still in his fleshly lusts *ad probaticam piscinam, expectantes aquae motum*[515] — at the pool that the Gospel speaketh of, beside the Temple, wherein they washed their sheep for the sacrifice, and they tarry to see the water stirred[516] — and when his good angel coming from God shall once begin to stir the water of his heart, and move him to the lowly meekness of a simple sheep, then if he call them to him, they will tell him another tale, and help to bear him and plunge him into the pool of penance over the hard ears.[517] But in the meanwhile, for fear lest when he would wax[518] never the better, he would wax much the worse — and from gentle, smooth, sweet, and courteous wax angry, rough, froward,[519] and sour, and thereupon be troublous and tedious[520] to the world — to make fair weather withal,[521] they give him fair words for the while, and put him in good comfort, and let him for the remnant stand at his own adventure.[522] And in such wise deal they with him as the mother doth sometimes with her child, which[523] when the little boy would not rise for her in time but lie still abed and slug,[524] and when he is up, weepeth because he hath lain so long, fearing to be beaten at school for his late coming thither, she telleth him it is but early days[525] and he shall come time enough,[526] and biddeth, "Go, good son; I warrant[527] thee, I have sent[528] to thy master myself; take thy bread and butter with thee; thou shalt not be beaten at all." And so thus she may send him merry forth at door,[529] that he weep not in her sight at home; she studieth[530] not much upon the matter, though he be taken tardy and beaten when he cometh to school. Surely thus, I fear me, fare[531] there many friars, and states'[532] chaplains too, in comfort-giving to great men when they be loath to displease them. I cannot commend their thus doing; but surely thus, I fear me, they do.

THE FIFTEENTH CHAPTER
Other objections

VINCENT: But yet, good Uncle, though that[533] some do thus, this answereth not full the matter. For we see that the whole Church, in the common service,[534] use diverse collects,[535] in which all men pray specially for the princes and prelates,[536] and generally every man for other, and for himself too, that God would vouchsafe[537] to send them all perpetual health and prosperity. And I can see no good man pray God send another sorrow, nor no such prayers are there put in the priest's porteous,[538] as far as I can hear.

And yet if it were as you say, good Uncle, that perpetual prosperity were to the soul so perilous, and tribulation thereto[539] so fruitful, then were, as meseemeth, every man bound of charity not only to pray God send their neighbors sorrow, but also to help thereto themselves; and when folk are sick, not pray God send them health, but when they come to comfort them, they should say, "I am glad, good gossip,[540] that ye be so sick; I pray God keep you long therein"; and neither should any man give any medicine to other, nor take any medicine himself neither, for by the diminishing of the tribulation, he taketh away part of the profit from his soul, which can by no bodily profit be sufficiently recompensed.

---

511 angry   **512** who   **513** risk
514 greatly, grievously   **515** "at the Sheep-Gate pool, [where] they await the movement of the water" — see Jn 5:2–3.
516 See Jn 5:2–9.   **517** *over … ears:* beyond the tips of his ears   **518** become, grow   **519** unruly, perverse   **520** irksome

521 *fair … withal:* a (feigned) good show of friendliness with him   **522** risk   **523** who (the mother)   **524** inactive   **525** *early days:* still early in the day   **526** *come time enough:* arrive in good time   **527** assure, promise   **528** sent word   **529** *forth at door:* out the door   **530** considers

531 behave   **532** noblemen's   **533** *though that:* even though   **534** *common service:* public prayer   **535** one of the prayers of the Mass   **536** bishops   **537** agree, be willing   **538** breviary, or any portable prayer book   **539** i.e., to the soul   **540** godparent; close friend

And also, this wot[541] ye well, good Uncle: that we read in Holy Scripture of men that were wealthy and rich, and yet very good withal.[542] Solomon was, ye wot well, the richest and wealthiest king that any man could in his time tell of, and yet was he well-beloved with God.

Job was also no beggar, pardie,[543] nor no wretch otherwise, nor lost his riches and his wealth for that[544] God would not that his friend should have wealth, but for the show of his patience, to the increase of his merit and confusion[545] of the devil. And for proof that prosperity may stand with God's favor, *Reddidit Deus Iob omnia duplicia* ("God restored him double of all that ever he lost"),[546] and gave him after[547] long life to take his pleasure long.[548] Abraham was eke,[549] ye wot well, a man of great substance,[550] and so continued all his life in honor and in wealth—yea, and when he died too, he went unto such wealth that Lazarus, which[551] died in tribulation and poverty, the best place that he came to was that rich man's bosom.[552] Finally, good Uncle, this we find at our eye,[553] and every day we perceive it by plain experience: that many a man is right wealthy, and yet therewith right good, and many a man a miserable wretch, as evil as he is wretched. And therefore it seemeth hard, good Uncle, that between prosperity and tribulation the matter should go thus, that tribulation should always be given by God to all those he loveth for a sign of salvation, and prosperity sent for displeasure as a token of eternal damnation.

THE SIXTEENTH CHAPTER
The answer to the objections

ANTONY: Either I said not, Cousin, or else meant I not to say, that for an undoubted rule worldly pleasure were always displeasant to God, or tribulation evermore wholesome to every man. For well wot[554] I that our Lord giveth in this world unto every sort of folk either sort of fortune: *Et facit solem suum oriri super bonos et malos, et pluit super iustos et iniustos* ("He maketh his sun to shine both upon the good and the bad, and the rain to rain both upon the just

and unjust").[555] And on the other side, *Flagellat omnem filium quem recipit* ("He scourgeth every son that he receiveth").[556] And yet he beateth not only good folk that he loveth, but *multa flagella peccatoris* too ("there are many scourges for sinners" also).[557]

He giveth evil folk good fortune in this world both to call them by kindness (and if they thereby come not, the more is their unkindness), and yet where wealth will not bring them, he giveth them sometimes sorrow. And some that in prosperity cannot to God creep forward, in tribulation they run toward him apace:[558] *Multiplicatae sunt infirmitates eorum, postea acceleraverunt* ("Their infirmities were multiplied," saith the prophet, "and after that, they made haste").[559]

To some that are good men, God showeth wealth here also, and they give him great thanks for his gift, and he rewardeth them for that thanks too. To some good folk he sendeth sorrow, and they thank him thereof too. If God should give the goods of this world only to evil folk, then would men ween[560] that God were not lord thereof; if God would give the goods only to good men, then would folk take occasion to serve him but for them.

Some will in wealth fall to folly: *Homo cum in honore esset non intellexit, comparatus est iumentis insipientibus, et similis factus est illis* ("When man was in honor, his understanding failed him; then was he compared with beasts and made like unto them").[561]

Some man with tribulation will fall into sin, and therefore saith the prophet, *Non relinquet Dominus virgam peccatorum super sortem iustorum ut non extendant iusti ad iniquitatem manus suas* ("God will not leave the rod of wicked men upon the lot of righteous men, lest the righteous peradventure hap[562] to extend and stretch out their hands to iniquity").[563]

So say I not nay but[564] that in either state—wealth or tribulation—may be matter of virtue and matter of vice also; but this is the point, lo, that standeth here in question between you and me: not whether every prosperity be a perilous token, but whether continual wealth in this world without any

541 know   **542** besides   **543** certainly; "by God" (from the French)   **544** because   **545** ruin; confounding   **546** *Reddidit... lost:* Job 42:10   **547** afterwards   **548** See Job 42:16–17.   **549** also   **550** wealth, property. See Gn 13:2.   **551** who   **552** See Lk 16:19–22.   **553** *at our eye:* before our eyes; at first glance   **554** know   **555** Mt 5:45   **556** Heb 12:6   **557** Ps 31(32):10   **558** with speed   **559** Ps 15(16):4   **560** think   **561** Ps 48(49):12   **562** *peradventure hap:* perhaps happen   **563** Ps 124(125):3   **564** *say... but:* I do not deny

tribulation be a fearful sign of God's indignation. And therefore, this[565] mark that we must shoot at set up well in our sight, we shall now mete[566] for the shot, and consider how near toward or how far off your arrows are from the prick.[567]

VINCENT: Some of my bolts,[568] Uncle, will I now take up myself, and prettily[569] put them under your belt again, for some of them, I see well, be not worth the meting; and no great marvel though[570] I shoot wide, while I somewhat mistake the mark.

ANTONY: These that make toward the mark and light[571] far too short, when the shot is met,[572] shall I take up for you. To prove that perpetual wealth should be no evil token, you lay[573] first that for princes and prelates, and every man for other, we pray all for perpetual prosperity, and that in the common prayers of the Church too.

Then say you secondly that if prosperity were so perilous, and tribulation so profitable, every man ought then to pray God to send others sorrow.

Thirdly, ye further your objections with examples of Solomon, Job, and Abraham.

And fourthly, in the end of all, you prove by experience of our own time daily before our face that some wealthy folk are good, and some needy very naught.[574] That last bolt,[575] since I lie the same[576] myself, you may be content to take up, it lieth so far wide.

VINCENT: That will I with good will, Uncle.

ANTONY: Well, do so then, Cousin, and we shall mete[577] for the remnant. First must you, Cousin, be sure that you look well to the mark, and that can you not but if[578] ye know what thing tribulation is, for since that is one of the things that we principally speak of; but if you consider well what thing that is, you may miss the mark again.

I suppose now that you will agree that tribulation is every such thing as troubleth and grieveth the man, either in body or in mind, and is as it were the prick of a thorn, a bramble, or a briar thrust into his flesh or into his mind. And surely, Cousin, the prick that very sore pricketh the mind as far almost passeth[579] in pain the grief that paineth the body as doth a thorn that sticketh in the heart pass and exceed in pain the thorn that is thrust in the heel.

Now, Cousin, if tribulation be this that I call it, then shall you soon consider this: that there be more kinds of tribulation than peradventure[580] ye thought on before. And thereupon it followeth also that, since every kind of tribulation is an interruption of wealth, prosperity (which is but of wealth another name) may be discontinued[581] by more ways than you would before have weened.[582]

Then say I thus unto you, Cousin: that since tribulation is not only such pains as pain the body, but every trouble also that grieveth the mind, many good men have many tribulations that every man marketh not, and consequently their wealth interrupted therewith when other men are not ware[583] — for trow[584] you, Cousin, that the temptations of the devil, the world, and the flesh, soliciting[585] the mind of a good man to sin, is not a great inward trouble and secret grief in his heart?

To such wretches as care not for their conscience, but like unreasonable beasts follow their foul affections, many of these temptations be no trouble at all, but matter of their beastly pleasure. But unto him, Cousin, that standeth in the dread of God, the tribulation of temptation is so painful that to be rid thereof or sure of the victory therein, be his substance[586] never so great, he would gladly give more than half.

Now if he that careth not for God think this trouble but a trifle, and with such tribulation prosperity not interrupted, let him cast in his mind if himself hap upon a fervent longing for the thing which get he cannot — and as a good man will not, as percase[587] his pleasure of some certain good woman that will not be naught — and then let him tell me whether the ruffle[588] of his desire shall so torment his mind as all the pleasure that he can take besides shall, for lack of that one, not please him of a pin.[589] And I dare be bold to warrant[590] him that the pain in resisting, and the great fear of falling, that many a good man hath in his temptation, is an anguish and a grief every deal as great as his.

---

565 having this   **566** measure   **567** bull's eye   **568** arrows   **569** quietly, unobtrusively   **570** if; that   **571** land   **572** measured   **573** allege, argue   **574** wicked   **575** arrow   **576** *lie the same:* am in the same place; agree with you   **577** measure   **578** *but if:* unless   **579** surpasses   **580** perhaps   **581** interrupted; broken off, withdrawn   **582** thought   **583** aware   **584** think; believe   **585** tempting   **586** possessions   **587** perhaps   **588** disturbance, turbulence   **589** *of a pin:* in the least   **590** guarantee, promise

Now say I further, Cousin, that if this be true (as in very deed, true it is) that such trouble is tribulation, and thereby consequently an interruption of prosperous wealth, no man precisely meaneth to pray for other[591] to keep him in continual prosperity, without any manner of discontinuance or change in this world; for that prayer, without any other condition added or implied, were inordinate and were very childish, for it were to pray that either they should never have temptation, or else that if they had, they might follow it and fulfill their affection.

Who dare, good Cousin, for shame or for sin, for himself or any man else, make this manner kind[592] of prayer? Besides this, Cousin, the Church, ye wot well, adviseth every man to fast, to watch,[593] and pray, both for taming of his fleshly lusts, and also to mourn and lament his sin before committed, and to bewail his offenses done against God—and as they did at the city of Nineveh[594] and as the prophet David did,[595] for their sin put affliction unto their flesh. And when a man so doth, Cousin, is this no tribulation to him because he doth it himself? For I wot well ye would agree that it were, if another man did it against his will. Then is tribulation, ye wot well, tribulation still, though it be taken well in worth[596]—yea, and though it be taken with very right good will, yet is pain, ye wot well, pain, and therefore so is it though a man do it himself.

Then, since the Church adviseth every man to take tribulation for his sin, whatsoever words you find in any prayer, they never mean, ye may be fast[597] and sure, to pray God to keep every good man, nor every bad man neither, from every manner kind of tribulation.

Now he that is not in some kind of tribulation (as peradventure in sickness, or in loss of goods) is not yet out of tribulation if he have his ease of body or of mind inquieted[598]—and thereby his wealth interrupted—with another kind of tribulation, as is either temptation to a good man, or voluntary affliction, either of body by penance, or of mind by contrition and heaviness[599] for his sin and offense against God.

And thus I say that for precise perpetual wealth and prosperity in this wretched world—that is to say, for the perpetual lack of all trouble and all tribulation—there is no wise man that either prayeth for himself or for any man else. And thus answer I your first objection.

Now before I meddle[600] with your second, your third will I join unto this, for upon this answer will the solution of your examples conveniently[601] depend. As for Solomon was, as you say, all his days a marvelous wealthy king, and much was he beloved with God, I wot well, in the beginning of his reign; but that the favor of God persevered with him as his prosperity did, that can I not tell. And therefore will I not warrant it. But surely we see that his continual wealth made him fall, first into such wanton[602] folly in multiplying wives to a horrible number, contrary to the commandment of God given in the law by Moses, and secondly taking to wife, among others, such as were infidels, contrary to another commandment of God's written law also; that finally, by the means of his miscreant[603] wife, he fell into the maintenance[604] of idolatry himself;[605] and of this find we none amendment or repentance, as we find of his father. And therefore, though he were buried where his father was, yet whether he went to the rest that his father did, through some secret sorrow for his sin at last—that is to say, by some kind of tribulation—I cannot tell, and am therefore content to trust well, and pray God he did so. But surely we be not sure. And therefore the example of Solomon can very little serve you; for you might as well lay it for a proof that God favored idolatry as that he favored prosperity, for Solomon was, ye wot well, in both.

As for Job, since our question hangeth upon perpetual prosperity, the wealth of Job, that was with so great adversity so sore interrupted, can (as yourself seeth) serve you for no example. And that God gave him here in this world all things double that he lost little toucheth my matter, which did deny not prosperity to be God's gift and given to some good men too, namely[606] such as have tribulation too.

But Abraham, Cousin, I suppose is all your chief hold,[607] because that you not only show riches and prosperity perpetual in him through the course of all his whole life in this world, but that after his death also, Lazarus—the poor man that lived in tribulation and died for pure hunger and thirst—had after his death his place, comfort, and rest in

591 another   592 *manner kind:* kind
593 keep vigil   594 See Jon 3:6–10.
595 See 2 Sm 12:1–24.   596 *well in worth:*

as valuable   597 certain   598 disquieted,
disturbed   599 sorrow   600 concern
myself   601 suitably   602 lustful,

unruly   603 unbelieving   604 support
605 See 1 Kgs 3:13–14; 10:14–27;
11:1–10.   606 especially   607 support

Abraham, the wealthy rich man's bosom. But here must you consider that Abraham had not such continual prosperity, but that it was discontinued with diverse tribulations. Was it nothing to him, trow[608] ye, to leave his own country, and at God's sending to go into a strange land which God promised him and his seed forever, but in all his whole life he gave himself[609] never a foot?[610]

Was it no trouble that his cousin[611] Lot and himself were fain[612] to part company because their servants could not agree together?[613]

Though he recovered Lot again from the three kings, was his taking[614] no trouble to him, trow you, in the meanwhile?[615]

Was the destruction of the five cities none heaviness[616] to his heart? A man would ween[617] "yes" that readeth in the story what labor he made to save them.[618]

His heart was, I dare say, in no little sorrow when he was fain to let Abimelech the king have his wife, whom though God provided to keep undefiled, and turned all to wealth, yet was it no little woe to him for the meantime.[619]

What a continual grief was it to his heart many a long day, that he had no child of his own body begotten? He that doubteth thereof shall find it in Genesis, of his own moan made unto God.[620]

No man doubteth but Ishmael was great comfort to him at his birth. And was it no grief then when he was cast out, the mother and the child both?[621]

Isaac, that was the child of promission,[622] although God kept his life, which was unlooked for, yet, while the loving father bound him and went about to behead him, and offer him up in sacrifice, who but himself can conceive what heaviness his heart had then?[623] I would ween in my mind — because you speak of Lazarus — that Lazarus's own death panged not him so sore.[624] Then, as Lazarus' pain was patiently borne, so was Abraham's taken not only patiently, but — which is a thing much more meritorious — of obedience willingly. And therefore, though Abraham had not, as he did indeed, far excel Lazarus in merit of reward for many other things besides — and specially for that he

was a special patriarch of the faith — yet had he far passed[625] him even by the merit of tribulation well taken here for God's sake too. And so serveth for your purpose no man less than Abraham.

But now, good Cousin, let us look a little longer here upon the rich Abraham and Lazarus the poor, and as we shall see Lazarus sit in wealth somewhat under the rich Abraham, so shall we see another rich man lie full low beneath Lazarus, crying and calling out of his fiery couch that Lazarus might, with a drop of water falling from his finger's end, a little cool and refresh the tip of his burning tongue.

Consider well, now, what Abraham answered to the rich wretch: *Fili, recordare quia recepisti bona in vita tua, et Lazarus similiter mala, nunc autem hic consolatur tu vero cruciaris* ("Son, remember that thou hast in thy life received wealth, and Lazarus in like wise pain; but now receiveth he comfort, and thou sorrow, pain, and torment").[626]

Christ describeth his wealth and his prosperity: gay[627] and soft apparel, with royal delicate fare[628] continually, day by day. *Epulabatur,* saith our Savior, *quotidie splendide* ("He did fare[629] royally every day")[630] — his wealth was continual, lo, no time of tribulation between. And Abraham telleth him[631] the same tale: that he had taken his wealth in this world, and Lazarus in like wise his pain, and that they had now changed each to the clean[632] contrary, poor Lazarus from tribulation into wealth, and the rich man from this continual prosperity into perpetual pain.

Here was laid expressly to Lazarus no very great virtue by name, nor to this rich glutton no great heinous crime but the taking of his own continual ease and pleasure, without any tribulation or grief. Whereof grew sloth and negligence to think upon the poor man's pain: for that ever himself saw Lazarus and wist him die for[633] hunger at his door, that laid neither Christ nor Abraham to his charge.[634] And therefore, Cousin, this story, lo, of which by occasion of Abraham and Lazarus you put me in remembrance, well declareth[635] what peril is in continual worldly wealth, and contrariwise what comfort cometh of tribulation. And thus, as your

---

608 think, suppose   609 i.e., Abraham himself   610 See Gn 12:1.   611 kinsman; nephew   612 forced   613 See Gn 13:5–11.   614 capture   615 See Gn 14:1–16, giving four not three kings.   616 grief, sorrow   617 suppose   618 See Gn 18:22–23.

619 See Gn 20:1–16.   620 See Gn 15:2–3.   621 See Gn 16:1–16; 21:1–21.   622 the promise   623 See Gn 22:1–15.   624 greatly, grievously   625 surpassed   626 Lk 16:25   627 brightly colored   628 food   629 dine   630 Lk 16:19

631 of him   632 complete   633 *wist… for:* knew him to be dying for   634 *that… charge:* neither Christ nor Abraham accused him of that   635 *declareth:* shows, makes clear

other examples of Solomon and Job nothing for the matter further you,[636] so your example of the rich Abraham and poor Lazarus have not a little hindered you.

THE SEVENTEENTH CHAPTER
An answer to the second objection

VINCENT: Surely, Uncle, you have shaken mine example sore, and have in meting[637] of your shot removed me these arrows, methinketh, farther from the prick[638] than methought they stuck when I shot them; and I shall now be content to take them up again. But yet meseemeth surely that my second shaft may stand: for of truth, if every kind of tribulation be so profitable that it be good to have it (as you say it is), I cannot see wherefore any man should wish or pray or any manner thing do to have any kind of tribulation withdrawn, either from himself or any friend of his.

ANTONY: I think in very deed tribulation so good and so profitable that I should haply[639] doubt as ye do, wherefore a man might labor or pray to be delivered of it, saving[640] that God, which teacheth us the one, teacheth us also the other, and as he biddeth us take our pain patiently, and exhort our neighbor to do also the same, so biddeth he us also not let[641] to do our devoir[642] to remove the pain from us both. And then when it is God that teacheth both, I shall not need to break my brain in devising wherefore he would bid us do both, the one seeming to resist the other.

If he send the scourge of scarcity and great famine, he will we shall[643] bear it patiently, but yet would he that we should eat our meat[644] when we can hap to get it.

If he send us the plague of pestilence, he will we shall patiently take it, but yet will he that we let[645] us blood and lay plasters to draw it,[646] and ripe it,[647] and lance it, and so get it away. Both these points teacheth God in Scripture in more than many places.

Fasting is better than eating, and more thanks hath of God, and yet will God that we shall eat. Praying is better than drinking, and much more pleasant to God, and yet will God that we drink. Waking in good business is much more acceptable to God than sleeping, and yet will God that we shall sleep.

God hath given us our bodies here to keep,[648] and will that we maintain them to do him service with, till he send for us hence. Now can we not surely tell how much tribulation may mar it, or peradventure[649] hurt the soul also; wherefore the Apostle,[650] after that he had commanded the Corinthians to deliver to the devil the abominable fornicator that forbore not[651] the bed of his own father's wife, yet after that he had been a while accursed and punished for his sin, the Apostle commanded them charitably to receive him again,[652] and give him consolation, *ut non a magnitudine doloris absorbeatur* ("that the greatness of his sorrow should not swallow him up").[653]

And therefore when God sendeth the tempest, he will that the shipmen shall get them to their tackling[654] and do the best they can for themselves, that the sea eat them not up; for help ourselves as well as we can, he can make his plague as sore[655] and as long-lasting as himself list.[656] And as he will that we do for ourselves, so will he that we do for our neighbor too, and that we shall in this world be each to other piteous,[657] and not *sine affectione*,[658] for which the Apostle rebuketh them that[659] lack their tender affections, so that of charity sorry should we be for their pains too, upon whom for cause necessary we be driven ourselves to put it. And whoso[660] saith that for pity of his neighbor's soul, he will have none of[661] his body, let him be sure that, as Saint John saith, "he that loveth not his neighbor, whom he seeth, loveth God but a little, whom he seeth not,"[662] so he that hath no pity on the pain that he feeleth his neighbor feel afore[663] him pitieth little, whatsoever he saith, the pain of his soul that he seeth not yet. God sendeth us also such tribulation sometimes because his pleasure is to have us pray unto him for help. And therefore when Saint Peter was in prison, the Scripture showeth that the whole Church without intermission prayed incessantly for

---

636 *nothing . . . you:* did not advance your argument at all   **637** measuring   **638** bull's-eye   **639** perhaps   **640** except   **641** hesitate   **642** task, duty   **643** *will we shall:* wants us to   **644** food   **645** draw, let out   **646** *lay plasters to draw it:* use curative applications to draw out the

disease   **647** *ripe it:* allow the pustules to fully swell   **648** take care of   **649** perhaps   **650** *the Apostle:* St. Paul   **651** *forbore not:* did not refrain from   **652** See 1 Cor 5:1–5.   **653** 2 Cor 2:7   **654** tackle, ship's rigging   **655** great, intense; grievous   **656** pleases   **657** compassionate, tender

658 *sine affectione:* "without affection." See Rom 1:28–32; 2 Tim 3:2–3.   **659** *them that:* whoever   **660** whoever   **661** *have none of:* take none (i.e., no pity) on   **662** 1 Jn 4:20   **663** in front of

him. And at their fervent prayer, God by miracle delivered him.[664]

When the disciples in the tempest stood in fear
of drowning, they prayed unto Christ and said,
Salva nos, Domine, perimus ("Save us, Lord, we perish");[665] and then, at their prayer, he shortly ceased
the tempest.[666] And now see we proved often that
in sore weather or sickness, by general processions[667]
God giveth gracious help. And many a man in his
great pain and sickness by calling upon God is marvelously made whole.

This is God's goodness, that, because in wealth we
remember him not but forget to pray to him, sendeth us sorrow and sickness to force us to draw toward him, and compelleth us to call upon him and
pray for release of our pain; whereby, when we learn
to know him and seek to him, we take a good occasion to fall after into a further grace.

THE EIGHTEENTH CHAPTER
Of them that in tribulation seek not unto God,
but some to the flesh, and some to the world,
and some to the devil himself

VINCENT: Verily,[668] good Uncle, with this good
answer am I well content.

ANTONY: Yea, Cousin, but many men are there,
with whom God is not content, which[669] abuse this
great high goodness of his, whom neither fair treating nor hard handling can cause them to remember
their Maker, but in wealth they be wanton,[670] forget
God and follow their lust, and when God with tribulation draweth them toward him, then wax they
wood[671] and draw back all that ever they may, and
rather run and seek help at any other hand than to
go fetch it at his.

Some for comfort seek to the flesh, some to the
world, and some to the devil himself.

Some man that in worldly prosperity is very full
of wealth, and hath deep stepped into many a sore[672]
sin—which sins, when he did them, he counted for
part of his pleasure—God, willing of his goodness
to call the man to grace, casteth a remorse into his
mind among[673] after his first sleep, and maketh him
lie a little while and bethink[674] him. Then beginneth he to remember his life, and from that he falleth to think upon his death, and how he must leave
all this worldly wealth within a while behind here
in this world and walk hence alone—he wotteth[675]
not whither, nor how soon he shall take his journey thither, nor can tell what company he shall
meet there. And then beginneth he to think that it
were good to make sure and to be merry so that we
be wise therewith, lest there hap to be such black
bugs[676] indeed as folk call devils, whose torments he
was wont[677] to take for poets' tales.

These thoughts, if they sink deep, are a sore tribulation, and surely if he take hold of the grace that
God therein offereth him, his tribulation is wholesome, and shall be full comfortable to remember
that God by this tribulation calleth him and biddeth him come home out of the country of sin that
he was bred and brought up so long in, and come
into the Land of Behest,[678] that floweth[679] milk and
honey. And then if he follow this calling (as many
one full well doth), joyful shall his sorrow be, and
glad shall he be to change his life, leave his wanton lusts, and do penance for his sins, bestowing
his time upon better business. But some men, now,
when this calling of God causeth them to be sad,
they be loath to leave their sinful lusts that hang
in their hearts; and specially if they have any such
kind of living as they must leave off or fall deeper
in sin, or if they have done so many great wrongs
that they have many amends to make that must (if
they follow God) diminish much their money, then
are those folk, alas, woefully bewrapped,[680] for God
pricketh upon them oft of his great goodness still,
and the grief of this great pang pincheth them by
the heart, and of wickedness they wry[681] away, and
from this tribulation they turn to their flesh for
help, and labor to shake off this thought. And then
they amend their pillow and lay their head softer,
and assay[682] to sleep; and when that will not be, then
they find a talk awhile with them that lie by them.
If that cannot be neither, then they lie and long for
day, and then get them forth about their worldly
wretchedness, the matter of their prosperity, the

664 See Acts 12:5–11.   **665** Mt 8:25
666 See Mt 8:23–27; Mk 4:35–39.
667 *general processions:* groups of people
praying while processing   **668** Truly
669 who   **670** undisciplined, unruly

671 *wax they wood:* they become senseless
or insane   **672** great, grievous   **673** occasionally; during the time   **674** think
about, consider   **675** knows   **676** *black
bugs:* bugbears; i.e., imaginary terrors

677 accustomed   **678** *Land of Behest:*
Promised Land   **679** flows with (e.g.,
Ex 3:8)   **680** involved   **681** turn, twist
682 attempt

selfsame sinful things with which they displease God most. And at length, with many times using this manner, God utterly casteth them off; and then they set nought neither by[683] God nor devil: *Peccator cum in profundum venerit, contemnit* ("When the sinner cometh into the depth, then he contemneth"),[684] and setteth nought by nothing saving[685] worldly fear that may fall by chance, or that needs must (they wot well) fall once by death.

But alas, when death cometh, then cometh again their sorrow: then will no soft bed serve, nor no company make him merry; then must he leave his outward worship[686] and comfort of his glory, and lie panting in his bed as he were on a pinebank.[687] Then cometh his fear of his evil life, and of his dreadful death; then cometh the torment of his cumbered[688] conscience and fear of his heavy judgment. Then the devil draweth him to despair with imagination of hell, and suffereth[689] him not then to take it for a fable. And yet if he do, then findeth it, the wretch, no fable. Ah, woe worth the while, that folk think not of this in time.

God sendeth to some man great trouble in his mind, and great tribulation about his worldly goods, because he would, of his goodness, take his delight and his confidence from them; and yet the man withdraweth no part of his fond fantasies,[690] but falleth more fervently to them than before, and setteth his whole heart, like a fool, more upon them; and then he taketh him all to the devices of his worldly counselors, and, without any counsel of God or any trust put in him, maketh many wise ways (as he weeneth), and all turn at length to folly, and one subtle drift[691] driveth another to naught.[692]

Some have I seen — even in their last sickness — sit up in their deathbed underpropped with pillows, take their playfellows to them, and comfort themselves with cards. And this, they said, did ease them well to put fantasies out of their head. And what fantasies, trow you?[693] Such as I told you right now: of their own lewd[694] life and peril of their soul, of heaven and of hell, that irked them to think of, and therefore cast it out with card-play as long as ever

they might, till the pure pangs of death pulled their heart from their play, and put them in the case[695] they could not reckon their game. And then left them their gamers and slyly slunk away, and long was it not ere[696] they galped[697] up the ghost. And what game they came then to, that God knoweth and not I. I pray God it were good, but I fear it very sore.[698]

Some men are there also that do as did King Saul: in their tribulation go seek unto the devil. This king had commanded all such to be destroyed as use the false abominable superstition of this ungracious[699] witchcraft and necromancy, and yet fell he to such folly afterward himself that ere he went to battle he sought unto a witch, and besought her to raise up a dead man to tell him how he should speed.[700]

Now had God showed him before by Samuel that he should come to naught, and he went about none amendment, but waxed[701] worse and worse, so that God list[702] not to look to him; and when he sought by the prophet[703] to have answer of God, there came none answer to him, which thing he thought strange, and because he was not with God heard at his pleasure, he made suit to the devil, desiring a woman by witchcraft to raise up dead Samuel. But speed[704] had he such thereof, as commonly they have all that[705] in their business meddle with such matters, for an evil answer had he, and an evil speed[706] thereafter: his army discomfit[707] and himself slain. And as it is rehearsed in Paralipomenon[708] (the tenth chapter of the First Book), one cause of his fall was for lack of trust in God, for which he left[709] to take counsel of God and fell to seek counsel of the witch, against God's prohibition in the law, and against his own good deed by which he punished and put out all witches so late afore.[710] Such speed let them look for that play the same part (as I see many do) that in a great loss send to seek a conjurer to get their gear[711] again, and marvelous things there they see sometimes, but never groat[712] of their goods.

And many fond fools are there that when they be sick will meddle with no physic, in no manner wise,[713] nor send his water to no cunning man, but

---

683 *set nought by:* care nothing about
684 views with contempt, scorns; Prv 18:3 **685** *setteth...saving:* has no concern about anything except **686** honor, renown, distinction **687** torturing rack **688** burdened **689** allows **690** *fond fantasies:* foolish delusions

691 *subtle drift:* clever scheme, plan **692** evil **693** *trow you:* do you suppose **694** wicked **695** condition **696** before **697** gave; vomited **698** grievous, bitter; painful **699** reprobate, wicked **700** fare **701** grew, became **702** chose **703** *the prophet:* i.e., Samuel **704** success

705 *they have all that:* all of them have who **706** outcome **707** defeated **708** Chronicles; see 1 Chr 10:13–14. **709** ceased **710** *late afore:* recently before; 1 Sm 28:3–19; 31:1–6 **711** possessions **712** a coin worth four pence; even a bit **713** *no manner wise:* any kind of way

send his cap or his hose to some wise woman,[714] otherwise called a witch. Then sendeth she word again that she hath spied in his hose where, when he took none heed, he was taken with a spirit between two doors as he went in the twilight, but the spirit would not let him feel it in five days after, and it hath the while festered in his body, and that is the grief that paineth him so sore; but let him go to no leechcraft,[715] nor any manner physic other than good meat and strong drink, for syrups should sour him up;[716] but he shall have five leaves of valerian,[717] that she enchanted with a charm and gathered with her left hand; let him lay those five leaves to his right thumb, not binded fast to,[718] but let it hang loose thereat, by a green thread; he shall never need to change it; look it fall not away, but let it hang till he be whole, and he shall need no more.

In such wise witches, and in such mad medicines, have their souls more faith a great deal than in God. And thus, Cousin, as I tell you, all these kind of folk in their tribulation call not upon God, but seek for their ease and help otherwise: to the flesh and the world and to the flinging fiend.[719] The tribulation that God's goodness sendeth them for good, themselves by their folly turn into their harm. And they that on the other side seek unto God therein, both comfort and profit they greatly take thereby.

THE NINETEENTH CHAPTER
Another objection, with the answer thereunto

VINCENT: I like well, good Uncle, all your answer herein. But one doubt yet remaineth there in my mind, which riseth upon[720] this answer that you make; and that doubt soiled,[721] I will as for this time, mine own good Uncle, encumber[722] you no further, for methink I do you very much wrong to give you occasion to labor yourself so much, in matter of some study, with long talking at once. I will therefore at this time move[723] you but one thing, and seek some other time for the remnant at your more ease.

My doubt, good Uncle, is this: I perceive well, by your answers gathered and considered together, that you will well agree that a man may both have

worldly wealth, and yet well go to God; and that on the other side a man may be miserable and live in tribulation, and yet go to the devil. And as a man may please God by patience in adversity, so may he please God by thanksgiving in prosperity.

Now since you grant these things to be such that either of them both may be matter of virtue or else matter of sin—matter of damnation or matter of salvation—they seem neither good nor bad of their own nature, but things of themselves equal and indifferent, turning to good or the contrary after as[724] they be taken. And then if this be thus, I can perceive no cause why you should give the preeminence unto tribulation, or wherefore you should reckon more cause of comfort therein than you should reckon to stand in prosperity, but rather a great deal less—by, in a manner,[725] half—since that in prosperity the man is well at ease, and may also by giving thanks to God get good unto his soul, whereas in tribulation, though he may merit by patience, as in abundance of worldly wealth the other may by thanks, yet lacketh he much comfort that the wealthy man hath, in that he is sore grieved with heaviness[726] and pain, besides this also: that a wealthy man, well at ease, may pray to God quietly and merrily, with alacrity and great quietness of mind, whereas he that lieth groaning in his grief cannot endure to pray, nor think almost upon nothing but upon his pain.

ANTONY: To begin, Cousin, where you leave[727]—the prayers of him that is in wealth and him that is in woe—if the men be both naught,[728] their prayers be both like. For neither hath the one list[729] to pray nor the other neither; and as the one is let[730] with his pain, so is the other with his pleasure, saving[731] that the pain stirreth him sometimes to call upon God in his grief, though the man be right bad, where[732] the pleasure pulleth his mind another way, though the man be meetly[733] good.

And this point I think there are few that can, if they say true, say that they find it otherwise. For in tribulation—which cometh, you wot[734] well, in many sundry kinds—any man that is not a dull beast or a desperate[735] wretch calleth upon God, not hoverly[736] but right heartily, and setteth his heart

---

714 *wise woman:* colloquial for any woman skilled in magic or hidden arts   715 *go to no leechcraft:* seek no medical remedy   716 *sour him up:* make him sad and bitter   717 a medicinal herb   718 *binded fast to:* tied tightly to it   719 *flinging fiend:* raging or ramping devil   720 *riseth upon:* arises from   721 resolved; cleared up   722 burden; impose upon   723 propose to   724 *after as:* according to how   725 *in a manner:* as it were; very nearly   726 sadness   727 *leave off*   728 wicked   729 desire   730 hindered   731 except   732 whereas   733 fairly   734 know   735 hopeless   736 lightly; inattentively

full whole upon his request, so sore he longeth for ease and help of his heaviness.

But when men are wealthy and well at their ease, while our tongue pattereth[737] upon our prayers apace,[738] good God, how many mad ways our mind wandereth the while.

Yet wot I well that in some tribulation, the while such sore sickness there is, or other grievous bodily pain, that hard it were for a man to say a long pair of Matins.[739] And yet some that lie a-dying say full devoutly the Seven Psalms[740] and other prayers with the priest at their own aneling.[741] But those that for the grief of their pain cannot endure to do it, or that be more tender and lack that strong heart and stomach[742] that some others have, God requireth no such long prayers of them; but the lifting up of their heart alone, without any word at all, is more acceptable to him of one in such case[743] than long service so said as folk use[744] to say it in health.

The martyrs in their agony made no long prayers aloud, but one inch of such a prayer so prayed in that pain was worth a whole ell[745] and more, even of their own prayers prayed at some other time.

Great learned men say that Christ, albeit that[746] he was very God, and as God was in eternal equal bliss with his Father, yet as man merited not for us only, but for himself too. For proof whereof they lay,[747] in these words, the authority of Saint Paul: *Christus humiliavit semet ipsum factus oboediens usque ad mortem, mortem autem crucis, propter quod et Deus exaltavit illum, et donavit illi nomen quod est super omne nomen, ut in nomine Iesu omne genu flectatur, caelestium, terrestrium, et infernorum, et omnis lingua confiteatur quia Dominus Iesus Christus in gloria est Dei Patris* ("Christ hath humbled himself, and became obedient unto the death, and that unto the death of the cross, for which thing God hath also exalted him and given him a name which is above all names, that in the name of Jesus every knee be bowed, both of the celestial creatures and the terrestrial, and of the infernal too, and that every tongue shall confess that our Lord Jesus Christ is in the glory of God his Father").[748]

Now, if it so be as these great learned men upon such authority of Holy Scripture say—that our Savior merited as man, and as man deserved reward not for us only, but for himself also—then were there in his deeds, as it seemeth, sundry degrees and difference of deserving, and not his Maundy[749] like merit as his Passion, nor his sleep like merit as his watch[750] and his prayer, no, nor his prayers peradventure[751] all of like merit neither, but though there none was nor none could be in his most blessed person but excellent and uncomparably passing[752] the prayer of any pure creature, yet his own not all alike, but some one far above some other. And then, if it thus be, of all his holy prayers the chief seemeth me those that he made in his great agony and pain of his bitter Passion.

The first, when he thrice fell prostrate in his agony[753]—when the heaviness of his heart with fear of death at hand so painful and so cruel as he well beheld it—made such a fervent commotion in his blessed body that the bloody sweat of his holy flesh dropped down on the ground.[754]

The others were the painful prayers that he made upon the cross, where, for all[755] the torment that he hanged in—of beating, nailing, and stretching out all his limbs, with the wresting of his sinews, and breaking of his tender veins, and the sharp crown of thorns so pricking him into the head that his blessed blood streamed down all his face—in all these hideous pains, in all their cruel despites,[756] yet two very devout and fervent prayers he made: the one for their pardon that so dispiteously[757] put him to this pain, and the other about his own deliverance, commending his own soul unto his holy Father in heaven. These prayers of his—among all that ever he made, made in his most pain—reckon I for the chief. And these prayers of our Savior at his bitter Passion, and of his holy martyrs in the fervor of their torment, shall serve us to see that there is no prayer made at pleasure so strong and effectual as in tribulation.

Now come I to the touching of the reason you make where you tell me that I grant you that both in wealth and in woe some man may be naught and offend God, the one by impatience, the other by fleshly lust; and on the other side, both in tribulation and prosperity too, some man may also do

737 mumbles, mutters 738 with speed 739 a part of the Divine Office said in the morning 740 *Seven Psalms:* known as the Penitential Psalms (Psalms 6, 32, 38, 51, 102, 130, 143) 741 anointing; last rites

742 considered the seat of courage and perseverance 743 condition 744 are accustomed 745 about forty-five inches 746 *albeit that:* although 747 put forward 748 Phil 2:8–11 749 Last

Supper 750 vigil-keeping 751 perhaps 752 surpassing 753 See Mt 26:36–46. 754 See Lk 22:40–44. 755 *for all:* despite 756 insults 757 cruelly

very well and deserve thanks of God by thanksgiving to God, as well of his gift of riches, worship, and wealth as of need, penury, prisonment, sickness, and pain; and that therefore you cannot see for what cause I should give any preeminence in comfort unto tribulation, but rather allow prosperity for the thing more comfortable, and that not a little, but in a manner by double, since therein hath the soul comfort and the body both — the soul by thanks given unto God for his gift, and then the body by being well at ease — where[758] the person pained in tribulation taketh no comfort but in his soul alone.

First, as for your double comfort, Cousin, you may cut off the one: for a man in prosperity, though he be bound to thank God of[759] his gift, wherein he feeleth ease, and may be glad also that he giveth thanks to God, yet for that[760] he taketh his ease here hath he little cause of comfort, except that[761] the sensual feeling of bodily pleasure you list for[762] to call by the name of comfort — nor I say not nay but that sometimes men use[763] so to take it when they say, "this good drink comforteth well my heart," but comfort, Cousin, is properly taken by them that take it right, rather for the consolation of good hope that men take in their heart of some good growing toward them than for a present pleasure with which the body is delighted and tickled for the while. Now, though a man without patience can have no reward for his pain, yet when his pain is patiently taken for God's sake, and his will conformed to God's pleasure therein, God rewardeth the sufferer after the rate[764] of his pain. And this thing appeareth by many a place in Scripture, of which some have I showed you, and yet shall I show you more. But never found I any place in Scripture that I remember in which, though the wealthy man thank God for his gift, our Lord promised any reward in heaven because the man took his ease and pleasure here. And therefore, since I speak but of such comfort as is very[765] comfort indeed, by which a man hath hope of God's favor and remission of his sins (with diminishing of his pain in purgatory, or reward else in heaven), and such comfort cometh of tribulation, and for tribulation well-taken, but not for pleasure, though it be well-taken — therefore of your comfort that you double by prosperity, you may, as I told you, cut very well away the half.

Now, why I give prerogative in comfort unto tribulation far above prosperity, though a man may do well in both, of this thing will I show you causes two or three, for (as I before have at length showed you) out of all question,[766] continual wealth interrupted with no tribulation is a very discomfortable token of everlasting damnation, whereupon it followeth that tribulation is one cause of comfort unto a man's heart, in that it dischargeth him of the discomfort that he might of reason take of overlong-lasting wealth.

Another is that Scripture much commendeth tribulation as occasion of more profit than wealth and prosperity, not to them only that are therein,[767] but to them too that resort[768] unto them. And therefore saith Ecclesiastes, *Melius est ire ad domum luctus quam ad domum convivii. In illa enim finis cunctorum admonetur hominum, et vivens cogitat quid futurum sit* ("Better it is to go to the house of weeping and wailing for some man's death than to the house of a feast: for in that house of heaviness[769] is a man put in remembrance of the end of every man, and while he yet liveth he thinketh what shall come after").[770] And yet he further saith, *Cor sapientium ubi tristitia est, et cor stultorum ubi laetitia* ("The heart of wise men is thereas[771] heaviness is, and the heart of fools is thereas is mirth and gladness").[772] And verily, thereas you shall hear worldly mirth seem to be commended in Scripture, it is either commonly spoken, as in the person of some worldly-disposed people, or understood of[773] rejoicing spiritual, or meant of some small moderate refreshing of the mind against a heavy discomfortable dullness.

Now whereas prosperity was to the children of Israel promised in the Old Law as a special gift of God, that was for their imperfection at that time, to draw them to God with gay[774] things and pleasant, as men, to make children learn, give them cake-bread and butter; for as the Scripture maketh mention, that people were much after the manner of children in lack of wit and in waywardness,[775] and therefore was their master Moses called *pedagogus*[776] — that

---

758 whereas **759** for **760** *for that:* because **761** *except that:* except for **762** *list for:* choose **763** are accustomed **764** *after the rate:* according to the amount

765 truly **766** *out of all question:* beyond all doubt **767** i.e., in suffering **768** turn **769** sorrow **770** Eccl 7:2 **771** in that place where **772** Eccl 7:4 **773** to mean

774 fine, beautiful; merry **775** Jer 3:14 **776** See Gal 3:24–5, although Moses himself is never actually called *pedagogus*.

is, a "teacher of children," or, as they call such one in the grammar schools, an "usher," or a "master of the petits";[777] for as Saint Paul saith, *Nihil ad perfectum duxit lex* ("The Old Law brought nothing to perfection").[778]

And God also threateneth folk with tribulation in this world for sin, not for that[779] worldly tribulation is evil, but for that we should be well ware[780] of the sickness of sin, for fear of that thing to follow, which,[781] though it be indeed a very good wholesome thing if we will well take it, is yet, because it is painful, the thing that we be loath to have.

But this I say yet again and again: that, as for the far better thing in this world toward the getting of the very good that God giveth in the world to come, the Scripture undoubtedly so commendeth tribulation that, in respect and comparison thereof, it discommendeth this worldly wretched wealth and discomfortable comfort utterly. For to what other thing soundeth the words of Ecclesiastes that I rehearsed[782] you now, that it is "better to be in the house of heaviness[783] than to be at a feast"? Whereto[784] soundeth this comparison of his, that "the wise man's heart draweth thither as[785] folk are in sadness, and the heart of a fool is thereas[786] he may find mirth"? Whereto draweth[787] this threat of the wise man, that he that delighteth in wealth shall fall into woe?[788] *Risus*, saith he, *dolore miscebitur, et extrema gaudii luctus occupat* ("Laughter shall be mingled with sorrow, and the end of mirth is taken up with heaviness").[789] And our Savior saith himself, *Vae vobis qui ridetis, quia lugebitis et flebitis* ("Woe be to you that laugh, for you shall weep and wail").[790] But he saith on the other side, *Beati qui lugent, quoniam illi consolabuntur* ("Blessed be they that weep and wail, for they shall be comforted");[791] and he saith to his disciples, *Mundus gaudebit, vos autem dolebitis, sed tristitia vestra vertetur in gaudium* ("The world shall joy, and you shall be sorry, but your sorrow shall be turned into joy");[792] and so is it, you wot well, now, and the mirth of many that then were in joy is now turned all to sorrow. And thus you see by the Scripture plain that in matter of

very comfort, tribulation is as far above prosperity as the day is above the night.

Another preeminence of tribulation over wealth in occasion of merit and reward shall well appear upon certain considerations well marked in them both.

Tribulation meriteth in patience, and in the obedient conforming of the man's will unto God, and in thanksgiving to God for his visitation.[793]

If you reckon me[794] now against these many other good deeds that a wealthy man may do — as[795] by riches give alms, by authority labor in doing many men justice, or if you find further any such other thing like — first I say that the patient person in tribulation hath, in all those virtues of a wealthy man, an occasion of merit too, the which a wealthy man hath not againward[796] in the fore-rehearsed[797] virtues of his; for it is easy for the person that is in tribulation to be well willing to do the selfsame if he could, and then shall his good will, where the power lacketh, go very near to the merit of the deed.

But now is not the wealthy man in a like case with the will of patience and conformity and thanks given to God for tribulation, since it is not so ready[798] for the wealthy man to be content to be in the tribulation that is the occasion of the patient's desert[799] as for the troubled to be content to be in prosperity to do the good deeds that the wealthy man doth.

Besides this, all that the wealthy man doth, though he could not do them without those things that are accounted for wealth and called by that name — as not do great alms without great riches, nor do those many men right by his labor without authority — yet may he do these things being not in wealth indeed, as where he taketh his wealth for no wealth, nor his riches for no riches, nor in heart setteth by neither nother,[800] but secretly liveth in a contrite heart and a life penitential, as many times did the prophet David, being a great king, so that worldly wealth was no wealth unto him.[801] And therefore it is not of necessity worldly wealth to be cause of these good deeds, since he may do them

777 small schoolboys   **778** Heb 7:19   **779** *for that:* because   **780** *well ware:* well aware; quite wary   **781** i.e., this tribulation   **782** quoted to   **783** sorrow, sadness   **784** To what   **785** *thither as:* to the place where   **786** where   **787** *Whereto draweth:* To what point tends   **788** See Prv 11:28.   **789** Prv 14:13   **790** Lk 6:25   **791** Mt 5:4   **792** Jn 16:20   **793** sending (of tribulation)   **794** *reckon me:* consider for me   **795** such as   **796** on the other hand; conversely   **797** previously mentioned   **798** likely, easy   **799** *patient's desert:* patient person's deserving   **800** *setteth by neither nother:* values neither the one nor the other   **801** See Ps 34(35):13–14; 2 Sm 12:13; 24:10.

and doth them best indeed to whom the thing that worldly folk call wealth is yet — for[802] his godly-set mind drawn from the delight thereof — no pleasure in manner[803] nor no wealth at all.

Finally, whensoever the wealthy man doth those good virtuous deeds, if we consider the nature of them right, we shall perceive that in the doing of them, he doth ever for the rate[804] and portion of those deeds diminish the matter of his worldly wealth — as in giving great alms, he departeth with[805] so much of his worldly goods, which are in that part the matter of his wealth. In laboring about the doing of many good deeds, his labor diminisheth his quiet and his rest, and for the rate of so much, it diminisheth his wealth — if pain and wealth be each to other contrary, as I ween[806] ye will agree they be.

Now whosoever then will well consider the thing, he shall, I doubt not, perceive and see therein — in these good deeds that the wealthy man doth — though he doth them by that that[807] his wealth maketh him able, yet in the doing of them he departeth for the portion[808] from the nature of wealth toward the nature of some part of tribulation. And therefore even in those good deeds themselves that prosperity doth in goodness, the prerogative of tribulation above wealth appears. Now, if it hap[809] that some man cannot perceive this point because the wealthy man, for all his alms, abideth rich still, and for all his good labor abideth still in his authority, let him consider that I speak but after[810] the portion. And because the portion of all that he giveth of his goods is very little in respect of that he leaveth, therefore is the reason haply[811] with some folk little perceived; but if[812] it so were that he went forth with giving till he had given out all and left himself nothing, then would a very blind man see it: for as he were from riches come to poverty, so were he from wealth willingly fallen into tribulation. And between labor and rest the reason goeth alike, which who can so consider shall see that for the portion in every good deed done by the wealthy man, the matter is all one. Then, since we have somewhat weighed the virtues of prosperity, let us consider on the other side the aforenamed

things that are the matter of merit and reward in tribulation: that is to wit,[813] patience, conformity, and thanks.

Patience the wealthy man hath not in that that[814] he is wealthy: for if he be pinched[815] in any point wherein he taketh patience, in that part he suffereth some tribulation; and so not by his prosperity, but by his tribulation hath the man that merit.

Like is it if we would say that the wealthy man hath another virtue in the stead[816] of patience: that is to wit, to keep himself from pride, and from such other sins as wealth would bring him to; for the resisting of such motions is, as I before told you, without any doubt a diminishing of fleshly wealth, and is a very true kind — and one of the most profitable kinds — of tribulation, so that all that good merit groweth to the wealthy man not by his wealth, but by the diminishing of his wealth with wholesome tribulation.

The most color of[817] comparison is in the other twain:[818] that is to wit, in the conformity of man's will unto God, and in the thanksgiving unto God; for like as the good man in tribulation sent him by God conformeth his will to God's will in that behalf,[819] and giveth God thanks therefor,[820] so doth the wealthy man, in his wealth which God giveth him, conform his will to God's in that point, since he is well content to take it of[821] his gift, and giveth God again[822] also right hearty thanks therefor.

And thus, as I said, in these two things may you catch the most color[823] to compare the wealthy man's merit with the merit of tribulation. But yet that they be not matches, you may soon see by this: For in tribulation can there none conform his will unto God's and give him thanks therefor but such a man as hath in that point a very special good mind. But he that is very naught,[824] or hath in his heart but very little good, may well be content to take wealth at God's hand and say, "Marry,[825] I thank you, sir, for this, with all mine heart, and will not fail to love you well while you let me fare no worse." *Confitebitur tibi cum benefeceris ei.*[826]

Now if the wealthy man be very good, yet in conformity of his will and thanks given to God for his

---

802 on account of   **803** *in manner:* very nearly; as it were   **804** amount   **805** *departeth with:* parts with   **806** think   **807** *that that:* that which   **808** *for the portion:* with regard to the part   **809** happens   **810** according to   **811** perhaps

812 *but if:* unless   **813** say   **814** *in that that:* insofar as   **815** afflicted   **816** place   **817** *most color of:* best ground for   **818** two   **819** *in that behalf:* with regard to that (tribulation)   **820** for it   **821** as   **822** in return   **823** *catch the most color:*

find the best grounds   **824** wicked; bad   **825** indeed; an exclamation, from "by Mary"   **826** "He will acknowledge you when you benefit him" (Ps 48(49):19).

wealth, his virtue is not like yet to his that doth the same in tribulation. For as the philosophers said in that thing very well of old, virtue standeth in things of hardness and difficulty.[827] And then, as I told you, much less hardness and less difficulty there is by a great deal to be content and to conform our will to God's will—and to give him thanks too—for our ease than for our pain, for our wealth than for our woe. And therefore is the conforming of our will unto God's, and the thanks that we give him for our tribulation, more worthy thanks again,[828] and more reward meriteth in the very fast[829] wealth and felicity of heaven, than our conformity with our thanks given for and in our worldly wealth here.

And this thing saw the devil when he said unto our Lord of Job that it was no marvel though[830] Job had a reverent fear unto God, God[831] had done so much for him and kept him in prosperity; but the devil wist[832] well that it was a hard thing for Job to be so loving and so to give thanks to God in tribulation and adversity. And therefore was he glad to get leave of[833] God to put him in tribulation, and thereby trusted to cause him murmur and grudge[834] against God with impatience.[835] But the devil had there a fall in his own turn. For the patience of Job in the short time of his adversity got him much more favor and thanks of God,[836] and more is he renowned and commended in Scripture[837] for that than for all the goodness of his long prosperous life.

Our Savior saith himself also that if we say well by them or yield them thanks that do us good, we do no great thing therein, and therefore can we with reason look for no great thanks again.

And thus have I showed you, lo, no little preeminence that tribulation hath in merit—and therefore no little preeminence of comfort in hope of heavenly reward—above the virtues, the merit, and cause of good hope and comfort that cometh of wealth and prosperity.

THE TWENTIETH CHAPTER
A summary: comfort of tribulation

ANTONY: And therefore, good Cousin, to finish our talking for this time, lest I should be too long a let[838] unto your other business: If we lay first, for a sure ground, a very fast[839] faith, whereby we believe to be true all that the Scripture saith—understanding truly, as the old holy doctors declare it, and as the Spirit of God instructeth his Catholic Church—then shall we consider tribulation as a gracious gift of God; a gift that he specially gave his special friends; the thing that in Scripture is highly commended and praised; a thing whereof the contrary long-continued is perilous; a thing which, but if[840] God send it, men have need by penance to put upon themselves and seek it; a thing that helpeth to purge our sins past; a thing that preserveth us from sin that else would come; a thing that causeth us set less by[841] the world; a thing that exciteth us to draw more toward God; a thing that much diminisheth our pains in purgatory; a thing that much increaseth our final reward in heaven; the thing by which our Savior entered his own kingdom; the thing with which all his apostles followed him thither; the thing which our Savior exhorteth all men to; the thing without which, he saith, we be not his disciples; the thing without which no man can get to heaven.

Whoso these things thinketh on, and remembereth well, shall in his tribulation neither murmur nor grudge, but first by patience take his pain in worth,[842] and then shall he grow in goodness and think himself well worthy, then shall he consider that God sendeth it for his weal,[843] and thereby shall he be moved to give God thanks therefor.

Therewith shall his grace increase, and God shall give him such comfort by considering that God is in his trouble evermore near unto him—*Quia Deus iuxta est iis qui tribulato sunt corde* ("God is near," saith the prophet, "to them that have their heart in trouble")[844]—that his joy thereof shall diminish much of his pain. And he shall not seek for vain comfort elsewhere, but specially trust in God and seek for help of him, submitting his own will wholly to God's

---

827 See Aristotle's *Nicomachean Ethics* 1105a 9–13; Seneca's *On Providence* 5.9–10. **828** *worthy . . . again:* deserving of thanks in return **829** secure, well assured **830** if **831** because God **832** knew **833** *leave of:* permission from **834** *murmur and grudge:* mutter complaints and grumble **835** See Job 1:8–12. **836** See Job 42:12. **837** See Jas 5:11. **838** hindrance **839** firm, steadfast **840** *but if:* unless **841** *set . . . by:* to value less **842** *in worth:* as worthwhile **843** well-being **844** Ps 33(34):19

pleasure, and pray to God in his heart, and pray his friends to pray for him, and specially the priests, as Saint James biddeth.[845] And begin first with confession, and make us clean to God and ready to depart and be glad to go to God, putting purgatory in his pleasure. If we this do, this dare I boldly say: we shall never live here the less of half an hour but shall with this comfort find our hearts lightened, and thereby the grief of our tribulation lessened, and the more likelihood to recover and to live the longer. Now, if God will we shall hence, then doth he much more for us, for he that this way taketh cannot go but well; for of him that is loath to leave this wretched world, mine heart is much in fear lest he die not well: hard it is for him to be welcome that cometh against his will, that saith unto God when he cometh to fetch him, "Welcome, my Maker, maugre my teeth,"[846] but he that so loveth him that he longeth to go to him, mine heart cannot give me but he shall be welcome, all were it[847] so that he should come ere[848] he were well purged, for "charity covereth a multitude of sins,"[849] and "he that trusteth in God cannot be confounded."[850] And Christ saith, "He that cometh to me, I will not cast him out."[851] And therefore let us never make our reckoning of long life; keep it while we may because God hath so commanded, but if God give the occasion that with his goodness we may go, let us be glad thereof and long to go to him. And then shall hope of heaven comfort our heaviness,[852] and out of our transitory tribulation shall we go to everlasting glory—to which, my good Cousin, I pray God bring us both.

VINCENT: Mine own good Uncle, I pray God reward you. And at this time will I no longer trouble you. I trow[853] I have this day done you much tribulation, with mine importune[854] objections of very little substance. And you have even showed me an example of sufferance[855] in bearing my folly so long and so patiently. And yet shall I be so bold upon you further as to seek some time to talk forth of the remnant: the most profitable point of tribulation, which you said you reserved to treat of last of all.

ANTONY: Let that be hardily[856] very shortly, Cousin, while this is fresh in mind.

VINCENT: I trust, good Uncle, so to put this in remembrance that it shall never be forgotten with me; our Lord send you such comfort as he knoweth to be best.

ANTONY: That is well said, good Cousin, and I pray the same good for you, and for all our other friends that have need of comfort—for whom, I think, more than for yourself, you needed of some counsel.

VINCENT: I shall, with this good counsel that I have heard of you, do[857] them some comfort, I trust in God—to whose keeping I commit you.

ANTONY: And I you also. Farewell, mine own good Cousin.

---

845 See Jas 5:14.　**846** *maugre my teeth: in spite of my resistance*　**847** *all were it: even if it were*　**848** before　**849** 1 Pt 4:8　**850** Rom 10:11　**851** Jn 6:37　**852** grief, sadness　**853** believe　**854** importunate; inopportune　**855** patient endurance　**856** certainly　**857** give

THE SECOND BOOK

PREFACE

VINCENT: It is to me, good Uncle, no little comfort that, as I came in here, I heard of[1] your folk that you have had since my last being here (God be thanked) meetly[2] good rest, and your stomach[3] somewhat more come to you. For verily, albeit[4] I had heard before that in respect of the great grief that for a month's space had holden you, you were a little before my last coming to you somewhat eased and relieved—for else would I not, for no good,[5] have put you to the pain to talk so much as you then did—yet after my departing from you, remembering how long we tarried together, and that we were all that while in talking, and all the labor yours in talking so long together without interpausing between,[6] and that of matter studious and displeasant, all of disease and sickness and other pain and tribulation, I was, in good faith, very sorry, and not a little wroth[7] with myself for mine own oversight, that I had so little considered your pain; and very feared I was, till I heard other word,[8] lest you should have waxed[9] weaker and more sick thereafter. But now I thank our Lord, that hath sent the contrary; for else a little casting back[10] were, in this great age of yours, no little danger and peril.

ANTONY: Nay, nay, good Cousin, to talk much, except some other pain let[11] me, is to me little grief. A fond[12] old man is often so full of words as a woman. It is, you wot[13] well, as some poets paint[14] us, all the lust[15] of an old fool's life to sit well and warm with a cup and a roasted crab and drivel[16] and drink and talk.

But in earnest,[17] Cousin, our talking was to me great comfort, and nothing displeasant at all, for though we communed[18] of sorrow and heaviness, yet was the thing that we chiefly thought upon not the tribulation itself, but the comfort that may grow thereon. And therefore am I now very glad that you be come to finish up the remnant.

VINCENT: Of truth, my good Uncle, it was comfortable to me, and hath been since to some others of your friends, to whom, as my poor wit and remembrance would serve me, I did—and not needless—report and rehearse[19] your most comfortable counsel; and now come I for the remnant, and am very joyful that I find you so well refreshed and so ready thereto. But yet this one thing, good Uncle, I beseech you heartily: that if I, for delight to hear you speak in the matter, forget myself and you both, and put you to too much pain, remember you your own ease, and when you list to leave,[20] command me to go my way and seek some other time.

ANTONY: Forsooth,[21] Cousin, many words, if a man were very weak, spoken (as you said right now) without interpausing, would peradventure[22] at length somewhat weary him. And therefore wished I the last time, after you were gone—when I felt myself, to say the truth, even a little weary—that I had not so told you still a long tale alone, but that we had more often interchanged words, and parted the talk between us with ofter enterparling[23] upon your part, in such manner as learned men use between the persons whom they devise disputing in their feigned dialogues. But yet in that point I soon excused you, and laid the lack[24] even where I found it, and that was even upon mine own neck. For I remembered that between you and me it fared as it did once between a nun and her brother.

Very virtuous was this lady, and of a very virtuous place—a close religion[25]—and therein had been long, in all which time she had never seen her brother, which[26] was in like wise very virtuous too, and had been far off at a university, and had there taken the degree of Doctor in Divinity. When he was come home, he went to see his sister, as he that[27] highly rejoiced in her virtue. So came she to the grate that they call, I trow,[28] the locutory.[29] And after their holy watchword spoken on both the sides, after the manner[30] used in that place, the one took the other

---

1 from   **2** fairly   **3** appetite   **4** *verily, albeit:* truly, although   **5** *for no good:* for anything   **6** *interpausing between:* pausing or resting at intervals   **7** angry **8** *other word:* word to the contrary **9** become, grown   **10** *casting back:*

relapse   **11** hinder   **12** foolish   **13** know **14** portray   **15** desire, wish; pleasure **16** *crab and drivel:* crab-apple and drool **17** seriousness   **18** talked   **19** tell; relate **20** *list . . . leave:* wish to leave off   **21** In truth   **22** perhaps   **23** taking part in the

conversation   **24** *laid the lack:* put the blame   **25** *close religion:* cloistered convent of a religious order   **26** who   **27** *as he that:* since he was someone who   **28** think **29** a grille allowing speech between the cloister and the public room   **30** custom

by the tip of the finger, for hand would there none be wrungen[31] through the grate; and forthwith[32] began my lady to give her brother a sermon of the wretchedness of this world, and the frailty of the flesh, and the subtle sleight[33] of the wicked fiend,[34] and gave him surely good counsel (saving[35] somewhat too long) how he should be well wary in his living, and master well his body for saving of his soul. And yet, ere[36] her own tale came all at an end, she began to find a little fault with him, and said, "In good faith, brother, I do somewhat marvel that you, that have been at learning so long, and are a doctor, and so learned in the law of God, do not now at our meeting (while we meet so seldom) to me, that am your sister and a simple unlearned soul, give of your charity some fruitful exhortation, and as I doubt not but you can say some good thing yourself." "By my troth,[37] good sister," quoth her brother, "I cannot for you, for your tongue hath never ceased, but said enough for us both." And so, Cousin, I remembered that when I was once fallen in,[38] I left you little space to say aught[39] between. But now will I therefore take another way with you, for I shall of our talking drive you to the one half.

Vincent: Now forsooth, Uncle, this was a merry tale. But now, if you make me take the one half, then shall you be contented far otherwise[40] than there was of late a kinswoman of your own — but which will I not tell you; guess her and[41] you can. Her husband had much pleasure in the manner and behavior of another honest man, and kept him therefore much company, by the reason whereof he was at his mealtime the more oft from home. So happed it on a time that his wife and he together dined or supped with that neighbor of theirs. And then she made a merry quarrel to him for making her husband so good cheer[42] out at door that she could not have him at home. "Forsooth,[43] mistress," quoth he (as he was a dry merry man), "in my company nothing keepeth him but one. Serve you him with the same, and he will never be from you." "What gay[44] thing may that be?" quoth our cousin[45] then. "Forsooth, mistress," quoth he, "your husband loveth well to

talk, and when he sitteth with me, I let him have all the words." "All the words?" quoth she. "Marry,[46] that am I content he shall have: all the words, with good will, as he hath ever had; but I speak them all myself, and give them all to him, and for aught that I care for them, so shall he have them still; but otherwise, to say that he shall have them all — you shall keep him still[47] rather than he get the half."

Antony: Forsooth, Cousin, I can soon guess which of our kin[48] she was. I would we had none therein, for all her merry words, that less would let their husbands for to talk.

Vincent: Forsooth, she is not so merry but she is as good.[49] But where you find fault, Uncle, that I speak not enough, I was in good faith ashamed that I spoke so much, and moved[50] you such questions, as I found upon your answer, might better have been spared, they were so little worth. But now, since I see you be so well-content that I shall not forbear[51] boldly to show my folly, I will be no more so shamefast,[52] but ask you what me list.[53]

THE FIRST CHAPTER
Whether a man may not in tribulation use some worldly recreation for his comfort

Vincent: And first, good Uncle, ere we proceed further, I will be bold to move[54] you one thing more of that we talked when I was here before. For when I revolved[55] in my mind again the things that were here concluded by you, methought you would in no wise[56] that in any tribulation men should seek for comfort either in worldly things or fleshly — which mind, Uncle, of yours seemeth somewhat hard. For a merry tale with a friend refresheth a man much, and without any harm lighteneth his mind and amendeth[57] his courage and his stomach,[58] so that it seemeth but well done to take such recreation. And Solomon saith, I trow,[59] that men should in heaviness[60] give the sorry[61] man wine to make him forget his sorrow.[62] And Saint Thomas saith that proper

31 squeezed; twisted   **32** immediately
33 trickery   **34** devil   **35** except
36 before   **37** faithfulness, truth
38 *when . . . fallen in:* once I'd gotten started
39 anything   **40** *far otherwise:* in a much
different way   **41** if   **42** *making . . .
cheer:* giving her husband such good

entertainment   **43** In truth   **44** fine;
enjoyable   **45** kinswoman   **46** exclamation (from "by Mary"), indeed   **47** *keep
him still:* still eat with him yourself
48 *our kin:* probably Lady Alice, More's
wife   **49** *she is . . . good:* she is every bit
as good as she is funny   **50** proposed to

51 hesitate   **52** embarrassed   **53** *me list:*
I wish   **54** propose to   **55** turned over,
considered   **56** *would in no wise:* would
in no way have it   **57** improves   **58** spirit
59 think, believe   **60** grief, sadness
61 sorrowing   **62** See Prv 31:6–7.

pleasant talking, which is called εὐτραπελία,[63] is a good virtue, serving to refresh the mind and make it quick and lusty[64] to labor and study again, where continual fatigation[65] would make it dull and deadly.[66]

ANTONY: Cousin, I forgot not that point, but I longed not much to touch[67] it. For neither might I well utterly forbear[68] it where the case might hap[69] to fall that it should not hurt, and on the other side,[70] if the case so should fall, methought yet it should little need to give any man counsel to it: folk are prone enough to such fancies of their own mind; you may see this by ourselves, which, coming now together to talk of as earnest sad[71] matter as men can devise, were fallen yet even[72] at the first into wanton[73] idle tales. And of truth, Cousin, as you know very well, myself am of nature even half a giglet[74] and more. I would I could as easily mend my fault as I well know it. But scant[75] can I refrain it, as old a fool as I am; howbeit,[76] so partial will I not be to my fault as to praise it. But for that you require[77] my mind in the matter, whether men in tribulation may not lawfully[78] seek recreation, and comfort themselves with some honest mirth: first agreed that our chief comfort must be of God—and that with him we must begin, and with him continue, and with him end also—a man to take now and then some honest worldly mirth, I dare not be so sore[79] as utterly to forbid it, since good men and well-learned have in some cases allowed it, specially for the diversity of diverse men's minds; for else,[80] if we were all such as I would God we were, and such as natural wisdom would we should[81] be (and is not all clean[82] excusable that we be not indeed), I would then put no doubt but that unto[83] any man the most comfortable talking that could be were to hear of heaven, whereas now (God help us) our wretchedness is such that in talking a while thereof, men wax[84] almost weary, and as though to hear of heaven were a heavy burden, they must refresh themselves after with a foolish tale.

Our affection toward heavenly joys waxeth[85]

wonderfully cold; if dread of hell were as far gone, very few would fear God, but that yet a little sticketh in our stomachs: mark me, Cousin, at the sermon, and commonly toward the end, somewhat the preacher speaketh of hell and of heaven; now, while he preacheth of the pains of hell, still they stand[86] and yet give him the hearing; but as soon as he cometh to the joys of heaven, they be busking them[87] backward and flockmeal[88] fall away. It is in the soul somewhat as it is in the body. Some are there, of nature or of evil custom, come to that point that a worse thing sometimes more steadeth them[89] than a better. Some man if he be sick can away with[90] no wholesome meat,[91] nor no medicine can go down with him but if[92] it be tempered[93] with some such thing for his fancy[94] as maketh the meat or the medicine less wholesome than it should be. And yet while[95] it will be no better, we must let him have it so.

Cassian,[96] that very good virtuous man, rehearseth in a certain collation[97] of his that a certain holy father, in making of a sermon, spoke of heaven and of heavenly things so celestially that much of his audience with the sweet sound thereof began to forget all the world and fall asleep; which when the father beheld, he dissembled[98] their sleeping and suddenly said unto them, "I shall tell you a merry tale," at which word they lift up their heads and hearkened unto that, and after the sleep therewith broken, heard him tell on of heaven again. In what wise that good father rebuked then their untoward[99] minds—so dull unto the thing that all our life we labor for, and so quick and lusty toward other trifles—I neither bear in mind nor shall here need to rehearse. But this much of that matter sufficeth for our purpose: that whereas you demand me whether in tribulation men may not sometimes refresh themselves with worldly mirth and recreation, I can no more say but he that cannot long endure to hold up his head and hear talking of heaven except he be now and then between (as though heaven were heaviness) refreshed with a foolish merry tale,

63 εὐτραπελία *(eutrapelia):* lively, witty conversation **64** desirous; vigorous **65** activity causing weariness **66** lifeless. *Summa theologica* 2-2, q. 168, art. 2 (referencing Aristotle's *Nicomachean Ethics* 2.7 and 4.8) **67** discuss **68** refrain from **69** happen **70** hand **71** serious **72** right **73** cheerful, frivolous, unrestrained **74** giggling child

75 barely, hardly **76** however, nevertheless **77** *for that you require:* because you ask **78** legitimately **79** severe, stern **80** otherwise **81** *would we should:* would have us **82** entirely **83** *but that unto:* that for **84** become **85** grows **86** stay **87** *busking them:* hustling themselves **88** in droves **89** *more steadeth them:* does them more good **90** *away with:*

tolerate **91** food **92** *but if:* unless **93** mixed, diluted **94** liking **95** as long as **96** St. John Cassian (*ca.* 360–435), a monk and theologian. What follows, however, is not from his *Collations.* For a somewhat similar story, see his *Institutes* 5.31. **97** discourse **98** pretended not to notice **99** perverse

there is none other remedy but you must let him have it; better would I wish it, but I cannot help it.

Howbeit, let us, by mine advice, at the leastwise make these kinds of recreation as short and seldom as we can; let them serve us but for sauce, and make them not our meat; and let us pray unto God, and all our good friends for us, that we may feel such a savor in[100] the delight of heaven that in respect of[101] the talking of the joys thereof, all worldly recreation be but a grief to think on. And be sure, Cousin, that if we might once purchase the grace to come to that point, we never of worldly recreation had so much comfort in a year as we should find in bethinking us of heaven in less than half an hour.

VINCENT: In faith, Uncle, I can well agree to this, and I pray God bring us once[102] to take such a savor in it. And surely, as you began the other day, by faith must we come to it, and to faith by prayer. But now I pray you, good Uncle, vouchsafe[103] to proceed in our principal matter.

THE SECOND CHAPTER
Of the short uncertain life in extreme age or sickness

ANTONY: Cousin, I have bethought me somewhat of this matter since we were last together, and I find it (if we should go some way to work)[104] a thing that would require many more days to treat of than we should haply[105] find meet[106] thereto in so few as myself ween[107] that I have now to live, while[108] every time is not like[109] with me, and among many painful[110] in which I look every day to depart; my mending days[111] come very seldom and are very shortly gone. For surely, Cousin, I cannot liken myself more meetly[112] now than to the snuff[113] of a candle that burneth within the candlestick nose:[114] for as that snuff burneth down so low that who[115] that looketh on it would ween it were quite out, and yet suddenly lifteth a leam[116] half an inch above the nose, and giveth a pretty short light again, and thus playeth diverse times till at last, ere it be looked for, out it goeth altogether, so have I, Cousin, diverse such days together, as every day of them I look

even for to die. And yet have I then after that some such few days again as you see me now have yourself, in which a man would ween that I might yet well continue. But I know my lingering not likely to last long, but out will my soul suddenly someday within a while. And therefore will I with God's help, seem I never so well amended,[117] nevertheless reckon every day for my last, for though that[118] to the repressing of the bold courage of blind youth there is a very true proverb that "as soon cometh a young sheep's skin to the market as an old," yet this difference there is at the least between them: that as the young man may hap sometimes to die soon, so the old man can never live long. And therefore, Cousin, in our matter here, leaving out many things that I would else[119] treat of, I shall for this time speak but of very few, howbeit[120] hereafter, if God send me more such days, then will we, when you list,[121] further talk of more.

THE THIRD CHAPTER
He divideth tribulation into three kinds;
of which three, the last he shortly passeth over

ANTONY: All manner of tribulation, Cousin, that any man can have, as far as for this time cometh to my mind, falleth under some one at the least of these three kinds: either is it such as himself willingly taketh, or secondly such as himself willingly suffereth, or finally such as he cannot put from him.

This third kind I purpose[122] not much more to speak of now, for thereof shall, as for this time, suffice these things that we have treated between us this other day; what kind of tribulation this is, I am sure yourself perceive. For sickness, imprisonment, loss of goods, loss of friends, or such bodily harm as a man hath already caught and can in no wise avoid — these things and such-like are the third kind of tribulation that I speak of, which a man neither willingly taketh in the beginning, nor can, though he would, put willingly away.

Now think I that as to the man that lacketh wit[123] and faith no comfort can serve, whatsoever counsel

---

100 *feel… in:* have such a taste for
101 *respect of:* comparison with   **102** someday   **103** be willing, agree   **104** *go… work:* go into it in any depth   **105** perhaps
106 equal, suitable   **107** *myself ween:* I

myself think   **108** when, since   **109** alike
110 painful times   **111** *my mending days:* days when I get better   **112** fittingly
113 wick   **114** socket   **115** whoever
116 gleam; flame   **117** improved,

recovered   **118** *though that:* even though
119 otherwise   **120** although   **121** wish
122 intend   **123** intelligence

be given, so to them that have both, I have as to this kind said in manner enough already.

And considering that suffer it needs he must while he can by no manner of means put it from him, the very necessity is half counsel enough to take it in good worth[124] and bear it patiently, and rather of his patience to take both ease and thanks than by fretting and by fuming to increase his present pain, and by murmur and grudge[125] to fall into further danger after, by displeasing of God with his froward[126] behavior. And yet, albeit that[127] I think that that[128] is said sufficeth, yet here and there I shall in the second kind show some such comforts as shall well serve unto this last kind too.

THE FOURTH CHAPTER

ANTONY: The first kind also will I shortly pass:[129] for the tribulation that a man taketh himself willingly, which no man putteth upon him against his own will, is, you wot[130] well, as I somewhat touched the last day, such affliction of the flesh or expense of his goods as a man taketh himself, or willingly bestoweth in punishment of his own sin and for devotion to God.

Now in this tribulation needeth the man none to comfort him; for while no man troubleth him but himself (which feeleth how far-forth he may conveniently bear,[131] and of reason and good discretion shall not pass[132] that—wherein if any doubt arise, counsel needeth,[133] and not comfort), the courage that for God's sake and his soul's health kindleth his heart and inflameth it thereto shall, by the same grace that put it in his mind, give him such comfort and such joy therein that the pleasure of his soul shall pass the pain of his body—yea, and while he hath in heart also some great heaviness[134] for his sin, yet when he considereth the joy that shall come of it, his soul shall not fail to feel then that strange case which my body felt once in a great fever.

VINCENT: What strange case was that, Uncle?

ANTONY: Forsooth,[135] Cousin, even in this same bed—it is now more than fifteen years ago—I lay in a tertian[136] and had passed,[137] I trow,[138] three or four fits.[139] But after[140] fell there on me one fit out of course so strange and so marvelous that I would in good faith have thought it impossible; for I suddenly felt myself verily[141] both hot and cold throughout all my body, not in some part the one and in some part the other (for that had been, you wot well, no very strange thing, to feel the head hot while the hands were cold), but the selfsame parts, I say, so God save my soul, I sensibly felt, and right painfully too, all in one instant both hot and cold at once.

VINCENT: By my faith, Uncle, this was a wonderful thing, and such as I never heard happen[142] any man else in my days. And few men are there of whose mouths I could have believed it.

ANTONY: Courtesy, Cousin, peradventure letteth[143] you to say that you believe it not yet of my mouth neither. And surely for fear of that, you should not have heard it of me neither, had there not happed me another thing soon after.

VINCENT: I pray you, what was that, Uncle?

ANTONY: Forsooth, Cousin, this: I asked a physician or twain that then looked unto me how this should be possible; and they twain told me both that it could not be so, but that I was fallen in some slumber and dreamed that I felt it so.

VINCENT: This hap hold I little cause[144] you to tell the tale the more boldly.

ANTONY: No, Cousin, that is true, lo; but then happed there another: that a young girl[145] here in this town—whom a kinsman of hers had begun to teach physic[146]—told me that there was such a kind of fever indeed.

---

124 *in good worth:* as valuable   125 *murmur and grudge:* muttering complaints and grumbling   126 rebellious, unruly   127 *albeit that:* although   128 *that that:* that which   129 go over   130 know   131 *which . . . bear:* and he himself

senses how much he can appropriately endure   132 go beyond   133 is needed   134 sorrow, sadness   135 In truth   136 *a tertian:* an intermittent fever   137 gone through   138 think, believe   139 bouts   140 afterwards   141 truly   142 happen to

143 *peradventure letteth:* perhaps prevents   144 *This hap . . . cause:* This occurrence I consider little reason for   145 Harpsfield says this is Margaret Giggs, More's adopted daughter (90–91).   146 medical science

VINCENT: By our Lady, Uncle, save for the credence of you,[147] the tale would I not tell again upon that hap of[148] the maid. For though I know her now for such as I durst[149] well believe her, it might hap her very well at that time to lie, because she would ye should[150] take her for cunning.[151]

ANTONY: Yea, but yet happed there another hap thereon, Cousin: that a work of Galen,[152] *De differentiis febrium*, is ready to be sold in the booksellers' shops, in which work she showed me then the chapter where Galen saith the same.[153]

VINCENT: Marry,[154] Uncle, as you say, that hap happed well, and that maid had, as hap was, in that one point more cunning than had both your physicians besides — and hath, I ween,[155] at this day in many points more.

ANTONY: In faith, so ween I too — and that is well-wared[156] on her. For she is very wise and well-learned, and very virtuous too. But see now, what age is, lo! I have been so long in my tale that I have almost forgotten for what purpose I told it. Oh, now I remember, lo: likewise, I say, as myself felt my body then both hot and cold at once, so he that is contrite and heavy[157] for his sin shall have cause to be, and shall be indeed, both sad and glad, and both twain[158] at once, and shall do as I remember holy Saint Jerome biddeth: *Et doleas et de dolore gaudeas* ("Both be thou sorry,"[159] saith he, "and be thou also of thy sorrow joyful");[160] and thus, as I began to say, of comfort to be given unto him that is in this tribulation (that is to wit,[161] in fruitful heaviness and penance for his sin) shall we none need to give, other than only to remember and consider well the goodness of God's excellent mercy, that infinitely passeth the malice of all men's sins, by which he is ready to receive every man, and did spread his arms abroad upon the cross lovingly to embrace all them that will come, and even there accepted the thief at his last end, that turned not to God till he might steal no longer,[162] and yet maketh more feast in heaven at one that from sin turneth than of fourscore and nineteen good men that sinned not at all.[163] And therefore of that first kind will I make no longer tale.

THE FIFTH CHAPTER
*An objection concerning them that turn not
to God till they come at the last cast*[164]

VINCENT: Forsooth,[165] Uncle, this is unto that kind comfort very great — and so great also that it may make many a man bold to abide in his sin even unto his end, trusting to be then saved as that thief was.

ANTONY: Very sooth you say, Cousin, that some wretches are there such that[166] in such wise abuse the great goodness of God, that the better that he is, the worse again[167] be they. But, Cousin, though there be more joy made of his turning that[168] from the point of perdition cometh to salvation — for pity that God had, and his saints all, of the peril of perishing that the man stood in — yet is he not set in like state in heaven as he should have been if he had lived better before, except it so fall[169] that he live so well after, and do so much good, that he therein outrun in the shorter time those good folk that yet did not so much in much longer.

As it proved in the blessed apostle Saint Paul, which[170] of a persecutor became an apostle, and last of all came in into that office, and yet in the labor of sowing the seed of Christ's faith outran all the remnant, and so far-forth[171] that he letted not[172] to say of himself, *Plus omnibus laboravi* ("I have labored more than all the remnant have").[173]

But yet, my Cousin, though God, I doubt not, be so merciful unto them that in any time of their life turn and ask his mercy and trust therein, though it be at the last end of a man's life, and hireth him as well for heaven that cometh to work in his vineyard

147 *save for the credence of you:* except for your credibility   **148** *hap of:* chance occurrence with   **149** dare   **150** *would ye should:* wanted you to   **151** *for cunning:* as knowledgeable   **152** a Greek physician and philosopher (AD 129–216)   **153** See *On the Different Kinds of Fever* 2.6.   **154** Indeed   **155** think   **156** *that...*

wared: that [compliment] is well-bestowed   **157** sorrowful   **158** together   **159** sorrowful   **160** In *Summa theologica* 3, q. 84, art. 9, this quotation is ascribed to St. Augustine. It is a paraphrase from *De vera et falsa poenitentia* (1.13.28), a work whose actual authorship is unknown.   **161** say   **162** See Lk 23:39–43.   **163** See Lk 15:3–7.

164 *at the last cast:* to the last chance, i.e., to death's door   **165** In truth   **166** who   **167** in return   **168** who   **169** *except it so fall:* unless it so happen   **170** who   **171** *so far-forth:* to such an extent   **172** *letted not:* did not hesitate   **173** 1 Cor 15:10

toward night, at such time as workmen leave work and go home, being then in will to work if the time would serve, as he hireth him that cometh in the morning,[174] yet may there no man upon the trust of this parable be bold all his life to lie still in sin. For let him remember that into God's vineyard there goeth no man but he that is called thither. Now he that in hope to be called toward night will sleep out the morning and drink out the day is full likely to pass at night unspoken to, and then shall he with shrewd[175] rest go supperless to bed.

They tell of one that was wont[176] always to say that all the while he lived he would do what he list;[177] for three words when he died should make all safe enough. But then so happed it that long ere he were old, his horse once stumbled upon a broken bridge; and as he labored to recover him, when he saw it would not be, but down into the flood head-long needs he should, in a sudden flight[178] he cried out in the falling, "Have all to the devil!" And there was he drowned—with his three words ere he died, whereon his hope hung all his wretched life. And therefore let no man sin in hope of grace; grace cometh but at God's will, and that mind may be the let[179] that grace of fruitful repenting shall never after be offered him, but that he shall either graceless go linger on careless, or with a care fruitless fall into despair.

THE SIXTH CHAPTER
An objection of them that say the tribulation of penance needeth not, but is a superstitious folly

VINCENT: Forsooth, Uncle, in this point methinketh you say very well. But then are there some again that say on the other side that heaviness[180] for our sins we shall need none at all, but only change our intent and purpose to do better, and for all that that[181] is past take no thought at all.

And as for fasting and other affliction of the body, they say we should not do it but only to tame the flesh when we feel it wax wanton[182] and begin to rebel; for fasting, they say, serveth to keep the body

in temperance. But for to fast for penance, or to do any other good work, alms-deed or other, toward satisfaction of our own sin, this thing they call plain injury to the Passion of Christ, by which only are our sins forgiven freely, without any recompense[183] of our own. And they that would do penance for their own sins look to be their own Christs and pay their own ransoms, and save their souls themselves. And with these reasons, in Saxony many cast fasting off, and all other bodily affliction, save[184] only where need requireth to bring the body to temperance; for other good, they say, can it none do to ourselves, and then to our neighbor can it do none at all. And therefore they condemn it for superstitious folly.

Now heaviness of heart and weeping for our sins, this they reckon shame almost and womanish peevishness[185]—howbeit,[186] thanked be God, their women wax[187] there now so mannish that they be not so peevish nor so poor of spirit, but[188] that they can sin on as men do, and be neither afeard nor ashamed, nor weep for their sins at all.

And surely, mine Uncle, I have marveled the less ever since I heard the manner of their preachers there; for, as you remember, when I was in Saxony these matters were, in manner,[189] but in a mammering;[190] nor Luther was not then wedded yet, nor religious men[191] out of their habit,[192] but suffered[193] were those that would be of the sect[194] freely to preach what they would unto the people. And forsooth, I heard a religious man there myself, one that had been reputed and taken for very good, and which, as far as the folk perceived, was of his own living somewhat austere and sharp.[195] But his preaching was wonderful; methink I hear him yet: his voice was so loud and shrill, his learning less than mean.[196] But whereas his matter was much part against fasting and all affliction for any penance, which he called men's inventions, he cried ever out upon them to keep well the laws of Christ, let go their peevish[197] penance and purpose them[198] to amend, and seek nothing to salvation but the death of Christ: "For he is our justice, and he is our Savior, and our whole satisfaction for all our deadly sins; he did full penance for us all upon his painful cross;

174 See Mt 20:1–16.   175 poor; not good   176 accustomed   177 wished, pleased, desired   178 state of agitation   179 hindrance, obstruction   180 sorrow   181 *that that:* that which   182 *wax wanton:* become unruly   183 reparation; satisfaction; atonement   184 except   185 foolishness, silliness   186 however, although   187 grow   188 except   189 *in manner:* so to speak   190 *but...mammering:* only in a state of doubt   191 *religious men:* religious-order priests   192 religious uniform   193 allowed   194 *those... sect:* those that later would be Lutherans   195 strict   196 average   197 foolish, silly   198 *purpose them:* make up their minds; resolve

he washed us there all clean with the water of his sweet side, and brought us out of the devil's danger with his dear precious blood! Leave therefore—leave, I beseech you—these inventions of men, your foolish Lenten fasts and your peevish penance! Diminish never Christ's thanks, nor look to save yourselves! It is Christ's death, I tell you, that must save us all! Christ's death, I tell you yet again, and not our own deeds! Leave your own fasting therefore and lean to[199] Christ alone, good Christian people, for Christ's dear bitter Passion!"

Now so loud and so shrill he cried "Christ" in their ears, and so thick he came forth with "Christ's bitter Passion," and that so bitterly[200] spoken, with the sweat dropping down his cheeks, that I marveled not though[201] I saw the poor women weep. For he made mine hair stand up upon mine head. And with such preaching were the people so brought in[202] that some fell to break the fasts on the fasting days, not of frailty or of malice first,[203] but almost of devotion, lest they should take from Christ the thanks of[204] his bitter Passion. But when they were a while nuzzled[205] in that point first, they could endure and abide after many things more, with which had he begun, they would have pulled him down.[206]

ANTONY: Cousin, God amend that man, whatsoever he be, and God keep all good folk from such manner of preachers. Such one preacher much more abuseth the name of Christ and of his bitter Passion than five hundred hazarders[207] that in their idle business swear and forswear[208] themselves by his holy bitter Passion at the dice.

They carry the minds of the people from the perceiving of their craft[209] by the continual naming of the name of Christ, and crying his Passion so shrilly into their ears.

They forget that the Church hath ever taught them that all our penance, without Christ's Passion, were not worth a pea. And they make the people ween that we[210] would be[211] saved by our own deeds without Christ's death, where[212] we confess that his only Passion[213] meriteth incomparably more for us than all our own deeds do. But his pleasure is that we shall also take pain our own selves with him. And therefore he biddeth all that will be his disciples take their crosses on their back as he did, and with their crosses follow him.[214]

And where they say that fasting serveth but for temperance, to tame the flesh and keep it from wantonness,[215] I would in good faith have went[216] that Moses had not been so wild that for taming of his flesh he should have needed to fast whole[217] forty days together.[218] No, nor Elijah neither,[219] nor yet our Savior himself, which began—and the apostles followed, and all Christendom have kept—the Lenten forty-days' fast that these folk now call so foolish.[220] King Ahab was not disposed to be wanton in his flesh when he fasted and went clothed in sackcloth and all besprent[221] with ashes.[222]

Nor no more was in Nineveh the king and all the city; but they wailed and did painful penance for their sin, to procure[223] God to pity them and withdraw his indignation.[224] Anna, that in her widowhood abode so many years with fasting and praying in the Temple till the birth of Christ, was not, I ween, in her old age so sore disposed to the wantonness of her flesh that she fasted all therefor.[225] Nor Saint Paul, that fasted so much, fasted not all therefor neither.[226] The Scripture is full of places that prove the fasting not to be the invention of man, but the institution of God, and that it hath many more profits than one.

And that the fasting of one man may do good to another, our Savior showeth himself, where he saith that some kinds of devils cannot be by one man cast out of another *nisi in oratione et ieiunio* ("without prayer and fasting").[227] And therefore I marvel that they take this way against fasting and other bodily penance.

And yet much more I marvel that they mislike the sorrow and heaviness and displeasure of mind that a man should take in forthinking[228] of his sin. The prophet saith, *Scindite corda vestra et non vestimenta* ("Tear your hearts," saith he, "and not your clothes").[229] And the prophet David saith, *Cor*

---

199 *lean to:* depend on   **200** *so bitterly:* with such intense emotion   **201** that   **202** *brought in:* taken in; deceived   **203** at first   **204** *thanks of:* gratitude for   **205** accustomed   **206** *pulled him down:* i.e., from the pulpit   **207** gamblers   **208** perjure   **209** fraud   **210** i.e., we who

do penance   **211** *would be:* want to be   **212** when   **213** *his only Passion:* his Passion alone   **214** See Mt 16:24; Lk 14:27.   **215** unruliness; lustfulness   **216** thought   **217** i.e., a whole   **218** See Ex 34:28.   **219** See 1 Kgs 19:1–8.   **220** See Lk 4:1–2; Mt 4:2.   **221** besprinkled   **222** See 1 Kgs

21:17–29.   **223** prevail upon; get   **224** See Jon 3:3–10.   **225** See Lk 2:36–38.   **226** See 2 Cor 11:27; Acts 9:9; 27:21–36.   **227** Mt 17:21   **228** regretting, repenting   **229** Jl 2:13

contritum et humiliatum Deus non despicies ("A contrite heart and a humbled"—that is to say, a heart broken, torn, and with tribulation of heaviness for his sin laid alow underfoot—"shall thou not, good Lord, despise").²³⁰ He saith also, of his own contrition, *Laboravi in gemitu meo, lavabo per singulas noctes lectum meum, lacrimis meis stratum meum rigabo* ("I have labored²³¹ in my wailing; I shall every night wash my bed with my tears; my couch will I water").²³²

But what should I need in this matter lay forth one place or twain?²³³ The Scripture is full of those places by which it plainly appeareth that God looketh of duty²³⁴ not only that we should amend and be better in the time to come, but also be sorry,²³⁵ and weep and bewail our sins committed before. And all the old holy doctors be full and whole of that mind: that men must have for their sins contrition and sorrow in heart.

THE SEVENTH CHAPTER
What if a man cannot weep, nor in his heart be sorry, for his sins?

VINCENT: Forsooth,²³⁶ Uncle, yet seemeth me this thing somewhat a sore sentence²³⁷—not for that²³⁸ I think otherwise but that there is good cause and great wherefore a man so should, but for that of truth some man cannot be sorry and heavy²³⁹ for his sin that he hath done, though he never so fain²⁴⁰ would. But though he can be content for God's sake to forbear it from thenceforth,²⁴¹ yet for every sin that is past can he not only not weep, but some were haply so wanton²⁴² that when he happeth to remember them, he can scantly forbear to laugh. Now, if contrition and sorrow of heart be so requisite of necessity to remission, many a man should stand, as it seemeth, in very perilous case.

ANTONY: Many so should indeed, Cousin, and indeed many so do; and the old saints write very sore²⁴³ in this point. Howbeit, *Misericordia Domini*

super omnia opera eius ("The mercy of God is above all his works"),²⁴⁴ and he standeth not bounden unto common rule; *Et ipse cognovit figmentum suum, et propitiatur infirmitatibus nostris* ("And he knoweth the frailty of his earthen vessel that is of his own making, and is merciful and hath pity upon our feeble infirmities"),²⁴⁵ and shall not exact of us above the thing that we may do.

But yet, Cousin, he that findeth himself in that case, in that²⁴⁶ he is minded to do well hereafter, let him give God thanks that he is no worse; but in that he cannot be sorry for his sin past, let him be sorry hardily²⁴⁷ that he is no better. And as Saint Jerome biddeth him that²⁴⁸ for his sin sorroweth in his heart be glad and rejoice in his sorrow, so would I counsel him that cannot be sad for his sin to be sorry yet at the least that he cannot be sorry.

Besides this, though I would in no wise any man should despair, yet would I counsel such a man, while that affection lasteth, not to be too bold of courage, but live in double fear.

First, for it is a token either of faint faith, or of a dull diligence; for surely if we well believe in God, and therewith deeply consider his majesty, with the peril of our sin and the great goodness of God also, either should dread make us tremble and break our stony heart, or love should for sorrow relent²⁴⁹ it into tears.

Besides this, since I can scant²⁵⁰ believe but since so little misliking of our old sin is an affection not very pure and clean, and none unclean thing shall enter into heaven,²⁵¹ cleansed shall it be and purified before that we come there. And therefore would I further advise one in that case the counsel which Master Gerson²⁵² giveth every man: that since the body and the soul together make the whole man, the less affliction that he feeleth in his soul, the more pain in recompense let him put upon his body, and purge the spirit by the affliction of the flesh.²⁵³ And he that so doth, I dare my life, shall have his hard heart after relent into tears, and his soul in a wholesome heaviness²⁵⁴ and heavenly gladness too—specially if (which must

230 Ps 50(51):17 **231** worn myself out **232** Ps 6:6 **233** *lay ... twain:* to cite one text or two **234** *looketh of duty:* expects as our duty **235** sorrowful; penitent **236** In truth **237** *sore sentence:* harsh opinion **238** *for that:* because **239** *sorry and heavy:* sorrowful and grieved **240** gladly; willingly **241** then on **242** *haply so wanton:* perhaps so excessive **243** strongly, severely **244** Ps 144(145):9 **245** See Ps 102(103):14; 102(103):3. **246** *in that:* seeing that; because **247** certainly, assuredly **248** who **249** soften **250** barely, hardly **251** See Rev 21:27. **252** *Master Gerson:* Jean Gerson (1363–1429), French scholar, theologian, and advocate of Church reform **253** *that since ... flesh:* This may be a reference to *The Imitation of Christ* (2.12), then attributed to Gerson. **254** sorrow

be joined with every good thing) he join faithful prayer therewith.

But, Cousin, as I told you the other day before, in these matters with these new men I will not dispute; but surely, for mine own part, I cannot well hold with them, for as far as mine own poor wit can perceive, the Holy Scripture of God is very plain against them. And the whole corps[255] of Christendom in every Christian region — and the very places in which they dwell themselves — have ever unto their own days clearly believed against them. And all the old holy doctors have evermore taught against them. And all the old holy interpreters have construed[256] the Scripture against them. And therefore, if these men have now perceived so late[257] that the Scripture hath been misunderstood all this while, and that of all those old holy doctors no man could understand it, then am I too old at this age to begin to study it now; and trust these men's cunning, Cousin, that dare I not in no wise, since I cannot see nor perceive no cause wherefore I should think that these men might not now in the understanding of Scripture as well be deceived themselves, as they bear us in hand,[258] that all those others have been all this while before.

Howbeit, Cousin, if it so be that their way be not wrong, but that they have found out so easy a way to heaven as to take no thought but make merry, nor take no penance at all, but sit them down and drink well for our Savior's sake — set cock a-hoop[259] and fill in all the cups at once, and then let Christ's Passion pay for all the scot[260] — I am not he that will envy their good hap;[261] but surely counsel dare I give no man to adventure[262] that way with them. But such as fear lest that way be not sure, and take upon them willingly tribulation of penance — what comfort they do take and well may take therein, that have I somewhat told you already. And since these other folk sit so merry without such tribulation, we need to talk to them, you wot[263] well, of no such manner comfort. And therefore of this kind of tribulation will I make an end.

THE EIGHTH CHAPTER
Of that kind of tribulation which, though they not willingly take, yet they willingly suffer

VINCENT: Verily, good Uncle, so may you well do, for you have brought it unto a very good pass.[264] And now I require[265] you to come to the other kind, of which you purposed always[266] to treat last.

ANTONY: That shall I, Cousin, very gladly do. The other kind is this, which I rehearsed[267] second, and, sorting out the other twain, have kept it for the last. This kind of tribulation is, you wot well, of them that willingly suffer tribulation, though that[268] of their own choice they took it not at the first. This kind, Cousin, divide we shall into twain. The first might we call temptation; the second, persecution. But here must you consider that I mean not every kind of persecution, but that kind only which, though the sufferer would be loath to fall in, yet will he rather abide[269] it and suffer it than by the flitting from it fall in the displeasure of God, or leave God's pleasure unprocured. Howbeit, if we well consider these two things, temptation and persecution, we may find that either of them is incident[270] to the other. For both by temptation the devil persecuteth us, and by persecution the devil also tempteth us; and as persecution is tribulation to every man, so is temptation tribulation to every good man. Now, though the devil, our spiritual enemy, fight against man in both, yet this difference hath the common temptation from the persecution: that temptation is, as it were, the fiend's train,[271] and persecution, his plain open fight. And therefore will I now call all this kind of tribulation here by the name of temptation, and that shall I divide into two parts. The first shall I call the devil's trains; the other, his open fight.

---

255 collective body   256 interpreted
257 *so late:* so recently; at such a late
date   258 *bear...in hand:* assert against
us   259 *set cock a-hoop:* turn on the tap

and let the liquor flow   260 tab, bill;
payment for entertainment   261 fortune
262 venture, risk taking   263 know
264 completion   265 ask   266 *purposed*

always: always intended   267 recounted
268 *though that:* even though
269 endure, put up with   270 related
271 snare, trap, deceit

THE NINTH CHAPTER
*First of temptation in general,
as it is common to both*

ANTONY: To speak of every kind of temptation particularly by itself, this were, ye wot well, in manner an infinite thing; for under that, as I told you, fall persecutions and all. And the devil hath of his trains[272] a thousand subtle ways, and of his open fight as many poisoned darts.

He tempteth us by the world; he tempteth us by our own flesh; he tempteth us by pleasure; he tempteth us by pain; he tempteth us by our foes; he tempteth us by our own friends—and under color[273] of kindred, he maketh many times our next[274] friends our most foes.[275] For as our Savior saith, *Inimici hominis domestici eius.*[276]

But in all manner of so diverse temptations, one marvelous comfort is this: that with the more we be tempted, the gladder have we cause to be; for as Saint James saith, *Omne gaudium existimate, fratres, cum in tentationes varias incideritis* ("Esteem it and take it," saith he, "my brethren, for a thing of all joy when you fall into diverse and sundry manner of temptations").[277] And no marvel, for there is in this world set up, as it were, a game of wrestling, wherein the people of God come in on the one side, and on the other side come mighty strong wrestlers and wily: that is to wit, the devils, the cursed proud damned spirits. For it is not our flesh alone that we must wrestle with, but with the devil too. *Non est nobis collectatio adversus carnem et sanguinem, sed adversus principes et potestates tenebrarum harum, adversus spiritalia nequitiae in caelestibus* ("Our wrestling is not here," saith Saint Paul, "against flesh and blood, but against the princes and potestates[278] of these dark regions, against the spiritual wicked ghosts of the air").[279]

But as God—unto them that on his[280] part give his adversary the fall—hath prepared a crown, so he that will not wrestle shall none have; for as Saint Paul saith, *Nemo coronabitur nisi qui legitime certaverit* ("There shall no man have the crown but he that doth his devoir[281] therefor, according to the law of the game").[282] And then, as holy Saint Bernard saith, how couldst thou fight or wrestle therefor, if there were no challenger against thee that would provoke thee thereto?[283] And therefore may it be a great comfort, as Saint James[284] saith, to every man that seeth himself challenged and provoked by temptation. For thereby perceiveth he that it cometh to his course[285] to wrestle, which shall be—but if[286] he willingly will play the coward or the fool—the matter of his eternal reward.

THE TENTH CHAPTER
A special comfort in all temptation

ANTONY: But now must this needs be to man an inestimable comfort in all temptation, if his faith fail him not: that is to wit, that he may be sure that God is always ready to give him strength against the devil's might, and wisdom against the devil's trains.[287] For as the prophet saith, *Fortitudo mea et laus mea est Dominus; factus est mihi in salutem* ("My strength and my praise is our Lord; he hath been my safeguard").[288] And the Scripture saith, *Pete a Deo sapientiam et dabit tibi* ("Ask wisdom of God and he shall give it thee")[289] *ut possitis,* as Saint Paul saith, *deprehendere omnes artes* ("that you may spy and perceive all the crafts").[290]

A great comfort may this be in all kinds of temptation: that God hath so his hand upon him that is willing to stand and will trust in him and call upon him, that he hath made him sure, by many faithful promises in Holy Scripture, that either he shall not fall, or if he sometimes through faintness of faith stagger or hap to fall, yet if he call upon God betimes,[291] his fall shall be no sore bruising to him, but as the Scripture saith, *Iustus si ceciderit non collidetur, quia Dominus supponit manum* ("The just man, though he fall, shall not be bruised, for our Lord holdeth under his hand").[292]

The prophet expresseth a plain comfortable promise of God against all temptation where he saith, *Qui habitat in adiutorio Altissimi, in protectione Dei caeli commorabitur* ("Whoso dwelleth in the help of the

---

272 traps, deceits   **273** the appearance, pretext   **274** nearest   **275** *most foes:* worst enemies   **276** "A man's enemies are [those] of his own household" (Mt 10:36). **277** Jas 1:2   **278** potentates; angelic powers   **279** Eph 6:12   **280** their (singular and plural pronouns were often mixed at this time)   **281** duty, task   **282** 2 Tim 2:5 **283** See St. Bernard's seventeenth sermon on the Song of Songs.   **284** *Saint James:* referring to the quote above (Jas 1:2) **285** turn   **286** *but if:* unless   **287** snares, deceits   **288** *Fortitudo...safeguard:* Ps 117(118):14   **289** See Jas 1:5.   **290** See Eph 3:18.   **291** in good time   **292** Ps 36(37):23–24

highest God, he shall abide in the protection or defense of the God of heaven").[293] Who dwelleth now, good Cousin, in the help of the high God? Surely he that through a good faith abideth in the trust and confidence of God's help, and never for lack of that faith and trust in his help falleth desperate of all help, nor departeth from the hope of his help to seek himself help[294] (as I told you the other day) of the flesh, the world, or the devil.

Now he then that by fast[295] faith and sure hope dwelleth in God's help and hangeth always thereupon, never falling from that hope, he shall, saith the prophet, "ever dwell and abide in God's defense and protection" — that is to say that, while he faileth not to believe well and hope well, God will never fail in all temptation to defend him. For unto such a faithful well-hoping man, the prophet in the same psalm saith further, *Scapulis suis obumbrabit tibi, et sub pennis eius sperabis* ("With his shoulders shall he shadow thee,[296] and under his feathers shalt thou trust").[297] Lo, here hath every faithful man a sure promise: that in the fervent[298] heat of temptation or tribulation (for as I have said diverse times before, they be in such wise coincident[299] that every tribulation the devil useth for temptation to bring us to impatience — and thereby to murmur and grudge[300] and blasphemy — and every kind of temptation, to a good man that fighteth against it and will not follow it, is a very painful tribulation) — in the fervent heat, I say therefore, of every temptation, God giveth the faithful man that hopeth in him the shadow of his holy shoulders, which are broad and large, sufficient to refrigerate[301] and refresh the man in that heat; and in every tribulation he putteth his shoulders for a defense between. And then what weapon of the devil may give us any deadly wound, while that impenetrable pavise[302] of the shoulder of God standeth always between?

Then goeth the verse further and saith unto such a faithful man, *Et sub pennis eius sperabis* ("Thine hope shall be under his feathers"): that is to wit, for the good hope thou hast in his help, he will take thee so near him into his protection that, as the hen, to keep her young chickens from the kite,[303] nestleth

them together under her own wings, so from the devil's claws — the ravenous kite of this dark air — will the God of heaven gather the faithful trusting folk near unto his own sides, and set them in surety, very well and warm, under the covering of his heavenly wings.

And of this defense and protection, our Savior spoke himself unto the Jews (as mention is made in the twenty-third chapter of Saint Matthew), to whom he said in this wise: *Ierusalem, Ierusalem, quae occidis prophetas et lapidas eos qui ad te missi sunt, quotiens volui congregare te quemadmodum gallina congregat pullos suos sub alas suas et noluisti* — that is to say, "Jerusalem, Jerusalem, that killest the prophets and stonest unto death them that are sent unto thee, how often would I have gathered thy sons together as the hen gathereth her chickens under her wings, and thou wouldst not?"[304]

Here are, Cousin Vincent, words of no little comfort unto every Christian man, by which we may see with how tender affection God of his great goodness longeth to gather under the protection of his wings, and how often like a loving hen he clucketh home unto him even those chickens of his that willfully walketh abroad into the kite's danger and will not come at his clucking; but ever the more he clucketh for them, the farther they go from him. And therefore can we not doubt if we will follow him, and with faithful hope come run to him, but that he shall, in all matter of temptation, take us near unto him and set us even under his wing. And then are we safe, if we will tarry there; for against our will can there no power pull us thence, nor hurt our souls there. *Pone me*, saith the prophet, *iuxta te, et cuiusvis manus pugnet contra me* ("Set me near unto thee, and fight against me whose hand that will").[305]

And to show the great safeguard and surety that we shall have while we sit under his heavenly feathers, the prophet saith yet a great deal further: *sub umbra alarum tuarum exsultabo*[306] — that is to wit, that we shall not only, when we sit by his sweet side under his holy wing, sit in safeguard, but that we shall also under the covering of his heavenly wings with great exultation rejoice.

293 Ps 90(91):1   **294** *himself help:* help for himself   **295** firm, steadfast   **296** *shadow thee:* give you shade   **297** Ps 90(91):4   **298** intense; burning   **299** the

same in such a way   **300** *murmur and grudge:* muttering complaints and grumbling   **301** cool   **302** a type of large shield   **303** a kind of hawk   **304** Mt

23:37   **305** *fight … will:* then the hand of anyone who wants to can fight against me; Job 17:3   **306** "Under the shadow of your wings I will exult" (Ps 62(63):7).

THE ELEVENTH CHAPTER
Of four kinds of temptation—and therein, both the parts of that kind of tribulation that men willingly suffer—touched in the two verses of the Psalter

ANTONY: Now, in the two next verses following, the prophet briefly comprehendeth[307] four kinds of temptation, and therein all the tribulation that we shall now speak of, and also some part of that which we have spoken of before. And therefore I shall peradventure, except any further thing fall in our way, with treating of those two verses finish and end all our matter.[308]

The prophet saith in the psalm, *Scuto circumdabit te veritas eius; non timebis a timore nocturne, a sagitta volante in die, a negotio perambulante in tenebris, ab incursu et daemonio meridiano* ("The truth of God shall compass thee about with a pavise; thou shalt not be afeard of the night's fear, nor of the arrow flying in the day, nor of the business walking about in the darknesses, nor of the incursion or invasion of the devil in the midday").[309]

First, Cousin, in these words, "the truth of God shall compass thee about with a pavise," the prophet, for the comfort of every good man in all temptation, and in all tribulation, beside those other things that he said before (that the shoulders of God should shadow them, and that also they should sit under his wing), here saith he further that "the truth of God shall compass thee with a pavise"—that is to wit, that as God hath faithfully promised to protect and defend those that faithfully will dwell in the trust of his help, so will he truly perform it. And thee, that such one art, will the truth of his promise defend,[310] not with a little round buckler[311] that scant[312] can cover the head, but with a long large pavise that covereth all along the body, made, as holy Saint Bernard saith, broad above with the Godhead, and narrow beneath with the manhood, so that this pavise is our Savior Christ himself.[313]

And yet is not this pavise like other pavises of this world, which are not made but in such wise as while it defendeth one part, the man may be wounded upon the other; but this pavise is such

that, as the prophet saith, it shall round about enclose and compass thee, so that thine enemy shall hurt thy soul on no side. For *scuto*, saith he, *circumdabit te veritas eius* ("with a pavise shall his truth environ and compass thee round about"). And then continently[314] following, to the intent that we should see that it is not without necessity that the pavise of God should compass us about upon every side, he showeth in what wise we be by the devil with trains[315] and assaults—by four kinds of temptations and tribulations—environed upon every side; against all which compass[316] of temptations and tribulations, that round compassing[317] pavise of God's truth shall in such wise defend us and keep us safe that we shall need to dread none of them all.

THE TWELFTH CHAPTER
The first kind of the four temptations

ANTONY: First he saith, *Non timebis a timore nocturno* ("Thou shalt not be afeard of the fear of the night"). By "the night" is there in Scripture sometimes understood tribulation, as appeareth in the thirty-fourth chapter of Job: *Novit enim Deus opera eorum, idcirco inducet noctem* ("God hath known the work of them, and therefore shall he bring night upon them")[318]—that is to wit, tribulation for their wickedness.

And well you wot that the night is of the nature of itself discomfortable and full of fear. And therefore by the "night's fear" here I understand the tribulations by which the devil, through the sufferance of God,[319] either by himself or others that are his instruments, tempteth good folk to impatience, as he did Job. But he that, as the prophet saith, dwelleth and continueth faithfully in the hope of God's help shall so be clipped in[320] on every side with the shield or pavise of God that he shall have no need to be afeard of such tribulation that is here called the night's fear. And it may be also conveniently[321] called the night's fear for two causes: the one, for that[322] many times the cause of his tribulation is, unto him that suffereth, dark and unknown, and therein varieth it and differeth from that tribulation by which

307 describes; includes **308** *all our matter:* our whole discussion **309** Ps 90(91):4–6 **310** *thee...defend:* the truth of His promise will defend you, who are such a one **311** shield **312** barely

313 See St. Bernard's *In Psalmum 90*, 5:2. **314** immediately **315** snares, deceits **316** artifice, crafty stratagem **317** surrounding **318** Job 34:25 **319** *the sufferance of God:* God's allowing

this **320** *clipped in:* closely surrounded **321** fittingly; appropriately **322** *for that:* because

the devil tempteth a man by open fight and assault for a good known thing from which he would withdraw him, or for some known evil thing into which he would drive him by force of such persecution.

5 Another cause for which it is called the night's fear may be for that that the night is so far out of courage,[323] and naturally so casteth folk in fear, that of everything whereof they perceive any manner dread, their fantasy doubleth their fear, and maketh them 10 often ween[324] that it were much worse than indeed it is. The prophet saith in the Psalter, *Posuisti tenebras, et facta est nox, in illa pertransibunt omnes bestiae silvarum, catuli leonum rugientes quaerentes a Deo escam sibi* ("Thou hast, good Lord, set the darkness, 15 and made was the night; and in the night walken all the beasts of the woods, the whelps[325] of the lions roaring and calling unto God for their meat").[326]

Now though that[327] the lions' whelps walk about roaring in the night and seek for their prey, yet can 20 they not get such meat as they would always, but must hold themselves content with such as God suffereth[328] to fall in their way. And though they be not ware[329] thereof, yet of God they ask it, and of him they have it.

25 And this may be comfort to all good men in their "night's fear," in their dark tribulation: that though they fall into the claws or the teeth of those lions' whelps, yet shall all that they[330] can do not pass beyond the body, which is but as the garment of the 30 soul. For the soul itself, which is the substance of the man, is so surely fenced in round about with the shield or pavise[331] of God that as long as he will abide faithfully in *adiutorio Altissimi* ("in the hope of God's help"),[332] the lions' whelps shall not be able 35 to hurt it; for the great lion himself could never be suffered to go further in the tribulation of Job than God from time to time gave him leave.[333] And therefore the deep darkness of the midnight maketh men that standeth out of[334] faith and out of good hope 40 in God to be in their tribulation far in the greater fear, for lack of the light of faith, whereby they might perceive that the uttermost of their peril is a far less thing than they take it for.

But we be so wont[335] to set so much by[336] our body, 45 which we see and feel, and in the feeding and fostering whereof we set our delight and our wealth,

and so little (alas) and so seldom we think upon our soul, because we cannot see that but by spiritual understanding, and most specially by the eye of our faith (in the meditation whereof we bestow, 50 God wot, little time), that the loss of our body we take for a sorer[337] thing, and for a greater tribulation a great deal, than we do the loss of our soul. And where[338] our Savior biddeth us that we should not fear those lions' whelps that can but kill our bodies, 55 and when that is done have no further thing in their power wherewith they can do us harm, but biddeth us stand in dread of him which, when he hath slain the body, is able then besides to cast the soul into everlasting fire, we be so blind in the dark night of 60 tribulation, for lack of full and fast[339] belief of God's word, that whereas in the day of prosperity we very little fear God for our soul, our night's fear of adversity maketh us very sore[340] to fear the lion and his whelps for dread of loss of our bodies. 65

And whereas Saint Paul in sundry places showeth us that our body is but as the garment of the soul, yet the faintness of our faith to the Scripture of God maketh us with the night's fear of tribulation more to dread not only the loss of our body than of 70 our soul[341] — that is to wit, of the clothing than of the substance that is clothed therewith — but also of the very outward goods that serve for the clothing of the body. And much more foolish are we in that dark night's fear than were he that would for- 75 get the saving of his body, for fear of losing of his old rain-beaten cloak that is but the covering of his gown or his coat.

Now consider further yet that the prophet, in the fore-rehearsed verses, saith not that in the night 80 walk only the lions' whelps, but also *omnes bestiae silvarum* ("all the beasts of the wood"). Now wot you well that if a man walk through the wood in the night, many things may make him afeard of which in the day he would not be afeard a whit. For 85 in the night, every bush, to him that waxeth[342] once afeard, seemeth a thief.

I remember that when I was a young man, I was once in the war with the king then my master (God assoil[343] his soul), and we were camped within 90 the Turk's ground, many a mile beyond Belgrade (which would God were ours now as well as it was

---

323 *far out of courage:* discouraging
324 think   325 cubs   326 Ps
103(104):20–21   327 *though that:* even
though   328 allows   329 aware   330 i.e.,

the lions' whelps   331 large shield   332 Ps
89(90):1   333 permission   334 *out of:*
without   335 accustomed   336 *set so
much by:* value so greatly   337 worse,

more grievous   338 whereas; given
that   339 firm, steadfast   340 grievously
341 See 1 Cor 15:51–55; 2 Cor 5:1–4.
342 becomes, grows   343 forgive

then); but so happed it that in our camp, about midnight, there suddenly rose a rumor and a scry[344] that the Turk's whole army was secretly stealing upon us, wherewith our whole host[345] was warned to arm them[346] in haste, and set themselves in array to fight; and then were the scourers[347] of ours that brought those sudden tidings examined more leisurely by the council, what surety, or what likelihood, they had perceived therein. Of whom, one showed that by the glimmering of the moon he had espied and perceived and seen them himself, coming on softly and soberly in a long range,[348] all in good order, not one farther forth than the other in the forefront, but as even as a thread, and in breadth farther than he could see in length.

His fellows, being examined, said that he was somewhat pricked forth before them,[349] and came so fast back to tell it them that they thought it rather time to make haste and give warning to the camp than to go nearer unto them.[350] For they were not so far off but that they had yet themselves somewhat an unperfect[351] sight of them too.

Thus stood we watching all the remnant of the night, evermore hearkening when we should hear them come, with "hush, stand still, methink I hear a trampling," so that at last many of us thought we heard them ourselves also. But when the day was sprungen[352] and that we saw no man, out was our scourer sent again, and some of our captains with him, to show whereabout the place was in which he perceived them. And when they came thither, they found that the great fearful army of the Turks so soberly coming on turned (God be thanked) into a fair long hedge standing even stone-still. And thus fareth it in the night's fear of tribulation, in which the devil, to bear down and overwhelm with dread the faithful hope that we should have in God, casteth in our imagination much more fear than cause; for while there walk in that night not only the lions' whelps, but over[353] that, all the beasts of the wood besides, the beast that we hear roar in the dark night of tribulation, and fear it for a lion, we sometimes find well afterward in the day that it was no lion at all, but a seely[354] rude roaring ass. And the thing that on the sea seemeth sometimes a rock

is indeed nothing else but a mist. Howbeit, as the prophet saith, he that faithfully dwelleth in the hope of God's help, the pavise of his truth shall so fence him round about that be it an ass, colt, or a lion's whelp, or a rock of stone, or a mist, *Non timebit a timore nocturno* ("The night's fear thereof shall he nothing need to dread").

THE THIRTEENTH CHAPTER
Of pusillanimity

ANTONY: Therefore find I that in the night's fear, one great part is the fault of pusillanimity—that is to wit, faint and feeble stomach[355]—by which a man, for faint heart, is afeard where he needeth not, by the reason whereof he fleeth oftentimes for fear of that thing of which, if he fled not, he should take none harm. And some man doth sometimes by his fleeing make his enemy bold on him, which[356] would, if he fled not, but durst[357] abide thereby, give over and flee from him.

This fault of pusillanimity maketh a man in his tribulation, for feeble heart, first impatient, and afterward oftentimes driveth him by impatience into a contrary affection, making him frowardly[358] stubborn and angry against God, and thereby to fall into blasphemy as do the damned souls in hell. This fault of pusillanimity and timorous mind letteth[359] a man also many times from the doing of many good things which, if he took a good stomach[360] to him in the trust of God's help, he were well able to do. But the devil casteth him in a cowardice, and maketh him take it for humility to think himself unmeet[361] and unable thereto, and therefore to leave the good thing undone whereof God offereth him occasion and had made him convenient[362] thereto.

But such folk have need to lift up their hearts and call upon God, and, by the counsel of other good ghostly[363] folk, cast away the cowardice of their own conceit[364] which the night's fear by the devil hath framed in their fantasy, and look in the Gospel upon him which[365] laid up his talent and left it unoccupied,[366] and therefore utterly lost it, with a great reproach of his pusillanimity, by which he had weened

---

344 clamor   **345** army   **346** themselves   **347** scouts   **348** row   **349** *was…before:* had galloped a little ahead of   **350** i.e., the Turks   **351** incomplete, partial; imperfect   **352** sprung; broken   **353** beyond

354 harmless; silly   **355** seat of courage and perseverance   **356** who (his enemy)   **357** dared   **358** perversely   **359** prevents   **360** courage   **361** unfit, unsuitable   **362** suitable, able   **363** spiritual

364 thinking; imagining   **365** *upon him which:* at that man who   **366** uninvested; Mt 25:14–30

he should have excused himself, in that he was afeard to put it forth in ure[367] and occupy[368] it; and all this fear cometh by the devil's drift,[369] wherein he taketh occasion of the faintness of our good and sure trust in God. And therefore let us faithfully dwell in the good hope of his help, and then shall the pavise of his truth so compass us about that of this night's fear we shall have no fear at all.

THE FOURTEENTH CHAPTER
Of the daughter of pusillanimity:
a scrupulous conscience

ANTONY: This pusillanimity bringeth forth by the night's fear a very timorous daughter: a seely[370] wretched girl and ever puling,[371] that is called scrupulosity, or a scrupulous conscience. This girl is a meetly[372] good pucelle[373] in a house, never idle, but ever occupied and busy; but albeit[374] she hath a very gentle mistress that loveth her well and is well content with that she doth — or if it be not all well (as all cannot always be well), content to pardon her, as she doth other of her fellows, and so letteth her know that she will — yet can this peevish[375] girl never cease whining and puling for fear lest her mistress be always angry with her, and that she shall shrewdly be shent.[376] Were her mistress, ween you,[377] like[378] to be content with this condition? Nay, surely.

I knew such one myself, whose mistress was a very wise woman and (which thing is in women very rare) very mild also and meek, and liked very well such service as she did her in the house. But this continual discomfortable fashion of hers she so much misliked that she would sometimes say, "Ay, what aileth this girl? The elvish urchin weeneth I were a devil, I trow.[379] Surely if she did me ten times better service than she doth, yet with this fantastical fear of hers I would be loath to have her in my house."

Thus fareth, lo, the scrupulous person, which frameth himself many times double the fear that he hath cause, and many times a great fear where there is no cause at all, and of that that[380] is indeed no sin, maketh a venial, and that that is venial, imagineth

to be deadly,[381] and yet, for all that, falleth in them being namely[382] of their nature such as no man long liveth without. And then he feareth that he be never full confessed, nor never fully contrite, and then that his sins be never full forgiven him; and then he confesseth and confesseth again, and cumbereth[383] himself and his confessor both; and then every prayer that he saith, though he say it as well as the frail infirmity of the man will suffer,[384] yet is he not satisfied but if[385] he say it again, and yet after that again; and when he hath said one thing thrice, as little is he satisfied at the last as with the first; and then is his heart evermore in heaviness, unquiet, and in fear — full of doubt and of dullness, without comfort or spiritual consolation.

With this night's fear the devil sore[386] troubleth the mind of many a right good man, and that doth he to bring him to some great inconvenience.[387] For he will, if he can, drive him so much to the minding of God's rigorous justice that he will keep him from the comfortable remembrance of God's great mighty mercy, and so make him do all his good works wearily, and without consolation or quickness.[388] Moreover, he maketh him to take for sin something that is none, and for deadly[389] some such as are but venial, to the intent that when he shall fall into them, he shall by reason of his scruple sin where else he should not, or sin deadly, while his conscience in the deed doing so gave[390] him, where indeed he had offended but venially. Yea, and further, the devil longeth to make all his good works and spiritual exercise so painful and so tedious unto him that with some other suggestion, or false wily doctrine of a false spiritual liberty, he should, for the false ease and pleasure that he should suddenly find therein, be easily conveyed from that evil fault into a much worse, and have his conscience as wide and as large after as ever it was narrow and strait before. For better is yet, of truth, a conscience a little too strait than a little too large.

My mother had, when I was a little boy, a good old woman that took heed to[391] her children; they called her Mother Maud — I trow you have heard of her?

VINCENT: Yea, yea, very much.

---

367 use   368 invest   369 scheme
370 poor, pitiable; silly   371 whimpering
372 fairly   373 maid   374 although
375 silly, foolish; capricious   376 *shrewdly*
be shent: be sharply scolded   377 *ween*

you: do you suppose   378 likely
379 suppose, believe   380 *that that:*
that which   381 mortal   382 *in them*
being namely: especially into those that
are   383 troubles   384 allow   385 *but*

if: unless   386 greatly, grievously
387 harm, trouble, disadvantage; immoral
or unseemly behavior   388 vitality, vigor
389 mortally   390 *so gave:* i.e., misgave
391 *heed to:* care of

ANTONY: She was wont,[392] when she sat by the fire with us, to tell us that were children many childish tales; but, as Pliny saith that there is no book lightly[393] so bad but that some good thing a man may pick out thereof,[394] so think I that there is almost no tale so foolish but that yet, in one matter or other, to some purpose it may hap to serve; for I remember me that among other of her fond[395] tales, she told us once that the ass and the wolf came upon a time to confession to the fox. The poor ass came to shrift[396] in the Shrovetide,[397] a day or two before Ash Wednesday; but the wolf would not come to confession till he saw first Palm Sunday past, and then foded yet forth[398] farther, till Good Friday. The fox asked the ass, before he began *Benedicite*,[399] wherefore[400] he came to confession before Lent began, so soon. The poor beast answered him again,[401] for fear of deadly sin, if he should lose his part of any of those prayers that the priest in the cleansing days[402] pray for them that are then confessed already. Then, in his shrift,[403] he had a marvelous grudge[404] in his inward conscience that he had one day given his master a cause of anger, in that that[405] with his rude roaring before his master arose, he had awaked him out of his sleep and bereaved him of his rest. The fox for that fault, like a good discreet[406] confessor, charged him to do so no more, but lie still and sleep like a good son himself till his master were up and ready to go to work, and so should he be sure that he should not wake him no more.

To tell you all the poor ass's confession, it were a long work; for everything that he did was deadly sin with[407] him, the poor soul was so scrupulous. But his wise wily confessor accounted them for trifles, as they were, and swore after unto the badger that he was so weary to sit so long and hear him that, saving for the manner sake,[408] he had liefer[409] have sitten all that while at breakfast with a good fat goose.

But when it came to the penance-giving, the fox found that the most weighty sin in all his shrift[410] was gluttony; and therefore he discreetly gave him in penance that he should never for greediness of his meat[411] do any other beast any harm or hindrance, and then eat his meat and study[412] for no more.

Now, as good Mother Maud told us, when the wolf came to Father Reynard[413] (that was, she said, the fox's name) to confession upon Good Friday, his confessor shook his great pair of beads[414] upon[415] him (almost as big as bowls) and asked him wherefore he came so late. "Forsooth,[416] Father Reynard," quoth he, "I must needs tell you the truth. I come, you wot well, therefor. I durst[417] come no sooner for fear lest you would for my gluttony have given me in penance to fast some part of this Lent." "Nay, nay," quoth Father Fox, "I am not so unreasonable; for I fast none of it myself. For I may say to thee, son— here in confession, between us twain— it is no commandment of God, this fasting, but an invention of man. The priests make folk fast, and put them to pain about the moonshine in the water,[418] and do but make folk fools; but they shall make me no such fool, I warrant[419] thee, son. For I eat flesh all this Lent myself, I. Howbeit[420] indeed, because I will not be occasion of slander, I therefore eat it secretly in my chamber,[421] out of sight of all such foolish brethren as for their weak scrupulous conscience would wax offended withal.[422] And so would I counsel you to do." "Forsooth, Father Fox," quoth the wolf, "and so, I thank God, I do, as near as I can; for when I go to my meat, I take none other company with me but such sure brethren as are of mine own nature— whose consciences are not weak, I warrant you, but their stomachs[423] as strong as mine." "Well then, no force,"[424] quoth Father Fox.

But when he heard after[425] by his confession that he was so great a ravener[426] that he devoured and spent sometimes so much victual[427] at one meal as the price thereof would well find[428] some poor man, with his wife and his children, almost all the week, then he prudently reproved that point in him, and preached him a process of[429] his own temperance, which[430] never used, as he said, to pass

---

392 accustomed   393 superficially
394 See Pliny, *Epistles* 3:5 (letter to Baebius Macer).   395 foolish   396 confession
397 the three days before Ash Wednesday
398 *foded yet forth:* put it off even
399 Confession commonly begins with "Bless me...for I have sinned."   400 why
401 in return, in reply   402 *the cleansing days:* Shrovetide   403 confession
404 scruple, doubt   405 *in that that:*

insofar as   406 sensible; judicious
407 to   408 *saving . . . sake:* except for the sake of appearances   409 *had liefer:* would rather   410 *all his shrift:* his whole confession   411 food   412 strive for; seek   413 alluding to Reynard the Fox, a popular beast-fable character   414 rosary beads   415 at   416 In truth   417 dared
418 *the moonshine in the water:* something unsubstantial or unreal   419 assure,

guarantee   420 However   421 bedroom, bedchamber   422 *wax offended withal:* become morally shocked by this
423 courage; appetites   424 *no force:* no matter   425 afterwards   426 voracious eater   427 food   428 provide for
429 *process of:* discourse or sermon about
430 who

upon himself[431] the value of sixpence at a meal—no, nor yet so much neither. "For when I bring home a goose," quoth he, "not out of the poulterer's shop—where folk find them out of the feathers ready plucked, and see which is the fattest, and yet for sixpence buy and choose the best—but out of the housewife's house, at the first hand, which may somewhat better cheap afford them,[432] you wot well, than the poulterer may; nor yet cannot be suffered[433] to see them plucked, and stand and choose them by day, but am fain[434] by night to take at a venture,[435] and when I come home, am fain to do the labor to pluck her myself too; yet for all this, though it be but lean, and I ween not well worth a groat,[436] serveth it me sometimes for all that both dinner and supper too. And therefore, as for that you live of ravin,[437] therein can I find no fault; you have used[438] it so long that I think you can do none other. And therefore were it folly to forbid it you, and to say the truth, against good conscience too; for live you must, I wot well, and other craft can you none.[439] And therefore (as reason is)[440] must you live by that. But yet, you wot well, too much is too much, and measure[441] is a merry mean, which I perceive by your shrift[442] you have never used to keep; and therefore surely this shall be your penance: that you shall all this year never pass upon yourself[443] the price of sixpence at a meal, as near as your conscience can guess the price."

Their shrift have I showed you as Mother Maud showed it us. But now serveth for our matter the conscience of them both in the true performing of their penance.

The poor ass, after his shrift, when he waxed a-hungered,[444] saw a sow lie with her pigs well lapped[445] in new straw; and near he drew, and thought to have eaten of the straw, but anon[446] his scrupulous conscience began therein to grudge[447] him: for while his penance was that, for greediness of his meat, he should do none other body none harm, he thought he might not eat one straw there, lest for lack of that straw, some of those pigs might hap to die for cold; so held he still his hunger till one[448] brought him meat;[449] but when he should fall thereto,[450] then fell he yet in a far further scruple. For then it came in his mind that he should yet break his penance if he should eat any of that either, since he was commanded by his ghostly[451] father that he should not for his own meat hinder any other beast; for he thought that if he ate not that meat, some other beast might hap to have it, and so should he, by the eating of it, peradventure[452] hinder another. And thus stood he, still fasting, till when he told the cause, his ghostly father came and informed him better; and then he cast off that scruple and fell mannerly[453] to his meat, and was a right honest ass many a fair day after.

The wolf, now, coming from shrift clean soiled[454] from his sins, went about to do as a shrewd[455] wife once told her husband that she would do when she came from shrift. "Be merry, man," quoth she now, "for this day, I thank God, was I well shriven;[456] and I purpose now therefore to leave off all mine old shrewdness and begin even afresh."

VINCENT: Ah, well, Uncle, can you report her so? That word heard I her speak, but she said it in sport, to make her husband laugh.

ANTONY: Indeed, it seemed she spoke it half in sport. For that she said she would cast away all her shrewdness, therein I trow[457] she sported; but in that she said she would begin it all afresh, her husband found that good earnest.[458]

VINCENT: Well, I shall show her what you say, I warrant[459] you.

ANTONY: Then will you make me make my word good;[460] but whatsoever she did, at the leastwise so fared now this wolf, which had cast out in confession all his old ravin;[461] and then hunger pricked[462]

---

431 *pass upon himself:* spend more on himself than   **432** *which...them:* who can offer them at a somewhat lower price   **433** *nor...suffered:* nor can I even stand   **434** obliged   **435** *at a venture:* at random   **436** a coin worth four pence   **437** *as for...ravin:* because you live by preying   **438** practiced   **439** *other...none:* you don't know any

other skill   **440** *as reason is:* as is right or reasonable   **441** moderation   **442** confession   **443** *pass...yourself:* exceed   **444** *waxed a-hungered:* became hungry   **445** covered   **446** at once, straightway   **447** trouble   **448** someone   **449** food   **450** *should fall thereto:* was about to start eating it   **451** spiritual   **452** perhaps   **453** properly, respectably   **454** *shrift clean*

soiled: confession completely absolved   **455** shrewish; given to fault-finding and scolding   **456** confessed; absolved   **457** believe   **458** *good earnest:* sincere; quite serious   **459** promise   **460** *make me...good:* make me prove that what I'm saying is true   **461** preying   **462** spurred

him forward that, as the shrewd wife said, he should begin all afresh. But yet the prick of conscience withdrew and held him back, because he would not, for breaking of his penance, take any prey for his mealtide[463] that should pass the price of sixpence.

It happed him then, as he walked prowling for his gear[464] about, he came where a man had in few days before cast off two old lean and lame horses, so sick that no flesh was there left upon them. And the one, when the wolf came by, could scant[465] stand on his legs, and the other already dead, and his skin ripped off and carried away. And as he looked upon them suddenly, he was first about to feed upon them and whet his teeth on their bones. But as he looked aside, he spied a fair cow in a close,[466] walking with her young calf by her side; and as soon as he saw them, his conscience began to grudge him against both those two horses. And then he sighed and said to himself, "Alas, wicked wretch that I am, I had almost broken my penance ere I was aware. For yonder dead horse—because I never saw dead horse sold in the market, and I should die therefor[467] by the way that my sinful soul shall to—I cannot devise[468] what price I should set upon him; but in my conscience I set him far above sixpence, and therefore I dare not meddle with him.

"Now, then, is yonder quick[469] horse of likelihood worth a great deal of money. For horses be dear[470] in this country—specially such soft amblers; for I see by his pace he trotteth not, nor can scant shift a foot; and therefore I may not meddle with him, for he very far passeth my sixpence. But kine[471] this country here hath enough, but money have they very little. And therefore, considering the plenty of the kine and the scarcity of the money, as for yonder peevish[472] cow, seemeth unto me, in my conscience, worth not past a groat and[473] she be worth so much. Now, then, as for her calf, is not so much as she by half; and therefore, while the cow is in my conscience worth but fourpence, my conscience cannot serve[474] me, for sin of my soul,

to praise[475] her calf above twopence; and so pass[476] they not sixpence between them both. And therefore they twain may I well eat at this one meal and break not my penance at all." And so thereupon[477] he did, without any scruple of conscience. If such beasts could speak now as Mother Maud said they could then, some of them would, I ween, tell a tale almost as wise as this; wherein, save[478] for the diminishing[479] of old Mother Maud's tale, else[480] would a shorter process[481] have served.

But yet, as peevish[482] as the parable is, in this it serveth for our purpose: that the night's fear of a conscience somewhat scrupulous, though it be painful and troublous to him that hath it (like as this poor ass had here), is less harm yet than a conscience overlarge,[483] or such as for his own fantasy the man list[484] to frame himself—now drawing it narrow, now stretching it in breadth, after the manner of a cheverel point,[485] to serve on every side for his own commodity[486]—as did here the wily wolf.

But such folk are out[487] of tribulation, and comfort need they none; and therefore are they out of our matter.

But those that are in the night's fear of their own scrupulous conscience, let them be well ware,[488] as I said, that the devil for weariness of the one draw them not into the other, and while he would flee from Scylla, drive him into Charybdis.[489] He must do as doth a ship that should come into a haven, in the mouth whereof lie secret[490] rocks under the water on both the sides: if he be by mishap entered in among them that are on the one side and cannot tell how to get out, he must get a substantial cunning[491] pilot that so can conduce him[492] from the rocks on that side that, yet he bring him not into those that are on the other side, but can guide him in the midway. Let them, I say, therefore that are in the troublous fear of their own scrupulous conscience submit the rule of their own conscience to the counsel of some other good man, which, after[493] the variety and the nature of the scruples, may temper the advice; yea, although a man be very

---

463 meal   **464** food   **465** hardly, barely   **466** enclosed field   **467** for that   **468** imagine   **469** live   **470** scarce; expensive   **471** cattle   **472** silly, worthless   **473** *groat if:* four pence if   **474** allow   **475** appraise   **476** exceed   **477** upon those grounds; directly after that   **478** except   **479** belittling

480 otherwise   **481** story, narrative   **482** silly   **483** too permissive   **484** pleases, chooses   **485** *cheverel point:* a strap made of a famously flexible kind of leather   **486** advantage   **487** outside   **488** aware; wary   **489** *Scylla . . . Charybdis:* a mythological monster living on one side of a narrow channel, and a whirlpool

on the other side of that same narrow channel. See Homer, *Odyssey*, Book 12.   **490** hidden   **491** *substantial cunning:* thoroughly knowledgeable   **492** *conduce him:* lead him away   **493** *which, after:* who, according to

well-learned himself, yet let him in this case learn the custom used among physicians. For be one of them never so cunning, yet in his own disease and sickness he never useth[494] to trust all to himself, but send for such of his fellows as he knoweth meet,[495] and putteth himself in their hands for many considerations whereof they assign[496] the causes. And one of the causes is fear—whereof, upon some tokens,[497] he may conceive in his own passion[498] a great deal more than needeth and than were good for his health, that for the time, that he knew no such thing at all.

I knew once in this town one of the most cunning men in that faculty,[499] and the best expert, and therewith the most famous too, and he that the greatest cures did upon other men. And yet when he was himself once very sore[500] sick, I heard his fellows that then looked unto him—of all which every one would in their own disease have used his help before any other man—wish yet that for the time of his own sickness, being so sore as it was, he had known no physic[501] at all: he took so great heed unto every suspicious token, and feared so far the worst, that his fear did him sometimes much more harm than the sickness gave him cause.

And therefore, as I say, whoso[502] hath such a trouble of his scrupulous conscience, let him for a while forbear the judgment of himself, and follow the counsel of some other whom he knoweth for well-learned and virtuous—and specially in the place of confession. For there is God specially present with his grace, assisting[503] his sacrament. And let him not doubt to acquiet[504] his mind, and follow that that[505] he is there bade,[506] and think for a while less of the fear of God's justice, and be more merry in remembrance of his mercy, and persevere in prayer for grace, and abide and dwell faithfully in the sure hope of his help; and then shall he find, without any doubt, that the pavise[507] of God's truth shall, as the prophet saith, so compass him about that he shall not dread the night's fear of scrupulosity, but shall have his conscience stablished in good quiet and rest.

THE FIFTEENTH CHAPTER
Another kind of the night's fear—another daughter of pusillanimity—that is to wit, that horrible temptation by which some folk are tempted to kill and destroy themselves

VINCENT: Verily, good Uncle, you have in my mind well declared[508] these kinds of the night's fear.

ANTONY: Surely, Cousin, but yet are there many more than I can either remember or find; howbeit,[509] one yet cometh now to my mind, of which I before nothing thought, and which is yet, in mine opinion, of all the other fears the most horrible: that is to wit, Cousin, where the devil tempteth a man to kill and destroy himself.

VINCENT: Undoubtedly this kind of tribulation is marvelous and strange, and the temptation is of such a sort that some men have opinion that such as once fall in that fantasy can never full cast it off.

ANTONY: Yes, yes, Cousin, many a hundred, and else God[510] forbid. But the thing that maketh men so say is because that of those which finally do destroy themselves, there is much speech and much wondering (as it is well worthy); but many a good man and woman hath sometimes—yea, diverse years, one after other continually—been tempted thereto, and yet have by grace and good counsel well and virtuously withstood it, and been in conclusion[511] clearly delivered of it, and their tribulation nothing known abroad, and therefore nothing talked of. But surely, Cousin, a horrible sore trouble it is to any man or woman that the devil tempteth therewith; many have I heard of, and with some have I talked myself, that have been sore cumbered[512] with that temptation; and marked have I not a little the manner of them.

VINCENT: I require[513] you, good Uncle, show me somewhat of such things as you perceive therein.

For first, where[514] you call this kind of temptation the daughter of pusillanimity and thereby so near of sib[515] unto the night's fear, methinketh on the other

---

494 makes it his practice   495 suitable, qualified   496 name   497 symptoms   498 suffering   499 profession   500 greatly, intensely, grievously   501 medical science

502 whoever   503 being present in   504 *doubt to acquiet:* hesitate to calm or acquit   505 *that that:* that which   506 bidden   507 large shield   508 explained   509 however   510 *and*

else God: if God does not   511 *in conclusion:* in the end, at last   512 *sore cumbered:* terribly burdened   513 ask   514 whereas   515 *near of sib:* closely akin

side that it is rather a thing that cometh of a great courage and boldness when they dare their[516] own hands put themselves to death, from which we see almost every man shrink and flee, and that[517] many such as we know by good proof and plain experience for men of great heart and excellent hardy courage.

ANTONY: I said, Cousin Vincent, that of pusillanimity cometh this temptation—and very truth it is that indeed so it doth—but I meant it not that of only faint heart and fear it cometh and groweth always; for the devil tempteth sundry folks by sundry ways. But the cause wherefore I spoke of none other kind of that temptation than of only that which is the daughter that the devil begetteth upon pusillanimity was for that that[518] those other kinds of that temptation fall not under the nature of tribulation and fear, and therefore fall they far out[519] of our matter here, and are such temptations as only need counsel and not comfort or consolation, for that the persons therewith tempted be with that kind of temptation not troubled in their mind, but verily well content both in the tempting and following. For some hath there been, Cousin, such that they have been tempted thereto by means of a foolish pride, and some by the means of anger, without any dread at all, and very glad to go thereto; to this I say not nay. But where you ween that none fall thereto by fear, but that they have all a strong mighty stomach[520]—that shall ye well see the contrary, and that peradventure in those of whom you would ween the stomach most strong and their heart and courage most hardy.

VINCENT: Yet is it marvel unto me that it should be as you say it is: that this temptation is unto them that do it for pride or for anger no tribulation, nor that they should need in so great a distress, and peril both of body and soul to be lost, no manner of good ghostly[521] comfort.

ANTONY: Let us therefore, Cousin, consider an example or two, for thereby shall we the better perceive it.

There was here in Buda, in King Ladislaus's[522]

days, a good poor honest man's wife. This woman was so fiendish that the devil, perceiving her nature, put her in the mind that she should anger her husband so sore that she might give him occasion to kill her, and then should he be hanged for her.

VINCENT: This was a strange temptation indeed—what the devil should she be the better then?

ANTONY: Nothing, but that it eased her shrewd stomach[523] before to think that her husband should be hanged after. And peradventure if you look about the world and consider it well, you shall find more such stomachs than a few. Have you never heard no furious body plainly say that to see some such man have a mischief,[524] he would with good will be content to lie as long in hell as God liveth in heaven?

VINCENT: Forsooth,[525] and some such have I heard of.

ANTONY: This mind of his was not much less mad than hers, but rather, haply,[526] the more mad of the twain; for the woman peradventure did not cast so far[527] peril therein. But to tell you now to what good pass[528] the charitable purpose came: as her husband (the man was a carpenter) stood hewing with his chip-axe upon a piece of timber, she began, after[529] her old guise,[530] so to revile him that the man waxed wroth[531] at last, and bade her get her in or he would lay the helm[532] of his axe about her back, and said also that it were little sin even with that axe-head to chop off that unhappy head of hers that carried such an ungracious tongue therein. At that word the devil took his time and whetted her tongue against her teeth; and when it was well sharped, she swore to him in very fierce anger, "By the Mass, whoreson husband, I would thou wouldst; here lieth mine head, lo"—and therewith, down she laid her head upon the same timber log—"if thou smite it not off, I beshrew[533] thine whoreson heart"; with that, likewise as[534] the devil stood at her elbow, so stood (as I heard say) his good angel at his, and gave him ghostly[535] courage, and bade him be bold and do it. And so the good man up with his chip-axe and at a

516 with their   **517** of those (who put themselves to death)   **518** *for that that:* because   **519** outside   **520** spirit, courage   **521** spiritual   **522** *King Ladislaus's:* St. Ladislaus I was King   of Hungary 1077–95.   **523** *shrewd stomach:* malicious disposition   **524** *have a mischief:* suffer a misfortune   **525** In truth   **526** perhaps   **527** *cast so far:* imagine so much   **528** outcome   **529** according to   **530** habit   **531** *waxed wroth:* grew irate   **532** flat side   **533** curse   **534** *likewise as:* just as if   **535** spiritual

chop chopped off her head indeed. There were standing other folk by, which had a good sport to hear her chide, but little they looked for this chance till it was done, ere they could let[536] it. They said they heard
5 her tongue babble in her head and call "Whoreson! Whoreson!" twice after that the head was from the body. At the leastwise, afterward unto the king thus they reported, all except only one — and that was a woman, and she said that she heard it not.

10 **VINCENT:** Forsooth, this was a wonderful work. What became, Uncle, of the man?

ANTONY: The king gave him his pardon.

VINCENT: Verily, he might in conscience do no less.

ANTONY: But then was further,[537] almost, at an-
15 other point: that there should have been a statute made that in such case there should never after pardon be granted, but, the truth being able to be proved, none husband should need any pardon, but should have leave by the law to follow the example
20 of the carpenter and do the same.

VINCENT: How happed it, Uncle, that that good law was left unmade?

ANTONY: How happed it? As it happeth, Cousin, that many more be left unmade as well as it, and
25 within a little as good as it too, both here and in other countries, and sometimes some worse made in their stead.[538] But as they say, the let[539] of that law was the queen's grace (God forgive her soul). It was the greatest thing, I ween, good lady, that she had to
30 answer for when she died. For surely, save[540] for that one thing, she was a full blessed woman.

But letting now that law pass, this temptation in procuring her own death was unto this carpenter's wife no tribulation at all, as far as ever men could
35 perceive: for it liked her well to think thereon, and she even longed therefor. And therefore if she had told you or me before her mind, and that she would so fain[541] bring it so to pass, we could have had none occasion to comfort her as one that were in tribula-
40 tion; but, marry,[542] counsel her (as I told you before)

we might, to refrain and amend that malicious devilish mind.

VINCENT: Verily, that is truth; but such as are well willing to do any purpose that is so shameful will never tell their mind to nobody, for very shame.   45

ANTONY: Some will not indeed; and yet are there some again that, be their intent never so shameful, find some yet whom their heart serveth[543] them to make of their counsel[544] therein. Some of my own folk here can tell you that no longer ago than even   50 yesterday, one that came out of Vienna showed us, among other talking, that a rich widow (but I forgot to ask him where it happed), having all her life a high proud mind[545] and a fell[546] (as those two virtues are wont[547] always to keep company together), was   55 at debate with another neighbor of hers in the town. And on a time[548] she made of her counsel a poor neighbor of hers, whom she thought for money she might induce to follow her mind.[549] With him she secretly broke[550] and offered him ten ducats for his   60 labor to do so much for her as in a morning, early, to come to her house, and with an axe — unknown, privily — strike off her head; and when he had so done, then convey the bloody axe into the house of him with whom she was at debate,[551] in some such   65 manner wise[552] as it might be thought that he had murdered her for malice; and then she thought she should be taken for a martyr. And yet had she further devised that another sum of money should after be sent to Rome, and there should be means made   70 to the Pope that she might in all haste be canonized.

This poor man promised, but intended not to perform it; howbeit, when he deferred it, she provided the axe herself, and he appointed[553] with her the morning when he should come and do it; and there-   75 upon, into her house he came. But then set he such other folk as he would should[554] know her frantic fantasy in such place appointed as they might well hear her and him talk together. And after that he had talked with her thereof what he would, so much as   80 he thought was enough, he made her lie down and took up the axe in his one hand, and with the other hand he felt the edge and found a fault, that it was not sharp, and that therefore he would in no wise

---

536 prevent   **537** *was … further:* was the matter developed further   **538** place   **539** prevention   **540** except   **541** willingly   **542** indeed   **543** allows

544 *make of their counsel:* take into their confidence   **545** disposition   **546** cruel   **547** accustomed   **548** *on a time:* one day   **549** purpose, intention   **550** disclosed

her thoughts   **551** strife, variance   **552** *manner wise:* kind of way   **553** agreed   **554** *would should:* wanted to

do it till he had grounden it sharper: he could not else, he said, for pity; it would put her to so much pain. And so, full sore[555] against her will, for that time she kept her head still; but because she would no more suffer any more deceive[556] her so, and feed her forth[557] with delays, ere it was very long after, she hanged herself with her own hands.

VINCENT: Forsooth, here was a tragical story whereof I never heard the like.

ANTONY: Forsooth, the party that told it me swore that he knew it for a truth. And himself is, I promise you, such as I reckon for right honest and of substantial truth.

Now here she letted not,[558] as shameful a mind as she had, to make one of her counsel yet — and yet, as I remember, another too, whom she trusted with the money that should procure her canonization.

And here I wot well that her temptation came not of fear, but of high malice and pride. But then was she so glad in the pleasant device thereof that, as I showed you, she took it for no tribulation, and therefore comforting of her could have no place; but if men should anything give her toward her help, it must have been, as I told you, good counsel. And therefore, as I said, this kind of temptation to a man's own destruction — which requireth[559] counsel, and is out[560] of tribulation — was out of our matter, that is to treat of comfort in tribulation.

THE SIXTEENTH CHAPTER
Of him that were moved to kill himself by illusion of the devil, which he reckoneth for a revelation

ANTONY: But lest you might reject both these examples, weening they were but feigned tales, I shall put you in remembrance of one which I reckon yourself have read in the *Collations* of Cassian[561] — and if you have not, there may you soon find it. For myself have half forgotten the thing, it is so long since I read it; but thus much I remember: that he telleth there of one that was many days a very special holy man in his living, and among the other virtuous monks and anchors[562] that lived there in wilderness was marvelously much esteemed, saving that some were not all out of fear of him[563] lest his "revelations," whereof he told many by himself, would prove illusions of the devil. And so proved it after indeed. For the man was by the devil's subtle suggestions brought into such a high spiritual pride that in conclusion[564] the devil brought him to that horrible point that he made him go kill himself. And (as far as my mind giveth me now, without new sight of the book) he brought him to it by this persuasion: that he made him believe that it was God's will he should so do, and that thereby should he go straight to heaven.

And then, if it were by that persuasion with which he took very great comfort in his own mind himself, then was it, as I said, out of our case, and needed not comfort, but counsel against giving credence to the devil's persuasion.

But marry,[565] if he made him first perceive how he had been deluded, and then tempted him to his own death by shame and by despair, then was it within our matter, lo; for then was his temptation fallen down from pride to pusillanimity, and was waxen[566] that kind of the "night's fear" that I spoke of, wherein a good part of the counsel that were to be given him should have need to stand in[567] good comforting. For then was he brought into right sore[568] tribulation.

But as I was about to tell you, strength of heart and courage is there none therein, not only for that very[569] strength, as it hath the name of virtue in a reasonable creature, can never be without prudence, but also for that, as I said, even in them that seem men of most hardiness it shall well appear — to them that well weigh the matter — that the mind whereby they be led to destroy themselves groweth of pusillanimity and very foolish fear.

Take for the example Cato Uticensis,[570] which in Africa killed himself after the great victory[571] that Julius Caesar had. Saint Augustine well declareth in his work *De civitate Dei*[572] that there was no strength nor magnanimity therein, but plain pusillanimity

---

555 *full sore:* very greatly **556** *suffer…deceive:* allow anyone to deceive **557** *feed her forth:* string her along **558** *letted not:* hesitated not **559** calls for **560** outside **561** See St. John Cassian, *Collationes* 2.5.

562 hermits, anchorites **563** *all…him:* entirely free of apprehension about him **564** *in conclusion:* in the end, at last **565** indeed **566** become **567** *stand in:* consist in **568** *right sore:* very great

or grievous **569** *for that very :* because true **570** *Cato Uticensis:* Cato the Younger (95–46 BC), a Stoic statesman **571** *great victory:* the Battle of Thapsus, April 6, 46 BC **572** See *City of God* 1.23.

and impotency of stomach,[573] whereby he was forced to the destruction of himself because his heart was too feeble for to bear the beholding of another man's glory, or the suffering of other worldly
5 calamities that he feared should fall on himself. So that, as Saint Augustine well proveth, that horrible deed is none act of strength, but an act of a mind either drawn from the consideration of itself with some devilish fantasy, wherein the man hath
10 need to be called home by good counsel, or else oppressed by faint heart and fear, wherein a good part of the counsel must stand in lifting up his courage with good consolation and comfort.

And therefore, if we found any such religious per-
15 son,[574] as was that father which Cassian writeth of, that were of such austerity and apparent ghostly[575] living that he were with such as well knew him reputed for a man of singular virtue, and that it were perceived that he had many strange visions ap-
20 pearing unto him, if it should now be perceived after that that the man went about secretly to destroy himself, whoso[576] should hap to come to the knowledge thereof, and intended to do his devoir in the let,[577] first must he find the means to search
25 and find out whether the man be in his manner and his countenance lightsome,[578] glad, and joyful, or dumpish,[579] heavy, and sad, and whether he go thereabout as one that were full of the glad hope of heaven, or as one that had his breast farced[580] full of
30 tediousness and weariness of the world. If he were found in the first fashion, it were a token that the devil hath by his fantastical apparitions puffed him up in such a peevish[581] pride that he hath finally persuaded him, by some illusion showed him for the
35 proof, that God's pleasure is that he shall for his[582] sake with his own hands kill himself.

VINCENT: Now, if a man so found it, Uncle, what counsel should a man give him then?

ANTONY: That were somewhat out[583] of our pur-
40 pose, Cousin, since, as I told you before, the man were not then in sorrow and tribulation—whereof

our matter speaketh[584]—but in a perilous merry mortal temptation, so that if we should, besides our own matter that we have in hand, enter into that too, we might make a longer work between them
45 both than we could well finish this day. Howbeit, to be short, it is soon seen that therein the sum and the effect of the counsel must in manner rest[585] in giving him warning of the devil's sleights;[586] and that must be done under such sweet pleasant manner
50 as the man should not abhor to hear it; for while it could lightly be none other but[587] that the man were rocked and sung asleep by the devil's craft, and his mind occupied, as it were, in a delectable dream, he should never have good audience for him
55 that[588] would rudely and boistously shog[589] him and wake him, and so shake him out thereof. Therefore must you fair and easily touch him, and with some pleasant speech awake him, so that he wax not wayward,[590] as children do that are waked ere they list
60 to rise.[591]

But when a man hath first begun with his praise (for if he be proud ye shall much better please him with a commendation than with a dirge), then, after favor won therewithal, a man may a little and lit-
65 tle insinuate[592] the doubt of such revelations—not at the first as[593] it were for any doubt of his,[594] but of some other's that men in some other places talk of. And peradventure it shall not miscontent himself to show[595] great perils that may fall therein in
70 another man's case than his own, and shall begin to preach upon it.

Or if you were a man that had not so very great scrupulous conscience of a harmless lie devised to do good withal—which kind Saint Augustine,[596]
75 though he take always for sin, yet he taketh but for venial, and Saint Jerome[597] (as by diverse places in his books appeareth) taketh not fully for so much—then may you feign some secret friend of yours to be in such case, and that yourself somewhat
80 fear his peril, and have made, of charity, this voyage[598] for his sake, to ask this good father's counsel. And in that communication, upon these words of Saint John, *Nolite omni spiritui credere, sed probate*

---

573 spirit, courage 574 *religious person:* person belonging to a religious order 575 spiritual 576 whoever 577 *devoir in the let:* utmost toward the prevention 578 lighthearted 579 down in the dumps 580 stuffed 581 foolish, silly 582 i.e., God's 583 outside 584 *whereof our matter speaketh:* which is what our

discussion is about 585 *in manner rest:* basically consist 586 cunning tricks 587 *lightly ... but:* hardly be otherwise than 588 *should ... that:* would never listen well to anyone 589 *boistously shog:* roughly shake 590 *wax not wayward:* not become recalcitrant 591 *ere ... rise:* before they want to get up 592 *a little*

and little insinuate: little by little bring up indirectly 593 as if 594 his revelations 595 *peradventure ... show:* perhaps he himself will not be unwilling to point out 596 See *On Lying* 24.25. 597 See *Commentary on the Epistle to the Galatians* 1.2. 598 undertaking

spiritus, si ex Deo sint ("Give not credence to every spirit, but prove[599] the spirits, whether they be of God"),[600] and these words of Saint Paul, *Angelus Satanae transfigurat se in angelum lucis* ("The angel of Satan transfigureth himself into the angel of light"),[601] you shall take occasion—the better if they hap to come in on his side; but yet not lack occasion neither if those texts, for lack of his offer, come in upon your own—occasion, I say, you shall not lack to inquire by what sure and undeceivable[602] tokens a man may discern the true revelations from the false illusions; whereof a man shall find many, both here and there in diverse other authors, and whole together diverse goodly treatises of that good godly doctor Master John Gerson entitled *De probatione spirituum*[603]—as whether the party be naturalwise, or anything seem fantastical, or whether the party be poor-spirited or proud (which will somewhat appear by his delight in his own praise), or, if of wiliness or of another pride for to[604] be praised of humility, he refuse to hear thereof yet[605] any little fault found in himself, or diffidence declared and mistrust of his own revelations and doubtful tokens told, wherefore himself should fear lest they be the devil's illusions—such things, as Master Gerson saith,[606] will make him spit out somewhat of his spirit if the devil lie in his breast.

Or if the devil be yet so subtle that he keep himself close[607] in his warm den, and blow out never a hot word, yet is it to be considered what end his revelations draw to: whether to any spiritual profit to himself or other folk, or only to vain marvels and wonders.

Also whether they withdraw him from such other good virtuous business as by the common rules of Christendom, or any rules of his profession, he was wont[608] to use or were bound to be occupied in.

Or whether he fall into any singularity of opinions against the Scripture of God, or against the common faith of Christ's Catholic Church.

Many other tokens are there in that work of Master Gerson spoken of to consider by whether the person—never having revelations of God nor illusions from the devil—do, either for winning of money or worldly favor, feign[609] his revelations himself and delude the people withal.[610] But now for our purpose: if among any of the marks by which the true revelations may be known from false illusions, that man himself bring forth for one mark the doing or teaching of anything against the Scripture of God or the common faith of the Church, then have you an entry made you by which, when you list,[611] you may enter into the special matter, wherein he can never well flit from you.

Or else may you yet, if you list, feign that your secret friend (for whose sake you come to him for counsel) is brought in that mind by a certain apparition showed unto him—as himself saith, by an angel; as you fear, by the devil—that he can be by you none otherwise persuaded as yet but that the pleasure of God is that he shall go kill himself, and that if he so do, then shall he be thereby so specially participant of Christ's Passion that he shall forthwith[612] be carried up with angels into heaven. For which is he so joyful that he firmly purposeth upon[613] it, no less glad to do it than another man would be glad to avoid it. And therefore may you desire his good counsel to instruct you with some substantial good advice wherewith you may turn him from this error, that he be not, under hope of God's true revelation, in body and soul destroyed by the devil's false illusion.

If he will in this thing study[614] and labor to instruct you, the things that himself shall find of his own invention, though they be less effectual, shall peradventure more work with himself toward his own amendment—since he shall of likelihood better like them—than shall double so substantial told him by another man.

If he be loath to think upon that side, and therefore shrink from the matter, then is there none other way but adventure,[615] after[616] the plain fashion, to fall into the matter and show what you hear, and to give him counsel and exhortation to the contrary—but if you list[617] to say that thus and thus hath the matter been reasoned already between your friend and you. And therein may you rehearse[618] such things as should prove that the vision which moveth him is no true revelation, but a very false illusion.

599 test   **600** 1 Jn 4:1   **601** 2 Cor 11:14   **602** incapable of deceiving; certain   **603** *De probatione spirituum: On the Testing of Spirits*   **604** *for to:* in order to   **605** even   **606** *Gerson saith:* See *On the Testing of Spirits* 3.39.   **607** concealed   **608** accustomed   **609** pretend   **610** with them   **611** choose, please, wish   **612** immediately   **613** *purposeth upon:* intends   **614** strive, seek   **615** to venture   **616** according to, following   **617** *but if . . . list:* unless you wish   **618** relate

VINCENT: Verily, Uncle, I well allow this: that a man should, as well in this thing as every other wherein he longeth to do another man good, seek such a pleasant way as the party should be likely to like, or at the leastwise, well to take in worth[619] his communication, and not so to enter in thereunto as he whom he would help should abhor him and be loath to hear him, and therefore take no profit by him. But now, Uncle, if it come, by the one way or the other, to the point that hear me he will or shall, what be the reasons effectual with which I should by my counsel convert him?

ANTONY: All those by which you may make him perceive that himself is deceived, and that his visions be no godly revelations, but very devilish illusions. And those reasons must you gather of the man, of the matter, and of the law of God, or of some one of these. Of the man, if you can peradventure show him that in such a point or such he is waxen worse, since such revelations have haunted him, than he was before — as in those that are deluded, whoso be well acquainted with them shall well mark and perceive: for they wax more proud, more wayward, more envious, suspicious, misjudging and depraving[620] other men, with the delight of their own praise and such other spiritual vices of the soul.

Of the matter may you gather if it have happed his revelations before to prove false, or that they be things rather strange than profitable, for that is a good mark between God's miracles and the devil's wonders; for Christ and his saints have their miracles always tending to fruit and profit; the devil and his witches and necromancers, all their wonderful works draw to no fruitful end, but to a fruitless ostentation and show, as[621] it were a juggler that would, for a show before the people, play masteries[622] at a feast.

Of the law of God you must draw your reasons in showing by the Scripture that the thing which he weeneth God by his angel biddeth, God hath his own mouth forbidden. And that is, you wot well, in the case that we speak of, so easy to find that I need not to rehearse it to you, since there is plain among the commandments forbidden the unlawful killing of any man — and therefore of himself (as Saint Augustine saith,[623] and all the Church teacheth), except[624] himself be no man.

VINCENT: This is very true, good Uncle, nor I will not dispute upon any glossing[625] of that prohibition; but since we find not the contrary, but that God may dispense with that commandment himself, and both license and command also, if himself list,[626] any man to go kill either another man or himself either, this man that is now by such a marvelous vision induced to believe that God so biddeth him, and therefore thinketh himself, in that case, of that prohibition discharged, and charged with the contrary commandment, with what reason may we make him perceive that his vision is but an illusion and not a true revelation?

ANTONY: Nay, Cousin Vincent, ye shall in this case not need to require[627] those reasons of me, but, taking the Scripture of God for a ground for this matter, you know very well yourself you shall go somewhat a shorter way to work if you ask this question of him: that since God hath once forbidden the thing himself, though he may dispense therewith if he will, yet since the devil may feign himself God, and with a marvelous vision delude one and make as though God did it, and since the devil is also more likely to speak against God's commandment than God against his own, you shall have good cause, I say, to demand of the man himself whereby he knoweth that his vision is God's true revelation and not the devil's false delusion.

VINCENT: Indeed, Uncle, I think that would be a hard question to him. May a man, Uncle, have in such a thing even a very sure knowledge of his own mind?

ANTONY: Yea, Cousin, God may cast into the mind of man, I suppose, such an inward light of understanding that he cannot fail but be sure thereof. And yet he that is deluded by the devil may think himself as sure, and yet be deceived indeed. And such a difference is there, in a manner,[628] between them as is between the sight of a thing while we be waking and look thereon and the sight with

---

619 *in worth:* as valuable   **620** disparaging, vilifying   **621** as if   **622** magic tricks   **623** See *City of God* 1.20.   **624** unless   **625** explaining away   **626** chooses, wishes   **627** ask   **628** *in a manner:* so to speak; very nearly

which we see a thing in our sleep while we dream thereof.

VINCENT: This is a pretty[629] similitude, Uncle, in this thing; and then is it easy for the monk that we speak of to declare how he knoweth his vision for a true revelation and not a false delusion, if there be so great difference between them.

ANTONY: Not so easy, Cousin, as you ween it were. For how can you now prove unto me that you be awake?

VINCENT: Marry, lo, do I not now wag my hand, shake my head, and stamp with my foot here in the floor?

ANTONY: Have you never dreamed ere this that you have done the same?

VINCENT: Yes, that have I, and more too than that; for I have ere this in my sleep dreamed that I doubted whether I were asleep or awake, and have, in good faith, thought that I did thereupon even the same things that I do now indeed, and thereby determined that I was not asleep. And yet have I dreamed, in good faith, further that I have been afterward at dinner, and there, making merry with good company, have told the same dream at the table, and laughed well thereat, that while I was asleep, I had, by such means of moving the parts of my body and considering thereof, so verily thought myself waking.

ANTONY: And will you not now soon, trow you,[630] when you wake and rise, laugh as well at yourself when you see that you lie now in your warm bed asleep again, and dream all this time while you ween so verily that you be waking and talking of these matters with me?

VINCENT: God's Lord, Uncle, you go now merrily to work with me indeed when you look and speak so sadly,[631] and would make me ween I were asleep.

ANTONY: It may be that you be so; for anything that you can say or do whereby you may, with any reason that you make, drive me to confess that yourself be sure of the contrary, since you can do nor say nothing now whereby you be sure to be waking but that you have ere this, or hereafter may, think yourself as surely to do the selfsame things indeed while you be all the while asleep, and nothing do but lie dreaming.

VINCENT: Well, well, Uncle, though I have ere this thought myself awake while I was indeed asleep, yet for[632] all that, this I know well enough: that I am awake now—and so do you too, though I cannot find the words by which I may with reason force you to confess it but that always you may drive me off by the example of my dream.

ANTONY: This is, Cousin, as meseemeth,[633] very true. And likewise seemeth me the manner and difference between some kinds of true revelations and some kinds of false illusions as it standeth between the things that are done waking and the things that in our dreams seem to be done while we be sleeping: that is to wit, that he which hath that kind of revelation from God is as sure of the truth as we be of our own deed while we be waking, and he that is illuded[634] by the devil is in such wise deceived, and worse too, than be they by their dream, and yet reckoneth for the time himself as sure as the other, saving[635] that the one falsely weeneth, the other truly knoweth.

But I say not, Cousin, that this kind of sure knowledge cometh in every kind of revelation, for there are many kinds—whereof were too long to talk now, but I say that God doth or may do to man in some thing certainly send some such.

VINCENT: Yet then may this religious man of whom we speak, when I show him the Scripture against his revelation, and therefore call it an illusion, bid me, with reason, go care for myself. For he knoweth well and surely himself that his revelation is very good and true and not any false illusion, since, for all the general commandment of God in the Scripture, God may dispense where he will and when he will, and may command him to do the contrary, as he commanded Abraham to kill his own son,[636] and as Samson had, by inspiration of God, commandment to kill himself with pulling down the house upon his own head at the feast of the Philistines.[637]

5   Now, if I would then do as you bade me right now—tell him that such apparitions may be illusions, and since God's word is in the Scripture against him plain for the prohibition, he must prove me the truth of his revelation, whereby that I may know it is not a false illusion—then shall he bid me 10 again[638] tell him whereby that I can prove myself to be awake and talk with him and not to be asleep and dream so, since in my dream I may as surely ween so as I know that I do so. And thus shall he drive me to the same bay[639] to which I would bring him.

15   **ANTONY:** This is well said, Cousin, but yet could he not escape you so. For the dispensation of God's common precept—which dispensation he must say that he hath by his private revelation—is a thing of such sort as showeth itself naught[640] and false. For 20 it never hath had any example like, since the world began unto now, that ever man hath read or heard of among faithful people commended.

First, in Abraham, touching the death of his son: God intended it not, but only tempted the toward- 25 ness[641] of the father's obedience. In Samson, all men make not the matter very sure whether he be saved or not, but yet therein some matter appeareth. For the Philistines being enemies to God, and using Samson for their mocking-stock[642] in scorn of 30 God, it is well likely that God gave him the mind to bestow his own life upon the revenging of the displeasure that those blasphemous Philistines did unto God. And that appeareth meetly[643] clear by this: that though his strength failed him when he 35 wanted his hair, yet had he not, as it seemeth, that strength evermore at hand while he had his hair, but at such times as it pleased God to give it him; which thing appeareth by these words that the Scripture (in some place) of that matter saith: *Irruit virtus* 40 *Domini in Samsonem* ("The power or might of God rushed into Samson").[644] And so, therefore, while this thing that he did, in the pulling down of the house, was done by the special gift of strength then at that point given him by God, it well declareth

that the strength of God, and therewith the Spirit 45 of God, entered into him therefor.

Saint Augustine also rehearseth[645] that certain holy virtuous virgins in time of persecution, being by God's enemious[646] infidels pursued upon to be deflowered by force, ran into a water and drowned 50 themselves rather than they would be bereaved of their virginity. And albeit that he thinketh it is not lawful for any other maid to follow their example— but rather suffer other[647] to do her any manner violence by force, and commit sin of his own upon 55 her against her will, than willingly, and thereby sinfully, herself become a homicide of herself—yet he thinketh that in them it happed by the special instinct[648] of the Spirit of God that, for causes seen unto himself, would rather that they should avoid it 60 with their own temporal death than abide the defiling and violation of their chastity.[649]

But now this good man neither hath any of God's enemies to be by his own death revenged on, nor any woman that violently pursue him by force to 65 bereave him of his virginity; nor never find we that God proved[650] any man's obedient mind by the commandment of his own slaughter of himself; therefore is his case both plain against God's open precept, and the dispensation strange and without 70 example, no cause appearing or well imaginable but if he would think that he could neither any longer live without him nor take him to him in such wise as he doth other men, but command him to come by a forbidden way, by which without other cause 75 we never heard that ever he bade[651] any man else before.

Now whether you think, if you should after this bid him tell you by what way he knoweth that his intent riseth upon a true revelation and not upon 80 a false illusion, he would bid you then again[652] tell him by what means you know that you be talking with him well waking[653] and not dream it sleeping, you may tell him again that men thus to talk together as you do, and in such manner wise,[654] and to 85 prove and perceive that they so do by the moving of themselves, with putting the question thereof unto themselves for their pleasure, and the marking and considering thereof, is in waking a daily common

---

637 See Jgs 16:23–30.   **638** in reply, in return   **639** situation with no way out   **640** wicked   **641** *tempted … towardness:* tested the willingness   **642** laughingstock

643 suitably   **644** See Jgs 14:6, 15:14.   **645** relates   **646** hostile   **647** another   **648** prompting   **649** See *City of God* 1.25–26.   **650** tested   **651** commanded

652 in return   **653** *well waking:* while you're fully awake   **654** *manner wise:* kinds of ways

thing that every man doth or may do when he will; and when they do it, they do it but of[655] pleasure; but in sleep it happeth very seldom that men dream they so do, nor in the dream never put the question but for doubt. And therefore it is more reason[656] that since his revelation is such also as happeth so seldom, and ofter[657] happeth that men dream of such than have such indeed—therefore it is more reason, you may tell him, that he show you whereby he knoweth in such a rare thing, and a thing more like a dream, that himself is not asleep, than you, in such a common thing among folk that are waking, and so seldom happing in a dream, should need to show him whereby you know that you be not asleep.

Besides this, himself, to whom you should show it, seeth and perceiveth the thing that he would bid you prove; but the thing that he would make you believe—the truth of his revelation, which you bid him prove—you see not, he wotteth[658] well himself. And therefore, ere you believe it against the Scripture, it were well consonant unto reason that he should show you whereby he knoweth it for a true waking revelation, and not a false dreaming delusion.

Vincent: Then shall he peradventure say to me again that whether I believe him or not maketh him no matter; the thing toucheth himself and not me, and himself is in himself as sure that it is a true revelation as that he can tell that he dreameth not but talketh with me waking.

Antony: Without doubt, Cousin, if he abide[659] at that point, and can be by no reason brought to do so much as doubt, nor can by no means be shogged[660] out of his deep sleep, but will needs take his dream for a very truth and, as some by night rise and walk about their chamber in their sleep, will so rise and hang himself, I can then none other way see but either bind him fast in his bed, or else assay[661] whether that might hap to help him with which the common tale goeth that a carver's wife in such a frantic fantasy helped her husband, to whom, when he would upon a Good Friday needs have killed himself for Christ's sake as Christ was killed for him, she would not in vain plead against his mind,

but well and wisely put him in remembrance that if he would die for Christ as Christ did for him, it were then convenient[662] for him to die even after the same fashion, and that might not be by his own hands, but by the hand of some other; for Christ, pardie,[663] killed not himself.

And because her husband should need to make no more of counsel[664] (for that would he not in no wise), she offered him that, for God's sake, she would secretly crucify him herself, upon a great cross that he had made to nail a new-carved crucifix upon; whereof when he was very glad, yet she bethought her that Christ was bounden to a pillar and beaten first, and after crowned with thorns; whereupon when she had by his own assent bound him fast[665] to a post, she left not beating, with holy exhortation to suffer, so much and so long that ere ever she left work and unbound him—praying[666] nevertheless that she might put on his head, and drive it well down, a crown of thorns that she had wreathen[667] for him and brought him—he said he thought this was enough for that year; he would pray God forbear[668] him of the remnant till Good Friday come again; but when it came again the next year, then was his lust[669] passed; he longed to follow Christ no farther.

Vincent: Indeed, Uncle, if this help him not, then will nothing help him, I trow.

Antony: And yet, Cousin, the devil may peradventure make him toward such a purpose first gladly to suffer other pain—yea, and diminish his feeling too therein—that he may thereby the less fear his death. And yet are peradventure sometimes such things, and many more, to be assayed;[670] for as the devil may hap to make him suffer, so may he hap to miss, namely[671] if his friends fall to prayer for him against his temptation—for that can himself never do while he taketh it for none. But for conclusion, if the man be surely proved so inflexibly set upon the purpose to destroy himself, as commanded thereto by God, that no good counsel that men can give him, nor any other thing that men may do to him, can refrain[672] him, but that he would surely shortly kill himself, then, except only good prayer by his friends made for him, I can find no further shift[673] but either have him ever in sight or bind him fast in his bed. And so must he needs of reason be content to be ordered. For though himself take his fantasy for a true revelation, yet since he cannot make us perceive it for such, likewise as he thinketh himself by his secret commandment bounden to follow it, so must he needs agree that, since it is against the plain open prohibition of God, we be by the plain open precept bounden to keep him from it.

VINCENT: In this point, Uncle, I can go no further. But now, if he were, upon the other side,[674] perceived to mind[675] his destruction and go thereabout with heaviness of heart and thought and dullness, what way were there to be used to him then?

ANTONY: Then were his temptation, as I told you before, properly pertaining to our matter, for then were he in a sore tribulation, and a very perilous; for then were it a token that the devil had either, by bringing him into some great sin, brought him in despair, or—peradventure by his revelations founden false and reproved, or by some secret sin of his deprehended[676] and divulged—cast him both in despair of heaven through fear and in a weariness of this life for shame, since he seeth his estimation lost among other folk, of whose praise he was wont to be proud. And therefore, Cousin, in such case as this is, the man is to be fair handled, and sweetly, and with douce[677] and tender loving words to be put in good courage and comfort in all that men goodly[678] may.

Here must they put him in mind that if he despair not, but pull up his courage and trust in God's great mercy, he shall have in conclusion great cause to be glad of this fall. For before, he stood in greater peril than he was aware of, while he took himself for better than he was. And God, for favor that he beareth him, hath suffered him to fall deep into the devil's danger to make him thereby know what he was while he took himself for so sure.[679] And therefore, as he suffered[680] him then to fall for a remedy against overbold pride, so will God now—if the man meek[681] himself, not with fruitless despair, but

with fruitful penance—so set him up again upon his feet, and so strengthen him with his grace, that for this one fall that the devil hath given him, he shall give the devil a hundred. And here must he be put in remembrance of Mary Magdalene, of the prophet David, and specially of Saint Peter, whose high bold courage took a foul fall; and yet, because he despaired not of God's mercy, but wept and called upon it, how highly God took him into his favor again in his Holy Scripture is well testified, and well through Christendom known.

And now shall it be charitably done if some good virtuous folk—such as himself somewhat esteemeth, and hath afore longed to stand in estimation with[682]—do resort sometimes unto him,[683] not only to give him counsel, but also to ask advice and counsel of him in some cases[684] of their own conscience, to let him thereby perceive that they no less esteem him now, but rather, more than they did before, since they think him now, by his fall, better expert of the devil's craft, and thereby not only better instructed himself, but also better able to give good advice and counsel unto others. This thing will, in my mind, well amend and lift up his courage from the peril of that desperate shame.

VINCENT: Methink, Uncle, that this were a perilous thing; for it may peradventure make him set the less by[685] his fall, and thereby cast him into his first pride or into his other sin again, the falling whereinto drove him into this despair.

ANTONY: I do not mean, Cousin, that every fool should at adventure[686] fall in hand with him; for so, lo, might it hap for to do harm indeed. But, Cousin, if a cunning physician have a man in hand, he can well discern when and how long some certain medicine is necessary, which at another time ministered, or at that time overlong continued, might put the patient to peril.

If he have his patient in an ague,[687] to the cure whereof he needeth his medicines in their working cold, yet if he hap ere that fever be full cured to fall into some such other disease as, except it were helped with hot medicines, were likely to kill the body before the fever could be cured, he would

---

673 expedient **674** hand **675** be troubled by **676** discovered **677** soothing, sweet **678** rightly, properly; gently, kindly **679** secure **680** allowed

681 humble, abase **682** *stand . . . with:* be respected by **683** *resort sometime unto him:* come see him sometimes **684** *in some cases:* about some matters **685** *set*

the less by: be less concerned about; make less of **686** random **687** an illness involving fever

for the while have his most care to the cure of that thing wherein were most present peril, and when that were once out of jeopardy, do then the more exact diligence after about the further cure of the fever.

And likewise, if the ship were in peril to fall into Scylla, the fear of falling into Charybdis[688] on the other side shall never let[689] any wise master thereof to draw him from Scylla toward Charybdis first, in all that ever he may. But when he hath him once so far away from Scylla that he seeth him safely out of that danger, then will he begin to take good heed to keep him well from the other. And in like wise, while this man is falling down to despair, and to the final destruction of himself, a good wise spiritual leech[690] will first look unto that, and by good comfort lift up his courage, and when he seeth that peril well past, care for the cure of his other faults after. Howbeit, even in the giving of his comfort, he may find ways enough in such wise to temper his words that the man may take occasion of good courage, and yet far from occasion giving of new recidivation[691] into his former sin, since the great part of his counsel shall be to courage him to amendment — and that is, pardie, far from falling unto sin again.

VINCENT: I think, Uncle, that folk fall into this ungracious mind through the devil's temptation by many more ways than one.

ANTONY: That is, Cousin, very true, for the devil taketh his occasions as he seeth them fall meet[692] for him. Some he stirreth to it for weariness of themselves after some great loss; some for fear of horrible bodily harm; and some, as I said, for fear of worldly shame. One wist[693] I myself that had been long reputed for a right honest man, which was fallen in such a fantasy that he was well-near worn away therewith; but what he was tempted to do, that would he not tell no man; but he told unto me that he was sore cumbered,[694] and that it always ran in his mind that folks' fantasies were fallen from him,[695] and that they esteemed not his wit as they

were wont to do, but ever his mind gave[696] him that the people began to take him for a fool. And folk of truth nothing so did at all, but reputed him both for wise and honest.

Two others knew I that were marvelous feared[697] that they should kill themselves and could tell me no cause wherefore they so feared it, but only that their own mind so gave them; neither loss had they any had, nor no such thing toward[698] them, nor none occasion of any worldly shame — the one in body very well-liking and lusty[699] — but wondrous weary were they both twain[700] of that mind.[701] And always they thought that do it they would not, for nothing. And nevertheless, ever they feared they should, and wherefore they so feared, neither of them both could tell; and the one, lest he should do it, desired his friends to bind him.

VINCENT: This is, Uncle, a marvelous strange manner.

ANTONY: Forsooth,[702] Cousin, I suppose many of them are in this case. The devil, as I said before, seeketh his occasions; for as Saint Peter saith, *Adversarius vester diabolus quasi leo rugiens circuit quaerens quem devoret* ("Your adversary the devil as a roaring lion goeth about, seeking whom he may devour").[703] He marketh well therefore the state and condition that every man standeth in, not only concerning these outward things — lands, possessions, goods, authority, fame, favor, or hatred of the world — but also men's complexions[704] within them: health or sickness, good humors[705] or bad, by which they be lighthearted or lumpish,[706] strong-hearted or faint and feeble of spirit, bold and hardy or timorous and fearful of courage. And after, as these things minister[707] him matter of temptation, so useth he[708] himself in the manner of his temptation.

Now likewise as such folk as are full of young warm lusty blood and other humors exciting the flesh to filthy[709] voluptuous living, the devil useth[710] to make those things his instruments in tempting them and provoking them thereunto. And where he findeth

---

688 *Scylla, Charybdis:* a mythological monster living on one side of a narrow channel, and a whirlpool on the other side of that same narrow channel. See Homer, *Odyssey,* Book 12.   689 prevent   690 physician, healer   691 relapse   692 suitable, favorable   693 knew   694 *sore cumbered:* terribly burdened   695 *folks'… him:* people didn't like him anymore   696 misgave; led him to believe   697 afraid   698 threatening   699 healthy, strong, vigorous; handsome   700 together   701 *of that mind:* by that thinking, disposition   702 In truth   703 1 Pt 5:8   704 temperaments, constitutions   705 four internal mood-producing physical elements   706 lethargic, melancholy   707 supply   708 *useth he:* he conducts   709 base, disgraceful   710 is accustomed

some folk full of hot blood and choler,[711] he maketh those humors his instruments to set their heart on fire in wrath and fierce furious anger, so where he findeth some folk which through some dull melancholious[712] humors are naturally disposed to fear, he casteth sometimes such a fearful imagination in their mind that without help of God they can never cast it out of their heart. Some, at the sudden falling of some horrible thought into their mind, have not only had a great abomination thereat (which abomination they well and virtuously had thereat), but the devil, using their malicious humor — and thereby their natural inclination to fear — for his instrument, hath caused them to conceive therewith such a deep dread besides that they ween[713] themselves with that abominable thought to be fallen into such an outrageous sin that they be ready to fall into despair of grace, weening that God hath given them over forever, whereas that thought, were it never so horrible and never so abominable, is yet unto them that never like it, but ever still abhor it and strive still thereagainst, matter of conscience and merit, and not any sin at all.

Some have, with holding a knife in their hand, suddenly thought upon the killing of themselves, and forthwith[714] in devising what a horrible thing it were if they should mishap so to do, have fallen in a fear that they should so do indeed, and have, with long and often thinking thereon, imprinted that fear so sore[715] in their imagination that some of them have not after cast it off without great difficulty, and some could never in their life be rid thereof, but have after in conclusion[716] miserably done it indeed. But likewise as where the devil useth the blood of a man's own body toward his purpose in provoking him to lechery, the man must and doth with grace and wisdom resist it, so must that man do whose malicious humors the devil abuseth toward the casting of such a desperate dread into his heart.

VINCENT: I pray you, Uncle, what advice were to be given him in such case?

ANTONY: Surely methinketh his help standeth in two things: counsel and prayer. First, as concerning counsel, likewise as it may be that he hath two things that hold him in his temptation — that is to wit, some evil humors of his own body, and the cursed devil that abuseth them to his pernicious purpose — so must he need against them twain[717] the counsel of two manner of folk: that is to wit, physicians for the body and physicians for the soul. The bodily physician shall consider what abundance the man hath of those evil humors that the devil maketh his instrument in moving the man toward that fearful affection, and as well by diet convenient[718] and medicines meet therefor,[719] to resist them, as by purgations to disburden the body of them.

Nor let no man think strange that I would advise a man to take counsel of a physician for the body in such a spiritual passion.[720] For since the soul and the body be so knit and joined together that they both make between them one person, the distemperance[721] of either other[722] engendereth sometimes the distemperance of both twain.

And therefore, like[723] as I would advise every man in every sickness of the body be shriven[724] and seek of a good spiritual physician the sure health of his soul, which shall not only serve against peril that may peradventure further grow by that sickness than in the beginning men would ween were likely, but the comfort thereof and God's favor increasing therewith, shall also do the body good — for which cause the blessed apostle Saint James exhorteth men that they shall in their bodily sickness induce[725] the priests, and saith that it shall do them good both in body and soul[726] — so would I sometimes advise some men in some sickness of the soul, besides their spiritual leech,[727] take also some counsel of the physician for the body. Some that are wretchedly disposed and yet long to be more vicious than they be go to physicians and apothecaries[728] and inquire what things may serve to make them more lusty to their foul fleshly delight. And were it then any folly upon the other side, if he that feeleth himself against his will much moved unto such uncleanness should inquire of the physician what thing, without diminishing of his health, were meet for the diminishing of such foul fleshly motion?

Of spiritual counsel, the first is to be shriven, that by reason of his other sins the devil have not the more power upon him.

711 anger; one of the four humors
712 gloomy   **713** believe   **714** at once   **715** strongly, grievously   **716** *in conclusion:* in the end, at last   **717** both   **718** appropriate   **719** *meet therefor:* suitable for this   **720** affliction, suffering   **721** disordered condition   **722** *either other:* either the one or the other   **723** just   **724** *be shriven:* to be absolved of sins through confession   **725** bring in; summon   **726** See Jas 5:14–15.   **727** physician, healer   **728** pharmacists

VINCENT: I have heard some say, Uncle, that when such folk have been at shrift,[729] their temptation hath been the more breme[730] upon them than it was before.

5   **ANTONY:** That think I very well; but that is a special token that shrift is wholesome for them, while the devil is with that most wroth. You find in some places of the Gospel that the devil the person whom he possessed did most trouble[731] when he saw that Christ would cast him out. We must else let the 10 devil do what he will if we fear his anger, for with every good deed will he wax angry.

    Then is it in his shrift to be showed him that he not only feareth more than he needeth, but also feareth where he needeth not, and over[732] that is sorry of 15 that thing whereof, but if he will willingly turn his good into his harm, he hath more cause to be glad.

    First, if he have cause to fear, yet feareth he more than he needeth. For there is no devil so diligent to destroy him as God is to preserve him, nor no devil 20 so near him to do him harm as God is to do him good, nor all the devils in hell so strong to invade and assault him as God is to defend him, if he distrust him not but faithfully put his trust in him.

    He feareth also where he needeth not; for where 25 he dreadeth that he were out of God's favor because such horrible thoughts fall in his mind against his will, they be not imputed unto him. He is, finally, sad of that[733] he may be glad. For since he taketh such thoughts displeasantly and striveth and fight- 30 eth against them, he hath thereby a good token that he is in God's favor, and that God assisteth him and helpeth him, and may make himself sure that so will God never cease to do but if[734] himself fail and fall from him first. And over that, this conflict that he 35 hath against his temptation shall (if he will not fall where he need not) be an occasion of his merit, and of a right great reward in heaven; and the pain that he taketh therein shall for so much (as Master Gerson well showeth)[735] stand him in stead[736] of his pur- 40 gatory. The manner of the fight against this temptation must stand in three things: that is to wit, in resisting, and in contemning,[737] and in the invocation of help.

Resist must a man for his own part with reason, 45 considering what a folly it were to fall where he need not, while he is not driven to it in avoiding of any other pain, or in hope of winning any manner of pleasure, but contrariwise should by that pain lose everlasting life and fall into everlasting pain. 50 And if it were in avoiding of other great pain, yet could he void[738] none so great thereby as he should thereby fall into.

He must also consider that a great part of this temptation is in effect but the fear of his own fan- 55 tasy: the dread that he hath lest he shall once be driven to it, which thing he may be sure that (but if[739] himself will, of his own folly) all the devils in hell can never drive him to; but his own foolish imagination may. For likewise as some man going 60 over a high bridge waxeth so feared through his own fantasy that he falleth down indeed, which[740] were else able enough to pass over without any danger; and as some man shall upon such a bridge, if folk call upon him, "You fall! You fall!", fall with the 65 fantasy that he taketh thereof, which bridge, if folk looked merrily upon him and said, "There is no danger therein," he would pass over well enough, and would not let[741] to run thereon if[742] it were but a foot from the ground—thus fareth it in this temp- 70 tation. The devil findeth the man of his own fond[743] fantasy afeard, and then crieth he in the ear of his heart, "Thou fallest! Thou fallest!" and maketh the fond man afeard that he should at every foot fall indeed. And the devil so wearieth him with that con- 75 tinual fear (if he give the ear of his heart unto him) that at the last he withdraweth his mind from due remembrance of God, and then driveth him to that deadly mischief indeed. Therefore, like as against the vice of the flesh the victory standeth[744] not all whole 80 in the fight, but sometimes also in the flight (saving that it is indeed a part of a wise warrior's fight, to flee from his enemy's trains),[745] so must a man in this temptation too not only resist it always with reasoning thereagainst, but sometimes set it clear at right 85 nought[746] and cast it off when it cometh, and not once regard it so much as to vouchsafe[747] to think thereon. Some folk have been clearly[748] rid of such pestilent fantasies with very full contempt thereof,

729 *at shrift:* to confession   **730** fierce, raging   **731** *the devil . . . trouble:* the devil gave the most trouble to the person whom he possessed. See Mk 1:23–6; 9:25–7; Mt 8:28–32; Lk 4:33–5.   **732** in addition to

733 *of that:* about that which unless   **735** See *Imitation of Christ* 1.24, then attributed to Gerson.   **736** place   **737** scorning, despising   **738** avoid   **739** *but if:* unless   **740** who   **741** hesitate

742 as if   **743** foolish   **744** consists   **745** traps, deceits   **746** *set clear at right nought:* regard as nothing at all, disregard entirely   **747** be willing   **748** entirely

making a cross upon their heart and bidding the devil avaunt,[749] and sometimes laugh him to scorn too, and then turn their mind to some other matter. And when the devil hath seen that they have set so little by him,[750] after certain assays,[751] made in such times as he thought most meet,[752] he hath given that temptation quite over, both for that[753] the proud spirit cannot endure to be mocked, and also lest with much tempting the man to the sin whereto he could not in conclusion bring him, he should much increase his merit.

The final fight is by invocation of help unto God: both praying for himself and desiring[754] others also to pray for him, both poor folk for his alms and other good folk of their charity, specially good priests in that holy sacred service of the Mass—and not only them, but also his own good angel and other holy saints such as his devotion specially stand unto; or if he be learned, use then the Litany[755] with the holy suffrages[756] that follow, which is a prayer in the Church of marvelous old antiquity, not made first, as some ween it were, by that holy man Saint Gregory (which opinion rose of that, that in[757] the time of a great pestilence in Rome, he caused the whole city go in solemn procession therewith), but it was in use in the Church many years before Saint Gregory's days, as well appeareth by the books of other holy doctors and saints that were dead hundreds of years before Saint Gregory was born. And holy Saint Bernard giveth counsel that every man should make suit unto[758] angels and saints to pray for him to God in the things that he would have sped at[759] his holy hand. If any man will stick at[760] that and say it need not, because God can hear us himself, and will also say that it is perilous so to do because, they say, we be not so counseled by no Scripture—I will not dispute the matter here; he that will not[761] do it, I let[762] him not to leave it undone. But yet for mine own part, I will as well trust to the counsel of Saint Bernard, and reckon him for as good and as well-learned in the Scripture as any man that I hear say the contrary. And better dare I jeopard[763] my soul with the soul of Saint Bernard than with his that findeth that fault in his doctrine.

Unto God himself every good man counseleth to have recourse above all, and in this temptation to have special remembrance of Christ's Passion, and pray him, for the honor of his death, the ground of man's salvation, keep this person thus tempted from that damnable death. Special verses may there be drawn out of the Psalter against the devil's wicked temptations, as for example, *Exsurgat Deus et dissipentur inimici eius, et fugiant qui oderunt eum a facie eius,*[764] and many others which are, in such horrible temptation, to God pleasant and to the devil very terrible. But none more terrible nor more odious to the devil than the words with which our Savior drove him away himself—*Vade, Satana*[765]—nor no prayer more acceptable unto God, nor more effectual for the matter, than those words which our Savior hath taught us himself: *Ne nos inducas in tentationem, sed libera nos a malo.*[766]

And I doubt not, by God's grace, but he that in such a temptation will use good counsel and prayer, and keep himself in good virtuous business and good virtuous company, and abide in the faithful hope of God's help, shall have the truth of God (as the prophet saith in the verse afore-rehearsed)[767] so compass him about with a pavise[768] that he shall not need to dread this night's fear of this wicked temptation. And thus will I finish this piece of the night's fear. And glad am I that we be past it and comen once unto the day, to those other words of the prophet, *a sagitta volante in die;*[769] for methinketh I have made it a long night.

VINCENT: Forsooth, Uncle, so have you; but we have not slept in it, but been very well occupied. But now I fear that except[770] you make here a pause till you have dined, you shall keep yourself from your dinner overlong.

ANTONY: Nay, nay, Cousin, for both broke I my fast even as you came in and also you shall find this night and this day like a winter day and a winter night: for as the winter hath short days and long nights, so shall you find that I made you not this fearful night so long, but I shall make you this light

---

749 to depart　**750** *set so little by him:* esteem him so little　**751** attempts　**752** suitable; favorable to him　**753** *for that:* because　**754** asking　**755** the Litany of the Saints　**756** intercessory prayers　**757** *rose...that in:* arose about that, because during　**758** *make suit unto:* ask　**759** *sped at:* prepared by　**760** *stick at:* object to　**761** *will not:* does not want to　**762** prevent　**763** risk　**764** "May God arise, and his enemies be scattered; and may those who hate him flee from his face" (Ps 67(68):1–2)　**765** "Begone, Satan" (Mt 4:10)　**766** "Do not lead us into temptation, but free us from evil" (Mt 6:13)　**767** *afore-rehearsed:* previously cited　**768** large shield　**769** "from the arrow that flies by day" (Ps 90(91):5)　**770** unless

courageous day as short. And so shall the matter require well[771] of itself indeed; for in those words of the prophet, *Scuto circumdabit te veritas eius a sagitta volante in die* ("The truth of God shall compass thee round about with a pavise from the arrow flying in the day"), I understand the arrow of pride, with which the devil tempteth a man not in the night (that is to wit, in tribulation and adversity), for that time is too discomfortable and too fearful for pride, but in the day (that is to wit, in prosperity), for that time is full of lightsome lust[772] and courage. But surely this worldly prosperity wherein a man so rejoiceth, and whereof the devil maketh him so proud, is but even a very short winter day.

For we begin, many, full poor and cold; and up we fly like an arrow that were shot up into the air; and yet, when we be suddenly shotten up into the highest, ere we be well warm there, down we come unto the cold ground again, and then even there stick we still. And yet for the short while that we be upward and aloft, Lord, how lusty[773] and how proud we be, buzzing above busily like as a bumblebee flieth about in summer, never aware that she shall die in winter. And so fare many of us (God help us), for in the short winter day of worldly wealth and prosperity, this flying arrow of the devil—this high spirit of pride, shot out of the devil's bow and piercing through our heart—beareth us up in our affection aloft into the clouds, where we ween we sit on the rainbow and overlook the world under us, accounting, in the regard of[774] our own glory, such other poor souls as were peradventure wont[775] to be our fellows for seely[776] poor pismires[777] and ants.

But this arrow of pride, fly it never so high in the clouds, and be the man that it carrieth up so high never so joyful thereof, yet let him remember that be this arrow never so light, it hath yet a heavy iron head, and therefore fly it never so high, down must it needs come, and on the ground must it light,[778] and falleth sometimes not in a very cleanly place, but the pride turneth into rebuke and shame, and there is then all the glory gone.

Of this arrow speaketh the Wise Man in the fifth chapter of Sapience,[779] where he saith in the person of them that in pride and vanity passed the time of this present life, and after that so spent, passed hence[780] into hell, *Quid profuit nobis superbia aut divitiarum iactantia, quid contulit nobis? Transierunt omnia illa tamquam umbra etc aut tamquam sagittae emissae in locum destinatum, divisus aer continuo in se reclusus est, ut ignoretur transitus illius. Sic et nos nati continuo desivimus esse, et virtutis quidem nullum signum valuimus ostendere; in malignitate autem nostra consumpti sumus. Talia dixerunt in inferno ii qui peccaverunt* ("'What hath pride profited us, or what good hath the glory of our riches done unto us? Passed are all those things like a shadow, or like an arrow shot out into the place appointed.[781] The air that was divided is by and by[782] returned into the place, and in such wise closed together again that the way is not perceived in which the arrow went. And in like wise we, as soon as we were born, be by and by vanished away, and have left no token of any good virtue behind us, but are consumed and wasted and come to nought in our malignity.'

"They, lo, that have lived here in sin, such words have they spoken when they lay in hell.")[783]

Here shall you, good Cousin, consider that whereas the Scripture here speaketh of the arrow shot into his place appointed or intended, in shooting of this arrow of pride there be diverse purposings and appointings; for the proud man himself hath no certain purpose or appointment at any mark, butt, or prick[784] upon earth whereat he determineth to shoot and there to stick and tarry, but ever he shooteth as children do that love to shoot up a-cop-high,[785] to see how high their arrow can fly up.

But now doth the devil intend and appoint a certain prick surely[786] set in a place into which he purposeth—fly this arrow never so high, and the proud heart thereon—to have them light[787] both at last. And that place is in the very pit of hell. There is set the devil's well-acquainted prick and his very just mark down, upon which prick, with his pricking shaft of pride, he hath by himself a plain proof and experience that—but if[788] it be stopped by some grace of God by the way—the soul that flieth up therewith can never fail to fall. For when himself was in heaven and began to fly up a-cop-high with

771 *require well:* well call for   **772** *lightsome lust:* lighthearted vigor or pleasure or appetite   **773** exhilarated, self-confident, merry   **774** *in the regard of:* in comparison with   **775** accustomed   **776** pitiful; helpless   **777** ants; insignificant persons   **778** land   **779** the Book of Wisdom   **780** from here   **781** aimed at   **782** *by and by:* immediately   **783** Wis 5:8–9, 12–14   **784** *mark, butt, or prick:* target, stand on which the target is set up, or bull's-eye of the target   **785** *a-cop-high:* high as can be   **786** securely   **787** land   **788** *but if:* unless

that lusty light flight of pride, saying, *Ascendam super astra, et ponam solium meum ad latera Aquilonis, et ero similis Altissimo* ("I will sty[789] up above the stars, and set my throne on the sides of the North, and will be like unto the Highest"),[790] long ere he could fly up half so high as he said in his heart he would, he was turned from a bright glorious angel into a dark deformed devil, and from flying any farther upward, down was he thrown into the deep dungeon of hell.

Now may it peradventure, Cousin, seem that since this kind of temptation of pride is no tribulation or pain, all this that we speak of this arrow of pride flying forth in the "day" of prosperity were beside our matter.

VINCENT: Verily, mine Uncle, and so seemed it unto me, and somewhat was I minded so to say to you too, saving[791] that were it properly pertaining to the present matter or somewhat digressing therefrom, good matter methought it was, and such as I had no lust to let.[792]

ANTONY: But now must you, Cousin, consider that though prosperity be contrary to tribulation, yet unto many a good man the devil's temptation unto pride in prosperity is a greater tribulation, and more need hath of good comfort and good counsel both than he that never felt it would ween.[793] And that is the thing, Cousin, that maketh me speak thereof as of a thing proper to this matter. For, Cousin, as it is a thing right hard to touch pitch and never file[794] the fingers, to put flax unto fire and yet keep them from burning, to keep a serpent in thy bosom and yet be safe from stinging, to put young men with young women without danger of foul fleshly desire, so is it hard for any person—either man or woman—in great worldly wealth and much prosperity, so to withstand the suggestions of the devil and occasions given by the world, that they keep themselves from the deadly desire of ambitious glory, whereupon there followeth (if a man fall thereto) a whole flood of all unhappy mischief: arrogant manner, high sullen solemn port,[795] overlooking the poor, in word and countenance displeasant, and disdainous

behavior, ravin,[796] extortion, oppression, hatred, and cruelty.

Now many a good man, Cousin, comen[797] into great authority, casting[798] in his mind the peril of such occasions of pride as the devil taketh of prosperity to make his instruments of, wherewith to move men to such high point of presumption as engendereth so many great inconveniences[799]—and feeling the devil therewith offering to themselves suggestions thereunto—they be sore troubled therewith, and some fall so feared thereof that even in the day of prosperity they fall into the night's fear of pusillanimity, and doubting[800] overmuch lest they should misuse themselves, leave the things undone wherein they might use themselves well, and mistrusting the aid and help of God in holding them upright in their temptations, give place to the devil in the contrary temptation, whereby for faint heart they leave off good business wherein they were well occupied, and under pretext (as it seemeth to themselves) of humble heart and meekness, and serving God in contemplation and silence, they seek their own ease and earthly rest unaware, wherewith (if it so be) God is not well content.

Howbeit, if it so be that a man feel himself such indeed as, by the experience that he hath of himself, he perceiveth that in wealth and authority he doth his own soul harm, and cannot do therein the good that to his part appertaineth, but seeth the things that he should set his hand to sustain decay through his default[801] and fall to ruin under him, and that to the amendment thereof he leaveth his own duty undone, then would I in any wise advise him to leave off that thing—be it spiritual benefice that he have (parsonage or bishopric) or temporal room[802] and authority—and rather give it over quite[803] and draw himself aside, and serve God, than take the worldly worship and commodity[804] for himself, with incommodity of them whom his duty were to profit. But on the other side, if he see not the contrary but that he may do his duty conveniently[805] well, and feareth nothing but that the temptations of ambition and pride may peradventure turn his good purpose and make him decline unto sin, I say not nay but that well done it is to stand in moderate fear

789 mount; ascend   **790** Is 14:13–14   **791** except   **792** *lust to let:* desire to prevent   **793** suppose   **794** defile, dirty   **795** bearing; importance   **796** plundering   **797** having come   **798** pondering   **799** unsuitable behaviors   **800** fearing   **801** neglect, failure   **802** *temporal room:* secular office or position   **803** completely   **804** *worship and commodity:* honor and advantage   **805** suitably always, whereof the Scripture saith, *Beatus homo qui semper est pavidus* ("Blessed is the man that is always fearful"),[806] and Saint Paul saith, *Qui stat videat ne cadat* ("He that standeth, let him look that he fall not");[807] yet is overmuch fear perilous, and draweth toward the mistrust of God's gracious help, which immoderate fear and faint heart Holy Scripture forbiddeth, saying, *Noli esse pusillanimis* ("Be not feeble-hearted or timorous").[808] Let such a man therefore temper his fear with good hope, and think that since God hath set him in that place (if he think that God have set him therein), God will assist him with his grace to the well using thereof. Howbeit, if he came thereto by simony[809] or some such other evil means, then were that thing one good reason wherefore he should the rather leave it off. But else[810] let him continue in his good business, and against the devil's provocation unto evil bless himself and call unto God and pray, and look what[811] thing the devil tempteth him to, lean the more to the contrary. Let him be piteous and comfortable to those that are in distress and affliction. I mean not to let every malefactor[812] pass forth unpunished and freely run out and rob at rovers,[813] but in his heart be sorry to see that, of necessity for fear of decaying the common weal, men are driven to put malefactors to pain. And yet where he findeth good tokens and likelihood of amendment, there, in all that he may, help that mercy may be had. There shall never lack desperately disposed wretches enough besides, upon whom, for example, justice may proceed. Let him think in his own heart every poor beggar his fellow.[814]

VINCENT: That will be very hard, Uncle, for an honorable man to do, when he beholdeth himself richly appareled and the beggar rigged in his rags.

ANTONY: If here were, Cousin, two men that were beggars both, and afterward a great rich man would take the one unto him and tell him that for a little time he would have him in his house, and thereupon arrayed him in silk and give him a great bag by his side filled even full of gold, but giving him this knot[815] therewith: that within a little while, out he should in his old rags again, and bear never a penny with him — if this beggar met his fellow now while his gay gown were on, might he not, for all his gay gear,[816] take him for his fellow still? And were he not a very fool if, for a wealth of a few weeks, he would ween himself far his better?

VINCENT: Yes, Uncle, if the difference of their state were none other.

ANTONY: Surely, Cousin, methinketh that in this world, between the richest and the most poor, the difference is scant[817] so much. For let the highest look on the most base, and consider how poor they came both into this world, and then consider further therewith, how rich soever he be now, he shall yet within a while, peradventure less than one week, walk out again as poor as that beggar shall. And then, by my troth,[818] methinketh this rich man much more than mad, if for the wealth of a little while, haply[819] less than one week, he reckon himself in earnest any better than the beggar's fellow. And less than thus can no man think that hath any natural wit and well useth it.

But now, a Christian man, Cousin, that hath the light of faith, he cannot fail to think on this thing much further. For he will not think only upon his bare coming hither and his bare going hence again, but also upon the dreadful judgment of God, and upon the fearful pains of hell, and the inestimable joys of heaven. And in the considering of these things, he will call to remembrance that peradventure when this beggar and he be both departed hence, the beggar may be suddenly set up in such royalty that well were himself that ever was he born if he might be made his fellow. And he that well bethinketh him, Cousin, upon these things, I verily think that the arrow of pride, flying forth in the "day" of worldly wealth, shall never so wound his heart that ever it shall bear him up one foot.

But now to the intent he may think on such things the better, let him use often[820] to resort to confession, and there open his heart, and by the mouth of some virtuous ghostly[821] father, have such things oft renewed in his remembrance.

Let him also choose himself some secret solitary place in his own house, as far from noise and

---

806 Prv 28:14   **807** 1 Cor 10:12   **808** Ecclus 7.9(7:10)   **809** buying a Church office   **810** otherwise   **811** *look*   *what:* whatever   **812** criminal   **813** *at rovers:* at will   **814** peer, equal   **815** binding condition   **816** apparel   **817** barely, hardly   **818** truth, faithfulness   **819** perhaps   **820** *use often:* make it a frequent practice   **821** spiritual

company as he conveniently can. And thither let him sometimes secretly resort alone, imagining himself as one going out of the world, even straight unto the giving up his reckoning unto God of his

5   sinful living. Then let him there before an altar or some pitiful image of Christ's bitter Passion — the beholding whereof may put him in remembrance of the thing and move him to devout compassion — kneel down or fall prostrate as at the feet of almighty

10   God, verily believing him to be there invisibly present, as without any doubt he is. There let him open his heart to God and confess his faults, such as he can call to mind, and pray God of forgiveness. Let him call to remembrance the benefits that God hath

15   given him, either in general among other men, or privately to himself, and give him humble hearty thanks therefor. There let him declare unto God the temptations of the devil, the suggestions of the flesh, the occasions of the world, and of his worldly

20   friends — much worse many times in drawing a man from God than are his most mortal enemies, which thing our Savior witnesseth himself where he saith, *Inimici hominis domestici eius* ("The enemies of a man are they that are his own familiars").[822]

25   There let him lament and bewail unto God his own frailty, negligence, and sloth in resisting and withstanding of temptation, his readiness and pronity[823] to fall thereunto.

There let him lamentably beseech God of[824] his

30   gracious aid and help to strengthen his infirmity withal,[825] both in keeping himself from falling, and, when he by his own fault misfortuneth to fall, then with the helping hand of his merciful grace to lift him up and set him on his feet in the state of his

35   grace again.

And let this man not doubt but that God heareth him and granteth him gladly his boon.[826] And so dwelling in the faithful trust of God's help, he shall well use his prosperity and persevere in his good

40   profitable business, and shall have therein the truth of God so compass him about with a pavise[827] of his heavenly defense that of the devil's arrow flying in the day of worldly wealth, he shall not need to dread.

45   **Vincent:** Forsooth, Uncle, I like this good counsel well, and I would ween that such as are in

prosperity and take such order therein may do, both to themselves and other folk about, much good.

Antony: I beseech our Lord, Cousin, put this and better in the mind of every man that need-

50   eth it. And now will I touch one word or twain of the third temptation, whereof the prophet speaketh in these words: *a negotio perambulante in tenebris* ("from the business walking in the darkness"). And then will we call for our dinner, leaving the

55   last temptation — that is to wit, *ab incursu et daemonio meridiano* ("from the incursion and the devil of the midday")[828] — till afternoon. And then shall we therewith, God willing, make an end of all this matter.

60

Vincent: Our Lord reward you, good Uncle, for your good labor with me. But for our Lord's sake, take good heed, Uncle, that you forbear not your dinner overlong.

Antony: Fear not that, Cousin, I warrant you, for 65 this piece will I make you but short.

THE SEVENTEENTH CHAPTER
Of the devil named negotium perambulans
in tenebris — *that is to wit, "business
walking in the darkness"*   70

Antony: The prophet saith in the said psalm, *Qui habitat in adiutorio Altissimi, in protectione Dei caeli commorabitur, scuto circumdabit te veritas eius; non timebis a timore, etc. A negotio perambulante in tenebris* ("He that dwelleth in the faithful hope of 75 God's help, he shall abide in the protection and safeguard of the God of heaven. And thou that art such one shall the truth of him so compass about with a pavise that thou shalt not be afeard of the business walking about in the darknesses").[829]   80

Negotium is here, Cousin, the name of a devil that is ever full of busyness in tempting folk to much evil business; his time of tempting is in the darknesses. For you wot well that besides the very full night, which is the deep dark, there are two times of dark- 85 nesses: the one ere the morning wax light, the other when the evening waxeth dark.

---

822 Mt 10:36   **823** inclination, proneness   of God's aid and help)   **826** favor   **829** Ps 90(91):1, 4–6
824 for   **825** with them (i.e., by means   **827** large shield   **828** Ps 90(91):6

Two times of like manner[830] darkness are there also in the soul of man: the one ere the light of grace be well in the heart sprungen up, the other when the light of grace out of the soul beginneth to walk fast away.

In these two darknesses the devil that is called Business busily walketh about, and such folk as will follow him, he carrieth about with him, and setteth them awork with many manner bumbling business.

He setteth, I say, some to seek the pleasures of the flesh: in eating, drinking, and other filthy[831] delight. And some he setteth about incessant seeking for these worldly goods.

And of such busy folk whom this devil called Business "walking about in the darkness" setteth awork with such business, our Savior saith in the Gospel, *Qui ambulat in tenebris nescit quo vadit* ("He that walketh in darkness wotteth not whither he goeth").[832] And surely in such case are they: they neither wot which way they go nor whither. For verily they walk round about, as it were, in a round maze; when they ween themselves at an end of their business, they be but at the beginning again. For is not the going about the serving of the flesh a business that hath none end, but evermore from the end cometh to the beginning again? Go they never so full-fed to bed, yet evermore on the morrow as new be they[833] to be fed again as they were the day before.

Thus fareth it by the belly; thus fareth it by those parts that are beneath the belly. And as for covetise,[834] fareth like the fire: the more wood that cometh thereto, the more fervent and the more greedy it is.

But now hath this maze a center or a middle place, into which sometimes they be conveyed suddenly when they ween they were not yet far from the brink.

The center or middle place of this maze is hell. And into that place be these busy folk that with this devil of Business walk about in this busy maze in the darkness suddenly sometimes conveyed, nothing ware[835] whither they be going, and even while they ween that they were not far walked from the beginning, and that they had yet a great way to walk about before they should come to the end.

But of these fleshly folk walking in this busy pleasant maze, the Scripture declareth the end: *Ducunt in bonis dies suos, et in puncto ad inferna descendunt* ("They lead their life in pleasure, and at a pop,[836] down they descend into hell").[837]

Of the covetous men saith Saint Paul, *Qui volunt divites fieri, incidunt in tentationem et in laqueum diaboli, et desideria multa inutilia et nociva, quae mergunt homines in interitum et perditionem* ("They that long to be rich do fall into temptation, and into the grin[838] of the devil, and into many desires unprofitable, and harmful, which drown men into death and into destruction").[839]

Lo, here is the middle place of this busy maze: the grin of the devil, the place of perdition and destruction that they fall and be caught and drowned in ere they be aware.

The covetous rich man also that our Savior speaketh of in the Gospel, that had so great plenty of corn that his barns would not receive it, but intended to make his barns larger, and said unto himself that he would make merry many days, had weened, you wot well, that he had had a great way yet to walk; but God said unto him, *Stulte, hac nocte tollent a te animam tuam; quae autem parasti, cuius erunt*? ("Fool, this night shall they take thy soul from thee; and then all this good that thou hast gathered, whose shall it be?")[840] Here you see that he fell suddenly into the deep center of this busy maze, so that he was fallen full therein long ere ever he had went he should have come near thereto.

Now this wot I very well, that those that are walking about in this busy maze take not their business for any tribulation. And yet are there many of them forwearied as sore,[841] and as sore panged and pained therein—their pleasures being so short, so little and so few, and their displeasures and their griefs so great, so continual and so many—that maketh me think upon a good worshipful[842] man which, when he diverse times beheld his wife,[843] what pain she took in strait[844] binding up her hair to make her a fair large forehead, and with strait bracing in her body to make her middle small (both twain[845] to her great pain, for the pride of a little foolish praise) he said unto her, "Forsooth, madam, if God give you not hell, he shall do you great wrong. For it

---

830 *like manner:* the same kind of
831 disgraceful, base   832 Jn 12:35
833 *as new be they:* they are as ready anew
834 lust, especially for wealth   835 aware,

wary   836 *at a pop:* in an instant, suddenly   837 Job 21:13   838 snare, trap
839 1 Tim 6:9   840 See Lk 12:16–20.
841 *forwearied as sore:* worn out as

grievously   842 honorable   843 Harpsfield says this is Lady Alice, More's wife
(94).   844 tightly   845 together

must needs be your own of very right, for you buy it very dear,[846] and take great pain therefor."

They that now lie in hell for their wretched living here do now perceive their folly in the more pain that they took here for the less pleasure. There confess they now their folly and cry out, *Lassati sumus in via iniquitatis* ("We have been wearied in the way of wickedness").[847] And yet while they were walking therein, they would not rest themselves but run on still in their weariness, and put themselves still unto more pain and more, for that little peevish[848] pleasure, short and soon gone, that they took all that labor and pain for, besides the everlasting pain that followed it for their further advantage after.

So help me God, and none otherwise but as I verily think that many a man buyeth hell here with so much pain that he might have bought heaven with less than the one half.

But yet, as I say, while these fleshly and worldly busy folk are walking about in this round busy maze of this devil that is called Business, that[849] walketh about in these two times of darkness, their wits are so by the secret enchantment of the devil bewitched that they mark not the great long miserable weariness and pain that the devil maketh them take and endure about nought;[850] and therefore they take it for no tribulation, so that they need no comfort; and therefore it is not for their sakes that I speak all this, saving[851] that it may serve them for counsel toward the perceiving of their own foolish misery through the good help of God's grace beginning to shine upon them again. But there are very good folk and virtuous that are in the daylight of grace, and yet because the devil tempteth them busily to such fleshly delight, and since they see plenty of worldly substance fall unto them, and feel the devil in like wise busily tempt them to set their heart thereupon, they be sore troubled therewith and begin to fear thereby that they be not with God in the light, but with this devil that the prophet calleth *Negotium* (that is to say, Business) walking about in these two times of darkness.

Howbeit, as I said before of those good folk and gracious that are in the worldly wealth of great power and authority, and thereby fear the devil's arrow of

pride, so say I now here again of these that stand in dread of fleshly foul sin and covetise:[852] since they be but tempted therewith and follow it not, albeit that they do well to stand ever in moderate fear, lest with waxing overbold and setting the thing overlight,[853] they might peradventure mishap[854] to fall in thereto, yet sore[855] to vex and trouble themselves with the fear of loss of God's favor therefor is without necessity and not always without peril. For as I said before, it withdraweth the mind of a man far from spiritual consolation of the good hope that he should have in God's help. And as for those temptations, while he that is tempted followeth them not, the fight against them serveth a man for matter of merit and reward in heaven, if he not only flee the deed, the consent, and the delectation,[856] but also (in that he conveniently[857] may) flee from all occasions thereof. And this point is, in those fleshly temptations, easy to perceive and meetly[858] plain enough. But in these worldly businesses pertaining unto covetise, therein is the thing somewhat more dark, and in the perceiving more difficulty. And very great troublous fear doth there oftentimes arise thereof in the hearts of very good folk, when the world falleth fast unto them, because of the sore[859] words and terrible threats that God in Holy Scripture speaketh against those that are rich, as where Saint Paul saith, *Qui volunt divites fieri incidunt in tentationem, et in laqueum diaboli* ("They that will be rich fall into temptation, and into the grin[860] of the devil"),[861] and where our Savior saith himself, *Facilius est camelum per foramen acus transire quam divitem intrare in regnum Dei* ("It is more easy for a camel" — or as some say, for *camelus* so signifieth in the Greek tongue, "for a great cable-rope" — "to go through a needle's eye than for a rich man to enter into the kingdom of God").[862]

No marvel now though[863] good folk that fear God take occasion of great dread at so dreadful words when they see the worldly goods fall to them. And some stand in doubt whether it be lawful for them to keep any goods or no. But evermore in all those places of Scripture, the having of the worldly goods is not the thing that is rebuked and threatened, but the affection that the haver unlawfully

---

846 *very dear:* at great cost   **847** Wis 5:7   **848** foolish   **849** who   **850** nothing   **851** except   **852** lust, esp. for wealth   **853** *waxing…overlight:*

growing overconfident and valuing the thing too lightly   **854** *peradventure mishap:* perhaps have the misfortune   **855** greatly, grievously   **856** enjoyment

857 suitably, appropriately   **858** fairly; quite   **859** severe, stern, harsh   **860** snare   **861** 1 Tm 6:9   **862** Mk 10:25   **863** if; that

beareth thereto. For where Saint Paul saith, *Qui volunt divites fieri*, etc. ("They that will be made rich"), he speaketh not of the having, but of the will and the desire and affection to have and the longing for it. For that cannot be lightly[864] without sin. For the thing that folk sore long for, they will make many shifts[865] to get and jeopard themselves therefor. And to declare[866] that the having of riches is not forbidden, but the inordinate affection of the mind sore set thereupon, the prophet saith, *Divitiae si affluant nolite cor apponere* ("If riches flow unto you, set not your heart thereupon").[867] And albeit that our Lord, by the said example of the camel or cable-rope to come through the needle's eye, said that it is not only hard but also impossible for a rich man to enter into the kingdom of heaven, yet he declared that though the rich man cannot get into heaven of himself, yet God, he said, can get him in well enough. For unto men, he said, it was impossible, but not unto God: "for unto God," he said, "all things are possible";[868] yet over that, he told of which manner rich men he meant that could not get into the Kingdom of Heaven, saying, *Filioli, quam difficile est confidentes in pecuniis regnum Dei introire* ("My babes, how hard is it for them that put their trust and confidence in their money to enter into the Kingdom of God").[869]

VINCENT: This I suppose very true, and else God forbid; for else were the world in a very hard case, if every rich man were in such danger and peril.

ANTONY: That were it, Cousin, indeed; and so, I ween, is it yet. For I fear me that to the multitude there be very few but that they long sore to be rich; and of those that so long to be, very few reserved[870] also but that they set their heart very sore thereon.

VINCENT: This is, Uncle, I fear me, very true, but yet not the thing that I was about to speak of. But the thing that I would have said was this: that I cannot well perceive (the world being such as it is, and so many poor people therein) how any man may be rich, and keep him rich, without danger of damnation therefor; for all the while that he seeth poor people so many that lack, while himself hath to give them, and whose necessity (while he hath therewith)[871] he is bound in such case of duty to relieve—so far-forth[872] that holy Saint Ambrose saith that whoso that die for default[873] where we might help them, we kill them[874]—I cannot see but that every rich man hath great cause to stand in great fear of damnation; nor I cannot perceive, as I say, how he can be delivered of that fear as long as he keepeth his riches. And therefore, though he might keep his riches if there lacked poor men, and yet stand in God's favor therewith—as Abraham did, and many another holy rich man since—yet in such abundance of poor men as there be now in every country, any man that keepeth any riches, it must needs be that he hath an inordinate affection thereunto, while he giveth it not out unto the poor needy persons, that the duty of charity bindeth and straineth[875] him to. And thus, Uncle, in this world, at this day, meseemeth[876] your comfort unto good men that are rich and troubled with fear of damnation for the keeping can very scantly[877] serve.

ANTONY: Hard is it, Cousin, in many manner things, to bid or forbid, affirm or deny, reprove or allow, a matter nakedly proposed[878] and put forth, or precisely to say "this thing is good," or "this thing is naught,"[879] without consideration of the circumstances.

Holy Saint Augustine telleth of a physician that gave a man a medicine in a certain disease that helped him. The selfsame man at another time in the selfsame disease took the selfsame medicine himself, and had thereof more harm than good; which thing when he showed unto the physician, and asked him whereof that harm should hap, "That medicine," quoth he, "did thee no good, but harm, because thou tookest it when I gave it thee not." This answer Saint Augustine very well alloweth. For that though[880] the medicine were one, yet might there be peradventure in the sickness some such difference as the patient perceived not—yea, or in the man himself, or in the place, or the time of the

---

864 *be lightly:* easily be   865 plans; efforts   866 make clear, show   867 Ps 61(62):10   868 Mk 10:27   869 Mk 10:24   870 excepted   871 company with him   872 *so far-forth:* so far forward; i.e., to such an extent   873 neglect, failure   874 Such a statement was commonly attributed to St. Ambrose during the Middle Ages (e.g., Gratian, *Decretals*, Part 1, Dist. 86, c. 21, and *Summa theologica* 2-2, q. 32, art. 5.)   The passage is actually from Zeno's *De justitia*.   875 constrains   876 it seems to me   877 scarcely   878 *nakedly proposed:* proposed in isolation   879 wicked   880 *For that though:* Because although

year—many things might make the let[881] for which the physician would not then have given him the selfsame medicine that he gave him before.[882] To peruse every circumstance that might, Cousin, in this matter be touched and were to be considered and weighed would indeed make this part of this devil of Business a very busy piece of work and a long. But I shall a little open[883] the point that you speak of, and shall show you what I think therein, with as few words as I conveniently[884] can—and then will we go to dinner.

First, Cousin, he that is a rich man and keepeth all his goods, he hath, I think, very good cause to be very feared[885] indeed. And yet I fear me that such folk fear least. For they be very far from the state of good men, since if they keep still all, then are they very far from charity, and do,[886] you wot well, alms either little or none at all. But now is our question, Cousin, not in what case the rich man standeth that keepeth all, but whether we should suffer men to stand in a perilous dread and fear for the keeping of any great part; for if that[887] by the keeping still of so much as maketh a rich man still, they stand in the state of damnation, then are the curates[888] bounden plainly to tell them so, according to the commandment of God given unto them all in the person of Ezekiel: *Si dicente me ad impium morte morieris non annuntiaveris ei*, etc. ("If when I say to the wicked man, 'Thou shalt die,' thou do not show it unto him, nor speak unto him, that he may be turned from his wicked way and may live, he shall soothly[889] die in his wickedness, and his blood shall I verily require of thine hand").[890]

But, Cousin, though God invited men unto the following of himself in willful poverty, by the leaving of altogether at once for his sake, as the thing whereby, with being out of the solicitude of worldly business and far from the desire of earthly commodities, they may the more speedily get and attain the state of spiritual perfection and the hungry desire and longing for celestial things, yet doth he not command every man so to do upon the peril of damnation. For where he saith, *Qui non renuntiaverit omnibus quae possidet non potest meus esse discipulus* ("He that forsake not all that ever he hath

cannot be my disciple"),[891] he declareth well, by other words of his own in the selfsame place a little before, what he meaneth: for there saith he more, *Si quis venit ad me, et non odit patrem suum et matrem, et uxorem et filios et fratres et sorores, adhuc autem et animam suam, non potest meus esse discipulus* ("He that cometh to me, and hateth not his father and his mother, and his wife and his children, and his brethren and his sisters—yea, and his own life too—cannot be my disciple").[892]

Here meaneth our Savior Christ that none can be his disciple but if he love him so far above all his kin, and above his own life too, that for the love of him, rather than to forsake him, he shall forsake them all. And so meaneth he by those other words that whosoever do not so renounce and forsake all that ever he hath in his own heart and affection that he will rather lose it all, and let it go every whit, than deadly displease God with the reserving of any one part thereof, he cannot be Christ's disciple, since Christ teacheth us to love God above all things, and he loveth not God above all things that contrary to God's pleasure keepeth any thing that he hath, for that thing he showeth himself to set more by than by God while[893] he is better content to lose God than it. But as I said, to give away all, or that no man should be rich or have substance,[894] that find I no commandment of. There are, as our Savior saith, in the house of his Father many mansions.[895] And happy shall he be that shall have the grace to dwell even in the lowest.

It seemeth verily by the Gospel that those which for God's sake patiently suffer penury shall not only dwell above those in heaven that live here in plenty in earth, but also that heaven in some manner of wise[896] more properly belongeth unto them, and is more specially prepared for them than it is for the rich, by that that[897] God in the Gospel counseleth the rich folk to buy, in a manner,[898] heaven of them, where he saith unto the rich men, *Facite vobis amicos de mammona iniquitatis, ut cum defeceritis recipiant vos in aeterna tabernacula* ("Make you friends of the wicked riches, that when you fail here, they may receive you into the everlasting tabernacles").[899]

But now, although this be thus in respect of the

---

881 *make the let:* constitute the obstacle
882 See Augustine, *Letter to Marcellinus* 1:3.
883 explain, clarify; declare my thoughts about 884 suitably 885 afraid 886 do

give 887 because 888 parish priests
889 truly 890 Ez 3:18 891 Lk 14:33
892 Lk 14:26 893 *set more…while:* value more than when 894 possessions, wealth

895 Jn 14:2 896 *manner of wise:* kind of way 897 *by that that:* for the reason that
898 *in a manner:* as it were; so to speak
899 Lk 16:9

riches and the poverty compared together, yet, they being good men both, there may be some other virtue besides wherein the rich man may so peradventure excel that he may in heaven be far above that poor man that was here in earth in other virtues far under him, as the proof appeareth clear in Lazarus and Abraham.⁹⁰⁰

Nor I say not this to the intent to comfort rich men in heaping up of riches. For a little comfort is bent⁹⁰¹ enough thereto for them that be not so proud-hearted and obstinate but that they would, I ween, to that counsel be with right little exhortation very conformable;⁹⁰² but I say this for that⁹⁰³ those good men — to whom God giveth substance⁹⁰⁴ and the mind to dispose it well, and yet not the mind to give it all away at once, but for good causes to keep some substance still — should not despair of God's favor for the not doing of the thing which God hath given them no commandment of, nor drawn by any special calling thereunto.

Zacchaeus, lo, that climbed up into the tree for desire that he had to behold our Savior, at such time as Christ called aloud unto him and said, "Zacchaeus, make haste and come down, for this day must I dwell in thine house,"⁹⁰⁵ was so glad thereof, and so touched inwardly with special grace to the profit of his soul, that whereas all the people murmured much that Christ would call him and be so familiar with him as of his own offer to come unto his house — considering that they knew him for the chief of the publicans, that were customers or toll-gatherers⁹⁰⁶ of the emperor's duties (all which whole company were among the people sore infamed of ravin,⁹⁰⁷ extortion, and bribery), and then Zacchaeus not only the chief of that fellowship, but also grown greatly rich, whereby the people accounted him in their own opinion for a man very sinful and naught — he forthwith,⁹⁰⁸ by the instinct⁹⁰⁹ of the Spirit of God, in reproach of all such temerarious,⁹¹⁰ bold, and blind judgment given upon a man whose inward mind and sudden change they cannot see, shortly proved them all deceived, and that our Lord had, at those few words outwardly spoken to him, so wrought in his heart within that whatsoever he was before, he was then,

unware⁹¹¹ unto them all, suddenly waxen good. For he made haste and came down, and gladly received Christ and said, "Lo, Lord, the one half of my goods here I give unto the poor people. And yet over that, if I have in anything deceived any man, here am I ready to recompense him fourfold as much."⁹¹²

VINCENT: This was, Uncle, a gracious hearing. But I marvel me somewhat wherefore Zacchaeus used his words in that manner of order. For methinketh he should first have spoken of making restitution unto those whom he had beguiled, and speak of giving of his alms after. For restitution is, you wot well, duty, and a thing of such necessity that in respect of⁹¹³ restitution, alms-deed is but voluntary. Therefore it might seem that to put men in mind of their duty in making restitution first and doing their alms after, Zacchaeus should have said more conveniently⁹¹⁴ if he had said first that he would make every man restitution whom he had wronged, and then give half in alms of that that⁹¹⁵ remained after, for only that might he call clearly his own.

ANTONY: This is true, Cousin, where a man hath not enough to suffice both. But he that hath is not bounden to leave his alms ungiven to the poor man that is at his hand, and peradventure calleth upon him, till he go seek up all his creditors and all those that he hath wronged — so far peradventure asunder⁹¹⁶ that, leaving the one good deed undone the while, he may, before they come together, change that good mind again and do neither the one nor the other. It is good always to be doing some good out of hand⁹¹⁷ while we think thereon; grace shall the better stand with us and increase also to go the farther in the other after. And this I answer if the man had there done the one out of hand — the giving, I mean, half in alms — and not so much as speak of restitution till after; whereas now, though he spoke the one in order before the other, and yet all at one time, the thing remained still in his liberty to put them both in execution after such order as he should then think expedient. But now, Cousin, did the Spirit of God temper the tongue of Zacchaeus in the utterance of these words, in such wise as it may

---

900 See Lk 16:19–31.   901 incentive
902 agreeable   903 *for that:* so that
904 wealth, possessions   905 Lk 19:5
906 *customers or toll-gatherers:* customs
agents or tax collectors   907 *sore infamed*

of ravin: strongly held in infamy for robbery   908 immediately   909 prompting
910 rash   911 unknown   912 See
Lk 19:1–10; esp. 19:8.   913 *in respect
of:* in comparison with   914 suitably,

appropriately   915 *that that:* that which
916 scattered; apart   917 *out of hand:* at
once

well appear the saying of the Wise Man to be verified in them where he saith, *Domini est gubernare
linguam* ("To God it belongeth to govern the
tongue").⁹¹⁸ For here—when he said he would give
half of his whole goods unto poor people, and yet
besides that not only recompense any man whom
he had wronged, but more than recompense him by
three times as much again—he doubly reproved⁹¹⁹
the false suspicion of the people that accounted him
for so evil that they reckoned in their mind all his
goods gotten in effect with wrong because he was
grown to substance⁹²⁰ in that office that was commonly misused extortiously.⁹²¹ But his words declared that he was ripe⁹²² enough in his reckoning
that if half his goods were given away, yet were he
well able to yield every man his duty with the other
half, and yet leave himself no beggar neither—for he
said not he would give away all.

Would God, Cousin, that every rich Christian
man that is reputed right worshipful⁹²³—yea, and
(which yet in my mind more is) reckoned for right
honest too—would and were able to do the thing
that little Zacchaeus, that same great publican (were
he Jew or were he paynim⁹²⁴), said: that is to wit,
with less than half his goods recompense every man
whom he had wronged four times as much; yea, yea,
Cousin, as much for as much, hardly. And then they
that shall receive it shall be content, I dare promise for them, to let the other thrice-as-much go and
forgive it, because it was one of the hard points of
the Old Law, whereas Christian men must be full
of forgiving and not use⁹²⁵ to require and exact their
amends to the uttermost. But now, for our purpose
here, notwithstanding that he promised not neither
to give away all, nor to become a beggar neither, no,
nor yet to leave off his office neither, which, albeit
that he had not used before peradventure in every
point so pure as Saint John the Baptist had taught
them the lesson—*Nihil amplius quam constitutum
est vobis faciatis* ("Do no more than is appointed
unto you")⁹²⁶—yet forasmuch as⁹²⁷ he might both
lawfully use his substance that he minded to reserve,
and lawfully might use his office too, in receiving
the prince's duty according to Christ's express commandment, *Reddite quae sunt Caesaris Caesari*
("Give the Emperor those things that be his"),⁹²⁸

refusing all extortion and bribery besides, our Lord,
well allowing his good purpose, and exacting no further forth of him concerning his worldly behavior,
answered and said, *Hodie salus facta est huic domui,
eo quod et ipse filius sit Abrahae* ("This day is health
comen to this house, for that⁹²⁹ he too is the son of
Abraham").⁹³⁰

But now forget I not, Cousin, that in effect thus
far you condescended unto⁹³¹ me, that a man may
be rich and yet not out of the state of grace, nor
out of God's favor. Howbeit, you think that though
it may be so in some time, or in some place, yet at
this time and in this place or any such other like,
wherein be so many poor people upon whom they
be (you think) bounden to bestow their goods, they
can keep no riches with conscience.⁹³²

Verily, Cousin, if that reason would hold, I ween
the world was never such anywhere in which any
man might have kept any substance without the
danger of damnation, as for⁹³³ since Christ's days
to the world's end, we have the witness of his own
word that there hath never lacked poor men, nor
never shall; for he said himself, *Pauperes semper
habebitis vobiscum, quibus cum vultis benefacere
potestis* ("Poor men shall you always have with you,
whom when you will you may do good unto").⁹³⁴ So
that, as I tell you, if your rule should hold, then were
there, I ween, no place in no time since Christ's days
hither—nor, as I think, in as long before that neither, nor never shall there hereafter—in which there
would abide any man rich without the danger of
eternal damnation even for his riches alone, though
he demeaned⁹³⁵ it never so well. But, Cousin, men of
substance must there be, for else more beggars shall
you have, pardie,⁹³⁶ than there be, and no man left
able to relieve another. For this I think in my mind a
very sure conclusion: that if all the money that is in
this country were tomorrow next brought together
out of every man's hand, and laid all upon one heap,
and then divided out unto every man alike, it would
be on the morrow after worse than it was the day before. For I suppose when it were all equally thus divided among all, the best should be left little better
then than almost a beggar is now. And yet he that
was a beggar before, all that he shall be the richer for
that⁹³⁷ he should thereby receive shall not make him

918 Prv 16:1   **919** proved wrong;
rebuked   **920** wealth   **921** for extortion
922 ready; able   **923** honorable
924 pagan   **925** accustom themselves;
make it their practice   **926** Lk 3:13
927 *forasmuch as:* seeing that, inasmuch
as   **928** Mk 12:17   **929** *for that:* because
930 Lk 19:9   **931** *condescended unto:*
agreed with   **932** a good conscience
933 *as for:* for   **934** Mk 14:7   **935** managed   **936** certainly   **937** what

much above a beggar still; but many one[938] of the rich men, if their riches stood but in movable substance,[939] shall be safe enough from riches haply[940] for all their life after.

Men cannot, you wot well, live here in this world but if that[941] some one man provide a means of living for some other many. Every man cannot have a ship of his own, nor every man be a merchant without a stock. And these things, you wot well, must needs be had; nor every man cannot have a plow by himself. And who might live by the tailor's craft, if no man were able to put a gown to make?[942] Who by the masonry, or who could live a[943] carpenter, if no man were able to build neither church nor house? Who should be the makers of any manner cloth, if there lacked men of substance to set sundry sorts awork? Some man that hath but two ducats in his house were better forbear[944] them both and leave himself not a farthing, but utterly lose all his own, than that some rich man by whom he is weekly set awork should of his money lose the one half, for then were himself like[945] to lack work. For surely the rich man's substance is the wellspring of the poor man's living. And therefore here would it fare by the poor man as it fared by[946] the woman in one of Aesop's fables, which[947] had a hen that laid her every day a golden egg, till on a day she thought she would have a great many eggs at once; and therefore she killed her hen, and found but one or twain in her belly, so that for a few, she lost many.

But now, Cousin, to come to your doubt how it may be that a man may with conscience keep riches with him when he seeth so many poor men upon whom he may bestow it; verily, that might he not with conscience do, if he must bestow it upon as many as he may. And so must of truth every rich man do, if all the poor folk that he seeth be so specially by God's commandment committed unto his charge alone that, because our Savior saith *omni petenti te da* ("give every man that asketh thee"),[948] therefore he be bounden to give out still to every beggar that will ask him, as long as any penny lasteth in his purse. But verily, Cousin, that saying hath (as Saint Augustine saith other places in Scripture hath) need of interpretation;[949] for as Saint Augustine saith, [*Omni petenti, inquit; non, omnia petenti*] ("Though Christ saith 'give every man that asketh thee,' he saith not, yet, 'give them all that they will ask thee'").[950] But surely all were one if he meant to bind me by commandment to give every man without exception somewhat, for so should I leave myself nothing.

Our Savior in that place of the sixth chapter of Saint Luke speaketh both of the contempt that we should in heart have of these worldly things, and also of the manner that men should use toward their enemies; for there he biddeth us love our enemies, give good words for evil, and not only suffer injuries patiently, both by taking away of our goods and harm done unto our body, but also be ready to suffer the double, and over[951] that to do them good again[952] that do us the harm.[953] And among these things he biddeth us "give every man that asketh," meaning that in the thing that we may conveniently do a man good, we should not refuse it, what manner of man soever he be, though he were our mortal enemy, namely[954] where we see that but if[955] we help him ourselves, the person of the man should stand in peril of perishing; and therefore saith, *Si esurierit inimicus tuus, da illi cibum* ("If thine enemy be in hunger, give him meat").[956] But now, though I be bound to give every manner man, in some manner, of his necessity—were he my friend or my foe, Christian man or heathen—yet am I not unto all men bound alike, nor unto any man in every case alike; but, as I began to tell you, the differences of the circumstances make great change in the matter. Saint Paul saith, *Qui non providet suis est infidelis deterior* ("He that provideth not for those that are his is worse than an infidel").[957] Those are ours that are belonging to our charge, either by nature or by law, or any commandment of God (by nature, as[958] our children; by law, as our servants in our household), so that, albeit these two sorts be not ours all alike, yet would I think that the least ours of the twain— that is to wit, our servants—if they need or lack, we be bounden to look to them and provide for their need, and see, so far-forth[959] as we may, that they

---

938 *many one:* many a one   **939** possessions   **940** perhaps   **941** *but if that:* unless   **942** *put a gown to make:* commission the making of a gown   **943** *live a:* make a living as a   **944** part with   **945** likely   **946** *fare by … fared by:* go with … as it went with   **947** who   **948** Lk 6:30   **949** The idea that Scripture is in need of interpretation is common in Augustine. See, for example, *City of God* 11.19.   **950** Augustine, *On the Sermon on the Mount* 2.20. More left a space here for the quotation to be added.   **951** in addition to   **952** in return   **953** See Lk 6:27–31.   **954** especially   **955** *but if:* unless   **956** Rom 12:20   **957** 1 Tm 5:8   **958** such as   **959** *so far-forth:* so far forward, i.e., to the extent

lack not the things that should serve for their necessity while they dwell in our service. Meseemeth also if they fall sick in our service, so that they cannot do the service that we retain them for, yet may we not in any wise turn them then out of doors, and cast them up comfortless while they be not able to labor and help themselves, for this were a thing against all humanity. And surely if he were but a wayfaring man that I received into my house as a guest, if he fall sick therein and his money gone, I reckon myself bounden to keep him still, and rather to beg about for his relief than cast him out in that case to the peril of his life, what loss soever I should hap to sustain in the keeping of him. For when God hath by such chance sent him to me, and there once matched me with him, I reckon myself surely charged with him, till I may without peril of his life be well and conveniently⁹⁶⁰ discharged of him.

By God's commandment are in our charge our parents, for by nature we be in theirs since, as Saint Paul saith, it is not the children's part to provide for the parents, but the parents' to provide for the children⁹⁶¹ — provide, I mean, conveniently⁹⁶² good learning, or good occupations to get their living by with truth and the favor of God, but not to make provision for them of such manner living as to Godward⁹⁶³ they should live the worse for; but rather, if they see by their manner that too much would make them naught, the father should then give them a great deal the less. But although that⁹⁶⁴ nature put not the parents in the charge of the children, yet not only God commandeth, but the order of nature also compelleth, that the children should both in reverent behavior honor their father and mother, and also in all their necessity maintain them. And yet as much as God and nature both bindeth us to the sustenance of our own father, his need may be so little (though it be somewhat), and a fremd⁹⁶⁵ man's so great, that both nature and God also would I should, in such unequal need, relieve that urgent necessity of a stranger — yea, my foe and God's enemy too, the very Turk or Saracen — before a little need, and unlikely to do great harm, in my father, and my mother too. For so ought they both twain themselves to be well content I should.

But now, Cousin, out⁹⁶⁶ of the case of such extreme needs well perceived and known unto myself, I am not bound to give every beggar that will ask, nor to believe every faitour⁹⁶⁷ that I meet in the street that will say himself that he is very sick, nor to reckon all the poor folk committed by God only so to my charge alone that none other man should give them nothing of his till I have first given out all mine, nor am not bounden neither to have so evil opinion of all other folk save myself as to think that but if⁹⁶⁸ I help, the poor folk shall all fail at once, for God hath left in all this quarter no more good folks now but me. I may think better by⁹⁶⁹ my neighbors and worse by myself than so, and yet come to heaven by God's grace well enough.

VINCENT: Marry,⁹⁷⁰ Uncle; but some man will peradventure be right well content in such case to think his neighbors very charitable, to the intent that he may think himself at liberty to give nothing at all.

ANTONY: That is, Cousin, very true; so will there some be content either to think or make⁹⁷¹ as though they thought — but those are they that are content to give nought because they be naught. But our question is, Cousin, not of them, but of good folk that by the keeping of worldly goods stand in great fear to offend God. For the acquieting⁹⁷² of their conscience speak we now, to the intent that they may perceive what manner of having of worldly goods and keeping thereof may stand with the state of grace. Now think I, Cousin, that if a man keep riches about him for a glory and royalty⁹⁷³ of the world, in the consideration whereof he taketh a great delight, and liketh himself therefor — taking the poorer, for the lack thereof, as one far worse than himself — such a mind is very vain foolish pride, and such a man is very naught indeed. But on the other side, if there be a man such (as would God were many) that hath unto riches no love, but having it fall abundantly unto him, taketh to his own part no great pleasure thereof, but as though he had it not, keepeth himself in like⁹⁷⁴ abstinence and penance privily as he would do in case he had it not, and in such things as he doth openly, bestow somewhat more liberally upon himself in his house after some manner of the world, lest he should give other folk occasion to marvel and muse and talk of his manner and misreport him for a hypocrite, therein between God and him doth truly protest and testify[975] as did the good queen Esther,[976] that he doth it not for any desire thereof in the satisfying of his own pleasure, but would with as good will or better forbear the possession of riches, saving[977] for the commodity[978] that other men have by his possessing thereof—as percase[979] in keeping a good household in good Christian order and fashion, and in setting other folk awork with such things as they gain their living the better by his means—this man's having of riches I might, methinketh, in merit match, in a manner, with another man's forsaking of all, if there were none other circumstance more pleasant unto God added further unto the forsaking besides— as percase for the more fervent contemplation, by reason of the solicitude of all worldly business left off, which was the thing that made Mary Magdalene's part the better. For else would Christ have canned[980] her much more thanks to go about and be busy in the helping her sister Martha to dress[981] his dinner than to take her stool and sit down at her ease and do nought.[982]

Now if he that have these goods and riches by him have not haply fully so perfect a mind, but somewhat loveth to keep himself from lack, and not, so fully as a pure Christian fashion requireth, determined to abandon his pleasure—well, what will you more? The man is so much the less perfect than I would he were, and haply than himself would wish if it were as easy to be it as to wish it, but yet not by and by[983] in state of damnation for all that—no more than every man is forthwith[984] in state of damnation that, forsaking all and entering into religion,[985] is not yet always so clear depured[986] from all worldly affections as he himself would very fain[987] he were and much bewaileth that he is not; of whom, some man that hath in the world willingly forsaken the likelihood of right worshipful rooms[988] hath afterward had much ado to keep himself from the desire of the office of cellarer or sexton,[989] to bear yet at the leastwise some rule and

authority, though it were but among the bells. But God is more merciful to man's imperfection—if the man know it and knowledge it and mislike it, and little and little[990] labor to amend it—than to reject and cast to the devil him that, after as[991] his frailty can bear and suffer, hath a general intent and purpose to please him, and to prefer or set by[992] nothing in all this world before him.

And therefore, Cousin, to make an end of this piece withal,[993] *a negotio perambulante in tenebris*— of this devil, I mean, that the prophet calleth "Business walking in the darkness"—if a man have a mind to serve God and please him, and rather lose all the goods he hath than wittingly[994] to do deadly sin, and would without murmur or grudge[995] give it every whit away in case that God should so command him, and intend to take it patiently if God would take it from him, and glad would be to use it unto God's pleasure, and do his diligence to know and to be taught what manner using thereof God would be pleased with, and therein from time to time be glad to follow the counsel of good virtuous men, though he neither give away all at once nor give every man that asketh him neither, let every man fear and think in this world that all the good that he doth or can do is a great deal too little, but yet for all[996] that fear let him dwell therewith in the faithful hope of God's help, and then shall the truth of God so compass him about (as the prophet saith) with a pavise[997] that he shall not so need to dread the trains[998] of and the temptations of the devil that the prophet calleth "Business walking about in the darkness," but that he shall, for all the having of riches and worldly substance, so avoid his trains and his temptations that he shall in conclusion,[999] by the great grace and almighty mercy of God, get into heaven well enough. And now was I, Cousin, about, lo, after this piece thus ended, to bid them bring in our dinner; but now shall I not need, lo, for here they come with it already.

VINCENT: Forsooth, good Uncle, God disposeth and timeth your matter and your dinner both, I

---

975 *truly … testify:* truthfully assert and attest **976** See Est 14:16–19. **977** except **978** benefit, advantage, profit **979** perhaps **980** given, expressed **981** prepare **982** See Lk 10:38–42. **983** *by and by:* on that account **984** immediately **985** a religious

order **986** *clear depured:* entirely purified **987** gladly (wish) **988** *right worshipful rooms:* very distinguished offices or positions **989** *cellarer or sexton:* officer in a monastery charged with storing and distributing food, officer assigned to grounds-keeping, grave-digging, and

bell-ringing **990** *little and little:* little by little **991** *after as:* according to what **992** *set by:* value **993** with **994** deliberately **995** *murmur or grudge:* complaint or grumbling **996** *for all:* despite **997** large shield **998** traps, deceits **999** *in conclusion:* in the end, at last trust. For the end of your good tale (for which our Lord reward you) and the beginning here of your good dinner too (from which it were more than pity that you should any longer have tarried) meet even at the close together.

ANTONY: Well, Cousin, now will we say grace, and then for a while will we leave talking, and assay[1] how our dinner shall like us, and how fair we can fall to feeding;[2] which done, you know my customable guise[3] (for "manner" I may not call it, because the guise is unmannerly) to bid you not farewell, but steal away from you to sleep. But, you wot well, I am not wont[4] at afternoon to sleep long, but even a little to forget the world; and when I wake, I will again come to you. And then is, God willing, all this long day ours, wherein we shall have time enough to talk much more than shall suffice for the finishing of this one part of our matter, which only now remaineth.

VINCENT: I pray you, good Uncle, keep your customable manner, for "manner" may you call it well enough: for as it were against good manner to look[5] that a man should kneel down for courtesy when his knee is sore, so is it very good manner that a man of your age, aggrieved with such sundry sicknesses besides that suffer you not always to sleep when you should, let this sleep not slip away, but take it when you may. And I will, Uncle, in the meanwhile steal[6] from you too, and speed[7] a little errand and return to you again.

ANTONY: Tarry while you will, and when you have dined, go at your pleasure—but I pray you tarry not long.

VINCENT: You shall not need, Uncle, to put me in mind of that, I would so fain have up[8] the remnant of our matter.

---

1 try   **2** *fall to feeding:* begin eating   practice   **4** accustomed   **5** expect   willingly take up
3 *customable guise:* customary   **6** depart   **7** carry out   **8** *fain have up:*

THE THIRD BOOK

The third and last book of consolation and
comfort in tribulation

PREFACE

5 **V**INCENT: Somewhat have I tarried the longer, Uncle, partly for that[1] I was loath to come oversoon, lest my soon coming might have happed[2] to have made you wake too soon, but specially by reason that I was letted with[3] one that showed me a 10 letter dated at Constantinople, by which letter it appeareth that the great Turk prepareth a marvelous mighty army. And yet whither he will therewith,[4] that can there yet no man tell. But I fear in good faith, Uncle, that his voyage shall be hither. How- 15 beit,[5] he that wrote the letter saith that it is secretly said in Constantinople that great part of his army shall be shipped and sent either into Naples or into Sicily.

ANTONY: It may fortune, Cousin, that the letter of 20 the Venetian dated at Constantinople was devised at Venice; from thence come there some among,[6] and sometimes from Rome too, and sometimes also from some other places, letters all farced[7] full of such tidings — that the Turk is ready to do some 25 great exploit which tidings they blow about for the furtherance of some such affairs as they then have themselves in hand.

The Turk hath also so many men of arms in his retinue at his continual charge that,[8] lest they 30 should lie still and do nothing but peradventure[9] fall in devising of some novelties among themselves, he is fain[10] yearly to make some assemblies, and some changing of them from one place to another, and part some sort asunder, that they wax not 35 overwell acquainted by dwelling overlong together.

By these ways also he maketh those that he mindeth[11] suddenly to invade indeed the less to look therefor — and thereby the less preparation to make before — while they see him so many times make 40 a great visage of war when he mindeth it not. But

then, at one time or other, they suddenly feel it when they fear it not.

Howbeit,[12] full likely, Cousin, it is of very truth that into this realm of Hungary he will not fail to come; for neither is there any country through 45 Christendom that lieth for him so meet,[13] nor never was there any time till now in which he might so well and surely win it.

For now call we him in ourselves (God save us), as Aesop telleth that the sheep took in the wolf unto 50 them to keep them from the dogs.[14]

VINCENT: Then are there very like,[15] good Uncle, all those tribulations to fall upon us here that I spoke of in the beginning of our first communication here the other day. 55

ANTONY: Very truth it is, Cousin, that so there will of likelihood in a while, but not forthwith[16] all at the first. For while he cometh under the color of aid for the one[17] against the other, he will somewhat see the proof[18] before he fully show himself. 60 But in conclusion, if he be able to get it for him,[19] you shall see him so handle it that he shall not fail to get it from him, and that forthwith out of hand,[20] ere[21] ever he suffer him settle himself over-sure therein. 65

VINCENT: Yet say they, Uncle, that he useth not[22] to force any man to forsake his faith.

ANTONY: Not any man, Cousin? They say more than they can make good that tell you so. He maketh a solemn oath among the ceremonies of the 70 feast in which he first taketh upon him the authority that he shall, in all that he possibly may, diminish the faith of Christ, and dilate[23] the faith of Muhammad. But yet hath he not used[24] to force every whole country at once to forsake their faith; for of 75

---

1 *for that:* because **2** happened **3** *letted with:* delayed by **4** *with that* **5** However **6** occasionally, now and again **7** stuffed **8** who **9** perhaps **10** obliged **11** intends **12** Nevertheless

13 suitable, useful **14** Erasmus's *Adagia* 1.4.10 is somewhat related. **15** likely **16** immediately **17** *color of aid for the one:* pretext of aiding one of the two kings vying for the rule of Hungary. See end of Preface,

Book 1. **18** *the proof:* outcome **19** *for him:* for that one king **20** *out of hand:* without delay **21** before **22** *useth not:* is not accustomed **23** increase; disperse, spread abroad **24** been accustomed

some countries hath he been content only to take a tribute yearly, and let them then live as they list.²⁵

Out of some he taketh the whole people away, dispersing them for slaves among many sundry countries of his very far from their own, without any sufferance of regress.²⁶

Some country, so great and populous that they cannot well be carried and conveyed thence, he destroyeth the gentlemen and giveth the lands, part to such as he bringeth, and part to such as willingly will renay²⁷ their faith, and keepeth the others in such misery that they were in manner as good be dead at once. In rest, he suffereth else no²⁸ Christian man almost, but those that resort²⁹ as merchants, or those that offer themselves to serve him in his war.

But as for those Christian countries that he useth not for only tributaries (as he doth Chios, Cyprus, or Candia),³⁰ but reckoneth for clear conquest and utterly taketh for his own (as Morea,³¹ Greece, and Macedonia, and such other like—and as I verily³² think he will Hungary, if he get it), in all those useth he Christian people after sundry fashions; he letteth them dwell there indeed, because they were too many to carry all away, and too many to kill them all too, but if³³ he should either leave the land dispeopled and desolate, or else some other countries of his own from whence he should (which would not well be done) convey the people thither to people that land withal.³⁴

There, lo, those that will not be turned from their faith, of which God keepeth (lauded be his holy name) very many, he suffereth³⁵ to dwell still in peace; but yet is their peace for all that not very peaceable. For lands he suffereth them to have none of their own; office or honest room³⁶ they bear none; with occasions of his wars he pilleth³⁷ them with taxes and tallages³⁸ unto the bare bones. Their children he chooseth where he list in their youth and taketh them from their parents, conveying them whither he list where their friends never see them after, and abuseth them as he list; some young maidens maketh harlots, some young men he bringeth up in war, and some young children he causeth to be gelded³⁹—not their stones cut out as the custom was of old, but cutteth off their whole

members by the body; how few escape and live he little forceth,⁴⁰ for he will have enough. And all that he so taketh young to any use of his own are betaken to such Turks or false renegates⁴¹ to keep that they be turned from the faith of Christ every one, or else so handled that, as for this world, they come to an evil chieving.⁴² For besides many other contumelies and despites⁴³ that the Turks and the false renegate Christians many times do to good Christian people that still persevere and abide by the faith, they find the means sometimes to make some false shrews⁴⁴ say that they heard such a Christian man speak opprobrious words against Muhammad. And upon that point falsely testified will they take occasion to compel him forsake the faith of Christ, and turn to the profession of their shameful superstitious sect, or else will they put him unto death with cruel intolerable torments.

Vincent: Our Lord, Uncle, for his mighty mercy, keep those wretches hence. For by my troth,⁴⁵ if they hap to come hither, methink I see many more tokens than one that we shall have of our own folk here ready to fall in unto them. For like as before a great storm, the sea beginneth sometimes to work and roar in itself ere ever⁴⁶ the wind waxeth boistous,⁴⁷ so methink I hear at mine ear some of our own here among us, which within these few years could no more have borne the name of a Turk than the name of the devil, begin now to find little fault therein—yea, and some to praise them too, little and little⁴⁸ as they may, more glad to find faults at every state of Christendom: priests, princes, rites, ceremonies, sacraments, laws and customs, spiritual, temporal, and all.

Antony: In good faith, Cousin, so begin we to fare here indeed, and that but even now of late. For since the title of the crown hath comen in question, the good rule of this realm hath very sore decayed, as little while as it is. And undoubtedly Hungary shall never do well as long as it standeth in this case: that men's minds hearken after novelties, and have their hearts hanging upon a change. And much the worse I like it when their words walk so large⁴⁹

---

25 please **26** return **27** renounce
28 *suffereth else no:* permits no other
29 go there **30** *Chios, Cyprus, or Candia:*
Candia is Crete; all are Greek islands.
31 the Peloponnese **32** truly **33** *but if:*

unless **34** with **35** allows **36** *honest*
room: position or office of honor **37** robs
38 taxes **39** castrated **40** cares
41 apostates, traitors **42** end, outcome
43 *contumelies and despites:* insults

and scornful actions **44** scoundrels
45 truth, faithfulness **46** *ere ever:* before
even **47** *waxeth boistous:* becomes loud or
violent **48** *little and little:* little by little
49 *walk so large:* tend so unrestrainedly

toward the favor of the Turk's sect, which they were ever wont[50] to have in so great abomination, as every true-minded Christian man and Christian woman too must have.

I am of such age as you see, and verily from as far as I can remember, it hath been marked and oftentimes proved true that when children have in Buda fallen in a fantasy by themselves to draw together, and in their playing make as it were corpses carried to church, and sing after their childish fashion the tune of the Dirge,[51] there hath great death there shortly followed after. And twice or thrice I may remember in my days when children in diverse parts of this realm have gathered themselves in sundry companies, and made as it were parties[52] and battles, and after their battles in sport (wherein some children have yet taken great hurt), there hath fallen very[53] battle and deadly war indeed.

These tokens were somewhat like your example of the sea, since they be of things that after follow tokens foregoing, through some secret motion or instinct, whereof the cause is unknown. But by Saint Mary, Cousin, these tokens like I much worse— these tokens, I say, not of children's plays, nor of children's songs, but old shrews' large[54] open words so boldly spoken in the favor of Muhammad's sect in this realm of Hungary, that hath been ever hitherto a very sure key of Christendom. And out of[55] doubt, if Hungary be lost, and that the Turk have it once fast in his possession, he shall, ere it be long after, have an open ready way into almost the remnant of all Christendom; though he win it not all in a week, the great part will be won after, I fear me, within very few years.

VINCENT: But yet evermore I trust in Christ, good Uncle, that he shall not suffer that abominable sect of his mortal enemies in such wise[56] to prevail against his Christian country.

ANTONY: That is very well said, Cousin. Let us have our sure hope in him, and then shall we be very sure that we shall not be deceived, for either shall we have the thing that we hope for, or a better

thing in the stead;[57] for as for the thing itself that we pray for, and hope to have, God will not always send us. And therefore, as I said in our first communication,[58] in all things save[59] only for heaven, our prayer nor our hope may never be too precise, although the thing be lawful to require.[60]

Verily, if we people of the Christian nations were such as would God we were, I would little fear all the preparations that the great Turk could make. No, nor yet being as bad as we be, I nothing doubt at all but that in conclusion,[61] how base soever Christendom be brought, it shall spring up again till the time be come very near to the Day of Doom,[62] whereof some tokens, as methinketh, are not comen yet. But somewhat before that time shall Christendom be striated sore,[63] and brought into so narrow a compass[64] that, according to Christ's words, *Filius hominis cum venerit putas inveniet fidem in terra?* ("When the Son of Man shall come again"—that is to wit,[65] to the day of general judgment—"weenest[66] thou that he shall find faith in the earth?"),[67] as who say,[68] but a little; for as appeareth in the Apocalypse and other places of Scripture,[69] the faith shall be at that time so far faded that he shall for the love of his elects,[70] lest they should fall and perish too, abridge those days and accelerate his coming.

But as I say, methinketh I miss yet in my mind some of those tokens that shall by the Scripture come a good while before that—and among others, the coming in of the Jews,[71] and the dilating[72] of Christendom again—before the world come to that strait. So that I say for mine own mind, I little doubt but that this ungracious sect of Muhammad shall have a foul fall, and Christendom spring and spread, flower and increase again. Howbeit, the pleasure and the comfort shall they see that shall be born after that we be buried, I fear me both twain.[73] For God giveth us great likelihood that, for our sinful wretched living, he goeth about to make these infidels, that are his open professed enemies, the sorrowful scourge of correction over evil Christian people that should be faithful, and are of truth his falsely professed friends. And surely, Cousin, albeit

---

50 accustomed   **51** *the Dirge:* the Psalms which make up the Office for the Dead   **52** sides in a battle; factions   **53** true   **54** unrestrained; intemperate   **55** *out of:* without a   **56** a way   **57** *the stead:* its place   **58** conversation   **59** except

60 ask for   **61** *in conclusion:* in the end   **62** *Day of Doom:* Judgment Day   **63** *straited sore:* grievously contracted   **64** *narrow a compass:* small an area   **65** *that is to wit:* that is to say; namely   **66** think   **67** Lk 18:8   **68** *as who*

say: that is to say   **69** See Rv 9:20; 13:5–10; 14:12; Mt 24:22.   **70** chosen ones   **71** See Rom 11:25–26.   **72** expanding   **73** together

that[74] methinketh I see diverse evil tokens of this misery coming to us, yet can there not in my mind be a worse prognostication[75] thereof than this ungracious token that you note here yourself. For undoubtedly, Cousin, this new manner here of men's favorable fashion in their language toward these ungracious Turks declareth plainly that not only their minds give them that hither in shall he come,[76] but also that they can be content both to live under him and, over[77] that, from the true faith of Christ, to fall into Muhammad's false abominable sect.

VINCENT: Verily, mine Uncle, as I go more about than you, so must I needs more hear—which is a heavy[78] hearing in mine ear—the manner of men in this matter, which increaseth about us here. I trust in other places of this realm by God's grace it is otherwise, but in this quarter here about us, many of these fellows that are meet[79] for the war, first were wont as it were in sport, and in a while after, half between game and earnest, and, by our Lady, now not far from fair[80] flat earnest indeed, talk as though they looked for a day when, with a turn unto the Turk's faith, they should be made masters here of true Christian men's bodies, and owners of all their goods.

ANTONY: Though I go little abroad, Cousin, yet hear I sometimes, when I say little, almost as much as that. But while there is no man to complain to for the redress, what remedy but patience, and fain[81] to sit still and hold my peace? For of these two that strive whether of them both shall reign upon us—and each of them calleth himself king, and both twain[82] put the people to pain—the one is, you wot[83] well, too far from our quarter here to help us in this behalf, and the other, while he looketh for the Turk's aid, either will not, or I ween well dare not, find any fault with them that favor the Turk and his sect. For of Turks natural[84] this country lacketh none now, which are here conversant[85] under diverse pretexts, and of everything advertise[86] the great Turk full surely. And therefore, Cousin, albeit I would advise every man pray still and call unto God to hold his gracious hand over us, and

keep away this wretchedness if his pleasure be, yet would I further advise every good Christian body to remember and consider that it is very likely to come, and therefore make his reckoning and cast his pennyworths[87] before, and every man and every woman both appoint[88] with God's help in their own mind beforehand what thing they intend to do if the very worst fall.

THE FIRST CHAPTER

Whether a man should cast in his mind and appoint in his heart before, that if he were taken with Turks, he would rather die than forsake the faith

VINCENT: Well fare your heart, good Uncle, for this good counsel of yours. For surely methinketh that this is marvelous good. But yet heard I once a right cunning[89] and a very good man say that it were great folly, and very perilous too, that a man should think upon any such thing, or imagine any such case in his mind, for fear of double peril that may follow thereupon: for either shall he be likely to answer himself, to that case put[90] by himself, that he will rather suffer any painful death than forsake his faith—and by that bold appointment[91] should he fall in the fault of Saint Peter, that[92] of oversight made a proud promise and soon had a foul fall—or else were he likely to think that, rather than abide the pain, he would forsake God indeed, and by that mind should sin deadly[93] through his own folly, whereas he needeth not, as he that shall peradventure[94] never come in the peril to be put thereunto. And that therefore it were most wisdom never to think upon any such manner case.

ANTONY: I believe well, Cousin, that you have heard some man that would so say. For I can show almost as much as that, left of a very good man and a great solemn doctor in writing. But yet, Cousin, although I should hap to find one or two more as good men, and as well-learned too, that would both twain say and write the same, yet would I not fear for my part to counsel my friend to the contrary; for, Cousin, if his mind answer him as Saint Peter

---

74 *albeit that:* although　**75** prophecy; prediction　**76** *not ... come:* not only do they think he will come in here　**77** beyond　**78** distressing, sorrowful, grievous　**79** suitable　**80** plain, open

81 willingly　**82** *both twain:* each separately　**83** know　**84** *Turks natural:* native Turks　**85** dwelling　**86** notify　**87** *cast his pennyworths:* consider what it will cost him　**88** determine, decide　**89** learned

90 *case put:* hypothetical scenario proposed　**91** decision, determination　**92** who　**93** mortally　**94** perhaps

answered Christ, that he would rather die than forsake him, though he say therein more unto himself
than he should be peradventure able to make good
if it came to the point, yet perceive I not that he
doth in that thought any deadly displeasure unto
God—nor Saint Peter, though he said more than
he could perform, yet in his so saying offended not
God greatly neither. But his offense was when he
did not after so well as he said before. But now may
this man be likely never to fall in the peril of breaking that appointment, since of some ten thousand
that so shall examine themselves, never one shall fall
in the peril; and yet to have that good purpose all
their life seemeth me no more harm the while than
a poor beggar that hath never a penny to think that
if he had great substance,⁹⁵ he would give great alms
for God's sake.

But now is all the peril, if the man answer himself that he would in such case rather forsake the
faith of Christ with his mouth, and keep it still in
his heart, than for the confessing of it to endure a
painful death; for by this mind he falleth in deadly
sin, which, while he never cometh in the case indeed, if he never had put himself the case, he never
had fallen in. But in good faith methinketh that he
which⁹⁶ upon that case put unto himself by himself will make himself that answer hath the habit of
faith so faint and so cold that, to the better knowledge of himself and of his necessity, to pray for more
strength of grace he had need to have the question
put him either by himself or some other man.

Besides this, to counsel a man never to think on
that case is in my mind as much reason⁹⁷ as the medicine that I have heard taught one for the toothache:
to go thrice about a churchyard and never think on
a foxtail. For if the counsel be not given them, it
cannot serve them; and if it be given them, it must
put the point of the matter in their mind, which
by and by⁹⁸ to reject and think therein neither one
thing nor other is a thing that may be sooner bidden than obeyed.

I ween also that very few men can escape it, but
that though they would never think thereon by
themselves, but that yet in one place or other where
they shall hap to come in company, they shall have
the question by adventure so proposed⁹⁹ and put

forth that, like¹⁰⁰ as while he heareth one talking to
him, he may well wink¹⁰¹ if he will, but he cannot
make himself sleep, so shall he, whether he will or
no, think one thing or other therein.

Finally, when Christ spoke so often and so plain
of the matter that every man should, upon pain of
damnation, openly confess his faith, if men took him
and by dread of death would drive him to the contrary,¹⁰² it seemeth me in a manner implied therein
that we be bounden conditionally to have evermore
that mind (actually¹⁰³ sometimes, and evermore habitually) that, if the case so should fall, then with
God's help so we would.

And thus much thinketh me necessary for every
man and woman to be always of this mind, and often to think thereupon, and where they find in the
thinking thereon their hearts agrise¹⁰⁴ and shrink
in the remembrance of the pain that their imagination representeth to the mind, then must they call
to mind and remember the great pain and torment
that Christ suffered for them, and heartily pray for
grace, that if the case should so fall, God should give
them strength to stand. And thus with exercise of
such meditation, though men should never stand
full out of fear of falling, yet must they persevere in
good hope, and in full purpose of standing.

And this seemeth me,¹⁰⁵ Cousin, so far-forth¹⁰⁶
the mind that every Christian man and woman
must needs have that methinketh every curate¹⁰⁷
should often counsel all his parishions,¹⁰⁸ and every
man and woman their servants and their children,
even beginning in their tender youth, to know this
point and think thereon, and little and little¹⁰⁹ from
their very childhood to accustom them dulcely¹¹⁰
and pleasantly in the meditation thereof; whereby
the goodness of God shall not fail so to aspire¹¹¹ the
grace of his Holy Spirit into their hearts, in reward
of that virtuous diligence, that through such ac-
tual¹¹² meditation he shall conserve them in such a
sure habit of spiritual faithful strength that all the
devils in hell, with all the wrestling that they can
make, shall never be able to wrest it out of their
heart.

VINCENT: By my troth, Uncle, methinketh that
you say very well.

---

95 wealth   **96** who   **97** *as much reason:*
as reasonable   **98** *by and by:* immediately,
at once   **99** *adventure so proposed:* chance
so proposed   **100** just   **101** shut his eyes

102 See Mt 10:32–33; Mk 8:38; Lk 9:26;
12:9.   **103** actively   **104** tremble; shudder
with terror   **105** *seemeth me:* it seems to
me   **106** *so far-forth:* to such an extent

107 pastor   **108** parishioners   **109** *little
and little:* little by little   **110** sweetly
111 breathe   **112** active

ANTONY: I say surely, Cousin, as I think; and yet all this have I said concerning them that dwell in such places as they be never like[113] in their lives to come in the danger to be put to the proof. Howbeit many a man may ween himself far therefrom that[114] yet may fortune by some one chance or other to fall in the case that either for the truth of faith, or for the truth of justice (which go almost all alike), he may fall in the case. But now be you and I, Cousin, and all our friends here, far in another point. For we be so likely to fall in the experience thereof so soon that it had been more time[115] for us (all other things set aside) to have devised[116] upon this matter, and firmly to have settled ourselves upon a fast point[117] long ago, than to begin to commune[118] and counsel upon it now.

VINCENT: In good faith, Uncle, you say therein very truth, and would God it had come sooner in my mind. But better is it yet late than never. And I trust God shall yet give us respite and time—whereof, Uncle, that we lose no part, I pray you proceed now with your good counsel therein.

ANTONY: Very gladly, Cousin, shall I now go forth in the fourth temptation, which only remaineth to be treated of, and properly pertaineth whole[119] unto this present purpose.

THE SECOND CHAPTER
Of the fourth temptation, which is persecution for the faith, touched in these words of the prophet:
ab incursu et daemonio meridiano[120]

ANTONY: The fourth temptation, Cousin, that the prophet speaketh of in the fore-remembered psalm, *Qui habitat in adiutorio Altissimi,*[121] etc., is plain open persecution, which is touched in these words: *ab incursu et daemonio meridiano.* And of all his temptations this is the most perilous, the most bitter sharp, and the most rigorous. For whereas in other temptations he useth either pleasant allectives[122] unto sin, or either secret sleights and trains,[123] and cometh in the night, and stealeth[124] on

in the dark unware,[125] or in some other part of the day flieth and passeth by like an arrow (so shaping himself, sometimes in one fashion, sometimes in another, and so dissimuling[126] himself and his high mortal malice, that a man is thereby so blinded and beguiled that he may not sometimes perceive well what he is), in this temptation, this plain open persecution for the faith, he cometh even in the very midday—that is to wit, even upon them that have a high light of faith shining in their heart—and openly suffereth[127] himself so plainly be perceived by his fierce malicious persecution against the faithful Christians for hatred of Christ's true Catholic faith that no man having faith can doubt what he is; for in this temptation he showeth himself such as the prophet nameth him, *daemonium meridianum* ("the midday devil"), he may be so lightsomely[128] seen with the eye of a faithful soul by his fierce furious assault and incursion; for therefore saith the prophet that the truth of God shall compass that man round about that[129] dwelleth in the faithful hope of his help with a pavise[130] *ab incursu et daemonio meridiano* ("from the incursion and the devil of the midday"), because this kind of persecution is not a wily temptation, but a furious force and a terrible incursion. In others of his temptations he stealeth on like a fox; but in this Turk's persecution for the faith, he runneth on roaring with assault like a ramping[131] lion.

This temptation is of all temptations also the most perilous: for whereas in temptations of prosperity he useth only delectable allectives to move a man to sin, and in other kinds of tribulation and adversity he useth only grief and pain to pull a man into murmur,[132] impatience, and blasphemy, in this kind of persecution for the faith of Christ he useth both twain—that is to wit, both his allective of quiet and rest by deliverance from death and pain, with other pleasures also of this present life, and besides that, the terror and infliction of intolerable pain and torment.

In other tribulation, as[133] loss, or sickness, or death of our friends, though the pain be peradventure as great and sometimes greater too, yet is not the peril nowhere nigh[134] half so much; for in other

---

113 likely   114 who   115 *more time:* more the time   116 decided, resolved 117 *fast point:* firm resolution   118 discuss together   119 entirely, completely 120 "From the incursion and devil of

the midday" (Ps 90(91):6)   121 "He who dwells in the help of the Most High" (Ps 90(91))   122 enticements 123 *sleights and trains:* sly tricks and snares   124 moves stealthily and

secretly   125 unnoticed   126 disguising 127 allows   128 clearly   129 who 130 large shield   131 rampaging, raging; 1 Pt 5:8   132 muttering complaints 133 such as   134 near

tribulations, as I said before, that necessity that the man must of fine force[135] abide and endure the pain, wax[136] he never so wroth[137] and impatient therewith, is a great reason to move him to keep his patience therein, and be content therewith, and thank God thereof, and of necessity to make a virtue, that he may be rewarded for. But in this temptation, this persecution for the faith, I mean not by fight in the field by which the faithful man standeth at his defense and putteth the faithless in half the fear and half the harm too, but where he is taken and in hold,[138] and may for the forswearing or the denying of his faith be delivered and suffered to live in rest and some in great worldly wealth also. In this case, I say, this thing—that he needeth not to suffer this trouble and pain but he will[139]—is a marvelous great occasion for him to fall into the sin that the devil would drive him to: that is to wit, the forsaking of the faith. And therefore as I say, of all the devil's temptations is this temptation, this persecution for the faith, the most perilous.

VINCENT: The more perilous, Uncle, that this temptation is, as indeed of all temptations the most perilous it is, the more need have they that stand in peril thereof to be before with substantial advice and good counsel well-armed against it, that we may, with the comfort and consolation thereof, the better bear that tribulation when it cometh, and the better withstand the temptation.

ANTONY: You say, Cousin Vincent, therein very truth, and I am content to fall therefore in hand with[140] it. But forasmuch, Cousin, as methinketh, that[141] of this tribulation somewhat you be more feared than I—and of truth somewhat more excusable it is in you than it were in me, mine age considered, and the sorrow that I have suffered already, with some other considerations upon my part besides—rehearse[142] you therefore the griefs and the pains that you think in this tribulation possible to fall unto you, and I shall against[143] each of them give you counsel, and rehearse you such occasion of comfort and consolation as my poor wit and learning can call unto my mind.

VINCENT: In good faith, Uncle, I am not all-thing afeard[144] in this case only for myself, but well you wot I have cause to care also for many more, and that folk of sundry sorts, men and women both, and that not all of one age.

ANTONY: All that you have cause to fear for, Cousin, for all them have I cause to fear with you too, since all your kinsfolk and allies within a little[145] be likewise unto me; howbeit,[146] to say the truth, every man hath cause in this case to fear both for himself and also for every other. For since, as the Scripture saith, *Unicuique dedit Deus curam de proximo suo* ("God hath given every man cure[147] and charge of his neighbor"),[148] there is no man that hath any spark of Christian love and charity in his breast but that[149] in a matter of such peril as this is, wherein the soul of man standeth in so great danger to be lost, he must needs care and take thought, not for his friends only, but also for his very foes; we shall therefore, Cousin, not rehearse your harms or mine that may befall in this persecution, but all the great harms in general, as near as we can call to mind, that may hap unto any man.

THE THIRD CHAPTER

ANTONY: Since a man is made of the body and the soul, all the harm that any man may take, it must needs be in one of these two, either immediately, or by the means of some such thing as serveth for the pleasure, weal, or commodity[150] of the one of these two. As for the soul, first, we shall need no rehearsal of any harm that by this kind of tribulation may attain thereto,[151] but if that[152] by some inordinate love and affection that the soul bear to the body, she consent to slide from the faith, and thereby doth her harm herself.

Now remain there the body and these outward things of fortune which serve for the maintenance of the body, and minister[153] matter of pleasure to the soul also, through the delight that she hath in the body for the while that she is matched therewith.

Consider then first the loss of those outward

---

135 *fine force:* simple necessity **136** grow
137 angry **138** custody, captivity
139 *but he will:* unless he chooses to
140 *fall in hand with:* deal with, consider
141 *forasmuch that:* seeing that **142** tell

143 with regard to **144** *not all-thing afeard:* not at all afraid **145** *allies... little:* close relatives **146** however **147** care
148 Ecclus 17:12 **149** *but that:* unless
150 *weal, or commodity:* well-being, or

advantage **151** *attain thereto:* happen to it (i.e., the soul) **152** *but if that:* unless
153 supply

things, as somewhat the less in weight than is the body itself. In them what may a man lose, and thereby what pain may he suffer?

VINCENT: He may lose, Uncle (of which I should somewhat lose myself), money, plate,[154] and other movable substance;[155] then offices, authority; and finally all the lands of his inheritance forever, that himself and his heirs perpetually might else[156] enjoy. And of all these things, Uncle, you wot[157] well that myself have some — little in respect of that that[158] some others have here, but somewhat more yet than he that hath most here would be well content to lose.

Upon the loss of these things follow neediness and poverty, the pain of lacking, the shame of begging (of which twain[159] I wot not well which is the most wretched necessity), besides the grief of heart and heaviness[160] in beholding good men and faithful, and his dear friends, bewrapped in like misery, and ungracious wretches and infidels, and his mortal enemies, enjoy the commodities that himself and his friends have lost.

Now for the body, very few words shall serve us. For therein I see none other harm but loss of liberty, labor, imprisonment, painful and shameful death.

ANTONY: There needeth not much more, Cousin, as the world is now, for I fear me that less than a fourth part of this will make many a man sore[161] stagger in his faith, and some fall quite therefrom, that[162] yet at this day, before he come to the proof, weeneth himself that he would stand very fast.[163] And I beseech our Lord that all they that so think, and would yet, when they were brought unto the point, swerve therefrom for fear or for pain, may get of God the grace to ween still as they do, and not to be brought to the assay,[164] where pain or fear should show them (as it showed Saint Peter) how far they be deceived now.

But now, Cousin, against these terrible things, what way shall we take in giving men counsel of comfort? If the faith were in our days as fervent as it hath been ere this in time before passed, little counsel and little comfort would suffice. We should

not much need with words and reasoning to extenuate and diminish the vigor and asperity of the pains, but the greater, the more bitter that the passion were, the more ready was of old time the fervor of faith to suffer it.

And surely, Cousin, I doubt it little in my mind but that if a man had in his heart so deep a desire and love-longing to be with God in heaven to have the fruition[165] of his glorious face, as had those holy men that were martyrs in old times, he would no more now stick at[166] the pain that he must pass between than at that time those old holy martyrs did. But alas, our faint and feeble faith, with our love to God less than lukewarm, by the fiery affection that we bear to our own filthy[167] flesh, make us so dull in the desire of heaven that the sudden dread of every bodily pain woundeth us to the heart and striketh our devotion dead. And therefore hath there every man, Cousin, as I said before, much the more need to think upon this thing many times and oft aforehand, ere any such peril fall; and by much devising[168] thereupon before they see cause to fear it — while the thing shall not appear so terrible unto them — reason shall better enter and, through grace working with their diligence, engender and set sure not a sudden slight affection of sufferance[169] for God's sake, but by a long continuance, a strong deep-rooted habit, not like a reed ready to wave with every wind, nor like a rootless tree scant up on end[170] in a loose heap of light sand, that will with a blast or two be blown down.

THE FOURTH CHAPTER

ANTONY: For if we now consider, Cousin, these causes of terror and dread that you have recited, which in this persecution for the faith, this midday devil, may by these Turks rear against us to make his incursion with, we shall well perceive, weighing them well with reason, that albeit[171] somewhat they be indeed, yet every part of the matter pondered, they shall well appear in conclusion things nothing so much to be dread and fled from as to folk at the first sight they do suddenly seem.

---

154 items of precious metal   **155** possessions   **156** otherwise   **157** know   **158** *that that:* that which   **159** two   **160** sadness   **161** greatly, grievously

162 who   **163** firm, steadfast   **164** test, trial   **165** enjoyment   **166** *stick at:* be deterred by; hesitate at   **167** base, disgraceful   **168** meditating

169 endurance   **170** *scant . . . end:* barely upright   **171** although

THE FIFTH CHAPTER
Of the loss of the goods of fortune

ANTONY: For first to begin at the outward goods, that neither are the proper goods of the soul nor of the body, but are called the goods of fortune, that serve for the substance and commodity[172] of man for the short season of this present life — as[173] worldly substance, offices, honor, and authority — what great good is there in these things of themselves, for which they were worthy so much as to bear the name by which the world of a worldly favor customably[174] calleth them? For if the having of strength make a man strong, and the having of heat make a man hot, and the having of virtue make a man virtuous, how can those things be verily and truly good which he that hath them may, by the having of them, as well be the worse as the better, and as experience proveth more oft is the worse than the better? What[175] should a good man greatly rejoice in that that[176] he daily seeth most abound in the hands of many that be naught?[177] Do not now the great Turk and his bashaws,[178] in all these advancements of fortune, surmount very far above any Christian estate,[179] and any lords living under him? And was there not yet hence upon twenty years[180] the great Soldan[181] of Syria, which many a year together[182] bore as great a port[183] as the great Turk? And after, in one summer, unto the great Turk the whole empire was lost. And so may all his empire now, and shall hereafter by God's grace, be lost into Christian men's hands likewise, when Christian people shall be mended and grow in God's favor again.

But when that whole kingdoms and mighty great empires are of so little surety to stand, but be so soon translated[184] from one man unto another, what great thing can you or I — yea, or any lord, the greatest in the land — reckon himself to have by the possession of a heap of silver or gold, white and yellow metals, not so profitable of their own nature, save[185] for a little glistering, as the rude rusty metal of iron?

THE SIXTH CHAPTER
Of the unsurety of lands and possessions

ANTONY: Lands and possessions many men yet much more esteem than money, because the lands seem not so casual[186] as money is or plate, for that[187] though their other substance may be stolen and taken away, yet evermore they think that their land will lie still where it lay. But what are we the better that our land cannot be stirred but will lie still where it lay, while ourselves may be removed and not suffered[188] to come near it?

What great difference is there to us whether our substance be movable or unmovable, since we be so movable ourselves that we may be removed from them both and lose them both twain,[189] saving that sometimes in the money is the surety somewhat more? For when we be fain[190] ourselves to flee, we may make shift[191] to carry some of our money with us, where of our land we cannot carry one inch.

If our land be of more surety than our money, how happeth it then that in this persecution we be more feared to lose it? For if it be a thing of more surety, then can it not so soon be lost.

In the translation[192] of these two great empires — Greece first (since myself was born), and after Syria (since you were born too) — the land was lost before the money was found.

O, Cousin Vincent, if the whole world were animated with a reasonable soul, as Plato had weened[193] it were, and that it had wit and understanding to mark and perceive all things — Lord God, how the ground on which a prince buildeth his palace would loud laugh his lord to scorn when he saw him proud of his possession, and heard him boast himself that he and his blood are forever the very lords and owners of that land; for then would the ground think the while in himself, "Ah, thou seely[194] poor soul, that weenest thou were half a god, and art amid thy glory but a man in a gay[195] gown. I that am the ground here, over whom thou art so proud, have had a hundred such owners of me as thou callest thyself, more than ever thou hast heard the names of. And some of them that proudly went over my

---

172 *substance and commodity:* wealth and advantage   **173** such as   **174** customarily   **175** Why   **176** *that that:* that which   **177** wicked   **178** high-ranking Turkish officers   **179** nobleman   **180** *hence upon twenty years:* twenty years ago

181 Sultan   **182** *a year together:* years in a row   **183** *bore as great a port:* had as high a standing   **184** transferred   **185** except   **186** precarious, subject to chance   **187** *for that:* because   **188** allowed   **189** together   **190** obliged   **191** efforts

192 transference of rule   **193** thought; cf. *Timaeus* 34a-37c   **194** foolish, pitiful   **195** fine, beautiful; brightly colored, showy, flamboyant

head lie now low in my belly, and my side lieth over them. And many one shall, as thou dost now, call himself mine owner after thee, that neither shall be sib[196] to thy blood, nor any word hear of thy name." Who ought[197] your castle, Cousin, three thousand years ago?

VINCENT: Three thousand, Uncle? Nay, nay; in any king, Christian or heathen, you may strike off a third part of that well enough, and as far as I ween, half of the remnant too. In far fewer years than three thousand, it may well fortune that a poor plowman's blood[198] may come up to a kingdom, and a king's right royal kin, on the other side,[199] fall down to the plow and cart, and neither that the king know that ever he came from the cart, nor the carter know that ever he came from the crown.

ANTONY: We find, Cousin Vincent, in full antique[200] stories, many strange changes as marvelous as that come about in the compass of very few years in effect. And be such things then in reason so greatly to be set by,[201] that we should esteem the loss at so great, when we see that in the keeping our surety is so little?

VINCENT: Marry,[202] Uncle, but the less surety that we have to keep it, since it is a great commodity[203] to have it, the fearder[204] by so much and the more loath we be to forgo it.

ANTONY: That reason shall I, Cousin, turn against yourself. For if it be so as you say, that since the things be commodious,[205] the less surety that you see you have of the keeping, the more cause you have to be afeard of the losing, then on the other side, the more that a thing is of his nature such that the commodity thereof bringeth a man little surety and much fear, that thing of reason the less have we cause to love. And then the less cause that we have to love a thing, the less cause have we to care therefor, or fear the loss thereof, or be loath to go therefrom.

THE SEVENTH CHAPTER
These outward goods or gifts of fortune are by two manner wise[206] to be considered

ANTONY: We shall yet, Cousin, consider in these outward goods of fortune — as[207] riches, good name, honest estimation, honorable fame, and authority — in all these things we shall, I say, consider that either we love them and set by them as things commodious unto us for the state and condition of this present life, or else as things that we purpose by the good use thereof to make them matter of our merit with God's help in the life after to come. Let us then first consider them as things set by and beloved for the pleasure and commodity of them for this present life.

THE EIGHTH CHAPTER
The little commodity of riches being set by but[208] for this present life

ANTONY: Now riches loved and set by for such, if we consider it well, the commodity that we take there thereof is not so great as our own fond[209] affection and fantasy maketh us imagine it. It maketh us (I say not nay) go much more gay and glorious in sight, garnished in silk; but cloth[210] is within a little[211] as warm. It maketh us have great plenty of many kinds of delicate[212] and delicious victual,[213] and thereby to make more excess; but less exquisite and less superfluous fare, with fewer surfeits[214] and fewer fevers growing thereonto, were within a little as wholesome. Then the labor in the getting, the fear in the keeping, and the pain in the parting from do more than counterpoise a great part of all the pleasure and commodity that they bring. Besides this, the riches is the thing that taketh many times from its master all his pleasure and his life too, for many a man is for his riches slain. And some that keep their riches as a thing pleasant and commodious for their life take none other pleasure in a manner thereof in all their life than as though they bore the key of another man's coffer, and rather are content to live in neediness miserably all their days than they could find in their heart to diminish their hoard, they have

---

196 akin   **197** owned   **198** kin
199 hand   **200** *full antique:* very old
201 *set by:* regarded, valued   **202** Indeed
203 benefit, advantage   **204** more afraid

205 advantageous, beneficial   **206** *manner wise:* kinds of ways   **207** such as
208 only   **209** foolish   **210** regular fabric
211 *within a little:* nearly   **212** pleasing,

luxurious   **213** food; provisions of any kind   **214** overindulgences

such fantasy to look thereon; yea and some men, for fear lest thieves should steal it from them, be their own thieves and steal it from themselves, while they dare not so much as let it lie where themselves may look thereon, but put it in a pot, and hide it in the ground, and there let it lie safe till they die, and sometimes seven years after—from which place, if the pot had been stolen away five years before his death, all the same five years that he lived after, weening always that his pot lay safe still, what had he been the poorer while he never occupied[215] it after?

VINCENT: By my troth, Uncle, not one penny, for aught[216] that I perceive.

THE NINTH CHAPTER
The little commodity of fame, being desired but for worldly pleasure

ANTONY: Let us now consider good name, honest estimation, and honorable fame, for these three things are of their own nature one, and take their difference, in effect, but of the manner of the common speech in diversity of degrees; for a "good name" may a man have be he never so poor; "honest estimation," in the common taking[217] of the people, belongeth not unto any man but him that is taken for one of some countenance and haviour,[218] and among his neighbors had in some reputation. In the word of "honorable fame," folk conceive the renown of great estates,[219] much and far spoken of by reason of their laudable acts.

Now all this gear[220] used as a thing pleasant and commodious for this present life, pleasant it may seem to him that fasteneth his fantasy therein, but of the nature of the thing itself, I perceive no great commodity that it hath. I say "of the nature of the thing itself" because it may be by chance some occasion of commodity, as if it hap that for the good name the poor man hath, or for the honest estimation that a man of some haviour and substance[221] standeth in among his neighbors, or for the honorable fame wherewith the great estate is renowned—if it hap, I say, that any man bearing them the better will[222] therefor do them therefore any good. And yet as for that, like as it may sometimes so hap (and

sometimes so happeth indeed), so may it hap sometimes on the other side (and on the other side so it sometimes happeth indeed) that such folk are of some others envied and hated, and as readily by them that envy them and hate them take harm as they take by them that love them good.

But now to speak of the thing itself in his own proper nature, what is it but a blast of another man's mouth, as soon passed as spoken, whereupon he that setteth his delight feedeth himself but with wind—whereof be he never so full, he hath little substance therein? And many times shall he much deceive himself, for he shall ween that many praise him that never speak word of him; and they that do, say it much less than he weeneth, and far more seldom too; for they spend not all the day, he may be sure, in talking of him alone. And whoso commend him most will yet, I ween, in every four-and-twenty hours wink[223] and forget him once; besides this, that while one talketh well of him in one place, another sitteth and saith as shrewdly[224] of him in another. And finally some that most praise him in his presence, behind his back mock him as fast,[225] and loud laugh him to scorn, and sometimes slyly to his own face too. And yet are there some fools so fed with this fond fantasy of fame that they rejoice and glory to think how they be continually praised all about, as though all the world did nothing else, day nor night, but ever sit and sing *Sanctus, Sanctus, Sanctus*[226] upon them.

THE TENTH CHAPTER
Of flattery

ANTONY: And into this pleasant frenzy of much foolish vainglory be there some men brought sometimes by such as themselves do in a manner hire to flatter them, and would not be content if a man should do otherwise, but would be right angry, not only if a man told them truth when they do nought[227] indeed, but also if they praise it but slenderly.

VINCENT: Forsooth,[228] Uncle, this is very truth. I have been ere this, and not very long ago, where I saw so proper experience of this point that I must stop your tale for so long while I tell you mine.

---

215 used, had possession of 216 anything
217 conception 218 *countenance and haviour:* position and possessions
219 positions 220 business; matter
221 wealth 222 regard, good will
223 close his eyes 224 wickedly, harshly
225 vigorously 226 Holy, Holy, Holy; a prayer sung at every Mass. See Is 6:1–3.
227 nothing 228 In truth

ANTONY: I pray you, Cousin, tell on.

VINCENT: When I was first in Almain,[229] Uncle, it happed me to be somewhat favored with a great man of the Church, and a great state,[230] one of the greatest in all that country there. And indeed whosoever might spend as much as he might in one thing and other were a right great estate in any country of Christendom. But glorious was he very far above all measure, and that was great pity, for it did harm, and made him abuse many great gifts that God had given him. Never was he satiate of hearing his own praise.

So happed it one day that he had in a great audience made an oration in a certain manner, wherein he liked himself so well that at his dinner he sat, him thought, on thorns till he might hear how they that sat with him at his board[231] would commend it. And when he had sat musing awhile, devising[232] (as I thought after) upon some pretty[233] proper way to bring it in withal, at the last, for lack of a better (lest he should have letted[234] the matter too long), he brought it even blunt forth, and asked us all that sat at his board's end (for at his own mess in the mids,[235] there sat but himself alone) how well we liked his oration that he had made that day.

But in faith, Uncle, when that problem was once proponed,[236] till it was fully answered, no man, I ween, ate one morsel of meat[237] more, every man was fallen in so deep a study for the finding of some exquisite praise. For he that should have brought out but a vulgar[238] and a common commendation would have thought himself shamed forever.

Then said we our sentences[239] by row as we sat, from the lowest unto the highest, in good order, as[240] it had been a great matter of the common weal in a right solemn council. When it came to my part (I will not say it, Uncle, for no boast), methought, by our Lady, for my part I quit[241] myself meetly[242] well; and I liked myself the better because methought my words, being but a stranger,[243] went yet with some grace in the Almain tongue, wherein, letting my Latin alone, me listed[244] to show my cunning. And

I hoped to be liked the better because I saw that he that sat next me and should say his sentence[245] after me was an unlearned priest, for he could speak no Latin at all. But when he came forth for his part with my lord's commendation, the wily fox had been so well accustomed in court with the craft of flattery that he went beyond me to too far. And then might I see by him what excellence a right mean[246] wit may come to in one craft, that in all his whole life studieth and busieth his wit about no more but that one. But I made after a solemn vow to myself that if ever he and I were matched together at that board again, when we should fall to our flattery, I would flatter in Latin, that he should not contend with me no more; for though I could be content to be outrun of a horse, yet would I no more abide it to be outrun of an ass.

But Uncle, here began now the game. He that sat highest, and was to speak last, was a great beneficed[247] man, and not a doctor[248] only, but also somewhat learned indeed in the laws of the Church. A world it was to see how he marked every man's word that spoke before him. And it seemed that every word, the more proper[249] that it was, the worse he liked, for the cumbrance[250] that he had to study out[251] a better to pass[252] it. The man even sweat with the labor, so that he was fain[253] in the while now and then to wipe his face. Howbeit,[254] in conclusion, when it came to his course,[255] we that had spoken before him had so taken up all among us before, that we had not left him one wise word to speak after.

ANTONY: Alas, good man, among so many of you, some good fellow should have lent him one.

VINCENT: It needed not, as hap was, Uncle, for he found out such a shift[256] that in his flattering he passed us all the many.

ANTONY: Why, what said he, Cousin?

VINCENT: By our Lady, Uncle, not one word. But like as, I trow,[257] Pliny telleth, that when Apelles[258]

---

229 Germany   **230** estate   **231** table
232 thinking   **233** clever, artful, elegant
234 hindered, delayed   **235** *mess in
the mids:* serving of food in the middle
236 proposed   **237** food   **238** ordinary,
undistinguished; unrefined   **239** opinions
240 as if   **241** acquitted   **242** fairly

243 foreigner   **244** desired, wished
245 opinion   **246** *right mean:* quite low
247 holding an ecclesiastical position
providing income   **248** theologian
249 apt   **250** *for . . . cumbrance:* on
account of the burden   **251** *study out:*
figure out   **252** surpass   **253** obliged

254 Nevertheless   **255** turn   **256** tactic
257 believe   **258** Apelles of Kos
(fourth c. BC); Pliny called him the greatest
painter of all time. However, the painting
of Iphigenia described here is attributed
by Pliny to Timanthes of Cythnus (also
fourth c. BC).

the painter, in the table[259] that he painted of the sacrifice and the death of Iphigenia, had, in the making of the sorrowful countenances of the other noblemen of Greece that beheld it, spent out so much his craft and his cunning[260] that, when he came to make the countenance of King Agamemnon, her father, which he reserved for the last — lest if he had made his visage before, he must in some of the others after either have made the visage less dolorous[261] than he could, and thereby have forborne[262] some part of his praise, or doing the uttermost of his craft, might have happed to make some other look more heavily[263] for the pity of her pain than her own father, which had been yet a far greater fault in his painting — when he came, I say, to the making of his face therefore last of all, he could devise no manner of new heavy cheer[264] or countenance for her father but that he had made there already in some of the others a much more heavy before. And therefore to the intent that no man should see what manner[265] countenance it was that her father had, the painter was fain[266] to paint him holding his face in his handkerchief.[267]

The like pageant,[268] in a manner, played us there this good ancient honorable flatterer; for when he saw that he could find no words of praise that would pass[269] all that had been spoken before already, the wily fox would speak never a word, but, as he that were ravished unto heavenward with the wonder of the wisdom and eloquence that my Lord's Grace had uttered in that oration, he fetched a long sigh with an "Oh!" from the bottom of his breast, and held up both his hands, and lifted up his head, and cast up his eyes into the welkin,[270] and wept.

ANTONY: Forsooth, Cousin, he played his part very properly.

But was that great prelate's oration, Cousin, anything praiseworthy? For you can tell, I see well. For you would not, I ween, play as Juvenal merrily describeth the blind senator, one of the flatterers of Tiberius the emperor, that among the remnant so magnified the great fish that the emperor had sent for them to show them — which this blind senator

(Montanus,[271] I trow, they called him) marveled of as much as any that marveled most; and many things he spoke thereof, with some of his words directed thereunto, looking himself toward his left side, while the fish lay on his right side[272] — you would not, I trow, Cousin, have taken upon you to praise it so but if[273] you had heard it.

VINCENT: I heard it, Uncle, indeed, and to say the truth, it was not to dispraise, howbeit[274] surely somewhat less praise might have served it by more a great deal than the half. But this am I sure: had it been the worst that ever was made, the praise had not been the less of one hair. For they that used[275] to praise him to his face never considered how much the thing deserved, but how great a laud and praise themselves could give his good Grace.

ANTONY: Surely, Cousin, as Terence saith, such folk make men of fools even stark mad,[276] and much cause have their lords to be right angry with them.

VINCENT: God hath indeed, and is, I ween. But as for their lords, Uncle, if they would after wax angry with them therefor, they should in my mind do them very great wrong, when it is one of the things that they specially keep them for; for those that are of such vainglorious mind (be they lords, or be they meaner men) can be much better contented to have their devices commended than amended; and require[277] they their servants and their friend never so specially[278] to tell them the very truth, yet shall they better please them if he speak them fair than if he telleth them truth. For they be in the case that Martial speaketh of in an epigram unto a friend of his that required his judgment, how he liked his verses. But he prayed[279] him in any wise to tell him even the very truth. To whom Martial made answer in this wise:

The very truth of me thou dost require.
The very truth is this, my friend dear:
The very truth thou wouldst not gladly hear.[280]

259 picture   **260** knowledge, skill
261 sorrowful-looking   **262** gone
without   **263** grief-stricken   **264** *heavy
cheer:* sorrowful expression   **265** kind
of   **266** obliged, forced   **267** *Pliny…
handkerchief:* See Pliny, *Natural History*

35.36.   **268** performance   **269** surpass
270 heavens   **271** Juvenal calls the
blind man Catullus, while Montanus is
a bystander.   **272** See Juvenal's *Satire* 4.
273 *but if:* unless   **274** although
275 made it their practice; accustomed

themselves   **276** *such…mad:* i.e., such
people turn fools into madmen; see
Terence, *The Eunuch* 2:254.   **277** request
278 explicitly   **279** asked   **280** *The
very…hear:* See Martial, *Epigrams* 8.76.

And in good faith, Uncle, the selfsame prelate that I told you my tale of—I dare be bold to swear it, I know it so surely—had on a time[281] made of his own drawing[282] a certain treatise that should serve for a league between that country and a great prince. In which treatise himself thought that he had devised his articles so wisely, and indited[283] them so well, that all the world would allow them; whereupon, longing sore to be praised, he called unto him a friend of his, a man well-learned and of good worship,[284] and very well expert in those matters, as he that had been diverse times ambassador for that country, and had made many such treatises himself. When he took him the treatise, and that he had read it, he asked him how he liked it, and said, "But I pray you heartily, tell me the very truth"; and that he spoke so heartily that the other had weened he would fain[285] have heard the truth. And in trust thereof, he told him a fault therein; at the hearing whereof, he swore in great anger, "By the Mass, thou art a very fool." The other afterward told me that he would never tell him truth again.

ANTONY: Without question, Cousin, I cannot greatly blame him. And thus themselves make every man mock them, flatter them, and deceive them— those, I say, that are of such vainglorious mind. For if they be content to hear the truth, let them then make much of them that tell them the truth, and withdraw their ear from them that falsely flatter them, and they shall be more truly served than with twenty requests praying[286] men to tell them true.

King Ladislaus,[287] our Lord assoil[288] his soul, used much this manner among his servants. When one of them praised any deed of his or any condition in him, if he perceived that they said but the truth, he would let it pass by, uncontrolled.[289] But when he saw that they set a gloss[290] upon it for his praise of their own making besides, then would he shortly[291] say unto them, "I pray thee, good fellow, when thou say grace at my board,[292] never bring in *Gloria Patri*[293] without a *sicut erat*.[294] Any act that ever I did, if thou report it again to mine honor with a *Gloria Patri*, never report it but with a *sicut erat*—that is to wit, even as it was, and none otherwise. And lift me not up with no lies, for I love it not."

If men would use this way with them that this noble king used, it would diminish much of their false flattery. I can well allow that men should commend (keeping them within the bonds[295] of truth) such things as they see praiseworthy in other men, to give them the greater courage to the increase thereof. For men keep still in that point one condition of children, that praise must prick[296] them forth. But better it were to do well and look for none. Howbeit, they that cannot find in their heart to commend another man's good deed show themselves either envious or else of nature very cold and dull.

But out of question,[297] he that putteth his pleasure in the praise of the people hath but a fond[298] fantasy; for if his finger do but ache of a hot blain,[299] a great many men's mouths blowing out his praise will scantly[300] do him among them all half so much ease as to have one boy blow upon his finger.

THE ELEVENTH CHAPTER
The little commodity that men have of rooms, offices, and authority, if they desire them but for their worldly commodity

ANTONY: Let us now consider in like wise what great worldly wealth ariseth unto men by great offices, rooms,[301] and authority—to those worldly-disposed people, I say, that desire them for no better purpose; for of them that desire them for better, we shall speak after anon.[302]

The great thing that they chief like all therein is that they may bear a rule, command and control other men, and live uncommanded and uncontrolled themselves. And yet this commodity took I so little heed of that I never was aware it was so great till a good friend of ours merrily told me once that his wife once in a great anger taught it him.[303] For when her husband had no list[304] to grow greatly upward in the world, nor neither would labor for

---

281 *on a time:* at some time   **282** drawing up   **283** composed; worded   **284** honor, distinction   **285** gladly   **286** asking   **287** St. Ladislaus I of Hungary (1040–95)   **288** absolve; i.e., rest   **289** undisputed   **290** interpretation   **291** curtly   **292** table

293 *Gloria Patri:* Glory to the Father   **294** *sicut erat:* as it was; both are parts of the same common prayer   **295** bounds   **296** spur   **297** *out of question:* beyond a doubt   **298** foolish   **299** inflammation   **300** hardly   **301** positions   **302** *after*

anon: directly, immediately after
303 Harpsfield identifies this as a personal remembrance of More's second wife, Dame Alice (94–95).   **304** desire, wish

office of authority, and over that forsook³⁰⁵ a right worshipful room³⁰⁶ when it was offered him, she fell in hand³⁰⁷ with him, he told me, and all-to rated³⁰⁸ him, and asked him, "What will you do, that you list not to put forth yourself as other folk do? Will you sit still by the fire and make goslings in the ashes with a stick as children do? Would God I were a man, and look what I would do."

"Why, wife," quoth her husband, "what would you do?"

"What? By God, go forward with the best; for as my mother was wont³⁰⁹ to say (God have mercy on her soul), it is evermore better to rule than to be ruled. And therefore, by God, I would not, I warrant³¹⁰ you, be so foolish to be ruled where I might rule."

"By my troth, wife," quoth her husband, "in this I dare say you say truth, for I never found you willing to be ruled yet."

VINCENT: Well, Uncle, I wot where you be now well enough: she is indeed a stout master woman. And in good faith, for aught that I can see, even that same womanish mind³¹¹ of hers is the greatest commodity³¹² that men reckon upon in rooms and offices of authority.

ANTONY: By my troth, and methinketh very few there are of them that attain any great commodity therein. For first there is in every kingdom but one that can have an office of such authority that no man may command him or control him; none officer can there stand in that case but the king himself, which only uncontrolled or uncommanded may control and command all. Now, of all the remnant, each is under him. And yet besides him, almost every one is under more commanders and controllers too than one. And some man that is in a great office commandeth fewer things and less labor to many men that are under him than some one that is over him commandeth him alone.

VINCENT: Yet it doth them good, Uncle, that men must make courtesy to them, and salute them with reverence, and stand barehead before them, or unto some of them kneel peradventure too.

ANTONY: Well, Cousin, in some part they do but play at gleek,³¹³ receive reverence, and to their cost pay honor again therefor; for except, as I said, only a king, the greatest in authority under him receiveth not so much reverence of no man as according to reason himself doth honor to him; nor twenty men's courtesies do him not so much pleasure as his own once kneeling doth him pain, if his knee hap to be sore.

And I wist³¹⁴ once a great officer of the king's say, and in good faith I ween he said but as he thought, that twenty men standing barehead before him kept not his head half so warm as to keep on his own cap. Nor he took never so much ease with their being barehead before him as he caught once grief with a cough that came upon him by standing barehead long before the king.

But let it be that these commodities be somewhat such as they be; yet then consider whether that any incommodities³¹⁵ be so joined therewith that a man were almost as good lack both as have both.³¹⁶

Goeth all things evermore as every one of them would have it? That were as hard as to please all the people at once with one weather, while in one house the husband would have fair weather for his corn, and his wife would have rain for her leeks. So while they that are in authority be not all evermore of one mind, but sometimes variance³¹⁷ among them, either for the respect³¹⁸ of profit, or for contention of rule, or for maintenance of matters — sundry parties for their sundry friends — it cannot be that both the parties can have their own mind; nor often are they content which³¹⁹ see their conclusion quail,³²⁰ but ten times they take the missing of their mind more displeasantly than other poor men do. And this goeth not only to men of mean³²¹ authority, but unto the very greatest. The princes themselves cannot have, you wot well, all their will. For how were it possible while each of them almost would, if he might, be lord over all the remnant? Then many men under their princes in authority are in that case that privy³²² malice and envy many bear them in heart, falsely speak them full fair and praise them with their mouth, which when there happeth any great fall unto them, bawl and bark and bite upon them like dogs.

---

305 turned down   306 *worshipful room:* distinguished office   307 *fell in hand:* dealt   308 *all-to rated:* soundly rebuked   309 accustomed   310 promise, guarantee

311 purpose; desire; wish; opinion   312 advantage, benefit   313 a card game   314 knew   315 disadvantages   316 *as good . . . have both:* as well off lacking both

as having both   317 (there is) dissension   318 consideration   319 who   320 fail   321 little   322 secret

Finally, the cost and charge, the danger and peril of war, wherein their part is more than a poor man's is, since the matter more dependeth upon them, and many a poor plowman may sit still by the fire, while they must arise and walk. And sometimes their authority falleth by change of their master's mind. And of that see we daily, in one place or other, examples such and so many that the parable of the philosopher can lack no testimony, which likened the servants of great princes unto the counters[323] with which men do cast a count.[324] For like as that counter that standeth sometimes for a farthing is suddenly set up and standeth for a thousand pounds, and after, as soon set down eftsoon[325] beneath, to stand for a farthing again, so fareth it, lo, sometimes with those that seek the way to rise and grow up in authority by the favor of great princes: that as they rise up high, so fall they down again as low.[326]

Howbeit, though a man escape all such adventures and abide in great authority till he die, yet then at the leastwise every man must leave it at the last. And that which we call "at last" hath no very long time to it. Let a man reckon his years that are passed of his age ere ever he can get up aloft, and let him, when he have it first in his fist, reckon how long he shall be like to live after, and I ween that then the most part shall have little cause to rejoice; they shall see the time likely to be so short that their honor and authority by nature shall endure, besides the manifold chances whereby they may lose it more soon. And then when they see that they must needs leave it, the thing which they did much more set their heart upon than ever they had reasonable cause—what sorrow they take therefor, that shall I not need to tell you.

And thus it seemeth unto me, Cousin, in good faith, that since in the having the profit is not great, and the displeasures neither small nor few, and of the losing so many sundry chances, and that by no means a man can keep it long, and that to part therefrom is such a painful grief, I can see no very great cause for which, as a high worldly commodity, men should greatly desire it.

THE TWELFTH CHAPTER

THE TWELFTH CHAPTER
That these outward goods, desired but for worldly wealth, be not only little good for the body, but are also much harm for the soul

ANTONY: And thus far have we considered hitherto, in these outward goods that are called the gifts of fortune, no further but the slender commodity that worldly-minded men have by them. But now if we consider further what harm to the soul they take by them that desire them but only for the wretched wealth of this world, then shall we well perceive how far more happy is he that well loseth them than he that evil[327] findeth them.

These things, though they be such as are of their own nature indifferent—that is to wit, of themselves things neither good nor bad, but are matter that may serve to the one or the other, after[328] as men will use them—yet need we little to doubt it but that they that desire them but for their worldly pleasure and for no further godly purpose, the devil shall soon turn them from things indifferent unto them and make them things very naught.[329] For though that[330] they be indifferent of their nature, yet cannot the use of them lightly[331] stand indifferent, but determinately[332] must either be good or bad; and therefore he that desireth them but for worldly pleasure desireth them not for any good; and for better purpose than he desireth them, to better use is he not likely to put them, and therefore not unto good, but consequently to naught.

As for example, first consider it in riches: he that longeth for them as for thing of temporal commodity, and not for any godly purpose, what good they shall do him Saint Paul declareth where he writeth unto Timothy, *Qui volunt divites fieri incidunt in tentationem, et in laqueum diaboli, et desideria multa inutilia et noxia, quae mergunt homines in interitum et perditionem* ("They that long to be rich fall into temptation, and into the grin[333] of the devil, and into many desires unprofitable and noyous,[334] which drown men into death and into perdition").[335] And the Holy Scripture saith also, in the twentieth chapter of the Proverbs, *Qui congregat thesauros impingetur ad laqueos mortis* ("He that gathereth treasures shall be shoved into the grin of death"),[336] so that whereas by the mouth of Saint

---

323 beads on an abacus or computing device **324** *cast a count:* tally up a total **325** soon afterwards, again **326** See Polybius, *Histories* 5:26:12–13. **327** wickedly **328** according **329** wicked **330** *though that:* even though **331** easily **332** definitely **333** snare **334** troublesome, harmful **335** 1 Tm 6:9 **336** Prv 21:6

Paul God saith that they shall fall into the devil's grin, he saith in the other place that they shall be pushed and shoved in by violence. And of truth, while a man desireth riches not for any good godly purpose, but for only worldly wealth, it must needs be that he shall have little conscience in the getting, but by all evil ways that he can invent shall labor to get them; and then shall he either niggardly[337] heap them up together (which is, you wot well, damnable) or wastefully misspend them about worldly pomp, pride, and gluttony, with occasion of many sins more. And that is yet much more damnable.

As for fame and glory desired but for worldly pleasure, doth[338] unto the soul inestimable harm, for that setteth men's hearts upon high devices and desires of such things as are immoderate and outrageous, and, by help of false flatterers, puff up a man in pride, and make a brotle[339] man lately made of earth—and that shall again shortly be laid full low in earth, and there lie and rot and turn again into earth—take himself in the meantime for a god here upon earth, and ween to win himself to be lord of all the earth.

This maketh battles between these great princes, and—with much trouble to much people, and great effusion of blood—one king to look to reign in five realms, that cannot well rule one. For how many hath now this great Turk, and yet aspireth to more? And those that he hath, he ordereth evil, and yet himself worse.

Then offices and rooms[340] of authority, if men desire them only for their worldly fantasies, who can look[341] that ever they shall occupy them well, but abuse their authority, and do thereby great hurt? For then shall they fall from indifferency[342] and maintain false matters of their friends, bear up[343] their servants and such as depend upon them with bearing down of[344] other innocent folk and not so able to do hurt, as easy to take harm. Then the laws that are made against malefactors shall they make, as an old philosopher said, to be much like unto cobwebs, in which the little gnats and flies stick still and hang fast, but the great humble-bees[345] break them and fly quite through.[346] And then the laws that are made as a buckler[347] in the defense of innocents, those shall they make serve for a sword to cut

and sore[348] wound them with, and therewith wound they their own souls sorer.

And thus you see, Cousin, that of all these outward goods which men call the goods of fortune, there is never one that unto them which long therefor, not for any godly purpose, but only for their worldly wealth, hath any great commodity[349] to the body; and yet are they all in such case besides that very deadly destruction unto the soul.

THE THIRTEENTH CHAPTER
Whether men desire these outward goods for their own worldly wealth or for any good virtuous purpose, this persecution of the Turk against the faith will declare, and the comfort that both twain may take in the losing them thus

VINCENT: Verily,[350] good Uncle, this thing is so plainly true that no man may by any good reason deny it. But I ween, Uncle, also that there will no man say nay; for I see no man that will for very shame confess that he desireth riches, honor, and renown, offices and rooms of authority, for his own worldly pleasure; for every man would fain[351] seem as holy as a horse, and therefore will every man say—and would it were believed too—that he desireth these things (though for his own worldly wealth a little so) yet principally to merit thereby, through doing some good therewith.

ANTONY: This is, Cousin, very sure so: that so doth every man say. But first, he that in the desire thereof hath his respect therein unto his worldly wealth, as you say, but a little so, so much as himself weeneth[352] were but a little may soon prove a great deal too much. And many men will say so too that have indeed their principal respect therein unto their worldly commodity,[353] and unto Godward therein little or nothing at all, and yet they pretend the contrary, and that unto their own harm: *quia Deus non irridetur* ("God cannot be mocked").[354]

And some peradventure[355] know not well their own affection themselves, but there lieth more imperfection secret in their affection than themselves are well aware of, which only God beholdeth; and

---

337 in miserly fashion   338 i.e., that or it doth   339 frail, brittle; mortal   340 positions   341 expect   342 impartiality   343 *bear up:* elevate   344 *with bearing*

down of: by oppressing   345 bumble-bees   346 See Plutarch, *Life of Solon* 5, where this saying is attributed to Anacharsis.   347 shield   348 greatly, grievously

349 benefit, advantage   350 Truly   351 gladly   352 thinks   353 benefit, advantage   354 Gal 6:7   355 perhaps

therefore saith the prophet unto God, *In perfectum meum viderunt oculi tui* ("Mine imperfection have thine eyes beholden");[356] for which the prophet prayeth, *Ab occultis meis munda me, Domine* ("From mine hidden sins cleanse thou me, good Lord").[357]

But now, Cousin, this tribulation of the Turk — if he so persecute us for the faith that those that will forsake their faith shall keep their goods, and those shall lose their goods that will not leave their faith — this manner of persecution, lo, shall like a touchstone try them, and show the feigned from the true-minded, and teach also them that ween they mean better than they do indeed, better to discern themselves. For some there are that ween they mean well while they frame themselves a conscience, and ever keep still a great heap of superfluous substance[358] by them, thinking ever still that they will bethink themselves upon[359] some good deed, whereon they will well bestow it once, or that else their executors shall. But now if they lie not unto themselves, but keep their goods for any good purpose to the pleasure of God indeed, then shall they in this persecution, for the pleasure of God in keeping of his faith, be glad to depart from them.

And therefore as for all these things — the loss, I mean, of all these outward things that men call the gifts of fortune — this is methinketh in this Turk's persecution for the faith consolation great and sufficient, that since every man that hath them either setteth by[360] them for the world or for God, he that setteth by them for the world hath, as I have showed you, little profit by them to the body, and great harm unto the soul, and therefore may well (if he be wise) reckon that he winneth by the loss, although he lost them but by some common chance — and much more happy then while he loseth them by such a meritorious means. And on the other side, he that keepeth them for some good purpose, intending to bestow them for the pleasure of God, the loss of them in this Turk's persecution, for keeping of the faith, can be no manner[361] grief unto him, since that by his so parting from them, he bestoweth them in such wise unto God's pleasure that at the time when he loseth them, by no way could he bestow them unto his high pleasure better. For though it had been peradventure better to have bestowed them well before, yet since he kept them for

some good purpose, he would not have left them unbestowed if he had foreknown the chance; but being now prevented so by persecution that he cannot bestow them in that other good way that he would, yet while he parteth from them because he will not part from the faith, though the devil's escheator[362] violently take them from him, yet willingly giveth he them to God.

THE FOURTEENTH CHAPTER
Another cause for which any man should be content to forgo his goods in the Turk's said persecution

VINCENT: I cannot in good faith, good Uncle, say nay to none of this. And indeed unto them that by the Turk's overrunning of the country were happed to be despoiled and robbed, and all their substance, movable and unmovable, bereft and lost already, their persons only fled and safe, I think that these considerations (considered therewith that, as you lately said, their sorrow could not amend their chance) might unto them be good occasion of comfort, and cause them, as you said, make a virtue of necessity. But in the case, Uncle, that we now speak of — that is to wit, where they have yet their substance untouched in their own hands, and that the keeping or the losing shall hang both in their own hands by the Turk's offer upon the retaining or the renouncing of the Christian faith — here, Uncle, I find it as you said, that this temptation is most sore[363] and most perilous, for I fear me that we shall find few of such as have much to lose that shall find in their hearts so suddenly to forsake their goods, with all those other things aforerehearsed, whereupon their worldly wealth dependeth.

ANTONY: That fear I much, Cousin, too; but thereby shall it well, as I said, appear that seemed they never so good and virtuous before, and flattered they themselves with never so gay a gloss[364] of good and gracious purpose that they keep their goods for, yet were their hearts inwardly in the deep sight of God not sound and sure such as they should be, and as peradventure some had themselves weened they had been, but like a puff ring of Paris,[365] hollow, light, and counterfeit indeed.

356 Ps 138(139):16   **357** Ps 18(19):13   **358** possessions, wealth   **359** *bethink themselves upon*: propose to   themselves; resolve upon   **360** *setteth by*: values   **361** kind of   **362** confiscator   **363** intense, grievous   **364** interpretation   **365** *puff... Paris*: a finger ring made of plaster of Paris (hollow)

And yet, they being even such, this would I fain[366] ask one of them—and I pray you, Cousin, take you his person upon you, and in this case answer for him—what letteth[367] you, would I ask (for we will take no small man for an example in this part, nor him that had little to lose; for such one were, methink, so far from all frame[368] that would cast away God for a little that he were not worthy to talk with), what letteth, I say therefore, your lordship, that you be not gladly content, without any deliberation at all, in this kind of persecution, rather than to leave your faith, to let go all that ever you have at once?

VINCENT: Since you put it, Uncle, unto me, to make the matter the more plain, that I should play that great man's part that is so wealthy and hath so much to lose, albeit I cannot be very sure of another man's mind, nor what another man would say, yet as far as mine own mind can conjecture, I shall answer in his person what I ween would be his let.[369]

And therefore, to your question I answer that there letteth me the thing that yourself may lightly[370] guess: the losing of the manifold commodities which I now have, riches and substance, lands and great possessions of inheritance, with great rule and authority here in my country, all which things the great Turk granteth me to keep still in peace, and have them enhanced too, so that[371] I will forsake the faith of Christ; yea, I may say to you, I have a motion[372] secretly made me further, to keep all this yet better cheap:[373] that is to wit, not be compelled utterly to forsake Christ, nor all the whole Christian faith, but only some such parts thereof as may not stand with Muhammad's law; and only granting Muhammad for a true prophet, and serving the Turk truly in his wars against all Christian kings, I shall not be letted to praise Christ also, and to call him a good man, and worship him and serve him too.

ANTONY: Nay, nay, my lord, Christ hath not so great need of your lordship as rather than to lose your service, he would fall at such covenants with you to take your service at halves, to serve him and his enemy both; he hath given you plain warning already, by Saint Paul, that he will have in your service

no parting fellow:[374] *Quae societas luci ad tenebras, Christi ad Belial*? ("What fellowship is there between light and darkness, between Christ and Belial?")[375] And he hath also plainly showed you himself by his own mouth, *Nemo potest duobus dominis servire* ("No man may serve two lords at once").[376] He will have you believe all that he telleth you, and do all that he biddeth you, and forbear all that he forbiddeth you, without any manner exception. Break one of his commandments and break all; forsake one point of his faith and forsake all, as for any thanks you get of him for the remnant.

And therefore if you devise as it were indentures[377] between God and you—what thing you will do for him and what thing you will not do, as though he should hold him content with such service of yours as yourself list to appoint[378] him—if you make, I say, such indentures, you shall seal both the parts yourself, and you get thereto none agreement of him.

And this I say though the Turk would make such an appointment[379] with you as you speak of, and would when he had made it keep it, whereas he would not, I warrant you, leave you so when he had once brought you so far-forth,[380] but would little and[381] little after, ere he left you, make you deny Christ altogether, and take Muhammad in his stead; and so doth he in the beginning, when he will not have you believe him to be God. For surely if he were not God, he were no good man neither, while he plainly said he was God.

But though he would never go so far-forth with you, yet Christ will (as I said) not take your service to halves, but will that you shall love him with all your whole heart. And because that[382] while he was living here fifteen hundred years ago, he foresaw this mind of yours that you have now, with which you would fain[383] serve him in some such fashion as you might keep your worldly substance[384] still, but rather forsake his service than put all your substance from you, he telleth you plain, fifteen hundred years ago, his[385] own mouth, that he will no such service of you, saying, *Non potestis servire Deo et mammonae* ("You cannot serve both God and your riches together").[386]

And therefore this thing established[387] for a plain

366 gladly; wish or desire to   **367** prevents
368 proper order   **369** obstacle, hindrance
370 easily   **371** *so that:* provided that
372 proposal   **373** *yet better cheap:* for
an even lower price   **374** *parting fellow:*
partner   **375** 2 Cor 6:14–15   **376** Mt
6:24   **377** contracts   **378** *list to appoint:*
wish to assign   **379** agreement   **380** far
forward   **381** by   **382** *because that:*
because   **383** gladly; wish or desire to
384 wealth, possessions, property   **385** by
his   **386** Lk 16:13   **387** is established

conclusion, which you must needs grant if you have faith; and if you be gone from that ground of faith already, then is all our disputation, you wot well, at an end. For whereto[388] should you then rather lose your goods than forsake your faith, if you have lost your faith and let it go already?

This point I say therefore put first for a ground between us both twain agreed: that you have yet the faith still, and intend to keep it always still in your heart, and are but in doubt whether you will lose all your worldly substance rather than forsake your faith in your only word;[389] now shall I reply to the point of your answer, wherein you tell me the loathness of your loss, and the comfort of the keeping, letteth you to forgo[390] them, and moveth you rather to forsake your faith.

I let pass all that I have spoken of the small commodity[391] of them unto your body, and of the great harm that the having of them do to your soul. And since the promise of the Turk made unto you for the keeping of them is the thing that moveth you and maketh you thus to doubt, I ask you first whereby you wot that when you have done all that he will have you do against Christ to the harm of your soul, whereby wot you, I say, that he will keep you his promise in these things that he promiseth you concerning the retaining of your well-beloved worldly wealth, for the pleasure of your body?

VINCENT: What surety can a man have of such a great prince but his promise, which for his own honor it cannot become[392] him to break?

ANTONY: I have known him and his father afore him to break more promises than five as great as this is that he should make with you. Who shall come and cast it in his teeth and tell him it is a shame for him to be so fickle and so false of his promise? And then what careth he for those words that he wotteth well he shall never hear? Not very much, although they were told him too. If you might come after and complain your grief unto his own person yourself, you should find him as shamefast[393] as a friend of mine, a merchant, found once the Soldan[394] of Syria, to whom, being certain years about his merchandise in that country, he gave a great sum of money for

a certain office meet[395] for him there for the while; which he scant[396] had him granted and put in his hand but that, ere ever it was aught[397] worth unto him, the Soldan suddenly sold it to another of his own sect, and put our Hungarian out. Then came he to him and humbly put him in remembrance of his grant passed[398] his own mouth and signed with his own hand, whereunto the Soldan answered him with a grim countenance, "I will thou wit it, losel,[399] that neither my mouth nor my hand shall be master over me, to bind all my body at their pleasure, but I will so be lord and master over them both that whatsoever the one say or the other write, I will be at mine own liberty to do what me list[400] myself, and ask them both no leave.[401] And therefore go get thee hence out of my country, knave."

Ween you[402] now, my lord, that Soldan and this Turk being both of one false sect, you may not find them both like[403] false of their promise?

VINCENT: That must I needs jeopard,[404] for other surety can there none be had.

ANTONY: An unwise jeoparding to put your soul in peril of damnation for the keeping of your bodily pleasures, and yet without surety thereof must jeopard them too.

But yet go a little further, lo. Suppose me that you might be very sure that the Turk would break no promise with you. Are you then sure enough to retain all your substance still?

VINCENT: Yea, then.

ANTONY: What if a man should ask you how long?

VINCENT: How long? As long as I live.

ANTONY: Well, let it be so, then. But yet as far as I can see, though the great Turk favor you never so much, and let you keep your goods as long as ever you live, yet if it hap that you be this day fifty years old, all the favor he can show you cannot make you one day younger tomorrow, but every day shall you wax elder[405] than other, and then within a while must you for[406] all his favor lose all.

---

388 to what end   389 *only word:* word alone   390 *letteth you to forgo:* prevents you from forgoing   391 benefit, advantage   392 suit, befit   393 ashamed

394 Sultan   395 suitable, appropriate
396 hardly   397 anything   398 passed
from   399 *I will … it, losel:* I'll have you
know, scoundrel   400 *me list:* pleases me

401 permission   402 *Ween you:* Don't you
think   403 similarly, equally   404 risk
405 *wax elder:* grow older   406 despite

VINCENT: Well, a man would be glad for all that, to be sure not to lack while he liveth.

ANTONY: Well then, if the great Turk give you your goods, can there then in all your life none other take them from you again?

VINCENT: Verily, I suppose no.

ANTONY: May he not lose this country again unto Christian men, and you, with the taking of this way, fall in the same peril then that you would now eschew?[407]

VINCENT: Forsooth, I think that if he get it once, he will never lose it again in our days.

ANTONY: Yes, by God's grace, but yet if he lose it after your days, there goeth your children's inheritance away again. But be it now that he could never lose it — could none take your substance from you then?

VINCENT: No, in good faith, none.

ANTONY: No? None at all? Not God?

VINCENT: God? What yes, pardie,[408] who doubteth of that?

ANTONY: Who? Marry, he that doubteth whether there be any God or no. And that there lacketh not some such, the prophet testifieth, where he saith, *Dixit insipiens in corde suo non est Deus* ("The fool hath said in his heart there is no God").[409] With the mouth the most foolish will forbear to say it unto other folk, but in the heart they let[410] not to say it softly to themselves. And I fear me there be many more such fools than every man would ween there were, and would not let to say it openly too, if they forbore it not more for dread or shame of men than for any fear of God. But now those that are so frantic foolish as to ween there were no God, and yet in their words confess him, though that,[411] as Saint Paul saith, in their deeds they deny him,[412] we shall let them pass till it please God show himself unto them, either inwardly betime[413] by his merciful grace,

or else outwardly, but overlate for them, by his terrible judgment.

But unto you, my lord, since you believe and confess (like as a wise man should) that though the Turk keep you promise[414] in letting you keep your substance because you do him pleasure in the forsaking of your faith, yet God, whose faith you forsake, and therein do him displeasure, may so take them from you that the great Turk with all the power that he hath is not able to keep you them, why will you be so unwise with the loss of your soul to please the great Turk for your goods, while you wot well that God, whom you displease therewith, may take them from you too?

Besides this, since you believe there is a God, you cannot but believe therewith that the great Turk cannot take your goods from you without his will or sufferance,[415] no more than the devil could from Job. And think you then that if he will suffer the Turk take away your goods albeit that[416] by the keeping and confessing of his faith you please him, he will, when you displease him by forsaking his faith, suffer[417] you of those goods that you get or keep thereby to rejoice or enjoy any benefit in?

VINCENT: God is gracious, and though that[418] men offend him, yet he suffereth them many times to live in prosperity long after.

ANTONY: Long after? Nay, by my troth, my lord, that doth he no man — for how can that be that he should suffer you live in prosperity long after, when your whole life is but short in altogether,[419] and either almost half thereof or more than half (you think yourself, I dare say) spent out already before? Can you burn out half a short candle, and then have a long one left of the remnant? There cannot be in this world a worse mind than that a man to delight and take comfort in any commodity[420] that he taketh by sinful means. For it is the very straight way toward the taking of boldness and courage in sin, and finally to fall into infidelity, and think that God careth not, nor regardeth not what things men do here, nor what mind we be of. But unto such-minded folk speaketh Holy Scripture in this wise: *Noli dicere, "Peccavi, et nihil mihi accidit triste," patiens enim redditor est Dominus* ("Say not, 'I have

---

407 avoid, escape   408 certainly   409 Ps 13(14):1   410 hesitate   411 *though that:* even though   412 See Tit 1:16.   413 in

time   414 *keep you promise:* keep his promise to you   415 allowance, sanction   416 *albeit that:* even if   417 allow

418 *though that:* even though   419 *in altogether:* as a whole   420 advantage, benefit, profit

sinned, and yet there hath happed me no harm," for God suffereth before he strike");[421] but as Saint Augustine saith, the longer that he tarrieth ere he strike, the sorer[422] is the stroke when he striketh.[423]

5 And therefore if ye will well do, reckon yourself very sure that when you deadly displease God for the getting or the keeping of your goods, God shall not suffer those goods to do you good, but either shall he take them shortly from you, or suffer[424] you 10 to keep them for a little while to your more harm, and after shall he, when you least look therefor, take you away from them. And then what a heap of heaviness[425] will there enter into your heart, when you shall see that you shall so suddenly go from your 15 goods, and leave them here in the earth in one place, and that your body shall be put in the earth in another place, and (which then shall be most heaviness of all) when you shall fear (and not without great cause) that your soul shall first forthwith,[426] 20 and after that at the final judgment your body too, be driven down deep toward the center of the earth into the very pit and dungeon of the devil of hell, there to tarry in torment world without end. What goods of the world can any man imagine, whereof 25 the pleasure and commodity could be such in a thousand years as were able to recompense that intolerable pain that there is to be suffered in one year, yea or one day, or one hour either? And then what a madness it is, for the poor pleasure of your worldly 30 goods of so few years, to cast yourself both body and soul into the everlasting fire of hell, whereof there is not diminished the mountenance[427] of a moment by the lying there the space of a hundred thousand years.

35 And therefore our Savior in few words concluded and confuted[428] all those follies of them that, for the short use of this worldly substance, forsake him and his faith and sell their souls unto the devil forever, where he saith, *Quid prodest homini si univer-* 40 *sum mundum lucretur, animae vero suae detrimentum patiatur*? ("What availeth it a man if he won all the whole world and lost his soul?")[429] This were methinketh cause and occasion enough to him that had never so much part of this world in his hand to 45 be content rather to lose it all than, for the retaining

or increasing of his worldly goods, to lose and destroy his soul.

VINCENT: This is, good Uncle, in good faith very true. And what other thing any of them that would not for this be content have for to allege in reason 50 for the defense of their folly, that can I not imagine, nor list[430] in this matter to play their part no longer, but I pray God give me the grace to play the contrary part indeed, and that I never, for any goods or substance[431] of this wretched world, forsake my 55 faith toward God, neither in heart nor tongue, as I trust in his great goodness I never shall.

THE FIFTEENTH CHAPTER
*This kind of tribulation trieth what mind men
have to their goods, which they that are wise* 60
*will, at the fame[432] thereof, see well and
wisely laid up safe before*

ANTONY: Methinketh, Cousin, that this persecution shall not only, as I said before, try men's hearts when it cometh, and make them know their own 65 affections, whether they have a corrupt greedy covetous mind or not, but also the very fame and expectation thereof may teach them this lesson ere ever the thing fall upon them itself, to their no little fruit,[433] if they have the wit and the grace to take it 70 in time while they may; for now may they find sure places to lay their treasure in, so that all the Turk's army shall never find it out.

VINCENT: Marry, Uncle, that way they will, I warrant you, not forget, as near as their wits will serve 75 them. But yet have I known some that have ere this thought that they had hid their money safe and sure enough, digging it full deep in the ground, and have missed it yet when they came again, and have found it digged out and carried away to their hands.[434] 80

ANTONY: Nay, "from their hands," I ween[435] you would say. And it was no marvel, for some such have I known too; but they have hid their goods foolishly, in such place as they were well warned before

---

421 Ecclus 5:4   **422** worse, more grievous, more painful   **423** See Augustine, Letter 138 (to Marcellinus) 2.14.   **424** allow   **425** sadness

426 immediately   **427** duration **428** *concluded and confuted:* overcame and refuted   **429** Mt 16:26   **430** (do I) desire, wish   **431** wealth   **432** rumor

433 profit, benefit, advantage   **434** *to their hands:* without exertion on their part **435** thought

that they should not. And that were they warned by him that they well knew for such one as wist[436] well enough what would come thereon.

VINCENT: Then were they more than mad. But did he tell them too where they should have hid it to have it sure?

ANTONY: Yea, by Saint Mary, did he, for else had he told them but half a tale; but he told them a whole tale, bidding them that they should in no wise hide their treasure in the ground; and he showed them a good cause, for there, thieves use[437] to dig it out and steal it away.

VINCENT: Why, where should they hide it then, said he? For thieves may hap to find it out in any place.

ANTONY: Forsooth,[438] he counseled them to hide their treasure in heaven, and there lay it up, for there it shall lie safe; for thither, he said, there can no thief come till he have left his theft[439] and be waxen[440] a true man first. And he that gave this counsel wist what he said well enough, for it was our Savior himself, which in the sixth chapter of Saint Matthew saith, *Nolite thesaurizare vobis thesauros in terra, ubi erugo et tinea demolitur, et ubi fures effodiunt et furantur. Thesaurizate vobis thesauros in caelo, ubi neque erugo neque tinea demolitur, et ubi fures non effodiunt nec furantur. Ubi enim est thesaurus tuus, ibi est et cor tuum* ("Hoard not up your treasures in earth, where the rust and the moth fret it out,[441] and where thieves dig it out and steal it away. But hoard up your treasures in heaven, where neither the rust and the moth fret them out, and where thieves dig them not out and steal them away; for whereas[442] is thy treasure, there is thine heart too").[443]

If we would well consider these words of our Savior Christ, we should, as methink, need no more counsel at all, nor no more comfort neither, concerning the loss of our temporal substance[444] in this Turk's persecution for the faith. For here our Lord in these words teacheth us where we may lay up our substance safe before the persecution come.

If we put it into the poor men's bosoms, there shall it lie safe. For who would go search a beggar's bag for money? If we deliver it to the poor for Christ's sake, we deliver it unto Christ himself. And then what persecutor can there be so strong as to take it out of his hand?

VINCENT: These things are, Uncle, undoubtedly so true that no man may with words wrestle therewith; but yet ever there hangeth in a man's heart a loathness[445] to lack a living.

ANTONY: There doth indeed, in theirs that either never or but seldom hear any good counsel thereagainst, and when they hear it, hearken it but as though they would an idle tale, rather for a pastime, or for the manner sake,[446] than for any substantial intent and purpose to follow good advertisement[447] and take any fruit thereby. But verily, if we would not only lay our ear, but also our heart thereto, and consider that the saying of our Savior Christ is not a poet's fable, nor a harper's song, but the very holy word of almighty God himself, we would, and well we might, be full sore[448] ashamed in ourselves, and full sorry too, when we felt in our affection those words to have in our hearts no more strength and weight but that we remain still of the same dull mind as we did before we heard them.

This manner of ours, in whose breasts the great good counsel of God no better settleth, nor taketh no better root, may well declare[449] us that the thorns and the briers and the brambles of our worldly substance grow so thick and spring up so high in the ground of our hearts that they strangle, as the Gospel saith, the word of God that was sown therein.[450] And therefore is God very good lord unto us when he causeth, like a good husbandman, his folk come on field (for the persecutors be his folk to this purpose) and with their hooks and their stocking irons[451] grub up[452] these wicked weeds and bushes of our earthly substance, and carry them quite away from us, that the word of God sown in our hearts may have room therein, and a glade round about for the warm sun of grace to come to it and make it grow; for surely those words of our Savior shall we find full

436 knew   437 are accustomed to   438 In truth   439 *left his theft:* quit his thieving   440 become   441 *fret it out:* eat it away   442 wherever   443 Mt 6:19–21   444 wealth, possessions   445 reluctance   446 *manner sake:* sake of appearances   447 advice   448 *full sore:* very greatly or grievously   449 show   450 See Mt 13:7–22; Lk 8:4–15.   451 *stocking irons:* iron tools for uprooting   452 *grub up:* dig up by the roots

true: *Ubi thesaurus tuus ibi est et cor tuum* ("Whereas thy treasure is, there is also thine heart");[453] if we lay up our treasures in earth, in earth shall be our hearts; if we send our treasure into heaven, in heaven shall we have our hearts. And surely the greatest comfort that any man may have in his tribulation is to have his heart in heaven.

If thine heart were indeed out of this world and in heaven, all the kinds of torment that all the world could devise could put thee to no pain here; let us then send our hearts hence thither, in such manner as we may, by sending thither our worldly substance hence. And let us never doubt it but we shall (that once done) find our hearts so conversant in heaven, with the glad consideration of our following the gracious counsel of Christ, that the comfort of his Holy Spirit, inspired[454] us therefor, shall mitigate, diminish, assuage, and in a manner quench the great furious fervor of the pain that we shall happen to have, by his loving sufferance,[455] for our further merit in our tribulation.

And therefore, like[456] as if we saw that we should be within a while driven out of this land and fain[457] to flee into another, we would ween that man were mad which would not be content to forbear[458] his goods here for the while, and send them into that land before him where he saw he should live all the remnant of his life, so may we verily think ourselves much more mad (seeing that we be sure it cannot be long ere we shall be sent, spite of our teeth,[459] out of this world) if the fear of a little lack, or the love to see our goods here about us, and the loathness to part from them for this little while which we may keep them here, shall be able to let[460] us from the sure sending them before us into the other world, in which we may be sure to live wealthily with them if we send them thither, or else shortly leave them here behind us, and then stand in great jeopardy there to live wretches forever.

VINCENT: In good faith, good Uncle, methinketh that concerning the loss of these outward things, these considerations are so sufficient comforts that for mine own part, save[461] only grace well to remember them, I would methink desire no more.

THE SIXTEENTH CHAPTER
Another comfort, and courage against the loss of worldly substance

ANTONY: Much less than this may serve, Cousin, with calling and trusting upon God's help, without which, much more than this cannot serve. But the fervor of the Christian faith so sore fainteth nowadays and decayeth, coming from hot unto lukewarm, and from lukewarm almost to key-cold,[462] that men must now be fain, as at a fire that is almost out, to lay many dry sticks thereto, and use much blowing thereat; but else[463] would I ween, by my troth, that unto a warm[464] faithful man, one thing alone, whereof we spoke yet no word, were comfort enough in this kind of persecution against the loss of all his goods.

VINCENT: What thing may that be, Uncle?

ANTONY: In good faith, Cousin, even the bare remembrance of the poverty that our Savior willingly suffered for us; for I verily suppose that if there were a great king that had so tender a love to a servant of his that he had, to help him out of danger, forsaken and left off all his worldly wealth and royalty, and become poor and needy for his sake, that servant could scant[465] be founden that were of such an unkind villain courage[466] that, if himself came after to some substance,[467] would not with better will lose it all again than shamefully to forsake such a master.

And therefore, as I say, I do surely suppose that if we would well remember and inwardly consider the great goodness of our Savior toward us, not yet being his poor sinful servants, but rather his adversaries and his enemies, and what wealth of this world that he willingly forsook for our sake, being indeed universal king thereof, and so having the power in his own hand to have used it if he had would[468]— instead whereof, to make us rich in heaven, he lived here in neediness and poverty all his life, and neither would have authority nor keep neither lands nor goods—the deep consideration and earnest advisement[469] of this one point alone were able to make any kind[470] Christian man or woman well content rather for his sake again[471] to give up all that ever

---

453 Mt 6:21   454 breathed into
455 allowance, sanction   456 just
457 forced   458 do without   459 *spite of our teeth:* despite all our efforts

460 prevent   461 excepting   462 cold as a key; i.e., without heat or fervor
463 otherwise   464 fervent   465 hardly, scarcely   466 *unkind villain courage:*

unnatural and base spirit   467 wealth
468 willed   469 *earnest advisement:* serious pondering   470 natural   471 in return

God hath lent them (and lent them hath he all that ever they have) than unkindly[472] and unfaithfully to forsake him. And him they forsake, if that for fear they forsake the confessing of his Christian faith.

And therefore to finish this piece withal,[473] concerning the dread of losing our outward worldly goods, let us consider the slender commodity[474] that they bring; with what labor they be bought; how little while they abide with whomsoever they abide longest; what pain their pleasure is mingled withal; what harm the love of them doth unto the soul; what loss is in the keeping, Christ's faith refused for them; what winning in the loss, if we lose them for God's sake; how much more profitable they be well given than evil kept; and finally what unkindness it were if we would not rather forsake them for Christ's sake than unfaithfully forsake Christ for them, which[475] while he lived for our sake forsook all the world, besides the suffering of shameful and painful death, whereof we shall speak after. If we these things, I say, will consider well, and will pray God with his holy hand to print them in our hearts, and will abide and dwell still in the hope of his help, his truth shall, as the prophet saith, so compass us about with a pavise[476] that we shall not need to be afeard *ab incursu et daemonio meridiano* ("of this incursion of this midday devil"),[477] this open plain persecution of the Turk, for any loss that we can take by the bereaving from us of our wretched worldly goods, for whose short and small pleasure in this life forborne, we shall be with heavenly substance everlastingly recompensed of God in joyful bliss and glory.

THE SEVENTEENTH CHAPTER

Of bodily pain, and that a man hath no cause to take discomfort in persecution, though he feel himself in a horror at the thinking upon bodily pain

VINCENT: Forsooth, Uncle, as for these outward goods, you have so far-forth[478] said that albeit[479] no man can be sure what strength he shall have or how faint and how feeble he may hap to find himself when he shall come to the point, and therefore I can make no warrantise[480] of myself seeing that Saint Peter so suddenly fainted at a woman's word

and so cowardly forsook his Master for whom he had so boldly fought within so few hours before, and by that fall in forsaking, well perceived that he had been too rash in his promise and was well worthy to take a fall for putting so full trust in himself. Yet, in good faith, methinketh now (and God shall, I trust, help me to keep this thought still) that if the Turk should take all that I have unto my very shirt, except I would forsake my faith, and offer it me all again with five times as much thereto to fall into his sect, I would not once stick[481] thereat rather to forsake it every whit than of Christ's holy faith to forsake any point. But surely, good Uncle, when I bethink me further on the grief and the pain that may turn unto my flesh, here find I the fear that forceth mine heart to tremble.

ANTONY: Neither have I cause thereof to marvel, nor you, Cousin, cause to be dismayed therefor. The great horror and the fear that our Savior had in his own flesh against[482] his painful Passion maketh me little to marvel, and may well make you take that comfort too, that for no such manner of grudging[483] felt in our sensual parts, the flesh shrinking at the meditation of pain and death, your reason shall give over, but resist it and manly master it, and though you would fain[484] flee from the painful death, and be loath to come thereto, yet may the meditation of his great grievous agony move you—and himself shall, if you so desire him, not fail to work with you therein, and get and give you the grace—that you shall submit and conform your will therein unto his, as he did his unto his Father, and shall thereupon be so comforted with the secret inward inspiration of his Holy Spirit, as he was with the personal presence of that angel that after his agony came and comforted him,[485] that you shall as his true disciple follow him, and with good will without grudge do as he did, and take your cross of pain and passion upon your back, and die for the truth with him, and thereby reign with him crowned in eternal glory. And this I say to give you warning of the thing that is truth, to the intent when a man feeleth such a horror of death in his heart, he should not thereby stand in outrageous fear that he were falling, for many a such man standeth for[486] all that fear full fast,[487] and finally better abideth the brunt,[488] when God is so good unto him as to bring him thereto and encourage him therein, than doth some other that in the beginning feeleth no fear at all. And yet may it be, and most often so it is, for God, having many mansions, and all wonderful wealthful in his Father's house,[489] exalteth not every good man up to the glory of a martyr, but foreseeing their infirmity—that though they be of good will before, and peradventure of right good courage too, would yet play Saint Peter if they were brought to the point, and thereby bring their souls into the peril of eternal damnation—he provideth otherwise for them before they come thereat, and either findeth a way that men shall not have the mind to lay any hands upon them (as he found for his disciples when himself was willingly taken),[490] or that if they set hands on them, they shall have no power to hold them (as he found for Saint John the Evangelist, which let his sheet fall from him; whereupon they caught hold, and so fled himself naked away and escaped from them),[491] or though they hold him and bring him to prison too, yet God sometimes delivereth them thence, as he did Saint Peter.[492] And sometimes he taketh them to him out of the prison into heaven, and suffereth[493] them not to come to their torment at all, as he hath done by many a good holy man. And some he suffereth to be brought into the torments, and yet suffereth them not to die therein, but live many years after and die their natural death (as he did by Saint John the Evangelist, and by many another more, as we may well see both by sundry stories and in the epistles of Saint Cyprian also).

And therefore, which way God will take with us, we cannot tell. But surely if we be true Christian men, this can we well tell: that without any bold warrantise[494] of ourselves, or foolish trust in our own strength, we be bound upon pain of damnation that we be not of the contrary mind, but that we will with his help, how loath soever we feel our flesh thereto, rather yet than forsake him or his faith afore the world (which if we do, he hath promised to forsake us afore his Father and all his holy company of heaven),[495] rather, I say, than we would so do, we would with his help endure and sustain for his sake all the tormentry that the devil with all his faithless tormentors in this world would devise. And then when we be of this mind, and

submit our will unto his, and call and pray for his grace, we can tell well enough that he will never suffer them to put more upon us than his grace will make us able to bear, but will also with their temptation provide for us a sure way. For *fidelis est Deus*, saith Saint Paul, *qui non patitur vos tentari supra id quod potestis sed dat etiam cum tentatione proventum ut possitis ferre* ("God is," saith the Apostle, "faithful, which suffereth you not to be tempted above that[496] you may bear, but giveth also with the temptation a way out").[497] For either, as I said, he will keep us out of their hands (though he before suffered us to be feared with[498] them to prove our faith withal)[499] that we may have by the examination of our own mind some comfort in hope of his grace, and some fear of our own frailty, to drive us to call for grace, or else if we fall in their hands, so that we fall not from the trust of him, nor cease to call for his help, his truth shall, as the prophet saith, so compass us about with a pavise[500] that we shall not need to fear this incursion of this midday devil; for either shall these Turks, his tormentors that shall enter this land and persecute us, either they shall, I say, not have the power to touch our bodies at all, or else the short pain that they shall put unto our bodies shall turn us to eternal profit, both in our souls and in our bodies too.

And therefore, Cousin, to begin with, let us be of good comfort. For since we be by our faith very sure that Holy Scripture is the very word of God, and that the word of God cannot be but true, and that we see that, both by the mouth of his holy prophet and by the mouth of his blessed apostle also, God hath made us so faithful promises—both that he will not suffer us to be tempted above our power, but will both provide a way out for us, and that he will also round about so compass us with his pavise, and defend us, that we shall have no cause to fear this midday devil with all his persecution—we cannot now but be very sure (except we be very shamefully cowardous of heart, and toward God in faith out of measure faint,[501] and in love less than lukewarm, or waxen even key-cold),[502] we may be very sure, I say, that either God shall not suffer the Turks to invade this land, or if they do, God shall provide such resistance that they shall not prevail. Or if they prevail, yet, if we take the way that I have told you,

---

489 See Jn 14:2. **490** See Jn 18:8–9. **491** See Mk 14:51–52. **492** See Acts 12:6–10. **493** permits **494** assurance

495 See Mt 10:33; Lk 12:9. **496** that which **497** 1 Cor 10:13 **498** *feared with:* frightened by **499** thereby

500 large shield **501** *out of measure:* exceedingly **502** *waxen even key-cold:* become ice-cold

we shall by their persecution take little harm, or rather none harm at all, but that that[503] shall seem harm shall indeed be to us none harm at all, but good. For if God make us and keep us good men, as he hath promised to do if we pray well therefor, then, saith Holy Scripture, *Bonis omnia cooperantur in bonum* ("Unto good folk, all things turn them to good").[504]

And therefore, Cousin, since that God knoweth what shall happen and not we, let us in the meanwhile, with a good hope in the help of God's grace, have a good purpose with us of sure standing by his holy faith against all persecutions. From which if we should (which our Lord forbid) hereafter either for fear or pain, for lack of his grace lost in our own default,[505] mishap to decline,[506] yet had we both won the well-spent time in this good purpose before, to the diminishment of our pain, and were also much the more likely that God should lift us up after our fall, and give us his grace again; howbeit, if this persecution come, we be, by this meditation and well-continued intent and purpose before, the better strengthened and confirmed, and much the more likely for to stand indeed. And if it so fortune (as with God's grace at men's good prayers and amendment of our evil lives, it may fortune full well) that the Turks shall either be well withstood and vanquished, or peradventure not invade us at all, then shall we, pardie,[507] by this good purpose get ourselves of God a very good cheap thanks.

And on the other side, while we now think thereon (as not to think thereon in so great likelihood thereof, I ween no wise man can), if we should for the fear of worldly loss, or bodily pain framed in our own minds, think that we would give over, and to save our goods and our lives, forsake our Savior by denial of his faith, then whether the Turks come or come not, we be gone from God the while. And then if they come not indeed, or come and be driven to flight, what a shame should this be to us before the face of God, in so shameful cowardous wise[508] to forsake him for fear of that pain that we never felt, nor never was falling toward us.

VINCENT: By my troth, Uncle, I thank you; methinketh that though you never said more in the matter, yet have you even with this that you have of the fear of bodily pain in this persecution spoken here already marvelously comforted mine heart.

ANTONY: I am glad, Cousin, if your heart have taken comfort thereby. But and if[509] you so have, give God the thanks and not me, for that work is his and not mine; for neither am I able any good thing to say but by him, nor all the good words in the world—no, not the holy words of God himself, and spoken also with his own holy mouth—can be able to profit the man with the sound entering at his ear but if[510] the Spirit of God therewith inwardly work in his soul; but that is his goodness ever ready to do, except the let[511] be through the untowardness[512] of our own froward[513] will.

THE EIGHTEENTH CHAPTER
Of comfort against bodily pain,
and first against captivity

ANTONY: And therefore, now being somewhat in comfort and courage before, whereby we may the more quietly consider everything—which is somewhat more hard and difficile[514] to do when the heart is before taken up and oppressed with the troublous affection of heavy[515] sorrowful fear—let us examine the weight and the substance of those bodily pains as the sorest[516] part of this persecution which you rehearsed before, which were, if I remember you right, thralldom,[517] imprisonment, painful and shameful death. And first let us (as reason is)[518] begin with the thralldom, for that was, as I remember, the first.

VINCENT: I pray you, good Uncle, say then somewhat thereof; for methinketh, Uncle, that captivity is a marvelous heavy thing, namely[519] when they shall (as they most commonly do) carry us far from home into a strange uncouth[520] land.

ANTONY: I cannot say nay but that grief it is, Cousin, indeed, but yet as unto me not half so much as it would be if they could carry me out into any such unknown country that God could not wit[521]

503 *that that:* that which   **504** Rom 8:28
505 *in . . . default:* through our own fault
506 *mishap to decline:* have the misfortune
to fall away   **507** certainly   **508** ways,
manner   **509** *and if:* if   **510** *but if:* unless
511 *except the let:* unless the hindrance
512 obstinacy   **513** perverse, unruly
514 difficult   **515** grievous   **516** most
grievous   **517** enslavement   **518** *as reason
is:* as is right or reasonable   **519** especially
520 unfamiliar   **521** know

where, nor find the means to come at me. But in good faith, Cousin, now if my transmigration into a strange country should be any great grief unto me, the fault should be much in myself; for since I am very sure that whithersoever men convey me, God is no more verily here than he shall be there, if I get (as I may if I will) the grace to set my whole heart upon him and long for nothing but him, it can then make me no great matter to my mind whether they carry me hence or leave me here. And then if I find my mind much offended therewith that I am not still in mine own country, I must consider that the cause of my grief is mine own wrong imagination, whereby I beguile myself with an untrue persuasion, weening that this were mine own country, whereas of truth it is not so. For as Saint Paul saith, *Non habemus hic civitatem manentem sed futuram inquirimus* ("We have here no city, nor dwelling country at all, but we seek for one that we shall come to").[522] And in what country soever we walk in this world, we be but as pilgrims and wayfaring men. And if I should take any country for mine own, it must be the country to which I come, and not the country from which I came.

That country that shall be to me then for a while so strange, shall yet, pardie,[523] be no more strange to me, nor longer strange to me neither, than was mine own native country when I came first into it. And therefore if that point, of my being far from hence,[524] be very grievous to me, and that I find it a great pain that I am not where I would[525] be, that grief shall great part grow for[526] lack of sure setting and settling my mind in God, where it should be; which fault of mine, when I mend, I shall soon ease my grief.

Now as for all other griefs and pains that are in captivity, thralldom, and bondage, I cannot deny but many there are and great. Howbeit, they seem yet somewhat (what say I somewhat? I may say a great deal) the more because we take our former liberty for more a great deal than indeed it was. Let us therefore consider the matter thus.

Captivity, bondage, or thralldom: what is it but the violent restraint of a man being so subdued under the dominion, rule, and power of another that he must do what the other list[527] to command him, and may not do at his liberty such things as he list himself?

Now when we shall be carried away with a Turk, and be fain[528] to be occupied about such things as he list to set us, here shall we lament the loss of our liberty, and think we bear a heavy burden of our servile condition. And so to do we shall have, I grant well, many times great occasion. But yet should we, I suppose, set thereby[529] somewhat the less if we would remember well what liberty that was that we lost, and take it for no larger than it was indeed. For we reckon as though we might before do what we would. But therein we deceive ourselves, for what free man is there so free that can be suffered[530] to do what him list? In many things God hath restrained us by his high commandment—so many that of those things which else we would do, I ween it be more than the half; howbeit, because (God forgive us) we let[531] so little therefor, but do what we list as though we heard him not, we reckon our liberty never the less for that.

But then is our liberty much restrained by the laws made by men, for the quiet and politic governance of the people. And these would, I ween, let[532] our liberty but a little neither, were it not for fear of the pains that fall thereupon.

Look then whether other men that have authority over us command us never no business which we dare not but do, and therefore do it full oft full sore[533] against our wills, of which things some service is sometimes so painful, and so perilous too, that no lord can lightly[534] command his bondman worse, nor seldom doth command him half so sore.

Let every free man that reckoneth his liberty to stand in doing what he list[535] consider well these points, and I ween he shall then find his liberty much less than he took it for before. And yet have I left untouched the bondage that almost every man is in that boasteth himself for free—the bondage, I mean, of sin, which to be a very bondage I shall have our Savior himself to bear me good record, for he saith, *Qui facit peccatum servus est peccati* ("He that committeth sin is the thrall or bondman of sin").[536] And then if this be thus (as it must needs be so, since God saith it is so), who is there then that may make so much boast of his liberty that he should take it for so sore a thing and so strange, to become through chance of war bond[537] unto a man, while he is already through sin become willingly thrall[538] and bond unto the devil?

Let us look well how many things and of what vile wretched sort the devil driveth us to do daily, through the rash braids[539] of our blind affections, which we be, for our faultful[540] lack of grace, fain[541] to follow, and are too feeble to refrain,[542] and then shall we find in our natural freedom our bondservice such that never was there any man lord of any so vile a villain that ever would for very shame command him so shameful service. And let us in the doing of our service to the man that we be slave unto remember what we were wont[543] to do about the same time of the day while we were at our free liberty before, and were well likely if we were at liberty to do the like again, and we shall peradventure perceive that it were better for us to do this business than that.

Now shall we have great occasion of comfort, if we consider that our servitude, though in the count[544] of the world it seem to come by chance of war, cometh yet in very deed unto us by the provident hand of God, and that for our great good, if we will take it well, both in remission of sins and also matter of our merit.

The greatest grief that is in bondage or captivity is this, as I trow, that we be forced to do such labor as with our good will we would not. But then against that grief Seneca teacheth us a good remedy: *Semper da operam ne quid invitus facias* ("Endeavor thyself evermore that thou do nothing against thy will").[545] But that thing that we see we shall needs do, let us use[546] always to put our good will thereto.

VINCENT: That is, Uncle, soon said, but it is hard to do.

ANTONY: Our froward[547] mind maketh every good thing hard, and that to our own more hurt and harm. But in this case if we will be good Christian men, we shall have great cause gladly to be content for[548] the great comfort that we may take thereby, while we remember that in the patient and glad doing of our service unto that man for God's sake — according to his high commandment by the mouth of Saint Paul, *Servi oboedite dominis*[549] — we shall have our thanks and our reward of God.

Finally, if we remember the great humble meekness of our Savior Christ himself — that he, being very almighty God, *humiliavit semet ipsum formam servi accipiens* ("humbled himself and took the form of a bondman or slave"),[550] rather than his Father should forsake us — we may think ourselves very unkind caitiffs[551] and very frantic fools too, if rather than to endure this worldly bondage for a while, we would forsake him that hath by his own death delivered us out of everlasting bondage of the devil, and will for our short bondage give us everlasting liberty.

VINCENT: Well fare you, good Uncle, this is very well said; albeit that[552] bondage is a condition that every man of any courage[553] would be glad to eschew[554] and very loath to fall in, yet have you well made it open[555] that it is a thing neither so strange nor so sore[556] as it before seemed unto me, and specially far from such as any man that any wit hath should for fear thereof shrink from the confession of his faith. And now therefore I pray you somewhat speak of your prisonment.[557]

THE NINETEENTH CHAPTER
Of imprisonment and comfort thereagainst

ANTONY: That shall I, Cousin, with good will. And first if we would consider what thing imprisonment is of his own nature, we should not methinketh have so great horror thereof; for of itself it is, pardie,[558] but a restraint of liberty which letteth[559] a man from going whither he would.

VINCENT: Yes, by Saint Mary, Uncle, methinketh it is much more sorrow than so; for besides the let[560] and restraint of liberty, it hath many more displeasures, and very sore griefs, knit and joined thereto.

ANTONY: That is, Cousin, very true indeed, and those pains, among many sorer[561] than those,

---

537 slave   **538** slave   **539** whims
540 culpable   **541** willing, glad
542 restrain   **543** accustomed
544 account; reckoning   **545** Seneca,
Letter 61.2–3   **546** make it our practice;

accustom ourselves   **547** unruly, perverse
548 on account of   **549** "Slaves, obey
your masters" (Eph 6:5).   **550** Phil
2:7   **551** *unkind caitiffs:* unnatural
wretches   **552** *albeit that:* although

553 spirit   **554** avoid   **555** clear, evident
556 grievous   **557** *your prisonment:* your
view of imprisonment   **558** certainly
559 prevents, hinders   **560** obstruction
561 worse, more grievous

thought I not after to forget. Howbeit, I purpose now to consider first imprisonment, but as imprisonment only, without any other incommodity[562] besides. For a man may be, pardie, imprisoned, and yet not set in the stocks nor collared fast by the neck; and a man may be let walk at large where he will, and yet a pair of fetters fast riveted on his legs; for in this country, ye wot well, and in Seville and Portugal too, so go all the slaves.

Howbeit, because that for such things men's hearts hath such horror thereof, albeit that I am not so mad as to go about to prove that bodily pain were no pain, yet since that because of these manner of pains, we so specially abhor the state and condition of prisoners, we should methinketh well perceive that a great part of our horror groweth of our own fantasy if we would call to mind and consider the state and condition of many other folk in whose state and condition we would wish ourselves to stand, taking them for no prisoners at all that[563] stand yet for all that in much part of the selfsame points that we abhor imprisonment for. Let us therefore consider these things in order.

And first as I thought to begin, because those other kinds of griefs that come with imprisonment are but accidents[564] thereunto — and yet neither such kinds of accidents as either be proper[565] thereunto, but that they may, almost all, fall unto a man without it, nor are not such accidents thereunto as are inseparable therefrom, but that imprisonment may fall to a man and none of all them therewith — we will, I say, therefore begin with the considering what manner pain or incommodity we should reckon imprisonment to be of himself and of his own nature alone. And then, in the course of our communication,[566] you shall as you list[567] increase and aggrieve[568] the cause of your horror with the terror of those painful accidents.

VINCENT: I am sorry that I did interrupt your tale. For you were about, I see well, to take an orderly way therein. And as yourself have devised, so I beseech you proceed; for though I reckon imprisonment much the sorer thing by sore and hard handling[569] therein, yet reckon I not the prisonment of itself any less than a thing very tedious, all were it[570] used

in the most favorable manner that it possibly might; for, Uncle, if it were a great prince that were taken prisoner upon the field and in the hand of a Christian king, which use[571] in such case (for the consideration of their former estate, and mutable chance of the war) to show much humanity to them and in very favorable wise[572] entreat them — for these infidel emperors handle oftentimes the princes that they take more villainously than they do the poorest men, as the great Tamburlaine kept the great Turk, when he had taken him, to tread on his back always while he leapt on horseback — but as I began to say by the example of a prince taken prisoner, were the imprisonment never so favorable, yet were it in my mind no little grief in itself for a man to be penned up, though not in a narrow chamber, but although his walk were right large and right fair gardens too therein, it could not but grieve his heart to be restrained by another man within certain limits and bounds, and lose the liberty to be where him list.

ANTONY: This is, Cousin, well considered of you, for in this you perceive well that imprisonment is of himself, and his own very nature alone, nothing else but the retaining of a man's person within the circuit of a certain space, narrower or larger as shall be limited unto him, restraining his liberty from the further going into any other place.

VINCENT: Very well said, as methinketh.

ANTONY: Yet forgot I, Cousin, to ask you one question.

VINCENT: What is that, Uncle?

ANTONY: This, lo: if there be two men kept in two several[573] chambers of one great castle, of which two chambers the one is much more larger than the other, whether be they prisoners both, or but the one that hath the less room to walk in?

VINCENT: What question is it, Uncle, but that they be prisoners both, as I said myself before, although[574] the one lay fast[575] locked in the stocks, and the other had all the whole castle to walk in?

---

562 harm, disadvantage   563 who
564 inessential attributes   565 *proper*
thereunto: exclusive to it

566 conversation   567 wish, please
568 make more grave or serious; exaggerate
569 *hard handling:* rough treatment

570 *all were it:* even if it were   571 are
accustomed   572 ways   573 separate
574 even if   575 securely

ANTONY: Methinketh verily, Cousin, that you say the truth. And then if imprisonment be such a thing as yourself here agree it is — that is to wit, but a lack of liberty to go if we list — now would I fain wit[576] of you what any one man you know that is at this day out of prison.

VINCENT: What one man, Uncle? Marry, I know almost none other, for surely prisoner am I none acquainted with, that I remember.

ANTONY: Then I see well you visit poor prisoners seldom.

VINCENT: No, by my troth,[577] Uncle, I cry God mercy. I send them sometimes mine alms, but by my troth I love not to come myself where I should see such misery.

ANTONY: In good faith, Cousin Vincent, though I say it before you, you have many good conditions;[578] but surely, though I say it before you too, that condition is none of them; which condition, if you would amend, then should you have yet the more good conditions by one, and peradventure[579] the more by three or four, for I assure you, it is hard to tell how much good to a man's soul the personal visiting to poor prisoners doth.

But now since you can name me none of them that are in prison, I pray you name some one of all them that you be, as you say, better acquainted with: men, I mean, that are out of prison; for I know, methinketh, as few of them as you know of the other.

VINCENT: That were, Uncle, a strange case, for every man is, Uncle, out of prison that may go where he will, though he be the poorest beggar in the town. And in good faith, Uncle (because you reckon imprisonment so small a matter of itself), the poor beggar that is at his liberty and may walk where he will is, as meseemeth,[580] in better case than is a king kept in prison that cannot go but where men give him leave.[581]

ANTONY: Well, Cousin, whether every way-walking[582] beggar be by this reason out of prison or no, we shall consider further when ye will,[583] but in the meanwhile, I can by this reason[584] see no prince that seemeth to be out of prison; for if the lack of liberty to go where a man will be imprisonment, as yourself say it is, then is the great Turk, by whom we so fear to be put in prison, in prison already himself, for he may not go where he will; for if he might, he would into Portugal, Italy, Spain, France, Almain,[585] and England, and as far on another quarter[586] too: both Prester John's land[587] and the Grand Khan's[588] too.

Now the beggar that you speak of, if he be (as you say he is) by reason of his liberty to go[589] where he will, in much better case than a king kept in prison, because he cannot go but where men give him leave, then is that beggar in better case not only than a prince in prison, but also than many a prince out of prison too, for I am sure there is many a beggar that may without let[590] walk further upon other men's ground than many a prince at his best liberty may walk upon his own. And as for walking out abroad upon other men's, that prince might hap to be said nay and holden fast where that beggar with his bag and his staff should be suffered[591] to go forth and hold on his way. But forasmuch, Cousin, as[592] neither the beggar nor the prince is at free liberty to walk where they will, but that if they would walk in some place, neither of them both should be suffered but men would withstand them and say them nay, therefore if imprisonment be (as you grant it is) a lack of liberty to go where we list,[593] I cannot see but as I say: the beggar and the prince, whom you reckon both at liberty, be by your own reason restrained in prison both.

VINCENT: Yea, but Uncle, both the one and the other have way enough to walk, the one in his own ground, the other in other men's or in the common highway, where they may walk till they be both weary of walking ere any man say them nay.

ANTONY: So may, Cousin, that king that had, as yourself put the case, all the whole castle to walk in, and yet you say not nay but that he is prisoner for[594] all that — though not so straitly[595] kept, yet as verily prisoner as he that lieth in the stocks.

---

576 know   **577** truth, faithfulness
578 qualities   **579** perhaps   **580** it seems to me   **581** permission   **582** vagrant
583 *when ye will:* whenever you want

584 reasoning   **585** Germany   **586** part of the globe   **587** *Prester John's land:* a legendary place generally identified with Ethiopia or India   **588** *the Great Khan's:*

i.e., China   **589** able to go   **590** hindrance   **591** allowed   **592** *forasmuch… as:* seeing that, inasmuch as   **593** wish, please   **594** despite   **595** narrowly

VINCENT: But they may go at the leastwise to every place that they need, or that is commodious[596] for them, and therefore they do not will to go but where they may go. And therefore be they at liberty to go where they will.

ANTONY: Me needeth not, Cousin, to spend the time about the impugning every part of this answer. For letting pass by that though a prisoner were with his keeper brought into every place where need required, yet since he might not when he would go where he would for his only pleasure, he were, ye wot well, a prisoner still; and letting pass over also this, that it were to this beggar need, and to this king commodious, to go into diverse places where neither of them both may come; and letting pass also that neither of them both is lightly[597] so temperately determined[598] but that they both fain so would do indeed; if this reason of yours put them out of prison, and set them at liberty and make them free (as I will well grant it doth) if they so do indeed— that is to wit, if they have no will to go but where they may go indeed—then let us look on our other prisoners enclosed within a castle, and we shall find that the straitest kept of them both, if he get the wisdom and the grace to quiet his own mind, and hold himself content with that place, and long not, like a woman with child for her lusts,[599] to be gadding out anywhere else, is by the same reason of yours, while his will is not longing to be anywhere else, he is, I say, at his free liberty to be where he will, and so is out of prison too.

And on the other side, if though his will be not longing to be anywhere else, yet because that if his will so were, he should not so be suffered, he is therefore not at his free liberty but a prisoner still, so since your free beggar that you speak of, and the prince that you call out of prison too, though they be (which I ween very few be) by some special wisdom so temperately disposed that they have not the will to be but where they see they may be suffered to be, yet since that if they would have that will, they could not then be where they would, they lack the effect of free liberty, and be both twain in prison too.

VINCENT: Well, Uncle, if every man universally be by this reason in prison already, after[600] the very propriety[601] of imprisonment, yet to be imprisoned in this special manner (which manner is only commonly called imprisonment) is a thing of great horror and fear, both for the straitness[602] of the keeping and the hard handling that many men have therein, of all which griefs and pains and displeasures, in this other general imprisonment that you speak of, we feel nothing at all. And therefore every man abhorreth the one, and would be loath to come into it, and no man abhorreth the other, for they feel none harm nor find no fault therein; wherefore, Uncle, in good faith, though I cannot find answers convenient[603] wherewith to avoid[604] your arguments, yet to be plain with you and tell you the very truth, my mind findeth not itself satisfied in this point, but that ever methinketh that these things wherewith you rather convince and conclude[605] me than induce a credence and persuade me, that every man is in prison already, be but sophistical fantasies, and that except those that are commonly called prisoners, other men are not in any prison at all.

ANTONY: Well fare thine heart, good Cousin Vincent. There was in good faith no word that you spoke since we talked of these matters that half so well liked[606] me as this that you speak now. For if you had assented in words, and in your mind departed unpersuaded, then if the thing be true that I say, yet had you lost the fruit,[607] and if it be peradventure false, and myself deceived therein, then while I should ween that it liked you too, you should have confirmed me in my folly; for in good faith, Cousin, such an old fool am I that this thing—in the persuading whereof unto you I had weened I had quit me[608] well, and when I have all done appeareth to your mind but a trifle and a sophistical fantasy—myself have so many years taken for so very substantial truth that as yet my mind cannot give me to think it any other. Wherefore lest I play as the French priest played, that had so long used[609] to say *Dominus* with the second syllable long that at last he thought it must needs be so and was ashamed to say it short, to the intent you may the better perceive me, or I the better myself, we shall here between us a little more consider the thing. And hardily spit well on your hands and take

---

596 beneficial   **597** probably   **598** disposed   **599** cravings   **600** according to   **601** nature   **602** narrowness, constriction

603 appropriate, suitable   **604** refute   **605** *convince and conclude:* overcome and force   **606** pleased   **607** benefit

608 *quit me:* acquitted myself   **609** been accustomed

good hold, and give it not over against your own mind. For then were we never the near.[610]

VINCENT: Nay, by my troth,[611] Uncle, that I intend not, nor nothing did yet since we began. And that may you well perceive by some things which, without any great cause save for the further satisfaction of mine own mind, I repeated and debated again.

ANTONY: That guise,[612] Cousin, hold on hardily[613] still, for in this matter I purpose to give over my part[614] except I make yourself perceive both that every man universally is a very[615] prisoner in very prison plainly, without any sophistication[616] at all, and that there is also no prince living upon earth but he is in worse case prisoner, by this general imprisonment that I speak of, than is many a lewd[617] simple wretch by that special imprisonment that you speak of; and over this, that in this general imprisonment that I speak of, men are for the time that they be therein so sore handled[618] and so hardly[619] and in such painful wise that men's hearts have with reason great cause as sore[620] to abhor the hard handling that is in this imprisonment as the other that is in that.

VINCENT: By my troth, Uncle, these things would I fain see well proved.

ANTONY: Tell me, then, Cousin, first by your troth, if there were a man attainted[621] of treason or felony, and after judgment given of his death, and that it were determined that he should die, only the time of his execution delayed till the king's further pleasure known, and he thereupon delivered to certain keepers, and put up in a sure place, out of which he could not escape, were this man a prisoner or no?

VINCENT: This man, quoth he? Yea, marry, that he were in very deed, if ever any man were.

ANTONY: But now, what if for the time that were mean[622] between his attainder[623] and his execution he were so favorably handled that he were suffered to do what he would as he was while he was abroad, and to have the use of his lands and his goods, and his wife and his children license to be with him, and his friends leave at liberty to resort unto him, and his servants not forbidden to bide[624] about him; and add yet thereunto that the place were a great castle royal, with parks and other pleasures therein a very great circuit about; yea, add yet and ye will that he were suffered to go and ride also, both when he would and whither he would, only this one point always provided and foreseen: that he should ever be surely seen to and safely kept from escaping, so that took he never so much of his own mind in the meanwhile all other ways save[625] escaping, yet he well knew that escape he could not, and that when he were called for, to death and execution he should? Now, Cousin Vincent, what would you call this man? A prisoner, because he is kept for execution? Or no prisoner, because he is in the meanwhile so favorably handled and suffered[626] to do all that he would save escape? And I bid you not here be hasty in your answer, but advise[627] it well, that you grant no such thing in haste as you would after mislike by leisure, and think yourself deceived.

VINCENT: Nay, by my troth, Uncle, this thing needeth no study at all in my mind, but that for all this favor showed him, and all this liberty lent him, yet being condemned to death, and being kept therefor, and kept with such sure watch laid upon him that he cannot escape, he is all that while a very plain prisoner still.

ANTONY: In good faith, Cousin, methinketh you say very true. But then one thing must I yet desire you, Cousin, to tell me a little further: if there were another laid in prison for a fray,[628] and through the jailer's displeasure were bolted and fettered and laid in a low dungeon in the stocks, where he might hap to lie peradventure for a while, and abide[629] in the mean season[630] some pain, but no danger of death at all, but that out again he should come well enough — whether[631] of these two prisoners stood in worse case, he that hath all this favor, or he that is thus hardly handled?[632]

---

610 nearer   611 truth, faithfulness
612 habit, practice   613 resolutely
614 *give over my part:* give up my side of the dispute; admit defeat   615 true
616 sophism; specious reasoning

617 uneducated; bungling; evil   618 *so sore handled:* treated so severely
619 roughly   620 greatly, intensely
621 convicted   622 intervening   623 sentence, condemnation   624 remain; reside

625 except   626 *handled and suffered:* treated and permitted   627 examine, consider, attend to   628 brawl   629 endure
630 *mean season:* meantime   631 which
632 *hardly handled:* roughly treated

VINCENT: By our Lady, Uncle, I ween the most part of men, if they should needs choose, had liefer[633] be such prisoners in every point[634] as he that so sorely lieth in the stocks than in every point such as he that at such liberty walketh about the park.

ANTONY: Consider then, Cousin, whether this thing seem any sophistry to you that I shall show you now, for it shall be such as seemeth, in good faith, substantial true to me. And if it so happen that you think otherwise, I will be very glad to perceive which of us both is beguiled. For it seemeth to me, Cousin, first, that every man coming into this world here upon earth, as he is created by God, so cometh he hither by the providence of God—is this any sophistry, first, or not?

VINCENT: Nay, verily, this is very substantial truth.

ANTONY: Now take I this also for very truth in my mind, that there cometh no man nor woman hither into the earth but that, ere ever they come quick[635] into the world out of the mother's womb, God condemneth them unto death, by his own sentence and judgment, for the original sin that they bring with them, contracted in the corrupted stock of our forefather Adam—is this, Cousin, think you, verily thus or not?

VINCENT: This is, Uncle, very true indeed.

ANTONY: Then seemeth this true, further, unto me, that God hath put every man here upon earth under so sure and under so safe keeping that of all the whole people living in this wide world there is neither man, woman, nor child, would they never so fain wander about and seek it, that possibly can find any way whereby they may escape from death—is this, Cousin, a fond[636] imagined fantasy, or is it very truth indeed?

VINCENT: Nay, this is none imagination, Uncle, but a thing so clearly proved true that no man is so mad to say nay.

ANTONY: Then need I no more, Cousin, for then is all the matter plain and open[637] evident truth which I said I took for truth—which is yet more a little now than I told you before, when you took my proof yet but for a sophistical fantasy, and said that for all my reasoning that every man is a prisoner, yet you thought that except these whom the common people call prisoners, there is else[638] no man a very prisoner indeed. And now you grant yourself again, for very substantial open truth, that every man is here (though he be the greatest king upon earth) set here by the ordinance of God in a place (be it never so large), a place, I say, yet (and you say the same) out of which no man can escape, but that therein is every man put under sure and safe keeping to be readily fetched forth when God calleth for him, and that then he shall surely die. And is not then, Cousin, by your own granting before, every man a very prisoner, when he is put in a place to be kept to be brought forth, when he would not, and himself wot not whither?

VINCENT: Yes, in good faith, Uncle, I cannot but well perceive this to be so.

ANTONY: This were, you wot well, true although[639] a man should be but taken by the arm and in fair manner led out of this world unto his judgment. But now, while we well know that there is no king so great but that all the while he walketh here, walk he never so loose,[640] ride he with never so strong an army for his defense, yet himself is very sure—though he seek in the mean season some other pastime to put it out of his mind—yet is he very sure, I say, that escape he cannot, and very well he knoweth that he hath already sentence given upon him to die, and that verily die he shall, and that himself, though he hope upon long respite[641] of his execution, yet can he not tell how soon; and therefore, but if[642] he be a fool, he can never be without fear that either on the morrow or on the selfsame day, the grisly cruel hangman Death, which from his first coming in hath ever hoved aloof[643] and looked toward him, and ever lain in a wait on him, shall, amid among[644] all his royalty and all his main strength, neither kneel before him, nor make him any reverence, nor with any good manner desire him to come forth, but rigorously and fiercely grip him by the very breast, and make all his bones rattle,

---

633 *had liefer:* would rather   **634** aspect
635 alive   **636** foolish   **637** clear
638 otherwise   **639** even if   **640** freely

641 *upon long respite:* for a long stay
642 *but if:* unless   **643** *hoved aloof:*

hovered at a distance   **644** *amid among:*
in the midst of

and so by long and diverse sore torments strike him stark dead in this prison, and then cause his body to be cast into the ground in a foul pit within some corner of the same, there to rot and be eaten with wretched worms of the earth, sending yet his soul out further unto a more fearful judgment, whereof at his temporal death his success is uncertain—and therefore, though by God's grace not out of good hope, yet for all that in the meanwhile in very sore dread and fear, and peradventure in peril inevitable of eternal fire.

Methinketh therefore, Cousin, that, as I told you, this keeping of every man in this wretched world for execution of death, it is a very plain imprisonment indeed, and that, as I say, such that the greatest king is in this prison in much worse case in all his wealth than many a man is by the other imprisonment that is therein sore and hardly handled; for whereas some of those lie not there attainted[645] nor condemned to death, the greatest man of this world and the most wealthy in this universal prison is laid in, to be kept undoubtedly for death.

VINCENT: But yet, Uncle, in that case is the other prisoner too, for he is as sure that he shall die too, pardie.

ANTONY: This is very true, Cousin, indeed, and well objected to. But then you must consider that he is not in danger of death by reason of that prison into which he is put peradventure but for a light fray,[646] but his danger of death is by the other imprisonment by which he is prisoner in the great prison of this whole earth, in which prison all the princes thereof be prisoners as well as he. If a man condemned to death were put up in a large prison, and while his execution were respited,[647] he were, for fighting with his fellows, put up in a strait[648] place, part of the same, he is in danger of death in that strait prison, but not by the being in that—for therein he is but for the fray—but his deadly imprisonment was the other: the larger, I say, into which he was put for death. So the prisoner that you speak of is, besides that narrow prison, a prisoner of the broad world, and all the princes thereof therein prisoners with him. And by that imprisonment, both they and he in like danger of death: not

by that strait imprisonment that is commonly called imprisonment, but by that imprisonment which, because of the large walk, men call it liberty—and which prison you therefore thought but a fantasy sophistical to prove it any prison at all. But now may you, methinketh, very plainly perceive that this whole earth is not only for all the whole kind[649] of man a very plain prison indeed, but also that every man without exception, even those that are most at their liberty therein, and reckon themselves great lords and possessioners of a very great parcel thereof, and thereby wax[650] with wantonness so forgetful of their own state that they ween they stand in great wealth, do stand for all that indeed, by the reason of that imprisonment in this large prison of the whole earth, in the selfsame condition that others do stand which[651] in the narrow prisons, which only be called prisons, and which only be reputed prisons in the opinion of the common people, stand in the most fearful and in the most odious case: that is to wit, condemned already to death.

And now, Cousin, if this thing that I tell you seem but a sophistical fantasy to your mind, I would be glad to know what moveth you so to think. For in good faith, as I have told you twice, I am no wiser but that I verily ween[652] that the thing is thus of very plain truth in very deed.

THE TWENTIETH CHAPTER

VINCENT: In good faith, Uncle, as for this farforth,[653] I not only can make with any reason no resistance thereagainst, but also see very clearly proved that it can be none otherwise but that every man is in this world a very prisoner, since we be all put here into a sure hold to be kept till we be put to execution, as folk already condemned all unto death. But yet, Uncle, that strait keeping, collaring, bolting, and stocking,[654] with lying in straw or on the cold ground—which manner of hard handling[655] is used in these special prisonments that only be called commonly by that name—must needs make that imprisonment, which only beareth among the people that name, much more odious and dreadful than the general imprisoning wherewith we be every man universally prisoned at large, walking where we

---

645 convicted   646 *light fray:* minor fight   647 stayed   648 enclosed, narrow   649 species, race   650 become, grow   651 who   652 *verily ween:* truly believe   653 *as . . . far-forth:* i.e., as for your argument thus far   654 *bolting,* *and stocking:* shackling, and putting in the stocks   655 *hard handling:* rough treatment

will round about the wide world—in which broad prison, out of[656] those narrow prisons, there is with the prisoners no such hard handling used.

ANTONY: I said, I trow,[657] Cousin, that I purposed to prove you further yet that in this general prison—the large prison, I mean, of this whole world—folk be for the time that they be therein as sore handled and as hardly, and wrenched and wrunged and breaked in such painful wise that our hearts (save that we consider it not) have with reason good and great cause to grudge[658] against and (as far-forth as pertaineth only to the respect of pain) as much horror to conceive against the hard handling that is in this prison as the other that is in that.

VINCENT: Indeed, Uncle, truth it is that this you said you would prove.

ANTONY: Nay, so much said I not, Cousin, but I said I would if I could, and if I could not, then would I therein give over my part.[659] But that trust I, Cousin, I shall not need to do, the thing seemeth me so plain; for Cousin, not only the prince and king, but also, though he hath both angels and devils that are jailers under him, yet the chief jailer over this whole broad prison, the world, is (as I take it) God. And that, I suppose, ye will grant me too.

VINCENT: That will I not, Uncle, deny.

ANTONY: If a man be, Cousin, committed to prison for no cause but to be kept, though there be never so great charge upon him, yet his keeper, if he be good and honest, is neither so cruel that would pain the man of[660] malice, nor so covetous that would put him to pain to make him seek his friends to pay for a pennyworth of ease; else,[661] if the place be such that he be sure to keep him safe otherwise, or that he can get surety for the recompense of more harm than he seeth he should have if he escaped, he will never handle him in any such hard fashion as we most abhor imprisonment for. But marry, if the place be such as the keeper cannot otherwise be sure, then is he compelled to keep him

after the rate the straiter.[662] And also, if the prisoner be unruly and fall to fighting with his fellows, or do some other manner of shrewd turns,[663] then useth the keeper[664] to punish him sundry wise,[665] in some of such fashions as yourself have spoken of.

So is it now, Cousin, that God—the chief jailer, as I say, of this broad prison, the world—is neither cruel nor covetous. And this prison is also so sure[666] and so subtly built that, albeit that it lieth open on every side without any wall in the world, yet wander we never so far about therein, the way to get out at shall we never find, so that he needeth not to collar us nor to stock us for any fear of escaping away. And therefore, except he see some other cause than our only keeping for death, he letteth us in the meanwhile (for as long as he list to respite[667] us) walk about in the prison, and do therein what we will, using ourselves in such wise as he hath by reason and revelation from time to time told us his pleasure.

And hereof it cometh, lo, that by reason of this favor, for a time we wax (as I said) so wanton[668] that we forget where we be—weening that we were lords at large, whereas we be indeed, if we would consider it, even seely[669] poor wretches in prison; for of very truth, our very prison this earth is. And yet thereof we cant[670] us out—part by covenants[671] that we make among us, and part by fraud, and part by violence too—diverse parts diversely to ourselves, and change the name thereof from the odious name of prison, and call it our own land and our livelihood.

Upon our prison we build our prison; we garnish it with gold and make it glorious. In this prison they buy and sell; in this prison they brawl and chide;[672] in this they run together and fight; in this they dice; in this they card. In this they pipe[673] and revel. In this they sing and dance. And in this prison many a man reputed right honest letteth not,[674] for his pleasure in the dark, privily[675] to play the knave.

And thus, while God, our king and our chief jailer too, suffereth[676] us and letteth us alone, we ween ourselves at liberty, and we abhor the state of those whom we call prisoners, taking ourselves for no prisoners at all.

In which false persuasion of wealth and forgetfulness of our own wretched state (which is but a

---

656 *out of:* outside   **657** think, believe   **658** complain   **659** *give over my part:* give up my side of the dispute; admit defeat   **660** out of   **661** otherwise   **662** *after the rate the straiter:* proportionately under

the tighter security   **663** *shrewd turns:* malicious deeds   **664** *useth the keeper:* the keeper is accustomed   **665** ways   **666** secure   **667** *list to respite:* chooses to reprieve   **668** lustful; unruly, unrestrained

669 pitiful; foolish   **670** parcel, apportion   **671** contracts   **672** wrangle, quarrel loudly   **673** play music   **674** *letteth not:* does not hesitate   **675** privately, secretly   **676** permits, endures

wandering about for a while in this prison of this world, till we be brought unto the execution of death), where we forget with our folly both ourselves and our jail, and our underjailers, angels and devils both, and our chief jailer, God, too—God, that forgetteth not us, but seeth us all the while well enough, and being sore[677] discontent to see so shrewd[678] rule kept in the jail, besides that he sendeth the hangman Death to put to execution here and there sometimes by the thousands at once, he handleth many of the remnant, whose execution he forbeareth[679] yet unto a further time, even as hardly,[680] and punisheth them as sore, in this common prison of the world as there are any handled in those special prisons, which for the hard handling used (you say) therein, your heart hath in such horror and so sore abhorreth.

VINCENT: The remnant will I not gainsay,[681] for methinketh I see it so indeed; but that God, our chief jailer in this world, useth any such prisonly fashion of punishment, that point must I needs deny, for I neither see him lay any man in the stocks or strike fetters on his legs, or so much as shut him up in a chamber either.

ANTONY: Is he no minstrel, Cousin, that playeth not on a harp? Maketh no man melody but he that playeth on a lute? He may be a minstrel and make melody, you wot well, with some other instrument, some strange-fashioned, peradventure, that never was seen before. God, our chief jailer, as himself is invisible, so useth he in his punishments invisible instruments, and therefore not of like fashion as the other jailers do, but yet of like effect, and as painful in feeling as those: for he layeth one of his prisoners with a hot fever, as evil at his ease in a warm bed as the other jailer layeth his on the cold ground; he wringeth them by the brows with a megrim;[682] he collareth them by the neck with a quinsy;[683] he bolteth[684] them by the arms with a palsy, that they cannot lift their hands to their head; he manacleth their hands with the gout in their fingers; he wringeth them by the legs with the cramp in their shins; he bindeth them to the bed-board with the crick in

the back, and layeth one there along,[685] and as unable to rise as though he lay by the feet fast in the stocks.

Some prisoner of another jail singeth and danceth in his two fetters, and feareth not his feet for stumbling[686] at a stone, while God's prisoner that hath his one foot fettered with the gout lieth groaning on a couch, and quaketh and crieth out if he fear there would fall on his foot no more but a cushion. And therefore, Cousin, as I said, if we consider it well, we shall find this general prison of this whole earth a place in which the prisoners be as sore handled[687] as they be in the other. And even in the other, some make as merry too, as there do some in this that are very merry at large out of that.

And surely, like as we ween ourselves out of prison now, so if there were some folk born and brought up in a prison that never came on the wall, nor looked out at the door, nor never heard of other world abroad, but saw some, for their shrewd turns[688] done among themselves, locked up in some straiter[689] room, and heard them only[690] called prisoners that were so served,[691] and themselves ever called free folk at large, the like opinion would they have there of themselves then that we have here of ourselves now. And when we take ourselves for other than prisoners now, as verily be we now deceived as those prisoners should there be then.

VINCENT: I cannot, Uncle, in good faith say nay but that you have performed all that you have promised. But yet since that for all this there appeareth no more but that as they be prisoners, so be we too, and that as some of them be sore handled, so be some of us too, since we wot well for all this that when we come to those prisons, we shall not fail to be in a straiter prison than we be now, and to have a door shut upon us where we have none shut on us now—this shall we be sure of at the leastwise, if there come no worse. And then may there come worse, ye wot well, it cometh there so commonly; wherefore, for all this, it is yet little marvel though men's hearts grudge[692] much there against.

ANTONY: Surely, Cousin, in this you say very well. Howbeit, somewhat had your words touched me the

677 very much, greatly   **678** poor, evil   **679** puts off   **680** roughly   **681** deny   **682** migraine   **683** swelling of the throat   **684** shackles   **685** at

full length   **686** *feareth…stumbling:* is not afraid his feet will stumble   **687** *sore handled:* severely treated   **688** *shrewd turns:* malicious deeds   **689** *straiter*

room: smaller space   **690** *heard them only:* heard only those ones   **691** treated   **692** grumble

nearer if I had said that imprisonment were no displeasure at all. But the thing that I say, Cousin, for our comfort therein, is that our fantasy frameth us a false opinion by which we deceive ourselves and take it for sorer[693] than it is. And that do we by the reason that we take ourselves before for more free than we be, and prisonment for a stranger thing to us than it is indeed. And thus far-forth,[694] as I said, have I proved very truth indeed. But now, the incommodities[695] that you repeat again, those, I say, that are proper to the imprisonment of their own nature—that is to wit, to have less room to walk in, and to have the door shut upon us—these are, methinketh, so very slender and slight that in so great a cause as to suffer for God's sake, we might be sore[696] ashamed so much as once to think upon them.

Many a good man there is, you wot well, which[697] without any force at all, or any necessity wherefore he should so do, suffereth these two things willingly of his own choice, with much other hardness more—holy monks, I mean, of the Charterhouse Order,[698] such as never pass their cells but only to the church set fast[699] by their cells, and thence to their cells again; and Saint Bridget's order, and Saint Clare's much like; and in a manner all close[700] religious houses, and yet anchors and anchoresses[701] most especially, all whose whole room[702] is less than a meetly[703] large chamber.[704] And yet are they there as well content many long years together as are other men (and better too) that walk about the world. And therefore you may see that the loathness of less room, and the door shut upon us, while so many folk are so well content therewith, and will for God's love lief[705] so to choose, is but a horror enhanced of our own fantasy.[706]

And indeed I wist[707] a woman once that came into a prison to visit of her charity a poor prisoner there, whom she found in a chamber, to say the truth, meetly fair; and at the leastwise it was strong enough. But with mats of straw the prisoner had made it so warm, both under the foot and round about the walls, that in these things, for keeping of his health, she was on his behalf glad and very well comforted. But among many other displeasures that for his sake she was sorry for, one she lamented much in her mind: that he should have the chamber door upon him by night made fast[708] by the jailer, that should shut him in. "For by my troth," [709] quoth she, "if the door should be shut upon me, I would ween it would stop up my breath." At that word of hers, the prisoner laughed in his mind, but he durst[710] not laugh aloud nor say nothing to her. For somewhat indeed he stood in awe of her, and had his finding[711] there much part of[712] her charity for alms; but he could not but laugh inwardly while he wist well enough that she used[713] on the inside to shut every night full surely[714] her own chamber to her, both door and windows too, and used not to open them of all the long night. And what difference then, as to the stopping of the breath, whether they were shut up within or without?[715]

And so surely, Cousin, these two things that you speak of are neither nother[716] of so great weight that in Christ's cause ought to move a Christian man; and the one of the twain is so very a childish fantasy that in a matter almost of three chips,[717] but if it were in chance of fire,[718] never should move any man.

As for those other accidents[719] of hard handling therein, so mad am I not to say they be no grief, but I say that our fear may imagine them much greater grief than they be. And I say that such as they be, many a man endureth them—yea, and many a woman too—that after[720] fare full well.

And then would I wit[721] what determination we take: whether for our Savior's sake to suffer some pain in our bodies, since he suffered in his blessed body so great pain for us, or else to give him warning to be at a point rather utterly to forsake him than suffer any pain at all? He that cometh in his mind unto this latter point—from which kind of unkindness God keep every man—comfort he none needeth, for he will flee the need; and counsel, I fear, availeth him little if grace be so far gone from him. But on the other side,[722] if rather than forsake our Savior we determine ourselves to suffer any pain at all, I cannot then see that the fear of hard handling should

---

693 worse, more grievous   **694** *thus far-forth:* this far; to this extent   **695** disadvantages; discomforts   **696** greatly, very much   **697** who   **698** *Charterhouse Order:* Carthusians   **699** right **700** cloistered   **701** *anchors and anchoresses:* monks and nuns who live in seclusion   **702** living space   **703** fairly

704 bedroom, bedchamber   **705** prefer **706** *enhanced of our own fantasy:* exaggerated by our own imagination   **707** knew **708** secure   **709** truth, faithfulness **710** dared   **711** upkeep, maintenance **712** *much part of:* by means of   **713** was accustomed   **714** securely   **715** Harpsfield identifies this as a personal anecdote

(98–99) and links it with Roper's famous account of Dame Alice's visit to the Tower. **716** *neither nother:* neither the one nor the other   **717** wood scraps   **718** *but...fire:* except in the event of fire   **719** incidental features (not belonging to imprisonment as such)   **720** afterwards   **721** *would I wit:* I want to know   **722** hand

anything stick with[723] us, and make us so to shrink as we rather would forsake his faith than to suffer for his sake so much as imprisonment, since the handling is neither such in prison but that many men many years, and many women too, live therewith and sustain it, and afterward yet fare full well; and yet that it may well fortune that besides the very bare imprisonment, there shall hap us no hard handling at all, nor that same haply[724] but for a short while neither, and yet besides all this, peradventure not at all; and specially since which of all these ways shall be taken with us lieth all in his will for whom we be content to take it, and which for that mind of ours favoreth us, and will suffer no man to put more pain unto us than he well wotteth we shall be well able to bear. For he will give us the strength thereto himself, as you have heard his promise already, by the mouth of Saint Paul: *Fidelis Deus qui non patitur vos tentari supra id quod potestis ferre sed dat etiam cum tentatione proventum* ("God is faithful, which[725] suffereth you not to be tempted above that you may bear, but giveth also with the temptation a way out").[726]

But now, if we have not lost our faith already, before we come to forsake it for fear, we know very well by our faith that by the forsaking of our faith we fall into the state to be cast into the prison of hell, and that can we not tell how soon, but as it may be that God will suffer us to live a while here upon earth, so may it be that he will throw us in that dungeon beneath before the time that the Turk shall once ask us the question. And therefore, if we fear imprisonment so sore,[727] we be much more than mad that we fear not most for the more sore: for out of that prison shall no man never get, and in this other shall no man abide but a while.

In prison was Joseph while his brethren were at large, and yet afterward were his brethren fain[728] to seek upon him for bread.[729]

In prison was Daniel, and the wild lions about him, and yet even here God kept him harmless,[730] and brought him safe out again.[731]

If we think that he will not do the likewise for us, let us not doubt but he will do for us either the like or better, for better may he do for us if he suffer us there to die.

Saint John the Baptist was, you wot well, in prison while Herod and Herodias sat full merry at the feast, and the daughter of Herodias delighted them with her dancing, till with her dancing she danced off Saint John's head;[732] and now sitteth he with great feast in heaven at God's board,[733] while Herod and Herodias full heavily[734] sit in hell burning both twain, and to make them sport withal, the devil with the damsel dance in the fire afore them.

Finally, Cousin, to finish this piece with: our Savior was himself taken prisoner for our sake; and prisoner was he carried; and prisoner was he kept; and prisoner was he brought forth before Annas; and prisoner from Annas carried unto Caiaphas; then prisoner was he carried from Caiaphas unto Pilate; and prisoner was he sent from Pilate to King Herod; prisoner from Herod unto Pilate again; and so kept as prisoner to the end of his Passion.[735]

The time of his imprisonment, I grant well, was not long, but as for hard handling (which our hearts most abhor), he had as much in that short while as many men among them all in much longer time. And surely then if we consider of what estate[736] he was, and therewith that he was prisoner in such wise for our sake, we shall, I trow (but if[737] we be worse than wretched beasts), never so shamefully play the unkind cowards as for fear of imprisonment sinfully to forsake him, nor so foolish neither as by forsaking of him to give him the occasion again to forsake us, and with the avoiding of an easier prison, fall into a worse, and instead of a prison that cannot keep us long, fall into that prison out of which we can never come, where the short prisonment would win us everlasting liberty.

THE TWENTY-FIRST CHAPTER
The fear of shameful and painful death

VINCENT: Forsooth,[738] Uncle—our Lord reward you therefor—if we feared not further, besides imprisonment, the terrible dart of shameful and painful death, as for imprisonment, I would verily trust that remembering these things which I have here heard of you, rather than I should forsake the faith of our Savior, I would with help of grace never shrink thereat.

---

723 *stick with:* deter **724** perhaps
725 who **726** 1 Cor 10:13 **727** greatly, grievously **728** obliged **729** See Gn 37:12–28; 39:6–23; 42:1–7; 43:1–15.

730 unharmed **731** See Dn 6:16–24.
732 See Mk 6:17–28; Mt 14:3–11.
733 table **734** sorrowfully **735** See Jn 18:12–14, 24, 28–29; Lk 23:6–16.

736 (high) rank **737** *but if:* unless
738 In truth

But now are we comen, Uncle, with much work at the last unto the last and uttermost point of the dread that maketh *incursum et daemonium meridianum* ("this incursion of this midday devil")—
5 this open invasion of the Turk, and his persecution against the faith—seem so terrible to men's minds that although the respect[739] of God vanquish all the remnant of the troubles that we have hitherto perused[740] (as[741] loss of goods, lands, and liberty),
10 yet, when we remember the terror of shameful and painful death, that point so suddenly putteth us in oblivion of all that should be our comfort that we feel, all men, I fear me, for the most part, the fervor of our faith wax[742] so cold, and our hearts so faint,
15 that we feel ourselves at the point to fall even therefrom for fear.

ANTONY: To this I say not nay, Cousin, but that indeed in this point is the sore pinch. And yet you see for all this that even this point too taketh increase
20 and diminishment of dread after[743] the difference of the affections that are before fixed and rooted in the mind, so far-forth[744] that you see some man set so much by[745] his worldly substance[746] that he less feareth the loss of his life than the loss of lands;
25 yea, some man shall you see that abideth deadly torment, and such as some other had liefer[747] die than endure, rather than he would bring forth the money that he hath hid.

And I doubt not but you have heard of many,
30 by right antique[748] stories, that some for one cause, some for other, have not letted[749] willingly to suffer death, diverse in diverse kinds, and some both with despiteful rebuke[750] and painful torment too. And therefore, as I say, we may see that the affections
35 of men's minds toward the increase or decrease of dread maketh much of the matter.

Now are the affections of men's minds imprinted by diverse means: one way, by the means of the bodily senses, moved by such things, pleasant or
40 displeasant, as are outwardly, through sensible[751] worldly things, offered and objected[752] unto them. And this manner of receiving of impression of affection is common unto men and beasts. Another

manner of receiving affections is by the means of reason, which both ordinately[753] tempereth those
45 affections that the bodily five wits[754] imprint, and also disposeth a man many times to some spiritual virtues very contrary to those affections that are fleshly and sensual. And those reasonable dispositions be the affections spiritual, and proper to the
50 nature of man, and above the nature of beast.

Now as our ghostly[755] enemy the devil enforceth[756] himself to make us lean[757] unto the sensual affections and beastly, so doth almighty God of his goodness by his Holy Spirit inspire[758] us good mo-
55 tions, with aid and help of his grace, toward the other affections spiritual, and by sundry means instructeth our reason to lean unto them, and not only to receive them as engendered and planted in our soul, but also in such wise water them with the
60 wise advertisement[759] of godly counsel and continual prayer that they may be habitually radicate[760] and surely take deep root therein. And after, as the one kind of affection or the other beareth the strength in our heart, so be we stronger or feebler
65 against the terror of death in this cause.

And therefore will we, Cousin, assay[761] to consider what things there are for which we have cause in reason to master that affection fearful and sensual, and though we cannot clean[762] avoid it and put
70 it away, yet in such wise to bridle it at the least that it run not out so far like a headstrong horse,[763] that spite of our teeth[764] it carry us out unto the devil.

Let us therefore now consider and well weigh this thing that we dread so sore,[765] that is to wit, shame-
75 ful and painful death.

THE TWENTY-SECOND CHAPTER
Of death considered by himself alone,
as a bare leaving of this life only

ANTONY: And first I perceive well by these two
80 things that you join unto death—that is to wit, "shameful" and "painful"—you would esteem[766] death so much the less if he shall come alone, without either shame or pain.

---

739 *although the respect:* even if the regard or consideration **740** examined **741** such as **742** grow **743** according to, following **744** *so far-forth:* to such a great extent **745** *set so much by:* value so greatly **746** possessions, wealth

747 rather **748** *right antique:* very old **749** hesitated **750** *despiteful rebuke:* insulting disgrace **751** perceptible by the senses **752** presented **753** in an ordered way **754** senses **755** spiritual **756** exerts **757** incline **758** breathe into

759 instruction **760** rooted **761** try **762** entirely **763** See Plato's *Phaedrus* 246, 253ff. **764** *spite of our teeth:* despite our resistance **765** greatly, grievously **766** account; appraise

VINCENT: Without doubt, Uncle, a great deal the less. But yet, though he should come without them both, by himself, whatsoever I would, I wot[767] well many a man would be for all that very loath to die.

ANTONY: That I believe well, Cousin, and the more pity it is, for that affection happeth in very few but that either the cause is lack of faith, lack of hope, or finally lack of wit.[768] They that believe not the life to come after this, and ween themselves here in wealth, are loath to leave this, for then they think they lose all. And thereof cometh the manifold foolish unfaithful words which are so rife in over many mouths: "This world we know, and the other we know not," and that some say in sport and think in earnest, "The devil is not so black as he is painted; and let him be as black as he will, he is no blacker than a crow," with many such other foolish fantasies of the same sort.

Some that believe well enough, yet through the lewdness[769] of living fall out of good hope of salvation, and then though they be loath to die, I very little marvel, howbeit[770] some that purpose to mend, and would fain[771] have some time left them longer to bestow somewhat better, may peradventure[772] be loath to die also by and by.[773] And that manner[774] loathness, albeit a very good will gladly to die and to be with God, were in my mind so thankful that it were well able to purchase as full remission both of sin and pain as peradventure he were like,[775] if he lived, to purchase in many years' penance — yet will I not say but that such kind of loathness to die may be before God allowable. Some are there also that are loath to die that are yet very glad to die, and long for to be dead.

VINCENT: That were, Uncle, a very strange case.

ANTONY: The case I fear me, Cousin, falleth not very often, but yet sometimes it doth, as where there is any man of that good mind that Saint Paul was, which for the longing that he had to be with God would fain have been dead, but for the profit of other folk was content to live here in pain, and defer and forbear for the while his inestimable bliss in heaven. *Cupio dissolvi et esse cum Christo; bonum autem mihi manere propter vos.*[776]

But of all these kinds, Cousin, of folks that are loath to die (except the first kind only, that lacketh faith), there is, I suppose, none but that, except the fear of shame or sharp pain joined unto death should be the let,[777] would else, for the bare respect of death alone, let[778] to depart hence with good will in this case of the faith — well witting,[779] by his faith, that his death taken for the faith should cleanse him clean of all his sins, and send him straight to heaven. And some of these (namely the last kind) are such that shame and pain both, joined unto death, were unlikely to make them loathe death or fear death so sore[780] but that they would suffer death in this case with good will, since they know well that the refusing of the faith for any cause in this world (were the cause never so good in sight)[781] should yet sever them from God — with whom, save[782] for other folks' profit, they so fain would be. And charity can it not be, for the profit of the whole world, deadly to displease him that made it.

Some are there, I say also, that are loath to die for lack of wit, which albeit that they believe the world that is to come, and hope also to come thither, yet they love so much the wealth of this world, and such things as delight them therein, that they would fain keep them as long as ever they might, even with tooth and nail. And when they may be suffered[783] in no wise to keep it no longer, but that death taketh them therefrom, then, if it may be no better, they will agree to be, as soon as they be hence, hanced[784] up in heaven and be with God by and by.[785]

These folk are as very nidiot[786] fools as he that had kept from his childhood a bag full of cherry stones, and cast such a fantasy thereto that he would not go from it for a bigger bag filled full of gold.

These folk fare, Cousin, as Aesop telleth in a fable that the snail did. For when Jupiter (whom the poets feign for[787] the great god) invited all poor worms of the earth to a great solemn feast that it pleased him (I have forgot upon what occasion) upon a time to prepare for them, the snail kept her at home, and would not come thereat. And when Jupiter asked her after wherefore she came not at his feast — where,

767 know **768** good sense; knowledge **769** wickedness **770** although **771** gladly **772** perhaps **773** *by and by:* right away **774** kind of **775** likely **776** "I long to be dissolved and to be with Christ; however, for you it is good for me to stay" (Phil 1:23–24). **777** obstacle **778** hesitate **779** knowing **780** greatly **781** *were…sight:* no matter how good the cause appeared to be **782** except **783** allowed **784** lifted, hoisted **785** *by and by:* directly **786** idiotic **787** *feign for:* pretend to be

he said, she should have been welcome, and have faren[788] well, and should have seen a goodly palace, and been delighted with many goodly pleasures— she answered him that she loved no place so well as her own house; with which answer Jupiter waxed so angry that he said since she loved her house so well, she should never after go from home, but should always bear her house upon her back wheresoever she went. And so hath she done ever since, as they say, and at the leastwise I wot well she doth so now, and hath done as long time as I can remember.

VINCENT: Forsooth, Uncle, I would ween the tale were not all feigned.[789] For I think verily that so much of your tale is true.

ANTONY: Aesop meant by that feigned fable to touch the folly of such folk as so set their fantasy upon some small simple pleasure that they cannot find in their heart to forbear it—neither for the pleasure of a better man, nor for the gaining of a better thing—by which their fond froward[790] fashion, they sometimes fall in great indignation, and take thereby no little harm.

And surely such Christian folk as by their foolish affection, which they have set like the snail upon their own house here in this earth, cannot for the loathness of leaving that house find in their heart with their good will to go to the great feast that God prepareth in heaven, and of his goodness so gently calleth them to, be like,[791] I fear me (but if[792] they amend that mind in time), to be served as the snail was, and yet much worse too. For they be like to have their house here, the earth, bound fast upon their backs forever, and not walk therewith where they will, as the snail creepeth about with hers, but lie fast bound in the mids[793] with the foul fire of hell about them.

For into this folly they bring themselves by their own fault, as the drunken man bringeth himself into drunkenness, whereby the evil that he doth in his drunkenness is not forgiven him for his folly, but to his pain imputed to his fault.

VINCENT: Surely, Uncle, this seemeth not unlikely, and by their fault they fall in such folly indeed. And

yet if this be folly indeed, there are then some folk fools that ween themselves right wise.

ANTONY: That ween themselves wise? Marry, I never saw fool yet that thought himself other than wise. For as it is one spark of soberness left in a drunken head when he perceive himself drunk and getteth him fair[794] to bed, so if a fool perceive himself a fool, that point is no folly, but a little spark of wit. But now, Cousin, as for these kind of fools, since they be loath to die for the love that they bear to their worldly fantasies, which they should[795] by their death leave behind them and forsake, they that would for that cause rather forsake the faith than die would rather forsake it than lose their worldly goods, though there were offered them no peril of death at all. And then, as touching those that are of that mind, we have, you wot well, said as much as yourself thought sufficient this afternoon herebefore.

VINCENT: Verily, Uncle, that is very true, and now have you rehearsed, as far as I can remember, all the other kinds of them that would be loath to die for any other respect[796] than the grievous qualities of shame and pain joined unto death. And of all these kinds except the kind of infidelity[797]—whom no comfort can help, but counsel only, to the attaining of faith, which faith must be to the receiving of comfort presupposed and had ready before, as you showed in the beginning of our communication[798] the first day that we talked of the matter—but else,[799] I say, except that one kind, there is none of the remnant of those that were before untouched which were likely to forsake their faith in the persecution for the fear and dread of death, save[800] for those grievous qualities (pain, I mean, and shame) that they see well would come therewith.

And therefore, Uncle, I pray you[801] give us some comfort against those twain. For in good faith, if death should come without them, in such a case as this is—wherein by the losing of this life we should find a far better—mine own reason giveth[802] me that save for the other griefs going before the change,[803] there would no man, that wit hath, anything stick[804] at all.

788 dined   **789** fictitious; made-up   **790** *fond froward:* foolish unruly   **791** likely   **792** *but if:* unless   **793** middle   **794** straight; directly   **795** would   **796** consideration   **797** *the kind of infidelity:* those without faith   **798** conversation   **799** otherwise   **800** except   **801** *pray you:* ask you to   **802** tells   **803** *the change:* the change from the one life to the other   **804** hesitate

ANTONY: Yes, peradventure suddenly,[805] before they gather their wits unto them and therewith well weigh the matter. But they, Cousin, that will consider the matter well, reason grounded upon the foundation of faith shall show them very great substantial causes for which the dread of those grievous qualities that they see shall come with death (shame, I mean, and pain also) shall not so sore abash[806] them as sinfully to drive them therefrom; for the proof whereof, let us first begin at the consideration of the shame.

THE TWENTY-THIRD CHAPTER
Of shame that is joined with the death
in the persecution for the faith

ANTONY: How can any faithful wise man dread the death so sore for any respect[807] of shame, when his reason and his faith together may shortly make him perceive that there is therein no piece[808] of very[809] shame at all? For how can that death be shameful that is glorious? Or how can that be but glorious to die for the faith of Christ, if we die both for the faith and in the faith joined with hope and charity, while the Scripture so plainly saith, *Pretiosa in conspectu Domini mors sanctorum eius* ("Precious is, in the sight of God, the death of his saints")?[810] Now if the death of his saints be glorious in the sight of God, it can never be shameful in very deed, how shameful soever it seem here in the sight of men. For here we may see and be sure that not at the death of Saint Stephen only, to whom it liked him to show himself with the heaven open over his head,[811] but at the death also of every man that so dieth for the faith, God with his heavenly company beholdeth his whole passion[812] and verily looketh on.

Now if it were so, Cousin, that ye should be brought through the broad high street of a great long city, and that all along the way that ye were going, there were on the one side of the way a rabble of ragged beggars and madmen that would despise you and dispraise[813] you with all the shameful names that they could call you and all the railing words that they could say to you, and that there were then, all along the other side of the same street where you

should come by, a goodly company, standing in a fair range a-row, of wise and worshipful[814] folk, allowing[815] and commending you, more than fifteen times as many as that rabble of ragged beggars and railing madmen are, would you let your way by your will,[816] weening that you went unto your shame for[817] the shameful jesting and railing of those mad foolish wretches, or hold on your way with a good cheer and a glad heart, thinking yourself much honored by the laud and approbation of that other honorable sort?

VINCENT: Nay, by my troth,[818] Uncle, there is no doubt but I would much regard the commendation of those commendable folk, and not regard a rush[819] the railing of all those ribalds.[820]

ANTONY: Then, Cousin, can there no man that hath faith account himself shamed here by any manner death that he suffereth for the faith of Christ, while how vile and how shameful soever it seem in the sight here of a few worldly wretches, it is allowed and approved for very precious and honorable in the sight of God, and of all the glorious company of heaven, which as perfectly stand and behold it as those peevish[821] people do, and are in number more than a hundred to one, and of that hundred, every one a hundred times more to be regarded and esteemed than of the other a hundred such whole rabbles.

And now if a man would be so mad as, for fear of the rebuke that he should have of such rebukeful[822] beasts, he would be ashamed to confess the faith of Christ, then with fleeing from a shadow of shame, he should fall into a very shame and a deadly painful shame indeed, for then hath our Savior made a sure promise that he will show himself ashamed of that man before the Father of heaven and all his holy angels, saying in the ninth chapter of Saint Luke, *Qui me erubuerit et meos sermones, hunc Filius hominis erubescet cum venerit in maiestate sua et Patris et sanctorum angelorum* ("He that is ashamed of me and of my words, of him shall the Son of Man be ashamed when he shall come in the majesty of himself and of his Father and of his holy angels").[823] And what manner a shameful shame shall that be

805 *peradventure suddenly:* perhaps at first   **806** *sore abash:* greatly confuse   **807** regard, consideration   **808** instance   **809** true   **810** Ps 115(116):15   **811** See

Acts 7:55–60.   **812** suffering   **813** disparage   **814** honorable   **815** approving of   **816** *let…will:* stop your journey voluntarily   **817** on account of   **818** truth,

faithfulness   **819** *regard a rush:* attach a straw's worth of importance to   **820** rascals, vagabonds   **821** foolish   **822** deserving of rebuke; shameful   **823** Lk 9:26

then. If a man's cheeks glow sometimes for shame in this world, they will fall on fire for shame when Christ shall show himself ashamed of them there.

To suffer the thing for Christ's faith that we worldly wretched fools ween were villainy[824] and shame, the blessed apostles reckoned for great glory; for they, when they were with despite[825] and shame scourged, and thereupon commanded to speak no more of the name of Christ, went their way from the council joyful and glad that God had vouchsafed[826] to do them the worship to suffer shameful despite for the name of Jesus. And so proud were they of that shame and villainous pain put unto them that, for all the forbidding of that great council assembled, they ceased not every day to preach out the name of Jesus still, not in the Temple only (out of which they were fetched and whipped for the same before), but also, to double it with, went preaching that name about from house to house too.[827]

I would, since we regard so greatly the estimation of worldly folk, we would, among many naughty[828] things that they use,[829] regard also some such as are good; for it is a manner[830] among them in many places that some by handicraft, some by merchandise, some by other kinds of living arise and come forward in the world; and commonly folk are in youth set forth to convenient[831] masters, under whom they are brought up and grow; but now whensoever they find a servant such as he disdaineth to do such things as he that is his master did while he was servant himself, that servant every man accounteth for a proud unthrift,[832] never like[833] to come to good proof.[834]

Let us, lo, mark and consider this, and weigh well therewithal[835] that our master, Christ—not the master only, but the maker too of all this whole world—was not so proud to disdain[836] for our sakes the most villainous and most shameful death, after[837] the worldly count,[838] that then was used in the world, and the most despiteful mocking therewith, joined to most grievous pain: as[839] crowning him with sharp thorns, that the blood ran down about his face; then they gave him a reed in his hand for a scepter, and knelt down to him and saluted him like a king in scorn, and beat then the reed upon the sharp thorns about his holy head.[840]

Now saith our Savior that the disciple or servant is not above his master.[841] And therefore since our Master endured so many kinds of painful shame, very proud beasts may we well think ourselves if we disdain to do as our Master did. And whereas he through shame ascended into glory, we would be so mad that we rather will fall into everlasting shame, both before heaven and hell, than for fear of a short worldly shame, to follow him into everlasting glory.

THE TWENTY-FOURTH CHAPTER
Of painful death to be suffered in the Turk's persecution for the faith

VINCENT: In good faith, Uncle, as for the shame, ye shall need to take no more pain, for I suppose surely that any man that hath reason in his head shall hold himself satisfied with this. But of truth, Uncle, all the pinch is in the pain; for as for shame, I perceive well enough a man may with wisdom so master it that it shall nothing move him at all, so farforth[842] that it is almost in every country become a common proverb that "shame is as it is taken."[843] But by God, Uncle, all the wisdom in this world can never so master pain but that pain will be painful, spite[844] of all the wit in this world.

ANTONY: Truth it is, Cousin, that no man can, with all the reason he hath, in such wise change the nature of pain that in the having of pain he feel it not; for but if[845] it be felt, it is, pardie,[846] no pain. And that is the natural cause, Cousin, for which a man may have his leg stricken off by the knee and grieve him not, if his head be off but half an hour before.

But reason may make a reasonable man, though he would not be so foolish as causeless to fall therein, yet upon good causes—either of gaining some kind of great profit, or avoiding of some great loss, or eschewing[847] thereby the suffering of far greater pain—not to shrink therefrom and refuse it to his more hurt and harm, but for his far greater

---

824 disgrace   **825** contempt
826 granted, agreed   **827** See Acts
5:12–42.   **828** wicked   **829** customarily
do   **830** custom   **831** appropriate,
suitable   **832** good-for-nothing

833 likely   **834** *come...proof:* turn
out well   **835** in comparison with that
836 *to disdain:* as to think it beneath him
837 according to   **838** reckoning; view
839 such as   **840** See Mt 27:27–30; Mk

15:16–20.   **841** See Mt 10:24; Lk 6:40; Jn
15:20.   **842** *so far-forth:* to such an extent
843 Whit S195; Til S274   **844** in spite
845 *but if:* unless   **846** "by God" (from the
French), certainly   **847** avoiding, escaping

advantage and commodity,[848] content and glad to sustain it.

And this doth reason alone in many cases where it hath much less help to take hold of than it hath in this matter of faith, for well you wot, to take a sour and a bitter potion is great grief and displeasure, and to be lanced and have the flesh cut is no little pain; now when such things shall be ministered unto a child, or to some childish man either, they will by their own wills rather let their sickness or their sore grow unto their more grief, till it become incurable, than abide the pain of the curing in time—and that for faint heart, joined with lack of discretion. But a man that hath more wisdom, though he would without cause no more abide the pain willingly than would the other, yet since reason showeth him what good he shall have by the suffering, and what harm by the refusing, this maketh him well content and glad also for to take it.

Now then, if reason alone be sufficient to move a man to take pain for the gaining of some worldly rest or pleasure, and for the avoiding of another pain though peradventure[849] more, yet endurable but for a short season, why should not reason grounded upon the sure foundation of faith, and helped also forward with aid of God's grace—as it ever is undoubtedly when folk for a good mind[850] in God's name comen together thereon, our Savior saying himself, *Ubi sunt duo vel tres congregati in nomine meo ibi et ego sum in medio eorum* ("Where there are two or three gathered together in my name, there am I also, even in the very midst of them")[851]—why should not then reason, I say, thus furthered with faith and grace, be much more able first to engender in us such an affection, and after, by long and deep meditation thereof, so to continue that affection that it shall turn into a habitual, fast,[852] and deep-rooted purpose of patient suffering the painful death of this body here in earth for the gaining of everlasting wealthy life in heaven, and avoiding of everlasting painful death in hell?

VINCENT: By my troth, Uncle, words can I none find that should have any reason with them—faith always presupposed, as you protested[853] in the beginning, for a ground—words, I say, can I none find wherewith I might reasonably counterplead[854] this that you have said here already.

But yet I remember the fable that Aesop telleth of a great old hart[855] that had fled from a little bitch[856] which had made suit[857] after him and chased him so long that she had lost him, and as he hoped, more than half given him over;[858] by occasion whereof, having then some time to talk, and meeting with another of his fellows, he fell in deliberation with him what were best for him to do: whether to run on still and fly further from her, or turn again and fight with her.

Whereunto the other hart advised him to fly no further, lest the bitch might happen to find him again at such time as he should, with the labor of farther flying, be fallen out of breath, and thereby all out of strength too; and so should he be killed lying where he could not stir him, whereas if he would turn and fight, he were in no peril at all: "For the man with whom she hunteth is more than a mile behind her, and she is but a little body, scant[859] half so much as thou, and thy horns may thrust her through before she can touch thy flesh by more than ten times her tooth length."

"By my troth," quoth the other hart, "I like your counsel well, and methinketh that the thing is even soothly[860] such as you say. But I fear me when I hear once that urchin[861] bitch bark, I shall fall to my feet[862] and forget altogether. But yet and[863] you will go back with me, then methink we shall be strong enough against that one bitch, between us both." Whereunto the other hart agreed, and so they both appointed them[864] thereon.

But even as they were about to busk them[865] forward to it, the bitch had found the foot[866] again, and on she came yearning[867] toward the place; whom as soon as the harts heard, they too go, both twain apace.[868]

And in good faith, Uncle, even so[869] I fear it would fare by[870] myself and many others too, which,[871] though we think it reason that you say,[872] and in our minds agree that we should do as you say—yea,

848 benefit 849 perhaps 850 intention, purpose 851 Mt 18:20 852 firm, steadfast 853 stipulated, asserted, insisted 854 argue against 855 deer 856 female dog 857 pursuit 858 *given him over:* given up on him 859 hardly 860 *even*

soothly: quite truly 861 ill-tempered 862 *fall to my feet:* take to my heels 863 if 864 *appointed them:* agreed between themselves 865 *busk them:* hurry themselves 866 *found the foot:* picked up the scent 867 baying, barking 868 *twain*

apace: together at full speed 869 *even so:* in just the same way 870 *fare by:* happen to 871 who 872 *it . . . say:* what you say is reasonable

and do peradventure[873] think also that we would in-deed do as ye say—yet as soon as we should once hear these hellhounds, these Turks, come yelping and bawling[874] upon us, our hearts should soon fall as clean[875] from us as those other harts fly from the hounds.

ANTONY: Cousin, in those days that Aesop speak-eth of, though[876] those harts and other brute beasts more had (if he saith sooth)[877] the power to speak and talk, and in their talking, power to talk reason too, yet to follow reason and rule them-selves thereby, thereto had they never given them the power. And in good faith, Cousin, as for such things as pertain toward the conducting of reason-able men to salvation, I think without help of grace, men's reasoning shall do little more.

But then are we sure, as I said before, that as for grace, if we desire it, God is at such reasoning al-ways present, and very ready to give it, and but if that[878] men will afterward willingly cast it away, he is ever still as ready to keep[879] it, and from time to time glad to increase it. And therefore biddeth us our Lord, by the mouth of the prophet, that we should not be like such brutish and unreasonable beasts as were those harts, and as are our horses and mules: *Nolite fieri sicut equus et mulus in quibus non est intellectus* ("Be not you like a horse and a mule, that hath none understanding").[880]

And therefore, Cousin, let us never dread but that if we will apply our minds to the gathering of comfort and courage against such persecutions, and hear reason, and let it sink into our heart, and cast it not out again, vomit it not up, nor even there choke it up and stifle it with pampering in and stuffing up our stomachs with a surfeit[881] of worldly vani-ties, God shall so well work therewith that we shall feel strength therein, and not in such wise have all such shameful cowardous hearts as to forsake our Savior, and thereby lose our own salvation and run into eternal fire for fear of death joined therewith, though bitter and sharp, yet short for all that, and in a manner a momentary pain.

VINCENT: Every man, Uncle, naturally grudgeth[882] at pain and is very loath to come at it.

ANTONY: That is very truth, nor no man holdeth[883] any man to go run into it but that if[884] he be taken and may not flee. Then we say that reason plainly telleth us that we should rather suffer and endure the less and shorter here than in hell the sorer[885] and so far the longer too.

VINCENT: I heard, Uncle, of late, where such a rea-son was made as you make me now—which reason seemeth undoubted[886] and inevitable unto me—yet heard I late, as I say, a man answer it thus: he said that if a man in this persecution should stand still[887] in the confession of his faith, and thereby fall into painful tormentry,[888] he might peradventure hap, for the sharpness and bitterness of the pain, to for-sake our Savior even in the midst, and die there with his sin, and so be damned forever; whereas by the forsaking of the faith in the beginning betime[889]— and for the time, and yet not but in word neither, keeping it still nevertheless in his heart—a man may save himself from that painful death, and after ask mercy, and have it, and live long and do many good deeds, and be saved as Saint Peter was.

ANTONY: That man's reason, Cousin, is like a three-footed stool, so tottering on every side that whoso sit thereon may soon take a foul fall. For these are the three feet of this tottering stool: fan-tastical fear, false faith, false flattering hope.

First, it is a fantastical fear that the man con-ceiveth that it should be perilous to stand[890] in the confession of the faith at the beginning lest he might afterward, through the bitterness of pain, fall to the forsaking, and so die there in the pain there-with out of hand,[891] and thereby be utterly damned, as though that if a man with pain were overcome, and so forsook his faith, God could not or would not as well give him grace to repent again, and thereupon give him forgiveness, as him that for-sook his faith in the beginning and did set so lit-tle by[892] him that he would rather forsake him than suffer for his sake any manner pain at all. As though the more pain that a man taketh for God's sake, the worse would God be to him.

If this reason were not unreasonable, then should our Savior not have said as he did, *Ne terreamini ab*

---

873 perhaps　**874** howling; shouting
875 completely　**876** even if　**877** truth
878 *but if that:* unless　**879** preserve
880 Ps 31(32):9　**881** overindulgence

882 complains; protests　**883** expects
884 *but that if:* unless　**885** worse
886 certainly correct　**887** firm
888 torture　**889** early on　**890** stand

firm　**891** *out of hand:* immediately
892 *set by:* value

his qui occidunt corpus et post haec non habent am-
plius quid faciant ("Be not afeard of them that kill
the body and after that have nothing that they can
do further").⁸⁹³ For he should by⁸⁹⁴ this reason have
said, "Dread and fear them that may slay the body,
for they may by the torment of painful death—but
if⁸⁹⁵ thou forsake me betimes,⁸⁹⁶ in the beginning,
and so save thy life and get of me thy pardon and
forgiveness after—make thee peradventure⁸⁹⁷ forsake me too late, and so to be damned forever."

The second foot of this tottering stool is a false
faith, for it is but a feigned faith for a man to say
to God secretly that he believeth him, trusteth him,
and loveth him, and then openly—where he should
to God's honor tell the same tale, and thereby prove
that he doth so—there, to God's dishonor, as much
as in him is,⁸⁹⁸ flatter God's enemies, and do them
pleasure and worldly worship⁸⁹⁹ with the forsaking
of God's faith before the world, and is either faithless in his heart too, or else wotteth well that he
doth God this despite⁹⁰⁰ even before his own face;
for except⁹⁰¹ he lack faith, he cannot but know that
our Lord is everywhere present, and while he so
shamefully forsaketh him, full angrily looketh on.

The third foot of this tottering stool is false flattering hope, for since the thing that he doth when
he forsaketh his faith for fear is by the mouth of
God (upon the pain of eternal death) forbidden,
though the goodness of God forgiveth many folk
the fault, yet to be the bolder in offending for the
hope of forgiving is a very false pestilent⁹⁰² hope,
wherewith a man flattereth himself toward his own
destruction.

He that in a sudden braid,⁹⁰³ for fear or other affection, unadvisedly falleth, and after⁹⁰⁴ in laboring to rise again, comforteth himself with hope of
God's gracious forgiveness, walketh in the ready
way toward his salvation. But he that with the hope
of God's mercy to follow doth encourage himself to
sin, and therewith offendeth God first—I have no
power to shut⁹⁰⁵ the hand of God from giving out
his pardon where he list,⁹⁰⁶ nor would if I could, but
rather help to pray therefor. But yet I very sore⁹⁰⁷
fear that such a man may miss the grace to require⁹⁰⁸

it in such effectual wise as to have it granted. Nor
I cannot suddenly now remember any example or
promise expressed in Holy Scripture that the offender in such a kind shall have the grace offered
after in such wise to seek for pardon that God hath
(by his other promises of remission promised to
penitents) bounden himself to grant it.

But this kind of presumption, under the pretext of
hope, seemeth rather to draw near on the one side, as
despair doth on the other side, toward the abominable sin of blasphemy against the Holy Ghost, against
which sin, concerning either the impossibility, or
at the least the great difficulty, of forgiveness, our
Savior hath showed himself in the twelfth chapter
of Saint Matthew and in the third chapter of Saint
Mark, where he saith that blasphemy against the
Holy Ghost shall never be forgiven, neither in this
world nor in the world to come.⁹⁰⁹

And where the man that you speak of took in
his reason an example of⁹¹⁰ Saint Peter, which forsook our Savior and got forgiveness after, let him
consider again on the other side⁹¹¹ that he forsook
him not upon the boldness of any such sinful trust,
but was overcome and vanquished upon a sudden
fear. And yet by the forsaking Saint Peter won but
little, for he did but delay his trouble but a little
while, you wot well; for besides that he repented
forthwith⁹¹² very sore that he had so done, and wept
therefor by and by⁹¹³ full bitterly,⁹¹⁴ he came forth at
the Whitsuntide ensuing,⁹¹⁵ and confessed his Master again; and soon after that, he was imprisoned
therefor; and not ceasing so, was thereupon sore
scourged for the confession of his faith; and yet after that, imprisoned again afresh; and being from
thence delivered, stinted⁹¹⁶ not to preach on still;⁹¹⁷
until that after manifold labors, travails, and troubles, he was at Rome crucified and with cruel torment slain.⁹¹⁸

And in like wise I ween I might, in a manner, well
warrant that there should no man which denieth
our Savior once, and after attaineth remission, escape through that denying one penny the better
cheap,⁹¹⁹ but that he shall, ere he come in heaven,
full surely pay therefor.

893 Lk 12:4 **894** according to **895** *but*
if: unless **896** early on **897** perhaps
898 *as much as in him is:* as much as he
possibly can **899** honor, distinction
900 insult **901** unless **902** pernicious;
deadly **903** attack **904** afterwards
905 hold back **906** chooses, pleases

907 greatly **908** request **909** See
Mt 12:31–32; Mk 3:28–29; Lk 12:10.
910 *took . . . of:* used in his argument as
an example **911** hand **912** at once
913 *by and by:* immediately **914** See Mt
26:69–75; Mk 14:66–72; Lk 22:54–62; Jn
18:15–17, 25–27. **915** *at the Whitsuntide*

ensuing: during the next season of
Pentecost **916** ceased **917** See Acts
2–5. **918** See Tertullian, *Adversus gnosticos*
Scorpice 15; Eusebius, *Church History* 3.1.
919 *better cheap:* more cheaply

VINCENT: He shall peradventure, Uncle, afterward work it out in the fruitful works of penance, prayer, and alms-deed done in true faith and due charity, and attain in such wise forgiveness well enough.

ANTONY: All his forgiveness goeth, Cousin, you see well, but by "perhaps." But as it may be perhaps yea, so may it be perhaps nay — and where is he then? And yet, you wot well, by no manner hap,[920] he shall never hap finally to escape from death, for fear of which he forsook his faith.

VINCENT: No, but he may die his natural death, and escape that violent death, and then he saveth himself from much pain, and so winneth therewith much ease. For evermore[921] a violent death is painful.

ANTONY: Peradventure he shall not avoid a violent death thereby, for God is without doubt displeased, and can bring him shortly to a death as violent by some other way.

Howbeit,[922] I see well that you reckon that whoso[923] dieth a natural death dieth like a wanton,[924] even at his ease; you make me remember a man that was once in a galley subtile[925] with us on the sea, which[926] while the sea was sore wrought,[927] and the waves rose very high, and he came never on the sea before, and lay tossed hither and thither, the poor soul groaned sore, and for pain he thought he would very fain[928] be dead, and ever he wished, "Would God I were on land, that I might die in rest." The waves so troubled him there, with tossing him up and down, to and fro, that he thought that trouble letted him to die,[929] because the waves would not let him rest. But if he might get once to land, he thought he should then die there even at his ease.

VINCENT: Nay, Uncle, this is no doubt, but that death is to every man painful, but yet is not the natural death so painful as is the violent.

ANTONY: By my troth, Cousin, methinketh that the death which men call commonly "natural" is a violent death to every man whom it fetcheth hence

by force against his will. And that is every man which when he dieth is loath to die, and fain would yet live longer if he might.

Howbeit, how small the pain is in the natural death, Cousin, fain would I wit[930] who hath told you. As far as I can perceive, those folk that commonly depart of[931] their natural death have ever one disease and sickness or other, whereof if the pain of that whole week or twain[932] in which they lie pining[933] in their bed were gathered together into so short a time as a man hath his pain that dieth a violent death, it would, I ween, make double the pain that that is, so that he that naturally dieth ofter[934] suffereth more pain than less, though he suffereth it in a longer time. And then would many a man be more loath to suffer so long lingering in pain than with a sharper to be sooner rid.[935]

And yet lieth many a man more days than one in well near as great pain continually as is the pain that with the violent death riddeth the man in less than half an hour, except[936] a man would ween that whereas the pain is great to have a knife cut his flesh on the outside from the skin inward, the pain would be much less if the knife might begin on the inside and cut from the mids[937] outward. Some we hear in their deathbed complain that they think they feel sharp knives cut a-two their heartstrings. Some cry out and think they feel within the brainpan their head pricked even full of pins. And they that lie in a pleurisy[938] think that every time they cough, they feel a sharp sword swap[939] them to the heart.

THE TWENTY-FIFTH CHAPTER

The consideration of the pains of hell, in which we fall if we forsake our Savior, may make us set all the painful death of this world at right nought[940]

ANTONY: Howbeit, what should we need to make any such comparison, between the natural death and the violent, for the matter that we be in hand with here? We may put it out of doubt[941] that he which for the fear of the violent death forsaketh the faith of Christ putteth himself in the peril to find

---

920 *by no manner hap:* by no way possible   921 always   922 However 923 whoever   924 pampered child 925 *galley subtile:* a long, narrow, low ship propelled by oars and sails   926 who

927 *sore wrought:* extremely turbulent 928 gladly   929 *letted . . . die:* prevented him from dying   930 know   931 by 932 two   933 suffering   934 more often 935 dispatched   936 unless   937 middle

938 disease resulting in pain in the chest or side   939 cut, cleave   940 *set at right nought:* regard as nothing at all, disregard completely   941 *put it out of doubt:* establish it without a doubt

his natural death more painful a thousand times, for his natural death hath his everlasting pain so suddenly[942] knit unto it that there is not one moment of an hour between, but the end of the one is the beginning of the other that after never shall have end. And therefore was it not without great cause that Christ gave us so good warning before, when he said, as Saint Luke in the twelfth chapter rehearseth, *Dico autem vobis amicis meis, ne terreamini ab his qui occidunt corpus, et post haec non habent amplius quid faciant. Ostendam autem vobis quem timeatis. Timete eum qui postquam occiderit, habet potestatem mittere in Gehennamta; ita dico vobis hunc timete* ("I say to you that are my friends, be not afeard of them that kill the body, and which[943] when that is done, are able to do no more. But I shall show you whom you should fear. Fear him which, when he hath killed, hath in his power further to cast him whom he killeth into everlasting fire. So I say to you, be afeard of him").[944]

God meaneth not here that we should nothing dread at all any man that can but kill the body, but he meaneth that we should not in such wise dread any such that we should for dread of them displease him that can everlastingly kill both body and soul, with a death ever dying and that yet never die. And therefore he addeth and repeateth in the end again the fear that we should have of him and saith, *Ita dico vobis hunc timete* ("So I say to you, fear him").

Oh, good God, Cousin, if a man would well weigh those words, and let them sink, as they should do, down deep into his heart, and often bethink himself thereon, it would, I doubt not, be able enough to make us set at nought all the great Turk's threats, and esteem[945] him not at a straw, but well content[946] to endure all the pain that all the world would put upon us, for so short while as all they[947] were able to make us dwell therein, rather than by the shrinking from those pains—though never so sharp,[948] yet but short—to cast ourselves into the pain of hell, a hundred thousand times more intolerable, and whereof there shall never come an end. A woeful death is that death in which folk shall evermore be dying and never can once be dead, whereof the Scripture saith, *Vocabunt mortem et mors fugiet ab eis* ("They

shall call and cry for death, and death shall fly from them").[949]

Oh, good Lord, if one of them were now put in choice of the both, they would rather suffer the whole year together[950] the most terrible death that all the Turks in Turkey could devise than the death that they lie in for the space of half an hour. In how wretched folly fall then those faithless or feeble-faithed folk that, to avoid the pain so far the less and so short, fall in the stead thereof into pain a thousand thousand times more horrible, and of which terrible torment they be sure they shall never have end.

This matter, Cousin, lacketh, as I believe, but[951] either full faith or sufficient minding,[952] for I think, on my faith, if we have the grace verily to believe it, and often to think well thereon, the fear of all the Turks' persecution, with all this midday devil were able to make them do in the forcing us to forsake our faith, should never be able to turn us.

VINCENT: By my troth,[953] Uncle, I think it be as you say, for surely if we would as often think on these pains of hell—as we be very loath to do, and seek us peevish[954] pastimes of[955] purpose to put such heavy[956] things out of our thought—this one point alone were able enough to make, I think, many a martyr.

THE TWENTY-SIXTH CHAPTER
The consideration of the joys of heaven should make us, for Christ's sake, abide and endure any painful death

ANTONY: Forsooth,[957] Cousin, if we were such as we should be, I would scant[958] for very shame, in exhortation to the keeping of Christ's faith, speak of the pains of hell. I would rather put us in mind of the joys of heaven, the pleasure whereof we should be more glad to get than we should be to flee and escape all the pains in hell.

But surely God, in that thing wherein he may seem most rigorous, is very merciful to us, and that is (which many men would little ween) in that he

---

942 directly   943 who   944 Lk 12:4–5
945 appraise; rate   946 *well content:*
(be) quite willing   947 *all they:* all of
them   948 *though…sharp:* no matter

how sharp they might be   949 Rv 9:6
950 without interruption   951 only
952 consideration, reflection   953 truth,
faithfulness   954 foolish   955 on

956 grave, troublesome, distressing
957 Truly   958 barely; hardly ever

provided hell. For I suppose very surely, Cousin, that many a man, and woman too, of whom there now sit some, and more shall hereafter sit, full gloriously crowned in heaven, had they not first been afraid of hell, would toward heaven never have set foot forward.

But yet, undoubtedly, were it so that we could as well conceive in our hearts the marvelous joys of heaven as we conceive the fearful pains of hell (howbeit[959] sufficiently we can conceive neither nother);[960] but if we would in our imagination draw as much toward the perceiving of the one as we may[961] toward the consideration of the other, we should not fail to be far more moved and stirred to the suffering for Christ's sake in this world, for the winning of the heavenly joys, than for the eschewing[962] of all those infernal pains.

But forasmuch as[963] the fleshly pleasures be far less pleasant than the fleshly pains be painful, therefore we fleshly folk that are so drowned in these fleshly pleasures, and in the desire thereof, that we can almost have no manner[964] savor or taste in any pleasure spiritual, have no cause to marvel that our fleshly affections be more abated[965] and refrained[966] by the dread and terror of hell than affections spiritual imprinted in us and pricked[967] forward with desire and joyful hope of heaven.

Howbeit, if we would somewhat set less by the filthy voluptuous[968] appetites of the flesh, and would by withdrawing from them, with help of prayer through the grace of God, draw near to the secret inward pleasure of the spirit, we should by the little sipping that our hearts should have here now, and that sudden taste thereof, have such an estimation of the incomparable and incogitable[969] joy that we shall have (if we will) in heaven by the very full draught[970] thereof — whereof it is written, *Satiabor cum apparuerit gloria tua* ("I shall be satiate[971] satisfied and fulfilled when thy glory, good Lord, shall appear,"[972] that is to wit, with the fruition[973] of the sight of God's glorious majesty face to face) — that the desire, expectation, and heavenly hope thereof shall more encourage us and make us strong to suffer and sustain for the love of God and salvation of our soul than ever we could be moved to suffer here worldly pain by the terrible dread of all the horrible pains that damned wretches have in hell.

Wherefore in the meantime for lack of such experimental[974] taste, as God giveth here sometimes to some of his special servants, to the intent we may draw toward spiritual exercise too — for which spiritual exercise, God with that gift, as with an earnest-penny[975] of their whole reward after in heaven, comforteth them here in earth — let us not so much with looking to have described what manner of joys they shall be, as with hearing what our Lord telleth us in Holy Scripture how marvelous great they shall be, labor by prayer to conceive in our hearts such a fervent longing for them that we may, for attaining to them, utterly set at nought[976] all fleshly delight, all worldly pleasures, all earthly losses, all bodily torment and pain.

Howbeit, some things are there in Scripture expressed of the manner of the pleasures and joys that we shall have in heaven, as where *fulgebunt iusti sicut sol, et qui erudiunt ad iustitiam tamquam scintillae in harundineto discurrent* ("righteous men shall shine as the sun, and shall run about like sparks of fire among reeds").[977]

Now tell some carnal-minded man of this manner pleasure, and he shall take little pleasure therein, and say he careth not to have his flesh shine, he, nor like a spark of fire to skip about in the sky.

Tell him that his body shall be impassible,[978] and never feel harm, yet if he think then therewith that he shall never be a-hungered nor athirst, and shall thereby forbear all his pleasure in eating and drinking, and that he shall never have lust[979] to sleep, and thereby lose the pleasure that he was wont[980] to take in slugging,[981] and that men and women shall there live together as angels without any manner mind or motion unto the carnal act of generation, and that he shall thereby not use there his old filthy voluptuous fashion, he will say he is better at ease already, and would not give this world for that; for as Saint Paul saith, *Animalis homo non percipit ea quae sunt Spiritus Dei, stultitia est enim ei.*[982]

But when the time shall come that these foul

959 although   **960** *neither nother:* neither the one nor the other   **961** can   **962** escaping   **963** *forasmuch as:* seeing that, inasmuch as   **964** kind of   **965** subdued   **966** restrained; held back   **967** spurred   **968** *set . . . voluptuous:* value less the base, sensual   **969** unthinkable; unimaginable   **970** drink   **971** completely   **972** Ps 16(17):15   **973** enjoyment   **974** experiential   **975** pledge, foretaste   **976** *set at nought:* regard as nothing   **977** Wis 3:7   **978** incapable of suffering   **979** desire   **980** accustomed   **981** lying around in bed   **982** "The bestial man does not perceive what is of the Spirit of God, for to him it is foolishness" (1 Cor 2:14).

filthy pleasures shall be so taken from him that it shall abhor his heart once to think on them—whereof every man hath among[983] a certain shadow of experience in the fervent grief of a sore painful sickness, while the stomach can scant[984] abide to look upon any meat,[985] and as for acts of the other foul filthy lust, is ready to vomit if it hap him to think thereon—when men shall, I say, after this life feel that horrible abomination in their heart at the remembrance of those voluptuous pleasures (of which abomination sickness hath here a shadow), for which voluptuous pleasures he would here be loath to change with the joys of heaven; when he shall, I say, after this life have[986] his fleshly pleasures in abomination, and shall, of those heavenly joys, which he set here so little by,[987] have there a glimmering, though far from a perfect sight—oh, good God, how fain[988] will he then be, with how good will and how glad will he then give this whole world, if it were his, to have the feeling of some little part of those joys.

And therefore let us all that cannot now conceive such delight in the consideration of them as we should have often in our eyes by reading, often in our ears by hearing, often in our mouths by rehearsing, often in our hearts by meditation and thinking, those joyful words of Holy Scripture by which we learn how wonderful, huge, and great those spiritual heavenly joys are, of which our carnal hearts hath so feeble and so faint a feeling, and our dull worldly wits so little able to conceive so much as a shadow of the right imagination. "A shadow," I say, for as for the thing as it is, that can not only no fleshly carnal fantasy conceive, but over[989] that, no spiritual ghostly[990] person peradventure neither that here is living still in this world. For since the very substance essential of all the celestial joy standeth in blessed beholding of the glorious Godhead face to face, there may no man presume or look to attain it in this life, for God hath so said himself: *Non videbit me homo et vivet* ("There shall no man here living behold me").[991] And therefore we may well know that for the state of this life, we be not only shut from the fruition[992] of the bliss of heaven, but also that the very best man living here upon earth (the best man, I mean, being no more but a man) cannot, I ween, attain the right imagination thereof, but those that are very virtuous are yet in a manner as far therefrom as the born-blind man from the right imagination of colors.

The words that Saint Paul rehearseth of the prophet Isaiah, prophesying of Christ's incarnation, may properly be verified of the joys of heaven: *Nec oculus vidit, nec auris audivit, nec in cor hominis ascendit, quae praeparavit Deus diligentibus se.*[993] For surely for this state of this world, the joys of heaven are by man's mouth unspeakable, to man's ears not audible, to men's hearts incogitable,[994] so far-forth[995] excel they all that ever men have heard of, all that ever men can speak of, and all that ever any man can by natural possibility think on. And yet where[996] the joys of heaven be such prepared for every saved soul, our Lord saith yet, by the mouth of Saint John, that he will give his holy martyrs, that suffer for his sake, many a special kind of joy. For he saith, *Vincenti dabo edere de ligno vitae* ("To him that overcometh, I shall give him to eat of the tree of life"),[997] and also, "he that overcometh shall be clothed in white clothes, and I shall confess his name before my Father and before his angels."[998] And also he saith, "fear none of those things that thou shalt suffer," etc., "but be faithful unto the death, and I shall give thee the crown of life. He that overcometh shall not be hurt of the second death."[999] He saith also, *Vincenti dabo manna absconditum, et dabo illi calculum candidum. Et in calculo nomen novum scriptum quod nemo scit nisi qui accipit* ("To him that overcometh will I give manna secret and hid. And I will give him a white suffrage,[1] and in[2] his suffrage a new name written, which no man knoweth but he that receiveth it").[3]

They used of old in Greece (where Saint John did write) to elect and choose men unto honorable rooms,[4] and every man's assent[5] was called his "suffrages," which in some place was by the voices, in some place by hands; and one kind of those suffrages was by certain things that are in Latin called *calculi*,[6] because that in some places they used thereto round stones. Now saith our Lord that unto him which overcometh, he will give a white suffrage, for those

983 now and then   **984** hardly, barely
985 food   **986** hold   **987** *set … by:* valued here so little   **988** glad, pleased
989 beyond   **990** devout   **991** Ex 33:20   **992** enjoyment   **993** "Eye has

not seen, nor ear heard, nor has it arisen in the heart of man, what God has prepared for those who love him" (1 Cor 2:9).
994 unthinkable; unimaginable   **995** *so far-forth:* to such an extent   **996** whereas

997 Rv 2:7; the name "Vincent" comes from here.   **998** Rv 3:5   **999** Rv 2:10–11
1 vote; an object, such as a pebble, used in casting votes   **2** on   **3** Rv 2:17
4 offices, positions   **5** vote   **6** "pebbles"

that were white signified approving, as the black signifieth reproving. And in those suffrages did they use to write the name of him to whom they gave their voice.[7] And now saith our Lord that unto him that overcometh, he will in the suffrage give him a new name, which no man knoweth but he that receiveth it.

He saith also, "He that overcometh, I will make him a pillar in the temple of my God, and he shall go no more out thereof; and I shall write upon him the name of my God and the name of the city of my God, the new Jerusalem, which descendeth from heaven from my God; and I shall write on him also my new name."[8]

If we should dilate[9] and were able to declare[10] these special gifts, with yet others more specified in the second and the third chapter of the Apocalypse,[11] there would it appear how far those heavenly joys shall surmount above all the comfort that ever came in the mind of any man living here upon earth.

The blessed apostle Saint Paul, that suffered so many perils and so many passions[12] — he that saith of himself that he hath been *in laboribus pluribus, in carceribus abundantius, in plagis supra modum,* etc. ("in many labors, in prisons ofter than others, in stripes above measure,[13] at point of death oftentimes; of the Jews had I, five times, forty stripes save one.[14] Thrice have I been beaten with rods; once was I stoned. Thrice have I been in shipwreck. A day and a night was I in the depth of the sea. In my journeys oft have I been in peril of floods, in peril of thieves, in perils by the Jews, in perils by the paynims,[15] in perils in the city, in perils in desert, in perils in the sea, perils by false brethren; in labor and misery, in many nights' watch, in hunger and thirst, in many fastings, in cold and nakedness; besides those things that are outward, my daily instant[16] labor, I mean my care and solicitude about all the churches"),[17] and yet saith he more of his tribulations, which for the length I let pass — this blessed apostle, I say, for all the tribulations that himself suffered in the continuance of so many years, calleth yet all the tribulations of this world but light and as short as a moment in respect of[18] the weighty glory that it after

this world winneth us: *Id enim quod in praesenti est momentaneum et leve tribulationis nostrae, supra modum in sublimitate aeternum gloriae pondus operatur in nobis, non contemplantibus nobis quae videntur sed quae non videntur, quae enim videntur temporalia sunt, quae autem non videntur aeterna sunt* ("This same short and momentary tribulation of ours, that is in this present time, worketh within us the weight of glory above measure—*in sublimitate*—on high, we beholding not those things that we see, but those things that we see not. For those things that we see be but temporal things, but those things that are not seen are eternal").[19]

Now to this great glory can there no man come headless. Our head is Christ,[20] and therefore to him must we be joined, and as members of his must we follow him if we will come thither. He is our guide to guide us thither and is entered in before us, and he therefore that will enter in after, *debet sicut ille ambulavit et ipse ambulare* ("the same way that Christ walked, the same way must he walk").[21] And what was the way by which he walked into heaven? Himself showeth what way it was that his Father had provided for him, where he said unto the two disciples going toward the castle[22] of Emmaus, *Nesciebatis quia oportebat Christum pati, et sic introire in regnum suum*? ("Knew ye not that Christ must suffer passion, and by that way enter into his kingdom?")[23] Who can for very shame desire to enter into the kingdom of Christ with ease, when himself entered not into his own without pain?

THE TWENTY-SEVENTH CHAPTER
The consideration of the painful death of Christ is sufficient to make us content to suffer painful death for his sake

ANTONY: Surely, Cousin, as I said before in[24] bearing the loss of worldly goods, in suffering of captivity, thralldom,[25] and imprisonment, and in the glad sustaining of worldly shame, that if we would in all those points deeply ponder the example of our Savior himself, it were of itself alone sufficient to encourage every kind[26] Christian man and woman to

---

7 support; proxy **8** Rv 3:12 **9** expand our scope **10** describe **11** Book of Revelation **12** sufferings, afflictions **13** *stripes above measure:* more floggings than can be counted **14** Thirty-nine lashes was a standard Jewish punishment, because forty was the absolute maximum; see Dt 25:3. **15** pagans **16** pressing, urgent **17** 2 Cor 11:23–28 **18** *in respect of:* in comparison with **19** 2 Cor 4:17–18 **20** See Col 1:18; Eph 1:22–23; 4:15–16. **21** 1 Jn 2:6 **22** village **23** See Lk 24:26. **24** about **25** enslavement **26** natural; loving; grateful

refuse none of all those calamities for his sake, so say I now for painful death also, that if we could and would with due compassion conceive in our minds a right imagination and remembrance of Christ's bitter painful Passion—of the many sore[27] bloody strokes that the cruel tormentors with rods and whips gave him upon every part of his holy tender body; the scornful crown of sharp thorns beaten down upon his holy head, so strait[28] and so deep that on every part his blessed blood issued out and streamed down; his lovely limbs drawn and stretched out upon the cross to the intolerable pain of his fore-beaten and sore-beaten veins and sinews, new feeling with the cruel stretching and straining pain far passing any cramp, in every part of his blessed body at once; then the great long nails cruelly driven with hammers through his holy hands and feet; and in this horrible pain, lift up and let hang with the peise[29] of all his body bearing down upon the painful wounded places so grievously pierced with nails; and in such torment (without pity, but not without many despites)[30] suffered to be pinned and pained the space of more than three long hours, till himself willingly gave up unto his Father his holy soul; after which yet, to show the mightiness of their malice after his holy soul departed, pierced his holy heart with a sharp spear, at which issued out the holy blood and water, whereof his holy sacraments have inestimable secret strength[31]—if we would, I say, remember these things in such wise, as would God we would, I verily suppose that the consideration of his incomparable kindness could not fail in such wise to inflame our key-cold[32] hearts, and set them on fire in his love, that we should find ourselves not only content, but also glad and desirous to suffer death for his sake, that[33] so marvelously lovingly letted[34] not to sustain so far passing painful death[35] for ours.[36]

Would God we would here, to the shame of our cold affection, again[37] toward God for such fervent love and inestimable kindness of God toward us—would God we would, I say, but consider what hot affection many of these fleshly lovers have borne, and daily do, to those upon whom they dote, how many of them have not letted to jeopard[38] their lives—and how many have willingly lost their lives indeed—without, either, great kindness showed them before. And afterward, you wot well, they could nothing win, but even that yet contented and satisfied their mind that by their death, their lover should clearly see how faithfully they loved; the delight whereof, imprinted in their fantasy, not assuaged only, but counterpoised also,[39] they thought, all their pain. Of these affections, with the wonderful dolorous effects following thereon, not only old written stories, but over[40] that, I think in every country, Christian and heathen both, experience giveth us proof enough. And is it not then a wonderful shame for us, for the dread of temporal death, to forsake our Savior, that willingly suffered so painful death rather than he would forsake us, considering that besides that, he shall for our suffering so highly reward us with everlasting wealth?

Oh, if he that is content to die for his love, of whom he looketh after[41] for no reward, and yet by his death goeth from her, might by his death be sure to come to her, and ever after in delight and pleasure to dwell with her, such a lover would not let here to die for her twice. And how cold lovers be we then unto God, if rather than die for him once, we will refuse him and forsake him forever, that both died for us before, and hath also provided that if we die here for him, we shall in heaven everlastingly both live and also reign with him? For as Saint Peter saith, *Si compatimur et conregnabimus* ("If we suffer with him, we shall reign with him").[42]

How many Romans, how many noble courages[43] of other sundry countries, have willingly given their own lives, and suffered great deadly pains and very painful deaths, for their countries, and the respect[44] of winning by their deaths the only reward of worldly renown and fame? And should we then shrink to suffer as much for eternal honor in heaven, and everlasting glory? The devil hath also some so obstinate heretics that endure willingly painful death for vain glory—and is it not then more than shame that Christ shall see his Catholics forsake his faith rather than suffer the same for heaven and very[45] glory?

Would God, as I many times have said, that the

---

27 great, grievous, painful   28 tight
29 weight   30 insults   31 hidden
power. See Mt 27:24–50; Mk 15:6–37; Lk
23:13–46; Jn 19:1–34.   32 without heat or
fervor   33 who   34 hesitated   35 *so . . .*
death: so far more extremely painful a death
36 our sake   37 in return, in response
38 *letted to jeopard:* hesitated to risk
39 *counterpoised also:* also compensated for
40 beyond   41 afterwards   42 See Rom
8:17; 2 Tim 2:11–12; 1 Pt 4:13.   43 spirits
44 consideration   45 true

remembrance of Christ's kindness in suffering his Passion for us, the consideration of hell that we should fall in by forsaking of him, the joyful meditation of eternal life in heaven that we shall win with this short temporal death patiently taken for him, had so deep a place in our breast as reason would they should, and as (if we would do our devoir⁴⁶ toward it and labor for it, and pray therefor) I verily think they should. For then should they so take up our mind, and ravish it⁴⁷ all another way, that as a man hurt in a fray⁴⁸ feeleth not sometimes his wound, nor yet is not ware⁴⁹ thereof till his mind fall more thereon, so far-forth⁵⁰ that sometimes another man showeth him that he hath lost a hand before that he perceiveth it himself, so the mind ravished in the thinking deeply of those other things—Christ's death, hell and heaven— were likely to diminish and put away of our painful death four parts⁵¹ of the feeling either of the fear or the pain. For of this am I very sure: if we had the fifteenth part of the love to Christ that he both had and hath to us, all the pain of this Turk's persecution could not keep us from him, but that there would be at this day as many martyrs here in Hungary as have been afore in other countries of old.

And of this point put I nothing doubt,⁵² but that if the Turk stood even here with all his whole army about him, and every one of them all were ready at our hand with all the terrible torments that they could imagine, and but if⁵³ we would forsake the faith were setting their torments to us, and to the increase of our terror, fell all at once in a shout with trumpets, tabrets, and timbrels⁵⁴ all blown up at once, and all their guns let go therewith, to make us a fearful noise, if there should suddenly then, on the other side, the ground quake and rive a-twain,⁵⁵ and the devils rise out of hell, and show themselves in such ugly shape as damned wretches shall see them, and with that hideous howling that those hellhounds should shriek, lay hell open on every side round about our feet, that as we stood, we should look down into that pestilent pit and see the swarm of seely⁵⁶ souls in the terrible torments there, we would wax so afeard⁵⁷ of that sight that, as for the Turk's host, we should scantly⁵⁸ remember we saw them.

And in good faith for all that, yet think I further this: that if there might then appear the glory of God, the Trinity in his high marvelous majesty, our Savior in his glorious manhood sitting on his throne, with his immaculate mother and all that glorious company calling us there unto them, and that yet our way should lie through marvelous painful death before we could come at them, upon the sight, I say, of that glory, there would I ween be no man that once would shrink thereat, but every man would run on toward them in all that ever he might, though there lay for malice to kill us by the way, both all the Turk's tormentors, and all the devils too.

And therefore, Cousin, let us well consider these things, and let us have sure hope in the help of God, and then I doubt not but that we shall be sure that as the prophet saith, the truth of his promise shall so compass us with a pavise⁵⁹ that of this incursion of this midday devil, this Turk's persecution, we shall never need to fear; for either if we trust in God well, and prepare us therefor, the Turk shall never meddle with us, or else if he do, harm shall he none do us, but instead of harm, inestimable good. Of whose gracious help wherefore⁶⁰ should we so sore⁶¹ now despair (except we were so mad men as to ween that either his power or his mercy were worn out already), when we see so many a thousand holy martyrs by his holy help suffered as much before as any man shall be put to now? Or what excuse can we have by the tenderness of our flesh, when we can be no more tender than were many of them, among whom were not only men of strength, but also weak women and children?

And since the strength of them all stood in the help of God, and that the very strongest of them all was never able of themselves, and with God's help the feeblest of them all was strong enough to stand against all the world, let us prepare ourselves with prayer, with our whole trust in his help, without any trust in our own strength. Let us think thereon and prepare us in our mind thereto long before; let us therein conform our will unto his, not desiring to be brought unto the peril of persecution (for it seemeth a proud high⁶² mind to desire martyrdom), but desiring help and strength of God if he suffer⁶³

---

46 best endeavor 47 *ravish it:* drag it by force 48 fight 49 aware 50 *so far-forth:* to such an extent 51 *four parts:* four times as much 52 *put I nothing*

doubt: I have no doubt at all 53 *but if:* unless 54 *tabrets and timbrels:* small drums and tamborines 55 *rive a-twain:* split in two 56 poor, pitiful 57 *wax so*

afeard: become so afraid 58 hardly, barely 59 shield 60 why 61 greatly, grievously 62 puffed-up; conceited 63 permit

us to come to the stress,[64] either being sought, founden, and brought out against our wills, or else being by his commandment for the comfort of our cure[65] bounden to abide.[66]

Let us fall to fasting, to prayer, to alms-deed in time, and give that unto God that may be taken from us; if the devil put in our mind the saving of our land and our goods, let us remember that we cannot save them long; if he fear[67] us with exile, and flying from our country, let us remember that we be born in the broad world, and not like a tree to stick still in one place, and that whithersoever we go God shall go with us.

If he threaten us with captivity, let us tell him again,[68] better is it to be thrall[69] unto man a while for the pleasure of God than by displeasing God be perpetual thrall unto the devil. If he threat us with imprisonment, let us tell him we will rather be man's prisoners a while here in earth than by forsaking the faith be his prisoners ever in hell.

If he put in our minds the terror of the Turks, let us consider his false sleight[70] therein. For this tale he telleth us to make us forget him. But let us remember well that in respect of himself,[71] the Turk is but a shadow, nor all that they all can do can be but a flea biting in comparison of the mischief that he goeth about. The Turks are but his tormentors, for himself doth the deed; our Lord saith in the Apocalypse, *Diabolus mittet aliquos vestrum in carcerem ut tentemini* ("The devil shall send some of you to prison, to tempt you");[72] he saith not that men shall, but that the devil shall himself, for without question, the devil's own deed it is to bring us by his temptation with fear and force thereof into eternal damnation. And therefore saith Saint Paul, *Non est nobis colluctatio adversus carnem et sanguinem*, etc. ("Our wrestling is not against flesh and blood,"[73] etc.). Thus may we see that in such persecutions it is the midday devil himself that maketh such incursion[74] upon us, by the men that are his ministers, to make us fall for fear. For till we fall, he can never hurt us. And therefore saith Saint Peter, *Resistite diabolo et fugiet a vobis* ("Stand against the devil, and he shall fly from you");[75] for

he never runneth upon a man to seize on him with his claws till he see him down on the ground willingly fallen himself, for his fashion[76] is to set his servants against us, and by them to make us for fear or for impatience to fall. And himself in the meanwhile compasseth[77] us, running and roaring like a ramping[78] lion about us, looking who will fall, that he then may devour him. *Adversarius vester diabolus*, saith Saint Peter, "*sicut leo rugiens circuit quaerens quem devoret*" ("Your adversary the devil like a roaring lion runneth about in circuit,[79] seeking whom he may devour").[80] The devil it is, therefore, that if we for fear of men will fall, is ready to run upon us and devour us. And is it wisdom, then, so much to think upon the Turks that we forget the devil? What madman is he, that when a lion were about to devour him, would vouchsafe[81] to regard the biting of a little fisting cur?[82] Therefore, when he roareth out upon us by the threats of mortal men, let us tell him that with our inward eye we see him well enough, and intend to stand and fight with him even hand to hand. If he threaten us that we be too weak, let us tell him that our captain Christ is with us, and that we shall fight with his strength that hath vanquished him already.

And let us fence us[83] with faith, and comfort us with hope, and smite the devil in the face with a firebrand of charity. For surely if we be of that tender loving mind that our Master was, and not hate them that kill us, but pity them and pray for them, with sorrow for the peril that they work unto themselves, that fire of charity thrown in his face striketh the devil suddenly so blind that he cannot see where to fasten a stroke[84] on us.

When we feel us too bold, remember our own feebleness; when we feel us too faint,[85] remember Christ's strength. In our fear, let us remember Christ's painful agony—that himself would for our comfort suffer before his Passion, to the intent that no fear should make us despair[86]—and ever call for his help, such as himself list[87] to send us. And then need we never to doubt but that either he shall keep us from the painful death, or shall not fail so to strengthen us in it that he shall joyously bring

---

64 hardship, affliction; suffering; trial
65 *our cure:* those we are responsible for
66 *bounden to abide:* obliged to remain
67 frighten 68 in return, in reply
69 slave 70 *false sleight:* treacherous trickery 71 *in respect of himself:* compared

to him 72 Rv 2:10 73 Eph 6:12
74 attack 75 actually Jam 4:7; but see
1 Pt 5:8–11. 76 custom, habitual practice
77 encircles 78 rampaging, raging
79 a circle 80 1 Pt 5:8 81 be willing
82 *fisting cur:* farting dog 83 *fence us:*

armor ourselves 84 *fasten a stroke:* land a blow 85 lacking in courage 86 *agony… despair:* See More's next and last book, *The Sadness of Christ.* 87 pleases, chooses us to heaven by it—and then doth he much more for us than if he kept us from it. For as God did more for poor Lazarus in helping him patiently to die for hunger at the rich man's door than if he had brought him to the door all the rich glutton's dinner,[88] so though he be gracious to a man whom he delivereth out of painful trouble, yet doth he much more for a man if through right painful death he deliver him from this wretched world into eternal bliss. From which whosoever shrink away with forsaking his faith, and falleth in the peril of everlasting fire, he shall be very sure to repent it ere it be long after. For I ween that whensoever he falleth sick next, he will wish that he had been killed for Christ's sake before.

What folly is it then for fear to flee from that death which thou seest thou shalt shortly after wish thou hadst died? Yea, I ween almost every good Christian man would very fain[89] this day that he had been for Christ's faith cruelly killed yesterday, even for the desire of heaven, though[90] there were none hell; but to fear while the pain is coming, there is all our let;[91] but then if we would remember hell's pain on the other side,[92] into which we fall while we flee from this, then should this short pain be no let at all. And yet should we be more pricked forward,[93] if we were faithful, by deep considering of the joys of heaven, of which the Apostle[94] saith, *Non sunt condignae passiones huius temporis ad futuram gloriam quae revelabitur in nobis* ("The passions[95] of this time be not worthy to the glory that is to come, which shall be showed in us").[96] We should not, I ween, Cousin, need much more in all this whole matter than that one text of Saint Paul, if we would consider it well. For surely, mine own good Cousin, remember that if it were possible for me and you alone to suffer as much trouble as the whole world doth together, all that were not worthy,[97] of itself, to bring us to the joy which we hope to have everlastingly. And there-

fore I pray you, let the consideration of that joy put out all worldly trouble out of your heart, and also pray that it may do the same in me. And even thus will I, good Cousin, with these words, make a sudden end of mine whole tale, and bid you farewell. For now begin I to feel myself somewhat weary.

VINCENT: Forsooth, good Uncle, this is a good end, and it is no marvel though you be waxen[98] weary. For I have this day put you to so much labor that, saving for the comfort that yourself may take of your time so well bestowed, and for the comfort that I have myself taken (and more shall, I trust) of your good counsel given, else would I be very sorry to have put you to so much pain. But now shall our Lord reward and recompense you therefor, and many shall, I trust, pray for you. For, to the intent that the more may take profit by you, I purpose, Uncle, as my poor wit and learning will serve me, to put your good counsel in remembrance, not in our language only, but in the Almain[99] tongue too. And thus, praying God to give me and all others that shall read it the grace to follow your good counsel therein, I shall commit you to God.

ANTONY: Since you be minded, Cousin, to bestow so much labor thereon, I would it had happed you[100] to fetch the counsel at[101] some wiser man, that could have given you better. But better men may set[102] more things, and better also thereto. And in the meantime, I beseech our Lord to breathe of his Holy Spirit into the reader's breast, which inwardly may teach him in heart, without whom little availeth all that all the mouths of the world were able to teach in men's ears. And thus, good Cousin, farewell, till God bring us together again, either here or in heaven. Amen.

Finis

---

88 See Lk 16:19–22. 89 gladly 90 even if 91 hindrance, obstacle 92 hand 93 *pricked forward:* spurred on 94 *the*

Apostle: Saint Paul 95 sufferings 96 Rom 8:18 97 enough to deserve 98 grown 99 German 100 *I would it*

had happed you: I wish you had happened 101 of 102 put in place, put down; add

The Sadness, the Weariness, the Fear, and the Prayer of Christ before He Was Taken Prisoner

Deprived of his writing materials on June 12, 1535, More wrote *De tristitia*, his last book, in the preceding weeks. Written on small gatherings of paper, this Latin commentary on Scripture was smuggled out of the Tower, probably by More's servant John-a-Wood or another visitor (*CW* 14: 717). The work was first published in the 1557 *Workes of Sir Thomas More, Knight*, in an English translation by Mary Basset, daughter of Margaret More Roper. The Latin text was first published in the 1565 Louvain edition of More's *Opera omnia*. The original manuscript, in More's own hand, was rediscovered in 1963 at the Royal College in Valencia; facsimiles of each page are given in *CW* 14, and provide an invaluable record of More's habits of composition and revision.

As Yale editor and translator Clarence Miller argues, the full title of this work, carefully chosen by More, indicates his three major concerns: first, the same "sadness" and "weariness" of emotional suffering that Christ experienced; second, the "fear," which informs More's meditation on martyrs; and finally, "the example Christ offered of reverent, attentive prayer" (*CW* 14: 740). Because "prayer is the only safeguard" against sadness and fear, More stresses the importance of this "fighting technique and battle plan" embodied in Christ's actions the night before his death.

Many of More's lifelong concerns as a writer remain in view throughout this last work, as the hourglass empties. More returns, for example, to the image of the ship in a storm as he considers anew the demands of bravery and prudence, as he did earlier in *Utopia*. He acknowledges being vexed by "mental wandering," reminiscent of struggles he discerned in *The Life of Pico* and elsewhere. His passages on Christ's example of friendship, extended to friends and enemies alike, recall earlier passages written by an author who was "born for friendship," according to Erasmus, and who now shares his commentary on these images of Christ's charity through writing which Louis Martz has called More's "last address to the world and to the self." Regarding More's choice of Latin for his final work, Martz concludes: "It is a moving and appropriate thought that in the somber close of his career More should have sought to communicate with the audience that had admired his *Utopia*."

After the text of *De tristitia*, readers will find a Catena (a "chain" or "connected series") of short texts that More compiled during his imprisonment. The text is a translation of twenty-eight handwritten pages that accompanied the Valencia manuscript (see *CW* 14: 626–81). As Clarence Miller observes, this gathering is "a catena of scriptural passages and some of his own brief reflections on the folly of refusing a martyr's death when the faith demanded it" (696).

The translation of *De tristitia* and notes are those of Clarence Miller, in consultation with the notes from Garry E. Haupt's edition of *The Tower Works* (New Haven: Yale University Press, 1980). Throughout *De tristitia*, More quotes from the *Monotessaron*, a Gospel harmony (a book that attempts to merge all four Gospels into one account) by John Gerson (1363–1429).

CONTENTS

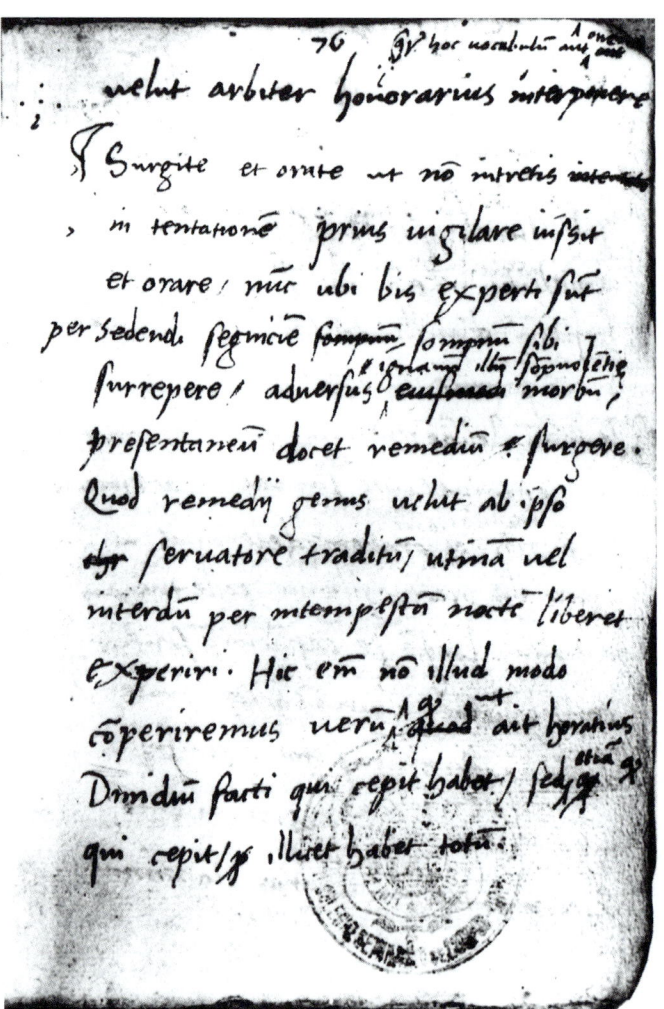

This facsimile (reduced) shows More's original manuscript of *The Sadness of Christ* (Fol. 76, Valencia MS. See *CW* 14: 302–3). At the top of the page is a note More makes to himself (*hoc vocabulum aut onerarius*) asking if the pun he intended (*honorarius/onerarius*) on the Ciceronian phrase *arbiter honorarius* should be made more obvious. At the bottom he quotes Horace from memory.

The Sadness, the Weariness, the Fear, and the Prayer of Christ before He Was Taken Prisoner

Matthew 26, Mark 14, Luke 22, John 18

When Jesus had said these things, they recited the hymn and went out to the Mount of Olives.[1]

Though he had spoken at length about holiness during the supper with his apostles, nevertheless he finished his discourses with a hymn when he was ready to leave. Alas, how different we are from Christ, though we call ourselves Christians: our conversation during meals is not only meaningless and inconsequential (and even for such negligence Christ warned us that we will have to render an accounting)[2] but often our table-talk is also vicious, and then finally, when we are bloated with food and drink, we leave the table without giving thanks to God for the banquets he has bestowed upon us, with never a thought for the gratitude we owe him.

[Paul of Saint Mary, Archbishop of] Burgos, a learned, holy man, and an outstanding investigator of sacred subjects, gives some convincing arguments to show that the hymn which Christ at that time recited with his apostles consisted of those six psalms which, taken together, are called by the Jews "The Great Alleluia" — namely Psalm 112[113] and the five following it. For from very ancient times the Jews have followed the custom of reciting these six psalms, under the name "Great Alleluia," as a prayer of thanksgiving at the Passover and certain other principal feasts, and even now they still go through the same hymn on the same feast days.

But as for us, though we used to say different hymns of thanksgiving and benediction at meals according to the different times of the year, each hymn suited to its season, we have now permitted almost all of them to fall out of use, and we rest content with saying two or three words, no matter what, before going away, and even those few words we mumble merely for form's sake, muttering through our yawns.

"They went out to the Mount of Olives," not to bed. The prophet says, "I arose in the middle of the night to pay homage to you,"[3] but Christ did not even lie down in bed. But as for us, I wish we could truly apply to ourselves even this text: "I thought of you as I lay in my bed."[4]

Moreover, it was not yet summer when Christ left the supper and went over to the mount. For it was not that much beyond the vernal equinox, and that the night was cold is clearly shown by the fact that the servants were warming themselves around charcoal fires in the courtyard of the high priest.[5] But this was not the first time that Christ had done this, as the evangelist clearly testifies when he says, "as he customarily did."[6] He went up a mountain to pray, teaching us by this sign that, when we prepare ourselves to pray, we must lift up our minds from the bustling confusion of human concerns to the contemplation of heavenly things.

Mount Olivet itself also has a mysterious significance, planted as it was with olive trees. For the olive branch was generally used as a symbol of peace, which Christ came to establish between God and man after their long alienation. Moreover, the oil which is produced from the olive represents the anointing by the Spirit, for Christ came and then returned to his Father in order to send the Holy Spirit upon the disciples so that his anointing might then teach them what they would not have been able to bear had it been told them only a short time before.[7]

Across the stream Cedron to the outlying estate named Gethsemani.[8]

The stream Cedron lies between the city of Jerusalem and the Mount of Olives, and the word "Cedron" in Hebrew means "sadness." The name "Gethsemani" in Hebrew means "most fertile valley" or

---

1 Mt 26:30 **2** Mt 12:36 **3** Ps 118(119):62 **4** Ps 62(63):62 **5** Jn 18:8 **6** Lk 22:39 **7** Jn 16:12–13 **8** Jn 18:1; Mt 26:36; Mk 14:32

"valley of olives." And so there is no reason for us to attribute it merely to chance that the evangelists recorded these place-names so carefully. For if that were the case, once they had reported that he went to the Mount of Olives, they would have considered that they had said quite enough, if it were not that God had veiled under these place-names some mysterious meanings which attentive men, with the help of the Holy Spirit, would try to uncover because the names were mentioned. And so, since not a single syllable can be thought inconsequential in a composition which was dictated by the Holy Spirit as the apostles wrote it, and since not a sparrow falls to the earth without God's direction,[9] I cannot think either that the evangelists mentioned those names accidentally or that the Jews assigned them to the places (whatever they themselves intended when they named them) without a secret plan (though unknown to the Jews themselves) of the Holy Spirit, who concealed in these names a store of sacred mysteries to be ferreted out sometime later.

But since "Cedron" means "sadness," and also "blackness," and since this same word is the name not only of the stream mentioned by the evangelists but also (as is sufficiently established) of the valley through which the stream flows and which separates the city from the estate Gethsemani, these names (if their effect is not blocked by our drowsiness) remind us that while we are exiled from the Lord (as the apostle says)[10] we must surely cross over, before we come to the fruitful Mount of Olives and the pleasant estate of Gethsemani, an estate which is not gloomy and ugly to look at but most fertile in every sort of joy, we must (I say) cross over the valley and stream of Cedron, a valley of tears and a stream of sadness whose waves can wash away the blackness and filth of our sins. But if we get so weary of pain and grief that we perversely attempt to change this world, this place of labor and penance, into a joyful haven of rest, if we seek heaven on earth, we cut ourselves off forever from true happiness, and will drown ourselves in penance when it is too late to do any good and in unbearable, unending tribulations as well.

This, then, is the very salutary lesson contained in these place-names, so fittingly chosen are they.

But as the words of Holy Scripture are not tied to one sense only but rather are teeming with various mysterious meanings, these place-names harmonize with the immediate context of Christ's Passion very well, as if for that reason alone God's eternal providence had seen to it that these places should long beforehand have been designated by such names as would prove to be, some centuries later, preordained tokens of his Passion, as the comparison of his deeds with the names would show. For, since "Cedron" means "blackened," does it not seem to recall that prediction of the prophet that Christ would work out his glory by means of inglorious torment, that he would be disfigured by dark bruises, gore, spittle, and dirt? — "There is nothing beautiful or handsome about his face."[11]

Then, too, the meaning of the stream he crossed — "sad" — was far from irrelevant as he himself testified when he said, "My soul is sad unto death."[12]

And his disciples also followed him.[13]

That is, the eleven who had remained followed him. As for the twelfth, the devil entered into him after the morsel and made off with him,[14] so that he did not follow the master as a disciple but pursued him as a traitor, and bore out only too well what Christ said: "He who is not with me is against me."[15] Against Christ he certainly was, since, at that very moment, he was preparing to spring his trap for him, while the other disciples were following after him to pray. Let us follow after Christ and pray to the Father together with him. Let us not emulate Judas by departing from Christ, after partaking of his favors and dining excellently with him, lest we should bear out that prophecy: "If you saw a thief you ran away with him."[16]

Judas, who betrayed him, also knew the place, because Jesus frequently went there with his disciples.[17]

Once again the evangelists take advantage of mentioning the betrayer to emphasize for us, and to recommend to us by such emphasis, Christ's holy custom of going together with his disciples to that place in order to pray. For if he had gone there only on some nights and not frequently, the betrayer would not have been so completely convinced he would find our Lord there that he could afford to

---

9 Mt 10:29   **10** 2 Cor 5:6   **11** Is 53:2   **14** Jn 13:27–30   **15** Mt 12:30; Lk 11:23
12 Mt 26:38; Mk 14:34   **13** Lk 22:39   **16** Ps 49(50):18   **17** Jn 18:2

bring the servants of the high priest and a Roman cohort there as if everything had been definitely arranged, for if they had found that it was not arranged, they would have thought he was playing a practical joke on them and would not have let him get away with it unscathed. Now where are those people who think they are men of stature, who are proud of themselves as if they had done something fine, if sometimes, on the vigil of a special feast, they either continue their prayers a little longer into the night or get up earlier for their morning prayers? Our Savior Christ had the habit of spending whole nights without sleep in order to pray.

Where are those who called him a glutton for food and wine because he did not refuse to go to the banquets of the publicans and did not think it beneath him to attend the celebrations of sinful men?[18] Where are those who thought that, by comparison with the strict regimen of the Pharisees, his morals were hardly better than those of the common rabble? But while these gloomy hypocrites were praying on the corners of the main thoroughfares so that they might be seen by men, he was eating lunch with sinners, calmly and kindly helping them to reform their lives. On the other hand, he used to spend the night praying under the open sky[19] while the hypocritical Pharisee was snoring away in his soft bed. How I wish that those of us who are prevented by our own laziness from imitating the illustrious example of our Savior might at least be willing to call to mind his all-night vigils when we turn over on the other side in our beds, half asleep, and that we might then, during the short time before we fall asleep again, offer him thanks, condemn our slothfulness, and pray for an increase of grace. Surely if we set out to make a habit of doing even the least little bit of good, I feel certain that God will soon set us forward a great way on the path of virtue.[20]

And he said, "Sit down here while I go over there to pray." And he took Peter and the two sons of Zebedee with him. He began to feel sorrow and grief and fear and weariness. Then he said to them, "My soul is sad unto death. Stay here and keep watch with me."[21]

Commanding the other eight to stop somewhat lower down, he went further on, taking with him Peter, John, and his brother James, the three whom he had always singled out from the rest of the apostles by a certain special privilege of intimacy. Now even if he had done this for no other reason than that he wanted to, no one ought to have been envious because of his generosity.[22] But still there were certain reasons for this which he might well have had in mind. For Peter was outstanding for his zealous faith and John for his virginity, and his brother James was to be the very first of all to suffer martyrdom in the name of Christ. Furthermore, these were the three to whom he had formerly granted the secret knowledge and open sight of his glorified body. It was only right, then, that those same three whom he had admitted to such an extraordinary vision and whom he had invigorated with a momentary flash of the eternal brilliance so that they ought to have been stronger than the others, should have assigned to them the role of his nearest supporters in the preliminary agony of his Passion. But when he had gone on a little way, he suddenly felt such a sharp and bitter attack of sadness, grief, fear, and weariness that he immediately uttered, even in their presence, those anguished words which gave expression to his overburdened feelings: "My soul is sad unto death."[23]

For a huge mass of troubles took possession of the tender and gentle body of our most holy Savior. He knew that his ordeal was now imminent and just about to overtake him: the treacherous betrayer, the bitter enemies, binding ropes, false accusations, slanders, blows, thorns, nails, the cross, and horrible tortures stretched out over many hours. Over and above these, he was tormented by the thought of his disciples' terror, the loss of the Jews, even the destruction of the very man who so disloyally betrayed him, and finally the ineffable grief of his beloved mother. The gathered storm of all these evils rushed into his most gentle heart and flooded it like the ocean sweeping through broken dikes.

Perhaps someone may wonder how it could be that our Savior Christ could feel sadness, sorrow, and grief, since he was truly God, equal to his all-powerful Father. Certainly he could not have felt them if he had been God (as he was) in such a way as not to be man also. But as a matter of fact, since he was no less really a man than he was really God, I see no reason for us to be surprised that, insofar as he was man, he had the ordinary feelings

18 See Mt 11:19.　**19** Lk 6:12　**20** See Mt 13:23.　**21** Mt 26:36–38; Mk 14:32–34　**22** Mt 20:15　**23** Mt 26:38

of mankind (though certainly no blameworthy ones)—no more than we should be surprised that, insofar as he was God, he performed stupendous miracles. For if we are surprised that Christ felt fear, weariness, and grief, simply on the grounds that he was God, why should we not also be surprised that he experienced hunger, thirst, and sleep, seeing that he was none the less divine for doing these things? But here, perhaps, you may object, "I am no longer surprised at his capacity for these emotions, but I cannot help being surprised at his desire to experience them. For he taught his disciples not to be afraid of those who can kill the body only and can do nothing beyond that;[24] and how can it be fitting that he himself should now be very much afraid of those same persons, especially since even his body could suffer nothing from them except what he himself allowed?

"Furthermore, since we know his martyrs rushed to their deaths eagerly and joyfully, triumphing over tyrants and torturers, how can it not seem inappropriate that Christ himself, the very prototype and leader of martyrs, the standard-bearer of them all, should be so terrified at the approach of pain, so shaken, so utterly downcast? Shouldn't he rather have been especially careful to set a good example in this matter, just as he had always let his deeds precede his precepts,[25] so that others might learn from his own example to undergo death eagerly for truth's sake, and so that those who afterwards would suffer death for the faith with fear and hesitation might not indulge their slackness by imagining that they are following Christ's precedent?—whereas, actually, their reluctance would both detract a great deal from the glory of their cause and discourage others who observe their sadness and fear." Those who bring up these objections and others of the same sort do not scrutinize carefully enough all the facets of this problem and do not pay enough attention to what Christ meant when he forbade his followers to fear death. For he hardly intended it to mean that they should never under any circumstances recoil from a violent death, but rather that they should not, out of fear, flee from a death which will not last, only to run, by denying the faith, into one which will be everlasting. For he wished his followers to be brave and prudent soldiers, not senseless and foolish. The brave man bears up under the blows which beset him; the senseless man simply does not feel them when they strike. Only a foolish man does not fear wounds, but a prudent man does not allow any fear of suffering to divert him from a holy way of life for that would be to refuse lesser pains at the expense of plunging himself into far more bitter ones.

When an afflicted part of the body is to be cut or cauterized, the doctor does not try to persuade the sick man not to feel any mental anguish at the thought of the pain the cutting or burning will cause, but rather encourages him to bear up under it. He admits it will be painful, but stresses that the pain will be outweighed by the pleasure of health and the avoidance of even more horrible pain. Indeed, though our Savior Christ commands us to suffer death (when it cannot be avoided) rather than fall away from him through a fear of death (and we do fall away from him when we publicly deny our faith in him), still he is so far from requiring us to do violence to our nature by not fearing death at all that he even leaves us free to flee from punishment (whenever this can be done without injury to his cause). "If you are persecuted in one city," he says, "flee to another."[26] This permission, this cautious advice of a prudent master, was followed by almost all the apostles and by almost all the illustrious martyrs in the many succeeding centuries: there is hardly one of them who did not use it at some time or other to save his life and extend it, with great profit to himself and others, until such a time as the hidden providence of God foresaw was more fitting.

On the other hand, some brave champions have taken the initiative by publicly professing their Christianity, though no one was trying to discover it, and by freely exposing themselves to death, though no one was demanding it. Thus God chose, according to his pleasure, to increase his glory sometimes by concealing the riches of the faith, so that those who set clever traps for his believers might be duped, sometimes by displaying them, so that those who cruelly persecuted his followers might be incensed by seeing all their hopes frustrated and finding, much to their outrage, that all their ferocity could not overcome martyrs who met death willingly. But God in his mercy does not command us to climb this steep and lofty peak of bravery, and

24 See Lk 12:4; Mt 10:28. **25** See Acts 1:1. **26** Mt 10:23.

hence it is not safe for just anyone to go rushing on heedlessly to the point where he cannot retrace his steps gradually but may be in danger of falling head over heels into the abyss if he cannot make it to the summit. As for those whom God calls to do this, let them choose their goal and pursue it successfully and they will reign in triumph.[27] He keeps hidden the times, the moments,[28] the causes of all things, and when the time is right he brings forth all things from the secret treasure-chest of his Wisdom, which penetrates all things irresistibly and disposes all things sweetly.[29]

And so, if anyone is brought to the point where he must either suffer torment or deny God, he need not doubt that it was God's will for him to be brought to this crisis. Therefore, he has very good reason to hope for the best. For God will either extricate him from the struggle, or else he will aid him in the fight and make him conquer so that he may crown him with the conqueror's wreath. "For God is trustworthy," the apostle says. "He does not allow you to be tempted beyond what you can stand, but with the temptation he also gives a way out so that you may be able to bear it."[30] Therefore, when things have come to the point of a hand-to-hand combat with the prince of this world, the devil,[31] and his cruel underlings, and there is no way left to withdraw without disgracing the cause, then I would think that a man ought to cast away fear and I would direct him to be completely calm, confident, and hopeful. "For," says the Scripture, "whoever lacks confidence on the day of tribulation, his courage will be lessened."[32]

But before the actual engagement, fear is not reprehensible, as long as reason does not cease to struggle against fear—a struggle which is not criminal or sinful but rather an immense opportunity for merit. For do you imagine that, since those most holy martyrs shed their blood for the faith, they had no fear at all of death and torments? On this point I will not pause to draw up a list; to me Paul may stand for a thousand others. Indeed, if David was worth ten thousand soldiers in the war against the Philistines,[33] then certainly Paul can also be considered worth ten thousand soldiers in the battle for the faith against faithless persecutors. And so this bravest of champions Paul, who was so far

advanced in hope and the love of Christ that he had no doubts about his heavenly reward, who said, "I have fought the good fight, I have finished the race, and now there remains for me a crown of justice,"[34] which he longed for so ardently that he said, "To me to live is Christ and to die is gain"[35] and "I long to be dissolved and to be with Christ,"[36] nevertheless this very same Paul not only managed skillfully to escape from the snares of the Jews by means of the tribune,[37] but also freed himself from prison by declaring that he was a Roman citizen,[38] and once again he eluded the cruelty of the Jews by appealing to Caesar,[39] and he escaped the hands of the impious King Aretas by being let down from the wall in a basket.[40]

But if anyone should contend that he was looking to the fruit that was to be planted afterwards through his efforts, and that throughout these events he was not frightened by any fear of death, certainly I will freely grant the first point, but I would not venture to assert the second. For that most brave heart of the apostle was not impervious to fear, as he himself clearly shows when he writes to the Corinthians, "For even when we came to Macedonia, our flesh had no rest, but suffered all manner of affliction, conflicts without, fears within."[41] And in another place he wrote to the same persons, "I was with you in weakness and fear and much trembling."[42] And once again, "For we do not wish you, brethren, to be ignorant of the affliction which came upon us in Asia, since we were burdened beyond measure, beyond our strength, so that we were weary even of life."[43] In these passages do you not hear from Paul's own mouth his fear, his trembling, his weariness more unbearable than death itself, so that his experience seems to call to mind that agony of Christ and to present, as it were, an image of it? Go ahead now and deny if you can that Christ's holy martyrs felt fear at the terrible prospect of death. But, on the other hand, no amount of terror, however great, could deter this same Paul from his program of advancing the faith, and no advice from the disciples could persuade him not to go to Jerusalem (to which he felt he was called by the spirit of God), even though the prophet Agabus had foretold that chains and certain dangers were awaiting him there.[44]

27 See Ps 44:5(45:4). **28** See Acts 1:7. **29** Wis 8:1 **30** 1 Cor 10:13 **31** Jn 12:31, 14:30, 16:11 **32** Prv 24:10 **33** 1 Sm 18:7–8; 21:11; 29:5 **34** 2 Tm 4:7–8 **35** Phil 1:21 **36** Phil 1:21, 23 **37** Acts 23:6–35 **38** Acts 22:25–29 **39** Acts 25:10–12 **40** 2 Cor 11:32–33; Acts 9:25 **41** 2 Cor 7:5 **42** 1 Cor 2:3 **43** 2 Cor 1:8 **44** Acts 21:10–13

And so the fear of death and torments carries no stigma of guilt but rather is an affliction of the sort Christ came to suffer, not to escape. We should not immediately consider it cowardice for someone to feel fear and horror at the thought of torments, not even if he prudently avoids dangers (provided he does not compromise himself); but to flee because of a fear of torture and death when the circumstances make it necessary to fight, or to give up all hope of victory and surrender to the enemy, that, to be sure, is a capital crime according to the military code.[45] But otherwise, no matter how much the heart of the soldier is agitated and stricken by fear, if he still comes forward at the command of the general, goes on, fights, and defeats the enemy, he has no reason to fear that his former fear might lessen his reward in any way. As a matter of fact, he ought to receive even more praise because of it, since he had to overcome not only the enemy but also his own fear, which is often harder to conquer than the enemy himself.

As for our Savior Christ, what happened a little later showed how far he was from letting his sadness, fear, and weariness prevent him from obeying his Father's command and keep him from carrying out with courage all those things which he had formerly regarded with a wise and wholesome fear. For the time being, however, he had more than one reason why he should choose to suffer fear, sadness, weariness, and grief—"choose" I say, not "be forced," for who could have forced God?[46] Quite the contrary, it was by his own marvelous arrangement that his divinity moderated its influence on his humanity for such a time and in such a way that he was able to yield to the passions of our frail humanity and to suffer them with such terrible intensity. But, as I was saying, Christ, in his wonderful generosity, chose to do this for a number of reasons.

First of all, in order to do that for which he came into the world—that is, to bear witness to the truth.[47] And then, although he was truly man and also truly God, still there have been some who, seeing the truth of his human nature in his hunger, thirst, sleep, weariness and suchlike, have falsely persuaded themselves that he was not true God—I do not mean the Jews and gentiles of his time, who rejected him, but rather the people of a much later time who even professed his name and his faith, namely heretics like Arrius and his followers, who denied that Christ was of one nature with the Father and thus embroiled the Church in great strife for many years. But against such plagues as this Christ provided a very powerful antidote, the endless supply of his miracles. But there also arose an equal danger on the other side, just as those who escaped Scylla had to cope with Charybdis.[48] For there were some who fixed their gaze so intently on the glory of his signs and powers that they were stunned and dazed by that immense brightness and went so far wrong as to deny altogether that he was truly a man. These people, too, growing from their original founder into a sect, did not hesitate to rend the holy unity of the Catholic Church and to tear it apart with their disgraceful sedition. This insane belief of theirs, which is no less dangerous than it is false, seeks to undermine and subvert completely (so far as lies within their power) the mystery of mankind's redemption, since it strives to utterly cut off and dry up the spring (as it were) from which the stream of our salvation flowed forth, namely the death and Passion of our Savior. And so, to cure this very deadly disease, the best and kindest of physicians chose to experience sadness, dread, weariness, and fear of tortures and thus to show by these very real signs of human frailty that he was really a man.

Moreover, because he came into the world to earn joy for us by his own sorrow, and since that future joy of ours was to be fulfilled in our souls as well as our bodies, so too he chose to experience not only the pain of torture in his body but also the most bitter feelings of sadness, fear, and weariness in his mind, partly in order to bind us to him all the more by reason of his greater sufferings for us, partly in order to admonish us how wrong it is for us either to refuse to suffer grief for his sake (since he freely bore so many and such immense griefs for us) or to tolerate grudgingly the punishment due to our sins, since we see our holy Savior himself endured by his own free choice such numerous and bitter kinds of torment, both bodily and mental—and that not because he deserved them through any fault of his own, but rather in order to do away with the wicked deeds which we alone committed.[49]

Finally, since nothing was hidden from his eternal

45 *Codex Justinianus* 12.45.1   **46** See Is 53:7; Jn 10:17–18.   **47** Jn 18:37   **48** See Homer's *Odyssey*, Book 12.   **49** See Is 53:5, 8, 12; 2 Cor 5:19–21.

foreknowledge, he foresaw that there would be people of various temperaments in the Church (which
is his own mystical body) — that his members (I say)
would differ considerably in their makeup.⁵⁰ And although nature alone, without the help of grace, is
quite incapable of enduring martyrdom (since, as
the apostle says, "no one can say 'Jesus is Lord' except
in the Spirit"),⁵¹ nevertheless God does not impart
grace to men in such a way as to suspend for the moment the functions and duties of nature, but instead
he either allows nature to accommodate itself to the
grace which is superadded to it, so that the good
deed may be performed with all the more ease, or
else, if nature is disposed to resist, so that this very resistance, overcome and put down by grace, may add
to the merit of the deed because it was difficult to do.

Therefore, since he foresaw that there would be
many people of such a delicate constitution that
they would be convulsed with terror at any danger
of being tortured, he chose to enhearten them by
the example of his own sorrow, his own sadness, his
own weariness and unequalled fear, lest they should
be so disheartened as they compare their own fearful state of mind with the boldness of the bravest
martyrs that they would yield freely what they fear
will be won from them by force. To such a person
as this, Christ wanted his own deed to speak out
(as it were) with his own living voice: "O faint of
heart, take courage and do not despair.⁵² You are
afraid, you are sad, you are stricken with weariness and dread of the torment with which you have
been cruelly threatened. Trust me. I conquered the
world,⁵³ and yet I suffered immeasurably more from
fear, I was sadder, more afflicted with weariness,
more horrified at the prospect of such cruel suffering drawing eagerly nearer and nearer. Let the brave
man have his high-spirited martyrs, let him rejoice
in imitating a thousand of them. But you, my timorous and feeble little sheep, be content to have me
alone as your shepherd,⁵⁴ follow my leadership; if
you do not trust yourself, place your trust in me.
See, I am walking ahead of you along this fearful
road. Take hold of the border of my garment and
you will feel going out from it a power which will
stay your heart's blood from issuing in vain fears,⁵⁵
and will make your mind more cheerful, especially

when you remember that you are following closely
in my footsteps (and I am to be trusted and will not
allow you to be tempted beyond what you can bear,
but I will give together with the temptation a way
out that you may be able to endure it)⁵⁶ and likewise
when you remember that this light and momentary
burden of tribulation will prepare for you a weight
of glory which is beyond all measure.⁵⁷ For the sufferings of this time are not worthy to be compared
with the glory to come which will be revealed in
you.⁵⁸ As you reflect on such things, take heart, and
use the sign of my cross to drive away this dread,
this sadness, fear, and weariness like vain specters
of the darkness. Advance successfully⁵⁹ and press
through all obstacles, firmly confident that I will
champion your cause⁶⁰ until you are victorious and
then in turn will reward you with the laurel crown
of victory."⁶¹

And so among the other reasons why our Savior deigned to take upon himself these feelings of
human weakness, this one I have spoken of is not
unworthy of consideration — I mean that, having
made himself weak for the sake of the weak, he
might take care of other weak men by means of his
own weakness.⁶² He had their welfare so much at
heart that this whole process of his agony seems designed for nothing more clearly than to lay down a
fighting technique and a battle code for the faint-
hearted soldier who needs to be swept along, as it
were, into martyrdom.

For, in order to teach anyone assailed by a fear of
imminent danger that he should both ask others
to watch and pray, and still place his trust in God
alone apart from the others, and likewise in order to signify that he would tread the bitter wine-
press of his cross alone without any companion,⁶³
he commanded those same three apostles whom he
had chosen from the other eight and taken on with
him almost to the foot of the mount, to stop there
and to bear up and watch with him; but he himself
withdrew from them about a stone's throw.⁶⁴

*And going on a little way he fell face down on the
earth and prayed that, if it were possible, the hour
might pass from him. And he said: "Abba, Father, to
you all things are possible. Take this cup away from*

50 See Eph 4:14–16; Jn 14:2.   **51** 1 Cor
12:3   **52** See Is 35:4; Ecclus 7:9.
53 Jn 16:33   **54** See Mt 26:31; Jn 10:14–16;

Jer 17:16; Zec 13:7.   **55** Mk 5:25–34; Lk
8:43–48   **56** 1 Cor 10:13   **57** 2 Cor 4:17
58 Rom 8:18   **59** See Ps 44:5(45:4).

60 See Is 19:20, 63:11.   **61** See 2 Tm
2:5; 1 Cor 9:25; 1 Cor 15:57; Heb 11:6.
62 1 Cor 9:22   **63** Is 63:3   **64** Lk 22:41

me, but yet not what I will, but what you will. My Father, if it is possible, let this cup pass away from me; yet not as I will, but as you will."[65]

First of all, Christ the commander teaches by his
5 own example that his soldier should take humility as his starting point, since it is the foundation (as it were) of all the virtues from which one may safely mount to higher levels. For, though his divinity is equal and identical to that of God the Father,
10 nevertheless because he is also man, he casts himself down humbly as a man, face down on the earth before God the Father.[66]

Reader, let us pause for a little at this point and contemplate with a devout mind our commander
15 lying on the ground in humble supplication. For if we do this carefully, a ray of that light which enlightens every man who comes into the world[67] will illuminate our minds so that we will see, recognize, deplore, and at long last correct, I will not say the
20 negligence, sloth, or apathy, but rather the feeble-mindedness, the insanity, the downright block-headed stupidity with which most of us approach the all-powerful God, and instead of praying reverently address him in a lazy and sleepy sort of way;
25 and by the same token I am very much afraid that instead of pleasing him and gaining his favor we exasperate him and sharply provoke his wrath.

I wish that sometime we would make a special effort, right after finishing our prayers, to run
30 over in our minds the whole sequence of time we spent praying. What follies will we see there? How much absurdity, and sometimes even foulness will we catch sight of? Indeed we will be amazed that it was at all possible for our minds to dissipate them-
35 selves in such a short time among so many places at such great distance from each other, among so many different affairs, such various, such manifold, such idle pursuits. For if someone, just as an experiment, should make a determined effort to make his mind
40 touch upon as many and as diverse objects as possible, I hardly think that in such a short time he could run through such disparate and numerous topics as the mind, left to its own devices, ranges through while the mouth negligently mumbles through the
45 hours of the office and other much used prayers.

And so if anyone wonders or has any doubts about what the mind is doing while dreams take

over our consciousness during sleep, I find no comparison that comes closer to the mark than to think
50 that the mind is occupied during sleep in exactly the same way as are the minds of those who are awake (if those who pray in this way can be said to be awake) but whose thoughts wander wildly during prayers, frantically flitting about in a throng of ab-
55 surd fantasies—with this difference, though, from the sleeping dreamer: some of the waking dreamer's strange sights, which his mind embraces in its foreign travels while his tongue runs rattling through his prayers as if they were mere sound without
60 sense,[68] some of these strange sights are such filthy and abominable monstrosities that if they had been seen during sleep, certainly no one, no matter how shameless, would have the nerve to recount such extravagant dreams after he woke up, not even in the
65 company of stable-boys.

And undoubtedly that old saying is very true, that our looks are a mirror of our minds.[69] For certainly such a wild and deranged state of mind is distinctly reflected in the eyes, in the cheeks, eyelids,
70 and eyebrows, in the hands, feet, and in short in the overall bearing of the entire body.[70] For just as our minds are inattentive when we set out to pray, so too we proceed to do so with an equally careless and sprawling deportment of our bodies.

75 True, we do pretend that the worship of God is our reason for wearing better than everyday clothes on feast days, but the negligence with which most of us pray makes it utterly clear that we have utterly failed to conceal the real motive, namely a haughty
80 desire to show off in the eyes of the world. Thus in our negligence we sometimes stroll around, sometimes sit down on a stool. And even when we kneel down, we either place our weight on one knee, raising up the other and resting it on our foot, or we
85 place a cushion under our knees, and sometimes (if we are especially spoiled) we even support our elbows on a cushion, looking for all the world like a propped up house that is threatening to tumble down.

90 And then our actions too, in how many ways do they betray that our minds are wandering miles away? We scratch our heads, clean our fingernails with a pocketknife, pick our noses with our fingers, meanwhile making the wrong responses. Having no

---

65 Mt 26:39; Mk 14:35–36   **66** See Phil   10.640   **69** Cicero, *De oratore* 3.221
2:5–7.   **67** Jn 1:9   **68** Vergil, *Aeneid*   **70** Cicero, *In Pisonem* 1.1

idea what we have already said and what we have not said, we make a wild guess as to what remains to be said. Are we not ashamed to pray in such a deranged state of mind and body—to beseech God's favor in a matter so crucial for us, to beg his forgiveness for so many monstrous misdeeds, to ask him to save us from eternal punishment?—so that even if we had not sinned before, we would still deserve tenfold eternal torments for having approached the majesty of God in such a contemptuous fashion.

Imagine, if you will, that you have committed a crime of high treason against some mortal prince or other who has your life in his hands but who is so merciful that he is prepared to temper his wrath because of your repentance and humble supplication, and to commute the death sentence into a monetary fine or even to suspend it completely if you give convincing signs of great shame and sorrow. Now, when you have been brought into the presence of the prince, go ahead and speak to him carelessly, casually, without the least concern. While he stays in one place and listens attentively, stroll around here and there as you run through your plea. Then, when you have had enough of walking up and down, sit down on a chair, or if courtesy seems to require that you condescend to kneel down, first command someone to come and place a cushion beneath your knees, or, better yet, to bring a prie-dieu with another cushion to lean your elbows on. Then yawn, stretch, sneeze, spit without giving it a thought, and belch up the fumes of your gluttony. In short, conduct yourself in such a way that he can clearly see from your face, your voice, your gestures, and your whole bodily deportment that while you are addressing him you are thinking about something else. Tell me now, what success could you hope for from such a plea as this?

Certainly we would consider it quite mad to defend ourselves in this way before a mortal prince against a charge that carries the death penalty. And yet such a prince, once he had destroyed our bodies, could do nothing further. And do we think it is reasonable, when we have been caught committing a whole series of far more serious crimes, to beg pardon so contemptuously from the king of all kings,[71] God himself, who, when he has destroyed our bodies, has the power to send both body and soul together to hell?[72]

Still I would not wish anyone to construe what I have said as meaning that I forbid anyone to pray while walking or sitting or even lying down. Indeed I wish that, whatever our bodies may be doing, we would at the same time constantly lift up our minds to God (which is the most acceptable form of prayer). For no matter where we may turn our steps, as long as our minds are directed to God, we clearly do not turn away from him who is present everywhere.[73] But just as the prophet who says to God, "I was mindful of you when I lay upon my bed"[74] did not rest content with that but also rose "in the middle of the night to pay homage to the Lord,"[75] so too I would require that, besides such prayers said while walking, we also occasionally say some prayers for which we prepare our minds more thoughtfully, for which we dispose our bodies more reverently, than we would if we were about to approach all the kings in the whole world sitting together in one place.

But of this much I can assure you: every time I think about this mental wandering, it vexes and plagues my mind.

Nevertheless, some ideas may be suggested to us during our prayers by an evil spirit or may creep into our imaginations through the normal functioning of our senses, and I would not assert that any one of these, not even if it is vile and quite horrible, must be immediately fatal, so long as we resist it and drive it away. But otherwise, if we accept it with pleasure or allow it through negligence to grow in intensity over a long period of time, I have not the slightest doubt that the force of it can become so aggravated as to be fatally destructive to the soul.

Certainly, when I consider the immeasurable glory of God's majesty, I am immediately compelled and forced to believe that if even these brief distractions of mind are not crimes punishable by death, it is only because God in his mercy and goodness deigns not to exact death for them, not because the wickedness inherent in their own nature does not deserve death—and for this reason: I simply cannot imagine how such thoughts can gain entrance into the minds of men when they are praying (that is, when they are speaking to God) unless it be through weakness of faith. Otherwise, since our minds do not go wool-gathering while we are addressing a mortal prince about some important matter or even speaking to one of his ministers who might be in a position of some influence with his master, certainly it could never happen that our minds should stray even the least bit while we are praying to God, certainly not, that is, if we believed with a strong and active faith that we are in the presence of God, who not only listens to our words and looks upon our facial features and bodily deportment as outward signs and indications from which our interior state of mind can be gathered, but who also pierces into the most secret and inward recesses of our hearts with a vision more penetrating than the eyes of Lynceus[76] and who illuminates everything with the immeasurable brightness of his majesty — it could not happen, I say, if we believed that God is present, God in whose glorious presence all the princes of the world in all their glory[77] must confess (unless they are out of their minds) that they are the merest mites and earth-creeping worms.

Therefore, since our Savior Christ saw that nothing is more profitable than prayer, but since he was also aware that this means of salvation would very often be fruitless because of the negligence of men and the malice of demons — so much so that it would very frequently be perverted into an instrument of destruction — he decided to take this opportunity, on the way to his death, to reinforce his teaching by his words and example, and to put the finishing touches on this most necessary point just as he did on the other parts of his teaching.

He wished us to know that we ought to serve God not only in soul but also in body, since he created both, and he wanted us to learn that a reverend attitude of the body, though it takes its origin and character from the soul, increases by a kind of reflex the soul's own reverence and devotion toward God. Hence he presented the most humble mode of subjection and venerated his heavenly Father in a bodily posture which no earthly prince has dared to demand, or even to accept if freely offered, except that drunken and debauched Macedonian [Alexander] and some other barbarians puffed up with success, who thought they ought to be venerated as gods.

For when he prayed he did not sit back or stand up or merely kneel down, but rather he threw his whole body face-forward and lay prostrate on the ground. Then, in that pitiable posture, he implored his Father's mercy and twice called his Father by name, begging him that, since all things are possible to him, he might be moved by his prayers to take away the cup of his Passion if this could be done, that is, if he had not imposed it on him by an immutable decree. But he also asked that his own will, as expressed in this prayer, might not be granted, if something else seemed better to his Father's will, which is absolutely best.

This passage should not lead you to think that the Son was ignorant of the will of the Father. Rather, because he wanted to instruct men, he also wanted to express the feelings of men. By saying the word "Father" twice, he wanted to remind us that all fatherhood proceeds from him, both in heaven and on earth.[78] Moreover, he also wanted to impress upon us that God the Father is his father in a double sense — namely by creation, which is a sort of fatherhood. (For we come from God, who created us from nothing, more truly than we do from the human father who begot us, since, in fact, God created beforehand that begetter himself and since he created and supplied beforehand all the matter out of which we were begotten.) But when Christ acknowledged God as his Father in this sense, he did so as a man. On the other hand, as God, he knows him as his natural and coeternal Father.

And yet another reason for his calling on his Father twice may not be far from the truth: he intended not only to acknowledge that God the Father is his natural father in heaven, but also to signify that he has no other father on earth, since he was conceived by a virgin mother according to the flesh, without any male seed, when the Holy Spirit came upon his mother — the Spirit, I say, both of the Father and of himself, whose works coexist in identity and cannot be radically distinguished by any human insight.[79]

Moreover, this forceful repetition of his Father's name, since it expresses an intense desire to gain what he asked for, might serve to teach us a very wholesome lesson: that when we pray for something without receiving it we should not give up like King Saul, who, because he did not immediately receive a prophecy from God, resorted to witchcraft and went off to the woman with a spirit, engaging

---

76 See 2 Chr 6:30; Jer 17:9–10. Lynceus, one of the Argonauts, was famed for the sharpness of his sight. **77** See Mt 6:29; Lk 12:27. **78** Eph 3:15 **79** See Jn 5:16–19.

in a practice forbidden by the law and formerly suppressed by his own decree.[80]

Christ teaches us that we should persevere in our prayers without murmuring at all if we do not obtain what we seek—and for good reason, since we see that the Son of God our Savior did not obtain the reprieve from death which he sought from his Father with such urgency, but always with the condition (and this is what we ought to imitate most of all) that his will was subject to the will of his Father.

And he went to his disciples and found them sleeping.[81]

Notice here how much greater one love is than another. Notice how Christ's love for his own was much greater than the love they gave him in return, even those who loved him most. For even the sadness, fear, dread, and weariness which so grievously assailed him as his most cruel torment drew near, could not keep him from going to see them. But they, on the other hand, however much they loved him (and undoubtedly they loved him intensely), even at the very time when such an enormous danger was threatening their loving master, could still give in to sleep.

And he said to Peter, "Simon, are you sleeping? Could you not stay awake one hour with me? Stay awake and pray that you may not enter into temptation. For the spirit indeed is willing, but the flesh is weak."[82]

This short speech of Christ is remarkably forceful: the words are mild, but their point is sharp and piercing. For by addressing him as Simon and reproaching him under that name for his sleepiness, Christ tacitly lets it be known that the name Peter, which Christ had previously given him because of his firmness, would hardly be altogether appropriate now because of this infirmity and sleep. Moreover, not only was the failure to use the name Peter (or rather, Cephas) a barbed omission, but the actual use of the name Simon also carries a sting. For in Hebrew, the language in which Christ was speaking to him, "Simon" means "listening" and also "obedient." But in fact, he was neither listening nor obedient, since he went to sleep against Christ's express wishes.

Over and above these, our Savior's gentle words to Peter seem to carry certain other barbed implications, which if he were chiding him more severely, would be something like this: "Simon, no longer Cephas, are you sleeping? For how do you deserve to be called Cephas, that is, rock? I singled you out by that name because of your firmness,[83] but now you show yourself to be so infirm that you cannot hold out even for an hour against the inroads of sleep. As for that old name of yours, Simon, certainly you live up to that remarkably well: can you be called listening when you are sleeping this way? or can you be called obedient when in spite of my instructions to stay awake, I am no sooner gone that you relax and doze and fall asleep? I always made much of you Simon, and yet Simon are you sleeping? I paid you many high honors, and yet Simon are you sleeping? A few moments ago you boasted that you would die with me,[84] and now Simon are you sleeping? Now I am pursued to the death by the Jews and the gentiles and by one worse than either of them, Judas, and Simon are you sleeping? Indeed, Satan is busily seeking to sift all of you like wheat,[85] and Simon are you sleeping? What can I expect from the others, when, in such great and pressing danger, not only to me but also to all of you, I find that you Simon, even you are sleeping?"

Then, lest this seem to be a matter which concerned Peter only, he turned and spoke to the others. "Stay awake and pray," he says, "that you may not enter into temptation. The Spirit indeed is willing, but the flesh is weak."[86]

Here we are enjoined to be constant in prayer, and we are informed that prayer is not only useful but also extremely necessary—for this reason: without it, the weakness of the flesh holds us back, somewhat in the way a remora-fish retards a ship, until our minds, no matter how willing to do good, are swept back into the evils of temptation. For whose spirit is more willing than Peter's was? And yet that he had great need of God's protection against the flesh is clear enough from this fact alone: when sleep kept him from praying and begging for God's help, he gave an opening to the devil, who not long afterwards used the weakness of Peter's flesh to blunt the eagerness of his spirit and impelled him to perjure himself by denying Christ.[87] Now if such things happened to the apostles, who were like flourishing green branches, that is, if they

80 1 Kgs 28:5–25   **81** Mt 26:40; Mk 14:37; Lk 22:45   **82** Mt 26:40–41; Mk 14:37–38   **83** 1 Jn 1:42   **84** Mk 14:31; Lk 22:33   **85** Lk 22:31   **86** Mt 26:44   **87** Mt 26:69–74; Mk 14:71

entered into temptation when they allowed sleep to interrupt their prayers, what will happen to us, who are like sapless sticks by comparison, if, when we are suddenly faced by danger (and when, I ask you, are we not in danger, since our enemy the devil constantly prowls like a roaring lion looking everywhere for someone who is ready to fall because of the weakness of the flesh, ready to pounce upon such a man and devour him)[88] in such great danger, I say, what will become of us if we do not follow Christ's advice by being steadfast in wakefulness and prayer?

Christ tells us to stay awake, but not for cards and dice, not for rowdy parties and drunken brawls, not for wine and women, but for prayer. He tells us to pray not occasionally, but constantly. "Pray," he says, "unceasingly."[89] He tells us to pray not only during the day (for it is hardly necessary to command anyone to stay awake during the day) but rather he exhorts us to devote to intense prayer a large part of that very time which most of us usually devote entirely to sleep. How much more, then, should we be ashamed of our miserable performance and recognize the enormous guilt we incur by saying no more than a short prayer or two, perhaps, during the day, and even those said as we doze and yawn. Finally our Savior tells us to pray, not that we may roll in wealth, not that we may live in a continuous round of pleasures, not that something awful may happen to our enemies, not that we may receive honor in this world, but rather that we may not enter into temptation. In fact, he wishes us to understand that all those worldly goods are either downright harmful, or else, by comparison with that one benefit, the merest trifles; and hence in his wisdom he placed this one petition at the end of the prayer which he had previously taught his disciples, as if it were a summary, in a way, of all the rest: "And lead us not into temptation, but deliver us from evil."[90]

And again he went away, for the second time, and said the same prayer over again, in these words: "My Father, if this cup cannot pass away without my drinking it, let your will be done." And he came again and found them sleeping, for their eyes were heavy. And they did not know what answer to make to him. And leaving them, he went away again and kneeling down said the same prayer, in these words: "Father, if you are willing, take this cup from me. Yet not my will but yours be done."[91]

Thus, after he had given his disciples this warning, he went back to pray again, and he repeated the same prayer he had said before, but still in such a way as to commit the whole matter once more to the will of the Father. Thus he teaches us to make our petitions earnest without being absolutely definite, but rather to trust the whole outcome to God, who desires our welfare no less than we ourselves do[92] and who knows what is likely to produce it a thousand times better than we do.

"My Father," he says, "if this cup cannot pass away without my drinking it, let your will be done." That pronoun "my" has a twofold effect: for it expresses great affection; and it makes it clear that God the Father is the father of Christ in a singular way—that is, not only by creation (for in this way he is the father of all things), not by adoption (in this way he is the father of Christians), but rather by nature he is God the Father of God the Son. And then he teaches the rest of us to pray thus: "Our Father who art in heaven." By these words we acknowledge that we are all brothers who have one Father in common, whereas Christ himself is the only one who can rightfully, because of his divinity, address the Father as he does here, "My Father." But if anyone is not content to be like other men[93] and is so proud as to imagine that he alone is governed by the secret spirit of God and that he has a different status from other men, it certainly seems to me that such a person arrogates to himself the language of Christ and prays with the invocation "My Father" instead of "Our Father," since he claims for himself as a private individual the spirit which God shares with all men, In fact, such a person is not much different from Lucifer, since he arrogates to himself God's language, just as Lucifer claimed God's place.[94] Christ's language here—"If this cup cannot pass away without my drinking it, let your will be done"—also makes it perfectly clear on what basis he calls a thing possible or impossible, namely on no other basis than the certain, immutable, unconstrained decision of his Father concerning his death. For otherwise, if he had thought that he was ineluctably and necessarily destined to die, either because

---

88 1 Pt 5:8   **89** 1 Thes; Lk 18:1   **90** Mt 6:13   **91** Mk 14:39–40; Mt 26:42–44   **92** See Mt 6:26.   **93** See Lk 18:11.   **94** See Is 14:13–14.

of the course of the heavenly bodies or because of some more abstract overall scheme of things such as fate, and if this had been the sense in which he said, "If this cup cannot pass away without my drinking it," then it would have been completely pointless for him to add the phrase "let your will be done." For how could he have left the matter to be decided by the Father if he believed that its outcome depended on something besides the Father, or if he thought that the Father had to make a certain choice necessarily, that is, willy-nilly?

But at the same time, while we examine the words with which Christ begged his Father to avert his death and humbly submitted everything to the will of his Father, we must also constantly bear in mind that, though he was both God and man, he said all these things not as God, but insofar as he was man. We ourselves provide a parallel: because we are composed of body and soul, we sometimes apply to our whole selves things which actually are true only of the soul and on the other hand we sometimes speak of ourselves when strict accuracy would require us to speak of our bodies alone. For we say that the martyrs go straight to heaven when they die, whereas actually only their souls are taken up to heaven. And, on the other hand, we say that men, however proud they may be, are still only dust and ashes and that when they have finished with this brief life they will rot in a common ordinary grave. We constantly talk this way, even though the soul does not enter into the grave or undergo death but rather outlives the body, either in miserable torment if it lived badly while in the body, or else in perpetual well-being if it lived well.

In a similar fashion, then, Christ speaks of what he did as God and what he did as man, not as if he were divided into two persons but as one and the same person, and that rightly, since he was one person; for in the omnipotent person of Christ humanity and divinity were joined and made one no less closely than his immortal soul was united to a body which could die. Thus because of his divinity he did not hesitate to say, "I and the Father are one"[95] and "Before Abraham came to be, I am."[96] Moreover, because of both his natures, he said, "I am with you all days even to the end of the world."[97] And, conversely, because of his humanity alone he

said, "The Father is greater than I"[98] and "A little while I am with you."[99] It is true, of course, that his glorious body is really present with us, and always will be till the end of the world, under the appearance of bread in the venerable sacrament of the Eucharist; but that bodily form in which he once associated with his disciples (and this is the kind of presence he had in mind when he said, "A little while I am with you") was taken away after Christ's ascension, unless he himself chooses to show it to someone, as he sometimes does.

Therefore, in this passage about Christ's agony, whichever of these deeds, sufferings, or prayers of his are so lowly that they seem quite incompatible with the lofty height of divinity, let us remember that the same Christ performed them as a man. Indeed some of them had their origin only in the lower part of his humanity. I mean the part concerned with sensation; and these served to proclaim the genuineness of his human nature and to relieve the natural fears of other men in later times. Nothing, then, in these words or in any of all the other things that the sequence of his agony presented as signs of his afflicted humanity, was considered by Christ to be unworthy of his glory; indeed so little did he think so that he himself took special care to see that they became widely known.

For, though everything written by all the apostles was dictated throughout by one and the same Spirit of Christ, still I find it hard to recall any of his other deeds which he took such particular pains to preserve in the memories of men. To be sure, he told his apostles about his intense sadness, so that they might be able to hand it down from him to posterity. But the words of his prayer to his Father they could hardly have heard even if they had been awake (since the nearest of them were a stone's throw away), and even if they had been present when it happened, they still could not have heard because they were asleep. Certainly they would have been even less able, at that time of night, to make out when he knelt down or when he threw himself face forward on the ground. As for those drops of blood which flowed like sweat from his whole body,[100] even if they had later clearly seen the stain left on the ground, I think they would have drawn almost any number of conclusions without guessing

95 Jn 10:30   **96** 3 Jn 8:58   **97** Mt 28:20   **98** Jn 14:28   **99** Jn 13:33   **100** Lk 22:44

the right one, since it was an unprecedented phenomenon for anyone to sweat blood.

Yet in the ensuing time before his death it seems unlikely that he spoke of these things either to his mother or to the apostles, unless one is willing to believe that he told the apostles the whole story of his agony when he left off praying and came back to them — that is, while they were either still sleeping or barely awake and quite drowsy — or else that he told them at the very time when the troops were at hand. The remaining alternative, then, and the one that seems most likely to be true, is that, after he rose from the dead and there could no longer be any doubt that he was God, his most loving mother and beloved disciples heard from his own most holy lips this detailed account, point by point, of his human suffering, the knowledge of which would benefit both them and (through them) others who would come after them, and which no one could have recounted except Christ himself. Therefore, to those whose hearts are troubled, meditation on this agony provides great consolation, and rightly so, since it was for this very purpose, to console the afflicted, that our Savior in his kindness made known his own affliction, which no one else knew or could have known.

Some may be concerned about another point: when Christ came back from that prayer to see his apostles and found them sleeping and so startled by his arrival that they did not know what to say, he left them, so that it might seem he had come only for the purpose of finding out whether they were awake, whereas he could not have lacked this knowledge (insofar as he was God) even before he came.

The answer to such persons, if there are any, should be this: nothing that he did was done in vain. It is true that his coming into their presence did not rouse them to complete vigilance but only to such a startled, half-waking drowsiness that they hardly raised their eyes to look at him, or else (what is worse yet) if his reproaches did wake them up completely, still they slipped back into sleep the moment he went away. Nevertheless, he himself both demonstrated his anxious concern for his disciples and also by his example gave to the future pastors of his Church a solemn injunction not to allow themselves the slightest wavering, out of sadness or weariness or fear, in their diligent care of their flock, but rather to conduct themselves so as to prove in actual fact that they are not so much concerned for themselves as for the welfare of their flock.

But perhaps some meticulous fussy dissector of the divine plan might say: "Either Christ wished the apostles to stay awake or he did not. If he did not, why did he give such an explicit command? If he did, what use was there in going back and forth so often? Since he was God, could he not at one and the same time speak the command and insure its execution?"

Doubtless he could have, my good man, since he was God, who carried out whatever he wished, who created all things with a word:[101] he spoke and it was done, he commanded and they were created.[102] He opened the eyes of a man blind from birth,[103] and could he not, then, find a way to open the eyes of a man who was asleep? Clearly, even someone who was not God could easily do that. For anyone can see that if you merely prick the eyes of sleepy men with a tiny pin they will stay awake and will certainly not go right back to sleep.

Doubtless Christ could have caused the apostles not to sleep at all but to stay awake, if that had been what he wished in an absolute and unqualified sense. But actually his wish was modified by a condition — namely that they themselves wish to do so, and wish it so effectually that each of them do his very best to comply with the outward command Christ himself gave and to cooperate with the promptings of his inward assistance. In this way he also wishes for all men to be saved[104] and for no one to suffer eternal torment, that is, always provided that we conform to his most loving will and do not set ourselves against it through our own willful malice. If someone stubbornly insists on doing this, God does not wish to waft him off to heaven against his will, as if he were in need of our services there and could not continue his glorious reign without our support. Indeed, if he could not reign without us, he would immediately punish many offenses which now, out of consideration for us, he tolerates and overlooks for a long time to see if his kindness and patience will bring us to repent. But we meanwhile abuse this great mercy of his by adding sins to sins,[105] thus heaping up for ourselves (as the apostle says) a treasure of wrath on the day of wrath.[106]

---

101 See Wis 9:1.　**102** Ps 32(33):9　**103** Jn 9:32　**104** 1 Tm 2:4　**105** See Ecclus 5:5; Is 30:1.　**106** Rom 2:5

Nevertheless, such is God's kindness that even when we are negligent and slumbering on the pillow of our sins, he disturbs us from time to time, shakes us, strikes us, and does his best to wake us up by means of tribulations. But still, even though he thus proves himself to be most loving even in his anger, most of us, in our gross human stupidity, misinterpret his action and imagine that such a great benefit is an injury, whereas actually (if we have any sense) we should feel bound to pray frequently and fervently that whenever we wander away from him he may use blows to drive us back to the right way, even though we are unwilling and struggle against him.

Thus we must first pray that we may see the way and with the Church we must say to God, "From blindness of heart, deliver us, O Lord."[107] And with the prophet we must say, "Teach me to do your will"[108] and "Show me your ways and teach me your paths."[109] Then we must intensely desire to run after you eagerly, O God, in the odor of your ointments,[110] in the most sweet scent of your spirit. But if we grow weary along the way (as we almost always do) and lag so far behind that we barely manage to follow at a distance,[111] let us immediately say to God, "Take my right hand"[112] and "Lead me along your path."[113]

Then if we are so overcome by weariness that we no longer have the heart to go on, if we are so soft and lazy that we are about to stop altogether, let us beg God to drag us along[114] even as we struggle not to go. Finally, if we resist when he draws us on gently, and are stiff-necked against the will of God, against our own salvation, utterly irrational like horses and mules which have no intellects,[115] we ought to beseech God humbly in the most fitting words of the prophet, "Hold my jaws hard, God, with a bridle and bit when I do not draw near to you."[116]

But then, since fondness for prayer is the first of our virtues to go when we are overtaken by sloth, and since we are reluctant to pray for anything (however useful) that we are reluctant to receive, certainly if we have any sense at all we ought to take this weakness into account, well in advance, before we fall into such sick and troubled states of mind—we ought, in other words, to pour out to God unceasingly such prayers as I have mentioned, and we should humbly implore him that, if at some later time we should ask for anything untoward—allured perhaps by the enticements of the flesh or seduced by a longing for worldly things or overthrown by the clever snares of the devils—he may be deaf to such prayers and avert what we pray for, showering upon us instead those things he knows will be good for us, however much we beg him to take them away. In fact, this is the way we normally act (if we are wise) when we are expecting a fever: we give advance warning to those who are to take care of us in our sickness that, even if we beg them, they should not give us any of those things which our diseased condition makes us perversely long for, though they are harmful to our health and only make the disease worse.

And when we are so fast asleep in our vices that even the calls and stirrings of divine mercy do not make us willing to rouse ourselves and wake up to virtuous living, we ourselves sometimes supply the reason why God goes away and leaves us to our vices; some he leaves so as never to come back again, but others he lets sleep only until another time, according as he sees fit in his wondrous kindness and the inscrutable depths of his wisdom.

Christ's action provided a sort of paradigm of this fact: when he went back to check on the apostles, they were unwilling to stay awake but rather went right on sleeping, and so he went away and left them. For "leaving them he went away again and kneeling down said the same prayer, in these words: 'Father, if you are willing, take this cup from me. Yet not my will but yours be done.'"[117]

Notice how he again asks the same thing, again adds the same condition, again sets us an example to show that when we fall into great danger, even for God's sake, we should not think we are not allowed to beg God urgently to provide us a way out[118] of that crisis. For one thing, it is quite possible that he permits us to be brought into such difficulties precisely because fear of danger makes us grow fervent in prayer when prosperity has made us cold, especially when it is a question of bodily danger—for most of us are not very warmly concerned about danger to our souls. Now as for those who are concerned (as they ought to be) about

107 part of the litany of the saints in the breviary of Salisbury   **108** Ps 142(143):10   **109** Ps 24(25):4   **110** See Sg 1:3.   **111** Mt 26:58; Mk 14:54; Lk 23:54   **112** See Ps 72:24(73:23); Is 42:6; 45:1.   **113** See Ps 5:9(8); 26(27):11; 138(139):24.   **114** See Sg 1:3; Jn 6:44; 12:32.   **115** Tob 6:17; Ps 31(32):9   **116** Ps 31(32):9   **117** Mt 26:42; Mk 14:39   **118** See 1 Cor 10:13.

their souls, unless someone is strengthened and inspired by God to undergo martyrdom—a condition which must be either directly experienced in an unexplainable way or else judged by appropriate indications—apart from such a case everyone has sufficient grounds to be afraid that he may grow weary under his burden and give in. Hence everyone, to avoid such overconfidence as Peter's,[119] ought to pray diligently that God in his goodness may deliver him from such a great danger to his soul. But it must be stressed again and again that no one should pray to escape danger so absolutely that he would not be willing to leave the whole matter up to God, ready in all obedience to endure what God has prepared for him.

These are some of the reasons, then, why Christ provided us with this salutary example of prayer, not that he himself was in any need of such prayer—nothing could be further from the truth. For, insofar as he was God, he was not inferior to the Father. Insofar as he was God, not only his power but also his will was the same as the Father's.[120] Certainly insofar as he was man, his power was infinitely less,[121] but then all power, both in heaven and on earth, was finally given to him by the Father.[122] And though his will, insofar as he was man, was not identical with the Father's, still it was in such complete conformity with the will of the Father that no disagreement was ever found between them.[123]

Thus the reasoning power of his soul, in obedience to the will of the Father, agrees to suffer that most bitter death, while at the same time, as a proof of his humanity, his bodily senses react to the prospect with revulsion and dread. His prayer expresses vividly both the fear and the obedience: "Father," he said, "if you are willing, take this cup from me. Yet not my will but yours be done."

His deeds, however, present this dual reaction even more clearly than his words. That his reasoning faculties never drew back from such horrible torture but rather remained obedient to the Father even to death, even to the death of the cross,[124] was demonstrated by the succeeding events of the Passion. And that his feelings were overwhelmed by an intense fear of his coming Passion is shown by the words which come next in the Gospel.

And there appeared to him an angel from heaven to strengthen him.[125]

Do you realize how intense his mental anguish must have been, that an angel should come from heaven to strengthen him?

But when I consider this passage, I cannot help wondering what pernicious nonsense has gotten into the heads of those who contend that it is futile for anyone to seek the intercession of any angel or departed saint, namely on the grounds that we can confidently address our prayers to God himself, not only because he alone is more present to us than all the angels and all the saints put together but also because he has the power to grant us more, and a greater desire to do so, than any of the saints in heaven, of whatever description.

With such trivial and groundless arguments as these, they express their envious displeasure at the glory of the saints, who are in turn equally displeased with such men; for they strive to undermine the loving homage we pay to the saints and the saving assistance they render to us. Why should these shameless men not follow the same line of reasoning here and argue that the angel's effort to offer consolation to our Savior Christ was utterly pointless and superfluous? For what angel of them all was as powerful as he himself or as near to him as God, since he himself was God? But in fact, just as he wished to undergo sadness and anxiety for our sake, so too for our sake he wished to have an angel console him, for a number of reasons: both to refute the foolish arguments of such men, and to make it clear that he was truly man (for just an angels ministered to him as God when he had triumphed over the temptations of the devil, so too an angel came to console him as man while he was making his lowly progress toward death) and moreover to give us hope that if we direct our prayers to God when we are in danger we cannot lack consolation, always provided we do not pray in a lazy and perfunctory way, but rather imitate Christ in this passage by sighing and praying from the bottom of our hearts.

For in his agony he prayed more earnestly, and his sweat became like drops of blood running down to the ground.[126]

---

119 Mt 26:33–35   **120** Jn 5:17–18   **121** Jn   5:30.   **124** See Phil 2:8.   **125** Lk 22:43
14:28   **122** Mt 11:27; 28:18   **123** See Jn   **126** Lk 22:44

Most scholars affirm that what Christ suffered for us was more painful than the suffering of any of all the martyrs, of whatever time or place, who underwent martyrdom for the faith. But others disagree, because there are various other sorts of torture than those to which Christ was subjected and some torments have been extended over a period of several days, a longer time than those of Christ lasted. Then, too, they think that, since one drop of Christ's precious blood, because of his infinite divinity, would have been far more than enough to redeem all mankind, therefore his ordeal was not ordained by God according to the standards of anyone else's suffering, but according to the proper measure of his own unfathomable wisdom. And since no one can know this measure with certainty, they hold that it is not prejudicial to the faith to believe that Christ's pain was less than that of some of the martyrs. But as for me, apart from the widespread opinion of the Church which fittingly applies to Christ Jeremiah's words about Jerusalem ("O all you who pass by the way, look and see if there is any sorrow like mine"),[127] certainly I find that this passage also provides very convincing reasons to believe that no martyr's torments could ever be compared with Christ's suffering, even on this point of the intensity of the pain.

Even if I should grant what I have good reasons to think need not be granted, namely that any of the martyrs was subjected to more kinds of torture, and greater ones, even (if you like) longer ones than Christ endured, still I find it not at all hard to believe that tortures which to all appearances may be considerably less fierce actually caused Christ to suffer more excruciating pain than someone might feel from tortures that seem much more grievous, and for this reason: I see that Christ, as the thought of his coming Passion was borne in upon him, was overwhelmed by mental anguish more bitter than any other mortal has ever experienced from the thought of coming torments. For who has ever felt such bitter anguish that a bloody sweat broke out all over his body and ran down in drops to the ground? The intensity of the actual pain itself, therefore, I estimate by this standard: I see that even the presentiment of it before it arrived was more bitter to Christ than such anticipation has ever been to anyone else.

Nor could this anguish of the mind ever have grown to sufficient intensity to cause the body to sweat blood if he had not, of his own free will, exercised his divine omnipotence, not only to refrain from alleviating this painful pressure, but even to add to its force and strength. This he did in order to prefigure the blood which future martyrs would be forced to pour forth on the ground, and at the same time to offer this unheard of, this marvelous example of profound anguish as a consolation to those who would be so fearful and alarmed at the thought of torture that they might otherwise interpret their fear as a sign of their downfall and thus yield to despair.

At this point, if someone should again bring up those martyrs who freely and eagerly exposed themselves to death because of their faith in Christ, and if he should offer his opinion that they are especially worthy of the laurels of triumph because with a joy that left no room for sorrow they betrayed no trace of sadness, no sign of fear, I am perfectly willing to go along with him on that point, so long as he does not go so far as to deny the triumph of those who do not rush forth of their own accord but who nevertheless do not hang back or withdraw once they have been seized, but rather go on in spite of their fearful anxiety and face the terrible prospect out of love for Christ.

Now if anyone should argue that the eager martyrs receive a greater share of glory than the others, I have no objection—he can have the argument all to himself. For I rest content with the fact that in heaven neither sort of martyr will lack a glory so great that while they were alive their eyes never saw the like, nor did their ears ever hear it, nor did it ever enter into their hearts [to conceive of it].[128] And even if someone does have a higher place in heaven, no one else envies him for it—quite the opposite, everyone enjoys the glory of everyone else because of their mutual love.

Besides, just who outranks whom in the glory assigned by God in heaven is not, I think, quite crystal-clear to us, groping as we are in the darkness of our mortality.

For, though I grant that God loves a cheerful giver,[129] still I have no doubt that he loved Tobias, and holy Job too. Now it is true that both of them bore their calamities bravely and patiently, but

neither of them, so far as I know, was exactly jumping with joy or clapping his hands out of happiness.

To expose one's self to death for Christ's sake
when the case clearly demands it or when God gives
a secret prompting to do so, this, I do not deny, is
a deed of preeminent virtue. But otherwise I do
not think it very safe to do so, and among those
who willingly suffered for Christ we find outstanding figures who were very much afraid, who were
deeply distressed, who even withdrew from death
more than once before they finally faced it bravely.

Certainly I do not mean to derogate from God's
power to inspire martyrs; indeed I believe that he
exercises it on occasion (either granting this favor to
holy persons as a reward for the labors of their past
lives or giving it purely and simply out of his own
generosity) by filling the whole mind of a martyr
with such joy that he not only wards off those grievous emotional disturbances but also keeps himself
completely free from what the Stoics call "incipi-
ent emotions," freely admitting that even their factitious wisemen are susceptible to them.

Since we often see it happen that some men do
not feel wounds inflicted in battle until their awareness, which had been displaced by strong feeling, returns to them and they notice the injury,[130] certainly
there is no reason why I should doubt that a mind
exulting in the high hopes of approaching glory can
be so rapt and transported beyond itself that it neither fears death nor feels torments.

But still, even if God did give someone this gift, I
would certainly be inclined to call it an unearned felicity or the recompense of past virtue, but not the
measure of future reward in heaven. Now I might
have believed that this future reward corresponds
to the pain suffered for Christ except that God in
his generosity bestows it in such good measure—
so full, so concentrated, so overflowing[131]—that the
sufferings of this time are by no means worthy to
be compared to that future glory which will be revealed in those[132] who loved God so dearly that they
spent their very life's blood for his glory, with such
mental agony and bodily torment. Besides it is not
possible that God in his goodness removes fear from
some persons not because he approves of or intends
to reward their boldness, but rather because he is
aware of their weakness and knows that they would

not be equal to facing fear. For some have yielded to
fear, even though they won out later when the actual tortures were inflicted.

Now as for the point that those who eagerly suffer
death encourage others by their example, I would
not deny that for many they provide a very useful
pattern. But on the other hand, since almost all of
us are fearful in the face of death, who can know
how many have also been helped by those whom we
see face death with fear and trembling but whom
we also observe as they break bravely through the
hindrances blocking their path, the obstacles bar-
ring their way with barriers harder than steel, that
is, their own weariness, fear, and anguish, and by
bursting these iron bars and triumphing over death
take heaven by storm?[133] Seeing them, will not weaklings who are, like them, cowardly and afraid take
heart so as not to yield under the stress of persecution even though they feel great sadness welling up
within them, and fear and weariness and horror at
the prospect of a ghastly death?

Thus the wisdom of God, which penetrates all
things irresistibly and disposes all things sweetly,[134]
foreseeing and contemplating in his ever-present
sight how the minds of men in different places
would be affected, suits his examples to various
times and places, choosing now one destiny, now
another, according as he sees which will be most
profitable. And so God proportions the temperaments of his martyrs according to his own providence in such a way that one rushes forth eagerly
to his death, another creeps out hesitantly and
fearfully, but for all that bears his death none the
less bravely—unless someone perhaps imagines he
ought to be thought less brave for having fought
down not only his other enemies but also his own
weariness, sadness, and fear—most strong feelings
and mighty enemies indeed.

But the whole drift of the present discussion finally comes to this: we should admire both kinds of
most holy martyrs, we should venerate both kinds,
praise God for both, we should imitate both when
the situation demands it, each according to his own
capacity and according to the grace God gives to
each.

But the person who is conscious of his own eagerness needs not so much encouragement to be daring

as perhaps a reminder to be afraid lest his presumption, like Peter's,[135] lead to a sudden relapse and fall. But if a person feels anxious, heavy-hearted, fearful, certainly he ought to be comforted and encouraged to take heart. For both sorts of martyrs this anguish of Christ is most salutary: it keeps the one from being over-exultant and it makes the other be of good hope when his spirit is crestfallen and downcast. For if anyone feels his mind swelling with ungovernable enthusiasm, perhaps when he recalls this lowly and anguished bearing of his commander, he will have reason to fear lest our sly enemy is lifting him up on high for a while so that a little later he can dash him to the ground all the harder.[136] But whoever is utterly crushed by feelings of anxiety and fear and is tortured by the fear that he may yield to despair, let him consider this agony of Christ, let him meditate on it constantly and turn it over in his mind, let him drink deep and health-giving draughts of consolation from this spring. For here he will see the loving shepherd lifting the weak lamb on his shoulders,[137] playing the same role as he himself does, expressing his very own feelings, and for this reason: so that anyone who later feels himself disturbed by similar feelings might take courage and not think that he must despair.

Therefore let us give him as many thanks as we can (for certainly we can never give him enough); and in our agony remembering his (with which no other can ever be compared) let us beg him with all our strength that he may deign to comfort us in our anguish by an insight into his; and when we urgently beseech him, because of our mental distress, to free us from danger, let us nevertheless follow his own most wholesome example by concluding our prayer with his own addition: "Yet not as I will but as you will." If we do these things diligently, I have no doubt at all that, just as an angel brought him consolation in answer to his prayer, so too each of our angels will bring us from his Spirit consolation that will give us the strength to persevere in those deeds that will lift us up to heaven. And in order to make us completely confident of this fact, Christ went there before us by the same method, by the same path. For after he had suffered this agony for a long time, his spirits were so restored that he arose,

returned to his apostles, and freely went out to meet the traitor and the tormentors who were seeking him to make him suffer. Then, when he had suffered (as was necessary) he entered into his glory,[138] preparing there a place also for those of us who follow in his footsteps.[139] And lest we should be deprived of it by our own dullness, may he himself because of his own agony deign to help us in ours.

And when he had arisen from prayer and come to his disciples, he found them sleeping for sadness, and he said to them, "Why are you sleeping?[140] Sleep on now and take your rest. That is enough. Get up and pray that you may not enter into temptation. Behold, the hour is coming when the Son of Man will be betrayed into the hands of sinners. Get up, let us go. Behold, the one who will betray me is near at hand."[141]

See now, when Christ comes back to his apostles for the third time, there they are, buried in sleep, though he commanded them to bear up with him and to stay awake and pray because of the impending danger; but Judas the traitor at the same time was so wide awake and intent on betraying the Lord that the very idea of sleep never entered his mind.

Does not this contrast between the traitor and the apostles present to us a clear and sharp mirror image (as it were), a sad and terrible view of what has happened through the ages from those times even to our own? Why do not bishops contemplate in this scene their own somnolence? Since they have succeeded in the place of the apostles, would that they would reproduce their virtues just as eagerly as they embrace their authority and as faithfully as they display their sloth and sleepiness! For very many are sleepy and apathetic in sowing virtues among the people and maintaining the truth, while the enemies of Christ in order to sow vices[142] and uproot the faith (that is, insofar as they can, to seize Christ and cruelly crucify him once again) are wide awake—so much wiser (as Christ says) are the sons of darkness in their generation than the sons of light.[143]

But although this comparison of the sleeping apostles applies very well to those bishops who sleep while virtue and the faith are placed in jeopardy, still it does not apply to all such prelates at

135 Mt 26:33–35, 69–75 **136** See Job 30:22; Ps 101:11(102:10); Claudian, *In Rufinum* 1.22. **137** See Lk 15:5; Jn 10:14. **138** Lk 24:26 **139** Jn 14:2; 1 Pt 2:21 **140** Lk 22:45–46 **141** Mt 26:45–46; Mk 14:41–42 **142** See Mt 13:24–29; Lk 8:5–15. **143** Lk 16:8

all points. For some of them—alas, far more than I could wish—do not drift into sleep through sadness and grief as the apostles did. Rather they are numbed and buried in destructive desires; that is, drunk with the new wine[144] of the devil, the flesh, and the world,[145] they sleep like pigs sprawling in the mire. Certainly the apostles' feeling of sadness because of the danger to their master was praiseworthy, but for them to be so overcome by sadness as to yield completely to sleep, that was certainly wrong. Even to grieve because the world is perishing or to weep because of the crimes of others bespeaks a reverent outlook, as was felt by the writer who said, "I sat by myself and groaned"[146] and also by the one who said, "I was sick at heart because of sinners abandoning your law."[147] Sadness of this sort I would place in the category of which he says, ["For the sorrow that is according to God produces repentance that surely tends to salvation, whereas the sorrow that is according to the world produces death"].[148] But I would place it there only if the feeling, however good, is checked by the rule and guidance of reason. For if this is not the case, if sorrow so grips the mind that its strength is sapped and reason gives up the reins,[149] if a bishop is so overcome by heavy-hearted sleep that he neglects to do what the duty of his office requires for the salvation of his flock—like a cowardly ship's captain who is so disheartened by the furious din of a storm that he deserts the helm, hides away cowering in some cranny, and abandons the ship to the waves—if a bishop does this, I would certainly not hesitate to juxtapose and compare his sadness with the sadness that leads, as [St. Paul][150] says, to hell; indeed, I would consider it far worse, since such sadness in religious matters seems to spring from a mind which despairs of God's help.

The next category, but a far worse one, consists of those who are not depressed by sadness at the danger of others but rather by a fear of injury to themselves, a fear which is so much the worse as its cause is the more contemptible, that is, when it is not a question of life or death but of money.[151]

And yet Christ commands us to contemn the loss of the body itself for his sake. "Do not be afraid," he says, "of those who destroy the body and after that can do nothing further. But I will show you the one you should fear, the one to fear: fear him who, when he has destroyed the body, has the power to send the soul also to hell. This, I tell you, is the one you must fear."[152]

And though he lays down this rule for everyone without exception when they have been seized and there is no way out, he attaches a separate charge over and above this to the high office of prelates: he does not allow them to be concerned only about their own souls or merely to take refuge in silence until they are dragged out and forced to choose between open profession or lying dissimulation, but he also wished them to come forth if they see that the flock entrusted to them is in danger and to face the danger of their own accord for the good of their flock. "The good shepherd," says Christ, "lays down his life for his sheep."[153] But if every good shepherd lays down his life for his sheep, certainly one who saves his own life to the detriment of his sheep, is not fulfilling the role of a good shepherd.

Therefore, just as one who loses his life for Christ (and he does this if he loses it for the flock of Christ entrusted to him) saves it for life everlasting, so too one who denies Christ (and this he does if he fails to profess the truth when his silence injures his flock) by saving his life, he actually proceeds to lose it.[154] Clearly, it is even worse if, driven by fear, he denies Christ openly in words and forsakes him publicly. Such prelates do not sleep like Peter; they make his waking denial. But under the kindly glance of Christ most of them through his grace will eventually wipe out that failure and save themselves by weeping, if only they respond to his glance and friendly call to repentance with bitterness of heart[155] and a new way of life, remembering his words and contemplating his Passion and leaving behind the shackles of evil which bound them in their sins.

But if anyone is so set in evil that he does not merely neglect to profess the truth out of fear but like Arrius and his ilk preaches false doctrine, whether for sordid gain or out of a corrupt ambition, such a person does not sleep like Peter, does not make Peter's denial, but rather stays awake with wicked Judas and like Judas persecutes Christ. This man's condition is far more dangerous than that of the others, as is shown by the sad and horrible end Judas came to.[156] But since there is no limit to the

---

144 See Acts 2:13. **145** See 1 Jn 2:15–16.
146 Lam 3:28 **147** Ps 118(119):53
148 More leaves a blank space here.

2 Cor 7:10 **149** Plato, *Phaedrus* 246,
254 **150** More leaves a blank space here.
151 See Terence, *Phormio* 631. **152** Lk

12:4–5; Mt 10:28 **153** Jn 10:11 **154** Mt
10:33, 39; Mk 8:35; Lk 9:24 **155** See Lk
22:61–62. **156** Mt 27:5; Acts 1:18

kindness of a merciful God, even this sort of sinner ought not to despair of forgiveness. Even to Judas God gave many opportunities of coming to his senses. He did not deny him his companionship. He did not take away from him the dignity of his apostleship. He did not even take the purse-strings from him, even though he was a thief.[157] He admitted the traitor to the fellowship of his beloved disciples at the last supper. He deigned to stoop down at the feet of the betrayer and to wash with his innocent and most sacred hands Judas' dirty feet, a most fit symbol of his filthy mind.[158] Moreover, with incomparable generosity, he gave him to eat, in the form of bread, that very body of his which the betrayer had already sold; and under the appearance of wine, he gave him that very blood to drink which, even while he was drinking it, the traitor was wickedly scheming to broach and set flowing.[159] Finally when Judas, coming with his crew to seize him, offered him a kiss, a kiss that was in fact the terrible token of his treachery, Christ received him calmly and gently.[160] who would not believe that any one of all these could have turned the traitor's mind, however hardened in crime, to better courses? Then too, even that beginning of repentance, when he admitted he had sinned, and gave back the pieces of silver, and threw them away when they were not accepted, crying out that he was a traitor and confessing that he had betrayed innocent blood[161] — I am inclined to believe that Christ prompted him thus far so that he might if possible — that is, if the traitor did not add despair to his treachery — save from ruin the very man who had so recently, so perfidiously betrayed him to death.

Therefore, since God showed his great mercy in so many ways even toward Judas, an apostle turned traitor, since he invited him to forgiveness so often and did not allow him to perish except through despair alone, certainly there is no reason why, in this life, anyone should despair of any imitator of Judas. Rather, according to that holy advice of the apostle "Pray for each other that you may be saved,"[162] if we see anyone wandering wildly from the right road, let us hope that he will one day return to the path, and meanwhile let us pray humbly and incessantly that God will hold out to him chances to come to his senses, and likewise that with God's help he will

eagerly seize them, and having seized them will hold fast and not throw them away out of malice or let them slip away from him through wretched sloth.

And so when Christ had found his apostles sleeping for the third time, he said to them, "Why are you sleeping?"[163] as if to say: "Now is not the time to sleep. Now is the crucial time for you to stay awake and pray, as I myself have already warned you twice before, only a little while ago." And as for them, since they did not know what to reply to him[164] when he found them sleeping for the second time, what suitable excuse could they possibly have devised now that they had been so quickly caught in the same fault for the third time? Could they use as an excuse what the evangelist mentions — that is, could they say they were sleeping because of their sadness? Certainly the fact is mentioned by Luke,[165] but it is also quite clear that he does not praise it. It is true, he does suggest that their sadness itself was praiseworthy, as it certainly was. Still, the sleep that followed from it was not free of moral blame. For the sort of sadness that is potentially worthy of great reward sometimes tends toward great evil. Certainly it does if we are so taken up by it that we render it useless — that is, if we do not have recourse to God with our petitions and prayers and seek comfort from him, but instead, in a certain downcast and desperate frame of mind, try to escape our awareness of sadness by looking for consolation in sleep. Nor will we find what we are looking for: losing in sleep the consolation we might have obtained from God by staying awake and praying, we feel the weary weight of a troubled mind even during sleep itself and also we stumble with our eyes closed into temptations and the traps set by the devil.

And so Christ, as if he intended to preclude any excuse for this sleepiness, said, "Why are you sleeping?[166] Sleep on now and take your rest. That is enough. Get up and pray that you may not enter into temptation. Behold, the hour has almost come when the Son of Man will be betrayed into the hands of sinners. Get up, let us go. Behold, the one who will betray me is near at hand. And while Jesus was still speaking, behold Judas Iscariot, etc."

Immediately after he had aroused the sleeping apostles for the third time, he undercut them with irony, not indeed that trivial and sportive variety

157 Jn 12:6; 13:29   **158** Jn 13:4–11   22:47–48   **161** Mt 27:3–5   **162** Jas 5:16   **165** Lk 22:45   **166** Lk 22:46
159 Lk 22:21   **160** Mt 26:48–50; Lk   **163** Lk 22:46   **164** Mk 14:40

with which idle men of wit are accustomed to amuse themselves, but rather a serious and weighty kind of irony. "Sleep on now," he said, "and take your rest. That is enough. Get up and pray that you may not enter into temptation. Behold, the hour has almost come when the Son of Man will be betrayed into the hands of sinners. Get up, let us go. Behold, the one who will betray me is near at hand. And while he was still speaking, Judas, etc."

Notice how he grants permission to sleep in such a way as clearly shows he means to take it away. For he had hardly said "Sleep" before he added "That is enough," as if to say: "Now there is no need for you to sleep any longer. It is enough that throughout the whole time you ought to have been staying awake, you have been sleeping—and that even against my direct orders. Now there is no time left to sleep, not even to sit down. You must get up immediately and pray that you may not enter into temptation, the temptation, perhaps, of deserting me and giving great scandal by doing so. Otherwise, so far as sleep is concerned, sleep on now and take your rest—you have my permission—that is, if you can. But you will certainly not be able to. For there are people coming—they are almost here—who will shake the yawning sleepiness out of you. For behold the hour has almost come when the Son of Man will be betrayed into the hands of sinners and behold the one who will betray me is near at hand. And he had hardly finished these few admonitions and was still speaking when, behold, Judas Iscariot, etc."[167]

I am not unaware that some learned and holy men do not allow this interpretation, though they admit that others, equally learned and holy, have found it agreeable. Not that those who do not accept this interpretation are shocked by this sort of irony, as some others are—also pious men to be sure, but not sufficiently versed in the figures of speech which Sacred Scripture customarily takes over from common speech. For if they were, they would have found irony in so many other places that they could not have found it offensive here.

What could be more pungent or witty than the irony with which the blessed apostle gracefully polishes off the Corinthians?—I mean where he asks pardon because he never burdened any of them with charges and expenses. "For how have I done any less for you than for the other churches, except this, that I have never been a burden to you? Pardon me for this injustice."[168] What could be more forceful or biting than the irony with which God's prophet ridiculed the prophets of Baal as they called upon the deaf statue of their god: "Call louder," he said, "for your god is asleep or perhaps has gone somewhere on a trip."[169] I have taken this occasion to bring up these instances in passing, because some readers, out of a certain pious simplicity, refuse to accept in Sacred Scripture (or at least do not notice there) these universally used forms of speech, and by neglecting the figures of speech they very often also miss the real sense of Scripture.

Now concerning this passage Saint Augustine says that he finds the interpretation I have given to be not unacceptable but also not necessary. He claims that the plain meaning without any figure is adequate. He presents such an interpretation of this passage in the work he wrote entitled *The Harmony of the Gospels*. "It seems," he says, "that the language of Matthew here is self-contradictory. For how could he say 'Sleep on now and take your rest' and then immediately add 'Get up, let us go'? Disturbed by this seeming inconsistency some try to set the tone of the words 'Sleep on now and take your rest' as reproachful rather than permissive. And this would be the right thing to do if it were necessary. But Mark reports it in such a way that when Christ had said 'Sleep on now and take your rest,' he added 'That is enough' and then went on to say 'The hour has come when the Son of Man will be betrayed.' Therefore it is surely at least implied that after he had said 'Sleep and take your rest' the Lord was silent for a while so that they could do what he had allowed them to do, and that he then went on to say 'Behold, the hour has almost come.' That is the reason why Mark includes 'That is enough,' that is, 'You have rested long enough.'"[170]

Subtle indeed this reasoning of the most blessed Augustine, as he always is; but I imagine that those of the opposite persuasion do not find it at all likely that, after Christ had already reproached them twice for sleeping when his capture was imminent, and after he had just rebuked them sternly by saying, "Why are you sleeping?" He should then have granted them time to sleep, especially at the very

---

167 Mt 26:45–47; Mk 14:41–43　　**170** Augustine, *De consensu evangelistarum*　*Latinorum* 43.282–83)
168 2 Cor 12:13　**169** 1 Kgs 18:27　(*Corpus Scriptorum Ecclesiasticorum*

time when the danger which was the reason they ought not to have slept before, was now pounding on the door, as they say. But now that I have presented both interpretations, everyone is free to choose whichever he likes. My purpose has been merely to recount both of them; it is not for such a nobody as me to render a decision like an official arbitrator.

Get up and pray that you may not enter into temptation.[171]

Before, he ordered them to watch and pray.[172] Now that they have twice learned by experience that the drowsy position of sitting lets sleep gradually slip up on them, he teaches an instant remedy for that sluggish disease of somnolence, namely to get up. Since this sort of remedy was handed down by our Savior himself, I heartily wish that we would occasionally be willing to try it out at the dead of night. For here we would discover not only that well begun is half done (as Horace says)[173] but that once begun is all done.

For when we are fighting against sleep, the first encounter is always the sharpest. Therefore, we should not try to conquer sleep by a prolonged struggle, but rather we should break with one thrust the grip of the alluring arms with which it embraces us and pulls us down, and we should dash away from it all of a sudden. Then, once we have cast off idle sleep, the very image of death,[174] life with its eagerness will resume its sway. Then, if we devote ourselves to meditation and prayer, the mind, collected and composed in that dark silence of the night,[175] will find that it is much more receptive to divine consolation than it is during the daytime, when the noisy bustle of business on all sides distracts the eyes, the ears, and the mind, and dissipates our energy in manifold activities, no less pointless than they are diverse. But Lord spare us, though thoughts about some trifling matter, some worldly matter at that, may sometimes interrupt our sleep and keep us awake for a long time and hardly let us go back to sleep at all, prayer does not keep us awake: in spite of the immense loss of spiritual benefits, in spite of the many traps set for us by our deadly enemy, in spite of the danger of being utterly undone, we do not wake up to pray but lie in a drugged sleep watching the dream-visions induced by mandragora.

But we must continually keep in mind that Christ did not command them simply to get up, but to get up in order to pray. For it is not enough to get up if we do not get up for a good purpose. If we do not, there would be far less sin in losing time through slothful drowsiness than in devoting waking time to the deliberate pursuit of malicious crimes.

Then, too, he does not merely order them to pray but shows them the need for it and teaches what they should have prayed for: "Pray," he says, "that you may not enter into temptation." Again and again he drove home this point to them,[176] that prayer is the only safeguard against temptation and that if someone refuses it entrance into the castle of his soul and shuts it out by yielding to sleep, through such negligence he permits the besieging troops of the devil (that is, temptations to evil) to break in.

Three times he admonished them verbally to pray. Then, to avoid the appearance of teaching merely by these words and in order to teach them by his example as well, he himself prayed three times, suggesting in this way that we ought to pray to the Trinity, namely to the unbegotten Father, to the co-equal Son begotten by him, and to the Spirit equal to each and proceeding from each of them. From these three we should likewise pray for three things: forgiveness for the past, grace to manage the present, and a prudent concern for the future. But we should pray for these things not lazily and carelessly but incessantly and fervently. Just how far from this kind of prayer nearly all of us are nowadays, everyone can judge privately from his own conscience and we may all publicly learn (God forbid) by the decreasing fruits of prayer, falling off gradually from day to day.

Nevertheless, since a little earlier I bore down on this point as vigorously as I could by attacking that sort of prayer in which the mind is not attentive but wandering and distracted among many ideas, it would be well at this point to propose an emollient from Gerson[177] to alleviate this sore point, lest I seem to be like a harsh surgeon touching this common sore too roughly, bringing to many tendersouled mortals not a healing medicine but rather

---

171 Lk 22:46   **172** Mt 26:41; Mk 14:38   **173** Horace, *Epistulae* 1.2.40   **174** See Ovid, *Amores* 2.9.41.   **175** See Vergil, *Aeneid* 4.123.   **176** Mt 6:13; 26:41; Mk 14:38; Lk 22:40, 46   **177** See Gerson's *De oratione et eius valore.*

pain, and taking away from them hope of attaining salvation. In order to cure these troublesome inflammations of the soul, Gerson uses certain palliatives which are analogous to those medications which doctors use to relieve bodily pain and which they call "anodynes."

And so this John Gerson, an outstanding scholar and a most gentle handler of troubled consciences, saw (I imagine) some people whom this distraction of mind made so terribly anxious that they repeated the individual words of their prayers one after the other with a belabored sort of babbling, and still got nowhere and sometimes were even less pleased with their prayer the third time than the first time. He saw that such people, through sheer weariness, lost all sense of consolation from their prayers and that some of them were ready to give up the habit of prayer as useless (if they were to pray in this way) or even harmful (as they feared). This kind man, then, in order to relieve them of their troublesome difficulty, pointed out three aspects of prayer: the act, the virtue, and the habit.

But to make his meaning clearer, he explains it by the example of a person setting out from France on a pilgrimage to Saint James [of Compostella].[178] For such a person sometimes goes forward on his journey and at the same time meditates on the holy saint and the purpose of the pilgrimage. And so this man throughout this whole time continues his pilgrimage by a double act, namely (and I shall use Gerson's own words) by a "natural continuity" and a "moral continuity": natural, because he actually and in fact proceeds toward that place; moral, because his thoughts are occupied with the matter of his pilgrimage. By "moral" he refers to that moral intention by which the act of setting out, otherwise indifferent, is perfected by the pious reason for setting out.

Sometimes, however, the pilgrim goes his way considering other matters, without thinking anything about the saint or the place, thinking perhaps about something even holier, such as God himself. In such a case he continues the act of his pilgrimage on a natural, but not on a moral level. For though he actually moves his feet along, he does not actually think about the reason for setting out nor perhaps even about the way he is going. But though the moral act of his pilgrimage does not continue,

its moral virtue does. For that whole natural act of walking is informed and imbued with a moral virtue because it is silently accompanied by the pious intention formed at the beginning, since all this motion follows from that first decision just as a stone continues on its course because of the original impetus, even though the hand which threw it has been withdrawn. Sometimes, however, the moral act takes place when there is no natural act, as, for example, whenever the person thinks about his pilgrimage when he is perhaps sitting and not walking. Finally, it often happens that both kinds of act are missing, as, for example, when we are sleeping, for then the pilgrim neither performs the natural act of walking nor the moral act of thinking about the pilgrimage; but still in the meantime the moral virtue, so long as it is not deliberately renounced, remains and persists habitually.

And so this pilgrimage is never truly interrupted in such a way that its merit does not continue and persist at least habitually, unless an opposite decision is made, either to give up the pilgrimage completely or at least to put it off until another time. And so by means of this comparison he draws the same conclusions about prayer, namely that once it has been begun attentively it can never afterwards be so interrupted that the virtue of the first intention does not remain and persist continuously— that is, either actually or habitually—so long as it is not relinquished by making a decision to stop nor cut off by turning away to mortal sin.

Hence he says that those words of Christ "You should pray always and not cease"[179] were not spoken figuratively but in a simple and straightforward sense, and that in fact they are actually and literally fulfilled by good men. He supports his opinion with that well-known adage of learned men "whoever lives well is always praying"—which is true, because whoever does everything according to the apostle's precept for the glory of God,[180] once he has begun praying attentively, never afterwards interrupts his prayer in such a way that its meritorious virtue does not persist, if not actually then at least habitually.

This is the explanation given by that most learned and virtuous man John Gerson in his short treatise entitled *Prayer and its Value.* But nevertheless he intends it as a consolation for those who are troubled and saddened because their attention slips away

---

178 Compostella is a Spanish city, traditionally considered the burial place of St. James the Greater.   **179** Lk 18:1   **180** 1 Cor 10:31

from them unawares during prayer, even though they are earnestly trying to pay attention; he does not intend that it should provide a flattering illusion of safety for those who out of careless laziness make no effort to think about their prayers. For when we perform such a grave duty negligently, we say prayers indeed, but we do not pray, and we do not (as I said before) render God favorable to us but drive him far from us in his wrath.

And why should anyone be surprised if God is angry when he sees himself addressed so contemptuously by a lowly human creature? And how can we imagine that a person does not approach and address God contemptuously when he says to God, "God, hear my prayer"[181] while his own mind all the time is turned away to other matters—vain and foolish and would that they were not sometimes also wicked matters—so that he does not even hear his own voice but murmurs his way by rote through well-worn prayers, his mind a complete blank, emitting (as Vergil says) sounds without sense.[182] Thus when we have finished our prayers and gone our way, very often we are immediately in need of other prayers to beg forgiveness for our former carelessness.

And so when Christ had said to his apostles, "Get up and pray that you may not enter into temptation," he immediately warned them how great the impending danger was, in order to show that no drowsy or lukewarm prayer would suffice: "Behold," he said, "the hour has almost come when the Son of Man will be betrayed into the hands of sinners,"[183] as if to include the following implications: "I predicted to you that I must be betrayed by one of you—you were shocked at the very words.[184] I foretold to you that Satan would seek you out to sift you like wheat—you heard this carelessly and made no response, as if his temptation were not much to be reckoned with.[185] So that you might know that temptation is not at all to be contemned, I predicted that you would all be scandalized in me—you all denied it. To him who denied it most of all, I predicted that he would deny me three times before the cock crowed—he absolutely insisted it would not be so and that he would rather die with me than deny me, and so you all said.[186] Lest you should consider temptation a thing to be taken lightly, I again and

again commanded you to watch and pray lest you enter into temptation—but you were always so far from recognizing the strength of temptation that you took no pains to pray against it or even to stay awake.

Perhaps you were encouraged to scorn the power of the devil's temptation by the fact that before, when I sent you out two by two to preach the faith, you came back and reported to me that even the demons were subject to you. But I, to whom the nature of demons, as well as your own nature, is more deeply known than either is to you, since indeed I established each of them, I immediately cautioned you not to glory in such vanity, because it was not your power that subjected the demons but rather I myself did it, and I did it not for your sakes but for the sake of others who were to be converted to the faith; and I admonished you rather to glory in a real source of joy, namely that your names are written in the book of life.[187] This really and truly belongs to you because once you have attained that joy you can never lose it, though all the ranks of the demons should struggle against you. But still the power you exerted against them at that time gave you such high confidence that you seem to scorn their temptations as matters of little moment.

"And so, though I foretold that there was danger impending on this very night, up to now you have still viewed these temptations as it were from a distance. But now I warn you that not only the very night but even the very hour is at hand. For behold, the hour has almost come when the Son of Man will be betrayed into the hands of sinners. Now, therefore, there is no more chance to sit and sleep. Now you will be forced to stay awake, and there is hardly a moment left to pray. Now, therefore, I no longer foretell future events, but I say to you right now, at this present moment, Get up, let us go—behold, the one who will betray me is at hand. If you are not willing to stay awake so that you might be able to pray, at least get up and go away quickly lest you be unable to escape. For, behold, the one who will betray me is at hand." Unless perhaps he did not say, "Get up, let us go" as intending that they should run away in fear, but rather that they should go forward with confidence. For he himself did so: he did not turn back in another direction but even as he spoke

181 Ps 54:2(55:1)   **182** Vergil, *Aeneid*   **184** Mt 26:21–22   **185** Lk 22:31–34
10.640   **183** Mt 26:45; Mk 14:41   **186** Mt 26:31–35   **187** Lk 10:17–20

he freely went on to encounter those butchers who were making their way toward him with murder in their hearts. While Jesus was still saying these things, behold, Judas Iscariot, one of the twelve, and with him a large crowd with swords and clubs, sent by the chief priests and the scribes and the elders of the people.[188]

Although nothing can contribute more effectively to salvation, and to the implanting of every sort of virtue in the Christian breast, than pious and fervent meditation on the successive events of Christ's Passion, still it would certainly be not unprofitable to take the story of that time when the apostles were sleeping as the Son of Man was being betrayed, and to apply it as a mysterious image of future times. For Christ, to redeem man truly became a son of man—that is, although he was conceived without male seed, he was nevertheless really descended from the first men and therefore truly became a son of Adam, so that by his Passion he might restore Adam's posterity, lost and cast off into wretchedness through the fault of our first parents, to a state of happiness even greater than their original one.[189] This is the reason that, in spite of his divinity, he constantly called himself the Son of Man (since he was also really a man), thus constantly suggesting, by mentioning that nature which alone was capable of death, the benefit we derive from his death. For, though God died, since he who was God died, nevertheless his divinity did not undergo death, but only his humanity, or actually only his body, if we consider the fact of nature more than the custom of language. For a man is said to die when the soul leaves the dead body, but the soul which departs is itself immortal. But since he did not merely delight in the phrase describing our nature but was also pleased to take upon himself our nature for our salvation, and then finally to unite with himself, in the structure of one body[190] (as it were), all of us whom he regenerated by his saving sacraments and by faith, granting us a share even of his names (since Scripture calls all the faithful both gods[191] and Christs),[192] I think we would not be far wrong if we were to fear that the time approaches when the Son of Man, Christ, will be betrayed into the hands of sinners, as often as we see an imminent danger that the mystical body of Christ,[193] the

Church of Christ, namely the Christian people, will be brought to ruin at the hands of wicked men. And this, alas, for some centuries now we have not failed to see happening somewhere, now in one place, now in another, while the cruel Turks invade some parts of the Christian dominion and other parts are torn asunder by the internal strife of manifold heretical sects.

Whenever we see such things or hear that they are beginning to happen, however far away, let us think that this is no time for us to sit and sleep but rather to get up immediately and bring relief to the danger of others in whatever way we can, by our prayers at least if in no other way. Nor is such danger to be taken lightly because it happens at some distance from us. Certainly if that saying of the comic poet is so highly approved, "Since I am a man, I consider nothing human to be foreign to me,"[194] how could it be anything but disgraceful for Christians to snore while other Christians are in danger? In order to suggest this, Christ directed his warning to watch and pray not only to those he had placed nearby but also to those he had caused to remain at some distance. Then, too, if we are perhaps unmoved by the misfortunes of others because they are at some distance from us, let us at least be moved by our own danger. For we have reason to fear that the destructive force will make its way from them to us, taught as we are by many examples how rapid the rushing force of a blaze can be and how terrible the contagion of a spreading plague. Since, therefore, all human safeguards are useless without the help of God to ward off evils, let us always remember these words from the Gospel and let us always imagine that Christ himself is again addressing to us over and over those words of his: "Why are you sleeping? Get up and pray that you may not enter into temptation."

At this juncture another point occurs to us: that Christ is also betrayed into the hands of sinners when his most holy body in the sacrament is consecrated and handled by unchaste, profligate, and sacrilegious priests. When we see such things happen (and they happen only too often, alas) let us imagine that Christ himself again says to us, "Why are you sleeping? Stay awake, get up, and pray that you may not enter into temptation, for the Son of

188 Mt 26:47; Mk 14:43 **189** See Rom 5:12–21. **190** See Jer 13:11. **191** Ex 22:8–9; Ps 81(82):6; Jn 10:34–35

192 Ps 104(105):15; Mk 9:40; 1 Chr 16:22 **193** 1 Cor 12:27 **194** Here More

quotes Terence (slightly inaccurately) from memory: *Heautontimoroumenos* 77.

Man is betrayed into the hands of sinners." From the example of bad priests the contamination of vice spreads easily among the people. And the less suitable for obtaining grace those persons are whose

5 duty it is to watch and pray for the people, the more necessary it is for the people to stay awake, get up, and pray all the more earnestly for themselves — and not only for themselves but also for priests of this sort. For it will be much to the advantage of the

10 people if bad priests improve.

Finally Christ is betrayed into the hands of sinners in a special way among those of a certain sect: these people, though they receive the venerable sacrament of the Eucharist more frequently and wish

15 to give the impression of honoring it more piously by receiving it under both species (contrary to public custom, without any necessity, but not without a great affront to the Catholic Church), nevertheless these people blaspheme against what they have

20 received under a show of honor, some of them by calling it true bread and true wine, some of them — and this is far worse — by calling it not only true but also mere bread and wine. For they altogether deny that the real body of Christ is contained in the sac-

25 rament, though they call it by that name. When at this late date they set out to do such a thing, against the most open passages of Scripture, against the clearest interpretations of all the saints, against the most constant faith of the whole Church for so

30 many centuries, against the truth most amply witnessed to by so many thousands of miracles — this group that labors under the second kind of infidelity (by far the worse), how little difference is there, I ask you, between them and those who took Christ

35 captive that night? How little difference between them and those troops of Pilate who in jest bent their knees before Christ as if they were honoring him while they insulted him and called him the king of the Jews, just as these people kneel before

40 the Eucharist and call it the body of Christ — which according to their own profession they no more believe than the soldiers of Pilate believed Christ was a king.

Therefore, whenever we hear that such evils have

45 befallen other peoples, no matter how distant, let us immediately imagine that Christ is urgently addressing us: "Why are you sleeping? Get up and pray that you may not enter into temptation." For

the fact is that wherever this plague rages today most fiercely, everyone did not catch the disease in 50 a single day. Rather the contagion spreads gradually and imperceptibly while those persons who despise it at first, afterwards can stand to hear it and respond to it with less than full scorn, then come to tolerate wicked discussions, and afterwards are car- 55 ried away into error, until like a cancer (as the apostle says) the creeping disease finally takes over the whole country.[195] Therefore let us stay awake, get up, and pray continually that all those who have fallen into this miserable folly through the wiles of Satan 60 may quickly come to their senses and that God may never suffer us to enter into this kind of temptation and may never allow the devil to roll the blasts of this storm of his to our shores. But so much for my digression into these mysteries; let us now return to 65 the historical events.

Judas, therefore, when he had received a cohort from the chief priests and servants from the Pharisees, came there with lanterns and torches.[196] And while Jesus was still speaking, behold, Judas Iscariot, one of the 70 twelve, and with him a large crowd with swords and clubs, sent by the chief priests and scribes and elders of the people. The traitor, however, had given them a sign, etc.[197]

I tend to believe that the cohort which, accord- 75 ing to the accounts of the evangelists, was handed over to the traitor by the high priests was a Roman cohort assigned to the high priests by Pilate. To it the Pharisees, scribes, and elders of the people had added their own servants, either because they did 80 not have enough confidence in the governor's soldiers or because they thought extra numbers would help prevent Christ from being rescued through some sudden confusion caused by the darkness, or perhaps for another reason, their desire to arrest at 85 the same time all the apostles, without letting any of them escape in the dark. They were prevented from executing this part of their plan by the power of Christ himself, who was himself captured only because he, and he alone wished to be taken. 90

They carry smoking torches and dim lanterns so that they might be able to discern through the darkness of sin the bright sun of justice,[198] not that they might be enlightened by the light of him who enlightens every man that comes into this world,[199] 95

195 2 Tm 2:17   196 Jn 18:3   197 Mt 26:47–48; Mk 14:43–44   198 Mal 4:2   199 Jn 1:9

but that they might put out that eternal light of his which can never be darkened. And like master like servant, for those who sent them strove to overthrow the law of God for the sake of their traditions. Even now some still follow in their footsteps and persecute Christ by striving mightily to overshadow the splendor of God's glory for the sake of their own glory. But in this passage it is worthwhile to pay close attention to the constant revolutions and vicissitudes of the human condition. For not six days before, even the gentiles had been eager to get a look at Christ, because of his remarkable miracles, together with the great holiness of his life.[200] But the Jews had welcomed him with truly extraordinary reverence as he rode into Jerusalem. But now the Jews, joining forces with the gentiles, come to arrest him like a thief; and not merely among them but at their head was a man worse than all the gentiles and Jews put together, Judas. Thus in his death Christ took care to provide this contrast as a notable warning to all men that no one should expect blind Fortune to stand still for him, and that no Christian especially, as one who hopes for heaven, should pursue the contemptible glory of this world.

The persons responsible for sending the crowd after Christ were priests—and not merely that, but princes of the priests—Pharisees, scribes and elders of the people. Here we see that whatever is best by nature turns out in the end to be the worst, once it begins to reverse its direction. Thus Lucifer, created by God as the most eminent among the angels in heaven, became the worst of the demons after he yielded to the pride which brought his downfall. So too, not the dregs of the crowd but the elders of the people, the scribes, Pharisees, priests, and high priests, the princes of the priests, whose duty it was to see that justice was done and to promote the affairs of God, these were the very ringleaders in a conspiracy to extinguish the sun of justice[201] and to destroy the only begotten Son of God—to such insane extremes of perversity were they driven by avarice, arrogance, and envy.

Another point should not be passed over lightly but should be given careful consideration: Judas, who in many other places is called by the infamous name traitor, is here also disgraced by the lofty title apostle. "Behold," he says, "Judas Iscariot, one of the twelve," Judas Iscariot, who was not one of the unbelieving pagans, not one of the Jewish enemies, not one of Christ's ordinary disciples (and even that would have been incredible enough), but (O the shame of it!) one of Christ's chosen apostles, can bear to hand over his Lord to be captured, and even to be the leader of the captors himself.

There is in this passage a lesson to be learned by all who exercise high public office: when they are addressed with solemn titles, they do not always have reason to be proud and congratulate themselves; rather, such titles are truly fitting only if those who bear them know in their hearts that they have in fact lived up to such honorific names by conscientiously performing their duties. For otherwise, they may very well be overcome with shame (unless they find pleasure in the empty jingle of words), since wicked men in high office—whether they be great men, princes, great lords, emperors, priests, bishops, it makes no difference as long as they are wicked—certainly ought to realize that whenever men titillate their ears by crooning their splendid titles of office, they do not do so sincerely, in order to pay them true honor, but rather to reproach them freely by seeming to praise those honors which they bear in so unpraiseworthy a fashion. So too, in the Gospel, when Judas is celebrated under his title of apostle in the phrase "Judas Iscariot, one of the twelve," the real intent is anything but praise, as is clear from the fact that in the next breath he is called a traitor. "For the traitor," according to the account, "had given them a signal, saying, 'whomever I kiss, that is the one. Seize him.'"[202]

At this point the usual question is why it was necessary for the traitor to give the crowd a signal identifying Jesus. To this some answer that they agreed on a signal because more than once before Christ had suddenly escaped from the hands of those who were trying to apprehend him. But since this usually happened in the daytime, when he was escaping from the hands of those who already recognized him, and since he did it by employing his divine power, either to disappear from their sight or to pass from their midst while they were in a state of shock, against this sort of escape giving a signal to identify him could not be of any use.

And so others say that one of the two James's looked very much like Christ—and for that reason, they think, he was called the brother of Christ[203]—so much so that unless you looked at them closely you could not tell them apart. But since they could have arrested both of them and taken both away with them to be identified later at their leisure by comparing them at close quarters, what need was there to worry about a signal?

The Gospel makes it clear that the night was far advanced, and, although daybreak was drawing near, it was still nighttime and quite dark, as is evident from the torches and lanterns they carried, which gave enough light to make them visible from some distance but hardly enough for them to discern anyone else from afar. And, although on that night they perhaps had the advantage of some faint light from the full moon, it could only have been enough to make out the shapes of bodies in the distance, not to get a good view of facial features and distinguish one person from another. Hence if they went rushing in at random in the hope of capturing all of them at once, each man choosing his victim without knowing who he was, they were afraid, and rightly so, that out of so many some (by all odds) might perhaps get away and that one of the fugitives might well be the very man they had come for. For those who are in the greatest danger are likely to be the quickest to look out for themselves.

Thus, whether they thought of this or whether Judas himself suggested it, they set their trap by having the betrayer go on ahead to single out the Lord by embracing and kissing him. In this way, when they had all fixed their eyes on him alone, each and every one of them could try to get his hands on him. After that, if any of the others got away, it would not be such a dangerous matter.

Therefore the traitor had given them a signal, saying, "Whomever I kiss, that is the one. Seize him and take him away carefully."[204]

O the lengths to which greed will go! Couldn't you be satisfied, you treacherous scoundrel, with betraying your Lord (who had raised you to the lofty office of an apostle) into the hands of impious men by the signal of a kiss, without also being so concerned that he should be taken away carefully, lest he might escape from his captors? You were hired to betray him; others were sent to take him, to guard him, to produce him in court. But you, as if your role in the crime were not important enough, go on

to meddle in the duties of the soldiers; and as if the villainous magistrates who sent them had not given them adequate instructions, there was a need for a circumspect man like you to add your own gratuitous cautions and commands, that they must lead him away carefully once he is captured. Were you afraid that, even though you had fully performed your criminal task by betraying Christ to his assassins, still if the soldiers had somehow been so remiss that Christ escaped through their carelessness or was rescued by force against their will — were you afraid that then your thirty pieces of silver, that illustrious reward of your heinous crime, would not be paid? Have no fear, they will be paid. But believe me, you are no more eager and greedy to get them now than you will be impatient and anxious to throw them away once you have gotten them. Meanwhile you will go on to complete a deed that brings pain to your Lord and death to you, but salvation to many.

He went ahead of them and came up to Jesus to kiss him. And when he had come, he went right up to him and said, "Rabbi, hail Rabbi," and he kissed him. Jesus said to him, "Friend, why have you come?"[205] *"Judas, are you betraying the Son of Man with a kiss?"*[206]

Though Judas really did, as a matter of historical fact, precede the crowd, still this also means in a spiritual sense that among those who share in the same sinful act, the one who has most reason to abstain takes precedence in God's judgment of their guilt.

"And he came up to him to kiss him. And when he had come, he went right up to him and said 'Rabbi, hail Rabbi.' And he kissed him." In this same way Christ is approached, greeted, called "Rabbi," kissed, by those who pretend to be disciples of Christ, professing his teaching in name but striving in fact to undermine it by crafty tricks and stratagems. In just this way Christ is greeted as "Rabbi" by anyone who calls him master and scorns his precepts. In just this way is he kissed by those priests who consecrate the most holy body of Christ and then put to death Christ's members, Christian souls, by their false teaching and wicked example. In just this way is Christ greeted and kissed by those who demand to be considered good and pious because at the persuasion of bad priests, they, though laymen, receive

204 Mk 14:44 **205** Mt 26:49–50; Mk 14:45 **206** Lk 22:48

the sacred body and blood of Christ under both species, without any real need for it, but not without great contempt for the whole Catholic Church and therefore not without grave sin. And this these latter-day saints do against the long-standing practice and custom of all Christians. And not only do they themselves do it (that we could somehow manage to put up with) but they condemn everyone who receives both substances under only one of the two species—that is, apart from themselves, all Christians everywhere for these many years. And still, though they hotly insist that both species are necessary for the laity, most of them—both laymen and priests—eliminate the reality, that is the body and blood, from both species, keeping only the words body and blood. In this respect, indeed, they are not unlike Pilate's guards, who mocked Christ by kneeling before him and saluting him as the king of the Jews. For these men likewise genuflect in veneration of the Eucharist and call it the body and blood of Christ though they no more believe it is the one or the other than the soldiers of Pilate believed Christ was a king.

Now all these groups which I have enumerated certainly bring to our minds the traitor Judas in that they combine a greeting and a kiss with treachery. But just as they renew an action of the past, so Joab (2 Kings 20)[207] once provided a prophetic figure of the future: for "when he had greeted Amasa thus, 'Greetings, my brother,' and had caressed Amasa's chin with his right hand" as if he were about to kiss him, he stealthily unsheathed a hidden sword and killed him with one stroke through his side,[208] and by a similar trick he had formerly killed Abner,[209] but later (as was only right) he justly paid with his life for his heinous deception.[210] Judas rightly calls to mind and represents Joab, whether you consider the status of the persons involved or the deceitful treachery of the crime, or the vengeance of God and the bad end both came to—with this difference, that Judas surpassed Joab in every respect.

Joab enjoyed great favor and influence with his prince; Judas had even more with an even greater prince. Joab killed Amasa who was his friend; Judas killed Jesus who was an even closer friend, not to say also his Lord. Joab was motivated by envy and ambition because he had heard that the king would promote Amasa above him;[211] but Judas, enticed by greed for a miserable reward, for a few pieces of silver, betrayed the Lord of the world to his death. In the same degree, therefore, as Judas' crime was worse, the vengeance exacted from him was the more devastating. For Joab was killed by another, but the most wretched Judas hanged himself with his own hand.

But in the treacherous pattern of their deception, there is a nice equivalence between the crimes of Joab and Judas. For just as Joab kills Amasa in the very act of courteously greeting him and preparing to kiss him, so too Judas approaches Christ affably, greets him reverently, kisses him lovingly and all the time the villainous wretch had nothing else in mind than to betray his Lord to his death. But Joab was able to deceive Amasa by flattery; not so Judas with Christ. He receives his advances, listens to his greeting, does not refuse his kiss, and, though aware of his abominable treachery, he nevertheless acted for a while as if he were completely ignorant of everything. Why did he do this? Was it to teach us to feign and dissemble, and with polite cunning to turn the deception back upon the deceiver? Hardly, but rather to teach us to bear patiently and gently all injuries and snares treacherously set for us, not to smolder with anger, not to seek revenge, not to give vent to our feelings by hurling back insults, not to find an empty pleasure in tripping up an enemy through some clever trick, but rather to set ourselves against deceitful injury with genuine courage, to conquer evil with good[212]—in fine, to make every effort by words both gentle and harsh, to insist both in season and out of season,[213] that the wicked may change their ways to good, so that if anyone should be suffering from a disease that does not respond to treatment, he may not blame the failure on our negligence but rather attribute it to the virulence of his own disease. And so Christ as a most conscientious physician tries both ways of effecting a cure. Employing first of all gentle words, he says, "Friend, why have you come?"

When he heard himself called "friend," the traitor was left hanging in doubt. For, since he was aware of his own crime, he was afraid that Christ used the title "friend" as a severe rebuke for his hostile unfriendliness. On the other hand, since criminals always flatter themselves with the hope that their crimes are unknown, he was blind and mad

---

207 i.e., 2 Sm 20　**208** 2 Sm 20:8–10　**209** 2 Sm 3:26–30　**210** 1 Kgs 2:28–35　**211** 2 Sm 19:13　**212** Rom 12:21　**213** See Tm 4:2.

enough to hope (even though he had often learned by personal experience that the thoughts of men lay open to Christ[214] and though his own treachery had been touched upon at the [last] supper),[215] nevertheless, I say, he was so demented and oblivious to everything as to hope that his villainous deed had escaped Christ's notice.

But because nothing could be more unwholesome for him than to be duped by such a futile hope (for nothing could work more strongly against his repentance than this), Christ in his goodness no longer allows him to be led on by a deceptive hope of deceiving but immediately adds in a grave tone, "Judas do you betray the Son of Man with a kiss?" He addresses him by the name he had ordinarily used—and for this reason, so that the memory of their old friendship might soften the heart of the traitor and move him to repent. He openly rebukes his treachery lest he should believe it is hidden and be ashamed to confess it. Moreover, he reviles the impious hypocrisy of the traitor: "With a kiss," he says, "do you betray the Son of Man?"

Among all the circumstances of a wicked deed it is not easy to find one more hateful to God than the perversion of the real nature of good things to make them into the instruments of our malice. Thus lying is hateful to God because words, which are ordained to express the meaning of the mind, are twisted to other deceitful purposes. Within this category of evil, it is a serious offense against God if anyone abuses the law to inflict the very injuries it was designed to prevent. And so Christ reproaches Judas sharply for this detestable kind of sin: "Judas," he says, "do you betray the Son of Man with a kiss? Either Judas, with betraying the Son of Man—indeed, I say, the son of that man through whom all men would have perished if this son of man, whom you imagine you are destroying, had not redeemed those who wish to be saved—was it not enough for you, I say, to betray this son of man without doing it with a kiss, thus turning the most sacred sign of charity into an instrument of betrayal? Certainly I am more favorably disposed toward this mob which attacks me with open force than toward you, Judas, who betray me to the attackers with a false kiss."

And so when Christ saw no sign of repentance in the traitor, wishing to show how much more willing he was to speak with open enemies than with a secret foe, having made it clear to the traitor that he cared not a whit for all his wicked stratagems, he immediately turned away from him and made his way, unarmed as he was, toward the armed crowd. For so the Gospel says: "And then Jesus, knowing everything that was to happen to him, went forward and said to them, 'whom do you seek?' They replied to him, 'Jesus of Nazareth.' Jesus said to them, 'I am he.' Now Judas, who betrayed him, was also standing with them. When therefore, he said to them, 'I am he,' they drew back and fell to the ground."[216]

O saving Christ, only a little while ago, you were so fearful that you lay face down in a most pitiable attitude and sweat blood as you begged your father to take away the chalice of your Passion. How is it that now, by a sudden reversal, you leap up and spring forth like a giant running his race[217] and come forward eagerly to meet those who seek to inflict that Passion upon you? How is it that you freely identify yourself to those who openly admit they are seeking you but who do not know that you are the one they are seeking? Hither, hither let all hasten who are faint of heart. Here let them take firm hold of an unwavering hope when they feel themselves struck by a horror of death. For just as they share Christ's agony, his fear, grief, anxiety, sadness, and sweat (provided that they pray, and persist in prayer, and submit themselves wholeheartedly to the will of God), they will also share this consolation, undoubtedly they will feel themselves helped by such consolation as Christ felt; and they will be so refreshed by the spirit of Christ that they will feel their hearts renewed as the old face of the earth is renewed by the dew from heaven,[218] and by means of the wood of Christ's cross let down into the water of their sorrow, the thought of death, once so bitter, will grow sweet,[219] eagerness will take the place of grief, mental strength and courage will replace dread, and finally they will long for the death they had viewed with horror, considering life a sad thing and death a gain, desiring to be dissolved and to be with Christ.[220]

"And so Christ coming up close to the crowd asks, 'whom do you seek?' They replied to him, 'Jesus of Nazareth.' Now Judas, who betrayed him, was standing with them. And Jesus said to them, 'I am

214 See Mt 9:4; 12:25.   **215** Mt 26:21-25   **218** Ps 103(104):5; Ex 16:13-14;   **219** See Ex 15:23-25.   **220** Phil 1:21-23
216 Jn 18:4-6   **217** See Ps 18:6(19:5).   Ps 132(133):3; Prv 19:12; Mi 5:7

he.' When, therefore, Jesus said to them, 'I am he,' they drew back and fell to the ground." If Christ's previous fear and anxiety lessened his standing in anyone's mind, the balance must now be redressed by the manly courage with which he fearlessly approaches that whole mass of armed men and, though he faces certain death ("for he knew everything which was to happen to him"),[221] betrays himself by his own act to those villains, who did not even know who he was, and thus offers himself freely as a victim to be cruelly slaughtered.

Certainly this sudden and drastic change would rightly be considered marvelous viewed simply as occurring in his venerable human nature. But what sort of estimate of him, how intense a reaction to him must be produced in the hearts of all the faithful by the force of divine power flashing so wonderfully through the weak body of a man? For how was it that none of his pursuers recognized him when he came up close to them? He had taught in the Temple, he had overturned the tables of the moneychangers, he had driven out the moneychangers themselves,[222] he had carried out his activities in public, he had confuted the Pharisees,[223] he had satisfied the sadducees,[224] he had refuted the scribes,[225] he eluded by a prudent answer the trick-question of the Herodian soldiers,[226] he had fed seven thousand men with five loaves,[227] he had healed the sick, raised the dead, made himself available to all sorts of men, Pharisees, tax-gatherers, the rich, the poor, just men, sinners, Jews, Samaritans, and gentiles, and now in this whole large crowd there was no one who recognized him by his face or voice as he addressed them near at hand, as if those who sent them had taken special care not to send anyone along who had ever seen beforehand the person they were then seeking.

Had no one even singled out Christ from his meeting with Judas, from the embrace and the sign Judas gave with a kiss? Even more, the traitor himself, who was at that time standing together with them, did he suddenly forget how to recognize the very person he had just betrayed by singling him out with a kiss? What was the source of this strange happening? Indeed, no one was able to recognize him for the very same reason that a little later Mary Magdalene, though she saw him, did not recognize

him until he revealed himself, and likewise neither one of the two disciples, though they were talking with him, knew who he was until he let them know, but rather the two disciples thought that he was a traveler and she thought he was a gardener.[228] Finally, then, if you want to know how it was that no one could recognize him when he came up to them, you should undoubtedly attribute it to the same cause you use to explain the fact that when he spoke no one could remain standing. "But when Jesus said, 'I am he,' they drew back and fell to the ground."

Here Christ proved that he truly is that word of God which pierces more sharply than any two-edged sword.[229] Thus a lightning bolt is said to be of such a nature that it liquefies a sword without damaging the sheath.[230] Certainly the mere voice of Christ, without damaging their bodies, so melted their souls that it deprived them of the strength to hold up their limbs.

Here the evangelist relates that Judas was standing together with them. For when he heard Jesus rebuke him openly as a traitor, whether overcome with shame or struck with fear (for he was acquainted with Peter's impulsiveness), he immediately withdrew and returned to his own kind. Thus the evangelist tells us he was standing together with them so that we may understand that like them he also fell down. And certainly the character of Judas was such that there was in that whole crowd no one worse or more worthy of being cast down. But the evangelist wished to impress upon everyone generally that they must be careful and cautious about the company they keep, for there is a danger that if they take their place with wicked men they will also fall together with them. It rarely happens that a person who is foolish enough to cast his lot with those who are headed for shipwreck in an unseaworthy vessel gets back to land alive after the others have drowned in the sea.

No one, I suppose, doubts that a person who could throw them all down with one word could easily have dashed them all down so forcibly that none of them could have gotten back up again. But Christ, who struck them down to let them know that they could inflict no suffering upon him

---

221 Jn 18:4   **222** Mk 11:15   **223** See Jn 8:21–47.   **224** Mk 2:6–12   **225** Mt 22:23–33   **226** See Mt 14:16–21; Mk 6:38–44; Lk 9:13–17; Jn 6:8–13.   **227** Mt 22:15–22   **228** See Jn 20:14–16; Lk 24:16–31.   **229** Heb 4:12   **230** See Seneca, *Naturales quaestiones* 2.31.

against his will, allowed them to get up again so that they could accomplish what he wished to endure. "And so, when they had gotten up, he asked them once more, 'whom do you seek?' And they said to him, 'Jesus of Nazareth.'"[231]

Here, too, anyone can see that they were so daunted, stunned and stupefied by their meeting with Christ that they seem almost to be out of their minds. For they might very well have known that at that time of night and in that place they would not find anyone who was not one of Christ's band of followers or else a friend of his and that the last thing in the world such a person would do would be to lead them to Christ. And yet, suddenly meeting a person whose identity was unknown to them as well as the reason for his question, right away they foolishly blurt out the heart of the whole affair, which they ought to have kept carefully concealed until they had carried it out. For as soon as he asked, "'Whom do you seek?' they replied, 'Jesus of Nazareth.' Jesus answered, 'I have told you I am he. If, therefore, you seek me, let these men go their way'"[232]—as if to say: If you are looking for me, now that I have approached you and let you know who I am by my own admission, why do you not arrest me on the spot? Surely the reason is that you are so far from being able to take me against my will that you cannot even remain standing at my mere words, as you have just learned by falling backwards. But now, if you have forgotten it so quickly, I again remind you that I am Jesus of Nazareth. "If, therefore, you seek me, let these men go their way."

By throwing them down, Christ made it very clear, I think, that his words "Let these men go their way" did not constitute a request. But sometimes it happens that those who are planning some great piece of villainy are not content with the bare crime alone but with perverse wantonness make a practice of adding certain trimmings, as it were, beyond what is required by the scope of the crime itself. Moreover, there are some ministers of crime who are so preposterously faithful that, to avoid the risk of omitting any evil deed that has been entrusted to them, they will add something extra on their own for good measure. Christ implicitly refers to each of these two types: "If you seek me," he says, "let these go their way." If my blood is what the chief priests, the scribes, Pharisees, and the elders of the people

are longing to drain away with such an eager thirst, behold, when you were seeking me I came to meet you; when you did not know me, I betrayed myself to you; when you were prostrate, I stood nearby; now that you are arising, I stand ready to be taken captive; and finally I myself hand myself over to you (which the traitor was not able to do) to keep my followers and you from imagining (as if it were not crime enough to kill me) that their blood must be added over and above mine. Therefore, "if you seek me, let these men go their way."

He commanded them to let them go, but he also forced them to do so against their will, and by seeing to it that all were saved by flight he frustrated their efforts to capture them. An indication of this outcome was what he intended by this prophetic statement of his—Let these men go their way—so that those words he had spoken might be fulfilled: "Of those you have given me, I have not lost anyone."[233] The words of Christ which the evangelist is talking about here are those words he spoke to his Father that same night at supper: "Holy Father, preserve in your name those whom you have given to me."[234] And afterwards: "I have guarded those whom you gave to me, and none of them has perished except the son of perdition, that the Scripture might be fulfilled."[235] See how Christ here, as he foretells that the disciples will be saved when he is taken captive, declares that he is their guardian. Hence the evangelist recalls this to the minds of his readers, wishing them to understand that, in spite of his words to the crowd—Let these men go their way—he himself by his hidden power had opened up a way for their escape.

The place in Scripture which predicts that Judas would perish is in Psalm 108[109], where the psalmist prophesies in the form of a prayer: "May his days be few and may another take over his ministry."[236] Although these prophetic words were spoken about the traitor Judas such a long time before the event, nevertheless it would be hard to say whether anyone, apart from the psalmist himself, knew that they referred to Judas until Christ made this clear and the event itself bore out the words. Even the prophets themselves did not see everything foreseen by other prophets. For the spirit of prophecy is measured out individually.[237] Certainly it seems clear to me that no one understands the

231 Jn 18:7   **232** Jn 18:8   **233** Jn 18:9   **234** Jn 17:11   **235** Jn 17:12   **236** Ps 108(109):8   **237** See Eph 4:7.

meaning of all scriptural passages so well that there are not many mysteries hidden there which are not yet understood, whether concerning the times of the Antichrist or the last judgment by Christ, and which will remain unknown until Elijah returns to explain them.[238] Therefore it seems to me that I can justly apply the apostle's exclamation about God's wisdom to Holy Scripture (in which God has hidden and laid up the vast stores of his wisdom): "O the depth of the riches of the wisdom and knowledge of God! How incomprehensible are his judgments and how unsearchable his ways!"[239]

And nevertheless nowadays, first in one place, then in another, there are springing up from day to day, almost like swarms of wasps or hornets, people who boast that they are "autodidacts" (to use Saint Jerome's word) and that, without the commentaries of the old doctors, they find clear, open, and easy all those things which all the ancient fathers confessed they found quite difficult — and the fathers were men of no less talent or training, of tireless energy, and as for that "spirit" which these moderns have as often on their lips as they do rarely in their hearts, here the fathers surpassed them no less than in holiness of life. But now these modern men, who have sprouted up overnight as theologians professing to know everything, not only disagree about the meaning of Scripture with all those men who led such heavenly lives, but also fail to agree among themselves concerning great dogmas of the Christian faith. Rather, each of them, whoever he may be, insisting that he sees the truth, conquers the rest and is in turn conquered by them. But they all are alike in opposing the catholic faith and all are alike in being conquered by it. He who dwells in the heavens laughs to scorn these wicked and vain attempts of theirs.[240] But I humbly pray that he may not so laugh them to scorn as to laugh also at their eternal ruination, but rather that he may inspire in them the health-giving grace of repentance so that these prodigal sons[241] who have wandered so long, alas, in exile may retrace their steps to the bosom of Mother Church and so that all of us together, united in the true faith of Christ and joined in mutual charity as true members of Christ, may attain to the glory of Christ our head,[242] which no one should ever be foolish enough to hope to arrive at

outside the body of Christ and without the true faith.

But, to return to what I was saying, the fact that this prophetic utterance applies to Judas was suggested by Christ,[243] was made clear by Judas' suicide, was afterwards made quite explicit by Peter,[244] and was fulfilled by all the apostles when Matthias was chosen by lot to take his place[245] and, thus, another took over his ministry. And to make the matter even clearer, after Matthias took Judas' place, no replacement was ever taken into that group of twelve (although bishops succeed in the place of the apostles in an uninterrupted line), but rather, as the apostleship was transmitted gradually to more persons, that sacred number came to an end once the prophecy had been fulfilled.

Therefore, when Christ said, "Let these men go their way," he was not begging for their permission, but rather declaring in veiled terms that he himself granted his disciples the power to leave, that he might fulfill those words he had spoken: "Father, I have guarded those whom you gave to me, and none of them has perished except the son of perdition."[246] I think it worthwhile to consider here for a moment how strongly Christ foretold in these words the contrast between the end of Judas and the end of the rest, the ruination of the traitor Judas and the success of the others. For he asserts each future outcome with such certainty that he announces them not as future happenings but as events that have already definitely taken place. "I have guarded," he says, "those whom you gave to me." They were not defended by their own strength, nor were they preserved by the mercy of the Jews, nor did they escape through the carelessness of the cohort, but rather "I guarded them. And none of them perished except the son of perdition." For he, too, Father, was among those whom you gave to me. Chosen by me, he received me, and to him as well as to the rest who received me I had given the power to become a son of God.[247] But when in his insane greed he went over to Satan, leaving me, betraying me treacherously, refusing to be saved, then he became a son of destruction in the very act of pursuing my destruction, and perished like a wretch in his wretchedness.

Infallibly certain about the fate of the traitor,

238 Mal 3:23   **239** Rom 11:33   **240** Ps   4:1–6.   **243** Jn 17:12   **244** Acts 1:20   **247** See Jn 1:12.
2:4   **241** See Lk 15:11–32.   **242** See Eph   **245** Acts 1:26   **246** Jn 17:12

Christ expresses his future ruin with such certainty that he asserts it as if it had already come to pass. And for all that, as Christ is being arrested, the unhappy traitor stands there as the ferocious leader and standard-bearer of Christ's captors, rejoicing and exulting, I imagine, in the danger of his fellow disciples and his master, for I am convinced he desired and hoped that all of them would be arrested and put to death. The raving madness and perversity of ingratitude manifests itself in this peculiarity: the ingrate desires the death of the very victim he has unjustly injured. So too, the person whose conscience is full of guilty sores is so sensitive that he views even the face of his victim as a reproach and shrinks from it with dread. Thus as the traitor rejoiced in the hope that all of them would be captured together, he was so stupidly sure of himself that nothing was further from his mind than the thought that the death sentence passed on him by God was hanging over his head like a dreadful noose ready to fall around his neck at any moment.

In this connection I am struck by the lamentable obscurity of the miserable human condition: often we are distressed and fearful, ignorant all the while that we are quite safe; often, on the other hand, we act as if we had not a care in the world, unaware that the death-dealing sword hangs over our heads. The other apostles were afraid they would be seized together with Christ and put to death, whereas actually they were all to escape. Judas, who had no fears for himself and took pleasure in their fears, perished only a few hours later. Cruel is the appetite which feeds on the misery of others. Nor is there any reason why a person should rejoice and congratulate himself on his good fortune because he has it in his power to cause another man's death, as the traitor thought he had by means of the cohort that had been delivered to him. For though a man may send someone else to his death, he himself is sure to follow him there. Even more, since the hour of death is uncertain, he himself may precede the very person he arrogantly imagines he has sent to death ahead of him.

Thus the death of the wretched Judas preceded that of Christ, whom he had betrayed to his death—a sad and terrible example to the whole world that the wrongdoer, however he may flout his arrogant impenitence, ought not to think he is safe from retribution. For against the wicked all creatures work together in harmony with their Creator.[248] The air longs to blow noxious vapors against the wicked man, the sea longs to overwhelm him in its waves, the mountains to fall upon him, the valleys to rise up against him, the earth to split open beneath him, hell to swallow him up after his headlong fall, the demons to plunge him into gulfs of ever-burning flames. All the while the only one who preserves the wretch is the God whom he deserted.

But if anyone is such a persistent imitator of Judas that God finally decides not to offer any longer the grace which has been offered and refused so often, this man is really and truly wretched: however he may flatter himself in the delusion that he is floating high in the air on the wings of felicity, he is actually wallowing in the utter depths of misery and calamity. Therefore let each of us pray to the most merciful Christ, each praying not only for himself but also for others, that we may not imitate Judas in his stubbornness but rather may eagerly accept the grace God offers us and may be restored once more to glory through penance and mercy.

THE SEVERING OF MALCHUS'S EAR, THE FLIGHT OF THE APOSTLES, AND THE CAPTURE OF CHRIST

The Severing of Malchus's Ear

The apostles had previously heard Christ foretelling the very things they were now seeing happen.[249] On that occasion, though they were saddened and grieved, they treated the matter with much less concern than now when they see it happening before their very eyes. Now that they see the whole cohort standing there and openly admitting that they are seeking Jesus of Nazareth, there is no more room for doubt that they are seeking him to take him captive.

When the apostles saw what was about to happen, their minds were overwhelmed by a sudden welter of different feelings: anxiety for their Lord whom they loved, fear for their own safety, and finally shame for that high-sounding promise[250] of theirs that they would all rather die than fail their master. Thus their impulses were divided between conflicting feelings. Their love of their master urged them not to flee; their fear for themselves, not to

---

248 Wis 5:21–24; 16:16–17; Cicero, *De finibus* 1.16.50–51   **249** Mt 16:21; Jn 16:6, 22   **250** Mt 26:33–35

remain. Fear of death impelled them to run away; shame for their promise, to stand fast.

Moreover, they remembered what Christ had said to them that very night: he told them that, whereas before he had forbidden any of them to carry so much as a staff to defend himself with,[251] now whoever did not have a sword should even sell his tunic to buy one.[252] Now they were struck with great fear as they saw massed against them the Roman cohort and the crowd of Jews, all of them armed with weapons, whereas there were only eleven of them, and even of those none had any weapons (apart perhaps from table-knives) except two who had swords. Nevertheless, they remembered that when they had said to Christ, "Look, here are two swords," he had replied, "That is enough."[253] Not understanding the great mystery contained in this reply, they suddenly and impulsively ask him whether he wants them to defend him with the sword, saying, "Lord, shall we strike with the sword?"[254]

But Peter's feelings boiled over so that he did not wait for a reply, but drew his sword, struck a blow at the servant of the high priest, and cut off his right ear — perhaps simply because this man happened to be standing near to Peter, perhaps because his fierce and haughty bearing made him conspicuous among the rest. At any rate he certainly seems to have been a notoriously wicked man, for the evangelists mention that he was the servant of the high priest, the chief and prince of all the priests. "The greater the house, the prouder the servants,"[255] as the satirist says, and men know from experience that everywhere in the world the servants of great lords are more arrogant and overbearing than their masters. That we might know that this man had some standing with the high priest and was for that reason all the more egregiously proud, John immediately adds his name. "The servant's name," he says, "was Malchus."[256] The evangelist does not ordinarily provide such information everywhere or without some special reason.

I imagine that this rascal, displaying such fierceness as he thrust himself forward, irked Peter, who chose this enemy to open the fight and who would have pressed the attack vigorously if Christ had not checked his course. For Christ immediately forbad the others to fight, declared Peter's zeal ineffectual,

and restored the ear of this miserable creature. These things he did because he came to suffer death, not to escape it; and even if he had not come to die, he would not have needed such assistance. To make this more manifest, he first gave his reply to the question put by the other apostles: "Let them go this far."[257] Still give them leave for a while. For I cast them all down with a mere word, and yet even I, as you see, allowed them to get up so that for the present they may accomplish whatever they wish. Since, then, I allow them to go so far, you must do the same. The time will shortly come when I will no longer allow them any power against me. Even now, in the meantime, I do not need your help.

Thus to the others he answered only, "Let them go this far." But turning to Peter separately, he said, "Put your sword away"[258] — as if to say, "I do not wish to be defended with the sword, and I have chosen you for the mission of fighting not with such a sword but with the sword of the word of God.[259] Therefore return the sword of iron to the sheath where it belongs — that is, to the hands of worldly princes to be used against evildoers. You who are the apostles of my flock have yet another sword far more terrible than any sword of iron, a sword by which a wicked man is sometimes cut off from the Church (like a rotten limb[260] removed from my mystical body) and handed over to Satan for the destruction of the flesh to save the spirit[261] (provided only that the man is of a mind to be healed) and to enable him once more to be joined and grafted into my body — though it sometimes happens that a man suffering from a hopeless disease is also handed over to the invisible death of the soul, lest he should infect the healthy members with his disease. But I am so far from wishing you to make use of that sword of iron (whose proper sheath, you must recognize, is the secular magistrate) that I do not think even that spiritual sword, whose use properly pertains to you, should be unsheathed very often. Rather, wield with vigor the sword of the word,[262] whose stroke, like that of a scalpel, lets the pus out and heals by wounding. As for that other heavy and dangerous sword of excommunication, I desire that it be kept hidden in the sheath of mercy unless some urgent and fearful necessity requires that it be withdrawn."

In answering the other apostles Christ contented

himself with three words, because they were more temperate, or perhaps merely more tepid, than Peter; but Peter's fiery and wild assault he controlled and checked at greater length. He not only ordered him to put up his sword, but also added the reason why he did not approve of his zeal, however pious. "Do you not wish me," he said, "to drink the chalice my Father gave me?"[263] Some time ago Christ had predicted to the apostles that "it would be necessary for him to go to Jerusalem and to suffer many things from the elders and scribes and princes of the priests, and to be killed and to rise on the third day. And taking him aside, Peter began to chide him, saying, 'Far be it from you, O Lord. This will not happen to you.' Christ turned and said to Peter, 'Get thee behind me, Satan, for you do not understand the things of God.'"[264] Notice how severely Christ here rebuked Peter.

Shortly before, when Peter had professed that Christ was the Son of God, Christ had said to him, "Blessed are you, Simon bar Jona, for flesh and blood have not revealed this to you, but rather my Father who is in heaven. And I say to you that you are Peter and upon this rock I will build my Church, and the gates of hell shall not prevail against it. And to you I will give the keys of heaven, and whatever you bind on earth will also be bound in heaven, etc."[265] But here he almost rejects this same Peter and thrusts him behind him and declares that he is a stumbling block to him and calls him Satan and asserts that he does not understand the things of God but rather those of men. And why does he do all this? Because Peter tried to persuade him not to die. Then he showed that it was necessary for him to follow through to his death, which was irrevocably decreed for him by his own will; and hence not only did he not want them to hinder his death, he even wanted them to follow him along the same road. "If anyone wishes to come after me," he said, "let him deny himself and take up his cross and follow me."[266] Not satisfied even with this, he went on to show that if anyone refuses to follow him on the road to death when the case requires it, he does not avoid death, but incurs a much worse death; on the other hand, whoever gives up his life does not lose it but exchanges it for a more vital life.[267] "Whoever wishes to save his life," he says, "will lose it. But whoever loses his life for my sake will find it. For what does it profit a man if he gain the whole world but suffer the loss of his own soul? Or what will a man give in exchange for his soul? For the Son of Man is to come with his angels in the glory of his Father, and then he will render to everyone according to his deeds."[268]

Perhaps I have devoted more time to this passage[269] than was necessary. But I ask you, who would not be led beyond the pale, as they say, by these words of Christ, so severe and threatening but also so effective in creating hope of eternal life? But the relevance of these words to the passage under discussion is this: here we see Peter earnestly admonished not to be misled by his zeal into further hindering the death of Christ. And yet see now how Peter is again carried away by this same zeal to oppose Christ's death, except that this time he does not limit himself to verbal dissuasion but tries to ward it off by fierce fighting. Still, because Peter meant well when he did what he did, and also because Christ bore himself with humility toward everyone as he drew near to his Passion, Christ chose not to reprove Peter sharply. Rather, he first rebuked him by giving a reason, then he declared Peter's act to be sinful, and finally he announced that even if he wished to avoid death he would not need Peter's protection or any other mortal assistance, since if he wished help he had only to ask his Father, who would not fail to aid him in his danger by sending a mighty and invincible array of angels against these puny mortals who were coming to take him captive.

First of all, then, as I said, he checks Peter's zeal to strike out by presenting a rational argument. He says, "Do you not wish me to drink the chalice which my Father gave me?" My whole life up to this point has been a pattern of obedience and a model of humility. What lessons have I taught more frequently or more forcefully than that magistrates ought to be obeyed,[270] that parents should be honored,[271] that what is Caesar's should be rendered to Caesar, what is God's to God.[272] And now, when I ought to be applying the finishing touches to bring my work to full perfection, now can you wish that I should refuse the chalice extended to me by my

263 Jn 18:11   **264** Mt 16:21–23   **265** Mt 16:17–19   **266** Mt 16:24   **267** See Cicero, *De amicitia* 6.22.   **268** Mt 16:25–27   **269** Mt 16:13–27   **270** See Rom 13:4–7; 1 Pt 2:17.   **271** See Ex 20:12; Eph 6:1; Col 3:20.   **272** Mt 22:21; Mk 12:17; Lk 20:25

Father, that the Son of Man should disobey God the Father, and thus unravel in a single moment all of that most beautiful fabric I have spent such a long time weaving?

Then he teaches Peter that he committed a sin by striking with the sword, and this he does by a parallel from the civil law. "For everyone who takes up the sword," he says, "will perish by the sword."[273] According to the Roman law, which also applied to the Jews at that time, any person discovered wearing a sword without legitimate authority for the purpose of killing a man was placed in almost the same category as the man who had killed his victim.[274] Naturally, therefore, a person who not only wore a sword but also drew it and struck a blow was in even greater legal jeopardy. Nor do I think that Peter, in that moment of confusion and alarm, was so self-possessed that he deliberately avoided hitting Malchus' head and aimed only at his ear, so as merely to frighten him but not kill him.

But if someone should perhaps maintain that everyone has the right to use even force in order to protect an innocent person from criminal assault, this objection would require a longer discussion than I could conveniently introduce in this place. This much is certain: however much Peter's offense was mitigated by his loyal affection for Christ, nevertheless, his lack of any legitimate authority to fight is made quite clear by the fact that on a previous occasion Christ had sharply warned him not to try to prevent his Passion and death, not even by verbal dissuasion, much less by actual fighting.

Next he checks Peter's attack by making another point: Peter's protection is quite unnecessary. "Do you not know," he says, "that I could ask my Father for help and he would immediately deliver to me more than twelve legions of angels?"[275]

About his own power he says nothing, but glories that he enjoys the favor of his Father. For as he drew near to his death, he wished to avoid lofty statements about himself or any assertion that his own power was equal to that of the Father. Rather, wishing to make it clear that he had no need of help from Peter or any other mortal, he declares that the assistance of the heavenly angels (if he chose to ask for it) would immediately be at hand, sent by his omnipotent Father. "Do you not know," he says, "that I could ask my Father for help and he would

immediately deliver to me more than twelve legions of angels?"—as if to say: You have just seen before your very eyes how I threw down, with a mere word, without even touching them, this whole crowd, such a large crowd that it would be sheer folly for you to think you are strong enough to defend me against them. If that could not convince you that I do not need your help, consider at least whose son you proclaimed me to be when I put the question "Who do you say I am?" and you immediately gave that heaven-inspired reply, "You are Christ, the son of the living God."[276] Therefore, since you know from God's own revelation that I am the Son of God, and since you must know that mortal parents do not fail their children, do you imagine that, if I were not going to my death of my own free will, my heavenly Father would choose to fail me? Do you not know that, if I chose to ask him, he would deliver to me more than twelve legions of angels, and that he would do so forthwith, without hesitation or delay? Against so many legions of angels, what resistance could be offered by this miserable cohort of puny mortals? Ten times twelve legions of creatures such as these would not dare even to look upon the angry frown of a single angel.

Then Christ returns to his first point, as the one closest to the central issue. "How, then," he says, "will the Scriptures be fulfilled that say this is the way it must be?"[277]

The Scriptures are full of prophecies concerning Christ's death, full of the mysteries of his Passion and of mankind's redemption which would not have happened without that Passion. Therefore, lest Peter or anyone else should mutter under his breath, "If you can obtain so many legions from your Father, Christ, why don't you ask for them?"—to counter this, Christ says, "How, then, will the Scriptures be fulfilled that say this is the way it must be?" Since you understand from the Scriptures that this is the only way chosen by the most just wisdom of God to restore the human race to its lost glory, if I should now successfully implore my Father to save me from death, what would I be doing but striving to undo the very thing I came to do? To call down from heaven angels to defend me, what effect would that have but precisely to exclude from heaven the whole human race, which I come to redeem and restore to the glory of heaven? With your sword,

---

273 Mt 26:52   **274** *Corpus juris civilis, digesta* 48.8.1   **275** Mt 26:53   **276** Mt 16:15–17   **277** Mt 26:54

therefore, you are not fighting against the wicked Jews but rather attacking the whole human race, inasmuch as you are setting yourself against the fulfillment of the Scriptures and desiring me not to drink the chalice given to me by my Father, that chalice by which I myself (unstained and undefiled) will wipe away that defiling stain of fallen nature.

But now behold the most gentle heart of Christ, who did not think it enough to check Peter's strokes but also touched the severed ear of his persecutor and made it sound again, in order to give us an example of rendering good for evil.

No one's body, I think, is so fully pervaded by his soul as the letter of Holy Scripture is pervaded by spiritual mysteries. Indeed, just as one cannot touch any part of the body in which the soul does not reside, providing life and sensation to even the smallest part, so too no factual account in all of Scripture is so gross and corporeal (so to speak) that it does not have life and breath from some spiritual mystery. Therefore, in considering how Malchus' ear was cut off by Peter's sword and restored by the hand of Christ, we should not feel bound to consider only the facts of the account, though even these can teach us salutary lessons, but let us look further for the saving mystery of the spirit veiled beneath the letter of the story.

Thus Malchus, whose name is the Hebrew word for "king," can appropriately be taken as a figure of reason. For in man reason ought to reign like a king, and it does truly reign when it makes itself loyally subject to faith and serves God. For to serve him is to reign. The high priest, on the other hand, together with his priests, with the Pharisees, scribes, and elders of the people, was given over to perverse superstitions, which he mixed into the law of God, and he used piety as a pretext to oppose piety and sought eagerly to eliminate the founder of true religion. Hence he together with his accomplices may rightly be taken to represent wicked heresiarchs, the chief priests of pernicious superstition, together with their followers.

And so whenever the rational mind rebels against the true faith of Christ and devotes itself to heresies, it becomes a fugitive from Christ and a servant of the heresiarch whom it follows, led astray by the devil and wandering down the byways of error.

Keeping, therefore, its left ear, with which it listens to sinister heresies, it loses its right ear, with which it ought to listen to the true faith. But this does not always happen from the same motivation or with the same effect. For some minds turn to heresies out of determined malice. Then the ear is not cut off by a swift stroke but rots slowly and gradually as the devil infuses his venom, until finally the purulent parts harden and block the passages with a clot so that nothing good can penetrate within. Such persons, alas, are hardly ever restored to health. For the parts eaten away by the ravaging cancer are completely gone and there is nothing left which can be put back in place.

But the ear cut off by a sudden stroke and sent whirling in one piece to the ground because of imprudent zeal, stands for those who turn from the truth to a false appearance of the truth because they are overcome by a sudden impulse; or it also represents those who are deceived by a well-meaning zeal, concerning whom Christ says, "The time will come when everyone who [kills you will think he is][278] performing a service for God."[279] Of this kind of person the apostle Paul was a typical figure.[280] Some of these, because their minds are confused by earthly feelings, allow the ear which has been cut off from heavenly doctrine to remain lying on the earth. But Christ often takes pity on the misery of such persons and with his own hand picks up from the earth the ear which has been cut off by a sudden impulse or by ill considered zeal and with his touch fastens it to the head again and makes it once more capable of listening to true doctrine. I know that the ancient fathers elicited various mysteries from this one passage, as each one, aided by the grace of the Holy Spirit, made his own particular discovery. But it is no part of my plan to review them all here because to do so would make too long an interruption in the account of the historical events.

But Jesus said to those princes of the priests and magistrates of the Temple and elders who had come, "You have come out with swords and clubs to seize me as if I were a robber, though I was with you every day in the Temple, and I sat teaching there and you did not detain me—you made no move to lay hands on me. But this is your hour and the power of darkness."[281]

---

278 Here More leaves a space and puts "etc."   **279** Jn 16:2   **280** Acts 9:1–2   **281** Lk 22:52–53; Mt 26:55; Mk 14:48–49

Christ said this to those princes of the priests and magistrates of the Temple and elders who had come. But here some readers are puzzled because the evangelist Luke reports that Jesus said these
5 things to the princes of the priests and the magistrates of the Temple and the elders of the people, while the other evangelists write in their accounts that these persons did not come themselves but sent the cohort and their servants.

10 Some solve the problem by saying that Jesus may indeed be said to have spoken to these persons because he spoke to those whom they had sent. In this sense princes ordinarily speak to one another through their ambassadors, and private persons ev-
15 erywhere speak to each other through messengers. Thus whatever we tell a servant who has been sent to us, we say to his master who sent him, for such servants will repeat to their master what they have been told.

20 Though I do not deny such a solution, I am certainly much more inclined to the opinion of those who think that Christ spoke face to face with the princes of the priests, magistrates of the Temple, and elders of the people. For Luke does not say that
25 Christ said these things to all the princes of the priests, or to all the magistrates of the Temple, or to all the elders of the people, but only to those "who had come." These words seem to indicate rather clearly that, although the cohort and servants had
30 been commissioned to seize Christ in the name of the whole assembly gathered together in council, still some members of each group—elders, Pharisees, and princes—also went along with them. This opinion agrees exactly with Luke's words and does
35 not contradict the accounts of the other evangelists.

Addressing, therefore, the princes of the priests, the Pharisees, and the elders of the people, Christ implicitly reminds them that they should not attribute his capture to their own strength or adroitness
40 and should not foolishly boast of it as a clever and ingenious achievement (according to that unfortunate tendency of those who are fortunate in evil). He lets them know that the foolish contrivances and maneuvers by which they labored to suppress
45 the truth were powerless to accomplish anything against him, but rather the profound wisdom of God had foreseen and set the time when the prince of this world[282] would be justly tricked into losing

his ill-gotten prey, the human race, even as he strove by unjust means to keep it. If this were not the case,
50 Christ explains to them, there would have been no need at all for them to pay for the services of the betrayer, to come at night with lanterns and torches, to make their approach surrounded by the dense ranks of the cohort and armed with swords and clubs,
55 since they had previously had many opportunities to arrest him as he sat teaching in the Temple and then they could have done it without expense, without any special effort, without spending a sleepless night, without any sabre-rattling at all.
60

But if they should take special credit for their prudent foresight and say that the arrest of Christ was no easy matter, as he claimed, but rather quite difficult because it necessarily brought with it the great danger of a popular uprising,[283] this difficulty,
65 for the most part, had arisen only recently, after the resurrection of Lazarus.[284] Before that event, it had happened more than once that, in spite of the people's great love of his virtues and their profound respect for him, he had had to use his own power to
70 escape from their midst.[285] On those occasions anyone attempting to capture and kill him would not have been in the least danger from the crowd but would have found them to be willing accomplices in crime. So unfailingly unreliable is the common
75 herd, always ready at a moment's notice to take the wrong side. Finally, what happened a little later showed how easy it is to brush aside the people's favor toward a person and any fear that might arise from it; as soon as he was arrested, the people were
80 no less furious at him as they cried out, "Away with him! Crucify him!" than they had formerly been eager to honor him when they cried, "Blessed is he who comes in the name of the lord!" and "Hosanna in the highest!"
85

And so up to that time God had caused the would-be captors of Christ to imagine purely fictitious grounds for fear and to tremble with dread where there was no reason to be afraid. But now that the proper time had come for all men (all,
90 that is, who truly desire it) to be redeemed by the bitter death of one man[286] and be restored to the sweetness of eternal life, these puny creatures stupidly imagined that they had achieved by clever planning what as a matter of fact God in his om-
95 nipotent providence (without which not a sparrow

falls to earth)²⁸⁷ had mercifully prescribed from all eternity. To show them how very wrong they were and to let them know that, without his own consent, the deceitfulness of the betrayer and their own cleverly laid snares and the power of the Romans would have been utterly ineffectual, Christ said, "But this is your hour and the power of darkness." These words of Christ are grounded firmly by what the evangelist says: "But all this was done so that the writings of the prophets might be fulfilled."²⁸⁸

Predictions of Christ's death are very frequent throughout the prophets: "He was led like a lamb to the slaughter, and his cry was not heard in the streets;"²⁸⁹ "They have pierced my hands and my feet;"²⁹⁰ "I was struck with these blows in the home of those who loved me;"²⁹¹ "And he was reckoned among the wicked;"²⁹² "Truly he bore our infirmities;"²⁹³ "By his bruises we have been healed;"²⁹⁴ "He has been brought to his death by the wickedness of my people."²⁹⁵ The prophets are full of very clear predictions of the death of Christ. In order that these might not remain unfulfilled, it was necessary that the matter depend not on human planning but rather on him who foresaw and prearranged from all eternity what would happen (that is, on the Father of Christ, and likewise on Christ himself, and on the Holy Spirit of both of them, for the actions of these three are always so harmoniously unified that there is no exterior act of anyone of them that does not belong equally to all three). The most suitable times of fulfillment, then, were already foreseen and prescribed. Therefore, while the high priests and the princes of the priests, the scribes, Pharisees and elders of the people, in short, all these accursed and wicked magistrates, were taking pride in their masterful plan for capturing Christ cleverly, they were nothing more than tools of God, eager in their ignorance, blind instruments of the most excellent and unchangeable will of almighty God, not only of the Father and the Holy Spirit, but also of Christ himself; thus, foolish and blind with malice, they did great harm to themselves and great good to others, they inflicted a temporary death on Christ but contributed to a most happy life for the human race, and they enhanced the everlasting glory of Christ.

And so Christ said to them, "This is your hour and the power of darkness." In the past, although you hated me intensely, although you longed to destroy me, although you could have done so at that time with less trouble (except that heavenly power prevented it), yet you did not detain me in the Temple—you did not even make a single move to lay hands on me. Why was this? It was because the time and the hour had not yet come, the hour fixed not by the heavenly bodies, not by your cleverness, but rather by the unsearchable plan of my Father, to which I too had given my consent. Would you like to know when he did this? Not only as long ago as the times of Abraham, but from all eternity. For from all eternity, together with the Father, before Abraham came to be, I am.²⁹⁶

"And so this is your hour and the power of darkness. This is the short hour allowed to you and the power granted to darkness, so that now in the dark you might do what you were not permitted to do in the daylight, flying in my face like winged creatures from the Stygian marsh,²⁹⁷ like harpies, like horned owls and screech-owls, like night-ravens and bats and nightowls, futilely swarming in a shrill uproar of beaks, talons, and teeth. You are in the dark when you ascribe my death to your strength. So too the governor Pilate will be in the dark when he takes pride in possessing the power to free me or to crucify me. For, even though my people and my high priests are about to hand me over to him, he would not have any power over me if it were not given to him from above. And for that very reason, those who will hand me over to him are the greater sinners.²⁹⁸

"But this is the hour and the brief power of darkness. A man who walks in the dark does not know where he is going.²⁹⁹ You also do not see or know what you are doing, and for that reason I myself will pray that you may be forgiven for what you are scheming to do to me.³⁰⁰ But not everyone will be forgiven. Blindness will not be an excuse for everyone. For you yourselves create your own darkness, you put out the light, you blind your own eyes first and then the eyes of others so that you are the blind leading the blind until both fall into a ditch.³⁰¹ This is your short hour. This is that mad and ungovernable power which brings you armed to take an unarmed man, which brings the fierce against the gentle, criminals against an innocent man, a traitor against his lord, puny mortals against God.

---

287 Mt 10:29 **288** Mt 26:56 **289** Is 53:7; Ps 43(44):11 **290** Ps 21(22):16 **291** Zec 13:6 **292** Lk 22:37; Is 53:12 **293** Is 53:4 **294** Is 53:5; 1 Pt 2:24 **295** Is 53:8, 12 **296** Jn 8:58 **297** *Stygian marsh:* classical underworld. See Vergil's *Aeneid* 6. **298** See Jn 19:10–11. **299** Jn 12:35 **300** See Lk 22:34. **301** Mt 15:14

"But this hour and this power of darkness are not only given to you now against me, but such an hour and such a brief power of darkness will also be given to other governors and other caesars against other disciples of mine. And this too will truly be the power of darkness. For whatever my disciples endure and whatever they say, they will not endure by their own strength or say of themselves, but conquering through my strength they will win their souls by their patience,[302] and it is my Father's spirit that will speak in them.[303] So too those who persecute and kill them will neither do nor speak anything of themselves. Rather, the prince of darkness who is already coming and who has no power over me[304] will instill his poison in the breasts of these tyrants and tormentors and will demonstrate and exercise his strength through them for the brief time allowed him. Hence my comrades-in-arms will be struggling not against flesh and blood but against princes and powers, against the rulers of the darkness of this world, against the spiritual forces of evil in high places.[305] Thus Nero is yet to be born, in whom the prince of darkness will kill Peter and to him will add Paul, who does not yet have that name and is still displaying his hatred of me. Through the prince of darkness other caesars and their governors will rise up against other disciples of my flock.

"But although the nations have raged and the people devised vain things, although the kings of the earth have risen up and the princes gathered together against the Lord and against his Christ, striving to break their chains and to cast off that most sweet yoke which a loving God, through his pastors, places upon their stubborn necks, then he who dwells in the heavens will laugh at them and the Lord will deride them. He sits not on a curule[306] throne like earthly princes, raised up a few feet above the earth, but rather he rises above the setting of the sun,[307] he sits above the cherubim,[308] the heavens are his throne, the earth is the footstool beneath his feet,[309] his name is the Lord.[310] He is the King of kings and the Lord of lords,[311] a terrible king who daunts the hearts of princes.[312] This king will speak to them in his anger, and in his rage he will throw them into confusion.[313] He will establish his Christ,

the son whom he has today begotten, as king on his holy mountain of Zion,[314] a mountain which will not be shaken.[315] He will cast all his enemies down before him like a footstool under his feet.[316] Those who tried to break his chains and cast off his yoke, he will rule against their will with a rod of iron, and he will shatter them like a potter's vessel.[317] Against them and their instigator, the prince of darkness, my disciples will be strengthened in the Lord.

"And putting on the armor of God, their loins girt with truth, wearing the breastplate of justice, shod in preparation to preach the Gospel of peace, taking up in all things the shield of faith and putting on the helmet of salvation and the sword of the spirit, which is the word of God,[318] they shall be clothed with power from on high.[319] And they will stand against the snares of the devil,[320] that is, against the soft speeches he will place on the lips of their persecutors to cajole them into leaving the way of truth. The open assaults of Satan they will also resist on the evil day:[321] compassed about by the shield of faith,[322] pouring forth tears in their prayers and shedding their blood in the agony of their suffering, they shall extinguish all the fiery darts hurled against them by the underlings of that monster of evil, Satan.[323] Thus, when they have taken up their cross to follow me,[324] when they have conquered the prince of darkness, the devil, when they have trod under foot the earthly minions of Satan, then finally, riding aloft on a triumphal chariot, the martyrs will enter into heaven in a magnificent and marvelous procession.

"But you who now give vent to your malice against me, and also that corrupt generation to come which will imitate your malice, that brood of vipers[325] which will assail my disciples with impenitent malice similar to yours, all of you, to your everlasting infamy, will be thrust down into the dark fires of hell. But in the meantime you are permitted to demonstrate and exercise your power. Still, lest you should take too much pride in it, remember that it must shortly come to an end. For the span of time allotted to your wanton arrogance is not endless but has been shortened to the span of a brief hour for the sake of the elect, that they might not be tried beyond their strength.[326]

302 Lk 21:19   **303** Mt 10:20   **304** Jn 14:30   **305** Eph 6:12   **306** a seat inlaid with ivory, used by the highest magistrates of Rome   **307** Ps 67:5(68:4)   **308** Ps 98(99):1; 79:2(80:1)   **309** Is 66:1   **310** Ps 67:5(68:4)   **311** 1 Tm 6:15   **312** Ps 75:12-13(76:11-12)   **313** Ps 2:5   **314** Ps 2:6-7   **315** Ps 124(125):1; 92(93):1, 95(96):10   **316** Ps 109(110):1; 1 Cor 15:25; Heb 1:13; 10:13   **317** Ps 2:3, 9   **318** Eph 6:10-17   **319** Lk 24:49   **320** Eph 6:11   **321** Eph 6:13   **322** See Ps 90:5(91:4)   **323** Eph 6:16   **324** Mt 10:38; 16:24; Mk 8:34   **325** See Mt 3:7; 12:34; 23:33; Lk 3:7.   **326** Mt 24:22; Mk 13:20; 1 Cor 10:13

"And so this hour of yours and this power of darkness are not long-lasting and enduring but quite as brief as the present moment to which they are limited, an instant of time always caught between a past that is gone and a future that has not arrived. Therefore, lest you should lose any of this hour of yours which is so short, proceed immediately to use it for your own evil purposes. Since you seek to destroy me, be quick about it,[327] arrest me without delay, but let these men go their way."

The Flight of the Disciples

Then all the disciples abandoned him and fled.[328]

From this passage it is easy to see how difficult and arduous a virtue patience is. For many can bring themselves to face certain death bravely provided they can strike back at their assailants and give vent to their feelings by inflicting wounds on those who attack them. But to suffer without any comfort from revenge, to meet death with a patience that not only refrains from striking back but also takes blows without returning so much as an angry word, that, I assure you, is such a lofty peak of heroic virtue that even the apostles were not yet strong enough to scale it. Remembering that grand promise of theirs that they would die together with him rather than desert him,[329] even they held out at least to the point of professing themselves ready to die providing that they had the chance to die fighting. And in deed as well as word Peter gave concrete evidence of this willingness by striking Malchus. But when out Savior denied them permission to fight and withheld the power to defend themselves, "they all abandoned him and fled."

I have sometimes asked myself this question: when Christ left off praying and returned to the apostles only to find them sleeping, did he go to both groups or only to those he had brought farther along and placed nearest to him? But when I consider these words of the evangelist, "All of them abandoned him and fled," I no longer have any doubt that it was all of them who fell asleep. While they should have been staying awake and praying that they might not enter into temptation (as Christ so often told them to do), instead they were sleeping and thus gave the tempter an opportunity

to weaken their wills with thoughtless drowsiness and make them far more inclined to fight or flee than to bear all with patience. And this was the reason that they all abandoned him and fled. And thus that saying of Christ was fulfilled, "This night you will all be scandalized in me," and also that prediction of the prophet, ["I will strike the shepherd and the sheep of the flock will be scattered"].[330]

But a certain young man was following him, having only a linen cloth wrapped about his naked body, and throwing it off, he fled from them naked.[331]

Just who this young man was has never been determined with certainty. Some think he was the James who was called the brother of the Lord and was distinguished by the epithet "the just." Others assert that he was the evangelist John, who always had a special place in our Lord's heart and who must have been still quite young, since he lived for so many years after Christ's death. For, according to Jerome, he died in the sixty-eighth year after our Lord's Passion.[332] But there are also some ancient writers who say that this young man was not one of the apostles at all but one of the servants in the household where Christ had celebrated the Passover that night. And certainly I myself find this opinion easier to accept. Apart from the fact that I find it unlikely for an apostle to be wearing nothing but a linen cloth, and even that so loosely fastened that it could be quickly thrown off, I am inclined to this opinion first of all by the sequence of historical events and then by the very words of the account.

Now, among those who think the young man was one of the apostles, the preponderance of opinion is for John. But this seems to me unlikely because of John's own words: "But Simon Peter was following Jesus and so was another disciple. Now that disciple was known to the high priest, and he entered the courtyard of the high priest together with Jesus. But Peter was standing outside at the gate. So the other disciple, who was known to the high priest, went out and spoke to the portress, and brought Peter in." Writers who assert that it was the blessed evangelist who followed Christ and fled when he was taken prisoner are faced with a slight hitch in their argument—namely, the fact that he threw off the linen cloth and fled naked. For this seems to conflict

---

327 Jn 13:27   **328** Mt 26:56, Mk 14:50   a blank space here.   **331** Mk 14:51–52   *Liber de viris illustribus* 9 (PL 23.625–26)
329 Mt 26:35   **330** Zec 13:7; More leaves   **332** *Adversus Jovinianum* 1.26 (PL 23.247),

with what follows—namely, that John entered the courtyard of the high priest, that he brought Peter in[333] (for everyone agrees that the disciple who did this was the evangelist), that he followed Christ all the way to the place of the crucifixion, and that he stood near the cross with Christ's most beloved mother (two pure virgins standing together), and that when Christ commended her to him he accepted her as his own mother from that day on.[334]

Now there can be no doubt that at all these times and in all these places John was wearing clothes. For he was a disciple of Christ, not of the cynic sect;[335] and therefore, though he had enough good sense not to avoid nakedness when circumstances required it or necessity demanded it, nevertheless I hardly think his virgin modesty would have allowed him to go out in public naked, for everyone to see, with no good reason at all. This difficulty they try to explain away by saying that he went somewhere else in the meantime and put on other clothes—a point I will not dispute, but it hardly seems likely to me, especially when I see in this passage that he continuously followed after Christ with Peter and that he entered the residence of Annas, the father-in-law of the high priest, together with Jesus.

Furthermore, another consideration that strongly persuades me to side with those who think that the young man was not one of the apostles but one of the servants of the inn is the sort of connection Mark makes between the apostles who ran away and the young man who stayed behind. "Then the disciples abandoned him and all of them ran away. But a certain young man was following him." Notice, he says not that some ran away but "all of them" and that the person who (unlike them) stayed behind and followed Christ was not anyone of the apostles (for all of them had already run away) but rather a "certain" young man, that is, it would seem, an unknown young man, whose name Mark either did not know or thought it not worthwhile to report.

Here, then, is how I would imagine it. This young man, who had previously been excited by Christ's fame and who now saw him in person as he was bringing in food to Christ and his disciples reclining at table, was touched by a secret breath of the spirit and felt the moving force of charity. Then, impelled to pursue a life of true devotion, he followed Christ when he left after dinner and continued to follow him, at a little distance, perhaps, from the apostles but still with them. And he sat down and got up again together with them until finally, when the mob came, he lost himself in the crowd. Furthermore, when all the apostles had escaped in terror from the hands of the sluggish soldiers this young man dared to remain behind, with all the more confidence because he knew that no one as yet was aware of the love he felt for Christ. But how hard it is to disguise the love we feel for someone! Although this young man had mingled with that crowd of people who hated Christ, still he betrayed himself by his gait and his bearing, making it clear to everyone that he pursued Christ (now deserted by the others) not as a persecutor but as a devoted follower. And so, when they finally noticed that the rest of Christ's band had fled and saw that this one had stayed behind and still dared to follow Christ, they quickly seized him.

This act of theirs convinces me that they also intended to seize all the apostles but were so taken by surprise that they lost their chance, and thus that prophetic command of Christ, "Let these men go their way," was indeed fulfilled. Christ did not intend this command to be limited to the apostles, whom he had chosen (though it was meant to apply principally to them), but he also wished to extend the riches of his kindness even more abundantly by making the command apply also to this young man, who, without being summoned, had followed him of his own accord and had slipped into the holy band of his apostles. And in this way Christ displayed his own secret power more clearly and at the same time exposed the weakness of the crowd more fully, because not only did they lose through negligence the eleven apostles, whose escape distressed them very much, but also they could not even detain this one young man whom they had already seized and who was (one may conjecture) completely walled in by their ranks; for "they seized him and he threw off the linen cloth and fled from them naked." Moreover, I have not the slightest doubt that this young man, who followed Christ that night and could not be torn away from him until the last possible moment, after all the apostles had fled—and even then it took manhandling and rough force—later took the first opportunity to return to Christ's flock and that even now he lives

---

333 Jn 18:15–16   **334** Jn 19:25–27   **335** Public shamelessness was recommended and practiced by some cynic philosophers.

with Christ in everlasting glory in heaven, where I hope and pray that we will one day live with him. Then he himself will tell us who he was, and we will get a most pleasant and full account of many other details of what happened that night which are not contained in Scripture.

In the meantime, in order to make our heavenward journey safer and easier, it will be of no small use for us to gather wholesome spiritual counsels from the flight of the disciples before they were captured and from the escape of this young man after he was captured: these counsels will be the provisions, as it were, for us to carry with us on the journey. The ancient fathers of the Church warn us not to be so sure of our strength as to place ourselves willingly and needlessly in danger of falling into sin. But if someone should happen to find himself in a situation where he recognizes an imminent danger that he will be driven by force to offend God, he ought to do what the apostles did—avoid capture by fleeing. I do not say this to suggest that the apostles' flight was praiseworthy, on the grounds that Christ, in his mercy (though he is indeed merciful) had permitted them to do so because of their weakness. Far from praising it, he had foretold it that very night as occasion of sin for them. But if we feel that our character is not strong enough, let us all imitate this flight of theirs insofar as we can, without sinning, flee the danger of falling into sin. For otherwise, if a person runs away when God commands him to stand and face the danger confidently, either for his own salvation or for that of those whom he sees have been entrusted to his care, then he is acting foolishly indeed, unless he does it out of concern for this present life—no, even then he acts foolishly. For what could be more stupid than to choose a brief time of misery over an eternity of happiness?

But if he does it because of the future life, with the idea that if he does not run away he may be forced to offend God, he compounds not only his folly but also his crime. For to desert one's post is itself a very serious crime, and if one adds to it the enormous gravity of despair, it is quite as serious as going over to the enemy's side. What worse offense could be imagined than to despair of God's help and by running away to hand over to the enemy the battle-station which God had assigned you

to guard? Furthermore, what greater madness could be conceived than to seek to avoid the possible sin that may happen if you stay, by committing the certain sin of running away? But when flight entails no offense against God, certainly the safer plan is to make haste to escape rather than to delay so long as to be captured and thus fall into the danger of committing a terrible sin. For it is easy and (where allowable) safe to run away in time, but it is difficult and dangerous to fight.

On the other hand, the example of this young man shows us what sort of person can afford to hold his ground longer with less danger and can easily escape from the hands of his captors if he should happen to be taken. For, although this young man stayed behind after all the others and followed Christ so long that they laid hands on him and held him, nevertheless, because he was not dressed in various garments but wore only a simple linen cloth—and even that not sewn together or buttoned on, but thrown carelessly over his naked body in such a way that he could easily shake it off—this young man suddenly threw off the cloth, leaving it there in the hands of his captors, and fled from them naked—taking the kernel, as it were, and leaving them holding the shell.[336] What is the figurative meaning of this? What else but this: just as a pot-bellied man, slowed down by his fat paunch,[337] or a man who goes around wearing a heavy load of clothes is hardly in a condition to run fast, so too the man who is hemmed in by a belt full of moneybags is hardly able to escape when troubles suddenly descend on him and put him in a bind. Neither will a man run very fast or very far if his clothing, however light it may be, is so tightly laced and knotted that he cannot breathe freely. For a man who is wearing a lot of clothing but can get rid of it quickly will find it easier to escape than a man who is wearing only a little but has it tied around his neck so tightly that he has to carry it with him wherever he runs. One sees rich men—less often, it is true, than I would like—but still, thank God, one sometimes sees exceedingly rich men who would rather lose everything they have than keep anything at all by offending God through sin. These men have many clothes, but they are not tightly confined by them, so that when they need to run away from danger, they escape easily by throwing off their clothes.

---

336 Plautus, *Captivi* 655   **337** See Juvenal 3.107.

On the other hand we see people — and far more of them than I would wish — who happen to have only light garments and quite skimpy outfits and yet have so welded their affections to those poor riches[338] of theirs that you could sooner strip skin from flesh than separate them from their goods. Such a person had better get going while there is still time. For once someone gets hold of his clothes, he will sooner die than leave his linen cloth behind. In summary, then, we learn from the example of this young man that we should always be prepared for troubles that arise suddenly, dangers that strike without warning and might make it necessary for us to run away; to be prepared, we ought not to be so loaded with various garments, or so buttoned up in even one, that in an emergency we are unable to throwaway our linen cloth and escape naked.

Now anyone who is willing to devote a little more attention to this deed of the young man can see that it offers us another teaching, even more forceful than the first. For the body is, as it were, the garment of the soul. The soul puts on the body when it comes into the world and takes off the body when it leaves the world at death. Hence, just as the clothes are worth much less than the body, so too the body is far less precious than the soul. Thus, to give away the soul to buy the body is the same kind of raving lunacy as to prefer the loss of a cloak to the loss of the body. Concerning the body, Christ did indeed say, "Is not the body worth more than its clothing?"[339] But concerning the soul he was far more emphatic: "What does it profit you if you gain the whole world but suffer the loss of your soul? or what will a man give in exchange for his soul?[340] But I say to you, my friends, do not be afraid of those who kill the body, and after that have nothing more that they can do. But I will show you the one to be afraid of. Fear him who, after he has killed, has the power to cast into hell. Yes, I say to you, fear him."[341] Thus, the example of this young man warns us about what sort of clothing for our souls our bodies ought to be when we are faced with such trials: they should not be obese from debauchery and flabby from dissolute living but thin like the linen cloth, with the fat worked off by fasting; and then we should not be so strongly attached to them that we cannot willingly cast them off when God's cause demands it. This is the lesson which that young man teaches us; when he was in the clutches of wicked men, he preferred to leave his linen cloth behind and flee from them naked rather than be forced to do or say anything which might impugn the honor of Christ.

In a similar way, another young man who lived long before this one, the holy and innocent patriarch Joseph, left to posterity a notable example, teaching that one should flee from the danger of unchaste defilement no less than if it were an attempted murder. Because he had a handsome face and was a fine figure of a man, the wife of Potiphar, in whose house he was the chief servant, cast her eyes on him and fell passionately in love with him. She was so carried away by the raving madness of her desire that she not only offered herself freely and shamelessly to the young man by her glances and words, enticing him to overcome his aversion, but also, when he refused, she went so far as to clutch his garment in her hands and presented the shameful spectacle of a woman wooing a man by force. But Joseph, who would rather have died than commit such a horrible sin and who also knew how dangerous it is to engage the embattled forces of Venus at close quarters and that against them the surest victory is flight, Joseph, I say, left his cloak in the hands of the adulteress and escaped by dashing out of doors.[342]

But, as I was saying, to avoid falling into grave sin we must throw off not merely a cloak or gown or shirt or any other such garment of the body but even the garment of the soul, the body itself. For if we strive to save the body by sin, we destroy it and we also lose the soul. But if we patiently endure the loss of the body for the love of God, then, just as the snake sloughs off its old skin (called, I think, its *senecta*) by rubbing it against thorns and thistles, and leaving it behind in the thick hedges comes forth young and shining, so too those of us who follow Christ's advice and become wise as serpents[343] will leave behind on earth our old bodies, rubbed off like a snake's old skin among the thorns of tribulation suffered for the love of God, and will quickly be carried up to heaven, shining and young and never more to feel the effects of old age.

338 See Horace, *Odes* 3.16.28; Ovid, *Metamorphoses* 3.466.   **339** Mt 6:25   **340** Mt 16:26   **341** Lk 12:4–5   **342** Gn 39:6–12   **343** Mt 10:16

The Capture of Christ

*Then they came up and laid hands on Jesus. The co-hort and the tribune and the servants of the Jews seized Jesus and holding him fast they bound him and took him first to Annas. For he was the father-in-law of Caiaphas. But it was Caiaphas who had advised the Jews that it is expedient that one man die for the people.*³⁴⁴ *And all the priests, scribes, Pharisees, and elders gathered together.*³⁴⁵

Exactly when they first laid hands on Jesus is a point on which the experts disagree. Among the interpreters of the Gospel accounts, which agree on the fact but vary in their way of presenting it (for one anticipates, another goes back to pick up a detail omitted earlier), some commentators follow one opinion, others another, though none of them impugn the historical truth of the accounts or deny that an opinion differing from their own may be the correct one. For Matthew and Mark relate the events in such an order as to allow the conjecture that they laid hands on Jesus immediately after Judas' kiss. And this is the opinion adopted not only by many celebrated doctors of the Church but also approved by that remarkable man John Gerson, who follows it in presenting the sequence of events in his work entitled *Monotessaron* (the work which I have generally followed in enumerating the events of the Passion in this discussion).

But in this one place I have departed from him and followed those interpreters (and they, too, are celebrated authorities) who are persuaded by very probable inferences from the accounts of Luke and John to adopt the opinion that only after Judas had given his kiss and returned to the cohort and the Jews, after Christ had thrown down the cohort merely by speaking to them, after the ear of the high priest's servant had been cut off and restored, after the other apostles had been forbidden to fight and Peter (who had already begun to fight) had been rebuked, after Christ had once more addressed the Jewish magistrates who were present at that time and had announced that they now had permission to do what they had not been able to do before — to take him captive — after all the apostles had escaped by running away, after the young man who had been seized but could not be held had saved himself by his active and eager acceptance of nakedness, only then, after all these events, did they lay hands on Jesus.

MORE'S CATENA³⁴⁶ OF SCRIPTURAL QUOTES AND REFLECTIONS

If your enemy should fall, do not be glad; let not your heart rejoice in his downfall, lest perhaps God should see and be displeased [Prv 24:17–18].

Do not return a curse for a curse [1 Pt 3:9].

Pray for those who persecute you [Mt 5:44].

Do not cool yourself in every breeze, and do not walk on every road. Be steadfast in the way of the Lord and in the truth of your judgment. Be meek in hearing the word of God that you may understand it, and make your reply with wisdom. If you understand the matter, give your neighbor an answer; but if not, put your hand over your mouth, lest you be caught saying something silly and be confounded. Never in your life be called a tale-bearer, and do not be tripped up and confounded by your tongue. But the tale-bearer shall have hatred and enmity and reproach. [Ws 5:11–17]

> All flesh is grass and all its glory is like the flower of the field. The grass has withered and its flower has fallen. But the word of the Lord endures forever. [1 Pt 1:24–25, quoting Is 40:6–8]

Whatever light and momentary affliction we now bear prepares for us an immeasurable and eternal weight of glory on high, while we contemplate not the things that are seen but the things that are not seen. For the things that are seen are temporal, but those that are not seen are eternal [2 Cor 4:17–18].

The sufferings of the present time are not worthy to be compared to the glory to come which will be revealed in us [Rm 8:18].

Eye has not seen nor ear heard nor has it entered into the heart of man, what things God has prepared for those who love him [1 Cor 2:9].

---

344 Jn 18:12–14   **345** Mt 26:57; Mk 14:53   **346** Catena means "chain" or "connected series." What follows is a translation of twenty-eight handwritten pages that accompanied the manuscript of *De tristitia* (CW 14: 626–81).

Cast your thoughts upon God and he will support you [Ps 54:23(55:22)].

Beloved, do not be startled at the trial by fire that is taking place among you to prove you, as if something strange were happening to you; but rejoice, insofar as you share in the sufferings of Christ, that you may also rejoice with exultation in the revelation of his glory [1 Pt 4:12–13].

Let those who suffer according to the will of God commend their souls to a faithful Creator [1 Pt 4:19].

Good men should be ashamed to be more timid in good deeds than wicked men are in wicked deeds: for one may hear thieves saying that a man is a coward to refuse seven years of pleasure to avoid a half hour of hanging, and should not a Christian man be ashamed to lose eternal life and happiness rather than be willing to suffer a quick death a little sooner, for he knows that he will have to suffer death a little later anyway and that unless he repents he will fall from a temporal death to an eternal death, one full of more grievous torments than any death whatever.
　　If you despair in the day of distress, your courage will be diminished [Prv 24:10].
　　Peter walked erect on the water with confidence, but when the wind rose and he began to lose his confidence and be afraid, he immediately began to sink. But when he called to Christ for help, Christ reached out his hand, saying, "O you of little faith, why did you doubt?" [See Mt 14:29–31.]

Christ was tempted not once but three times, and also afterwards. For as Luke testifies, the tempter left him "until the time" [Lk 4:13].

God is faithful and does not permit you to be tempted beyond what you can bear, but with the temptation also gives a way out [1 Cor 10:13].

Consider it nothing but joy, my brothers, when you fall into various trials, knowing that the trying of your faith produces patience. But let your patience have its perfect work, that you may be whole and perfect. [Js 1:2–4]

Whoever wishes to be my disciple, let him take up his cross and follow me [Mt 16:24; Mk 8:34; Lk 9:23; 14:27].

They have crucified their flesh with its vices and desires [Gal 5:24].

The world is crucified to me and I to the world [Gal 6:14].

Strong as death is love [Sg 8:6].

I long to be dissolved and to be with Christ [Phil 1:23].

For me to live is Christ and to die is gain [Phil 1:21].

As the hind longs for springs of water, so my soul longs for you, O God. My soul has thirsted for God, the living spring. When shall I come and appear before the face of God? [Ps 41:2–3(42:1–2)]

I say to you, my friends, do not be afraid of those who can kill the body and after that have nothing more that they can do. But I will show you whom you ought to be afraid of. Fear him who, when he has killed, has the power to cast into hell. Yes, I say to you, fear him. [Lk 12:4–5]

Your adversary the devil goes about like a roaring lion, seeking someone to devour [1 Pt 5:8]. Bernard:[347] I give thanks to that great Lion of the tribe of Judah [Rv 5:5]. He can roar but he cannot bite. However much he may threaten, let us not be beasts that an empty roar should lay us low. For that man is truly a beast, truly lacking reason, who is so fainthearted that fear alone makes him yield, who even before the battle is conquered simply by an exaggerated notion of the effort to come and is laid low not by a weapon but by a war-trumpet. "For you have not yet resisted as far as blood," says that vigorous leader who knew that the roar of this lion is futile [Heb 12:4] and another leader says, "Resist the devil and he will flee from you" [Js 4:7]. "Resist him, steadfast in the faith" [1 Pt 5:9].

---

347 See St. Bernard of Clairvaux, *Sermo 13 in psalmum "Qui habitat"* [Ps 90].

He chose a glorious death over a hateful life [2 Mc 6:19]. If a man saves his life by offending God, he will find the life he has saved in this way to be hateful. For if you save your life in this way, on the very next day you yourself will find your life hateful and you will be very sorry indeed that you did not suffer death the day before. For you will remember that death still awaits you, though you do not know what sort it will be nor how quickly it will come. And you have good reason to fear that this delayed death will be followed by the torments of hell, where men will long to die and death will flee from them [Rv 9:6], whereas the death you fled from would have been followed by the eternal glory of heaven.

Your adversary the devil goes about like a raging lion, seeking someone to devour [1 Pt 5:8]. This lion is the prince of this world, nor is there any power on earth like him. The strongest and most savage of men, compared with this lion, would be like a Maltese lapdog. A roaring and rapacious lion [Ps 21:14(22:13)] is attacking me, seeking to devour me, and do I have time to give even a thought to the bite of a little dog? If a person could see even one of these demons who are waiting for us in great numbers to torture us eternally, he would consider the combined threats of all mortals a mere trifle by comparison with the fear inspired by that one devil. And how much less would he think of these threats if he could see the heavens opened and Jesus standing there as blessed Stephen saw him? [Acts 7:55–56]. How foolish is it to avoid a temporary death by incurring an eternal one! and not even to avoid the temporary one, but merely to put it off for a little while! For if you avoid death for the time being, can you always be as successful? Will you die at another time without pain? Perhaps even you are threatened by the same danger that Christ declared to the rich man who promised himself a long life: "Fool, this night they will snatch from you your soul" [Lk 12:20]. But this much you know for certain, that you must die some time and, considering the brevity of human life, you cannot live long. Finally, you are doubtless aware that when the fatal disease arrives and your anguish begins to grow worse in the throes of death, you will wish you had died long before when you could have saved your soul, no matter how excruciating the death might have been. Therefore you should not be so

desperately afraid of what might happen, since you know that a little later you will wish that that very thing had happened.

Sadness

He is affected with sadness... bad health...

The sadness that is according to God produces repentance that surely tends toward salvation, but the sadness of this world produces death [2 Cor 7:10; Jas 5:13].

My soul is sad even unto death [Mt 26:38; Mk 14:34].

For I would not have you ignorant, brothers, of the tribulation which came upon us in Asia, for we were burdened beyond measure, so that we were weary even of life [2 Cor 1:8].

As the sufferings of Christ abound in us, so also through Christ does our comfort abound [2 Cor 1:5]. Part of the sufferings of Christ was fear and sadness. Then, because of his weariness and fear, in the anguish of his agony, drops of his blood dripped on the ground. [See Lk 22:44.]

Isaiah predicts that [those who] abandon [hope in] God [and take refuge in] human assistance [will perish] together with their assistance [Is 31:3]. Thus perished King Saul, who, murmuring impatiently and despairing of God's help because he had not been heard immediately, went over to consult a witch, although formerly he had commanded by a public edict that all witches should be punished [1 Sm 28:5–25; 1 Chr 10:13–14].

Naked you came into the world [and you will take] nothing away with you [1 Tm 6:7; Eccl 5:14].

The Lord gave, the Lord has taken away. As it pleased the Lord, so has it been done. [Jb 1:21]

... of Christ... this man [was led] who in all things... nor once opened his mouth [Acts 8:32; Is 53:7]... [not] a word of complaint or excuse or threat or curse [1 Pt 2:23] would he speak against those cursed dogs [Ps 21:17(22:16)], but his very last act was to pour forth a word of blessing on his enemies, such as was never heard from the beginning of the world [Jn 9:32]: Father, forgive them for they know not what they do [Lk 23:34].

Blessed be God and the Father of our Lord Jesus Christ, who according to his mercy has begotten us again, through the resurrection of Jesus Christ from the dead, unto a living hope, unto an incor-
5 ruptible inheritance, undefiled and unfading, reserved in heaven for you, who are guarded by the power of God through faith unto salvation, the salvation made ready to be revealed in the last days. In this you will rejoice, though you must now be sad-
10 dened for a little while by various temptations, that the trial of your faith may be far more precious than gold which is tried by fire, that it may be discovered unto praise and glory and honor at the revelation of Jesus Christ. Him, though you have not seen, you
15 love. In him, though you do not see him now, you believe, and believing, you will rejoice with a joy inexpressible and triumphant, receiving as the final issue of your faith the salvation of your souls. [1 Pt 1:3–9]

20 Fear God. Honor the king. Servants, be subject to your masters in all fear, not only to the good and moderate, but also to the bad-tempered. For this is indeed a grace, if for consciousness of God anyone endures sorrows, suffering unjustly. For how is it a
25 grace if when you sin and are buffeted you endure it? But if, when you do right, you suffer patiently, this is indeed a grace in the eyes of God. For to this you have been called, because Christ too suffered for us, leaving us an example that we might follow
30 in his footsteps. "He committed no sin, nor was deceit found in his mouth" [Is 53:9]. When he was cursed, he did not curse. When he suffered, he did not threaten but handed himself over to him who judged him unjustly. He himself bore our sins in his
35 body on the cross that we, having died to sin, might live to justice. By his bruises we were healed. [1 Pt 2:17–24]

Be all of one mind in the faith, compassionate, loving your brothers, merciful, modest, humble, not re-
40 turning evil for evil or curse for curse, but contrariwise, blessing. For to this you were called that you might inherit a blessing. [1 Pt 3:8–9]

Who is there to harm you if you are zealous for what is good? But even if you suffer anything for
45 the sake of justice, blessed are you. But have no fear of their fear that you may not be troubled, but in your hearts declare the holiness of the Lord, always ready to satisfy anyone who asks you the reason for the hope that is in you. But do so with modesty and fear, having a good conscience, so that those who 50 unjustly blame your good behavior in Christ may be put to shame for the detractions they have brought against you. For it is better, if such is the will of God, that we should suffer for doing good than for doing evil. For Christ, too, once died for our sins, 55 the just for the unjust, that he might offer us to God as men dead indeed in the flesh, but brought to life in the spirit. [1 Pt 3:13–18]

But the end of all things will draw near. Therefore, be prudent and watchful in prayers. But above all, 60 have a constant mutual charity among yourselves, for charity covers a multitude of sins. [1 Pt 4:7–8]

Beloved, do not be startled at the trial by fire that is taking place among you to prove you, as if something strange were happening to you; but rejoice, in- 65 sofar as you share in the sufferings of Christ, that you may also rejoice with exultation in the revelation of his glory. If you are reproached in the name of Christ, blessed shall you be because the honor, glory, and power of God and his Spirit rest upon 70 you. But let none of you suffer as a murderer or thief or a slanderer or as one who covets what belongs to others. But if he suffers as a Christian, let him not be ashamed, but let him glorify God under that name. For the time is at hand for the judgment to begin 75 with the household of God. But if it begins first with us, what will be the end of those who do not believe the Gospel? For if the just man will barely be saved, what will happen to the wicked man and the sinner? Therefore let those who suffer according to 80 the will of God commend their souls to a faithful Creator by doing good deeds. [1 Pt 4:12–19]

And you became imitators of us and of the Lord, receiving the Word in great tribulation, with joy of the Holy Spirit [1 Thes 1:6]. 85

As a helper, then, we exhort you not to receive the grace of God in vain. For he says, "In an acceptable time I have heard you and in the day of salvation I have helped you" [Is 49:8]. Behold, now is the acceptable time. Behold, now is the day of sal- 90 vation. Giving offense to no one, so that our ministry may not be blamed, let us rather show ourselves in all things to be the ministers of God, in much patience in tribulations, in hardships, in distress, in blows, in prisons, in tumults, in labors, in sleepless nights, in fasting, in innocence, in knowledge, in long-suffering, in kindness, in the Holy Spirit, in unfeigned charity, in the Word of truth, in the power of God, with the armor of justice on the right hand and on the left, in honor and dishonor, in evil report and good report, as deceivers and yet truthful, as unknown and yet well known, as dying and behold we live, as chastised but not killed, as sorrowful yet always rejoicing, as poor yet enriching many, as having nothing yet possessing all things. [2 Cor 6:1–10]

God, who commanded light to shine out of darkness, has himself shone in our hearts to give enlightenment concerning the knowledge of the glory of God, shining in the face of Jesus Christ. But we carry this treasure in vessels of clay, to show that the abundance of power is God's and not ours. In all things we suffer tribulation but we are not distressed; we are shaken but we are not destitute; we suffer persecution but we are not forsaken; we are humiliated but not put to shame; we are cast down but we do not perish; always bearing about in our body the dying of Jesus so that the life also of Jesus may be made manifest in our bodies. For we the living are always being handed over to death for the sake of Jesus, so that the life also of Jesus may be made manifest in our mortal flesh. [2 Cor 4:6–11]

For we know that if the earthly house in which we dwell be destroyed, we have a building from God, a house not made by human hands but eternal in the heavens. For even in this present state we groan, longing to be clothed over with that habitation of ours which is from heaven, if indeed we shall be found clothed and not naked. For even we who are in this tent groan and are burdened, because we do not wish to be unclothed but rather clothed over, that what is mortal might be swallowed up by life. Now he who made us for this very thing is God, who gave us the Spirit as its pledge. Always full of courage, then, and knowing that while we are in the body we are exiled from the Lord—for we walk by faith and not by sight—we have the courage and the greatest willingness to be even more exiled from the body and to be in the presence of God. And therefore we strive, whether in the body or out of it, to please him. For all of us must be made manifest before the tribunal of Christ, so that each one may receive what he has won through the body, according to his works, whether good or evil. [2 Cor 5:1–10]

For you know the graciousness of our Lord Jesus Christ—how being rich, he became poor for your sakes, that by his poverty you might become rich [2 Cor 8:9]. He does not say "having been rich" he became poor, but "being rich" he took on poverty without losing his riches—inwardly rich, outwardly poor, having the hidden riches of divinity but appearing in the poverty of humanity. All of us, then, become rich by believing in the poor Christ. Therefore, let no poor man in his hut look down on himself. Rich in his conscience, he sleeps more securely on the ground than the man rich in gold does on his regal coverlet. And so do not be afraid to come like a poor beggar before him who, clothing himself in our poverty, enriched us by impoverishing himself.

If anyone does not obey our word by this letter, note that man and do not associate with him, that he may be put to shame. And do not regard him as an enemy, but admonish him as a brother. But may the God of peace himself give you everlasting peace in every place. [2 Thes 3:14–16]

How good is the God of Israel to those who are upright of heart. But my feet almost wavered, my steps almost slipped. [Ps 72(73):1–2]

Direct my steps according to your word, and do not let any injustice rule over me [Ps 118(119):133].

O God, you know my folly, and my offenses are not hidden from you. Let not those who are waiting for you be put to shame because of me, O Lord, Lord of hosts. Let those who seek you not be confounded because of me, O God of Israel. [Ps 68:6–7(69):5–6]

Blessed be the Lord, the God of Israel, who alone does wondrous things. And blessed be the name of his majesty forever, and the whole earth shall be filled with his majesty. So be it! So be it! [Ps 71(72):18–19]

Tribulation and distress have found me out; your commandments are my meditation [Ps 118(119):143].

This facsimile, actual size, shows the careful revisions that More made to his manuscript penned in prison. He alludes to Plato's figure of the unruly horses with *infrenet* and *habenas*, and then to the figure of the cowardly helmsman with *gubernet*. See Clarence Miller's commentary on such revisions in *CW* 14: 789–999.

Letters: Prison Years, 1534–35

CONTENTS

The prefatory number of each letter corresponds to *The Correspondence of Sir Thomas More* [*Corr*], ed. Elizabeth F. Rogers (Princeton, NJ: Princeton UP, 1947). The symbols < > indicate uncertainty about the date or place.

neïther, after so many wyse mē whō ye
take foʒ no saumple, but if I should say
like M.Harry: why shold you refuse to
swere father foʒ I haue swoʒn my self.
At this he laughed & sayde. That woʒd
was like Eue too, foʒ she offered Apā ꝺo
woʒse fruit than she had eaten her self.
But yet father ꝙ I by my trouth, I fere
me very soʒe, ŷ this matter will bʒynge
you in merueilous heauy truoble. You
know wel ŷ as I shewed you, M.Secre-
tary sent you woʒd as your very frend,
to remēber, ŷ the parlement lasteth yet.
Margaret ꝙ my father, I thanke hym
right hertely. But as I shewed you thā
agayn, I left not this geare vnthought
on. And albeit I knowe well that if
they would make a lawe to doo me any
harme, that lawe coulde neuer be law-
full

She tok ethe othe with this excepciō as farre as would stande with the law of god.

This side note (given in standardized English, and correcting the typesetter's error) comments about Margaret Roper: "She took the oath with this excepted: as far as would stand with the law of God." The bishops took the same "exception" in January 1531 when they were asked to acknowledge Henry VIII as head of the Church in England. The text above is from the 1557 *Workes*, p. 1441 (but here, enlarged). In this *Essential Works* edition, it would appear next to lines 8–14 of Letter 206 on p. 1319.

Letters: Prison Years, 1534–35

200. To Margaret Roper

<Tower of London, *ca.* 17 April 1534>

Sir Thomas More, upon warning¹ given him, came be-
fore the King's Commissioners² at the Archbishop of
Canterbury's place at Lambeth (the Monday the thir-
teenth day of April in the year of our Lord 1534, and
in the latter end of the twenty-fifth year of the reign
of King Henry the Eighth), where he refused the oath³
then offered unto him. And thereupon was he deliv-
ered to the Abbot of Westminster⁴ to be kept as a pris-
oner, with whom he remained till Friday following,
and then was sent prisoner to the Tower of London.
And shortly after his coming thither, he wrote a let-
ter and sent unto his eldest daughter Mistress Mar-
garet Roper, the copy whereof here followeth. [Workes
1428]⁵

When I was before the Lords at Lambeth, I was
the first that was called in, albeit⁶ Master Doctor
the Vicar of Croydon⁷ was come before me, and diverse others. After the cause of my sending-for de-
clared⁸ unto me (whereof I somewhat marveled in
my mind, considering that they sent for no more
temporal men⁹ but me), I desired the sight of the
oath, which they showed me under the Great Seal.
Then desired I the sight of the Act of the Succession, which was delivered me in a printed roll. After which read secretly¹⁰ by myself, and the oath
considered with the act, I showed unto them that
my purpose was not to put any fault either in the
act or any man that made it, or in the oath or any
man that swore it, nor to condemn the conscience
of any other man. But as for myself, in good faith
my conscience so moved me in the matter that
though I would not deny to swear to the succession, yet unto the oath that there was offered me, I
could not swear without the jeoparding¹¹ of my soul
to perpetual damnation. And that if they doubted

whether I did refuse the oath only for the grudge¹²
of my conscience, or for any other fantasy,¹³ I was
ready therein to satisfy them by mine oath. Which
if they trusted not, what should they be the better to give me any oath? And if they trusted that
I would therein swear true, then trusted I that of
their goodness they would not move¹⁴ me to swear
the oath that they offered me, perceiving that for to
swear it was against my conscience.

Unto this my Lord Chancellor¹⁵ said, that they all
were sorry to hear me say thus, and see me thus refuse the oath. And they said all that on their faith I
was the very first that ever refused it, which would
cause the King's Highness to conceive great suspicion of me and great indignation toward me. And
therewith they showed me the roll, and let me see
the names of the lords and the commons which had
sworn and subscribed their names already. Which
notwithstanding when they saw that I refused to
swear the same myself, not blaming any other man
that had sworn, I was in conclusion commanded to
go down into the garden, and thereupon I tarried in
the old burned chamber that looketh into the garden, and would not go down because of the heat. In
that time saw I Master Doctor Latimer¹⁶ come into
the garden, and there walked he with diverse other
doctors and chaplains of my Lord of Canterbury,¹⁷
and very merry I saw him, for he laughed, and took
one or twain¹⁸ about the neck so handsomely that,
if they had been women, I would have weened¹⁹ he
had been waxen wanton.²⁰ After that came Master Doctor Wilson²¹ forth from the lords and was
with two gentlemen brought by me, and gentle-
manly sent straight unto the Tower. What time my
Lord of Rochester²² was called in before them, that
cannot I tell. But at night I heard that he had been
before them, but where he remained that night,
and so forth till he was sent hither, I never heard.
I heard also that Master Vicar of Croydon, and all

1 summons **2** Archbishop Cranmer,
Lord Chancellor Audley, and the Dukes
of Norfolk and of Suffolk **3** the Oath of
Succession required by the Act of Succession **4** *Abbot of Westminster:* William
Benson **5** These introductory notes
appeared in the 1557 *Workes of Sir Thomas*

More Knight. **6** although **7** *Vicar of*
Croydon: Rowland Phillips, who agreed to
swear the oath **8** was declared **9** *tempo-*
ral men: laymen **10** privately **11** endan-
gering, jeopardizing **12** uneasiness,
misgiving; scruple **13** whim; imagining
14 urge **15** Sir Thomas Audley **16** Hugh

Latimer (1492?–1555) **17** Archbishop
Thomas Cranmer **18** two **19** supposed,
thought **20** *waxen wanton:* grown lustful
21 Fr. Nicholas Wilson was imprisoned a
week before More for refusing the same
oath. **22** *Lord of Rochester:* John Fisher,
Bishop of Rochester

the remnant of the priests of London that were sent for, were sworn, and that they had such favor at the Council's hand that they were not lingered[23] nor made to dance any long attendance[24] to their travail and cost (as suitors were sometime wont to be), but were sped apace[25] to their great comfort so far-forth[26] that Master Vicar of Croydon, either for gladness or for dryness, or else that it might be seen (*quod ille notus erat pontifici*),[27] went to my Lord's[28] buttery-bar,[29] and called for drink, and drank (*valde familiariter*).[30]

When they had played their pageant[31] and were gone out of the place, then was I called in again. And then was it declared unto me, what a number had sworn, even since I went aside, gladly, without any sticking.[32] Wherein I laid no blame in no man, but for mine own self answered as before. Now as well before as then, they somewhat laid unto me for obstinacy, that whereas before, since I refused to swear, I would not declare any special part of that oath that grudged[33] my conscience, and open the cause wherefore. For thereunto I had said to them, that I feared lest the King's Highness would, as they said, take displeasure enough toward me for the only[34] refusal of the oath. And that if I should open and disclose the causes why, I should therewith but further exasperate his Highness, which I would in no wise[35] do, but rather would I abide all the danger and harm that might come toward me than give his Highness any occasion of further displeasure than the offering of the oath unto me of pure necessity constrained me. Howbeit,[36] when they diverse times imputed this to me for stubbornness and obstinacy—that I would neither swear the oath nor yet declare the causes why—I declined[37] thus far toward them: that rather than I would be accounted for obstinate, I would, upon[38] the King's gracious license[39] or rather his such commandment had,[40] as might be my sufficient warrant,[41] that my declaration should not offend his Highness, nor put me in the danger of any of his statutes, I would be content to declare the causes in writing and, over[42] that, to give an oath in the

beginning that if I might find those causes by any man in such wise answered as I might think mine own conscience satisfied, I would after that with all mine heart swear the principal oath too.

To this I was answered that though the King would give me license under his letters patent,[43] yet would it not serve against the statute. Whereto I said that yet, if I had them, I would stand unto the trust of his honor at my peril for the remnant. But yet it thinketh me,[44] lo, that if I may not declare the causes without peril, then to leave them undeclared is no obstinacy.

My Lord of Canterbury, taking hold upon that that[45] I said, that I condemned not the conscience of them that swore, said unto me that it appeared well that I did not take it for a very sure thing and a certain that I might not lawfully swear it, but rather as a thing uncertain and doubtful. "But then," said my Lord, "you know for a certainty, and a thing without doubt, that you be bounden to obey your sovereign lord your King. And therefore are ye bounden to leave off the doubt of your unsure conscience in refusing the oath, and take the sure way in obeying of your Prince,[46] and swear it." Now all was it[47] so that in mine own mind methought myself not concluded,[48] yet this argument seemed me[49] suddenly so subtle—and namely[50] with such authority, coming out of so noble a prelate's mouth—that I could again answer nothing thereto but only that I thought myself I might not well do so, because that[51] in my conscience this was one of the cases in which I was bounden that I should not obey my Prince, since that whatsoever other folk thought in the matter (whose conscience and learning I would not condemn nor take upon me to judge), yet in my conscience the truth seemed on the other side. Wherein I had not informed my conscience neither suddenly nor[52] slightly, but by long leisure and diligent search for the matter. And of truth if that reason may conclude, then have we a ready way to avoid all perplexities. For in whatsoever matters the doctors[53] stand in great doubt, the King's

---

23 made to wait   **24** *dance…attendance:* ready attendance; stand waiting in an antechamber   **25** *sped apace:* expedited   **26** *so far-forth:* to such an extent   **27** *quod… pontifici:* "because he was known to the high priest." See Peter's denial of Christ, Jn 18:15–16.   **28** Archbishop Cranmer's   **29** a sideboard for serving liquor   **30** *valde*

familiariter: "very familiarly"   **31** stageplay, show   **32** hesitation; scruple   **33** troubled   **34** only for the refusal   **35** way   **36** however   **37** acceded, gave in   **38** as soon as   **39** permission   **40** *his…had:* having such commandment   **41** safeguard   **42** in addition to   **43** *letters patent:* open letters to put an

agreement on record   **44** *it thinketh me:* I think   **45** *that that:* that which   **46** King   **47** *all was it:* even if it were   **48** convinced   **49** to me   **50** especially   **51** *because that:* because   **52** *not…nor:* More commonly uses a double negative where modern English would use "not…either…or"   **53** i.e., of the Church

commandment, given upon whither[54] side he list,[55] soileth[56] all the doubts.

Then said my Lord of Westminster[57] to me that howsoever the matter seemed unto mine own mind, I had cause to fear that mine own mind was erroneous when I see the great Council of the realm determine of my mind the contrary, and that therefore I ought to change my conscience. To that I answered that if there were no more but myself upon my side, and the whole Parliament upon the other, I would be sore[58] afraid to lean to mine own mind only against so many. But on the other side,[59] if it so be that, in some things for which I refuse the oath, I have (as I think I have) upon my part[60] as great a council and a greater too, I am not then bounden to change my conscience and conform it to the council of one realm against the General Council[61] of Christendom. Upon this, Master Secretary[62] (as he that tenderly favoreth me)[63] said and swore a great oath that he had liefer[64] that his own only son (which is of truth a goodly[65] young gentleman, and shall, I trust, come to much worship[66]) had lost his head than that I should thus have refused the oath. For surely the King's Highness would now conceive a great suspicion against me, and think that the matter of the nun of Canterbury[67] was all contrived by my drift.[68] To which I said that the contrary was true and well known, and whatsoever should mishap[69] me, it lay not in my power to help it without peril of my soul. Then did my Lord Chancellor repeat before me my refusal unto Master Secretary, as to him that was going unto the King's Grace. And in the rehearsing,[70] his Lordship repeated again that I denied not but was content to swear to the succession. Whereunto I said that as for that point, I would be content so that I might see my oath in that point so framed in such a manner as might stand with my conscience.

Then said my Lord, "Marry,[71] Master Secretary, mark that too, that he will not swear that neither,[72] but under some certain manner." "Verily[73] no, my Lord," quoth I, "but that I will see it made in such wise first, as I shall myself see, that[74] I shall neither be forsworn[75] nor swear against my conscience.

Surely as to swear to the succession I see no peril, but I thought and think it reason that to mine own oath I look well myself, and be of counsel also in the fashion, and never intended to swear for a piece[76] and set my hand to the whole oath. Howbeit (as help me God), as touching the whole oath, I never withdrew any man from it, nor never advised any to refuse it, nor never put, nor will, any scruple in any man's head, but leave every man to his own conscience. And methinketh in good faith that so were it good reason that every man should leave me to mine."

201. To Margaret Roper
Tower of London, <April–May? 1534>

A letter written with a coal by Sir Thomas More to his daughter Mistress Margaret Roper, within a while after he was prisoner in the Tower. [Workes 1430]

Mine own good daughter.

Our Lord be thanked, I am in good health of body, and in good quiet of mind; and of worldly things I no more desire than I have. I beseech him make you all merry in the hope of heaven. And such things as I somewhat longed to talk with you all, concerning the world to come, our Lord put them into your minds, as I trust he doth, and better too, by his Holy Spirit, who bless you and preserve you all. Written with a coal by your tender loving father, who in his poor prayers forgetteth none of you all, nor your babes, nor your nurses, nor your good husbands, nor your good husbands' shrewd[77] wives, nor your father's shrewd wife neither, nor our other friends. And thus fare you heartily well for lack of paper.

Thomas More, Knight

Our Lord keep me continually true, faithful, and plain; to the contrary whereof I beseech him heartily never to suffer me live. For as for long life (as I have often told thee, Meg), I neither look for, nor long for, but am well content to go if God call me

54 whichever   **55** pleases, chooses
56 resolves   **57** *Lord of Westminster:*
the Abbot   **58** greatly   **59** hand
60 side   **61** *General Council:* a meeting
of all the world's bishops approved by
the Pope   **62** *Master Secretary:* Thomas

Cromwell   **63** *as . . . me:* like someone
kindly indulging me   **64** *had liefer:*
would rather   **65** virtuous; distinguished;
comely   **66** honor, renown, distinction
67 *nun of Canterbury:* Elizabeth Barton
68 plotting   **69** happen unfortunately to

70 telling, relating   **71** Indeed (an
expression of surprise, from "By Mary!")
72 *not . . . neither:* not either   **73** Truly
74 so that   **75** sworn to something untrue
76 *for a piece:* to a part   **77** cunning

hence tomorrow. And I thank our Lord I know no person living that I would had one fillip[78] for my sake; of which mind I am more glad than of all the world beside.

Recommend me to your shrewd Will and mine other sons, and to John Harris my friend, and yourself knoweth to whom else, and to my shrewd wife above all; and God preserve you all, and make and keep you his servants all.

202. To Margaret Roper
Tower of London, <May? 1534>

Within a while after Sir Thomas More was in prison in the Tower, his daughter Mistress Margaret Roper wrote and sent unto him a letter,[79] wherein she seemed somewhat to labor to persuade him to take the oath (though she nothing so thought) to win thereby credence[80] with Master Thomas Cromwell, that she might the rather get liberty to have free resort[81] unto her father (which she only[82] had for the most time of his imprisonment) unto which letter her father wrote an answer, the copy whereof here followeth. [Workes 1431]

Our Lord bless you all.

If I had not been, my dearly beloved daughter, at a firm and fast[83] point (I trust in God's great mercy), this good great while before, your lamentable[84] letter had not a little abashed[85] me, surely far above all other things, of which I hear diverse times not a few terrible toward me. But surely they all touched me never so near, nor were so grievous unto me, as to see you, my well-beloved child, in such vehement piteous manner labor to persuade unto me that thing wherein I have of pure necessity for respect unto mine own soul so often given you so precise answer before. Wherein as touching the points of your letter, I can make none answer, for I doubt not but you well remember that the matters which move my conscience (without declaration whereof I can nothing touch the points) I have sundry times showed you that I will disclose them to no man. And therefore, daughter Margaret, I can

in this thing no further but, like as you labor[86] me again to follow your mind, to desire and pray you both again to leave off such labor and with my former answers to hold yourself content.

A deadly grief unto me, and much more deadly than to hear of mine own death (for the fear thereof, I thank our Lord, the fear of hell, the hope of heaven and the Passion of Christ daily more and more assuage), is that I perceive my good son your husband, and you my good daughter, and my good wife, and mine other good children and innocent friends, in great displeasure and danger of great harm thereby. The let[87] whereof, while it lieth not in my hand, I can no further but commit all unto God. *Nam in manu Dei*, saith the Scripture, *cor regis est, et sicut divisiones aquarum quocumque voluerit, impellit illud.*[88] Whose high goodness I most humbly beseech to incline the noble heart of the King's Highness to the tender favor of you all, and to favor me no better than God and myself know that my faithful heart toward him and my daily prayer for him do deserve. For surely if his Highness might inwardly see my true mind such as God knoweth it is, it would (I trust) soon assuage his high displeasure. Which while I can in this world never in such wise show but that his Grace may be persuaded to believe the contrary of me, I can no further go but put all in the hands of him for fear of whose displeasure for the safeguard of my soul stirred by mine own conscience (without insectation[89] or reproach laying to any other man's) I suffer and endure this trouble. Out of which I beseech him to bring me, when his will shall be, into his endless bliss of heaven, and in the meanwhile, give me grace and you both, in all our agonies and troubles, devoutly to resort prostrate unto the remembrance of that bitter agony, which our Savior suffered before his Passion at the Mount.[90] And if we diligently so do, I verily[91] trust we shall find therein great comfort and consolation. And thus, my dear daughter, the blessed spirit of Christ for his tender mercy govern and guide you all, to his pleasure and your weal[92] and comforts both body and soul.

Your tender loving father,
Thomas More, Knight

---

78 a small tap with the finger
79 Margaret Roper's letter is not extant   80 confidence, trust   81 access
82 alone   83 steadfast   84 distressing

85 disconcerted   86 urge   87 hindrance, stoppage   88 "For in the hand of God is the heart of the king, and as the divisions of waters, he moves it wherever he

wills"—similar to Prv 21:1; also quoted in Letters 208, 210, 213.   89 pursuing with words, railing   90 Mt 26:36–46
91 truly   92 well-being

203. From Margaret Roper
<May? 1534>

To this last letter, Mistress Margaret Roper wrote an answer and sent it to Sir Thomas More her father; the copy whereof here followeth. [Workes 1432]

Mine own good father.

It is to me no little comfort, since I cannot talk with you by such means as I would, at the least way to delight myself among[93] in this bitter time of your absence by such means as I may, by as often writing to you as shall be expedient[94] and by reading again and again your most fruitful and delectable letter, the faithful messenger of your very virtuous and ghostly[95] mind, rid from all corrupt love of worldly things, and fast knit only in the love of God, and desire of heaven, as becometh a very true worshiper and a faithful servant of God, which,[96] I doubt not, good Father, holdeth his holy hand over you and shall (as he hath) preserve you both body and soul (*ut sit mens sana in corpore sano*)[97] and namely[98] now, when you have abjected[99] all earthly consolations and resigned yourself willingly, gladly and fully for his love, to his holy protection.

Father, what think you hath been our comfort since your departing from us? Surely the experience we have had of your life past and godly conversation, and wholesome counsel, and virtuous example, and a surety[100] not only of the continuance of the same, but also a great increase by the goodness of our Lord to the great rest and gladness of your heart devoid of all earthly dregs and garnished with the noble vesture of heavenly virtues, a pleasant palace for the Holy Spirit of God to rest in, who defend you (as I doubt not, good father, but of his goodness he will) from all trouble of mind and of body, and give me your most loving obedient daughter and handmaid, and all us your children and friends, to follow that that[101] we praise in you, and, to[102] our only comfort, remember and commune[103] together of you, that we may in conclusion[104] meet with you, mine own dear father, in the bliss of heaven, to which our most merciful Lord hath bought us with his precious blood.

Your own most loving obedient daughter and beadswoman,[105] Margaret Roper, which desireth above all worldly things to be in John Wood's[106] stead to do you some service. But we live in hope that we shall shortly receive you again; I pray God heartily we may, if it be his holy will.

204. To All His Friends
Tower of London, <1534>

Within a while after Sir Thomas More had been in prison in the Tower, his daughter Mistress Margaret Roper obtained license of the King that she might resort unto her father in the Tower, which she did. And thereupon he wrote with a coal[107] a letter to all his friends, whereof the copy followeth. [Workes 1432]

To all my loving friends.

For as much as being in prison I cannot tell what need I may have, or what necessity I may hap[108] to stand in, I heartily beseech you all that, if my well-beloved daughter Margaret Roper (which only of all my friends hath by the King's gracious favor license to resort to me) do anything desire of any of you, of such things as I shall hap to need, that it may like you no less to regard and tender[109] it than if I moved it unto you and required[110] it of you personally present myself. And I beseech you all to pray for me, and I shall pray for you.

Your faithful lover and poor beadsman,[111]
Thomas More, Knight, prisoner

205. Alice Alington to Margaret Roper
17 August <1534>

In August in the year of our Lord 1534, and in the twenty-sixth year of the reign of King Henry the Eighth, the Lady Alice Alington (wife to Sir Giles Alington, Knight, and daughter to Sir Thomas More's second and last wife) wrote a letter to Mistress Margaret Roper, the copy whereof here followeth. [Workes 1433]

---

93 from time to time   **94** appropriate   **95** spiritual   **96** who (God)   **97** *ut sit … sano:* "that the mind may be sound in a sound body," Juvenal's *Satire* 10.356. See Letter 106, where More quoted the same passage.   **98** especially   **99** renounced,

rejected   **100** pledge, guarantee   **101** *that that:* that which   **102** as   **103** talk, confer   **104** *in conclusion:* finally, eventually   **105** a woman who prays for another; named from the beads of a rosary   **106** *John Wood:* More's personal servant, who

continued to serve More in the Tower   **107** charcoal used for writing   **108** happen   **109** attend to   **110** asked   **111** one who prays for another

Sister Roper, with all my heart I recommend me unto you, thanking you for all kindness.

The cause of my writing at this time is to show[112] you that at my coming home, within two hours after, my Lord Chancellor did come to take a course at[113] a buck in our park, the which was to my husband a great comfort that it would please him so to do. Then when he had taken his pleasure and killed his deer, he went unto Sir Thomas Barmeston to bed, where I was the next day with him at his desire, the which I could not say nay to, for methought he did bid me heartily, and most specially because I would speak to him for my father.

And when I saw my time, I did desire[114] him as humbly as I could that he would, as I have heard say that he hath been, be still good lord unto my father. And he said it did appear very well when the matter of the nun[115] was laid to his charge. And as for this other matter,[116] he marveled that my father is so obstinate in his own conceit,[117] as that[118] everybody went forthwithal[119] save only the blind bishop[120] and he. "And in good faith," said my Lord, "I am very glad that I have no learning but in a few of Aesop's fables, of the which I shall tell you one. There was a country in the which there were almost none but fools, saving a few which were wise. And they by their wisdom knew that there should fall a great rain, the which should make them all fools that[121] should so be fouled or wet therewith. They, seeing that, made them[122] caves under the ground till all the rain was past. Then they came forth, thinking to make the fools to do what they list,[123] and to rule them as they would. But the fools would none of that, but would have the rule themselves, for all[124] their craft. And when the wise men saw they could not obtain their purpose, they wished that they had been in the rain, and had defouled[125] their clothes with them."

When this tale was told, my Lord did laugh very merrily. Then I said to him that for all his merry fable I did put no doubts but that he would be good lord unto my father when he saw his time. He said, "I would not have your father so scrupulous of his conscience." And then he told me another fable of a lion, an ass, and a wolf, and of their confession. First the lion confessed him that he had devoured all the beasts that he could come by. His confessor assoiled[126] him because he was a king and also it was his nature so to do. Then came the poor ass and said that he took but one straw out of his master's shoe for hunger, by the means whereof he thought that his master did take cold. His confessor could not assoil this great trespass, but by and by[127] sent him to the bishop. Then came the wolf and made his confession, and he was straitly[128] commanded that he should not pass six pence at a meal. But when this said wolf had used this diet a little while, he waxed[129] very hungry, insomuch that on a day when he saw a cow with her calf come by him he said to himself, "I am very hungry and fain[130] would I eat, but[131] that I am bounden by my ghostly[132] father. Notwithstanding that, my conscience shall judge me. And then if it be so, then shall my conscience be thus: that the cow doth seem to me now but worth a groat,[133] and then if the cow be but worth a groat, then is the calf but worth two pence." So did the wolf eat both the cow and the calf. Now good sister, hath not my lord told me two pretty fables? In good faith, they pleased me nothing, nor I wist[134] not what to say for I was abashed of[135] this answer. And I see no better suit than to almighty God, for he is the comforter of all sorrows, and will not fail to send his comfort to his servants when they have most need. Thus fare ye well, mine own good sister.

Written the Monday after Saint Lawrence in haste by

Your sister Dame,
Alice Alington

206. Margaret Roper to Alice Alington
<August 1534>

When Mistress Roper had received a letter from her sister Lady Alice Alington, she, at her next repair[136] to her father, showed him the letter. And what communication was thereupon between her father and her, ye shall perceive by an answer here following (as written

112 tell   113 *take a course at:* hunt
114 ask   115 Elizabeth Barton; see Letter
200 above.   116 *other matter:* More's
refusal to take the oath   117 notion,
conception, idea   118 *as that:* since

119 immediately   120 *blind bishop:*
John Fisher   121 who   122 themselves   123 wanted   124 *for all:* in
spite of, notwithstanding   125 dirtied
126 absolved, forgave   127 *by and by:*

immediately   128 strictly   129 became
130 gladly   131 except   132 spiritual
133 a coin worth four pence   134 knew
135 *abashed of:* confused or disconcerted by
136 visit

to the Lady Alington). But whether this answer were written by Sir Thomas More in his daughter Roper's name or by herself, it is not certainly known. [Workes 1434]

When I came next unto my father after, methought it both convenient and necessary to show him your letter: convenient,¹³⁷ that he might thereby see your loving labor taken for him; necessary, that since he might perceive thereby that if he stand still in this scruple of his conscience (as it is at the leastwise called by many that are his friends and wise), all his friends that seem most able to do him good either shall finally forsake him, or peradventure¹³⁸ not be able indeed to do him any good at all.

And for these causes, at my next being with him after your letter received, when I had a while talked with him, first of his diseases—both in his breast of old, and his reins¹³⁹ now by reason of gravel and stone¹⁴⁰—and of the cramp also that diverse nights grippeth him in his legs, and that¹⁴¹ I found by his words that they were not much increased but continued after their manner that they did before, sometimes very sore¹⁴² and sometimes little grief, and that¹⁴³ at that time I found him out of pain, and (as one in his case might) meetly¹⁴⁴ well-minded, after our seven psalms¹⁴⁵ and the litany¹⁴⁶ said,¹⁴⁷ to sit and talk and be merry, beginning first with other things of the good comfort of my mother, and the good order of my brother, and all my sisters, disposing themselves every day more and more to set little by the world, and draw more and more to God, and that his household, his neighbors, and other good friends abroad¹⁴⁸ diligently remembered him in their prayers, I added unto this: "I pray God, good father, that their prayers and ours, and your own therewith, may purchase of God the grace that you may in this great matter—for which you stand in this trouble and, for your trouble, all we also that love you—take such a way betime¹⁴⁹ as, standing with the pleasure of God, may content and please the King, whom ye have always founden so singularly gracious unto you that if ye should stiffly refuse to do the thing that were his pleasure—which, God not displeased, you might do (as many great wise and well-learned men say that in this thing you

may)—it would both be a great blot in your worship¹⁵⁰ in every wise man's opinion and, as myself have heard some say (such as yourself have always taken for well-learned and good), a peril unto your soul also. But as for that point, father, will I not be bold to dispute upon, since I trust in God and your good mind that ye will look surely thereto. And your learning I know for such that I wot¹⁵¹ well you can. But one thing is there which I and other your friends find and perceive abroad, which, but if¹⁵² it be showed you, you may—peradventure to your great peril—mistake and hope for less harm (for as for good I wot well in this world of this matter ye look for none) than, I sore fear me, shall be likely to fall to you. For I assure you, father, I have received a letter of late from my sister Alington, by which I see well that if ye change not your mind, you are likely to lose all those friends that are able to do you any good. Or if ye lose not their good wills, ye shall at the leastwise lose the effect thereof, for any good that they shall be able to do you."

With this, my father smiled upon me and said: "What, Mistress Eve (as I called you when you came first), hath my daughter Alington played the serpent with you, and with a letter set you awork to come tempt your father again¹⁵³ and, for the favor that you bear him, labor to make him swear against his conscience, and so send him to the devil?" And after that, he looked sadly again, and earnestly said unto me: "Daughter Margaret, we two have talked of this thing ofter¹⁵⁴ than twice or thrice, and that same tale, in effect, that you tell me now therein, and the same fear too, have you twice told me before; and I have twice answered you too that in this matter if it were possible for me to do the thing that might content the King's Grace, and God therewith not offended, there hath no man taken this oath already more gladly than I would do, as he that reckoneth himself more deeply bounden unto the King's Highness for his most singular bounty, many ways showed and declared, than any of them all besides. But since, standing¹⁵⁵ my conscience, I can in no wise¹⁵⁶ do it—and that for the instruction of my conscience in the matter, I have not slightly looked, but by many years studied and advisedly considered, and never could yet see nor hear that thing,

---

137 appropriate 138 perhaps 139 kidneys 140 *gravel and stone:* kidney stones 141 when 142 much 143 when 144 suitably 145 *seven psalms:* the penitential psalms, i.e., Pss 6, 31(32), 37(38), 50(51), 101(102), 129(130), & 142(143) 146 the Litany of the Saints 147 had been said 148 outside (the Tower) 149 in good time 150 reputation 151 know 152 *but if:* unless 153 See Gn 3. 154 more often 155 continuing or remaining with 156 way

nor I think I never shall, that could induce mine own mind to think otherwise than I do—I have no manner[157] remedy but God hath given me to the strait:[158] that either I must deadly displease him, or abide any worldly harm that he shall for mine other sins, under name of this thing, suffer[159] to fall upon me. Whereof[160] (as I before this have told you too) I have, ere[161] I came here, not left unbethought nor unconsidered the very worst and the uttermost that can by possibility fall. And albeit that[162] I know mine own frailty full well and the natural faintness of mine own heart, yet if I had not trusted that God should give me strength rather to endure all things than offend him by swearing ungodly against mine own conscience, you may be very sure I would not have come here. And since I look in this matter but only unto God, it maketh me little matter though men call it as it pleaseth them and say it is no conscience but a foolish scruple."

At this word I took a good occasion, and said unto him thus: "In good faith, father, for my part I neither do, nor it cannot become me, either to mistrust your good mind or your learning. But because you speak of that—that some call it but a scruple— I assure you, you shall see my sister's letter, that one of the greatest estates[163] in this realm, and a man learned too, and (as I dare say yourself shall think when you know him, and as you have already right effectually proved him) your tender friend and very special good lord, accounteth your conscience in this matter for a right simple scruple; and you may be sure he saith it of good mind and layeth[164] no little cause.[165] For he saith that where you say your conscience moveth you to this, all the nobles of this realm, and almost all other men too, go boldly forth with the contrary and stick[166] not thereat, save only yourself and one other man,[167] whom, though he be right good and very well-learned too, yet would I ween[168] few that love you give you the counsel, against all other men, to lean to his mind alone."

And with this word I took him your letter that he might see my words were not feigned, but spoken of his mouth whom he much loveth and esteemeth highly. Thereupon he read over your letter.

And when he came to the end, he began it afresh and read it over again. And in the reading he made no manner haste, but advised[169] it leisurely and pointed[170] every word.

And after that he paused, and then thus he said: "Forsooth,[171] daughter Margaret, I find my daughter Alington such as I have ever found her, and I trust ever shall, as naturally minding me as you that are mine own. Howbeit,[172] her take I verily[173] for mine own too, since I have married her mother, and brought up her of[174] a child as I have brought up you, in other things and learning both, wherein, I thank God, she findeth now some fruit, and bringeth her own up very virtuously and well. Whereof[175] God, I thank him, hath sent her good store; our Lord preserve them and send her much joy of them and my good son her gentle husband too, and have mercy on the soul of mine other good son her first;[176] I am daily beadsman[177] (and so write her) for them all.

"In this matter she hath used[178] herself like herself: wisely and like a very daughter toward me, and in the end of her letter, giveth as good counsel as any man that wit hath would wish; God give me grace to follow it and God reward her for it. Now, daughter Margaret, as for my Lord, I not only think, but have also found it, that he is undoubtedly my singular good lord. And in mine other business concerning the seely[179] nun,[180] as my cause was good and clear, so was he my good lord therein, and Master Secretary[181] my good master too, for which I shall never cease to be faithful beadsman for them both and daily do I, by my troth,[182] pray for them as I do for myself. And whensoever it should happen (which I trust in God shall never happen) that I be found other than a true man to my Prince, let them never favor me—neither of them both—nor of truth no more it could become them to do.

"But in this matter, Meg, to tell the truth between thee and me, my Lord's Aesop's fables do not greatly move me. But as his Wisdom,[183] for his pastime, told them merrily to mine one daughter, so shall I, for my pastime, answer them to thee, Meg, that art mine other daughter. The first fable, of the rain that washed away all their wits that[184] stood

---

157 kind of   **158** narrow place   **159** allow
160 Of that [harm]   **161** before
162 *albeit that:* although   **163** noblemen
164 puts forward   **165** reasoning
166 hesitate; scruple   **167** Bishop John
Fisher   **168** think   **169** examined

170 marked, noted   **171** Indeed
172 However   **173** truly   **174** since
175 of which (children)   **176** her deceased
first husband, Thomas Elrington   **177** one
who prays for another   **178** conducted
179 pitiable, foolish   **180** Elizabeth

Barton   **181** Thomas Cromwell
182 truthfulness, faithfulness   **183** Audley,
the Lord Chancellor   **184** *their wits that:*
the wits of those who

abroad[185] when it fell, I have heard often ere this. It was a tale so often told among the King's Council by my Lord Cardinal[186] when his Grace was chancellor that I cannot lightly forget it. For of troth, in times past, when variance began to fall between the Emperor[187] and the French King[188] in such wise that they were likely and did indeed fall together at war, and that there were in the Council here sometimes sundry opinions—in which some were of the mind that they thought it wisdom that we should sit still and let them alone, but evermore against that way—my Lord used this fable of those wise men that,[189] because they would not be washed with the rain that should make all the people fools, went themselves into caves and hid them[190] under the ground. But when the rain had once made all the remnant fools and that they[191] come out of their caves and would utter their wisdom, the fools agreed together against them, and there all-to[192] beat them. And so said his Grace that if we would be so wise that we would sit in peace while the fools fought, they would not fail after[193] to make peace and agree and fall at length all upon us. I will not dispute upon his Grace's counsel, and I trust we never made war but as reason would. But yet this fable, for his part, did in his days help the King and the realm to spend many a fair penny. But that gear[194] is passed and his Grace is gone, our Lord assoil[195] his soul.

"And therefore shall I now come to this Aesop's fable, as my Lord full merrily laid it forth for me. If those wise men, Meg, when the rain was gone at their coming abroad—where they found all men fools—wished themselves fools too because they could not rule them, then seemeth it that the foolish rain was so sore[196] a shower that, even through the ground, it sank into their caves, and poured down upon their heads, and wet them to the skin, and made them more noddies[197] than them that stood abroad. For if they had had any wit, they might well see that, though they had been fools too, that thing would not have sufficed to make them the rulers over the other fools, no more than the other fools over them; and of so many fools all might not be rulers. Now when they longed so sore to bear a rule

among fools—that so they, they so might[198]—they would be glad to lose their wit and be fools too, the foolish rain had washed them meetly[199] well. Howbeit, to say the truth, before the rain came, if they thought that all the remnant should turn into fools and then either were so foolish that they would or so mad to think that they should, so few, rule so many fools and had not so much wit as to consider that there are none so unruly as they that lack wit and are fools, then were these wise men stark fools before the rain came. Howbeit, daughter Roper, whom my Lord taketh here for the wise men and whom he meaneth to be fools, I cannot very well guess; I cannot well read such riddles. For as Davus saith in Terence, *Non sum Oedipus,*[200] I may say, you wot[201] well, *Non sum Oedipus, sed Morus,*[202] which name of mine, what it signifieth in Greek, I need not tell you. But I trust my Lord reckoneth me among the fools, and so reckon I myself, as my name is in Greek. And I find, I thank God, causes not a few, wherefore I so should in very deed.

"But surely among those that long to be rulers, God and mine own conscience clearly knoweth that no man may truly number and reckon me. And I ween each other man's conscience can tell himself the same, since it is so well known that, of the King's great goodness, I was one of the greatest rulers in this noble realm and that, at mine own great labor by his great goodness, discharged. But whomsoever my Lord meaneth for the wise men, and whomsoever his Lordship take for the fools, and whosoever long for the rule, and whosoever long for none, I beseech our Lord make us all so wise as that we may, every man here, so wisely rule ourselves in this time of tears, this vale of misery, this simple wretched world—in which, as Boethius saith, one man to be proud that he beareth rule over other men is much like as one mouse would be proud to bear a rule over other mice in a barn[203]—God, I say, give us the grace so wisely to rule ourselves here that when we shall hence in haste to meet the great Spouse, we be not taken sleepers and, for lack of light in our lamps, shut out of heaven among the five foolish virgins.[204]

---

185 outside   **186** Cardinal Wolsey, More's predecessor as Lord Chancellor   **187** Charles V, Holy Roman Emperor   **188** Francis I   **189** who   **190** themselves   **191** *that they:* if they (the wisemen)   **192** utterly, completely   **193** afterwards

194 matter, talk   **195** absolve, forgive   **196** great   **197** fools   **198** *that so they, they so might:* that in whatever way they (were able to obtain rule), they would (obtain it)   **199** fairly; quite   **200** *Non sum Oedipus:* "I am not Oedipus." See

Terence's *Andria* 1.2.23. Oedipus famously solved the riddle of the Sphinx.   **201** know   **202** *sed Morus:* "but More"; in Greek, *Morus* means "fool."   **203** *one man … in a barn:* Boethius, *The Consolation of Philosophy,* 2. Pr. 6.147   **204** Mt 25:1–13

"The second fable, Marget, seemeth not to be Aesop's. For by that[205] the matter goeth all upon confession, it seemeth to be feigned since Christendom began. For in Greece before Christ's days they used not confession, no more the men then than the beasts now. And Aesop was a Greek, and died long ere Christ was born. But what? Who made it, maketh little matter. Nor I envy not[206] that Aesop hath the name.[207] But surely it is somewhat too subtle for me. For whom his Lordship understandeth by the lion and the wolf (which both twain[208] confessed themselves of ravin[209] and devouring of all that came to their hands, and the one enlarged his conscience at his pleasure in the construction[210] of his penance), nor whom by the good discreet confessor (that enjoined the one a little penance, and the other none at all, and sent the poor ass to the bishop)—of all these things can I nothing tell. But by the foolish scrupulous ass (that had so sore[211] a conscience, for the taking of a straw for hunger out of his master's shoe), my Lord's other words of my scruple declare that his Lordship merrily meant that by me, signifying (as it seemeth by that similitude) that of oversight and folly my scrupulous conscience taketh for a great perilous thing toward my soul if I should swear this oath, which thing, as his Lordship thinketh, were indeed but a trifle. And I suppose well, Margaret, as you told me right now, that so thinketh many more beside, as well spiritual as temporal,[212] and that even of those that, for their learning and their virtue, myself not a little esteem. And yet albeit that[213] I suppose this to be true, yet believe I not even very surely that every man so thinketh that so saith. But though they did, daughter, that would not make much to me, not though I should see my Lord of Rochester[214] say the same, and swear the oath himself before me too.

"For whereas you told me right now that such as love me would not advise me that, against all other men, I should lean unto his mind alone, verily, daughter, no more I do. For albeit that, of very truth, I have him in that reverent estimation that I reckon in this realm no one man—in wisdom, learning, and long-approved virtue together—meet[215] to be matched and compared with him, yet, that in this matter I was not led by him very well and plainly appeareth both in that I refused the oath before it was offered him and in that also that his Lordship was content to have sworn of that oath (as I perceived since by[216] you when you moved me to the same) either somewhat more, or in some other manner than ever I minded to do. Verily, daughter, I never intend (God being my good lord) to pin my soul at another man's back, not even the best man that I know this day living, for I know not whither he may hap[217] to carry it. There is no man living of whom, while he liveth, I may make myself sure. Some may do for favor, and some may do for fear, and so might they carry my soul a wrong way. And some might hap to frame himself a conscience and think that, while he did it for fear, God would forgive it. And some may peradventure[218] think that they will repent, and be shriven[219] thereof, and that so God shall remit it them. And some may be peradventure of that mind that, if they say one thing and think the while the contrary, God more regardeth their heart than their tongue, and that therefore their oath goeth upon that they think and not upon that they say, as a woman reasoned once—I trow,[220] daughter, you were by. But in good faith, Marget, I can use no such ways in so great a matter; but like[221] as if mine own conscience served me, I would not let[222] to do it though other men refused, so though others refuse it not, I dare not do it, mine own conscience standing against it. If I had (as I told you) looked but lightly for[223] the matter, I should have cause to fear. But now have I so looked for it, and so long, that I purpose at the leastwise to have no less regard unto my soul than had once a poor honest man of the country that was called Company."

And with this, he told me a tale. I ween[224] I can scant[225] tell it you again, because it hangeth upon some terms and ceremonies of the law. But as far as I can call to mind, my father's tale was this: That there is a court belonging of course[226] unto every fair, to do justice in such things as happen within the same. This court hath a pretty fond[227] name, but I cannot happen upon it, but it beginneth with a pie, and the

205 *by that:* inasmuch as   **206** *Nor … not:* Nor am I envious (the double negative was standard at More's time)   **207** fame, glory   **208** *both twain:* both the two   **209** the act of taking prey   **210** construing   **211** distressed   **212** *as well … temporal:* clergy as well as laymen   **213** although   **214** *Lord of Rochester:* Bishop Fisher, the only bishop who refused to swear the oath   **215** suitable, worthy   **216** *perceived since by:* learned subsequently from   **217** happen   **218** perhaps   **219** forgiven in the sacrament of confession   **220** believe   **221** just   **222** hesitate   **223** into   **224** think   **225** hardly, scarcely   **226** *of course:* routinely   **227** silly

remnant goeth much like the name of a knight that I have known, iwis[228] (and I trow you too, for he hath been at my father's often ere this, at such time as you were there), a meetly tall black[229] man; his name was Sir William Pounder. But tut,[230] let the name of the court go for this once, or call it, if ye will, a court of pie Sir William Pounder.[231] But this was the matter, lo: That upon a time, at such a court held at Bartholomew Fair,[232] there was an escheator[233] of London that had arrested a man that was outlawed,[234] and had seized his goods that he had brought into the fair, tolling[235] him out of the fair by a train.[236] The man that was arrested and his goods seized was a northern man, which, by[237] his friends, made the escheator within the fair to be arrested upon an action[238] (I wot nere[239] what), and so was he brought before the judge of the court of pie Sir William Pounder, and at the last, the matter came to a certain ceremony to be tried by a quest[240] of twelve men, a jury, as I remember they call it, or else a perjury.

Now had the clothman,[241] by friendship of the officers, founden the means to have all the quest, almost, made of the northern men, such as had their booths there standing in the fair. Now was it come to the last day[242] in the afternoon, and the twelve men had heard both the parties and their counsel tell their tales at the bar, and were, from the bar, had into a place to talk and commune[243] and agree upon their sentence. Nay, let me speak better in my terms yet: I trow the judge giveth the sentence and the quest's tale is called a verdict. They were scant[244] come in together, but the northern men were agreed — and in effect all the others too — to cast[245] our London escheator. They thought they needed no more to prove that he did wrong than even the name[246] of his bare office alone. But then, was there then (as the devil would) this honest man of another quarter, that was called Company. And because the fellow seemed but a fool and sat still and said nothing, they made no reckoning of him, but said, "We be agreed now; come, let us go give our verdict."

Then when the poor fellow saw that they made such haste, and his mind nothing gave him that way that theirs did (if their minds gave them that way that they said), he prayed[247] them to tarry[248] and talk upon the matter and tell him such reason therein, that he might think as they did; and when he so should do, he would be glad to say with them, or else, he said, they must pardon him. For since he had a soul of his own to keep as they had, he must say as he thought for his, as they must for theirs. When they heard this, they were half angry with him. "What, good fellow?" quoth one of the northern men. "Where wonnest thou?[249] Be not we eleven here and you but ene la alene,[250] and all we agreed? Whereto[251] shouldst you stick?[252] What is thy name, gude[253] fellow?" "Masters," quoth he, "my name is called Company." "Company," quoth they, "now by thy troth,[254] gude fellow, play then the gude companion; come thereon[255] forth with us and pass,[256] even for gude company." "Would God, good masters," quoth the man again, "that there lay no more weight[257] thereby. But now when we shall hence and come before God, and that he shall send you to heaven for doing according to your conscience, and me to the devil for doing against mine, in passing[258] at your request here for good company now, by God, Master Dickenson" (that was one of the northern men's name), "if I shall then say to all you again, 'Masters, I went once for good company with you, which is the cause that I go now to hell, play you the good fellows now again with me; as I went then for good company with you, so some of you go now for good company with me.' Would ye go, Master Dickenson? Nay, nay, by our Lady, nor never one of you all. And therefore must ye pardon me from passing as you pass; but if[259] I thought in the matter as you do, I dare not in such a matter pass for good company. For the passage of my poor soul passeth[260] all good company."

And when my father had told me this tale, then said he further thus: "I pray thee now, good Marget,

---

228 indeed, certainly **229** black hair or eyes; dark-complexioned **230** no matter **231** *pie Sir William Pounder:* The court at an English fair is called a "Court of Piepowders" from French *pieds poudrés* (dusty feet), as justice was administered without delay to all who came, dusty as they were from traveling. **232** a fair that was held annually from 1133 to 1855, at West Smithfield **233** a law officer **234** a technical legal term meaning (in this case) that he had been

stripped of his property rights by a court **235** debarring (a legal action) **236** course of action; deceit **237** *which, by:* who, by the help of **238** a legal suit or warrant **239** *wot nere:* know not **240** a legally established board **241** the defendant, who was at the fair to sell cloth **242** a legal term for a court session **243** discuss, confer **244** hardly **245** defeat in a legal action **246** The officer was called both an "escheator" and a "cheator" at this time.

247 asked **248** wait **249** *Where wonnest thou?:* Where do you live? ("Wonnest" is a word of northern England's dialect) **250** *ene la alene:* northern dialect for "one all alone" **251** For what reason? **252** persist; remain fixed **253** northern dialect for "good" **254** truth, faithfulness **255** on that subject **256** render a verdict (legal term) **257** *lay weight:* were attached importance **258** voting for a verdict **259** *but if:* unless **260** surpasses

tell me this: wouldst you wish thy poor father, being at the leastwise somewhat learned, less to regard the peril of his soul than did there the honest unlearned man? I meddle not (you wot[261] well) with the conscience of any man that hath sworn; nor I take not upon me to be their judge. But now if they do well, and that their conscience grudge[262] them not, if I, with my conscience to the contrary, should for good company pass on with them and swear as they do, when all our souls hereafter shall pass out of this world and stand in judgment at the bar before the high Judge, if he judge them to heaven and me to the devil because I did as they did, not thinking as they thought, if I should then say (as the good man Company said): 'Mine old good lords and friends (naming such a lord and such; yea, and some bishops peradventure of such as I love best), I swore because you swore and went that way that you went; do likewise for me now; let me not go alone; if there be any good fellowship with you, some of you come with me,' by my troth, Marget, I may say to thee — in secret counsel, here between us twain (but let it go no farther, I beseech thee heartily) — I find the friendship of this wretched world so fickle that for anything that I could treat[263] or pray, that would for good fellowship go to the devil with me, among them all I ween[264] I should not find one. And then, by God, Marget, if you think so too, best it is, I suppose, that for[265] any respect of them all, were they twice as many more as they be, I have myself a respect to mine own soul.'"

"Surely, father," quoth I, "without any scruple at all you may be bold, I dare say, for to swear that. But father, they that think you should not refuse to swear the thing that you see so many so good men, and so well-learned, swear before you, mean not that you should swear to bear them fellowship, nor to pass with them for good company, but that the credence that you may with reason give to their persons for their aforesaid qualities should well move you to think the oath such of itself as every man may well swear without peril of their soul, if their own private conscience to the contrary be not the let,[266] and that ye well ought and have good cause to change your own conscience, in conforming your own conscience to the conscience of so many others, namely[267] being such as you know they be. And since it is also by a law made by the Parliament commanded, they think that you be, upon the peril of your soul, bounden to change and reform your conscience, and conform your own, as I said, to other men's."

"Marry,[268] Marget," quoth my father again, "for the part that you play, you play it not much amiss. But, Margaret, first, as for the law of the land, though every man being born and inhabiting therein is bounden to the keeping in every case upon some temporal pain and in many cases upon pain of God's displeasure too, yet is there no man bounden to swear that every law is well made, nor bounden upon the pain of God's displeasure to perform any such point of the law as were indeed unlawful. Of which manner kind, that there may such hap[269] to be made in any part of Christendom, I suppose no man doubteth, the General Council of the whole body of Christendom evermore in that point except,[270] which,[271] though it may make some things better than others and some things may grow to that point that by another law they may need to be reformed, yet to institute anything in such wise, to God's displeasure, as at the making might not lawfully be performed, the Spirit of God, that governeth his Church, never hath yet suffered,[272] nor never hereafter shall, his whole Catholic Church lawfully gathered together in a General Council — as Christ hath made plain promises in Scripture.

"Now if it so hap that, in any particular part of Christendom, there be a law made that be such as, for[273] some part thereof, some men think that the law of God cannot bear it, and some other think yes (the thing being in such manner in question that through diverse quarters of Christendom some that are good men and cunning,[274] both of our own days and before our days, think some one way, and some other of like learning and goodness think the contrary), in this case he that thinketh against the law neither may swear that law lawfully was made, standing his own conscience to the contrary, nor is bounden upon pain of God's displeasure to change his own conscience therein for any particular law made anywhere, other than by the General Council or by a general faith grown by the working of God universally through all Christian nations — nor other authority than one of these twain[275] (except special revelation and express commandment of

261 know   262 trouble, disturb   268 Indeed (from "by Mary")   (Council)   272 permitted   273 because
263 entreat   264 think   265 despite   269 happen   270 excepted   271 that   of   274 learned; clever   275 two
266 hindrance   267 especially

God), since the contrary opinions of good men and well-learned, as I put you the case, made the understanding of the Scriptures doubtful, I can see none that lawfully may command and compel any man to change his own opinion and to translate[276] his own conscience from the one side to the other.

"For an example of some such manner things, I have, I trow,[277] before this time told you that, whether our Blessed Lady were conceived in original sin or not, was some time in great question among the great learned men of Christendom. And whether it be yet decided and determined by any General Council, I remember not. But this I remember well, that notwithstanding that the feast[278] of her conception was then celebrated in the Church (at the leastwise in diverse provinces), yet was holy Saint Bernard—which, as his manifold books made in the laud and praise of our Lady do declare, was of as devout affection toward all things sounding toward her commendation that he thought might well be verified or suffered as any man was living—yet, I say, was that holy devout man against that part of her praise, as appeareth well by an epistle of his wherein he right sore[279] and with great reason argueth thereagainst and approveth not the institution of that feast neither. Nor he was not of this mind alone, but many other well-learned men with him, and right holy men too. Now was there on the other side the blessed holy bishop Saint Anselm, and he not alone neither, but many well-learned and very virtuous also with him. And they be both twain holy saints in heaven, and many more that were on either side. Nor neither part was there bounden to change their opinion for the other, nor for any provincial council either.

"But like as, after the determination of a well assembled General Council, every man had been bounden to give credence that way and conform their own conscience to the determination of the Council General, and then all they that held the contrary before were for that holding out of blame, so if before such decision a man had against his own conscience sworn to maintain and defend the other side, he had not failed to offend God very sore. But, marry, if on the other side a man would in a matter take away[280]—by himself upon his own mind alone, or with some few, or with never so many—against

an evident truth appearing by the common faith of Christendom, this conscience is very damnable; yea, or if it be not even fully so plain and evident, yet if he see but himself with far the fewer part think the one way, against far the more part (of as well-learned and as good as those are that affirm the thing that he thinketh) thinking and affirming the contrary, and that of such folk as he hath no reasonable cause wherefore he should not in that matter suppose that those which say they think against his mind affirm the thing that they say for none other cause but for[281] that they so think indeed: this is, of very truth, a very good occasion to move him, and yet not to compel him, to conform his mind and conscience unto theirs.

"But Margaret, for what causes I refuse the oath, the thing (as I have often told you) I will never show you, neither you nor nobody else, except the King's Highness should like to command me. Which if his Grace did, I have ere[282] this told you therein how obediently I have said. But surely, daughter, I have refused it and do, for more causes than one. And for what causes soever I refuse it, this am I sure: that it is well known that, of them that have sworn it, some of the best-learned, before the oath given them, said and plain affirmed the contrary of some such things as they have now sworn in the oath—and that upon their troth, and their learning then, and that not in haste nor suddenly, but often and after great diligence done to seek and find out the truth."

"That might be, father," quoth I.

"And yet since they might see more, I will not," quoth he, "dispute, daughter Margaret, against that, nor misjudge any other man's conscience, which lieth in their own heart, far out of my sight. But this will I say, that I never heard myself the cause of their change, by any new further thing founden of authority, than as far as I perceive they had looked on, and as I suppose, very well weighed before. Now, if the selfsame things that they saw before seem some otherwise unto them now than they did before, I am, for their sakes, the gladder a great deal. But anything that ever I saw before, yet at this day to me they seem but as they did. And therefore, though they may do otherwise than they might, yet, daughter, I may not. As for such things as some men would haply[283] say that I might with reason the less regard

276 convey; transfer **277** trust **278** of the Immaculate Conception **279** *right* *sore:* very strongly **280** from its actual condition **281** *but for:* except **282** before **283** perhaps

their change, for any example of them to be taken to the change of my conscience because that the keeping of the Prince's pleasure and the avoiding of his indignation, the fear of the losing of their worldly substance,[284] with regard unto the discomfort of their kindred and their friends, might hap make some men either swear otherwise than they think or frame their conscience afresh to think otherwise than they thought — any such opinion as this is, will I not conceive of them; I have better hope of their goodness than to think of them so. For if such things should have turned them, the same things had been likely to make me do the same; for, in good faith, I knew few so fainthearted as myself. Therefore will I, Margaret, by my will, think no worse of other folk in the thing that I know not, than I find in myself. But, as I know well mine only conscience[285] causeth me to refuse the oath, so will I trust in God that according to their conscience they have received it and sworn.

"But whereas you think, Marget, that they[286] be so many more than there are on the other side that think in this thing as I think, surely for your own comfort — that you shall not take thought, thinking that your father casteth himself away so like a fool that he would jeopard[287] the loss of his substance, and peradventure[288] his body, without any cause why he so should for peril of his soul, but rather his soul in peril thereby too — to this shall I say to thee, Marget, that in some of my causes I nothing doubt at all but that, though not in this realm, yet in Christendom about, of those well-learned men and virtuous that are yet alive, they be not the fewer part that are of my mind. Besides that, that it were,[289] ye wot[290] well, possible that some men in this realm too, think not so clear the contrary, as by the oath received they have sworn to say.

"Now this far-forth[291] I say for them that are yet alive. But go we now to them that are dead before and that are, I trust, in heaven; I am sure that it is not the fewer part of them that, all the time while they lived, thought in some of the things the way that I think now. I am also, Margaret, of this thing sure enough, that of those holy doctors and saints, which to be with God in heaven long ago no Christian man doubteth, whose books yet at this day remain here in men's hands, there thought in

some such things as I think now. I say not that they thought all so, but surely such and so many (as will well appear by their writing) that I pray God give me the grace that my soul may follow theirs. And yet I show you not all, Margaret, that I have for myself in the sure discharge of my conscience. But for the conclusion, daughter Margaret, of all this matter, as I have often told you, I take not upon me neither to define nor dispute in these matters; nor I rebuke not nor impugn any other man's deed, nor I never wrote, nor so much as spoke in any company, any word of reproach in anything that the Parliament had passed; nor I meddled not with the conscience of any other man that either thinketh or saith he thinketh contrary unto mine. But as concerning mine own self, for thy comfort shall I say, daughter, to thee, that mine own conscience in this matter (I damn none other man's) is such as may well stand with mine own salvation; thereof am I, Meg, so sure, as that is, God is in heaven. And therefore as for all the remnant — goods, lands, and life both (if the chance should so fortune) — since this conscience is sure for me, I verily trust in God, he shall rather strengthen me to bear the loss, than against this conscience to swear and put my soul in peril, since all the causes that I perceive move other men to the contrary seem not such unto me as in my conscience make any change."

When he saw me sit with this[292] very sad — as I promise you, sister, my heart was full heavy[293] for the peril of his person; for in faith I fear not his soul — he smiled upon me and said: "How now, daughter Marget? What how, mother Eve? Where is your mind now? Sit not musing with some serpent in your breast, upon some new persuasion, to offer father Adam the apple yet once again?"

"In good faith, father," quoth I, "I can no further go, but am (as I trow[294] Cressida saith in Chaucer)[295] comen to dulcarnon,[296] even at my wit's end. For since the example of so many wise men cannot in this matter move you, I see not what to say more, but if[297] I should look to persuade you with the reason that Master Harry Patenson[298] made. For he met one day one of our men, and when he had asked where you were and heard that you were in the Tower still, he waxed even[299] angry with you

---

284 wealth, property   **285** *mine only conscience:* my conscience alone   **286** those who have sworn   **287** jeopardize, risk   **288** perhaps   **289** *that it were:* it could be

290 know   **291** to a great extent   **292** *me sit with this:* that this made me   **293** sad, distressed   **294** believe   **295** *Cressida saith in Chaucer: Troilus and Criseyde,*

3.930–31   **296** a point of perplexity   **297** *but if:* except, unless   **298** *Harry Patenson:* More's household jester   **299** *waxed even:* became quite

and said, 'Why? What aileth him that he will not swear? Wherefore[300] should he stick[301] to swear? I have sworn the oath myself.' And so I can in good faith go now no further neither, after so many wise men whom ye take for no example, but if I should say like Master Harry: Why should you refuse to swear, father? For I have sworn myself."[302]

At this he laughed and said, "That word was like Eve too, for she offered Adam no worse fruit than she had eaten herself."

"But yet father, " quoth I, "by my troth, I fear me very sore[303] that this matter will bring you in marvelous heavy trouble. You know well that, as I showed you, Master Secretary sent you word as your very[304] friend to remember that the Parliament lasteth yet."[305]

"Margaret," quoth my father, "I thank him right heartily. But as I showed you then again, I left not this gear[306] unthought on. And albeit[307] I know well that if they would make a law to do me any harm, that law could never be lawful, but that[308] God shall I trust keep me in that grace, that concerning my duty to my prince, no man shall do me hurt but if he do me wrong (and then, as I told you, this is like a riddle, a case in which a man may lose his head and have no harm), and notwithstanding also that I have good hope that God shall never suffer[309] so good and wise a prince in such wise to requite the long service of his true faithful servant, yet since there is nothing impossible to fall,[310] I forgot not in this matter the counsel of Christ in the Gospel[311] that ere I should begin to build this castle for the safeguard of mine own soul, I should sit and reckon what the charge would be. I counted, Marget, full surely many a restless night—while my wife slept, and weened[312] that I had slept too—what peril was possible for to fall to me, so far-forth that I am sure there can come none above. And in devising,[313] daughter, thereupon, I had a full heavy heart. But yet—I thank our Lord—for all that, I never thought to change, though the very uttermost should hap[314] me that my fear ran upon."

"No, father," quoth I, "it is not like[315] to think upon a thing that may be, and to see a thing that shall be, as ye should (our Lord save you) if the chance should so fortune.[316] And then should[317] you peradventure[318] think that you think not now and yet then peradventure it would be too late."

"Too late, daughter" (quoth my father) "Margaret? I beseech our Lord that if ever I make such a change, it may be too late indeed. For well I wot the change cannot be good for my soul, that change, I say, that should grow but by fear. And therefore I pray God that in this world I never have good[319] of such change. For so much as I take harm here, I shall have at the leastwise the less therefore when I am hence. And if so were[320] that I wist[321] well now that I should[322] faint and fall, and for fear swear hereafter, yet would I wish to take harm by the refusing first, for so should I have the better hope for grace to rise again.

"And albeit, Marget, that I wot well my lewdness[323] hath been such that I know myself well worthy that God should let me slip, yet can I not but trust in his merciful goodness, that as his grace hath strengthened me hitherto, and made me content in my heart to lose goods, land, and life too, rather than to swear against my conscience, and hath also put in the King toward me that[324] good and gracious mind that as yet he hath taken from me nothing but my liberty—wherewith[325] (as help me God) his Grace hath done me so great good by the spiritual profit that I trust I take thereby, that among all his great benefits heaped upon me so thick, I reckon upon my faith my prisonment even the very chief—I cannot, I say, therefore mistrust the grace of God, but that either he shall conserve and keep the King in that gracious mind still to do me none hurt, or else, if his pleasure be, that for mine other sins I shall suffer in such a case in sight[326] as I shall not deserve, his grace shall give me the strength to take it patiently, and peradventure somewhat gladly too, whereby his high goodness shall (by the merits of his bitter Passion joined thereunto, and far surmounting in merit for me, all that I can suffer myself) make it serve for release of my pain in purgatory and, over[327] that, for increase of some reward in heaven.

"Mistrust him, Meg, will I not; though I feel me faint, yea, and though I should feel my fear even at

---

300 Why   **301** hesitate; scruple
302 After this line in the 1557 *Workes*, a marginal note reads: "She toke the othe with this excepcion [:] as farre as would stande with the law of god" (1441).
303 greatly   **304** true   **305** *lasteth*

yet: is still in session   **306** matter
307 although   **308** *but that:* but (notwithstanding)   **309** allow; permit
310 happen   **311** Lk 14:28   **312** thought
313 thinking out; examining   **314** happen to   **315** the same   **316** *the chance…*

fortune: it does happen to turn out that way
317 might   **318** perhaps   **319** benefit
320 *so were:* it was the case   **321** knew
322 would   **323** sinfulness   **324** such a
325 by doing so   **326** *in sight:* apparently
327 in addition to

point to overthrow me too, yet shall I remember
how Saint Peter, with a blast of wind, began to sink
for his faint faith, and shall do as he did: call upon
Christ and pray him to help.[328] And then I trust he
5   shall set his holy hand unto me, and in the stormy
seas hold me up from drowning. Yea and if he suffer[329] me to play St. Peter further, and to fall full[330]
to the ground and swear and forswear too—which
our Lord, for his tender Passion, keep me from, and
10   let me lose if it so fall,[331] and never win thereby—yet
after shall I trust that his goodness will cast upon
me his tender piteous eye,[332] as he did upon St. Peter,
and make me stand up again and confess the truth
of my conscience afresh, and abide the shame and
15   harm here of mine own fault.

    "And finally, Marget, this wot I well, that without
my fault[333] he will not let me be lost. I shall therefore with good hope commit myself wholly to him.
And if he suffer me for my faults to perish, yet shall
20   I then serve for a praise of his justice. But in good
faith, Meg, I trust that his tender pity shall keep my
poor soul safe and make me commend[334] his mercy.
And therefore, mine own good daughter, never
trouble thy mind for anything that ever shall hap
25   me in this world. Nothing can come but that that[335]
God will. And I make me very sure that whatsoever
that be, seem it never so bad in sight, it shall indeed
be the best. And with this, my good child, I pray you
heartily, be you and all your sisters and my sons too
30   comfortable[336] and serviceable to your good mother
my wife. And of your good husbands' minds I have
no manner[337] doubt. Commend me to them all, and
to my good daughter Alington, and to all my other
friends, sisters, nieces, nephews, and allies,[338] and
35   unto all our servants—man, woman, and child—
and all my good neighbors, and our acquaintance
abroad. And I right heartily pray both you and
them to serve God and be merry and rejoice in him.
And if anything hap me that you would be loath,
40   pray to God for me, but trouble not yourself, as I
shall full heartily pray for us all, that we may meet
together once in heaven, where we shall make merry
forever, and never have trouble after."

207. To Dr. Nicholas Wilson
Tower of London, 1534   45

*A letter written and sent by Sir T. More to Master
Doctor Nicholas Wilson*[339] *(then both prisoners in
the Tower of London) in the year of our Lord God
1534, and in the twenty-sixth year of the reign of King
Henry the Eighth.* [Workes 1443]   50

Our Lord be your comfort and whereas I perceive
by sundry means that you have promised to swear
the oath, I beseech our Lord give you thereof good
luck. I never gave any man counsel to the contrary
in my days nor never used any ways to put any scru-   55
ple in other folks' conscience concerning the matter. And whereas I perceive that you would gladly
know what I intend to do, you wot[340] well that I
told you when we were both abroad that I would
therein neither know your mind nor no man's else,   60
nor you nor no man else should therein know mine,
for I would be no part taker[341] with no man nor of
troth[342] never I will, but leaving every other man to
their own conscience myself will with good grace
follow mine. For against mine own to swear were   65
peril of my damnation and what mine own shall
be tomorrow myself cannot be sure and whether I
shall have finally the grace to do according to mine
own conscience or not hangeth in God's goodness
and not in mine, to whom I beseech you heartily re-   70
member me in your devout prayers and I shall and
daily do remember you in mine, such as they be, and
as long as my poor short life shall last, any thing that
I have, your part shall be therein.

208. To Dr. Nicholas Wilson   75
Tower of London, 1534

*Another letter written and sent by Sir Thomas More
to Master Doctor Wilson (then both prisoners in
the Tower) in the year of our Lord 1534, and in the
twenty-sixth year of the reign of King Henry the   80
Eighth.* [Workes 1443]

328 *St. Peter...help:* Mt 14:30   **329** permit; allow   **330** *fall full:* Mt 26:69–75
331 happen   **332** *cast...eye:* Lk 22:61
333 failing, sin   **334** praise   **335** *but that
that:* except that which   **336** encouraging,
supporting   **337** kind of   **338** in-laws
339 *Nicholas Wilson:* (d. 1548) B.A.

Cambridge (Christ's College) 1508/9,
D.D. 1533, was chaplain and confessor
to the King, held Church preferments,
and in 1533 was Master of Michaelhouse,
Cambridge. In Convocation he was in the
minority which thought that the Pope
could dispense for the marriage of Henry

with his brother's widow. After two years'
imprisonment in the Tower, he took the
oath to the Succession and was released.
340 know   **341** partisan   **342** *of troth:*
in truth

Master Wilson in my right hearty wise[343] I recommend me to you.

And very sorry am I to see you — besides the trouble that you be in by this imprisonment with loss of liberty, goods, revenues of your livelihood, and comfort of your friends' company — fallen also into such agony and vexation of mind through doubts falling in your mind that diversely[344] to and fro toss and trouble your conscience to your great heaviness of heart as I (to no little grief of mine own mind for your sake) perceive. And so much am I for you, good Master Doctor, the more sorry for that it lieth not in me to give you such kind of comfort as meseemeth[345] you somewhat desire and look for at mine hand.

For whereas you would somewhat hear of my mind in your doubts, I am a man at this day very little meet[346] therefor. For this you know well, good Master Doctor, that at such time as the matter came in such manner in question as mine opinion was asked therein amongst others and yet you made privy thereunto before me, you remember well that at that time you and I many things talked together thereof. And by all the time after by which I did at the King's gracious commandment both seek out and read and commune[347] with all such as I knew made privy to the matter to perceive what I might therein upon both sides and by indifferent[348] weighing of everything as near as my poor wit and learning would serve to see to which side my conscience could incline and, as my own mind should give me, so to make his Highness report which way myself should hap to think therein. For other commandment had I never of his Grace in good faith, saving that this knot[349] his Highness added thereto that I should therein look first unto God and after God unto him, which word was also the first lesson that his Grace gave me what time I came first into his noble service and neither a more indifferent commandment nor a more gracious lesson could there in my mind never King give his counselor or any his other servant.[350]

But as I began to tell you by all this long time,[351] I cannot now tell how many years, of all those that I talked with of the matter and with whom I most conferred[352] those places of Scripture and of the old holy doctors that touched either the one side or the other, with the councils and laws on either side, that speak thereof also, the most, as I trow you wot[353] well, was yourself. For with no man communed I so much and so often thereof as with you, both for your substantial learning and for your mature judgment, and for that[354] I well perceived ever in you that no man had or lightly could have a more faithful respect unto the King's honor and surety[355] both of body and soul than I ever saw that you had.

And yet among many other things which I well liked in you, one specially was that I well perceived in the thing that the King's Grace did put you in trust with,[356] your substantial[357] secret manner. For where I had heard (I wot not now of whom) that you had written his Highness a book of that matter from Paris before, yet in all those years of our long acquaintance and often talking and reasoning upon the thing, I never heard you so much as make once any mention of that book. But else (except[358] there were any other things in that book that you peradventure[359] thought not on) I suppose that all that ever came to your mind, that might in the matter make for the one side or the other comprised[360] either in the Scripture or in the old ancient doctors, I verily[361] think in my mind that you did communicate with[362] me and I likewise with you and at the least wise I remember well that of those points which you call now newly to your remembrance there was none at that time forgotten.

I remember well also by your often conference[363] in the matter that by all the time in which I studied about it, you and I were in every point both twain[364] of one opinion and remember well that the laws and councils and the words of Saint Augustine's *De civitate Dei* and the epistle of Saint Ambrose *Ad paternum* and the epistle of Saint Basil translated out of Greek and the writing of Saint Gregory you and I read together and over that the places of the Scripture itself both in Leviticus and in the Deuteronomy and in the Gospel and in Saint Paul's epistles[365] and, over[366] this, in that other place of Saint Augustine that you remember now and, beside that, other places of his wherein he properly toucheth[367] the matter expressly with the words of Saint Jerome

---

343 manner **344** in diverse ways **345** it seems to me **346** suitable **347** confer, discuss **348** impartial **349** bond, obligation **350** unless **351** *any . . . servant:* any other servant of his **352** *by . . . time:* in all this long time **353** compared **354** *trow you wot:* think you know **355** *for that:* because **356** security **357** *that . . . with:* in which the King's Grace trusted you **358** essentially **359** possibly **360** perceived **361** truly **362** *communicate with:* impart to **363** action of taking counsel **364** together **365** See Lv 20:21; Dt 25:5; Mk 10; Mt 19; 1 Cor 7; 1 Tim 5:14. **366** in addition to **367** treats

and of Saint Chrysostom too, and I cannot now remember of how many more. But I verily think that on your part, and I am very sure that on my part, albeit that[368] it had been peradventure over-long to show and read with you every man's book that I read by myself (whereto the parties peradventure that trusted me therewith gave me no leave to show their books further as you peradventure used the like manner with me) yet in good faith as it was of reason my part in that case to do, you and I having both one commandment indifferently[369] to consider the matter, everything of Scripture and of the doctors, I faithfully communed[370] with you and, as I suppose, verily so did you with me too so that of me, good Master Doctor, though I had all the points as ripe in mind now as I had then and had still all the books about me that I then had, and were as willing to meddle[371] in the matter as any man could be, yet could you now no new thing hear of me more than you have, I ween,[372] heard often before nor, I ween, I of you neither.

But now standeth it with me in far other case. For afterward when I had signified unto the King's Highness mine own poor opinion in the matter, which his Highness very graciously took in good part, and that I saw further progress in the matter wherein to do his Grace service to his pleasure I could not, and anything meddle against his pleasure I would not, I determined utterly with myself to discharge[373] my mind of any further studying or musing of the matter and thereupon I sent home again such books as I had saving[374] that some I burned by the consent of the owner that was minded[375] as myself was no more to meddle of[376] the matter, and therefore now, good Master Doctor, I could not be sufficient and able to reason those points again though I were minded thereto since many things are out of my mind which I never purpose to look for again nor though I would were never like to find again while I live. Besides this, all that ever I looked for was, you wot well, concerning two or three questions to be pondered and weighed by the study of Scripture and the interpreters of the same, save for somewhat that hath been touched in the same by the canon laws of the Church.

But then were there at that time in the matter other things more, diverse faults found in the bull[377] of the dispensation,[378] by which the King's Council learned in the spiritual law reckoned the bull vicious, partly for untrue suggestion,[379] partly by reason of unsufficient suggestion. Now concerning those points I never meddled. For I neither understand the doctors of the law nor well can turn their books. And many things have there since in this great matter grown in question wherein I neither am sufficiently learned in the law nor full informed of the fact, and therefore I am not he that either murmur or grudge,[380] make assertions, hold opinions or keep dispicions[381] in the matter, but like the King's true poor humble subject daily pray for the preservation of his Grace and the Queen's Grace and their noble issue and of all the realm, without harm doing or intending, I thank our Lord, unto any man living.

Finally as touching the oath, the causes for which I refused it, no man wotteth what they be for they be secret in mine own conscience, some other peradventure than those that other men would ween, and such as I never disclosed unto any man yet nor never intend to do while I live. Finally as I said unto you, before the oath offered unto us when we met in London at adventure,[382] I would be no part taker[383] in the matter but for mine own self follow mine own conscience, for which myself must make answer unto God, and shall leave every other man to his own, so say to you still and I dare say further that no more never intended you neither.[384] Many things every man learned[385] wotteth well there are, in which every man is at liberty without peril of damnation to think which way him list[386] till the one part be determined for necessary to be believed by a General Council and I am not he that take upon me to define or determine of what kind or nature everything is that the oath containeth, nor am so bold or presumptuous to blame or dispraise the conscience of other men, their truth nor their learning neither, nor I meddle with no man but of myself, nor of no man's conscience else will I meddle but of mine own. And in mine own conscience I cry God mercy; I find of mine own life, matters enough to think on.

---

368 *albeit that:* although   **369** impartially   **370** conferred, discussed   **371** concern myself   **372** think, suppose   **373** disburden   **374** except   **375** disposed   **376** in   **377** pope's edict, with leaden bulla or seal   **378** ecclesiastical license to do what is otherwise forbidden by canon law   **379** complaints; accusations   **380** grumble   **381** disputations   **382** by chance   **383** partisan   **384** *no … neither:* neither did you intend more   **385** *man learned:* learned man   **386** desires

I have lived, methinks, a long life and now neither I look nor I long to live much longer. I have since I came in the Tower looked once or twice to have given up my ghost ere[387] this and in good faith mine

5 heart waxed[388] the lighter with hope thereof. Yet forget I not that I have a long reckoning and a great to give account of, but I put my trust in God and in the merits of his bitter Passion, and I beseech him give me and keep me the mind to long to be out of this

10 world and to be with him. For I can never but trust that who so long to be with him shall be welcome to him and on the other side my mind giveth me verily that any that ever shall come to him shall full heartily wish to be with him or[389] ever he shall come at[390]

15 him. And I beseech him heartily to set your heart at such rest and quiet as may be to his pleasure and eternal weal[391] of your soul and so I verily trust that he shortly shall and shall also if it be his pleasure incline the King's noble heart to be gracious and fa-

20 vorable to you and me both, since we be both twain of true faithful mind unto him, whether we be in this matter of one mind both, or of diverse. *Sicut divisiones aquarum, ita cor regis in manu Domini, quocumque voluerit, inclinabit illud.*[392] And if the

25 pleasure of God be on any of us both otherwise to dispose,[393] I need to give you no counsel nor advice.

But for myself I most humbly beseech him to give me the grace in such wise patiently to conform my mind unto his high pleasure therein, that, after

30 the troublous storm of this my tempestuous time, his great mercy may conduct me into the sure haven of the joyful bliss of heaven, and after at his further pleasure (if I have any) all mine enemies too; for there shall we love together well enough and I thank

35 our Lord for my part so do I here too. Be not angry now though I pray not like for you; you be sure enough I would my friends fare no worse than they, nor yet they, so help me God, no worse than myself.

For our Lord's sake, good Master Wilson, pray

40 for me for I pray for you daily and sometimes when I would be sorry but if I thought you were asleep. Comfort yourself, good Master Doctor, with remembering God's great mercy and the King's accustomed goodness, and by my troth[394] I think that

all his Grace's Council favoreth you in their hearts.
45 I cannot judge in my mind any one of them so evil as to be of the mind that you should do otherwise than well. And for conclusion, in God is all. *Spes non confundit.*[395] I pray you pardon my scribbling for I cannot always so well endure to write as
50 I might sometime. And I pray you when ye see time convenient at your pleasure, send me this rude bill again. *Quia quamquam nihil inest mali, tamen propter ministrum nolim rescire.*[396]

209. Margaret Roper to More
1534

A letter written and sent by Mistress Margaret Roper, to her father Sir Thomas More then shut up in close prison in the Tower, written in the year of our Lord God 1534, and in the twenty-sixth year of the reign of King Henry the Eighth, answering to a letter which her father had sent unto her. [Workes 1446]

Mine own most entirely beloved father.

I think myself never able to give you sufficient thanks, for the inestimable comfort my poor heart
65 received in the reading of your most loving and godly letter, representing to me the clear shining brightness of your soul, the pure temple of the Holy Spirit of God, which I doubt not shall perpetually rest in you and you in him. Father, if all the world
70 had been given to me, as I be saved, it had been a small pleasure, in comparison of the pleasure I conceived of the treasure of your letter, which though it were written with a coal is worthy in mine opinion to be written in letters of gold.
75

Father, what moved them to shut you up again, we can nothing hear. But surely I conjecture that when they considered that you were of so temperate mind that you were contented to abide there
80 all your life with such liberty, they thought it were never possible to incline you to their will, except it were by restraining you from the church, and the company of my good mother, your dear wife, and us your children and beadsfolk.[397] But, father, this

---

387 *given . . . ere:* to have died before **388** grew **389** before **390** to **391** well-being **392** "As the divisions of waters, so the heart of the king is in the hand of God: whithersoever he will, he shall turn it" (Prv 21:1). **393** *both . . . dispose:* i.e., to dispose

otherwise for either of us **394** faithfulness; truthfulness **395** "Hope does not disappoint" (Rom 5:5). **396** "Because, although there is nothing evil [disloyal or treasonous] in it, yet on account of the servant I would not wish them to discover

it." George Golde, the Lieutenant's servant, carried letters for prisoners. More wished to keep letters to prove their harmlessness, but Golde said there was no better keeper than the fire and burned them. **397** people who pray for others

chance was not strange[398] to you. For I shall not forget how you told us, when we were with you in the garden, that these things were like enough to chance shortly after. Father, I have many times rehearsed to mine own comfort, and diverse others, your fashion and words ye had to us when we were last with you: for which I trust, by the grace of God, to be the better while I live, and when I am departed out of this frail life, which, I pray God, I may pass and end in his true obedient service, after the wholesome counsel and fruitful example of living I have had (good father) of you, whom I pray God give me grace to follow, which I shall the better through the assistance of your devout prayers, the special stay[399] of my frailty. Father, I am sorry I have no longer leisure at this time to talk with you, the chief comfort of my life; I trust to have occasion to write again shortly. I trust I have your daily prayer and blessing.

Your most loving obedient daughter and beadswoman Margaret Roper, which daily and hourly is bound to pray for you, for whom she prayeth in this wise,[400] that our Lord of his infinite mercy give you of his heavenly comfort, and so to assist you with his special grace, that ye never in anything decline from his blessed will, but live and die his true obedient servant. Amen.

210. To Margaret Roper
Tower of London, 1534

A letter written and sent by Sir Thomas More to his daughter Mistress Roper, answering her letter here next before.[401] [*Workes* 1446]

The Holy Spirit of God be with you.

If I would with my writing, mine own good daughter, declare how much pleasure and comfort your daughterly loving letters were unto me, a peck of coals would not suffice to make me the pens. And other pens have I, good Margaret, none here, and therefore can I write you no long process,[402] nor dare adventure,[403] good daughter, to write often.

The cause of my close keeping[404] again did of likelihood grow of my negligent[405] and very plain true word which you remember. And verily[406] where as my mind gave me (as I told you in the garden) that some such thing were likely to happen, so doth my mind always give me that some folk yet ween[407] that I was not so poor as it appeared in the search, and that it may therefore happen that yet eftsoon ofter[408] than once, some new sudden searches may hap to be made in every house of ours as narrowly as is possible. Which thing if ever it so should hap can make but game[409] to us that know the truth of my poverty but if[410] they find out my wife's gay girdle and her golden beads. Howbeit,[411] I verily believe in good faith that the King's Grace of his benign pity will take nothing from her.

I thought and yet think that it may be that I was shut up again upon some new causeless suspicion, grown peradventure[412] upon some secret sinister information, whereby some folk haply[413] thought that there should be found out against me some other greater things. But I thank our Lord whensoever this conjecture hath fallen in my mind, the clearness of my conscience hath made my heart hop for joy. For one thing am I very sure of hitherto, and trust in God's mercy to be while I live, that, as often I have said unto you, I shall for anything toward my Prince never take great harm but if I take great wrong, in the sight of God I say, howsoever it shall seem in the sight of men. For to the world, wrong may seem right sometimes by false conjecturing, sometimes by false witnesses, as that good Lord said unto you, which is I dare say my very good lord in his mind, and said it of very good will. Before the world also, my refusing of this oath is accounted a heinous[414] offense, and my religious fear[415] toward God is called obstinacy toward my Prince. But my lords of the Council, before whom I refused it, might well perceive by the heaviness of my heart appearing well more ways than one unto them that all sturdy stubbornness whereof obstinacy groweth was very far from my mind. For the clearer proof whereof, since they seemed to take for one argument of obstinacy in me that refusing of the oath, I would not declare the causes why, I offered with a full heavy heart, that albeit[416] I rather would endure all the pain and peril of the statute than, by declaring of the causes, give any occasion of exasperation unto my most dread Sovereign Lord and Prince, yet,

398 unknown; unfamiliar 399 support
400 way, manner 401 *letter . . . before:*
i.e., her previous letter 402 narrative
403 try 404 strict confinement.

See reasons given by Harpsfield, 174.
405 careless 406 truly 407 think
408 *eftsoon ofter:* again more often
409 sport 410 *but if:* unless

411 However 412 perhaps 413 by
chance 414 criminal 415 mingled feeling of dread and reverence 416 although

rather than his Highness should for not disclosing the causes account me for stubborn and obstinate, I would upon such his gracious license and commandment as should discharge me of his displeasure and peril of any statute declare those points that letted[417] my poor conscience to receive that oath; and would over[418] that be sworn before, that, if I should after the causes disclosed and declared find them so answered as my conscience should think itself satisfied, I would thereupon swear the oath that I there refused. To this, Master Secretary[419] answered me that though the King's Grace gave me such a license, yet it could not discharge me against[420] the statutes in saying anything that were by them upon heinous[421] pains prohibited. In this good warning he showed himself my special tender friend.

And now you see well, Margaret, that it is no obstinacy to leave the causes undeclared, while I could not declare them without peril. But now is it accounted great obstinacy that I refuse the oath, whatsoever my causes be, considering that of so many wiser and better men none sticked[422] thereat. And Master Secretary of a great zeal that he bore unto me swore there before them a great oath that for the displeasure that he thought the King's Highness would bear me, and the suspicion that his Grace would conceive of me, which would now think in his mind that all the Nun's business was wrought and devised by me, he had liefer[423] than I should have refused the oath that his own only son (which is a goodly young gentleman of whom our Lord send him much joy) had had his head stricken off. This word Margaret, as it was a marvelous declaration of Master Secretary's great good mind and favor toward me, so was it a heavy hearing to me that the King's Grace, my most dread Sovereign Lord, were likely to conceive such high suspicion of me and bear such grievous indignation toward me, for the thing which, without the danger and peril of my poor soul, lay not in my hand to help, nor doth.

Now have I heard since that some say that this obstinate manner of mine in still refusing the oath shall peradventure force and drive the King's Grace to make a further law[424] for me. I cannot let[425] such a law to be made. But I am very sure that if I died by such a law, I should die for that point innocent afore God. And albeit, good daughter, that I think our Lord that "hath the hearts of kings in his hand"[426] would never suffer[427] of his high goodness, so gracious a prince, and so many honorable men, and so many good men as be in the Parliament to make such an unlawful law, as that should be if it so misshaped,[428] yet lest I note that point unthought upon, but many times more than one revolved and cast in my mind before my coming hither, both that peril and all others that might put my body in peril of death by the refusing of this oath. In devising whereupon, albeit, mine own good daughter, that I found myself—I cry God mercy—very sensual[429] and my flesh much more shrinking from pain and from death than methought it the part of a faithful Christian man, in such a case as my conscience gave me, that in the saving of my body should stand the loss of my soul, yet I thank our Lord, that in that conflict the Spirit had in conclusion the mastery, and reason with help of faith finally concluded that for to be put to death wrongfully for doing well (as I am very sure I do, in refusing to swear against mine own conscience, being such as I am not upon peril of my soul bounden to change whether my death should come without law, or by color[430] of a law), it is a case in which a man may lose his head and yet have none harm, but instead of harm inestimable good at the hand of God.

And I thank our Lord, Meg, since I am come hither I set by[431] death every day less than other. For though a man lose of his years in this world, it is more than manifold recompensed by coming the sooner to heaven. And though it be a pain to die while a man is in health, yet see I very few that in sickness die with ease. And finally, very sure am I that whensoever the time shall come that may hap to come, God wot[432] how soon, in which I should lie sick in my deathbed by nature, I shall then think that God had done much for me, if he had suffered me to die before by the color[433] of such a law. And therefore my reason showeth me, Margaret, that it were great folly for me to be sorry to come to that death, which I would after wish that I had died. Beside that, that a man may hap with less thanks of

417 prevented   **418** in addition to
419 Thomas Cromwell   **420** *discharge me against:* exempt me from   **421** severe
422 hesitated; scrupled   **423** rather

424 In November 1534, Parliament did pass new laws.   **425** prevent   **426** As in Letters 202, 208, and 213, More refers to Prv 21:1.   **427** permit; allow   **428** misshapened,

deformed   **429** depending on the senses only and not on the intellect or spirit
430 *by color:* under the pretext   **431** *set by:* value   **432** knows   **433** pretext

God and more adventure[434] of his soul to die as violently and as painfully by many other chances as by enemies or thieves. And therefore, mine own good daughter, I assure you—thanks be to God—the thinking of any such albeit it hath grieved me ere[435] this, yet at this day grieveth me nothing. And yet I know well for all this mine own frailty, and that Saint Peter which feared it much less than I, fell in such fear soon after that at the word of a simple girl he forsook and forswore[436] our Savior.[437] And therefore am I not, Meg, so mad as to warrant[438] myself to stand. But I shall pray, and I pray thee, mine own good daughter, to pray with me, that it may please God that hath given me this mind, to give me the grace to keep it.

And thus have I, mine own good daughter, disclosed unto you the very secret bottom of my mind, referring the order thereof only to the goodness of God, and that so fully that I assure you, Margaret, on my faith, I never have prayed God to bring me hence nor deliver me from death, but referring all things whole unto his only pleasure, as to him that seeth better what is best for me than myself doth. Nor never longed I since I came hither to set my foot in mine own house, for any desire of or pleasure of my house, but gladly would I sometime somewhat talk with my friends, and specially my wife and you that pertain to my charge. But since that God otherwise disposeth,[439] I commit all wholly to his goodness and take daily great comfort in that I perceive that you live together so charitably and so quietly; I beseech our Lord continue it. And thus, mine own good daughter, putting you finally in remembrance that albeit if the necessity so should require, I thank our Lord in this quiet and comfort is mine heart at this day, and I trust in God's goodness so shall have grace to continue, yet (as I said before) I verily trust that God shall so inspire and govern the King's heart that he shall not suffer his noble heart and courage to requite my true faithful heart and service with such extreme unlawful and uncharitable dealing, only for the displeasure that I cannot think so as others do. But his true subject will I live and die, and truly pray for him will I, both here and in the other world too.

And thus, mine own good daughter, have me recommended to my good bedfellow and all my chil-

dren, men, women and all, with all your babes and your nurses and all the maids and all the servants, and all our kin, and all our other friends abroad. And I beseech our Lord to save them all and keep them. And I pray you all pray for me, and I shall pray for you all. And take no thought for me whatsoever you shall hap to hear, but be merry in God.

211. To Margaret Roper
Tower of London, 1534

Another letter written and sent by Sir Thomas More (in the year of our Lord 1534 and in the twenty-sixth year of King Henry the Eighth) to his daughter Mistress Roper, answering a letter[440] which she wrote and sent unto him. [Workes 1449]

The Holy Spirit of God be with you.

Your daughterly loving letter, my dearly beloved child, was and is, I faithfully assure you, much more inward comfort unto me than my pen can well express you, for diverse things that I marked therein but of all things most especially for that[441] God of his high goodness giveth you the grace to consider the incomparable difference between the wretched estate of this present life and the wealthy[442] state of the life to come for them that die in God; and to pray God in such a good Christian fashion that it may please him, it doth me good here to rehearse your own words: "of his tender pity so firmly to rest our love in him, with little regard of this world, and so to flee sin and embrace virtue that we may say with Saint Paul, *Mihi vivere Christus est et mori luchrum. And this, Cupio dissolui et esse cum Christo.*"[443] I beseech our Lord, my dearly beloved daughter, that wholesome prayer that he hath put in your mind, it may like him to give your father the grace daily to remember and pray, and yourself as you have written it even so daily devoutly to kneel and pray it. For surely if God give us that, he giveth us and will give us therewith all that ever we can well wish. And therefore, good Marget, when you pray it, pray it for us both, and I shall on my part the like, in such manner[444] as it shall like our Lord to give me, poor wretch, the grace that likewise as in this wretched world I have been very glad

---

434 peril   **435** before   **436** denied
437 Mt 26:69–75   **438** pledge
439 ordains   **440** Margaret's letter is lost

441 *for that:* because   **442** possessing
well-being   **443** Phil 1:21, 23: "For me to

live is Christ and to die is gain. . . . I desire to
depart and to be with Christ."   **444** a way

of your company and you of mine, and yet would if it might be (as natural charity bindeth the father and the child) so we may rejoice and enjoy each other's company with our other kinsfolk, allies,[445] and friends everlastingly in the glorious bliss of heaven, and in the meantime with good counsel and prayer, each help other thitherward.

And where you write these words of yourself—"But good father, I wretch am far, far, farthest of all others from such point of perfection; our Lord send me the grace to amend my life, and continually to have an eye to mine end, without grudge[446] of death, which to them that die in God is the gate of a wealthy life to which God of his infinite mercy bring us all. Amen. Good father, strengthen my frailty with your devout prayers." The father of heaven mote[447] strengthen thy frailty, my good daughter, and the frailty of thy frail father too. And let us not doubt but he so will, if we will not be slack in calling upon him therefor. Of my poor prayers, such as they be, ye may be bold to reckon. For Christian charity and natural love and your very daughterly dealing (*funiculo triplici*, as saith the Scripture, *difficile rumpitur*)[448] both bind me and strain me thereto. And of yours I put as little doubt.

That you fear your own frailty, Marget, nothing misliketh me.[449] God give us both twain[450] the grace to despair of our own self, and wholly to depend and hang upon the hope and strength of God. The blessed apostle Saint Paul found such lack of strength in himself that in his own temptation he was fain[451] thrice to call and cry out unto God to take that temptation from him. And yet sped[452] he not of his prayer, in the manner that he required.[453] For God of his high wisdom, seeing that it was (as himself saith) necessary for him to keep him from pride that else he might peradventure[454] have fallen in, would not at his thrice praying, by and by[455] take it from him, but suffered him to be panged[456] in the pain and fear thereof, giving him yet at the last this comfort against his fear of falling: *Sufficit tibi gratia mea.*[457] By which words it well seemeth that the temptation was so strong (whatsoever kind of temptation it was) that he was very feared of falling,

through the feebleness of resisting that he began to feel in himself. Wherefore for his comfort God answered, *Sufficit tibi gratia mea*, putting him in surety that were he of himself never so feeble and faint, nor never so likely to fall, yet the grace of God was sufficient to keep him up and make him stand. And our Lord said further, *Virtus in infirmitate proficitur.*[458] The more weak that man is, the more is the strength of God in his safeguard declared. And so Saint Paul saith, *Omnia possum in eo qui me confortat.*[459]

Surely, Meg, a fainter heart than thy frail father hath, canst you not have. And yet I verily[460] trust in the great mercy of God that he shall of his goodness so stay[461] me with his holy hand that he shall not finally suffer me to fall wretchedly from his favor. And the like trust, dear daughter, in his high goodness I verily conceive of you. And so much the more in that there is neither of us both but that, if we call his benefits to mind and give him oft thanks for them, we may find tokens[462] many to give us good hope for all our manifold offenses toward him, that his great mercy, when we will heartily call therefor, shall not be withdrawn from us. And verily, my dear daughter, in this is my great comfort, that albeit[463] I am of nature so shrinking from pain that I am almost afeard of a fillip,[464] yet in all the agonies that I have had whereof before my coming hither (as I have showed you ere this), I have had neither small nor few, with heavy fearful heart, forecasting[465] all such perils and painful deaths, as by any manner of possibility might after fall unto me, and in such thought lain long restless and waking, while my wife had weened[466] I had slept, yet in any such fear and heavy pensiveness[467] (I thank the mighty mercy of God), I never in my mind intended to consent that I would for the enduring of the uttermost do any such thing as I should in mine own conscience (for with other men's I am not a man meet[468] to take upon me to meddle) think to be to myself such as should damnably cast me in the displeasure of God. And this is the least point that any man may with his salvation come to, as far as I can see, and is bounden if he see peril to examine his conscience surely by learning and by good counsel and be sure

---

445 relatives by marriage   446 fear
447 must   448 Eccl 4:12 ("a threefold cord is not quickly broken")
449 *nothing misliketh me:* I do not disapprove   450 together   451 obliged
452 succeeded   453 requested

454 possibly   455 straightway
456 afflicted   457 2 Cor 12:7–10 ("My grace is sufficient for you.")   458 2 Cor 12:9 ("Strength is made perfect in weakness.")   459 Phil 4:13 ("I can do all things in him who strengthens me.")

460 truly   461 support   462 signs of divine power   463 although   464 a small tap with the finger   465 imagining beforehand   466 thought   467 thoughtfulness; melancholy   468 fit

that his conscience be such as it may stand with his salvation, or else reform it. And if the matter be such as both the parties may stand with salvation, then on whither[469] side his conscience fall, he is safe enough before God. But that mine own may stand with my own salvation, thereof I thank our Lord I am very sure. I beseech our Lord bring all parts[470] to his bliss.

It is now, my good daughter, late. And therefore thus I commend you to the holy Trinity, to guide you, comfort you and direct you with his Holy Spirit, and all yours and my wife with all my children and all our other friends.

Thomas More, Knight

212. Lady More to Henry VIII
<*ca.* Christmas 1534>

In lamentable wise, beseech your most noble Grace your most humble subjects and continual beadsfolk,[471] the poor miserable wife and children of your true, poor, heavy subject and beadsman Sir Thomas More, Knight, that whereas the same Sir Thomas, being your Grace's prisoner in your Tower of London by the space of eight months and above, in great continual sickness of body and heaviness of heart, during all which space notwithstanding that the same Sir Thomas More had by refusing of the oath forfeited unto your most noble Grace all his goods and cattles[472] and the profit of all his lands, annuities[473] and fees[474] that as well himself as your said beadswoman his wife should live by, yet your most gracious Highness, of your most blessed disposition, suffered[475] your said beadswoman, his poor wife, to retain and keep still his moveable goods and the revenues of his lands to keep her said husband and her poor household with.

So it is now, most gracious Sovereign, that now late,[476] by reason of a new act or twain[477] made in this last past prorogation[478] of your Parliament, not only the said former forfeiture is confirmed, but also the inheritance of all such lands and tenements[479] as the same Sir Thomas had of your most

bountiful gift, amounting to the yearly value sixty pounds, is forfeited also. And thus (except your merciful favor be showed) your said poor beadswoman his wife, which brought fair substance[480] to him—which is all spent in your Grace's service—is likely to be utterly undone; and his poor son, one of your said humble suppliants, standing charged and bounden for the payment of great sums of money due by the said Sir Thomas unto your Grace, standeth in danger to be cast away and undone in this world also. But over all this, the said Sir Thomas himself, after his long true service—to his power[481] diligently done to your Grace—is likely to be in his age and continual sickness, for lack of comfort and good keeping, to be shortly destroyed, to the woeful heaviness and deadly discomfort of all your said sorrowful suppliants.

In consideration of the premises, for that his offense is grown not of any malice or obstinate mind but of such a long-continued and deep-rooted scruple as passeth his power to avoid and put away, it may like your most noble Majesty, of your most abundant grace, to remit and pardon your most grievous displeasure to the said Sir Thomas and to have tender pity and compassion upon his long distress and great heaviness, and, for the tender mercy of God, to deliver him out of prison and suffer him quietly to live the remnant of his life with your said poor beadswoman his wife and other of your poor suppliants his children, with only such entertainment[482] of living as it shall like your most noble Majesty, of your gracious alms and pity, to appoint him. And this in the way of mercy and pity, and all your said poor beadsfolk shall daily during their lives pray to God for the preservation of your most royal estate.

213. To Master Leder
Tower of London, Saturday, 16 January 1534/5

A letter written by Sir Thomas More to one Master Leder,[483] a virtuous priest, the sixteenth day of January in the year of our Lord 1534 after the computation[484]

469 whichever **470** sides in the contention; parties **471** people who pray for others **472** chattels, property **473** annual amounts due from a particular person **474** inheritable estates **475** permitted **476** just recently

477 two **478** the time between sessions of Parliament **479** *lands and tenements:* real property **480** *which...substance:* who brought to him (when she married him) considerable wealth. Her legal point is that, as a widow, she had independent

title to her property, and thus the King is confiscating not only her husband's property, but hers too. **481** *to his power:* to the extent of his ability **482** provision for support **483** Master Leder seems not otherwise known. **484** reckoning

of the Church of England, and in the twenty-sixth year of the reign of King Henry the Eighth. [Workes 1450]

The tale that is reported, albeit[485] I cannot but thank you though you would it were true, yet I thank God it is a very vanity. I trust in the great goodness of God that he shall never suffer it to be true. If my mind had been obstinate indeed, I would not let[486] for any rebuke or worldly shame plainly to confess the truth. For I purpose not to depend upon the fame of the world. But I thank our Lord that the thing that I do is not for obstinacy but for the salvation of my soul, because I cannot induce mine own mind otherwise to think than I do concerning the oath.

As for other men's consciences, I will be no judge of, nor I never advised any man neither to swear nor to refuse, but as for mine own self if ever I should mishap[487] to receive the oath (which I trust our Lord shall never suffer me), ye may reckon sure that it were expressed and extorted by duresse[488] and hard handling.[489] For as for all the goods of this world, I thank our Lord I set not much more by, than I do by dust.[490] And I trust both that they will use no violent forcible ways and also that, if they would, God would of his grace and the rather a great deal through good folks' prayers give me strength to stand. *Fidelis Deus,* saith Saint Paul, *qui non patitur vos tentari supra id quod potestis ferre, sed dat cum tentatione proventum ut possitis sustinere.*[491] For this I am very sure, that if ever I should swear it, I should swear deadly against mine own conscience. For I am very sure in my mind that I shall never be able to change mine own conscience to the contrary; as for other men's, I will not meddle of.

It hath been showed me that I am reckoned willful and obstinate because that since my coming hither I have not written unto the King's Highness and by mine own writing made some suit unto his Grace. But in good faith I do not forbear it of any obstinacy, but rather of a lowly mind and a reverent,

because that I see nothing that I could write but that I fear me sore[492] that his Grace were likely rather to take displeasure with me for it than otherwise, while his Grace believeth me not that my conscience is the cause but rather obstinate willfulness. But surely that my let[493] is but my conscience, that knoweth God to whose order I commit the whole matter. *In cuius manu corda regum sunt.*[494] I beseech our Lord that all may prove as true faithful subjects to the King that have sworn as I am in my mind very sure that they be, which have refused to swear.

In haste, the Saturday the sixteenth day of January by the hand of your beadsman,[495]

Thomas More, Knight and prisoner

214. To Margaret Roper
Tower of London, 2 or 3 May 1535

A letter written and sent by Sir Thomas More to his daughter Mistress Roper, written the second or third day of May, in the year of our Lord 1535 and in the twenty-seventh year of the reign of King Henry the Eighth. [Workes 1451]

Our Lord bless you, my dearly beloved daughter.

I doubt not but by the reason of the councillors resorting hither — in this time (in which our Lord be their comfort) these fathers of the Charterhouse[496] and Master Reynolds[497] of Syon that be now judged to death for treason (whose matters and causes I know not) — may hap to put you in trouble and fear of mind concerning my being here prisoner, specially for that[498] it is not unlikely but that you have heard that I was brought also before the Council here myself. I have thought it necessary to advertise[499] you of the very truth, to the end that you neither conceive more hope than the matter giveth, lest upon other turn it might aggrieve your heaviness,[500] nor more grief and fear than the matter giveth of, on the other side. Wherefore shortly ye shall understand that on

---

485 although   **486** refrain   **487** have the misfortune   **488** compulsion   **489** More feared that he would be tortured. **490** *set . . . dust:* value them as worth no more than I do value dust   **491** 1 Cor 10:13: "God is faithful and will not permit you to be tempted beyond your strength, but with the temptation will also give you a way out that you may be able to bear it." **492** greatly   **493** hindrance   **494** "In

his hand are the hearts of kings," alluding to Prv 21:1   **495** one who prays for another   **496** *fathers of the Charterhouse:* Three Carthusian monks, John Houghton, prior of the London Charterhouse; Robert Lawrence, prior of the Beauvale Charterhouse; and Augustine Weber, prior of our Lady of Melwood Charterhouse. They were all in London to confer about whether to take the oath. When they refused,

they were arrested and tried. They were hanged, drawn, and quartered on May 4. **497** *Master Reynolds:* Richard Reynolds, a Bridgettine monk of Syon Abbey at Isleworth, near London, was tried and executed with the Carthusians.   **498** *for that:* since   **499** warn   **500** anxiety, burden

Friday the last day of April in the afternoon, Master Lieutenant[501] came in here unto me and showed me that Master Secretary[502] would speak with me. Whereupon I shifted[503] my gown and went out with Master Lieutenant into the gallery to him, where I met many, some known and some unknown, in the way. And in conclusion coming into the chamber where his Mastership[504] sat with Master Attorney,[505] Master Solicitor,[506] Master Bedyll,[507] and Master Doctor Tregonwell,[508] I was offered to sit with them, which in no wise I would.

Whereupon Master Secretary showed unto me that he doubted not but that I had by such friends as hither had resorted to me seen the new statutes made at the last sitting of the Parliament. Whereunto I answered: "Yea, verily.[509] Howbeit[510] forasmuch as being here, I have no conversation with any people, I thought it little need for me to bestow much time upon them, and therefore I redelivered the book shortly, and the effect of the statutes I never marked nor studied to put in remembrance." Then he asked me whether I had not read the first statute of them, of the King being head of the Church. Whereunto I answered, "Yes." Then his Mastership declared unto me that since it was now by Act of Parliament ordained that his Highness and his heirs be, and ever of right have been, and perpetually should be Supreme Head in earth of the Church of England under Christ, the King's pleasure was that those of his Council there assembled should demand mine opinion, and what my mind was therein. Whereunto I answered that in good faith I had well trusted that the King's Highness would never have commanded any such question to be demanded of me, considering that I ever from the beginning well and truly from time to time declared my mind unto his Highness, and since that time I had, I said, "unto your Mastership Master Secretary also, both by mouth and by writing. And now I have in good faith discharged my mind of all such matters, and neither will dispute kings' titles nor popes', but the King's true faithful subject I am and will be, and daily I pray for him and for all his, and for you all that are of his honorable Council, and for all the realm, and otherwise than thus I never intend to meddle."

Whereunto Master Secretary answered that he thought this manner[511] answer should not satisfy nor content the King's Highness, but that his Grace would exact a more full answer. And his Mastership added thereunto that the King's Highness was a prince not of rigor, but of mercy and pity, and though that[512] he had found obstinacy at some time in any of his subjects, yet when he should find them at another time conformable and submit themselves, his Grace would show mercy. And that concerning myself, his Highness would be glad to see me take such conformable ways, as[513] I might be abroad in the world again among other men as I have been before.

Whereunto I shortly (after the inward affection[514] of my mind) answered for a very truth that I would never meddle in the world again, to have the world given me. And to the remnant of the matter, I answered in effect as before, showing that I had fully determined with myself neither to study nor meddle with any matter of this world, but that my whole study should be upon the Passion of Christ and mine own passage out of this world.

Upon this I was commanded to go forth for a while, and after called in again. At which time Master Secretary said unto me that though I was prisoner and condemned to perpetual prison, yet I was not thereby discharged of mine obedience and allegiance unto the King's Highness. And thereupon demanded me whether that I thought that the King's Grace might exact of me such things as are contained in the statutes, and upon like pains as he might of other men. Whereto I answered that I would not say the contrary. Whereto he said that likewise as the King's Highness would be gracious to them that he found conformable, so his Grace would follow the course of his laws toward such as he shall find obstinate. And his Mastership said further that my demeanor in that matter was of a thing that of likelihood made now other men so stiff therein as they be.

Whereto I answered that I give no man occasion to hold any point one or other, nor never gave any man advice or counsel therein one way or other. And for conclusion I could no further go, whatsoever pain should come thereof. "I am," quoth I, "the

---

501 Sir Edmund Walsingham
502 Thomas Cromwell **503** changed
504 *his Mastership:* Cromwell **505** Sir
Christopher Hales, Attorney-General
506 Richard Rich, Solicitor-General;

his testimony was an important part of
More's treason trial. **507** Thomas Bedyll,
Clerk of the Privy Council **508** Sir
John Tregonwell, member of the Privy
Council and head judge of the Court of

Admiralty **509** truly **510** However
511 kind of **512** *though that:* even though
513 such that **514** disposition; emotion;
inclination

King's true faithful subject and daily beadsman[515] and pray for his Highness and all his and all the realm. I do nobody harm, I say none harm, I think none harm, but wish everybody good. And if this be not enough to keep a man alive, in good faith I long not to live. And I am dying already, and have, since I came here, been diverse times in the case that I thought to die within one hour, and I thank our Lord I was never sorry for it, but rather sorry when I saw the pang past. And therefore my poor body is at the King's pleasure; would God my death might do him good."

After this Master Secretary said: "Well ye find no fault in that statute; find you any in any of the other statutes after?" Whereto I answered, "Sir, whatsoever thing should seem to me other than good, in any of the statutes or in that statute either, I would not declare what fault I found, nor speak thereof." Whereunto finally his Mastership said full gently that of anything that I had spoken, there should none advantage be taken; and whether he said further that there be none to be taken, I am not well remembered. But he said that report should be made unto the King's Highness, and his gracious pleasure known.

Whereupon I was delivered again to Master Lieutenant, which was then called in, and so was I by Master Lieutenant brought again into my chamber, and here am I yet in such case as I was, neither better nor worse. That that[516] shall follow lieth in the hand of God, whom I beseech to put in the King's Grace's mind that thing that may be to his high pleasure, and in mine, to mind only the weal[517] of my soul, with little regard of my body.

And you with all yours, and my wife and all my children and all our other friends both bodily and ghostly,[518] heartily well to fare. And I pray you and all them, pray for me, and take no thought whatsoever shall happen me. For I verily trust in the goodness of God; seem it never so evil to this world, it shall indeed in another world be for the best.

Your loving father,
Thomas More, Knight

215. Lady More to Thomas Cromwell
May 1535

Right Honorable, and my especial good Master Secretary.

In my most humble wise I recommend me unto your good Mastership, acknowledging myself to be most deeply bounden to your good Mastership for your manifold goodness and loving favor, both before this time and yet daily now also, showed toward my poor husband and me. I pray almighty God continue your goodness so still, for thereupon hangeth the greatest part of my poor husband's comfort and mine.

The cause of my writing at this time is to certify your especial good Mastership of my great and extreme necessity, which, on and besides the charge of mine own house, do pay weekly 15 shillings for the board-wages of my poor husband and his servant; for the maintaining whereof, I have been compelled of very necessity to sell part of mine apparel for lack of other substance to make money of. Wherefore my most humble petition and suit to your Mastership at this time is to desire your Mastership's favorable advice and counsel, whether I may be so bold to attend upon the King's most gracious Highness. I trust there is no doubt in the cause of my impediment, for the young man, being a ploughman, had been diseased with the ague by the space of three years before that he departed. And besides this, it is now five weeks since he departed, and no other person diseased in the house since that time; wherefore I most humbly beseech your especial good Mastership (as my only trust is, and else know not what to do, but utterly in this world to be undone), for the love of God to consider the premises, and thereupon, of your most abundant goodness, to show your most favorable help to the comforting of my poor husband and me in this our great heaviness,[519] extreme age, and necessity. And thus we, and all ours, shall daily, during our lives, pray to God for the prosperous success of your right honorable dignity.

By your poor continual oratrix,[520]
Dame Alice More

---

515 one who prays for another   **516** *That that:* That which   **517** well-being   **518** spiritually   **519** grief; sadness   **520** a female plaintiff or petitioner

216. To Margaret Roper
<Tower of London, 3 June 1535>

*Another letter written and sent by Sir Thomas More
to his daughter Mistress Roper, written in the year of
our Lord 1535, and in the twenty-seventh year of the
reign of King Henry the Eighth.* [Workes 1452]

Our Lord bless you and all yours.

Forasmuch, dearly beloved daughter, as it is likely
that you either have heard or shortly shall hear that
the Council was here this day, and that I was before
them, I have thought it necessary to send you word
how the matter standeth. And verily[521] to be short I
perceive little difference between this time and the
last, for as far as I can see the whole purpose is either
to drive me to say precisely the one way, or else precisely the other.

Here sat my Lord of Canterbury,[522] my Lord
Chancellor,[523] my Lord of Suffolk,[524] my Lord of
Wiltshire[525] and Master Secretary.[526] And after
my coming, Master Secretary made rehearsal[527] in
what wise he had reported unto the King's Highness what had been said by his Grace's Council to
me, and what had been answered by me to them at
mine other being before them last. Which thing his
Mastership rehearsed in good faith very well, as I
acknowledged and confessed and heartily thanked
him therefor. Whereupon he added thereunto that
the King's Highness was nothing content nor satisfied with mine answer, but thought that by my demeanor[528] I had been occasion[529] of much grudge[530]
and harm in the realm, and that I had an obstinate
mind and an evil toward him and that my duty was
being his subject, and so he had sent them now in
his name upon mine allegiance to command me
to make a plain and terminate[531] answer whether I
thought the statute lawful or not, and that I should
either acknowledge and confess it lawful that his
Highness should be Supreme Head of the Church
of England or else to utter plainly my malignity.

Whereto I answered that I had no malignity and
therefore I could none utter. And as to the matter, I could none other answer make than I had before made, which answer his Mastership had there

rehearsed. Very heavy I was that the King's Highness should have any such opinion of me. Howbeit[532] if there were one that had informed his
Highness many evil things of me that were untrue, to which his Highness for the time gave credence, I would be very sorry that he should have
that opinion of me the space of one day. Howbeit
if I were sure that other should come on the morrow by whom his Grace should know the truth of
mine innocency, I should in the meanwhile comfort
myself with consideration of that. And in like wise
now though it be great heaviness[533] to me that his
Highness have such opinion of me for the while, yet
have I no remedy to help it, but only to comfort myself with this consideration: that I know very well
that the time shall come when God shall declare
my troth[534] toward his Grace before him and all the
world. And whereas it might haply[535] seem to be but
small cause of comfort because I might take harm
here first in the meanwhile, I thanked God that my
case was such in this matter through the clearness
of mine own conscience that though I might have
pain, I could not have harm, for a man may in such
case lose his head and have no harm. For I was very
sure that I had no corrupt affection, but that I had
always from the beginning truly used[536] myself to
looking first upon God and next upon the King according to the lesson that his Highness taught me
at my first coming to his noble service, the most
virtuous lesson that ever prince taught his servant;
whose Highness to have of me such opinion is my
great heaviness, but I have no means, as I said, to
help it but only comfort myself in the meantime
with the hope of that joyful day in which my troth
toward him shall well be known. And in this matter further I could not go, nor other answer thereto
I could not make.

To this it was said by my Lord Chancellor and
Master Secretary both that the King might by his
laws compel me to make a plain answer thereto, either the one way or the other.

Whereunto I answered I would not dispute the
King's authority, what his Highness might do in
such case, but I said that verily under correction[537]
it[538] seemed to me somewhat hard. For if it so were

521 truly   **522** Archbishop Thomas
Cranmer   **523** Sir Thomas Audley
524 Charles Brandon, Duke of
Suffolk   **525** Thomas Boleyn, Earl of
Wiltshire, Lord Privy Seal   **526** Thomas

Cromwell   **527** *made rehearsal:*
repeated   **528** conduct   **529** the
source; cause   **530** discontent; ill will
531 determined, definite   **532** However
533 grief   **534** faithfulness; truthfulness

535 perhaps   **536** accustomed, trained
537 *under correction:* subject to punishment   **538** swearing the oath

that my conscience gave me against the statutes (wherein how my mind giveth me I make no declaration), then I nothing doing nor nothing saying against the statute it were a very hard thing to compel me to say either precisely with it, against my conscience to the loss of my soul, or precisely against it to the destruction of my body.

To this Master Secretary said that I had ere[539] this, when I was chancellor, examined heretics and thieves and other malefactors, and gave me a great praise (above my deserving) in that behalf. And he said that I then (as he thought, and at the least-wise bishops) did use to examine heretics whether they believed the pope to be head of the Church, and used to compel them to make a precise answer thereto. And why should not then the King, since it is a law made here that his Grace is head of the Church, here compel men to answer precisely to the law here as they did then concerning the pope.

I answered and said that I protested that I intended not to defend any part or stand in contention, but I said there was a difference between those two cases because that at that time, as well here as elsewhere through the corps[540] of Christendom, the pope's power was recognized for an undoubted thing which seemeth not like a thing agreed in this realm and the contrary taken for truth in other realms; whereunto Master Secretary answered that they were as well burned for the denying of that as they be beheaded for denying of this, and therefore as good reason to compel them to make precise answer to the one as to the other.

Whereto I answered that since in this case a man is not by a law of one realm so bound in his conscience where there is a law of the whole corps of Christendom to the contrary in matter touching belief, as he is by a law of the whole corps though there hap to be made in some place a law local to the contrary, the reasonableness or the unreasonableness in binding a man to precise answer standeth not in the respect[541] or difference between heading[542] or burning, but, because of the difference in charge of conscience, the difference standeth between heading and hell.

Much was there answered unto this both by Master Secretary and my Lord Chancellor, overlong to rehearse. And in conclusion they offered me an oath by which I should be sworn to make true answer to such things as should be asked me on the King's behalf, concerning the King's own person.

Whereto I answered that verily I never purposed[543] to swear any book oath[544] more while I lived. Then they said that was very obstinate if I would refuse that, for every man doth it in the Star Chamber and everywhere. I said that was true, but I had not so little foresight but that I might well conjecture what should be part of my interrogatory, and as good it was to refuse it at the first as afterward.

Whereto my Lord Chancellor answered that he thought I guessed truth, for I should see them; and so they were showed me, and they were but twain:[545] the first whether I had seen the statute; the other whether I believed that it were a lawful made interrogatory or not. Whereupon I refused the oath and said further by mouth that the first I had before confessed, and to the second I would make none answer.

Which was the end of the communication and I was thereupon sent away. In the communication before, it was said that it was marveled that I stuck so much in my conscience while at the uttermost[546] I was not sure therein. Whereto I said that I was very sure that mine own conscience, so informed as it is by such diligence as I have so long taken therein, may stand with mine own salvation. I meddle not with the conscience of them that think otherwise; every man *suo domino stat et cadit*.[547] I am no man's judge. It was also said unto me that if I had as lief[548] be out of the world as in it, as I had there said, why did I not speak even out plain against the statute? It appeared well I was not content to die though I said so. Whereto I answered, as the truth is, that I have not been a man of such holy living as I might be bold to offer myself to death, lest God for my presumption might suffer[549] me to fall, and therefore I put not myself forward, but draw back. Howbeit if God draw me to it himself, then trust I in his great mercy that he shall not fail to give me grace and strength.

In conclusion Master Secretary said that he liked me this day much worse than he did the last time, for then he said he pitied me much, and now he thought that I meant not well; but God and I know both that I mean well and so I pray God do by me.[550]

---

539 before **540** body **541** point, consideration **542** beheading **543** intended **544** *book oath:* an oath sworn on the Bible **545** two **546** *at the uttermost:* in the end **547** *suo … cadit:* "before his own lord he stands and falls" (Rom 14:4) **548** *had as* *lief:* were as willing to **549** permit; allow **550** *so … do by me:* so deal with me

I pray you, be you and mine other friends of good cheer whatsoever fall of me, and take no thought for me but pray for me as I do and shall do for you and all them.

Your tender loving father,
Thomas More, Knight

217. To Antonio Bonvisi
Tower of London, 1535

Sir Thomas More, a little before he was arraigned, was condemned (in the year of our Lord 1535, and in the twenty-seventh year of the reign of King Henry the Eighth), being shut up so close in prison in the Tower that he had no pen nor ink, wrote with a coal an epistle in Latin to Master Anthony Bonvisi (merchant of Lucca and then dwelling in London), his old and dear friend, and sent it unto him, the copy whereof here followeth. [Workes 1455]

To the most friendly of friends, and deservedly dearest to me, greetings.[551]

Since my mind has a presentiment (perhaps a false one, but still a presentiment) that before very long I will be unable to write to you, I have decided, while I may, to show by this little letter, at least, how much I am refreshed by the pleasantness of your friendship now that fortune has abandoned me.

To be sure, most excellent sir, in the past I have always been wonderfully delighted by this love of yours for me, but when I remembered that for almost forty years now I have been, not a guest, but a continual habitué of the Bonvisi household, and that in all this time I have not proven to be a friend in repaying my debt to you, but only a barren lover, my sense of shame truly made that genuine sweetness, which I otherwise enjoyed in thinking about the friendship of the Bonvisis, turn a little bit sour because I felt somehow awkward and ashamed, as if I had neglected to do my part. But certainly I now console myself with the thought that there never arose any opportunity for me to pay you back, since your fortune was so large that there was no way left for me to do anything for you. And so I am aware that I did not fail to pay you back through any neglect of my duty toward you, but because there was no opportunity. But now that even the hope of

recompense is taken away, when I see you persist in loving and obliging me, nay rather, when I see you push on in your friendship and run the race unwearied, so that few men court their fortunate friends as much as you favor, love, cherish, and regard your More—overthrown as he is, cast aside, struck down, and sentenced to prison—then I not only absolve myself from whatever bitter shame I felt before but also find peace in the sweetness of this wonderful friendship of yours. And my good fortune in having such a faithful friend as you seems somehow—I don't know how—almost to counterbalance this unfortunate shipwreck of my fleet. Certainly, apart from the indignation of the Prince, whom I love no less than I ought to fear him, for the rest, your friendship almost outweighs my losses, since they, after all, are to be counted among the evils of fortune.

But if I were to count the possession of such a constant friendship—which such an unfavorable fall of fortune has not snatched away, but rather cemented more strongly—among the fleeting goods of fortune, truly I should be out of my mind. For the happiness of a friendship so faithful, and so constant against the contrary blast of fortune, is a rare favor, and without a doubt is a higher good, and a more exalted one, arising from a certain special loving-kindness of God. Certainly I do not otherwise accept or understand it than as something arranged by the unparalleled mercy of God, that among my poor little friends, a person such as you, so great a friend, was prepared so long beforehand, who might assuage and lighten by your consolation a great part of that distress which the weight of fortune rushing headlong against me has brought upon me. Therefore, my dear Antonio, dearest of all mortals to me, with all my strength I pray (the only thing I can do) to Almighty God, who provided you for me, that, since he gave you such a debtor, who will never be able to discharge his debt, he himself for his loving-kindness vouchsafe to requite you for those deeds of kindness of yours which you daily expend so profusely upon me; then that he bring us, for his great mercy, from this wretched and stormy world to his peace, where there will be no need for letters, where no wall will separate us, where no porter will prevent us from talking together, but with God the Father unbegotten, and his only-begotten Son, our Lord and Redeemer Jesus Christ, and the Holy Spirit of

551 Elizabeth McCutcheon's translation from *Moreana* nos. 71–72 (Nov. 1981): 55–56; used with permission.

them both, the Comforter proceeding from them both, we shall fully enjoy eternal joy. Meanwhile may Almighty God bring it about that you, my dear Antonio, and I, and would that all mortals, and everyone everywhere, may hold cheap all the riches of this world, all the glory of the whole universe, and even the sweetness of life itself, for the ardent desire of that joy. Most trusty of all friends, and most beloved by me, and (as I am now long accustomed to call you) the apple of my eye: goodbye. May Christ keep unharmed your whole household, so very like the head of the family in their affection for me.

T. More: If I put down "yours," I'll have done so in vain. For you cannot now not know this, when you have bought it by so many deeds of kindness. Nor am I now such, that it matters whose I am.

218. To Margaret Roper
Tower of London, 5 July 1535

Sir Thomas More was beheaded at the Tower Hill in London, on Tuesday the sixth day of July in the year of our Lord 1535, and in the twenty-seventh year of the reign of King Henry the Eighth. And on the day next before, being Monday and the fifth day of July, he wrote with a coal[552] *a letter to his daughter Mistress Roper, and sent it to her (which was the last thing that ever he wrote). The copy whereof here followeth.*
[Workes 1457]

Our Lord bless you, good daughter, and your good husband and your little boy and all yours and all my children and all my godchildren and all our friends. Recommend[553] me when you may to my good daughter Cecily,[554] whom I beseech our Lord to comfort, and I send her my blessing and to all her children and pray her to pray for me. I send her a handkerchief and God comfort my good son her husband. My good daughter Daunce[555] hath the picture in parchment that you delivered me from my Lady Conyers; her name is on the back side. Show her that I heartily pray her that you may send it in my name to her again for a token from me to pray for me.

I like special[556] well Dorothy Coly;[557] I pray you be good unto her. I would wit[558] whether this be she that you wrote me of. If not, I pray you be good to the other as you may in her affliction and to my good daughter Joan Aleyn[559] to give her I pray you some kind answer, for she sued[560] hither to me this day to pray you be good to her.

I cumber[561] you, good Margaret, much but I would be sorry if it should be any longer than tomorrow, for it is Saint Thomas Even and the Utas of Saint Peter[562] and therefore tomorrow long I to go to God; it were a day very meet and convenient[563] for me. I never liked your manner toward me better than when[564] you kissed me last for I love when daughterly love and dear charity hath no leisure to look to worldly courtesy.

Farewell, my dear child, and pray for me, and I shall for you and all your friends that we may merrily meet in heaven. I thank you for your great cost.

I send now unto my good daughter Clement[565] her algorism stone[566] and I send her and my good son and all hers God's blessing and mine.

I pray you at time convenient recommend me to my good son John More.[567] I liked well his natural fashion. Our Lord bless him and his good wife, my loving daughter,[568] to whom I pray him be good, as he hath great cause, and that if the land of mine come to his hand, he break not my will concerning his sister Daunce. And our Lord bless Thomas and Austen[569] and all that they shall have.

---

552 charcoal pencil   **553** commend   **554** Cecily (1507–39 [?]) was More's third and youngest daughter, who married in 1525 Giles Heron, wealthy heir of Sir John Heron, treasurer of the chamber of Henry VIII. He was a member of Parliament, but was later attainted by Parliament for treason in 1540 and hung, drawn, and quartered—his lands going to Cromwell and Rich. Giles had brought the message about the fire at Chelsea; More was his ward from 1522 to 1525, and gave a judgment against him in court.   **555** Elizabeth (1506–64), More's second daughter, married William Daunce, son of Sir John Daunce, Knight of the Body to Henry VIII, in 1525.   **556** specially   **557** Margaret Roper's maid. Margaret sent her to the Tower every day during More's imprisonment, often with gifts. She married John Harris, More's secretary. Together they preserved many of More's letters and took them to the Low Countries in their exile.   **558** know   **559** Another of Margaret Roper's maids. She had been educated in More's "School" and so is called "daughter."   **560** appealed   **561** trouble   **562** The eve of the translation of the relics of St. Thomas of Canterbury (Becket), kept in England on July 7, octave of the feast of St. Peter, June 29.   **563** *meet and convenient:* fitting and appropriate   **564** when she embraced her father on Tower Wharf, on his return from Westminster Hall after conviction and sentence   **565** Margaret Giggs, his foster daughter, now wife of John Clement. The algorism stone was for arithmetic—undoubtedly a slate, needed when he had few writing materials in prison.   **566** *algorism stone:* a counter used to perform calculations   **567** John More had knelt to ask his father's blessing when he came from judgment.   **568** Anne Cresacre   **569** *Thomas and Austen:* the children of John More and Anne Cresacre

In More's own hand at the top and bottom of this page of his prayer book are the first two lines of his "Godly Meditation," written while imprisoned in the Tower of London, 1534–35.

Instructions, Meditations, and Prayers
made and collected by Sir Thomas More, Knight, while he was prisoner in the Tower

Our major source for this collection and for their individual titles is the 1557 *Workes*, except for "A Godly Meditation." That most famous prayer we have written in More's own hand in the upper and lower margins of his prayer book, along with almost 400 of his marginal markings that include 151 written comments, 161 lines, and 71 staves that look like musical notes. (See the facing and following pages for examples.) That prayer book, composed of More's *Book of Hours* and his *Psalter,* is in the Beinecke Library at Yale University, and a facsimile of its annotated pages was published as *Thomas More's Prayer Book* (New Haven: Yale University Press, 1969) with transcription, translation, and introduction by Louis L. Martz and Richard S. Sylvester.

Each "Godly Instruction" is just that: a surprisingly impersonal, even light-heartedly logical, presentation of principles. Neither impersonal nor devoid of emotion is "Imploring Divine Help against Temptation." This is an intricately constructed "cento prayer," that is, a "unifed prayer consisting of psalm verses" (*CW* 13: cliii) — a traditional prayer that Antony refers to in *A Dialogue of Comfort against Tribulation* when he recommends to Vincent that "special verses . . . be drawn out of the Psalter" in times of great spiritual need. This cento prayer, although in Latin, was considered to be so important by More's early editors that it was first published in the collection of More's English writings, the 1557 *Workes of Sir Thomas More Knight,* and then in the 1565, 1566, and 1689 *Opera Omnia.* Adding to the psalmist's fluctuations of emotion are More's own marginal comments in his psalter.

The most recent and detailed editor of this complex prayer, Garry E. Haupt, suggests that "More's Psalter marginalia . . . are an integral part of [More's] meditation" (*CW* 13: 302), and so this corresponding marginalia is included in square brackets in the pages that follow.

The last prayer More wrote was "A Devout Prayer before Death" — at least according to the 1557 editorial note, which dates it between More's trial on July 1 and his execution by beheading on Tower Hill July 6, 1535. More was expecting to suffer the harshest of deaths. According to the official court account, he was to "be dragged through the midst of the city of London directly to the gallows of Tyburn and hanged upon those gallows, and while alive be cast upon the earth and his entrails be taken from his belly and burned, with him still alive, and his head be struck off and his body divided into four parts, and his head and quarters be placed where the Lord King shall wish to assign them." When that harsh and public death was commuted to the less public and less painful beheading is not known, but it was on July 5 that Henry VIII signed the official execution warrant. On July 5 More wrote Letter 218 to his daughter Margaret, expressing his desire to die the next day, an anniversary honoring Saint Thomas Becket. At his execution the following day, according to the Paris Newsletter of August 4, 1535, "he asked those present to pray to God for him and he would do the same for them. He then besought them earnestly to pray to God to give the King good counsel, protesting that he died his good servant, and God's first [*son bon serviteur et de Dieu premierement*]."

CONTENTS

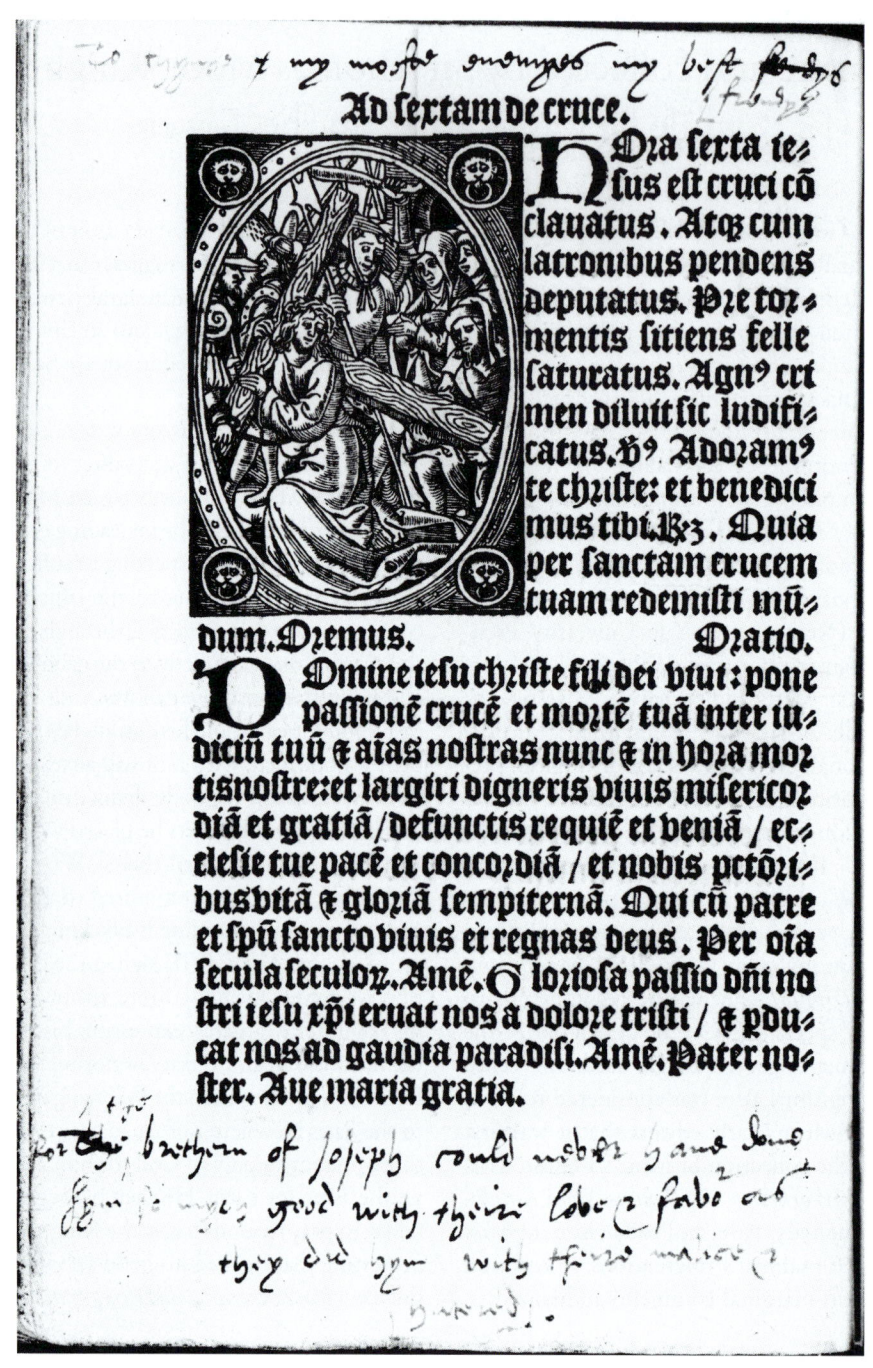

to tygres & my mortal enymyes my best frendys

Ad sextam de cruce.

Hora sexta iesus est cruci conclauatus. Atqz cum latronibus pendens deputatus. Pre tormentis sitiens felle saturatus. Agnus crimen diluit sic ludificatus. R. Adoramus te christe: et benedicimus tibi. R. z. Quia per sanctam crucem tuam redemisti mundum. Oremus.

Oratio.

Domine iesu christe fili dei viui: pone passione cruce et morte tua inter iudiciu tuu & aias nostras nunc & in hora mortisnostre:et largiri digneris viuis misericordia et gratia / defunctis requie et venia / ecclesie tue pace et concordia / et nobis pctoribusbita & gloria sempiterna. Qui cu patre et spu sancto viuis et regnas deus. Per oia secula seculor. Ame. O loriosa passio dni nostri iesu xpi eruat nos a dolore tristi / & pducat nos ad gaudia paradisi. Ame. Pater noster. Aue maria gratia.

for the brethern of Joseph could never have done
him so myche good with their love & favor as
they did hym with their malice &
hatred.

This page of More's prayer book shows, in More's own hand, lines 48–52 of "A Godly Meditation."

Instructions, Meditations, and Prayers
made and collected by Sir Thomas More, Knight, while he was prisoner in the Tower

A GODLY INSTRUCTION
*written by Sir Thomas More, Knight, within
a while after he was prisoner in the Tower of
London, in the year of our Lord 1534*

Bear no malice nor evil will to no man living.
For either the man is good or naught.[1] If he be
good, and I hate him, then am I naught.

If he be naught, either he shall amend and die
good and go to God, or abide[2] naught and die
naught and go the devil. And then let me remember that if he shall be saved, he shall not fail (if I be
saved too, as I trust to be) to love me very heartily,
and I shall then in like wise love him.

And why should I now then hate one for this
while[3] which shall hereafter love me for evermore,
and why should I be now, then, enemy to him with
whom I shall in time coming be coupled in eternal friendship? And on the other side, if he shall
continue naught and be damned, then is there so
outrageous eternal sorrow toward[4] him that I may
well think myself a deadly cruel wretch if I would
not now rather pity his pain than malign his person. If one would say that we may well with good
conscience wish an evil man harm, lest he should do
harm to such other folk as are innocent and good, I
will not now dispute upon that point, for that root
hath more branches to be well weighed and considered than I can now conveniently write (having
none other pen than a coal). But verily thus will I
say that I will give counsel to every good friend of
mine, but if[5] he be put in such a room[6] as to punish an evil man lieth[7] in his charge by reason of his
office, else leave the desire of punishing unto God
and unto such other folk as are so grounded in charity, and so fast cleave to God, that no secret shrewd[8]
cruel affection,[9] under the cloak of a just and a virtuous zeal, can creep in and undermine them. But

let us that are no better than men of a mean[10] sort
ever pray for such merciful amendment in other
folk as our own conscience showeth us that we have
need in ourselves.

A GODLY INSTRUCTION
*written in Latin[11] by Sir Thomas More, Knight,
while he was prisoner in the Tower of London,
in the year of our Lord 1534*

Whosoever so saveth his life that he displeaseth
God thereby shall soon after, to his no little
grief, full sore[12] mislike the same. For if thou so sav-
est thy life, thou shalt on the morrow so deadly hate
thy life that at the heart full heavy[13] shalt thou be
that the day before thou didst not lose thy life. For
that certainly die thou must, shalt thou full surely[14]
remember; but how, or how soon, that wottest[15]
thou not at all. And just cause hast thou to fear lest
upon the such delay of that death may haply[16] ensue
the everlasting torments in hell, where "men shall
sore long to die, and death shall flee from them,"[17]
whereas by the enduring of that death which thou
so much abhorrest, there should have undoubtedly
followed the everlasting joys of heaven.

What folly is it for thee, then, to avoid this temporal death as thereby to fall in peril to purchase
thyself eternal death? And yet therewith not to escape thy temporal death, but perhaps for a while
only to delay thy death.

For put case thou mightest for that while eschew[18]
the danger of death. Art thou sure, therefore, either
to continue thy life forever, or at another time to
die and feel no pain? Nay, rather it may fortune[19] to
fare with thee as it fared with the rich man that assuredly reckoned himself to live full many a year —
to whom Christ said, "This night, thou fool, shall

---

1 wicked **2** remain **3** period of time
4 facing **5** *but if:* unless **6** office,
position **7** who lieth **8** malicious,
wicked **9** inclination **10** mediocre;

common; poor **11** The translation that
follows appeared in the 1557 *Workes.*
12 *full sore:* very greatly **13** sorry **14** *full
surely:* with complete certainty **15** *wottest*

thou: you know **16** perhaps **17** Rv 9:6
18 escape; avoid **19** happen

they bereave thee of thy life."[20] And again, this art thou well assured of: that both die once thou shalt and also (for that[21] so shortly man's life here passeth away) that long here live thou canst not.

Finally hereof,[22] as I suppose, doubtest thou never a deal:[23] that when the time shall come in which thou shalt lie sick on thy deathbed, and therewith begin to feel the painful pangs of death so dreadfully[24] drawing on, then wilt thou heartily wish, for the saving of thy soul, thou hadst died a most sharp and cruel death many a day before. Then cause hast thou none, pardie,[25] so sore[26] to fear that thing to fall which, as thou knowest thyself right well, thou wouldst within a while after have wished to have fallen unto thee before. Whosoever suffer any trouble or adversity, according to the will of God, must wholly commit their souls into the hands of God, their trusty and faithful Creator. "Be not discouraged, my well-beloved brethren," saith Saint Peter, "by reason of the extreme persecution that is amongst you (which is sent you for a proof[27] of your patience), as though some strange thing were befallen unto you; but inasmuch as ye be partakers[28] of Christ's pains and Passion, full heartily rejoice, that thou mayest likewise rejoice at the revelation of his glory."[29]

Well may good men be ashamed to have less courage to do good than evil men have to do evil. For a man may hear thieves not let[30] to say that he hath a faint stomach[31] that will stick[32] for half an hour's hanging to live seven years in pleasure. And what a shame were it then for a Christian man to be content rather to lose the life and bliss everlasting than suffer a short death somewhat before his time — which he is so well assured that needs suffer he shall, and that within a while after and, but if[33] he repent him in time, straight upon his temporal death fall into eternal death, and the same so horrible and painful that it far exceedeth all other kinds of death.

If it were possible for a man, with his corporeal eyes, to behold one of those grisly fiends which in so great a number daily look and long for us in hell forever to torment us: the fear of him alone would make him not to regard a rush[34] all the terrible threats that any man could imagine. And how much less would he regard them, then, if he might possibly see heaven open and Jesus Christ there standing, as did the blessed Saint Stephen?[35]

"Your adversary the devil," saith Saint Peter, "like a roaring lion runneth about, seeking whom he may devour."[36] But hark what Saint Bernard saith:[37] "I humbly thank that mighty Lion of the tribe of Judah; well roar may this lion, but bite me he cannot. Threateneth he us never so much, let us not be such beastly cowards that for his only[38] rude roaring, we fall down flat to the ground.

"For a very beast is he, and hath no reason indeed, which[39] is either so feeble-spirited that for fear alone giveth over, or so discomfited upon a vain imagination of the pains that he may hap to suffer, that at the bare blast of the trumpet, before the battle begin, he is quite and clean overthrown, without any stroke at all.

"'Ye have not resisted as yet to the shedding of your blood,'[40] saith that valiant Captain, which knew right well that the roaring of this lion was nothing to be passed on.[41] And another saith, 'Stand stiff against the devil, and he will flee from you.'"[42]

Stand stiff, I say, with a "strong and steadfast faith";[43] for Isaiah giveth us warning[44] before that "they that, having no hope of God's help, fly for succor to man's help, shall both themselves and their helpers with them come to utter confusion."[45]

So came King Saul to naught,[46] who, because he was not by and by[47] of God heard at his pleasure, murmured, grudged[48] and distrusted God and so fell in conclusion to seek counsel of a witch — whereas for the punishment of all witches, he himself had given generally[49] so precise[50] commandment before.[51] My firm hope is that he which[52] so dearly bought[53] me will not, without mine own damnable fault, lose me to his most malicious enemy.[54]

---

20 Lk 12:20   **21** *for that:* because   **22** of this   **23** a bit   **24** fearfully   **25** "by God" (from the French); certainly   **26** greatly   **27** testing   **28** sharers   **29** 1 Pt 4:12–13   **30** hesitate   **31** spirit, courage   **32** hesitate   **33** *but if:* unless   **34** *regard a rush:* attach a straw's worth of importance to   **35** Acts 7:55–56   **36** 1 Pt 5:8   **37** These next paragraphs are from Saint Bernard's thirteenth sermon on Psalm 90(91).   **38** *for his only:* just because of his   **39** who   **40** Heb 12:4   **41** *passed on:* paid any attention to   **42** Jas 4:7   **43** 1 Pt 5:9   **44** Is 31:1, 3   **45** *confusion:* ruin, destruction   **46** wickedness   **47** immediately   **48** grumbled, complained   **49** all inclusive, without exception   **50** strict   **51** 1 Chr 10:13–14   **52** who   **53** *so dearly bought:* at such great cost ransomed or redeemed. See 1 Cor 6:20.   **54** This concluding sentence follows the Latin prayer in *Workes*, p. 1407.

These are two pages from Thomas More's Psalter, showing his marginalia.
Next to Ps 5:11, More writes: *contra insidias demonum* ("against the snares of the devil")
Next to Ps 6:2: *Imploratio veniae pro peccatis* ("a prayer imploring pardon for one's sins")
Next to Ps 7:2: *contra spiritales nequitias* ("against the spiritual hosts of wickedness")

IMPLORING DIVINE HELP AGAINST TEMPTATION WHILE SCORNING DEMONS THROUGH HOPE AND CONFIDENCE IN GOD

5 *A devout prayer collected out of the Psalms of David by Sir Thomas More Knight, while a prisoner in the Tower of London*

PSALM 3

Why, O Lord, are they multiplied that afflict me?
10   Many are they who rise up against me.[55]
Many say to my soul, "There is no salvation for him in his God."
But thou, O Lord, art my protector, my glory, and the lifter up of my head.
15 I have slept and taken my rest, and I have risen up, because the Lord hath protected me.[56]
I will not fear thousands of the people, surrounding me. Arise, O Lord; save me, O my God.[57]

PSALM 5

20 Conduct me, O Lord, in thy justice; because of my enemies, direct my way in thy sight.
For there is no truth in their mouth; their heart is vain.
Their throat is an open sepulchre; judge them,
25   O God.
Let them fall from their devices; according to the multitude of their wickedness cast them out, for they have provoked thee, O Lord.
But let all them be glad that hope in thee; they
30   shall rejoice forever, and thou shalt dwell in them.
O Lord, thou hast crowned us, as with a shield of thy good will.[58]

PSALM 7

35 O Lord my God, in thee have I put my trust; save me from all them that persecute me, and deliver me.[59]
Lest at any time he seize upon my soul like a lion, while there is no one to redeem me, nor to save.

Rise up, O Lord, in thy anger, and be thou exalted   40
in the borders of my enemies.[60]
The enemy pursues[61] my soul; let them take it, and tread down my life on the earth, and bring down my glory to the dust.
He hath bent his bow and made it ready. And in it   45
he hath prepared the instruments of death; he hath made ready his arrows for them that burn.
Behold, he hath been in labor with injustice; he hath conceived sorrow, and brought forth iniquity.   50
He hath opened a pit and dug it, and he is fallen into the hole he made.[62]
His sorrow shall be turned on his own head, and his iniquity shall come down upon his crown.
I will give glory to the Lord according to his jus-   55
tice, and will sing to the name of the Lord, the most high.[63]

PSALM 4

In peace, in the selfsame, I will sleep and I will rest.
For thou, O Lord, singularly hast settled me in   60
hope.[64]

PSALM 9

Have mercy on me, O Lord; see my humiliation which I suffer from my enemies.
And let them trust in thee who know thy name,   65
for thou hast not forsaken them that seek thee, O Lord.
And the Lord is become a refuge for the poor, a helper in due time in tribulation.
Why, O Lord, hast thou retired afar off? Why   70
dost thou slight us in our wants, in the time of trouble?
For the poor man shall not be forgotten to the end; the patience of the poor shall not perish forever. Arise, O Lord God; let thy hand be   75
exalted; forget not the poor.
To thee is the poor man left; thou wilt be a helper to the orphan.
The Lord hath heard the desire of the poor; thy ear hath heard the preparation of their heart.[65]   80

---

55 Here in the margin of his Psalter, More writes "the soul recovering from sin." Below, these handwritten comments of More are given in square brackets. For examples of this marginalia, see the previous page, as well as *Thomas More's Prayer Book* (New Haven: Yale University Press, 1969), which gives a facsimile of each page along with R. S. Sylvester's translations of the marginalia given here. See also Garry Houpt's detailed commentary in *CW* 13.   **56** [he who rises up from sin]   **57** [a challenge against demons] Ps 3:2–4, 6–7 (3:1–3, 5–7).   **58** Ps 5:9–13 (5:8–12)   **59** [against the spiritual hosts of wickedness]   **60** [against demons]   **61** As Garry Haupt points out, More changes the verb form — to present indicative, making "the passage extremely relevant to More's situation in the Tower" (*CW* 13: 312).   **62** [against the demon]   **63** Ps 7:2–3, 7, 6, 13–18 (7:1–2, 6, 5, 12–17)   **64** Ps 4:9–10 (4:8)   **65** Ps 9:14, 11, 10, 22, 19, 33, 35, 38 (9:13, 10, 9; 10:1; 9:18; 10:12, 14, 17)

PSALM 10

The Lord is in his holy temple; the Lord's throne is
    in heaven.

His eyes look on the poor man; his eyelids examine
5   the sons of men.[66]

PSALM 11

"By reason of the misery of the needy, and the
    groans of the poor, now will I arise," saith the
    Lord.[67]

PSALM 7

10

O Lord my God, in thee have I put my trust; save
    me from all them that persecute me, and deliver
    me.[68]

PSALM 12

15 How long, O Lord, wilt thou forget me unto the
    end? How long dost thou turn away thy face
    from me?[69]

How long shall I take counsels in my soul, sorrow
    in my heart all the day?

20 How long shall my enemy be exalted over
    me? Consider, and hear me, O Lord my God.

Enlighten my eyes that I never sleep in death, lest
    at any time my enemy say, "I have prevailed
    against him."

25 They that trouble me will rejoice when I am
    moved, but I have trusted in thy mercy.

My heart shall rejoice in thy salvation; I will sing to
    the Lord, who giveth me good things; yea I will
    sing to the name of the Lord the most high.[70]

PSALM 15

30

Preserve me, O Lord, for I have put my trust in
    thee. I have said to the Lord, "Thou art my
    God," for thou hast no need of my goods.[71]

PSALM 16

35 Perfect thou my goings in thy paths, that my foot-
    steps be not moved.[72]

Show forth thy wonderful mercies; thou who
    savest them that trust in thee.[73]

PSALM 15

I set the Lord always in my sight, for he is at my
    right hand, that I be not moved.[74]   40

Therefore my heart hath been glad, and my tongue
    hath rejoiced; moreover my flesh also shall rest
    in hope.[75]

PSALM 17

45

Thou lightest my lamp, O Lord. O my God,
    enlighten my darkness.

For by thee I shall be delivered from temptation,
    and through my God I shall go over a wall.

As for my God, his way is undefiled; the words of   50
    the Lord are fire-tried; he is the protector of all
    that trust in him.

For who is God but the Lord? Or who is God but
    our God?[76]

PSALM 21

55

But I am a worm, and no man, the reproach of
    men, and the outcast of the people.[77]

All they that saw me have laughed me to scorn;
    they have spoken with the lips, and wagged the
    head.   60

Thou art he that hast drawn me out of the womb,
    my hope from the breasts of my mother. I was
    cast upon thee from the womb.

From my mother's womb thou art my God; depart
    not from me.   65

But thou, O Lord, remove not thy help to a dis-
    tance from me; look toward my defense.[78]

PSALM 22

Though I should walk in the midst of the shadow
    of death, I will fear no evils, for thou art with   70
    me.[79]

Thy rod and thy staff, they have comforted me.[80]

PSALM 24

To thee, O Lord, have I lifted up my soul. In
    thee, O my God, I put my trust; let me not be   75
    ashamed.

Neither let my enemies laugh at me,[81] for none of
    them that wait on thee shall be confounded.

---

66 Ps 10:5 (11:4)   **67** Ps 11:6 (12:5)   (13:1–6)   **71** Ps 15:1–2 (16:1–2)   **72** [he   **77** [in the time of suffering with disgrace]
68 [against the spiritual hosts of darkness]   prays that he may not falter in the time   **78** [against demons] Ps 21:7–8, 10–12, 20
Ps 7:2 (7:1)   **69** [He who has scruples in   of temptation]   **73** Ps 16:5, 7 (17:5, 7)   (22:6–7, 9–11, 19)   **79** [trust]   **80** [tribu-
confession and is not satisfied in his own   **74** [comfort in tribulation]   **75** Ps 15:8–9   lation] Ps 22:4 (23:4)   **81** [demons]
soul should pray this psalm]   **70** Ps 12:1–6   (16:8–9)   **76** Ps 17:29–32 (18:28–31)

The sins of my youth and my ignorances do not remember.[82]

According to thy mercy remember thou me, for thy goodness' sake, O Lord.

5 For thy name's sake, O Lord, thou wilt pardon my sin, for it is great.[83]

My eyes are ever toward the Lord, for he shall pluck my feet out of the snare.[84]

The troubles of my heart are multiplied; deliver me

10 from my necessities.

See my abjection and my labor, and forgive me all my sins.[85]

PSALM 26

The Lord is my light and my salvation: whom shall

15 I fear?[86]

The Lord is the protector of my life: of whom shall I be afraid?

If armies in camp should stand together against me, my heart shall not fear.

20 If a battle should rise up against me, in this will I be confident.

One thing I have asked of the Lord, this will I seek after: that I may dwell in the house of the Lord all the days of my life.

25 That I may see the delight of the Lord, and may visit his temple.

Hear, O Lord, my voice, with which I have cried to thee; have mercy on me and hear me.

My heart hath said to thee, "My face hath sought

30 thee." Thy face, O Lord, will I still seek.

Turn not away thy face from me; decline not in thy wrath from thy servant.

Be thou my helper; forsake me not; do not thou despise me, O God my Savior.

35 I believe to see the good things of the Lord in the land of the living.[87]

Expect the Lord; do manfully, and let thy heart take courage, and wait thou for the Lord.[88]

PSALM 27

40 Unto thee will I cry, O Lord. O my God, be not thou silent to me, lest if thou be silent to me, I become like them that go down into the pit.[89]

PSALM 29

Sing to the Lord, O ye his saints, and give praise to the memory of his holiness.   45

For wrath is in his indignation, and life in his good will.

In the evening weeping shall have place, and in the morning gladness.

Thou turnedst away thy face from me, and I be-   50 came troubled.[90]

To thee, O Lord, will I cry, and I will make suppli- cation to my God.

What profit is there in my blood, whilst I go down to corruption?[91]   55

PSALM 30

In thee, O Lord, have I hoped; let me never be confounded; deliver me in thy justice.

Bow down thy ear to me; make haste to deliver me.

Be thou unto me a God, a protector, and a house   60 of refuge, to save me.

For thou art my strength and my refuge, and for thy name's sake thou wilt lead me, and nourish me.

Thou wilt bring me out of this snare, which they   65 have hidden for me, for thou art my protector.[92]

Into thy hands I commend my spirit; thou hast redeemed me, O Lord, the God of truth.

Have mercy on me, O Lord, for I am afflicted; my eye is troubled with wrath, my soul, and my   70 belly.

For my life is wasted with grief, and my years in sighs.

My strength is weakened through poverty and my bones are disturbed.   75

I am become a reproach among all my enemies and very much to my neighbors, and a fear to my acquaintance.[93]

They that saw me without fled from me. I am for- gotten as one dead from the heart.   80

I am become as a vessel that is destroyed, for I have heard the blame of many that dwell round about. While they assembled together against me, they consulted to take away my life.

But I have put my trust in thee, O Lord. I said,   85 "Thou art my God." My lots are in thy hands.

---

82 [for one's sins]   83 [for one's sins]   84 [rescue from sin or prison; tribulation]   85 Ps 24(25):1–3, 7, 11, 15, 17–18   86 [trust]   87 [hope and trust]   88 [patience] Ps 26(27):1, 3–4, 7–9, 13–14   89 Ps 27(28):1   90 [tribulation]   91 Ps 29:5–6, 8–10 (30:4–5, 7–9)   92 [against the snares of demons]   93 [in infamy and danger]

Make thy face to shine upon thy servant; save
    me in thy mercy. Let me not be confounded,
    O Lord, for I have called upon thee.
O how great is the multitude of thy sweetness,
5   O Lord, which thou hast hidden for them that
    fear thee.[94]

PSALM 32

Behold, the eyes of the Lord are on them that fear
    him, and on them that hope in his mercy.
10 To deliver their souls from death, and feed them in
    famine.
Our soul waiteth for the Lord, for he is our helper
    and protector.
For in him our heart shall rejoice, and in his holy
15   name we have trusted.
Let thy mercy, O Lord, be upon us, as we have
    hoped in thee.[95]

PSALM 33

Come ye to him, and be enlightened, and your
20   faces shall not be confounded.
The angel of the Lord shall encamp round about
    them that fear him, and shall deliver them.
O taste, and see that the Lord is sweet; blessed is
    the man that hopeth in him.
25 Fear the Lord, all ye his saints, for there is no want
    to them that fear him.
The rich have wanted, and have suffered hunger,
    but they that seek the Lord shall not be de-
    prived of any good.
30 The Lord is nigh unto them that are of a contrite
    heart, and he will save the humble of spirit.[96]

PSALM 35

But the children of men shall put their trust under
    the covert of thy wings. They shall be inebriated
35   with the plenty of thy house.
For with thee is the fountain of life, and in thy
    light we shall see light.[97]

PSALM 37

Rebuke me not, O Lord, in thy indignation, nor
    chastise me in thy wrath.[98]   40
For thy arrows are fastened in me, and thy hand
    hath been strong upon me.
There is no health in my flesh, because of thy
    wrath; there is no peace for my bones, because
    of my sins.   45
For my iniquities are gone over my head, and as a
    heavy burden are become heavy upon me.
My sores are putrified and corrupted, because of
    my foolishness.
I am become miserable, and am bowed down even 50
    to the end. I walked sorrowful all the day long.
For my loins are filled with illusions, and there is
    no health in my flesh.
I am afflicted and humbled exceedingly; I roared
    with the groaning of my heart.   55
Lord, all my desire is before thee, and my groaning
    is not hidden from thee.
My heart is troubled; my strength hath left me,
    and the light of my eyes itself is not with me.
My friends and my neighbors have drawn near, and 60
    stood against me.
And they that were near me stood afar off, and
    they that sought my soul used violence.
And they that sought evils to me spoke vain things,
    and studied deceits all the day long.   65
But I, as a deaf man heard not, and as a dumb man
    not opening his mouth.[99]
And I became as a man that heareth not, and that
    hath no reproofs in his mouth.
For in thee, O Lord, have I hoped; thou wilt hear 70
    me, O Lord my God.
For I said, "Lest at any time my enemies rejoice
    over me, and whilst my feet are moved, they
    speak great things against me."
For I am ready for scourges, and my sorrow is 75
    continually before me.
For I will declare my iniquity, and I will think for
    my sin.
But my enemies live, and are stronger than I; and
    they that hate me wrongfully are multiplied. 80
They that render evil for good have detracted me,
    because I followed goodness.

---

94 [consolation for the soul in tribulation]
Ps 30:2–6, 10–18, 20 (31:1–5, 9–17, 19)
95 Ps 32(33):18–22 **96** Ps 33:6, 8–11, 19
(34:5, 7–10, 18) **97** Ps 35:8–10 (36:7–9)
98 [a good psalm for obtaining pardon]

99 [a meek man ought to behave in this
way during tribulation; he should neither
speak proudly himself nor retort to what
is spoken wickedly, but should bless those
who speak evil of him and suffer willingly,

either for justice's sake if he has deserved
it or for God's sake if he has deserved
nothing]

Forsake me not, O Lord my God; do not thou depart from me.

Attend unto my help, O Lord, the God of my salvation.[100]

PSALM 38

5

I said, "I will take heed to my ways, that I sin not with my tongue.

"I have set guard to my mouth,[101] when the sinner stood against me."

10 I was dumb, and was humbled, and kept silence from good things, and my sorrow was renewed.

My heart grew hot within me, and in my meditation a fire shall flame out.

I spoke with my tongue, "O Lord, make me know

15 my end.

And what is the number of my days, that I may know what is wanting to me."

Behold, thou hast made my days measurable, and my substance is as nothing before thee.

20 And indeed all things are vanity, every man living.

Surely man passeth as an image; yea, and he is disquieted in vain.

He storeth up, and he knoweth not for whom he shall gather these things.

25 And now what is my hope? Is it not the Lord? And my substance is with thee.

Deliver thou me from all my iniquities; thou hast made me a reproach to the fool.

I was dumb, and I opened not my mouth, because

30 thou hast done it. Remove thy scourges from me.

The strength of thy hand hath made me faint in rebukes. Thou hast corrected man for iniquity.

And thou hast made his soul to waste away like a

35 spider; surely in vain is any man disquieted.

Hear my prayer, O Lord, and my supplication; give ear to my tears.

Be not silent, for I am a stranger with thee, and a sojourner as all my fathers were.

40 O forgive me, that I may be refreshed before I go hence, and be no more.[102]

PSALM 39

Blessed is the man whose trust is in the name of the Lord, and who hath not had regard to vanities, and lying follies.

45 Thou hast multiplied thy wonderful works, O Lord my God, and in thy thoughts there is no one like to thee.

Withhold not thou, O Lord, thy tender mercies from me; thy mercy and thy truth have always

50 upheld me.

For evils without number have surrounded me; my iniquities have overtaken me, and I was not able to see.

They are multiplied above the hairs of my head,

55 and my heart hath forsaken me.

Be pleased, O Lord, to deliver me; look down, O Lord, to help me.

Let all that seek thee rejoice and be glad in thee, and let such as love thy salvation say always,

60 "The Lord be magnified!"

But I am a beggar and poor; the Lord is careful for me.

Thou art my helper and my protector; O my God,

65 be not slack.[103]

PSALM 41

As the hart panteth after the fountains of water, so my soul panteth after thee, O God.[104]

My soul hath thirsted after the strong living God.

70 When shall I come and appear before the face of God?

My tears have been my bread day and night, whilst it is said to me daily, "Where is thy God?"

These things I remembered, and poured out my

75 soul in me, for I shall go over into the place of the wonderful tabernacle, even to the house of God.

With the voice of joy and praise, the noise of one feasting.

80 Why art thou sad, O my soul? And why dost thou trouble me?[105]

Hope in God, for I will still give praise to him, the salvation of my countenance, and my God.

My soul is troubled within myself; therefore will

85 I remember thee from the land of Jordan and Hermoniim, from the little hill.

100 Ps 37:2–23 (38:1–22)   **101** [evil words   (39:1–13)   **103** Ps 39:5–6, 12–14, 17–18   the man who can say this from his soul]
are not to be employed]   **102** Ps 38:2–14   (40:4–5, 11–13, 16–17)   **104** [happy   **105** [in tribulation]

Deep calleth on deep, at the noise of thy
    flood-gates.

All thy heights and thy billows have passed over
    me.

5 In the daytime the Lord hath commanded his
    mercy, and a canticle to him in the night.

With me is prayer to the God of my life. I will say
    to God, "Thou art my support.

Why hast thou forgotten me? And why go I

10   mourning, whilst my enemy afflicteth me?"

Whilst my bones are broken, my enemies who
    trouble me have reproached me.

Whilst they say to me day by day, "Where is thy
    God?"

15 Why art thou cast down, O my soul? And why
    dost thou disquiet me?

Hope thou in God, for I will still give praise to
    him, the salvation of my countenance, and my
    God.[106]

PSALM 45

20

Our God is our refuge and strength, a helper in
    troubles, which have found us exceedingly.[107]

Therefore we will not fear, when the earth shall be
    troubled, and the mountains shall be removed

25   into the heart of the sea.

Their waters roared and were troubled; the moun-
    tains were troubled with his strength.

The stream of the river maketh the city of God
    joyful; the Most High hath sanctified his own

30   tabernacle.

God is in the midst thereof; it shall not be moved;
    God will help it in the morning early.[108]

PSALM 50

Have mercy on me, O God, according to thy great

35   mercy.

And according to the multitude of thy tender mer-
    cies, blot out my iniquity.

Wash me yet more from my iniquity, and cleanse
    me from my sin.

40 For I know my iniquity, and my sin is always be-
    fore me.

To thee only have I sinned, and have done evil be-
    fore thee, that thou mayst be justified in thy
    words and mayst overcome when thou art

45   judged.

For behold I was conceived in iniquities, and in
    sins did my mother conceive me.

For behold thou hast loved truth; the uncertain
    and hidden things of thy wisdom thou hast
    made manifest to me.   50

Thou shalt sprinkle me with hyssop, and I shall
    be cleansed; thou shalt wash me, and I shall be
    made whiter than snow.

To my hearing thou shalt give joy and gladness, and
    the bones that have been humbled shall rejoice.   55

Turn away thy face from my sins, and blot out all
    my iniquities.

Create a clean heart in me, O God, and renew a
    right spirit within my bowels.

Cast me not away from thy face, and take not thy   60
    holy spirit from me.

Restore unto me the joy of thy salvation, and
    strengthen me with a perfect spirit.

I will teach the unjust thy ways, and the wicked
    shall be converted to thee.   65

Deliver me from blood, O God, thou God of my
    salvation, and my tongue shall extol thy justice.

O Lord, thou wilt open my lips, and my mouth
    shall declare thy praise.

For if thou hadst desired sacrifice, I would indeed   70
    have given it; with burnt offerings thou wilt not
    be delighted.

A sacrifice to God is an afflicted spirit; a con-
    trite and humbled heart, O God, thou wilt not
    despise.   75

Deal favorably, O Lord, in thy good will with Zion,
    that the walls of Jerusalem may be built up.

Then shalt thou accept the sacrifice of justice, obla-
    tions and whole burnt offerings; then shall they
    lay calves upon thy altar.[109]   80

PSALM 54

Hear, O God, my prayer, and despise not my sup-
    plication. Be attentive to me and hear me.[110]

My heart is troubled within me, and the fear of
    death is fallen upon me.   85

Fear and trembling are come upon me, and dark-
    ness hath covered me.

And I said, "Who will give me wings like a dove,
    and I will fly and be at rest?"

Cast thy care upon the Lord, and he shall sustain   90
    thee.[111]

106 Ps 41:2–12 (42:1–11)   **107** [trust   2–6 (46:1–5)   **109** Ps 50:3–21 (51:1–19)   **111** Ps 54:2–3, 5–7, 23 (55:1–2, 4–6, 22)
in God against tribulation]   **108** Ps 45:   **110** [in tribulation]

PSALM 61

Shall not my soul be subject to God? For from him
    is my salvation.[112]

For he is my God and my savior; he is my protec-
    tor; I shall be moved no more.

How long do you rush in upon a man? You all kill,
    as if you were thrusting down a leaning wall,
    and a tottering fence.

But be thou, O my soul, subject to God, for from
    him is my patience.[113]

For he is my God and my savior; he is my helper, I
    shall not be moved.

In God is my salvation and my glory; he is the God
    of my help, and my hope is in God.

Trust in him, all ye congregation of people; pour
    out your hearts before him. God is our helper
    forever.

God hath spoken once; these two things have I
    heard: that power belongeth to God, and mercy
    to thee, O Lord, for thou wilt render to every
    man according to his works.[114]

PSALM 62

O God, my God, to thee do I watch at break of day.

For thee my soul hath thirsted, for thee my flesh —
    O how many ways![115]

In a desert land, and where there is no way and no
    water, so in the sanctuary have I come before
    thee, to see thy power and thy glory.

For thy mercy is better than lives; thee my lips will
    praise.[116]

Thus will I bless thee all my life long, and in thy
    name I will lift up my hands.

Let my soul be filled as with marrow and fatness,
    and my mouth shall praise thee with joyful
    lips.

If I have remembered thee upon my bed, I will
    meditate on thee in the morning, because thou
    hast been my helper.

And I will rejoice under the covert of thy wings;
    my soul hath stuck close to thee; thy right hand
    hath received me.

But they have sought my soul in vain; they shall go
    into the lower parts of the earth; they shall be
    delivered into the hands of the sword; they shall
    be the portions of foxes.

But the king shall rejoice in God; all they shall be
    praised that swear by him, because the mouth is
    stopped of them that speak wicked things.[117]

PSALM 66

May God have mercy on us, and bless us; may he
    cause the light of his countenance to shine upon
    us, and may he have mercy on us.

That we may know thy way upon earth, thy salva-
    tion in all nations.

Let people confess to thee, O God; let all people
    give praise to thee.

Let the nations be glad and rejoice, for thou judg-
    est the people with justice, and directest the
    nations upon earth.

Let the people, O God, confess to thee; let all the
    people give praise to thee; the earth hath yielded
    her fruit.

May God, our God, bless us. May God bless us,
    and all the ends of the earth fear him.[118]

---

112 [patience in tribulation, or I shall not commit such a sin again] **113** [patience] **114** Ps 61:2–4, 6–9, 12–13 (62:1–3, 5–8, 11–12) **115** [longing for God] **116** [in tribulation and fear of death] **117** Ps 62:2–12 (63:1–11) **118** Ps 66:2–8 (67:1–7)

A GODLY MEDITATION

written by Sir Thomas More, Knight,
while he was prisoner in the Tower of London
in the year of our Lord 1534

5   Give me thy grace, good Lord,
       To set the world at nought;[119]

       To set my mind fast[120] upon thee,
          And not to hang upon the blast
          of men's mouths;

10   To be content to be solitary,
          Not to long for worldly company;

       Little and[121] little utterly to cast off the world,
          And rid my mind of all the
          business thereof;

15   Not to long to hear of any worldly things,
          But that the hearing of worldly fantasies
          may be to me displeasant;

       Gladly to be thinking of God;
       Piteously to call for his help;

20   To lean unto the comfort of God;
       Busily to labor to love him;

       To know mine own vility[122] and wretchedness;
       To humble and meeken myself under the
          mighty hand of God;

25   To bewail my sins passed;
       For the purging of them, patiently to
          suffer adversity;

       Gladly to bear my purgatory here;
       To be joyful of tribulations;

       To walk the narrow way that leadeth to life;   30
       To bear the cross with Christ;

       To have the last things in remembrance;
       To have ever afore mine eye my death that is
          ever at hand;

       To make death no stranger to me;
       To foresee and consider the everlasting   35
          fire of hell;

       To pray for pardon before the judge come;
       To have continually in mind the Passion that
          Christ suffered for me;

       For his benefits incessantly to give him thanks; 40
       To buy[123] the time again that I before have lost;

       To abstain from vain confabulations;[124]
       To eschew[125] light foolish mirth and gladness;

       Recreations not necessary, to cut off;
          Of worldly substance, friends, liberty, life,   45
          and all-to set the loss at right nought[126] for
          the winning of Christ;

       To think my most[127] enemies my best friends,
          For the brethren of Joseph[128] could never
          have done him so much good with their   50
          love and favor as they did him with their
          malice and hatred.

       These minds[129] are more to be desired of every
       man than all the treasure of all the princes and
       kings, Christian and heathen, were it gathered   55
       and laid together all upon one heap.

---

119 *set at nought:* regard as nothing   **123** redeem   **124** familiar conversations;   **127** greatest, worst   **128** Gn 37, 41
120 firmly; steadfastly   **121** by   chats   **125** avoid   **126** *set . . . nought:*   **129** thoughts; intentions; dispositions
122 lowness of condition; moral baseness   regard the loss as nothing at all

A Devout Prayer

made by Sir Thomas More, Knight, after he was
condemned to die, and before he was put to death;
who was condemned the Thursday the first day of
July in the year of our Lord God 1535, and in the
twenty-seventh year of the reign of King Henry
the Eighth, and was beheaded at the Tower Hill
at London the Tuesday following

Paternoster, Ave Maria, Credo.[130]

O Holy Trinity: the Father, the Son, and the Holy Ghost—three equal and coeternal persons, and one almighty God—have mercy on me, vile, abject, abominable, sinful wretch, meekly acknowledging before thine high majesty my long-continued sinful life, even from my very childhead[131] hitherto.

In my childhead in this point and that point, etc.

After my childhead in this point and that point, etc., and so forth by every age.

Now, good gracious Lord, as thou givest me thy grace to acknowledge them, so give me thy grace, not in only word but in heart also, with very sorrowful contrition to repent them, and utterly to forsake them. And forgive me those sins also in which by mine own default,[132] through evil affections[133] and evil custom,[134] my reason is with sensuality so blinded that I cannot discern them for sin. And illumine, good Lord, mine heart, and give me thy grace to know them and to acknowledge them, and forgive me my sins negligently forgotten, and bring them to my mind with grace to be purely confessed of them.

Glorious God, give me from henceforth the grace, with little respect unto the world, so to set and fix firmly mine heart upon thee that I may say with thy blessed apostle Saint Paul, *Mundus mihi crucifixus est, et ego mundo. Mihi vivere Christus est et mori lucrum. Cupio dissolvi et esse cum Christo.*[135]

Give me the grace to amend my life and to have an eye to mine end without grudge[136] of death, which to them that die in thee, good Lord, is the gate of a wealthy[137] life.

Almighty God: *Doce me facere voluntatem tuam. Fac me currere in odore unguentorum tuorum. Apprehende manum meam dexteram, et deduc me in via recta propter inimicos meos. Trahe me post te. In chamo et freno maxillas meas constringe, cum non approximo ad te.*[138]

O glorious God, all sinful fear, all sinful sorrow and pensiveness, all sinful hope, all sinful mirth and gladness take from me. And on the other side, concerning such fear, such sorrow, such heaviness,[139] such comfort, consolation, and gladness as shall be profitable for my soul, *Fac mecum secundum magnam bonitatem tuam Domine.*[140]

Good Lord, give me the grace in all my fear and agony to have recourse to that great fear and wonderful agony that thou my sweet Savior hadst at the Mount of Olivet before thy most bitter Passion, and in the meditation thereof to conceive ghostly[141] comfort and consolation profitable for my soul.

Almighty God, take from me all vainglorious minds,[142] all appetites of mine own praise, all envy, covetise,[143] gluttony, sloth and lechery, all wrathful affections, all appetite of revenging, all desire or delight of other folks' harm, all pleasure in provoking any person to wrath and anger, all delight of exprobration[144] or insultation[145] against any person in their affliction and calamity.

And give me, good Lord, a humble, lowly, quiet, peaceable, patient, charitable, kind, tender, and pitiful mind, with all my works, and all my words, and all my thoughts to have a taste of thy holy blessed Spirit.

Give me, good Lord, a full faith, a firm hope, and a fervent charity, a love to thee, good Lord, incomparable[146] above the love to myself, and that I love nothing to thy displeasure, but everything in an order to[147] thee.

130 This rubric indicates one should pray the Our Father, Hail Mary, and the Creed. **131** childhood **132** misdeed **133** dispositions **134** habit **135** "The world is crucified to me, and I to the world. For to me to live is Christ and to die is gain. I wish to be dissolved and be with Christ." See Gal 6:14 and Phil 1:21–23. **136** complaint; being discontent **137** possessing well-being **138** "Teach me to do your will. Make me run in the scent of thy ointments. Take my right hand, and lead me in the right path because of my enemies. Draw me after you. With a bit and bridle bind fast my jaws when I come not near unto thee." See Ps 142(143):10; Sg 1:3; Ps 72(73):24; Ps 26(27):11; Ps 31(32):9. **139** grief **140** "Deal with me according to your great goodness, O Lord." See Ps 118(119):124. **141** spiritual **142** dispositions; intentions **143** covetousness **144** reproaching **145** insult; scornful triumph or boasting **146** incomparably **147** *in … to*: ordered to

Give me, good Lord, a longing to be with thee, not for the avoiding of the calamities of this wretched world, nor so much for the avoiding of the pains of purgatory, nor of the pains of hell neither, nor so much for the attaining of the joys of heaven, in respect of mine own commodity,[148] as even for a very[149] love to thee.

And bear me, good Lord, thy love and favor, which thing my love to thee-ward[150] (were it never so great) could not but of thy great goodness deserve.

And pardon me, good Lord, that I am so bold to ask so high petitions, being so vile a sinful wretch and so unworthy to attain the lowest. But yet, good Lord, such they be as I am bounden to wish and should be nearer the effectual desire of them if my manifold sins were not the let.[151] From which, O glorious Trinity, vouchsafe[152] of thy goodness to wash me with that blessed blood that issued out of thy tender body (O sweet Savior Christ) in the diverse torments of thy most bitter Passion.

Take from me, good Lord, this lukewarm fashion, or rather key-cold[153] manner of meditation, and this dullness in praying unto thee. And give me warmth, delight, and quickness in thinking upon thee, and give me thy grace to long for thine holy sacraments, and specially to rejoice in the presence of thy very blessed body, sweet Savior Christ, in the holy Sacrament of the altar, and duly to thank thee for thy gracious visitation therewith, and at that high memorial, with tender compassion to remember and consider thy most bitter Passion.

Make us all, good Lord, virtually[154] participant of that holy Sacrament this day, and every day make us all lively members, sweet Savior Christ, of thine holy mystical body, thy Catholic Church.

Dignare Domine die isto sine peccato nos custodire.[155]
Miserere nostri Domine, miserere nostri.[156]
Fiat misericordia tua Domine super nos, quemadmodum speravimus in te.[157]
In te Domine speravi, non confundar in aeternum.[158]
Ora pro nobis, sancta Dei genetrix, ut digni efficiamur promissionibus Christi.[159]

Pro Amicis[160]

Almighty God, have mercy on N.[161] and N., etc., with special meditation and consideration of every friend, as godly affection and occasion requireth.

Pro Inimicis[162]

Almighty God, have mercy on N. and N., etc., and on all that bear me evil will, and would me harm; and their faults and mine together, by such easy tender merciful means as thine infinite wisdom best can devise, vouchsafe to amend and redress, and make us saved souls in heaven together, where we may ever live and love together with thee and thy blessed saints. O glorious Trinity, for the bitter Passion of our sweet Savior Christ, Amen.

Lord, give me patience in tribulation, and grace in everything to conform my will to thine, that I may truly say: *Fiat voluntas tua, sicut in caelo, et in terra.*[163]

The things, good Lord, that I pray for, give me the grace to labor for. Amen.

---

148 benefit **149** true **150** *to theeward:* toward thee **151** hindrance **152** grant **153** cold as a key; without heat or fervor **154** with spiritual effect **155** "Deign, O Lord, on that day to preserve us without sin." This and the following psalms comprise the last stanza of the *Te Deum,* a hymn of thanksgiving. **156** "Have mercy upon us, O Lord, have mercy upon us." See Ps 122(123):3. **157** "Let your mercy, O Lord, be upon us, just as we have hoped in you." See Ps 32(33):22. **158** "In you, O Lord, have I hoped, let me never be confounded." See Ps 30(31):2. **159** "Pray for us, holy mother of God, that we may be made worthy of the promises of Christ" (from the prayer *Salve regina*). **160** "For Friends" **161** The liturgical abbreviation for the Latin *nomen* ("name"), providing for one to add names appropriate to one's own prayer. **162** "For Enemies" **163** "Thy will be done on earth, as it is in heaven" (Mt 6:10).

This memo of Secretary Thomas Cromwell, written in the hand of a clerk *ca.* June 18, 1535, is entitled "Remembraunces at my next goyng to the Courte." Three items pertain directly to Thomas More. [1] The fifth "Item" reads: "to knowe his [Henry's] pleasure touchyng Maister More," and then Cromwell adds in his own hand: "and to declare the oppynyon of the Judges theron, & what shalbe the kynge pleasure." [2] The twelfth "Item" reads: "when Maister Fissher shall go to execucion with also the other," followed by [3] the thirteenth: "Item what shalbe done farther touching Maister More." "Item" 11 reads: "to remember S[i]r Wa[l]ter Hungerford in his well doynges"; Hungerford was a juror at Fisher's June 17 trial as well as the foreman of the jury for the April 28–29 trial of the three Carthusian priors (including More's friend John Houghton) and Dr. Richard Reynolds of the Bridgettine monastery of Sion.

Thomas More's Trial Reconstructed

Thomas More's trial in Westminster Hall on July 1, 1535, is among the more famous trials in Western history. The reconstruction given here is taken from *Thomas More's Trial by Jury* (Boydell and Brewer, 2011), which gives the existing accounts, official documents, and other documentary evidence of More's trial, including the Latin texts with translations. After "Thomas More's Trial Reconstructed" there follows a selection of the acts, oaths, and laws relevant to More's trial. The earliest published account, the *Paris Newsletter*, is given in the next section, "Earliest Biographical Accounts."

More had first been imprisoned in April 1534 for refusing to take the oath required by the Act of Succession, the statute whereby Queen Anne Boleyn's children were recognized as legal heirs of the throne, and as such were due the "faith, truth, and obedience" of their subjects. As Peter Marshall maintains, More's difficulty was not so much with the succession claim itself as with the oath, most likely the words pronouncing Anne the King's "entirely beloved *lawful* wife" (emphasis added) and especially the oath's implied rejection of any "foreign authority or potentate," a reference to Rome and the pope (*CC* 121–23). In late 1534, instead of a trial, More was subject to an Act of Attainder, a legislative bill passed by the English Parliament for the purpose of "attainting" or convicting More of misprision of treason, with the punishment of life imprisonment.

When More was brought to trial over six months later, he was formally charged with violating two new statutes, the Act of Supremacy and the Treasons Act, which Parliament had passed in late 1534. The Act of Supremacy gave official "corroboration and confirmation" of what the Bishops' Convocations had already in effect granted through the Submission of the Clergy earlier in 1532: "that the King, our sovereign lord, his heirs and successors, kings of this realm, shall be taken, accepted, and reputed the only Supreme Head in earth of the Church of England, called *Anglicana Ecclesia*...." The second statute More allegedly violated was the Treasons Act, which made it high treason, the penalty for which was death, for anyone to "maliciously wish, will or desire, by words or writing, or by craft imagine, invent, practice, or attempt any bodily harm to be done or committed to the King's most royal person, the Queen's, or their heirs apparent, or to deprive them or any of them of their dignity, title, or name of their royal estates, or slanderously and maliciously publish and pronounce, by express writing or words, that the King our sovereign lord should be heretic, schismatic, tyrant, infidel, or usurper of the crown...."

The indictment accuses More of high treason for depriving the English King of his title, Supreme Head, in three ways: first, by persevering in malicious silence when authorities demanded he affirm the King's title; second, by maliciously conspiring with Bishop John Fisher, also imprisoned, to deny the King's title; and third, by maliciously telling Richard Rich in a conversation that an act of Parliament could not make the King Supreme Head of the Church in England. More argued against the first two charges, but Richard Rich's sworn testimony regarding a conversation between himself and More was taken as proof enough in support of the third charge. While it has been widely accepted that More was convicted on the third count of the indictment alone, Henry Kelly concludes in his procedural review of the trial in *Thomas More's Trial by Jury* that More was convicted on the whole indictment, and he points out that there are two extant accounts of the fateful conversation between Rich and More: the first version by Rich, the second by Roper, More's son-in-law. In any event, after the dramatic exchanges reconstructed here, More was condemned for high treason and sentenced to death by being drawn and quartered. That sentence was later commuted to beheading.

CONTENTS

TIMELINE: IMPORTANT DATES AND LEGAL CONTEXT

Acts, Oaths, Interrogations, and Trial

September 1530	Archbishop Cranmer presents *Collectanea satis copiosa* [*Determinations of the Universities*] arguing for the English king's divine right and imperial status.
January 1531	King Henry charges the clergy with Praemunire and requires they recognize him as head of the English Church; they do so "as far as Christ's law allows" and pay £100,000 penalty.
30 March 1531	Henry has More report *Collectanea* to the Parliament.
February 1532	Warham, Archbishop of Canterbury, formally dissociates himself from anticlerical laws since 1529.
19 March 1532	Conditional Restraint of Annates Act (23 H8 c. 20) passes House of Lords after Henry VIII visits three times; all bishops, two abbots and Earl of Arundel opposed (*LP* 5, 879).
26 March 1532	Conditional Restraint of Annates Act (23 H8 c. 20) passes House of Commons after Henry VIII "causes the House to divide" for the first time in English history (*LP* 5, 898).
14 May 1532	Henry dismisses Parliament after it refuses, under More, to pass Submission of the Clergy Act.
15 May 1532	Submission of the Clergy Act (*LP* 5, 1023) accepted by some in Upper House of Convocation after disbanding Lower House; More resigns 16 May.
Summer 1532	More has epitaph for his tomb engraved, installed — the text sent to Erasmus to publish (Letter 191).
Feb–Mar 1533	Act in Restraint of Appeals (24 H8 c. 12): Henry as emperor and as head of the Church.
March 1534	– Act of Submission of the Clergy (25 H8 c. 19): Parliament formalizes 1532 Convocation statute; all appeals of Church law now to go to King's Court of Chancery
	– Act Restraining Annates (25 H8 c. 20) confirms 1532 Conditional Act; abbots and bishops now appointed by Henry VIII
	– Act of Succession (25 H8 c. 22), effective 1 May 1534, penalty of high treason for writing or acting against it, and misprision of treason for refusing an oath concerning it
13 April 1534	More interrogated at Lambeth Palace; imprisoned on 17th (Letter 200). **Interrogation #1**
August 1534	Chancellor Audley sends warning to More (Letters 205–6).
Nov–Dec 1534	– Act Recognizing the King as Supreme Head of the Church in England (26 H8 c.1)
	– Act Ratifying the Oath to the Succession (26 H8 c. 2)
	– Treason Act (26 H8 c. 13): makes it high treason to maliciously deprive the King and Queen of the dignity, title, or name of their royal estates, by word or deed; effective 1 February 1535
	– Act of Attainder of Thomas More: misprision of treason for refusing the oath of Succession (26 H8 c. 23)
30 April 1535	Cromwell and others interrogate More (Letter 214; Indictment §4). **Interrogation #2**
3 June 1535	More and Fisher interrogated separately; both remain silent and speak of "two-edged sword" (Indictment §7, §9, *LP* 8, 814; Letter 216). **Interrogation #3**
12 June 1535	Richard Rich removes books and writing materials; has disputed conversation with More.
14 June 1535	More interrogated again (*LP* 8, 867). **Interrogation #4**
25 June 1535	Henry VIII orders the guilt of Fisher and More to be publicized (*LP* 8, 921).
28 June 1535	Grand Jury meets; they accept the state's Indictment (Indictment §12).
1 July 1535	More's trial at Westminster Hall; More invokes Magna Carta and the King's Coronation Oath.
6 July 1535	More's execution by beheading.

Thomas More's Trial[1]
Reconstructed

NARRATOR: On Saturday, June 26, 1535, a special commission of oyer[2] and terminer[3] met at Westminster and summoned a grand jury to meet on Monday, June 28; on that day the justices presented the jury with an indictment against Sir Thomas More. The jury found it a true bill.[4]

The indictment charged More with high treason under the Act of Treasons concerning the King's supremacy of the English Church, in that he sought to deprive the King of this title in the following ways:

1) by maliciously remaining silent when asked to affirm it;
2) by maliciously conspiring with Bishop Fisher to deny the title; and
3) by maliciously asserting to Richard Rich that Parliament did not have power to grant the King this title.[5]

On Wednesday, June 30, the Commissioners ordered the constable of the Tower to present Sir Thomas More before them at Westminster on the following day. On that day, Thursday, July 1, Audley ordered the Sheriff of Middlesex to have a petty jury[6] before them that very day. Sir Thomas More was brought to the bar by Sir Edmund Walsingham, lieutenant of Sir William Kingston, constable of the Tower.[7]

Thereupon "Thomas More, recently chancellor of the Kingdom of England, after being confined in prison for fifteen months, was brought before the magistrates and judges appointed by the King. When he was present, the accusations against him were publicly recited."[8]

DUKE OF NORFOLK: "More, you see that you have gravely offended against the royal Majesty in this matter. Nevertheless, we have confidence in his clemency and bounty that if you should be willing to repent and change for the better this rash opinion of yours, which you have so pertinaciously adhered to, you will easily gain forgiveness of your fault from him."[9]

SIR THOMAS MORE: "Noble sirs, my very great thanks to you for your exceeding benevolence to me. But I ask only this of the great good God, that by his help I may be able to persevere in my right opinion until death. But as for what concerns the accusations with which I am charged, I fear that neither my mental ability, nor memory, nor words will suffice to explain them, because I am impeded not only by the prolixity and extensiveness of the articles, but also by my long detention in prison and the illness and bodily weakness that now afflict me."[10]

ONE OF THE JUDGES: The prisoner requires a chair for his feebleness.[11]

LORD CHANCELLOR THOMAS AUDLEY (*when other judges nod in agreement*): Let the prisoner have a chair.

1 This reconstruction is from *Thomas More's Trial by Jury: A Procedural and Legal Review with a Collection of Documents*, ed. Henry Ansgar Kelly, Louis W. Karlin, and Gerard B. Wegemer (Woodbridge, Suffolk: Boydell Press, 2011). The footnotes that follow refer to this collection and its section numbers. A list of the original sources is given at the end of this section. **2** "to hear" **3** "to determine" **4** Bag of Secrets **5** More's Indictment 4–11 **6** *petty jury:* a trial jury (as opposed to a grand jury) **7** Bag of Secrets **8** Guildhall Report 1.a **9** Guildhall Report 1.b **10** Guildhall Report 1.c **11** Guildhall Report 2.a

MORE (*after being seated*): "As for what pertains to the first part of the accusation, which has it that, to show the greatest possible malice of my mind against the King, I was a constant opponent in the contention over his second marriage, I have nothing to say other than what I have said before; and that is, that whatever I spoke in that matter, I did it at the urging of my conscience. For it did not behoove me, nor did I wish it, to conceal the truth from my prince. If I had not acted so, I would have been an enemy to him, not a faithful servant. Now for this sin, if it is proper to call it a sin, I was adjudged to perpetual imprisonment, in which I have now been detained for fifteen months, and my goods besides confiscated."[12]

In regard to the indictment, I openly declare that I would abide upon[13] it in law, were it not that I would thereby be driven to confess of myself the very matter, which is, the denial of the King's supremacy, which is untrue. Wherefore I plead thereto not guilty.[14]

I place myself for good or ill upon my country.[15]

And I reserve unto myself advantage to be taken of the body of the matter, after verdict, to a-void this indictment. But here I say that if only those odious terms, "maliciously, traitorously, and diabolically" were put out of the indictment, I see therein nothing justly wherewith to charge me.[16]

NARRATOR: The judges assigned the same day for More's trial and remanded him to Walsingham's custody until the petty jury is assembled and sworn.[17]

"Immediately twelve men were called by the Public Minister, after the custom of the British nation, to whom were given the chapters of accusation."[18]

More was called again to the bar.[19]

ATTORNEY GENERAL CHRISTOPHER HALES: Sir Thomas More, I challenge you to reply to the charges in the indictment.

MORE: "I reply only to the main heading of the first accusation. You say that I have merited the penalty inflicted by the statute passed in the last Parliament of our leaders, for which I was now held in custody, for the reason that, with malicious, false, and faithless mind, I injured the royal Majesty and name and titles and honor and dignity which they in the aforesaid Parliament or Council attributed to the King, by which he is considered to be Supreme Head after Jesus Christ of the English Church; and, above all, that you object to me that I wished to answer nothing to the Secretary of the King and to the honorable Council of the royal Majesty, when he asked me what my opinion was about that statute, other than that, because I was now dead to the world, I did not occupy myself with such things but only meditated on the Passion of our Lord Jesus Christ."[20]

"To which I clearly respond to you that it is not lawful for me to be judged to death for such silence on my part, because neither your statute nor anything in the laws of the whole world can rightly afflict anyone with punishment, unless one has committed a crime in word or deed, since laws have constituted no penalty for silence."[21]

HALES: "Such silence was a sure indication and a not obscure sign of some malign thinking about the statute, because all subjects, being faithful to their prince, when interrogated on their view concerning the statute, are obliged to respond openly, and without dissimulation, that it is good and holy.[22]

JUDGES: Malice! Malice![23]

MORE: "But if it is true what universal law says, 'One who keeps silent seems to consent,' then that silence of mine gave approval to that statute of yours more than it weakened it. But as for all the faithful being bound and obliged to make response, etc., I answer that there is a much greater obligation on the part of a good man and faithful subject to consult his own conscience and eternal salvation, and to follow the prescriptions of reason, than to take account of any other thing, especially since the kind of conscience that I have offers no offense to its prince and stirs up no sedition — asserting this to you, that my conscience had not been opened to any mortal."[24]

"As for what I am accused of in the second part, that I contravened the statute and worked for its abolition in writings to the Bishop of Rochester, by means of eight letters in which I fortified him against your statute: again and again I wished for

12 Guildhall Report 2.a **13** *abide upon:* act in accordance with **14** Roper 3 **15** Bag of Secrets **16** Roper 3 **17** Bag of Secrets **18** Guildhall Report 7 **19** Bag of Secrets **20** Guildhall Report 2.b **21** Guildhall Report 2.c **22** Guildhall Report 3 **23** Pole 6 **24** Guildhall Report 4

those letters to have been publicly recited. But since, as you tell me, they were burned by the said Bishop, I myself will sum up for you their contents. Some of them dealt with familiar matters, such as our old custom and friendship called for. One of them responded to his request to know how I answered when first examined on the statute. I replied that I had exonerated my conscience and followed reason, and I urged him to do the same. This was, so help me God, the purport of my letters, and there is nothing on their account that should be judged worthy of death under your statute."[25]

"As for what pertains to the third article, which says that when I was interrogated by the Council I responded that your statute is like a two-edged sword, so that one who obeyed it imperiled the salvation of his soul, while one who opposed it would lose his life; and that the Bishop of Rochester (you say) responded in the same way, from which it should appear that this was done by agreement between us, both of us responding in the same way: to this part of the accusation I respond that I was not speaking straightforwardly but only conditionally; that is, if there should be some statute that was like a two-edged sword, how could any person take care against coming up against one edge or the other? But what the Bishop of Rochester responded, I do not know. It may be that he responded in the same way, but it was not done through any conspiracy, but rather it occurred because of our similar minds and education. But believe me most assuredly on this point, that I never said or did anything maliciously against your statute. In the meantime, however, it could be that many things have been viciously and maliciously spoken about me to arouse hatred against me on the part of his royal Majesty."[26]

NARRATOR: "And for proof to the jury that Sir Thomas More was guilty of this treason, Master Solicitor Rich was called forth to give evidence unto them upon his oath, as he did."[27]

RICHARD RICH: My lords, I, being sent to Sir Thomas More into the Tower, along with Sir Richard Southwell and Master Palmer, servant to Secretary Cromwell, to fetch away his books from him, while Sir Richard and Master Palmer were busy in the trussing up of his books, spoke with him thus.[28]

I asked him, if it were enacted by the authority of Parliament that if I myself, that is, Richard Rich, were king, and that it would be treason if anyone denied it, what would be the offense in the said Thomas More if the same Thomas said that the said Richard Rich was king? Certainly (I continued further), there would be no offense in his conscience, but rather the said Thomas More was obliged to say so and accept the same Richard, because the consent of the said Thomas More was obligated by the act of Parliament. The said Thomas More then and there responded and said that he would indeed commit an offense if he denied it, since he was able to give his consent to it. But he said that this case will be a trivial case.[29]

"Therefore, the same Thomas then and there said to [me] that he would propose a more lofty case, saying thus: 'Let us say that it was enacted by Parliament that God was not God, and that if anyone wished to impugn that act, it would be treason; if the question were put to you, Richard Rich, "Do you wish to say that God is not God," in accord with the statute, and you said yes, would you not commit an offense?'"[30]

"To which [I said]…, 'Yes, certainly, because it is impossible to bring it about that God be not God. And because your case is on such a high level, I will propose to you this middle case: You know that our Lord King has been constituted as Supreme Head on earth of the English Church; and why should not you, Master More, affirm and accept him as such in this case, just as in the foregoing case in which I was selected to be king? In that case you concede that you would be obligated to affirm and accept me as king.'"[31]

"To this the said Thomas More… responded to [me] that those cases are not like, because a king can be made by Parliament, and can be deprived by Parliament, to which act any subject being at the Parliament may give his consent; but to the case of a primacy, the subject cannot be bound, because he cannot give his consent from him in Parliament. And although the king were generally accepted as such in England, yet most outer parts do not affirm it."[32]

AUDLEY: Let the prisoner be sworn to answer concerning the witness's testimony.

25 Guildhall Report 5 **26** Guildhall Report 6 **27** Roper 4 **28** Roper 1   **29** More's Indictment 11b **30** More's Indictment 11c **31** More's Indictment 11d   **32** More's Indictment 11e

MORE (*after being sworn specifically to respond to Rich's allegations*): "If I were a man, my lords, that did not regard an oath, I needed not, as it is well known, in this place, at this time, nor in this case, to 5 stand here as an accused person."[33]

"And if this oath of yours, Master Rich, be true, then pray I that I never see God in the face; which I would not say, were it otherwise, to win the whole world."[34]

10 My lords, I will here recite to you the discourse of all our communication in the Tower, according to the truth.[35]

Master Rich said unto me, "Forasmuch as it is well known, Master More, that you are a man both 15 wise and well-learned as well in the laws of the realm as otherwise, I pray you therefore, sir, let me be so bold as of good will to put unto you this case. Admit there were, sir, . . . an act of Parliament that all the realm should take me for king. Would not 20 you, Master More, take me for king?"

To which I replied: "Yes, sir, that would I."

"I put case further," quoth Master Rich, "that there were an act of Parliament that all the realm should take me for pope. Would not you, then, 25 Master More, take me for pope?"

"For answer, sir," quoth I, "to your first case: the Parliament may well, Master Rich, meddle with the state of temporal princes. But to make answer to your other case, I will put you this case: suppose the 30 Parliament would make a law that God should not be God. Would you then, Master Rich, say that God were not God?"

"No, sir," quoth he, "that would I not, since no Parliament may make any such law."

35 "No more," said I, "could the Parliament make the king Supreme Head of the Church [i.e., pope]."[36]

NARRATOR: Thus, having shown how Master Rich changed cases, from speaking about Rich being declared pope to speaking about King Henry 40 being declared Head of the English Church, More addressed Master Rich directly:

MORE: "In good faith, Master Rich, I am sorrier for your perjury than for my own peril. And you shall understand that neither I nor no man else to 45 my knowledge ever took you to be a man of such credit as in any matter of importance, aye, or any other, would at any time vouchsafe to communicate with you. And I, as you know, for no small while have been acquainted with you and your conversa- 50 tion, who have known you from your youth hitherto. For we long dwelled both in one parish together, where, as yourself can tell (I am sorry you compel me so to say), you were esteemed very light of your tongue, a great dicer, and of no commend- 55 able fame. And so in your house at the Temple, where hath been your chief bringing up, were you likewise accounted."[37]

NARRATOR: Sir Thomas More then addressed the judges:

MORE: "Can it therefore seem likely unto your 60 honorable lordships that I would, in so weighty a cause, so unadvisedly overshoot myself as to trust Master Rich, a man of me always reputed for one of so little truth, as your lordships have heard, so far above my sovereign lord the King, or any of his no- 65 ble councilors, that I would unto him utter the secrets of my conscience touching the king's supremacy, the special point and only mark at my hands so long sought for? A thing which I never did, nor never would, after the statute thereof made, reveal, 70 either to the King's Highness himself, or to any of his honorable councilors, as it is not unknown to your honors at sundry several times sent from his Grace's own person unto the Tower unto me for none other purpose. Can this in your judgments, 75 my lords, seem likely to be true?"[38]

"And yet, if I had so done in deed, my lords, as Master Rich hath sworn, seeing it was spoken but in familiar secret talk, nothing affirming, and only in putting of cases, without other displeasant cir- 80 cumstances, it cannot justly be taken to be spoken maliciously. And where there is no malice, there can be no offense. And over this I can never think, my lords, that so many worthy bishops, so many honorable personages, and so many other worshipful, vir- 85 tuous, wise, and well-learned men as at the making of that law were in the Parliament assembled, ever meant to have any man punished by death in whom there could be found no malice, taking *malitia* for *malevolentia*. For if *malitia* be generally taken 90 for 'sin,' no man is there then that can thereof excuse himself; *quia,* '*Si dixerimus quod peccatum non habemus, nosmetipsos seducimus, et veritas in nobis non est* ["If we should say that we do not have sin, we deceive ourselves, and the truth is not in us"].³⁹ And only this word *maliciously* is in the statute material, as this term *forcible* is in the Statute of Forcible Entries. By which statute, if a man enter peaceably and put not his adversary out forcibly, it is no offense. But if he put him out forcibly, then by the statute it is an offense, and so shall he be punished by this term *forcibly*."⁴⁰

"Besides this, the manifold goodness of the King's Highness himself, that hath been so many ways my singular good lord and gracious sovereign, that hath so dearly loved and trusted me, even at my very first coming into his noble service with the dignity of his honorable Privy Council vouchsafing to admit me, and to offices of great credit and worship most liberally advance me, and finally with that weighty room of his Grace's high chancellor—the like whereof he never did to temporal man before—next to his own royal person the highest officer in this noble realm, so far above my merits or qualities able and meet therefore, of his incomparable benignity honored and exalted me, by the space of twenty years and more showing his continual favor towards me, and (until at my own poor suit, it pleased his Highness, giving me license, with his Majesty's favor, to bestow the residue of my life for the provision of my soul in the service of God, of his especial goodness thereof to discharge and unburden me), most benignly heaped honors continually more and more upon me. All this his Highness's goodness, I say, so long thus bountifully extended towards me, were, in my mind, my lords, matter sufficient to convince this slanderous surmise by this man so wrongfully imagined against me."⁴¹

NARRATOR: "Master Rich, seeing himself so disproved, and his credit so foully defaced, caused Sir Richard Southwell and Master Palmer, that at the time of their communication were in the chamber, to be sworn what words had passed between them."⁴²

MASTER PALMER: My lords, I "was so busy about the trussing up of Sir Thomas More's books in a sack, that [I] took no heed to their talk."⁴³

SIR RICHARD SOUTHWELL: My lords, I "was appointed only to look unto the conveyance of his books, [and therefore I] gave no ear unto them."⁴⁴

NARRATOR: "After this were there many other reasons by Sir Thomas More in his own defense alleged, to the discredit of Master Rich's aforesaid evidence, and proof of the clearness of his own conscience."⁴⁵

AUDLEY: Let the jury now make deliberation over the accusations laid against the prisoner.

NARRATOR: "Now the twelve men, who according to the custom of our country have the power of life and death in trials, were called forward. And these men, since they had the word *malice*, which had sounded throughout the whole courtroom, fixed in their ears and minds, made no delay—in fact, it was a wonder that they could so quickly come to agreement."⁴⁶

The jury, "sitting about a quarter of an hour, after deliberation [having been] had among them . . . returned to the sight of the princes and judges delegate."⁴⁷

AUDLEY: How does the jury find? Is the prisoner guilty or not guilty of sinning maliciously against the statute?⁴⁸

SPOKESMAN OF THE JURY: We find upon our oath that Thomas More is guilty of the treason imputed to him; and we find also that he possesses no lands or holdings or goods or chattels."⁴⁹

ATTORNEY GENERAL HALES AND SERGEANTS-AT-LAW: We demand that judgment and execution be given against Thomas More according to the form of law.⁵⁰

AUDLEY: We, the commissioned justices, having seen and understood all and singular of what has gone before, are ready to pronounce judgment of high treason against Thomas More.⁵¹

MORE (*interrupting*): "My lord, when I was toward the law, the manner in such case was to ask the prisoner before judgment why judgment should not be given against him."⁵²

AUDLEY: What are you able to say to the contrary of such judgment?

MORE: "Forasmuch as, my lord, . . . this indictment is grounded upon an act of Parliament directly repugnant to the laws of God and his holy Church,

39 1 Jn 1:8   **40** Roper 10   **41** Roper 11   **45** Roper 13   **46** Pole 6   **47** Guildhall   **49** Bag of Secrets   **50** Bag of Secrets
42 Roper 12   **43** Roper 12   **44** Roper 12   Report 7   **48** Guildhall Report 7   **51** Bag of Secrets   **52** Roper 14

the supreme government of which, or of any part whereof, may no temporal prince presume by any law to take upon him, as rightfully belonging to the see of Rome, a spiritual preeminence by the mouth of our Savior himself, personally present upon the earth, only to Saint Peter and his successors, bishops of the same see, by special prerogative granted; it is therefore in law amongst Christian men insufficient to charge any Christian man."

"This realm, being but one member and small part of the Church, may not make a particular law disagreeable with the general law of Christ's universal Catholic Church, no more than the city of London, being but one poor member in respect of the whole realm, may make a law against an act of Parliament to bind the whole realm.... It [is] contrary both to the laws and statutes of our own land yet unrepealed, as [you] might evidently perceive in Magna Carta: *Quod Ecclesia Anglicana libera sit et habeat omnia iura sua integra et libertates suas illaesas* — ["That the English Church be free and have all of its rights whole and its liberties uninjured"]; and also contrary to that sacred oath which the King's Highness himself and every other Christian prince always with great solemnity receive at their coronations.... No more might this realm of England refuse obedience to the see of Rome than might the child refuse obedience to his own natural father. For, as Saint Paul said of the Corinthians, 'I have regenerated you, my children in Christ.' So might Saint Gregory, Pope of Rome, of whom, by Saint Augustine, his messenger, we first received the Christian faith, of us Englishmen truly say: 'You are my children, because I have given to you everlasting salvation, a far higher and better inheritance than any carnal father can leave to his child, and by regeneration made you my spiritual children in Christ.'"[53]

AUDLEY: But seeing that "all the bishops, universities, and best learned of this realm have to this act agreed," I much marvel that you "alone against them all do so stiffly stick thereat, and so vehemently argue thereagainst."[54]

MORE: "If the number of bishops and universities be so material as your lordship seemeth to take it, then see I little cause, my lord, why that thing in my conscience should make any change. For I nothing doubt but that, though not in this realm, yet in Christendom about, of these well-learned bishops and virtuous men that are yet alive, they be not the fewer part that be of my mind therein. But if I should speak of those which already be dead, of whom many be now holy saints in heaven, I am very sure it is the far greater part of them that, all the while they lived, thought in this case that way that I think now. And therefore am I not bound, my lord, to conform my conscience to the counsel of one realm against the general counsel of Christendom."[55]

NARRATOR: Sir Thomas More added thereto many other exceptions, objections, and reasons for the voiding of the Indictment. Then "the Lord Chancellor, loath to have the burden of that judgment wholly to depend upon himself, there openly asked the advice of the Lord FitzJames, then Lord Chief Justice of the King's Bench, and joined in commission with him.[56]

AUDLEY: My Lord Chief Justice, I put it to you, is "this indictment sufficient" in law?[57]

LORD CHIEF JUSTICE FITZJAMES: "My lords all, by Saint Julian,... I must needs confess that, if the act of Parliament be not unlawful, then is not the Indictment, in my conscience, insufficient."[58]

AUDLEY: "Lo, my lords, lo, you hear what my Lord Chief Justice says. [I therefore give] judgment against him."[59]

In accord with the Statute of Treasons, therefore, we adjudge you, Thomas More, lawfully convict of high treason, to be led by Deputy Constable Sir Edmund Walsingham "to the Tower of London, and thence dragged through the midst of the city of London directly to the gallows of Tyburn and hanged upon those gallows, and while alive to be cast upon the earth and your entrails be taken from your belly and burned, you being still alive, and your head to be struck off and your body divided into four parts, and that your head and quarters be placed where the Lord King shall wish to assign them."[60]

SIR JOHN SPELMAN (*aside to his fellow justices*): I sum up the case thus for my reports: Sir Thomas More, Knight, one-time chancellor of England,

53 Roper 15   **54** Roper 16   **55** Roper 17   **59** Roper 19   **60** Bag of Secrets (with
56 Roper 18   **57** Roper 18   **58** Roper 18   pronouns adjusted)

having been "arraigned before the said chancellor, Sir Thomas Audley, and the other commissioners, for treason, in that he was an aider, counselor, and abettor to the Bishop, and also for that he falsely, maliciously, and traitorously desiring, willing, and scheming, contrived, practiced, and attempted to deprive the King of his dignity, name, and title of Supreme Head on earth of the Church of England, [is] found guilty, and the said chancellor gave judgment."[61]

OTHER JUDGES: Sir Thomas, have you anything else to add in your defense? We will be favorably attentive to whatever you have to say.[62]

MORE: My lords, "since I have been adjudged to death, whether rightly or wrongly, God knows, for the exonerating of my conscience I would willingly say some words to you concerning your statute. I affirm that I have spent all my study during the whole of the last seven years, and I have never found an approved doctor of the Church to hold that any layman is the head of an ecclesiastical order."[63]

SPELMAN (*aside*): He stands firmly against the statute, holding that "Parliament could not make the king Supreme Head" of the English Church.[64]

AUDLEY (*interrupting More's statement*): "Do you wish to be more prudent and religious than all the bishops, the whole nobility, and all of the people who are subjects of the King and his kingdom?"[65]

MORE: "For one bishop who agrees with you, I have easily a hundred, including some who are among the saints. And for your one council, Parliament, and your statute—what it is worth the great good God knows—on my side are all the general councils celebrated during the last thousand years. And for one kingdom, the kingdom of France and all other kingdoms of the Christian world agree with me."[66]

NORFOLK: "More, now you are plainly revealing your mind's stubborn malice."[67]

MORE: "What I say, I say because necessity compels me, for I wish to exonerate my conscience and not weigh down my soul. I call on God, the searcher of hearts, as witness."[68]

"I add this besides, that your statute was wrongly made, because you deliberately swore your oaths against the Church, which alone is whole and undivided through the whole Christian world. And you alone have no power to enact anything, without the consent of all other Christians, which is contrary to the unity and concord of the Christian religion."[69]

I am now for the first time revealing my opinion concerning this law by which the king has been appointed Head of the Church in England. I have not done so before this, to avoid giving my enemies further opportunity of lashing out against me, and it would have hindered my defense here today. But I speak out now, "being mindful of my care for England, lest any person therein should imprudently and ignorantly favor this pestiferous law. This law is in contradiction to all human and divine laws. It will be more pernicious to anyone who assents to it than it has been to me, who stand condemned to capital punishment for having dissented from it."[70]

One final word, my lords: "I am not unaware of the reason for which you have adjudged me to death. The one single cause is that I have been unwilling over the past years to consent to the second marriage of the King."[71]

NARRATOR: Now More addressed all present.

MORE: "Here indeed is a place of discord, dissension, and tumult, but I go now to where the root of all strife and dissension is removed, where love, peace, concord, and tranquility will live in all."[72]

"But still I have great hope in the divine clemency and goodness that, as we read that Saint Paul persecuted Blessed Stephen,[73] but they are now together in heaven, so all of us, though we disagree in this life, will nevertheless agree in another life with perfect charity. I therefore pray the great good God to guard the King, conserve him, and make him safe, and send him salutary counsel."[74]

NARRATOR: More turned back to the judges.

MORE: "More have I not to say, my lords, but that... I verily trust, and shall therefore right heartily pray, that though your lordships have now here in earth been judges to my condemnation, we may yet hereafter in heaven merrily all meet together, to our everlasting salvation."[75]

61 Spelman Report   **62** Roper 20   **63** Guildhall Report 8   **64** Spelman Report   **65** Guildhall Report 9   **66** Guildhall Report 10   **67** Guildhall Report 11   **68** Guildhall Report 11   **69** Guildhall Report 12   **70** Pole 8   **71** Guildhall Report 12   **72** Pole 9   **73** See Acts 6-9.   **74** Guildhall Report 13   **75** Roper 20

NARRATOR: "Now after this arraignment, departed he from the bar to the Tower again, led by Sir William Kingston, a tall, strong, and comely knight, constable of the Tower, and his very dear friend, who, when he had brought him from Westminster to the Old Swan towards the Tower, with a heavy heart, the tears running down his cheeks," spoke to him:

SIR WILLIAM KINGSTON: My old friend, I here bid you farewell.

MORE: "Good Master Kingston, trouble not yourself, but be of good cheer; for I will pray for you, and my good lady, your wife, that we may meet in heaven together, where we shall be merry forever and ever."[76]

NARRATOR: Then, "before he arrived at the prison, one of his daughters, named Margaret, rushing through the midst of the crowd of guards and soldiers, burning with great desire for her parent, taking no care for herself or the public place or those standing by, she barely broke through at last to her father, and there, embracing his neck with pitiable weeping she bore witness to her extreme grief. And after she held onto him tightly for some time, with sorrow completely overcoming her voice, her father with the guards' permission consoled her thus:

MORE: "Margaret, be of strong spirit, and do not torment yourself further; this is God's will. You have long known all the secrets of my mind."[77]

NARRATOR: "Then, when her father had scarcely been taken away another ten or twelve steps, she again fell upon him and once more threw her arms around her father's neck. Thereupon More, shedding no tears, and showing no distress of countenance or mind, said only this:

MORE: "Farewell, and pray to God for the salvation of my soul."[78]

NARRATOR: "On the day before[79] the Nones[80] of July, his head was struck off in the great field before the royal Tower, and he spoke a few words before he was beheaded simply asking the crowd to pray for him in this life and he in turn would intercede for them in another life. Finally he strongly exhorted them and urged them to pray to God for the King, that he would grant him right counsel and good mind; openly protesting and declaring that he died a faithful minister to him, yet first of all to God Almighty."[81]

ABBREVIATIONS OF SOURCES

Bag of Secrets   PRO KB 8/7, part 3 (Bag of Secrets) in The National Archives, Kew: Trial of Thomas More, 26 June–1 July 1535.

Guildhall Report   Guildhall MS 1231, as recovered from the composite Latin text in J. Duncan Derrett's "Neglected Versions of the Contemporary Account of the Trial of Sir Thomas More," *Bulletin of the Institute of Historical Research* 33 (1960): 214–23, trans. H. A. Kelly.

More's Indictment   Nicholas Harpsfield's *The Life and Death of Sir Thomas Moore, Knight*, ed. Elsie Vaughan Hitchcock (London: The Early English Text Society, 1932): 267–76, trans. H. A. Kelly.

Pole   Reginald Pole's *Pole's Defense of the Unity of the Church,* trans. Joseph G. Dwyer (Westminster, Maryland: Newman Press, 1965): 217–27.

Roper   William Roper's *The Life of Sir Thomas Moore, Knight*, ed. Elsie Vaughan Hitchcock (London: The Early English Text Society, 1935): 84–97.

Spelman Report   *The Reports of Sir John Spelman*, 1:58, ed. J. H. Baker (London: Publications of the Seldon Society, 1977).

---

76 Roper 22   **77** Guildhall Report 14   **79** *day before:* July 6   **80** the ninth day before the ides: i.e., July 7   **81** Guildhall Report 15–16
78 Guildhall Report 14

Laws, Acts, and Oaths Related to
Thomas More's Trial

1. *Magna Carta Libertatem* ("The Great Charter of Liberty"), Article 1, 1215

5 *During his trial, More appealed to this provision of the* Magna Carta. *The translation below is taken from* G. R. C. Davis, Magna Carta, *Revised Edition (London: British Library, 1989).*

First, we have granted[1] to God, and by this present
10 charter have confirmed for us and our heirs in perpetuity, that the English Church shall be free, and shall have its rights undiminished, and its liberties unimpaired. That we wish this so to be observed, appears from the fact that of our own free will, be-
15 fore the outbreak of the present dispute between us and our barons, we granted and confirmed by charter the freedom of the Church's elections—a right reckoned to be of the greatest necessity and importance to it—and caused this to be confirmed by
20 Pope Innocent III. This freedom we shall observe ourselves, and desire to be observed in good faith by our heirs in perpetuity.

To all free men of our kingdom we have also granted, for us and our heirs for ever, all the liber-
25 ties written out below, to have and to keep for them and their heirs, of us and our heirs

2. King's Coronation Oath, 1308

During his trial, Thomas More also invoked the kings' Coronation Oath, which dates back in some form to
30 *the 900s with the Anglo-Saxon kings. At least since the coronation of Edward II in 1308, the oath was administered, traditionally by the Archbishop of Canterbury, in the form of question and answer given here (Statutes of the Realm 1.168). The text of that 1308*
35 *oath follows, taken from* Sources of English Constitutional History, *ed. C. Stephenson and F. G. Marcham (New York: Harper Brothers, 1937). A manuscript copy of this Coronation Oath, with striking changes proposed in Henry's own hand, survives and*
40 *dates likely from the early 1530s.*

ARCHBISHOP: "Sire, will you grant and keep and by your oath confirm to the people of England the laws and customs given to them by the previous just and God-fearing kings, your ancestors, and especially the laws, customs, and liberties granted to the 45 clergy and people by the glorious king, the sainted Edward, your predecessor?"

KING: "I grant and promise them."

ARCHBISHOP: "Sire, will you in all your judgments, so far as in you lies, preserve to God and 50 Holy Church, and to the people and clergy, entire peace and concord before God?"

KING: "I will preserve them."

ARCHBISHOP: "Sire will you so far as in you lies, cause justice to be rendered rightly, impartially, and 55 wisely, in compassion and in truth?"

KING: "I will do so."

ARCHBISHOP: "Sire, do you grant to be held and observed the just laws and customs that the community of your realm shall determine, and will you, 60 so far as in you lies, defend and strengthen them to the honor of God?"

KING: "I grant and promise them."

3. Oath of the Act of Succession, 1534

In April 1534, Sir Thomas More and others were ar- 65 *rested for refusing to take an oath required but not formulated by Parliament's First Act of Succession (March 1534, 25 Henry VIII c. 22). In the November–December session of Parliament, that oath was formulated in what is now known as the Second Act of* 70 *Succession (26 Henry VIII c. 2). Misprision of treason (life imprisonment and loss of all property) was the automatic penalty for refusal to take this oath. The source for this and the following texts are* Documents Illustrative of English Church History, *ed. Henry* 75 *Gee and William John Hardy (London: Macmillan, 1896).*

---

1 The Latin is *concessisse,* meaning to "concede" or "assent."

Where at the last session of this present Parliament, in the Act then made for the establishment of the succession of the heirs of the King's highness in the imperial crown of this realm, it is contained, amongst other things, that all and singular the King's subjects, as well the nobles spiritual and temporal as other, should make and take a corporal oath, whensoever it should please the King's majesty, or his heirs, to appoint, that they should truly, firmly, and constantly, without fraud or guile, observe, fulfil, maintain, defend, and keep, to their cunning, wit, and uttermost of their powers, the whole effects and contents of the said Act, as in the same Act, among other things, more plainly appeareth.

And at the day of the last prorogation of this present Parliament, as well the nobles spiritual and temporal as other the Commons of this present Parliament, most lovingly accepted and took such oath as then was devised in writing for maintenance and defence of the said Act, and meant and intended at that time that every other the King's subjects should be bound to accept and take the same, upon the pains contained in the said Act, the tenor of which oath hereafter ensueth:

Ye shall swear to bear faith, truth, and obedience alonely to the King's majesty, and to his heirs of his body of his most dear and entirely beloved lawful wife Queen Anne, begotten and to be begotten, and further to the heirs of our said sovereign lord according to the limitation in the statute made for surety of his succession in the crown of this realm, mentioned and contained, and not to any other within this realm, for foreign authority or potentate: and in case any oath be made, or has been made, by you, to any person or persons, that then ye repute the same as vain and annihilate; and that, to your cunning, wit, and uttermost of your power, without guile, fraud, or other undue means, you shall observe, keep, maintain, and defend the said Act of Succession, and all the whole effects and contents thereof, and all other Acts and statutes made in confirmation, or for the execution of the same, or of anything therein contained; and this ye shall do against all manner of persons, of what estate, dignity, degree, or condition soever they be, and in no wise do or attempt, nor to your power suffer to be done or attempted, directly or indirectly, any thing or things privily or apartly to the let, hindrance, damage, or derogation thereof, or of any part of the same, by any manner of means, or for any manner of pretense; so help you God, all saints, and the holy Evangelists.

And forasmuch as it is convenient for the sure maintenance and defence of the same Act that the said oath should not only be authorized by authority of Parliament, but also be interpreted and expounded by the whole assent of this present Parliament, that is was meant and intended by the King's majesty, the Lords and Commons of the Parliament, at the said day of the said last prorogation, that every subject should be bounden to take the same oath, according to the tenor and effect thereof, upon the pains and penalties contained in the said Act:

Therefore be it enacted by authority of this present Parliament that the said oath above rehearsed shall be interpreted, expounded, reputed, accepted, and adjudged the very oath that the King's highness, the lords spiritual and temporal, and the Commons of this present Parliament meant and intended that every subject of this realm should be obliged and bounden to take and accept, for maintenance and defence of the same Act, upon the pains contained in the said Act, and that every of the King's subjects, upon the said pains, shall be obliged to accept and take the said oath. And be it further enacted by authority aforesaid that the commissioners that hereafter shall be appointed to receive such oath of the King's subjects, or two of them at least, shall have power and authority to certify into the King's Bench, by writing under their seals, every refusal that hereafter shall be made afore them of the same oath by any person or persons coming before them to take the same oath; and that every such certificate to be made by such commissioners, as is aforesaid, shall be taken as strong and as available in the law as an indictment of twelve men lawfully found of the said refusal; so that the person and persons, against whom any such certificate shall be made, shall be compelled to answer hereunto as if they were indicted; and that such process, judgement, execution, and every other thing shall be had, used, and ministered, of and upon every such certificate against the offenders, as if they had been lawfully indicted of such offenses by the due course and order of the common laws of this realm.

4. Act of Supremacy, November 1534

This statute decreed that the English monarch is the "Supreme Head of the Church of England" (26 Henry VIII, c. 1; Statutes of the Realm 3.492). Accordingly, More was indicted with high treason for having "falsely, traitorously, and maliciously by craft schemed, contrived, practiced, and attempted to fundamentally deprive" King Henry of "his dignity, title, and name of Supreme Head on earth of the English Church."

Albeit the King's Majesty justly and rightfully is and ought to be the Supreme Head of the Church of England, and so is recognized by the clergy of this realm in their Convocations, yet nevertheless, for corroboration and confirmation thereof, and for increase of virtue in Christ's religion within this realm of England, and to repress and extirpate all errors, heresies, and other enormities and abuses heretofore used in the same, be it enacted, by authority of this present Parliament, that the King, our sovereign lord, his heirs and successors, kings of this realm, shall be taken, accepted, and reputed the only Supreme Head in earth of the Church of England, called *Anglicana Ecclesia*; and shall have and enjoy, annexed and united to the imperial crown of this realm, as well the title and style thereof, as all honors, dignities, preeminences, jurisdictions, privileges, authorities, immunities, profits, and commodities to the said dignity of the Supreme Head of the same Church belonging and appertaining; and that our said sovereign lord, his heirs and successors, kings of this realm, shall have full power and authority from time to time to visit, repress, redress, record, order, correct, restrain, and amend all such errors, heresies, abuses, offenses, contempts and enormities, whatsoever they be, which by any manner of spiritual authority or jurisdiction ought or may lawfully be reformed, repressed, ordered, redressed, corrected, restrained, or amended, most to the pleasure of almighty God, the increase of virtue in Christ's religion, and for the conservation of the peace, unity, and tranquility of this realm; any usage, custom, foreign land, foreign authority, prescription, or any other thing or things to the contrary hereof notwithstanding.

5. Act of Attainder[2] of Sir Thomas More, Nov/Dec 1534

More was imprisoned in April 1534 and was to be tried for violating the Act of Succession whereby the crime would be misprison of treason and the penalty life imprisonment. Instead of a trial, the November/ December Parliament declared More guilty of misprison by this Act of Attainder for his "obstinate refusal" to take the oath required by the Act of Succession (26 Henry VIII, c. 23). An Act of Attainder is a legislative bill "introduced or passed in the English Parliament (first in 1459) for attainting any one without a judicial trial" (OED). An excerpt is given here from Statutes of the Realm 3.528.

... And forasmuch as the said Sir Thomas More, contrary to the trust and confidence aforesaid, being lawfully and duly required, since the first day of May last past unnaturally and contrary to his duty of allegiance, intending to sow and make sedition, murmur, and grudge within this the King's realm among the true obedient and faithful subjects of the same, hath obstinately, forwardly and contemptuously refused to make and receive such corporal oath as was ordained to be accepted of every subject of this realm for the surety and establishment of the succession of our said sovereign lord in the imperial crown of this realm. And for that he has unkindly and ungratefully served our said sovereign lord by diverse and sundry ways, means, and conditions contrary to his trust and confidence....

... And further be it enacted by the authority of this present Parliament, that forasmuch as the said Sir Thomas More, by the obstinate refusal of the said oath, has committed and done misprision of high treason, that the same Sir Thomas More for his offenses aforesaid shall stand and be attainted convicted of misprision of high treason, in such manner and form as if he were attainted for the same offense of misprision of high treason by the due order of the common law, and shall suffer such pains of imprisonment of his body, and losses of his goods, chattels, debts, leases for years, states of freehold, and other forfeitures and penalties contained, specified, and provided in the statute of succession of the crown of this realm for offenses of misprision of high treason, in such manner, form, and condition

---

2 An Act of Attainder is a legislative bill "introduced or passed in the English Parliament (first in 1459) for attainting any one without a judicial trial" *(OED).*

to all intents and purpose as if the said Sir Thomas More for the same offense of misprision of high treason were lawfully attainted by order of the common law upon the same....

6. The Treasons Act, 1534

To enforce the First and Second Acts of Succession, Parliament also passed the Treasons Act (26 Henry VIII, c. 13; Statutes of the Realm 3.508) at the November/December session, to be in effect as of February 1, 1535. At his July 1 trial, More was found guilty of high treason as defined by this Act, guilty of malicious action to deprive the King of his legislatively conferred new powers. An excerpt is given here.

... Be it therefore enacted by the assent and consent of our sovereign lord the King, and the lords spiritual and temporal, and Commons in this present Parliament assembled, and by the authority of the same, that if any person or persons, after the first day of February next coming, do maliciously wish, will or desire, by words or writing, or by craft imagine, invent, practice, or attempt any bodily harm to be done or committed to the King's most royal person, the Queen's, or their heirs apparent, or to deprive them or any of them of their dignity, title, or name of their royal estates, or slanderously and maliciously publish and pronounce, by express writing or words, that the King our sovereign lord should be heretic, schismatic, tyrant, infidel, or usurper of the crown, or rebelliously do detain, keep, or withhold from our said sovereign lord, his heirs or successors, any of his or their castles, fortresses, fortalices, or holds within this realm, or in any other the King's dominions or marches, or rebelliously detain, keep, or withhold from the King's said Highness, his heirs or successors, any of his or their ships, ordnances, artillery, or other munitions or fortifications of war, and do not humbly render and give up to our said sovereign lord, his heirs or successors, or to such persons as shall be deputed by them, such castles, fortresses, fortalices, holds, ships, ordnances, artillery, and other munitions and fortifications of war, rebelliously kept or detained, within six days next after they shall be commanded by our said sovereign lord, his heirs or successors, by open proclamation under the great seal:

That then every such person and persons so offending in any the premises, after the said first day of February, their aiders, counselors, consenters, and abettors, being thereof lawfully convicted according to the laws and customs of this realm, shall be adjudged traitors, and that every such offense in any the premises, that shall be committed or done after the said first day of February, shall be reputed, accepted, and adjudged high treason, and the offenders therein and their aiders, consenters, counselors, and abettors, being lawfully convicted of any such offense as is aforesaid, shall have and suffer such pains of death and other penalties, as is limited and accustomed in cases of high treason....

The Earliest Biographical Accounts and Collected Editions, 1506–95

These early documents offer a representative range of responses to More and date from roughly 1506-56. They articulate and anticipate the debate over More's life and legacy, which began in his own time and the years following his death for high treason. More recently, debate over More intensified with the work of revisionist historians and biographers such as Geoffrey Elton, Alistair Fox, and Richard Marius, and responses to their accounts by scholars such as John Guy, Eamon Duffy, Cathy Curtis, Travis Curtright, Richard Rex, and Joanne Paul. Considering this complex debate, John Guy asks at the beginning of his *Thomas More*, "Is there an historical Thomas More? Which of the many characterizations that have attached to his name, some blatantly incompatible, are upheld by the sources?" (Oxford: Oxford University Press, 2000, ix).

Two recent accounts of More's complex legacy are Anne Lake Prescott's essay, "Afterlives," in the *Cambridge Companion to Thomas More* (2011), and Travis Curtright's "Iconic Thomas Mores on Trial," the conclusion of his study *The One Thomas More* (2012). For a thorough cataloguing of the many references to Thomas More in early modern England, see *Sir Thomas More in the English Renaissance: An Annotated Catalogue* (Binghamton, NY: Medieval and Renaissance Texts and Studies, 1994). For accounts of the various biographies of Thomas More, see Germain Marc'hadour's "Latin Lives of Thomas More," and Michael Ackland's "Modern Biographies of Sir Thomas More," both published in *A Companion to Thomas More*, ed. A.D. Cousins and Damian Grace (Madison: Farleigh Dickinson University Press, 2009).

CONTENTS

In this painting that Erasmus sent to Thomas More (see Plate 9c) as a sign of friendship, artist Quentin Matsys gives a good imitation of Erasmus's handwriting. On the right-hand side, Erasmus is paraphrasing the epistle of St. Paul to the Romans. The Latin, reconstructed, is:

<table>
<tr><td>IN EPISTOLAM AD RO-
MANOS PARIPHASIS
ERASMI ROTERO
DAME
PAulus ego ille e Sau
lo factus, e turbulem
te pacificus, nuper obnox-
ius legi mosaice. nunc
Moisi Libertus. seruus au-
tem factus Iesus.</td><td>On the LETTER TO THE ROMANS:
A PARAPHRASE OF
ERASMUS OF ROTTERDAM
I, the Paul who once was Saul,
once a turbulent man,
but now a man of peace, lately
subject to the Mosaic law, but now,
as Moses' Freedman, having become
the servant of
Jesus . . . .</td></tr>
</table>

On the left-hand page is the word *Gratia* or "grace," a key term of Paul's epistle. Erasmus wears a signet ring (a gift from More) and is using a reed pen, his favorite writing instrument.

Earliest Accounts and Editions

ERASMUS ON THOMAS MORE

191. To Richard Whitford[1]
From the country, 1 May 1506

Erasmus of Rotterdam to his delightful friend, the
English scholar Richard Whitford.
    After being quite immersed in Greek literature
for some years now, my dear Richard, I have recently
turned to writing Latin declamations, just for the
sake of getting on familiar terms again with that language. This I did at the suggestion of Thomas More,
who is, as you are aware, so full of eloquence that
he could not fail to carry any argument, even with
an enemy, and whom I regard with such affection
that, even if he ordered me to join the rope-circle
and dance,[2] I should obey him without hesitation.
He himself tackles the same theme,[3] with such thoroughness too that there is not a single point he fails
to investigate and account for. And I believe (unless
I am deluded by the intensity of the love I bear him)
that nature never created a livelier mind, or one
quicker, more discerning, or clearer—in short, more
perfectly endowed with all the talents—than his;
and his intelligence is matched by his power of expression. Moreover, he has an exceptionally charming disposition and a great deal of wit; yet the wit is
good-natured; so you could not find him lacking in
a single one of the qualities needed by the perfect
barrister.
    Consequently it was not my intention, when I
undertook to write this, either to rival or to outdo
such a skillful practitioner, but merely to wrestle, as
it were, in this contest of wits with the most congenial of all my friends, in whose company I enjoy
combining jest and earnest; and I have done so all
the more willingly because I am most anxious that
this sort of exercise, which I regard as the most
profitable of all, should someday be revived in our
schools. The lack of it is, I believe, the sole reason
why in this age of ours, in spite of the myriads who
peruse the pages of the most eloquent authors, there
are nevertheless so few who do not seem totally in-
articulate when the occasion calls for an orator. But
if we were to follow the precepts of Cicero and
Quintilian, and also the general practice of antiquity, and carefully train ourselves from boyhood onwards in exercises of this kind, I believe there would
be less of the poverty of expression, the pitiful lack
of style, and the disgraceful stammering we see even
among public professors of the art of oratory.
    Please bear in mind, as you read my declamation,
that I did not compose it but merely threw it off as a
recreation within a very few days. At the same time
I request you also to compare it with More's, and
in this way judge if there be any difference in style
between two authors whom you used to describe
as so similar in mind, character, outlook, and pursuits that, you said, no pair of twins on earth could
be more alike. One thing is sure; as you love both
of them equally, so you in turn are equally beloved
of them both. Farewell, my sweet and most charming Richard.

In the country, 1 May 1506

999. To Ulrich von Hutten[4]
Antwerp, 23 July 1519

Erasmus of Rotterdam to the Honorable Ulrich
von Hutten, Knight, greetings.
    The affection—one might almost say, the passion
—that you feel for that gifted man Thomas More,[5]
fired as of course you are by reading his books, which
you rightly call as brilliant as they are scholarly—
all this, believe me my dear Hutten, you share with
many of us, and between you and More it works
both ways: he in his turn is so delighted with the
originality of your own work that I am almost jealous of you. Surely this is an example of that wisdom

---

[1] Translation by R. A. B. Mynors, from
CWE 2: 112–13. Whitford was a close friend
of both More and Erasmus; at that time
he was chaplain to Bishop Foxe. [2] See
Terence, *Adelphoe* 752. [3] See above
in "Lucian Translations and Response."
[4] Translation by R. A. B. Mynors, from
CWE 7: 16–25. Von Hutten (1488–1523)
was a German poet, scholar, satirist, and
humanist who eventually allied himself
with Luther and turned against Erasmus.
[5] More is forty-one and has completed his
first year in Henry VIII's service. Erasmus
and More first met in 1499, when More was
twenty-one.

which Plato calls the most desirable of all things, which rouses far more passionate desire in mortal hearts than the most splendid physical beauty. The eyes of the body cannot perceive it, but the mind has its own eyes, so that here too we find the truth of the old Greek saying that the eye is the gateway to the heart. They are the means through which the most cordial affection sometimes unites men who have never exchanged a word or set bodily eyes on one another. It is a common experience that for some obscure reason one man is captivated by this form of beauty and another by something different; and in the same way between one man's spirit and another's there seems to be a kind of unspoken kinship, which makes us take great delight in certain special people, and less in others.

Be that as it may, you ask me to draw a picture of More for you at full length, and I wish I were as skillful as you are eager. For me too it would be nothing but a pleasure to spend a little time thinking about the friend I love best. But there are difficulties: it is not everyone can appreciate all More's gifts, and I doubt if he would endure to be depicted by any and every artist. It is, I suspect, no easier to produce a portrait of More than one of Alexander the Great or Achilles, nor did they deserve their immortality any more than he does. Such a sitter demands the skill of an Apelles, and I fear there is less of Apelles in me than of Fulvius or Rutuba. I will try, however, to do you not so much a picture as an outline sketch of the whole man, based on long-standing and intimate acquaintance, as far as my observation or memory will serve. Should any mission overseas eventually bring you together, you will realize what an incompetent artist you have selected for this task, and I am afraid that you will think me either envious or purblind—too blind to detect, or too envious to be willing to record more than a few of all his good qualities.

To begin with one aspect of More which is quite unknown to you, in stature and habit of body he is not tall, without being noticeably short, but the general harmony of his proportions is such that nothing seems amiss. He has a fair skin; his complexion tends to be warm rather than pale, though with no tendency to a high color, except for a very delicate flush which suffuses it all. His hair blackish-brown, or brownish-black if you prefer; beard somewhat thin; eyes rather greyish-blue, with a kind of fleck in them, the sort that usually indicates a gifted

intelligence, and among the English is thought attractive, while our own people prefer dark eyes. No kind of eye, they say, is so immune from defects. His expression shows the sort of man he is, always friendly and cheerful, with something of the air of one who smiles easily, and (to speak frankly) disposed to be merry rather than serious or solemn, but without a hint of the fool or the buffoon. His right shoulder looks a little higher than his left, especially when walking, not by nature but from force of habit, like so many human tricks. Otherwise there is nothing to criticize in his physique. Only his hands are a trifle coarse, at least if one compares them with his other bodily features. As for the care of his personal appearance, he has taken absolutely no heed of it ever since boyhood, to the extent of devoting very little care even to those niceties allotted to the gentlemen by Ovid. How good-looking he was as a young man, one can guess even now by what remains—though I knew him myself when he was not more than three-and-twenty, for even now he is scarcely past his fortieth year.

He enjoys good, but not rude, health, adequate at any rate to support all the duties of a good citizen, and is subject to no complaints or very few; there is every hope that he will enjoy long life, for his father is still alive at a great age, but wonderfully active and vigorous for his years. I have never seen a man less particular about his food. Until he reached manhood he was content to drink nothing but water, a habit inherited from his father. Only, for fear of causing any embarrassment in this regard, he used to drink his beer out of a pewter tankard, so that the guests did not know—small beer next door to water, and often just water. As for wine, the habit in those parts being to invite your neighbor to drink in his turn from the same cup, he sometimes barely sipped it, so as not to seem entirely to dislike it, and at the same time to learn to follow common usage. Beef, salt fish, and coarse bread with much yeast in it he preferred to the dishes of which most people are fond, though in other ways he was by no means averse from all the things that bring harmless pleasure, be it only to the body. Dairy produce and all the fruit which grows on trees have always had a great attraction for him, and he is particularly devoted to eggs. His voice is not loud, yet not particularly soft, but of a sort to strike clearly on the ear; no music in it, no subtlety, a straightforward speaking voice, for he does not seem framed by nature to be a singer, though he is fond of music of all kinds. His language is remarkably clear and precise, without a trace of hurry or hesitation.

Simple clothes please him best, and he never wears silk or scarlet or a gold chain, except when it is not open to him to lay it aside. He sets surprisingly little store by the ceremonies which ordinary men regard as a touchstone of good breeding; these he neither demands from other people nor tenders meticulously himself either in public assemblies or in private parties, although he is familiar with them should he wish to use them. But he thinks it effeminate and unworthy of a man to waste a good part of his time in such frivolities.

Court life and the friendship of princes were formerly not to his taste, for he has always had a special hatred of tyranny and a corresponding love for equality. You will hardly find any court, however modest, that is not full of turmoil and self-seeking, of pretense and luxury, and is really free from any taint of despotic power. Even the court of Henry VIII he could not be induced to enter except by great efforts, although it would be difficult to wish for anything more cultured and more unassuming than the present king. By nature he has a great love of liberty and leisure; but dearly as he loves to enjoy leisure when he can, no one displays more energy or more endurance at the call of duty.

Friendship he seems born and designed for; no one is more open-hearted in making friends or more tenacious in keeping them, nor has he any fear of that plethora of friendships against which Hesiod warns us. The road to a secure place in his affections is open to anyone. In the choice of friends he is never difficult to please, in keeping up with them the most compliant of men, and in retaining them the most unfailing. If by any chance he has picked on someone whose faults he cannot mend, he waits for an opportunity to be quit of him, loosening the knot of friendship and not breaking it off. When he finds open-hearted people naturally suited to him, he enjoys their company and conversation so much that one would think he reckoned such things the chief pleasure in life. For ball games, games of chance, and cards he hates, and all the other pastimes with which the common run of grandees normally beguile their tedious hours. Besides which, though somewhat negligent in his own affairs, no

one could take more trouble in furthering the business of his friends. In a word, whoever desires a perfect example of true friendship, will seek it nowhere to better purpose than in More.

In society he shows such rare courtesy and sweetness of disposition that there is no man so melancholy by nature that More does not enliven him, no disaster so great that he does not dissipate its unpleasantness. From boyhood he has taken such pleasure in jesting that he might seem born for it, but in this he never goes as far as buffoonery, and he has never liked bitterness. In his youth he both wrote brief comedies and acted in them. Any remark with more wit in it than ordinary always gave him pleasure, even if directed against himself—such is his delight in witty sayings that betray a lively mind. Hence his trying his hand as a young man at epigrams, and his special devotion to Lucian; in fact it was he (yes, he can make the camel dance) who persuaded me to write my *In Praise of Folly*.

In fact there is nothing in human life to which he cannot look for entertainment, even in most serious moments. If he has to do with educated and intelligent people, he enjoys their gifts; if they are ignorant and stupid, he is amused by their absurdity. He has no objection to professional buffoons, such is the skill with which he adapts himself to the mood of anyone. With women as a rule, and even with his wife, he confines himself to humor and pleasantry. You would think him Democritus[6] reborn, or rather that Pythagorean philosopher who strolled unthinking through the market-place watching the crowds of people buying and selling. Nobody is less swayed by public opinion, and yet nobody is closer to the feelings of ordinary men.

He takes a particular pleasure in contemplating the shapes, character, and behavior of different living creatures. Thus there is hardly any kind of bird of which he does not keep one in his household, and the same with any animal that as a rule is rarely seen, such as monkey, fox, ferret, weasel, and the like. Besides these, if he sees anything outlandish or otherwise remarkable, he buys it greedily, and has his house stocked with such things from all sources, so that everywhere you may see something to attract the eyes of the visitor; and when he sees other people pleased, his own pleasure begins anew. In his younger days he was not averse from affairs with

6 Democritus (fifth century BC) was known as the laughing philosopher.

young women, but always without dishonor, enjoying such things when they came his way without going out to seek them, and attracted by the mingling of minds rather than bodies.

A liberal education he had imbibed from his very earliest years. As a young man he devoted himself to the study of Greek literature and philosophy, with so little support from his father, a man in other respects of good sense and high character, that his efforts were deprived of all outside help and he was treated almost as if disinherited because he was thought to be deserting his father's profession, for his father is a specialist in English law. The law as a profession has little in common with literature truly so called, but in England those who have made themselves authorities in that subject are in the first rank for eminence and distinction. Nor is it easy in that country to find any other career more likely to lead to wealth and reputation, and in fact most of the nobility of the island owes its rank to studies of this kind. In the law, they say, no one can perfect himself without many years of hard work. So it was not surprising that, when he was a young man, More's nature should swerve away from the law, being made for better things; but after a taste of the subjects studied at the university, he betook himself to it with such good effect that there was no one whose advice was more freely sought by litigants, nor was a larger income made by any of those who gave their whole time to the law. Such was the force and quickness of his intelligence.

Besides this he devoted himself actively to reading the works of the orthodox Fathers. On St Augustine's *City of God* he gave public lectures before large audiences while still quite a young man;[7] priests and old men were not ashamed to seek instruction in holy things from a young man and a layman, or sorry they had done so. And all the time he applied his whole mind to the pursuit of piety, with vigils and fasts and prayer and similar exercises preparing himself for the priesthood. In this indeed he showed not a little more sense than those who plunge headlong into so exacting a vocation without first making trial of themselves. Nor did anything stand in the way of his devoting himself to this kind of life, except that he could not shake off the desire to get married. And so he chose to be a god-fearing husband rather than an immoral priest.

However, he chose for his wife[8] an unmarried girl who was still very young, of good family, and quite inexperienced as yet, having always lived in the country with her parents and her sisters, which gave him the more opportunity to mold her character to match his own. He arranged for her education and made her skilled in music of every kind, and had (it is clear) almost succeeded in making her a person with whom he would gladly have shared his whole life, had not an early death removed her from the scene, after she had borne him several children. Of these there survive three daughters, Margaret, Alice, and Cecily, and one son, John. Nor did he endure to remain a widower for very long, though the advice of his friends urged a different course. A few months[9] after his wife's death, he married a widow, more to have someone to look after his household than for his own pleasure, for she was neither beautiful nor in her first youth, as he used to remark in jest, but a capable and watchful housewife, though they lived on as close and affectionate terms as if she had been a girl of the most winning appearance. Few husbands secure as much obedience from their wives by severity and giving them orders as he did by his kindness and his merry humor. He could make her do anything: did he not cause a woman already past the prime of life, of a far from elastic disposition, and devoted to her household affairs, to learn to play the zither, the lute, the monochord, and the recorder, and in this department to produce a set piece of work every day to please her exacting husband?

He shows the same geniality in the management of his household, in which there are no troubles and no disputes. If anything should go wrong, he puts it right promptly or makes them agree; nor has he ever dismissed anyone as a result of ill feeling on either side. In fact his household seems to enjoy a kind of natural felicity, for no one has ever been a member of it without bettering his fortune later, and no one has ever earned the least shadow on his reputation. Indeed you would hardly find such close relations anywhere between a man and his mother as exists between him and his stepmother; for his father had now remarried for the second time, and he loved them both as if they had been his own mother. The

---

7 More's teacher William Grocyn invited More to give these lectures at Grocyn's church (*ca.* 1501), at St. Lawrence Jewry.

8 Joanna Colt, from Netherhall, Essex
9 In fact, More married Alice Middleton

thirty days after Joanna's death, in the summer of 1511.

father[10] has lately remarried a third time, and More solemnly swears that he has never seen a better person. Such moreover is his affection for his kinsmen, his children, and his sisters that his relations with them are never oppressive, nor yet does he ever fall short in his family duties.

From any love of filthy lucre he is absolutely free. To provide for his children he has earmarked as much of his resources as he considers sufficient for them, and the rest he spends liberally. In the days when he was still dependent on the income from his clients, he gave everyone helpful and reliable advice, thinking much more of their advantage than of his own; the majority he used to persuade to settle their actions, on the ground that this would save them expense. If that was not successful, he then tried to show them how to carry on their litigation at the least cost to themselves, for some men are so made that they actually enjoy going to law. In the city of London, in which he was born, he has for some years acted as judge in civil cases.[11] This office is by no means onerous, for the court sits only on Thursdays until dinner-time, but it carries much prestige. No one ever determined more cases, and no one showed more absolute integrity. Many people have had the money returned to them which according to precedent must be paid by litigants; for before the action comes into court, the plaintiff must deposit three drachmas, and the defendant the same, nor is it permissible to demand any more. The result of this behavior was that his native city held him in deep affection.

He had made up his mind to be content with this station in life, which gave him quite sufficient standing and at the same time was not exposed to serious risks. More than once he was forced to go on a diplomatic mission, and as he conducted these with great intelligence, his serene Majesty King Henry VIII would not rest until he had dragged the man to his court. I use the word "dragged" advisedly, for no man was ever more consumed with ambition to enter a court than he was to avoid it. But since that excellent king had it in mind to fill his household with learned, wise, intelligent, and upright men, he summoned a great many others, and especially More, whom he keeps so close to him that he never allows him leave to go. If serious business is afoot, no better counselor than he; if the King

wishes to relax his mind with more cheerful topics, no man's company more gay. Often difficult issues demand an authoritative and able judge, and More can settle these in such a way that both parties are grateful. Yet no one has succeeded in persuading him to take a present from anybody. Happy indeed a commonwealth would be, if the prince would appoint to each post a magistrate like More. And all the time no pride has touched him.

Amidst such masses of business he does not forget his old and ordinary friends, and returns to his beloved literature from time to time. Whatever power his station gives him, whatever his influence can do with so powerful a king, is all devoted to the good of the commonwealth and of his friends. His disposition was always most ready to do good unto all men, and wonderfully prone to show mercy, and he now gives it more play, because he has more power to do good. Some men he helps with money, to some he gives the protection of his authority, others he advances in life by his recommendation. Those whom he cannot help in any other way he aids with good advice. He has never sent anyone away with a long face. You might call More the general resource of everyone who needs help. He thinks some great stroke of luck has come his way if he has been able to relieve the oppressed, to help the perplexed and entangled out of their troubles, or to reconcile the parties to a quarrel. No one more enjoys doing a kindness or less demands gratitude for doing one. And yet, though he is very fortunate on so many counts, and though good fortune is often accompanied by self-conceit, it has never yet been my fortune to see a man more free from that fault than he.

But to return to tell of his literary pursuits, which have been the chief bond between More and myself in both directions. His earlier years were exercised principally in poetry; after that came a long struggle to acquire a more supple style in prose by practicing his pen in every sort of writing. What his style is like now, I need not set down, especially for your benefit, for you have his books always in your hands. He has taken delight especially in declamations, and, in that department, in paradoxical themes, as offering more lively practice to one's ingenuity. As a youth he even worked on a dialogue in which he supported Plato's doctrine of communalism, extending it even to wives. He wrote an answer to Lucian's

10 Sir John More married four times, his last wife being Alice Clerk.   **11** More was undersheriff of London from 1510 to 1518.

Tyrannicida, on which topic it was his wish to have me as an opponent, to test more accurately what progress he had made in this sort of composition. *Utopia* he published with the purpose of showing the reasons for the shortcomings of a commonwealth, but he represented the English commonwealth in particular, because he had studied it and knew it best. The second book he had written earlier, when at leisure; at a later opportunity he added the first in the heat of the moment. Hence there is a certain unevenness in the style.

It would be difficult to find a more felicitous extempore speaker, so fertile are both his mind and the tongue that does its bidding. His mind is always ready, ever passing nimbly to the next point; his memory always at his elbow, and as everything in it is held, so to say, in ready cash, it puts forward promptly and without hesitation whatever time or place demand. In disputations nothing more acute can be imagined, so that he has often taken on even the most eminent theologians in their own field and been almost too much for them. John Colet, a sensitive and experienced critic, used to say sometimes in conversation that there was only one able man in the whole of England, though the island is blessed with so many men of outstanding ability.

True piety finds in him a practicing follower, though far removed from all superstition. He has his fixed hours at which he says his prayers, and they are not conventional but come from the heart. When he talks with friends about the life after death, you recognize that he is speaking from conviction, and not without good hope. And More is like this even at court. What becomes then of those people who think that Christians are not to be found except in monasteries?

Such are the men whom that most intelligent king admits to his household and his privy chamber; admits, yes, and invites, and even forces them to come. These are the continual spectators and witnesses of the way he lives; these form his council; these are the companions of his journeys. He rejoices to have them round him rather than young men or women dissolute and vicious, or even rich men in their splendid collars, or all the blandishments of insincerity, where one man would divert him to aimless pleasures, another would heat his

blood with thoughts of tyranny, another put forward fresh tricks with which to fleece his people. Had you lived in this court, my dear Hutten, I have no doubt you would quite rewrite your *Aula*, and cease to be a professed enemy of court life, though you too live with as honorable a prince as you could wish, nor do you lack men who look for a better state of things, such as Stromer and Kopp. But what are the few that you have in comparison with such a company of distinguished men: Mountjoy, Linacre, Pace, Colet, Stokesley, Latimer, More, Tunstall, Clerk, and others like them? Whichever you choose to name, you will have mentioned in one word a world of all the virtues and all learning. I myself, however, have hopes of no common kind that Albert, the one ornament of our native Germany at this time, may gather more men like himself into his household, and may set an important precedent for all the other princes, encouraging them too to wish to do the same, each in his own court.

There is the portrait, the best of sitters ill done by the worst of artists. You will like it less when you have the good fortune to know More better. But I have done it to protect myself for the moment to stop your complaining that I have not done what you asked, and your constant objections that my letters are too short. Though this has not seemed to me longer than usual in the writing, nor will you find it, I am sure, long-winded in the reading; my dear More's charm will see to that.

Farewell.

Erasmus

1233. To Guillaume Budé[12]
Andelecht, <*ca.* September> 1521

Erasmus of Rotterdam to his friend, Guillaume Budé, greetings.

… More is to be congratulated. He neither aimed at it nor asked for it, but the king has promoted him to a very honorable post, with a salary by no means to be despised: he is his prince's treasurer. This office in England is in the first rank of grandeur and distinction, but is not unduly exposed either to unpopularity or to tedious press of business. He had a rival for it, a fairly influential man who wanted the office

---

12 Translated by R. A. B. Mynors, from *CWE* 8:295–99. Budé was a leading French humanist who contributed a letter to More's *Utopia* (see above).

so badly that he would not object to holding it at his own costs and charges. But that admirable king gave the clearest proof of his high opinion of More, in that he went so far as to give him a salary when he did not want the post, rather than accept an official who did not need to be paid. Not content with that, this most generous prince has also knighted him, nor can there be any doubt that some day he will honor him with yet greater distinctions when the occasion presents itself; for normally princes show a much greater tendency to promote bachelors. But More is so deeply embedded in the ranks of married men, that not even his wife's death has given him his freedom. For having buried his first wife, who was a girl when he married her, the widower has now taken unto himself a widow.

I am the more delighted for More's sake at this attitude of his prince toward him for this reason, that whatever increase in authority or influence accrues to him, accrues, I believe, to the study of the humanities, of which he is such a keen supporter that, were his resources equal to his wishes, the English would find their gifted minds in no lack of an open-hearted and generous Maecenas. The courts of princes usually behave like the physician who first evacuates the body of the patient entrusted to him and then fills it up and restores its energy; and I do not doubt that our friend More has had some such experience hitherto. How it has gone in your case you know better than I do. And yet gifted men have enjoyed his bounty, in the days when not only was he far from having plenty to give away, he was burdened with debt.

But to be a good scholar himself and give generous support to all other scholars is not the only way in which he honors liberal studies. He takes pains to give his whole household an education in good literature, setting thereby a new precedent which, if I mistake not, will soon be widely followed, so happy is the outcome. He has three daughters, of whom Margaret, the eldest, is already married to a young man who is well off, has a most honorable and modest character, and besides that is no stranger to our literary pursuits. All of them from their earliest years he has had properly and strictly brought up in point of character, and has given them a liberal education. To his three daughters he has added a fourth girl,[13] whom he maintains as a piece of generosity to be a playmate for them. He also has a step-daughter[14] of great beauty and exceptional gifts, married for some years now to a young man not without education and of truly golden character. And he has a son[15] by his first wife, now a boy of about thirteen, who is the youngest of his children.

About a year ago, More took it into his head to give me a demonstration of the progress of their education. He told them all to write to me, each of them independently. No subject was supplied them, nor was what they wrote corrected in any way. When they had shown their drafts to their father for criticism, he told them, as though he took exception to their bad writing, to make a cleaner and more careful copy of the same words; and when they had done that, he did not alter a syllable, but sealed up the letters and sent them off to me. Believe me, my dear Budé, I never saw anything so admirable. In what they said there was nothing foolish or childish, and the language made one feel that they must be making daily progress. This charming group, with the husbands of two of them, he keeps under his own roof. There you never see one of the girls idle, or busied with the trifles that women enjoy; they have a Livy in their hands. They have made such progress that they can read and understand authors of that class without anyone to explain them, unless they come upon some word that might have held up even me or someone like me.

His wife, whose strength lies in mother-wit and experience rather than book-learning, controls the whole institution with remarkable skill, acting as a kind of overseer who gives each one her task and sees that she performs it and allows no idleness or frivolous occupations.

You are wont to complain in your letters from time to time that in your case classical study has acquired a bad name for having brought two bad things into your life, poor health and pecuniary loss. The result of More's activity on the other hand, is to make it acceptable to everyone concerned on every count, for he says he owes to his literary studies his much better health, his popularity and influence with an excellent prince and all men both friends and strangers, his easier circumstances, his own greater happiness and the happiness he gives his friends, the services he can now render to his country and his relations and kinsfolk, his increased

13 Margaret Giggs 14 Alice Middleton 15 John More

adaptability to court society, to life among the nobility, and to the whole way of life that he now leads,
and a greater ease in pleasing heaven. At first liberal studies had a bad name for depriving their devoted adherents of the common touch. There is no
journey, no business however voluminous or difficult, that can take the book out of More's hand; and
yet it would be hard to find anyone who was more
truly a man for all seasons[16] and all men, who was
more ready to oblige, more easily available for meeting, more lively in conversation, or who combined
so much real wisdom with such charm of character.
The result is that, while only a few days ago a love
of literature was thought to be of no practical or
ornamental value, there is now hardly one of our
great nobles who would reckon his children worthy
of their ancestry if they had no education in liberal
studies. Monarchs themselves are thought to lack a
good share of the qualities proper to a king if their
knowledge of literature leaves much to be desired.

Again, scarcely any mortal man was not under the
conviction that, for the female sex, education had
nothing to offer in the way of either virtue or reputation. Nor was I myself in the old days completely free
of this opinion, but More has quite put it out of my
head. For two things in particular are perilous to a
girl's virtue, idleness and improper amusements, and
against both of these the love of literature is a protection. There is no better way to maintain a spotless reputation than faultless behavior, and no woman's chastity is more secure than hers who is chaste
by deliberate choice. Not that I disapprove the ideas
of those who plan to protect their daughters' honor
by teaching them the domestic arts, but nothing so
occupies a girl's whole heart as the love of reading.
And besides this advantage, that the mind is kept
from pernicious idleness, this is the way to absorb
the highest principles, which can both instruct and
inspire the mind in the pursuit of virtue. Many have
been exposed to the loss of their maidenhead by inexperience and ignorance of the world, before they
know what the things are that put that great treasure
at risk. Nor do I see why husbands need fear that if
they have educated wives they will have wives who
are less obedient, unless they are the kind of men
who wish to demand from a wife what ought not
to be demanded of respectable married women. In

my opinion, on the other hand, nothing is more in-
tractable than ignorance. At least, a mind developed
and exercised by reading has this advantage, that it
can recognize good and just reasons for what they
are, and perceive what conduct is proper and what
is profitable. Why, the man who has taught her the
facts has almost converted her. Besides which, what
makes wedlock delightful and lasting is more the
good will between mind and mind than any physical
passion, so that far stronger bonds unite those who
are joined by mutual affection of minds as well, and
a wife has more respect for a husband whom she acknowledges as a teacher also. Devotion will not be
less because there is less unreason in it. Personally, I
would rather have one talent of pure gold than three
contaminated heavily with lead and dross.

We often hear other women returning from
church quite ready to say that the preacher gave
them a wonderful sermon, and they provide a lively
account of his expression. Beyond that, they are
quite unable to report what he said or what it was
like. These young ladies recount nearly the whole
sermon to you in order, though not without some
selection; if the preacher let fall anything foolish or
irreligious or off the point, as we see not seldom happens nowadays, they know how to make fun of it or
ignore it or protest against it. This, and only this, is
what listening to a sermon means. One can really enjoy the society of girls like this. I differ profoundly
from those who keep a wife for no purpose except
physical satisfaction, for which half-witted females
are better fitted. A woman must have intelligence
if she is to keep her household up to its duties, to
form and mold her children's characters, and meet
her husband's needs in every way. Apart from that,
when I was talking to More recently, I put the objection that if anything should happen, as the way of all
flesh is, he would be the more tormented by grief for
the loss of them, inasmuch as he had spent all that
effort on their upbringing; and he replied, "If anything inevitable were to happen, I would rather they
died educated than uneducated." And I was then reminded of that remark of Phocion, I think it was,
who was about to drink the hemlock, and when his
wife cried out, "O my husband, you will die an innocent man," his answer was, "What of it, my dear
wife? Would you rather I died guilty?"

---

16 Erasmus first comments on this phrase,
omnium horarum homo, in the first edition
of his *Adages* (1508): "The man who suits

himself to seriousness and jesting alike, and
whose company is always delightful — that
is the man the ancients call 'a man for all

hours.'" Robert Whittington translates
this phrase as "a man for all seasons" in his
Vulgaria (see ahead, p. 1381).

In the meantime the idea has come into my head of matching you two together as two outstanding leaders in the field, much as a man might compare Camillus and Scipio Africanus.[17] You have been fighting the enemies of good letters for more years and in an age more unfavorable to them, and in this respect at least you are ahead of More. At the same time, what you have been trying to do with your sons only and in your brothers, he does not hesitate in his wives and daughters too, with a brave contempt for the criticism excited by this new idea; and under this head, conversely, he is superior to you. Again, in published books you have done more for the supply in both languages than he has, and will do more still, I promise myself, in the future, if you can once start bringing forth the riches you have filed away and sharing them with the public. Not but what our younger men have great expectations of More too, for he is still a long way from old age and has a father aged, I suppose, not much less than eighty, whose old age is wonderfully green— you could hardly find anyone who carries his years with a better grace. This allows one to hope for a ripe old age for More likewise. I perceive one thing in which you might render a very great service to Greek studies, if you were to make a really full lexicon, not only listing the words but explaining the idioms and turns of speech peculiar to Greek when these are not generally known and obvious. It is a rather humdrum subject, I admit, and unworthy of your position, but I believe that a man of principle should be ready to demean himself to some extent for the public benefit, as Plato expects of his wise men....

Farewell.

Erasmus

2750. To John Faber[18]
<Freiburg, late 1532>

How fast has the rumor flown, all the way here: the news that the distinguished Sir Thomas More has been removed from the office of chancellor, and that he has been succeeded by another noble, who then immediately set free the men More had sent to prison for their contentious teachings. Both Homer and Vergil lift "rumor" to the sky as a flying bird, all covered with feathers, to show that nothing is faster. But the speed of any winged creature seems slow and sluggish to me, compared with the swiftness of this rumor which has suddenly spread so widely: lightning flashing into every quarter of the globe would hardly be faster. And although this story has been flying through everyone's lips constantly, and although I have not received any letters from Britain (Thomas More's letter, which I am now forwarding to you, had been held up several months in Saxony), nevertheless I was "more certain than certain" that all this talk was the emptiest gossip. For I knew very well the character of that most humane ruler, with what constancy he cherishes friends once he has decided to take them to his heart, with what reluctance he removes anyone from his favor, even when he has detected some human error in them. On the other hand, I also knew Thomas More's honesty, his skillfulness in handling matters both large and small, the vigilance of that extraordinary prudence of his, so free from the habit of "turning a blind eye." In fact, the King's benevolent attitude toward More became clearer to me when he freed him from that office—a most prestigious office, yes, but also fraught with burden and danger—than when he conferred the honor on him in the first place. When the King, in spite of More's protests, saddled him with that heavy load, the King showed his love of country, and was only looking out for his own and the realm's best interests; when, at More's request, the King removed that load, he showed his love of More. When he appointed him, he merited praise and universal acclaim for his beneficence and wisdom in entrusting a most difficult post to the man best qualified in the realm for bearing so heavy a burden; when he released him, he earned high praise for his humanity by letting his own judgment and concern for the common good yield a bit to the pleas of a friend asking for the kind of leisurely retirement Cassiodorus once obtained from his ruler.[19] And I have no doubt that More was brought by very solid

---

17 These are Roman statesmen: the first defeated the Gauls, *ca.* 387 BC; the second conquered Carthage in 202 BC.
18 Translated by Gerald Malsbary with the collaboration of Mary Taneyhill, © CTMS

2016, with the first four paragraphs based on a translation by Marcus A. Haworth, S.J., which appeared in *Erasmus and His Age: Selected Letters of Desiderius Erasmus,* ed. Hans J. Hillerbrand (New

York: Harper & Row, 1970). Faber was an Austrian humanist; later, Bishop of Vienna.
19 Theodoric the Ostrogoth, King of Italy 493–526 AD

reasons to plead with the King for that release. Otherwise, neither would he ever have been so bold as to ask for a discharge so soon, nor would the King have been so compliant as to grant his request for just any excuse.

The King knew that the status of his entire domain depended for the most part upon the integrity, learning, and wisdom of the chancellor. For this office of chancellor is not, as it is in some countries, merely that of a secretary. In dignity, the office ranks next to the crown, so that, when the chancellor appears in public, to his right is displayed a golden scepter, topped by a golden imperial crown, and to his left, a book. The one symbolizes supreme power under the king, the other, knowledge of the laws. For he is chief justice of the whole British dominion, the right eye, so to speak, and the right hand of the king and of the royal council. A very wise leader would never have entrusted such a lofty responsibility to someone who had not been tested. Hardly anyone else saw more deeply, or loved more seriously, the rare and almost divine endowments of More's nature. In fact, even the Cardinal of York,[20] despite his own misfortune, was no fool: when he realized that he himself had no hope of returning to his former power, he declared that no man in the entire island, other than More alone, was equal to so great an office. And this was no mere "favorable recommendation" or vote of confidence. When the Cardinal was still alive, he was hardly just toward More; and more truly feared him than loved him. The judgment of the people was not otherwise. And so, just as he entered upon his office with such congratulations of the whole realm as no man had received before, so did he resign it with the deep sorrow of all the wise and good. For he resigned after he had earned the most wonderful praise of all: that none of his predecessors had administered the office more skillfully or with greater justice. And you know how critical the people usually are of top civil officials, especially during their first years in office. Even so, I could easily convince you of what I am saying if I could show you the letters of the most eminent men expressing their congratulations to the King, to the realm, to More himself, and even to me, in my enthusiasm about More's acceptance of the office; and then, by contrast, the letters written by the same men, deploring the fact that the commonwealth had lost such a judge and "counsel-giver" — *boulēphóros,* to use Homer's word for him.

I do not doubt that the King has replaced More by someone distinguished, although he is utterly unknown to me. Now, with regard to the luster of his own family's heritage, Thomas More, with his clearly philosophical character, never pursued it much, nor boasted of it. He was born in London, that most famous of all cities, and to be born and educated in that city is regarded by the English as bringing a good deal of nobility along with it. His father was by no means obscure, being a doctor of British law, a profession of the highest distinction among the English, and said to be the origin of a large part of the nobility of that island. Young More followed in his father's footsteps, and did it so well, that the father, though competent in every way and illustrious in his own right, was overshadowed by the son. Of course, nobody more truly casts a light upon his ancestors than when he overshadows them like this.

I shall pass over the titles of honor with which both were decorated — and not through solicited or purchased favor, but through the free decision of the King — unless perhaps, we are to think that true nobility is won only by strenuous and repeated exploits in war, while distinguished service to the commonwealth in times of peace, and accomplished by intelligence rather than arms, deserves no honor at all. The better the general condition of a commonwealth, the less need it has for military exertions. But the services of men who excel in learning, good judgment, and jurisprudence are always necessary to kings and kingdoms, both in times of war and in times of peace. We hear the oracular voice of the Scripture that says: "By me kings reign."[21] And yet it is not the voice of the military but of wisdom that keeps war from breaking out in the first place, and, when war cannot be avoided, to make sure that it be waged with the least possible damage to the commonwealth. It is a greater blessing to avoid war altogether than carry it out bravely.

Peace, in turn, cannot long endure, and if it is lasting, only engenders bad morals in the people unless it be directed by the counsels of the prudent. If Torquatus became famous through ripping the collar from a Gallic enemy's neck, will another man not win fame who for many years has furnished himself to his native land as a just judge and loyal counselor? The earliest Roman emperors thought far otherwise: they conferred the highest honors on their legal ssistants, who were renowned for their knowledge of the law. In fact, they even decreed that teachers of grammar and logic and professors of law who had been exemplars of learning and integrity for twenty years should be decorated with the same honorary insignia as were the imperial deputies, and the rank of imperial deputy was equal to the rank of the emperor's attendants and generals. The twelfth chapter of Justinian's Code, "On Professors," attests to this.[22] Today, however, people are counted "noble" only when their blood bestows the insignia of nobility, and not if they are given (you might say "sold") these titles by the ruler. But I would think that the honor conferred by a ruler of the state upon those who have served the state well counts as a double nobility, since in this case the authority of the ruler comes in addition to virtue, and virtue is the parent of all true nobility. If ancient family origin is lacking, it is more glorious to earn nobility than to receive it from one's forefathers.

But I know this praise is of only the slightest importance to More, who would rather bequeath love of piety to his posterity than the honor of a distinguished rank. And as for what they are saying about prisons, whether it is true or not, I do not know. This point is certain: that most mild-natured man was not troublesome to anyone who, after being admonished by him, would be willing to return to their senses from the contagion of a sect. Do such critics demand that the highest judge of so great a kingdom not have any prisons? The man hates the seditious teachings by which, sadly, the world is now so shaken. He does not hide this feeling, nor does he want it to be secret, being so devoted to piety that, if he leaned the slightest bit toward one side or the other of two extremes, he would seem to be closer to superstition than to impiety. Yet this is pretty good proof of an extraordinary kind of mercifulness: the fact that under him as chancellor no one has suffered capital punishment for disapproved teachings,[23] while so many have been

put to death in both Germany and France. Is this not a merciful hatred of the impious, when someone, though having the legal right to execute them, is so eager to heal their faults that he leaves their persons remain unharmed? Surely the critics are not demanding that, while representing the king, he favor a new, seditious, movement against the opinion of the King and bishops? Let us suppose that he was not at all repulsed by strange teachings (a thing far from the case): he would still either have to resign from the office that he held, or else only pretend to be enjoying the royal support.

Finally — to set aside, for now, any conflict about doctrines — who can be unaware how many amateurish and quarrelsome people would be prepared, under these circumstances, to get away with all kinds of wickedness, were it not for the strictness of public officials keeping such ever-growing audacity in check? And are they indignant that in England the kingdom's highest judge has done what a parliament has been sometimes forced to do in states that have changed their religion? And if it had not been done, false preachers would long since have burst into the chambers and libraries of the rich, and anyone who had something would be considered a papist. But so great is the audacity of so many, so out of control their malice, that even the originators and sponsors of the new doctrines are wielding their own pens fiercely against them. And did they want the supreme judge of England to look the other way, while such filth flooded the kingdom with impunity? A kingdom flourishing in wealth, talent, and especially religion? It can, of course, be true that some are being granted release from the prisons to please the new chancellor, persons who were harmless, or imprisoned on relatively light charges: the sort of thing that normally happens when new kings succeed to the throne, simply to please the multitude. The same thing happened, I suppose, when More himself first took office. But what are those *Triptolemi*[24] doing, who sow such tales? Is it to convince people that a haven has been prepared among the English for sects and supporters of sects? And yet judging by the letters of many by no means unimportant men, it is clear to me that the King is somewhat less friendly toward the new teachings than the Bishop or priests.

---

22 *Codex Justinianus* 12.15 **23** Actually six individuals were executed for "seditious treason" under More's chancellorship. Under his successor, Thomas Audley, there were fifteen or sixteen. **24** *Triptolemus*, ancient Greek hero and god of agriculture, was taught by Demeter and famous for spreading the art of agriculture around the world. Erasmus plays on the agricultural metaphor with the verb *serunt* ("they sow").

No pious man does not hope for a correction of the Church's morals; but no prudent man thinks we should accept universal confusion.

When I heard that Thomas More had been raised to the highest dignity, since it seemed to me that I understood something of his talent, thanks to our long acquaintance, I wrote that I publicly congratulated the King and country, but did not privately congratulate the man himself. Now, however, I sincerely do so because, with the utmost favor of his ruler, with the entire nation's most honorable testimony, it has speedily become his good fortune to extricate himself from the labyrinths of civil affairs, an opportunity given neither to Scipio Africanus, nor Pompey the Great nor Marcus Tullius Cicero. Octavian Augustus hoped to put down the burden of empire, but never had the chance. Now in the fullness of his lifetime Thomas More has attained with dignity the kind of life to which he has been inclined since his youth, so that now he might freely have leisure with his own family (for if anyone loves his family,[25] he does) for worthwhile pursuits and religious devotion. He has built, by the Thames river, not far from the city of London, a country-seat that is by no means primitive, yet not so magnificent as to cause envy, but still comfortable: there he spends time with the intimate company of his wife, his son and daughter-in-law, his three daughters and as many sons-in-law, making altogether eleven with his grandchildren so far. He has, by the favor of Christ, seen his children's children, and is going to see the ones to be born from them. For since all of them are in the bloom of life, it is likely that a numerous progeny will come. But even he himself could still be the father of many children if his wife had not already ceased to bear children by reason of age. He married her as a widow, and has not raised any children by her. The children he does have, he begot by his former wife, whom he lost while still a young girl with several children. But although his wife be sterile, and advanced in age, he loves and cherishes her no otherwise than if she were a girl fifteen years old. Hardly anyone else now living loves his children more, nor does he see any difference between a matron and a girl: but such is the kindliness of his disposition, or rather, to say it better, such is his piety and wisdom, that whatever

comes his way that cannot be corrected, he comes to love just as wholeheartedly as if nothing better could have happened to him. You could say that his house is another Platonic Academy. But I dishonor his home when I liken it to Plato's Academy, where they discussed numbers and geometric figures, and on occasion moral virtues; this home of More's you could more rightly call a school and gymnasium of the Christian religion. There is no man or woman there who does not have leisure to study the liberal arts and worthwhile reading, although the chief and primary concern is for piety. No quarrel or nagging word is to be heard there, no lazy person to be seen. But such good family discipline is not secured through scolding or arrogance, but with courtesy and benevolence. All are busy about their duty, but there is liveliness there and no lack of self-possessed merriment.

In the church of his neighborhood he erected a common tomb for himself and his family, and brought the remains of his former wife there, since any kind of divorce from her displeased him. The wall has an inscribed tablet, testifying to the fortune and manner of life of the man; my servant has written this down word-for-word. You will receive a copy with this letter.[26] I see that I have been rather loquacious, but it gladdens me to talk about a friend to a friend. By addressing the people frequently, you are acting like a true bishop — a thing most pleasing to all good people. May your example encourage many imitators.

The things you wrote me about King Ferdinand's affairs were most welcome to me. After such preambles I am called to have good hope, that someday fortune will correspond to the virtues of the best and holiest ruler. Farewell.

ERASMUS'S FINAL COMMENTS
ABOUT THOMAS MORE, 1535[27]

3036. From the Preface to Erasmus's *Ecclesiastes*
August 1535

And therefore, what could be more cruel than this moment in time, which has deprived me of so many tried and true friends? First there was William War-

---

25 Erasmus uses the Greek word *philost-orgos*, "one who likes family affection."

26 More sent Erasmus a copy with Epistle 2831 (Allen edition). See above, Letter 191.

27 The following passages were translated by Dr. Gerald Malsbary, © CTMS 2017.

ham, the Archbishop of Canterbury; and just now William Mountjoy, the Bishop of Rochester, and Thomas More, who was the highest judge of the land, with a heart purer than driven snow, a talent

5 such as England never had before nor will ever have again, even though it is a country otherwise most abundant in talents. (lines 100–104)

3048. To Bartholomew Latomus[28]
Basel, 24 August 1535

10 The capital penalty was suffered by certain monks, among whom there was a Bridgettine brother, who was dragged on the ground, then hanged, and finally, after having his heart pulled out, torn into four pieces. There is steady rumor here, which is

15 quite believable, that when the King heard that the Bishop of Rochester[29] had been appointed by Pope Paul III to the College of Cardinals, he brought him out of prison all the sooner to have him beheaded, and thereby gave him his red Cardinal's hat.

20 It is true of course that Thomas More has long been in prison, his personal possessions confiscated by the crown. He too, it has been said, was executed, but I still do not have certain news of it. How I wish he had stayed out of such a dangerous business, and

25 had left theological disputes to the theologians. Other friends of mine, who have been kind enough to write to me and help me, now write or send me nothing at all, nor are they receiving anything from anybody: as if a scorpion slept under every rock!

30 (lines 50–63)

3049. To Peter Tomiczki[30]
Basel, 31 August 1535

From the fragment of the letter I am sending to you, you will learn what happened to the Bishop of Rochester and Thomas More—a pair of human be- 35 ings that are England's holiest and best possession. When More died I seem to have died myself: because we were a single soul as Pythagoras once said. But such is the tide of human affairs. (lines 160–64)

3052. To Conrad Goclenius[31] 40
Basel, 2 September 1535

Aleander has published another angry book under the name "Doletus": he therein takes revenge on Thomas More, whom he had heard was in prison. He makes the masterful, commanding [*imperio-* 45 *sum*][32] More speak timidly. (lines 26–30)

ROBERT WHITTINGTON
ON THOMAS MORE[33]
(1519–20)

a man for all seasons[34] 50
More is a man of an angel's wit and singular learning. He is a man of many excellent virtues; if I should say as it is, I know not his fellow. For where is the man (in whom is so many goodly virtues) of that gentleness, lowliness, and affability? And as 55 time requires, a man of marvelous mirth and pastimes, and sometime of sad gravity—as who say, a man for all seasons. (*Vulgaria*, 1520)

---

28 Bartholomew Latomus taught Latin at the College de France.　**29** John Fisher　**30** Peter Tomiczki was the Bishop of Cracow.　**31** Conrad Goclenius taught Latin at the University of Louvain. **32** Boethius uses the same term to describe Lady Philosophy (1.1 Prose, 44–8, *Consolation of Philosophy*). Common definitions of *imperiosus* are "exercising authority, possessed of command, powerful, far-ruling, commanding." **33** Richard Whittington (*ca.* 1480–*ca.* 1553) was a grammarian and schoolmaster.

His high praise of More, even greater in his two Latin poems about More, is somewhat surprising given the "grammar war" he started by attacking More's friend William Lily, who collaborated in the "Progymnasmata" prefaced to More's *Epigrams*. See R. S. Sylvester's "The 'Man for All Seasons' Again: Robert Whittington's Verses to Thomas More," *Huntington Library Quarterly* 26.2 (Feb. 1963): 147–54. **34** For this passage, see *The Vulgaria of John Stanbridge and the Vulgaria of Robert Whittington* (London: Early English Text

Society, 1932), 64. The equivalent of this famous phrase was first used by Erasmus to describe More in Latin (*omnia horarum homo*), and Whittington probably had Erasmus's phrase in mind when writing this passage for his grammar students. Erasmus explains the phrase in his 1508 edition of *Adagia* (*CWE* 31: 304) and applies it to More in his 1509 prefatory letter to *Praise of Folly* (1509, Letter 7 above; *CWE* 2: 163, *EE* 222/20–21), and later again in his 1521 letter to Budé describing More (given above; *CWE* 8: 297, *EE* 1233/94).

WILLIAM TYNDALE ON THOMAS MORE[35]
(1530–31)

From *The Practice of Prelates:* Whether the King's grace may be separated from his queen because she was his brother's wife (1530)

This is Sir Thomas More[36]

Moreover the proctor of purgatory saith in his dialogue, *Quoth I, and quoth he, and quoth your friend,* how that the foresaid Duke of Gloucester was a noble man and a great clerk, and so wise that he could spy false miracles, and disclose them, and judge them from the true.[37] (297)

Then come in the ambassadors of France, and money, a few prelates, and certain other the King's play-fellows, that be sworn with them to betray both the King and the realm too, and then is peace concluded. But outwardly there is nothing save a truce taken for half a year, till our soldiers be at home again, for fear lest they would not be content. Then cometh the whole host home beggared, both great and small, and the poor, that cannot suddenly get work, fall to stealing, and be hanged at home. This could More tell in his *Utopia*, before he was the Cardinal's sworn secretary, and fallen at his feet to betray the truth for to get promotion. (302)

[I]t is concluded that the Queen is not his[38] wife, and the cause why they be not divorced is peradventure[39] that our prelates are afraid. If they could have brought any marriage about, to join us unto France, it had been done long since; but because they cannot (for the French king's sister knew too much of Christ to consent unto such wickedness), haply they would it were undone. I doubt not but they bear the King's Grace in hand that the Pope dare not confirm it for fear of the Emperor; but I doubt not, if they feared not the Emperor and the lords and commons, it had been done already.

After that my lord Cardinal with More, his sworn secretary, and the Bishop[40] of London, that still Saturn, the imaginer of all mischief, went to France to juggle secretly, and carried with him more than he brought home again. This is of a truth, that he carried great treasure with him. (320–21)

Cardinal Wolsey preferred More to be chancellor

[Cardinal Wolsey] set up in his room,[41] to minister forth and to fight against God as he had begun, the chiefest of all his secretaries, one nothing inferior unto his master in lying, feigning, and bearing two faces in one hood; a whelp that goeth not out of kind from his sire; the chiefest teasel[42] wherewith the Cardinal caught the King's Grace, whom he called unto the confirmation of all that he intended to persuade, saying, "If it like your Grace, More is a learned man, and knoweth it, and is also a layman, wherefore he will not say otherwise than it is, for any partiality to us-ward," which secretary yet must first deserve it with writing against Martin,[43] and against *The Obedience*, and *Mammon*, and become the proctor of purgatory, to write against *The Supplication of Beggars.*[44] (335)

Thomas More is proved a liar

And More, among his other blasphemies in his dialogue,[45] saith, that none of us dare abide by our faith unto the death. But shortly thereafter God, to prove More that he hath ever been a false liar, gave strength unto his servant Sir Thomas Hitton to confess, and that unto the death, the faith of his holy Son Jesus; which Thomas[46] the bishops of Canterbury and Rochester, after they had dieted and tormented him secretly, murdered at Maidstone most cruelly. (340)

---

35 All works of Tyndale quoted here, except for the last, are from the Cambridge University editions of 1848 and 1849 entitled respectively: *Doctrinal Treatises and Introductions to Different Portions of Holy Scripture by William Tyndale, Martyr, 1536* and *Expositions of Scripture and Practice of Prelates,* both edited by Henry Walter. **36** What are given here and below as subtitles appeared as marginal notes. **37** Here Tyndale refers to More's *Dialogue of Sir Thomas More, Knight,* 1.14, where More praises the Duke of Gloucester. Shakespeare dramatizes this same incident in *Henry VI.2,* 2.1. The reference to "proctor of purgatory," however, refers to More's *Supplication of Souls.* **38** King Henry VIII's **39** perhaps **40** Cuthbert Tunstall **41** office, position **42** a plant with hooked prickles **43** Luther **44** *The Supplication of Beggars* was written by Simon Fish and answered by Thomas More's *Supplication of Souls.* **45** See *Dialogue of Sir Thomas More, Knight* 2.4 above. **46** 1849 note: This sufferer is here called Sir Thomas, after the usual manner of styling priests in Tyndale's time; but Foxe only calls Hitton "an honest poor man and religious." The Archbishop of Canterbury was Warham; the Bishop of Rochester was Fisher. The date of Hitton's marytrdom is said by Foxe to have been February 20, 1529.

From *An Exposition of the First Epistle of St. John* (1531)

These hypocrites laid to Wycliffe's charge, and do yet, that his doctrine caused insurrection. But they, 5 to quench the truth of his preaching, slew the right king, and set up three false kings a row:[47] by which mischievous sedition they caused half England to be slain up, and brought the realm into such ruin and desolation that Master More could say, in his 10 Utopia, that as Englishmen were wont to eat sheep, even so their sheep now eat up them by whole parishes at once, besides other inconveniences that he then saw. And so the hypocrites say now likewise, that God's Word causeth insurrection: but ye shall 15 see shortly that these hypocrites themselves, after their old wont and examples, in quenching the truth that uttereth their juggling, shall cause all realms Christian to rise one against another, and some against themselves. (224–25)

From *An Exposition upon the Fifth, Sixth, and Seventh Chapters of Matthew* (ca. 1531–32)

Covetousness blinded the eyes and hardened the heart of Sir Thomas More

Covetousness maketh many, whom the truth 25 pleaseth at the beginning, to cast it up again and to be afterward the most cruel enemies thereof, after the example of Simon Magus; yea, and after the example of Sir Thomas More, Knight, which knew the truth, and for covetousness forsook it again, 30 and conspired first with the Cardinal to deceive the King, and to lead him in darkness: and afterward, when the light was sprung upon them, and had driven them clean out of the Scripture, and had delivered it out of their tyranny, and had expelled 35 the dark stinking mist of their devilish glosses, and had wiped away the cobwebs, which those poisoned spiders had spread upon the face of the clear text, so that the spiritualty (as they call themselves) were ashamed of their part, as shameless as they

be; yet for all that, covetousness blinded the eyes 40 of that gleering fox more and more, and hardened his heart against the truth, with the confidence of his painted poetry, babbling eloquence, and juggling arguments of subtle sophistry, grounded on his "unwritten verities," as true and as authentic as 45 his story of Utopia. (100)

From William Tyndale's *An Answer unto Sir Thomas More's Dialogue*[48] (1531)

MASTER MORE: Christ lived chaste and exhorteth us to chastity. 50

TYNDALE: We be not all of Christ's complexion; neither exhorteth he to other chastity than wedlock, save at a time to serve our neighbors. Now the pope's chastity is not to serve a man's neighbor, but to run to riot and to carry away with him the living 55 of the poor and of the true preacher, even the tithes of five or six parishes and to go and either dwell by a stew or to carry a stews with him, or to corrupt other men's wives.

Pannutius, a man that never proved[49] marriage, 60 is praised in the stories for resisting such doctrine with God's word in a general council before the pope was a god. And now Master More, a man that hath proved it twice, is magnified for defending it with sophistry. And again me seemeth that it is a 65 great oversight of Master More to think that Christ, though he was never married, would not more accept the service of a married man that would more say truth for him than they that abhor wedlock: inasmuch as the spiritualty accept his humble ser- 70 vice and reward his merits with so high honor, because he can better fain[50] for them, than any of their unchaste — I would say any chaste people though he be bigamous and past the grace of his neck-verse.[51]

And finally, if Master More look so much on the 75 pleasure that is in marriage, why setteth he not his eyes on the thanksgiving for that pleasure and on the patience of other displeasures? (166–67)

---

47 1849 note: See *Exposition upon Matthew*, p. 53. Tyndale charges the popish clergy with what he accounted the guilt of deposing Richard II, and of transferring the crown to the house of Lancaster, when the hereditary right had devolved to the house of York. **48** See Anne O'Donnell's and Jared Wick's edition (Washington, DC: Catholic University of America Press, 2000), but the spelling and punctuation have been adjusted, 166–67. **49** experienced **50** be glad **51** a Latin verse printed in black letter formerly set before a person claiming benefit of clergy, by reading which he might prove his clerical status and hence save his neck (*OED*)

THE PARIS NEWSLETTER[52]
On More's Trial and Execution (1535)

This account of More's July 1 trial and July 6 execution was the earliest and most widely known, having left London within ten days or so after More's execution. A translation of this account, from French to Latin, had already been done in Paris by or on July 23, 1535.[53] Word traveled fast, since a trip from London to Paris generally took, at best, seven to ten days.

On the 1st July 1535, Master Thomas More, Chancellor of England, was brought before the judges and the accusations against him read in his presence. The Chancellor and the Duke of Norfolk turned to him and said, "You, Master More, have gravely erred against the King; nevertheless we hope by his clemency that if you repent and correct your obstinate opinion in which you have so rashly persevered, you will receive pardon." He replied, "My lords, I thank you very heartily for your good will. I pray God preserve me in my just opinion even to death. As to the accusation against me, I fear words, memory, and judgment would alike fail me to reply to such a length of articles, especially considering my present imprisonment and great infirmity." A chair was then ordered to be placed for him, and he proceeded as follows.

"As to the first article, charging me with having always maliciously opposed the King's second marriage, I will only answer that what I have said has been according to my conscience. I never wished to conceal the truth, and if I had, I should have been a traitor. For this error, if error it should be called, I have been condemned to perpetual imprisonment, which I have already suffered for fifteen months, and my goods confiscated. For this reason I will only reply to the principal charge against me, that I have incurred the penalty of the statute made in the last Parliament since I was in prison, by refusing to the King his title of Supreme Head of the Church, in proof of which you allege my reply to the Secretary and Council, that as I was dead to the world, I did not care to think of such things, but only of the Passion of Christ. I reply that your statute cannot condemn me to death for such silence, for neither your statute nor any laws in the world punish

people except for words or deed—surely not for keeping silence." To this the King's proctor replied that such silence was a certain proof of malice intended against the statute, especially as every faithful subject, on being questioned about the statute, was obliged to answer categorically that the statute was good and wholesome. "Surely," replied More, "if what the common law says is true, that he who is silent seems to consent, my silence should rather be taken as approval than contempt of your statute. You say that all good subjects are obliged to reply; but I say that the faithful subject is more bound to his conscience and his soul than to anything else in the world, provided his conscience, like mine, does not raise scandal or sedition, and I assure you that I have never discovered what is in my conscience to any person living.

"As to the second article, that I have conspired against the statute by writing eight letters to the Bishop of Rochester, advising him to disobey it, I could wish these letters had been read in public, but as you say the Bishop has burnt them, I will tell you the substance of them. Some were about private matters connected with our old friendship. Another was a reply to one of his asking how I had answered in the Tower to the first examination about the statute. I said that I had informed my conscience, and so he also ought to do the same. I swear that this was the tenor of the letters, for which I cannot be condemned by your statute.

"Touching the third article, that when I was examined by the Council, I answered that your statute was like a two-edged sword, for he who approved it would ruin his soul, and he who contradicted it, his body; and that the Bishop of Rochester answered similarly, showing that we were confederates, I reply that I only answered thus conditionally, that if the statute cut both ways like a two-edged sword, how could a man behave so as not to incur either danger? I do not know how the Bishop replied, but if he answered like me, it must have been from the agreement between us in opinion, but not because we had ever arranged it between us. Be assured I never did or said anything maliciously against the statute, but it may be that this has been maliciously reported to the King."

Then they ordered an usher to summon twelve

52 This translation is from *LP* 8:996, with the adjustment noted at the end. For the original French, see Harpsfield 258–66.

53 See J. D. M. Derrett, "Neglected Versions of the Contemporary Account of the Trial of Sir Thomas More," *Bulletin of the Institute of Historical Research* 33: 202–23.

men according to the custom of the country, and these articles were given to them that they might judge whether More had maliciously contravened the statute. After a quarter of an hour's absence they declared him guilty of death, and sentence was pronounced by the Chancellor *selon la lettre de la nouvelle loy*.[54]

More then spoke as follows: "Since I am condemned, and God knows how, I wish to speak freely of your statute, for the discharge of my conscience. For the seven years that I have studied the matter, I have not read in any approved doctor of the Church that a temporal lord could or ought to be head of the spiritualty." The Chancellor interrupting him, said, "What, More, you wish to be considered wiser and of better conscience than all the bishops and nobles of the realm?" To this More replied, "My lord, for one bishop of your opinion I have a hundred saints of mine; and for one parliament of yours, and God knows of what kind, I have all the General Councils for 1,000 years, and for one kingdom I have France and all the kingdoms of Christendom." Norfolk told him that now his malice was clear. More replied, "What I say is necessary for discharge of my conscience and satisfaction of my soul, and to this I call God to witness, the sole Searcher of human hearts. I say further, that your statute is ill made, because you have sworn never to do anything against the Church, which through all Christendom is one and undivided, and you have no authority, without the common consent of all Christians, to make a law or act of Parliament or Council against the union of Christendom. I know well that the reason why you have condemned me is because I have never been willing to consent to the King's second marriage, but I hope in the divine goodness and mercy, that as St. Paul and St. Stephen whom he persecuted are now friends in Paradise, so we, though differing in this world, shall be united in perfect charity in the other. I pray God to protect the King and give him good counsel."

On his way to the Tower one of his daughters, named Margaret, pushed through the archers and guards, and held him in her embrace some time without being able to speak. Afterwards More, asking leave of the archers, bade her have patience, for it was God's will, and she had long known the secret of his heart. After going ten or twelve steps she returned and embraced him again, to which he said nothing, except to bid her pray to God for his soul, and this without tears or change of color. On the Tuesday following he was beheaded in the open space in front of the Tower. A little before his death he asked those present to pray to God for him and he would do the same for them [in the other world.][55] He then besought them earnestly to pray to God to give the King good counsel, protesting that he died his faithful servant, and God's first.[56]

REGINALD POLE[57] ON THOMAS MORE
(1536)

Oh! England! What do you say here?...Rather do you not know that you were deprived of your own parent in this finest and most loving citizen of yours? Furthermore, if anyone ever deserved from you the name of "Father of his Country," it was this man....

But you, Oh! City of London! All of these things happened within your view. You saw him when he was led out from jail to plead against this charge of treason. You recall that a short time thereafter he was convicted of treason before your tribunal. You beheld him as a boy, a youth, a man, and finally in his later years as he advanced up the steps of the highest honors with the very great praise and approval of all, due to his most unusual virtues. Finally, you saw him ascend to the most renowned position; and because he was your citizen and your native son, you witnessed this with a certain feeling of joy.... (229–30)

Though I myself write these things concerning his death, separated by such a great distance, I have not only many private reasons for loving him but I have rather loved and cherished him especially because of his virtue and uprighteousness, on account of which I knew him to be most useful to his native land.... Though indeed, [London], by nature he

54 "according to the tenor of the new law" **55** from the Spanish translation of this letter **56** The French of this last phrase is *qu'il mouroit son bon serviteur et de Dieu premierement*. **57** A cousin (by both the Plantagenet and Tudor lines) and one-time close friend of Henry VIII, Reginald Pole (1500–1558) wrote this personal appeal to the King in the year after More's death. This excerpt is taken from Pole's *Defense of the Unity of the Church*, trans. Joseph Dwyer (Westminster, MD: Newman Press, 1965).

was your son through his citizenship; by his benefits, however, he was your father. He displayed more
signs of paternal affection toward you than a most
indulgent father showed toward his one and dearest son. But in no greater way did he show that he
was your parent than by his death. He lost his life
for the very special reason that he would not betray
your security.

Wherefore we read in the histories of the Greeks
that Socrates was assailed in an unjust trial by the
Athenians, even as it is now well known that More
was condemned to death by you. A short while
later, in a theatre where people had assembled for
a spectacle, these words were read aloud from a certain tragedy: "You have killed, you have killed the
best man of all the Greeks!" Immediately at these
words the bitter memory of the murder of Socrates
went through the minds of all.... [B]y how much
more just anger and compassion should you, City
of London, be stirred? You did not hear these words
uttered by chance just once in a theatre in you country by some actor, but you were compelled to hear
this charge: "You have killed, you have killed the
best of all Englishmen!" brought against you by the
most serious men at a time when they were speaking most seriously in every place now Christian in
name.... (230–31)

...Perhaps [a critic of More and Fisher] would
say that they did not see any truth at all by divine
light or by the light of reason. He would say that
by some kind of obstinacy from the very beginning
their minds began to defend a false opinion. He
would say that it seems they decided to die rather
than abandon this opinion.

Truly, my Prince, I beseech you! Examine the record for a moment. Consider the words of those
who spoke in this manner. But first, you yourself
who knew these men, examine them! See to it that
you consider what they were like during the rest of
their lives. However, I ask only this of you; I ask
whether you remember anyone who ever accused
these men of imprudence prior to the time when
this question began to be discussed publicly.

Now I am speaking of More alone. Was anyone
in all your realm considered more prudent than
More during his lifetime? Manifestly, no one, in the
opinion of all who knew him, can be mentioned

as comparable to him in talent and prudence. He
excelled in prudence; therefore, when it happened
in his case that he could have avoided all inconvenience and troubles, and also could have surpassed
all others in honors and in favor with you—if he
would only withdraw from his opinion—he deprived himself of these honors and your favor. Can
we believe he acted imprudently? (311)

EDWARD HALL ON THOMAS MORE[58]

1517 May Day Riot

With these opinions was the Recorder sent to
the Cardinal before eight of the clock, and then he,
with such as were of the King's Council at his place,
commanded that in no wise[59] watch should be kept,
but that every man should repair to his own house,
and there to keep him and his servants till seven of
the clock of the morning, with which commandment the said Richard Brook, serjeant at the law
and recorder, and Sir Thomas More, late undersheriff of London, and then of the King's Council,
came to the Guildhall half hour and before nine of
the clock, and there showed the commandment of
the King's Council. Then in all haste, every alderman sent to his ward[60] that no man should stir after nine of the clock out of his house, but to keep
his doors shut, and his servants within till seven
of the clock in the morning. After this commandment, Sir John Mundy, alderman, came from his
ward, and found two young men in Cheap[61] playing at bucklers,[62] and a great company of young
men looking on them, for the commandment was
then scarce known, for then it was but nine of the
clock. Master Mundy seeing that, bade them leave,
and the one young man asked him, "Why?" and
then he said, "Thou shalt know," and took him by
the arm to have had him to the counter.[63] Then all
the young men resisted the alderman, and took
him from Master Mundy, and cried, "Apprentices
and clubs!" Then out at every door came clubs and
weapons and the alderman fled, and was in great
danger. Then more people arose out of every quarter, and out came serving-men, and watermen and

---

58 All references are to Edward Hall, *Hall's Chronicle* (London, 1809). **59** way **60** district **61** a street in London **62** *playing at bucklers:* fencing, sword-fighting **63** prison

courtiers, and by an eleven of the clock there were in Cheap six or seven hundred. And out of Paul's Churchyard came three hundred, which wist[64] not of the other, and so out of all places they gathered, and broke up the counters, and took out the prisoners, that the Mayor had thither committed for hurting of the strangers, and came to Newgate[65] and took out Studley and Petyt, committed thither for that cause. The Mayor and sheriffs were there present, and made proclamation in the King's name, but nothing was obeyed. Thus they ran a plump[66] through Saint Nicholas Shambles,[67] and at Saint Martin's gate, there met with them Sir Thomas More and others, desiring them to go to their lodgings. And as they were entreating, and had almost brought them to a stay, the people of Saint Martin's threw out stones and bats, and hurt diverse honest persons, that were persuading the riotous people to cease, and they bade them hold their hands, but still they threw out bricks and hot water. Then a sergeant of armes called Nicholas Downes, which[68] was there with Master More entreating them, being sore[69] hurt, in a fury cried, "Down with them!" Then all the misruled[70] persons ran to the doors and windows of Saint Martin, and spoiled all that they found, and cast it into the street, and left few houses unspoiled. (588–89)

1518 Oration for London

And about three of the clock at afternoon on the twenty-ninth day of July the said legate entered the city, and in Southwark met him all the clergy of London with crosses, censers, and copes and censed[71] him with great reverence. The Mayor and aldermen, and all the occupations of the city in their best liveries[72] stood in the streets, and him highly honored, to whom Sir Thomas More made a brief oration in the name of the city. (593)

1522 Oration before King and Charles V

In the way, the Mayor John Milborne and his brethren, in fine scarlet and well-horsed, met with the Emperor and the King where one Sir Thomas More, Knight and well-learned, made to them an eloquent oration, in the praise of the two princes, and of the peace and love between them, and what comfort it was to their subjects to see them in such

amity, and how that the Mayor and citizens offered any pleasure of service that in them lay, next their Sovereign Lord. (637)

1523 Speaker of the House of Commons

According to this instruction the Commons departed to the Common House and chose for their speaker Sir Thomas More, Knight, and presented him the Saturday after in the Parliament chamber, where he according to the old usage disabled himself[73] both in wit, learning, and discretion to speak before the King, and brought in for his purpose how one Phormio desired Hannibal to come to his reading, which[74] thereto assented, and when Hannibal was come, he began to read, *de re militaire*, that is "of chivalry"; when Hannibal perceived him, he called him arrogant fool, because he would presume to teach him which was master of chivalry in the feats of war. So the speaker said, if he should speak before the King of learning and ordering of a commonwealth and such other like, the King being so well learned and of such prudence and experience might say to him as Hannibal said to Phormio. Wherefore he desired his Grace that the Commons might choose another speaker. The Cardinal answered that the King knew his wit, learning, and discretion by long experience in his service, wherefore he thought that the Commons had chosen him as the most meetest[75] of all, and so he did admit him. Then Sir Thomas More gave to the King his most humble thanks, and desired of him two petitions—the one, if he should be sent from the Commons to the King on message and mistake their intent, that he might with the King's pleasure resort again[76] to the Commons for the knowledge of their true meaning; the other was, if in communication and reasoning any man in the Common House should speak more largely[77] than of duty he ought to do, that all such offenses should be pardoned, and that to be entered of record—which two petitions were granted, and so thus began the Parliament and continued as you shall hear. (652–53)

1525 Oration before King and Ambassadors

The twenty-eighth day of April, in the beginning of this eighteenth year, came to the Court

64 knew 65 a famous prison in London   unruly 71 anointed 72 clothes   incapable 74 who 75 fittest 76 back
66 *a plump:* in a group, band 67 a church 73 *disabled himself:* pronounced himself   77 copiously, abundantly
68 who 69 greatly, badly 70 disorderly;

to Greenwich Monsieur Brenion, chief president of Roan, and John Jokyn now called Monsieur de Vaux, which President of Roan before the King, set in a throne, and accompanied with all his no-
5 bles, and the ambassadors of Rome, of the Emperor, of Venice, and Florence, being there present, made in the Latin tongue a solemn oration, the effect whereof was that he showed how dreadful the wars had been between the realms of England and
10 France, what great loss the realm of France had sustained by the said wars. He declared further of what power the King of England was of and what conquest he might have made in France, the King being prisoner, and acknowledged the King of England's
15 right in the wars, and their wrongs, where he humbly thanked him, of his pity and compassion that he had on them in their necessity and affliction, that he would consent to peace. To this oration the Chancellor of the Duchy of Lancaster, by name Sir
20 Thomas More, made answer, saying that it much rejoiced the King that they first considered how by his power he might have oppressed, and how by his pity he had relieved them; wherefore he would[78] hereafter that for kindness, they should show him
25 none unkindness, but inviolately to keep that league which was concluded. (711–12)

1529 Chosen as Lord Chancellor

The twenty and three day of October, the King came to his manor of Greenwich, and there much
30 consulted with his Council, for a meet[79] man to be his chancellor, so that in no wise[80] he were no man of the spirualty,[81] and so after long debate, the King resoluted himself upon Sir Thomas More, Knight, Chancellor of the Duchy of Lancaster, a man well-
35 learned in the tongues, and also in the common law, whose wit was fine, and full of imaginations, by reason whereof, he was too much given to mocking, which was to his gravity a great blemish. And then on the Sunday, the twenty and four day of the same
40 month, the King made him his chancellor, and delivered him the Great Seal, which Lord Chancellor, the next morrow after, was led into the Chancery by the two dukes of Norfolk and Suffolk, and there sworn, and then the mace was borne before
45 him. (761)

1529 Opening Speech as Lord Chancellor

The King with all the lords of the Parliament, and Commons which were summoned to appear at that day came into the Parliament chamber, where the King sat in his throne, or seat royal, and Sir Thomas
50 More his chancellor standing on the right hand of the King behind the bar made an eloquent oration, declaring that like[82] as a good shepherd which not alonely keepeth and attendeth well his sheep, but also forseeth and provideth for all things, which
55 either may be hurtful or noisome[83] to his flock, or may preserve and defend the same against all perils that may chance to come, so the King which was the shepherd, ruler, and governor of his realm, vigilantly forseeing things to come, considered how di-
60 verse laws before this time were made now by long continuance of time and mutation of things, very insufficient, and unperfect; and also by the frail condition of man diverse new enormities were sprung amongst the people, for the which no law was yet
65 made to reform the same, which was the very cause why at that time the King had summoned his high court of Parliament. And he resembled the King to a shepherd, or herdsman for this cause: "For if a prince be compared to his riches, he is but a rich
70 man, if a prince be compared to his honor, he is but an honorable man; but compare him to the multitude of his people and the number of his flock, then he is a ruler, a governor of might and puissance, so that his people maketh him a prince, as of the
75 multitude of sheep, cometh the name of a shepherd. And as you see that amongst a great flock of sheep some be rotten and faulty, which the good shepherd sendeth from the good sheep, so the great wether[84] which is of late fallen, as you all know, so craftily,
80 so scabbedly,[85] yea and so untruly juggled[86] with the King, that all men must needs guess and think that[87] he thought in himself, that he had no wit to perceive his crafty doing, or else that he presumed that the King would not see nor know his fraudu-
85 lent juggling and attempts; but he was deceived, for his Grace's sight was so quick and penetrable, that he saw him, yea and saw through him, both within and without, so that all things to him was open, and according to his desert he hath had a gentle correc-
90 tion, which small punishment the King will[88] not to

---

78 wanted   79 fit, fair   80 way, manner   84 ram   85 basely   86 cheated, deceived
81 clergy   82 just   83 harmful, injurious   87 that which   88 wants

be an example to other offenders, but clearly declareth that whosoever hereafter shall make like[89] attempt to commit like offense, shall not escape with like punishment, and because you of the Common House be a gross multitude, and cannot speak all at one time. Therefore the King's pleasure is, that you shall resort to the Nether House,[90] and there amongst yourselves according to the old and ancient custom to choose an able person to be your common mouth and speaker, and after your election so made to advertise[91] his Grace thereof, which will declare to you his pleasure what day he will have him present in this place. (764)

1531 Opinions on Divorce Presented to Parliament

While the Parliament sat, on the thirtieth day of March at afternoon there came into the Common House the Lord Chancellor and diverse lords of the spiritualty and temporalty[92] to the number of twelve, and there the Lord Chancellor said, "You of this worshipful house I am sure be not so ignorant but you know well that the King, our sovereign lord hath married his brother's wife, for she was both wedded and bedded with his brother Prince Arthur, and therefore you may surely say that he hath married his brother's wife; if this marriage be good or no, many clerkes do doubt. Wherefore the King like a virtuous prince willing to be satisfied in his conscience, and also for the surety[93] of his realm, hath with great deliberation consulted with great clerks, and hath sent my Lord of London here present to the chief universities of all Christendom to know their opinion and judgment in that behalf. And although that the Universities of Cambridge and Oxford had been sufficient to discuss the cause, yet because they be in his realm and to avoid all suspicion of partiality he hath sent into the realm of France, Italy, the Pope's dominions, and Venetians to know their judgment in that behalf, which have concluded, written and sealed their determinations according as you shall hear read." Then Sir Brian Tuke took out of a box twelve writings sealed, and read them word-by-word, as after ensueth translated out of Latin into the English tongue....

Then the Chancellor said, "Now you of this Common House may report in your countries[94] what you

have seen and heard, and then all men shall openly perceive that the King hath not attempted this matter of[95] will or pleasure, as some strangers report, but only for the discharge of his conscience and surety of the succession of his realm. This is the cause of our repair[96] hither to you, and now we will depart."

When these determinations were published, all wise men in the realm much abhorred that marriage, but women, and such as were more wilful than wise or learned, spoke against the determination, and said that the universities were corrupt and enticed so to do, which is not to be thought. (775, 780)

1532 Resignation

The opening of these oaths was one of the occasions why the Pope, within two years following, lost all his jurisdiction in England, as you shall hear afterward. The fourteenth day [of May] the Parliament was prorogued,[97] till the fourteenth day of February next ensuing. After which prorogation, Sir Thomas More, Chancellor of England, after long suits made to the King to be discharged of that office, the sixteenth day of May he delivered to the King at Westminster, the Great Seal of England, and was with the King's favor discharged, which Seal the King kept till Whitsuntide following, and on the Monday in Whitsun week, he dubbed Thomas Audley, Speaker of the Parliament, Knight, and made him Lord Keeper of the Great Seal, and so was he called. (789)

1534 Imprisonment

The thirtieth day of March, the Parliament was prorogued, and there every lord and burgess and all others were sworn to the Act of Succession, and subscribed their hands to a parchment fixed to the same oath. This Parliament was prorogued till the third day of November next. After this, commissions were sent over all England to take the oath of all men and women to the Act of Succession, at which few repined,[98] except Doctor John Fisher; Sir Thomas More, knight, late Lord Chancellor; and Doctor Nicholas Wilson, parson of Saint Thomas Apostles in London, wherfore these three persons, after long exhortation to them made by the Bishop of Canterbury at Lambeth, and express denial

89 a similar 90 House of Commons 91 inform 92 *spiritualty and temporalty:* 93 safety, security 94 regions 95 from, out of 96 return 97 deferred, postponed 98 complained

of them to be sworn, they were sent to the Tower where they remained and were oftentimes motioned to be sworn; but the Bishop and Sir Thomas More said that they had in their writings written the Princess-Dowager "queen," and therfore they might not go against that, and the Doctor said that he in preaching called her "queen," which he would not withsay; howbeit[99] at length he was very well contented, and dissembled the matter and so escaped. But the other twain[100] stood against all the realm in their opinion. (814)

1535 Execution

Also the sixth day of July was Sir Thomas More beheaded for the like treason before rehearsed,[101] which as you have heard was for the denying of the King's Majesty's supremity. This man was also accounted learned, and as you have heard before he was Lord Chancellor of England, and in that time a great persecutor of such as detested the supremacy of the Bishop of Rome, which he himself so highly favored that he stood to it till he was brought to the scaffold on the Tower Hill where on a block his head was stricken from his shoulders and had no more harm. I cannot tell whether I should call him a foolish wiseman, or a wise foolishman, for undoubtedly he, besides his learning, had a great wit, but it was so mingled with taunting and mocking that it seemed to them that best knew him that he thought nothing to be well spoken except[102] he had ministred some mock in the communication, insomuch as at his coming to the Tower, one of the officers demanded his upper garment for his fee, meaning his gown, and he answered, he should have it, and took him his cap, saying it was the uppermost garment that he had. Likewise, even going to his death at the Tower gate, a poor woman called unto him and besought him to declare that he had certain evidences of hers in[103] the time that he was in office (which after he was apprehended she could not come by) and that he would entreat she might have them again, or else she was undone. He answered, "Good woman, have patience a little while, for the King is good unto me that even within this half hour he will discharge me of all businesses, and help thee himself." Also when he went up the stair

on the scaffold, he desired one of the sheriff's officers to give him his hand to help him up, and said, "When I come down again, let me shift for myself as well as I can." Also the hangman kneeled down to him, asking him forgiveness of his death (as the manner is) to whom he said, "I forgive thee, but I promise thee that thou shalt never have honesty[104] of the striking off my head; my neck is so short." Also even when he should lay down his head on the block, he having a great gray beard, striked out his beard and said to the hangman, "I pray you let me lay my beard over the block, lest ye should cut it." Thus with a mock he ended his life. (815–16)

THE LIFE OF
SIR THOMAS MORE[105]
by William Roper (*ca.* 1556)

Forasmuch as Sir Thomas More, Knight, sometime[106] Lord Chancellor of England, a man of singular virtue and of a clear unspotted conscience, as witnesseth Erasmus, more pure and white than the whitest snow, and of such an angelical wit as England, he saith, never had the like before, nor never shall again, universally, as well in the laws of our own realm (a study in effect able to occupy the whole life of a man), as in all other sciences, right well studied, was in his days accounted a man worthy of perpetual famous memory: I, William Roper, though most unworthy, his son-in-law by marriage to his eldest daughter,[107] knowing at this day no one man living that of him and of his doings understood so much as myself, for that[108] I was continually resident in his house by the space of sixteen years and more, thought it therefore my part to set forth such matters touching his life as I could at this present call to remembrance. Among which things, very many notable things (not meet[109] to have been forgotten) through negligence and long continuance of time are slipped out of my mind. Yet, to the intent the same should not all utterly perish, I have at the desire of diverse worshipful friends of mine (though very far from the grace and worthiness of them, nevertheless as far-forth[110] as my mean wit,

---

99 however   **100** two   **101** recounted
102 unless   **103** from   **104** honor; credit
105 The critical edition of this work is *The*

Lyfe of Sir Thomas Moore, knight, ed. E. V. Hitchcock (London: Early English Text Society, 1935).   **106** at a certain time;

formerly   **107** Roper married Margaret More on July 2, 1521.   **108** *for that:* because
109 proper, fitting   **110** to the extent

memory and knowledge would serve me) declared so much thereof as in my poor judgment seemed worthy to be remembered.

This Sir Thomas More, after he had been brought up in the Latin tongue at Saint Anthony's in London, was by his father's[111] procurement received into the house of the right reverend, wise, and learned prelate Cardinal Morton,[112] where, though he was young of years, yet would he at Christmastide suddenly sometimes step in among the players, and never studying for the matter, make a part of his own there presently among them, which made the lookers-on more sport than all the players besides. In whose[113] wit and towardness[114] the Cardinal, much delighting, would often say of him unto the nobles that diverse times dined with him, "This child here waiting at the table, whosoever shall live to see it, will prove a marvelous man."

Whereupon for his better furtherance in learning, he placed him at Oxford, where, when he was both in the Greek[115] and Latin tongue sufficiently instructed, he was then for the study of the law of the realm put to an Inn of Chancery called New Inn, where for his time he very well prospered. And from thence was admitted to Lincoln's Inn, with very small allowance, continuing there his study until he was made and accounted a worthy utter barrister.

After this, to his great commendation, he read for a good space a public lecture of Saint Augustine's *De civitate Dei,* in the Church of Saint Lawrence in the Old Jewry, whereunto there resorted Doctor Grocyn an excellent cunning[116] man, and all[117] the chief learned of the City of London.

Then was he made reader at Furnival's Inn, so remaining by the space of three years and more.

After which time he gave himself to devotion and prayer in the Charterhouse of London, religiously living there, without vow, about four years, until he resorted to the house of one Master Colt, a gentleman of Essex, that had oft invited him thither, having three daughters, whose honest conversation and virtuous education provoked him there specially to set his affection. And albeit[118] his mind most served[119] him to the second daughter, for that[120] he thought her the fairest and best favored, yet when he considered that it would be both great grief and

William Roper completed in 1556 his account of More's life to provide his own memories as source material for Nicholas Harpsfield, who was asked by Roper to write his famous father-in-law's biography. Roper's *Life* was first published in the edition shown here, in 1626, but at the press of the Jesuit college at St. Omer, not in Paris.

111 John More (*ca.* 1451–1530)   **112** Lord Chancellor of England, 1487–1500; Archbishop of Canterbury, 1486–1500; made a cardinal in 1493. More entered Morton's household in 1490, at Lambeth Palace.   **113** his (More's)   **114** natural aptitude and good disposition   **115** More indicates in his 1501 letter to John Holt that he began the serious study of Greek after his years at Oxford.   **116** learned   **117** of all   **118** although   **119** conduced   **120** *for that:* because

some shame also to the eldest to see her younger sister in marriage preferred before her, he then of a certain pity framed his fancy toward her, and soon after married her, never the more discontinuing his study of the law at Lincoln's Inn, but applying still the same until he was called to the bench, and had read[121] twice, which is as often as ordinarily any judge of the law doth read.

Before which time he had placed himself and his wife at Bucklersbury in London, where he had by her three daughters and one son, in virtue and learning brought up from their youth, whom he would often exhort to take virtue and learning for their meat, and play for their sauce.

Who,[122] ere[123] ever he had been reader in Court, was in the latter time of King Henry VII made a burgess of the Parliament, wherein there were by the King demanded (as I have heard reported) about three-fifteenths[124] for the marriage of his eldest daughter, that then should be the Scottish queen. At the last debating whereof he[125] made such arguments and reasons thereagainst, that the King's demands thereby were clean overthrown. So that one of the King's Privy Chamber named Master Tyler, being present thereat, brought word to the King out of the Parliament House that a beardless boy had disappointed all his purpose. Whereupon the King, conceiving great indignation toward him, could not be satisfied until he had some way revenged it. And, forasmuch as he nothing having, nothing could lose, his Grace devised a causeless quarrel against his father, keeping him in the Tower until he had made him pay to him a hundred pounds fine.

Shortly thereupon it fortuned that this Sir Thomas More, coming in a suit to Doctor Fox, Bishop of Winchester (one of the King's Privy Council), the Bishop called him aside, and, pretending great favor toward him, promised him that, if he would be ruled by him, he would not fail into the King's favor again to restore him, meaning (as it was after conjectured) to cause him thereby to confess his offense against the King, whereby his Highness might with the better color have occasion to revenge his displeasure against him. But when he came from the Bishop, he fell in communication with one Master Whitford, his familiar friend, then chaplain to that Bishop, and after a father of Syon,[126] and showed him what the Bishop had said unto him, desiring to have his advice therein, who for the Passion of God, prayed him in no wise[127] to follow his counsel. "For my lord, my master," quoth he, "to serve the King's turn, will not stick[128] to agree to his own father's death." So Sir Thomas More returned to the Bishop no more. And had not the King soon after died,[129] he was determined to have gone over the sea, thinking that, being in the King's indignation, he could not live in England without great danger.

After this he was made one of the undersheriffs of London, by which office and his learning together (as I have heard him say), he gained without grief not so little as four hundred pounds[130] by the year, since there was at that time in none of the prince's courts of the laws of this realm any matter of importance in controversy wherein he was not with the one part of counsel. Of whom, for his learning, wisdom, knowledge, and experience, men had such estimation that, before he came to the service of King Henry VIII, at the suit and instance[131] of the English merchants, he was by the King's consent made twice ambassador in certain great causes between them and merchants of the Steelyard: whose wise and discreet dealing therein, to his high commendation, coming to the King's understanding, provoked his Highness to cause Cardinal Wolsey (then Lord Chancellor) to procure him to his service. And albeit[132] the Cardinal, according to the King's request, earnestly travailed[133] with him therefore, among many other his[134] persuasions alleging unto him how dear his service must needs be unto his Majesty, which could not, with his honor, with less than he should yearly lose thereby, seem to recompense him. Yet he, loath to change his estate, made such means to the King, by the Cardinal, to the contrary, that his Grace, for that time, was well satisfied.

Now happened there after this, a great ship of his that then was Pope to arrive at Southampton, which the King claiming for a forfeiture, the Pope's ambassador, by suit unto his Grace, obtained that he might for his master the Pope have counsel learned in the laws of this realm, and the matter in his own presence (being himself a singular[135] civilian) in some

---

121 given a series of lectures   122 He (a continuative relative)   123 before 124 a property tax that amounted to three-fifteenths of the property's value

125 More   126 a Bridgettine monastery in Middlesex   127 way   128 hesitate, delay   129 April 1509   130 An ordinary worker earned roughly ten pounds per

year.   131 urgent entreaty, solicitation 132 although   133 labored   134 *many other his:* his many other   135 eminent, distinguished

public place to be openly heard and discussed. At which time there could none of our law be found so meet[136] to be of counsel with this ambassador as Sir Thomas More, who could report to the ambassador in Latin all the reasons and arguments by the learned counsel on both sides alleged. Upon this the counselors of either part, in presence of the Lord Chancellor and other the judges, in the Star Chamber had audience accordingly. Where Sir Thomas More not only declared to the ambassador the whole effect of all their opinions, but also, in defense of the Pope's side, argued so learnedly himself, that both was the aforesaid forfeiture to the Pope restored, and himself among all the hearers, for his upright and commendable demeanor therein, so greatly renowned, that for no entreaty would the King from thenceforth be induced any longer to forbear his service. At whose first entry thereunto he made him Master of the Requests (having then no better room void[137]) and within a month after, Knight and one of his Privy Council.

And so from time to time was he by the Prince advanced, continuing in his singular favor and trusty service twenty years and above, a good part whereof used the King upon holy-days, when he had done his own devotions, to send for him into his traverse,[138] and there sometimes in matters of astronomy, geometry, divinity, and such other faculties, and sometimes of his worldly affairs, to sit and confer with him. And other whiles would he, in the night, have him up into his leads,[139] there for to consider with him the diversities, courses, motions, and operations of the stars and planets. And because he was of a pleasant disposition, it pleased the King and the Queen, after the Council had supped, at the time of their supper, for their pleasure, commonly to call for him to be merry with them. Whom when he perceived so much in his talk to delight, that he could not once in a month get leave to go home to his wife and children (whose company he most desired) and to be absent from the Court two days together, but that he should be thither sent for again, he, much misliking this restraint of his liberty, began thereupon somewhat to dissemble his nature, and so by little and little from his former accustomed mirth to disuse[140] himself, that he was of

them from thenceforth at such seasons no more so ordinarily sent for.

Then died one Master Weston, Treasurer of the Exchequer, whose office, after his death, the King of his own offer, without any asking, freely gave unto Sir Thomas More.[141]

In the fourteenth year of his Grace's reign was there a Parliament holden, whereof Sir Thomas More was chosen Speaker, who, being very loath to take that room upon him, made an oration (not now extant)[142] to the King's Highness for his discharge thereof; whereunto when the King would not consent, he spoke unto his Grace in form following:

Since I perceive, most redoubled Sovereign, that it standeth not with your high pleasure to reform this election and cause it to be changed, but have by the mouth of the most reverend father in God, the legate, your Highness's Chancellor, thereunto given your most royal assent, and have of your benignity determined, far above that I may bear, to enable me and for this office to repute me meet[143] rather than you should seem to impute unto your Commons that they have unmeetly chosen, I am therefore, and always shall be, ready obediently to conform myself to the accomplishment of your high commandment, in my most humble wise[144] beseeching your most noble Majesty that I may with your Grace's favor, before I farther enter thereunto, make mine humble intercession unto your Highness for two lowly petitions: the one privately concerning myself, the other the whole assembly of your Common House.

For myself, gracious Sovereign, that if it mishap me in anything hereafter that is on the behalf of your Commons in your high presence to be declared, to mistake my message, and in the lack of good utterance, by my misrehearsal,[145] to pervert or impair their prudent instructions, it may then like your most noble Majesty, of your abundant grace, with the eye of your accustomed pity, to pardon my simpleness, giving me leave to repair again to the Common House, and there to confer with them, and to take their substantial advice what thing and in what wise I shall on their behalf utter and speak before your noble Grace, to

136 fitting, appropriate 137 *room void:* office vacant 138 small screened-off portion of a larger room 139 flat roof covered with lead 140 disengage 141 Here Roper errs. More was made undertreasurer of the Exchequer, and his predecessor was John Castle, not Weston. 142 See Edward Hall's summary of that speech above, p. 1387. 143 declare me fit 144 way, manner 145 misrepresentation

the intent their prudent devices[146] and affairs be not by my simpleness and folly hindered or impaired: which thing, if it should so mishap, as it were well likely to mishap in me, if your gracious benignity relieved not my oversight, it could not fail to be during my life a perpetual grudge and heaviness to my heart, the help and remedy whereof, in manner aforesaid remembered,[147] is, most gracious Sovereign, my first lowly suit and humble petition unto your most noble Grace.

Mine other humble request, most excellent Prince, is this: forasmuch as there be of your Commons, here by your high commandment assembled for your Parliament, a great number which are, after the accustomed manner, appointed in the Common House to treat and advise of the common affairs among themselves apart, and albeit, most dear liege Lord, that according to your prudent advice, by your honorable writs everywhere declared, there hath been as due diligence used in sending up to your Highness's Court of Parliament the most discreet persons out of every quarter that men could esteem meet thereunto, whereby it is not to be doubted but that there is a very substantial assembly of right wise and politic persons; yet, most victorious Prince, since among so many wise men neither is every man wise alike, nor among so many men, like well-witted, every man like well-spoken, and it often happeneth that, likewise as much folly is uttered with painted polished speech, so many, boisterous and rude in language, see deep indeed, and give right substantial counsel; and since also in matters of great importance, the mind is often so occupied in the matter that a man rather studieth what to say than how, by reason whereof the wisest man and the best spoken in a whole country fortuneth among, while his mind is fervent in the matter, somewhat to speak in such wise[148] as he would afterward wish to have been uttered otherwise, and yet no worse will had when he spoke it, than he hath when he would so gladly change it; therefore, most gracious Sovereign, considering that in your High Court of Parliament is nothing entreated[149] but matter of weight and importance concerning your realm and your own royal estate, it could not fail to let[150] and put to silence

from the giving of their advice and counsel many of your discreet Commons, to the great hindrance of the common affairs, except that every of your Commons were utterly discharged of all doubt and fear how anything that it should happen them to speak, should happen of your Highness to be taken. And in this point, though your well known and proved benignity putteth every man in right good hope, yet such is the weight of the matter, such is the reverend dread that the timorous hearts of your natural subjects conceive toward your High Majesty, our most redoubled King and undoubted Sovereign, that they cannot in this point find themselves satisfied, except[151] your gracious bounty therein declared put away the scruple of their timorous minds, and animate and encourage them, and put them out of doubt. It may therefore like your most abundant Grace, our most benign and godly King, to give to all your Commons here assembled your most gracious licence and pardon, freely, without doubt of your dreadful displeasure, every man to discharge his conscience, and boldly in everything incident among us to declare his advice, and whatsoever happen any man to say, that it may like your noble Majesty, or your inestimable goodness, to take all in good part,[152] interpreting every man's words, how uncunningly[153] soever they be couched, to proceed yet of good zeal toward the profit of your realm and honor of your royal person, the prosperous estate and preservation whereof, most excellent Sovereign, is the thing which we all, your most humble loving subjects, according to the most bounden duty of our natural allegiance, most highly desire and pray for.

At this Parliament Cardinal Wolsey found himself much grieved with the Burgesses thereof, for that[154] nothing was so soon done or spoken therein but that it was immediately blown abroad in every alehouse. It fortuned at that Parliament a very great subsidy to be demanded, which the Cardinal fearing would not pass the Common House, determined for the furtherance thereof to be there personally present himself. Before whose coming, after long debating there, whether it were better but with a few of his lords (as the most opinion of the House

---

146 opinions; plans　**147** recounted　　**148** a way　**149** treated　**150** hinder　　**151** unless　**152** *in good part:* favorably, without offense　**153** unskillfully　　**154** *for that:* because

was) or with his whole train royally to receive him there amongst them.

"Masters," quoth Sir Thomas More, "forasmuch as my Lord Cardinal lately, you wot[155] well, laid to our charge the lightness of our tongues for things uttered out of this House, it shall not in my mind be amiss with all his pomp to receive him, with his maces, his pillars, his pole-axes, his crosses, his hat, and Great Seal too — to the intent, if he find the like fault with us hereafter, we may be the bolder from ourselves to lay the blame on those that his Grace bringeth hither with him." Whereunto the House wholly agreeing, he was received accordingly.

Where, after that he had in solemn oration by many reasons proved how necessary it was the demand there moved to be granted, and further showed that less would not serve to maintain the Prince's purpose, he, seeing the company sitting still silent, and thereunto nothing answering, and contrary to his expectation showing in themselves toward his request no towardness of inclination, said unto them: "Masters, you have many wise and learned men among you, and since I am from the King's own person sent hither unto you for the preservation of yourselves and the realm, I think it meet[156] you give me some reasonable answer." Whereat, every man holding his peace, then began he to speak to one Master Marney (after Lord Marney): "How say you," quoth he, "Master Marney?" Who making no answer neither, he severally asked the same question of diverse others accounted the wisest of the company.

To whom, when none of them all would give so much as one word, being before agreed, as the custom was, by their Speaker to make answer, "Masters," quoth the Cardinal, "unless it be the manner of your House, as of likelihood it is, by the mouth of your Speaker, whom you have chosen for trusty and wise, as indeed he is, in such cases to utter your minds, here is without doubt a marvelous obstinate silence."

And thereupon he required an answer of Master Speaker, who first reverently upon his knees excusing the silence of the House, abashed at the presence of so noble a personage, able to amaze the wisest and best learned in a realm, and after by many probable arguments proving that for them to make answer was it neither expedient nor agreeable with the ancient liberty of the House, in conclusion for himself showed that though they had all with their voices trusted him, yet except[157] every one of them could put into his one head all their several wits, he alone in so weighty a matter was unmeet to make his Grace answer.

Whereupon the Cardinal, displeased with Sir Thomas More, that had not in this Parliament in all things satisfied his desire, suddenly arose and departed.

And after the Parliament ended, in his gallery at Whitehall in Westminster, uttered unto him his griefs, saying, "Would to God you had been at Rome, Master More, when I made you Speaker." "Your Grace not offended, so would I too, my lord," quoth he. And to wind such quarrels out of the Cardinal's head, he began to talk of that gallery, and said, "I like this gallery of yours, my lord, much better than your gallery at Hampton Court." Wherewith so wisely broke he off the Cardinal's displeasant talk that the Cardinal at that present, as it seemed, wist[158] not what more to say to him. But for the revengement of his displeasure, counseled the King to send him ambassador into Spain, commending to his Highness his wisdom, learning, and meetness for that voyage; and the difficulty of the cause considered, none was there, he said, so well able to serve his Grace therein. Which, when the King had broken to Sir Thomas More, and that he had declared unto his Grace how unfit a journey it was for him, the nature of the country and disposition of his complexion so disagreeing together that he should never be likely to do his Grace acceptable service there, knowing right well that if his Grace sent him thither, he should send him to his grave, but showing himself nevertheless ready, according to his duty (all were it with the loss of his life), to fulfill his Grace's pleasure in that behalf, the King, allowing[159] well his answer, said unto him, "It is not our meaning, Master More, to do you hurt, but to do you good would we be glad; we will this purpose devise[160] upon some other, and employ your service otherwise."

And such entire favor did the King bear him that he made him Chancellor of the Duchy of Lancaster, upon the death of Sir Richard Wingfield, who had that office before.

And for the pleasure he took in his company, would his Grace suddenly sometimes come home to

155 know   **156** fitting, appropriate   **157** unless   **158** knew   **159** accepting   **160** assign

his house at Chelsea, to be merry with him; whither on a time, unlooked for, he came to dinner to him, and after dinner, in a fair garden of his, walked with him by the space of an hour, holding his arm about
5 his neck. As soon as his Grace was gone, I, rejoicing thereat, told Sir Thomas More how happy he was, whom the King had so familiarly entertained, as I never had seen him to do to any other except Cardinal Wolsey, whom I saw his Grace once walk with,
10 arm in arm. "I thank our Lord, son," quoth he, "I find his Grace my very good lord indeed, and I believe he doth as singularly favor me as any subject within this realm. Howbeit,[161] son Roper, I may tell thee I have no cause to be proud thereof, for if my
15 head could win him a castle in France (for then was there war between us) it should not fail to go."

This Sir Thomas More, among all other his virtues, was of such meekness that if it had fortuned him with any learned man resorting to him from
20 Oxford, Cambridge, or elsewhere, as there did diverse, some for desire of his acquaintance, some for the famous report of his wisdom and learning, and some for suits of the universities, to have entered into argument (wherein few were comparable
25 unto him) and so far to have discoursed with them therein that he might perceive they could not, without some inconvenience, hold out much further disputation against him, then, lest he should discomfort them, as he that sought not his own glory,
30 but rather would seem conquered than to discourage students in their studies, ever showing himself more desirous to learn than to teach, would he by some witty device courteously break off into some other matter, and give over.
35 Of whom, for his wisdom and learning, had the King such an opinion, that at such time as he attended upon his Highness, taking his progress either to Oxford or Cambridge, where he was received with very eloquent orations, his Grace
40 would always assign him, as one that was prompt and ready therein, *ex tempore* to make answer thereunto. Whose manner was, whensoever he had occasion, either here or beyond the sea, to be in any university, not only to be present at the readings and
45 disputations there commonly used, but also learnedly to dispute among them himself.

Who, being Chancellor of the Duchy, was made ambassador twice, joined in commission with Cardinal Wolsey, once to the Emperor Charles into Flanders, the other time to the French King into
50 France.

Not long after this, the Water-bailiff of London, sometime[162] his servant, hearing, where he had been at dinner, certain merchants liberally to rail against his old master, waxed[163] so discontented therewith
55 that he hastily came to him and told him what he had heard. "And were I you, sir," quoth he, "in such favor and authority with my Prince as you are, such men surely should not be suffered so villainously and falsely to misreport and slander me. Wherefore
60 I would wish you to call them before you, and to their shame for their lewd[164] malice punish them."

Who, smiling upon him, said, "Why, Master Water-bailiff, would you have me punish those by whom I receive more benefit than by you all that
65 be my friends? Let them, a[165] God's name, speak as lewdly as they list of me, and shoot never so many arrows at me, as long as they do not hit me, what am I the worse? But if they should once hit me, then would it indeed not a little trouble me. Howbeit,
70 I trust, by God's help, there shall none of them all once be able to touch me. I have more cause, I assure thee, Master Water-bailiff, to pity them than to be angry with them." Such fruitful communication had he oftentimes with his familiar friends.
75 So on a time, walking with me along the Thames-side at Chelsea, in talking of other things he said unto me, "Now would to our Lord, son Roper, upon condition that three things were well established in Christendom, I were put into a sack, and
80 here presently cast into the Thames."

"What great things be those, sir," quoth I, "that should move you so to wish?"

"Wouldst thou know what they be, son Roper?" quoth he.
85 "Yea, marry,[166] with good will, sir, if it please you," quoth I.

"In faith, Son, they be these," said he. "The first is, that where the most part of Christian princes be at mortal war, they were all at a universal peace. The
90 second, that where the Church of Christ is at this present sore[167] afflicted with many errors and heresies, it were settled in a perfect uniformity of religion. The third, that where the King's matter of his marriage is now come in question, it were to the
95 glory of God and quietness of all parties brought to

---

161 However **162** at one time **163** became **164** ignorant; wicked **165** in **166** indeed, from "by Mary" **167** greatly

a good conclusion." Whereby, as I could gather, he judged that otherwise it would be a disturbance to a great part of Christendom.

Thus did it by his doings throughout the whole course of his life appear that all his travail[168] and pains, without respect of earthly commodities, either to himself, or any of his, were only upon the service of God, the prince, and the realm, wholly bestowed and employed, whom I heard in his later time to say that he never asked the King himself the value of one penny.

As Sir Thomas More's custom was daily, if he were at home, besides his private prayers, with his children to say the Seven Psalms, litany and suffrages following, so was his guise[169] nightly, before he went to bed, with his wife, children, and household, to go to his chapel and there upon his knees ordinarily to say certain psalms and collects with them. And because he was desirous for godly purposes sometime to be solitary, and sequester himself from worldly company, a good distance from his mansion house builded he a place called the New Building, wherein there was a chapel, a library, and a gallery, in which, as his use was upon other days to occupy himself in prayer and study together, so on the Friday there usually continued he from morning till evening, spending his time only in devout prayers and spiritual exercises.

And to provoke his wife and children to the desire of heavenly things, he would sometimes use these words unto them:

It is now no mastery[170] for you children to go to heaven, for everybody giveth you good counsel, everybody giveth you good example; you see virtue rewarded and vice punished, so that you are carried up to heaven even by the chins. But if you live the time that no man will give you good counsel, nor no man will give you good example, when you shall see virtue punished and vice rewarded, if you will then stand fast and firmly stick to God, upon pain of my life, though you be but half good, God will allow you for whole good.

If his wife or any of his children had been diseased or troubled, he would say unto them:

We may not look[171] at our pleasure to go to heaven in featherbeds; it is not the way, for our Lord himself went thither with great pain and by many tribulations, which was the path wherein he walked thither, for the servant may not look to be in better case[172] than his master.

And as he would in this sort persuade them to take their troubles patiently, so would he in like sort teach them to withstand the devil and his temptations valiantly, saying,

Whosoever will mark the devil and his temptations shall find him therein much like to an ape. For like as an ape, not well looked unto, will be busy and bold to do shrewd turns,[173] and contrariwise, being spied, will suddenly leap back and adventure no farther, so the devil, finding a man idle, slothful, and without resistance ready to receive his temptations, waxeth[174] so hardy that he will not fail still to continue with him, until to his purpose he have thoroughly brought him. But on the other side, if he see a man with diligence persevere to prevent and withstand his temptations, he waxeth so weary that in conclusion he utterly forsaketh him. For as the devil of disposition is a spirit of so high a pride that he cannot abide to be mocked, so is he of nature so envious that he feareth any more to assault him, lest he should thereby not only catch a foul fall himself, but also minister[175] to the man more matter of merit.

Thus delighted he evermore not only in virtuous exercises to be occupied himself, but also to exhort his wife, children, and household to embrace and follow the same.

To whom, for his notable virtue and godliness, God showed, as it seemed, a manifest miraculous token of his special favor toward him, at such time as my wife, as many others that year were, was sick of the sweating sickness; who, lying in so great extremity of that disease as by no invention or devices that physicians in such cases commonly use (of whom she had diverse both expert, wise, and well-learned, then continually attendant about her) she could be kept from sleep, so that both physicians and all others there despaired of her recovery, and gave her over; her father, as he that most entirely tendered her, being in no small heaviness[176]

168 labor **169** custom **170** achievement, victory **171** expect **172** condition **173** *shrewd turns:* harmful tricks **174** becomes **175** supply **176** sadness

for her, by prayer at God's hand sought to get her remedy.

Whereupon going up, after his usual manner, into his foresaid New Building, there in his chapel, upon his knees, with tears most devoutly besought almighty God that it would like his goodness, unto whom nothing was impossible, if it were his blessed will, at his mediation to vouchsafe graciously to hear his humble petition. Where incontinent[177] came into his mind that a glister[178] should be the only way to help her. Which, when he told the physicians, they by and by[179] confessed that, if there were any hope of health, that was the very best help indeed, much marveling of themselves that they had not before remembered it.

Then was it immediately ministered unto her sleeping, which she could by no means have been brought unto waking. And albeit[180] after that she was thereby thoroughly awaked, God's marks,[181] an evident undoubted token of death, plainly appeared upon her, yet she, contrary to all their expectations, was, as it was thought, by her father's fervent prayer miraculously recovered, and at length again to perfect health restored. Whom, if it had pleased God at that time to have taken to his mercy, her father said he would never have meddled with worldly matters after.

Now while Sir Thomas More was Chancellor of the Duchy, the See of Rome chanced to be void, which was cause of much trouble. For Cardinal Wolsey, a man very ambitious, and desirous (as good hope and likelihood he had) to aspire unto that dignity, perceiving himself of his expectation disappointed, by means of the Emperor Charles so highly commending one Cardinal Adrian, sometime[182] his schoolmaster, to the cardinals of Rome, in the time of their election, for his virtue and worthiness, that thereupon was he chosen pope, who from Spain, where he was then resident, coming on foot to Rome, before his entry into the city, did put off his hose and shoes, barefoot and barelegged passing through the streets toward his palace, with such humbleness that all the people had him in great reverence. Cardinal Wolsey, I say, waxed so wood[183] therewith, that he studied to invent all ways of revengement of his grief against the Emperor, which, as it was the beginning

of a lamentable tragedy, so some part of it as not impertinent to my present purpose, I reckoned requisite here to put in remembrance.

This Cardinal therefore, not ignorant of the King's inconstant and mutable disposition, soon inclined to withdraw his devotion from his own most noble, virtuous, and lawful wife, Queen Catherine, aunt to the Emperor, upon every light occasion, and upon other,[184] to her in nobility, wisdom, virtue, favor, and beauty, far incomparable, to fix his affection, meaning to make this his so light disposition an instrument to bring about his ungodly intent, devised to allure the King (then already, contrary to his mind, nothing less looking for, falling in love with the Lady Anne Boleyn) to cast fantasy to one of the French King's sisters, which thing, because of the enmity and war that was at that time between the French King and the Emperor (whom, for the cause afore-remembered,[185] he mortally maligned) he was very desirous to procure. And for the better achieving thereof, [Wolsey] requested Longland, Bishop of Lincoln, and ghostly[186] father to the King, to put a scruple into his Grace's head, that it was not lawful for him to marry his brother's wife, which the King, not sorry to hear of, opened it first to Sir Thomas More, whose counsel he required[187] therein, showing him certain places of Scripture that somewhat seemed to serve his appetite; which, when he had perused, and thereupon, as one that had never professed the study of divinity, himself excused to be unmeet[188] many ways to meddle with such matters. The King, not satisfied with this answer, so sore[189] still pressed upon him therefore, that in conclusion he condescended to his Grace's motion. And further, forasmuch as the case was of such importance as needed great advisement and deliberation, he besought his Grace of sufficient respite advisedly to consider of it. Wherewith the King, well contented, said unto him that Tunstall and Clerk, Bishops of Durham and Bath, with other learned of his Privy Council, should also be dealers therein.

So Sir Thomas More departing, conferred[190] those places of Scripture with expositions of diverse of the old holy doctors, and at his coming to the Court, in talking with his Grace of the aforesaid matter, he said,

---

177 immediately   178 enema   182 at one time, formerly   183 *waxed*   187 asked   188 unfit   189 intensely
179 immediately   180 although   *so wood:* became so angry   184 another   190 collected, compared
181 *God's marks:* visible signs of the plague   185 aforementioned   186 spiritual

To be plain with your Grace, neither my Lord of Durham, nor my Lord of Bath, though I know them both to be wise, virtuous, learned, and honorable prelates, nor myself, with the rest of your Council, being all your Grace's own servants, for your manifold benefits daily bestowed on us so most bounden to you, be, in my judgment, meet counselors for your Grace herein. But if your Grace mind to understand the truth, such counselors may you have devised, as neither for respect of their own worldly commodity,[191] nor for fear of your princely authority, will be inclined to deceive you.

To whom he named then Saint Jerome, Saint Augustine, and diverse other old holy doctors, both Greeks and Latins, and moreover showed him what authorities he had gathered out of them, which although the King (as disagreeable with his desire) did not very well like of, yet were they by Sir Thomas More, who in all his communication with the King in that matter had always most discreetly behaved himself, so wisely tempered, that he both presently took them in good part,[192] and oftentimes had thereof conference with him again.

After this were there certain questions among his Council propounded, whether the King needed in this case to have any scruple at all, and if he had, what way were best to be taken to deliver him of it. The most part of whom were of opinion that there was good cause of scruple, and that for discharging of it, suit were meet to be made to the See of Rome, where the King hoped by liberality to obtain his purpose, wherein, as it after appeared, he was far deceived.

Then was there for the trial and examination of this matrimony procured from Rome a commission in which Cardinal Campeggio and Cardinal Wolsey were joined commissioners, who for the determination thereof, sat at the Blackfriars in London where a libel[193] was put in for the annulling of the said matrimony, alleging the marriage between the King and Queen to be unlawful. And for proof of the marriage to be lawful, was there brought in a dispensation, in which, after diverse disputations thereon holden, there appeared an imperfection, which, by an instrument or brief,[194] upon

search found in the Treasury of Spain, and sent to the commissioners in England, was supplied. And so should judgment have been given by the Pope accordingly, had not the King, upon intelligence thereof, before the same judgment, appealed to the next General Council. After whose application the Cardinal upon that matter sat no longer.

It fortuned before the matter of the said matrimony brought in question, when I, in talk with Sir Thomas More, of[195] a certain joy commended unto him the happy estate of this realm that had so Catholic a prince that no heretic durst[196] show his face, so virtuous and learned a clergy, so grave and sound a nobility, and so loving, obedient subjects, all in one faith agreeing together.

"Truth it is indeed, son Roper," quoth he, and in commending all degrees and estates of the same went far beyond me. "And yet, son Roper, pray God," said he, "that some of us, as high as we seem to sit upon the mountains, treading heretics under our feet like ants, live not the day that we gladly would wish to be at league and composition[197] with them, to let them have their churches quietly to themselves, so that they would be content to let us have ours quietly to ourselves." After that I had told him many considerations why he had no cause so to say. "Well," said he, "I pray God, son Roper, some of us live not till that day," showing me no reason why he should put any doubt therein. To whom I said, "By my troth,[198] Sir, it is very desperately spoken." That vile term, I cry God mercy, did I give him. Who, by these words, perceiving me in a fume, said merrily unto me, "Well, well, son Roper, it shall not be so, it shall not be so." Whom, in sixteen years and more being in house conversant with him, I could never perceive as much as once in a fume.

But now to return again where I left. After the supplying of the imperfections of the dispensation sent (as before rehearsed[199]) to the commissioners into England, the King, taking the matter for ended, and then meaning no farther to proceed in that matter, assigned the Bishop of Durham and Sir Thomas More to go[200] ambassadors to Cambrai, a place neither Imperial nor French, to treat a peace between the Emperor, the French King, and him. In the concluding whereof Sir Thomas More so worthily handled himself, procuring in our league far

191 benefit   192 *in good part:* favorably, without offense   193 plaintiff's statement   194 *instrument or brief:* formal legal   document or royal letter   195 out of   196 dared   197 mutual agreement   198 faithfulness; truthfulness; integrity   199 related   200 go as

more benefits unto this realm than at that time by the King or his Council was thought possible to be compassed,[201] that for his good service in that voyage, the King, when he after made him Lord Chancellor, caused the Duke of Norfolk openly to declare unto the people (as you shall hear hereafter more at large) how much all England was bound unto him.

Now upon the coming home of the Bishop of Durham and Sir Thomas More from Cambrai, the King was as earnest in persuading Sir Thomas More to agree unto the matter of his marriage as before, by many and diverse ways provoking him thereunto. For the which cause, as it was thought, he the rather soon after made him Lord Chancellor, and further declaring unto him that, though at his going overseas to Cambrai he was in utter despair thereof, yet he had conceived since some good hope to compass it. For albeit[202] his marriage, being against the positive laws of the Church and the written laws of God, was helped by the dispensation, yet was there another thing found out of late, he said, whereby his marriage appeared to be so directly against the law of nature that it could in no wise[203] by the Church be dispensable, as Doctor Stokesley (whom he then preferred to be Bishop of London, and in that case chiefly credited) was able to instruct him, with whom he prayed him in that point to confer.[204] But for all his conference with him, he saw nothing of such force as could induce him to change his opinion therein, which notwithstanding the Bishop showed in his report of him to the King's Highness so good and favorable that he said he found him in his Grace's cause very toward,[205] and desirous to find some good matter wherewith he might truly serve his Grace to his contentment.

This Bishop Stokesley, being by the Cardinal not long before in the Star Chamber openly put to rebuke and awarded[206] to the Fleet, not brooking[207] his contumelious[208] usage, and thinking that forasmuch as the Cardinal, for lack of such forwardness in setting forth the King's divorce as his Grace looked for, was out of his Highness's favor, he had now a good occasion offered him to revenge his quarrel against him, further to incense the King's displeasure toward him, busily travailed[209] to invent some colorable[210] device for the King's furtherance in that behalf, which (as before is mentioned) he to his Grace revealed, hoping thereby to bring the King to the better liking of himself, and the more misliking of the Cardinal, whom his Highness therefore soon after of his office displaced, and to Sir Thomas More, the rather to move him to incline to his side, the same in his stead committed.

Who, between the Dukes of Norfolk and Suffolk, being brought through Westminster Hall to his place in the Chancery, the Duke of Norfolk, in audience of all the people there assembled, showed that he was from the King himself straightly charged, by special commission, there openly, in the presence of them all, to make declaration how much all England was beholding[211] to Sir Thomas More for his good service, and how worthy he was to have the highest room[212] in the realm, and how dearly his Grace loved and trusted him, for which, said the Duke, he had great cause to rejoice. Whereunto Sir Thomas More, among many other his humble and wise sayings not now in my memory, answered: that although he had good cause to take comfort of his Highness's singular favor toward him, that he had, far above his deserts, so highly commended him, to whom therefore he acknowledged himself most deeply bounden, yet, nevertheless, he must of his own part needs confess, that in all things by his Grace alleged he had done no more than was his duty, and further disabled himself as unmeet[213] for that room, wherein, considering how wise and honorable a prelate had lately before taken so great a fall, he had, he said, thereof no cause to rejoice. And as they had before, on the King's behalf, charged him uprightly to minister indifferent[214] justice to the people, without corruption or affection,[215] so did he likewise charge them again that, if they saw him, at any time, in any thing, digress from any part of his duty in that honorable office, even as they would discharge their own duty and fidelity to God and the King, so should they not fail to disclose it to his Grace, who otherwise might have just occasion to lay his fault wholly to their charge.

While he was Lord Chancellor, being at leisure (as seldom he was), one of his sons-in-law[216] on a time said merrily unto him, "When Cardinal

201 contrived, devised   **202** although
203 way, manner   **204** agree   **205** agreeable   **206** sentenced   **207** enduring
208 reproachful   **209** labored

210 plausible, reasonable   **211** obliged
212 office   **213** unfit, unsuitable
214 *minister indifferent:* give impartial
215 bias   **216** William Daunce married

More's second daughter, Elizabeth on September 29, 1525. Cecily More and Giles Heron married on the same day during the same ceremony.

Wolsey was Lord Chancellor, not only diverse of his privy chamber, but such also as were his doorkeepers got great gain." And since he had married one of his daughters, and gave still attendance upon him, he thought he might of reason look for some, where he indeed, because he was so ready himself to hear every man, poor and rich, and kept no doors shut from them, could find none, which was to him a great discourage. And whereas else, some for friendship, some for kindred, and some for profit, would gladly have had his furtherance in bringing them to his presence, if he should now take anything of them, he knew, he said, he should do them great wrong, for that[217] they might do as much for themselves as he could do for them, which condition, although he thought in Sir Thomas More very commendable, yet to him, being his son, he found it nothing profitable.

When he had told him this tale: "You say well, son," quoth he. "I do not mislike that you are of conscience so scrupulous, but many other ways be there, Son, that I may both do yourself good and pleasure your friend also. For sometimes may I by my word stand your friend in stead, and sometimes may I by my letter help him, or if he have a cause depending before me, at your request I may hear him before another. Or if his cause be not all the best, yet may I move the parties to fall to some reasonable end by arbitrament. Howbeit,[218] this one thing, Son, I assure thee on my faith, that if the parties will at my hands call for justice, then, all were it[219] my father stood on the one side and the devil on the other, his cause being good, the devil should have right." So offered he his son, as he thought, he said, as much favor as with reason he could require.[220]

And that he would for no respect digress from justice, well appeared by a plain example of another of his sons-in-law called Master Heron.[221] For when he, having a matter before him in Chancery, and presuming too much of his favor, would by him in no wise[222] be persuaded to agree to any indifferent[223] order, then made he in conclusion a flat decree against him.

This Lord Chancellor used commonly every afternoon to sit in his open hall, to the intent that, if any persons had suit unto him, they might the more boldly come to his presence and there open their complaints before him, whose manner[224] was also to read every bill himself ere[225] he would award any subpoena, which bearing matter sufficient worthy a subpoena, would he set his hand unto or else cancel it.

Whensoever he passed through Westminster Hall to his place in the Chancery by the court of the King's Bench, if his father, one of the judges thereof, had been sat ere he came, he would go into the same court, and there reverently kneeling down in the sight of them all, duly ask his father's blessing. And if it fortuned that his father and he, at readings in Lincoln's Inn, met together, as they sometimes did, notwithstanding his high office, he would offer in argument the preeminence to his father, though he, for his office's sake, would refuse to take it. And for the better declaration of his natural affection toward his father, he not only, while he lay on his deathbed, according to his duty, ofttimes with comfortable words most kindly came to visit him, but also at his departure out of the world with tears taking him about the neck, most lovingly kissed and embraced him, commending him into the merciful hands of Almighty God, and so departed from him.

And as few injunctions as he granted while he was Lord Chancellor, yet were they by some of the judges of the law misliked, which I understanding, declared the same to Sir Thomas More, who answered me that they should have little cause to find fault with him therefor. And thereupon caused he one Master Crooke, chief of the six clerks, to make a docket containing the whole number and causes of all such injunctions as either in his time had already passed, or at that present depended in any of the King's Courts at Westminster before him. Which done, he invited all the judges to dine with him in the Council Chamber at Westminster, where, after dinner, when he had broken with[226] them what complaints he had heard of his injunctions, and moreover showed them both the number of causes of every one of them, in order, so plainly that, upon full debating of those matters, they were all enforced to confess that they, in like case, could have done no otherwise themselves. Then offered he this unto them: that if the justices of every court (unto whom the reformation of the rigor of the law, by reason of their office, most especially appertained)

217 *for that:* because   218 However
219 *all were it:* even if   220 ask
221 married to More's third daughter, Cecily   222 way   223 impartial
224 custom   225 before   226 *broken with:* told

would, upon reasonable considerations, by their own discretions (as they were, he thought, in conscience bound), mitigate and reform the rigor of the law themselves, there should from thenceforth by him no more injunctions be granted. Whereunto when they refused to condescend,[227] then said he unto them, "Forasmuch as yourselves, my lords, drive me to that necessity for awarding out injunctions to relieve the people's injury, you cannot hereafter any more justly blame me." After that he said secretly unto me, "I perceive, Son, why they like not so to do, for they see that they may by the verdict of the jury cast off all quarrels from themselves upon them, which they account their chief defense, and therefore am I compelled to abide the adventure of all such reports."

And as little leisure as he had to be occupied in the study of Holy Scripture and controversies upon religion and such other virtuous exercises, being in manner continually busied about the affairs of the King and the realm, yet such watch[228] and pain in setting forth of diverse profitable works, in defense of the true Christian religion, against heresies secretly sown abroad in the realm, assuredly sustained[229] he, that the bishops, to whose pastoral cure[230] the reformation thereof principally appertained, thinking themselves by his travail,[231] wherein by their own confession they were not able with him to make comparison, of their duties in that behalf discharged; and considering that for all his prince's favor he was no rich man, nor in yearly revenues advanced as his worthiness deserved, therefore at a convocation among themselves and others of the clergy, they agreed together and concluded upon a sum of four or five thousand pounds, at the least, to my remembrance, for his pains to recompense him. To the payment whereof every bishop, abbot, and the rest of the clergy were — after the rate of their abilities — liberal contributories, hoping this portion should be to his contentation.[232]

Whereupon Tunstall, Bishop of Durham, Clerk, Bishop of Bath, and, as far as I can call to mind, Veysey, Bishop of Exeter, repaired unto him, declaring how thankfully his travails, to their discharge in God's cause bestowed, they reckoned themselves bounden to consider him. And that albeit[233] they could not, according to his deserts so worthily as they gladly would, requite him therefore, but must reserve that only to the goodness of God, yet for a small part of recompense, in respect of his estate so unequal to his worthiness, in the name of their whole convocation, they presented unto him that sum, which they desired him to take in good part.

Who, forsaking[234] it, said, that like as it was no small comfort unto him that so wise and learned men so well accepted his simple doings, for which he never intended to receive reward but at the hands of God only, to whom alone was the thanks thereof chiefly to be ascribed, so gave he most humble thanks to their honors all for their so bountiful and friendly consideration.

When they, for all their importunate pressing upon him, that few would have went[235] he could have refused it, could by no means make him to take it, then besought they him to be content yet that they might bestow it upon his wife and children. "Not so, my lords," quoth he, "I had rather see it all cast into the Thames than I, or any of mine, should have thereof the worth of one penny. For though your offer, my lords, be indeed very friendly and honorable, yet set I so much by my pleasure and so little by my profit that I would not, in good faith, for so much, and much more too, have lost the rest of so many nights' sleep as was spent upon the same. And yet wish would I, for all that, upon condition that all heresies were suppressed, that all my books were burned and my labor utterly lost."

Thus departing, were they fain[236] to restore unto every man his own again.

This Lord Chancellor, albeit he was to God and the world well known of notable virtue (though not so of every man considered) yet, for the avoiding of singularity,[237] would he appear none otherwise than other men in his apparel and other behavior. And albeit outwardly he appeared honorable like one of his calling, yet inwardly he no such vanities esteeming, secretly next his body wore a shirt of hair, which my sister More, a young gentlewoman,[238] in the summer, as he sat at supper singly in his doublet and hose, wearing thereupon a plain shirt without ruff or collar, chancing to spy it, began to laugh at it. My wife, not ignorant of his manner, perceiving the same, privily told him of it, and he, being sorry that she saw it, presently amended it.

---

227 agree   228 vigilance   229 maintained   230 charge, duty   231 labor   232 satisfaction   233 although   234 declining   235 thought   236 glad; obliged, forced   237 personal gain; distinction   238 Anne Cresacre, who married More's son, John, in 1529

He used also sometimes to punish his body with whips, the cords knotted, which was known only to my wife, his eldest daughter, whom for her secrecy above all others he specially trusted, causing her, as need required, to wash the same shirt of hair.

Now shortly upon his entry into the high office of the Chancellorship, the King yet eftsoons[239] again moved him to weigh and consider his great matter, who, falling down upon his knees, humbly besought his Highness to stand his gracious Sovereign, as he ever since his entry into his Grace's service had found him, saying there was nothing in the world had been so grievous unto his heart as to remember that he was not able, as he willingly would, with the loss of one of his limbs, for that matter anything to find whereby he could, with his conscience, safely serve his Grace's contentation,[240] as he that always bore in mind the most godly words that his Highness spoke unto him at his first coming into his noble service, the most virtuous lesson that ever prince taught his servant, willing him first to look unto God, and after God to him, as, in good faith, he said he did, or else might his Grace well account him his most unworthy servant. To this the King answered, that if he could not therein with his conscience serve him, he was content to accept his service otherwise, and using the advice of others of his learned Council, whose consciences could well enough agree therewith, would nevertheless continue his gracious favor toward him, and never with that matter molest his conscience after.

But Sir Thomas More, in process of time, seeing the King fully determined to proceed forth in the marriage of Queen Anne, and when he, with the bishops and nobles of the Higher House of the Parliament, were, for the furtherance of that marriage, commanded by the King to go down to the Common House to show unto them both what the universities, as well as of other parts beyond the seas as of Oxford and Cambridge, had done in that behalf,[241] and their seals also testifying the same—all which matters, at the King's request, not showing of what mind himself was therein, he opened to the Lower House of the Parliament—nevertheless, doubting[242] lest further attempts after should follow, which, contrary to his conscience, by reason of his office, he was likely to be put unto, he made suit

unto the Duke of Norfolk, his singular dear friend, to be a means to the King that he might, with his Grace's favor, be discharged of that chargeable room[243] of the chancellorship, wherein, for certain infirmities of his body, he pretended himself unable any longer to serve.

This Duke, coming on a time to Chelsea to dine with him, fortuned to find him at the church, singing in the choir, with a surplice[244] on his back; to whom, after service, as they went homeward together, arm in arm, the Duke said, "God body! God body! My Lord Chancellor, a parish clerk, a parish clerk! You dishonor the King and his office." "Nay," quoth Sir Thomas More, smiling upon the Duke, "your Grace may not think that the King, your master and mine, will with me, for serving of God his master, be offended, or thereby count his office dishonored."

When the Duke, being thereunto often solicited, by importunate suit had at length of the King obtained for Sir Thomas More a clear discharge of his office, then, at a time convenient, by his Highness's appointment, repaired he to his Grace to yield up unto him the Great Seal. Which, as his Grace, with thanks and praise for his worthy service in that office, courteously at his hands received, so pleased it his Highness further to say unto him that, for the service that he before had done him, in any suit which he should after have unto him that either should concern his honor (for that word it liked his Highness to use unto him) or that should appertain unto his profit, he should find his Highness good and gracious lord unto him.

After he had thus given over the chancellorship, and placed all his gentlemen and yeomen with bishops and noblemen, and his eight watermen with the Lord Audley, that in the same office succeeded him, to whom also he gave his great barge, then, calling us all that were his children unto him and asking our advice how we might now, in this decay of his ability (by the surrender of his office so impaired that he could not, as he was wont, and gladly would, bear out the whole charge[245] of them all himself) from thenceforth be able to live and continue together, as he wished we should; when he saw us silent, and in that case not ready to show our opinions to him, "Then will I," said he, "show my poor

---

239 soon afterwards   **240** satisfaction   **243** office   **244** a loose vestment of white
241 *Collectanea satis copiosa*   **242** fearing   linen worn by choristers   **245** expense

mind unto you. I have been brought up," quoth he, "at Oxford, at an Inn of Chancery, at Lincoln's Inn and also in the King's Court, and so forth from the lowest degree to the highest, and yet have I in yearly revenues at this present left me little above a hundred pounds by the year,[246] so that now must we hereafter, if we like to live together, be contented to become contributories together. But, by my counsel, it shall not be best for us to fall to the lowest fare first. We will not therefore descend to Oxford fare, nor to the fare of New Inn, but we will begin with Lincoln's Inn diet, where many right worshipful[247] and of good years do live full well; which, if we find not ourselves the first year able to maintain, then will we the next year go one step down to New Inn fare, wherewith many an honest man is well contented. If that exceed our ability too, then will we the next year after descend to Oxford fare, where many grave, learned, and ancient fathers be continually conversant, which if our power stretch not to maintain neither, then may we yet, with bags and wallets, go a begging together, and hoping that for pity some good folk will give us their charity, at every man's door to sing *Salve Regina,* and so still keep company and be merry together."

And whereas you have heard before, he was by the King from a very worshipful living taken into his Grace's service, with whom, in all the great and weighty causes that concerned his Highness or the realm, he consumed and spent with painful cares, travels and troubles, as well beyond the seas as within the realm, in effect the whole substance of his life, yet with all the gain he got thereby, being never wasteful spender thereof, was he not able, after the resignation of his office of Lord Chancellor, for the maintenance of himself and such as necessarily belonged unto him, sufficiently to find meat, drink, fuel, apparel, and such other necessary charges. All the land that ever he purchased, which also he purchased before he was Lord Chancellor, was not, I am well assured, above the value of twenty marks by the year. And after his debts paid, he had not, I know, his chain excepted, in gold and silver left him the worth of one hundred pounds.

And whereas upon the holy days during his High Chancellorship, one of his gentlemen, when service at the church was done, ordinarily used to come to my lady his wife's pew and say unto her, "Madame, my lord is gone," the next holy day after the surrender of his office and departure of his gentleman, he came unto my lady his wife's pew himself, and making a low curtsy, said unto her, "Madame, my lord is gone."

In the time somewhat before his trouble, he would talk with his wife and children of the joys of heaven and the pains of hell, of the lives of holy martyrs, of their grievous martyrdoms, of their marvelous patience, and of their passions and deaths that they suffered rather than they would offend God. And what a happy and blessed thing it was, for the love of God, to suffer loss of goods, imprisonment, loss of lands, and life also. He would further say unto them that, upon his faith, if he might perceive his wife and children would encourage him to die in a good cause, it should so comfort him that, for very joy thereof, it would make him merrily run to death. He showed unto them afore what trouble might after fall unto him, wherewith and the like virtuous talk he had so long before his trouble encouraged them, that when he after fell into trouble indeed, his trouble to them was a great deal the less. *Quia spicula previsa minus laedunt.*[248]

Now upon this resignment of his office, came Master Thomas Cromwell, then in the King's high favor, to Chelsea to him with a message from the King. Wherein when they had thoroughly communed[249] together, "Master Cromwell," quoth he, "you are now entered into the service of a most noble, wise, and liberal prince. If you will follow my poor advice, you shall, in your counsel-giving unto his Grace, ever tell him what he ought to do, but never what he is able to do. So shall you show yourself a true faithful servant and a right worthy Counselor. For if a lion knew his own strength, hard were it for any man to rule him."

Shortly thereupon was there a commission directed to Cranmer, then Archbishop of Canterbury, to determine the matter of the matrimony between the King and Queen Catherine, at Saint Albans, where, according to the King's mind, it was thoroughly determined, who, pretending he had no justice at the Pope's hands, from thenceforth sequestered himself from the See of Rome, and so married the Lady Anne Boleyn; which, Sir Thomas More

---

246 Sir Thomas retained his salary of 100 pounds a year as counselor until March 1534. **247** honorable **248** "Because spears foreseen hurt less" **249** talked, conferred

understanding, said unto me, "God give grace, Son, that these matters within a while be not confirmed with oaths." I, at that time seeing no likelihood thereof, yet fearing lest his forespeaking it would the sooner come to pass, waxed[250] therefore for his so saying much offended with him.

It fortuned not long before the coming of Queen Anne through the streets of London from the Tower to Westminster to her coronation, that he received a letter from the bishops of Durham, Bath and Winchester,[251] requesting him both to keep them company from the Tower to the coronation, and also to take twenty pounds that by the bearer thereof they had sent him to buy him a gown with, which he thankfully receiving, and at home still tarrying, at their next meeting said merrily unto them:

My lords, in the letters which you lately sent me, you required[252] two things of me, the one whereof, since I was so well content to grant you, the other therefore I thought I might be the bolder to deny you. And like as the one, because I took you for no beggars, and myself I knew to be no rich man, I thought I might the rather fulfill, so the other did put me in remembrance of an emperor[253] that had ordained a law that whosoever committed a certain offense (which I now remember not) except[254] it were a virgin, should suffer the pains of death, such a reverence had he for virginity. Now so it happened that the first committer of that offense was indeed a virgin, whereof the Emperor hearing was in no small perplexity, as he that by some example fain[255] would have had that law to have been put in execution. Whereupon when his Council had sat long, solemnly debating this case, suddenly arose there up one of his Council, a good plain man, among them, and said, "Why make you so much ado,[256] my lords, about so small a matter? Let her first be deflowered, and then after may she be devoured." And so though your lordships have in the matter of the matrimony hitherto kept yourselves pure virgins, yet take good heed, my lords, that you keep your virginity still. For some there be that by procuring your lordships first at the coronation to be present, and next to preach for the setting forth of it, and finally to write books to all the world in defense thereof, are desirous to deflower you; and when they have deflowered you, then will they not fail soon after to devour you. Now my lords, quoth he, it lieth not in my power but that they may devour me; but God being my good lord, I will provide that they shall never deflower me.

In continuance, when the King saw that he could by no manner of benefits win him on his side, then, lo, went he about by terrors and threats to drive him thereunto. The beginning of which trouble grew by occasion of a certain nun dwelling in Canterbury, for her virtue and holiness among people not a little esteemed; unto whom, for that cause, many religious persons, doctors of divinity, and diverse others of good worship[257] of the laity used to resort; who, affirming that she had revelations from God to give the King warning of his wicked life, and of the abuse of the sword and authority committed unto him by God, and understanding my Lord of Rochester, Bishop Fisher, to be a man of notable virtuous living and learning, repaired to Rochester, and there disclosed to him all her revelations, desiring his advice and counsel therein; which the Bishop perceiving might well stand with the laws of God and his holy Church, advised her (as she before had warning and intended) to go to the King herself, and to let him understand the whole circumstance thereof. Whereupon she went to the King, and told him all her revelations, and so returned home again. And in short space after, she, making a voyage to the nuns of Syon, by means of one Master Reynolds, a father of the same house, there fortuned concerning such secrets as had been revealed unto her (some part whereof seemed to touch the matter of the King's supremacy and marriage, which shortly thereupon followed) to enter into talk with Sir Thomas More, who, notwithstanding he might well, at that time, without danger of any law (though after, as himself had prognosticated before, those matters were established by statutes and confirmed by oaths) freely and safely have talked with her therein; nevertheless, in all the communication between them (as in process[258] appeared) had always so discreetly demeaned[259] himself that he deserved not to be blamed, but contrariwise to be commended and praised.

---

250 became **251** Cuthbert Tunstall, John Clerk, Stephen Gardiner **252** asked **253** See Tacitus, *Annales* 6.5.9, about Emperor Tiberius's execution of Sejanus's young daughter. **254** unless **255** gladly **256** trouble **257** honor, renown **258** the course of time **259** conducted

And had he not been one that in all his great offices and doings for the King and the realm, so many years together, had from all corruption of wrong-doing or bribes-taking kept himself so clear that no man was able therewith once to blemish him or make just quarrel against him, it would, without doubt, in this troublous time of the King's indignation toward him, have been deeply laid to his charge, and of the King's Highness most favorably accepted, as in the case of one Parnell it most manifestly appeared; against whom, because Sir Thomas More, while he was Lord Chancellor, at the suit of one Vaughan, his adversary, had made a decree. This Parnell to his Highness most grievously complained that Sir Thomas More, for making the same decree, had of the same Vaughan (unable for the gout to travel abroad himself) by the hands of his wife taken a fair great gilt cup for a bribe. Who thereupon, by the King's appointment, being called before the whole Council, where that matter was heinously laid to his charge, forthwith[260] confessed that forasmuch as that cup was, long after the aforesaid decree, brought him for a New Year's gift, he, upon her importunate pressing upon him therefore, of courtesy, refused not to receive it.

Then the Lord of Wiltshire[261] (for hatred of his religion preferrer of this suit) with much rejoicing said unto the lords, "Lo, did I not tell you, my lords, that you should find this matter true?" Whereupon Sir Thomas More desired their lordships that as they had courteously heard him tell the one part of his tale, so they would vouchsafe of their honors indifferently to hear the other. After which obtained, he further declared unto them that, albeit[262] he had indeed, with much work, received that cup, yet immediately thereupon he caused his butler to fill it with wine, and of that cup drank to her, and that when he had so done, and she pledged him, then as freely as her husband had given it to him, even so freely gave her the same unto her again, to give unto her husband as his New Year's gift, which, at his instant request, though much against her will, at length yet she was fain[263] to receive, as herself, and certain others there, presently before them deposed.[264] Thus was the great mountain turned scant[265] to a little molehill.

So I remember that at another time, upon a New Year's day, there came to him one Mistress Crocker, a rich widow, for whom with no small pain he had made a decree in the Chancery against the Lord Arundel, to present him with a pair of gloves, and forty pounds in angels[266] in them for a New Year's gift. Of whom he thankfully receiving the gloves, but refusing the money, said unto her, "Mistress, since it were against good manners to forsake a gentlewoman's New Year's gift, I am content to take your gloves, but as for your money I utterly refuse." So, much against her mind,[267] enforced he her to take her gold again.

And one Master Gresham likewise, having at the same time a cause depending in the Chancery before him, sent him for a New Year's gift a fair gilt cup, the fashion whereof he very well liking, caused one of his own (though not in his fantasy of so good a fashion, yet better in value) to be brought him out of his chamber, which he willed the messenger, in recompense, to deliver to his master, and under other conditions would he in no wise[268] receive it.

Many things more of like[269] effect, for the declaration of his innocency and clearness from all corruption or evil affection, could I rehearse[270] besides, which for tediousness omitting, I refer to the readers by these few before remembered examples, with their own judgments wisely to weigh and consider the same.

At the Parliament following, was there put into the Lords' House a bill to attaint the nun and diverse other religious persons[271] of high treason, and the Bishop of Rochester, Sir Thomas More, and certain others, of misprision of treason,[272] the King presupposing of likelihood that this bill would be to Sir Thomas More so troublous and terrible that it would force him to relent and condescend[273] to his request — wherein his Grace was much deceived. To which bill Sir Thomas More was a suitor personally to be received in his own defense to make answer. But the King, not liking that, assigned the Archbishop of Canterbury, the Lord Chancellor, the Duke of Norfolk and Master Cromwell, at a day and place appointed, to call Sir Thomas More before them. At which time, I, thinking that I had

260 immediately   **261** Sir Thomas Boleyn, who was father of Queen Anne   **262** although   **263** glad; obliged, forced   **264** testified   **265** hardly, barely

266 gold coins   **267** intent, purpose   **268** way   **269** similar   **270** recount, tell   **271** *religious persons:* members of the clergy   **272** *misprision of treason:* an offense akin to

treason but punishable by life imprisonment and loss of goods, not death; usually it involved concealing one's knowledge of a treasonable act   **273** agree

a good opportunity, earnestly advised him to labor unto those lords for the help of his discharge out of that Parliament bill. Who answered me he would.

And at his coming before them, according to their appointment, they entertained him very friendly, willing him to sit down with them, which in no wise he would. Then began the Lord Chancellor to declare unto him how many ways the King had showed his love and favor toward him, how fain[274] he would have had him continue in his office, how glad he would have been to have heaped more benefits upon him, and finally how he could ask no worldly honor nor profit at his Highness's hands that were likely to be denied him, hoping, by the declaration of the King's kindness and affection toward him, to provoke him to recompense his Grace with the like again, and unto those things that the Parliament, the bishops and the universities had already passed, to add his consent.

To this Sir Thomas More mildly made answer, saying,

No man living is there, my lords, that would with better will do the thing that should be acceptable to the King's Highness than I, which must needs confess his manifold goodness and bountiful benefits most benignly bestowed on me. Howbeit,[275] I verily[276] hoped that I should never have heard of this matter more, considering that I have, from time to time, always from the beginning, so plainly and truly declared my mind unto his Grace, which his Highness to me ever seemed, like a most gracious prince, very well to accept, never minding, as he said, to molest me more therewith; since which time any further thing that was able to move me to any change could I never find, and if I could, there is none in all the world that would have been gladder of it than I.

Many things more were there of like[277] sort uttered on both sides. But in the end, when they saw they could by no manner of persuasions remove him from his former determination, then began they more terribly to touch him, telling him that the King's Highness had given them in commandment, if they could by no gentleness win him, in his name with his great ingratitude to charge him, that never was there servant to his sovereign so villainous, nor subject to his prince so traitorous as he, for he, by his subtle sinister slights most unnaturally procuring and provoking him to set forth a book of *The Assertion of the Seven Sacraments* and maintenance of the Pope's authority, had caused him, to his dishonor throughout all Christendom, to put a sword into the Pope's hands to fight against himself.

When they had thus laid forth all the terrors they could imagine against him, "My lords," quoth he, "these terrors be arguments for children, and not for me. But to answer that wherewith you do chiefly burden me, I believe the King's Highness of his honor will never lay that to my charge. For none is there that can in that point say in my excuse more than his Highness himself, who right well knoweth that I never was procurer[278] nor counselor of his Majesty thereunto. But after it was finished, by his Grace's appointment and consent of the makers of the same, only a sorter-out and placer of the principal matters therein contained. Wherein when I found the pope's authority highly advanced and with strong arguments mightily defended, I said unto his Grace, 'I must put your Highness in remembrance of one thing, and that is this. The pope, as your Grace knoweth, is a prince as you are, and in league with all other Christian princes. It may hereafter so fall out that your Grace and he may vary upon some points of the league, whereupon may grow breach of amity and war between you both. I think it best therefore that that place be amended, and his authority more slenderly touched.'

"'Nay,' quoth his Grace, 'that shall it not. We are so much bounden unto the See of Rome that we cannot do too much honor unto it.'

"Then did I further put him in remembrance of the Statute of Praemunire, whereby a good part of the pope's pastoral cure[279] here was pared away.

"To that answered his Highness, 'Whatsoever impediment be to the contrary, we will set forth that authority to the uttermost. For we received from that See our crown imperial' — which, till his Grace with his own mouth told it me, I never heard of before. So that I trust, when his Grace shall be once truly informed of this, and call to his gracious remembrance my doing in that behalf, his Highness will never speak of it more, but clear me thoroughly therein himself."

And thus displeasantly departed they.

---

274 gladly; willingly   **275** However   **276** truly   **277** similar   **278** agent; advocate   **279** charge, jurisdiction

Then took Sir Thomas More his boat toward his house at Chelsea, wherein by the way he was very merry, and for that I was nothing sorry, hoping that he had got himself discharged out of the Parliament bill. When he was landed and come home, then walked we twain[280] alone in his garden together, where I, desirous to know how he had sped, said, "I trust, sir, that all is well because you be so merry."

"It is so indeed, son Roper, I thank God," quoth he.

"Are you then put out of the Parliament bill?" said I.

"By my troth,[281] son Roper," quoth he, "I never remembered it."

"Never remembered it, sir?!" said I, "a case that toucheth yourself so near, and us all for your sake?! I am sorry to hear it, for I verily[282] trusted, when I saw you so merry, that all had been well."

Then said he, "Wilt thou know, son Roper, why I was so merry?"

"That would I gladly, sir," quoth I.

"In good faith, I rejoiced, Son," quoth he, "that I had given the devil a foul fall, and that with those lords I had gone so far, as without great shame I could never go back again."

At which words waxed[283] I very sad, for though himself liked it well, yet liked it me but a little.

Now upon the report made by the Lord Chancellor and the other lords to the King of all their whole discourse had with Sir Thomas More, the King was so highly offended with him that he plainly told them he was fully determined that the aforesaid Parliament bill should undoubtedly proceed forth against him. To whom the Lord Chancellor and the rest of the lords said that they perceived the lords of the Upper House so precisely bent to hear him, in his own defense, make answer himself, that if he were not put out of the bill, it would without fail be utterly an overthrow of all. But, for all this, needs would the King have his own will therein, or else he said that at the passing thereof, he would be personally present himself.

Then the Lord Audley and the rest, seeing him so vehemently set thereupon, on their knees most humbly besought his Grace to forbear the same, considering that if he should, in his own presence receive an overthrow, it would not only encourage his subjects forever after to condemn him, but also throughout all Christendom redound to his dishonor forever, adding thereunto that they mistrusted not in time against him to find some meeter[284] matter to serve his turn better. For in this case of the nun, he was accounted, they said, so innocent and clear, that for his dealing therein, men reckoned him far worthier of praise than reproof. Whereupon at length, through their earnest persuasion, he was content to condescend[285] to their petition.

And on the morrow, Master Cromwell, meeting me in the Parliament House, willed me to tell my father that he was put out of the Parliament bill. But because I had appointed to dine that day in London, I sent the message by my servant to my wife to Chelsea. Whereof when she informed her father, "In faith, Meg," quoth he, "*quod differtur, non aufertur.*"[286]

After this, as the Duke of Norfolk and Sir Thomas More chanced to fall in familiar talk together, the Duke said unto him, "By the Mass, Master More, it is perilous striving with princes. And therefore I would wish you somewhat to incline to the King's pleasure, for, by God's body, Master More, *indignatio principis mors est.*"[287]

"Is that all, my lord?" quoth he. "Then in good faith is there no more difference between your Grace and me, but that I shall die today and you tomorrow."

So fell it out, within a month or thereabouts after the making of the statute for the Oath of the Supremacy and Matrimony, that all the priests of London and Westminster, and no temporal man but he, were sent for to appear at Lambeth before the Bishop of Canterbury, the Lord Chancellor, and Secretary Cromwell, commissioners appointed there to tender the oath unto them.

Then Sir Thomas More, as his accustomed manner was always, ere[288] he entered into any matter of importance, as when he was first chosen of the King's Privy Council, when he was sent ambassador, appointed Speaker of the Parliament, made Lord Chancellor, or when he took any like[289] weighty matter upon him, to go to church and be confessed, to hear Mass and be houseled[290] so did he likewise

280 two   **281** faithfulness; truthfulness   **282** truly   **283** became   **284** fitter, more appropriate   **285** agree   **286** "what is put off is not put aside"   **287** "the indignation of the prince is death"   **288** before   **289** similar   **290** *be houseled:* receive the Eucharist

in the morning early the selfsame day that he was summoned to appear before the lords at Lambeth. And whereas he evermore used before at his departure from his wife and children, whom he tenderly loved, to have them bring him to his boat, and there to kiss them all, and bid them farewell, then would he suffer[291] none of them forth of the gate to follow him, but pulled the wicket after him, and shut them all from him, and with a heavy heart, as by his countenance[292] it appeared, with me and our four servants there took he his boat toward Lambeth. Wherein sitting still sadly a while, at last he suddenly rounded[293] me in the ear, and said, "Son Roper, I thank our Lord, the field is won." What he meant thereby I then wist[294] not, yet loath to seem ignorant, I answered: "Sir, I am thereof glad." But as I conjectured afterwards, it was for that[295] the love he had to God wrought in him so effectually that it conquered all his carnal affections utterly.

Now at his coming to Lambeth, how wisely he behaved himself before the commissioners, at the ministration of the oath unto him, may be found in certain letters sent to my wife remaining in a great book of his works.[296] Where, by the space of four days he was betaken to the custody of the Abbot of Westminster, during which time the King consulted with his Council what order were meet to be taken with him. And albeit[297] in the beginning they were resolved that with an oath not to be acknowledged whether he had to the Supremacy been sworn, or what he thought thereof, he should be discharged, yet did Queen Anne, by her importunate clamor, so sore[298] exasperate the King against him, that contrary to his former resolution, he caused the said Oath of the Supremacy to be administered unto him. Who, albeit he made a discreet qualified answer, nevertheless was forthwith[299] committed to the Tower.

Whom, as he was going thitherward, wearing, as he commonly did, a chain of gold about his neck, Sir Richard Cromwell, that had the charge of his conveyance thither, advised him to send home his chain to his wife, or to some of his children. "Nay, sir," quoth he, "that I will not, for if I were taken in the field by my enemies, I would they should somewhat fare the better by me."

At whose landing Master Lieutenant at the Tower Gate was ready to receive him, where the porter demanded of him his upper garment. "Master Porter," quoth he, "here it is," and took off his cap and delivered it him saying, "I am sorry it is no better for you." "No, sir," quoth the porter, "I must have your gown."

And so was he by Master Lieutenant conveyed to his lodging, where he called unto him one John a Wood, his own servant, there appointed to attend upon him, who could neither write nor read, and swore him before the Lieutenant that if he should hear or see him, at any time, speak or write any manner of thing against the King, the Council, or the state of the realm, he should open it to the Lieutenant, that the Lieutenant might incontinent[300] reveal it to the Council.

Now when he had remained in the Tower a little more than a month, my wife, longing to see her father, by her earnest suit at length got leave to go to him. At whose coming, after the Seven Psalms[301] and litany said (which, whensoever she came to him, ere[302] he fell in talk of any worldly matters, he used accustomably[303] to say with her) among other communication he said unto her, "I believe, Meg, that they that put me here, ween[304] they have done me a high displeasure. But I assure thee, on my faith, my own good daughter, if it had not been for my wife and you that be my children, whom I account the chief part of my charge, I would not have failed long ere this to have closed myself in as strait[305] a room, and straiter too. But since I am come hither without mine own desert, I trust that God of his goodness will discharge me of my care, and with his gracious help supply my lack among you. I find no cause, I thank God, Meg, to reckon myself in worse case[306] here than in my own house. For methinketh God maketh me a wanton,[307] and setteth me on his lap and dandleth[308] me." Thus by his gracious demeanor in tribulation appeared it that all the troubles that ever chanced unto him, by his patient sufferance thereof, were to him no painful punishments, but of his patience, profitable exercises.

And at another time, when he had first questioned with my wife a while of the order of his wife, children, and state of his house in his absence, he asked her how Queen Anne did. "In faith, Father," quoth

---

291 allow   **292** face; demeanor
293 whispered   **294** knew   **295** *for that:* because   **296** More's 1557 *Workes*
297 although   **298** greatly

299 immediately   **300** immediately
301 the Penitential Psalms: 6, 31(32), 37(38), 50(51), 101(102), 129(130), 142(143)
302 before   **303** usually   **304** think

305 tight   **306** situation   **307** spoiled child   **308** moves (a child) lightly up and down in the arms or on the knee

she, "never better." "Never better! Meg," quoth he. "Alas! Meg, alas! It pitieth me to remember into what misery, poor soul, she shall shortly come."

After this, Master Lieutenant, coming into his chamber to visit him, rehearsed[309] the benefits and friendship that he had many ways received at his hands, and how much bounden he was therefore friendly to entertain him and make him good cheer, which, since the case standing as it did, he could not do without the King's indignations, he trusted, he said, he would accept his good will, and such poor cheer as he had. "Master Lieutenant," quoth he again, "I verily[310] believe, as you may, so you are my good friend indeed, and would, as you say, with your best cheer entertain me, for the which I most heartily thank you, and assure yourself, Master Lieutenant, I do not mislike my cheer, but whensoever I do, then thrust me out of your doors."

Whereas the oath confirming the supremacy and matrimony was by the first statute in few words comprised, the Lord Chancellor and Master Secretary did of their own heads add more words unto it, to make it appear unto the King's ears more pleasant and plausible. And that oath, so amplified, caused they to be ministered to Sir Thomas More, and to all other throughout the realm. Which Sir Thomas More perceiving, said unto my wife, "I may tell thee, Meg, they that have committed me hither, for refusing of this oath not agreeable to the statute, are not by their own law able to justify my imprisonment. And surely, daughter, it is great pity that any Christian prince should by a flexible Council ready to follow his affections, and by a weak clergy lacking grace constantly to stand to their learning, with flattery be so shamefully abused." But at length the Lord Chancellor and Master Secretary, espying their own oversight in that behalf, were fain[311] afterwards to find the means that another statute should be made for the confirmation of the oath so amplified with their additions.

After Sir Thomas More had given over his office and all other worldly doings therewith, to the intent he might from thenceforth the more quietly settle himself to the service of God, then made he a conveyance for the disposition[312] of all his lands, reserving to himself an estate thereof only for the term of his own life, and after his decease assuring some part of the same to his wife, some to his son's wife for a jointure in consideration that she was an inheritrix in possession of more than a hundred pounds land by the year, and some to me and my wife in recompense of our marriage money, with diverse remainders over. All which conveyance[313] and assurance was perfectly finished long before that matter whereupon he was attainted was made an offense, and yet after by statute clearly avoided.[314] And so were all his lands, that he had to his wife and children by the said conveyance in such sort assured, contrary to the order of law, taken away from them, and brought into the King's hands, saving that portion which he had appointed to my wife and me, which, although he had in the foresaid conveyance reserved, as he did the rest, for term of life to himself, nevertheless, upon further consideration, two days after, by another conveyance, he gave the same immediately to my wife and me in possession. And so because the statute had undone only the first conveyance, giving no more to the King but so much as passed by that, the second conveyance, whereby it was given to my wife and me, being dated two days after, was without[315] the compass of the statute. And so was our portion to us by that means clearly reserved.

As Sir Thomas More in the Tower chanced on a time, looking out of his window, to behold one Master Reynolds, a religious, learned, and virtuous father of Syon, and three monks of the Charterhouse, for the matters of the matrimony and supremacy, going out of the Tower to execution, he, as one longing in that journey to have accompanied them, said unto my wife, then standing there beside him, "Lo, dost thou not see, Meg, that these blessed fathers be now as cheerfully going to their deaths as bridegrooms to their marriage? Wherefore mayest thou see, mine own good daughter, what a great difference there is between such as have in effect spent all their days in a straight, hard, penitential, and painful life religiously, and such as have in the world, like worldly wretches, as thy poor father hath done, consumed all their time in pleasure and ease licentiously. For God, considering their long-continued life in most sore and grievous penance, will no longer suffer them to remain here in this vale of misery and iniquity, but speedily hence

---

309 recounted, told   **310** truly   **313** legal transference   **314** made void
311 obliged, inclined   **312** disposal   **315** *without the compass:* beyond the bounds

taketh them to the fruition of his everlasting deity, whereas thy silly father, Meg, that like a most wicked caitiff[316] hath passed forth the whole course of his miserable life most sinfully, God, thinking him not worthy so soon to come to that eternal felicity, leaveth him here yet still in the world, further to be plunged and turmoiled with misery."

Within a while after, Master Secretary,[317] coming to him into the Tower from the King, pretended much friendship toward him, and for his comfort told him that the King's Highness was his good and gracious lord, and minded not with any matter wherein he should have cause of scruple, from henceforth to trouble his conscience. As soon as Master Secretary was gone, to express what comfort he conceived of his words, he wrote with a coal, for ink then had he none, these verses following:

Eye-flattering fortune, look thou never so fair,
Nor never so pleasantly begin to smile,
As though thou wouldst my ruin all repair,
During my life thou shalt not me beguile.
Trust I shall God, to enter in a while
His haven of heaven, sure[318] and uniform;
Ever after thy calm, look I for a storm.

When Sir Thomas More had continued a good while in the Tower, my lady, his wife, obtained license to see him, who, at her first coming, like a simple ignorant woman, and somewhat worldly too, with this manner of salutation bluntly saluted him:

"What the good year,[319] Master More," quoth she. "I marvel that you, that have been always hitherto taken for so wise a man, will now so play the fool to lie here in this close,[320] filthy prison, and be content thus to be shut up amongst mice and rats, when you might be abroad at your liberty, and with the favor and good will both of the King and his Council, if you would but do as all the bishops and best learned of this realm have done. And seeing you have at Chelsea a right fair house, your library, your books, your gallery, your garden, your orchard, and all other necessaries so handsome about you, where you might in the company of me your wife, your children, and household be merry, I muse what, a[321] God's name, you mean here still thus fondly[322] to tarry."

After he had a while quietly heard her, with a cheerful countenance he said unto her, "I pray thee, good Mistress Alice, tell me one thing."

"What is that?" quoth she.

"Is not this house," quoth he, "as nigh[323] heaven as my own?"

To whom she, after her accustomed homely[324] fashion, not liking such talk, answered, "Tilly-vally,[325] tilly-vally!"

"How say you, Mistress Alice," quoth he, "is it not so?"

"*Bone deus, bone deus,* man, will this gear[326] never be left?" quoth she.

"Well then, Mistress Alice, if it be so," quoth he, "it is very well. For I see no great cause why I should much joy either of my gay house or of anything belonging thereunto, when, if I should but seven years lie buried under the ground, and then arise and come thither again, I should not fail to find some therein that would bid me get out of doors, and tell me it were none of mine. What cause have I then to like such an house as would so soon forget his master?"

So her persuasions moved him but a little.

Not long after came there to him the Lord Chancellor, the Dukes of Norfolk and Suffolk with Master Secretary, and certain other of the Privy Council, at two several times, by all policies possible procuring[327] him, either precisely to confess the Supremacy, or precisely to deny it; whereunto, as appeareth by his examinations in the said great book,[328] they could never bring him.

Shortly hereupon, Master Rich (afterwards Lord Rich), then newly made the King's Solicitor, Sir Richard Southwell, and one Master Palmer, servant to the Secretary, were sent to Sir Thomas More into the Tower to fetch away his books from him. And while Sir Richard Southwell and Master Palmer were busy in the trussing[329] up of his books, Master Rich, pretending friendly talk with him, among other things, of[330] a set course, as it seemed, said thus unto him:

"Forasmuch as it is well known, Master More, that you are a man both wise and well-learned as well in the laws of the realm as otherwise, I pray you therefore, sir, let me be so bold as of good will to put unto you this case. Admit there were, sir," quoth he,

316 wretch   **317** Thomas Cromwell   **318** secure, safe   **319** an expression that connotes impatience   **320** enclosed,   confined   **321** in   **322** foolishly   **323** near   **324** domestic; ordinary, simple   **325** "Nonsense!"   **326** business; matter   **327** urging   **328** More's 1557 *Workes*   **329** packing   **330** from, out of

"an act of Parliament that all the realm should take me for king. Would not you, Master More, take me for king?"

"Yes, sir," quoth Sir Thomas More, "that would I."

"I put case further," quoth Master Rich, "that there were an act of Parliament that all the realm should take me for pope. Would not you then, Master More, take me for pope?"

"For answer, sir," quoth Sir Thomas More, "to your first case, the Parliament may well, Master Rich, meddle with the state of temporal princes. But to make answer to your other cause, I will put you this case: Suppose the Parliament would make a law that God should not be God. Would you then, Master Rich, say that God were not God?"

"No, sir," quoth he, "that would I not, since no Parliament may make any such law."

"No more," said Sir Thomas More, as Master Rich reported him, "could the Parliament make the king supreme head of the Church."

Upon whose only report was Sir Thomas More indicted of treason upon the statute whereby it was made treason to deny the King to be supreme head of the Church. Into which indictment were put these heinous words—"maliciously, traitorously, and diabolically."

When Sir Thomas More was brought from the Tower to Westminster Hall to answer the indictment, and at the King's Bench bar before the judges thereupon arraigned, he openly told them that he would upon that indictment have abidden[331] in law, but that he thereby should have been driven to confess of himself the matter indeed, that was the denial of the King's supremacy, which he protested was untrue. Wherefore he thereto pleaded not guilty; and so reserved unto himself advantage to be taken of the body of the matter, after verdict, to avoid that indictment, and moreover added that if those only odious terms, "maliciously, traitorously, and diabolically," were put out of the indictment he saw therein nothing justly to charge him.

And for proof to the jury that Sir Thomas More was guilty of this treason, Master Rich was called forth to give evidence unto them upon his oath, as he did. Against whom thus sworn, Sir Thomas More began in this wise[332] to say, "If I were a man, my lords, that did not regard an oath, I needed not, as it is well known, in this place, at this time, nor in

this case, to stand here as an accused person. And if this oath of yours, Master Rich, be true, then pray I that I never see God in the face, which I would not say, were it otherwise, to win the whole world." Then recited he to the court the discourse of all their communication in the Tower, according to the truth, and said:

In good faith, Master Rich, I am sorrier for your perjury than for my own peril. And you shall understand that neither I, nor no man else to my knowledge, ever took you to be a man of such credit as in any matter of importance I, or any other, would at any time vouchsafe to communicate with you. And I, as you know, of no small while have been acquainted with you and your conversation, who have known you from your youth hitherto. For we have long dwelled both in one parish together, where, as yourself can tell (I am sorry you compel me so to say) you were esteemed very light[333] of your tongue, a great dicer, and of no commendable fame. And so in your house at the Temple,[334] where hath been your chief bringing up, were you likewise accounted.

Can it therefore seem likely unto your honorable lordships that I would, in so weighty a cause, so unadvisedly overshoot myself as to trust Master Rich, a man of me always reputed for one of so little truth, as your lordships have heard, so far above my Sovereign Lord the King, or any of his noble councilors, that I would unto him utter the secrets of my conscience touching the King's supremacy, the special point and only mark at my hands so long sought for, a thing which I never did, nor never would, after the statute thereof made, reveal either to the King's Highness himself, or to any of his honorable councilors, as it is not unknown to your honors, at sundry several times sent from his Grace's own person unto the Tower unto me for none other purpose? Can this in your judgments, my lords, seem likely to be true? And yet, if I had so done indeed, my lords, as Master Rich hath sworn, seeing it was spoken but in familiar secret talk, nothing affirming, and only putting of cases, without other displeasant circumstances, it cannot justly be taken to be spoken maliciously, and where there is no malice, there can be no offense. And over[335] this

331 remained   332 way   333 heedless   334 the Middle Temple, one of the inns of court   335 in addition to

I can never think, my lords, that so many worthy bishops, so many honorable personages, and so many other worshipful,[336] virtuous, wise, and well-learned men as at the making of that law were in Parliament assembled, ever meant to have any man punished by death in whom there could be found no malice, taking *malitia* for *malevolentia*. For if *malitia* be generally taken for "sin," no man is there then that can thereof excuse himself. *Quia si dixerimus quod peccatum non habemus, nosmet ipsos seducimus, et veritas in nobis non est.*[337] And only this word "maliciously" is in the statute material, as this term "forcible" is in the statute of forcible entries, by which statute, if a man enter peaceably, and put not his adversary out forcibly, it is no offense. But if he put him out forcibly, then by that statute it is an offense, and so shall he be punished by this term "forcibly."

Besides this, the manifold goodness of the King's Highness himself, that hath been so many ways my singular good lord and gracious sovereign, that hath so dearly loved and trusted me, even at my very first coming into his noble service with the dignity of his honorable Privy Council vouchsafing to admit me, and to offices of great credit and worship most liberally advanced me, and finally with that weighty room of his Grace's High Chancellor (the like whereof he never did to temporal man before), next to his own royal person the highest officer in this noble realm, so far above my merits or qualities able and meet[338] therefor, of his incomparable benignity honored and exalted me, by the space of twenty years and more showing his continual favor toward me, and (until at my own poor suit, it pleased his Highness, giving me license, with his Majesty's favor, to bestow the residue of my life for the provision of my soul in the service of God, of his especial goodness thereof to discharge and unburden me) most benignly heaped honors continually more and more upon me — all this his Highness's goodness, I say, so long thus bountifully extended toward me, were in my mind, my lords, matter sufficient to convince this slanderous surmise by this man so wrongfully imagined against me.

Master Rich, seeing himself so disproved, and his credit so foul defaced, caused Sir Richard Southwell and Master Palmer, that at the time of their communication were in the chamber, to be sworn what words had passed between them. Whereupon Master Palmer, upon his deposition, said that he was so busy about the trussing[339] up of Sir Thomas More's books in a sack, that he took no heed to their talk. Sir Richard Southwell likewise, upon his deposition, said that because he was appointed only to look unto the conveyance of his books, he gave no ear unto them.

After this were there many other reasons, not now to my remembrance, by Sir Thomas More in his own defense alleged, to the discredit of Master Rich's aforesaid evidence, and proof of the clearness of his own conscience. All which notwithstanding, the jury found him guilty. And incontinent upon[340] their verdict, the Lord Chancellor, for that matter chief commissioner, beginning to proceed in judgment against him, Sir Thomas More said to him: "My lord, when I was toward[341] the law, the manner in such case was to ask the prisoner before judgment, why judgment should not be given against him." Whereupon the Lord Chancellor, staying his judgment, wherein he had partly proceeded, demanded of him what he was able to say to the contrary. Who then in this sort most humbly made answer:

"Forasmuch as, my lord," quoth he, "this indictment is grounded upon an act of Parliament directly repugnant to the laws of God and his Holy Church, the supreme government of which, or of any part whereof, may no temporal prince presume by any law to take upon him, as rightfully belonging to the See of Rome, a spiritual preeminence by the mouth of our Savior himself, personally present upon the earth, only to Saint Peter and his successors, bishops of the same See, by special prerogative granted, it is therefore in law amongst Christian men insufficient to charge any Christian man."

And for proof thereof, like as, among diverse other reasons and authorities, he declared that this realm, being but one member and small part of the Church, might not make a particular law disagreeable with the general law of Christ's universal Catholic Church, no more than the city of London, being but one poor member in respect of the whole realm, might make a law against an act of Parliament to bind the whole realm. So farther showed he that it was contrary both to the laws and statutes of our own land yet unrepealed, as they might evidently perceive in Magna Carta, *Quod ecclesia Anglicana libera sit, et habeat omnia iura sua integra et libertates suas illaesas.*[342] And also contrary to that sacred oath[343] which the King's Highness himself and every other Christian prince always with great solemnity received at their coronations, alleging moreover that no more might this realm of England refuse obedience to the See of Rome than might a child refuse obedience to his own natural father. For as Saint Paul said to the Corinthians, "I have regenerated you, my children, in Christ."[344] So might Saint Gregory, pope of Rome, of whom by Saint Augustine, his messenger, we first received the Christian faith, of us Englishmen truly say, "You are my children, because I have given to you everlasting salvation, a far higher and better inheritance than any carnal father can leave to his child, and by regeneration made you my spiritual children in Christ."

Then was it by the Lord Chancellor thereunto answered that seeing all the bishops, universities, and best learned of this realm had to this act agreed, it was much marveled that he alone against them all would so stiffly stick thereat, and so vehemently argue thereagainst.

To that Sir Thomas More replied, saying, "If the number of bishops and universities be so material as your lordship seemeth to take it, then see I little cause, my lord, why that thing in my conscience should make any change. For I nothing doubt[345] but that, though not in this realm, yet in Christendom about,[346] of these well-learned bishops and virtuous men that are yet alive, they be not the fewer part that be of my mind therein. But if I should speak of those which already be dead, of whom many be now holy saints in heaven, I am very sure it is the far greater part of them that, all the while they lived, thought in this case that way that I think now. And

therefore am I not bound, my lord, to conform my conscience to the Council of one realm against the General Council of Christendom."

Now when Sir Thomas More, for the voiding of the indictment, had taken as many exceptions as he thought meet,[347] and many more reasons than I can now remember alleged, the Lord Chancellor, loath to have the burden of that judgment wholly to depend upon himself, there openly asked advice of the Lord Fitz-James, then Lord Chief Justice of the King's Bench, and joined in commission with him, whether this indictment were sufficient or not. Who, like a wise man, answered, "My lords all, by Saint Julian" (that was ever his oath), "I must needs confess that if the act of Parliament be not unlawful, then is not the indictment in my conscience insufficient."

Whereupon the Lord Chancellor said to the rest of the lords: "Lo, my Lords, you hear what my Lord Chief Justice saith," and so immediately gave he judgment against him.

After which ended, the commissioners yet further courteously offered him, if he had anything else to allege for his defense, to grant him favorable audience. Who answered, "More have I not to say, my lords, but that like the blessed apostle Saint Paul, as we read in the Acts of the Apostles, was present, and consented to the death of Saint Stephen, and kept their clothes that stoned him to death,[348] and yet be they now both twain[349] holy saints in heaven, and shall continue there friends forever, so I verily[350] trust, and shall therefore right heartily pray, that though your lordships have now here in earth been judges to my condemnation, we may yet hereafter in heaven merrily all meet together, to our everlasting salvation."

This much touching Sir Thomas More's arraignment, being not thereat present myself, have I by credible report, partly of the right worshipful Sir Anthony St. Leger, Knight, and partly of Richard Heywood and John Webbe, gentlemen, with others of good credit, at the hearing thereof present themselves, as far as my poor wit and memory would serve me, here truly rehearsed[351] unto you.

Now, after this arraignment, departed he from the bar to the Tower again, led by Sir William King-

---

342 "That the English Church may be free, and that it may exist with all its laws uncorrupted and its liberties unviolated" is the first right listed in the Magna Carta. **343** This Coronation Oath required the king to confirm "especially the laws, customs, and liberties granted the clergy and the people." **344** See 1 Cor 3:1, 4:15–16. **345** fear **346** abroad **347** fit; fair **348** See Acts 7:54–60. **349** two **350** truly **351** recounted, told

ston, a tall, strong, and comely knight, Constable of the Tower, and his very dear friend. Who, when he had brought him from Westminster to the Old Swan toward the Tower, there with a heavy heart, the tears running down by his cheeks, bade him farewell. Sir Thomas More, seeing him so sorrowful, comforted him with as good words as he could, saying: "Good Master Kingston, trouble not yourself, but be of good cheer; for I will pray for you, and my good lady, your wife, that we may meet in heaven together, where we shall be merry for ever and ever."

Soon after, Sir William Kingston, talking with me of Sir Thomas More, said, "In good faith, Master Roper, I was ashamed of myself, that, at my departing from your father, I found my heart so feeble, and his so strong, that he was fain[352] to comfort me, which should rather have comforted him."

When Sir Thomas More came from Westminster to the Towerward again, his daughter, my wife, desirous to see her father, whom she thought she should never see in this world after, and also to have his final blessing, gave attendance about the Tower Wharf, where she knew he would pass by, before he could enter into the Tower, there tarrying for his coming home. As soon as she saw him, after his blessing on her knees reverently received, she hastening toward him, and, without consideration or care of herself, pressing in among the midst of the throng and company of the guard, that with halberds and bills[353] went round about him, hastily ran to him, and there openly, in the sight of all, embraced him, took him about the neck, and kissed him. Who, well liking her most natural and dear daughterly affection toward him, gave her his fatherly blessing and many goodly words of comfort besides. From whom after she was departed, she, not satisfied with the former sight of him, and like one that had forgotten herself, being all ravished[354] with the entire love of her dear father, having respect neither to herself, nor to the press of the people and multitude that were there about him, suddenly turned back again, ran to him as before, took him about the neck, and diverse times together most lovingly kissed him, and at last, with a full heavy heart, was fain[355] to depart from him. The beholding whereof was to many of them that were present thereat so lamentable that it made them for very sorrow thereof to mourn and weep.

So remained Sir Thomas More in the Tower more than a seven-night[356] after his judgment. From whence, the day before he suffered, he sent his shirt of hair (not willing to have it seen) to my wife, his dearly beloved daughter, and a letter written with a coal, contained in the aforesaid book of his works,[357] plainly expressing the fervent desire he had to suffer on the morrow, in these words following:

I cumber[358] you, good Margaret, much, but I would be sorry if it should be any longer than tomorrow, for tomorrow is Saint Thomas's Even, and the Utas of Saint Peter.[359] And therefore tomorrow long I to go to God; it were a day very meet and convenient[360] for me, etc. I never liked your manner toward me better than when you kissed me last. For I like when daughterly love and dear charity have no leisure to look to worldly courtesy.

And so upon the next morrow, being Tuesday, Saint Thomas's Eve, and the Utas of Saint Peter, in the year of our Lord, one thousand five hundred thirty and five (according as he in his letter the day before had wished) early in the morning came to him Sir Thomas Pope, his singular friend, on message from the King and his Council, that he should before nine of the clock the same morning suffer death, and that therefore forthwith[361] he should prepare himself thereunto.

"Master Pope," quoth he, "for your good tidings I most heartily thank you. I have been always much bounden to the King's Highness for the benefits and honors that he hath still from time to time most bountifully heaped upon me, and yet more bound am I to his Grace for putting me into this place, where I have had convenient time and space to have remembrance of my end. And so help me, God, most of all, Master Pope, am I bound to his Highness that it pleaseth him so shortly to rid me out of the miseries of this wretched world. And therefore will I not fail earnestly to pray for his Grace, both here and also in another world."

"The King's pleasure is further," quoth Master

352 forced; obliged **353** *halberds and bills:* battle-axes and broadswords **354** carried away **355** obliged **356** More's trial was actually July 1 and his execution, July 6. **357** More's 1557 *Workes* **358** trouble **359** July 7 was the feast of St. Thomas Becket and the octave of St. Peter's feast, observed on June 29. **360** *meet and convenient:* fit and appropriate **361** immediately

Pope, "that at your execution you shall not use many words."

"Master Pope," quoth he, "you do well to give me warning of his Grace's pleasure, for otherwise I had purposed at that time somewhat[362] to have spoken, but of no matter wherewith his Grace, or any other, should have had cause to be offended. Nevertheless, whatsoever I intended, I am ready obediently to conform myself to his Grace's commandments. And I beseech you, good Master Pope, to be a mean[363] unto his Highness that my daughter Margaret may be at my burial."

"The King is content already," quoth Master Pope, "that your wife, children, and other your friends shall have liberty to be present thereat."

"O, how much beholden then," said Sir Thomas More, "am I to his Grace that unto my poor burial vouchsafeth to have so gracious consideration."

Wherewithal Master Pope, taking his leave of him, could not refrain from weeping. Which Sir Thomas More perceiving, comforted him in this wise, "Quiet yourself, good Master Pope, and be not discomforted, for I trust that we shall, once in heaven, see each other full merrily, where we shall be sure to live and love together, in joyful bliss eternally."

Upon whose departure, Sir Thomas More, as one that had been invited to some solemn feast, changed himself into his best apparel, which Master Lieutenant espying, advised him to put it off, saying that he that should have it was but a javel.[364]

"What, Master Lieutenant," quoth he, "shall I account him a javel that shall do me this day so singular a benefit? Nay, I assure you, were it cloth of gold, I would account it well bestowed on him, as St. Cyprian did, who gave his executioner thirty pieces of gold." And albeit at length, through Master Lieutenant's importunate persuasion, he altered his apparel, yet after the example of Saint Cyprian, did he, of that little money that was left him, send one angel of gold to his executioner.

And so was he by Master Lieutenant brought out of the Tower, and from thence led toward the place of execution. Where, going up the scaffold, which was so weak that it was ready to fall, he said merrily to Master Lieutenant, "I pray you, Master Lieutenant, see me safe up, and for my coming down, let me shift for myself."

Then desired he all the people thereabout to pray for him, and to bear witness with him that he should now there suffer death in and for the faith of the holy Catholic Church. Which done, he knelt down, and after his prayers said, turned to the executioner and with a cheerful countenance spake thus to him: "Pluck up thy spirits, man, and be not afraid to do thine office; my neck is very short; take heed therefore thou strike not awry, for saving of thine honesty."

So passed Sir Thomas More out of this world to God, upon the very same day in which himself had most desired.

Soon after whose death came intelligence thereof to the Emperor Charles. Whereupon he sent for Sir Thomas Elyot, our English ambassador, and said unto him: "My Lord Ambassador, we understand that the King, your master, hath put his faithful servant and grave wise councilor, Sir Thomas More, to death." Whereunto Sir Thomas Elyot answered that he understood nothing thereof. "Well," said the Emperor, "it is too true. And this will we say, that if we had been master of such a servant, of whose doings our self have had these many years no small experience, we would rather have lost the best city of our dominions than have lost such a worthy councilor." Which matter was by the same Sir Thomas Elyot to myself, to my wife, to Master Clement and his wife, to Master John Heywood and his wife, and unto diverse other his friends accordingly reported.

Finis. Deo gratias.

---

362 something   **363** intermediary   **364** rascal; worthless person

WORKES OF SIR THOMAS MORE KNIGHT

(1557)

This 1,490-page book is the first one-volume collection of More's English works, edited by William Rastell, who was More's nephew and from 1529 to 1534 the printer of More's polemical books. As Rastell says in the prefatory letter to Queen Mary that follows, he "did diligently collect and gather together, as many of those his works, books, letters, and other writings, printed and unprinted in the English tongue, as I could come by," as he prepared More's *Workes* for publication. Rastell's letter also praises More's writing for showing the "eloquence and property of the English tongue," in the service of "true doctrine" and the "moral virtues that appertain to the framing and forming of men's manners and consciences, to live a virtuous and devout Christian life." Rastell's "commodious and profitable book" would be followed by one-volume editions of More's Latin writings later in the sixteenth century.

To the moste hygh and

vertuous Princeſſe, MARY by the grace of GOD, quene of
Englande, Spayne, Fraunce, both Sicilles, Ieruſalem, and Ireland, defen-
dour of the fayth, Archeducheſſe of Auſtria, Ducheſſe of Burgondy,
Myllayne, and Brabant, Counteſſe of Haſpurge, Flaunders, and
Tyroll, her highneſſe moſte humble and obedient ſubiect,
VVyllyam Raſtell ſeriant at lawe, wiſſheth health,
wealth, honour, and felicitie, worldely and
euerlaſtyngly.

Hen I conſidered with my ſelfe (mooſt
gratious ſoueraigne) what greate eloquence, excellent learninge, and morall
vertues, were and be conteyned in the
workes and bookes, that the wyſe and
godlie man, ſir Thomas More knighte,
ſometyme lorde Chauncellour of England (my dere vncle) wrote in the En-
glyſh tonge, ſo many, and ſo well, as no
one Engliſhman (I ſuppoſe) euer wrote
the like, whereby his workes be worthy to be hadde and redde of euerye
Engliſhe man, that is ſtudious or deſirous to know and learne, not onelye
the eloquence and propertie of the Engliſh tongē, but alſo the trewe do-
ctryne of Chriſtes catholike fayth, the confutacion of deteſtable hereſyes,
or the godly morall vertues that appertaine to the framinge and four-
minge of mennes maners and conſciences, to liue a vertuous and deuout
chriſten life, and when I further conſidered, that thoſe workes of his
were not yet all imprinted, and thoſe that were imprinted, were in ſeue-
rall volumes and bokes, whereby it were likely, that aſwell thoſe bokes
of his that were already abrode in print, as thoſe ỹ were yet vnprinted,
ſhould in time percaſe periſh and vtterly vaniſh away (to the great loſſe
and detriment of many) vnleſſe they were gathered together and printed
in one whole volume, for theſe cauſes (my moſt gracious liege Lady) I dyd
diligētly collect and gather together, as many of thoſe his workes, bokes,
letters, and other writinges, printed and vnprinted in ỹ Engliſh tonge, as
I could come by, and the ſame (certain yeres in the euil world paſt, keping
in my handes, very ſurely and ſafely) now lately haue cauſed to be imprin

C.ii.   ted

ted in this one volume, to thintent, not onely that euery man ẙ will now
in our dayes, maye haue and take commoditie by them, but also that they
may be preserued for the profit like wise of our posteritie. VVhich workes
who so will take paines diligently and aduisedly to peruse and rede, shall
therby shortly attain gret knowledge, aswel for the incresing of al kindes
of godly vertues and holy liuinge, as for the confirming of his owne faith,
and eschuing and confuting of all peruerse opinions, false doctrine, and de
uillyshe heresies, if he be not vtterly destitute of Gods grace, and blinded
both with obstinate and stubburne malice, and also with proude and arrogant presumptiō. And this volume thus finished the last day of Aprill
in this yeare of oure Lorde G O D. 1557. I youre graces humble obediēte
and faithfull subiect, do dedicate vnto your most excellent maiestie, as to
that person, to whom specially of all worldelye creatures, I truste this
boke shalbe moste acceptable, both for that (I thinke) that it beinge red
of many, as it is likely to be, shall much helpe forwarde youre Maiesties
most godly purpose, in purging this youre realme of all wicked heresies,
(which are, thankes be to almighty God, thorowe his great goodnes and
your Maiesties meanes, very much abated, and as I trust, if it may please
god to graunt your highnes lōg to reigne ouer vs, which I beseche him of
his most mercifull goodnes to do, in time shalbe clearely extinct) and for
that also that syr Thomas More(the auethor of these workes) whyle he
lyued, dyd beare towardes your highnesse a speciall zeale, an entier affection, and reuerent deuocion: and on thother syde lyke wyse your grace (as
it is well knowen)had towardes him in his life time, a beneuolent mynde
and synguler fauoure, not onelye for his great learnynge, but also for his
moch more vertue. And I am fully perswaded, ẙ your highnes good affe-
ctiō towardes him, is no whyt mynysshed now after his death, but rather
by his worthy workes and godly ende more and more encreased, who now
(beynge with almyghtie G O D, and lyuynge in heauen with hym)with
muche greater zeale and deuocion towardes your maiestie, than he had
whyle he lyued here in earth, ceaseth not to praye to God for the kinges
maiestie, for your hyghnesse, your subiectes, your realmes, and domynions,
and for the common welth, and catholyke religion of the same, and for
all christen realmes also. And this cōmodious and profytable boke thus
beynge dedicated vnto your hyghnes, I your obedient subiect most hum-
blye praye and beseche your maiestie, to be the patrone and defendour of
the same, wherby I am well assured, it shall muche the rather, be ioyously
enbrased and had in estymacion of all trew Englyshe hartes.

LIFE AND DEATH OF SIR THOMAS MORE, KNIGHT

by Nicholas Harpsfield (*ca.* 1557)

This manuscript copy of Nicholas Harpsfield's *Life and Death of Sir Thomas More* was taken, as indicated by the note at top, "from Mr. Thomas More's study among other books at Greenstreet, Mr. Wayfarer's house, when Mr. More [of Barnborough, grandson of Sir Thomas More] was apprehended the xiiith of April 1582." Although Harpsfield completed this biography *ca.* 1557, it was not published until 1932. Indebted to William Roper's recollections, Harpsfield's *Life* presents More as both a spiritual and secular figure. Harpsfield's More is the first English martyr among the laity, who serves as an "ambassador" and "messenger" to them. In his conclusion, Harpsfield connects the sight of More's severed head on London Bridge to the death of Cicero centuries earlier: "A rueful and a pitiful spectacle for all good Citizens and other good Christians — and much more lamentable — to see their Christian English Cicero's head in such sort, then it was to the Romans to see the head of Marcus Tullius Cicero set up in the same City and place where he had, by his great eloquent orations, preserved many an innocent from imminent danger and peril, and had preserved the whole City, by his great industry, from the mischievous conspiracy of Catiline and his seditious accomplices."

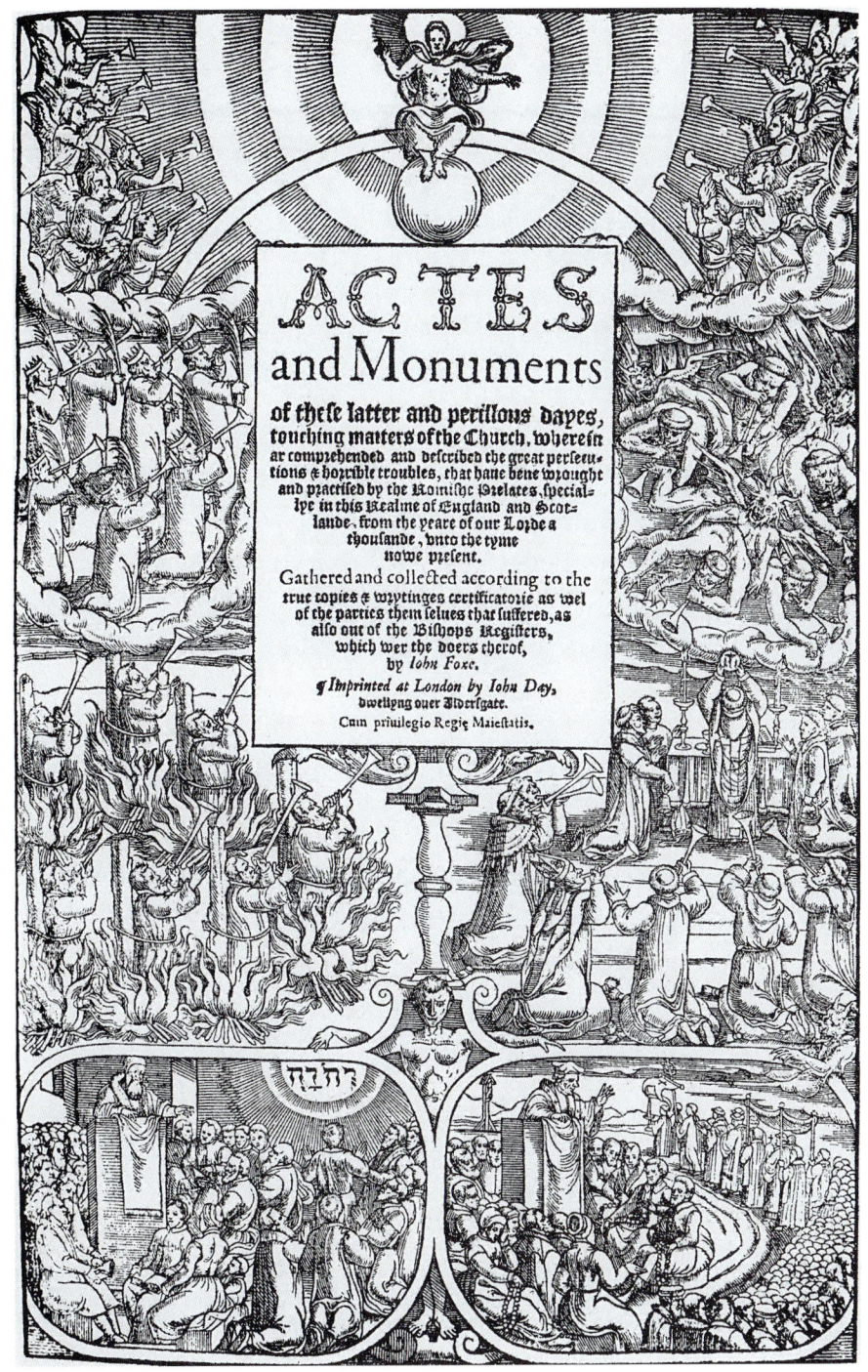

ACTS AND MONUMENTS

by John Foxe (1563–83)

John Foxe's *Acts and Monuments*, commonly known as Foxe's *Book of Martyrs,* was published in English in 1563, 1570, 1576, and 1583, in editions ranging from 1,800 large folio pages to 2,300 pages. Foxe presents Thomas More as a "hunter of heretics" whose "blind devotion" eventually brought the axe down "upon his own neck." Foxe's More is a tragic "over-reacher," "full of imaginations" and "too much given to mocking," a man who "could not tell his tale without laughing." Foxe withdrew, however, his harshest criticisms of More from his second edition, acknowledging those charges as false. He strongly maintained, however, that More pretended "falsely to face us out" about Thomas Bilney's recanting at his death, a death More authorized as Lord Chancellor. Despite his criticisms, Foxe called More "a man otherwise of pregnant wit . . . for his learning above the common sort of his estate: esteemed industrious no less in his studies than well exercised in his pen."

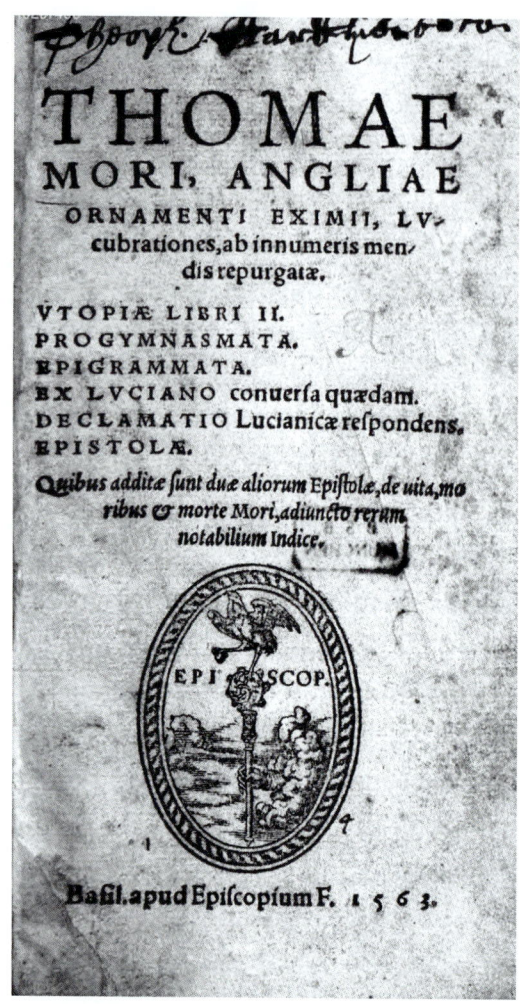

THOMAE MORI LUCUBRATIONES

(1563)

Printed at Basle by the Froben Press in 1563, this first edition of
Thomas More's Latin works included the most famous literary works,
except *Richard III,* and sixteen letters mostly of Erasmus and More.
A folio of 608 pages from Erasmus's famous printer, *Lucrubrations* has
been said to represent the "Erasmian, humanist More." It contains the
first printed edition of More's 1515 *Letter to Dorp,* defending Erasmus.

THOMÆ MORI

ANGLI, VIRI ERVDI-
TIONIS PARITER AC VIR-
TVTIS NOMINE CLARISSI-
MI, ANGLIÆQVE OLIM
CANCELLARII,

Omnia, quæ hucuſque ad manus noſtras peruenerunt, Latina Operai
quorum aliqua nunc primum in lucem prodeunt, reliqua
verò multo quàm antea caſti-
gatiora.

HORVM OMNIVM ELENCHVM
Pagina duodecima commonſtrabit.

LOVANII;
Apud Ioannem Bogardum ſub Biblijs
Aureis, Anno **1565.**

THOMAE MORI OPERA OMNIA
(1565, 1566)

Thomas More's Latin works were published in Louvain in 1565 and again in 1566. The next and only other collected edition of the Latin works was printed in Frankfurt, Germany, in 1689. The title above in translation is THOMAS MORE / THE ENGLISHMAN, A MAN / FOR BOTH LEARNING AND VIRTUE / MOST RENOWNED, AND FORMERLY / CHANCELLOR OF ENGLAND: / All his Latin writings which have up until now come into our hands; / of which some are now published for the first time, and the rest / much more correctly printed than before / OF ALL THESE WORKS A COMPLETE INDEX / *Is displayed, beginning on page twelve.* LOUVAIN / Johannes Bogardus, "Golden Books" / 1565 A.D.

TRES THOMAE.

SEV

De S. THOMÆ Apostoli rebus gestis.

De S. THOMA Archiepiscopo Can-
tuariensi & Martyre.

D. THOMÆ MORI Angliæ quon-
dam Cancellarij VITA.

*His adiecta est ORATIO FVNEBRIS
in laudem R. P. Arnoldi de Ganthois
Abbatis Marchennensis.*

AVTHORE
THOMA STAPLETONO ANGLO
S. Theolog. Doctore.

*Summa rerum singularium CAPITA pag. post epistolam
dedicatoriam proxima indicantur.*

DVACI,
Ex officina Ioannis Bogardi
CIƆ. IƆ. LXXXVIII.

VITA THOMAE MORI
by Thomas Stapleton (1588)

In 1588, Thomas Stapleton published the biographies of *Three Thomases:* the apostle St. Thomas, the English Archbishop St. Thomas Becket, and the "sometime English Chancellor" Thomas More. Stapleton had access to the More family, and this biography is the sole source for many of the personal letters that Thomas More wrote. Stapleton's goal is to display "the greatness of More" and his "high excellence in all virtue and knowledge," through a "thoroughly authentic account of Thomas More's life, and the true cause, the manner, and the circumstances of his martyrdom." Drawing on "abundant authentic information" and written after a review of "all contemporary writers" who commented on More's life, Stapleton describes his book as "a complete and even worthy history" of More, one that manifests "the power of truth, the radiance of piety, and the light of justice." Stapleton argues that More is his country's "chief glory," and Stapleton's *Life* would be one of the sources of the Elizabethan play *Sir Thomas More*.

The Book of Sir Thomas More[1]

by Anthony Munday, Henry Chettle,
Thomas Decker, Thomas Heywood, William Shakespeare

[*Censor Edmund Tilney, Master of Revels, writes:*]
*Leave out the insurrection wholly and the cause
thereof, and begin with Sir Thomas More at the
Mayor's sessions, with a report afterwards of his good
service done being Sheriff of London upon a mutiny
against the Lombards—only a short report, and not
otherwise, at your own perils.*

E. Tilney

I.1

*Enter at one end John Lincoln with George Betts
and clown Ralph Betts together; at the other end
enters Francis de Barde, and Doll Williamson,
a lusty woman, he haling her by the arm.*

DOLL
Whither wilt thou hale[2] me?

BARDE
Whither I please; thou art my prize and I plead
purchase of thee.

DOLL
Purchase of me? Away ye rascal! I am an honest,
plain carpenter's wife and though I have no beauty
to like a husband, yet whatsoever is mine scorns to
stoop to a stranger. Hand off then when I bid thee!

BARDE
Go with me quietly, or I'll compel thee.

DOLL
Compel me, ye dog's face? Thou think'st thou
hast the goldsmith's wife in hand, whom thou
enticed'st from her husband with all his plate, and
when thou turned'st her home to him again, mad'st
him, like an ass, pay for his wife's board.

BARDE
So will I make thy husband too, if please me.
*Enter Caveler with a pair of doves, Williamson
the carpenter and Sherwin following him.*

DOLL
Here he comes himself; tell him so if thou dar'st.

CAVELER [*To Williamson.*]
Follow me no further; I say thou shalt not have
them.

WILLIAMSON
I bought them in Cheapside,[3] and paid my money
for them.

SHERWIN
He did, sir, indeed, and you offer him wrong,
both to take them from him and not restore him
his money neither.

CAVELER
If he paid for them, let it suffice that I possess
them. Beef and brewis[4] may serve such hinds. Are
pigeons meat for a coarse[5] carpenter?

LINCOLN [*Aside to George Betts.*]
It is hard when Englishmen's patience must be
thus jetted[6] on by strangers, and they not dare to
revenge their own wrongs.

GEORGE BETTS [*Aside to Lincoln.*]
Lincoln, let's beat them down, and bear no more
of these abuses.

LINCOLN [*Aside to George Betts.*]
We may not, Betts. Be patient and hear more.

DOLL
How now, husband? What, one stranger take thy
food from thee, and another thy wife? By'r Lady,
flesh and blood, I think, can hardly brook that.

LINCOLN
Will this gear[7] never be otherwise? Must these
wrongs be thus endured?

GEORGE BETTS
Let us step in, and help to revenge their injury.

---

1 The primary basis for this edition is
W. W. Greg's *The Book of Sir Thomas More*
(Oxford: Oxford University Press, 1911).

For the best scholarly edition, see John
Jowett's *Sir Thomas More* (London: Arden
Shakespeare, 2011). 2 pull along forcibly

3 London's main food market 4 broth
or broth-soaked bread 5 common
6 encroached upon 7 business

BARDE

What art thou that talkst of revenge? My Lord Ambassador shall once more make your Mayor have a check if he punish thee not for this saucy presumption.

WILLIAMSON

Indeed, my Lord Mayor, on the Ambassador's complaint, sent me to Newgate[8] one day because (against my will) I took the wall[9] of a stranger. You may do anything. The goldsmith's wife, and mine now, must be at your commandment.

GEORGE BETTS

The more patient fools are ye both to suffer it.

BARDE

Suffer it? Mend it thou or he if ye can or dare. I tell thee, fellow, an[10] she were the Mayor of London's wife, had I her once in my possession, I would keep her in spite of him that durst say nay.

GEORGE BETTS

I tell thee, Lombard, these words should cost thy best cap,[11] were I not curbed by duty and obedience. The Mayor of London's wife? O God, shall it be thus?

DOLL

Why, Betts, am not I as dear to my husband as my Lord Mayor's wife to him? [*To Williamson.*] And wilt thou so neglectly suffer thine own shame? [*To de Barde.*] Hands off, proud stranger, or by him that bought me, if men's milky hearts dare not strike a stranger, yet women will beat them down, ere they bear these abuses.

BARDE

Mistress, I say you shall along with me.

DOLL

Touch not Doll Williamson, lest she lay thee along on God's dear earth. [*To Caveler.*] And you, sir, that allow such coarse cates[12] to carpenters, whilst pigeons which they pay for must serve your dainty appetite: deliver them back to my husband again or I'll call so many women to mine assistance, as we'll not leave one inch untorn of thee. If our husbands must be bridled by law, and forced to bear your wrongs, their wives will be a little lawless, and soundly beat ye.

CAVELER

Come away, de Bard, and let us go complain to my Lord Ambassador.   *Exeunt both.*

DOLL

Ay, go, and send him among us, and we'll give him his welcome too. I am ashamed that freeborn Englishmen, having beaten strangers within their own bounds, should thus be braved and abused by them at home.

SHERWIN

It is not our lack of courage in the cause, but the strict obedience that we are bound to. I am the goldsmith whose wrongs you talked of, but how to redress yours or mine own is a matter beyond all our abilities.

LINCOLN

Not so, not so, my good friends. I, though a mean man, a broker by profession and named John Lincoln, have long time winked at these vile enormities with mighty impatience, and, as these two brethren here, Bettses by name, can witness, with loss of mine own life would gladly remedy them.

GEORGE BETTS

And he is in a good forwardness,[13] I tell ye, if all hit right.

DOLL

As how, I prithee? Tell it to Doll Williamson.

LINCOLN

You know the Spital sermons[14] begin the next week. I have drawn a bill of our wrongs, and the strangers' insolencies.

GEORGE BETTS

Which he means the preachers shall there openly publish in the pulpit.

WILLIAMSON

Oh, but that they would! I'faith it would tickle[15] our strangers thoroughly.

DOLL

Ay, and if you men durst not undertake it, before

---

8 London's main prison **9** i.e., took the privilege of walking near the wall (the cleaner and safer side of the pavement) **10** if **11** *best cap:* head **12** provisions **13** eagerness **14** *Spital sermons:* Sermons preached on Easter Monday and Tuesday from a special pulpit at St. Mary's Spital outside of Bishopsgate, London **15** vex, provoke

God we women will. Take an honest woman from her husband? Why, it is intolerable!

SHERWIN [*To Lincoln.*]
105   But how find ye the preachers affected to it?

LINCOLN
Master Doctor Standish [will not meddle with such matter in his sermon, but Master Doctor Beale promised that he will undertake to][16] reform it and doubts not but happy success will ensue upon our
110   wrongs. You shall perceive there's no hurt in the bill; here's a copy of it. I pray ye hear it.

ALL
With all our hearts; for God's sake, read it.

LINCOLN (*Reads.*)
"To you all the worshipful lords and masters of this city that will take compassion over the poor
115   people your neighbors, and also of the great importable hurts, losses, and hindrances whereof proceedeth extreme poverty to all the King's subjects that inhabit within this city and surburbs of the same. For so it is that aliens and strangers eat the bread
120   from the fatherless children, and take the living from all the artificers, and the intercourse from all merchants, whereby poverty is so much increased that every man bewaileth the misery of other, for craftsmen be brought to beggary, and merchants to
125   neediness. Wherefore, the premises considered, the redress must be of the commons,[17] knit and united to one part. And as the hurt and damage grieveth all men, so must all men set to their willing power for remedy, and not suffer the said aliens in their
130   wealth, and the natural born men of this region to come to confusion."

DOLL
Before God, 'tis excellent, and I'll maintain the suit to be honest.

SHERWIN
Well, say 'tis read, what is your further meaning
135   in the matter?

GEORGE BETTS
What? Marry, list to me. No doubt but this will store us with friends enough, whose names we will

closely keep in writing, and on May Day[18] next in the morning we'll go forth a-Maying, but make it the worst May Day for the strangers that ever they   140 saw. How say ye? Do ye subscribe, or are ye faint-hearted revolters?

DOLL
Hold thee, George Betts, there's my hand and my heart; by the Lord, I'll make a captain among ye, and do somewhat to be talk of[19] for ever after.   145

WILLIAMSON
My masters, ere we part, let's friendly go and drink together, and swear true secrecy upon our lives.

GEORGE BETTS
There spake an angel; come, let us along then.
Exeunt.

1.2
An arras is drawn, and behind it (as in sessions)
sit the Lord Mayor, Justice Suresby, and other
justices, Sheriff More and the other sheriff
sitting by; Smart is the plaintiff,
Lifter the prisoner at the bar.

LORD MAYOR
Having dispatched our weightier businesses,
We may give ear to petty felonies.
Master Sheriff More, what is this fellow?

MORE
My lord, he stands indicted for a purse.
He hath been tried; the jury is together.   5

LORD MAYOR
Who sent him in?

SURESBY
                That did I, my lord.
Had he had right, he had been hanged ere this,
The only captain of the cutpurse crew.

LORD MAYOR
What is his name?

SURESBY
As his profession is: Lifter, my lord,   10
One that can lift a purse right cunningly.

16 This emendation follows Vittorio Gabrieli and Giorgio Melchiori's reconstruction in *Sir Thomas More* (Manchester: Manchester University Press, 1990). Here and occasionally throughout, a portion of the manuscript is missing or damaged. 17 commoners 18 *May Day:* the first of May. This particular May-Day would come to be known as Ill or Evil May-Day, as is indicated later at 2.1. 19 *somewhat to be talk of:* something to be talked about

LORD MAYOR

And is that he[20] accuses him?

SURESBY

The same, my lord, whom, by your honor's leave,
I must say somewhat to,[21] because I find
15   In some respects he is well worthy blame.

LORD MAYOR

Good Master Justice Suresby, speak your mind.
We are well pleased to give you audience.

SURESBY

Hear me, Smart. Thou art a foolish fellow.
If Lifter be convicted by the law,
20   As I see not how the jury can acquit him,
I'll stand to't thou art guilty of his death.

MORE [*To Lord Mayor.*]

My lord, that's worth the hearing.

LORD MAYOR

Listen then, good Master More.

SURESBY [*To Smart.*]

I tell thee plain, it is a shame for thee
25   With such a sum to tempt necessity.
No less than ten pounds, sir, will serve your turn
To carry in your purse about with ye,
To crack and brag in taverns of your money?
I promise ye, a man that goes abroad
30   With an intent of truth, meeting such a booty,
May be provoked to that he never meant.
What makes so many pilferers and felons
But such fond baits that foolish people lay
To tempt the needy miserable wretch?
35   Ten pounds odd[22] money, this is a pretty sum
To bear about, which were more safe at home.
          Lord Mayor and More whisper.
'Fore God, 'twere well to fine ye as much more
To the relief of the poor prisoners,
To teach ye be [more mindful of][23] your own.

MORE

40   Good my lord, soothe a [little jest][24] for once,
Only to try conclusions in this case.

MAYOR

Content, good Master More. We'll rise awhile
And till the jury can return their verdict
Walk in the garden. How say ye, justices?

ALL JUSTICES

We like it well, my lord; we'll follow ye.   45
          Exeunt Lord Mayor and justices.

MORE

Nay, plaintiff, go you too;
                              Exit Smart.
                    and, officers,
Stand you aside, and leave the prisoner
To me awhile.   *Exeunt all but More and Lifter*
          Lifter, come hither.

LIFTER

What is your worship's pleasure?

MORE

Sirrah, you know that you are known to me   50
And I have often saved ye from this place
Since first I came in office. Thou seest beside
That Justice Suresby is thy heavy friend,
For all the blame that he pretends to Smart
For tempting thee with such a sum of money.   55
I tell thee what: devise me but a means
To pick or cut his purse, and on my credit
And as I am a Christian and a man,
I will procure thy pardon for that jest.

LIFTER

Good Master Shrieve,[25] seek not my overthrow.   60
You know, sir, I have many heavy friends
And more indictments like to come upon me.
You are too deep for me to deal withal;
You are known to be one of the wisest men
That is in England. I pray ye, Master Sheriff,   65
Go not about to undermine my life.

MORE

Lifter, I am true subject to my king.
Thou much mistak'st me, and for thou shalt not
    think
I mean by this to hurt thy life at all,
I will maintain[26] the act when thou hast done it.   70
Thou knowst there are such matters in my hands
As, if I pleased to give them to the jury,
I should not need this way to circumvent[27] thee.
All that I aim at is a merry jest.
Perform it, Lifter, and expect my best.   75

LIFTER

I thank your worship; God preserve your life.

---

20 he who **21** *somewhat to:* something about **22** or so **23** John Shirley's emendation in *Sir Thomas More* (Goulden, 1938) **24** Shirley's emendation **25** Sheriff **26** uphold **27** entrap

But Master Justice Suresby is gone in;
I know not how to come near where he is.

MORE
Let me alone for that; I'll be thy setter.²⁸

80   I'll send him hither to thee presently
Under the color of thine own request
Of private matters to acquaint him with.

LIFTER
If ye do so, sir, then let me alone.
Forty to one but then his purse is gone.

MORE
85   Well said, but see that thou diminish not
One penny of the money, but give it me.
It is the cunning act that credits thee.

LIFTER
I will, good Master Sheriff; I assure ye.
                              Exit More.

I see the purpose of this gentleman
90   Is but to check the folly of the Justice
For blaming others in a desperate case
Wherein himself may fall as soon as any.
To save my life it is a good adventure.²⁹
Silence there, ho! Now doth the Justice enter.
                    Enter Justice Suresby.

SURESBY
95   Now, sirrah, now what is your will with me?
Wilt thou discharge thy conscience like an honest
    man?
What sayst to me, sirrah? Be brief, be brief.

LIFTER
As brief, sir, as I can.
(*Aside.*) If ye stand fair, I will be brief anon.

SURESBY
Speak out and mumble not. What sayst thou,
100   sirrah?

LIFTER
Sir, I am charged, as God shall be my comfort,
With more than's true —

SURESBY
Sir, sir, ye are indeed, "with more than's true,"
For you are flatly charged with felony.
You're charged with more than truth, and that is
105   theft,

More than a true man should be charged withal.
Thou art a varlet;³⁰ that's no more than true.
Trifle not with me; do not, do not, sirrah;
Confess but what thou knowest. I ask no more.

LIFTER
There be, sir, there be, if't shall please your
    worship —   110

SURESBY
"There be," Varlet? What be there? Tell me what
    there be.
Come off or on. "There be," what be there, knave?

LIFTER
There be, sir, diverse very cunning fellows
That while you stand and look them in the face
Will have your purse.   115

SURESBY
Th'art an honest knave.
Tell me what are they? Where they may be
    caught?
Ay, those are they I look for.

LIFTER
                    You talk of me, sir. —
Alas, I am a puny.³¹ There's one, indeed,
Goes by my name; he puts down all for purses   120
[   ]
[   ]

SURESBY
Be as familiar as thou wilt, my knave.
'Tis this I long to know.

LIFTER (*Aside.*)
And you shall have your longing ere ye go.   125
This fellow, sir, perhaps will meet ye thus,
          (*Action [of greeting, embracing].*)
Or thus, or thus, and in kind compliment
Pretend acquaintance, somewhat doubtfully,
And these embraces serve —

SURESBY (*Shrugging gladly.*)
                    Ay, marry, Lifter,
Wherefore serve they?

LIFTER
                    Only to feel   130
Whether you go full under sail or no,
Or that your lading be aboard your bark.³²

28 decoy for a swindler **29** venture **30** rogue **31** unimportant person **32** *lading be aboard your bark:* freight be on your vessel

SURESBY
In plainer English, Lifter, if my purse
Be stored[33] or no?

LIFTER
                         Ye have it, sir.

SURESBY
                              Excellent, excellent.

LIFTER
135   Then, sir, you cannot but for manners' sake
Walk on with him, for he will walk your way,
Alleging either you have much forgot him,
Or he mistakes you.

SURESBY
But in this time has he my purse or no?

LIFTER
140   Not yet, sir, fie! [*Aside.*] No, nor I have not yours.
      [*He takes Suresby's purse.*]
           Enter Lord Mayor, etc.
But now we must forbear; my lords return.

SURESBY
A murrain[34] on't! Lifter, we'll more anon.
Ay, thou sayst true; there are shrewd knaves
     indeed.
               He sits down.
But let them gull me, widgeon me, rook me, fop
     me,[35]
145   I'faith, i'faith, they are too short for me.
Knaves and fools meet when purses go;
Wise men look to their purses well enough.

MORE (*Aside.*)
Lifter, is it done?

LIFTER (*Aside.*)
               Done, Master Shrieve, and there it is.

MORE (*Aside.*)
Then build upon my word, I'll save thy life.

RECORDER
150   Lifter, stand to the bar.
The jury have returned thee guilty; thou must die.
According to the custom, look to it, Master
     Shrieve.

MAYOR
Then gentlemen, as you are wont to do,
Because as yet we have no burial place,

What charity your meaning's to bestow   155
Toward burial of the prisoners now condemned,
Let it be given. There is first for me.

RECORDER
And there's for me.

ANOTHER
                         And me.

SURESBY
Body of me, my purse is gone!

MORE
Gone, sir? What, here? How can that be?   160

MAYOR
Against all reason, sitting on the bench?

SURESBY
Lifter, I talked with you. You have not lifted me,
     ha?

LIFTER
Suspect ye me, sir? Oh what a world is this!

MORE
But hear ye, Master Suresby, are ye sure
Ye had a purse about ye?   165

SURESBY
Sure, Master Shrieve? As sure as you are there,
And in it seven pounds odd money, on my
     faith.

MORE
Seven pounds odd money? What, were you so
     mad,
Being a wise man and a magistrate,
To trust your purse with such a liberal sum?   170
Seven pounds odd money? 'Fore God it is a
     shame
With such a sum to tempt necessity.
I promise ye, a man that goes abroad
With an intent of truth, meeting such a booty,[36]
May be provoked to that he never thought.   175
What makes so many pilferers and felons,
But these fond baits that foolish people lay
To tempt the needy miserable wretch?
Should he be taken now that has your purse,
I'd stand to't, you are guilty of his death,   180
For questionless he would be cast by law.
'Twere a good deed to fine ye as much more

33 full   **34** plague   **35** *gull...fop me:* i.e., defraud me   **36** prize

To the relief of the poor prisoners,
To teach ye lock your money up at home.

SURESBY

185 Well, Master More, you are a merry man.
I find[37] ye, sir, I find ye well enough.

MORE

Nay, ye shall see, sir, trusting thus your money,
And Lifter here in trial for like case,
But that the poor man is a prisoner,
190 It would be now suspected that he had it.
Thus may ye see what mischief often comes
By the fond carriage of such needless sums.

MAYOR

Believe me, Master Suresby, this is strange.
You, being a man so settled in assurance,
195 Will fall in that which you condemned in other.

MORE

Well, Master Suresby, there's your purse again,
And all your money. Fear nothing of More:
Wisdom still [doth bid ye watch][38] the door.
Exeunt.

1.3

Enter the Earls of Shrewsbury and Surrey,
Sir Thomas Palmer and Sir Roger Cholmley.

SHREWSBURY

My Lord of Surrey, and Sir Thomas Palmer,
Might I with patience tempt your grave advice?
I tell ye true, that in these dangerous times
I do not like this frowning vulgar brow.
5 My searching eye did never entertain
A more distracted countenance of grief
Than I have late observed
In the displeasèd commons of the city.

SURREY

'Tis strange, that from his princely clemency,
10 So well a tempered mercy and a grace
To all the aliens in this fruitful land,
That this high crested[39] insolence should spring
From them that breathe from his majestic bounty,
That, fattened with the traffic[40] of our country,
15 Already leap into his subjects' face.

PALMER

Yet Sherwin, hindered to commence his suit
Against de Bard, by the Ambassador
By supplication made unto the King,
Who, having first enticed away his wife
20 And got his plate, near worth four hundred
pound,
To grieve some wronged citizens that found
This vile disgrace oft cast into their teeth,
Of late sues Sherwin, and arrested him
For money for the boarding of his wife.

SURREY

25 The more knave Barde, that, using Sherwin's
goods,
Doth ask him interest for the occupation.[41]
I like not that, my Lord of Shrewsbury.
He's ill bestead[42] that lends a well paced horse
Unto a man that will not find him meat.

CHOLMLEY

30 My Lord of Surrey will be pleasant still.

PALMER

I being then employed by your honors
To stay the broil[43] that fell about the same,
Where by persuasion I enforced the wrongs
And urged the grief of the displeasèd city,
35 He answered me, and with a solemn oath,
That, if he had the Mayor of London's wife,
He would keep her in despite of any English.[44]

SURREY

'Tis good, Sir Thomas, then, for you and me
Your wife is dead and I a bachelor.
40 If no man can possess his wife alone,
I am glad, Sir Thomas Palmer, I have none.

CHOLMLEY

If 'a[45] take my wife, 'a shall find her meat.

SURREY

And reason good, Sir Roger Cholmley, too.
If these hot Frenchmen needsly[46] will have sport,
45 They should in kindness yet defray the charge.
'Tis hard when men possess our wives in quiet
And yet leave us in to discharge[47] their diet.

SHREWSBURY

My lord, our caters[48] shall not use the market

---

37 understand   38 Shirley's emendation
39 proud   40 commerce   41 use
42 situated   43 quarrel   44 Tilney strikes
out "English" and adds "man."   45 he
46 necessarily   47 pay for   48 servants in
charge of ordering supplies for a household

For our provision, but some stranger[49] now
50   Will take the victuals from him he hath bought.
A carpenter, as I was late informed,
Who, having bought a pair of doves in Cheap,
Immediately a Frenchman[50] took them from him
And beat the poor man for resisting him;
55   And when the fellow did complain his wrongs,
He was severely punished for his labour.

SURREY
But if the English blood be once but up,
As I perceive their hearts already full,
I fear me much, before their spleens be cold,
60   Some of these saucy aliens for their pride
Will pay for't soundly, wheresoe'er it lights.
This tide of rage, that with the eddy strives,
I fear me much will drown too many lives.

CHOLMLEY
Now afore God, your honors, pardon me.
65   Men of your place and greatness are to blame—
I tell ye true, my lords—in that his Majesty
Is not informal[51] of this base abuse,
And daily wrongs are offered to his subjects,
For if he were, I know his gracious wisdom
70   Would soon redress it.
                            Enter a messenger.

SHREWSBURY
Sirrah, what news?

CHOLMLEY
                            None good, I fear.

MESSENGER
My lord, ill news, and worse I fear will follow
If speedily it be not looked unto.
The city is in an uproar and the Mayor
75   Is threatened if he come out of his house.
A number of poor artificers[52] [are out
Inflamed to kill the hated aliens.][53]

[CHOLMLEY]
['Twas to be] feared what this would come unto.
This follows on the doctor's publishing
80   The bill of wrongs in public at the Spital.

SHREWSBURY
That Doctor Beale may chance beshrew[54] himself
For reading of the bill.

PALMER
Let us go gather forces to the Mayor
For quick suppressing this rebellious rout.

SURREY
Now I bethink myself of Master More,   85
One of the sheriffs, a wise and learned gentleman,
And in especial favor with the people.
He, backed with other grave and sober men,
May by his gentle and persuasive speech
Perhaps prevail more than we can with power.   90

SHREWSBURY
Believe me but your honor well advises.
Let us make haste, or I do greatly fear
Some to their graves this morning's work will
   bear.   *Exeunt.*

2.1
Enter Lincoln, George and Clown Bettses,
Williamson, Sherwin and other armed, Doll in
a shirt of mail, a headpiece, sword and buckler,
a crew attending.

CLOWN BETTS
Come, come; we'll tickle their turnips; we'll butter their boxes![55] Shall strangers rule the roost? Yes,
but we'll baste the roast. Come, come; a flaunt, a
flaunt.[56]

GEORGE BETTS
Brother, give place and hear John Lincoln speak.   5

CLOWN BETTS
Ay, Lincoln my leader,
And Doll my true breeder,
With the rest of our crew
Shall ran-tan-tarra-ran.
Do all they what they can,   10
Shall we be bobbed, braved?[57] No.
Shall we be held under? No.
We are free-born
And do take scorn
To be used so!   15

DOLL
Peace there, I say! Hear Captain Lincoln speak!
Keep silence till we know his mind at large.

49 Tilney adds "Lombard" and strikes out "stranger."   **50** Tilney adds "Lombard" and strikes out "Frenchman."   **51** informed   **52** craftsmen   **53** Shirley's emendation, and the next   **54** blame   **55** *tickle…boxes:* beat them up   **56** display   oneself ostentatiously   **57** *bobbed, braved:* beaten

Clown Betts [*To Lincoln.*]

Then largely deliver. Speak, bully,[58] and he that presumes to interrupt thee in thy oration, this for
20   him!

Lincoln

Then, gallant bloods, you whose free souls do scorn
To bear th'enforcèd wrongs of aliens,
Add rage to resolution; fire the houses
Of these audacious strangers! This is St. Martin's,
25   And yonder dwells Meautis, a wealthy Picardy,
At the Green Gate,
De Bard, Peter van Hollock, Adrian Martin,
With many more outlandish fugitives.
Shall these enjoy more privilege than we
In our own country? Let's then become their
30   slaves!
Since justice keeps not them in greater awe,
We'll be ourselves rough ministers at law.

Clown Betts

Use no more swords,
Nor no more words,
35   But fire the houses!
Brave Captain Courageous,
Fire me their houses!

Doll

Ay, for we may as well make bonfires on May Day
as at Midsummer[59]; we'll alter the day in the calen-
40   dar, and set it down in flaming letters.

Sherwin

Stay! That would much endanger the whole city,
whereto I would not the least prejudice.

Doll

No, nor I neither—so may mine own house be
burned for company. I'll tell ye what: we'll drag the
45   strangers out into Moorfields, and there bombast
them till they stink again.

Clown Betts

And that's soon done, for they smell for fear
already.

George Betts

Let some of us enter the strangers' houses,
50   And if we find them there, then bring them forth.

Doll

But if ye bring them forth ere ye find them, I'll
never allow of that.

Clown Betts

Now, Mars, for thy honor,
Dutch or French,
So it be a wench,   55
I'll upon her.

[*Exeunt Clown, Sherwin, and others.*]

Williamson

Now lads, how shall we labor in our safety?
I hear the Mayor hath gathered men in arms
And that Shrieve More an hour ago received
Some of the Privy Council in at Ludgate.   60
Force now must make our peace or else we fall.
'Twill soon be known we are the principal.[60]

Doll

And what of that? If thou be'st afraid, husband,
go home again and hide thy head for, by the Lord,
I'll have a little sport now I am at it.   65

George Betts

Let's stand upon our guard, and if they come
Receive them as they were our enemies.

Enter Sherwin and the rest.

Clown Betts

A purchase, a purchase![61] We have found, we ha'
found—

Doll

What?   70

Clown Betts

Nothing, not a French Fleming nor a Fleming
French to be found, but all fled, in plain English.

Lincoln

How now, have you found any?

Sherwin

No, not one; they're all fled.

Lincoln

Then fire the houses, that, the Mayor being busy   75
About the quenching of them, we may 'scape.
Burn down their kennels; let us, straight away,
Lest this day prove to us an ill May Day.

---

58 a term of endearment   **59** June 24, when lighting bonfires was traditional   **60** main persons responsible   **61** plundered prize

CLOWN BETTS

Fire, fire! I'll be the first.

80　If hanging come, 'tis welcome; that's the worst.

Exeunt.

2.2

Enter Sheriff More and the Lord Mayor.

MAYOR

What, Sir John Munday, are you hurt?

SIR JOHN

A little knock, my lord. There was even now

A sort of prentices playing at cudgels.

I did command them to their masters' houses,

5　But one of them, backed by the other crew,

Wounded me in the forehead with his cudgel;

And now, I fear me, they are gone to join

With Lincoln, Sherwin, and their dangerous

train.[62]

MORE

The captains of this insurrection

10　Have ta'en themselves to arms, and came but now

To both the Counters,[63] where they have released

Sundry indebted prisoners, and from thence

I hear that they are gone into St Martin's,

Where they intend to offer violence

15　To the amazed Lombards. Therefore, my lord,

If we expect the safety of the city,

'Tis time that force or parley do encounter

With these displeasèd men.

Enter a messenger.

MAYOR

How now, what news?

MESSENGER

My lord, the rebels have broke open Newgate,

20　From whence they have delivered many prisoners,

Both felons and notorious murderers,

That desperately cleave to their lawless train.

MAYOR

Up with the drawbridge; gather some forces

To Cornhill and Cheapside. And, gentlemen,

25　If diligence be used on every side,

A quiet ebb will follow this rough tide.

Enter Shrewsbury, Surrey, Palmer, Cholmley.

SHREWSBURY

Lord Mayor, his Majesty, receiving notice

Of this most dangerous insurrection,

Hath sent my Lord of Surrey and myself,

Sir Thomas Palmer and our followers　　　30

To add unto your forces our best means

For pacifying of this mutiny.

In God's name, then, set on with happy speed.[64]

The King laments if one true subject bleed.

SURREY

I hear they mean to fire the Lombards' houses.　35

O power, what art thou in a madman's eyes?

Thou mak'st the plodding idiot bloody-wise.

MORE

My lords, I doubt not but we shall appease

With a calm breath this flux[65] of discontent.

PALMER

To call them to a parley questionless　　　40

May fall out good. 'Tis well said, Master More.

MORE

Let's to these simple men, for many sweat

Under this act that knows not the law's debt

Which hangs upon their lives. For silly[66] men

Plod on they know not how; like a fool's pen　45

That ending shows not any sentence writ

Linked but to common reason or slightest wit.

These follow for no harm, but yet incur

Self penalty with those that raised this stir.

I' God's name on, to calm our private foes　50

With breath of gravity, not dangerous blows.

Exeunt.

2.3[67]

Enter Lincoln, Doll, Clown Betts, George Betts,
[Sherwin,] Williamson, others,
[and a sergeant-at-arms].

LINCOLN

Peace, hear me! He that will not see a red herring

at a Harry groat,[68] butter at eleven pence a pound,

meal at nine shillings a bushel, and beef at four no-

bles[69] a stone, list to me.

---

62 Tilney marks these opening lines for deletion.　**63** debtors' prisons in London　**64** success　**65** flow　**66** defenseless; ignorant; deserving of pity　**67** This scene is widely accepted to be in Shakespeare's hand.　**68** *Harry groat:* a type of coin minted by Henry VIII　**69** English gold coins

GEORGE BETTS

5 It will come to that pass, if strangers be suffered.
Mark him!

LINCOLN

Our country is a great eating country; *argo*,[70] they
eat more in our country than they do in their own.

CLOWN BETTS

By a halfpenny loaf a day, troy weight.

LINCOLN

10 They bring in strange roots, which is merely to the
undoing of our poor prentices,[71] for what's a sorry
parsnip to a good heart?

WILLIAMSON

Trash, trash! They breed sore eyes, and 'tis enough
to infect the city with the palsy.

LINCOLN

15 Nay, it has infected it with the palsy, for these bastards of dung—as you know they grow in dung—
have infected us, and it is our infection will make
the city shake, which partly comes through the
eating of parsnips.

CLOWN BETTS

20 True, and pumpkins together.

SERGEANT

What say you to the mercy of the King?
Do you refuse it?

LINCOLN

You would have us upon th' hip,[72] would you? No,
marry, do we not. We accept of the King's mercy,
25 but we will show no mercy upon the strangers.

SERGEANT

You are the simplest things that ever stood
In such a question.

LINCOLN

How say you now? Prentices "simple"? Down
with him!

ALL

30 Prentices simple? Prentices simple?
Enter the Lord Mayor, the Earl of Surrey,
and the Earl of Shrewsbury.

SHERIFF

Hold, in the King's name, hold!

SURREY

Friends, masters, countrymen—

MAYOR

Peace ho, peace! I charge you, keep the peace.

SHREWSBURY

My masters, countrymen—

SHERWIN

The noble Earl of Shrewsbury, let's hear him.

GEORGE BETTS

We'll hear the Earl of Surrey.   35

LINCOLN

The Earl of Shrewsbury.

GEORGE BETTS

We'll hear both.

ALL

Both, both, both, both!

LINCOLN

Peace, I say peace! Are you men of wisdom, or
what are you?   40

SURREY

What you will have them, but not men of wisdom.

SOME

We'll not hear my Lord of Surrey.

OTHERS

No, no, no, no, no! Shrewsbury, Shrewsbury!

MORE

Whiles they are o'er the bank of their obedience,
Thus will they bear down all things.   45

LINCOLN

Shrieve[73] More speaks. Shall we hear Shrieve More
speak?

DOLL

Let's hear him. 'A[74] keeps a plentiful shrievaltry,[75]
and 'a made my brother Arthur Watchins Sergeant
Safe's yeoman. Let's hear Shrieve More!   50

ALL

Shrieve More, More, More, Shrieve More!

---

70 Lincoln's mistake for the Latin
ergo (therefore) **71** apprentices

72 *upon th' hip*: at a disadvantage
73 Sheriff **74** He **75** Doll

mispronounces "shrievalty," which is "the
office of sheriff."

MORE

Even by the rule you have among yourselves,
Command still audience.

SOME

Surrey, Surrey!

OTHERS

55 More, More!

LINCOLN AND GEORGE BETTS

Peace! Peace! Silence! Peace!

MORE

You that have voice and credit with the number,
Command them to a stillness.

LINCOLN

A plague on them, they will not hold their peace.
60 The devil cannot rule them.

MORE

Then what a rough and riotous charge have you,
To lead those that the devil cannot rule.
Good masters, hear me speak.

DOLL

Ay, by th' Mass, will we. More, thou'rt a good
65 housekeeper, and I thank thy good worship for my
brother Arthur Watchins.

ALL

Peace, peace!

MORE

Look! What you do offend you cry upon:
That is, the peace. Not one of you here present,
70 Had there such fellows lived when you were babes
That could have topped[76] the peace as now you
    would,
The peace wherein you have till now grown up
Had been ta'en from you, and the bloody times
Could not have brought you to the state of
    men.
75 Alas, poor things; what is it you have got,
Although we grant you get the thing you seek?

GEORGE BETTS

Marry, the removing of the strangers,[77] which
cannot choose but much advantage the poor handicrafts[78] of the city.

MORE

Grant them removed, and grant that this your
    noise   80
Hath chid down all the majesty of England.
Imagine that you see the wretched strangers,
Their babies at their backs, with their poor
    luggage
Plodding to th' ports and coasts for transportation,
And that you sit as kings in your desires,   85
Authority quite silenced by your brawl,
And you in ruff[79] of your opinions clothed:
What had you got? I'll tell you. You had taught
How insolence and strong hand should prevail,
How order should be quelled, and by this pattern 90
Not one of you should live an aged man,
For other ruffians, as their fancies wrought —
With selfsame hand, self reasons, and self right —
Would shark[80] on you, and men, like ravenous
    fishes,
Would feed on one another.   95

DOLL

Before God, that's as true as the Gospel.

LINCOLN

Nay, this' a sound fellow, I tell you. Let's mark
him.

MORE

Let me set up before your thoughts, good friends,
One supposition, which if you will mark   100
You shall perceive how horrible a shape
Your innovation[81] bears. First, 'tis a sin
Which oft th'apostle did forewarn us of,
Urging obedience to authority;
And 'twere no error if I told you all   105
You were in arms 'gainst God.

ALL

Marry, God forbid that!

MORE

Nay, certainly you are.
For, to the king, God hath his office lent
Of dread,[82] of justice, power, and command,   110
Hath bid him rule, and willed you to obey;
And to add ampler majesty to this,
He hath not only lent the king his figure,
His throne and sword, but given him his own
    name,

---

76 beheaded; killed or destroyed   **79** vainglory **80** prey **81** insurrection;
77 foreigners **78** makers of handicrafts   rebellion **82** respect, reverence

Calls him a god on earth. What do you, then,
Rising 'gainst him that God himself installs,
But rise 'gainst God? What do you to your souls
In doing this? Oh, desperate as you are,
Wash your foul minds with tears, and those same
    hands
That you, like rebels, lift against the peace
Lift up for peace, and your unreverent knees,
Make them your feet. To kneel to be forgiven
Is safer wars than ever you can make,
Whose discipline is riot.[83]
In, in, to your obedience! Why, even your hurly[84]
Cannot proceed but by obedience.
Tell me but this: What rebel captain,
As mutinies are incident,[85] by his name
Can still the rout? Who will obey a traitor?
Or how can well that proclamation sound
When there is no addition[86] but "a rebel"
To qualify[87] a rebel? You'll put down strangers,
Kill them, cut their throats, possess their houses,
And lead the majesty of law in lyam[88]
To slip[89] him like a hound — alas, alas!
Say now the King,
As he is clement if th'offender mourn,
Should so much come too short of your great
    trespass
As but to banish you: whither would you go?
What country, by the nature of your error,
Should give you harbor? Go you to France or
    Flanders,
To any German province, Spain or Portugal,
Nay, anywhere that not adheres to England —
Why, you must needs be strangers. Would you be
    pleased
To find a nation of such barbarous temper
That, breaking out in hideous violence,
Would not afford you an abode on earth,
Whet their detested knives against your throats,
Spurn you like dogs, and like as if that God
Owed[90] not nor made not you, nor that the
    elements
Were not all appropriate to your comforts,
But chartered unto[91] them? What would you
    think
To be thus used? This is the strangers' case,
And this your mountainish inhumanity.

ALL
Faith, 'a says true. Let's do as we may be done
    by.[92]

LINCOLN
We'll be ruled by you, Master More, if you'll stand
our friend to procure our pardon.

MORE
Submit you to these noble gentlemen,
Entreat their mediation to the King,
Give up yourself to form, obey the magistrate,
And there's no doubt but mercy may be found,
If you so seek it.

ALL
We yield, and desire his Highness' mercy.
They lay by their weapons.

MORE
No doubt his Majesty will grant it you.
But you must yield to go to several prisons,
Till that his Highness' will be further known.

ALL
Most willingly, whither you will have us.

SHREWSBURY
Lord Mayor, let them be sent to several prisons,
And there in any case be well entreated.[93]
My Lord of Surrey, please you to take horse
And ride to Cheapside, where the aldermen
Are with their several companies in arms.
Will them to go unto their several wards,[94]
Both for the stay[95] of further mutiny,
And for the apprehending of such persons
As shall contend.

SURREY
        I go, my noble lord.
                           Exit.

SHREWSBURY
We'll straight go tell his Highness these good
    news.
Withal,[96] Shrieve More, I'll tell him how your
    breath
Hath ransomed many a subject from sad death.
    Exeunt Shrewsbury and Cholmley.

---

83 *To kneel … riot:* i.e., To repent your lack of discipline is the sounder war to wage. **84** commotion, tumult **85** likely to occur **86** identifying mark of one's occupation or rank **87** give recognized status to **88** a leash for hounds **89** release a hunting animal from a leash **90** owned **91** *chartered unto:* licensed to **92** See Mt 7:12. **93** treated **94** districts **95** prevention **96** Moreover

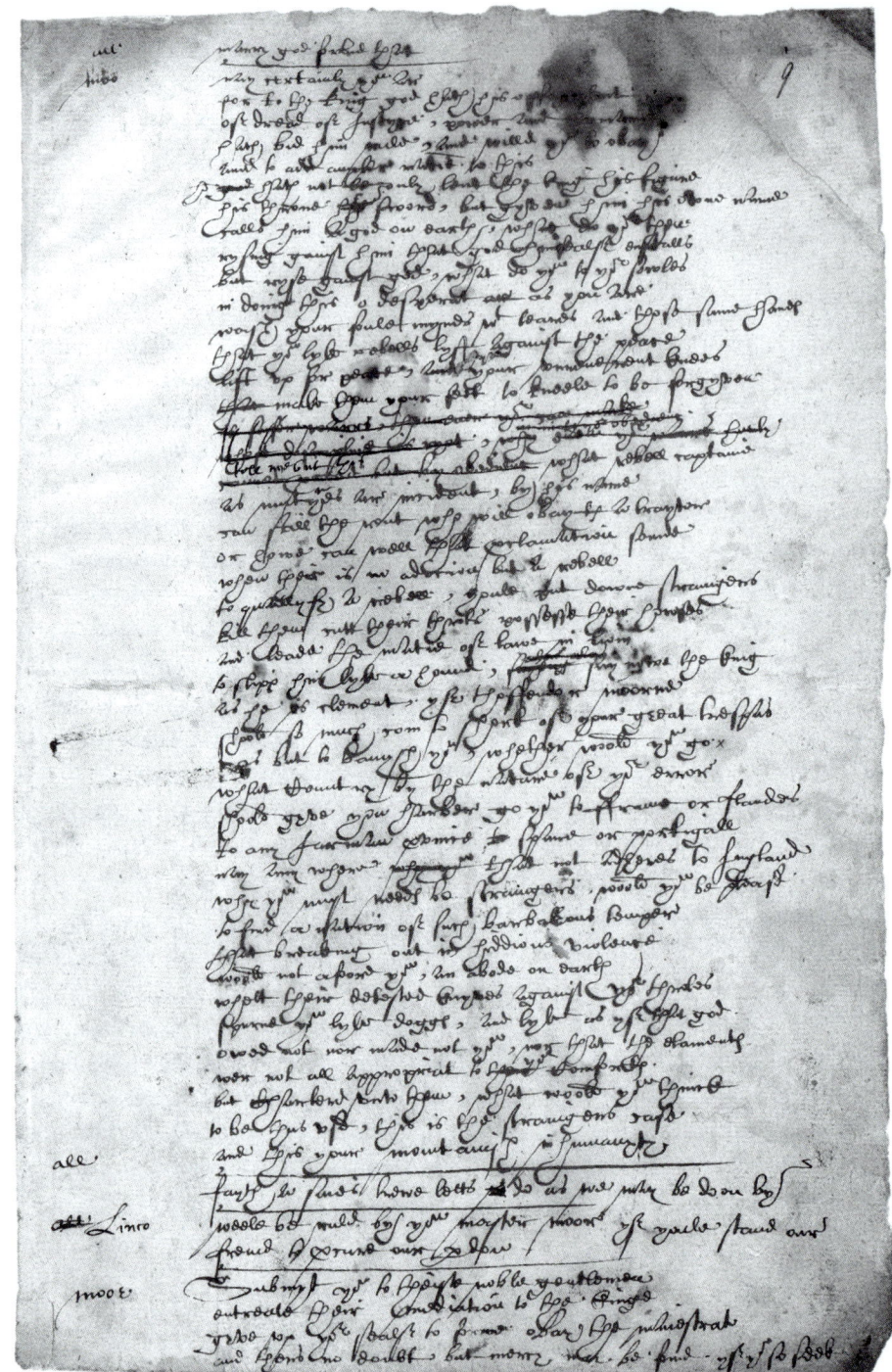

This scene in which Thomas More quells a London riot in *The Booke of Sir Thomas Moore* (*ca.* 1592–95) is attributed to Shakespeare, here in his own handwriting. The underscored lines at the bottom read:

	and this your momtanish [mountainish] inhumanyty
all	faith, 'a saies trewe. letts us do as we may be doon by
Linco[ln]	weele [We'll] be rul'd by yo͏ᵘ master moor yf you'le stand our
	friend t' pcure [procure] our pdon [pardon]

This prompt book is in the hands of five London playwrights believed to be Anthony Munday, Henry Chettle, Thomas Dekker, Thomas Heywood, and William Shakespeare. It was first transcribed and published in 1911; for the most complete edition, see John Jowett's *Sir Thomas More* (London: Arden Shakespeare, 2011).

MAYOR

180 Lincoln and Sherwin, you shall both to Newgate,
the rest unto the Counters.

PALMER

Go, guard them hence. A little breath well spent
Cheats expectation in his fair'st event.

DOLL

Well, Sheriff More, thou hast done more with thy
185 good words than all they could with their weapons.
Give me thy hand; keep thy promise now for the
King's pardon, or, by the Lord, I'll call thee a plain
cony-catcher.[97]

LINCOLN

Farewell, Shrieve More, and as we yield by thee,
190 So make our peace; then thou deal'st honestly.

CLOWN BETTS

Ay, and save us from the gallows, else 'a deals double honestly.[98]

They are led away.

MAYOR

Master Shrieve More, you have preserved the city
From a most dangerous fierce commotion,
195 For if this limb of riot here in St. Martin's
Had joined with other branches of the city
That did begin to kindle, 'twould have bred
Great rage. That rage much murder would have
fed.

PALMER

Not steel but eloquence hath wrought this good.
You have redeemed us from much threatened
200 blood.

MORE

My lord and brethren, what I here have spoke,
My country's love and next the city's care
Enjoined[99] me to; which, since it thus prevails,
Think God hath made weak More his instrument
205 To thwart sedition's violent intent.
I think 'twere best, my lord, some two hours
hence
We meet at the Guildhall, and there determine
That through every ward the watch be clad
In armor, but especially provide
210 That at the city gates, selected men,

Substantial citizens, do ward tonight,
For fear of further mischief.

MAYOR

                                   It shall be so.
Enter Shrewsbury.
But yond methink's my Lord of Shrewsbury.

SHREWSBURY

My lord, his Majesty sends loving thanks
To you, your brethren, and his faithful subjects,   215
Your careful[100] citizens. But Master More, to you
A rougher, yet as kind a salutation:
Your name is yet too short; nay, you must kneel.
            [*More kneels.*]
A knight's creation is this knightly steel.
            [*He knights More.*]
Rise up, Sir Thomas More.   220

MORE

I thank his Highness for thus honoring me.

SHREWSBURY

This is but first taste of his princely favor,
For it hath pleased his high Majesty,
Noting your wisdom and deserving merit,
To put this staff of honor in your hand,   225
For he hath chose you of his Privy Council.
            [*He gives More a staff of office.*]

MORE

My lord, for to deny my Sovereign's bounty
Were to drop precious stones into the heaps
Whence first they came.
To urge my imperfections in excuse,   230
Were all as stale as custom. No, my lord,
My service is my King's — good reason why,
Since life or death hangs on our Sovereign's eye.

MAYOR

His Majesty hath honored much the city
In this his princely choice.

MORE

                                   My lord and brethren,   235
Though I depart for [Court] my love shall rest
[True to the home wherewith my youth was
blessed.][101]
I now must sleep in Court; sound sleeps
forbear:

---

97 cheat   **98** *double honestly:* not
honestly at all (as in double-dealing)

99 Compelled   **100** solicitous; concerned
101 Shirley's emendation

The chamberlain to state is public care.

240 Yet in this rising of my private blood,[102]

My studious thoughts shall tend the city's good.

Enter Crofts.

SHREWSBURY

How now, Crofts? What news?

CROFTS

My lord, his Highness sends express command

That a record be entered of this riot,

245 And that the chief and capital offenders

Be thereon straight arraigned, for himself intends

To sit in person on the rest tomorrow

At Westminster.

SHREWSBURY

Lord Mayor, you hear your charge.

Come, good Sir Thomas More, to Court let's

250 hie:[103]

You are th'appeaser of this mutiny.

MORE [*To Mayor.*]

My lord, farewell. New days begets new tides;

Life whirls 'bout fate, then to a grave it slides.

Exeunt severally.

2.4

Enter Sheriff and meet a messenger.

SHERIFF

Messenger, what news?

MESSENGER

Is execution yet performed?

SHERIFF

Not yet; the carts stand ready at the stairs,

And they shall presently away to Tyburn.

MESSENGER

Stay, Master Shrieve; it is the Council's pleasure,

5   For more example in so bad a case,

A gibbet[104] be erected in Cheapside,

Hard by the Standard, whither you must bring

Lincoln and those that were the chief with him

To suffer death, and that immediately.

Enter Officers.

SHERIFF

It shall be done, sir.

Exit messenger.

Officers, be speedy.   10

Call for a gibbet; see it be erected.

Others make haste to Newgate; bid them bring

The prisoners hither, for they here must die.

Away, I say, and see no time be slacked.

OFFICERS

We go, sir.   15

Exeunt some severally; others set up the gibbet.

SHERIFF

That's well said, fellows; now you do your duty.

God, for his pity, help these troublous times.

The street's stopped up with gazing multitudes;

Command our armèd officers with halberds

Make way for entrance of the prisoners.   20

Let proclamation once again be made

That every householder, on pain of death,

Keep in his prentices, and every man

Stand with a weapon ready at his door,

As he will answer to the contrary.   25

OFFICER

I'll see it done, sir.   *Exit.*

Enter another officer.

SHERIFF

Bring them away to execution.

The writ is come above two hours since;

The city will be fined for this neglect.

OFFICER

There's such a press and multitude at Newgate,   30

They cannot bring the carts unto the stairs

To take the prisoners in.

SHERIFF

Then let them come on foot.

We may not dally time with great command.

OFFICER

Some of the Bench, sir, think it very fit

That stay be made and give it out abroad   35

The execution is deferred till morning,

And when the streets shall be a little cleared,

To chain them up, and suddenly dispatch it.

The prisoners are brought in well guarded.

---

102 *private blood:* common origins   **103** go quickly   **104** gallows

SHERIFF

    Stay, in meantime methinks they come along.

40   See, they are coming, so, 'tis very well.

    Bring Lincoln there, the first unto the tree.[105]

CLOWN BETTS

    Ay, for I cry lag,[106] sir.

LINCOLN

    I knew the first, sir, did belong to me.

    This the old proverb now complete doth make:

    That "Lincoln should be hanged for London's

45   sake."

    I' God's name, let's to work:

    [*To Hangman.*]   Fellow, dispatch.

                He goes up.

    I was the foremost man in this rebellion,

    And I the foremost that must die for it.

DOLL

    Bravely, John Lincoln, let thy death express

50   That, as thou lived'st a man, thou died'st no less.

LINCOLN

    Doll Williamson, thine eyes shall witness it.

    Then, to all you that come to view mine end,

    I must confess I had no ill intent,

    But against such as wronged us overmuch.

55   And now I can perceive it was not fit

    That private men should carve out their redress,

    Which way they list.[107] No, learn it now by me:

    Obedience is the best in each degree.

    And asking mercy meekly of my King,

60   I patiently submit me to the law.

    But God forgive them that were cause of it,

    And, as a Christian truly from my heart,

    I likewise crave they would forgive me too.

    [   ]

65   That others by example of the same

    Henceforth be warnèd to attempt[108] the like

    'Gainst any alien that repaireth[109] hither.

    Fare ye well, all; the next time that we meet

    I trust in heaven we shall each other greet.

                He leaps off.

DOLL

70   Farewell, John Lincoln; say all what they can:

    Thou lived'st a good fellow, and died'st an honest

    man.

CLOWN BETTS

    Would I were so far on my journey; the first

    stretch is the worst, methinks.

SHERIFF

    Bring Williamson there forward.

DOLL

    Good Master Shrieve, I have an earnest suit,   75

    And, as you are a man, deny't me not.

SHERIFF

    Woman, what is it? Be it in my power,

    Thou shalt obtain it.

DOLL

    Let me die next, sir; that is all I crave.

    You know not what a comfort you shall bring   80

    To my poor heart to die before my husband.

SHERIFF

    Bring her to death; she shall have her desire.

CLOWN BETTS

    Sir, and I have a suit to you too.

SHERIFF

    What is it?

CLOWN BETTS

    That as you have hanged Lincoln first and will   85

    hang her next, so you will not hang me at all.

SHERIFF

    Nay, you set ope[110] the Counter gates and you

    must hang chiefly.[111]

CLOWN BETTS

    Well then, so much for that.

DOLL [*To Sheriff.*]

    Sir, your free bounty much contents my mind.   90

    Commend me to that good shrieve Master More,

    And tell him, had't not been for his persuasion,

    John Lincoln had not hung here as he does.

    We would first have locked up[112] in Leadenhall

    And there been burned to ashes with the roof.   95

SHERIFF

    Woman, what Master More did was a subject's

        duty,

    And hath so pleased our gracious lord the King

105 gallows **106** *cry lag:* request to be last **107** wish **108** *to attempt:* against   attempting **109** comes **110** open **111** especially **112** *have locked up:*   have been locked up

That he is hence removed to higher place,
And made of Council to his Majesty.

DOLL

100 Well is he worthy of it, by my troth:
An honest, wise, well-spoken gentleman;
Yet would I praise his honesty much more
If he had kept his word and saved our lives.
But let that pass; men are but men, and so
105 Words are but words, and pays not what men
owe.
Now, husband, since perhaps the world may say
That through my means thou comest thus to thy
end,
Here I begin this cup of death to thee,
Because thou shalt be sure to taste no worse
110 Than I have taken, that must go before thee.
What though I be a woman? That's no matter.
I do owe God a death, and I must pay him.
Husband, give me thy hand; be not dismayed.
This chore being chored, then all our debt is paid.
115 Only, two little babes we leave behind us,
And all I can bequeath them at this time
Is but the love of some good honest friend
To bring them up in charitable sort.
What, masters? He goes upright that never halts,
120 And they may live to mend their parents' faults.

WILLIAMSON

Why, well said, wife; i'faith thou cheer'st my
heart.
Give me thy hand; let's kiss, and so let's part.
He kisses her on the ladder.

DOLL

The next kiss, Williamson, shall be in heaven.
Now cheerly lads, George Betts, a hand with thee,
And thine too, Ralph, and thine, good honest
125 Sherwin.
Now let me tell the women of this town
No stranger yet brought Doll to lying down.
So long as I an Englishman can see,
Nor French nor Dutch shall get a kiss of me.
130 And when that I am dead, for me yet say
I died in scorn to be a stranger's prey.
A great shout and noise.
[Voices] within.
Pardon, pardon, pardon, pardon!
Room for the Earl of Surrey! Room there, room!
Enter Surrey.

SURREY

Save the man's life, if it be possible.

SHERIFF

It is too late, my lord; he's dead already. 135

SURREY

I tell ye, Master Sheriff, you are too forward
To make such haste with men unto their death.
I think your pains will merit little thanks
Since that his Highness is so merciful
As not to spill the blood of any subject. 140

SHERIFF

My noble lord, would we so much had known.
The Council's warrant hastened our dispatch;
It had not else been done so suddenly.

SURREY

Sir Thomas More humbly upon his knee
Did beg the lives of all, since on his word 145
They did so gently yield. The King hath granted it
And made him Lord High Chancellor of
England,
According as he worthily deserves.
Since Lincoln's life cannot be had again,
Then for the rest, from my dread[113] Sovereign's
lips, 150
I here pronounce free pardon for them all.

ALL (*Flinging up caps.*)
God save the King! God save the King,
My good Lord Chancellor and the Earl of Surrey!

DOLL

And Doll desires it from her very heart
More's name may live for this right noble part. 155
And whensoe'er we talk of ill May Day
Praise More whose [word did sin and judgment
stay].[114]

SURREY

In hope his Highness' clemency and mercy,
Which in the arms of mild and meek compassion
Would rather clip[115] you, as the loving nurse 160
Oft doth the wayward infant, than to leave you
To the sharp rod of justice, so to draw you
To shun such lewd[116] assemblies as beget
Unlawful riots and such traitorous acts
That striking with the hand of private[117] hate, 165
Maim your dear country with a public wound.
O God, that mercy, whose majestic brow

113 revered **114** Shirley's emendation **115** gently correct **116** ignorant, wicked **117** personal, factional

Should be unwrinkled, and that awe-full justice
Which looketh through a veil of sufferance
170 Upon the frailty of the multitude,
Should with the clamors of outrageous wrongs
Be stirred and wakened thus to punishment!
But your deservèd death he doth forgive,
Who gives you life, pray all he long may live.

ALL

175 God save the King! God save the King,
My good Lord Chancellor, and the Earl of Surrey!
Exeunt.

3.1

A table being covered with a green carpet, a state cushion on it, and the purse and mace lying thereon. Enter Sir Thomas More.

MORE[118]

It is in heaven that I am thus and thus,
And that which we profanely[119] term our fortunes
Is the provision of the power above,
Fitted and shaped just to that strength of nature
Which we are born with. Good God, good
    God,
5 That I from such an humble bench[120] of birth
Should step, as 'twere, up to my country's head
And give the law out there; I, in my father's life,
To take prerogative and tithe[121] of knees
10 From elder kinsmen, and him, bind by my place
To give the smooth and dexter[122] way to me
That owe it him by nature: sure these things,
Not physicked by respect,[123] might turn our
    blood
To much corruption. But More, the more thou
    hast
15 Either of honor, office, wealth, and calling,
Which might accite[124] thee to embrace and hug
    them,
The more do thou in serpents' natures think
    them;
Fear their gay skins, with thought of their sharp
    state,
And let this be thy maxim: to be great
20 Is, when the thread of hazard is once spun,
A bottom[125] great wound up, greatly undone.

Enter his man Randall attired like him.
Come on, sir, are you ready?

RANDALL

Yes, my lord, I stand[126] but on a few points. I shall have done presently. Before God, I have practised your lordship's shift[127] so well that I think I shall 25 grow proud, my lord.

MORE

'Tis fit thou shouldst wax[128] proud, or else thou'lt
    ne'er
Be near allied to greatness. Observe me, sirrah:
The learned clerk Erasmus is arrived
30 Within our English Court. Last night I hear
He feasted with our honored English poet
The Earl of Surrey, and I learned today
The famous clerk of Rotterdam will visit
Sir Thomas More. Therefore, sir, take my seat:
You are lord chancellor. [*Randall sits.*]
                    Dress[129] your behavior 35
According to my carriage,[130] but beware
You talk not over much, for 'twill betray thee.
Who prates[131] not much seems wise, his wit few
    scan,[132]
While the tongue blabs tales of the imperfect
    man.
40 I'll see if great Erasmus can distinguish
Merit and outward ceremony.

RANDALL

If I do not deserve a share for playing of your lordship well, let me be yeoman usher to your sumpter,[133] and be banished from wearing of a gold chain for ever. 45

MORE

Well, sir, I'll hide our motion.[134] Act my part
With a firm boldness, and thou winst my heart.
*Enter the Sheriff with Falkner (a ruffian)
and officers.*
How now? What's the matter?

FALKNER [*To Officers.*]

Tug me not; I'm no bear. 'Sblood,[135] if all the dogs in Paris Garden hung at my tail, I'd shake 'em off 50 with this: that I'll appear before no king christened but my good Lord Chancellor.

---

118 This soliloquy is generally thought to be by Shakespeare. **119** impiously **120** situation **121** tribute **122** right hand (a position of honor) **123** *physicked by respect:* tempered by reflection **124** excite; induce **125** a ball of wound thread **126** wait **127** contrivance **128** grow **129** arrange **130** demeanor **131** talks foolishly **132** discern **133** *let... sumpter:* let me be demoted to serving your lowliest servant **134** show, entertainment **135** God's blood

SHERIFF

We'll christen you, sirrah. Bring him forward.

MORE [*To Falkner.*]

How now, what tumults make you?

FALKNER

55   The azured heavens protect my noble Lord
Chancellor.

MORE [*To Sheriff.*]

What fellow's this?

SHERIFF

A ruffian, my lord, that hath set half the city in
an uproar.

FALKNER

60   My lord —

SHERIFF

There was a fray in Paternoster Row, and because
they would not be parted, the street was choked up
with carts.

FALKNER

My noble lord, Panyer Alley's throat was open.

MORE

65   Sirrah, hold your peace.

FALKNER

I'll prove the street was not choked, but is as well
as ever it was since it was a street.

SHERIFF

This fellow was a principal broacher[136] of the
broil —

FALKNER

70   'Sblood, I broached none.[137] It was broached and
half run out before I had a lick at it.

SHERIFF

—and would be brought before no justice but
your honor.

FALKNER

I am haled,[138] my noble lord.

MORE [*To Sheriff.*]

75   No ear to choose for every trivial noise
But mine, and in so full[139] a time? Away.

You wrong me, Master Shrieve. Dispose of him
At your own pleasure. Send the knave to Newgate.

FALKNER

To Newgate? 'Sblood, Sir Thomas More, I appeal,
I appeal; from Newgate to any of the two worship-   80
ful Counters.[140]

MORE

Fellow, whose man are you that are thus lusty?[141]

FALKNER

My name's Jack Falkner. I serve, next under God
and my prince, Master Morris, secretary to my Lord
of Winchester.   85

MORE

A fellow of your hair[142] is very fit
To be a secretary's follower!

FALKNER

I hope so, my lord. The fray was between the Bishops' men of Ely and Winchester, and I could not in
honor but part them. I thought it stood not with my   90
reputation and degree[143] to come to my questions
and answers before a city justice. I knew I should to
the pot.[144]

MORE

Thou hast been there, it seems, too late already.[145]

FALKNER

I know your honor is wise and so forth, and I de-   95
sire to be only catechized[146] or examined by you, my
noble Lord Chancellor.

MORE

Sirrah, sirrah, you are a busy[147] dangerous ruffian.

FALKNER

Ruffian?

MORE

How long have you worn this hair?   100

FALKNER

I have worn this hair ever since I was born.

MORE

You know that's not my question. But how long
Hath this shag fleece hung dangling on thy
        head?

---

136 instigator   137 drew no liquor
(playing on another sense of the word)
138 pulled along forcibly   139 busy
140 debtors' prisons in London

141 insolent   142 double meaning of
physical hair and other sense of the word
as "kind" or "type"   143 position   144 *to
the pot:* be ruined or destroyed   145 *been*

there...already: More plays on the sense
of a pot for drinking.   146 instructed
147 meddlesome

FALKNER

How long, my lord? Why, sometimes thus long,
105   sometimes lower, as the Fates and humors please.

MORE

So quick, sir, with me, ha? I see, good fellow,
Thou lovest plain dealing. Sirrah, tell me now,
When were you last at barber's? How long time
Have you upon your head worn this shag hair?

FALKNER

110   My lord, Jack Falkner tells no Aesop's fables.
Troth, I was not at barber's this three years. I have
not been cut, nor will not be cut, upon a foolish
vow which, as the destinies shall direct, I am sworn
to keep.

MORE

115   When comes that vow out?

FALKNER

Why, when the humors are purged:[148] not these
three years.

MORE

Vows are recorded in the court of heaven,
For they are holy acts. Young man, I charge thee,
120   And do advise thee, start[149] not from that vow,
And for[150] I will be sure thou shalt not shear,
Besides, because it is an odious sight
To see a man thus hairy, thou shalt lie
In Newgate till thy vow and thy three years
Be full expired. Away with him.

FALKNER

125   My lord—

MORE

Cut off this fleece, and lie there but a month.

FALKNER

I'll not lose a hair to be lord chancellor of Europe.

MORE

To Newgate then. Sirrah, great sins are bred
In all that body where there's a foul head.
130   Away with him.

Exeunt [all except Randall].
Enter Surrey, Erasmus, and attendants.

SURREY

Now, great Erasmus, you approach the presence
Of a most worthy learned gentleman.
This little isle holds not a truer friend
Unto the arts, nor doth his greatness add
A feignèd flourish[151] to his worthy parts.   135
He's great in study: that's the statist's grace,[152]
That gains more reverence than the outward
    place.

ERASMUS

Report, my lord, hath crossed the narrow seas
And to the several parts of Christendom
Hath borne the fame of your lord chancellor.   140
I long to see him whom with loving thoughts
I in my study oft have visited.
Is that Sir Thomas More?

SURREY

                                        It is, Erasmus.
Now shall you view the honorablest scholar,
The most religious politician,   145
The worthiest counselor that tends our state.
That study is the general watch of England;
In it, the prince's safety and the peace
That shines upon our commonwealth are forged
By loyal industry.   150

ERASMUS

                                I doubt him not
To be as near the life of excellence
As you proclaim him, when his meanest servants
Are of some weight. You saw, my lord, his porter
Give entertainment to us at the gate
In Latin good phrase. What's the master then,   155
When such good parts shine in his meanest men?

SURREY

His lordship hath some weighty business,
For see, as yet he takes no notice of us.

ERASMUS

I think 'twere best I did my duty to him
In a short Latin speech: 160
[Taking off his hat, Erasmus addresses Randall.]
Qui in celeberrima patria natus est et gloriosa plus
habet negotii ut in lucem veniat quam qui—[153]

---

148 *humors are purged:* dispositions
are purified   **149** break   **150** in order
that   **151** *feigned flourish:* counterfeited
embellishment   **152** *statist's grace:* statesman's virtue or excellence   **153** "Someone
born in a very famous and glorious country
has more difficulty in becoming famous
than one who…."

RANDALL

I pray thee, good Erasmus, be covered.[154] I have forsworn speaking of Latin, else, as I am true councilor, I'd tickle[155] you with a speech. Nay, sit, Erasmus; sit, good my Lord of Surrey. I'll make my lady

165 come to you anon,[156] if she will, and give you good entertainment.

ERASMUS

Is this Sir Thomas More?

SURREY

                    O good Erasmus,
You must conceive his vein:[157] he's ever furnished
With these conceits.

RANDALL

170 Yes, faith, my learned poet doth not lie for that matter. I am neither more nor less merry Sir Thomas always. Wilt sup with me? By God, I love a parlous[158] wise fellow that smells of a politician better than a long progress.[159]

Enter Sir Thomas More.

SURREY

175 We are deluded. This is not his lordship.

RANDALL

I pray you, Erasmus, how long will the Holland cheese in your country keep without maggots?

MORE

Fool, painted barbarism, retire thyself
Into thy first creation.   [*Exit Randall.*]
                    Thus you see,
180 My loving learned friends, how far respect
Waits often on the ceremonious train
Of base, illiterate wealth, whilst men of schools,
Shrouded in poverty, are counted fools.
Pardon, thou reverend German. I have mixed
185 So slight a jest to the fair entertainment
Of thy most worthy self. For know, Erasmus,
Mirth wrinkles up my face, and I still crave,
When that forsakes me, I may hug my grave.

ERASMUS

Your honor's merry humor is best physic[160]
190 Unto your able body, for we learn,

Where melancholy chokes the passages
Of blood and breath, the erected spirit still
Lengthens our days with sportful exercise.
Study should be the saddest[161] time of life;
The rest, a sport exempt from thought of strife.   195

MORE

Erasmus preacheth gospel against physic.
My noble poet —

SURREY

                    O my lord, you tax[162] me
In that word "poet" of much idleness.
It is a study that makes poor our fate;
Poets were ever thought unfit for state.   200

MORE

Oh, give not up fair poesy, sweet lord,
To such contempt. That I may speak my heart,
It is the sweetest heraldry of art
That sets a difference 'tween the tough sharp holly
And tender bay tree.

SURREY

                    Yet, my lord,   205
It is become the very lag i'number[163]
To all mechanic sciences.[164]

MORE

                    Why, I'll show the reason.
This is no age for poets: they should sing,
To the loud canon,[165] *heroica facta*
Qui faciunt reges heroica carmina laudant;[166]   210
And as great subjects of their pen decay,
Even so, unphysicked,[167] they do melt away.
                    Enter Master Morris.
Come, will your lordship in? My dear Erasmus —
I'll hear you, Master Morris presently.
My lord, I make you master of my house;   215
We'll banquet here with fresh and staid[168]
     delights;
The Muses' music here shall cheer our sprites;[169]
The cates[170] must be but mean where scholars sit,
For they're made all with courses of neat[171] wit.
                    [*Exeunt Surrey, Erasmus, and attendants.*]
How now, Master Morris?   220

---

154 *be covered:* put your hat back on
155 delight; beat up; make an end of
something   156 presently   157 *conceive*
his vein: understand his style   158 shrewd;
mischievous   159 a journey made by a

royal personage   160 medicine   161 most
serious or grave   162 blame   163 *lag*
i'number: last in order   164 *mechanic*
sciences: non-liberal disciplines; practical
skills and arts   165 musical composition;

law or rule; standard of judgment
166 "Heroic poems praise the heroic deeds
that kings perform."   167 unnurtured
168 free from extravagance   169 spirits
170 provisions   171 refined, well selected

MORRIS

I am a suitor to your lordship in behalf of a servant of mine.

MORE

The fellow with long hair, good Master Morris? Come to me three years hence and then I'll hear you.

MORRIS

225 I understand, your honor, but the foolish knave has submitted himself to the mercy of a barber, and is without, ready to make a new vow before your lordship, hereafter to live civil.

MORE

Nay then, let's talk with him. Pray, call him in.

Enter Falkner and officers.

FALKNER

230 Bless your honor: a new man, my lord.

MORE

Why, sure, this' not he.

FALKNER

An[172] your lordship will, the barber shall give you a sample of my head. I am he in faith, my lord, I am *ipse*.[173]

MORE

235 Why, now thy face is like an honest man's. Thou hast played well at this new cut,[174] and won.

FALKNER

No, my lord. Lost all that ever God sent me.

MORE

God sent thee into the world as thou art now, with short hair. How quickly are three years run 240 out in Newgate.

FALKNER

I think so, my lord, for there was but a hair's length between my going thither and so long time.

MORE

Because I see some grace in thee, go free. Discharge him, fellows. Farewell, Master Morris. 245 Thy head is for thy shoulders now more fit: Thou hast less hair upon it but more wit.   *Exit.*

MORRIS

Did not I tell thee always of these locks?

FALKNER

An the locks were on again, all the goldsmiths in Cheapside should not pick them open. 'Sheart![175] If my hair stand not on end when I look for my face in 250 a glass,[176] I am a polecat.[177] Here's a lousy jest. But if I notch[178] not that rogue Tom barber that makes me look thus like a Brownist,[179] hang me. I'll be worse to the nittical[180] knave than ten tooth-drawings.[181] Here's a head with a pox!   255

MORRIS

What ail'st thou? Art thou mad now?

FALKNER

Mad, now? 'Nails![182] If loss of hair cannot mad a man, what can? I am deposed; my crown is taken from me. More had been better a' scoured Moorditch than a' notched me thus. Does he begin sheep-   260 shearing with Jack Falkner?

MORRIS

Nay, an you feed this vein, sir, fare you well.

FALKNER

Why, farewell, frost! I'll go hang myself out for the poll[183] head. Make a Sar'cen of Jack?

MORRIS

Thou desperate knave, for that I see the devil   265 wholly gets hold of thee.

FALKNER

The devil's a damned rascal.

MORRIS

I charge thee wait on me no more; no more Call me thy master.

FALKNER

Why then, a word, Master Morris.   270

MORRIS

I'll hear no words, sir. Fare you well.

FALKNER

'Sblood! Farewell?

MORRIS

Why dost thou follow me?

FALKNER

Because I'm an ass. Do you set your shavers[184]
275 upon me, and then cast me off? Must I condole?[185]
Have the Fates played the fools? [*Weeps.*] Am I their
cut? Now the poor sconce[186] is taken, must Jack
march with bag and baggage?

MORRIS

You coxcomb![187]

FALKNER

280 Nay, you ha'[188] poached me; you ha' given me a
hair. It's here, here.

MORRIS

Away, you kind ass. Come, sir, dry your eyes.
Keep your old place, and mend these fooleries.

FALKNER

I care not to be turned off,[189] and 'twere a ladder,
285 so it be in my humor, or the Fates beckon to me.
Nay, pray, sir, if the Destinies spin me a fine thread,
Falkner flies another pitch. And to avoid the headache, hereafter before I'll be a hairmonger I'll be a
whoremonger.   *Exeunt.*

3.2

Enter a messenger to More.

MESSENGER

My honorable lord, the Mayor of London,
Accompanied with his lady and her train,
Are coming hither, and are hard at hand,
To feast with you. A sergeant's come before
5 To tell your lordship of their near approach.

MORE

Why, this is cheerful news. Friends go and come;
Reverend Erasmus, whose delicious words
Express the very soul and life of wit,
Newly took sad leave of me, with tears
10 Troubled the silver channel of the Thames,
Which, glad of such a burden, proudly swelled
And on her bosom bore him toward the sea.
He's gone to Rotterdam; peace go with him.
He left me heavy when he went from hence,
15 But this recomforts me: the kind Lord Mayor,
His brethren aldermen with their fair wives,

Will feast this night with us. Why, so't should be;
More's merry heart lives by good company.
[*Enter Master Roper and servingmen.*]
Good gentlemen, be careful; give great charge
Our diet be made dainty for the taste,   20
For of all people that the earth affords
The Londoners fare richest at their boards.[190]
Come, my good fellows, stir, be diligent!
Sloth is an idle fellow; leave him now.
The time requires your expeditious service.   25
Place me here stools to set the ladies on.
[*Servingmen set stools.*]
Son Roper, you have given order for the banquet?

ROPER

I have, my lord, and everything is ready.
Enter Lady More.

MORE

O welcome, wife. Give you direction
How women should be placed. You know it best.   30
For my Lord Mayor, his brethren, and the rest,
Let me alone: men best can order men.

LADY MORE

I warrant ye, my lord, all shall be well.
There's one without that stays to speak with ye,
And bade me tell ye that he is a player.   35

MORE

A player, wife? One of ye bid him come in.
Exit one [servingman].
Nay, stir there, fellows. Fie; ye are too slow.
See that your lights be in a readiness;
The banquet shall be here. God's me,[191] madam,
Leave my Lady Mayoress? Both of us from the
  board?   40
And my son Roper too? What may our guests
  think?

LADY MORE

My lord, they are risen and sitting by the fire.

MORE

Why, yet go you and keep them company.
It is not meet[192] we should be absent both.
Exit Lady.
Enter Player.
Welcome, good friend. What is your will with
  me?   45

---

184 razors; swindlers **185** grieve **186** a
jocular term for head **187** fool; ludicrous

term for the head **188** have **189** *turned
off:* dismissed; turned off the ladder to be

hanged **190** tables **191** *God's me:* God
bless me **192** appropriate

PLAYER
My lord, my fellows and myself
Are come to tender[193] ye our willing service,
So please you to command us.

MORE
                              What, for a play, you mean?
Whom do you serve?

PLAYER
                              My Lord Cardinal's grace.

MORE
My Lord Cardinal's players? Now trust me,
50   welcome.
You happen hither in a lucky time
To pleasure me and benefit yourselves.
The mayor of London and some aldermen,
His lady and their wives, are my kind guests
55   This night at supper. Now, to have a play
Before the banquet will be excellent.
How think you, son Roper?

ROPER
                              'Twill do well, my lord,
And be right pleasing pastime to your guests.

MORE
I prithee tell me, what plays have ye?

PLAYER
60   Diverse, my lord: *The Cradle of Security,*
Hit Nail o' th' Head, Impatient Poverty,
The Play of Four Ps, Dives and Lazarus,
Lusty Juventus, and *The Marriage of Wit and*
Wisdom.

MORE
The Marriage of Wit and Wisdom? That, my lads.
65   I'll none but that. The theme is very good,
And may maintain a liberal[194] argument.
To marry wit to wisdom asks some cunning;[195]
Many have wit that may come short of wisdom.
We'll see how Master Poet plays his part,
70   And whether wit or wisdom grace his art.
[*To Servingmen.*] Go, make him drink, and all his
      fellows too.
[*To Player.*] How many are ye?

PLAYER
                              Four men and a boy, sir.

MORE
But one boy? Then I see,
There's but few women in the play.

PLAYER
Three, my lord: Dame Science, Lady Vanity,   75
And Wisdom, she herself.

MORE
And one boy play them all? By'r Lady, he's loaden.
Well, my good fellow, get ye straight together
And make ye ready with what haste ye may.
[*To Servingmen.*] Provide their supper 'gainst[196]
      the play be done,   80
Else shall we stay our guests here overlong.
[*To Player.*] Make haste, I pray ye.

PLAYER
                              We will, my lord.
      Exeunt Servingmen and Player.

MORE
Where are the waits?[197] [*To Roper.*] Go, bid them
      play,
To spend the time awhile.
      Enter Lady More.
                              How now, madam?

LADY MORE
My lord, they're coming hither.   85

MORE
They're welcome. Wife, I'll tell ye one thing:
Our sport is somewhat mended; we shall have
A play tonight, *The Marriage of Wit and*
      Wisdom,
And acted by my good Lord Cardinal's players.
How like ye that, wife?

LADY MORE
                              My lord, I like it well.   90
See, they are coming.
      Waits play hautbois.[198] Enter Lord Mayor,
      so many aldermen as may, the Lady Mayoress
      in scarlet, with other ladies and
      Sir Thomas More's daughters, servants
      carrying lighted torches by them.

MORE
Once again, welcome. Welcome, my good Lord
      Mayor,
And brethren all, for once I was your brother

193 offer   **194** humanistic   **195** skill   **196** when   **197** musicians   **198** oboe-like instruments

And so am still in heart. It is not state[199]
95 That can our love from London separate.
[There be, as I have oft of late espied,
In whom Dame Fortune's gifts breed][200] nought
    but pride,
But they that cast an eye still whence they came,
Know how they rose, and how to use the same.

MAYOR
100 My lord, you set a gloss[201] on London's fame,
And make it happy ever by your name.
Needs must we say when we remember More,
'Twas he that drove rebellion from our door,
With grave discretion's mild and gentle breath
105 Shielding a many subjects' lives from death.
Oh, how our city is by you renowned,
And with your virtues our endeavors crowned.

MORE
No more, my good Lord Mayor; but thanks to all
That on so short a summons you would come
110 To visit him that holds your kindness dear.
[*To Lady More.*] Madam, you are not merry with
    my Lady Mayoress,
And these fair ladies; pray ye seat them all.
[*To Mayor.*] And here, my lord, let me appoint
    your place,
The rest to seat themselves. Nay, I'll weary ye;
115 You will not long in haste to visit me.

LADY MORE
Good madam, sit; in sooth you shall sit here.

MAYORESS
Good madam, pardon me; it may not be.

LADY MORE
In troth, I'll have it so; I'll sit here by ye.
Good ladies, sit; more stools here, ho!

MAYORESS
120 It is your favor, madam, makes me thus
Presume above my merit.

LADY MORE
                        When we come to you,
Then shall you rule us as we rule you here.
            [*They sit.*]
Now must I tell ye, madam, we have a play
To welcome ye withal;[202] how good soe'er
125 That know not I; my lord will have it so.

MORE [*Aside.*]
Wife, hope the best; I am sure they'll do their
    best.
They that would better comes not at their feast.
[*Aloud.*] My good Lord Cardinal's players, I
    thank them for it.
Play us a play, to lengthen out your welcome.
They say it is *The Marriage of Wit and Wisdom*,   130
A theme of some import, howe'er it prove;
But if art fail, we'll inch it out with love.
What, are they ready?

SERVANT
My lord, one of the players craves to speak with
you.   135

MORE
With me? Where is he?
        Enter Inclination, the Vice, ready
        [*with bridle in hand*].

INCLINATION
Here, my lord.

MORE
How now, what's the matter?

INCLINATION
We would desire your honor but to stay a little;
one of my fellows is but run to Ogle's for a long   140
beard for young Wit, and he'll be here presently.

MORE
A long beard for young Wit? Why, man, he may
be without a beard till he come to marriage, for wit
goes not all by the hair. When comes Wit in?

INCLINATION
In the second scene, next to the prologue, my   145
lord.

MORE
Why, play on till that scene come, and by that
time Wit's beard will be grown, or else the fellow
returned with it. And what part playst thou?

INCLINATION
Inclination, the Vice, my lord.   150

MORE
Gramercies,[203] now I may take the Vice if I list.[204]
And wherefore hast thou that bridle in thy hand?

199 rank   **200** Shirley's emendation   **201** glow   **202** as well   **203** Many thanks   **204** wish to

INCLINATION

I must be bridled anon, my lord.

MORE

An thou be'st not saddled too, it makes no matter,
155 for then Wit's Inclination may gallop so fast that he
will outstrip wisdom and fall to folly.

INCLINATION

Indeed, so he does to Lady Vanity; but we have
no Folly in our play.

MORE

Then there's no wit in't, I'll be sworn. Folly waits
160 on wit as the shadow on the body, and where wit
is ripest, there folly still is readiest. But begin, I
prithee; we'll rather allow a beardless Wit than Wit,
all beard, to have no brain.

INCLINATION

Nay, he has his apparel on too, my lord, and there-
165 fore he is the readier to enter.

MORE

Then, good Inclination, begin at a venture.²⁰⁵
                          Exit [*Inclination*].
My Lord Mayor, Wit lacks a beard, or else they
    would begin.
I'd lend him mine, but that it is too thin.
Silence, they come.
            The trumpet sounds. Enter the Prologue.

PROLOGUE

170 Now forasmuch as in these latter days
Throughout the whole world in every land
Vice doth increase and virtue decays,
Iniquity having the upper hand,
We therefore intend, good gentle audience,
175 A pretty, short interlude to play at this present,
Desiring your leave and quiet silence
To show the same as is meet and expedient.
It is called *The Marriage of Wit and Wisdom*,
A matter right pithy and pleasing to hear,
180 Whereof in brief we will show the whole sum.
But I must be gone, for Wit doth appear.   *Exit.*
    *Enter Wit ruffling*²⁰⁶ *and Inclination, the Vice.*

WIT

In an arbor green, asleep whereas I lay,
The birds sang sweetly in the midst of the day;

I dreamed fast of mirth and play:
In youth is pleasure, in youth is pleasure.   185
    Methought I walked still to and fro,
    And from her company I could not go,
    But when I waked it was not so:
In youth is pleasure, in youth is pleasure.
    Therefore my heart is surely plight²⁰⁷   190
    Of her alone to have a sight
    Which is my joy and heart's delight:
In youth is pleasure, in youth is pleasure.

MORE [*To Mayor.*]

Mark ye, my lord, this is Wit without a beard;
what will he be by that time he comes to the com- 195
modity of a beard?

INCLINATION

O sir, the ground is the better on which she
    doth go.
For she will make better cheer with a little she can
    get
Than many a one can with a great banquet of
    meat.

WIT

And is her name Wisdom?

INCLINATION

                        Ay, sir, a wife most fit   200
For you, my good master, my dainty sweet Wit.

WIT

To be in her company, my heart it is set.
Therefore I prithee to let us be gone,
For unto Wisdom, Wit hath inclination.

INCLINATION

O sir, she will come herself even anon,   205
For I told her before where we would stand,
And then she said she would beck²⁰⁸ us with her
    hand.
            Flourishing his dagger.
Back with those boys and saucy great knaves.
What, stand ye here so big in your braves?²⁰⁹
My dagger about your coxcombs²¹⁰ shall walk   210
If I may but so much as hear ye chat or talk.

WIT

But will she take pains to come for us hither?

---

205 *at a venture:* without further concern **206** swaggering **207** pledged **208** beckon, call **209** brave talk; bravado **210** heads

INCLINATION

I warrant[211] ye; therefore, you must be familiar
  with her.
        When she cometh in place,
215   You must her embrace
        Somewhat handsomely,
        Lest she think it danger,
        Because you are a stranger,
        To come in your company.

WIT

220   I warrant thee, Inclination, I will be busy.
    Oh, how Wit longs to be in Wisdom's company.
        Enter Lady Vanity singing
        and beckoning with her hand.

VANITY

    Come hither, come hither, come hither, come!
    Such cheer as I have, thou shalt have some.

MORE

    This is Lady Vanity, I'll hold[212] my life.
225   Beware, good Wit, you take not her to wife.

INCLINATION [*To Vanity.*]

    What, Unknown Honesty, a word in your ear.
        She offers to depart.
    You shall not be gone as yet, I swear.
    Here's none but your friends; you need not to
      fray.[213]
    This young gentleman loves ye; therefore, you
      must stay.

WIT

230   I trust in me she will think no danger,
    For I love well the company of fair women;
    And though to you I am a stranger,
    Yet Wit may pleasure you now and then.

VANITY

    Who, you? Nay, you are such a holy man,
235   That to touch one you dare not be bold.
    I think you would not kiss a young woman
    If one would give ye twenty pound in gold.

WIT

    Yes, in good sadness,[214] lady, that I would.
    I could find in my heart to kiss you in your smock.

VANITY

    My back is broad enough to bear that mock,   240
    For it hath been told me many a time
    That you would be seen in no such company as
      mine.

WIT

    Not Wit in the company of Lady Wisdom?
    O Jove, for what do I hither come?

INCLINATION

    Sir, she did this nothing else but to prove   245
    Whether a little thing would you move
    To be angry and fret.
        What an if one said so?
        Let such trifling matters go,
    And with a kind kiss come out of her debt.   250
        Enter another player.

PLAYER OF INCLINATION

    Is Luggins come yet with the beard?

PLAYER

    No, faith, he is not come. Alas, what shall we do?

PLAYER OF INCLINATION [*To More.*]

    Forsooth, we can go no further till our fellow
    Luggins come, for he plays Good Counsel, and now
    he should enter to admonish Wit that this is Lady   255
    Vanity and not Lady Wisdom.

MORE

    Nay, an[215] it be no more but so, ye shall not tarry at
    a stand[216] for that. We'll not have our play marred for
    lack of a little good counsel. Till your fellow come,
    I'll give him the best counsel that I can. Pardon me,   260
    my Lord Mayor — I love to be merry.

MORE [*As Good Counsel.*]

    O good Mother Wit, thou art now on the bow
      hand,[217]
    And blindly in thine own opinion dost stand.
    I tell thee, this naughty lewd Inclination
    Does lead thee amiss in a very strange fashion.   265
    This is not Wisdom, but Lady Vanity;
    Therefore list[218] to Good Counsel, and be ruled
      by me.

PLAYER OF INCLINATION

    In troth, my lord, it is as right to Luggins's part as
    can be. Speak, Wit.

---

211 assure **212** stake **213** fear **214** *in*   **216** *tarry at a stand:* remain at a standstill   **218** listen
good sadness: in earnest; seriously **215** if   **217** *on the bow hand:* wide of the mark

MORE

270   Nay, we will not have our audience disappointed, if I can help it.

WIT

Art thou Good Counsel, and wilt tell me so?
Wouldst thou have Wit from Lady Wisdom to
        go?
Thou art some deceiver, I tell thee verily,
275   In saying that this is Lady Vanity.

MORE [*As Good Counsel.*]

Wit, judge not things by the outward show;
The eye oft mistakes, right well you do know.
Good Counsel assures thee upon his honesty
That this is not Wisdom, but Lady Vanity.
        Enter Luggins with the beard.

INCLINATION

280   O my lord, he is come; now we shall go forward.

MORE [*To Luggins.*]

Art thou come? Well, fellow, I have holp[219] to
save thine honesty[220] a little. Now, if thou canst give
Wit any better counsel than I have done, spare not.
There I leave him to thy mercy.
285   But by this time I am sure our banquet's ready.
My lord and ladies, we will taste that first
And then they shall begin the play again,
Which, through the fellow's absence, and by me,
Instead of helping, hath been hindered.
[*To Servants.*] Prepare against we come.[221] Lights
290   there, I say.
Thus fools oft times do help to mar the play.
        Exeunt all but the players.

WIT

Fie, fellow Luggins, you serve us handsomely; do ye not, think ye?

LUGGINS

Why, Ogle was not within, and his wife would
295   not let me have the beard, and, by my troth, I ran so fast that I sweat again.

INCLINATION

Do ye hear, fellows? Would not my lord make a rare player? Oh, he would uphold a company beyond all ho,[222] better than Mason among the King's
300   players. Did ye mark how extemp'rically he fell to the matter, and spake Luggins's part almost as it is in the very book set down?

WIT

Peace! Do ye know what ye say? My lord, a player? Let us not meddle with any such matters. Yet I may be a little proud that my lord hath answered me in   305 my part. But come, let us go and be ready to begin the play again.

LUGGINS

Ay, that's the best, for now we lack nothing.
        Enter a servingman to reward the players.

SERVINGMAN

Where be these players?

ALL

Here, sir.   310

SERVINGMAN

My lord is sent for to the Court,
And all the guests do after supper part.
And for he will not trouble you again,
By me for your reward 'a sends eight angels[223]
With many thanks. But sup before you go.   315
It is his will you should be fairly entreated.
Follow, I pray ye.

WIT

                        This, Luggins, is your negligence.
Wanting Wit's beard brought things into
        dislike,[224]
For otherwise the play had been all seen,
Where now some curious citizen disgraced it   320
And, discommending it, all is dismissed.

INCLINATION

'Fore God, 'a says true. But hear ye, sirs, eight angels? Ha! My lord would never give's eight angels, more or less for twelvepence. Either it should be three pounds, five pounds or ten pounds. There's   325 twenty shillings wanting, sure.

WIT

Twenty to one 'tis so. I have a trick. — My lord comes; stand aside.
        Enter More with attendants with purse and mace.

MORE

In haste, to Council? What's the business now,

---

219 helped   **220** good name; honor   [after dinner]   **222** pause, intermission
221 *against . . . come:* for when we come   **223** gold coins   **224** discord

330 That all so late his Highness sends for me?
What seek'st thou, fellow?

WIT

Nay, nothing. Your lordship sent eight angels by
   your man,
And I have lost two of them in the rushes.

MORE

Wit, look to that. Eight angels? I did send them
   Ten.
335 Who gave it them?

SERVINGMAN

I, my lord. I had no more about me,
But by and by they shall receive the rest.

MORE

Well, Wit, 'twas wisely done; thou playest Wit
   well indeed,
Not to be thus deceivèd of thy right.
340 Am I a man by office truly ordained
Equally to divide true right his own,
And shall I have deceivers in my house?
Then what avails my bounty, when such servants
Deceive the poor of what the master gives?
345 Go one and pull his coat over his ears.
There are too many such. Give them their right.
Wit, let thy fellows thank thee; 'twas well done.
Thou now deservest to match[225] with Lady
   Wisdom.
                              [*Exit with attendants.*]

INCLINATION

God a' mercy, Wit. [*To the servingman.*] Sir, you
350 had a master, Sir Thomas More. More? But now we
shall have more.

LUGGINS

God bless him. I would there were more of his
mind. 'A loves our quality, and yet he's a learned
man and knows what the world is.

INCLINATION

355 Well, a kind man and more loving than many
other, but I think we ha' met with the first —

LUGGINS

First served his man that had our angels, and he
may chance dine with Duke Humphrey tomorrow,
being turned away today. Come, let's go.

INCLINATION

And many such rewards would make us all ride   360
and horse us with the best nags in Smithfield.
                              [*Exeunt.*]

4.1

*Enter the Earls of Shrewsbury and Surrey, the
Bishop of Rochester and other lords, severally,
doing courtesy to each other, the Clerk of
the Council waiting bareheaded.*

SURREY

Good morrow to my Lord of Shrewsbury.

SHREWSBURY

The like unto the honored Earl of Surrey.
Yond comes my Lord of Rochester.

ROCHESTER

Good morrow, my good lords.

SURREY

                              Clerk of the Council,
What time is't of day?

CLERK

                              Past eight of clock, my lord.   5

SHREWSBURY

I wonder that my good Lord Chancellor
Doth stay so long, considering there's matters
Of high importance to be scanned upon.[226]

SURREY

Clerk of the Council, certify his lordship
The lords expect him here.

ROCHESTER

                              It shall not need;   10
Yond comes his lordship.
         *Enter Sir Thomas More,
   with purse and mace borne before him.*

MORE

Good morrow to this fair assembly.
Come, my good lords, let's sit.
                              They sit.
                              O serious square,[227]
Upon this little board is daily scanned
The health and preservation of the land.   15
We, the physicians, that effect this good,
Now by choice diet, anon[228] by letting blood.

---

225 marry   **226** *scanned upon:* examined   **227** *serious square:* grave table (at which the Council sits)   **228** straightway

Our toil and careful watching brings the King
In league with slumbers, to which peace doth
   sing.
20 —Avoid the room there!
What business, lords, today?

SHREWSBURY
                  This, my good lord:
About the entertainment[229] of the Emperor
'Gainst the perfidious French into our pay.

SURREY
My lords, as 'tis the custom in this place
25 The youngest should speak first, so if I chance
In this case to speak youngly, pardon me.
I will agree France now hath her full strength,
As having new recovered the pale blood
Which war sluiced forth,[230] and I consent to this:
30 That the conjunction of our English forces
With arms of Germany may sooner bring
This prize of conquest in. But then, my lords,
As in the moral hunting 'twixt the lion
And other beasts, force joined [with guile][231]
35 Frighted the weaker sharers from their parts,
So if the Empire's Sovereign chance to put
His plea of partnership into war's court,
Swords should decide the difference, and our
   blood
In private tears lament his entertainment.

SHREWSBURY
40 To doubt[232] the worst is still the wise man's shield
That arms him safely; but the world knows this:
The Emperor is a man of royal faith.
His love unto our Sovereign brings him down
From his imperial seat, to march in pay
45 Under our English flag, and wear the cross
Like some high order[233] on his manly breast.
Thus serving, he's not master of himself,
But like a colonel, commanding other,
Is by the general over-awed himself.

ROCHESTER
Yet, my good lord—

SHREWSBURY
50   Let me conclude my speech.
As subjects share no portion in the conquest
Of their true sovereign, other than the merit

That from the sovereign guerdons[234] the true
   subject,
So the good Emperor, in a friendly league
Of amity with England, will not soil   55
His honor with the theft of English spoil.

MORE
There is no question but this entertainment
Will be most honorable, most commodious.[235]
I have oft heard good captains wish to have
Rich soldiers to attend them, such as would fight   60
Both for their lives and livings. Such a one
Is the good Emperor. I would to God
We had ten thousand of such able men.
Ha! Then there would appear no court, no city,
But, where the wars were, they would pay
   themselves.   65
Then to prevent in French wars England's loss,
Let German flags wave with our English cross.
      Enter Sir Thomas Palmer.

PALMER
My lords, his Majesty hath sent by me
These articles enclosed, first to be viewed
And then to be subscribed to.   70
(*With great reverence.*) I tender[236] them
In that due reverence which befits this place.

MORE
Subscribe these articles? Stay, let us pause.
Our conscience first shall parley[237] with our laws.
My Lord of Rochester, view you the paper.   75

ROCHESTER
Subscribe to these? Now, good Sir Thomas
   Palmer,
Beseech the King that he will pardon me.
My heart will check my hand whilst I do write:
Subscribing so, I were an hypocrite.

PALMER
Do you refuse it then, my lord?[238]

ROCHESTER
               I do, Sir Thomas.   80

PALMER
Then here I summon you forthwith t'appear
Before his Majesty, to answer there
This capital contempt.

---

229 employment   **230** *sluiced forth:*
drew out   **231** Shirley's emendation
232 fear   **233** honor   **234** rewards

235 advantageous   **236** offer for
formal acceptance   **237** hold conference

238 The following section (lines 82–104)
was crossed out by Edmund Tilney.

ROCHESTER

                       I rise and part,
In lieu of this, to tender him my heart.
He rises.

PALMER

85   Will't please your honor to subscribe, my lord?

MORE

Sir, tell his Highness I entreat
Some time for to bethink me of this task.
In the meanwhile I do resign mine office
Into my Sovereign's hands.

PALMER

                        Then, my lord,
90   Hear the preparèd order from the King.
On your refusal, you shall straight depart
Unto your house at Chelsea, till you know
Our Sovereign's further pleasure.

MORE

                      Most willingly I go.
My lords, if you will visit me at Chelsea,
95   We'll go a-fishing, and with a cunning[239] net,
Not like weak film, we'll catch none but the great.
Farewell, my noble lords. Why, this is right.
Good morrow to the sun, to state goodnight.
Exit.

PALMER

Will you subscribe, my lords?

SURREY

                    Instantly, good Sir Thomas.
They write.
100   We'll bring the writing unto our Sovereign.

PALMER

My Lord of Rochester,
You must with me, to answer this contempt.

ROCHESTER

This is the worst;
Who's freed from life, is from all care exempt.
Exeunt Rochester and Palmer.

SURREY

105   Now let us [bear this][240] to our Sovereign.
'Tis strange that my Lord Chancellor should
    refuse

The duty that the law of God bequeaths
Unto the King.

SHREWSBURY

               Come, let us in. No doubt
His mind will alter, and the bishop's too.
Error in learned heads hath much to do.   110

[Exeunt.]

4.2

*Enter the Lady More, her two daughters,
and Master Roper, as walking.*

ROPER

Madam, what ails ye for to look so sad?

LADY MORE

Troth, son, I know not what. I am not sick,
And yet I am not well. I would be merry,
But somewhat[241] lies so heavy on my heart,
I cannot choose but sigh. You are a scholar.   5
I pray ye tell me, may one credit[242] dreams?

ROPER

Why ask you that, dear madam?

LADY MORE

Because tonight I had the strangest dream
That e'er my sleep was troubled with.
Methought 'twas night,   10
And that the King and Queen went on the
    Thames
In barges to hear music. My lord and I
Were in a little boat, methought. Lord, Lord,
What strange things live in slumbers! And being
    near,
We grappled[243] to the barge that bare the King.   15
But after many pleasing voices spent
In that still-moving music house, methought
The violence of the stream did sever us
Quite from the golden fleet, and hurried us
Unto the Bridge,[244] which with unusèd[245] horror   20
We entered at full tide; thence some flight-
    shoot[246]
Being carried by the waves, our boat stood still
Just opposite the Tower, and there it turned
And turned about, as when a whirlpool sucks
The circled waters. Methought that we both cried   25
Till that we sunk, where arm in arm we died.

---

239 skillfully made   **240** Shirley's emendation   **241** something   **242** trust   **243** attached our boats   **244** London Bridge   **245** unusual   **246** swift rush of water

ROPER

Give no respect,[247] dear madam, to fond dreams;
They are but slight illusions of the blood.

LADY MORE

Tell me not all are so, for often dreams
30   Are true diviners,[248] either of good or ill.
I cannot be in quiet[249] till I hear
How my lord fares.

ROPER (*Aside.*)

                        Nor I. [*Aside to his wife.*]
                              Come hither, wife.
I will not fright thy mother to interpret
The nature of a dream; but trust me, sweet,
35   This night I have been troubled with thy father
Beyond all thought.

ROPER'S WIFE [*Aside to Roper.*]

                        Truly, and so have I.
Methought I saw him here in Chelsea church,
Standing upon the rood loft, now defaced,
And whilst he kneeled and prayed before the image,
40   It fell with him into the upper choir,
Where my poor father lay all stained in blood.

ROPER [*Aside to his wife.*]

Our dreams all meet in one conclusion:
Fatal, I fear.

LADY MORE

What's that you talk? I pray ye let me know it.

ROPER'S WIFE

45   Nothing, good mother.

LADY MORE

This is your fashion still; I must know nothing.
Call Master Catesby; he shall straight to Court
And see how my lord does. I shall not rest
Until my heart lean panting on his breast.
Enter Sir Thomas More merrily, servants attending.

SECOND DAUGHTER

50   See where my father comes, joyful and merry.

MORE

As seamen, having passed a troubled storm,
Dance on the pleasant shore, so I — Oh, I could speak
Now like a poet. Now, afore God, I am passing light.[250]
Wife, give me kind welcome. [*Kissing her.*]
                              Thou wast wont to blame
My kissing, when my beard was in the stubble,   55
But I have been trimmed of late; I have had
A smooth Court shaving, in good faith I have.
Daughters kneel.
God bless ye. Son Roper, give me your hand.

ROPER

Your honor's welcome home.

MORE

                              Honor? Ha, ha!
And how dost, wife?

ROPER

                  He bears himself most strangely.   60

LADY MORE

Will your lordship in?

MORE

                  Lordship? No, wife, that's gone.
The ground was slight that we did lean upon.

LADY MORE

Lord, that your honor ne'er will leave these jests!
In faith, it ill becomes ye.

MORE

                  O good wife,
Honor and jests are both together fled;   65
The merriest councilor of England's dead.

LADY MORE

Who's that, my lord?

MORE

            Still "lord?" The Lord Chancellor, wife.

LADY MORE

That's you.

MORE

            Certain, but I have changed my life.
Am I not leaner than I was before?
The fat is gone; my title's only "More."   70
Contented with one style,[251] I'll live at rest.
They that have many names are not still[252] best.
I have resigned mine office; count'st me not wise?

247 regard   **248** prophets, omens   **249** peace   **250** light-hearted   **251** title   **252** always

LADY MORE

O God!

MORE

75 Come, breed not female children in your eyes.
The King will have it so.

LADY MORE

What's the offense?

MORE

Tush, let that pass; we'll talk of that anon.
The King seems a physician to my fate;
His princely mind would train me back to state.

ROPER

80 Then be his patient, my most honored father.

MORE

O son Roper,
Ubi turpis est medicina, sanari piget.[253]
No, wife, be merry, and be merry all.
You smiled at rising; weep not at my fall.
85 Let's in, and here joy[254] like to private friends,
Since days of pleasure have repentant ends.
The light of greatness is with triumph borne;
It sets at midday oft, with public scorn.   *Exeunt.*

4.3

*Enter the Bishop of Rochester, Surrey,
Shrewsbury, Lieutenant of the Tower
and warders with weapons.*

ROCHESTER

Your kind persuasions, honorable lords,
I can but thank ye for, but in this breast
There lives a soul that aims at higher things
Than temporary pleasing earthly kings.
5 God bless his Highness, even with all my heart;
We shall meet one day, though that now we part.

SURREY

We not misdoubt[255] your wisdom can discern
What best befits it; yet in love and zeal
We could entreat it might be otherwise.

SHREWSBURY

10 No doubt your fatherhood will by yourself
Consider better of the present case,
And grow as great in favor as before.

ROCHESTER

For that, as pleaseth God, in my restraint
From worldly causes, I shall better see
Into myself than at proud liberty.   15
The Tower and I will privately confer
Of things wherein at freedom I may err.
But I am troublesome unto your honors,
And hold ye longer than becomes my duty.
Master Lieutenant, I am now your charge,   20
And though you keep my body, yet my love
Waits on my king and you while Fisher lives.

SURREY

Farewell, my Lord of Rochester. We'll pray
For your release, and labor't as we may.

SHREWSBURY

Thereof assure yourself. So do we leave ye,   25
And to your happy private thoughts bequeath ye.
Exeunt lords.

ROCHESTER

Now, Master Lieutenant, on; i' God's name, go.
And with as glad a mind go I with you,
As ever truant bade the school adieu.
Exeunt.

4.4

*Enter Sir Thomas More, his Lady, daughters,
Master Roper, gentlemen and servants,
as in his house at Chelsea. Low stools.*

MORE

Good morrow, good son Roper. [*To Lady More.*]
Sit, good madam,
Upon an humble seat; the time so craves.
Rest your good heart on earth, the roof of graves.
You see the floor of greatness is uneven,
The cricket[256] and high throne alike near heaven.   5
Now, daughters, you that like to branches
    spread
And give best shadow to a private house,
Be comforted, my girls. Your hopes stand fair:
Virtue breeds gentry; she makes the best heir.

DAUGHTERS

Good morrow to your honor.

---

253 Creon's words to King Oedipus from Seneca's *Oedipus*, 517: "When the remedy is shameful, one hates being cured." Tilney crossed out this quotation.   **254** *joy . . . to:* have joy characteristic of   **255** (do not) doubt   **256** low stool

MORE

10   Nay, good night rather.
Your honor's crestfall'n with your happy father.

ROPER

O, what formality, what square[257] observance
Lives in a little room! Here public care
Gags[258] not the eyes of slumber; here fierce riot
15   Ruffles[259] not proudly in a coat of trust,
Whilst like a pawn at chess he keeps in rank
With kings and mighty fellows. Yet indeed
Those men that stand on tiptoe smile to see
Him pawn his fortunes.

MORE

                              True, son, here['s not so,][260]
20   Nor does the wanton tongue[261] here screw itself
Into the ear, that like a vice drinks up
The iron instrument.

LADY MORE

                         We are here at peace.

MORE

Then peace,[262] good wife.

LADY MORE

For keeping still in compass — a strange point
25   In time's new navigation — we have sailed
Beyond our course.

MORE

                         Have done.

LADY MORE

We are exiled the Court.

MORE

                              Still thou harp'st on that.
'Tis sin for to deserve that banishment;
But he that ne'er knew Court, courts sweet
    content.

LADY MORE

O, but, dear husband —

MORE

                              I will not hear thee, wife.
30   The winding labyrinth of thy strange discourse
Will ne'er have end. Sit still and, my good wife,
Entreat thy tongue be still, or credit me,

Thou shalt not understand a word we speak;
We'll talk in Latin.
[*To Roper.*] *Humida vallis raros patitur fulminis*   35
    ictus.[263]
More rest enjoys the subject meanly bred
Than he that bears the kingdom in his head.
Great men are still musicians, else the world lies:
They learn low strains after the notes that rise.   40

ROPER

Good sir, be still yourself, and but remember
How in this general court of short-lived pleasure,
The world, creation is the ample food
That is digested in the maw[264] of time.
If man himself be subject to such ruin,   45
How shall his garment then, or the loose points
That tie respect unto his awe-full place,
Avoid destruction? Most honored father-in-law,
The blood you have bequeathed these several
    hearts
To nourish your posterity stands firm,   50
And as with joy you led us first to rise,
So with like hearts we'll lock preferment's eyes.[265]

MORE

Now will I speak like More in melancholy:
For if grief's power could with her sharpest darts
Pierce my firm bosom, here's sufficient cause   55
To take my farewell of mirth's hurtless laws.
Poor humbled lady, thou that wert of late
Placed with the noblest women of the land,
Invited to their angel companies,
Seeming a bright star in the courtly sphere: 60
Why shouldst thou like a widow sit thus low
And all thy fair consorts move from the clouds
That overdrip thy beauty and thy worth?
I'll tell thee the true cause: the Court, like heaven,
Examines not the anger of the prince,   65
And being more frail compos'd of gilded earth,
Shines upon them on whom the King doth shine,
Smiles if he smile, declines if he decline.
Yet seeing both are mortal, Court and King,
Shed not one tear for any earthly thing;   70
For, so God pardon me, in my saddest hour
Thou hast no more occasion to lament —
Nor these, nor those — my exile from the Court,
No, nor this body's torture were't imposed —

257 solemn, precise   258 props open
259 swaggers   260 Gabrieli and Melchiori's emendation   261 *wanton tongue:*

lawless or insolent speech   262 hold your
peace   263 From Seneca's *Hippolytus,*
lines 1132–33: "The soggy lowland is

rarely hit by lightning bolts."   264 belly
265 *lock preferment's eyes:* close the eyes to
advancement

75   As commonly disgraces of great men
      Are the forewarnings of a hasty death —
      Than to behold me after many a toil
      Honor'd with endless rest. Perchance the King,
      Seeing the Court is full of vanity,
80   Has pity lest our souls should be misled,
      And sends us to a life contemplative.
      O, happy banishment from worldly pride,
      When souls by private life are sanctified.

LADY MORE
      O, but I fear some plot against your life!

MORE
85   Why then, 'tis thus: the King of his high grace,
      Seeing my faithful service to his state,
      Intends to send me to the King of heaven
      For a rich present, where my soul shall prove
      A true rememb'rer of his Majesty.
      Come, prithee mourn not; the worst chance is
90   death,
      And that brings endless joy for fickle breath.

LADY MORE
      Ah, but your children!

MORE
                            Tush, let them alone.
      Say they be stripped from this poor painted cloth,
      This outside of the earth, left houseless, bare;
95   They have minds instructed how to gather more.
      There's no man that's ingenuous can be poor.
      And therefore, do not weep, my little ones,
      Though you lose all the earth; keep your souls
          even
      And you shall find inheritance in heaven.
100   But for my servants, there's my chiefest care.
      [*To Catesby.*] Come hither, faithful steward. Be
          not griev'd
      That in thy person I discharge both thee
      And all thy other fellow officers,
      For my great master hath discharged me.
105   If thou by serving me hast suffer'd loss,
      Then benefit thyself by leaving me.
      I hope thou hast not, for such times as these
      Bring gain to officers, whoever leese.[266]
      Great lords have only name, but in their fall
110   Lord Spend-All's steward's Master Gathers-All.
      But I suspect not thee. Admit thou hast.

It's good the servants save when masters waste.
But you, poor gentlemen, that had no place
T'enrich yourselves but by loathed bribery,
Which I abhorred and never found you loved,   115
Think, when an oak falls, underwood shrinks
    down
And yet may live, though bruised. I pray ye, strive
To shun my ruin, for the axe is set
Even at my root, to fell me to the ground.
The best I can do to prefer you all   120
With my mean store expect, for Heaven can tell
That More loves all his followers more than well.
          Enter a servant.

SERVANT
My lord, there are new-lighted[267] at the gate
The Earls of Surrey and of Shrewsbury,
And they expect you in the inner court.   125

MORE
Entreat their lordships come into the hall.

LADY MORE
O God, what news with them?

MORE
                            Why, how now, wife?
They are but come to visit their old friend.

LADY MORE
O God, I fear, I fear.

MORE
What shouldst thou fear, fond[268] woman?   130
*Iustum si fractus illabatur orbis, impavidum
    ferient ruinae.*[269]
Here let me live estranged from great men's looks:
They are like golden flies on leaden hooks.
          *Enter the Earls of Surrey and Shrewsbury,
          Downes with his mace, and attendants.*

SHREWSBURY
Good morrow, good Sir Thomas.

SURREY [*To Lady More.*]
Good day, good madam.   (*Kind salutations.*)

MORE
                            Welcome, my good lords.   135
What ails your lordships look so melancholy?
Oh, I know: you live in Court, and the Court diet
Is only friend to physic.[270]

---

266 lose   **267** just dismounted
268 foolish   **269** "Even if the world falls

apart, the ruin will not strike fear in the
heart of the just man." See Horace's ode

on "Justice and Steadfastness of Purpose,"
3.3.1, 7–8.   **270** medicine

SURREY

               O Sir Thomas,
Our words are now the King's, and our sad[271]
   looks
140 The interest[272] of your love. We are sent to you
From our mild Sovereign, once more to demand
If you'll subscribe unto those articles
He sent ye th'other day. Be well advised,
For on mine honor, lord, grave Doctor Fisher,
145 Bishop of Rochester, at the self-same instant
Attached[273] with you, is sent unto the Tower
For the like obstinacy; his Majesty
Hath only sent you prisoner to your house.
But if you now refuse for to subscribe,
A stricter course will follow.

LADY MORE

150   O dear husband!
        Kneeling and weeping.

DAUGHTERS
Dear Father!

MORE
         See, my lords,
This partner and these subjects to my flesh
Prove rebels to my conscience. But, my good
   lords,
If I refuse, must I unto the Tower?

SHREWSBURY
155 You must, my lord. Here is an officer
Ready for to arrest you of high treason.

LADY MORE AND DAUGHTERS
O God, O God!

ROPER
         Be patient, good madam.

MORE
Ay, Downes, is't thou? I once did save thy life,
When else by cruel riotous assault
160 Thou hadst been torn in pieces. Thou art reserved
To be my summoner to yond spiritual court.
Give me thy hand, good fellow. Smooth thy
   face.[274]
The diet that thou drink'st is spiced with mace,[275]
And I could ne'er abide it. 'Twill not disgest;
165 'Twill lie too heavy, man, on my weak breast.

SHREWSBURY
Be brief, my lord, for we are limited
Unto an hour.

MORE
        Unto an hour? 'Tis well,
The bell, earth's thunder, soon shall toll my
   knell.[276]

LADY MORE (*Kneeling.*)
Dear loving husband, if you respect[277] not me,
Yet think upon your daughters.

MORE
                 Wife, stand up.   170
I have bethought me,
And I'll now satisfy the King's good pleasure.

DAUGHTERS
Oh, happy alteration!

SHREWSBURY
          Come then, subscribe, my lord.

SURREY
I am right glad of this your fair conversion.

MORE
Oh, pardon me,   175
I will subscribe to go unto the Tower
With all submissive willingness, and thereto add
My bones to strengthen the foundation
Of Julius Caesar's palace. Now, my lord,
I'll satisfy the King even with my blood,   180
Nor will I wrong your patience. Friend, do thine
   office.[278]

DOWNES
Sir Thomas More, Lord Chancellor of England,
I arrest you in the King's name of high treason.

MORE
Gramercies,[279] friend.
To a great prison, to discharge[280] the strife   185
Commenced 'twixt conscience and my frailer life,
More now must march. Chelsea, adieu, adieu.
Strange farewell; thou shalt ne'er more see More
   true,
For I shall ne'er see thee more. Servants, farewell.
Wife, mar not thine indifferent[281] face; be wise.   190
More's widow's husband, he must make thee rise.

---

271 grave; unhappy **272** concern for;
claim upon **273** arrested **274** *smooth
thy face*: take a calm expression **275** a
nutmeg spice; swindling **276** the toll
of a funeral bell; death knell **277** show
consideration for **278** duty **279** Great
thanks **280** relieve **281** unemotional

Daughters, […] what's here, what's here?
Mine eye had almost parted with a tear.
Dear son, possess my virtue, that I ne'er gave.
195 Grave More thus lightly walks to a quick grave.

ROPER

Curae leves loquuntur, ingentes stupent.[282]

MORE

You that way in; mind you my course in prayer.
By water I to prison, to heaven through air.

Exeunt.

5.1

Enter the Warders of the Tower with halberds.

FIRST WARDER

Ho, make a guard there!

SECOND WARDER

Master Lieutenant gives a strait command
The people be avoided[283] from the bridge.

THIRD WARDER

From whence is he committed,[284] who can tell?

FIRST WARDER

5 From Durham House, I hear.

SECOND WARDER

The guard were waiting there an hour ago.

THIRD WARDER

If he stay long, he'll not get near the wharf,
There's such a crowd of boats upon the Thames.

FIRST WARDER

Well, be it spoken without offense to any,
10 A wiser or more virtuous gentleman
Was never bred in England.

SECOND WARDER

I think the poor will bury him in tears.
I never heard a man since I was born
So generally bewailed of everyone.

Enter a poor woman.

THIRD WARDER

What means this woman? — Whither dost thou
15 press?

FIRST WARDER

This woman will be trod to death anon.

SECOND WARDER

What makest thou here?

WOMAN

To speak with that good man Sir Thomas More.

FIRST WARDER

To speak with him? He's not Lord Chancellor.

WOMAN

The more's the pity, sir, if it pleased God. 20

FIRST WARDER

Therefore if thou hast a petition to deliver,
Thou mayst keep it now, for anything I know.

WOMAN

I am a poor woman, and have had, God knows,
A suit this two year in the Chancery,[285]
And he hath all the evidence I have, 25
Which should I lose, I am utterly undone.

FIRST WARDER

Faith, and I fear thou'lt hardly come by 'em now.
I am sorry for thee even with all my heart.

*Enter the Lords of Shrewsbury and Surrey with
Sir Thomas More and attendants, and enter
Lieutenant and Gentleman Porter.*

SECOND WARDER

Woman, stand back; you must avoid this place.
The lords must pass this way into the Tower. 30

MORE

I thank your lordships for your pains thus far
To my strong house.

WOMAN

Now, good Sir Thomas More, for Christ's dear
sake,
Deliver me my writings back again
That do concern my title. 35

MORE

What, my old client, art thou got hither too?
Poor silly[286] wretch, I must confess indeed
I had such writings as concern thee near,
But the King has ta'en the matter into his own
hand;

---

282 Seneca's *Hippolytus*, 607: "Silly worries speak, serious ones are silent."   **283** removed   **284** imprisoned   **285** i.e., in the court of the Lord Chancellor   **286** deserving of pity

40   He has all I had. Then, woman, sue to him.
     I cannot help thee; thou must bear with me.

WOMAN
     Ah, gentle heart, my soul for thee is sad.
     Farewell, the best friend that the poor e'er had.
                                        Exit.

GENTLEMAN PORTER
     Before you enter through the Tower gate,
45   Your upper garment, sir, belongs to me.

MORE
     Sir, you shall have it; there it is.
                    He gives him his cap.

GENTLEMAN PORTER
     The upmost on your back, sir. You mistake me.

MORE
     Sir, now I understand ye very well.
     But that you name my back,
                    [*He gives him his cloak.*]
50   Sure else my cap had been the uppermost.

SHREWSBURY
     Farewell, kind lord. God send us merry meeting.

MORE
     Amen, my lord.

SURREY
     Farewell, dear friend. I hope your safe return.

MORE
     My lord, and my dear fellow in the Muses,
55   Farewell. Farewell, most noble poet.

LIEUTENANT
     Adieu, most honored lords.
                              Exeunt lords.

MORE
     Fair prison, welcome. Yet methinks,
     For thy fair building, 'tis too foul a name.
     Many a guilty soul, and many an innocent,
60   Have breathed their farewell to thy hollow rooms.
     I oft have entered into thee this way,
     Yet, I thank God, ne'er with a clearer conscience
     Than at this hour.
     This is my comfort yet: how hard soe'er
65   My lodging prove, the cry of the poor suitor,
     Fatherless orphan or distressèd widow

Shall not disturb me in my quiet sleep.
On then, i' God's name, to our close[287] abode;
God is as strong here as he is abroad.   *Exeunt.*

5.2
*Enter Butler, Brewer, Porter, and Horsekeeper
several ways.*

BUTLER
     Robin Brewer, how now, man? What cheer, what
cheer?

BREWER
     Faith, Ned Butler, sick of thy disease, and these
our other fellows here, Ralph Horsekeeper and Giles
Porter: sad, sad. They say my lord goes to his trial   5
today.

HORSEKEEPER
     To it, man? Why, he is now at it. God send him
well to speed.[288]

PORTER
     Amen. Even as I wish to mine own soul, so speed
it with my honorable lord and master, Sir Thomas   10
More.

BUTLER
     I cannot tell; I have nothing to do with matters
above my capacity,[289] but as God judge me, if I
might speak my mind, I think there lives not a more
harmless gentleman in the universal world.   15

BREWER
     Nor a wiser, nor a merrier, nor an honester. Go
to; I'll put that in upon mine own knowledge.

PORTER
     Nay, an ye bate him his due of[290] his housekeeping,
hang ye all. Have ye many lord chancellors comes in
debt at the year's end, and for very housekeeping?   20

HORSEKEEPER
     Well, he was too good a lord for us, and therefore,
I fear, God himself will take him. But I'll be hanged
if ever I have such another service.

BREWER
     Soft, man, we are not discharged yet. My lord may
come home again and all will be well.   25

287 closed up, secret, hidden **288** success; ability **290** *an...due of:* if you don't give
good fortune **289** competence, mental him credit for

BUTLER

I much mistrust[291] it; when they go to 'raigning[292]
once, there's ever foul weather for a great while after.

Enter Gough and Catesby with a paper.

But soft, here comes Master Gough and Master
Catesby. Now we shall hear more.

HORSEKEEPER

30   Before God, they are very sad; I doubt[293] my lord
is condemned.

PORTER

God bless his soul, and a fig[294] then for all worldly
condemnation!

GOUGH

Well said, Giles Porter; I commend thee for it;
35   'Twas spoken like a well-affected[295] servant
Of him that was a kind lord to us all.

CATESBY

Which now no more he shall be, for, dear fellows,
Now we are masterless. Though he may live
So long as please the King, but law hath made him
A dead man to the world, and given the axe his
40   head,
But his sweet soul to live among the saints.

GOUGH

Let us entreat ye to go call together
The rest of your sad fellows — by the roll
You're just seven score[296] — and tell them what ye
        hear
45   A virtuous honorable lord hath done
Even for the meanest follower that he had.
This writing found my lady in his study
This instant[297] morning, wherein is set down
Each servant's name, according to his place
50   And office in the house. On every man
He frankly[298] hath bestown twenty nobles,
The best and worst together, all alike,
Which Master Catesby here forth will pay ye.

CATESBY

Take it, as it is meant, a kind remembrance
55   Of a far kinder lord, with whose sad fall
He gives up house, and farewell to us all.
Thus the fair-spreading oak falls not alone,
But all the neighbor plants and under-trees

Are crushed down with his weight. No more of
    this,
Come and receive your due, and after go   60
Fellow-like hence, co-partners of one woe.

Exeunt.

5.3

*Enter Sir Thomas More, the lieutenant, and a
servant attending, as in his chamber in the Tower.*

MORE

Master Lieutenant, is the warrant come?
If it be so, i' God's name, let us know it.

LIEUTENANT

My lord, it is.

MORE

'Tis welcome, sir, to me, with all my heart.
His blessed will be done.   5

LIEUTENANT

Your wisdom, sir, hath been so well approved,[299]
And your fair patience in imprisonment
Hath ever shown such constancy of mind
And Christian resolution in all troubles,
As warrants us you are not unprepared.   10

MORE

No, Master Lieutenant, I thank my God
I have peace of conscience, though the world
    and I
Are at a little odds. But we'll be even now, I hope,
Ere long. When is the execution[300] of your
    warrant?

LIEUTENANT

Tomorrow morning.

MORE

               So, sir, I thank ye.   15
I have not lived so ill I fear to die.
Master Lieutenant,
I have had a sore fit of the stone[301] tonight,
But the King hath sent me such a rare receipt,[302]
I thank him, as I shall not need to fear it much.   20

LIEUTENANT

In life and death, still merry Sir Thomas More.

291 doubt   **292** arraigning, trying; puns
on raining   **293** fear   **294** *a fig:* term
of contempt   **295** cherished   **296** *seven*

score: 140   **297** very same   **298** freely
299 demonstrated   **300** issuance
(with pun on a warrant of execution)

301 *sore . . . stone:* grievous pain from kidney
stones   **302** prescription

MORE [*To Servant.*]

Sirrah, fellow, reach me the urinal.

He gives it him.

Ha, let me see. [There's]³⁰³ gravel in the water,

[Faith, there's no instant jeopardy in that.]

25   The man were likely to live long enough,

So pleased the King. Here, fellow, take it.

SERVANT

Shall I go with it to the doctor, sir?

MORE

No, save thy labor; we'll cozen³⁰⁴ him of a fee.

Thou shalt see me take a dram³⁰⁵ tomorrow

morning

30   Shall cure the stone I warrant, doubt it not.

Master Lieutenant, what news of my Lord of

Rochester?

LIEUTENANT

Yesterday morning was he put to death.

MORE

The peace of soul sleep with him.

He was a learned and a reverend prelate,

35   And a rich man, believe me.

LIEUTENANT

If he were rich, what is Sir Thomas More,

That all this while hath been Lord Chancellor?

MORE

Say ye so, Master Lieutenant? What do you think

A man that with my time had held my place

40   Might purchase?³⁰⁶

LIEUTENANT

Perhaps, my lord, two thousand pound a year.

MORE

Master Lieutenant, I protest to you

I never had the means in all my life

To purchase one poor hundred pound a year.

45   I think I am the poorest chancellor

That ever was in England, though I could wish,

For credit of the place, that my estate were better.

LIEUTENANT

It's very strange.

MORE

It will be found as true.

I think, sir, that with most part of my coin

I have purchased as strange commodities   50

As ever you heard tell of in your life.

LIEUTENANT

Commodities, my lord?

Might I, without offense, enquire of them?

MORE

Crutches, Master Lieutenant, and bare³⁰⁷ cloaks,

For halting soldiers and poor needy scholars,   55

Have had my gettings in the Chancery.

To think but what acheat³⁰⁸ the Crown shall have

By my attainder!³⁰⁹

I prithee, if thou beest a gentleman,

Get but a copy of my inventory.   60

That part of poet that was given me

Made me a very unthrift;

For this is the disease attends us all:

Poets were never thrifty, never shall.

Enter Lady More mourning,

daughters, Master Roper.

LIEUTENANT

O noble More—   65

My lord, your wife, your son-in-law, and

daughters.

MORE

Son Roper, welcome; welcome, wife and girls.

Why do you weep? Because I live at ease?

Did you not see, when I was chancellor,

I was so cloyed³¹⁰ with suitors every hour   70

I could not sleep, nor dine, nor sup in quiet?

Here's none of this; here I can sit and talk

With my honest keeper half a day together,

Laugh and be merry. Why then should you weep?

ROPER

These tears, my lord, for this your long restraint   75

Hope had dried up with comfort that we yet,

Although imprisoned, might have had your life.

MORE

To live in prison, what a life were that?

The King, I thank him, loves me more than so.

Tomorrow I shall be at liberty   80

---

303 Shirley's emendation, and the next   304 cheat   305 draught of medicine   306 acquire   307 threadbare   308 escheat; reversion of property to a feudal lord   309 legal consequences of a treason conviction—in this case, forfeiture of property   310 encumbered

To go even whither I can,
After I have dispatched my business.

LADY MORE
Ah husband, husband, yet submit yourself.
Have care of your poor wife and children.

MORE
85   Wife, so I have, and I do leave you all
To his protection hath the power to keep
You safer than I can,
The father of the widow and the orphan.

ROPER
The world, my lord, hath ever held you wise,
90   And 't shall be no distaste unto your wisdom
To yield to the opinion of the state.

MORE
I have deceived myself, I must acknowledge;
And as you say, son Roper, to confess the same
It will be no disparagement at all.

LADY MORE
95   His Highness shall be certified[311] thereof,
immediately.   *Offering to depart.*

MORE
Nay, hear me, wife; first let me tell ye how
I thought to have had a barber for my beard.
Now I remember that were labor lost:
The headsman now shall cut off head and all.

ROPER'S WIFE
100   Father, his Majesty upon your meek submission
Will yet, they say, receive you to his grace
In as great credit[312] as you were before.

MORE
['Tis so indeed,][313] wench. Faith, my lord the
King
Has appointed me to do a little business.
105   If that were past, my girl, thou then shouldst see
What I would say to him about that matter.
But I shall be so busy until then, I shall not
tend it.

DAUGHTERS
Ah, my dear father.

LADY MORE
Dear lord and husband.

MORE
Be comforted, good wife, to live and love my
children,
For with thee leave I all my care of them.   110
Son Roper, for my sake that have loved thee well,
And for her virtue's sake, cherish my child.
Girl, be not proud, but of[314] thy husband's love
Ever retain thy virtuous modesty.
That modesty is such a comely garment   115
As it is never out of fashion, sits as fair
Upon the meaner woman as the empress.
No stuff that gold can buy is half so rich,
Nor ornament that so becomes a woman.
Live all, and love together, and thereby   120
You give your father a rich obsequy.

DAUGHTERS
Your blessing, dear father.

MORE
                              I must be gone —
God bless you — to talk with God, who now doth
call.

LADY MORE
Ah, my dear husband!

MORE
                 Sweet wife, good night, good night.
God send us all his everlasting light.   125

ROPER
I think before this hour,
More heavy hearts ne'er parted in the Tower.
                                   Exeunt.

5.4
*Enter the sheriffs of London and their officers at one
door, the warders with their halberds at another.*

FIRST SHERIFF
Officers, what time of day is 't?

OFFICER
                        Almost eight o'clock.

SECOND SHERIFF
We must make haste then, lest we stay too long.

FIRST WARDER
Good morrow, Master Shrieves of London.
Master Lieutenant

311 informed   **312** favor   **313** Shirley's emendation   **314** on account of

Wills ye repair to the limits of the Tower,
5   There to receive your prisoner.

FIRST SHERIFF [*To Officer.*]
Go back, and tell his Worship we are ready.

SECOND SHERIFF
Go bid the officers make clear the way,
There may be passage for the prisoner.
    Enter Lieutenant and his guard with More.

MORE
Yet God be thanked; here's a fair day toward[315]
10   To take our journey in. Master Lieutenant,
It were fair walking on the Tower leads.

LIEUTENANT
An so it might have liked my Sovereign Lord,
I would to God you might have walked there
    still.   *He weeps.*

MORE
Sir, we are walking to a better place.
15   O sir, your kind and loving tears
Are like sweet odors to embalm your friend.
Thank your good lady; since I was your guest
She has made me a very wanton,[316] in good sooth.

LIEUTENANT
Oh, I had hoped we should not yet have parted.

MORE
20   But I must leave ye for a little while.
Within an hour or two you may look for me,
But there will be so many come to see me
That I shall be so proud I will not speak.
And sure my memory is grown so ill
25   I fear I shall forget my head behind me.

LIEUTENANT
God and his blessed angels be about ye.
Here, Master Shrieves, receive your prisoner.

MORE
Good morrow, Master Shrieves of London, to ye
    both.
I thank ye that ye will vouchsafe[317] to meet me.
30   I see by this you have not quite forgot
That I was in times past as you are now:
A sheriff of London.

FIRST SHERIFF
Sir, then you know our duty doth require it.

MORE
I know it well, sir, else I would have been glad
You might have saved a labor at this time.   35
[*To Second Sheriff.*] Ah, Master Sheriff,
You and I have been of old acquaintance.
You were a patient auditor[318] of mine
When I read the divinity lecture at Saint
    Lawrence's.[319]

SECOND SHERIFF
Sir Thomas More,   40
I have heard you oft, as many other did,
To our great comfort.

MORE
Pray God, you may so now, with all my heart.
And, as I call to mind,
When I studied the law in Lincoln's Inn,   45
I was of counsel[320] with ye in a cause.

[FIRST] SHERIFF
I was about to say so, good Sir Thomas.
[   ][321]

MORE
Oh, is this the place?
I promise ye, it is a goodly scaffold.   50
In sooth, I am come about a headless errand,
For I have not much to say, now I am here.
Well, let's ascend, i' God's name.
[*To the Hangman.*] In troth, methinks your stair
    is somewhat weak.
I prithee, honest friend, lend me thy hand   55
To help me up. As for my coming down,
Let me alone; I'll look to that myself.
        As he is going up the stairs,
    enters the Earls of Surrey and Shrewsbury.

MORE
My lords of Surrey and of Shrewsbury, give me
your hands yet before we part. Ye see, though it
pleaseth the King to raise me thus high, yet I am not   60
proud, for the higher I mount, the better I can see
my friends about me. I am now on a far voyage, and
this strange wooden horse must bear me thither;
yet I perceive by your looks you like my bargain so

315 coming, about to be   316 spoilt
child   317 graciously agree   318 listener   319 More's delivered lectures on
Augustine's *City of God*, at St. Lawrence
Jewry in 1501.   320 *of counsel:* worked
together in a legal capacity   321 This line
was lost due to manuscript damage.

65 ill that there's not one of ye all dare venture with me. (*Walking.*) Truly, here's a most sweet gallery; I like the air of it better than my garden at Chelsea. By your patience, good people that have pressed thus into my bedchamber, if you'll not trouble me, 70 I'll take a sound sleep here.

SHREWSBURY

My lord, 'twere good you'd publish[322] to the world
Your great offense unto his Majesty.

MORE

My lord, I'll bequeath this legacy to the hangman, and do it instantly. (*Gives him his gown.*) I confess his 75 Majesty hath been ever good to me, and my offense to his Highness makes me, of[323] a state pleader, a stage player (though I am old, and have a bad voice) to act this last scene of my tragedy. I'll send him for my trespass a reverent head, somewhat bald, for it 80 is not requisite any head should stand covered to so high majesty. If that content him not, because I think my body will then do me small pleasure, let him but bury it and take it.

SURREY

My lord, my lord, hold conference with your soul. 85 You see, my lord, the time of life is short.

MORE

I see it, my good lord; I dispatched that business the last night. I come hither only to be let blood;[324] my doctor here tells me it is good for the headache.

HANGMAN

I beseech ye, my lord, forgive me.

MORE

90 Forgive thee, honest fellow? Why?

HANGMAN

For your death, my lord.

MORE

Oh, my death. I had rather it were in thy power to forgive me, for thou hast the sharpest action against me. The law, my honest friend, lies in thy hands now. 95 ([*Gives*] *his purse.*) Here's thy fee, and, my good fellow, let my suit be dispatched presently; for 'tis all one pain to die a lingering death and to live in the continual mill of a lawsuit. But I can tell thee, my

neck is so short that if thou shouldst behead an hundred noblemen like myself, thou wouldst ne'er get 100 credit[325] by it. Therefore—look ye, sir—do it handsomely,[326] or of my word thou shalt never deal with me hereafter.

HANGMAN

I'll take an order for that, my lord.

MORE

One thing more: take heed thou cut'st not off my 105 beard. Oh, I forgot; execution passed upon that last night, and the body of it lies buried in the Tower.—Stay. Is't not possible to make a scape[327] from all this strong guard? It is.
There is a thing within me that will raise 110
And elevate my better part 'bove sight
Of these same weaker eyes. And, Master Shrieves,
For all this troop of steel that tends[328] my death,
I shall break from you, and fly up to heaven.
Let's seek the means for this. 115

HANGMAN

My lord, I pray ye, put off your doublet.

MORE

Speak not so coldly to me; I am hoarse already;
I would be loath, good fellow, to take more.
Point me the block; I ne'er was here before.

HANGMAN

To the east side, my lord.

MORE

                                  Then to the east, 120
We go to sigh; that o'er, to sleep in rest.
Here More forsakes all mirth, good reason why:
The fool of flesh must with her frail life die.
No eye salute my trunk[329] with a sad tear.
Our birth to heaven should be thus: void of fear. 125
                                          Exit.

SURREY

A very learned worthy gentleman
Seals error with his blood. Come, we'll to Court.
Let's sadly hence to perfect[330] unknown fates,
Whilst he tends progress[331] to the state of states.
                                  [*Exeunt.*]

                    FINIS.

---

322 formally acknowledge **323** out of, i.e., from having been **324** *let blood:* releasing blood was a common prescription for

ill patients **325** payment; appreciation **326** properly **327** escape **328** attends **329** headless body **330** fulfill **331** *tends*

progress: makes his way—alluding to a royal progress or journey

ONLINE RESOURCES

See the companion website, www.essentialmore.org, for supporting materials, including:

Study Materials
An ongoing collection of materials developed and used by experienced teachers

Timelines
Detailed accounts of each year from 1529 to 1535, linked to primary sources

E-texts
Full English texts not contained in this volume:
A Response to Luther
The Confutation of Tyndale's Answer 1–9
The Debellation of Salem and Bizance
Nicholas Harpsfield's *Life and Death of Sir Thomas More*

Full Latin texts not contained in this volume:
Lucian Latin texts
Historia Richardi Tertii
Utopia
Epigrammata
Responsio ad Lutherum

Concordances
For each individual book contained in the Yale CW and for Roger's 1947 *Correspondence*
A cumulative concordance of More's English works
A cumulative concordance of More's Latin works
A cumulative concordance of More's complete works

Bibliographies
Links to major international bibliographies and Moreana archive materials for over 10,000 items

Thomas More's London
Interactive color map

This facsimile and the ones on the following two pages continue from page xvi Thomas More's handwritten letter of 5 March <1534> to King Henry VIII. For a full transcription see pages 381 to 382.

beene, & will be tell) dye, how so ever y^r pleasure be to do by me.
Howe be it if in the considering of my cause y^r high wysedome & groyouse
goodnes perceyve (as I veryly trust in god you shall) that I more
otherwise have demeaned my self, than well may stand w^t my bounden
dutie of faithfullnes toward y^r royall maiestie than in my most
humble wyse I beseech y^r moste noble grace, that the knowoledge of
y^r trew gracyouse persuasion in that byhalfe, may withe the turmoile
of my present heavynesse, conceyved of the drede & feare (by that I sawe
such a goodnesse bill put by y^r lerned councell in to ye high cort of
parliament agaynst me) lest y^r grace myght by some sinistre informacion
be induced any thyng to thinke the contrary. which if y^r highnes do not
(as I trust in god & y^r great goodnes the mater by y^r alone high
prudence examined & consydered you will not) then in my most
humble maner I beseech y^r highnes further (albeit that in respecte
of my former requeste the other thyng ye very sleight) yet sith
y^r highnes hath here before of y^r more habundant goodnes heped
& accumulated uppon me (though I was therto very far unworthy
fro tyme to tyme bothe worshippe & great honor to my selfe) now seme.
lefte of all such thinges, and nothing seke or desyre but the lyfe to
come, & in the meane while pray for y^r grace, it may lyke y^r highnes
of y^r accustumed benignitie somewhat to tendre my poore honestie,
and never suffre by the meanes of such a bill put forth agaynst me
any man to take occasion here after agaynst the trouth to slaundre
me. which thyng shold yit by the peryll of theyre alone soules
do theym selfe more hurt than me which shall I trust settle myn
harte with y^r gracyouse favor to depend uppon the comfort of
the trouth & hope of hevyn, and not uppon the fallible opinion
or some spoken wordes, & hoyst & some chaungeable people. And that

most dredde & most dere soverayn lord I beseche the blessed trinite
preserve yo' moost noble grace both in body & soule, and all
that are yo' well willers, and amend all the contrary. among
whome if Nor I be one or ever have bene one, then pray I god that he may with
myn open shame & destruction declare it. At my pore howse
in chelchith the fifeth day of march by the knowen rude hand
of

BRITISH MUSEUM

yo' moste humble & moste heby
faithfull subgiett & bedeman

Tho. More Kt.

WRITINGS OF THOMAS MORE